WISDEN

CRICKETERS' ALMANACK

2020

EDITED BY LAWRENCE BOOTH

WISDEN

CRICKETERS' ALMANACK

2020

157th EDITION

John Wisden & Co

An imprint of Bloomsbury Publishing Plc

WISDEN
Bloomsbury Publishing Plc
50 Bedford Square, London, WC1B 3DP, UK

BLOOMSBURY, WISDEN and the wood-engraving device are trademarks of
Bloomsbury Publishing Plc

First published in Great Britain 2020

WISDEN CRICKETERS' ALMANACK
Editor **Lawrence Booth**
Co-editor **Hugh Chevallier**
International editor **Steven Lynch**
Statistical editor **Harriet Monkhouse**
Digital editor **Richard Whitehead**
Production co-ordinator **Matt Boulton**
Statisticians **Philip Bailey** and **Andrew Samson**
Proofreader **Charles Barr**
Database and typesetting **James Parsisson**
Publisher **Katy McAdam**
Consultant publisher **Christopher Lane**

Reader feedback: almanack@wisden.com
www.wisdenalmanack.com
www.wisdenrecords.com
Follow Wisden on Twitter @WisdenAlmanack
and on Facebook at Wisden Sports

A catalogue record for this book is available from the British Library

Library of Congress Cataloguing-in-Publication data has been applied for

Hardback 978-1-4729-7285-9 £55

Soft cover 978-1-4729-7288-0 £55

Large format 978-1-4729-7286-6 £75

Leatherbound 978-1-4729-7287-3 £295

The Shorter Wisden (eBook) 978-1-4729-7638-3 £9.99

2 4 6 8 10 9 7 5 3 1

A Taste of Wisden 2020

Bob Willis himself was late only once: for his funeral, when the hearse got stuck in traffic in Barnes. He should have gone by bus.
Bob Willis, 1949–2019, page 30

* * *

It appeared the ECB were desperate to use any picture, as long as it did not come from a game of cricket.
The Birth of The Hundred, page 49

* * *

December's BBC Sports Personality of the Year award became not so much about who would win, but about who would finish second and third.
The Leading Cricketer in the World in 2019, page 63

* * *

Instead of letting his passengers alight, the driver gave them an unwanted tour of Cumbrian byways for 50 minutes, at one stage returning south down the M6.
County outgrounds, page 100

* * *

I try to trick myself to sleep, not by counting sheep, but by replaying in my mind the 100th century of the cricketing hero of my Yorkshire childhood, Geoffrey Boycott.
Cricket and mental health, page 106

* * *

"He always had to bowl long spells into the wind and uphill, apart from Thursday afternoons between lunch and tea when Trevor was filing his column for the *Financial Times*."
Obituaries, page 219

* * *

There were 25 times more British eyes on Lyon (France) for the semi-final between England and the USA than on Lyon (Nathan) for the semi-final between England and Australia.
The ICC men's World Cup in 2019, page 252

* * *

One batsman couldn't watch, the other could barely see.
England v Australia in 2019, Third Test, page 402

6

LIST OF CONTRIBUTORS

Ujjwal Acharya
Andrew Alderson
Tanya Aldred
Paul Allott
Jofra Archer
Chris Aspin
Philip August
Jonny Bairstow
Vaneisa Baksh
Sambit Bal
Benedict Bermange
Edward Bevan
Paul Bird
Paul Bolton
Daniel Brettig
Liam Brickhill
Gideon Brooks
Colin Bryden
Andy Bull
Jos Buttler
Ian Callender
Brian Carpenter
Daniel Cherny
Rex Clementine
Adam Collins
Patrick Collins
James Coyne
John Crace
Liam Cromar
Jon Culley
John Curtis
Debasish Datta
Martin Davies
Geoffrey Dean
Bertus de Jong
Peter Della Penna
William Dick
George Dobell
Rory Dollard
Paul Edwards
Syd Egan
Vithushan Ehantharajah
Mark Eklid
Matthew Engel
Peter English
John Etheridge
Melinda Farrell

Sebastian Faulks
Fidel Fernando
Jonathan Foulkes
Warwick Franks
Daniel Gallan
Alan Gardner
Mark Geenty
Richard Gibson
Haydn Gill
James Gingell
Gideon Haigh
Kevin Hand
Graham Hardcastle
David Hardy
Shahid Hashmi
Douglas Henderson
Andrew Hignell
Paul Hiscock
Jon Hotten
Nick Hoult
Mishal Husain
Howard Jacobson
Emma John
Miles Jupp
Abid Ali Kazi
Malcolm Knox
Zaffar Kunial
Peter Lalor
Richard Latham
Mark Lawson
Geoff Lemon
Jonathan Liew
Will Macpherson
Neil Manthorp
Vic Marks
Ali Martin
Alex Massie
Kalika Mehta
Sam Mendes
Peter Miller
Mohammad Isam
R. Mohan
Sidharth Monga
Benj Moorehead
Eoin Morgan
Sam Morshead
Kritika Naidu

Chetan Narula
Raf Nicholson
Andrew Nixon
Mark Pennell
Liam Plunkett
Paul Radley
Richard Rae
Adil Rashid
Charles Reynolds
Tim Rice
Joe Root
Jason Roy
Osman Samiuddin
Helge Schutz
Neville Scott
Jack Shantry
Colin Shindler
Utpal Shuvro
Simon Sinclair
Richard Spiller
John Stern
Fraser Stewart
Andy Stockhausen
Chris Stocks
Ben Stokes
Santosh Suri
Pat Symes
Bruce Talbot
Sa'adi Thawfeeq
Dave Tickner
Sharda Ugra
Anand Vasu
Phil Walker
John Ward
Isabelle Westbury
Tim Wigmore
Freddie Wilde
Simon Wilde
Barry Wilkinson
Marcus Williams
Dean Wilson
Alex Winter
Chris Woakes
Mark Wood
Andrew Wu
Lungani Zama

Cartoons by Nick Newman. Contributors to **Cricket Round the World** are listed after their articles.

The editor also acknowledges with gratitude assistance from the following: Robin Abrahams, Clare Adams, Derek Barnard, Chris Barron, Peter Bather, Mike Bechley, David Bishop, Nick Bramall, Duncan Calow, Derek Carlaw, Stephen Chalke, Stuart Clarke, Charles Colvile, Brian Croudy, Stephen Cubitt, Prakash Dahatonde, Nigel Davies, Andrew Dawson, Tony Debenham, Patrick Eagar, Gulu Ezekiel, M. L. Fernando, Ric Finlay, Alan Fordham, David Frith, Christabel Gurney, Jo Halpin, Robert Hands, Clive Hitchcock, Julia and John Hunt, David Kendix, Rajesh Kumar, Daniel Lightman, Valentine Low, Nirav Malavi, Peter Martin, Rob Outram, Trevor Owens, Michael Owen-Smith, Rachel Pagan, Francis Payne, Qamar Ahmed, Matthew Reynolds, Eva Rice, David Rimmer, Neil Robinson, Steven Stern, Claire Taylor, Chris Walmsley, Chris and Jean Whipps.

The production of *Wisden* would not be possible without the support and co-operation of many other cricket officials, county scorers, writers and lovers of the game. To them all, many thanks.

PREFACE

If you haven't heard of Max Heron-Maxwell, it's partly *Wisden's* fault. She deserved an obituary in the 1956 Almanack, but didn't get one, so we've tried to make amends on page 200 – the first of our tributes to cricketing women who have been unfairly overlooked. There will be some good stories to come.

Women have often set the pace. In 1973, two years earlier than the men, they staged a World Cup, Rachael Heyhoe Flint lifting the trophy 46 years before Eoin Morgan (last summer's tournament gets its own section in these pages). And the ICC awarded Twenty20 international status to all their Associate Member women's teams six months before the men, who joined in at the start of 2019. We have done our best to reflect the changing landscape, without it overwhelming us.

In January 2020, *Wisden* lost an old friend. Terry Cooper first wrote for the Almanack in 1968, and was Middlesex correspondent for two decades; his obituary will appear next year. He was the kind of unsung hero on which the book relies. Another, Edward Bevan, has notched up 30 years as our man in Glamorgan, the longest-serving of our current county reporters.

Wisden thrives beyond book form – only a couple of clicks away. On wisdenalmanack.com, you can download a useful index covering every edition since 1985. And on wisden.com, you can find an array of major articles from our archive. Do browse at your leisure.

This year's book was another labour of love, and I'm grateful to more than I can mention here. The editorial team of Hugh Chevallier, Harriet Monkhouse, Steven Lynch and Richard Whitehead played their customary blinder, and we were fortunate that our new production coordinator, Matt Boulton, slipped so smoothly into the shoes of Peter Bather, who stepped down after 43 editions. I thought of Peter last year when the Indian board put out a press release to "condone" the death of a bigwig; had he seen the infelicity on a proof, he would have quietly crossed out the "n", replaced it with an "l", reworked the syntax, and handed it back, eyebrow raised.

Thanks, too, to our proofreader Charles Barr, who would also have spotted the error; to Christopher Lane, our consultant publisher; to James Parsisson, typesetting supremo at DLxml; to Katy McAdam, Lizzy Ewer and Katherine Macpherson at Bloomsbury; and to my colleagues at the *Daily Mail* and *The Mail on Sunday*, Marc Padgett, Mike Richards, Paul Newman and Richard Gibson, who always support my Almanack-related absences. Clare Adams at MCC was invaluable in organising our photograph competition, which needs a sponsor. Please get in touch if you can help.

My parents, Philip and Vreni, stoically accommodated my family for two months over Christmas while our house underwent refurbishments; a lot of these pages were edited at theirs. My wife, Anjali, was – as ever – a rock. Our two-year-old daughter, Aleya, seemed to absorb something of the summer. One bedtime, she whispered: "Come on, Ben Stokes."

LAWRENCE BOOTH
Barnes, February 2020

CONTENTS

Part One – Comment

Part Two – The Wisden Review

Part Three – The ICC Men's World Cup

Part Four – English International Cricket

Part Five – English Domestic Cricket

STATISTICS

SPECSAVERS COUNTY CHAMPIONSHIP

ONE-DAY COUNTY COMPETITIONS

OTHER ENGLISH CRICKET

Part Six – Overseas Cricket

Part Seven – Overseas Twenty20 Franchise Cricket

Part Eight – Women's Cricket

Part Nine – Records and Registers

Part Ten – The Almanack

SYMBOLS AND ABBREVIATIONS

*	In full scorecards and lists of tour parties signifies the captain. In short scorecards, averages and records signifies not out.
†	In full scorecards signifies the designated wicketkeeper. In averages signifies a left-handed batsman.
‡	In short scorecards signifies the team who won the toss.
MoM/PoM	In short scorecards signifies the Man/Player of the Match.
MoS/PoS	In short scorecards signifies the Man/Player of the Series.
DLS	Signifies where the result of a curtailed match has been determined under the Duckworth/Lewis/Stern method.

Other uses of symbols are explained in notes where they appear.

First-class matches   Men's matches of three or more days are first-class unless otherwise stated. All other matches are not first-class, including one-day and T20 internationals.

Scorecards   Where full scorecards are not provided in this book, they can be found at Cricket Archive (www.cricketarchive.co.uk) or ESPNcricinfo (www.cricinfo.com). Full scorecards from matches played overseas can also be found in the relevant *ACS Overseas First-Class Annuals*. In Twenty20 scorecards, the second figure in a bowling analysis refers to dot balls, and not maidens (as in first-class or List A games).

Records   The Records section (pages 1220–1365) is online at www.wisdenrecords.com. The database is regularly updated and, in many instances, more detailed than in *Wisden 2020*. Further information on past winners of tournaments covered in this book can be found at www.wisden.com/almanacklinks.

PART ONE

Comment

Wisden Honours

THE LEADING CRICKETERS IN THE WORLD

Ben Stokes (page 63)
Ellyse Perry (page 65)

The Leading Cricketers in the World are chosen by the editor of *Wisden* in consultation with some of the world's most experienced writers and commentators. Selection is based on a player's class and form in all cricket during the calendar year, and is merely guided by statistics rather than governed by them. There is no limit to how many times a player may be chosen. A list of winners can be found on pages 64 and 65. A list of notional past winners, backdated to 1900, appeared on page 35 of *Wisden 2007*.

THE LEADING TWENTY20 CRICKETER IN THE WORLD

Andre Russell (page 1129)

This award exactly mirrors those above, but is based solely on performances in Twenty20 cricket, both international and domestic – and may be won by a male or female player.

FIVE CRICKETERS OF THE YEAR

Jofra Archer (page 67)
Pat Cummins (page 69)
Simon Harmer (page 71)
Marnus Labuschagne (page 73)
Ellyse Perry (page 75)

The Five Cricketers of the Year are chosen by the editor of *Wisden*, and represent a tradition that dates back to 1889, making this the oldest individual award in cricket. Excellence in and/or influence on the previous English summer are the major criteria for inclusion. No one can be chosen more than once. A list of past winners can be found on page 1466.

WISDEN SCHOOLS CRICKETER OF THE YEAR

Tawanda Muyeye (page 821)

The Schools Cricketer of the Year, based on first-team performances during the previous English summer, is chosen by *Wisden's* schools correspondent in consultation with the editor and other experienced observers. The winner's school must be in the UK, play cricket to a standard approved by *Wisden*, and provide reports to this Almanack. A list of past winners can be found on page 820.

WISDEN BOOK OF THE YEAR

Cricket 2.0 by Tim Wigmore and Freddie Wilde (page 134)

The Book of the Year is selected by *Wisden's* guest reviewer; all cricket books published in the previous calendar year and submitted to *Wisden* for possible review are eligible. A list of past winners can be found on page 134.

WISDEN–MCC CRICKET PHOTOGRAPH OF THE YEAR

was won by Gareth Copley (whose entry appears opposite page 64)

The Wisden–MCC Cricket Photograph of the Year is chosen by a panel of independent experts; all images on a cricket theme photographed in the previous calendar year are eligible.

WISDEN'S WRITING COMPETITION

was won by Jonathan Foulkes (page 61)

Wisden's Writing Competition is open to anyone (other than previous winners) who has not been commissioned to write for, or has a working relationship with, the Almanack. Full details on page 62.

NOTES BY THE EDITOR

If you thought it was going to be straightforward, you hadn't been paying attention: English sporting triumphs rarely are. As Jos Buttler demolished the stumps at the Pavilion End on a fantastical evening at Lord's, running out Martin Guptill and clinching the World Cup, the ghosts of cock-ups and sob stories past seemed less haunting. That opening stand between Brearley and Boycott, Gatting's reverse sweep, Pringle's lbw shouts against Javed Miandad, the Stokes over to Brathwaite... Not banished, just easier to brush off. England's men had always wondered how it felt to be one-day world champions. Now they knew.

The moment arrived amid the kind of knuckle-chewing drama for which precedent had prepared us, but with two differences. One, it was more fraught than ever. Two, the breaks – for once – went in England's favour, as if a higher force had ruled on humanitarian grounds against another tale of woe.

Not everyone saw it that way. With the trophy decided on boundary countback – as random as tossing a coin, minus the tension – cricket took note of the zeitgeist, and split into irreconcilable camps. This was either the greatest injustice known to man, a view held mainly in India and Australia, though not New Zealand, where they've never resented the British with such fervour. Or it was a glorious inversion of the way sport is meant to be, a view held in England. The more paranoid still wonder if the ICC will demand the trophy back, and fly it to Auckland.

Even those upset on the New Zealanders' behalf – more or less everyone – could agree they had just witnessed the most tumultuous few seconds in the history of English cricket. Yet, magically, the final had been more than that. As millions caught their breath, the game felt like all the things we always want it to be, and too often isn't. Bodies littered the outfield, like the morning after a raucous house party. England's joy rubbed shoulders with New Zealand's despair, and each was considerate of the other. Briefly, St John's Wood was the centre of the universe, exerting its own gravitational pull.

Then there were the tales for the grandchildren. Jofra Archer had veered off alone to backward point, before team-mates mobbed him – a metaphor for the start of his international career two months earlier, and perhaps for his relationship with much of the country. Eoin Morgan, the Dubliner-turned-Londoner who had masterminded England's one-day *volte-face*, cavorted with colleagues of various races, religions and backgrounds (there was a lesson there somewhere).

Ben Stokes, less than a year after he might have gone to prison, burst into tears. Jason Roy fell to his knees, having just avoided a lifetime of self-recrimination after two errors in the super over. Buttler, hurling the ball skywards, later said he might not have been able to play again had he botched the run-out. Jonny Bairstow picked up Joe Root, who pummelled him in the chest, a show of affection in Yorkshire. It was a scene full of humanity. In Bayeux, they'd have made a tapestry.

All the while, Guptill lay flat on the turf, for ever a few feet from glory (Chris Woakes wanted to help him up; Jimmy Neesham thanked Woakes for the thought). And there was Kane Williamson, a picture of pain and poise, one of the tournament's defining images. There was a risk of fetishising the New Zealanders: for all the fine words about their good grace, they were distraught. Yet there was no ill feeling, as there might have been – just a mutual acknowledgment of the absurdity of it all. Separated only by an arcane regulation, England took the spoils, their opponents the sympathy.

Fourteen years earlier, Michael Vaughan's Ashes winners had soaked up the sunshine and adulation in Trafalgar Square, a moment of nationwide celebration that was immediately undermined when English cricket vanished behind a paywall. Now, thanks to Sky's decision to share the final with Channel 4, the England team belonged to the whole country once more. Social media clips, likes and memes come and go. But it is *live* sporting drama, freely available, that makes an impact, instant and lasting.

Some England players had been underwhelmed as the World Cup progressed: stadiums were generally full, yet could not mask a broader indifference. Advertising was aimed at Indian TV, not ticket-holders. Visiting teams and journalists were appalled to learn they could follow neutral games only if their hotel owned a satellite dish.

In response to a question about whether the final should be broadcast free-to-air if it involved England, their fast bowler Liam Plunkett suggested it was "always nice to be on a bigger platform". That seemed hard to argue with, but he quickly fell back into line, thanking Sky on Twitter for their investment in cricket, using language that smacked of corporate intervention. It was no coincidence that several of England's new world champions spoke of 2005 as their source of childhood inspiration. Now, they dared imagine playing a similar role.

The sense of togetherness was fleeting. When England next took the field, for the Lord's Test against Ireland ten days later, they were back behind the paywall. The genie, though, was out of the bottle. The ECB calculated that almost a third of the 15.4m who at some point tuned in to Channel 4's coverage were watching cricket for the first time – and it would have been higher still if the Wimbledon men's singles final that afternoon hadn't been another epic. (Intriguingly, the super over finished 15-all.)

The argument that no one watches TV any more sounded odder than ever; and the rule of thumb by which 10% of viewers are under 18 meant more than 1.5m potential young converts. When the UK next hosts the World Cup, the government must insist that England's games can be watched by the man and woman on the street, not just those who can afford the subscription. It's a forlorn hope.

There will, it's true, be more free-to-air cricket this summer, thanks to The Hundred. But the new competition will clash with the Royal London One-Day Cup, relegating a format in which England's men and women are reigning world champions to the status of what a senior ECB official called a "developmental competition". (To hasten its demise, this summer's county final will be the first not to take place at Lord's.) Watching the England players pinch themselves on the podium, one wondered why cricket needed anything new at all.

Butterfly defect

Boundary countback is one of those regulations that angers no one until it comes into play, at which point it is plain daft. (See: beating your carpet in the street after 8am, illegal in parts of England since 1839.) When the ICC scrapped the rule three months later, sensibly replacing it with a further super over, it was regarded in darker corners of the web as proof – proof! – that New Zealand had been robbed. This was silly and simplistic, classic post-rationalisation. Yet there was no denying cricket had been left with a bit of a philosophical poser, in which England appeared to have won and tied simultaneously, and New Zealand to have tied and lost – Schrödinger's bat, perhaps.

It was ludicrous that the game's showpiece should be decided by the small print. Yet both sides knew the deal: New Zealand needed to score 16 off Archer's over, England to deny them. And it was damning that the umpires didn't know the Law about overthrows: during the final over of the chase, Stokes should have been awarded five runs, not six, after the ball deflected off his bat to the boundary, leaving Adil Rashid on strike, and four runs, not three, needed off two.

But it was wrong to suggest England's victory was tarnished, or that they owed anyone an apology – as if sport isn't littered with famous injustices. (For an example of the chaos that can ensue when a game strives for absolute fairness, witness football's VAR.) Morgan could hardly refuse the trophy on moral grounds.

Still, let's indulge the what-if brigade. Had Rashid faced the penultimate ball of England's 50th over – as he should – he might reasonably have been expected to take a single. Stokes might then have walloped Trent Boult's leg-stump full toss towards Regent's Park. Instead, he played the percentages, pushing to long-on, and guaranteeing, at worst, a tie. Similarly, had England been defending 15, not 16, Archer would have tried to run out Neesham from the fifth ball of the super over; he might have succeeded. And Guptill would have needed three, not two, off the last; he might have succeeded, too.

That's the thing about chaos theory: change the flap of a butterfly's wing, and the tsunami never happens. It's understandable some think justice wasn't done. But we'll go mad trying to second-guess a parallel universe.

Wilde thing

To lose one super over may be regarded as a misfortune. But four? Such was New Zealand's fate, as if stuck in a recurring nightmare, somewhere between Sisyphus's boulder and Tantalus's fruit. At Auckland in November, when they lost their second super over to England, this time in a Twenty20 game, stand-in captain Tim Southee half-joked: "Hopefully it's a case of third time lucky, if there's another." Southee had bowled that one, which – with Boult in the team – seemed odd. Then, against India in the new year, New Zealand messed up two T20 chases in three days: two more super overs, both bowled by Southee, both lost. When they win one, we'll all breathe more freely.

Best of breed?

Every so often, an England cricketer joins the national conversation. First among equals is W. G. Grace, because he put the sport on the map. But others have kept it there: Hobbs, Hutton, Compton, Botham, Flintoff, Pietersen and now Ben Stokes. Of the three modern all-rounders, Stokes can be the greatest.

Last year, these pages urged him to rediscover his mongrel as a matter of national urgency. He did, and more: in the World Cup final and the Headingley Test, he was playing fantasy cricket. In between came an Ashes hundred at Lord's – normally a career highlight, scarcely a tremor on the Stokesograph.

It is tempting to see him as the heir to Botham and Flintoff. He is, as far as the story goes. But we're barely halfway through: Stokes turns 29 this summer, and his summit may still be to come. By that age, the others were already on the downward slope. After Botham's 29th birthday, his Test batting average was 25 (with one hundred, a nostalgic romp at Brisbane), his bowling average 37. Flintoff – 28 with the bat, 40 with the ball – was fading too. Both had lived the high life, and paid the price. Stokes, given a glimpse of other possibilities by his appearance in court, has turned into England's rock. At Cape Town, he began 2020 like a man enjoying the taste of responsibility.

He may never match Botham's early years with the ball, but he is already more rounded with the bat, craftsman as much as hitter. And by the end of the South Africa series, he had more hundreds and five-wicket hauls (from 16 fewer Tests) than Flintoff. Stokes refuses to believe his own publicity, insisting at Newlands that the match award he had won belonged to Dominic Sibley. When he says what matters is the team, we hear sincerity, not a soundbite.

In 2019, Stokes's value was measured not just by the stirring victories that excite the public, but by the defiance appreciated by team-mates. When England stumbled during the World Cup, losing to Sri Lanka and Australia, he stood tall. Without him, this Almanack might have been another English hard-luck story. Instead, it's a celebration. Stokes is their all-weather cricketer, a giant come rain or shine. The next few years should be fun.

The very model of a modern great at Headingley

In any sane year, events on the fourth and final day of the Third Ashes Test at Headingley would have had pride of place. But Stokes's unbeaten 135, Jack Leach's unbeaten one, and England's one-wicket win, were – by the barest of margins – only the second-most astonishing twist of 2019. It was like awarding a silver medal to Steve Redgrave.

Cricket loves to classify, and debate raged: where in the pantheon did Stokes's innings belong? It was arbitrary to proclaim it the greatest of all time: months earlier at Durban, Sri Lanka's Kusal Perera had scored 153 not out after a last-wicket stand of 78 (Stokes and Leach added 76). That said, if casual observers who overlooked Perera, they could hardly be blamed: the series was watched by one man and his Rhodesian ridgeback.

But *England's* greatest Test innings? Stokes certainly had all the ingredients. Unlike Graham Gooch's 154 not out against West Indies at Headingley in

1991, the series was at stake. Unlike Mike Atherton's Johannesburg vigil in 1995-96, it led to a win. Unlike Ian Botham's own Headingley heist, it was sudden death. Unlike Kevin Pietersen's 186 at Mumbai in 2012-13, it was talked about next day up and down the land. Unlike Gilbert Jessop's 104 at The Oval in 1902, it survives beyond a few written words.

Stokes's innings was a modern hybrid: Test tempo as he saw out the third day; something approaching one-day mode, in partnership with Bairstow; finally, pure Twenty20. Two days earlier, after England had folded for 67, their relationship with white-ball cricket was branded toxic. Now, it was agreed their win might never have happened without the limited-overs game.

Of England Test innings that have been reported on widely enough to merit inclusion here, arguably only two can challenge Stokes: Pietersen's 158 at The Oval on the last afternoon of the 2005 Ashes, and – a few weeks after Headingley – Botham's 118 off 102 balls at Old Trafford, where he hooked Dennis Lillee without a helmet. The argument may one day be settled by another innings, and Stokes will doubtless play it.

Tight versus might

Headingley was the latest example of a strange phenomenon. In Tests between the sides decided by one or two wickets, or by fewer than 20 runs, England lead Australia 13–5. Australia last clinched an Ashes nailbiter nearly a century ago, recovering from 119 for six to 489 at Adelaide in January 1925, and winning by 11 runs. Maybe they have grown used to having things their own way, and regard close finishes as a threat. Maybe England have learned to believe nothing is impossible. Attitudes can become self-fulfilling.

But is there something else at play? In Australia, cricket is the national sport, a means of self-affirmation. Remorselessness is prized – Steve Smith last summer, Marnus Labuschagne over the winter. It's about being the best, again and again (overall, Australia lead England 146–110). In England, cricket has to shout for attention: the Test team's hard-fought rise up the rankings in 2011 was never going to make as many headlines as the rousing one-off. Perhaps both countries are simply giving their people what they want.

Look after the pennies

Six months after consummating their new love affair with 50-over cricket, England rekindled an old flame. The Test match had been lavished with less attention during Trevor Bayliss's four years in charge: you win one, you lose one, and – as he liked to put it – the sun rises next day. It was fitting that he signed off both with a World Cup, magnificently fulfilling his brief, and an exhilarating, messy 2–2 Ashes draw. With Chris Silverwood has come a change of emphasis. The talk is of platforms laid and totals built: where Bayliss tore down orthodoxy, Silverwood seeks reconstruction.

After defeat in New Zealand, England won in South Africa, a pick-me-up for the new coach, and a tonic for the captaincy of Root. Thanks to global economics and sporting politics, their opponents are not what they were. But after England lost the Boxing Day Test at Centurion, the new South African management team of Graeme Smith, Mark Boucher and Jacques Kallis were hailed as saviours. By contrast, the assurances that Root would lead the side to Australia in 2021-22 were beginning to smack of entitlement.

With a quiet, considered demeanour at odds with his former (brief) incarnation as England's fastest bowler, Silverwood did not waver. His catchphrase was more down-to-earth than Bayliss's, and more practical: he wanted round pegs for round holes, which meant Sibley as an opener, not Roy. He wanted a top order that respected the rhythms of Test cricket, which meant first-day totals of 241 for four at Mount Maunganui, and 224 for four at Port Elizabeth. Above all, he wanted method, not madness – fewer nights out, more evenings in with cocoa and Netflix.

Silverwood was right to resort to basics: for the first time since 1999, England had gone through a calendar year without winning a Test series. And when they did win the odd game, there was always a caveat. St Lucia was a consolation, since West Indies were 2–0 up. Victory over Ireland came after England had been humbled for 85. At Headingley, they needed a miracle; at The Oval, Australia had already retained the urn. They were living off scraps, which was fair enough: the banquet had come in the one-day game.

In New Zealand, England sowed seeds, scoring 353 and 476. Then, after Centurion's stony ground, they put down roots: 391 for eight at Cape Town, 499 for nine at Port Elizabeth, 400 at Johannesburg. For the first time in two years, they made 400 – Silverwood's *sine qua non* – in successive first innings.

Faith was placed in youngsters, and repaid. Sibley made 133 not out at Cape Town, and Ollie Pope an undefeated 135 at Port Elizabeth so accomplished that several good judges anointed him England's best since Root. Dominic Bess returned from nowhere to spin his way to five wickets. Sibley and Zak Crawley began batting though entire sessions, riches after almost a decade of rags. With Rory Burns set to return from injury, England faced an unusual dilemma: too many openers. Throw in the pace of Archer and the born-again Mark Wood, and Root looked spoiled for choice.

There are no guarantees of anything, and the next two winters bring five-Test series in India and Australia. But, after a year in which those trips loomed terrifyingly, there was lightness in the air.

Pleading the fifth

In early January, the South African board expressed their support for four-day Tests. Their timing had presumably been learned at the School for Cricket Administrators: a few hours later, Newlands was rejoicing in one of the most memorable of fifth days. In fairness to Cricket South Africa, they were only toeing the line: their English and Australian counterparts had already backed the idea, "cautiously" in the case of the ECB, which sounded like a sop. It was an age-old malaise: even while the suits bang on about how much they treasure the Test match, they steadily enfeeble it.

Cricket is already full of limited-overs formats and, thanks to The Hundred, is about to gain another. Uniquely, the five-day Test incorporates timelessness:

more than any other sporting contest, it reveals character. A game can be unfinished and majestic, like La Sagrada Familia, or hurry to its demise, like a row of dominoes. Test cricket is merciless, fragile and fascinating. To lose a day would be to lose its essence. Cricket has had enough of dumbing down.

Four-day Tests do make sense in certain circumstances: England v Ireland last summer worked fine. But there are practical issues which the game shows no sign of resolving. Administrators believe, for instance, that players can get through 98 overs a day, when 90 is an endangered species. Then there's the rain. Shorten the Test match, and cricket's greatest gift to civilisation will disappear for good. And for what? A little more space in the calendar, quickly filled by the next frippery.

"[insert team name] 'til we die!"

The Hundred begins in July. *Wisden* laid out its position a year ago, since when nothing has diluted the fear that – to borrow from Kierkegaard – our summer sport risks being tranquillised by the trivial.

English cricket has bet the house on its new creation, so it would help if we didn't keep wincing. Attempting to manufacture something from nothing, the ECB ascribed ready-made characteristics to non-existent tribes. Welsh Fire, who are supposed to represent Somerset and Gloucestershire, as well as Glamorgan, were determined to get their retaliation in first: "Burning bright with intense passion and relentless energy, their hunger will prove the haters wrong." London Spirit, flying the flag for Middlesex, Essex and, er, Northamptonshire, have a "unique ability to conjure something special". That may be news to Southern Brave (Hampshire and Sussex, seldom bosom buddies), who "go boldly where others shy away".

Then there was the absence of a single home-grown head coach from the eight men's teams, demolishing a crucial pillar of the argument that The Hundred would benefit the English game. One of the new coaches, Gary Kirsten, posted a tweet that included a generic "[insert team name]". Another was Shane Warne, who used to tell us coaches were a means of transport.

We haven't even mentioned the junk-food sponsorship, or a draft which stripped some counties of their assets (Sussex contributed 11 players), and left others feeling ignored (Leicestershire contributed none). It all smacked of contrivance, carelessness and expediency. And yet, for the sake of English cricket's finances, it has to work.

Turn for the worse

The decision to punish Somerset because of their pitch for the Championship decider against Essex was in keeping with English cricket's proud mistrust of the turning ball. Officially, it was "excessive unevenness of bounce", though everyone knew Taunton was on the blacklist because of the help for spinners. While almost every other team in the country have, for years, got away with greentops that inflate the medium-pacer, spook the batsman, and defang the slow bowler, Somerset have dared to be different. Occasionally, they have gone too far, but the game is big enough to cope: domestic cricket needs variety if it is to breed Test players. The point has been made before: Northamptonshire once produced Graeme Swann and Monty Panesar, before the ECB clamped down on their turning pitches. Since then, *nada*. Somerset, meanwhile, have helped make Test bowlers of Leach and Bess. Let's not scare Taunton as we did Wantage Road.

Imaginary numbers

The news that Test players would have names and numbers on their shirts was greeted by some as an affront, as if the format should remain a secret to all but the connoisseur. But, as coaches like to say of the miscue to long-off, it was a good idea, just poorly executed.

If conditions demanded a sweater, as they often do in England, the details were obscured. And when they were visible, they were obscure – the names too small to read from a distance, the numbers legible but random. Thus, on the first day at Lord's, Australia's cordon went: 7 PAINE, [woolly sweater], 49 SMITH, 43 BANCROFT, [woolly sweater].

What did it all mean? A marketing guru in Australia argued that a player's choice of number needed to be "articulated" to the fans, who required help to "tangibilise the sport experience". No doubt tangibilisation levels went through the roof when Smith explained that 49 "doesn't have any significance – I just like it as a number". Bancroft's loyalty to 43 was unexplained. Only Paine's 7 made sense: it's his place in the batting order – an idea so simple it will never catch on.

It all adds up

In the idyllic surroundings of Prior Park College near Bath last summer, former England all-rounder Chris Lewis was in reflective mood. The school were staging a play about his time in prison for smuggling cocaine. Behind bars, he had done some thinking, and the conversation turned to loaded language. He recalled scoring a double-century for Nottinghamshire. Walking off, he heard a spectator remark: "Well struck." A harmless compliment? To Lewis, it was "subtly different". He added: "It was as if you've *bulldozed* your way to it."

The suggestion that he, a black man, had "struck" his way to 200 – rather than stroked, caressed or even batted – was not, in Lewis's view, racist. But it stemmed, he agreed, from an "unconscious bias", which is as explicit as some minorities feel they can be without angering the white mainstream.

Last year, English cricket couldn't shake off the suspicion that unconscious bias is part of the furniture. First there was Jofra Archer, regarded in some quarters as an interloper, until he helped win a World Cup, when he became a national hero. Then, as soon as his pace dropped, or he struggled on heartless pitches in New Zealand with the Kookaburra, his motivation was questioned. Out came the stereotypes: he was too cold; he was too laid-back; he was a natural athlete, so why couldn't he bowl at 95mph on demand? It was the sort of inquisition the injury-prone Mark Wood has never had to face.

Then there was Moeen Ali, whose religion helps him see cricket for what it is. When he flourishes, the English game applauds. When he doesn't, it whispers about Anglo-Saxon work ethics. Ali confessed to feeling a scapegoat. He looked, as some may see him, like an outsider.

We could go on. Adil Rashid has been suspected by Yorkshire fans of not caring. Before him, Usman Afzaal was flashy, and Alex Tudor frustrating. Before them, Devon Malcolm had a wonky radar, and Phil DeFreitas kept being dropped. In isolation, these labels might be unremarkable; together, they grow ugly. Lewis knows it's unhelpful to call it racism. But there are times when English cricket seems unwilling to call it anything at all.

Pakistan, zindabad!

Last summer disguised the fact, but in 2019 the international game rarely covered itself in glory. South Africa and Zimbabwe remained a mess; Bangladesh and Sri Lanka laboured under corruption scandals; the Indian board reverted to cronyism; Afghanistan had to change their Tudor base in India because Dehradun lacked a five-star hotel; Ireland's Test honeymoon was cut short by financial reality, since they couldn't afford to host many others, and not many others could afford to host them.

So thank goodness for the Rawalpindi Test between Pakistan and Sri Lanka in December – the first Pakistan had hosted since the Lahore terrorist attack in March 2009. Their UAE exile has always felt synthetic, games in the desert watched by administrators, journalists and men in fluorescent bibs. Mercifully, the passion back in Pakistan never died.

Re-righting history

The ICC's decision to award international status to all Twenty20 matches between member countries corroborates the bit in their mission statement about spreading the game. And it would be self-absorbed of a cricket annual to grumble about the knock-on effects for statisticians. After all, the stories this has thrown up – "Turkey roasted again", "Maldives make double figures" – are right up our street. But the move highlights an ongoing nonsense. Fifty years ago, the British government's cancellation of a tour by the cricketers of apartheid South Africa led to a five-match series between England and the Rest of the World (whose team included, needless to say, several South Africans). These games were sold to the public as Test matches, despite misgivings at the ICC. *Wisden* treated them as Tests until 1980, when the relevant stats were reluctantly removed from our records.

It would be perverse to reinstate them without common agreement. Yet it reflects poorly on cricket's ability to organise itself that the deeds of the World XI – one of the greatest teams to play in this country – have no validity beyond the first-class records, while the well-meaning Associate nations get the bells and whistles. Deep down, the ICC must know the five games should be reclassified: in October 2005, they handed Test status to their own World XI's one-off match against Australia. It's time they reconsidered 1970.

Fiddling while Australia burns

It was unedifying and yet oddly reassuring to see Australian prime minister Scott Morrison seek solace in cricket while bushfires ravaged the landscape. The people, he argued before the Sydney Test against New Zealand, would be "inspired by the great feats of our cricketers, and encouraged by the spirit shown by Australians, and the way that people have gone about remembering the terrible things that other Australians are dealing with at the moment". Gibberish, of course. But it was also a reminder of cricket's place in Australian society: it was hard to conceive of his British counterpart citing Root and Co during an apocalyptic flood. If politicians truly believe cricket can cheer everyone up, perhaps not all is lost. Morrison's views on climate change are another matter.

The height of her powers

In February, Ellyse Perry was reminded of her place in the world by the front page of an Australian newspaper. She and David Warner, the men's opener, had just won gongs at Australian cricket's awards night, yet the cut-out images used by the paper to plug the story suggested Warner was easily the taller, when the opposite is true.

Unlike Warner, Perry had enjoyed an English summer to cherish. And unlike Steve Smith, her team won the Ashes (there's no need to write in: Australia's men *retained* the urn, but still haven't won a Test series in England since 2001). Smith's appetite for runs was astonishing, but Perry was even more dominant, and is entering a class of her own. By the start of the T20 World Cup earlier this year, her Test batting and bowling averages were 78 and 18; in one-day internationals, it was 52 and 24; in T20s, 29 and 18. Sixty-four of her 171 innings for Australia were unbeaten. We are watching history at work.

A sight for four eyes?

When a bespectacled South African fan rushed across the grassy banks at the Wanderers in January to address Stokes after he was dismissed in the Fourth Test, Stokes did not take kindly to being likened to pop star Ed Sheeran. But what to make of the fact that his retort included the epithet "four-eyed"? Truly, it was as if he had forgotten that Leach, his faithful sidekick during the Headingley climax, was a four-eyed so-and-so himself.

Right, you've seen off the shine…

At Port Elizabeth, England became the first team to play 500 Tests away from home. At Johannesburg a few days later, they became the first to score half a million runs (an unknown number during batting collapses). The Test team have always been there, battling away in the background, often in the dead of night, infuriating us, bringing us joy. As we brace ourselves for The Hundred, here's to the day England notch up a million.

WISDEN'S CHAMPION COUNTY

Red Rose to the top

JON HOTTEN

Late last year, and with a heavy heart, I was rereading Bob Willis's *Diary of a Cricket Season*, written in 1978. After only three paragraphs, Bob was in off the long run: "The early weeks are absurdly cluttered with one-day cricket; you either seem to be playing 55-over games or 40-over games; the Championship gets lost until almost the end of May."

It reminded me of an email I had received from *Wisden*. They too had been taking stock of an era passed. This one had begun in 1963 when a second competition joined the Championship, and ended in 2019, with the announcement of The Hundred, the first domestic tournament not to feature the counties. The Almanack had compiled a spreadsheet of those 57 summers, tracking the performance of every side in each competition, and awarded points to the winners, runners-up and – where applicable – semi-finalists. The system weighted the Championship above the others, but aimed to keep things simple.

How had 1978 played out? County Champions: Kent. Gillette Cup: Sussex. John Player League: Hampshire. Benson and Hedges Cup: Kent. More from Bob's diary, Sunday, May 14: "Kent have never been my favourite bunch of blokes, and I liked them even less when they beat us in the Sunday League… We had them in a lot of bother until John Shepherd saw them home." The next April, Shepherd was one of the *Wisden* Five, along with Gower, Lever, Old and Radley.

I looked at the spreadsheet again. Each entry, I realised, was not simply an outcome: it was a story, a day, a week, a season in the life, in many lives. Eras formed, teams rose and fell.

- Late-1970s **Somerset**, always at Lord's, with Beefy, Viv and Joel, Dasher Denning and the Demon of Frome.
- **Middlesex's** three Championships in the first half of the 1980s: Brearley, Gatting, Emburey, Edmonds, *Daniel* – what a bowler the Diamond was.
- **Warwickshire** in 1994 and '95, a treble, then a double: Reeve, Small, Brown, Munton, Donald, the Smiths, *Lara* – greatest few weeks of batting ever.

WISDEN CHAMPION COUNTY – SCORING OF POINTS

	Championship	Knockout	League
Winner.....................	14	8	8
Runners-up	10	6	6
Third........................	6	–	4
Fourth......................	2	–	2
Beaten semi-finalists	–	3	–

Wisden's champion county: Lancashire celebrate the 1998 NatWest Trophy. Gary Yates, Peter Martin, Ian Austin, Neil Fairbrother, Mike Atherton (partially hidden), Wasim Akram, Mark Chilton (partially hidden), John Crawley, Andrew Flintoff, Warren Hegg, Glen Chapple and Graham Lloyd.

- **Gloucestershire** around 2000, unbeatable at the short stuff: Russell, Alleyne, Barnett, Snape, *Harvey* – the "Freak", with his supernatural slower one.
- Further forward, the **Sussex** of Mushy and Goodwin, the **Surrey** of Hollioake and the noble Ramprakash…

The effect of overseas players was visible. Uniquely, **Nottinghamshire** recorded a Eurovision-style *nul points* decade, in the 1970s, despite the presence for several years of Garry Sobers. Then came Clive Rice and Richard Hadlee, who arrived in 1978 but *landed* in 1981, with 105 wickets at 14, as Nottinghamshire swept to the Championship title. There was another in 1987, when Hadlee took 97 at 11, the Trent Bridge greentop now feared throughout the country. Meanwhile, **Sussex** managed no Championship top-four finishes in the 1990s, when they mustered 14 points in all competitions – and then found Mushtaq Ahmed. In 85 first-class games, he claimed 478 wickets at 25, and Sussex had their first three Championship crowns.

It tripped the memory, this chart, revealing the most successful team of each decade:

- 1960s: **Yorkshire**
- 1970s: **Kent** (by a mile, with the highest tally of any side in any decade)
- 1980s: **Middlesex** (by a hair, from Essex)
- 1990s: **Lancashire** and **Warwickshire** (a tie!)
- 2000s: **Sussex** (pipping Lancashire and Surrey)
- 2010s: **Somerset** (despite the agonies of a Championship blank; a sharing of power, rather than a concentration of it)

There were 322 points between the bottom county – chin up, Derbyshire – and the first, but only 42 between the top four: Kent in fourth with 364, Essex with 375, Warwickshire with 393, and – breasting the tape – **Lancashire** with 406.

Some Moneyballing of the top-line stats underlined old truths. Lancashire were not a pre-eminent Championship team, accruing only one title (in 2011), and just 114 of their points, in the longest form. On that score, they were trumped by seven counties, with Middlesex top (though only sixth overall). They, Essex and Yorkshire accounted for 22 titles, nearly two-fifths of the total.

Lancashire's power came in limited-overs cricket. According to the points system, they have been the second-most successful side in the Gillette Cup and its successors (behind Warwickshire), second in the B&H (behind Kent), third in the Sunday League (behind Essex and Kent), and joint-first in T20 (with Somerset). In all, their 17 short-form titles bested Warwickshire's 13, and the 11 by Kent and Essex. Kent's extraordinary record as runners-up – five times in both knockout cups, four times in the Sunday League, once in the T20 Cup – showed their depth and consistency.

Doctor Who and the Beatles live on, the current prime minister was not yet born

But it has been the Red Rose era, a dynastic span started by Jack Bond, who captained Lancashire to their first five one-day titles. Bond could call on Farokh Engineer and Clive Lloyd, the proto-one-day spinner in Jack Simmons, a blueprint of wicketkeeper-batsmen, middle-order power and containing bowlers that still holds good. The key was succession, from David Hughes in the dying of the light through John Abrahams, Neil Fairbrother, Mike Watkinson, John Crawley, Warren Hegg, the eternal Glen Chapple, a northern brew of the home-grown and the glorious import: Wasim Akram, Stuart Law, Carl Hooper. Everyone has done it, but no one has done it quite like Lancashire.

The spreadsheet measured change, too. The prime minister during the 1963 season was Harold Macmillan, born in 1894, when Grace was in his autumn. That summer had not just the new Gillette Cup, but the first Doctor Who and Beatles album, and the Great Train Robbery. The distance between then and now seems mutable: Doctor Who and the Beatles live on, the current prime minister was not yet born. Cricket has got both longer (four days) and shorter (20 overs). There has been evolution in the competitions, and a flow of sponsors, from cigarettes to insurance, redolent of changes in how we live. There has been a revolution in playing technique, especially from 2003 and the introduction of the Twenty20 Cup. That idea has become the game's second Big Bang, its expansion into global franchises ushering in The Hundred, and its centralisation of power and talent.

In 2015, there was a refocusing of English cricket. It turned the way the wind was blowing, and won a World Cup. What a day it was, and what a team they are. But England's Test side paid a price: 2019 was the first year this millennium they had not won a series, the cry for players with more durable skills echoing back into a Championship programme shunted to either end of what is now a white-ball season.

Sweeping the 1970s: Kent dominated the decade like no one since. Derek Underwood (partially hidden), David Nicholls, John Shepherd, Asif Iqbal, Graham Johnson, Norman Graham, Richard Elms (partially hidden), Bob Woolmer, Mike Denness, Alan Ealham, Colin Cowdrey and Alan Knott.

There's a glinting uncertainty to the summer of 2020, and those beyond. Crisp-sponsored franchises lack the hinterland that comes alive with the names and competitions scattered across decades. And yet the sport has always been in one kind of flux or other, as Bob's *Diary of a Season* showed. Cricket is a slow game in an accelerating world, and things get left behind as the future rushes in. Exactly what we have lost is the question.

Jon Hotten is the author of six books, including The Elements of Cricket, *to be published in 2020.*

WISDEN COUNTY TABLE, 1963–2019

		Championship	Limited-overs Cup	Benson and Hedges	League	Twenty20	Total
1	Lancashire	114	116	62	82	**32**	406
2	Warwickshire	141	**137**	40	52	23	393
3	Essex	156	48	55	**96**	20	375
4	Kent	132	58	**69**	88	17	364
5	Surrey	144	76	54	22	29	325
6	Middlesex	**170**	68	28	36	8	310
7	Worcestershire	108	62	44	78	14	306
8	Somerset	92	89	34	50	**32**	297
9	Yorkshire	152	60	38	28	9	287
10	Hampshire	86	82	25	55	31	279
11	Nottinghamshire	116	42	26	44	23	251
12	Sussex	77	91	**6**	45	20	239
13	Leicestershire	92	**21**	45	50	30	238
14	Northamptonshire	54	55	29	22	25	185
15	Gloucestershire	46	63	33	26	9	177
16	Glamorgan	66	**21**	9	26	6	128
17	Durham	62	25	–	**4**	9	100
18	Derbyshire	**16**	26	23	16	**3**	84

WISDEN COUNTY TABLE, BY DECADE

	1st	2nd	3rd	4th	5th	Last
1960s	**Yorks (74)**	Worcs (50)	Warwicks (38)	Glam (36)	Kent (30)	Essex (4)
1970s	**Kent (145)**	Lancs (81)	Leics (75)	*Middx (64)	*Essex (64)	Notts (0)
1980s	**Middx (136)**	Essex (132)	Notts (100)	Worcs (71)	Hants (54)	Glam (3)
1990s	†Lancs (118)	†Warwicks (118)	Essex (76)	Kent (71)	Leics (69)	‡Sussex (14)
2000s	**Sussex (93)**	Lancs (89)	Surrey (86)	Warwicks (73)	Glos (64)	Derbys (3)
2010s	**Somerset (96)**	Warwicks (81)	Yorks (75)	Notts (64)	Hants (62)	Derbys (3)

In this context, 1960s means 1963–69.   *   *4th equal.*   †   *1st equal.*
‡   *Durham became the 18th first-class county in 1992. They finished the 1990s with 0pts.*

WISDEN COUNTY TABLE, BY DECADE AND COMPETITION

	Championship	Limited-overs Cup	Benson & Hedges	League	Twenty20
1960s	Yorks (58)	Sussex (28)		Lancs (8)	
	Worcs (38)	Warwicks (25)		Hants (6)	
	Glam (36)	Yorks (16)		Essex (4)	
1970s	Kent (54)	Lancs (47)	Kent (30)	Kent (44)	
	Middx (32)	Somerset (23)	Leics (22)	Leics (32)	
	Hants/Surrey (30)	Sussex (23)	Surrey (17)	Essex (26)	
1980s	Middx (66)	Middx (36)	Essex (27)	Essex (34)	
	Essex (60)	Surrey (20)	Middx (22)	Sussex (22)	
	Notts (48)	Warwicks (17)	Kent (21)	Worcs (22)	
1990s	Leics (44)	Warwicks (34)	Lancs (36)	Lancs (36)	
	Middx (40)	Lancs (24)	Worcs (23)	Warwicks (30)	
	Warwicks (40)	Northants (23)	Kent (18)	Kent (28)	
2000s	Sussex (48)	Glos (27)	Glos (14)	Essex (22)	Leics (22)
	Surrey (44)	Hants (21)	Surrey (11)	Sussex (20)	Surrey (20)
	Durham (38)	Lancs/Warwicks (21)	Warwicks (8)	Glam/Worcs (18)	Kent (17)
2010s	Yorks (54)	Warwicks (28)			Hants (31)
	Somerset (52)	Somerset (26)			Northants (24)
	Warwicks (36)	Surrey (26)			Lancs (20)

In this context, 1960s means 1963–69. The limited-overs cup has had various guises, from the Gillette Cup in 1963 to the Royal London One-Day Cup in 2019.
The League began in 1969; the points for the 1960s reflect the top three in that year. It ended in 2009.
The B&H began in 1972 and ended in 2002.   The Twenty20 competition began in 2003.

BOB WILLIS, 1949–2019

"I must have been bloody mad"

PAUL ALLOTT

There are some things you cannot be late for. Rushing to see Bob for the last time, I nearly missed him, thanks to the vagaries of South Western Railway's service to Putney. That would have tickled him, for he was a champion of public transport. He knew every bus route, every underground line, every station; he even knew the timetables (he was more informative than Transport for London). I arrived at his home with – it turned out – seven minutes to spare, enough for one final hand squeeze. Bob himself was late only once: two weeks later, for his funeral, when the hearse got stuck in traffic in Barnes. He should have gone by bus.

Our friendship had begun towards the end of his playing days, and endured nearly four decades of broadcasting, travelling and holidaying together. We became the best of pals. It all started at Old Trafford, during the 1981 Ashes series which ultimately defined him. I was freshly selected, not yet 25, and in awe of the dressing-room. They were heroes, never mind team-mates: Brearley, Boycott, Botham, Knott – and Willis, well established as England's premier fast bowler, and more than seven years my senior. I thought of him as stern, unapproachable and a little frightening. Yet he welcomed me with a smile and, after practice, was the first to buy me a beer in The Romper. My preconceptions probably stemmed from a deep respect, and a sense of not wanting to let him down.

Before we bowled together, however, we batted together, and put on an improbable 56 for the tenth wicket, at which point Bob tried to hit Dennis Lillee back over his head. The partnership may have inspired Brearley to keep us in tandem with the new ball. I was a novice, but I had a maiden fifty and my home crowd behind me: there was little time for nerves. Between us, we took four wickets in seven deliveries: Bob ripped out John Dyson, Kim Hughes and Graham Yallop, and I got my first Test wicket, Graeme Wood. We didn't play many Tests together, but he was instrumental in my success in both my first and his last, against West Indies at Headingley in 1984, when I took my best figures of six for 61.

Bob always cared, and had a mission, largely unfulfilled, to bring about a slimmed-down county structure. It began on the boundary at Nagpur during a four-month tour of India in 1981-82 – my first England trip, his tenth. Sheets of foolscap were filled by a new domestic schedule, with four-day matches separated from one-day cricket to allow rest and practice; some Tests were standalone fixtures. Bob was 20 years ahead of his time. Later, he co-founded the Cricket Reform Group, which championed the game's restructuring. We even had an audience with an intrigued Duncan Fletcher in Bulawayo in late 2004. In the end, though, Bob was forced to concede there were too many interests at work.

Lauren Clark

Bowled together, batted together, drank together: Bob Willis and Paul Allott on holiday in Sussex.

We also shared a love of beer, the fast bowler's time-honoured staple; Bob was an honorary member of CAMRA. He later educated me in the world's wines, with one exception: life was too short, he argued, to drink Italian. Dylan and Wagner almost exclusively sustained his musical tastes; Dylan I loved, but he took mercy on me with Wagner. Golf proved a frustration, not through want of trying. He was an entertaining partner, though, because you never quite knew what was coming: he could play four sublime holes, then five-putt for no apparent reason.

Our travels gave us our best experiences, some with an unexpected twist. After months of meticulous planning of our route around the winelands of Central Otago, Marlborough and Hawke's Bay, Bob decided within a day of landing in Auckland that he would be teetotal for the entire tour. He suffered from insomnia, and thought six weeks off the booze would restore his sleep. Needless to say, it did not, though at least it provided me with a driver. It also emphasised his strength of will, and the stubborn streak that sustained his career.

After simultaneous operations on both knees, and a withering assessment of his fitness from Tony Greig following the Centenary Test at Melbourne in

1976-77, Bob embarked on a regime of slow-paced distance running. It prolonged and rejuvenated his bowling. He advocated the method for all aspiring quicks, and remained convinced the modern breed spent too much time in the gym.

Perhaps he could have spared himself at least some of the effort. Not long ago, when we were commentating at Taunton, he marked out his run, all 43 paces. He got to the end, a yard or two inside the boundary, looked back at the stumps, and said: "I must have been bloody mad!"

If there was one thing he could have changed, it would not have been his high-stepping, idiosyncratic run-up, which became the most mimicked in the game, or his awkward, angular delivery. (He thought he bowled with a perfect sideways action, like Fred Trueman, until he saw himself on TV, and was mortified.) No, it would have been his penchant for no-balls. He delivered 939 in Test cricket, more than any other bowler, which added about 50 miles to the Willis clock, and probably deprived him of 20 wickets. Little wonder he thought himself mad. (In those days, no-balls didn't count against the bowler. If they had, Sky Sports statistician Benedict Bermange reckons his Test bowling average would have risen from 25 to 28.)

I often wondered how viciously he would have admonished himself for overstepping so frequently, in his guise as Sky's hanging judge on "The Verdict", which he made required viewing. If Bob's TV persona was carefully constructed, there was no disguising his apoplexy at England's Test frailties – although in real life he was more usually caring, funny, shy and determined. And, deep down, he enjoyed nothing better than watching England succeed. The players knew that too, even those watching from behind the sofa.

Bob was undoubtedly a great bowler. When he reached 300 Test wickets, only three others had beaten him to it: Trueman, Lance Gibbs and Lillee. He was at his best when he bowled fast, angling the ball into the right-hander and getting steep bounce from a length. His best spell will always resonate, yet he nearly missed Headingley '81 altogether. He had been ill the week before, and out of form, so the selectors picked Mike Hendrick instead. But Bob insisted he was fit, and they changed their minds. Hendrick's invitation (we received letters from the TCCB in those days) was pinched from the postman's sack by an astute secretary at Derbyshire. And a hastily arranged Warwickshire Second XI game gave him a chance of bowling some overs. On the morning of the Test, Brearley wanted Willis ahead of off-spinner John Emburey. Botham's Ashes, yes, but with due deference to Willis's Headingley, where he seemed entranced – as he so often did. He regarded sledging as unnecessary.

He had a wonderful, self-deprecating sense of humour, masking a long battle with depression, which only those close to him knew about. Once, we went to pick up our accreditation in Melbourne, only to find no pass for Bob. There was, though, one for Bruce Willis, which he wore uncomplainingly for the next couple of months. Bob would have been the last person to think of himself as an all-action hero, but it described my old friend better than he ever knew.

Paul Allott played six of his 13 Tests alongside Bob Willis, and took 652 first-class and 321 one-day wickets in a career spanning 16 years.

MEMORIES OF THE SUPER OVER

"Whatever happens will not define you"

Joe Root

There wasn't the normal Lord's hum, but pockets of pin-drop silence, like a game of snooker. Jofra was unlucky when the first ball was called wide, and he got quite animated. To keep his composure after that was a credit to him. When Neesham hit that six, I thought back to Eden Gardens in 2016 – this surely can't happen again. Watching the ball sail into the stands was a sinking feeling.

But Jof has such strong self-belief. From the penultimate delivery, he fielded off his own bowling, and I screamed: "Hold it!" If he had hit the stumps with a shy, Neesham would have been run out – but if he had missed, it would have handed New Zealand an extra run.

When Jos took the bails off next ball, I had a great view from midwicket. Straight behind him, on the balcony, all the support staff and coaches were bouncing around, and to the left were the families. Jofra ran off and did a Klinsmann dive, but everyone hurried after Jos, wheeling away into the bottom corner of the ground.

Seeing my parents up above us, with my grandfather, little boy, wife and friends, was really special. Jonny Bairstow picked me up. I punched him in the chest, and screamed in his face: "World Cup! World Cup!" The other squad members were soon on the field too. I have never seen Moeen Ali run so fast. It was pure elation.

Jofra Archer

When Woody got run out off the last ball of our 50 overs, everyone was so confused about what came next. But the waiting period got us all fired up, especially me. At one point, I didn't think we were even going to tie the game, so to be given another life meant everyone had that little bit more fight.

I wanted to bowl the super over, but didn't get confirmation until about two minutes before we warmed up. I usually bowl at the death of a 50-over innings, so I thought it was likely to be me, but I wouldn't have been too upset if it hadn't: at least I wouldn't have been responsible if we'd lost.

When the umpire signalled a wide on the tramline first ball, I asked Morgs to review it. He said, "You can't with a wide, Jof, I'm sorry," and we laughed. Even when I was hit for six, I was not worried. You have to accept you are probably going to go for a boundary. We had the misfield, but kept our heads, and limited them to ones and twos.

When Jos completed the run-out, I set off in the opposite direction to the others, and did a chest slide. Then we all joined up, and people started jumping on me. It was the sweetest moment I've had on a cricket field. I'll be honest: it almost brought a tear to my eye. As someone who has always loved the game,

Consolation prize: Chris Woakes comforts Martin Guptill after victory evades New Zealand.

it still feels surreal to be a World Cup winner. I can only imagine how special it feels for the others, because they were on that journey for four years. They went through what happened in 2015. In fact, I feel happier for them than I do for myself.

Chris Woakes

Like all the others, I enjoyed a minute of utter madness, picking up Mark Wood and tossing him in the air. Then I saw Martin Guptill still lying on the ground. I've always felt that the only thing worse than a sore loser is a sore winner. I'm sure people could understand why we were all running around like headless chickens, but going over to commiserate seemed the right thing to do. It probably helped that we've always got on well with the New Zealanders.

Jimmy Neesham was there too, and I said: "Hard luck, lads, great game." I half-tried to pick Guptill off the turf, but he wasn't budging. Neesham just said: "Nah, we're all good, mate. Congratulations." It wasn't until I saw the photo later of me and Guptill that I thought back to 2005 and the image of Andrew Flintoff with Brett Lee at Edgbaston. I was there that day on the groundstaff. Now, here I was as a player, in a moment I'll never forget.

Mark Wood

Umpire Aleem Dar came into the dressing-room, and Eoin Morgan told him: "Woody's torn his side." Even throwing a ball was going to hurt, so Aleem said a substitute fielder was fine. I watched from the bench with the physio and the doctor.

Ben was so intense: he had that eye-of-the-tiger look. He headed out the back to gather himself. Jos Buttler is someone who's normally really calm, yet he was quite animated. At one point, he was on his haunches, hitting the physio bed with his fists, shouting expletives. That's definitely not like him. But when he and Stokesy went back out, they were both in the zone.

I felt sick the whole time but, when Jos hit that last ball for four, it settled me down. I thought 15 was a great score. During their over, I was biting my nails, unable to stand still. Moeen Ali and I were guessing every ball what Jofra was going to do; I'm not sure we got any right.

Jos Buttler

I was excited to have another chance to affect things. I had got out at a crucial time, and it was tough watching, but suddenly I was back in the game. I started to pad up, because I assumed it would be me – and wanted it to be me. I'd been involved in a few super overs, so I knew what to expect.

Trent Boult bowled a good over, and it did feel like we had to scramble hard. Stokesy skewed one over third man, then I hit one to deep cover that the fielder didn't pick up, so we managed two. After I hit the last ball for four, Stokesy gave me a massive fist-bump: we got 15, which felt like a decent effort, plus we had Jofra to bowl, and no one had got him away in the regular innings.

As we walked back out, Rash said we had Allah with us, and Morgs spoke about the luck of the Irish. We had definitely enjoyed some good fortune – when the ball deflected off Stokesy's bat to the boundary, that must be how it feels to win the lottery.

I've watched the super over back on TV and, when Neesham hits the six, you think the game is over. But on the field it never felt lost. We knew how good Jofra was. I just thought: do your job, don't get ahead of yourself. That was the same right down to the run-out.

People have often asked whether I thought I might be about to drop the World Cup, but it never entered my mind: there was no time. It was a simple bit of fielding. The ball goes straight to Jason, and when he throws it in, you know the bounce at Lord's will be true: just catch it, and break the stumps. I knew as soon as Guptill had hit it that I was going to have time, and he was a long way short.

Then I remember the biggest and best feeling of pure emotion for 30 seconds or a minute, with everyone running around, and me throwing my gloves in the air. I don't remember anyone saying anything, just running and hugging…

Eoin Morgan

The only moment I felt rushed all day was when we batted in the super over. The plan before the game, in the unlikely event of one happening, had been to send out Jason with Jos, but because Ben had played so well – and almost everyone else so terribly – we thought he had to go out again. I asked him if that was all right, and he said he'd be fine, even though he could barely breathe.

When Boult started bowling yorkers from the Nursery End, I thought that, if a wicket fell, it would be tough for a right-hander to hit him up the hill. So I hurried to get my pads on. It was the biggest panic of the day.

After the 2016 World T20 final, you never think you have enough runs, but Jofra is the best, and we felt we could defend 15. Marais Erasmus called us over as we were walking out to field, to tell us about boundary countback: 15's a win, he said, 16 a defeat. But when Neesham hit that six, New Zealand needed seven off four. It was theirs to lose.

I was talking to Jofra every ball. What matters as a captain is that you receive a response which makes sense. If the bowler's talking gibberish, or his eyes are glazed over, you need to take more time, and ask him what he's doing. The only time he wasn't thinking clearly was when he wanted DRS for the first-ball wide! But his presence of mind was extraordinary. From the fifth ball, which was supposed to be a bouncer, he decided not to try to run Neesham out: if he'd missed, it would have been game over.

The last delivery to Guptill was superb. We only had three fielders on the off side: short third man, point and cover. So Jofra had to follow him if he tried to create room. I was at the bowler's end as Jason gathered the ball at deep midwicket, and Guptill was just turning for the second: he had no chance. It was a good throw, not a great one, and Jos did unbelievable work at the stumps.

We were all running around, trying to grab each other as fast as we could. It was brilliant. That feeling didn't stop. Even now, I still think about it.

Liam Plunkett

I remember listening to Petr Cech, the former Chelsea goalkeeper, talking about the penalty shootout in the 2012 Champions League final, and how each one felt as if it was happening in slow motion. That's how it was for me, like I was in a film. Adil Rashid and I covered the areas behind the wicket – I was at short third man – and we chatted about what we were doing. We just wanted to protect our areas.

Even though Jofra got hit for six, I always felt we were going to win. For some reason, I was never worried. I knew how skilful he was: he'd missed one ball, but didn't usually miss many. When I saw J-Roy get to the last ball quickly, all I could think was: "Get it in Jos's hands." The feeling when the bails came off was insane. I met Morgs on my celebratory run, and he jumped on me. It was perfect, after the way we had come through the campaign, that we were all out there on the field together.

Jason Roy

Morgs told me and Jos to get our pads on, but then there was a discussion. More thought went into the fact that the shorter boundary from the Nursery End was downhill for a left-hander. Ben had been in a long time, and had the pace of the wicket. He was exhausted, but we were saying to him: "Come on, mate, get a Red Bull down you, and get back out there."

Because I had been a member of the team that lost the World Twenty20 final when Carlos Brathwaite had his day out, at no stage did I think we had won. I knew Jof was going to try to hit the hole, and the ball was likely to come my way at cow corner. The third did, but it took a slight bobble, and I stood up too quickly as I went to collect it. I thought: "How the hell have I done that?" Maybe I was over-keen to laser it in. They pinched two.

I thought I had got to the next ball quick enough to throw it to the bowler's end. They were my nearest stumps, but not the ones I should have been aiming for: that's what pressure does. My thinking was not as clear as it should have been. Two more.

Thankfully, I found a happy medium for the final ball. I visualised it coming to me, and didn't have the level of anxiety you might expect. I was more on edge watching it back – which I didn't do until Christmas. For months, I had been saying to myself: "Imagine if I'd fumbled!" It would have been catastrophic – and tough to come back from.

At the time, though, I knew I had to do what I had trained for. You can always overthink things: "If I don't get this ball in, we lose." I actually took longer to gather it than I had the previous ones – I knew that if Guptill was at that far end as I was picking it up, there was no way he was getting back.

Luckily it was somewhere near Jos. I can't remember the next few seconds very well. I set off running, then stopped, fell to my knees, and thought "Holy shhh…".

Adil Rashid

About five minutes before our bowling over started, there were a lot of balls being thrown into mitts, and we were buzzing. Morgs asked: "What have you got for me, Rash? What do you reckon?" I told him: "Don't worry. Allah's with us." "Yes, he is," he said. Later, Morgs told me he must have been with us, because we'd had the rub of the green – although I wasn't expecting our conversation to be revealed in the press conference, or to go viral.

As we warmed up, I couldn't stop thinking what our celebrations would be like. There was a lot of talk among the lads. Were we going to hug each other? Which direction were we going to run? Me and Mo said that, if we won, we would run to each other.

I was at short fine leg, talking to Puds [Liam Plunkett] and Jos. I sensed excitement, not nerves. We knew we couldn't let four years of hard work go to waste. At the end, it was an emotional time. Part of that, I'm sure, was because the win had not come easy. We will all cherish it for the rest of our lives.

Jonny Bairstow

Woody turned like the *QE2* as he went for what would have been the winning run, and we were all wondering why he was wearing chest and thigh pads, plus an arm-guard; even he chuckled about it afterwards. There was disbelief when the scores were tied. Nobody really knew the rules. When it became clear we were having a super over, the questions started. Which end? New ball or old?

Uprooted: Jonny Bairstow and Joe Root, companions since the age of 12.

Who's bowling for them, who's batting for us? All the batters wanted a go, but there was no disappointment: we had to remain calm.

When Neesham hit that one, the crowd behind me were shouting that the ball was coming my way. They were not wrong: I watched the six fly straight over my head. The atmosphere was electric. No one could remember Lord's that loud, ever.

For the last ball, I was on the fence at deep square but, by the time Jos had taken off the bails, I had sprinted past the umpire. As soon as Jason's pick-up was clean, I knew the throw would be fine. Suddenly we were all at the bottom of the hill going crazy. Rooty jumped on me, and started whacking me, and shouting. Joe and I have been through plenty since we first met on the Yorkshire Academy aged 12. It was amazing.

Ben Stokes

"Whatever happens will not define you as a cricketer." I thought it was important for Jofra to hear those words from me as we walked out again. If there was anyone who understood the pressure of defending a score in a global final, it was me. After being on the receiving end of Carlos Brathwaite, I knew how things could go wrong.

I was angry it had come to this, that I had not been able to finish the job in regulation time. As Mark Wood and I left the field, I kicked my bat in frustration. I told Eoin Morgan I thought Jason Roy and Jos Buttler should bat in the super over, because of the way they had played throughout the tournament. But he said he wanted a left-hand/right-hand combination. "Sweet," I said, accepting it was a good point.

It meant I had to get my game head on again. I went out the back into the toilets to separate myself from all that had gone on, and enter a different place mentally. I wanted to get rid of the feelings that had built up over a crazy couple of hours. I wanted a little bit of me time.

When Jos hit the last delivery of our over through midwicket for four, I thought we'd won the World Cup there and then. I jumped in the air, arms aloft. I was going nuts, because I couldn't see New Zealand getting 16 off Jofra.

In normal circumstances, I would have been fielding at deep midwicket. But I was sore and tired, so I asked J-Roy to switch with me. The decisive moment in New Zealand's over was not the six struck by Neesham, but a stroke of luck from the penultimate ball. Jofra bowled a bumper, and an under-edge crashed into Neesham's boot. Instead of the ball leaking behind square leg for two, it dribbled for a single.

A few seconds later, as Jofra entered his delivery stride for a perfectly executed yorker, I was 15 yards off the boundary, walking in to put pressure on the batsmen. Realising that J-Roy's throw had beaten Martin Guptill's dive, I pushed off on a run to join my team-mates, lost my footing and ended up on my backside. Then something weird happened: I started crying. The more I tried to stop the flow, the more the tears leaked. I never thought I would cry on a cricket field. But, on a day like that, I couldn't have cared less.

Interviews by Richard Gibson, Will Macpherson and Lawrence Booth.

WOMEN AT MCC

Minority report

EMMA JOHN

Your first mistake is buying beer at the Long Room bar during a T20 game. Turns out there's an ancient statute – or perhaps a curse, you're still not quite clear – that means your drinks can never leave the room, much like the Holy Grail in *Indiana Jones and the Last Crusade*. So you down them, and follow directions to the Bowlers' Bar. Where you buy more beers, then discover you can't take those outside either. So you down them, and walk shakily back to your seat. You aren't sure how many overs you've missed, but in the meantime the numbers on the scorecard have turned to squiggles, and you've sort of forgotten who's playing. One of them's Middlesex, right?

Wait, that *isn't* your first mistake. Your first mistake was showing up an hour before the start of play. You thought that left plenty of time to get a seat, but the Pavilion benches had been entirely papered over: *Telegraphs*, *Timeses*, spread proprietorially from the front row to the upper balcony. The sole remaining spot was next to a stinky bin and behind a pillar that obscured the slip cordon. You sat down on the bench. It was like a packing crate. You should have brought a cushion. Rookie error #3.

*   *   *

In 1998, seized by a rare fit of liberality, Marylebone Cricket Club finally opened their doors to women. I was one of the first to put my name down and, last year, one of the first to graduate from the notoriously long waiting list. There were 134 women elected to full membership in 2019; we were the largest female intake the club had seen. Although, to offer perspective, there are currently 18,000 full members of MCC.

Some see membership as a cynical way to guarantee a seat for every day of the Lord's Tests. Well, let's not pretend. Unfettered access to the ground, its historic Pavilion, and its exclusive members-and-friends stands, at the ridiculously good value of £600 per annum, is precisely what makes a 20-year wait worthwhile. But there are other privileges: a say in the future of the most prestigious cricket venue in the world; use of facilities that include a peerless indoor school and a real-tennis court; plus, of course, an excuse to wear those eye-watering club colours.

*   *   *

My red pass lands on my doormat in March, embossed in gold, and stiff as a brigadier's upper lip. Twenty years is half my lifetime. When you've been waiting that long for something, it doesn't occur that you may not be ready.

Front of the queue: the number of women joining MCC is growing.

You've been in the Pavilion before – it's not new to you. Or is it? So many rooms you're now allowed into, but are too nervous to enter; staircases you can't tell apart; corridors that don't join up; unmarked doors that usher you into a display of vintage tour blazers; a parlour of white-linened tables that smells like school, where men in grey suits and navy ties sit alone, chewing carefully on bacon rolls. Even the ground you know so well looks alien from this angle. Of course it does – you can't see Victorian brick.

You've never experienced the Long Room like this, either. Never walked in during a game, seen the rows of empty stools, wondered if you're brave enough to sit on one. Decided you're not. Hovered, instead, in no man's land, holding your breath, hoping a steward won't demand you move. An echo amplifies the softest shuffle, turns a hallway into a cathedral. Maybe that's why no one speaks. Portraits of cricketing grandees stare down. They should put candles in front of them. Send up prayers to St Grace.

There's a shout from the middle, a distant cheer, a smatter of applause. You see the batsman heading in, and you're terrified of being in the way, desperate to get out of this room, this room you were once so eager to conquer. So you spin round, straight into his replacement.

*   *   *

There is solidarity in being a minority. It was at my second game that I met Olivia, whom I sat beside, I'll admit, entirely on the basis of gender. She described her first visit as "horrendous" – the horror of arriving at a party where you know nobody. Since then, some of the female members have taken matters into their own hands and created a Facebook group. If you are planning to be at a game, you can post a message and find out who else is going. A digital response to the old boys' network.

I joined immediately. I also discovered the library. It wasn't as grand as I'd imagined – just a small room next to the museum, modestly furnished, walls stacked floor to ceiling with what appeared to be every cricket book ever published. Unthreatening and, most of the time, uninhabited. Not as sociable, perhaps, as joining the bridge or chess or backgammon societies, whose existence I learned of in the club newsletter. But it made me feel, for the first time, at home.

* * *

Thursday. First day of the Ashes Test. OK, it's not, not strictly – the first day was a Wednesday washout – but it feels like it. Bright green outfield, bright blue sky. Pat Cummins reaches his mark, and every conversation in the ground pauses. Nothing is as quiet as the silence of 30,000 people.

Four and a half hours you've been here. By 6.30am, the line of egg-and-bacon ties was nearing the end of St John's Wood Road, about to turn the corner towards the hospital. A thermos of coffee and two slices of toast, kept warm in tin foil, saw you through until the gates opened. No wonder members are caught napping in the afternoon session. Queuing is brutal.

But the cricket is electric. And next to you is Robbie, a nice bloke you knew at college who has offered to help you acclimatise, teach you the seat-bagging etiquette, stop you repeating the beer mistake. He played for the club before he became a member, and even he found the place intimidating. It's easy to assume everyone is old, or posh, or not your kind of person, says Robbie. But you find your people. Then you're friends until you die.

You fall in with his rituals, which are comfortingly alcoholic. Only diehards want to sit on those bum-numbing Pavilion benches, so you're on the plushy tip-up seats in the new Warner Stand. You're heading to the bar when a couple of chaps – maybe ten years older than you, maybe 20 – summon you over as if you're their waitress. They've spotted the MCC colours on your hat.

"Can I just say?" The dominant male is speaking. "Can I just say? I voted against women the first time round. But the second time, I voted for you." There's a pause, which you sense you're supposed to fill with gratitude. Instead you ask what changed his mind. He smirks at his friend. "Good-looking women like you!"

* * *

Several of our Facebook group were playing members, which meant they had bypassed the epic waiting list and been given the freedom of Lord's years ago. In the early days, some of these veterans had been accosted by strangers and asked: "What are you doing here?" Being patronised or pawed was an occupational hazard. My own induction came early in the season, trying to

Sarah Williams

Inner sanctum: watching the denouement of the World Cup final from the committee room.

resist an unwanted hug from a stranger on the Pavilion steps. ("It's OK," he told me boozily, "we can have a cuddle.")

In the wake of #metoo, MCC were serious about changing the culture. A senior executive had resigned after an investigation into his conduct. One man was expelled from the club after verbally abusing a fellow member simply for being female. And at the AGM in May 2019, as a woman revealed she had been assaulted during a major match, the membership voted through their first official code of conduct. We were told there were disciplinary panels to investigate breaches, and urged to report incidents straightaway.

A letter had gone out from the president, too, celebrating MCC's increasing diversity, and encouraging everyone to make new female members feel welcome. Over the course of the summer, I could sense the goodwill efforts: the smiles and nods; the awkward-yet-well-meant conversation starters from the men sitting alongside me; the gentle helpfulness of the stewards. It was these gestures, as much as anything, that persuaded me the only way to feel like a member was to act like one.

So I did. I went along to a members' forum, where a red-faced gentleman roared about the lack of QUALITY REFRESHMENTS in the Long Room, and demanded the beer be served at a RELEVANT TEMPERATURE. I booked an induction session at the real-tennis court, where I discovered that the trajectory of a heavy, hand-stitched cloth ball is as difficult to predict as Murali's mystery spin. And before long, I started running into people whose names I knew – people, dare I say, I started to call friends.

*   *   *

Last day of the season. Rain's been pouring down all morning, but you cycled through it anyway. Which is why you're now standing in the ladies, holding your skirt under the hand dryer and wondering whether the mud spots on your tights violate the dress code.

A woman with a grey bob comes in to fix her make-up. Liz. Two hours, it's taken her, to get here from home, but she couldn't miss the last day. Never thought she'd have the privilege of watching from this end, after all. Upstairs, over a cup of tea, she tells you how, years ago, a friend suggested she apply. "And I thought, why would they want me? I've got no fancy connections, I wouldn't fit in." She looks around her. "Best thing I've ever done."

A series of loud creaks emanates from the end of the corridor. Eleven men are moving heavily down the stairs. Liz heads to the benches, but you make for the empty Writing Room. From an armchair, you can watch the game through a vast open window that frames the wicket, as though it were another of the artworks. It's your new favourite place.

The bowler runs in, arms and legs pumping like he's Tom Cruise about to hurl himself between buildings. The ball slides down leg, and the batsman tucks it round the corner. There's a tut from another armchair – you're not quite alone. You can't see his face, just the *Playfair* on the table next to him. But you can tell, over the course of the afternoon, that he really doesn't like the Middlesex bowling. The Writing Room was somewhere for quiet retreat. It used to have its own postbox; at its desks, the old-timers worked on their correspondence. Plum Warner. Perhaps Lord Harris. They must have heard these same sounds: the background burble of the spectators; the vowels of encouragement from the fielders; the rasp of the pendulum from the wall clock. They watched the field expand and contract, as you do. Maybe they, too, saw an autumn leaf fall from a steel-grey sky.

But the view they knew is long gone. And the evolution of Lord's continues, right now, right in front of you. Even as play goes on, diggers are at work on the Compton Stand. Tearing down hunks of concrete. Making way for the future. Change at both ends.

Emma John is the author of Following On, *Wisden Book of the Year in 2017.*

THE BIRTH OF THE HUNDRED

Saviour – or monster?

N ICK H OULT

Desert Springs, a five-star golf resort in southern Spain, is not the obvious place to start an English cricket revolution. In late October 2017, ECB chief executive Tom Harrison, chairman Colin Graves, and Andrew Strauss, director of the England team, had flown in to size up the venue as a winter training centre. But their trip took a twist. Called together by Sanjay Patel, then the board's chief commercial officer, they were soon listening to the latest idea from his department. It was a meeting that changed the sport, possibly for ever.

Patel's PowerPoint presentation described a new game comprising 100 balls per side – shorter than Twenty20 and, in his opinion, simpler to understand for the new audience the board were desperate to attract. It is not known who first dreamed up The Hundred. Patel will say only that it was born out of many discussions; even Graves is unsure. "Sanjay came out with this presentation," he says. "We all looked at one another, and said: 'How the heck is that going to work?' To give him his due, Sanjay said: 'Don't prejudge it. Just go away and have a think.' He had the vision – and he stuck with it."

So began one of the most rancorous periods in the history of English domestic cricket. It led to accusations of betrayal and bullying; included PR blunders that damaged the game's reputation; pitted the board against their richest county; stirred impassioned resistance from the sport's supporter base; sparked constitutional change that dramatically reduced the influence of the 18 first-class counties; and triggered fears about a widening of the gap between the so-called super clubs at the Test-match grounds, and the rest.

Graves stands down in November 2020, after The Hundred's first season: the job of making it work in the long term will be his successor's task. But he will leave office convinced a new format was needed. With Test cricket on the wane around the world, the ECB fear it will lose value even in England. And, in 2018, they received a jolt as they set about trying to renew their Indian broadcast deal, only for Star Sports – who had recently spent $2.55bn on the IPL – to cut ties. It left Sony to pick up the five-year contract, for what sources have described as "tens of millions" lower than the Star deal. It was the first serious sign that Test-match rights cannot be banked ad infinitum. The hole needed filling.

The Hundred is owned by the ECB, which means they now have a property to sell to global broadcasters; each county (and MCC) have a nineteenth share. If, for the sake of argument, a rich Indian investor wanted to buy a team, the board – and thus the counties – would earn a windfall. Without The Hundred, Graves believes, there would have been no £1.3bn television deal with Sky, no £1.3m extra annual payment to the counties, no cricket on free-to-air television. In their first live coverage for two decades, the BBC are set to show ten games

In his hands: Sanjay Patel, the ECB's managing director of The Hundred, makes his case.

a summer between 2020 and 2024: eight in The Hundred, and two T20 internationals.

"Cricket does not stand still," says Graves. "A lot of people talk about tradition, and say we cannot change this or that. It is rubbish. If we sit and do nothing, we will get left behind. We have created something that is different. When we launched T20, we missed a trick. We should have patented it and, if the rest of the world wanted it, said: 'Cough up.' We gave them T20, and a lot of countries did it better than us.

"Not many at the ECB believed in T20. They thought it was a gimmick, so we did not get behind it. Not this time. We do not want to miss an opportunity with The Hundred. If we do it properly, we will have something unique, and worth a lot of money. Yes, we have had a rough ride, and some of that was of our own making. But, behind the scenes, the guys have been determined to develop something good for cricket."

You may argue that a rough ride is a choppy ferry crossing from Dover to Calais, or a day stuck in traffic on the M1. What the ECB and English cricket have experienced over the past two years, ever since The Hundred was made public in April 2018, would have had the hardiest traveller reaching for the sickness pills. Yet, whatever your view, it has been an incredible feat to pull off such radical change within a sport renowned for conservatism. To shepherd 18 counties and MCC down the same road took planning, focus and ruthless decision-making. And it has left feelings of anger and bitterness.

The counties can roughly be split into three groups. There are those who simply need the money: the annual payout will sustain the likes of Derbyshire, Leicestershire and Northamptonshire through the dark winter months. From those at Test venues, including Lancashire, Nottinghamshire, Warwickshire and Yorkshire, there was wholehearted backing: they will be hosts, and central to the tournament. The final group were either openly against the idea – such as Essex, Kent, Middlesex and Surrey – or privately lukewarm but reluctant to make enemies at the board.

It is at Somerset where a sense of betrayal lingered, so much so that they sought legal advice about suing the board over what they perceived as a broken promise. Originally, Andy Nash, chairman for ten years, had voted in favour of the new competition, believing Somerset – a well-run club at the heart of local life – would be a host venue. In a letter in April 2017, received before a crucial meeting of the Somerset committee, Graves had described Taunton as a "key part of the future of the game, with an opportunity to stage matches like all other major venues in England & Wales".

Ambiguous? Yes – and carefully worded. Graves strongly denies assurances were given that Taunton would be one of the eight host grounds, and points to an email he received in August 2016 in which Nash had stated his support for an "EPL [English Premier League] with six to eight teams. Set criteria for qualification, e.g. 10,000 min capacity. Counties/ECB own the sides, and profits distributed fairly across the game." Later, Nash and Graves fell out badly; when Nash resigned from the ECB board, he published a stinging letter criticising Graves's leadership. But the Somerset committee had already taken Graves's letter as confirmation that he would be at the top table in any new competition, and voted in support when it was agreed – 38 to three – by the ECB's members in April 2017. Once it became clear from meetings with the ECB later in the year that Taunton would not be a host venue, Somerset were incensed.

Bloodier battles lay ahead. To introduce a competition not featuring the first-class counties required constitutional change, and a two-thirds majority: the ECB's articles of association stated that all 18 had to be involved in any tournament at professional level. The ECB's legal department realised the voter base could also include the Minor Counties, diluting the 18. Their representative on the ECB board is Devon's Jim Wood, who is close to Graves. With extra revenue promised to the Minor Counties – now, after 124 years, rebranded the National Counties Cricket Association – they pledged support. The dissenters had been neutered, the two-thirds majority achieved.

Graves believes part of the difficulty of selling The Hundred to the counties has been the turnover of chairmen: in his five years, he says he has dealt with 37. It takes chairmen at least a year to bed into the job, in which time they also have to assess decisions that have a wider impact. Critics of The Hundred believe that is why some fell into line so quickly: it is hard to rock the boat when new to a business. But it works both ways: Graves feels he had to start all over again with counties who had already agreed to his reforms.

"I never threatened anybody," he says. "But I said: 'If you don't support this, you are going to have a problem, because going forward I cannot guarantee you anything financially. Where is your revenue going to come from? If the television deal goes down, some of you are at risk.' ECB revenue has to keep rising for the counties to survive."

The Hundred was worked on quietly behind the scenes for six months after Desert Springs, but not revealed to the counties until a meeting at Lord's on

The Hundred, but no thousands… At Nottingham in September 2018, the ECB organised a trial of the game's fourth format.

April 19, 2018. No agenda was issued in advance. The meeting lasted two hours. Patel presented his idea to the counties, who were told a press release would be released immediately: badly burned by the Kevin Pietersen saga, the ECB were suspicious of leaks. It is understood senior voices at Sky begged them not to go public. Details were still too vague: let the leaks happen, but keep quiet officially until everything is fleshed out, then launch in style. The ECB ignored the advice. Journalists learned of the plans over a chaotic conference call with Harrison, Patel and Clare Connor, head of women's cricket. Beyond the innings lasting 100 balls, there was little that was concrete.

"There was no consultation," says Surrey chief executive Richard Gould. "The county CEOs were brought into a room, and told The Hundred was happening. It was released to the media ten minutes later, while we were still in the room. It was delivered as a fait accompli. The ECB then used all their leverage to make their dream become a reality."

It was now that the mud started to fly. Harrison did not give a media interview for the rest of the year. And, as the ECB fell silent, their critics filled the void, and fed the news cycle.

The original message was that The Hundred was for new fans, not existing supporters. This left some county followers, and those who pay good money for Test tickets, feeling abandoned. The board undertook market research, but it would be another 12 months before they made any of it public. When they did, it was light on detail. The policy of silence was also an error. "People were asking questions, rightfully so, but we had nothing to say because we had not finished building it," says Graves. "It was conceptual. That was difficult. If we had been able to keep it confidential, it would have gone a lot quicker and smoother."

All the while, the relationship with Surrey, the richest county, was disintegrating. They challenged the ECB's perception of the average fan as pale, male and stale – a central plank of the board's argument that cricket needed a new demographic. "Fifty-two per cent of our ticket purchasers last year had never bought tickets before, and our membership has doubled in the last eight," says Gould. "We sell out most of our games, even though we don't play Yorkshire or Lancashire." That is why Surrey instead supported a two-divisional model for a new Twenty20 tournament.

When Nash chaired the ECB's Domestic Structure Steering Group in 2016, he had proposed precisely that, with the top clubs in the Premier Division, plus promotion and relegation. But while Deloitte valued the annual broadcast rights for a two-tier county T20 tournament at £4.7m, their figure for a competition with eight new teams was six times higher, at £28.7m. Four years on, those valuations remain a sore point. The ECB issued non-disclosure agreements, so county chief executives – forbidden to discuss the details – could not get a second opinion. The board say this protected their commercial interests; counties felt gagged and bullied. Mutual suspicion reigned.

Nash believes The Hundred is the start of a takeover by the Test-match counties. "We don't play cricket for money, but you cannot play cricket without it," he says. "For those counties struggling to remain solvent, the guarantee of seven-figure sums over a five-year period would be extremely hard to resist. But it will be the end of the T20 Blast. Fewer professional counties will assume greater power. Once you unleash the forces of Darwin, the market will do the rest. It will be interesting to see at what stage the counties decide their lack of representation on the national governing body's board necessitates steps to ensure they can protect their own interests, as in soccer and rugby union."

The media can be misleading, and PR plans sunk by outside influences, but there is no doubt The Hundred has been beset by self-inflicted wounds. When the ECB announced their long-awaited data at Lord's in April 2018, they revealed research showing that ticket buyers for professional matches were male (82%), white British (94%), and had an average age of 50. But officials were secretive under questioning, partly because most of their research painted a bad picture of cricket: it is not good business to slam your product in public, even when building a case for change.

Harrison admitted mistakes had been made, and tried to reassure existing fans they were part of the new concept. But the board blundered when it emerged that the image used to launch the home page of the Hundred website had been taken from a rap concert in Miami, and depicted an almost entirely male crowd. To compound the error, it was then replaced with one from a football match. It appeared the ECB were desperate to use any picture, as long as it did not come from a game of cricket.

The board then used the eve of England's important World Cup match against India to slip out the fact that the tournament would be sponsored by KP Snacks. It seemed like a good day to bury questionable news, but the decision came back to haunt them. Healthy-eating charities and obesity campaigners, including the outgoing chief medical officer of England,

THE HUNDRED DRAFT

Eyes down!

VITHUSHAN EHANTHARAJAH

There have been many unkept promises in English cricket. So when talk emerged of The Hundred getting the full Sky Sports treatment for a draft, the like of which had never been seen before in British sport, it came with trepidation. In the event, there were no Texans bearing Perspex boxes full of fake cash.

Hosted in Sky's swanky complex in Isleworth on October 20, the draft was a bold step for a competition taking a giant leap. While each of the eight teams went about their business, the broadcaster's established talent – Nasser Hussain, Ian Ward, Isa Guha and Rob Key – were seated front and centre on a curved couch, steering the programme live.

The format was simple-ish: every team had two 100-second windows in each of the seven rounds to make their picks, though three cricketers per team had already been allocated – two local icons, and an England Test player. Each team were allowed up to three overseas players, and there were seven salary bands, ranging from £30,000 to £125,000 (and from £3,600 to £15,000 for the women).

Now came the science. Each team had a plinth with two representatives from their coaching set-up, plus another, generally an analyst. Oval Invincibles had a boffin from data-intelligence company CricViz, while Southern Brave, based at Hampshire's Rose Bowl, had Mark Nicholas.

High up in the studio were a host of players assembled to provide colour from a café/green-room hybrid. At first they seemed oblivious to the cameras, catching themselves on screen, and tailoring their conversation accordingly, particularly when a questionable decision was made. "What the fuck are they playing at?!" laughed one England international at the string of picks from Manchester Originals, who proved the butt of many jokes.

Oddly, players felt safer in the media area, situated in another building entirely. "It's a bit weird with the cameras right there in your face," noted Jos Buttler, an Originals man, whose perplexed reaction to his side's selection of Lancashire captain Dane Vilas as a top-tier £125,000 pick went viral. Afterwards, it emerged Vilas was chosen because the Originals had been thrown by Birmingham Phoenix's selection of Liam Livingstone.

This was the peak of the drama. Rashid Khan had been the first choice, Luke Wright the last – both for Trent Rockets – but once the higher-profile names were out of the way early, interest dissipated. Even TV started to spend less time on the main event, instead rattling through interviews, while a ticker at the bottom of the screen kept viewers posted on the five-figure dealings – though not on which players were left, nor how teams needed to balance their squads. At times it felt like being at the bingo without a card.

The chat was stale, though the women players were more engaging, and told their stories well. But since the best-paid woman would earn half as much as the lowest-paid man, it felt like rubbing it in when the camera panned to them.

On the whole, this was a smooth operation, perhaps too smooth: the draft finished more than half an hour ahead of schedule on Sky Sports, which meant more filler. Sky One's two-hour broadcast ended after one, at 9pm, catching many viewers unaware. But it was all far less tedious than other auctions. Now to the real thing.

Vithushan Ehantharajah is The Independent's *sports feature writer.*

THE HUNDRED – FRANCHISE SQUADS

	Birmingham Phoenix	London Spirit	Manchester Originals	Northern Superchargers
ETCC	Chris Woakes	Rory Burns	Jos Buttler	Ben Stokes
£125,000	Liam Livingstone	†Glenn Maxwell	†Imran Tahir	†Aaron Finch
£125,000	*Moeen Ali	*Eoin Morgan	Dane Vilas	†Mujeeb Zadran
£100,000	†Kane Williamson	†Mohammad Nabi	Phil Salt	†Chris Lynn
£100,000	Ravi Bopara	†Mohammad Amir	Tom Abell	*Adil Rashid
£75,000	Benny Howell	R. E. van der Merwe	*Matt Parkinson	Adam Lyth
£75,000	Tom Helm	Mark Wood	*Saqib Mahmood	*David Willey
£60,000	†Shaheen Afridi	Joe Denly	†Daniel Christian	Richard Gleeson
£60,000	*Pat Brown	†Dan Lawrence	Wayne Madsen	Ben Foakes
£50,000	Adam Hose	Mason Crane	Wayne Parnell	T. Köhler-Cadmore
£50,000	Cameron Delport	Kyle Abbott	†Mitchell Santner	David Wiese
£40,000	Henry Brookes	Adam Rossington	Joe Clarke	Nathan Rimmington
£40,000	†Adam Zampa	Zak Crawley	Marchant de Lange	Brydon Carse
£30,000	Riki Wessels	Jade Dernbach	Ed Pollock	Ed Barnard
£30,000	Chris Cooke	Luis Reece	Ed Byrom	John Simpson

	Oval Invincibles	Southern Brave	Trent Rockets	Welsh Fire
ETCC	Sam Curran	Jofra Archer	Joe Root	Jonny Bairstow
£125,000	†Sunil Narine	†Andre Russell	†Rashid Khan	†Mitchell Starc
£125,000	*Jason Roy	†David Warner	†D'Arcy Short	*Steve Smith
£100,000	Sam Billings	Liam Dawson	Lewis Gregory	*Colin Ingram
£100,000	†S. Lamichhane	*James Vince	*Alex Hales	*Tom Banton
£75,000	Rilee Rossouw	†Shadab Khan	†Nathan Coulter-Nile	Ben Duckett
£75,000	*Tom Curran	*Chris Jordan	*Harry Gurney	Ravi Rampaul
£60,000	Reece Topley	Tymal Mills	Steven Mullaney	Simon Harmer
£60,000	Hardus Viljoen	Ross Whiteley	Matthew Carter	*Qais Ahmed
£50,000	†Fabian Allen	Delray Rawlins	Luke Wood	Liam Plunkett
£50,000	Alex Blake	Ollie Pope	Tom Moores	Ryan ten Doeschate
£40,000	Will Jacks	George Garton	Dawid Malan	David Payne
£40,000	Chris Wood	Alex Davies	Ben Cox	Ryan Higgins
£30,000	Nathan Sowter	Max Waller	Luke Fletcher	Danny Briggs
£30,000	Laurie Evans	Craig Overton	Luke Wright	Leus du Plooy

ETCC *England Test central contract.*   * *Local icon.*   † *Overseas player.*

Teams have the option to draft a T20 Blast wildcard for £30,000 nearer the start of the tournament.

Snack attack: Kate Cross and Joe Root sport their crisp new kit.

lined up to criticise the ECB when the tournament's kits were launched in October, replete with branding from McCoy's, Skips, Kettle Chips and others. In January, KP Snacks announced their branding would be absent from children's replica shirts, making Butterkist and Pom-Bear for adult consumption only.

And on it went. When all the head coaches turned out to be foreigners, the argument that the competition would promote English talent fell flat. One of the coaches, South African Gary Kirsten, added to the haplessness. "Can't wait for The Hundred Draft and to pick the [insert team name] squad on Sunday at 7pm," he obligingly tweeted.

Harrison was rightly praised for landing the £1.3bn rights deal with Sky and the BBC: ten games on free-to-air television, plus publicity on the BBC's multiple platforms, is a crumb of comfort for the critics of the sport's disappearance behind a paywall in 2006. Sky are satisfied too: they preserved their cricket content, and will show the lion's share of the new competition. And while other sports have suffered a decrease in the valuation of television rights, the ECB have bucked the trend. Patel is confident The Hundred will make money in its first year, which would be a remarkable achievement given the board have said they will be happy with ground occupation of 60–65%. He also defends the junk-food deal.

"The easiest thing for us to do would have been to bring in a financial services brand," he says. "What we did was get a household brand who understand families better than we ever will, because they sell to them on a daily basis. That sort of insight is so valuable to us. Also, if you reach a different audience, the people who come to the cricket are going to relate to those brands."

The women's Hundred, which replaces the Kia Super League, will be marketed alongside the men's, and hosted by the smaller counties, who have every motivation to get behind it.

"The game needs this for a number of reasons," says Patel. "People think the driving motivation is money. That is wrong. It is about getting more people to pick up a bat and a ball. It is going to be brilliant cricket. Get behind it, and support it. If people do, and the existing county fans embrace it, we will absolutely be the envy of the world. I hope that is the passion they can share. It will jump us ahead of the curve."

And what about those existing supporters? It is never wise to read too much into social media, but on Twitter and Facebook the response to The Hundred has usually been cutting – less so on Instagram, mainly used by a younger age group. The ECB believe most of the criticism comes from fans in the South-East and South-West, where the anti-Hundred counties are largely based.

But supporters share Nash's fear of the growth of super counties, and worry that those who host the new teams will be able to poach the best talent by offering Hundred deals alongside traditional contracts. In December, Lancashire took down from their website an "inadvertently misleading" letter from Manchester Originals head coach, Australian Simon Katich, who said his squad were an "extension of this great county". The hope had been to encourage Lancashire supporters to back the Originals, yet many considered it proof that lines were already blurred.

Meanwhile, a Twitter account called @Opposethe100 had more than 3,000 followers by the end of 2019, amid fears the tournament would kill the character of the cricket they love. Annie Chave, a Somerset fan, is a vocal critic. "We are going to have 50-over games with seven of our squad missing at The Hundred," she says. "It must be hard to keep continuity going when you lose that many. And it will cause division. How is it going to work in the dressing-room if one guy is on £125k from The Hundred, and another is just on a county contract? You are making players into mercenaries, not caring who they play for, and that is a dangerous thing. White-ball cricket is exciting and exhilarating, but it is not the form of the game that made me fall in love with cricket. I go to cricket to relax, not sit on the edge of my seat." Sussex, losing 11, are even more affected.

The player draft, shown on Sky Sports in October, made the tournament feel more of a reality, though some ECB officials were frustrated when Chris Gayle went unsigned. While they saw potential ticket sales, the clubs saw an ageing star no longer worth the money.

The Hundred is inevitable, but the counties will not go quietly. At the end of 2019, Surrey commissioned a report entitled "One Million & Rising". It recommended a two-division Blast, expanded beyond England with an attempt to build partnerships with IPL teams, and a governance structure separate from the ECB. "An updated Blast is still very much on the cards, perhaps with two or three divisions, and new teams from Scotland, Ireland and Europe," says Gould. "The counties know there will be significant broadcast interest in T20 when the next rights cycle arrives. Ultimately, it will be up to them to decide. There are lots of options available, and there is no doubt T20 will remain the most important global brand for short-form cricket for the next 20 years or so."

The Hundred begins at The Oval on July 17, when Oval Invincibles play Welsh Fire. It is the start of a new era, but not the end of the story.

Nick Hoult is chief cricket correspondent of The Daily Telegraph.

THE ECB FACE THE POLITICIANS

Enough to make the silver blush

JOHN CRACE

It's come to something when the two most eloquent performers are inanimate. Yet not even being flanked by the pomp and circumstance of the men's and women's World Cup trophies could save Colin Graves and Tom Harrison from two excruciating hours in October before the select committee for Digital, Culture, Media and Sport.

Any hopes the chairman and chief executive of the ECB might have had of the silverware providing diplomatic immunity were disabused within ten minutes. After a few niceties, during which Harrison enthused it was a "very exciting time for cricket", committee chair Damian Collins (Conservative, Folkestone and Hythe) got down to business.

Why, he wondered, was 2005 – one of English cricket's *anni mirabiles* – not its breakthrough year? Could it possibly have had something to do with that being the last summer the sport was broadcast free to air? Neither Graves nor Harrison could quite believe what they were hearing. That was a ludicrous suggestion. Sky money had done nothing but wonders for cricket. Stadium upgrades and increased salaries all round for players and administrators at the top of the game. Everything was being done to protect cricket's growth.

"That's odd," said Ian C. Lucas (Labour, Wrexham). "Grass-roots participation has fallen by almost 50%." Harrison shook his head sadly. That was just one of those things. An outlier. Sometimes you had to take one step backward to take two forward. Just look at the two trophies. (The trophies blushed a little.) Everything the ECB had been doing since 2005 had been about making England world champions. It had been a brilliant and cunning strategy: the team had deliberately been useless in previous World Cups, just so they could power home after a super over at Lord's.

But now was the time to let bygones be bygones. After a lot of protests from ordinary fans, the 2019 World Cup final had been shown on Channel 4 – though Harrison could not conceal a hint of regret that it had escaped Sky's exclusive clutches – and cricket was now coming back to free-to-air TV. From 2020, the BBC would be broadcasting live coverage of a couple of men's and women's Twenty20 internationals, and some games from the new format, The Hundred.

At the mention of this, Harrison began to purr. The most exciting development in modern cricket for more than a decade, with city franchises – whoops, teams, definitely teams! – playing matches of ten ten-ball overs. The committee were rather more sceptical. Weren't the current T20, 50-over and Test formats all fit for purpose? Why bother to change something that wasn't broken?

Here the proceedings grew steadily trickier for the ECB's two top bods, their answers more evasive and brusque. The board had done considerable research on The Hundred, and could prove both that it was necessary and would be a

Parliament TV

Cupbearers: Lord Patel, Colin Graves, Tom Harrison, Clare Connor and a pair of trophies.

sure-fire success. Would they care to share this research, the committee wondered, and estimate how much it had cost? No, they would not. The research was all theirs, and so overwhelmingly positive it could not be published.

Had the politicians been better prepared, things could have got even more awkward for Graves and Harrison. As it was, they were lucky to escape questioning on the counties' scepticism over the competition's viability, or on the £1.3m payout each received to get them on board. Even so, the two men had to endure another hour of slow torture.

Harrison all but admitted that the ECB's main motivation for the new tournament was that they had failed to capitalise on the introduction of T20, and were taking an expensive punt – The Hundred stands to lose about £20m in its first year – on a brand-new format that may or may not take off globally. He also tried to make out that the ECB had been fighting off major sponsors, and had chosen Butterkist popcorn and Pom-Bear crisps only to appear down with the kids. The committee were unconvinced, observing that junk-food brands didn't exactly promote cricket as a healthy lifestyle, and suspecting the sole reason they had been selected was because they had made the best – and only – offers.

There were similar prevarications and evasions over logistics. How did the ECB square wanting to increase exposure to the game with restricting the men's matches to seven major cities? They didn't. "OK," said Clive Efford (Labour, Eltham). "How do you see The Hundred developing? What would a successful outcome look like?" "We want to be on 'The One Show' and CBeebies," Harrison replied cheerfully. That may not be every cricket lover's benchmark of success. But each to their own.

Maybe he and Graves can return in a year's time to update the select committee on the progress of The Hundred. And maybe the committee will give them an even tougher ride.

John Crace is the political sketchwriter for The Guardian.

WATCHING THE WORLD CUP FINAL

Abandoning Bairstow for Beyoncé

Miles Jupp

I wasn't even looking for a ticket, but two days before the final I got an email from a friend saying he just happened to have a spare, and would I possibly be interested in shelling out the cost of 29½ hours of childcare? Until then, I had followed the tournament only in print and on the radio. It would be the first match I had actually seen.

I got to Lord's early in the hope of soaking up an excited atmosphere, but everything felt nervily restrained. A sense of gloomy realism seemed to have settled on the crowds of English fans walking up Wellington Road. Our seats were in the Warner Stand, four rows back. There was a deluge of corporate entertainment, and then we were off.

From the first ball, there was the sense that England were behind; nearly 100 overs later, they were still behind. And there was constant confusion. Trent Boult stood on the rope just yards in front of us, but I didn't realise it had happened: I was watching his hands. As England's 50th over began, the lady to my left suddenly said: "I don't want to be here." I didn't realise the ball had ricocheted off Stokes's bat: I was watching the line.

When the scores were level after 50 overs, I couldn't have told you where our last 15 runs had come from, and I didn't know what a super over was. All I knew was that my heart was racing, and that the lyrics of "Sweet Caroline" came to me with surprising ease. And then we had won. We didn't quite deserve to, but we had. In the words of Max Boyce: "I was there."

Miles Jupp is an actor and writer.

Mishal Husain

Sunday tends to be a working day for me in the BBC newsroom, and so it was that afternoon. I left the family huddled on the sofa, watching the match, and headed to New Broadcasting House, wondering idly if we'd have a result in time for the early-evening news bulletin on BBC One.

Almost everyone in the newsroom had at least one eye on sport – either Lord's or Wimbledon, where Novak Djokovic was locked in battle with Roger Federer in what turned out to be the longest singles final in the tournament's history. Our bulletin was due to follow the tennis and, as the match went on and on, the main preoccupation was practical: how delayed would we be, and how much might our airtime be cut in the scramble to get the channel back on track?

Simultaneously, the action at Lord's began to reach fever pitch. From an earlier assumption that England wouldn't win, and the World Cup was therefore unlikely to be our top story, everything started to feel different.

Mishal Husain.

Perhaps this *was* our lead, depending on where the game had reached by the time we finally got on air. We'll know any minute, I thought, as I watched Ben Stokes edge closer to the New Zealand total – and I can get on with writing the headlines.

Then came the tie, and the super over. All over the newsroom, producers were standing up and scratching their heads: "How does this work?"... "Can anyone explain a super over?"... "What on earth is going on?" And I still didn't know what to put in the headlines. Meanwhile, at Wimbledon, they were also in the endgame. The efficiency of the All England Club meant the prize-giving would be set up in a jiffy, the tennis coverage would wrap up, and it would be over to us. Even the short time it takes to move from my desk in the newsroom to the presenter's seat in the studio, getting earpiece and microphone set up along the way, would be a crucial period unplugged from the live action.

The gods smiled on us. With minutes to spare before the on-air time we were finally given by BBC One, we had a result. The newsroom erupted alongside the country – and I had my headlines. No fancy turn of phrase, no play on words. Just the simplest of sentences, and a tale to make the heart sing: "England have won the World Cup."

Mishal Husain presents BBC One news bulletins, and the Today *programme on Radio 4.*

Tim Rice

I left Lord's as England began their reply to New Zealand's useful, but not overpowering, 241. I had no wish to depart, but on the other hand I had no reason to suppose that the remainder of the day's play would be anything out of the ordinary; the previous World Cup final at Lord's, in 1999, when Australia waltzed to victory over Pakistan, had not been a gripper. But I had to attend the European premiere of the *Lion King* movie. The wise folk at Disney had clearly not factored cricket into their plans to promote their latest blockbuster, a remake of the 1994 cartoon version, for which I had co-written the songs with Sir Elton John.

So I abandoned Bairstow for Beyoncé, Morgan for Mufasa. Thus unravelled the greatest sporting disappointment of my cricketing life as a spectator – I have had far too many as a player. By five o'clock, I was standing in my dinner jacket in a line of A-listers (and lesser mortals) in an increasingly warm cinema foyer in Leicester Square, wishing I had attended the Los Angeles world premiere a week earlier instead. My brother, Jonathan, was updating me with the score as Harry and Meghan were introduced to the team behind the film. It was becoming annoyingly clear this was no rerun of 1999.

By the time HRH got to me, he was glad to be informed that Ben Stokes and Jos Buttler were going strong. As we took our seats, it was apparent we were heading for one of the tightest finishes since W. G. Grace was a lad. The lights dimmed, and as Lebo M's immortal opening chant to "Circle of Life" took flight, England needed 24 from two overs. At this point, an alert usher – quite correctly – ordered me to switch off my phone. Nearly two hours later, I learned what I had missed.

Tim Rice is a lyricist and a former president of MCC.

Howard Jacobson

I had decided, well in advance, that I wouldn't be watching. England weren't going to reach the final anyway and, while India v Australia would be enthralling, I am too sore a loser to take pleasure in the skills of teams we should have beaten. Alternatively, we'd make the final, only to go down ignominiously to one or other of those teams. Either way, there could be only pain. So, a couple of weeks before, I invited friends round to watch Wimbledon, making my wife a solemn promise that, whatever transpired, I wouldn't keep switching channels to get the cricket score.

On the day, I made the same promise to myself. Playing New Zealand doesn't fill me with the unease that playing Australia does. I can bear to see us lose to New Zealand. I like their game. They keep their humour. But I still knew I couldn't watch. I have necromantic powers over cricket matches. I go to the ground and an English wicket falls. I turn on the television and two English wickets fall. I owed it to my country to stay away, and cheer on Federer against Djokovic, neither of whom I warm to, though I warm to Djokovic less. From which it should be clear that I implicate myself in sport in ways that are unhealthy. I keep forgetting it is not about me.

Federer wouldn't have thanked me for my support. He lost. Already despondent, I asked my friends if they minded my quickly changing channels, and when I did I was just in time to catch the now infamous overthrow off Stokes's bat. "That's lucky," opined a tactless friend. "Everything's lucky or unlucky," was my answer. But I wondered. Six weeks later, watching Lyon's fumbling the run-out at Headingley, I was wondering again: have we actually won anything? I'm not just a sore loser. I'm a sore winner.

Howard Jacobson's latest novel, Live a Little, *is published by Jonathan Cape.*

Sebastian Faulks

I had been lucky enough to get a ticket to the semi-final at Edgbaston on the Thursday, where I sat among the Barmy Army in the Eric Hollies Stand, and got showered with beer. I hoped something might turn up for Sunday, but it didn't. So by ten o'clock, I was installed on the sofa with the dog at home in west London.

I didn't think any of our bowlers did as well in their first spells as they had at Birmingham, but the wickets came with a comforting regularity. To me, it seemed as though New Zealand were always a little behind. My feeling (quite wrong) was that 260–270 was where the action would be. The dog and I took lunch with cautious optimism and a small glass of wine.

It was not until New Zealand bowled that it became clear what a difficult pitch it was – not an ideal track for an ODI, to be honest, because so many great strokemakers were unable to time the ball (though England had struggled throughout the tournament to come to terms with English conditions). How well New Zealand bowled and fielded. But what impiety had they shown towards the gods of cricket that they should so spit on them?

England were finished when Buttler was out, surely. We lacked the impetus that one big over would have given. We were always tantalisingly short, until that insane ricochet…

Then, as Neesham swiped Archer for six in the super over, we were dead again. Shouldn't we have bowled Woakes or Plunkett? And then redemption for Jason Roy, so deserved, with that fizzing flat

David M. Benett/Getty Images

Sebastian Faulks.

throw… Buttler's safe hands, and heartbreak, so undeserved, for the Kiwis. It was a tie. Two winners. Believe me: I wasn't there. I was dancing with the dog.

Sebastian Faulks's most recent novel, Paris Echo, *is published by Vintage.*

Sam Mendes

I have a memory of a late summer day, some time in the 1970s: Middlesex against Worcestershire at Lord's. I was there on my own, having climbed over the locked iron gates behind the old red-brick Grand Stand and found my way into a hospitality box. I sat there, watching an untroubled Glenn Turner. It remains my most vivid memory of Lord's, despite many visits since, and I occasionally wonder how the scene might have looked as a reverse shot: the stand empty, except for a solitary small boy – a tiny smudge – as the shadows lengthened across the grass.

During the World Cup final, I was sitting in almost exactly the same spot and, although nearly everything had changed, I was surrounded by the past. Either side were two England captains from my boyhood, Brearley and Gatting, bantering about whose World Cup final defeat had been more avoidable: 1979 or 1987? (A clue: the loser was polishing off a pork pie.) A few seats away was Theresa May, in her last days in office – a sad, haunted figure. Behind me, John Major chatted with Ashley Giles. We had come to see England win, and we saw probably the greatest one-day match of all time. Well, at least *they* did.

Some months before, I had agreed to do a small event in Cheltenham for my lovely wife, the classical trumpeter Alison Balsom. She was running the music festival, and I wanted to show my support. For some reason, I had chosen that Sunday. Despite having been a member of the World Cup's directorial board, and having crafted the shooting schedule for my movie *1917* with half an eye on the fixture list, I had contrived a situation where I had to leave Lord's at five o'clock.

And so I did, just as Ben Stokes came out to bat. I listened in a car on the M40, and arrived at Cheltenham Town Hall just as Jofra Archer began his super over. Had you been in Cheltenham Imperial Gardens that day, you might have seen a solitary figure punching the air and happily shedding a tear, as the shadows lengthened across the grass.

Sam Mendes is a film and theatre director.

WISDEN WRITING COMPETITION IN 2019

When Sussex wept for Alan Wells

JONATHAN FOULKES

There is a place in Sussex where the road falls away so suddenly and unexpectedly that, just for a moment, unsuspecting drivers must feel they have driven over the edge of a cliff. Locals slow almost to a stop, while cars coming the other way, straining up the hill as they shunt through the gears, approach the summit at a similar speed. Much like commuters on the underground, travelling up and down the escalators, motorists get to enjoy a good old gander at their opposite number as they pass slowly by. It was on just such an occasion that I listened to the entirety of Alan Wells's debut Test innings.

I was the barman of an old pub at the foot of Windover Hill, across the fields from Alfriston. There were views to the west, and we were assured by a regular that, on Midsummer's Eve, the sun would set over the spire of Berwick Church. It didn't – but, as he pointed out, it rather depended where you stood.

I was thrilled to discover Alan was a near neighbour, and occasional visitor. He was the swashbuckling captain of Sussex, a run machine with an unwanted sobriquet: "Best Batsman Never to Have Played for England." We were delighted when, in 1995, he was at last selected. But we hadn't reckoned on Curtly Ambrose. Only once did I see Ambrose in the flesh, four years earlier at The Oval, the day before Ian Botham couldn't get his leg over. It was Botham I'd gone to see – but it was the easy rolling action of Ambrose that caught my eye. I was side on to the wicket, and able to watch that sinuous run-up, seemingly effortless, with no suggestion of haste or hurry, the ball released again and again from an apex well in excess of eight feet. I was smitten.

Ambrose was beginning that run-up as I started the climb. By the time I had reached the top, Alan was walking back to the pavilion. Somewhere in between, he had faced his first ball, and gloved it to Sherwin Campbell at short leg. Meanwhile, in one of those lovely moments of shared experience, I and the driver coming down the hill had simultaneously thrown our heads in our hands as we listened to the disaster unfold on *TMS*. We exchanged looks, shook our heads, and drove on. The whole county felt his pain: that day, Sussex wept for Alan Wells.

It was among the shorter Test careers, though he did make three not out in the second innings. Later that week, he joined us for a beer. A farm worker who did odd jobs around the place called over: "That fencing, Alan – is it to keep the ducks out?" As jokes go, it was lame, but it broke the ice. Alan laughed. I poured his pint, and he told us all about it: the day he played for England.

Jonathan Foulkes is a university administrator living in Ely. Under the pen name Eric Wark, he is the author of "Behind the Sky", a little-read blog of Suffolk walks, Russia, and found photographs, at www.ericwark.com.

THE COMPETITION

Wisden received more than 80 entries for its eighth writing competition. As always, the geographical range of the entrants was impressive – they came, as you might expect, from Australia, India and New Zealand, but also from Bermuda, the United States, the UAE, and that cricketing stronghold Valencia. As always, the standard was high. Wisden appreciates the imagination and hard work of all entrants. The first submissions began to arrive in June; others were rather closer to the deadline at the end of November. All were equally welcome, and all read by the editorial team. Judging the competition gets no easier. The prize remains the same: publication, adulation, and an invitation to the launch dinner, held at Lord's in April.

The rules are also unchanged. Anyone who has never been commissioned by Wisden can take part. Entries, which should not have been submitted before (and are restricted to a maximum of two per person), must be:

1. the entrant's own work
2. unpublished in any medium
3. received by the end of 30 November, 2020
4. between 480 and 500 words (excluding the title)
5. neither libellous nor offensive
6. related to cricket, but not a match report

Articles should be sent to competitions@wisdenalmanack.com, with "Writing Competition 2020" as the subject line. (Those without access to email may post their entry to Writing Competition 2020, John Wisden & Co, 13 Old Aylesfield, Golden Pot, Alton, Hampshire GU34 4BY, *though email is much preferred*.) Please provide your name, address and telephone number. All entrants will be contacted by the end of 2020, and the winner informed by the end of January 2021. (Please contact Wisden if your entry has not been acknowledged by the end of December.) Past winners of this competition, Bloomsbury staff and those who in the editor's opinion have a working relationship with Wisden are ineligible. The editor's decision is final. We much look forward to receiving your contributions.

THE 2019 ENTRANTS

Benjamin Bard, Mike Battrum, Ed Bayliss, Matt Becker, Faraz Beg, James Belfast, Lucy Burch, Paul Caswell, Sarthak Chugh, Ian Clay, Mark Cowan, Jonathan Farmer, Tony Fishwick, Daniel Forman, Jonathan Foulkes, David Fraser, Simon Freeman, Alan Garley, Toby Fraser-Gausden, Mark Gannaway, Ian Gent, Riddhi Goel, Nick Gormack, Steve Green, The Grumbler, Rob Hamill, Philip Hardman, Mike Harfield, Andy Heafield, Tony Hodges, Tony Hutton, Daniel Jason, Neil Joynson, Asmi Kartikeya, Hasinuddin Kazi, John Kirby, Laurence Klein, Joel Lamy, James McGee, Zeeshan Mahmud, Josh Marks, Andy Millar, Avijit Mishra, Rhod Morgan, Neil Nelson, Jerome Pailing, Richard Pierce, Andrew Price, Gordon Price, David Potter, Sanjay Rangharajhan, Richard Reardon, John Rigg, Kenneth Rignall, John Roberts, Steve Robinson, Mark Sanderson, Apurv Sardeshmukh, Niall Sellar, Michael Sexton, Christopher Sharp, David Sim, John Slade, John Sleigh, Chris Sowton, Owen Teakle, Ram Teja, Seth Thomas, David Thornton, Nick Treby, Barry Turner, Charles Ullathorne, G. Venkatesh, David Walsh, Stephen Ward, Nick Wilkinson, Graham Willard, John Winnifrith, James Woodroof.

WINNERS

2012	Brian Carpenter	2016	John Pitt
2013	Liam Cromar	2017	Robert Stanier
2014	Peter Casterton	2018	Nick Campion
2015	Will Beaudouin	**2019**	**Jonathan Foulkes**

THE LEADING CRICKETER IN THE WORLD IN 2019

Ben Stokes

RICHARD GIBSON

It was an image that summed up the greatest year of his career: head back, shoulders arched, a guttural eruption towards the Headingley sky. At the end of an epic battle – and with apologies to Jack Leach – Ben Stokes really was the last man standing.

As he soaked in the atmosphere, he was cheered on by an increasingly adoring public. Not just the 17,000 lucky so-and-sos who had witnessed a heist to trump Ian Botham and 1981, but others who had been part of the peak (free-to-air) television audience of 8m for the World Cup final six weeks earlier, been converted by its drama, and now followed the Third Ashes Test from afar. Like Lord's, Headingley had been slipping from England's grasp until Stokes's extraordinary intervention had the country glued. Thanks to him, cricket was thrust back into the nation's conscience. December's BBC Sports Personality of the Year award became not so much about who would win, but about who would finish second and third.

While cricket is a game of numbers, his impact went well beyond his batting stats – though they were impressive. Across the calendar year, he hit 821 Test runs at 45, including an Ashes hundred at Lord's, and 719 in one-day internationals, at almost 60. Rivals dwarfed his 50-over tally, and scored at a faster lick: Stokes's one-day strike-rate of 92 was the lowest of England's established top six. But those two landmark innings… 84 and 135, both unbeaten, the first propelling his country to a maiden World Cup, the second inspiring a national record Test chase of 359. They alone were feats worthy of breaking Virat Kohli's three-year monopoly as *Wisden's* Leading Cricketer in the World; in the award's 17 years, only one other Englishman – Andrew Flintoff in 2005 – has prevailed. As he underlined during England's 3–1 Test win in South Africa in early 2020, when he averaged 45 with the bat and 22 with the ball, Stokes was the first name in a World XI.

It was a year in which he habitually came up with the right answer. Invited to join a podcast hosted by his Test colleague Stuart Broad, Stokes listened to a story in which Broad spoke of the pride he felt at seeing fellow passengers on the Tube read newspapers with his mate's face grinning out from front and back pages. Stokes quipped: "That's not what you were saying two years ago!"

The allusion to the Bristol street fracas in September 2017, leading to a court appearance on charges of affray (and a not-guilty verdict), was a reminder of how he had repaired his image. Yet this was no redemption story. He has not been motivated by atonement, but by an unwavering desire to win matches for England.

It's true that increased maturity has become a feature of his play – naturally enough, perhaps, for a man who turns 30 next year. The instinctive see-ball, hit-ball batsman who struck a hundred at Perth in 2013-14, and England's fastest double-century at Newlands two winters later, has metamorphosed into a player who visualises innings in advance. At Leeds, he assessed the situation as he sat in the dressing-room on the third afternoon, and concluded he had to be there at the close if England were to have any chance of preventing Australia retaining the urn with two games in hand. He finished the day with two from 50 balls.

"When you realise what's at stake, and you have an opportunity to influence a match, it focuses the mind," he says. "At times like those, I have come to understand I have a responsibility to try to do something that allows us to win. I am thinking about the game and situations a lot more – including an understanding that batting is always a lot easier the longer you spend in the middle."

Stokes struggles to chart exactly when his mindset altered, but recalls finishing unbeaten on 71 to marshal a one-day chase of 341 against Pakistan at Trent Bridge shortly before the World Cup. "The experience of being in that situation, not out at the end, told me I could do it."

There has been a similarly pragmatic approach to his one-day bowling, his modus operandi switching from hunting wickets to drying up runs. Though regularly featuring as England's third- or fourth-change bowler during the World Cup, his economy-rate of 4.83 was the eighth-best in the tournament of those who sent down at least 50 overs (and, unlike Stokes, the seven above him were all hit for at least one six).

In Tests, he took 22 wickets at 35, which – again – didn't quite tell the whole story. At Leeds, as if a precursor to his heroics with the bat, he refused to give up until the task of dismissing the Australians in their second innings was done. In all, he delivered 24.2 overs, interrupted only by an incomplete over from the cramping Jofra Archer, and the second-day close.

"I have just always wanted to be contributing to a successful team," he says. "When I look back at 2019, it will always be about the things we achieved as a group. There were a couple of individual things that I am obviously very proud of, and will always hold on to, but the memories of our celebrations will last for ever. It was the summer of cricket."

And Stokes was its heartbeat.

THE LEADING CRICKETER IN THE WORLD

2003	Ricky Ponting (Australia)	2012	Michael Clarke (Australia)
2004	Shane Warne (Australia)	2013	Dale Steyn (South Africa)
2005	Andrew Flintoff (England)	2014	Kumar Sangakkara (Sri Lanka)
2006	Muttiah Muralitharan (Sri Lanka)	2015	Kane Williamson (New Zealand)
2007	Jacques Kallis (South Africa)	2016	Virat Kohli (India)
2008	Virender Sehwag (India)	2017	Virat Kohli (India)
2009	Virender Sehwag (India)	2018	Virat Kohli (India)
2010	Sachin Tendulkar (India)	**2019**	**Ben Stokes (England)**
2011	Kumar Sangakkara (Sri Lanka)		

A list of notional past winners from 1900 appeared in Wisden 2007, *page 32.*

THE WISDEN–MCC CRICKET PHOTOGRAPH OF 2019 Gareth Copley wins the award for his picture of Ben Stokes seconds after England clinch the Headingley Ashes Test, August 25. STOKES IS ALSO THE LEADING CRICKETER IN THE WORLD.

The tenth Wisden–MCC Cricket Photograph of the Year attracted over 650 entries. First prize was £2,000; the two runners-up received £1,000, and the eight other shortlisted entries £250 each. Any image with a cricket theme taken during 2019 was eligible. The independent judging panel, chaired by former *Sunday Times* chief photographer Chris Smith, comprised award-winning photographer Patrick Eagar, ex-England cricketer Claire Taylor, Martin Devereux of the British Postal Museum and Nigel Davies, the former art director of *The Cricketer*. For more details, go to www.lords.org/photooftheyear

THE WISDEN-MCC CRICKET PHOTOGRAPH OF 2019   Kieran Hanlon is one of two runners-up, for his early-morning shot of the County Ground at Taunton, December 30.

THE WISDEN–MCC CRICKET PHOTOGRAPH OF 2019   The other runner-up is Tom Jenkins, who captured the moment Jos Buttler broke the stumps to run out Martin Guptill – and win the World Cup for England. Lord's, July 14.

FIVE CRICKETERS OF THE YEAR   Jofra Archer

FIVE CRICKETERS OF THE YEAR   Pat Cummins

FIVE CRICKETERS OF THE YEAR   Simon Harmer

FIVE CRICKETERS OF THE YEAR   Marnus Labuschagne

FIVE CRICKETERS OF THE YEAR, AND LEADING WOMAN CRICKETER IN THE WORLD   Ellyse Perry

LEADING WOMAN CRICKETER IN THE WORLD IN 2019

Ellyse Perry

RAF NICHOLSON

It is rare that a player achieves the double of Leading Cricketer in the World and one of the Five Cricketers of the Year in the same Almanack. Three men have done it: Kumar Sangakkara, Kane Williamson and Virat Kohli. But it is fitting that Ellyse Perry – one of the great all-rounders – becomes the first woman.

Perry is also the first to be named the Leading Woman Cricketer in the World twice, having previously won the award for 2016. Back then, *Wisden* summarised her performances thus: "If consistency is the mark of greatness, Perry raised the bar." In 2019, she raised it still higher, scoring a century (plus 76 not out) in her only Test, and two more (both unbeaten) in ODIs, where she averaged 73. From six Twenty20 international innings, she was dismissed once, averaging a ridiculous 150. On top of that were 21 one-day wickets at 13 apiece, and six in T20s. Quite simply, there was only one winner.

Her year began with an unbeaten century against New Zealand at Adelaide, featured a seven-for at Canterbury, and a Player of the Match performance in the Ashes Test at Taunton in July, before ending with a record-breaking unbroken opening partnership of 199 with Alyssa Healy for Sydney Sixers in the Big Bash League, in which she averaged 93. In December, she even published a book, *Perspective*. She also became the first (male or female) to achieve the double of 1,000 runs and 100 wickets in T20 internationals.

That is a telling statistic, since Perry was now succeeding where she once struggled. She had made her debut back in 2007 as a seamer but, as her batting came to the fore, her bowling couldn't always keep up. The strength of the Australian top order also meant she had to wait her turn: not until August 2013 did she appear as high as No. 5 in a one-day international. But since becoming the regular No. 4 early in 2016, she has made the spot her own, averaging 69 by the end of last year, with 39 innings producing 18 scores of 50 or more, and 15 not-outs. In T20s, she was equally hard to budge, unbeaten in 28 of her 64 innings overall. All the while, she has usually opened the bowling.

Her performance in the third Ashes one-dayer at Canterbury was particularly breathtaking: her swing, seam and pace embarrassed England, making a world-class batting line-up look as if they had never faced fast bowling. Perry took seven for 22. The first two matches of the series had been competitive, but in the space of half an hour she dictated the course of the summer.

As a result, the former England captain Charlotte Edwards labelled Perry "the greatest female player we're ever going to see". Few would argue.

WISDEN'S LEADING WOMAN CRICKETER IN THE WORLD

2014 Meg Lanning (Australia)	2016 Ellyse Perry (Australia)	2018 Smriti Mandhana (India)
2015 Suzie Bates (NZ)	2017 Mithali Raj (India)	2019 **Ellyse Perry (Australia)**

FIVE CRICKETERS OF THE YEAR

The Five Cricketers of the Year represent a tradition that dates back in Wisden *to 1889, making this the oldest individual award in cricket. The Five are picked by the editor, and the selection is based, primarily but not exclusively, on the players' influence on the previous English season. No one can be chosen more than once. A list of past Cricketers of the Year appears on page 1466.*

THE TRICKIEST OF SELECTIONS

Apologies, then, to Josh Hazlewood, Jack Leach, Jason Roy, Rohit Sharma and Mitchell Starc. In another year, they might have made a compelling Five. But the summer of 2019 – World Cup, Ashes and all – was always likely to throw up a crowded list of candidates; not every drop of cream could rise to the top.

Cricketers of the Year have been chosen by *Wisden* since 1889, usually in clumps of five (though there has also been a nine, a six, a four and three ones), and rarely without the editor's sanity being questioned. But there is, in theory, a method to the madness: a player is picked only once, a quirk which is part of the award's charm and distinctiveness; and, according to Almanack rubric (see page 14), the selection is made on the basis of "excellence in and/or influence on the previous English summer".

Winners have not always ticked both boxes, but the bar for admission to the class of 2020 was necessarily high. Leach, for instance, achieved near-cult status for his nightwatchman's 92 against Ireland, his one not out at Headingley, and his sweaty specs; he even spawned his own mask. Had he bowled Somerset to their first Championship title on the last day of the season, who knows? But an Ashes haul of 12 wickets was unexceptional. In the end, his influence outdid his excellence.

Sharma hit a record five World Cup hundreds, which in any other year would have guaranteed a place at high table. But India lost their semi-final to New Zealand (Sharma c Latham b Henry 1), and he was not the only opener to make hay. Roy's return from injury gave England's stuttering World Cup the shot of adrenalin it needed, then he struggled in the Ashes. Starc also broke a World Cup record (27 wickets), but was entrusted by Australia's selectors with a single Ashes Test; come mid-September, he felt sidelined. Hazlewood was superb, but not even his side's best bowler.

For the chosen Five, there were few such quibbles. Jofra Archer vied with Ben Stokes (selected in 2016, and so ineligible) as the all-format player of the summer. Pat Cummins was relentless with white ball and red, the Platonic ideal of a fast bowler. Simon Harmer's off-breaks (as well as his occasional captaincy and lower-order hitting) inspired Essex to a unique Championship/Twenty20 double. Marnus Labuschagne piled up runs for Glamorgan, then somehow ensured Australia's batting lost little for the absence of Steve Smith (like Stokes, a winner in 2016). Ellyse Perry bestrode the (women's) Ashes like a colossus, or possibly a colossa. Excellence, influence: you name it, they displayed it.

Was there a case for plucking the Five solely from those involved in the World Cup and the (men's) Ashes, the summer's two highest-profile events? Perhaps, but the credentials of Harmer and Perry seemed stronger. County cricket and the women's game did not deserve to be ignored.

The Five Cricketers have never claimed to represent the five best players of the previous summer; there are plenty of awards for that. Instead, they represent a one-off invitation to a hall of fame that now includes over 600 members. It's possible no set of Five has set such high standards. LAWRENCE BOOTH

Jofra Archer

WILL MACPHERSON

It wasn't one of his 20 World Cup wickets, or even the trophy-sealing super over. And it wasn't either of the six-wicket hauls in Ashes victories at Headingley or The Oval, nor flooring Steve Smith, the leading Test batsman of the era, in one of the quickest spells Lord's had seen. No, the moment Jofra Archer instantly recalls from his first summer in international cricket came during a rain-ruined one-day game in early May against Pakistan, his third match for England. He bowled four beautiful, pacy overs, and took one for six. "That was one of the days I felt best with ball in hand," he says. "Who knows what would have happened if it hadn't rained?"

In the months that followed, Archer became a sensation, and contributed to a resurgence in cricket's popularity. He is a 25-year-old of his time: a voracious player of "Fortnite" and "Call of Duty" on his beloved Xbox, and a compulsive tweeter, his account a mix of memes, random thoughts (will the wifi work in Port Elizabeth?) and – the further back you dig – entertaining observations on cricket.

The West Indian-born Archer was only a few weeks qualified when he first played for England, a one-dayer in Dublin, where Ireland's No. 8 Mark Adair became his first international victim. His Test debut at Lord's three months later (he had missed the Ashes opener with a side injury) was England's most anticipated since Kevin Pietersen 14 years earlier. He left quite a mark. "It was comforting to debut in England, and Lord's was the best place to do it," he says. "I loved that home support, and was very grateful."

He had already got used to special moments. During the World Cup, he bowled Bangladesh's Soumya Sarkar at Cardiff with a ball that flew off the stumps and over the boundary – on the full. In the semi-final at Edgbaston, he dismissed Australia's Glenn Maxwell with a perfect knuckle ball. Then came the super over, where he held his nerve after New Zealand's Jimmy Neesham hit him for six. In his first two Tests – searing pace at Lord's, supreme swing at Leeds – he showed his sophistication. (England fans loved his personality too: when a Headingley steward confiscated an inflatable watermelon, Archer ran 50 yards to return it to the raucous Western Terrace.)

Of his spell at Lord's, which ruled Smith out of three innings with concussion, he says: "No one can bowl as fast as that every single time. It's impossible. At Headingley, it was dark and chilly, and I had to bowl to conditions." There were a few grumbles when his pace dropped once more, at Old Trafford; tours of New Zealand and South Africa were not easy, despite another five-for, at Centurion, and Joe Root's handling of him was regular fodder for the pundits. But 30 wickets in his first seven Tests spoke for itself.

JOFRA CHIOKE ARCHER was born in Bridgetown, Barbados, on April 1, 1995, the son of an English father, Frank Archer (who was born in Catford, south-east London, and was a Tube driver), and a Bajan mother, Joelle Waithe. Growing up on the island, he believes, fostered his competitive spirit. "I was always outside, always playing," he says. If it was not cricket, a love fostered by his stepfather, Patrick, it was football or athletics. And when it was cricket, it wasn't just fast bowling. Restlessly waiting his turn to bat or bowl, Archer would practise spin with his other arm; even now, he warms up by bowling serviceable left-arm orthodox.

Pace bowling had begun at 13, but he wasn't "strong or fast enough, and didn't stand out against my peers". Despite that, Nhamo Winn, his coach at Christchurch Foundation School, just up from Oistins Fish Fry, remembers that Archer was regularly touching 80mph within two years. Yet Archer says he still does not feel quick. "You see the speed gun, but you never really know. I would like to face myself to find out."

As a schoolboy in 2010, he was at the Kensington Oval to watch Paul Collingwood's England win the World T20. His favourite player was Craig Kieswetter: Archer now wears his No. 22 jersey. The idea of representing England (his only passport is British) crystallised in 2015, when he was still stewing over his omission from the West Indies Under-19 World Cup squad the previous year. Chris Jordan, his friend and fellow Bajan, introduced him to Sussex.

"I knew I had a British passport, so it was always a thought," says Archer. "But I thought it was too far away. I often said to myself I wouldn't play for England because I had played for Windies Under-19s, and the guys in England had a head start. They would pick their own. Seeing CJ do well, I started to believe it could be possible."

Moving to Sussex, where he played for Middleton, was not simple: "Having to leave where you are familiar with, to start another life away from your family and friends, is daunting." A stress fracture caused him to remodel his now famously relaxed run-up, and things took off in 2016. Having played for Sussex Seconds, he was handed a first-class debut against the touring Pakistanis at Hove, and picked up five wickets. A run in the Championship side followed: in 20 first-class matches in 2016 and 2017, he collected 89 wickets at 26, and scored six half-centuries.

In September 2016, Archer had been preparing to return to Barbados. "I was about to pack up my stuff and go home for the winter, when Sussex said: 'You can't leave. We need to put you through winter training.' My mum found it harder than anyone. I had to tell her I wasn't coming home." It proved worthwhile. His county performances led to Twenty20 gigs in Bangladesh, Australia and Pakistan, then an IPL contract with Rajasthan Royals. His status as one of the planet's most exciting talents was assured.

Archer was happy to wait seven years, until he was 27, to qualify for England on residency grounds. But, in November 2018, the qualification period was reduced to three years, in line with other countries, opening up the possibility of a debut in early 2019. Archer could not hide his excitement, even if some in the Caribbean questioned his motivation. In England, others – including squad members – wondered whether he would disrupt a settled team. "There was some uproar," he says. "And that did upset me." He was not upset for long, and spent the summer living up to the hype. "It's all been amazing."

Pat Cummins

Daniel Brettig

Among several nicknames, Pat Cummins last year found himself answering to "Winx", after one of Australia's favourite thoroughbreds. And there was a thrill to match any of Winx's triumphs when Cummins burst through the defences of Joe Root on the penultimate evening of the pivotal Fourth Test at Old Trafford, which ended with Australia retaining the Ashes in England for the first time since 2001.

The moment had been a long time in the planning. Cummins had been visiting England most years since 2012, fit to play or not, and gained knowledge about the Dukes ball and northern-summer conditions. When Australia's cricketers convened for a pre-Ashes camp in Southampton following their loss to England in the World Cup semi-final at Edgbaston, the agenda was clear.

"We sat down and mapped out the statistics that JL [coach Justin Langer], Painey [captain Tim Paine] and Dene Hills, our analyst, had come up with," says Cummins. "They said: 'Right, this is our blueprint. Everyone's got their theories about swinging the ball big in England and bowling full, but the hard data says aim for the top of off stump, be super disciplined, and let the ball do the rest.' It was something we all bought into, although there were times we had to keep each other accountable, and stick to our plan."

In Manchester that early September evening, the plan came together in a way Cummins, his team-mates and most of the Australian public will long remember. Root, for all his struggles, remained the prized wicket. "I don't think I could bowl a much better ball than that," says Cummins. "The plan for him was to bowl well in his first ten, 20, 30 balls, so he doesn't get away from us. He's done that a few times: if he gets away early, it tends to be when he scores his big runs. To get him first ball, late in the day, knowing we were going to go to bed with them a couple down and Joe Root already in the shed, and we can turn up next day with a chance to retain the Ashes – that was one of my career highlights."

Born in the Sydney suburb of Westmead on May 8, 1993, PATRICK JAMES CUMMINS grew up in the Blue Mountains, west of the city. When he was four, he tried to burst into the bathroom at home to give his younger sister, Laura, a bag of sweets; she slammed the door on him, slicing off the tip of his right middle finger, which still lacks a nail. But the shortened finger has never impeded his mastery of seam or swing. Meanwhile, his love of cricket grew as he became accustomed to seeing Australia win in England. After the 2005 epic, he was upset, but not crestfallen: after all, normal service would soon be resumed, right?

"For basically my whole childhood, we'd beaten England. You go: 'Oh, we'll win the next one over there.' Then we'd lose again, which happened three or four times. Something we spoke about last year was that we hadn't won there for 18 years."

Cummins had made his Test debut at Johannesburg in November 2011, aged 18, and took six for 79 to help set up a two-wicket win. But a series of back problems intervened, and he did not play another Test for five and a half years. In 2013, he had been a travelling spectator in England ahead of the third of Australia's four successive away Ashes defeats. Two years later, they lost again; Cummins was a late replacement for the retired Ryan Harris, but didn't play a Test. All the while, having also visited England on limited-overs and A-tours, he was working out how to bowl there, and his body was learning how to cope with the rigours of fast bowling. He is one of Cricket Australia's shrewdest investments. "I'd never played many first-class games over there, but I felt like I'd had eight or nine years of experience bowling with the Dukes, and talking to a lot of other guys about it."

In January 2019, he was chosen – along with batsman Travis Head – as one of Paine's vice-captains, in part because of his intelligence and his handle on what matters in the game, and in life. And he is certain the Australians stood up to the slings and arrows of the most watchable Ashes since 2005 because they had the right plans and the right attitude.

The highest figure fetched by a non-Indian in IPL history

"It was serious stuff, but more importantly we were enjoying the tour. We made a real effort to avoid unnecessary media: there were no newspapers on the buses, and a lot of the boys came off social media. It really helped: we had a 17-man squad that felt really tight, like our own little sanctuary."

Of course, things might have been more straightforward without the intervention of Ben Stokes at Headingley. "That last day, he was batting out of his skin, but it was probably the only time I felt the wicket and the ball weren't bowler-friendly," says Cummins. "It just seemed more like one-day cricket."

At Old Trafford, the Australians proved resilient, finding enough batting in support of the incomparable Steve Smith, then charging in at an England line-up that, Stokes aside, had been steadily worn down. Cummins, in contrast to his faltering early steps as a teenager, when he tried to bowl fast without collapsing in a heap, had the confidence in his body to hurl rocket after rocket. But he also trusted others to step up if he did get injured. There was no need: alone among Australia's quick bowlers, he played all five Tests, bowling nearly 36 more overs than the next busiest seamer on either side, Stuart Broad.

As the series swung one way, then the other, culminating in England's win at The Oval and a 2–2 draw, his durability paid off, often at the times of Australia's greatest need. Cummins struck in every innings, and finished with 29 wickets at 19, the biggest haul in a Test series without a five-for. Such reliable brilliance has already marked him as one of the finest fast bowlers of his, or any, generation. In December, he was picked up at the IPL auction by Kolkata Knight Riders for Rs15.5 crore (nearly £1.7m) – the highest figure fetched by a non-Indian in the tournament's history.

But that mattered less than the events of a few months earlier, when – at Old Trafford – he lifted his eyes and sprinted for the line. Australia's thoroughbred brought the Ashes home, where in his childhood he had remembered them resting.

Simon Harmer

ALAN GARDNER

It was the defining week of the best season of Simon Harmer's career. But, at the end, his overriding emotion was relief. Spin-bowling spearhead of Essex's Championship challenge, as well as captain of the Twenty20 side making their first finals-day appearance since 2013, Harmer admits he felt "extremely anxious" as the county took aim at an unprecedented double. He need not have worried.

Twice in six days he lived up to his billing as domestic cricket's premier spinner, and guided Essex to silverware; individual accolades would come too, as well as a fitting amount of fizz for a man who loves to give his off-breaks a rip. These were rewards for a career marked by hard work and sacrifice, though Harmer still had plenty he wanted to prove.

His central role in Essex's second Championship in three years was no great surprise, though a haul of 83 wickets at 18 apiece surpassed even the 72 at 19 he had managed in 2017. But T20 success – the club's first, after more than a decade and a half of trying – bore a more personal stamp. Harmer had only just taken the reins, and saw his team manage two wins from their first ten games, before striking a vein of form. On finals day, Essex's armoury could not have been more Harmer-y: figures of four for 19 and three for 16 (his two best hauls in the format) kept Derbyshire and Worcestershire tied down. But someone had to finish the job with the bat. Step forward the captain, to hit the winning runs from the last ball. "The stars aligned," he says. "The way I played at finals day will be something I look back on for many years."

Less than 48 hours later, Essex were at Taunton, looking to dampen Somerset's hopes of a maiden Championship title. They were helped by the weather, but there was enough time for Harmer to claim his tenth five-wicket haul of the season (the most since Mushtaq Ahmed's 11 for Sussex in 2006). With Somerset unable to force the win they needed, Essex's players could start popping the champagne corks again.

SIMON ROSS HARMER was born on February 10, 1989, in Pretoria, the administrative capital of South Africa, where he spent his "whole life" – at least until he finished at Pretoria Boys High School. The son of a geologist, Jock, and a tennis coach, Barbara, he developed his love for cricket by playing with his older brother, Matthew, in the backyard (and bowling seam-up until the age of 15). Despite being more interested in sport than homework, Harmer embarked on a law degree at Nelson Mandela Metropolitan University, which also allowed him to pursue cricket with Eastern Province. "My dad and I packed the car and the trailer, and made the ten-hour trip down to Port Elizabeth. I'd never been before in my life." It wouldn't be his last step into the unknown.

Before long, he broke into the franchise system with Warriors (his degree remains unfinished, but Harmer wants to complete it via distance learning). In 2015, he performed respectably in five Tests for South Africa, and even had the West Indian limpet Shivnarine Chanderpaul stumped, one of only two bowlers – with New Zealand's Mark Craig – to do so in Tests. Yet, as transformation targets reshaped the sport at home, Harmer remained uncertain about his future.

Having gained promotion in the Championship in 2016, Essex were looking for a spinner, and offered him the chance to turn Kolpak – even if an initial six-month contract worth £30,000 hardly guaranteed long-term riches. But, given an opportunity, he grabbed it with one of those bear-like paws, raising the possibility of a return to international cricket, this time for England, though his ability to meet the qualification requirements was tangled in Home Office red tape – not to mention the tendrils of Brexit. Adding to the sense of flux is the fact that he can't buy property, while his girlfriend can't work in the UK.

"I'm very much a cricketing nomad," he says. "I pack up my life, put it in boxes, store them and move on to the next place. It's extremely frustrating because, as much as I love Essex, I feel like I don't belong, because I don't have somewhere to come back to."

Not that he is complaining. "Excuse my language, but some cricketers are kissed on the cock, and things come easy. I feel like I'm a late bloomer in life and cricket: I've had to do things the hard way. I've had to put myself under pressure, which I think I quite enjoy. It's just the way things have worked out."

At Essex, things could hardly have worked out better. Tall and imposingly solid for an off-spinner, with fingers that look as if they could rip off a doorknob, he has, since his arrival at Chelmsford, claimed more Championship wickets (212) than anyone. Before the 2019 season, he had resolved to step things up still further.

"I felt more responsibility," he says. "In the first year, I was just happy to be there, trying my nuts off to contribute. Then everyone's talking about second-year syndrome: 'Is he going to be effective?' We didn't play our best cricket as a team. So last year, I just wanted to be the best I possibly could be – taking responsibility for the attack, putting pressure on myself to be the guy that bowled from one end."

That competitor's spirit is what drives him, and motivates him to prove wrong those who doubted his ability, or his decision to quit South Africa. It is what prompts him to speak openly about wanting to play for England, or believing himself to be among the best off-spinners in the world. He says he would love to compete against the likes of Nathan Lyon and Ravichandran Ashwin, "and see how I fare".

Whatever comes next, Harmer seems well-equipped to forge his own path. "You're always going to have people with an opinion, a lot of them ill-informed: people on social media, old coaches who didn't really support me. When you turn your back on international cricket, you wonder: were you good enough, did you make the right decision? To come over here, and be the best spinner in England, makes me feel a lot happier."

Marnus Labuschagne

Malcolm Knox

Marnus Labuschagne spent four days of what became his Ashes debut wearing an orange vest, and running drinks, towels and gloves to his team-mates. Like everyone at Lord's on the fourth afternoon, a Saturday, he was gripped by tension as Jofra Archer sent down the fastest spell of 2019 at the inevitable Steve Smith. "I was at ground level, sitting on the edge of my chair," says Labuschagne. "He was bombarding Steve, bowling really quick. From the way Steve was ducking and weaving, I realised it was a really fast spell. I looked up at the scoreboard: it was 93mph, then 95…"

Even when Smith was felled by a bouncer, Labuschagne had no thought of joining the game. He continued to play the reserve's role, taking a drink to Pat Cummins at the non-striker's end, and watching Smith receive medical attention. Smith would retire hurt, then return, before falling for 92. But Labuschagne slept well that night, thinking Smith would play next day.

"I never really thought I'd be out there, but my mind did start to work," he says. "I reckoned I was probably the most like-for-like in the team. But when he came out and batted again, I thought he'd be fine. That meant I didn't overthink things, or get nervous. Then, next morning, Tim Paine came over to the nets and said: 'Mate, I think you're playing.'"

Labuschagne had been given his footnote as Test cricket's first concussion substitute. Even then, he expected a limited role on a field where he had played only once, a one-day appearance for Glamorgan against Middlesex earlier in the summer. On the Sunday, England resumed on 96 for four, only 104 ahead; the match seemed unlikely to shrug off the burden of time lost to rain. But Ben Stokes made a hundred, and Australia began losing wickets. Labuschagne was now able to taste Archer's ferocious pace for himself.

"His second ball was right on the money, and hit me on the grille. I remember thinking it was one of the fastest I'd faced: it hit me before I could move. But once you get hit, you're up and about. It gets you going. You start watching the ball a bit harder. I was less nervous playing than I had been watching. When you're out there, you can do something about it."

Labuschagne batted 30 overs to help save a match for which he had not been selected. Like Shirley MacLaine in *The Pajama Game* on Broadway, the understudy turned into a star. Through the remaining three Tests, he became the nearest thing to a like-for-like replacement for the irreplaceable. And by the end of 2019, he was even outscoring Smith: he hit 896 runs in five home Tests against Pakistan and New Zealand, culminating in 215 at the SCG, his fourth hundred of the Australian summer.

MARNUS LABUSCHAGNE was born in Klerksdorp, a mining town in South Africa's North West province, on June 22, 1994, the elder of two children of mining executive Andre and home economics teacher Alta. In 2004, Andre's employer, DRDGold, offered him a three-year posting to run a new mine in Queensland. The Labuschagnes liked Brisbane enough to stay.

Attending Cleveland State School, then Brisbane State High School, Marnus showed talent as a scrum-half, and a good deal more as a cricketer. Gifted enough to be picked for Queensland age-group teams, he was not quite among the country's best teenage players, but was already showing the obsessive work ethic that would become his signature. At 18, he beat a path to Neil D'Costa, the Sydney batting coach who had mentored Michael Clarke and Phillip Hughes. D'Costa changed everything: grip, stance, backlift, attitude, even diet and training. "I was doing everything I could to become a professional cricketer," says Labuschagne. "I wouldn't say I had no doubt I would get there, but I hadn't left myself any other options."

He continued to obey the textbook, spending summers in England with Plymouth CC and Kent's Sandwich Town. While learning how to bat and bowl leg-spin in diverse conditions, he also got a name as the ultimate nuffie, the player who kept others awake with the tap of his bat on his hotel-room floor, who never stopped eating, drinking or talking cricket. Back in Australia, his downtime was spent with friends improvising cricketish activities – backyard pitches made of bodyboards angled so the ball reared from a length, kitchen games that involved catching pieces of corn as they flew off a chopping board.

He was also collecting his own catalogue of footnotes. A club cricketer called in as a substitute fielder, he took a spectacular diving short-leg catch to dismiss India's Varun Aaron at Brisbane in 2014-15. In September 2017, during a one-day match for Queensland, he became the first to give away a five-run penalty under a new fake-throwing rule, designed to stop fielders tricking batsmen into thinking they have the ball. "I'd been doing it for years," he admits. "I got caught for not adapting quick enough."

Even when unexpectedly selected for Australia as a batsman on the tour of the UAE in 2018-19, Labuschagne had the mark of a curio cricketer, used more for his leg-spin than for the batting which had yet to reach great heights for Queensland. But the selectors saw something they liked. He was back in the Test team late that summer, and his thousand runs for Glamorgan in early 2019 thrust him out of a thicket of contenders.

A week after Lord's, Labuschagne made 74 – out of 179 – and 80 at Headingley. "The first innings was my best in the series. It was overcast, and nipping and swinging about, but sometimes you get a feeling you're picking the ball up early, and it's going to be really hard to get out." In the end, he was undone by a Stokes full toss.

At Old Trafford, he became the fourth player – after Herbie Collins, Herbert Sutcliffe and Mike Hussey – to reach 50 in his first four Ashes innings. Riding in the front seat of Australia's 2019 rollercoaster, he then produced a moment of magic with the ball in the lengthening shadows to end Jack Leach's two hours of defence in two northern cities, and hasten the retention of the urn.

"To crack them open and win the Test like that was awesome," says Labuschagne, before changing the subject to talk about someone else. There is no such thing as a like-for-like replacement, but with leg-spin and bat, by day and by night, he was becoming at least an echo of the nonpareil Smith.

Ellyse Perry

MELINDA FARRELL

Perhaps the only surprise about Ellyse Perry's inclusion as one of *Wisden's* Five was that it had not happened before. Since becoming Australia's youngest debutante in 2007, aged 16, she has so often played a pivotal role that it is easy to take her for granted. Whether opening the bowling, batting at No. 4 or shining in the field, she has made the exceptional seem routine.

The seventh female Cricketer of the Year was the first from outside England. The 2019 women's Ashes provided a typical snapshot of Perry's dominance, the multi-format nature of the series an ideal vehicle for showcasing one of cricket's great all-rounders. During Australia's 3–0 whitewash of the one-dayers, she bookended a stylish half-century with two outstanding bowling performances: three for 43 at Leicester, followed by seven for 22 – Australia's best one-day figures, and the fourth-best overall – as she scythed through a deflated England at Canterbury. In the Twenty20 matches, she excelled once more, taking two for 11 at Chelmsford, before notching 47 at Hove and 60 at Bristol, both unbeaten.

In between those two sets of games, Perry was named Player of the Match in the lone Test, at Taunton. It's just a shame this was only her eighth: she appears to revel in the extended fight. In her seventh, against England at North Sydney Oval in November 2017, she had scored a marathon 213 not out. At Taunton, she made 116 and 76 not out in a display of patience and technical mastery, leaving her with a Test average of 78. All her batting figures over the past two years include a lavish number of asterisks; the question of how to capture Perry's wicket hovers over all her opponents.

It is difficult to overstate the quality of her Test batting, especially as women play little multi-day domestic cricket: the red ball, Kookaburra or Dukes, is a novelty. Watching her conquer it, whether bowling or batting, was one of the delights of the season.

"I love the challenge of spending a lot of time at the crease, and going through different periods while you're out there – those tough spells of bowling you've got to face," she says. "We all really enjoy the opportunity to play those Test matches. They're the pinnacle of our sport, particularly with the Baggy Green being involved. It's such an important symbol of Australian cricket history, so it's a huge honour and thrill when those matches come around."

Perry's batting last summer also illustrated her development. She has always played in the classical mould, solid in defence and proficient in the V. In the shorter formats, she often started conservatively, then accelerated. And while she still relies on technical skill, she has grown more aggressive, especially in Twenty20: years of strength and conditioning work have endowed her with power to augment her timing. The 2019 model had a more hardened, muscular physique than the lithe, naturally talented teenager who first exploded on to the international scene. "Rather than play the same shot along the ground, I've now got the ability to play it in the air. The strokeplay is still similar – it's probably just at a higher intensity."

Bowling had been Perry's first calling card, and it continued to plague England. Top-order batters were chief among her victims but, even when she wasn't taking wickets, she was showing off a combination of pace (she remains one of the quickest in the women's game) and nagging control of subtle swing and seam. In recent years, she has captained Sydney Sixers in the women's Big Bash League, making her even cannier with the ball. Throughout, she has hungered for the thick of battle. Whether turning at the top of her mark, taking guard, or firing the ball back to the stumps, Perry is consistently at the heart of the action.

ELLYSE ALEXANDRA PERRY was born in Wahroonga, Sydney, on November 3, 1990. Her mother, Kathy, is a GP, and her practice is run by her husband Mark, formerly a maths teacher. Perry's earliest cricket memory is of trying to work out how to bowl with her father (who played squash for Australia) and older brother, Damien, in the family lounge. Next day, she was bowling in the backyard, and Mark has been her coach ever since. She describes her sport-filled childhood as that of a "typical Aussie kid". And sport continues to run in the family: in 2015, she married rugby union international Matt Toomua.

A natural athlete, she excelled across the board, but concentrated on cricket and football, eventually representing her country in both; she holds the rare distinction of being a dual-sport World Cup player. Identified as an exceptional talent in her early teens, she vaulted into the Australian side even before she had played a domestic senior match, taking two wickets on debut against New Zealand. A fortnight later, she made her first appearance for the national football team. Despite being a defender, she scored within two minutes of an Olympic qualifying match against Hong Kong. She went on to win 18 caps.

For several years, she juggled them both, before committing to cricket – and featured prominently from the start. Off the last ball of the 2010 World T20 final against New Zealand at Bridgetown, she combined the skills of her two sports to give Australia the trophy: with Sophie Devine needing four to tie, Perry deflected a fierce straight-drive with her right boot to mid-on, limiting the damage to a single. And in the final of the 50-over World Cup in 2013, against West Indies at Mumbai, she overcame an ankle injury, hobbling her way to three wickets, and setting up an Australian victory. She is arguably the most talented all-rounder women's cricket has ever seen, at a time when increased professionalism has dramatically raised standards.

"The exciting thing is, we don't know where it's going to go next," she says. "It's probably about trying to keep evolving, to stay in line with the trends." Can she possibly contribute more? "In everything. On and off the field, as a leader and as a player, with the fans as well. I think you can always be a better person in any environment. You can always be a better player, too."

Ellyse Perry is only 29. It is sobering to imagine what her thirties will bring.

ENGLAND'S MULTICULTURAL WORLD CUP WINNERS

Different strokes for different folks

Eoin Morgan

As we took the field to defend 15 in the super over in the World Cup final last summer, Jos Buttler told me he hoped I had a couple of shamrocks in my pocket. I laughed, and turned to Adil Rashid: "Allah's with us, isn't he?" Rash agreed he was. Later, at the end of a crazy day, I mentioned that comment in the post-match press conference, because it seemed to sum up the kind of team we had become: a team of different backgrounds, races and religions, a team which derived strength from diversity, and represented the best of our country.

That's right: *our* country. I've lived in London longer than in Ireland. It's my home, and has been for a long time – longer than many realise. And the fact that I've experienced so many cultures here makes me feel as if England's World Cup winners stand for us all.

Last summer, that feeling mattered as much as ever. Until the 2016 EU referendum, most of us probably thought life in the UK was pretty harmonious. Since then, it's become completely divided, which is sad. But sport, I think, generally gets it right, because it is driven by a common goal. Most of the time, people are committed to that, and so they have to be honest with each other. In sport, you can't get away with lies – at least not for long. It's more important than it's ever been that the national side epitomise the culture we live in.

In that final, Jason Roy (born in South Africa), Ben Stokes (New Zealand), Jofra Archer (Barbados) and I all started life somewhere else. Rash is Muslim, and so is Moeen Ali, who didn't play at Lord's but was an important part of the squad. Let's be honest: the England team have never really been made up of 11 white Christians, anyway; these days more people seem comfortable about that.

Attitudes have changed even during my time. When I first played for England in 2009, I remember being told by someone that, with all the money that goes into the county academies, the cost of producing a home-grown

Culture of success: the diverse England team who lifted the World Cup. Ben Stokes, Jofra Archer, Jos Buttler, Joe Root, Mark Wood, Eoin Morgan, Jonny Bairstow, Adil Rashid, Liam Plunkett, Chris Woakes and Jason Roy.

ICC/Getty Images

player like Stuart Broad, who has gone through the system, was about £6m – that's the rough figure you reach, in other words, if you divide the money that goes into the academies by the number of England players the system produces. The implication was that the figure was higher than it would have been had the national side been made up of 11 born-and-bred Englishmen.

For a while, there was a stigma about being born abroad and playing cricket for England, especially when there was an influx of South African guys coming here to make a living. When I started out, we had Kevin Pietersen and Jonathan Trott, as well as players who were born in South Africa but bred in England, like Andrew Strauss and Matt Prior. English cricket didn't fully embrace the influx – and that was the biggest mistake it could have made. That kind of attitude just creates a bigger divide between the players and their public.

> I'm not religious, but I can see the importance of faith for others

I was struck during the World Cup by the different ethnicities who turned up to cheer us on. I never thought, for example, that we'd have so many England-based Indian fans supporting us but, when you look at the footage from the tournament, you can see how many were wearing England shirts. It was amazing, and a change for the better.

My own approach has undergone a bit of a transformation, too. When I played for Ireland, I never sang the national anthem when the teams lined up before a game. It wasn't something that got me excited or fired up and, when I threw in my lot with England, I felt exactly the same – despite our coach Andy Flower asking us to sing along during the World Twenty20 in 2009, which we were hosting. I didn't think it was an issue, although others obviously did – especially during the 2015 World Cup, when my decision was met with a real song and dance, so to speak.

What eventually made me choose to sing "God Save the Queen" was a chat over a beer with a couple of friends, who are both English, but of Irish heritage. They told me how passionate they get about the anthem – one sings the British, the other the Irish. It opened my eyes to what an anthem can mean, and after that I made a conscious decision to join in. That said, if I stopped singing it now, I don't think a fuss would be made. I reckon we've moved on.

I also think the players have matured in terms of the discussions we have about our backgrounds. Take the question of religion, which isn't always the easiest subject. I'm not religious these days: I guess I believe in human beings, and their potential. But I can also see the importance of faith for guys like Mo and Rash: it helps them put things in perspective, and that sense of calm can rub off on team-mates.

I understand where they're coming from, having grown up in Catholic Ireland, where the church was so important and the idea of respecting your elders built into the way of life. Islam is similar, and I fully respect that. It helps me understand the dynamics of the relationship between Mo and Rash, and informs the way I talk to them to get the best out of them.

A lot of people I know claim to be religious, but aren't – it's just that the branding suits them. But with Mo, you can feel his faith in everything he does. He's never uptight or tense. His faith brings the best out of him, and helps

Shoulder to shoulder: Chris Woakes, Jofra Archer, Adil Rashid and Moeen Ali during England's opening-day victory over South Africa.

relieve the pressures of daily life. Because he has that grounding, that belief in a higher purpose, he brings a different perspective to the team. It's the same with Rash, and it's priceless in a situation like the World Cup final. That's why I said what I did at the press conference. I wasn't being flippant: I was trying to articulate something that had become central to our dressing-room.

As I grew up, religion was placed on the back burner. Travelling the world to play cricket made me more interested in people than in a higher being. In a way, I wish I had taken more interest in religions other than Catholicism, and chosen one or two to delve into. Perhaps that's why I'm inquisitive about what makes Mo and Rash tick. When they asked if we could get photos out of the way at the end of games before everyone starts spraying champagne, the lads agreed without hesitation.

Does having different nationalities help us bond too? I think it does – and in some ways it's easier to talk about than religion. You ask each other questions. You get to know each other. You become closer precisely because of your differences. Jason Roy can tell us what it was like growing up with the Durban beach on your doorstep. I can regale the guys with stories of cold, dark Irish winters. And Jofra is from a different climate altogether.

I generally try to stay away from the chatter outside the dressing-room, especially during the build-up to something as important as the World Cup. But I made sure I stayed in the loop about the guys' thoughts on the potential inclusion of Jofra in our 15-man squad. Dave Willey and Chris Woakes were quoted out of context on the subject and, as soon as I spoke to them, I realised it wasn't an issue.

We then had a pre-tournament camp in Glamorgan, where the backroom staff were able to get a handle on what it was like having Jofra around. Did it create angst, or was it good for the team? It was unequivocally the latter.

Usually in a six-horse race, which is effectively what was going on with the bowlers who were trying to secure a place in the final 15, one ends up lagging behind. But not after Jofra came in. Thanks to the presence of a so-called outsider, everyone's standards rose. If anything, the mood around the camp did too. Multiculturalism made us stronger.

England's football team went through an interesting time last year, travelling around the corners of Europe and dealing with racism. But that is what society is going through. You don't sit back and apologise, and you don't shy away from it: you need to go through it, and get out the other side. Last summer, I was proud that our cricketers did such a great job – and that the nation responded.

Eoin Morgan played 23 one-day internationals for Ireland from August 2006, before first appearing for England in May 2009. He was talking to Lawrence Booth.

INDIAN CRICKET'S GREATEST NURSERY

In search of the new Kohli

ANAND VASU

Early on an October morning in Bangalore, southern India, the skies are dark grey, and rain has collected in muddy puddles by the roadside. Over a hundred children – some in whites, some in coloured clothing, some under umbrellas held by anxious parents, some blissfully drenched – wait at the gates of the Karnataka Institute of Cricket. They will open, as they always do, at six.

Anywhere else, there would be no queues, for the unseasonal all-night downpour would have made cricket impossible. Here, it's just another day. The rain has stopped for the moment, and the groundsmen are doing their bit, refreshing the run-ups on the artificial turf with gravel chips, removing the covers, and mopping up the edges where water has seeped in. Then, as if receiving an invisible sign, a choreographed dance begins.

There are never enough nets for practice – and there are more nets here (36 in all) than at any other private facility in the world. Even most Test grounds do not have 36 that can be used simultaneously. KIOC opened on April 19, 1996, and have not shut for a single day since. This is not an exaggeration: there are no holidays, no Christmas, no Eid, no Diwali. For nearly 25 years, they have operated day in, day out. The average daily footfall is over 1,500, though never more than 2,000, which feels too crowded. There

Drills and spills: a choreographed dance begins.

is nowhere quite like it in India (Mumbai's Shivaji Park is more of a shared public space), and almost certainly nowhere quite like it anywhere else.

It's a serious business – as serious as cricket gets. KIOC employ 75 full-time coaches, and usually have between 15 and 20 on call. Over the years, they have produced more than 100 players who have gone on to represent Karnataka at various levels, and international cricketers, male and female, for India, the United States of America, even England.

There is a delicious circle in operation. Young hopefuls come here because they believe the institute can set them on a path – competitive club cricket first, then age-group representative cricket, eventually first-class cricket. As thousands churn through, the cream rises. And when they succeed, they become poster boys or girls (the split is roughly 85–15, which is less one-sided than most Indian coaching centres). They in turn drive ever more young aspirants back in the institute's direction. So much so that KIOC need to downplay expectations: every child walking through the door dreams of becoming the next Sachin Tendulkar or Virat Kohli.

> **He'll get thrown in the deep end, and soon we will know if he can swim or not**

The man behind it all is Irfan Sait, a Level 3 certified coach who has been involved with cricket in Karnataka – the state of Erapalli Prasanna and Gundappa Viswanath, Anil Kumble and Rahul Dravid – since the 1980s. He is also the gatekeeper. "We sit parents across the table, and tell them not to put pressure on the child about selections, Karnataka and India and all that," he says. "Let the child enjoy the game first. A time will come when we will be able to sit back and say that this boy has the potential and the skill to play at a higher level.

"As they say, if talent doesn't work hard, hard work will beat talent. There will be someone who is less skilful, but he can overtake. A time comes when you have to push further with fitness, speed, skills, agility. Till such time, enjoy your child's cricket. It's a sporting event, not some kind of race to be selected."

Irfan needs to maintain a balance, for he cannot talk his academy down. After all, kids do not come here for recreational sport. The hope of being picked by the Karnataka state team, who have won the Ranji Trophy eight times (only Mumbai have won more), or for the Twenty20 Karnataka Premier League, is on the minds of ambitious youngsters and pushy parents alike. "We keep them grounded," says Irfan. "Not everyone who wears pads and picks up a bat is going to play like Kohli."

While that should be obvious, for parents who funnel their children into such institutes, there is a certain roll of the dice. "I know my son has the potential to go far," says I. B. Raj, father of 12-year-old Rakshit, who is enrolled full-time. "But we had to test this. The only way to do that was to put him in a place like this. He'll get thrown in the deep end, and soon we will know if he can swim or not."

Rakshit appears to be enjoying the experience. "See, I never got a chance to play cricket all day before this," he says. "From morning to evening I am here. In other places, I would do a net or two, then go home. Here, I finish my session, then hang around. Even if I can't bat, I can bowl in any net. And there is always someone watching me and helping, even when I'm bowling my left-arm spin rather than batting. I'd rather bowl than simply sit at home."

The financial investment is significant. A child enrolled in the weekend classes alone will pay Rs22,000 (about £235) a year. Those who push harder, taking in two sessions a day, five days a week, pay double. This may not sound like a fortune, but in India it is not easy for middle-class parents, especially when your child may never reach the heights. Throw in the cost of kit, which probably exceeds the coaching fee, and it is quite a commitment.

KIOC have found ways to ease the burden. Once a cricketer is earmarked as a serious prospect, the fee is removed. And if he or she is from outside Bangalore – and many are,

No one says no: Irfan Sait.

even from outside Karnataka – accommodation and meals are free too. The idea is that the investment will eventually pay off: successful and recognised players stay loyal to the academy, promote it on social media, and attract the next crop.

Irfan concedes cricket has become an expensive sport, but adds: "There is no sport today that is cheap, if you pursue it seriously. Any coaching comes with a cost. There are ways we can help, if a player is good. We have our own equipment store. All the manufacturers and dealers are with us. We speak to one of them, and explain that so-and-so is good, but comes from a background where he can't afford the best of equipment: can you sponsor him? When we tell manufacturers a player is likely to make it to a certain level, we are taken seriously. Not a single manufacturer has said no to us."

KIOC can also offer the enticement of teams in all five divisions of the Karnataka League: in total, they own, manage or run 13. And they have multiple grounds in the city, so they can organise practice matches for their wards, giving coaches a chance to assess players in game situations.

The other thing KIOC have done well is to rope in big names. Not long after he finished as coach of the Indian team, Gary Kirsten ran a half-day session, followed by interactions with the players and the media, bringing the academy profile and stature. Cynics may dismiss this as a marketing ploy, but it can take unexpected turns. When the former New Zealand captain Martin Crowe was working in Bangalore as a media pundit for ESPNcricinfo, he agreed to run a session. And what was meant to be a one-off turned into something else altogether. Crowe was so taken with the sheer number of players, and their enthusiasm, that he began turning up for whole afternoons, free of charge, just watching batsmen, offering a word here and there, and sharing his knowledge with youngsters still finding their feet.

Look who's dropped in: Virat Kohli and a crowd of happy students.

"Martin Crowe was always floral in his compliments," says Irfan. "The day he walked in here, he told me he had never seen anything like this, anywhere in the world. What struck him most was the intensity and passion of our youngsters. The word he used was awestruck. Someone like Crowe had gone around the world, but the passion, the way young kids work, some of them training and practising the whole day… he really was awestruck."

While thousands of cricketers have passed through KIOC, several high-profile internationals have publicly acknowledged its contribution to their own careers, including Indian women internationals Mamatha Maben, Karuna Jain, Nooshin Al Khadeer, Veda Krishnamurthy and Vellaswamy Vanitha. Then there are USA captain Sindhu Sriharsha, Akshatha Rao (also of the USA) and Sonia Odedra, who played a Test for England in 2014. In the men's game, the biggest names are Robin Uthappa, Manish Pandey, Mayank Agarwal and Shreyas Gopal; from the current crop, Devdutt Padikkal and Shubhang Hegde are making waves.

Agarwal, who was averaging 67 from his nine Tests by the end of 2019, put it like this: "The sun never sets on KIOC." He was referring to the fact that when the gates close at 10pm, the first ball is being bowled in a satellite academy, more than 8,500 miles away in San Francisco.

Whether anyone will say so explicitly, the hunt for the next Kohli is well under way.

Anand Vasu has written about cricket for 20 years.

A HISTORY OF LEFT-HANDED BATTING

Maladroit, sinister and gauche?

ANDY BULL

February 2019 in Durban: Kusal Perera cuts the winning runs in Sri Lanka's one-wicket victory against South Africa, one of the greatest Tests ever played. July at Lord's: Ben Stokes follows an unbeaten 84 with eight more in the super over as the World Cup reaches its improbable climax. August at Headingley: Stokes is closing in on a century, with Jack Leach at the other end, in the final moments of one of England's most breathless wins. September at Taunton: Leach is bowling, Alastair Cook batting, in the last twist of a classic County Championship. November at Adelaide: David Warner punches to cover, the final single in his monumental unbeaten 335.

There's another world in which none of these things happened – not the way we saw them, anyway – a parallel timeline where 2019 is mapped out by another set of landmarks, and the game looks very different. In the summer of 1913, while the nation worried about women's suffrage, Irish Home Rule, and mass strikes in the Black Country, English cricket was in the midst of its own little crisis. Everyone who cared for it was fretting, again, about its health. And *The Times*, that stately paper of record, had a "revolutionary" proposal to fix it.

Ban the left-handers.

Not immediately: that, the paper allowed, would be "absurd". But from now on, all boys should be taught to bat right-handed, leading – in a decade or so – to "the painless extinction of the left-handed batsman".

The Times were so keen that they returned to the idea when the debate about the state of the game restarted after the war: "The left-handed batsman is a thorough nuisance and a cause of waste of time." From 1925 onwards, none of the breed should "come into cricket". *The Times* were tapping into the prejudice against the left-handed: the good sheep, remember, sit at God's right hand, the wicked goats at his left. It was an old stigma, but it found new currency in the schools and factories of Victorian England.

The Manchester Guardian were sympathetic, since "the left-hander tries patience, and tends to upset the poise and movement of the game". But, the paper concluded, "they put into the game as much as they take from it". *Wisden* described the plan as "fatuous" and "foolish"; *Punch* called it "monstrous", "treacherous" and "infidel".

Imagine if the idea had taken root at the MCC's advisory committee meeting. In that world, Mahela Jayawardene holds the Test record (374), and Hanif Mohammad the first-class (499); Ravi Shastri is the first to hit six sixes, and Graeme Pollock's curtailed Test career isn't a what-if, but a never-was; David Gower does not pull his first ball for four, and Sanath Jayasuriya does not tear up the 1996 World Cup. Five of Test cricket's ten leading run-scorers have been scrubbed from the books, and six of its ten highest scores.

That covers it: Garry Sobers drives elegantly, during the Oval Test of 1973, watched by Alan Knott and Frank Hayes.

You begin to feel the size of the void. It would have been largest in the last decade: there are more left-handers coming into Test cricket than ever before. Of all the men who made their Test debuts in the 2010s, 30% bat left-handed. That's an increase of 4% on the 2000s, 9% on the 1990s, 13% on the 1980s, and – going much further back – 21% on the 1910s. The common estimate is that around 11% of us are left-handed. In contemporary cricket, then, left-handers are hugely over-represented.

To understand why, you first need to understand exactly what we're talking about. Because while left and right may seem a binary divide, it's actually a bit of a muddle. That's not just because of the odd ambidextrous player, such as David Warner, who could bat so well both ways that, according to team-mates from his teenage years, it was unclear which he would settle for.

The point is that a lot of great left-handed cricketers bat right-handed (Sachin Tendulkar, Michael Clarke, Kane Williamson), and a lot of great right-handed cricketers bat left-handed (Gower, Cook, Brian Lara). In *An Endangered Species*, Gower describes himself as "a right-handed person in pretty much everything I do" – except the one thing he's most famous for. So you have to distinguish between the genuinely left-handed, such as Garry Sobers, and left-handers who simply learned to bat that way. (Even then, there's an old story that a busybody teacher tried to make Sobers bat right-handed. It isn't true. But he did try to make him hold his pen with his right hand.)

The stance doesn't depend so much on whether a player is right- or left-handed, but on the position of the dominant hand. According to a study published in *Sports Medicine* in 2016, elite players are seven times more likely to bat with their dominant hand on top of the handle than the rest of us. If you're right-handed, that means a left-handed stance. As Gower writes: "Being a left-hander allows my right side to dominate, as it is my right eye, and more importantly my right hand, that leads." He isn't alone. Richard Hutton taught his right-handed son Ben, once the captain of Middlesex, to bat left-handed, because "it means your top hand on the bat handle is your stronger hand, and gives you more control".

Other right-handers ended up switching for more everyday reasons: Sourav Ganguly because he inherited left-handed gloves from his older brother; Mike Hussey because he wanted to copy Allan Border after watching him in the 1982 Boxing Day Test against England; Sadiq Mohammad because his oldest brother, Wazir, told him the Pakistan team lacked lefties.

For a game with a reputation for being hidebound by technique, cricket is oddly flexible about the fundamental question of which way round to hold the bat. And it always has been. In the 1851 edition of *The Science of Cricket*, James Pycroft (another leftie) included an annotated list of 71 "famous left-handed cricketers".

> He taught Richard Nyren all the skill and judgment that the noble general possessed

He describes 20 as having either "batted left, but bowled right", "batted right, but bowled left", "batted right, threw left" or – like Leach – "batted left, but threw right".

The first in the list was Richard Newland, "the father of serious cricket", according to E. V. Lucas. Newland was a farmer from Slindon in Sussex, where the church still has a tablet on the wall in his honour. He captained All-England in the 1740s, and features both on cricket's oldest surviving scorecard and in its first match report, or at least the nearest thing we have to one – James Love's poem about a game between Kent and England at the Honourable Artillery Ground on June 8, 1744.

Newland matters, too, because of his famous nephew, who would captain Hambledon. "He taught Richard Nyren all the skill and judgment that the noble general possessed," Lucas wrote. "Nyren communicated his knowledge to the Hambledon XI, and the game was made." The nephew, like the uncle, was a left-hander, and so was his son, John, who wrote the book on the club, *The Cricketers of My Time*. So there is a left-handed lineage running through the sport's earliest years. It was the method practised, and propounded, by the men who shaped cricket's development.

In *The Game of Life*, Scyld Berry estimates that a third of 18th-century batsmen we know about batted left-handed. There were enough, certainly, for a first-class match between left-handers and right-handers at the original Lord's ground in 1790, held for a 1,000-guinea stake. The right-handers were odds-on favourites, but lost by 39 runs.

According to Pycroft, the left-handed players were "almost all severe hitters" – one of the first of their stereotypes. Pycroft thought it was because "they can

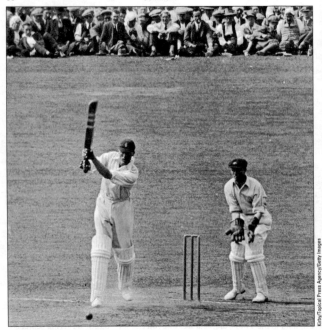

Kirby/Topical Press Agency/Getty Images

Not right: Frank Woolley was the first left-hander to hit a Test hundred for England. Here, he bats at Leeds in 1926, with Australia's Bert Oldfield keeping wicket.

generally use both arms well", and have "a certain square and powerful build". A century later, Graeme Pollock had a better explanation. "Left-handers are probably fortunate because most bowlers tend to move the ball away from us," he wrote. "This gives you lots of room in which to play your shot, whereas with the ball coming into the body you are inclined to become cramped." The flipside, Pollock argued, is that the concentration of bowling in that channel means left-handers often get a reputation for being weak outside off stump.

Which may have been one reason why, even as Pycroft was finishing his list, left-handed batting started to disappear from English cricket. The left-handers played the right-handers twice in the 1820s and 1830s, losing by 226 runs and an innings and 87. The game took place once more, in 1870 – another innings drubbing. W. G. Grace, who took nine wickets and scored 35, complained it wasn't much of a contest because the "left didn't show". *Baily's Magazine* complained "there is not now a first-class left-handed batsman in England".

The Test team felt the lack. The Australians had produced Joe Darling, who scored three Ashes centuries in 1897-98, and Clem Hill, who scored another in that series, the first of seven. By 1905, *The Manchester Guardian* were complaining that some English captains were so "dismayed by the advent of a left-hander" that they had no idea how to set the field. It got worse: the summer of 1909 was dominated by two Australian lefties, Warren Bardsley and Vernon Ransford. England were still waiting for one of their own to score a Test century.

Berry puts the decline down to "stern and inflexible Victorian mores, demanding conformity". There is a hint of this in an essay by Theodore Andrea Cook, an Edwardian critic: "The use of the right hand has been encouraged, perhaps from the idea that left-handed batting is awkward in style, or gauche." Gauche is one of those borrowed words referring to the left side that has taken on negative connotations, like maladroit or sinister.

> Woolley, the first famously graceful left-hander, still is the nonpareil

Later, Sir William Dobbie, who played three first-class matches for the Europeans in India before he became Governor of Malta, felt so strongly that he said he "would beat a son of mine who tried to bowl with the wrong arm".

Cook argued that "Bardsley and Hill seem graceful in spite of their left-handedness," which is an inversion of today's cliché that left-handers tend to be elegant, like Gower or Moeen Ali. And if they're not elegant, they're bound to be nuggety, like Justin Langer or Graeme Smith, as if their lack of elegance is all the more conspicuous because it contrasts so starkly with our expectations. We still tend to split left-handers into these two groups, each in opposition to the other. The real difference may just be that one lot love to play the cover-drive, despite its risks, and the other lot do not.

The oddly moral injunction against using your left hand meant anyone who did inevitably came across as a dilettante. Take Frank Woolley, who finally scored England's first left-handed Test century, in their 120th Test, at Sydney in 1911-12. If Newland was the first great left-hander, Woolley was the first famously graceful one. There were other candidates: Middlesex's F. G. J. Ford was "a wizard", according to Lucas, but Woolley was, still is, the nonpareil.

Neville Cardus made sure of that, with lashings of purple prose. "Cricket belongs entirely to summer every time that Woolley bats an innings," he wrote. "His cricket is compounded of soft airs and fresh flavours. And the very brevity of summer is in it too, making for loveliness. Woolley, so the statisticians tell us, often plays a long innings. But Time's a cheat, as the old song sings. Fleeter he seems in his stay than in his flight. The brevity in Woolley's batting is a thing of pulse or spirit, not to be checked by clocks, but only to be apprehended by imagination. He is always about to lose his wicket."

Woolley himself would point out, more prosaically, that if it seemed he was always about to lose his wicket, it was because "a left-hand bat has to cope with the bowler's rough". But Cardus had done his talking for him, apparently inventing the stereotype of the stylish but flawed left-hander, which lingers today.

In the end, Woolley's cover-drive, thing of beauty as it was, was the single best argument against the *Times's* proposal. The paper had a point when they argued "that a boy at the beginning of his cricket career, even if he be naturally left-handed, can be taught to bat just as well right-handed in the same way that many boys who are naturally right-handed have been taught, or have taught themselves, to bowl left-handed". Jofra Archer has done exactly that, and warms up by bowling left-arm spin because, he says, it's a fun way to stretch that side of his body.

Where the paper got it wildly wrong, though, was in leaping from that to this: "Thus if left-handed batting had never been allowed at cricket, there would have been no hardship." Oh, there'd have been less hardship for the bowlers, no doubt. But what a loss for the rest of us.

Andy Bull writes on sport for The Guardian.

CRICKET AND GENDER

A fraught battleground

Tanya Aldred

Career controversialist Katie Hopkins tweeting about cricket? There must be a bandwagon rolling into town. Sure enough, there it was – pulling into Lord's, brazen, klaxon at full volume.

When Maxine Blythin was named Kent's woman Player of the Year in September, all hell broke loose on social media. This was because she was born a boy, but transitioned in her teens. When it comes to trans women in women's sport, nuance and empathy can disappear: Hopkins called Blythin's award "another kick in the ovaries for biological females everywhere".

It is a battleground where inclusion flips the bird at equality, trans activists square up to gender-critical feminists, and science faces off against identity politics. It is also an issue that revolves around female sport, both biological women (sometimes referred to as cis women) and trans women (men who have transitioned into females). Trans men do not threaten male sport in any meaningful way.

For some trans activists, it is straightforward: a trans woman is a woman, and has a right to be included in women's spaces, including sport. For others, a trans woman who has gone through male puberty should not play against biological females. Between the two positions lies an ocean of grey. (Caster Semenya, the South African middle-distance runner, is a cause célèbre for a different category altogether: intersex, where a person is born with characteristics that are not typically male or female.)

In the UK, especially, debate has been poisonous, catalysed by proposed changes to the 2004 Gender Recognition Act. Former British Olympic swimmer Sharron Davies and nine-times Wimbledon champion Martina Navratilova have been accused of transphobia, after talking about the advantage of the male body, and in many places discussion has effectively been shut down – freedom of speech losing out to accusations of hate crime. In January, Selina Todd, a gender-critical feminist professor, was given two security guards by Oxford University after threats from trans activists. Meanwhile, cricket's administrators are torn.

Predictably, the picture portrayed of Blythin on social media was incomplete. A softly spoken trans woman who works in finance, she wasn't trying to trick anyone, and had written to the ECB before she started playing for Kent, explaining her position and offering her testosterone results. She was forced by the subsequent publicity to come out to everyone she knew. She is also a red herring of sorts.

Blythin, who was backed in the Twitter storm by her Kent captain, England batsman Tammy Beaumont, says she was born with very low testosterone levels; she is waiting for doctors to confirm her condition. Crucially, she says

The long and the short of it: Maxine Blythin bats for Kent; Lauren Winfield keeps for Yorkshire.

she didn't go through male puberty, and started living as a female in her teens. After taking oestrogen, she then went through female puberty.

Last year, her debut season for Kent's women, she averaged 33, and was their third-highest scorer. She also played for St Lawrence & Highland Court's women's team (and averaged 127) and Chesham Second XI, a men's team (and averaged 11). Mixed cricket is not unusual for good female players, because it gives them further experience: in 2011, England batsman Arran Brindle scored the first century, in Lincolnshire, by a woman in a men's Premier League match for Louth; in 2015, England seamer Kate Cross took eight for 47 in the Lancashire League.

"The papers make out that I'm this massive hench guy," says Blythin. "Yes, I'm six foot four on my tippy toes, but my dad is taller, and my sister is tall. I've never had to shave. I have pretty much zero testosterone."

Does she think being born a man gives her an edge? "None at all. People will point to my height, but it brings advantages and disadvantages. A long reach can be really useful, but when you're smaller you can get away with angles. There are girls in my team who can hit the ball harder, and have bigger hands – though I've got the longest legs. I get the arguments against trans women in sport, and I think it needs to be done on a case-by-case basis, though once you've transitioned medically, you lose that advantage, by and large."

Nicola Williams is director of Fair Play for Women, who monitor the impact of transgender policy on women and girls in the UK. "Pre-puberty, there is little difference between the sexes," she says. "It is male puberty that brings huge and irreversible advantages. Sex matters in sport. Female-only categories exist because of the large and well-known performance advantage enjoyed by males. If we didn't divide categories by sex, women would never win, or even get selected to play. The purpose of female-only is to keep female sport safe and competitive. Sporting clubs are letting that understanding slip away. They are opening up the women's game in the name of inclusion, but failing to acknowledge how this directly excludes females from their own teams. They've not found a way to solve the conundrum, which is why groups like FPFW exist."

The ICC's transgender policy is based on International Olympic Committee guidelines, and allows trans women to play women's cricket at international level if their testosterone level has been under ten nanomoles per litre for at least 12 months, and stays that way during competition (typically, male testosterone levels are between 7.7 and 29.4, while Blythin says hers were always below five). All ICC member countries must abide by this in international competition, but the ECB and Cricket Australia have their own policies for domestic cricket.

> Blythin says her testosterone levels were always below five

Australia launched their transgender and gender-diverse policy in August 2019, backed by former Australian captain Alex Blackwell and her team-mate at the Universities Women's Cricket Club in Sydney, transgender woman Erica James, who returned to the sport after transition, and became a poster girl for the new CA policy. Elite domestic cricket (including the Women's Big Bash League) shadows the ICC testosterone rule, with the possibility of a referral to an expert panel on issues of "strength, stamina or physique".

At recreational level, Australian players are allowed to self-ID – determine their own gender, without any medical assessment or treatment – with the onus on umpires or local associations to rule if there is too much disparity. In the current febrile atmosphere, it is easy to imagine this becoming problematic – for someone raising an objection, and also for the decision-maker. At both elite and recreational level, transgender players must "demonstrate a commitment to their gender identity, as nominated for the purpose of this policy, being consistent with their gender identity in other aspects of everyday life".

The ECB use the self-ID model up to and including county cricket and The Hundred (though no trans women have been drafted into the women's competition for 2020), despite the ICC recommending that their medicalised model be followed "at the level of national championships or similar". Clare Connor, the ECB's managing director of women's cricket, has hinted that the board may look at a change for The Hundred for 2021, but nothing concrete had been heard in the meantime.

For any professional clubs or England pathway teams, the ECB's head of policy development can "decide whether the transgender woman should receive clearance to play in the requested competition(s) and match(es)". But at recreational level, the only advice to clubs is that, "a transgender woman may compete in any open competition, league or match or any female-only competition, league or match, and should be accepted in the gender in which they present".

Cricket is played on many levels. It requires concentration, tactical nous, and skill. But it is also a game based on strength and speed, which is why women use a lighter, smaller ball than men, and play with shorter boundaries. The fastest ball bowled by a man is 100mph, by Shoaib Akhtar; the fastest by a woman 77mph, by Cathryn Fitzpatrick. Some men hit the ball 100 metres; Raphael Brandon, the ECB's head of science and medicine, said in 2017 that the best women might soon clear 80.

Reducing testosterone to level the playing field is controversial. The IOC – and ICC – limit of 10nmol/l is seen by some as far too high, considering women's testosterone levels tend to range between 0.12 and 1.79. There was talk of the IOC reducing the limit to five before this year's Tokyo Olympics, but scientists were unable to agree a policy. And recent research suggests that, though reducing testosterone has an effect on transgender women, it doesn't reduce all the advantages of male puberty.

Tommy Lundberg works at the Karolinska Institute in Stockholm. According to his research, after one year of gender-affirming treatment a trans woman typically loses 5% of muscle mass ("quite a small amount"), but no strength. "Few sports are based purely on muscle mass," he says. "They usually include endurance and technique as well. However, I would say that, with hitting, throwing and sprinting, muscle mass and strength are important variables, so this matters in cricket. Some of the trans women lost far more than 5% of their muscle mass, some lost almost zero, and god knows what would happen if you were actually training during that period. We just don't have all the answers yet."

He is backed by evidence from exercise scientist Professor Gregory Brown for a lawsuit brought by Connecticut schoolgirl runners, who sued after transgender girls were allowed to run against them. Brown concluded that, at elite level, biological-male physiology is the basis for the advantage that men or adolescent boys post-puberty have over women or adolescent girls in almost all athletic contests, and that it was not undone by gender treatment. He details "more muscle mass, greater muscle strength, less body fat, higher bone mineral density, greater bone strength, higher haemoglobin concentrations, larger hearts and larger coronary blood vessels, and larger overall statures than women and adolescent girls".

Joanna Harper, a medical physicist, adviser to the IOC and a trans woman, was the first to do quantitative analysis of transgender athletes. Her study of eight transgender female athletes showed that, when runners took hormone-suppressing medication, collectively they ran much slower, and did not outperform other women. Harper concedes her study isn't considered high-quality research, though it was revolutionary. She also agrees that, even after hormone treatment, trans women are bigger and stronger than the typical

At the vanguard? Transgender cricketer Erica James is flanked by Kevin Roberts, CEO of Cricket Australia, and Dr David Hughes, chief medical officer at the Australian Institute of Sport.

woman. "But there are two things I would add," she says. "They have a larger frame and a reduced muscle mass, which is a disadvantage. Also, we allow advantage in sport: we allow, for example, left-handed fencers to compete against right-handed fencers.

"The jury is still out on the science: there is a balance to be struck. If one is being totally honest, there is a small infringement on cis women, but to suggest that sporting organisations have ignored cis women is not true. Nor have women's sports disappeared since the Olympic committee first allowed transgender athletes to compete in 2004, or when they dropped the demand for reassignment surgery in 2016. Trans women undergo hormone therapy because it makes us more feminine. If they choose not to, they should do men's sports, except in cases of self-ID at recreational level. At higher levels, self-ID is absolutely problematic."

Does she think the ECB's policy of allowing trans women to self-ID all the way to the top of the domestic game is fair? "It's difficult. Where do you draw the line? I'm no cricket expert. I don't feel qualified to answer." Blythin sees possible problems, too: "Obviously, you can't have Jofra Archer rocking up after a two-week self-ID period – I get that – but lots of the talk tends to be fear-mongering."

Where, then, from these murky waters? The ICC, CA and ECB all say their rules are subject to review. Fair Play for Women believe the answer is for trans women to play in a category appropriate to their sex. They also believe there should be a protected category for those born female, and an open category for everyone else. "I don't want to see trans women excluded, but they can play in the open game," says Williams. "There should be no stigma for a trans woman playing at the top level in the open game. Men don't need their own protected category, so it makes sense that the men's category should become more inclusive, not the female one."

If the science seems to point in one direction, the desire for inclusion looks in another. Yet inclusion of whom? The ECB drew up their transgender strategy in consultation with Gendered Intelligence (who work with the trans community) and Stonewall, an LGBT-rights charity. But they spoke to no representatives of exclusively female groups. The prioritising of gender identity over sex also results in the curious ECB rule that a non-binary person – described by the ECB as "someone whose gender identity doesn't sit comfortably with man or woman" – is forbidden to play in the female-only competition. This includes a biological woman.

Women's cricket has come on so much, in investment, media coverage, standards. A career as a professional, once unthinkable, is now feasible. But, even today, girls are not socialised to play sport in the same way as boys, and their participation drops off considerably at puberty. A trans woman playing women's cricket means a biological girl or woman misses out.

Harper disputes this. "In a social sense, trans women are women. It is only because people suggest that trans women are really men that this argument is still being had. One in 150 people are trans. You wouldn't ever suggest a red-headed woman is preventing someone of another hair colour playing."

Sport can be so many brilliant things, improving mental and physical wellbeing, and bringing people together. For those suffering the torment of gender dysmorphia, playing alongside others of the same gender may prove a lifeline. It is also true that trans women are not swamping female cricket at any level, and blood testing at recreational level would be impossible.

What value kindness, compassion? Then again, what value safety – at 90mph – or the protected status of women's sport? And that's before even touching on the vexed issue of women's private spaces. At the elite level, tiny differences in performance can make or break a career. We are all constrained by our biology, and sport is, ultimately, a biological test: the gap between men and women is real.

"I don't envy the people making these decisions," says Lundberg. "What is their priority: to be inclusive, or to protect the female category?" All voices in the debate need to be heard; women's voices, disregarded in sport for so long, must not be ignored again. For, whatever the question, the answer has never been lots of people shouting at each other, fingers in ears.

Tanya Aldred is a freelance writer and editor.

LORD'S MEMORIES   Jonny Bairstow shares a moment with his mother, Janet, after England win the World Cup. A few weeks earlier, it is India South who come out on top, in the final of the Street Child Cricket World Cup.

PLAYING HIS OWN GAME Steve Smith does as he pleases during his twin hundreds in the First Ashes Test at Edgbaston.

Stu Forster, Getty Images

IMPACT ASSESSMENT   Marnus Labuschagne, struck by Jofra Archer at Lord's, and Ben Stokes, by Josh Hazlewood at Headingley, get close to the action.

FLYING AUSSIES Athleticism from Rachael Haynes and Kurtis Patterson brings the wickets of Anya Shrubsole, in the women's Ashes, and Diruwan Perera, in a Test against Sri Lanka.

FLYING BRITS   Chris Woakes catches India's Rishabh Pant during a World Cup game at Edgbaston and, at Radcliffe on Trent, Dan Blatherwick of Papplewick & Linby CC leaps among the willows.

TRAINING SESSION... NET SESSION Passengers in Dhaka keep track of the cricket, while boys at Fishery Ghat, Chittagong, find room for a game.

MAKING THEIR PITCH Hardy souls in Sweden defy (or ignore) the elements on the lake at Västlandasjön; meanwhile Extinction Rebellion protesters take a break for a game in front of Westminster Abbey.

IN FOR THE LONG HAUL   Spectators at Swansea come prepared for a June heatwave; at Kew in south-west London, cricket has a sepulchral quality.

COUNTY OUTGROUNDS

In search of cricket's soul

PAUL EDWARDS

Early on June 30 last year, queues appeared outside two grounds. The first, at Edgbaston, was what you would expect: England were playing India in the World Cup. There was more surprise, and some delight, when followers of Lancashire and Durham formed a line on Sedbergh's Loftus Hill, waiting patiently to bag the best seats on a ground that would soon claim to possess domestic cricket's most spectacular first-class setting.

Sedbergh School was only one of five venues that hosted their maiden Championship match in 2019. Almost a fortnight before that morning in the Howgill Fells, Yorkshire had played Warwickshire at York's effortlessly classy Clifton Park, their first match there since 1890. In May, Hampshire visited the Isle of Wight for the first time since 1962, hosting Nottinghamshire at the wonderful Newclose. It had been no more than pasture barely a decade before, until the late Brian Gardener spent £2m on his dream of bringing first-class cricket back to the island.

Hampshire won comfortably, though Liam Dawson missed the last three days in the abundant Medina Valley because he had been called up to England's World Cup squad. And so, for nearly two months, the season offered parallel narratives: while the world's best 50-over cricketers went about their business in the stadiums, the Championship visited many outgrounds, reminding older spectators of distant summers, when almost all counties took the game back to the schools and clubs that had provided them with players in the first place.

Thus Middlesex played at Radlett and at Merchant Taylors' School, Northwood; Lancashire went to Aigburth, as well as Sedbergh; and Nottinghamshire's return match against Hampshire, a rain-wrecked affair, took place at Sookholme, home of Welbeck CC (Nottinghamshire's outgrounds tour also included Grantham, Tunbridge Wells and Scarborough). In May, Glamorgan went back to Newport after an absence of 53 years, entertaining Gloucestershire at Spytty Park, where the local club had moved in the early 1990s following the sale of Rodney Parade.

Glamorgan are a good example of a county who use outgrounds as much from preference as necessity: they play at Colwyn Bay and Swansea partly because they feel Wales's first-class county should take games to the north and the west. Yorkshire members voted recently to double the number of four-day games at Scarborough (the attendance for the second day against Nottinghamshire was nearly 5,000), and Gloucestershire's season would be duller (and less profitable) without the Cheltenham Festival. Last summer, that loyalty was repaid with two thrilling victories in three games.

Of course, there was charm – and naturally there were cock-ups. Lancashire's attempt to ease the burden on spectators travelling to Sedbergh by offering free

Sight for sore eyes: Lancashire v Durham at Sedbergh.

Nathan Stirk, Getty Images

return journeys by coach was marred when one vehicle arrived at the ground on the first day with over an hour to spare, but missed the turning into the car park, and found nowhere to stop in the small town. Instead of letting his passengers alight, the driver gave them an unwanted tour of Cumbrian byways for 50 minutes, at one stage returning south down the M6. For the Lancashire members who felt Sedbergh was a long haul from Manchester anyway, this did not help (although 1,486 spectators turned up on that first day, more than for any of the days of Lancashire's subsequent Championship game, against Sussex at Old Trafford).

Play was occasionally held up by people using the public footpath adjoining St Andrew's churchyard, behind the bowler's arm. The school had decided the match was an event to be shared with the community, and did not request that the path be closed during the game. Home supporters concluded that, since spectators could sit there and watch without paying a penny, perhaps it should be renamed the Yorkshire End. (The town was in the county until boundary changes in 1974, and is still within the Yorkshire Dales National Park.)

There is a danger that such gentle intimacies might be misinterpreted as make-do-and-mend amateurism. Nothing could be further from the truth: the volunteers who organise outground matches perfectly understand their obligations, and venues are aware of the danger of losing a fixture because of a substandard pitch. Every aspect of infrastructure must be considered, and the catering for players and corporate guests professionally handled. Hosting a first-class match is both a privilege and a money-making opportunity: witness the vast marquee down one side of Clifton Park, and the tented village behind it, where York's staff – keen to reciprocate the honour paid them – treated players and officials generously. In fact, many outground staff take a week's holiday to work 14-hour days for nothing.

A dozen counties left their headquarters in 2019, and four-day games were played at 18 outgrounds. It would have been 17 but, when New Road flooded in June, Worcestershire moved their matches against Sussex and Derbyshire to Kidderminster, which had not hosted first-class cricket since 2008. They went off with few problems, and the resourcefulness of the Chester Road staff was widely praised. Other outground officials might have been praying they are never given such short notice: planning for most games begins in December, at the latest.

It remains to be seen whether 2019 represents no more than a spike in a long-term trend. In 1965, Championship cricket took place at 51 outgrounds; Essex, Kent and Yorkshire each used six, and were effectively peripatetic. Only Middlesex (who in 2019 played host at five different venues) and Surrey stayed put. For spectators in the larger counties who found it difficult to make the journey to, say, Leeds, Manchester or Taunton, it was a golden age.

The decrease in outgrounds can be explained partly by the reduction in the Championship programme. Back in 1965, each county played 28 three-day games, which allowed most to take cricket away from HQ. Twenty years later, when each county played four fewer matches, 35 outgrounds were used. In 2000, after the counties first split into two divisions, each playing 16 four-day games, the figure was 21.

John Sutton

Close to perfect: Hampshire host Nottinghamshire at the Newclose ground, on the Isle of Wight.

This summer, only nine are scheduled for Championship use (the same as in 2018). However, many counties, particularly those with Test grounds, will play their 50-over cricket away from their base, because the big stadiums will be needed for The Hundred. Once again, the smaller venues will answer the call. Should the Championship in future seasons clash with the 100-ball jamboree, the outgrounds may yet be required on something like the scale of 2019 – and the high-summer months are more suitable for such games than the margins of the season.

If a few county executives would only realise it, there is a pleasing symbiosis here. The redevelopment of many stadiums – the distinction between a stadium and a ground seems ever more important – was not undertaken with four-day cricket in mind. Old Trafford and Edgbaston rock with excitement during major Tests or T20 clashes. Yet on the second afternoon of a Championship game, the atmosphere is slightly quieter. Why not take it to a place where it would be an event rather than a routine fixture? Certainly, most players enjoy outgrounds, not least because of the proximity of appreciative crowds. No one is arguing for the return of wandering counties, but many are intrigued by the possibility that each first-class side might play at least one four-day game away from their base.

In doing so, they would be following the example set by New Zealand, who decided to stage England's Tests over the winter at Mount Maunganui and Hamilton, two boutique venues. "The atmosphere at both will be akin to outground matches in the County Championship, and first-class cricket can be all the better for that," wrote Mike Atherton in *The Times*. "Cricket was not

Home of the white rose: Yorkshire v Warwickshire at York.

designed to emulate football." Atherton's last point should receive consideration from one or two executives who know the cost of an outground match to the last penny, but not its value. Yet spending a few bob taking a game away from headquarters does more for a club's long-term health than Kolpacking the squad with former internationals.

In a decade's time, none of this may matter. Should the domestic game become the monopoly of an urban elite, the notion of county cricket will seem a quaint anachronism, and this article a romantic reverie. Already one or two counties are discreetly dropping the word "county" from their publicity, as if embarrassed by their history and *raison d'être*.

But if The Hundred is indeed the advance guard for a broader assault, then something precious will be gone for good. The first-class counties are much more than their headquarters and academies: they are an expression of local pride, for schools where the game is still played, and for thousands of clubs. It seems good manners for the counties to play the odd game in the sticks.

Few who watched Championship cricket at an outground last season thought they were being short-changed. They were content to follow the World Cup on their radios, or watch the evening highlights. In The Dalesman, the Sedbergh pub which became an unofficial mess for Lancashire's match against Durham, players, spectators, scorers, umpires and even the odd journalist mixed happily. On those blessed midsummer evenings, it seemed they were sharing something more than a pint and their love of a game. "I only went out for a walk, and finally concluded to stay out till sundown," wrote the naturalist John Muir, "for going out, I found, was really going in."

Paul Edwards is a freelance cricket writer who works for, among others, The Times *and the* Southport Visiter. *He has been a member of Southport & Birkdale CC since 1981.*

CRICKET AND MENTAL HEALTH

A healing at Lord's

Mark Lawson

Where is the best place to go after your mother has died? Many must head for the sanctuaries of church, wood, pub or home. On an awkward empty day before mum's funeral in September, I found myself drawn to Lord's, where Middlesex were playing Derbyshire in the final round of the Championship. *Supposed* to be playing: it rained. Not long after her death, another loved one was admitted as a surgical emergency – the third in just over a year – to Northampton General Hospital. One day, between visiting hours, I went to watch Northamptonshire against Durham – or would have done, had the covers not been on, the umbrellas up.

Neither visit saw a ball bowled, but both saw victories: sitting in the stands raised my spirits and restored my equilibrium. This was no surprise. I recently learned that cricket grounds are as effective as antidepressants, and equal to cathedrals, as places for recuperative meditation.

So although I understand the cricketing objections to last season's unusually late finish, it proved a boon to me. If the family death or hospitalisation had happened on those dates a few seasons earlier, no pilgrimage to Lord's or Wantage Road would have been possible. And cricket would not have been able to steady my life as, five years previously, the game had, I believe, saved it.

Mum's local church, where her requiem mass took place, was called Our Lady of Lourdes. Her slightly hybrid vowels – she had lived, successively, in the North-East, London, Leeds and Hertfordshire – meant she pronounced the French shrine "Lords", creating an overlap between the world's most revered cricket ground and the shrine where the desperate pray for a miracle (England and Middlesex supporters, insert your own joke here). My mother would have found it mildly blasphemous to refer to being healed at Lord's, but been pleased it happened.

In the spring of 2014, I very publicly and abruptly left BBC Radio, following editorial disagreements. A fuller account should await the book I may one day publish; the events are relevant here only to establish the perilous position that preceded my recovery. Distorted reporting, encouraged by a morbid obsession with the Corporation in parts of the media, coincided with another crisis: on the day the story broke, the family member who provides so much work for surgeons was undergoing a 14-hour operation.

My mental health, fragile for some years, collapsed. One morning, I was unable to get out of bed, or to stop writhing and perspiring. Another symptom was an inability to concentrate, so I shakily scribbled down all 14 physical signs, including insomnia and palpitations. The only symptom I omitted, for fear of being sectioned, was a vivid sensation of having lost a future tense. Presumably from aggregated experience, my excellent GP seemed confident

Solace in the solitary: a spectator at Lord's.

I could get through it, while warning it could take months. To the standard question about self-harm, I responded with a joke about experiencing homicidal thoughts only towards certain BBC executives. In truth, I more expected to die from the effects of the stress and worry than by my own hand. I was signed off on sick leave – for a freelance, a theoretical and terrifying status.

Two months into the illness, I was able to read and write again, but those activities were part of my work. Urged to spend time on something more distracting, I thought of sport, which has been a large part of my life. Most Saturdays and many Tuesdays, from August to May, I go to football matches, but following Northampton Town would be risky for anyone suffering from depressive illness even in the best of seasons, which 2013-14 was not; Northampton were bottom of Division Two, apparently doomed to relegation from the Football League. There were other local clubs, the lesser personal investment reducing the pressure, but any football ground felt too noisy, crowded and relentlessly tense. Nor did the traditional match-day smell of urine and fried onions serve as aromatherapy.

My sense that cricket might be a better balm was not just a hunch. A few years before, when I had two tickets for the Friday of an Ashes Test at Lord's, the friend I was going with rang to say a relative had died, and the funeral was scheduled for the day of our outing. Just as I was wondering who might go instead, another friend texted to reveal that he, too, had suffered a bereavement, in a sudden and terrible way. My first thought was that it was my moral duty to miss England v Australia, and spend the day with him; my second, not much later, was that the cricket might do him good. Amazingly, thrillingly, it helped him: new to the sport, he found the outing therapeutic and purgative.

If there is a cricket cure, how might it work? Doctors often advise the mentally unwell to get outside, time-honoured belief in the merits of fresh air combining with more recent intelligence about sunshine and Vitamin D. My friend commented on how Lord's felt surprisingly "rural" (as it would have done when the first match was played there in 1814). He was startled by the smell of grass, and other summer scents.

Mark Twain supposedly described golf as a good walk spoiled; cricket, I think, is a long walk stalled. Grounds are often surrounded by trees, flowers, rivers, while stands are open-topped or open-backed, admitting the breeze in a way rarely found at football stadiums, roofed and walled to keep the crowds apart and the weather at bay.

Equally significant is the rhythm. As detractors are prone to note, no other game, except chess, proceeds so slowly or with such regular breaks: overs, wickets, drinks, meals – and now the Decision Review System. But this pace is soothing for the fragile mind, leaving time for rest and reflection. Watching a game live with radio commentary playing in my ear reminded me of the mindfulness tapes (in which a voice purrs calming thoughts) that were another part of my treatment.

The structure of cricket gives a good lesson for the struggling. Especially in its proper, longer form, the game is built on the idea of a second chance, and the possibility of recovery, even from the worst position. A duck can be followed by a century, a dropped catch redeemed by a flying one-hander. Failure can be extreme and exposing, but there will be a chance to make amends.

The journalistic consensus that it was "redemption" to play two of the greatest-ever innings, a year after standing trial in a case that could have ended his career, has been rejected by Ben Stokes himself. Yet his sport is the most inherently redemptive of all. It has helped to think of the time since my breakdown as a second innings.

The idea of indomitability has helped too. Boxing champions may retire undefeated, and baseball pitchers may strike out, denying the batters a single run. One of cricket's special pleasures is the match-winning innings no bowler can end. It is fitting that the three most famous modern English turnarounds – Ian Botham's 149 at Headingley in 1981, Stokes's 84 in last summer's World Cup final, soon followed by his 135 at Headingley – all had asterisks. "Not out" is a good motivational slogan for the unwell.

Similarly, while a drawn five-day game may seem boring to those who believe sport should have a winner and a loser, the concept can be inspirational to those who fear their state of mind may prove the final outcome. To shake hands, draw stumps and move on – aware the contest may merely be deferred – is a useful goal for tested minds. And bodies. Watching relatives and friends go

Marc Atkins, Getty Images

Comfort in the ordinary: Northampton's Wantage Road prepares for a resumption of play.

through cancer treatment, it has struck me that the draw – in which neither the disease nor the patient decisively wins, but a pause is achieved – is a useful parallel for the new tumour-limiting treatments in modern oncology, which allow even those with final-stage diagnoses to remain in the game, knowing further tests will come. Try telling them that the lack of a decisive outcome is boring.

Another key part of the Lord's cure will be more pleasing to the NHS than the ECB. At my worst, a Test match or one-day international would have been too crowded or loud, hence the county games. The almost complete emptiness of the stands for a Championship fixture – though ominous for the economics of four-day cricket – give even Lord's the reflective silence of a religious retreat. At a midweek, mid-table game, you can almost literally be alone with your thoughts. Even when it rained at those late-season matches, the effect was not reduced: it simply felt like being in a church when there is no service.

> On a good night,
> I am generally
> asleep after
> about two hours
> of Boycott

Cricket helps me long after the day's close. Waking at 3am with the sudden, stubborn insomnia that is a common consequence of anxiety and depression, I try to trick myself to sleep, not by counting sheep, but by replaying in my mind the 100th century of the cricketing hero of my Yorkshire childhood, Geoffrey Boycott, for England against Australia at Headingley on August 11, 1977. It took him 232 balls. On a bad night, I reach the moment, on 80, when he edges Ray Bright, and have another thing to worry about: if DRS had existed, Boycott would surely have been out, and history different. On a good night, I am generally asleep after about two hours, as he nudges the ball off his legs for a single to move into the late twenties just before lunch. And because England's winter Test series often take place in polarised time zones, radio commentary from Australia or New Zealand has helped me through many wakeful nights.

But if, for listeners and viewers, cricket can be a cure for depression, there is compelling evidence that, for players, it may be the cause. This was first explored in David Frith's *By His Own Hand*, a study of cricketing suicides. My edition has, poignantly, a foreword by Peter Roebuck, later described by multiple witnesses in a posthumous biography, *Chasing Shadows*, as a "troubled soul", whose fatal fall from a South African hotel, though still disputed, may have made him a candidate for a future edition of Frith's book.

Candid autobiographies from Marcus Trescothick, Jonathan Trott, Graeme Fowler, Simon Jones and Jonny Bairstow, which reflect on either direct or observed experience of mental pressures, reveal a level of depressive illness in the sport, possibly because cricket is a team game that places individuals in situations of terrifying and pivotal isolation.

Those troublesome case studies made me feel even luckier as my therapy continued. And what brought me back to Lord's last September had, oddly, a cricketing context. I had arranged to visit my mother on August 26, the last Bank Holiday Monday of the summer. At 2pm the day before, I phoned to sort out lunch plans. There was no answer. I tried again at half-hour intervals, while watching the Headingley Test on television. Each time, the ringing tone

Morpheus: Geoffrey Boycott, bringer of sleep, reaches his 100th hundred.

Patrick Eagar, Popperfoto/Getty Images

continued until I hung up. This meant my Sunday afternoon fluctuated between the ecstatic impossibility of Stokes's last-wicket stand with Jack Leach, and mounting fear at the likeliest reason for mum's silence.

Around 6pm, as the triumphantly shattered batsmen struggled to find breath for post-victory interviews, my sister, Geraldine, rang to ask if I'd been in touch with mum, as she had tried all day too. Speaking hands-free, while she drove up ten M1 junctions from London, and I travelled down five from Northamptonshire, we assumed our mother was dead. Paramedics, though, found her unwell but conscious, suspecting either a vascular event or infection.

Next day, while she dozed in hospital, I was reading a newspaper. Waking, she asked: "Is that Stokes?" His face was on every front page. Mum had little interest in cricket, but now made an exception because Stokes was not only connected with County Durham (her birthplace), but looked uncannily like her father. It was he who had introduced me to cricket. Since he was a retired Durham coalminer who had left school at 12, I have always resisted the easy view that it is an upper-class sport. He was staying with us in July 1981, and we watched the Third Test together. As England struggled in the follow-on, my mum, a teacher on school holidays, put her head round the door: "Do you want a cup of tea, Da?"

"*By*," he said – a common Northern prologue to dismay, popularised by the plays of Alan Bennett. "After that batting, I need something stronger." Mum complied: it was the only time I saw him drink beer before lunch. We then witnessed, through the willpower batting and bowling of Botham and Willis, a cricketing miracle, unmatched until the one achieved by the player with my Granda's face, a few days before mum died, gently, after a long and remarkable life, her twin children each holding one of her hands.

So it seemed even more fitting to go to Lord's and, when I was summoned to a second hospital a few days later, to the County Ground. Around half the symptoms listed to my GP five years before had returned, though less severely. That September week, in which I again took the cricket cure, coincided with the retirement of Trescothick. His book, *Coming Back To Me*, launched a subgenre of cricket literature that makes it impossible now to watch a game without wondering how many of those displaying physical prowess might mentally be struggling.

Yet I also hope the stands contain many others who, through the lulling outdoor rhythms of a game designed always to give the players another go, achieve a healing at Lord's.

Mark Lawson is a journalist, broadcaster, novelist and playwright. He writes about culture for The Guardian, *and is theatre critic of* The Tablet. *He was* Wisden's *book reviewer in 1999.*

STOP THE SEVENTY TOUR

Cancel – or be damned

COLIN SHINDLER

When Brian Johnston died in January 1994, *Test Match Special's* lunchtime interview "A View from the Boundary" passed to Jonathan Agnew. South Africa would be touring England for the first time since readmission – and playing their first Test at Lord's since 1965. With commendable eagerness, Agnew thought it would be a good idea if his guest on the Saturday were Neath MP Peter Hain who, as chairman of the Stop the Seventy Tour committee 24 years earlier, had been a bête noire of the English cricket authorities.

TMS's long-standing producer, Peter Baxter, was not initially as keen as Agnew had hoped. Baxter had joined the BBC in 1966, and remembered only too well the events of 1970, when the invitation to the South Africa Cricket Association was withdrawn 12 days before their players were due to land. He thought the BBC hierarchy would remember, too, and treated Agnew's bold idea with circumspection. Had Johnston been alive, Baxter believed, he would have rejected Hain (who had been brought up in South Africa), or insisted another broadcaster interview him. For Johnston, Hain remained the sideburned 19-year-old student who had wantonly destroyed a summer's cricket.

Eventually, recognising Agnew's enthusiasm, Baxter relented, and the invitation to Hain was despatched and accepted. As play began that Saturday, Trevor Bailey – one of the *TMS* summarisers – took Baxter aside and quietly requested a schedule that would not require him either side of lunch: Bailey wanted to avoid any contact with Hain, whom he had not forgiven for what he still regarded as a sorry episode.

Looking back 50 years, one is struck by the similarity to events in the UK following the 2016 referendum on membership of the European Union. Passions were inflamed, and people who had previously shown little interest in cricket or politics grew exercised; families were divided, friendships destroyed. There had been controversy in 1968, of course, in the wake of John Vorster's refusal to allow Basil D'Oliveira to enter South Africa as part of the MCC touring squad, but in the public mind that was a predictable decision taken by a foreign government determined to protect apartheid. MCC had been criticised in liberal quarters for what appeared to be a spineless move not to include D'Oliveira in the original party, though the club's membership had voted in support of the committee. As far as they were concerned, that was the end of the matter. It wasn't: middle-class opinion in Britain had been offended, and the impact would be felt in 1970.

The wider events of 1968 had changed the world's social and political landscape. The Tet Offensive in Vietnam had convinced Walter Cronkite and other American commentators that the conflict could not be won; anti-war

Taking a stand: Peter Hain in March 1970. With him are Jeff Crawford (secretary of the West Indian Standing Conference), Mike Brearley and Mike Craft, an STST committee member.

protests intensified accordingly. In March, British television audiences were horrified by the spectacle of policemen beating up anti-war demonstrators outside the US Embassy in the genteel surroundings of Grosvenor Square. Meanwhile, the assassination of Martin Luther King in April confirmed to civil-rights campaigners the belief that non-violent protest had to be replaced by the more radical actions advocated by Stokely Carmichael, Huey Newton and the Black Panthers. Letters to *The Guardian* from Hampstead protesting about the iniquities of apartheid were never going to cause a moment's discomfort to Vorster: direct action, it seemed, was the best way of bringing home to South Africa's players and their admirers exactly what a large number of British people felt.

The main objective of Stop the Seventy Tour, formed in 1969, was to force MCC into withdrawing their invitation to SACA, but as fate would have it the Rugby Football Union had arranged a tour of the British Isles by the Springboks for the winter of 1969-70. Cricket and tennis in South Africa were played largely by the descendants of British settlers; rugby was the sport of the Afrikaners, the originators of apartheid. The Springboks were to play 26 matches in three months, including one against each of the four home nations, but from the moment they arrived in London in October 1969, they faced the full wrath of Britain's Anti-Apartheid Movement. MCC looked on with trepidation: whatever happened now would likely be replicated at the cricket the following summer. Their worst fears were realised.

The AAM were a loose alliance of students, trade unionists, politicians and churchmen, and their more militant members got to work: they invaded the rugby matches, hijacked the team bus, and handcuffed themselves to Twickenham's goalposts. Scarcely a match was uninterrupted, and the impact on the South Africans was significant: they were beaten by Oxford University and lost two of their internationals, a failure that disconcerted the public back home – not just on a sporting level. Everyone knew that if an 80-minute game of rugby could not be defended by the police, a five-day Test match could hardly be protected either, except by a large security force costing more than cricket's authorities could afford. And if the match took place behind barbed wire while being patrolled by guard dogs, what sort of atmosphere was that?

Between the Springboks' internationals against Ireland and Wales, attention suddenly focused on the forthcoming cricket tour. On the night of January 19, in a co-ordinated attack organised by a covert anti-apartheid group, ten county grounds were broken into. At Bristol, weedkiller was poured on the pitch, and slogans painted on the glass-fronted Jessop scoreboard. At Hove, the covers and heavy roller were daubed in paint. At Northlands Road, Southampton, the scoreboard was defaced, and walls graffitied. At Cardiff, Wilf Wooller's notoriously short temper was not improved when he discovered that, in addition to digging up the pitch and pouring tin tacks into the hole, the "hooligans" had given his car a fresh coat of paint. A small fire was started at Lord's, and there was damage at The Oval, Headingley, Old Trafford, Grace Road and Taunton.

> "I want to see you behind bars, and I am going to make sure that happens"

Hain carefully distanced himself from those events: despite his belief in direct action, he was uncomfortable with violence. Yet some MCC members regarded him with suspicion. "I met E. W. Swanton when I encountered him during the course of the STST campaign, and of course I read what he wrote," says Hain. "He was extremely courteous and engaging, which I didn't expect, whereas Wilf Wooller was not. Billy Griffith, who was conservative with a big C and a small c, was polite whenever I handed him a letter. He had a clipped politeness, which was very much not the case with Wooller, who was extremely aggressive towards me. The first thing he said was: 'I want to see you behind bars, and I am going to make sure that happens.'"

The events of January 19, widely condemned as gratuitous violence, simply confirmed the opinions of MCC and the Cricket Council (MCC in all but name) that South Africa's visit had to go ahead, if only to show that decent people could not be bullied. The Council ascertained that playing cricket in England was a legal pursuit; preventing it, therefore, was not. The tour, according to opinion polls, was still supported by the great majority of Britons. In the Council's view, cancellation would be bowing to the pressure of hooligans and fascists. If the tour was going to be called off, the government would have to do it. The rule of a minority, many of whom, it was believed by *Daily Telegraph* readers, did not wash as often as they should, was not part of the British way of life.

The Council did indeed suggest the counties invest in barbed wire, searchlights and guard dogs. Nottinghamshire informed Lord's it would cost £250 to install lights at Trent Bridge, adding £6 a week to the electricity bill.

If you could see their national sport, you might be less keen to see their cricket.

Anti-Apartheid Movement, 89 Charlotte Street, London W1.

Painting a grim picture: Wilf Wooller, secretary of Glamorgan, surveys his car; a poster published by the Anti-Apartheid Movement.

At Edgbaston, Warwickshire put the cost at £300, plus £120 a week to pay security patrols. At Lord's, MCC had already spent £200 on Dannert wire, a form of toughened barbed wire. When a much-anticipated Cricket Council meeting took place in the Long Room on a cold, dark February evening, it was possible to look through the windows and see, not the run stealers flicker to and fro, but the barbed wire silhouetted against the snow-covered turf. Watchtowers and guard dogs added to the impression that the long shadows on county grounds were now of concentration camps. In a sense, the grounds had resumed some of their wartime appearance, when Lord's was commandeered as an air-crew receiving centre, The Oval made ready for prisoners of war, and Headingley taken over by the Royal Army Medical Corps and used as a mortuary. In defence of liberty and freedom, the cricket authorities seemed prepared to turn grounds back into the fortified camps everyone assumed had been consigned to history.

At the meeting, the counties and MCC backed the tour, while cutting the number of fixtures from 28 to 12. Instead of coming at the end of April, the South Africans would now arrive at the start of June; and instead of playing every county, they would play mainly at the major city grounds – the six Test venues, plus Bramall Lane and Swansea – where it was easier to maintain security. Artificial pitches would be prepared in case of vandalism.

The recently formed Professional Cricketers' Association (regarded by some as the only trade union whose members were more right-wing than their employers) voted overwhelmingly in favour of the tour, despite a passionate speech from their president, John Arlott, advocating cancellation. The cricketers were not interested in politics, and wished only to be allowed to play – an attitude that chimed with the arguments employed at Lord's.

Mike Brearley was one of a handful of players who voted against the tour, but he understood why the majority of his colleagues felt as they did. "I wasn't surprised at the PCA vote," he says. "Many players made a living out of South Africa. They went there during the winter, coached out there, and maybe played league cricket or even for a state side. They saw businessmen and actors going there and doing well out of it, and they didn't see why they should take the brunt of it, even if they were sympathetic to the Anti-Apartheid Movement."

As views became entrenched, news arrived of some glorious cricket taking place in South Africa: Barry Richards, Mike Procter, Eddie Barlow, Graeme Pollock and the rest had whitewashed Australia 4–0. The prospect of seeing them in England whetted the appetite, and a fund was set up to raise £200,000 for security. The right-wing papers supported the tour; the more liberal papers did not. Tempers continued to fray.

David Sheppard, Bishop of Woolwich and an advocate of cancellation, attempted to arrange a conciliatory meeting; Peter May, his Cambridge friend and former England colleague, replied bluntly that they had nothing to talk about. When Arlott wrote in *The Guardian* that he would not broadcast on *TMS* if the tour went ahead, he received a large postbag, mostly in agreement, but some severely critical. According to his son, Tim, the most unpleasant was written by May, who was held in great regard by many, not just for his batting but for his decency. Yet on South Africa, he was uncharacteristically intemperate. His relationship with Sheppard never recovered.

The Labour government were reluctant to issue a direct order to cancel the tour, but a general election was approaching. Stop the Seventy Tour was adept at attracting television crews to their stunts, and the government feared news broadcasts featuring large-scale disruptions on streets and cricket grounds, just as the Conservatives were making law and order a central part of their manifesto. On May 14, an emergency debate was called in the House of Commons. The prime minister, Harold Wilson, detested South Africa, and – to the fury of his political opponents and MCC – let it be known in various interviews that he would look favourably on peaceful protests. By now, even Swanton believed the tour would not be in the interests of cricket. South Africa were expelled from the Olympic movement, and 13 African countries announced that, if the tour were to proceed, they would boycott the Commonwealth Games in Edinburgh in July. Even the well-heeled residents of St John's Wood, fearing trouble in the streets, pleaded with Lord's to call it off.

Faced with overwhelming pressure, and with the South Africans due to get under way against Southern Counties at Lord's on June 6, the Cricket Council met on May 18. The following day, Griffith read a long-winded, self-serving statement confirming the tour. Having called an election for June 18, the government ran out of patience. The home secretary, James Callaghan, summoned the Council and told them the tour had to be cancelled. It was over. On May 22, the Council announced that, with deep regret, they had no option but to comply.

MCC and their supporters had claimed it was more beneficial for non-white South Africans for bridges to be built and windows to be opened so that positive contact could be maintained. Their opponents believed sporting

Taking it to the wire: pitch preparation at The Oval in March 1970.

isolation was much more likely to force political change. It took another 20 years, but history has shown which side was right.

The opponents for the five scheduled Tests became a Rest of the World team captained by Garry Sobers. Yet taking the field in the first match were Richards, Procter, Barlow, and Graeme Pollock; in the third, they were joined by Peter Pollock. *Wisden 1971* included one article on the matches, written by the editor, Norman Preston, and another on the tour's cancellation, for which he commissioned the statistician Irving Rosenwater, rather than Arlott, the obvious candidate and a regular contributor. Rosenwater wrote a measured piece, but his political sympathies were apparent as he described the mayhem of the protests in terms of arrests made and policemen injured. It added little lustre to the Almanack. Robert Winder, the book's historian, wrote in 2013 that an article by Arlott "would have cemented *Wisden's* moral authority around the world. As it was, it put a question mark over the idea that cricket even knew the meaning of the 'fair play' culture it so keenly espoused."

Perhaps we should not be too censorious. Fifty years from now, it is possible historians will wonder how we made such a meal of Brexit.

Colin Shindler's book on the events of 1970, Barbed Wire and Cucumber Sandwiches, *is published this summer.*

PART TWO

The Wisden Review

CRICKET BOOKS IN 2019

Rhymes with rhododendron

ALEX MASSIE

Alastair Cook is one answer to the question "Can you be a great cricketer but not a great batsman (or bowler)?" And if you don't believe me when I say it's possible, perhaps you will be convinced by the man himself. This is the subtext to **Alastair Cook: The Autobiography**. The Cook paradox is a good one: no one has scored more runs more forgettably. This is not a criticism, merely a statement of fact. His gifts, and virtues, lay elsewhere.

So much so that the book is in large part a glorious humblebrag – a series of modest statements that actually draw attention to his feats. So he stresses how he lacked the talents given to others. But he made it work, more than anyone else in English cricket. There are times when this book, like its author, threatens to go on and on. It does the job, though, and before you know it you've reached the final chapter, and begun to realise all over again just how much England will miss him.

"There's a lot of talk about mental toughness, but what does that really mean?" asks Cook. "To me, it involves wringing the maximum out of your natural ability at the most important moments on the biggest stages. Opening is suited to the more literal thinker, the individual who can place an innings, good or bad, in a box and hide the key. Failure must never be allowed to fester."

Cricket is a game for tough guys, not just talented ones. Cook talks of the "intangible force" players must feel within if they are to make a true success of themselves. Those without that force, that drive, will never make it. That mental edge is everything. No wonder the game can chew people up.

It was rarely a pretty business; even at the end, that sun-dappled century against India, his batting occasioned more respect than gushing admiration. As a player and a servant, Cook earned fondness. He was a very English kind of hero.

His job was to "soak it up" and see off the opposition. He was the setter of scenes, the man who made life easier for those who followed. He has a keen awareness of his strengths and limitations. Not for nothing is Graham Gooch his hero: fancy stuff is suspicious, hard work its own reward. When you hit a boundary, take a single next ball, and let the other batsman do his bit. Self-knowledge is key. Cook's greatest gift was the ability to wipe the previous delivery from his memory, and focus on the ball to come. Playing for England, not reaching personal milestones, was what drove him. And he shows insight, too: "There's nothing you can do about the saddest fact of a cricketer's life, that you wish you knew at 21 what you know at 35."

This is typical of a book that is stronger, not on the good times, but on the lean, when the sheer bloody hardness of the game is its most significant, unchanging, feature. It ends with what I take to be the expression of a peak-Cook sensibility. Cricket's lessons can be summed up thus: "Don't be found wanting."

Well, quite. "If there was a brunt around, he was there to bear it," wrote Gideon Haigh of Cook in one of his columns assembled in **The Standard Bearers**. Ostensibly, this is a record of Australia's 12 months after the sandpaper incident; in reality, it is the latest inquiry into the wellbeing and future of the sport. Haigh, as always, is elegant and to the point, the finest writer of his kind in the world today. He has a generous sympathy for the players, but less time for the administrators, who feature in this collection more frequently than is healthy for cricket or, I imagine, cheerful for Haigh to contemplate.

He also writes the introduction to **A Field of Tents and Waving Colours**, a collection of Neville Cardus's greatest hits. By definition, there is little new here, save Haigh's essay, which notes: "For a long time, Sir Neville Cardus was regarded as cricket's greatest writer. Then he wasn't." Fashions come and go but, 45 years after his death, I fancy Cardus is back in vogue.

Indeed, for a certain kind of cricket lover, his perfumed prose gains value when contrasted with the style favoured in press boxes today. Moreover, as statistical analysis expands, there is something to be said for a reminder that numbers are only part of the matter. Or, as Cardus put it: "The great batsman lifts us out of our utilitarian selves: we admire his work for its beauty, not merely for its value in runs." The how is just as important as the how many. "What is a critic to say of Mozart at his most felicitous?" he asked. "The purer the music, the less there is to say about it." A similar point might be made of Cardus. The work largely speaks for itself.

The first difficulty with books about journalists is that, even to other journalists, they are usually less interesting than the people and events they write about. This is so even when, as here, the journalist is a rum cove. The second – and, in the case of Cardus, more pressing – problem is that a writer whose prose is essentially a matter of style and mood resists deep analysis.

If Duncan Hamilton's **The Great Romantic: Cricket and the Golden Age of Neville Cardus** doesn't quite solve these problems, it is not for lack of effort. It is a labour of long gestation, a project which Hamilton, on and off, tinkered with for seven years. A long wait, but worthwhile.

The chief knock on Cardus is that – frankly – he made things up. So he did, but what you got was A Day At The Cricket: the sense of an English summer was more vital than an adherence to what actually occurred. As Hamilton concludes: "The admission Cardus made about tampering with quotes damages him irreparably as a scrupulous nuts-and-bolts news reporter, but never as a critic – and certainly not as a master of descriptive prose." That seems wise and fair. If Cardus is read now, it is for his ability to conjure a certain idea of cricket. And anyway, as *The Man Who Shot Liberty Valance* reminds us: "When the legend becomes fact, print the legend."

Cardus is the game's great romantic, a chronicler of a golden age that never quite existed. That is an achievement unparalleled in the history of cricket writing. Hamilton concludes: "Nowadays you realise that, without him, the game's past – and some of the names in it – would be nothing more than ghostly smoke and a murmur of voices." Read Hamilton on Cardus, but read Cardus too.

He spent the war years in Australia, chiefly writing about music, his other great passion, for the Sydney prints. Although the post-war explosion in sporting attendance disguised the fact – Britons thirsted for any entertainment available after all the privation – the glory years, for Cardus, were mainly confined to before the war. The sense of an era closing, unavoidably

> He became a
> resolute critic
> of Margaret
> Thatcher's
> economic policies

if shatteringly, permeates Christopher Sandford's **The Final Innings: The Cricketers of Summer 1939**, a companion to an earlier book that catalogued the season before the lights went out across the continent in 1914. There is plenty to admire. Sandford captures the shadows lengthening over cricket – and everything else – in late-1930s England. Above all, how can you maintain the appearance of normality in abnormal times? The answer, it becomes clear, is: you can't.

No English cricketer of the post-war period enjoyed a greater hinterland than the Reverend David Sheppard. If he was not quite the last amateur captain of England, he remains the player who did most with his life *after* cricket. As Bishop of Liverpool for 22 years from 1975, he – and his Roman Catholic counterpart Derek Worlock – provided the moral leadership the city needed during a difficult period in its history. Had the cards been dealt otherwise, he might have succeeded Robert Runcie as Archbishop of Canterbury. Since Sheppard died in 2005, aged 75, it is a curiosity that no comprehensive biography has been published, until now. Andrew Bradstock's **Batting for the Poor** makes up for lost time. This impeccably researched book does ample justice to Sheppard's remarkable life as cricketer and clergyman.

He declined to play against the South Africans, and became a leading figure in the Anti-Apartheid Movement, doing his best to "persuade cricketers that the age-old sportsman's defence – 'No religion! No politics!' – is an escape from reality". In Liverpool, where employment fell by a third in the late 1970s and early 1980s, he became a resolute critic of Margaret Thatcher's economic policies.

Sheppard described his voyage through life as "not that of a natural-born cricketer, nor of a ready-made bishop". Diligence paid off: "I really did make the most of my talents." Be that as it may, Robin Marlar, a team-mate at Cambridge and Sussex, thought Sheppard comfortably the outstanding player of their generation. Had he devoted his entire career to cricket, he might have

joined a select group of batsmen with 100 first-class centuries. As it was, he was restricted to 22 Tests between 1950 and 1963.

The promise was evident early. In 1950, Sheppard made a flawless 227 for Cambridge against the touring West Indians, earning an England debut at The Oval and a tour of Australia. At university, he discovered religion; cricket was a passion, faith a conviction. A natural leader, he took Sussex to second in the Championship in 1953, then their joint-best finish. The next year, in the absence of the exhausted Len Hutton, he twice captained England against Pakistan, prompting speculation he might lead them in Australia.

Sheppard made clear he was willing to tour if offered the captaincy – a duty he was bound to accept, rather than a choice of his own – but not otherwise. Geoffrey Fisher, Archbishop of Canterbury, regarded the possibility of Sheppard leading England as "a piece of what I should regard as direct service to the wider interests of the Kingdom of God". Besides, "as I understand it, there really is a crying need for someone to bring back into the higher ranks of English cricket a moral decisiveness which has been slipping". Hutton, however, had fully recovered, and was restored to the role.

That was not quite the end of Sheppard's career, but it marked the moment the church supplanted cricket. If you will forgive me, Lord's loss was the Lord's gain, and Bradstock's compelling biography is an excellent account of a decent man's life.

Berkmann's Cricketing Miscellany offers an abundance of bon mots, trivia, and stories, most of them good, some even fairly fresh. This is not a criticism: a loo book is no place for novelty. But if you are the sort of person who likes to know that Hugh Tayfield and Bill Edrich share the record for being married more often than any other Test cricketer (five times each), or that John Betjeman once rhymed Patsy Hendren with "rhododendron", this is the book for you. I am only a little bit ashamed to admit I am that sort of person.

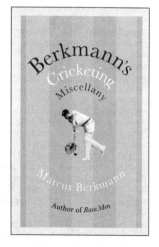

Berkmann also informs us that Jimmy Anderson holds the record for the most consecutive innings by an England player without reaching six: 18, though 12 were not-outs. Anderson does not include this factoid – despite being true, it cannot quite rise to the level of a fact – in his latest work, **Bowl. Sleep. Repeat.** It is a scrapbook of items devoted to everything from dressing-room superstitions to his tour kit (just two bats, apparently), golf (he plays off six) and the general business of being Jimmy Anderson.

Somehow it comes off, even though I suspect it shouldn't. Anderson has a good line in self-deprecation. Contrasting the on-field fast-bowling competitor with his "intensely socially awkward" nature off it, he recalls an early date with his wife. "We were sitting in a pub in Maida Vale. I thought it was going relatively well. An hour into the admittedly stunted conversation, she snapped and looked me square in the eye: 'Look, you're going to have to speak.'"

Best of all, however, are Anderson's reflections on his friendships with Graeme Swann, Stuart Broad and Alastair Cook. As you might expect, there's plenty of ribbing and joshing, but rather more than that. These relationships go beyond camaraderie, and enter the realm of something like love, even if they may find it embarrassing to regard their lives in such terms. You come away from these passages thinking more of all of them.

Marks takes self-effacement to heroic lengths

If Anderson's book can be recommended, the latest to roll off the Henry Blofeld production line cannot. **My A–Z of Cricket** is as idle and clichéd as the tired format suggests. Even Blofeld admits this is little more than a collection of offcuts, refashioned into a book that is barely serviceable.

Alas, it will not do. I dare say the Dear Old Thing's many admirers won't care, but consider this. D is for The Draw, of which Blowers says: "I now propose to blow out of the water for ever the ridiculous belief that a drawn cricket match is a waste of time. It is a myth that has been propagated for far too long by our American friends when they deign to consider the workings of cricket. It is none of their business anyway." With whom does he think he is arguing? Not a single purchaser will disagree.

A disproportionate number of those of us who began following cricket around 1981 became lifelong supporters of Somerset. There were four reasons: Ian Botham, Viv Richards, Joel Garner, and the fact that (limited-overs) cricket was always on television. Vic Marks was a vital, if underrated, part of that team. **Original Spin: Misadventures in Cricket** is a very Marksian book: gentle, often knowing, usually charming. Marks can never quite believe his luck. A career with Oxford, Somerset, Western Australia and England, before becoming – as we all know – an avuncular presence on *Test Match Special*, and a wise old owl at *The Observer* and more recently *The Guardian*. That's pretty good going.

Sometimes he takes self-effacement to heroic lengths. Somerset's 1985 season was a disaster, but Marks concedes: "Our solitary victory demands a mention since it coincided with my career-best figures. On a worn pitch at Bath, I took eight for 17; the ball spun a lot, and I must have bowled well as Lancashire were dismissed for 89." Nice one, Victor.

Marks was Somerset's official captain for only a season, and a lot of trauma could have been avoided if it had been for longer. That's also the view of Brian Rose. **Rosey: My Life in Somerset Cricket** is aptly titled, for he is one of those servants all counties need. He led Somerset in most of the glory years, when they won five one-day trophies and were runners-up in as many more. Unavoidably, the sackings of Richards and Garner, which spelled Botham's departure, prove more arresting than the more standard tales. It was a difficult situation, handled ineptly by the committee. Rose was never asked his opinion and, whereas Marks has some sympathy for the predicament in which Peter Roebuck, the new captain, found himself, Rose is withering. Roebuck, he writes, "could be abrupt, acid, self-centred and sometimes deliberately provocative. I think he saw himself as some sort of guru, to whom everyone ought to look up."

Rose's book is among the last published by Fairfield Books, whose founder, Stephen Chalke, is drawing stumps. He will be much missed, and this autobiography, charming and poignant, reminds you why. He was an accidental author, and even more accidental publisher. His first project, *Runs in the Memory*, was based on a simple premise: tell the story of 1950s county cricket by teasing out the recollections of those who played it. (The result was a magnificent book, perhaps surpassed only by Chalke's magisterial history of the Championship, *Summer's Crown*.) As no commercial publisher would take it, he published it himself. In all, Fairfield produced 42 books, most of which would never have seen the day but for Chalke. He tells this tale, and that of his life, with typical lyricism and panache. **Through The Remembered Gate** has an elegiac quality, but Chalke, a great preserver of the game's oral history, is also an optimist: "Cricket has so much power to do good in the world, to bring people of different cultures together, to inculcate good manners and respect." The game is so busy hurtling towards the future, it sometimes forgets to care about the present; Chalke's reminder that we need to look after its memory is more valuable than ever.

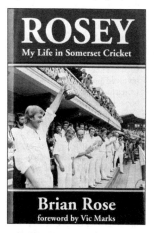

County cricket is always under threat but, he argues, it has been unstable almost from its creation. Despite a reputation for conservatism, it has constantly reinvented itself to survive. The question of how many first-class counties there should be has never disappeared. Those who would reduce the number should consider the elevation of Durham. In **Five Trophies and a Funeral**, Stuart Rayner has spoken to everyone, and produced a highly readable history of their rise, their near-demise and, it is hoped, their recovery.

"Those who dared cross Don Bradman had a habit of disappearing" is a splendid opening line, and **Pep: The Story of Cec Pepper, the Best Cricketer Never to Represent Australia** was one of the year's most unexpected treats. Cecil Pepper, Ken Piesse reminds us, was a garrulous, profane, six-smashing, leg-spinning all-rounder, who collected more than 14,000 runs and 1,800 wickets in the Lancashire Leagues. His greatest hours came in the Victory Tests of 1945, when – alongside Keith Miller – he starred for the Australian

STEPHEN CHALKE RETIRES

The accidental publisher

Richard Whitehead

It was while pushing Fred Rumsey in his wheelchair through demonstrators in London last autumn that Stephen Chalke realised he had made the right decision to retire. Rumsey weighs 18 stone, and Chalke's burden was augmented by a box of books on his lap. The Extinction Rebellion protests meant he had been forced to park more than a mile away from the National Liberal Club, where the two men were speaking to a meeting of the Cricket Society.

At 71, and after 23 unexpectedly rewarding years as a writer and publisher, Chalke knew it was time to call it a day. Of course, not every engagement involved pushing the wheelchair of a former England seamer, but he was increasingly taxed by the miles spent promoting his works. "The boxes of books seemed to be getting heavier," he says.

Chalke's story goes deeper than the acclaim of critics, or the collecting of awards. In gathering the memories of a generation of unsung cricketers – mainly from the 1950s and 1960s – he gave a voice to players who would otherwise have been forgotten. The writer Paul Coupar compared him to Alan Lomax, the American musicologist whose recordings ensured the preservation of folk songs, and the anecdotes of their performers. The association delighted Chalke: "It was one of the nicest things anyone ever said."

In his mid-forties, keen to add a few more years to his career as a club player, he had attended coaching sessions with the former Somerset bowler Ken Biddulph. Over a drink, Chalke was enraptured by Biddulph's tales from the county circuit. When he was made redundant from his work in adult education, Chalke was tempted by the idea of becoming an author. A creative-writing course fired his imagination. He talked to Biddulph about his favourite match, and wrote it up in the style that would become his trademark: warm, generous, evocative, but never sentimental.

Similar conversations led in 1998 to *Runs in the Memory: County Cricket in the 1950s*, his first book and – just as significantly in the long term – the first produced by his own company, Fairfield Books (the name came from the road he lives on in Bath). He had sent the manuscript to publishers, and received polite rejection slips, so he decided to go it alone. It was a leap in the dark but, after endorsements from Frank Keating and Michael Parkinson, the book sold.

Some of his best work came in collaborative efforts with former players: the larger-than-life Bomber Wells, the initially reserved Bob Appleyard, the idealistic Tom Cartwright, and the far-sighted Micky Stewart. Chalke developed a genre that was neither biography nor ghosted autobiography. He gave his subjects ample scope for speaking, but drove the story in his own words: "I prefer to call it oral history."

College outing: Stephen Chalke and Bomber Wells at Cheltenham.

The Appleyard production, *No Coward Soul*, was *Wisden's* Book of the Year in 2004, and became Fairfield's best-seller. Appleyard had begun to work with the journalist Derek Hodgson, but the project had stalled. Slowly, Chalke teased from him an extraordinary backstory. Appleyard's mother had left home when he was seven, his sister died when he was 13. But he had never spoken of how, in the days after war was declared in 1939, he had returned home from his grandparents' to find that his father had gassed himself, his second wife and their two daughters.

Another award winner was *Summer's Crown*, a handsomely illustrated history of the County Championship, published in 2015. In the course of his exhaustive research, Chalke concluded that the domestic game had almost always been in one form of crisis or another.

Careless reviewers would sometimes call his work "nostalgic", but the term makes him uncomfortable. "I don't want people to think that I believe the world was a better place than it is now. I don't want to be the champion of the way things used to be."

After publishing 42 books, 19 as author, he decided enough was enough. He had managed to make a small living, suffering only one major financial setback with too large a print run for *Supercat*, Simon Lister's otherwise successful biography of Clive Lloyd. Rumsey's autobiography, *Sense of Humour, Sense of Justice*, was one of four titles that came out in a burst of activity in 2019. At the Cricket Writers' Club annual lunch, Chalke was given the Peter Smith Award for services to the promotion of cricket. His final book, *Through the Remembered Gate*, was a memoir, reflecting on the remarkable success of a project that had begun over a pint with Biddulph in a leisure-centre bar in Stroud.

Services XI. On their tour of Britain, he averaged 42 with the bat and 27 with his leggies and flippers.

The defining moment in his career, such as it was, came soon after the Services XI returned home. At Adelaide in December 1945, they played South Australia. Pepper bowled to Bradman and, according to legend, had him plumb lbw twice in an over (both with the flipper) only to be denied on each occasion. "What do you have to do to get the little bastard out?" Pepper asked the umpire, before – perhaps ill-advisedly – suggesting: "You're a fucking cheat." That was that, and Pepper, as the subtitle says, never did play for Australia. Piesse is protective of his subject, and fiercely partisan; the result is extremely entertaining.

Tatenda Taibu's **Keeper of Faith** is less amusing. The first black man to captain Zimbabwe should have an inspiring tale to tell; instead it is largely miserable. Taibu now lives in exile in Liverpool, a victim – like so many of his compatriots – of his country's interminable corruption. In Zimbabwe, he writes, "you cannot separate" sport from politics, "as desirable as it may be". He was a township boy and so, unavoidably, a symbol of cricket's racial transformation. Given that, it is little surprise that Taibu, though a protégé of Andy Flower, also sympathised with the goals, if not the means, of Robert Mugabe's land-reform agenda. He struggled to see the advantage in Flower and Henry Olonga's black-armband protest at the 2003 World Cup that mourned the "death of democracy" in their country. "African politics has its own rules," writes Taibu, "and what they did wasn't going to change that."

Nor, though, could he navigate the system. Leading Zimbabwe aged just 20, he was soon at loggerheads with the board, demanding better pay for his players. Such independence of thought and action was not welcome. When he stood down as captain, he was handed an envelope containing photographs of dead bodies. No wonder Taibu writes: "Throughout much of my career as an international cricketer, I felt as though I was living in hiding, wondering whether certain eyes were watching my every move." And it was his faith that sustained him. He wearily concludes: "In all my years in Zimbabwean cricket, little has changed."

And now for something completely different. Monty Panesar's **The Full Monty** is a superbly odd book, every bit as idiosyncratic as you might expect. A far from untypical line reads: "If you want someone to bowl out Sachin Tendulkar, I'm your man. But eggs? That's not really my Luis Boa Morte." That was Panesar on *Celebrity Masterchef* which, compared with a painful appearance on *Celebrity Mastermind*, was a triumph. *Mastermind* was "like the *Titanic* ramming the *Hindenburg*", which, if nothing else, is a metaphor to make you think. Or take this: "Friedrich Nietzsche said 'What doesn't kill you makes you stronger,' but he'd never been touring with Peter Moores."

Panesar is entertaining company: Monty cannot help being Monty. But amid the laughs and the eccentricity is pathos aplenty. He chronicles his descent into mental illness – paranoid schizophrenia, according to one diagnosis – with brutal, compelling candour. Sessions with Mike Brearley helped, and so did rediscovering the consolations of religion. Through it all, you find yourself rooting for him. He concludes: "When you're at your lowest,

you'll realise people have an overwhelming desire to help you. Don't be afraid to ask them."

Just as moving, and sometimes as terrifying, is Robin Smith's admirable **The Judge**. The discrepancy between the on-field Smith, one of the few batsmen who truly loved the fastest bowling, and the off-field Smith, whose life after cricket fell apart, wracked by mental illness, alcohol addiction and family breakdown, is pitiful. As he observes: "Cricket was my comfort zone, and I had little idea how to function outside it." The cricketing Smith was a "fearless warrior", the non-cricketing Smith a "frantic worrier", whose identity had been suppressed for most of his adult life. He eventually discovered he couldn't run from it.

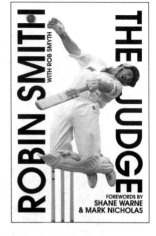

Even a move from Hampshire to Western Australia provided no kind of fresh start: suicide became a near-constant background hum. "I knew that one day… I would wake up and know instinctively that I was about to get out of bed for the last time." The voices in Smith's head were insistent: "Do it, Judge. Everyone will be better off without you." What saved Smith was, in a word, love. Or, as Martin Crowe told him: "We are given these challenges to move on from old unhelpful ways. We are given a chance to regenerate and, for cricketers like us, that is a must, as the game takes us too far away from our true reality."

Graeme Fowler's autobiography, *Absolutely Foxed*, has spawned a sequel, **Mind Over Batter: Mental Strategies for Sport and Life**, which is stuffed with tales from his Lancashire and England career, and – more significantly – sage advice on how best to "enjoy being yourself". It is bookended by sessions with, once again, Brearley, whose wisdom is abundant. Fowler's depressive tendencies are traced to a terrible relationship with his mother, who beat him mercilessly and without reason. When root causes are identified, Brearley tells Fowler and, by extension, all of us: "You now have a choice. You now know what causes your depression and, knowing you, in most situations you will find a solution. And if there is no solution, you'll know that and, therefore, it shouldn't upset you. Because it's the not knowing, or trying to find a solution when there isn't one, that really gets you down." Fowler's book, however, is no misery memoir: it is warm, acutely insightful and offers something not too far from hope.

The most academic cricket publication of the year was also among the most interesting. Prashant Kidambi is associate professor of colonial urban history at the University of Leicester and, in **Cricket Country: An Indian Odyssey in the Age of Empire**, he tells the story of the 1911 tour of the British Isles by

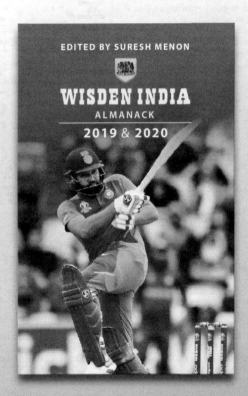

the first socially representative team of Indian cricketers to visit the UK. Less successful visits had been made by teams of Parsis from Bombay, but the 16-man expedition included Hindus and Muslims, as well as a Sikh. The party ranged from princes to, remarkably, a pair of Dalits – "untouchables".

Although ostensibly writing about the tour, Kidambi is more interested in the development of a pan-Indian consciousness, and the interplay between colonial Britain and colonised India. A flavour can be gleaned from an English writer's reaction to the defeat of the Bombay Gymkhana club by a team of Parsis in 1890: "We rule in India by conquest, by strength, by prestige, and we cannot afford that these three bonds of empire should be loosened even through the medium of so trivial an affair as a game of cricket." This is a richly detailed, rewarding, fascinating book.

The rules of tragedy are straightforward: the protagonist must, thanks to some flaw, deserve his or her fate. As in the theatre, so on the cricket field. Michael Bates was for some years considered the best wicketkeeper in England. He was a contemporary of Jos Buttler and Joe Root, and his excellence behind the stumps – notably when standing up to quicker bowlers – was a core part of Hampshire's winning two one-day trophies in 2012. A glittering future seemed likely. There was just one problem: Bates couldn't bat.

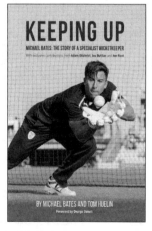

KEEPING UP

MICHAEL BATES: THE STORY OF A SPECIALIST WICKETKEEPER

With exclusive contributions from Adam Gilchrist, Jos Buttler and Joe Root

BY MICHAEL BATES AND TOM HUELIN

Foreword by George Dobell

Or rather, given a first-class average of a shade under 20, he could not bat to the standard demanded nowadays. **Keeping Up** is his story, told in partnership with Tom Huelin. Bates is mournful about his troubles with the bat, and melancholy about his glovework: though universally acknowledged, it was not enough to give him the career it merited. He was an anachronism. It is impossible to read this and not think that cricket loses out if there is no place for the genuine wicketkeeper.

As Jimmy Adams, Hampshire captain when Bates was released in 2014, says: "If someone had asked me, 'Who was the best keeper you played with?' I'd say Michael Bates. But he's not playing any more, and that's a very strange thing." Bates retired from first-class cricket aged 25. He has found solace in coaching; writing this book, one imagines, provided consolation, perhaps even closure.

Notionally, the shorter the format, the more room for a specialist wicketkeeper. That was Bates's hope once. For if your No. 11 is unlikely to bat, and you have a couple of bowlers who really can hit the ball, why not a top-class keeper down the order? It hasn't quite worked out like that, but the

theory remains sound: one who, like Bates, can stand up to the stumps, even for quicks, puts the batsman under more pressure than one who cannot.

Tim Wigmore and Freddie Wilde's **Cricket 2.0: Inside the T20 Revolution** shows there may still be room for the specialist keeper. One problem is that there is no statistical measure of their contribution. But as cricket, and especially T20, becomes more data-driven, that may change. Fielding stats are the next frontier.

This book is really the first history of a cricketing revolution. Twenty20 might have begun as a bit of a joke, a piece of whack and giggle not to be confused with the real thing. But in 15 or so years, it has become the game's pulsating driving force. There is, as the authors make clear, no going back.

The sport changed irrevocably in 2008, when Brendon McCullum smashed 158 off 73 deliveries for Kolkata Knight Riders in the IPL's first match. New avenues of possibility opened up. Nothing has ever been the same. *Cricket 2.0* is plainly influenced by Michael Lewis's *Moneyball,* and Wigmore and Wilde are right in arguing that the shorter the format, the narrower the advantages a side can gain. Every decision carries more weight than in the first-class game: data is more, not less, vital.

> They have got under the skin of how T20 is played, and why

Wigmore, a journalist for *The Daily Telegraph*, and Wilde, a data analyst for CricViz, have produced a fascinating book, essential for anyone who wishes to understand cricket's new age. It is peppered with arresting statistics. Chris Gayle intimidates bowlers into delivering a wide or a no-ball every 19 deliveries; the average for other batsmen is one in 35. Full tosses typically go for ten an over, and take a wicket once every 20 deliveries; for Lasith Malinga, the figures are 7.75 and 13. A decade ago, batsmen hit a six once in 28 balls; in 2018, it was once in 20. Everything is changing, and everything – even slow bowling – is getting faster. Shane Warne averaged a delivery speed of 49mph, Rashid Khan 57.

If there are moments when Wigmore and Wilde are in danger of allowing modernity to run away with itself, this matters little in the greater scheme. The authors take us inside IPL franchises, explaining why – in a format designed to enhance parity – some are consistently more successful. They have spoken to dozens and dozens of the world's leading cricketers and, more than any other book, got under the skin of how T20 is played, and why.

It is perhaps a question of mindset. As Eoin Morgan says: "Every decision in T20 cricket should be aggressive." This takes courage, because "it goes against human reactions. We have a safe nature." The short game elevates and concentrates risk and reward, and almost everything you learned about traditional cricket must be unlearned for T20. Batsman cannot afford to fear dismissal; they must run towards risk. Bowlers, who prize consistency in first-class games, must appreciate it translates into predictability in T20 cricket, which will get you killed. When there are only 24 deliveries to play with, the job is to be consistently inconsistent.

The ultimate takeaway – you realise by the end of this intelligent, absorbing, detailed survey of where and how we have reached this moment in the history of the game – is that soon, perhaps sooner than we think, T20 and Test cricket, already diverging, will be seen as cousins rather than siblings. Cricket 2.0 will not be with us for long; 3.0 is already in development. While we wait, *Cricket 2.0* is the Wisden Book of the Year.

Alex Massie writes a political column for The Times *and* The Sunday Times.

WISDEN BOOK OF THE YEAR

Since 2003, *Wisden's* reviewer has selected a Book of the Year. The winners have been:

2003   *Bodyline Autopsy* by David Frith
2004   *No Coward Soul* by Stephen Chalke and Derek Hodgson
2005   *On and Off the Field* by Ed Smith
2006   *Ashes 2005* by Gideon Haigh
2007   *Brim Full of Passion* by Wasim Khan
2008   *Tom Cartwright: The Flame Still Burns* by Stephen Chalke
2009   *Sweet Summers: The Classic Cricket Writing of J. M. Kilburn* edited by Duncan Hamilton
2010   *Harold Larwood: The Authorised Biography of the World's Fastest Bowler* by Duncan Hamilton
2011   *The Cricketer's Progress: Meadowland to Mumbai* by Eric Midwinter
2012   *Fred Trueman: The Authorised Biography* by Chris Waters
2013   *Bookie Gambler Fixer Spy: A Journey to the Heart of Cricket's Underworld* by Ed Hawkins
2014   *Driving Ambition* by Andrew Strauss
2015   *Wounded Tiger: A History of Cricket in Pakistan* by Peter Oborne
2016   *The Test: My Life, and the Inside Story of the Greatest Ashes Series* by Simon Jones and Jon Hotten
2017   *Following On: A Memoir of Teenage Obsession and Terrible Cricket* by Emma John
2018   *A Clear Blue Sky* by Jonny Bairstow and Duncan Hamilton
2019   *Steve Smith's Men: Behind Australian Cricket's Fall* by Geoff Lemon
2020   *Cricket 2.0: Inside the T20 Revolution* by Tim Wigmore and Freddie Wilde

OTHER AWARDS

The Cricket Society Literary Award has been presented since 1970 to the author of the cricket book judged best of the year. The 2019 award, made by the Cricket Society in association with MCC, was won in April by Geoff Lemon for **Steve Smith's Men** (Hardie Grant); he received £3,000. The book also won the Cricket Writers' Club award in October.

In June, Stephen Fay and David Kynaston won the cricket category at the British Sports Book Awards for **Arlott, Swanton and the Soul of English Cricket** (Bloomsbury).

In December, Duncan Hamilton won the William Hill Sports Book of the Year and a £30,000 prize for **The Great Romantic**, his biography of Neville Cardus.

BOOKS RECEIVED IN 2019

GENERAL

Arnot, Chris **The Festive Soul of English Cricket** From Tunbridge Wells to Scarborough (Takahe, paperback, £11.95)
Battersby, David **The Auckland Single-Wicket Competition 1968 to 1973** (limited-edition paperback; details from dave@talbot.force9.co.uk)
Berkmann, Marcus **Berkmann's Cricketing Miscellany** (Little, Brown, £14.99)
Bose, Mihir **The Nine Waves** The Extraordinary Story of Indian Cricket (Aleph, Rs999)
Blofeld, Henry **My A–Z of Cricket** A Personal Celebration of our Glorious Game (Hodder & Stoughton, £20)

Brettig, Daniel **Bradman & Packer** The deal that changed cricket (Slattery Media Group, paperback, $A24.95). *Slim but fascinating account of the part played by Sir Donald Bradman in brokering the peace deal between World Series Cricket and the Australian board.*

Goulstone, John **On the Level** Cricket and Society in 18th-Century Brighton (Sussex Cricket Museum, limited-edition hardback £80, paperback £20; details from sharp554@btinternet.com)

Haigh, Gideon **The Standard Bearers** Australia v India, Pakistan and Sri Lanka 2018-19 (Wilkinson Publishing, paperback, £23.99).

Hignell, Andrew **Glamorgan Cricketers 1889–1920** (Halsgrove, £16.99)

Kidambi, Prashant **Cricket Country** An Indian Odyssey in the Age of Empire (OUP, £25)

Lonsdale, Jeremy **A Game Sustained** The impact of the First World War on cricket in Yorkshire 1914–20 (ACS, paperback, £15)

Midwinter, Eric **'His Captain's hand on his shoulder smote'** The incidence and influence of cricket in schoolboy stories (ACS, paperback, £15)

Murphy, Patrick **The Greatest Season** Warwickshire in the Summer of 1994 Photographs by Graham Morris, foreword by Ian Bell (Fairfield Books, £20). *Warwickshire's treble-winning season of 1994 revisited by most of the key witnesses. A brisk, lively read.*

Northall, Jonathan **Ruling the World** The Story of the 1992 Cricket World Cup Foreword by Kepler Wessels (Pitch, £19.99). *Detailed account of the first multi-coloured World Cup, won by Imran Khan's Cornered Tigers; also the first to feature South Africa.*

Rayner, Stuart **Five Trophies and a Funeral** The Building and Rebuilding of Durham County Cricket Club Foreword by Paul Collingwood (Pitch, £19.99)

Rice, Jonathan **Stories of Cricket's Finest Painting: Kent v Lancashire 1906** (Pitch, £18.99). *Everything you wanted to know about Albert Chevallier Tayler's painting depicting county cricket in all its Edwardian glory.*

Roberts, Andrew **A History and Guide to the Cricket World Cup** (White Owl, paperback, £12.99)

Sandford, Christopher **The Final Innings** The Cricketers of Summer 1939 (The History Press, £20)

Schofield, John **Sticky Wicket** Over 150 Years of Cricket on Vancouver Island (Northwind Ink, paperback, £10.62)

Whitehead, Richard, ed. **The Times: England's World Cup** The Full Story of the 2019 Tournament Foreword by Mike Atherton (The History Press, £20). *A chance to relive the tournament as it happened, through the paper's reports. Some fascinating features, too.*

Wigmore, Tim, and Wilde, Freddie **Cricket 2.0** Inside the T20 Revolution Forewords by Harsha Bhogle and Michael Vaughan (Polaris, £17.99)

BIOGRAPHY

Battersby, David **The Early Years of Gilbert Laird Jessop** (privately published, paperback, £12; details from dave@talbot.force9.co.uk)

Battersby, David **The Sporting Solicitor: Hugh Murray Ingledew** (privately published, paperback, £6.50; details from dave@talbot.force9.co.uk)

Bonnell, Max **Dainty** The Bert Ironmonger Story (£25 plus p&p; details from www.cricketbooks.com.au). *Well-researched biography, with many unseen photographs, of the left-arm spinner who made his Test debut for Australia at 46, and played in the 1932-33 Bodyline series aged 50.*

Bradstock, Andrew **David Sheppard: Batting for the Poor** The authorised biography of the celebrated cricketer and bishop Foreword by Desmond Tutu (SPCK, £19.99)

Hamilton, Duncan **The Great Romantic** Cricket and the Golden Age of Neville Cardus (Hodder & Stoughton, £20)

Harte, Wesley **Bert Sutcliffe** A Kiwi Champion (privately published, paperback, £15; details from robert.phipps2@ntlworld.com)

Harte, Wesley **John Reid** A Mighty Force (privately published, paperback, £12; details from robert.phipps2@ntlworld.com)

Hedges, Stephen **Bernard Hedges** The Player from 'Ponty' (St David's Press, paperback, £19.99). *Son's tribute to an unsung Glamorgan batsman who scored more than 2,000 runs in 1961.*

Piesse, Ken **Pep** The Story of Cec Pepper, the Best Cricketer Never to Represent Australia Foreword by Arthur Morris (published by the author, $A50; details from kenpiesse@ozemail.com.au)

Sandford, Christopher **Keeper of Style** John Murray: The King of Lord's (Pitch, £18.99). *Overdue memories of a wicketkeeper who deserved more than his 21 Tests, although his rivals are perhaps underestimated. Sadly, Murray died while the book was being written.*

Sandford, Keith A. P., **Sir Garfield Sobers: The Bayland's Favourite Son** (limited-edition hardback £100, paperback £15; details from mckenziecricket@btconnect.com). *Insight into the great all-rounder's early years, written by a classmate at his first school in Barbados.*

Tebay, K. Martin **"Mr. Scorer" Lunt** Samuel Lunt, Official scorer, Lancashire CCC 1887–1911 (Red Rose Cricket Books, £5.99)

AUTOBIOGRAPHY

Anderson, Jimmy, with White, Felix **Bowl. Sleep. Repeat.** Inside the World of England's Greatest-Ever Bowler (Cassell, £20)

Bates, Michael and Huelin, Tom **Keeping Up** Michael Bates: The Story of a Specialist Wicketkeeper (Into Words, paperback, £11.99)

Chalke, Stephen **Through The Remembered Gate** (Fairfield Books, £16)

Cook, Alastair, with Calvin, Michael **The Autobiography** (Michael Joseph, £20)

Fowler, Graeme **Mind Over Batter** Mental Strategies for Sport and Life (Simon & Schuster, £20)

Marks, Vic **Original Spin** Misadventures in Cricket (Allen & Unwin, £20)

Panesar, Monty, with Atkins, Fred **The Full Monty** Foreword by Andrew Flintoff (White Owl, £20)

Rose, Brian **Rosey** My Life in Somerset Cricket Foreword by Vic Marks (Fairfield Books, £16)

Rumsey, Fred **Sense of Humour, Sense of Justice** (Fairfield Books, £16). *Entertaining story of a man who took the new ball in a Test with Fred Trueman, helped set up the Cricketers' Association, and was instrumental in dragging cricket into a more commercial mindset.*

Smith, Robin, with Smyth, Rob **The Judge** Forewords by Shane Warne and Mark Nicholas (Yellow Jersey Press, £20)

Stephenson, Franklyn, with Bracegirdle, Dave **My Song Shall Be Cricket** Foreword by Sir Garfield Sobers (Pitch, £19.99). *Formidable county all-rounder whose career was defined by his decision to join a West Indian rebel tour of South Africa.*

Taibu, Tatenda **Keeper of Faith** Cricket, Conflict and God in Zimbabwe's Age of Extremes (deCoubertin Books, paperback, £12.99)

ILLUSTRATED

Akel, Jules **Cricket Tickets** Lord's Ground Tickets 1993–2018 (Christopher Saunders, £20 + p&p). *Beautifully presented celebration of the witty and imaginative tickets the author produced for Lord's over 25 years. See Wisden 2019, page 97.*

FICTION

Redfern, David **Lord Hawke's Cufflinks** (privately published, paperback, £8.99; more details from garryart123@gmail.com)

POETRY

Kunial, Zaffar **Six** Cricket Poems (Faber& Faber, paperback, £6)

ANTHOLOGIES

Cardus, Neville **A Field of Tents and Waving Colours** Neville Cardus writing on Cricket Foreword by Gideon Haigh (Safe Haven, £14.99)

STATISTICAL

Bryant, John, ed. **First-Class Matches: Pakistan 1980/81 to 1983/84** (ACS, paperback, £27)

Lawton Smith, Julian, ed. **The Minor Counties Championship 1913** (ACS, paperback, £17)

HANDBOOKS AND ANNUALS

Bailey, Philip, ed. **ACS International Cricket Year Book 2019** (ACS, paperback, £32)

Bryant, John, ed. **ACS Overseas First-Class Annual 2019** (ACS, paperback, £70)
  Full scorecards for first-class matches outside England in 2018-19.

Bryden, Colin, ed. **South African Cricket Annual 2019** (Blue Weaver, R270, info@blueweaver.co.za)

Hignell, Andrew, Clayton, Howard, and Gerrish, Keith ed. **First-Class Counties Second Eleven Annual 2019** (ACS, paperback, £13)

Colliver, Lawrie, ed. **Australian Cricket Digest 2019-20** (paperback, $A35; details from lawrie.colliver@gmail.com)

Easdown, Craig, ed. **Ireland Cricket: 2019 season guide** (New Century, €5/£4)

Marshall, Ian, ed. **Playfair Cricket Annual 2019** (Headline, paperback, £9.99)

Moorehead, Benj, ed. **The Cricketers' Who's Who 2019** Foreword by Gareth Batty (Jellyfish, £19.99, ebook £10)

Payne, Francis and Smith, Ian, ed. **2019 New Zealand Cricket Almanack** (Upstart Press, $NZ55)

Piesse, Ken, ed. **Pavilion 2020** (Australian Cricket Society, paperback, $A10, www.cricketbooks.com.au)

PERIODICALS

Catalogue 200 (J. W. McKenzie, paperback, no charge)

The Cricketer (monthly) ed. Simon Hughes (The Cricketer Publishing, £5.50; £44.99 for 12 print issues, £44.99 digital, £49.99 print & digital. Subscriptions: www.thecricketer.com)

The Cricket Paper (weekly) ed. Jon Couch (Greenways Publishing, £1.50; £20 for ten issues inc p&p, £49.99 for one year digital, www.thecricketpaper.com)

The Cricket Statistician (quarterly) ed. Simon Sweetman (ACS, £3.50 to non-members)

The Journal of the Cricket Society ed. Nigel Hancock (twice yearly) (from D. Seymour, 13 Ewhurst Road, Crofton Park, London SE4 1AG, £5 to non-members, details from nigelhancock@cricketsociety.com)

The Nightwatchman The Wisden Cricket Quarterly ed. Tanya Aldred, Jon Hotten and Benj Moorehead (TriNorth, £10 print, £5 digital; £29.95 for four print issues exc p&p, £15 digital, www.thenightwatchman.net)

Wisden Cricket Monthly ed. Phil Walker (TriNorth, £4.95; £39.99 for 12 print issues, £17.99 digital. Subscriptions: www.wisdensubs.com)

CRICKET AND THE MEDIA IN 2019

The ultimate spectacles

Patrick Collins

On a Tuesday afternoon in June, before a capacity crowd at Lord's, Australia beat England by 64 runs at the World Cup. Kevin Pietersen reacted with a mixture of alarm and spite. "Oh no, Eoin Morgan looked scared!" he tweeted. "That Is A Horror Sign… The England captain stepping to square leg when Starc bowled his first delivery to him made me think England could have a little problem over the next week or so. I hope not, but I've not seen a captain show such weakness for a while."

Michael Vaughan was equally scathing: "I've been involved in a couple of atrocious World Cups," he told BBC Radio. "If they're not careful, this could turn out to be top of the tree." Vaughan had been passably positive a few weeks earlier. Indeed, he had promised: "It's gonna be an aggressive World Cup, cos the batsmen are just gonna go out there and aggress." But now the tone had changed.

Jonny Bairstow was asked what he thought of the criticism. "People were waiting for us to fail," he said. "They are not willing us on to win… It's a typical English thing to do, in every sport." Vaughan promptly took to Instagram to describe Bairstow's reaction as "negative and pathetic". England's subsequent recovery captivated the public, yet hatchets had not been buried. After a classy hundred against New Zealand, Bairstow made great play of removing his cap and rubbing his hair. This was apparently a jibe at Vaughan.

A few days before the semi-final Australia's coach, Justin Langer, led his team on a barefoot stroll around the Edgbaston outfield. The aim, it seems, was to give the players a "feel" for the ground. This was all a bit New Age for *The Sun*, which bellowed its derision. A spoof report from "Graham Bunions" announced: "This is the bonkers barefoot ritual the batty Aussies believe will help KO England. But the toezos from Down Under have such an appalling record at Edgbaston that Thursday's World Cup semi-final will surely end in glorious DEFEET for them."

And, of course, it did. And the newspapers rejoiced. *The Sun* had England "smashing the old enemy", *The Guardian* spoke of a "hammering", while *The Daily Telegraph* ran a leader entitled "The drama and glory of cricket". There would be more drama, and more glory, before the summer was done.

The details of the World Cup final remain warmly familiar. The batting of Ben Stokes had played a crucial role in England's progress, and he now soared to the occasion with an assertive 84 not out, followed by a thumping contribution to the super over. Jonathan Agnew described the conclusion with a brilliant stream-of-consciousness commentary for BBC Radio: "It's come to this. Here's the last ball of the World Cup final. Archer bowls it. It's clipped away to the leg side. They're going to come back for the second! The throw is

picked up, they throw to the wicketkeeper's end. He's run out – is he?, I think! I think he's run out! England think he's run out! England are convinced he's been run out!"

We listen breathlessly until the TV umpire mumbles his message. "That tells you that England have won the World Cup!"

The country acclaimed the new champions. The newspapers published special supplements, more than one bearing the headline "Champagne Super Over". Vaughan called it the "greatest day I have had in cricket", and Scyld Berry in *The Telegraph* captured the moment beautifully: "On what basis did England win after two ties? That they had hit more boundaries on the day than New Zealand. It seems arcane, even cruel, perhaps absurd, but there had to be a tie-breaker. Otherwise the contest between the two countries… would have continued until the sun had set on the most dramatic day ever known at Lord's."

The previous day, deep in his irony-free zone, Pietersen had turned again to Twitter: "The reason I've been so supportive of England throughout this cricket World Cup is purely because of the way they've changed the way 50-over cricket is played globally." Somewhere, a glass in one hand and the World Cup in the other, Morgan was trying not to chuckle.

Meanwhile, the man who delivered that memorable piece of commentary was in the throes of a bizarre controversy. Shortly before the start of the tournament, Agnew had publicly pondered the wisdom of allowing the Barbados-born Jofra Archer to play for England, arguing that it was a "huge call", and wondering if it might affect "morale and camaraderie". In a devastating article for *The Independent*, Jonathan Liew clinically dismantled this assertion, and concluded by throwing Agnew's comment back in his face: "Who doesn't love morale and camaraderie, after all? Until you begin to ask why Archer is deemed such a grave threat to it... There's an incendiary word you could posit to describe all this, but I'm not going to use it."

The charge was serious. Agnew had heard enough. There are people who can recite his late-night Twitter outburst – written as private direct messages to Liew, who later went public – word for four-letter word. It began: "Fucking disgraceful. You have massive chips on your shoulder... you are a racist." On it went, approaching a demented crescendo: "You are so strange I don't know if you'd be upset to know those who think you are a cunt... I'm SO angry... Book yourself in somewhere... You need help... Who the fuck are you?"

It was shocking, of course, yet reminiscent of one of Basil Fawlty's tirades: "I'm trying to run a hotel here! Have you any idea of how much there is to do... Well, let me tell you something. This is exactly how Nazi Germany started: a lot of layabouts with nothing better to do than to cause trouble!"

The onslaught subsided until, in late August, Agnew posted a series of semi-coherent tweets, again late at night. Liew complained to the BBC, and Agnew deleted his Twitter account. Which was probably wise.

At least he survived with his job. David Gower was less fortunate: after 20 years at Sky Sports, he left their commentary box at the end of the Ashes, and made way for Isa Guha, once ranked the world's No. 1 female bowler. The 62-year-old Gower was clearly distressed by the decision, and with reason. An incisive reader of the game, he was one of Sky's shining lights. In an interview in the *Daily Mail*, he put on his bravest face. "I have no intention of retiring to a hilltop in Peru yet," he assured us. To his credit, he went on to cover the series with effortless distinction, yet his sense of injustice was never far from the surface.

For her part, Ms Guha enjoyed a solidly capable summer. In fact, if we are to believe a mischievously sexist tale from Nigel Farndale in *The Times*, her impact was rather greater: "As well as being wise and witty she is also easy on the eye and her doddery old male colleagues are clearly smitten by her. The Bothams, Gowers and Bumbles have all started dressing in trendier clothes, brushing their hair, and checking the freshness of their breath in cupped hands before going on air and trying to impress her with their bants."

Gower was in post on the first morning of the Ashes, as the Sky coverage sought its line and length. Naturally, there were bumps in the road: Sir Ian Botham – also beginning his last series as a Sky pundit – often wore the air of a man who would have been far happier on a golf course, while David Lloyd was acutely perceptive when the mood took him, but all too often fell back on the pantomime persona of Bumble.

Test Match Special faced similar problems. Agnew, his humour mercifully restored, was in dazzling form, while the dependable Jim Maxwell took raucous delight in describing the first couple of centuries from Steve Smith. But Phil Tufnell, with the experience of 42 Test matches to impart, instinctively resorted to his Tuffers caricature. And then there was Dan Norcross.

CRICKET PODCASTS IN 2019

And the final word goes to…

JAMES GINGELL

Various forms exist of the internet's Rule 34, but the essential idea is this: if you can imagine it, there's a porn film of it. The podcasting world is much the same. Tiny barriers to entry allow huge variety: with no one to say no to new approaches, all that's needed is a mike and a broadband connection – and hey presto! A niche internet radio show.

Andy Zaltzman enjoys the freedom more than most. He has been the nerdy, wordy host of cult-favourite satire **The Bugle** since 2007, and now has two cricket podcasts to further explore his galactic imagination: **The Urnbelievable Ashes** (with Felicity Ward) and **The Cricket Sadist Hour** (with Jarrod Kimber). It's excellent stuff, if frustratingly infrequent. Funnier still are Dave Edwards, Ian Higgins and Sam Perry, the millennial Australians behind **The Grade Cricketer**. They roast the mores and morons at every level of the game, and earn the right by holding such obvious affection for them all.

Tailenders occupies much the same space, with James Anderson, Greg James and Felix White the blokes with the jokes. The real joy is listening to Anderson. So often caught scowling and swearing on the field, here he giggles and joshes, while also being vulnerable enough to reveal he was a target for bullies at school. It's probably not for people who read almanacks – Radio 1's James sets the tempo – but it knows its crowd and keeps them smiling.

If Tailenders made a mistake, it was inspiring one of Anderson's colleagues to think anyone can do it. Amid the tedium of listening to **Broad and Fry**, the mind drifts. (Mine alighted on 1990s action film *Double Team*, which threw together Jean-Claude Van Damme and basketball's Dennis Rodman for no reason or benefit to anyone.) We're treated to some blistering anecdotes: Laurence Olivier once said fuck; Nottinghamshire had a physio who looked like *Where's Wally?* Stephen Fry is off form, but it's Stuart Broad who bores most. He reads an advert offering free cases of beer in a manner that makes you want to order one and down the lot.

For those after weightier punditry, a clutch of magazine shows are provided by the usual suspects. **The Analyst** (from *The Cricketer*), **Switch Hit** (ESPNcricinfo), **The Spin** (*The Guardian*), **Wisden Cricket Podcast**, and **Sky Sports Cricket Podcast** are all tonal relatives of the discussions that tend to be broadcast during Test-match rain breaks. No bad thing, but **The Doosra** (Radio 5 Live), presented by Isa Guha and Aatif Nawaz, tailors itself expertly to a British-Asian audience.

Far the best of the serious ones is the **The Final Word**, from Australian duo Adam Collins and Geoff Lemon. In other hands, an hour-long discussion of the whys and wherefores of Mankading in the aftermath of Jos Buttler's latest mishap would be unlistenable. But their inquisitive minds and liquid delivery ensure constant engagement. The Final Word's long-form interviews are also a delight, an exhibition of sympathy in the subject; Kate Cross, Glenn Maxwell and Jimmy Neesham are all charmed enough to bare their souls. Collins and Lemon even find depth to a pre-sandpaper David Warner, who hinted he might fancy a career in politics after his cricket days are over. Quite what attracts him to an industry of manufactured bullying is left unexplored.

James Gingell is a civil servant whose only partiality is to Somerset CCC.

In an earlier life, Dan was surely a Butlin's Redcoat, organising treasure hunts and knobbly-knees contests. He brings the same brand of relentless jollity to *TMS*. Midway through that First Test, Dan struck a purple patch. "We've had an email: 'Have England ever before fielded a side including six players whose names begin with the letter J?'" He was off and running. At one point, the umpires were asked to check the ball, and produced a pair of calipers. "Where do they come from?" demanded Dan. "Is it from an umpires' shop?"

Dan saw comedy gold in the notion of an umpire's shop. He asked for a suitable shop name. An emailer offered an umporium. "Very good," said Dan. "Do keep 'em coming." He began to read out more messages from listeners. Each was greeted with helpless hilarity. He was still giggling when Geoffrey Boycott made his entrance. "We're talking about an umpire's shop, Geoffrey," he spluttered. Geoffrey merely grunted: "Been a little bored, have you, Dan?"

> "This is killing Test cricket. They should round up all the pads and bats and burn them…"

Simon Mann was back in the *TMS* box for the Lord's Test. He was serious, eloquent and unassuming, a latter-day Christopher Martin-Jenkins, and his professionalism lit up a rain-tainted draw.

Along came Headingley, where the series exploded after England were dismissed in their first innings for 67. The newspapers were predictably severe, but for sheer foot-stamping, mouth-foaming, totally confected fury, one Andy Jacobs of Talksport took the palm. "This is absolutely killing Test cricket," he ranted. "They should round up all the pads and bats and burn them… It's a farce! It's pitiful! Hopeless!"

Then came the historic run-chase, the innings for the ages from Stokes, and the determination of Jack Leach. And out came the superlatives. Paul Newman, the *Mail's* experienced cricket correspondent, called it "surely the greatest Test innings of all time". Alastair Cook, promising on the punditry front, declared it the "most extraordinary innings ever played by an Englishman". And Alyson Rudd pronounced in *The Times*: "Never in the history of sport has a heavily padded man wiping his spectacles seemed so heroic."

Reports were splashed across front and back pages. *The Times* featured Michael Atherton quoting Thomas Babington Macaulay: "Now who will stand on either hand, and keep the bridge with me?" *The Sun* preferred "Go Urn My Son!" They also toasted Stokes's "heroic one-man stand", and spoke of a possible knighthood for the nation's hero. Scarcely three weeks later, the same newspaper ran an appalling story on its front page, concerning his family and a tragic incident which took place three years before he was born. Stokes called it "low and despicable behaviour, disguised as journalism", and the barrage of criticism prompted a defence so feebly transparent you could almost feel sorry for the *Sun* spokesperson obliged to deliver it. Almost.

After the drama of Headingley, it seemed inevitable that the Fourth Test in Manchester would prove an anticlimax in English eyes. Smith, returning after concussion, effectively ended England's hopes with a monstrous 211 in the first innings, and in Marnus Labuschagne he found an able ally. Australia had

retained the Ashes, and the back pages sang a different song. "Outfought. Out-thought. Outclassed", said *The Telegraph*. "Ashes to Ashes", reflected *The Guardian*. "Cold Trafford", mourned the *Daily Mirror*, while *The Sun* ran pictures of a celebrating Smith beneath the expressive headline: "XXXX It!"

A lingering memory is of Sky's Ian Ward interrogating Smith and Labuschagne with questions culled from the football handbook: "Steve, how special is that?… Marnus, how are you feeling?" Both somehow avoided: "Over the moon." Joe Root came in for criticism in the wake of defeat, but he will surely have been encouraged by Vic Marks's honest attempt at a kindly summary in *The Guardian*: "Root may not be a brilliant captain, but he is not crap."

Before the final Test, Boycott received a knighthood in Theresa May's Resignation Honours. Inevitably, this provoked a media storm, in view of his conviction in 1998 for assault on a former girlfriend. Equally inevitably, Boycott managed to inflame matters still further. Interviewed by Martha Kearney for the *Today* programme on Radio 4, Boycott was asked to comment on the hostile reaction to his honour from the chief executive of Women's Aid. "I don't give a toss about her, love," he replied, claiming – quite erroneously – that the legal system in France rested on the principle of "guilt until proven innocent". This, he said, was one of the reasons he didn't vote Remain in the EU referendum. There may well have been greater public relations disasters, but they didn't come clamouring to mind.

Boycott returned to *TMS* for the Fifth Test at The Oval, and he watched England save a memorable series. Gideon Haigh, the superb Australian stylist, summed it up in *The Times*: "The Ashes series that was too close to call has proved just that… This final afternoon was England's… Root called it a 'blueprint' for how he would like England to play. A strange time to produce it, when the house is complete, but better late than never."

Gower and Botham said farewell to Sky; Gower was typically urbane, while Botham, in cut-down jeans and fishing shirt, resembled a member of The Wurzels, the noted Scrumpy and Western band from Somerset. And Vaughan, happily converted to the joys of the English game, told *The Telegraph*: "This summer has brought a new audience to cricket. In ten or 15 years' time, we will be hearing from young England players who fell in love with cricket in 2019… The sport needed this summer."

So glasses were raised, and glad memories stored. And if many reflected that a resurgent sport needed a far wider audience than Sky, for all its excellence, could provide, then that was a subject for another day. Better to cherish the deeds of Ben Stokes, Steve Smith and Jack Leach, and the glowing memories of the golden summer of 2019.

For 33 years, Patrick Collins was the chief sportswriter for The Mail on Sunday. *He is the winner of five Sports Journalist of the Year awards.*

CRICKET AND SOCIAL MEDIA

The prophecies of Jofradamus

D AVE T ICKNER

Another year, another 12 months of poison, bile and unpleasantness on social media, where the trend remains a worrying/terrifying/apocalyptic amplification of the worst people and opinions.

But for #CricketTwitter, it was a great year. Heaven help us, it was at times a happy year. It would be wrong to pretend absolutely all was well, but the theme of cricket's best social-media stories in 2019 was hope and positivity. Let's say it: the theme was love. For once, in this small, poisonous corner of the internet, love won – without recourse to boundary countback.

One problem for young professional sportspeople is that they were using social media before they were old enough to know better. Many have been caught saying stupid teenager things when they were stupid teenagers, and many more will. But when Jofra Archer's old tweets turned up, the news stories that accompanied them did not include phrases such as "issued an apology" or "closed his account on the popular micro-blogging hellscape". His old tweets were innocent and funny – and they appeared to predict everything that would ever happen in the sport. Jofradamus was born.

Archer's Twitter skill set – surely more valuable than rattling helmets at 95mph – is simple: he spent much of his formative years watching cricket, and tweeting prolifically yet succinctly. It has left a treasure trove of 40,000 tweets containing just enough content, and little enough context, to be repurposed for any circumstance. This peaked during England's World Cup semi-final win over Australia, with entire match reports concocted from ancient tweets about Glenn Maxwell, and six-year-old advice – unheeded by the Aussie lower order – to "watch that googly, man". For the run-out of Steve Smith, there was an unimprovable "Nutmeg". He had tweeted it in 2014.

A tweet from May that year read: "Want to go to lords". To Lord's he went. Were there old tweets about super overs and Ben Stokes and Trent Boult? Like Jofradamus, you already know. There was even one – "16 from 6" – for the target New Zealand missed by the barest of margins.

So many are about stars Archer now finds himself playing with and against. The tweets had few interactions, until rediscovered by Twitter's army of online wags. Here was a young man watching every possible minute of cricket, and second-screening it at a million miles an hour, not because he had a large audience, but because he could. None of us is likely to win a World Cup, or fell Smith, yet here was a direct connection with Archer: we've all tweeted our frustration, delight, nervousness and joy about this stupid sport we adore.

Not even Jofradamus could predict the year's other Twitter hero, as Pavel Florin went viral for his village-level bowling at the European Cricket League. First came mockery – proof for those who wanted it of the poor standard of the

CRICKET AND BLOGS IN 2019

Tattoed euphoria

Brian Carpenter

Cricket in England spent the year oscillating between breathless, disbelieving joy – and suspicion of the future. Either way, it continued to stimulate a range of emotions: optimism, pessimism, serenity, anger. In 2019, cricket's blogs reflected all this.

Matt Becker, at *Limited Overs* (**limitedovers.wordpress.com**), gave his customary, deeply felt, American take on events at Lord's on July 14. "Stokes, shaking off Bristol once and for all. Stokes, so tired at the end he could barely lift his arms. Stokes, leaning on his bat, in the shadows of a London late afternoon… begging for his chance to win it for his adopted country, only to fall just short. And then a few minutes later, walking out to bat the super over, his kit grass-stained and filthy, ready to give just a little bit more."

For all the day's drama, and the unprecedented nature of its conclusion, James Morgan at *The Full Toss* (**thefulltoss.com**) adopted a more nuanced position. Amid the celebrations and the peculiar experience of talking about cricket to people who have never shown any interest, he spoke for those of us who felt conflicted about the match and its outcome. "Why did England have the opportunity to bat first?" he asked. "It's just an unfair technicality. It's written in the rules that the team batting second in the main event gets to bat first in the super over. Why this should be the case, nobody knows. It just is. And there's no rhyme or reason for it… Ultimately an outrageous fluke and a random technicality determined the outcome."

He continued: "So did England deserve to win yesterday's World Cup final? In my opinion, no. But are they worthy world champions? Oh yes. Undoubtedly. This tournament was a marathon not a sprint. And we outlasted every other team through pure talent and immense character."

When Ben Stokes consolidated his legend at Headingley in late August, Rick Walton (**cricketmanwales.com**) captured his sense of place and time, and his amazement, at what we had just witnessed. "Ben Stokes. Crazy, wonderful, tattooed euphoria… How in god's name did it actually happen? From Buttler/Woakes, how the hell did that happen?"

Meanwhile, The Hundred hung like a spectre over the game. Steve Dolman, at *Peakfan's Blog* (**derbyshirecricket.blogspot.com**), spoke for many: "Since it was first touted, the marketing and publicity behind this competition has been a shambles. From saying it was not aimed at the traditional fan (silly) to simplifying it for mums and kids (patronising) to choosing Test grounds to host it, but not Durham (absurd), it has been pathetic."

Away from the discontent, Marco Jackson (**frominsideright.wordpress.com**) provided an evocative, elegant reminder of the gentler emotions the game can stir, with a series of "Trips in Cricket". One of his posts about a visit to the St Lawrence Ground in Canterbury was so good it seems invidious to reproduce any extracts in isolation. However, he did leave the reader with an admirable piece of cricket-watching philosophy.

"By now, the peak of summer is come and gone, the greens turned brown, the upright grasses now bent and bowed by harvest and harvester," he wrote. "The days themselves may still be golden, but the fields tell the story of an autumn that will soon be upon them. Enjoy the summer while it lasts, they say, and I intended to do just that; make cricketing hay while the sun shines."

Brian Carpenter was the inaugural winner of Wisden's *writing competition, in 2013.*

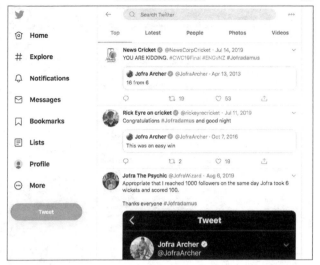

game outside the traditional hotbeds. Gradually, the tone shifted, as more details emerged. Florin was the only born-and-bred Romanian in his Cluj side, and it became clear his infectious love of the game would put even 2014 Jofra to shame. Cynically, we waited for the backlash to the backlash. It never came. Florin was a bona fide Twitter phenomenon, and soon a full international, thanks to the expansion of Twenty20.

Continuing the love theme, the year also saw England World Cup winners Katherine Brunt and Nat Sciver announce their engagement on Instagram. Inevitably, Jofra was the first to congratulate them, all the way back in 2013: "Congrats! Treat her well."

Dave Tickner is editor of Cricket365.com, and can generally be found posting the same three or four tired jokes on Twitter as @tickerscricket.

Mulling it all over: Marcus Trescothick on Test debut, August 2000.

Patrick Eagar, Popperfoto/Getty Images

RETIREMENTS IN 2019

Banger, the butcher of Taunton

Jack Shantry

There's an old line in show business. You only ever perform twice at the same venue: once on the way up, and once on the way down. When **Marcus Trescothick**, aged 43, took his final bow in 2019 – save for a cameo as twelfth man in the title decider against Essex – it was for Somerset's Second XI, 28 seasons after his first game for them.

In between, he enjoyed one heck of a career: 76 Tests (two as captain), 123 one-day internationals (plus three Twenty20s), 391 first-class matches, over 26,000 runs, and 66 centuries. He was never dropped by England – from his first cap, in 2000, to his last, in 2006 – and he averaged not far off 44 in Tests: how England yearn for a player of his calibre at the top of the order. His international career was cut short by a mental-health condition; his 2008 autobiography, detailing his struggles, led to other cricketers coming forward to speak about their own. He has stayed on at Taunton as assistant coach.

A free-flowing batsman who caught the selectors' eye with imperious off-drives and a simple but sound technique against fast bowling, Trescothick was earmarked early on for success. Duncan Fletcher famously plucked him from county cricket, along with Michael Vaughan, placing the evidence of his own eyes above modest stats: in September 1999, Trescothick had butchered 167 from 187 balls against Glamorgan, whom Fletcher was coaching. He became part of the England side that regained the Ashes in 2005, and set the ball rolling with a punishing 90 on the first day of the pivotal Second Test at Edgbaston.

A frequent lament is what might have been, had Trescothick not suffered mental-health issues, especially on tour. Many county pros bemoaned their luck that a player as good as "Banger" was instead destroying domestic attacks up and down the country. After his international retirement, he scored 1,000 first-class runs in a season eight times. I once took to singing Wurzels songs at him between deliveries in a bid to break his concentration in a game at New Road. I took his wicket, too. He made 203.

Adam Riley was once touted as England's off-spinning successor to Graeme Swann. Andrew Strauss led the calls for him to be fast-tracked to international honours after he enjoyed a successful 2014 season with Kent, taking 57 first-class wickets. But he struggled to repeat that performance, and retired at 27, when most spinners are yet to peak. Many, including his former county coach Matt Walker, put his loss of form down to an England Lions tour of South Africa in 2015, when coaches tried to make significant changes to his action.

Will Smith is part of an elite club, having won four County Championships, one with Nottinghamshire (while completing a degree in biochemistry) and three with Durham, captaining them to glory in 2009. He had a spell with Hampshire, where his occasional off-breaks became an important part of their T20 plans. Smith returned to Chester-le-Street for a second stint in 2018.

MOST COUNTY CHAMPIONSHIP MEDALS IN THE 21ST CENTURY

5	R. J. Sidebottom	Yorkshire (2001, 2014, 2015); Nottinghamshire (2005, 2010)
4	Mushtaq Ahmed	Surrey (2002); Sussex (2003, 2006, 2007)
4	**W. R. Smith** . . .	**Nottinghamshire (2005); Durham (2008, 2009, 2013)**
4	A. J. Hodd	Sussex (2006, 2007); Yorkshire (2014, 2015)
4	L. E. Plunkett . .	Durham (2008, 2009); Yorkshire (2014, 2015)
4	M. D. Stoneman	Durham (2008, 2009, 2013); Surrey (2018)

The Australian **Michael Klinger** was made to wait for his international debut – a Twenty20 call-up at the age of 36. That his late-career form was so strong owed much to a long spell in county cricket. After a year at Worcestershire in 2012, he moved down the M5 to Gloucestershire, where he replaced Alex Gidman as captain, and enjoyed seven stellar seasons. His List A and T20 records – he averaged 49 and 34 – are particularly impressive. He was quickly appointed coach of Melbourne Renegades in the Big Bash League.

Will Tavaré never reached the same heights as his uncle Chris, but did score 1,000 first-class runs for Gloucestershire in 2014. There was a stylistic resemblance, and 54 first-class appearances brought him six hundreds.

Jack Shantry made 255 appearances in a ten-year career for Worcestershire. He retired in 2018, aged 30, and has taken up umpiring.

CAREER FIGURES

Players not expected to appear in county cricket in 2020

(minimum 30 first-class appearances)

BATTING

	M	I	NO	R	HS	100	Avge	1,000r/ season
M. T. Coles	116	154	23	2,624	103*	1	20.03	–
N. J. Dexter	162	270	30	8,316	180	18	34.65	–
A. Harinath	75	131	6	3,870	154	6	30.96	–
A. Javid	43	70	6	1,503	143	3	23.48	–
M. Klinger.	182	321	33	11,320	255	30	39.30	1+2
C. J. Liddle	34	36	18	208	53	–	11.55	–
R. D. Pringle	40	63	8	1,336	99	–	24.29	–
O. P. Rayner	151	201	32	3,432	143*	2	20.30	–
A. E. N. Riley	61	75	28	495	34	–	10.53	–
D. Smit	137	208	37	6,077	156*	9	35.53	–
W. R. Smith	183	313	22	9,541	210	18	32.78	1
W. A. Tavaré	54	92	6	2,721	139	6	31.63	1
M. E. Trescothick	391	675	36	26,234	284	66	41.05	8

1+2 indicates one season in England and two in Australia.

BOWLING

	R	W	BB	Avge	5I	10M	Ct/St
M. T. Coles	10,553	358	6-51	29.47	12	2	62
N. J. Dexter	5,813	169	6-63	34.39	6	–	98
A. Harinath	195	5	2-1	39.00	–	–	20
A. Javid	441	5	1-1	88.20	–	–	18
M. Klinger.	3	0	0-3	–	–	–	179
C. J. Liddle	2,326	48	3-42	48.45	–	–	8
R. D. Pringle	2,401	63	7-107	38.11	2	1	24
O. P. Rayner	10,411	313	8-46	33.26	10	1	196
A. E. N. Riley	4,776	128	7-150	37.31	5	–	37
D. Smit	3,501	106	7-27	33.02	3	–	362/22
W. R. Smith	1,629	32	3-34	50.90	–	–	115
W. A. Tavaré	82	0	0-1	–	–	–	36
M. E. Trescothick	1,551	36	4-36	43.08	–	–	560

Winter sports: L. S. Lowry's *A Cricket Match* – not the traditional depiction of the English game.

CRICKETANA IN 2019

Strapped for cash

MARCUS WILLIAMS

While the wider world of cricket awaited, with varying levels of anticipation, The Hundred, the world of cricketana celebrated the million. More precisely, it celebrated the £1.155m paid for an L. S. Lowry painting of children playing a makeshift game in a deprived part of Manchester. It was the monetary high spot of a year which also saw the most notorious bat of the modern era come to market, as well as furniture, rare books and players' equipment designed for the head – and for elsewhere.

Lowry's *A Cricket Match*, a 24in × 18in canvas painted in 1938, went under the hammer at a packed Sotheby's in London as part of a sale of modern and post-war British art, alongside works by Henry Moore, Graham Sutherland and Winston Churchill. It had been part of a private collection in America, and now went to an anonymous telephone purchaser, whose bid of £950,000 ultimately exceeded £1m thanks to buyer's premium. The setting is an area of waste ground behind a run-down tenement building in Broughton, a suburb of Salford. The backdrop is as much the subject as the children playing cricket, as are the others who watch from behind a wall or have their back to the activity.

This painting had sold for £282,000 in 1996, then a record for a Lowry, though that figure has since been left far behind. In 2011, two separate works, *The Football Match* and *Piccadilly Circus*, fetched £5.6m each. Cricket was not a subject especially close to Lowry's heart – gritty landscapes and the working classes were his well-known inspiration – but a close friend, Alick Leggat, was Lancashire's honorary treasurer, and advised him on aspects of the game. In January 2020, *The Mill, Pendlebury*, also featuring children playing cricket, made £2.65m at Christie's in London.

These aside, there are only a few other cricket paintings by Lowry. The MCC collection contains a 1940 pencil drawing of work-mates playing with bat and ball outside a mill, while a 1952 piece, also titled *A Cricket Match* but set in a school playground dwarfed by a large factory, fetched nearly £770,000 at Christie's in 2008; it was once owned by Sir Paul Getty.

The aluminium bat that caused a change in the Laws

Lowry's only depiction of more formal cricket is a painting from the 1960s, latterly titled *Lancashire League Cricket Match*, though it takes place in a generic setting. Accompanied by *Crowd Round a Cricket Sight Board* – a section of the original canvas detached by the artist after he had difficulty in "reconciling the two portions" – it sold for £677,250 in 2004.

A very different artwork featured in a sale held by Chorleys of Gloucestershire. A late-Victorian chest of drawers with a cricket scene painted on the front sold for £2,728, more than ten times its estimate, even though it was in far from perfect condition. In contrast to Lowry's figures, the players – from an earlier era, and with tricorn hats, billowing white shirts and cream breeches – are playing in front of a country house with trees, picket fences, a candy-striped tent and spectators dining in a marquee.

The protagonists in one of modern cricket's more infamous episodes have doubtless dined out on tales of the aluminium bat that caused a change in the Laws. Known as the ComBat, and made in Australia, it was used by Dennis Lillee in the Perth Test against England in December 1979. After complaints from both captains, Greg Chappell and Mike Brearley, Chappell lost patience and walked out to hand Lillee a traditional willow.

There followed protracted debate with the umpires, and eventually Lillee – having hurled the ComBat some distance away – reluctantly complied. "I now hold the record for throwing an aluminium bat the furthest in a Test, and I know it will stand for ever," he said later. (The second innings of this game would make history in a less combative way, when it produced the immortal scorecard entry: Lillee c Willey b Dilley 19.)

Lillee gave it to the English batmaker Duncan Fearnley (with whom, in theory, he had an exclusive contract at the time), and in July it was bought for £6,136 by a telephone bidder at a John Goodwin auction in Malvern. Other items from Fearnley's collection were sold: the bat belonging to Graeme Hick when he scored 1,000 runs before the end of May 1988 realised £4,484; one of the three wielded by Ian Botham in the summer of 1981 made £3,776; and another, used by Sunil Gavaskar against England at Lord's in 1979, made

John Goodwin

Tools of the trade: the back of the ComBat is on the left; other Duncan Fearnleys include bats used by Graeme Hick, Glenn Turner and David Steele.

£2,360. This last was also banned because, like Lillee's, it had holes drilled in it to make it lighter – and these were reckoned to damage the ball.

At the same sale was a bronze bust of Viv Richards, believed to be one of only two cast by Neale Andrew, son of former England wicketkeeper Keith, and which made £1,770. An 1885 terracotta figure of an earlier giant of the game, W. G. Grace, leaning on a bat, attracted fierce bidding at Canterbury Auction Galleries, and fetched £12,400 – more than ten times estimate.

Though not in the same league as a Yankees baseball shirt worn by Babe Ruth (which soared to £4.4m at auction in New York in June), items of kit once belonging to international cricketers proved popular. Off-spinner Lance Gibbs's West Indies cap made £620 at Mullock's, and the England cap belonging to Kent's Harry Wood, who played four Tests in the late 19th century, £786 in a Graham Budd sale.

There was a bizarre offering in a Moore Allen & Innocent auction in Cirencester: a framed jockstrap said to have belonged to Allan Lamb, together with a "certificate of authenticity" asserting it had been worn in "The Ball-Tampering Test" at Karachi in January 1991. At that time, England and Lamb were actually playing in Australia, so it was clearly a case of *caveat emptor*. Nonetheless, the *emptor* in question parted with £62 for a lot which also included two old bats and some leather cases.

On more revered ground, a copy of the rare *A Correct Account of All The Cricket Matches Played by The Nottingham Old Cricket Club from 1771 to 1829* by William North, together with the *1830–35* follow-up edition, far exceeded the £100 estimate at the Richard Winterton sale in Lichfield. It sold for £7,936. Its battered nature was in contrast to a pristine set of the limited-edition, leatherbound modern *Wisdens* (1995–2018), which fetched £4,464 at Dominic Winter Auctions, Cirencester.

During 2019, J. W. McKenzie, the renowned Surrey-based cricket bookseller and publisher, issued his 200th catalogue. Having started out from his parents' house in 1972, he now runs the only shop premises specialising solely in cricket books and memorabilia. He first came to prominence by selling a complete run of *Wisdens* to Tim Rice, and now issues four detailed catalogues each year, as well as reprints of many rare cricket titles. As he says: "It really has been a labour of love."

CRICKET AND THE WEATHER IN 2019

Humberto echo and the Spanish plume

ANDREW HIGNELL

The World Cup suffered a record four washouts, and the Manchester semi-final fell back on a reserve day. Perhaps the portents were there on May 29, the day of the glitzy launch in London, when 27 hours were lost in the seven Championship matches taking place around the country.

From mid-June, however, the tournament benefited from a phenomenon known as the Spanish plume: high pressure built up over the Bay of Biscay and brought a mini-heatwave. Championship cricket also flourished in warm, dry conditions, since a restructuring of the calendar meant more first-class matches were played in midsummer than in previous years. Inevitably, though, the heat gave way to violent thunderstorms – one reason 2019 lost much more time than the year before.

Another factor was the miserable conclusion to the Championship season in late September, when the remnants of tropical storm Humberto spiralled across the country. All 18 counties were involved, with the destiny of the pennant at stake. But bands of heavy rain meant every game lost more than half its scheduled playing time: 154.75 hours out of a possible 216 fell foul of the grim autumnal weather.

The T20 Blast was shunted later in the season and, like the World Cup, endured a soggy start: only one of the seven games on July 19, the second day of competition, was uninterrupted, and four were abandoned. Friday, August 16 was worse still: not a ball was bowled in any of the eight matches.

HOURS LOST TO THE WEATHER IN THE 2019 CHAMPIONSHIP

	Home	Away	2019	2018	Difference
Derbyshire	6.75	26.25	33.00	35.00	–2.00
Durham	33.50	7.00	40.50	41.50	–1.00
Essex	10.50	32.00	42.50	53.25	**–10.75**
Glamorgan	6.25	41.25	47.50	37.25	10.25
Gloucestershire	38.50	9.75	48.25	50.00	–1.75
Hampshire	**5.50**	**50.50**	56.00	42.75	13.25
Kent	44.00	10.75	54.75	22.75	32.00
Lancashire	7.00	49.00	56.00	**17.75**	38.25
Leicestershire	**44.25**	17.75	62.00	23.25	**38.75**
Middlesex	30.75	34.50	**65.25**	38.25	27.00
Northamptonshire	14.50	33.00	47.50	**58.25**	**–10.75**
Nottinghamshire	18.75	22.75	41.50	32.00	9.50
Somerset	26.00	22.00	48.00	25.50	22.50
Surrey	40.00	11.25	51.25	32.50	18.75
Sussex	38.50	12.25	50.75	32.50	18.25
Warwickshire	26.50	**3.00**	**29.50**	21.75	7.75
Worcestershire	30.75	22.00	52.75	25.75	27.00
Yorkshire	16.75	33.75	50.50	57.00	–6.50
	438.75	438.75	877.50	647.00	230.50

CRICKET PEOPLE

Not the retiring kind

RICHARD WHITEHEAD

It takes **Ian Gould** less than ten seconds to shrug off a question about how he is enjoying international retirement. "Well, I'm off to South Africa tomorrow to umpire in the Under-19 World Cup," he says. An email had arrived from the ICC a few days earlier, asking if he would be willing to stand in the tournament, six months after his official farewell at the World Cup game between India and Sri Lanka at Headingley. "I thought it was daft not to," he says. "I like the idea of mentoring the next generation of officials – and getting some sunshine." But he's not about to become the Frank Sinatra of umpires. "It's just a one-off. I have definitely retired."

Gould stumbled into umpiring: after a playing career with Middlesex and Sussex that also brought 18 ODI caps, he was coach of Middlesex Second XI when, one day, an umpire was late arriving. He pulled on a white coat, and relished the experience. He joined the first-class list in 2001, took charge of the first of 140 ODIs in 2006, and the first of 74 Tests two years later. With his quick wit and affability, he soon became one of the most popular officials in the world. "The secret is to be polite, and explain your decisions. And people know I am a stickler for the Laws."

He was widely known as "Gunner", because of a spell as a young goalkeeper with Arsenal, and his unwavering support for the club. He was 62 in August, but age had nothing to do with his decision. "In fact, I'd just had probably my best year," he says. "But I was fed up of the travelling, and I wanted to go out on my own terms." He has experienced at first hand a revolution in the umpire's role, but embraced the introduction of technology. "I think TV viewers and spectators at the ground enjoy it," he says. "It has brought a bit of theatre to the game. If a change is better for those who watch the game, then bring it on."

His lowest moment was during a Test in the Caribbean in 2018, when Sri Lanka refused to come out on the third morning after being punished for ball-tampering. "I was a bit miffed. I thought the game should be abandoned – but that probably had something to do with it being in St Lucia."

When his team-mates in the Durham Under-19 squad began to forge careers in first-class cricket, **Iain Nairn** wondered about his own future. A developmental issue caused his right leg to be amputated when he was six months, but a prosthetic limb did not stop him playing alongside the likes of Mark Davies and Gary Pratt in the county's age-group teams.

"I didn't think of myself as being different – I was just playing cricket with the lads," he says. "Until that age, I was just about able to keep up, but then they went off to start county careers." Nairn played Premier League club cricket with Chester-le-Street, until the creation of the England Physical Disability team in 2012 changed everything. He made his debut for them in 2013, and took over the captaincy the following year. From then, until his retirement after a triangular tournament last summer, he has achieved more than he thought possible: "To captain your country is the biggest privilege you could have."

In 2014, he led England to victory in the first physical disability competition, held in Bangladesh. It remains a highlight. "No one can take away that I was the first winning captain in a PD tournament." And he fondly recalls an innings against Pakistan in Dubai in 2016. "We were 20 for three, and I made 69. Kevin Pietersen was there watching, and that meant a lot."

At 39, and with a new generation of players emerging, he felt it was time to go. Now he can give more attention to his work as an insolvency practitioner in Durham, though he is keen to help raise the profile of PD cricket. "It's a game that can be adapted to people's mobility needs," he says. "I want to encourage more disabled people to play cricket."

After his part in South Africa's calamitous defeat by Australia in the 1999 semi-final, no one would have blamed **Steve Elworthy** if he had wanted nothing to do with another World Cup in the British Isles. Instead, when the tournament returned last summer, he was in charge. On that day at Edgbaston 20 years earlier, his ten wicketless overs went for 59, and he was ninth out as South Africa crashed and burned. He retired from the game after failing to make the squad for the 2003 competition.

But the end of his playing career was just the beginning of Elworthy's story. Within five years, his success in piloting the first World Twenty20 in South Africa had made him the go-to man for global tournaments. He joined the ECB soon after, and organised the 2009 World T20, two Champions Trophies and a women's World Cup. In 2018, he picked up an MBE. Last summer came "the pinnacle", as managing director of the World Cup. "I always felt this was the biggest tournament I would run," he says. He now has a new role with the ECB as director of events; he will play a key role in the presentation of The Hundred.

Years of hard work by Elworthy, now 55, and his team of around 120 ensured the World Cup was an administrative success, apart from a ticketing fiasco on the second day, when thousands of spectators were unable to get into Trent Bridge until the match between Pakistan and West Indies was practically over. "It was a perfect storm," he says. "I was mortified, but we made changes overnight to allow people to print tickets at home."

Early on the morning of the final, he gathered his colleagues together, and told them to make the most of the day. Hours later, as the match reached its dizzying conclusion, he tried to brief the VIP party on the details of the presentation ceremony. "They weren't listening. I decided it could wait until we were all down on the outfield." At least he found time to enjoy the drama. "Watching from the Pavilion was the most incredible hour of my life."

CRICKET AND THE COURTS IN 2019

County player jailed for rape

Worcestershire's Australian all-rounder Alex Hepburn, 24, was jailed for five years at Hereford Crown Court on April 30 after being found of guilty of rape. Hepburn was convicted of oral rape at a flat in Worcester in April 2017. The incident happened after the woman had had consensual sex with his team-mate Joe Clarke, who had passed out in the bathroom.

The prosecution said that, days before the attack, Hepburn had sent the rules of a competition to find the "top shagger" to a few friends on WhatsApp. His messages included a reference to rape.

This game, Miranda Moore, QC, told the jury, had "precious little to do with cricket… The 'score' that he hoped to make may well help you in the explanation as to what he was doing to her. He saw that girl asleep in the bed and decided to take advantage." Michelle Heeley, QC, defending, said the woman's memories were hazy, and the sex consensual.

At an earlier trial, the jury had been discharged after failing to reach a verdict. At the retrial, Hepburn was acquitted on one count but, after nearly 11 hours' deliberation, unanimously found guilty on the second. Judge Jim Tindal described Hepburn's contest as a "pathetic sexist game", adding: "You probably thought it was laddish behaviour at the time. In truth, it was foul sexism. It demeaned women and trivialised rape – a word you personally threw around lightly. Only now do you realise how serious rape is."

Hepburn played five List A and two Twenty20 matches for Worcestershire, taking five for 24 in a T20 game against Nottinghamshire in 2017. His contract was ended after he was charged.

BLIND CRICKETER CAN'T JOIN IPL

The Indian Supreme Court rejected a petition from a partially sighted cricketer who said it was discriminatory not to let him play in the Indian Premier League. Ratendra Singh Jayara from Uttar Pradesh has played in several national-level blind competitions; he asked to join the IPL, but was refused. In a filing to the court, Jayara cited the Right to Equality in the Indian constitution and the Rights of Persons with Disabilities Act 2016. Chief Justice Ranjan Gogi said the case was "devoid of merit".

WORLD CUP WIN COSTS CRICKET FAN LICENCE AND JOB

A Derbyshire driver swerved towards the kerb in what he said was excitement while listening to the end of England's World Cup win at Lord's. He was, however, seen by police, who breathalysed him: he registered more than double the alcohol limit. Andrew Lodge, from Barlborough, pleaded guilty and was banned from driving for 20 months by Chesterfield magistrates; he also had to pay a fine and costs, totalling £516. The court heard the imminent ban had cost Lodge his job as a mortgage adviser.

LASHINGS OFFICIAL ADMITS FRAUD

James Honey-Green, a former executive with the celebrity team Lashings, diverted money into his own bank account. The fraud came to light when ex-England player Darren Maddy met Lashings captain David Smith at an event, and said he had not received match fees. Other discrepancies were then discovered.

Honey-Green, the club's operations manager, admitted three charges of fraud, and was given a ten-month suspended sentence at Maidstone Crown Court in April. He was ordered to repay £9,000, and placed under a three-month curfew. Lashings was founded in 1984 as a pub team, but is now a business – "the Harlem Globetrotters of cricket," says the website – and turns out teams of ageing cricketers to play allcomers.

VILLAGE CLUB LOSE VAT APPEAL

An Oxfordshire village club have had their appeal against paying VAT on a new pavilion dismissed by judges after a four-year legal battle. Eynsham CC were contesting an HM Revenue and Customs decision forcing them to pay £37,000 in tax, contending there were charitable purposes involved. In what was described as a "very complex" case, an upper tribunal ruled in October 2019 that the club were "not established for charitable purposes and hence cannot be a charity". In 2015, David Cameron, then the prime minister and Eynsham's local MP, raised the matter with his Chancellor of the Exchequer, George Osborne. Cameron had told the club the situation was "not promising".

DRIVING, WARNIE

Shane Warne was banned from driving for 12 months by Wimbledon magistrates in September, after admitting his sixth speeding offence in two years. He was clocked doing 47mph in a hired Jaguar on a 40mph slip road on to the A40 in west London. Deputy District Judge Adrian Turner said that, while each incident on its own may have been serious, "for points-disqualification purposes, the triviality of the offences is not to be taken into account". Warne was also fined £1,845.

CRICKET AND THE LAWS IN 2019

Cross-checking

FRASER STEWART

It wouldn't be cricket if things were simple. And so, at a vital moment of the gripping World Cup final, the year's largest Laws-related spanner was thrown into the works. The details of the deflection off Ben Stokes's bat, sending the ball to the boundary, are well known. The key issue was whether the batsmen had crossed on the second run at the instant Martin Guptill threw the ball in from deep midwicket. Law 19.8 is clear but, under the ICC's protocols, the umpires were not allowed to refer that decision to their TV colleague. As it turned out, Stokes and Adil Rashid were well short of crossing, which – in the heat of the moment – the umpires failed to spot. Only five runs should have been credited to England, rather than six, and Stokes told he was at the non-striker's end for the next delivery.

As convention (rather than Law) dictates, Stokes did not attempt more runs after the deflection, holding his hand up in apology. However, once the ball crosses the rope, the runs for the boundary must count. The ball has to remain live after any contact with batsmen, otherwise fielders could deliberately throw it at them to prevent further runs. And, once a ball that is live crosses the boundary, four must be credited.

Some questioned the rationale of using the moment of the throw for deciding the number of runs scored, suggesting that the moment it passes the wicket, or crosses the boundary, would be better. But not all overthrows pass the stumps; some slip backwards out of the fielder's hand, even going behind them over the boundary. And it would be too generous to credit batsmen with runs taken while the overthrow is travelling towards the rope; this doesn't happen with a normal boundary, and the same principle applies. The moment of the throw is regarded as a fair compromise, with umpires required to be aware of this in each instance, in case the overthrow reaches the boundary.

During the Fourth Ashes Test at Old Trafford, there was a more straightforward problem: it was so windy the umpires decided play would continue without bails. A heavy set was apparently unavailable, but the first attempt at a solution seemed more suited to the village green: a handyman inserted screws into the ends of the normal bails, for extra weight. This failed to solve the problem, so the umpires enacted Law 8.5, removing both sets of bails. For the wicket to be put down in such circumstances, the umpires must simply be satisfied that suitable contact with the stumps has been made.

In a World Cup match at Edgbaston, India referred a not-out lbw decision against Bangladesh's Soumya Sarkar. Replays seemed to show the ball had hit bat and pad at the same time. Since the introduction of DRS, the Law has been altered to cater for judgments too fine for the naked eye. Consequently, Law 36.2.2 states that "if the ball makes contact with the striker's person and bat simultaneously, this shall be considered as the ball having first touched the bat". India's review was unsuccessful.

Earlier in the year, there was controversy at the Indian Premier League, where Jos Buttler was run out at the non-striker's end by Ravichandran Ashwin before he delivered the ball. Buttler was clearly out of his ground when the wicket was put down but, at the moment Ashwin reached the position when he would have been expected to release the ball, Buttler was still in – just. Ashwin paused, before Buttler's momentum as he backed up took him out of his ground, and Ashwin removed the bails. It was given out – the second time Buttler has been dismissed this way in professional cricket. While non-strikers who leave the crease early put themselves as risk of dismissal, MCC stated that, in this instance, they felt Ashwin's pause had been too long, almost as if he was waiting for Buttler to leave his ground, and that the dismissal was contrary to the spirit of the game.

In another IPL game, between Sunrisers Hyderabad and Delhi Capitals, there was drama in the final over, when Amit Mishra was given out obstructing the field as he scampered for a single, having been called through for a bye by the non-striker. The wicketkeeper's throw missed the stumps, and the ball ended up mid-pitch with the bowler, Khaleel Ahmed. Mishra, a right-handed batsman, was running along the edge of the cut strip to his leg side but, having passed the bowler, he veered on to the pitch and ran directly between him and the non-striker's stumps. Khaleel's shy hit Mishra, who had clearly attempted to block the throw. The decision by the TV umpire to give him out was justified.

MCC were pleased the ICC introduced concussion replacements. It is something they have called for in the professional game, where medical expertise and like-for-like replacements are usually on hand. Such luxuries are not normally available in recreational cricket, but the Laws do allow for replacement players – for any reason, not just concussion – with the consent of the opposition captain.

The amateur game, increasingly streamed or recorded, also throws up some interesting conundrums. One was caught on camera at Sanderstead CC in Surrey. The striker missed the ball, which clipped the outside of off stump. The off bail jumped up, and was dislodged from its groove, before coming to rest on top of the stump. Heads were scratched, but the umpires correctly gave it not out: under Law 29.1.1, a bail must be completely removed from the top of the stumps. A photo and interpretation of that exact scenario had already been included in the new edition of Tom Smith's *Cricket Umpiring & Scoring*, which was released in 2019. An e-book version, containing video clips, was due for publication in early 2020.

Fraser Stewart is Laws Manager at MCC.

CRICKET AND THE THEATRE IN 2019

The Long Walk Back

HUGH CHEVALLIER

Cricket is a game of expanse: sunlit turf, spread-out fields, endless possibility. A prison cell is a place of enclosure: grey walls, hemmed-in bars, dwindling possibility. In both, time oozes unknown into the future – delicious for the cricketer or spectator, desperate for the new inmate. The worlds rarely collide, but in 2008 Chris Lewis, the England player of the 1990s, slipped from one into the other.

Even with maximum remission, he was facing a term of six and a half years after being caught smuggling £140,000 worth of liquid cocaine from St Lucia into Britain. It is a truism that sport at the highest level demands psychological toughness. But how does an international cricketer – Lewis played 32 Tests and 53 ODIs, including a World Cup final – cope with life inside? Does that inner steel fortify him, or does the lack of daily purpose bring mental disintegration? It's the goings-on in Lewis's head that playwright Dougie Blaxland and director Shane Morgan explore in *The Long Walk Back*.

That comes as no surprise for those who saw their previous cricket collaboration. *When The Eye Has Gone* charted the decline of Colin Milburn, another England player of exceptional talent who never quite fulfilled his potential. Milburn and Lewis affected a confident, bluff exterior, but beneath the carapace were insecure men struggling with demons. There is, though, a difference. While Milburn drank himself to an early death, aged 48, Lewis sought out the prison gym, which became a place of spiritual as well as physical salvation.

Not that there is much sign of redemption when we first see the actors. Before the play starts, Martin Edwards and Scott Bayliss play out a series of restless tableaux in a stark cell to a menacing soundtrack. The opening scene, so quick you almost miss it, takes us to St Lucia, where Lewis and an accomplice are about to board the plane, drugs in their cases. The next thing we know, we're in a cell in Staffordshire, in Dovegate Prison. And in despair.

Blaxland shuns a chronological structure, and it works – though you need your wits about you to follow the shifts of time, scene and character. This is not meant to be easy. While Edwards remains Lewis pretty much throughout, Bayliss's role is protean. The script calls him "The Other Man", and as such he leaps from fellow smuggler to chairman of the Surrey committee, customs official, radio commentator, judge – and more besides.

His main role, though, is as Lewis's alter ego, and the conversation between these two, the dialogue of the mind, forms the core of the drama. It's where the play strides boldly into issues of emotional health, and where Lewis ultimately proves resilient. It's also where sport comes in. Blaxland has said cricket was essentially his entrée into a psychological exploration,

Lisa Hounsome

Long-term partners: Martin Edwards (Chris Lewis) and Scott Bayliss (The Other Man).

yet it feels integral to the plot. Lewis, who claims never to have made a plan in his life, is coaxed into describing how he out-thought Javed Miandad at Lord's in 1992. Later, he comes to see his greatest sporting failure – a first-baller in the World Cup final earlier that year – as a Kiplingesque stepping-stone to mental fortitude. There follows an understanding of the nature and consequences of his crime. His recovery is not painless, but he emerges a stronger, better person.

Yet there are questions. As Lewis's conscience/alter ego, The Other Man is a one-dimensional creation defined by wise counsel. Early on, we witness Lewis's dark night of the soul – he contemplates killing himself – but the other voice administers a dose of common sense, and the crisis passes. Is that how the desperate mind works? While Lewis changes and develops, The Other Man does not. And while Bayliss's character challenges and tests Lewis, the converse never happens. So in one sequence, Lewis is persuaded that the £50,000 he stood to gain was a poor return when spread over six and a half years and shared between the 15 people affected by his conviction. Never does he counter that being caught was not in the plan.

Such observations are cavils, though, and the overall effect is compelling and uplifting. So is the reaction from audiences. After an early performance at Portland Prison, the mother of a young offender contacted Lewis – there to do a Q&A session with the inmates – to say her son had been so moved that his outlook on life had radically altered. That must be the most eloquent review.

Dougie Blaxland is the nom de plume of Jim Graham-Brown, who played 30 first-class and 27 one-day games for Kent, Derbyshire and Dorset between 1974 and 1991.

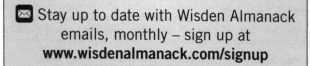

CRICKET AND TECHNOLOGY IN 2019

Data protection

LIAM CROMAR

Jos Buttler's shot selection has always been eye-catching but, during England's tour of the UAE in 2015-16, so was his choice of kit. Footage showed him wearing a sports bra – or did it? As Mark Wood explained via video blog, the players were now wearing activity trackers. It was the most noticeable example of wearable technology in cricket, and quickly became an accepted part of the top players' apparel.

Wearables in sport are not new. Rugby and football were already well down the corridor before cricket joined them, and it is surprising the ECB took so long to begin their trial; meanwhile, the first IPL team to use them, Rajasthan Royals, started only in 2019.

The technology uses GPS sensors to pinpoint location, accelerometers to measure change in movement, and gyroscopes to identify orientation, all of which you can find in your smartphone. Because biometrics are hard to do on the field of play, the focus – explains Raph Brandon, the ECB's head of science, medicine and innovation – is on micromovements, such as running speed, body rotation in degrees per second, and trunk flexion or extension.

The key is not collecting the data, but interpreting it. To do so, the measurements are crunched by algorithms to detect patterns, which identify when the subject is sprinting, walking, at rest and so on. We have learned, for example, that Stuart Broad might cover 15 miles in a day's Test cricket. Yet the information goes deeper: the wearables differentiate between high- and low-intensity actions, allowing staff to see how far players push their bodies.

Other algorithms then identify cricket-specific movements, such as fast-bowling actions. With the help of a library of video footage, the ECB and sport-sensors company Catapult are able to detect the pattern of movements that build up into a delivery. As a result, it is possible to determine exactly how many balls are bowled by each player, across matches and training. The strain placed on different parts of the body can then be revealed.

This has yielded a new metric of player load, which reflects the physical stresses affecting each bowler. As this has been found to correlate with ball speed, training can be carefully managed. Rather than Ben Stokes turning up to nets and trying to reach 90mph for 24 deliveries (a full T20 spell), he can be instructed to send down only four at that pace, so lessening the risk of burnout or injury. "Everything is monitored," says Steffan Jones, bowling coach for Rajasthan Royals. Specific requirements for power hitting, throwing and running between the wickets have been identified, allowing the workload of batsmen and fielders to be managed too.

"In terms of the specific preparation of a player going into a series, we're not guessing any more," says Brandon. "And that's helping with our injuries."

Once a player's baseline performance has been established, the coaching team can calculate the level of training needed to reach optimal level – or decide whether a player is match-fit, especially after an injury. With such a small number of cricketers using the technology, conclusions are tricky. But anecdotal results are positive. "I'd say there's definitely an injury reduction," says Jones. "The injury rate for Rajasthan Royals [in IPL 2019] was very low. We were in a good physical condition all the way through."

England's women have made good use of wearables, too. In the semi-final of the 2017 World Cup, a trophy they went on to win, it emerged that some of their players were running faster than they had ever been measured: their physical performance was peaking at the right time.

Jones has also employed the technology effectively in the school game, having pioneered the cricket application of Motus wearables, used primarily in American sports. It consists of a sleeve, measuring arm speed and torque, that can be worn during a match, with the coach monitoring proceedings on an iPad; this yields the hard data to help achieve more pace. And by tracking trunk-rotational speed, and speed drop-off before the back foot lands at the point of delivery, Catapult can reveal technical flaws in bowling actions, and aid remedial work.

As the game continues to expand, so do the challenges of tracking: if a cricketer plays in an overseas league, their temporary employers may not have the technology. The market is dominated by two companies: Catapult, used by England and Australia, and STATSports, whose clients include the Indian team. But if a franchise is well-equipped, players – already broadly accommodating of the technology – may take greater ownership of their data, and use their smartphone to fine-tune their training. It is likely that real-time tracking will be rolled out: at the moment, players typically have their wearable data downloaded at the end of a session, but instant transmission would allow staff to monitor micromovements on the field.

More and more aspects of the game are being tracked, recorded and analysed. Last year, Kookaburra announced in-ball tracking with its new SmartBall, claiming it would allow data on revolution and speed, and in time assist with adjudication of low catches and nicks.

During the World Cup, optical tracking of fielders was part of the TV coverage, showing their position on the ground in a computer-game style display. The main challenge to the users of tracking technology will be not in the gathering of data, but in its application. As Jones warns, there is the danger of "paralysis by analysis", with the numbers obscuring the actual performance. But for those who can avoid the trap, wearable technology is already proving to be the right track.

CRICKET AND THE ENVIRONMENT IN 2019

Australia's burning

T ANYA A LDRED

If 2019 was the year the climate crisis regularly hit the headlines, thanks to Greta Thunberg, school strikes and Extinction Rebellion, it was also the year the penny began to drop for cricket. The game was not immune from a fracturing environment: the crisis was now, and in the most iconic places. As 2020 coughed into life, Australia burned, with mass evacuations down the east coast and a state of disaster announced in Victoria. At the Sydney Test against New Zealand, players wore black armbands to honour the emergency services, several of whom had died tackling the flames.

Two reports on cricket and climate centred on temperature. The first, *Hit for Six*, published at Lord's in September, was a follow-up to 2018's *Game Changer*. It drilled deep into climate data, examining the effects of the crisis on cricket nations, and focused on the impact on the players, especially of extreme heat.

The report commissioned a series of experiments undertaken by the University of Portsmouth, showing the risk to batsmen jogging between the wickets at the equivalent of 5mph. The risk, it turned out, was considerable: from cramp to life-endangering heatstroke. "Above 35°C, the body runs out of options to cool itself," said Mike Tipton, professor of Human & Applied Physiology, and one of the report's authors. "For batsmen and wicketkeepers, even sweating has limited impact, as the heavy protective cladding creates a highly humid microclimate next to their bodies." This was no idle theorising: in Antigua in September, Australia's Beth Mooney retired ill because of heat stress.

Hit for Six also found that extreme heat affects the brain, in particular "vigilance (the ability to maintain attention, for example, when batting), short-term/working memory (a bowler remembering how the ball bounced off the pitch) and dual tasks (a batter keeping an eye on an incoming delivery while simultaneously manoeuvring to take a shot)". It pointed out that umpires are just as vulnerable.

Before it was released, the report went before the MCC World Cricket Committee, where it caught the eye of Shane Warne. "Before I'd seen the report, I hadn't really thought about how [the climate crisis] would impact cricket," he told *The Guardian*. "Some of the stuff we were presented with – how hot it was for the players at certain times, up to 50° in the middle, and how dangerous it was – was scary." Warne's surprise intervention attracted some equally surprised media attention, and he subsequently auctioned his Baggy Green, raising over $A1m to help Australia's firefighters; Harbhajan Singh, Virender Sehwag and Jimmy Neesham also expressed concern about the climate crisis on Twitter.

Australia is still the only country to use a heat-stress index to protect their professional players, which was praised by *Hit for Six*. It called for boards to

DELHI SMOG

In the air tonight, oh Lord…

SIDHARTH MONGA

"What is the cost of lies? It's not that we will mistake them for truth. The real danger is that if we hear enough lies, we no longer recognise truth at all."

In the first week of November, two boards, their national teams, the ICC and about 20,000 fans all either failed, or refused, to recognise the truth, bringing to mind the first words spoken in the TV mini-series *Chernobyl*. This was the weekend after Diwali, when crop stubble burned in the neighbouring states of land-locked Delhi combined with fireworks to form deadly clouds of smog, taking the air quality to hazardous levels. Diwali and stubble are just the seasonal triggers that remind us we have pushed the environment almost to a point of no return.

Around this time, health authorities tend to issue instructions: avoid stepping outdoors if possible, and eliminate strenuous activity, lest one end up with irreversible lung damage. And cricket in Delhi is routinely affected: in 2016, Ranji Trophy matches were moved out of the capital, in 2017 a Test was stalled, and in 2018 a batsman wore a pollution mask.

Yet in June 2019, the Indian board scheduled for November a Twenty20 international there against Bangladesh, who agreed (the ICC remained a bystander). The BCCI allot matches based on rotation, but venues have the option to swap fixtures. Despite previous lessons, nobody at the board, or in Delhi, raised a red flag until days before the match.

The afternoon made everyone nervous: Sunday, November 3 was straight from a disaster movie. Thick smog settled, making visibility poor; by 3pm, the Air Quality Index was 912 (over 200 is considered unsuitable for strenuous outdoor activity). Eyes stung after a few minutes. Delhi-bound flights were instructed not to take off, while those waiting to land kept circling, and 37 were made to land elsewhere. Schools had already been told to stay shut until Tuesday.

While the ICC match referee is mandated to take players off if conditions are unsafe, it is rarely a good idea to embarrass the BCCI. Miraculously, the AQI dropped to 563 at 4pm, and to 492 an hour later. Visibility improved. Flights began to land. One commentator, a former Test cricketer, suggested that Ranji Trophy cricket had been played in such Delhi "weather" before. Not that the locals needed convincing: a near full house queued up outside Feroz Shah Kotla two hours before the toss. Just after it, the Delhi government issued a health advisory, asking people to reschedule all outdoor activity.

In such conditions, 22 fine young men and a few others on the bench undertook an activity that requires explosive bursts of energy at regular intervals for close to four hours. During it, their lungs pumped in more foul air, and more particulate matter, than is healthy. The cheering crowds, the workers who make matches happen, the on-duty police, all put their health on the line.

Two players vomited on the field, but that didn't make the broadcast. BCCI president Sourav Ganguly, who had assumed the role in the week of the match, thanked the teams for playing in difficult conditions, becoming the only member of the board even to acknowledge something was unusual. Hopefully, cricket had learned its lesson; the human race may be a different story.

Bad light stops play: at Canberra on December 21, smoke from bushfires ends play between Sydney Thunder and Adelaide Strikers in the Big Bash League. Sydney's Alex Hales walks off.

safeguard their cricketers, particularly juniors, reduce carbon emissions, consider climate mitigation – from replacing trousers with shorts, to lengthening tours to ensure greater acclimatisation – and establish an ICC global climate-disaster fund. Just three months after its publication, Australia was in the midst of what the Climate Council, an independent, non-profit organisation, called the "terrible trifecta of heatwaves, drought and bushfires". It was both the hottest and driest year in the country's history. The land was tinder-ready.

By the end of 2019, around 4.4m hectares (11m acres) had been burned in Queensland, New South Wales, South Australia and Victoria: the equivalent of a square stretching from Cardiff to London, and from Liverpool to the Lincolnshire Wolds. The usual bushfire season had not even begun. At least 25 people were dead, and many more suffered heatstroke or breathing difficulties. Tens of millions of animals perished. Prime minister Scott Morrison, a renowned climate-change sceptic, was under severe pressure to change his government's policy, especially an over-reliance on coal.

In December, the Royal Australian College of General Practitioners had called climate change a health emergency. In early January, data suggested the fires had released about 350m tonnes of CO_2 since August, two-thirds the country's usual annual emission. Meanwhile, Australia was accused of cheating at the UN climate talks in Madrid. But cricket – at least those games not abandoned because of heat, pollution or fires – played on.

A heatwave warning had been issued the night before the First Test against New Zealand at Perth. Tim Paine, Australia's captain, said: "It's a real advantage. We thrive on these conditions." He was right: Australia won by 296 runs. But with temperatures of 43°C forecast ahead of the Second, at

Melbourne, New Zealand cancelled the first day of their warm-up match against a Victoria XI.

New South Wales and Queensland had already played a Sheffield Shield match at the SCG through a veil of smoke, that famous blue sky absent, dangerously ill. Spinner Steve O'Keefe likened the air quality to "smoking 80 cigarettes a day", and added: "It's not healthy. It's toxic. I don't have kids, but if I did, they'd be locked up inside." A Big Bash game between Sydney Thunder and Adelaide Strikers at Canberra was suspended, then called off, after smoke from nearby fires drifted over the ground, forcing children in the crowd to use clothes as masks.

Then, as the Boxing Day Test got under way, the Australian Conservation Foundation launched a report questioning the fixture's future in a world where the number of extreme-heat days in December is likely to increase. They suggested moving the game to November or March, splitting a day's play in two, or making it a day/night match.

The report also homed in on one Victorian cricket association, Red Cliffs in Mildura, where average daytime January temperatures have increased by 2.7°C in 40 years. Red Cliffs are playing shorter games, and moving training sessions to the pool. They desperately need to increase shading, but for that they need money. And with more games called off because of the heat, there are fewer takings at the bar or the barbeque. The choking air is also a huge risk, especially for those exercising, and the young. But in that, Australia was not alone.

Five major cricketing cities in the list of ten most polluted

The World Health Organisation estimate that 7m people a year die early from exposure to air pollution, with the World Bank calculating the cost to the global economy in lost labour as $225bn. A December report by University College London said cutting pollution to legal EU levels would prevent 15% of depression cases worldwide. In November, the world air-quality index rankings placed five major cricketing cities in the ten most polluted. Delhi was top, followed by Lahore (second, with Pakistan prime minister Imran Khan describing the air as a silent killer), Karachi (fourth), Kolkata (seventh) and Dhaka (eighth). In Kabul, Afghanistan, more than 3,000 die from pollution-induced illness every year; London also regularly busts legal limits.

There were, at last, positive signs of action from individual boards. After much internal lobbying, major announcements on climate-crisis policies were expected in 2020 from both the ECB and Cricket Australia, covering carbon reduction and mitigation. Discussion in Australia about whether, under the Australian Corporations Act, company directors could be held legally responsible if they continued to ignore climate risk, floated usefully in the background.

But substantial guidance, or money, from the ICC still seemed a distance away. The promised new 2019 strategy never emerged, after a new CEO was appointed, though a launch was scheduled for early 2020. It was expected to contain corporate social-responsibility targets aligned with the UN's sustainable development goals, but not to produce any firm rules on heat or air pollution, with match officials on the ground simply instructed to work within guidelines.

Nor has there been any great leadership from the players' unions. "This is very clearly an important topic," the Professional Cricketers' Association told *Wisden*. "However, we do not believe we have a fair reflection of our membership's views, or a particular stance on the areas you mention." A spokesperson for the Australian Cricketers' Association wrote: "Climate change hasn't been front of mind for us... we do have a joint CA/ACA occupational health and safety committee that discusses risks to players and officials, which I believe operates well, but I admit we don't discuss issues that have a broader impact on the environment."

Meanwhile, photographs of a blood-red sky, and evacuation from the beaches of Mallacoota, Victoria, went viral. All over the cricket world, similarly apocalyptic scenes were being played out: drought in southern Africa had by December turned Victoria Falls into a trickle, and threatened the livelihood of millions; it has also left 2m people in Zambia (an ICC Associate Member) in need of food aid. But it was happening to less publicity, and in front of fewer cameras.

As Kevin Mitchell, the prime minister of Grenada, wrote in the *Game Changer* foreword: "Climate change is real. It's as simple as that. Every ball bowled at us is currently a bouncer. We're ducking so much, we're struggling to build an innings that will ensure a safe, secure and sustainable future for our people."

Tanya Aldred is a freelance cricket writer and founder of @TheNextTest.

CRICKET AND FILM IN 2019

Flower arrangements

GEOFF LEMON

Out of focus, in the distance, a figure runs along an empty beach towards the camera. This isn't romantic – there's an urgency. The skies above are dull grey. As he comes into focus, he fills the frame, puffing, resting hands on knees. It's England's record wicket-taker, James Anderson.

In the past, it was hard for an audience to be sure of sincerity from cricketers. There would be memoirs written long after the fact, with all the bloodless distance of the page, and the convenient plasticity of memory. Books can delve into detail, and array evidence too complex for the screen. Film, though, can draw characters in a few frames, with body language or gestures or shifts in expression of voice or face that carry so much information. Even sincere writing lacks this immediacy.

Immediacy is what two of last year's cinematic productions offer, in greatly varied form. *The Edge* is a tautly constructed feature film, 90 minutes of artfully arranged narrative and visual metaphor that track the rise and fall of an England Test team. *Cricket Fever* is a sprawling Netflix series that spends eight episodes behind the scenes of a stuttering Mumbai campaign in the Indian Premier League.

Cricket isn't a cinematic sport. So much of it is about waiting, patience, a gradual shift. Highlight reels of wickets and boundaries miss most of the story. But director Barney Douglas turns **The Edge** into a work of art. In part, that's because he's armed with a trove of outstanding original footage that he shot on England's victorious 2010-11 Ashes tour, before the idea for this film had formed. And in part because it's his willingness to diverge from standard documentary form.

The opening image of Anderson on the beach unfolds its symbolic meaning as the film progresses: in showing the physical toil, the isolation, the need to provide one's own drive, it tells a story about professional cricket. This is a game where so many players suffocate in silos, but admitting to the problem rarely comes until retirement.

Early in the film, we see a long shot of an off-guard Monty Panesar cleaning his glasses while awaiting his interview; it captures his vulnerability in devastatingly simple fashion. Jonathan Trott is pictured trapped below water, struggling for air in his full England kit, and later striding into a vast sunlit field to mark his guard, a tiny figure among a mown row of wheat. One sequence starts with 2009's new captain Andrew Strauss sitting thunderstruck in a press conference after his team have been routed by West Indies for 51. What follows is a triumph of editing, flickering from dismissals to news footage to the participants' later reactions, in a staccato collage that surges with energy.

Body of work: Barney Douglas, director of *The Edge*.

The story follows their rise from that Caribbean low: under new coach Andy Flower, England went to No. 1 in the world, won in Australia and India, and disintegrated during the Ashes whitewash of 2013-14. More impressive than its visual artistry is how the film wins the trust of its subjects. Anderson, Trott, Flower, Panesar, Strauss, Kevin Pietersen, Graeme Swann, Stuart Broad, Matt Prior, Tim Bresnan, Steven Finn, Alastair Cook, Paul Collingwood and Ian Bell all speak, most with a surprising frankness about the human cost of pursuing lofty goals.

Finn speaks of breaking down whenever he thought about bowling, Panesar of hiding in his room to stuff himself with room-service junk. Pietersen speaks of the exhaustion of touring, crying in the dressing-room between his rage-fuelled century at Leeds and his falling-out with Strauss. Swann couldn't feel his fingers when injury ended his career, Prior hid a torn Achilles tendon from team-mates for months to prolong his. Bresnan was lost when England reached the coveted No. 1 spot: "It was like – fuck, now what?"

Most prominent, in film and team, is the experience of Trott, a batting perfectionist who became frozen by anxiety until he had to walk out of the game. "I pushed myself so hard, basically to breaking point," he says. You sense claustrophobia as he plunges into the water, and isolation as he walks into the wheat field, both representing his former state of mind.

Not that this film is all dark. Bresnan leads the comedy bill with his perfect descriptive anecdote of meeting Flower: "I didn't really know him from a bar of soap, to be honest. We were having this chat, and he like – he punched me. Like, straight there [in the chest]. So I just went, 'Fuck off mate, what are you giving it?' [and punched him back]. He was just like, 'Ya. I like you. Ya.'"

There is plentiful handycam footage from tours, mostly centred on Swann, memorably described by Trott as "a Mars Bar: you don't want one every day".

We return to the players' joyous moments, and there is a wistful sincerity as they separately recall the highs and camaraderie. Ultimately the film is about joy, and how its transience makes it all the more vital.

Cricket Fever can't match that emotional arc, since Mumbai Indians come together only for a few weeks at a time, rather than a few years. Auctions take place annualy; the team are always changing. Little-known locals mix with big foreign stars. The IPL is a land of instant results, so there is consternation as this expensive franchise crash to five losses in their first six games in 2018. The rest of the season becomes a tightrope walk through the group stage.

What the series offers is access. The camp is laced with microphones and cameras, and it's compelling to see how the team are assembled and prepared. Regular interviews give the players' perspective. Viewers who have never been interested in the IPL might be drawn in, as squad members – from millionaire to fringe – become familiar. It's hard not to invest in their stories.

Sri Lanka legend Mahela Jayawardene is one of the stars of the show, the kindly coach forever putting an arm around his players. "You're getting the money because you're good," he reassures Krunal Pandya, before trying to calm Evin Lewis's injury nerves, and Ishan Kishan's compulsive slogging. Under the glare of the spotlight, in the game's most capricious format, we see players doubting themselves after one bad day.

Jasprit Bumrah is a fascinating study. Filmed before his breakthrough year as a Test bowler, the series shows how well he already knows his craft. He has complete confidence talking over ideas with coach Shane Bond, and is always ready to make suggestions to other bowlers. He thinks through everything: the pitch, the player, the wind, the size of the boundary. Even in 2018, he was ready to be a leader.

The audience rides with Bumrah to his mother's house; with the Pandya brothers to their shared childhood bedroom; with Rohit Sharma to his club on the maidan. Stories of humble origins sit in contrast to the team's owners: business mogul Mukesh Ambani first handed over the running of Mumbai Indians to his wife, Nita, then their son, Akash. In photos from the early seasons, Akash is a child, but by 26 he is supposedly in charge. Most of his input is about superstitions involving red socks or torn jeans. There are many unelucidated lessons from the IPL about the buying of prestige through sport, and the fantasy of merit in a society controlled by wealth.

Where *The Edge* and *Cricket Fever* create intimacy, Sam Lockyer's film **501 Not Out** pulls us back to the boundary. It is based on Brian Lara's innings for Warwickshire against Durham in 1994, though Lara himself appears only in historical footage. This works for the best, however, as the film is about adoration from the spectator.

An unabashed fan, Lockyer was swept up in Lara fever that county season. A quarter-century later, he speaks to a broad range of contributors in Trinidad and England to trace how an unglamorous club obtained the signature of the hottest property in the game just before his then Test record score of 375.

The trawl through file footage has turned up some gems, with pride of place to the arrival press conference that features Lara in an oversized suit jacket and turtleneck in the style of Arsenio Hall, the outfit topped off with a flat-brim

Warwickshire cap, the player sprawling for photos on the bonnet of a sponsored Peugeot with the number plate L375 ARA.

The raft of photographers tells a story by their numbers. The film is partly about the feat: how could one player possibly score a quintuple-century? But it's more about the emergence of cricket's first true worldwide star. There is a surprising aptness years later when Barack Obama describes Lara as the Michael Jordan of cricket. Back in 1994, and his most prolific feats, his interviews hint at the issue that our other films make explicit: Lara's struggle to hold himself together when so many people want a piece. To this day, he remains a publicly reserved and guarded figure.

The three films sit in contrast. *The Edge* is visually symphonic, thanks to director Douglas playing conductor alongside Felix White's original score. *Cricket Fever* is confessional, an omnipresent camera hovering unseen over a shoulder, a long-forgotten lapel microphone strapped to coaches at training. *501 Not Out* is archival, revivifying an era through the lens of hindsight. Each, in its own way, brings us face to face with the game.

Geoff Lemon is a writer and cricket commentator from Melbourne.

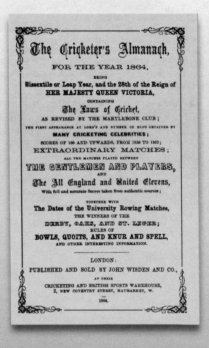

OBITUARIES

ABDUL QADIR KHAN died on September 6, aged 63. If Abdul Qadir had done nothing but take leg-spin bowling out of a dusty museum cabinet and repurpose it for the modern age, he would have earned the lasting gratitude of purists. But he did much more. With his prancing approach to the crease, whirring delivery and beseeching appeals, he turned the arcane world of the leg-break and googly into a theatrical experience; no off-spinner or slow left-armer ever created such spectacle. Qadir also changed the perception that an attacking spinner could not flourish in the shorter format. Every leg-spinning hired gun in Twenty20 franchise cricket is in his debt. "He was a genius," said his former captain Imran Khan. "He brightened Pakistan's name in the cricket world."

After pace had dominated for years, Qadir's arrival on the scene early in 1978 was a breath of fresh air. Aged 22, and in his second Test, he took six for 44 against England at Hyderabad. "He bowled beautifully," wrote John Woodcock in *The Times*. "He has a well-disguised googly, is a genuine spinner of the ball and gives very little away." But it was a while before Qadir became the master of all the weapons in his armoury; his best days were still to come.

Qadir grew up as one of four children in the Dharampura area of Lahore. His father earned a pittance reciting prayers at a local mosque; food was not always plentiful on the family table. Aged 22, and in his second Test, he took six for 44 against England at fire did not play cricket until he was 11 and, though no prodigy, improved steadily during his teens as a batsman and seamer. He worked on a bookstall to help the family, but his friends paid the stallholder to release him for matches. In the nets, he discovered a new talent: spin in abundance. And he became consumed. "I used to go to bed with a cricket ball, and as I was falling asleep I used to imagine various grips and what the ball would do," he recalled. Qadir joined the Dharampura Gymkhana club, and progressed to the Water and Power Development Authority, then to a first-class debut for Habib Bank in September 1975. Finally given a chance as their sixth bowler, he took six for 67.

Before Pakistan's tour of England in 1982, Imran persuaded him to grow a goatee beard, to enhance the air of a mysterious figure from the East. At Lord's, he took six in the match, as Pakistan won by ten wickets. Later that year, he claimed 22 in three home Tests against Australia, including 11 for 218 at Faisalabad. It was Pakistan's first series whitewash, and Imran was praised for backing Qadir, despite a media campaign against his selection. A bond of trust formed with his captain.

But he was not immune to controversy. He missed a series against India when the Pakistan board took umbrage after he asked for a loan to finance a house purchase in Lahore. In New Zealand in 1984-85, he was disciplined for lacklustre fielding in a tour match. He refused to pay the fine, criticised his team-mates in a TV interview, and was sent home. Three years later in the Caribbean, as Pakistan pushed for a series-clinching win in Barbados, he was enraged when an umpire turned down an appeal for a bat–pad catch off Jeff Dujon. Qadir stormed off to field on the boundary, where he was jeered by

BEST TEST FIGURES FOR PAKISTAN

9-56	Abdul Qadir	v England at Lahore	1987-88
9-86	Sarfraz Nawaz	v Australia at Melbourne	1978-79
8-41	Yasir Shah	v New Zealand at Dubai	2018-19
8-58	Imran Khan	v Sri Lanka at Lahore	1981-82
8-60	Imran Khan	v India at Karachi	1982-83
8-69	Sikander Bakht	v India at Delhi	1979-80
8-164	Saqlain Mushtaq	v England at Lahore	2000-01
7-40	Imran Khan	v England at Leeds	1987
7-42	Fazal Mahmood	v India at Lucknow	1952-53
7-49	Iqbal Qasim	v Australia at Karachi	1979-80

Paragon of prestidigitation: Abdul Qadir bowls to Bob Taylor in the Third Test, at Karachi, in January 1978; the non-striker is Graham Roope.

the crowd. He climbed the fence, and punched one of his abusers. The team management paid the victim $1,000 not to press charges.

He missed the start of the 1987 tour of England because his wife was ill, and after a late arrival took just one wicket in his first three Tests. But in the Fifth at The Oval, with Pakistan needing to avoid defeat to win their first series in England, he had first-innings figures of seven for 96, enabling the follow-on. England saved the match, but not the series. Qadir's finest hour came in the return, three months later. In the First Test at Lahore, he was close to unplayable, bowling unchanged for 37 overs in the first innings to take nine for 56 – still Pakistan's best Test figures. "The little paragon of prestidigitation, the sultan of spin, made sure of a page in the history books," wrote Mike Selvey in *The Guardian*. In the second innings, he took four for 45 to secure an innings win. At Faisalabad – infamous for Mike Gatting's spat with Shakoor Rana – Qadir added seven wickets, followed by ten at Karachi. In all, he had taken 30 wickets at 14, and flummoxed England.

Like many wrist-spinners, Qadir liked to cloak his art in layers of mystery. He admitted his hyperactive run-up was designed to create anxiety. Though only 5ft 5in, he delivered with a jump and a high arm that gave the ball natural loop. He had two googlies and two top-spinners, one from wider on the crease. David Gower recalled him asking, "Did you pick my googly?", while Graham Gooch was a confirmed admirer. "He'd show you a googly you could read, then he would bowl one you suspected of being a googly, but weren't sure about. Then he'd send down one you'd be completely bamboozled by, but it would usually turn out to be another googly. These were all bowled with a different action, to complement his leg-break, top-spinner and flipper." Over dinner, Qadir amazed Richie Benaud by demonstrating how he used three fingers to spin the ball, rather than two. "With three you get more power, more turn, and it's easier to bowl the googly," he said. "To be a leg-spinner, above all you need courage."

After the high point of 1987-88, Qadir was seldom as potent. He played his 67th and final Test in December 1990, finishing with 236 wickets at 32, still fifth on Pakistan's all-time list. But his record was markedly different outside Pakistan: in 27 Tests abroad, he took 68 wickets at 47, compared with 168 at 26 in 40 at home. And he did much better against England (82 wickets in 16 matches) than against India (27 in 16), whose batsmen did not buy into his aura, supposedly calling out "googly" or "leg-break" after each ball.

He had made his one-day debut during the 1983 World Cup in England, and in 104 matches took 132 wickets with an economy-rate just over four. But by the time Pakistan lifted the trophy in 1992, he had been succeeded by Mushtaq Ahmed, one of his protégés. Qadir was a useful batsman, hitting two first-class hundreds. In a group game in the 1987 World Cup, he clouted 13 off the final over from Courtney Walsh to beat West Indies.

After retiring, he ran a cricket school in Lahore, and was Pakistan's chief selector for six months in 2008-09. In 2008 he was one of the subjects of a *Wisden* feature on five great players who were never a Cricketer of the Year. "In the pantheon of wrist-spinners he surely ranks near the very top," wrote Woodcock. Qadir's sons – Rehman, Imran, Sulaman and Usman – all played first-class cricket. Usman, the youngest, has played for Western Australia, and was called up by Pakistan for their tour of Australia shortly after his father died. He also had two daughters, Noor Aamina (who married the Pakistan Test player Umar Akmal) and Noor Fatima.

Qadir did not inspire only Pakistani youngsters. In the Melbourne suburbs, a young Shane Warne tried to copy his hero in backyard games with his brother: "He was the guy we looked up to." During Australia's tour of Pakistan in 1994-95, the journalist Qamar Ahmed arranged for Warne to go to Qadir's home. They ended up spinning an orange to each other across the sitting-room carpet. "That was an education," said Warne. "One of the most interesting nights of my life." Gooch was in no doubt that Qadir was the more awkward to face: "Reading him is one thing; playing him is another."

ABID BUTT, MOHAMMAD, who died of a heart attack on August 28, aged 52, played two matches as a leg-spinner for Pakistan's Allied Bank, taking his only wicket in his first over. He later managed the Sui Northern Gas team which won the Quaid-e-Azam Trophy three times in four seasons from 2013-14.

ACHREKAR, RAMAKANT VITHAL, who died on January 2, aged 86, played one first-class match, for the State Bank of India in October 1963, but was better known as a coach and mentor. A legend around Mumbai, he brought on a number of Test cricketers, most notably Sachin Tendulkar, who always referred to him as Achrekar Sir. "Had it not been for Sir, I would not be the cricketer I turned out to be," he wrote. In a game for Shardashram Vidyamandir School in February 1988 – he had moved there because that was where Sir coached – the 13-year-old Tendulkar put on 664 with another star pupil, Vinod Kambli, who called Achrekar "the man who gave birth to my cricketing career".

AGHA AKBAR, MOHAMMAD KHAN, who died on May 19, aged 62, was a prominent writer from Lahore, who covered cricket World Cups, as well as Olympic and Asian Games. After spells as sports editor of *The Nation* and *Pakistan Today*, he proved a popular and approachable media manager for the Pakistan board between 2013 and 2017.

AKHTAR SARFRAZ, who died of colon cancer on June 10, aged 43, was a powerful left-hander from Peshawar who played four one-day internationals for Pakistan, never surpassing the 25 he made on debut against West Indies in Sharjah in December 1997. After starting his first-class career with nine single-figure scores, he made 134 not out in his tenth innings, and 162 – the highest of his eventual 13 centuries – in the next, against

Karachi Whites in December 1995. Later he was a coach, and helped select the Pakistan women's team. "He was a great human being," said Imran Khan. "A good coach and manager, and a great friend."

APTE, MADHAVRAO LAXMANRAO, died on September 23, aged 86. A stylish batsman who played Kanga League cricket in Mumbai into his seventies, Madhav Apte appeared in seven Tests for India, all in 1952-53, and averaged a tick under 50. The highlight came in Trinidad, where his 163 not out in almost ten hours prevented any possibility of defeat in the Third Test. "I was on 99, and got very anxious to score that one run," he said. "Frank Worrell from the slips told me: 'Cool it, young man. Don't throw away your innings. Have patience.' It was very sporting of him." Apte remained a heavy scorer for Bombay into the 1960s but, at a time when Indian selection was frequently mysterious, never played another Test after his successful West Indian tour. He had his own theory: the chairman of selectors, Lala Amarnath, asked Apte's father if he could become the Delhi distributor for the family's textile company. "He politely declined. Lala continued to be chairman for a few years. I was never selected again!" Late in life, Apte produced a lavish autobiography, *As Luck Would Have It*, which featured a picture of himself on the cover, in MCC sweater. His younger brother, Arvind, who died in 2014, also prospered for Bombay, and played one Test, in England in 1959.

ARNOTT, DONALD BRIAN, died on April 11, aged 83. Don Arnott was a polished wicketkeeper who played 28 first-class matches for Rhodesia from 1954-55, having represented South Africa Schools the previous season. His debut, aged 18, was delayed by a match after he lost a tooth standing up in the nets to Joe Partridge, who later opened the bowling for South Africa. When England toured in 1956-57, Arnott was called in as cover for the Third Test when the regular keeper, John Waite, picked up an injury – but he recovered, and Arnott never won a cap. He became a tobacco farmer, before a stint as the Zimbabwe Cricket Union's first chief executive from 1994 to 1998. His son, Kevin, opened the batting in Zimbabwe's first four Tests, in 1992-93.

ASHIQ HUSSAIN QURESHI, who died on November 1, aged 70, had run the Pakistan Veterans Cricket Association since 1990. Formerly a successful club player, he was a close friend of Imran Khan; he helped him establish a cancer hospital in Lahore. A distinguished diplomat, he was later one of the founder members of Imran's Pakistan Tehreek-e-Insaf political party.

BALOCH, Dr KHADIM HUSSAIN, died on September 9, aged 80. Originally from Karachi, where he had been a keen club cricketer, "Kim" Baloch settled down as a doctor in rural Essex. He was an avid collector of cricket books, and compiled several himself, including accounts of Pakistan's tours of England in 1987, 1992 and 1996, and an exhaustive encyclopedia of the sport in his native country. "He was the man I called if I wanted an authoritative answer about something in Pakistan cricket," said fellow historian David Frith.

BARKER, EDNA, who died on March 25, aged 82, was an all-rounder from Surrey who appeared in 15 Tests between 1957-58 and 1968-69 – a period in which England's women played only 22 in all. Barker started as an off-spinner, taking seven for 18 against Somerset in 1956, and was a superb fielder with a strong throw. On her Test debut in 1957-58, at Christchurch, she had returns of 38–19–50–1 and 25–11–46–1. Later in the tour, at Adelaide, she scored a maiden fifty during a last-wicket partnership of 78 with Helene Hegarty, which remained a Test record until 2005. Her batting gradually took over, and in January 1969 – by now England's vice-captain – she hit 100 in 138 minutes against Australia in Melbourne, sharing a stand of 137 with Rachael Heyhoe, the captain. In 1999, Barker was among the first group of ten women given honorary membership of MCC.

BARTLETT, CHRISTOPHER JOHN, died on September 6, aged 88. A founder member of the Association of Cricket Statisticians, Kit Bartlett was an assiduous researcher who edited several ACS publications, some of which he wrote; he co-authored the booklet on John Wisden in their "Famous Cricketers" series. A former personnel officer with London Transport, Bartlett watched first-class cricket on more than 100 grounds.

BASSON, BRIAN CLIFTON, who died on August 30, aged 76, moved from umpiring – he stood in 14 first-class matches – to become the general manager of cricket operations for the South African board. Ali Bacher, the chief executive at the time, called him "meticulous, super-efficient, unassuming and humble – in his field, he had no equal in world cricket".

BECCA, LASCELLES ANTHONY, died on February 28, aged 78. Through both the glory days and the sad decline, Tony Becca comprised half the press corps – alongside the better-known Tony Cozier – who followed the West Indian team round the

A study in concentration: Edna Barker at the Sydney Cricket Ground in 1958.

Frank Burke, Fairfax Media/Getty Images

cricketing world. Becca was a Jamaican, educated at Wolmer's Boys' School in Kingston, where he developed into a solid batsman. After a stint on the *Jamaica Daily News*, which closed, he joined its rival, *The Gleaner*, and became both sports editor and lead sportswriter, covering cricket above all. He was a member (and eventually president) of the Melbourne Cricket Club in Kingston, where he played with the young Michael Holding, and became friends with just about every Jamaican cricketer from George Headley to Chris Gayle. His work was syndicated across the Caribbean, and he was respected everywhere for his honest opinions and his quiet, sometimes despairing, passion for the game there. On a tour of South Africa in 1998, he, West Indies board president Pat Rousseau, and Rousseau's wife, Hester, were robbed at gunpoint in Soweto. "It was then that I saw St Peter," said Becca. "If Tony Cozier was the distinctive voice of West Indian cricket," wrote Pat Gibson, former chairman of the Cricket Writers' Club, "Tony Becca was its softly spoken soul."

BECK, REV. GEOFFREY EDWARD, who died on March 5, aged 100, played three matches for Oxford University while a theology student in 1946. He scored 50 against Surrey in his first innings, defying Alec Bedser and Alf Gover at Guildford, but then never exceeded ten. Three years earlier, he hit 60 against Cambridge in a one-day wartime Varsity Match at Lord's. Beck became a Congregational minister, ending up at the Central Free Church in Brighton (1971–84) after a spell as a warden at Coventry Cathedral. He co-founded the Adam von Trott Memorial Appeal, commemorating an Oxford graduate who was part of the plot to assassinate Adolf Hitler in 1944; some 70 years later, Beck was awarded the Order of Merit by Angela Merkel's government for his efforts to improve Anglo-German relations.

BHATTACHARYYA, PROFESSOR LORD (Sushantha Kumar), CBE, FRS, who died on March 1, aged 78, was an academic who set up the Warwick Manufacturing Group, based at Warwick University where he was a lecturer, with the main aim of forging better links between industry and academia. Happy to be known informally as "Lord Battery Charger" after receiving a peerage in 2004, he was an adviser to Tory and Labour governments, and in 2007 brokered the takeover of British Steel by the Indian Tata conglomerate. Bhattacharyya had arrived from India in 1962 with, according to *The Times*, "little more than his books and his cricket kit". Despite finding the food inedible and the weather intolerable, he loved Britain – and cricket – and stayed on. He liked to point out to visitors that the research facilities at Warwick were built on a cricket ground on which he used to showcase his skills.

BLAIR, WAYNE LESLIE, who died on January 11, aged 70, was a left-hander with Otago: he made his debut at 18, over Christmas 1967, and played fitfully until 1982-83. Eight years later, by then 42, he had another season in the Plunket Shield. He hit two centuries, including a career-best 140 following on against Canterbury in 1980-81, after top-scoring with 88 in the first innings. He often played alongside his brother, Bruce, who won 14 one-day caps for New Zealand. "His philosophy was, if it wasn't hitting the wickets, he could smash it," said the former Test spinner Stephen Boock. "He was a bold batsman, and good fun. He never lost his boyishness. He just enjoyed having adventures. It was like being part of the Famous Five."

BOND, JOHN DAVID, died on July 11, aged 87. In February 1968, Lancashire were in turmoil. Still without a captain after Brian Statham's resignation the previous summer, they had approached Garry Sobers, who signed instead for Nottinghamshire. Another candidate, A. C. Smith, chose to stay with Warwickshire. Lancashire turned to a former captain, Bob Barber, who had left in 1962. He told them the right man was already on the staff: Jack Bond, despite soon turning 36, and being unsure of his place. "They asked me on a caretaker basis," said Bond. "There was no long-term job being offered."

The appointment marked a turning point in Lancashire's history. Bond became one of the club's greatest captains, leading them to five one-day titles in four years, and dramatically improving their fortunes in the Championship. At 5ft 6in, he was not a commanding figure, and his batting was modest, but he was a shrewd tactician and a canny man-manager. "He was," said Farokh Engineer, "the best captain I ever played under."

His elevation was perfectly timed. A group of young cricketers, untainted by failure, were being blooded, and Clive Lloyd arrived as a second overseas player, a year after Engineer. Bond was initially pragmatic. "The first thing he did was ensure we did not lose so often," said David Lloyd. "He wanted us to get out of the habit." After years of dressing-room rancour and dwindling support, Bond also hit on a winning formula in one-day cricket, bringing trophies and capacity crowds to Old Trafford.

The son of cotton-mill workers in Bolton, he had made his debut in 1955, having developed his game in the leagues, before a newspaper talent-spotting contest brought him to Lancashire's attention. His first game was against Surrey at Old Trafford,

Sound, but unspectacular: Jack Bond at The Oval in 1958; the wicketkeeper is Roy Swetman.

Dennis Oulds; Hulton Archive/Getty Images

where Tony Lock dismissed him for nought and one. "If poor young Bond had ever wondered what first-class cricket was about, he was to learn a great deal in an unpleasantly short time," wrote Denys Rowbotham in *The Manchester Guardian*. Under the captaincy of the haughty Cyril Washbrook, it was not an easy time for a raw recruit. "There was quite a lot of professional jealousy," Bond recalled. "You didn't really have any friends."

Progress was slow. He did not score a century until 1959, or become a regular until 1961. But in 1962, when he was selected for MCC against the champion county, his sound, unspectacular technique earned him 2,125 runs at 36, including five hundreds. Early the following summer, however, Wes Hall broke his wrist during Lancashire's match against the West Indians. Bond attempted a comeback too quickly, and struggled to recapture his form: in five seasons, his best aggregate was 743. By the late 1960s, he was in and out of the team, fretting about his contract.

It was a bleak decade at Old Trafford. Lancashire finished in the bottom half of the table seven years in a row, and changed captain frequently: Barber (two seasons) was followed by Joe Blackledge (one) and Ken Grieves (two). An advertisement in *The Times* failed to produce a suitable candidate, and a reluctant Statham took on the job for three summers. Bond had enjoyed some success captaining the Second XI and, on his promotion in 1968, demanded hard work, loyalty and fitness. He also asked his team to perform with zest, and win over a disillusioned membership: "If you enjoy playing, the public will enjoy watching you."

Lancashire rose to sixth in the Championship, and Bond set a selfless example. At Northampton in July, he declared seven short of his first century for three years, allowing Ken Higgs and Ken Shuttleworth a half-hour burst with the new ball; next day, Lancashire completed a ten-wicket win. In 1969, Bond led them to the John Player's County League title, in the competition's first summer. Some considered the 40-over Sunday-afternoon matches a gimmick, but Bond's young team – schooled in Saturday league cricket – attacked them with gusto. Fielding standards rocketed. "He told us, 'If your whites are not dirty when you come back in, I want to know why,'" said spinner Jack Simmons.

They retained the title in 1970, added the Gillette Cup by beating Sussex at Lord's, and finished third in the Championship. He had been a founder member of the Professional Cricketers' Association in 1967, and shared their first Player of the Year award with Mike Procter in 1970. Bond was named a Wisden Cricketer of the Year in 1971 aged 38, and that summer hit the winning run in the celebrated Gillette Cup semi-final against Gloucestershire in the Old Trafford gloom. The final against Kent was an epic, bringing together the best two one-day sides. Asif Iqbal looked set to carry Kent to victory, but Bond turned the match with a leaping, one-handed grab at extra cover. "You can't possibly see a better catch than that in a final," exclaimed Jim Laker on TV. "Bondy was fantastic," said fast bowler Peter Lever. "Once we had one trophy, there was no stopping us."

Bond's leadership style was quiet but firm. "He was a father figure to all of us," said David Lloyd. "We loved to play for him. If he pulled you over and told you off, you hung your head a bit: it was like letting your parents down." A devout Methodist – though he enjoyed a drink – he went to church before every Sunday League fixture. If there was no Methodist church nearby, he was happy to attend another denomination, and sang hymns with a vim that belied his diminutive frame. The organ at his home church in Bolton was often played by the Blackpool and England footballer Jimmy Armfield.

His one-day formula was simple, but ahead of its time. "He always wanted us to have wickets in hand to go for broke in the last ten overs," said Lloyd. "When we were bowling, it was pace up front, then he'd want the spinners, Jack Simmons and David Hughes, to squeeze the opposition in the middle overs." Two fleet-footed runners were deployed on either side of the wicket. "We were the first team to go in for sliding stops, and diving to prevent boundaries," said Lever. A dazzling Clive Lloyd century illuminated the 1972 Gillette Cup final against Warwickshire, when Lancashire completed a hat-trick. Their vociferous support had helped turn Lord's finals into something akin to big football matches, but the fans recognised Bond's understated qualities. "Jack for PM," read one banner.

Now aged 40, he retired to a coaching role, although he was enticed back to lead Nottinghamshire in 1974, with modest results. He was an England selector that summer,

Sunday best: Jack Bond receives a cheque after Lancashire win the first John Player's County League, at Nuneaton in 1969; Warwickshire captain Tom Cartwright wipes a speck from his eye.

then moved to the Isle of Man to become coach and groundsman at King William's College. In 1979, Bond returned to Old Trafford as manager. Lancashire won the Benson and Hedges Cup in 1984 but, after a wretched season in 1986, he was summoned to a meeting with chairman Cedric Rhoades. "I'm sorry, I think it's time to call it a day," said Rhoades. Bond replied: "I don't really think so, chairman. I think you're doing a grand job." "Not me," said Rhoades. "I mean thee."

Bond joined the first-class umpires list in 1988, and remained on it until 1997. His commitment to Lancashire never waned, and he turned up to help the groundstaff until a hip operation in 2014. At his funeral, his coffin was carried by former team-mates Barry Wood, David Lloyd, Simmons and Hughes, plus Mike Atherton and Warren Hegg, two of his last signings as manager. They entered the Methodist church in Walkden, Stafford, to the team's 1972 cup-final song, "We Will Always Stick Together". The service was conducted by the club historian, the Rev. Malcolm Lorimer. "I can think of no other Lancashire player," he said, "who was held in such high esteem by his fellow players, which is remarkable because there were greater batsmen and bowlers – but no greater man."

BOOKER, CHRISTOPHER JOHN PENRICE, who died on July 3, aged 81, was the founding editor of the satirical magazine *Private Eye*, and was a contributor until his death. Possessing a restless mind, he also wrote several books, and had a weekly column in *The Sunday Telegraph* for around 30 years (always, according to *The Guardian*, barking up the wrong tree). He was also a fanatical Somerset supporter, and liked to make arcane points to *Wisden*'s editor, especially about the six-hitting exploits of Arthur Wellard. He was the "guest" book reviewer for the 1995 Almanack.

BOYD, WILLIAM ROBERT, died on March 8, aged 80. A former chairman of the Northern Cricket Union, and a passionate supporter of cricket in Ireland, Billy Boyd was credited with defusing tensions in the annual matches between Lurgan, his club, and Waringstown, which often attracted big boisterous crowds. He chaired the organising committee for Ireland's first official one-day international against England, at Stormont in 2006.

Passing muster: taking guard in the Regent's Park nets in 1934 is the ten-year-old Dwin Bramall, one of three boys from Gibbs Preparatory School given prizes by Douglas Jardine.

BRAMALL, Field Marshal Lord (Edwin Noel Westby), KG, GCB, OBE, MC, JP, DL, who died on November 12, aged 95, was president of MCC in 1988–89. During his tenure, the club approved new guidelines about their role in the game – which would, Dwin Bramall hoped, see them act as "the constitutional monarch of English cricket". A long-serving army officer, he took part in the Normandy Landings in 1943, and rose to become Chief of the Defence Staff from 1982 until his retirement in 1985. After the Falklands conflict in 1982, he would say to returning servicemen: "In the years ahead when you are old men, you will be able to say – as they said after Waterloo, after Alamein and Arnhem – 'I marched and fought and won in the Falklands, and showed the world the incomparable quality of professionalism of the British Army.'" He concluded, wryly: "No doubt you will bore successive generations of children and grandchildren into the bargain, but such is life." Before joining up, he had captained the unbeaten Eton team in 1942, and later that year scored 55 for Lord's Schools against The Rest, skippered by Trevor Bailey. He made occasional appearances for Army sides, and went on an MCC tour of the Netherlands in 1948, keeping wicket to Gubby Allen and Ian Peebles. When he was 51, and commander of the British forces in Hong Kong, Bramall made the last century on the Victoria ground. His later years were clouded by unfounded allegations of sexual abuse, from a man eventually jailed for his malicious accusations.

BROOKER, Mervyn Edward William, who died on January 23, aged 64, was a Cambridge Blue in 1976, after a few matches two years previously. He took four for 58 with his seamers against Leicestershire at Fenner's, but managed only one wicket in the Varsity Match – in the first over. Brooker's most memorable performance had come earlier in 1976 in the Benson and Hedges Cup, when his three for 44 helped the Combined Universities – captained by Vic Marks, and including Paul Parker, Peter Roebuck and Chris Tavaré – to restrict Yorkshire to 185 for seven in their 55 overs on a stodgy pitch at Barnsley. The students gleefully knocked off their target. "One could sense the eyebrows of the PA man heading northwards as he announced bowlers such as A. R. Wingfield

Digby and R. le Q. Savage at the home ground of Dickie Bird and Michael Parkinson," remembered Marks. Brooker later played for Staffordshire and Cambridgeshire. A teacher, he became headmaster of King Edward VI Camp Hill School in Birmingham in 1995, and of Bolton School in 2003.

BURDEN, DAVID LOUIS, who died on June 26, aged 73, umpired Minor Counties matches for around 20 years after retiring from playing – he kept wicket for Surrey's Second XI. He had a spell as chairman of the Association of Cricket Umpires and Scorers. Berkshire CCC instituted an award in his honour for contributions to youth cricket.

BUTCHER, BASIL FITZHERBERT, who died on December 16, aged 86, was a bulwark of the West Indian middle order in the 1960s, restraining his attacking instincts to allow the likes of Rohan Kanhai and Garry Sobers to play their natural games. But Butcher was an elegant batsman himself, strong on the cut, and harsh on anything overpitched. He was seen as an lbw candidate, as he sometimes played across the line. "My bat comes down from somewhere about mid-off," he said. "Maybe if I'd had a coach, I'd only have been clean bowled." He still averaged 43 in Tests, and just below 50 in first-class matches.

Butcher was born in the sugar-producing village of Port Mourant, in British Guiana (now Guyana). His mother was an Amerindian, making him the first player of native descent known to have represented West Indies. Kanhai lived 200 yards down the road, while Joe Solomon – another steady Test performer – was not much further away. They were among the first from outside the capital, Georgetown, to make a mark on the region's cricket.

The first signs of Butcher's talent became apparent in October 1956: an unbeaten 154 against Jamaica, whose attack included the tearaway fast bowler Roy Gilchrist, as well as Test spinners Alf Valentine and Collie Smith. There was another hundred against the 1957-58 Pakistan tourists, but Butcher had to wait until the following season's trip to the subcontinent – West Indies' first since the war without any of the Three Ws – for a cap. He grabbed it eagerly, hitting 103 in the Third Test against India, and 142 in the Fourth.

He was sidelined for a while when Frank Worrell and Clyde Walcott returned, and missed the 1960-61 Australian tour but, buoyed by success in the Lancashire League, was

Caribbean lavishness: Basil Butcher at Lord's in September 1966; his West Indies colleague Deryck Murray keeps for the Rest of the World during the Rothmans World Cricket Cup.

recalled for the trip to England in 1963. And Butcher made sure he would not be left out again, hitting a superb 133 at Lord's, despite going in shortly after opening a letter from his wife, Pam, telling him she had suffered a miscarriage. Of Butcher's performance, Alan Ross wrote: "Predominantly an on-side innings, it had a West Indian lavishness to it… swinging from the studious to the impulsive." It gave West Indies enough runs to attack on the final day of a drawn Test made famous by Colin Cowdrey's late emergence with a broken arm.

Without him, West Indies might well have lost: three years later, in the Third Test at Trent Bridge, he went one better, transforming probable defeat into victory with a career-best unbeaten 209 in the second innings, although he was dropped five times. West Indies had been 65 for two when he came in, still 25 behind, but Butcher shared careful century stands with Kanhai and Seymour Nurse, then added another 173, rather more quickly, with Sobers.

After a slow start to the 1967-68 home series against England, Butcher made 86 and 60 in the Third Test, then unexpectedly enlivened the Fourth. Asked to send down his flighty leg-breaks, he nabbed England's captain Colin Cowdrey for 148, and polished off the tail to finish with five for 34, the only wickets of his Test career (though England won after Sobers's notorious declaration). "He delivers a googly which is easy to read but turns considerably," said the watching Brian Close.

Back in England in 1969, Butcher had a quiet time until the Third and final Test, at Headingley. Needing 303 to square the series, West Indies seemed set fair at 219 for three, with Butcher 91 – but he was given out caught behind off Derek Underwood and, after Sobers fell for a duck, they ended up 30 short. His team-mates were sure Butcher hadn't hit it, but he was sanguine: "I was out. The umpire said so." He topped the tour first-class averages with 61, and was named a Wisden Cricketer of the Year in 1970. Jack Barker's accompanying essay observed: "He has been known to smile during an innings, but rarely before the 400th run."

There was one other indelible memory of that tour. With Sobers and vice-captain Lance Gibbs given the match off, Butcher took charge for the game against Ireland, the day after the Lord's Test. On a pudding of a pitch at Sion Mills, he decided to bat first, despite recent rain, and the West Indians were skittled for 25. The Jamaican journalist L. D. "Strebor" Roberts noted the tourists' flag was flying upside down: "Half-mast might have been more appropriate."

Butcher played no more international cricket, but there was still time for an undefeated 203 for Guyana against Barbados in March 1970, and a last hurrah of 162 against Trinidad the following year. He remained in Guyana, mainly working in public relations, and had a spell as a Test selector, before moving late in life to the United States. "He was very reliable – calm, and an excellent player of pace and spin," said Clive Lloyd. "In many ways, he was the Mr Dependable of that era."

CARLISLE, JOHN RUSSELL, who died on February 18, aged 76, was a Conservative MP from 1979 to 1997, who functioned as an unusual kind of populist: most of his causes had already ceased to be popular. He was, for instance, staunchly in favour of hanging, and against homosexuality ("sick and depraved"). Above all, he was parliament's fiercest defender of white-run South Africa; he was particularly opposed to the sporting boycott, and was a vocal supporter of the rebel tours that convulsed world cricket between 1982 and 1990. Though he notionally represented Luton, he was often known as "the member for Bloemfontein"; it was assumed that, like the cricketers, he was being quietly funded by the apartheid government. Carlisle himself was never quiet, and was brave enough to make his case on university campuses. He also had charm and an impish wit: when protesters marched through Luton to mark the still-imprisoned Nelson Mandela's 70th birthday in 1988, he handed the leaders bottles of wine – South African, of course. He was quoted incessantly in the South African papers, whose readers assumed he was influential: he wasn't. Although Margaret Thatcher might have privately sympathised with some of his thoughts, she knew they were politically toxic.

CAUSBY, JOHN PHILLIP, died on June 8, aged 76. An outstanding batsman at Adelaide's Prince Alfred College, Causby played first-grade cricket at 15, and for South Australia in 1960-61 at 18. A local journalist noted his "concentration and unruffled temperament", but it took him ten matches over several seasons to nail down a place. He finally did so with 137 against New South Wales at Adelaide in 1967-68, during an opening partnership with Les Favell of 281, a state record until Henry Hunt and Jake Weatherald put on 293 against Tasmania in November 2019. Causby peaked with 773 runs at 48 in 1968-69, but diminishing returns led to his retirement from both first-class and grade cricket in 1973-74.

CHANDRASEKHAR, VAKKADAI BIKSHESWARAN, was found hanged on August 15, aged 57, after running into financial difficulties. "VB" had been a dashing batsman for Tamil Nadu, often opening with the equally attacking Kris Srikkanth. In the Irani Trophy match against the Rest of India in Madras in October 1988, they began a successful chase of 340 by piling on 154: Chandrasekhar finished with 118 from 78 balls, with eight sixes. He later played for Goa, carrying his bat for 237 against Kerala in 1995-96 in an uncharacteristically restrained innings lasting over 12 hours. "He was an outstanding attacking batsman," said Srikkanth. "It's unfortunate he did not play more for India." Chandrasekhar did win seven one-day caps, but 53 against New Zealand at Indore in 1988-89 – again opening with Srikkanth – was his only score above ten. He also helped younger players. "I taught him how to sweep," he liked to say about Rahul Dravid. Chandrasekhar took on various roles in cricket after retiring, including a spell as a national selector and some TV commentary. He managed Chennai Super Kings in the first three seasons of the IPL, and secured M. S. Dhoni's services for the franchise, making the winning bid at the inaugural auction. "His consistent efforts made it possible to set the right foundation of the CSK team," said Suresh Raina, another shrewd signing.

CHINGOKA, PETER FARAI, who died on August 22, aged 65, was president (and later chairman) of the Zimbabwe Cricket Union from 1992 to 2014. His reign included the acquisition of Test status, and the racial integration of cricket in the country – but he also presided over several damaging disputes that led to the break-up of the team that had done well at the 1999 World Cup. The ICC paid tribute to a man who "significantly contributed to the game's development across Africa", but this told only part of the story: Chingoka was linked to the often vicious Mugabe regime, and for a time was banned from entering Britain and Australia. "Basically, I think he was a good man who was somewhat corrupted and used by extremists," said a seasoned observer in Harare. "They probably said, in effect, join us, and you get to stay on and join in the benefits. Oppose us, and we will remove you." Others were less forgiving. "He was a pawn of the government, who robbed Zimbabwe cricket blind," said one. "He finished a rich man, despite claiming he only earned $20,000 a year." A fast bowler in his youth, Chingoka was one of the first black cricketers to make a mark in what was then Rhodesia, and captained an African XI in two List A matches in South Africa in the mid-1970s, dismissing Barry Richards for 12.

Integration... then disintegration: the fortunes of Zimbabwe cricket fluctuated while Peter Chingoka was in charge.

Tom Shaw, Getty Images

CLARK, CHARLES FRANCIS BURNETT, who died of cancer on June 21, aged 59, had been Somerset's chairman since January 2018. An auctioneer and land agent, he was married to Rebecca Pow, the Conservative MP for Taunton Deane. Although ill, Clark made it to Lord's to see Somerset win the Royal London Cup in May. "He was a Somerset man through and through," said club president Brian Rose.

COOPER, LEWIS DALE, OAM, died on April 11, aged 81. Lew Cooper kept wicket in 34 matches for Queensland over a decade from 1958-59, usually when Wally Grout was on Test duty. At first, he was not much of a batsman, managing 15 runs in 11 innings in 1959-60, but he became irritatingly hard to dislodge, and averaged 18 over his final two seasons. He played for the University club in Brisbane, and was secretary of the Queensland Cricket Association from 1969 to 1974.

DE COSTA, KESARA. M. AMITHA, who died on June 8, aged 70, was a determined opening batsman from Colombo's Nomads club who played an unofficial Test for Sri Lanka against a strong Indian side in 1975-76. Three seasons earlier, he made his first-class debut against Tony Lewis's England tourists, surviving for an hour as his side were bowled out for 86.

DE LANGE, CON DE WET, died of a brain tumour on April 18, aged 38. Con de Lange began his career playing for Boland against the touring Sri Lankans in his native South Africa, and ended it playing for Scotland in a one-day international against Papua New Guinea in the UAE. In the intervening 19 years, he represented a variety of teams, embraced many cultures, and made scores of friends. "One of the greatest blokes you will ever meet," said Alex Wakely, his captain at Northamptonshire in 2012. An all-rounder who batted right-handed and bowled slow left-arm, de Lange represented five South African provinces, making his only first-class hundred for Boland against an Easterns attack led by Andre Nel and Andrew Hall at Paarl in 2003-04. His best figures, seven for 48, also came that season, against Gauteng at Randjesfontein. After a summer of mainly white-ball matches for Northamptonshire, de Lange switched to club cricket in Scotland, where he improved his coaching credentials, and eventually qualified for the national team by residence. At the Ferguslie club in Paisley, he met his future wife, Claire; they had two children. He made his debut for Scotland in 2015, in all earning 13 one-day and eight T20 caps; his best bowling, five for 60, came in a victory over Zimbabwe at Edinburgh in 2017, Scotland's first against a Test nation in an official ODI. After de Lange was diagnosed in 2018, Cricket Scotland launched an appeal to fund his cancer treatment. "He was a great servant to cricket in Scotland, as well as South Africa and elsewhere," said their chairman Tony Brian, "not just in the national team, but also at regional and club level, with his infectious and inspirational commitment."

Great servant: Con de Lange plays for Scotland, July 2016.

Andy Buchanan, AFP/Getty Images

DE ZOYSA, MICHAEL JOHN, who died on September 29, the day before his 73rd birthday, was a Sri Lankan businessman whose administrative roles included a spell as the national team's manager. His tenure included the World Twenty20 in 2014, which Sri Lanka won, and the 2015 World Cup. "We have lost a passionate stalwart and lover of cricket, Ceylon tea and the Sinhalese Sports Club," said Kumar Sangakkara. The team wore black armbands in his honour during a one-day international in Karachi.

DHARMALINGAM, P. K., who died on June 2, aged 84, was an all-rounder who played for Services while in the Indian Air Force, and later for Madras: he was, according to a team-mate, "a dependable batsman, a handy leg-spinner and a top-class fielder with lightning reflexes". Dharmalingam hit 162 from No. 7 for Services against Southern Punjab in Delhi in 1966-67, two years after wrapping up a victory over Northern Punjab with five for 38, which remained career-best figures. He later coached, among others, the Indian spinner Ravichandran Ashwin, who recalled "a man who spent his entire life for the sport. His *Cricket Kanavugal* [Cricket Dreams] programme on TV will always be remembered by the kids from the '90s."

DOTIWALLA, DARA NADIRSHAH, who died on January 30, aged 85, was an Indian umpire who stood in six Tests, including the tie against Australia at Madras in 1986-87. With the scores level, his colleague V. Vikramraju gave Maninder Singh out lbw to a ball most of the players thought he had edged. Three years earlier, Dotiwalla had enraged Viv Richards when adjudging him leg-before to Kapil Dev in a Test at Delhi: "During the tea interval, Richards told us, 'You Indian umpires are cheats.' We complained to our board president, and decided not to come out on the field the next day. But the West Indian captain Clive Lloyd promised us an apology, so we started play." Dotiwalla also stood in eight one-day internationals and 43 other first-class matches.

DOWNES, LESLIE WILLIAM, died on November 9, aged 74. Some felt Les Downes had the talent to keep wicket for New Zealand, based on his displays for Manawatu in the Hawke Cup, the competition for the country's minor associations. But his province, Central Districts, were well stocked with keepers, and he was restricted to a single Plunket Shield season, in 1975-76, when he was 30. He started with 52 not out against Wellington, and added an unbeaten 89 against a Canterbury attack containing two Hadlees and the future Test spinner Stephen Boock; in eight matches, he averaged 35 and made 26 dismissals. His father, Eddie, was a first-class umpire.

DRABBLE, DAVID, who died on October 17, aged 82, was the co-founder (with his father, George) of the Sheffield Cricket Lovers' Society, who celebrate their 60th anniversary in 2020. A former Yorkshire committee member, he received an ICC medal for services to cricket in 2010.

EAGAR, MICHAEL ANTONY, died on August 24, aged 85. From a landed Anglo-Irish family, Mike Eagar was an attractive middle-order batsman who in the late 1950s was a mainstay of one of the strongest teams fielded by Oxford University. He came late to first-class cricket, having completed his national service after Rugby School, where *Wisden* noted his potential as a "decidedly useful" batsman. The Navy posted him to the Ministry of Defence, which conveniently ensured he was often available for their hockey team. He had learned Russian at school, and was given the job of making notes on high-ranking naval officers by reading the communist propaganda newspaper *Pravda*. "If I saw one with a drink in his hand, I'd write: 'Probably an alcoholic.' My successor told me he couldn't read my handwriting, and had to start again." He won Blues for hockey and cricket in 1956, and in only his third match made 125 against Free Foresters. Soon after, he hit 35 and 58 against the Australians. An uncle on the Gloucestershire committee brought him to the club (with a hint at the captaincy), and he made four Championship appearances in July 1957, having already played two non-first-class games for Ireland against West Indies, catching Garry Sobers. But he found county cricket a different world.

Where Eagars dare: at the Parks in June 1957, Mike plays for Oxford University against Hampshire, captained by a cousin, Desmond (far left). On the right is Colonel Edward, father of Desmond and grandfather of the cricket photographer, Patrick. The photographer is Edward's wife, Elaine.

"It struck me immediately that I'd walked out of a conservatory and into a working business," he told the writer Stephen Chalke. Gloucestershire's skipper George Emmett advised him not to pursue the captaincy. Instead, he returned to enjoy success with Oxford, although he was summoned from a teaching post at Eton to make two more modest appearances for Gloucestershire in 1961. And he played one first-class match for MCC against Ireland in 1966. He ran the cricket at Shrewsbury School for a decade, and was later headmaster of Abbey Gate College in Chester.

EDWARDS, ALLAN ROBERT, OAM, who died on May 30, aged 97, was the last surviving player from Western Australia's long-delayed Sheffield Shield debut, an innings victory over South Australia at Perth in November 1947. For the next decade, the left-handed Edwards provided much-needed ballast to a sometimes frail line-up. Watchful, but strong square of the wicket, he was the first WA batsman to score two centuries in a match – against Queensland in 1950-51 – and was later their first to pass 2,000 runs. After retiring, he was an assiduous state selector for nearly 30 years from 1960-61, during which time they won the Shield ten times. Even in his nineties, he rarely missed a home game.

EELE, PETER JOHN, who died on January 25, aged 83, was a diminutive wicketkeeper, and left-handed batsman, who was born within a mile of the County Ground in Taunton. He spent a decade on the Somerset staff from 1955, joining straight from school. But with Harold Stephenson entrenched behind the stumps, he had to be patient. A chance came in 1958, when Stephenson picked up an injury, and Eele kept capably in 17 matches. He took eight catches against Northamptonshire at Glastonbury, and top-scored with 30 against an attack including Frank Tyson – but that was the highest of a summer in which he averaged nine. He made occasional first-team appearances over the next five seasons, scoring a maiden century in 1963 against a Pakistan Eaglets touring side containing three of the Mohammad brothers, but finally became first choice the following summer after Stephenson retired. Eele again gave little away behind the stumps, but managed only 201

Line judge: Peter Eele studies Jeff Thomson's feet, Middlesex v Essex at Lord's, May 1981.

runs in 26 matches, and lost his place in 1965 when Geoff Clayton moved to Taunton after falling out with Lancashire. "He felt let down," wrote Peter Roebuck in his Somerset history, "as if he had been used as a reserve by men never intending to give him a proper chance." Eele left the club at the end of 1965, and played for Devon until 1972. After working in a bank, he spent six seasons on the first-class umpires' list.

ENTWISTLE, ROBERT, died on July 11, aged 77. Bob Entwistle played 48 matches for Lancashire between 1962 and 1966, without establishing himself: he reached 50 on 14 occasions, but never three figures, his highest score 85 against MCC in 1964. The year before, he was the first batsman dismissed in official List A cricket, hitting his own wicket against Leicestershire in the inaugural Gillette Cup. He liked to attack: at Old Trafford, remembered David Lloyd, "he would regularly hit the ball into the adjacent railway track with his forte shot, the pull. He was the only one I saw do it regularly." Entwistle had first played for his native Burnley in the Lancashire League when he was 15, but his best seasons came in the Northern League, in which he amassed 15,674 runs at 51 for four different clubs. He was known as the "Run Machine". A regular in Minor Counties cricket for Cumberland, he scored nearly 8,000, including a satisfying unbeaten 139 out of 259 after Lancashire's Second XI had been skittled for 66 at Kendal in 1970.

FALKSON, RODNEY JACK, who died on August 9, aged 77, was a seam-bowling all-rounder from Pretoria, who took seven for 40 for North Eastern Transvaal against Border in 1970-71, two years after hitting 95 against them, also in East London. He served successively as player, captain, manager and selector.

FENTON, RONALD ALBERT, died on February 20, aged 62. For several years, Ron Fenton was the press-box steward at Lord's, initially in the Warner Stand, then in the new media centre at the Nursery End. A proud Scot, he once conjured up a breakfast of Arbroath Smokies for Ian Botham.

FERRANDI, JOHN HEYNES, who died on September 16, aged 89, was a neat wicketkeeper who had a long career for South Africa's Western Province. He came close to selection for the England tours of 1955 and 1960, but missed out to better batsmen: his highest score was

89, when WP followed on against Natal at Pietermaritzburg in 1955-56. Two years later, he played for a South African XI against the Australian tourists and, after making 62 in the first innings, added 30 in the second – but still failed to crack the Test side.

FORD, DOUGLAS ALLAN, died on June 30, aged 90. A wicketkeeper from the Mosman club in Sydney, Doug Ford was a surprise choice to make his debut for New South Wales in 1957-58. He had been the Second XI's third-choice keeper the previous year, but was promoted when Ossie Lambert was unavailable – and remained in place for seven successful seasons. New South Wales were exceedingly powerful at the time: in 1961-62, a season with no internationals to distract from the Sheffield Shield, they used only 12 players, ten of them Test caps. Ford was one of the exceptions, but his position was never questioned. Keeping to an attack which often boasted three or four high-class spinners gave him every chance to show off his slick glovework: almost a third of his 179 first-class dismissals were stumpings. There had been a few uncomfortable moments in his first season, when the tearaway fast bowler Gordon Rorke sprayed three of his first four deliveries past the diving Ford for four byes. His last summer, 1963-64, was arguably his best. He hit his highest score of 36 not out, while his season's-best 33 victims included nine (five stumped) against Victoria. "Reliability was Doug's keynote," said Brian Booth, one of Ford's more celebrated team-mates. "There was nothing flashy about his work. He was a wonderful team man who was always encouraging us from behind the stumps, even through the toughest days."

GANGADHARAN, HAREESH, died while playing in a club match in New Zealand on February 2. He was 33, and complained of shortness of breath after bowling two overs for Green Island in Dunedin.

GHODGE, RAJESH DHAMODAR, collapsed and died at the non-striker's end during a club match in Goa on January 13, two days before his 44th birthday. Ghodge played a pair of Ranji Trophy matches for Goa in November 1999, and eight one-day games, making 63 against Karnataka in 1998-99. Former team-mates formed a long guard of honour with their bats at his funeral.

GILL, JAMES ALLAN, died on June 30, aged 91. A wicketkeeper and handy left-hand batsman, Jim Gill played 16 Plunket Shield matches for Otago in a decade from 1953-54. His highest score of 91 came against Canterbury on Christmas Day in 1954.

HALL, MICHAEL JOHN, died on August 10, aged 84. After five seasons on the staff at Trent Bridge, Mike Hall finally got a first-team chance in 1958. It was an inauspicious start: stumped for a duck in his first innings, against Essex, and bowled for another in the next game. Hall never reproduced the form that brought him runs for the Retford club, managing only two first-class fifties. His highest score was 72 against Cambridge University in 1959, when he shared a stand of 128 with Keith Miller, making a one-off appearance for Nottinghamshire. Hall later captained the Second XI, and led Retford to five league titles. His father, John, also played for Nottinghamshire.

HALLIDAY, ALEXANDER JAMES TOLLEMACHE, who died of cancer on November 5, 2018, aged 46, was a prominent club batsman who scored 49 centuries, and captained Eastbourne to the national club knockout title at Lord's in 1997. A schoolteacher, he ran the cricket at Radley College, and later became senior master at The Pilgrims' School in Winchester, where the new pavilion has been named after him.

HARCHARAN SINGH, who died on October 9, aged 81, was a tall, hard-hitting opener and tidy wicketkeeper who played 50 first-class matches in India, chiefly for Southern Punjab and Services. He made five centuries, the highest 177 in what turned out to be his last game, for Services against Jammu & Kashmir in 1968-69. "He was the finest hooker I've known," said the former Indian captain Bishan Bedi. "And I'm talking of the times when not many of the top-notch Indian batsmen relished the short-pitched delivery."

Stand, and deliver: John Harris is the umpire, Lancashire's Jack Simmons the bowler, 1984.

HARRIS, JOHN HENRY, who died on March 28, aged 83, became Somerset's youngest player, at 16 years 101 days in 1952, although he failed to take a wicket against Glamorgan. The grandson of Somerset's groundsman, he had joined the staff at Taunton the previous year, not long after abandoning off-spin in favour of seam-up, but never became a regular: three for 29 against Worcestershire in 1959, his last season, were his best figures. He became a coach and groundsman, and after spells at several schools joined Devon's Sidmouth CC in 1966, achieving a unique 2,000-run/100-wicket double six years later. Harris eventually became an umpire, and joined the first-class panel in 1983. When he retired in 2000, he had stood in nearly 600 county games, 288 first-class. "John had a nice action, and I opened the bowling with him when he got his career-best," remembered Ken Palmer, a colleague as player and umpire. "Over the years, we stood together in a lot of games. I always enjoyed his company."

HAWES, JOAN LILLIAN, who died on December 6, aged 86, was a London-born medium-pacer from Surrey's Redoubtables club. She toured Australasia in 1957-58, and played in three of the Tests, taking four for 36 at Auckland on debut, and adding six wickets in Australia to finish with ten at 17. Along with Edna Barker, who also died in 2019, she was part of Betty Wilson's hat-trick – the first in women's Tests – in Melbourne. In June 1956, Hawes had taken five for seven as Surrey Women bowled Sussex out for 20 at Richmond. Armed with a degree in nuclear physics, she became a schoolteacher. After retiring, she compiled *The Golden Triangle*, a history of the first 50 years of women's Test cricket.

HAWKE, ROBERT JAMES LEE, AC, GCL, who died on May 16, aged 89, was prime minister of Australia from 1983 to 1991. Only Sir Robert Menzies and John Howard have held the job longer and, like Bob Hawke, they were cricket enthusiasts. But Hawke was much the most talented player: as a Rhodes scholar at Oxford, he appeared in the 1954 university trial. Though he understandably failed to make a batting line-up that included Colin Cowdrey and M. J. K. Smith, he is said to have been twelfth man three times. He also played first-grade cricket while studying in both Perth and Canberra, often keeping wicket: his favourite moment was getting Bill Alderman (father of Terry) caught and stumped off the same ball in a prearranged leg-side ploy for the University of Western Australia against Subiaco.

His best-known achievement at Oxford was drinking a yard of ale (two and a half pints) in 11 seconds. As he became a successful trade union leader and then prime minister, this feat remained a significant part of the Hawke legend (he cut back on the drinking, but failed to curb a roving eye). He played the role of the ultimate Aussie – manly, sporty, matey – and functioned as the nation's chief sporting cheerleader, most famously when proclaiming, after Australia sensationally won yachting's America's Cup: "Any boss who sacks anyone for not turning up today is a bum."

His most public appearance as a cricketer was less successful: aged 54, Hawke was hit in the eye – his glasses were smashed – and taken to hospital in a match between his staff and the Canberra press. But five years after that, he still led out his own all-star team against an Aboriginal side. He also resurrected the annual Prime Minister's XI match against the touring team in Canberra after a 19-year gap. Hawke was fundamentally a serious politician who presided over an era of prosperity and progressive policies, and restored Australian Labor as a serious party of government. But he was always "Good ol' Bob" and, at quiet moments, much of his conversation with staffers concerned the day's horse racing. Aged 88, at the Sydney New Year Test in 2018, he downed a beer in full view of the TV cameras, egged on by Shane Warne. Not quite as fast as in the 1950s, but impressive nonetheless.

HAYE, WILLIAM, died on March 18, aged 70, after he was shot by intruders at his home in Jamaica, which was then set on fire. An opening bowler, Haye played seven first-class matches in the early 1970s with little success, although he did score 60 against the 1970-71 Indian tourists at Sabina Park.

HEATH, MALCOLM BREWSTER, who died on December 17, aged 85, was part of Hampshire's first Championship-winning side, in 1961, when he contributed 63 wickets. By then, Heath had lost his role as Derek Shackleton's new-ball partner to the pacier Butch White, but was still a valued member of a small, tight-knit squad. He was also one of the few prepared to travel in the car driven by their captain, the ebullient Colin Ingleby-Mackenzie. Hampshire might have won the title three years earlier. They were top of the table in mid-August 1958, but came a cropper against Derbyshire on a rain-affected pitch at Burton-on-Trent, where 39 wickets tumbled on the second day; Heath took 13 for 87, including his 100th of the season, but Hampshire were skittled for 23 and 55 by Les Jackson and Harold Rhodes. Surrey finished the season more strongly, and took the last of their seven successive titles.

Heath had played for the Second XI as a 15-year-old in 1949, after which his lean frame was built up in an unusual way: along with other aspiring fast bowlers, such as Middlesex's Alan Moss, he spent winters doing manual labour at the Stuart Surridge bat-making company's willow plantation. "It was so healthy, out in the fresh air," he told the writer Stephen Chalke. "They've got a wonderful keep-fit suite at Lord's, but I doubt it makes them as fit as that tree-felling made me."

A more robust Heath made his first-team debut in 1954. His height, allied to added pace, helped the ball jump off a length, and he made an early mark with five for 40 against Yorkshire at Bournemouth, where he dismissed Len Hutton in both innings. Three years later, he was capped during a season that produced 76 wickets, with seven for 55 (and 11 in the match) as Somerset were walloped at Bath. He peaked in 1958, his 126 victims including those 13 at Burton, and 13 more against Sussex at Portsmouth, with a career-best eight for 43. But a troublesome hip started to bother him: Heath was released after a dozen matches in 1962, and a testimonial the following season. The day the committee were discussing his future, he ran laps of the ground in his tracksuit to show how fit he was – to no avail. "Next thing I was in the secretary's office. To me, it felt like the end of the world." A genial man with a ready smile – some thought him too nice to be a fast bowler – he became a coach and mentor at St Paul's School next to Hammersmith Bridge, and often coached at Lord's.

THE WOMEN WISDEN MISSED

Living life to the Max

HERON-MAXWELL, FRANCES JANE, MBE, died on July 5, 1955, aged 90. For Frances Heron-Maxwell – or Max as she was usually known – it was not enough to be a driving force in the expansion of women's cricket. Her promotion of the game, and women's sport in general, extended to establishing her own ground. As with most things, she was an enthusiast.

In 1903, she and her husband, Patrick Heron-Maxwell, moved to Great Comp, near Sevenoaks, where she turned a meadow into a cricket ground, complete with a thatched pavilion containing a gym. Often referred to as "the Oval", it hosted many of the early matches played by teams representing the Women's Cricket Association. The Australian women visited for a practice match on their 1937 tour, and the Netherlands women played there in 1936 and 1938. At the start of the Second World War, it was given over to vegetable growing, and never reinstated, but it is believed to be the only ground in the world owned by a woman.

Women's Cricket Association/MCC

Max Heron-Maxwell in the late 1930s.

In shirt and tie, tweed trousers and a trilby, Heron-Maxwell cut quite a figure. She was born Frances Cockburn in Suffolk in 1864, one of seven daughters of Rear Admiral James Horsford Cockburn, who served in the Crimean War. She married in 1886, and they lived at Newton Stewart in Wigtownshire, before moving to Kent.

She was an indefatigable campaigner for women's rights. In Scotland, she established a branch of the Women's Emancipation Union, and in 1908 formed the Forward Suffrage Union, a group within the Women's Liberal Federation. In 1913, Heron-Maxwell co-founded the Liberal Women's Suffrage Society. She chaired the meeting that led to the foundation of the WCA at the Ex-Servicewomen's Club in London in October 1926, and unsurprisingly emerged as the first chairman, a position she held until 1938. She oversaw a huge expansion in women's cricket: by the start of the war, 123 clubs and 82 schools were affiliated to the WCA. She was president from 1945 until her death.

The WCA remained her pet project. "Her encouragement of enterprise, her dislike of lethargy, her organising powers, her graciousness and courtesy, her ability to draw the best out of anyone, have made their sure mark on our Association and will not be forgotten by her countless friends and colleagues," wrote Netta Rheinberg.

President of the All England Women's Hockey Association from 1912 until 1923, she served on the committee of the Women's Alpine Club, and was high up in the National Federation of Women's Institutes. In 1918, she was appointed MBE for her work in organising the Women's Land Army in Kent. She died in Switzerland while on her annual holiday with her friend Vera Cox – a fellow founder member of the WCA and a former England hockey captain – who lived with the Heron-Maxwells.

Heron-Maxwell's attire raised eyebrows, and was an important part of her campaigning life: she was secretary of the Rational Dress League, an organisation founded in 1881 "to promote the adoption, according to individual taste and convenience, of a style of dress based on considerations of health, comfort and beauty". She recalled: "In those days, women played hockey in long, heavy skirts and wore sailor hats and heavy boots. There is no doubt that the women of today have succeeded in evolving 'rational dress' suitable for the occasion."

For too long, these obituaries largely ignored women's cricket. In the coming years, Wisden *will publish details of significant figures whose death was overlooked.*

HENDERSON, DEREK, who died on June 13, aged 93, played 11 matches for Oxford University in 1949 and 1950, winning a Blue in his second year, not long after taking a career-best four for 39 (and seven in the match) against Surrey with his seamers. In 1944, he had played for the Public Schools against a select XI at Lord's, and dismissed two Test players – Jack MacBryan and David Townsend. In 1964, he and Hugh Watts (a Cambridge Blue) founded Moor Park preparatory school in Shropshire, where Henderson was headmaster until he retired in 1988. His son, Stephen, captained Cambridge University in 1983, and also played for Worcestershire and Glamorgan.

HÉROYS, NICHOLAS, died on January 26, aged 81. Nick Héroys played one first-class match, for a strong Cambridge University side – including Tony Lewis and Roger Prideaux – against Hampshire in 1960, scoring nought and ten. During a long business career, he briefly became chairman of John Wisden & Co., after it was taken over by McCorquodales in 1985. Héroys played club cricket, especially for the Band of Brothers, served on the Kent committee for over 30 years, and was their president in 1995-96. He represented Old Tonbridgians in six Cricketer Cup finals, captaining in five: he finished on the winning side in 1972 and 1976 (along with Colin Cowdrey) and 1979 (when the Cowdrey at No. 3 was Chris).

HITCHCOCK, RAYMOND EDWARD, died on September 8, aged 89. Bespectacled left-hander Ray Hitchcock was the last survivor of Warwickshire's Championship-winning side in 1951, when he made 974 runs in his first full season. Although he did not manage a century, there were several important contributions: a vital run-out against Nottinghamshire, a 38-minute half-century against Gloucestershire – to seal a fifth consecutive victory – and 60 against Northamptonshire at Coventry in the match that clinched the title.

A New Zealander who had played two matches for Canterbury in 1947-48, Hitchcock worked his passage to England, and joined compatriot Tom Pritchard at Edgbaston. After a couple of quiet seasons, he prospered in 1955, making four centuries – including an unbeaten 121 against champions Surrey – on the way to 1,695 runs, many from thumping hooks and pulls. Another fallow period ensued, but he passed 1,000 four years running from 1961, with 1,840 in 1961, and a career-best unbeaten 153 – out of 230 while he was at the crease – against Derbyshire at Chesterfield the following year. Hitchcock was a handy leg-spinner: he claimed 45 wickets in 1955, and took six for 27 to set up victory over Glamorgan at Edgbaston in 1962. M. J. K. Smith, latterly his captain, recalled: "Anyone who could be persuaded to play back to his leg-breaks was usually lbw."

Hitchcock was one of the founders of the Warwick Pool financial initiative in 1953, which made Warwickshire the richest club in England for a considerable time. After retirement, he ran a sports shop in Solihull for over 30 years, and bred horses.

HOLDER, ADZIL HARCOURT, who died on March 21, aged 87, had some success for Barbados in the 1950s, taking seven for 38 against Trinidad at Georgetown in October 1956. He made a career-best 52 when Barbados batted, but could not add to his haul in Trinidad's second innings, when another left-arm spinner – the young Garry Sobers – claimed four for 24. With the Jamaican Alf Valentine seemingly a fixture in the West Indies team, Holder followed the well-trodden path to league cricket in Britain. He was a popular professional in Scotland over a dozen years from 1958, before returning to Barbados. In his first season, he took eight for seven for Clackmannanshire against Forfarshire, and two years later was an integral part of their first league championship win since 1924. Holder later played for Ferguslie and Clydesdale, and was a noted coach. His charges included the young Andrew Neil, yet to become a feared political interviewer, who remembered "the wonderful Adzil Holder from the Windies".

HOOKER, RONALD WILLIAM, died on February 22, his 84th birthday. At a packed Bat and Ball ground at Gravesend one Saturday in May 1959, Ron Hooker showed off his destructive power. He hit 137 for Middlesex against Kent, his maiden century, with 26 fours and three sixes, and shared a rampaging stand of 133 with Fred Titmus. Hooker

Wholehearted: Middlesex's Ron Hooker, 1968.

made a lasting impression on the press corps. "Your correspondent will remember him by the hole in the windscreen of his car, inflicted by the second of Hooker's three sixes," wrote R. L. Hollands in *The Sunday Times*. In an era when the game was desperate to entertain a declining audience, his approach was welcome. "Anyone who will try and hit a six when in his nineties, as Hooker did, has his heart in the right place," said Hollands.

Hooker was a hard-working all-rounder who made 300 first-class appearances for Middlesex between 1955 and 1969. He bowled medium-pace awayswing, and batted aggressively, but perhaps his greatest contribution was in the field. Crouching at backward short leg, he was a key member of a close-catching unit – wicketkeeper John Murray, Peter Parfitt at slip, Bob Gale in the gully – that snapped up hundreds of wickets for Titmus. Early on, his constant diving earned him the nickname "Coco", after the clown, but he soon won over team-mates. "He was brave, and he stood very close," said Clive Radley. "He took a few blows, but he was agile and held lots of catches."

Born in Lower Clapton, east London, Hooker went to school in Hendon and trained in electrical engineering at Harrow Technical College. He captained Middlesex Schools, and made his county debut, aged 21, in May 1956. It was a sensational start. Batting at No. 6, he put on 139 with Bill Edrich, who made the last double-century of his career. Overcoming a nervous start, Hooker kept pace with his partner, and finished with 77 not out. Then, bowling second change, he took two for 22. He did not establish himself until 1959, when he had his most prolific year with the bat – 1,449 runs at 30. As well as his hundred at Gravesend, he made 12 fifties. He passed 1,000 runs again in 1963, but it was his occasional pyrotechnics that stayed in the memory. "He was belligerent," said Radley. "I remember him getting after Derek Underwood a couple of times when the rest of us could barely lay bat on ball." Against Somerset at Weston-super-Mare in July 1966, he hit an 89-minute hundred after coming in at 110 for five. On a dry, turning pitch, only one other batsman passed 50 in the match.

His best year as a bowler was 1965, when he took 90 wickets at 24, including a career-best seven for 18 against Worcestershire at New Road. "Swinging the ball in a cross-wind and bringing it back off the seam, Hooker dismissed the top three batsmen for 16 runs, and then became practically unplayable," reported *The Times*. The champions were bowled out for 77, and Middlesex moved top of the table. "He is what we call a 'strangler' as a bowler," wrote Titmus. "You put Ron on to break a big partnership, he sends down a full toss or a long hop, then something peculiar happens and he takes a wicket. And he gets quite a lot of wickets, so there is obviously more to it than luck."

His game was well suited to one-day cricket. In a Gillette Cup semi-final against Warwickshire at Lord's in 1968, he made an unbeaten 43 and took four for 20. The following summer – his last before retirement – he took six for six in eight overs in the Sunday League against Surrey. After leaving Middlesex, he became general manager and a director of a precision engineering company in Harrow. He played in the Minor Counties Championship for Buckinghamshire and, in 1975, made a nostalgic return to Lord's in the first round of the Gillette Cup. The scorecard proved unsentimental: Hooker lbw b Titmus 0.

HUDSON, GEORGE TIMOTHY, died on December 14, aged 79. For a brief psychedelic period in the mid-1980s, "Lord Tim" Hudson was a familiar figure on the sports pages. It was often difficult to separate fact from fiction, but Hudson – schooled in Scotland, where he enjoyed cricket – had blustered his way to celebrity in America, chiefly as an English disc jockey at the time of Beatlemania, his in-vogue accent also bringing him voice parts in the Disney films *The Jungle Book* and *The Aristocats*. In 1982, he bought Birtles Hall in Cheshire, established a cricket ground, and embarked on an attempt to make the sport more glamorous: "Colours, music playing all the time, pretty, pretty girls, and playing for money," he told Sky TV's Charles Colvile in 2018. Hudson assured Ian Botham that he could become a movie star, and replaced the old-school Reg Hayter as his agent; Botham and Viv Richards were soon pictured sporting the garish Birtles colours. Plans for a long stay buttering up Hollywood moguls were hampered by inconvenient England Test tours, and the big studios never did come calling. Predictably, it ended in tears. Hudson stumbled out of a party in Malibu to be asked for a quote about his client, who had been accused of smoking cannabis. His headline-grabbing reply – "Doesn't everyone?" – gave Botham (and his increasingly alarmed advisers) an excuse to fire him. "I wasn't the only one sucked in," Botham told *The Guardian* in 2007. "It took me a while, but when I had that final moment of revelation and saw through him, I realised that for everything he promised, it was all about him at the end of the day. He's off his rocker." The Birtles Bowl was abandoned after Hudson fell out with the local council, and he returned to California, where he wrote a book (*From the Beatles to Botham*), did more radio work, and took up painting. Mick Middles, a music journalist and Birtles regular, wrote: "I remember the words of my editor at the *Evening News*. 'We need the Hudsons of this world... they sell newspapers... they make life interesting.'"

HUGHES, PETER CLOWE, who died on February 5, aged 96, was an actor who appeared in classic sitcoms such as *Steptoe and Son*, as *Bergerac's* bank manager, and as General Franco in Alan Parker's film of the musical *Evita*. In the 1987 wartime film *Hope and Glory*, he was able to combine work with his other passion, helping director John Boorman stage a cricket scene. Between jobs in the 1970s, he ran an indoor school at Chiswick, coaching there and at the Ealing club – where he helped set up the colts section – for many years. He passed on his love of the game to his son Simon, who was later part of the successful Middlesex team of the 1980s, and a writer, commentator and editor of *The Cricketer*. Peter always watched Middlesex home games from the same seat in the Warner Stand. "My no-balls got his goat more than anything," said Simon. "When I dismissed Geoffrey Boycott for nought in what turned out to be his last innings at Lord's, only for it to be called a no-ball, he didn't speak to me for two days."

INDER DEV, GOKUL, who died on May 14, aged 80, was a leg-spinning all-rounder unlucky not to catch the selectors' eyes during a long career in India, mainly for Services (he rose to become a colonel in the Indian army). He took 302 wickets at 21, and hit seven centuries, the highest 131 against Punjab in Delhi in 1974-75. With the ball he could sometimes be irresistible. At Srinagar in 1964-65, he reaped 14 wickets after Jammu & Kashmir had started with an opening stand of 158; against the same opposition four years later, he improved his career-best to eight for 37. In 1972-73, playing for a North Zone side captained by Bishan Bedi against the England tourists, Inder Dev cheaply disposed of Graham Roope, Tony Greig and Alan Knott. "He was no mug with the bat, but he was primarily a leg-spinner, rubbing shoulders with the best in the country," said Bedi. "I would often call him 'Jokul' in appreciation of his very lively humour."

JACOBS, DENNIS HARRY, died on May 7, aged 85. "Eier" Jacobs was an exceptional all-round sportsman who played rugby for South Africa's non-white team, and cricket for Griqualand West's. He was one of the stars from the apartheid era honoured with a special representative blazer after unification.

JAITLEY, ARUN, who died on August 24, aged 66, was an Indian politician who served in Narendra Modi's government as defence and finance minister. In 1999, he had become the president of the Delhi Cricket Association, overseeing a renaissance that culminated in the Ranji Trophy title – Delhi's first for 16 years – in 2007-08. "He was a gem," said the former Test opener Virender Sehwag. "He backed the players – helped them get jobs, met their medical expenses, organised travel by air for all age groups." The Indian team wore black armbands in Jaitley's memory on the third day of the First Test against West Indies in Antigua, and in September the Feroz Shah Kotla ground in Delhi was officially renamed after him.

JAMES, LLOYD, who died on April 15, aged 82, was a batsman whose unbeaten 173 for St George's in the 1962 Cup Match remained a record for Bermuda's big game until 2001. Ten years later, he made his only first-class appearance, against the New Zealand tourists, but failed to reach double figures. He later became an MP in Bermuda.

JOHN, KOPI, who died of tuberculosis on August 27, aged 25, was a promising batsman for the Lewas, the Papua New Guinea women's team. "Skinny" John opened throughout the Twenty20 World Cup Qualifier in the Netherlands in 2018, scoring 40 to help set up a victory over the hosts.

JONES, RONALD, died on April 30, aged 80. Wolverhampton-born Ron Jones was just 16 when he became Worcestershire's third-youngest player, in 1955. It was not a success: he made two and 23 in an innings defeat by Cambridge University at New Road. Hampered by a knee injury, he never played for the first team again, though he continued to turn out for Stourbridge CC.

JONES, TREFOR GEORGE, who died on June 16, aged 77, was a familiar face at Lord's, after starting work there in 1961. He managed MCC's Club Office from 1975 to 1989, before stepping down with stress-related problems; the job's two main responsibilities – tickets and membership – were split soon afterwards. Later, as an honorary life member, he rekindled his love of cricket from a favourite seat in the Pavilion. Jones also had an encyclopedic knowledge of football, and compiled several books about Watford, his favourite team; he had stood on the Vicarage Road terraces with Reg Dwight, before he became Elton John.

KAMRAN ALAM FAZLI, who died on January 16, aged 63, was a left-arm seamer who played one first-class match for Pakistan's Public Works Department in 1974-75, taking two for 18 in a 427-run defeat of Sukkur. He later joined the Tablighi Jamaat missionary movement, which urges Muslims to adopt traditional Sunni Islamic traditions and dress.

KLEINVELDT, JONATHAN DAVID, died on May 30, aged 61. Combative all-rounder Johnny Kleinveldt played 15 matches now considered first-class for the non-white teams of Western Province and Transvaal; he usually took the new ball, and had figures of seven for 75 in his second game for WP, against Natal in 1979-80. In the mid-1980s, he was invited to play for Pinelands, a prominent Cape Town club which had previously been whites-only. Kleinveldt's family persuaded him not to join, citing cricket administrator Hassan Howa's mantra: "No normal sport in an abnormal society." His son Matthew, born in England while Kleinveldt was coaching there, has played for WP, while nephew Rory played four Tests and 16 white-ball internationals for South Africa.

KUNDU, SOUMENDRANATH, who died on July 11, aged 77, had great success with his leg-breaks in India, finishing with 127 wickets at 16. He took 14 as Bengal walloped Assam in December 1960, and a few weeks later eight for 104 against Delhi. Said team-mate Raju Mukherjee: "He got big turn, with a deceptive googly. He was more successful on the hard wickets in the north when he shifted to Railways. He was a real team man, and extremely popular due to his tremendous sense of humour."

Élan and empathy: Andrew Longmore.

LINEHAN, ALPHONSUS JAMES, died on June 25, aged 74. A powerful batsman, Alfie Linehan rarely reproduced his Downpatrick club form for the Irish national team. He played 11 times – six as captain – with a highest score of 61 not out to save the match against Denmark at Aalborg in 1971. The previous year, he had found time to play in Downpatrick's league game against Lurgan between his wedding and the reception. Linehan later became a coach, managed the national side, and was president of the Irish Cricket Union in 1993. His niece, Anne, played a Test and 60 one-day internationals for Ireland.

LONGMORE, ANDREW NIGEL MURRAY, who died in his sleep during a walking holiday in France on April 11, aged 65, played two first-class matches for Oxford University, in 1973 and 1975. He soon realised that his notion of becoming a county wicketkeeper might be ambitious, and switched to journalism, gravitating from the *Bracknell News* to *The Cricketer*, as Christopher Martin-Jenkins's assistant. Longmore could have made a brilliant cricket correspondent for any of the quality papers. Instead, after five years at the magazine, he spent the next 30 ranging far and wide: as tennis correspondent of *The Times*, chief sportswriter of *The Independent on Sunday*, and finally as the *Sunday Times's* utility player, covering anything and everything with élan and empathy. His books included an anthology, *Moments of Greatness, Touches of Class*, produced to raise funds for the Romanian Orphanage Trust after he had covered a Davis Cup tie in Bucharest amid poverty and chaos in the wake of the 1989 revolution. He was sunny and instinctively generous.

LUTHRA, SURESH, who died on February 12, aged 74, was a left-armer who took 262 wickets at 16 for various Indian teams. He swung the ball at a decent pace, but his Test chances were stymied by concerns about his action, and he was eventually called for throwing four times by the Test umpire Piloo Reporter in a Ranji Trophy match in 1975-76. "Everyone in the domestic circuit knew Luthra chucked," Reporter said, "yet no umpire had called him, for reasons unexplained or unknown." In 1972-73, Luthra had taken six wickets in each innings for Delhi against his native Haryana, then started the next match, against Railways, with six more. Four years later, against Services at Delhi, he took the first nine in the innings, before Rakesh Shukla ended his chances of all ten. He was also a handy batsman, who hit 101 for Northern Punjab against Services at Ludhiana in 1965-66, his first season. After retirement he was successively Delhi's coach, manager and selector, and remained committed to cricket. "He even played a local match on his wedding day," said clubmate Sarkar Talwar.

McDONALD, Dr IAN HAMILTON, died on February 5, aged 95. The older brother of the Test opener Colin, Ian McDonald kept wicket stylishly and securely for Victoria for five seasons from 1948-49. His 131 dismissals included 53 stumpings, a reflection of the strengths of an attack which included Test spinners Ian Johnson, Doug Ring and the two Jacks, Iverson and Hill. After 32 victims in 1951-52 – his best season – McDonald was rewarded with a place in the Australian XI for a warm-up match against the 1952-53 South Africans.

Chances of further recognition ended when he won a Nuffield Fellowship to Oxford University for postgraduate study in anaesthetics. His skill and empathy with young patients were such that McDonald became the leading figure in paediatric anaesthetics in Victoria. He accompanied his brother to India and Pakistan in 1959-60 as the Australian team's medical officer, and had a busy time: Gordon Rorke and Lindsay Kline had to be sent home after falling ill, while Gavin Stevens contracted hepatitis. He was hospitalised in Madras, came close to death, and never played first-class cricket again. "My brother not only had the satisfaction of fielding as substitute in one game at Bangalore," remembered Colin, "but the much greater satisfaction of preventing an actual fatality among four on the tour who were seriously ill."

McDonald was a member of the Melbourne Cricket Club for 79 years. He ended up as a guide to visitors to the MCG, having played cricket and hockey for the club. He was also a founding member of the associated XXIX Club, whose qualifications included an alleged age of 29 and a love of cricket, plus a willingness to contribute to good causes.

McFARLANE, LESLIE LEOPOLD, died on May 27, aged 66. An energetic Jamaican seamer, Les McFarlane rekindled his first-class career by taking 62 wickets at 16 for Bedfordshire in the 1981 Minor Counties Championship. He had already made a name for himself around Northampton, sharing a feared new-ball partnership for the United Social club with his brother Carl. He had played eight times for Northamptonshire in 1979, with little success – 13 wickets, and no runs at all – but joined Lancashire for 1982. His best performance came in a remarkable match against Warwickshire at Southport that July. He had taken two quick wickets, before Alvin Kallicharran and Geoff Humpage put on 470; Lancashire's reply left them more than 100 adrift, but McFarlane claimed six for 59 as Warwickshire were bundled out for 111, then Graeme Fowler and David Lloyd knocked off a target of 221. "He was a really nice chap, bowled brisk outswing," said Lloyd. "In that game everything fell perfectly – nothing untoward was happening, but suddenly Les started swinging the ball late, and he and Steve O'Shaughnessy bowled the oppo out." McFarlane faded away after two more years at Old Trafford, and finished with a low-key season for Glamorgan.

Life after Bedfordshire: Les McFarlane.

McKNOULTY, JOHN NOEL, AM, who died on May 11, aged 87, was president of Queensland Cricket from 1994 to 2002, during which time they finally won the Sheffield Shield after almost 80 years of trying. He was made a Member of the Order of Australia in 2003 for "service to the administration of sport, particularly cricket".

MANN, ANTHONY LONGFORD, died on November 15, aged 74. Leg-spinner Tony "Rocket" Mann made his debut for Western Australia in 1963-64 but, after 32 first-class matches spread across 13 years,

Alan Purcell, Fairfax Media/Getty Images

Mann of the century: in his last Test innings, against India, Tony Mann falls for nought, but he had a match-winning hundred to his name.

he had only 814 runs at a touch under 20, and 80 wickets at 38. There had been glimpses of talent: three five-wicket hauls among his 25 victims in 1969-70, and a rapid 110 after going in as nightwatchman against Ray Illingworth's MCC tourists the following season. He was also a fine fielder in the covers, where his aggressive returns to the keeper earned him his nickname.

But 1977-78 was the season Kerry Packer changed everything. Most of Australia's first-choice cricketers were playing for their new master, and unavailable for the Test series against India. Among the Packer recruits was the incumbent Test leg-spinner, Kerry O'Keeffe, so the selectors turned to Mann, who was 32 but in reasonable form, having taken 19 wickets in four Sheffield Shield matches. But India's batsmen, brought up on spin, found his bowling easy to read, and by now he was mainly delivering googlies. Still, Mann had his day in the sun, at home in the Second Test at Perth, after Australia were set 339. In the closing moments of the fourth day, Bob Simpson sent him in as nightwatchman, and next day he dominated a third-wicket stand of 139 with David Ogilvie, which set a platform for a narrow victory. "We felt the Indian spinners were not as effective against left-handers," said Simpson. "This proved the case as Mann scored a dynamic 105 to pull the game out of the fire." He was just the second nightwatchman to reach three figures in a Test, after Nasim-ul-Ghani of Pakistan at Lord's in 1962; only Jason Gillespie (against Bangladesh in 2005-06) has done it since for Australia. "I couldn't hang around," Mann told the *West Australian* newspaper shortly before his death. "We needed more than 300 on the last day and I had to get on with it."

After a pair in the Fourth Test, he was replaced by his state team-mate Bruce Yardley for the Fifth. He never played for Australia again, but remained close to the game, continuing at club level after his first-class career finished – with a round 200 wickets – in

1983-84. He also did a lot of coaching. Brad Hogg, who later played for Australia as a left-arm wrist-spinner, paid tribute: "He changed my life by asking me to bowl leg-spin – and never giving up on me even when I gave up on myself."

Mann had a running gag with Shane Warne, which would involve him introducing the pair of them with: "We've got 712 Test wickets and one Test century between us. He's got 708 of the wickets – but he hasn't got the century."

MASSEY, EILEEN MABEL (later Mrs Uebergang), who died on January 22, aged 83, spent her early years in Western Australia, but her cricket really developed after the family moved to Melbourne. In her first Test, against New Zealand at Adelaide in 1956-57, she made a useful 32, partnering Joyce Christ in a seventh-wicket stand of 81. Massey then claimed two wickets with the new ball as the visitors struggled to 98 all out. In her other three Tests, against the 1957-58 England tourists, she played alongside her younger sister Nell, a wicketkeeper.

MILLER, ROY SAMUEL, who died on August 21, 2014, was a fast bowler who played one Test for West Indies, against India at Georgetown early in 1953. On a spin-friendly pitch, he sent down 16 wicketless overs in the first innings, but could not bowl in the second after straining his back going for a big hit while batting. He played only seven other first-class matches, and never took more than three wickets in an innings, although he did hit 86 against British Guiana a few months before his Test. He moved to the United States, where his death escaped the notice of the cricket community for a time.

MITRA, SHYAM SUNDAR, who died on June 27, aged 82, was a solid batsman from Calcutta who never played a Test, despite a first-class average above 50. His seven centuries all came for Bengal, the highest 155 against Assam at Eden Gardens in 1965-66. "He was distinctly unlucky not to play for India," wrote Raju Mukherjee, a former team-mate. "It's said he was omitted by the East Zone representative in the national selection committee because he did not wish to transfer to the selector's club, Sporting Union. Whether this is authentic or not, the fact remains that all those [from Calcutta] who played for India in the 1950s, '60s and early '70s were from Sporting Union."

MORGAN, LESLEY JACQUELINE, who died on August 9, aged 74, was an industrious scorer for Andover CC and Wiltshire in the Minor Counties Championship; she also kept the book for three matches at Lord's. She had a spell as Andover's president, and helped train other would-be scorers.

MORTON, WILLIAM, died of a heart attack on July 19, aged 58. A left-arm spinner from Stirling, Willie Morton made several appearances for Scotland before a brief flirtation with county cricket for Warwickshire. His two years at Edgbaston were affected by a back injury, though he did take four for 85 against Glamorgan in 1984, outperforming a more seasoned slow left-armer in 44-year-old Norman Gifford (one for 80). Morton returned to league cricket in Scotland for Watsonians, Stirling County and Penicuik, where he played alongside his son, Keith, in the 2008 Scottish Cup final. He had worked as a gravedigger on leaving school, and returned to the soil as a popular groundsman and coach at George Watson's College in Edinburgh. "He had a huge influence on many young Scottish players and the wider cricket community," said the former national captain Craig Wright.

MOSS, ALAN EDWARD, died on March 12, aged 88. Alan Moss notched up over half a century of service to Middlesex, filling so many roles it became easier to list the positions he had not held. "Others may have scored more runs or taken more wickets for Middlesex, but few, if any, have given more time and thought to the club," said Angus Fraser, their managing director of cricket. But it was as a tall, wholehearted seamer, charging in from the Pavilion End, that a generation of supporters remember him. Moss's misfortune was to play in a golden age of English fast bowlers: but for Fred Trueman, Brian Statham, Frank Tyson and Peter Loader, he would almost certainly have appeared in more than nine Tests.

A policeman's son from Tottenham, Moss came late to cricket. At 16, he joined the north London nomadic club West Willesden Ramblers, who glimpsed enough potential to put him forward for the London Colts scheme run by *Evening News* journalist E. M. Wellings (Brian Taylor, a future Essex wicketkeeper, also emerged from that year's intake). At Alf Gover's indoor school, Moss was taught the value of accuracy to complement his natural pace. He was an apprentice carpenter in Wembley, but a successful outing at Lord's brought a career change. "I was approached by two or three counties, and I had to decide whether I was going to play cricket or carry on with carpentry," he said. "Thank God I made the right decision."

He made his debut against Lancashire at Lord's in June 1950 – Cyril Washbrook was a notable first victim – but played just four times that season, and had begun national service by the start of the next. When Middlesex enquired about his availability, he told them he had saved up 40 days' leave. In 19 first-class matches, he took 55 wickets at 26, but Lord's had its frustrations. "It was difficult because you were on your own," he told the writer John Stern in 2013. "The nets were in the evenings, and you would bowl to the members and to amateur players

In the gather: Alan Moss prepares to bowl, 1960.

Central Press/Hulton Archive/Getty Images

like Freddie Brown and Norman Yardley, who worked in the City. There was the Honourable Luke White, who had played in one of the Victory Tests – I broke his jaw in the nets. That got me in trouble."

After turning professional at the end of his military service, he took 95 wickets at 23 in his first full season, in 1952. Well built and not easily discouraged, he gave Middlesex a cutting edge. "He was not as fast as Fred, Brian or Frank," said his team-mate Peter Parfitt. "But he was about the same pace as Peter Loader, and certainly quicker than Ken Preston of Essex or Fred Ridgway of Kent." The Lord's slope discombobulated some fast bowlers, but Moss, a keen learner, used his classical action and high arm to harness it to his advantage. "He swung the ball in, so bowling from the Pavilion End he used the slope and the ridge," said Parfitt. In another 90-wicket summer in 1953, his reputation spread beyond

1,000 FIRST-CLASS WICKETS FOR MIDDLESEX

		M	Runs	BB	5I	10M	Avge	Career
2,361	F. J. Titmus	642	50,225	9-52	146	23	21.27	1949–82
2,093	J. T. Hearne	453	38,166	9-32	171	39	18.23	1888–1923
1,438	J. W. Hearne	465	33,309	9-61	88	20	23.16	1909–36
1,257	J. M. Sims	381	31,708	9-92	77	14	25.22	1929–52
1,250	J. E. Emburey	376	30,116	8-40	58	12	24.09	1973–95
1,182	J. A. Young	292	22,707	8-31	70	14	19.21	1933–56
1,178	F. J. Durston	349	25,877	8-27	65	8	21.96	1919–33
1,088	**A. E. Moss**	**307**	**21,556**	**8-31**	**59**	**13**	**19.81**	**1950–63**
1,005	F. A. Tarrant	206	17,518	9-41	89	24	17.43	1904–14

Winter harvest: Alan Moss and Surrey captain Stuart Surridge at work in the Surridge family willow plantations in Essex, 1952.

the capital. With Trueman, Statham and Trevor Bailey, he was chosen to tour the Caribbean, Len Hutton's first overseas assignment as captain.

In a warm-up game against Combined Parishes at Spanish Town, Jamaica, Moss calmed the local frenzy about George Headley's possible Test recall by dismissing him twice in three balls. He was part of a four-pronged pace attack in the First Test at Sabina Park, where Everton Weekes was his maiden Test wicket, but he took only one more in a heavy England defeat, and sat out the rest of the series. He still finished second in the tour averages, with 18 wickets at 27, his enthusiasm and work ethic impressing Hutton.

A prolific start to the 1956 season earned him a call-up for the First Ashes Test at Trent Bridge, but he suffered a pelvic injury in the field, and was out for two months. Some thought he never quite regained his pace but, after returning in 1957, he took more than 100 wickets in four of the next five seasons (and 96 in the other). "Mossy would have 30 wickets by the end of May, and Fred Titmus would not be in double figures," said Parfitt. "But by the time we got to August, Fred would charge ahead."

Moss played in three Tests against India in 1959, and two more on a second trip to the Caribbean that winter. Peter May's tour report praised his qualities as a team man, but noted: "Lost a great deal of pace." Yet 1960 proved his most productive summer – 136 wickets at 13 – and he made a final pair of Test appearances, against South Africa, taking four for 35 in the first innings at Lord's. Twice that season he established career-best figures: at Neath in June, he took eight for 37 against Glamorgan, bettered six weeks later by eight for 31 against Northamptonshire at Kettering.

In 1962, Moss took over as captain when Ian Bedford was injured. Although his own form suffered, he led the side well and was thought likely to be appointed permanently. But the Middlesex committee opted for an amateur, the former Oxford University captain Colin Drybrough. The class divide remained strong. "We played at The Oval when J. J. Warr was captain and I was in the pros' dressing-room," said Moss. "I was the senior pro, and JJ said to me: 'There's no room in there, come on in with us.' So I took my bags in and put them down. Then Peter May walked in, took him aside and said: 'I'm sorry, JJ, Mossy can't stay in here.'"

He retired from county cricket in 1963 with 1,088 wickets for Middlesex, eighth on their all-time list, at a shade under 20. He went into the printing industry, eventually becoming managing director of the British Printing and Communications Corporation. The company was taken over by Robert Maxwell; when Moss joined a long list of sacked executives, he drove to Maxwell's home in Oxford to confront him. The meeting was fruitless, but he went on to establish his own printing company.

At Middlesex, he was treasurer between 1984 and 1995, chairman from 1996 to 1999, and president from 2003 to 2005. He sat on the committee in two spells between 1976 and 2010, and was chairman of the Middlesex Cricket Board from 1996 to 2010. As treasurer, he was involved in a furious dressing-room row over pay with Phil Edmonds. "It was like watching two huge stags rutting," said Fraser. He took a keen interest in all the club's fast bowlers, sharing his experience with Fraser and, later, Steven Finn. "He was always willing to help, to come and watch you bowl in practice and to give advice," Fraser recalled. He also had views on dealing with the physical stress of the job. "If your back's sore, go and kick a door – that will take the pain away."

MOTTRAM, THOMAS JAMES, died on July 26, aged 79. Tom Mottram was a lanky seamer whose spare frame and distinctive gait led his Hampshire team-mates to nickname him the Pink Panther. He had arrived at Southampton with a sketchy CV, amounting to a handful of Second XI appearances for Hampshire and his native Lancashire. But after a few matches in 1972, he played a big part in winning the Championship the following year, taking 57 wickets at 22, with a best of six for 63 to send Warwickshire packing at Coventry. Almost as memorable, for a usually statuesque fielder, was his swooping return catch to account for Roy Virgin in a top-of-the-table clash with Northamptonshire in August. It left team-mates lying on the ground in laughter, temporarily incapable of celebrating a Mottram wicket, as was their wont, by humming a few bars of Henry Mancini's *Pink Panther* theme. "I think Tom did well for two reasons," said his captain, Richard Gilliat. "First, batsmen did not rate him, and took undue risks. More importantly, on account of his height, he bowled with a different trajectory to others, and the bounce he obtained, allied to his accuracy, got him a lot of wickets." The arrival of Andy Roberts in 1974 restricted Mottram's first-class opportunities, but he remained an important part of Hampshire's one-day team until 1977, after which he returned to his career as an architect. It emerged after his death that he had knocked five years off his age to help secure a county contract, and was actually 32 when he made his debut, against the 1972 Australian tourists.

Patrick Eagar, Popperfoto/Getty Images

Youth policy? Tom Mottram, 1977.

MUGABE, ROBERT GABRIEL, who died on September 6, aged 95, was the president of Zimbabwe from 1980 to 2017. His overthrow, after an often violent regime, was at least peaceful: *Wisden* reported that a first-class match at the Harare Sports Club, across the road from his official residence, was unaffected. Touring teams were often introduced to the president: Mark Nicholas, captaining England A early in 1990, told Mugabe that meeting him had "made this the greatest day of my life". ("Trouble was," wrote

Derek Pringle, another tourist, "MCJ had already had two 'greatest days of my life' that trip.") Seven years later, when England played their first Test in Zimbabwe, Michael Atherton also had to shake his hand – but by 2004-05, when the realities of life under Mugabe were becoming ever more clear, the ECB stipulated that their team would not meet any government official. Although he preferred tennis, Mugabe once said: "Cricket civilises people and creates good gentlemen. I want everyone to play cricket in Zimbabwe. I want ours to be a nation of gentlemen." Much of his reign, however, was far from gentlemanly, and contributed to cricket's decline in the country.

MUNTON, SALLY ANN, who died on January 25, aged 66, played an important if unsung part in the history of Wisden in the decade (1993–2003) when it was owned by the philanthropist Sir Paul Getty. Munton, as Sir Paul's personal assistant, was the efficient, friendly link between the company's staff and their benign but remote employer. And, armed with the best contacts book in London, she handed out invitations to matches at Getty's bespoke ground, Wormsley, and his box in the Mound Stand at Lord's. She contracted breast cancer and was intermittently ill for many years. She was a founder of the Shocking Pink Party Appeal, which raised money for research at the Royal Marsden Hospital.

MURRAY, BRUCE KEIR, who died on July 30, aged 80, was a university professor who produced several learned books about South African sport, including *Caught Behind: Race and Politics in Springbok Cricket*, the definitive account of the 1968 D'Oliveira Affair, while his *Empire and Cricket 1884–1914* covered relations between British and Afrikaner cricketers, as well as black and white people. An outspoken opponent of apartheid, Murray joined the teaching staff at Witwatersrand University in Johannesburg in 1970, eventually becoming professor of Edwardian British history. "He was an accomplished academic," said his colleague Rob Sharman, "and chairman – later president – of the cricket club, which in 1983 and '84 won everything in the Transvaal, as it was then known."

NASEEM SHEIKH, who collapsed and died during a club game in Karachi on October 7, aged 56, was a prominent local umpire who took time off from his butcher's shop to officiate.

NASH, MALCOLM ANDREW, died on July 30, aged 74, after being taken ill at a function at Lord's. Had life worked out differently, Malcolm Nash might have been remembered for a five-for against the Australians to set up a famous Glamorgan victory at Swansea in 1968. Or as the county's fifth-highest wicket-taker, and their leading bowler when they won the Championship in 1969. Instead, his death provided an excuse to dust off a few minutes of grainy film. It showed him as the fall guy in one of sport's greatest episodes.

On Saturday, August 31, 1968, nearly four weeks after the humbling of the Australians, Nash returned to St Helen's for the final home Championship match of the season, against Nottinghamshire. He bowled well, taking four of the five wickets to have fallen. Garry Sobers had arrived at the crease at around 5pm, irritated that his team were scoring too slowly. The best batsman in the world had dropped down to No. 7 to fit in a trip to the bookies, and wanted quick runs to set up a declaration. Nash would be talking about what happened next for the rest of his life.

He usually bowled left-arm seam and swing, but had been experimenting with brisk spin, in the style of Derek Underwood (who four days earlier had bowled England to a famous Ashes victory at The Oval). With the match drifting, Nash decided there was no harm in giving his new style a public airing. Sobers smashed the first ball over wide long-on, and out of the ground. The second sailed in roughly the same direction, bouncing off the roof of The Cricketers pub. The third, over long-off, clattered into the wooden benches in front of the pavilion. Glamorgan's captain, Tony Lewis, advised Nash to switch back to his usual style: "Whack it in the blockhole, like you normally do." He was ignored. The fourth disappeared high over deep midwicket. Amid mounting excitement in the crowd, and with thousands watching on BBC Wales, Sobers crashed Nash's fifth ball towards long-off, where Roger Davis caught it, before toppling backwards. Sobers

Scene of the crime: Malcolm Nash bowls for Glamorgan against Kent at Swansea in 1973, five years after *that* over.

began to walk off, but Glamorgan's Tony Cordle indicated that Davis had carried the ball over the rope.

For the final ball, Nash reverted to seam-up, but continued round the wicket. It was invitingly short, and Sobers hammered it over midwicket – and out of the ground. The Glamorgan secretary, Wilf Wooller, moonlighting for the BBC, had ignored orders to hand back to London, and now enjoyed his moment of commentating immortality: "He's done it! He's done it! And, my goodness, it's gone way down to Swansea!"

Six sixes in an over was cricket's four-minute mile – it had never been done before – and Sobers's feat was front-page news. Nash did not resent the spotlight. "I suppose I can gain some consolation from the fact that my name will be permanently in the record books," he said. And he remained philosophical. To mark the 50th anniversary, in 2018, he published an autobiography – *Not Only, But Also* – that highlighted his other achievements, yet acknowledged his inextricable link with Sobers. "There's no point in moaning and groaning and crying about it," he said. "Garry and I had a few beers that night, and I wasn't glum."

Nash was born in Abergavenny, and introduced to cricket by his father, a stalwart of the local club. He went to Wells Cathedral School in Somerset, where he excelled at cricket and hockey, in which he represented Wales Under-21. When he arrived at Glamorgan, his initials – MAN – and unabashed self-confidence earned the nickname "Super". He made his first-class debut in 1966, and blossomed in 1968, claiming six for 25 against Gloucestershire, then seven for 15 as Somerset were bowled out for 40. In the win over the Australians, Ian Redpath and Bob Cowper were among his first-day victims. "He has more pace than is at once apparent, makes the ball cut some odd curves through the air, and occasionally brings it back sharply from the pitch," wrote John Arlott in his *Guardian* match report. Nash bowled off about 12 paces. "He had a whippy action and got close to the stumps," said Lewis. "He pitched the ball up, made the batsman play, and got late swing."

Glamorgan started poorly in 1969, but gathered momentum. In August, they faced Gloucestershire in a top-of-the-table showdown at Cheltenham. On the opening day, Nash was close to unplayable. "Line, length and stamina, together with the ability to cut the odd ball away from the right-handers, helped him to finish with six for 37," wrote John Woodcock in *The Times*.

Assisted by a formidable group of close catchers, Nash was key to Glamorgan's strategy. "He was one of the best attacking bowlers in the country," said Lewis. "And he got good batsmen out." He finished the season with 71 Championship wickets at 18. Nash remained a consistent performer, but in 1977 – almost nine years to the day from Sobers's assault – Lancashire's Frank Hayes hit him for 34 in an over, again at Swansea (a four off the second ball prevented a gruesome double). He took it on the chin. "I'd say: 'So I'm in the *Guinness Book of Records* at No. 1 and No. 2. You tell me who's managed that.'" His best season was 1975, when his 85 wickets included 14 against Hampshire at Basingstoke. The following summer he was chosen for a Test trial at Bristol, but that was the closest he came to international recognition. His lack of pace may have concerned selectors, but Lewis said: "In this country, he would have been successful."

750 FIRST-CLASS WICKETS FOR GLAMORGAN

		M	Runs	BB	5I	10M	Avge	Career
2,174	D. J. Shepherd	647	45,571	9-42	122	28	20.96	1950–72
1,460	J. Mercer	412	34,058	10-51	98	16	23.32	1922–39
1,292	J. C. Clay	358	25,181	9-54	105	28	19.48	1921–49
1,055	R. D. B. Croft	364	37,534	8-66	46	8	35.57	1989–2012
991	**M. A. Nash**	**335**	**25,601**	**9-56**	**45**	**5**	**25.83**	**1966–83**
913	F. P. Ryan	215	19,053	8-41	79	17	20.86	1922–31
887	W. Wooller	400	23,511	8-45	40	5	26.50	1938–62
885	D. E. Davies	612	26,030	6-24	32	2	29.41	1924–54
861	S. L. Watkin	250	23,802	8-59	31	4	27.64	1986–2001
799	J. E. McConnon	243	15,656	8-36	49	12	19.59	1950–61
774	A. J. Watkins	407	17,684	7-28	25	0	22.84	1939–61
771	P. M. Walker	437	21,652	7-58	22	2	28.08	1956–72

Nash was also a hard-hitting tailender. In 1976, he cracked a hundred before lunch against Surrey at The Oval. Nine days later, he raced to another, off 61 balls, in a Benson and Hedges Cup game against Hampshire at Swansea – Glamorgan's first century in the competition. He was club captain in 1980 and 1981, but they were not happy years. Nash retired in 1983, and spent two seasons playing for Shropshire. He lived in America for a while, working in sports marketing and later as a school bus driver, but returned to Wales in 2013 after being diagnosed with a heart condition.

In 2006, an Indian company had paid more than £26,000 at auction for the ball Sobers had smashed "down to Swansea". It was a Dukes, yet Glamorgan had always used a Stuart Surridge; the popular theory was that Sobers had unwittingly handed over the wrong ball. Nash stopped short of criticising him, but was "getting somewhat irritated that my reputation and integrity are being called into question".

Above all, he was never allowed to forget that late-August afternoon at St Helen's. "I don't think it changed my character too much," he said. "I've got fairly broad shoulders. But I didn't bowl slow left-arm again for a while."

NEAME, ROBERT HARRY BEALE, CBE, DL, died on November 15, aged 85. The Old Harrovian Bobby Neame was a director of the Kent brewers Shepherd Neame – Britain's oldest, formed in 1698 – for 50 years, serving as chairman from 1970; he became their first president after handing over to his son in 2005. He was also Kent CCC's president in 2003. "He was a dominant force in so many aspects of Kent life," said Jamie Clifford, their former chief executive. "He was a big supporter of the club – and Shepherd Neame have been faithful sponsors for decades." Neame's younger brother, Rex, played a few matches for Kent in the 1950s.

NOTLEY, BERNARR, died on January 22, four months after becoming the first Nottinghamshire player to reach 100 years of age. An off-spinning all-rounder, "Bill" Notley took nine for 86 (and 14 in the match) for the Second XI against Warwickshire in 1949, and a few days later made his only first-class appearance, against Surrey at The Oval. He took one wicket, but was dismissed by Alec Bedser for a duck. Notley continued to turn out for the Seconds, often as captain.

NURSE, SEYMOUR MacDONALD, who died on May 6, aged 85, made the highest score by a batsman in his final Test innings, 258 for West Indies against New Zealand in 1968-69. A big man who liked to hit the ball hard, Nurse lit up a cloudy Christchurch day with his trademark thumping back-foot drives. "It was some achievement on New Zealand pitches, which tend to favour the bowlers more than in the West Indies or Australia," said Garry Sobers, his captain and fellow Bajan. "He should have played on much longer than he did."

However, disillusioned by the West Indians' poor performances in Australia just before, Nurse had already announced his impending retirement. His own form, if not the team's, recovered spectacularly: 137 in the final Test at Sydney was followed by 95 and 168 at Auckland, before the Christchurch double gave him an unmatched average, for a player's last six Test innings, of 115. Sobers had persuaded him to carry on to New Zealand, but failed to convince him to go to England later in 1969 (West Indies lost 2–0). Nurse was worried he would look indecisive if he returned, but also wanted, at 35, to go out on his own terms, after what he felt were earlier injustices in selection. Many years later, he declined to take part in a reunion of the 1960-61 tied-Test squads, which some suspected revealed an antipathy to Frank Worrell, the otherwise popular leader on that trip.

Born in 1933 in the exotic-sounding Jack-My-Nanny Gap (later renamed more prosaically as Wavell Avenue), Nurse was a late starter in first-class cricket. Hamstrung by the need to earn a living, he was also faced with a Barbados team containing Sobers and the Three Ws. His game advanced when he joined one of the Ws, Everton Weekes, at Bridgetown's Empire club, and he finally made his debut for Barbados in 1958, aged 24. Nurse made up for lost time with 128 not out in his second match, against Jamaica at Kingston, and 131 in the fourth, against British Guiana at Bridgetown. And in his next, in 1959-60, he put his name firmly in the selectors' sights, hammering 213 – and adding 306 with Sobers – in a ten-wicket win over the England tourists. It signalled, according to E. W. Swanton, "the arrival of a batsman with obvious pretensions to the top flight".

Nurse made his debut in the Third Test, and scored 70 at Kingston, where he and Sobers shared another century partnership. But he was left out of the next match when Clyde Walcott was recalled, and dropped again soon after another 70 in his second Test, in Australia in 1960-61. Restricted by injury in England in 1963, he had won only five caps by the time the Australians toured the Caribbean two years later, but finally cemented his place, extending his maiden century, at home in Bridgetown, to 201. The watching Richie Benaud enjoyed Nurse "several times playing that magnificent cover-drive that he hits between point and cover, and playing it so well that the Australians applauded every time".

HIGHEST SCORE IN FINAL TEST

325	A. Sandham	England v West Indies at Kingston	1929-30
266	W. H. Ponsford	Australia v England at The Oval	1934
258†	**S. M. Nurse**	**West Indies v New Zealand at Christchurch**	**1968-69**
206†	P. A. de Silva	Sri Lanka v Bangladesh at Colombo (PSO)	2002
201*†	J. N. Gillespie	Australia v Bangladesh at Chittagong (ZAC)	2005-06
196	G. B. Legge	England v New Zealand at Auckland	1929-30
187†	M. Leyland	England v Australia at The Oval	1938
182†	G. S. Chappell	Australia v Pakistan at Sydney	1983-84
154†	V. M. Merchant	India v England at Delhi	1951-52

† *In final innings. Current players are not included.*

At the top of his game: Seymour Nurse in 1966, when he was chosen as one of *Wisden's* Five.

In England in 1966, Nurse added 137 at Headingley, where he and Sobers rescued West Indies with a fifth-wicket stand of 265. He had also made an important 93 on the first day of the previous match, at Trent Bridge, and finished that famous series with 501 runs; only Sobers (722) made more. A keen footballer, Nurse attended several World Cup matches, including the final between England and West Germany. He did enough to be named as one of the Wisden Cricketers of the Year. The accompanying essay observed: "He established himself in the eyes of the English followers as a strokemaker fit to line up with credit beside the likes of George Headley, Frank Worrell and Everton Weekes."

Another productive time followed at home in 1967-68, even though he opened in four of the Tests: in the Fourth, back at No. 3, he hit 136, this time sharing a stand of 273 with Rohan Kanhai. Nurse was more restrained than usual, "content to leave the stage to his dapper and brilliant partner", according to John Woodcock in *The Times*. However, Sobers's capricious declaration handed England the series 1–0. The cracks were beginning to show in what had been a successful team; little more than a year later, Nurse had retired.

He played a few more matches for Barbados, bowing out with 76 (and a duck) against the 1971-72 New Zealand tourists. He went into coaching, was a Test selector for a time, and managed the West Indian Under-19 side. Desmond Haynes, one of his charges, recalled: "We used to walk like Seymour, try to bat like him, and try to talk like him."

Sobers had no hesitation in naming Nurse at No. 4 in his best West Indian side for a 1988 book. At the time, Nurse was 53, and still playing Over-40s cricket. "I reckon he is still good enough to play for Barbados," said Sobers, "so good is his technique."

PARKER, JOHN FRANCIS, who died on October 7, 2018, aged 82, brought up his sole Sheffield Shield century with a six, on the way to a breezy undefeated 139 against a New South Wales attack containing five Test bowlers at the WACA in February 1964. Parker also played two notable innings against Australian sides on their way to England, in the days when they would depart by ship from Fremantle. In 1961, he collected an uncharacteristically subdued 52, and in 1964 (the last time the Australians travelled to England by sea) a studied 84.

PATNAIK, SIDHANTA, who died of cancer on May 31, aged 34, was an Indian journalist with a passion for the game's lesser lights. "International cricket can look after itself," he said, and instead concentrated on juniors, under-19s and, above all, the women's game. Shortly before his death he completed *The Fire Burns Blue*, a comprehensive history of women's cricket in India, co-authored with Karunya Keshav. Patnaik worked for the Indian edition of *Wisden*, whose editor, Suresh Menon, remembered: "I was in England on the India tour [in 2018] when I received a message saying he had been given two hours to live. When I met him on my return, the doctors told me he had asked them to extend his life by ten days so he could complete his Almanack work." He survived almost another year. "Cricket is my source of energy," he wrote in his final article.

PEARSON, LAUNCELOT ROBERT, died on July 20, aged 82. A tall batsman who usually opened, Lance Pearson played 31 matches for Otago, hitting 140 against Auckland at Carisbrook in December 1969. He was also a prominent basketball player and administrator.

PETERS, NICHOLAS HOWARD, died of cancer on May 20, aged 51. Tall, dark and handsome – his good looks earned him the nickname "Bondy" – seamer Nick Peters played 16 matches for Surrey in 1988 and 1989, obtaining good pace and bounce from a shortish run-up. In one of his early games, he took six for 31 (and ten for 67 in the match) against Warwickshire at The Oval; it was, said local journalist Richard Spiller, "one of the few occasions on which batsmen appeared to prefer facing Sylvester Clarke". But full-time cricket was not a priority, and after leaving the Surrey staff Peters had a spell as a teacher, before qualifying as a psychotherapist. "He was such a nice guy," remembered team-mate Adam Hollioake. "In all honesty, that usually doesn't blend well with professional sport, and I wasn't surprised to see him retire young."

PINNOCK, RENFORD AUGUSTUS, who died on November 1, aged 82, was a neat and stylish batsman, who sometimes kept wicket. In only his second match for Jamaica, he defied the fearsome Barbados new-ball pair of Wes Hall and Charlie Griffith to score 68 and 106, and made five other centuries, the highest a rapid 176 against Sussex at Hove in August 1970. Pinnock also hit 175 against Barbados at Kensington Oval in 1968-69, which helped Jamaica secure the regional title. He later took up umpiring, and also coached.

PLAYLE, WILLIAM RODGER, died on February 27, aged 80. Bill Playle was selected for New Zealand's 1958 tour of England on the strength of a century for Auckland against Central Districts in January, a month after his 19th birthday. The tour, though, was a sodden disaster – although the weather did prevent the New Zealanders from a 5–0 whitewash by ruining the final Test. Playle began well, with 96 against Leicestershire, but then found English conditions so difficult that he failed to reach double figures in 21 of his 36 innings. *Wisden* noted sympathetically that he "possessed possibilities as a stylish batsman, and must have done better in a drier summer".

In the second innings of the Headingley Test, he resisted inevitable defeat for 194 minutes in making 18, with only seven scoring shots. What John Clarke of the *Evening News* called "a kind of Leeds lullaby" earned Playle a place on Test slow-scoring lists. His defensive demonstration was evocatively described by John Arlott: "Playing with the shallow pendulum of a very straight bat, refusing all temptation, batting with both eyes fixed on the ball, but his mind, apparently, on eternity." Almost five years later, Playle made 65, his only Test half-century, against England at Wellington.

In May 1965, his job took him to Perth, where he was immediately drafted into the Western Australian side. He made 642 runs in his first season, with centuries against Victoria and Queensland, his batting still marked by its trademark solidity, but now spiced by a more positive attitude. However, he was dropped after a poor start the following summer.

Playle moved in 1976 to New South Wales, where he had two more seasons of grade cricket before opening a consultancy specialising in industrial and commercial cleaning systems. He continued to coach junior players. A person of understated humour and charm, he was known to fellow cricketers as "Buckets", after his name appeared on an Australian scoreboard as "Pail".

PRESTON, KENNETH CHARLES, died on January 6, aged 93. Ken Preston was an indefatigable mainstay of the Essex seam attack from the late 1940s to the mid-1960s. He was a skilled operator, swinging the ball, deploying cutters and testing batsmen's patience with his accuracy. But when he first appeared, in 1948, he had an even greater asset – raw speed. He was erratic and unpredictable but, in taking 42 Championship wickets at 28, he regularly jarred bat handles; *Wisden* warmed to his "considerable promise". The following winter, however, he suffered a double fracture of his left leg playing football: his pace was never the same. After a long rehabilitation, he emerged a different bowler.

But Preston's value transcended the averages. "He was the best possible example of 'team spirit' in the true sense of that much misused and overworked phrase," wrote Essex captain Doug Insole. His cheery magnanimity even extended to driving the county's kit van up and down the country. Insole's successor, Trevor Bailey, said he could not have asked for a better senior pro.

Take cover: Essex colleagues Bill Greensmith, Barry Knight, Ken Preston, Trevor Bailey and Brian Taylor (crouching), at the Old Blue Rugby Club, Fairlop, in 1962.

Preston was born in Goodmayes, near Romford. In 1943, aged 18, he joined the Royal Navy. On D-Day, he crewed one of the hundreds of landing craft that carried Allied troops to the Normandy beaches. Just over a week later, he was on the vessel that took the exiled Charles de Gaulle back to France; in 2015, Preston was among the British veterans awarded the *Légion d'Honneur* by the French government.

He did not make his first-class debut until he had turned 22, but soon made an impression in a country desperate to unearth pace bowlers. But the football injury changed the course of his career. The recovery was slow: he missed the whole of 1949, and in 1950 he had still not regained full fitness. Confidence and form returned the following season, and he passed 80 wickets for the first of three successive years.

But after struggling again in 1954, he was dropped. Preston had already cut his run-up and now, forced to reinvent himself in the Second XI, he ceased searching for his old pace, mastering cutters and concentrating on accuracy. In 1955, he took 94 wickets, and passed 90 again in 1956, including a career-best seven for 55 against Northamptonshire at Peterborough. His peak came in 1957, with 140 wickets at 20; only five bowlers in the country took more. Preston was also a superb slip fielder – his 344 catches placed him fourth on Essex's all-time list – and a useful lower-order batsman.

He continued to perform consistently into the early 1960s, and became a kindly mentor to a new generation of Essex players. "He was quiet, a fatherly figure," said Robin Hobbs. "He was the ultimate senior pro, and he really enjoyed that role. Young pros would always go to Ken rather than Trevor if they had a problem." On the 18-year-old Keith Fletcher's debut, Preston took ten wickets against Glamorgan at Ebbw Vale. "He was strict and firm, with set ideas on how the game should be played," Fletcher recalled. "But he was always fair to us youngsters, and nobody could trample on us when he was around."

In the winters he worked for the Essex Supporters' Association, raising funds for a hard-up county. He later became coach at Brentwood School. And the team always came before individual glory. "He always had to bowl long spells into the wind and uphill," said Hobbs, "apart from Thursday afternoons between lunch and tea, when Trevor was filing his column for the *Financial Times*."

PUCKERIN, LIVINGSTONE KENNETH, who died of cancer on September 18, 2018, aged 49, was a wicketkeeper-batsman who played 18 first-class matches for Barbados, never exceeding his 79 on debut against Trinidad at Bridgetown in January 1989. In the Barbados Cricket League, mainly for the old-established Spartan club, he amassed more than 7,500 runs – with ten centuries – and 439 dismissals, including 168 stumpings. "He was a very inspirational cricketer and captain," said the former Test opener Philo Wallace, a team-mate at Spartan. "He was a clinical player, and did everything from the heart."

RAINE, BRIAN, who died on October 6, aged 66, had been the voice of The Oval – manning the public-address system – for around 20 years, although his association with the club stretched back twice as long, and included spells in the ticket office and running the electronic scoreboards. Long days at the cricket – usually followed by a trip home to Leicestershire – were alleviated by moments of humour, such as when he was forced to make an announcement asking a cigarette (a man in costume for an advertising campaign) not to walk behind the bowler's arm.

READE, LAWRENCE BURNARD, died on August 21, aged 88. Opening batsman Lawrie Reade played 24 matches for Central Districts, hitting 163 – his only century – against Northern Districts in 1960-61. He was part of the Nelson team that held the Hawke Cup, for New Zealand's minor associations, for six years from 1958-59; only team-mate Ian Leggat has scored more runs in the competition than Reade's 1,951.

RIAZUDDIN, who died of a heart attack on June 11, aged 60, was an umpire from Karachi who oversaw 12 Tests between 1990-91 and 2001-02, his last being Pakistan's first in the UAE. He also stood in 12 one-day internationals, and was an early member of the ICC elite panel. In all, Riazuddin officiated in 310 first-class matches – a Pakistan record – before retiring at the end of 2018. "He was an institution," said his former colleague Khizer Hayat. "Very good umpire and fine human being." The Pakistan team wore black armbands in his honour during their World Cup match against Australia.

ROBINSON, BARRY DAVID, who died on January 16, aged 86, was a good all-round sportsman who played 87 matches for Bedfordshire between 1957 and 1973, scoring 2,222 runs, with two centuries. He was part of the side that won the Minor Counties Championship in 1970, and captained Luton Town CC from 1962 to 1978.

ROUSSEAU, PATRICK HOPPNER ORLA, died on April 16, aged 85. Pat Rousseau was an influential president of the West Indies Cricket Board between 1996 and 2001, his term including a successful bid to stage the 2007 World Cup in the Caribbean. A lawyer who did much for sport in Jamaica – he played hockey for them in his youth – Rousseau had "a sharp legal and business mind", according to Ricky Skerritt, who became the board's president in 2019.

ROXBURGHE, THE 10TH DUKE OF, died of cancer on August 29, aged 64. Guy David Innes-Ker, then known by his courtesy title the Marquis of Bowmont, top-scored in both innings (27 and 53 not out) as captain of Eton against Harrow at Lord's in 1973. A year later, he inherited the dukedom, Floors Castle, and a 52,000-acre estate in the Scottish Borders. The duke was variously described as a "driving force in the modernisation of land ownership", someone "who did not suffer fools lightly", and "a Corinthian". He listed five sports as his hobbies, none cricket, though he was the patron of the local Kelso club.

SALEEM, SULTAN, who died on August 21, aged 73, was a stylish batsman with a ready smile who played 44 first-class matches for various Indian teams. Most were for Hyderabad; he hit 90 against Bombay at the Brabourne Stadium in 1972-73. But he never fulfilled the promise expected after he slammed 201 and 312 in the same game for All Saints High School: there were only four other fifties, and he averaged just over 20. "He had a relatively quiet Ranji Trophy career, in and out of a talented side including Abbas Ali Baig, M. A. K. Pataudi, M. L. Jaisimha and Abid Ali," remembered team-mate V. Ramnarayan. "But with his slim physique, uncreased flannels and elegant batting, he was no way behind the Test stars in the glamour department."

SCARLETT, REGINALD OSMOND, died on August 14, the day before his 85th birthday. Hulking and hirsute, Reg Scarlett first played for his native Jamaica in 1951-52 and, two seasons later, took eight wickets in two matches against Len Hutton's England tourists. In July 1958, he claimed 14 more in two games against Barbados and, when England toured again in 1959-60, he played in three of the Tests. Alan Ross described him as "a Bedser-size off-spinner", but Scarlett managed only two wickets, and did little with the bat. As it turned out, they were his last first-class matches: he started playing as a professional in Britain, first in Scotland then, for a decade, in the hard school of the Lancashire leagues. With Lance Gibbs seemingly a fixture in the West Indian side, there was no room for Scarlett, although he remained close to his former team-mates. In 1973, he and Garry Sobers staggered out of a nightclub at 4am during the Lord's Test; after a shower and another drink or two to freshen up, Sobers returned to the crease and extended his final Test century to 150 not out.

Scarlett became better known as a coach, setting up the acclaimed Haringey (later London) Cricket College, which produced several county players, many from underprivileged backgrounds. Adrian Rollins, who would score 13 first-class hundreds for Derbyshire and Northamptonshire, said: "If it hadn't been for the London Cricket College, I'd probably have been in prison." Scarlett eventually returned to the Caribbean in 1997, as West Indies' first director of coaching. "In his pomp, Reg was a bear of a bloke, with the heart and soul of a lion," said the journalist Stephen Thorpe. "As a vintage man of cricket, here's one who actually merited a knighthood for services to the game."

SCHANSCHIEFF, SIMON GEORGE, OBE, DL, who died on November 15, aged 81, was Northamptonshire's chairman from 2000 to 2007, and also sat on ECB committees. He followed his father, Brian, as committee man and president (1974–77), and his son, Guy, has also served on the board of directors: the committee room at the County Ground was renamed the Schanschieff Room in recognition of the family's contribution to the club over six decades. An accountant and long-serving magistrate, he had a keen interest in healthcare, and in 1986 produced a report into unnecessary dental treatment. He played cricket and hockey for Northampton Saints in his younger days.

SCOTT, ANDREW ARCHIBALD STEELE, died on November 1, aged 101, the first Scotland cricketer to make it to three figures. Archie Scott, whose father and uncle both played international rugby, made one appearance for the country's cricket team, in Ireland in 1947, not long after an eventful war: he took part in 11 battles, and once looked down to find his heel on the hinge of a mine. He played in Edinburgh for the Grange club, but work in the whisky trade restricted his cricket. Scott remained active: married for 68 years, he published a memoir called *96 Not Out*, four years before buying a new car when he reached 100.

SETALVAD, ANANT, who died on August 4, aged 84, was a well-known presence on All India Radio for over 20 years from the mid-1960s, describing international and domestic cricket in what *The Hindu* called a "pleasant baritone voice". Raju Bharatan, a former colleague, said: "He was easy in delivery, accurate in description."

SEYMOUR, MICHAEL ARTHUR, died on February 18, aged 82. Off-spinner "Kelly" Seymour – the name derived from a nanny's inability to pronounce Michael – won seven caps for South Africa, the first four in Australia in 1963-64. He had come to prominence two years before, with seven for 80 (a career-best) and 12 in the match for South African Universities against the New Zealand tourists. "He was a very nice, quiet, reserved guy," said Peter Pollock, South Africa's pace spearhead. "The selectors believed off-spinners were the answer in Australia because of Hugh Tayfield's success in the early 1950s. So they picked two – Kelly and David Pithey." But they had got it wrong, as the captain Trevor Goddard admitted: "What we needed out there was not off-spinners, but someone who could spin the ball away from the bat." Pithey failed to take a wicket in three Tests, while Seymour managed five – three in the closing stages of the series, when finally given a long bowl. He flew home before the New Zealand leg to sit his final medical exams, but appeared in the first two Tests against England in 1964-65, again proving tidy but unthreatening. Medicine took precedence for a while but, after figures of five for 70 for Western Province against Natal early in 1969-70, Seymour received a surprise call for the First Test against Australia at Cape Town, joining his captain Ali Bacher as the second doctor in the side. The track was expected to turn, but he claimed only one wicket in each innings, and John Traicos – younger, and a superb fielder – was preferred for the remaining Tests as South Africa cruised to a clean sweep.

SHAH, JAWAHIR NATHOO, who died on September 15, aged 77, was a Kenyan batsman from Nairobi's Gymkhana club. He came to prominence in August 1967 with 96 and 134 in a match against the Indian tourists, on their way home from England. That October, he made 74 against Warwickshire. In 1975, he was one of the East African side which took part in the first World Cup, despite being controversially replaced as captain shortly beforehand; four years later, he played in the inaugural ICC Trophy. He played three first-class matches for East Africa in three different years in three different countries.

SHAMIM KABIR, who died on July 29, aged 74, captained Bangladesh in their first representative match, against a touring MCC side in Dacca in January 1977. A tall opening batsman who sometimes kept wicket, he had played 15 first-class matches before Bangladesh gained independence, with a top score of 89 for East Pakistan Greens against Railways in 1967-68. Four years earlier, he hit 64 for Dacca University against a Pakistan

International Airlines side containing several Test players. Shamim later became an administrator, and managed the national team in the ICC Trophy in 1982 and 1986. "He was a pioneer," said the current board president Nazmul Hassan. "He captained Bangladesh when times were difficult for cricket, and the game had very limited resources."

SHUKLA, RAKESH CHANDRA, who died on June 29, aged 71, was a long-serving all-rounder, mainly for Delhi in the Ranji Trophy. Although his strongest suit was his leg-spin – he took 295 first-class wickets at 24 – he was a useful batsman, who made six centuries. His best-remembered knock, however, was 69 not out, during a ninth-wicket stand of 118 with Rajesh Peter that spirited Delhi to 707 for eight, past Karnataka's 705, to win the 1981-82 Ranji final on first innings. The previous year, he had scored 120 in the final. Shukla was on the fringe of the Indian team for many years, but won only one Test cap, against Sri Lanka at Madras in 1982-83, by which time he was 34. He took two important wickets, teasing out Roy Dias (97) and Duleep Mendis (105) after a century partnership in the second innings. "He was a good middle-order batsman and an attacking spinner," said Delhi team-mate Vinay Lamba. "He did not turn the ball much, but had a lethal googly. He should have got his chance much earlier." Shukla's older brother, Anand, also had a long first-class career.

SILK, DENNIS RAOUL WHITEHALL, CBE, JP, who died on June 19, aged 87, announced himself by hitting hundreds in successive Varsity Matches. In 1953, he guided Cambridge to an against-the-clock victory with a thrilling assault on Oxford's bowling; a less eye-catching innings the following year was more true to type. "He was stubborn," said his opening partner Mike Bushby. "He sold his wicket dearly." Silk went into teaching, but played for Somerset in the holidays. Had he been available full-time, he would almost certainly have become captain. "He was a man of gentle voice, charm and authority," wrote the Somerset historian David Foot.

In 1968, Silk became warden (headmaster) of Radley College in Oxfordshire. It was at a low ebb, but he transformed it into one of the leading private schools in the country: John Rae, his counterpart at Westminster, said Radley became "after Eton, the most sought-after school in England". Silk maintained his links with cricket and, a prominent MCC committee member, supported ties with South Africa; he later became the first president to serve for two years, in a short-lived experiment. In the mid-1990s, he was chairman of the Test and County Cricket Board (the predecessor of the ECB) at a time when England were in perpetual crisis.

He was born in Eureka, California, where his father was working as a medical missionary to the Hupa Indians. His Spanish mother died when he was a small boy, and he was brought up by his grandmother in north London. Silk was educated at Christ's Hospital, West Sussex, where he was head boy and a talented sportsman. He first opened the batting with Bushby in two schools matches at Lord's in August 1949. It was the beginning of a lifelong friendship.

At Cambridge, where he studied history at Sidney Sussex College, Silk won a Blue at rugby and a half-Blue at fives – John Pretlove, later of Kent, was a regular doubles partner – and made his first-class debut against Free Foresters in 1952, his only appearance that summer. The following year, he made centuries against Free Foresters and MCC (a career-best 126). But it was his performance in the Varsity Match that made headlines. On the last day, he batted five and a quarter hours for an unbeaten 116, but Cambridge's apparent reluctance to chase 238 produced slow handclaps. With eight wickets down – and his captain Robin Marlar, fresh to the crease, telling him to play for a draw – he went on the attack. "Silk, all at once emerging from his protective shell, now pressed Cambridge past the post in a furious assault of driving completely out of context with all that had gone before," wrote Geoffrey Green in *The Times*. Cambridge won with three minutes to spare. In 1954, he made a hundred against the county champions, Surrey, and hit his second Varsity Match century in a draw dominated by M. J. K. Smith's

"A man of gentle voice, charm and authority": Dennis Silk and Jack Cheetham, captains of Cambridge University and South Africa, at the toss, Fenner's, 1955.

unbeaten 201. Silk was captain of Cambridge in 1955, leading them to wins over Sussex, Warwickshire and Worcestershire.

For a time he lived with an aunt in Somerset, which enabled him to qualify for the county. He made his debut in 1956, and instantly felt at home. "He loved playing for Somerset," said Bushby. "He loved the humour and banter of the professionals." In later life, Silk's after-dinner speeches frequently included stories about colourful team-mates such as Bill Alley or Maurice Tremlett. "He mixed well with the rest of us and, unlike most amateurs, he was worth his place," said off-spinner Brian Langford. "The greatest compliment I can pay Dennis is that the rest of the team treated him like a professional." Silk advised the Somerset committee that Tremlett should be appointed captain in 1956, rather than the amateur Alan Shirreff.

He led MCC tours to North America in 1959 and New Zealand in 1960-61, displaying his easy talent for bringing people together. "He was popular, and also liked by the opposition because they all enjoyed his speeches," said Bob Barber, who went on both tours. Silk was a dogged, front-foot player, but became more expansive. "He was very determined – and he carried that into every aspect of his life," said Barber. He played for Somerset until 1960, making just one hundred, against Glamorgan at Cardiff Arms Park in 1956. In his last first-class match in England, he scored 119 for the Gentlemen against the Players at Scarborough.

While at Cambridge, Silk was introduced to the poet Siegfried Sassoon, and the friendship blossomed after he took up his first teaching post at Marlborough College. Sassoon developed Silk's love of English literature, and he passed it on to his pupils. He once asked for an example of alliteration: a young Christopher Martin-Jenkins proffered "Stupendous Statham skittles Springboks", from that morning's *Daily Express*. Silk confessed he was hoping for something more literary. He began to reshape Radley on arrival, impressing the staff at first meeting because he had memorised their names and duties. Against some opposition, he approved a fly-on-the-wall BBC documentary – possibly remembering a short promotional film during his time at Marlborough, when he banged a gong at the start, in the manner of the Rank films, clad only in his jockstrap.

He joined the MCC committee in 1966, and defended the club when the D'Oliveira Affair erupted four years later. At short notice, he was asked to speak at the special general meeting called by a group of rebel members, led by David Sheppard, one of his closest friends at university. "We do not stand as the social conscience of Great Britain any more than our government stands as the social conscience of the world," said Silk. In *The Guardian*, John Arlott wrote: "Dennis Silk introduced a note of personal acrimony towards David Sheppard, which if one sensed the feeling of the meeting aright, did the committee's case very little good with the audience in the hall." MCC won all three votes that night; the rift between the two men was healed soon afterwards.

Silk became TCCB chairman in October 1994, months after Ray Illingworth had been made chairman of selectors. He was a supporter of Illingworth's attempt to expand his influence, which meant the sacking of England manager Keith Fletcher after the 3–1 Ashes defeat in 1994-95. "I was disappointed about the lack of progress some of our players were making, and felt you were sometimes too kind to them," he wrote to Fletcher. But Silk stood down after two years because he lacked support for a national academy. "Surely the best of the elite can be developed so much better at a centre," he said. "South Africa, New Zealand and Sri Lanka all have them. Areas like technique, fitness, nutrition could be explored. It seems self-evident." His departure came months after England's abysmal performance at the 1996 World Cup. "If our team keeps going the way it has been, then our game will die," he said. "All you will have left behind will be village and club cricket."

But he did not lose his love for the sport, or his popularity. Bushby said it became impossible for him and Silk to chat during a day at a match. "Everybody wanted a bit of him – everywhere you went, he knew people."

SLADE, WILLIAM DOUGLAS, died on December 22, aged 78. Billy Slade made his debut for Glamorgan's Second XI as a 17-year-old in 1959, and went on to play 67 matches for the first team. A middle-order batsman, handy change seamer and superb fielder, he never improved on the 370 runs he made in his maiden first-class season of 1961. He took five catches at Bournemouth that year to help defeat eventual champions Hampshire, all off Don Shepherd, who rated him one of the best close fielders he had seen. One of those catches, to dismiss opener Jimmy Gray, was described by Basil Easterbrook in the *Western Mail*: "The batsman struck the ball like a projectile towards the youngster, but Slade stood his ground and completed a searing catch, as if Gray had gently tossed him an apple." Two years later, Slade made his highest score, an unbeaten 73 against Derbyshire at Swansea, and in 1964 was part of the Glamorgan team which defeated the touring Australians. In 1979, he played for Wales in the ICC Trophy.

SRINIVASAN, MUTHUSWAMI, who died on September 5, aged 94, was a wicketkeeper from Madras who played 18 first-class matches, including one for South Zone against the 1958-59 West Indian tourists. He finished with 12 catches and 12 stumpings – and a highest score of 12.

STEWART, RICHARD WILLIAM, died on June 15, aged 74. "Wes" Stewart was a Jamaican-born seamer who spent three seasons with Middlesex in the 1960s. However, it was another half-century before he came to national prominence – as one of many innocent victims of the *Windrush* scandal. Six years before he died, Stewart discovered that, though he had lived in Britain since he was ten, he had no official status, was ineligible for a British passport, and at risk of deportation. The problem arose from a trip he had made to Jamaica in 1968 to visit his dying mother. By the time he was able to return, his British passport had expired, and he had come back on a Jamaican passport; he was thus wrongly classed, along with many others, as an illegal immigrant. After years of bureaucratic delays, Stewart was given a new British passport before he died, but none of the promised compensation for the errors made by the Home Office. His son, who really was called Wesley, said his father had been worn down by the stress of his situation, and that "it was blatant discrimination."

His father's nickname was perhaps ironic since, unlike Wes Hall, he was not lightning fast. "He was not much above medium pace, but very accurate, a very decent bowler," recalled Mike Brearley, who just overlapped with him. "He was a likeable chap too, unpretentious, with a sly grin." Stewart played a single match for Gloucestershire against Oxford University in 1966 before Middlesex snapped him up, and he took six for 65 on his Championship debut to thwart a Glamorgan run-chase at Lord's. That year, he took 70 wickets, averaging 22, and another 49 in 1967. His form dipped and, when Middlesex signed the Australian fast bowler Alan Connolly for 1969, there was no place for Stewart. He later worked as a painter and decorator.

STODDART, PETER LAURENCE BOWRING, who died on April 19, aged 84, was a stylish batsman, schooled at Eton, who captained Buckinghamshire in the Minor Counties Championship from 1959 to 1965. That included their first match in the Gillette Cup, at Lord's in 1965, when Stoddart was run out without facing. He played one first-class match, for MCC against Ireland in 1958. He was a merchant banker.

STOTHER, HELEN JOY, who died on October 8, aged 64, was a Lancashire-born medium-pacer who played seven Tests and 12 one-day internationals for England in the 1980s. Her debut came in the 1981-82 World Cup in New Zealand – she and wicketkeeper Shirley Hodges were the only England players who had to take unpaid leave to participate – although Stother missed the final, which England lost to Australia. The week before her Test debut, against New Zealand in 1984, she took five for 14 for Middlesex Women against Sussex at Lewes. A PE teacher, she also played representative hockey.

SUTTON, MICHAEL ANTONY, who died on June 28, aged 98, had been Somerset's oldest surviving player. Tony Sutton had driven a tank during the D-Day landings, and studied at Oxford after the war. An off-spinner, he removed Len Hutton on his first-class debut for the university; later in 1946, he took five for 63 against Leicestershire, and eight in the next game, against Middlesex, to secure a Blue. He did less well the following year, and missed the Varsity Match, but in 1948 made his one appearance for Somerset, against Oxford. He became a solicitor – and a member of the Magic Circle – and played cricket and rugby in Devon for many years. Sutton once took all ten wickets in an innings for the Devon Dumplings, and also had the unusual experience of reading his own obituary, after *The Cricketer* included him by mistake in 1993. They sent champagne by way of apology, which was duly consumed at a special Obituary Party at Sutton's home.

TAYLOR, JAMES ROBERT NIVEN, died on July 14, aged 89. Jim Taylor played one game for Scotland, against Ireland in 1949, while studying at Edinburgh University. He then returned to India, where he was born, and played three Ranji Trophy matches for Bengal, making 41 against Bihar at Eden Gardens in Calcutta. He later moved to Canada.

THEUNISSEN-FOURIE, ELRIESA, died in a car accident in Stilfontein, in South Africa's North West province, on April 5. She was 25, and about to give birth to her first child. An all-rounder who hit 94 for North West in a T20 game against Easterns in 2012-13, she played three one-day internationals – including one in the 2012-13 World Cup – and a T20 match for South Africa.

THOMAS, HUGH RONALD, who died on February 13, aged 88, was a schoolmaster with a passion for Sussex cricket: he was chairman and later president of Horsham CC and, after retiring from Hurstpierpoint College, became a qualified umpire. He was one of

Trevor Dallen, Fairfax Media/Getty Images

Better than dairy: Sam Trimble, 1970.

the first recipients of an ECB OSCA, for outstanding service to cricket. In his younger days, Thomas played ten Minor Counties Championship matches for Shropshire as a slow left-armer, taking seven wickets in the last, a narrow victory over Lincolnshire in 1961.

TRIMBLE, SAMUEL CHRISTY, MBE, died on July 28, aged 84. Sam Trimble once topped the list of Sheffield Shield batsmen who never played Test cricket, with 9,647 runs. Although more matches take place now, only four batsmen have surpassed him – Jamie Cox, Jamie Siddons, Michael Di Venuto and Jimmy Maher. Trimble was also unfortunate that, as a top-order batsman, his best years coincided with Australia's settled opening pair of Bob Simpson and Bill Lawry. Trimble was handicapped, too, by playing for Queensland, seen as an unfashionable outpost in the days when Australian cricket was still dominated by Victoria and New South Wales. He was actually born in NSW – but in the far north, 500 miles from Sydney and only 125 from Brisbane, where he would find fame. He was raised on one of the area's then-plentiful dairy farms, but preferred cricket: "It sure beat chasing cows around a paddock."

After a few outings for junior NSW sides produced little interest, Trimble made his debut for Queensland in 1959-60. He was dismissed by a Sydney paper as "no stylist" – but opponents noted a strong square-cut, a legacy of learning the game on fast, bouncy concrete pitches topped by coir matting. In 1963-64, "Slammin' Sam" piled up 1,006 runs in nine matches, with five centuries, including his highest score, a chanceless eight-hour 252 not out against NSW to wipe out a deficit of 328 at Sydney. Two seasons later, he toured the West Indies as reserve opener, but rose no higher than twelfth man in the First Test.

Consolation of a kind came at the end of the 1969-70 season, when Trimble was appointed captain of what would now be called an A-team, in New Zealand. It was a mixture of promising younger players such as Greg Chappell and Dennis Lillee, and elders in the form of Trimble and John Inverarity. Trimble showed his capacity for the long haul by making 213 in a four-day representative match at Wellington – the next-highest score was 27 – but Keith Stackpole's success as an opener in the 1970-71 Ashes put paid to any faint hopes of a Test cap.

Trimble captained Queensland from 1968-69, but his side never did win that elusive Shield; he finally retired, aged 41, in 1976. When Queensland's team of the century were named in 2000, Trimble was the only uncapped member. He ran an indoor school in Brisbane, and was awarded an MBE for services to cricket in 1975. His son Glenn, a hard-driving batsman and back-up medium-pacer, did play for Australia, in two one-day internationals in 1985-86.

VAN ANDERSON, KEITH FITZHERBERT CARLTON, died on May 16, aged 67. Usually equipped with a hat in MCC colours, plus club tie, pipe, and an elegant cricket ball walking stick, the dapper van Anderson – often known simply as "Pipe Man" – was an instantly recognisable figure. A local government official originally from Guyana, he attended every Test at Lord's for more than 40 years after watching West Indies win there in 1973, and was invariably at the head of the members' queue, having arrived before dawn. After some years as a steward he was elected in 1993, and felt his red MCC membership pass was "more important than a passport. I once used it at a Guyana bank." He often watched the practice days, too, and his charm rubbed off on the players. "I always enjoyed my chats with him," said Curtly Ambrose; Stuart Broad and Bishan Bedi were among many others to pay tribute.

Dressed for the occasion: Keith van Anderson at Lord's.

VIJAY KUMAR, VIJAYALAPUR SESHADRI, who died on May 31, aged 73, was part of the first Karnataka side to win the Ranji Trophy, in 1973-74. He took a career-best four for nine in the final with his seamers, including Rajasthan's captain Hanumant Singh for 83, but was much better known as an attacking opening batsman – he also hit 66 in that final – who paved the way for the likes of Gundappa Viswanath and Brijesh Patel. Vijay Kumar made four first-class centuries, the highest 158 against Kerala in 1969-70. Three seasons later, he scored 94 in both innings against Rajasthan. He had made his first-class debut for Mysore (as Karnataka were then called) in the same game as Viswanath, who remembered: "I spent a lot of time with him, as I would go to his house after practice for almost five years. He was a very good cricketer, and I loved watching him drive the ball."

WADHWANEY, KISHIN ROCHIRAM, who died on October 24, aged 90, was the former sports editor (and aviation correspondent) of *The Indian Express*. He wrote more than 30 books, many on cricket, including biographies of Lala Amarnath, Sunil Gavaskar and the Nawab of Pataudi. Born in Karachi, he settled in Lucknow after Partition, and was a useful club cricketer: he claimed to have twice been chosen to play for Uttar Pradesh, only for his selection to be vetoed by the Maharajkumar of Vizianagram. Wadhwaney was the father-in-law of Indian Test wicketkeeper Vijay Dahiya.

WALES, PETER JOHN, who died on October 3, 2018, aged 89, played just one first-class match for Sussex in 1951 – against Hampshire at Worthing – but made it count: he had match figures of 13–9–13–5 with his seamers and, after opening the batting in both innings, was at the crease when Sussex completed a ten-wicket victory. But he was training to be an accountant, and could not agree terms with Sussex, who were short of money. He played club cricket for Brighton & Hove, and fitted in football and table tennis, too. Members of the Sussex Cricket Society recalled an evening when Wales and wicketkeeper Rupert Webb were the guest speakers; the one-match wonder spoke for well over an hour, leaving Webb about five minutes for the highlights of his own 256-game career.

WETTIMUNY, MITHRA DE SILVA, who died on January 20, aged 67, was a member of a famous Sri Lankan cricketing family: brother Sunil played in the first World Cup, in 1975, and Sidath, another brother, scored the country's first Test century. Mithra did not hit their heights, but did play two Tests, in New Zealand in 1982-83, opening with Sidath in both, before returning to his accountancy practice. His entire first-class career

BROTHERS OPENING THE BATTING IN A TEST

E. M. and W. G. Grace	England v Australia at The Oval	1880
Hanif and Sadiq Mohammad . .	Pakistan v New Zealand at Karachi	1969-70
M. D. and S. Wettimuny . . .	**Sri Lanka v NZ at Christchurch and Wellington**	**1982-83**
G. and P. N. Kirsten†	South Africa v England at The Oval	1994

† *Half-brothers.*

---

encompassed nine matches in four countries – Zimbabwe, Sri Lanka, Australia and New Zealand – in the space of 127 days; he never bettered his 55 on debut at Bulawayo in November 1982. A dozen years earlier, Wettimuny had scored 102 while skippering a Ceylon Schools side (containing future Test captains Bandula Warnapura and Duleep Mendis) against India Schools at Eden Gardens in Calcutta.

WILLIAMS, LORD (Charles Cuthbert Powell), CBE, PC, who died on December 30, aged 86, was a high-powered banker, chairman of the Prices Commission, and later an improbably grand Labour peer, having been recommended by fellow cricket-lover Roy Hattersley. He also wrote several books, including biographies of Harold Macmillan, General de Gaulle, Konrad Adenauer – and Don Bradman. Williams's 1996 volume, subtitled *An Australian Hero*, was a lively attempt to place Bradman at the heart of Australia's rise to maturity as a nation, and also dissected his unusual batting technique. Later, Williams wrote *Gentlemen and Players: The Death of Amateurism in Cricket*, which described – with a pinch of regret – the events which led to the abolition of the amateur in 1963. He was well qualified to tackle this subject: he had played for the Gentlemen in 1956, although he managed just one run in two innings.

Williams was a solid batsman, who scored four centuries for Oxford University, two in 1954, the second of his three years as a Blue. Against Lancashire, he put on 173 with his captain, Colin Cowdrey, the highest partnership in first-class cricket between two future members of the House of Lords. Williams succeeded Cowdrey in 1955, and was followed in 1956 by another England captain, M. J. K. Smith, who remembered an "orthodox batsman – very much one of the leading players at Oxford". In the 1955 Varsity Match, they put on 109 in 90 minutes as Oxford chased a tall target; when Smith was out, Williams battened down the hatches with 47 not out. In his history of the matches, George Chesterton summed up: "Like Leonidas against the Persians, the Oxford captain barred the way."

There were also intermittent appearances for Essex, with another century – during a stand of 200 with Doug Insole – against Leicestershire in 1955. Had Williams been able to devote himself to county cricket, thought the Essex historian David Lemmon, "he would have been a batsman of real quality. As it was, he was of immense value whenever available." Geoff Smith, who played alongside him at Essex, recalled "a nice man, although I suffered when he came down from Oxford, as one of us youngsters in the side had to drop out. That happened quite often in those days, in every county. But Charles was good enough for you to think: 'That's fair enough, he's a good player.'"

WILLIS, ROBERT GEORGE DYLAN, MBE, died on December 4, aged 70. On July 11, 1981, five days before the start of the Headingley Test, Bob Willis was watching his Warwickshire team-mates at The Oval when a call came through from the chairman of selectors, Alec Bedser. It was bad news. He was being left out of the side that would be captained by the returning Mike Brearley. Willis had ended the Lord's Test earlier that week with a chest infection, and had not played since. The selectors thought him a risk.

The next few minutes were among the most important of Willis's career. He persuaded Bedser he had recovered, and would play next day in the Sunday League to prove it. When the squad was announced, Mike Hendrick, part of the original 12, had been left out. Willis was in. He had bowled poorly at Lord's – including 24 no-balls in Australia's first innings

Raw pace: Bob Willis hits Iqbal Qasim at Edgbaston, 1978. Three years later, at Headingley, the unseen Willis uproots Ray Bright's middle stump, bringing England's most famous Test victory.

– and some in the media thought that, at 32, and after knee surgery, he was a spent force. And he was included at Headingley at the last moment, ahead of John Emburey, when Brearley opted for an all-seam attack. First-innings figures of 30–8–72–0 hardly endorsed the judgment.

Back at the team hotel on the Monday evening, after Ian Botham's bravura innings had given England slim hope, Brearley, Botham and Graham Gooch urged Willis to run in with more intent, focus on line not length, and forget about no-balls. "At that point in his career, he was definitely concerned he had lost some of his potency," said Brearley. "He wondered if he should cut his pace, and concentrate on accuracy. It was fortunate for him that he had that shit-or-bust spell at Headingley."

After five fruitless overs up the hill, Willis persuaded Brearley to give him a chance from the Kirkstall Lane End, with the wind at his back. "Normally he didn't like bowling at that end, because of the slope and the problems with no-balls," said Chris Old. Half an hour before lunch, and with Australia cruising at 48 for one in pursuit of 130, Willis clicked: batsmen began flinching like boxers on the ropes. He took three wickets before the break, and five more on a frenzied afternoon. The denouement – one of the most replayed moments in British sport – came when he plucked out Ray Bright's middle stump with a yorker. Figures of eight for 43 would always be attached to his name.

Throughout, Willis remained in a trance-like state, barely celebrating or acknowledging team-mates. "As the wickets went down, everyone congregated, but he was looking through people," said Old. "He didn't want anyone around him – he just wanted to get on with the job." After bowling Bright, he raised his arms triumphantly, circled as if unsure where to go, then turned and sprinted for the dressing-room through the crowd. Still stony-faced in a TV interview with Peter West, he attacked the media: "The standard of journalism in this country has gone down the nick completely." He later regretted that – "foolish, petulant, immature," he said – but the significance of his achievement sank in only during his exhausted journey back down the M1, when radio bulletins led on the cricket.

A turning point had come in 1977, days after the Centenary Test, when Willis attended a barbecue at the Sydney home of the hypnotherapist Arthur Jackson. In conversation with England captain Tony Greig, Willis expressed admiration for Dennis Lillee. "You should be able to bowl like that, too," snapped Greig. "But you're always knackered after five overs." Coming after a successful tour of India, Willis took umbrage, but he knew Greig's remarks contained a grain of truth. Jackson recommended hypnosis to improve his fragile mental state, and the theories of Ernst van Aaken, pioneer of the concept of slow distance running to improve stamina. Willis instantly saw the benefits of hypnosis. And, after initial scepticism, he reaped the rewards of van Aaken's regime on his battle-scarred knees.

The effect was immediate. In the 1977 Ashes, he took 27 wickets at 19, as England won 3–0. The following summer, against Pakistan and New Zealand, there were 25 more, then 20 in the Ashes defence of 1978-79, and 29 in 1981. Through hard work, and frequently defying pain, he became one of the world's leading strike bowlers.

Willis may have lacked the aesthetic of Harold Larwood, the theatricality of Fred Trueman, or the guile of James Anderson, but he was among England's fast-bowling greats. In his era, he lost nothing in hostility to Lillee, Jeff Thomson or the West Indians. Standing 6ft 6in, he charged in off a long, curving run, and delivered in a tangle of hair and arms, which flapped behind him, earning the nickname "Goose". He had an open-chested action. "If it was swinging, he would swing it in; if it was seaming, he would move it away," said Brearley. He was not engrossed in mechanics, but could be analytical. "He would talk about length and direction. He would ask if he looked all right, and talk to the wicketkeeper about how the ball was hitting the gloves."

The son of a journalist, Willis was born in Sunderland, but left Wearside aged six weeks when work took his father to Manchester. He spent five years there, long enough to fall under cricket's spell after an uncle took him and his brother, David, to the 1953 Ashes Test at Old Trafford. The family next moved to Stoke d'Abernon, near Guildford, when Willis senior took up a post with the BBC. To the appreciation of Surrey commuters, Bob and David would post the latest Test score on a blackboard in their window. He attended the Royal Grammar School, Guildford, and played for the Under-15s two years early. Winter afternoons on the rugby field imbued a lifelong dislike of the game, but he enjoyed football, and later kept goal for Corinthian-Casuals.

He was a truculent teenager, and an infatuation with Bob Dylan did not endear him to the school staff; at the height of his obsession, he added Dylan as a middle name. Despite poor O-levels, he was determined to go to university, but his A-levels also fell short. Cricket was another matter. By 16, he was 6ft 4in, and coaches encouraged him to bowl fast. He went on a tour of Pakistan with Surrey and Middlesex Young Cricketers, and spent the rest of the winter manning a petrol pump.

Ignoring fierce parental opposition, he accepted a summer trial with Surrey in 1969, but was unprepared for the rigours of professional cricket, and contemplated giving up. Things improved, however, and he made his first-class debut against Scotland in August. He took his first five-for at Trent Bridge, although Garry Sobers spoiled his figures. And, on the rest day of a Championship match against Hampshire, he may have been the only county cricketer to watch Dylan's Isle of Wight festival performance.

In 1970, he picked up 28 Championship wickets in 11 matches. When Alan Ward was injured early on that winter's Ashes tour, captain Ray Illingworth wanted someone to match his pace. He had never seen Willis, but John Edrich endorsed him, and he was soon on the plane. When Ken Shuttleworth was injured before the Fourth Test at Sydney, the gangly 21-year-old Willis – a "two-iron with ears", according to Bill O'Reilly – made his debut.

He played in four Tests, plus another in New Zealand, and returned home with 14 wickets at 28, plus an unlikely reputation as a sharp close-to-the-wicket fielder. But little in Willis's career was straightforward. Instead of a hero's welcome at The Oval, he found Surrey unwilling to award his county cap. Although he contributed 31 wickets to their Championship triumph in 1971, he resolved to leave; Geoff Arnold and Robin Jackman were ahead in the pecking order, and the Oval wickets discouragingly flat. Lancashire and Leicestershire were interested, but Warwickshire doubled his money. The TCCB, keen to discourage a transfer market, suspended him for two months, but he still took eight for 44 (including a hat-trick) against Derbyshire, and won a second consecutive Championship.

The selectors, meanwhile, appeared to have forgotten him: Willis did not play another Test until August 1973. He earned a place in Mike Denness's side for the tour of the

Tearaway: Bob Willis at Old Trafford, 1977.

Caribbean, but enjoyed little success, and appeared in only two home Tests in 1974. Then John Snow was omitted from the 1974-75 Ashes, leaving Willis as the main retaliatory weapon to Lillee and Thomson. He took 15 wickets in the first three Tests, before his knees gave in. Old recalled: "He would bowl an opening spell, but if I was twelfth man I knew I'd be coming on the field at some stage for Bob." Ian Chappell said Willis was a force to be reckoned with before lunch, but there for the taking after tea.

In 1975, he submitted to surgery on both knees, and a long rehabilitation, spending the winter on the dole, bleakly contemplating his future. He played only sporadically in 1976, though a six-for in a tour match at Edgbaston meant a recall against West Indies, and he took eight wickets on his return at Headingley. Conventional wisdom was that fast bowlers were excess baggage in India, but Willis prospered under Greig's ebullient leadership in 1976-77, and bowled superbly in a 3–1 win. That did not prevent Greig's rebuke in Sydney, and Willis was even better as England regained the Ashes. After long deliberation, he turned down Kerry Packer – and soon became a vocal critic of World Series Cricket.

He was a Wisden Cricketer of the Year in 1978. That summer, he attracted criticism for hitting Pakistan tailender Iqbal Qasim in the mouth with a round-the-wicket bouncer at Edgbaston. Willis was unrepentant: Qasim had been sent in at No. 3 as a nightwatchman, and been batting for 45 minutes that morning. Willis's only regret was going back to his mark without checking on his wellbeing.

Surprisingly, in view of his Test commitments, he was appointed Warwickshire captain in 1980. Despite a sharp cricket brain, he had never been regarded as leadership material. Warwickshire immediately won the Sunday League, but struggled in the Championship, and in 1981 finished bottom. Willis took 13 wickets in seven games. "It was of limited comfort to suffering supporters that he was putting on match-winning performances against Australia," huffed *Wisden*. There was grumbling among the Warwickshire members. Once, when he brought himself on, a spectator called out: "Bowler's name?"

Early in the 1982 season, after the sacking of Keith Fletcher as England captain, Willis received a call from chairman of selectors Peter May, asking him to take over. The team had been denuded by suspensions following the rebel tour of South Africa – a team Willis had turned down the chance to lead. The England job was another matter: "It represented the pinnacle of all my years in the game."

England beat India and Pakistan at home (Willis missed the only Test defeat), but lost in Australia that winter, when he paid the price for bowling first at Adelaide. He felt let down by some senior players, and dismayed by the lack of application among the youngsters. England reached the semi-finals of the 1983 World Cup, and beat New Zealand 3–1, but a few months later they lost a series to them for the first time, and were 1–0 down in Pakistan when Willis was incapacitated by illness. It was the end of his captaincy, after 18 Tests, seven wins and five defeats. He was keen to play on against West Indies in 1984, despite not having fully recovered from the virus picked up in Pakistan. After being

---

MOST TEST WICKETS AS ENGLAND CAPTAIN

		M	Avge	Span
77	R. G. D. Willis	18	21.59	**1982 to 1983-84**
51	R. Illingworth	31	35.96	1969 to 1973
42	G. O. B. Allen	11	25.26	1936 to 1947-48
37	J. W. H. T. Douglas	18	30.91	1911-12 to 1924
35	I. T. Botham	12	33.08	1980 to 1981
34	A. Flintoff	11	34.44	2005-06 to 2006-07
33	E. R. Dexter	30	41.69	1961-62 to 1964
30	F. R. Brown	15	30.76	1949 to 1951
27	A. E. R. Gilligan	9	31.14	1924 to 1924-25
24	A. W. Greig	14	42.37	1975 to 1976-77

---

thrashed around Headingley by Michael Holding in the Third Test, he withdrew from the Fourth. Within weeks, he had announced his retirement, after feeling ill throughout Warwickshire's Benson and Hedges Cup final defeat by Lancashire. He had 325 Test wickets at 25; at that point, only Lillee had more.

Willis did broadcasting work for the BBC, quickly realising he could not hold back from criticising old team-mates, and was an early signing for Sky, Rupert Murdoch's new satellite venture. He became one of their key commentators, though his monotone attracted criticism: Tim de Lisle likened it to the drone of a lawnmower. But colleague Charles Colvile was kinder: "People overlooked the fact that he was a fine wordsmith."

After Sky acquired exclusive rights to England's home Tests in 2006, Willis moved to an early-evening discussion programme. Hosted by Colvile, "The Verdict" (later "The Debate") proved a natural home for his opinions, sometimes hammed in, rarely unfair. "When we got to the studio, he knew what he was going to say, and he would rehearse it," said Colvile. "But I didn't want him to tell me. I wanted to react to it." Willis's "Well, Charles" preamble became a catchphrase. "He was as professional about his broadcasting as he had been about his fast bowling," said Colvile.

Willis's death, after several years of suffering with cancer, had an impact beyond the cricket community – the *Daily Mail* had six pages of coverage – and underlined the place of Headingley '81 in the national consciousness. As Willis once said: "The sight of Ray Bright's middle stump going over will probably be the last memory I take to my grave."

WILLSON, RONALD HENRY, who died on January 3, 2017, aged 83, was an all-rounder from a Romany background who made his debut for Sussex's Second XI aged 15, in 1949. He went on to play 19 matches for the first team, following three successive ducks with 113 not out – his only century – in what turned out to be his last game for them, against Somerset in a friendly at Hove in 1957. He then moved to southern Africa, and appeared three times for Rhodesia in 1961-62, twice dismissing Everton Weekes (playing for an International XI) with his slow left-armers, which had claimed only one previous first-class wicket. He had an eventful private life, outliving his fourth wife; one son – who thought Willson was his older brother – met him only twice.

WITHERDEN, EDWIN GEORGE, died on May 6, five days after his 97th birthday. Ted Witherden was 31 in the summer of 1953 but, in only his fourth Championship match, he gave a glimpse of what might have been. With Peter Loader running riot for Surrey at Blackheath, Witherden top-scored with 26 not out in Kent's measly first-innings 63. He then batted 310 minutes for an unbeaten 125 to save the game. His next match brought 51 against Warwickshire at Maidstone; the following day, still at Mote Park, he took a century off Worcestershire. "Witherden is not a stylist, but he can hit the ball, hit it true and place it perfectly without apparent effort," wrote Gordon Ross in *The Sunday Times*. It was the end of Witherden's brief purple patch, but he made 22 appearances in 1954, and 40 in all, before moving into Minor Counties cricket with Norfolk in 1956. There he was a prolific scorer, and took useful wickets with his off-breaks until the early 1960s, when he became the professional at Bishop's Stortford College. The son of a Sandwich policeman, Witherden initially had an unsuccessful trial with Kent in the 1930s. During the war, he served first on the home front – one of his duties was guarding Churchill at Chartwell – before seeing active service in the Far East. He had another Kent trial in 1947, but was judged too old, though he performed so well in isolated appearances for the Second XI that he was offered a place on the staff in 1951. His granddaughters Becky and Lucy have both played for Hertfordshire.

YARDLEY, BRUCE, who died on March 27, aged 71, was a late bloomer who made his Test debut at 30, one of several tried as replacements for the players signed by Kerry Packer for World Series Cricket. Unlike many of the newcomers, Yardley prospered after peace was brokered, and was Australia's International Cricketer of the Year in 1981-82. He bowled off-breaks with an unusual grip from a longish run, a relic of his days as a seamer. "He had been a good baseball pitcher," remembered former team-mate John Inverarity. "He developed a very effective 'drop ball' by placing it between his index and middle fingers, and spinning it hard. By imparting high revs he gained drop, bounce and turn." His brisk deliveries often jumped at unsuspecting batsmen, and he finished with 126 wickets in 33 Tests.

Yardley was also an attacking batsman, whose antics enraged the West Indians in Bridgetown in 1977-78, and earned a beamer from the usually placid Joel Garner. Yardley cut the next ball for six, which worried his batting partner even more. "Take it easy, mate," said Steve Rixon. "You'll get us all killed!" But Yardley careered on, reaching his half-century with another six, from just 29 balls – the fastest in Tests by an Australian until David Warner got there in 23 in January 2017 – and eventually perished for a Test-best 74. His team-mates remained in awe. "I just blocked and blocked," remembered last man Jim Higgs, "and he was trying to hit Colin Croft over cover."

To complete the set, Yardley was an athletic close fielder, especially in the gully, where he took a screamer off a Gordon Greenidge square-drive at Sydney in 1981-82. His personality led to the nickname "Roo": he could not be tied down for long. The historian Warwick Franks summed up: "In an era when Australian cricketers seemed to regard Test cricket as trench warfare with a reduced ration of mustard gas, he managed to convey a sense of enjoying the game with relish."

Yardley started with the Midland-Guildford club in Perth, where the first-team captain was the uncompromising Englishman Tony Lock. He made his debut for Western Australia in

MOST TEST WICKETS WITHOUT ANY IN ENGLAND

		T	*Runs*	*5I*	*10M*	*Avge*	*Debut*
208	S. C. G. MacGill (Australia)	44	6,038	12	2	29.02	1997-98
156	M. D. K. Perera (Sri Lanka)	41	5,512	8	2	35.33	2013-14
131	M. Dillon (West Indies)	38	4,398	2	0	33.57	1996-97
126	**B. Yardley (Australia)**	**33**	**3,986**	**6**	**1**	**31.63**	**1977-78**
113	B. A. Reid (Australia)	27	2,784	5	2	24.63	1985-86
113	P. P. Ojha (India)	24	3,420	7	1	30.26	2009-10
106	Taijul Islam (Bangladesh)	27	3,475	7	1	32.78	2014-15
102	N. S. Yadav (India)	35	3,580	3	0	35.09	1979-80
100	I. K. Pathan (India)	29	3,226	7	2	32.26	2003-04
100	N. Boje (South Africa)	43	4,265	3	0	42.65	1999-2000

Untiedownable: Bruce Yardley bowls against England in the Third Test at Adelaide, 1982-83.

1966-67, taking one wicket in an innings victory, but did not feature for another four years. Eventually his club coach Keith Slater, a former Test player, suggested he try off-spin. It worked. In 1977-78, as the selectors cast around in the wake of the Packer signings, Yardley was called up after taking seven for 44 – which remained a career-best – for WA against South Australia at Adelaide. His Test debut, also at Adelaide, was the final act of an exciting series against India. Despite injuring a finger in the nets just before the start, Yardley took four second-innings wickets, including top-scorers Mohinder Amarnath and Dilip Vengsarkar, and made 48 runs in a match Australia won by 47, to pinch the series 3–2.

It earned him a trip to the West Indies, where he took 41 wickets, 15 in the Tests. He was, out of the blue, called for throwing in a tour game against Jamaica by Douglas Sang Hue, West Indies' leading umpire but a World Series Cricket employee; the tourists, led by the veteran Bob Simpson, suspected a conspiracy, as they had reservations about the legality of a couple of the West Indian bowlers. Yardley's action was never queried again, but some wondered whether lingering doubts might have been behind his omission from the 1981 Ashes tour. However, he had also lost form, playing only two of the six Tests in the preceding Australian summer.

Yardley bounced back in 1981-82. He took seven for 187 from a marathon 66 overs as Pakistan reached 500 at the MCG, then improved his Test-best with seven for 98 – and ten in the match – against West Indies at Sydney a few weeks later. In all, he collected 38 wickets at 22 that season, to earn his player of the year award. The following summer he took 22 wickets as the Ashes were won, but announced his retirement shortly after being overlooked for the 1983 World Cup in England (oddly, for such an attacking player, he won only seven one-day caps). Yardley put his retirement down to his age – 36 – but made a surprise return to first-class cricket seven seasons later, playing five matches for WA, before bowing out for good when he was unavailable because of a prearranged TV commentary stint. Then came a coaching career: Yardley took charge of Sri Lanka for a while, his work interrupted by an operation in 1997 to remove his left eye, which had a cancerous growth behind it. He seemed to recover, but later faced further problems with cancer.

"He had the ability to settle everyone down in a pressure situation," remembered team-mate Geoff Marsh. "He was a very funny man, and had a real passion for the game."

YORK, STUART ERNEST, who died on August 23, aged 80, played for Buckinghamshire throughout the 1970s, and was their president at the time of his death. A batsman from High Wycombe CC, in June 1975 he made a plucky 73 not out in a Gillette Cup match at Lord's against a Middlesex attack boasting six Test players, and a month later hit an undefeated 118 against Hertfordshire.

ZULFIQAR ALI BOKHARI, SYED, who died on January 4, aged 85, was chairman of the Pakistan Cricket Board from 1995 to 1998, his tenure including the 1996 World Cup on the subcontinent. Ehsan Mani, the current chairman, said: "He was a thorough gentleman and a solid administrator, who cared about cricket and loved it from the heart."

The obituaries section includes those who died, or whose deaths were notified, in 2019. Wisden always welcomes information about those who might be included: please send details to almanack@wisden.com, or to John Wisden & Co, 13 Old Aylesfield, Golden Pot, Alton, Hampshire GU34 4BY.

BRIEFLY NOTED

The following, whose deaths were noted during 2019, played or umpired in a small number of first/class (fc) matches.

	Died	*Age*	*Main team(s)*
ABRAHAMS, Shukri	3.2.2019	50	Eastern Province B

Bowler on the fringe of Eastern Province's side in the 1980s, later a coach; killed in car accident.

| **ALTAF HUSSAIN** | 27.2.2019 | 75 | East Pakistan |

Medium-pacer who took six wickets in six fc matches before Bangladesh gained independence.

| **BLUETT**, John Douglas Jeremy | 23.8.2019 | 89 | Kent |

Batsman from Bromley CC: two fc matches in 1950, after two hundreds for the Second XI.

| **CHOWDHURY**, Bikash Kumar | 23.11.2019 | 81 | Bengal |

Five fc matches: 90 on debut against Assam on New Year's Eve, 1959.

| **D'ARCY-EVANS**, Eyre James | 2.9.2018 | 83 | Umpire |

Stood in 14 men's fc matches, and one women's Test (1976-77), all in Perth.

| **DOBLE**, Alan William | 15.12.2019 | 76 | Victoria |

Tall, quick left-armer from North Melbourne; fell away after a promising start in 1964-65.

| **EDWARDS**, Daniel Rudolph Valentine ("Franklyn") | 7.6.2019 | 81 | Leeward Islands |

Batsman from Montserrat: three fc matches, 52 against 1961-62 Indian tourists.

| **HARRY**, Rex Alexander | 15.4.2019 | 82 | Victoria |

North Melbourne leg-spinner: one fc match in 1961-62, taking the final wicket to beat Tasmania.

| **HENDERSON**, John Duncan | 26.1.2019 | 90 | Central Districts |

Seamer who played three fc matches in 1960-61.

| **KARHADKAR**, Vilas Vasudev | 13.3.2019 | 60 | Umpire |

Baroda official who stood in eight fc matches in India.

| **KING**, Horace Arlington | 15.11.2016 | 87 | Barbados |

Slow left-armer who took four wickets in three fc matches between 1948-49 and 1952-53.

| **KUKRETI**, Rahul | 12.8.2019 | 43 | United States |

Wicketkeeper who emigrated from India to Texas, and played five times for the USA.

| **KURUPPU**, Aubrey | 11.10.2019 | 74 | Ceylon |

Batsman who played two fc matches; later secretary of the Kandy District Cricket Association.

| **McARLEY**, Vernon Aubrey Clinton | 4.7.2019 | 95 | Otago |

Seamer: six fc matches, with 31–11–41–3 in the last, against Canterbury in 1957-58.

| **MORGAN**, Howard William | 16.3.2019 | 87 | Glamorgan |

Off-spinner from Maesteg: two fc matches in 1958.

| **RAMAN**, G. K. | 15.9.2019 | 89 | Umpire |

Madras official who stood in 23 fc matches, and a women's Test against Australia in 1983-84.

RHODES, Brian Leslie   28.6.2019   68   New South Wales
Opened the bowling for Western Suburbs club in Sydney aged 15; one fc match in 1971-72.

ROBERTS, John Francis Esdale   2.12.2019   86   Lancashire
Seamer from Kearsley, near Bolton: two fc matches in 1957, without taking a wicket.

ROCK, Kingsley   23.10.2019   81   Leeward Islands
Batsman from Montserrat who played two fc matches, one against the 1959-60 England tourists.

RODWELL, Gary   29.6.2019   60   Griqualand West
Prominent local sportsman: five fc matches in 1980-81.

SYME, Ian Alexander Hastie   26.12.2018   88   Scotland
Stirling County seamer who played one fc match in 1950, against Ireland.

WAINWRIGHT, Thomas Dodsworth ("Dod")   28.5.2019   78   Col. L. C. Stevens' XI
One fc match v Cambridge in 1961, not long after leaving Eastbourne College: later lived in the USA.

A LIFE IN NUMBERS

	Runs	Avge	Wkts	Avge		Runs	Avge	Wkts	Avge
Abdul Qadir	3,740	18.33	960	23.24	Longmore, A. N. M.	28	9.33	–	–
Abid Butt	8	8.00	1	37.00	Luthra, S.	1,014	16.35	262	16.92
Achrekar, R. V.	28	14.00	–	–	McDonald, I. H.	843	16.86	0	–
Akhtar Sarfraz	5,720	36.43	4	58.50	McFarlane, L. L.	127	5.77	102	40.58
Apte, M. L.	3,336	38.79	4	24.25	**Mann, A. L.**	2,544	24.22	200	34.54
Arnott, D. B.	458	14.77	–	–	**Miller, R. S.**	231	25.66	14	45.35
Beck, G. E.	72	12.00	–	–	Mitra, S.	3,058	50.13	15	70.20
Blair, W. L.	3,698	26.04	0	–	Morton, W.	57	5.70	29	34.58
Bond, J. D.	12,125	25.90	0	–	**Moss, A. E.**	1,671	6.96	1,301	20.78
Brooker, M. E. W.	43	3.30	25	45.96	Mottram, T. J.	95	5.58	111	24.11
Butcher, B. F.	11,628	49.90	40	30.42	Nash, A. M.	7,129	17.73	993	25.87
Causby, J. P.	3,067	28.93	0	–	Notley, B.	0	0.00	1	90.00
Chandrasekhar, V. B.	4,999	43.09	0	–	**Nurse, S. M.**	9,489	43.93	12	32.41
Cooper, L. D.	462	14.00	–	–	Parker, J. F.	1,480	30.20	0	–
de Costa, K. M. A.	230	16.42	–	–	Pearson, L. R.	1,348	23.64	1	70.00
de Lange, C. D.	2,888	22.92	183	38.39	Peters, N. H.	101	10.10	40	31.15
Dharmalingam, P. K.	1,132	28.30	44	20.50	Pinnock, R. A.	2,662	40.33	1	52.00
Downes, L. E.	287	35.87	–	–	**Playle, W. R.**	2,888	21.87	1	94.00
Eagar, M. A.	2,465	25.41	0	–	Preston, K. C.	3,053	10.17	1,160	26.32
Edwards, A. R.	2,370	32.46	14	24.71	Puckerin, L. K.	610	21.78	–	–
Eele, P. J.	612	12.24	–	–	Reade, L. B.	1,106	25.72	0	–
Entwistle, R.	1,612	20.93	–	–	Saleem, S.	1,124	20.43	2	91.50
Falkson, R. J.	948	23.12	66	28.67	**Scarlett, R. O.**	477	23.85	48	34.12
Ferrandi, J. H.	2,012	23.39	–	–	Scott, A. S.	12	6.00	–	–
Ford, D. A.	575	13.37	–	–	**Seymour, M. A.**	569	14.22	111	29.52
Ghodge, R. D.	76	19.00	–	–	Shah, J. N.	141	23.50	0	–
Gill, J. A.	458	16.96	–	–	Shamim Kabir	411	17.86	0	–
Hall, M. J.	430	14.82	–	–	**Shukla, R. C.**	3,798	31.91	295	24.53
Harcharan Singh	2,495	31.18	0	–	Silk, D. R. W.	3,845	29.80	1	240.00
Harris, J. H.	154	11.00	19	32.05	Slade, W. D.	1,482	14.11	32	46.65
Haye, W.	198	24.75	6	47.83	Srinivasan, M.	41	5.85	–	–
Heath, M. B.	569	5.86	527	25.11	Stewart, R. W.	107	4.28	131	23.91
Henderson, D.	131	10.91	34	30.55	Stoddart, P. L. B.	22	11.00	–	–
Héroys, N.	10	5.00	–	–	Sutton, M. A.	144	8.00	47	25.91
Hitchcock, R. E.	12,473	27.84	196	29.82	Taylor, J. R. N.	129	18.42	–	–
Holder, A. H.	251	20.91	26	34.92	Trimble, S. C.	10,282	41.79	3	59.00
Hooker, R. W.	8,222	22.16	490	27.46	Vijay Kumar, V. S.	2,891	31.42	46	36.73
Inder Dev, G.	3,485	29.53	302	21.39	Wales, P. J.	38	38.00	5	2.60
James, L.	10	5.00	–	–	**Wettimuny, M. D.**	268	17.86	0	–
Jones, R.	25	12.50	–	–	Williams, C. C. P.	4,090	28.20	1	61.00
Kamran Alam	2	–	2	14.00	**Willis, R. G. D.**	2,690	14.30	899	24.99
Kleinveldt, J. D.	186	10.33	44	16.63	Willson, R. H.	411	14.17	4	97.50
Kundu, S.	128	8.53	127	16.81	Witherden, E. G.	1,380	22.25	9	41.22
Linehan, A. J.	29	7.25	–	–	**Yardley, B.**	2,738	20.58	344	28.19

Test players are in bold; their career figures can be found on page 1366.

Arnott made 40 catches and 11 stumpings; Blair 66 and two; Cooper 84 and 18; de Costa one and three; Downes 24 and two; Eele 87 and 19; Ferrandi 122 and 32; Ford 122 and 57; Gill 18 and five; Harcharan Singh 59 and 36; Longmore three and none; McDonald 78 and 53; Pinnock 26 and five; Puckerin 19 and one; Srinivasan 12 and 12.

PART THREE

The Men's World Cup

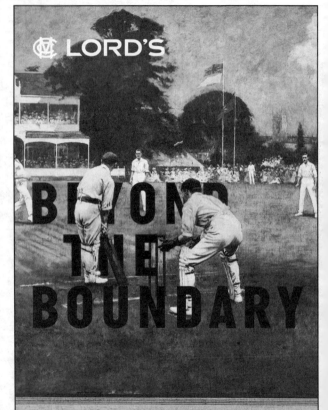

THE ICC MEN'S WORLD CUP IN 2019

REVIEW BY HUGH CHEVALLIER

1 England   2 New Zealand   3= Australia, India

At 7.30 on the evening of July 14, there came a strange sight. As the golden midsummer sun suffused Lord's with a glow fit for fables, a man, dressed all in blue, pummelled his fists into the emerald grass. He was in delirium, his flailing of limbs the only outlet for his ecstasy. Another crazy moment on the craziest of days.

Jofra Archer had just coped with more pressure than most will experience in a lifetime, and tension was finding release. After England made 15 from their super over, he limited New Zealand to 15 from theirs. Tied after 100 overs, tied after two more. But the next separator was clear-cut: New Zealand hit 17 boundaries, England 27. Lord's was on its feet. At the 12th attempt, England had done something many thought would never happen. They had won the World Cup.

Wind back a few minutes, and other heroes peopled the stage. Set 242, England were 227 for eight, and up against it. Four years' graft had boiled down to six balls and 15 runs. Fortunately for them, Ben Stokes was on strike. But he could not trust a new partner to belt the boundaries that were the only path to glory and, with Trent Boult summoning off-side yorkers, he declined two singles: 15 from four.

On this stage, on this pitch, against this bowler, the task was gargantuan. But Boult shortened his length, and Stokes connected. The task, still gargantuan, was six smaller. Then came the luckiest – cruellest – moment. Martin Guptill hurled the ball from deep midwicket as Stokes, aiming to complete a hairy but essential second, dived headlong for safety. The ball pinged off his bat and to the third-man boundary for what *The Times* called "The Miracle of the Deflected Overthrow". After consulting, the umpires awarded six runs. This, it transpired, was more mistake than miracle: by the letter of Law 19.8, it should have been five; Adil Rashid should have been on strike, with four needed from two. But that happened in a parallel universe. In ours, in something that had to be reality though seemed anything but, they needed only three: Stokes snatched two singles, twice losing a partner as he attempted a second, to set up the überdrama of the super over – and Archer raining blows on wormholes.

If the climax of the final justified every superlative, the earlier exchanges had been a little flatter. The last day of the tournament, then, was the 2019 World Cup in microcosm.

In terms of combatants, this was the smallest since 1992, when there were nine. Now there were ten, four down on 2014-15, to allow an all-play-all format. So Full Members Ireland and Zimbabwe dropped out, as did Scotland and the United Arab Emirates. It showed the ICC's true colours: keener on monetising big beasts such as India than evangelising the 50-over game. This structure guaranteed everyone, regardless of performance, at least nine fixtures.

Cloud nine: England are buoyant at their first World Cup success.

The first was in late May, and it confirmed why England were favourites. They cast aside South Africa with a familiar swagger that included a catch by Stokes so absurdly athletic it grabbed front-page headlines. The match also set a couple of hares running. One came from the second ball of the tournament, when Jonny Bairstow fell to Imran Tahir's leg-spin; the other when England passed 300 for the fifth ODI in a row. It was easy to read too much into both.

Spin played a subdued role over the next six weeks. And when the ICC announced their Team of the Tournament, the only slow bowler was Shakib Al Hasan, batting at No. 5 and selected as much for 606 runs at 86 as his 11 wickets. Of the 29 bowlers to take at least ten, only five were spinners. The most was 12, by India's leg-spinner Yuzvendra Chahal; 17 seamers seized 13 or more. Though many pitches took a little turn, it rarely defined the game.

The other hare was what constituted a decent total, a subject that could run and run – if not as far as some predicted. Before the tournament, Virat Kohli, India's talkative captain, joined in a conversation about England targeting 500, a notion more rooted in mind games than reality. More perceptively, he forecast that, as pressure rose, scores would fall.

And then there were the pitches. The 2015 competition had been criticised for first-innings totals of 300-plus and one-sided games. Though the 11 venues used in 2019 all behaved differently, the surfaces, prepared under the ICC's supervision, tended to be slow. England, and the crowds, had to get used to lower totals. Pitches often lost pace even in the course of a game.

For the first three weeks, a captain calling correctly would usually field; in only four of the first 21 completed games did he buck the trend. Bowling at 10.30 on a grey morning, and batsmen knowing the size of the chase – these were tempting options. Not that winning the toss conferred much advantage: in 11 of the 21, it led to defeat.

Tied down: New Zealand, meanwhile, experience a familiar sinking feeling.

Those first three weeks did bring a discernible pattern, however. With one exception – Pakistan's defeat of England – whenever India, Australia, England or New Zealand met any of the other six, they prevailed, often by a comfortable margin. The tournament was acquiring a humdrum feel, alleviated more by individual acts of brilliance than memorable matches. Sheldon Cottrell's boundary dash to dismiss Steve Smith, as Australia dug deep against West Indies, was the equal of Stokes's wondercatch. The weather wasn't helping, either. There were no reserve days until the knockouts – when New Zealand took advantage of their semi-final against India spilling on to a second day – and rain filched four group matches, making it the wettest World Cup. Another talking-point was the Zing bails, which became the batsman's friend. Five times in the first 13 games they lit up, only to stay put. The ICC said they would not be changed, yet oddly the phantom illuminations stopped. But the biggest worry was that the group stage would descend into a series of dead rubbers.

And then, on the summer solstice, **England** met Sri Lanka at Leeds. Even on a comatose strip, a target of 233 would have been within the hosts' ambit 99 times out of 100. But this was the World Cup, Lasith Malinga opened old scars, and confidence evaporated. It was just what the tournament, if not England, needed: one of the breakaway group was wounded, and the pack picked up the scent. Now there was a sense of jeopardy and, though the Fab Four did ultimately progress, getting there turned out to be fun after all.

The Headingley hiccup reinforced a change in strategy. As stakes grew higher, and pitches stodgier, so the value of runs in the bank rose. From the Australia v Bangladesh match at Nottingham on June 20 until the final, captains opted to bat 18 times out of 23, including the last nine. Results bore out the hunch: in those 23 games, the team batting first won 17 times, with one tied.

ICC TEAM OF THE TOURNAMENT

R. G. Sharma (India)	†A. T. Carey (Australia)
J. J. Roy (England)	M. A. Starc (Australia)
*K. S. Williamson (New Zealand)	J. C. Archer (England)
J. E. Root (England)	L. H. Ferguson (New Zealand)
Shakib Al Hasan (Bangladesh)	J. J. Bumrah (India)
B. A. Stokes (England)	T. A. Boult (New Zealand) (*twelfth man*)

That whiff of vulnerability became stronger when England crumbled again, to Australia at Lord's. They had beaten three of the weaker teams batting first, but chasing – so long their modus operandi – was turning out to be a different prospect. Victory over a flimsy West Indies aside, they had lost to Pakistan, Sri Lanka, and now Australia. Still to come were India and New Zealand, the last two unbeaten teams. It looked horribly like a crisis: a slip in either game could – indeed would – have proved terminal.

Having begun the tournament No. 1, England had briefly lost top spot to India after their third defeat. Integral to their wellbeing were the opening pair of Jason Roy and Bairstow. But Roy had pulled a hamstring against West Indies, and the wheels worked loose. Against India, England risked him, though not fully fit. He transformed the team, and they inflicted on India their only defeat of the league stage. They had to do it all over again against New Zealand – and did. First-wicket stands of 160 and 123 stamped authority on the matches after Morgan had twice won the toss.

In three games with stand-in opener James Vince, Bairstow had twice cracked; reunited with Roy, he twice cracked hundreds. It may have helped that he worked himself into a lather after perceived slights from Michael Vaughan: "People were waiting for us to fail," said Bairstow. "They are not willing us on to win… they are waiting for you to get that loss so they can jump on your throat. It's a typical English thing to do, in every sport."

The fielding and bowling clicked too. Chris Woakes woke from a decent tournament to be the epitome of control in the opening games. Against India, he did not concede a run until his 19th ball. Another important cog was Liam Plunkett, blessed with the knack of breaking through in the middle overs. His seven matches ended in victory (or at least not in defeat), and only against Afghanistan did England win without him. To a man, his 11 victims were from the top six. With the pace of Archer and Mark Wood, the leg-spin of Rashid and Stokes's back-up seam, England boasted the competition's most balanced attack. None averaged more than 5.71 an over; no other side could claim such consistency.

England's late surge whooshed them to third, and a semi at Edgbaston. Aaron Finch chose to bat, and faint hearts sagged. Moments later, Australia were 14 for three, never to make a full recovery. England, who had not beaten them at the World Cup since 1992, walloped them into Worcestershire.

Just as they did four years earlier, **Australia** had the leading wicket-taker. On both occasions it was Mitchell Starc, who in 2015 was joint top with fellow left-armer Boult. This time Starc took 27 wickets at 18, and his total from two

BACK FOR MORE

Players who appeared in the 2007 and 2019 World Cups:

	Previous tournaments
M. S. Dhoni (India)	2007, 2011, 2015
C. H. Gayle (West Indies)	2003, 2007, 2011, 2015
S. L. Malinga (Sri Lanka)	2007, 2011, 2015
Mashrafe bin Mortaza (Bangladesh)	2003, 2007, 2015
Mohammad Hafeez (Pakistan).	2007, 2011
E. J. G. Morgan (Ireland and England)	2007, 2011, 2015
Mushfiqur Rahim (Bangladesh).	2007, 2011, 2015
L. E. Plunkett (England)	2007
Shakib Al Hasan (Bangladesh)	2007, 2011, 2015
Shoaib Malik (Pakistan).	2007
Tamim Iqbal (Bangladesh)	2007, 2011, 2015
L. R. P. L. Taylor (New Zealand)	2007, 2011, 2015

K. D. Karthik was in India's squad in 2007 but made his World Cup debut in 2019.

World Cups to 49. His dismissal of Stokes in the group game at Lord's, a vicious, whistling yorker homing in on the stumps, was the ball of the competition. The right-arm pace of Pat Cummins was a useful foil, more parsimonious if less penetrative. Finch used them in short bursts, and the ploy usually brought heads on a plate.

Australia were first to book a place in the knockouts. Their strength, pace apart, lay at the top of the order. In Finch and David Warner, they had an opening pair who could challenge England's. Finch smashed 507, but there was a post-sandpaper caution to Warner, who hit more runs than four years before, at a lower strike-rate: 647 at 89 rather than 345 at 120. While Steve Smith and Usman Khawaja were steady, Glenn Maxwell – the vaunted engine-room – was not, totalling 177 from ten innings. Instead, wicketkeeper-batsman Alex Carey burnished his reputation.

The Australians lost twice in the league stage. Unexpected defeat by a demoralised South Africa in the last game meant their semi would be at Edgbaston, where they were yet to play. The less surprising defeat was at the hands of **India**, who in the group stages looked the most complete team. Their first match was delayed because the Lodha Commission had requested a window of at least 15 days between the IPL final and India's next international. Perhaps the rest did them good. Though they lost Shikhar Dhawan after Cummins broke his thumb, fellow opener Rohit Sharma proved nigh unstoppable. Drop him in haste, repent at leisure: South Africa, Australia, England and Bangladesh gave him a life in single figures, and all but Australia (when he made 57) watched him sail past 100. He hit an unprecedented five centuries, ending as the tournament's highest run-maker, with 648.

MOST WORLD CUP FIVE-FORS

M	BB			M	BB	
3	**18**	**6-28**	**M. A. Starc (Australia)**	2	9	5-32	A. L. F. de Mel (Sri Lanka)
2	6-14	G. J. Gilmour (Australia)		2	27	5-16	Shahid Afridi (Pakistan)
2	6	5-33	V. C. Drakes (West Indies)	2	39	7-15	G. D. McGrath (Australia)
2	**8**	**5-59**	**Mustafizur Rahman (Bang)**				

A HISTORY OF TIE-BREAKERS

Boundary rider

SIMON WILDE

"I don't know how they won it," said Kane Williamson. "What was it, boundaries or something?" He spoke for many. Until the World Cup final unfolded, many observers were ignorant of the super-over clause; fewer still had any idea about boundary countback. Random? Yes. But how do you settle a tied – or washed-out – one-day match? It is a problem with which administrators have long wrestled.

English one-day cricket was a year old when, in 1964, Somerset beat Nottinghamshire in the Gillette Cup by virtue of losing fewer wickets following a tie. In 1981, Derbyshire benefited from the rule to win both the semi-final and the final, each time batting second. But when Leicestershire beat Hampshire in 1995, a secondary tie-breaker was required: score after 30 overs.

Resolving rain-ruined games has proved trickier. Originally, umpires could order a ten-over match, but even that was not possible in the Middlesex–Gloucestershire Benson and Hedges Cup quarter-final of 1983, triggering the toss of a coin. Mike Gatting planned to call heads, but switched with the coin mid-air – and won. Middlesex went on to lift the trophy. After that, a form of countback was introduced: the team whose bowlers had achieved the better strike-rate in the group stage would progress, allowing Gatting's Middlesex to beat Worcestershire in the 1985 B&H quarters.

Then came the bowl-out, probably inspired by the popularity of football's penalty shoot-outs. In the 1991 NatWest Trophy, Derbyshire hit the stumps only once in ten attempts, and lost to Hertfordshire; on the same day, Surrey beat Oxfordshire in the Oval's indoor nets. Derbyshire were better prepared for their 1993 B&H quarter-final, deploying several batsmen as bowlers, and beating Somerset 6–3. At the same stage in 1994, Warwickshire – en route to a treble – beat Kent 5–4. And in 2009, Somerset beat Lancashire 5–1 after a Twenty20 Cup quarter-final at Old Trafford was washed out on three successive days. The bowl-out also resolved ties: in 2005, in another Twenty20 Cup quarter-final, it concluded a contentious encounter when, after 9pm, Tim Murtagh helped Surrey prevail over Warwickshire.

Eventually, international cricket joined the fun. After the epic World Cup semi-final tie of 1999, Australia pipped South Africa by the gossamer-fine virtue of finishing higher in the Super Six table – on net run-rate. The first bowl-out came at Auckland in February 2006, when New Zealand beat West Indies in a T20 game.

The super over was sanctioned by the ICC in 2008, and first used that year in a T20 international, again at Auckland, where West Indies scored a world-record 25, all by Chris Gayle. New Zealand lost two more super overs during the World T20 in 2012-13. Both semi-finals of the Friends Life t20 in 2011 went to super overs. And six of England's World Cup winners featured in their only previous super over, in Sharjah in 2015-16, when Chris Jordan restricted Pakistan to three runs.

Boundary countback was first used to settle a T20 match in the Caribbean in 2010, when sixes were the determining factor, and was available at the 2011 World Cup and for the 2015 World Cup final.

As if New Zealand hadn't suffered enough, in October the ICC abolished the countback rule. While group games at global events could now include a super over, the game would be tied if the super over finished level. For knockout matches, the super over would now be repeated until it proved decisive – a proposal several pundits suggested after the 2019 final. In all, ten games have been decided by some form of boundary countback:

†Australia beat England at Basseterre (Women's World Twenty20)	2010
†Barbados beat Combined Campuses & Colleges at Bridgetown (Caribbean T20)	2010
Otago Volts beat Lions at Jaipur (Champions League)	2013-14
Rajasthan Royals beat Kolkata Knight Riders at Abu Dhabi (IPL)	2013-14
Lions beat Knights at Potchefstroom (Ram Slam Challenge)	2014-15
Sydney Thunder beat Sydney Sixers at Sydney (Women's Big Bash)	2016-17
Melbourne Stars beat Melbourne Renegades at Melbourne (Women's Big Bash)	2017-18
Colombo District beat Kandy District at Colombo (RPS) (Super Four Provincial T20)	2018
Gujarat beat Rajasthan at Surat (Syed Mushtaq Ali Trophy)	2018-19
England beat New Zealand at Lord's (World Cup final)	2019

†   *Decided on sixes; Australia hit the only one of the match, while Barbados won 10–8.*

Well armed: Mitchell Starc, the most successful bowler at consecutive World Cups.

Kohli had hit 19 ODI centuries since the previous World Cup, so his was an odd string of scores, five times reaching 66, never passing 82. His captaincy was little tested while India kept winning, which suggested he wasn't doing a bad job. But he waxed prickly after the England defeat, carping about a short boundary, as if it affected one team more than the other. And selection issues dogged him and coach Ravi Shastri. They struggled to find a settled combination at Nos 4 and 5, positions that did not contribute a half-century. And the repeated exclusion of Ravindra Jadeja – peerless in the field, handy with bat or ball – remained one of life's unsolved mysteries, as impenetrable as the Bermuda Triangle or Voynich Manuscript.

The captain, the coach and the nation appeared to retain faith in M. S. Dhoni, but at 38 he was a waning force. In both defeats, he was culpable. Against England, his 31-ball 42 sounded brisk, though he never took the game by the scruff; against New Zealand in the semi, his 72-ball 50 was shown up by Jadeja, in his second game, who powered 77 off 59. Dhoni's strike-rate of 87 was 15 lower than in 2015; his 2019 strike-rate of 45 against slow bowling was the lowest of any player to face at least 50 balls of spin.

Jasprit Bumrah spearheaded the attack, with Kohli deploying him as Finch did Starc, in bursts. In a tournament marked by variation as much as pace, disguise as much as movement, Bumrah was masterful: slower-ball bouncers, fast-ball bouncers, knuckle balls, scrambled seams, full balls outside off, inswinging yorkers, off-cutters, leg-cutters… Underlying them all was finesse.

LEADING RUN-SCORER AT EACH WORLD CUP

		M	I	NO	Runs	HS	100	Avge	SR
1975	G. M. Turner (NZ)..	4	4	2	333	171*	1	166.50	68.51
1979	C. G. Greenidge (WI)	4	4	1	253	106*	1	84.33	62.31
1983	D. I. Gower (E)	7	7	2	384	130	1	76.80	84.95
1987-88	G. A. Gooch (E)....	8	8	0	471	115	1	58.87	70.29
1991-92	M. D. Crowe (NZ)..	9	9	5	456	100*	1	114.00	90.65
1995-96	S. R. Tendulkar (I)..	7	7	1	523	137	2	87.16	85.87
1999	R. Dravid (I)......	8	8	1	461	145	2	65.85	85.52
2002-03	S. R. Tendulkar (I)..	11	11	0	673	152	1	61.18	89.25
2006-07	M. L. Hayden (A)..	11	10	1	659	158	3	73.22	101.07
2010-11	T. M. Dilshan (SL) ..	9	9	1	500	144	2	62.50	90.74
2014-15	M. J. Guptill (NZ) ..	9	9	1	547	237*	2	68.37	104.58
2019	**R. G. Sharma (I)...**	**9**	**9**	**1**	**648**	**140**	**5**	**81.00**	**98.33**

He clogged up the start, middle and end of an innings and, while he fetched 18 wickets, an economy-rate of just 4.41 also bought them for others. Mohammed Shami could thank Bumrah for many of his 14.

If the shock of the shebang was **New Zealand** shoving India aside in the first semi-final, perhaps it shouldn't have been. They are perennial World Cup overachievers, and in the phlegmatic Kane Williamson had the Player of the Tournament, the holist-in-chief who extracted more from his team than seemed possible. But in the group stage they peaked early, flirted with elimination after losing their last three, and progressed, intriguingly, courtesy of a tie-breaker that favoured net run-rate over head-to-head results. It was to Williamson's credit that, with a little help from a sticky Old Trafford pitch, he roused his side against India.

Few sportsmen could have faced the horror of going undefeated in the final – and missing out on the trophy – with such equanimity. But Williamson was more than just dignity and grace. With a nod to greatness and yet another dab to third man, he hit 578 from No. 3, almost 27% of New Zealand's runs. On six occasions, he was batting before the total was 13. Against South Africa, he masterminded the overhaul of 241 (a score that came back to bite them) with the calm of a Zen master. Against West Indies, he built a monumental 148 from the first-over ruins of seven for two. No colleague made a century, no one approached his average of 82 (Ross Taylor's 38 was next). The biggest disappointment was Guptill: leading run-scorer in 2015 with 547, a lowly 45th in 2019 with 186.

By the end, New Zealand had totted up 2,154 – over 1,000 behind England. Their only player in the top 18 run-makers was Williamson, but there were four in the top 14 wicket-takers. Their prowess lay in bowling first and limiting opponents to low scores (though they defended their own modest total in the semi-final, and came within an ace of repeating the trick in the final). The zippy Lockie Ferguson claimed 21 wickets, while Boult, another of the left-arm army, and Matt Henry found early breakthroughs; Jimmy Neesham epitomised New Zealand's can-do attitude, allying 15 wickets with 232 runs. Boult had another string to his bow, his catch at long-on bringing a breathless victory over West Indies when a pace backwards would, it turned out, have

Cut above: India's Rohit Sharma was the leading run-scorer.

brought an early exit. It was tough, then, that almost his only error came at an even more crucial juncture, when he trod on the boundary late in the Lord's final, reprieving Stokes and handing England six.

It was as if **Pakistan** had set out to tick every box marked stereotype. Mercurial batting, inconsistent bowling, unpredictable fielding: all the old favourites, all valid. They had lost ten of their previous 11 ODIs – the other was a no-result – so expectations were modest. Their opening fixture was against West Indies, who seemed to offer a short cut to winning ways. Instead, Pakistan came the almightiest of croppers. Bounced out for 105 in 22 overs, they were flattened inside 14 more. If their pride was punctured, the lasting damage was to their net run-rate: after one game, it read –5.80. The full grimness of that figure would not become clear for another five weeks. Given that they had lost to West Indies, how would they fare against England, who had just brushed them aside 4–0? Daft question, really. Pakistan won.

If that apparently confirmed there was no pattern to their performances, the next three fixtures – a washout against Sri Lanka, defeats by Australia and India – persuaded some that, far from random, the sequence was preordained. At the 1992 World Cup, Imran Khan's Pakistan had endured an identical start: heavy defeat (by West Indies), victory, no-result, defeat, defeat.

Even though Sarfraz Ahmed's 2019 team lost to India, incurable optimists took heart from the fact that an unbroken string of victories had sped Imran to cricketing immortality. The correlation was extraordinary, and Pakistan did indeed win all their remaining games. But there the parallel ended. They began their last match knowing that, though they could (and did) tie with the fourth-

WORLD CUP NOTES...

As the gripping climax to New Zealand v West Indies unfolded at Old Trafford, 11,000 miles away in Wellington, a morning flight to Auckland was waiting to take off. On board was Kieran McAnulty, a cricket-loving New Zealand MP. "The expectation was that we would commence taxi to the runway – but we didn't," he said. "There was no reason for any delay, so we just kept playing the game would complete before we started." When Trent Boult caught Carlos Brathwaite, passengers erupted. "As the cheers and applause died down only then did the plane start to move."

The Royal Mail celebrated England's victory – and, belatedly, England women's World Cup win in 2017 – by issuing a commemorative set of stamps and painting a postbox white and gold in each of the host towns or cities. To initial bemusement, blue postboxes had appeared near World Cup grounds ahead of the tournament. The makeover went unexplained until they were decorated with World Cup logos.

An unexpected media star emerged during the three games at Taunton. Brian the cat first appeared at the County Ground in 2013 but, when television cottoned on, his fame quickly spread; he was even the subject of a video profile on the ICC website. Brian, a ginger described as "feisty", has his own Twitter account, but rarely granted a selfie.

Jaykishan Plaha, a 23-year-old bowler from Osterley CC, suffered a fractured skull after being struck by a drive from David Warner while bowling in the nets at The Oval the day before Australia's match against India. "Dave was pretty shaken up," said captain Aaron Finch. Plaha made a swift recovery, and met Warner a week later: "He said, 'Big man, I'm sorry.' He spoke to my mum and apologised to her."

Afghanistan had some high-level support in their game against England at Old Trafford: Ashraf Ghani, the country's president, took time out from an official trip to the UK to meet the team. The president encouraged the players to do well in the remaining matches, and they all promised to put up a good show," said an Afghanistan Cricket Board official.

Police were called to a Manchester restaurant where Afghanistan players were eating on the eve of their match against England. According to *The Sun*, the players objected to a member of the public trying to film them at Akbar's Indian restaurant. Police confirmed they were called to an "altercation" at around 11.15, but no arrests were made.

The ICC were taking no chances with the names of non-tournament sponsors appearing anywhere at grounds. The OCS Stand at The Oval was renamed the Kennington Stand, and white seats that spell out OCS were removed. At the Ageas Bowl – which became the Hampshire Bowl – tape was placed over sponsors' names in the lifts.

When Sanath Jayasuriya was spotted in the Headingley crowd during Sri Lanka's match against India, the ICC warned the Sri Lankan team that he must not be allowed into official areas, or mix with players or their families. Jayasuriya, who played 582 times for his country across all formats, was serving a two-year ban for breaches of anti-corruption regulations.

A no-fly zone was put in place over Old Trafford before India's semi-final against New Zealand. Planes displaying political banners had flown over Headingley during the matches between Afghanistan and Pakistan, and India and Sri Lanka. The ICC said it was "incredibly disappointed" that West Yorkshire Police had failed to stop the second protest, although the force insisted the protests were a matter of free speech.

Afghanistan seamer Aftab Alam was sent home and suspended for a year after a series of disciplinary breaches. Aftab was withdrawn under "exceptional circumstances", said a statement. There were allegations of misbehaviour with a female guest at the team's hotel in Southampton. He was also reported to have turned up with friends and demanded VIP access at the India–Pakistan match. The group got into one of the hospitality areas, but were asked to leave.

Srikanta Maity, a 33-year-old Kolkata cycle-shop owner, collapsed while watching M. S. Dhoni's run-out in India's semi-final defeat by New Zealand. He was taken to hospital, but declared dead on arrival.

Medical staff at a Kolkata hospital were said to be more interested in watching the semi-final than in helping a man who had lost a fingertip in a motorcycle accident. Chemical engineer Nilotpal Chakraborty had managed to keep the fingertip and took it to the hospital. But by the time he was ready for surgery it had gone missing. Chakraborty's wife alleged it was lost because the staff were engrossed in events at Old Trafford.

New Zealand all-rounder Jimmy Neesham had a distraction before the group match against England at Chester-le-Street. He had to sit a communications exam as part of a course back home at Massey University. Team manager Mike Sandle took on the role of invigilator. "The wrist got a bit sore from all the writing," Neesham said. "I haven't written for two hours straight for quite a few years. I'd rather fail the exam and win the World Cup."

...AND QUOTES

"No way! No, no way! You cannot do that, Ben Stokes. That is remarkable. That is one of the greatest catches of all time!"   *Nasser Hussain's TV commentary on Stokes's catch against South Africa*

"I really hope they don't get too much stick. We all make mistakes. We are human beings and we have feelings. I know deep down they are probably really good people. I just hope they get treated decently."
    Moeen Ali calls for calm as Steve Smith and David Warner return from their ban

"Just because there's so many Indian fans here, I didn't want them to set a bad example, because he didn't do anything to be booed, in my opinion. I felt bad, because if I was in a position where something had happened with me and I had apologised, accepted it and came back, and still I would get booed, I wouldn't like it, either."
    Virat Kohli after asking Indian fans to stop booing Smith at The Oval

"I don't think I could do anything, or should do anything, to try to influence the fans to change their minds. They have committed something and they have served their penalty. It doesn't necessarily mean they are welcomed back with open arms into the cricket community. Regaining trust takes a lot of time. Who knows how long it will take?"   *Eoin Morgan before England v Australia at Lord's*

"It's helpful for the environment and for the animals, too. So it's good for everyone, but on the field I'm definitely lighter for it, that's for sure."
    Australian leg-spinner Adam Zampa on his vegan diet

"Every time we get hit on our pad the finger goes up. When we hit the opposition on their pad, the finger stays down."   *Carlos Brathwaite on the umpiring in West Indies' defeat by Australia*

"I saw some stats which said the soccer World Cup final attracted 1.6bn viewers. Tomorrow is likely to get 1.5bn. It doesn't get bigger than that."
    Pakistan coach Mickey Arthur before the game against India

"I have played against Kagiso many times, and if anything needs to be said we can discuss it man to man."   *Virat Kohli on being called "immature" by Kagiso Rabada*

"Ricky Ponting was rooming about ten rooms up from me the other day and said: 'Were you batting at seven o'clock this morning?' He could hear me tapping on the ground."
    Steve Smith on his batting obsession

"We put men on the moon, so why can't we have a reserve day?"
    Bangladesh coach Steve Rhodes after another washout

"The thing that kept me going was my wife and kids. She's disciplined, selfless, she got me out of bed a lot in those first 12 weeks, got me back running and training hard."
    David Warner pays tribute to Candice after his century against Pakistan

"He's English, so no."
    Jason Holder on whether Barbados-born Jofra Archer would make the West Indies team

"I didn't bowl at him much in the nets, though. A lot of guys don't want to face me or Oshane Thomas."
    Jofra Archer on his IPL friendship with Steve Smith

"When Kevin Pietersen comes out with a comment, it's very similar to comments I address from Geoffrey Boycott. They are not ones that are considered good for a team environment and don't have the best interests of the team or the player at heart. Guys are trying their heart out to do well for their country, trying to learn, trying to get better."   *Eoin Morgan*

RUNS BY OPENERS

	M	I	Runs	HS	Avge	SR	100	50	0	4	6
Australia	10	20	1,154	166	60.73	94.51	5	6	1	113	26
England.	11	22	1,115	153	53.09	101.17	4	6	3	134	23
India	9	18	1,097	140	64.52	91.34	7	3	1	112	18
South Africa . . .	9	18	587	80*	39.13	77.54	0	5	0	60	5
Pakistan.	8	16	491	100	30.68	78.30	1	2	2	55	4
Sri Lanka.	7	14	470	97	36.15	87.85	0	5	1	51	1
West Indies . . .	9	16	421	87	26.31	84.53	0	4	1	42	16
Afghanistan. . . .	9	18	418	62	23.22	77.55	0	1	3	53	3
Bangladesh	8	16	414	62	25.87	82.96	0	1	0	51	2
New Zealand. . .	10	20	402	73*	22.33	80.72	0	3	4	47	6

place side, New Zealand, on points and wins, their net run-rate was beyond rescue. Their coach, Mickey Arthur, suggested the head-to-head result might be a fairer means of separation, especially since they had won that clash. There were no complaints from New Zealand. Not about this tie-breaker – nor, to be fair, the one in the final.

Babar Azam defied stereotype and made at least 45 in six of his eight innings, while Imam-ul-Haq was almost as dependable. As so often, the stars were the left-arm quicks. Despite only five wickets from his previous 15 ODIs, Mohammad Amir was a wild-card choice for the squad, provoking the jilted Junaid Khan into posting a photograph of himself with tape over his mouth. Amir and the 19-year-old Shaheen Shah Afridi, who against Bangladesh became the youngest to take a World Cup five-for, shared 33.

Also unhappy about tie-breaks were **Sri Lanka**. Having resuscitated the tournament from looming lifelessness at Leeds, they started their penultimate game theoretically able to match England on points. But, victims of two washouts, they could not swell their number of wins beyond England's, and so were eliminated, come what may. Their preparations had been shambolic, epitomised by the choice of captain: Dimuth Karunaratne had not played an ODI between March 2015 and May 2019. Routed by New Zealand, they almost lost to Afghanistan and, after Headingley, the good news went no further than victory over West Indies.

South Africa endured their worst World Cup, which was saying something. It was pretty much downhill from that second ball dismissal of Bairstow, when the 40-year-old Tahir tore off on a celebratory circuit of The Oval. But England won at a canter, and Faf du Plessis's side lost their first three games. So much for the captain's relaxed regime, aimed to guard against choking... Successes against Afghanistan and Sri Lanka were scant cause for junketing, and some likened the defeat of Australia to a dead-cat bounce. They were not helped by the risky selection of Dale Steyn, whose shoulder injury prevented him taking the field, or by fellow fast bowler Lungi Ngidi being sidelined for five matches after pulling a hamstring. Then there was Hashim Amla, whose strike-rate of 64 was the lowest by anyone to make 200 runs (which he did by just three). And in an extraordinary intervention, former captain A. B. de Villiers had suggested an 11th-hour return, despite retiring from international cricket in March 2018. South Africa rejected what they saw as a destabilising move.

High flyers: Ravindra Jadeja, from India, and Pakistan's Shaheen Shah Afridi rose to the occasion.

The **Bangladesh** story was essentially Shakib – consistency incarnate at No. 3. Eight innings produced a forty and seven fifties, two of which blossomed into hundreds, while his left-arm spin was typically tidy. He was the only player outside the semi-finalists to make the ICC Team of the Tournament. Bangladesh began by beating South Africa, which engendered more hope than it probably merited, though in Mushfiqur Rahim and Mustafizur Rahman they had batting experience and, at the death, fizzing seam. Victory over West Indies came thanks to the second-highest successful run-chase in World Cup history. But for Mashrafe bin Mortaza – stalwart, captain and member of parliament – figures of one for 361 told a salutary tale.

And then there were the sides who had come through the qualifiers. At around midday on June 6, **West Indies** looked like champions: after crushing Pakistan, they had Australia 79 for five. But they couldn't convert it into victory, and thereafter enjoyed only flashes of brilliance. By a matter of inches, Carlos Brathwaite failed to hit the six that would have given them a famous win over New Zealand, and kept their hopes alive. They also had to contend with the distraction of the Chris Gayle sideshow, which produced many slow starts and only two fifties.

Afghanistan lost all nine matches, but won a few friends. Not that relations within the camp were cordial. Like Sri Lanka, they appointed a new captain, Gulbadeen Naib, in the run-up to the World Cup, while coach Phil Simmons threatened to detail the fraught goings-on after wicketkeeper Mohammad Shahzad was sent home with a damaged knee, only to claim the injury was a fiction. Not short on self-assurance, Gulbadeen opened the batting (and bowled at the death) with more swash than buckle. They gave genuine frights to India and Pakistan, but suffered their own against England, when Morgan eviscerated Rashid Khan. It took immense character to come back from conceding 110 (and 11 sixes), but stick at it he did.

So, was the 46-day jamboree a roaring success? There were roars, all right, whenever a subcontinental team were involved. Even the smattering of Afghan supporters ensured a crackling atmosphere, though during the Pakistan match at Leeds they were involved in scuffles. Indian fans outnumbered all others, England's included. With India v Pakistan in mind, Old Trafford erected a mammoth temporary stand comprising 47km of scaffolding, and seating 8,500. It made little impression on the 800,000 who had apparently applied for tickets. Without the vibrancy and volume that accompanied the Asian teams, some clashes felt bloodless.

Despite the winners, the impact of the final was hard to gauge. The only World Cup behind a TV paywall in the host country, it was scandalously invisible in the UK. Though the organisers staged it after the domestic football season, they underestimated the profile of the women's World Cup, with which it clashed, and which hogged attention. So there were 25 times more British eyes on Lyon (France) for the semi-final between England and the USA than on Lyon (Nathan) for the semi-final between England and Australia. The sobering figures were 11.7m v 465,000.

Redemption, though, was on hand in the unexpected form of Sky TV, and the improved form of the England team. Sky promised that if Morgan's side reached the final, they would share the rights with a free-to-air broadcaster. So Channel 4 cleared the airtime decks. Out went *A Place in the Sun*; in came a place at the crease. Few swaps in life are as delicious. The tournament locomotive pootling down the branch line to Bognor now had clearance for the tracks used by the Bullet Train. The figures were good – all told, 8.7m watched the Lord's denouement – but not that good. The concurrent Wimbledon men's final attracted 9.6m. More encouraging was the performance of the BBC website, which saw 39.7m page views, the largest for a live event of any sort.

The BBC ran with it the next day, too, and cricket took over Radio 4, especially the flagship *Today* programme. ESPNcricinfo appeared on a review of the papers and websites, while the lead item on the news and sports bulletins, the theme of Thought for the Day and the subject of the exalted 8.10 slot were

QUALIFYING TABLE

	P	W	L	NR/A	Pts	NRR
INDIA	9	7	1	1	15	0.80
AUSTRALIA	9	7	2	0	14	0.86
ENGLAND	9	6	3	0	12	1.15
NEW ZEALAND	9	5	3	1	11	0.17
Pakistan	9	5	3	1	11	-0.43
Sri Lanka	9	3	4	2	8	-0.91
South Africa	9	3	5	1	7	-0.03
Bangladesh	9	3	5	1	7	-0.41
West Indies	9	2	6	1	5	-0.22
Afghanistan	9	0	9	0	0	-1.32

all England's triumph. One of the presenters, Justin Webb, said: "The next hour of this programme will be one elongated super over."

There were gripes. Why on earth did the ICC need to introduce away strips when, for centuries, 22 players dressed in white have avoided mistaking an opponent for a colleague? Could the "cricketarists", strumming riffs at the fall of each wicket, have had a wider repertoire? Did it really need a team of 21 to hold up three flags before each game? And – no question mark here – there is a limit to the number of times any human being can listen to yet another snatch of Loryn & Rudimental singing "Stand By", the ubiquitous World Cup anthem.

And yet, and yet, and yet. In the end, it was truly, madly, utterly brilliant.

2019 WORLD CUP STATISTICS

Leading run-scorers

	M	I	NO	R	HS	100	Avge	SR	4	6
R. G. Sharma (I)	9	9	1	648	140	5	81.00	98.33	67	14
†D. A. Warner (A)	10	10	1	647	166	3	71.88	89.36	66	8
†Shakib Al Hasan (B).	8	8	1	606	124*	2	86.57	96.03	60	2
K. S. Williamson (NZ)	9	9	2	578	148	2	82.57	74.96	50	3
J. E. Root (E)	11	11	2	556	107	2	61.77	89.53	48	2
J. M. Bairstow (E)	11	11	0	532	111	2	48.36	92.84	67	11
A. J. Finch (A)	10	10	0	507	153	2	50.70	102.01	47	18
Babar Azam (P)	8	8	1	474	101*	1	67.71	87.77	50	2
†B. A. Stokes (E)	11	10	3	465	89	0	66.42	93.18	38	11
J. J. Roy (E)	8	7	0	443	153	1	63.28	115.36	51	12
V. Kohli (I).	9	9	1	443	82	0	55.37	94.05	38	2
F. du Plessis (SA).	9	8	2	387	100	1	64.50	89.58	36	4
S. P. D. Smith (A).	10	10	0	379	85	0	37.90	85.94	33	2
†A. T. Carey (A).	10	9	3	375	85	0	62.50	104.16	46	2
†E. J. G. Morgan (E).	11	10	1	371	148	1	41.22	111.07	26	22
†N. Pooran (WI).	9	8	1	367	118	1	52.42	100.27	33	10
Mushfiqur Rahim (B)	8	8	1	367	102*	1	52.42	92.67	30	2
K. L. Rahul (I)	9	9	1	361	111	1	45.12	77.46	31	5
L. R. P. L. Taylor (NZ).	10	9	0	350	82	0	38.88	75.26	29	2

Sharma's five centuries were a World Cup record, beating four by K. C. Sangakkara for Sri Lanka in 2014-15. Only two men had previously scored 600 runs in a World Cup: S. R. Tendulkar (India) 673 in 2002-03, and M. L. Hayden (Australia) 659 in 2006-07.

Highest individual scores

Runs	Balls	4	6	SR		
166	147	14	5	112.92	D. A. Warner	Australia v Bangladesh at Nottingham.
153	121	14	5	126.44	J. J. Roy	England v Bangladesh at Cardiff.
153	132	15	5	115.90	A. J. Finch	Australia v Sri Lanka at The Oval.
148	71	4	17	208.45	E. J. G. Morgan	England v Afghanistan at Manchester.
148	154	14	1	96.10	K. S. Williamson	New Zealand v W. Indies at Manchester.
140	113	14	3	123.89	R. G. Sharma	India v Pakistan at Manchester.
124*	99	16	0	125.25	Shakib Al Hasan	Bangladesh v W. Indies at Taunton.
122*	144	13	2	84.72	R. G. Sharma	India v South Africa at Southampton.
122	117	15	2	104.27	D. A. Warner	Australia v South Africa at Manchester.
121	119	12	1	101.68	Shakib Al Hasan	Bangladesh v England at Cardiff.
118	103	11	4	114.56	N. Pooran	W. Indies v Sri Lanka at Chester-le-Street.
117	109	16	0	107.33	S. Dhawan	India v Australia at The Oval.
113	128	10	2	88.28	A. D. Mathews	Sri Lanka v India at Leeds.
111	109	10	6	101.83	J. M. Bairstow	England v India at Birmingham.
111	118	11	1	94.06	K. L. Rahul	India v Sri Lanka at Leeds.

There were 16 other hundreds, making 31; the only World Cup with more was 2014-15, with 38.

Best strike-rates

	SR	Runs		SR	Runs
G. J. Maxwell (A)	150.00	177	C. R. Brathwaite (WI)......	106.20	154
J. C. Buttler (E)	122.83	312	W. I. A. Fernando (SL)......	105.72	203
Imad Wasim (P)	118.24	162	A. T. Carey (A)............	104.16	375
J. J. Roy (E)...............	115.36	443	A. J. Finch (A)..............	102.01	507
H. H. Pandya (I)	112.43	226	S. O. Hetmyer (WI)........	101.58	257
E. J. G. Morgan (E)........	111.07	371	Soumya Sarkar (B)	101.21	166
M. D. K. J. Perera (SL).....	110.97	273	C. de Grandhomme (NZ) ...	100.52	190
Liton Das (B)	110.17	184	N. Pooran (WI)	100.27	367
J. O. Holder (WI)	108.97	170			

Minimum 150 runs.

Leading wicket-takers

	Style	O	M	R	W	BB	4I	Avge	SR	ER
M. A. Starc (A)	LF	92.2	5	502	27	5-26	4	18.59	20.51	5.43
L. H. Ferguson (NZ)	RF	83.4	3	409	21	4-37	1	19.47	23.90	4.88
J. C. Archer (E)	RF	100.5	8	461	20	3-27	0	23.05	30.25	4.57
Mustafizur Rahman (B).......	LFM	72.1	2	484	20	5-59	2	24.20	21.65	6.70
J. J. Bumrah (I)	RF	84	9	371	18	4-55	1	20.61	28.00	4.41
M. A. Wood (E).............	RF	89.4	2	463	18	3-18	0	25.72	29.88	5.16
Mohammad Amir (P).........	LFM	73	5	358	17	5-30	1	21.05	25.76	4.90
T. A. Boult (NZ)	LFM	99	4	479	17	4-30	2	28.17	34.94	4.83
Shaheen Shah Afridi (P)	LFM	47.1	3	234	16	6-35	2	14.62	17.68	4.96
C. R. Woakes (E)............	RFM	85	6	446	16	3-20	0	27.87	31.87	5.24
J. D. S. Neesham (NZ).......	RFM	54.3	2	292	15	5-31	1	19.46	21.80	5.35
Mohammed Shami (I)	RFM	35.1	2	193	14	5-69	3	13.78	15.07	5.48
M. J. Henry (NZ)	RFM	80.2	5	392	14	4-47	1	28.00	34.42	4.87
P. J. Cummins (A)............	RF	86.1	6	427	14	3-33	0	30.50	36.92	4.95
C. H. Morris (SA)	RFM	63.4	5	341	13	3-13	0	26.23	29.38	5.35
S. L. Malinga (SL)...........	RFM	61.4	4	373	13	4-43	1	28.69	28.46	6.04
Mohammad Saifuddin (B).....	RFM	62	2	417	13	3-72	0	32.07	26.76	7.18
S. S. Cottrell (WI)	LFM	67	2	392	12	4-56	1	32.66	33.50	5.85
Y. S. Chahal (I)	LB	74	0	442	12	4-51	1	36.83	37.00	5.97

Starc, who was also the joint-leading wicket-taker (with Boult) in 2014-15 with 22, broke the record for the most in a World Cup, previously G. D. McGrath's 26 for Australia in 2006-07.

Best bowling analyses

6-35	Shaheen Shah Afridi...........	Pakistan v Bangladesh at Lord's.
5-26	M. A. Starc	Australia v New Zealand at Lord's.
5-29	Shakib Al Hasan................	Bangladesh v Afghanistan at Southampton.
5-30	Mohammad Amir...............	Pakistan v Australia at Taunton.
5-31	J. D. S. Neesham...............	New Zealand v Afghanistan at Taunton.
5-44	J. P. Behrendorff..............	Australia v England at Lord's.
5-46	M. A. Starc	Australia v West Indies at Nottingham.
5-59	Mustafizur Rahman............	Bangladesh v India at Birmingham.
5-69	Mohammed Shami	India v England at Birmingham.
5-75	Mustafizur Rahman............	Bangladesh v Pakistan at Lord's.

Most economical bowlers

	ER	Overs		ER	Overs
K. A. J. Roach (WI)	3.66	33	M. J. Santner (NZ)	4.82	67
R. A. Jadeja (I)	3.70	20	T. A. Boult (NZ)	4.83	99
D. Pretorius (SA)	4.08	23	B. A. Stokes (E)	4.83	50.5
C. de Grandhomme (NZ)	4.15	51	L. E. Plunkett (E)	4.85	56
J. J. Bumrah (I)	4.41	84	M. J. Henry (NZ)	4.87	80.2
Mujeeb Zadran (Afg)	4.47	57.5	L. H. Ferguson (NZ)	4.88	83.4
J. C. Archer (E)	4.57	100.5	Mohammad Amir (P)	4.90	73
Mohammad Nabi (Afg)	4.61	72.4	Imran Tahir (SA)	4.92	76
Hamid Hassan (Afg)	4.69	26	P. J. Cummins (A)	4.95	86.1
Imad Wasim (P)	4.82	39	Shaheen Shah Afridi (P)	4.96	47.1

Minimum 20 overs. Of the 59 who bowled at least 30, Stokes was alone in not conceding a six.

Leading wicketkeepers

	Dis	M		Dis	M
T. W. M. Latham (NZ)	21 (21 ct)	10	Mushfiqur Rahim (B)	10 (8 ct, 2 st)	8
A. T. Carey (A)	20 (18 ct, 2 st)	10	M. S. Dhoni (I)	10 (7 ct, 3 st)	9
S. D. Hope (WI)	16 (16 ct)	9	Q. de Kock (SA)	9 (9 ct)	9
Sarfraz Ahmed (P)	14 (13 ct, 1 st)	8	M. D. K. J. Perera (SL)	8 (8 ct)	7
J. C. Buttler (E)	14 (12 ct, 2 st)	10			

Latham equalled the record for dismissals, set by A. C. Gilchrist (21 ct) for Australia in 2002-03.
Buttler played in 11 games, but did not keep wicket in one because of injury.

Most dismissals in a match

A. T. Carey	5 (4 ct, 1 st)	Australia v Afghanistan at Bristol.
T. W. M. Latham	5 (5 ct)	New Zealand v Afghanistan at Taunton.
J. M. Bairstow	4 (4ct)	England v Bangladesh at Cardiff.
A. T. Carey	4 (4 ct)	Australia v Pakistan at Taunton.
A. T. Carey	4 (4 ct)	Australia v Sri Lanka at The Oval.
M. S. Dhoni	4 (3ct, 1st)	India v Sri Lanka at Leeds.
S. D. Hope	4 (4 ct)	West Indies v Pakistan at Nottingham.
S. D. Hope	4 (4 ct)	West Indies v Australia at Nottingham.
S. D. Hope	4 (4 ct)	West Indies v India at Manchester.
T. W. M. Latham	4 (4 ct)	New Zealand v West Indies at Manchester.
M. D. K. J. Perera	4 (4 ct)	Sri Lanka v England at Leeds.

Bairstow was deputising as wicketkeeper.

Leading fielders

	Ct	M		Ct	M
J. E. Root (E)	13	11	Soumya Sarkar (B)	7	8
F. du Plessis (SA)	10	9	T. A. Boult (NZ)	7	10
S. S. Cottrell (WI)	8	9	J. O. Holder (WI)	6	9
M. J. Guptill (NZ)	8	10	V. Kohli (I)	6	9
C. R. Woakes (E)	8	11	K. S. Williamson (NZ)	6	10

Root broke the record for outfield catches, previously 11 by R. T. Ponting (A) in 2002-03. J. M. Bairstow (E) took nine catches, but four were while deputising as wicketkeeper.

Highest totals

397-6	England v Afghanistan at Manchester.	334-7	Australia v Sri Lanka at The Oval.
386-6	England v Bangladesh at Cardiff.	334-9	England v Pakistan at Nottingham.
381-5	Australia v Bangladesh at Nottingham.	333-8	Bangladesh v Australia at Nottingham.
352-5	India v Australia at The Oval.	330-6	Bangladesh v South Africa at The Oval.
348-8	Pakistan v England at Nottingham.	325-6	South Africa v Australia at Manchester.
338-6	Sri Lanka v W. Indies at Chester-le-Street.	322-3	Bangladesh v West Indies at Taunton.
337-7	England v India at Birmingham.	321-8	West Indies v Bangladesh at Taunton.
336-5	India v Pakistan at Manchester.		

All from 50 overs, except Bangladesh's 322-3 (41.3). There were 12 other totals of 300 or more.

Lowest completed totals

105	Pakistan v West Indies at Nottingham.	152	Afghanistan v Sri Lanka at Cardiff.
125	Afghanistan v South Africa at Cardiff.	157	New Zealand v Australia at Lord's.
136	Sri Lanka v New Zealand at Cardiff.	172	Afghanistan v New Zealand at Taunton.
143	West Indies v India at Manchester.	186	NZ v England at Chester-le-Street.

A list of all-time World Cup records can be found on page 1344.

NATIONAL SQUADS

* *Captain.* † *Did not play.*

Afghanistan *Gulbadeen Naib, Aftab Alam, Asghar Afghan, Dawlat Zadran, Hamid Hassan, Hashmatullah Shahidi, Hazratullah Zazai, Ikram Alikhil, Mohammad Nabi, Mohammad Shahzad, Mujeeb Zadran, Najibullah Zadran, Noor Ali Zadran, Rahmat Shah, Rashid Khan, Samiullah Shenwari, Sayed Shirzad. *Coach:* P. V. Simmons.

Mohammad Shahzad suffered a knee injury, and was replaced on June 6 by Ikram Alikhil. Aftab Alam was sent home for disciplinary reasons and replaced on June 27 by Sayed Shirzad.

Australia *A. J. Finch, J. P. Behrendorff, A. T. Carey, N. M. Coulter-Nile, P. J. Cummins, P. S. P. Handscomb, U. T. Khawaja, N. M. Lyon, S. E. Marsh, G. J. Maxwell, K. W. Richardson, S. P. D. Smith, M. A. Starc, M. P. Stoinis, †M. S. Wade, D. A. Warner, A. Zampa. *Coach:* J. L. Langer.

J. A. Richardson was originally selected, but failed to recover from a shoulder injury; K. W. Richardson replaced him. Marsh broke his right arm in the nets, and was replaced on July 4 by Handscomb. Khawaja injured his hamstring during the last group game, and was replaced on July 10 by Wade.

Bangladesh *Mashrafe bin Mortaza, †Abu Jayed, Liton Das, Mahmudullah, Mehedi Hasan, Mithun Ali, Mohammad Saifuddin, Mosaddek Hossain, Mushfiqur Rahim, Mustafizur Rahman, Rubel Hossain, Sabbir Rahman, Shakib Al Hasan, Soumya Sarkar, Tamim Iqbal. *Coach:* S. J. Rhodes.

England *E. J. G. Morgan, M. M. Ali, J. C. Archer, J. M. Bairstow, J. C. Buttler, †T. K. Curran, †L. A. Dawson, L. E. Plunkett, A. U. Rashid, J. E. Root, J. J. Roy, B. A. Stokes, J. M. Vince, C. R. Woakes, M. A. Wood. *Coach:* T. H. Bayliss.

A. D. Hales was originally named, but was dropped after receiving a domestic ban for recreational drug use, while J. L. Denly and D. J. Willey – also in the preliminary squad – were replaced before the deadline for finalising teams. Archer, Dawson and Vince were preferred.

India *V. Kohli, †M. A. Agarwal, Bhuvneshwar Kumar, J. J. Bumrah, Y. S. Chahal, S. Dhawan, M. S. Dhoni, R. A. Jadeja, K. M. Jadhav, K. D. Karthik, Mohammed Shami, H. H. Pandya, R. R. Pant, K. L. Rahul, V. Shankar, R. G. Sharma, K. Yadav. *Coach:* R. J. Shastri.

Dhawan's left thumb was broken during the match against Australia on June 9; he was replaced on June 19 by Pant. Shankar suffered a toe injury, and was replaced on July 1 by Agarwal.

New Zealand *K. S. Williamson, †T. A. Blundell, T. A. Boult, C. de Grandhomme, L. H. Ferguson, M. J. Guptill, M. J. Henry, T. W. M. Latham, C. Munro, J. D. S. Neesham, H. M. Nicholls, M. J. Santner, I. S. Sodhi, T. G. Southee, L. R. P. L. Taylor. *Coach:* G. R. Stead.

Pakistan *Sarfraz Ahmed, Asif Ali, Babar Azam, Fakhar Zaman, Haris Sohail, Hasan Ali, Imad Wasim, Imam-ul-Haq, Mohammad Amir, Mohammad Hafeez, †Mohammad Hasnain, Shadab Khan, Shaheen Shah Afridi, Shoaib Malik, Wahab Riaz. *Coach:* J. M. Arthur.
Abid Ali, Fahim Ashraf and Junaid Khan were named in the original squad, but replaced by Asif Ali, Mohammad Amir and Wahab Riaz before the deadline.

South Africa *F. du Plessis, H. M. Amla, Q. de Kock, J-P. Duminy, B. E. Hendricks, Imran Tahir, A. K. Markram, D. A. Miller, C. H. Morris, L. T. Ngidi, A. M. Phehlukwayo, D. Pretorius, K. Rabada, T. Shamsi, †D. W. Steyn, H. E. van der Dussen. *Coach:* O. D. Gibson.
A. A. Nortje was originally selected, but broke his right thumb and was replaced by Morris. Steyn failed to recover from a shoulder injury, and on June 4 Hendricks was called up.

Sri Lanka *F. D. M. Karunaratne, D. M. de Silva, A. N. P. R. Fernando, W. I. A. Fernando, R. A. S. Lakmal, S. L. Malinga, A. D. Mathews, B. K. G. Mendis, B. M. A. J. Mendis, M. D. K. J. Perera, N. L. T. C. Perera, C. A. K. Rajitha, T. A. M. Siriwardene, H. D. R. L. Thirimanne, I. Udana, J. D. F. Vandersay. *Coach:* U. C. Hathurusinghe.
A. N. P. R. Fernando went down with chickenpox, and was replaced on June 29 by Rajitha.

West Indies *J. O. Holder, F. A. Allen, S. W. Ambris, C. R. Brathwaite, D. M. Bravo, S. S. Cottrell, S. T. Gabriel, C. H. Gayle, S. O. Hetmyer, S. D. Hope, E. Lewis, A. R. Nurse, N. Pooran, K. A. J. Roach, A. D. Russell, O. R. Thomas. *Coach:* F. L. Reifer.
Russell aggravated a knee injury, and was replaced on June 24 by Ambris.

ENGLAND v SOUTH AFRICA

At The Oval, May 30. England won by 104 runs. Toss: South Africa.

Ben Stokes was cursing himself as Phehlukwayo nailed a slog-sweep. He had strayed in from the midwicket fence: a six seemed inevitable. But instinct took him backwards and sideways. He twisted his body as he leapt for the sky, and somehow emerged clutching the ball in his right hand. As The Oval erupted, the World Cup sprang to life. It was the champagne moment of an England victory built on responsible batting, the fluid bowling of Archer, and Stokes's all-round vivacity. His first contribution had been an intelligent 89 off 79 balls, his highest international score since returning from suspension in February 2018. That followed fifties from Roy, Root and Morgan, who was winning an England-record 200th one-day international cap (there were also 23 for Ireland), and passed 7,000 ODI runs. But a total of 311 required hard work. Bairstow had fallen to the day's second ball, bowled – in a cute move from du Plessis – by leg-spinner Imran Tahir, and the last 15 overs produced a modest 111 for five, as South Africa's seamers exploited slower deliveries on a grudging pitch. Archer then purred into action, forcing Amla off for a concussion test after hitting his helmet (he returned later, to little avail), and beating Markram and du Plessis for pace. De Kock rallied, though on 25 Rashid's googly brushed his off stump without dislodging one of the briefly illuminated bails. But when Plunkett persuaded de Kock to shovel a long hop to long leg, South Africa disintegrated, losing eight for 78. That included the run-out of Pretorius by Stokes from deep extra cover – and that catch. By the time he wrapped things up with two wickets in two balls, the match award had long been decided. A full house disappeared into the south London evening talking of the miracle at midwicket. LAWRENCE BOOTH

Player of the Match: B. A. Stokes. *Attendance:* 21,821.

England

J. J. Roy c du Plessis b Phehlukwayo	54	L. E. Plunkett not out		9
J. M. Bairstow c de Kock b Imran Tahir	0	J. C. Archer not out		7
J. E. Root c Duminy b Rabada	51	Lb 2, w 8		10
*E. J. G. Morgan c Markram b Imran Tahir	57			
B. A. Stokes c Amla b Ngidi	89	1/1 (2) 2/107 (1)	(8 wkts, 50 overs)	311
†J. C. Buttler b Ngidi	18	3/111 (3) 4/217 (4)		
M. M. Ali c du Plessis b Ngidi	3	5/247 (6) 6/260 (7)		
C. R. Woakes c du Plessis b Rabada	13	7/285 (8) 8/300 (5)	10 overs: 60-1	

A. U. Rashid did not bat.

Imran Tahir 10–0–61–2; Ngidi 10–0–66–3; Rabada 10–0–66–2; Pretorius 7–0–42–0; Phehlukwayo 8–0–44–1; Duminy 2–0–14–0; Markram 3–0–16–0.

South Africa

†Q. de Kock c Root b Plunkett	68	L. T. Ngidi not out		6
H. M. Amla c Buttler b Plunkett	13	Imran Tahir c Root b Stokes		0
A. K. Markram c Root b Archer	11			
*F. du Plessis c Ali b Archer	5	B 4, lb 5, w 1		10
H. E. van der Dussen c Ali b Archer	50			
J-P. Duminy c Stokes b Ali	8	1/36 (3) 2/44 (4)	(39.5 overs)	207
D. Pretorius run out (Stokes/Morgan)	1	3/129 (1) 4/142 (6) 5/144 (7)		
A. L. Phehlukwayo c Stokes b Rashid	24	6/167 (5) 7/180 (8) 8/193 (2)		
K. Rabada c Plunkett b Stokes	11	9/207 (9) 10/207 (11)	10 overs: 44-2	

Amla, when 5, retired hurt at 14-0 and resumed at 167-6.

Woakes 5–0–24–0; Archer 7–1–27–3; Rashid 8–0–35–1; Ali 10–0–63–1; Plunkett 7–0–37–2; Stokes 2.5–0–12–2.

Umpires: H. D. P. K. Dharmasena and B. N. J. Oxenford.   Third umpire: P. R. Reiffel.
Referee: D. C. Boon.

PAKISTAN v WEST INDIES

At Nottingham, May 31. West Indies won by seven wickets. Toss: West Indies.

The talk beforehand, given Trent Bridge's run-soaked reputation, was of the 500 barrier being breached for the first time in a one-day international. Instead, on a springy surface beneath overcast skies, Pakistan staggered past 100, thanks to their last pair. The match

---

SHORTEST COMPLETED WORLD CUP MATCHES

Balls		
140	Sri Lanka (37-1 in 4.4 overs) beat Canada (36 in 18.4) at Paarl	2002-03
187	West Indies (59-1 in 12.2) beat Bangladesh (58 in 18.5) at Mirpur	2010-11
191	New Zealand (72-0 in 8) beat Kenya (69 in 23.5) at Chennai	2010-11
212	**West Indies (108-3 in 13.4) beat Pakistan (105 in 21.4) at Nottingham**	**2019**
226	Sri Lanka (81-2 in 10) beat Ireland (77 in 27.4) at St George's, Grenada	2006-07
246	Australia (133-3 in 15.2) beat Scotland (130 in 25.4) at Hobart	2014-15
250	West Indies (70-2 in 10.1) beat Scotland (68 in 31.3) at Leicester	1999
254	Australia (92-1 in 12.2) beat Ireland (91 in 30) at Bridgetown	2006-07
273	**New Zealand (137-0 in 16.1) beat Sri Lanka (136 in 29.2) at Cardiff**	**2019**
274	New Zealand (125-2 in 12.2) beat England (123 in 33.2) at Wellington	2014-15

Excludes matches in which the number of overs was reduced.

Soar point: an airborne Andre Russell tears into Pakistan.

was over before the scheduled mid-innings break. In a throwback to the West Indian fast bowlers' heyday, a succession of batsmen flapped at short deliveries that targeted their throats: Pakistan's fans began by protesting these were wides, but became less vocal as the barrage continued and the umpires kept their arms down. Fakhar Zaman had started aggressively – Holder's first two overs cost 20 – but fell to the fifth ball from Russell, who had played only two ODIs since the previous World Cup. He made up for lost time, repeatedly digging the ball in, and later grumbled good-naturedly: "When my name comes on the big screen it says 'medium-pacer'. I show them I can bowl 90." Russell sent down only three overs, but also nabbed Haris Sohail. Then Thomas kept Pakistan on the back foot: he removed Babar Azam – who was averaging 102 against West Indies – thanks to the best of Hope's four catches, as six wickets cascaded for 21. Although Mohammad Amir made two quick strikes, Gayle ensured Pakistan's 11th successive ODI defeat with a 34-ball 50. The first of three sixes was his 38th in the World Cup, breaking A. B. de Villiers's record. Pooran, after one luscious, Lara-like, square-driven four, ended proceedings at 1.54 with a six. Many spectators missed a lot of the action because of problems with the ticketing system. The ICC refunded anyone whose passes were issued after the start, and enabled print-at-home tickets for future games.   STEVEN LYNCH

Player of the Match: O. R. Thomas.   *Attendance:* 11,278.

Pakistan

Imam-ul-Haq c Hope b Cottrell	2	Wahab Riaz b Thomas	18
Fakhar Zaman b Russell	22	Mohammad Amir not out	3
Babar Azam c Hope b Thomas	22		
Haris Sohail c Hope b Russell	8	W 2, nb 2	4
*†Sarfraz Ahmed c Hope b Holder	8		—
Mohammad Hafeez c Cottrell b Thomas	16	1/17 (1) 2/35 (2) 3/45 (4) (21.4 overs)	105
Imad Wasim c Gayle b Holder	1	4/62 (3) 5/75 (5) 6/77 (7)	
Shadab Khan lbw b Thomas	0	7/78 (8) 8/81 (9) 9/83 (6)	
Hasan Ali c Cottrell b Holder	1	10/105 (10)	10 overs: 45-3

Cottrell 4–0–18–1; Holder 5–0–42–3; Russell 3–1–4–2; Brathwaite 4–0–14–0; Thomas 5.4–0–27–4.

West Indies

C. H. Gayle c Shadab Khan		N. Pooran not out	34
b Mohammad Amir	50	S. O. Hetmyer not out	7
†S. D. Hope c Mohammad Hafeez		Lb 3, w 3	6
b Mohammad Amir	11		
D. M. Bravo c Babar Azam		1/36 (2) 2/46 (3) (3 wkts, 13.4 overs)	108
b Mohammad Amir	0	3/77 (1)	10 overs: 71-2

*J. O. Holder, A. D. Russell, C. R. Brathwaite, A. R. Nurse, S. S. Cottrell and O. R. Thomas did not bat.

Mohammad Amir 6–0–26–3; Hasan Ali 4–0–39–0; Wahab Riaz 3.4–1–40–0.

Umpires: M. Erasmus and C. B. Gaffaney.   Third umpire: S. Ravi.
Referee: J. J. Crowe.

NEW ZEALAND v SRI LANKA

At Cardiff, June 1. New Zealand won by ten wickets. Toss: New Zealand.

There were gasps as groundstaff unveiled a green mamba pitch but, by the time the match was completed in 45.3 overs, New Zealand had found an antidote to the venom. The toss was crucial, and their pace bowlers were hungry; few had more of an appetite than Henry. A late calf injury to Tim Southee had given him the chance to make up for figures of 9–0–107–2 during a warm-up game against West Indies, and he responded with three for 29 in seven unchanged overs, restricting Sri Lanka to 136. The Pereras – Kusal and Tissara – had their moments, but opener and captain Karunaratne alone offered prolonged resistance. He made 52 off 84 balls, becoming the second player to carry his bat at a World Cup, after West Indies' Ridley Jacobs against Australia at Old Trafford in 1999. No one else passed seven, while three New Zealanders – Henry, Ferguson and de Grandhomme – struck in their first over. They were helped by fielders pursuing the ball as if it had scampered off with their wallet. Munro also seized on a late recall, as Henry Nicholls nursed a hamstring. He made 58 from 47 balls, alongside Guptill's 73 from 51, in an unbroken stand of 137. Sri Lanka's first ten-wicket defeat at a World Cup was New Zealand's third such victory – a record.   ANDREW ALDERSON

Player of the Match: M. J. Henry.   *Attendance:* 11,659.

Sri Lanka

H. D. R. L. Thirimanne lbw b Henry	4	I. Udana c Henry b Neesham		0
*F. D. M. Karunaratne not out	52	R. A. S. Lakmal c Santner b Boult		7
†M. D. K. J. Perera c de Grandhomme		S. L. Malinga b Ferguson		1
b Henry	29	B 1, w 8, nb 2		11
B. K. G. Mendis c Guptill b Henry	0			
D. M. de Silva lbw b Ferguson	4	1/4 (1) 2/46 (3) 3/46 (4)	(29.2 overs)	136
A. D. Mathews c Latham b de Grandhomme	0	4/53 (5) 5/59 (6) 6/60 (7)		
B. M. A. J. Mendis c Neesham b Ferguson	1	7/112 (8) 8/114 (9) 9/130 (10)		
N. L. T. C. Perera c Boult b Santner	27	10/136 (11)	10 overs: 51-3	

Henry 7–0–29–3; Boult 9–0–44–1; Ferguson 6.2–0–22–3; de Grandhomme 2–0–14–1; Neesham 3–0–21–1; Santner 2–0–5–1.

New Zealand

M. J. Guptill not out	73
C. Munro not out	58
Lb 3, w 2, nb 1	6
	—
(no wkt, 16.1 overs)	137
	10 overs: 77-0

*K. S. Williamson, L. R. P. L. Taylor, †T. W. M. Latham, J. D. S. Neesham, C. de Grandhomme, M. J. Santner, M. J. Henry, L. H. Ferguson and T. A. Boult did not bat.

Malinga 5–0–46–0; Lakmal 4–0–28–0; Udana 3–0–24–0; N. L. T. C. Perera 3–0–25–0; B. M. A. J. Mendis 1.1–0–11–0.

Umpires: I. J. Gould and R. J. Tucker.   Third umpire: N. J. Llong.
Referee: A. J. Pycroft.

AFGHANISTAN v AUSTRALIA

At Bristol, June 1 (day/night). Australia won by seven wickets. Toss: Afghanistan.

Try as they might, the Nevil Road crowd could not jeer the Australians off their stride. This was the first official international appearance by Smith and Warner since their shenanigans in Cape Town 434 days earlier, and the locals were in no mood to forgive, let alone forget. Both were barracked as they walked out to bat, while a small section of the crowd noisily scratched pieces of sandpaper. Warner admitted to early nerves as Australia set about chasing 208, and might have been caught on ten, then stumped on 19. But Finch's punishing 66 from 49 balls allowed Warner to bide his time. He played out two maidens from Hamid Hassan, and brought up his fifty from 74 deliveries, the slowest of his 32 ODI half-centuries; when Maxwell thumped his first ball over mid-off for the winning four, Warner was still there on 89 from 114. Smith, meanwhile, had just departed, caught at short third man for 18 – giving spectators one more chance for a beery pantomime boo. After choosing to bat in the tournament's first day/nighter (though the lights were barely needed), Afghanistan had lost Mohammad Shahzad third ball to a Starc yorker. After that it was trial by bouncer, which made for frenetic fare. Afghanistan simply hit out at everything: Najibullah Zadran clubbed Zampa for 20 in four balls, and Rashid Khan hit Stoinis for 20 in five. But too many others had a heave, leading to three of Carey's five dismissals and curtailing the innings with nearly 12 overs unused.   LAWRENCE BOOTH

Player of the Match: D. A. Warner.   Attendance: 7,964.

Afghanistan

†Mohammad Shahzad b Starc	0	
Hazratullah Zazai c Carey b Cummins	0	
Rahmat Shah c Smith b Zampa	43	
Hashmatullah Shahidi st Carey b Zampa	18	
Mohammad Nabi run out (Smith/Carey)	7	
*Gulbadeen Naib c Carey b Stoinis	31	
Najibullah Zadran c Carey b Stoinis	51	
Rashid Khan lbw b Zampa	27	
Dawlat Zadran c Carey b Cummins	4	

Mujeeb Zadran b Cummins 13
Hamid Hassan not out 1

Lb 3, w 8, nb 1 12
———
1/0 (1)   2/5 (2)   3/56 (4)   (38.2 overs) 207
4/75 (3)   5/77 (5)   6/160 (6)
7/162 (7)   8/166 (9)   9/205 (8)
10/207 (10)   10 overs: 37-2

Starc 7–1–31–1; Cummins 8.2–0–40–3; Coulter-Nile 8–1–36–0; Stoinis 7–1–37–2; Zampa 8–0–60–3.

Australia

*A. J. Finch c Mujeeb Zadran b Gulbadeen Naib	66	
D. A. Warner not out	89	
U. T. Khawaja lbw b Rashid Khan	15	
S. P. D. Smith c Hazratullah Zazai b Mujeeb Zadran	18	

G. J. Maxwell not out 4

Lb 1, w 14, nb 2 17
———
1/96 (1)   2/156 (3)   (3 wkts, 34.5 overs) 209
3/205 (4)   10 overs: 55-0

M. P. Stoinis, †A. T. Carey, N. M. Coulter-Nile, P. J. Cummins, M. A. Starc and A. Zampa did not bat.

Mujeeb Zadran 4.5–0–45–1; Hamid Hassan 6–2–15–0; Dawlat Zadran 5–0–32–0; Gulbadeen Naib 5–0–32–1; Mohammad Nabi 6–0–32–0; Rashid Khan 8–0–52–1.

Umpires: Aleem Dar and R. K. Illingworth.   Third umpire: M. A. Gough.
Referee: R. S. Madugalle.

BANGLADESH v SOUTH AFRICA

At The Oval, June 2. Bangladesh won by 21 runs. Toss: South Africa.

After three games in which an Asian team had batted first and lost by plenty, Bangladesh thrillingly broke the sequence. Grateful to be inserted on a used pitch, they racked up their then highest one-day total (beating 329 for six against Pakistan at Mirpur in April 2015), before exploiting South Africa's hesitancy. While the Bangladesh fans rejoiced in a resounding win, du Plessis grimly dissected his side's second defeat in four days, and reflected on a mounting injury crisis. Already missing Dale Steyn (shoulder) and Hashim Amla (suffering a delayed reaction to a blow from Jofra Archer), South Africa lost Ngidi after just four overs because of a hamstring strain. It left their attack underpowered – but they were outmanoeuvred too. The Bangladesh innings had three phases. Soumya Sarkar supplied the early oomph, cracking nine fours in a 30-ball 42, before Shakib Al Hasan and Mushfiqur Rahim put on 142 for the third wicket, briefly their country's highest World Cup partnership. Mahmudullah then supervised the addition of 70 in the last six overs as South Africa grew sloppy. Their reply wasn't much better. De Kock was run out by an alert Mushfiqur, and du Plessis bowled on the charge by Mehedi Hasan for 62. The asking-rate grew, and the pressure told. Mohammad Saifuddin bowled the dangerous van der Dussen, and left-armer Mustafizur Rahman disposed of Morris and Duminy in successive overs; the spinners were miserly. This was only Bangladesh's fourth win in 21 ODIs against these opponents, though it was now 2–2 at World Cups, and their dominance meant it hardly felt like an upset. Already, the South Africans were fighting for their lives.   Lawrence Booth

Player of the Match: Shakib Al Hasan.   *Attendance:* 20,596.

Bangladesh

Tamim Iqbal c de Kock b Phehlukwayo	...	16
Soumya Sarkar c de Kock b Morris	......	42
Shakib Al Hasan b Imran Tahir	....	75
†Mushfiqur Rahim c van der Dussen		
	b Phehlukwayo	78
Mithun Ali b Imran Tahir	....	21
Mahmudullah not out	....	46

Mosaddek Hossain c Phehlukwayo b Morris	26
Mehedi Hasan not out	....	5
Lb 9, w 12	....	21
1/60 (1) 2/75 (2)	(6 wkts, 50 overs) 330
3/217 (3) 4/242 (5)	
5/250 (4) 6/316 (7)	10 overs: 65-1

Mohammad Saifuddin, *Mashrafe bin Mortaza and Mustafizur Rahman did not bat.

Ngidi 4–0–34–0; Rabada 10–0–57–0; Phehlukwayo 10–1–52–2; Morris 10–0–73–2; Markram 5–0–38–0; Imran Tahir 10–0–57–2; Duminy 1–0–10–0.

South Africa

†Q. de Kock run out (Mushfiqur Rahim)	...	23
A. K. Markram b Shakib Al Hasan	....	45
*F. du Plessis b Mehedi Hasan	....	62
D. A. Miller c Mehedi Hasan		
	b Mustafizur Rahman	38
H. E. van der Dussen		
	b Mohammad Saifuddin	41
J-P. Duminy b Mustafizur Rahman	.....	45
A. L. Phehlukwayo c Shakib Al Hasan		
	b Mohammad Saifuddin	8

C. H. Morris c Soumya Sarkar		
	b Mustafizur Rahman	10
K. Rabada not out	....	13
Imran Tahir not out	....	10
B 4, w 9, nb 1	....	14
1/49 (1) 2/102 (2)	(8 wkts, 50 overs) 309
3/147 (3) 4/202 (4)	
5/228 (5) 6/252 (7)	
7/275 (8) 8/287 (6)	10 overs: 51-1

L. T. Ngidi did not bat.

Mustafizur Rahman 10–0–67–3; Mehedi Hasan 10–0–44–1; Mohammad Saifuddin 8–1–57–2; Shakib Al Hasan 10–0–50–1; Mashrafe bin Mortaza 6–0–49–0; Mosaddek Hossain 6–0–38–0.

Umpires: P. R. Reiffel and J. S. Wilson. Third umpire: H. D. P. K. Dharmasena.
Referee: D. C. Boon.

ENGLAND v PAKISTAN

At Nottingham, June 3. Pakistan won by 14 runs. Toss: England.

If Bangladesh lit a spark under the tournament, Pakistan doused it in petrol. Roared on by their raucous support, they rediscovered the untrammelled qualities that make them so compelling, and put a dent in England's self-esteem. It made for a stunning spectacle – and there was even a sprinkling of combustible moments, invoking the historic enmity that defines this fixture. After 11 ODI defeats in a row, including a 4–0 thumping by England, Pakistan would have been entitled to feel cowed. But there was a mood swing in the first over, when one of two fours hit by Fakhar Zaman off Woakes came via a misfield by Morgan. It set the tone for a slipshod fielding display. The nadir came when Roy grassed a skyer at long-off after Mohammad Hafeez, on 14, mistimed Rashid. Hafeez went on to hit 84, while Babar Azam and Sarfraz Ahmed also contributed half-centuries; Woakes's four catches were an England ODI record for a non-wicketkeeper. Such was England's form – they had not failed in a home run-chase since September 2015 – that a target of 349 did not seem terrifying. Taking a leaf out of South Africa's book, Pakistan opened with a leg-spinner, and in his second over Shadab Khan trapped Roy on the sweep, a wasted review compounding the error. But from 118 for four, Root and Buttler put on 130 in 17 overs, both reaching hundreds, the first of the tournament – Root from 97

FASTEST WORLD CUP HUNDREDS

Balls

50	K. J. O'Brien (113)............	Ireland v England at Bangalore............	2010-11
51	G. J. Maxwell (102)...........	Australia v Sri Lanka at Sydney............	2014-15
52	A. B. de Villiers (162*).......	South Africa v West Indies at Sydney.......	2014-15
57	**E. J. G. Morgan (148)**........	**England v Afghanistan at Manchester**....	**2019**
66	M. L. Hayden (101)..........	Australia v South Africa at Basseterre.......	2006-07
67	J. M. Davison (111)..........	Canada v West Indies at Centurion.........	2002-03
70	P. R. Stirling (101)..........	Ireland v Netherlands at Kolkata..........	2010-11
70	K. C. Sangakkara (117*).....	Sri Lanka v England at Wellington.........	2014-15
72	A. C. Gilchrist (149)........	Australia v Sri Lanka at Bridgetown†	2006-07
73	K. C. Sangakkara (105*).....	Sri Lanka v Bangladesh at Melbourne......	2014-15
75	**J. C. Buttler (103)**...........	**England v Pakistan at Nottingham**.......	**2019**

† *World Cup final.*

balls, Buttler from 75 (for 15 days, England's fastest at a World Cup). But both fell soon after and, with Pakistan's fans cranking up the volume, their bowlers suffocated England's late middle order. Both sides were warned for throwing the ball in on the bounce, prompting Root and Buttler to mutter about its condition. It really was just like old times.   RICHARD WHITEHEAD

Player of the Match: Mohammad Hafeez.   *Attendance:* 14,882.

Pakistan

Imam-ul-Haq c Woakes b Ali..........	44
Fakhar Zaman st Buttler b Ali..........	36
Babar Azam c Woakes b Ali..........	63
Mohammad Hafeez c Woakes b Wood....	84
*†Sarfraz Ahmed c and b Woakes........	55
Asif Ali c Bairstow b Wood	14
Shoaib Malik c Morgan b Woakes........	8
Wahab Riaz c Root b Woakes...........	4

Mohammad Amir did not bat.

Hasan Ali not out....................	10
Shadab Khan not out	10
B 1, lb 8, w 11	20

1/82 (2) 2/111 (1)   (8 wkts, 50 overs) 348
3/199 (3) 4/279 (4)
5/311 (6) 6/319 (5)
7/325 (8) 8/337 (7)   10 overs: 69-0

Woakes 8–1–71–3; Archer 10–0–79–0; Ali 10–0–50–3; Wood 10–0–53–2; Stokes 7–0–43–0; Rashid 5–0–43–0.

England

J. J. Roy lbw b Shadab Khan............	8
J. M. Bairstow c Sarfraz Ahmed	
b Wahab Riaz.	32
J. E. Root c Mohammad Hafeez	
b Shadab Khan.	107
*E. J. G. Morgan b Mohammad Hafeez	9
B. A. Stokes c Sarfraz Ahmed	
b Shoaib Malik.	13
†J. C. Buttler c Wahab Riaz	
b Mohammad Amir.	103
M. M. Ali c Fakhar Zaman b Wahab Riaz .	19
C. R. Woakes c Sarfraz Ahmed	
b Wahab Riaz.	21

J. C. Archer c Wahab Riaz	
b Mohammad Amir.	1
A. U. Rashid not out	3
M. A. Wood not out	10
Lb 3, w 5	8

1/12 (1) 2/60 (2)   (9 wkts, 50 overs) 334
3/86 (4) 4/118 (5)
5/248 (3) 6/288 (6)
7/320 (7) 8/320 (8)
9/322 (9)   10 overs: 62-2

Shadab Khan 10–0–63–2; Mohammad Amir 10–0–67–2; Wahab Riaz 10–0–82–3; Hasan Ali 10–0–66–0; Mohammad Hafeez 7–0–43–1; Shoaib Malik 3–0–10–1.

Umpires: M. Erasmus and S. Ravi.   Third umpire: R. S. A. Palliyaguruge.
Referee: J. J. Crowe.

Off the record: Mohammad Nabi took four for 30 against Sri Lanka with his off-breaks, the best World Cup figures for Afghanistan.

AFGHANISTAN v SRI LANKA

At Cardiff, June 4. Sri Lanka won by 34 runs (DLS). Toss: Afghanistan.

The tournament was not a week old, yet this already felt like a scramble to avoid the wooden spoon. Both teams, crushed in their opening fixture, knew flawed opponents represented their best chance of victory. Inserted under skies of Cambrian slate, Sri Lanka began with unexpected sparkle: the openers feasted on wayward fare, especially from Hamid Hassan, and 50 came up in the fifth. By the 21st, it was 144 for one, and thoughts turned to the stronghold such foundations would support. It turned out to be a castle in the air. Brick by brick, Sri Lanka demolished their own platform, abetted by Mohammad Nabi, Afghanistan's canny off-spinner. Despite modest turn, he bowled Thirimanne, then had Mendis and Mathews held at slip – all in the 22nd over. A revitalised Hamid removed de Silva in the next, before Tissara Perera ran himself out, and Udana missed a slog. The roof fell in when Kusal Perera nicked a reverse-sweep, ending a vital innings. At 180 for eight, seven had gone for 36. After a three-hour rain delay, it became a 41-over affair – not that Sri Lanka used all theirs. Second-highest contribution came from Extras, including 22 in wides. Needing a revised 187, Afghanistan also set off at full pelt, but the accuracy of Pradeep Fernando, the only change for either side, highlighted the difference between them. So did a phenomenal catch from Tissara Perera, hurtling round the fine-leg boundary to dismiss the free-scoring Hazratullah Zazai. There was still the odd Chuckle Brothers moment: one shot was misfielded by three Sri Lankans on its way for four. But once Malinga rediscovered his inswinging yorkers, the game, watched by a meagre crowd, was up. HUGH CHEVALLIER

Player of the Match: A. N. P. R. Fernando. *Attendance:* 4,382.

Sri Lanka

*F. D. M. Karunaratne c Najibullah Zadran		
b Mohammad Nabi .	30	
†M. D. K. J. Perera c Mohammad Shahzad		
b Rashid Khan .	78	
H. D. R. L. Thirimanne b Mohammad Nabi	25	
B. K. G. Mendis c Rahmat Shah		
b Mohammad Nabi .	2	
A. D. Mathews c Rahmat Shah		
b Mohammad Nabi .	0	
D. M. de Silva c Mohammad Shahzad		
b Hamid Hassan .	0	
N. L. T. C. Perera run out (Hashmatullah		
Shahidi/Mohammad Shahzad) .	2	

I. Udana b Dawlat Zadran .	10
R. A. S. Lakmal not out.	15
S. L. Malinga b Dawlat Zadran .	4
A. N. P. R. Fernando b Rashid Khan.	0
Lb 10, w 22, nb 3 .	35

1/92 (1) 2/144 (3)   (36.5 overs) 201
3/146 (4) 4/146 (5)
5/149 (6) 6/159 (7)
7/178 (8) 8/180 (2)
9/199 (10) 10/201 (11)   10 overs: 79-0

Dawlat Zadran 6–0–34–2; Hamid Hassan 7–0–53–1; Mujeeb Zadran 3–0–19–0; Mohammad Nabi 9–0–30–4; Gulbadeen Naib 4–0–38–0; Rashid Khan 7.5–1–17–2.

Afghanistan

†Mohammad Shahzad c Karunaratne		
b Malinga .	7	
Hazratullah Zazai c N. L. T. C. Perera		
b Fernando .	30	
Rahmat Shah c Mathews b Udana.	2	
Hashmatullah Shahidi c M. D. K. J. Perera		
b Fernando .	4	
Mohammad Nabi b N. L. T. C. Perera .	11	
*Gulbadeen Naib lbw b Fernando.	23	
Najibullah Zadran run out (Karunaratne) .	43	

Rashid Khan b Fernando .	2
Dawlat Zadran b Malinga .	6
Hamid Hassan b Malinga .	6
Mujeeb Zadran not out .	1
B 1, w 15, nb 1 .	17

1/34 (1) 2/42 (3) 3/44 (2)   (32.4 overs) 152
4/57 (4) 5/57 (5) 6/121 (6)
7/123 (8) 8/136 (9) 9/145 (7)
10/152 (10)   8 overs: 43-2

Malinga 6.4–0–39–3; Lakmal 6–0–27–0; Udana 6–0–28–1; Fernando 9–1–31–4; N. L. T. C. Perera 4–0–19–1; de Silva 1–0–7–0.

Umpires: N. J. Llong and P. Wilson.   Third umpire: R. J. Tucker.
Referee: A. J. Pycroft.

INDIA v SOUTH AFRICA

At Southampton, June 5. India won by six wickets. Toss: South Africa.

India made a belated first appearance, and performed like old hands. Bumrah disposed of the openers, Chahal flummoxed the middle order, and Sharma ticked off his 23rd ODI century. For South Africa, it was a third defeat in seven days – a scenario so wearingly familiar that du Plessis, their captain, skipped the post-match press conference, sending Morris instead. Without Dale Steyn, who was now out of the tournament because of his shoulder, and Lungi Ngidi, nursing his hamstring, du Plessis had chosen to bat in testing conditions. That must have delighted India. First the relentless Bumrah brushed aside Amla – back after concussion – and de Kock. Then Chahal bowled van der Dussen, reverse sweeping, in the same over, and du Plessis through the gate. Morris rallied, but 227 felt like a white flag. Still, with a bit more luck, South Africa's bowlers might have made life tricky. Du Plessis, running forward from second slip, spilled Sharma off Rabada on one, and both openers gloved lifters just over gully. Rabada did get Dhawan, but not even the wicket of Kohli – superbly pouched by de Kock off Phehlukwayo for 18 – could change the game. Sharma was unflustered, adding 85 with Rahul and 74 with Dhoni, and surviving on 107 when Miller dropped a dolly at cover off an incredulous Rabada. It was the mistake of a team whose spirit was breaking.   LAWRENCE BOOTH

Player of the Match: R. G. Sharma.   Attendance: 14,322.

South Africa

H. M. Amla c Sharma b Bumrah	6	Imran Tahir c Jadhav	
†Q. de Kock c Kohli b Bumrah	10	b Bhuvneshwar Kumar	0
*F. du Plessis b Chahal	38		
H. E. van der Dussen b Chahal	22	B 1, lb 3, w 6	10
D. A. Miller c and b Chahal	31		
J-P. Duminy lbw b Yadav	3	1/11 (1) 2/24 (2) (9 wkts, 50 overs) 227	
A. L. Phehlukwayo st Dhoni b Chahal	34	3/78 (4) 4/80 (3)	
C. H. Morris c Kohli b Bhuvneshwar Kumar	42	5/89 (6) 6/135 (5) 7/158 (7)	
K. Rabada not out	31	8/224 (8) 9/227 (10) 10 overs: 34-2	

T. Shamsi did not bat.

Bhuvneshwar Kumar 10–0–44–2; Bumrah 10–1–35–2; Pandya 6–0–31–0; Yadav 10–0–46–1; Chahal 10–0–51–4; Jadhav 4–0–16–0.

India

S. Dhawan c de Kock b Rabada	8	H. H. Pandya not out	15
R. G. Sharma not out	122	Lb 3, w 4	7
*V. Kohli c de Kock b Phehlukwayo	18		
K. L. Rahul c du Plessis b Rabada	26	1/13 (1) 2/54 (3) (4 wkts, 47.3 overs) 230	
†M. S. Dhoni c and b Morris	34	3/139 (4) 4/213 (5) 10 overs: 34-1	

K. M. Jadhav, Bhuvneshwar Kumar, K. Yadav, Y. S. Chahal and J. J. Bumrah did not bat.

Imran Tahir 10–0–58–0; Rabada 10–1–39–2; Morris 10–3–36–1; Phehlukwayo 8.3–0–40–1; Shamsi 9–0–54–0.

Umpires: M. A. Gough and R. A. Kettleborough. Third umpire: R. K. Illingworth.
Referee: R. S. Madugalle.

BANGLADESH v NEW ZEALAND

At The Oval, June 5 (day/night). New Zealand won by two wickets. Toss: New Zealand.

At 160 for two after 31 overs, chasing a modest 245, New Zealand seemed to be coasting to victory. Williamson had survived a run-out chance on eight, when Mushfiqur Rahim dislodged the bails with his arm before collecting the ball, and put on 105 with Taylor, their 13th century stand in one-day internationals. But he hoisted an attempted flick off Mehedi Hasan to deep midwicket, and was followed in the same over by Latham. A single frame spared Neesham from a run-out in Mehedi's next, but the fall of Taylor, to a leg-side tickle after a measured 82 from 91 balls, sent the largely green-clad crowd wild again. "There were times out there I thought I was in Chittagong or Dhaka," said Taylor. Big hitters de Grandhomme and Neesham departed in successive overs; then, with seven wanted, Henry was castled by a Mohammad Saifuddin full toss. The pressure eased with two wides, before Ferguson jammed down on a yorker; it scudded away for four to level the scores. Santner had earlier dispensed no gifts during a tight spell, and now – glasses glinting beneath the lights – he eased Mustafizur Rahman through the covers. Bangladesh's innings, which had started under clouds, had been notable for New Zealand's discipline: only 37 runs came between the 30th and 40th overs, while Mahmudullah and Mosaddek Hossain faced 63 balls without a boundary. Of the main bowlers only Henry, who took four wickets, went for more than five an over. STEVEN LYNCH

Player of the Match: L. R. P. L. Taylor. *Attendance:* 17,219.

Bangladesh

Tamim Iqbal c Boult b Ferguson	24	Mehedi Hasan c Latham b Boult	7
Soumya Sarkar b Henry	25	*Mashrafe bin Mortaza c Boult b Henry	1
Shakib Al Hasan c Latham		Mustafizur Rahman not out	0
b de Grandhomme	64	B 1, lb 8, w 9	18
†Mushfiqur Rahim run out (Guptill/Latham)	19		
Mithun Ali c de Grandhomme b Henry	26	1/45 (2) 2/60 (1)	(49.2 overs) 244
Mahmudullah c Williamson b Santner	20	3/110 (4) 4/151 (3) 5/179 (5)	
Mosaddek Hossain c Guptill b Boult	11	6/197 (6) 7/224 (7) 8/235 (9)	
Mohammad Saifuddin b Henry	29	9/244 (10) 10/244 (8)	10 overs: 49-1

Henry 9.2–0–47–4; Boult 10–0–44–2; Ferguson 10–0–40–1; de Grandhomme 8–0–39–1; Neesham 2–0–24–0; Santner 10–1–41–1.

New Zealand

M. J. Guptill c Tamim Iqbal		C. de Grandhomme c Mushfiqur Rahim	
b Shakib Al Hasan	25	b Mohammad Saifuddin	15
C. Munro c Mehedi Hasan		M. J. Santner not out	17
b Shakib Al Hasan	24	M. J. Henry b Mohammad Saifuddin	6
*K. S. Williamson c Mosaddek Hossain		L. H. Ferguson not out	4
b Mehedi Hasan	40		
L. R. P. L. Taylor c Mushfiqur Rahim		W 9, nb 1	10
b Mosaddek Hossain	82		
†T. W. M. Latham c Mohammad Saifuddin		1/35 (1) 2/55 (2)	(8 wkts, 47.1 overs) 248
b Mehedi Hasan	0	3/160 (3) 4/162 (5)	
J. D. S. Neesham c Soumya Sarkar		5/191 (4) 6/218 (7)	
b Mosaddek Hossain	25	7/218 (6) 8/238 (9)	10 overs: 55-2

T. A. Boult did not bat.

Mashrafe bin Mortaza 5–0–32–0; Mehedi Hasan 10–0–47–2; Mustafizur Rahman 7.1–0–48–0; Shakib Al Hasan 10–0–47–2; Mohammad Saifuddin 7–0–41–2; Mosaddek Hossain 8–0–33–2.

Umpires: B. N. J. Oxenford and P. R. Reiffel.   Third umpire: J. S. Wilson.
Referee: D. C. Boon.

AUSTRALIA v WEST INDIES

At Nottingham, June 6. Australia won by 15 runs. Toss: West Indies.

When Stoinis bunted to midwicket, leaving Australia 79 for five, it seemed West Indies were carrying on where they left off against Pakistan. Their tall fast bowlers were digging it in again: Khawaja, struck on the helmet by Thomas, backed away after being hit by Russell, and toe-ended to the diving Hope. Smith settled in, though a gettable target was

HIGHEST SCORE FROM No. 8 IN ODIs

95*	C. R. Woakes	England v Sri Lanka at Nottingham	2016
92	**N. M. Coulter-Nile**	**Australia v West Indies at Nottingham**	**2019**
84	T. M. Odoyo	Kenya v Bangladesh at Nairobi (Gymkhana)	2006
83	L. Klusener	South Africa v Australia at Johannesburg	2001-02
83	D. L. Vettori	New Zealand v Australia at Christchurch	2004-05
83	J. D. P. Oram	New Zealand v Bangladesh at Napier	2009-10
80	T. T. Bresnan	England v Australia at Centurion	2009-10

The previous-highest in the World Cup was 72*, by H. H. Streak for Zimbabwe v New Zealand at Bloemfontein in 2002-03; in the 2019 semi-final at Manchester, R. A. Jadeja would make 77 for India v New Zealand.

still possible when Russell, in between feeling his troublesome knee, found Carey's edge after an adventurous 45. But West Indies were about to discover the sauce of the Coulter-Nile. After a sketchy start, he motored past his previous bests in international (34) and domestic cricket (64). He chipped Russell off his legs for six, clonked three more, and dominated a seventh-wicket stand of 102, which ended when Smith flicked Thomas to deep square. Six? No. Cottrell steamed round the boundary, clasped the ball in his outstretched left hand, and tossed it up as he skipped over the rope; he collected it back on the field and gave a gleeful salute. West Indies' chase of 289 had a frenetic start. After Lewis fell in the second over, Gayle was given out three times by Chris Gaffaney in five balls from Starc. Gayle reviewed all three: the first (for caught behind) had kissed stump rather than bat, the next (lbw) was missing leg, but the third was just flicking. West Indian outrage at what Michael Holding called "atrocious" umpiring (two decisions against Holder were later overturned) was amplified when replays showed the delivery before the final lbw was a huge uncalled no-ball, so Gayle should have been contemplating a free hit. Hope settled in, but chipped tamely to mid-on after 68 from 105 balls, and West Indies lost their way. Holder also fell to Starc, his 150th wicket in 77 ODIs, one quicker than the Pakistan off-spinner Saqlain Mushtaq. The tail could not prevent Australia's tenth successive one-day victory, despite Nurse – strangely inactive in the previous two overs – smacking the last four balls, from Coulter-Nile, to the boundary.   STEVEN LYNCH

Player of the Match: N. M. Coulter-Nile.   *Attendance:* 16,328.

Australia

D. A. Warner c Hetmyer b Cottrell	3	M. A. Starc c Holder b Brathwaite		8
*A. J. Finch c Hope b Thomas	6	A. Zampa not out		0
U. T. Khawaja c Hope b Russell	13			
S. P. D. Smith c Cottrell b Thomas	73	B 1, lb 1, w 24, nb 1		27
G. J. Maxwell c Hope b Cottrell	0			
M. P. Stoinis c Pooran b Holder	19	1/15 (2) 2/26 (1) 3/36 (3) (49 overs)	288
†A. T. Carey c Hope b Russell	45	4/38 (5) 5/79 (6) 6/147 (7)	
N. M. Coulter-Nile c Holder b Brathwaite	92	7/249 (4) 8/268 (9) 9/284 (8)	
P. J. Cummins c Cottrell b Brathwaite	2	10/288 (10)	10 overs: 48-4

Thomas 10–0–63–2; Cottrell 9–0–56–2; Russell 8–0–41–2; Brathwaite 10–0–67–3; Holder 7–2–28–1; Nurse 5–0–31–0.

West Indies

C. H. Gayle lbw b Starc	21	S. S. Cottrell b Starc		1
E. Lewis c Smith b Cummins	1	O. R. Thomas not out		0
†S. D. Hope c Khawaja b Cummins	68			
N. Pooran c Finch b Zampa	40	Lb 9, w 11		20
S. O. Hetmyer run out (Cummins/Maxwell)	21			
*J. O. Holder c Zampa b Starc	51	1/7 (2) 2/31 (1) (9 wkts, 50 overs)	273
A. D. Russell c Maxwell b Starc	15	3/99 (4) 4/149 (5)	
C. R. Brathwaite c Finch b Starc	16	5/190 (3) 6/216 (7) 7/252 (8)	
A. R. Nurse not out	19	8/252 (6) 9/256 (10)	10 overs: 54-2

Starc 10–1–46–5; Cummins 10–3–41–2; Coulter-Nile 10–0–70–0; Maxwell 6–1–31–0; Zampa 10–0–58–1; Stoinis 4–0–18–0.

Umpires: C. B. Gaffaney and R. S. A. Palliyaguruge.   Third umpire: M. Erasmus.
Referee: J. J. Crowe.

PAKISTAN v SRI LANKA

At Bristol, June 7. Abandoned.

This was only the second complete washout of a World Cup match in England: the previous instance came at The Oval in 1979 when, despite the tournament having reserve days, Sri Lanka v West Indies never got as far as the toss. The only other World Cup abandonment was Australia v Bangladesh at Brisbane in 2014-15, although India v Sri Lanka at Mackay in 1991-92 lasted just two balls.

ENGLAND v BANGLADESH

At Cardiff, June 8. England won by 106 runs. Toss: Bangladesh.

Borne along by the power of Roy and the pace of Archer, England served up a stinging riposte to their defeat by Pakistan. Both had been fined for poor behaviour in Nottingham, but now competed with a near-gale in South Wales to blow away Bangladesh. Roy crashed a superlative 153 from 121 balls out of 235 while he was in, eventually falling as he tried to hit Mehedi Hasan for a fourth successive six. Then, the wind behind him, Archer unleashed a five-over spell peaking at 95.1mph; excluding deliberate slower balls, he averaged 90.7, the fastest opening burst by an England one-day bowler since these things were first measured regularly in 2006. Wood actually sent down the day's quickest delivery (95.7), but Archer its most dramatic, the ball clipping the top of Soumya Sarkar's off stump and flying on the full over the boundary by the River Taff. England had looked untroubled after Roy and Bairstow began with their eighth century stand, and Buttler kept up the pace with a punishing 64 from 44. When Woakes and Plunkett carted 45 from the last 16 balls, they had what was briefly their highest World Cup total, well beyond 338 for eight in a tie against India at Bangalore in 2011. Led by Shakib Al Hasan, Bangladesh reached a respectable 169 for two, but in nearly 29 overs. Two wickets in four balls – one to Plunkett, who had replaced Moeen Ali – set them back. By the time Stokes, en route to his best ODI figures since January 2014, yorked Shakib for a classy 121, the required rate had climbed to 16. Bairstow kept wicket because Buttler had bruised his hip, and held four catches, while Archer returned to dock the tail, and lift English spirits. LAWRENCE BOOTH

Player of the Match: J. J. Roy. *Attendance:* 13,741.

England

J. J. Roy c Mashrafe bin Mortaza	B. A. Stokes c Mashrafe bin Mortaza	
b Mehedi Hasan . 153	b Mustafizur Rahman .	6
J. M. Bairstow c Mehedi Hasan	C. R. Woakes not out	18
b Mashrafe bin Mortaza . 51	L. E. Plunkett not out.	27
J. E. Root b Mohammad Saifuddin 21	Lb 3, w 7, nb 1.	11
†J. C. Buttler c Soumya Sarkar		
b Mohammad Saifuddin . 64	1/128 (2) 2/205 (3) (6 wkts, 50 overs) 386	
*E. J. G. Morgan c Soumya Sarkar	3/235 (1) 4/330 (4)	
b Mehedi Hasan . 35	5/340 (5) 6/341 (6) 10 overs: 67-0	

J. C. Archer, A. U. Rashid and M. A. Wood did not bat.

Shakib Al Hasan 10–0–71–0; Mashrafe bin Mortaza 10–0–68–1; Mohammad Saifuddin 9–0–78–2; Mustafizur Rahman 9–0–75–1; Mehedi Hasan 10–0–67–2; Mosaddek Hossain 2–0–24–0.

Bangladesh

Tamim Iqbal c Morgan b Wood 19	*Mashrafe bin Mortaza not out	4
Soumya Sarkar b Archer 2	Mustafizur Rahman c †Bairstow b Archer .	0
Shakib Al Hasan b Stokes 121		
†Mushfiqur Rahim c Roy b Plunkett 44	Lb 9, w 10	19
Mithun Ali c †Bairstow b Rashid 0		
Mahmudullah c †Bairstow b Wood 28	1/8 (2) 2/63 (1) 3/169 (4) (48.5 overs) 280	
Mosaddek Hossain c Archer b Stokes 26	4/170 (5) 5/219 (3) 6/254 (7)	
Mohammad Saifuddin b Stokes. 5	7/261 (6) 8/264 (8) 9/280 (9)	
Mehedi Hasan c †Bairstow b Archer. 12	10/280 (11) 10 overs: 48-1	

Woakes 8–0–67–0; Archer 8.5–2–29–3; Plunkett 8–0–36–1; Wood 8–0–52–2; Rashid 10–0–64–1; Stokes 6–1–23–3.

Umpires: H. D. P. K. Dharmasena and J. S. Wilson.   Third umpire: B. N. J. Oxenford.
Referee: D. C. Boon.

AFGHANISTAN v NEW ZEALAND

At Taunton, June 8 (day/night). New Zealand won by seven wickets. Toss: New Zealand.

New Zealand ensured they extracted the maximum benefit from their soft launch to the tournament with a third successive victory. After the harum-scarum conclusion to their win over Bangladesh, this was a return to traditional values: calm, calculated and completed with the minimum of fuss. For Afghanistan, who suffered a third straight defeat, there were few positives. Wicketkeeper-batsman Mohammad Shahzad had been sent home with a knee injury; he later claimed the first he heard of it was in an ICC press release (and that he was fit). Their batting was brittle, and a groggy Rashid Khan did not bowl after ducking into one from Ferguson that ricocheted via helmet on to stumps. For ten gloriously entertaining overs, it had been a different story, as openers Hazratullah Zazai and Noor Ali Zadran – apparently channelling Taunton's big-hitting heritage – charged to 61. "Relax, buddy!" shouted one anxious supporter in a large Afghan contingent as another lofted shot landed between fielders. It seemed too good to last, and so it proved: 66 without loss became 70 for four. Neesham, whose two overs against Bangladesh had cost 24, was the chief beneficiary, collecting a maiden ODI five-for. There were also four for the fiery Ferguson. Hashmatullah Shahidi was last out for a more measured 59. Aftab Alam surprised Guptill with bounce from the first ball of the reply, but Williamson made sure New Zealand progressed at their own, largely untroubled, pace.   RICHARD WHITEHEAD

Player of the Match: J. D. S. Neesham.   *Attendance:* 6,617.

Afghanistan

Hazratullah Zazai c Munro b Neesham	34	Aftab Alam c Latham b Ferguson 14
Noor Ali Zadran c Latham b Ferguson	31	Hamid Hassan not out 7
Rahmat Shah c Guptill b Neesham	0	
Hashmatullah Shahidi c Henry b Ferguson	59	Lb 6, w 2 8
*Gulbadeen Naib c Latham b Neesham	4	
Mohammad Nabi c Latham b Neesham	9	1/66 (1) 2/66 (2) 3/66 (3) (41.1 overs) 172
Najibullah Zadran c Latham b Neesham	4	4/70 (5) 5/105 (6) 6/109 (7)
Ikram Alikhil c Guptill b de Grandhomme	2	7/130 (8) 8/131 (9) 9/147 (10)
Rashid Khan b Ferguson	0	10/172 (4) 10 overs: 61-0

Henry 8–0–50–0; Boult 10–0–34–0; Ferguson 9.1–3–37–4; Neesham 10–1–31–5; de Grandhomme 4–1–14–1.

New Zealand

M. J. Guptill c Najibullah Zadran		†T. W. M. Latham not out 13
b Aftab Alam .	0	Lb 4, w 6, nb 1 11
C. Munro c Hamid Hassan b Aftab Alam	22	
K. S. Williamson not out	79	1/0 (1) 2/41 (2) (3 wkts, 32.1 overs) 173
L. R. P. L. Taylor b Aftab Alam	48	3/130 (4) 10 overs: 52-2

J. D. S. Neesham, C. de Grandhomme, M. J. Santner, M. J. Henry, L. H. Ferguson and T. A. Boult did not bat.

Aftab Alam 8.1–0–45–3; Hamid Hassan 7–0–30–0; Gulbadeen Naib 9–1–55–0; Mohammad Nabi 3–0–18–0; Rahmat Shah 5–0–21–0.

Umpires: Aleem Dar and M. A. Gough.   Third umpire: R. A. Kettleborough.
Referee: R. S. Madugalle.

THE INDIAN FAN PHENOMENON

Making themselves at home

ANAND VASU

India might not have won the World Cup, but their fans lorded it over the tournament. This was clear from their first game, against South Africa at Southampton, when a train full of blue jerseys headed south from Waterloo. In the stands, the effect was more extreme, and fans could be divided broadly into three categories – Indians from India, Indians from the UK, and Indians from America and elsewhere.

Indians from India have not always travelled abroad in large groups, but the Bharat Army have changed that. Despite ICC figures suggesting only 4% of World Cup ticket buyers lived in India, this group were the most vociferous – the likeliest to wear masks of nationalist prime minister Narendra Modi, and chant "*Mandir Yahin Banegi*" ("the temple will be built here"), a reference to right-wing Hindus wanting to develop the site of the demolished Babri Masjid mosque in Ayodhya, Uttar Pradesh.

British Indians tended to be found in smaller clusters, and lingered longer in the beer tents. Those from America (home to another 4% of buyers) gave themselves away by their accents. But whatever their origin, they turned up in huge numbers. Four days later, against Australia at The Oval, the joke was that the only yellow in the crowd came from the fluorescent jackets of the stewards. Officially, 32% of all tickets were bought by supporters of India.

How did they become so dominant? Mostly, it seems, through old-fashioned doggedness and innovation. Take Akshay Natarajan, an investment banker from London who extended his sabbatical to watch the World Cup. Before it began, there were two ballot windows, but he failed to get tickets in either. "I could not stand the thought of a World Cup in my backyard without going to an India match, so I stumped up £750 for a hospitality ticket for India–Australia," he says. But his luck improved, and he eventually attended nine league games (including India's first five), their semi and the final.

"I got my tickets mainly by patrolling the ICC resale website," says Akshay, who discovered there was most liquidity in the top-end (platinum) and lowest-end (bronze) tickets. "You had to check it every 15 minutes or so and, when you did get in a queue, it took as long as five hours for your turn to actually buy a ticket. I did this because I had the time and inclination, but there were entire Indian families living here who did it as a business. Every member of the family would be logged on, in shifts, and as soon as tickets became available they would add to their basket and put them up for sale on a WhatsApp group."

Akshay monitored three such groups, which had as many as 500 members. But getting to so many matches came at a price: tickets at face value, food and drink, and train travel all added up to nearly £2,500.

Others paid touts far more. One young man from Delhi wanted to propose to his girlfriend in the stands at India v Pakistan, and paid £10,000 for a pair of tickets (she says yes). Another, on a work trip in Europe, took a week out to attend five matches, each in a different city. When he arrived home, in San Francisco, he discovered a ticket had become available for the Pakistan game, so flew to Manchester on the morning of the match, then flew straight back after the last ball.

Sheer bloody-mindedness – that was the story behind India's fans reverse-colonising England, one ground at a time.

AUSTRALIA v INDIA

At The Oval, June 9. India won by 36 runs. Toss: India.

Four years previously, Australia had bossed India in the World Cup semi-final at Sydney. Now, before a noisy, partisan crowd, India dominated from the second over, after Sharma's airy chip off Starc was put down by Coulter-Nile, diving at short midwicket. Apart from that, the only discomfort the openers felt while putting on 127 in 22 overs was when Cummins rapped Dhawan on the left thumb, causing a hairline fracture (despite initial optimism, he was eventually ruled out of the tournament). Sharma parried a catch behind, but Kohli was at his most businesslike, tucking into some precision pulls against Australia's anaemic change bowling. Dhawan, who lives near Melbourne, sailed to his third hundred in five one-day internationals at The Oval, finally holing out to deep midwicket just after smashing Starc straight for his 16th four. Kohli took a back seat while Pandya (dropped first ball by Carey off Coulter-Nile) bashed and Dhoni lashed; his six off Starc was caught in the back row of the stand at square leg. In all, 116 came from the last ten overs. Once Finch was carelessly run out in the 14th, Australia never really threatened. Warner edged Bumrah's opening delivery into his stumps, but survived when the Zing bails stayed put – the tournament's fifth such instance. Warner continued to 56, but again found timing elusive: for the second time in nine days, he registered his slowest ODI fifty – 77 balls – and 48 of the 84 he faced overall were dots, including 14 in a row. Under cloud, and against testing seam bowling, Smith buckled down for a run-a-ball 69 before he was trapped by Bhuvneshwar Kumar. Carey slugged a 25-ball half-century, but in vain. Dhoni had accepted an ICC ruling that he should stop wearing gloves bearing military insignia, while Zampa briefly excited those looking for another Australian tampering scandal when he pulled something from his pocket and appeared to rub it on the ball. It turned out to be a hand-warmer. STEVEN LYNCH

Player of the Match: S. Dhawan. *Attendance:* 23,605.

India

R. G. Sharma c Carey b Coulter-Nile	57	K. M. Jadhav not out	0
S. Dhawan c sub (N. M. Lyon) b Starc	117	Lb 3, w 7	10
V. Kohli c Cummins b Stoinis	82		
H. H. Pandya c Finch b Cummins	48	1/127 (1) 2/220 (2) (5 wkts, 50 overs)	352
M. S. Dhoni c and b Stoinis	27	3/301 (4) 4/338 (5)	
K. L. Rahul not out	11	5/348 (3) 10 overs: 41-0	

Bhuvneshwar Kumar, K. Yadav, Y. S. Chahal and J. J. Bumrah did not bat.

Cummins 10–0–55–1; Starc 10–0–74–1; Coulter-Nile 10–1–63–1; Maxwell 7–0–45–0; Zampa 6–0–50–0; Stoinis 7–0–62–2.

Australia

D. A. Warner c Bhuvneshwar Kumar b Chahal	56	M. A. Starc run out (sub V. Shankar/ Bhuvneshwar Kumar)	3
A. J. Finch run out (Jadhav/Pandya)	36	A. Zampa c sub (R. A. Jadeja) b Bhuvneshwar Kumar	1
S. P. D. Smith lbw b Bhuvneshwar Kumar	69	B 3, lb 3, w 7, nb 1	14
U. T. Khawaja b Bumrah	42		
G. J. Maxwell c sub (R. A. Jadeja) b Chahal	28	1/61 (2) 2/133 (1) 3/202 (4) (50 overs)	316
M. P. Stoinis b Bhuvneshwar Kumar	0	4/238 (3) 5/238 (6) 6/244 (5)	
A. T. Carey not out	55	7/283 (8) 8/300 (9) 9/313 (10)	
N. M. Coulter-Nile c Kohli b Bumrah	4	10/316 (11) 10 overs: 48-0	
P. J. Cummins c Dhoni b Bumrah	8		

Bhuvneshwar Kumar 10–0–50–3; Bumrah 10–1–61–3; Pandya 10–0–68–0; Yadav 9–0–55–0; Chahal 10–0–62–2; Jadhav 1–0–14–0.

Umpires: C. B. Gaffaney and I. J. Gould. Third umpire: N. J. Llong.
Referee: A. J. Pycroft.

SOUTH AFRICA v WEST INDIES

At Southampton, June 10. No result. Toss: West Indies.

The forecast was so dreadful many stayed away. Those who did turn up shivered through 38 minutes' play – time enough for Cottrell to unfurl his trademark march-and-salute celebration twice more. South Africa gained their first point of the tournament, but realistically needed two to have a chance of the knockouts.   HUGH CHEVALLIER

South Africa

†Q. de Kock not out.	17
H. M. Amla c Gayle b Cottrell	6
A. K. Markram c Hope b Cottrell	5
*F. du Plessis not out.	0
W 1	1

1/11 (2) 2/28 (3)   (2 wkts, 7.3 overs)   29

H. E. van der Dussen, D. A. Miller, A. L. Phehlukwayo, C. H. Morris, K. Rabada, B. E. Hendricks and Imran Tahir did not bat.

Cottrell 4–1–18–2; Roach 3–0–10–0; Thomas 0.3–0–1–0.

West Indies

C. H. Gayle, †S. D. Hope, D. M. Bravo, N. Pooran, S. O. Hetmyer, *J. O. Holder, C. R. Brathwaite, A. R. Nurse, K. A. J. Roach, S. S. Cottrell, O. R. Thomas.

Umpires: R. J. Tucker and P. Wilson.   Third umpire: S. Ravi.
Referee: D. C. Boon.

BANGLADESH v SRI LANKA

At Bristol, June 11. Abandoned.

This was the second match to be washed out at Bristol in five days, both involving Sri Lanka.

AUSTRALIA v PAKISTAN

At Taunton, June 12. Australia won by 41 runs. Toss: Pakistan.

Pakistan twice came back from the dead, only to flatline at the crucial moment. First Mohammad Amir rattled through the middle order after Australia had reached 189 for one, to leave an achievable target of 308, then Hasan Ali and Wahab Riaz gave them an unexpected chance with the bat. Ultimately, though, the Pakistan fans who had flocked to Taunton in wintry conditions were left disappointed – and their team's World Cup hopes hanging by a thread. Australia had struggled against the nibble and swing of Amir, who routinely beat Finch and Warner early on; Wahab, meanwhile, had Finch dropped in the slips by Asif Ali on 26. Once the pitch settled, however, so did the Australians. The openers paced their innings superbly, upping the aggression against the part-time off-breaks of Mohammad Hafeez and Shoaib Malik, both playing ahead of frontline leg-spinner Shadab Khan. Finch fell for 82, but Warner went on to a century – his first in international cricket since the Boxing Day Ashes Test of 2017, and his first in 37 innings in England. He later admitted wondering during his ball-tampering exile whether he would ever score another for his country. Amir collected five for 30, his first such haul in ODIs but lacked support: his team-mates managed five for 267. Then, despite Imam-ul-Haq's diligent half-century, Pakistan were struggling for oxygen at 160 for six after 30 overs. Sarfraz Ahmed held firm, and lusty blows from Hasan and Wahab lifted them to 264 for seven with 35 balls left. But Wahab was given out on review after edging Starc to Carey, and the end followed swiftly – to Australia's relief. SAM MORSHEAD

Player of the Match: D. A. Warner. *Attendance:* 6,476.

Australia

*A. J. Finch c Mohammad Hafeez b Mohammad Amir .	82	N. M. Coulter-Nile c Sarfraz Ahmed b Wahab Riaz .	2
D. A. Warner c Imam-ul-Haq b Shaheen Shah Afridi .	107	P. J. Cummins c Sarfraz Ahmed b Hasan Ali	2
S. P. D. Smith c Asif Ali b Mohammad Hafeez .	10	M. A. Starc c Shoaib Malik b Mohammad Amir .	3
G. J. Maxwell b Shaheen Shah Afridi .	20	K. W. Richardson not out .	1
S. E. Marsh c Shoaib Malik b Mohammad Amir .	23	Lb 10, w 6, nb 3 .	19
U. T. Khawaja c Wahab Riaz b Mohammad Amir.	18	1/146 (1) 2/189 (3) (49 overs)	307
†A. T. Carey lbw b Mohammad Amir.	20	3/223 (4) 4/242 (2) 5/277 (6) 6/288 (5) 7/299 (8) 8/302 (9) 9/304 (7) 10/307 (10) 10 overs: 56-0	

Mohammad Amir 10-2-30-5; Shaheen Shah Afridi 10-0-70-2; Hasan Ali 10-0-67-1; Wahab Riaz 8-0-44-1; Mohammad Hafeez 7-0-60-1; Shoaib Malik 4-0-26-0.

Pakistan

Imam-ul-Haq c Carey b Cummins .	53	Mohammad Amir b Starc .	0
Fakhar Zaman c Richardson b Cummins .	0	Shaheen Shah Afridi not out .	1
Babar Azam c Richardson b Coulter-Nile. .	30		
Mohammad Hafeez c Starc b Finch .	46	Lb 4, w 9, nb 1.	14
†Sarfraz Ahmed run out (Maxwell) .	40		
Shoaib Malik c Carey b Cummins. .	0	1/2 (2) 2/56 (3) 3/136 (1) (45.4 overs)	266
Asif Ali c Carey b Richardson. .	5	4/146 (4) 5/147 (6) 6/160 (7)	
Hasan Ali c Khawaja b Richardson. .	32	7/200 (8) 8/264 (9) 9/265 (10)	
Wahab Riaz c Carey b Starc .	45	10/266 (5) 10 overs: 51-1	

Cummins 10-0-33-3; Starc 9-1-43-2; Richardson 8.4-0-62-2; Coulter-Nile 9-0-53-1; Maxwell 7-0-58-0; Finch 2-0-13-1.

Umpires: N. J. Llong and R. S. A. Palliyaguruge.   Third umpire: I. J. Gould.
Referee: A. J. Pycroft.

INDIA v NEW ZEALAND

At Nottingham, June 13. Abandoned.

The tournament's two unbeaten teams arrived at Trent Bridge – and left unbeaten too, after the third washout inside a week, more than in all the previous World Cups put together. Onlookers began to fear that the English weather in not-so-flaming June might ruin the competition. But this proved the last of the abandonments.

ENGLAND v WEST INDIES

At Southampton, June 14. England won by eight wickets. Toss: England.

On paper, this was a tricky assignment for England: they had lost to Pakistan, whom West Indies had crushed. England's luck, though, was in from the moment Morgan won the toss under familiar clouds – yet with the prospect of afternoon sun. Woakes put iffy form behind him to remove the left-handed Lewis with an inswinger in the third over and, had Wood not shelled a tough but holdable chance at third man, would have had Gayle for 15 in the seventh. It was not too costly: a slower ball from Plunkett forced an error, and

Bairstow held the skyer. Moments later, England shrewdly reviewed Wood's lbw shout against Hope. From a rickety 55 for three, West Indies pieced together a recovery thanks to rising stars Pooran and Hetmyer. They had added 89 when the breakthrough came via an unlikely Root. His little-seen, if honest, off-breaks-cum-gentle-seam inveigled both Hetmyer and Holder into giving return catches, and his first ODI wickets for 17 months had West Indies teetering at 156 for five. Archer, against the team he might have represented, slammed the escape hatch, another smart review confirming Buttler's belief that Pooran had gloved a snorter; the rest followed meekly. Yet there had been an unexpected cost: Roy (hamstring) and Morgan (back spasm) limped off. It meant the adaptable Root opened, with Woakes coming in at first drop: new England roles for both in white-ball cricket. Against an anodyne attack – on this slow surface, West Indies' demolition of Pakistan was a hazy memory – Root strode towards his third World Cup hundred, a national record. Bairstow, who wafted straight to third man, and Woakes hit uncomplicated forties, and England strolled to victory. HUGH CHEVALLIER

Player of the Match: J. E. Root. *Attendance:* 16,391.

West Indies

C. H. Gayle c Bairstow b Plunkett	36		O. R. Thomas not out		0
E. Lewis b Woakes	2		S. T. Gabriel b Wood		0
†S. D. Hope lbw b Wood	11				
N. Pooran c Buttler b Archer	63		Lb 5, w 12		17
S. O. Hetmyer c and b Root	39				
*J. O. Holder c and b Root	9		1/4 (2) 2/54 (1) 3/55 (3)	(44.4 overs)	212
A. D. Russell c Woakes b Wood	21		4/144 (5) 5/156 (6) 6/188 (7)		
C. R. Brathwaite c Buttler b Archer	14		7/202 (4) 8/202 (9) 9/211 (8)		
S. S. Cottrell lbw b Archer	0		10/212 (11)	10 overs: 41-1	

Woakes 5–2–16–1; Archer 9–1–30–3; Plunkett 5–0–30–1; Wood 6.4–0–18–3; Stokes 4–0–25–0; Rashid 10–0–61–0; Root 5–0–27–2.

England

J. M. Bairstow c Brathwaite b Gabriel	45
J. E. Root not out	100
C. R. Woakes c sub (F. A. Allen) b Gabriel	40
B. A. Stokes not out	10
Lb 2, w 15, nb 1	18

1/95 (1) 2/199 (3)   (2 wkts, 33.1 overs) 213
10 overs: 62-0

J. J. Roy, *E. J. G. Morgan, †J. C. Buttler, L. E. Plunkett, J. C. Archer, A. U. Rashid and M. A. Wood did not bat.

Cottrell 3–0–17–0; Thomas 6–0–43–0; Gabriel 7–0–49–2; Russell 2–0–14–0; Holder 5.1–0–31–0; Brathwaite 5–0–35–0; Gayle 5–0–22–0.

Umpires: H. D. P. K. Dharmasena and S. Ravi.   Third umpire: R. J. Tucker.
Referee: D. C. Boon.

AUSTRALIA v SRI LANKA

At The Oval, June 15. Australia won by 87 runs. Toss: Sri Lanka.

Sri Lanka began and ended the game in a foul mood, alleviated only by a breezy interlude. While Karunaratne and Kusal Perera started a pursuit of 335 with 115 in 15 overs, dressing-room anger over "very unfair" treatment by the ICC subsided. Team manager Ashantha de Mel had written to them to complain about a number of issues, including the green pitches his side had faced in Cardiff, and the absence of a swimming pool at their hotel in Bristol. The ICC dismissed the grumble, which might have explained why – after a collapse of eight for 61 – the Sri Lankans declined to send anyone to the press conference. Not that much analysis was needed: with the exception of two late run-outs in three balls by Udana off his own bowling, their fielding had been abysmal, allowing Finch to proceed to a powerful 153 from 132 balls. It was the highest score by an Australian captain at a World Cup, beating Ricky Ponting's 140 not out in the 2002-03 final against India at Johannesburg. Finch added 173 for the third wicket with Smith, before Maxwell provided the icing. Sri Lanka's openers opted for valour above caution, taking 12 off the first over, from Starc, racing past 50 in the seventh, and 100 in the 13th; Perera's half-century needed just 33 deliveries. But after he was bowled by Starc, the runs slowed against the off-breaks of Maxwell. When he caught Karunaratne for 97, Sri Lanka caved in to Starc and Richardson, handing Australia their fourth win out of five, and top spot in the table.   LAWRENCE BOOTH

Player of the Match: A. J. Finch.   *Attendance:* 20,826.

Australia

D. A. Warner b de Silva	26	P. J. Cummins run out (Udana)	0
*A. J. Finch c Karunaratne b Udana	153	M. A. Starc not out	5
U. T. Khawaja c Udana b de Silva	10	Lb 4, w 9, nb 1	14
S. P. D. Smith b Malinga	73		
G. J. Maxwell not out	46	1/80 (1) 2/100 (3) (7 wkts, 50 overs)	334
S. E. Marsh c Siriwardene b Udana	3	3/273 (2) 4/278 (4)	
†A. T. Carey run out (Udana)	4	5/310 (6) 6/317 (7) 7/320 (8) 10 overs: 53-0	

J. P. Behrendorff and K. W. Richardson did not bat.

Malinga 10-1-61-1; Fernando 10-0-88-0; Udana 10-0-57-2; N. L. T. C. Perera 10-0-67-0; de Silva 8-0-40-2; Siriwardene 2-0-17-0.

Sri Lanka

*F. D. M. Karunaratne c Maxwell b Richardson	97	I. Udana c Finch b Richardson	8
†M. D. K. J. Perera b Starc	52	S. L. Malinga c Khawaja b Richardson	1
H. D. R. L. Thirimanne c Carey b Behrendorff	16	A. N. P. R. Fernando c Carey b Cummins	0
B. K. G. Mendis c Carey b Starc	30	Lb 2, w 6	8
A. D. Mathews c Carey b Cummins	9	1/115 (2) 2/153 (3) (45.5 overs)	247
T. A. M. Siriwardene b Starc	3	3/186 (1) 4/205 (5) 5/209 (6)	
N. L. T. C. Perera c Warner b Starc	7	6/217 (7) 7/222 (4) 8/236 (9)	
D. M. de Silva not out	16	9/237 (10) 10/247 (11) 10 overs: 87-0	

Starc 10-0-55-4; Cummins 7.5-0-38-2; Behrendorff 9-0-59-1; Richardson 9-1-47-3; Maxwell 10-0-46-0.

Umpires: Aleem Dar and R. K. Illingworth.   Third umpire: M. A. Gough.
Referee: J. J. Crowe.

AFGHANISTAN v SOUTH AFRICA

At Cardiff, June 15 (day/night). South Africa won by nine wickets (DLS). Toss: South Africa.
    South Africa finally won, defying two weather interruptions to cruise home with almost 20 overs to spare. Put in, Afghanistan had reached 69 for two before the hour-long second break, then donated five for eight after the restart. One of those was Asghar Afghan, playing his first match as he was now fully fit, according to his successor, Gulbadeen Naib; bafflingly, the man to make way was Najibullah Zadran, Afghanistan's leading scorer in the tournament. Imran Tahir was the destroyer, castling Noor Ali with a first-ball googly, and catching Asghar for a duck off his own bowling four deliveries later. It took a muscular 35 from Rashid Khan to lift the total into three figures. After the target was

tweaked to 127 off 48 overs, de Kock collected 68 and put on 104 with Amla, South Africa's first ODI century opening stand for 20 months. Desperate for time in the middle, Amla laboured to 41 from 83 balls, a curious innings given South Africa needed to repair their net run-rate. Phehlukwayo, having bowled tightly, was promoted to No. 3, and ended the match by walloping Mohammad Nabi straight for six.   LUNGANI ZAMA

Player of the Match: Imran Tahir.   *Attendance:* 10,103.

Afghanistan

Hazratullah Zazai c van der Dussen		Rashid Khan c van der Dussen b Imran Tahir	35
b Rabada.	22	Hamid Hassan c du Plessis b Morris	0
Noor Ali Zadran b Imran Tahir	32	Aftab Alam not out	0
Rahmat Shah lbw b Morris	6		
Hashmatullah Shahidi c du Plessis		Lb 4, w 3	7
b Phehlukwayo.	8		—
Asghar Afghan c and b Imran Tahir	0	1/39 (1) 2/56 (3) 3/69 (4) (34.1 overs)	125
Mohammad Nabi b Phehlukwayo	1	4/69 (2) 5/70 (5) 6/70 (6)	
†Ikram Alikhil c Amla b Morris	9	7/77 (8) 8/111 (7) 9/125 (9)	
*Gulbadeen Naib c Markram b Imran Tahir	5	10/125 (10)	10 overs: 43-1

Rabada 8–1–36–1; Hendricks 5–1–25–0; Phehlukwayo 8–1–18–2; Morris 6.1–2–13–3; Imran Tahir 7–0–29–4.

South Africa

H. M. Amla not out	41		
†Q. de Kock c Mohammad Nabi			
b Gulbadeen Naib.	68		
A. L. Phehlukwayo not out	17		
Lb 1, w 4	5		
	—		
1/104 (2) (1 wkt, 28.4 overs)	131		
10 overs: 35-0			

A. K. Markram, *F. du Plessis, H. E. van der Dussen, D. A. Miller, C. H. Morris, K. Rabada, B. E. Hendricks and Imran Tahir did not bat.

Aftab Alam 5–1–16–0; Hamid Hassan 4–1–11–0; Rashid Khan 7–0–45–0; Gulbadeen Naib 6–0–29–1; Mohammad Nabi 6.4–0–29–0.

Umpires: C. B. Gaffaney and R. S. A. Palliyaguruge.   Third umpire: I. J. Gould.
Referee: A. J. Pycroft.

INDIA v PAKISTAN

At Manchester, June 16. India won by 89 runs (DLS). Toss: Pakistan.

Around a third of a billion were estimated to have tuned in to a match that never scaled the heights demanded by a pounding Manchester crowd. It had roughly three times the viewers of the most-watched Super Bowl, but a combination of leaden skies, Pakistan's inferiority complex and Sharma's effortless majesty produced a game with little drama. After Sarfraz Ahmed invited India's new-look opening partnership of Rahul and Sharma to have first go, it did not take long for erratic bowling – especially from Hasan Ali and Wahab Riaz – to suck the life from the contest. Rahul registered a serene fifty, before Sharma breezed to another hundred. It seemed he might reach his fourth ODI double, only to loft Hasan to short fine leg in the 39th. Kohli took over, but with 15 deliveries left and a century possible, he flapped at a bouncer from Mohammad Amir – a beacon of quality in a threadbare attack – and walked. Replays showed no edge, and Kohli later blamed a

WICKET WITH FIRST BALL IN THE WORLD CUP

Bowler	*Batsman*		
M. A. Ealham	H. P. Tillekeratne	England v Sri Lanka at Lord's	1999
I. J. Harvey	Salim Elahi	Australia v Pakistan at Johannesburg.	2002-03
M. O. Jones	R. V. Uthappa	Bermuda v India at Port-of-Spain . .	2006-07
Mohammad Yousuf† . .	C. B. Mpofu	Pakistan v Zimbabwe at Kingston . . .	2006-07
N. L. T. C. Perera	J. M. Davison	Sri Lanka v Canada at Hambantota . .	2010-11
J. O. Ngoche	R. Gunasekera‡	Kenya v Canada at Delhi	2010-11
Dawlat Zadran	H. D. R. L. Thirimanne	Afghanistan v Sri Lanka at Dunedin .	2014-15
V. Shankar	**Imam-ul-Haq**	**India v Pakistan at Manchester**	**2019**

† *His only delivery in the World Cup.* ‡ *Stumped off a wide.*
For New Zealand against England at Gros Islet in 2006-07, J. E. C. Franklin dismissed E. C. Joyce
with his first legal delivery, after a no-ball.
Ball-by-ball data is not available for several matches prior to 1999.

clicky bat handle. No matter: Pakistan were never in the hunt. Imam-ul-Haq fell to Shankar's first ball, after Bhuvneshwar Kumar pulled a hamstring mid-over, and even a 104-run stand for the second wicket between Fakhar Zaman and Babar Azam was a mishmash of style and desperation. When Kuldeep Yadav dismissed them in consecutive overs, Pakistan's slim chances evaporated. Then came another lengthy rain delay. With evening approaching and many fans having left, the teams retook the field for a farcical five-over spell in which Pakistan needed another 136. Victory put India 7–0 ahead in World Cup clashes. Few had been as emphatic. PHIL WALKER

Player of the Match: R. G. Sharma. *Attendance:* 22,865.

India

K. L. Rahul c Babar Azam b Wahab Riaz .	57	V. Shankar not out.	15
R. G. Sharma c Wahab Riaz b Hasan Ali . .	140	K. M. Jadhav not out.	9
*V. Kohli c Sarfraz Ahmed			
b Mohammad Amir .	77	B 1, lb 1, w 9	11
H. H. Pandya c Babar Azam			—
b Mohammad Amir .	26	1/136 (1) 2/234 (2) (5 wkts, 50 overs)	336
M. S. Dhoni c Sarfraz Ahmed		3/285 (4) 4/298 (5)	
b Mohammad Amir .	1	5/314 (3) 10 overs: 53-0	

Bhuvneshwar Kumar, K. Yadav, J. J. Bumrah and Y. S. Chahal did not bat.

Mohammad Amir 10–1–47–3; Hasan Ali 9–0–84–1; Wahab Riaz 10–0–71–1; Imad Wasim 10–0–49–0; Shadab Khan 9–0–61–0; Shoaib Malik 1–0–11–0; Mohammad Hafeez 1–0–11–0.

Pakistan

Imam-ul-Haq lbw b Shankar	7	Shadab Khan not out	20
Fakhar Zaman c Chahal b Yadav	62		
Babar Azam b Yadav	48	Lb 1, w 6, nb 1	8
Mohammad Hafeez c Shankar b Pandya. . .	9		—
*Sarfraz Ahmed b Shankar.	12	1/13 (1) 2/117 (3) (6 wkts, 40 overs)	212
Shoaib Malik b Pandya	0	3/126 (2) 4/129 (4)	
Imad Wasim not out	46	5/129 (6) 6/165 (5) 10 overs: 38-1	

Hasan Ali, Wahab Riaz and Mohammad Amir did not bat.

Bhuvneshwar Kumar 2.4–0–8–0; Bumrah 8–0–52–0; Shankar 5.2–0–22–2; Pandya 8–0–44–2; Yadav 9–1–32–2; Chahal 7–0–53–0.

Umpires: M. Erasmus and B. N. J. Oxenford. Third umpire: J. S. Wilson.
Referee: R. S. Madugalle.

BANGLADESH v WEST INDIES

At Taunton, June 17. Bangladesh won by seven wickets. Toss: Bangladesh.

At the halfway point of the qualifying stage, these teams arrived at a critical moment. The winners would stay in the mix, the losers would glance nervously at airline schedules. Bangladesh handled the pressure, and sashayed home to complete the second-highest successful World Cup run-chase. At the heart of a stirring triumph was Shakib Al Hasan. Gathering records like a wealthy vinyl collector, he hit his second successive hundred, in the process reaching an ODI double of 6,000 runs and 250 wickets in 92 fewer matches than the next fastest (Shahid Afridi). With Liton Das – celebrating his call-up with an immaculately constructed 94 from 69 balls – he put on an unbeaten 189, a national World Cup record. Despite mounting evidence that the tactic was not working, West Indies kept bowling short;

HIGHEST SUCCESSFUL WORLD CUP RUN-CHASES

Total	Overs		
329-7	49.1	Ireland v England (327-8) at Bangalore	2010-11
322-3	**41.3**	**Bangladesh v West Indies (321-8) at Taunton**	**2019**
322-4	48.1	Bangladesh v Scotland (318-8) at Nelson	2014-15
313-7	49.2	Sri Lanka v Zimbabwe (312-4) at New Plymouth	1991-92
312-1	47.2	Sri Lanka v England (309-6) at Wellington	2014-15
307-4	47.4	Ireland v Netherlands (306) at Kolkata.	2010-11
307-6	45.5	Ireland v West Indies (304-7) at Nelson	2014-15
301-9	49.5	England v West Indies (300) at Bridgetown.	2006-07
300-7	49.4	South Africa v India (296) at Nagpur	2010-11

Bangladesh were unfazed. But the plotline was not straightforward. Holder rued an incident in the 23rd over, when Shakib swung lazily at Russell and the ball landed between Gabriel, snoozing at fine leg, and Hope, haring back from behind the stumps. That would have been 148 for four, and given West Indies an opening. Their own innings had been a stop–start affair: Hope may have batted too long (121 balls) for 96, others not long enough, although Lewis belatedly made his mark with 70 off 67. In one passage of rollicking entertainment, 60 came between the 35th and 38th overs, with Hetmyer, who holed out after reaching 50 in 25 deliveries, striking the ball beautifully. Cottrell provided one other highlight: swooping on Tamim Iqbal's firmly struck drive in his follow-through, he hurled the ball back in a flash, beating Tamim's dive to complete a thrilling run-out. RICHARD WHITEHEAD

Player of the Match: Shakib Al Hasan.　*Attendance:* 6,613.

West Indies

C. H. Gayle c Mushfiqur Rahim b Mohammad Saifuddin .	0	*J. O. Holder c Mahmudullah b Mohammad Saifuddin .	33
E. Lewis c sub (Sabbir Rahman) b Shakib Al Hasan .	70	D. M. Bravo b Mohammad Saifuddin	19
†S. D. Hope c Liton Das b Mustafizur Rahman .	96	O. R. Thomas not out	6
N. Pooran c Soumya Sarkar b Shakib Al Hasan .	25	Lb 6, w 16	22
S. O. Hetmyer c Tamim Iqbal b Mustafizur Rahman .	50	1/6 (1) 2/122 (2) (8 wkts, 50 overs) 321	
A. D. Russell c Mushfiqur Rahim b Mustafizur Rahman .	0	3/159 (4) 4/242 (5) 5/243 (6) 6/282 (7) 7/297 (3) 8/321 (8)	

S. S. Cottrell and S. T. Gabriel did not bat.

10 overs: 32-1

Mashrafe bin Mortaza 8–1–37–0; Mohammad Saifuddin 10–1–72–3; Mustafizur Rahman 9–0–59–3; Mehedi Hasan 9–0–57–0; Mosaddek Hossain 6–0–36–0; Shakib Al Hasan 8–0–54–2.

Bangladesh

Tamim Iqbal run out (Cottrell)	48
Soumya Sarkar c Gayle b Russell	29
Shakib Al Hasan not out	124
†Mushfiqur Rahim c Hope b Thomas	1
Liton Das not out	94
B 1, w 25	26

1/52 (2) 2/121 (1)   (3 wkts, 41.3 overs) 322
3/133 (4)   10 overs: 70-1

Mahmudullah, Mosaddek Hossain, Mohammad Saifuddin, Mehedi Hasan, *Mashrafe bin Mortaza and Mustafizur Rahman did not bat.

Cottrell 10–0–65–0; Holder 9–0–62–0; Russell 6–0–42–1; Gabriel 8.3–0–78–0; Thomas 6–0–52–1; Gayle 2–0–22–0.

Umpires: S. Ravi and R. J. Tucker.   Third umpire: P. Wilson.
Referee: D. C. Boon.

ENGLAND v AFGHANISTAN

At Manchester, June 18. England won by 150 runs. Toss: England.

Untroubled by his dodgy back, and obliged to go for it after choosing not to promote Buttler, Morgan embarked on the biggest six-hitting spree in the history of international cricket. There were 17 in total, all between long-off and midwicket, all out of the middle; he later admitted he didn't think he had the innings in him. On a less-than-fluent pitch, England had been aiming for 280–290, but Morgan's assault meant they could target 400. Among Afghanistan's bowlers, only Mujeeb Zadran's clever off-breaks were spared, while Rashid Khan's leg-spin suffered most. Having never conceded more than two sixes in an

RECORDS SET AT OLD TRAFFORD

17	Sixes by Eoin Morgan, beating the previous one-day international record of 16, set by Rohit Sharma in 2013-14, and equalled by A. B. de Villiers and Chris Gayle in 2014-15. No one has hit more sixes in any international format, and only D'Arcy Short, with 23 in his 257 for Western Australia v Queensland in Sydney in 2018-19, has hit more in a List A innings.
25	Sixes by England, beating their own ODI record of 24, against West Indies in Grenada in February 2019.
33	Sixes in the match, a World Cup record – previously 31, by New Zealand (15) and West Indies (16) at Wellington in 2014-15. Overall, only two ODIs have featured more sixes: the most is 46, by England (24) and West Indies (22) in Grenada in 2018-19.
57	Balls for Morgan's century, England's fastest in the World Cup – previously 75, by Jos Buttler against Pakistan at Nottingham 15 days earlier.
110	Runs conceded (from nine overs) by Rashid Khan, the most in a World Cup innings – previously 105 (from 12 overs, including a maiden) by New Zealand's Martin Snedden against England at The Oval in 1983. Only Mick Lewis, with 0-113 for Australia v South Africa at Johannesburg in 2005-06, had conceded more in an ODI innings.
189	Runs added by Joe Root and Morgan, an England record for any wicket in the World Cup, beating 176 for the second by Dennis Amiss and Keith Fletcher against India on the opening day of the first World Cup in 1975.
247	Afghanistan's highest World Cup total at the time, beating 232 against Sri Lanka at Dunedin in 2014-15.
397	England's highest World Cup total, beating 386 for six against Bangladesh at Cardiff ten days previously.

STEVEN LYNCH

ODI innings, he went for a world-record 11; seven were by Morgan, a record for one batsman against one bowler, though Rashid ought to have dismissed him for 28, only for Dawlat Zadran to misjudge the catch at deep midwicket. Rashid's nine overs cost 110. Morgan's eventual 148 from 71 balls was the highest of his 13 ODI centuries, and overshadowed two near misses: 90 from Bairstow (opening with Vince because Jason Roy had hamstring trouble) and 88 from Root. A nine-ball 31 from Ali, recalled in place of Liam Plunkett, took England's tally of sixes to 25, another world record, and more than they had hit in total at any previous World Cup. The last 20 overs produced 233. Noor Ali Zadran dragged on for a duck against Archer, but England missed the chance to run through Afghanistan when Bairstow at slip dropped Rahmat Shah on six off Woakes. Instead, the batsmen knuckled down, while Hashmatullah Shahidi overcame a nasty blow on the helmet from Wood to make 76, ignoring medical advice to leave the field because he didn't want to concern his family. When the Afghans survived 50 overs for the first time in the tournament, it was a crumb of comfort on a day when England tucked in.   LAWRENCE BOOTH

Player of the Match: E. J. G. Morgan.   *Attendance:* 21,737.

England

J. M. Vince c Mujeeb Zadran		B. A. Stokes b Dawlat Zadran	2
b Dawlat Zadran .	26	M. M. Ali not out.	31
J. M. Bairstow c and b Gulbadeen Naib . . .	90	C. R. Woakes not out	1
J. E. Root c Rahmat Shah b Gulbadeen Naib	88	Lb 1, w 7, nb 1	9
*E. J. G. Morgan c Rahmat Shah			
b Gulbadeen Naib .	148	1/44 (1) 2/164 (2) (6 wkts, 50 overs)	397
†J. C. Buttler c Mohammad Nabi		3/353 (3) 4/359 (4)	
b Dawlat Zadran .	2	5/362 (5) 6/378 (6) 10 overs: 46-1	

A. U. Rashid, J. C. Archer and M. A. Wood did not bat.

Mujeeb Zadran 10–0–44–0; Dawlat Zadran 10–0–85–3; Mohammad Nabi 9–0–70–0; Gulbadeen Naib 10–0–68–3; Rahmat Shah 2–0–19–0; Rashid Khan 9–0–110–0.

Afghanistan

Noor Ali Zadran b Archer	0	†Ikram Alikhil not out	3
*Gulbadeen Naib c Buttler b Wood	37	Dawlat Zadran not out	0
Rahmat Shah c Bairstow b Rashid	46	Lb 1, w 8	9
Hashmatullah Shahidi b Archer.	76		
Asghar Afghan c Root b Rashid	44	1/4 (1) 2/52 (2) (8 wkts, 50 overs)	247
Mohammad Nabi c Stokes b Rashid	9	3/104 (3) 4/198 (5)	
Najibullah Zadran b Wood	15	5/210 (6) 6/234 (4)	
Rashid Khan c Bairstow b Archer.	8	7/234 (7) 8/247 (8) 10 overs: 48-1	

Mujeeb Zadran did not bat.

Woakes 9–0–41–0; Archer 10–1–52–3; Ali 7–0–35–0; Wood 10–1–40–2; Stokes 4–0–12–0; Rashid 10–0–66–3.

Umpires: P. R. Reiffel and J. S. Wilson.   Third umpire: M. Erasmus.
Referee: R. S. Madugalle.

NEW ZEALAND v SOUTH AFRICA

At Birmingham, June 19. New Zealand won by four wickets. Toss: New Zealand.

At last came the gripping finish the World Cup craved, but amid the tumult Williamson was as cool as a hired gun. Needing 12 from seven balls, New Zealand were in danger of making a hash of the chase, while South Africa sensed a shot at redemption. But

The glance that brought a thousand runs? Kane Williamson deflects another to third man.

Williamson steered a surgically precise four past short third man and, having regained the strike, lofted Phehlukwayo into the Hollies Stand for the first six of a magnificent innings. It seemed incidental that it also brought up his hundred. Next ball, he threaded another late dab between fielders to finish the job. South Africa had passed up chances to revive their car crash of a tournament. In the 38th over – Imran Tahir's last – Miller failed to cling on when de Grandhomme offered a difficult chance. More grievously, Tahir attracted no support when he thought Williamson, on 76, had edged to de Kock; replays showed Tahir was right. The list of gaffes grew when Miller bungled a chance to run Williamson out. After a sodden outfield had reduced the match to 49 overs a side, South Africa batted like a team hobbled by fear. Only van der Dussen, with an unbeaten 67 off 64 balls, showed much urgency. The pitch was tricky rather than treacherous, and de Grandhomme – whose ten overs had cost only 33 – shrewdly deployed the local knowledge gained in two spells with Warwickshire. He hit an occasionally brutal 60 off 47 balls, and added 91 with Williamson. RICHARD WHITEHEAD

Player of the Match: K. S. Williamson. *Attendance:* 20,252.

LEADING THEM HOME

Highest scores by captains in successful World Cup run-chases:

134*	S. P. Fleming	New Zealand v South Africa at Johannesburg	2002-03
120*	S. R. Waugh	Australia v South Africa at Leeds	1999
114*	G. M. Turner	New Zealand v India at Manchester	1975
107*	S. C. Ganguly	India v Kenya at Cape Town	2002-03
106*	**K. S. Williamson**	**New Zealand v South Africa at Birmingham**	**2019**
102*	S. P. Fleming	New Zealand v Bangladesh at North Sound	2006-07

South Africa

†Q. de Kock b Boult	5	C. H. Morris not out	6
H. M. Amla b Santner	55		
*F. du Plessis b Ferguson	23		
A. K. Markram c Munro b de Grandhomme	38	Lb 7, w 4	11
H. E. van der Dussen not out	67		
D. A. Miller c Boult b Ferguson	36	1/9 (1) 2/59 (3) (6 wkts, 49 overs) 241	
A. L. Phehlukwayo c Williamson		3/111 (2) 4/136 (4)	
b Ferguson	0	5/208 (6) 6/218 (7) 10 overs: 40-1	

K. Rabada, L. T. Ngidi and Imran Tahir did not bat.

Henry 10–2–34–0; Boult 10–0–63–1; Ferguson 10–0–59–3; de Grandhomme 10–0–33–1; Santner 9–0–45–1.

New Zealand

M. J. Guptill hit wkt b Phehlukwayo	35	M. J. Santner not out	2
C. Munro c and b Rabada	9		
*K. S. Williamson not out	106	Lb 1, w 6, nb 1	8
L. R. P. L. Taylor c de Kock b Morris	1		
†T. W. M. Latham c de Kock b Morris	1	1/12 (2) 2/72 (1) (6 wkts, 48.3 overs) 245	
J. D. S. Neesham c Amla b Morris	23	3/74 (4) 4/80 (5)	
C. de Grandhomme c du Plessis b Ngidi	60	5/137 (6) 6/228 (7) 10 overs: 43-1	

M. J. Henry, L. H. Ferguson and T. A. Boult did not bat.

Rabada 10–0–42–1; Ngidi 10–1–47–1; Morris 10–0–49–3; Phehlukwayo 8.3–0–73–1; Imran Tahir 10–0–33–0.

Umpires: I. J. Gould and N. J. Llong.   Third umpire: R. J. Tucker.
Referee: R. B. Richardson.

AUSTRALIA v BANGLADESH

At Nottingham, June 20. Australia won by 48 runs. Toss: Australia.

At no stage did the head say Bangladesh were going to pull off their mammoth chase. But the heart? It yearned for them to come good. Not simply because Warner 2.0 (now with extra sobriety!) had made Australia no more likeable for the neutral, but because anything else threatened to leave the World Cup's breakaway quartet out of sight. Ultimately, if entertainingly, the underdogs failed. Finch had won his first toss of the tournament and, on the strip where a year and a day earlier Australia had leaked 481, opted to bat. The openers scampered off, Finch a little faster than Warner; soon after raising their hundred stand, they passed 500 together for the competition. Without the injured Mohammad Saifuddin, Bangladesh struggled for control, so tried the part-time medium-pace of Soumya Sarkar; from his fifth ball, Finch dollied to short third man. Warner and the under-scrutiny Khawaja knuckled down, Warner cutting loose only after reaching his 16th ODI hundred. He made 166, and the pair added 192, both records for this World Cup. Runs gushed; 400 beckoned until Khawaja declined a call from a rampant Maxwell, stitched up for a ten-ball 32. The reply suffered an early run-out, bringing the in-form Shakib Al Hasan – and an almighty roar from a green-and-red crowd. A leading edge ended his attractive 41, heaping pressure on his team-mates. Tamim Iqbal dragged on for 62, and Liton Das fell lbw for 20. After 37 overs, Australia had been 218 for one; Bangladesh were 219 for four, but with no Maxwell of their own. A terrier-like century from Mushfiqur Rahim and a punchier fifty from Mahmudullah exhilarated the spectators, and took Bangladesh to their highest ODI total for the second time in 19 days – though Australia knew they were safe.   HUGH CHEVALLIER

Player of the Match: D. A. Warner.   *Attendance:* 15,421.

Australia

D. A. Warner c Rubel Hossain		S. P. D. Smith lbw b Mustafizur Rahman . .	1
b Soumya Sarkar. 166		†A. T. Carey not out	11
*A. J. Finch c Rubel Hossain			
b Soumya Sarkar. 53		B 1, lb 5, w 5, nb 1	12
U. T. Khawaja c Mushfiqur Rahim			
b Soumya Sarkar. 89		1/121 (2) 2/313 (1) (5 wkts, 50 overs) 381	
G. J. Maxwell run out (Rubel Hossain). . . . 32		3/352 (4) 4/353 (3)	
M. P. Stoinis not out 17		5/354 (6) 10 overs: 53-0	

N. M. Coulter-Nile, P. J. Cummins, M. A. Starc and A. Zampa did not bat.

Mashrafe bin Mortaza 8–0–56–0; Mustafizur Rahman 9–0–69–1; Shakib Al Hasan 6–0–50–0; Rubel Hossain 9–0–83–0; Mehedi Hasan 10–0–59–0; Soumya Sarkar 8–0–58–3.

Bangladesh

Tamim Iqbal b Starc 62		*Mashrafe bin Mortaza c Maxwell b Stoinis 6	
Soumya Sarkar run out (Finch) 10			
Shakib Al Hasan c Warner b Stoinis 41		B 4, lb 4, w 9	17
†Mushfiqur Rahim not out. 102			
Liton Das lbw b Zampa. 20		1/23 (2) 2/102 (3) (8 wkts, 50 overs) 333	
Mahmudullah c Cummins b Coulter-Nile . . 69		3/144 (1) 4/175 (5)	
Sabbir Rahman b Coulter-Nile 0		5/302 (6) 6/302 (7)	
Mehedi Hasan c Warner b Starc 6		7/323 (8) 8/333 (9) 10 overs: 53-1	

Rubel Hossain and Mustafizur Rahman did not bat.

Starc 10–0–55–2; Cummins 10–1–65–0; Maxwell 3–0–25–0; Coulter-Nile 10–0–58–2; Stoinis 8–0–54–2; Zampa 9–0–68–1.

Umpires: M. A. Gough and R. A. Kettleborough.   Third umpire: R. K. Illingworth.
Referee: J. J. Crowe.

ENGLAND v SRI LANKA

At Leeds, June 21. Sri Lanka won by 20 runs. Toss: Sri Lanka.

No one saw this coming – least of all England. At 127 for three in the 31st over, with Root ticking off his fifth score of 50 or more, they were on course for a win that would leave them in striking distance of the semis. But the pitch was slow, and so was their progress. When Malinga, having earlier disposed of the openers, returned to have Root caught down the leg side on review, then Buttler trapped by a trademark yorker, Sri Lanka perked up. Stokes stayed calm, but his partners panicked. The ball after slog-sweeping de Silva for six, Ali picked out long-off, a stroke described by Michael Vaughan as "completely pathetic"; in de Silva's next over, Woakes and Rashid were both caught behind trying to cut; Archer heaved to long-on. As Wood trudged out, England required 47 off 38 – and Stokes had to make the bulk. He brought the crowd to life with successive sixes off Udana, then successive fours off Pradeep Fernando, only for Wood to edge the last ball of the 47th over. Five years earlier, Sri Lanka had won a gripping Leeds Test after important runs from Mathews. Here, he chiselled out an unbeaten 85 from 115 deliveries to repair a scoreboard that had read three for two, and later 133 for five, with Rashid on a hat-trick. Other contributions had come from Avishka Fernando, who counter-attacked on his World Cup debut, twice pulling Archer for six, and Kusal Mendis. Still, England

Roar power: Lasith Malinga dismisses Jos Buttler, and Sri Lanka head for victory.

hadn't failed to chase anything lower than 233 since January 2014. They wouldn't stumble now, would they? Yes, they would, leaving Buttler to bemoan a lack of intent, and others to draw comparisons to the 2017 Champions Trophy semi-final defeat by Pakistan in Cardiff.   LAWRENCE BOOTH

   Player of the Match: S. L. Malinga.   *Attendance:* 15,847.

Sri Lanka

*F. D. M. Karunaratne c Buttler b Archer	1	S. L. Malinga b Wood	1
†M. D. K. J. Perera c Ali b Woakes	2	A. N. P. R. Fernando not out	1
W. I. A. Fernando c Rashid b Wood	49		
B. K. G. Mendis c Morgan b Rashid	46	Lb 4, w 6	10
A. D. Mathews not out	85		
B. M. A. J. Mendis c and b Rashid	0	(9 wkts, 50 overs)	232
D. M. de Silva c Root b Archer	29		
N. L. T. C. Perera c Rashid b Archer	2		
I. Udana c Root b Wood	6		

1/3 (1) 2/3 (2) 3/62 (3) 4/133 (4) 5/133 (6) 6/190 (7) 7/200 (8) 8/209 (9) 9/220 (10) 10 overs: 48-2

Woakes 5–0–22–1; Archer 10–2–52–3; Wood 8–0–40–3; Stokes 5–0–16–0; Ali 10–0–40–0; Rashid 10–0–45–2; Root 2–0–13–0.

England

J. M. Vince c B. K. G. Mendis b Malinga	14	J. C. Archer c N. L. T. C. Perera b Udana	3
J. M. Bairstow lbw b Malinga	0	M. A. Wood c M. D. K. J. Perera	
J. E. Root c M. D. K. J. Perera b Malinga	57	b A. N. P. R. Fernando	0
*E. J. G. Morgan c and b Udana	21	Lb 1, w 5	6
B. A. Stokes not out	82		
†J. C. Buttler lbw b Malinga	10	(47 overs)	212
M. M. Ali c Udana b de Silva	16		
C. R. Woakes c M. D. K. J. Perera b de Silva	2		
A. U. Rashid c M. D. K. J. Perera b de Silva	1		

1/1 (2) 2/26 (1) 3/73 (4) 4/127 (3) 5/144 (6) 6/170 (7) 7/176 (9) 8/178 (9) 9/186 (10) 10/212 (11) 10 overs: 38-2

Malinga 10–1–43–4; A. N. P. R. Fernando 10–1–38–1; de Silva 8–0–32–3; N. L. T. C. Perera 8–0–34–0; Udana 8–0–41–2; B. M. A. J. Mendis 3–0–23–0.

Umpires: M. Erasmus and P. Wilson.   Third umpire: B. N. J. Oxenford.
Referee: R. B. Richardson.

AFGHANISTAN v INDIA

At Southampton, June 22. India won by 11 runs. Toss: India.

The sun beat down, and a game some feared would be a drab drubbing turned into a vivid thriller. One side had not lost, the other had not won, yet it was often impossible to gauge which was which, despite Afghanistan having conceded 397 against England. India chose to bat, and a pale, dry pitch showed its true colours: it was a curmudgeonly turner. In the fifth over, Mujeeb Zadran slipped a googly past a bamboozled Sharma. The first Indian to fall to spin in the tournament, he had made one from ten. With a single glorious, predictable, exception, no one found the going easy. Kohli played with a studiously straight bat and, until he miscued Mohammad Nabi to short third man for 67, his placement was exquisite, his running exemplary. Distrust of the surface unsettled others, easy singles were spurned, and between the 31st and 45th overs Dhoni and Jadhav scraped 57. A total of 224 felt vulnerable. While Afghanistan boasted a fearsome spin attack, India fielded a gifted pace battery: Bhuvneshwar Kumar was injured, yet his replacement, Mohammed Shami, tore in at 90mph, and the runs would not come. But neither did wickets and, at 98 for two after 26, Kohli brought back Bumrah, whose seventh ball struck Rahmat Shah on the pad. When Aleem Dar declined the appeal – India had used up their review – Kohli's fury earned a fine and a demerit point. But the fiery over did dismiss two batsmen, and India were on top. Nabi, though, was his cussed, combative self and, with Afghanistan needing 24 from three, an upset of seismic proportions was on – only for Shami to snuff out resistance with a hat-trick, India's second in the World Cup. The Afghan storm had been weathered. But it was close.   HUGH CHEVALLIER

Player of the Match: J. J. Bumrah.   Attendance: 16,808.

India

K. L. Rahul c Hazratullah Zazai		Mohammed Shami b Gulbadeen Naib	1
b Mohammad Nabi.	30	K. Yadav not out	1
R. G. Sharma b Mujeeb Zadran	1	J. J. Bumrah not out	1
*V. Kohli c Rahmat Shah b Mohammad Nabi	67	W 7	7
V. Shankar lbw b Rahmat Shah	29		
†M. S. Dhoni st Ikram Alikhil b Rashid Khan	28	1/7 (2) 2/64 (1) (8 wkts, 50 overs) 224	
K. M. Jadhav c sub (Noor Ali Zadran)		3/122 (4) 4/135 (3)	
b Gulbadeen Naib.	52	5/192 (5) 6/217 (7)	
H. H. Pandya c Ikram Alikhil b Aftab Alam	7	7/222 (8) 8/223 (6) 10 overs: 41-1	
Y. S. Chahal did not bat.			

Mujeeb Zadran 10–0–26–1; Aftab Alam 7–1–54–1; Gulbadeen Naib 9–0–51–2; Mohammad Nabi 9–0–33–2; Rashid Khan 10–0–38–1; Rahmat Shah 5–0–22–1.

Afghanistan

Hazratullah Zazai b Mohammed Shami	10	†Ikram Alikhil not out	7
*Gulbadeen Naib c Shankar b Pandya	27	Aftab Alam b Mohammed Shami	0
Rahmat Shah c Chahal b Bumrah	36	Mujeeb Zadran b Mohammed Shami	0
Hashmatullah Shahidi c and b Bumrah	21	B 4, lb 4, w 9	17
Asghar Afghan b Chahal	8		
Mohammad Nabi c Pandya		1/20 (1) 2/64 (2) (49.5 overs) 213	
b Mohammed Shami.	52	3/106 (3) 4/106 (4) 5/130 (5)	
Najibullah Zadran c Chahal b Pandya	21	6/166 (7) 7/190 (8) 8/213 (6)	
Rashid Khan st Dhoni b Chahal	14	9/213 (10) 10/213 (11) 10 overs: 37-1	

Mohammed Shami 9.5–1–40–4; Bumrah 10–1–39–2; Chahal 10–0–36–2; Pandya 10–1–51–2; Yadav 10–0–39–0.

Umpires: Aleem Dar and R. K. Illingworth.   Third umpire: R. A. Kettleborough.
Referee: B. C. Broad.

NEW ZEALAND v WEST INDIES

The mighty fallen: Carlos Brathwaite's innings
ends in despair – caught by Trent Boult.

Michael Steele, Getty Images

At Manchester, June 22 (day/night). New Zealand won by five runs. Toss: West Indies.

A couple of feet made all the difference. With West Indies needing six to win, Carlos Brathwaite was caught at long-on by Boult from the last ball of the penultimate over, bowled by Neesham, who had conjured up four dots from the first five deliveries. Neesham knew the ball hadn't quite been middled, because "it makes a distinct sound when the West Indians do that". Brathwaite thought he had enough on it, before sinking to his knees, and being consoled by the New Zealanders, led by Taylor; even a maiden international century could not make up for the near miss. "Inches away from being Colossus Brathwaite," said broadcaster Alan Wilkins. He had rebuilt his side's hopes after the loss of five for 22 in 29 balls, then scored all 41 in a tenth-wicket partnership with Thomas, who faced just four. The 48th over looked to have swung the match in West Indies' favour: Henry couldn't find his length as Brathwaite, evoking memories of his last-over assault on Ben Stokes in the 2016 World T20 final, crunched 25, including three successive sixes. (Next day he enquired via Twitter where he could get a bat fixed in Manchester.) New Zealand had fought back, too, after losing both openers for golden ducks to Cottrell. The nerveless Williamson responded with 148, his 13th and highest ODI century, taking his sequence between dismissals to 333, and putting on 160 for the third wicket with Taylor. As West Indies set about chasing 292, Boult removed Hope and Pooran for a single apiece, before Gayle, who biffed six sixes in his 87, and Hetmyer added 122. But at 164 for seven, West Indies seemed out of it. Then came Brathwaite.   ANDREW ALDERSON

Player of the Match: K. S. Williamson.   *Attendance:* 21,895.

OUT FIRST BALL OF A WORLD CUP INNINGS

Batsman	Bowler		
Aamir Sohail	D. K. Morrison	P v NZ at Christchurch	1991-92
G. A. Gooch	E. A. Brandes	E v Zim at Albury	1991-92
G. Kirsten	N. C. Johnson	SA v Zim at Chelmsford	1999
R. Walters	H. H. Streak	Namibia v Zim at Harare	2002-03
Hannan Sarkar	W. P. U. J. C. Vaas	Bang v SL at Pietermaritzburg	2002-03
B. R. M. Taylor	Khurram Chauhan	Zim v Canada at Nagpur	2010-11
W. T. S. Porterfield	J. M. Anderson	Ire v E at Bangalore	2010-11
H. D. R. L. Thirimanne	Dawlat Zadran	SL v Afg at Dunedin	2014-15
M. J. Guptill	**Aftab Alam**	**NZ v Afg at Taunton**	**2019**
M. J. Guptill	**S. S. Cottrell**	**NZ v WI at Manchester**	**2019**
F. D. M. Karunaratne	**K. Rabada**	**SL v SA at Chester-le-Street**	**2019**

Sarkar, Taylor, Guptill (at Manchester) and Karunaratne fell to the first ball of the match.
J. G. Wright of New Zealand was dismissed by the first legal delivery of the 1991-92 World Cup, at Auckland, though C. J. McDermott (Australia) had started with two wides.

ON TOP OF THE WORLD   Ben Stokes and Jofra Archer ooze happiness at Lord's.

TWO STOKES OF LUCK   Trent Boult catches Stokes, only to realise he's treading on the foam, before a throw from Martin Guptill pings off his bat and races to the boundary.

THE HEIGHT OF SUMMER   The greatest one-day international reaches its climax, and Lord's erupts.

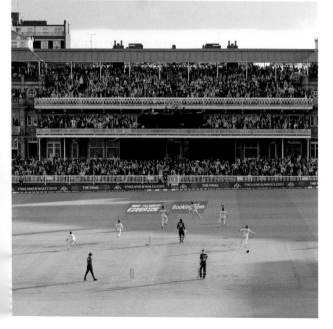

NOT BAD FOR STARTERS The first game of the World Cup ignites after a breathtaking catch by Stokes to dismiss South Africa's Andile Phehlukwayo, while Jonny Bairstow regularly got England off to a flyer.

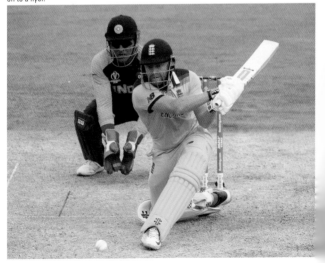

SOME YOU WIN, SOME YOU DON'T   Australia's David Warner, who made 647 runs in the tournament, survives the ball hitting the base of his stumps, against India; South African captain, Faf du Plessis, fails to hide his gloom at another defeat.

LOWS AND HIGHS   When Stokes falls to an inswinging yorker from Australia's Mitchell Starc – the ball of the season – England seem to have run aground. Bangladesh's Shakib Al Hasan, here against West Indies, enjoyed a stellar few weeks.

THE EYES HAVE IT Sheldon Cottrell's celebratory salute after taking a wicket masks a faltering West Indian performance, while the expression of Virat Kohli tells a tale in the first semi-final.

UMBRELLA STAND Old Trafford hosts the rain-affected India–Pakistan clash, a drabber affair on the pitch than off.

New Zealand

M. J. Guptill lbw b Cottrell	0	M. J. Henry not out		0
C. Munro b Cottrell	0			
*K. S. Williamson c Hope b Cottrell	148	Lb 4, w 3, nb 1		8
L. R. P. L. Taylor c Holder b Gayle	69			
†T. W. M. Latham c and b Cottrell	12	1/0 (1) 2/7 (2)	(8 wkts, 50 overs)	291
J. D. S. Neesham c Cottrell b Brathwaite	28	3/167 (4) 4/210 (5)		
C. de Grandhomme run out (Cottrell)	16	5/251 (3) 6/270 (7)		
M. J. Santner c Cottrell b Brathwaite	10	7/291 (8) 8/291 (6)	10 overs: 30-2	

L. H. Ferguson and T. A. Boult did not bat.

Cottrell 10–1–56–4; Roach 10–2–38–0; Holder 7–0–42–0; Thomas 6–0–30–0; Brathwaite 6–0–58–2; Nurse 9–0–55–0; Gayle 2–0–8–1.

West Indies

C. H. Gayle c Boult b de Grandhomme	87	S. S. Cottrell b Ferguson		15
†S. D. Hope b Boult	1	O. R. Thomas not out		0
N. Pooran c Latham b Boult	1			
S. O. Hetmyer b Ferguson	54	Lb 3, w 9		12
*J. O. Holder c Latham b Ferguson	0			
C. R. Brathwaite c Boult b Neesham	101	1/3 (2) 2/20 (3) 3/142 (4)	(49 overs)	286
A. R. Nurse c Latham b Boult	1	4/142 (5) 5/152 (1) 6/163 (7)		
E. Lewis c Neesham b Boult	0	7/164 (8) 8/211 (9) 9/245 (10)		
K. A. J. Roach c Latham b Henry	14	10/286 (6)	10 overs: 59-2	

Boult 10–1–30–4; Henry 9–0–76–1; Ferguson 10–0–59–3; Neesham 6–0–35–1; Santner 10–1–61–0; de Grandhomme 4–0–22–1.

Umpires: I. J. Gould and R. S. A. Palliyaguruge. Third umpire: N. J. Llong.
Referee: D. C. Boon.

PAKISTAN v SOUTH AFRICA

At Lord's, June 23. Pakistan won by 49 runs. Toss: Pakistan.

A grey day at Lord's, staging its first game of the tournament, was brightened by the greenery of Pakistan's fans and the batting of Haris Sohail. Dropped after his side's opening-game mauling by West Indies, he conjured a delightful 89 from 59 balls, before the Pakistan attack – inspired by two left-armers and a leg-spinner – kept them in the hunt, just, for the semi-finals. For South Africa, a fifth defeat really did mean curtains; du Plessis, searching for the *mot juste*, settled on "embarrassing". Five of his team passed 30, but none could better his 63, ended by the vibrant Mohammad Amir, who had removed Amla with his first ball and whose first seven overs yielded two for 19. Shadab Khan's leg-breaks troubled the middle order, before Wahab Riaz hit the tailenders' stumps – a prudent option, since Pakistan dropped six catches (three by Amir). After Sarfraz Ahmed had bravely chosen to bat, the openers each contributed 44, while Babar Azam compiled an unruffled 69. But Haris stole the show, on-driving Rabada for four, then carving his next ball into the Grand Stand for six. Earlier, the sight of du Plessis arguing with the umpires over their soft signal of not out after Imran Tahir claimed a catch in the deep off Fakhar Zaman summed up South Africa's World Cup: frustrating, fractious and entirely fruitless. LAWRENCE BOOTH

Player of the Match: Haris Sohail. *Attendance:* 23,849.

Pakistan

Imam-ul-Haq c and b Imran Tahir	44	*†Sarfraz Ahmed not out		2
Fakhar Zaman c Amla b Imran Tahir	44	Shadab Khan not out		1
Babar Azam c Ngidi b Phehlukwayo	69	Lb 6, w 5, nb 1		12
Mohammad Hafeez lbw b Markram	20			
Haris Sohail c de Kock b Ngidi	89	1/81 (2) 2/98 (1)	(7 wkts, 50 overs)	308
Imad Wasim c sub (J-P. Duminy) b Ngidi	23	3/143 (4) 4/224 (3)		
Wahab Riaz b Ngidi	4	5/295 (6) 6/304 (7) 7/307 (5)	10 overs: 58-0	

Mohammad Amir and Shaheen Shah Afridi did not bat.

Rabada 10–0–65–0; Ngidi 9–0–64–3; Morris 9–0–61–0; Phehlukwayo 8–0–49–1; Imran Tahir 10–0–41–2; Markram 4–0–22–1.

South Africa

H. M. Amla lbw b Mohammad Amir	2	K. Rabada b Wahab Riaz		3
†Q. de Kock c Imam-ul-Haq b Shadab Khan	47	L. T. Ngidi b Wahab Riaz		1
*F. du Plessis c Sarfraz Ahmed		Imran Tahir not out		1
b Mohammad Amir.	63			
A. K. Markram b Shadab Khan	7	Lb 1, w 5		6
H. E. van der Dussen c Mohammad Hafeez				
b Shadab Khan.	36	1/4 (1) 2/91 (2)	(9 wkts, 50 overs)	259
D. A. Miller b Shaheen Shah Afridi	31	3/103 (4) 4/136 (3)		
A. L. Phehlukwayo not out	46	5/189 (5) 6/192 (6) 7/222 (8)		
C. H. Morris b Wahab Riaz	16	8/239 (9) 9/246 (10)	10 overs: 38-1	

Mohammad Hafeez 2–0–11–0; Mohammad Amir 10–1–49–2; Shaheen Shah Afridi 8–0–54–1; Imad Wasim 10–0–48–0; Wahab Riaz 10–0–46–3; Shadab Khan 10–1–50–3.

Umpires: H. D. P. K. Dharmasena and J. S. Wilson.   Third umpire: C. B. Gaffaney.
Referee: R. S. Madugalle.

AFGHANISTAN v BANGLADESH

At Southampton, June 24. Bangladesh won by 62 runs. Toss: Afghanistan.

There may be no truth in the rumour that Clark Kent dons a Shakib Al Hasan shirt during his downtime in Metropolis, but Shakib continued his run of superhero performances to maintain Bangladesh's ambitions of gatecrashing the semi-finals. After hitting his fifth 50-plus score of the competition, he intelligently exploited a helpful pitch to take five for 29, then the best figures of the tournament, and Bangladesh's first World Cup five-for. Only India's Yuvraj Singh – against Ireland at Bangalore in 2010-11 – had previously hit a fifty and claimed five in the same World Cup match. Bangladesh's cool professionalism contrasted sharply with a disappointing Afghanistan display. Captain Gulbadeen Naib rued his team's shoddy fielding, and his bowlers' inability to locate the right lengths, but their malaise ran deeper: they looked like a side waking up to the realities of international sport. Put in on a used pitch, Bangladesh had proceeded unhurriedly towards a total they calculated would be out of reach, though Mujeeb Zadran – opening the bowling with his off-breaks – kept things tight. Mushfiqur Rahim continued his good form with 83 from 87 balls, and later completed two stumpings. Afghanistan negotiated the first powerplay without mishap, then foundered against Shakib: after seven overs, he had four for ten. Samiullah Shenwari's attractive unbeaten 49 off 51 raised questions about why this was his first game of the tournament. RICHARD WHITEHEAD

Player of the Match: Shakib Al Hasan.   *Attendance:* 15,103.

Bangladesh

Liton Das c Hashmatullah Shahidi		Mosaddek Hossain b Gulbadeen Naib	35
b Mujeeb Zadran	16	Mohammad Saifuddin not out	2
Tamim Iqbal b Mohammad Nabi	36		
Shakib Al Hasan lbw b Mujeeb Zadran	51		
†Mushfiqur Rahim c Mohammad Nabi		W 9	9
b Dawlat Zadran	83		
Soumya Sarkar lbw b Mujeeb Zadran	3	1/23 (1) 2/82 (2) (7 wkts, 50 overs)	262
Mahmudullah c Mohammad Nabi		3/143 (3) 4/151 (5)	
b Gulbadeen Naib	27	5/207 (6) 6/251 (4) 7/262 (7) 10 overs: 44-1	

Mehedi Hasan, *Mashrafe bin Mortaza and Mustafizur Rahman did not bat.

Mujeeb Zadran 10–0–39–3; Dawlat Zadran 9–0–64–1; Mohammad Nabi 10–0–44–1; Gulbadeen Naib 10–1–56–2; Rashid Khan 10–0–52–0; Rahmat Shah 1–0–7–0.

Afghanistan

*Gulbadeen Naib c Liton Das		Rashid Khan c Mashrafe bin Mortaza	
b Shakib Al Hasan	47	b Mustafizur Rahman	2
Rahmat Shah c Tamim Iqbal		Dawlat Zadran c Mushfiqur Rahim	
b Shakib Al Hasan	24	b Mustafizur Rahman	0
Hashmatullah Shahidi b Mosaddek Hossain	11	Mujeeb Zadran b Mohammad Saifuddin	0
Asghar Afghan c sub (Sabbir Rahman)			
b Shakib Al Hasan	20	B 1, lb 6, w 6	13
Mohammad Nabi b Shakib Al Hasan	0		
Samiullah Shenwari not out	49	1/49 (2) 2/79 (3) 3/104 (1) (47 overs)	200
†Ikram Alikhil run out (Liton Das)	11	4/104 (5) 5/117 (4) 6/132 (7)	
Najibullah Zadran st Mushfiqur Rahim		7/188 (8) 8/191 (9) 9/195 (10)	
b Shakib Al Hasan	23	10/200 (11) 10 overs: 48-0	

Mashrafe bin Mortaza 7–0–37–0; Mustafizur Rahman 8–1–32–2; Mohammad Saifuddin 8–0–33–1; Shakib Al Hasan 10–1–29–5; Mehedi Hasan 8–0–37–0; Mosaddek Hossain 6–0–25–1.

Umpires: M. A. Gough and R. A. Kettleborough.   Third umpire: Aleem Dar.
Referee: R. B. Richardson.

ENGLAND v AUSTRALIA

At Lord's, June 25. Australia won by 64 runs. Toss: England.

England's defeat by Sri Lanka had left their fans twitchy. Now, after a hammering by Australia – whom they had beaten in ten of their previous 11 ODIs – those fans began to wonder: could a place in the semi-finals really be slipping through England's fingers? Morgan's decision to bowl, on a cloudy morning after an overnight deluge, made sense. But while lavish movement helped Woakes repeatedly pass Warner's bat, Archer and Wood dropped too short. The openers took grateful advantage, and brought up their fifth successive stand of 60 or more, gold dust in the circumstances. They extended it to 123 before Warner miscued Ali to point, having become the first in the tournament to reach 500. Finch completed his 15th ODI hundred (and seventh against England), but Australia's progress slowed against Stokes and Rashid: 285 for seven was fewer than had seemed likely at 162 for one after 30 overs. Still, England needed a solid start; within six overs, they were in pieces. The unassuming left-armer Behrendorff, handed the new ball ahead of Cummins and a brief to pitch it up, swung his second delivery through Vince's prod, before Starc trapped Root with another full-length inswinger. When Morgan top-edged

Starc to fine leg, England were 26 for three, and in need of heroics. Instead, Bairstow and Buttler both picked out fielders in the deep, leaving Stokes alone on the burning deck, as he had been four days earlier against Sri Lanka. Two sixes in three balls off Maxwell roused the crowd, but an unplayable, laser-guided yorker from Starc ended his resistance on 89. Stokes dropped his bat, kicked it, and dragged himself off, taking England's fading hopes with him. Behrendorff cleaned up to claim a maiden ODI five-for, and Starc finished with four. Australia were the first side into the semi-final, their eighth in all World Cups. England were contemplating the unthinkable.   LAWRENCE BOOTH

Player of the Match: A. J. Finch.   *Attendance:* 26,305.

Australia

*A. J. Finch c Woakes b Archer	100	P. J. Cummins c Buttler b Woakes	1
D. A. Warner c Root b Ali	53	M. A. Starc not out	4
U. T. Khawaja b Stokes	23		
S. P. D. Smith c Archer b Woakes	38	Lb 4, w 4	8
G. J. Maxwell c Buttler b Wood	12		
M. P. Stoinis		1/123 (2) 2/173 (3) (7 wkts, 50 overs)	285
run out (Bairstow/Rashid/Buttler)	8	3/185 (1) 4/213 (5)	
†A. T. Carey not out	38	5/228 (6) 6/250 (4) 7/259 (8) 10 overs: 44-0	

N. M. Lyon and J. P. Behrendorff did not bat.

Woakes 10–0–46–2; Archer 9–0–56–1; Wood 9–0–59–1; Stokes 6–0–29–1; Ali 6–0–42–1; Rashid 10–0–49–0.

England

J. M. Vince b Behrendorff	0	J. C. Archer c Warner b Behrendorff	1
J. M. Bairstow c Cummins b Behrendorff	27	M. A. Wood not out	1
J. E. Root lbw b Starc	8		
*E. J. G. Morgan c Cummins b Starc	4	B 1, lb 5, w 3	9
B. A. Stokes b Starc	89		
†J. C. Buttler c Khawaja b Stoinis	25	1/0 (1) 2/15 (3) 3/26 (4) (44.4 overs)	221
C. R. Woakes c Finch b Behrendorff	26	4/53 (2) 5/124 (6) 6/177 (5)	
M. M. Ali c Carey b Behrendorff	6	7/189 (8) 8/202 (7) 9/211 (10)	
A. U. Rashid c Stoinis b Starc	25	10/221 (9) 10 overs: 39-3	

Behrendorff 10–0–44–5; Starc 8.4–1–43–4; Cummins 8–1–41–0; Lyon 9–0–43–0; Stoinis 7–0–29–1; Maxwell 2–0–15–0.

Umpires: C. B. Gaffaney and S. Ravi.   Third umpire: H. D. P. K. Dharmasena.
Referee: R. S. Madugalle.

NEW ZEALAND v PAKISTAN

At Birmingham, June 26. Pakistan won by six wickets. Toss: New Zealand.

In a frenzied atmosphere, Pakistan continued their rehabilitation and inflicted on New Zealand their first defeat. Amid the whistles-and-horns cacophony outside Edgbaston afterwards, the chatter was about the growing list of parallels with 1992, when Pakistan won their only World Cup – as if a sequence of results could be deciphered like the symbols on the tomb of an ancient king. Now, as then, their first seven results read: defeat (by West Indies), victory, washout, defeat, defeat, victory, victory. But this was a triumph for Pakistani pragmatism as well as passion: on a used pitch, they managed an awkward chase with such precision that the winning boundary came off the first ball of the final over. Babar Azam, basking in the adulation, made a brilliant unbeaten 101. He won a compelling battle with Boult, and shared a soothing fourth-wicket stand of 126 with Haris Sohail. After a delayed start, the match burst into life like the opening scene of a Hollywood blockbuster, when Mohammad Amir's first ball induced a drag-on by Guptill, prompting a volcanic eruption of noise. But it was Shaheen Shah Afridi who did most to undermine New Zealand, with the wickets of Munro, Taylor – athletically caught by Sarfraz Ahmed – and Latham, at a cost of five runs in 20 balls. Williamson failed to reach 50 for the first time in four innings but, from 83 for five, Neesham and de Grandhomme doggedly fought back, putting on 132, New Zealand's first sixth-wicket century partnership in a World Cup. Ferguson was brisk and hostile but, on a surface which might have helped leg-spinner Ish Sodhi, Williamson had deployed his own part-time off-breaks. The result piled more pressure on England, who now led Pakistan by only a point.　RICHARD WHITEHEAD

　　Player of the Match: Babar Azam.　*Attendance:* 20,871.

New Zealand

M. J. Guptill b Mohammad Amir	5	C. de Grandhomme	
C. Munro c Haris Sohail		run out (Mohammad Amir/Sarfraz Ahmed)	64
b Shaheen Shah Afridi	12	M. J. Santner not out	5
*K. S. Williamson c Sarfraz Ahmed			
b Shadab Khan	41	B 2, lb 3, w 4	9
L. R. P. L. Taylor c Sarfraz Ahmed			
b Shaheen Shah Afridi	3	1/5 (1) 2/24 (2) 3/38 (4) (6 wkts, 50 overs)	237
†T. W. M. Latham c Sarfraz Ahmed		4/46 (5) 5/83 (3)	
b Shaheen Shah Afridi	1	6/215 (7)	
J. D. S. Neesham not out	97		10 overs: 44-3

M. J. Henry, L. H. Ferguson and T. A. Boult did not bat.

Mohammad Hafeez 7–0–22–0; Mohammad Amir 10–0–67–1; Shaheen Shah Afridi 10–3–28–3; Imad Wasim 3–0–17–0; Shadab Khan 10–0–43–1; Wahab Riaz 10–0–55–0.

Pakistan

Imam-ul-Haq c Guptill b Ferguson	19	*†Sarfraz Ahmed not out	5
Fakhar Zaman c Guptill b Boult	9		
Babar Azam not out	101	W 7	7
Mohammad Hafeez c Ferguson			
b Williamson	32	1/19 (2) 2/44 (1) (4 wkts, 49.1 overs)	241
Haris Sohail run out (Guptill)	68	3/110 (4) 4/236 (5)	
		10 overs: 43-1	

Imad Wasim, Wahab Riaz, Shadab Khan, Mohammad Amir and Shaheen Shah Afridi did not bat.

Boult 10–0–48–1; Henry 7–0–25–0; Ferguson 8.1–0–50–1; de Grandhomme 2–0–12–0; Santner 10–0–38–0; Neesham 3–0–20–0; Williamson 8–0–39–1; Munro 1–0–9–0.

　　Umpires: B. N. J. Oxenford and P. R. Reiffel.　Third umpire: P. Wilson.
　　　　　　　　　Referee: R. B. Richardson.

INDIA v WEST INDIES

At Manchester, June 27. India won by 125 runs. Toss: India.

　　On the ground where, in 1983, India inflicted West Indies' first defeat in any World Cup, they did it again, but more emphatically and predictably. It meant West Indies were eliminated, while India – having returned to the top of the one-day rankings following England's defeat by Australia – marched on to the ubiquitous beat of the Bharat Army drums, the only unbeaten side in the tournament. On the same pitch used for West Indies' narrow defeat by New Zealand five days earlier, India's batsmen were mostly kept in check by disciplined bowling, with Holder sending down 46 dot balls. But Holder's decision to exhaust his and Roach's allocations before the closing overs exposed his side's limitations: an assault from Pandya, and Dhoni's first fifty of the World Cup, brought 81 off the last nine. Kohli's fourth successive half-century, meanwhile, had taken him past 20,000 international runs in all formats. From 417 innings, he was the fastest of the 12 to get there, and the third Indian (after Tendulkar and Dravid). However satisfied West Indies might have felt at limiting their target to 269, they needed a substantial contribution from Gayle, but he was quickly bounced out by Mohammed Shami. Two overs later, Hope, having bungled an easy chance to stump Dhoni, was bowled through the gate by an inswinger from Shami, who took his figures for the tournament to eight for 56, in two games. The innings never got going – Bumrah had two for nine in six overs – and West Indies lost their last eight for 72. JOHN STERN

Player of the Match: V. Kohli. *Attendance:* 21,836.

India

K. L. Rahul b Holder	48	Mohammed Shami c Hope b Cottrell	0
R. G. Sharma c Hope b Roach	18	K. Yadav not out	0
*V. Kohli c sub (D. M. Bravo) b Holder	72	B 1, w 6	7
V. Shankar c Hope b Roach	14		
K. M. Jadhav c Hope b Roach	7		(7 wkts, 50 overs) 268
†M. S. Dhoni not out	56		
H. H. Pandya c Allen b Cottrell	46		

1/29 (2) 2/98 (1)   (7 wkts, 50 overs) 268
3/126 (4) 4/140 (5)
5/180 (3) 6/250 (7) 7/252 (8)   10 overs: 47-1

J. J. Bumrah and Y. S. Chahal did not bat.

Cottrell 10–0–50–2; Roach 10–0–36–3; Thomas 7–0–63–0; Allen 10–0–52–0; Holder 10–2–33–2; Brathwaite 3–0–33–0.

West Indies

C. H. Gayle c Jadhav b Mohammed Shami	6	S. S. Cottrell lbw b Chahal	10
S. W. Ambris lbw b Pandya	31	O. R. Thomas c Sharma	
†S. D. Hope b Mohammed Shami	5	b Mohammed Shami	6
N. Pooran c Mohammed Shami b Yadav	28	B 9, lb 3, w 5, nb 1	18
S. O. Hetmyer c Rahul b Mohammed Shami	18		
*J. O. Holder c Jadhav b Chahal	6		
C. R. Brathwaite c Dhoni b Bumrah	1		
F. A. Allen lbw b Bumrah	0		
K. A. J. Roach not out	14		

1/10 (1) 2/16 (3) 3/71 (2)   (34.2 overs) 143
4/80 (4) 5/98 (6) 6/107 (7)
7/107 (8) 8/112 (5) 9/124 (10)
10/143 (11)   10 overs: 29-2

Mohammed Shami 6.2–0–16–4; Bumrah 6–1–9–2; Pandya 5–0–28–1; Yadav 9–1–35–1; Jadhav 1–0–4–0; Chahal 7–0–39–2.

Umpires: R. K. Illingworth and R. A. Kettleborough.   Third umpire: M. A. Gough.
Referee: B. C. Broad.

SOUTH AFRICA v SRI LANKA

At Chester-le-Street, June 28. South Africa won by nine wickets. Toss: South Africa.
South Africa finally found their touch, displaying a full range of skills to wallop Sri Lanka, whose hopes were all but ended. The tone was set when du Plessis chose to bowl, and caught his opposite number, Karunaratne, off the first ball. Though Sri Lanka scored 67 in the first powerplay, South Africa never let them get away, and no one topped 30. The pace attack bowled clinically, with all-rounder Pretorius, who had returned in place of Lungi Ngidi for his first game since the opener against England four weeks earlier, claiming three for 25. South Africa needed over 204; Malinga fired a yorker through de Kock's defences, but it was Sri Lanka's only success, and du Plessis finished on 96 as he and Amla cruised to an unbroken stand of 175. The day's most memorable image came when the players fell to the ground to avoid a swarm of bees that invaded the field towards the end of Sri Lanka's innings. Bees had also interrupted a one-day match between these teams at Johannesburg two years earlier. LUNGANI ZAMA

Player of the Match: D. Pretorius. *Attendance:* 12,520.

Sri Lanka

*F. D. M. Karunaratne c du Plessis b Rabada	0	R. A. S. Lakmal not out............	5
†M. D. K. J. Perera b Pretorius...........	30	S. L. Malinga c du Plessis b Morris......	4
W. I. A. Fernando c du Plessis b Pretorius .	30		
B. K. G. Mendis c Morris b Pretorius.....	23	B 4, lb 3, w 13...............	20
A. D. Mathews b Morris...............	11		
D. M. de Silva b Duminy..............	24	1/0 (1) 2/67 (3) 3/72 (2)	(49.3 overs) 203
B. M. A. J. Mendis c Pretorius b Morris...	18	4/100 (5) 5/111 (4) 6/135 (6)	
N. L. T. C. Perera c Rabada b Phehlukwayo	21	7/163 (7) 8/184 (8) 9/197 (9)	
I. Udana c and b Rabada..............	17	10/203 (11)	10 overs: 67-2

Rabada 10–2–36–2; Morris 9.3–0–46–3; Pretorius 10–2–25–3; Phehlukwayo 8–0–38–1; Imran Tahir 10–0–36–0; Duminy 2–0–15–1.

South Africa

†Q. de Kock b Malinga................	15
H. M. Amla not out..................	80
*F. du Plessis not out................	96
Lb 1, w 14....................	15

1/31 (1)   (1 wkt, 37.2 overs) 206
                              10 overs: 53-1

A. K. Markram, H. E. van der Dussen, J-P. Duminy, D. Pretorius, A. L. Phehlukwayo, C. H. Morris, K. Rabada and Imran Tahir did not bat.

Malinga 10–1–47–1; de Silva 4–0–18–0; Lakmal 6–0–47–0; N. L. T. C. Perera 5.2–1–28–0; B. M. A. J. Mendis 7–0–36–0; Udana 5–0–29–0.

Umpires: S. Ravi and R. J. Tucker.   Third umpire: B. N. J. Oxenford.
Referee: D. C. Boon.

AFGHANISTAN v PAKISTAN

At Leeds, June 29. Pakistan won by three wickets. Toss: Afghanistan.

The first World Cup meeting between these neighbours was marred by off-field violence. A mass charge at the gates on St Michael's Lane was repelled, but fans attempting to circumvent security (and the price of admission) succeeded in scaling the walls behind the Western Terrace. Rival supporters scuffled and hurled objects at each other, in full view of the pitch, and there were numerous ejections. The authorities had hired 60 extra stewards, but seemed to have underestimated the mutual animosity. This derived not only from border tensions, but from the fact that, though most of their players had learned the game as refugees in Pakistan, the Afghanistan team had grown closer to India, who host their home fixtures. The clashes intensified after a small plane towing banners reading "Justice for Balochistan" (a province of Pakistan, which has accused Afghanistan of harbouring Baloch insurgents) and "Help end disappearances in Pakistan" flew over the ground. The unpleasantness detracted from a nerve-jangling contest apparently heading Afghanistan's way until its final throes. Having used his spinners to strangle the scoring – Mohammad Nabi's two for 23 remained the tournament's meanest ten-over analysis – Gulbadeen Naib inexplicably brought himself on with 46 required from 30 deliveries. An increase in pace and misdirection produced 18 in the over, mostly to the clean striking of Imad Wasim. It was the turning point – although Gulbadeen later pointed to a hamstring injury restricting seamer Hamid Hassan to 12 balls, in what he had said would be his last international. Imad sealed victory in the final over (Gulbadeen again), flashing his fifth four through the covers, to propel Pakistan above England into fourth place. A week after their near miss against India, Afghanistan remained winless, despite a return to form for their recently deposed captain, Asghar Afghan. RICHARD GIBSON

Player of the Match: Imad Wasim.   *Attendance:* 17,334.

Afghanistan

Rahmat Shah c Babar Azam b Imad Wasim	35
*Gulbadeen Naib c Sarfraz Ahmed	
b Shaheen Shah Afridi .	15
Hashmatullah Shahidi c Imad Wasim	
b Shaheen Shah Afridi .	0
†Ikram Alikhil c Mohammad Hafeez	
b Imad Wasim .	24
Asghar Afghan b Shadab Khan	42
Mohammad Nabi c Mohammad Amir	
b Wahab Riaz .	16
Najibullah Zadran b Shaheen Shah Afridi .	42

Samiullah Shenwari not out.	19
Rashid Khan c Fakhar Zaman	
b Shaheen Shah Afridi .	8
Hamid Hassan b Wahab Riaz	1
Mujeeb Zadran not out	7
Lb 8, w 10	18

1/27 (2)　2/27 (3)　　　(9 wkts, 50 overs) 227
3/57 (1)　4/121 (5)
5/125 (4)　6/167 (6)　7/202 (7)
8/210 (9)　9/219 (10)　　10 overs: 46-2

Imad Wasim 10–0–48–2; Mohammad Amir 10–1–41–0; Shaheen Shah Afridi 10–0–47–4; Mohammad Hafeez 2–0–10–0; Wahab Riaz 8–0–29–2; Shadab Khan 10–0–44–1.

Pakistan

Fakhar Zaman lbw b Mujeeb Zadran	0
Imam-ul-Haq st Ikram Alikhil	
b Mohammad Nabi.	36
Babar Azam b Mohammad Nabi	45
Mohammad Hafeez	
c Hashmatullah Shahidi b Mujeeb Zadran .	19
Haris Sohail lbw b Rashid Khan	27
*†Sarfraz Ahmed	
run out (Najibullah Zadran/Ikram Alikhil) .	18

Imad Wasim not out	49
Shadab Khan	
run out (Gulbadeen Naib/Ikram Alikhil).	11
Wahab Riaz not out	15
B 1, lb 4, w 5	10

1/0 (1)　2/72 (2)　　(7 wkts, 49.4 overs) 230
3/81 (3)　4/121 (4)
5/142 (5)　6/156 (6)　7/206 (8)　　10 overs: 49-1

Mohammad Amir and Shaheen Shah Afridi did not bat.

Mujeeb Zadran 10–1–34–2; Hamid Hassan 2–0–13–0; Gulbadeen Naib 9.4–0–73–0; Mohammad Nabi 10–0–23–2; Rashid Khan 10–0–50–1; Samiullah Shenwari 8–0–32–0.

Umpires: N. J. Llong and P. Wilson.　Third umpire: C. B. Gaffaney.
Referee: B. C. Broad.

AUSTRALIA v NEW ZEALAND

At Lord's, June 29 (day/night). Australia won by 86 runs. Toss: Australia.

A replay of the 2015 final proved similarly one-sided. On a baking hot day, the men in black really felt the heat when Starc returned to remove their talisman, Williamson. He had none for 16 before that, but finished with five for 26, then the best figures in a one-day international at Lord's. Earlier, things had looked brighter for New Zealand. With a pitch already used for the England–Australia match proving sluggish, and affording occasional turn and bounce, they reduced Australia to 92 for five. Finch was pinned by Boult, and

BEST ODI FIGURES AT LORD'S

6-35	Shaheen Shah Afridi	Pakistan v Bangladesh	2019
5-26	M. A. Starc	Australia v New Zealand	2019
5-30	D. L. Vettori	New Zealand v West Indies	2004
5-34	M. Muralitharan	Sri Lanka v England	1998
5-38†	J. Garner	West Indies v England	1979
5-41	B. Lee	Australia v England	2005
5-44	D. Gough	England v Australia	1997
5-44	J. P. Behrendorff	Australia v England	2019
5-45	F. H. Edwards	West Indies v England	2007
5-47	M. S. Kasprowicz	Australia v Pakistan	2004
5-48	G. J. Gilmour	Australia v West Indies (World Cup final)	1975
5-49	B. Lee	Australia v England	2009
5-75	Mustafizur Rahman	Bangladesh v Pakistan	2019

Warner gloved a screamer from Ferguson. He then had a disbelieving Smith caught off a full-blooded pull at leg gully by the flying Guptill, who had already dropped two tough chances, including Khawaja on nought. But Australia were rescued by Carey, who thumped 11 fours in a forthright career-best, and the adhesive Khawaja, who lasted 129 balls. He was part of Boult's final-over hat-trick, his second in ODIs but New Zealand's first in the World Cup. Williamson might have turned to him earlier during a sixth-wicket stand of 107; instead, with spinners Santner and Sodhi lacking control, he fiddled through seven overs of off-breaks himself. New Zealand navigated Starc's first spell, creeping to 29 before Nicholls fell to Behrendorff in the tenth over, but they couldn't survive his later bursts. Williamson, usually clinical in his nurdles to third man, feathered to the keeper, and Taylor skyed Cummins; the dangerous de Grandhomme then obligingly pounded his first ball to long-off, to become Smith's first victim in ODIs since November 2014 (he was one of 15 bowlers used, equalling a World Cup record). As New Zealand stuttered towards a second successive defeat, it was a rare attacking shot among the dots, of which there were 172.   Steven Lynch

Player of the Match: A. T. Carey.   *Attendance:* 23,539.

Australia

D. A. Warner c Latham b Ferguson	16		J. P. Behrendorff lbw b Boult		0
*A. J. Finch lbw b Boult	8		N. M. Lyon not out		0
U. T. Khawaja b Boult	88				
S. P. D. Smith c Guptill b Ferguson	5		Lb 3, w 7		10
M. P. Stoinis c Latham b Neesham	21				
G. J. Maxwell c and b Neesham	1			(9 wkts, 50 overs)	243
†A. T. Carey c Guptill b Williamson	71				
P. J. Cummins not out	23				
M. A. Starc b Boult	0				

1/15 (2) 2/38 (1)   (9 wkts, 50 overs) 243
3/46 (4) 4/81 (5)
5/92 (6) 6/199 (7) 7/243 (3)
8/243 (9) 9/243 (10)   10 overs: 40-2

Boult 10–1–51–4; de Grandhomme 8–1–29–0; Ferguson 10–0–49–2; Sodhi 6–0–35–0; Neesham 6–0–28–2; Santner 3–0–23–0; Williamson 7–0–25–1.

New Zealand

M. J. Guptill lbw b Behrendorff	20		L. H. Ferguson b Starc		0
H. M. Nicholls c Carey b Behrendorff	8		T. A. Boult not out		2
*K. S. Williamson c Carey b Starc	40				
L. R. P. L. Taylor c Carey b Cummins	30		B 4, lb 3, w 10		17
†T. W. M. Latham b Smith b Starc	14				
C. de Grandhomme c Khawaja b Smith	0			(43.4 overs)	157
J. D. S. Neesham c and b Lyon	9				
M. J. Santner c Behrendorff b Starc	12				
I. S. Sodhi lbw b Starc	5				

1/29 (2) 2/42 (1) 3/97 (3)   (43.4 overs) 157
4/118 (4) 5/118 (6) 6/125 (5)
7/131 (7) 8/141 (9) 9/144 (10)
10/157 (8)   10 overs: 31-1

Behrendorff 9–0–31–2; Starc 9.4–1–26–5; Cummins 6–1–14–1; Lyon 10–0–36–1; Smith 2–0–6–1; Finch 1–0–7–0; Stoinis 2–0–12–0; Maxwell 4–0–18–0.

Umpires: R. K. Illingworth and J. S. Wilson.   Third umpire: R. A. Kettleborough.
Referee: R. B. Richardson.

ENGLAND v INDIA

At Birmingham, June 30. England won by 31 runs. Toss: England.
The return of Roy transmuted England from base metal to burnished silver. Under intense – if self-inflicted – pressure, they won: beat New Zealand, and they would reach the semis, while India were still odds-on to progress. Back for James Vince, Roy had not batted for three weeks, but the message in two first-over boundaries was clear: normal service had been resumed. The most swaggering opening pair in cricket rode their luck. Twice Bairstow inside-edged Mohammed Shami for four, while Roy survived gloving Pandya down the leg side on 21. Kohli declined a review – there would be none all day –

WATCHING THE WORLD CUP
The final free for all

Ali Martin

As well as the packed house at Lord's, the thrilling climax to England's World Cup final victory over New Zealand was watched live by a UK television audience of 8.7m. This peak figure topped even the high point of the 2005 Ashes: 8.4m viewed the fourth day of the Trent Bridge Test on Channel 4. And the reason? For the first time since that giddy summer, you could watch England playing cricket on a terrestrial channel, after Sky Sports shared their broadcast with Channel 4. It was a bold but sensible move, tacit acceptance that Sky's reach alone was not enough for this once-in-a-generation match.

The journey to this point was a subplot in itself. After a limp opening ceremony, Ben Stokes fired the starting gun with his catch against South Africa. Replays spread across the internet like wildfire, photographs claimed front pages and back, and Stokes was on the BBC News for the right reasons.

But as Eoin Morgan's side stuttered through the group stage, and bad weather created time for reflection, many wondered whether the live action, hidden behind a paywall, was penetrating the national consciousness as a home World Cup should. With 37% of ticket sales going to first-time buyers, there was clearly demand beyond Sky's customers or their pay-as-you-go streaming service, Now TV. The tournament also saw 39.7m access the BBC Sport website for cricket, where they could watch near-live clips; and *Test Match Special* claimed 10.7m listeners via their online platforms alone. The ICC reported 4.6bn global views of their digital video content.

Terrestrial television coverage in UK was limited to a daily hour of highlights on Channel 4, pushed late into the night by the requirement for a three-hour delay after Sky's live transmission. With official sponsors making little effort outside the grounds – their focus was the Indian TV market – cricket's visibility felt limited. At the women's football World Cup in France, by contrast, England's Lionesses had drawn a BBC One audience of 6.1m for their opening win over Scotland. That week, the highest figure on Sky for the cricket was 1.3m, for England's defeat by Pakistan.

Sky maintained it was unfair to compare a 90-minute sport played at prime time with eight hours of 50-over cricket; the ECB, wary of upsetting their broadcast partners, claimed it was a question for the ICC.

The debate came to a head after England secured a semi-final place with victory over New Zealand, the day after a peak audience of 11.7m had watched the Lionesses lose their own semi, to the USA. Asked by BBC Five Live whether the team would lobby for the final to be shown on free-to-air, England seamer Liam Plunkett replied: "I'm not sure they're going to do it. But it would be great for everybody to be able to watch that. Playing for England, you're the pride of the country, and you want people to be able to access that."

Plunkett quickly took to social media to claim his words had been "twisted", but change was afoot. Next day, it was announced that, should England reach the final, Sky would make their broadcast "available to everyone, so the whole country can be part of a rare and special big sporting moment". Channel 4 were soon on board.

On the day, the ratings were won by the Wimbledon men's final between Roger Federer and Novak Djokovic, with a peak of 9.6m viewers on BBC One, while 3.5m watched Channel 4's British Grand Prix coverage (the cricket moved to More4 during the race). But the World Cup's denouement caused 5.2m to flock to Channel 4. And with 3.5m watching on Sky's platforms, England's cricket team were – fleetingly, but for the first time in 14 years – the whole nation's once more.

and the openers cuffed another 111 in 11 overs. Reluctant to test Roy's hamstring too much, they exploited a short boundary, happily depositing wrist-spinners Chahal and Yadav into the Drayton Manor Stand. Eventually, sub fielder Ravindra Jadeja nimbly caught Roy for an exhilarating 66. A score of 160 in 22 hinted at riches, but Root was unusually leaden on a slowish surface, and Shami, en route to a career-best five-for, enjoyed a spell of 3–1–3–2. His first wicket was Bairstow, whose steely century made amends for having bizarrely accused some players-turned-pundits of wanting England to fail. Even so, it needed Stokes's third successive score of 79-plus to pull them past 300. After Bumrah took death bowling to new heights, Woakes began with three maidens, limiting India to 28 for one from ten. Sharma, dropped on four by Root off Archer at second slip, and Kohli accelerated; at 146 in the 29th, the game was on. But for the fifth match running, Kohli failed to transform a fifty into a century. Woakes came back to remove Sharma, who had now converted three out of four, then held an outrageous diving catch to end a breathless innings from Pant. And when Plunkett, in for Moeen Ali, claimed the hard-hitting Pandya, India needed 71 from 31 – tricky, but not impossible. Yet Dhoni chose discretion over valour, singles over boundaries, triggering accusations of deliberately sabotaging Pakistan's late charge towards the knockouts. Whatever India's motivation, their actions did not look good.   HUGH CHEVALLIER

Player of the Match: J. M. Bairstow.   *Attendance:* 23,645.

England

J. J. Roy c sub (R. A. Jadeja) b Yadav	66	L. E. Plunkett not out	1
J. M. Bairstow c Pant b Mohammed Shami	111	J. C. Archer not out	0
J. E. Root c Pandya b Mohammed Shami	44		
*E. J. G. Morgan c Jadhav			
b Mohammed Shami	1	B 2, lb 2, w 4	8
B. A. Stokes c sub (R. A. Jadeja) b Bumrah	79		
†J. C. Buttler c and b Mohammed Shami	20	1/160 (1) 2/205 (2) (7 wkts, 50 overs)	337
C. R. Woakes c Sharma		3/207 (4) 4/277 (3)	
b Mohammed Shami	7	5/310 (6) 6/319 (7) 7/336 (5) 10 overs: 47-0	

A. U. Rashid and M. A. Wood did not bat.

Mohammed Shami 10–1–69–5; Bumrah 10–1–44–1; Chahal 10–0–88–0; Pandya 10–0–60–0; Yadav 10–0–72–1.

India

K. L. Rahul c and b Woakes	0	K. M. Jadhav not out	12
R. G. Sharma c Buttler b Woakes	102	Lb 1, w 6	7
*V. Kohli c sub (J. M. Vince) b Plunkett	66		
R. R. Pant c Woakes b Plunkett	32	1/8 (1) 2/146 (3) (5 wkts, 50 overs)	306
H. H. Pandya c sub (J. M. Vince) b Plunkett	45	3/198 (2) 4/226 (4)	
†M. S. Dhoni not out	42	5/267 (5) 10 overs: 28-1	

Mohammed Shami, K. Yadav, J. J. Bumrah and Y. S. Chahal did not bat.

Woakes 10–3–58–2; Archer 10–0–45–0; Plunkett 10–0–55–3; Wood 10–0–73–0; Rashid 6–0–40–0; Stokes 4–0–34–0.

Umpires: Aleem Dar and H. D. P. K. Dharmasena.   Third umpire: R. S. A. Palliyaguruge.
Referee: R. S. Madugalle.

SRI LANKA v WEST INDIES

At Chester-le-Street, July 1. Sri Lanka won by 23 runs. Toss: West Indies.

Two stylish maiden one-day centuries imbued the tournament's first officially dead match with class, passion and unexpected tension. The lack of meaningful context did

YOUNGEST WORLD CUP CENTURY-MAKERS

Yrs	Days			
20	196	P. R. Stirling (101)	Ireland v Netherlands at Kolkata	2010-11
21	76	R. T. Ponting (102)	Australia v West Indies at Jaipur	1995-96
21	**87**	**W. I. A. Fernando (104)** .	**Sri Lanka v West Indies at Chester-le-Street**	**2019**
22	106	V. Kohli (100*)	India v Bangladesh at Mirpur	2010-11
22	300	S. R. Tendulkar (127*) ...	India v Kenya at Cuttack	1995-96
23	52	A. B. de Villiers (146)...	South Africa v West Indies at St George's	2006-07
23	164	C. H. Gayle (119)	West Indies v Kenya at Kimberley	2002-03
23	**205**	**Imam-ul-Haq (100)**	**Pakistan v Bangladesh at Lord's**	**2019**
23	**272**	**N. Pooran (118)**	**West Indies v Sri Lanka at Chester-le-Street**	**2019**
23	301	A. Flower (115*)........	Zimbabwe v Sri Lanka at New Plymouth	1991-92

Tendulkar hit a second World Cup hundred 13 days later.

---

not dampen the atmosphere at Riverside. Sri Lankan flags flew proudly in a stiff breeze, and attention turned later to the sight of the Bajan pop star Rihanna – a schoolmate of Brathwaite – cheering them on from a hospitality box as West Indies fought back. Fernando, 21, and Pooran, 23, each shone in their ninth ODI. Fernando, compact, fluent and reminiscent of Mahela Jayawardene, became Sri Lanka's youngest World Cup centurion as they reached 250 for the first time in the tournament. West Indies' melancholic body language and feckless outcricket did not suggest a purposeful pursuit; nor did the opening overs of their reply. Gayle threatened briefly but, at 84 for four, the match looked over. The left-handed Pooran had other ideas, bringing to fruition all the hours of Brian Lara worship, and adding 83 in ten overs for the seventh wicket with Allen. Even when Allen fell for a 32-ball 51 – one of three run-outs involving Pooran – West Indies still had hope. That evaporated, though, when Pooran was caught behind off Mathews's first ball in an ODI since December 2017. JOHN STERN

Player of the Match: W. I. A. Fernando. *Attendance:* 12,096.

Sri Lanka

*F. D. M. Karunaratne c Hope b Holder	32	I. Udana c Holder b Thomas	3	
†M. D. K. J. Perera		D. M. de Silva not out	6	
run out (Cottrell/Brathwaite).	64	B 4, lb 5, w 5, nb 5	19	
W. I. A. Fernando c Allen b Cottrell	104			
B. K. G. Mendis c and b Allen	39	1/93 (1) 2/104 (2) (6 wkts, 50 overs)	338	
A. D. Mathews b Holder	26	3/189 (4) 4/247 (5)		
H. D. R. L. Thirimanne not out	45	5/314 (3) 6/327 (7) 10 overs: 49-0		

J. D. F. Vandersay, S. L. Malinga and C. A. K. Rajitha did not bat.

Cottrell 10–0–69–1; Thomas 10–1–58–1; Gabriel 5–0–46–0; Holder 10–0–59–2; Brathwaite 7–0–53–0; Allen 8–0–44–1.

West Indies

C. H. Gayle c Vandersay b Rajitha	35	S. S. Cottrell not out	7	
S. W. Ambris c Perera b Malinga	5	O. R. Thomas lbw b Malinga	1	
†S. D. Hope b Malinga	5	S. T. Gabriel not out	3	
S. O. Hetmyer run out (de Silva)........	29	B 3, lb 2, w 20, nb 2	27	
N. Pooran c Perera b Mathews	118			
*J. O. Holder c sub (B. M. A. J. Mendis)		1/12 (2) 2/22 (3) (9 wkts, 50 overs)	315	
b Vandersay.	26	3/71 (1) 4/84 (4)		
C. R. Brathwaite run out (Udana)	8	5/145 (6) 6/199 (7) 7/282 (8)		
F. A. Allen run out (Rajitha/Udana)	51	8/308 (5) 9/311 (10) 10 overs: 37-2		

Malinga 10–0–55–3; de Silva 10–0–49–0; Udana 10–0–67–0; Rajitha 10–0–76–1; Vandersay 7–0–50–1; Karunaratne 1–0–7–0; Mathews 2–0–6–1.

Umpires: B. N. J. Oxenford and P. R. Reiffel.   Third umpire: S. Ravi.
Referee: D. C. Boon.

BANGLADESH v INDIA

At Birmingham, July 2. India won by 28 runs. Toss: India.

In front of a sea of national flags, India rubber-stamped their semi-final place, and eliminated Bangladesh. On the ground where his side had managed a single six to England's 13 two days earlier, Sharma hoisted one in the first over, and another in the sixth. By then he had been badly dropped, on nine, by Tamim Iqbal at deep midwicket. As against England, Sharma took full advantage of the early reprieve, hitting his fourth century of the World Cup; he heaved three more sixes while putting on 180 with Rahul. When they were parted in the 30th over, a massive total looked likely, but Bangladesh clawed their way back. Kohli perished on the boundary he had labelled too short against England, ending a sequence of five fifties; and although Pant clattered 48, there were three wickets in the final over – one a run-out – as Mustafizur Rahman finished with five. Tamim looked determined to make up for his fielding error, but dragged on in the tenth, then Kohli questioned the umpires after India lost their review following an lbw appeal: it was unclear whether Soumya Sarkar had got an inside edge. Four overs later, Soumya drove straight to extra cover: Kohli caught it, raised a finger, and mouthed "Out!" Also deceived by a tricky surface, Mushfiqur Rahim and Liton Das followed sumptuous boundaries with simple catches, and Bangladesh looked done for when Shakib Al Hasan went after a calm 66, a second sitter for Karthik, making his World Cup debut nearly 15 years after his first one-day international. Sabbir Rahman and Mohammad Saifuddin put on 66, creaming Mohammed Shami for four fours in an over, but Bumrah returned to soothe any Indian nerves, rolling his fingers across a series of pitch-perfect yorkers, including two from the game's final two deliveries. STEVEN LYNCH

Player of the Match: R. G. Sharma.   *Attendance:* 20,427.

India

K. L. Rahul c Mushfiqur Rahim			Bhuvneshwar Kumar run out		
b Rubel Hossain	.	77	(Mushfiqur Rahim/Mustafizur Rahman)	.	2
R. G. Sharma c Liton Das b Soumya Sarkar		104	Mohammed Shami b Mustafizur Rahman	. .	1
*V. Kohli c Rubel Hossain			J. J. Bumrah not out	. . . .	0
b Mustafizur Rahman	.	26			
R. R. Pant c Mosaddek Hossain			Lb 6, w 6, nb 1	. . . .	13
b Shakib Al Hasan	.	48			
H. H. Pandya c Soumya Sarkar			1/180 (2) 2/195 (1) (9 wkts, 50 overs)		314
b Mustafizur Rahman	.	0	3/237 (4) 4/237 (5)		
*M. S. Dhoni c Shakib Al Hasan			5/277 (4) 6/298 (7)		
b Mustafizur Rahman	.	35	7/311 (6) 8/314 (8)		
K. D. Karthik c Mosaddek Hossain			9/314 (9)	10 overs: 69-0	
b Mustafizur Rahman	.	8			

Y. S. Chahal did not bat.

Mashrafe bin Mortaza 5–0–36–0; Mohammad Saifuddin 7–0–59–0; Mustafizur Rahman 10–1–59–5; Shakib Al Hasan 10–0–41–1; Mosaddek Hossain 4–0–32–0; Rubel Hossain 8–0–48–1; Soumya Sarkar 6–0–33–1.

Bangladesh

Tamim Iqbal b Mohammed Shami	22	Rubel Hossain b Bumrah	9
Soumya Sarkar c Kohli b Pandya	33	Mustafizur Rahman b Bumrah	0
Shakib Al Hasan c Karthik b Pandya	66		
†Mushfiqur Rahim c Mohammed Shami b Chahal	24	B 1, lb 1, w 10	12
Liton Das c Karthik b Pandya	22		
Mosaddek Hossain b Bumrah	3	1/39 (1) 2/74 (2)	(48 overs) 286
Sabbir Rahman b Bumrah	36	3/121 (4) 4/162 (5)	
Mohammad Saifuddin not out	51	5/173 (6) 6/179 (3)	
*Mashrafe bin Mortaza c Dhoni b Bhuvneshwar Kumar	8	7/245 (7) 8/257 (9) 9/286 (10) 10/286 (11)	10 overs: 40-1

Bhuvneshwar Kumar 9–0–51–1; Bumrah 10–1–55–4; Mohammed Shami 9–0–68–1; Chahal 10–0–50–1; Pandya 10–0–60–3.

Umpires: M. Erasmus and R. S. A. Palliyaguruge. Third umpire: Aleem Dar.
Referee: R. S. Madugalle.

ENGLAND v NEW ZEALAND

At Chester-le-Street, July 3. England won by 119 runs. Toss: England.

England got the breaks, and the points, to qualify for their first World Cup semi-final since 1992. With their third successive defeat, New Zealand limped haplessly towards the last four, knowing a Pakistan miracle 48 hours later was the only obstacle in their way. Had this been a must-win game for them – as it was for England – they might have risked Lockie Ferguson, their fastest bowler and one of the stars of the tournament. But they protected his hamstring and brought back Southee, who had destroyed England in the 2015 World Cup, but whose previous competitive match had been ten weeks earlier at the

Finger-lickin' good: Mark Wood kisses the fingertips that spelled the end of Kane Williamson.

IPL. His cobwebs were brutally blown away by Bairstow, who launched his third and fourth balls through the covers, and took 13 off his next over. He and Roy brought up a third consecutive century stand, inside 15 overs, before New Zealand fought back. From 194 for one after 30, with Bairstow completing his second hundred in a row, England managed only another 111 for seven as the pitch slowed dramatically, and the bowlers took pace off the ball. But New Zealand's pursuit never gained momentum, and England had all the luck: Nicholls failed to review an lbw shout from Woakes that was going over the top, before Williamson was run out backing up when Taylor's drive received the merest deflection off Wood's fingertips. Wood's version of events was typically eccentric: "He doesn't know how unlucky he is, because I've got the smallest hands for a bloke you've ever seen." Next over, Taylor was run out too, chancing a second to Rashid at deep backward square. Latham found form at last, but no one could stay with him, and Wood picked up three on his home ground to confirm England's first World Cup win over New Zealand since 1983.   JOHN STERN

Player of the Match: J. M. Bairstow.   *Attendance:* 12,828.

England

J. J. Roy c Santner b Neesham	60	A. U. Rashid b Southee		16
J. M. Bairstow b Henry	106	J. C. Archer not out		1
J. E. Root c Latham b Boult	24	B 4, lb 4, w 7		15
†J. C. Buttler c Williamson b Boult	11			
*E. J. G. Morgan c Santner b Henry	42	1/123 (1) 2/194 (3)	(8 wkts, 50 overs)	305
B. A. Stokes c Henry b Santner	11	3/206 (2) 4/214 (4)		
C. R. Woakes c Williamson b Neesham	4	5/248 (6) 6/259 (7)		
L. E. Plunkett not out	15	7/272 (5) 8/301 (9)	10 overs: 67-0	

M. A. Wood did not bat.

Santner 10–0–65–1; Boult 10–0–56–2; Southee 9–0–70–1; Henry 10–0–54–2; de Grandhomme 1–0–11–0; Neesham 10–1–41–2.

New Zealand

M. J. Guptill c Buttler b Archer	8	M. J. Henry b Wood		7
H. M. Nicholls lbw b Woakes	0	T. A. Boult st Buttler b Rashid		4
*K. S. Williamson run out (Wood)	27			
L. R. P. L. Taylor run out (Rashid/Buttler)	28	B 2, lb 6, w 6		14
†T. W. M. Latham c Buttler b Plunkett	57			
J. D. S. Neesham b Wood	19	1/2 (2) 2/14 (1) 3/61 (3)	(45 overs)	186
C. de Grandhomme c Root b Stokes	3	4/69 (4) 5/123 (6) 6/128 (7)		
M. J. Santner lbw b Wood	12	7/164 (5) 8/166 (8) 9/181 (10)		
T. G. Southee not out	7	10/186 (11)	10 overs: 37-2	

Woakes 8–0–44–1; Archer 7–1–17–1; Plunkett 8–0–28–1; Wood 9–0–34–3; Root 3–0–15–0; Rashid 5–0–30–1; Stokes 5–0–10–1.

Umpires: S. Ravi and R. J. Tucker.   Third umpire: P. R. Reiffel.
Referee: D. C. Boon.

AFGHANISTAN v WEST INDIES

At Leeds, July 4. West Indies won by 23 runs. Toss: West Indies.

An enjoyable match that had no bearing on the knockouts felt at times like a testimonial for Gayle, playing his 35th and last World Cup game. The two sides who battled through qualifying had long since been eliminated – and you could see why, especially in the field. Yet there were also glimpses of class. West Indies passed 300, not thanks to Gayle, who backed away to Dawlat Zadran and edged behind for seven, but to players who may be in their prime come 2023. Hope, dropped on five by Rashid Khan at midwicket, anchored the innings with 77. Then came pyrotechnics from Hetmyer, Pooran and Holder; in all, six

HIGHEST WORLD CUP SCORES BY TEENAGERS

	Yrs	Days			
86	18	278	Ikram Alikhil	Afghanistan v West Indies at Leeds	2019
84	18	323	S. R. Tendulkar.	India v New Zealand at Dunedin	1991-92
81	18	318	S. R. Tendulkar.	India v Zimbabwe at Hamilton	1991-92
60	19	172	Abdul Razzaq	Pakistan v Australia at Leeds	1999
59	19	23	Ijaz Ahmed	Pakistan v England at Rawalpindi	1987-88
56*	18	197	Mushfiqur Rahim	Bangladesh v India at Port-of-Spain	2006-07
56	18	170	Mohammad Ashraful . . .	Bangladesh v New Zealand at Kimberley . . .	2002-03
54*	18	315	S. R. Tendulkar.	India v Pakistan at Sydney	1991-92
54	18	356	B. Zuiderent	Netherlands v England at Peshawar.	1995-96
54	19	218	H. Patel	Canada v Australia at Bangalore	2010-11

players contributed to West Indies' tally of 12 sixes. A target of 312 was tough: Afghanistan had never successfully chased more than 274. But Rahmat Shah and Ikram Alikhil – the 18-year-old wicketkeeper who had batted at No. 9 earlier in the competition, and boasted an ODI best of 24 – put on 133 for the second wicket; Alikhil's 86 contained sumptuous timing and straight-drives. At 189 for two, the game was nicely poised. But Gayle trapped Alikhil, Najibullah Zadran was run out two balls later and, when Mohammad Nabi fell cheaply, Afghanistan's hopes of recording a victory in the tournament were vanishing. The lower order kept swinging, and Brathwaite grabbed four. West Indies won their first game since routing Pakistan in May – and Gayle led them from the field.   Tim Wigmore

Player of the Match: S. D. Hope.   *Attendance:* 14,238.

West Indies

C. H. Gayle c Ikram Alikhil b Dawlat Zadran	7	C. R. Brathwaite not out 14
E. Lewis c Mohammad Nabi b Rashid Khan	58	F. A. Allen not out. 0
†S. D. Hope c Rashid Khan		
b Mohammad Nabi .	77	
S. O. Hetmyer c sub (Noor Ali Zadran)		
b Dawlat Zadran .	39	Lb 4, w 9 13
N. Pooran run out (Ikram Alikhil/		
Sayed Shirzad) .	58	1/21 (1) 2/109 (2) (6 wkts, 50 overs) 311
*J. O. Holder c Dawlat Zadran		3/174 (4) 4/192 (3)
b Sayed Shirzad .	45	5/297 (5) 6/297 (6) 10 overs: 43-1

K. A. J. Roach, S. S. Cottrell and O. R. Thomas did not bat.

Mujeeb Zadran 10–0–52–0; Dawlat Zadran 9–1–73–2; Sayed Shirzad 8–0–56–1; Gulbadeen Naib 3–0–18–0; Mohammad Nabi 10–0–56–1; Rashid Khan 10–0–52–1.

Afghanistan

*Gulbadeen Naib c Lewis b Roach	5	Dawlat Zadran c Cottrell b Brathwaite 1
Rahmat Shah c Gayle b Brathwaite	62	Sayed Shirzad c Allen b Thomas 25
†Ikram Alikhil lbw b Gayle.	86	Mujeeb Zadran not out 7
Najibullah Zadran run out (Hetmyer/		Lb 2, w 10, nb 2. 14
Brathwaite) .	31	
Asghar Afghan c Holder b Brathwaite	40	1/5 (1) 2/138 (2) 3/189 (3) (50 overs) 288
Mohammad Nabi c Allen b Roach	2	4/194 (4) 5/201 (6) 6/227 (7)
Samiullah Shenwari c Hetmyer b Roach. . .	6	7/244 (5) 8/255 (9) 9/260 (8)
Rashid Khan c Holder b Brathwaite	9	10/288 (10) 10 overs: 44-1

Cottrell 7–0–43–0; Roach 10.2–2–37–3; Thomas 7–0–43–1; Holder 8–0–46–0; Allen 3–0–26–0; Brathwaite 9–0–63–4; Gayle 6–0–28–1.

Umpires: C. B. Gaffaney and N. J. Llong.   Third umpire: I. J. Gould.
Referee: B. C. Broad.

BANGLADESH v PAKISTAN

At Lord's, July 5. Pakistan won by 94 runs. Toss: Pakistan.

New Zealand's stumble had given Pakistan a tantalising glimpse of the semi-finals – trouble was, they had to win by more than 300 runs to qualify on net run-rate. Perhaps bothered by the ramifications of losing to the former East Pakistan, they didn't show enough intent, pottering to 38 for one in the powerplay and 115 by halfway, even though the second-wicket pair were sharing a stand eventually worth 157. Babar Azam went for 96 after easing Mohammad Saifuddin for consecutive fours, but Imam-ul-Haq completed the World Cup century that had eluded his more famous uncle, Inzamam, watching from a hospitality box. Next ball, he trod on his stumps. Imad Wasim sparkled, but also forced his captain, Sarfraz Ahmed, to retire briefly after smashing him on the arm with a straight-drive. Mustafizur Rahman collected a second successive five-for, while off-

BEST WORLD CUP FIGURES FOR PAKISTAN

6-35	**Shaheen Shah Afridi**	**v Bangladesh at Lord's**	**2019**
5-16	Shahid Afridi	v Kenya at Hambantota	2010-11
5-23	Shahid Afridi	v Canada at Colombo (RPS)	2010-11
5-28	Wasim Akram	v Namibia at Kimberley	2002-03
5-30	**Mohammad Amir**	**v Australia at Taunton**	**2019**
5-35	Saqlain Mushtaq	v Bangladesh at Northampton	1999
5-44	Abdul Qadir	v Sri Lanka at Leeds	1983
5-46	Wahab Riaz	v India at Mohali	2010-11
5-55	Sohail Khan	v India at Adelaide	2014-15

spinner Mehedi Hasan whirred through ten overs without conceding a boundary, apart from his own wild throw that beat the keeper. Pakistan needed to bowl Bangladesh out for seven to qualify and, after a maiden prolonged the agony, were officially eliminated in the second over. But Bangladesh, playing their first ODI at Lord's, were never on terms. Shakib Al Hasan alone made much impression, taking his tournament aggregate to 606. He fell in the 33rd over, a third victim for Shaheen Shah Afridi, the first teenager to take a World Cup five-for. With members showing little interest in tickets, MCC – anxious to avoid negative publicity about a half-empty Pavilion – invited in more than 200 children from local state schools.   STEVEN LYNCH

Player of the Match: Shaheen Shah Afridi.   *Attendance:* 23,305.

Pakistan

Fakhar Zaman c Mehedi Hasan		Wahab Riaz b Mohammad Saifuddin	2
b Mohammad Saifuddin	13	Shadab Khan c and b Mustafizur Rahman	1
Imam-ul-Haq hit wkt b Mustafizur Rahman	100	Mohammad Amir c Mushfiqur Rahim	
Babar Azam lbw b Mohammad Saifuddin	96	b Mustafizur Rahman	8
Mohammad Hafeez c Shakib Al Hasan		Shaheen Shah Afridi not out	0
b Mehedi Hasan	27	Lb 3, w 12, nb 1	16
Haris Sohail c Soumya Sarkar			
b Mustafizur Rahman	6	1/23 (1) 2/180 (3) (9 wkts, 50 overs)	315
Imad Wasim c Mahmudullah		3/246 (4) 4/248 (4)	
b Mustafizur Rahman	43	5/255 (5) 6/288 (8) 7/289 (9)	
*†Sarfraz Ahmed not out	3	8/314 (6) 9/314 (10) 10 overs: 38-1	

Sarfraz Ahmed, when 2, retired hurt at 267-5 and resumed at 314-9.

Mehedi Hasan 10–0–30–1; Mohammad Saifuddin 9–0–77–3; Mustafizur Rahman 10–0–75–5; Mashrafe bin Mortaza 7–0–46–0; Shakib Al Hasan 10–0–57–0; Mosaddek Hossain 4–0–27–0.

Bangladesh

Tamim Iqbal b Shaheen Shah Afridi	8
Soumya Sarkar c Fakhar Zaman b Mohammad Amir	22
Shakib Al Hasan c Sarfraz Ahmed b Shaheen Shah Afridi	64
†Mushfiqur Rahim b Wahab Riaz	16
Liton Das c Haris Sohail b Shaheen Shah Afridi	32
Mahmudullah b Shaheen Shah Afridi	29
Mosaddek Hossain c Babar Azam b Shadab Khan	16
Mohammad Saifuddin c Mohammad Amir b Shaheen Shah Afridi	0
Mehedi Hasan not out	7
*Mashrafe bin Mortaza st Sarfraz Ahmed b Shadab Khan	15
Mustafizur Rahman b Shaheen Shah Afridi	1
Lb 5, w 6	11

1/26 (2) 2/48 (1) (44.1 overs) 221
3/78 (4) 4/136 (5)
5/154 (3) 6/197 (7)
7/197 (8) 8/198 (6)
9/219 (10) 10/221 (11) 10 overs: 47-1

Mohammad Hafeez 6–1–32–0; Mohammad Amir 7–0–31–1; Shaheen Shah Afridi 9.1–0–35–6; Wahab Riaz 7–0–33–1; Imad Wasim 6–0–26–0; Shadab Khan 9–0–59–2.

Umpires: M. A. Gough and R. A. Kettleborough.   Third umpire: R. K. Illingworth.
Referee: R. B. Richardson.

INDIA v SRI LANKA

At Leeds, July 6. India won by seven wickets. Toss: Sri Lanka.

India ended their league engagements with a comprehensive win. With seven victories, a washout and a defeat, they topped the table with 15 points. But they had to wait a few hours to find out whether Australia could overtake them by beating South Africa: they could not, leaving India with a semi-final against New Zealand at Old Trafford. The man behind their success was Sharma, who scored his fifth century of the tournament, beating Kumar Sangakkara's World Cup record of four in 2014-15. Sharma powered a 189-run

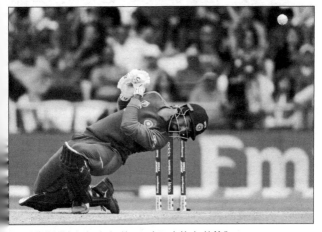

Short shrift: K. L. Rahul, a hundred to his name, is toppled by Lasith Malinga.

it's who you play with /

opening partnership in pursuit of 265, and Rahul later brought up his second ODI hundred. By the time he was dismissed, India needed just 21. Sri Lanka had chosen to bat, but were pushed on the back foot by Bumrah, who removed the openers; at 55 for four, they were on the edge. A painstaking 113 from Mathews and fifty from Thirimanne put a score on the board, if not one likely to trouble India. A week after a plane towing a political message disrupted Pakistan's match here with Afghanistan, there was another airborne protest, this time opposing India's rule in the disputed region of Kashmir. The game was Ian Gould's last as an international umpire, after 74 Tests, 140 ODIs and 37 Twenty20s. ANAND VASU

Player of the Match: R. G. Sharma.   *Attendance:* 15,985.

Sri Lanka

*F. D. M. Karunaratne c Dhoni b Bumrah	. .	10	I. Udana not out	1
†M. D. K. J. Perera c Dhoni b Bumrah	. . . . .	18		
W. I. A. Fernando c Dhoni b Pandya	. . . . .	20		
B. K. G. Mendis st Dhoni b Jadeja	. . . .	3	B 4, lb 2, w 8, nb 1	15
A. D. Mathews c Sharma b Bumrah	. . . . . .	113		
H. D. R. L. Thirimanne c Jadeja b Yadav	. .	53	1/17 (1) 2/40 (2) (7 wkts, 50 overs)	264
D. M. de Silva not out	. . . .	29	3/53 (4) 4/55 (3)	
N. L. T. C. Perera c Pandya			5/179 (6) 6/253 (5)	
	b Bhuvneshwar Kumar .	2	7/260 (8) 10 overs: 52-2	

S. L. Malinga and C. A. K. Rajitha did not bat.

Bhuvneshwar Kumar 10–0–73–1; Bumrah 10–2–37–3; Pandya 10–0–50–1; Jadeja 10–0–40–1; Yadav 10–0–58–1.

India

K. L. Rahul c M. D. K. J. Perera b Malinga	111			
R. G. Sharma c Mathews b Rajitha	. . . .	103		
*V. Kohli not out	34			
R. R. Pant lbw b Udana	4			
H. H. Pandya not out	7			
Lb 1, w 5	6			

1/189 (2) 2/244 (1)   (3 wkts, 43.3 overs)   265
3/253 (4)   10 overs: 59-0

†M. S. Dhoni, K. D. Karthik, R. A. Jadeja, Bhuvneshwar Kumar, K. Yadav and J. J. Bumrah did not bat.

Malinga 10–1–82–1; Rajitha 8–0–47–1; Udana 9.3–0–50–1; N. L. T. C. Perera 10–0–34–0; de Silva 6–0–51–0.

Umpires: I. J. Gould and P. Wilson.   Third umpire: C. B. Gaffaney.
Referee: B. C. Broad.

AUSTRALIA v SOUTH AFRICA

At Manchester, July 6 (day/night). South Africa won by ten runs. Toss: South Africa.

South Africa's disappointing World Cup ended not with a whimper but a bang: written off beforehand, and missing Hashim Amla with a knee injury, they joined the party, far too late. Defeat cost Australia top spot in the table, consigning them to a semi-final against England rather than New Zealand, who would now face India. The script went awry from the start: Markram caressed two fours in Starc's first over, which cost 14, and there were 12 boundaries in the powerplay – the joint-most in the tournament – as the openers zipped to 73. Lyon eventually teased out both, but du Plessis took over, belting Cummins and Lyon for huge sixes. He put on 151 with van der Dussen, who was initially ponderous against spin but dismissive against pace: van der Dussen perished last ball of the innings, deftly caught by Maxwell on the midwicket boundary just short of a six and a maiden one-day international century. But he had lifted the total to 325, which looked even better when Finch departed in the third over and Smith – lbw to Pretorius's third ball – in the seventh. Khawaja pulled a hamstring (he resumed later, but missed the semi-final), before Stoinis was run out by a superb backhand flick from de Kock, who then leapt high to snare Maxwell. Australia were kept afloat by Warner, who might have been run out himself in the first over, but scurried to 122 – his 17th ODI hundred and third of this World Cup – before sending a flying catch to Morris at wide mid-on. He put on 108 with the increasingly impressive Carey, whose career-best 85 was ended by another good catch at deep cover. The tail went down slugging, but could not prevent the 16th win by the side batting first in the last 20 matches of the qualifying stage. STEVEN LYNCH

Player of the Match: F. du Plessis.   *Attendance:* 21,102.

South Africa

A. K. Markram st Carey b Lyon	34	A. L. Phehlukwayo not out	4
†Q. de Kock c Starc b Lyon	52	B 1, lb 10, w 13	24
*F. du Plessis c Starc b Behrendorff	100		
H. E. van der Dussen c Maxwell b Cummins	95	1/79 (1) 2/114 (2) (6 wkts, 50 overs)	325
J-P. Duminy c Stoinis b Starc	14	3/265 (3) 4/295 (5)	
D. Pretorius b Starc	2	5/317 (6) 6/325 (4) 10 overs: 73-0	

C. H. Morris, K. Rabada, Imran Tahir and T. Shamsi did not bat.

Starc 9–0–59–2; Behrendorff 8–0–55–1; Lyon 10–0–53–2; Cummins 9–0–66–1; Smith 1–0–5–0; Stoinis 3–0–19–0; Maxwell 10–0–57–0.

Australia

D. A. Warner c Morris b Pretorius	122	J. P. Behrendorff not out	11
*A. J. Finch c Markram b Imran Tahir	3	N. M. Lyon c Markram b Phehlukwayo	3
U. T. Khawaja b Rabada	18		
S. P. D. Smith lbw b Pretorius	7	Lb 4, w 3	7
M. P. Stoinis run out (Rabada/de Kock)	22		
G. J. Maxwell c de Kock b Rabada	12	1/5 (2) 2/33 (4) 3/95 (5) (49.5 overs)	315
†A. T. Carey c Markram b Morris	85	4/119 (6) 5/227 (1) 6/272 (8)	
P. J. Cummins c Duminy b Phehlukwayo	9	7/275 (7) 8/301 (3) 9/306 (9)	
M. A. Starc b Rabada	16	10/315 (11) 10 overs: 44-2	

Khawaja, when 6, retired hurt at 20-1 and resumed at 275-7.

Imran Tahir 9–0–59–1; Rabada 10–0–56–3; Pretorius 6–2–27–2; Morris 9–0–63–1; Shamsi 9–0–62–0; Phehlukwayo 2.5–0–22–2; Duminy 4–0–22–0.

Umpires: Aleem Dar and H. D. P. K. Dharmasena.   Third umpire: S. Ravi.
Referee: R. S. Madugalle.

SEMI-FINALS

INDIA v NEW ZEALAND

At Manchester, July 9–10. New Zealand won by 18 runs. Toss: New Zealand.

"Forty-five minutes of bad cricket," lamented Kohli. They came as India started their chase of 240 and slipped to 24 for four, their musketeers Sharma, Kohli himself and Rahul going all for one, unique in international cricket for a top three. Henry started the rot, but Boult bent a ball in to Kohli, who had also fallen for a single in the 2015 semi-final defeat by Australia. After Richard Illingworth raised his finger, the inevitable review showed a bail-clipping umpire's call. The collapse was enough to see table-toppers India dumped out, despite a stirring comeback orchestrated by Jadeja, batting for the first time in the tournament after inexplicably missing most of the group games (except when he was an electric substitute fielder). From 92 for six, he dominated a World Cup-record seventh-wicket stand of 116 with Dhoni, whose share was only 32. Jadeja hoisted four sweet sixes before, with the rate still rising – Santner's first eight overs cost only 15 – skying to mid-off. Jadeja's 77 ("his best knock, according to me," said Kohli) followed ten tight overs of his left-arm spin, a direct-hit run-out from the boundary and a nonchalant running catch. It wasn't a bad return for a "bits and pieces player," as he had been described by the former Indian batsman Sanjay Manjrekar. Jadeja's celebrations on reaching his half-century had included a pointed gesture towards the media centre, where Manjrekar was commentating. Forced to hit out, Dhoni cracked a six over point before, hustling for two, he was narrowly beaten by Guptill's exocet from the edge of the 30-yard circle. It was the final flash of fielding brilliance – Neesham's earlier catch at backward point was another – to swing a match which spilled into two days when rain washed out the first afternoon; had a late restart been possible, India might have been contemplating a DLS target of 148 in 20 overs. New Zealand, after three defeats, had made a sticky start. Guptill survived an lbw review from the first ball of the game (India later lost their batting review to its last), but soon became the first to fall for a single, and the scoring-rate seemed sluggish. Williamson's 67 took 95 deliveries, while Taylor grafted to 74 from 90 – but it was pragmatic stuff under leaden skies on a grudging pitch offering occasional turn. New Zealand managed 28 more from 23 balls when play resumed next morning – then embarked on those fateful 45 minutes that broke a billion Indian hearts. STEVEN LYNCH

Player of the Match: M. J. Henry.   *Attendance:* 20,760.
Close of play: first day, New Zealand 211-5 (46.1 overs) (Taylor 67, Latham 3).

New Zealand

M. J. Guptill c Kohli b Bumrah	1	M. J. Santner not out	9
H. M. Nicholls b Jadeja	28	M. J. Henry c Kohli b Bhuvneshwar Kumar	1
*K. S. Williamson c Jadeja b Chahal	67	T. A. Boult not out	3
L. R. P. L. Taylor run out (Jadeja)	74	Lb 5, w 13	18
J. D. S. Neesham c Karthik b Pandya	12		
C. de Grandhomme c Dhoni		1/1 (1) 2/69 (2) (8 wkts, 50 overs) 239	
b Bhuvneshwar Kumar	16	3/134 (4) 4/162 (5)	
†T. W. M. Latham c Jadeja		5/200 (6) 6/225 (4)	
b Bhuvneshwar Kumar	10	7/225 (7) 8/232 (9) 10 overs: 27-1	

L. H. Ferguson did not bat.

Bhuvneshwar Kumar 10–1–43–3; Bumrah 10–1–39–1; Pandya 10–0–55–1; Jadeja 10–0–34–1; Chahal 10–0–63–1.

India

K. L. Rahul c Latham b Henry	1	Y. S. Chahal c Latham b Neesham	5
R. G. Sharma c Latham b Henry	1	J. J. Bumrah not out	0
*V. Kohli lbw b Boult	1		
R. R. Pant c de Grandhomme b Santner	32	Lb 3, w 13	16
K. D. Karthik c Neesham b Henry	6		
H. H. Pandya c Williamson b Santner	32	1/4 (2) 2/5 (3) 3/5 (1) (49.3 overs) 221	
M. S. Dhoni run out (Guptill)	50	4/24 (5) 5/71 (4) 6/92 (6)	
R. A. Jadeja c Williamson b Boult	77	7/208 (8) 8/216 (7) 9/217 (9)	
Bhuvneshwar Kumar b Ferguson	0	10/221 (10) 10 overs: 24-4	

Boult 10–2–42–2; Henry 10–1–37–3; Ferguson 10–0–43–1; de Grandhomme 2–0–13–0; Neesham 7.3–0–49–1; Santner 10–2–34–2.

Umpires: R. K. Illingworth and R. A. Kettleborough.   Third umpire: R. J. Tucker.
Referee: D. C. Boon.

Roy of the overs: Jason Roy crashes Steve Smith for a third successive straight six.

ENGLAND v AUSTRALIA

At Birmingham, July 11. England won by eight wickets. Toss: Australia.

In the build-up to England's first World Cup semi-final for a generation, the Australian squad walked barefoot on the Birmingham grass, ostensibly to draw positive energy from the earth. In the game itself, England made that connection deeper still: they buried them. Finch inevitably chose to bat, since England's three hiccups had come chasing. Proceedings began with Warner driving a Woakes half-volley through the covers, but the bowlers hit back. Archer's first-ball inswinger trapped Finch for a golden duck, then Woakes had Warner taken at second slip with one that bounced and left him. And when a wobbly Handscomb – on World Cup debut because of injury to Usman Khawaja – was castled by Woakes, it was 14 for three. Only the quickest of thinking from Carey, promoted to No. 5, prevented it becoming 19 for four: a vicious ball from Archer dislodged his helmet which, had he not caught it, seemed to be heading for the stumps. Despite a deep cut to the chin, Carey maintained his composure and, together with the hyper-fidgety Smith, set a recovery in train. Neither rapid nor pretty, it was effective: first Australia's hundred, then the century stand. Rashid's variations held no mystery, and his first 25 balls yielded 30 risk-free runs. But then Carey, looking to clear deep midwicket, found the fielder. The lapse reinvigorated England: Rashid claimed two more, both with googlies, and Archer's exquisite knuckle ball made a fool of Maxwell, who dollied to cover. A feisty Smith–Starc alliance battled on, eventually ended by dazzling athleticism and a dollop of luck: a blink-of-an-eye pick-up-and-throw from Buttler threaded Smith's legs as he tore down the wicket. His cussed classic gave Australia a scrap of hope: 224 was three more than England had managed against them a fortnight earlier, 12 more than against Sri Lanka. But now there was the Roy factor. Undaunted by reputation or pressure, he held back, then pulled out the pin. Starc was first to suffer: ten off his second over, and a flick over fine leg for six in his third. Would spin stem the flow? No chance. Lyon's first delivery sailed over his head for another six. Where should Finch turn? Smith's leg-breaks? Mistake. After two singles and a wide came three more monstrous Roy sixes, the last almost clearing Edgbaston's huge new South Stand. The savaging of Smith brought the openers their 11th century partnership. And although Starc did remove Bairstow in the 18th, the Australian goose was already on a plate, with roast potatoes. Two overs later, Kumar Dharmasena detected a non-existent leg-side edge and gave Roy out. Bairstow had squandered the review, and Roy's indignation earned him a 30% fine and two demerit points. Root and Morgan then hastened Australia's first World Cup semi-final defeat out of eight – ensuring a new name would be on the trophy. England travelled to their first final since 1992 brimming with brio, their fear of chasing laid to rest.   HUGH CHEVALLIER

Player of the Match: C. R. Woakes.   *Attendance:* 22,100.

Australia

D. A. Warner c Bairstow b Woakes		9
*A. J. Finch lbw b Archer		0
S. P. D. Smith run out (Buttler)		85
P. S. P. Handscomb b Woakes		4
†A. T. Carey c sub (J. M. Vince) b Rashid		46
M. P. Stoinis lbw b Rashid		0
G. J. Maxwell c Morgan b Archer		22
P. J. Cummins c Root b Rashid		6
M. A. Starc c Buttler b Woakes		29

J. P. Behrendorff b Wood	1
N. M. Lyon not out	5
Lb 6, w 10	16
(49 overs)	**223**

1/4 (2) 2/10 (1) 3/14 (4)   (49 overs) 223
4/117 (5) 5/118 (6) 6/157 (7)
7/166 (8) 8/217 (3) 9/217 (9)
10/223 (10)   10 overs: 27-3

Woakes 8–0–20–3; Archer 10–0–32–2; Stokes 4–0–22–0; Wood 9–0–45–1; Plunkett 8–0–44–0; Rashid 10–0–54–3.

England

J. J. Roy c Carey b Cummins	85
J. M. Bairstow lbw b Starc	34
J. E. Root not out	49
*E. J. G. Morgan not out	45
Lb 1, w 12	13

1/124 (2) 2/147 (1) (2 wkts, 32.1 overs) 226
10 overs: 50-0

B. A. Stokes, †J. C. Buttler, C. R. Woakes, L. E. Plunkett, J. C. Archer, A. U. Rashid and M. A. Wood did not bat.

Behrendorff 8.1–2–38–0; Starc 9–0–70–1; Cummins 7–0–34–1; Lyon 5–0–49–0; Smith 1–0–21–0; Stoinis 2–0–13–0.

Umpires: H. D. P. K. Dharmasena and M. Erasmus.   Third umpire: C. B. Gaffaney.
Referee: R. S. Madugalle.

> ❝'Can I just say?' The dominant male is speaking. 'Can I just say? I voted against women the first time round. But the second time, I voted for you.' There's a pause, which you sense you're supposed to fill with gratitude. Instead you ask what changed his mind. He smirks at his friend. 'Good-looking women like you!'"
> Women at MCC, page 42

THE FINAL

Notes...

Australian bookmaker Sportsbet refunded money to those who had bet on a New Zealand win: "For a World Cup final to be decided in that manner is an absolute disgrace, and the punters shouldn't have to pay for the ineptness of the ICC."

Less than a week after the final, Ben Stokes was nominated for the New Zealander of the Year award. Cameron Bennett, chief judge, said: "He might not have been playing for the Black Caps but, having been born in Christchurch, where his parents now live, and with Maori ancestry, there's clearly a few Kiwis about who think we can still claim him." Stokes said he was flattered, but withdrew his name because it did not "sit right", and championed Kane Williamson instead.

There were shades of 2005 when the England team were invited to Downing Street the day after their victory. No one urinated in the garden but, according to *The Daily Telegraph*, the players began a chant of "Allez, allez, allez" before they emerged into the street to pose for the trophy with the prime minister. The statesmanlike Eoin Morgan told them to calm down.

...and Quotes

"Kids, don't take up sport. Take up baking or something. Die at 60 really fat and happy."
Tweet by Jimmy Neesham

"I just remember it being so much fun. Myself and Ben, we'd get to the end of an over and be like, 'How good is this atmosphere?'" *Jos Buttler on his partnership with Ben Stokes*

"Hopefully everyone at home will want to be the next Ben Stokes." *Eoin Morgan*

"This is the moment – it's Archer to Guptill. Two to win. Guptill's got to push for two, they've gotta go! The throw's gotta go to the keeper's end. He's got it! England have won the World Cup – by the barest of margins. By the barest of all margins. Absolute ecstasy for England. Agony, agony for New Zealand. Wow. It's all yours Nasser – it's your cup."
Ian Smith commentates on the climax

"We actually had quite a good party. Obviously it was quite a sombre mood for a while, but then we realised we were part of one of the greatest games in cricket history, so we got over it fairly quickly."
Martin Guptill

"There was a lot of singing, as the English like to do. They can string a few words together, unlike the Aussies, who just go 'Oi, Oi, Oi!'" *Trevor Bayliss*

"I wasn't sure it was possible for England to win the World Cup when I started, but I thought I'd give it a go." *Bayliss*

"I don't want this taken out of context, but he is a real fighter." *Bayliss pays tribute to Stokes*

"I'm probably the most hated father in New Zealand." *Ged Stokes*

"I went to bed just after four and I couldn't sleep. I was up for three hours just thinking, trying to understand what happened in the game... and absolutely none of it has sunk in."
Eoin Morgan a few days later

"What was scaring me was, if we lost, I didn't know how I'd play cricket again." *Jos Buttler*

"We still have our WhatsApp group, where each day we greet each other with 'Morning, champions'." *Mark Wood*

"My little boy has suddenly gone cricket mad. He's in the garden until the sun goes down saying, 'Dad, can you bowl a few at me?'" *Golfer Justin Rose*

"I'm gonna go home for the first time in about four months. Probably gonna walk my dog along the beach and try and put it aside. I'm sure he won't be too angry at me." *Trent Boult*

FINAL

ENGLAND v NEW ZEALAND

Lawrence Booth

At Lord's, July 14. England won by virtue of hitting more boundaries, after both the match and the super over were tied. Toss: New Zealand.

Words were not enough, but the captains tried anyway. "Extraordinary," said Morgan. "Gutted," said Williamson. More or less everyone else was speechless. England had won their first men's World Cup on an obscure technicality, after tying not once with New Zealand, but twice: 241 apiece after 50 overs, then 15-all after the super over. But because they had hit more boundaries overall (27 to 17), England were declared the winners. It was slightly random, and possibly unjust. Yet the drama was unsurpassable, outdoing even the 1999 semi-final between Australia and South Africa at Edgbaston. Neither side deserved to lose, but someone had to win.

Morgan, born in Dublin, was asked if England had enjoyed the "luck of the Irish". Drawing on his team's multiculturalism, he quoted Rashid, his leg-spinner, who had suggested "Allah was definitely with us". Whatever the source of their fortune, England enjoyed plenty. Taylor had been given lbw to one that was going over (Guptill had wasted the review). Then, from the first ball of the chase, Roy survived a huge shout by Boult: not out, said Marais Erasmus; umpire's call on leg stump, said DRS, though another millimetre or two would have overturned the decision. A few hours later, with England needing 22 off nine, Stokes was caught at long-on by Boult, who didn't realise how close he was to the boundary, and stepped on it. Standing nearby, waiting for the relay catch, Guptill forlornly but sportingly signalled six.

The drama was far from over. England, now eight down, required 15 from four when Stokes smeared Boult for six: nine off three. He pulled the next ball to deep midwicket, and hared back for the second, his dive coinciding with the arrival of Guptill's powerful throw. Astonishingly, the ball ricocheted off Stokes's outstretched bat, and scooted off up the hill to the third-man boundary, with de Grandhomme in vain pursuit; everyone looked aghast, even Stokes. After a confab with Erasmus, umpire Dharmasena used his fingers to signal six: two runs, four overthrows. The equation was three off two… but should it have been *four* off two? Hours later, someone discovered Law 19.8, the one about boundaries from overthrows. The batsmen, it transpired, had to have crossed "at the instant of the throw or act" for the "run in progress" to count. Stokes and Rashid had not crossed at the moment Guptill released the ball, so England should have scored five, not six, and Rashid, not Stokes, should have been on strike. Four elite-panel umpires were on duty, yet none noticed the error. Conceivably, it cost New Zealand the World Cup.

Still, Stokes played the next two deliveries in the knowledge that two runs would mean a super over, regardless of wickets lost. He pushed the fifth ball to long-off for an easy single, but a tricky two: Santner's return beat Rashid, though he should probably have aimed for the striker's end and run out Stokes. One ball to go: one run for a super over, two for instant glory. Boult produced a leg-stump full toss, which Stokes might have hit for six had he needed to. But, as he said later, this was a moment for pragmatism, not heroics. A bunt to long-on brought the scores level, before Neesham's throw did for Wood – like Rashid, run out without facing. Stokes kicked his bat, then dragged himself back to the dressing-room, and found a quiet spot in the shower. He emerged to learn he would soon be returning to the middle with Buttler, because Morgan wanted a left–right combination. Lord's was chaos.

The super overs were impossibly tense. England took 15 off Boult, including a last-ball four to midwicket by Buttler. Archer began with the narrowest of off-side wides and, when Neesham pulled his second legitimate delivery into the Tavern for six, New Zealand needed seven off four. But Archer held his nerve, obliging Guptill – on strike for the first

THE FINAL PRESS CONFERENCE
Civilised citizen Kane

SAMBIT BAL

"Laugh or cry – it's your choice, isn't it?" Barely an hour after apparently being consigned
to a lifetime of hurt, Kane Williamson sat smiling in the real-tennis court behind the
Lord's Pavilion, bearing not the faintest resemblance to a man whose spirit has been
crushed. He was not burning with indignation or anger; he was not even a little bitter
or begrudging.

Williamson was not the first World Cup-losing captain to face a press conference, but
who else has lost the World Cup without actually losing? If it was an evening of providential
deliverance for England, it was also the cruellest for New Zealand. They had lost their
second successive World Cup final, not by the slenderest of margins, but by the travesty of
a regulation mandating that fours and sixes counted more than their actual value.

Even before it came to the ties and the tie-breaker, there was the case of a dismissal
turning into a six, when Trent Boult back-pedalled on to the ropes, and the misfortune of
another six along the carpet via a ricochet off the bat. Had the umpires been more vigilant,
this should have been a five, leaving England's No. 10 on strike with four to get off
two balls.

Distance brings perspective, and time heals pain but, despite the rawness of the moment,
Williamson – who had not so much led New Zealand's World Cup campaign as carried it
– was wise enough to concede that the tie-breaker rule existed before the tournament
began, and the overthrow rule since eternity, and that the match hadn't been won or lost
in any single moment. He spoke of the uncontrollables – umpiring decisions, reviews and
rules – without blaming any.

There was only a hint of wistfulness when he mentioned his disappointment. "It's hard to
swallow" came up a few times. But even the acknowledgment that luck had gone England's
way came with the recognition that this was inevitable in a match of no margins. Whichever
side had won would have felt fortunate, he said. "So, yeah, it's one of those things."

Grace, poise, magnanimity – and let's add enlightenment. That luck, human errors, the
thinnest of margins are as intrinsic to the game as skill and athletic prowess is common
knowledge. But what level of calm it must have taken to arrive at this.

The journalist who asked the last question said he was standing up out of reverence for
Williamson's conduct. "Should everyone be a gentleman like you?" he asked. Williamson
laughed again. "Everybody is allowed to be themselves. That is a good thing about the
world. And everybody should be a little bit different as well." He paused, and surveyed
the room. "That is probably my best answer. Just be yourself and try and enjoy what you
do." Another laugh, echoed by the whole room.

As he started walking off, the applause began. I don't know who was first to clap, but
soon Williamson was receiving a standing ovation from the most cynical bunch of cricket
followers, trained not to let emotion get in the way.

Only twice before had I seen cricketers applauded at a press conference: Steve Waugh
at Sydney in 2004, then M. S. Dhoni and Yuvraj Singh after India's World Cup win at
Mumbai in 2011. In the first instance, it was mainly Australian journalists, saying goodbye
to an iconic captain; in the second, it was only Indian journalists, moved by a first World
Cup win in 28 years.

With only a handful of New Zealanders present, this was no stirring of national passion
for Williamson. It was something much higher: a spontaneous outbreak of warmth,
appreciation and gratitude for a man whose dignity and empathy and loveliness had
provided the magnificent finish to an unforgettable day.

time – to score two off the last. Despite his lack of runs, he had been chosen for the task, said Williamson, because of his speed, but Roy's throw from deep midwicket was too quick even for him. Buttler, cool as you like, broke the stumps moments before Guptill slid in. England went berserk, though Woakes found the time to comfort Guptill, who had barely picked himself off the turf. The 4,192nd one-day international was the most improbable of the lot.

The final had begun more sedately (and 15 minutes late because of overnight rain). As in the group game at Chester-le-Street 11 days earlier, Nicholls was wrongly given lbw to Woakes on nought, but this time asked for a review. Woakes did then trap Guptill, who had tried to hit his way back into form. But, as Nicholls and Williamson settled in on a pitch that was green and slow, New Zealand's decision to bat threatened to assume a critical air.

Yet this was a game that kept confounding expectations. Plunkett had Williamson caught behind on review for 30, and bowled Nicholls off an inside edge for 55. Latham managed 47 but, in all, the last 28 overs produced 139 for seven, with Archer's five overs at the death costing just 24. When Santner ducked under the final ball of the innings, an Archer bouncer, it seemed insignificant at the time. Woakes and Plunkett finished with three wickets each.

England's target of 242 sounded straightforward, but only three higher totals had successfully been chased all tournament. Erasmus turned down Boult's first-ball appeal against Roy, and England's openers got to 28 before Roy fiddled at Henry. Root's torturous 30-ball seven ended with a swipe at de Grandhomme's economical medium-pacers. When Bairstow played on against Ferguson, and Morgan scythed Neesham to deep point, where Ferguson dived forward to hold a superb catch, England were 86 for four in the 24th, and in danger of suffocating.

THE SUPER OVERS, BALL-BY-BALL

England's over – Trent Boult bowling

Ball 1	A Stokes heave flies off the edge over short third man towards the Pavilion	**3**
Ball 2	Buttler smears full-length delivery to deep midwicket	**1**
Ball 3	Stokes bisects fielders on leg-side boundary with slog-sweep on one knee	**4**
Ball 4	Full toss outside off; Stokes aims to steer through the ring, but picks out cover . .	**1**
Ball 5	Buttler drives full-length ball to deep extra cover.	**2**
Ball 6	Another full toss, on leg stump; Buttler shovels it over midwicket	**4**

Stokes 8*, Buttler 7*; Boult 1–0–15–0 **15-0**

New Zealand's over – Jofra Archer bowling

Ball 1	Dharmasena signals wide as full-length ball is fractionally too far outside off. . . .	**1**
Ball 1	Neesham cloths near-yorker to long-off	**2**
Ball 2	Length ball allows Neesham to free his arms and swing into the Mound Stand . . .	**6**
Ball 3	Neesham mows full ball to deep midwicket; fumble by Roy allows a second	**2**
Ball 4	Near repeat: Roy throws to non-striker's end, with Buttler ready at the other	**2**
Ball 5	Neesham, in a tangle to a short-of-a-length delivery, mistimes pull. The ball dribbles in front of him; Archer does not shy at non-striker's end for fear of overthrows . . .	**1**
Ball 6	Full ball just outside leg; Guptill drives to deep midwicket. Roy picks out Buttler, who gathers the ball, lunges, and demolishes stumps	**1(W)**

Neesham 13*, Guptill 1, Extras 1; Archer 1–0–15–0 **15-1**

England win on boundary count.

England: 22 fours and three sixes* (50 overs) + two fours (super over) = 27
New Zealand: 14 fours and two sixes (50 overs) + one six (super over) = 17

*   Includes the six involving four overthrows deflected off Stokes's bat.

With Woakes at No. 7, the onus was on Stokes and Buttler. They responded magnificently, adding 110 in 21 overs. Buttler batted as fluently as anyone all match, cutting Ferguson, straight-driving Neesham, then ramping Henry, all for four. But when he fell to a world-class tumbling catch at deep point by substitute fielder Southee, England required 46 from 31. Stokes was exhausted and struggling for timing, while the lower order could not get going. It looked like New Zealand's trophy. The equation ticked down, the rate crept up, as if in slow motion: 39 off four overs, 34 off three, 24 off two. Up in the dressing-room, Bairstow remarked that England needed three sixes. With a generous helping of luck, Stokes obliged. Soon, Morgan was lifting the trophy, too delighted to wonder how on earth England had won and, in all likelihood, too delighted to care.

Player of the Match: B. A. Stokes. *Attendance:* 26,970.

Player of the Tournament: K. S. Williamson.

New Zealand

M. J. Guptill lbw b Woakes	19	M. J. Santner not out	5
H. M. Nicholls b Plunkett	55	M. J. Henry b Archer	4
*K. S. Williamson c Buttler b Plunkett	30	T. A. Boult not out	1
L. R. P. L. Taylor lbw b Wood	15	Lb 12, w 17, nb 1	30
†T. W. M. Latham c sub (J. M. Vince)			
b Woakes	47	1/29 (1) 2/103 (3)	(8 wkts, 50 overs) 241
J. D. S. Neesham c Root b Plunkett	19	3/118 (2) 4/141 (4)	
C. de Grandhomme c sub (J. M. Vince)		5/173 (6) 6/219 (7)	
b Woakes	16	7/232 (5) 8/240 (9)	10 overs: 33-1

L. H. Ferguson did not bat.

Woakes 9–0–37–3; Archer 10–0–42–1; Plunkett 10–0–42–3; Wood 10–1–49–1; Rashid 8–0–39–0; Stokes 3–0–20–0.

England

J. J. Roy c Latham b Henry	17	A. U. Rashid run out (Santner/Boult)	0
J. M. Bairstow b Ferguson	36	M. A. Wood run out (Neesham/Boult)	0
J. E. Root c Latham b de Grandhomme	7		
*E. J. G. Morgan c Ferguson b Neesham	9	B 2, lb 3, w 12	17
B. A. Stokes not out	84		
†J. C. Buttler c sub (T. G. Southee) b Ferguson	59	1/28 (1) 2/59 (3) 3/71 (2)	(50 overs) 241
C. R. Woakes c Latham b Ferguson	2	4/86 (4) 5/196 (6) 6/203 (7)	
L. E. Plunkett c Boult b Neesham	10	7/220 (8) 8/227 (9) 9/240 (10)	
J. C. Archer b Neesham	0	10/241 (11)	10 overs: 39-1

Boult 10–0–67–0; Henry 10–2–40–1; de Grandhomme 10–2–25–1; Ferguson 10–0–50–3; Neesham 7–0–43–3; Santner 3–0–11–0.

Umpires: H. D. P. K. Dharmasena and M. Erasmus. Third umpire: R. J. Tucker. Referee: R. S. Madugalle.

English
International
Cricket

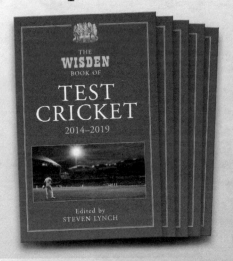

THE ENGLAND TEAM IN 2019

Moore, Johnson… and Morgan

TIM WIGMORE

At Wembley in 1966, it was a goal that even now provokes argument. At Sydney in 2003, it was a drop goal with 26 seconds to go in extra time. So perhaps it was inevitable that, when the England men's cricketers finally joined the footballers and rugby players in winning a World Cup, they would do so in wildly oscillating, electrifying fashion. Inside an hour on the evening of July 14 came a series of moments that were, each in their own right, extraordinary: Trent Boult stepping on the rope after catching Ben Stokes; Martin Guptill's throw deflecting off Stokes's bat for an incorrectly awarded six; the first World Cup final tie; then another in the super over. Taken together, they amounted to a denouement that, for sheer ludicrousness, surpassed both 1966 and 2003.

It was 7.30 at an enraptured, sun-kissed Lord's, when Jos Buttler collected a throw from Jason Roy and, in one smooth motion, broke the stumps.

ENGLAND IN 2019

Tests	Played	Won	Lost	Drawn/No result
Tests	12	4	6	2
One-day internationals	22	14	5	3
Twenty20 internationals	9	6	2	1

JANUARY		
FEBRUARY	3 Tests, 5 ODIs and 3 T20Is (a) v West Indies	(page 337)
MARCH		
APRIL		
MAY	1 ODI (a) v Ireland	(page 364)
	5 ODIs and 1 T20I (h) v Pakistan	(page 366)
JUNE	World Cup	(page 237)
JULY	1 Test (h) v Ireland	(page 374)
AUGUST	5 Tests (h) v Australia	(page 381)
SEPTEMBER		
OCTOBER		
NOVEMBER	2 Tests and 5 T20Is (a) v New Zealand	(page 420)
DECEMBER		
JANUARY	4 Tests, 3 ODIs and 3 T20Is (a) v South Africa	(page 440)
FEBRUARY		

England's World Cup… in the hands of Irishman Eoin Morgan and Australian Trevor Bayliss.

So England won one of the most stupendous matches of all time, even if it seemed unfair that New Zealand – who over the day had scored the same number of runs, while losing fewer wickets – had lost.

In England, though, it felt as if a new generation of fans had been won, too. Following frantic negotiations between the ECB, ICC, Sky Sports and Channel 4, the final was the first England international broadcast live on free-to-air television since the last Test of the 2005 Ashes, and was enjoyed by a peak audience of 8.3m. The odds of such a conclusion to the match were infinitesimal. It was an opportunity for cricket to capture the nation anew.

The road to Lord's had begun four years earlier, at the start of Andrew Strauss's stint as director of cricket. Riled by their status as perpetual ODI jokes, Strauss decided white-ball cricket would no longer be regarded as an inconvenience. Instead, for the first time in England's history, it became a priority. This spirit ran through all the crucial decisions of the Strauss years: appointing Trevor Bayliss as coach; creating white-ball central contracts; and encouraging England players to go to the IPL.

Before the super over, Jofra Archer had declared: "I presume I'm bowling it." It was an indication of how quickly he had become attack leader. He just about came through the trial, ending a tournament in which his 20 wickets snared through a combination of venomous new-ball bowling and late-innings variations honed in the IPL, marked him out as one of the most thrilling sights in the world game. It was remarkable to think Archer had made his international debut less than a month before the World Cup; even more that some considered his selection controversial. To captain Eoin Morgan and national selector Ed Smith, his talents brooked no argument.

Archer was the first English player given a debut, in large part, because of his IPL performances; he had more Big Bash and IPL appearances than all but three of the other 21 in the World Cup final. Indeed, the super over distilled English cricket's debt to the franchise tournament: Buttler, Stokes and Archer are three of England's most successful IPL exports.

Had they lost at Lord's, England would have missed their moment, but still rejuvenated their image. As much as the glory itself, Morgan's crowning achievement was to invert the standing of a team renowned for staid and timid play, and to turn them into cavaliers. Their victory was all the more commendable for coming on pitches of a different character from those that had helped them to a mountain of runs in the previous four years: tackier, and harder to score on, they forced batsmen to adapt, and led to the ditching of Moeen Ali as second spinner. The recall of Liam Plunkett, and his mid-innings bite – England won all seven of the World Cup games he played – was crucial. But, as the next T20 World Cup, in Australia in October 2020, loomed into view, Plunkett was ruthlessly discarded. That spoke of England's enviable depth in the white-ball forms, illustrated by a 3–2 victory with a shadow side in a T20 series in New Zealand in November – sealed, naturally, by a super over.

If vindication of English cricket's rebooting arrived that evening at Lord's, payback came 56 days later, when Josh Hazlewood trapped Craig Overton in the Fourth Ashes Test at Old Trafford. The urn was staying put. England had been impeded by the single-minded brilliance of Steve Smith, the doughtiness of his mini-me Marnus Labuschagne, and the remorseless Australian attack. Yet England had also been impeded by their own administrators.

Set against the World Cup, their Ashes seemed like collateral damage. Australia had been preparing for it for three years, ever since swapping the Kookaburra ball with the Dukes in the last half of the Sheffield Shield season. England had been preparing for barely three weeks, so short was the gap between the World Cup final and the First Test at Edgbaston. The way Australia's quick bowlers were managed – Hazlewood sat out the World Cup to ensure peak fitness for the Ashes – summed up their planning, and perhaps their priorities. Maybe neither country was wrong: England had never won the World Cup, while Australia had won three since last leaving England with the urn.

In the circumstances – and with James Anderson missing all bar four overs through injury – a 2–2 draw was a respectable effort, especially given how Australia later crushed allcomers back home. The result owed much to Stokes's Headingley heist, a performance arguably even more improbable than the World Cup final. It wasn't quite enough to win the series, but it did remove a source of existential angst for the English game: 2019 ended with Stokes named BBC Sports Personality of the Year, the first cricketer to win the award since Andrew Flintoff in 2005. Stokes, along with Bayliss, also received an OBE. There were CBEs for Morgan – which didn't please everyone in Ireland – and board chairman Colin Graves, and MBEs for Buttler and Joe Root.

Such acclaim could not conceal the fact that, for those who continued to judge English cricket by their Test team, it was a wretched year. The seeds

The storm before the balm: the Leeds scoreboard spells out the gory details of England's first innings.

were sown in the Caribbean in January. Rather arrogantly, given England's record of one series win there since 1967-68, many had expected a cruise. Instead, the batting was eviscerated, bundled out in the first two Tests for 77, 246, 187 and 132 by West Indies' unrelenting pace; victory in St Lucia, inspired by the speed of Mark Wood, was no more than a consolation. The series was the latest reincarnation of the England batting collapse, one species assuredly safe from the effects of climate change.

A new nadir took place at Lord's only ten days after the World Cup final, when England were skittled for 85 by Ireland. Had the Irish gone into the game with more practice – their home season had been decimated by rain – England might not have been able to recover as they did. And it was thanks only to Stokes's unbeaten 135 at Leeds that the first-innings humiliation of 67 all out could be swept under the carpet.

After a run of eight victories in nine Tests in 2018, this was a year of stagnation. As 2019 ended with a series defeat in New Zealand, then an emphatic loss at Centurion to a previously crisis-stricken South Africa, England's prospects of reaching the inaugural World Test Championship final, in June 2021, already looked remote – though they pulled things round emphatically to take the series 3–1. Whether this spoke of England recovery of South African decline was a moot point.

Yet while their struggles to take 20 wickets abroad at an acceptable cost had – until South Africa – loomed as large as ever. England's batting was little better. The decade had begun with a top seven who all averaged at least 40. Across England's 12 Tests in 2019, only Stokes did so. Buttler averaged 25, Roy – a disaster as a Test opener after his scintillating World Cup – and Jonny Bairstow both 18, and Ali just ten. It was galling that one of the few batting successes, Rory Burns, who passed 50 seven times, had his winter cut short by an ankle injury sustained during one of the team's games of football. And it said much about a lowering of standards that Joe Denly's haul of 651 Test runs at 31 – with no hundred in 21 innings – was felt to have provided the top order with stability. But Dom Sibley, after struggling in his maiden Test series, in New Zealand, and at Centurion, gave hope for the future with a superb unbeaten 133 to set up the Newlands triumph. And, in the next game, Ollie Pope underlined his potential with an unbeaten 135.

All the while, Root continued to slip away from the other members of the big four – Smith, Kohli and Williamson. He was beginning to look like Andy Murray in the company of Federer, Nadal and Djokovic. And as his batting faded – he had averaged 50 in 2017, his first calendar year as captain, 41 in his second, and now 37 – so the grumbling about his leadership grew. There were valid criticisms: the overuse and misuse of Archer, who averaged nearly 40 overs a Test before an elbow injury ruled him out of the last three in South Africa; the distrust of spin, and lack of faith in Ali; the apparent absence of tactical flair; and, of course, Root's own shortage of runs. But critics had to reckon both with how he had been encumbered by the system, and the lack of plausible alternatives. England know all about the folly of entrusting the armband to their talismanic all-rounders.

Under Bayliss, they had lost 24 one-day internationals and 25 Tests, offset by victory in 63 ODIs and 27 Tests. Indeed, had England lost at The Oval, where Australia looked distracted after retaining the urn, and chose to bowl, Bayliss's Test record would have been 26–26, reinforcing the sense that the team had made no progress at all. The appointment of Chris Silverwood partly reflected the desire of Ashley Giles, the new director of men's cricket, to have an English supremo. But it was also born of a belief that Silverwood would rebalance priorities in favour of the red-ball game.

Yet the fundamental barriers to Test consistency went far beyond the identity of the coach: a lack of reliable top-order batsmen emerging from county cricket; a paucity of spin at domestic level; and the bowlers' ineffectiveness with the Kookaburra. These were not new problems, yet they felt more severe than ever.

Modernisers and traditionalists could at least agree on one truth: never had England's white-ball side been so far ahead of their red-ball peers. Whether the gap widens with the launch of The Hundred, and its stretching of the domestic schedule to absurdity, remained to be seen.

But, for fans weaned on failure, none of this uncertainty could dim the afterglow of Morgan, the Irishman from Rush CC, becoming the third England captain in a major men's team sport, after Bobby Moore and Martin Johnson, to lift a World Cup. He lost nothing by comparison, such was his cocktail of tactical savvy, clear-sightedness and the calm, unemotional way in which he led his players. As Morgan lifted the World Cup trophy, his team had provided all England fans with a sight to be treasured until the end of their days.

English cricket's hope was that this image – of renewed success on the pitch, and a freshly captivated nation off it – was a harbinger of what was to come. It was, if nothing else, a nice idea.

ENGLAND PLAYERS IN 2019

LAWRENCE BOOTH

The following 38 players (there were 35 in 2018, and 33 in 2017) appeared in 2019, when England played 12 Tests, 22 one-day internationals and nine Twenty20 internationals. Statistics refer to the calendar year, not the 2019 season.

MOEEN ALI   Worcestershire

So exhausted was Ali after five years of batting and bowling in all three formats that, in September, prompted by the loss of his Test central contract, he took an indefinite break from red-ball cricket. It was a brave decision, but sad too – and he later admitted he often felt a scapegoat. He had become peripheral at the World Cup, not playing in England's last four matches, and was then dropped from the Test side after the Ashes opener. His batting had disintegrated: a Test haul of 90 runs in nine innings included 60 in Antigua, seven single-figure dismissals and four ducks (with two more in ODIs). The decline in his bowling was less steep, but still alarming. In the 12 months before the Ireland Test, he had been the world's leading wicket-taker. Now, encumbered by a sore spinning finger, he signed off with three for 172 against Australia on a turning pitch at Edgbaston.

   5 Tests: 90 runs @ 10.00; 18 wickets @ 28.88.
   14 ODIs: 145 runs @ 18.12, SR 97.97; 6 wickets @ 98.00, ER 6.39.

JAMES ANDERSON   Lancashire

His year was defined as much by what he didn't do as what he did, after injury limited his Ashes to four overs. The mishap occurred two days after his 37th birthday, prompting fresh speculation that the end was nigh. But Anderson spoke of his desire to make the return trip to Australia in 2021-22, and recovered in time for South Africa. At Centurion, he struck with his first ball back (a leg-side looser), then helped square the series at Cape Town with an England record 28th Test five-for, before his body let him down again. Figures of 30–13–46–5 at Bridgetown in January 2019 felt a distant memory.

   5 Tests: 12 runs @ 3.00; 12 wickets @ 30.16.

JOFRA ARCHER   Sussex

Two balls at Lord's, a few weeks apart, encapsulated Archer's first summer on the big stage. The first, a yorker near leg stump, limited Martin Guptill to a single from the last ball of the World Cup final super over, when New Zealand needed two. The second, a searing bouncer, knocked Steve Smith to the turf during the Ashes. In all, five World Cup three-fors and two Ashes six-fors added up to England's most exciting fast-bowling talent in a generation, and exposed the early-season debate over whether to leapfrog him into the World Cup squad as the nonsense it was. New Zealand's less pliant pitches quietened the hype, and Root occasionally seemed unsure how to manage him (Archer's batting, too, was a letdown). There was an expensive five-for at Centurion, before injury intervened. But he had time on his side – and, when he found his rhythm, pace to die for.

    7 Tests: 97 runs @ 8.08; 30 wickets @ 27.40.
    14 ODIs: 13 runs @ 3.25, SR 59.09; 23 wickets @ 24.73, ER 4.63.
    1 T20I: did not bat; 2 wickets @ 14.50, ER 7.25.

JONNY BAIRSTOW   Yorkshire

It was strange to witness the discrepancy between the buccaneering white-ball opener who struck hundreds in the crucial World Cup games against India and New Zealand, and the uncertain Test batsman who pogoed around the order in search of meaning. Experts discerned too much white-ball technique in his red-ball dismissals, and a Test average of 18 – including a pair against Ireland – hardly disproved them. Just as painful for Bairstow was his omission from the Test squad in New Zealand. When illness to Pope ahead of the Boxing Day Test in South Africa allowed him a way back, it was as a specialist batsman; he failed twice, and was left out again. If he felt messed around, he was also increasingly short of sympathy.

    10 Tests: 334 runs @ 18.55; 24 catches as wicketkeeper, 4 stumpings.
    20 ODIs: 844 runs @ 46.88, SR 102.92; 4 catches as wicketkeeper.
    7 T20Is: 207 runs @ 29.57, SR 153.33; 5 catches as wicketkeeper.

SAM BILLINGS   Kent

A typically inventive 87 off 47 balls in a T20 at Basseterre in March augured well, but Billings's World Cup hopes were dashed by a dislocated shoulder. Later, England tossed him a juicy bone: the vice-captaincy for the 20-over series in New Zealand. A total of 34 runs off 34 balls did not repay the faith.

    8 T20Is: 139 runs @ 34.75, SR 143.29; 2 catches as wicketkeeper.

STUART BROAD   Nottinghamshire

Broad's merciless Ashes dissection of David Warner formed the centrepiece of an excellent year, in which his willingness to pitch the ball up, and go round the wicket, silenced those who thought him over the hill. Controversially omitted from England's first Test of 2019, at Bridgetown, he set about reminding sceptics of his class. There were six hauls of four or more, and an overall set of figures to compare with any in his 12-year career (though the less said about his batting, the better). But he derived the greatest pleasure from his one-sided duels with Warner, whom he removed seven times at a personal cost of 35 runs. By the end of the South Africa series, Broad had 485 Test wickets, seventh in the all-time list, with Courtney Walsh's 519 creeping into view.

    11 Tests: 94 runs @ 7.83; 43 wickets @ 25.11.

RORY BURNS   Surrey

Of the 17 bona fide openers tried by England since the retirement of Andrew Strauss, Burns looked the most convincing. An Ashes century at Edgbaston was a test of character – there were plays and misses aplenty – and so was the Australians' liberal use of the short ball. Ill at ease at first, Burns found a remedy, averaging almost 40 in a series where no other opener could buy a run, then scoring his second Test hundred, at Hamilton. In 2019, only Marnus

Labuschagne faced more balls in Test cricket than Burns's 1,882. Amid a prolonged drought for English openers, it felt like a deluge, though he couldn't shake a tendency to give it away when set. It was cruel when an ankle injury sustained while playing football ended his tour of South Africa after only one Test.

12 Tests: 824 runs @ 35.82.

JOS BUTTLER   Lancashire

Buttler's greatest deed came on the biggest stage: 59 off 60 balls on a stodgy Lord's pitch to keep England in the hunt in the World Cup final. Soon, he was whipping off the bails to run out Guptill, and secure the trophy. It all made up for a quiet tournament in which he rarely repeated the fireworks that had brought him 150 off 77 in Grenada in February. His Test batting proceeded in fits and starts: a pair of half-centuries in St Lucia, then a strong finish to the Ashes. During the first three Tests against Australia, though, he looked drained following the World Cup, leading to renewed questions about his red-ball future. They were partly answered when the selectors handed him the gloves in New Zealand and South Africa, but few believed it a permanent solution, especially when nine innings produced an average of 17.

10 Tests: 502 runs @ 25.10; 6 catches as wicketkeeper.
20 ODIs: 667 runs @ 47.64, SR 135.56; 18 catches as wicketkeeper, 6 stumpings.

SAM CURRAN   Surrey

His Test batting had less impact than in 2018, but his bowling – after he was miscast with the new ball at Bridgetown – went up a notch. Ignored in the Ashes until The Oval, he responded with three for 46 (and had Steve Smith dropped), then elbowed aside Woakes at Mount Maunganui (where he winkled out Kane Williamson). A first-innings four-for at Centurion confirmed his rise. By opening the bowling with success during the Twenty20s in New Zealand, he had already added another string to his bow. It was no longer fair to patronise him as a player who "makes things happen".

7 Tests: 206 runs @ 20.60; 18 wickets @ 33.55.
5 T20Is: 35 runs @ 11.66, SR 152.17; 6 wickets @ 25.50, ER 8.50.

TOM CURRAN   Surrey

His all-round chutzpah and seam-bowling variations earned him a place (though not a game) at the World Cup, then the new ball – with brother Sam – during the New Zealand T20s. Everything he did, starting with an unbeaten 47 to help beat Ireland at Malahide, had the edge a captain loves.

6 ODIs: 107 runs @ 35.66, SR 102.88; 9 wickets @ 32.22, ER 6.54.
8 T20Is: 28 runs @ 28.00, SR 133.33; 9 wickets @ 20.33, ER 7.95.

JOE DENLY   Kent

Until the second innings of the Third Ashes Test at Leeds, it was hard to argue with the naysayers who regarded Denly as the pet project of national selector Ed Smith. Already ousted from the World Cup squad by Liam Dawson, he had passed 30 once in 11 Test innings. But 50 in almost four hours against the Australians hinted at something more substantial (and paved the way for

Stokes). It was the first of five half-centuries in eight innings, despite his being moved around a fluid top order. He was soon looking like the closest thing England had to solidity, only to spoil the effect slightly by managing a lone fifty in South Africa.

11 Tests: 651 runs @ 31.00; no wicket for 148 runs.

4 ODIs: 25 runs @ 12.50, SR 65.78; 1 wicket @ 60.00, ER 5.45.

4 T20Is: 52 runs @ 26.00, SR 110.63; 2 wickets @ 28.50, ER 9.50.

BEN FOAKES   Surrey

Some regarded Foakes as a cause célèbre, unjustly ditched as England's wicketkeeper in the Caribbean to accommodate the whims of Bairstow. And while he endured a middling summer with Surrey, he was good enough to exploit his one chance at international level – an unbeaten 61 to avert trouble at Malahide. After his heroics at Galle in November 2018, that made him the first England player to win the match awards in both his first Test and ODI. It was hard to imagine he wouldn't get another opportunity.

2 Tests: 55 runs @ 13.75; 2 catches as wicketkeeper.

1 ODI: 61 runs without dismissal, SR 80.26; 2 catches as wicketkeeper, 1 stumping.

1 T20I: did not bat; 1 catch as wicketkeeper.

ALEX HALES   Nottinghamshire

Hales hit the buffers in April, when it emerged he was serving a 21-day ban after twice testing positive for recreational drugs. Soon after, England cut him adrift: his chance to be first batting reserve at the World Cup, a role four years in the making, was gone. What international cricket he did play had already been squeezed into a fortnight in the Caribbean, where he made 82 off 73 balls in a one-dayer in Grenada, before tailing off.

3 ODIs: 105 runs @ 52.50, SR 97.22.

3 T20Is: 39 runs @ 13.00, SR 156.00.

CHRIS JORDAN   Sussex

It was tempting to suggest that Jordan's biggest contribution was the support he offered Archer, his fellow Sussex Bajan. But that would overlook his importance to the 20-over team. In March, he took four for six in St Kitts, England's best Twenty20 figures; in November, he dragged the series decider at Auckland into a super over by hitting 12 from three balls, then clinched victory by bowling the over himself. His 14 wickets in the format were five clear of England's next best, Tom Curran.

8 T20Is: 48 runs @ 48.00, SR 218.18; 14 wickets @ 12.85, ER 7.55.

JACK LEACH   Somerset

Picked for his tidy left-arm spin, Leach instead made cult-hero headlines with the bat. After chiselling out 92 as a nightwatchman-opener to turn the Lord's Test against Ireland, he helped Stokes put on 76 for the last wicket (Leach: one not out) to pull off the miracle at Headingley. Another fighting innings almost saved the next Test, at Old Trafford, where he looked more organised than some of his top-order colleagues. It was a shame his bowling lacked bite, especially on pitches that demanded more than consistency, and he was dropped after the First Test in New Zealand in a winter dogged by poor health.

6 Tests: 165 runs @ 27.50; 14 wickets @ 34.92.

DAWID MALAN   Middlesex/Yorkshire

Malan's best moment – a punishing century in 48 deliveries at the Napier T20 – was immediately followed by a slap-down from Morgan, who questioned why he hadn't attempted a last-ball bye. If that sounded harsh, it also said something about Malan's dressing-room standing – despite a T20 record that now boasted six scores of 50 more in his first nine innings.

1 ODI: 24 runs @ 24.00, SR 80.00.
4 T20Is: 208 runs @ 69.33, SR 163.77.

EOIN MORGAN   Middlesex

It was the year Morgan joined Bobby Moore and Martin Johnson as an England World Cup-winning captain (with apologies to Paul Collingwood, who in 2010 lifted the less prestigious World T20). He was no figurehead, either, personifying his team's aggression: his one-day strike-rate of 112 was his best in a calendar year, his average of 52 and aggregate of 791 each his second-best. Morgan hit 60 white-ball sixes – more than anyone in the world – including an international-record 17 against Afghanistan. As a captain, he kept growing in stature, calmly leading his crew through the choppy waters of World Cup defeats by Sri Lanka and Australia, and to the winner's podium. No one would have begrudged him early retirement, but the 20-over series in New Zealand reminded him he still loved the job – and the T20 World Cup in Australia looked a beguiling opportunity to do the double.

21 ODIs: 791 runs @ 52.73, SR 112.19.
9 T20Is: 268 runs @ 44.66, SR 172.90.

LIAM PLUNKETT   Surrey

He began the World Cup amid whispers that he had lost his cutting edge, and rounded it off with the wicket of Kane Williamson. Despite Plunkett's slow start to the summer, Morgan's faith in his ability to control the middle overs was a handy insurance policy. As the tournament progressed, his back-of-a-length cross-seamers proved as valuable as ever – his dismissal of Virat Kohli set up victory over India at Edgbaston – so it seemed ruthless when he lost his limited-overs contract only two months after it finished. At 34, he still had international ambitions, and was exploring qualification for the USA (his wife, Emeleah, is from Pennsylvania).

15 ODIs: 64 runs @ 32.00, SR 145.45; 20 wickets @ 29.30, ER 5.52.
2 T20Is: did not bat; 2 wickets @ 26.00, ER 7.60.

ADIL RASHID   Yorkshire

Even while nursing a sore shoulder through the World Cup with steroid injections, Rashid was central to England's prospects, drawing on his experience in the semi-final against Australia to remove Alex Carey and Marcus Stoinis in the same over. If he lacked some of the incision of 2018, it was in part because the injury made his googly harder to bowl: more than usual, batsmen knew what was coming. After a wicketless Test at Bridgetown, his red-ball international career was put on hold.

1 Test: 13 runs @ 6.50; no wicket for 117 runs.
21 ODIs: 74 runs @ 12.33, SR 101.36; 24 wickets @ 38.62, ER 6.10.
7 T20Is: 4 runs @ 4.00, SR 66.66; 8 wickets @ 22.75, ER 7.58.

JOE ROOT   Yorkshire

Not even an abstemious double-hundred at Hamilton in December could disguise the fact that Root was spurning the chance to go down as a Test great. Before that innings, his average had been 27 for the year and, for the first time as captain, had dropped below 40. Once, the problem had been turning fifties into hundreds; now it was reaching 30, which he managed only eight times in 23 innings. Too many fiddles outside off stump, and three Ashes ducks (including two first-ballers), suggested the cares of office were getting to him, before a young team responded superbly in South Africa. Some of his bowling changes, meanwhile, were puzzling. As a one-day player – without leadership to worry about – he remained crucial, especially during the first half of the World Cup. But his desire to crack the 20-over game felt like one spinning plate too many.

12 Tests: 851 runs @ 37.00; 4 wickets @ 74.75.
22 ODIs: 910 runs @ 50.55, SR 92.85; 2 wickets @ 32.50, ER 5.41.
4 T20Is: 106 runs @ 35.33, SR 111.57.

JASON ROY   Surrey

Famine followed feast. Roy's one-day form was electric, full of fast hands and big scores – and England's World Cup prospects suffered when injury forced him to miss two games. His return was as if someone had switched on the lights: 66 off 57 against India, 60 off 61 against New Zealand, and 85 off 65 in the semi-final against Australia, when only an umpiring blunder spoiled the fun. And, from the tournament's last ball, his throw from the deep brought the trophy. Hopes of turning him into a David Warner-style Test batsman began well, with 72 on a treacherous Lord's surface against Ireland, but against Australia he averaged just 13, even after moving down the order. He wasn't the only opener to struggle during the Ashes (ask Warner), but his tendency to lunge at the red ball suggested a curious inability to adapt from the white.

5 Tests: 187 runs @ 18.70.
14 ODIs: 845 runs @ 70.41, SR 118.18.

DOMINIC SIBLEY   Warwickshire

His domestic form was irresistible. By facing over 1,000 balls more than anyone else in Division One of the County Championship, Sibley forced his way into a Test team crying out for top-order resolve. And in three of his first five innings, in New Zealand and South Africa, he lasted at least an hour and a half. That was enough time for the pundits to query a leg-side technique, and a frailty against spin, but his riposte spoke volumes: an unbeaten 133 to underpin England's victory at Cape Town, and 324 runs in the series, more than any of his team-mates.

3 Tests: 71 runs @ 14.20.

BEN STOKES   **Durham**

Less than ten months after his trip to court, Stokes embarked on the summer of his life. He began with a twisting boundary catch at The Oval to kickstart the World Cup, and barely paused for breath. While team-mates wilted, Stokes bloomed, hitting eighties in the defeats by Sri Lanka and Australia (the lowest of his seven ODI half-centuries in 2019 was 71 not out). Then, with 15 needed off four balls in the final, he earned a tie with a mix of brawn, brain and luck. Needless to say, he was soon out in the middle again, batting in the super over. Yet his work was only half done. As if an unbeaten Ashes hundred at Lord's was not enough, a week later he produced arguably the greatest Test innings of all time to turn certain defeat into fabled victory at Leeds (where he bowled an almost-uninterrupted spell of 24.2 overs). All the while, he was nursing one injury or another: nothing, it seemed, could break him. He became the first cricketer since Andrew Flintoff in 2005 to win the BBC Sports Personality of the Year award, pocketed an OBE, then took the Newlands Test in January 2020 – and, it turned out, the whole South Africa series – by its scruff.

    11 Tests: 821 runs @ 45.61; 22 wickets @ 35.45.
    20 ODIs: 719 runs @ 59.91, SR 92.53; 12 wickets @ 44.50, ER 5.69.

JAMES VINCE   **Hampshire**

A dozen white-ball games produced six scores of 20 or more, but only one half-century – and familiar murmurs about unfulfilled talent. The sense of anticlimax was most acute during the World Cup when, in three innings as a replacement for the injured Roy, he totalled 40, including a second-ball duck against Australia. Though popular among influential team-mates, he was running out of chances.

    7 ODIs: 134 runs @ 22.33, SR 89.93.
    5 T20Is: 146 runs @ 29.20, SR 132.72.

DAVID WILLEY   **Yorkshire**

Willey reacted sportingly to the slight, but his year ended when he was squeezed out of the World Cup 15 by Archer. Figures of one for 86 at Headingley during the ODI series against Pakistan didn't help; nor did a general absence of swing with the white Kookaburra. T20 figures of four for seven at Basseterre in March faded into the footnotes.

    4 ODIs: 34 runs @ 17.00, SR 69.38; 4 wickets @ 56.00, ER 6.40.
    4 T20Is: 14 runs without dismissal, SR 116.66; 6 wickets @ 11.66, ER 6.36.

CHRIS WOAKES   **Warwickshire**

Woakes's most impressive achievement while managing a knee niggle was to play a central role at the business end of the World Cup. As India chased a big score at Edgbaston, he began with three maidens, then picked up thrifty three-fors in the semi-final and final. His overall ODI haul of 29 was England's best. In Tests, he was underbowled during the Ashes, but rarely less than probing – even with the Kookaburra on a flat one at Hamilton – and against Ireland picked up England's joint-cheapest six-for since Derek Underwood in 1970-71.

His batting was unusually ineffective, especially against the short ball, but there was no doubting his popularity.

6 Tests: 133 runs @ 14.77; 20 wickets @ 23.85.
19 ODIs: 147 runs @ 14.70, SR 85.96; 29 wickets @ 29.79, ER 5.95.

MARK WOOD   Durham

If England had an unsung World Cup hero, it was Wood. Only once, during the high-scoring defeat of India, did he fail to contribute with the ball, while his tournament tally of 18 was – among team-mates – second only to Archer. In the final group game, against New Zealand, he was outstanding. Above all, Wood was being spoken of once more as a bowler of genuine pace, following a lightning spell to demolish West Indies in the St Lucia Test in February. With Archer, he lent England's attack a two-edged menace they had not enjoyed for years. As ever, injury intervened – a side strain this time, picked up during the World Cup final. But the vulnerability was easily forgiven, especially when two Tests in South Africa in January 2020 produced 12 wickets at 13, and some meaty blows with the bat.

1 Test: 6 runs @ 6.00; 6 wickets @ 15.50.
16 ODIs: 12 runs @ 6.00, SR 80.00; 27 wickets @ 27.25, ER 5.54.
1 T20I: did not bat; 3 wickets @ 3.00, ER 3.00.

AND THE REST...

Keaton Jennings (Lancashire; 2 Tests) was dropped, then recalled in the Caribbean, but kept squirting drives into the cordon. **Ollie Pope** (Surrey; 2 Tests) followed two horrible dismissals at Mount Maunganui with a studious 75 at Hamilton, where he was burdened with the gloves. But in South Africa, he sparkled, scoring his first Test century, at Port Elizabeth, and averaging 88. **Olly Stone** (Warwickshire; 1 Test) bowled with pace and hostility on Test debut against Ireland, before his season was ended by a back injury. **Zak Crawley** (Kent; 1 Test) struggled in his first Test, at Hamilton, having earned a last-minute debut because of injury to Buttler. Burns's injury in Cape Town gave him another chance, and he formed a useful alliance with Sibley. **Craig Overton** (Somerset; 1 Test) almost saved the Old Trafford Test with the bat, but – like his fellow seamers – struggled in blustery conditions. **Lewis Gregory** (Somerset; 5 T20Is) was given the full 20-over series in New Zealand, but made little impression, beyond taking a wicket with his first ball. In the same series, **Pat Brown** (Worcestershire; 4 T20Is) couldn't quite reproduce his county form, though he enjoyed little luck with dropped catches. Fellow first-time tourist **Tom Banton** (Somerset; 3 T20Is) flickered attractively, earning not entirely fanciful comparisons with Kevin Pietersen. England had high hopes for **Saqib Mahmood** (Lancashire; 3 T20Is), but he went for 11.50 an over in New Zealand, and didn't rattle the speed gun as expected. **Matt Parkinson** (Lancashire; 2 T20Is) was steady under fire at Napier, floating up his leg-breaks to take four wickets. **Ben Duckett** (Nottinghamshire; 1 T20I) made only nine in the T20 game against Pakistan at Cardiff, his first international for two and a half years.

ENGLAND TEST AVERAGES
IN CALENDAR YEAR 2019

BATTING AND FIELDING

		T	I	NO	R	HS	100	50	Avge	SR	Ct/St
1	†B. A. Stokes	11	21	3	821	135*	2	4	45.61	52.66	13
2	J. E. Root	12	23	0	851	226	2	4	37.00	46.32	25
3	O. J. D. Pope	2	3	0	110	75	0	1	36.66	39.00	3
4	†R. J. Burns	12	23	0	824	133	2	5	35.82	43.78	11
5	J. L. Denly	11	21	0	651	94	0	6	31.00	41.54	5
6	†M. J. Leach	6	11	5	165	92	0	1	27.50	40.74	3
7	J. C. Buttler	10	20	0	502	70	0	3	25.10	48.45	16
8	†S. M. Curran	7	13	3	206	37	0	0	20.60	76.86	2
9	J. J. Roy	5	10	0	187	72	0	1	18.70	58.80	1
10	J. M. Bairstow	10	19	1	334	52	0	2	18.55	50.45	27/4
11	†K. K. Jennings	2	4	0	62	23	0	0	15.50	23.84	2
12	C. R. Woakes	6	10	1	133	37*	0	0	14.77	48.71	1
13	D. P. Sibley	3	5	0	71	29	0	0	14.20	28.74	3
14	B. T. Foakes	2	4	0	55	35	0	0	13.75	44.00	2
15	C. Overton	1	2	0	26	21	0	0	13.00	21.66	0
16	†M. M. Ali	5	9	0	90	60	0	1	10.00	44.55	1
17	O. P. Stone	1	2	0	19	19	0	0	9.50	65.51	0
18	J. C. Archer	7	12	0	97	30	0	0	8.08	49.74	1
19	†S. C. J. Broad	11	19	7	94	29	0	0	7.83	44.54	3
20	A. U. Rashid	1	2	0	13	12	0	0	6.50	54.16	0
21	M. A. Wood	1	1	0	6	6	0	0	6.00	150.00	1
22	†J. M. Anderson	5	9	5	12	4*	0	0	3.00	18.46	4
23	Z. Crawley	1	1	0	1	1	0	0	1.00	16.66	0

BOWLING

		Style	O	M	R	W	BB	5I	Avge	SR
1	O. P. Stone	RF	12	3	29	3	3-29	0	9.66	24.00
2	M. A. Wood	RF	20.2	3	93	6	5-41	1	15.50	20.33
3	C. R. Woakes	RFM	154.4	31	477	20	6-17	1	23.85	46.40
4	S. C. J. Broad	RFM	367.4	89	1,080	43	5-86	1	25.11	51.30
5	J. C. Archer	RF	274	63	822	30	6-45	3	27.40	54.80
6	M. M. Ali	OB	139.2	18	520	18	4-36	0	28.88	46.44
7	J. M. Anderson	RFM	135.1	35	362	12	5-46	1	30.16	67.58
8	S. M. Curran	LFM	183.5	40	604	18	4-58	0	33.55	61.27
9	M. J. Leach	SLA	151.4	27	489	14	4-49	0	34.92	65.00
10	B. A. Stokes	RFM	242.3	42	780	22	4-59	0	35.45	66.13
11	C. Overton	RFM	33.5	4	107	2	2-85	0	53.50	101.50
12	J. E. Root	OB/LB	72	6	299	4	2-26	0	74.75	108.00
13	K. K. Jennings	RM	4.1	0	29	0	0-29	0	–	–
14	A. U. Rashid	LB	26	1	117	0	0-56	0	–	–
15	J. L. Denly	LB	40	6	148	0	0-0	0	–	–

ENGLAND ONE-DAY INTERNATIONAL AVERAGES
IN CALENDAR YEAR 2019

BATTING AND FIELDING

		M	I	NO	R	HS	100	50	Avge	SR	Ct/St
1	J. J. Roy	14	12	0	845	153	3	6	70.41	118.18	4
2	†B. A. Stokes	20	17	5	719	89	0	7	59.91	92.53	7
3	†E. J. G. Morgan	21	18	3	791	148	2	5	52.73	112.19	7
4	A. D. Hales	3	2	0	105	82	0	1	52.50	97.22	2
5	J. E. Root	22	20	2	910	107	3	4	50.55	92.85	18
6	J. C. Buttler	20	16	2	667	150	3	2	47.64	135.56	18/6
7	J. M. Bairstow	20	18	0	844	128	3	4	46.88	102.92	11
8	T. K. Curran	6	5	2	107	47*	0	0	35.66	102.88	0
9	L. E. Plunkett	15	6	4	64	27*	0	0	32.00	145.45	2
10	†D. J. Malan	1	1	0	24	24	0	0	24.00	80.00	0
11	J. M. Vince	7	6	0	134	43	0	0	22.33	89.93	0
12	†M. M. Ali	14	11	3	145	46*	0	0	18.12	97.97	6
13	†D. J. Willey	4	2	0	34	20	0	0	17.00	69.38	2
14	C. R. Woakes	19	12	2	147	40	0	0	14.70	85.96	10
15	J. L. Denly	4	2	0	25	17	0	0	12.50	65.78	2
16	A. U. Rashid	21	9	3	74	25	0	0	12.33	101.36	6
17	M. A. Wood	16	6	4	12	10*	0	0	6.00	80.00	2
18	J. C. Archer	14	7	3	13	7*	0	0	3.25	59.09	4
19	B. T. Foakes	1	1	1	61	61*	0	1	–	80.26	2/1

BOWLING

		Style	O	M	R	W	BB	4I	Avge	SR	ER
1	J. C. Archer	RF	122.5	10	569	23	3-27	0	24.73	32.04	4.63
2	M. A. Wood	RF	132.4	2	736	27	4-60	1	27.25	29.48	5.54
3	L. E. Plunkett	RFM	106	0	586	20	4-35	1	29.30	31.80	5.52
4	C. R. Woakes	RFM	145	8	864	29	5-54	2	29.79	30.00	5.95
5	T. K. Curran	RFM	44.2	1	290	9	4-75	1	32.22	29.55	6.54
6	J. E. Root	OB	12	0	65	2	2-27	0	32.50	36.00	5.41
7	A. U. Rashid	LB	151.5	0	927	24	5-85	1	38.62	37.95	6.10
8	B. A. Stokes	RFM	93.5	2	534	12	3-23	0	44.50	46.91	5.69
9	D. J. Willey	LFM	35	2	224	4	2-57	0	56.00	52.50	6.40
10	J. L. Denly	LB	11	0	60	1	1-24	0	60.00	66.00	5.45
11	M. M. Ali	OB	92	0	588	6	3-50	0	98.00	92.00	6.39

ENGLAND TWENTY20 INTERNATIONAL AVERAGES IN CALENDAR YEAR 2019

BATTING AND FIELDING

		M	I	NO	R	HS	50	Avge	SR	4	6	Ct
1	C. J. Jordan	8	2	1	48	36	0	48.00	**218.18**	4	4	7
2	†E. J. G. Morgan	9	9	3	268	91	2	44.66	**172.90**	22	19	3
3	T. Banton	3	3	0	56	31	0	18.66	**164.70**	6	3	4
4	†D. J. Malan	4	4	1	208	103*	2	69.33	**163.77**	21	9	1
5	A. D. Hales	3	3	0	39	20	0	13.00	**156.00**	4	3	1
6	J. M. Bairstow	7	7	0	207	68	1	29.57	**153.33**	23	10	7
7	†S. M. Curran	5	3	0	35	24	0	11.66	**152.17**	3	2	0
8	S. W. Billings	8	7	3	139	87	1	34.75	**143.29**	14	3	4
9	T. K. Curran	8	3	2	28	14*	0	28.00	**133.33**	0	2	2
10	J. M. Vince	5	5	0	146	59	1	29.20	**132.72**	14	4	5
11	†B. M. Duckett	1	1	0	9	9	0	9.00	**128.57**	1	0	0
12	†D. J. Willey	4	2	2	14	13*	0	–	**116.66**	0	1	3
13	J. E. Root	4	4	1	106	55	1	35.33	**111.57**	12	0	3
14	J. L. Denly	4	3	1	52	30	0	26.00	**110.63**	6	1	2
15	L. Gregory	5	3	0	21	15	0	7.00	**110.52**	0	2	0
16	S. Mahmood	3	2	1	7	4	0	7.00	**100.00**	1	0	1
17	A. U. Rashid	7	1	0	4	4	0	4.00	**66.66**	0	0	0
18	P. R. Brown	4	1	1	4	4*	0	–	**44.44**	0	0	2
19	J. C. Archer	1	0	0	0	0	0	–	–	0	0	0
20	B. T. Foakes	1	0	0	0	0	0	–	–	0	0	1
21	M. W. Parkinson	2	0	0	0	0	0	–	–	0	0	0
22	L. E. Plunkett	2	0	0	0	0	0	–	–	0	0	1
23	M. A. Wood	1	0	0	0	0	0	–	–	0	0	0

BOWLING

		Style	O	Dots	R	W	BB	4I	Avge	SR	ER
1	M. A. Wood	RF	3	12	9	3	3-9	0	3.00	6.00	**3.00**
2	D. J. Willey	LFM	11	35	70	6	4-7	1	11.66	11.00	**6.36**
3	J. C. Archer	RF	4	9	29	2	2-29	0	14.50	12.00	**7.25**
4	L. Gregory	RFM	4	9	29	1	1-10	0	29.00	24.00	**7.25**
5	C. J. Jordan	RFM	23.5	63	180	14	4-6	1	12.85	10.21	**7.55**
6	A. U. Rashid	LB	24	52	182	8	2-12	0	22.75	18.00	**7.58**
7	L. E. Plunkett	RFM	6.5	19	52	2	2-8	0	26.00	20.50	**7.60**
8	T. K. Curran	RFM	23	52	183	9	4-36	1	20.33	15.33	**7.95**
9	S. M. Curran	LFM	18	37	153	6	2-22	0	25.50	18.00	**8.50**
10	J. L. Denly	LB	6	10	57	2	1-14	0	28.50	18.00	**9.50**
11	P. R. Brown	RFM	13	20	128	3	1-29	0	42.66	26.00	**9.84**
12	M. W. Parkinson	LB	6	14	61	5	4-47	1	12.20	7.20	**10.16**
13	S. Mahmood	RFM	10	14	115	3	1-20	0	38.33	20.00	**11.50**

WEST INDIES v ENGLAND IN 2018-19

Review by George Dobell

Test matches (3): West Indies 2, England 1
One-day internationals (5): West Indies 2, England 2
Twenty20 internationals (3): West Indies 0, England 3

The pre-tour narrative was familiar. Caribbean cricket was in terminal decline, spectators were losing interest, the best players had other priorities. Memories of West Indies' glory days were not so much an inspiration to the modern generation as a yardstick against which they could only fail. The fire in Babylon had long since gone out. England would win with ease.

By the time they flew home, having surrendered the Wisden Trophy and won only one of the three series – the Twenty20s, against an understrength side – there were grounds for a tentative belief that cricket in the Caribbean was enjoying a resurgence. To see West Indies win a Test series on the basis of their pace bowling, to see the emergence of a new generation of strokemakers – among them Shimron Hetmyer, a gloriously uncomplicated talent with whom the world could fall in love – was to be reminded of another age. Any cricket lover, even the throngs of England supporters, could rejoice in that.

Perhaps we shouldn't have been surprised. England had won just one Test series in the West Indies in more than 50 years, under Michael Vaughan in 2003-04. And while Ashes tours have two or three first-class warm-up games, this had none. Still, that didn't stop bold predictions. Four years earlier, ECB

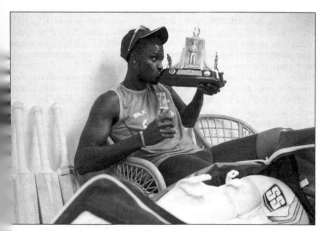

The new holder: West Indies captain Jason Holder relishes the return of the Wisden Trophy.

chairman-elect Colin Graves had denounced West Indies as "mediocre" – a comment pinned to their dressing-room door as a motivational tool, before England were held to a 1–1 draw. This time, fellow Yorkshireman Geoff Boycott wrote in his newspaper column that England should be "far too good" for a team of "very ordinary, average cricketers".

To some extent, the confidence was understandable. West Indies hadn't won a Test series against anyone other than Bangladesh or Zimbabwe since beating New Zealand at home in 2012, and had slipped to eighth in the rankings; only once in the 21st century (at home, in 2008-09) had they won against England. They also had an interim head coach, Richard Pybus, who had not proved especially popular during a three-year stint as West Indies' director of cricket that ended in 2016, and who appeared to have been appointed by Cricket West Indies president Dave Cameron despite the reservations of Jimmy Adams, Pybus's successor. (By early April, Cameron was out of a job, while Pybus had resumed running the academy.) England, meanwhile, had just completed a historic 3–0 whitewash in Sri Lanka, and were ranked third.

Neither was there anything in the pair of two-day (non-first-class) warm-up games to suggest a shock. England twice overwhelmed a Board President's XI: in the first, the hosts lost 19 wickets for 203 runs on the second day, with Stuart Broad, operating off a shorter run-up, claiming a hat-trick. The only cloud on England's horizon was the return home of Warwickshire fast bowler Olly Stone because of a stress fracture in his lower back. But the games lacked intensity, and were played on painfully slow surfaces. On the quicker tracks produced during the Test series, against more organised and motivated opponents, England were 2–0 down before they were able to adapt.

That was, in part, reward for some brave decisions by West Indies. The former coaching regime, led by Stuart Law, wanted to play the Tests with a Kookaburra ball, on slow, low pitches, to negate the skill of England's experienced seam attack. They also favoured venues such as Guyana, which might have proved a little less comfortable for England's players, and would have attracted fewer travelling supporters, lessening the sense that the tourists were playing at home. But all that was overruled by CWI chief executive Johnny Grave. He reasoned that West Indies would play more entertaining cricket on quicker surfaces and with a Dukes; an adaptation of the ball used in England, it retained its shape and shine. Grave hoped this might help coax back home supporters. The venues were largely decided by economics, with Caribbean governments bidding to host in the knowledge that England fans would come if the destinations were attractive. The three islands chosen for the Tests – Barbados, Antigua, St Lucia – really did represent something approaching paradise, and fans crossed the Atlantic in their thousands.

Most of all, there was the leadership of Jason Holder. An all-rounder good enough to win a place in the top ten of the ICC's bowling rankings, and score a series-defining double-century in the First Test in Barbados, his home island, he gave West Indies depth and balance, and was a wonderfully focused captain. It was no coincidence that, when he was suspended from the final Test because of a string of over-rate violations, they lost. Captaining this side through defeats and tribulations cannot have been easy, but he did it without complaint.

Philip Brown, Popperfoto/Getty Images

Hurry up: Ben Stokes's discomfort against the short ball was typical of England's unease.

– and with calm authority. Comparisons with Clive Lloyd were inevitable but, when Holder reacted to news of South African fast bowler Duanne Olivier's Kolpak registration with Yorkshire by calling on the ICC and players' unions to introduce a global minimum wage, you wondered if he might develop into a statesman of Frank Worrell's stature. A future in leadership outside cricket would be no surprise.

The excellence of West Indies' seamers was a major theme of the Tests. Blessed with pace, skill and stamina, they were devastating, preying on a line-up that lacked the discipline to resist. Kemar Roach demonstrated his improved fitness, and won the series award after claiming 18 wickets at 13; Shannon Gabriel's figures – nine at 31 – did not reflect the hostility he generated or the pressure he built. Holder and Alzarri Joseph provided relentless support. Their batsmen were impressive, too. John Campbell and Kraigg Brathwaite became the first West Indian openers to add 50 or more four times in a series since Phil Simmons and Desmond Haynes in England in 1991, protecting their colleagues from the ball at its hardest and the bowlers at their freshest.

England's opening pair progressed beyond 35 just once, and their batsmen failed to reach 250 until the Third Test, by which time it was too late. And if their first-innings 77 in Barbados stood out, their second-innings 246 was arguably even more lamentable. To lose eight wickets against Roston Chase's tidy but unthreatening off-spin, on a pitch offering him nothing, represented a collapse as soft as any in recent years; Chase didn't take another wicket in the series, though he made a classy rearguard hundred in a lost cause in St Lucia.

There was some mitigation for England's batting malaise. The bowlers benefited from helpful conditions, and the surface in Antigua – subsequently sanctioned by the ICC – was especially tough. Even so, totals of 187 and 132 did nothing to alter the suspicion that their batsmen lacked patience, and Joe

Root raised eyebrows by suggesting "you don't win games by batting long periods of time". Yet Bravo and Co had won the Antigua Test by doing exactly that. For England, by contrast, only Ben Stokes averaged over 30, and only Root – after 55 runs in his first five innings – scored a century. Before the tour was out, batting coach Mark Ramprakash was sacked.

The tourists had little idea about their best side. Keaton Jennings was dropped for Antigua, then recalled for St Lucia, while Jonny Bairstow was restored to No. 7, only three Tests after making a century as the new No. 3, in

---

FIVE STATS YOU MAY HAVE MISSED

BENEDICT BERMANGE

- In Barbados, Jason Holder made only the third Test double-century by a No. 8. The highest scores from No. 8 or lower are:

257*	Wasim Akram	Pakistan v Zimbabwe at Sheikhupura	1996-97
209	Imtiaz Ahmed	Pakistan v New Zealand at Lahore	1955-56
202*	**J. O. Holder**	**West Indies v England at Bridgetown**	**2018-19**
173	I. D. S. Smith	New Zealand v India at Auckland	1989-90
169	S. C. J. Broad	England v Pakistan at Lord's	2010

Smith and Broad went in at No. 9, the others at No. 8.

- The third day at Bridgetown, when West Indies moved from 127 for six to 415 for six, and England made 56 without loss, provided only the second instance of no wickets falling on a day on which both sides batted and more than 250 runs were scored. The other occasion was the fourth day at Calcutta in 1978-79, when India moved from 70 for one to 361 for one, and West Indies made 15 without loss. The day before at Bridgetown, 18 wickets had gone down, more than in any Test to include a wicketless full day.

- Roston Chase was only the fifth player to score a century and take eight wickets in an innings during the same Test series:

L. C. Braund (102 and 8-81)	England in Australia	1903-04
A. W. Greig (148, 121 and 8-86)	England in the West Indies	1973-74
I. T. Botham (100, 108 and 8-34)	England v Pakistan	1978
Imran Khan (117 and 8-60)	Pakistan v India	1982-83
R. L. Chase (102* and 8-60)	**West Indies v England**	**2018-19**

- Shimron Hetmyer failed to clear the boundary in his first innings at Gros Islet, bringing to an end a record-equalling sequence of seven successive Test innings with at least one six. The others to achieve the feat are Imran Khan (Pakistan) in 1988-89 and 1989-90 and Chris Cairns (New Zealand) in 1999-2000.

- There were 38 extras from wides in St Lucia, a Test record:

38	**West Indies (conceded 24) v England (14) at Gros Islet**	**2018-19**
34	West Indies (26) v Australia (8) at Bridgetown	2007-08
33	South Africa (18) v India (15) at Johannesburg	2017-18
31	South Africa (22) v India (9) at Johannesburg	2013-14
30	Pakistan (22) v India (8) at Faisalabad	1989-90
30	South Africa (18) v Australia (12) at Centurion	2013-14

This includes all runs accrued from wides; 18 deliveries were called wide at Gros Islet.

Benedict Bermange is the statistician for Sky Sports.

Downbeat: Jonny Bairstow, Moeen Ali, Joe Root and James Anderson after England's ten-wicket defeat at Antigua.

Colombo. That meant his wicketkeeping rival Ben Foakes, Player of the Series in Sri Lanka, had to be left out. Broad was omitted on a Barbados track that might have been made for him – England instead picked two spinners and three seamers – while Sam Curran's stock fell as his lack of pace was exposed. When Ashley Giles, the new director of the England men's teams, described the selection as "a bit funky", he didn't mean it as a compliment. And there was no sign that England were any closer to finding an opening pair – Rory Burns reached 30 once in six innings – or a permanent No. 3, despite Joe Denly's stylish 69 in St Lucia. Chris Woakes was not deemed fit for the Tests because of a long-standing knee problem.

The one-day series was dominated by the 39-year-old Chris Gayle. Having announced his intention to retire from the format after the World Cup, he hit 135, 50, 162 and 77, and batted as well as ever. He ate up many dot balls, could barely move between the wickets – 74% of his runs came from boundaries – and was a liability in the field, but his hitting was so devastating that he helped West Indies defy the gap in the rankings (first v ninth), and secure a 2–2 draw. His 39 sixes – a record in any series or tournament – came at a rate of one every eight deliveries.

England's batsmen enjoyed some good moments, too. Jos Buttler made a magnificent 150 in Grenada, while Eoin Morgan and Jason Roy also flourished, although Roy's tour was cut short by a hamstring strain and the impending birth of his first child. But when they were bowled out for 113 in the final game in St Lucia, England showed a familiar failure to adapt to anything other than perfect batting conditions. It was the struggle of the bowlers, however, that rang alarm bells ahead of the World Cup. The pitches were flat, and the boundaries short, but too often they simply had no answer to Gayle. Inevitably, the clamour grew for the inclusion of the Barbados-born Jofra Archer, who qualified for selection shortly after the tour.

England clawed back some ground in the Twenty20s, skittling West Indies for 45 and 71. But there was a sense that the serious business had already taken place. England rested key players, while West Indies picked their one-day squad, with a view to the World Cup. Those games did reinforce one impression. During the early days of the tour, England supporters outnumbered locals, yet the ratio changed as belief in the home side grew. With fast bowlers tearing in, fearless young batsmen making runs, and locals turning up to watch, it felt as if the embers of that fire in Babylon were starting to flame.

ENGLAND TOURING PARTY

*J. E. Root (Yorkshire; T/50/20), M. M. Ali (Worcestershire; T/50), J. M. Anderson (Lancashire; T), J. M. Bairstow (Yorkshire; T/50/20), S. W. Billings (Kent; 20), S. C. J. Broad (Nottinghamshire; T), R. J. Burns (Surrey; T), J. C. Buttler (Lancashire; T/50), S. M. Curran (Surrey; T/20), T. K. Curran (Surrey; 50/20), J. L. Denly (Kent; T/50/20), B. T. Foakes (Surrey; T), A. D. Hales (Nottinghamshire; 50/20), K. K. Jennings (Lancashire; T), C. J. Jordan (Sussex; 20), M. J. Leach (Somerset; T), D. J. Malan (Middlesex; 20), E. J. G. Morgan (Middlesex; 50/20), L. E. Plunkett (Surrey; 50/20), A. U. Rashid (Yorkshire; T/50/20), J. J. Roy (Surrey; 50), B. A. Stokes (Durham; T/50), O. P. Stone (Warwickshire; T), D. J. Willey (Yorkshire; 50/20), C. R. Woakes (Warwickshire; T/50), M. A. Wood (Durham; T/50/20).

Morgan captained in the white-ball matches. Stone was diagnosed with a stress fracture of the back after the first warm-up match and returned home; Wood was added to the Test squad. Ali was originally named in the T20 squad, but was then rested; S. M. Curran replaced him.

Coach: T. H. Bayliss (T/50/20). *Assistant coach:* P. Farbrace (T/50/20). *Batting coach:* M. R. Ramprakash (T), G. P. Thorpe (50/20). *Fast-bowling coach:* C. E. W. Silverwood (T/50/20). *Consultant coach:* P. D. Collingwood (T). *Wicketkeeping coach:* B. N. French (T). *Fielding coach:* C. D. Hopkinson (50). *Spin consultant:* Saqlain Mushtaq (T/50). *Operations manager:* A. W. Bentley (T/50/20). *Analyst:* G. Lindsay (T), N. A. Leamon (50/20). *Doctor:* Gurjit Bhogal (T), M. G. Wotherspoon (50/20), G. Rae (50/20). *Physiotherapist:* C. A. de Weymarn (T/50/20). *Masseur:* M. Saxby (T/50/20). *Strength and conditioning:* P. C. F. Scott (T/50/20). *Security manager:* R. C. Dickason (T), W. Carr (50/20). *Head of team communications:* D. M. Reuben (T/50/20).

TEST MATCH AVERAGES

WEST INDIES – BATTING AND FIELDING

	T	I	NO	R	HS	100	50	Avge	Ct/St
J. O. Holder	2	3	1	229	202*	1	0	114.50	4
S. O. Dowrich	3	5	1	204	116*	1	0	51.00	8
R. L. Chase	3	5	1	160	102*	1	1	40.00	0
†J. D. Campbell	3	6	1	176	47	0	0	35.20	3
†S. O. Hetmyer	3	5	0	160	81	0	1	32.00	2
K. C. Brathwaite	3	6	1	138	49	0	0	27.60	1
S. D. Hope	3	5	0	119	57	0	1	23.80	4/1
K. A. J. Roach	3	4	1	51	29	0	0	17.00	0
†D. M. Bravo	3	5	0	59	50	0	1	11.80	3
A. S. Joseph	3	4	0	43	34	0	0	10.75	4
S. T. Gabriel	3	4	2	8	4	0	0	4.00	1

Played in one Test: K. M. A. Paul 9, 12 (1 ct).

BOWLING

	Style	O	M	R	W	BB	5I	Avge
K. A. J. Roach	RFM	96.5	34	250	18	5-17	1	13.88
J. O. Holder	RFM	45.1	16	125	7	4-43	0	17.85
K. M. A. Paul	RFM	26	8	69	3	2-58	0	23.00
A. S. Joseph	RFM	66.2	16	238	10	2-12	0	23.80
R. L. Chase.................	OB	70.4	4	223	8	8-60	1	27.87
S. T. Gabriel...............	RF	96.1	19	281	9	3-45	0	31.22

Also bowled: K. C. Brathwaite (OB) 16–2–29–0; J. D. Campbell (OB) 4.1–0–10–0.

ENGLAND – BATTING AND FIELDING

	T	I	NO	R	HS	100	50	Avge	Ct/St
†B. A. Stokes	3	6	1	186	79	0	1	37.20	6
J. C. Buttler	3	6	0	178	67	0	2	29.66	5
J. E. Root	3	6	0	177	122	1	0	29.50	6
J. L. Denly	2	4	0	112	69	0	1	28.00	0
†R. J. Burns................	3	6	0	145	84	0	1	24.16	3
J. M. Bairstow	3	5	0	110	52	0	1	22.00	3/2
†S. M. Curran	2	4	1	50	17	0	0	16.66	0
†K. K. Jennings	2	4	0	62	23	0	0	15.50	2
†M. M. Ali	3	5	0	77	60	0	1	15.40	1
B. T. Foakes...............	2	4	0	55	35	0	0	13.75	2
†J. M. Anderson............	3	5	2	5	4*	0	0	1.66	4
‡S. C. J. Broad	2	3	2	0	0*	0	0	0.00	2

Played in one Test: A. U. Rashid 12, 1; M. A. Wood 6 (1 ct).

BOWLING

	Style	O	M	R	W	BB	5I	Avge
M. A. Wood	RF	20.2	3	93	6	5-41	1	15.50
B. A. Stokes	RFM	86.2	15	228	10	4-59	0	22.80
M. M. Ali	OB	93	13	334	14	4-36	0	23.85
J. M. Anderson.............	RFM	98.1	27	245	10	5-46	1	24.50
S. C. J. Broad	RFM	66	26	123	4	3-53	0	30.75

Also bowled: S. M. Curran (LFM) 42–4–161–1; J. L. Denly (LB) 4–0–17–0; K. K. Jennings (RM) 4.1–0–29–0; A. U. Rashid (LB) 26–1–117–0; J. E. Root (OB) 15–0–47–0.

At Bridgetown (Three Ws Oval), Barbados, January 15–16, 2019. **Drawn. England XI 317-10 dec** (87 overs) (J. E. Root 87, B. A. Stokes 56; C. K. Holder 3-67, B. N. L. Charles 5-10); ‡**West Indies Board President's XI 203-19** (79.5 overs) (J. M. Anderson 4-12, S. C. J. Broad 4-19, J. E. Root 3-12). *The hardest-working people at the Three Ws Oval for this non-first-class practice game (the ECB had turned down the West Indian board's suggestion of a proper four-day match) were the scorers, especially on the second day, when eight of the President's XI batted twice as they lost 19 wickets for 203 on an untrustworthy pitch (Keaton Jennings did so for England). The Jamaican opener John Campbell twice fell for a single, but still made his Test debut a few days later; there was a hat-trick for Stuart Broad, while Jimmy Anderson had figures of 11–4–12–4. Things had been more routine on the first day, which England treated as a net: Rory Burns batted for more than two hours for 35, only to be outdone for diligence by Ben Stokes, who made 56 in 143 minutes. Joe Root scored a sprightly 87 at a run a ball.*

At Bridgetown (Three Ws Oval), Barbados, January 17–18, 2019. **Drawn. ‡England XI 379** (86.4 overs) (R. J. Burns 68, J. M. Bairstow 98; R. A. Reifer 3-39, J. D. Campbell 3-58); **West Indies Board President's XI 233-11** (73 overs) (S. W. Ambris 94; C. R. Woakes 3-31). *A second failure for Keaton Jennings – out for seven after making ten and 15* in the first match – was a worry* *ahead of the Tests, but Burns and Jonny Bairstow showed good form in adding 118 for the second wicket. Later Sam Curran (47), Chris Woakes (43) and Adil Rashid (48) took England close to 400. Broad started the second day by trapping Devon Thomas first ball (he reappeared later and made 10*), and the bowlers enjoyed a gentle workout, only Rashid (19–3–53–2) sending down more than 12 overs. Sunil Ambris battled three hours for 94; the next-highest score was 22.*

WEST INDIES v ENGLAND

First Test

ALI MARTIN

At Bridgetown, Barbados, January 23–26, 2019. West Indies won by 381 runs. Toss: West Indies. Test debut: J. D. Campbell.

When the prime minister of Barbados, Mia Mottley, stood by the boundary and applauded the West Indians off the field at a jubilant Kensington Oval, few were inclined to grumble that she was cashing in on reflected glory. This had been a famous victory, as Bajan as a plate of flying fish and cou cou, or a bottle of Mount Gay rum. All six players who hailed from the island had contributed to a performance that was ruthless and hostile – inflicting on England their heaviest defeat by runs in the Caribbean, and leaving more than a whiff of nostalgia in the air.

Holder, the gentle giant who had spent more than three years dutifully leading a struggling side, stood – at 6ft 7in – head and shoulders above them all. He had just been chosen as the all-rounder in the ICC's Test team of 2018, and his remorseless 202 not out

BEST TEST FIGURES FOR WEST INDIES

9-95	J. M. Noreiga	v India at Port-of-Spain	1970-71
8-29	C. E. H. Croft	v Pakistan at Port-of-Spain	1976-77
8-38	L. R. Gibbs	v India at Bridgetown	1961-62
8-45	C. E. L. Ambrose	v England at Bridgetown	1989-90
8-49	D. Bishoo	v Pakistan at Dubai	2016-17
8-60	**R. L. Chase**	**v England at Bridgetown**	**2018-19**
8-62	S. T. Gabriel	v Sri Lanka at Gros Islet	2018
8-92	M. A. Holding	v England at The Oval	1976
8-104†	A. L. Valentine	v England at Manchester	1950

† *On debut.*

from No. 8 in West Indies' second innings had dominated an unbroken stand of 295 with Dowrich, his wicketkeeper and fellow countryman. It was the third-highest seventh-wicket partnership in Test history, and left England needing 628 over the best part of seven sessions. West Indies had never set a higher target.

Chase, another Bajan, inflicted the *coup de grâce* on the fourth day, when he picked up eight wickets with his non-turning off-breaks to dispose of a frazzled England for 246. But it was Roach, yet another local, who had set this First Test on an irreversible path. His spell of five for four in 27 balls on the second afternoon filleted a side who, not long after winning 3–0 in Sri Lanka, crumbled to 77. Had Jennings departed shortly after lunch rather than shortly before, England might have lost all ten in a session for the fourth time in three years – a fate they had not previously suffered since the Second World War.

Broad appeal: Kemar Roach traps Ben Stokes for a duck to leave England 48 for 5.

Root, on losing his first toss in nine and being asked to field, named an attack of three seamers and two spinners, which left many scratching their heads. Where, above all, was Stuart Broad? The surfaces in Sri Lanka before Christmas had not been his bag, nor Anderson's. But Bridgetown? His omission smacked of overthink, and England's limitations were exposed, with Curran now a frontline seamer. A green, marbled pitch watered 24 hours earlier had led Root, coach Trevor Bayliss and national selector Ed Smith to conclude that Ali's off-spin needed augmenting with Rashid's leg-breaks. Instead, it was Anderson and Stokes who offered most threat, sharing nine wickets as West Indies began with a workable 289.

Brathwaite's three-hour 40 and watchful half-centuries from Hope and Chase had kicked off the Bajan contribution; before that, Jamaican opener John Campbell served up a breakneck 44 on debut, beaming throughout after being presented with his maroon cap by Garfield Sobers. Hetmyer, meanwhile, the stylish Guyanese left-hander, top-scored from No. 6 with 81, and was last out on the second morning. By then, Anderson had added two more milestones to his CV. The wicket of Chase on the first evening was the 1,000th claimed in total by him (567) and Broad (433); that of Joseph on the next morning brought

ENGLAND'S LOWEST TOTALS AGAINST WEST INDIES

46	Port-of-Spain	1993-94	93	Manchester	1988
51	Kingston	2008-09	103†	Kingston	1934-35
71	Manchester	1976	103	The Oval	1950
77	**Bridgetown**	**2018-19**	107	Port-of-Spain	1934-35
89†	Birmingham	1995	111	Georgetown	1947-48

† *One man absent hurt.*

MASTER OF BOTH TRADES

Players who have scored a double-century and taken ten wickets in a match during their Test career:

	200	10M	Completed		200	10M	Completed
M. H. Mankad (I)	2	2	1955-56	Wasim Akram (P) ..	1	5	1996-97
I. T. Botham (E) .	1	4	1982	Shakib Al Hasan (B)	1	2	2016-17
A. R. Border (A) .	2	1	1988-89	**J. O. Holder (WI)** ..	**1**	**1**	**2018-19**

up his 27th Test five-for, equalling Ian Botham's England record. The last six had fallen for 49.

Any sense of an English foothold soon vanished, however, as the West Indies bowlers got to work. After Jennings squirted Holder to gully for 17, Roach – in his second spell – breathed fire. He was meant to have lost the raw pace of his youth following a car crash in 2014, but here he was irresistible. Burns and Bairstow played on – Bairstow, retained as a specialist No. 3, via his elbow – and a strokeless Stokes was pinned lbw from wide of the crease for a 17-ball duck. Ali fell to his first delivery, lazily top-edging a pull to long leg, before a snorter had Buttler caught behind off the splice.

In between, Holder knocked over Root, lbw to one that jagged back and exploited skittish footwork. With Joseph and Gabriel, the fastest of the quartet, extinguishing Foakes and the tail, West Indies had a first-innings lead of 212. Three days plus a session remained, but Holder eschewed the follow-on in favour of tightening the ligature. That evening, to their credit, England staged a mini-fightback: Stokes and Ali shared five for nine in 28 deliveries, before Curran finally struck, removing Hetmyer. But, even at 127 for six, West Indies led by 339 – more than England had made to win a Test.

Rashid and Ali lacked control, and Curran his captain's trust, so Root bowled Anderson and Stokes into the ground. When Holder reached his double-century – the second-highest score by a West Indian captain against England, after Brian Lara's unbeaten 400 in April 2004 – he held his arms outstretched in ecstasy, soaked up the adulation, then declared, presenting his guests with a task to make Sisyphus quail.

England's openers held firm on the third evening. But next morning came a second heinous collapse. To be blown away by the quicks was one thing; to allow Chase's part-time spin to grab the sixth-best figures in West Indian history quite another. Only Jennings, removed by Joseph in a leaden-footed repeat of his first-innings dismissal, and Bairstow, glancing behind off the fired-up Gabriel, escaped his clutches.

Chase, in fairness, prompted indecision over whether to play forward or back. Burns, so positive against the seamers during a Test-best 84 full of cuts and drives, was first to be sucked in, bowled through the gate in the final over before lunch. Root, roughed up by Gabriel, who bounced him out off a no-ball, poked tamely to slip on 22. Just before tea, Stokes was lbw playing outside a straighter ball, then Ali completed a sorry pair, guiding to slip.

The force was with West Indies. Campbell's flying catch at short midwicket to dismiss Buttler gave Chase his fifth, a sweep from Foakes into short leg's midriff his sixth, and Rashid's flail to deep midwicket his seventh. Local support at the Kensington Oval had built during the day and, when Curran was last out, stumped by Hope (deputising for

---

❝ Kent have never been my favourite bunch of blokes, and I liked them even less when they beat us in the Sunday League… We had them in a lot of bother until John Shepherd saw them home."
Wisden's champion county, page 25

Minor tweak: Roston Chase's seemingly innocuous off-breaks hurried West Indies to victory.

Dowrich, who had a stiff back), they witnessed the conclusion of a performance that had flipped predictions on their heads. For England, it was an inglorious start to a year in which they were targeting World Cup and Ashes glory; for West Indies, a rare chance to celebrate.

Player of the Match: J. O. Holder.

Close of play: first day, West Indies 264-8 (Hetmyer 56); second day, West Indies 127-6 (Dowrich 27, Holder 7); third day, England 56-0 (Burns 39, Jennings 11).

West Indies

K. C. Brathwaite c Root b Stokes	40	– lbw b Ali	24
J. D. Campbell lbw b Ali	44	– c Jennings b Stokes	33
S. D. Hope c Foakes b Anderson	57	– c Jennings b Stokes	3
D. M. Bravo lbw b Stokes	2	– c Stokes b Ali	1
R. L. Chase c Root b Anderson	54	– c Stokes b Ali	0
S. O. Hetmyer c Foakes b Stokes	81	– c Buttler b Curran	31
S. O. Dowrich c Buttler b Anderson	0	– not out	116
J. O. Holder c and b Anderson	5	– not out	202
K. A. J. Roach c Root b Stokes	0		
A. S. Joseph c Buttler b Anderson	0		
S. T. Gabriel not out	0		
Lb 5, nb 1	6	B 1, lb 1, nb 3	5

1/53 (2) 2/126 (1) 3/128 (4)   (101.3 overs) 289   1/52 (1)   (6 wkts dec, 103.1 overs) 415
4/174 (3) 5/240 (5) 6/250 (7)   2/60 (2) 3/61 (4)
7/261 (8) 8/264 (9) 9/289 (10) 10/289 (6)   4/61 (5) 5/61 (3) 6/120 (6)

Anderson 30–13–46–5; Curran 12–3–54–0; Stokes 25.3–2–59–4; Ali 12–1–59–1; Rashid 17–1–56–0; Root 5–0–10–0. *Second innings*—Anderson 18–4–58–0; Curran 17–1–69–1; Ali 20–3–78–3; Stokes 25–3–81–2; Rashid 9–0–61–0; Root 10–0–37–0; Jennings 4.1–0–29–0.

England

R. J. Burns b Roach	2	– b Chase	84
K. K. Jennings c Hope b Holder	17	– c Holder b Joseph	14
J. M. Bairstow b Roach	12	– c †Hope b Gabriel	30
*J. E. Root lbw b Holder	4	– c Bravo b Chase	22
B. A. Stokes lbw b Roach	0	– lbw b Chase	34
J. C. Buttler c Dowrich b Roach	4	– c Campbell b Chase	26
M. M. Ali c Joseph b Roach	0	– c Holder b Chase	0
†B. T. Foakes c Dowrich b Joseph	2	– c Hetmyer b Chase	5
S. M. Curran c Hope b Gabriel	14	– st †Hope b Chase	17
A. U. Rashid c Holder b Joseph	12	– c Brathwaite b Chase	1
J. M. Anderson not out	0	– not out	4
B 4, lb 6	10	B 4, w 3, nb 2	9
	77		**246**

1/23 (2) 2/35 (1) 3/44 (3) (30.2 overs) 77
4/44 (4) 5/48 (5) 6/48 (7)
7/49 (6) 8/61 (8) 9/73 (9) 10/77 (10)

1/85 (2) 2/134 (1) (80.4 overs) 246
3/143 (3) 4/167 (4)
5/215 (5) 6/217 (7) 7/218 (6)
8/228 (8) 9/234 (10) 10/246 (9)

Roach 11–7–17–5; Gabriel 7–2–15–1; Holder 8–3–15–2; Joseph 4.2–1–20–2. *Second innings*—Roach 14–3–58–0; Gabriel 16.5–2–55–1; Holder 12–6–24–0; Chase 21.4–2–60–8; Joseph 12–4–35–1; Campbell 4.1–0–10–0.

Umpires: C. B. Gaffaney and R. J. Tucker.   Third umpire: H. D. P. K. Dharmasena.
Referee: J. J. Crowe.

WEST INDIES v ENGLAND

Second Test

John Etheridge

At North Sound, Antigua, January 31–February 2, 2019. West Indies won by ten wickets. Toss: West Indies. Test debut: J. L. Denly.

The script was similar to the First Test, only more brutal. Like the first innings in Barbados, this match resembled a throwback to the 1980s, when West Indies ruled the world with speed, skill and intimidation. After the embarrassment of losing eight wickets to an unheralded, scarcely turning spinner, England now lost all 20 to fast bowlers. It was a fearful going-over. And, for the first time since 1993-94, they had lost successive Tests to West Indies in the same series.

It was hard to avoid comparisons – and refreshing simply to be able to make them. For Malcolm Marshall, read Roach; for Colin Croft, read Gabriel; for Michael Holding, read Joseph. The modern incarnations might not have been quite as devastating as their predecessors, but it was a close-run thing. And for Clive Lloyd, read Holder. As captain, he retained the pressure and oversaw a cohesive, committed team; as a fourth prong to the pace attack, he was invaluable, his match haul of five wickets including Buttler twice. The only blot was that Holder didn't appear worried how quickly he dispensed his team's ferocity, and he was banned from the next Test because of a slow over-rate. In fact, with West Indies winning by ten wickets inside three days, and England's two innings lasting

Another day in paradise: Stuart Broad endured a frustrating time after his recall.

total of 103.1 overs, it seemed speedy work by his bowlers. West Indies had regained the Wisden Trophy – which they had last held a decade earlier – with a match to spare.

For England, the stats were damning. In this series they had now lost a wicket every 32 balls, at an average cost of 16. At that point, they were their worst batting figures in a series since 1888. Head coach Trevor Bayliss was not amused: "We haven't seemed to have the will to fight. There have been some loose shots, and other guys have been very tentative. We have a white-ball team that plays aggressively, and sometimes I feel the message between one-day and Test cricket becomes a little muddled." Root was no less despondent: "We have to be better. I can't bat for 11 guys. The responsibility is down to the individual. I wouldn't say it was a fair contest between bat and ball, but West Indies managed the conditions better than us."

England appeared taken aback by the hostility and accuracy of the West Indian quartet, and spooked by the spiteful nature of the pitch; it was later rated "below average" by ICC match referee Jeff Crowe, costing the Sir Vivian Richards Stadium a demerit point. Even so, England perished to some terrible shots. While they showed little heart for the battle, West Indies displayed the discipline their batting had often lacked in recent years – none more so than Darren Bravo, who took 215 balls over his half-century. After a pair of failures at Bridgetown, he fully vindicated the decision by the selectors to recall him after an absence of two years.

Put in to bat, England soon found their bodies and heads targeted. Painful moments included Stokes leaping in agony after taking a blow on the hand, Ali being hit on the helmet, Foakes falling to a ball that deflected off his glove on to the stumps, and which also prevented him from keeping. The bowler each time was Gabriel. Root received a near-unplayable delivery which trampolined off the pitch and flew from his bat handle to third slip, where Campbell parried the chance, and Hope ran in from gully to catch the rebound. There was uneven bounce – mainly steepling, sometimes low – and the fast bowlers were merciless.

There was swing, too. Roach moved the ball at decent pace and enjoyed success against England's left-handers from around the wicket; only two of his eight victims were right-handers. Gabriel, aggressive and distinctly unangelic, engaged in a couple of verbal exchanges in which Stokes, of all people, was the pacifier. Joseph's action was fluid, his pace slippery; Holder exploited the variations in the surface. Later, Joseph insisted on bowling in England's second innings, even though his mother had died overnight after a long illness.

In the first, Bairstow had made a counter-attacking 52 out of 74 while he was at the wicket; but when he was pinned by Roach, England were in trouble at 78 for five. Ali later top-scored with 60, following a pair in Barbados; it was his highest score for 25 Test innings. But only two others reached double figures, and the last four fell for nine after Ali and Foakes had added a careful 85.

Joe Denly had been chosen ahead of Keaton Jennings and, aged 32 years 321 days, became the oldest England batsman to make his Test debut since 33-year-old Alan Wells against West Indies at The Oval in 1995. Wells had been dismissed by Curtly Ambrose for a golden duck in his first innings, and Denly might easily have registered a pair: in the first innings, he survived an lbw review from Roach by the thickness of a blade of grass;

SLOWEST TEST HALF-CENTURIES

Mins	Balls			
357	350	T. E. Bailey (68)	England v Australia at Brisbane	1958-59
350	236	C. J. Tavaré (82)	England v Pakistan at Lord's	1982
340	**215**	**D. M. Bravo (50)**	**West Indies v England at North Sound**	**2018-19**
333	229	B. A. Young (51)	New Zealand v South Africa at Durban	1994-95
326		S. M. Gavaskar (51)	India v Sri Lanka at Colombo (SSC)	1985-86
318	209	Ramiz Raja (62)	Pakistan v West Indies at Karachi	1986-87
316		C. P. S. Chauhan (61)	India v Pakistan at Kanpur	1979-80
315	229	Shoaib Mohammad (53*)	Pakistan v Zimbabwe at Lahore	1993-94
313	343	D. J. McGlew (70)	South Africa v Australia at Johannesburg	1957-58
312	212	J. J. Crowe (120*)	New Zealand v Sri Lanka at Colombo (CCC)	1986-87

Balls faced not known for some innings.

in the second, he was dropped at fine leg by Brathwaite off Gabriel. His two dismissals were ugly, too. He toe-ended a waft at a wide long hop to give Joseph a wicket with his first ball in Test cricket on his home island, and was then bowled by Joseph offering no shot. Denly was the 17th opener – including Alastair Cook and a nightwatchman – tried by England since the retirement of Andrew Strauss in 2012.

It then took them more than 33 overs to break through with the ball, which meant – following the big stand between Holder and Dowrich in Barbados – they had gone wicketless for 101. The lowest score among West Indies' resolute top four was 44, and their total of 306 spanned 131 overs, with Bravo last out, having batted 78 – and more than five and a half hours – for exactly 50.

West Indies secured a lead of 119, at which point England did little more than wave the white flag, their resolve evaporating against a diet of bouncers and rising deliveries that threatened their welfare and challenged their courage. The procession began when Burns part-wafted, part-uppercut a catch into the slips, before Bairstow departed in familiar fashion, bowled aiming an expansive drive. Denly shouldered arms, Stokes dragged on after he had been dropped on nought, and Ali was also bowled trying to drive. These were poor dismissals, the sort of shots they might play on a flat pitch against a white ball. Buttler top-scored with 24. West Indies needed just 14, and the game ended with Campbell pulling Anderson for six. Their win was utterly emphatic, and richly deserved.

Player of the Match: K. A. J. Roach.

Close of play: first day, West Indies 30-0 (Brathwaite 11, Campbell 16); second day, West Indies 272-6 (Bravo 33, Holder 19).

England

R. J. Burns c Holder b Roach	4	– c Campbell b Holder	16
J. L. Denly c Dowrich b Joseph	6	– b Joseph	17
J. M. Bairstow lbw b Roach	52	– b Holder	14
*J. E. Root c Hope b Joseph	7	– c Dowrich b Joseph	7
J. C. Buttler c Campbell b Holder	1	– lbw b Holder	24
B. A. Stokes c Dowrich b Gabriel	14	– b Roach	11
M. M. Ali c Gabriel b Roach	60	– b Roach	4
†B. T. Foakes b Gabriel	35	– lbw b Roach	13
S. M. Curran b sub (S. S. J. Brooks) b Roach	6	– not out	13
S. C. J. Broad not out	0	– lbw b Roach	0
J. M. Anderson b Gabriel	1	– c Joseph b Holder	0
W 1	1	Lb 3, w 10	13

1/4 (1) 2/16 (2) 3/34 (4) (61 overs) 187 1/35 (1) 2/49 (3) (42.1 overs) 132
4/55 (5) 5/78 (3) 6/93 (6) 3/56 (4) 4/59 (2)
7/178 (7) 8/186 (8) 9/186 (9) 10/187 (11) 5/88 (6) 6/96 (7) 7/118 (8)
8/118 (5) 9/125 (10) 10/132 (11)

Roach 15–5–30–4; Gabriel 15–5–45–3; Joseph 10–3–38–2; Holder 13–5–43–1; Chase 8–1–31–0. *Second innings*—Roach 13–2–52–4; Gabriel 10–3–22–0; Holder 12.1–2–43–4; Joseph 7–4–12–2.

West Indies

K. C. Brathwaite c sub (K. K. Jennings) b Ali	49	– not out	5
J. D. Campbell c Buttler b Stokes	47	– not out	11
S. D. Hope c †Bairstow b Broad	44		
D. M. Bravo st †Bairstow b Ali	50		
R. L. Chase b Broad	4		
S. O. Hetmyer c Anderson b Ali	21		
†S. O. Dowrich c Buttler b Broad	31		
*J. O. Holder c †Bairstow b Anderson	22		
K. A. J. Roach c Stokes b Anderson	6		
A. S. Joseph c Burns b Stokes	7		
S. T. Gabriel not out	1		
B 8, lb 13, w 1, nb 2	24	Lb 1	1

1/70 (2) 2/133 (1) 3/151 (3) (131 overs) 306 (no wkt, 2.1 overs) 17
4/155 (5) 5/186 (6) 6/236 (7)
7/281 (8) 8/289 (9) 9/298 (10) 10/306 (4)

Anderson 29–5–73–2; Broad 36–16–53–3; Stokes 27–8–58–2; Curran 13–0–38–0; Ali 25–4–62–3; Denly 1–0–1–0. *Second innings*—Anderson 1.1–0–10–0; Broad 1–0–6–0.

Umpires: H. D. P. K. Dharmasena and C. B. Gaffaney. Third umpire: R. J. Tucker.
Referee: J. J. Crowe.

> **❝** The lights dimmed, and as Lebo M's immortal opening chant to 'Circle of Life' took flight, England needed 24 from two overs. At this point, an alert usher – quite correctly – ordered me to switch off my phone. Nearly two hours later, I learned what I had missed."
>
> Watching the World Cup final, page 58

WEST INDIES v ENGLAND

Third Test

J O N A T H A N   L I E W

At Gros Islet, St Lucia, February 9–12, 2019. England won by 232 runs. Toss: West Indies.

Shortly after tea on the second day, with West Indies six down in their first innings, Wood was preparing to start a new over when Ali strolled over for a chat. Paul had just slapped him back over his head, and Ali asked if Wood wanted a man at mid-on. Wood said he thought he already had one. Ali fixed him with a look: "You haven't had a mid-on for five or six overs."

This was the point, perhaps, at which it began to dawn on Wood that something out of the ordinary was occurring; that he was inhabiting the vague and rarefied plane of sporting achievement popularly described as "the zone", where minor details – the field, the crowd, the score, the day, the month and very possibly the year – no longer seem to register; that his 13th Test cap, nine months after his 12th, and almost four years after his first, would not be like the others. "It was the adrenalin coursing through me," he said later. "All I could really see was the batter."

Not, though, for long. Four West Indians fell to Wood in the space of 22 balls and, by the time he led England off the field, the Dukes held aloft, the wider significance of his feat was already apparent. Having bowled Gabriel with the second delivery of his second spell, he had completed his first five-wicket haul in Tests. It was a burst that essentially won the game for England, and resurrected Wood's fragile international career after a litany of injuries. But it was more. On a warm, balmy afternoon, with a brisk easterly blowing over the party stand, and the series already decided, it was the moment English cricket rekindled its love affair with express pace.

Staggering: Mark Wood hurls himself at West Indies during England's quickest spell for a decade.

RAGS TO RICHES

Players who followed a golden duck with a century in a Test:

J. H. Sinclair (0 and 104).	South Africa v Australia at Cape Town.	1902-03
D. G. Bradman (0 and 103*).	Australia v England at Melbourne.	1932-33
G. S. Sobers (0 and 113*)	West Indies v England at Kingston	1967-68
R. B. McCosker (0 and 105)	Australia v Pakistan at Melbourne.	1976-77
D. L. Haynes (0 and 122)	West Indies v New Zealand at Christchurch	1979-80
I. T. Botham (0 and 118).	England v Australia at Manchester	1981
M. Azharuddin (0 and 109).	India v Pakistan at Faisalabad	1989-90
F. du Plessis (0 and 120)	South Africa v Australia at Johannesburg	2017-18
R. L. Chase (0 and 102*)	**West Indies v England at Gros Islet**	**2018-19**

A fleeting affair it's been, to be sure: list England's fastest half-dozen bowlers – say, Kortright, Larwood, Tyson, Snow, Malcolm and Harmison – and there is a sense of something transitory. And if it seems a touch hyperbolic to number Wood among their company, then it is simply a measure of the rarity of the species. His hat-trick delivery, survived by Hetmyer, was clocked at 94.6mph – the fastest recorded by an England bowler since Andrew Flintoff hit 95.1 at Lord's during the 2009 Ashes.

And so, at the end of a series dominated by pace, England finally made their mark, aided in part by Brathwaite's hubris. It was hard to blame an emboldened West Indies, on winning the toss, for wanting first dig at an England line-up given yet another shuffle: Ben Foakes was omitted, allowing Bairstow to reclaim the gloves and bat at No. 7, and Jennings to return as opener, while pushing Denly down a place. But in retrospect, and given the suspension of Holder for over-rate offences, Brathwaite was probably over-confident. Holder's absence deprived them not of one cricketer, but four: a talismanic leader, an in-form lower-order batsman, a world-class seamer, and a man mountain who would almost certainly have grabbed a flying chance in the slips when Buttler was on nought.

England's luck caught up with them on the second morning, as six wickets fell for 45. Bairstow's return to his favoured position met an unhappy, protracted end: two runs in 75 minutes, plus a blow on the helmet from Gabriel. Dowrich took a magnificent 30-yard running catch to claim Stokes for 79 off the top edge, Roach mopped up the tail and, when the doughty Brathwaite and the combative Campbell hewed West Indies to 57 without loss, the game was in the balance.

It was Ali who made the initial breakthroughs, prising out the openers in two balls. At which point: enter Wood. Root and Stokes later said they couldn't remember the last time they had stood so far back behind the wicket. Wood's first three balls fizzed past the outside edge. His fourth was a searing 90mph bumper that put Hope on his knees. His fifth and sixth – 92mph – were edged to Burns in the gully by Hope and Chase. Seldom can the roles of hunter and hunted have switched so abruptly or as spectacularly.

For Wood, the rest of the afternoon may have passed in a blur. He was bowled a little too long by an enraptured Root – eight overs either side of tea – but by the time he returned to finish the innings, his fizzing energy had already changed the mood of the game. Ali had taken his third and fourth wickets in the meantime, with Joseph falling to a stunning grab by Broad, furiously backpedalling from mid-off, sticking out a single, hopeful hand, and miraculously rising with the ball.

Having been blown this way and that during the first two Tests, England now had a lead of 123: space to breathe, time to bat. A quadriceps injury to Paul left West Indies' attack badly stretched and, in balmy, benign conditions, Root capitalised. In recent months, he had become susceptible to full balls swinging into the stumps, and over the course of two hours in the nets with batting coach Mark Ramprakash earlier in the week had worked on the problem, keeping his front pad inside the line, avoiding getting sucked across his stumps. This, his 16th Test century, was his reward, even if it was not his finest vintage.

Accompanied by Denly's pleasant 69 and another brawny half-century from Buttler, Root eased England into an impregnable position early on the fourth day, setting a target of 485. When Anderson reduced West Indies to ten for three – which included the 100th time he had taken the first wicket of a Test innings (Glenn McGrath was next, with 97) – it seemed they had finally run out of puff. It was to their credit that, with only pride to play for, they continued to compete; West Indies sides of the recent past would not necessarily have shown the same fight. While Hetmyer and Dowrich, then Roach and Joseph, swung merrily at the other end, the underrated Chase played an innings of controlled aggression and impressive maturity. He reached 98 when the fall of the ninth wicket – with Paul still convalescing in the dressing-room – apparently left him stranded.

But after a few moments, and to warm applause, Paul limped down the steps and out to the wicket, blocking the final ball of the over and allowing Chase to reach his fifth Test century with a dismissive cut off Denly. And so, even in a convincing defeat, a modicum of satisfaction for West Indies: the knowledge that, against their oldest enemy, with the series won and their captain absent, there remained enough character to flash a defiant eye.

The other talking point was the homophobic slur aimed by Gabriel at Root on the third day, for which he was fined 75% of his match fee and banned for four one-day internationals. "Root was looking at me intensely as I prepared to bowl, which may have been the usual psychological strategy with which all Test cricketers are familiar," Gabriel said. "I recognise now that I was attempting to break through my own tension when I said to Root: 'Why are you smiling? Do you like boys?'"

Gabriel's jibe was not picked up on the stump microphones. But Root's instinctive response was. "Don't use it as an insult," he said. There's nothing wrong with being gay". It earned him widespread admiration in England, and made the evening news. And if Gabriel's comment was a sour moment at the end of a series played largely in the right spirit, then Root's riposte was a reminder that, while sport's self-contained conflict is the basis of its appeal, now and again it offers a canvas for more important battles.

Player of the Match: M. A. Wood.   *Player of the Series:* K. A. J. Roach.
Close of play: first day, England 231-4 (Buttler 67, Stokes 62); second day, England 19-0 (Burns 10, Jennings 8); third day, England 325-4 (Root 111, Stokes 29).

Off and running: Joe Root drives on his way to a redemptive century in England's consolation victory.

England

R. J. Burns lbw b Paul	29	c Joseph b Paul	10
K. K. Jennings c Bravo b Paul	8	b Joseph	23
J. L. Denly lbw b Gabriel	20	c Dowrich b Gabriel	69
*J. E. Root c Dowrich b Joseph	15	c Hetmyer b Gabriel	122
J. C. Buttler b Gabriel	67	b Roach	56
B. A. Stokes c Dowrich b Roach	79	not out	48
†J. M. Bairstow b Roach	2		
M. M. Ali c Bravo b Paul	13		
M. A. Wood c Joseph b Roach	6		
S. C. J. Broad not out	0		
J. M. Anderson c Paul b Roach	0		
B 5, lb 11, w 16, nb 6	38	B 13, lb 9, w 8, nb 3	33

1/30 (2) 2/69 (1) 3/69 (3)   (101.5 overs) 277
4/107 (4) 5/232 (5) 6/256 (6)
7/270 (7) 8/275 (8) 9/277 (9) 10/277 (11)

1/19 (1)   (5 wkts dec, 105.2 overs) 361
2/73 (2) 3/147 (3)
4/254 (5) 5/361 (4)

Roach 25.5–11–48–4; Gabriel 24–6–49–2; Joseph 17–2–61–2; Paul 21–7–58–2; Chase 10–0–40–0; Brathwaite 4–0–5–0. *Second innings*—Roach 18–6–45–1; Gabriel 23.2–1–95–2; Paul 5–1–11–1; Joseph 16–2–72–1; Chase 31–1–92–0; Brathwaite 12–2–24–0.

West Indies

*K. C. Brathwaite c Anderson b Ali	12	c Stokes b Anderson	8
J. D. Campbell lbw b Ali	41	c Ali b Anderson	0
S. D. Hope c Burns b Wood	1	c Broad b Wood	14
D. M. Bravo c Root b Wood	6	c Root b Anderson	0
R. L. Chase c Burns b Wood	0	not out	102
S. O. Hetmyer c Root b Wood	8	run out (Denly/Bairstow)	19
*S. O. Dowrich lbw b Broad	38	c Stokes b Ali	19
K. M. A. Paul st Bairstow b Ali	9	(11) c b Stokes	12
K. A. J. Roach not out	16	(8) c Wood b Ali	29
A. S. Joseph c Broad b Ali	2	(9) c Anderson b Ali	34
S. T. Gabriel b Wood	4	(10) c Bairstow b Stokes	3
Lb 4, w 10, nb 3	17	B 1, lb 5, w 4, nb 2	12

1/57 (1) 2/57 (2) 3/59 (3)   (47.2 overs) 154
4/59 (5) 5/74 (6) 6/79 (4)
7/104 (8) 8/145 (7) 9/148 (10) 10/154 (11)

1/5 (2) 2/10 (1)   (69.5 overs) 252
3/10 (4) 4/31 (3)
5/76 (6) 6/110 (7) 7/156 (8)
8/212 (9) 9/236 (10) 10/252 (11)

Anderson 9–3–31–0; Broad 15–4–42–1; Ali 15–4–36–4; Wood 8.2–2–41–5. *Second innings*—Anderson 11.2–2–27–3; Broad 14–6–22–0; Stokes 8.5–2–30–2; Wood 12–1–52–1; Ali 21–1–99–3; Denly 3–0–16–0.

Umpires: H. D. P. K. Dharmasena and R. J. Tucker.   Third umpire: C. B. Gaffaney.
Referee: J. J. Crowe.

At Bridgetown (Three Ws Oval), Barbados, February 17, 2019. **England XI won by 171 runs. England XI 371-7** (50 overs) (J. J. Roy 110, J. E. Root 114); ‡**University of West Indies Vice-Chancellor's XI 200** (43.5 overs). *Jason Roy and Jonny Bairstow (46) piled on 129 in the first 18.2 overs; Roy eventually retired out after facing 82 balls. Joe Root took over, hitting four sixes and 11 fours from 81. It was all too much for the inexperienced Vice-Chancellor's XI, although their captain, local man Kyle Corbin, made a bright start; with wicketkeeper Amir Jangoo, he took the score to 91-1 in the 15th over before the spinners applied the brakes. An England fan was treated by the team doctor after being hit in the face trying to catch a six struck by Moeen Ali.*

LIMITED-OVERS INTERNATIONAL REPORTS BY RORY DOLLARD

WEST INDIES v ENGLAND

First One-Day International

At Bridgetown, Barbados, February 20, 2019 (day/night). England won by six wickets. Toss: West Indies. One-day international debuts: J. D. Campbell, N. Pooran.

Chris Gayle emerged from a seven-month international hiatus with a typically hard-hit century, only to cede the spotlight as England launched a record chase. A couple of days after announcing his plans to retire from one-day internationals after the World Cup (plans he would rescind during the tournament itself), the 39-year-old Gayle got off to a characteristically ponderous start. He had ambled to nine off 32 deliveries when he was badly dropped by Roy off Plunkett, and didn't reach or clear the fence until the 15th over. But he then exploited a short leg-side boundary and an inviting breeze, swatting a dozen sixes and losing several balls, as Ali – who disappeared over the ropes nine times in all – and Plunkett drifted into his hitting arc. The first of the 12 took Gayle clear of Shahid Afridi's 476 sixes in all internationals, and he finished with 135 from 129 balls, then his highest score against England; he hit only three fours. When Nurse launched the last ball of the innings, from Rashid, over long-on, West Indies' tally of sixes rose to 23, breaking New Zealand's world record, set against West Indies at Queenstown in January 2014, though from only 21 overs. For a week it was also their highest total against England. It was explosive stuff, but also flawed: there were 143 dot balls, compared with 98 in England's unflustered reply. Roy set the tone against the new-ball pairing of Bishoo and Thomas, and sprinted to three figures in 65 balls (Gayle had used up 76 reaching fifty). He added 114 for the second wicket with Root, who then put on 116 for the third with Morgan, making 102 – and passing 5,000 runs in ODIs – before holing out with the scores tied. West Indies might have gone closer had they taken one of several chances offered by the centurions. Instead, England could celebrate their highest successful one-day chase, beating 350 for three against New Zealand at Trent Bridge in 2015.

Player of the Match: J. J. Roy.

West Indies

C. H. Gayle b Stokes	135	A. R. Nurse not out		25
J. D. Campbell c Ali b Woakes	30	D. Bishoo not out		9
†S. D. Hope c Rashid b Stokes	64	B 1, lb 1, w 15, nb 1		18
S. O. Hetmyer c Roy b Woakes	20			
N. Pooran c Roy b Rashid	0	1/38 (2) 2/169 (3)	(8 wkts, 50 overs)	360
D. M. Bravo c Woakes b Rashid	40	3/229 (4) 4/230 (5)		
*J. O. Holder st Buttler b Rashid	16	5/294 (6) 6/317 (1)		
C. R. Brathwaite c Buttler b Stokes	3	7/322 (7) 8/343 (8)	10 overs: 49-1	

O. R. Thomas did not bat.

Woakes 10–0–59–2; Wood 7–0–49–0; Ali 10–0–85–0; Plunkett 6–0–54–0; Stokes 8–0–37–3; Rashid 9–0–74–3.

England

J. J. Roy c Bravo b Bishoo	123	†J. C. Buttler not out		4
J. M. Bairstow c Hope b Holder	34	Lb 3, w 13		16
J. E. Root c Pooran b Holder	102			
*E. J. G. Morgan c Holder b Thomas	65	1/91 (2) 2/205 (1)	(4 wkts, 48.4 overs)	364
B. A. Stokes not out	20	3/321 (4) 4/360 (3)	10 overs: 88-0	

M. M. Ali, C. R. Woakes, A. U. Rashid, L. E. Plunkett and M. A. Wood did not bat.

Bishoo 10–0–78–1; Thomas 9–0–72–1; Holder 9.4–0–63–2; Brathwaite 9–0–66–0; Nurse 10–0–69–0; Campbell 1–0–13–0.

Umpires: L. S. Reifer and P. Wilson.   Third umpire: B. N. J. Oxenford.
Referee: A. J. Pycroft.

WEST INDIES v ENGLAND

Second One-Day International

At Bridgetown, Barbados, February 22, 2019. West Indies won by 26 runs. Toss: England.

Just 48 hours after watching England make light work of chasing 361, West Indies returned to the Kensington Oval to mount a spirited defence of a much skinnier total. England were complicit in their own downfall, losing six for 35 in the closing stages to fritter away a hard-won platform, but this was primarily a success story. Success for Hetmyer, whose classy century confirmed his status as the brightest young star in the West Indian firmament. Success for Holder, who dragged his side back from the brink with an inspired late spell. And success for Cottrell, a Jamaican soldier who earned five opportunities to indulge his theatrical military celebration – a march and salute for each batsman who fell to his skilful left-arm swing. Hetmyer, batting variously in a helmet or a wide-brimmed sunhat, or with his bleached golden hair on full display, fluently anchored the innings after Gayle had hit four more sixes in his 50, and stage-managed a neat finale by reaching his hundred from the penultimate ball. Moments earlier, Stokes had overstepped, to end a sequence of two years, 43 ODIs and over 11,000 deliveries without a front-foot no-ball by an England bowler. Cottrell cut the reply off at the roots, taking out Bairstow and Roy with the new ball, and drew a loose shot from Morgan in full flow. He then held his nerve as England fumbled at the death. A responsible knock from Stokes and a series of sweet strikes from Buttler had left them needing 62 from 61 balls with six wickets in hand. But Holder induced an edge from Stokes, then removed Buttler and Curran in successive deliveries. Gregory Brathwaite's decision to give Curran out leg-before was horrible – the ball was comfortably missing leg stump – but Stokes had wasted England's review, and the series was all square.

Player of the Match: S. O. Hetmyer.

West Indies

C. H. Gayle b Rashid	50	A. R. Nurse not out		13
J. D. Campbell c Ali b Plunkett	23			
†S. D. Hope c Bairstow b Stokes	33	Lb 9, w 13, nb 3		25
D. M. Bravo run out (Rashid)	25			
S. O. Hetmyer not out	104	1/61 (2) 2/98 (1)	(6 wkts, 50 overs)	289
*J. O. Holder run out (Roy)	3	3/121 (3) 4/197 (4)		
C. R. Brathwaite b Wood	13	5/207 (6) 6/237 (7)	10 overs: 49-0	

D. Bishoo, S. S. Cottrell and O. R. Thomas did not bat.

Wood 10–0–38–1; Curran 10–0–62–0; Ali 7–0–51–0; Plunkett 7–0–39–1; Stokes 10–1–62–1; Rashid 6–0–28–1.

England

J. J. Roy b Cottrell	2	L. E. Plunkett c Holder b Brathwaite		2
J. M. Bairstow lbw b Cottrell	0	M. A. Wood not out		1
J. E. Root c Hope b Thomas	36			
*E. J. G. Morgan c Hetmyer b Cottrell	70	Lb 3, w 9		12
B. A. Stokes c Hope b Holder	79			
†J. C. Buttler c Hetmyer b Holder	34	1/1 (2) 2/10 (1) 3/60 (3)	(47.4 overs)	263
M. M. Ali b Cottrell	12	4/159 (4) 5/228 (5) 6/233 (6)		
T. K. Curran lbw b Holder	0	7/233 (8) 8/260 (9) 9/261 (7)		
A. U. Rashid c Hope b Cottrell	15	10/263 (10)	10 overs: 42-2	

Cottrell 9–0–46–5; Holder 10–1–53–3; Thomas 5–0–32–1; Nurse 6–0–28–0; Bishoo 10–0–49–0; Gayle 2–0–15–0; Brathwaite 5.4–0–37–1.

Umpires: G. O. Brathwaite and B. N. J. Oxenford. Third umpire: P. Wilson.
Referee: A. J. Pycroft.

For World Cup records, see page 1344

Greatest hits: Jos Buttler blasts one of 12 sixes during his 150 at Grenada. Chris Gayle thrashed a belligerent 135 in the first match at Barbados.

WEST INDIES v ENGLAND

Third One-Day International

At St George's, Grenada, February 25, 2019. Abandoned. Toss: England.

Almost four years after Grenada last hosted men's international cricket, their big day fell foul of rain, though it did mean the end of a lengthy dry spell. Local fans were grateful they had been afforded a second game, part of a lopsided itinerary in which Guyana, Jamaica and Trinidad all went unvisited. This one counted as a match, as the toss was made.

West Indies

C. H. Gayle, J. D. Campbell, †S. D. Hope, D. M. Bravo, S. O. Hetmyer, *J. O. Holder, C. R. Brathwaite, A. R. Nurse, D. Bishoo, S. S. Cottrell, O. R. Thomas.

England

J. J. Roy, J. M. Bairstow, A. D. Hales, J. E. Root, *E. J. G. Morgan, †J. C. Buttler, M. M. Ali, C. R. Woakes, A. U. Rashid, L. E. Plunkett, M. A. Wood.

Umpires: N. Duguid and P. Wilson.   Third umpire: B. N. J. Oxenford.
Referee: A. J. Pycroft.

WEST INDIES v ENGLAND

Fourth One-Day International

At St George's, Grenada, February 27, 2019. England won by 29 runs. Toss: West Indies.

With the skies mercifully clear and the stands enthusiastically filled, the 100th ODI between the sides became a circus of ball-striking. There were 807 runs in all, comprising the two highest totals in this fixture. There were also 46 sixes, which smashed the previous record of 38; England pinched

West Indies' week-old record by hitting 24. Buttler alone hit 12, only for Gayle to trump him, with 14; Woakes conceded seven, and Holder six (his seven overs cost 88). England's batsmen had touched the accelerator immediately, as Bairstow and Hales – playing because Jason Roy had a hamstring injury – thrashed 89 in the powerplay. But the dam did not burst until the final ten overs, when Buttler vaulted from 45 to 150 in 32 deliveries, ten in a row launched for four or six. He finished with a career-best 150 from 77 balls, and offered Cottrell a return salute. Morgan cheerfully settled for second billing, and became the first to pass 6,000 one-day runs for England. By topping 400 for the fourth time in their history, England gave themselves acres of leeway, much of it devoured by Gayle, who victimised Woakes, Stokes and Ali as he ticked off a shopping-list of landmarks: 10,000 ODI runs; 500 international sixes; and a 55-ball century, the second-fastest for West Indies, after Brian Lara took 45 against Bangladesh at Dhaka in October 1999. At 220 for two after 23 overs, they were on course, but Wood – who had begun by removing Campbell and Hope – returned to snare Bravo with the first ball of a new spell, and offered Cottrell a return salute. Morgan cheerfully settled for second billing, and offered Cottrell a return salute. Plunkett nudged the brakes, before Stokes conquered a tiring Gayle, bowled for a 97-ball 162. Rashid quickly removed Holder, but Carlos Brathwaite and Nurse rallied, leaving an equation of 32 from three overs. Rashid, though, provided one final twist with four wickets in five balls, to finish with the most expensive ODI five-for. Morgan, not prone to hyperbole, called the match "a pure, intense, crazy type of cricket". Few could disagree.

Player of the Match: J. C. Buttler.

England

J. M. Bairstow b Thomas	56		M. M. Ali not out	0		
A. D. Hales c Hetmyer b Nurse	82		B 1, lb 1, w 7, nb 2	11		
J. E. Root c Hope b Thomas	5					
*E. J. G. Morgan c Holder b Cottrell	103		1/100 (1) 2/120 (3)	(6 wkts, 50 overs) 418		
†J. C. Buttler b Brathwaite	150		3/165 (2) 4/369 (4)			
B. A. Stokes c Hetmyer b Brathwaite	11		5/417 (5) 6/418 (6)	10 overs: 89-0		

C. R. Woakes, A. U. Rashid, L. E. Plunkett and M. A. Wood did not bat.

Cottrell 9–0–64–1; Holder 7–0–88–0; Nurse 10–0–68–1; Bishoo 4–0–43–0; Brathwaite 10–0–69–2; Thomas 10–0–84–2.

West Indies

C. H. Gayle b Stokes	162		S. S. Cottrell not out	0	
J. D. Campbell c Root b Wood	15		O. R. Thomas st Buttler b Rashid	0	
S. D. Hope c Buttler b Wood	5				
D. M. Bravo c Stokes b Wood	61		Lb 5, w 12, nb 1	18	
S. O. Hetmyer c Hales b Wood	6				
†J. O. Holder st Buttler b Rashid	29		1/24 (2) 2/44 (3) 3/220 (4)	(48 overs) 389	
C. R. Brathwaite c Morgan b Rashid	50		4/226 (5) 5/295 (1) 6/301 (6)		
A. R. Nurse c Plunkett b Rashid	43		7/389 (8) 8/389 (7) 9/389 (9)		
D. Bishoo c Hales b Rashid	0		10/389 (11)	10 overs: 75-2	

Woakes 10–0–91–0; Wood 10–0–60–4; Plunkett 8–0–40–0; Stokes 8–0–77–1; Rashid 10–0–85–5; Ali 2–0–31–0.

Umpires: G. O. Brathwaite and B. N. J. Oxenford. Third umpire: P. Wilson.
Referee: A. J. Pycroft.

WEST INDIES v ENGLAND

Fifth One-Day International

At Gros Islet, St Lucia, March 2, 2019 (day/night). West Indies won by seven wickets. Toss: West Indies.

West Indies conjured a perfect storm in St Lucia, ensuring a dramatic series ended with the exclamation mark, and the result, it deserved. Pace and bounce were back on the menu, resetting the balance between bat and ball, but only one side were up for the challenge. Technically and temperamentally, England were wholly unprepared. Trevor Bayliss described the experience as "macabre", venturing outside standard cricketing vernacular after seeing his team swept away with 358 of the game's deliveries unused. Flatly refusing to tailor their gung-ho approach to conditions, England had followed their best total against West Indies with their worst. Their previous nadir (114) had come in March 1986, against an attack of Garner, Patterson, Marshall and Holding; here, it was the inexperienced Jamaican Oshane Thomas who did the damage, exploiting his height and trajectory on a springy track. When he splayed Curran's stumps with a yorker, he had the first five-wicket haul of his professional career; England's last five had fallen for two runs. Gayle seemed to regard the

MOST SIXES IN ONE-DAY SERIES AND TOURNAMENTS

6	M			
39	**5**	C. H. Gayle	**West Indies v England**	**2018-19**
26	6	C. H. Gayle	West Indies (World Cup)	2014-15
23	6	R. G. Sharma	India v Australia	2013-14
22	**11**	**E. J. G. Morgan**	**England (World Cup)**	**2019**
21	8	A. B. de Villiers	South Africa (World Cup)	2014-15
20	3	S. R. Watson	Australia in Bangladesh	2010-11
20	5	A. B. de Villiers	South Africa in India	2015-16

target as a personal affront. He treated Woakes with violent disdain, swinging for the stands en route to a 19-ball half-century, the fastest by a West Indian in ODIs (Darren Sammy needed 20 against South Africa in Antigua in May 2010). Gayle reeled off nine more sixes; even his exit – after losing his off stump to Wood for a 27-ball 77 – took on a triumphant feel as he bade farewell to an adoring crowd. When Hetmyer hit the winning boundary in the 13th over, the match had occupied only a couple of balls more than a Twenty20, but nobody felt short-changed.

Player of the Match: O. R. Thomas. *Player of the Series:* C. H. Gayle.

England

J. M. Bairstow b Cottrell	11		A. U. Rashid c Hope b Holder	0
A. D. Hales c Hope b Brathwaite	23		M. A. Wood not out	0
J. E. Root c Cottrell b Holder	1			
*E. J. G. Morgan c Cottrell b Thomas.....	18		W 9, nb 1	10
B. A. Stokes c Hope b Brathwaite.......	15			—
†J. C. Buttler c Cottrell b Thomas.......	23		1/16 (1) 2/18 (3) 3/57 (2) (28.1 overs)	113
M. M. Ali c Hope b Thomas	12		4/63 (4) 5/88 (5) 6/111 (7)	
C. R. Woakes c Brathwaite b Thomas.....	0		7/111 (8) 8/113 (6) 9/113 (10)	
T. K. Curran b Thomas	0		10/113 (9) 10 overs: 55-2	

Cottrell 4–0–23–1; Holder 7–2–28–2; Brathwaite 8–1–17–2; Thomas 5.1–0–21–5; Nurse 4–0–24–0.

West Indies

C. H. Gayle b Wood	77
J. D. Campbell b Wood	1
†S. D. Hope b Woakes	13
D. M. Bravo not out	7
S. O. Hetmyer not out	11
W 5, nb 1	6

1/40 (2) 2/93 (1) (3 wkts, 12.1 overs) 115
3/95 (3) 10 overs: 97-3

*J. O. Holder, C. R. Brathwaite, A. R. Nurse, D. Bishoo, S. S. Cottrell and O. R. Thomas did not bat.

Woakes 6–0–56–1; Wood 6–0–55–2; Curran 0.1–0–4–0.

Umpires: N. Duguid and P. Wilson. Third umpire: B. N. J. Oxenford.
Referee: A. J. Pycroft.

WEST INDIES v ENGLAND

First Twenty20 International

At Gros Islet, St Lucia, March 5, 2019 (floodlit). England won by four wickets. Toss: England.

While England committed early to a selection gamble for the final leg of their trip – Jos Buttler, Ben Stokes and Moeen Ali were all rested ahead of the IPL, while Jason Roy was offered parental leave – West Indies did not confirm their squad until the eve of the match. In the end, they retained their 50-over team en masse, with Holder continuing as captain instead of regular T20 skipper Carlos Brathwaite, but they could not replicate their victory here three days earlier. Tom Curran benefited from hopeful hitting at the start and end of the West Indian innings to bank a career-best four-for. But he was outshone by the meticulous Rashid, who conceded just 15 runs (and one boundary, from an overthrow), and removed the dangerous Brathwaite for a six-ball duck. Jordan also excelled, claiming Gayle with a wide yorker and pouncing for a wonderful caught and bowled to see off Bravo. It needed another career-best, 58 from Pooran, to lift the total to 160. Questions over England's revamped top order were answered forcefully by the versatile Bairstow, who was shunted up to open for the first time in 28 matches, and responded with 68 from 40 balls, yet another career-best. A half-century stand between the Kent pair of Denly and Billings all but sealed the win.

Player of the Match: J. M. Bairstow.

West Indies

		B	4/6
1 †S. D. Hope *c 3 b 8*	6	5	1
2 C. H. Gayle *c 11 b 9*	15	12	0/2
3 S. O. Hetmyer *c 10 b 8*	14	11	1/1
4 D. M. Bravo *c and b 9*	28	30	1/2
5 N. Pooran *b 8*	58	37	3/4
6 C. R. Brathwaite *c 2 b 11*	0	6	0
7 F. A. Allen *c 9 b 5*	8	6	0/1
8 *J. O. Holder *c 6 b 8*	7	5	1
9 A. R. Nurse *not out*	13	8	2
B 1, w 10	11		

6 overs: 43-3   (20 overs) 160-8

1/7 2/31 3/37 4/101 5/102 6/127 7/137 8/160

10 S. S. Cottrell and 11 O. R. Thomas did not bat.

Willey 2–6–20–0; Curran 4–11–36–4; Jordan 3–10–16–2; Rashid 4–13–15–1; Plunkett 4–7–44–0; Denly 3–6–28–1.

England

		B	4/6
1 A. D. Hales *b 10*	11	5	1/1
2 †J. M. Bairstow *c 6 b 9*	68	40	9/2
3 J. E. Root *lbw b 10*	0	2	0
4 *E. J. G. Morgan *c 2 b 6*	8	16	1
5 J. L. Denly *c 5 b 8*	30	29	4
6 S. W. Billings *b 10*	18	16	1
7 D. J. Willey *not out*	1	3	0
8 T. K. Curran *not out*	2	2	0
B 8, lb 7, w 8	23		

6 overs: 62-2   (18.5 overs) 161-6

1/17 2/32 3/83 4/103 5/153 6/154

9 C. J. Jordan, 10 L. E. Plunkett and 11 A. U. Rashid did not bat.

Cottrell 3.5–11–29–3; Thomas 2–7–18–0; Nurse 4–8–32–1; Holder 4–8–26–1; Brathwaite 4–9–33–1; Allen 1–2–8–0.

Umpires: G. O. Brathwaite and N. Duguid.   Third umpire: L. S. Reifer.

Referee: A. J. Pycroft.

WEST INDIES v ENGLAND

Second Twenty20 International

At Basseterre, St Kitts, March 8, 2019 (floodlit). England won by 137 runs. Toss: West Indies. Twenty20 international debut: O. C. McCoy.

With the Wisden Trophy safely tucked away, and the one-dayers squared, it was not until West Indies reached the supposedly safe ground of Twenty20 that the wheels fell off. They were mown down for 45, the second-lowest total in T20 internationals, behind the Netherlands' 39 against Sri Lanka at Chittagong in March 2014. It was an act of collective irresponsibility; only Hetmyer and Brathwaite squeaked into double figures, and the innings did not last 12 overs. Jordan, in particular, cashed in, taking four for six – England's best T20 return – and reinvigorating his chances of World Cup consideration. Things had started awkwardly for England, who slipped to 32 for four, before

BEST BOWLING FOR ENGLAND IN T20 INTERNATIONALS

4-6	**C. J. Jordan**	**v West Indies at Basseterre**	**2018-19**
4-7	**D. J. Willey**	**v West Indies at Basseterre**	**2018-19**
4-10	R. S. Bopara	v West Indies at The Oval	2011
4-19	J. L. Denly	v Sri Lanka at Colombo (RPS)	2018-19
4-22	P. D. Collingwood	v Sri Lanka at Southampton	2006
4-22	J. W. Dernbach	v India at Manchester	2011
4-24	J Lewis	v Australia at Southampton	2005
4-24	S. C. J. Broad	v New Zealand at Auckland	2012-13
4-28	C. J. Jordan	v Sri Lanka at Delhi	2015-16
4-36	**T. K. Curran**	**v West Indies at Gros Islet**	**2018-19**
4-47	**M. W. Parkinson**	**v New Zealand at Napier**	**2019-20**

Root and Billings rebuilt. Root reached his first half-century in the format since the World Twenty20 final against West Indies at Kolkata almost three years earlier; Billings lifted a decent score to a decadent one, thrashing 53 in 15 balls after Root was run out, and finishing with 87, his highest score in international cricket. It provided enough padding to help England to their record victory by runs, surpassing 116 against Afghanistan in Colombo during the 2012 World T20.

Player of the Match: S. W. Billings.

England

	B	4/6
1 A. D. Hales *c 8 b 7*	8	7	0/1
2 †J. M. Bairstow *c 9 b 10*	12	8	2
3 J. E. Root *run out (7/2)*	55	40	7
4 *E. J. G. Morgan *c 2 b 8*	1	3	0
5 J. L. Denly *b 7*	2	6	0
6 S. W. Billings *c 2 b 11*	87	47	10/3
7 D. J. Willey *not out*	13	9	0/1
Lb 2, w 2	4		

6 overs: 39-4   (20 overs) 182-6

1/15 2/27 3/29 4/32 5/114 6/182

8 T. K. Curran, 9 C. J. Jordan, 10 L. E. Plunkett and 11 A. U. Rashid did not bat.

Cottrell 3–8–28–1; Holder 4–9–29–0; Allen 4–7–29–2; Brathwaite 4–7–33–1; Bishoo 2–1–17–0; McCoy 3–3–44–1.

West Indies

	B	4/6
1 C. H. Gayle *c 3 b 7*	5	4	1
2 †S. D. Hope *c 4 b 7*	7	12	1
3 S. O. Hetmyer *c 7 b 10*	10	11	1
4 D. M. Bravo *c 2 b 9*	0	4	0
5 *J. O. Holder *lbw b 9*	0	1	0
6 N. Pooran *c 2 b 9*	1	4	0
7 F. A. Allen *c 3 b 9*	1	3	0
8 C. R. Brathwaite *c 7 b 11*	10	4	0/1
9 D. Bishoo *c 6 b 10*	8	20	1
10 S. S. Cottrell *b 11*	2	4	0
11 O. C. McCoy *not out*	1	4	0

6 overs: 25-6   (11.5 overs) 45

1/12 2/13 3/14 4/14 5/20 6/22 7/33 8/35 9/39

Willey 3–9–18–2; Curran 1–5–1–0; Jordan 2–8–6–4; Rashid 3–11–12–2; Plunkett 2.5–12–8–2.

Umpires: G. O. Brathwaite and L. S. Reifer.   Third umpire: N. Duguid.
Referee: A. J. Pycroft.

WEST INDIES v ENGLAND

Third Twenty20 International

At Basseterre, St Kitts, March 10, 2019 (floodlit). England won by eight wickets. Toss: West Indies. Twenty20 international debut: J. D. Campbell.

The tour finale took place against a backdrop of a bush fire near Warner Park, with ash blowing across the ground. The scene was ripe for metaphor; obligingly, Holder's side went up in smoke. There was a carelessness to their strokeplay that brought to mind the early detractions of T20 cricket as "hit and giggle" – though laughter was in short supply as they made it 20 wickets for 116 since arriving in St Kitts. Willey, for his part, burned bright, which was just as well: with Jofra Archer soon to become available for England, Willey had questioned the wisdom of incorporating a newcomer so late in a World Cup cycle. But he ripped out West Indies' top order with a heady blend of swing and attacking lengths; his figures of four for seven were the second-best for England, behind

Jordan's effort two days earlier. Wood took three for nine, also a career-best, while West Indies had recorded two of their three lowest all-out T20 totals in successive matches. When Hales pounded 15 runs off his first five deliveries from Cottrell, the only real issue was whether England would beat the clock on their fastest completed chase. Morgan made sure they did, thumping Bishoo for six, then sweeping him for four to secure a 3–0 win with 57 balls remaining.

Player of the Match: D. J. Willey.   *Player of the Series:* C. J. Jordan.

West Indies

		B	4/6
1 †S. D. Hope *c 1 b 7*	0	1	0
2 J. D. Campbell *c 5 b 7*	11	14	2
3 S. O. Hetmyer *c 9 b 7*	8	7	1
4 D. M. Bravo *c 2 b 7*	4	5	1
5 *J. O. Holder *c 9 b 5*	11	13	0/1
6 N. Pooran *c 9 b 11*	11	17	0
7 F. A. Allen *b 10*	7	4	0/1
8 C. R. Brathwaite *c 2 b 11*	0	5	0
9 D. Bishoo *not out*	3	3	0
10 S. S. Cottrell *b 11*	4	3	1
11 O. C. McCoy *b 10*	10	6	1/1
B 1, w 1	2		

6 overs: 30-4   (13 overs) 71

1/0 2/10 3/24 4/24 5/45 6/48 7/54 8/56 9/60

Willey 3–14–7–4; Curran 1–2–8–0; Jordan 2–5–14–0; Denly 2–3–14–1; Wood 3–12–9–3; Rashid 2–7–18–2.

England

		B	4/6
1 A. D. Hales *c 2 b 5*	20	13	3/1
2 †J. M. Bairstow *b 9*	37	31	4/2
3 J. E. Root *not out*	4	11	0
4 *E. J. G. Morgan *not out*	10	8	1/1
W 1	1		

6 overs: 39-1   (10.3 overs) 72-2

1/28 2/60

5 J. L. Denly, 6 S. W. Billings, 7 D. J. Willey, 8 T. K. Curran, 9 C. J. Jordan, 10 A. U. Rashid and 11 M. A. Wood did not bat.

Cottrell 1–1–16–0; Allen 4–16–25–0; Holder 3–8–19–1; Bishoo 1.3–6–11–1; Campbell 1–5–1–0.

Umpires: N. Duguid and L. S. Reifer.   Third umpire: G. O. Brathwaite.
Referee: A. J. Pycroft.

IRELAND v ENGLAND IN 2019

One-Day International

CHRIS STOCKS

At Malahide, May 3. England won by four wickets. Toss: England. One-day international debuts: M. R. Adair, J. B. Little, L. J. Tucker; J. C. Archer, B. T. Foakes, D. J. Malan.

This match saw the highly anticipated England debut of Jofra Archer, the Barbados-born fast bowler who had qualified for his adopted country seven weeks earlier. But it was Ben Foakes, also on his one-day international debut, who made the decisive contribution. Having excelled with the bat in his first Test, at Galle in November, he repeated the trick here. His unbeaten 61 from 76 balls rescued an understrength England, missing seven first-choice players – as well as Alex Hales, who

MATCH AWARD ON INTERNATIONAL DEBUT IN TWO FORMATS

Elias Sunny (Bangladesh)	Test v West Indies (2011-12), T20I v Ireland (2012)
Mustafizur Rahman (Bangladesh)	Test v South Africa, ODI v India (both 2015)
L. T. Ngidi (South Africa)	Test v India (2017-18), T20I v Sri Lanka (2016-17)
B. T. Foakes (England)	**Test v Sri Lanka (2018-19), ODI v Ireland (2019)**

had been dropped after news broke that he had failed two drugs tests. Foakes was playing because Sam Billings had dislocated his shoulder with Kent, while England's other wicketkeepers, Jos Buttler and Jonny Bairstow, were rested following the IPL. In a contest reduced to 45 overs a side because of a wet outfield, yet another debutant – Ireland's lively 19-year-old left-arm seamer Josh Little – took four wickets as England slipped to 101 for six in pursuit of 199. A repeat of the previous year's upset against Scotland loomed, before Foakes added a calm, unbroken 98 with his Surrey team-mate Tom Curran. Foakes had earlier shown his expertise with the gloves, waiting for Balbirnie to

Star starters: Josh Little and Ben Foakes excel on their one-day international debuts.

overbalance after he missed a sweep, and whipping off the bails when his back foot was momentarily raised; Ireland were unhappy, arguing the ball should have been called dead. Archer did produce one moment to savour – an eye-catching 90mph yorker to uproot Mark Adair's off stump. Plunkett claimed four wickets and Curran three as Ireland subsided from 55 without loss in the 12th over, but it was Foakes who stole the show.

Player of the Match: B. T. Foakes.

Ireland

*W. T. S. Porterfield c Foakes b Plunkett	17	J. B. Little b Curran		9
P. R. Stirling c Archer b Curran	33	W. B. Rankin not out		5
A. Balbirnie st Foakes b Denly	29			
L. J. Tucker c Morgan b Plunkett	7	B 4, lb 7, w 7		18
K. J. O'Brien c Denly b Curran	4			
†G. C. Wilson c Root b Rashid	8	1/55 (2) 2/60 (1) 3/70 (4)	(43.1 overs)	198
G. H. Dockrell c Morgan b Plunkett	24	4/77 (5) 5/110 (6) 6/111 (3)		
M. R. Adair b Archer	32	7/157 (8) 8/183 (9) 9/183 (7)		
T. J. Murtagh c Foakes b Plunkett	12	10/198 (10)	9 overs: 46-0	

Willey 6–1–26–0; Archer 8–0–40–1; Curran 8.1–1–35–3; Plunkett 7–0–35–4; Rashid 9–0–27–1; Denly 5–0–24–1.

England

J. M. Vince c Dockrell b Little	18	T. K. Curran not out		47
D. J. Malan c Wilson b Little	24			
J. E. Root lbw b Murtagh	7	Lb 5, w 8, nb 1		14
*E. J. G. Morgan c Wilson b Little	0			
J. L. Denly c O'Brien b Rankin	8	1/34 (1) 2/41 (3)	(6 wkts, 42 overs)	199
†B. T. Foakes not out	61	3/46 (4) 4/62 (2)		
D. J. Willey c Adair b Little	20	5/66 (5) 6/101 (7)	9 overs: 41-2	

J. C. Archer, A. U. Rashid and L. E. Plunkett did not bat.

Murtagh 9–1–29–1; Adair 8–0–48–0; Little 8–0–45–4; Rankin 6–0–38–1; O'Brien 2–0–7–0; Dockrell 9–0–27–0.

Umpires: H. D. P. K. Dharmasena and P. A. Reynolds. Third umpire: Aleem Dar.
Referee: R. B. Richardson.

ENGLAND v PAKISTAN IN 2019

Dean Wilson

Twenty20 international (1); England 1, Pakistan 0
One-day internationals (5): England 4, Pakistan 0

Rarely can Pakistan have arrived in England for a series in which the results seemed so inconsequential. That is not to say the matches were uncompetitive, or didn't produce high-quality cricket. Quite the opposite. But the tour's unusually low relevance stemmed from its position in the summer: next up was the World Cup, in which every game would hold the significance of a life's work.

Pakistan's last limited-overs foray to the UK had been a happy one: victory at the 2017 Champions Trophy, including a semi-final win over England. Before that, Pakistan's recent record against them had been poor – four wins in the previous 20 ODIs. By the time the 50-over series was done, they had not added to the tally.

Pakistan comfortably won their three warm-up matches – one-day games against Kent and Northamptonshire, and a T20 against Leicestershire – and their squad was packed with well-known internationals. But, after naming 17 players, they ended up without two familiar faces. Leg-spinner Shadab Khan was struck down with a mystery virus, later confirmed as hepatitis C, supposedly contracted during dental treatment in Rawalpindi. Mohammad Amir, meanwhile, who had struggled for form since the Champions Trophy, caught chickenpox, and missed out on a proper chance to push for a World Cup place (though he was eventually selected).

And pushing for a World Cup place was where the series derived its meaning. No player exemplified this more than Jofra Archer, the Barbados-born fast bowler with an English father and a British passport. Newly eligible for selection after a change in the ECB's residential qualification period, from seven years to three, he now had the opportunity to leapfrog his way into the World Cup 15.

England had also named a one-day squad of 17, including Chris Jordan, Archer's friend and fellow Sussex Bajan. Alex Hales was originally chosen, but dropped after news broke that he had failed two tests for recreational drug use, allowing James Vince to take his place. Scores of 43 and 33 were enough to earn him a World Cup spot, but for others there was less security. Kent's Joe Denly was hoping to show off his versatility: his batting, leg-spin and athletic fielding had long persuaded national selector Ed Smith of his merits. Yet in three ODIs he batted only once and bowled just six overs.

From the outset, Archer's skill and pace left no doubt he would graduate to the World Cup. In four overs on a rain-spoiled day at The Oval, he sent down two maidens and claimed one for six in a spell that had spectators mesmerised. But the question of who would lose out dogged every other fast bowler, and not all of them sounded thrilled at the prospect.

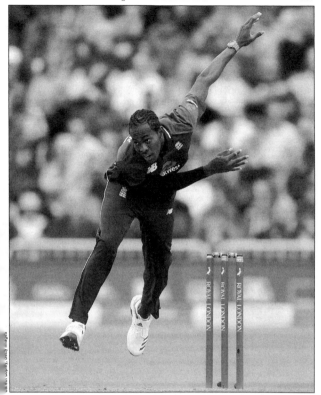

Leaps and bounds: Jofra Archer tears into Pakistan.

Back in March, in the Caribbean, David Willey had questioned the wisdom of disrupting the squad so close to the World Cup. In April, Mark Wood half-jokingly wondered whether Archer might become England's Faustino Asprilla, the Colombian footballer who joined Newcastle United in February 1996, after which their Premier League challenge fell away. Next day, Chris Woakes got his words in a tangle, telling the BBC that it would "not be fair morally" for Archer to replace a player who had helped England to the top of the rankings. All three claimed they were misquoted, but there was no denying the tension.

Eventually, the selectors dispensed with Willey. After four years in and around the side, he had paid the price for an inescapable truth, underlined during this series: the white ball in England simply did not swing. For a player who relied on it, this was bad news.

Not that many bowlers enjoyed themselves during the four ODIs that survived the rain. Seven of the eight innings reached 340, while the eighth – Pakistan's chase at Headingley, where they struggled in vain to avoid a 4–0 defeat – was 297. England averaged 61 per wicket, Pakistan 41. Of the regular bowlers, the meanest was Woakes, with an economy-rate of 6.23 (Archer went at 4.85, but from only 14 overs). In all, 12 players passed 50. It was carnage, which suited England down to the ground.

PAKISTAN TOURING PARTY

*Sarfraz Ahmed, Abid Ali, Asif Ali, Babar Azam, Fahim Ashraf, Fakhar Zaman, Haris Sohail, Hasan Ali, Imad Wasim, Imam-ul-Haq, Junaid Khan, Mohammad Amir, Mohammad Hafeez, Mohammad Hasnain, Shaheen Shah Afridi, Shoaib Malik, Yasir Shah. *Coach:* J. M. Arthur.

Shadab Khan withdrew from the tour with illness, and was replaced by Yasir Shah. Mohammad Amir appeared in only two games before going down with chickenpox.

At Beckenham, April 27. **Pakistanis won by 100 runs.** ‡Pakistanis 358-7 (50 overs) (Imam-ul-Haq 39, Fakhar Zaman 76, Haris Sohail 75, Imad Wasim 117*; I. Qayyum 4-45); **Kent 258** (44.1 overs) (O. G. Robinson 49, A. J. Blake 89; Yasir Shah 3-90). *County debuts:* J. M. Cox, S. Snater. *Imam-ul-Haq and Fakhar Zaman gave the Pakistanis' innings a good start on a chilly morning, with 92 in 14.4 overs. But the real warming-up was supplied by No. 7 Imad Wasim, who belted 117* from 78 balls. Kent's new-ball pair of James Harris (borrowed from Middlesex) and Dutchman Fred Klaassen finished with 1-87 and 1-86; earlier, left-arm spinner Imran Qayyum had slowed the rate with four wickets. An inexperienced Kent side dipped to 10-2 in the seventh, and never got close, although Alex Blake's 48-ball 89, which included six sixes and six fours, dented his former Kent colleague Yasir Shah's figures.*

At Northampton, April 29. **Pakistanis won by eight wickets.** ‡Northamptonshire 273-6 (50 overs) (J. J. Cobb 146*); **Pakistanis 275-2** (41 overs) (Imam-ul-Haq 71, Fakhar Zaman 101, Babar Azam 68*, Sarfraz Ahmed 30*). *Skipper Josh Cobb's seventh and highest List A century – his first for four years – propelled Northamptonshire to a handy score. But the tourists steamed past it with nine overs to spare; the openers flourished again, putting on 157 in 22 overs before Fakhar fell for 101 from 81 balls. Ricardo Vasconcelos had retired hurt (1*) shortly after being hit on the head by Mohammad Hasnain, and played no further part in the match.*

At Leicester, May 1 (floodlit). **Pakistanis won by 58 runs. Pakistanis 200-6** (20 overs) (Fakhar Zaman 52, Babar Azam 101; B. W. M. Mike 3-38); ‡Leicestershire 142 (19.2 overs) (B. W. M. Mike 37). *County debut:* H. G. Munsey. *Babar Azam went in first with Fakhar, and scorched to 101 in 63 balls; the openers put on 104 in 11 overs. Leicestershire made a poor start, losing the Scotland international George Munsey in the first over. They were 39-4 after six, and later 81-8, before Ben Mike and Callum Parkinson (27) shared a face-saving stand of 59.*

ENGLAND v PAKISTAN

Twenty20 International

At Cardiff, May 5. England won by seven wickets. Toss: Pakistan. Twenty20 international debuts: J. C. Archer, B. M. Duckett, B. T. Foakes; Imam-ul-Haq, Mohammad Hasnain.

At any other time, a T20 match between England and Pakistan would have been a box-office affair. Yet this was never going to be anything more than an *amuse-bouche*. After Pakistan chose to bat, Babar Azam once again confirmed his status as the format's No. 1 batsman, hitting 65 from 42 balls and adding an innings-defining 103 with Haris Sohail. All eyes, though, were on Archer, in his first international on English soil. His pace-filled two for 29 was exactly what fans had hoped for, and he also ran out Babar off his own bowling. England needed 174, but quickly lost Duckett, making his T20I debut because Dawid Malan had injured his groin two days earlier in Dublin; it was Duckett's first senior international since the Test series in India in late 2016. Vince fell for 36, but

Root hit a steady 47, and Morgan proved he still had the skills to mix it with the new boys, his pugnacious 57 not out taking England home in the final over, in the company of Denly. Earlier, Willey was lucky to avoid serious injury when his left boot disappeared briefly through a small drainage cover a couple of strides before he bowled the first ball of his second over.

Player of the Match: E. J. G. Morgan.　*Attendance:* 10,235.

Pakistan

		B	4/6
1 Fakhar Zaman c 4 b 8	7	6	1
2 Babar Azam *run out (9)*	65	42	5/3
3 Imam-ul-Haq c 6 b 9	7	10	0
4 Haris Sohail c 7 b 9	50	36	5/1
5 Asif Ali *run out (10)*	3	3	0
6 Imad Wasim *not out*	18	13	3
7 Fahim Ashraf c 5 b 10	17	10	1/1
8 Hasan Ali *not out*	0	0	0
Lb 3, w 3	6		

6 overs: 38-2　　(20 overs)　173-6

1/16 2/31 3/134 4/135 5/139 6/165

9 *†Sarfraz Ahmed, 10 Shaheen Shah Afridi and 11 Mohammad Hasnain did not bat.

Willey 3–6–25–0; Curran 4–9–28–1; Archer 4–9–29–2; Jordan 4–9–41–1; Rashid 4–4–32–0; Denly 1–1–15–0.

England

		B	4/6
1 J. M. Vince c 9 b 6	36	27	3/1
2 B. M. Duckett c 6 b 10	9	7	1
3 J. E. Root c 9 b 8	47	42	5
4 *E. J. G. Morgan *not out*	57	29	5/3
5 J. L. Denly *not out*	20	12	2/1
Lb 2, w 3, nb 1	6		

6 overs: 48-1　　(19.2 overs)　175-3

1/21 2/66 3/131

6 †B. T. Foakes, 7 D. J. Willey, 8 T. K. Curran, 9 J. C. Archer, 10 C. J. Jordan and 11 A. U. Rashid did not bat.

Imad Wasim 4–7–24–1; Fahim Ashraf 3.2–5–43–0; Shaheen Shah Afridi 4–7–35–1; Mohammad Hasnain 4–9–29–0; Hasan Ali 4–4–42–1.

Umpires: M. A. Gough and A. G. Wharf.　Third umpire: R. T. Robinson.
Referee: R. B. Richardson.

ENGLAND v PAKISTAN

First One-Day International

At The Oval, May 8 (day/night). No result. Toss: England.

Rarely do cricket's "I was there" moments come in an abandoned match, but the four overs bowled by Archer of the 19 England sent down before rain called a halt shortly before 4.30 were an exception. Devastatingly quick, he took one for six, with Fakhar Zaman edging Archer's 11th ball to second slip, where Root held a juggling catch. Not until his 15th delivery, a wide, did he concede a run. Babar Azam nibbled at Plunkett, but the bad weather that had delayed the start by 75 minutes returned, and Archer's fire and brimstone gave way to rain and hailstones.

Attendance: 22,503.

Pakistan

Imam-ul-Haq *not out*	42
Fakhar Zaman c Root b Archer	3
Babar Azam c Buttler b Plunkett	16
Haris Sohail *not out*	14
Lb 2, w 3	5

1/10 (2)　2/45 (3)　　(2 wkts, 19 overs)　80
　　　　　　　　　　10 overs: 35-1

Asif Ali, *†Sarfraz Ahmed, Imad Wasim, Fahim Ashraf, Hasan Ali, Shaheen Shah Afridi and Mohammad Amir did not bat.

Woakes 5–0–19–0; Archer 4–2–6–1; Plunkett 4–0–27–1; Stokes 3–0–13–0; Root 2–0–10–0; Rashid 1–0–3–0.

England

J. M. Vince, J. M. Bairstow, J. E. Root, *E. J. G. Morgan, B. A. Stokes, †J. C. Buttler, J. L. Denly,
C. R. Woakes, A. U. Rashid, J. C. Archer, L. E. Plunkett.

Umpires: R. J. Bailey and P. R. Reiffel.   Third umpire: C. B. Gaffaney.
Referee: R. B. Richardson.

ENGLAND v PAKISTAN

Second One-Day International

At Southampton, May 11. England won by 12 runs. Toss: Pakistan.

This game set the tone for a high-scoring series, with Buttler thrashing a 50-ball century, before
Pakistan came close, thanks to a potent response from Fakhar Zaman. Only Buttler himself had
scored a faster ODI hundred for England (46 balls, also against Pakistan, in Dubai in November
2015). He celebrated with the baby-rocking gesture favoured by footballers: his first child, Georgia,
had been born a fortnight earlier. Buttler had raced to 15 after four balls from Yasir Shah, and later
butchered 42 off the last 12 he received from Hasan Ali. In all, he faced 55 deliveries, and hit six
fours and nine sixes; he added an unbroken 162 for the fourth wicket in 14.5 overs with Morgan,
who was no slouch either, carving 71 from 48. "I don't know how you bowl to him," said Pakistan
coach Mickey Arthur. His team, though, did know how to bat. Despite never having chased more
than 327 to win an ODI, they reached 227 for one in the 33rd over, before Fakhar toe-ended Woakes
and was given out on review for 138 from 106. Babar Azam and Asif Ali each hit 51, and Sarfraz
Ahmed took the pursuit deep. But Willey, bowling wide yorkers from round the wicket to the right-
handers, collected two for 17 in a crucial three-over burst, and Plunkett kept his nerve. Earlier, Roy
and Bairstow had fired the ball to all parts in an opening stand of 115 in 19 overs, but Buttler outdid
even them.

Player of the Match: J. C. Buttler.   *Attendance:* 17,028.

England

J. J. Roy c Imad Wasim b Hasan Ali	87	†J. C. Buttler not out	110
J. M. Bairstow c Fakhar Zaman		B 1, lb 3, w 10	14
b Shaheen Shah Afridi	51		
J. E. Root c Haris Sohail b Yasir Shah	40	1/115 (2) 2/177 (1) (3 wkts, 50 overs)	373
*E. J. G. Morgan not out	71	3/211 (3) 10 overs: 57-0	

B. A. Stokes, M. M. Ali, C. R. Woakes, D. J. Willey, A. U. Rashid and L. E. Plunkett did not bat.

Shaheen Shah Afridi 10–0–80–1; Fahim Ashraf 10–0–69–0; Imad Wasim 10–0–63–0; Hasan Ali
10–1–81–1; Yasir Shah 7–0–60–1; Haris Sohail 3–0–16–0.

Pakistan

Imam-ul-Haq c and b Ali	35	Fahim Ashraf c Stokes b Plunkett	3
Fakhar Zaman c Buttler b Woakes	138	Hasan Ali not out	4
Babar Azam c and b Rashid	51	B 2, lb 4, w 10	16
Asif Ali c Stokes b Willey	51		
Haris Sohail c Bairstow b Plunkett	14	1/92 (1) 2/227 (2) (7 wkts, 50 overs)	361
*†Sarfraz Ahmed not out	41	3/233 (4) 4/274 (5)	
Imad Wasim c Buttler b Willey	8	5/323 (4) 6/345 (7) 7/353 (8) 10 overs: 66-0	

Yasir Shah and Shaheen Shah Afridi did not bat.

Woakes 9–0–72–1; Willey 10–0–57–2; Ali 10–0–66–1; Plunkett 9–0–64–2; Rashid 10–0–81–1;
Stokes 2–0–15–0.

Umpires: C. B. Gaffaney and R. T. Robinson.   Third umpire: P. R. Reiffel.
Referee: R. B. Richardson.

ENGLAND v PAKISTAN

Third One-Day International

At Bristol, May 14 (day/night). England won by six wickets. Toss: England.

It said everything about the strides England's one-day cricket had made that the opposition could post 358 for nine and still lose by six wickets with time to spare. As the fans left Nevil Road, it was as if they had just witnessed the most natural thing in the world. In fact, only once before – at Bridgetown in February, when they were set 361 – had England overhauled a higher total. The architects of their latest success were Bairstow and Roy, who put on 159 inside 18 overs to shred a target built on the shoulders of Pakistan opener Imam-ul-Haq's brilliant career-best 151. In the circumstances, Woakes's four for 67 were

---

ENGLAND'S HIGHEST SUCCESSFUL ODI RUN-CHASES

	Overs		
364-4	**48.4**	**v West Indies (360-8) at Bridgetown**	**2018-19**
359-4	**44.5**	**v Pakistan (358-9) at Bristol**	**2019**
350-3	44	v New Zealand (349-7) at Nottingham	2015
341-7	**49.3**	**v Pakistan (340-7) at Nottingham**	**2019**
314-4	44.4	v Australia (310-8) at Chester-le-Street.	2018
309-4	40.1	v Sri Lanka (305-5 in 42 overs) at The Oval	2016
308-2	47.2	v Bangladesh (305-6) at The Oval.	2017
308-5	48.5	v Australia (304-8) at Melbourne	2017-18
306-5	47.2	v Pakistan (304-9) at Karachi	2000-01
304-7	48.2	v Australia (299-7) at Leeds	2015
301-9	49.5	v West Indies (300) at Bridgetown	2006-07

---

near-miraculous. England's high-octane approach never let up, despite Jos Buttler taking a break and allowing Bairstow to keep wicket, in case he had to at the World Cup. Roy, badly dropped on 21 at mid-off by Shaheen Shah Afridi off Hasan Ali, eventually fell for 76 off 55, while Bairstow finished with 128 off 93. In a light reshuffle, Stokes and Ali went in ahead of Morgan, who later learned he would be suspended for a match because of England's poor over-rate. The Pakistan innings included only seven overs of spin, despite Denly supposedly there to audition for the World Cup role of back-up slow bowler to Ali and Adil Rashid. He bowled just one over of leg-breaks, which did not augur well for his prospects.

Player of the Match: J. M. Bairstow.   *Attendance:* 7,883.

Pakistan

Imam-ul-Haq b Curran 151	Hasan Ali not out. 18
Fakhar Zaman c Root b Woakes 2	Shaheen Shah Afridi c and b Willey 7
Babar Azam b Woakes 15	Junaid Khan not out. 0
Haris Sohail run out (Curran) 41	Lb 1, w 9 10
*†Sarfraz Ahmed c sub (C. J. Jordan)	
b Plunkett . 27	1/7 (2) 2/27 (3) (9 wkts, 50 overs) 358
Asif Ali c Roy b Woakes. 52	3/95 (4) 4/162 (5)
Imad Wasim c and b Woakes 22	5/287 (6) 6/310 (1) 7/322 (7)
Fahim Ashraf lbw b Curran. 13	8/335 (8) 9/348 (10) 10 overs: 59-2

Woakes 10–0–67–4; Willey 10–0–86–1; Ali 6–0–32–0; Plunkett 9–0–55–1; Curran 10–0–74–2; Stokes 4–0–34–0; Denly 1–0–9–0.

England

J. J. Roy c Asif Ali b Fahim Ashraf 76	*E. J. G. Morgan not out 17
J. M. Bairstow b Junaid Khan 128	Lb 3, w 8, nb 1 12
J. E. Root c Babar Azam b Imad Wasim . . . 43	
B. A. Stokes run out (Shaheen Shah Afridi) 37	1/159 (1) 2/234 (2) (4 wkts, 44.5 overs) 359
M. M. Ali not out. 46	3/278 (3) 4/324 (4) 10 overs: 74-0

J. L. Denly, C. R. Woakes, D. J. Willey, T. K. Curran and L. E. Plunkett did not bat.

Junaid Khan 8–0–57–1; Shaheen Shah Afridi 10–0–83–0; Hasan Ali 8–0–55–0; Imad Wasim 7–0–58–1; Fahim Ashraf 9–0–75–1; Haris Sohail 2–0–19–0; Asif Ali 0.5–0–9–0.

Umpires: M. A. Gough and P. R. Reiffel.　Third umpire: C. B. Gaffaney.
Referee: R. B. Richardson.

ENGLAND v PAKISTAN

Fourth One-Day International

At Nottingham, May 17 (day/night). England won by three wickets. Toss: England.

Another game, another big target, another win for the hosts – this time with just three balls to spare. Once more, with the World Cup in mind, England made a switch: Vince came in for Jonny Bairstow, and put on 94 in just 13.3 overs with Roy, who went on to his eighth ODI hundred. He later revealed he had almost missed the game after spending the night in hospital with his baby daughter, Everly, who had a stomach infection. She was fine by the morning, and Roy looked in rude health too, striking 114 from 89 balls to set up England's 17th successful chase at home in a row. It wasn't as though Pakistan played badly. Imam-ul-Haq retired hurt on three following a blow to the left elbow from Wood, playing his first international in more than two months after ankle trouble, and registering 92mph in his first over. But Babar Azam hit 115, and was well supported by fifties from Fakhar Zaman and Mohammad Hafeez. Even so, from 220 for one with more than 13 overs to go, Pakistan's eventual 340 for seven felt a touch light. Their bowlers kept them in the hunt, reducing England from 201 for one in the 28th to 258 for six after 40, including stand-in captain Buttler (Eoin Morgan was serving his over-rate ban) and Ali for ducks. But Stokes held things together, and received handy support from Tom Curran, who had earlier taken four wickets, and Rashid. Had Pakistan appealed for a run-out when Curran was on seven, the technology would have backed them up – to make it 272 for seven. Instead, England headed for Leeds planning to wrap up the series 4–0.

Player of the Match: J. J. Roy.　*Attendance:* 16,273.

Pakistan

Imam-ul-Haq not out	6	*†Sarfraz Ahmed not out	21
Fakhar Zaman c Wood b Curran	57	Hasan Ali c Denly b Curran	1
Babar Azam c Archer b Curran	115			
Mohammad Hafeez c sub (C. J. Jordan) b Wood	59	Lb 4, w 7	11
Shoaib Malik hit wkt b Wood	41	1/116 (2) 2/220 (4) (7 wkts, 50 overs) 340
Asif Ali c Wood b Archer	17	3/249 (3) 4/280 (6)
Imad Wasim b Curran	12	5/298 (7) 6/316 (5) 7/319 (9) 10 overs: 63-0

Junaid Khan and Mohammad Hasnain did not bat.

Imam-ul-Haq, when 3, retired hurt at 9-0 and resumed at 319-7.

Archer 10–0–62–1; Wood 10–0–71–2; Denly 5–0–27–0; Curran 10–0–75–4; Rashid 7–0–49–0; Stokes 4–0–22–0; Ali 4–0–30–0.

England

J. J. Roy c Sarfraz Ahmed b Mohammad Hasnain	114	J. L. Denly c and b Junaid Khan	17
J. M. Vince b Mohammad Hasnain	43	T. K. Curran b Hasan Ali	31
J. E. Root c Mohammad Hafeez b Imad Wasim	36	A. U. Rashid not out	12
B. A. Stokes not out	71	Lb 5, w 12	17
*†J. C. Buttler c Mohammad Hasnain b Imad Wasim	0	1/94 (2) 2/201 (1) (7 wkts, 49.3 overs) 341
M. M. Ali c Fakhar Zaman b Shoaib Malik	0	3/208 (3) 4/208 (5)
		5/216 (6) 6/258 (7) 7/319 (8) 10 overs: 68-0

J. C. Archer and M. A. Wood did not bat.

Junaid Khan 10–0–85–1; Hasan Ali 9.3–0–57–1; Imad Wasim 10–0–62–2; Mohammad Hasnain 10–0–80–2; Mohammad Hafeez 8–0–48–0; Shoaib Malik 2–0–4–1.

Umpires: C. B. Gaffaney and A. G. Wharf.　Third umpire: P. R. Reiffel.
Referee: R. B. Richardson.

ENGLAND v PAKISTAN

Fifth One-Day International

At Leeds, May 19. England won by 54 runs. Toss: England.

England finished with another tour de force, racking up 351 for nine – the highest score at Headingley in 41 ODIs spread across 46 years. No one made a hundred, but it didn't matter: Root led the way on his home ground with 84 off 73, while the returning Morgan smashed five sixes in his 64-ball 76. Five others passed 20, with Curran's late flurry – an unbeaten 29 from 15 – taking them beyond their 339 for six against South Africa here two years earlier. Pakistan's reply was instantly on life support after a triple-wicket burst from Woakes, before Babar Azam and Sarfraz Ahmed restored some competitiveness in a stand of 146. But both were run out by quick-witted fielding. Babar had 80 when he set off for a sharp single, only to be sent back by Sarfraz, the striker; Buttler ran round to short square leg to gather the ball and return it to Rashid, who – his back to the stumps – executed a clever no-look direct hit. After Rashid then produced a superb left-handed return catch to dismiss Shoaib Malik, Sarfraz was outsmarted on 97: Buttler intercepted a dab off Moeen Ali with his right boot, then broke the stumps before Sarfraz, having left his crease, could scramble back. Woakes completed his third ODI haul of five or more, before No. 11 Mohammad Hasnain scored 28, his first runs in senior cricket, after four ducks and a nought not out in 16 previous matches.

Player of the Match: C. R. Woakes.   *Attendance:* 13,504.

Player of the Series: J. J. Roy.

England

J. M. Vince c Fakhar Zaman		
b Shaheen Shah Afridi .	33	
J. M. Bairstow c Shaheen Shah Afridi		
b Imad Wasim .	32	
J. E. Root c Asif Ali b Mohammad Hasnain	84	
*E. J. G. Morgan c Abid Ali		
b Shaheen Shah Afridi .	76	

D. J. Willey b Shaheen Shah Afridi 14
T. K. Curran not out 29
A. U. Rashid not out 2

Lb 2, w 10, nb 1 13

†J. C. Buttler c Babar Azam b Imad Wasim 34
B. A. Stokes c Fakhar Zaman b Hasan Ali . 21
M. M. Ali lbw b Imad Wasim 0
C. R. Woakes c Babar Azam
      b Shaheen Shah Afridi . 13

1/63 (1) 2/105 (2) (9 wkts, 50 overs) 351
3/222 (4) 4/257 (3)
5/272 (5) 6/272 (7)
7/295 (8) 8/310 (6)
9/336 (9)

10 overs: 95-1

Hasan Ali 10–0–70–1; Shaheen Shah Afridi 10–0–82–4; Mohammad Hasnain 8–0–67–1; Imad Wasim 10–0–53–3; Fakhar Zaman 4–0–23–0; Shoaib Malik 4–0–29–0; Mohammad Hafeez 4–0–25–0.

Pakistan

Fakhar Zaman c Root b Woakes 0
Abid Ali lbw b Woakes 5
Babar Azam run out (Buttler/Rashid) 80
Mohammad Hafeez lbw b Woakes 0
*†Sarfraz Ahmed run out (Buttler)........ 97
Shoaib Malik c and b Rashid............ 4
Asif Ali c Stokes b Willey.............. 22
Imad Wasim c Buttler b Woakes......... 25
Hasan Ali c Willey b Woakes 11

Shaheen Shah Afridi not out 19
Mohammad Hasnain st Buttler b Rashid... 28

Lb 3, w 3 6

1/0 (1) 2/6 (2) 3/6 (4) (46.5 overs) 297
4/152 (3) 5/189 (6) 6/193 (5)
7/232 (8) 8/250 (7) 9/250 (9)
10/297 (11)

10 overs: 55-3

Woakes 10–2–54–5; Willey 9–1–55–1; Curran 6–0–40–0; Stokes 4–0–28–0; Ali 10–0–63–0; Rashid 7.5–0–54–2.

Umpires: M. A. Gough and P. R. Reiffel.   Third umpire: C. B. Gaffaney.
Referee: R. B. Richardson.

ENGLAND v IRELAND IN 2019

Hugh Chevallier

Test match (1): England 1, Ireland 0

Ten days earlier, an Irishman had raised the World Cup to an ecstatic Lord's. But Eoin Morgan was captain of England, and it felt as if, at least for 2019, that might be as close as Irish cricket came to glory. Not a bit of it. On a scorching July morning, Tim Murtagh – 13 seasons a mucker of Morgan's at Middlesex – gave an undercooked England a roasting, all out for 85. No one knew this ground like he did; no one had taken a cheaper Test five-for at Lord's than his five for 13. Though he could not engineer perhaps the biggest Test upset of all, his control was sublime. Not brisk, not brazen, not brash, Murtagh destroyed England – just as Stuart Broad and Chris Woakes did Ireland 48 hours later.

Ireland had every right to be fired up. Unwanted at the World Cup because the ICC preferred to milk the cash cows of Indian and English cricket rather than cultivate the wider 50-over game; up against a weakened team; and given only a four-day Test, they responded in a manner befitting the most eloquent of nations. This was the first Test in England scheduled for fewer than five days since 1949, and only the second, after South Africa v Zimbabwe in December 2017, since the ICC sanctioned a reduced duration – as long as both sides agreed.

Much of the talk beforehand was about which of England's white-ball heroes would be fit and willing to return to St John's Wood. Ben Stokes, Jos Buttler and Adil Rashid opted for rest, while Jofra Archer and Mark Wood were nursing side strains. Happy to play were Joe Root and Jonny Bairstow (Test captain and Test keeper), Chris Woakes and Moeen Ali, whose iffy form had seen him dropped from the second half of the World Cup. Jason Roy, named as an opener in the team of the tournament, joined his Surrey colleague Rory Burns at the top of the order. Might they see off the new ball more effectively than the myriad combinations tried by England since the retirement of Andrew Strauss in 2012? Their other debutant was Olly Stone,

CHEAPEST TEST FIVE-FORS AT LORD'S

5-13	T. J. Murtagh	**Ireland v England**	**2019**
5-15	E. S. H. Giddins	England v Zimbabwe	2000
5-16	F. R. Foster	England v South Africa	1912
5-16	A. R. Caddick	England v West Indies	2000
6-17	**C. R. Woakes**	**England v Ireland**	**2019**
5-17	G. A. R. Lock	England v New Zealand	1958
5-20	D. L. Underwood	England v Pakistan	1974
5-20	J. M. Anderson	England v India	2018
5-21	C. M. Old	England v India	1974
6-22	B. A. Stokes	England v West Indies	2017
5-25	S. F. Barnes	England v South Africa	1912

England drew against Pakistan, and won every other Test.

Philip Brown, Popperfoto/Getty Images

Stirling castled: Chris Woakes removes Paul Stirling, and the Irish collapse gathers pace.

capable of 90mph, but worryingly injury-prone. His opportunity arose because Jimmy Anderson had not fully recovered from a torn calf muscle. Jack Leach and Sam Curran were given the chance to reinvigorate fledgling Test careers. Somerset's Lewis Gregory was also in the squad, but missed out on a Test debut.

Ireland had endured a narrow defeat at home by Pakistan 14 months before, and a heavier one by Afghanistan in India in March 2019. Those Tests were in Malahide and Dehradun, so this was an altogether bigger stage. Intriguingly, though, the Irish had more first-class appearances at Lord's than England: helped by Murtagh and Paul Stirling being Middlesex regulars, they edged it 93–88. Most of their side had county experience, including debutant seamer Mark Adair who – like the captain, William Porterfield – had turned out for Warwickshire.

The six England players uninvolved in the World Cup had all recently taken part in first-class matches. Not so the Irish, whose red-ball preparation amounted to a two-day game against Middlesex Seconds at Merchant Taylors' School, Northwood; Ireland were unable to bat because of rain. But for much of the Test, it felt as if England were the novices.

IRELAND TOURING PARTY

*W. T. S. Porterfield, M. R. Adair, A. Balbirnie, A. R. McBrine, J. A. McCollum, T. J. Murtagh, K. J. O'Brien, W. B. Rankin, S. Singh, P. R. Stirling, S. R. Thompson, L. J. Tucker, G. C. Wilson, C. A. Young. *Coach:* G. X. Ford. *Assistant coach:* R. J. Cassell. *Batting and fielding coach:* B. F. Smith. *Manager:* C. M. Siddell. *Analyst:* S. D. Irvine. *Head of medical services and physiotherapy:* M. Rausa. *Strength and conditioning coach:* B. A. Connor. *Media manager:* C. D. Easdown.

ENGLAND v IRELAND

Only Specsavers Test

At Lord's, July 24–26. England won by 143 runs. Toss: England. Test debuts: J. J. Roy, O. P. Stone; M. R. Adair.

What was the world coming to? On the first day, a new prime minister sacked more cabinet ministers than anyone knew could hugger-mugger round a table; on the second, the UK recorded its hottest-ever temperature, 38.7°C (101.7°F), in Cambridge; and on the last, fleetingly, there was a distinct chance that Ireland, in their third Test, would beat England, in their 1,011th. In the event, an absurd match took a different course, and Ireland vaporised for 38, the lowest Test offering at Lord's, beating 42 by India in 1974. If only climate change and one or two other problems facing the Boris Johnson administration would melt away quite so quickly.

After almost seven weeks of the World Cup, the sight of 13 players clad in white, and a ball clad in red, felt strangely novel. It did not take long for a sold-out Lord's to get back in the swing. Root opted to bat, despite the pitch having an appropriately emerald tinge, and a Surrey pair strode out. In the second over, Roy was plumb lbw to fellow Test debutant Mark Adair, only to be saved by umpire Palliyaguruge's shout of no-ball. The reprieve lasted three deliveries. Murtagh, once a Surrey man himself, but long of the St John's Wood parish, clipped Roy's bat, and Stirling at first slip didn't so much catch the ball as sandwich it between his wrists. They all count.

TWO SURREY PLAYERS OPENING FOR ENGLAND IN A TEST

T. W. Hayward and J. B. Hobbs (1) v Australia at Lord's	1909
J. B. Hobbs and D. R. Jardine (1) v Australia at Melbourne	1928-29
M. J. Stewart and J. H. Edrich (2) v West Indies at Manchester	1963
J. H. Edrich and K. F. Barrington (2) v India at Leeds	1967
M. A. Butcher and A. J. Stewart (3) v Australia at Sydney	1998-99
R. J. Burns and J. J. Roy (4) v Ireland at Lord's	**2019**

Only first instance is shown; figures in brackets indicate number of Tests for the partnership.

After briefly looking a million dollars, Denly then looked a bit of a chump, falling to the Adair nip-backer. Survival for 28 balls did not give Denly's uncertain international renaissance the lift it needed. However, set amid the rubble of the England innings, it came to resemble a beacon of permanence, as batsman after batsman tripped over each other in an undefying rush to and from the Pavilion.

The surface was tricky, to be sure, but this tricky? In 28 deliveries, 36 for one became 43 for seven. If the pitch was not perfect, Murtagh was. Not Glenn McGrath's match for height or pace, he was his equal for accuracy. He hit a precise, fullish length on off, moved it both ways at about 77mph, and never allowed the batsmen to settle. So when Bairstow was distracted by something and backed away with Murtagh mid-delivery, it was inevitable that the ball clipped the off bail. None of the England line-up knew how to cope, playing round their pads or with hard hands. Bairstow resorted to standing so far outside his crease the umpires intervened, telling him he was in danger of damaging the protected area, as prohibited by Law 41. Not that he hung around long enough: Murtagh bowled him through the gate for a six-ball duck. After 78 minutes, he had a five-for.

The introduction of Thompson let the tension slip, before Rankin, against the team he had played for at Sydney in 2013-14, helped administer the last rites. England were bowled out for 85 in 23.4 overs, their shortest Test innings at home. There can have been few more ignominious falls from grace: world champions one week, humbled by neophytes the next. Despite Ireland's over-rate being as execrable as England's batting, the bloodbath

How's that for starters? Tim Murtagh ends Jason Roy's brief first Test innings.

was complete before the end of an extended first session: as part of the revised playing hours of a four-day Test, lunch was at 1.15 and tea 4.10.

The Ireland openers saw out 12 anodyne overs before Porterfield flapped Curran's first ball, an arrant half-tracker, to midwicket. Six overs later, McCollum dragged on, but his colleagues took advantage of two drops, both off Broad. Bairstow, who had spent the World Cup haring round the boundary, seemed to forget his station behind the stumps, and watched an edge from Balbirnie, on ten, sail past for four; soon afterwards, Root was culpable, spilling a low but catchable chance at first slip when Stirling had 17. Until now, Woakes's Test record at Lord's had been exceptional: 18 wickets at ten, plus 261 runs at 130. But he followed a silver duck with a spell of utter ordinariness. Leach was distinctly worse, bowling full toss after full toss in his first home Test, though his unexpected moment in an unpredictable game would come.

At tea, the score was 127 for two, and England were facing a long evening. But once again wickets started to tumble. Stirling had the worse of a tight lbw call – Broad wisely removing fielders from the equation – and Balbirnie his middle stump uprooted by an 89mph inswinger from Stone, who quickly accounted for Wilson with a vicious ball he deflected to slip. Once Thompson had foolishly shouldered arms to Broad, and Adair edged Curran into his stumps, Ireland were 149 for seven; five had gone for 17, and a sweet day was turning a little sour. But O'Brien was still there, and with the tail he kept runs coming. Murtagh was particularly frisky, and four unorthodox cross-bat thwacks brought 16, three more than he had conceded in nine overs. As strains of the Blarney Army singing "Cockles and mussels, alive, alive-o!" rang around Lord's, Rankin missed a heave at Ali, and the day's 20th wicket was the first (and last) for spin. Not since 1912, when South Africa lost at The Oval, had so many fallen on the first day of a Test in the UK. Ireland led by 122.

England had endured an absolute stinker and, with an over to face, there was scope for it to get worse. Unwilling to expose Roy, they sent in Leach, ten places higher than his

ENGLAND'S SHORTEST TEST INNINGS AT HOME

Balls	Overs	Score		
142	**23.4**	**85**	**v Ireland at Lord's**	**2019**
167	**27.5**	**67**	**v Australia at Leeds**	**2019**
180	30	89†	v West Indies at Birmingham	1995
188	47*	62	v Australia at Lord's	1888
197	32.5	71	v West Indies at Manchester	1976
200	50*	53	v Australia at Lord's	1888
203	33.5	102	v Australia at Leeds	2009
219	36.3	76	v South Africa at Leeds	1907
220	55*	77	v Australia at The Oval	1882
222	37	112	v Australia at Nottingham	1921
222	37	103	v Australia at Lord's	2015

* *Four-ball overs.* † *One man absent.* *England won both Tests in 2019 and the one in 1907, and lost the rest.*

---

natural home. Since last reaching double figures, in Sri Lanka in November 2018, he had totted up 56 runs in 19 innings at an average below four. (It was only the second time, after Harry Butt for England against South Africa at Port Elizabeth in 1895-96, that anyone had batted at No. 11 and No. 1 on the same day in a Test.) Against the odds, Leach survived Murtagh's over. Next morning, Burns departed for a twitchy six, just as he had the day before. The sun beat down, the mercury rose, the crowd broiled; life melted from the pitch. Leach and Roy grew into their partnership, the nightwatchman standing taller with every boundary. And there were quite a few: straight-drives, caresses through cover – and the occasional miscue.

Leach had an unusual problem. Because he batted in glasses, he struggled to stop them steaming up once his headband had become drenched with sweat. But on he went: by lunch England had wiped out the deficit; soon after came the century stand. Leach outlasted Roy, who did a Denly: for every shot that brought an argh, there were three or four that brought an ahh. He seemed destined for a maiden century after twice being dropped, on 72 and 92. But three balls after the second life, Adair did cling on, and the dream lay shattered. Leach had at least increased his first-class career-best from the 66 he made against Lancashire in 2018.

England hadn't collapsed for, oh, well over a session, so one was overdue. Root helped out, thinking better of a single and selling Denly down the river, before Bairstow, all at sea, failed to overturn an lbw call that had him sinking to his first Test pair, and his fifth duck in seven Test innings at home. In heat that peaked in London at over 35°C, the Irish bowlers were industry personified. England's decline from 171 for one to 248 for eight, though not their most precipitous, was alarming, given the lead stood at 126. Then Curran,

---

LOWEST FIRST-INNINGS TOTALS TO WIN A TEST

45	England beat Australia by 13 runs at Sydney...................	1886-87
63	Australia beat England by seven runs at The Oval..............	1882
75	England beat Australia by 94 runs at Melbourne	1894-95
76	England beat South Africa by 53 runs at Leeds	1907
85	**England beat Ireland by 143 runs at Lord's**	**2019**
92	England beat South Africa by 210 runs at Cape Town...........	1898-99
99	Pakistan beat England by 71 runs at Dubai	2011-12
102	Pakistan beat New Zealand by 65 runs at Faisalabad...........	1990-91
104	India beat Australia by 13 runs at Mumbai....................	2004-05
112	Australia beat England by 229 runs at Melbourne	1901-02
113	England beat Australia by 126 runs at Sydney.................	1887-88

Totals are the first of four innings.

The last shall be first... Jack Leach, No. 11 in England's first innings, bats at No. 1 in the second.

reprising his lower-order heroics from 2018, crashed 37 from 29 balls. England were 303 for nine when an electrical storm scurried the players from the field; the first two innings had been completed on the opening day, and the third spanned three. Just.

First ball next morning, Thompson ran in, and Stone's leg stump cartwheeled towards the Nursery Ground. That inswinger delivered a warning: batsmen beware! England had never successfully defended a target as low as 182 at Lord's, yet the atmospherics – dreich skies, mugginess, occasional mizzle – suggested they might make a fist of it. And how.

The players had trooped on and off after just one ball, then rain interrupted Ireland's innings after seven. Following the resumption, they made it to a streaky, creaky 11 before Woakes broke through, Porterfield the victim. As abject as England were on day one, they were adroit on day three. Behind the stumps, Bairstow swapped cumbersome for lissom, while in front Broad and Woakes allied a perfect length with constant movement – in the air and off the seam. No batsman stayed long enough to develop an innings, and Ireland hurtled not to the triumph that had seemed so possible the previous evening, but to humiliation. Their heart, their hard work, their courage deserved better. In the end, Woakes took a career-best six for 17 and Broad four for 19, as Ireland were poleaxed for 38. After the cheapest Lord's five-for came the cheapest six-for.

Oddities abounded: for the first time, both keepers got pairs; for the first time in 132 years, both teams were dismissed in a session; only once in 2,352 Tests had an innings lasted fewer than Ireland's 94 balls, when South Africa were filleted in 75 at Edgbaston in 1924; in eight innings, Nos 6 and 7 collected 13 runs – a record low that included six ducks. Summing it up was the fact that the match award went to a No. 11 for his batting at the top of the order.

Player of the Match: M. J. Leach.   *Attendance:* 77,162.

Close of play: first day, England 0-0 (Leach 0, Burns 0); second day, England 303-9 (Broad 21, Stone 0).

England

R. J. Burns c Wilson b Murtagh	6	– (2) c Wilson b Rankin	6
J. J. Roy c Stirling b Murtagh	5	– (3) b Thompson	72
J. L. Denly lbw b Adair	23	– (4) run out (O'Brien/McBride)	10
*J. E. Root lbw b Adair	2	– (5) c Wilson b Adair	31
†J. M. Bairstow b Murtagh	0	– (6) lbw b Adair	0
M. M. Ali c Wilson b Murtagh	0	– (7) c Wilson b Rankin	9
C. R. Woakes lbw b Murtagh	0	– (8) c Balbirnie b Adair	13
S. M. Curran c McCollum b Rankin	18	– (9) c McCollum b Thompson	37
S. C. J. Broad c Wilson b Rankin	3	– (10) not out	21
O. P. Stone b Adair	19	– (11) b Thompson	0
M. J. Leach not out	1	– (1) c Adair b Murtagh	92
Lb 5, w 1, nb 2	8	B 1, lb 7, nb 4	12

1/8 (2) 2/36 (3) 3/36 (1)   (23.4 overs) 85
4/42 (4) 5/42 (5) 6/42 (7)
7/43 (6) 8/58 (9) 9/67 (8) 10/85 (10)

1/26 (2) 2/171 (3)   (77.5 overs) 303
3/182 (1) 4/194 (4)
5/194 (6) 6/219 (7) 7/239 (5)
8/248 (8) 9/293 (9) 10/303 (11)

Murtagh 9–2–13–5; Adair 7.4–1–32–3; Thompson 4–1–30–0; Rankin 3–1–5–2. *Second innings*—Murtagh 18–3–52–1; Adair 20–7–66–3; Rankin 17–1–86–2; Thompson 12.5–0–44–3; McBride 10–1–47–0.

Ireland

*W. T. S. Porterfield c Leach b Curran	14	– c Bairstow b Woakes	2
J. A. McCollum b Curran	19	– c Root b Woakes	11
A. Balbirnie b Stone	55	– c Root b Broad	5
P. R. Stirling lbw b Broad	36	– b Woakes	0
K. J. O'Brien not out	28	– lbw b Broad	4
†G. C. Wilson c Root b Stone	0	– lbw b Woakes	0
S. R. Thompson b Broad	0	– c Root b Woakes	4
M. R. Adair b Curran	3	– b Broad	8
A. R. McBride b Broad	11	– c Root b Woakes	0
T. J. Murtagh c Burns b Stone	16	– b Woakes	2
W. B. Rankin b Ali	7	– not out	0
B 10, lb 6, w 2	18	B 1, lb 1	2

1/32 (1) 2/45 (2) 3/132 (4)   (58.2 overs) 207
4/138 (3) 5/138 (6) 6/141 (7)
7/149 (8) 8/174 (9) 9/195 (10) 10/207 (11)

1/11 (1) 2/18 (3)   (15.4 overs) 38
3/19 (4) 4/24 (2)
5/24 (6) 6/24 (5) 7/32 (8)
8/36 (7) 9/36 (9) 10/38 (10)

Broad 19–5–60–3; Woakes 10–2–34–0; Stone 12–3–29–3; Curran 10–3–28–3; Leach 3–0–26–0; Ali 4.2–1–14–1. *Second innings*—Broad 8–3–19–4; Woakes 7.4–2–17–6.

Umpires: Aleem Dar and R. S. A. Palliyaguruge.   Third umpire: P. Wilson.
Referee: A. J. Pycroft.

ENGLAND v AUSTRALIA IN 2019

REVIEW BY GEOFF LEMON

Test matches (5): England 2 (56pts), Australia 2 (56pts)

Before a contest, the participants often scuffle for the designation of underdog. There is a power to being unfancied: it lessens expectation and, especially in team sports, cultivates a sense of embattlement that can help form solidarity, a group against the world. Where boxers are obliged to talk themselves up, captains tend to talk themselves down, citing the (inevitably world-class) quality of their opponents, lacing their speech with qualifiers, pleading that their own side can hope to win only by completing to perfection every step of an undisclosed process.

In the Ashes of 2019, both England and Australia seemed like underdogs. That may defy the dictates of logic, but in advance each team appeared irretrievably flawed, straining against their own shortcomings even before the opposition arrived to exert any force the other way. With each passing Test, this apprehension was borne out. A series win for either side would have come in spite of limitations, not by transcending them. A draw, the first in the Ashes since 1972, felt entirely apt (though the new ICC Test Championship scored it 56 points apiece).

Yet this was no dull stalemate. It was exhilarating. The lasting impression was not of poor quality, but of pure anarchic fun. Sporting audiences say they want to see the best standard of play, but most of all they want to see a level fight. Here were teams evenly matched. And in their struggle came a few truly outstanding performances worthy of any era. Each of the first four Tests was defined by a single player: Steven Smith at Edgbaston, Jofra Archer at Lord's, Ben Stokes at Headingley, Smith again at Old Trafford, his return after concussion ensuring the urn's destination.

The flaws, it must be emphasised, were strictly in the batting. Ahead of the series, each team boasted a blue-chip bowling attack. England had the vast experience of James Anderson and Stuart Broad, both enjoying a late-career bloom, and a class operator of swing in Chris Woakes. Losing Anderson to

MOST TEST WICKETS IN A SERIES WITHOUT A FIVE-FOR

	Avge			
29	19.62	P. J. Cummins	Australia v England	2019
28	25.03	W. M. Clark	Australia v India	1977-78
27	16.14	J. Garner	West Indies v England	1985-86
27	17.85	M. D. Marshall	West Indies v England	1985-86
26	14.26	J. Garner	West Indies v England	1980
26	17.03	S. R. Clark	Australia v England	2006-07
25	23.84	D. K. Lillee	Australia v England	1974-75
25	25.08	M. Ntini	South Africa v England	2004-05
25	27.52	J. Garner	West Indies v Pakistan	1976-77

All five-Test series apart from Lillee (six).

Arms control: the Australians celebrate the moment at Old Trafford when they retain the Ashes.

injury after just four overs was a blow, but then came Archer – a revelation after qualifying from his native Barbados just in time for the World Cup, where in a few games he had become England's most important short-form bowler. His big-stage delivery, and record in first-class cricket, accurately predicted he was just as capable of an impact in Tests.

Australia, meanwhile, had finally got the band together. For several years, there had been a messianic promise of an unprecedented bounty of pace – proper pace, nostril-tingling stuff, via four young quicks who had been tracked through school ranks and on to the international scene. James Pattinson, furious outswingers, a five-for on Test debut; Mitchell Starc, the left-arm equivalent, crashing through the 2015 World Cup; Josh Hazlewood, the most accurate, using his height for extra bounce and movement; Patrick Cummins, perhaps the fastest at first, maturing into the most dangerous and relentless of the lot.

Never, though, had all been available at once. Each had missed years to injury – stress fractures of the back most commonly, the market price of pace, but also muscle strains and broken toes and training mishaps, their bodies pushed to the limit. Not until the 2017-18 Ashes had even three been available – Starc, Cummins and Hazlewood demolished England 4–0. Finally, in the last year of the decade that had begun with talk of them, all four were fit. Add the canny Peter Siddle after a productive summer and a half at Essex, and off-spinner Nathan Lyon, poised to pass Dennis Lillee's 355 Test wickets, and Australia had a formidable ensemble.

The two attacks would take on batting orders made of rice paper: fragile, soluble and, like the wrapping of a Vietnamese roll, transparently unable to conceal the raw jumble within. England had been searching for Alastair Cook's new opening partner ever since Andrew Strauss retired in 2012; in the end, Cook retired too, leaving them in need of two replacements. The No. 3 spot had lacked a regular tenant since Jonathan Trott in 2013. All three places had seen a flood of contenders.

For 2019, Surrey captain Rory Burns rose to the surface, a left-hander who faced up with a mangled stance that suggested he had just tumbled down three flights of stairs, and Jason Roy, whose buccaneering had worked wonders in the World Cup, but didn't translate to Tests. Joe Root as captain was most comfortable at four, but now bowed to the Australian orthodoxy of his coach, Trevor Bayliss, that the best player must bat at three. Joe Denly, initially in the frame as a Twenty20 handyman, somehow took Root's old spot, before displacing Roy as an opener. Then came a flurry of all-rounders: Stokes was a certainty, but his best position wasn't clear; Moeen Ali tended to freeze in Australian headlights, and was dropped after the First Test; Jonny Bairstow and Jos Buttler were wicketkeepers and attacking batsmen who seemed like luxury picks on their own, never mind together. Bairstow's Test form had waned, but he curled a lip territorially at suggestions he might concentrate on one discipline, and give up the gloves. He averaged 23, and was later omitted from the Test squad for New Zealand.

For Australia, Smith and David Warner were a different kind of gamble. The former captain and vice-captain had been banned after their 2018 ball-tampering adventure, and first returned for the World Cup, where Warner in particular flourished. Neither had played a Test in 16 months. But their records – 44 centuries between them – demanded inclusion. Their Cape Town collaborator, Cameron Bancroft, was recalled on the less convincing grounds of second-division county runs and a squad practice match.

The other batsmen starting at Edgbaston were Usman Khawaja, who had never imposed himself on the Ashes in a decade of trying; Travis Head, routinely loose outside off stump; and Matthew Wade, picked as a specialist for the first time, having previously been dropped as a wicketkeeper for want of runs. His then-replacement, Tim Paine, had in the interim become Test captain, but boasted only one first-class century in a career dating back to 2005. Spare in the squad were Marcus Harris and Marnus Labuschagne, both without a Test hundred, and Mitchell Marsh, whose two in 2017-18 had been a brief flash among years of batting mediocrity.

AN OPEN-AND-SHUT CASE

The lowest average opening partnership (by both teams) in a series of five or more Tests:

		T	I	NO	R	HS	100	50	
12.55	England v Australia	5	20	0	251	54	0	1	2019
14.15	South Africa v England	5	19	0	269	70	0	1	1905-06
18.66	Australia v England	6	25	0	448	65	0	3	1978-79
19.05	England v West Indies	5	17	0	324	53	0	1	1966
20.05	Australia v England	5	18	0	361	53	0	1	1936-37
20.15	Australia v England	5	19	0	383	74	0	1	1950-51
21.05	South Africa v West Indies	5	20	0	421	97	0	4	1998-99
21.06	Australia v India	5	16	0	337	124	1	0	1947-48
21.26	Australia v England	5	19	0	404	98	0	2	1894-95
21.66	Australia v England	5	19	1	390	61	0	1	1884-85

Opening balance: England's new-ball pair of Stuart Broad and Jofra Archer shared 45 wickets.

The mismatch of capability between bat and ball was clear on the field. Each opening partnership was a handful of dust. Broad monstered Warner (who scored 61 of his series aggregate of 95 in one innings); every Australian bowler monstered Roy (who shifted down the order, then out of the side altogether). At Birmingham, Burns made one of the luckiest hundreds seen in Tests, a loose collage of false shots. Bancroft was dropped after two games for Harris, who played even worse, but had no one left to replace him. The original No. 3s fared little better: Khawaja was ousted by Labuschagne, who at Lord's had initially been Smith's (and Test cricket's first) concussion substitute; Root, having never made a golden duck in Tests, made two in three, and in between fell second ball, also for nought.

England were shot out for 146 at Edgbaston and 67 at Headingley. Australia avoided such abject scores thanks only to Smith, who top-scored six times in seven attempts: three centuries, three near enough. He missed three innings with concussion and still finished with 774 runs; only Don Bradman (twice), Viv Richards and Everton Weekes had scored more in a series from so few innings. Not until the end was he prised out for under 80.

Stokes carried England more dramatically, if less consistently: some epic bowling spells, two fifties, two unbeaten hundreds, including – with the improbable help of the bespectacled No. 11, Jack Leach – the miracle to flip the Headingley embarrassment. No matter the destruction Australia's bowlers had wrought in the first innings: their batting without Smith couldn't close England out. The thrills of that final day sent electricity coursing through the series: Stokes in glorious sunshine, with zero margin for error, launched six after six into the Western Terrace as though mistiming a ball was a concept he had never come across. Panicking, the Australians bowled erratically and challenged decisions incorrectly; Harris missed a tricky catch, and Lyon a simple run-out that would have given them the game – and the series. Despite England needing 73 when their ninth wicket fell, Stokes charged down 359, joint-ninth-highest successful chase in Test history.

Support for both champions came via scattered cameos. Root made four fifties among the ducks. Though Burns often failed, he sometimes found a way, and averaged 39. Labuschagne, having enjoyed a prolific stint with Glamorgan, filled in creditably for Smith, scoring four half-centuries in a row. Wade bookended the series with hundreds, though in between scarcely found a run.

A final aspect that stayed with the observer was the spirit of play, manifestly better than in so many previous Ashes. There was still the odd flashpoint but, given the worldwide chastisement of Australia's cricket culture after Cape Town, and the damning results of cultural reviews commissioned by their

IF AT FIRST YOU DON'T SUCCEED...

Fewest runs by an opener with at least ten innings in a series:

Runs		M	I	NO	HS	50	Avge		
95	D. A. Warner...	5	10	0	61	1	9.50	Australia v England	2019
136	J. W. D'Arcy....	5	10	0	33	0	13.60	New Zealand v England ..	1958
164	P. H. Punjabi....	5	10	0	33	0	16.40	India v Pakistan	1954-55
173	C. Washbrook...	5	10	0	34	0	17.30	England v Australia	1950-51
174	A. D. Gaekwad ..	6	11	0	48	0	15.81	India v West Indies......	1983-84
176	D. L. Haynes....	6	10	0	55	1	17.60	West Indies v India......	1983-84
179	Pankaj Roy.....	5	10	0	54	1	17.90	India v England	1959
181	P. V. Simmons ..	5	10	0	38	0	18.10	West Indies v England ..	1991
187	S. L. Campbell..	5	10	0	79	2	18.70	West Indies v Australia ..	2000-01
189	D. J. McGlew ...	5	10	1	45	0	21.00	South Africa v England...	1960

administrators, a public-relations effort had to be made. Paine pursued it with determination, and set a standard. Some moments still grated, like Wade's tasteless chuntering into the stump microphones, and the Australians' belligerent celebrations after retaining the Ashes at Old Trafford. But it was an improvement on the pantomime aggro that had marred 2017-18.

Often, a post-mortem is unduly affected by how the chips fall. Plenty of scribes had written that England were much the better team in 2013 – though Australia had lost two likely wins to rain. This time, after Australia went 2–1 up, various outlets in both countries argued they had been demonstrably better. But for the Stokes miracle, they said, the scoreline would have been 3–0.

Yet, without two days of rain at Lord's, England would probably have won there; had Smith not been present, they might have won everywhere. Effectively, an Australian team with one-and-a-half batsmen took on an England team with one-and-a-few-different-halves of a batsman. Neither was better than the other, but Australia could retain the trophy with a draw, and they managed not to lose their nerve in the Fourth Test after fumbling so drastically in the Third.

So what was the wash-up? If England had managed one more win in the first four matches, the teams could have gone into the fifth for a winner-takes-

Seeing it like a metaphor: Steve Smith batted as if against a beach ball all series. At Old Trafford, he did.

the-urn contest, and the series might have been a classic. Had England then won, it would have sat alongside their delirious escape in the World Cup final. Had Australia held England off at The Oval, retaining the trophy would have felt more like victory than anticlimax.

Instead, Australia's defeat there ensured the series was neither one thing nor the other. Taking the Ashes home was a major coup, given that stronger teams had failed on four previous visits. It was especially significant for Paine, who had been appointed emergency captain when Smith was suddenly sacked, yet a year and a half later had made the team his own. A player of modest ability, but a person of substantial calibre, proved the leader Australia needed. His biggest achievement was making sure his team didn't fall apart after conceding the Headingley Test, where Lyon's blunder could have thrown them into disarray. On the contrary, the Australians held their nerve when England took the next Test, in Manchester, into the final hour. While some commentators blew up the significance of Smith influencing field settings, Paine's ownership of the team went well beyond on-field tactics.

Those losing Australian sides from 2005 onwards, though, had also faced a far stronger England than this one. The triumphant summer of English dream – an Ashes–World Cup double – had not been realised, but England could still say that no visiting Australian team had won since 2001. The span is guaranteed to grow to at least 22 years.

Transcending the dross or sense of anticlimax, though, were moments of awe. Smith, on the first day of the series, walking back into the hardest format of the game after more than a year out, taking on a swinging ball and a heckling crowd – and rescuing a collapsing team – to make the best hundred of his career, an innings that swelled in authority and flourish as the sun grew lower. Stokes at Headingley, words that will long evoke the mayhem and glory of the last day. Smith again in Manchester, batting for so long that only he could initiate his dismissal, reverse-sweeping part-time spin. (When told he had twice been out to Root that way, following Lord's in 2015, Smith cheerfully fired back that both dismissals had come after a double-century.) Cummins and Hazlewood, also in Manchester, never letting batsmen draw breath, unleashing a tireless bombardment despite the aches, and finally dislodging England on the fifth evening when a draw was in sight.

Perhaps most of all, there was Archer: his lithe run and casual menace in one of cricket's most memorable debuts, just when Smith looked set to make another match his own. He produced a spell – one of the fastest recorded for England – that first thrilled, then frightened, pushing batsmen to the limit and the speed gun past 96mph. It shocked a Lord's crowd into silence under dramatic skies, and left Smith face down on the turf. Cricket lives in the moment: slow-motion electricity, for those who were there to pass on to those

---

FIVE STATS YOU MAY HAVE MISSED

- Leeds, England were dismissed for 67, their third total of 85 or fewer in 2019, after Bridgetown (77 v West Indies) and Lord's (85 v Ireland). Five other sides have endured a similar fate in a calendar year:

1888	Australia (six times)	2000	West Indies
1889	South Africa	2010	Pakistan
1958	New Zealand (four times)	**2019**	**England**

- In the first innings there, Joe Denly made 12, the lowest top-score in any completed England Test innings.

12 (out of 67)	J. L. Denly	v **Australia at Leeds**	**2019**
15 (99) †	W. G. Quaife	v Australia at Sydney	1901-02
15 (99) †	G. L. Jessop	v Australia at Sydney	1901-02
15 (110)	N. Hussain	v South Africa at Lord's	1998

† *The same innings.*

- Australia's No. 4 top-scored in nine successive innings. The previous record for one position was five:

9	**No. 4**	**Australia (S. P. D. Smith, M. Labuschagne) v England**	**2019**
5	No. 1	South Africa (E. A. B. Rowan) v England	1951
5	No. 4	South Africa (J. H. Kallis, J. A. Rudolph) v England	2004-05
5	No. 5	West Indies (S. Chanderpaul) v England, South Africa . .	2007 to 2007-08
5	No. 3	Sri Lanka (K. C. Sangakkara) v Bangladesh, England . . .	2013-14 to 2014

- David Warner made eight single-figure scores, equalling the record for a top-seven batsman in a Test series. Another Warner, England's Pelham, had eight in South Africa in 1905-06.

- Stuart Broad has more Test wickets at home for England against Australia than anyone:

	T	W	5I	Avge		T	W	5I	Avge
S. C. J. Broad	20	84	6	26.19	J. C. Laker	11	64	4	17.59
I. T. Botham	18	79	6	26.96	A. V. Bedser	10	57	5	24.03
W. Rhodes	21	67	3	20.97	R. G. D. Willis	11	56	4	21.42

Steady as he goes: Joe Denly shores up the England batting at The Oval.

who will hear about it in years to come. Beyond struggles or failures or a drawn scoreline, these are the parts that will live on.

AUSTRALIA TOURING PARTY

*T. D. Paine, C. T. Bancroft, P. J. Cummins, M. S. Harris, J. R. Hazlewood, T. M. Head, U. T. Khawaja, M. Labuschagne, N. M. Lyon, M. R. Marsh, M. G. Neser, J. L. Pattinson, P. M. Siddle, S. P. D. Smith, M. A. Starc, M. S. Wade, D. A. Warner.

A. T. Carey played against Derbyshire to allow Paine to rest before the Fourth Test.

Coach: J. L. Langer. *Manager:* G. Dovey. *Selector:* T. V. Hohns. *Assistant coaches:* T. J. Cooley, B. J. Haddin, G. A. Hick, S. Sridharan. *Analyst:* D. F. Hills. *Videographer:* A. Mauger. *Strength and conditioning coach:* A. D. Kellett. *Physiotherapist:* D. Beakley. *Massage therapist:* A. Mackenzie. *Doctor:* R. Saw. *Psychologist:* M. Lloyd. *Operations and logistics:* S. Allport. *Security manager:* F. A. Dimasi. *Media managers:* B. H. Murgatroyd and M. Conn. *Mentor:* S. R. Waugh.

TEST MATCH AVERAGES

ENGLAND – BATTING AND FIELDING

	T	I	NO	R	HS	100	50	Avge	Ct/St
†B. A. Stokes	5	10	2	441	135*	2	2	55.12	4
†R. J. Burns	5	10	0	390	133	1	2	39.00	6
J. E. Root	5	10	0	325	77	0	4	32.50	7
J. L. Denly	5	10	0	312	94	0	3	31.20	4
J. C. Buttler	5	10	0	247	70	0	1	24.70	5
J. M. Bairstow	5	10	1	214	52	0	1	23.77	20/2
C. R. Woakes	4	7	1	120	37*	0	0	20.00	0
J. J. Roy	4	8	0	110	31	0	0	13.75	1
†M. J. Leach	4	7	3	54	21	0	0	13.50	1
†S. C. J. Broad	5	9	4	61	29	0	0	12.20	0
J. C. Archer	4	7	0	48	15	0	0	6.85	0

Played in one Test: †M. M. Ali 0, 4; †J. M. Anderson 3, 4*; †S. M. Curran 15, 17; C. Overton 5, 21

BOWLING

	Style	O	M	R	W	BB	5I	Avge
J. C. Archer	RF	156	34	446	22	6-45	2	20.27
S. M. Curran	LFM	25	9	68	3	3-46	0	22.66
M. J. Leach	SLA	101.4	20	310	12	4-49	0	25.83
S. C. J. Broad	RFM	175.1	29	613	23	5-86	1	26.65
C. R. Woakes	RFM	95	17	331	10	3-58	0	33.10
J. E. Root	OB	28	2	122	3	2-26	0	40.66
B. A. Stokes	RFM	95.1	15	362	8	3-56	0	45.25
M. M. Ali	OB	42	4	172	3	2-130	0	57.33

Also bowled: J. M. Anderson (RFM) 4–3–1–0; J. L. Denly (LB) 21–5–87–0; C. Overton (RFM) 33.5–4–107–2.

AUSTRALIA – BATTING AND FIELDING

	T	I	NO	R	HS	100	50	Avge	Ct
S. P. D. Smith	4	7	0	774	211	3	3	110.57	12
M. Labuschagne	4	7	0	353	80	0	4	50.42	3
†M. S. Wade	5	10	0	337	117	2	0	33.70	3
P. M. Siddle	3	4	1	84	44	0	0	28.00	2
†T. M. Head	4	8	1	191	51	0	1	27.28	2
‡J. L. Pattinson	2	4	1	69	47*	0	0	23.00	1
‡U. T. Khawaja	3	6	0	122	40	0	0	20.33	3
T. D. Paine	5	10	1	180	58	0	1	20.00	20
N. M. Lyon	5	7	2	80	26*	0	0	16.00	2
C. T. Bancroft	2	4	0	44	16	0	0	11.00	5
P. J. Cummins	5	9	2	71	26*	0	0	10.14	2
*M. S. Harris	3	6	0	58	19	0	0	9.66	0
*D. A. Warner	5	10	0	95	61	0	1	9.50	8
J. R. Hazlewood	4	5	4	9	4*	0	0	9.00	2

Played in one Test: M. R. Marsh 17, 24 (1 ct); †M. A. Starc 54*, 3*.

BOWLING

	Style	O	M	R	W	BB	5I	Avge
M. R. Marsh	RFM	29.2	5	86	7	5-46	1	12.28
P. J. Cummins	RF	211	61	569	29	4-32	0	19.62
J. R. Hazlewood	RFM	161.2	43	437	20	5-30	1	21.85
M. A. Starc	LF	38	9	126	4	3-80	0	31.50
N. M. Lyon	OB	242.3	44	668	20	6-49	1	33.40
J. L. Pattinson	RFM	65	15	167	5	2-9	0	33.40
P. M. Siddle	RFM	97	21	295	7	2-52	0	42.14

Also bowled: T. M. Head (OB) 3–2–7–0; M. Labuschagne (LB) 18–2–56–1; S. P. D. Smith (LB) 5–1–15–0; M. S. Wade (RM) 1–0–7–0.

‡At Southampton, July 23–25 (not first-class). **G. A. Hick's XII won by five wickets. B. J. Haddin's XII 105** (42.5 overs) (M. Labuschagne 41; M. G. Neser 4-18, J. M. Bird 3-28) **and 170** (55.2 overs) (D. A. Warner 58, W. J. Pucovski 37; J. L. Pattinson 3-19, M. R. Marsh 5-34); ‡**G. A. Hick's XII 120** (45.1 overs) (P. M. Siddle 4-31, P. J. Cummins 5-24) **and 156-5** (60 overs) (C. A. Bancroft 93*). *In order to finalise their squad, the Australians called up several players from the A-team who were also touring England, split themselves into two sides of 12, and asked for a green pitch. Whether they wanted quite such seam and bounce was another matter. By the end of the first day, Graeme Hick's team were 96-7, in answer to 105 by Brad Haddin's. Conditions eased a little, and Cameron Bancroft steered them to victory – and himself into the side for the First Test – with 93*. In a sign of things to come, there were runs for Marnus Labuschagne and wickets for Pat Cummins.*

Fixed intent: Rory Burns battles to a hundred on Ashes debut at Birmingham.

ENGLAND v AUSTRALIA

First Specsavers Test

JAMES COYNE

At Birmingham, August 1–5. Australia won by 251 runs. Australia 24pts. Toss: Australia.

England pitched up aiming to channel years of noisy dominance at Edgbaston into their own Gabbatoir – a Brummie kneecapping right out of *Peaky Blinders*. But the feeling at the end was that, unless the ball moved around, it didn't matter where the Ashes were played: for all England's graft, Australia would probably win.

The phoney war had been shorter and less personal than usual, partly because of Australia's post-sandpaper makeover and England's World Cup triumph. But amateur psychology still made an appearance. Embarking on his first Ashes Test as captain, Paine attempted to invoke the spirit of Winston Churchill, though his chosen quote – "Behaviour doesn't lie" – was attributed by a gleeful media to conspiracy theorist David Icke. A more appropriate Churchill quote might have applied to Smith: for England, he really was a riddle, wrapped in a mystery, inside an enigma.

All manner of suggestions were proffered as to how to get him out. But, if anything, he was better than ever at stepping across, waiting for the bad ball and persuading it into a gap of his choosing. With England lacking the express pace of Jofra Archer or Olly Stone – both injured – their best bet looked to be to hang it outside off and hope for a nick.

On the first afternoon, Smith almost single-handedly held the bowlers at bay, his 144 the highest score on the opening day of an Ashes series in England (beating Johnny

Tyldesley's 138, also at Birmingham, in 1902); his average on the first day of all Tests, meanwhile, rose to 116. By the time his second hundred had England flat on the canvas, he had centuries from six of his last ten Ashes innings. To achieve all this in his first Test after a year's ban, with near-constant booing from the Hollies Stand, confirmed an unparalleled ability to block everything out.

At the start of a series that appeared to rest on key bowlers, the runes were reading better for Australia. They had the luxury of keeping up their sleeve two previous tormentors of England, Josh Hazlewood and Mitchell Starc, and of backing Pattinson and Siddle to transfer their form from county stints. Anderson, by contrast, had not played for a month since limping off with a calf tear in a Championship game. Root maintained he had passed all the fitness tests. And so Anderson, at 37, became the oldest to take the new ball for England in the Ashes since Les Jackson, the Whitwell collier, who was 40 in 1961. Instead, he pulled up four overs into his first spell: England were down to ten men – and Anderson would not bowl again in anger until Boxing Day.

Meanwhile, his old accomplice Broad – wearing the No. 8 shirt of a combative central midfielder, in the first Test since the ICC introduced names and numbers – removed both openers, to give his own career a shot in the arm. Aleem Dar had reprieved Warner despite a faint under-edge down the leg side, before raising his finger for a dubious lbw

---

BATTING ON ALL FIVE DAYS OF A TEST

M. L. Jaisimha (20*, 74)	India v Australia at Calcutta	1959-60
G. Boycott (107, 80*)	England v Australia at Nottingham	1977
K. J. Hughes (117, 84)	Australia v England at Lord's	1980
A. J. Lamb (23, 110)	England v West Indies at Lord's	1984
R. J. Shastri (111, 7*)	India v Australia at Calcutta	1984-85
A. F. G. Griffith (114, 18)	West Indies v New Zealand at Hamilton	1999-2000
A. Flintoff (70, 51)	England v India at Mohali	2005-06
A. N. Petersen (156, 39)	South Africa v New Zealand at Wellington	2011-12
C. A. Pujara (52, 22)	India v Sri Lanka at Kolkata	2017-18
R. J. Burns (133, 11)	**England v Australia at Birmingham**	**2019**

---

which Warner didn't contest. Broad thought he had the other decisive wicket, too, when Smith, on 34, padded up to a nip-backer. Dar reckoned it was clipping off stump; DRS ruled otherwise.

Dar was stung by a wasp later in the day, forcing a stoppage for antihistamine, but his match slowly improved. Not so for his junior partner, Joel Wilson, elevated to the ICC elite panel a few games earlier, but regularly wincing at the big screen: eight of his decisions were overturned. As the Australians charged to victory on the last day, with men round the bat and challenging everything at Wilson's end, Dar walked over to pat his colleague on the bum when he got one right. It was tough to watch such a public humiliation, but necessary if the ICC were to address the issue of a small and overburdened set of umpires, especially when it came to Ashes Tests: all but five of the 12 were English or Australian, and so ineligible.

The Hollies Stand cared little for all that, as the umpiring hokey-cokey helped give England a foothold. By five o'clock, Smith had faced more balls than the rest of the top nine put together. At first the pitch was fresh enough, but Edgbaston's efficient drainage gradually produced a surface on which he could prosper. When England commissioned a special batch of Dukes balls to be pumped off the Walthamstow factory line, they did not imagine they would find less swing here than in any home Test since CricViz started measuring it 13 years earlier. Emboldened, Smith enlisted the stubborn Siddle and Lyon to add 162 for the last two wickets; no Test team had previously made as many as 284 after losing eight wickets for as few as 122.

Insatiable: Steve Smith lets his bat do the talking, time and time again.

Broad finished with five (and 100 Ashes wickets), but England were suddenly in a scrap, and the situation demanded they bat time – a Test-match tradition unfamiliar to many of them. That they made such a good fist of it owed much to the steely Burns. A week earlier, Ireland's Tim Murtagh had left him on the rack at Lord's. But Burns returned to his childhood mentor, Neil Stewart (brother of Alec), who urged him to rediscover the balance at the crease that had delivered so many runs for Surrey. His method was still crabby: the shimmer off the stickers on the back of his bat could be seen by the bowler at the top of his mark. But, despite numerous plays and misses, he kept Root company, taking England into the calm waters of 150 for one for the second Test in a row (they had not previously got there in Root's tenure). Root did enjoy one moment of fortune, on nine, when Pattinson clipped his off stump without dislodging the bail; hearing a noise, Wilson gave him out caught behind, only for technology to reveal the truth.

Burns completed his maiden Test hundred on the second evening, which was just as well, since England's middle order, for so long their muscle, had become their soft underbelly. They were not helped by a change of ball. The new batch had not swung as much as the 2018 model, which – both teams had twigged – now made up the box of replacements. As soon as Australia had persuaded the umpires the ball had gone out of shape, its successor hooped through Denly and Buttler. Next morning, Stokes was fifth

TWO CENTURIES IN AN ASHES TEST

136 and 130	W. Bardsley (Australia)	The Oval	1909
176 and 127	H. Sutcliffe (England)	Melbourne	1924-2
119* and 177	W. R. Hammond (England)	Adelaide	1928-2*
147 and 103*	D. C. S. Compton (England)	Adelaide	1946-4
122 and 124*	A. R. Morris (Australia)	Adelaide	1946-4
108 and 116	S. R. Waugh (Australia)	Manchester	199
197 and 103	M. L. Hayden (Australia)	Brisbane	2002-0
144 and 142	**S. P. D. Smith (Australia)**	**Birmingham**	**201**

out, for 50, with England still trailing by two; three wickets quickly followed, before judicious swiping from Woakes and Broad pilfered a lead of 90. But, with Anderson unavailable, that was more impressive on paper than on grass.

This time, Smith would need to work his magic with Australia three down – including Warner, a 450th Test wicket for Broad – and still 15 behind. Yet no challenge seemed too great. The match was on a knife-edge as Head clung on until the end of the third day, and it all boiled down to how quickly England could strike next morning, when play resumed with Australia effectively 34 for three. Broad came close, but the game soon ran away.

If Pat Howard, Cricket Australia's former high performance manager, was watching, he deserved a little credit. Before he was culled in the ball-tampering fallout, he had lobbied for a lengthy A-team tour to precede the Ashes, giving Australia's less-feted batsmen a rare recce of the conditions. Sure enough, Head and Wade, two counter-attacking left-handers, grew in confidence the longer they stayed with Smith, who went on to become only the second player, after Marcus Trescothick against West Indies in 2004, to score two hundreds in a Test at Edgbaston.

England's confidence, on the other hand, was deserting them. Root ignored Woakes on the fourth morning and, on a pitch now turning, Ali's off-spin was disintegrating fast. Stokes ran in hard, and some feared he was being overbowled. For Paine, it was all coming up rosy. He had challenged his side to bat first in the swingiest period, only to be suckered into holing out, then dropped a couple of catches. Now he had the space to regain some form, and keep his opponents in the field until the lead was 397. After much pleading, England succeeded in changing the ball, but only after Pattinson had landed it in a spectator's beer – one of his four sixes.

Sent in on the fourth evening, England needed rain, or for Australia to lose patience. Neither happened. Siddle built up the pressure, Cummins homed in on the stumps at express pace, and Lyon – with rough to exploit – was devilishly difficult. From the moment Roy danced down the track to him on the final morning and was bowled through the gate, the collapse gathered pace like a runaway train. Lyon finished with six for 49 – fourth-innings figures bettered by an Australian in England only by Fred Spofforth (seven for 44 in the 1882 Oval Test that spawned the Ashes) and Bill O'Reilly (seven for 54 at Trent

---

EDGBASTON NOTES AND QUOTES

Joe Root was said not to be keen on any pre-series handshakes. Tim Paine had introduced the ritual, borrowed from football, as a way of improving Australia's image in the wake of the ball-tampering scandal. Root and coach Trevor Bayliss were apparently surprised when ICC match referee Ranjan Madugalle briefed them – and in the event it didn't take place.

Paine brushed aside the Edgbaston factor, despite England having lost just one Test there since 2001. Asked if there were a more intimidating ground in world cricket, he replied: "Than this? I could name you 15." He declined to list them. Stuart Broad said after the first day: "One thing's for sure, that atmosphere was lively today. It was loud. Certainly in my top 15." Afterwards, Paine admitted: "You try to deflect as much as you can heading into a game of this magnitude, and we were fully aware of how the crowd is here. It was a little bit of a bluff."

This was the first Test worldwide in which the players wore names and numbers on the back of their shirts, to help spectators distinguish between them (and possibly to sell merchandise). Australia plumped for a heavy font. The England players' names were printed in a lighter face, barely legible from the boundary. Not until the second day did the printed scorecards at Edgbaston list the players' numbers next to their names.

A hot July led to a surge in the wasp population, and a nest had to be removed above a window in the R. E. S. Wyatt Stand. Paul Williams, a spectator, tweeted that a number of people in the area had been stung on the first day, "a lady rather badly under her eye". Several were given different seats.

Bridge in 1934). He also moved past 350 Test wickets, and got rid of Ali for the ninth time in 11 innings.

To think that after all that sweat – Smith had gone through more than 20 pairs of gloves over the course of 11 hours' batting – victory was worth just 24 points for Australia in the ICC's new World Test Championship, of which this was the first game. With 120 available for each series, Sri Lanka and New Zealand would soon pocket 60 each for a 1–1 draw.

And yet, in an age when everything needs to be quantified, the purest joy lay in watching the supreme Test batsman of his time defy whatever England could throw at him.

Player of the Match: S. P. D. Smith.   *Attendance:* 108,614.

Close of play: first day, England 10-0 (Burns 4, Roy 6); second day, England 267-4 (Burns 125, Stokes 38); third day, Australia 124-3 (Smith 46, Head 21); fourth day, England 13-0 (Burns 7, Roy 6).

Australia

C. T. Bancroft c Root b Broad	8	– c Buttler b Ali	7
D. A. Warner lbw b Broad	2	– c Bairstow b Broad	8
U. T. Khawaja c Bairstow b Woakes	13	– c Bairstow b Stokes	40
S. P. D. Smith b Broad	144	– c Bairstow b Woakes	142
T. M. Head lbw b Woakes	35	– c Bairstow b Stokes	51
M. S. Wade lbw b Woakes	1	– c Denly b Stokes	110
*†T. D. Paine c Burns b Broad	5	– b Ali	34
J. L. Pattinson lbw b Broad	0	– not out	47
P. J. Cummins lbw b Stokes	5	– not out	26
P. M. Siddle c Buttler b Ali	44		
N. M. Lyon not out	12		
Lb 13, w 2	15	B 11, lb 2, w 3, nb 6	22

1/2 (2) 2/17 (1) 3/35 (3)   (80.4 overs) 284   1/13 (2)   (7 wkts dec, 112 overs) 487
4/99 (5) 5/105 (6) 6/122 (7)   2/27 (1) 3/75 (3)
7/112 (8) 8/122 (9) 9/210 (10) 10/284 (4)   4/205 (5) 5/331 (4) 6/407 (6) 7/409 (7)

Anderson 4–3–1–0; Broad 22.4–4–86–5; Woakes 21–2–58–3; Stokes 18–1–77–1; Ali 13–3–42–1; Denly 2–1–7–0. *Second innings*—Broad 22–2–91–1; Woakes 13–1–46–1; Ali 29–1–130–2; Root 12–1–50–0; Stokes 22–5–85–3; Denly 14–1–72–0.

England

R. J. Burns c Paine b Lyon	133	– c Lyon b Cummins	11
J. J. Roy c Smith b Pattinson	10	– b Lyon	28
*J. E. Root c and b Siddle	57	– c Bancroft b Lyon	28
J. L. Denly lbw b Pattinson	18	– c Bancroft b Lyon	11
J. C. Buttler c Bancroft b Cummins	5	– b Cummins	1
B. A. Stokes c Paine b Cummins	50	– c Paine b Lyon	6
†J. M. Bairstow c Warner b Siddle	8	– c Bancroft b Cummins	6
M. M. Ali b Lyon	0	– c Warner b Lyon	4
C. R. Woakes not out	37	– c Smith b Cummins	37
S. C. J. Broad c Pattinson b Cummins	29	– c Smith b Lyon	0
J. M. Anderson c Cummins b Lyon	3	– not out	4
B 10, lb 11, w 2, nb 1	24	B 4, lb 4, nb 2	10

1/22 (2) 2/154 (3) 3/189 (4)   (135.5 overs) 374   1/19 (1) 2/60 (2)   (52.3 overs) 146
4/194 (5) 5/282 (6) 6/296 (1)   3/80 (4) 4/85 (3)
7/300 (8) 8/300 (7) 9/365 (10) 10/374 (11)   5/85 (5) 6/97 (7) 7/97 (6)
                                                           8/136 (8) 9/136 (10) 10/146 (9)

Cummins 33–9–84–3; Pattinson 27–3–82–2; Siddle 27–8–52–2; Lyon 43.5–8–112–3; Wade 1–0–7–0; Head 2–1–7–0; Smith 2–0–9–0. *Second innings*—Siddle 12–2–28–0; Lyon 20–5–49–6; Pattinson 8–1–29–0; Cummins 11.3–3–32–4; Smith 1–1–0–0.

Umpires: Aleem Dar and J. S. Wilson.   Third umpire: C. B. Gaffaney.
Referee: R. S. Madugalle.

WORCESTERSHIRE v AUSTRALIANS

At Worcester, August 7–9. Drawn. Toss: Worcestershire. First-class debut: J. A. Haynes.

Buoyed by a come-from-behind victory in the First Test, the Australians made the familiar trip to New Road, if a little later than traditional. Or at least most did: the coach, Justin Langer, as well as Cummins, Lyon, Smith and Warner, went to London instead. Paine stayed in charge, but handed the gloves to Wade, and surveyed proceedings from mid-on. What he saw didn't necessarily answer the pressing question: should Starc or Hazlewood, or both, elbow their way into the Test attack? Before that, there was some batting to be done. Harris was bowled shouldering arms, though there were decent runs for Khawaja and Head, and a so-so 33 for Bancroft. Others fared less well, but Paine declared at 266 for five on the first evening. Starc promptly removed Fell, and Hazlewood got Dell, both for ducks, but Jack Haynes, on first-class debut, clipped Starc for four fours. He was trapped by Hazlewood, who proved more miserly and, with Worcestershire 75 for eight, the bowlers seemed to have done the job. Then fifties from Milton and Morris – his first – oversaw a recovery that raised questions about Australian ruthlessness, and allowed Leach his own declaration. Harris helped his prospects with a crisp half-century, before rain permitted only 13 overs on the last day.

Close of play: first day, Worcestershire 31-3 (Ferguson 6, Wessels 0); second day, Australians 92-1 (Harris 62, Marsh 22).

Australians

C. T. Bancroft b Tongue	33	– c Milton b Morris	7
M. S. Harris b Finch	14	– lbw b Leach	67
U. T. Khawaja c Milton b Tongue	57		
T. M. Head not out	109		
M. Labuschagne c Fell b Morris	15	– (4) not out	9
M. R. Marsh lbw b Morris	13	– (3) not out	39
†M. S. Wade not out	20		
B 1, lb 2, nb 2	5	Lb 1, nb 1	2

1/36 (2) 2/58 (1)   (5 wkts dec, 75 overs) 266   1/31 (1)   (2 wkts, 39 overs) 124
3/159 (3) 4/201 (5) 5/227 (6)   2/103 (2)

*T. D. Paine, M. G. Neser, M. A. Starc and J. R. Hazlewood did not bat.

Leach 15–3–32–0; Tongue 13–2–46–2; Morris 16–4–57–2; Finch 16–2–75–1; Rhodes 15–0–53–0. *Second innings*—Leach 11–3–32–1; Tongue 11–5–34–0; Morris 8–1–33–1; Finch 9–3–24–0.

Worcestershire

T. C. Fell lbw b Starc	0	J. C. Tongue c and b Labuschagne	2
J. J. Dell b Hazlewood	0	C. A. J. Morris not out	53
C. J. Ferguson c Labuschagne b Starc	6	A. W. Finch not out	18
J. A. Haynes lbw b Hazlewood	24	Lb 2, nb 2	4
M. H. Wessels c Labuschagne b Hazlewood	9		
A. G. Milton c Starc b Labuschagne	74	1/0 (1) 2/0 (2) (9 wkts dec, 62.5 overs) 201	
G. H. Rhodes lbw b Neser	11	3/29 (4) 4/31 (3)	
J. Leach c Wade b Neser	0	5/43 (5) 6/72 (7) 7/72 (8) 8/75 (9) 9/163 (6)	

Starc 15.5–3–56–2; Hazlewood 15–4–34–3; Neser 12–1–32–2; Marsh 7–3–24–0; Labuschagne 11–3–37–2; Head 2–0–16–0.

Umpires: Hassan Adnan and N. A. Mallender.

> **"**In the summer of 1913, while the nation worried about women's suffrage, Irish Home Rule, and mass strikes in the Black Country, English cricket was in the midst of its own little crisis."
> A History of Left-Handed Batting, page 85

ENGLAND v AUSTRALIA

Second Specsavers Test

S T E V E N   L Y N C H

At Lord's, August 14–18. Drawn. Toss: Australia. England 8pts, Australia 8pts. Test debut: J. C. Archer.

In the end it was a draw, as had seemed likely once the first day and most of the third were washed away. But in between, a pulsating match unfolded, and perhaps only the loss of ten overs on the final morning prevented England from squaring the series. The clouds had a silver lining: Jofra Archer confirmed his arrival as a genuine star with red ball as well as white. A month after clinching the World Cup with a super over, he now conjured several super-fast overs, usually over 90mph, occasionally touching 96. And, during a lightning fourth-day spell, he roused Lord's to a frenzy, then reduced it to stunned silence when he slammed Steve Smith on the neck. Smith recovered, although delayed concussion kept him out of the second innings of this game, and all the next.

Archer had sat out the First Test after picking up a side strain in the World Cup. But now he replaced the injured James Anderson, and became England's 693rd Test cricketer; he and 98 others – one in seven – had not been born in England. (Leach also returned, for the out-of-form Moeen Ali.) Archer's Sussex team-mate and close friend Chris Jordan presented his cap, and he quickly became Root's go-to man, so much so there were immediate fears about his workload.

It all looked so easy: the run-up more of a jog, a dozen relaxed strides, before the arm whirled over, the wrist snapped, and the batsman tried to get out of the way. The simplicity – and the searing pace – brought to mind Michael Holding, the last to bowl so fast with such apparent economy of effort. Twelve direct hits were recorded on Australian bodies or helmets, 11 inflicted by Archer. He finished with five for 91 from 44 overs, in the most stunning England debut since Kevin Pietersen in the 2005 Ashes.

Here we go again: Stuart Broad dismisses David Warner, for three.

After an anticlimactic first-day washout, things began in earnest on the sunny second. It was an emotional occasion: Lord's had gone red for the charity foundation set up by the former England captain Andrew Strauss in memory of his wife, Ruth, who died of cancer late in 2018. Their young sons rang the bell at the start; the stumps, adverts and player numbers were all red, as were many of the spectators, even in the Pavilion – not that MCC members needed encouragement to pull on crimson chinos.

Paine, who had made his Test debut alongside Smith at Lord's against Pakistan in 2010, decided to bowl, and was rewarded when Hazlewood – back in the side in place of James Pattinson – removed Roy for a duck, after a third speculative swish, then pinned Root in the fifth over of a high-quality spell. Burns flashed Siddle into the gully, but the ball hit Khawaja on the chest and went down. He survived another chance, to Paine, before being superbly taken one-handed by the diving Bancroft at short leg for 53, a good follow-up to his Edgbaston century. Just before that, Denly had become Hazlewood's third wicket after a handy stand of 66, although the watching Geoff Boycott was frustrated: "Pretty little thirties don't win Test matches."

> Broad got Warner with a peach that seamed up the hill and flicked the bails

After suffering two drops, Siddle removed Buttler and, when Stokes missed a sweep against Lyon, it was 138 for six. Bairstow and Woakes gritted the total past 200, before Woakes was caught behind off Cummins, two balls after being clanged on the helmet. Archer shrugged off several short-pitched deliveries as Cummins got his retaliation in first, and Bairstow was last out for 52, slogging Lyon to deep square. England's 258 was at least something to play with.

Broad, who had failed to dismiss Warner in the previous two Ashes series, now got him for the third time in 29 balls, and once more from round the wicket, with a peach that seamed up the hill and flicked the bails. Bancroft and Khawaja survived to the close, before falling in successive overs on a grey third morning. Trapped by a nip-backer, Bancroft was Archer's first Test victim. Broad soon had Head lbw with one hitting halfway up middle stump, although it had to be confirmed on review, as Aleem Dar – standing in his 128th Test, equalling Steve Bucknor's record – imagined an inside edge. That was almost it for the day, as rain set in on the stroke of lunch. With five blank sessions out of nine, a draw seemed assured and, when Smith settled in next morning, it felt even more likely. Broad had suggested England could win if they knocked Australia over by lunch – but the only casualty of the opening session was Wade, well taken low at third slip.

And then Archer returned. Paine bat-padded to short leg in his first over after lunch, before Smith felt the heat. Old ball? Batsman well set? Bowler into his 24th over? Pitch

---

LORD'S NOTES AND QUOTES

An announcement at St John's Wood tube station, read out by *Test Match Special* commentator Jonathan Agnew, implored any spectators who knew how to get Steve Smith out to report to the England dressing-room.

An MCC member was ejected from the Pavilion for shouting "Disgrace!" and "Cheat!" as Smith walked through the Long Room after being dismissed for 92 on the fourth day. The "egg-and-bacon blazered boo-boy," as *The Sun* described him, was disciplined under a new code of conduct introduced at MCC's annual meeting in May.

Australian prime minister Scott Morrison weighed in, posting online that it was "a total Ashes foul for the crowd at Lord's to boo Steve Smith. His performance on the pitch during his return to Test match cricket in the UK demands nothing other than respect."

The world's longest-lived Test cricketer, 107-year-old Eileen Ash, was at Lord's on the fourth day for the unveiling of her portrait, by Alex Chamberlin. "It's marvellous," she said. "I think it's absolutely brilliant, and I feel 200 years old." She made her Test debut for England in 1937.

Phillip Brown, Popperfoto/Getty Images

Blowing hot – and hotter: Steve Smith is struck by a ball from Jofra Archer, a blow that echoed through the Ashes.

on the sluggish side? Watch out. Smith was hit on the elbow, then smashed on his unprotected forearm. He stayed on, but looked hurried – not surprising since Archer, stirred by the arrival of Cummins, sent down an over which averaged more than 90mph. The crowd were lapping it up, and the noise was incredible – until everything went silent in the 77th over. Smith, on 80, crumpled to the floor. The TV cameras kept a respectful distance as he flopped, starfish-like, on to his back; eventually, replays showed the ball thumping into his neck close to the spot that had proved fatal for his former team-mate Phillip Hughes in 2014.

Smith was soon on his feet, and reluctantly escorted off by the team doctor for concussion tests, which he passed. He had been using a helmet without the neck-guards introduced after the Hughes tragedy, as he found them uncomfortable. It was a shock when he returned to the crease 40 minutes later, after Woakes got Siddle. Many felt he should not have been allowed to continue, although Cricket Australia pointed out that the correct protocols had been followed. Justin Langer, the coach, said the players were like his sons – but that he couldn't prevent him from going out again. Smith apparently insisted: "I can't get on the honours board if I'm not batting."

But, mind probably scrambled, he didn't quite make it. Even more skittish than usual, he heaved Woakes for four, then edged to third man for another. Finally, on 92, Smith padded up to a straight one, and seemed to start trudging off even before the finger was raised; he stopped, reviewed the decision… and kept walking. That ended his participation: next morning he woke with a headache, failed further concussion tests, and was withdrawn from the match. New regulations allowed a like-for-like replacement, so Marnus Labuschagne became Test cricket's first full substitute.

By then England, leading by just eight, had made another stuttering start. Roy lasted into the fifth over this time, and was followed immediately by Root, who bagged his first golden duck, in his 153rd Test innings. It was Paine's 100th dismissal, in his 23rd match; only Adam Gilchrist and Quinton de Kock had got there more quickly. Burns and Denly managed another fifty partnership, although they needed luck: Denly was dropped by Warner at slip, and nearly run out, while Burns would have gone had Paine reviewed Lyon's lbw shout in his second over. Later, Buttler had a similar escape.

England were four down and a wobbly 104 ahead by the close, but enjoyed the abbreviated fifth morning: Stokes and Buttler reprised their World Cup final heroics, adding an unbroken 61 as thoughts of defeat receded. Buttler swatted to long leg soon after lunch, but Stokes surged on. He swung Lyon for two sixes in an over, not long after Bairstow had shown him how, and reached his seventh Test century. Stokes celebrated by smashing Siddle for four and six, before Root's declaration set Australia 267 in 48 overs.

Could England do it? It was a job for Jofra. Warner edged low to fourth slip in Archer's second over, and Khawaja nicked to the keeper in his next. In came Labuschagne, only to be smacked on the grille second ball by a wicked bouncer that knocked him down too. Luckily, the concussion substitute didn't need a sub himself, and he settled in, showing the form that had already produced 1,114 Championship runs in ten matches for Glamorgan.

Four wickets left, but only seven overs to go

In front of an animated full house, Leach struck in the first over after tea, Bancroft playing across the line to one that kept low, but Labuschagne and Head – initially at sea against Leach – seemed to make things safe with a stand of 85. It looked a different game when Archer was not bowling, and England's last chance had apparently disappeared when Roy, at second slip, shelled a straightforward catch off Stokes when Head had 22.

In the third over of the last hour, Labuschagne flicked firmly at Leach; the ball ballooned off Buttler's left thigh at short leg to midwicket, where Root took a low catch that survived scrutiny by TV, much to the Australians' chagrin. Wade soon gloved Leach to Buttler, and suddenly a result was back on. In roared Archer: Paine was hit, beaten, hit; he then ducked before jabbing to short leg, who shied at the stumps. In Archer's next over, he connected with a pull, only to be acrobatically caught, one-handed, by Denly at square leg. Four wickets left, but only seven overs to go, and Head and Cummins clung on, despite a cluster of close catchers; Burns, at a very silly point, nearly clasped Cummins with 18 deliveries remaining, but the ball squirmed away.

And so, at 7.22, it ended in a draw, the first in England for 21 Tests, and only the second in the last 35. Stokes won the match award, but the man of the moment was already the most famous Archer in England since Robin Hood.

Player of the Match: B. A. Stokes.　*Attendance*: 113,684.

Close of play: first day, no play; second day, Australia 30-1 (Bancroft 5, Khawaja 18); third day, Australia 80-4 (Smith 13, Wade 0); fourth day, England 96-4 (Stokes 16, Buttler 10).

England

R. J. Burns c Bancroft b Cummins	53	– c Paine b Siddle 29
J. J. Roy c Paine b Hazlewood	0	– c and b Cummins 2
*J. E. Root lbw b Hazlewood	14	– c Paine b Cummins 0
J. L. Denly c Paine b Hazlewood	30	– c and b Siddle................ 26
J. C. Buttler c Paine b Siddle	12	– (6) c Hazlewood b Cummins 31
B. A. Stokes lbw b Lyon	13	– (5) not out 115
†J. M. Bairstow c Khawaja b Lyon	52	– not out 30
C. R. Woakes c Paine b Cummins	32	
J. C. Archer c Khawaja b Cummins	12	
S. C. J. Broad b Lyon	11	
M. J. Leach not out	6	
B 12, lb 5, w 6	23	B 5, lb 19, nb 1 25

1/0 (2)　2/26 (3)　3/92 (4)　　　　　　(77.1 overs) 258　　1/9 (2)　　(5 wkts dec, 71 overs) 258
4/116 (1)　5/136 (5)　6/138 (6)　　　　　　　　　　　　　2/9 (3)　3/64 (4)
7/210 (8)　8/230 (9)　9/251 (10)　10/258 (7)　　　　　　4/71 (1)　5/161 (6)

Cummins 21–8–61–3; Hazlewood 22–6–58–3; Siddle 13–2–48–1; Lyon 19.1–2–68–3; Smith 2–0–6–0. *Second innings*—Cummins 17–6–35–3; Hazlewood 13–1–43–0; Siddle 15–4–54–2; Lyon 26–3–102–0.

Australia

C. T. Bancroft lbw b Archer	13	– lbw b Leach		16
D. A. Warner b Broad	3	– c Burns b Archer		5
U. T. Khawaja c Bairstow b Woakes	36	– c Bairstow b Archer		2
S. P. D. Smith lbw b Woakes	92			
T. M. Head lbw b Broad	7	– not out		42
M. S. Wade c Burns b Broad	4	– c Buttler b Leach		1
*†T. D. Paine c Buttler b Archer	23	– c Denly b Archer		4
P. J. Cummins c Bairstow b Broad	20	– not out		1
P. M. Siddle c Bairstow b Woakes	9			
N. M. Lyon lbw b Leach	6			
J. R. Hazlewood not out	3			
M. Labuschagne (did not bat)		– (4) c Root b Leach		59
B 17, lb 12, w 2, nb 1	32	B 8, lb 14, w 1, nb 1		24

1/11 (2) 2/60 (1) 3/60 (3)   (94.3 overs) 250   1/13 (2)   (6 wkts, 47.3 overs) 154
4/71 (5) 5/102 (6) 6/162 (7)   2/19 (3) 3/47 (1)
7/218 (9) 8/234 (4) 9/246 (10) 10/250 (8)   4/132 (4) 5/138 (6) 6/149 (7)

In the first innings Smith, when 80, retired hurt at 203-6 and resumed at 218-7. Labuschagne replaced Smith, as a concussion substitute.

Broad 27.3–7–65–4; Archer 29–11–59–2; Woakes 19–6–61–3; Stokes 8–1–17–0; Leach 11–3–19–1. *Second innings*—Broad 7–0–29–0; Archer 15.2–2–32–3; Woakes 3–0–11–0; Leach 16.3–5–37–3; Stokes 3–1–16–0; Root 1–0–7–0; Denly 2–2–0–0.

Umpires: Aleem Dar and C. B. Gaffaney. Third umpire: J. S. Wilson.
Referee: R. S. Madugalle.

ENGLAND v AUSTRALIA

Third Specsavers Test

Lawrence Booth

At Leeds, August 22–25. England won by one wicket. England 24pts. Toss: England.

Long after Headingley had emptied, an animated figure out in the middle was taking team-mates through what he apparently saw as the crucial few seconds of an extraordinary day. The figure was not Ben Stokes, who had just entered folklore with an unbeaten 135. It was Jack Leach, England's No. 11, who had described himself as a "village cricketer" on account of his bald head and spectacles, but was not far from folklore status himself. Re-enacting the single he had pinched to level the scores, he scampered down the pitch from the Kirkstall Lane End with a thrill that spoke for a nation. It was a simple, touching scene, the calm after the storm.

When Leach joined Stokes at 3.17 on the fourth afternoon, England's hopes had, by any sensible measure, turned to dust. Bowled out in their first innings for 67, they had just lost five for 41 in their second. To keep the Ashes alive, they needed 73 to win (or 72 to tie). And they were chasing 359, which was 27 more than they had ever managed to win a Test.

England could clutch at two straws. One was Stokes, who six weeks earlier had bent the World Cup final to his will. The other was Headingley, for ever associated in the English psyche – and possibly the Australian – with the summer of '81. Ian Botham was in the commentary box this time, but in spirit he was out there too, doubtless urging Stokes to "give it some humpty", as he had Graham Dilley all those summers ago. Leach had recently made 92 as nightwatchman against Ireland, but he was no Dilley. Stokes, on 61, knew it was up to him and, for most of the 17 deliveries his partner negotiated, he rested helplessly on his haunches, staring at the turf. Leach was having trouble focusing,

Number's up: Jason Roy falls to Josh Hazlewood, and England spiral towards 67 all out.

repeatedly wiping sweat from his glasses. One batsman couldn't watch, the other could barely see. It did not have the makings of a miracle.

Stokes preferred not to not to get 'em in singles. He launched Lyon straight for six, and repeated the dose in his next over, before playing an outrageous reverse mow into the Western Terrace. He scooped Cummins for six more, then pulled the previously unhittable Hazlewood through midwicket, reaching an Ashes hundred for the second Sunday in succession. Stokes did not raise his bat: his eye was on the bigger prize.

England needed 33. He paddled a low full toss from Hazlewood for another six, then pulled the next ball for yet another, briefly interesting two of the nine men on the fence. With 17 required, Stokes made his first mistake, miscuing Cummins towards third man: Harris ran in, but spilled a tumbling catch – shades of Simon Jones at Edgbaston in 2005. Australia's wound was instantly salted: a pull for four, then a majestic back-foot force down the ground. Nine wanted.

Countless anecdotes over the next few days would reveal that the country had come to a standstill. After Stokes pushed a single to long-off, Cummins had two balls at Leach. The first was a harmless bouncer, but the second struck the pad, prompting a discussion that would cost Australia the Test. Cummins thought Leach had edged a ball that pitched in line; Paine hadn't seen an edge, but reckoned it pitched outside leg. Somehow, this added up to a review. But Paine was right – and Australia were out of challenges.

Stokes carried on. Another straight six off Lyon just cleared Labuschagne at long-off: two needed, Headingley delirious. The field came in – and the protagonists panicked. After failing to force Lyon through the covers, Stokes played a reverse sweep, but picked out Cummins at short third man. Leach hared out of the traps, Stokes sent him back, Cummins threw gently to the non-striker's end. Leach was yards out, but Lyon – the stumps at his mercy, the Ashes in his grasp – dropped the ball. It was a clanger for the ages.

LAST-WICKET STANDS TO BRING A TEST VICTORY

78	Sri Lanka (191 and 304-9) beat South Africa (235 and 259) at Durban	**2018-19**
76	**England (67 and 362-9) beat Australia (179 and 246) at Leeds**	**2019**
57	Pakistan (256 and 315-9) beat Australia (337 and 232) at Karachi	1994-95
48	South Africa (91 and 287-9) beat England (184 and 190) at Johannesburg	1905-06
39	England (382 and 282-9) beat Australia (266 and 397) at Melbourne	1907-08
38	Australia (216 and 260-9) beat West Indies (272 and 203) at Melbourne	1951-52
19	West Indies (273 and 216-9) beat Pakistan (269 and 219) at St John's	1999-2000
15	England (183 and 263-9) beat Australia (324 and 121) at The Oval	1902
11	India (405 and 216-9) beat Australia (428 and 192) at Mohali	2010-11
9	West Indies (329 and 311-9) beat Australia (490 and 146) at Bridgetown	1998-99
5	England (183 and 173-9) beat South Africa (113 and 242) at Cape Town	1922-23
5	Pakistan (175 and 262-9) beat Bangladesh (281 and 154) at Multan	2003
4	New Zealand (249 and 104-9) beat West Indies (140 and 212) at Dunedin.	1979-80
2	Sri Lanka (321 and 352-9) beat South Africa (361 and 311) at Colombo (PSO)...	2006

Next ball, Stokes missed a sweep, and Lyon – sensing immediate redemption, but with Australia out of reviews – bellowed for leg-before. Umpire Joel Wilson shook his head; Hawk-Eye suggested he should have nodded, though Stokes later disputed the accuracy of the technology.

Amid the chaos, it went almost unnoticed that, for the first time in their partnership, Leach would begin an over on strike. Third ball, he tucked Cummins off his hip, and was called through for the single he later relived in the gathering gloom. The scores were level for as long as it took Stokes to hammer the next delivery through the covers. Headingley erupted, Stokes arched his back, letting out a primal roar, and the batsmen embraced; Stokes called it the best kiss of his life. One by one, the Australians half-hugged him, too stunned to go the whole hog, but conscious they had witnessed one of the greatest innings. England's last pair had added 76 in 62 balls, and Stokes had made 74. It was 1–1. The series was alive.

The temptation was to regard everything that came before as a sideshow, yet it was far from that. On an opening day limited by showers to 52 overs, and played out under lights and louring cloud, Australia were put in by Root – and dismissed for 179. Archer, in his first first-class game at Headingley, removed Harris (who had replaced Cameron Bancroft), and Broad strangled Khawaja down leg. But after a couple of breaks for the weather, Warner and Labuschagne (Steve Smith had failed to recover from concussion) exploited some horrible stuff from Woakes and Stokes to put on 111 in 23 overs.

England yearned for inspiration, and it came from a predictable source. Archer, bowling within himself, he later said, because the conditions required accuracy rather than hostility,

LOWEST FIRST-INNINGS TOTALS THAT LED TO TEST WINS

45	England (second inns: 184) beat Australia (119 and 97) at Sydney	1886-87
63	Australia (122) beat England (101 and 77) at The Oval	1882
67	**England (362-9) beat Australia (179 and 246) at Leeds**	**2019**
75	England (475) beat Australia (123 and 333) at Melbourne	1894-95
75	Australia (336-5) beat South Africa (311 and 99) at Durban	1949-50
76	England (162) beat South Africa (110 and 75) at Leeds	1907
81-7 dec	England (75-6) beat West Indies (102 and 51-6 dec) at Bridgetown.	1934-35
85	**England (303) beat Ireland (207 and 38) at Lord's.**	**2019**
91	South Africa (287-9) beat England (184 and 190) at Johannesburg	1905-06
92	England (330) beat South Africa (177 and 35) at Cape Town.	1898-99
94	New Zealand (160-6) beat India (99 and 154) at Hamilton	2002-03
96	South Africa (236-2) beat Australia (284 and 47) at Cape Town	2011-12
99	Pakistan (365) beat England (141 and 252) at Dubai	2011-12

At Centurion in 1999-2000, England (0-0 dec and 251-8) beat South Africa (248-8 dec and forfeited second innings).

WHAT THEY SAID

Walking off there at the end, when the whole of Headingley was standing up and celebrating, was a very special moment and something I had to try and take in. Moments like that don't come along very often. It was amazing to be part of.

Ben Stokes

A knock-off Nando's and two bars of Yorkie biscuit and raisin.

Stokes explains what he ate the night before

He's a bit of a freak.

Joe Root

It was probably the best Test innings I've seen, and the rest of the team thought the same thing. It was an unbelievable innings. He was too good for us.   *Tim Paine*

Forget this nonsense about teams being a collective and a tight group: England won that match because of one man.   *Michael Vaughan*

I've seen some remarkable cricket moments in my life, but that is the best I've seen in over 50 years.

Geoffrey Boycott

The greatest ever innings by an Englishman.

Alastair Cook

The most incredible performance by anyone, ever.

David Gower

Oh god, that will haunt me for ever, even though we won. I thought, with one ball after that one, we would be really looking to squeeze in a single on that ball, but Stokes was looking to finish the game that over. I would say it was miscommunication, although Stokesy afterwards was like: "What were you doing?!"

Jack Leach on the near run-out that almost cost England

You want him in the trenches with you. He is a special talent and an amazing cricketer.

Shane Warne

He's the Special One and I intend to call him that for the rest of his career.

Ian Botham

Do we need to bother with any other contenders for Sports Personality of The Year?

Gary Lineker

Just come off stage to the news. Cannot believe I missed it, but cannot believe there was such a match!!! #Ashes2019 #BenStokes Test cricket is the gift that does not know how to stop giving. #speechless #radiantwithhappiness

Stephen Fry on Twitter

The Ashes is a Test cricket series played between Ben Stokes and Australia.

Briefly modified Wikipedia entry

Ben Stokes can play centre-half for us next week, that's for sure.

Newcastle United manager Steve Bruce

Star of the summer: Ben Stokes and Jack Leach at the moment of an extraordinary victory.

had Warner caught behind for 61, his only score in this series above 11. Broad trimmed Head's off bail, before Archer bowled Wade round his legs via thigh pad, both for ducks. The innings deteriorated with the light, Labuschagne's vigil ending when he missed a Stokes full toss. Archer pocketed six for 45, England's best Ashes figures at Leeds since 1981, when Bob Willis, that other maker of Headingley miracles, took eight for 43.

Friday dawned bright, like a cosmic joke at Australia's expense. Yet 15 minutes before lunch, England were 45 for six, victims of Hazlewood's metronomics and their own wretchedness; no one played a worse shot than Stokes, who edged a near-wide from Pattinson (in for Peter Siddle) to slip, where Warner held the third of his six catches in the game. Woakes fell first ball after the break, and England were soon rumbled for 67, their lowest at Headingley, and their lowest anywhere against Australia since 1948, when they made 52 at The Oval in Bradman's last Test. Hazlewood gobbled up five for 30, and Australia led by 112. Not for the last time in the game, they had one hand on the Ashes.

Broad got rid of Warner cheaply again (a record 45th Test wicket at Headingley, passing Fred Trueman), and Leach bowled Harris with his first delivery, a beauty that spun back through the left-hander's gate. But Root spilled Labuschagne on 14 at slip off Stokes, who later had him caught behind off a no-ball on 35, then dropped by Bairstow on 42. Meanwhile, Archer limped off mid-over with cramp. England chipped away, but by stumps Australia were 171 for six, leading by 283, which already felt like plenty. Interrupted only by Archer's incomplete over, Stokes had bowled 15 on the trot, but he wasn't finished. By the time Australia had been dismissed for 246 on the third morning (though not before Labuschagne was reprieved for the fourth time, by Bairstow off Broad on 60), Stokes had three for 56 from 24.2 more-or-less unbroken overs. It was heroic, all right, but no one believed it would make any odds.

Burns and Roy came and went with the score on 15, hastening thoughts of a three-day finish; Denly, whose first-innings 12 was still England's best score of the Test, did not suggest permanence. Bit by bit, the mood changed. Denly shelved the flashy drives, and Root, having avoided a third successive duck, went in search of England's mislaid Test-match tempo. Finally, after a stand of 126 encompassing 53 overs – nearly twice as long as their entire first innings – Denly was bounced out by Hazlewood.

Enter Stokes, for an innings in three acts. From his first 73 balls, spanning the third evening and fourth morning, he scored three singles – like Geoffrey Boycott, only more

ENGLAND'S HIGHEST SUCCESSFUL TEST RUN-CHASES

362-9	**v Australia at Leeds**	**2019**	284-6	v NZ at Nottingham	2004
332-7	v Australia at Melbourne	1928-29	282-9	v Australia at Melbourne	1907-08
315-4	v Australia at Leeds	2001	282-3	v NZ at Lord's	2004
307-6	v NZ at Christchurch	1996-97	263-9	v Australia at The Oval	1902
298-4	v Australia at Melbourne	1894-95	251-8	v SA at Centurion	1999-2000
294-4	v NZ at Manchester	2008	247-2	v SA at Nottingham	1998

dogged. By the time Stokes eased Lyon through midwicket, Root had gone for 77, charging Lyon but edging on to his pad and falling to another superb slip catch by Warner (Lyon moved to 356 Test wickets, one ahead of Dennis Lillee). Against the second new ball, Stokes batted normally, while Bairstow counter-attacked. At lunch, England needed 121 runs, Australia six wickets.

Perhaps the prospect of more Headingley magic spooked the English. Bairstow carved to slip, Buttler fell to a dodgy call by Stokes, and Woakes drove straight to short extra. Archer butchered three fours before launching Lyon straight to deep midwicket, and it was 286 for nine when Pattinson trapped Broad. Out walked Leach.

The middle phase of Stokes's innings had produced 58 runs off 101 balls, but his last 74 came from 45. Only two players had scored more for England in a victorious fourth-innings chase: Mark Butcher made an unbeaten 173 in another mad Ashes win at Headingley, in 2001, and Jack Brown 140 at Melbourne in March 1895. Stokes's total of eight sixes beat Kevin Pietersen's Ashes record of seven, at The Oval in 2005.

The question now was whether 2019 could go on to rival that summer. As the sun set over Yorkshire, it was a possibility no one dared discount.

Player of the Match: B. A. Stokes. *Attendance:* 69,739.

Close of play: first day, Australia 179; second day, Australia 171-6 (Labuschagne 53, Pattinson 2); third day, England 156-3 (Root 75, Stokes 2).

HEADINGLEY NOTES AND QUOTES

Test sponsors Specsavers responded to a suggestion from Ben Stokes by promising to supply Jack Leach with free glasses for life. Leach had repeatedly cleaned his glasses during his hour-long innings with a small black cloth, bought from Bristol optometrist Amar Shah. Tracked down on holiday in Mallorca by the *Bristol Post*, Shah – who has worked with the England rugby team, Arsenal, Gloucestershire and Somerset – said Leach's spectacles were steam-proof, and that he was cleaning them to buy Stokes some time. "I thought to myself: 'That's my little cleaning wipe,'" he said. "I should have made the logo bigger, so people could see it!"

Australian captain Tim Paine could hardly bring himself to discuss umpire Joel Wilson's rejection of Nathan Lyon's lbw shout against Stokes with two runs needed. "I saw it live, that's all," he said. "I don't need to see a replay. I don't want to watch that again." Paine did admit he was in no position to criticise the umpires after using up his side's reviews, though Stokes didn't think he was out anyway. "I thought as soon as it hit me it was sliding down leg because there was no spin," he said. "I still can't believe it was three reds."

Five days after the Test, Stokes was sent a Tottenham Hotspur shirt by a fan, with his name and number (55) on the back. "Never supported a club, always wanted to, but never loved football enough really," he tweeted. "My first ever football top was actually a Tottenham one, it was the blue and yellow kit with Thomson on the front. But after getting sent this I guess I'm now officially a Spurs fan."

On the second day, the Australians wore black armbands following the death of Yvonne Conn, mother of their media liaison officer, Malcolm, who had previously made his name as the hard-hitting cricket correspondent of *The Australian*.

Australia

D. A. Warner c Bairstow b Archer	61	– (2) lbw b Broad	0
M. S. Harris c Bairstow b Archer	8	– (1) b Leach	19
U. T. Khawaja c Bairstow b Broad	8	– c Roy b Woakes	23
M. Labuschagne lbw b Stokes	74	– run out (Denly/Bairstow)	80
T. M. Head b Broad	0	– b Stokes	25
M. S. Wade b Archer	0	– c Bairstow b Stokes	33
*†T. D. Paine lbw b Woakes	11	– c Denly b Broad	0
J. L. Pattinson c Root b Archer	2	– c Root b Archer	20
P. J. Cummins c Bairstow b Archer	0	– b Stokes	6
N. M. Lyon lbw b Archer	1	– b Archer	9
J. R. Hazlewood not out	1	– not out	4
B 4, lb 2, w 5, nb 2	13	B 5, lb 13, w 2, nb 7	27

1/12 (2)	2/25 (3)	3/136 (1)	(52.1 overs) 179	1/10 (2)	2/36 (1)	(75.2 overs) 246
4/138 (5)	5/139 (6)	6/162 (7)		3/52 (4)	4/97 (5)	
7/173 (8)	8/174 (9)	9/177 (4) 10/179 (10)		5/163 (6)	6/164 (7) 7/215 (8)	
				8/226 (9)	9/237 (4) 10/246 (10)	

Broad 14–4–32–2; Archer 17.1–3–45–6; Woakes 12–4–51–1; Stokes 9–0–45–1. *Second innings—* Archer 14–2–40–2; Broad 16–2–52–2; Woakes 10–1–34–1; Leach 11–0–46–1; Stokes 24.2–7–56–3.

England

R. J. Burns c Paine b Cummins	9	– c Warner b Hazlewood	7
J. J. Roy c Warner b Hazlewood	9	– b Cummins	8
*J. E. Root c Warner b Hazlewood	0	– c Warner b Lyon	77
J. L. Denly c Paine b Pattinson	12	– c Paine b Hazlewood	50
B. A. Stokes c Warner b Pattinson	8	– not out	135
†J. M. Bairstow c Warner b Hazlewood	4	– c Labuschagne b Hazlewood	36
J. C. Buttler c Khawaja b Hazlewood	5	– run out (Head)	1
C. R. Woakes c Paine b Cummins	5	– c Wade b Hazlewood	1
J. C. Archer c Paine b Cummins	7	– c Head b Lyon	15
S. C. J. Broad not out	4	– lbw b Pattinson	0
M. J. Leach b Hazlewood	1	– not out	1
Lb 3	3	B 5, lb 15, w 10, nb 1	31

1/10 (2)	2/10 (3)	3/20 (1)	(27.5 overs) 67	1/15 (1)	(9 wkts, 124.4 overs) 362
4/34 (5)	5/45 (4)	6/45 (6)		2/15 (2)	3/141 (4)
7/54 (8)	8/56 (7)	9/66 (9) 10/67 (11)		4/159 (3)	5/245 (6) 6/253 (7)
				7/261 (8)	8/286 (9) 9/286 (10)

Cummins 9–4–23–3; Hazlewood 12.5–2–30–5; Lyon 1–0–2–0; Pattinson 5–2–9–2. *Second innings—*Cummins 24.4–5–80–1; Hazlewood 31–11–85–4; Lyon 39–5–114–2; Pattinson 25–9–47–1; Labuschagne 6–0–16–0.

Umpires: C. B. Gaffaney and J. S. Wilson.   Third umpire: H. D. P. K. Dharmasena.
Referee: J. Srinath.

DERBYSHIRE v AUSTRALIANS

At Derby, August 29–31. Australians won by an innings and 54 runs. Toss: Derbyshire. First-class debut: D. R. Melton.

All eyes were on Smith, absent when England levelled the series at Headingley because of the lingering effects of concussion. He had nothing to prove other than his fitness, and the fact that he played here was always going to speak louder than his performance, which proved anticlimactic. His innings ended on 23, when he pulled leg-spinner Critchley straight to a fielder in the deep, and had no bearing on what was coming in the Old Trafford Test or on this match, which the Australians won with predictable ease. Starc furthered his case for a recall to the Test side with seven wickets in the match, while Harris and Khawaja teased the selectors: one would make way for Smith, but neither could convert a half-century (nor could Marsh). The game's highest score came from Derbyshire's du Plooy, who played neatly for his first-innings 86; he top-scored in the second, too. Otherwise, despite a slow pitch, they were hurried out twice. Dustin Melton, a Zimbabwe-born seamer, contributed neither wicket nor run, but did remove Harris with a direct hit from cover.

Close of play: first day, Australians 77-0 (Harris 52, Khawaja 18); second day, Derbyshire 53-3 (du Plooy 9, Hughes 11).

Derbyshire

L. M. Reece c Bancroft b Neser	28	– (2) c Wade b Siddle	14
*B. A. Godleman c Wade b Neser	0	– (1) b Starc	13
A. K. Dal c Carey b Neser	0	– lbw b Starc	1
J. L. du Plooy b Siddle	86	– lbw b Marsh	37
A. L. Hughes c Marsh b Labuschagne	9	– b Neser	11
†H. R. Hosein c Carey b Marsh	19	– c Carey b Siddle	8
M. J. J. Critchley c Carey b Starc	11	– not out	17
A. F. Gleadall b Starc	0	– b Marsh	0
A. P. Palladino b Starc	0	– absent hurt	
Hamidullah Qadri c Siddle b Labuschagne	5	– (9) c Wade b Starc	0
D. R. Melton not out	0	– (10) b Starc	0
Lb 9, w 5	14	B 8, lb 3	11

1/0 (2) 2/0 (3) 3/66 (1)　　　　　(57.2 overs) 172　　1/14 (1) 2/22 (3)　　　　(36.4 overs) 112
4/89 (5) 5/136 (6) 6/151 (7)　　　　　　　　　　　　3/37 (2) 4/58 (5) 5/85 (6)
7/151 (8) 8/151 (9) 9/172 (4) 10/172 (10)　　　　　6/99 (4) 7/99 (8) 8/112 (9) 9/112 (10)

Starc 16–5–46–3; Neser 11–4–31–3; Marsh 11–1–33–1; Siddle 8–3–11–1; Labuschagne 10.2–2–37–2; Smith 1–0–5–0. *Second innings*—Starc 10.4–2–39–4; Neser 8–3–14–1; Labuschagne 4–0–22–0; Siddle 8–2–21–2; Marsh 6–3–5–2.

Australians

M. S. Harris run out (Melton)	64	M. Labuschagne not out	39
*U. T. Khawaja b Dal	72		
M. R. Marsh c Dal b Critchley	74	B 14, w 1, nb 3	18
S. P. D. Smith c Hamidullah Qadri b Critchley	23		
		1/106 (1)　　(5 wkts dec, 92 overs) 338	
M. S. Wade c Hamidullah Qadri b du Plooy	12	2/179 (2) 3/237 (4)	
C. T. Bancroft not out	36	4/254 (3) 5/262 (5)	

†A. T. Carey, M. A. Starc, P. M. Siddle and M. G. Neser did not bat.

Palladino 13–3–34–0; Melton 14–4–55–0; Gleadall 12–0–60–0; Hamidullah Qadri 22–4–79–0; Hughes 3–0–8–0; Dal 12–1–33–1; Critchley 13–0–47–2; du Plooy 3–0–8–1.

Umpires: N. L. Bainton and N. Pratt.

ENGLAND v AUSTRALIA

Fourth Specsavers Test

Gideon Haigh

At Manchester, September 4–8. Australia won by 185 runs. Australia 24pts. Toss: Australia. With the ninth delivery of the last hour of the final day, Australia retained the Ashes in England for the first time in 18 years. As part of a dogged but unavailing retreat, Overton had held them at bay for nearly three hours, until Hazlewood hit him on the pad. A review confirmed his demise – and a 2–1 lead for Australia, with only The Oval to come.

So ended a struggle in which they had held the ascendancy more or less throughout, at least from the moment Smith – back from concussion – walked out on the first day with his team 28 for two. His 211 in more than eight and a half hours was his 26th Test century, and arguably most significant. By the end of the match, his summer's tally stood at 671 from only three Tests, with Don Bradman's 974 in 1930 conceivably within reach. Only Bradman had scored a double-hundred in more Ashes series than Smith's three.

At Chris Woakes's expense, Overton had been England's sole change, while Starc returned for his first game of the series, ahead of James Pattinson. Home confidence had boomed after Stokes's coup in the sun in Leeds, but conditions in Manchester could hardly

TEST DOUBLE-HUNDREDS AT OLD TRAFFORD

311	R. B. Simpson	Australia v England	1964
256	K. F. Barrington	England v Australia	1964
254	J. E. Root	England v Pakistan	2016
223	C. G. Greenidge	West Indies v England	1984
211	**S. P. D. Smith**	**Australia v England**	**2019**
210	G. Kirsten	South Africa v England	1998
205	Aamir Sohail	Pakistan v England	1992

have been less similar. On the first day, restricted to 44 overs, rain was seldom far away, the cold bitter, the crosswind ceaseless, the dark relieved by the floodlights. Australia's bowlers must have welcomed Paine's success at the toss; four of their countrymen in the crowd were treated for exposure.

Broad removed Warner for another duck, and soon had Harris too. But, looking more orthodox for the idiosyncratic company, Labuschagne helped Smith get established in a patient third-wicket partnership of 116, before his fourth consecutive half-century was ended by a skilful nip-backer from Overton. Thereafter, Smith seemed to bat with impunity, adapting superbly as England defaulted to shorter lengths: 90 of his runs came behind the wicket. He even disposed firmly of a beach ball that blew across the ground. Archer and Stokes, game changers at Headingley, were innocuous. On the second morning, Archer – whose pace was down – missed a sharp caught-and-bowled offered by Smith, on 65, while Stokes was withdrawn from the attack in the afternoon because of a shoulder injury. At times, England seemed more concerned with battling the elements than their opponents.

Potentially their best session, after lunch on the second day, soured into their worst. Twice they spared Paine: on nine, when Roy was the culprit at second slip, and on 49, when substitute Sam Curran spilled a low chance at mid-on. In between – and worst of all – Smith edged Leach to Stokes on 118. It would have left Australia 273 for six, had the third umpire not established that Leach had somehow overstepped in the process of his hop, skip and jump. Root looked furious, inconsolable, and barked at his players. Smith quickly recovered his sangfroid. In a session in which England might have re-established themselves, they leaked runs like Uber leaks money: 124 in 32 wicketless overs. Smith's partnership with Paine was ended first ball after tea by Overton, but – at 145 – it would prove the highest of the series.

After the break, Australia took complete mastery of the match. Smith, Starc and Lyon added 110 in 21 overs for the eighth and ninth wickets, before Cummins removed the newly promoted Denly in the ten left by Paine's declaration. Smith's departure had been suitably eccentric: having found gaps with unerring precision in the course of 319 balls that included 24 fours and two sixes, he picked out backward point with a reverse sweep from Root's part-time spin. By the time Starc hit seven fours and two sixes, Australia's first innings had swollen to nearly 500; had Leach not transgressed, it might have been closer to 300.

AUSTRALIAN OPENERS MAKING A PAIR IN A TEST

A. C. Bannerman	v England at Lord's	1888
V. T. Trumper	v England at Melbourne	1907-08
J. H. W. Fingleton	v England at Adelaide	1932-33
V. Y. Richardson	v England at Sydney	1932-33
J. Moroney	v England at Brisbane	1950-51
R. Edwards	v England at Leeds	1972
K. R. Stackpole	v New Zealand at Auckland	1973-74
G. M. Wood	v New Zealand at Perth	1980-81
M. A. Taylor	v Pakistan at Karachi	1994-95
D. A. Warner	**v England at Manchester**	**2019**

Rain swirled again on the third day, wiping out the morning. But, after the early loss of nightwatchman Overton (a 100th Test catch for Smith), batting conditions remained benign, and Root bedded in with Burns to restore English heart. Starc proved wayward, except for a delivery that bisected Root and shattered his protector; Lyon, struggling with a split spinning finger, posed little threat; Paine permutated limited options as best he could. The partnership grew to 141 in 53 overs, England's highest of the series. Their eventual collapse came as a form of delayed concussion. Either side of tea, Cummins had bowled a relentless spell of 10–2–22–0, seeing a chance from Root, on 54, fly between keeper and first slip, and otherwise challenging both edges at high speed. He was succeeded in the last hour by Hazlewood, who promptly swept away Burns, Root and the increasingly hapless Roy, now in the middle order after swapping spots with Denly, but still lunging at the ball as if he were opening at the World Cup. The spell effectively ended England's hopes of arriving in south London all square.

On the fourth day, Starc justified his inclusion, bowling Bairstow through the gate, locating a testing length to remove Stokes, and castling Broad. England just achieved their immediate task of avoiding the follow-on, thanks mainly to some calculated blows by Buttler, although no thanks to Archer, who might have been languidly run out first ball, then perished to a wretched waft. He atoned when Australia batted again, cranking up his speeds beyond 90mph, at last getting the better of the adhesive Labuschagne, and bowling the sketchy Head.

At Root's instigation, Stokes had addressed England's team huddle before the innings began. It appeared to have an effect. Broad again proved his lethality to left-handers, trapping both Warner and Harris; Warner's pair was his first, prolonging his agonies to seven single-figure scores in eight innings. But with Australia 50 for four, Root turned to Overton and Leach, and resumed with them after tea; in ten overs, England's effort

OLD TRAFFORD NOTES AND QUOTES

After Jofra Archer's quiet performance in Australia's first innings, England fast-bowling coach Chris Silverwood urged critics to "cut him a bit of slack". He added: "I think we're just going to be careful with Jofra. He's still finding his way into international cricket. He's figuring out what it's all about."

Two Australian fans were thrown out of the ground by police on the opening day after shouting, "Jofra, show us your passport" while he was fielding. Archer has a British passport.

The Australians caused a stir with their post-match celebrations on the outfield. After chanting, among other things, "Who did we beat? England. How did we do it? Easy", they dropped to the turf for some press-ups. Steve Smith was photographed wearing glasses, widely interpreted as mockery of Jack Leach – though Cricket Australia insisted he was doing an impression of the bespectacled former Australian Test opener Chris Rogers, whose name had barely been mentioned all summer.

Surrender: Jos Buttler's error of judgment against Josh Hazlewood hastens England's defeat.

tapered, and Smith surged again. By his exalted standards, his 82 was not a great innings: there were some dazzling improvisations and madcap capers, including one delivery from Archer from which he toppled back and ended up shaping to play from a supine position. But it accentuated the difference between Smith and the rest: he looked to be sunbathing on a rock to which everyone else was desperately clinging beneath smashing waves. His fifth-wicket stand with Wade was worth 105, before he miscued a big drive off Leach, who this time stayed behind the line. Paine then expedited his second declaration of the game with four neat boundaries in 18 deliveries.

The closure, with an English target of 383 in a day and 30 minutes, paid off at once: with the third and fourth deliveries of the innings, Cummins swept aside Burns and Root, whose third duck of the series came courtesy of a near-perfect delivery that kissed the outside of the top of off. England entered the final day needing to bat a minimum 98 overs to save the match. It was a tribute to their determination that, at various stages, this looked almost possible.

Overnight batsmen Denly and Roy hung in, respectively, for nearly three hours and nearly two. But Cummins saw off Roy and Stokes, before Denly – having ground out a half-century – perished to a short-leg catch off Lyon to leave England 93 for five shortly after lunch. The pitch, however, was slow and true, and the crowd greeted each passing over with patriotic rapture. Australia needed to find two searching deliveries after tea: Hazlewood bent a 75-over-old ball back to end Buttler's two-and-a-half-hour resistance as the batsman abjured a stroke; then Labuschagne, brought opportunistically into the attack, spun one sharply from the rough to force a bat-pad catch from Leach after an hour's defence. Overton followed moments later.

Strung out for nearly 92 overs, England's effort was decidedly gripping. Root took comfort from it, reiterating his commitment to leading them into the future: "It's tough to take, losing the Ashes. But when you find yourself in a situation like today, you learn a lot about your team and the guys."

Paine, who had an excellent match, with two good innings, two sharp catches, two well-timed declarations and 30 last-day bowling changes, admitted to some anxiety as England's resistance extended. "There were a few nervous moments there, coming off Headingley," he said. "But I thought we learned from that, held our nerve and bowled really well against a team that fought really hard, like we knew they would." Defeat in the Third Test had been of a kind to "break a lot of teams", but in the collective effort Paine took a good tradesman's satisfaction: "We turned up here and did our job, like good sports teams do."

All that remained now for Australia was to win a series in England for the first time since Steve Waugh's side in 2001.

Player of the Match: S. P. D. Smith. *Attendance:* 116,857.

Close of play: first day, Australia 170-3 (Smith 60, Head 18); second day, England 23-1 (Burns 15, Overton 3); third day, England 200-5 (Stokes 7, Bairstow 2); fourth day, England 18-2 (Denly 10, Roy 8).

Australia

M. S. Harris lbw b Broad	13	– (2) lbw b Broad		6
D. A. Warner c Bairstow b Broad	0	– (1) lbw b Broad		0
M. Labuschagne b Overton	67	– lbw b Archer		11
S. P. D. Smith c Denly b Root	211	– c Stokes b Leach		82
T. M. Head lbw b Broad	19	– b Archer		12
M. S. Wade c Root b Leach	16	– c Bairstow b Archer		34
*†T. D. Paine c Bairstow b Overton	58	– not out		23
P. J. Cummins c Stokes b Leach	4			
M. A. Starc not out	54	– (8) not out		3
N. M. Lyon not out	26			
B 8, lb 14, w 3, nb 4	29	B 5, lb 2, w 7, nb 1		15

1/1 (2) 2/28 (1) (8 wkts dec, 126 overs) 497   1/0 (1) (6 wkts dec, 42.5 overs) 186
3/144 (3) 4/183 (5) 5/224 (6)   2/16 (2) 3/24 (3)
6/369 (7) 7/387 (8) 8/438 (4)   4/44 (5) 5/149 (4) 6/158 (6)

J. R. Hazlewood did not bat.

Broad 25-2-97-3; Archer 27-3-97-0; Stokes 10.5-0-66-0; Leach 26.1-3-83-2; Overton 28-3-85-2; Denly 3-1-8-0; Root 6-0-39-1. *Second innings*—Broad 14-4-54-2; Archer 14-2-45-3; Overton 5.5-1-22-0; Leach 9-0-58-1.

England

R. J. Burns c Smith b Hazlewood	81	– c Head b Cummins		0
J. L. Denly c Wade b Cummins	4	– c Labuschagne b Lyon		53
C. Overton c Smith b Hazlewood	5	– (8) lbw b Hazlewood		21
*J. E. Root lbw b Hazlewood	71	– (3) b Cummins		0
J. J. Roy b Hazlewood	22	– (4) b Cummins		31
B. A. Stokes c Smith b Starc	26	– (5) c Paine b Cummins		1
†J. M. Bairstow b Starc	17	– (6) lbw b Starc		25
J. C. Buttler b Cummins	41	– b Hazlewood		34
J. C. Archer c Paine b Cummins	1	– lbw b Lyon		1
S. C. J. Broad b Starc	5	– (11) not out		0
M. J. Leach not out	4	– (10) c Wade b Labuschagne		12
B 4, lb 11, w 5, nb 4	24	B 9, lb 8, nb 2		19

1/10 (2) 2/25 (3) 3/166 (1) (107 overs) 301   1/0 (1) 2/0 (3) (91.3 overs) 197
4/175 (4) 5/196 (5) 6/228 (7)   3/66 (4) 4/74 (5)
7/243 (6) 8/256 (9) 9/283 (10) 10/301 (8)   5/93 (2) 6/138 (6) 7/172 (7)
    8/173 (9) 9/196 (10) 10/197 (8)

Starc 22-7-80-3; Hazlewood 25-6-57-4; Cummins 24-6-60-3; Lyon 36-4-89-0. *Second innings*—Cummins 29-9-43-4; Hazlewood 17.3-5-31-2; Lyon 29-12-51-2; Starc 16-2-46-1; Labuschagne 4-1-9-1; Head 1-1-0-0.

Umpires: H. D. P. K. Dharmasena and M. Erasmus.   Third umpire: R. S. A. Palliyaguruge.
Referee: J. Srinath.

ENGLAND v AUSTRALIA

Fifth Specsavers Test

RICHARD WHITEHEAD

At The Oval, September 12–15. England won by 135 runs. England 24 pts. Toss: Australia.

In the closing moments of his 24th international match of the summer, Root scooted eagerly across the Oval outfield as if it were early May, back in Malahide, where it had begun. After he positioned himself at square leg, Lyon obligingly swept Leach straight into his waiting palms. Next ball, on the other side of the pitch for the left-handed Hazlewood, he dived low at midwicket to grasp an uppish clip and complete a victory that ensured the first drawn Ashes series since 1972.

Beforehand, at the end of the most gruelling home season undertaken by an England player, Root had appeared weary. Now, the boyish grin and puppyish enthusiasm were back: as he put it, 2–2 sounded a lot better than 3–1. England deserved credit for rousing themselves for one last push. But they also benefited from muddle-headed Australian selection, and shoddy catching on the first day, which suggested the tourists had celebrated a little too lustily at Old Trafford. Preferring Siddle to Mitchell Starc seemed perverse,

---

IT'S PERSONAL

Bowler dismissing one batsman seven times in a Test series:

Bowler	Batsman	Balls	R	W	Avge	
S. C. J. Broad (E)	**D. A. Warner (A)**.	**104**	**35**	**7**	**5.00**	**2019**
J. B. Statham (E)	T. L. Goddard (SA)	215	76	7	10.85	1960
G. D. McGrath (A)	M. A. Atherton (E)	190	84	7	12.00	1997
C. V. Grimmett (A)	I. J. Siedle (SA)	261	85	7	12.14	1935-36
N. M. Lyon (A)	M. M. Ali (E)	218	90	7	12.85	2017-18
G. F. Lawson (A)	D. I. Gower (E)	201	139	7	19.85	1989

Benedict Bermange.

---

even before he was hampered by a hip injury – especially with Mitchell Marsh replacing Travis Head to purvey Siddle-esque seam. The same applied to Paine's decision to bowl, an error compounded by the fielding. Paine, who broke his thumb near the end, admitted to "a couple of regrets", though he surely had more.

After Manchester's icy blasts, it was possible to consult forecasts without worrying about the wind chill. The latest Test ever staged in England basked in four days of balmy sunshine, ensuring the ECB got away with a piece of high-risk scheduling. Encouraged by Paine's munificence, England compiled what was then the highest opening stand of the series – 27 – before Denly drove loosely at Cummins. It took Smith three attempts to cling on, a taste of what lay ahead.

Root was dropped on 24, 25 and 30 – most culpably by Siddle at fine leg – and reached 7,000 Test runs with a delightful square-drive off Hazlewood, which suggested he was relocating his fluency. But, after Burns fell to a poorly executed pull on 47, Root was bowled for 57 by a beauty from Cummins, and from 170 for three England subsided to 226 for eight. The sequence included the wicket of Sam Curran, the talisman of 2018 making his first appearance of the Ashes – in place of Jason Roy – because Stokes's shoulder injury meant he could not bowl. The damage was done not by Cummins or Hazlewood, but by Marsh, making expert use of the inswinging yorker. Paine's gamble at the toss was beginning to look shrewd.

OVAL TIME

Zaffar Kunial

I forget that cricket grounds exist in winter
seeing out snow and floating in fog.
I forget that the ground's been there almost forever
and curling around it like a finger
pointing at the wrought-iron gasholder, a buried river
leaving a curve, the Effra.
A road like a brooch around an opal.
The Kennington Oval.

The O of a cambered surface that drains the water
like an upturned saucer, keeping the clay dry
in the middle. The filled O of the rolled field, its funky
four-tone tartan. Green. Green. Green. And green.
The O of a crowd in the shade. The eternal
O of a roped boundary. The O

of a century. A double century. Bradman's duck.
The O of their open mouths watching
a last innings. A last Test. Of not knowing
how many summers you'll have left.
Of the tilted earth, of an arc, of orbiting the sun
around an invisible seam. The long repeating

wide-brimmed O, as a river of white sunhats streams
in summer from the Vauxhall tube. The shaken
O of an unstopped urn, as a life's dust is tipped over
the stumpless wicket, in winter, and atoms drift and turn
up towards the gods, towards the favourite seats
where days happened and stuck.

Time unfolds again and again from the crease. Fielders
stand with their well-ironed shadows. Grace
takes guard, where a bearded man he can't see called Ali
takes a hat-trick. An event horizon where Richards
has more time at the crease, sees the ball a nano-
second sooner. Where twitchy Smith stares into history

and bobs like a bird, a wagtail or a dipper
half sitting, half standing as if stubbornly over
an egg. Sure as an egg timer. Over and over. The O
of a decommissioned gasholder, of a crowd's open silence,
of a NO shouted at the non-striker's end. The O
behind that held-up, white, skeletal glove.
NO. STAY THERE.
The O of that palm, creased like a river.

*Zaffar Kunial was poet in residence at The Oval during the Fifth Test, as part
of the nationwide Places of Poetry festival (placesofpoetry.org.uk).*

Face-off: neither Matthew Wade nor Jofra Archer yields an inch.

Buttler, however, got the crowd going with a thrilling counter-thrust. Having started cautiously to 29, he hit Hazlewood for successive straight sixes, and went past a maiden Ashes fifty (at the 17th attempt) with a third, over square leg. His partnership with his old Somerset colleague Leach was worth 68 when it was ended by Cummins, armed with the new ball on the second morning. Marsh bowled Leach to complete his first Test five-for but, on a pitch already taking turn, England had the upper hand.

There was a twist to a familiar plot when Warner, flailing desperately at a wide ball, fell to Archer, not Broad, for five – making him the first opener in Test history to suffer eight single-figure dismissals in a series. There appeared to be daylight between bat and ball, but Ultra Edge detected the slightest contact. Archer also snared Harris and Labuschagne, two short of another fifty, but – as so often – Smith was playing a different game. Against Curran, he offered a series of exaggerated leaves, but showed everything was in good working order by lofting Leach over long-on for six to bring up his tenth successive Ashes fifty, a record for a Test batsman against one opponent, beating Inzamam-ul-Haq's nine against England between 2001 and 2006.

On 66, he was dropped by Root at slip off Curran – a difficult chance, high and fast to his right – but Curran is seldom discouraged, and soon claimed Paine and Cummins in two balls. While Smith remained, Australia could always forge ahead, hence the incredulity when he missed a straight one from Woakes (replacing Overton) on 80, his lowest score of the series so far.

Archer put an end to some swiping from Lyon and – with the help of a stunning slip catch by Burns – Siddle, becoming the first England bowler to take two six-fors in an Ashes since Ian Botham in 1981. It was reward for his consistently challenging line, as much as his pace. With England's lead a handy but not definitive 69, Burns and Denly (late to the ground that morning after becoming a father for the second time) faced an awkward 20 minutes before the close. They clung on, just. Denly, on nought, survived a straightforward slip catch, though in fairness to Harris the ground was deep in shadow, and Burns overturned a leg-before decision off the day's last ball.

Next morning, conditions were less challenging. Denly was confident enough to lift Lyon for ten off two balls, and doubled his first-innings opening partnership with Burns,

who then feathered a cut off Lyon. Root was greeted by some extended vocals from Australia's agitator-in-chief Wade, salty enough for the umpires to intervene. Denly, meanwhile, was subjected to a more conventional working-over: he was hit twice by Siddle, then by Cummins in the box. The crowd winced; Root giggled. Denly went to his third fifty in five innings with a crisp clip off his legs, and enjoyed a let-off on 54 when Australia opted not to review an lbw appeal from Marsh that would have hit leg.

It was hard to shake the feeling that a collapse would leave England susceptible to an Adelaide 2006-style heist (then, their first-innings lead had been 38), but the partnership to soothe fears came when Stokes joined Denly. Stokes's final innings of a summer with which he will always be synonymous contained some lovely strokes, and they had put on 127 when he was bowled by a ripper from Lyon. Attention turned to whether Denly could wet the baby's head with a first Test hundred, but on 94 he edged a Siddle outswinger: Paine had moved up to the stumps, and the ball pinged off his thigh to Smith at first slip. Buttler reprised his first-innings role with an invaluable 47.

The Australian fielding had sharpened up. From successive balls, Smith took a brilliant diving goalkeeper's catch – his sixth of the Test – to remove Woakes, before Buttler fell to Labuschagne's headlong dash from deep square leg. When the last two wickets went down on the fourth morning, though not before Broad had forearm-smashed two sixes off Cummins, Australia needed 399. A sign of Smith's stature was that it did not seem beyond the realms of possibility. Broad was having none of it. He sent Harris's off stump cartwheeling in his third over, and in his next induced Warner to edge to third slip. It was the seventh time he had dismissed him in the series; he also became the first England bowler to take 20 or more wickets in four separate Ashes.

Smith and his new accomplice Labuschagne carried Australian hopes. But Labuschagne was smartly stumped by Bairstow to give Leach his first wicket, and Smith athletically held by Stokes at leg slip off Broad for 23, a dismissal England had waited for the entire summer. It produced a full-throated roar, followed by a standing ovation. After all the booing, Smith's oddball genius had earned enduring respect. An aggregate of 774 runs, more than twice any of his team-mates', and an average of 110: both spoke of greatness.

Expectations of an early finish reckoned without Wade, described by Bairstow on his arrival at the crease as the "shit-stirrer". Revelling in the invective, he played an innings full of booming drives and up-yours defiance. The backchat as the players left the field at

---

OVAL NOTES AND QUOTES

In the build-up to his last match, there were warm words for England head coach Trevor Bayliss, and some unusual farewell gifts from the media. George Dobell, senior correspondent at ESPNcricinfo, presented him with a hip flask inscribed "Drink positively", a candle and a CD – a reference to a column in which Dobell suggested that Bayliss's laid-back approach could be replicated by "a couple of scented candles, a yucca plant and a CD of ambient whale noises."

Former prime minister Theresa May attended on the second day. Earlier in the week, her resignation honours list included Geoffrey Boycott and Andrew Strauss, both at the Test on media duty.

David Gower's final match as part of the Sky Sports team was enlivened when he was caught swearing on air at the end of the lunch interval on Saturday. Gower was handing back from the outfield when he was prompted to name the waiting commentators. He forgot to press the mute button: "Let's take you now to the commentary box and… ain't got a fucking clue." It led to what may have been a first – Shane Warne apologising for an expletive.

Following events at Old Trafford, where Steve Smith had appeared to mock Jack Leach's glasses, both posed for a photograph… wearing glasses. "He came up to me to let me know that it wasn't about me," said Leach. "I was kind of hoping it was, and thought it was a good laugh. I was very embarrassed after Headingley when the video came out of me doing my one not out. I think I deserved that, to be honest."

TOP-SCORER IN MOST CONSECUTIVE TEST INNINGS

7	S. Chanderpaul (WI)	69 (v P), 74, 50, 116*, 136*, 70 (v E), 104 (v SA) ..	2006-07 to 2007-08
6	G. A. Headley (WI) ..	93, 53, 270*, 106, 107, 51 (v E)	1934-35 to 1939
6	**S. P. D. Smith (A).**	**144, 142, 92, 211, 82, 80 (v E)**	**2019**
5	V. S. Hazare (I)	52, 40, 122 (v WI), 164*, 155 (v E)..........	1948-49 to 1951-52
5	E. A. B. Rowan (SA)	57, 236, 60*, 55, 45 (v E)	1951
5	I. V. A. Richards (WI)	101, 50, 98 (v A), 142, 130 (v I)	1975-76
5	B. C. Lara (WI)	87, 145, 152, 20, 179 (v E)	1995
5	G. P. Thorpe (E) ...	46, 113*, 32* (v SL), 80, 138 (v P)	2000-01 to 2001
5	A. J. Strauss (E).	126, 94*, 25, 136, 45 (v SA)	2004-05
5	S. Chanderpaul (WI) .	94, 68, 69 (v A), 87*, 91 (v E)..............	2011-12 to 2012
5	K. C. Sangakkara (SL)	319, 105 (v B), 147, 61, 79 (v E)	2013-14 to 2014

tea prompted the umpires to speak to both captains, but didn't trouble Wade. He was soon involved in a compelling confrontation with Archer, who bowled eight overs unchanged from the Pavilion End and, galvanised by the sight of his Hobart Hurricanes captain, put the pedal to the metal. There were stare-outs that belonged to the weigh-in before a title fight (although boxers are usually better matched in stature), and at one point an extraordinary field, with three men on the leg-side boundary, and Stokes on the ropes at long stop.

But Wade would not be shifted, at least not until he had completed his second hundred of the series. Root eventually got him via Bairstow's second stumping. After that, it was a question of whether Australia could take the game into the fifth day, remarkably destined to be another sell-out. But Leach mopped up, and Paine joined Ricky Ponting (Edgbaston 2005) as the only Australian captains to lose after opting to bowl in England.

Paine kissed a replica urn amid a shower of green and gold ticker tape, but the ECB marketeers ensured the words "Series drawn" appeared prominently behind the Australians – perhaps a riposte to the giant hands indicating 4–0 on the podium at Sydney in January 2018. "What a summer of cricket it has been," said Root. No one disagreed.

Player of the Match: J. C. Archer. *Attendance:* 95,918.

Players of the Series: England – B. A. Stokes; Australia – S. P. D. Smith.
Compton–Miller Medal: S. P. D. Smith.
Close of play: first day, England 271-8 (Buttler 64, Leach 10); second day, England 9-0 (Burns 4, Denly 1); third day, England 313-8 (Archer 3, Leach 5).

England

R. J. Burns c Marsh b Hazlewood	47	– c Paine b Lyon	20
J. L. Denly c Smith b Cummins................	14	– c Smith b Siddle..............	94
*J. E. Root c Cummins......................	57	– c Smith b Lyon...............	21
B. A. Stokes c Lyon b Marsh.................	20	– b Lyon	67
†J. M. Bairstow lbw b Marsh.................	22	– c Smith b Marsh..............	14
J. C. Buttler b Cummins....................	70	– c Labuschagne b Siddle	47
S. M. Curran c Smith b Marsh...............	15	– c Paine b Cummins	17
C. R. Woakes lbw b Marsh..................	2	– c Smith b Marsh..............	6
J. C. Archer c Paine b Hazlewood	9	– c Paine b Cummins	3
M. J. Leach b Marsh.......................	21	– c Hazlewood b Lyon	9
S. C. J. Broad not out.....................	0	– not out	12
B 3, lb 7, w 5, nb 2	17	B 7, lb 11, nb 1.............	19

1/27 (2) 2/103 (1) 3/130 (4)   (87.1 overs) 294   1/54 (1) 2/87 (3)   (95.3 overs) 329
4/170 (3) 5/176 (5) 6/199 (7)   3/214 (4) 4/222 (2)
7/205 (8) 8/226 (9) 9/294 (6) 10/294 (10)   5/249 (5) 6/279 (7) 7/305 (8)
8/305 (6) 9/317 (9) 10/329 (10)

Cummins 25.5–6–84–3; Hazlewood 21–7–76–2; Siddle 17–1–61–0; Marsh 18.2–4–46–5; Lyon 4–0–12–0; Labuschagne 1–0–5–0. *Second innings*—Cummins 21.5–5–67–2; Hazlewood 19–5–57–0; Lyon 24.3–5–69–4; Siddle 13–4–52–2; Marsh 11–1–40–2; Labuschagne 7–1–26–0.

Australia

D. A. Warner c Bairstow b Archer	5	– (2) c Burns b Broad	11
M. S. Harris c Stokes b Archer	3	– (1) b Broad	9
M. Labuschagne lbw b Archer	48	– st Bairstow b Leach	14
S. P. D. Smith lbw b Woakes	80	– c Stokes b Broad	23
M. S. Wade lbw b Curran	19	– st Bairstow b Root	117
M. R. Marsh c Leach b Archer	17	– c Buttler b Root	24
*†T. D. Paine c Bairstow b Curran	1	– lbw b Leach	21
P. J. Cummins lbw b Curran	0	– c Bairstow b Broad	9
P. M. Siddle c Burns b Archer	18	– not out	13
N. M. Lyon b Archer	25	– c Root b Leach	1
J. R. Hazlewood not out	1	– c Root b Leach	0
B 1, lb 2, w 5	8	B 2, lb 12, nb 2, p 5	21

1/5 (1) 2/14 (2) 3/83 (3)   (68.5 overs) 225
4/118 (5) 5/160 (6) 6/166 (7)
7/166 (8) 8/187 (4) 9/224 (10) 10/225 (9)

1/18 (1) 2/29 (2)   (77 overs) 263
3/56 (3) 4/85 (4)
5/148 (6) 6/200 (7) 7/244 (8)
8/260 (5) 9/263 (10) 10/263 (11)

Broad 12–3–45–0; Archer 23.5–9–62–6; Curran 17–6–46–3; Woakes 10–2–51–1; Leach 6–1–18–0. *Second innings*—Broad 15–1–62–4; Archer 16–2–66–0; Curran 8–3–22–0; Leach 22–8–49–4; Woakes 7–1–19–0; Root 9–1–26–2.

Umpires: H. D. P. K. Dharmasena and M. Erasmus.   Third umpire: R. S. A. Palliyaguruge.
Referee: J. Srinath.

NEW ZEALAND v ENGLAND IN 2019-20

REVIEW BY LAWRENCE BOOTH

Twenty20 internationals (5): New Zealand 2, England 3
Test matches (2): New Zealand 1, England 0

A little over three months after their heart-stopping World Cup final, the sides were thrown together again for a tour that rarely set the pulse racing, though was not entirely devoid of drama. With England resting several senior players for the five Twenty20 games, and the Tests sitting outside the new ICC World Championship (drawn up after the schedule for this trip had been agreed), the cricket struggled for context. The presence on the fixture list of Saxton Oval in Nelson and the equally idyllic Bay Oval in Mount Maunganui provided some consolation, while adding to the holiday atmosphere.

Attempts to hype the 20-over matches as New Zealand's chance for revenge were unconvincing, mainly because the teams got on so well. Yet, incredibly, the decider at Eden Park went to another super over, with England again the victors, though this time without a second tie-breaker. A slow-moving Test series deservedly went New Zealand's way, allowing some restoration of national pride, which had been further dented a few weeks earlier, when England dumped the All Blacks out of the rugby World Cup in Japan.

For England's new head coach Chris Silverwood, victory in the Twenty20s, achieved from 2–1 down following a collapse at Nelson, was a bonus, but the two-Test series provided a weary reminder of deficiencies away from home. The way some players spoke about the Kookaburra, they might as well have been bowling with one of the local oranges, which were only just out of season: for the first time in England's 20 Test trips to New Zealand, games started in late spring. (Their earliest previous Test here had begun on January 10, on their first visit, in 1930; this time, the Mount Maunganui Test got going on November 21. Only once had New Zealand played an earlier home Test, against Pakistan on November 17, 2016.)

The upshot was England's tenth overseas series out of 12 which they failed to win since upsetting India in 2012-13. They also equalled their longest winless streak – seven Tests – in New Zealand, though the two previous sequences had consisted of 13 draws and only one defeat. There was nothing as drastic as the 58 all out at Auckland that had marred their previous visit, early in 2018, but that

NEW ZEALAND'S HIGHEST TOTALS AGAINST ENGLAND

615-9 dec	**Mount Maunganui** .	**2019-20**	476	Lord's	1994
551-9 dec	Lord's	1973	470	Hamilton	2007-08
537	Wellington	1983-84	469-9 dec	Lord's	1931
523	Lord's	2015	462-9 dec	Lord's	1990
512-6 dec	Wellington	1987-88	460-9 dec	Dunedin	2012-13
496-9 dec	Auckland	1983-84	454-8 dec	Leeds	2015
496-9 dec	Manchester	1999	451	Christchurch	2001-02
484	Lord's	1949	443	Auckland	2012-13

Gareth Copley, Getty Images

Ebbing away: England lose nightwatchman Jack Leach on the fourth evening, and New Zealand scent blood at Mount Maunganui.

was scarcely cause for celebration. England's bowlers kept things tight, but were as far away as ever from dismissing good teams in thankless conditions.

Results aside, English interest centred on two men. Joe Root's captaincy had been all but rubber-stamped until the 2021-22 Ashes, with director of cricket Ashley Giles seeking stability for a side in need of direction. When Root fell in the First Test for two and 11, playing what he cheerfully described as a pair of "horrendous" dabs outside off stump, his position came under unprecedented scrutiny; for the first time since replacing Alastair Cook in 2017, he was averaging below 40 as captain. But he responded like a champion, making 226 on a sluggish track at Hamilton's Seddon Park. If he never stopped smiling, there were times when it looked a bit rictus.

Jofra Archer, meanwhile, returned to terra firma after a summer on cloud nine, taking only two wickets at 104 apiece in 82 overs, and finishing bottom of England's averages. Dropped catches didn't help: a blunder by Joe Denly on the final day at Hamilton instantly qualified as one of England's worst. But it was clear Archer had lots to learn if he was to supply Root with the cutting edge he craved overseas.

The relationship between captain and star bowler had the air of a soap opera, every gesture being pored over. At different moments, Root stood accused both of overbowling Archer (in the First Test, he sent down 42 overs, 12 more than in any first-class innings) and of ignoring him altogether. He also made it clear he wanted Archer to summon the pace that had unsettled the Australians a couple of months earlier. The speed-gun readings were not in his favour, though Archer nursed a theory that the machinery was defective. Some racist heckling from a spectator at Mount Maunganui – who was later banned from attending games in New Zealand for two years – added to an uncomfortable first tour.

After the inconsistency of the Trevor Bayliss years, Silverwood had laid out a disarmingly concise wish list. He wanted batsmen to place a premium on their wickets, and rack up match-defining first-innings totals, preferably 500. And he wanted bowlers to find a way of taking 20 wickets without the aid of green grass and a red Dukes. Both requests sounded like the basic requirements of the five-day game, home or abroad; that they needed saying at all reflected the chaotic nature of England's recent Test cricket.

The players responded in patches. A first-day score of 241 for four at Mount Maunganui boded well, but it was followed by a surrender triggered by the gung-ho dismissal of Ben Stokes. New Zealand's doughty wicketkeeper B-J. Watling showed them how it should be done, compiling 205 in more than 11 hours, and adding 261 with Mitchell Santner, who scored a maiden Test hundred. England then batted fecklessly, and lost by an innings. In the Second Test, they again spurned the chance to put the game beyond New Zealand, and lost their last five wickets for 21 after reaching 455 for five. Quite simply, they lacked their opponents' ruthlessness, and possibly their patience.

The bowling – minus the recuperating Jimmy Anderson and Mark Wood, as well as Moeen Ali, who had taken a break from Tests – ranged from the

---

FIVE STATS YOU MAY HAVE MISSED

BENEDICT BERMANGE

- At Mount Maunganui, England's bowlers conceded 21 runs from wides, equalling the record for a Test innings, set by West Indies in Australia's total of 251 at Bridgetown in 2007-08.

- Mitchell Santner was only the fourth man to follow a Test century by dismissing the first three batsmen in the next innings of the match:

S. A. Durani	India v West Indies at Port-of-Spain	1961-62
A. W. Greig	England v West Indies at Bridgetown	1973-74
K. P. Pietersen.	England v South Africa at Leeds	2012
M. J. Santner.	**New Zealand v England at Mount Maunganui** .	**2019-20**

Greig took the first four wickets.

- At Hamilton, Joe Root became only the second England outfielder to catch the first three batsmen in a Test innings, after Len Hutton, who caught Sidney Barnes, Don Bradman and Arthur Morris in the 1948 Ashes Test at Lord's.

- In New Zealand's second innings, Ross Taylor became the sixth batsman known to have completed a Test century with successive sixes:

S. R. Waugh (103*)	Australia v Pakistan at Sharjah	2002-03
B. C. Lara (130)	West Indies v Pakistan at Bridgetown	2004-05
P. J. Hughes (115).	Australia v South Africa at Durban	2008-09
A. B. de Villiers (129)	South Africa v India at Centurion	2010-11
B. A. Stokes (112)	England v South Africa at The Oval	2017
L. R. P. L. Taylor (105*) . .	**New Zealand v England at Hamilton**	**2019-20**

Hughes's century was his first, in his second Test. Stokes hit the next ball for six as well.

- Neil Wagner became the first New Zealander to claim two five-wicket hauls in a home series against England.

perseveringto the anodyne. In both games, New Zealand were five down for fewer than 200, yet England could not sustain the pressure, and grew fixated on the refusal of the ball to deviate from the straight and narrow. Sam Curran, preferred for the First Test to Chris Woakes (who returned for the Second in place of spinner Jack Leach, with some success), was the leading wicket-taker. Yet his modest tally of six included two lbws which would have been overturned on review.

Marty Melville, AFP/Getty Images

Unarmed combat: the bat slips from Dawid Malan's grasp in the Napier T20, but his hundred brings victory.

Rory Burns built on a good Ashes with scores of 52, 31 and 101, while Denly exemplified the new quest for solidity, twice hanging around at Mount Maunganui. But debutant opener Dom Sibley had technical issues, both outside off stump and against spin, while Zak Crawley – drafted in for the Second Test after Jos Buttler hurt his back – lasted only six balls.

The sense that not everyone was treating the tour with the utmost urgency was compounded by another unintended consequence of Buttler's injury: with Jonny Bairstow dropped (and Ben Foakes ignored altogether), the gloves passed to Ollie Pope, the 21-year-old Surrey batsman who had kept wicket in only five first-class games, and was trying to re-establish himself as a Test No. 6. He batted well (from No. 7) to make 75 at Seddon Park, and kept tidily enough, until he dropped Kane Williamson on the last morning. And while Pope had been nominated in advance as the reserve keeper, England hadn't in reality expected to use him.

New Zealand – who boasted five centuries in the Tests to England's two – looked what they were: second in the rankings. This was their 11th series win at home in the last 13. After Watling's marathon, six of their top seven could claim a Test average of at least 40 (England had only Root), while Tim Southee's expert use of the width of the crease was an object lesson in how to tackle grudging surfaces. Neil Wagner, the left-arm seamer with the stamina of a Duracell bunny, once more circumvented conditions by banging it in short, and was rewarded with a pair of five-fors and 13 wickets, six more than his nearest rival. England lacked anyone with either his engine or imagination.

It symbolised New Zealand's quiet control of the Tests that, when a deluge cut short the last day in Hamilton, Williamson and Ross Taylor both had unbeaten centuries. Their partnership of 213 left England with a haul of 21 wickets at 58 apiece, their worst in a series of more than one Test.

The pitches, it's true, were not designed for thrill-a-minute cricket. Hosting its first Test, Bay Oval was so flat it left Root with little option but to become only the second captain to bat first in New Zealand since January 2011 (South Africa's. Faf du Plessis did so twice). But the hosts' innings win, completed in the final session, meant England could hardly grumble about conditions. The surface at Seddon Park, though, was a shocker: slow and lifeless, it sucked the joy out of batsmen, bowlers and spectators. The downpour put everyone out of their misery.

The 20-over matches – both teams were eyeing up the Twenty20 World Cup in Australia in October – had given Silverwood and Eoin Morgan a chance to look at fringe players and fresh blood, while the likes of Root, Buttler, Stokes, Ali and Jason Roy were rested.

Dawid Malan produced the knock of the series, a 51-ball 103 not out at Napier, but earned a rebuke from Morgan after declining to risk a bye from the last delivery of the innings. James Vince faded after starring in the first game, at Christchurch's Hagley Oval and, when England needed two batsmen for the super over at Auckland, they turned without hesitation to Morgan and Bairstow. Next in would have been Chris Jordan, who had earned the tie by hitting Jimmy Neesham's last three balls for 12, and who then bowled the super over, confirming his role as leader of an otherwise young attack.

Others flickered. Somerset opener Tom Banton played strokes of genuine pedigree; Lancashire leg-spinner Matt Parkinson tossed the ball up; Worcestershire seamer Pat Brown rummaged around his box of tricks; the Curran brothers, Tom and Sam, formed a probing new-ball attack. But Sam Billings, generously awarded the vice-captaincy – in part because it had been decided he would keep wicket in every game – made little impact, and first-time tourists Lewis Gregory and Saqib Mahmood were peripheral.

In that respect, they embodied the tour as a whole, with Root taking the chance to explain away another overseas defeat as a valuable opportunity to learn. It was true that the newness of his partnership with Silverwood bought him time as England embarked on yet another attempt to reinvent their Test cricket. But with only three Test tours between this and the Ashes – which loomed like an obsession over the dressing-room – time was running out.

ENGLAND TOURING PARTY

*J. E. Root (Yorkshire; T), J. C. Archer (Sussex; T), J. M. Bairstow (Yorkshire; 20), T. Banton (Somerset; 20), S. W. Billings (Kent; 20), S. C. J. Broad (Nottinghamshire; T), P. R. Brown (Worcestershire; 20), R. J. Burns (Surrey; T), J. C. Buttler (Lancashire; T), Z. Crawley (Kent; T), S. M. Curran (Surrey; T/20), T. K. Curran (Surrey; 20), J. L. Denly (Kent; T/20), L. Gregory (Somerset; 20), C. J. Jordan (Sussex; 20), M. J. Leach (Somerset; T), S. Mahmood (Lancashire; T/20), D. J. Malan (Middlesex; 20), E. J. G. Morgan (Middlesex; 20), M. W. Parkinson (Lancashire; T/20), O. J. D. Pope (Surrey; T), A. U. Rashid (Yorkshire; 20), D. P. Sibley (Warwickshire; T), B. A. Stokes (Durham; T), J. M. Vince (Hampshire; 20), C. R. Woakes (Warwickshire; T).

Morgan captained in the T20s. Bairstow, originally omitted from the Test squad, was initially retained as cover after Denly injured his ankle, which prevented him playing in the T20s.

Coach: C. E. W. Silverwood (T/20). *Assistant coaches:* G. P. Thorpe (T/20), P. D. Collingwood (T/20). *Fast bowling consultant:* D. Gough (T). *Spin consultant:* J. S. Patel (20). *Wicketkeeping coach:* B. N. French (T). *Fielding coach:* C. D. Hopkinson (20). *Team manager:* P. A. Neale (T/20). *Analyst:* G. Lindsay (T/20). *Doctors:* Moiz Moghal (20), J. D. Williams (T). *Physiotherapist:* C. A. de Weymarn (T/20). *Masseur:* M. Saxby (T/20). *Strength and conditioning:* P. C. F. Scott (T/20). *Psychologist:* D. J. Young (T). *Security manager:* S. Dickason (T/20). *Head of team communications:* D. M. Reuben (T/20). *Digital editor:* G. R. Stobart (T/20).

At Lincoln, October 27, 2019. **England XI won by six wickets. New Zealand XI 172-4** (20 overs) (A. P. Devcich 62, A. K. Kitchen 50*); ‡**England XI 178-4** (18.1 overs) (J. M. Bairstow 78*; L. H. Ferguson 3-32). *Jonny Bairstow hurried England to victory in their tour opener with 78* from 45 balls, launching the left-arm wrist-spin of Blake Coburn for three straight sixes in a row to make light of a testing chase. Lockie Ferguson had reduced them to 51-3, including Tom Banton for 11 on his senior debut, and Joe Denly for a third-ball duck. But Bairstow, in his first innings since being dropped from the Test side, put on 61 with Sam Billings (28) and 66* with Sam Curran (28*). As a gale swirled around the Bert Sutcliffe Oval, the tourists had earlier dropped three catches, Saqib Mahmood twice the culprit at third man off fellow newcomer Pat Brown. Half-centuries from Anton Devcich and Anaru Kitchen had given the New Zealanders a chance, but Bairstow had other ideas.*

At Lincoln, October 29, 2019. **New Zealand XI won by eight wickets.** ‡**England XI 188-5** (20 overs) (J. M. Vince 46, J. L. Denly 39*; A. Verma 3-46); **New Zealand XI 191-2** (18.3 overs) (C. Munro 107*, A. K. Kitchen 48*). *Colin Munro gave England pause for thought ahead of the internationals, walloping 107* from 57 balls, and adding 138* in 66 with Kitchen, to seal victory with nine to spare. Fortunate to survive a leg-before shout on 25 from Matt Parkinson, who had removed Anton Devcich with his third ball in England colours, Munro cracked seven sixes; only Tom Curran (0-27) escaped punishment, though he dropped Munro on 93 off Parkinson at deep backward square. England had stumbled mid-innings against the seam of Anurag Verma, before Lewis Gregory – another newcomer – launched him for 24 in the 19th over.*

Twenty20 International reports by Ali Martin

NEW ZEALAND v ENGLAND

First Twenty20 International

At Christchurch, November 1, 2019. England won by seven wickets. Toss: England. Twenty20 international debuts: P. R. Brown, S. M. Curran, L. Gregory.

Hagley Oval hosted its first international since the terrorist attack in March that led to the deaths of 51 worshippers at two local mosques. During a minute's silence before the game, the teams were joined by relatives of the victims. The cricketing headlines went to Vince, whose 38-ball 59 was his maiden half-century in Twenty20 internationals, and broke the back of England's pursuit of 154. Bairstow had taken Kuggeleijn for 18 in the third over, while Morgan confirmed a winning start for new head coach Chris Silverwood when he heaved Southee over midwicket. Morgan claimed afterwards he felt in terrible form at the crease, and credited his varied attack as the difference between the sides on a two-paced pitch. New Zealand had never recovered from scoring just seven in their first three overs, despite late impetus from Taylor and Mitchell. The Currans had become the first brothers to share the new ball for England: Sam, on T20 international debut, bowled Guptill in his second over, while Tom began with a maiden. Jordan removed Munro and Seifert with low full tosses, and Pat Brown – like Lewis Gregory, making his England debut – conceded only six from the last over, in which he removed Taylor with a smart off-cutter.

Player of the Match: J. M. Vince.

BROTHERS SHARING THE NEW BALL IN INTERNATIONAL CRICKET

D. R. and R. J. Hadlee (New Zealand)	1 Test	1973-74
A. O. and M. A. Suji (Kenya)	8 ODIs	1997-98 to 1999
P. T. Collins and F. H. Edwards (West Indies)†	4 Tests	2003-04
J. A. and M. Morkel (Africa XI)	1 ODI	2007
J. O. Ngoche and N. N. Odhiambo (Kenya)	2 ODIs	2011-12
J. O. and S. O. Ngoche (Kenya)	1 T20I	2012-13
N. N. Odhiambo and L. N. Onyango (Kenya)	1 ODI	2013-14
Aftab Alam and Karim Sadiq (Afghanistan)	1 T20I	2015-16
S. M. and T. K. Curran (England)	4 T20Is	**2019-20**

† *Half-brothers.*

New Zealand

		B	4/6
1 M. J. Guptill b 6	2	7	0
2 C. Munro c 4 b 9	21	20	1/2
3 †T. L. Seifert c 1 b 9	32	26	1/1
4 C. de Grandhomme c 3 b 10	19	14	1/1
5 L. R. P. L. Taylor c 1 b 11	44	35	3/1
6 D. J. Mitchell not out	30	17	1/2
7 M. J. Santner not out	1	1	0
Lb 3, w 1	4		

6 overs: 39-2   (20 overs) 153-5

1/6 2/39 3/72 4/93 5/149

8 S. C. Kuggeleijn, 9 *T. G. Southee, 10 I. S. Sodhi and 11 L. H. Ferguson did not bat.

S. M. Curran 4–8–33–1; T. K. Curran 4–10–25–0; Jordan 4–9–28–2; Rashid 4–3–31–1; Brown 4–5–33–1.

England

		B	4/6
1 J. M. Bairstow c 1 b 7	35	28	5/1
2 D. J. Malan c 10 b 7	11	13	2
3 J. M. Vince c 1 b 7	59	38	7/2
4 *E. J. G. Morgan not out	34	21	4/1
5 †S. W. Billings not out	14	11	2
W 1	1		

6 overs: 42-1   (18.3 overs) 154-3

1/37 2/68 3/122

6 S. M. Curran, 7 L. Gregory, 8 T. K. Curran, 9 C. J. Jordan, 10 A. U. Rashid and 11 P. R. Brown did not bat.

Southee 3.3–11–30–0; Ferguson 4–11–28–0; Kuggeleijn 3–5–35–0; Santner 4–10–23–3; Sodhi 4–5–38–0.

Umpires: S. B. Haig and W. R. Knights.   Third umpire: A. Mehrotra.

Referee: A. J. Pycroft.

NEW ZEALAND v ENGLAND

Second Twenty20 International

At Wellington (Westpac Stadium), November 3, 2019. New Zealand won by 21 runs. Toss: England. Twenty20 international debut: S. Mahmood.

For the second time in less than 24 hours, an England team suffered defeat on a rugby field. After an evening spent watching the rugby players lose the World Cup final to South Africa in Yokohama, the cricketers served up an error-strewn performance of their own on the drop-in pitch at the Cake Tin, home of Wellington Lions. This was New Zealand's sixth straight T20 win here (and England's first

WICKET WITH FIRST BALL FOR ENGLAND

Bowler	Batsman		
W. M. Bradley	F. J. Laver (Australia)	Manchester	1899
E. G. Arnold	V. T. Trumper (Australia)	Sydney	1903-04
J. N. Crawford	A. E. E. Vogler (South Africa)	Johannesburg	1905-06
G. G. Macaulay	G. A. L. Hearne (South Africa)	Cape Town	1922-23
M. W. Tate	M. J. Susskind (South Africa)	Birmingham	1924
R. Howorth	D. V. Dyer (South Africa)	The Oval	1947
R. Clarke	Imran Nazir (Pakistan)	Manchester	2003
J. L. Denly	G. C. Smith (South Africa)	Centurion	2009-10
L. Gregory	**C. de Grandhomme (New Zealand)**	**Wellington (Westpac)**	**2019-20**

The first six were in Tests, Clarke in an ODI, and Denly and Gregory in T20Is. R. K. Illingworth took a wicket with his first ball in a Test, in 1991, but had already bowled in ODIs; G. G. Arnold struck with his first delivery in ODIs, in 1972, but had already bowled in Tests.

defeat in seven anywhere), and the hosts made good use of their knowledge of the ground's unusual dimensions. Chasing 177, England lost Bairstow first ball, chipping Southee to mid-on, while five others – restricted by New Zealand's fuller lengths – also perished hitting to the long straight boundary. Spinners Santner and Sodhi set the traps; when they were sprung, de Grandhomme and Guptill caught impeccably in the deep. The target might have been smaller had England not dropped four chances (five, said the harsher judges), with Vince responsible for two (possibly three), and Billings and Malan one each; rueful looks at the sun left Morgan unimpressed. Most damagingly, Vince put down the recalled

Neesham at deep midwicket off Rashid only four runs into a rapid 42. Vince's dozy day was summed up when he walked out to bat with two left-handed gloves. One of the few bright spots for England came when Gregory bowled de Grandhomme with his first delivery in international cricket.

Player of the Match: M. J. Santner.

New Zealand

		B	4/6
1 M. J. Guptill *c 3 b 9*	41	28	3/2
2 C. Munro *lbw b 6*	7	5	0/1
3 †T. L. Seifert *c 5 b 10*	16	15	1/1
4 C. de Grandhomme *b 7*	28	12	1/3
5 L. R. P. L. Taylor *lbw b 8*	28	24	2/1
6 D. J. Mitchell *c 8 b 6*	5	9	0
7 J. D. S. Neesham *c 3 b 8*	42	22	2/4
8 M. J. Santner *c 11 b 8*	0	2	0
9 *T. G. Southee *not out*	4	3	0
Lb 3, w 2	5		

6 overs: 53-1 (20 overs) 176-8

1/23 2/57 3/85 4/96 5/121 6/151 7/151 8/176

10 I. S. Sodhi and 11 L. H. Ferguson did not bat.

Curran 4–9–22–2; Mahmood 4–5–46–1; Jordan 4–13–23–3; Brown 2–1–32–0; Rashid 4–9–40–1; Gregory 2–5–10–1.

England

		B	4/6
1 J. M. Bairstow *c 6 b 9*	0	1	0
2 D. J. Malan *c 1 b 10*	39	29	2/2
3 J. M. Vince *c 8 b 11*	1	4	0
4 *E. J. G. Morgan *c 4 b 8*	32	17	3/3
5 †S. W. Billings *c 4 b 10*	8	10	0
6 S. M. Curran *c 4 b 8*	9	6	1
7 L. Gregory *c 4 b 9*	15	15	0/1
8 C. J. Jordan *c 1 b 8*	36	19	3/3
9 A. U. Rashid *b 6*	4	6	0
10 S. Mahmood *c 9 b 11*	4	3	1
11 P. R. Brown *not out*	4	9	0
Lb 2, w 1	3		

6 overs: 49-3 (19.5 overs) 155

1/0 2/3 3/40 4/64 5/91 6/93 7/134 8/144 9/148

Southee 4–11–25–2; Ferguson 4–12–34–2; Santner 4–12–25–3; Neesham 2–1–23–0; Sodhi 4–7–37–2; Mitchell 1.5–5–9–1.

Umpires: S. B. Haig and W. R. Knights.   Third umpire: A. Mehrotra.

Referee: A. J. Pycroft.

NEW ZEALAND v ENGLAND

Third Twenty20 International

At Nelson, November 5, 2019. New Zealand won by 14 runs. Toss: New Zealand. Twenty20 international debuts: T. Banton, M. W. Parkinson.

Morgan bemoaned a lack of experience after his side collapsed at Saxton Oval. But while it was true that, without the rested Jonny Bairstow and Chris Jordan, a combined 142 T20 caps going into the match was nearly 1,000 fewer than the opposing side had accumulated by July's World Cup final, his diagnosis did not entirely stack up. With Morgan part of a top five including three county captains – Malan, Vince and Billings – England's target of 181 should have been a stroll after they had reduced the equation to 42 from 31 deliveries with eight wickets in hand. Malan had fallen after a 29-ball half-century, but Vince and Morgan were well set. Yet when Morgan holed out attempting a third six from Santner's final over, it sparked a cascade of five for ten in 19 balls. New Zealand squeezed England superbly. Billings was run out from point after rethinking a suicidal single, and Vince flapped meekly to mid-off. Ferguson, earlier whipped for six by the debutant Tom Banton, then removed Gregory and Sam Curran in three balls to leave the tail an impossible task. New Zealand's innings had included some meaty blows from de Grandhomme, and a wicket with his fifth delivery at international level for leg-spinner Matt Parkinson, who bowled Seifert through his legs as he attempted a reverse sweep.

Player of the Match: C. de Grandhomme.

New Zealand

	B	4/6
1 C. Munro *c 9 b 8* 6	8	0
2 M. J. Guptill *c 8 b 11* 33	17	7
3 †T. L. Seifert *b 10* 7	12	1
4 C. de Grandhomme *c 1 b 8* 55	35	5/3
5 L. R. P. L. Taylor *lbw b 9* 27	24	2/1
6 J. D. S. Neesham *b 6* 20	15	2/1
7 M. J. Santner *run out (5)* 15	9	2
8 *T. G. Southee *not out* 1	2	0
Lb 6, w 8, nb 2 16		

6 overs: 52-2		(20 overs)		180-7

1/40 2/42 3/69 4/135 5/162 6/171 7/180

9 I. S. Sodhi, 10 L. H. Ferguson and 11 B. M. Tickner did not bat.

S. M. Curran 4–8–29–1; T. K. Curran 4–9–29–2; Mahmood 4–6–49–1; Brown 4–10–34–1; Parkinson 2–5–14–1; Gregory 2–4–19–0.

England

	B	4/6
1 T. Banton *b 11* 18	10	2/1
2 D. J. Malan *c 2 b 9* 55	34	8/1
3 J. M. Vince *c 8 b 11* 49	39	4/1
4 *E. J. G. Morgan *c 1 b 7* 18	13	0/2
5 †S. W. Billings *run out (1)* 1	2	0
6 S. M. Curran *c 1 b 10* 2	6	0
7 L. Gregory *b 10* 0	2	0
8 T. K. Curran *not out* 14	10	0/1
9 S. Mahmood *not out* 3	4	0
Lb 1, w 5 6		

6 overs: 46-1		(20 overs)		166-7

1/27 2/90 3/139 4/142 5/147 6/148 7/149

10 M. W. Parkinson and 11 P. R. Brown did not bat.

Southee 4–9–28–0; Ferguson 4–11–25–2; Tickner 4–11–25–2; Sodhi 3–4–30–1; Santner 4–7–41–1; Neesham 1–0–16–0.

Umpires: C. M. Brown and W. R. Knights.		Third umpire: S. B. Haig.
Referee: A. J. Pycroft.

NEW ZEALAND v ENGLAND

Fourth Twenty20 International

At Napier, November 8, 2019 (floodlit). England won by 76 runs. Toss: New Zealand.

Back on another rugby ground, England learned from the mistakes of Wellington, as Malan's unbeaten 103 from 51 balls, and Morgan's 91 from 41, sent the scoreboard spinning like a fruit machine. Their stand of 182 was an England T20 record for any wicket, while a total of 241 for three was their highest, beating 230 for eight against South Africa at Mumbai at the 2016 World T20. Morgan's half-century from 21 balls was another national record – one better than Jos Buttler against Australia at Edgbaston in 2018. When Malan launched a Boult full toss out of the ground, he became England's second T20 centurion, after Alex Hales; though from 48 balls to Hales's 60 (against Sri Lanka at Chittagong in March 2014). England had stuttered to 18 for one from four overs after Southee opted to bowl, but Banton seized the initiative. Malan and Morgan, until recently Middlesex team-mates, then embarked on a firework display. New Zealand didn't help themselves: Morgan was caught off no-balls above waist height on 51 and 59. And, though Guptill and Munro brought up 50 in 25 in reply, Parkinson and England's outfielders exploited the urgency, and set up a decider. Afterwards, Morgan criticised Malan's decision not to attempt a risky bye off the last ball of the England innings: "If we get guys that are not running off the last ball because they want to get a not-out, there's something to address."

Player of the Match: D. J. Malan.

England

		B	4/6
1 T. Banton *lbw b 7*	31	20	4/1
2 J. M. Bairstow *c 6 b 7*	8	9	1
3 D. J. Malan *not out*	103	51	9/6
4 *E. J. G. Morgan *c 6 b 8*	91	41	7/7
5 †S. W. Billings *not out*	0	1	0
Lb 3, w 3, nb 2	8		

6 overs: 48-1   (20 overs) 241-3

1/16 2/58 3/240

6 S. M. Curran, 7 L. Gregory, 8 T. K. Curran,
9 C. J. Jordan, 10 M. W. Parkinson and 11 P. R.
Brown did not bat.

Boult 4–11–35–0; Southee 4–5–47–1; Santner
4–10–32–2; Tickner 4–5–50–0; Sodhi
3–1–49–0; Mitchell 1–1–25–0.

New Zealand

		B	4/6
1 M. J. Guptill *c 3 b 8*	27	14	1/3
2 C. Munro *c 11 b 10*	30	21	3
3 †T. L. Seifert *c 8 b 9*	3	4	0
4 C. de Grandhomme *c 1 b 10*	7	3	0/1
5 L. R. P. L. Taylor *c 1 b 11*	14	10	0/1
6 D. J. Mitchell *c 9 b 10*	2	5	0
7 M. J. Santner *c 5 b 6*	10	8	1
8 *T. G. Southee *lbw b 10*	39	15	2/4
9 I. S. Sodhi *run out (9)*	9	7	0/1
10 T. A. Boult *b 9*	8	8	1
11 B. M. Tickner *not out*	5	6	0
Lb 3, w 8	11		

6 overs: 61-2   (16.5 overs) 165

1/54 2/59 3/70 4/70 5/78 6/89 7/138 8/144 9/154

S. M. Curran 4–8–36–1; T. K. Curran
3–3–26–1; Jordan 2.5–7–24–2; Parkinson
4–9–47–4; Brown 3–4–29–1.

Umpires: C. B. Gaffaney and S. B. Haig.   Third umpire: W. R. Knights.
Referee: A. J. Pycroft.

NEW ZEALAND v ENGLAND

Fifth Twenty20 International

At Auckland, November 10, 2019. England won the super over, after a tie. Toss: England.

The World Cup final had haunted New Zealand all series. Now, it came back more clearly than
ever in the guise of another super over. In a game reduced by rain to 11 overs a side, Jordan had
forced the tie-breaker by taking 12 from Neesham's last three balls. Then, after Morgan and Bairstow

Banking on Jordan: with bat and ball, Chris Jordan saw England home in the deciding T20.

struck a six apiece to set New Zealand 18, Jordan conceded just eight, and removed Seifert fourth ball when Morgan held a spectacular diving catch over his shoulder at extra cover. "Hopefully it's a case of third time lucky if there's another," joked Southee. In truth, this super over was an anticlimax, after a six-hitting frenzy on a ground where the straight boundaries are barely a sand wedge away. Guptill and Munro had begun with a blaze of 83 from 31 deliveries, before Seifert's 39 off 16 lit the afterburners. Overs such as the sixth, from Rashid (five runs and the wicket of Guptill), and the seventh, from Mahmood (seven and the wicket of de Grandhomme), were like gold dust. England's reply did not begin well: Banton fell lbw to Boult, and Vince's exasperating tour ended second ball. But Bairstow's bristling 47 off 18, including three successive straight bunts for six off Sodhi, and cameos from Morgan and Sam Curran, got them back on track. After Billings and Tom Curran gummed up the works, England needed Jordan's calm, with bat and ball, to seal a 3–2 win.

Player of the Match: J. M. Bairstow. *Player of the Series:* M. J. Santner.

New Zealand

	B	4/6
1 M. J. Guptill *c 1 b 10*.	50	20 3/5
2 C. Munro *c 3 b 5*	46	21 2/4
3 C. de Grandhomme *c 3 b 11* . .	6	5 1
4 †T. L. Seifert *b 8*	39	16 1/5
5 J. D. S. Neesham *not out*	1	1 0
6 L. R. P. L. Taylor *run out (5/6)*. .	3	3 0
Lb 1	1	
3 overs: 55-0 (11 overs) 146-5		

1/83 2/93 3/120 4/143 5/146

7 M. J. Santner, 8 S. C. Kuggeleijn, 9 *T. G. Southee, 10 I. S. Sodhi and 11 T. A. Boult did not bat.

S. M. Curran 2–4–33–1; T. K. Curran 2–3–30–1; Jordan 2–2–28–0; Rashid 3–5–34–1; Mahmood 2–3–20–1.

England

	B	4/6
1 T. Banton *lbw b 11*	7	4 0/1
2 J. M. Bairstow *c 4 b 5*	47	18 2/5
3 J. M. Vince *c 8 b 9*.	1	2 0
4 *E. J. G. Morgan *c 8 b 11*	17	7 1/2
5 S. M. Curran *st 4 b 7*	24	11 2/2
6 †S. W. Billings *not out*	11	10 1
7 L. Gregory *c 9 b 7*	6	2 0/1
8 T. K. Curran *c 3 b 5*.	12	9 0/1
9 C. J. Jordan *not out*	12	3 1/1
Lb 2, w 7	9	
3 overs: 39-3 (11 overs) 146-7		

1/8 2/9 3/39 4/100 5/101 6/107 7/134

10 A. U. Rashid and 11 S. Mahmood did not bat.

Boult 3–9–35–2; Southee 2–3–22–1; Santner 2–3–20–2; Kuggeleijn 1–2–20–0; Sodhi 1–0–22–0; Neesham 2–3–25–2.

Super over: **England 17-0** (Bairstow 8*, Morgan 9*; Southee 1–0–17–0); **New Zealand 8-1** (Seifert 6, Guptill 1*, de Grandhomme 0*; Extras 1; Jordan 1–3–8–1).

Umpires: C. B. Gaffaney and W. R. Knights. Third umpire: C. M. Brown.

Referee: A. J. Pycroft.

At Whangarei, November 12–13, 2019 (not first-class). **Drawn. England XI 376-5 dec** (87 overs) (D. P. Sibley 100, Z. Crawley 103); **New Zealand XI 285-5** (75 overs) (J. J. N. P. Bhula 61, F. H. Allen 104, S. K. Patel 56*). *Dom Sibley and Zak Crawley both retired following hundreds on their representative England debuts in the first of two warm-up games at Cobham Oval. With no toss taking place, the plan had been for England – who chose from 13 players to the New Zealanders' 12 – to bat and bowl for a day each, though they extended their innings for 21 overs into the second morning after rain had delayed the first-day start until 2.27; Ben Stokes cracked 30* from 20 balls. Jofra Archer struck twice in his first outing with the red Kookaburra, before Finn Allen, a 20-year-old Aucklander with a first-class average of 22, made a composed century.*

NEW ZEALAND A v ENGLAND XI

At Whangarei, November 15–17, 2019. Drawn. Toss: New Zealand A.

England were denied victory in this first-class fixture by a stubborn unbeaten ninth-wicket stand of 40 in almost 23 overs between New Zealand A spinners Somerville and Patel. Three wickets for Curran – preferred, in a sign of England's thinking ahead of the First Test, to Chris Woakes – had helped reduce them to 129 for eight. Earlier, Phillips scored a composed hundred after emerging from a spell by Archer which he described as the quickest he had ever faced (Archer also hit Rutherford on the head during his first-innings 59, prompting the use of Kuggeleijn as a concussion substitute). England slipped to 105 for five, but Pope put on 90 with Denly, back after injuring his right ankle before the T20 series, and 114 with Buttler, who completed only his sixth first-class hundred. In all, the last five wickets added 300, before Archer removed both openers. England, though, couldn't finish the job.

Close of play: first day, England XI 26-1 (Sibley 6, Leach 2); second day, England XI 355-8 (Buttler 88, Archer 17).

New Zealand A

H. D. Rutherford c Buttler b Archer	59			
R. Ravindra lbw b Broad	12	– (1) c Sibley b Archer	22
G. D. Phillips c Pope b Leach	116	– c Buttler b Curran	36
T. L. Seifert c Denly b Stokes	24	– (2) c Sibley b Archer	0
J. D. S. Neesham c Buttler b Stokes	0	– c Buttler b Curran	9
*†T. A. Blundell c Burns b Archer	60	– c Sibley b Archer	8
D. J. Mitchell not out	19	– (4) lbw b Broad	22
K. A. Jamieson (did not bat)		– (7) c Buttler b Stokes	4
S. C. Kuggeleijn (did not bat)		– (8) b Curran	19
W. E. R. Somerville (did not bat)		– (9) not out	32
A. Y. Patel (did not bat)		– (10) not out	10
Lb 5, w 2, nb 5	12	B 2, lb 4, nb 1	7

1/17 (2) 2/124 (1)	(6 wkts dec, 84 overs) 302	1/2 (2) 2/33 (1)	(8 wkts, 68 overs) 169
3/165 (4) 4/167 (5)		3/70 (3) 4/86 (5)	
5/255 (3) 6/302 (6)		5/92 (4) 6/99 (6) 7/104 (7) 8/129 (8)	

B. M. Tickner did not bat.

Kuggeleijn replaced Rutherford, as a concussion substitute.

Broad 16–2–66–1; Archer 17–1–58–2; Curran 15–1–53–0; Leach 26–7–56–1; Stokes 10–0–64–2. *Second innings*—Broad 12–5–25–1; Archer 14–4–34–3; Leach 15–2–37–0; Curran 13–1–42–3; Stokes 9–2–20–1; Root 5–3–5–0.

England XI

R. J. Burns c Somerville b Jamieson	14	J. C. Archer not out	41
D. P. Sibley c Patel b Tickner	14	S. C. J. Broad c Ravindra b Kuggeleijn	0
M. J. Leach c Tickner b Mitchell	22		
J. L. Denly c Mitchell b Tickner	68	B 10, lb 6, w 12, nb 2	30
*J. E. Root lbw b Mitchell	2		
B. A. Stokes c Mitchell b Neesham	3	1/24 (1) 2/53 (2)	(117.5 overs) 405
O. J. D. Pope c Kuggeleijn b Patel	88	3/93 (3) 4/102 (5)	
†J. C. Buttler c Blundell b Kuggeleijn	110	5/105 (6) 6/195 (4) 7/309 (7)	
S. M. Curran c Tickner b Kuggeleijn	13	8/334 (9) 9/405 (8) 10/405 (11)	

Jamieson 24–5–70–1; Tickner 19–2–63–2; Mitchell 10–4–34–2; Neesham 10–3–40–1; Kuggeleijn 13.5–3–46–3; Patel 25–5–68–1; Somerville 16–0–68–0.

Umpires: C. M. Brown and W. R. Knights.   Referee: R. A. Dykes.

> ❝ Twitter was predictably judgmental, with Florin ridiculed, then feted; both seemed wide of the mark. 'My bowling isn't beautiful,' he said. 'But I'm a slow bowler. Is it a problem? I think not.'"
> *Cricket Round the World*, page 1123

Bay of plenty: Mount Maunganui's first Test brings New Zealand an innings victory.

NEW ZEALAND v ENGLAND

First Test

SIMON WILDE

At Mount Maunganui, November 21–25, 2019. New Zealand won by an innings and 65 runs. Toss: England. Test debut: D. P. Sibley.

England were intent on turning over a new leaf in Test cricket, but ended up repeating old errors. For head coach Chris Silverwood, New Zealand on their own soil were every bit as tough to crack as South Africa at Johannesburg in 1999-2000 for Duncan Fletcher, and West Indies in Jamaica in 2008-09 for Andy Flower, in their first matches in the job. Like those games, this ended in an innings defeat.

Root's torture was exquisite: with scores of two and 11, he experienced his least productive Test as captain when batting twice, and was condemned to 14 hours in the field before New Zealand declared on 615 for nine, their highest total against England. The largely unheralded Watling, meanwhile, became the first wicketkeeper to score a Test double-hundred against them.

The match followed a grimly familiar pattern for Root and other senior players who had toured India and Australia in recent winters: England's first innings, though not without substance, was effortlessly eclipsed. Instead, the novelty resided in the setting: the Bay Oval in Mount Maunganui was staging its inaugural Test, and a fine job it did, making an eloquent case for the boutique outground over the hell of another concrete bowl. Several of the New Zealand team had properties in the area: in every sense, they were at home.

The only discordant note came on the final afternoon when, with England slipping to defeat, Archer was racially abused by a spectator as he left the field. He reported the incident to a steward, before expressing his disappointment several hours later on social media. New Zealand Cricket were mortified this had occurred on their watch, launched an investigation and made a full apology to Archer and the England team. They subsequently banned the spectator from home grounds for two years.

England had often begun overseas Test series poorly. But this time they had stressed their desire to amass big first-innings totals, however long it took, and picked Warwickshire's adhesive Dom Sibley – the tenth player to debut for England as an opener since 2015 – with precisely that brief. So it was galling that they failed quite so comprehensively to deliver. The first day had been promising enough: Sibley clipped his first ball through midwicket, and the top order moved sensibly to 241 for four. There were painstaking half-centuries from Burns and Denly, who looked comfortable at No. 3 following Root's decision to drop back to No. 4, and Stokes, who at stumps was well poised on 67.

But things unravelled fast, despite a surface designed to blunt the bowlers. England's remaining 16 wickets would fall for 273, several to rash shots against a disciplined and experienced New Zealand attack. Their varied tactics paid dividends: prolonged spells of accuracy, bouts of hanging the ball wide and, in Wagner's case, hammering in bouncer after bouncer.

The collapse started when Stokes, on 91, advanced down the pitch at Southee, chased a bit of width, and was brilliantly caught by Taylor, who had put him down the previous evening on 63. Pope, Curran (first ball) and Archer followed in the space of six deliveries.

TEST DOUBLE-HUNDREDS BY A WICKETKEEPER

232*	A. Flower	Zimbabwe v India at Nagpur	2000-01
230	K. C. Sangakkara	Sri Lanka v Pakistan at Lahore	2001-02
224	M. S. Dhoni	India v Australia at Chennai	2012-13
219*	Mushfiqur Rahim	Bangladesh v Zimbabwe at Mirpur	2018-19
210*	Taslim Arif	Pakistan v Australia at Faisalabad	1979-80
209	Imtiaz Ahmed	Pakistan v New Zealand at Lahore	1955-56
205	**B-J. Watling**	**New Zealand v England at Mount Maunganui**	**2019-20**
204*	A. C. Gilchrist	Australia v South Africa at Johannesburg	2001-02
201*†	D. S. B. P. Kuruppu	Sri Lanka v New Zealand at Colombo (CCC)	1986-87
200	Mushfiqur Rahim	Bangladesh v Sri Lanka at Galle	2012-13

† *Test debut.*

Southee was involved in all four wickets – three as bowler, one as fielder – and it took a ninth-wicket stand of 52 between Buttler and Leach to hoist England towards 353, at least 100 below par, probably more.

For the rest of the second day, battle was closely fought, but England had the edge at stumps, with New Zealand 144 for four. Latham had fallen lbw in Curran's first over, though Hot Spot detected a thin inside edge, while Raval was all at sea against Leach. But it was the departures of Taylor and Williamson that really lifted England. Taylor was caught in the deep aiming an ugly smear against Stokes, while Williamson was surprised by a ball from Curran that leapt off a length, and seduced England into imagining the pitch would play more tricks. Shortly before the close, Archer – used in shorter bursts than during the Ashes, with instructions to rattle the speed gun and bowl short – struck Nicholls a heavy blow on the side of the head. He resolutely saw out the session.

The game turned on the third day, as England floundered against batsmen prepared to break their spirits. Root declined to start with Archer, surely the bowler Nicholls least wanted to face; nor did he give him the second new ball, preferring Curran and Broad. Late in the morning, Stokes put down Watling at slip on 31 off Root, a mistake initially overshadowed when Root removed Nicholls in the same over.

Dive-bomb: B-J. Watling makes his ground during his 11-hour double-hundred.

But that was England's last success until the first ball after tea, when de Grandhomme was well held at gully by Sibley, ending a sixth-wicket partnership of 119 that brought New Zealand to within 37. Archer sent down a ferocious burst in mid-afternoon, during which he topped 94mph, but Santner kept Watling company for the final session, and England were confined to two wickets in the day. They conceded only 250 in 90 overs, but New Zealand were well placed to build a commanding lead.

This they did. By remaining patient against tight bowling on the fourth morning, Watling and Santner created scope to push on later. Only 58 were added in 30 overs before lunch, but no wicket was lost, and in the afternoon, as Santner cut loose en route to a maiden Test century, 138 were plundered from 27. Shortly before tea, Santner holed out at long-on, ending a stand of 261, a record for New Zealand's seventh wicket (beating 225 between Chris Cairns and Jacob Oram against South Africa at Auckland in 2003-04). Shortly after, Watling's marathon innings, spanning 667 minutes and 473 balls, ended with a catch at the wicket off Archer. His 205 was the highest score by a New Zealand No. 6 (beating Jeremy Coney's unbeaten 174 against England at Wellington in 1983-84), and highest by a No. 6 against England, after Don Bradman's 234 at Sydney in 1946-47. New Zealand declared with a lead of 262, leaving England – exhausted in body and mind after spending more than 200 overs in the field for only the third time this century – almost four sessions to survive.

Santner was not done for the day. He had claimed only 34 wickets in his 19 Tests, while the previous 101 taken by New Zealand bowlers at home had all fallen to seamers. But he now struck three times in 18 balls. Sibley, uncomfortable against spin, edged a wide one; Burns top-edged a slog-sweep; and nightwatchman Leach was caught at short leg in the day's last over (replays suggested he hadn't touched it).

England believed they could save the game, and well into the final afternoon that optimism seemed justified. By then, only one more wicket had fallen: Root, after almost

HIGHEST TOTAL IN A GROUND'S FIRST TEST

849	England v West Indies........	Sabina Park, Kingston..............	1929-30
674-6 dec	Australia v England...........	Sophia Gardens, Cardiff...........	2009
648-9 dec	West Indies v Bangladesh.....	Sheikh Abu Naser Stadium, Khulna	2012-13
631	West Indies v India...........	Feroz Shah Kotla, Delhi...........	1948-49
629-6 dec	West Indies v India...........	Brabourne Stadium, Bombay.......	1948-49
615-9 dec	**New Zealand v England**	**Bay Oval, Mount Maunganui**.......	**2019-20**
610-3 dec	India v Bangladesh..........	Shere Bangla Stadium, Mirpur.......	2007
608	England v South Africa.......	Ellis Park, Johannesburg..........	1948-49
604-6 dec	West Indies v India..........	Wankhede Stadium, Bombay.......	1974-75
603-9 dec	India v Australia.............	Jharkhand State CA Oval, Ranchi....	2016-17

an hour of stout defence, was caught in two minds by a ball of width from de Grandhomme, and steered it to gully. Moreover, Boult had left the field one over into his first spell of the day, reporting pain in his ribs.

But the day changed 35 minutes after lunch, when Stokes – playing at one he could have ignored – chopped on against Southee. Twenty minutes later, Wagner, embarking on a passage of play that saw him claim the last five wickets, produced extra bounce to have Denly, after spending 215 minutes over 35, caught off the bottom of his glove. Pope practically threw himself off his feet reaching a low full toss, and was brilliantly caught by a diving Santner at cover, before Buttler was bowled playing no shot at the first delivery from the second new ball.

Curran and Archer showed survival was possible, staying together more than an hour, before Archer aimed one big hit too many. With Broad falling first ball, England's last six wickets had tumbled in less than 28 overs, after only one had gone down in the day's first 41. Williamson was happy with the conditions, saying the pitch had deteriorated more than many he had played on in New Zealand. Root remained remarkably sanguine. "We want to play in a way very different to how we've played in our conditions," he said. "It's going to take time."

Player of the Match: B-J. Watling.

Close of play: first day, England 241-4 (Stokes 67, Pope 18); second day, New Zealand 144-4 (Nicholls 26, Watling 6); third day, New Zealand 394-6 (Watling 119, Santner 31); fourth day, England 55-3 (Denly 7).

England

R. J. Burns c Watling b de Grandhomme........	52	– c de Grandhomme b Santner	31
D. P. Sibley c Taylor b de Grandhomme.........	22	– c Watling b Santner	12
J. L. Denly c Watling b Southee	74	– c Watling b Wagner	35
*J. E. Root c Southee b Wagner.................	2	– (5) c Latham b de Grandhomme	11
B. A. Stokes c Taylor b Southee	91	– (6) b Southee	28
O. J. D. Pope c Watling b Southee.............	29	– (7) c Santner b Wagner	6
†J. C. Buttler c Santner b Wagner	43	– (8) b Wagner	0
S. M. Curran lbw b Southee	0	– (9) not out................	29
J. C. Archer c Southee b Boult............	4	– (10) c sub (M. J. Henry) b Wagner ..	30
M. J. Leach not out	18	– (4) c Latham b Santner...........	0
S. C. J. Broad b Wagner....................	1	– lbw b Wagner...............	0
B 2, lb 11, w 3, nb 1...............	17	B 12, lb 1, w 1, nb 1.......	15

1/52 (2) 2/113 (1) 3/120 (4)   (124 overs) 353   1/48 (2) 2/53 (1)   (96.2 overs) 197
4/203 (3) 5/277 (5) 6/286 (6)   3/55 (4) 4/69 (5)
7/286 (8) 8/295 (9) 9/347 (7) 10/353 (11)   5/121 (6) 6/132 (3) 7/133 (7)
                                         8/138 (8) 9/197 (10) 10/197 (11)

Boult 31–6–97–1; Southee 32–7–88–4; de Grandhomme 23–5–41–2; Wagner 32–7–90–3; Santner 6–1–24–0. *Second innings*—Southee 20–4–60–1; Boult 6–4–6–0; de Grandhomme 10–3–15–1; Santner 40–19–53–3; Wagner 19.2–6–44–5; Williamson 1–0–6–0.

New Zealand

J. A. Raval c Denly b Leach	19	N. Wagner not out	11
T. W. M. Latham lbw b Curran	8	T. A. Boult not out	1
*K. S. Williamson c Stokes b Curran	51		
L. R. P. L. Taylor c Pope b Stokes	25	B 22, lb 9, w 21, nb 2	54
H. M. Nicholls lbw b Root	41		
†B-J. Watling c Buttler b Archer	205	1/18 (2)	(9 wkts dec, 201 overs) 615
C. de Grandhomme c Sibley b Stokes	65	2/72 (1) 3/106 (4)	
M. J. Santner c Pope b Curran	126	4/127 (3) 5/197 (5) 6/316 (7)	
T. G. Southee c and b Leach	9	7/577 (8) 8/598 (9) 9/603 (6)	

Broad 33–13–64–0; Archer 42–15–107–1; Curran 35–7–119–3; Leach 47–7–153–2; Stokes 26–5–74–2; Root 18–3–67–1.

Umpires: H. D. P. K. Dharmasena and B. N. J. Oxenford.   Third umpire: P. Wilson.
Referee: J. Srinath.

NEW ZEALAND v ENGLAND

Second Test

George Dobell

At Hamilton, November 29–December 3, 2019. Drawn. Toss: England. Test debuts: D. J. Mitchell; Z. Crawley.

There's an old joke about a pilot landing in New Zealand and recommending his passengers set their watches back 40 years. It's unfair, of course. As England – and the thousands of supporters they brought with them – were reminded, New Zealand offers the perfect touring destination, with sophisticated infrastructure allied to a warm welcome.

But as the second match in succession crawled along at a funereal rate, it was hard to avoid the suspicion that this style of cricket – testing players' patience and discipline as much as their skill and technique – belonged to an earlier age, when distractions were fewer, attention spans longer and expectations lower. Put simply, this was a painfully

Blade runner: Joe Root flourishes at Hamilton.

slow surface which, combined with the Kookaburra ball, only grudgingly gave crumbs of entertainment.

That partly explained why England didn't come close to claiming the 20 wickets they required to level the series. There was, though, some consolation, as Root returned to form with his third Test double-century. At Mount Maunganui, his average for the year had fallen to 27. He was in need of a significant contribution to quieten the voices questioning his position. And how he responded. In batting more than ten and a half hours – 441 balls – he produced the longest innings of his career, taking England to their highest score since the Boxing Day Ashes Test of 2017-18, and their longest innings (in overs) since 2015-16. More than that, he demonstrated to his team the style of play – tougher, more prosaic – he had asked of them. Gone was talk of taking the attack to the bowler; in its place was talk of ruthlessness and converting starts into match-defining positions. A man known for his wide range of strokes took 259 deliveries over his first hundred runs, and at one stage went 30 overs without a boundary.

New Zealand were without Trent Boult and Colin de Grandhomme, who sustained side and abdominal injuries respectively in the First Test, while England were forced into a late switch when Jos Buttler, their first-choice keeper, suffered a back spasm in the gym the day before. That meant a debut for 21-year-old Zak Crawley, who had scored a century in one of the warm-ups, and a chance for Pope to keep wicket. Having previously done so in just five first-class games, he became England's least experienced wicketkeeper since the bespectacled Dick Young, who had kept in only four when he took the gloves at Sydney in 1907-08.

It raised questions about the wisdom of the tour selection, and the absence of Ben Foakes, Pope's Surrey colleague, in particular. England also dropped Jack Leach, and so went into a Test without a specialist spinner for the first time since Leeds 2012, against South Africa. (Leach was subsequently admitted to hospital suffering from gastroenteritis, complicated by long-standing issues with Crohn's disease.) Woakes came in as part of a five-man seam attack, though there were murmurs of concerns about Stokes's left knee, which seemed to be borne out when he clutched it, grimacing, during one of only two overs he bowled on the first day. He recovered sufficiently to send down 27 in the match but, not for the first time, his fitness was a worry.

New Zealand recalled Henry, preferred to Lockie Ferguson, and handed a Test debut to Hamilton-born all-rounder Daryl Mitchell, whose father, John, had been England's defence coach at the recent rugby World Cup. England's coach, Chris Silverwood, meanwhile, flew home after the second day following the death of his father-in-law. England fielded a Test side containing three (Pope, Crawley and Curran) aged under 22 for the first time, and five (Archer and Sibley were the others) aged 24 or below for only the fourth time in 50 years.

When New Zealand reached 155 for two towards the end of a first day limited to 54.3 overs by rain, it looked as if Root's decision to put them in had backfired. Latham, dropped at slip by Stokes off Archer on 66, batted especially well to record his fifth century in ten Test innings, while Taylor and – on the second day – Watling also got stuck in. But bowling first was not, England's management explained, based on the surface's green tinge on the eve of the game, when it had 16mm covering of grass (in England, it is usually

TEST DOUBLE-HUNDREDS BY AN ENGLAND CAPTAIN

333	G. A. Gooch	v India at Lord's	1990
285*	P. B. H. May	v West Indies at Birmingham	1957
263	A. N. Cook	v Pakistan at Abu Dhabi	2015-16
240	W. R. Hammond	v Australia at Lord's	1938
226	**J. E. Root**	**v New Zealand at Hamilton**	**2019-20**
215	D. I. Gower	v Australia at Birmingham	1985
205	L. Hutton	v West Indies at Kingston	1953-54
205	E. R. Dexter	v Pakistan at Karachi	1961-62

English International Cricket

Not infallible: Ollie Pope gives Kane Williamson a reprieve on the final morning.

4–8mm). Rather, they expected conditions to improve for batsmen on the second and third days, and wanted to take advantage.

And so it proved. Despite Mitchell's assured half-century, Woakes made an impressive return, and Broad, employing all his experience and variations, helped England work their way through the batting. At 315 for five in the last over before tea on the second afternoon, New Zealand were set to take control. But Broad surprised Watling with extra bounce, the catalyst for a collapse of five for 60 as England made good use of the short ball.

In reply, Sibley and Denly fell quickly, while Burns rode some early luck, dropped on ten and 19 as England reached 39 for two that evening. Next day, he registered his second Test century, only to run himself out two balls later after dawdling over the first run, then failing to resist Root's demand for a second. It was a lame end to a measured stand of 177 in nearly 64 overs, and New Zealand briefly took heart: Stokes poked Southee to slip, before Crawley dangled his bat at Wagner and was caught behind for a single. On the fourth day, though, Pope reined in his natural aggression, and batted over four hours for a maiden Test fifty, to help his captain add 193 for the sixth wicket.

Most of all, there was Root. During his chanceless innings, he overtook Wally Hammond's 7,249 to move into the top ten of England Test run-scorers (none had a higher average), and became the first overseas captain to register a double-century in New Zealand. And while the attempt to accelerate and set up a declaration led to a collapse – the last five fell for 21, handing Wagner a five-wicket haul for the fourth successive Test – England still took a lead of 101.

When New Zealand quickly lost their openers after tea on the fourth day, England had a sniff of victory. But they had to take every chance that came their way. As it was, with New Zealand still two behind on the final morning, Pope dropped Williamson on 39 – a relatively straightforward catch – down the leg side off Stokes. Then, with Williamson on 62, Denly made a fearsome hash of an absolute dolly at short midwicket. The unfortunate bowler, Archer, let out a cry of anguish that could be heard around the ground. It was understandable he had just deceived one of the world's best batsmen with a brilliantly disguised knuckle ball, and was on his way to averaging more than 100 per wicket in the series.

By then, the grass banks were almost deserted, and the first spots of rain beginning to fall. Not long after lunch, Taylor thrashed successive balls from Root through midwicket for four, six and six to complete his sixth century in 12 Tests at Seddon Park; almost immediately, play was suspended for the final time. Williamson and Taylor had posted an unbroken 213-run stand to make the game and the series safe. Williamson recorded his 21st Test century, and Taylor his 19th, becoming the second New Zealander, after Stephen Fleming, to pass 7,000 Test runs. It was indicative of his side's burgeoning confidence and the balance of power when Williamson hinted it was New Zealand, leading by 140, who had been thwarted by the rain.

Player of the Match: J. E. Root. *Player of the Series:* N. Wagner.

Close of play: first day, New Zealand 173-3 (Latham 101, Nicholls 5); second day, England 39-2 (Burns 24, Root 6); third day, England 269-5 (Root 114, Pope 4); fourth day, New Zealand 96-2 (Williamson 37, Taylor 31).

New Zealand

J. A. Raval c Root b Broad	5	– (2) lbw b Curran	0
T. W. M. Latham b Broad	105	– (1) c Root b Woakes	18
*K. S. Williamson c Root b Woakes	4	– not out	104
L. R. P. L. Taylor c Root b Woakes	53	– not out	105
H. M. Nicholls c Broad b Curran	16		
†B-J. Watling c Burns b Broad	55		
D. J. Mitchell c Archer b Broad	73		
M. J. Santner c Woakes b Archer	23		
T. G. Southee c Pope b Woakes	18		
M. J. Henry not out	5		
N. Wagner c Sibley b Curran	0		
B 15, lb 3	18	B 2, lb 3, w 3, nb 1, p 5	14

1/16 (1) 2/39 (3) 3/155 (4) (129.1 overs) 375   1/2 (2) 2/28 (1) (2 wkts, 75 overs) 241
4/182 (2) 5/191 (5) 6/315 (6)
7/330 (7) 8/357 (9) 9/375 (8) 10/375 (11)

Broad 28–7–73–4; Archer 28–8–75–1; Woakes 31–6–83–3; Curran 23.1–7–63–2; Root 3–0–14–0; Stokes 13–5–36–0; Denly 3–0–13–0. *Second innings*—Broad 9–0–28–0; Curran 16–2–56–1; Archer 12–1–27–0; Woakes 11–4–12–1; Stokes 14–1–58–0; Denly 9–1–27–0; Root 4–1–23–0.

England

R. J. Burns run out (Raval/Watling)	101	J. C. Archer b Wagner	8
D. P. Sibley lbw b Southee	4	S. C. J. Broad b Wagner	0
J. L. Denly c Watling b Henry	4		
J. E. Root c Nicholls b Santner	226	B 4, lb 14, w 1, nb 1	20
B. A. Stokes c Taylor b Southee	26		
Z. Crawley c Watling b Wagner	1	1/11 (2) 2/24 (3) (162.5 overs) 476
O. J. D. Pope c Raval b Wagner	75	3/201 (1) 4/245 (5)
S. M. Curran not out	11	5/262 (6) 6/455 (7) 7/458 (4)
C. R. Woakes c Watling b Wagner	0	8/460 (9) 9/476 (10) 10/476 (11)

Southee 37–4–90–2; Henry 33–6–87–1; Wagner 35.5–3–124–5; Mitchell 22–5–69–0; Santner 35–4–88–1.

Umpires: H. D. P. K. Dharmasena and P. Wilson. Third umpire: B. N. J. Oxenford.
Referee: J. Srinath.

SOUTH AFRICA v ENGLAND IN 2019-20

Review by Rory Dollard

Test matches (4): South Africa 1 (24pts), England 3 (90pts)
One-day internationals (3): South Africa 1, England 1
Twenty20 internationals (3): South Africa 1, England 2

As the calamities piled up for England in their early days in South Africa, Ben Stokes revealed that the squad had begun to speak of the "cursed tour". By the time the Test series was in the books, it had taken on the form of a blessing – rebirth for the team, renewal for individuals, and the restatement of a project being gently remoulded to Joe Root's specifications.

A series win for England might not have seemed an outlandish prediction: they had beaten a much stiffer South Africa side on their previous visit, four years earlier, then easily retained the Basil D'Oliveira Trophy at home in 2017. But circumstances made this a result to savour. Illness had swept the camp from the moment they touched down in Johannesburg, with symptoms of flu and gastroenteritis working their way through the squad. In a vain attempt to contain the spread, net sessions were depleted, daily health bulletins posted by the media manager on the travelling journalists' WhatsApp group, and quarantine rooms established at the team hotels and training grounds.

Head coach Chris Silverwood had hoped to cure England's reputation as slow starters, dialling up the intensity with a first-class match against a strong South Africa A side. Instead, he was forced into requesting the fixture be downgraded to knockabout status. A sorely underprepared squad were defeated in the First Test at Centurion, by the end of which 11 players and six backroom staff had been affected. Root was among those stricken mid-match, as was Stokes, whose participation in that game came under intolerable emotional strain: his father, Ged, had been taken seriously ill two days before Christmas, rallying sufficiently in intensive care to tell his son he had to play.

Stokes's standing was already established and, on the eve of the Third Test, he was crowned ICC Cricketer of the Year. But his performances during this series – 318 runs, ten wickets, 12 catches – told of a deep well of resolve. Numbers alone were enough to earn him Player of the Series, though the intangibles were just as compelling: how and when he contributed, the tone he set, and the psychological impact his mere presence had on South Africa.

Yet England's misfortunes lingered long enough to ensure they were not once able to pick their preferred side. Rory Burns injured an ankle playing football before the Second Test at Cape Town, where James Anderson broke a rib while returning match figures of 37–15–63–7; Jack Leach endured a doomed fitness battle, and Jofra Archer was limited to one Test after hurting his elbow. But the stand-ins proved more than able, and England's strategies sufficiently nimble, for the setbacks to be worn lightly.

Root's captaincy was both a cause, and a beneficiary, of this success. Winning all four tosses helped, but overseas victories are not the preserve of

Stu Forster, Getty Images

Poise and promise: Ollie Pope enjoyed a breakthrough tour.

lucky generals. He showed stoicism when things veered off course, sensibly enforced the follow-on at Port Elizabeth, and wisely declined to do so at Johannesburg. Even while using 16 players, he managed to retain team unity and tactical cohesion. For the second time – after Sri Lanka in 2018-19 – Root had captained England to three successive away wins, a feat beyond either of his predecessors, Alastair Cook and Andrew Strauss. And, after all the talk of their aversion to the Kookaburra, England bowled out South Africa in all eight innings. The biggest challenge of Root's reign could still be carving out the right space for Archer, who continued to inspire intrigue even when he was unfit, though there was no temptation to press him into action when his body pushed back, and an assurance from Root that he would be handled with care.

For South Africa, and particularly their careworn captain, Faf du Plessis, English talk of a curse must have sounded like a fuss about nothing. Stomach bugs clear, bones and muscles heal, but some problems run deeper. Already hobbled by Kolpak, Cricket South Africa were swamped by backstage chaos in the days leading up to England's arrival. Key commercial partners abandoned ship, and there was an accreditation row with domestic media, before the cavalry emerged in the form of Graeme Smith, Mark Boucher and Jacques Kallis. Their respective appointments as acting-director of cricket, head coach and batting consultant brought instant credibility, and injected a dose of awe into the dressing-room. But, allied to the return of Jacques Faul as acting-CEO, some detected a managerial "whitewash". A day after the final Twenty20, du Plessis (who missed both limited-overs series) announced he was stepping down, having first led the white-ball teams in 2012-13, and the Test side in August 2016. Following a Test series in which he had averaged 18 and often looked frazzled, he spoke of a "new direction" and of "putting the team first".

Before then, the murmurs grew as transformation targets – which are supposed to average out over the course of a year to six players of colour in each XI, including two black Africans – were missed in all four matches. Temba Bavuma, as is his fate, became a lightning rod for the racial debates, his name cropping up more than any other; he made his solitary appearance in the final Test. Explaining Bavuma's non-selection at Newlands, du Plessis suggested the national side "don't see colour". It was a laudable sentiment, but not easy to take for large sections of South African cricket. Enoch Nkwe, who swallowed his ego to accept a demotion – from interim head coach to Boucher's assistant – could emerge as one of the set-up's wisest counsellors.

South Africa fielded five debutants, at least one in each match, with Beuran Hendricks, aged 29, the youngest. The short-term results were mixed, the long-range investment uncertain. England preferred fresher blood. There was 22-year-old Dom Bess, a late arrival as cover for Leach; he locked down an end at Cape Town, then took the first five wickets at Port Elizabeth. There was

YOU NAME IT, HE DID IT

Players with 300 runs, ten wickets and ten catches in the same Test series:

Runs	Wkts	Ct	M			
442	23	15	5	J. M. Gregory	Australia v England	1920-21
333	15	12	5	T. L. Goddard	South Africa v England	1956-57
430	15	12	5	G. S. Sobers	West Indies v Australia	1960-61
424	23	11	5	G. S. Sobers	West Indies v India	1961-62
722	20	10	5	G. S. Sobers	West Indies v England	1966
446	17	12	6	A. W. Greig	England v Australia	1974-75
399	34	12	6	I. T. Botham	England v Australia	1981
318	**10**	**12**	**4**	**B. A. Stokes**	**England v South Africa**	**2019-20**

24-year-old Dom Sibley: his maiden hundred, a tireless unbeaten 133 to underpin England's second-innings charge at Cape Town, brought out the paternal side in Stokes, who stuffed his trophy for the match award in Sibley's kitbag. With 324 runs, he was England's top scorer, pipping Stokes and Root. There was 21-year-old Zak Crawley and his bold talk of "taking down" Kagiso Rabada. Most of all, there was Ollie Pope, who had just turned 22.

His reputation as a coming man had long been foretold, starting at Surrey, then swelling to a consensus across the county game; his out-of-position debut in 2018 against India had been a false start, his return in New Zealand a palate cleanser. But this was proof of his quality. Pope's three first-innings efforts – he missed the Centurion Test through illness – made a persuasive body of work: he top-scored with an unbeaten 61 in the Second Test, went through the gears to hit a staggeringly accomplished 135 not out in the Third, and outscored Root during a century stand in the Fourth. His strokeplay was pleasing enough to earn comparisons – inside and outside the dressing-room – to the previous generation's premier classicist, Ian Bell, yet his repertoire may be even broader. A selection of ramps, flips and flicks after he had reached his maiden hundred were as eye-catching as his sweet blows through extra cover, and gave a thrilling hint of his range.

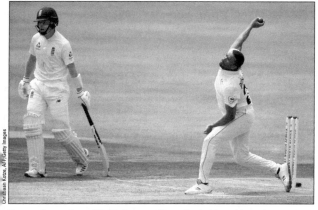

Next stop, Taunton: Vernon Philander bows out of international cricket at Johannesburg, to pursue a Kolpak career with Somerset.

Of course, England were by no means a kindergarten. Led by Root and Stokes in their peak years, and still leaning on Anderson's and Stuart Broad's combined tally – by the end of the series – of 289 caps and 1,069 wickets, there was also room for the return of a thirtysomething with the Tiggerish enthusiasm of a first-timer. Almost six months after tearing his side in the World Cup final, Mark Wood bounded back for the last two Tests, rattling batsmen with his pace and trajectory, and sweeping up 12 wickets at 13. He had spent long enough out of action over the years to wonder if every 90mph bouncer, and every cartwheeling stump might be his last. It showed. For good measure, he hit eight sixes.

South African optimism was thinner on the ground, particularly when it was announced that the venerable Vernon Philander would be their latest star trading an international career for a Kolpak deal. His first spell after breaking the news, at Centurion, began with five maidens; in mockery of his planned departure for Somerset, he banked figures of four for 16. But his influence faded, and only sentiment prevented him from being rested from at least one Test. His lethargic swansongs at Port Elizabeth and Johannesburg might easily have been bettered by those waiting in the wings, but the skills which brought him 224 wickets at 22 will be harder to replace.

There were bright spots. Quinton de Kock and Anrich Nortje were the series' leading run-scorer (380) and wicket-taker (18). De Kock was still prone to loose dismissals, but was comfortably South Africa's best batsman, not that he faced much competition: their eight innings produced a best of 284, and an average of 241. He also held 23 catches behind the stumps. Already one-day captain, he seemed well placed for the Test job, too, following du Plessis's resignation. Nortje established himself as a Test cricketer of merit. Over the

FIVE STATS YOU MAY HAVE MISSED

BENEDICT BERMANGE

- At Centurion, Rassie van der Dussen became the first to make a half-century in his first match in each of the three formats. He had scored 56 against Zimbabwe at East London in his first T20 international in October 2018, then 93 against Pakistan at Port Elizabeth on ODI debut in January 2019. In his first Test he added six and 51.

- Quinton de Kock was the fourth wicketkeeper to dismiss the top five in a Test innings:

R. C. Russell	England v Australia at Melbourne	1990-91
B-J. Watling	New Zealand v India at Auckland	2013-14
B. J. Haddin	Australia v India at Brisbane	2014-15
Q. de Kock	**South Africa v England at Centurion**	**2019-20**

- At Cape Town, Ben Stokes became the third man to score 100 runs, take three wickets and hold six catches in the same Test:

F. E. Woolley (133*, 11; 2-1, 1-36; 6 ct)	England v Australia at Sydney	1911-12
J. H. Kallis (224; 3-35; 6 ct)	South Africa v Sri Lanka at Cape Town	2011-12
B. A. Stokes (47, 72; 0-34, 3-35; 6 ct)	**England v South Africa at Cape Town**	**2019-20**

- Towards the end of South Africa's second innings at Cape Town, they went 70 successive deliveries without a run, their longest such sequence in Tests.

- In the Third Test, Anrich Nortje became the second nightwatchman to bat for at least two hours twice in a series, after India's Syed Kirmani against Australia in 1979-80. Nortje survived for 127 minutes at Centurion, and 191 at Port Elizabeth; Kirmani had managed 235 at Madras, and 306 at Bombay, where he made 101 not out.

course of the series, he did his best to put flesh on the bones of bowling coach Charl Langeveldt's description of him as "a proper Dutchman", which seems destined to stick. He charged in combatively and whole-heartedly, always fast and only occasionally furious. His willingness to embrace the role of nightwatchman, and wear the bruises, marked him out as another pillar of the future. For the moment, though, the South Africans – who had lost to Sri Lanka in February 2019 – were nursing successive home Test series defeats for the first time since 1948-49 (against England) and 1949-50 (Australia).

Match referee Andy Pycroft had a busy few weeks doling out fines and demerit points – one leading to the suspension of Rabada from the Fourth Test – but his hand was forced mostly by bad language rather than bad blood. By the final evening, the players had come together in the traditional style, an entertaining and hard-fought contest put to rest over drinks.

Gideon Brooks writes: With the next World Cup not until 2023, the first half of the white-ball series lacked context, beyond being a first victory lap for England's world champions, seven months on from the drama of Lord's. The three super-over stars that day were all missing: Stokes and Jos Buttler (after a disappointing Test series) were rested, Archer injured. Conversely, with the T20 World Cup in Australia only eight months away, the 20-over series was a belter. It showcased the talents of two well-matched sides, and suggested England's World Cup win had added self-belief to their armoury.

MOST SIXES IN TWENTY20 INTERNATIONALS

		M	*Runs*	*Avge*	*SR*
127	R. G. Sharma (India)	108	2,773	32.62	138.78
119	M. J. Guptill (New Zealand)	88	2,536	32.51	134.60
107	C. Munro (New Zealand)	65	1,724	31.34	156.44
105	C. H. Gayle (West Indies)	58	1,627	32.54	142.84
105	E. J. G. Morgan (England)	89	2,138	30.98	137.49
91	B. B. McCullum (New Zealand)	71	2,140	35.66	136.21
90	A. J. Finch (Australia)	58	1,878	38.32	156.50
86	D. A. Warner (Australia)	76	2,079	30.57	140.85
83	S. R. Watson (Australia)	58	1,462	29.24	145.32
81	G. J. Maxwell (Australia)	61	1,576	35.02	160.00

Silverwood and captain Eoin Morgan had viewed the ODIs as a vehicle to find out about fringe players; it was not, they said, about putting out their best XI. In the first two matches – the second, at Kingsmead, was spoiled by rain – leg-spinner Matt Parkinson and Sam Curran rather proved their point, failing to push their cases. With England 1–0 down after a brilliant century from de Kock at Cape Town, the management brought in Adil Rashid and Moeen Ali at the Wanderers. They helped secure a 1–1 draw, and preserve an unbeaten record in bilateral one-day series stretching back to March 2017 in the West Indies. Joe Denly was England's leading run-scorer, with 153, though he was less successful in the T20s.

In three terrific games, which saw 1,207 runs scored – a record for a three-match T20 series – Morgan, Jonny Bairstow and Jason Roy came to the fore for England, while openers de Kock and Bavuma matched them for South Africa, sharing stands of 48 in 4.1 overs, 92 in 7.5, and 84 in 7.4. Lungi Ngidi bowled the hosts to victory in the first game, at East London, after England failed to score seven from their last seven balls. But Tom Curran responded with wickets from the last two of the next game, at Durban, as South Africa lost by two runs. A late flourish from Morgan then inspired his side to chase down 223 in the decider. His seven sixes in that game made him the first England batsman, and the fifth in all, to hit 100 in T20 internationals (next, on 55, were Buttler and Alex Hales). It meant England had come back from behind in each of the three formats, ending a memorable tour on a high.

ENGLAND TOURING PARTY

*J. E. Root (Yorkshire; T/50), M. M. Ali (Worcestershire; 50/20), J. M. Anderson (Lancashire; T), J. C. Archer (Sussex; T), J. M. Bairstow (Yorkshire; T/50/20), T. Banton (Somerset; 50), D. M. Bess (Somerset; T), S. C. J. Broad (Nottinghamshire; T), R. J. Burns (Surrey; T), J. C. Buttler (Lancashire; T/20), Z. Crawley (Kent; T), S. M. Curran (Surrey; T/50/20), T. K. Curran (Surrey; 50/20), J. L. Denly (Kent; T/50/20), C. J. Jordan (Sussex; 50/20), M. J. Leach (Somerset; T), S. Mahmood (Lancashire; 50/20), D. J. Malan (Yorkshire; 50/20), E. J. G. Morgan (Middlesex; 50/20), C. Overton (Somerset; T), M. W. Parkinson (Lancashire; T/50/20), O. J. D. Pope (Surrey; T), A. U. Rashid (Yorkshire; 50/20), J. J. Roy (Surrey; 50/20), D. P. Sibley (Warwickshire; T), B. A. Stokes (Durham; T/20), C. R. Woakes (Warwickshire; T/50), M. A. Wood (Durham; T/20).

Bess and Overton were added to the Test squad as cover for illness and injury. Anderson (broken rib), Burns (injured ankle) and Leach (various ailments) returned home after the Second Test. P. R. Brown (Worcestershire) was originally named in the white-ball squads, but withdrew with a lumbar stress fracture. Archer was originally chosen for the T20s, but was withdrawn because of an elbow problem, and replaced by Mahmood. Morgan captained in the white-ball matches.

Head coach: C. E. W. Silverwood (T/50/20). *Assistant coaches:* G. P. Thorpe (T/50), P. D. Collingwood (T/50/20). *Batting consultant:* M. E. Trescothick (20). *Spin consultant:* J. S. Patel (T/50/20). *Wicketkeeping coach:* B. N. French (T). *Fielding coach:* C. D. Hopkinson (T/20). *Team manager:* A. W. Bentley (T/50/20). *Analyst:* R. Lewis (T), N. A. Leamon (50/20). *Doctor:* A. Biswas (T), Moiz Moghal (50/20). *Physiotherapist:* C. A. de Weymarn (T), B. Langley (50/20). *Masseur:* M. Saxby (T/50). *Strength and conditioning:* P. C. F. Scott (T), R. Ahmun (50/20). *Nutritionist:* E. Gardner (T/50). *Psychologist:* D. J. Young (T). *Security managers:* S. Dickason (T), J. Shaw (T/50/20). *Head of team communications:* D. M. Reuben (T/50/20). *Digital editor:* G. R. Stobart (T), W. Turner (50/20).

TEST MATCH AVERAGES

SOUTH AFRICA – BATTING AND FIELDING

	T	I	NO	R	HS	100	50	Avge	Ct
†Q. de Kock	4	8	0	380	95	0	4	47.50	23
D. Paterson	2	4	3	43	39*	0	0	43.00	1
H. E. van der Dussen	4	8	0	274	98	0	3	34.25	8
†D. Elgar	4	8	0	244	88	0	1	30.50	6
P. J. Malan	3	6	0	156	84	0	1	26.00	3
V. D. Philander	4	8	1	160	46	0	0	22.85	0
F. du Plessis	4	8	0	151	36	0	0	18.87	3
K. A. Maharaj	3	6	0	94	71	0	1	15.66	2
D. Pretorius	3	6	0	83	37	0	0	13.83	2
M. Z. Hamza	3	6	0	78	39	0	0	13.00	3
†K. Rabada	3	6	2	48	16*	0	0	12.00	1
A. A. Nortje	4	8	1	77	40	0	0	11.00	1

Played in one Test: T. Bavuma 6, 27; †B. E. Hendricks 5*, 4; A. K. Markram 20, 2.

BOWLING

	Style	O	M	R	W	BB	5I	Avge
V. D. Philander	RFM	101.5	34	213	8	4-16	0	26.62
A. A. Nortje	RF	125	16	488	18	5-110	1	27.11
K. Rabada	RF	106.5	16	405	14	4-103	0	28.92
B. E. Hendricks	LFM	38.3	5	175	6	5-64	1	29.16
D. Pretorius	RFM	80	22	252	7	2-26	0	36.00
D. Paterson	RFM	57.5	11	166	4	2-86	0	41.50
K. A. Maharaj	SLA	148	34	463	10	5-180	1	46.30

Also bowled: D. Elgar (SLA) 1–0–6–0; P. J. Malan (RM) 2–0–5–0.

ENGLAND – BATTING AND FIELDING

	T	I	NO	R	HS	100	50	Avge	Ct
O. J. D. Pope	3	5	2	266	135*	1	2	88.66	7
D. P. Sibley	4	7	1	324	133*	1	0	54.00	2
M. A. Wood	2	3	1	95	42	0	0	47.50	2
†B. A. Stokes	4	7	0	318	120	1	1	45.42	12
J. E. Root	4	7	0	317	61	0	3	45.28	7
Z. Crawley	3	5	0	163	66	0	1	32.60	3
J. L. Denly	4	7	0	210	50	0	1	30.00	2
†S. M. Curran	4	7	0	130	44	0	0	18.57	3
J. C. Buttler	4	7	0	115	29	0	0	16.42	14
†S. C. J. Broad	4	6	2	61	43	0	0	15.25	3
†J. M. Anderson	2	3	2	4	4	0	0	4.00	1
D. M. Bess	2	3	0	1	1	0	0	0.33	1

Played in one Test: J. C. Archer 3, 4; J. M. Bairstow 1, 9 (3 ct); †R. J. Burns 9, 84; C. R. Woakes 32, 0 (2 ct).

BOWLING

	Style	O	M	R	W	BB	5I	Avge
M. A. Wood	RF	58.3	15	163	12	5-46	1	13.58
S. C. J. Broad	RFM	118.1	35	272	14	4-58	0	19.42
J. M. Anderson..............	RFM	70	20	179	9	5-40	1	19.88
B. A. Stokes	RFM	77.4	17	220	10	3-35	0	22.00
D. M. Bess	OB	113	40	206	8	5-51	1	25.75
J. C. Archer	RF	36	5	167	6	5-102	1	27.83
C. R. Woakes	RFM	31	10	85	3	2-38	0	28.33
S. M. Curran	LFM	101.4	23	326	10	4-58	0	32.60
J. E. Root	OB	60	19	190	4	4-87	0	47.50

Also bowled: J. L. Denly (LB) 28–5–75–2.

At Benoni, December 17–18, 2019 (not first-class). **Drawn. ‡England XI 309-7 dec** (90 overs) (D. P. Sibley 58, J. L. Denly 60, J. E. Root 72); **South African Invitation XI 289** (68 overs) (K. W. Sekhukhune 65, G. J. Snyman 79, D. S. Rosier 70; C. R. Woakes 3-48). *Dom Sibley, Joe Denly and Joe Root all retired out not long after reaching half-centuries in this gentle pipe-opener. All nine England batsmen reached double figures. Sam Curran took two quick wickets on the second morning, but Kabelo Sekhukhune and Jacques Snyman put on 133, before the Invitation XI captain Diego Rosier added 70 against an England attack lacking Jofra Archer and Stuart Broad, who had fallen ill.*

At Benoni, December 20–22, 2019 (not first-class). **Drawn. ‡England XI 456-7 dec** (109.3 overs) (R. J. Burns 56, J. L. Denly 103, O. J. D. Pope 132; A. L. Phehlukwayo 3-55); **South Africa A 325-5** (93.2 overs) (K. D. Petersen 111, R. S. Second 55, K. Verreynne 74; J. M. Anderson 3-41). *This was originally scheduled to be a first-class game, but was downgraded at England's request after illness swept through the tour party. They chose from 12 players, and South Africa A from 14. Denly made his first century in an England shirt on the first day, and Ollie Pope (70* overnight) completed his on the second. Ben Stokes made 47, not long after joining the tour late, having been given permission to collect his BBC Sports Personality of the Year trophy in Aberdeen. With several of the tourists confined to the hotel, the captains shook hands on the draw before tea on the third day, shortly after Keegan Petersen completed a century that propelled him into South Africa's Test squad. Jimmy Anderson had encouraging figures of 19–7–41–3. "He looks in great shape," said Root, "probably as strong as we've seen him."*

SOUTH AFRICA v ENGLAND

First Test

NEIL MANTHORP

At Centurion, December 26–29, 2019. South Africa won by 107 runs. South Africa 30pts. Toss: England. Test debuts: D. Pretorius, H. E. van der Dussen.

The sickness wracking the England squad had shown no signs of abating by the time the series began. There was chaos from the start – and it never let up. Bairstow took Ollie Pope's place at No. 6, and significant time was spent off the field by Root and Stokes. On the third day, Bairstow also took the gloves, while Buttler was receiving treatment. The instability proved a metaphor for their performance.

Debilitated and dehydrated, the tourists still refused to use the bug as an excuse, and maintained a stiff upper lip – in contrast to their bowels. Not that Root could blame his bizarre decision to bowl first on being unwell: locals, including his opposite number, du Plessis, were delighted South Africa would not be batting last on a pitch renowned for deteriorating. Root had been part of the previous England team to play at Centurion, four years earlier, when – after South Africa batted first – successive totals were 475, 342, 248 for five and 101. That made his call even more peculiar. There was nothing, visual or anecdotal, to suggest this pitch would be any different.

England's omission of a spinner was also curious, but their problems were more fundamental: a pair of all-too-familiar collapses (seven for 39, and seven for 64), wasteful new-ball bowling, and a failure to locate a top-of-off-stump length in conditions routinely offering rewards for doing so. De Kock's attacking 95 in the first innings was the greatest statistical difference between the sides, but other – less easily quantifiable – passages of play shaped the game just as much.

Broad and Anderson – one sick, the other without a meaningful match for five months – began with too many unthreatening balls, even if Anderson struck with his opening delivery, a leg-stump half-tracker feathered by Elgar, his first Test scalp since St Lucia in February. Then, despite South Africa slumping to 111 for five, Archer led a concerted short-pitched attack – uncomfortable for the batsmen, but unrewarded. Despite just one success, when du Plessis paddle-pulled a bouncer to fine leg in the second innings, Archer stuck to the plan throughout. Words were continually exchanged with batsmen, and it looked obvious he had been drawn into a battle of egos. This was no surprise: South Africa's new head coach Mark Boucher had said his team would be targeting him.

WICKET WITH THE FIRST BALL OF A TEST FOR ENGLAND

Bowler	*Batsman*		
M. W. Tate	W. Bardsley	v Australia at Leeds	1926
G. G. Arnold	S. M. Gavaskar	v India at Birmingham	1974
G. G. Arnold	J. F. M. Morrison	v New Zealand at Christchurch	1974-75
R. J. Sidebottom	D. Ganga	v West Indies at Chester-le-Street	2007
J. M. Anderson	**D. Elgar**	**v South Africa at Centurion**	**2019-20**

There have been 32 instances in all Tests.

De Kock scored so freely that his fifty came from 45 deliveries, and a century beckoned, until Curran produced just enough old-ball movement to find the edge – from the right length. South Africa's decision to play 30-year-old debutant Dwaine Pretorius as an extra all-rounder along with Philander paid off, with both men making solid thirties. (Pretorius had agreed Kolpak terms with Nottinghamshire a couple of weeks earlier, but former captain Graeme Smith, newly installed as Cricket South Africa's inaugural director of cricket, persuaded him to change his mind.) England were satisfied with dismissing their hosts for under 300, with Broad and Curran, who collected a career-best, both picking up four. But locals knew better. In the preceding three years, on some spiteful Centurion pitches, a collection of twenties and thirties – South Africa's innings included five – had often proved match-winning.

Philander opened with five maidens, which included the wicket of Burns, nibbling outside off; by the end of the spell, Sibley had gone too, undone by a brute from Rabada. Yet, as meticulously accurate as Philander was, England made little attempt to rotate the strike: Denly, whose latest Test fifty contained nine fours, managed only 14 runs from his other 102 deliveries. The nature of the pitch, and South Africa's probing length, was confirmed by six catches for de Kock, three off Philander, who finished with four for 16 from 14.2 overs. He had bowled well in what he had already announced would be his last Test series. But England's passivity meant he could do as he wished. And, from 142 for three, they played a series of woeful strokes, seven wickets falling in 15.4 overs.

Near-Centurion: Quinton de Kock hits a vital 95 on the first day of the series.

A deficit of 103 was a huge handicap, but they fought their way back into the contest as South Africa wobbled to 62 for four. Anderson struck in the first over again – Markram, this time – while Archer claimed two prized wickets. Elgar inside-edged an effort ball, before du Plessis played his curious scoop. England's best hope was cool heads and patience, but Archer opted for explosives and a quick fix. Boundaries began to flow as England dropped short. And if strokes were not always from the middle of the bat, it seemed clear the bowlers had got their lengths horribly wrong.

Not only did Nortje survive 23 minutes on the second evening as nightwatchman, he lasted another 20 overs on the third day, and shared a match-changing stand of 91 with van der Dussen. Like Pretorius, van der Dussen was making his debut at the age of 30, and immediately looked comfortable. Nortje did not, but he knew how to survive against deliveries aimed at his head and body. Archer persisted with bouncers, determined to see his plan succeed, but he was a gambler chasing his debts. It allowed van der Dussen to score more quickly than usual, while Nortje collected six boundaries and twice as many bruises, as Archer attacked from round the wicket with a Bodyline field. By the time van der Dussen was trapped leg-before, South Africa were 256 ahead, and England required the final five wickets quickly to have any chance. Instead, de Kock hooked his third and fourth balls, from Archer, for six, and reached lunch on 30 from 17. The lead was 300, and his side had entered safe waters. Philander's composed 46 was welcome insurance, but hardly necessary. Archer's five for 102 from 17 overs was, by economy-rate, Test cricket's fourth-most expensive five-for.

England needed 376, and Sibley showed his potential against the seamers during an opening stand of 92, until he chipped a tame catch back to left-arm spinner Maharaj. But, at 121 for one going into the fourth day, there was a genuine belief they might duplicate their epic chase at Headingley. After all, Stokes was still to come.

Before lunch, England added just 50, for the loss of Burns, who had looked as assured as anyone in the match until, frustrated by a period of inactivity, he miscued a hook off

DISMISSED BY THE FIRST BALL OF A TEST SERIES

Batsman	Bowler		
H. Sutcliffe	F. T. Badcock	England v New Zealand at Christchurch	1932-33
T. S. Worthington	E. L. McCormick	England v Australia at Brisbane	1936-37
S. J. Cook†	Kapil Dev	South Africa v India at Durban†	1992-93
Hannan Sarkar	P. T. Collins	Bangladesh v West Indies at Dhaka	2002-03
Hannan Sarkar	P. T. Collins	Bangladesh v West Indies at Gros Islet	2003-04
Wasim Jaffer	Mashrafe bin Mortaza	India v Bangladesh at Chittagong	2007
T. G. McIntosh	Mohammad Amir	New Zealand v Pakistan at Dunedin	2009-10
K. L. Rahul	R. A. S. Lakmal	India v Sri Lanka at Kolkata	2017-18
D. Elgar	**J. M. Anderson**	**v South Africa at Centurion**	**2019-20**

† *Test debut.*   *Research: Benedict Bermange*

the rapid Nortje. Denly was then trapped by Pretorius. Superstitious statisticians were all a dither when Stokes walked out, with 218 needed and seven wickets in hand – the exact scenario he had faced at Leeds. And, as then, he attempted to play himself in with a barrage of blocks, reaching four from 42 balls, before clobbering a couple of fours off Maharaj.

But with the total 204, and England beginning to wonder, Maharaj caught him in two minds – somewhere between a back-foot punch and a late cut – and the ball deflected off the bottom edge on to the stumps. Bairstow flashed a wild drive into the cordon and, when Root edged another top-of-off delivery from Nortje, the game was up. Rabada was never at his best but, like all champions, he found a way to deliver, taking three of the last four.

England, you sensed, were more interested in heading for recuperation in the Cape than dissecting a match in which they did themselves no favours. South Africa, on the other hand, had snapped a five-Test losing streak with a smart plan based on the rotation of two genuinely fast strike bowlers, two frustratingly accurate medium-pacers, and a spinner. They had also been prepared to out-scrap their opponents with the bat. Thanks to England's failure to read the conditions, they didn't need to.

Player of the Match: Q. de Kock.

Close of play: first day, South Africa 277-9 (Philander 28); second day, South Africa 72-4 (van der Dussen 17, Nortje 4); third day, England 121-1 (Burns 77, Denly 10).

South Africa

D. Elgar c Buttler b Anderson	0	– (2) c Buttler b Archer	22
A. K. Markram c Bairstow b Curran	20	– (1) lbw b Anderson	2
M. Z. Hamza c Stokes b Broad	39	– c Buttler b Broad	4
*F. du Plessis c Root b Broad	29	– c Curran b Archer	20
H. E. van der Dussen c Root b Curran	6	– lbw b Archer	51
†Q. de Kock c Buttler b Curran	95	– (7) c Bairstow b Stokes	34
D. Pretorius c Root b Curran	33	– (8) c Sibley b Stokes	7
V. D. Philander c Buttler b Broad	35	– (9) c Bairstow b Curran	46
K. A. Maharaj c Stokes b Archer	6	– (10) c Curran b Archer	11
K. Rabada b Broad	12	– (11) not out	16
A. A. Nortje not out	0	– (6) c sub (Z. Crawley) b Archer	40
Lb 4, w 3, nb 2	9	B 5, lb 3, w 9, nb 2	19

1/0 (1) 2/32 (2) 3/71 (3)   (84.3 overs) 284   1/2 (1) 2/25 (3)   (61.4 overs) 272
4/97 (5) 5/111 (4) 6/198 (7)   3/29 (2) 4/62 (4)
7/245 (6) 8/252 (9) 9/277 (10) 10/284 (8)   5/153 (5) 6/170 (6) 7/177 (8)
                                                         8/220 (7) 9/250 (10) 10/272 (9)

Anderson 20–4–69–1; Broad 18.3–4–58–4; Curran 20–5–58–4; Archer 19–4–65–1; Root 4–0–26–0; Denly 3–0–4–0. *Second innings*—Anderson 13–1–47–1; Broad 11–2–42–1; Archer 17–1–102–5; Curran 12.4–3–51–1; Stokes 8–1–22–2.

England

R. J. Burns c de Kock b Philander	9	– c Rabada b Nortje	84
D. P. Sibley c de Kock b Rabada	4	– c and b Maharaj	29
J. L. Denly c de Kock b Pretorius	50	– lbw b Pretorius	31
*J. E. Root c de Kock b Philander	29	– c de Kock b Nortje	48
B. A. Stokes c de Kock b Nortje	35	– b Maharaj	14
J. M. Bairstow b Nortje	1	– c Hamza b Rabada	9
†J. C. Buttler c de Kock b Philander	12	– c Pretorius b Rabada	22
S. M. Curran c Hamza b Rabada	20	– c de Kock b Rabada	9
J. C. Archer b Philander	3	– c van der Dussen b Nortje	4
S. C. J. Broad c Elgar b Rabada	2	– b Rabada	6
J. M. Anderson not out	0	– not out	0
B 4, lb 5, w 5, nb 2	16	B 8, lb 3, w 1	12
	181		268

1/11 (1) 2/15 (2) 3/70 (4)   (53.2 overs) 181   1/92 (2) 2/139 (1)   (93 overs) 268
4/142 (3) 5/143 (6) 6/150 (5)   3/158 (3) 4/204 (5)
7/176 (8) 8/176 (7) 9/181 (10) 10/181 (9)   5/222 (6) 6/232 (4) 7/251 (8)
8/256 (9) 9/262 (7) 10/268 (10)

Rabada 15–1–68–3; Philander 14.2–8–16–4; Pretorius 8–2–23–1; Nortje 12–2–47–2; Maharaj 4–1–18–0. *Second innings*—Rabada 24–3–103–4; Philander 20–8–35–0; Nortje 17–4–56–3; Pretorius 16–6–26–1; Maharaj 16–3–37–2.

Umpires: C. B. Gaffaney and P. R. Reiffel.   Third umpire: H. D. P. K. Dharmasena.
Referee: A. J. Pycroft.

SOUTH AFRICA v ENGLAND

Second Test

Vic Marks

At Cape Town, January 3–7, 2020. England won by 189 runs. England 30pts. Toss: England. Test debut: P. J. Malan.

England's margin of victory in a memorable Test sounded straightforward. But add into the mix the fact that there were only 50 balls remaining when the final South African wicket fell, and it was clear why this was hailed as the perfect advert for the five-day game. The match took place not only against the glorious backdrop of Table Mountain, but with a debate about the length of Tests rumbling on behind the scenes. An ICC proposal that they should become four-day contests prompted passionate debate. It transpired that those present – and there were lots of them, as the stands were sold out for three days, and busy on the last two – witnessed the best possible argument against the idea. That view was also volunteered after the game by both Root and Stokes.

The Test ebbed and flowed deliciously in sublime sunshine. South Africa seemed to be in charge after the first day. By the end of the third, England were in the ascendancy. Then South Africa rallied obstinately in the fourth innings, to the extent that they still had five wickets intact at tea on the final day. With 13 overs left, England needed three for victory, whereupon Root summoned his *deus ex machina*. As the tail dug in, he tossed the ball to Stokes, who had yet to take a wicket in the match. Not that he had been idle: in South Africa's first innings, he had held five catches, a Test record by an England outfielder; in England's second, he had blasted 72 from 47 balls, allowing Root to declare earlier than anticipated, and creating extra time to bowl the opposition out.

In that final session, Stokes moved in like a predator circling his prey. It was not obvious exactly how he was going to remove the last three South Africans on a pitch that seemed ever more benign. But it was obvious he was going to do it through sheer force of will, like Ian Botham in his pomp. He needed some help from his team-mates, and received it

Taking strides: Dom Sibley reverse-sweeps after reaching a maiden Test hundred.

in the form of flawless slip catching. The last three fell in 26 balls, and soon Stokes was being crowned man of an exceptional match – once again.

Upon receiving the award, he was quick to praise his colleagues after a magnificent team performance. Anderson had taken seven for 63 from 37 overs, a critical contribution, despite being unable to bowl at the end because of a rib injury that would finish his winter. Sibley rejoiced in his maiden Test century, batting in the second innings for 497 minutes and 311 balls to make an unbeaten 133 – a potential watershed for him, and just the sort of innings he had been enlisted to play. Moreover, victory – the first at Newlands since readmission by a touring team other than Australia, and the first there by England since 1956-57 – was achieved by a team containing four players under 23, another England first.

This emphasis on youth came more by accident than design. Indeed, as the players were preparing for the Test, it seemed England's nightmare start to the tour was about to continue. Having just shaken off the flu epidemic, the squad were now afflicted by more conventional setbacks. One of them, though, occurred in a controversial manner. On the eve of the match, Rory Burns was injured playing football at the start of practice. This is an activity the players love, as it promotes cheerful arguments and endless rivalry on a long tour. Burns tore ligaments in his left ankle, and was soon ruled out of the tour of Sri Lanka in March, let alone the rest of this one. Football was promptly banned by the management.

Jofra Archer was also unfit, because of an elbow problem. So England brought in three youngsters to join the 21-year-old Curran: Crawley for Burns, Bess for Archer, and Pope, back after the flu, for Jonny Bairstow. South Africa made one enforced change, with the 30-year-old opener Pieter Malan making his debut in place of Aiden Markram, who had broken a finger in the field at Centurion.

Root unhesitatingly chose to bat, but endured the frustration of seeing five of his top seven – including himself – getting starts, then getting out, with scores ranging from 29 to 47. The only exceptions were Crawley, dismissed for four, and Pope, unbeaten on 61 when

MOST FIVE-FORS IN TESTS

		T	Wkts			T	Wkts
67	M. Muralitharan (Sri Lanka/Wld) .	133	800	27	R. Ashwin (India)	70	362
37	S. K. Warne (Australia)	145	708	27	I. T. Botham (England) . . .	102	383
36	R. J. Hadlee (New Zealand)	86	431	26	D. W. Steyn (South Africa)	93	439
35	A. Kumble (India)	132	619	25	Wasim Akram (Pakistan) . .	104	414
34	H. M. R. K. B. Herath (Sri Lanka)	93	433	25	Harbhajan Singh (India) . . .	103	417
29	G. D. McGrath (Australia)	124	563	24	S. F. Barnes (England)	27	189
28	**J. M. Anderson (England)**	**151**	**584**				

England were bowled out for 269 on the second morning. In the circumstances, his last-wicket partnership of 35 with Anderson was significant.

Even so, it seemed as if England had squandered an opportunity to dominate the game. But perhaps the surface was not so benign as it first appeared. And, on the second day, they produced some excellent cricket, their senior citizens to the fore. Broad made the early incisions, before Elgar, the most fluent of the South African batsmen, and van der Dussen countered with a resolute stand of 117 in almost 49 overs – though van der Dussen was spared on 16, when he was caught behind off a Broad snorter, only for replays to reveal a clear no-ball.

Then Anderson intervened, with critical help from the youngsters. Curran, innocuous in his first spell, snatched the vital wickets of de Kock and van der Dussen, after Bess, who bowled 27 overs for only 62 runs, dismissed Elgar, who was trying to loft him back over his head. He had not played since September, yet Bess bowled with maturity and control throughout the match, if for slim rewards. By disposing of the tail, Anderson completed his 28th Test five-for, passing Botham's England record (though from 49 more matches).

England led by 46, and now Sibley dug in with increasing assurance, adding a careful 73 with Denly; Root was more inventive in a partnership of 116. On the fourth morning, Stokes signalled his intentions with a straight six off Pretorius, then an audacious reverse slap for four next ball. He scored 45 of the first 50 in a stand ultimately worth 92, and his aggression allowed Sibley to move sedately towards three figures.

Buttler hit two sixes in his 23 before falling to his one-day ramp, and Root was able to declare with a lead of 437, and 146 overs remaining. It soon became evident his team would need most of those to bowl South Africa out again, and Malan batted for more than six hours, with great determination and a solid, uncomplicated technique, for 84. For a while, Elgar was on song too, until he became Denly's first Test victim, given out caught behind after reviewing unsuccessfully, and departing still unconvinced he had touched the ball. Anderson removed Hamza in the day's penultimate over, after Stokes had softened him up with a short-ball barrage, and England required eight wickets on the last.

Anderson quickly despatched nightwatchman Maharaj, while Bess and Denly were gifted wickets by poorly executed attacking shots from du Plessis and de Kock. In between, Curran removed Malan. But the obdurate van der Dussen took some shifting. Increasingly, all the fielders were hovering around the bat and, when Broad was bowling, someone decided to move Anderson from silly mid-on to leg slip. Broad's next delivery was wide of leg stump – wider than intended, he later explained – and van der Dussen, having blocked his way to 17 from 139 balls, helped it straight into Anderson's hands.

Tensions remained high. The usually placid Buttler was caught on the stump mike giving Philander a piece of his mind, believing he had obscured his view of a return throw; he was later fined 15% of his match fee. But the door was now open for Stokes's recall. In he steamed from the Wynberg End. An edge from Pretorius was neatly held low down by Root at first slip; the next delivery, to Nortje, found a thicker edge, and the chance flew into the cordon, where Crawley contrived a spectacular catch. He parried the ball with an outstretched right hand, before falling backwards to the ground, from where he calmly collected it with his left. By now, Stokes was an irresistible force. He found steep lift from

Calm and collected: Zak Crawley holds the catch that dismisses Anrich Nortje, and England are one wicket from victory.

a crack just outside of off stump that seemed to have disappeared for a day or two, and Philander edged high into the gully. The series was level.

"He's a golden nugget, isn't he?" said Root. No one privileged to be at Newlands over the five days was inclined to disagree.

Player of the Match: B. A. Stokes.

Close of play: first day, England 262-9 (Pope 56, Anderson 3); second day, South Africa 215-8 (Philander 13); third day, England 218-4 (Sibley 85); fourth day, South Africa 126-2 (Malan 63, Maharaj 2).

England

Z. Crawley c de Kock b Philander	4	– c de Kock b Rabada	25
D. P. Sibley c de Kock b Rabada	34	– not out	133
J. L. Denly b Maharaj	38	– c Pretorius b Nortje	31
*J. E. Root c de Kock b Nortje	35	– c du Plessis b Pretorius	61
B. A. Stokes c Elgar b Nortje	47	– (6) c van der Dussen b Maharaj	72
O. J. D. Pope not out	61	– (7) b Rabada	3
†J. C. Buttler c de Kock b Pretorius	29	– (8) c de Kock b Nortje	23
S. M. Curran b Pretorius	9	– (9) c Hamza b Maharaj	13
D. M. Bess c de Kock b Philander	0	– (5) c de Kock b Nortje	0
S. C. J. Broad b Rabada	1	– not out	8
J. M. Anderson c van der Dussen b Rabada	4		
B 4, lb 1, w 1, nb 1	7	B 18, lb 3, w 1	22

1/8 (1) 2/63 (2) 3/105 (4)	(91.5 overs)	269
4/127 (3) 5/185 (5) 6/221 (7)		
7/231 (8) 8/231 (9) 9/234 (10) 10/269 (11)		

1/28 (1)	(8 wkts dec, 111 overs)	391
2/101 (3) 3/217 (4)		
4/218 (5) 5/310 (6)		
6/315 (7) 7/356 (8) 8/375 (9)		

Philander 16–3–46–2; Rabada 19.5–5–68–3; Nortje 18–2–56–2; Maharaj 27–6–68–1; Pretorius 11–5–26–2. *Second innings*—Rabada 20–3–69–2; Philander 14–7–24–0; Nortje 18–2–61–3; Pretorius 16–4–56–1; Maharaj 43–9–160–2.

South Africa

D. Elgar c Root b Bess	88	– (2) c Buttler b Denly	34
P. J. Malan c Root b Broad	5	– (1) c Stokes b Curran	84
M. Z. Hamza c Stokes b Broad	5	– c Buttler b Anderson	18
*F. du Plessis c Stokes b Anderson	1	– (5) c Denly b Bess	19
H. E. van der Dussen c Stokes b Curran	68	– (6) c Anderson b Broad	17
†Q. de Kock c Anderson b Curran	20	– (7) c Crawley b Denly	50
V. D. Philander not out	17	– (8) c Pope b Stokes	8
D. Pretorius c Stokes b Anderson	4	– (9) c Root b Stokes	0
K. A. Maharaj c Sibley b Anderson	4	– (4) lbw b Anderson	2
K. Rabada c Buttler b Anderson	4	– (11) not out	3
A. A. Nortje c Stokes b Anderson	4	– (10) c Crawley b Stokes	0
B 4, lb 2, nb 1	7	B 4, lb 2, w 2, nb 5	13

1/26 (2) 2/38 (3) 3/40 (4)   (89 overs) 223   1/71 (2) 2/123 (3)   (137.4 overs) 248
4/157 (1) 5/191 (6) 6/200 (5)   3/129 (4) 4/164 (5)
7/207 (8) 8/215 (9) 9/215 (10) 10/223 (11)   5/171 (4) 6/237 (7) 7/237 (6)
                                                    8/241 (9) 9/241 (10) 10/248 (8)

Anderson 19–6–40–5; Broad 18–6–38–2; Curran 13–3–39–2; Bess 27–3–62–1; Stokes 9–0–34–0; Root 3–1–4–0. *Second innings*—Anderson 18–9–23–2; Broad 23–8–37–1; Bess 33–14–57–1; Curran 16–4–37–1; Denly 18–4–42–2; Root 6–0–11–0; Stokes 23.4–8–35–3.

Umpires: H. D. P. K. Dharmasena and P. R. Reiffel.   Third umpire: C. B. Gaffaney.
Referee: A. J. Pycroft.

SOUTH AFRICA v ENGLAND

Third Test

DANIEL GALLAN

At Port Elizabeth, January 16–20, 2020. England won by an innings and 53 runs. England 30pts. Toss: England. Test debut: D. Paterson.

A lot needs to go wrong for a team to lose by an innings at home. A lot did: barring one session on the first day, South Africa were a distant third in a two-horse race. At Cape Town, their final-day rearguard was hailed by some as a morale boost, despite the margin of defeat. England had won the battle, but South Africa's resilience had the potential – went the argument – to trigger a recovery. Newlands would be du Plessis's Thermopylae, a gutsy last stand to inspire future triumphs. Instead, it proved a precursor of more heartache.

It didn't help that he lost his sixth toss in a row. Root gleefully chose to bat: even by the standards of St George's Park, the pitch was flat. But playing both Philander and debutant Dane Paterson – who replaced Dwaine Pretorius – was a mistake, since both offered much the same: discipline, a wobbly seam, not much pace. Rumours of reverse swing had been circling, and Paterson was touted as the man to exploit it. Bowling coach Charl Langeveldt, meanwhile, later admitted South Africa's decision-makers knew conditions would not be conducive to Philander's skills. If he failed to strike with the new ball, he would be reduced to a slow-moving fielder. Sentiment, rather than logic, governed his involvement.

Space invader: Kagiso Rabada's celebration of Joe Root's wicket triggered a one-Test ban.

Philander began with a tight over, conceding a single, at which point everyone in the ground, including England's openers, collected their breath in anticipation of Rabada's fury. It never came. Astonishingly, the second over went to Paterson. Where was the promised hostility? Had the fight from Cape Town dissipated? Had it been mere talk?

Crawley and Sibley had played six Tests between them. They had graduated through the county system, facing Dukes balls delivered by bowlers as quick as Paterson and Philander, but on tougher pitches. What they hadn't faced much was 90mph rockets around their nostrils, with a man at short leg, and a murder of slips hovering like carrion fowl. Six overs into a Test in South Africa, de Kock was standing up to the stumps. Crawley and Sibley must have felt like men given a last-minute reprieve on their way to the gallows. They remained unscathed until lunch, with 61 on the board – the first time England had not lost a wicket in the opening session of a Test since Alastair Cook and Andrew Strauss against India at The Oval in 2011.

South Africa straightened their lines after the break, and had both openers caught at backward square leg. Four overs after tea, a becalmed Denly – whose 25 had taken two hours – was trapped by Maharaj, playing back to a skidding delivery. When Rabada knocked back Root's off stump three overs later, England were in a spot of bother at 148 for four, and had taken nearly 65 overs to get there.

South Africa's progress, however, came at a price. Anger has always fuelled fast bowlers: like apex predators, they charge in with gnashing teeth, growling their intent. But no sooner had the bails hit the turf than Rabada galloped towards Root. He stopped within touching distance, crouched low, and let out an earth-quaking roar. Root held his tongue as he trudged off, later claiming his side "go about things the right way". Rabada had crossed a line. Match referee Andy Pycroft agreed, and handed him a demerit point – his fourth in two years, which meant a one-Test suspension. Pope and Stokes, meanwhile, steered England to the close on an old-fashioned 224 for four.

Stokes began the second day full of intent, twice crunching Rabada through midwicket to bring up his fifty. Pope followed him soon after, with a scythe past gully off Philander.

ENGLAND'S ROAD TO 500

STEVEN LYNCH

Port Elizabeth witnessed England's 500th overseas Test match, nearly 143 years after the first, at Melbourne. No other country has played as many (Australia were next with 404, then West Indies on 295). The first 100 took 52 years, but things have speeded up: the last 100 took just over 16. In all, England have won exactly 30% of their away Tests – but lost over 36%.

Tests 1–100 (1876-77 to 1928-29) **W 47** **L 47** **D 6**

England gave as good as they got in their first overseas century, thanks to a 19–10 lead in 33 matches in South Africa, which made up for trailing 38–27 in 67 in Australia. Jack Hobbs scored 3,475 runs in this period, more than twice as many as any other Englishman (Wilfred Rhodes was next, with 1,547). S. F. Barnes took 126 wickets in 17 matches, and George Lohmann 76 from nine.

101–200 (1929-30 to 1961-62) **W 29** **L 29** **D 42**

England's second 100 away matches again finished all square. Despite Don Bradman, they closed the gap on Australia to 16–10 (from 30 matches), but also trailed West Indies 7–5 (22 matches) and were level with India (3–3 from 13). They led New Zealand 5–0 (with eight draws), and Pakistan 1–0, with one draw (their 200th match, in Dacca). Len Hutton scored 3,041 runs, 22 more than Wally Hammond. Brian Statham led the bowlers with 91 wickets, five ahead of Bill Voce.

201–300 (1961-62 to 1982-83) **W 25** **L 21** **D 54**

The third 100 featured more draws than results, with ten draws out of ten in Pakistan – and was the only set in which they won more than they lost. Ashes victories in 1970-71 and 1978-79 meant England were their closest to Australia, trailing 13–10 (with 12 draws). They led everyone else except West Indies (3–2 down, with nine draws). Geoff Boycott amassed 3,758 runs – he played 51 of the matches – while Derek Underwood took 152 wickets, Bob Willis 130 and Ian Botham 117.

301–400 (1982-83 to 2003-04) **W 21** **L 41** **D 38**

This chunk, which started with a pulsating three-run win at Melbourne, and finished with a win at Dhaka in 2003-04, was England's worst in terms of results. It included dominant times for Australia (who led 14–6, with eight draws) and West Indies (13–3, plus four draws). Alec Stewart collected 3,813 runs from 59 of the matches, and Mike Atherton 3,012; Andy Caddick took 106 wickets, and Darren Gough 105.

401–500 (2003-04 to 2019-20) **W 28** **L 44** **D 28**

England redressed the balance a little, although Australia were untouchable, leading 15–3 at home (only two draws). Pakistan (7–0, two draws) and India (7–3, four) also had big leads. Jimmy Anderson took 216 wickets in 67 overseas Tests; Stuart Broad had 178 and Graeme Swann 135. Alastair Cook dwarfed everyone else with 5,904 runs (Kevin Pietersen was next with 3,644). Port Elizabeth was their 150th away win.

THE BREAKDOWN

	First	P	W	L	D	%W	%L	%D
v Australia	1876-77	180	57	95	28	31.66	52.77	15.55
v South Africa.................	1888-89	84	33	20	31	39.28	23.80	36.90
v New Zealand	1929-30	51	18	6	27	35.29	11.76	52.94
v West Indies	1929-30	71	15	27	29	21.12	38.02	40.84
v India	1933-34	60	13	19	28	21.66	31.66	46.66
v Pakistan....................	1961-62	30	2	9	19	6.66	30.00	63.33
v Sri Lanka	1981-82	16	7	5	4	43.75	31.25	25.00
v Zimbabwe	1996-97	2	0	0	2	0.00	0.00	100.00
v Bangladesh.................	2003-04	6	5	1	0	83.33	16.66	0.00
		500	**150**	**182**	**168**	**30.00**	**36.40**	**33.60**

YOUNGEST ENGLAND TEST CENTURY-MAKERS

Yrs	Days			
20	19	D. C. S. Compton (102).	v Australia at Nottingham	1938
20	324	J. W. Hearne (114)	v Australia at Melbourne	1911-12
21	31	L. Hutton (100)	v New Zealand at Manchester	1937
21	69	A. N. Cook† (104*).	v India at Nagpur	2005-06
21	118	D. I. Gower (111)	v New Zealand at The Oval	1978
21	209	P. B. H. May† (138)	v South Africa at Leeds	1951
22	7	M. C. Cowdrey (102)	v Australia at Melbourne	1954-55
22	**15**	**O. J. D. Pope (135*). . . . .**	**v South Africa at Port Elizabeth. . . .**	**2019-20**
22	81	M. A. Atherton (151).	v New Zealand at Nottingham	1990
22	91	J. Briggs (121).	v Australia at Melbourne	1884-85
22	93	I. T. Botham (103).	v New Zealand at Christchurch	1977-78
22	145	J. E. Root (104)	v New Zealand at Leeds.	2013
22	196	B. A. Stokes (120).	v Australia at Perth.	2013-14

† *On debut. Only the first instance is shown for each batsman.*

When Stokes clattered Maharaj for six over cow corner, the pair had set a record fifth-wicket partnership at Port Elizabeth, beating the unbeaten 126 of Jacques Kallis and Jonty Rhodes against England in 1999-2000. But they were just getting started. Pope threaded the field, and Stokes hit boundaries – particularly off Maharaj – both at will. By lunch, England had scored 111 in the session, and Stokes his ninth Test century, as well as 4,000 runs. Pope's maiden ton looked a formality.

The interval broke Stokes's rhythm, and he struggled for fluency against defensive fields and a sixth-stump line. The plan worked, up to a point: when he flashed to Elgar at backward point, Paterson had his first Test wicket. Trouble was, the stand had been worth 203, England's highest for the fifth wicket in South Africa, beating 154 by Percy Fender and Phil Mead at Durban in 1922-23, and the best for any wicket at Port Elizabeth.

One brought two, Buttler's torrid tour continuing as he popped a gentle return catch to Maharaj. Then the fun began. Curran hit 44 off 50 balls, and Wood – who had replaced the injured James Anderson, England's only change from Cape Town – bludgeoned 42 off 23, with five sixes. Amid the carnage, Pope raised his bat as a centurion for the first time in a Test, before opening up too. Two reverse paddles off Rabada showed off his all-round game; a classic technique, coupled with a contemporary 360-degree approach, suggested a bright future. Wood had been caught on 25 off Rabada, prompting Root to declare on 467 – only for replays to reveal a no-ball and Root to recant. When Wood was finally out, Root declared again, on 499 for nine, with Pope unbeaten on 135. Maharaj finished with five for 180, the most expensive five-for in South Africa's history.

YOUNGEST ENGLAND SPINNERS TO TAKE A TEST FIVE-FOR

Yrs	Days			
21	32	J. N. Crawford (5-79)	v Australia at Melbourne	1907-08
21	260	P. I. Pocock (6-79)	v Australia at Manchester	1968
22	68	D. L. Underwood (5-52).	v Pakistan at Nottingham	1967
22	**180**	**D. M. Bess (5-51). . . . .**	**v South Africa at Port Elizabeth . . . .**	**2019-20**
22	212	I. A. R. Peebles (5-204).	v Australia at The Oval.	1930
22	256	W. E. Hollies (7-50)	v West Indies at Georgetown	1934-35
22	325	J. W. Hearne (5-49).	v South Africa at Johannesburg	1913-14
23	164	M. J. Hilton (5-61)	v India at Kanpur	1951-52
23	290	J. Briggs (5-29).	v Australia at Lord's.	1886
24	41	M. S. Panesar (5-78)	v Sri Lanka at Nottingham	2006
24	44	G. A. R. Lock (5-45).	v Australia at The Oval.	1953

Crawford is usually described as a medium-paced off-spinner.
Only the first instance is shown for each bowler.

Strange things happen to batsmen when they're staring at a mountain, and better teams than South Africa have crumbled while craning their necks. Elgar and Malan did reach 50 without fuss, but that was as good as it got. In dying light on the second day, Bess held on to a simple return from Malan, and had Hamza caught at short leg. A late call-up to the squad, Bess looked like he belonged, even if he was helped by South African stage fright.

Du Plessis made it clear that the way to combat spin, and exorcise the demons that had haunted his side since their tour of India in 2015-16, was to be aggressive. Bess would be treated with the respect a rookie deserved. Yet, apart from nightwatchman Nortje, who faced 136 balls – second only in the innings to de Kock's 139 – Bess dismissed all of South Africa's regular top five. He was the first English spinner to take the first five wickets in a Test since Derek Underwood, who took the first seven at Adelaide in 1974-75. Du Plessis's recklessness stood out: after bunting consecutive deliveries off Bess for four, he charged at him again, and provided Pope with a sharp catch at short leg.

De Kock and Philander gave South Africa breathing space, adding 54 for the seventh wicket by the close of a third day limited by the weather to 64 overs. But hubris plagued them next morning, as the last four wickets fell for one run – Broad took three – amid a succession of rash shots. All out for 209, a deficit of 290, they were asked to follow on. The carnage continued, and this time it was Wood's searing pace that caused grief. He upended

Speed Test: Dean Elgar is done for pace by Mark Wood.

Elgar's off stump with a blistering full ball, and ruffled Hamza with the short stuff, forcing a tickle down leg. Then, as if to underline the South Africans' ineptitude against the turning ball, Root brought himself on, and bagged four wickets before stumps, having never previously taken more than two in a Test innings. South Africa closed at 102 for six, down and all but out.

It took three balls on the final morning for Broad to remove Philander, caught at short mid-on by Pope, who became only the sixth to take six outfield catches and score a hundred in the same Test. Rabada and Nortje followed quickly and, with the die cast, Maharaj heaved at anything near him, and hammered three sixes and ten fours, including 24 in a Root over costing 28, equalling the Test record. Paterson also threw his hands around, and collected 39 in a last-wicket stand of 99. The pantomime ended when Maharaj was run out by Curran at mid-on: England had retained the Basil D'Oliveira Trophy.

South Africa had suffered their first innings defeat at home since England won at Durban more than a decade earlier, and – following the disastrous tour of India – their third, home and away, in five Tests. It was also their 27th consecutive Test without a draw, a world record (Zimbabwe had 26 between 2005 and 2017), and a 14th defeat. For a team once renowned for their stubborn resistance, it was a damning statistic.

Du Plessis wore a tired expression. He had endured a horrendous 2019, and his 2020 was off to a difficult start: two crushing defeats, senior players losing their heads, and a legacy being tarnished. He was committed to the cause, but one wondered how much fight he had left.

Player of the Match: O. J. D. Pope.

Close of play: first day, England 224-4 (Stokes 38, Pope 39); second day, South Africa 60-2 (Elgar 42, Nortje 0); third day, South Africa 208-6 (de Kock 63, Philander 27); fourth day, South Africa 102-6 (Philander 13, Maharaj 5).

England

Z. Crawley c van der Dussen b Nortje	44	D. M. Bess c Malan b Maharaj 1
D. P. Sibley c Elgar b Rabada	36	M. A. Wood c Nortje b Maharaj 42
J. L. Denly lbw b Maharaj	25	B 2, lb 14, w 4, nb 4 24
*J. E. Root b Rabada	27	
B. A. Stokes c Elgar b Paterson	120	1/70 (2) (9 wkts dec, 152 overs) 499
O. J. D. Pope not out	135	2/103 (1) 3/134 (3)
†J. C. Buttler c and b Maharaj	1	4/148 (4) 5/351 (5) 6/354 (7)
S. M. Curran c Elgar b Maharaj	44	7/413 (6) 8/426 (9) 9/499 (10)

S. C. J. Broad did not bat.

Philander 16–5–41–0; Paterson 24–3–62–1; Rabada 28–6–97–2; Nortje 25–4–97–1; Maharaj 58–15–180–5; Elgar 1–0–6–0.

South Africa

D. Elgar c Pope b Bess	35	– (2) b Wood	15
P. J. Malan c and b Bess	18	– (1) lbw b Root	12
M. Z. Hamza c Pope b Bess	10	– c Buttler b Wood	2
A. A. Nortje c Root b Stokes	18	– (10) b Bess	5
*F. du Plessis c Pope b Bess	8	– (4) c Pope b Root	36
H. E. van der Dussen b Bess	24	– (5) c Pope b Root	10
†Q. de Kock b Curran	63	– (6) c Wood b Root	3
V. D. Philander b Broad	27	– (7) c Pope b Broad	13
K. A. Maharaj b Broad	0	– (8) run out (Curran)	71
K. Rabada c Wood b Broad	1	– (9) c Broad b Wood	16
D. Paterson not out	0	– not out	39
B 4, w 1	5	B 12, lb 1, w 1, nb 1	15

1/50 (2) 2/60 (3) 3/63 (1)	(86.4 overs)	209	1/18 (2) 2/22 (3)	(88.5 overs) 237
4/71 (5) 5/109 (6) 6/154 (4)			3/44 (1) 4/66 (5)	
7/208 (8) 8/208 (7) 9/208 (9) 10/209 (10)			5/74 (6) 6/83 (4) 7/102 (7)	
			8/128 (9) 9/138 (10) 10/237 (8)	

Broad 13.4–6–30–3; Curran 11–2–32–1; Bess 31–12–51–5; Wood 11–4–31–0; Denly 4–1–10–0; Root 11–4–25–0; Stokes 5–1–26–1. *Second innings*—Broad 10–5–14–1; Curran 6–0–46–0; Wood 16.5–6–32–3; Bess 22–11–36–1; Stokes 5–2–9–0; Root 29–13–87–4.

Umpires: B. N. J. Oxenford and R. J. Tucker.   Third umpire: J. S. Wilson.
Referee: A. J. Pycroft.

SOUTH AFRICA v ENGLAND

Fourth Test

NICK HOULT

At Johannesburg, January 24–27, 2020. England won by 191 runs. England 30pts, South Africa –6pts. Toss: England. Test debut: B. E. Hendricks.

Root cited his team's three guiding principles – courage, unity and respect – as he reflected on a crushing victory in the final Test. "We have shown those in abundance throughout this trip," he said, "and it has made a massive difference to our performances." According to Root, courage had come in recovering from 1–0 down, and coping with the loss of injured players, which continued when Jofra Archer broke down in the warm-up having looked fit the day before. Unity referred to the consistent application of the new Test strategy, in particular the patience shown by Sibley and Crawley during a century

Strike force: Mark Wood leads England from the field after taking five for 46.

opening stand. Respect? That was trickier, since two players were fined for shouting obscenities: Stokes at a supporter, Broad at du Plessis.

Yet Root's pride was well placed – and England were ruthless. Pope oozed class as their first innings was wavering, and a knockabout tenth-wicket stand between Wood and Broad took the last gasps of wind from South African sails. England's seamers bowled as a unit, earning each other wickets, and wearing down their opponents. Playing back-to-back Tests for the first time since July 2017 (also against South Africa), Wood finished with nine for 100, the best overseas figures by an England seamer since Ryan Sidebottom's ten for 139 against New Zealand at Hamilton in March 2008. He had opened up the South African first innings by removing Malan, and later shattered a bail bowling de Kock.

It all prompted Stokes to suggest England had found a template for winning back the Ashes, though presumably the master plan did not include getting sucked in to a ruckus with a fan. Moments after his tame dismissal on the first day, he had been striding towards the players' tunnel that connects the pitch and the dressing-rooms, when – according to eyewitnesses – a South Africa supporter mocked his ginger hair, comparing him to the singer Ed Sheeran. Stokes offered to see him round the back of the stands – not for a selfie – and swore. He later apologised, while team director Ashley Giles called for extra security, even as he admitted Stokes's reaction had been unacceptable. Match referee Andy Pycroft fined him 15% of his fee, and gave him a demerit point. Stokes reflected: "A grown man comes 50 yards to say something. Let's just say we were both immature."

Philander, meanwhile, exited Test cricket a forlorn figure, diminished by his side's defeat, a hamstring strain that restricted him to nine balls in the second innings, and a fine for giving Buttler a send-off. A message on the giant screen – "Thanks Vern" – was in danger of seeming sarcastic.

After complaining of a slight groin strain, Wood had been given the all-clear only on the day of the match, once he and Archer had undergone pitchside fitness tests. But while Wood looked ready, Archer – supposedly recovered from an elbow problem – was soon slumped on the ground, in tears. As team-mates consoled him, the management had no option but to leave him out. With Woakes picked for his first game of the series, in place of Dom Bess, and South Africa dropping slow left-armer Keshav Maharaj, it meant both teams had five seamers. But, with Kagiso Rabada suspended, South Africa looked toothless: other than the fading Philander, the recalled Pretorius was playing only his third Test, Paterson his second, and left-armer Beuran Hendricks his first. For all Nortje's efforts (and this was only his sixth), the hosts could not match England's firepower or skill.

In fact, South Africa – who also drafted in Bavuma to the middle order, having dropped the struggling Zubayr Hamza – were beaten in all departments. Set 466, they were bowled out an hour after tea on a fractious fourth day, when England harried them, not only with the ball, but aggressive posturing. "This batting line-up needs guidance," said du Plessis. "Bowling, we competed. But it's tough to ask guys making their debut to compete against guys with 500 wickets."

Rain had delayed the toss until 1pm and, after Root called correctly for the fourth time in the series, England batted again. Crawley was the more impressive of the openers: standing tall, he drove on top of the bounce, and left on length, as if he had been playing at the Wanderers for years; he ticked off his highest Test score for the fifth successive innings. Sibley was less fluent, though his growing confidence was reflected by a more expansive off-side game. At the interval, England were 100 without loss, the first time their openers had shared a century stand since Alastair Cook and Keaton Jennings at Chennai in December 2016. That was 70 innings ago – their longest such streak.

WINNING A FOUR-TEST SERIES 3–1 FROM 0–1 DOWN

West Indies beat England in England	1950
South Africa beat Australia in South Africa	2017-18
England beat South Africa in South Africa	**2019-20**

South Africa had been poor, but came out fighting after tea. Du Plessis set more exacting fields, and his bowlers kept the slips interested. Sibley was caught down the leg side – a maiden Test scalp for Hendricks – before Crawley fenced at Philander. Denly was dropped twice, then edged behind, and Stokes drove hard to slip, before wandering off for his altercation. At 157 for four, Root and Pope faced South African bowlers with their tails up, for what turned out to be the game's most competitive spell. Pope limboed out of the way of a Nortje bouncer, but otherwise looked assured, helping England to 192 without further damage before bad light intervened.

Next morning, the pitch had quickened, and the pair extended their stand to 101 in 24 overs, as South Africa fed their cuts and pulls. Again, the hosts regrouped: Pope fell first ball after drinks to Nortje, who then removed Root – failing to convert another fifty – and Curran with successive deliveries. When he later dismissed Woakes, he sheepishly held up the ball to acknowledge his first Test five-for. England, having lost five for 60, were 318 for nine. But Nortje needed a break, and the last pair cashed in. Wood and Broad walloped seven sixes, eventually adding 82 in 50 balls as South Africa lost control. A total of 400 was about 100 more than England's estimate of par.

Emboldened by his batting, Wood then pierced a stubborn opening stand, sending down short balls to Malan in excess of 90mph, before pitching up the next, and finding his edge. At 94.4mph, it was the second-fastest wicket-taking ball recorded for England, after one of Steve Harmison's at Perth in 2006-07, which was somewhat wasted on Glenn McGrath. Curran removed van der Dussen, promoted to No. 3, for a duck; Stokes took care of Elgar, and Woakes won a marginal lbw against du Plessis. When Wood did for Bavuma and nightwatchman Nortje, South Africa staggered to the close at 88 for six. The game was all but over. De Kock and Pretorius rallied next day, but Wood finished with five for 46, and – despite a lead of 217 – Root chose not to enforce the follow-on, preferring to give his fast bowlers a break before the final push.

Heating up: Faf du Plessis, the embattled South African captain, exchanges words with Stuart Broad. Jos Buttler listens in.

The third innings was about subplots. After another decent opening stand, 56 this time, Denly – with one half-century all series – had the ideal platform for a big score. Instead, he scratched around for eight, before edging Paterson on to his stumps. Also in need of runs was Buttler, but he too managed only eight; he trudged off knowing his Test career was on the line, Philander's send-off ringing in his ears. Another half-century from Root, and a cameo 35 off 29 from Curran, took England to 248 at stumps on the third day, compiled at four an over; Hendricks's five-wicket haul on debut owed much to cavalier batting.

For a while, England were made to sweat, as van der Dussen and du Plessis took South Africa to 181 for two on a sweltering fourth afternoon. The tourists metaphorically lost their cool too, getting stuck in to du Plessis for picking up the ball after a forward defensive: they suspected he was attempting to make it sweaty, and scupper their hopes of reverse swing. Curran soon hurled it in the batsman's direction, while Broad used language that would cost him 15% of his match fee; riled, du Plessis appeared to bump into Buttler with his shoulder. The next delivery he faced, from Stokes – in the middle of one of those spells where he demanded the ball – cannoned off the bottom edge on to the stumps. England later claimed they had broken his concentration; du Plessis pointed out it had kept low. Both were true. Either way, England had their breakthrough.

Having avoided a pair when he overturned an lbw shout from Woakes, van der Dussen had batted courageously against high pace on an up-and-down pitch. A maiden Test hundred was in sight when – seven balls after the demise of du Plessis, and two overs before tea – he was suckered by Wood. With men in catching positions on the leg side, and van der Dussen on 98, he stayed back, expecting the bouncer. Wood pitched it up, and an off-balance van der Dussen drove to Broad at short extra cover.

Bavuma flayed six fours, before gloving a vicious short one from Broad, who quickly bounced out Pretorius. Philander was caught down the leg side off Wood, a limp end to his international career. De Kock characteristically counterpunched, but fell driving wildly, before Hendricks was run out, and Nortje strangled down leg. A review confirmed

England's triumph. South Africa were docked six World Championship points for a slow over-rate. But the pain of their defeat, the first time since 1913-14 they had lost three Tests in a home series to a side other than Australia, would take longer to subside.

Player of the Match: M. A. Wood.   *Player of the Series:* B. A. Stokes.

Close of play: first day, England 192-4 (Root 25, Pope 22); second day, South Africa 88-6 (de Kock 32); third day, England 248.

England

Z. Crawley c van der Dussen b Philander	66	– c de Kock b Pretorius	24
D. P. Sibley c de Kock b Hendricks	44	– c Malan b Hendricks	44
J. L. Denly c van der Dussen b Paterson	27	– b Paterson	8
*J. E. Root c de Kock b Nortje	59	– c du Plessis b Hendricks	58
B. A. Stokes c van der Dussen b Nortje	2	– c van der Dussen b Hendricks	28
O. J. D. Pope b Nortje	56	– c de Kock b Nortje	11
†J. C. Buttler c Elgar b Philander	20	– c de Kock b Nortje	8
S. M. Curran c de Kock b Nortje	0	– c Paterson b Hendricks	35
C. R. Woakes c du Plessis b Nortje	32	– c de Kock b Hendricks	0
M. A. Wood not out	35	– b Pretorius	18
S. C. J. Broad c Malan b Paterson	43	– not out	1
Lb 9, w 4, nb 3	16	B 4, lb 8, w 1	13
	400		**248**

1/107 (2) 2/116 (1) 3/150 (3) (98.2 overs) 400   1/56 (1) 2/75 (3) (61.3 overs) 248
4/157 (5) 5/258 (6) 6/269 (4)   3/92 (2) 4/136 (5)
7/269 (8) 8/309 (7) 9/318 (9) 10/400 (11)   5/150 (6) 6/160 (7) 7/206 (8)
8/206 (9) 9/240 (10) 10/248 (4)

Philander 20–2–50–2; Hendricks 23–3–111–1; Nortje 24–1–110–5; Paterson 20.2–3–86–2; Pretorius 11–3–34–0. *Second innings*—Philander 1.3–1–1–0; Nortje 11–1–61–2; Paterson 13.3–5–18–1; Hendricks 15.3–2–64–5; Pretorius 18–2–87–2; Malan 2–0–5–0.

South Africa

D. Elgar c Woakes b Stokes	26	– (2) c and b Stokes	24
P. J. Malan c Buttler b Wood	15	– (1) c Stokes b Woakes	22
H. E. van der Dussen c Stokes b Curran	0	– c Broad b Wood	98
*F. du Plessis lbw b Woakes	3	– b Stokes	35
†Q. de Kock b Wood	76	– c Woakes b Wood	39
T. Bavuma c Stokes b Wood	6	– c Buttler b Broad	27
A. A. Nortje c Denly b Wood	6	– (9) c Buttler b Wood	4
V. D. Philander c Broad b Woakes	4	– c Buttler b Wood	10
D. Pretorius c Crawley b Stokes	37	– (7) c Curran b Broad	2
B. E. Hendricks not out	5	– run out (Sibley/Buttler)	4
D. Paterson c Buttler b Wood	4	– not out	0
W 1	1	B 4, lb 2, w 3	9
	183		**274**

1/29 (2) 2/37 (3) 3/43 (1) (68.3 overs) 183   1/39 (1) 2/89 (2) (77.1 overs) 274
4/60 (4) 5/74 (6) 6/88 (7)   3/181 (4) 4/187 (3)
7/93 (8) 8/172 (9) 9/174 (5) 10/183 (11)   5/235 (6) 6/239 (7) 7/260 (8)
8/267 (5) 9/273 (10) 10/274 (9)

Broad 14–3–27–0; Curran 12–4–25–1; Woakes 17–7–38–2; Wood 14.3–2–46–5; Stokes 11–1–47–2. *Second innings*—Broad 10.1–1–26–2; Curran 11–2–38–0; Wood 16.1–3–54–4; Woakes 14–3–47–1; Stokes 16–4–47–2; Root 7–1–37–0; Denly 3–0–19–0.

Umpires: R. J. Tucker and J. S. Wilson.   Third umpire: B. N. J. Oxenford.
Referee: A. J. Pycroft.

At Paarl, January 31, 2020. **England XI won by 77 runs.** ‡**England XI 240** (44.1 overs) (J. J. Roy 104); **South African Invitation XI 163** (38.4 overs) (G. J. Snyman 65). *England lost two wickets i Stefan Tait's opening over, and in the fourth Eoin Morgan left for a duck to make it 16-3. Jason Ro made light of a tricky pitch to cruise to a 94-ball century, although he wasn't sure he had got there* *as the scoreboard had been hit by a power cut. Led by Jacques Snyman, the Invitation XI reached 91-1, but then lost nine for 72 as England's bowlers got to work: there were seven single-figure scores. Both sides chose from 13 players.*

At Paarl, February 1, 2020. **South African Invitation XI won by three wickets** (DLS). ‡**England XI 346-8** (50 overs) (J. M. Bairstow 100, J. E. Root 91, J. L. Denly 85; S. Tait 4-56); **South African Invitation XI 193-7** (30 overs) (K. W. Sekhukhune 54; M. W. Parkinson 3-9). *After Dawid Malan collected a duck, Jonny Bairstow and Joe Root put on 157 in 21 overs, then Joe Denly hit five sixes in a 63-ball 85. A total of 346 looked huge, and England were sailing to victory with the home side 103-3 after 20. But the England management wanted a more testing scenario for the battles ahead, and the target was reset to a further 85 off ten overs. Snyman, out for 29 earlier, came in again and belted 38 off 16, and the Invitation XI won with two balls to spare when Andile Mogakane carved Tom Curran for four (the final two deliveries were bowled anyway, and he managed another four off the last). The Invitation XI chose from 14 players, and England from 12.*

LIMITED-OVERS INTERNATIONAL REPORTS BY GIDEON BROOKS

SOUTH AFRICA v ENGLAND

First One-Day International

At Cape Town, February 4, 2020 (day/night). South Africa won by seven wickets. Toss: South Africa. One-day international debuts: L. L. Sipamla, J. T. Smuts; T. Banton, M. W. Parkinson.

England found their hosts no respecter of title or reputation in their first one-day international since the World Cup final nearly seven months earlier. And while they were missing six of their Lord's heroes, Morgan offered no excuses, admitting his side had been "outplayed in all three departments". De Kock, in his first game as South Africa's permanent one-day captain (he had previously led them in two ODIs and two T20s), enjoyed his day rather more, restricting England to an underpowered 258 for eight after putting them in, then hitting 107 to inspire what was, surprisingly, a record successful chase for the ground. His match-winning partnership of 173 with Bavuma, who in only his third ODI was eventually trapped for 98 by Jordan (playing his first since September 2016), was a second-wicket record against England for South Africa. Bowling first had looked a brave call from de Kock: only eight teams had won here batting second from 32 previous floodlit matches. But England's batsmen struggled for timing, especially when South Africa took pace off the ball. Roy and Bairstow combined for a scratchy partnership of 51, but England then lost six for 80 in 18.3 overs. Left-arm wrist-spinner Shamsi was the pick, with three for 38, including debutant Tom Banton for 18, and England were thankful for Denly's 87 from 103 balls. His stand of 91 with Woakes at least gave the bowlers something to defend. Woakes then removed Reeza Hendricks cheaply, but de Kock, with his 15th ODI hundred, and Bavuma had little trouble against lethargic bowling.

Player of the Match: Q. de Kock.

England

J. J. Roy c R. R. Hendricks b Smuts	32	T. K. Curran not out	15
J. M. Bairstow c Sipamla b Phehlukwayo	19	C. J. Jordan not out	1
J. E. Root run out (van der Dussen)	17		
E. J. G. Morgan c Bavuma b Shamsi	11	Lb 2, w 8, nb 1	11
J. L. Denly c R. R. Hendricks b B. E. Hendricks	87	1/51 (1) 2/53 (2) (8 wkts, 50 overs) 258
T. Banton lbw b Shamsi	18	3/83 (3) 4/83 (4)
S. M. Curran b Shamsi	7	5/108 (6) 6/131 (7)
C. R. Woakes c Miller b Sipamla	40	7/222 (8) 8/254 (5)

M. W. Parkinson did not bat.

B. E. Hendricks 8-0-46-1; Ngidi 7-0-42-0; Smuts 10-0-43-1; Phehlukwayo 8-0-47-1; Shamsi 10-0-38-3; Sipamla 7-0-40-1.

10 overs: 52-1

South Africa

*†Q. de Kock b Root	107
R. R. Hendricks c Bairstow b Woakes	6
T. Bavuma lbw b Jordan	98
H. E. van der Dussen not out	38
J. T. Smuts not out	7
Lb 2, w 1	3

1/25 (2) 2/198 (1)   (3 wkts, 47.4 overs) 259
3/234 (3)   10 overs: 41-1

D. A. Miller, A. L. Phehlukwayo, B. E. Hendricks, L. L. Sipamla, L. T. Ngidi and T. Shamsi did not bat.

Woakes 9–0–36–1; S. M. Curran 5–0–28–0; Root 7–0–35–1; T. K. Curran 7–0–38–0; Parkinson 8.4–0–48–0; Jordan 5–0–31–1; Denly 6–0–41–0.

Umpires: G. O. Brathwaite and S. George.   Third umpire: Aleem Dar.
Referee: D. C. Boon.

SOUTH AFRICA v ENGLAND

Second One-Day International

At Durban, February 7, 2020 (day/night). No result. Toss: England. One-day international debut: B. C. Fortuin.

Only 11.2 overs survived rain, just enough time for England to achieve what they had failed to do in Cape Town, and cheaply dismiss de Kock and Bavuma. A delayed start saw the match reduced to 45 overs a side, then – after a three-hour interruption – 26. In the first mini-session, Root bowled de Kock. And, from what turned out to be the final ball of the match, Jordan trapped Bavuma. Both dismissals were a repeat of Newlands.

South Africa

*†Q. de Kock b Root	11
R. R. Hendricks not out	35
T. Bavuma lbw b Jordan	21
B 1, lb 1, w 2	4

1/32 (1)   (2 wkts, 11.2 overs) 71
2/71 (3)   6.3 overs: 38-1

H. E. van der Dussen, J. T. Smuts, D. A. Miller, A. L. Phehlukwayo, B. E. Hendricks, B. C. Fortuin, L. L. Sipamla and T. Shamsi did not bat.

Woakes 4–0–21–0; S. M. Curran 2–0–16–0; Root 1–0–4–1; T. K. Curran 2–0–13–0; Parkinson 2–0–15–0; Jordan 0.2–0–0–1.

England

J. J. Roy, †J. M. Bairstow, J. E. Root, *E. J. G. Morgan, J. L. Denly, T. Banton, S. M. Curran, C. R. Woakes, T. K. Curran, C. J. Jordan, M. W. Parkinson.

Umpires: Aleem Dar and A. Paleker.   Third umpire: G. O. Brathwaite.
Referee: D. C. Boon.

SOUTH AFRICA v ENGLAND

Third One-Day International

At Johannesburg, February 9, 2020. England won by two wickets. Toss: England. One-day international debut: S. Mahmood.

Having used the first two matches to assess his fringe players, Morgan opted for the tried and tested as he sought to avoid a first bilateral series defeat for three years. Rashid's three for 51 – taking him above Ian Botham's ODI tally of 145, and fifth on England's all-time table – had squeezed South Africa at a ground not high on spinners' bucket lists. He might have had four, only for the scalp of van der Dussen to be taken from him: TV umpire Aleem Dar decided to reinstate a review most thought had been burned by Bavuma's failed challenge against an lbw shout the ball before. Dar reasoned that, because Ultra Edge had not worked during Bavuma's review (even though there had clearly been no edge), it should remain intact. When a grinning van der Dussen walked back to the middle, and used the review, technology had the ball missing leg. If England were confused, they were hardly inconvenienced: in his first international appearance since the First Ashes Test in August, Ali bowled van der Dussen in the next over. Rashid also bowled de Kock, for 69, and it needed an unbroken stand of 52 between Miller (whose 69 came from 53 balls) and Lutho Sipamla to give South Africa a total to defend. Earlier, Saqib Mahmood had struck in the fourth over of his ODI debut, trimming Reeza Hendricks's off bail with a beauty. In reply, England got off to a flyer, as Bairstow's 23-ball 43 punished an error-strewn display from Ngidi and Beuran Hendricks. Root and Denly built on the platform, and Banton added a layer. With 25 needed, England carelessly lost four for 20, before Ali settled the matter with 40 balls to spare.

Player of the Match: A. U. Rashid. *Player of the Series:* Q. de Kock.

South Africa

*†Q. de Kock b Rashid	69	
R. R. Hendricks b Mahmood	11	
T. Bavuma lbw b Rashid	29	
H. E. van der Dussen b Ali	5	
J. T. Smuts run out (Banton/Bairstow)	31	
D. A. Miller not out	69	
A. L. Phehlukwayo lbw b Rashid	14	

B. E. Hendricks run out (Rashid/Morgan)	3
L. L. Sipamla not out	10
B 1, lb 6, w 8	15

1/23 (2) 2/89 (3)   (7 wkts, 50 overs) 256
3/94 (4) 4/140 (1)
5/155 (5) 6/188 (7) 7/204 (8)   10 overs: 36-1

L. T. Ngidi and T. Shamsi did not bat.

Curran 9–1–38–0; Mahmood 5–1–17–1; Jordan 9–0–59–0; Root 7–0–42–0; Ali 10–0–42–1; Rashid 10–0–51–3.

England

J. J. Roy c Ngidi b B. E. Hendricks	21	
J. M. Bairstow c Phehlukwayo b Sipamla	43	
J. E. Root c Bavuma b Shamsi	49	
E. J. G. Morgan c and b B. E. Hendricks	9	
J. L. Denly c Phehlukwayo b Ngidi	66	
T. Banton c de Kock b B. E. Hendricks	32	
M. M. Ali not out	17	
T. K. Curran b Bavuma b Ngidi	5	

A. U. Rashid c de Kock b Ngidi	2
C. J. Jordan not out	0
W 13	13

1/61 (2) 2/69 (1)   (8 wkts, 43.2 overs) 257
3/86 (4) 4/162 (3)
5/232 (5) 6/232 (6)
7/241 (8) 8/252 (9)   10 overs: 77-2

S. Mahmood did not bat.

Ngidi 9–2–63–3; B. E. Hendricks 10–0–59–3; Sipamla 9.2–1–42–1; Shamsi 10–0–58–1; Smuts 3–0–12–0; Phehlukwayo 2–0–23–0.

Umpires: G. O. Brathwaite and S. George.   Third umpire: Aleem Dar.
Referee: D. C. Boon.

For World Cup records, see page 1344

SOUTH AFRICA v ENGLAND

First Twenty20 International

At East London, February 12, 2020 (floodlit). South Africa won by one run. Toss: England.

England contrived to spurn victory with clinical precision. Chasing 178 at a Buffalo Park ground whipped throughout by a stiff crossfield wind, they needed seven from seven balls with five wickets in hand, only for a combination of excessive aggression and skilful bowling from Ngidi to cost them four wickets and the game. Ali and Rashid were the last two to fall, having earlier squeezed South Africa with two for 45 in eight overs of spin. It meant the hosts failed to exploit a position of 105 for one after ten, and the last two overs produced just eight runs for the loss of four wickets, with Jordan's yorkers lethal. In reply, Roy raced to the joint-second-fastest T20 half-century for England, from 22 balls, to put them in control. After he miscued a wide long hop from Hendricks to short fine leg, Morgan took over, and appeared to have won it when he pummelled Hendricks for 14 in three balls in the 19th over. But he swung the next to long-on, and Tom Curran followed suit in the 20th, delivered by Ngidi. Ali scrambled two off the fourth ball, but was bowled by the fifth, before Rashid – needing two for a super over – could manage only a single. "With all the games I've played and the experience I have, I would have liked to see it through," said Morgan.

Player of the Match: L. T. Ngidi.

South Africa		B	4/6
1 T. Bavuma c 7 b 10		43	27 5
2 *†Q. de Kock c 5 b 7		31	15 3/2
3 H. E. van der Dussen c 3 b 6		31	26 3/1
4 D. A. Miller c 9 b 8		16	14 1
5 J. T. Smuts c 6 b 11		20	20 2
6 A. L. Phehlukwayo run out (9)		18	15 0/2
7 D. Pretorius b 9		1	2 0
8 B. E. Hendricks b 9		0	1 0
9 D. W. Steyn not out		5	2 1
B 2, lb 5, w 3, nb 2		12	
6 overs: 68-1 (20 overs)		177-8	

1/48 2/111 3/113 4/135 5/170 6/172 7/172 8/177

10 L. T. Ngidi and 11 T. Shamsi did not bat.

Ali 4–9–22–1; Curran 3–4–41–1; Wood 3–5–32–1; Jordan 3–7–28–2; Rashid 4–9–23–1; Stokes 3–4–24–1.

England		B	4/6
1 J. J. Roy c 10 b 8		70	38 7/3
2 †J. C. Buttler c 4 b 9		15	10 3
3 J. M. Bairstow lbw b 6		23	19 3
4 *E. J. G. Morgan c 1 b 8		52	34 7/1
5 J. L. Denly c 3 b 6		3	4 0
6 B. A. Stokes c 4 b 10		4	7 0
7 M. M. Ali b 10		5	5 0
8 T. K. Curran c 4 b 10		2	2 0
9 C. J. Jordan not out		0	0 0
10 A. U. Rashid run out (9/2)		1	1 0
Lb 1		1	
6 overs: 68-1 (20 overs)		176-9	

1/19 2/91 3/132 4/137 5/152 6/171 7/173 8/175 9/176

11 M. A. Wood did not bat.

Steyn 4–9–33–1; Ngidi 4–9–30–3; Smuts 1–1–22–0; Phehlukwayo 4–3–32–2; Shamsi 4–6–25–0; Hendricks 3–5–33–2.

Umpires: A. T. Holdstock and B. P. Jele.   Third umpire: A. Paleker.
Referee: D. C. Boon.

SOUTH AFRICA v ENGLAND

Second Twenty20 International

At Durban, February 14, 2020 (floodlit). England won by two runs. Toss: South Africa.

A second consecutive nailbiter this time went the tourists' way, after South Africa – like England two days earlier – failed to score three from the last two balls. Thanks to Tom Curran, both produced wickets: Pretorius was pinned by a yorker, then Fortuin ramped a back-of-the-hand slower ball to short fine leg. Even then, England had to wait for victory to be confirmed, as the third umpire checked whether Rashid, who had back-pedalled to take the catch, had left the inner ring before the moment of delivery. He hadn't – just – and the series was level. England had climbed to 204, for two days their highest T20 score in South Africa (beating 202 for six at Johannesburg in November 2009). Ali's 11-ball 39 was the highlight, after big hitting from Roy and Bairstow; Stokes held it all together with 47 not out. But South Africa's response was led by de Kock, who reached his half century in a national-record 17 balls, eclipsing 21, which he shared with A. B. de Villiers, against England at Johannesburg four years earlier. He fell for a classy 22-ball 65, including eight sixes, to end an opening stand of 92 inside eight overs with Bavuma. Jordan later yorked Smuts and Phehlukwayo with successive balls in the 17th over to leave South Africa needing 47 off 20, but van der Dussen and Pretorius managed 44 before Curran's late intervention.

Player of the Match: M. M. Ali.

England

		B	4/6
1 J. J. Roy *c 3 b 11*	40	29	3/2
2 †J. C. Buttler *c 2 b 10*	2	4	0
3 J. M. Bairstow *b 6*	35	17	2/3
4 *E. J. G. Morgan *c 1 b 7*	27	24	2/1
5 B. A. Stokes *not out*	47	30	4/2
6 J. L. Denly *b 6*	1	2	0
7 M. M. Ali *c 1 b 10*	39	11	3/4
8 C. J. Jordan *c 1 b 10*	7	3	0/1
9 T. K. Curran *not out*	0	0	
Lb 2, w 4	6		

6 overs: 55-1   (20 overs)   204-7

1/17 2/69 3/90 4/123 5/125 6/176 7/194

10 A. U. Rashid and 11 M. A. Wood did not bat.

Fortuin 2–5–15–0; Hendricks 3–4–45–0; Ngidi 4–8–48–3; Phehlukwayo 4–5–47–2; Shamsi 4–7–30–1; Pretorius 3–6–17–1.

South Africa

		B	4/6
1 T. Bavuma *c 2 b 11*	31	29	2
2 *†Q. de Kock *c 5 b 11*	65	22	2/8
3 D. A. Miller *c 8 b 5*	21	16	1/2
4 H. E. van der Dussen *not out*	43	26	2/3
5 J. T. Smuts *b 8*	13	12	0/1
6 A. L. Phehlukwayo *b 8*	0	1	0
7 D. Pretorius *lbw b 9*	25	13	2/1
8 B. C. Fortuin *c 10 b 9*	0	1	0
Lb 1, w 3	4		

6 overs: 69-0   (20 overs)   202-7

1/92 2/101 3/123 4/158 5/158 6/202 7/202

9 B. E. Hendricks, 10 L. T. Ngidi and 11 T. Shamsi did not bat.

Ali 3–5–36–0; Curran 4–8–45–2; Jordan 4–6–31–2; Rashid 3–5–34–0; Wood 4–8–39–2; Stokes 2–4–16–1.

Umpires: B. P. Jele and A. Paleker.   Third umpire: A. T. Holdstock.

Referee: D. C. Boon.

SOUTH AFRICA v ENGLAND

Third Twenty20 International

At Centurion, February 16, 2020. England won by five wickets. Toss: South Africa.

A third consecutive thriller in a terrific series went England's way, as Morgan steered them to the fourth-highest successful run-chase in a T20 international. Set 223, they got there with five balls to spare, after he blitzed 57 not out off 22, with seven sixes, equalling the England record for a T20 innings (there had now been six instances of seven, and Morgan had four). It was a body blow for South Africa, who had been given another electric start by Bavuma and de Kock (84 this time, inside

KEEP ON RUNNING

Highest runs per over in a bilateral Twenty20 series (minimum three matches):

	Runs		
10.12	1,207	**South Africa v England**	**2019-20**
10.00	1,172	**India v West Indies**	**2019-20**
9.70	1,051	Afghanistan v Ireland in India	2016-17
9.52	1,121	South Africa v West Indies	2014-15
9.49	1,682	**New Zealand v England** (*5 matches*)	**2019-20**
9.45	1,128	Afghanistan v Ireland in India	2018-19
9.42	796	New Zealand v West Indies	2017-18
9.33	853	**West Indies v Ireland**	**2019-20**
9.29	1,098	New Zealand v India	2018-19
9.24	975	Bangladesh v West Indies	2018-19
9.20	1,092	South Africa v India	2017-18
9.12	1,083	South Africa v Australia	2015-16
9.01	1,077	Australia v India	2015-16

eight overs), before Klaasen pummelled 66 off 33 in his first game of the series. Tom Curran and Stokes proved the only bowlers from either side to keep their economy-rates below ten. In reply, Buttler and Bairstow put on 91 for the second wicket, but when Malan, also appearing for the first time in the series following an illness to Joe Denly, fell for 11, it was 145 for four in the 14th over. Stokes responded with 22 in 12, and Morgan's 21-ball half-century – equalling his own record for England's quickest, set at Napier three months earlier – gave them the series. Only once before, against South Africa at Mumbai during the 2016 World T20, had they knocked off more to win.

Player of the Match: E. J. G. Morgan.   *Player of the Series:* E. J. G. Morgan.

South Africa

		B	4/6
1 T. Bavuma *b 10*	49	24	4/3
2 *†Q. de Kock *c 3 b 6*	35	24	1/4
3 H. E. van der Dussen *c 9 b 6*	11	9	1
4 H. Klaasen *c 6 b 9*	66	33	4/4
5 D. A. Miller *not out*	35	20	3/2
6 D. Pretorius *c 2 b 9*	11	7	2
7 A. L. Phehlukwayo *c 6 b 11*	1	3	0
8 B. C. Fortuin *not out*	0	0	0
Lb 5, w 9	14		

6 overs: 64-0   (20 overs) 222-6

1/84 2/86 3/113 4/177 5/202 6/214

9 D. W. Steyn, 10 L. T. Ngidi and 11 T. Shamsi did not bat.

12th man: B. E. Hendricks.

Ali 1–1–11–0; Curran 4–9–33–2; Wood 3–4–47–1; Jordan 4–7–49–0; Rashid 4–3–42–1; Stokes 4–5–35–2.

England

		B	4/6
1 J. J. Roy *c 11 b 10*	7	4	0/1
2 †J. C. Buttler *c 11 b 6*	57	29	9/2
3 J. M. Bairstow *b 7*	64	34	7/3
4 D. J. Malan *c 2 b 11*	11	12	1
5 *E. J. G. Morgan *not out*	57	22	0/7
6 B. A. Stokes *c 12 b 10*	22	12	1/2
7 M. M. Ali *not out*	5	2	1
W 3	3		

6 overs: 62-1   (19.1 overs) 226-5

1/15 2/106 3/140 4/145 5/206

8 C. J. Jordan, 9 T. K. Curran, 10 A. U. Rashid and 11 M. A. Wood did not bat.

Steyn 4–9–43–0; Ngidi 4–6–55–2; Phehlukwayo 3.1–6–34–1; Shamsi 3–3–40–1; Pretorius 4–5–40–1; Fortuin 1–1–14–0.

Umpires: A. T. Holdstock and A. Paleker.   Third umpire: B. P. Jele.
Referee: D. C. Boon.

PART FIVE

English Domestic Cricket

FIRST-CLASS AVERAGES IN 2019

These include MCC v Surrey at Dubai.

BATTING AND FIELDING

(Qualification: 10 innings)

		M	I	NO	R	HS	100	50	Avge	Ct/St
1	D. J. Vilas (*Lancs*)	14	17	4	1,036	266	2	7	79.69	47/1
2	D. P. Sibley (*MCC, Warwicks & Eng Lions*)	15	25	2	1,575	244	6	6	68.47	8
3	M. Labuschagne (*Glam & Australians*)	16	28	3	1,530	182	5	9	61.20	18
4	R. F. Higgins (*Glos*)	14	21	5	958	199	4	3	59.87	4
5	†M. H. Azad (*Leics & Loughborough MCCU*)	16	28	4	1,353	139	4	8	56.37	9
6	†B. A. Stokes (*England*)	5	10	4	441	135*	2	2	55.12	4
7	†T. M. Head (*Australia A & Australians*)	7	12	3	485	139*	1	2	53.88	2
8	S. R. Hain (*Warwicks & England Lions*)	13	21	4	914	129*	2	4	53.76	17
9	L. A. Dawson (*Hants*)	9	13	1	643	103	1	6	53.58	6
10	†A. N. Cook (*Essex*)	15	25	5	1,063	150*	2	7	53.15	17
11	J. J. Bohannon (*Lancs*)	11	12	3	472	174	1	2	52.44	4
12	S. A. Northeast (*Hants & England Lions*)	15	25	3	1,123	169	4	5	51.04	6
13	J. M. Vince (*Hants*)	7	11	1	504	142	2	1	50.40	4
14	†S. van Zyl (*Sussex*)	13	22	3	931	173	3	4	49.00	4
15	†D. J. Malan (*Middx*)	14	23	1	1,059	199	4	3	48.13	17
16	†C. D. J. Dent (*Glos*)	14	24	1	1,087	176	4	4	47.26	8
17	S. J. Croft (*Lancs*)	11	12	2	472	78	0	4	47.20	4
18	J. E. Root (*Yorks & England*)	8	15	1	655	130*	1	6	46.78	14
19	†G. S. Ballance (*Yorks*)	15	24	2	1,014	159	5	3	46.09	4
20	L. S. Livingstone (*Lancs*)	11	14	1	599	114	1	5	46.07	7
21	C. B. Cooke (*Glam*)	7	10	2	368	96	0	2	46.00	18/2
22	T. Köhler-Cadmore (*Yorks*)	15	23	1	1,004	176	3	3	45.63	33
23	B. C. Brown (*Sussex*)	15	24	4	908	156	3	5	45.40	54/1
24	T. van der Gugten (*Glam*)	8	10	7	135	30*	0	0	45.00	2
25	†R. S. Vasconcelos (*Northants*)	11	20	2	805	184	2	3	44.72	16
26	†J. A. Simpson (*Middx*)	15	24	4	853	167*	2	5	42.65	37
27	†J. L. du Plooy (*Derbys*)	11	19	3	677	118	2	3	42.31	9
28	A. M. Rossington (*Northants*)	14	21	2	803	82	0	8	42.26	34/2
29	J. J. Cobb (*Northants*)	7	11	0	453	139	1	3	41.18	3
30	J. L. Denly (*Kent & England*)	12	23	2	849	167*	2	4	40.42	5
31	†M. S. Wade (*Australian XI & Australians*)	8	14	2	485	117	3	0	40.41	7
32	E. J. H. Eckersley (*Durham*)	13	22	4	720	118	1	4	40.00	42
33	A. H. T. Donald (*Hants*)	9	15	1	554	173	1	2	39.57	4
34	T. C. Lace (*Derbys & Middx*)	12	23	1	865	143	3	4	39.31	11
35	D. W. Lawrence (*MCC & Essex*)	15	24	4	785	147	1	6	39.25	11
36	C. T. Bancroft (*Durham & Australians*)	13	24	2	846	158	2	3	38.45	22
37	W. L. Madsen (*Derbys*)	14	25	1	917	204*	2	3	38.20	26
38	R. S. Bopara (*Essex*)	11	16	1	570	135	2	3	38.00	10
39	D. J. Bell-Drummond (*Kent*)	15	28	2	987	166	1	6	37.96	4
40	T. Bavuma (*Northants*)	8	15	0	566	134	2	1	37.73	7
41	R. Ashwin (*Notts*)	5	10	1	339	66*	0	2	37.66	3
42	S. D. Robson (*Middx*)	15	25	1	900	140*	2	4	37.50	10
43	†A. Z. Lees (*Durham*)	15	27	1	973	181	3	4	37.42	11
44	†L. A. Procter (*Northants*)	15	23	8	559	86*	0	2	37.26	4
45	†B. M. Duckett (*Notts*)	14	25	0	928	216	2	3	37.12	8
46	R. P. Jones (*Lancs*)	14	19	2	624	122	1	4	36.70	11
47	†W. T. Root (*Glam*)	14	22	1	768	229	2	1	36.57	4
48	A. G. Wakely (*Northants*)	12	16	1	548	102	1	2	36.53	12
49	G. L. van Buuren (*Glos*)	10	13	3	363	93	0	2	36.30	4
50	†B. A. Godleman (*Derbys*)	16	30	0	1,087	227	4	2	36.23	2

	M	I	NO	R	HS	100	50	Avge	Ct/St
51 †W. M. H. Rhodes (*MCC & Warwicks*)	15	25	0	904	109	1	6	36.16	14
52 †D. M. W. Rawlins (*Sussex*)	7	12	1	397	100	1	3	36.09	5
53 J. A. R. Harris (*Middx*)	10	17	4	469	80	0	3	36.07	2
54 A. L. Davies (*Lancs*)	10	14	1	468	147	1	2	36.00	0
55 C. N. Ackermann (*Leics*)	14	25	6	675	70*	0	7	35.52	19
56 T. N. Cullen (*Glam*)	9	12	3	319	63	0	0	35.44	29
57 R. I. Keogh (*Northants*)	15	23	0	811	150	2	3	35.26	4
58 †R. J. Burns (*Surrey & England*)	15	29	0	1,017	133	2	4	35.06	15
59 †M. J. Cosgrove (*Leics*)	13	23	3	697	107*	1	6	34.85	2
60 Z. Crawley (*Kent & England Lions*)	15	28	0	974	111	2	6	34.78	17
61 †R. R. Rossouw (*Hants*)	11	19	1	620	92	0	5	34.44	2
62 T. Westley (*MCC & Essex*)	15	25	1	822	141	1	3	34.25	11
63 F. J. Hudson-Prentice (*Derbys*)	7	12	2	342	99	0	2	34.20	1
64 N. J. Selman (*Glam*)	14	24	2	752	150	1	5	34.18	10
65 {†A. Lyth (*Yorks*)	15	26	2	816	95	0	7	34.00	27
{†M. S. Harris (*Australia A & Australians*) . .	7	13	1	408	109	1	3	34.00	2
67 N. J. Dexter (*Leics*)	9	13	0	441	180	1	2	33.92	1
68 R. Clarke (*Surrey*)	15	26	6	678	88	0	3	33.90	18
69 †J. R. Bracey (*Glos & England Lions*)	14	24	2	745	152	2	2	33.86	23
70 †B. J. Curran (*Northants*)	8	13	2	368	64	0	2	33.45	3
71 J. L. Smith (*Surrey*)	9	15	1	465	127	1	2	33.21	5/2
72 P. D. Salt (*Sussex*)	12	23	1	727	122	2	4	33.04	13
73 J. A. Tattersall (*Yorks*)	15	22	2	658	135*	1	3	32.90	36/4
74 O. G. Robinson (*Kent*)	15	26	2	786	143	2	3	32.75	54
75 †S. M. Curran (*Surrey, Eng Lions & England*)	8	15	1	458	80	0	4	32.71	1
76 H. R. Hosein (*Derbys*)	16	28	4	783	138*	1	5	32.62	33/2
77 G. G. Wagg (*Glam*)	16	26	3	418	100	1	3	32.15	2
78 C. R. Hemphrey (*Glam*)	10	18	1	546	75	0	5	32.11	7
79 N. L. Buck (*Northants*)	11	14	5	287	53	0	3	31.88	2
80 I. G. Holland (*Hants*)	9	16	1	478	143	1	3	31.86	5
81 S. R. Dickson (*Kent*)	12	23	2	668	161	3	1	31.80	13
82 D. Wiese (*Sussex*)	15	21	0	666	139	1	5	31.71	1
83 S. J. Mullaney (*Notts*)	14	26	0	824	179	2	4	31.69	14
84 D. A. Douthwaite (*Cardiff MCCU & Glam*).	9	15	1	443	100*	1	1	31.64	1
85 †L. M. Reece (*Derbys*)	16	30	0	944	184	2	2	31.46	6
86 D. I. Stevens (*Kent*)	13	20	1	597	237	1	2	31.42	3
87 G. H. Roderick (*Glos*)	14	24	3	654	158	1	2	31.14	41/1
88 P. M. Siddle (*Essex & Australians*)	12	15	5	311	60	0	1	31.10	5
89 †K. K. Jennings (*Lancs*)	14	21	2	588	97	0	6	30.94	17
90 G. A. Bartlett (*Somerset*)	15	26	1	772	137	2	3	30.88	1
91 T. B. Abell (*MCC & Somerset*)	15	27	1	797	101	1	5	30.65	13
92 D. L. Lloyd (*Glam*)	14	23	1	668	97	0	4	30.36	16
93 †S. G. Borthwick (*Surrey*)	14	24	0	721	137	2	2	30.04	16
94 †R. M. Yates (*Warwicks*)	12	19	0	570	141	1	2	30.00	10
95 C. J. Ferguson (*Worcs*)	10	18	1	509	127	1	3	29.94	8
96 W. A. T. Beer (*Sussex*)	11	17	3	417	97	0	3	29.78	1
97 L. D. McManus (*Hants*)	7	10	1	267	61	0	1	29.66	20/1
98 T. Banton (*Somerset*)	10	18	0	533	79	0	5	29.61	6
99 C. J. Jordan (*Sussex*)	12	17	2	444	166	1	1	29.60	18
100 †N. L. J. Browne (*Essex*)	15	25	1	710	163	1	3	29.58	13
101 †M. D. Stoneman (*Surrey*)	14	24	0	706	100	1	4	29.41	5
102 J. C. Hildreth (*Somerset*)	15	26	1	731	158*	2	3	29.24	17
103 J. M. Clarke (*Notts*)	13	23	1	643	125	3	1	29.22	6
104 †D. Elgar (*Surrey*)	10	19	0	555	103	1	5	29.21	6
105 {C. D. Nash (*Notts*)	13	24	1	667	85	0	6	29.00	4
{N. J. Rimmington (*Durham*)	7	10	2	232	92	0	2	29.00	3
107 P. J. Horton (*Leics*)	15	27	1	751	100*	1	3	28.88	13
108 R. I. Newton (*Northants*)	11	20	2	514	118	2	1	28.55	1
109 H. Hameed (*Lancs*)	10	15	3	341	117	1	1	28.41	5
110 W. A. R. Fraine (*Yorks*)	8	15	1	393	106	1	0	28.07	8

	M	I	NO	R	HS	100	50	Avge	Ct/St
111 M. G. Hogan (*Glam*)	11	12	6	166	54	0	1	27.66	3
112 †S. M. Davies (*Somerset*)	15	26	1	688	109	1	3	27.52	48/3
113 M. H. Wessels (*Worcs*)	15	24	2	602	118	1	3	27.36	21
114 L. Gregory (*Somerset & England Lions*)	13	20	2	491	129*	1	3	27.27	11
115 F. S. Organ (*Hants*)	6	11	0	300	100	1	2	27.27	4
116 J. T. A. Burnham (*Durham*)	13	23	1	598	86	0	4	27.18	4
117 G. J. Harte (*Durham*)	12	23	2	569	108*	1	3	27.09	2
118 R. N. ten Doeschate (*Essex*)	14	19	1	483	130	2	1	26.83	8
119 †K. H. D. Barker (*Hants*)	14	19	4	401	64	0	1	26.73	2
120 O. B. Cox (*MCC & Worcs*)	15	23	2	558	100*	1	3	26.57	38/1
121 W. G. Jacks (*Surrey*)	11	17	0	447	120	1	3	26.29	14
122 J. A. Leaning (*Yorks*)	9	13	1	315	77*	0	3	26.25	4
123 J. J. Weatherley (*Hants*)	9	15	2	341	66	0	2	26.23	8
124 D. M. Bess (*MCC, Yorks & Somerset*)	12	19	4	393	91*	0	1	26.20	4
125 †R. A. Whiteley (*Worcs*)	10	16	1	391	88	0	3	26.06	4
126 †N. R. T. Gubbins (*Middx*)	15	26	0	668	105	1	3	25.69	4
127 A. J. A. Wheater (*Essex*)	11	13	1	307	130	1	0	25.58	29/3
128 L. J. Carey (*Glam*)	9	12	3	230	62*	0	2	25.55	0
129 D. K. H. Mitchell (*Worcs*)	14	24	2	559	139	2	2	25.40	18
130 H. G. Kuhn (*Kent*)	14	24	0	605	95	0	5	25.20	11
131 A. L. Hughes (*Derbys*)	13	24	1	578	109*	1	1	25.13	12
132 †B. T. Slater (*Notts*)	14	25	1	601	130	1	1	25.04	6
133 Azhar Ali (*Somerset*)	10	18	2	399	79	0	3	24.93	3
134 †L. W. P. Wells (*Sussex*)	16	29	4	620	98*	0	3	24.80	6
135 J. Leach (*Worcs*)	13	21	4	420	54*	0	2	24.70	1
136 J. C. Buttler (*England*)	5	10	0	247	70	0	1	24.70	5
137 B. A. C. Howell (*Glos*)	10	15	0	369	76	0	2	24.60	12
138 B. T. Foakes (*Surrey & England Lions*)	14	25	1	590	69	0	5	24.58	41/6
139 †L. Trevaskis (*Durham*)	10	17	1	392	64	0	2	24.50	2
140 J. Clark (*Surrey*)	9	15	4	268	54	0	1	24.36	1
141 { S. S. Eskinazi (*Middx*)	13	22	0	528	125	1	1	24.00	13
141 { T. S. Roland-Jones (*Middx*)	12	18	4	336	54	0	2	24.00	3
143 A. M. Rahane (*Hants*)	7	13	0	307	119	1	1	23.61	6
144 †T. P. Alsop (*Hants*)	11	18	3	353	150	1	1	23.53	14
145 M. J. J. Critchley (*Derbys*)	16	27	4	540	79*	0	3	23.47	14
146 †R. S. Patel (*Surrey*)	9	15	1	328	100*	1	1	23.42	3
147 L. J. Hill (*Leics*)	8	12	2	232	67	0	1	23.20	28/1
148 S. R. Patel (*Notts & Glam*)	14	24	2	506	66	0	3	23.00	4
149 E. G. Barnard (*Worcs*)	14	21	2	429	56	0	2	22.57	11
150 M. D. Taylor (*Glos*)	9	10	7	67	28*	0	0	22.33	4
151 B. A. Raine (*Durham*)	15	24	2	486	82	0	2	22.09	1
152 B. W. M. Mike (*Leics & Warwicks*)	7	11	2	197	72	0	1	21.88	0
153 H. C. Brook (*Yorks*)	11	17	0	370	101	1	0	21.76	7
154 L. J. Evans (*Sussex*)	8	13	0	282	113	1	1	21.69	6
155 D. Olivier (*Yorks*)	14	17	11	130	24	0	0	21.66	3
156 †H. E. Dearden (*Leics*)	14	20	0	431	61	0	2	21.55	7
157 J. M. R. Taylor (*Glos*)	9	13	0	279	99	0	1	21.46	3
158 C. A. J. Morris (*Worcs*)	12	16	9	149	53*	0	1	21.28	0
159 S. R. Harmer (*Essex*)	15	21	3	382	62	0	2	21.22	16
160 O. E. Robinson (*Sussex & England Lions*)	13	18	5	275	59	0	1	21.15	5
161 †T. J. Haines (*Sussex*)	7	12	0	252	93	0	1	21.00	2
162 T. E. Bailey (*Lancs*)	9	10	0	207	68	0	2	20.70	5
163 B. A. Carse (*Durham*)	10	15	3	246	77*	0	1	20.50	1
164 G. F. B. Scott (*Middx*)	7	11	1	204	55	0	1	20.40	3
165 J. S. Patel (*Warwicks*)	14	22	4	365	70*	0	2	20.27	8
166 T. R. Ambrose (*Warwicks*)	12	20	0	399	107	1	0	19.95	39/3
167 T. D. Paine (*Australia A & Australians*)	8	13	1	238	58	0	1	19.83	29/1
168 A. K. Dal (*Derbys*)	11	19	4	295	92	0	2	19.66	7
169 †J. L. Pattinson (*Notts, Aus A & Australia*)	6	10	3	137	47*	0	0	19.57	1
170 J. M. Bairstow (*England*)	6	12	1	214	52	0	1	19.45	21/2

		M	I	NO	R	HS	100	50	Avge	Ct/St
171	{†M. A. H. Hammond (*Glos*)	14	23	1	418	82	0	2	19.00	14
	H. J. H. Brookes (*Warwicks*)	11	17	2	285	84	0	1	19.00	4
173	J. D. Libby (*Notts*)	5	10	0	189	77	0	1	18.90	3
174	J. J. Roy (*England*)	5	10	0	187	72	0	1	18.70	1
175	D. A. Payne (*Glos*)	12	15	4	205	43	0	0	18.63	4
176	C. Overton (*Somerset & England*)	12	18	1	314	58	0	1	18.47	12
177	J. Overton (*Northants & Somerset*)	10	17	2	277	52*	0	1	18.46	18
178	B. A. Hutton (*Northants*)	10	15	4	203	34*	0	0	18.45	9
179	N. A. Sowter (*Middx*)	7	11	1	184	57*	0	2	18.40	4
180	G. H. Rhodes (*Worcs & Leics*)	7	13	2	198	61*	0	1	18.00	1
181	H. W. Podmore (*Kent*)	15	22	6	279	54*	0	1	17.43	4
182	B. O. Coad (*Yorks*)	12	15	3	206	48	0	0	17.16	0
183	†L. Wood (*Notts & Northants*)	10	16	3	222	66	0	2	17.07	3
184	{A. J. Hose (*Warwicks*)	11	20	0	340	111	1	0	17.00	3
	S. Mahmood (*Lancs*)	9	10	2	136	34	0	0	17.00	1
186	L. Banks (*Warwicks*)	8	13	0	220	50	0	1	16.92	14
187	H. J. Swindells (*Leics*)	7	10	0	168	37	0	0	16.80	12/1
188	C. J. C. Wright (*Leics*)	15	21	3	295	60	0	1	16.38	3
189	K. J. Abbott (*Hants*)	14	18	4	229	72	0	1	16.35	1
190	S. A. Patterson (*Yorks*)	15	21	2	310	60	0	1	16.31	6
191	W. S. Davis (*Leics*)	11	17	8	142	39*	0	0	15.77	1
192	O. P. Rayner (*Middx & Kent*)	10	14	2	181	40*	0	0	15.08	7
193	B. W. Sanderson (*Northants*)	15	17	6	162	28	0	0	14.72	0
194	†M. E. Trescothick (*Somerset*)	6	10	0	145	37	0	0	14.50	10
195	{M. de Lange (*Glam*)	8	10	1	127	45*	0	0	14.11	2
	L. V. van Beek (*Derbys*)	9	12	3	127	34*	0	0	14.11	5
197	†T. J. Moores (*Notts*)	14	25	0	347	48	0	0	13.88	31/1
198	†A. J. Blake (*Kent*)	6	10	0	137	34	0	0	13.70	2
199	O. C. Soames (*Hants*)	6	11	0	148	62	0	1	13.45	2
200	C. T. Steel (*Durham*)	6	10	0	133	39	0	0	13.30	2
201	†R. Rampaul (*Derbys*)	13	19	5	186	30	0	0	13.28	2
202	{J. J. Dell (*Worcs*)	7	12	0	158	61	0	1	13.16	5
	J. A. Brooks (*Somerset*)	9	13	7	79	35*	0	0	13.16	2
204	M. E. Milnes (*Kent*)	15	20	6	183	31	0	0	13.07	6
205	†S. C. J. Broad (*MCC, Notts & England*)	14	25	9	209	30	0	0	13.06	5
206	†T. J. Murtagh (*Middx & Ireland*)	13	17	4	167	33	0	0	12.84	2
207	†M. J. Leach (*Somerset, Eng Lions & England*)	16	24	8	203	92	0	1	12.68	12
208	†M. D. E. Holden (*Middx*)	10	18	0	227	54	0	1	12.61	1
209	A. W. Finch (*Worcs*)	8	10	5	61	18*	0	0	12.20	0
210	H. Z. Finch (*Sussex*)	9	16	1	179	48	0	0	11.93	12
211	G. J. Batty (*Surrey*)	8	15	4	123	29	0	0	11.18	2
212	J. T. Ball (*Notts*)	11	17	11	67	15*	0	0	11.16	3
213	J. H. Davey (*Somerset*)	6	10	1	99	36	0	0	11.00	1
214	A. P. Palladino (*Derbys*)	11	16	3	134	58	0	1	10.30	0
215	J. Shaw (*Glos & Yorks*)	10	13	2	113	38*	0	0	10.27	3
216	†O. J. Hannon-Dalby (*Warwicks*)	12	15	5	102	17*	0	0	10.20	2
217	T. D. Groenewald (*Somerset*)	7	13	3	100	17	0	0	10.00	3
218	L. J. Fletcher (*Notts*)	13	22	1	209	25*	0	0	9.95	2
219	†D. A. Warner (*Australia*)	5	10	0	95	61	0	1	9.50	8
220	G. K. Berg (*Hants & Northants*)	9	13	1	103	33	0	0	8.58	1
221	M. E. T. Salisbury (*Durham*)	5	10	1	76	23	0	0	8.44	0
222	A. Sakande (*Sussex*)	7	10	4	47	15	0	0	7.83	2
223	E. R. Bamber (*Middx & Glos*)	7	11	3	60	15	0	0	7.50	0
224	G. Onions (*Lancs*)	10	10	1	65	18	0	0	7.22	1
225	S. J. Cook (*MCC & Essex*)	10	11	3	54	37*	0	0	6.75	2
226	†M. Morkel (*Surrey*)	15	23	3	134	27	0	0	6.70	3
227	C. Rushworth (*Durham*)	15	20	9	66	12*	0	0	6.00	4
228	F. H. Edwards (*Hants*)	15	17	9	32	8*	0	0	4.00	3
229	J. A. Porter (*Essex & England Lions*)	15	16	5	32	17	0	0	2.90	3
230	Mohammad Abbas (*Leics*)	9	11	3	22	11	0	0	2.75	4

BOWLING

(Qualification: 10 wickets)

		Style	O	M	R	W	BB	5I	Avge
1	J. M. Anderson (*Lancs & England*)	RFM	163.4	64	282	30	5-18	2	9.40
2	J. H. Davey (*Somerset*)	RFM	123.5	30	341	22	5-21	1	15.50
3	T. J. Murtagh (*Middx & Ireland*)	RFM	348.3	113	857	55	6-51	5	15.58
4	L. Gregory (*Somerset & England Lions*)	RFM	332	97	927	59	6-32	4	15.71
5	K. J. Abbott (*Hants*)	RFM	376.5	79	1,163	72	9-40	6	16.15
6	M. R. Marsh (*Aus XI & Australians*)	RFM	71.2	16	201	12	5-46	1	16.75
7	D. I. Stevens (*Kent*)	RM	422	134	937	54	5-20	5	17.35
8	C. Rushworth (*Durham*)	RFM	505.4	134	1,317	75	6-39	4	17.56
9	R. E. van der Merwe (*Somerset*)	SLA	66.5	21	177	10	4-41	0	17.70
10	S. R. Harmer (*Essex*)	OB	617.5	181	1,561	86	8-98	10	18.15
11	M. G. Neser (*Aus A & Australians*)	RFM	76	18	218	12	3-31	0	18.16
12	T. H. S. Pettman (*Oxford MCCU & Univ*)	RFM	97	29	264	14	5-19	1	18.85
13	K. A. Maharaj (*Yorks*)	SLA	266	76	719	38	7-52	4	18.92
14	O. E. Robinson (*Sussex & England Lions*)	RM/OB	427.3	92	1,211	64	8-34	6	18.92
15	M. W. Parkinson (*Lancs*)	LB	143.5	33	381	20	6-23	1	19.05
16	L. M. Reece (*Derbys*)	LFM	386	109	1,071	55	6-58	3	19.47
17	G. Onions (*Lancs*)	RFM	306.1	66	881	45	5-38	3	19.57
18	P. J. Cummins (*Australia*)	RF	211	61	569	29	4-32	0	19.62
19	B. W. Sanderson (*Northants*)	RFM	460.2	122	1,197	61	6-37	3	19.62
20	G. S. Virdi (*Surrey*)	OB	140	34	452	23	8-61	2	19.65
21	B. A. Hutton (*Northants*)	RFM	263.3	72	700	35	6-57	2	20.00
22	R. J. Gleeson (*Lancs*)	RFM	273.1	61	948	47	6-43	5	20.17
23	J. C. Archer (*England*)	RF	156	34	446	22	6-45	2	20.27
24	C. Overton (*Somerset & England*)	RFM	331.4	70	956	47	6-24	3	20.34
25	B. A. Raine (*Durham*)	RFM	486.3	130	1,230	60	6-27	3	20.50
25	T. A. I. Taylor (*Leics*)	RFM	127.2	26	410	20	6-47	1	20.50
25	G. J. Maxwell (*Lancs*)	OB	109.5	27	287	14	5-40	1	20.50
28	M. A. Starc (*Australians*)	LF	80.3	19	267	13	4-39	0	20.53
29	T. E. Bailey (*Lancs*)	RFM	289.2	81	777	37	5-41	1	21.00
29	L. A. Patterson-White (*Notts*)	SLA	134.5	17	420	20	5-73	1	21.00
31	J. C. Tongue (*Worcs*)	RFM	137.3	30	402	19	5-37	1	21.15
32	M. G. Hogan (*Glam*)	RFM	349	85	974	46	5-62	1	21.17
33	M. P. Dunn (*Surrey*)	RFM	90.2	18	277	13	5-43	1	21.30
34	A. P. Beard (*Essex*)	RFM	129	22	450	21	4-23	0	21.42
35	J. Overton (*Northants & Somerset*)	RFM	212.1	32	744	34	5-70	1	21.88
36	S. J. Cook (*MCC & Essex*)	RFM	258.5	65	748	34	7-23	3	22.00
37	C. A. J. Morris (*Worcs*)	RFM	317	72	1,035	47	7-45	3	22.02
38	M. J. Leach (*Somerset, Eng Lions & Eng*)	SLA	409	97	1,128	51	6-36	3	22.11
39	E. G. Barnard (*Worcs*)	RFM	371	100	993	44	6-42	1	22.56
40	J. R. Hazlewood (*Aus A & Australians*)	RFM	201.2	56	524	23	5-30	1	22.78
41	P. M. Siddle (*Essex & Australians*)	RFM	376.4	98	1,010	44	6-104	2	22.95
42	W. D. Parnell (*Worcs*)	LFM	157.4	42	507	22	5-47	1	23.04
43	F. J. Hudson-Prentice (*Derbys*)	RFM	148	38	465	20	3-27	0	23.25
44	S. M. Curran (*Surrey, Eng Lions & Eng*)	LFM	225.5	45	727	31	6-95	1	23.45
45	M. E. T. Salisbury (*Durham*)	RFM	137.1	27	448	19	4-67	0	23.57
46	R. F. Higgins (*Glos*)	RM	453.4	110	1,182	50	5-54	2	23.64
47	Clark. Clarke (*Surrey*)	RFM	352	83	1,065	45	7-74	2	23.66
48	C. R. Woakes (*England*)	RFM	112.4	21	382	16	6-17	1	23.87
49	J. L. Pattinson (*Notts, Aus A & Australia*)	RFM	165.4	33	479	20	6-73	1	23.95
50	T. B. Abell (*MCC & Somerset*)	RM	103.2	30	313	13	4-39	0	24.07
51	R. Rampaul (*Derbys*)	RFM	393	87	1,180	49	5-77	2	24.08
52	B. O. Coad (*Yorks*)	RFM	366.5	91	1,013	42	6-52	1	24.11
53	M. J. Waite (*Yorks*)	RFM	84	15	292	12	5-16	1	24.33
54	M. E. Claydon (*Kent*)	RFM	130.2	20	466	19	5-46	1	24.52
55	R. Ashwin (*Notts*)	OB	297.4	73	836	34	6-69	3	24.58
56	N. J. Rimmington (*Durham*)	RFM	158.2	31	446	18	4-42	0	24.77

		Style	O	M	R	W	BB	5I	Avge
57	L. S. Livingstone (*Lancs*)	LB	135.1	42	249	10	2-17	0	24.90
58	T. G. Helm (*Middx*)	RFM	208	39	600	24	5-36	2	25.00
59	F. H. Edwards (*Hants*)	RFM	366.1	57	1,266	50	5-49	4	25.32
60	J. Shaw (*Glos & Yorks*)	RFM	233.2	46	761	30	4-33	0	25.36
61	A. P. Palladino (*Derbys*)	RFM	295.5	102	686	27	5-29	1	25.40
62	M. E. Milnes (*Kent*)	RFM	408.2	70	1,478	58	5-68	2	25.48
63	O. J. Hannon-Dalby (*Warwicks*)	RFM	399	108	1,129	44	5-18	2	25.65
64	L. C. Norwell (*Warwicks*)	RFM	110.5	30	360	14	7-41	1	25.71
65	Mohammad Abbas (*Leics*)	RFM	281.5	81	747	29	4-72	0	25.75
66	D. A. Payne (*Glos*)	LFM	403.5	94	1,113	43	4-40	0	25.88
67	J. A. Porter (*Essex & England Lions*)	RFM	443.1	97	1,376	53	5-51	2	25.96
68	G. J. Batty (*Surrey*)	OB	234.3	43	678	26	8-64	1	26.07
69	M. D. Fisher (*Yorks*)	RFM	82	16	288	11	3-59	0	26.18
70	S. C. J. Broad (*MCC, Notts & England*)	RFM	417.5	88	1,284	49	5-73	2	26.20
71	M. D. Taylor (*Glos*)	LM	245	43	760	29	5-57	1	26.20
72	T. D. Groenewald (*Somerset*)	RFM	163.3	32	472	18	5-51	1	26.22
73	K. H. D. Barker (*Hants*)	LFM	362	85	1,001	38	5-48	1	26.34
74	Mir Hamza (*Sussex*)	LFM	212	51	633	24	4-51	0	26.37
75	L. J. Fletcher (*Notts*)	RFM	326.4	68	926	35	5-50	2	26.45
76	H. W. Podmore (*Kent*)	RFM	499.3	114	1,444	54	5-41	2	26.74
77	J. S. Patel (*Warwicks*)	OB	635.1	182	1,712	64	8-36	4	26.75
78	B. A. Carse (*Durham*)	RF	250.4	42	940	35	6-26	3	26.85
79	J. A. Brooks (*Somerset*)	RFM	228.1	53	762	28	5-33	1	27.21
80	J. Leach (*Worcs*)	RFM	410.4	89	1,145	42	6-79	1	27.26
81	G. K. Berg (*Hants & Northants*)	RFM	186.3	50	518	19	2-4	0	27.26
82	G. J. Harte (*Durham*)	RM	94	23	281	10	4-15	0	28.10
83	T. S. Roland-Jones (*Middx*)	RFM	328.5	64	1,044	37	7-52	3	28.21
84	D. J. Willey (*Yorks*)	LFM	88.2	21	316	11	3-71	0	28.72
85	D. Klein (*Leics*)	LFM	112	15	467	16	4-113	0	29.18
86	C. J. C. Wright (*Leics*)	RFM	450.2	90	1,501	51	5-30	2	29.43
87	S. A. Patterson (*Yorks*)	RFM	415.4	118	1,095	37	5-81	1	29.59
88	M. T. Coles (*Essex & Northants*)	RFM	82	16	298	10	3-51	0	29.80
89	O. P. Stone (*Warwicks & England*)	RF	78.3	13	299	10	5-93	1	29.90
90	S. T. Finn (*Middx*)	RFM	171.4	29	600	20	5-75	1	30.00
91	J. Clark (*Surrey*)	RM	151.4	17	636	21	5-77	1	30.28
92	W. M. H. Rhodes (*MCC & Warwicks*)	RFM	165.1	38	489	16	5-17	1	30.56
93	P. W. A. Mulder (*Kent*)	RFM	91.5	22	307	10	4-118	0	30.70
94	E. R. Bamber (*Middx & Glos*)	RFM	210.3	46	587	19	5-93	1	30.89
95	M. Morkel (*Surrey*)	RF	439	99	1,360	44	4-43	0	30.90
96	L. Wood (*Notts & Northants*)	LFM	216.1	36	712	23	5-67	2	30.95
97	D. Olivier (*Yorks*)	RF	390.3	75	1,458	47	5-96	2	31.02
98	D. M. Bess (*MCC, Yorks & Somerset*)	OB	300.4	69	840	27	5-59	1	31.11
99	C. J. Jordan (*Sussex*)	RFM	311	65	972	31	5-53	1	31.35
100	S. Mahmood (*Lancs*)	RFM	196.3	31	660	21	4-48	0	31.42
101	O. P. Rayner (*Middx & Kent*)	OB	238.3	92	475	15	4-58	0	31.66
102	C. N. Miles (*Warwicks*)	RFM	118.4	14	542	17	5-91	1	31.88
103	S. R. Patel (*Notts & Glam*)	SLA	251	62	704	22	4-58	0	32.00
104	W. S. Davis (*Leics*)	RFM	288.5	63	954	29	4-73	0	32.89
105	N. M. Lyon (*Australia*)	OB	242.3	44	668	20	6-49	1	33.40
106	N. L. Buck (*Northants*)	RFM	219.1	41	842	25	5-54	1	33.68
107	G. Stewart (*Kent*)	RFM	135.3	16	514	15	3-37	0	34.26
108	D. Wiese (*Sussex*)	RFM	346.1	69	1,082	31	5-26	2	34.90
109	M. M. Ali (*England & Worcs*)	OB/RM	101.5	15	396	11	3-126	0	36.00
110	C. J. Sayers (*Glos*)	RFM	149.4	39	400	11	3-60	0	36.36
111	M. Labuschagne (*Glam & Australians*)	LB	235.4	23	876	24	3-52	0	36.50
112	M. de Lange (*Glam*)	RF	244.4	33	950	26	4-64	0	36.53
113	L. W. P. Wells (*Sussex*)	LB	167.4	25	571	15	5-63	1	38.06
114	L. V. van Beek (*Derbys*)	RFM	219.2	34	726	19	3-20	0	38.21
115	S. J. Mullaney (*Notts*)	RM	173	36	545	14	4-48	0	38.92
116	L. A. Dawson (*Hants*)	SLA	224.1	48	549	14	4-11	0	39.21

		Style	O	M	R	W	BB	5I	Avge
117	D. M. W. Rawlins (*Sussex*)	SLA	109	12	396	10	3-19	0	39.60
118	B. L. D'Oliveira (*Worcs*)	LB	170.4	22	556	14	7-92	1	39.71
119	G. T. Griffiths (*Leics*)	RFM	128.2	24	439	11	3-71	0	39.90
120	L. J. Carey (*Glam*)	RFM	242.3	50	766	19	4-54	0	40.31
121	J. A. R. Harris (*Middx*)	RFM	273	45	932	23	4-98	0	40.52
122	M. J. J. Critchley (*Derbys*)	LB	256.5	29	935	23	4-107	0	40.65
123	C. McKerr (*Surrey*)	RFM	106	16	416	10	3-40	0	41.60
124	H. J. H. Brookes (*Warwicks*)	RFM	315.3	52	1,350	32	3-100	0	42.18
125	L. A. Procter (*Northants*)	RM	217.1	49	722	17	4-26	0	42.47
126	D. A. Douthwaite (*Cardiff MCCU & Glam*)	RFM	190.1	16	902	21	4-48	0	42.95
127	A. Sakande (*Sussex*)	RFM	146.3	21	568	13	3-74	0	43.69
128	D. L. Lloyd (*Glam*)	RM	128.1	22	437	10	2-35	0	43.70
129	G. G. Wagg (*Glam*)	SLA/LM	236	35	789	17	3-59	0	46.41
130	N. A. Sowter (*Middx*)	LB	180.4	23	650	14	3-42	0	46.42
131	T. van der Gugten (*Glam*)	RFM	198	26	705	15	3-44	0	47.00
132	R. I. Keogh (*Northants*)	OB	234.4	39	819	17	4-15	0	48.17
133	J. T. Ball (*Notts*)	RFM	259.5	46	904	18	3-26	0	50.22
134	P. Coughlin (*Notts*)	RFM	144.4	19	582	11	3-37	0	52.90
135	B. W. M. Mike (*Leics & Warwicks*)	RFM	140.3	15	649	12	3-41	0	54.08
136	A. W. Finch (*Worcs*)	RM	177.2	31	682	12	2-23	0	56.83
137	C. N. Ackermann (*Leics*)	OB	180	22	703	12	5-69	1	58.58

BOWLING STYLES

LB	Leg-breaks (7)		**RF**	Right-arm fast (7)
LF	Left-arm fast (1)		**RFM**	Right-arm fast medium (82)
LFM	Left-arm fast medium (9)		**RM**	Right-arm medium (11)
LM	Left-arm medium (2)		**SLA**	Slow left-arm (8)
OB	Off-breaks (13)			

Note: The total comes to 140 because M. M. Ali, O. E. Robinson and G. G. Wagg have two styles of bowling.

INDIVIDUAL SCORES OF 100 AND OVER

There were **205** three-figure innings in 149 first-class matches in 2019, which was 39 more than in 2018, when 147 matches were played. Of these, 11 were double-hundreds, compared with six in 2018. The list includes 164 in the County Championship, compared with 136 in 2018.

D. P. Sibley (6)
128 MCC v Surrey, Dubai
132 Warwicks v Kent, Birmingham
109* Warwicks v Hants, Birmingham
244 Warwicks v Kent, Canterbury
215* } Warwicks v Notts, Nottingham
109

G. S. Ballance (5)
101* Yorks v Notts, Nottingham
148 Yorks v Hants, Southampton
159 Yorks v Kent, Canterbury
100 Yorks v Hants, Leeds
111 Yorks v Somerset, Leeds

M. Labuschagne (5)
121 Glam v Northants, Cardiff
137 Glam v Glos, Newport
182 Glam v Sussex, Hove
106 } Glam v Worcs, Cardiff
100

M. H. Azad (4)
139 Leics v Loughborough MCCU, Leicester
137 } Leics v Glos, Leicester
100*
121 Leics v Glos, Cheltenham

C. D. J. Dent (4)
176 Glos v Leics, Leicester
105 Glos v Glam, Bristol
125 Glos v Leics, Cheltenham
169 Glos v Derbys, Derby

B. A. Godleman (4)
227 Derbys v Glam, Swansea
102 Derbys v Middx, Derby
111 Derbys v Lancs, Manchester
106 Derbys v Sussex, Derby

R. J. Higgins (4)
103 Glos v Glam, Newport
119* Glos v Sussex, Arundel
199 Glos v Leics, Leicester
101 Glos v Derbys, Derby

D. J. Malan (4)
160* Middx v Northants, Northampton
124 Middx v Worcs, Worcester
199 Middx v Derbys, Derby
166 Middx v Glam, Cardiff

S. A. Northeast (4)
118 Hants v Oxford MCCU, Oxford
169 Hants v Essex, Southampton
133 Hants v Notts, Newclose
101 Hants v Somerset, Taunton

S. W. Billings (3)
100 Kent v Notts, Nottingham
138 } Kent v Yorks, Leeds
122*

B. C. Brown (3)
156 Sussex v Northants, Northampton
131 Sussex v Glam, Hove
107 Sussex v Middx, Lord's

J. M. Clarke (3)
112 Notts v Yorks, Nottingham
125 } Notts v Warwicks, Nottingham
112

S. R. Dickson (3)
108* Kent v Loughborough MCCU, Canterbury
128 Kent v Surrey, Beckenham
161 Kent v Warwicks, Canterbury

T. Köhler-Cadmore (3)
176 Yorks v Leeds/Bradford MCCU, Leeds
102 Yorks v Somerset, Leeds
165* Yorks v Warwicks, Birmingham

T. C. Lace (3)
143 Derbys v Glam, Swansea
132* Derbys v Worcs, Kidderminster
125 Derbys v Glos, Derby

A. Z. Lees (3)
107* Durham v Derbys, Chester-le-Street
143 Durham v Sussex, Hove
181 Durham v Leics, Chester-le-Street

O. J. D. Pope (3)
251 Surrey v MCC, Dubai
221* Surrey v Hants, The Oval
106 Surrey v Notts, The Oval

S. P. D. Smith (3)
144 } Australia v England, Birmingham
142
211 Australia v England, Manchester

S. van Zyl (3)
103   Sussex v Cardiff MCCU, Hove
101* Sussex v Durham, Chester-le-Street
173   Sussex v Middx, Lord's

M. S. Wade (3)
114   Australian XI v England Lions, Canterbury
110   Australia v England, Birmingham
117   Australia v England, The Oval

C. T. Bancroft (2)
158   Durham v Sussex, Hove
109   Durham v Leics, Leicester

G. A. Bartlett (2)
133   Somerset v Notts, Nottingham
137   Somerset v Surrey, Guildford

T. Bavuma (2)
103   Northants v Lancs, Northampton
134   Northants v Derbys, Chesterfield

R. S. Bopara (2)
107   Essex v Hants, Southampton
135   Essex v Notts, Nottingham

S. G. Borthwick (2)
100   Surrey v Hants, The Oval
137   Surrey v Notts, The Oval

J. R. Bracey (2)
152   Glos v Glam, Newport
116* Glos v Derbys, Derby

R. J. Burns (2)
107   Surrey v Somerset, Taunton
133   England v Australia, Birmingham

A. N. Cook (2)
150* Essex v Cambridge MCCU, Cambridge
125   Essex v Kent, Chelmsford

Z. Crawley (2)
108   Kent v Warwicks, Birmingham
111   Kent v Notts, Tunbridge Wells

J. L. Denly (2)
167* Kent v Notts, Tunbridge Wells
154   Kent v Hants, Southampton

B. M. Duckett (2)
216   Notts v Cambridge MCCU, Cambridge
140   Notts v Warwicks, Birmingham

J. L. du Plooy (2)
118   Derbys v Middx, Derby
100* Derbys v Middx, Lord's

S. R. Hain (2)
129*⎫
104 ⎬ Warwicks v Hants, Southampton

T. M. Head (2)
139* Australian XI v England Lions, Canterbury
109* Australians v Worcs, Worcester

J. C. Hildreth (2)
158* Somerset v Cardiff MCCU, Taunton
105   Somerset v Hants, Taunton

R. I. Keogh (2)
150   Northants v Glam, Cardiff
132   Northants v Leics, Leicester

W. L. Madsen (2)
123   Derbys v Leeds/Bradford MCCU, Derby
204* Derbys v Glos, Bristol

D. K. H. Mitchell (2)
114   Worcs v Leics, Leicester
139   Worcs v Glam, Worcester

S. J. Mullaney (2)
102   Notts v Hants, Newclose
179   Notts v Warwicks, Nottingham

R. I. Newton (2)
118   Northants v Durham MCCU, Northampton
105   Northants v Glam, Cardiff

L. M. Reece (2)
111   Derbys v Glam, Derby
184   Derbys v Sussex, Derby

O. G. Robinson (2)
143   Kent v Warwicks, Birmingham
103   Kent v Yorks, Canterbury

S. D. Robson (2)
107   Middx v Glam, Radlett
140* Middx v Glam, Cardiff

W. T. Root (2)
126   Glam v Northants, Cardiff
229   Glam v Northants, Northampton

P. D. Salt (2)
122   Sussex v Northants, Northampton
103   Sussex v Glam, Hove

J. A. Simpson (2)
115   Middx v Derbys, Derby
167* Middx v Lancs, Manchester

B. A. Stokes (2)
115* England v Australia, Lord's
135* England v Australia, Leeds

R. N. ten Doeschate (2)
130 Essex v Surrey, The Oval
103 Essex v Surrey, Chelmsford

D. J. Vilas (2)
132* Lancs v Sussex, Manchester
266 Lancs v Glam, Colwyn Bay

R. S. Vasconcelos (2)
184 Northants v Glam, Cardiff
105* Northants v Durham, Chester-le-Street

J. M. Vince (2)
139 Hants v Oxford MCCU, Oxford
142 Hants v Somerset, Southampton

The following each played one three-figure innings:

T. B. Abell, 101, Somerset v Notts, Nottingham; T. P. Alsop, 150, Hants v Warwicks, Birmingham; T. R. Ambrose, 107, Warwicks v Kent, Birmingham.

D. J. Bell-Drummond, 166, Kent v Warwicks, Canterbury; J. J. Bohannon, 174, Lancs v Derbys, Manchester; K. C. Brathwaite, 103*, Glam v Leics, Cardiff; H. C. Brook, 101, Yorks v Somerset, Leeds; N. L. J. Browne, 163, Essex v Notts, Nottingham; J. A. Burns, 133, Australia A v Sussex, Arundel; E. J. Byrom, 115*, Somerset v Cardiff MCCU, Taunton.

K. S. Carlson, 111, Glam v Northants, Cardiff; J. J. Cobb, 139, Northants v Durham MCCU, Northampton; M. J. Cosgrove, 107*, Leics v Durham, Chester-le-Street; O. B. Cox, 100*, Worcs v Leics, Leicester.

A. L. Davies, 147, Lancs v Northants, Northampton; S. M. Davies, 109, Somerset v Warwicks, Birmingham; L. A. Dawson, 103, Hants v Somerset, Southampton; N. J. Dexter, 180, Leics v Glos, Leicester; B. L. D'Oliveira, 103, Worcs v Glam, Cardiff; A. H. T. Donald, 173, Hants v Warwicks, Southampton; D. A. Douthwaite, 100*, Cardiff MCCU v Sussex, Hove.

E. J. H. Eckersley, 118, Durham v Sussex, Hove; D. Elgar, 103, Surrey v Somerset, Taunton; S. S. Eskinazi, 125, Middx v Oxford MCCU, Northwood; L. J. Evans, 113, Sussex v Worcs, Kidderminster.

C. J. Ferguson, 127, Worcs v Derbys, Kidderminster; W. A. R. Fraine, 106, Yorks v Surrey, Scarborough.

L. Gregory, 129*, Somerset v Surrey, Taunton; N. R. T. Gubbins, 105, Middx v Oxford MCCU, Northwood.

H. Hameed, 117, Lancs v Middx, Lord's; G. T. Hargrave, 146, Oxford Univ v Cambridge Univ, Cambridge; M. S. Harris, 109, Australia A v Sussex, Arundel; G. J. Harte, 108*, Durham v Durham MCCU, Chester-le-Street; I. G. Holland, 143, Hants v Warwicks, Southampton; P. J. Horton, 100*, Leics v Glos, Leicester; A. J. Hose, 111, Warwicks v Notts, Birmingham; H. R. Hosein, 138*, Derbys v Leeds/Bradford MCCU, Derby; A. L. Hughes, 109*, Derbys v Glos, Bristol.

W. G. Jacks, 120, Surrey v Kent, Beckenham; A. Javid, 143, Leics v Loughborough MCCU, Leicester; R. P. Jones, 122, Lancs v Middx, Lord's; C. J. Jordan, 166, Sussex v Northants, Northampton.

M. J. Lamb, 173, Warwicks v Essex, Birmingham; D. W. Lawrence, 147, Essex v Surrey, Chelmsford; L. S. Livingstone, 114, Lancs v Leics, Liverpool.

F. S. Organ, 100, Hants v Kent, Southampton.

R. S. Patel, 100*, Surrey v Essex, The Oval; D. Pretorius, 111, Northants v Worcs, Northampton.

A. M. Rahane, 119, Hants v Notts, Newclose; D. M. W. Rawlins, 100, Sussex v Lancs, Manchester; W. M. H. Rhodes, 109, Warwicks v Kent, Canterbury; G. H. Roderick, 158, Glos v Sussex, Arundel; J. E. Root, 130*, Yorks v Notts, Nottingham; H. D. Rutherford, 123, Worcs v Leics, Leicester.

N. J. Selman, 150, Glam v Glos, Newport; B. T. Slater, 130, Notts v Cambridge MCCU, Cambridge; J. L. Smith, 127, Surrey v MCC, Dubai; W. R. Smith, 179, Durham v Durham MCCU, Chester-le-Street; D. I. Stevens, 237, Kent v Yorks, Leeds; P. R. Stirling, 138, Middx v Glam, Radlett; M. D. Stoneman, 100, Surrey v Yorks, Scarborough.

J. A. Tattersall, 135*, Yorks v Leeds/Bradford MCCU, Leeds.

G. G. Wagg, 100, Glam v Derbys, Swansea; A. G. Wakely, 102, Northants v Worcs, Northampton; B-J. Watling, 104*, Durham v Glam, Chester-le-Street; M. H. Wessels, 118, Worcs v Durham, Worcester; T. Westley, 141, Essex v Warwicks, Birmingham; A. J. A. Wheater, 130, Essex v Cambridge MCCU, Cambridge; D. Wiese, 139, Sussex v Cardiff MCCU, Hove.

R. M. Yates, 141, Warwicks v Somerset, Birmingham.

FASTEST HUNDREDS BY BALLS...

Balls
80	D. Wiese	Sussex v Cardiff MCCU, Hove.
89	R. F. Higgins	Gloucestershire v Glamorgan, Newport.
90	P. D. Salt	Sussex v Northamptonshire, Northampton.
93	S. J. Mullaney	Nottinghamshire v Warwickshire, Nottingham.
95	B. M. Duckett	Nottinghamshire v Cambridge MCCU, Cambridge.
99	D. M. W. Rawlins	Sussex v Lancashire, Manchester.

...AND THE SLOWEST

Balls
277	R. S. Patel	Surrey v Essex, The Oval.
266	T. C. Lace	Derbyshire v Worcestershire, Kidderminster.
261	M. J. Cosgrove	Leicestershire v Durham, Chester-le-Street.
256	M. H. Azad	Leicestershire v Gloucestershire, Cheltenham.
250	N. L. J. Browne	Essex v Nottinghamshire, Nottingham.

TEN WICKETS IN A MATCH

There were **23** instances of bowlers taking ten or more wickets in a first-class match in 2019, the same as in 2018. All were in the County Championship.

O. E. Robinson (3)
10-148 Sussex v Middx, Lord's
10-132 Sussex v Northants, Hove
14-135 Sussex v Middx, Hove

K. A. Maharaj (2)
10-127 Yorks v Somerset, Leeds
10-176 Yorks v Somerset, Taunton

S. R. Harmer (2)
11-170 Essex v Kent, Chelmsford
12-61   Essex v Hants, Chelmsford

J. S. Patel (2)
12-89   Warwicks v Surrey, Birmingham
10-88   Warwicks v Notts, Birmingham

The following each took ten wickets in a match on one occasion:

K. J. Abbott, 17-86, Hants v Somerset, Southampton; R. Ashwin, 12-144, Notts v Surrey, Nottingham.
T. E. Bailey, 10-119, Lancs v Middx, Manchester; G. J. Batty, 10-111, Surrey v Warwicks, Birmingham.
S. J. Cook, 12-65, Essex v Kent, Canterbury.
R. J. Gleeson, 10-113, Lancs v Northants, Manchester; L. Gregory, 11-53, Somerset v Kent, Canterbury.
M. W. Parkinson, 10-165, Lancs v Sussex, Manchester.
T. S. Roland-Jones, 10-79, Middx v Glos, Northwood; C. Rushworth, 10-67, Durham v Worcestershire, Chester-le-Street.
B. W. Sanderson, 10-55, Northants v Sussex, Hove; D. I. Stevens, 10-92, Kent v Notts, Nottingham.
T. A. I. Taylor, 10-122, Leics v Sussex, Hove.
G. S. Virdi, 14-139, Surrey v Notts, Nottingham.

SPECSAVERS COUNTY CHAMPIONSHIP IN 2019

Neville Scott

***Division One** 1 Essex 2 Somerset*
***Division Two** 1 Lancashire 2 Northamptonshire 3 Gloucestershire*

Even as Essex and Somerset prepared to meet in a title-deciding showdown to a gripping campaign, the legal representative of one former prime minister, John Major, was arguing his case in the Supreme Court against the incumbent, Boris Johnson, for misleading the monarch in order to prorogue parliament. The improbable barristers deployed in a uniquely improbable case included Lord Pannick and Lord Keen, names apparently borrowed from the pages of pantomime or restoration farce.

Johnson lost that battle. But, three months on, he resoundingly won the war, with a landslide at the polls. And by then, the absurdity had advanced into cricket. Somerset, already thwarted by Taunton rain as **Essex** claimed the crown, were later – 53 days later – held by an ECB Cricket Discipline Commission panel to have produced a "poor pitch". The verdict carried a 12-point penalty for the 2020 campaign, with another 12 suspended for two years. Not until December 13, on the day Johnson celebrated victory, did the matter finally rest, as Somerset announced they would not appeal, lamenting the

COUNTY CHAMPIONSHIP TABLES

Division One

		M	W	L	D	Bonus pts		Pen	Pts
						Bat	Bowl		
1	Essex (**3**)	14	9	1	4	26	38	0	228
2	Somerset (**2**)	14	9	3	2	25	38	0	217
3	Hampshire (**5**)	14	5	3	6	31	36	1	176
4	Kent (**2**)	14	5	5	4	36	36	0	172
5	Yorkshire (**4**)	14	5	4	5	24	36	0	165
6	Surrey (**1**)	14	2	6	6	33	38	0	133
7	Warwickshire (*1*)	14	3	6	5	26	32	0	131
8	Nottinghamshire (**6**) . . .	14	0	10	4	16	32	1	67

Division Two

		M	W	L	D	Bonus pts		Pen	Pts
						Bat	Bowl		
1	Lancashire (**7**)	14	8	0	6	34	41	0	233
2	Northamptonshire (*9*) . . .	14	5	2	7	35	38	0	188
3	Gloucestershire (*5*)	14	5	3	6	36	36	0	182
4	Glamorgan (*10*)	14	4	3	7	35	34	1	167
5	Durham (*8*)	14	5	5	4	21	36	0	157
6	Sussex (*3*)	14	4	5	5	32	35	0	156
7	Derbyshire (*7*)	14	4	6	4	23	38	0	145
8	Middlesex (*4*)	14	3	5	6	24	33	2	133
9	Worcestershire (**8**)	14	3	7	4	20	37	0	125
10	Leicestershire (*6*)	14	1	6	7	24	32	0	107

2018 positions are shown in brackets: Division One in bold, Division Two in italic.
Win = 16pts; tie = 8pts; draw = 5pts. **Penalties for slow over-rates.**

"heavy burden of proof" demanded to overturn the decision. The voice of the ECB seemed to dictate their final comment: "The club notes the strong message the panel ruling sends to all first-class counties."

One hopes they are right. Cricket had narrowly escaped becoming a laughing stock, and the danger persists. Had Somerset, amid high media interest, claimed a historic maiden Championship title, prompting open-top bus parades around the county, they would presumably have been stripped of the honour, like some wretched subaltern publicly cashiered.

The pitch problem, compounded by fixtures perennially banished to April and autumn, remains the most unenviable to resolve. But, for years, penalties have been applied too sparingly; real deterrence has been lacking. A sanction of 12 points (four fewer than the reward for a win) hardly seems condign, while pitch preparation for pivotal matches in the final few rounds could surely be more closely monitored. The Championship, already marginalised and devalued, flirted with farce in 2019. It may not elude ridicule next time.

The penalty meant that key Taunton game, eagerly awaited for over two months, was in retrospect not key at all. It was, anyway, largely washed out – unsurprisingly, since it began on the autumn equinox. Despite forfeiting an innings on the final evening, and bidding to dismiss Essex in just over an hour, **Somerset** were foiled again, runners-up for the fifth time in ten seasons. They are one of only three counties never to have taken the title.

Sixteen weeks earlier, on the anniversary of D-Day, their hopes were high: there was a sense of "it's June, it's Guildford, it must be the decider" when they beat Surrey to go top. In the previous two summers, results at Woodbridge Road around this time had proved the turning point. **Surrey**, sitting champions, suffered a second successive defeat, and were evidently in decline; injuries, England calls and a disappointing season for Morne Morkel mocked their early status as favourites. Newly tagged as prospective champions, Somerset's main challengers now seemed to be Hampshire and Yorkshire, not Essex. Next round, when they became the sole side to cheat widespread downpours, beating Kent away in the equivalent of four sessions, their lead extended further: June 13 found Essex fourth, 50 points behind, though with a game in hand.

A month earlier, in dry conditions, Ilkley Moor was on fire. So, too, were **Yorkshire**. Wins in two of their first three games, and three for **Hampshire** in their opening four, had set the pace, until both slipped back. Yorkshire, fielding an expensive, but too often blunt, spearhead in Kolpak player Duanne Olivier, continued to move away from the home-grown side that had brought consecutive titles four years earlier, and Hampshire remained a team who only inconsistently translated their reliance on imported talent into victory. Each, though, retained the capacity to scupper Somerset, who, for all their early success, still had to meet both sides, plus Essex, away in their final eight games. Decisively, each of these three fixtures would be lost.

Essex enjoyed their game in hand, hammering Hampshire by an innings, the momentum on home soil picking up. It proved unstoppable: they won every match at Chelmsford. With pitches to suit his off-spin, Simon Harmer, the South African Kolpak who as in 2017 was their man of the season, claimed 56 wickets there at 13 (against 27 at 28 away), despite Essex winning just one

Philip Brown, Popperfoto/Getty Images

Cut-out for glory: the triumphant Essex team, plus cardboard figure of Peter Siddle, at Taunton.

toss all summer. That was in the next game, when it was Alastair Cook who determined the first of Somerset's three critical away defeats. After raging thunderstorms overnight, he completed scores of 80 and 47 in a contest that saw a best of 40 in the other 42 innings. On June 26, with all first-division sides exactly halfway through, the Somerset advantage had been cut to 13 points.

Three rounds later, in mid-July, Essex took the lead. In a catastrophic visit to Leeds, Somerset exercised their right to field, conceded 520 and, following on, emerged with a solitary point from an innings defeat. Keshav Maharaj's left-arm spin claimed half their wickets. From the start, following a uniquely dry and hot February, there had been signs that spin would become a theme of the summer: in early April, the occasional off-breaks of Glenn Maxwell and Colin Ackermann had brought maiden five-wicket bags, and wins for Lancashire and Leicestershire respectively. At the end of May, Warwickshire inflicted the first of Surrey's six defeats when, on the final day at Edgbaston, both Gareth Batty and Jeetan Patel claimed career-best eight-fors. And in mid-July, four spinners – Harmer, Maharaj, Ravichandran Ashwin and Amar Virdi – shared 44 wickets in three games.

Glaringly, just two of this octet were English: Batty and Virdi, who – four days before turning 21 – became the first spinner to take 14 or more in a match for Surrey since 1968, as they inflicted the fourth of seven consecutive Nottinghamshire defeats. Somerset's own main spinner, Jack Leach, missed the Leeds debacle after selection for England Lions, and Test call-ups meant he missed five matches in all; England duties also claimed Craig Overton and Lewis Gregory in a season where Essex remained almost wholly unaffected.

When Essex prevailed in 2017, Harmer was crucially supported by Jamie Porter's pace; the 2019 triumph was more patently inspired by Harmer alone. Not since Sussex's twin successes of 2006 – when Mushtaq Ahmed was the last bowler to take 100 wickets in a season – and 2007 had a Championship been so conclusively determined by spin. It proved central to relegation, too. With only one team due to go down as the ECB altered the balance between the divisions, the 64 wickets claimed by Patel, also an outstanding leader, willed injury-ravaged Warwickshire to avoid the drop, whereas Ashwin's 34 from five late appearances could not rescue Nottinghamshire, by then shot in mind and spirit. It remains a crippling deficiency of the English game that, by importing quality spinners, a county can almost guarantee wickets against home batsmen denied any real exposure to the art; yet English spinners fail to emerge because the ECB insistently consign four-day play to the margins, reserving high summer for instant cricket alone.

On top at last on July 16, fifty years after Apollo 11 took off for the moon, Essex had landed. Or so it seemed. In fact, they maintained their supremacy for only two rounds before Somerset regained the lead, though that was in September, on the other side of the yawning T20 gap. In the intervening one-off August round, Essex somehow beat Kent amid yet more carnage at Canterbury: on the third (and last) day of a rain-affected game, 26 wickets fell, 12 lbw, on a pitch keeping low. Despite a first-innings deficit of 112, Essex dismissed Kent for 40, their lowest Championship total since 1952, and scraped home by three wickets. That kept them two points ahead but, when the race resumed, they drew in Birmingham while Somerset were winning in Taunton, to lead by eight entering their penultimate match. Another South African Kolpak then sealed their fate.

Kyle Abbott collected 17 Somerset wickets for 86, the fourth-best match figures in a Championship game, and the best in first-class cricket since Jim Laker's Ashes return of 19 for 90 in 1956. That was not all: coming in at 103 for eight, with Hampshire only 157 ahead in their second innings, he batted 28.4 overs, mostly in support of James Vince, to help set a target of 281, far beyond Somerset's reach.

That they should be sunk by overseas influence seemed harsh; it was no surprise that they also signed a quality Kolpak, Vernon Philander, in the new year. And Essex, too, had nurtured rich local talent, players who grew up with the mutual obligation and commitment that long association may instil; the same ethos had rewarded Surrey in 2018, Yorkshire three years earlier, Lancashire and Durham before that. But the pivotal performers over the last three seasons have been Kolpaks: Harmer in 2017 and 2019, Morkel in 2018. Each added one decisive final piece. Foreign talent has become fundamental, one more factor threatening to make Championships the preserve of the wealthy alone. With little apparent concern for poorer counties, whose best players soon decamp, the ECB feed the suspicion that a cull will one day come, perhaps to a dozen teams.

Johnson's election win, however, may close the Kolpak route. As he steered the United Kingdom out of the European Union, the ECB wrote to the counties advising them that, on their current understanding, they expected Kolpaks to remain eligible as local players in 2020, under the EU law that would still apply during the government transition period; by implication, that status was likely to disappear after December 31. The Professional Cricketers' Association

responded by backing calls for counties to be allowed two official o
players, to protect the contracts of their Kolpak members. It would be a sur
if the ECB resisted this; performance-related payments to counties who ha
promoted home cricketers and resisted the import route have never been
lucrative enough to influence club policies. And Kolpaks are just part of it:
overall, around 30% of all Championship appearances in the last decade have
been made by players whose formative cricket, before they turned 16, was
learned abroad – a lamentable reflection on the extent to which the grassroots
game (outside private schools) has been allowed to atrophy in Britain. Foreign
players, recruited for county and England cricket, are but symptoms, and
deserve no blame. It is the ECB who have evaded the real issue: the decline of
cricket across the wider community at home.

Meanwhile, unfancied **Kent** flew the flag for lesser brethren with a 433-run
victory in Leeds, the fourth-most emphatic by runs in Championship history,
which left Yorkshire fifth in the final table. Kent ended fourth, four points
behind Hampshire, whom they met in a final fixture that also fell foul of those
equinoctal storms. **Warwickshire**, so depleted that they required 14 seamers,
came through with immense character to finish seventh, two points behind
Surrey – and with almost double the 67 managed by winless **Nottinghamshire**,
who went into the campaign full of hope, vigour, and recruits from other
teams, but emerged a relegated rabble.

If the title race was tense, the fight to escape Division Two became a mass
brawl. **Lancashire**, for whom Jimmy Anderson claimed 30 scalps at 9.36 –
the lowest Championship average in history for any bowler with more than 16
wickets – were unassailable. But, in a restless migration up and down the table,
every other side retained hopes of promotion. **Northamptonshire**, bottom of
the pile at the halfway stage, finished second, and **Gloucestershire** jumped
from next to bottom after eight games to third, following excellent back-to-
back wins in tight finishes at Cheltenham. Both counties were a credit to their
understated coaches, David Ripley and Richard Dawson; it felt like one in the
eye for the ECB when they snatched the remaining promotion berths, but they
will start as relegation favourites this year. **Glamorgan**, awash with runs from
Marnus Labuschagne on docile home pitches, but conceding even more per
wicket than they scored, declined to fourth once he joined Australia, and
Durham, fifth, never quite overcame defeats in their opening four games.

For **Sussex**, Will Beer batted 461 minutes beside the castle at Arundel,
only to miss the slowest hundred in all English first-class cricket when he
departed, three short of a maiden century. It still eludes him, and in a hit-and-
miss season his side finished sixth. At the summer's start, **Derbyshire**
maintained an unchanged team through four games for only the second time
in 42 years, winning two. They ended seventh, ahead of an underperforming
Middlesex side that clearly had deep problems with team culture. **Worcestershire** were among the eight contenders who occupied one of the three
promotion places at some stage in the summer but, losing five times in the
second half, ended ninth. **Leicestershire**, second only to Glamorgan in
reliance on second-rank overseas players, reverted to their traditional role this
decade as holders of the wooden spoon.

...g (best available prices): *Division One* – 5-2 Surrey; 9-2 ESSEX; 15-2 ...e; 8-1 Hampshire, Somerset and Yorkshire; 9-1 Warwickshire; 20-1 Kent. *Division* ...LANCASHIRE; 3-1 Middlesex; 4-1 Sussex; 8-1 Worcestershire; 20-1 Leicestershire; ...am and Gloucestershire; 28-1 Derbyshire; 33-1 Glamorgan and Northamptonshire.

Prize money

Division One
£532,100 for winners: ESSEX.
£221,020 for runners-up: SOMERSET.
£103,022 for third: HAMPSHIRE.
£32,121 for fourth: KENT.
£24,000 for fifth: YORKSHIRE.

Division Two
£111,050 for winners: LANCASHIRE.
£51,052 for runners-up: NORTHAMPTONSHIRE.

Leaders: *Division One* – from April 8 Hampshire; April 13 Somerset; May 30 Hampshire; June 6 Somerset; July 16 Essex; September 12 Somerset; September 18 Essex; Essex became champions on September 26.
Division Two – from April 8 Leicestershire; April 14 Derbyshire; May 17 Worcestershire; May 22 Lancashire; June 26 Glamorgan; July 10 Lancashire; Lancashire became champions on September 16.
Bottom place: *Division One* – from April 14 Warwickshire; May 30 Nottinghamshire.
Division Two – from April 14 Durham; June 27 Northamptonshire; July 2 Middlesex; July 9 Leicestershire.

Scoring of Points

(a) For a win, 16 points plus any points scored in the first innings.
(b) In a tie, each side score eight points, plus any points scored in the first innings.
(c) In a drawn match, each side score five points, plus any points scored in the first innings.
(d) If the scores are equal in a drawn match, the side batting in the fourth innings score eight points, plus any points scored in the first innings, and the opposing side score five points, plus any points scored in the first innings.
(e) First-innings points (awarded only for performances in the first 110 overs of each first innings and retained whatever the result of the match):
 (i) A maximum of five batting points to be available: 200 to 249 runs – 1 point; 250 to 299 runs – 2 points; 300 to 349 runs – 3 points; 350 to 399 runs – 4 points; 400 runs or over – 5 points. Penalty runs awarded within the first 110 overs of each first innings count towards the award of bonus points.
 (ii) A maximum of three bowling points to be available: 3 to 5 wickets taken – 1 point; 6 to 8 wickets taken – 2 points; 9 to 10 wickets taken – 3 points.
(f) If a match is abandoned without a ball being bowled, each side score five points.
(g) The side who have the highest aggregate of points shall be the champion county of their respective division. Should any sides in the Championship table be equal on points, the following tie-breakers will be applied in the order stated: most wins, fewest losses, team achieving most points in head-to-head contests, most wickets taken, most runs scored.
(h) The minimum over-rate to be achieved by counties will be 16 overs per hour. Overs will be calculated at the end of the match, and penalties applied on a match-by-match basis. For each over (ignoring fractions) that a side have bowled short of the target number, one point will be deducted from their Championship total.
(i) Penalties for poor and unfit pitches are at the discretion of the Cricket Discipline Commission.

Under ECB playing conditions, two extras were scored for every no-ball bowled, whether scored off or not, and one for every wide. Any runs scored off the bat were credited to the batsman, while byes and leg-byes were counted as no-balls or wides, as appropriate, in accordance with Law 24.13, in addition to the initial penalty.

CONSTITUTION OF COUNTY CHAMPIONSHIP

At least four possible dates have been given for the start of county cricket in England. The first, patchy, references began in 1825. The earliest mention in any cricket publication is in 1864, and eight counties have come to be regarded as first-class from that date, including Cambridgeshire, who dropped out after 1871. For many years, the County Championship was considered to have started in 1873, when regulations governing qualification first applied; indeed, a special commemorative stamp was issued by the Post Office in 1973. However, the Championship was not formally organised until 1890, and before then champions were proclaimed by the press; sometimes publications differed in their views, and no definitive list of champions can start before that date. Eight teams contested the 1890 competition – Gloucestershire, Kent, Lancashire, Middlesex, Nottinghamshire, Surrey, Sussex and Yorkshire. Somerset joined the following year, and in 1895 the Championship began to acquire something of its modern shape, when Derbyshire, Essex, Hampshire, Leicestershire and Warwickshire were added. At that point, MCC officially recognised the competition's existence. Worcestershire, Northamptonshire and Glamorgan were admitted in 1899, 1905 and 1921 respectively, and are regarded as first-class from these dates. An invitation in 1921 to Buckinghamshire to enter the Championship was declined, owing to the lack of necessary playing facilities, and an application by Devon in 1948 was unsuccessful. Durham were admitted in 1992, and granted first-class status prior to their pre-season tour of Zimbabwe.

In 2000, the Championship was split for the first time into two divisions, on the basis of counties' standings in the 1999 competition. From 2000 onwards, the bottom three teams in Division One were relegated at the end of the season, and the top three teams in Division Two promoted. From 2006, this was changed to two teams relegated and two promoted. In 2016, two were relegated and one promoted, to create divisions of eight and ten teams. In 2019, one was relegated and three promoted, to change the balance to ten teams in Division One and eight in Division Two.

COUNTY CHAMPIONS

The title of champion county is unreliable before 1890. In 1963, *Wisden* formally accepted the list of champions "most generally selected" by contemporaries, as researched by Rowland Bowen (see *Wisden 1959*, page 91). This appears to be the most accurate available list but has no official status. The county champions from 1864 to 1889 were, according to Bowen: 1864 Surrey; 1865 Nottinghamshire; 1866 Middlesex; 1867 Yorkshire; 1868 Nottinghamshire; 1869 Nottinghamshire and Yorkshire; 1870 Yorkshire; 1871 Nottinghamshire; 1872 Nottinghamshire; 1873 Gloucestershire and Nottinghamshire; 1874 Gloucestershire; 1875 Nottinghamshire; 1876 Gloucestershire; 1877 Gloucestershire; 1878 undecided; 1879 Lancashire and Nottinghamshire; 1880 Nottinghamshire; 1881 Lancashire; 1882 Lancashire and Nottinghamshire; 1883 Nottinghamshire; 1884 Nottinghamshire; 1885 Nottinghamshire; 1886 Nottinghamshire; 1887 Surrey; 1888 Surrey; 1889 Lancashire, Nottinghamshire and Surrey.

1890	Surrey	1910	Kent	1934	Lancashire
1891	Surrey	1911	Warwickshire	1935	Yorkshire
1892	Surrey	1912	Yorkshire	1936	Derbyshire
1893	Yorkshire	1913	Kent	1937	Yorkshire
1894	Surrey	1914	Surrey	1938	Yorkshire
1895	Surrey	1919	Yorkshire	1939	Yorkshire
1896	Yorkshire	1920	Middlesex	1946	Yorkshire
1897	Lancashire	1921	Middlesex	1947	Middlesex
1898	Yorkshire	1922	Yorkshire	1948	Glamorgan
1899	Surrey	1923	Yorkshire	1949 {	Middlesex
1900	Yorkshire	1924	Yorkshire		Yorkshire
1901	Yorkshire	1925	Yorkshire	1950 {	Lancashire
1902	Yorkshire	1926	Lancashire		Surrey
1903	Middlesex	1927	Lancashire	1951	Warwickshire
1904	Lancashire	1928	Lancashire	1952	Surrey
1905	Yorkshire	1929	Nottinghamshire	1953	Surrey
1906	Kent	1930	Lancashire	1954	Surrey
1907	Nottinghamshire	1931	Yorkshire	1955	Surrey
1908	Yorkshire	1932	Yorkshire	1956	Surrey
1909	Kent	1933	Yorkshire	1957	Surrey

1958 Surrey	1978 Kent	1999 Surrey
1959 Yorkshire	1979 Essex	2000 Surrey
1960 Yorkshire	1980 Middlesex	2001 Yorkshire
1961 Hampshire	1981 Nottinghamshire	2002 Surrey
1962 Yorkshire	1982 Middlesex	2003 Sussex
1963 Yorkshire	1983 Essex	2004 Warwickshire
1964 Worcestershire	1984 Essex	2005 Nottinghamshire
1965 Worcestershire	1985 Middlesex	2006 Sussex
1966 Yorkshire	1986 Essex	2007 Sussex
1967 Yorkshire	1987 Nottinghamshire	2008 Durham
1968 Yorkshire	1988 Worcestershire	2009 Durham
1969 Glamorgan	1989 Worcestershire	2010 Nottinghamshire
1970 Kent	1990 Middlesex	2011 Lancashire
1971 Surrey	1991 Essex	2012 Warwickshire
1972 Warwickshire	1992 Essex	2013 Durham
1973 Hampshire	1993 Middlesex	2014 Yorkshire
1974 Worcestershire	1994 Warwickshire	2015 Yorkshire
1975 Leicestershire	1995 Warwickshire	2016 Middlesex
1976 Middlesex	1996 Leicestershire	2017 Essex
1977 { Middlesex / Kent }	1997 Glamorgan	2018 Surrey
	1998 Leicestershire	2019 Essex

Notes: Since the Championship was constituted in 1890, it has been won outright as follows: Yorkshire 32 times, Surrey 19, Middlesex 11, Essex and Lancashire 8, Warwickshire 7, Kent and Nottinghamshire 6, Worcestershire 5, Durham, Glamorgan, Leicestershire and Sussex 3, Hampshire 2, Derbyshire 1. Gloucestershire, Northamptonshire and Somerset have never won.

The title has been shared three times since 1890, involving Middlesex twice, Kent, Lancashire, Surrey and Yorkshire.

Wooden spoons: Since the major expansion of the Championship from nine teams to 14 in 1895, the counties have finished outright bottom as follows: Derbyshire 16, Leicestershire 14, Somerset 12, Glamorgan and Northamptonshire 11, Gloucestershire 9, Nottinghamshire and Sussex 8, Worcestershire 6, Durham and Hampshire 5, Warwickshire 3, Essex and Kent 2, Yorkshire 1. Lancashire, Middlesex and Surrey have never finished bottom. Leicestershire have also shared bottom place twice, once with Hampshire and once with Somerset.

From 1977 to 1983 the Championship was sponsored by Schweppes, from 1984 to 1998 by Britannic Assurance, from 1999 to 2000 by PPP healthcare, in 2001 by Cricinfo, from 2002 to 2005 by Frizzell, from 2006 to 2015 by Liverpool Victoria (LV), and from 2016 by Specsavers.

COUNTY CHAMPIONSHIP – FINAL POSITIONS, 1890–2019

	Derbyshire	Durham	Essex	Glamorgan	Gloucestershire	Hampshire	Kent	Lancashire	Leicestershire	Middlesex	Northamptonshire	Nottinghamshire	Somerset	Surrey	Sussex	Warwickshire	Worcestershire	Yorkshire
1890	–	–	–	–	6	–	3	2	–	7	–	5	–	1	8	–	–	3
1891	–	–	–	–	9	–	5	2	–	3	–	4	5	1	7	–	–	8
1892	–	–	–	–	7	–	7	4	–	5	–	2	3	1	9	–	–	6
1893	–	–	–	–	9	–	4	2	–	3	–	6	8	5	7	–	–	1
1894	–	–	–	–	9	–	4	4	–	3	–	7	6	1	8	–	–	2
1895	5	–	9	–	4	10	14	2	12	6	–	12	8	1	11	6	–	1
1896	7	–	5	–	10	8	9	2	13	3	–	6	11	4	14	12	–	1
1897	14	–	3	–	5	9	12	1	13	8	–	10	11	2	6	7	–	4
1898	9	–	5	–	3	12	7	6	13	2	–	8	13	4	9	9	–	1
1899	15	–	6	–	9	10	8	4	13	2	–	10	13	1	5	7	12	3
1900	13	–	10	–	7	15	3	2	14	7	–	5	11	7	3	6	12	1
1901	15	–	10	–	14	7	7	3	12	2	–	9	12	6	4	5	11	1
1902	10	–	13	–	14	15	7	5	11	12	–	3	7	4	2	6	9	1

	Derbyshire	Durham	Essex	Glamorgan	Gloucestershire	Hampshire	Kent	Lancashire	Leicestershire	Middlesex	Northamptonshire	Nottinghamshire	Somerset	Surrey	Sussex	Warwickshire	Worcestershire	Yorkshire
1903	12	–	8	–	13	14	8	4	14	1	–	5	10	11	2	7	6	3
1904	10	–	14	–	9	15	3	1	7	4	–	5	12	11	6	7	13	2
1905	14	–	12	–	8	16	6	2	5	11	13	10	15	4	3	7	8	1
1906	16	–	7	–	9	8	1	4	15	11	11	5	11	3	10	6	14	2
1907	16	–	7	–	10	12	8	6	11	5	15	1	14	4	13	9	2	2
1908	14	–	11	–	10	9	2	7	13	4	15	8	16	3	5	12	6	1
1909	15	–	14	–	16	8	1	2	13	6	7	10	11	5	4	12	8	3
1910	15	–	11	–	12	6	1	4	10	3	9	5	16	2	7	14	13	8
1911	14	–	6	–	12	11	2	4	15	3	10	8	16	5	13	1	9	7
1912	12	–	15	–	11	6	3	4	13	5	2	8	14	7	10	9	16	1
1913	13	–	15	–	9	10	1	8	14	6	4	5	16	3	7	11	12	2
1914	12	–	8	–	16	5	3	11	13	2	9	10	15	1	6	7	14	4
1919	9	–	14	–	8	7	2	5	9	13	12	3	5	4	11	15	–	1
1920	16	–	9	–	8	11	5	2	13	1	14	7	10	3	6	12	15	4
1921	12	–	15	17	7	6	4	5	11	1	13	8	10	2	9	16	14	3
1922	11	–	8	16	13	6	4	5	14	7	15	2	10	3	9	12	17	1
1923	10	–	13	16	11	7	5	3	14	8	17	2	9	4	6	12	15	1
1924	17	–	15	13	6	12	5	4	11	2	16	6	8	3	10	9	14	1
1925	14	–	7	17	10	9	5	3	12	6	11	4	15	2	13	8	16	1
1926	11	–	9	8	15	7	3	1	13	6	14	4	14	5	10	12	17	2
1927	5	–	8	15	12	13	4	1	7	9	16	2	14	6	10	11	17	3
1928	10	–	16	15	5	12	2	1	9	8	13	3	14	6	7	11	17	4
1929	7	–	12	17	4	11	8	2	9	6	13	1	15	10	4	14	16	2
1930	9	–	6	11	2	13	5	1	12	16	17	4	13	8	7	15	10	3
1931	7	–	10	15	2	12	3	6	16	11	17	5	13	8	4	9	14	1
1932	10	–	14	15	13	8	3	6	12	10	16	4	7	5	2	9	17	1
1933	6	–	4	16	10	14	3	5	17	12	13	8	11	9	2	7	15	1
1934	3	–	8	13	7	14	5	1	12	10	17	9	15	11	2	4	16	5
1935	2	–	9	13	15	16	10	4	6	3	17	5	14	11	7	8	12	1
1936	1	–	9	16	4	10	8	11	15	2	17	5	7	6	14	13	12	3
1937	3	–	6	7	4	14	12	9	16	2	17	10	13	8	5	11	15	1
1938	5	–	6	16	10	14	9	4	15	2	17	12	7	3	8	13	11	1
1939	9	–	4	13	3	15	5	6	17	2	16	12	14	8	10	11	7	1
1946	15	–	8	6	5	16	4	3	11	2	16	13	4	11	17	14	8	1
1947	5	–	11	9	2	16	4	3	14	1	17	11	11	6	9	15	7	7
1948	6	–	13	1	8	9	15	5	11	3	17	14	12	2	16	7	10	4
1949	15	–	9	8	7	16	13	11	17	1	6	11	9	5	13	4	3	1
1950	5	–	17	11	7	12	9	1	16	14	10	15	7	1	13	4	6	3
1951	11	–	8	5	12	9	16	3	15	7	13	17	14	6	10	1	4	2
1952	4	–	10	7	9	12	15	3	6	5	8	16	17	1	13	10	14	2
1953	6	–	12	10	6	14	16	3	3	5	11	8	17	1	2	9	15	12
1954	3	–	15	4	13	14	11	10	16	7	7	5	17	1	9	6	11	2
1955	8	–	14	16	12	3	13	9	6	5	7	11	17	1	4	9	15	2
1956	12	–	11	13	3	6	16	2	17	5	4	8	15	1	9	14	9	7
1957	4	–	5	9	12	13	14	6	17	7	2	15	8	1	9	11	16	3
1958	5	–	6	15	14	2	8	7	12	10	4	17	3	1	13	16	9	11
1959	7	–	9	6	2	8	13	5	16	10	11	17	12	3	15	4	14	1
1960	5	–	6	11	8	12	10	2	17	3	9	16	14	7	4	15	13	1
1961	7	–	6	14	5	1	11	13	9	3	16	17	10	15	8	12	4	2
1962	7	–	9	14	4	10	11	16	17	13	8	15	6	5	12	3	2	1
1963	17	–	12	2	8	10	13	15	16	6	7	9	3	11	4	4	14	1
1964	12	–	10	11	17	12	7	14	16	6	3	15	8	4	9	2	1	5
1965	9	–	15	3	10	12	5	13	14	6	2	17	7	8	16	11	1	4
1966	9	–	16	14	15	11	4	12	8	12	5	17	3	7	10	6	2	1

	Derbyshire	Durham	Essex	Glamorgan	Gloucestershire	Hampshire	Kent	Lancashire	Leicestershire	Middlesex	Northamptonshire	Nottinghamshire	Somerset	Surrey	Sussex	Warwickshire	Worcestershire	Yorkshire
1967	6	–	15	14	17	12	2	11	2	7	9	15	8	4	13	10	5	1
1968	8	–	14	3	16	5	2	6	9	10	13	4	12	15	17	11	7	1
1969	16	–	6	1	2	5	10	15	14	11	9	8	17	3	7	4	12	13
1970	7	–	12	2	17	10	1	3	15	16	14	11	13	5	9	7	6	4
1971	17	–	10	16	8	9	4	3	5	6	14	12	7	1	11	2	15	13
1972	17	–	5	13	3	9	2	15	6	8	4	14	11	12	16	1	7	10
1973	16	–	8	11	5	1	4	12	9	13	3	17	10	2	15	7	6	14
1974	17	–	12	16	14	2	10	8	4	6	3	15	5	7	13	9	1	11
1975	15	–	7	9	16	3	5	4	1	11	8	13	12	6	17	14	10	2
1976	15	–	6	17	3	12	14	16	4	1	2	13	7	9	10	5	11	8
1977	7	–	6	14	3	11	1	16	5	1	9	17	4	14	8	10	13	12
1978	14	–	2	13	10	8	1	12	6	3	17	7	5	16	9	11	15	4
1979	16	–	1	17	10	12	5	13	6	14	11	9	8	3	4	15	2	7
1980	9	–	8	13	7	17	16	15	10	1	12	3	5	2	4	14	11	6
1981	12	–	5	14	13	7	9	16	8	4	15	1	3	6	2	17	11	10
1982	11	–	7	16	15	13	3	13	12	2	1	9	4	6	5	8	17	14
1983	9	–	1	15	12	3	7	12	4	2	6	14	10	8	11	5	16	17
1984	12	–	1	13	17	15	5	16	4	3	11	2	7	8	6	9	10	14
1985	13	–	4	12	3	2	9	14	16	1	10	8	17	6	7	15	5	11
1986	11	–	1	17	2	6	8	15	7	12	9	4	16	3	14	12	5	10
1987	6	–	12	13	10	5	14	2	3	16	7	1	11	4	17	15	9	8
1988	14	–	3	17	10	15	2	9	8	7	12	5	11	4	16	6	1	13
1989	6	–	2	17	9	6	15	4	13	3	5	11	14	12	10	8	1	16
1990	12	–	2	8	13	3	16	6	7	1	11	10	13	15	9	17	5	14
1991	3	–	1	12	13	9	6	8	16	15	10	4	17	5	11	2	6	14
1992	5	18	1	14	10	15	2	12	8	11	3	4	9	13	7	6	17	16
1993	15	18	11	3	17	13	8	13	9	1	4	7	5	6	10	16	2	12
1994	17	16	6	18	12	13	9	10	2	4	5	3	11	7	8	1	15	13
1995	14	17	5	16	6	13	18	4	7	2	3	11	9	12	15	1	10	8
1996	2	18	5	10	13	14	4	15	1	9	16	17	11	3	12	8	7	6
1997	16	17	18	1	7	14	2	11	10	4	15	13	12	8	18	4	5	6
1998	10	14	18	12	4	6	11	2	1	17	15	16	9	5	7	8	13	3
1999	9	8	12	14	18	7	5	2	3	16	13	17	4	1	11	10	15	6
2000	*9*	*8*	**2**	*3*	**4**	**6**	**2**	**4**	*8*	**1**	*7*	**5**	**1**	*9*	*6*	*5*	**1**	*1*
2001	*9*	*8*	**9**	*8*	**4**	**2**	*3*	**6**	*5*	**5**	*7*	*7*	**2**	*4*	*1*	*3*	*6*	**1**
2002	*6*	**9**	**1**	*5*	*8*	*7*	**3**	**4**	*5*	**2**	*7*	*3*	*8*	**1**	**6**	**2**	*4*	**9**
2003	*9*	**6**	**7**	*5*	*3*	*8*	**4**	**2**	*9*	**6**	*2*	*8*	*7*	**3**	**1**	*5*	*1*	*4*
2004	*8*	**9**	*5*	*3*	**6**	**2**	**8**	**6**	*4*	**9**	*1*	*4*	**3**	*5*	**1**	*7*	*7*	*7*
2005	*9*	**2**	*5*	*9*	*8*	**2**	*5*	*1*	*7*	**6**	*4*	**1**	*8*	*7*	**3**	*4*	**6**	*3*
2006	*5*	**7**	*3*	*3*	*8*	*7*	**3**	*5*	*2*	*4*	**6**	**8**	**9**	*1*	*1*	**4**	*2*	**6**
2007	*6*	**2**	*4*	*9*	*7*	**5**	*7*	**3**	*8*	*3*	*5*	**2**	*1*	**4**	*1*	**8**	**9**	**6**
2008	*6*	**1**	*5*	*8*	*9*	**3**	*8*	**5**	*7*	*3*	*4*	**2**	*4*	**9**	**6**	*1*	*2*	**7**
2009	*6*	**1**	*2*	*5*	*4*	**6**	*1*	**4**	*9*	*8*	*8*	**2**	**3**	*7*	**8**	*5*	**9**	**7**
2010	*9*	**5**	**9**	*3*	*3*	**4**	*8*	**1**	*4*	**9**	*8*	*6*	**1**	*7*	**8**	**4**	*7*	**6**
2011	*5*	**3**	*7*	*6*	*9*	**4**	*3*	**1**	*9*	**1**	*3*	*6*	**4**	*2*	**5**	**2**	*7*	**8**
2012	*1*	**6**	*5*	*6*	*9*	*4*	*3*	**8**	*7*	**3**	*8*	**5**	**2**	**9**	**4**	**1**	*9*	**2**
2013	**8**	**1**	*3*	*8*	*6*	**4**	*7*	*1*	*9*	**5**	*2*	*7*	**6**	**9**	**3**	**4**	*5*	**2**
2014	*4*	**5**	*3*	*8*	*7*	*1*	*6*	**8**	*9*	**7**	*9*	**4**	**6**	**5**	**3**	**2**	*2*	**1**
2015	*8*	**4**	*3*	*4*	*6*	*8*	*7*	**2**	*9*	**2**	*5*	**3**	**6**	*1*	**8**	**5**	*9*	**1**
2016	*9*	**4**	*1*	*8*	*6*	*8*	**2**	**7**	*7*	**1**	*5*	**9**	**2**	**5**	**4**	**6**	*3*	**3**
2017	*8*	*9*	**1**	*7*	*6*	**5**	*5*	**2**	*10*	**7**	*3*	*2*	**6**	**3**	**4**	**8**	**1**	**4**
2018	*7*	*8*	**3**	*10*	*3*	**3**	*7*	*6*	*4*	**9**	*6*	**2**	**1**	*3*	**1**	*3*	**1**	**8**
2019	*7*	*5*	**1**	*4*	*3*	**3**	*4*	*1*	*10*	**8**	*2*	**8**	**2**	*6*	**6**	*7*	*9*	**5**

For the 2000–2019 Championships, Division One placings are in bold, Division Two in italic.

MATCH RESULTS, 1864–2019

County	Years of Play	Played	Won	Lost	Drawn	Tied	% Won
Derbyshire	1871–87; 1895–2019	2,587	633	957	996	1	24.46
Durham	1992–2019	451	124	187	140	0	27.49
Essex	1895–2019	2,551	757	732	1,056	6	29.67
Glamorgan	1921–2019	2,077	456	721	900	0	21.95
Gloucestershire	1870–2019	2,830	829	1,035	964	2	29.29
Hampshire	1864–85; 1895–2019	2,660	701	889	1,066	4	26.35
Kent	1864–2019	2,945	1,053	879	1,008	5	35.75
Lancashire	1865–2019	3,022	1,114	628	1,276	4	36.86
Leicestershire	1895–2019	2,517	559	923	1,034	1	22.20
Middlesex	1864–2019	2,727	990	695	1,037	5	36.30
Northamptonshire	1905–2019	2,284	576	778	927	3	25.21
Nottinghamshire	1864–2019	2,857	862	788	1,206	1	30.17
Somerset	1882–85; 1891–2019	2,559	628	980	947	4	24.54
Surrey	1864–2019	3,102	1,207	692	1,199	4	38.91
Sussex	1864–2019	2,996	858	1,015	1,117	6	28.63
Warwickshire	1895–2019	2,532	709	722	1,099	2	28.00
Worcestershire	1899–2019	2,469	638	865	964	2	25.84
Yorkshire	1864–2019	3,125	1,349	557	1,217	2	43.16
Cambridgeshire	1864–69; 1871	19	8	8	3	0	42.10
		23,155	14,051	14,051	9,078	26	

Matches abandoned without a ball bowled are wholly excluded.

Counties participated in the years shown, except that there were no matches in 1915–1918 and 1940–1945; Hampshire did not play inter-county matches in 1868–1869, 1871–1874 and 1879; Worcestershire did not take part in the Championship in 1919.

COUNTY CHAMPIONSHIP STATISTICS FOR 2019

County	For			Runs scored	Against		
	Runs	Wickets	Avge	per 100 balls	Runs	Wickets	Avge
Derbyshire (7)	7,040	233	30.21	55.72	6,132	212	28.92
Durham (5)	6,123	231	26.50	48.86	5,831	227	25.68
Essex (1)	5,505	187	29.43	50.23	5,476	235	23.30
Glamorgan (4)	7,100	202	35.14	61.74	7,364	204	36.09
Gloucestershire (3)	6,128	194	31.58	54.39	6,434	202	31.85
Hampshire (3)	6,637	209	31.75	59.98	6,013	206	29.18
Kent (4)	6,882	224	30.72	59.97	6,382	232	27.50
Lancashire (1)	5,676	160	35.47	55.72	5,507	245	22.47
Leicestershire (10)	6,140	217	28.29	46.78	6,539	179	36.53
Middlesex (8)	6,270	224	27.99	53.49	5,846	192	30.44
Northamptonshire (2)	6,670	199	33.51	57.97	6,196	198	31.29
Nottinghamshire (8)	5,558	243	22.87	50.83	6,922	181	38.24
Somerset (2)	5,823	233	24.99	58.67	5,419	255	21.25
Surrey (6)	6,787	235	28.88	53.12	6,217	208	29.88
Sussex (6)	6,351	209	30.38	58.09	6,782	206	32.92
Warwickshire (7)	6,503	212	30.67	49.00	7,349	217	33.86
Worcestershire (9)	5,393	214	25.20	51.26	6,260	218	28.71
Yorkshire (5)	6,524	205	31.82	54.39	6,441	214	30.09
	113,110	3,831	29.52	54.29	113,110	3,831	29.52

2019 Championship positions are shown in brackets; Division One in bold, Division Two in italic.

For World Cup records, see page 1344

ECB PITCHES TABLE OF MERIT IN 2019

	First-class	One-day		First-class	One-day
Derbyshire	4.78	5.09	Middlesex	5.00	5.86
Durham	5.25	5.36	Northamptonshire	5.13	5.75
Essex	4.00	5.69	Nottinghamshire	5.14	5.77
Glamorgan	5.00	6.00	Somerset	4.89	6.00
Gloucestershire	4.88	5.60	Surrey	4.89	5.40
Hampshire	4.38	5.57	Sussex	5.11	5.72
Kent	4.78	5.79	Warwickshire	5.33	5.00
Lancashire	5.13	5.62	Worcestershire	4.88	5.54
Leicestershire	5.38	5.87	Yorkshire	5.75	5.93

Each umpire in a match marks the pitch on the following scale: 6 – Very good; 5 – Good; 4 – Above average; 3 – Below average; 2 – Poor; 1 – Unfit.

The tables, provided by the ECB, cover major matches, including Tests, Under-19 internationals, women's internationals and MCCU games, played on grounds under the county's jurisdiction. Middlesex pitches at Lord's are the responsibility of MCC. The "First-class" column includes women's and Under-19 Tests.

Yorkshire had the highest mark for first-class cricket, while Glamorgan and Somerset had the best for one-day cricket, though the ECB point out that the tables of merit are not a direct assessment of the groundsmen's ability. Marks may be affected by many factors, including weather, soil conditions and the resources available.

COUNTY CAPS AWARDED IN 2019

Derbyshire	M. J. J. Critchley, R. Rampaul, L. M. Reece.
Glamorgan*	M. de Lange, M. Labuschagne, D. L. Lloyd.
Gloucestershire*	B. M. J. Allison, E. R. Bamber, S. T. Gabriel, H. J. Hankins, C. J. Sayers.
Hampshire	S. A. Northeast.
Kent	Z. Crawley, A. F. Milne, H. W. Podmore.
Lancashire	J. P. Faulkner, M. W. Parkinson.
Leicestershire	C. N. Ackermann.
Middlesex	T. G. Helm.
Northamptonshire	R. I. Keogh, A. M. Rossington.
Nottinghamshire	R. Ashwin.
Somerset	Azhar Ali, J. Overton.
Sussex	O. E. Robinson, S. van Zyl.
Warwickshire	O. J. Hannon-Dalby, D. P. Sibley.
Worcestershire*	J. J. Dell, C. J. Ferguson, A. W. Finch, J. A. Haynes, H. D. Rutherford, M. H. Wessels.
Yorkshire	T. Köhler-Cadmore.

* Glamorgan's capping system is now based on a player's number of appearances. Gloucestershire now award caps to all first-class players. Worcestershire have replaced caps with colours awarded to all Championship players. Durham abolished their capping system after 2005.

No caps were awarded by Essex or Surrey.

COUNTY TESTIMONIALS AWARDED FOR 2020

Glamorgan	M. G. Hogan.	Northamptonshire	A. G. Wakely.
Lancashire	S. D. Parry.	Yorkshire	A. Lyth.
Middlesex	E. J. G. Morgan.		

None of the other 13 counties awarded a testimonial for 2020.

DERBYSHIRE

It's a Blast for Cork

Mark Eklid

Success at Derbyshire is usually measured in relative terms, and the relative success of the summer of 2019 came from the least likely source. After 16 years of underachievement in Twenty20 cricket, in which they were the only county never to reach finals day, Derbyshire earned an invitation to the Vitality Blast party.

Their third appearance in the quarter-finals had proved the charm and, even though their semi-final ended in defeat by Essex, the eventual winners, simply being there was a triumph. The signs had been less than promising. Before the T20 campaign, both Derbyshire's choices for their second overseas player withdrew – Kane Richardson because he was called into Australia's World Cup squad, and his countryman Billy Stanlake through injury. A potential move for a late replacement was ruled out for financial reasons after a summer pop concert at the County Ground was cancelled.

But in his first year in overall charge of T20 coaching, former captain Dominic Cork turned adversity into a source of collective inspiration: as so often in his playing career, his side defied the odds. Derbyshire's strength was the sum of their parts. A settled top four of Billy Godleman, Luis Reece, Wayne Madsen and Leus du Plooy consistently delivered runs, while Ravi Rampaul finished as the top wicket-taker in the country, with 23; leg-spinner Matt Critchley's 17 victims equalled the previous Derbyshire best for a season.

Cork confirmed on finals day that he wanted to return to complete his "unfinished business" in the competition, and his contract was later extended by a year. It may not be too much of a stretch to suggest Derbyshire should be considered serious contenders in 2020. Over the last three seasons, only Nottinghamshire, Somerset and Lancashire have managed more than their 20 group-stage wins.

If the Blast provided the highlight of the season, the County Championship was the biggest source of regret. With three promotion spots available (a one-off arrangement to expand Division One), Derbyshire had a real opportunity, but their challenge never took off. Two defeats which might have ended in victory, had they shown greater composure on the last day – at home to Glamorgan and away to Durham – were especially damaging.

There were individual successes. The captain, Godleman, became the first Englishman since Chris Adams and Kim Barnett in 1996 to score more than 2,000 runs in a season in all matches for Derbyshire. He was the leading run-scorer for any county in the Royal London Cup, with 521, including three successive centuries; he made another four in the Championship, with a career-best 227 at Swansea, and was one of only six batsmen in Division Two to pass 1,000, even though his first eight innings had accrued a mere 101.

DERBYSHIRE AT 150

Many of the county's most influential figures gathered on November 4, 1870, at the Guildhall in Derby to hear Walter Boden, a partner in a local lace business who had played one first-class match for the Gentlemen of the North in 1859, propose the formation of a Derbyshire County Club. With limited resources of finance and talent, times were tough for the new club but. A century and a half later, it is still going strong.

1871   Derbyshire's first match, at Old Trafford, ended in victory by an innings and 11 runs after they dismissed Lancashire for 25, with Dove Gregory taking six for nine. The return match, at the Racecourse in Derby three months later, was won by Lancashire.

1884   In a bid to bring in extra revenue through the winter, the cricket club formed Derby County Football Club, who played at the Racecourse until 1895. The ground became the first outside London to host an FA Cup final, in 1886, a replay in which West Bromwich Albion beat Blackburn Rovers 2–0. It was also used for an international between England and Ireland in 1895.

1896   George Davidson scored 274 against Lancashire at Old Trafford, still Derbyshire's highest score.

1921   Billy Bestwick took ten for 40 before lunch at Cardiff, still the county's best figures. He was 46, the oldest first-class bowler to take all ten. A burly former miner, he had been cleared of manslaughter after a pub brawl in 1907, but sacked by Derbyshire two years later because of a voracious thirst, then re-engaged after the war.

1936   Derbyshire won their only County Championship, led by Arthur Richardson. With 140 wickets from Bill Copson and 116 from Tommy Mitchell, supported by more than 1,000 runs from each of Stan Worthington, Leslie Townsend, Denis Smith and Albert Alderman, they held off Middlesex and Yorkshire.

1952   Donald Carr became Derbyshire's only England Test captain, deputising for Nigel Howard, who had pleurisy. His sole match in charge, at Madras, ended in their first defeat by India.

1963   Les Jackson played his 394th and last match for Derbyshire, against Middlesex at Lord's, and took his 1,670th first-class wicket, a county record.

1978   Four Derbyshire players appeared in the First Test between England and New Zealand at Wellington – Bob Taylor, Geoff Miller and Mike Hendrick for the tourists, and John Wright for New Zealand, who beat England for the first time.

1981   A scrambled single off the last ball brought Derbyshire their first one-day title: they levelled the scores in the NatWest Trophy final against Northamptonshire, and won because they had lost fewer wickets.

1990   Derbyshire clinched the Refuge Assurance Sunday League title by beating Essex at Derby in the last round. They later lost the final of the Refuge Assurance Cup to Middlesex.

1993   More one-day success: an unbeaten 92 from 21-year-old Dominic Cork earned the Gold Award in a six-run victory over Lancashire in the Benson and Hedges Cup final.

1998   Kim Barnett played his last game for Derbyshire, and left holding the county records for first-class runs (23,854), first-class centuries (53), one-day runs (12,358) and one-day centuries (13).

2004   Derbyshire became only the third first-class county to install permanent floodlights.

2012   Led by Wayne Madsen, Derbyshire won Division Two of the County Championship, and their first promotion.

2019   After 16 years trying, Derbyshire made their debut at Twenty20 finals day – the last of the first-class counties to get there.

Madsen's Championship aggregate was down on recent years, but his white-ball form took him to the second-best season of his career across all formats, with 1,835 runs. His continued value in the field was measured by 45 catches, the most in the outfield for Derbyshire since Mike Page's 49 in 1967.

Gareth Copley, Getty Images

Ravi Rampaul

The heaviest workload fell on Reece, who usually opened the batting and occasionally the bowling. His 1,579 runs and 70 wickets in all matches were the best all-round return for the county since Eddie Barlow's 1,897 and 80 in 1976. Understandably, Derbyshire were quick to offer him a contract extension; he signed to stay until 2023. Reece's 52 Championship wickets put him eight ahead of Rampaul, whose high standards at the age of 34 earned him the county's Player of the Year award.

Two players recruited after the season began indicated they could play valuable roles. Du Plooy, a stylish South African batsman who arrived on Kolpak terms, scored 1,326 runs in all, despite a spell out with a dislocated finger, while Fynn Hudson-Prentice, an energetic seamer and aggressive batsman released by Sussex in 2016, joined after two years on the MCC Young Cricketers staff.

Tom Lace, on loan from Middlesex, hit three hundreds and led the batting averages. His season ended in August, when he needed surgery on a broken finger, but he showed immense promise, whether it is to be fulfilled at Lord's or Derby. Wicketkeeper Harvey Hosein made advances with the gloves and the bat in his first full Championship season.

The winter recruitment wish-list of David Houghton, Derbyshire's head of cricket, focused on finding an overseas strike bowler. New Zealander Logan van Beek had been unable to fill this role; though his commitment was unquestioned, he was limited by a knee problem and his returns were modest. Australian international seamer Sean Abbott joined for up to ten Championship games and the Blast, after Michael Cohen, a young left-arm pace bowler from Western Province with a European passport, signed in October. Tasmanian batsman Ben McDermott, son of Craig, will play white-ball cricket. Houghton also needed to coax Critchley to bowl with greater consistency in first-class cricket, especially following the loss of England Under-19 off-spinner Hamidullah Qadri to Kent.

That departure highlighted another area for concern. Qadri was one of 14 players who had emerged through the county's age-group system to represent the first team in 2017 – but only two, Hosein and Alex Hughes, remained at the club by the start of 2020. Of the rest, only Qadri and Ben Slater left of their own volition. It is a problem which a county with such limited resources as Derbyshire must address if relative success is to be turned into the real thing.

Championship attendance: 11,788.

DERBYSHIRE RESULTS

All first-class matches – Played 16: Won 5, Lost 7, Drawn 4.
County Championship matches – Played 14: Won 4, Lost 6, Drawn 4.

Specsavers County Championship, 7th in Division 2;
Vitality Blast, semi-finalists; Royal London One-Day Cup, 5th in North Group.

COUNTY CHAMPIONSHIP AVERAGES, BATTING AND FIELDING

Cap		Birthplace	M	I	NO	R	HS	100	Avge	Ct/St
	T. C. Lace	Hammersmith	10	19	1	780	143	3	43.33	10
2015	†J. L. du Plooy†† ...	Pretoria, SA.....	10	17	3	554	118	2	39.57	9
2015	†B. A. Godleman....	Islington	14	26	0	1,008	227	4	38.76	2
2011	W. L. Madsen	Durban, SA	13	24	1	794	204*	1	34.52	21
	F. J. Hudson-Prentice	Haywards Heath ..	7	12	2	342	99	0	34.20	1
2019	†L. M. Reece	Taunton	14	26	0	785	184	2	30.19	5
	H. R. Hosein......	Chesterfield‡....	14	25	3	618	91*	0	28.09	30/2
2017	A. L. Hughes	Wordsley	11	20	1	510	109*	1	26.84	11
2019	M. J. J. Critchley....	Preston	14	23	2	461	79*	0	21.95	14
	A. K. Dal	Newcastle-u-Tyne .	9	16	3	278	92	0	21.38	5
	L. V. van Beek¶...	Christchurch, NZ..	9	12	3	127	34*	0	14.11	5
2019	†R. Rampaul††.....	Preysal, Trinidad .	12	19	5	186	30	0	13.28	2
	Hamidullah Qadri...	Kandahar, Afg...	2	4	2	23	17*	0	11.50	0
2012	A. P. Palladino....	Tower Hamlets ...	10	15	3	134	58	0	11.16	0

Also batted: S. Conners (*Nottingham*) (2 matches) 14, 6*; M. H. McKiernan (*Billinge*) (1 match) 0, 7 (3 ct); D. R. Melton (*Harare, Zimbabwe*) (2 matches) 1*, 0 (1 ct).

‡ *Born in Derbyshire.* ¶ *Official overseas player.* †† *Other non-England-qualified.*

BOWLING

	Style	O	M	R	W	BB	5I	Avge
L. M. Reece	LFM	371	105	1,022	52	6-58	3	19.65
F. J. Hudson-Prentice.................	RFM	148	38	465	20	3-27	0	23.25
A. P. Palladino	RFM	282.5	99	652	27	5-29	1	24.14
R. Rampaul	RFM	374	79	1,139	44	5-77	2	25.88
L. V. van Beek....................	RFM	219.2	34	726	19	3-20	0	38.21
M. J. J. Critchley	LB	229.1	26	841	19	4-107	0	44.26

Also bowled: S. Conners (RFM) 23–3–77–2; A. K. Dal (RFM) 45.4–8–142–7; J. L. du Plooy (SLA) 46.3–2–182–4; Hamidullah Qadri (OB) 31.3–3–140–5; A. L. Hughes (RM) 81–14–219–3; W. L. Madsen (OB) 59–12–188–4; D. R. Melton (RFM) 17.5–1–94–2.

LEADING ROYAL LONDON CUP AVERAGES (100 runs/4 wickets)

Batting	Runs	HS	Avge	SR	Ct	Bowling	W	BB	Avge	ER
B. A. Godleman .	521	116	74.42	88.30	2	R. Rampaul.......	8	2-25	33.37	5.23
M. J. J. Critchley .	208	64*	69.33	113.04	2	A. L. Hughes	7	4-44	37.71	6.28
W. L. Madsen ...	406	119*	58.00	106.84	6	L. V. van Beek ...	7	3-50	37.71	7.13
J. L. du Plooy....	222	75	55.50	108.29	1	M. R. J. Watt	6	2-32	45.83	5.93
L. M. Reece.....	310	128	38.75	95.67	3	M. J. J. Critchley .	5	3-73	62.60	6.26
A. L. Hughes	139	69	27.80	108.59	4	L. M. Reece	5	2-59	66.80	6.30
T. C. Lace	108	48	18.00	85.03	2					

LEADING VITALITY BLAST AVERAGES (90 runs/15 overs)

Batting	Runs	HS	Avge	SR	Ct
W. L. Madsen....	464	69	46.40	**146.83**	17
J. L. du Plooy....	312	70	39.00	**133.33**	9
L. M. Reece	325	61	25.00	**126.95**	6
B. A. Godleman.	453	92	41.18	**115.85**	10
F. J. Hudson-Prentice	94	31*	18.80	**111.90**	3
M. J. J. Critchley .	94	21	10.44	**100.00**	5

Bowling	W	BB	Avge	ER
R. Rampaul.......	23	3-17	15.73	**6.70**
A. L. Hughes......	10	3-13	24.90	**6.91**
M. J. J. Critchley...	17	4-36	18.52	**7.13**
L. M. Reece.......	10	2-9	27.00	**7.94**
L. V. van Beek	9	4-17	29.33	**8.51**
F. J. Hudson-Prentice	11	2-2	29.09	**8.64**
M. R. J. Watt......	7	4-19	25.85	**9.05**

FIRST-CLASS COUNTY RECORDS

Highest score for	274	G. A. Davidson v Lancashire at Manchester	1896
Highest score against	343*	P. A. Perrin (Essex) at Chesterfield	1904
Leading run-scorer	23,854	K. J. Barnett (avge 41.12).	1979–98
Best bowling for	10-40	W. Bestwick v Glamorgan at Cardiff............	1921
Best bowling against	10-45	R. L. Johnson (Middlesex) at Derby.............	1994
Leading wicket-taker	1,670	H. L. Jackson (avge 17.11).....................	1947–63
Highest total for	801-8 dec	v Somerset at Taunton	2007
Highest total against	677-7 dec	by Yorkshire at Leeds.........................	2013
Lowest total for	16	v Nottinghamshire at Nottingham	1879
Lowest total against	23	by Hampshire at Burton-upon-Trent	1958

LIST A COUNTY RECORDS

Highest score for	173*	M. J. Di Venuto v Derbys County Board at Derby .	2000
Highest score against	158	R. K. Rao (Sussex) at Derby....................	1997
Leading run-scorer	12,358	K. J. Barnett (avge 36.67).....................	1979–98
Best bowling for	8-21	M. A. Holding v Sussex at Hove	1988
Best bowling against	8-66	S. R. G. Francis (Somerset) at Derby	2004
Leading wicket-taker	246	A. E. Warner (avge 27.13).....................	1985–95
Highest total for	366-4	v Combined Universities at Oxford	1991
Highest total against	369-6	by New Zealanders at Derby	1999
Lowest total for	60	v Kent at Canterbury	2008
Lowest total against	42	by Glamorgan at Swansea	1979

TWENTY20 COUNTY RECORDS

Highest score for	111	W. J. Durston v Nottinghamshire at Nottingham ...	2010
Highest score against	158*	B. B. McCullum (Warwickshire) at Birmingham...	2015
Leading run-scorer	**2,806**	**W. L. Madsen** (avge 31.17, SR 134.06)........	**2010–19**
Best bowling for	5-27	T. Lungley v Leicestershire at Leicester..........	2009
Best bowling against	5-14	P. D. Collingwood (Durham) at Chester-le-Street ..	2008
Leading wicket-taker	51	T. D. Groenewald (avge 27.52, ER 7.85).........	2009–14
Highest total for	{222-5 {222-5	v Yorkshire at Leeds.......................... v Nottinghamshire at Nottingham	2010 2017
Highest total against	249-8	by Hampshire at Derby........................	2017
Lowest total for	72	v Leicestershire at Derby	2013
Lowest total against	84	by West Indians at Derby	2007

ADDRESS

The Pattonair County Ground, Nottingham Road, Derby DE21 6DA; 01332 388 101; info@derby-shireccc.com; www.derbyshireccc.com.

OFFICIALS

Captain B. A. Godleman	**President** H. J. Rhodes
Head of cricket D. L. Houghton	**Chairman** R. I. Morgan
Head of talent pathway D. Smit	**Chief executive** R. Duckett
Assistant coach (batting) M. B. Loye	**Head groundsman** N. Godrich
(bowling) S. P. Kirby	**Scorer** J. M. Brown
Twenty20 coach D. G. Cork	

DERBYSHIRE v LEEDS/BRADFORD MCCU

At Derby, March 26–28. Derbyshire won by 336 runs. Toss: Derbyshire. First-class debuts: S. Conners; S. T. Ashraf, O. R. Batchelor, S. Cantwell, T. R. Cornall, A. E. C. Dahl, J. B. Fallows, J. L. Haynes, J. B. R. Holling, D. A. Ironside, A. J. Neal.

Derbyshire's first first-class fixture in March resulted in their fourth-highest victory by runs, against a Leeds/Bradford side in which all but wicketkeeper Jonny Read were making their first-class debuts. Centuries from Madsen and Hosein – his highest score – gave them control; aggression from last man Stephen Cantwell, outscored only by Extras, hauled the students to 200, barely half the county's total. Having given more batsmen time in the middle, Derbyshire set themselves two sessions to take ten wickets, and did so comfortably, with 18-year-old seamer James Taylor improving his career-best figures for the second time in the match.

Close of play: first day, Derbyshire 398-5 (Hosein 138, Critchley 39); second day, Derbyshire 95-1 (Reece 43, Hughes 9).

Derbyshire

L. M. Reece c Cantwell b Neal	21	– lbw b Dahl	96
*B. A. Godleman c Ashraf b Holling	27	– c Dahl b Haynes	39
W. L. Madsen c Read b Holling	123		
T. C. Lace c Read b Cantwell	30	– (6) c Haynes b Dahl	0
A. L. Hughes c Cornall b Holling	0	– (3) c Cornall b Haynes	48
†H. R. Hosein not out	138		
M. J. J. Critchley not out	39	– (5) c Read b Haynes	12
A. K. Dal (did not bat)		– (4) not out	16
J. P. A. Taylor (did not bat)		– (7) not out	11
B 2, lb 6, nb 12	20	Lb 4, w 2, nb 4	10

1/39 (1) 2/54 (2)   (5 wkts dec, 103 overs) 398   1/76 (2)   (5 wkts dec, 65 overs) 232
3/118 (4) 4/123 (5) 5/310 (3)   2/193 (3) 3/193 (1)
                                 4/212 (5) 5/215 (6)

S. Conners and R. Rampaul did not bat.

Cantwell 21–4–67–1; Fallows 17–2–68–0; Neal 19–3–84–1; Holling 13–0–56–3; Haynes 18–3–62–0; Dahl 12–3–33–0; Ironside 3–0–20–0. *Second innings*—Cantwell 10-2–30–0; Fallows 10–1–44–0; Neal 10–2–38–0; Holling 8–1–38–0; Haynes 15–1–37–3; Dahl 12–1–41–2.

Leeds/Bradford MCCU

J. L. Haynes b Rampaul	0	– lbw b Rampaul	0
T. R. Cornall c Lace b Rampaul	19	– c Madsen b Rampaul	5
O. R. Batchelor c Madsen b Reece	21	– c Madsen b Rampaul	0
*A. E. C. Dahl c Madsen b Conners	14	– c Reece b Taylor	10
S. T. Ashraf lbw b Taylor	13	– c Hughes b Conners	10
D. A. Ironside lbw b Taylor	10	– c Hosein b Taylor	24
†J. Read c Madsen b Reece	14	– b Conners	0
A. J. Neal c Hosein b Taylor	9	– c Hosein b Dal	4
J. B. Fallows not out	12	– b Taylor	19
J. B. R. Holling lbw b Reece	0	– lbw b Critchley	3
S. Cantwell c Dal b Critchley	43	– not out	8
B 12, lb 9, nb 24	45	B 4, lb 5, nb 2	11

1/0 (1) 2/49 (2) 3/53 (3)   (61.2 overs) 200   1/0 (1) 2/0 (3)   (37.2 overs) 94
4/85 (4) 5/101 (6) 6/106 (5)   3/19 (2) 4/19 (4)
7/128 (8) 8/132 (7) 9/136 (10) 10/200 (11)   5/33 (5) 6/33 (7) 7/38 (8)
                                   8/33 (9) 9/84 (6) 10/94 (10)

Rampaul 14–5–34–2; Taylor 12–3–48–3; Reece 15–4–49–3; Conners 8–2–23–1; Hughes 5–2–10–0; Critchley 7.2–3–15–1. *Second innings*—Rampaul 5-3–7–3; Taylor 11–3–26–3; Conners 6–1–13–2; Dal 5–2–5–1; Hughes 3–1–2–0; Critchley 7.2–0–32–1.

Umpires: Hassan Adnan and S. J. O'Shaughnessy.

DERBYSHIRE v DURHAM

At Derby, April 5–8. Derbyshire won by 125 runs. Derbyshire 19pts, Durham 3pts. Toss: Derbyshire. County debut: L. V. van Beek.

Losing wickets to the first and third balls of the new Championship season was hardly the most promising start – especially after Derbyshire had chosen to bat – but they recovered to build a winning position. A battling 78 from Hosein, and the medium-pace swing of Reece, who followed up seven for 20 in the final game of 2018 with five for 47 here, gave them a slim first-innings lead of 26. Then sloppy early-season catching from Durham and resolute batting from Lace, a 20-year-old on loan from Middlesex who completed a maiden fifty, and Hosein again set the platform for the lower order. Critchley, in particular, piled on the punishment as they stretched the target to an unlikely 361. Openers Harte and Lees put on 83, but leg-spinner Critchley struck twice with successive deliveries, and Durham's challenge slipped away as the last seven wickets fell for 58. Derbyshire's victory came just before a delayed tea interval on the final day.

Close of play: first day, Durham 41-3 (Lees 12, Salisbury 0); second day, Derbyshire 107-3 (Lace 41, Hughes 7); third day, Durham 10-0 (Harte 4, Lees 6).

Derbyshire

L. M. Reece c Richardson b Rushworth	0	– c Richardson b Salisbury	10
*B. A. Godleman c Lees b Raine	19	– c Poynter b Raine	19
W. L. Madsen b Rushworth	0	– c Lees b Salisbury	30
T. C. Lace c Richardson b Raine	8	– c Richardson b Harte	61
A. L. Hughes c Smith b Weighell	16	– c Poynter b Harte	39
†H. R. Hosein run out (Raine)	78	– c Lees b Trevaskis	62
M. J. J. Critchley lbw b Harte	24	– lbw b Rushworth	51
A. K. Dal c Poynter b Weighell	17	– c Lees b Weighell	6
L. V. van Beek b Raine	8	– not out	19
A. P. Palladino b Weighell	0	– c Richardson b Weighell	5
R. Rampaul not out	0	– c Burnham b Salisbury	24
B 9, lb 13, w 1, nb 4	27	Lb 8	8

1/0 (1) 2/0 (3) 3/27 (4)   (72.1 overs) 197   1/25 (1) 2/33 (2)   (111.2 overs) 334
4/36 (2) 5/63 (5) 6/119 (7)   3/83 (3) 4/149 (4)
7/169 (8) 8/192 (9) 9/193 (10) 10/197 (6)   5/210 (5) 6/273 (7) 7/282 (6)
                                         8/296 (9) 9/308 (10) 10/334 (11)

Rushworth 16–6–28–2; Salisbury 13–3–29–0; Raine 17–2–48–3; Weighell 14.1–2–49–3; Harte 7–1–15–1; Trevaskis 5–3–6–0. *Second innings*—Rushworth 20.7–4–71; Salisbury 17.2–2–65–3; Raine 24–4–64–1; Weighell 17–4–55–2; Harte 17–6–32–2; Trevaskis 14–1–53–1; Smith 2–1–10–0.

Durham

G. J. Harte c Hughes b Reece	14	– b van Beek	69
*A. Z. Lees lbw b Rampaul	32	– c Lace b Critchley	59
W. R. Smith lbw b Reece	4	– c Madsen b Critchley	0
M. J. Richardson c Lace b van Beek	7	– b Rampaul	5
M. E. T. Salisbury c Dal b Rampaul	12	– (10) c Madsen b Rampaul	4
J. T. A. Burnham c Hosein b Reece	31	– (5) c van Beek b Madsen	32
†S. W. Poynter lbw b Palladino	8	– (6) c Hosein b van Beek	7
L. Trevaskis c Madsen b Rampaul	15	– (7) not out	27
B. A. Raine c Lace b Reece	20	– (8) c and b Critchley	5
W. J. Weighell c Madsen b Reece	8	– (9) run out (Reece)	4
C. Rushworth not out	0	– lbw b Reece	6
B 12, lb 2, nb 6	20	B 7, lb 10	17

1/19 (1) 2/25 (3) 3/41 (4)   (67.1 overs) 171   1/83 (2) 2/83 (3)   (92 overs) 235
4/76 (5) 5/83 (2) 6/103 (7)   3/120 (4) 4/177 (5)
7/143 (6) 8/143 (8) 9/154 (10) 10/171 (9)   5/185 (1) 6/186 (6) 7/195 (8)
                                         8/199 (9) 9/209 (10) 10/235 (11)

Rampaul 20–5–47–3; Palladino 17–7–27–1; Reece 17.1–5–47–5; van Beek 13–3–36–1. *Second innings*—Rampaul 22–7–43–2; Palladino 14–5–26–0; van Beek 15–2–43–2; Reece 8–2–21–1; Madsen 14–6–31–1; Critchley 19–6–54–3.

Umpires: R. T. Robinson and B. V. Taylor.

At Bristol, April 11–14. DERBYSHIRE drew with GLOUCESTERSHIRE. *Wayne Madsen scores 204*, his 30th first-class hundred.*

DERBYSHIRE v GLAMORGAN

At Derby, May 19–22. Glamorgan won by two wickets. Glamorgan 22pts, Derbyshire 7pts. Toss: Derbyshire. Championship debut: D. A. Douthwaite.

Cullen's unbeaten maiden fifty helped Glamorgan edge a close contest. Reece scored the only century, on the opening day, adding 104 with Hughes, who reached 3,000 first-class runs before Carey bowled him during a career-best four for 61. For Glamorgan, Hemphrey responded with his third successive half-century, and Root scored a valuable 68 on the day the ECB announced his suspension from bowling because of a suspect action. But Rampaul's first five-wicket haul for Derbyshire ensured a 32-run lead. They seemed to be wasting that when they lost eight for 66 on the third evening, with all-rounder Dan Douthwaite picking up four in 23 balls on Championship debut; he also played two solid innings. Then last-wicket pair Dal and Rampaul combined for their second fifty partnership of the match to leave a target of 246, one more than Glamorgan's highest successful fourth-innings chase against Derbyshire, at Cardiff Arms Park in 1949. It looked tricky at 162 for seven – but Cullen put on 55 with Salter, called up on the first day after Kieran Bull suffered a back spasm. Salter atoned for a first-innings duck and no wickets, helping to tip the balance Glamorgan's way.

Close of play: first day, Derbyshire 253-5 (Hughes 63, Critchley 6); second day, Glamorgan 214-4 (Root 53, Lawlor 4); third day, Derbyshire 171-9 (Dal 6, Rampaul 8).

Derbyshire

L. M. Reece c Lawlor b Douthwaite	111	– c Selman b Lloyd	31
*B. A. Godleman lbw b Hogan	11	– c Cullen b Hogan	9
W. L. Madsen c Cullen b Hogan	37	– c Selman b Lloyd	47
T. C. Lace c Hemphrey b Carey	6	– b Douthwaite	29
A. L. Hughes b Carey	82	– c Lawlor b Carey	6
†H. R. Hosein b Labuschagne	1	– c Cullen b Douthwaite	4
M. J. J. Critchley c Selman b Douthwaite	15	– lbw b Douthwaite	11
A. K. Dal b Hogan	64	– not out	23
L. V. van Beek b Carey	4	– c Cullen b Douthwaite	1
A. P. Palladino c Lawlor b Carey	10	– b Hogan	4
R. Rampaul not out	11	– b Labuschagne	30
B 8, lb 9, w 1, nb 8	26	B 2, lb 9, w 1, nb 6	18

1/19 (2) 2/107 (3) 3/127 (4)   (104.1 overs) 378
4/231 (1) 5/235 (6) 6/276 (7)
7/290 (5) 8/304 (9) 9/328 (10) 10/378 (8)

1/16 (2) 2/96 (3)   (63.5 overs) 213
3/111 (1) 4/126 (5)
5/136 (6) 6/149 (4) 7/150 (7)
8/156 (9) 9/162 (10) 10/213 (11)

Hogan 22.1–7–55–3; Carey 21–4–61–4; Douthwaite 20–1–89–2; Lloyd 11–1–46–0; Lawlor 6–1–15–0; Salter 12–1–49–0; Labuschagne 12–1–46–1. *Second innings*—Carey 11–2–28–1; Hogan 17–2–55–2; Douthwaite 15–1–48–4; Salter 12–3–31–0; Lloyd 8–1–35–2; Labuschagne 0.5–0–5–1.

Glamorgan

N. J. Selman c Critchley b Palladino	21	– c Hosein b Palladino 2
C. R. Hemphrey lbw b van Beek	75	– lbw b Rampaul..................... 4
M. Labuschagne lbw b Rampaul	14	– c van Beek b Rampaul 32
*D. L. Lloyd c Dal b Reece	26	– lbw b Palladino................... 37
W. T. Root lbw b Reece	68	– lbw b Rampaul 26
J. L. Lawlor lbw b Rampaul	10	– c Reece b Critchley 25
D. A. Douthwaite c Hosein b Rampaul	39	– c and b Madsen 31
†T. N. Cullen b Rampaul	40	– not out 51
A. G. Salter c Hughes b Reece	0	– c Madsen b Reece 26
L. J. Carey c Lace b Rampaul	24	– not out 9
M. G. Hogan not out	4	
Lb 19, nb 6	25	Lb 3, nb 2................ 5

1/44 (1) 2/70 (3) 3/121 (4)   (112.3 overs) 346   1/2 (1)   (8 wkts, 78.5 overs) 248
4/189 (2) 5/225 (6) 6/235 (5)   2/14 (2) 3/47 (3)
7/307 (7) 8/318 (8) 9/320 (9)   4/89 (5) 5/114 (4)
10/346 (10)   110 overs: 321-9   6/146 (6) 7/162 (7) 8/217 (9)

Rampaul 24.3–5–94–5; Palladino 24–12–34–1; van Beek 23–3–65–1; Reece 22–9–53–3; Hughes 9–0–50–0; Critchley 8–1–28–0; Madsen 2–0–3–0. *Second innings*—Palladino 11–2–40–2; Rampaul 15–4–55–3; Reece 12–5–33–1; van Beek 17–2–57–0; Madsen 8–2–14–1; Critchley 15.5–2–46–1.

Umpires: M. J. Saggers and B. V. Taylor.

At Leicester, May 27–30. DERBYSHIRE beat LEICESTERSHIRE by 65 runs.

At Chester-le-Street, June 3–6. DERBYSHIRE lost to DURHAM by 29 runs.

At Swansea, June 11–14. DERBYSHIRE drew with GLAMORGAN.

DERBYSHIRE v LANCASHIRE

At Derby, June 17–19. Lancashire won by ten wickets. Lancashire 20pts, Derbyshire 3pts. Toss: uncontested. Championship debut: S. Conners.
   The stars aligned for division leaders Lancashire, who needed less than two days' playing time to complete their fourth Championship victory. After a blank first morning, Vilas opted to bowl under heavy cloud cover on a green, seaming wicket, underprepared thanks to days of rain. He could hardly have had two bowlers better able to exploit the conditions than Anderson and Onions, both 36, who overwhelmed Derbyshire with a combined 17 for 104 in 60 overs. In between, Reece riposted with six against his old county, but Croft scored the game's only half-century to ensure Lancashire led by 83. Then Onions claimed his 700th first-class wicket, and Anderson advanced to 948 as they tore through the batting again. Derbyshire avoided an innings defeat on the third morning, when last man Rampaul ran two off his first ball; he was bowled by his second, and Lancashire needed two to win. Jennings struck the next delivery to the boundary. On the opening day, Derbyshire had handed in the wrong teamsheet, mistakenly including Tony Palladino; after the umpires consulted with Vilas, Championship newcomer Sam Conners was allowed to replace him.
   Close of play: first day, Lancashire 8-1 (Davies 1, Mahmood 7); second day, Derbyshire 19-4 (Hughes 0, Hosein 0).

Derbyshire

L. M. Reece b Anderson	2	(8) c Jennings b Mahmood	0
*B. A. Godleman c Jones b Onions	4	lbw b Anderson	5
W. L. Madsen c Jennings b Onions	4	b Onions	9
T. C. Lace lbw b Onions	4	(1) c Vilas b Onions	3
A. L. Hughes b Anderson	32	c Vilas b Anderson	16
†H. R. Hosein lbw b Anderson	7	c Vilas b Onions	29
M. J. J. Critchley c Vilas b Anderson	30	lbw b Anderson	2
J. L. du Plooy not out	38	(4) lbw b Onions	1
L. V. van Beek lbw b Anderson	0	c Jones b Anderson	1
S. Conners c Hameed b Bohannon	14	not out	6
R. Rampaul c Bohannon b Mahmood	13	b Onions	2
Lb 3, nb 2	5	B 8, lb 2	10

1/6 (2) 2/10 (3) 3/14 (4)   (51.4 overs) 153   1/3 (1) 2/17 (3)   (35 overs) 84
4/16 (1) 5/24 (6) 6/86 (7)   3/17 (2) 4/19 (4)
7/91 (5) 8/91 (9) 9/139 (10) 10/153 (11)   5/59 (5) 6/61 (7) 7/62 (8)
     8/67 (9) 9/82 (6) 10/84 (11)

Anderson 17–7–18–5; Onions 14–4–19–3; Bohannon 9–0–40–1; Mahmood 10.4–0–63–1; Livingstone 1–0–10–0. *Second innings*—Anderson 16–6–29–4; Onions 13–3–38–5; Mahmood 6–1–7–1.

Lancashire

K. K. Jennings lbw b Reece	0	not out	4
A. L. Davies c Hughes b Reece	41	not out	0
S. Mahmood c Hosein b Reece	20		
H. Hameed c Hughes b Reece	9		
R. P. Jones lbw b Conners	13		
L. S. Livingstone c Hughes b van Beek	29		
*†D. J. Vilas b Reece	32		
S. J. Croft not out	53		
J. J. Bohannon c Critchley b Reece	0		
G. Onions c Lace b Rampaul	18		
J. M. Anderson lbw b Rampaul	6		
B 1, lb 6, nb 8	15		

1/0 (1) 2/46 (3) 3/69 (2)   (69.4 overs) 236   (no wkt, 0.1 overs) 4
4/76 (4) 5/112 (6) 6/134 (5)
7/184 (7) 8/186 (9) 9/215 (10) 10/236 (11)

Reece 22–7–58–6; Rampaul 16.4–3–57–2; van Beek 10–2–47–1; Conners 11–2–36–1; Hughes 7–1–19–0; Critchley 3–1–12–0. *Second innings*—Reece 0.1–0–4–0.

Umpires: I. D. Blackwell and N. G. B. Cook.

At Derby, June 23. DERBYSHIRE lost to AUSTRALIA A by seven wickets (see Australia A tour section).

DERBYSHIRE v MIDDLESEX

At Derby, June 30–July 3. Drawn. Derbyshire 12pts, Middlesex 9pts. Toss: uncontested.

Early second-innings wickets left Derbyshire flirting with the possibility of defeat on the last day, but du Plooy and Hosein reasserted the dominance of the bat in a match of landmarks and near misses. Derbyshire had never before reached 500 against Middlesex; here, they surged past, thanks to five scores of 90 or more, a unique achievement for the county. There were hundreds for Godleman and du Plooy (his first in the Championship), though Hudson-Prentice and Dal both fell just short of maiden first-class centuries. Hudson-Prentice, on his first-class county debut, later became the fifth bowler to take a wicket with his first delivery for Derbyshire, and Middlesex were in danger of following on at 250 for six. Then Malan and Simpson plundered a stand of 224, extinguishing home hopes of a substantial lead. Malan's dismissal left him one short of a first double-century, and the partnership one short of the all-time seventh-wicket record against Derbyshire.

Close of play: first day, Derbyshire 372-4 (du Plooy 50, Dal 12); second day, Middlesex 135-3 (Malan 39, Finn 0); third day, Middlesex 436-6 (Malan 177, Simpson 91).

Derbyshire

L. M. Reece c Roland-Jones b Scott	96	– lbw b Sowter	14
*B. A. Godleman c Simpson b Sowter	102	– c Simpson b Helm	18
F. J. Hudson-Prentice c Finn b Helm	99	– run out (Malan)	0
J. L. du Plooy c Sowter b Scott	118	– not out	69
A. L. Hughes c Simpson b Helm	0	– c Simpson b Sowter	0
A. K. Dal c Finn b Roland-Jones	92	– (8) not out	6
†H. R. Hosein not out	32	– (6) lbw b Sowter	61
M. J. J. Critchley (did not bat)		– (7) lbw b Malan	1
B 1, lb 7, nb 10	18	B 4, lb 1, nb 4	9

1/167 (2) 2/222 (1) (6 wkts dec, 144.2 overs) 557   1/23 (2) (6 wkts dec, 47 overs) 178
3/347 (3) 4/349 (5)   2/25 (3) 3/39 (1)
5/482 (4) 6/557 (6)   4/39 (5) 5/160 (6) 6/161 (7)
110 overs: 414-4

L. V. van Beek, A. P. Palladino and R. Rampaul did not bat.

Helm 30–4–112–2; Roland-Jones 30.2–6–107–1; Finn 28–3–111–0; Sowter 39–2–156–1; Scott 14–1–49–2; Malan 3–0–14–0. *Second innings*—Helm 10.2–2–32–1; Roland-Jones 11–2–72–0; Sowter 18–1–89–3; Robson 3–0–19–0; Malan 5–0–11–1.

Middlesex

S. D. Robson c du Plooy b Palladino	34	T. S. Roland-Jones not out	19
S. S. Eskinazi c Critchley b Reece	23	T. G. Helm lbw b du Plooy	1
N. R. T. Gubbins lbw b Reece	37	N. A. Sowter b Palladino	13
*D. J. Malan c and b Critchley	199	B 12, lb 8, nb 8	28
S. T. Finn b van Beek	18		
M. D. E. Holden c Hosein		1/53 (2) 2/65 (1) (167.3 overs) 520	
b Hudson-Prentice	10	3/132 (3) 4/159 (5) 5/204 (6)	
G. F. B. Scott c Critchley b Rampaul	23	6/250 (7) 7/474 (4) 8/488 (8)	
†J. A. Simpson b du Plooy	115	9/492 (10) 10/520 (11) 110 overs: 321-6	

Palladino 27.3–12–44–2; Rampaul 29–6–94–1; Reece 26–5–87–2; van Beek 18–2–72–1; Critchley 31–1–113–1; Hudson-Prentice 17–4–42–1; Hughes 6–1–6–0; du Plooy 13–0–42–2.

Umpires: P. J. Hartley and C. M. Watts.

At Kidderminster, July 7–10. DERBYSHIRE beat WORCESTERSHIRE by 82 runs.

DERBYSHIRE v NORTHAMPTONSHIRE

At Chesterfield, July 14–16. Northamptonshire won by 72 runs. Northamptonshire 22pts, Derbyshire 3pts. Toss: Northamptonshire.

Ill-judged batting on an inconsistent Queen's Park pitch produced 24 wickets on the second day and condensed the match into less than seven sessions. Appropriately, the one outstanding performance with the bat proved decisive: in the last game of his shift at Northamptonshire, South Africa's Bavuma demonstrated resolve and technique a class above much of what followed. His measured aggression brought him a second century in successive games, supported by cavalier thirties from Rossington, Cobb and Zaib, to put the visitors in a strong position on the first afternoon. Their control grew as Sanderson claimed five wickets, and Derbyshire were bowled out 196 behind, despite Hudson-Prentice's bullish unbeaten half-century. Northamptonshire chose not to enforce the follow-on, but in the second innings their application in tough conditions was also poor, with Hudson-Prentice and Palladino reducing them to 39 for five. Chasing 319, however, Derbyshire slipped to 155 for five by the close, and it was all over before lunch on day three.

Close of play: first day, Derbyshire 34-1 (Godleman 7, Madsen 22); second day, Derbyshire 155-5 (Lace 34, Hosein 6).

Northamptonshire

R. S. Vasconcelos lbw b Reece	30	– run out (Hudson-Prentice)	11
R. I. Newton c du Plooy b Rampaul	11	– lbw b Hudson-Prentice	9
L. A. Procter c Madsen b Hudson-Prentice	1	– lbw b Hudson-Prentice	7
T. Bavuma lbw b Critchley	134	– c Lace b Palladino	31
R. I. Keogh c du Plooy b Reece	28	– lbw b Palladino	3
*†A. M. Rossington c and b Critchley	38	– c Hosein b Palladino	0
J. J. Cobb c Hudson-Prentice b Critchley	30	– c Reece b Critchley	24
S. A. Zaib b Hamidullah Qadri	31	– c du Plooy b Hamidullah Qadri	17
B. A. Hutton c Madsen b Hamidullah Qadri	10	– (10) lbw b Palladino	5
M. T. Coles c Rampaul b Critchley	26	– (9) b Hamidullah Qadri	3
B. W. Sanderson not out	0	– not out	10
Lb 1, nb 2	3	Lb 2	2

1/28 (2) 2/43 (3) 3/45 (1) (81.1 overs) 342
4/126 (5) 5/202 (6) 6/258 (7)
7/299 (4) 8/311 (8) 9/342 (10) 10/342 (9)

1/19 (2) 2/20 (1) (30.2 overs) 122
3/30 (3) 4/39 (5)
5/39 (6) 6/86 (7) 7/86 (4)
8/91 (9) 9/102 (10) 10/122 (8)

Palladino 12–5–33–0; Rampaul 12–3–47–1; Hudson-Prentice 8–1–31–1; Reece 14–5–50–2; Hamidullah Qadri 11.1–2–46–2; Critchley 18–0–107–4; du Plooy 6–0–27–0. *Second innings*—Palladino 12–3–33–4; Rampaul 6–0–19–0; Hudson-Prentice 6–1–30–2; Critchley 2–0–14–1; Hamidullah Qadri 4.2–0–24–2.

Derbyshire

L. M. Reece b Hutton	5	– lbw b Keogh	33
*B. A. Godleman c Rossington b Sanderson	22	– st Rossington b Sanderson	25
W. L. Madsen lbw b Hutton	25	– b Coles	27
T. C. Lace lbw b Sanderson	0	– c Bavuma b Hutton	41
J. L. du Plooy lbw b Sanderson	1	– c Hutton b Procter	18
†H. R. Hosein c Rossington b Sanderson	6	– (7) lbw b Procter	22
M. J. J. Critchley lbw b Coles	10	– (8) b Coles	19
F. J. Hudson-Prentice not out	55	– (9) not out	26
A. P. Palladino c Coles b Keogh	16	– (10) c Rossington b Procter	1
Hamidullah Qadri b Sanderson	6	– (6) b Procter	0
R. Rampaul b Keogh	0	– c Bavuma b Sanderson	20
B 4, lb 8, nb 2	14		

1/5 (1) 2/43 (3) 3/48 (4) (47.5 overs) 146
4/52 (5) 5/59 (6) 6/60 (6)
7/95 (7) 8/121 (9) 9/129 (10) 10/146 (11)

1/41 (2) 2/85 (3) (50 overs) 246
3/97 (1) 4/134 (5)
5/134 (6) 6/168 (4) 7/182 (7)
8/206 (8) 9/217 (10) 10/246 (11)

Sanderson 19–5–46–5; Hutton 13–4–22–2; Keogh 8.5–1–47–2; Coles 3–0–15–1; Zaib 4–0–16–0. *Second innings*—Sanderson 11–0–43–2; Hutton 7–0–38–1; Keogh 11–2–48–1; Coles 12–1–79–2; Procter 9–0–26–4.

Umpires: I. D. Blackwell and N. A. Mallender.

DERBYSHIRE v GLOUCESTERSHIRE

At Derby, August 18–21. Gloucestershire won by eight wickets. Gloucestershire 23pts, Derbyshire 3pts. Toss: uncontested. First-class debut: B. M. J. Allison.

Gloucestershire capitalised on a generous fourth-day invitation, when Godleman challenged them to score 263 in 49 overs on an increasingly placid surface. Bracey overcame illness to make a unbeaten century, steering them to their highest successful run-chase against Derbyshire, with 11 balls to spare. To add injury to insult, Lace broke a finger trying to catch him, and was ruled out for the rest of the summer. Earlier in the day, Lace had completed his third Championship hundred of 2019. Derbyshire had struggled to 61 for five on the first morning, and Higgins finished with five for 54; he followed up by adding 221 with Dent, a sixth-wicket record for this fixture, and reaching his fourth century of the season. Facing a deficit of 219, Derbyshire's top order produced a much stronger performance, building a platform from which they could have ruled out defeat. But they gambled, trying to get back into the promotion race, and Gloucestershire took advantage to move into second place.

Close of play: first day, Gloucestershire 46-2 (Dent 20, Hammond 16); second day, Gloucestershire 396-7 (Taylor 12, Payne 13); third day, Derbyshire 305-3 (Lace 69, du Plooy 27).

Derbyshire

L. M. Reece c Roderick b Higgins	3	– (2) lbw b Shaw	38
*B. A. Godleman c Roderick b Payne	0	– (1) c Roderick b Allison	86
W. L. Madsen b Higgins	21	– c Dent b Allison	69
T. C. Lace lbw b Higgins	16	– c Roderick b Allison	125
J. L. du Plooy c Bracey b Shaw	15	– c Higgins b Smith	67
A. L. Hughes b Higgins	39	– b Smith	28
†H. R. Hosein c Hammond b Higgins	6	– not out	29
M. J. J. Critchley lbw b Allison	5		
F. J. Hudson-Prentice c Roderick b Shaw	38		
L. V. van Beek not out	34		
R. Rampaul c Bracey b Shaw	5	– (8) not out	17
Lb 12, w 2, nb 4	18	B 9, lb 4, w 1, nb 8	22

1/3 (2) 2/5 (1) 3/34 (3) (74.5 overs) 200
4/57 (5) 5/61 (4) 6/75 (7)
7/95 (8) 8/150 (6) 9/164 (9) 10/200 (11)

1/71 (2) (6 wkts dec, 130 overs) 481
2/177 (1) 3/245 (3)
4/402 (4) 5/404 (5) 6/455 (6)

Payne 20–3–45–1; Higgins 22–8–54–5; Shaw 17.5–3–50–3; Allison 12–3–30–1; Charlesworth 2–1–8–0; Smith 1–0–1–0. *Second innings*—Payne 20–3–68–0; Higgins 33–7–88–0; Shaw 26–6–102–1; Allison 29–6–109–3; Smith 18–2–73–2; Charlesworth 2–0–16–0; Hammond 2–0–12–0.

Gloucestershire

J. R. Bracey c Hosein b Reece	5	– not out	116
C. D. J. Dent c Hosein b van Beek	169	– c du Plooy b Rampaul	62
G. H. Roderick c Critchley b Rampaul	0	– c Reece b Critchley	48
M. A. H. Hammond c Hosein b Rampaul	36		
T. M. J. Smith b Critchley	32		
B. G. Charlesworth c Hosein b Rampaul	1		
R. F. Higgins lbw b van Beek	101	– (4) not out	21
J. M. R. Taylor b Reece	17		
*D. A. Payne not out	26		
J. Shaw lbw b Reece	4		
B. M. J. Allison b Reece	0		
B 9, lb 12, w 1, nb 6	28	B 1, lb 10, w 1, nb 4	16

1/23 (1) 2/24 (3) 3/77 (4) (123.4 overs) 419
4/142 (5) 5/143 (6) 6/364 (2)
7/367 (7) 8/405 (8) 9/419 (10)
10/419 (11)

1/133 (2) (2 wkts, 47.1 overs) 263
2/227 (3)

110 overs: 379-7

Rampaul 30–5–88–3; Reece 27.4–4–91–4; van Beek 16–2–59–2; Hudson-Prentice 17–6–54–0; Critchley 17–2–55–1; Hughes 10–2–16–0; du Plooy 6–0–35–0. *Second innings*—Rampaul 1–2–52–1; Reece 4–1–14–0; van Beek 4–0–27–0; Critchley 17.1–0–108–1; Madsen 9–1–33–0; Hudson-Prentice 2–0–18–0.

Umpires: J. W. Lloyds and T. Lungley.

At Derby, August 29–31. DERBYSHIRE lost to AUSTRALIANS by an innings and 54 runs (see Australian tour section).

At Manchester, September 10–12. DERBYSHIRE lost to LANCASHIRE by an innings and 45 runs.

DERBYSHIRE v SUSSEX

At Derby, September 16–18. Derbyshire won by 181 runs. Derbyshire 19pts, Sussex 4pts. Toss: uncontested. First-class debut: M. H. McKiernan. Championship debut: D. R. Melton.

A memorable day for Reece set up Derbyshire's first win in four Championship games, and ended Sussex's hopes of promotion. The visitors had finished the opening day only 22 behind with seven wickets left, but next morning Reece took his haul to five, limiting the deficit to 93. He was awarded his county cap at lunch, then dismantled the Sussex attack with clinical fluency in a career-best 184 from 189 balls, including 32 fours and a six. Reece was only the second Derbyshire player to score 150 and take five in an innings in the same match (Garnet Lee did it twice, in 1926 and 1928); his opening stand of 274 with Godleman was an all-wicket county record against Sussex. Five wickets from Robinson and four from Topley, playing his first first-class match in more than two years, kept the target down to 345. But, despite an injury which prevented Palladino bowling, Sussex meekly fell away, and lost with a day to spare.

Close of play: first day, Sussex 116-3 (van Zyl 49, Rawlins 26); second day, Derbyshire 360-2 (Godleman 106, Dal 3).

Derbyshire

L. M. Reece c Robinson b Jordan	0	– run out (Topley)	184
*B. A. Godleman c Salt b Topley	22	– c Salt b Robinson	106
W. L. Madsen c Garton b Jordan	20	– c Brown b Topley	42
J. L. du Plooy c Salt b Topley	24	– (5) lbw b Topley	28
†H. R. Hosein b Wiese	7	– (6) lbw b Robinson	0
M. J. J. Critchley c Rawlins b Wiese	0	– (7) c Brown b Robinson	10
M. H. McKiernan b Wiese	0	– (8) c Salt b Robinson	7
F. J. Hudson-Prentice c Wells b Robinson	14	– (9) c Garton b Topley	17
A. K. Dal c Brown b Wiese	35	– (4) c Brown b Robinson	9
A. P. Palladino c Rawlins b Garton	3	– not out	0
D. R. Melton not out	1	– lbw b Topley	0
Lb 8, nb 4	12	B 9, lb 7, nb 18	34

1/1 (1) 2/43 (2) 3/44 (3)   (46.1 overs) 138
4/59 (5) 5/75 (6) 6/75 (7)
7/83 (4) 8/101 (8) 9/109 (10) 10/138 (9)

1/274 (1) 2/351 (3)   (98.3 overs) 437
3/360 (2) 4/371 (4)
5/371 (6) 6/383 (7) 7/397 (8)
8/432 (5) 9/437 (9) 10/437 (11)

Robinson 10-2-25-1; Jordan 13-1-51-2; Topley 8-2-23-2; Wiese 10.1-5-18-4; Garton 5-1-13-1. *Second innings*—Robinson 24-5-88-5; Jordan 17-4-73-0; Wiese 13-2-61-0; Topley 14.3-2-58-4; Rawlins 11-0-57-0; Garton 7-0-41-0; Wells 4-0-21-0; Beer 8-1-22-0.

Sussex

P. D. Salt c Critchley b Reece	3	– c Madsen b Dal	38
L. W. P. Wells b Reece	5	– c McKiernan b Hudson-Prentice	5
W. A. T. Beer lbw b Hudson-Prentice	9	– lbw b Dal	19
S. van Zyl lbw b Reece	60	– c Hosein b Hudson-Prentice	27
D. M. W. Rawlins c Melton b Reece	34	– c Godleman b Dal	11
*†B. C. Brown c Hosein b Reece	0	– not out	29
D. Wiese c McKiernan b Hudson-Prentice	24	– c Hosein b Hudson-Prentice	0
C. J. Jordan c Hosein b Hudson-Prentice	3	– c sub (L. V. van Beek) b Melton	4
G. H. S. Garton c McKiernan b Melton	50	– b Critchley	2
O. E. Robinson lbw b Madsen	16	– b Critchley	7
R. J. W. Topley not out	1	– lbw b Critchley	5
B 2, lb 9, w 5, nb 10	26	B 1, lb 3, nb 12	16

1/7 (1) 2/16 (2) 3/25 (3)   (60.5 overs) 231
4/128 (5) 5/128 (6) 6/145 (4)
7/152 (8) 8/169 (7) 9/202 (10) 10/231 (9)

1/30 (2) 2/67 (3)   (52.2 overs) 163
3/72 (1) 4/90 (5)
5/120 (4) 6/120 (7) 7/134 (8)
8/145 (9) 9/153 (10) 10/163 (11)

Palladino 12–1–44–0; Reece 20–4–63–5; Hudson-Prentice 15–3–47–3; Melton 3.5–0–24–1; Madsen 5–2–16–1; Critchley 5–0–26–0. *Second innings*—Reece 15–1–61–0; Hudson-Prentice 14–4–36–3; Melton 9–1–30–1; Dal 6–2–11–3; Critchley 5.2–1–9–3; Madsen 3–0–12–0.

Umpires: B. J. Debenham and P. R. Pollard.

At Lord's, September 23–26. DERBYSHIRE drew with MIDDLESEX.

DURHAM

Ready to roar again?

SIMON SINCLAIR

Durham proclaimed a new era when they rebranded their badge, kit and name in early 2019. A snarling lion's head emerging from the letter D replaced the heraldic shield on their limited-overs shirts – now blue for 50-over cricket, yellow for Twenty20 – and the team were officially named Durham Cricket across all formats, dropping the Jets nickname. The new look accompanied a new management team, who oversaw a year of strides forward, slides back and, ultimately, widespread frustration.

The director of cricket, former Australian batsman Marcus North, had begun his reign by hiring New Zealander James Franklin to replace Jon Lewis as head coach. It was a bold decision: this was Franklin's first senior coaching role – he was still playing white-ball cricket for Middlesex in 2018 – although assistants Neil Killeen and Alan Walker provided continuity in the backroom staff.

Eyebrows rose at the signing of Australia's Cameron Bancroft, who had just served a nine-month ban for his role in the ball-tampering incident at Cape Town; they rose even further when it was announced he would succeed Paul Collingwood as captain. But, despite local scepticism, Bancroft proved his worth with 726 Championship runs at 45, plus four wins. The only snag was that his form was so strong he forced his way into the Ashes squad; by the end of July, he was gone.

Bancroft had also been made to wait for his county debut, after Cricket Australia told him to stay in Perth for Western Australia's end-of-season dinner. By the time he reached the UK, Durham were well on their way to losing the opening Championship match, at Derby. There was no improvement when he did play at Chester-le-Street a few days later: Sussex won by six wickets. Defeats by Worcestershire and Gloucestershire followed in May.

Four losses represented Durham's worst start to a Championship season. Familiar batting woes and a lack of ruthlessness were to blame, but Franklin was not deterred. He insisted time was needed to overcome ingrained mental issues that had plagued the team since they were relegated at the end of 2016, the penalty for requiring a financial rescue by the ECB.

The Royal London One-Day Cup provided a welcome interruption. Bancroft broke his team out of their slump, scoring back-to-back centuries to orchestrate victories over Northamptonshire and Leicestershire. Durham enjoyed a strong run, until their attempts to reach the knockouts were blighted by washouts in the last two matches; they finished fourth in the North Group.

They used their one-day momentum to reboot the Championship campaign, beginning with an incredible turnaround against Derbyshire at Riverside in June. Durham looked beaten on day four, only to grab four wickets in eight deliveries – a dramatic triumph to get off the mark.

That began an eight-match unbeaten run, including five wins, which lifted them from the bottom of Division Two to fourth place, and an unlikely promotion bid. With Bancroft now gone, North and Franklin had to scramble for overseas replacements in the form of Peter Handscomb and B-J. Watling. Ned Eckersley, who had joined from Leicestershire, stepped up as captain for the last four Championship games; he could claim to be Durham's signing of the season for his performances with the gloves (42 catches) and lower-order batting (720 runs). Defeat by Northamptonshire in

Cameron Bancroft

the penultimate round ended the charge – and again left them ruing that shoddy start.

Durham could well have surged into the knockouts in the Vitality Blast. They had pulled off a coup by signing Australia's D'Arcy Short, who in September was named the tournament's Most Valuable Player for his devastating batting – he formed a powerful opening partnership with 20-year-old Scott Steel – and his left-arm wrist-spin. Middle-order collapses against Worcestershire and Yorkshire cost Durham victory in successive home matches. They were unable to recover, wasting Short's outstanding contribution by ending up three points off the pace in the North Group. He turned down a deal for 2020, and moved to Surrey.

As Franklin admitted, Durham had only themselves to blame for missing out in the Championship and the Blast. But there were signs of recovery around Riverside. Three years since their relegation, and the financial sanctions that cost them several key players, Durham looked to be on their way back to becoming a competitive side in all three formats. Bancroft's return in 2020 should be a huge boost, providing consistency at the top of the order alongside opener Alex Lees – the leading Championship run-scorer with 899 – as well as leadership skills.

Chris Rushworth's brilliance with the red ball continued: turning 33 in July, he took 69 Championship wickets at 18. Back in the North-East after six seasons at Leicester, Ben Raine collected 54, while adding valuable late-order runs. Pace bowler Brydon Carse finally got on top of his injury problems to flourish in all forms of the game. His upward trajectory was highlighted when he was selected by Northern Superchargers in the Hundred draft; in December, he was picked for the England Lions tour of Australia. And all-rounder Paul Coughlin was to return from Nottingham in 2020.

Durham ended a season of change with renewed hopes that they could advance from the foundations laid by North and Franklin to regain Division One status, and recreate past glories.

Championship attendance: 16,225.

DURHAM RESULTS

All first-class matches – Played 15: Won 6, Lost 5, Drawn 4.
County Championship matches – Played 14: Won 5, Lost 5, Drawn 4.

Specsavers County Championship, 5th in Division 2;
Vitality Blast, 6th in North Group; Royal London One-Day Cup, 4th in North Group.

COUNTY CHAMPIONSHIP AVERAGES, BATTING AND FIELDING

	Birthplace	M	I	NO	R	HS	100	Avge	Ct
C. T. Bancroft¶	Attadale, Australia	9	17	1	726	158	2	45.37	16
E. J. H. Eckersley	Oxford	13	22	4	720	118	1	40.00	42
†A. Z. Lees	Halifax	14	25	1	899	181	3	37.45	10
N. J. Rimmington††	Redcliffe, Australia	6	9	2	210	92	0	30.00	3
J. T. A. Burnham	Durham‡	13	23	1	598	86	0	27.18	4
†L. Trevaskis	Carlisle	10	17	1	392	64	0	24.50	2
G. J. Harte	Johannesburg, SA	11	21	1	459	77	0	22.95	2
B. A. Raine	Sunderland‡	14	23	2	464	82	0	22.09	0
B. A. Carse	Port Elizabeth, SA	10	15	3	246	77*	0	20.50	1
A. J. Robson	Darlinghurst, Australia	4	6	0	97	64	0	16.16	6
C. T. Steel	Greenbrae, USA	6	10	0	133	39	0	13.30	2
S. Steel	Durham‡	2	4	0	48	39	0	12.00	1
M. J. Potts	Sunderland‡	3	5	1	46	20	0	11.50	1
G. Clark	Whitehaven	4	8	1	79	26	0	11.28	4
R. D. Pringle	Sunderland‡	2	4	0	41	30	0	10.25	1
M. E. T. Salisbury	Chelmsford	5	10	1	76	23	0	8.44	0
W. J. Weighell	Middlesbrough	3	5	0	37	24	0	7.40	1
C. Rushworth	Sunderland‡	14	19	8	56	12*	0	5.09	3

Also batted: S. J. D. Bell (*Newcastle-upon-Tyne*) (1 match) 1; J. O. I. Campbell (*Portsmouth*) (1 match) 0*; P. S. P. Handscomb¶ (*Box Hill, Australia*) (2 matches) 29, 54, 3 (4 ct); M. A. Jones (*Ormskirk*) (2 matches) 0, 9, 0; S. W. Poynter†† (*Hammersmith*) (1 match) 8, 7 (3 ct); M. J. Richardson (*Port Elizabeth, SA*) (1 match) 7, 5 (5 ct); W. R. Smith (*Luton*) (1 match) 4, 0 (1 ct); B-J. Watling¶ (*Durban, SA*) (2 matches) 0, 35, 104* (1 ct).

‡ *Born in Durham.*   ¶ *Official overseas player.*   †† *Other non-England-qualified.*

Durham ceased to award caps after 2005.

BOWLING

	Style	O	M	R	W	BB	5I	Avge
C. Rushworth	RFM	486.4	127	1,271	69	6-39	4	18.42
B. A. Raine	RFM	463.4	122	1,179	54	6-27	3	21.83
M. E. T. Salisbury	RFM	137.1	27	448	19	4-67	0	23.57
N. J. Rimmington	RFM	140.2	29	392	16	4-42	0	24.50
G. J. Harte	RM	91	23	256	10	4-15	0	25.60
B. A. Carse	RF	250.4	42	940	35	6-26	3	26.85

Also bowled: J. T. A. Burnham (RM) 10.1–2–17–0; J. O. I. Campbell (LFM) 28–3–87–1; G. Clark (LB) 2–0–7–0; A. Z. Lees (LB) 0.1–0–0–0; M. J. Potts (RFM) 68–13–213–2; R. D. Pringle (OB) 2–0–6–0; W. R. Smith (OB) 2–1–10–0; C. T. Steel (LB) 10–1–35–2; S. Steel (OB) 7–3–16–0; L. Trevaskis (SLA) 149.3–36–410–6; W. J. Weighell (RM) 75.1–17–222–9.

LEADING ROYAL LONDON CUP AVERAGES (80 runs/4 wickets)

Batting

	Runs	HS	Avge	SR	Ct
C. T. Bancroft	377	151*	94.25	95.44	9
A. Z. Lees	361	115	90.25	83.37	2
M. J. Richardson	215	102	71.66	91.88	0
S. Steel	227	68	32.42	80.78	3
G. Clark	89	66	14.83	80.90	3

Bowling

	W	BB	Avge	Ec
B. A. Carse	10	3-52	22.30	5.4
M. J. Potts	10	4-62	23.60	5.3
L. Trevaskis	7	2-27	26.71	4.4
M. E. T. Salisbury	9	3-51	31.00	5.3
B. A. Raine	7	2-25	31.42	4.6

LEADING VITALITY BLAST AVERAGES (100 runs/15 overs)

Batting	Runs	HS	Avge	SR	Ct		Bowling	W	BB	Avge	ER
D. J. M. Short....	483	77*	43.90	**139.59**	5		S. Steel	5	1-6	19.80	**6.18**
S. Steel	369	70	33.54	**136.66**	1		N. J. Rimmington.	16	3-15	19.06	**6.95**
G. Clark	196	59*	21.77	**134.24**	7		L. Trevaskis......	12	3-16	23.41	**6.99**
P. S. P. Handscomb	206	65*	34.33	**120.46**	4		D. J. M. Short...	13	2-19	24.46	**7.88**
A. Z. Lees.......	128	44	25.60	**107.56**	3		M. J. Potts	17	3-22	19.52	**8.33**
							B. A. Carse	7	1-21	42.00	**8.90**

FIRST-CLASS COUNTY RECORDS

Highest score for	273	M. L. Love v Hampshire at Chester-le-Street....	2003
Highest score against	501*	B. C. Lara (Warwickshire) at Birmingham	1994
Leading run-scorer	12,030	P. D. Collingwood (avge 33.98).............	1996–2018
Best bowling for	10-47	O. D. Gibson v Hampshire at Chester-le-Street ..	2007
Best bowling against	9-34	J. A. R. Harris (Middlesex) at Lord's..........	2015
Leading wicket-taker	527	G. Onions (avge 25.58)...................	2004–17
Highest total for	648-5 dec	v Nottinghamshire at Chester-le-Street.......	2009
Highest total against	810-4 dec	by Warwickshire at Birmingham	1994
Lowest total for	61	v Leicestershire at Leicester..............	2018
Lowest total against	18	by Durham MCCU at Chester-le-Street........	2012

LIST A COUNTY RECORDS

Highest score for	164	B. A. Stokes v Nottinghamshire at Chester-le-St .	2014
Highest score against	174	J. M. Bairstow (Yorkshire) at Leeds..........	2017
Leading run-scorer	6,007	P. D. Collingwood (avge 33.00).............	1995–2018
Best bowling for	7-32	S. P. Davis v Lancashire at Chester-le-Street....	1983
Best bowling against	6-22	A. Dale (Glamorgan) at Colwyn Bay	1993
Leading wicket-taker	298	N. Killeen (avge 23.96)...................	1995–2010
Highest total for	353-8	v Nottinghamshire at Chester-le-Street.......	2014
Highest total against	361-7	by Essex at Chelmsford	1996
Lowest total for	72	v Warwickshire at Birmingham	2002
Lowest total against	63	by Hertfordshire at Darlington	1964

TWENTY20 COUNTY RECORDS

Highest score for	108*	P. D. Collingwood v Worcestershire at Worcester..	2017
Highest score against	127	T. Köhler-Cadmore (Worcs) at Worcester	2016
Leading run-scorer	3,206	P. Mustard (avge 25.04, SR 121.99)	2003–16
Best bowling for	5-6	P. D. Collingwood v Northants at Chester-le-St...	2011
Best bowling against	5-11	J. W. Shutt (Yorkshire) at Chester-le-Street ...	2019
Leading wicket-taker	93	G. R. Breese (avge 21.56, ER 6.76).........	2004–14
Highest total for	225-2	v Leicestershire at Chester-le-Street.........	2010
Highest total against	225-6	by Worcestershire at Worcester.............	2016
Lowest total for	78	v Lancashire at Chester-le-Street	2018
Lowest total against	47	by Northamptonshire at Chester-le-Street......	2011

ADDRESS

Emirates Riverside, Chester-le-Street, County Durham DH3 3QR; 0191 387 1717; reception @durhamcricket.co.uk; www. durhamcricket.co.uk.

OFFICIALS

Captain C. T. Bancroft
  (Twenty20) S. W. Poynter
Director of cricket M. J. North
High performance coach J. E. C. Franklin
Academy coach J. B. Windows

Chairman Sir Ian Botham
Chief operating officer R. Dowson
Chief executive T. J. Bostock
Head groundsman V. Demain
Scorer W. R. Dobson

DURHAM v DURHAM MCCU

At Chester-le-Street, March 26–28. Durham won by 296 runs. Toss: Durham. First-class debuts: R. L. Greenwell; L. Bedford, C. G. Benjamin, J. O. I. Campbell, A. H. J. Dewes, T. B. Powe, C. F. B. Scott, B. D. Sidwell.

Durham dominated the students in the first first-class fixture played in March at Chester-le-Street. Will Smith laid the groundwork in a seven-hour 179, sharing century stands with acting-captain Lees and No. 9 Harding. Then Rushworth, with three for nine in nine overs, and Raine, with four on his return to Durham after six seasons with Leicestershire, took charge. Poynter held six catches, one short of the county record, before adding 118 with Harte as Durham extended their lead to 502. Rushworth and Co drove them home by dismissing the students again in the last two sessions.

Close of play: first day, Durham 331-7 (Smith 148, Harding 35); second day, Durham 65-1 (Harte 44, Greenwell 20).

Durham

G. J. Harte c Singh b Owen	2	– not out 108
*A. Z. Lees run out (Sidwell)	74	– c Sookias b Owen 0
R. L. Greenwell c Sookias b Owen	4	– sub (J. Subramanyan) b Graves... 31
W. R. Smith c Dewes b Graves	179	– (5) not out................. 15
†S. W. Poynter lbw b Singh	0	– (4) b Dewes 80
R. D. Pringle lbw b Owen	3	
B. A. Raine c and b Singh	22	
J. Coughlin c Sookias b Singh	24	
G. H. I. Harding b Sidwell	36	
N. J. Rimmington lbw b Graves	22	
C. Rushworth not out	10	
B 10, lb 11	21	W 1, nb 2 3

1/4 (1) 2/14 (3) 3/130 (2)   (121.2 overs) 399   1/1 (2)   (3 wkts dec, 63 overs) 237
4/132 (5) 5/147 (6) 6/184 (7)   2/95 (3) 3/213 (4)
7/236 (8) 8/337 (9) 9/385 (4) 10/399 (10)

Owen 21–7–60–3; Campbell 28–5–87–0; Sidwell 30–10–58–1; Singh 26–1–117–3; Graves 16.2–3–56–2. *Second innings*—Owen 6.4–1–20–1; Campbell 7–2–24–0; Singh 15–1–69–0; Sidwell 9.2–1–26–0; Graves 17–3–62–1; Dewes 7–0–33–1; Powe 1–0–3–0.

Durham MCCU

L. Bedford c and b Rushworth	0	– b Rushworth.................... 0
A. H. J. Dewes lbw b Rushworth	5	– c Poynter b Rimmington ... 6
T. B. Powe c Poynter b Rushworth	33	– lbw b Raine 15
*B. W. M. Graves c Poynter b Raine	9	– c Poynter b Rimmington ... 66
C. F. B. Scott c Lees b Raine	32	– b Coughlin 4
C. G. Benjamin c Poynter b Harding	13	– b Rimmington 33
†J. H. Sookias c Poynter b Coughlin	1	– lbw b Raine 0
A. R. Singh c Poynter b Raine	31	– c Poynter b Rushworth..... 2
B. D. Sidwell c Poynter b Harding	3	– not out 42
X. G. Owen not out	7	– c Raine b Pringle 24
J. O. I. Campbell b Raine	0	– c and b Pringle 2
		B 5, lb 7 12

1/4 (1) 2/9 (2) 3/41 (4)   (59.5 overs) 134   1/0 (1) 2/8 (2)   (57.4 overs) 206
4/60 (3) 5/87 (5) 6/90 (7)   3/43 (3) 4/48 (5)
7/107 (6) 8/115 (9) 9/130 (8) 10/134 (11)   5/123 (6) 6/124 (7) 7/127 (8)
                                         8/150 (4) 9/204 (10) 10/206 (11)

Rushworth 9–7–9–3; Coughlin 13–3–39–1; Raine 11.5–3–30–4; Rimmington 9–1–28–0; Pringle 10–3–19–0; Harding 7–4–9–2. *Second innings*—Rushworth 10–0–37–3; Rimmington 9–1–26–2; Coughlin 8–2–28–1; Raine 11–5–21–2; Smith 5–1–21–0; Harte 3–0–25–0; Pringle 7.4–3–16–2; Harding 4–0–20–0.

Umpires: N. A. Mallender and N. Pratt.

At Derby, April 5–8. DURHAM lost to DERBYSHIRE by 125 runs.

DURHAM v SUSSEX

At Chester-le-Street, April 11–14. Sussex won by six wickets. Sussex 20pts, Durham 4pts. Toss: uncontested. County debuts: C. T. Bancroft, E. J. H. Eckersley.

When Sussex were 71 for seven on the second day, it looked as if Durham's new captain, Cameron Bancroft, might begin with a win. Another incomer, Ned Eckersley from Leicestershire, had rescued the home side from 97 for five, almost doubling the score with Trevaskis, who reached a maiden fifty, and their eventual total of 224 was beginning to look solid. But Wells dug Sussex out of trouble, bringing the deficit down to 22 before he ran out of partners on 98, and Wiese's savvy seam ripped through Durham's lower order. Needing 212, Sussex still had plenty of work to do, especially when Rushworth and Raine reduced them to 16 for two. But van Zyl – who had put on 376 with Wells during Durham's visit to Hove in 2017 – saw them home van a brilliant unbeaten century.

Close of play: first day, Durham 210-8 (Raine 12, Salisbury 2); second day, Durham 31-1 (Lees 14, Bancroft 14); third day, Sussex 144-3 (van Zyl 66, Evans 21).

Durham

C. T. Steel b Robinson	3	– lbw b Robinson	0
A. Z. Lees b Mir Hamza	12	– c Brown b Wiese	14
*C. T. Bancroft c Jordan b Wiese	33	– c Brown b Mir Hamza	22
G. J. Harte b Robinson	18	– not out	74
J. T. A. Burnham lbw b Robinson	0	– b Mir Hamza	5
†E. J. H. Eckersley c Brown b Jordan	40	– c Evans b Haines	21
L. Trevaskis b Jordan	54	– c Brown b Wiese	0
B. A. Raine c van Zyl b Wiese	16	– c Brown b Wiese	0
W. J. Weighell lbw b Jordan	0	– c Salt b Wiese	24
M. E. T. Salisbury not out	7	– c Jordan b Wiese	1
C. Rushworth lbw b Robinson	3	– b Jordan	9
B 8, lb 18, nb 12	38	B 4, lb 9, nb 6	19

1/8 (1) 2/17 (2) 3/63 (4) (102.4 overs) 224
4/63 (5) 5/97 (3) 6/190 (6)
7/201 (7) 8/201 (9) 9/214 (8) 10/224 (11)

1/0 (1) 2/32 (2) (66 overs) 189
3/62 (3) 4/70 (5)
5/105 (6) 6/106 (7) 7/106 (8)
8/150 (9) 9/152 (10) 10/189 (11)

Robinson 29.4–10–53–4; Mir Hamza 16–7–21–1; Wiese 23–7–49–2; Haines 13–3–30–0; Jordan 19–6–38–3; Wells 2–0–7–0. *Second innings*—Robinson 13–2–41–1; Mir Hamza 14–5–34–2; Jordan 16–3–42–1; Wiese 16–2–43–5; Haines 3–1–9–1; Wells 4–1–7–0.

Sussex

P. D. Salt c Lees b Rushworth	2	– c Weighell b Rushworth	2
T. J. Haines c Bancroft b Raine	22	– c Bancroft b Raine	8
L. W. P. Wells not out	98	– lbw b Salisbury	41
S. van Zyl c Bancroft b Weighell	1	– not out	101
L. J. Evans b Weighell	10	– lbw b Salisbury	51
†B. C. Brown lbw b Weighell	0	– not out	1
M. G. K. Burgess b Rushworth	9		
D. Wiese b Rushworth	1		
C. J. Jordan run out (Raine/Eckersley)	25		
O. E. Robinson b Salisbury	14		
Mir Hamza b Rushworth	0		
B 3, lb 5, w 2, nb 2	12	B 1, lb 4, w 1, nb 2	8

1/3 (1) 2/38 (2) 3/39 (4) (68 overs) 202
4/49 (5) 5/49 (6) 6/67 (7)
7/71 (8) 8/119 (9) 9/159 (10) 10/202 (11)

1/8 (1) (4 wkts, 66.4 overs) 212
2/16 (2) 3/99 (3)
4/211 (5)

Rushworth 18–4–41–4; Salisbury 15.3–5–53–1; Raine 16–3–41–1; Weighell 11–1–41–3; Trevaskis 4–0–7–0; Harte 3–0–11–0. *Second innings*—Rushworth 18–3–40–1; Salisbury 14.4–0–62–2; Raine 20–4–57–1; Weighell 10–2–30–0; Trevaskis 4–0–18–0.

Umpires: G. D. Lloyd and R. J. Warren.

at Worcester, May 14–17. DURHAM lost to WORCESTERSHIRE by five wickets.

DURHAM v GLOUCESTERSHIRE

At Chester-le-Street, May 20–22. Gloucestershire won by six wickets. Gloucestershire 19pts, Durham 3pts. Toss: uncontested.

Gloucestershire exposed Durham's batting frailties to condemn them to their fourth successive Championship defeat. In a devastating spell of 8–3–11–3, Payne removed Bancroft, Lees and Harte as they lurched to 17 for four. Burnham and Raine revived the innings, but Durham had to settle for 158. Gloucestershire lost their sixth wicket at 120 at the start of the second day but, despite tight bowling from Rushworth and Salisbury the last four wickets added 54 to edge them ahead. An early onslaught from Shaw – Harte completed a pair – left Durham's second innings effectively 27 for four, before Bancroft and Trevaskis began to rebuild, but Bancroft's run-out prompted another collapse, and Gloucestershire required only 117 to win. Dent and Hammond whittled that down by half that evening, with the game's only fifty stand, and next day Bracey steered his side to their first win of the season, with five sessions to spare.

Close of play: first day, Gloucestershire 120-5 (Howell 27, Shaw 8); second day, Gloucestershire 64-1 (Hammond 30, Shaw 0).

Durham

A. Z. Lees c and b Payne	4	– lbw b Payne	0
R. D. Pringle lbw b Higgins	9	– c Payne b Shaw	30
*C. T. Bancroft c Bracey b Payne	0	– run out (van Buuren)	40
G. J. Harte b Payne	0	– b Shaw	0
J. T. A. Burnham c Dent b Taylor	43	– b Shaw	0
L. Trevaskis c Higgins b Taylor	10	– c Bracey b Payne	21
†E. J. H. Eckersley lbw b Higgins	12	– c Howell b Higgins	21
B. A. Raine c Bracey b Shaw	42	– c Bracey b Taylor	7
B. A. Carse c Bracey b Shaw	0	– c Bracey b Higgins	8
M. E. T. Salisbury b Payne	23	– b Taylor	0
C. Rushworth not out	4	– not out	0
Lb 7, nb 4	11	B 4, w 1	5

1/12 (2) 2/13 (3) 3/14 (1) (56.4 overs) 158
4/17 (4) 5/31 (6) 6/62 (7)
7/108 (5) 8/109 (9) 9/138 (8) 10/158 (10)

1/0 (1) 2/39 (2) (50.4 overs) 132
3/43 (4) 4/43 (5)
5/91 (6) 6/97 (6) 7/120 (8)
8/131 (9) 9/132 (10) 10/132 (7)

Payne 19.4–5–40–4; Higgins 15–6–35–2; Shaw 13–1–36–2; Taylor 9–1–40–2. *Second innings*—Payne 14–1–48–2; Shaw 14–5–31–3; Higgins 11.4–3–13–2; Taylor 9–2–28–2; Howell 2–0–8–0.

Gloucestershire

M. A. H. Hammond lbw b Carse	14	– (2) c Eckersley b Salisbury	36
*C. D. J. Dent c Eckersley b Salisbury	23	– (1) c Eckersley b Salisbury	29
†J. R. Bracey c Eckersley b Rushworth	35	– (4) not out	25
G. T. Hankins b Salisbury	0	– (5) b Salisbury	14
G. H. Roderick lbw b Salisbury	1	– (6) not out	3
B. A. C. Howell c Bancroft b Raine	27		
J. Shaw b Rushworth	18	– (3) c Eckersley b Rushworth	0
R. F. Higgins c Carse b Rushworth	3		
G. L. van Buuren c Eckersley b Carse	17		
D. A. Payne c Eckersley b Carse	7		
M. D. Taylor not out	14		
B 4, lb 7, nb 4	15	B 4, lb 4, nb 4	12

1/27 (1) 2/59 (2) 3/65 (4) (56.5 overs) 174
4/67 (5) 5/102 (3) 6/120 (6)
7/133 (8) 8/144 (7) 9/151 (9) 10/174 (10)

1/60 (1) (4 wkts, 40.3 overs) 119
2/64 (3) 3/82 (2)
4/112 (5)

Rushworth 18–5–39–3; Raine 15–4–43–1; Carse 11.5–0–51–3; Salisbury 12–2–30–3. *Second innings*—Rushworth 8–3–16–1; Raine 12–4–34–0; Salisbury 11–2–41–3; Carse 9–3–20–0; Burnham 0.3–0–0–0.

Umpires: P. K. Baldwin and N. G. B. Cook.

DURHAM v DERBYSHIRE

At Chester-le-Street, June 3–6. Durham won by 29 runs. Durham 21pts, Derbyshire 5pts. Toss: uncontested. Championship debut: J. L. du Plooy.

Durham snatched their first Championship victory since September 2018 in a dramatic finish. With five overs to go, Derbyshire needed 34; they had four wickets left and Critchley going strong on 71. But ambition got the better of him, and he was caught on the boundary, going for a big hit off Rushworth. Hosein was run out, van Beek bowled and, when Raine bowled Palladino, the last four had fallen in eight deliveries. On the first day, Jones – Lees's fourth opening partner in five matches (following Harte, Steel and Pringle) – had failed to score, but sixties from Lees and Burnham set up Durham's biggest total of the season to date. Rampaul claimed his best Championship figures, thanks to two quality new-ball spells. Derbyshire then struggled to 128 for six before Critchley, exploiting a life on 28, compiled an unbeaten 79, which left them only 25 behind. They surged back into the contest. Rampaul and Reece reduced Durham to 86 for five, which would have been six had Madsen held Lees on 34. Instead, Lees added 123 with Eckersley and carried his bat for nearly six hours in his first first-class century since leaving Yorkshire. The target was a competitive 268; Critchley's second innings almost pulled it off.

Close of play: first day, Durham 254-8 (Eckersley 5, Potts 3); second day, Derbyshire 181-6 (Critchley 38, du Plooy 10); third day, Durham 160-5 (Lees 63, Eckersley 33).

Durham

A. Z. Lees c Hughes b Reece	63	– not out 107
M. A. Jones c Hosein b Rampaul	0	– c Hughes b Rampaul 9
*C. T. Bancroft lbw b Rampaul	18	– c Hughes b Reece 3
G. J. Harte lbw b Palladino	24	– c Critchley b Rampaul 26
J. T. A. Burnham lbw b Rampaul	67	– c and b Rampaul 0
L. Trevaskis c du Plooy b Critchley	40	– b Reece 2
†E. J. H. Eckersley not out	26	– c van Beek b Critchley 52
B. A. Raine lbw b Rampaul	0	– c Godleman b Critchley 0
B. A. Carse c Hughes b Reece	10	– c Lace b van Beek 4
M. J. Potts b Palladino	14	– c du Plooy b van Beek 0
C. Rushworth c Lace b Rampaul	4	– run out (Godleman) 2
B 5, lb 7, w 5, nb 10	27	B 10, lb 18, w 5, nb 4 37

1/0 (2) 2/30 (3) 3/87 (4)   (106.5 overs) 293
4/140 (1) 5/226 (6) 6/233 (5)
7/233 (8) 8/250 (9) 9/270 (10) 10/293 (11)

1/12 (2) 2/26 (3)   (84.5 overs) 242
5/86 (6) 6/209 (7) 7/211 (8)
8/227 (9) 9/232 (10) 10/242 (11)

Palladino 26–11–58–2; Rampaul 29.5–6–77–5; van Beek 17–4–50–0; Reece 17–6–28–2; Hughes 5–1–22–0; Madsen 4–0–21–0; Critchley 8–0–25–1. *Second innings*—Palladino 20–4–47–0; Rampaul 21–5–53–3; Reece 13–5–17–2; van Beek 19–2–62–2; Critchley 9.5–1–32–2; Hughes 2–1–3–0.

Derbyshire

L. M. Reece c Eckersley b Raine	34	– c Eckersley b Potts 21
*B. A. Godleman b Harte	66	– lbw b Rushworth 42
W. L. Madsen c Eckersley b Raine	0	– lbw b Raine 0
T. C. Lace b Harte	21	– b Raine 24
A. L. Hughes c Bancroft b Rushworth	0	– b Carse 40
H. R. Hosein b Harte	0	– (8) run out (Potts) 8
M. J. J. Critchley not out	79	– (6) c Trevaskis b Rushworth 71
J. L. du Plooy c Eckersley b Reece	17	– (7) c Eckersley b Raine 19
L. V. van Beek b Harte	12	– b Rushworth 0
A. P. Palladino c Trevaskis b Raine	6	– b Raine 0
R. Rampaul c Eckersley b Rushworth	12	– not out 4
B 1, lb 6, nb 14	21	Lb 7, nb 2 9

1/83 (1) 2/83 (3) 3/117 (2)   (87.5 overs) 268
4/128 (4) 5/128 (6) 6/128 (5)
7/199 (8) 8/229 (9) 9/245 (10) 10/268 (11)

1/55 (1) 2/60 (3)   (71.2 overs) 238
3/78 (2) 4/96 (4)
5/181 (5) 6/214 (7) 7/234 (6)
8/234 (8) 9/234 (9) 10/238 (10)

Rushworth 22.5–5–96–2; Carse 11–1–65–0; Raine 26–11–46–4; Potts 18–5–39–0; Harte 10–6–15–4. *Second innings*—Rushworth 18–2–55–3; Carse 11–1–44–1; Potts 13–2–47–1; Raine 18.2–4–44–4; Harte 8–3–21–0; Trevaskis 3–0–20–0.

Umpires: R. J. Bailey and P. R. Pollard.

DURHAM v NORTHAMPTONSHIRE

At Chester-le-Street, June 10–13. Drawn. Durham 9pts, Northamptonshire 10pts. Toss: uncontested. County debut: M. T. Coles.

Rain washed out the final two days of what had been shaping up as a fascinating bottom-of-the-table contest. Northamptonshire had just passed Durham's first-innings 253, thanks to Vasconcelos, who reached three figures by hooking Carse for six. Rossington, in charge after Wakely's resignation a few days earlier, had inserted Durham, who were soon 18 for four, with the top three bowled by Sanderson, and Matt Coles — on loan from Essex — finding Harte's edge. Raine and Carse came together in mid-afternoon, at 81 for seven, when even one batting point seemed unthinkable – but Durham ended up with two. Both made career-bests as they put on 154, a county eighth-wicket record, beating 147 by Phil Mustard and Liam Plunkett at Headingley in 2009. Northamptonshire's batsmen benefited from poor catching: most expensively, Vasconcelos was dropped by Burnham at slip on ten, and went on to add 99 with Bavuma and an unbroken 80 with Hutton, either side of a burst of three in seven balls from Rushworth.

Close of play: first day, Durham 209-7 (Raine 75, Carse 47); second day, Northamptonshire 254-6 (Vasconcelos 105, Hutton 34); third day, no play.

Durham

A. Z. Lees b Sanderson	8	B. A. Carse not out	77
M. A. Jones b Sanderson	0	M. J. Potts c Hutton b Sanderson	3
*C. T. Bancroft b Sanderson	2	C. Rushworth lbw b Hutton	4
G. J. Harte c Vasconcelos b Coles	6	Lb 7	7
J. T. A. Burnham lbw b Buck	12		
L. Trevaskis c Curran b Buck	26	1/1 (2) 2/5 (3) 3/16 (1) (107.3 overs)	253
†E. J. H. Eckersley c Rossington b Coles	26	4/18 (4) 5/46 (5) 6/81 (7)	
B. A. Raine lbw b Hutton	82	7/81 (6) 8/235 (8) 9/244 (10) 10/253 (11)	

Sanderson 28–11–55–4; Hutton 22.3–9–42–2; Coles 17–5–37–2; Buck 20–3–68–2; Procter 10–4–27–0; Keogh 9–3–15–0; Bavuma 1–0–2–0.

Northamptonshire

B. J. Curran b Carse	32	B. A. Hutton not out	34
R. S. Vasconcelos not out	105		
A. G. Wakely c Bancroft b Carse	0	B 8, lb 15, w 1, nb 6	30
T. Bavuma c Eckersley b Carse	43		
R. I. Keogh lbw b Rushworth	0	1/46 (1) 2/54 (3) (6 wkts, 71 overs)	254
*†A. M. Rossington c Eckersley b Rushworth	10	3/153 (4) 4/162 (5)	
L. A. Procter c Eckersley b Rushworth	0	5/174 (6) 6/174 (7)	

M. T. Coles, N. L. Buck and B. W. Sanderson did not bat.

Rushworth 21–5–45–3; Carse 17–2–62–3; Raine 14–2–55–0; Trevaskis 1–0–5–0; Potts 16–3–52–0; Harte 2–0–12–0.

Umpires: J. H. Evans and P. J. Hartley.

At Hove, June 24–27. DURHAM beat SUSSEX by 196 runs.

At Sedbergh, June 30–July 3. DURHAM drew with LANCASHIRE.

At Leicester, July 7–10. DURHAM beat LEICESTERSHIRE by 119 runs.

DURHAM v WORCESTERSHIRE

At Chester-le-Street, July 13–16. Durham won by 109 runs. Durham 20pts, Worcestershire 3pts. Toss: uncontested.

Rushworth bowled Durham to their third win in four games, which put them one point behind Northamptonshire and the third promotion slot. They had made a dreadful start on the first morning – 47 for six against quality bowling, before rain caused a lengthy break. But Eckersley and Raine salvaged the innings between showers, taking their partnership to 115 next day. Raine, stranded on 78 as Barnard finished with four wickets, then combined with Rushworth to skittle Worcestershire for 151, handing Durham a healthy advantage of 61. Burnham led a confident second-innings effort which stretched that to 351, before Bancroft – in his last match before joining Australia – declared on the third evening. Rushworth struck in successive overs to reduce Worcestershire to 11 for three; though Cox and D'Oliveira offered resistance on the final day, he continued to whittle away at the line-up, his persistence claiming six for 39, and ten for 67 in the match.

Close of play: first day, Durham 122-6 (Eckersley 39, Raine 25); second day, Durham 26-0 (Bancroft 11, Lees 5); third day, Worcestershire 31-3 (Ferguson 15, Whiteley 14).

Durham

*C. T. Bancroft lbw b Pennington	8	– c Cox b Barnard	28
A. Z. Lees b Morris	12	– b Pennington	40
G. J. Harte lbw b Leach	4	– b Barnard	19
J. T. A. Burnham lbw b Leach	0	– c Ferguson b Whiteley	76
G. Clark c Cox b Morris	12	– b Barnard	6
R. D. Pringle c Dell b Barnard	1	– lbw b Morris	1
†E. J. H. Eckersley b Wessels b Barnard	50	– b Barnard	33
B. A. Raine not out	78	– b Leach	28
B. A. Carse c Mitchell b Whiteley	17	– not out	11
N. J. Rimmington c Cox b Barnard	2	– not out	21
C. Rushworth lbw b Barnard	0		
B 14, lb 12, nb 2	28	B 8, lb 12, w 1, nb 6	27

1/19 (1) 2/26 (3) 3/26 (4)   (75.4 overs) 212   1/56 (1)   (8 wkts dec, 96 overs) 290
4/38 (2) 5/43 (6) 6/47 (5)   2/103 (2) 3/131 (3)
7/162 (7) 8/209 (9) 9/212 (10) 10/212 (11)   4/141 (5) 5/142 (6)
6/205 (4) 7/255 (8) 8/259 (7)

Leach 24–7–68–2; Pennington 18–8–29–1; Morris 14–3–37–2; Barnard 16.4–3–42–4; Whiteley 3–0–10–1. *Second innings*—Leach 25–7–42–1; Pennington 15–2–38–1; Barnard 25–5–79–4; Morris 15–6–48–1; Whiteley 10–0–52–1; D'Oliveira 6–0–11–0.

Worcestershire

D. K. H. Mitchell lbw b Rushworth	0	– b Rushworth	1
M. H. Wessels b Harte	33	– b Rushworth	0
C. J. Ferguson lbw b Raine	11	– c Clark b Rushworth	30
J. J. Dell lbw b Rushworth	15	– lbw b Rushworth	0
R. A. Whiteley c Eckersley b Carse	18	– b Rushworth	18
E. G. Barnard b Raine	7	– lbw b Rimmington	43
O. B. Cox lbw b Rushworth	24	– c Pringle b Carse	62
B. L. D'Oliveira b Rimmington	5	– not out	45
J. Leach lbw b Rushworth	19	– c Eckersley b Carse	3
D. Y. Pennington b Raine	3	– c Clark b Rimmington	7
C. A. J. Morris not out	0	– b Rushworth	14
B 1, lb 11, nb 4	16	B 1, lb 16, nb 2	19

1/0 (1) 2/31 (3) 3/53 (2)   (52.2 overs) 151   1/2 (1) 2/9 (2)   (84.4 overs) 242
4/77 (4) 5/83 (5) 6/94 (6)   3/11 (4) 4/43 (5)
7/113 (8) 8/144 (7) 9/151 (9) 10/151 (10)   5/56 (3) 6/152 (6) 7/172 (7)
8/184 (9) 9/199 (10) 10/242 (11)

Rushworth 15–4–28–4; Carse 11–0–47–1; Raine 12.2–3–31–3; Rimmington 11–4–24–1; Harte 3–0–9–1. *Second innings*—Rushworth 24.4–10–39–6; Raine 22–4–59–0; Rimmington 18–2–53–2; Carse 15–2–49–2; Harte 3–0–19–0; Pringle 2–0–6–0.

Umpires: B. J. Debenham and J. D. Middlebrook.

DURHAM v LEICESTERSHIRE

At Chester-le-Street, August 18–21. Drawn. Durham 13pts, Leicestershire 8pts. Toss: uncontested. County debut: A. J. Robson.

A resilient century from Cosgrove saved Leicestershire after Durham had controlled most of the game. Asked to bat, Durham had amassed 544, their highest total for more than three years, and their biggest against these opponents. A composed 181 from Lees, who added 147 with Burnham, provided the platform; Eckersley, appointed captain in Cameron Bancroft's absence, responded with an unbeaten 71, securing maximum batting points for Durham for the first time since August 2017. Carse helped him steam past 500 in a ninth-wicket stand of 93, then used his pace to tear through Leicestershire for a career-best six for 63. After openers Azad and Horton had put on 100, they lost all ten for 136 and followed on, 308 behind. Despite another solid opening partnership, they were three down again by the close. But, surviving an odd moment when he deliberately headed away a bouncer to first slip, Cosgrove defied the home attack throughout the final day, until bad light intervened with ten overs remaining and Durham two wickets short of victory.

Close of play: first day, Durham 368-5 (Trevaskis 10, Rimmington 5); second day, Leicestershire 152-4 (Ackermann 7, Wright 5); third day, Leicestershire 153-3 (Cosgrove 21).

Durham

A. Z. Lees lbw b Mohammad Abbas	181	B. A. Raine lbw b Wright		11
C. T. Steel c Ackermann b Griffiths	24	B. A. Carse run out (Wright)		43
A. J. Robson lbw b Davis	16	B 9, lb 6, w 2, nb 4		21
P. S. P. Handscomb lbw b Wright	29			
J. T. A. Burnham c Swindells b Davis	86	1/75 (2) (9 wkts dec, 139.3 overs)		544
L. Trevaskis lbw b Griffiths	37	2/118 (3) 3/195 (4)		
N. J. Rimmington b Davis	25	4/342 (1) 5/361 (5) 6/394 (7) 9/430 (6)		
*†E. J. H. Eckersley not out	71	8/451 (9) 9/544 (10) 110 overs: 410-6		

C. Rushworth did not bat.

Mohammad Abbas 30–3–94–1; Wright 23–4–105–2; Griffiths 23–3–80–2; Davis 28–4–100–3; Ackermann 17–2–84–0; Dexter 18.3–4–66–0.

Leicestershire

M. H. Azad c Handscomb b Carse	53	– c Eckersley b Carse	57
*P. J. Horton c Robson b Carse	52	– c Eckersley b Raine	35
N. J. Dexter c Eckersley b Carse	0	– lbw b Steel	24
M. J. Cosgrove b Trevaskis	21	– not out	107
C. N. Ackermann c Handscomb b Raine	13	– c Handscomb b Trevaskis	56
C. J. C. Wright c Eckersley b Carse	27	– (9) b Steel	5
H. E. Dearden lbw b Carse	22	– b Raine	8
†H. J. Swindells lbw b Rushworth	24	– (7) lbw b Rimmington	15
G. T. Griffiths b Rushworth	1	– (8) c Handscomb b Trevaskis	5
W. S. Davis c Rimmington b Carse	1	– not out	5
Mohammad Abbas not out	0		
B 8, lb 4, nb 10	22	B 21, lb 9, nb 16	46

1/100 (2) 2/100 (3) 3/140 (4) (84.4 overs) 236   1/93 (2) (8 wkts, 145 overs) 36
4/143 (1) 5/166 (5) 6/184 (6)   2/114 (1) 3/153 (3)
7/234 (8) 8/234 (7) 9/236 (10) 10/236 (9)   4/257 (5) 5/278 (6)
   6/303 (7) 7/338 (8) 8/345 (9)

Rushworth 24.4–6–61–2; Carse 20–5–63–6; Raine 20–8–46–1; Rimmington 11–0–30–0; Trevaskis 7–1–20–1; Burnham 2–0–4–0. *Second innings*—Rushworth 27–10–52–0; Carse 26–9–73–1; Raine 22–5–53–2; Rimmington 13–5–19–1; Trevaskis 44–14–96–2; Steel 10–1–35–2; Burnham 3–1–5–0.

Umpires: S. J. O'Shaughnessy and C. M. Watts.

At Lord's, September 10–12. DURHAM beat MIDDLESEX by 44 runs.

At Northampton, September 16–19. DURHAM lost to NORTHAMPTONSHIRE by 169 runs.

DURHAM v GLAMORGAN

At Chester-le-Street, September 23–26. Drawn. Durham 7pts, Glamorgan 7pts. Toss: uncontested. First-class debut: S. J. D. Bell.

Less than 87 overs survived heavy rain at Riverside, which washed away Glamorgan's slim chance of promotion. The start of the match was delayed 90 minutes, after a leak in the covers wrecked the designated pitch; a new one was hastily prepared on the edge of the square. Trailing third-placed Gloucestershire by 16 points, Glamorgan desperately needed a win. But New Zealand keeper Watling, in his second game as Durham's overseas player, blunted their hopes, reaching a century shortly before the rain returned an hour into day two. The pitch was soon waterlogged, and the match abandoned early on the final morning, prompting celebrations in Bristol.

Close of play: first day, Durham 197-6 (Watling 83, Raine 26); second day, Durham 262-8 (Watling 104, Rimmington 8); third day, no play.

Durham

A. Z. Lees lbw b Hogan	45	B. A. Carse c Cooke b de Lange	27
C. T. Steel lbw b Hogan	1	N. J. Rimmington not out	8
A. J. Robson c Brathwaite b Carey	7		
B-J. Watling not out	104	Lb 15, w 5	20
J. T. A. Burnham c Root b Lloyd	16		
S. J. D. Bell b Hogan	1	1/7 (2) 2/33 (3) (8 wkts, 86.4 overs)	262
*†E. J. H. Eckersley lbw b Hogan	7	3/95 (1) 4/140 (5)	
B. A. Raine b de Lange	26	5/143 (6) 6/161 (7) 7/198 (8) 8/238 (9)	

C. Rushworth did not bat.

Hogan 19–8–35–4; Carey 22–5–49–1; van der Gugten 14–0–57–0; de Lange 16–2–68–2; Lloyd 13–3–33–1; Patel 2.4–1–5–0.

Glamorgan

N. J. Selman, K. C. Brathwaite, D. L. Lloyd, S. R. Patel, W. T. Root, *†C. B. Cooke, T. N. Cullen, M. de Lange, T. van der Gugten, L. J. Carey, M. G. Hogan.

Umpires: P. J. Hartley and N. A. Mallender.

ESSEX

From disaster to delight – twice

P A U L   H I S C O C K

A season that began on a subdued note ended in unparalleled success, as Essex became the first side to lift the County Championship and the Twenty20 Cup in the same year.

April had been something of a disaster, with an innings defeat at Southampton soon followed by three successive setbacks in the Royal London Cup, more or less scuppering hopes of qualification (they finished eighth in the group). But under the astute leadership of Ryan ten Doeschate, Essex allied resilience to belief, and began to sweep the opposition aside in the Championship in breathtaking style.

By mid-September, they were lying second with two matches left. But while they overwhelmed defending champions Surrey at Chelmsford – Essex won all home games, another unique achievement – leaders Somerset lost to Hampshire, for whom Kyle Abbott took 17 wickets. Soon after, the Essex Twitter feed jokingly named him their player of the month for September. It meant Essex found themselves 12 points in front, and needed only to avoid defeat in the final game, at Taunton, which they achieved with ease, helped by the weather.

A second Championship trophy in three years also owed much to the calm hand on the tiller of coach Anthony McGrath. He had been Chris Silverwood's assistant during the 2017 title-winning season, and took over when Silverwood joined the England set-up later that year. McGrath had bolstered his backroom staff with the addition of Andre Nel, the former South African firebrand who had appeared for Essex for three summers in the 2000s. Nel's input was most obvious in the way the pacemen performed.

After his retirement from Test cricket in 2018, it was not surprising that Alastair Cook was Essex's leading run-getter. He warmed up with an unbeaten 150 against Cambridge MCCU in his first match since being knighted, but was steady rather than spectacular in the Championship: he finished with 913 runs, but only one century, against Kent. Overall, the batting lacked fluency, and Cook alone averaged over 40. Tom Westley fell just short of 800, and Dan Lawrence made 725 but, like Cook, they reached three figures only once each. In all, six players made centuries in the Championship, with ten Doeschate and Ravi Bopara managing two apiece. There was relief at Chelmsford when ten Doeschate, who turns 40 in June, agreed a new one-year contract, although he passed the captaincy to Westley.

Off-spinner Simon Harmer was the kingpin of the attack, finishing with 83 wickets at 18, including ten five-fors and two hauls of ten. His tally was 12 more than anyone else in the Championship, and took his aggregate since joining Essex in 2017 as a Kolpak player to 212 at a touch over 20. Of those

132 had come at Chelmsford. But the seamers played their part: Essex bowled the opposition out twice in each of their nine Championship wins, removing the need for any delicate declarations. Jamie Porter had another good season, with 48 Championship wickets – in all first-class matches, he passed 50 for the fifth season running – while the popular Australian Peter Siddle claimed 34 in eight, and Sam Cook 32; Aaron Beard showed promise when asked to fill in. Mohammad Amir, the other overseas player, made only one appearance in the Championship, when his six wickets

Nick Wood, Getty Images

Peter Siddle

helped set up an important victory over Kent at Canterbury. Siddle announced his retirement from international cricket in December, which should mean he is available throughout 2020.

The Blast, in which Harmer led the side, looked a lost cause by mid-August: after ten matches, Essex had two victories, four defeats and four washouts. But they sneaked through to the quarter-finals by winning three and tying one of their last four. Victory over Lancashire in the quarter-final was followed by two fine performances on finals day, with Harmer to the fore: he took four wickets in the semi, then three more in the final, before hitting the winning runs off the last ball. At the end of the season, he expressed a desire to play for England – although, as he has already played five Tests for South Africa, during 2015, he admitted, "there are quite a lot of hoops I'd need to jump through".

Ravi Bopara did well in his new role as a one-day finisher, despite not being keen on the idea. He was also briefly left out of the side in mid-season – Essex were unhappy at his request to play in the Euro T20 Slam, which was eventually cancelled – and decided to leave Chelmsford after 18 seasons, having made his debut as a 17-year-old, and scored almost 20,000 runs in all formats. He signed for Sussex, and was ambitiously targeting an international return in the Twenty20 format. "It's very sad to be leaving my boyhood club," he said. "I'm not giving up red-ball cricket, but I want to take the opportunity to focus on T20 for now – I think I can really improve my game and take it to the next level."

Adam Zampa, the Australian leg-spinner, took a dozen wickets in the Blast, and will return in 2020. He missed finals day, though – he and Amir were represented in the Edgbaston dressing-room by cardboard cut-outs – and Essex fielded nine home-grown players in the last three Championship games, which bodes well for the future.

Championship attendance: 34,813.

ESSEX RESULTS

All first-class matches – Played 15: Won 10, Lost 1, Drawn 4.
County Championship matches – Played 14: Won 9, Lost 1, Drawn 4.

Specsavers County Championship, winners of Division 1;
Vitality Blast, winners; Royal London One-Day Cup, 8th in South Group.

COUNTY CHAMPIONSHIP AVERAGES, BATTING AND FIELDING

Cap		Birthplace	M	I	NO	R	HS	100	Avge	Ct/St
2005	†A. N. Cook.........	Gloucester.......	14	24	4	913	125	1	45.65	15
2005	R. S. Bopara........	Forest Gate‡.....	10	14	1	514	135	2	39.53	9
2017	D. W. Lawrence....	Leytonstone‡......	14	22	3	725	147	1	38.15	9
2013	T. Westley	Cambridge	14	23	1	794	141	1	36.09	11
	P. M. Siddle¶.......	Traralgon, Aust...	8	11	4	227	60	0	32.42	2
2015	†N. L. J. Browne	Leytonstone‡......	14	23	1	604	163	1	27.45	11
2006	R. N. ten Doeschate††	Port Elizabeth, SA .	14	19	1	483	130	2	26.83	8
	†A. P. Beard........	Chelmsford‡	7	9	4	112	41	0	22.40	3
2018	S. R. Harmer††.....	Pretoria, SA	14	19	2	340	62	0	20.00	15
	R. K. Patel	Chigwell‡	4	5	0	87	35	0	17.40	1
	A. J. A. Wheater....	Leytonstone‡......	10	12	1	177	30*	0	16.09	26/3
	M. R. Quinn††	Auckland, NZ	3	5	2	23	10	0	7.66	0
	S. J. Cook	Chelmsford‡	9	10	2	54	37*	0	6.75	2
2015	J. A. Porter........	Leytonstone‡......	13	15	5	31	17	0	3.10	3

Also batted: W. E. L. Buttleman (*Chelmsford‡*) (1 match) 0 (3 ct); †Mohammad Amir¶ (*Gujar Khan, Pakistan*) (1 match) 28, 4*; †A. S. S. Nijjar (*Goodmayes‡*) (1 match) 2; M. S. Pepper (*Harlow‡*) (1 match) 1, 7 (6 ct); R. G. White (*Ealing*) (2 matches) 39, 2 (4 ct, 2 st).

‡ *Born in Essex.*   ¶ *Official overseas player.*   †† *Other non-England-qualified.*

BOWLING

	Style	O	M	R	W	BB	5I	Avge
S. R. Harmer	OB	595.5	175	1,518	83	8-98	10	18.28
P. M. Siddle	RFM	263.4	72	683	34	6-104	2	20.08
S. J. Cook	RFM	235.5	61	673	32	7-23	1	21.03
A. P. Beard	RFM	114	18	406	17	4-23	0	23.88
J. A. Porter	RFM	391.2	83	1,234	48	5-51	2	25.70

Also bowled: R. S. Bopara (RM) 69–12–222–6; D. W. Lawrence (OB) 23.4–4–52–0; Mohammad Amir (LFM) 30–8–64–6; A. S. S. Nijjar (SLA) 4.4–0–18–1; M. R. Quinn (RFM) 89–12–327–5; R. N. ten Doeschate (RM) 7–0–21–0; T. Westley (OB) 15.2–2–58–0.

LEADING ROYAL LONDON CUP AVERAGES (100 runs/4 wickets)

Batting	Runs	HS	Avge	SR	Ct		Bowling	W	BB	Avge	ER
V. Chopra	421	156	84.20	88.25	3		P. M. Siddle	12	4-60	22.08	5.40
T. Westley	373	77	46.62	99.20	2		M. T. Coles.......	9	4-48	28.00	7.48
R. N. ten Doeschate	227	89	37.83	128.97	1		S. J. Cook	6	3-37	29.83	5.77
D. W. Lawrence..	270	56	33.75	95.74	2		R. S. Bopara	8	3-26	40.75	6.03
A. N. Cook	204	53	25.50	85.35	2		D. W. Lawrence ..	5	2-52	54.00	6.50
R. S. Bopara.....	179	89	22.37	95.72	0		S. R. Harmer	4	2-44	59.25	5.78
							J. A. Porter	4	2-44	63.00	5.04

LEADING VITALITY BLAST AVERAGES (100 runs/15 overs)

Batting	Runs	HS	Avge	SR	Ct/St
C. S. Delport	409	129	29.21	167.62	2
R. S. Bopara	291	70*	48.50	162.56	9
D. W. Lawrence	386	69	35.09	152.56	4
T. Westley	363	86*	30.25	130.57	7
R. N. ten Doeschate	269	74*	33.62	120.62	3
A. J. A. Wheater	178	39	16.18	112.65	5/4

Bowling	W	BB	Avge	ER
Mohammad Amir	10	4-29	20.10	7.44
R. S. Bopara	12	3-18	21.75	7.45
A. Zampa	12	2-31	28.91	8.06
S. R. Harmer	17	4-19	20.47	8.15
A. P. Beard	6	2-31	32.16	9.65

FIRST-CLASS COUNTY RECORDS

Highest score for	343*	P. A. Perrin v Derbyshire at Chesterfield	1904
Highest score against	332	W. H. Ashdown (Kent) at Brentwood	1934
Leading run-scorer	30,701	G. A. Gooch (avge 51.77)	1973–97
Best bowling for	10-32	H. Pickett v Leicestershire at Leyton	1895
Best bowling against	10-40	E. G. Dennett (Gloucestershire) at Bristol	1906
Leading wicket-taker	1,610	T. P. B. Smith (avge 26.68)	1929–51
Highest total for	761-6 dec	v Leicestershire at Chelmsford	1990
Highest total against	803-4 dec	by Kent at Brentwood	1934
Lowest total for	20	v Lancashire at Chelmsford	2013
Lowest total against	14	by Surrey at Chelmsford	1983

LIST A COUNTY RECORDS

Highest score for	201*	R. S. Bopara v Leicestershire at Leicester	2008
Highest score against	158*	M. W. Goodwin (Sussex) at Chelmsford	2006
Leading run-scorer	16,536	G. A. Gooch (avge 40.93)	1973–97
Best bowling for	8-26	K. D. Boyce v Lancashire at Manchester	1971
Best bowling against	7-29	D. A. Payne (Gloucestershire) at Chelmsford	2010
Leading wicket-taker	616	J. K. Lever (avge 19.04)	1968–89
Highest total for	391-5	v Surrey at The Oval	2008
Highest total against	373-5	by Nottinghamshire at Chelmsford	2017
Lowest total for	57	v Lancashire at Lord's	1996
Lowest total against	{ 41	by Middlesex at Westcliff-on-Sea	1972
	41	by Shropshire at Wellington	1974

TWENTY20 COUNTY RECORDS

Highest score for	152*	G. R. Napier v Sussex at Chelmsford	2008
Highest score against	153*	L. J. Wright (Sussex) at Chelmsford	2014
Leading run-scorer	**3,405**	**R. S. Bopara (avge 28.85, SR 129.36)**	**2003–19**
Best bowling for	6-16	T. G. Southee v Glamorgan at Chelmsford	2011
Best bowling against	{ 5-11	Mushtaq Ahmed (Sussex) at Hove	2005
	5-11	T. G. Helm (Middlesex) at Lord's	2017
Leading wicket-taker	**126**	**R. S. Bopara (avge 25.66, ER 7.57)**	**2003–19**
Highest total for	242-3	v Sussex at Chelmsford	2008
Highest total against	226-3	by Sussex at Chelmsford	2014
Lowest total for	74	v Middlesex at Chelmsford	2013
Lowest total against	82	by Gloucestershire at Chelmsford	2011

ADDRESS

The Cloudfm County Ground, New Writtle Street, Chelmsford CM2 0PG; 01245 252420; administration@essexcricket.co.uk; www.essexcricket.org.uk.

OFFICIALS

Captain 2019 R. N. ten Doeschate
(Twenty20) S. R. Harmer
2020 T. Westley
(Twenty20) S. R. Harmer
Head coach A. McGrath
President D. L. Acfield

Chairman J. F. Faragher
Chief executive D. W. Bowden
Chairman, cricket advisory group R. C. Irani
Head groundsman S. G. Kerrison
Scorer A. E. Choat

At Cambridge, March 26–28. ESSEX beat CAMBRIDGE MCCU by 286 runs. *Alastair Cook scores 150* in his first innings since being knighted.*

At Southampton, April 5–8. ESSEX lost to HAMPSHIRE by an innings and 87 runs.

At The Oval, April 11–14. ESSEX drew with SURREY.

ESSEX v NOTTINGHAMSHIRE

At Chelmsford, May 14–16. Essex won by eight wickets. Essex 20pts, Nottinghamshire 3pts. Toss: Nottinghamshire.

In June 2018, Essex lost this fixture by 301 runs – Nottinghamshire had not won since – but now they atoned with a convincing victory on a pitch offering bounce and turn. Wickets fell in clumps: on the first day, Nottinghamshire lost four for 21 mid-innings, then their last three for four. When Essex batted, the dismissal of Browne – whose 67 in 207 minutes was the game's only half-century – was part of a collapse in which six fell for 34. There were five victims for Fletcher, and two for Broad in, rather surprisingly, his first Championship appearance at Chelmsford. But Harmer and Siddle, who had earlier taken his 100th Championship wicket, took Essex into the lead during an invaluable stand of 81. "We played and missed a hundred times," admitted Harmer, "but we didn't nick them." They then got to work with the ball. Harmer finished with six for 60 as the visiting batsmen struggled after a decent start; the openers put on 70, before six wickets clattered for 16. Cook anchored the chase, which was completed with more than four sessions to spare.

Close of play: first day, Essex 68-0 (Browne 34, A. N. Cook 29); second day, Nottinghamshire 90-6 (Nash 13, Moores 2).

Nottinghamshire

B. T. Slater c White b Porter	45	– lbw b Porter	31
B. M. Duckett lbw b Porter	7	– c Porter b Harmer	37
C. D. Nash c sub (J. H. Plom) b S. J. Cook	26	– c Lawrence b Harmer	32
J. M. Clarke b Porter	48	– c A. N. Cook b Harmer	1
*S. J. Mullaney c Browne b S. J. Cook	6	– c ten Doeschate b Harmer	2
S. R. Patel c White b Siddle	3	– c ten Doeschate b Harmer	0
†T. J. Moores c Browne b Harmer	10	– (8) st White b Harmer	22
L. J. Fletcher c S. J. Cook b Harmer	24	– (9) c Harmer b Porter	15
S. C. J. Broad not out	11	– (10) b Porter	9
Z. J. Chappell c Westley b Harmer	0	– (11) not out	2
M. Carter c Westley b Siddle	0	– (7) lbw b Siddle	2
B 3, lb 2, nb 2	7	B 3, lb 2	5

1/9 (2) 2/38 (1) 3/118 (1)   (72.3 overs) 187   1/70 (2) 2/70 (1)   (54.3 overs) 158
4/131 (4) 5/137 (6) 6/139 (5)   3/71 (4) 4/79 (5)
7/155 (7) 8/183 (8) 9/187 (10) 10/187 (11)   5/79 (6) 6/86 (7) 7/116 (3)
    8/143 (8) 9/153 (9) 10/158 (10)

Porter 18–3–75–4; S. J. Cook 19–5–49–2; Siddle 17.3–8–31–2; Harmer 17–9–20–2; ten Doeschate 1–0–7–0. *Second innings*—Porter 12.3–3–41–3; S. J. Cook 5–1–18–0; Siddle 15–3–34–1; Harmer 22–5–60–6.

Essex

N. L. J. Browne c Patel b Carter	67	– run out (Fletcher)		1
A. N. Cook c Mullaney b Broad	31	– not out		40
T. Westley lbw b Broad	12	– c Clarke b Patel		49
D. W. Lawrence c Moores b Fletcher	19	– not out		7
R. K. Patel c Carter b Fletcher	5			
*R. N. ten Doeschate lbw b Fletcher	0			
†R. G. White c Slater b Carter	2			
S. R. Harmer lbw b Fletcher	43			
J. A. Porter c Slater b Carter	2			
P. M. Siddle not out	40			
S. J. Cook b Fletcher	0			
B 5, lb 7, w 2, nb 6	20	B 4, lb 2, w 2		8

1/78 (2) 2/98 (3) 3/124 (4) (82.1 overs) 241   1/1 (1) (2 wkts, 34.4 overs) 105
4/136 (5) 5/140 (1) 6/144 (6)   2/86 (3)
7/146 (7) 8/158 (9) 9/239 (8) 10/241 (11)

Fletcher 24.1–8–50–5; Broad 20–2–50–2; Chappell 12–1–44–0; Mullaney 2–0–9–0; Carter 20–3–68–3; Patel 4–0–8–0. *Second innings*—Carter 12.4–2–34–0; Broad 8–2–15–0; Fletcher 4–0–21–0; Patel 6.4–2–18–1; Chappell 3.2–0–11–0.

Umpires: J. W. Lloyds and N. A. Mallender.

ESSEX v KENT

At Chelmsford, May 27–30. Essex won by 113 runs. Essex 22pts, Kent 3pts. Toss: uncontested.

In his 100th first-class match for Essex, Alastair Cook continued his good early-season form, with two high-quality innings setting up another victory. He batted for most of the first day for 125, his 65th first-class century but first in the Championship since June 2017; several team-mates got themselves out when established, although Bopara did help him add 130. Cook, who reached three figures with consecutive boundaries off Denly – captaining Kent after being dropped from England's World Cup squad – was finally run out, for the first time in Championship cricket. Kent lost Dickson in the first over, and never mastered the bowling; wicketkeeper Pepper pocketed five in his only match of the season. The one man not caught in the cordon was Milnes, whose last-wicket stand of 45 with Qayyum was the highest of the innings. Cook was soon at it again as Essex built on a lead of 131, making an unhurried 90, while no one else could exceed 22. After rain shortened the third day, Kent were set 338 in 90 overs, but only Bell-Drummond defied Harmer's wily off-breaks for long. He put on 75 with Kuhn and 47 with Stevens, but was eventually last out after 203 minutes – Harmer's eighth victim of the innings, and 11th of the match.

Close of play: first day, Essex 303-8 (Harmer 0, Porter 1); second day, Kent 182; third day, Essex 181-6 (Pepper 5, Harmer 0).

Essex

N. L. J. Browne c Robinson b Stevens	24	– lbw b Stevens		19
A. N. Cook run out (Dickson)	125	– c Dickson b Mulder		90
T. Westley c Stevens b Milnes	12	– lbw b Milnes		20
D. W. Lawrence c Milnes	42	– c Crawley b Podmore		15
R. S. Bopara lbw b Stevens	61	– c Crawley b Podmore		0
R. N. ten Doeschate c Dickson b Podmore	12	– lbw b Denly		22
M. S. Pepper c Robinson b Stevens	1	– lbw b Milnes		7
S. R. Harmer lbw b Milnes	10	– not out		20
P. M. Siddle c Robinson b Milnes	1	– not out		3
J. A. Porter lbw b Podmore	1			
S. J. Cook not out	0			
B 7, lb 11, nb 6	24	B 1, lb 3, w 2, nb 4		10

1/41 (1) 2/71 (3) 3/145 (2) (101.2 overs) 313   1/55 (1) (7 wkts dec, 63 overs) 206
4/275 (2) 5/298 (6) 6/299 (7)   2/89 (3) 3/130 (4)
7/300 (5) 8/301 (9) 9/303 (10) 10/313 (8)   4/130 (5) 5/169 (6) 6/175 (2) 7/193 (7)

Podmore 27–7–77–2; Stevens 24–5–53–3; Milnes 21.2–7–61–4; Mulder 17–3–55–0; Qayyum 6–0–24–0; Denly 6–0–25–0. *Second innings*—Podmore 15–3–62–2; Stevens 15–6–26–1; Mulder 15–5–40–1; Milnes 12–1–47–2; Qayyum 2–0–19–0; Denly 4–1–8–1.

Kent

S. R. Dickson c Harmer b Porter	0	– c Harmer b Siddle	19
Z. Crawley b Bopara b Harmer	15	– lbw b Harmer	18
*J. L. Denly c Pepper b Harmer	20	– c Browne b Harmer	11
D. J. Bell-Drummond c Pepper b S. J. Cook	28	– b Harmer	81
H. G. Kuhn c Pepper b Siddle	20	– lbw b Harmer	36
†O. G. Robinson c Pepper b Porter	22	– c Bopara b Harmer	9
P. W. A. Mulder c Bopara b Harmer	19	– c Pepper b S. J. Cook	0
D. I. Stevens c Bopara b Siddle	0	– c Lawrence b Harmer	32
H. W. Podmore c Pepper b Siddle	2	– c S. J. Cook b Harmer	8
M. E. Milnes b S. J. Cook	23	– c Bopara b Harmer	0
I. Qayyum not out	14	– not out	1
B 9, lb 10	19	B 5, lb 4	9

1/0 (1) 2/29 (3) 3/42 (2)   (88.2 overs) 182   1/34 (2) 2/50 (3)   (73.5 overs) 224
4/79 (5) 5/98 (4) 6/127 (6)   3/51 (1) 4/126 (5)
7/129 (8) 8/133 (7) 9/137 (9) 10/182 (10)   5/162 (6) 6/163 (7) 7/210 (8)
                                          8/220 (9) 9/223 (10) 10/224 (4)

Porter 20–10–34–2; S. J. Cook 16.2–6–28–2; Siddle 17–5–29–3; Harmer 35–7–72–3. *Second innings*—Porter 13–1–52–0; S. J. Cook 14–3–45–1; Harmer 32.5–8–98–8; Siddle 13–5–17–1; Westley 1–0–3–0.

Umpires: M. Burns and R. T. Robinson.

At Leeds, June 3–6. ESSEX drew with YORKSHIRE.

ESSEX v HAMPSHIRE

At Chelmsford, June 16–17. Essex won by an innings and eight runs. Essex 20pts, Hampshire 2pts (after 1pt penalty). Toss: Hampshire.

Essex strolled to victory in less than five sessions – and one of those lost 12 overs to rain. The main architect, once again, was Harmer, who followed five for 23 as Hampshire were skittled for 118 on the first day with seven for 38 in their meagre second innings of 88. Although the pitch did allow some turn, it was hardly a minefield – Rossouw alone got to 30 for the visitors, while their Indian Test batsman Rahane bagged a three-ball pair. Weatherley carried his bat in the second innings for 29, the lowest by a player achieving the feat for Hampshire (previously Neville Rogers's 32 against Leicestershire at Loughborough in 1953). Essex were in front by the end of the first day, but faltered on the second: a fourth-wicket stand of 105 between Lawrence and Bopara provided almost half the eventual total of 214. Half the match's 30 wickets fell to lbws, while Crane – one of only two batsmen to reach 20 in Hampshire's second innings – was caught by ten Doeschate at leg slip after keeper Wheater dropped a sharp chance but volleyed the ball sideways with his foot another victim for Harmer. An "Essex Pride" concert in the adjacent Central Park provided background music throughout the opening day.

Close of play: first day, Essex 147-3 (Lawrence 34, Bopara 50).

Hampshire

J. J. Weatherley lbw b Porter	2	– not out	29
†T. P. Alsop c Lawrence b S. J. Cook	6	– lbw b Porter	2
A. M. Rahane c Wheater b Porter	0	– c Wheater b Porter	0
*S. A. Northeast lbw b Harmer	18	– st Wheater b Harmer	3
R. R. Rossouw st Wheater b Harmer	34	– c Beard b Harmer	4
A. H. T. Donald b S. J. Cook	25	– c Beard b Harmer	4
J. K. Fuller c ten Doeschate b Harmer	8	– lbw b Harmer	4
K. H. D. Barker lbw b Harmer	3	– c A. N. Cook b Harmer	0
K. J. Abbott lbw b S. J. Cook	10	– c ten Doeschate b Beard	18
M. S. Crane lbw b Harmer	7	– c ten Doeschate b Harmer	20
F. H. Edwards not out	0	– lbw b Porter	0
Lb 1	1	Lb 4	4

1/6 (1) 2/8 (3) 3/8 (2)   (34 overs) 118
4/53 (4) 5/70 (5) 6/94 (6)
7/94 (7) 8/105 (9) 9/107 (8) 10/118 (10)

1/5 (2) 2/5 (3)   (29.5 overs) 88
3/12 (4) 4/16 (5)
5/26 (6) 6/32 (7) 7/32 (8)
8/61 (9) 9/88 (10) 10/88 (11)

Porter 12–3–44–2; S. J. Cook 11–2–50–3; Harmer 11–4–23–5. *Second innings—*Porter 10–2–19–2; S. J. Cook 1.4–1–4–0; Harmer 13.1–3–38–7; Beard 5–0–23–1.

Essex

N. L. J. Browne lbw b Barker	31	A. P. Beard b Edwards	2
A. N. Cook lbw b Fuller	15	J. A. Porter not out	0
T. Westley b Barker	8	S. J. Cook lbw b Abbott	1
D. W. Lawrence lbw b Abbott	57	B 4, lb 11, nb 6	21
R. S. Bopara lbw b Fuller	59		
*R. N. ten Doeschate c Alsop b Edwards	12	1/53 (2) 2/53 (1) 3/64 (3) (73.1 overs) 214
†A. J. A. Wheater lbw b Abbott	4	4/169 (5) 5/195 (4) 6/199 (7)
S. R. Harmer lbw b Abbott	4	7/203 (8) 8/210 (9) 9/213 (6) 10/214 (11)

Barker 18–7–38–2; Abbott 19.1–2–54–4; Edwards 15–4–31–2; Fuller 16–4–43–2; Crane 5–0–33–0.

Umpires: P. J. Hartley and B. V. Taylor.

ESSEX v SOMERSET

At Chelmsford, June 23–25. Essex won by 151 runs. Essex 20pts, Somerset 3pts. Toss: Essex.

This was billed as a battle of the spinners – Harmer, who had taken 31 wickets in Essex's first three home games, and Leach for Somerset – but the seamers held sway, accounting for 35 of the 40 wickets as Essex pulled off a fourth home win in a row. It was Somerset's first defeat, although they stayed top. Essex's bowling heroes were Porter, who finished with nine for 73, and Beard, playing because Sam Cook had injured his side in the previous match; he started with four wickets in his first 15 balls. Somerset tottered from 54 for one to 74 for six, and to 131; it made Essex's first-day 216, in which Cook top-scored with a four-hour 80, look commanding. Armed with a lead of 85, Essex struggled again once the openers were separated after putting on 43, with Groenewald claiming five wickets. Somerset never threatened a target of 269. Porter removed Abell and Azhar Ali in his first eight balls, and Beard wrapped things up with three in 13. Gregory had clumped Harmer for four sixes during a rapid 40, but was bowled by a ball from Beard which snapped the middle stump and shattered a bail.

Close of play: first day, Somerset 32-1 (Abell 22, Groenewald 0); second day, Essex 164-6 (Wheater 22, Harmer 0).

Essex

N. L. J. Browne b Overton	29	– c Gregory b Groenewald	29
A. N. Cook c Overton b Groenewald	80	– c Overton b Groenewald	47
T. Westley c Davies b Overton	36	– c Leach b Overton	12
D. W. Lawrence lbw b Gregory	5	– c Davies b Gregory	21
R. S. Bopara c Brooks b Gregory	7	– sub (D. M. Bess) b Overton	18
*R. N. ten Doeschate lbw b Overton	10	– c Davies b Groenewald	2
†A. J. A. Wheater c Davies b Groenewald	21	– c Overton b Gregory	30
S. R. Harmer c Davies b Leach	15	– b Groenewald	0
P. M. Siddle lbw b Leach	2	– c Leach b Gregory	1
A. P. Beard not out	2	– not out	9
J. A. Porter c Davies b Leach	0	– c Overton b Groenewald	1
Lb 3, w 2, nb 4	9	Lb 4, w 7, nb 2	13

1/50 (1) 2/126 (3) 3/138 (4)	(77.3 overs) 216
4/147 (5) 5/166 (6) 6/182 (2)	
7/197 (7) 8/211 (9) 9/216 (8) 10/216 (11)	

1/43 (1) 2/72 (3)	(53.3 overs) 183
3/104 (2) 4/125 (2)	
5/134 (6) 6/163 (5) 7/166 (8)	
8/167 (9) 9/182 (7) 10/183 (11)	

Gregory 17–4–48–2; Brooks 12–3–47–0; Leach 16.3–6–30–3; Overton 15–3–43–3; Groenewald 17–1–45–2. *Second innings*—Gregory 15–3–37–3; Brooks 6–0–33–0; Groenewald 14.3–2–51–5; Overton 7–0–20–2; Leach 11–1–38–0.

Somerset

*T. B. Abell lbw b Porter	36	– c and b Porter	0
Azhar Ali c Wheater b Porter	8	– c Westley b Porter	1
T. D. Groenewald c Westley b Beard	6	– (9) c Browne b Beard	7
J. C. Hildreth c Browne b Beard	8	– (3) c Wheater b Siddle	32
T. Banton c Wheater b Beard	2	– (4) c Browne b Harmer	24
G. A. Bartlett lbw b Siddle	25	– (5) c Lawrence b Porter	8
†S. M. Davies c ten Doeschate b Beard	6	– (6) c Cook b Harmer	0
L. Gregory c Harmer b Porter	14	– (7) b Beard	40
J. Overton c Browne b Porter	10	– (8) c Browne b Porter	0
M. J. Leach not out	3	– not out	2
J. A. Brooks b Porter	1	– b Beard	2
B 1, lb 9, nb 2	12	Lb 1	1

1/25 (2) 2/54 (1) 3/63 (3)	(48.5 overs) 131
4/66 (4) 5/68 (5) 6/74 (7)	
7/114 (8) 8/120 (6) 9/128 (9) 10/131 (11)	

1/0 (1) 2/7 (2)	(32.2 overs) 117
3/46 (4) 4/64 (3)	
5/65 (6) 6/67 (5) 7/73 (8)	
8/110 (7) 9/113 (9) 10/117 (11)	

Porter 19.5–3–51–5; Siddle 18–5–39–1; Harmer 6–3–8–0; Beard 5–1–23–4. *Second innings*—Porter 9–2–22–4; Siddle 8–1–29–1; Beard 4.2–0–22–3; Harmer 11–1–43–2.

Umpires: N. G. B. Cook and G. D. Lloyd.

At Nottingham, June 30–July 3. ESSEX beat NOTTINGHAMSHIRE by an innings and 123 runs.

ESSEX v YORKSHIRE

At Chelmsford, July 7–9. Essex won by eight wickets. Essex 22pts, Yorkshire 3pts. Toss: Yorkshire.

Harmer took advantage of Chelmsford's driest pitch of the summer – it had already staged two one-day games – to collect five wickets on the first day. Five Yorkshire batsmen reached the twenties but, amid some undistinguished strokeplay, the highest was Brook's 46. Patterson had won their 11th successive contested toss, but admitted: "We haven't played [Harmer] well enough." Essex never lost control. A disciplined 269-minute innings from Westley took them almost level, before a more attacking knock from ten Doeschate – who put on 75 for the ninth wicket with Beard – left them 120 in front. Yorkshire were soon in tatters at 81 for six, though a belligerent 85 from Maharaj (the next-best was 18) averted an innings defeat. He launched five sixes, four off Harmer, his fellow South African, before becoming a fourth victim for Siddle, who had earlier dropped a screamer off Harmer at midwicket that flew away for four. Porter finished the innings with his 300th first-class wicket for Essex. They knocked off their target before tea on the third day, and effectively reduced the Championship to a two-horse race: they ended this round 15 points behind Somerset, but 40 ahead of Yorkshire and Hampshire.

Close of play: first day, Essex 122-3 (Westley 52, Patel 10); second day, Yorkshire 38-3 (Lyth 9, Brook 4).

Yorkshire

A. Lyth c Browne b Porter	5	– lbw b Porter	14
W. A. R. Fraine c Wheater b Porter	29	– b Siddle	3
G. S. Ballance b Siddle	8	– c Wheater b Siddle	4
T. Köhler-Cadmore lbw b Harmer	16	– lbw b Harmer	8
H. C. Brook b Harmer	46	– lbw b Siddle	12
†J. A. Tattersall c Wheater b Harmer	23	– c Lawrence b Harmer	14
M. D. Fisher lbw b Harmer	25	– lbw b Harmer	16
K. A. Maharaj lbw b Harmer	26	– b Siddle	85
*S. A. Patterson b Siddle	7	– c Cook b Porter	4
B. O. Coad c Wheater b Beard	14	– c Cook b Porter	18
D. Olivier not out	1	– not out	7
Lb 6, nb 2	8	B 8, lb 16, nb 2	26

1/18 (1) 2/37 (3) 3/43 (2) (49.3 overs) 208 1/10 (2) 2/14 (3) (72.4 overs) 211
4/69 (4) 5/128 (5) 6/129 (6) 3/30 (4) 4/52 (1)
7/177 (8) 8/184 (9) 9/206 (10) 10/208 (7) 5/58 (5) 6/81 (6) 7/110 (7)
8/129 (9) 9/193 (8) 10/211 (10)

Porter 11–1–40–2; Siddle 14–1–71–2; Harmer 18.3–2–76–5; Beard 6–2–15–1. *Second innings*— Porter 18.4–2–62–3; Siddle 21–8–32–4; Harmer 24–8–72–3; Beard 8–2–17–0; Westley 1–0–4–0.

Essex

N. L. J. Browne c and b Fisher	8	– not out	33
A. N. Cook c Tattersall b Patterson	27	– c Köhler-Cadmore b Patterson	6
T. Westley lbw b Olivier	81	– st Tattersall b Maharaj	31
D. W. Lawrence c Maharaj b Olivier	15	– not out	18
R. K. Patel c Fraine b Fisher	35		
*R. N. ten Doeschate not out	70		
†A. J. A. Wheater c Tattersall b Coad	6		
S. R. Harmer b Fisher	3		
P. M. Siddle b Maharaj	19		
A. P. Beard b Maharaj	41		
J. A. Porter c Köhler-Cadmore b Maharaj	0		
B 1, lb 16, nb 6	23	B 2, lb 4	6

1/11 (1) 2/57 (2) 3/101 (4) (117 overs) 328 1/22 (2) (2 wkts, 21.5 overs) 94
4/169 (5) 5/202 (3) 6/219 (7) 2/61 (3)
7/222 (8) 8/253 (9) 9/328 (10)
10/328 (11) 110 overs: 308-8

Coad 19–4–56–1; Fisher 22–4–59–3; Patterson 17–7–22–1; Maharaj 36–11–93–3; Olivier 19–1–76–2; Lyth 4–2–5–0. *Second innings*—Fisher 3–1–13–0; Patterson 8–3–19–1; Maharaj 8–2–35–1; Olivier 2.5–0–21–0.

Umpires: R. J. Bailey and P. R. Pollard.

ESSEX v WARWICKSHIRE

At Chelmsford, July 13–16. Essex won by 187 runs. Essex 20pts, Warwickshire 3pts. Toss: uncontested. First-class debut: D. R. Mousley. County debut: M. G. K. Burgess.

Essex went top of the table after their fifth successive victory, as Siddle and Harmer shared 15 wickets. While Cook and Lawrence were putting on 116 on the first day, they had looked set for a big total, but both fell in quick succession to the medium-pace of Rhodes. After one previous Championship wicket in 2019, he now claimed a career-best five for 17 in 14.3 overs. But Beard lifted Essex to 245, and Warwickshire were soon in trouble next morning at 33 for four; Ambrose and the newcomer Michael Burgess (another wicketkeeper signed from Sussex) led a fightback, ended by Siddle in a lively spell of four for four in 23 balls. Cook inflated Essex's lead with a three-hour 83, then Lawrence and Harmer helped push the advantage to 400, despite four more scalps for Rhodes. Liam Banks scored a maiden half-century, before five quick wickets – Harmer took four for two in 20 balls – left Warwickshire 112 for six. Burgess and Brookes put on 51, but both fell victim to Will Buttleman, keeping wicket as a substitute after Wheater injured his thumb. This match was originally scheduled for Worcester (Edgbaston was unavailable because of the World Cup), but flooding meant it was relocated, with the counties' September meeting switched to Birmingham.

Close of play: first day, Essex 245; second day, Essex 73-1 (Cook 34, Quinn 0); third day, Warwickshire 67-1 (Banks 36, Yates 4).

Essex

N. L. J. Browne c Yates b Brookes	6	– lbw b Rhodes	38
A. N. Cook c Patel b Rhodes	84	– lbw b Rhodes	83
T. Westley c Burgess b Brookes	8	– (4) c Ambrose b Rhodes.	4
D. W. Lawrence c Ambrose b Rhodes	61	– (5) c Ambrose b Rhodes.	74
R. K. Patel c Banks b Rhodes	1	– (6) c Banks b Brookes	15
*R. N. ten Doeschate c Ambrose b Stone	26	– (7) b Brookes	5
†A. J. A. Wheater c Stone b Rhodes	0	– (8) c Rhodes b Patel	21
S. R. Harmer lbw b Hannon-Dalby	0	– (9) c Banks b Patel	43
P. M. Siddle b Stone	17	– (11) not out.	10
A. P. Beard c Ambrose b Rhodes	29	– not out	6
M. R. Quinn not out	4	– (3) c Ambrose b Patel.	9
Lb 3, w 2, nb 4	9	B 4, lb 1, w 1, nb 2	8

1/27 (1) 2/41 (3) 3/157 (2)   (93.3 overs) 245   1/72 (1)   (9 wkts dec, 97.1 overs) 316
4/164 (5) 5/171 (5) 6/171 (7)   2/135 (2) 3/139 (4)
7/178 (8) 8/197 (6) 9/211 (9) 10/245 (10)   4/139 (3) 5/169 (6) 6/177 (7)
     7/215 (8) 8/299 (5) 9/299 (9)

Hannon-Dalby 21–9–35–1; Stone 19–4–64–2; Brookes 18–2–69–2; Patel 21–6–57–0; Rhodes 14.3–6–17–5. *Second innings*—Hannon-Dalby 5–1–11–0; Stone 18–2–77–0; Patel 37–6–97–3; Brookes 17–3–81–2; Rhodes 18.1–6–38–4; Banks 2–0–7–0.

Warwickshire

W. M. H. Rhodes lbw b Siddle	3	– lbw b Beard	25
L. Banks b Quinn	8	– c Westley b Siddle	50
R. M. Yates lbw b Harmer	32	– c Cook b Harmer	13
A. J. Hose c Cook b Beard	0	– c Patel b Harmer.	13
D. R. Mousley c Wheater b Harmer	3	– c Cook b Harmer	0
†T. R. Ambrose c Westley b Siddle	38	– c Lawrence b Harmer.	8
M. G. K. Burgess c Westley b Siddle	35	– c sub (†W. E. L. Buttleman) b Harmer	64
H. J. H. Brookes c ten Doeschate b Siddle	1	– c sub (†W. E. L. Buttleman) b Quinn	27
*J. S. Patel b Beard	23	– c Harmer b Siddle	6
O. P. Stone c Wheater b Siddle	0	– c sub (†W. E. L. Buttleman) b Harmer	1
O. J. Hannon-Dalby not out	7	– not out	0
B 8, w 1, nb 2	11	B 2, lb 2, nb 2	6

1/6 (1) 2/14 (2) 3/21 (4)   (66.4 overs) 161   1/56 (1) 2/83 (2)   (65.1 overs) 213
4/33 (5) 5/62 (3) 6/126 (6)   3/93 (3) 4/93 (5)
7/127 (7) 8/134 (8) 9/134 (10) 10/161 (9)   5/107 (6) 6/112 (4) 7/163 (8)
     8/183 (9) 9/200 (10) 10/213 (7)

Siddle 17–7–33–5; Quinn 11–3–33–1; Harmer 27–7–68–2; Beard 10.4–3–18–2; ten Doeschate 1–0–1–0. *Second innings*—Siddle 14–2–47–2; Quinn 11–1–43–1; Harmer 29.1–12–75–6; Beard 11–1–44–1.

Umpires: P. K. Baldwin and S. J. O'Shaughnessy.

At Canterbury, August 18–20. ESSEX beat KENT by three wickets.

At Birmingham, September 10–13. ESSEX drew with WARWICKSHIRE.

ESSEX v SURREY

At Chelmsford, September 16–18. Essex won by an innings and 40 runs. Essex 23pts, Surrey 3pts. Toss: Surrey.

Another thumping victory was Essex's seventh out of seven at home in 2019, and left them 12 points clear in the table ahead of a visit to second-placed Somerset. This win was set up by Porter and Sam Cook, who both grabbed five-fors as Surrey were skittled, their last six wickets managing only 37 in little more than an hour on the second morning. When Porter castled Plunkett, he reached 50 first-class wickets for the fifth successive season. Lawrence, driving powerfully, made a vigilant 147, and put on 173 in 40 overs with ten Doeschate, who timed the ball well during his fourth Championship century against Surrey. Harmer thrashed a 46-ball fifty as the lead swelled to 221, then returned to his stronger suit. He extracted the first five wickets, including Pope and Jacks (gated through an expansive drive) with successive balls, and finally bowled the swiping Morkel to finish with seven for 58, his ninth haul of five or more for the summer. The 2018 champions were swept aside with a day to spare.

Close of play: first day, Surrey 137-4 (Foakes 31, Jacks 12); second day, Essex 302-6 (ten Doeschate 78, Wheater 0).

Surrey

M. D. Stoneman lbw b Porter	16	–	lbw b Harmer	26
S. G. Borthwick c Wheater b Porter	21	–	c Browne b Harmer	9
J. L. Smith c Harmer b S. J. Cook	34	–	lbw b Harmer	10
O. J. D. Pope lbw b S. J. Cook	23	–	c Beard b Harmer	30
*†B. T. Foakes b S. J. Cook	34	–	lbw b Harmer	15
W. G. Jacks c Wheater b S. J. Cook	28	–	b Harmer	0
R. Clarke c Harmer b Porter	3	–	c Harmer b Porter	19
J. Clark b S. J. Cook	8	–	c Wheater b Bopara	33
L. E. Plunkett b Porter	0	–	c Wheater b Porter	21
M. Morkel b Porter	1	–	b Harmer	21
G. S. Virdi not out	2	–	not out	12
B 4	4		Lb 4	4

1/36 (1) 2/37 (2) 3/88 (4)   (61.3 overs) 174
4/99 (3) 5/152 (5) 6/155 (7)
7/159 (6) 8/160 (9) 9/170 (10) 10/174 (8)

1/35 (1) 2/36 (2)   (77.2 overs) 181
3/63 (3) 4/80 (4)
5/80 (6) 6/111 (7) 7/115 (5)
8/118 (9) 9/161 (8) 10/181 (10)

Porter 21–8–62–5; S. J. Cook 18.3–4–53–5; Harmer 15–4–30–0; Beard 7–2–25–0. *Second innings*—Porter 17–4–41–2; S. J. Cook 7–1–33–0; Harmer 34.2–14–58–7; Lawrence 2–1–2–0; Beard 11–3–28–0; Bopara 6–2–15–1.

Essex

N. L. J. Browne b Clark	2	A. P. Beard c Pope b Clarke	3
A. N. Cook lbw b Clark	24	S. J. Cook c Borthwick b Virdi	6
T. Westley lbw b Clark	4		
D. W. Lawrence c Borthwick b Morkel	147	Lb 6, nb 10	16
R. S. Bopara b Morkel	34		
*R. N. ten Doeschate c Clarke b Virdi	103	1/16 (1) 2/26 (3) (109.1 overs) 395	
J. A. Porter lbw b Clarke	0	3/53 (2) 4/125 (5)	
ʻA. J. A. Wheater st Foakes b Virdi	6	5/298 (4) 6/301 (7) 7/334 (6)	
S. R. Harmer not out	50	8/335 (8) 9/354 (10) 10/395 (11)	

Morkel 22–6–62–2; Clarke 22–4–65–2; Clark 15.2–2–52–3; Virdi 32.1–6–116–3; Plunkett 11–0–61–0; Borthwick 7–0–33–0.

Umpires: I. J. Gould and M. J. Saggers.

At Taunton, September 23–26. ESSEX drew with SOMERSET. *Essex clinch the Championship.*

GLAMORGAN

Marnus a plus

EDWARD BEVAN

By the middle of the season, Glamorgan's players and supporters were entertaining thoughts of a return to Division One for the first time since 2005. After winning three of their first nine matches, they topped the table going into July, with three promotion spots available, and a 40-point cushion over fourth place. But it all unravelled: there was only one more victory, and it was Glamorgan who ended up fourth. While that was a let-down after the early promise, it was still their best finish for four years, and a vast improvement on the previous season's wooden spoon.

Glamorgan collected 35 batting points; only Gloucestershire and Kent, with 36, had more. Much of that could be put down to the superb form of Marnus Labuschagne, who amassed 1,114 runs in ten Championship appearances before joining the Australian tourists for the Ashes, where he prospered too. Glamorgan won only one of the four games he missed, and lost two heavily; there was great delight when he agreed to return for another two years, although that may be scuppered if he cements a place in Australia's one-day team. Labuschagne made five centuries, while his team-mates managed six between them – two by Billy Root, whose 768 runs included a maiden double-hundred against Northamptonshire (after a rare failure from Labuschagne). That helped Glamorgan recover from 120 for five to a towering 547, and set up an innings victory. But it was not all good news for Root: despite playing every Championship match, he was dropped during the T20 Blast.

Nick Selman and David Lloyd were also ever-present in the Championship, but struggled to convert half-centuries (11 between them) into hundreds (the only one was Selman's 150 against Gloucestershire). There was a promising start for Charlie Hemphrey, born in Doncaster but raised in Kent, before moving to Queensland, whom he has represented in the Sheffield Shield. But ambitious plans to field more Welsh-born players were hampered by the indifferent form of Kiran Carlson, who also picked up an injury, and Jeremy Lawlor, who was released at the end of the season. Pembrokeshire-born left-hander Jack Murphy did not feature all summer: he was eventually forced to retire – aged only 24 – by a chronic knee injury.

Among the bowlers, the 38-year-old Michael Hogan was again a steadying influence. He finished with 46 wickets at 21, and might have had more, but for a surprising decision to convert the seamers early on. Hogan relies on rhythm, so looked undercooked at times. Marchant de Lange was a disappointment in the Championship, although he did produce some encouraging white-ball spells, and was rewarded with another two-year contract. Timm van der Gugten, Glamorgan's Player of the Season in 2018, was hampered by back trouble, and picked up only 15 wickets in eight Championship matches.

Glamorgan's spin attack looked threadbare, at least until the end of the season, when Samit Patel joined on loan from Nottinghamshire. Off-spinner Andrew Salter played only two four-day games, but topped the county's averages in the T20 Blast with 14 wickets at 19.

Charlie Hemphrey

The progress in the Championship was not replicated in white-ball cricket, where Glamorgan lurched from average in the Royal London Cup to hopeless in the Vitality Blast. They won only one of their 14 T20 matches – the last, against Hampshire – and, embarrassingly, were bowled out at The Oval for 44, the lowest score in 17 seasons of English Twenty20 cricket. Glamorgan were hampered by problems with their overseas signings, never managing to field both at once. The Marsh brothers were the original choices, but Shaun dislocated his shoulder, and Mitchell was called up for the Ashes. Pakistan opener Fakhar Zaman averaged 16 in seven games before returning home early, while South African Colin Ingram, one of the most destructive T20 batsmen in recent years, totalled just 261. Still, only Lloyd (358) scored more, with Chris Cooke (196) the one other player to make it into three figures.

There were signs that fortunes in the shorter formats could improve. The Second XI won their T20 competition, beating Hampshire in the final. Dan Douthwaite, signed after making a century against Sussex and 95 against Glamorgan for Cardiff MCCU in April, hit 52 in the successful Royal London chase of 348 at Hove, while wicketkeeper Tom Cullen forced his way into the Championship side.

The season ended amid worries that Matthew Maynard, the interim coach, might move on, as he sought assurances about the future. Director of cricket Mark Wallace – like Maynard, a former Glamorgan captain – took his time over a review of the summer, but eventually decided he should be offered the post full-time. "The side showed a great deal of improvement across two of the three formats under his leadership, and came very close to gaining promotion in the Championship," said Wallace. It will be a second period at the helm for Maynard, who was director of cricket between 2008 and 2010. "I love being a part of this club," he said. "There is lots of talent within the squad, and we have a good mix of young players and experienced heads."

Off the field, Glamorgan's financial position continued to improve, and should be further helped by the ECB's decision to make Sophia Gardens a centre for The Hundred.

Championship attendance: 16,295.

GLAMORGAN RESULTS

All first-class matches – Played 14: Won 4, Lost 3, Drawn 7.
County Championship matches – Played 14: Won 4, Lost 3, Drawn 7.

Specsavers County Championship, 4th in Division 2;
Vitality Blast, 9th in South Group; Royal London One-Day Cup, 6th in South Group.

COUNTY CHAMPIONSHIP AVERAGES, BATTING AND FIELDING

Cap		Birthplace	M	I	NO	R	HS	100	Avge	Ct/St
2019	M. Labuschagne¶ ...	Klerksdorp, SA ...	10	18	1	1,114	182	5	65.52	12
	K. C. Brathwaite¶ ..	Belfield, Barbados .	3	4	1	166	103*	1	55.33	2
2016	C. B. Cooke	Johannesburg, SA .	7	10	2	368	96	0	46.00	18/2
2018	T. van der Gugten†† .	Sydney, Australia .	8	10	7	135	30*	0	45.00	2
	W. T. Root	Sheffield	14	22	1	768	229	2	36.57	4
	T. N. Cullen	Perth, Australia ...	9	12	3	319	63	0	35.44	29
	N. J. Selman	Brisbane, Australia	14	24	2	752	150	1	34.18	10
	K. S. Carlson	Cardiff‡	3	4	0	130	111	1	32.50	2
2013	G. G. Wagg	Rugby	10	16	3	418	100	1	32.15	2
	C. R. Hemphrey	Doncaster	10	18	1	546	75	0	32.11	7
	S. R. Patel	Leicester	4	6	0	187	66	0	31.16	1
2019	D. L. Lloyd	St Asaph‡	14	23	1	668	97	0	30.36	16
2013	M. G. Hogan††	Newcastle, Aust ...	11	12	6	166	54	0	27.66	3
	L. J. Carey	Carmarthen‡	9	12	3	230	62*	0	25.55	0
	D. A. Douthwaite ...	Kingston-u-Thames	7	12	0	298	63	0	24.83	1
	J. L. Lawlor	Cardiff‡	2	4	0	74	25	0	18.50	3
	A. O. Morgan	Swansea‡	4	6	1	82	43	0	16.40	1
2019	M. de Lange††	Tzaneen, SA	8	10	1	127	45*	0	14.11	2
	R. A. J. Smith	Glasgow	3	5	0	35	18	0	7.00	1

Also batted: K. A. Bull (*Haverfordwest‡*) (1 match) 2, 5 (1 ct); †S. E. Marsh¶ (*Narrogin, Australia*) (1 match) 8, 9 (1 ct); A. G. Salter (*Haverfordwest‡*) (2 matches) 0, 26, 21.

‡ *Born in Wales.* ¶ *Official overseas player.* †† *Other non-England-qualified.*

BOWLING

	Style	O	M	R	W	BB	5I	Avge
M. G. Hogan	RFM	349	85	974	46	5-62	1	21.17
S. R. Patel	SLA	122.1	40	292	12	4-58	0	24.33
D. A. Douthwaite	RFM	132.1	10	612	17	4-48	0	36.00
M. de Lange	RF	244.4	33	950	26	4-64	0	36.53
M. Labuschagne	LB	192.2	16	724	19	3-52	0	38.10
L. J. Carey	RFM	242.3	50	766	19	4-54	0	40.31
D. L. Lloyd	RM	128.1	22	437	10	2-35	0	43.70
G. G. Wagg	SLA/LM	236	35	789	17	3-59	0	46.41
T. van der Gugten	RFM	198	26	705	15	3-44	0	47.00

Also bowled: K. A. Bull (OB) 36–6–100–2; K. S. Carlson (OB) 15–2–52–0; C. R. Hemphrey (OB) 43–4–163–2; J. L. Lawlor (RM) 6–1–15–0; A. O. Morgan (SLA) 31–2–108–0; W. T. Root (OB) 19–4–69–0; A. G. Salter (OB) 45–12–103–4; N. J. Selman (RM) 3.3–0–22–1; R. A. J. Smith (RM) 67–11–224–7.

LEADING ROYAL LONDON CUP AVERAGES (125 runs/4 wickets)

Batting	Runs	HS	Avge	SR	Ct/St
W. T. Root	386	113*	64.33	95.30	4
C. B. Cooke ...	337	161	42.12	96.01	7/2
D. L. Lloyd ...	240	84	34.28	93.02	4
M. de Lange ...	159	58*	31.80	152.88	4
G. G. Wagg ...	207	68	29.57	102.47	2
J. L. Lawlor...	129	48	25.80	74.13	2
C. R. Hemphrey	134	87	22.33	93.70	4

Bowling	W	BB	Avge	ER
M. de Lange	16	4-63	26.31	6.70
G. G. Wagg	9	3-46	36.33	6.22
T. van der Gugten	2	2-63	47.50	5.90
M. Labuschagne .	7	3-46	48.57	5.86
L. J. Carey......	4	2-64	62.75	5.22

LEADING VITALITY BLAST AVERAGES (90 runs/15 overs)

Batting	Runs	HS	Avge	SR	Ct/St
C. B. Cooke	196	45	21.77	**145.18**	9/1
C. A. Ingram ...	261	50*	26.10	**145.00**	2
N. J. Selman...	93	40	31.00	**143.07**	1
D. L. Lloyd	358	63	32.54	139.84	2
Fakhar Zaman ..	99	58	16.50	**93.39**	3

Bowling	W	BB	Avge	ER
G. G. Wagg......	5	2-28	34.00	**7.39**
A. G. Salter......	14	4-12	19.21	**7.91**
D. A. Douthwaite .	3	1-25	51.33	**9.05**
M. de Lange	13	4-26	23.38	**9.16**
L. J. Carey	2	1-15	74.00	**9.25**

FIRST-CLASS COUNTY RECORDS

Highest score for	309*	S. P. James v Sussex at Colwyn Bay.............	2000
Highest score against	322*	M. B. Loye (Northamptonshire) at Northampton ...	1998
Leading run-scorer	34,056	A. Jones (avge 33.03).......................	1957–83
Best bowling for	10-51	J. Mercer v Worcestershire at Worcester.........	1936
Best bowling against	10-18	G. Geary (Leicestershire) at Pontypridd.........	1929
Leading wicket-taker	2,174	D. J. Shepherd (avge 20.95)...................	1950–72
Highest total for	718-3 dec	v Sussex at Colwyn Bay......................	2000
Highest total against	750	**by Northamptonshire at Cardiff**.............	**2019**
Lowest total for	22	v Lancashire at Liverpool.....................	1924
Lowest total against	33	by Leicestershire at Ebbw Vale................	1965

LIST A COUNTY RECORDS

Highest score for	169*	J. A. Rudolph v Sussex at Hove...............	2014
Highest score against	268	A. D. Brown (Surrey) at The Oval..............	2002
Leading run-scorer	12,278	M. P. Maynard (avge 37.66)	1985–2005
Best bowling for	7-16	S. D. Thomas v Surrey at Swansea	1998
Best bowling against	7-30	M. P. Bicknell (Surrey) at The Oval	1999
Leading wicket-taker	356	R. D. B. Croft (avge 31.96)...................	1989–2012
Highest total for	429	v Surrey at The Oval	2002
Highest total against	438-5	by Surrey at The Oval	2002
Lowest total for	42	v Derbyshire at Swansea	1979
Lowest total against {	59	by Combined Universities at Cambridge........	1983
	59	by Sussex at Hove	1996

TWENTY20 COUNTY RECORDS

Highest score for	116*	I. J. Thomas v Somerset at Taunton............	2004
Highest score against	117	M. J. Prior (Sussex) at Hove	2010
Leading run-scorer	**2,031**	**C. A. Ingram (avge 38.32, SR 159.29)**	**2015–19**
Best bowling for	5-14	G. G. Wagg v Worcestershire at Worcester.......	2013
Best bowling against	6-5	A. V. Suppiah (Somerset) at Cardiff	2011
Leading wicket-taker	100	D. A. Cosker (avge 30.32, ER 7.79)...........	2003–16
Highest total for	240-3	v Surrey at The Oval	2015
Highest total against	239-5	by Sussex at Hove	2010
Lowest total for	**44**	**v Surrey at The Oval**	**2019**
Lowest total against	81	by Gloucestershire at Bristol	2011

ADDRESS

Sophia Gardens, Cardiff CF11 9XR; 029 2040 9380; info@glamorgancricket. co.uk; www.glam-organcricket.com.

OFFICIALS

Captain C. B. Cooke
 2019 (Twenty20) C. A. Ingram
 2020 (50-over) D. L. Lloyd
Head coach M. P. Maynard
Director of cricket M. A. Wallace
Head of talent development R. V. Almond

President G. Elias
Chairman G. Williams
Chief executive H. Morris
Head groundsman R. Saxton
Scorer/archivist A. K. Hignell

At Cardiff, April 5–7 (not first-class). Drawn. ‡Glamorgan 253-8 dec (69 overs) (W. T. Root 108*, G. G. Wagg 59; B. N. Evans 4-65) **and 110-2 dec** (25 overs); **Cardiff MCCU 230** (61.5 overs) (D. A. Douthwaite 95; T. van der Gugten 3-51, C. A. J. Meschede 3-34). *County debuts:* C. R. Hemphrey, M. Labuschagne, W. T. Root. *After the first day was washed out, Billy Root made a century in his first match for his new county, while Brad Evans, a Zimbabwe-born seamer, took four wickets. When the students batted, the Glamorgan regular Kiran Carlson made 25, far outshone by Dan Douthwaite from Surrey. He was crestfallen to be given lbw five short of a century, but had impressed Glamorgan enough to be offered a three-year contract.*

GLAMORGAN v NORTHAMPTONSHIRE

At Cardiff, April 11–14. Drawn. Glamorgan 11pts, Northamptonshire 11pts. Toss: Glamorgan. Championship debuts: C. R. Hemphrey, M. Labuschagne; B. Muzarabani.

This dreary encounter, which produced 1,390 runs and 19 wickets, was a poor advertisement for Championship cricket. The pitch was slow and low, and batsmen made hay: Labuschagne, the new overseas signing from Australia, and Root both hit centuries in their first Championship match for Glamorgan, then Carlson added another as full batting points were secured in the 92nd over. Northamptonshire's openers responded with a stand of 303 in five and a half hours, with Vasconcelos going on to a career-best 184; Keogh then batted for more than six hours for 150. Wakely, the visitors' captain, was reluctant to engineer a run-chase with little chance of a result, as his bowlers had spent a lot of time in the field in their previous game, when they asked Middlesex to follow on. Northamptonshire ground their way to 750, a total they had exceeded only once, with 781 for seven against Nottinghamshire at Wantage Road in 1995. It was the highest at Sophia Gardens, beating Surrey's 701 for nine in 2001. By the end of the match, only 27 spectators and a handful of hospitality guests remained.

Close of play: first day, Glamorgan 433-4 (Root 126, Carlson 101); second day, Northamptonshire 234-0 (Vasconcelos 125, Newton 85); third day, Northamptonshire 522-4 (Keogh 73, Rossington 32).

Glamorgan

N. J. Selman c Wakely b Buck	10	– b Cobb	22
C. R. Hemphrey c Rossington b Holder	28	– not out	17
M. Labuschagne c Vasconcelos b Muzarabani	121	– not out	27
D. L. Lloyd c Vasconcelos b Muzarabani	31		
W. T. Root c Vasconcelos b Procter	126		
K. S. Carlson c Wakely b Buck	111		
*†C. B. Cooke not out	70		
G. G. Wagg b Sanderson	14		
M. de Lange c Muzarabani b Holder	12		
T. van der Gugten not out	21		
B 3, lb 14, w 3, nb 6	26	B 4	4

1/27 (1) 2/62 (2)		(8 wkts dec, 125 overs) 570	1/37 (1)		(1 wkt, 18 overs) 70
3/126 (4) 4/261 (3) 5/433 (5)
6/457 (6) 7/480 (8) 8/511 (9)				110 overs: 471-6

M. G. Hogan did not bat.

Sanderson 24–7–70–1; Buck 21–3–80–2; Holder 21–2–79–2; Muzarabani 22–2–113–2; Procter 17–2–72–1; Keogh 15–0–108–0; Cobb 5–0–31–0. *Second innings*—Procter 4–1–16–0; Cobb 8–0–21–1; Rossington 5–0–20–0; Vasconcelos 1–0–9–0.

Northamptonshire

R. S. Vasconcelos lbw b Labuschagne 184	N. L. Buck lbw b Root 53
R. I. Newton c Cooke b van der Gugten ... 105	B. W. Sanderson c Cooke b Selman 18
*A. G. Wakely c Cooke b Wagg.......... 18	B. Muzarabani not out.................. 1
J. J. Cobb c Wagg b Root 60	B 18, lb 25, w 2, nb 16 61
R. I. Keogh c and b Labuschagne 150	
†A. M. Rossington c Hemphrey	1/303 (2) 2/343 (3) (227.3 overs) 750
b Labuschagne . 70	3/353 (1) 4/453 (4) 5/622 (6)
J. O. Holder b Hemphrey............... 3	6/629 (7) 7/661 (5) 8/683 (8)
L. A. Procter c Lloyd b Wagg 27	9/748 (9) 10/750 (10) 110 overs: 376-3

Hogan 28–8–56–0; Wagg 35–8–84–2; de Lange 21–3–94–0; van der Gugten 24–4–91–1; Lloyd 23–4–75–0; Labuschagne 44–6–122–3; Hemphrey 17–4–48–1; Root 17–3–63–2; Carlson 15–2–52–0; Selman 3.3–0–22–1.

Umpires: N. L. Bainton and I. D. Blackwell.

GLAMORGAN v GLOUCESTERSHIRE

At Newport, May 14–17. Drawn. Glamorgan 9pts, Gloucestershire 13pts. Toss: Gloucestershire.

With Cardiff being prepared for the World Cup, Spytty Park became Glamorgan's latest first-class venue: this was the first Championship match in Newport since 1965, when Warwickshire played at Rodney Parade. Gloucestershire made most of the running, forcing Glamorgan to follow on. However, after Selman and Labuschagne both scored centuries during a stand of 231, the visitors were in some peril at 41 for four on a cloudy final afternoon; Roderick, who gritted out 19 in 105 minutes, and Howell ensured the draw. Such an ending had looked unlikely when Gloucestershire were motoring in their first innings: after Bracey made 152 – his fourth first-class century, and third against Glamorgan – Higgins added an 89-ball hundred. Career-best figures for the 20-year-old off-spinner Drissell helped dismantle Glamorgan for 250 – a deficit of 213 – but they fared much better in the follow-on. Payne, Gloucestershire's left-arm seamer, was lucky to escape injury when the

Payne relief: A Spytty Park sightscreen falls on Gloucestershire's David Payne, who was unhurt.

sightscreen collapsed around him while he was trying to adjust it. Lloyd was awarded his county cap at lunch on the first day, and took over as captain on the second after Cooke twisted his ankle while batting. From Denbighshire, Lloyd was the first player born in North Wales to be capped by Glamorgan since Wilf Wooller in 1939.

Close of play: first day, Gloucestershire 360-6 (Higgins 25, van Buuren 21); second day, Glamorgan 241-8 (Wagg 45, van der Gugten 9); third day, Glamorgan 359-1 (Selman 148, Labuschagne 128).

Gloucestershire

M. A. H. Hammond c Bull b de Lange	0	– (2) c sub (T. N. Cullen) b de Lange	14
*C. D. J. Dent lbw b Wagg	14	– (1) c Selman b van der Gugten	1
J. R. Bracey c Hemphrey b de Lange	152	– c Selman b Wagg	22
G. T. Hankins b Lloyd	3	– b Bull	2
†G. H. Roderick lbw b van der Gugten	88	– c sub (T. N. Cullen) b Labuschagne	19
B. A. C. Howell b de Lange	35	– c Lloyd b Bull	44
R. F. Higgins c Labuschagne b Lloyd	103	– not out	15
G. L. van Buuren lbw b van der Gugten	25	– not out	15
G. S. Drissell c Cooke b de Lange	1		
D. A. Payne c Labuschagne b Wagg	8		
M. D. Taylor not out	5		
B 9, lb 2, w 2, nb 16	29	Lb 1, nb 4	5

1/0 (1) 2/50 (2) 3/55 (4)   (118.1 overs) 463   1/1 (1) 2/27 (2) (6 wkts, 50 overs) 137
4/254 (5) 5/309 (6) 6/314 (3)   3/39 (3) 4/41 (4)
7/410 (8) 8/413 (9) 9/432 (10)   5/103 (6) 6/107 (5)
10/463 (7)   110 overs: 426-8

De Lange 25-1-116-4; van der Gugten 28-4-96-2; Lloyd 14.1-3-48-2; Wagg 21-3-83-2; Bull 16-0-58-0; Labuschagne 14-0-51-0. *Second innings*—de Lange 8-1-23-1; van der Gugten 6-1-20-1; Wagg 7-0-30-1; Bull 20-6-42-2; Labuschagne 9-4-21-1.

Glamorgan

N. J. Selman lbw b Payne	14	– c Roderick b Payne	150
C. R. Hemphrey lbw b Drissell	60	– c Roderick b Taylor	58
M. Labuschagne c Roderick b Payne	0	– lbw b Taylor	137
D. L. Lloyd st Roderick b Drissell	37	– lbw b Payne	34
W. T. Root b Taylor	18	– c and b Higgins	17
J. L. Lawlor lbw b Taylor	18	– b Howell	21
*†C. B. Cooke retired hurt	23		
G. G. Wagg c Hammond b Drissell	50	– (7) not out	27
M. de Lange b Higgins	8	– (8) c Howell b Payne	4
K. A. Bull c Roderick b Drissell	2	– (9) c Roderick b Payne	5
T. van der Gugten not out	13	– (10) not out	3
B 1, lb 2, nb 4	7	B 8, lb 7, nb 10	25

1/14 (1) 2/14 (3) 3/109 (4)   (75.1 overs) 250   1/133 (2)   (8 wkts dec, 132 overs) 481
4/124 (2) 5/140 (5) 6/159 (6)   2/364 (1) 3/388 (3)
7/208 (9) 8/217 (10) 9/250 (8)   4/410 (4) 5/432 (5)
                                                        6/442 (6) 7/446 (8) 8/476 (9)

In the first innings Cooke retired hurt at 195-6.

Payne 15-4-45-2; Taylor 13-0-54-2; Higgins 13-3-35-1; Howell 7-3-14-0; Drissell 22.1-3-83-4; van Buuren 5-0-16-0. *Second innings*—Payne 36-7-121-4; Taylor 29-7-91-2; Higgins 18-6-42-1; Howell 18-1-75-1; Drissell 19-2-91-0; van Buuren 9-1-33-0; Hammond 3-0-13-0.

Umpires: G. D. Lloyd and R. J. Warren.

At Derby, May 19–22. GLAMORGAN beat DERBYSHIRE by two wickets.

At Hove, May 27–30. GLAMORGAN drew with SUSSEX.

At Northampton, June 2–5. GLAMORGAN beat NORTHAMPTONSHIRE by an innings and 143 runs. *Billy Root scores 229.*

GLAMORGAN v DERBYSHIRE

At Swansea, June 11–14. Drawn. Glamorgan 10pts, Derbyshire 13pts. Toss: uncontested.

Bad weather cost 84 overs and prevented much chance of a result. Batsmen held sway – after Selman's first-over dismissal, anyway – although Glamorgan were indebted to Wagg and Carey, who set a ninth-wicket record for this fixture of 167. Wagg hit four sixes – one an audacious scoop over the keeper off Palladino – in his 101-ball century, his first for three years, while Carey struck 11 fours in a career-best unbeaten 62. Glamorgan started optimistically by posting five slips for Hogan, but they were soon deployed elsewhere. Derbyshire's reply also centred on a big stand, 291 for the third wicket between Godleman, who went on a career-best of his own, and Tom Lace, on loan from Middlesex, who extended his maiden century to 143 before falling to a spectacular one-handed catch by the diving Morgan at deep square. On the final day, Godleman decided to bat on, and the lead extended past 200 before he declared with a draw all but certain, leaving Hosein stranded on 91.

Close of play: first day, Glamorgan 167-5 (Morgan 24, Douthwaite 5); second day, Derbyshire 221-2 (Godleman 86, Lace 78); third day, Derbyshire 504-4 (Godleman 211, Hosein 53).

Glamorgan

N. J. Selman lbw b Palladino	0	– not out	70
C. R. Hemphrey lbw b Palladino	32	– b Rampaul	19
M. Labuschagne c Hughes b Reece	37	– st Hosein b Hughes	83
*D. L. Lloyd c Lace b van Beek	32	– not out	8
W. T. Root c Madsen b Reece	28		
A. O. Morgan b Palladino	43		
D. A. Douthwaite c Madsen b van Beek	27		
†T. N. Cullen c Critchley b Reece	6		
G. G. Wagg c Reece b du Plooy	100		
L. J. Carey not out	62		
M. G. Hogan st Hosein b du Plooy	1		
B 4, lb 16, w 2, nb 4	26	B 4	4

1/0 (1) 2/54 (3) 3/101 (2) (95.3 overs) 394   1/30 (2) (2 wkts, 40 overs) 184
4/114 (4) 5/157 (5) 6/194 (6)   2/172 (3)
7/215 (7) 8/217 (8) 9/384 (9) 10/394 (11)

Palladino 23–5–104–3; Rampaul 23–4–86–0; Reece 14–5–40–3; van Beek 16–1–71–2; Hughes 8–0–29–0; Critchley 6–1–20–0; du Plooy 5.3–0–24–2. *Second innings*—Palladino 5–0–26–0; Rampaul 6–0–17–1; Reece 3–1–18–0; van Beek 2–0–9–0; Critchley 9–0–44–0; du Plooy 4–0–30–0; Madsen 3–0–23–0; Hughes 8–1–13–1.

Derbyshire

L. M. Reece c Wagg b Douthwaite	29	M. J. J. Critchley not out	34
*B. A. Godleman lbw b Carey	227	B 10, lb 12, nb 10	32
W. L. Madsen c Lloyd b Carey	20		
T. C. Lace c Morgan b Wagg	143	1/52 (1) (5 wkts dec, 131 overs) 598
A. L. Hughes lbw b Hogan	22	2/74 (3) 3/365 (4)
†H. R. Hosein not out	91	4/394 (5) 5/529 (2) 110 overs: 489-4

J. L. du Plooy, L. V. van Beek, A. P. Palladino and R. Rampaul did not bat.

Hogan 21–0–120–1; Carey 27–3–99–2; Douthwaite 18–0–95–1; Wagg 19–5–65–1; Morgan 16–0–62–0; Labuschagne 18–0–90–0; Lloyd 4–0–16–0; Hemphrey 8–0–29–0.

Umpires: M. Burns and R. J. Warren.

At Radlett, June 16–19. GLAMORGAN drew with MIDDLESEX.

At Bristol, June 23–26. GLAMORGAN beat GLOUCESTERSHIRE by four wickets.

GLAMORGAN v WORCESTERSHIRE

At Cardiff, June 30–July 3. Drawn. Glamorgan 13pts, Worcestershire 10pts. Toss: uncontested.

On another pitch offering little to the bowlers, Glamorgan did enough to remain top of the table, although hopes of a win were stymied when Worcestershire showed no interest in a target of 326 in 66 overs. Glamorgan had sewn up full batting points, mainly thanks to Labuschagne and Lloyd, who shared a stand of 138. Leg-spinner D'Oliveira persisted gamely for his best figures, and, after superb bowling by Hogan, hit his first century, from No. 9, for nearly two years to restrict the lead to 79. He dominated a last-wicket stand of 68 with 19-year-old Adam Finch. When Glamorgan batted again, Labuschagne – who received his county cap from Alan Jones at lunch on the third day – added his second hundred of the game, having passed 1,000 runs for the season. He was the second in the country to get there, two minutes after Warwickshire's Dom Sibley (whose tally included the MCC–Surrey match in Dubai).

Close of play: first day, Glamorgan 354-6 (Cullen 26, Wagg 0); second day, Worcestershire 191-5 (Barnard 27, Morris 2); third day, Glamorgan 137-1 (Selman 42, Labuschagne 90).

Glamorgan

N. J. Selman c Wessels b Barnard		67	– b D'Oliveira	58
A. O. Morgan c Wessels b Finch		28	– c Cox b Leach	0
M. Labuschagne c and b D'Oliveira		106	– c Barnard b D'Oliveira	100
*D. L. Lloyd c Wessels b D'Oliveira		97	– c Cox b Morris	12
W. T. Root b D'Oliveira		0	– not out	25
D. A. Douthwaite lbw b D'Oliveira		0	– lbw b Barnard	40
†T. N. Cullen b D'Oliveira		51	– not out	2
G. G. Wagg c Ferguson b Finch		4		
L. J. Carey b D'Oliveira		23		
T. van der Gugten not out		22		
M. G. Hogan c Ferguson b D'Oliveira		19		
B 6, lb 4, nb 22		32	Lb 5, w 2, nb 2	9

1/80 (2) 2/155 (1) 3/293 (3)   (120.5 overs) 449   1/1 (2)   (5 wkts dec, 66 overs) 246
4/295 (5) 5/295 (6) 6/350 (4)   2/157 (3) 3/178 (1)
7/365 (8) 8/404 (9) 9/413 (7)   4/182 (4) 5/240 (6)
10/449 (11)   110 overs: 403-7

Leach 21–5–80–0; Finch 25–4–102–2; Morris 18–4–59–0; Barnard 19–3–67–1; Whiteley 9–1–35–0; D'Oliveira 26.5–0–92–7; Mitchell 2–1–4–0. *Second innings*—Leach 13–1–48–1; Finch 4–0–18–0; Morris 14–2–52–1; D'Oliveira 26–1–90–2; Barnard 8–1–32–1; Mitchell 1–0–1–0.

Worcestershire

D. K. H. Mitchell c Cullen b Hogan	43	– not out	64
J. J. Dell c Cullen b Lloyd	36	– lbw b Carey	1
C. J. Ferguson b Douthwaite	29	– not out	70
M. H. Wessels c Selman b Wagg	9		
R. A. Whiteley b Hogan	17		
E. G. Barnard lbw b Hogan	56		
C. A. J. Morris run out (Root/Cullen)	7		
†O. B. Cox c Cullen b Douthwaite	12		
B. L. D'Oliveira c and b Hogan	103		
*J. Leach c Cullen b Hogan	16		
A. W. Finch not out	5		
B 4, lb 5, w 6, nb 22	37	Lb 1, w 1, nb 6	8

1/83 (2) 2/104 (1) 3/127 (4)   (128.5 overs) 370   1/8 (2)   (1 wkt, 51 overs) 143
4/139 (3) 5/183 (5) 6/203 (7)
7/234 (6) 8/267 (8) 9/302 (10)
10/370 (9)   110 overs: 318-9

Carey 18–3–46–0; Hogan 29.5–9–62–5; Wagg 24–4–63–1; van der Gugten 19–4–55–0; Labuschagne 21–2–67–0; Lloyd 5–0–12–1; Douthwaite 12–1–56–2. *Second innings*—Hogan 8–0–20–0; Carey 14.5–5–29–1; van der Gugten 5–1–16–0; Wagg 8–1–19–0; Labuschagne 5–0–29–0; Morgan 11–2–29–0.

Umpires: J. H. Evans and T. Lungley.

GLAMORGAN v MIDDLESEX

At Cardiff, July 13–16. Middlesex won by 256 runs. Middlesex 23pts, Glamorgan 2pts (after 1pt penalty). Toss: Middlesex.

Glamorgan surrendered their unbeaten record with a thumping defeat – their biggest by runs by Middlesex (previously 254 at Lord's in 1960). Malan's fourth century of the season had underpinned the visitors' innings; dropped by Lloyd at first slip off Carey when 43, he was last out for 166, sharing late stands of 95 with Roland-Jones and 115 with Sowter, who briefly retired hurt for treatment on a hand hit by Wagg. Helm's spell of four for five in 14 balls reduced Glamorgan to 24 for four on the first evening, in a session enlivened by a flock of seagulls – an unusual sight at a non-seaside ground – feasting on flying ants in the outfield. Glamorgan were all out next day 213 behind and, after reducing Middlesex to 49 for three, were subdued by Robson, who carried his bat to extend the lead to 555. Hemphrey survived five and a quarter hours for 72. Labuschagne ended his highly successful Championship season with 1,114 runs before joining Australia's Ashes tourists. But Roland-Jones, who finished with nine wickets in the match, and leg-spinner Sowter worked their way through, completing victory half an hour before lunch on the final day. Glamorgan were docked a point for being one ball short of the required over-rate.

Close of play: first day, Glamorgan 25-4 (Lloyd 0, Root 0); second day, Middlesex 189-5 (Robson 73); third day, Glamorgan 171-6 (Hemphrey 52, Wagg 7).

Middlesex

S. D. Robson c Cooke b Carey	7	– (2) not out	140
S. S. Eskinazi c Cooke b Wagg	36	– (1) c Hemphrey b Carey	5
N. R. T. Gubbins c Labuschagne b Carey	0	– c Lloyd b Hogan	13
*D. J. Malan c Labuschagne b Carey	166	– run out (Wagg)	6
G. F. B. Scott lbw b Hogan	1	– b Douthwaite	23
†J. A. Simpson c Cooke b Hogan	24	– c Root b de Lange	56
R. G. White b Hogan	2	– c Cooke b Hogan	1
T. S. Roland-Jones c de Lange b Labuschagne	54	– c Cooke b de Lange	1
T. G. Helm c Cooke b Carey	6	– c and b Labuschagne	38
N. A. Sowter not out	57	– c Lloyd b Hemphrey	3
T. J. Murtagh c Douthwaite b Wagg	8	– c de Lange b Labuschagne	33
B 8, lb 1, nb 14	23	Lb 14, w 1, nb 8	23

1/29 (1) 2/35 (3) 3/64 (2)   (84.1 overs) 384
4/65 (5) 5/123 (6) 6/131 (7)
7/226 (8) 8/243 (9) 9/384 (11) 10/384 (4)

1/8 (1) 2/33 (3)   (78.4 overs) 342
3/49 (4) 4/82 (5)
5/189 (6) 6/190 (7) 7/191 (8)
8/259 (9) 9/266 (10) 10/342 (11)

In the first innings Sowter, when 57, retired hurt at 358-8 and resumed at 384-9.

De Lange 15–3–75–0; Carey 16.1–3–54–4; Hogan 18–1–75–3; Wagg 15–2–61–2; Douthwaite 5–0–31–0; Lloyd 3–0–21–0; Labuschagne 9–1–40–1; Hemphrey 3–0–18–0. *Second innings—* Carey 13–2–53–1; Hogan 15–2–56–2; de Lange 17–1–69–2; Wagg 10–3–29–0; Douthwaite 7–0–44–1; Lloyd 5–1–22–0; Hemphrey 5–0–17–1; Labuschagne 6.4–0–38–2.

Glamorgan

N. J. Selman c Malan b Helm	7	– c Simpson b Helm	4
C. R. Hemphrey b Helm	4	– c Simpson b Roland-Jones	72
L. J. Carey c Simpson b Helm	0	– (10) b Roland-Jones	7
M. Labuschagne b Helm	6	– (3) lbw b Roland-Jones	51
D. L. Lloyd c Simpson b Roland-Jones	67	– (4) lbw b Sowter	19
W. T. Root c Malan b Roland-Jones	32	– (5) lbw b Hogan	4
*†C. B. Cooke b Roland-Jones	19	– (6) lbw b Murtagh	3
D. A. Douthwaite c Scott b Murtagh	2	– (7) lbw b Sowter	9
G. G. Wagg c Malan b Roland-Jones	10	– (8) c Malan b Roland-Jones	40
M. de Lange b Helm	10	– (9) not out	45
M. G. Hogan not out	8	– c Scott b Sowter	22
B 4, lb 4, nb 4	12	B 8, lb 6, nb 4, p 5	23

1/7 (1) 2/7 (3) 3/21 (4)   (53.3 overs) 171
4/24 (2) 5/83 (6) 6/143 (7)
7/148 (8) 8/148 (5) 9/153 (9) 10/171 (10)

1/9 (1) 2/106 (3)   (90.4 overs) 299
3/141 (4) 4/150 (5)
5/153 (6) 6/163 (7) 7/225 (2)
8/250 (8) 9/264 (10) 10/299 (11)

Murtagh 18–4–53–1; Helm 16.3–0–53–5; Roland-Jones 15–3–45–4; Scott 3–0–10–0; Sowter 1–0–2–0. *Second innings—* Murtagh 16–4–59–1; Helm 19–6–37–1; Roland-Jones 22–6–68–5; Sowter 29.4–2–100–3; Malan 4–1–16–0.

Umpires: P. R. Pollard and M. J. Saggers.

GLAMORGAN v LANCASHIRE

At Colwyn Bay, August 18–20. Lancashire won by an innings and 150 runs. Lancashire 24pts, Glamorgan 4pts. Toss: Glamorgan. County debut: S. R. Patel.

Lancashire extended their lead to 29 points, while Glamorgan's promotion prospects took a hit with a second successive defeat; allied to a disastrous T20 season, it meant they had not won a competitive match for two months. Glamorgan knew they had underachieved on a perfect batting pitch after a patchy first-innings display: they were rescued from 145 for eight by the former England all-rounder Samit Patel, playing his first match on loan from Nottinghamshire, and a last-ditch stand of 52 in five overs between Carey and Hogan. Medium-pacer Danny Lamb took his first four first-class wickets, including Wagg and Smith with consecutive deliveries. Vilas then put Glamorgan's total of 257 into perspective, exceeding himself in a career-best 266 that included 35 fours and six sixes from 240 balls – it was the highest score of the season. He shared century stands with Jones and Lamb as the last five wickets added 316, and Lamb then removed both openers on the third morning; there was no comeback from 40 for four. Shaun Marsh, who like Lamb was playing his only Championship match of the season, was trapped twice in single figures by Bailey. For Glamorgan, defeat was doubly costly: with Colwyn Bay easily accessible from Manchester, all three days were well attended, and the fourth had been expected to produce around £15,000.

Close of play: first day, Lancashire 85-1 (Jennings 46, Bohannon 6); second day, Lancashire 544-9 (Mahmood 8, Gleeson 1).

Glamorgan

N. J. Selman c Vilas b Bailey............	1	– lbw b Lamb	18
C. R. Hemphrey lbw b Lamb............	56	– lbw b Lamb	14
S. E. Marsh lbw b Bailey	8	– lbw b Bailey...............	9
D. L. Lloyd lbw b Lamb	17	– c Vilas b Gleeson	5
W. T. Root lbw b Bailey	32	– c Vilas b Gleeson	0
S. R. Patel c Vilas b Bailey	54	– lbw b Mahmood	22
*†C. B. Cooke c Vilas b Gleeson	4	– lbw b Mahmood	41
G. G. Wagg c Vilas b Lamb...........	0	– c Jones b Bailey	9
R. A. J. Smith b Lamb	0	– b Mahmood	1
L. J. Carey not out	51	– b Bailey	8
M. G. Hogan b Mahmood	32	– not out	0
Lb 2	2	B 4, lb 5, nb 2.............	11

1/2 (1) 2/12 (3) 3/44 (4) (60.4 overs) 257
4/94 (5) 5/139 (2) 6/144 (7)
7/145 (8) 8/145 (9) 9/205 (6) 10/257 (11)

1/28 (1) 2/33 (2) (51.1 overs) 138
3/40 (4) 4/40 (5)
5/54 (3) 6/96 (6) 7/123 (8)
8/127 (7) 9/138 (10) 10/138 (9)

Bailey 14–6–50–4; Gleeson 16–3–73–1; Mahmood 12.4–3–45–1; Lamb 15–2–70–4; Maxwell 3–0–17–0. *Second innings*—Bailey 15–5–44–3; Gleeson 12–4–24–2; Mahmood 13.1–3–42–3; Lamb 11–3–19–2.

Lancashire

K. K. Jennings lbw b Wagg...........	86	S. Mahmood c Lloyd b Patel...........	8
A. L. Davies lbw b Smith	32	R. J. Gleeson not out	2
J. J. Bohannon c Cooke b Hogan........	6		
L. S. Livingstone c Marsh b Hogan.......	3	B 7, lb 16, nb 2	25
G. J. Maxwell c Selman b Carey	31		
*†D. J. Vilas b Lloyd	266	1/59 (2) 2/89 (3) (127.4 overs) 545
R. P. Jones run out (Hemphrey)	33	3/93 (4) 4/137 (5) 5/229 (1)
D. J. Lamb b Wagg	49	6/344 (7) 7/455 (8) 8/484 (9)
T. E. Bailey st Cooke b Patel..........	4	9/539 (6) 10/545 (10) 110 overs: 459-7

Hogan 24–7–64–2; Carey 22–2–125–1; Wagg 21–1–86–2; Smith 24–1–87–1; Patel 25.4–7–104–2; Lloyd 7–3–27–1; Hemphrey 4–0–29–0.

Umpires: G. D. Lloyd and J. D. Middlebrook.

At Worcester, September 10–12. GLAMORGAN lost to WORCESTERSHIRE by 155 runs.

GLAMORGAN v LEICESTERSHIRE

At Cardiff, September 16–19. Glamorgan won by 291 runs. Glamorgan 24pts, Leicestershire 4pts. Toss: uncontested.

Glamorgan bounced back after three heavy defeats with a convincing victory over wooden-spoonists Leicestershire, which gave them an outside chance of promotion if they could beat Durham in their final match. A worn, green pitch encouraged Horton to bowl first, but Glamorgan's batsmen applied themselves well, contriving six fifty partnerships, and gaining maximum batting points in the last possible over. Wright and Griffiths stuck at it with the ball, but the others made little impression. Leicestershire's openers gave them a decent start, putting on 85, but they lost five for two, three in a dozen balls from Patel. A swashbuckling 60 from Wright, who clouted ten fours and a six, and added 92 with last man Davis, lifted the total to 263, but they still conceded a lead of 172. Cooke waived the follow-on, and the West Indian opener Brathwaite anchored the second innings with a maiden Championship century. Chasing an unlikely 424, Leicestershire lost two quick wickets to Carey on the third evening, and were 44 for four early next day. Cosgrove settled in for 200 minutes for 28, but spinners Patel and Salter, who both finished with striking figures, exploited a helpful surface; Glamorgan won with more than 40 overs to spare.

Close of play: first day, Glamorgan 300-4 (Root 27, Cooke 25); second day, Leicestershire 191-9 (Wright 26, Davis 6); third day, Leicestershire 32-2 (Azad 15, Cosgrove 3).

Glamorgan

N. J. Selman c Davis b Mike	36	– lbw b Griffiths	8
K. C. Brathwaite lbw b Griffiths	44	– not out	103
D. L. Lloyd b Wright	66	– c Swindells b Davis	25
S. R. Patel c Ackermann b Mike	66	– lbw b Ackermann	33
W. T. Root c Ackermann b Griffiths	36	– lbw b Wright	19
*†C. B. Cooke b Wright	96	– b Wright	43
G. G. Wagg lbw b Griffiths	3	– not out	2
A. G. Salter c Swindells b Wright	21		
R. A. J. Smith b Wright	12		
L. J. Carey c Dearden b Wright	6		
M. G. Hogan not out	1		
B 23, lb 16, w 1, nb 8	48	B 2, lb 13, w 3	18

1/62 (1) 2/143 (2) 3/196 (3) (116.4 overs) 435
4/255 (4) 5/322 (5) 6/330 (7)
7/406 (8) 8/413 (6) 9/434 (9)
10/435 (10) 110 overs: 406-6

1/24 (1) (5 wkts dec, 61.3 overs) 251
2/60 (3) 3/125 (4)
4/164 (5) 5/244 (6)

Wright 25.4–8–64–5; Griffiths 27–7–71–3; Davis 25–6–87–0; Mike 22–5–99–2; Ackermann 11–1–56–0; Rhodes 1–0–3–0; Cosgrove 5–1–16–0. *Second innings*—Griffiths 14.5–5–36–1; Wright 14.3–2–67–2; Davis 10–2–38–1; Mike 6–0–20–0; Ackermann 16–0–75–1; Cosgrove 0.1–0–0–0.

Leicestershire

M. H. Azad c Root b Patel	28	– lbw b Hogan	16
*P. J. Horton b Hogan	49	– c Cooke b Carey	7
C. N. Ackermann lbw b Patel	1	– c Lloyd b Carey	1
M. J. Cosgrove b Patel	0	– run out (Root)	28
G. H. Rhodes b Smith	0	– b Hogan	4
H. E. Dearden lbw b Salter	9	– lbw b Salter	37
†H. J. Swindells c Cooke b Hogan	29	– c Lloyd b Patel	2
B. W. M. Mike lbw b Smith	16	– not out	15
C. J. C. Wright st Cooke b Patel	60	– c Lloyd b Salter	6
G. T. Griffiths lbw b Smith	3	– (11) c Lloyd b Patel	1
W. S. Davis not out	39	– (10) c Hogan b Salter	0
B 20, lb 6, w 1, nb 2	29	B 8, lb 4, w 1, nb 2	15

1/85 (2) 2/86 (3) 3/86 (4) (82.1 overs) 263
4/87 (5) 5/87 (1) 6/111 (6)
7/146 (7) 8/167 (8) 9/171 (10) 10/263 (9)

1/14 (2) 2/18 (3) (70.4 overs) 132
3/40 (1) 4/44 (5)
5/99 (6) 6/104 (7) 7/110 (4)
8/125 (9) 9/125 (10) 10/132 (11)

Hogan 18–3–66–2; Wagg 6–0–27–0; Carey 6–0–26–0; Patel 26.1–9–58–4; Smith 15–4–43–3; Salter 11–3–17–1. *Second innings*—Hogan 16–6–39–2; Carey 13–7–14–2; Patel 24.4–12–45–2; Smith 1–0–10–0; Wagg 5–3–6–0; Salter 10–5–6–3; Root 1–1–0–0.

Umpires: N. L. Bainton and B. V. Taylor.

At Chester-le-Street, September 23–26. GLAMORGAN drew with DURHAM.

GLOUCESTERSHIRE

Overcoming home disadvantage

ANDY STOCKHAUSEN

Gloucestershire exceeded all expectations. Most importantly, they won promotion after 14 seasons in the Championship's lower division, but they also reached the quarter-finals of the Vitality Blast, and missed the knockout stages of the Royal London Cup only on net run-rate. It all represented a personal triumph for head coach Richard Dawson, who had overseen steady improvement since his appointment in 2015. Though it's true Gloucestershire benefited from a restructuring of the Championship that – for one year – allowed three teams to go up, there was no question they had become more consistent and more competitive.

Success was achieved against the odds. A small budget limited them to a small squad, so injury hurt Gloucestershire more than most. Australian Dan Worrall was signed for the entire season, but damaged his back in his second game, and the county did not field an overseas player in the Championship until Chadd Sayers, another seamer from South Australia, in June. All-rounder Benny Howell pulled a hamstring in August, and missed the rest of the summer. Asked to shoulder a heavy workload, left-arm seamer Matt Taylor broke down during the Cheltenham Festival, placing further strain on a depleted attack.

Dawson reduced the impact of injuries, however, by making shrewd use of the loan market. Seam bowlers Josh Shaw and Ethan Bamber arrived from Yorkshire and Middlesex, while one-time England Under-19 international Ben Allison was given a first-class debut at Derby, continuing Gloucestershire's commitment to blooding talented young domestic cricketers. Sayers proved a reasonable locum, picking up 11 wickets at 36, but West Indian pace bowler Shannon Gabriel found life trickier, and managed two at 90.

In one – worrying – respect, the 2019 season maintained a trend. Gloucestershire find it much harder to win Championship matches at Bristol, where they play most of their fixtures, than at Cheltenham. Since the start of 2015, they have won three of their 26 games at Nevil Road, and seven out of 11 at the College. Both home victories in 2019 came at their festival base; at HQ, the record was two defeats and two draws. They fared better on the road, and prevailed at Chester-le-Street, Derby and Worcester.

Gloucestershire's determination to be tougher opponents bore fruit, and they went unbeaten in their opening six matches, winning one, to establish a solid foundation. But back-to-back defeats by Glamorgan and Middlesex left them with ground to make up during the last third of the season. Favoured, if counter-intuitively, by a fixture list that kept them away from Bristol for almost three months, they staged a grandstand finish, and won four out of five; as the final round began, they were third, 16 points above nearest rivals Glamorgan.

Ryan Higgins

A damp draw suited them and their opponents, Northamptonshire, who also gained promotion.

The youth-cum-loan policy also paid off. Bamber, aged 20, played a part in Cheltenham's cliffhanger wins over Leicestershire and Worcestershire; the 19-year-old Allison took four wickets in a dramatic victory over Derbyshire (when Gloucestershire scored 263 in 49 overs); and Shaw, a little older at 23 and now back on a permanent deal, bolstered the attack during the run-in.

It was not all down to the youngsters, though. The ever-present captain, Chris Dent, was prepared to bat time if neccesary, and he set a superb example at the top of the order, hitting four hundreds – and passing 1,000 runs for the fourth time. When he played well, so did Gloucestershire. It was a tougher season for Miles Hammond, who began as Dent's partner, but shuffled down a place or two; a total of 418 at 19 summed up his travails. James Bracey, who replaced Hammond as an opener, and wicketkeeper Gareth Roderick enjoyed decent returns of around 650 runs at an average in the thirties.

In a testament to his stamina and fitness, all-rounder Ryan Higgins, still only 24, missed just one match in the entire season – a limited-overs game against Australia A. In the Championship, he took 50 wickets at 23 and hit 958 runs at a shade under 60. He topped both averages, and was arguably Division Two's player of the season. Left-arm seam bowler David Payne proved a model of consistency, and claimed 43 victims (plus 16 in the Blast).

Given that key players were safely under contract, the immediate future looked encouraging. The club bolstered their attack by signing veteran West Indies fast bowler Jerome Taylor to play in all formats on a Kolpak deal, and also 19-year-old Afghanistan leg-spinner Qais Ahmad for six Championship matches and the Blast. Should the luckless Worrall prove his fitness, he could return for a third stint.

Gloucestershire rose from seventh in their RLODC group to fourth, edged out of the knockouts by eventual winners Somerset. Proving his ability to excel in all formats, Bracey hit 333 runs at 55; Howell took 12 wickets. In the Vitality Blast, they were beaten quarter-finalists for the third time in four years, Australians Michael Klinger (371 runs) and Andrew Tye (15 wickets) helping secure second place in their group. Defeat by Derbyshire in the last eight denied Klinger a finals-day swansong before he headed into retirement, and a coaching role with Melbourne Renegades. His record of 2,949 T20 runs was comfortably the most for Gloucestershire, and he hit seven of their 12 hundreds. In his seven years at Bristol, Klinger was also a major influence on young players, and he left a huge gap.

Championship attendance: 23,803.

GLOUCESTERSHIRE RESULTS

All first-class matches – Played 14: Won 5, Lost 3, Drawn 6.
County Championship matches – Played 14: Won 5, Lost 3, Drawn 6.

Specsavers County Championship, 3rd in Division 2;
Vitality Blast, quarter-finalists; Royal London One-Day Cup, 4th in South Group.

COUNTY CHAMPIONSHIP AVERAGES, BATTING AND FIELDING

Cap		Birthplace	M	I	NO	R	HS	100	Avge	Ct/St
2018	R. F. Higgins	Harare, Zimbabwe	14	21	5	958	199	4	59.87	4
2010	†C. D. J. Dent	Bristol	14	24	1	1,087	176	4	47.26	8
2016	G. L. van Buuren†† .	Pretoria, SA	10	13	3	363	93	0	36.30	4
2016	†J. R. Bracey.	Bristol	13	22	2	677	152	2	33.85	23
2013	T. M. J. Smith.	Eastbourne	5	8	0	261	84	0	32.62	3
2013	G. H. Roderick†† . . .	Durban, SA	14	24	3	654	158	1	31.14	41/1
2012	B. A. C. Howell	Bordeaux, France .	10	15	0	369	76	0	24.60	12
2018	†B. G. Charlesworth .	Oxford	5	7	1	145	77*	0	24.16	3
2013	M. D. Taylor.	Banbury	9	10	7	67	28*	0	22.33	0
2010	J. M. R. Taylor	Banbury	9	13	0	279	99	0	21.46	3
2013	†M. A. H. Hammond .	Cheltenham‡ . . .	14	23	1	418	82	0	19.00	14
2011	D. A. Payne	Poole	12	15	4	205	43	0	18.63	4
2019	C. J. Sayers¶.	Henley Beach, Aust	4	4	1	55	33*	0	18.33	0
2016	J. Shaw	Wakefield	9	12	2	107	38*	0	10.70	3
2016	G. T. Hankins	Bath	4	6	0	23	14	0	3.83	0

Also batted: B. M. J. Allison (*Colchester*) (cap 2019) (1 match) 0; E. R. Bamber (cap 2019) (*Westminster*) (2 matches) 15, 3, 12*; G. S. Drissell (*Bristol*) (cap 2017) (1 match) 1; S. T. Gabriel¶ (*Trinidad*) (cap 2019) (3 matches) 1, 2, 2*; H. J. Hankins (*Bath*) (cap 2019) (1 match) 9.

‡ *Born in Gloucestershire.* ¶ *Official overseas player.* †† *Other non-England-qualified.*

BOWLING

	Style	O	M	R	W	BB	5I	Avge
R. F. Higgins	RM	453.4	110	1,182	50	5-54	2	23.64
J. Shaw.	RFM	225.2	43	737	30	4-33	0	24.56
D. A. Payne	LFM	403.5	94	1,113	43	4-40	0	25.88
M. D. Taylor	LM	245	43	760	29	5-57	1	26.20
C. J. Sayers.	RFM	149.4	39	400	11	3-60	0	36.36

Also bowled: B. M. J. Allison (RFM) 41–9–139–4; E. R. Bamber (RFM) 85.3–15–206–8; J. R. Bracey (RM) 10–0–35–0; B. G. Charlesworth (RM) 18–1–84–3; C. D. J. Dent (SLA) 2.2–0–18–1; G. S. Drissell (OB) 41.1–5–174–4; S. T. Gabriel (RF) 32.5–0–180–2; M. A. H. Hammond (OB) 22–0–121–0; H. J. Hankins (RFM) 33–4–101–0; B. A. C. Howell (RM) 97.2–23–262–7; T. M. J. Smith (SLA) 76–14–217–4; J. M. R. Taylor (OB) 9–0–51–0; G. L. van Buuren (SLA) 119–16–343–3.

LEADING ROYAL LONDON CUP AVERAGES (100 runs/3 wickets)

Batting	Runs	HS	Avge	SR	Ct
J. R. Bracey	333	113*	55.50	106.38	3
J. M. R. Taylor . .	253	75	50.60	108.58	6
G. H. Roderick . .	302	100*	43.14	89.34	8
C. D. J. Dent	345	89	43.12	81.94	4
M. A. H. Hammond	165	95	41.25	73.66	1
R. F. Higgins	180	45	30.00	111.80	2
G. L. van Buuren	120	61	30.00	80.00	1
B. A. C. Howell .	190	55	27.14	86.75	3

Bowling	W	BB	Avge	ER
D. J. Worrall	4	2-22	13.00	5.20
B. A. C. Howell . . .	12	3-45	26.58	6.05
C. J. Liddle	9	4-66	34.55	7.40
T. M. J. Smith	8	3-7	35.37	5.05
M. D. Taylor	5	3-39	35.80	4.83
R. F. Higgins	8	2-55	38.00	5.08
D. A. Payne	9	2-30	39.22	6.41
G. L. van Buuren . .	4	1-19	55.25	5.02

LEADING VITALITY BLAST AVERAGES (100 runs/15 overs)

Batting	Runs	HS	Avge	SR	Ct/St		Bowling	W	BB	Avge	ER
B. A. C. Howell	106	33	26.50	145.20	2		B. A. C. Howell	10	5-18	17.30	6.65
M. A. H. Hammond	322	63	26.83	140.61	5		D. A. Payne	16	3-32	21.68	7.38
R. F. Higgins	206	77*	25.75	137.33	2		A. J. Tye	15	2-23	25.06	7.59
J. M. R. Taylor	193	42	24.12	134.96	4		T. M. J. Smith	8	3-19	39.00	7.80
M. Klinger	371	102*	33.72	122.44	10		C. J. Liddle	11	3-25	16.72	7.94
I. A. Cockbain	277	61*	34.62	120.96	7		R. F. Higgins	8	3-36	30.12	8.50
J. R. Bracey	245	64	20.41	118.35	7/3		G. L. van Buuren	4	2-27	38.50	9.05

FIRST-CLASS COUNTY RECORDS

Highest score for	341	C. M. Spearman v Middlesex at Gloucester	2004
Highest score against	319	C. J. L. Rogers (Northants) at Northampton	2006
Leading run-scorer	33,664	W. R. Hammond (avge 57.05)	1920–51
Best bowling for	10-40	E. G. Dennett v Essex at Bristol	1906
Best bowling against	10-66	A. A. Mailey (Australians) at Cheltenham	1921
	10-66	K. Smales (Nottinghamshire) at Stroud	1956
Leading wicket-taker	3,170	C. W. L. Parker (avge 19.43)	1903–35
Highest total for	695-9 dec	v Middlesex at Gloucester	2004
Highest total against	774-7 dec	by Australians at Bristol	1948
Lowest total for	17	v Australians at Cheltenham	1896
Lowest total against	12	by Northamptonshire at Gloucester	1907

LIST A COUNTY RECORDS

Highest score for	177	A. J. Wright v Scotland at Bristol	1997
Highest score against	190	J. M. Vince (Hampshire) at Southampton	2019
Leading run-scorer	7,825	M. W. Alleyne (avge 26.89)	1986–2005
Best bowling for	7-29	D. A. Payne v Essex at Chelmsford	2010
Best bowling against	6-16	Shoaib Akhtar (Worcestershire) at Worcester	2005
Leading wicket-taker	393	M. W. Alleyne (avge 29.88)	1986–2005
Highest total for	401-7	v Buckinghamshire at Wing	2003
Highest total against	496-4	by Surrey at The Oval	2007
Lowest total for	49	v Middlesex at Bristol	1978
Lowest total against	48	by Middlesex at Lydney	1973

TWENTY20 COUNTY RECORDS

Highest score for	126*	M. Klinger v Essex at Bristol	2015
Highest score against	116*	C. L. White (Somerset) at Taunton	2006
Leading run-scorer	2,949	M. Klinger (avge 42.12, SR 128.10)	2013–19
Best bowling for	5-18	B. A. C. Howell v Glamorgan at Cheltenham	2019
Best bowling against	5-16	R. E. Watkins (Glamorgan) at Cardiff	2009
Leading wicket-taker	109	B. A. C. Howell (avge 18.80, ER 7.02)	2012–19
Highest total for	254-3	v Middlesex at Uxbridge	2011
Highest total against	250-3	by Somerset at Taunton	2006
Lowest total for	68	v Hampshire at Bristol	2010
Lowest total against	97	by Surrey at The Oval	2010

ADDRESS

County Ground, Nevil Road, Bristol BS7 9EJ; 0117 910 8000; reception@glosccc.co.uk; www.gloscricket.co.uk.

OFFICIALS

Captain (first-class) C. D. J. Dent
    2019 (Twenty20) M. Klinger
Head coach R. K. J. Dawson
Assistant head coach I. J. Harvey
Head of talent pathway T. H. C. Hancock

President R. A. Gibbons
Chairman J. A. Hollingdale
Chief executive W. G. Brown
Head groundsman S. P. Williams
Scorer A. J. Bull

At Bristol, April 5–7 (not first-class). **Drawn. Gloucestershire 466-7 dec** (112 overs) (G. H. Roderick 115, G. T. Hankins 118, B. A. C. Howell 87*, R. F. Higgins 74*; A. R. Wilkinson 3-85) **and 33-0** (10 overs) (T. D. Heathfield 71 overs) (T. D. Heathfield 85; M. D. Taylor 3-60, R. F. Higgins 3-30, B. A. C. Howell 3-37). *County debut: H. J. Hankins. With the Championship round the corner, Gloucestershire hit enough runs and bowled enough balls to gain useful practice. But, in a match interrupted by rain, they could not defeat the students, whose modest attack dismissed the top three in single figures. Roderick and Hankins redressed the balance, each making a century before retiring; Howell then scored a brisk 87*, and Higgins an even faster 74*, from 51 balls, as their opponents tired. The eighth-wicket stand had reached 131* from 17 overs at the declaration. Left-armer Alex Wilkinson had three wickets. Survival represented the height of the students' batting ambitions, and opener Tom Heathfield made a watchful 85 from 199 balls. A trio of Gloucestershire bowlers took three wickets, while debutant seamer Harry Hankins – younger brother of George – claimed the other. Late on the last day, Dent chose not to enforce the follow-on, despite a lead of 291.*

GLOUCESTERSHIRE v DERBYSHIRE

At Bristol, April 11–14. Drawn. Gloucestershire 11pts, Derbyshire 9pts. Toss: Gloucestershire. First-class debut: H. J. Hankins.

A painstaking unbeaten 204 by Madsen blocked Gloucestershire's path towards victory on the last day of a slow-moving contest, played out on an unresponsive surface. It also took him past 15,000 runs in all cricket for Derbyshire. After forging a handy lead of 59, Gloucestershire had dismissed openers Reece and Godleman before stumps on the third day. Lace fell for 57 next morning, but Madsen and Hughes slammed the door on West Country ambition by diligently compiling an unbroken 278, a fourth-wicket record in this fixture. Madsen batted for seven and a half hours, and Hughes four hours 20 minutes, allowing Derbyshire to declare at 388 for three, the game long since safe. After negotiating 237 balls, Roderick had earlier fallen in sight of a first hundred since July 2016. He put on 118 for the sixth wicket with Higgins, who contributed 74 – and was also the pick of Gloucestershire's injury-hit attack.

Close of play: first day, Derbyshire 256-7 (Dal 1, van Beek 0); second day, Gloucestershire 202-5 (Roderick 33, Higgins 33); third day, Derbyshire 97-2 (Madsen 41, Lace 48).

Derbyshire

L. M. Reece c Roderick b Shaw	39	– c Roderick b Taylor	0
*B. A. Godleman b Higgins	7	– c Roderick b Higgins	6
W. L. Madsen lbw b Taylor	15	– not out	204
T. C. Lace c Roderick b Shaw	83	– b Dent b Howell	57
A. L. Hughes c Howell b Higgins	26	– not out	109
†H. R. Hosein b Howell	41		
M. J. J. Critchley lbw b Shaw	39		
A. K. Dal lbw b Higgins	3		
L. V. van Beek b Taylor	7		
A. P. Palladino not out	9		
R. Rampaul c Dent b Howell	9		
B 5, lb 5, w 1, nb 2	13	B 2, lb 7, w 1, nb 2	12

1/16 (2) 2/48 (3) 3/95 (1)   (109.2 overs) 291   1/0 (1)   (3 wkts dec, 123 overs) 388
4/168 (4) 5/184 (5) 6/255 (7)   2/18 (2) 3/110 (4)
7/255 (6) 8/258 (8) 9/266 (9) 10/291 (11)

Taylor 27–6–85–3; Higgins 29–13–52–3; H. J. Hankins 15–2–50–0; Shaw 20–3–65–2; Howell 14.2–7–19–2; van Buuren 4–0–10–0. *Second innings*—Taylor 21–3–55–1; Higgins 27–9–57–1; Shaw 3–2–4–0; H. J. Hankins 18–2–51–0; Howell 18–4–48–1; van Buuren 22–1–89–0; Hammond 11–0–70–0; Bracey 3–0–5–0.

Gloucestershire

M. A. H. Hammond c Madsen b Reece	6	M. D. Taylor not out		8
*C. D. J. Dent b Hughes	33	H. J. Hankins c Dal b van Beek		9
J. R. Bracey c Dal b Palladino	65			
G. T. Hankins c Lace b Reece	0	B 4, lb 3, nb 4		11
†G. H. Roderick c Hosein b van Beek	98			—
B. A. C. Howell c Critchley b van Beek	25	1/12 (1) 2/96 (2)	(129.2 overs)	350
R. F. Higgins b Reece	74	3/97 (4) 4/111 (3) 5/157 (6)		
G. L. van Buuren lbw b Rampaul	15	6/275 (7) 7/311 (8) 8/325 (9)		
J. Shaw c van Beek b Rampaul	6	9/332 (5) 10/350 (11)	110 overs: 303-6	

Rampaul 25–4–86–2; Palladino 20–10–32–1; Reece 23–6–60–3; van Beek 22.2–4–75–3; Hughes 21–6–49–1; Madsen 3–1–4–0; Critchley 13–4–29–0; Dal 2–0–8–0.

Umpires: B. J. Debenham and D. J. Millns.

At Newport, May 14–17. GLOUCESTERSHIRE drew with GLAMORGAN.

At Chester-le-Street, May 20–22. GLOUCESTERSHIRE beat DURHAM by six wickets.

GLOUCESTERSHIRE v LANCASHIRE

At Cheltenham, May 27–30. Drawn. Gloucestershire 9pts, Lancashire 9pts. Toss: uncontested.

A draw was inevitable after rain prevented any play on the second or third day. Even so, the contest produced some notable performances. Cheltenham-born opener Hammond was given a stern examination by Anderson and, though Hammond fell to him in the end, his 82 proved the game's highest score. Jack Taylor offered robust support, and Gloucestershire – inserted on a dry pitch – made 205, with Dent passing 8,000 first-class runs. The highly regarded Mahmood had claimed the first three wickets by Anderson and, finished with four for 48. In reply, Jennings and Jones hit fifties, and Lancashire were well placed at 105 for two, before being restricted to a lead of 39. Matt Taylor took five for 57, his best Championship figures.

Close of play: first day, Lancashire 47-2 (Jennings 26, Jones 14); second day, no play; third day, no play.

Gloucestershire

M. A. H. Hammond b Anderson	82	– (2) c Jones b Bailey	6
*C. D. J. Dent c Vilas b Mahmood	23	– (1) not out	30
J. R. Bracey c Vilas b Mahmood	4	– c Vilas b Gleeson	16
†G. H. Roderick b Mahmood	10	– not out	10
B. A. C. Howell c Hameed b Bailey	4		
J. M. R. Taylor c Jennings b Livingstone	42		
R. F. Higgins b Livingstone	0		
G. L. van Buuren b Mahmood	23		
D. A. Payne run out (Anderson)	7		
J. Shaw b Anderson	0		
M. D. Taylor not out	0		
Lb 2, nb 8	10	Nb 6	6

1/55 (2) 2/63 (3) 3/77 (4)	(69.1 overs) 205	1/24 (2)	(2 wkts, 21 overs) 68
4/84 (5) 5/168 (6) 6/168 (7)		2/56 (3)	
7/189 (1) 8/205 (8) 9/205 (9) 10/205 (10)			

Anderson 14.1–8–25–2; Bailey 19–4–52–1; Gleeson 12–0–55–0; Mahmood 14–2–48–4; Livingstone 10–1–23–2. *Second innings—*Anderson 4–1–12–0; Bailey 6–4–10–1; Mahmood 4–0–21–0; Gleeson 4–0–14–1; Livingstone 3–0–11–0.

Lancashire

K. K. Jennings c Howell b M. D. Taylor. . .	52	S. Mahmood c Roderick b M. D. Taylor. . .	0
H. Hameed run out (M. D. Taylor)	7	R. J. Gleeson c Howell b Payne	10
J. S. Lehmann b Payne	0	J. M. Anderson not out	9
R. P. Jones c Roderick b M. D. Taylor . .	53	B 8, lb 5, nb 6	19
L. S. Livingstone c Hammond b Shaw	28		
*†D. J. Vilas c Roderick b M. D. Taylor. . . .	0	1/16 (2) 2/24 (3) 3/105 (4) (72.5 overs) 244
S. J. Croft c Payne b Higgins.	35	4/124 (1) 5/126 (6) 6/153 (5)
T. E. Bailey b M. D. Taylor.	31	7/211 (8) 8/213 (9) 9/223 (7) 10/244 (10)

Payne 21.5–11–32–2; Higgins 18–2–58–1; Shaw 17–2–84–1; M. D. Taylor 15–4–57–5; van Buuren 1–1–0–0.

Umpires: J. H. Evans and P. R. Pollard.

At Arundel, June 11–14. GLOUCESTERSHIRE drew with SUSSEX.

At Leicester, June 17–20. GLOUCESTERSHIRE drew with LEICESTERSHIRE. *Chris Dent and Ryan Higgins put on 318, a sixth-wicket record for this fixture.*

GLOUCESTERSHIRE v GLAMORGAN

At Bristol, June 23–26. Glamorgan won by four wickets. Glamorgan 21pts, Gloucestershire 6pts. Toss: uncontested.

Two Australian imports, Hogan and Labuschagne, consigned Gloucestershire to their first defeat since the previous August – and took Glamorgan top of the table. At the start of the last day, the hosts had been reasonably placed: 67 ahead with eight wickets in hand. But they succumbed to Hogan, who cut a swathe through their second innings with four for 22 in 18 overs. Having removed Dent, a first-innings centurion, on the third evening, he dismissed Roderick next morning, before instigating a post-lunch collapse in which the last five wickets fell for 16. It meant Gloucestershire could set a target of only 188 in 49 overs. Labuschagne then crafted a second half-century of the match, his assured 82 crucial in guiding Glamorgan home with seven overs to spare. At 176 for one, Gloucestershire had been even better placed on the second morning, but Hogan made inroads – his match figures were seven for 73 – to limit the total to 313. The Glamorgan reply followed a similar trajectory: 153 for one led to 287 all out.

Close of play: first day, Gloucestershire 168-1 (Dent 82, Bracey 21); second day, Glamorgan 187-4 (Labuschagne 56); third day, Gloucestershire 41-2 (Bracey 14, Roderick 0).

Gloucestershire

M. A. H. Hammond c Labuschagne b Lloyd	61	– (2) b Douthwaite	21
*C. D. J. Dent c Cullen b Douthwaite	105	– (1) c Lloyd b Hogan	2
J. R. Bracey c Lloyd b Hogan	28	– lbw b Douthwaite	33
*G. H. Roderick b Hogan.	22	– c Selman b Hogan	20
B. A. C. Howell c Cullen b Wagg	2	– b Hogan	33
J. M. R. Taylor c Selman b Wagg	13	– lbw b Lloyd	16
R. F. Higgins c Cullen b Hogan.	18	– c Cullen b Hogan.	6
G. L. van Buuren c Cullen b Wagg	17	– c Cullen de Lange	9
D. A. Payne b de Lange	9	– c Cullen b Wagg.	1
J. Shaw not out	18	– c Labuschagne b Wagg	0
M. D. Taylor c Cullen b Douthwaite	1	– not out	2
Lb 1, w 1, nb 10	12	B 5, lb 2, w 1, nb 10.	18

1/127 (1) 2/176 (3) 3/210 (2) (96.1 overs) 313	1/3 (1) 2/35 (2) (62.2 overs) 161
4/215 (5) 5/233 (6) 6/266 (4)	3/64 (4) 4/95 (3)
7/267 (7) 8/280 (9) 9/312 (8) 10/313 (11)	5/129 (6) 6/145 (7) 7/149 (5)
	8/153 (9) 9/155 (10) 10/161 (8)

De Lange 27–5–91–1; Hogan 25–6–51–3; Wagg 15–1–59–3; Hemphrey 2–0–7–0; Douthwaite 11.1–0–49–2; Labuschagne 7–0–35–0; Lloyd 9–2–20–1. *Second innings*—de Lange 16.2–4–51–1; Hogan 18–6–22–4; Douthwaite 9–3–35–2; Wagg 12–2–35–2; Lloyd 7–2–11–1.

Glamorgan

N. J. Selman c Howell b Shaw	73	– c J. M. R. Taylor b Payne	6
C. R. Hemphrey c Roderick b Shaw	28	– c Dent b Shaw	15
M. Labuschagne c Roderick b Payne	65	– c Roderick b Payne	82
*D. L. Lloyd c Roderick b Higgins	1	– b M. D. Taylor	8
W. T. Root b M. D. Taylor	21	– c Dent b Shaw	31
A. O. Morgan c Hammond b Payne	5	– (8) not out	6
D. A. Douthwaite lbw b Higgins	23	– (6) c van Buuren b Shaw	14
†T. N. Cullen c Bracey b Shaw	7		
G. G. Wagg c Payne b Higgins	33	– (7) not out	15
M. de Lange c Roderick b Payne	8		
M. G. Hogan not out	0		
B 4, lb 13, nb 6	23	B 2, lb 7, nb 2	11

1/58 (2) 2/153 (1) 3/156 (4)	(93.1 overs) 287	1/6 (1)	(6 wkts, 42.1 overs) 188
4/187 (5) 5/201 (3) 6/204 (6)		2/68 (2) 3/85 (4)	
7/215 (8) 8/264 (7) 9/287 (10) 10/287 (9)		4/147 (5) 5/153 (3) 6/179 (6)	

Payne 29–3–90–3; Higgins 25.1–4–63–3; M. D. Taylor 15–2–44–1; Shaw 19–3–61–3; Howell 5–1–12–0. *Second innings*—Payne 16–1–58–2; Higgins 9–1–49–0; Shaw 10.1–1–41–3; M. D. Taylor 5–0–21–1; van Buuren 2–0–10–0.

Umpires: R. J. Bailey and U. V. Gandhe.

At Bristol, June 30. GLOUCESTERSHIRE lost to AUSTRALIA A by five wickets (see Australia A tour section).

At Bristol, July 2. GLOUCESTERSHIRE lost to AUSTRALIA A by nine runs (see Australia A tour section).

At Northwood, July 7–9. GLOUCESTERSHIRE lost to MIDDLESEX by 78 runs.

GLOUCESTERSHIRE v LEICESTERSHIRE

At Cheltenham, July 15–18. Gloucestershire won by six wickets. Gloucestershire 22pts, Leicestershire 4pts. Toss: Leicestershire. County debut: E. R. Bamber.

Roderick plundered a towering six over point to give Gloucestershire, chasing 48 in eight overs, a nailbiting victory with three balls to spare. Azad's dogged resistance had looked as if it might save Leicestershire, but his dismissal to the first delivery after tea, his 302nd, was the start of a collapse from 255 for four to 299 all out. Higgins finished with five for 71, reward for his control. A Gloucestershire victory had been on the cards ever since Dent and Tom Smith added 195 for the third wicket; Dent hit his third century of a productive summer, while Smith – in his first Championship appearance since 2017, and batting higher than usual at No. 4 – made a career-best 84. Jack Taylor and Howell built on the platform in a seventh-wicket stand of 157, and allowed Dent to declare on exactly twice Leicestershire's first-innings 252. Their batting had been denuded by the loss of Mark Cosgrove, struck on the head in the nets before the match. Dexter did his best to glue things together on day one, when Bamber – on loan from Middlesex – and Matt Taylor took three wickets each.

Close of play: first day, Leicestershire 252; second day, Gloucestershire 275-6 (J. M. R. Taylor 15, Howell 0); third day, Leicestershire 78-2 (Azad 38, Ackermann 8).

Leicestershire

M. H. Azad c Roderick b Bamber	1	– c Hammond b Bamber	121
*P. J. Horton lbw b M. D. Taylor	47	– lbw b Higgins	26
N. J. Dexter c Hammond b Sayers	56	– c Hammond b Higgins	0
C. N. Ackermann c van Buuren b M. D. Taylor	21	– c Roderick b M. D. Taylor	41
H. E. Dearden b Higgins	7	– b Higgins	19
B. W. M. Mike b Howell	7	– c Roderick b M. D. Taylor	14
†H. J. Swindells lbw b Higgins	32	– c Howell b Higgins	12
C. F. Parkinson c b M. D. Taylor	19	– c Hammond b Sayers	17
C. J. C. Wright b Bamber	30	– b Sayers	2
W. S. Davis not out	8	– lbw b Higgins	0
Mohammad Abbas c Smith b Bamber	3	– not out	1
B 4, lb 5, nb 12	21	B 12, lb 2, nb 20	46

1/1 (1) 2/74 (2) 3/124 (4)   (95.3 overs) 252
4/132 (5) 5/143 (6) 6/151 (3)
7/197 (8) 8/226 (7) 9/246 (9) 10/252 (11)

1/48 (2) 2/56 (3)   (119.1 overs) 299
3/169 (4) 4/213 (5)
5/255 (1) 6/259 (6) 7/292 (7)
8/292 (8) 9/293 (10) 10/299 (9)

Sayers 24–4–77–1; Bamber 22.3–2–53–3; M. D. Taylor 18–4–39–3; Higgins 17–4–44–2; Smith 8–3–16–0; Howell 6–1–14–1. *Second innings*—Sayers 25.1–7–49–2; Bamber 22–4–50–1; Higgins 24–2–71–5; M. D. Taylor 27–7–56–2; Smith 16–4–38–0; van Buuren 5–2–9–0.

Gloucestershire

M. A. H. Hammond c Ackermann b Mohammad Abbas	0	– (2) c sub (G. T. Griffiths) b Wright	12
*C. D. J. Dent c Swindells b Wright	125	– (1) b Wright	6
†G. H. Roderick run out (Dexter)	22	– (6) not out	8
T. M. J. Smith b Wright	84		
R. F. Higgins b Davis	14	– (3) not out	13
G. L. van Buuren c Ackermann b Wright	0		
J. M. R. Taylor b Davis	99	– (4) c Dearden b Mohammad Abbas	8
B. A. C. Howell lbw b Davis	76	– (5) run out (Davis)	1
C. J. Sayers not out	33		
E. R. Bamber st Swindells b Parkinson	15		
B 9, lb 9, nb 18	36		

1/0 (1) 2/46 (3)   (9 wkts dec, 154.1 overs) 504
3/241 (2) 4/252 (4)
5/252 (6) 6/273 (5) 7/430 (7)
8/463 (8) 9/504 (10)
110 overs: 323-6

1/9 (1)   (4 wkts, 7.3 overs) 48
2/24 (2) 3/33 (4)
4/40 (5)

M. D. Taylor did not bat.

Mohammad Abbas 29–8–82–1; Wright 31–3–89–3; Davis 29–8–73–3; Dexter 17–2–53–0; Mike 18–2–82–0; Parkinson 21.1–3–74–1; Ackermann 9–2–33–0. *Second innings*—Mohammad Abbas 4–0–22–1; Wright 3.3–0–26–2.

Umpires: N. G. B. Cook and R. J. Warren.

GLOUCESTERSHIRE v WORCESTERSHIRE

At Cheltenham, July 21–24. Gloucestershire won by 13 runs. Gloucestershire 23pts, Worcestershire 5pts. Toss: uncontested.

Higgins shone again, this time taking four for 64, as a resurgent Gloucestershire held their nerve in another last-ditch victory at Cheltenham. Buoyed by Ferguson's half-century, Worcestershire seemed on their way to a target of 246 after reaching 229 for seven, with the experienced Parnell at the crease, and Gloucestershire a seamer down because Matt Taylor had suffered a side strain. But Higgins bowled Parnell and Pennington in three balls, and Finch edged Payne to second slip. Worcestershire were left to rue their decision on the final morning to deploy D'Oliveira's leg-spin against tailenders Payne and Bamber, who extended their vital ninth-wicket partnership to 40.

Despite Leach's first-innings six-for, Gloucestershire had laid solid foundations thanks to three half-centuries, including an unfettered 59-ball 76 from Higgins. Whiteley and D'Oliveira rescued the reply from a precarious 68 for five in a restrained stand worth 146, but Worcestershire still conceded a lead of 61; on a surface of variable bounce that kept the seamers interested, neither team ever pulled away. Successive Festival victories had taken Gloucestershire from ninth to third.

Close of play: first day, Gloucestershire 339-7 (Smith 79, Payne 4); second day, Worcestershire 232-6 (D'Oliveira 66, Parnell 10); third day, Gloucestershire 149-8 (Payne 1, Bamber 5).

Gloucestershire

M. A. H. Hammond c Cox b Leach	0	– (2) lbw b Barnard	17
*C. D. J. Dent c Cox b Leach	58	– (1) c Cox b Leach	0
G. H. Roderick c Ferguson b Pennington	40	– b Parnell	12
†J. R. Bracey c Wessels b Leach	8	– b Parnell	16
T. M. J. Smith c Barnard b Leach	83	– c Wessels b Parnell	25
R. F. Higgins c Cox b D'Oliveira	76	– c Wessels b Pennington	36
J. M. R. Taylor c Parnell b D'Oliveira	10	– c Cox b Barnard	20
B. A. C. Howell c Barnard b Parnell	36	– c Parnell b D'Oliveira	4
D. A. Payne b Leach	8	– c Mitchell b Barnard	22
E. R. Bamber c Cox b Leach	3	– not out	12
M. D. Taylor not out	4	– c Cox b Finch	1
B 5, lb 2, w 5, nb 16	28	B 5, lb 4, nb 10	19

1/0 (1) 2/70 (3) 3/92 (4)   (103.2 overs) 354
4/125 (2) 5/253 (6) 6/271 (7)
7/329 (8) 8/345 (9) 9/349 (10) 10/354 (5)

1/0 (1) 2/21 (3)   (76.3 overs) 184
3/35 (2) 4/47 (4)
5/103 (6) 6/132 (5) 7/143 (7)
8/143 (8) 9/183 (9) 10/184 (11)

Leach 24.2–4–79–6; Pennington 21–5–55–1; Finch 14–0–74–0; Parnell 15–5–47–1; Barnard 14–2–46–0; D'Oliveira 15–2–46–2. *Second innings*—Leach 12–3–27–1; Pennington 9–3–13–1; Parnell 17–5–37–3; Barnard 15–6–17–3; Finch 9.3–2–41–1; D'Oliveira 14–6–40–1.

Worcestershire

D. K. H. Mitchell c Bracey b Higgins	18	– c Bracey b Payne	0
M. H. Wessels c Howell b Bamber	12	– c Bracey b Smith	42
C. J. Ferguson c Hammond b Payne	1	– c Bracey b Howell	63
E. G. Barnard c Bracey b Higgins	6	– c Bracey b Higgins	10
R. A. Whiteley c Howell b M. D. Taylor	88	– lbw b Higgins	0
†O. B. Cox c Howell b Payne	13	– c Higgins b Bamber	42
B. L. D'Oliveira c Hammond b Bamber	68	– c sub (G. T. Hankins) b Howell	11
W. D. Parnell c Bracey b Bamber	17	– b Higgins	15
*J. Leach b Higgins	38	– not out	15
D. Y. Pennington lbw b Payne	1	– b Higgins	0
A. W. Finch not out	8	– c sub (G. T. Hankins) b Payne	0
B 1, lb 10, nb 12	23	B 5, lb 18, w 1, nb 10	34

1/24 (2) 2/25 (3) 3/41 (4)   (113 overs) 293
4/44 (1) 5/68 (6) 6/214 (5) 7/240 (8)
8/245 (7) 9/246 (10) 10/293 (9)

1/0 (1) 2/73 (2)   (75.1 overs) 232
3/96 (4) 4/100 (5)
5/181 (6) 6/189 (3) 7/198 (7)
8/229 (8) 9/229 (10) 10/232 (11)

110 overs: 291-9

Payne 27.1–9–73–3; Bamber 24–6–59–3; M. D. Taylor 15.5–3–50–1; Higgins 24–5–52–3; Howell 7–2–11–0; Smith 15–2–37–0. *Second innings*—Payne 19.1–4–55–2; Bamber 17–3–44–1; Higgins 21–6–64–4; Howell 12–4–32–2; Smith 6–1–14–1.

Umpires: R. K. Illingworth and G. D. Lloyd.

At Derby, August 18–21. GLOUCESTERSHIRE beat DERBYSHIRE by eight wickets. *Ryan Higgins takes 5-54 and hits 101.*

GLOUCESTERSHIRE v SUSSEX

At Bristol, September 10–13. Sussex won by eight wickets. Sussex 23pts, Gloucestershire 4pts. Toss: uncontested. County debut: S. T. Gabriel.

On a bowler-friendly pitch made trickier by overhead conditions, Sussex's greater discipline was rewarded with a hard-earned victory that steered them back towards promotion contention. Inserted on a low and slow wicket, Gloucestershire were guilty of poor shot selection and impatience, and laboured to 200. By contrast, Sussex showed far more application, a string of contributions building into handy partnerships – a lead of 170. Gloucestershire scarcely helped themselves, with 46 in no-balls swelling Extras to 60. Higgins and West Indies Test quick Shannon Gabriel, who proved costly on county debut, were the culprits; the only bowler to pose a threat was Payne. During his second-innings 72, Dent passed 1,000 runs for the fourth time, but too many colleagues were guilty of revisiting past sins, and perished to ill-advised strokes. The Sussex seamers shared the wickets, with Wiese again proving an invaluable all-rounder. Knocking off a target of 74 was straightforward, and Gloucestershire's rise up the table came to a halt.

Close of play: first day, Sussex 73-0 (Salt 53, Wells 6); second day, Sussex 313-7 (Wiese 40, Beer 28); third day, Gloucestershire 197-6 (Higgins 24, J. M. R. Taylor 10).

Gloucestershire

J. R. Bracey c Brown b Jordan	61	– c Brown b Wiese	18
*C. D. J. Dent c Jordan b Haines	7	– c Brown b Garton	72
†G. H. Roderick b Wiese	0	– c Haines b Wiese	8
M. A. H. Hammond c Rawlins b Garton	16	– c Jordan b Rawlins	10
T. M. J. Smith b Jordan	0	– c Beer b Robinson	23
B. G. Charlesworth c Brown b Jordan	28	– lbw b Robinson	15
R. F. Higgins c Salt b Wiese	22	– c Robinson b Jordan	27
J. M. R. Taylor c Jordan b Robinson	26	– c Brown b Jordan	10
D. A. Payne not out	22	– c Jordan b Rawlins	13
M. D. Taylor b Beer	4	– not out	28
S. T. Gabriel c Wiese b Garton	1	– b Rawlins	2
B 1, lb 10, nb 2	13	B 4, lb 7, nb 6	17

1/48 (2) 2/63 (3) 3/97 (1)   (77.5 overs) 200   1/48 (1) 2/64 (3)   (80.4 overs) 243
4/97 (5) 5/102 (4) 6/133 (7)   3/112 (4) 4/128 (2)
7/173 (6) 8/177 (8) 9/189 (10) 10/200 (11)   5/151 (5) 6/170 (6) 7/200 (8)
                                           8/201 (7) 9/239 (9) 10/243 (11)

Robinson 21–6–29–1; Jordan 20–3–49–3; Haines 6–0–17–1; Wiese 13–4–34–2; Rawlins 4–1–16–0; Beer 6–2–15–1; Garton 7.5–0–29–2. *Second innings*—Robinson 21–5–50–2; Jordan 18–5–51–2; Wiese 6–1–29–2; Haines 3–0–14–0; Garton 11–1–24–1; Rawlins 10.4–0–36–3; Wells 6–3–13–0; Beer 5–1–15–0.

Sussex

P. D. Salt c Bracey b Payne	64	– not out	30
L. W. P. Wells c Bracey b Payne	42	– c Charlesworth b Payne	2
T. J. Haines c Bracey b Smith	22	– c Bracey b M. D. Taylor	10
S. van Zyl lbw b M. D. Taylor	28	– not out	30
D. M. W. Rawlins c Roderick b Payne	10		
†B. C. Brown c Hammond b Charlesworth	24		
D. Wiese c Charlesworth b Higgins	67		
*C. J. Jordan c Roderick b Charlesworth	6		
W. A. T. Beer hit wkt b Payne	40		
G. H. S. Garton not out	1		
O. E. Robinson c J. M. R. Taylor b Higgins	6		
B 7, lb 7, nb 46	60	Nb 2	2

1/100 (1) 2/151 (3) 3/161 (2)   (101.5 overs) 370   1/13 (2)   (2 wkts, 23.1 overs) 74
4/177 (5) 5/221 (4) 6/259 (6)   2/33 (3)
7/267 (8) 8/359 (7) 9/359 (9) 10/370 (11)

Payne 29–10–59–4; Gabriel 20–0–121–0; Higgins 23.5–6–73–2; M. D. Taylor 11–1–38–1; Smith 12–2–38–1; Charlesworth 6–0–27–2. *Second innings*—Payne 6–0–13–1; Higgins 6–0–11–0; Charlesworth 5–0–19–0; M. D. Taylor 5.1–0–19–1; J. M. R. Taylor 1–0–12–0.

Umpires: B. J. Debenham and S. J. O'Shaughnessy.

At Worcester, September 16–18. GLOUCESTERSHIRE beat WORCESTERSHIRE by six wickets.

GLOUCESTERSHIRE v NORTHAMPTONSHIRE

At Bristol, September 23–26. Drawn. Gloucestershire 6pts, Northamptonshire 7pts. Toss: uncontested. First-class debut: E. N. Gay.

Frustration at being able to complete only 73 overs was forgotten once it became clear a draw had secured promotion for both sides. In truth, that was always the likeliest outcome, since Glamorgan, the only team who could have interfered, had to win at Chester-le-Street to have any chance of going up – and rain fell in Durham too. Gloucestershire, on the cusp of playing in Division One for the first time since 2005, were edgy after being inserted beneath low cloud. Sanderson made the most of conditions, claiming the 59th and 60th wickets of a superb Championship season, and a mixture of steady Northamptonshire bowling, poor batting, feckless running and ill luck (the second run-out came thanks to a deflection on to the non-striker's stumps) reduced Gloucestershire to 67 for six before lunch. Rain soon set in, and play did not resume until the third afternoon, when Charlesworth and van Buuren took their stand to 151. The weather interrupted again, and next morning the game was called off. It proved an uneventful debut for Northamptonshire's Emilio Gay, a 19-year-old left-hander from Bedford, whose involvement was limited to a catch, though he did join post-match celebrations in which both teams drank to their common success.

Close of play: first day, Gloucestershire 80-6 (Charlesworth 35, van Buuren 5); second day, no play; third day, Gloucestershire 220-7 (Charlesworth 77, Payne 1).

Gloucestershire

†J. R. Bracey c Rossington b Sanderson	8	G. L. van Buuren c Rossington b Berg	93
*C. D. J. Dent run out (Procter)	15	D. A. Payne not out	1
M. A. H. Hammond c Hutton b Berg	5	Lb 12, nb 6	18
G. H. Roderick c Rossington b Sanderson	2		
B. G. Charlesworth not out	77	1/27 (1) 2/28 (3) (7 wkts, 73 overs)	220
G. T. Hankins run out (Bracewell)	4	3/30 (2) 4/32 (4)	
R. F. Higgins c Gay b Bracewell	1	5/56 (6) 6/67 (7) 7/218 (8)	

J. Shaw and S. T. Gabriel did not bat.

Hutton 14–4–42–0; Sanderson 14–3–33–2; Berg 13–3–35–2; Bracewell 9–0–42–1; Procter 7–1–17–0; Keogh 16–4–39–0.

Northamptonshire

B. J. Curran, E. N. Gay, A. G. Wakely, R. I. Keogh, R. E. Levi, *†A. M. Rossington, L. A. Procter, D. A. J. Bracewell, G. K. Berg, B. A. Hutton, B. W. Sanderson.

Umpires: M. Burns and D. J. Millns.

HAMPSHIRE

Southern powerhouse?

PAT SYMES

Hampshire could look back on 2019 as a qualified success: third in the Championship (they had not finished as high since 2008), runners-up in the Royal London Cup and probable quarter-finalists in the T20 Blast – until they were beaten in their last group match.

It might have been better. Hampshire won three of their first four Championship games, inflicting on Essex their only defeat of the summer, and two of their last three. But somewhere in the middle they lost their way, and were never serious rivals for Essex, the eventual champions, or gallant runners-up Somerset.

Their mid-season meandering may be partly explained by the loss to England's World Cup squad of James Vince and Liam Dawson, captain and key all-rounder. An influential figure on the domestic stage, Vince played only six Championship games, and Dawson eight. Despite the sterling efforts of stand-in captain Sam Northeast and the Herculean performance of pace bowler Kyle Abbott, their absence was keenly felt.

Hampshire missed them – and South African opener Aiden Markram, also on World Cup duty – at the climax of the Royal London. All three had been instrumental in taking the holders to another final, the last at Lord's. Vince was outstanding: 509 runs at 72, including a county-record 190 against Gloucestershire, 95 against Glamorgan and 79 in the home semi against Lancashire. Dawson took 18 wickets and made 108 to help defeat Surrey, while Markram scored 130, 88 twice and 61 in group matches.

Since the World Cup had not begun, Hampshire asked if they could play Vince and Dawson in the final against Somerset, but were refused. They went down to a six-wicket defeat, with 39 balls to spare; three weeks earlier, they had won the qualifying match at Taunton by seven wickets and 111 balls. Other contributions on the road to Lord's included five for 26 by Gareth Berg in the semi, and two Tom Alsop centuries. Berg, aged 38, joined Northamptonshire in September.

Hampshire's crushing of Essex by an innings and 87 runs in the chill of early April proved a Championship highlight. An influential figure in that victory was Northeast, who made 169, his highest score of a season that brought 1,123 first-class runs at 51. He hit four centuries (one at the Parks), led the side capably while Vince was away, and finished fourth in the list of highest scorers. Vince and Dawson also averaged above 50, and Aneurin Donald a fraction below 40 (though knee surgery was set to rule him out for most of the 2020 season).

Yet this was deceptive: Hampshire rarely enjoyed the sound starts a stroke-making middle order required. Young openers Alsop, Felix Organ, Ollie

Aiden Markram

Soames and Joe Weatherley showed flashes of potential, but none averaged 30. Weatherley, though, deserved praise for carrying his bat for 29 in a two-day rout at Chelmsford.

Of the overseas players, Markram was superb during his short stay, but neither Ajinkya Rahane nor Chris Morris (T20 only) had the same impact, even though Rahane began with a century in the home win against Nottinghamshire, when, for the first time since 1962, first-class cricket crossed the Solent to the Isle of Wight; enthusiastic crowds of more than 1,000 a day greeted Hampshire's trip to the splendid Newclose arena.

The T20 Blast typified their season: bright individual performances, and a few inexplicable results. In a tight group, they finished seventh, though had they beaten winless Glamorgan, they would have progressed at the expense of Essex, the eventual champions, whom Hampshire trounced at Chelmsford (and tied with at the Rose Bowl). Vince hit four half-centuries, and Northeast two.

Player of the season was, without question, Abbott, the South African Kolpak. In an extraordinary summer, he claimed 112 wickets, 71 in the Championship and 20 each in the white-ball competitions (and one against Oxford). In all three, he took more than any other team-mate. His 17 for 86 against Somerset was the best return for Hampshire, the best in all first-class cricket since Jim Laker's 19 for 90 in 1956, and the fourth-best in Championship history. Abbott signed a contract keeping him at Southampton until 2022.

He took skilful advantage of some lively surfaces. In 2020, they will be prepared by Simon Lee, recruited from Taunton, allowing Nigel Gray to return to the retirement he left when his successor, Karl McDermott, joined Lord's. Abbott was ably supported by the experienced pair of Fidel Edwards, who claimed 48 Championship wickets, and Keith Barker, who took 37. Barker also weighed in with 357 runs, and proved a useful signing from Warwickshire. If there is a concern about the Hampshire attack, it is that the powerhouse of Abbott, Edwards and Barker are all 32 or older. Edwards, Hampshire's only ever-present in the Championship, will be 38 on his return in 2020.

The slow bowlers were a disappointment. Dawson took ten Championship wickets at 53, and leg-spinner Mason Crane, recovered from the back injury that ended his summer in 2018, managed only five at 107, in six appearances. He was more effective elsewhere, claiming 14 in the Royal London and 11 in the Blast, rekindling hopes of a return to the form that won him an England cap. The signing of Australian Test off-spinner Nathan Lyon should help everyone.

Hampshire used 26 players in all competitions, including Harry Came, who was a concussion substitute against Surrey and made an unbeaten 23. He is one of many promising young cricketers, whose potential was illustrated by Hampshire winning the Second XI Championship for the first time since 2001.

Championship attendance: 25,897.

HAMPSHIRE RESULTS

All first-class matches – Played 15: Won 5, Lost 3, Drawn 7.
County Championship matches – Played 14: Won 5, Lost 3, Drawn 6.

Specsavers County Championship, 3rd in Division 1;
Vitality Blast, 7th in South Group; Royal London One-Day Cup, finalists.

COUNTY CHAMPIONSHIP AVERAGES, BATTING AND FIELDING

Cap		Birthplace	M	I	NO	R	HS	100	Avge	Ct/St
2019	S. A. Northeast	Ashford, Kent	13	22	3	969	169	3	51.00	5
2013	L. A. Dawson	Swindon	8	12	1	561	103	1	51.00	6
2013	J. M. Vince	Cuckfield	6	10	1	365	142	1	40.55	3
	A. H. T. Donald	Swansea	9	15	1	554	173	1	39.57	4
	†R. R. Rossouw††	Bloemfontein, SA	10	17	1	595	92	0	37.18	2
	J. K. Fuller	Cape Town, SA	4	5	1	138	54*	0	34.50	1
	I. G. Holland††	Stevens Point, USA	9	16	1	478	143	1	31.86	5
	L. D. McManus	Poole	7	10	1	267	61	0	29.66	20/1
	J. J. Weatherley	Winchester‡	8	13	2	322	66	0	29.27	8
	F. S. Organ	Sydney, Australia	6	11	0	300	100	1	27.27	4
	†T. P. Alsop	Wycombe	10	16	3	347	150	1	26.69	11
	†K. H. D. Barker	Manchester	13	18	4	357	64	0	25.50	2
	A. M. Rahane¶	Ashwi Khurd, India	7	13	0	307	119	1	23.61	6
2017	K. J. Abbott††	Empangeni, SA	13	16	2	207	72	0	14.78	1
	O. C. Soames	Kingston-u-Thames	5	9	0	124	62	0	13.77	2
2016	G. K. Berg	Cape Town, SA	5	8	0	79	33	0	9.87	1
	M. S. Crane	Shoreham-by-Sea	6	8	1	65	20	0	9.28	0
2018	F. H. Edwards††	St Peter, Barbados	14	17	9	32	8*	0	4.00	3

Also batted: H. R. C. Came (*Basingstoke*) (1 match) 23*; A. K. Markram¶ (*Pretoria, SA*) (2 matches) 63, 45, 7; R. A. Stevenson (*Torquay*) (1 match) 51 (1 ct).

‡ *Born in Hampshire.* ¶ *Official overseas player.* †† *Other non-England-qualified.*

BOWLING

	Style	O	M	R	W	BB	5I	Avge
K. J. Abbott	RFM	362.5	78	1,117	71	9-40	6	15.73
F. H. Edwards	RFM	353.1	55	1,240	48	5-49	4	25.83
K. H. D. Barker	LFM	348	78	984	37	5-48	1	26.59
L. A. Dawson	SLA	210.1	39	538	10	3-184	0	53.80

Also bowled: T. P. Alsop (SLA) 1–0–3–0; G. K. Berg (RFM) 116–24–361–9; M. S. Crane (LB) 106.5–8–539–5; J. K. Fuller (RFM) 80.4–15–302–9; I. G. Holland (RFM) 146.1–33–378–5; F. S. Organ (OB) 45.5–9–125–8; R. A. Stevenson (RFM) 25–1–87–1; J. M. Vince (RM) 6–0–17–0; J. J. Weatherley (OB) 16–0–67–1.

LEADING ROYAL LONDON CUP AVERAGES (150 runs/4 wickets)

Batting	Runs	HS	Avge	SR	Ct/St
J. M. Vince	509	190	72.71	110.89	6
A. K. Markram	466	130	58.25	101.96	3
R. R. Rossouw	388	93	48.50	111.17	2
L. A. Dawson	274	108	45.66	102.62	5
S. A. Northeast	280	105*	40.00	81.15	5
T. P. Alsop	351	130*	39.00	90.00	14/5
J. K. Fuller	162	55*	27.00	120.89	6

Bowling	W	BB	Avge	ER
L. A. Dawson	18	3-37	20.33	4.11
A. K. Markram	5	3-39	23.40	4.50
K. J. Abbott	20	3-36	23.55	5.75
G. K. Berg	9	5-26	31.00	5.19
M. S. Crane	14	3-42	31.85	6.01
F. H. Edwards	5	3-69	33.00	6.73
J. K. Fuller	5	2-55	68.00	7.08

LEADING VITALITY BLAST AVERAGES (100 runs/15 overs)

Batting	Runs	HS	Avge	SR	Ct/St
L. D. McManus .	107	32	26.75	**157.35**	5/3
A. H. T. Donald .	203	51	20.30	**138.09**	7
J. M. Vince	407	87*	40.70	**132.14**	5
R. R. Rossouw . .	174	60	17.40	**124.28**	4
S. A. Northeast . .	273	73	22.75	**107.90**	5
L. A. Dawson . . .	232	47*	33.14	**107.40**	6

Bowling	W	BB	Avge	ER
L. A. Dawson	10	3-11	30.80	**6.62**
M. S. Crane	11	3-22	16.63	**7.03**
C. H. Morris	12	3-22	24.75	**7.81**
C. P. Wood	14	2-18	25.92	**7.94**
K. J. Abbott	20	3-15	17.80	**8.18**
T. Shamsi	3	1-32	47.00	**9.40**

FIRST-CLASS COUNTY RECORDS

Highest score for	316	R. H. Moore v Warwickshire at Bournemouth	1937
Highest score against	303*	G. A. Hick (Worcestershire) at Southampton	1997
Leading run-scorer	48,892	C. P. Mead (avge 48.84)	1905–36
Best bowling for	9-25	R. M. H. Cottam v Lancashire at Manchester	1965
Best bowling against	10-46	W. Hickton (Lancashire) at Manchester	1870
Leading wicket-taker	2,669	D. Shackleton (avge 18.23)	1948–69
Highest total for	714-5 dec	v Nottinghamshire at Southampton	2005
Highest total against	742	by Surrey at The Oval	1909
Lowest total for	15	v Warwickshire at Birmingham	1922
Lowest total against	23	by Yorkshire at Middlesbrough	1965

LIST A COUNTY RECORDS

Highest score for	190	J. M. Vince v Gloucestershire at Southampton .	**2019**
Highest score against	203	A. D. Brown (Surrey) at Guildford	1997
Leading run-scorer	12,034	R. A. Smith (avge 42.97)	1983–2003
Best bowling for	7-30	P. J. Sainsbury v Norfolk at Southampton	1965
Best bowling against	7-22	J. R. Thomson (Middlesex) at Lord's	1981
Leading wicket-taker	411	C. A. Connor (avge 25.07)	1984–98
Highest total for	371-4	v Glamorgan at Southampton	1975
Highest total against	360-7	by Somerset at Southampton	2018
Lowest total for	43	v Essex at Basingstoke	1972
Lowest total against {	61	by Somerset at Bath	1973
	61	by Derbyshire at Portsmouth	1990

TWENTY20 COUNTY RECORDS

Highest score for	124*	M. J. Lumb v Essex v Southampton	2009
Highest score against	116*	L. J. Wright (Sussex) at Southampton	2014
Leading run-scorer	3,837	J. M. Vince (avge 32.79, SR 135.77)	**2010–19**
Best bowling for	5-14	A. D. Mascarenhas v Sussex at Hove	2004
Best bowling against	6-28	J. K. Fuller (Middlesex) at Southampton	2018
Leading wicket-taker	131	C. P. Wood (avge 25.97, ER 8.30)	**2010–19**
Highest total for	249-8	v Derbyshire at Derby	2017
Highest total against	220-4	by Somerset at Taunton	2010
Lowest total for	85	v Sussex at Southampton	2008
Lowest total against	67	by Sussex at Hove	2004

ADDRESS

The Ageas Bowl, Botley Road, West End, Southampton SO30 3XH; 023 8047 2002
enquiries@ageasbowl.com; www.ageasbowl.com.

OFFICIALS

Captain J. M. Vince	**Chairman** R. G. Bransgrove
Cricket operations manager T. M. Tremlett	**Chief executive** D. Mann
Director of cricket G. W. White	**Head groundsman 2019** N. Gray
First-team coach A. V. Birrell	**2020** S. Lee
Head of player development C. R. M. Freeston	**Scorer** K. R. Baker
President N. E. J. Pocock	

At Oxford, March 31–April 2. HAMPSHIRE drew with OXFORD MCCU.

HAMPSHIRE v ESSEX

At Southampton, April 5–8. Hampshire won by an innings and 87 runs. Hampshire 24pts, Essex 1pt. Toss: uncontested. County debut: A. K. Markram.

Sir Alastair Cook became the first cricketing knight to play in the Championship, but had little else to celebrate. He managed a gritty half-century, before being twice dismissed by Abbott on the third day, as ten Doeschate rued not asking for a toss. Instead, he let Hampshire gorge on a benign pitch. They amassed 525 for eight, their highest total against Essex since 1996, with four batsmen – including South Africa Test opener Markram – exceeding 60. Northeast made his fifth century against his favourite opposition, and four bowlers conceded at least 100. Essex, who lost Wheater with an injured right hand, found batting trickier, and were shot out for 164, trailing by 361. They fared a little better in the follow-on, but 12 wickets fell on the third day. Edwards had done the damage in the first innings – four of his five victims were bowled – while Abbott took five in the second. Bopara fought hardest, hitting a combative century, though he could only delay the inevitable. Injury forced both sides to use three wicketkeepers: Wheater, Lawrence and substitute Will Buttleman for Essex; Alsop (who also hurt his hand), Vince and substitute Lewis McManus for Hampshire.

Close of play: first day, Hampshire 303-4 (Northeast 94, Dawson 10); second day, Essex 25-1 (A. N. Cook 17, Westley 7); third day, Essex 132-4 (Bopara 60, ten Doeschate 18).

Hampshire

J. J. Weatherley c Westley b Quinn	13	G. K. Berg c Bopara b Harmer 33
*J. M. Vince lbw b Bopara	40	K. H. D. Barker not out 31
A. K. Markram c †Lawrence b Quinn	63	B 8, lb 2, nb 2 12
S. A. Northeast lbw b Bopara	169	
R. R. Rossouw c Harmer b Porter	76	1/40 (1) (8 wkts dec, 130.5 overs) 525
L. A. Dawson c sub (*W. E. L. Buttleman)		2/71 (2) 3/146 (3)
b Quinn	64	4/263 (5) 5/428 (4) 6/445 (6)
†T. P. Alsop c A. N. Cook b Harmer	24	7/479 (7) 8/525 (8) 110 overs: 441-5

K. J. Abbott and F. H. Edwards did not bat.

Porter 25–4–112–1; S. J. Cook 27–5–105–0; Quinn 29–3–104–3; Bopara 16–0–54–2; Harmer 31.5–3–134–2; Lawrence 2–0–6–0.

Essex

N. L. J. Browne b Edwards	1	1 – lbw b Barker	7
A. N. Cook c Vince b Abbott	50	c sub (†L. D. McManus) b Abbott	8
T. Westley b Abbott	16	c sub (†L. D. McManus) b Edwards	24
D. W. Lawrence b Edwards	31	lbw b Abbott	6
R. S. Bopara not out	37	c sub (†L. D. McManus) b Abbott	107
R. N. ten Doeschate lbw b Edwards	6	c sub (†L. D. McManus) b Edwards	36
S. R. Harmer b Edwards	0	lbw b Edwards	62
J. A. Porter lbw b Barker	17	c Dawson b Abbott	0
S. J. Cook lbw b Barker	1	b Abbott	3
M. R. Quinn b Edwards	0	not out	0
A. J. A. Wheater absent hurt		absent hurt	
Lb 3, nb 2	5	B 7, lb 11, w 1, nb 2	21

1/13 (1) 2/40 (3) 3/90 (2)	(58.3 overs) 164	1/14 (1) 2/17 (2)	(89.1 overs) 274
4/108 (4) 5/122 (6) 6/122 (7)		3/27 (4) 4/94 (5) 5/158 (6)	
7/152 (8) 8/154 (9) 9/164 (10)		6/269 (5) 7/271 (7) 8/273 (8) 9/274 (9)	

Barker 12–3–30–2; Edwards 14.3–1–51–5; Abbott 15–3–38–2; Berg 9–3–24–0; Dawson 2–2–18–0. *Second innings*—Barker 13–3–41–1; Edwards 17–3–49–3; Abbott 19.1–3–77–5; Berg 10–2–28–0; Dawson 23–5–43–0; Weatherley 1–0–1–0; Vince 6–0–17–0.

Umpires: N. A. Mallender and M. J. Saggers.

HAMPSHIRE v YORKSHIRE

At Southampton, April 11–14. Yorkshire won by an innings and 44 runs. Yorkshire 23pts, Hampshire 4pts. Toss: Yorkshire.

Yorkshire overwhelmed Hampshire in much the way Hampshire had crushed Essex here a week earlier. After Patterson chose to bat on an easy-paced wicket, Yorkshire made hay, and compiled a formidable 554 for seven, which spanned 164 overs. Once again, Ballance enjoyed his trip to the south coast: his previous two games at the Rose Bowl had produced three centuries (one a double), and now he struck another. Lyth, meanwhile, passed 10,000 first-class runs. Dawson's left arm bore the brunt of the work, sending down 60 overs; on only six occasions had a Hampshire bowler conceded more than his 184. He did claim three wickets, including Root, to end a third-wicket stand of 182 with Ballance. Dawson then contributed 57 in reply, and Northeast 99, but there was no avoiding the follow-on. Batting again, 252 behind, the hosts slumped to 59 for eight. Dawson and Barker saved some face by adding 131, a Hampshire ninth-wicket record against Yorkshire, but could not prevent an innings defeat. Holland had earlier become the county's first concussion substitute after McManus was ruled unfit; he fell first ball.

Close of play: first day, Yorkshire 310-3 (Ballance 120, Patterson 5); second day, Hampshire 74-3 (Northeast 19, Abbott 1); third day, Hampshire 54-5 (Rossouw 2, Dawson 12).

Yorkshire

A. Lyth c McManus b Edwards	67	M. J. Waite not out	5
H. C. Brook b Edwards	5		
G. S. Ballance c McManus b Berg	148	B 4, lb 17, w 4, nb 6	31
J. E. Root b Dawson	94		
*S. A. Patterson c Dawson b Berg	34	1/21 (2) (7 wkts dec, 164 overs)	554
T. Köhler-Cadmore lbw b Dawson	41	2/109 (1) 3/291 (4)	
J. A. Leaning not out	77	4/371 (3) 5/374 (5)	
†J. A. Tattersall c Vince b Dawson	52	6/445 (6) 7/540 (8) 110 overs: 371-3	

B. O. Coad and D. Olivier did not bat.

Edwards 21–3–78–2; Abbott 25–5–84–0; Barker 30–6–90–0; Berg 27–3–92–2; Dawson 60–4–184–3; Weatherley 1–0–5–0.

Hampshire

J. J. Weatherley c Tattersall b Olivier	2	– c Köhler-Cadmore b Patterson	9
*J. M. Vince c Köhler-Cadmore b Coad	5	– lbw b Patterson	11
A. K. Markram c Ballance b Leaning	45	– c Tattersall b Waite	7
S. A. Northeast c Tattersall b Olivier	99	– c Köhler-Cadmore b Patterson	0
K. J. Abbott c Ballance b Coad	1	– (6) b Waite	5
R. R. Rossouw b Waite	33	– (5) lbw b Coad	3
L. A. Dawson c Root b Leaning	57	– c Köhler-Cadmore b Olivier	92
†L. D. McManus c Köhler-Cadmore b Patterson	27		
G. K. Berg c Tattersall b Olivier	0	– (8) c Köhler-Cadmore b Coad	0
K. H. D. Barker not out	9	– c Tattersall b Patterson	64
F. H. Edwards c Köhler-Cadmore b Patterson	0	– not out	0
I. G. Holland (did not bat)		– (9) lbw b Coad	0
B 14, nb 10	24	B 4, lb 6, w 1, nb 6	17

1/7 (2) 2/11 (1) 3/70 (3)	(94.3 overs) 302	1/22 (1) 2/23 (2)	(71.4 overs) 208
4/87 (5) 5/138 (6) 6/247 (7)		3/29 (4) 4/31 (3)	
7/264 (4) 8/274 (9) 9/302 (8) 10/302 (11)		5/41 (6) 6/55 (5) 7/59 (8)	
		8/59 (9) 9/190 (10) 10/208 (7)	

Holland replaced McManus, as a concussion substitute.

Coad 23–6–65–2; Olivier 21–3–89–3; Patterson 19.3–8–36–2; Waite 10–0–35–1; Root 12–0–43–0; Leaning 9–2–20–2. *Second innings*—Coad 17–8–27–3; Olivier 16.4–5–50–1; Patterson 18–5–47–4; Waite 11–1–38–2; Root 8–0–31–0; Leaning 1–0–5–0.

Umpires: J. H. Evans and A. G. Wharf.

At Birmingham, May 14–17. HAMPSHIRE beat WARWICKSHIRE by 314 runs.

HAMPSHIRE v NOTTINGHAMSHIRE

At Newclose, May 20–23. Hampshire won by 244 runs. Hampshire 22pts, Nottinghamshire 4pts. Toss: uncontested. County debut: A. M. Rahane.

First-class cricket returned to the Isle of Wight for the first time since 1962. Back then, Hampshire had hosted Worcestershire at J. Samuel White's Ground in Cowes; now they welcomed Nottinghamshire to Newclose, a well-appointed venue on the outskirts of Newport, around six miles south. A first-class fixture had been the dream of the late Brian Gardener, who poured £2m into the development of what until 2007 was farmland. Hampshire, whose Rose Bowl headquarters were being readied for the World Cup, helped spectators cross from the mainland, and healthy crowds of 1,000 or more turned up each day. Hampshire's young openers enjoyed a century partnership on the first, but no one stamped their authority on the innings. Without Mullaney's defiance, Nottinghamshire would have been in serious trouble, but they trailed by 71 all the same. This time, the home openers went quickly, but India Test batsman Rahane added 257 with Northeast to cement the advantage. Set 439, Nottinghamshire were two down by the third-evening close. Next day, the pace trio of Abbott, Barker and Edwards shared the wickets, as they had in the first innings, and a third victory in four took Hampshire to within two points of leaders Somerset. After the first day, Dawson was added to England's World Cup squad, with Crane replacing him as a full substitute.

Close of play: first day, Hampshire 288-6 (Donald 35, Holland 24); second day, Hampshire 3-1 (Soames 0, Rahane 0); third day, Nottinghamshire 42-2 (Nash 20, Carter 8).

Hampshire

J. J. Weatherley c Moores b Ball	66	– lbw b Fletcher	2
O. C. Soames c Carter b Ball	44	– c Moores b Broad	2
A. M. Rahane c Nash b Broad	10	– b Carter	119
*S. A. Northeast lbw b Mullaney	33	– c Broad b Mullaney	133
L. A. Dawson b Fletcher	25		
†T. P. Alsop c Moores b Mullaney	9	– (5) not out	51
A. H. T. Donald c Moores b Broad	46	– (6) b Mullaney	3
I. G. Holland c Moores b Fletcher	27	– (7) not out	39
K. H. D. Barker c Carter b Fletcher	0		
K. J. Abbott not out	6		
F. H. Edwards c Clarke b Fletcher	1		
B 12, lb 16, w 1, nb 14	43	B 14, lb 3, w 1	18

1/112 (1) 2/134 (3) 3/161 (2)	(103.3 overs) 310	1/3 (1)	(5 wkts dec, 85 overs) 367
4/193 (4) 5/205 (6) 6/245 (5)		2/9 (3) 3/266 (3)	
7/295 (8) 8/295 (9) 9/305 (7) 10/310 (11)		4/272 (4) 5/279 (6)	

M. S. Crane replaced Dawson, who left to join England's World Cup squad.

Fletcher 24.3–4–79–4; Broad 26–6–76–2; Ball 21–6–57–2; Mullaney 24–12–42–2; Carter 8–0–28–0. *Second innings*—Fletcher 14–3–39–1; Broad 13–4–31–1; Mullaney 22–4–78–2; Ball 12–0–42–0; Carter 22–0–140–1; Libby 2–0–20–0.

Nottinghamshire

B. T. Slater c Alsop b Abbott	9	– c Alsop b Edwards	12
B. M. Duckett b Barker	19	– lbw b Barker	0
C. D. Nash c Northeast b Abbott	10	– lbw b Abbott	60
J. M. Clarke b Abbott	29	– (5) c Alsop b Abbott	0
J. D. Libby lbw b Barker	4	– (6) c Soames b Edwards	17
*S. J. Mullaney c and b Holland	102	– (7) b Barker	12
†T. J. Moores c Alsop b Edwards	34	– (8) lbw b Abbott	5
L. J. Fletcher lbw b Barker	2	– (9) not out	25
S. C. J. Broad b Edwards	1	– (10) c Rahane b Edwards	9
M. Carter lbw b Edwards	14	– (4) lbw b Barker	23
J. T. Ball not out	0	– c Donald b Crane	0
B 2, lb 5, nb 8	15	B 21, lb 6, nb 4	31

1/24 (2) 2/28 (1) 3/61 (3) (77.1 overs) 239
4/72 (4) 5/72 (5) 6/151 (7)
7/156 (8) 8/159 (9) 9/239 (10) 10/239 (6)

1/6 (2) 2/22 (1) (66.5 overs) 194
3/75 (4) 4/78 (5)
5/122 (6) 6/132 (3) 7/144 (8)
8/165 (7) 9/189 (10) 10/194 (11)

Abbott 18–6–61–3; Edwards 19–2–49–3; Barker 16–3–46–3; Holland 13.1–4–25–1; Crane 11–2–51–0. *Second innings*—Abbott 16–2–46–3; Barker 18–5–42–3; Edwards 14–6–37–3; Holland 6–3–6–0; Crane 12.5–2–36–1.

Umpires: M. Burns and D. J. Millns.

At Leeds, May 27–30. HAMPSHIRE drew with YORKSHIRE.

At Sookholme, June 9–12. HAMPSHIRE drew with NOTTINGHAMSHIRE.

At Chelmsford, June 16–17. HAMPSHIRE lost to ESSEX by an innings and eight runs.

At Taunton, June 30–July 3. HAMPSHIRE lost to SOMERSET by 313 runs.

HAMPSHIRE v WARWICKSHIRE

At Southampton, July 6–9. Drawn. Hampshire 12pts, Warwickshire 9pts. Toss: uncontested.

After four away games had produced two draws and two heavy defeats, Hampshire began the final day in sight of a restorative victory – but could not manage the seven wickets they needed. They were frustrated by Hain who, having gone three years without a Championship century, hit his second of the match. It proved crucial, rescuing Warwickshire after Abbott reduced them to 52 for five. Hain found a staunch ally in Mike, who helped him soak up more than 40 overs on a lifeless pitch, and hit a maiden fifty. Brookes and the free-scoring Patel then added an unbroken 112. The turning point had been the first ball of the day, when Hain, on nine, was put down at the wicket; he was missed again in the slips. Although Stone, like Abbott, had found something in the surface, Hampshire dominated almost from the start, thanks to a hundred from stand-in opener Holland, who sailed past a previous best of 58 not out. He and the ferocious Donald added 262, a Hampshire fifth-wicket record, beating 235 by Gerry Hill and Donald Walker against Sussex at Portsmouth in 1937;

HIGHEST HAMPSHIRE TOTALS AT THE ROSE BOWL

714-5 dec.	v Nottinghamshire	2005	**539**	v Warwickshire	**2019**
599-3 dec.	v Yorkshire	2011	**525-8 dec**	v Essex	**2019**
576-6 dec.	v Warwickshire	2005	515	v Warwickshire	2017
553-7 dec.	v Kent	2010	512	v Somerset	2010
548	v Somerset	2009	505	v Warwickshire	2009
548-6 dec.	v Lancashire	2016	500-9 dec.	v Worcestershire	2013
545	v Northamptonshire	2013			

it was also Donald's first century for three years. Despite a lead of 232, Northeast declined the follow-on, a decision that seemed justified – until Hain made the most of the dropped catches.

Close of play: first day, Hampshire 450-6 (Berg 12); second day, Warwickshire 198-3 (Hain 68, Hose 6); third day, Warwickshire 31-3 (Yates 10, Hain 9).

Hampshire

F. S. Organ c Hain b Stone	1	– b Patel	18
I. G. Holland c Ambrose b Stone	143	– b Hannon-Dalby	26
A. M. Rahane c Rhodes b Stone	4	– lbw b Hannon-Dalby	3
*S. A. Northeast c Ambrose b Hannon-Dalby	59	– not out	36
R. R. Rossouw b Patel	34	– c Hose b Hannon-Dalby	1
A. H. T. Donald c Hose b Brookes	173	– c Ambrose b Patel	52
G. K. Berg b Hannon-Dalby	15	– st Ambrose b Patel	5
†L. D. McManus not out	41	– c Yates b Brookes	20
K. H. D. Barker c Hose b Mike	35	– c Ambrose b Brookes	6
K. J. Abbott lbw b Stone	1		
F. H. Edwards c Yates b Stone	4		
B 5, lb 15, w 2, nb 2, p 5	29	Lb 2, nb 2	4

1/9 (1) 2/13 (3) 3/111 (4) (115.3 overs) 539   1/46 (2) (8 wkts dec, 35.5 overs) 171
4/168 (5) 5/430 (2) 6/450 (6)   2/46 (1) 3/50 (3)
7/473 (8) 8/533 (9) 9/535 (10)   4/52 (5) 5/123 (6)
10/539 (11)   110 overs: 513-7   6/133 (7) 7/158 (8) 8/171 (9)

Hannon-Dalby 24–6–62–2; Stone 21.3–3–93–5; Brookes 22–1–111–1; Mike 17–0–75–1; Patel 24–2–141–1; Rhodes 7–1–32–0. *Second innings*—Stone 8–1–36–0; Brookes 6.5–0–33–2; Patel 14–0–71–3; Hannon-Dalby 7–0–29–3.

Warwickshire

W. M. H. Rhodes c McManus b Abbott	9	– c Rahane b Abbott	10
D. P. Sibley c Rossouw b Abbott	16	– b Abbott	2
R. M. Yates c Berg b Organ	91	– b Abbott	14
S. R. Hain not out	129	– (5) b Organ	104
A. J. Hose lbw b Edwards	14	– (6) b Abbott	2
†T. R. Ambrose c McManus b Barker	2	– (7) c Rahane b Barker	14
B. W. M. Mike c McManus b Berg	0	– (8) c McManus b Holland	72
H. J. H. Brookes c McManus b Berg	0	– (9) not out	36
*J. S. Patel b Edwards	4	– (10) not out	70
O. P. Stone run out (Rahane)	21	– (4) b Abbott	0
O. J. Hannon-Dalby c Rahane b Organ	4		
B 5, lb 1, nb 4	10	B 7, lb 4, nb 12	23

1/15 (1) 2/39 (2) 3/181 (3) (118.5 overs) 307 1/4 (2) (8 wkts, 106.5 overs) 347
4/229 (5) 5/235 (6) 6/254 (7)   2/21 (1) 3/21 (4)
7/254 (8) 8/259 (9) 9/294 (10)   6/103 (7) 7/223 (8) 8/235 (5)
10/307 (11)   110 overs: 287-8   6/103 (7) 7/223 (8) 8/235 (5)

Edwards 29–8–88–2; Abbott 24–6–53–2; Berg 23–6–62–2; Barker 22–6–65–1; Holland 11–5–14–0; Organ 9.5–2–19–2. *Second innings*—Edwards 20.5–3–85–0; Abbott 23–4–78–5; Barker 13–1–47–1; Berg 12–2–31–0; Organ 24–5–64–1; Holland 14–3–31–1.

Umpires: J. H. Evans and A. G. Wharf.

HAMPSHIRE v KENT

At Southampton, July 13–16. Drawn. Hampshire 11pts, Kent 12pts. Toss: Hampshire. First-class debut: J. M. Cox.

When Hampshire lost their last four second-innings wickets for 28, Kent sniffed an unlikely victory. They needed 153 from 17 overs and, as it happened, had Blake – a specialist Twenty20 six-hitter – in the side after Kuhn suffered concussion. The task, though, was beyond them, and they agreed a draw on 57 for three from 50 balls. The game was yet another high-scoring affair on a placid Rose Bowl strip. Hampshire declared at 409 for nine, with Felix Organ – born in Sydney, schooled in Dorset – reaching a maiden century on his third appearance, then departing next delivery. Stevens, the old workhorse, claimed five wickets, including a burst of three for none in seven balls. He hit his first fifty of the season, too, before becoming one of five scalps for Edwards, another stalwart. Denly had led the assault on the Hampshire attack – adding 206 for the third wicket with Bell-Drummond – and Kent were 146 in front. Hampshire began the last day two down and 27 behind, but Holland and Rossouw dug in, before the late collapse briefly raised Kentish hopes.

Close of play: first day, Hampshire 340-6 (McManus 20, Barker 1); second day, Kent 319-3 (Denly 138, Kuhn 28); third day, Hampshire 119-2 (Holland 37, Rossouw 37).

Hampshire

F. S. Organ c Robinson b Stevens	100	– lbw b Stevens	3
I. G. Holland c Dickson b Podmore	60	– c Robinson b Rayner	69
A. M. Rahane c Bell-Drummond b Milnes	1	– b Stewart	42
R. R. Rossouw c Dickson b Rayner	92	– c Bell-Drummond b Denly	66
A. H. T. Donald c Denly b Stewart	40	– c Bell-Drummond b Milnes	43
G. K. Berg b Stevens	0	– lbw b Denly	0
†L. D. McManus c Robinson b Stevens	49	– c Dickson b Stevens	10
K. H. D. Barker not out	35	– not out	37
*K. J. Abbott lbw b Stevens	0	– lbw b Denly	8
M. S. Crane c Dickson b Stevens	0	– c Cox b Stewart	7
F. H. Edwards not out	0	– c Robinson b Stewart	0
B 9, lb 12, w 3, nb 8	32	B 4, lb 5, nb 4	13

1/95 (2) 2/96 (3)   (9 wkts dec, 115 overs) 409   1/7 (1) 2/66 (3)   (115.4 overs) 298
3/262 (4) 4/286 (1)   3/184 (4) 4/185 (2)
5/286 (6) 6/318 (5) 7/391 (7)   5/186 (6) 6/207 (7) 7/270 (5)
8/391 (9) 9/391 (10)   8/285 (9) 9/298 (10) 10/298 (11)
                      110 overs: 391-8

Podmore 21–4–57–1; Stevens 25–8–68–5; Milnes 21–4–67–1; Stewart 15–1–88–1; Rayner 21–7–51–1; Denly 5–1–24–0; Bell-Drummond 7–1–33–0. *Second innings*—Podmore 15–3–43–0; Stevens 23–9–33–2; Milnes 16–1–70–1; Stewart 13.4–2–57–3; Rayner 23–14–38–1; Denly 25–8–48–3.

Kent

S. R. Dickson lbw b Abbott	15	– c Organ b Barker	4
J. M. Cox c McManus b Barker	27		
J. L. Denly lbw b Barker	154	– (2) not out	29
D. J. Bell-Drummond b Edwards	94	– b Abbott	2
*H. G. Kuhn b Edwards	95		
†O. G. Robinson b Edwards	29	– (5) not out	1
G. Stewart b Edwards	0		
D. I. Stevens c Donald b Edwards	60		
O. P. Rayner c Rahane b Berg	26		
H. W. Podmore not out	21		
M. E. Milnes c Organ b Berg	1		
A. J. Blake (did not bat)		– (3) c McManus b Edwards	15
B 4, lb 11, nb 18	33	Lb 1, w 1, nb 4	6

1/34 (1) 2/62 (2) 3/268 (4)   (131.1 overs) 555   1/9 (1)   (3 wkts, 8.2 overs) 57
4/345 (3) 5/400 (6) 6/410 (7)   2/53 (4) 3/56 (4)
7/502 (8) 8/511 (5) 9/543 (9)
10/555 (11)   110 overs: 460-6

Blake replaced Kuhn, as a concussion substitute.

Edwards 27–3–118–5; Abbott 20–3–74–1; Berg 14.1–1–67–2; Barker 24–4–78–2; Holland 24–3–77–0; Crane 22–1–126–0. *Second innings*—Abbott 4.2–0–20–1; Barker 3–0–29–1; Edwards 1–0–7–1.

Umpires: G. D. Lloyd and J. W. Lloyds.

At The Oval, August 18–21. HAMPSHIRE drew with SURREY.

HAMPSHIRE v SURREY

At Southampton, September 10–12. Hampshire won by 272 runs. Hampshire 19pts, Surrey 3pts. Toss: Hampshire.

A greentop provided extravagant movement for the seam bowlers: 17 wickets fell on the first day and another five before lunch on the second. It suited Rikki Clarke in particular, whose seventh five-for helped him to 500 first-class wickets, in his 251st match. With support from his near-namesake, Jordan Clark, he demolished Hampshire for 149. Pope and the versatile Clarke inspired Surrey to a narrow lead, before a more convincing batting display took the match from them. Vince top-scored with a brutal 59-ball 91, and there were four other half-centuries as Hampshire built a formidable total on a surface reverting to type. Surrey's target was 424 and, although Pope fought hard, they soon fell to heavy defeat. On the third day, the umpires ruled the light too poor for a pace attack, so Vince was obliged to turn to Organ, an occasional off-spinner, to complement Dawson's slow left-arm. His four previous matches had yielded three wickets, but he ran through the Surrey middle order to finish with five for 25. It gave Hampshire their first victory in eight, and their first at home against Surrey for 25 years.

Close of play: first day, Surrey 143-7 (Clarke 35); second day, Hampshire 296-6 (Dawson 39, McManus 14).

Hampshire

F. S. Organ c Elgar b Clarke	6	– c Clarke b McKerr	54
I. G. Holland b Clark	9	– b Morkel	4
T. P. Alsop b Clarke	3	– c Foakes b Clark	6
S. A. Northeast c Borthwick b Clarke	4	– c Clarke b Clark	73
*J. M. Vince c Smith b Clark	15	– c Clarke b Virdi	91
L. A. Dawson c Foakes b McKerr	12	– c Clarke b Morkel	88
A. H. T. Donald c McKerr b Clarke	27	– b Virdi	8
*L. D. McManus lbw b Morkel	27	– c Pope b McKerr	61
K. H. D. Barker c Pope b Clarke	1	– c Foakes b Morkel	18
K. J. Abbott b Clark	27	– st Foakes b Virdi	16
F. H. Edwards not out	8	– not out	0
B 1, w 1, nb 8	10	Lb 3, w 1, nb 8, p 5	17

1/18 (2) 2/18 (1) 3/21 (3)   (46.2 overs) 149   1/5 (2) 2/39 (3)   (92.4 overs) 436
4/26 (4) 5/42 (5) 6/69 (6)   3/84 (1) 4/213 (5)
7/81 (7) 8/90 (9) 9/135 (10) 10/149 (8)   5/257 (4) 6/272 (7) 7/388 (6)
                                                        8/400 (8) 9/428 (10) 10/436 (9)

Morkel 12.2–6–41–1; McKerr 12–3–36–1; Clarke 11–5–21–5; Clark 11–2–50–3. *Second innings*— Morkel 20.4–7–75–3; McKerr 16–3–72–2; Clark 19–0–95–2; Clarke 15–4–73–0; Virdi 21–3–110–3; Borthwick 1–0–3–0.

Surrey

M. D. Stoneman c Vince b Edwards	2 – (2) b Holland	12
D. Elgar c McManus b Abbott	11 – (1) c McManus b Barker	1
S. G. Borthwick c Dawson b Barker	7 – c McManus b Abbott	7
O. J. D. Pope lbw b Holland	68 – c McManus b Abbott	40
J. L. Smith c Dawson b Barker	2 – st McManus b Organ	34
*†B. T. Foakes b Barker	5 – c Northeast b Organ	15
R. Clarke lbw b Abbott	40 – c Holland b Organ	9
C. McKerr lbw b Abbott	6 – (9) lbw b Organ	1
J. Clark not out	13 – (8) c Edwards b Organ	6
M. Morkel run out (Alsop)	0 – b Dawson	4
G. S. Virdi b Barker	0 – not out	14
B 1, lb 7	8	Lb 7, w 1	8

1/9 (1) 2/15 (2) 3/37 (3)   (52 overs) 162
4/43 (5) 5/61 (6) 6/133 (4)
7/143 (8) 8/158 (7) 9/161 (10) 10/162 (11)

1/1 (1) 2/12 (3)   (49.2 overs) 151
3/37 (2) 4/77 (4)
5/117 (6) 6/122 (5) 7/131 (7)
8/132 (9) 9/137 (8) 10/151 (10)

Abbott 17–5–31–3; Edwards 7–0–45–1; Barker 16–5–38–4; Holland 6–0–27–1; Dawson 6–0–13–0. *Second innings*—Abbott 10.1–1–44–2; Barker 9–3–29–1; Holland 5–2–14–1; Edwards 5–0–15–0; Dawson 11.2–4–14–1; Alsop 1–0–3–0; Organ 8–2–25–5.

Umpires: M. Burns and I. J. Gould.

HAMPSHIRE v SOMERSET

At Southampton, September 16–18. Hampshire won by 136 runs. Hampshire 19pts, Somerset 3pts. Toss: Hampshire.

Many neutrals hoped this match would take Somerset within touching distance of a historic first Championship. There was history, all right, but for Kyle Abbott's mastery, not Tom Abell's Somerset. Abbott was unplayable, twice running through the visitors and condemning them to a demoralising defeat that left them 12 points adrift of Essex (whom they would host in the final fixture). Abbott's figures, and his control, were astonishing. He followed nine wickets in the first innings with eight in the second, and his eventual 17 for 86 – the seventh-best return in first-class cricket – was unmatched since Jim Laker took 19 for 90 for England against Australia at Manchester in 1956. A lively pitch offered generous seam movement and disconcerting pace from the first morning, and Somerset made an encouraging start: Hampshire, after choosing to bat, tottered to 24 for five. But Dawson hit his first century in over three years, Barker made 40, and a total of 196 looked competitive. Next came the first instalment of the Abbott show, which delivered a handy 54-run lead. When Hampshire

---

BEST MATCH FIGURES FOR HAMPSHIRE

17-86	K. J. Abbott	v Somerset at Southampton	2019
16-88	J. A. Newman	v Somerset at Weston-super-Mare	1927
15-116	A. S. Kennedy	v Somerset at Bath	1922
15-142	H. Baldwin	v Sussex at Hove	1898
14-29	D. Shackleton	v Somerset at Weston-super-Mare	1955
14-54	A. Jaques	v Somerset at Bath	1914
14-87	A. S. Kennedy	v Glamorgan at Swansea	1929
14-99	D. Shackleton	v Warwickshire at Bournemouth	1965
14-105	A. Jaques	v Derbyshire at Basingstoke	1914
14-111	D. Shackleton	v Lancashire at Manchester	1957

There are five more instances of a Hampshire bowler taking 14 wickets.

slipped to ten for three, it looked as if they would need it. And at 103 for eight, the force seemed with Somerset. But Abbott joined Vince, then on 46, and added 119; Vince's superb 142 was almost two-thirds of the total. Somerset required 281, and Vijay and Davies weathered the early Abbott storm to reach 86 without loss. Time for the second instalment: Abbott removed Vijay, sparking a collapse of seven for 14 in ten overs. Gregory scrapped, but this match was all about one man.

Close of play: first day, Somerset 30-2 (Abell 15, Hildreth 0); second day, Hampshire 176-8 (Vince 102, Abbott 17).

Hampshire

F. S. Organ c Hildreth b Gregory	0	– c Davies b Gregory 3
I. G. Holland c Vijay b Overton	4	– c Vijay b Davey 7
T. P. Alsop b Davey	3	– c van der Merwe b Davey 0
S. A. Northeast c van der Merwe b Gregory	6	– lbw b Overton 22
*J. M. Vince b Gregory	6	– c Davies b Overton 142
L. A. Dawson c Davies b Abell	103	– lbw b Gregory 2
A. H. T. Donald c Overton b Davey	9	– b Overton 1
†L. D. McManus c Bess b Overton	11	– lbw b van der Merwe 10
K. H. D. Barker lbw b Bess	40	– lbw b Abell 9
K. J. Abbott not out	7	– c Gregory b Davey 25
F. H. Edwards b Abell	0	– not out 0
B 2, lb 5	7	B 2, lb 3 5

1/0 (1) 2/3 (3) 3/12 (4)   (58.4 overs) 196   1/10 (2) 2/10 (3)   (61.3 overs) 226
4/18 (5) 5/24 (4) 6/57 (7)   3/10 (1) 4/34 (4)
7/88 (8) 8/180 (9) 9/190 (6) 10/196 (11)   5/40 (6) 6/45 (7) 7/90 (8)
     8/103 (9) 9/222 (5) 10/226 (10)

Gregory 15–2–63–3; Davey 13–4–34–2; Overton 15–3–46–2; Abell 7.4–1–25–2; Bess 8–1–21–1. *Second innings*—Gregory 19–9–58–2; Davey 11.3–5–22–3; Overton 19–3–74–3; van der Merwe 9–0–45–1; Abell 3–0–22–1.

Somerset

M. Vijay lbw b Abbott	0	– c Donald b Abbott 29
†S. M. Davies b Abbott	10	– c McManus b Abbott 51
*T. B. Abell b Abbott	20	– c McManus b Abbott 2
J. C. Hildreth c McManus b Abbott	2	– b Dawson 0
T. Banton c McManus b Edwards	6	– lbw b Abbott 2
G. A. Bartlett lbw b Abbott	9	– lbw b Abbott 0
L. Gregory lbw b Abbott	0	– not out 34
D. M. Bess c Donald b Abbott	37	– lbw b Abbott 0
C. Overton b Abbott	4	– c Dawson b Abbott 10
R. E. van der Merwe not out	29	– c Abbott b Dawson 2
J. H. Davey c McManus b Abbott	10	– b Abbott 0
B 4, lb 3, nb 8	15	B 4, lb 2, nb 8 14

1/12 (1) 2/23 (2) 3/38 (3)   (48.4 overs) 142   1/86 (1) 2/91 (3)   (48.4 overs) 144
4/45 (5) 5/45 (4) 6/58 (6)   3/92 (4) 4/95 (5)
7/59 (7) 8/65 (9) 9/132 (8) 10/142 (11)   5/95 (6) 6/96 (2) 7/100 (8)
     8/140 (9) 9/143 (10) 10/144 (11)

Abbott 18.4–9–40–9; Barker 12–0–44–0; Edwards 13–2–42–1; Holland 4–0–8–0; Dawson 1–0–1–0. *Second innings*—Abbott 17.4–3–46–8; Barker 5–1–22–0; Edwards 9–0–26–0; Dawson 13–5–21–2; Holland 2–0–14–0; Organ 2–0–9–0.

Umpires: G. D. Lloyd and N. A. Mallender.

At Canterbury, September 23–26. KENT drew with HAMPSHIRE.

KENT

All hail, Stevo!

Mark Pennell

In late July, Kent caused uproar when they announced that Darren Stevens, in his 15th summer at the club, would be released at the end of the season. He was 43, and with Marcus Trescothick the oldest in the county game. In a press briefing headed "All good things must come to an end", they reasoned it was time to encourage younger bowlers and, at a members' forum soon after, explained their belief that Stevens lacked impact with a softer, older ball, and that his invaluable late-middle-order runs had dried up.

After suffering a poor Royal London Cup – three games brought 41 runs and three expensive wickets – Stevens was omitted from the T20 Blast squad for the second year in a row. He joined Derbyshire on loan, and played a minor role in their run to finals day. His first-class batting was iffy, and by mid-June he had managed only 131 runs at 14. His bowling was handier, collecting 17 wickets at 26, but he was dropped from the four-day side who beat Nottinghamshire in Tunbridge Wells. Though restored for the next game – a high-scoring draw with Warwickshire at Canterbury – he added four runs and one more wicket.

Stevens realised he was falling lbw too often, even if no one at Kent had noticed. A chance meeting on the golf course with former head coach Simon Willis led to an extended net session, with Willis quickly working out what was going wrong. "Simon was instrumental in bringing me to the club in 2005, and knows my game inside and out," said Stevens. "I came away feeling a million dollars." With three Championship fixtures left, he embarked upon a career-saving patch of deepest purple.

At Trent Bridge, Stevens clubbed 88 from 90 balls and, for the second time, claimed ten wickets in the match. Then, at Headingley, he enjoyed the performance of his life. Having hit a career-best 237 off 225 balls, he took match figures of seven for 70, including five for 20 in the second innings to set up a 433-run victory. The only other Kent player to combine a double-hundred and a five-for was Frank Woolley, against Somerset in 1925.

Kent gathered 46 points from those two wins, and had a chance of grabbing third until rain ruined the last match. Even so, fourth place – their best since 2004 – was significantly better than all but the most diehard supporters had expected. And amid the rain came news that the county had seen the light: Stevens was offered a contract for 2020, when the club celebrate the 150th anniversary of their merger with the Canterbury-based Beverley Kent Cricket Club.

Stevens finished with 52 Championship victims at 17, which put him top of the Kent averages, though he was not the leading wicket-taker. Matt Milnes, one of five to appear in all 14 games, proved a shrewd signing.

Having managed 11 wickets for Nottinghamshire with his brisk seam in 2018, he scooped up 55 – and earned a winter Lions selection. The third workhorse was Harry Podmore, who like Stevens took 52. The last time three Kent bowlers had passed 50 Championship wickets in a season was 1985 – Derek Underwood, Eldine Baptiste and Kevin Jarvis.

Ollie Robinson

Inevitably, Stevens was the supporters' Player of the Year at the end-of-season awards, where Zak Crawley picked up three prizes. He hit two first-class hundreds and one in the Royal London, and made his Test debut in New Zealand. All told, seven players hit 500 runs in the Championship, Daniel Bell-Drummond leading the way with 892 at 35. Kent saw little of Joe Denly, whose international career was belatedly taking off, or club captain Sam Billings, who dislocated his shoulder in April – though when they did play, they tended to prosper.

That injury allowed understudy wicketkeeper Ollie Robinson an extended go, and he did so well – two centuries, 765 nuggety runs and 54 catches – that he retained the gloves when Billings returned in August. There were short visits from South Africans Wiaan Mulder and Faf du Plessis, neither of whom made much impression. Nor did Australian international Matt Renshaw; he did not manage a fifty in the Championship, but did hit a Royal London hundred in a losing cause.

Kent endured an abysmal 50-over campaign. Although Crawley collected 394 runs, and Milnes 16 wickets, there was little support, and a record of two wins consigned them to seventh. A crumb of comfort was the emergence as a handy all-rounder of Bell-Drummond, combining 184 runs with five cheap wickets and an economy-rate of 4.47.

The Spitfires made a superb start to the T20 Blast, winning six of their first seven games to head their group, thanks in part to strong overseas reinforcements. Adam Milne, the rapid New Zealand seamer, claimed ten wickets, while Mohammad Nabi – who had been playing for Afghanistan in the World Cup – and Hardus Viljoen, a South African Kolpak, made telling contributions. But once Nabi left, and Milne suffered an ankle injury, the wins dried up: the last seven games produced five defeats and two washouts, and Kent finished fifth, just outside the knockouts.

Late in the summer, the county announced the release of Adam Riley, who retired, and Mitch Claydon, who joined Sussex. They gave contracts to two young off-spinners: Academy graduate Marcus O'Riordan (like Crawley, educated at Tonbridge School) and England Under-19 player Hamidullah Qadri, recruited from Derbyshire. Jack Leaning joined from Yorkshire to bolster the batting, while the 36-year-old Tim Groenewald came from Somerset, perhaps – or perhaps not – to fill the boots of Stevens.

Championship attendance: 25,859.

KENT RESULTS

All first-class matches – Played 15: Won 5, Lost 5, Drawn 5.
County Championship matches – Played 14: Won 5, Lost 5, Drawn 4.

Specsavers County Championship, 4th in Division 1;
Vitality Blast, 5th in South Group; Royal London One-Day Cup, 7th in South Group.

COUNTY CHAMPIONSHIP AVERAGES, BATTING AND FIELDING

Cap		Birthplace	M	I	NO	R	HS	100	Avge	Ct
2015	S. W. Billings	Pembury‡	4	7	1	366	138	3	61.00	1
2008	J. L. Denly	Canterbury‡	6	11	2	504	167*	2	56.00	1
2015	D. J. Bell-Drummond	Lewisham‡	14	26	1	892	166	1	35.68	4
2019	Z. Crawley	Bromley‡	13	24	0	820	111	2	34.16	16
	O. G. Robinson	Sidcup‡	14	25	2	765	143	1	33.26	54
2005	D. I. Stevens	Leicester	12	19	1	597	237	1	33.16	2
	P. W. A. Mulder¶	Johannesburg, SA	3	6	2	114	68*	0	28.50	0
	S. R. Dickson††	Johannesburg, SA	11	21	0	557	161	2	26.52	13
2018	H. G. Kuhn††	Piet Retief, SA	14	24	0	605	95	0	25.20	11
	†M. T. Renshaw	Middlesbrough	3	6	1	118	48*	0	23.60	3
	G. Stewart††	Kalgoorlie, Australia	5	7	2	113	59	0	22.60	0
	J. M. Cox	Margate‡	3	4	0	71	27	0	17.75	1
2019	H. W. Podmore	Hammersmith	14	21	6	265	54*	0	17.66	4
	O. P. Rayner	Walsrode, Germany	8	10	1	152	40*	0	16.88	5
2016	†M. E. Claydon	Fairfield, Australia	6	7	4	50	13*	0	16.66	0
2017	†A. J. Blake	Farnborough‡	5	9	0	136	34	0	15.11	2
	M. E. Milnes	Nottingham	14	19	6	174	31	0	13.38	5

Also batted: F. du Plessis¶ (*Pretoria, SA*) (1 match) 0, 36 (3 ct); F. J. Klaassen (*Haywards Heath*) (1 match) 10, 13 (1 ct); M. K. O'Riordan (*Pembury*‡) (1 match) 12, 9; I. Qayyum (*Ealing*) (1 match) 14*, 1*; A. E. N. Riley (*Sidcup*‡) (2 matches) 3*, 0*, 7 (4 ct).

‡ *Born in Kent.* ¶ *Official overseas player.* †† *Other non-England-qualified.*

BOWLING

	Style	O	M	R	W	BB	5I	Avge
D. I. Stevens	RM	403	126	914	52	5-20	5	17.57
M. E. Claydon	RFM	130.2	20	466	19	5-46	1	24.52
M. E. Milnes	RFM	386.4	68	1,383	55	5-68	2	25.14
H. W. Podmore	RFM	473.3	105	1,380	52	5-41	2	26.53
O. P. Rayner	OB	166.3	76	292	10	2-7	0	29.20
P. W. A. Mulder	RFM	91.5	22	307	10	4-118	0	30.70
G. Stewart	RFM	135.3	16	514	15	3-37	0	34.26

Also bowled: D. J. Bell-Drummond (RM) 60.2–11–163–6; A. J. Blake (OB) 1–0–9–0; Z. Crawley (OB) 11–2–33–0; J. L. Denly (LB) 72–20–184–4; S. R. Dickson (RM) 4–0–9–0; F. J. Klaassen (LFM) 29–0–132–2; M. K. O'Riordan (OB) 7–0–33–0; I. Qayyum (SLA) 8–0–43–0; M. T. Renshaw (OB) 16–2–53–0; A. E. N. Riley (OB) 56–10–182–2.

LEADING ROYAL LONDON CUP AVERAGES (100 runs/4 wickets)

Batting	Runs	HS	Avge	SR	Ct/St
D. J. Bell-Drummond	184	120*	61.33	87.20	1
Z. Crawley	394	120	56.28	87.55	4
M. T. Renshaw	213	109	42.60	90.25	6
H. G. Kuhn	116	36*	29.00	109.43	2
A. J. Blake	112	43	22.40	83.58	4
A. P. Rouse	111	45*	22.20	85.38	7/1
H. W. Podmore	103	40	20.60	94.49	5

Bowling	W	BB	Avge	ER
D. J. Bell-Drummond	5	2-22	20.60	4.47
M. E. Milnes	16	5-79	30.87	6.87
F. J. Klaassen	7	2-17	34.71	6.02
H. W. Podmore	8	2-54	51.37	5.78
I. Qayyum	5	2-37	61.60	5.81

LEADING VITALITY BLAST AVERAGES (100 runs/15 overs)

Batting	Runs	HS	Avge	SR	Ct/St		Bowling	W	BB	Avge	ER
Mohammad Nabi	147	43*	18.37	153.12	3		Mohammad Nabi	8	2-32	28.00	7.22
A. J. Blake	204	66*	22.66	148.90	3		I. Qayyum	12	5-21	18.83	7.49
Z. Crawley	307	89	27.90	144.81	5		A. F. Milne	10	3-21	24.20	7.68
H. G. Kuhn	255	55*	42.50	132.12	10		G. C. Viljoen ...	18	3-15	19.72	7.83
D. J. Bell-Drummond	317	64	26.41	119.62	4		M. E. Claydon ...	1	1-37	134.00	8.93
O. G. Robinson .	139	53	13.90	104.51	6/2		F. J. Klaassen....	10	2-24	38.40	9.32

FIRST-CLASS COUNTY RECORDS

Highest score for	332	W. H. Ashdown v Essex at Brentwood	1934
Highest score against	344	W. G. Grace (MCC) at Canterbury	1876
Leading run-scorer	47,868	F. E. Woolley (avge 41.77)	1906–38
Best bowling for	10-30	C. Blythe v Northamptonshire at Northampton.....	1907
Best bowling against	10-48	C. H. G. Bland (Sussex) at Tonbridge............	1899
Leading wicket-taker	3,340	A. P. Freeman (avge 17.64)	1914–36
Highest total for	803-4 dec	v Essex at Brentwood	1934
Highest total against	676	by Australians at Canterbury	1921
Lowest total for	18	v Sussex at Gravesend	1867
Lowest total against	16	by Warwickshire at Tonbridge..................	1913

LIST A COUNTY RECORDS

Highest score for	150*	J. L. Denly v Glamorgan at Canterbury...........	2018
Highest score against	167*	P. Johnson (Nottinghamshire) at Nottingham	1993
Leading run-scorer	7,814	M. R. Benson (avge 31.89)	1980–95
Best bowling for	8-31	D. L. Underwood v Scotland at Edinburgh	1987
Best bowling against	6-5	A. G. Wharf (Glamorgan) at Cardiff	2004
Leading wicket-taker	530	D. L. Underwood (avge 18.93)	1963–87
Highest total for	{ 384-6	v Berkshire at Finchampstead	1994
	{ 384-8	v Surrey at Beckenham	2018
Highest total against	380-5	by Middlesex at Canterbury	2019
Lowest total for	60	v Somerset at Taunton	1979
Lowest total against	60	by Derbyshire at Canterbury	2008

TWENTY20 COUNTY RECORDS

Highest score for	127	J. L. Denly v Essex at Chelmsford...............	2017
Highest score against	151*	C. H. Gayle (Somerset) at Taunton	2015
Leading run-scorer	3,358	J. L. Denly (avge 30.25, SR 126.86)	2004–18
Best bowling for	5-11	A. F. Milne v Somerset at Taunton	2017
Best bowling against	5-17	G. M. Smith (Essex) at Chelmsford..............	2012
Leading wicket-taker	119	J. C. Tredwell (avge 28.46, ER 7.32).	2003–17
Highest total for	{ 231-7	v Surrey at The Oval	2015
	{ 231-5	v Somerset at Canterbury	2018
Highest total against	250-6	by Surrey at Canterbury	2018
Lowest total for	72	v Hampshire at Southampton	2011
Lowest total against	82	by Somerset at Taunton	2010

ADDRESS

The Spitfire Ground, St Lawrence, Old Dover Road, Canterbury CT1 3NZ; 01227 456886; kent@ecb.co.uk; www.kentcricket.co.uk.

OFFICIALS

Captain S. W. Billings
Director of cricket P. R. Downton
Head coach M. J. Walker
High performance director 2019 J. R. Weaver
Head of talent pathway 2020 M. M. Patel

President 2019 C. R. Swadkin
President 2020 Sir Timothy Laurence
Chairman S. R. C. Philip
Chief executive S. Storey
Head groundsman A. Llong
Scorer L. A. R. Hart

KENT v LOUGHBOROUGH MCCU

At Canterbury, March 31–April 2. Drawn. Toss: Loughborough MCCU. First-class-debut: F. J. Klaassen. County debut: M. E. Milnes.

A five-hour unbeaten hundred from Dickson and four other half-centuries were the modest batting highlights of a match that lost much of its last day to showers and bad light. Dickson was the mainstay of a total of 247 for eight; no one else passed 40, as seamers Will Pereira and Alex Evans took three wickets each. The students batted sensibly in reply, and declared one run to the good after sixties from Louis Kimber and Adam Tillcock, the captain. It was the only instance of an MCCU team gaining a first-innings lead over a county in 2019. Kimber had gained a reprieve on 26 when he was dropped in the cordon off Dutch international Fred Klaassen, one of two Kent debutants. The other, Matt Milnes, claimed three for 95 in his first game since leaving his native Nottinghamshire. Fifties from Crawley and Bell-Drummond gave Kent a decent lead before the end.

Close of play: first day, Loughborough MCCU 27-1 (Azad 17, Kimber 2); second day, Kent 44-0 (Crawley 25, Bell-Drummond 12).

Kent

S. R. Dickson not out............................	108	– retired hurt...................................		3
Z. Crawley lbw b Evans........................	9	– c Azad b Kimber..............................		87
*D. J. Bell-Drummond c King b Evans...........	40	– not out..		55
†A. P. Rouse b Evans............................	0			
A. J. Blake lbw b Pereira.......................	1			
D. I. Stevens lbw b Pereira.....................	0			
O. G. Robinson b Pereira.......................	21			
H. W. Podmore lbw b Sanders..................	14			
M. E. Milnes run out (Welch)...................	9			
F. J. Klaassen not out...........................	14			
Lb 5, nb 26..................................	31	Lb 4..................................		4

1/33 (2) 2/119 (3)   (8 wkts dec, 73 overs) 247   1/149 (2)   (1 wkt, 44.3 overs) 149
3/123 (4) 4/134 (5)
5/134 (6) 6/168 (7) 7/186 (8) 8/223 (9)

A. E. N. Riley did not bat.

In the second innings Dickson retired hurt at 8-0.

Sanders 19–4–72–1; Pereira 19–5–61–3; Evans 19–4–49–3; Bhabra 12–1–48–0; Tillcock 4–0–12–0. *Second innings*—Evans 16–6–37–0; Pereira 4–0–19–0; Sanders 2–1–5–0; Bhabra 0.4–0–0–0; Tillcock 13.2–0–50–0; Kimber 8.3–0–34–1.

Loughborough MCCU

N. R. Welch b Stevens	5	W. J. N. Pereira c Crawley b Milnes...... 4
M. H. Azad lbw b Stevens..............	25	H. A. Evans not out...................... 7
L. P. J. Kimber c Rouse b Milnes	62	B 4, lb 10, w 3, nb 4 21
*A. D. Tillcock c Stevens b Bell-Drummond	60	
J. S. Kendall lbw b Bell-Drummond	33	1/6 (1) 2/36 (2) (9 wkts dec, 93.4 overs) 248
†A. E. King c Milnes b Podmore.........	13	3/146 (3) 4/192 (4)
C. W. G. Sanders c Klaassen b Milnes	18	5/200 (5) 6/233 (6)
B. J. Bhabra c Rouse b Podmore	0	7/233 (8) 8/237 (7) 9/248 (9)

N. A. Hammond did not bat.

Podmore 26–9–64–2; Stevens 19–8–23–2; Klaassen 16–2–38–0; Milnes 21.4–2–95–3; Bell-Drummond 7–2–6–2; Riley 4–1–8–0.

Umpires: M. J. Saggers and C. M. Watts.

At Taunton, April 5–8. KENT lost to SOMERSET by 74 runs.

At Birmingham, April 11–14. KENT beat WARWICKSHIRE by eight wickets.

At Beckenham, April 27. KENT lost to PAKISTANIS by 100 runs (see Pakistan tour section).

KENT v YORKSHIRE

At Canterbury, May 14–17. Yorkshire won by 172 runs. Yorkshire 20pts, Kent 5pts. Toss: Yorkshire. County debut: D. M. Bess. Championship debut: F. J. Klaassen.

In the last hour of the game, Yorkshire overcame spirited defiance from Kent's lower order, and narrowed the gap on leaders Somerset. They had started shakily, shot out inside two sessions: six batsmen, plus Extras, made it into the twenties, but none beyond, as Milnes led the way with three wickets. Kent tumbled to 71 for four on the first evening too, thanks to the talented young pair of Crawley and Robinson, reached 261 for five, and were eyeing a big lead. Instead, they subsided for 296, and a less convincing advantage of 86. Köhler-Cadmore became only the second Yorkshire player, after Ellis Robinson against Leicestershire at Bradford in 1938, to hold six outfield catches. On an easing pitch, the visitors then batted with greater resolve. Ballance hit 25 runs in 159, his fourth Championship hundred in four games stretching back to September 2018. Requiring 384, Kent were three down at the end of the third day and – despite a dogged 13 in 110 balls from nightwatchman Klaassen, and a similarly determined 41 by Bell-Drummond – could not salvage a draw. Bess, on loan from Somerset, had a quiet match, but Coad's six-for helped bring Yorkshire their first Championship win in Kent since 2001.

Close of play: first day, Kent 130-4 (Crawley 73, Robinson 14); second day, Yorkshire 166-3 (Ballance 57, Leaning 11); third day, Kent 34-3 (Klaassen 3, Bell-Drummond 0).

Yorkshire

A. Lyth c Renshaw b Podmore	0	– c Robinson b Claydon 44
H. C. Brook b Podmore	29	– c Robinson b Klaassen 13
G. S. Ballance c Robinson b Klaassen	11	– b Bell-Drummond 159
T. Köhler-Cadmore c Podmore b Milnes	28	– c Crawley b Bell-Drummond 28
J. A. Leaning run out (Kuhn)	17	– lbw b Milnes 69
J. A. Tattersall lbw b Claydon	29	– c Robinson b Milnes 19
T. T. Bresnan c Crawley b Milnes	0	– b Claydon 23
D. M. Bess b Milnes	25	– c Klaassen b Podmore 34
*S. A. Patterson run out (Claydon)	23	– b Claydon 0
B. O. Coad c Crawley b Bell-Drummond	7	– c Dickson b Podmore 35
D. Olivier not out	21	– not out 0
B 4, lb 6, nb 10	20	B 13, lb 11, w 1, nb 20 45

1/0 (1) 2/35 (3) 3/47 (2)   (56.2 overs) 210
4/87 (5) 5/96 (4) 6/96 (7)
7/126 (8) 8/166 (6) 9/181 (10) 10/210 (9)

1/33 (2) 2/82 (1)   (131.1 overs) 469
3/139 (4) 4/327 (5)
5/361 (3) 6/374 (6) 7/416 (7)
8/416 (9) 9/460 (8) 10/469 (10)

Podmore 15–5–33–2; Milnes 16–5–63–3; Klaassen 10–0–44–1; Claydon 11.2–1–51–1; Bell-Drummond 4–2–9–1. *Second innings*—Podmore 32.1–11–89–2; Milnes 28–4–107–2; Claydon 27–5–83–3; Klaassen 19–0–88–1; Bell-Drummond 13–2–35–2; Renshaw 11–2–34–0; Blake 1–0–9–0.

Kent

S. R. Dickson b Olivier	5	c Brook b Olivier	1
Z. Crawley c and b Patterson	81	lbw b Coad	9
M. T. Renshaw c Köhler-Cadmore b Coad	16	b Coad	13
D. J. Bell-Drummond c Köhler-Cadmore b Bresnan	3	(5) lbw b Patterson	41
*H. G. Kuhn c Köhler-Cadmore b Bresnan	15	(6) c Lyth b Coad	0
†O. G. Robinson c Patterson b Coad	103	(7) c Ballance b Coad	35
A. J. Blake c Köhler-Cadmore b Olivier	34	(8) lbw b Leaning	22
H. W. Podmore c Köhler-Cadmore b Bess	9	(9) b Coad	29
M. E. Milnes c Tattersall b Olivier	0	(10) not out	14
F. J. Klaassen c Köhler-Cadmore b Coad	10	(4) c Lyth b Olivier	13
M. E. Claydon not out	3	c Brook b Coad	4
B 6, lb 1, nb 10	17	B 3, lb 7, nb 20	30

1/9 (1) 2/38 (3) 3/51 (4)   (87 overs) 296
4/71 (5) 5/157 (2) 6/261 (7)
7/272 (8) 8/272 (9) 9/293 (6) 10/296 (10)

1/3 (1) 2/19 (2)   (88.5 overs) 211
3/30 (3) 4/84 (4)
5/89 (6) 6/118 (5) 7/142 (7)
8/179 (8) 9/207 (9) 10/211 (11)

Coad 21–7–66–3; Olivier 21–4–82–3; Bresnan 17–5–47–2; Patterson 15–5–42–1; Bess 13–0–52–1. *Second innings*—Coad 24.5–6–52–6; Olivier 25–4–92–2; Patterson 19–10–35–1; Bresnan 2–2–0–0; Bess 16–6–41–0; Leaning 2–0–8–1.

Umpires: M. Burns and P. R. Pollard.

KENT v SURREY

At Beckenham, May 20–23. Drawn. Kent 10pts, Surrey 13pts. Toss: Surrey. County debut: P. W. A. Mulder.

Wiaan Mulder, a South African all-rounder making his county debut, helped thwart Surrey's victory tilt. He and compatriots Dickson and Kuhn scored half-centuries, and all survived at least 100 balls, together forming the cornerstone of Kent's resistance, which lasted 113 overs. Batting first, Surrey had recovered from 65 for five to make 439, thanks to contributions from an English-born trio. Borthwick and Jacks, whose maiden first-class century featured 20 fours, added 175 – a sixth-wicket record for Surrey in this fixture – before Clarke hit a combative 88. Mulder finished with four victims. In contrast, Kent began strongly: the openers put on 128, and the second wicket did not fall until 197. But despite Dickson's hundred (following a triple on his last Championship visit to Beckenham, in 2017), the rest fell away, and Kent conceded a lead of 145. Another half-century from Borthwick and a brisk 80 from Curran upped the tempo as Surrey's lead reached 425. They removed Crawley in the 17 overs available on the third evening, but could take only seven wickets on the last day, as one South African after another dug in against an attack containing – in Morkel, McKerr and Elgar – three more.

Close of play: first day, Surrey 420-9 (Clarke 87, McKerr 1); second day, Surrey 11-0 (Burns 6, Stoneman 4); third day, Kent 46-1 (Dickson 27, Riley 4).

Surrey

*R. J. Burns c Robinson b Podmore	14	c Robinson b Stevens	15
M. D. Stoneman run out (Mulder)	19	c Riley b Milnes	13
S. G. Borthwick lbw b Riley	95	b Riley	58
D. Elgar c Robinson b Milnes	4	lbw b Podmore	13
†B. T. Foakes c Dickson b Mulder	5	c Robinson b Podmore	44
S. M. Curran b Riley b Mulder	4	c Blake b Milnes	80
W. G. Jacks c Robinson b Mulder	120	c Robinson b Mulder	4
R. Clarke c Dickson b Podmore	88	c and b Milnes	35
M. Morkel c Blake b Mulder	17	(10) not out	4
G. J. Batty c Robinson b Stevens	24	(9) lbw b Podmore	6
C. McKerr not out	17	b Milnes	1
B 4, lb 9, w 5, nb 14	32	Lb 4, w 1, nb 2	7

1/29 (2) 2/37 (1) 3/45 (4)   (98.1 overs) 439
4/60 (5) 5/65 (6) 6/240 (3)
7/314 (8) 8/362 (9) 9/390 (10) 10/439 (8)

1/21 (1) 2/29 (2)   (79.5 overs) 280
3/59 (4) 4/134 (5)
5/163 (3) 6/176 (7) 7/261 (6)
8/274 (9) 9/278 (8) 10/280 (11)

Podmore 19.1–3–79–2; Stevens 23–6–63–1; Mulder 22–3–118–4; Milnes 21–5–110–1; Riley 13–1–56–1. *Second innings*—Podmore 22–5–66–3; Stevens 16–6–50–1; Milnes 17.5–3–74–4; Riley 12–1–45–1; Mulder 12–2–41–1.

Kent

S. R. Dickson c Foakes b Curran	128	– c Foakes b Clarke	91
Z. Crawley b Clarke	63	– c Borthwick b Morkel	9
D. J. Bell-Drummond b Batty	37	– (4) lbw b Clarke	7
*H. G. Kuhn c Foakes b Batty	15	– (5) c Foakes b Morkel	81
†O. G. Robinson c Clarke b Batty	0	– (6) c Batty b Morkel	34
P. W. A. Mulder c Jacks b Curran	7	– (7) not out	68
A. J. Blake c Jacks b Clarke	0	– (8) c Jacks b Elgar	8
D. I. Stevens lbw b Clarke	12	– (9) c Foakes b Clarke	5
H. W. Podmore c Jacks b Morkel	11	– (10) not out	4
M. E. Milnes c Clarke b Curran	7		
A. E. N. Riley not out	0	– (3) b Curran	7
B 4, lb 6, nb 4	14	B 12, lb 14, w 4, nb 8	38

1/128 (2) 2/197 (3) 3/227 (4)   (85.5 overs) 294   1/23 (2)   (8 wkts, 113 overs) 352
4/227 (5) 5/236 (6) 6/238 (7)   2/69 (3) 3/90 (4)
7/260 (8) 8/272 (1) 9/290 (10) 10/294 (9)   4/172 (1) 5/242 (6)
                                                6/263 (5) 7/308 (8) 8/333 (9)

Morkel 18.5–3–41–1; Curran 20–5–54–3; McKerr 16–1–70–0; Clarke 19–2–70–3; Batty 12–0–49–3. *Second innings*—Curran 8.1–2–21–1; Morkel 27–4–86–3; Clarke 25–6–67–3; McKerr 19–1–63–0; Batty 25.5–5–72–0; Elgar 8–2–17–1.

Umpires: G. D. Lloyd and A. G. Wharf. B. J. Debenham replaced Wharf on the fourth day.

At Chelmsford, May 27–30. KENT lost to ESSEX by 113 runs.

KENT v SOMERSET

At Canterbury, June 10–13. Somerset won by ten wickets. Somerset 19pts, Kent 3pts. Toss: uncontested.

Gregory returned career-best figures of 11 for 53 as Somerset won handsomely, despite the first and third days being washed out. When play got under way on the second, the ball swerved, and 22 wickets tumbled. First Kent were bundled out for 139 in 41 overs, with Gregory claiming six for 32, also a career-best. Somerset then crashed to 35 for four before Banton, whose maiden fifty was the only score in the match above 37, helped secure a lead of 30. The downfall of Jamie Overton had provided a comic moment: unaware of the ball's whereabouts after playing it into the pitch, he turned round, saw it falling behind him, panicked, and kicked it into leg stump. The fortunate bowler was

---

SHORTEST CHAMPIONSHIP MATCHES INVOLVING KENT

Overs
125.2*	Middx (68 and 44) lost to Kent (120) by an innings and eight runs at Lord's	1891
106.5	Derbys (78 and 37) lost to Kent (215) by an innings and 100 runs at Chesterfield	1907
109.5	Northants (69 and 86) lost to Kent (167) by an innings and 12 runs at Chesterfield	1999
110.3	Leics (25 and 155) lost to Kent (110 and 72-2) by eight wickets at Leicester	1912
112	Kent (187) beat Worcs (25 and 61) by an innings and 101 runs at Tunbridge Wells	1960
119.2	Surrey (148 and 60) lost to Kent (134 and 78-0) by ten wickets at Beckenham	1905
120	Glos (96 and 62) lost to Kent (154 and 8-0) by ten wickets at Gravesend	1920
120.1	**Kent (139 and 59) lost to Somerset (169 and 30-0) by ten wickets at Canterbury**	**2019**
121.1	Warwicks (111 and 78) lost to Kent (110 and 79-1) by nine wickets at Birmingham	1914
122	Leics (66 and 101) lost to Kent (127 and 44-2) by eight wickets at Leicester	1907

* *Five-ball overs, equating to 104.3 six-ball overs.*

Excluding single-innings matches, those with forfeitures, or those affected by rain.

Stewart, one of three home seamers to claim three wickets. Kent slid to 24 for two before an eventful day watched by over 1,000 schoolchildren was done. When the game resumed after lunch on the final afternoon, so did the carnage. Gregory, ending with five for 21, and Craig Overton (three for seven) ran amok, blowing their opponents away for 59. Only once before had Kent made fewer against Somerset: 55 at Tonbridge in 1926. The Somerset openers whizzed to victory, and their fifth win – Kent's fourth defeat – increased the lead over Hampshire at the top to 26 points.

Close of play: first day, no play; second day, Kent 24-2 (Dickson 17, Podmore 0); third day, no play.

Kent

S. R. Dickson lbw b Brooks	0	– c Hildreth b C. Overton	22	
Z. Crawley c Brooks b Gregory	10	– lbw b Gregory	3	
*J. L. Denly lbw b C. Overton	4	– b J. Overton	1	
D. J. Bell-Drummond lbw b Brooks	12	– (5) c C. Overton b Gregory	0	
H. G. Kuhn c Davies b J. Overton	6	– (6) c C. Overton b Gregory	2	
†O. G. Robinson lbw b Gregory	37	– (7) c Davies b Gregory	8	
A. J. Blake c J. Overton b Gregory	28	– (8) c J. Overton b Gregory	1	
D. I. Stevens lbw b Gregory	0	– (9) lbw b C. Overton	10	
G. Stewart b Gregory	28	– (10) lbw b C. Overton	0	
H. W. Podmore not out	1	– (4) lbw b Brooks	6	
M. E. Milnes b Gregory	0	– not out	0	
B 4, lb 2, w 5, nb 2	13	Lb 4, nb 2	6	

1/5 (1) 2/10 (3) 3/27 (4)   (41 overs) 139
4/43 (5) 5/45 (2) 6/101 (7)
7/101 (8) 8/126 (6) 9/139 (9) 10/139 (11)

1/7 (2) 2/24 (3)   (26.1 overs) 59
3/32 (4) 4/37 (5)
5/39 (6) 6/39 (1) 7/40 (8)
8/59 (9) 9/59 (10) 10/59 (7)

C. Overton 5.5–1–26–1; Brooks 12–5–22–2; J. Overton 7–1–29–1; Gregory 13.1–6–32–6; Abell 3–0–24–0. *Second innings*—Gregory 13.1–6–21–5; Brooks 7–2–27–1; J. Overton 2–2–0–1; C. Overton 4–1–7–3.

Somerset

*T. B. Abell lbw b Podmore	3	– not out	15	
Azhar Ali lbw b Stevens	0	– not out	13	
J. C. Hildreth c Robinson b Podmore	0			
T. Banton c Milnes b Stewart	63			
G. A. Bartlett c Robinson b Podmore	9			
†S. M. Davies c Kuhn b Milnes	31			
L. Gregory lbw b Milnes	26			
C. Overton b Stewart	0			
J. Overton b Stewart	9			
M. J. Leach lbw b Milnes	5			
J. A. Brooks not out	0			
B 9, lb 5, w 1, nb 8	23	Nb 2	2	

1/2 (2) 2/5 (3) 3/14 (1)   (46.2 overs) 169
4/35 (5) 5/97 (6) 6/139 (4)
7/139 (8) 8/163 (7) 9/169 (9) 10/169 (10)

(no wkt, 6.4 overs) 30

Podmore 13–4–37–3; Stevens 11–4–42–1; Stewart 12–2–37–3; Milnes 10.2–1–39–3. *Second innings*—Podmore 1–0–13–0; Stevens 3–1–3–0; Stewart 2.4–0–14–0.

Umpires: M. J. Saggers and B. V. Taylor.

> 66 India slipped to 24 for four, their musketeers Sharma, Kohli and Rahul going all for one, unique in international cricket for a top three."
> India v New Zealand, World Cup semi-final, page 310

KENT v NOTTINGHAMSHIRE

At Tunbridge Wells, June 17–20. Kent won by 285 runs. Kent 22pts, Nottinghamshire 5pts. Toss: uncontested. County debut: O. P. Rayner.

Kuhn, captain because Denly was concentrating on his batting before the Ashes, led Kent to an emphatic victory, their only home win of an otherwise encouraging Championship season. A steadfast 111 from Crawley, plus tail-wagging from Stewart and Podmore, helped them recover from 119 for six; that included Robinson, caught at first slip by Duckett after the chance was spilled by Mullaney at third, then parried by Carter at second. Pattinson, another with the Ashes on his mind, did most damage with six for 73. When Nottinghamshire replied, Milnes claimed his maiden five-for, against his former club, and Mulder a handy three for 35. But it was Podmore's only wicket that caused debate: Nash, caught behind, said he had been distracted by a white cloth falling from the bowler's waistband. The innings followed the opposite trajectory, with Nottinghamshire squandering a healthy position of 207 for three. Kent extended their 42-run lead thanks to a timely 167 not out from Denly, and the declaration – nine overs into the final day – set Nottinghamshire 406 in 85. Rayner, on loan from Middlesex, took the wickets of Slater and Pattinson in a post-lunch stint of 16–12–13–2; Podmore bagged five for 41, as they were blown away for 120 by tea.

Close of play: first day, Nottinghamshire 30-0 (Slater 13, Duckett 17); second day, Nottinghamshire 208-4 (Patel 42, Mullaney 1); third day, Kent 277-3 (Denly 111, Kuhn 22).

Kent

S. R. Dickson c Moores b Pattinson	4	– (2) c Moores b Pattinson	1
Z. Crawley b Pattinson	111	– (1) c Duckett b Ball	37
J. L. Denly lbw b Pattinson	8	– not out	167
D. J. Bell-Drummond lbw b Fletcher	9	– c Moores b Pattinson	79
*H. G. Kuhn b Fletcher	9	– b Carter	42
†O. G. Robinson c Duckett b Ball	9	– c Carter b Mullaney	1
P. W. A. Mulder lbw b Pattinson	13	– not out	7
G. Stewart b Pattinson	59		
O. P. Rayner lbw b Pattinson	0		
H. W. Podmore not out	49		
M. E. Milnes c Duckett b Ball	13		
B 5, lb 11, w 1, nb 8	25	B 5, lb 10, nb 14	29

1/4 (1) 2/31 (3) 3/69 (4) (83.1 overs) 309
4/81 (5) 5/100 (6) 6/119 (7)
7/219 (8) 8/225 (9) 9/254 (2) 10/309 (11)

1/19 (2) (5 wkts dec, 76 overs) 363
2/94 (1) 3/246 (4)
4/319 (5) 5/328 (6)

Pattinson 21–5–73–6; Fletcher 19–2–77–2; Ball 19.1–4–59–2; Mullaney 16–4–48–0; Carter 8–1–36–0. *Second innings*—Pattinson 17–1–67–2; Fletcher 12–1–53–0; Mullaney 18–2–85–1; Ball 12–1–47–1; Patel 5–0–29–0; Carter 12–0–67–1.

Nottinghamshire

B. T. Slater c Robinson b Mulder	34	– c Robinson b Rayner	20
B. M. Duckett lbw b Milnes	33	– c Robinson b Podmore	23
C. D. Nash c Robinson b Podmore	67	– c Robinson b Podmore	7
J. M. Clarke c Robinson b Milnes	12	– lbw b Podmore	0
S. R. Patel lbw b Milnes	52	– c Bell-Drummond b Stewart	6
*S. J. Mullaney b Milnes	13	– lbw b Mulder	11
†T. J. Moores lbw b Stewart	13	– lbw b Milnes	11
J. L. Pattinson c Dickson b Milnes	0	– c Kuhn b Rayner	8
L. J. Fletcher c Dickson b Mulder	3	– c Kuhn b Stewart	18
M. Carter c Dickson b Mulder	6	– c Dickson b Podmore	6
J. T. Ball not out	7	– not out	8
B 4, lb 6, w 1, nb 16	27	Lb 2	2

1/58 (2) 2/74 (1) 3/117 (4) (102.5 overs) 267
4/207 (3) 5/228 (6) 6/243 (5)
7/243 (8) 8/253 (9) 9/255 (7) 10/267 (10)

1/27 (2) 2/43 (3) (60.1 overs) 120
3/43 (4) 4/52 (5)
5/65 (1) 6/73 (6) 7/88 (7)
8/94 (8) 9/101 (10) 10/120 (9)

Podmore 27–8–71–1; Stewart 22–4–64–1; Rayner 10–4–10–0; Milnes 23–2–68–5; Mulder 16.5–7–35–3; Denly 4–1–9–0. *Second innings*—Podmore 16–5–41–5; Milnes 6–2–20–0; Stewart 9.1–2–12–2; Mulder 9–2–18–1; Rayner 16–12–13–2; Denly 4–2–14–0.

Umpires: N. A. Mallender and S. J. O'Shaughnessy.

KENT v WARWICKSHIRE

At Canterbury, June 30–July 3. Drawn. Kent 10pts, Warwickshire 9pts. Toss: Kent. First-class debut: J. C. Wainman. County debut: B. W. M. Mike.

With six frontline bowlers injured or unavailable, Warwickshire were forced to play two loanees in Toby Lester (from Lancashire) and Ben Mike (Leicestershire), and give a first-class debut to James Wainman, a 26-year-old left-armer from Yorkshire. Kent took advantage of the inexperience, and of a Canterbury featherbed. After Dickson had put on 132 with Crawley, he and Bell-Drummond added 197 for the third wicket, both eventually falling in the 160s to Wainman. Patel bowled cannily, though he suffered late punishment from Robinson and Stewart, and his only wicket prompted the declaration at 585 for seven. Life was no easier for Kent's more settled attack:

DOMINIC SIBLEY v KENT

Since joining Warwickshire in 2017, Dominic Sibley has (usually) enjoyed batting against Kent:

Runs	Balls	Mins	4	Cumulative Average		
1	17	31	–	1.00	at Tunbridge Wells	2018
104	258	356	9	52.50	at Tunbridge Wells	2018
119	287	383	12	74.66	at Birmingham.	2018
132	315	400	15	89.00	at Birmingham.	2019
5	19	32	1	72.20	at Birmingham.	2019
244	491	640	34	100.83	at Canterbury	2019
605	1,387	1,842	71	100.83		

Rhodes and Sibley began with 221, a Warwickshire first-wicket record in this fixture, and Sibley ground resolutely on. When he reached 175, he became the first to 1,000 first-class runs, beating Glamorgan's Marnus Labuschagne by a couple of minutes (though Sibley's total included the MCC–Surrey match at Dubai in March). The game was condemned to stalemate long before Sibley swept Bell-Drummond to short fine leg for a career-best 244. It was his seventh hundred for Warwickshire, with four coming against Kent, and – at 640 minutes – the eighth-longest in Championship history. Warwickshire's innings was their second-longest, after 222 overs against Yorkshire at Birmingham in 1929.

Close of play: first day, Kent 338-2 (Dickson 146, Bell-Drummond 68); second day, Warwickshire 142-0 (Rhodes 70, Sibley 60); third day, Warwickshire 400-3 (Sibley 207, Hose 18).

Kent

Z. Crawley lbw b Rhodes	72	D. I. Stevens c Hain b Patel.	4
S. R. Dickson c Patel b Wainman	161		
J. L. Denly c Patel b Lamb	22	B 8, lb 7, w 1, nb 26	42
D. J. Bell-Drummond c Ambrose			
b Wainman .	166	1/132 (1) (7 wkts dec, 144.1 overs)	585
*H. G. Kuhn c sub (A. G. Oxley) b Wainman	17	2/186 (3) 3/383 (2)	
†O. G. Robinson c Rhodes b Lester	78	4/427 (5) 5/513 (4)	
G. Stewart not out	23	6/569 (6) 7/585 (8)	110 overs: 410-3

O. P. Rayner, H. W. Podmore and M. E. Milnes did not bat.

Lester 23–3–104–1; Mike 19–1–88–0; Rhodes 20–7–50–1; Wainman 23–4–112–3; Lamb 16–1–81–1; Patel 43.1–9–135–1.

Warwickshire

W. M. H. Rhodes c Robinson b Stewart	109	*J. S. Patel not out	29
D. P. Sibley c Kuhn b Bell-Drummond	244		
R. M. Yates c Kuhn b Stevens	3	B 21, lb 9, nb 8	38
S. R. Hain c Robinson b Podmore	40		—
A. J. Hose lbw b Rayner	21	1/221 (1) (7 wkts dec, 218 overs)	574
M. J. Lamb lbw b Stewart	6	2/233 (3) 3/341 (4)	
†T. R. Ambrose run out (Kuhn)	39	4/416 (5) 5/433 (6)	
B. W. M. Mike not out	45	6/457 (2) 7/512 (7) 110 overs: 311-2	

T. J. Lester and J. C. Wainman did not bat.

Podmore 35–4–119–1; Stevens 33–15–52–1; Rayner 43–20–74–1; Milnes 20–4–51–0; Stewart 34–4–120–2; Denly 24–7–56–0; Bell-Drummond 14–1–30–1; Crawley 11–2–33–0; Dickson 4–0–9–0.

Umpires: N. G. B. Cook and B. J. Debenham.

At The Oval, July 7–10. KENT beat SURREY by five wickets.

At Southampton, July 13–16. KENT drew with HAMPSHIRE.

KENT v ESSEX

At Canterbury, August 18–20. Essex won by three wickets. Essex 19pts, Kent 4pts. Toss: uncontested.
In a match of muddle-headed batting, Essex routed Kent for 40 to storm to a dramatic three-day win that kept them top. With the ball moving, though not extravagantly, Sam Cook was persistence incarnate, following up five for 42 with seven for 23; eight of his victims fell lbw, and a ninth was bowled. On a rain-marred opening day, there were few signs of what was to come, even if Kent reached the close at a shaky 125 for six, kept afloat by Bell-Drummond. On the second – also curtailed by the weather – a brisk half-century from Podmore guided them to 226, which looked

LOWEST CHAMPIONSHIP TOTALS BY KENT

32	v Hampshire at Southampton	1952	43	v Surrey at Catford	1895
35	v Sussex at Catford	1894	43	v Essex at Southend	1925
39	v Yorkshire at Sheffield	1936	43	v Middlesex at Lord's	1953
40	**v Essex at Canterbury**	**2019**	43	v Middlesex at Dover	1957
42	v Lancashire at Manchester	1904	45	v Surrey at The Oval	1891
42	v Warwickshire at Birmingham	1925	45	v Gloucestershire at Cheltenham	1956

decisive once Essex were shot out for 114 on the third, with Podmore and Stevens, in his 300th first-class match, doing the damage. The fun and games, though, had hardly started: Kent's second innings lasted a mere 86 minutes as Cook, aided by Mohammad Amir, polished them off in 109 balls; no one reached double figures. Essex added to the tension by losing seven wickets in pursuit of 153, with Lawrence and Bopara both completing pairs, before Wheater's combative, unbeaten 30 saw them over the line. Three mad sessions had seen 26 wickets and 275 runs.
Close of play: first day, Kent 125-6 (Stevens 2, Rayner 4); second day, Essex 32-1 (A. N. Cook 8, Westley 10).

Kent

Z. Crawley b Mohammad Amir	5	– lbw b S. J. Cook	3
S. R. Dickson lbw b S. J. Cook	8	– lbw b S. J. Cook	0
D. J. Bell-Drummond b Mohammad Amir	55	– c Harmer b Mohammad Amir	4
*S. W. Billings lbw b S. J. Cook	1	– c Wheater b Mohammad Amir	0
H. G. Kuhn b S. J. Cook	6	– c Wheater b S. J. Cook	5
†O. G. Robinson b Mohammad Amir	35	– c Westley b S. J. Cook	2
D. I. Stevens lbw b S. J. Cook	6	– lbw b S. J. Cook	4
O. P. Rayner b Mohammad Amir	5	– lbw b S. J. Cook	9
H. W. Podmore not out	54	– lbw b S. J. Cook	0
M. E. Milnes c A. N. Cook b Bopara	31	– b Porter	9
M. E. Claydon c Westley b S. J. Cook	9	– not out	4
B 2, lb 7, nb 2	11		

1/7 (1) 2/23 (2) 3/29 (4)	(80.4 overs) 226	1/0 (2) 2/7 (3) (18.1 overs) 40
4/49 (5) 5/117 (3) 6/118 (6)		3/7 (4) 4/7 (1)
7/128 (8) 8/138 (7) 9/203 (10) 10/226 (11)		5/9 (6) 6/18 (5) 7/19 (7)
		8/23 (9) 9/36 (8) 10/40 (10)

Porter 22–5–61–0; Mohammad Amir 23–6–48–4; S. J. Cook 18.4–5–42–5; Harmer 14–1–46–0; Bopara 3–0–20–1. *Second innings*—Mohammad Amir 7–2–16–2; S. J. Cook 9–2–23–7; Porter 2.1–1–1–1.

Essex

N. L. J. Browne c Rayner b Podmore	6	– c Crawley b Stevens	3
A. N. Cook lbw b Stevens	12	– c Rayner b Milnes	29
T. Westley lbw b Stevens	17	– b Claydon	25
D. W. Lawrence lbw b Podmore	0	– lbw b Milnes	0
R. S. Bopara c Rayner b Podmore	0	– c Robinson b Stevens	0
*R. N. ten Doeschate lbw b Stevens	6	– c Robinson b Claydon	17
†A. J. A. Wheater c Robinson b Podmore	20	– not out	30
S. R. Harmer lbw b Claydon	5	– lbw b Claydon	30
Mohammad Amir c Kuhn b Rayner	28	– not out	4
S. J. Cook c Billings b Rayner	2		
J. A. Porter not out	0		
B 4, lb 8, nb 6	18	B 3, lb 3, w 1, nb 8	15

1/8 (1) 2/40 (2) 3/41 (4)	(47.3 overs) 114	1/5 (1) (7 wkts, 42.1 overs) 153
4/41 (5) 5/49 (3) 6/58 (6)		2/51 (2) 3/51 (4)
7/67 (8) 8/110 (9) 9/110 (7) 10/114 (10)		4/52 (5) 5/82 (3) 6/84 (6) 7/141 (8)

Podmore 18–5–34–4; Stevens 15–8–17–3; Milnes 7–1–24–0; Claydon 4–0–20–1; Rayner 3.3–0–7–2. *Second innings*—Podmore 10–0–46–0; Stevens 14–6–30–2; Milnes 11.1–1–50–2; Claydon 7–1–21–3.

Umpires: P. K. Baldwin and I. D. Blackwell.

At Nottingham, September 10–12. KENT beat NOTTINGHAMSHIRE by 227 runs. *At the age of 43, Darren Stevens becomes the oldest seamer to take ten wickets in a match since 1968.*

At Leeds, September 16–19. KENT beat YORKSHIRE by 433 runs. *Stevens becomes the second-oldest to combine a double-hundred and a five-for in a first-class match.*

KENT v HAMPSHIRE

At Canterbury, September 23–26. Drawn. Kent 6pts, Hampshire 8pts. Toss: uncontested.

In this tussle for third place, Kent's hopes were washed away by the rain that stole the last three days. A soggy draw meant Hampshire noses stayed ahead, and they picked up the bigger cheque. What little action there was – the opening day also lost 29 overs – saw Kent stumble to 147. Abbott had crushed Somerset in the previous game, but now he was outbowled by Barker; Bell-Drummond and Rayner each hit 39. It looked as if Hampshire were heading for a first-innings lead before they traipsed off for bad light on the first evening, but they never had a chance to build on 80 for three. The day after the scheduled finish, Crawley – named in England's tour party for New Zealand on the first day – and Podmore were given their Kent caps.

Close of play: first day, Hampshire 80-3 (Northeast 11, Vince 7); second day, no play; third day, no play.

Kent

Z. Crawley b Abbott	0	H. W. Podmore b Barker	2
D. J. Bell-Drummond lbw b Abbott	39	M. E. Milnes c Holland b Dawson	11
†O. G. Robinson b Barker	2	M. E. Claydon not out	10
*S. W. Billings c McManus b Abbott	1	B 6, lb 1, nb 4	11
H. G. Kuhn c Edwards b Barker	13		
J. M. Cox b Barker	2	1/0 (1) 2/3 (3) 3/4 (4) (43.5 overs) 147
D. I. Stevens lbw b Barker	17	4/25 (5) 5/42 (6) 6/77 (2)
O. P. Rayner c Organ b Edwards	39	7/87 (7) 8/111 (9) 9/129 (8) 10/147 (10)

Abbott 14–3–49–3; Barker 17–3–48–5; Edwards 8–0–31–1; Holland 4–1–12–0; Dawson 0.5–0–0–1.

Hampshire

F. S. Organ lbw b Stevens	12
I. G. Holland c Crawley b Podmore	0
T. P. Alsop lbw b Stevens	40
S. A. Northeast not out	11
*J. M. Vince not out	7
Lb 8, nb 2	10

1/7 (2) 2/56 (1) (3 wkts, 21 overs) 80
3/67 (3)

L. A. Dawson, A. H. T. Donald, †L. D. McManus, K. H. D. Barker, K. J. Abbott and F. H. Edwards did not bat.

Podmore 5–0–28–1; Stevens 10–2–27–2; Milnes 6–1–17–0.

Umpires: B. J. Debenham and I. J. Gould.

LANCASHIRE

Great Dane provides fearsome bite

PAUL EDWARDS

Lancashire were comfortably the best team in Division Two in 2019. Their success owed everything to good cricket, and nothing to the fickle breeze of fortune: neither the weather nor an asymmetric fixture list eased their progress to the title. If anything, they could feel a trifle hard done by. Had not water got under the covers at Cheltenham in May, or rain spoiled the games against Leicestershire and Worcestershire in June, Lancashire's third promotion in seven years might have been secured well before the second week in September. As it was, a third successive innings victory clinched their main objective, and the division title followed a week later with the defeat of Middlesex. They were 45 points ahead of the pack, claiming eight wins to the five apiece by Northamptonshire and Gloucestershire, who were promoted with them. At no point did they come near to losing a four-day game.

There was sufficient reason to think the squad would thrive on their return to the top tier but, should standards falter, Dane Vilas will be asking some questions. Lancashire's new captain combined leadership with inspiration. He played in every game across all formats, and scored 1,036 first-class runs, over 400 more than any team-mate; he also took on the wicketkeeping duties for most of the season after Alex Davies broke his finger at Lord's in the first Championship match. Directors of cricket and coaches can sign players, encourage them and dish out rollickings, but it is the captain who establishes and maintains his team's approach. From the moment of his appointment, Vilas looked a fine choice. His value was reinforced during the draft for The Hundred, when he was a surprise pick for Manchester Originals at £125,000, the top bracket. It was a savage irony that his one clanger – the decision to bowl Liam Livingstone in the 19th over of the Vitality Blast quarter-final against Essex – probably cost his team the match, and an appearance at finals day. Typically, Vilas admitted his error.

Lancashire's seam attack were perhaps the best in either division: they dropped only one of a possible 42 bowling points. Freed of international calls early in the season, James Anderson took 30 wickets in six matches, before injury at Sedbergh wrecked his summer. Graham Onions, who turned 37 in September, took 45 batsmen in ten and remained an admirable influence on his colleagues, no doubt colouring Lancashire's decision to offer him a 12-month contract extension. Richard Gleeson was the leading wicket-taker with 47. Despite a knee injury, Tom Bailey confirmed his reputation, while Saqib Mahmood's 21 wickets earned him a place on England's tour of New Zealand. But the crucial factor was that the presence of five quicker bowlers allowed players to be rested, with negligible loss of bite: none of the quintet appeared in more than ten games. This advantage should be reinforced by the signing of Luke Wood from Nottinghamshire.

Neither Lancashire's spin bowling nor their batting was as impressive – though there were many occasions when, once the quick bowlers had completed their work, there was little for the twirlers to do. Australia's Glenn Maxwell was available either side of the World Cup, but six of his 14 first-class wickets were taken in the opening game, against Middlesex. Leg-spinner Matt Parkinson played only four Championship matches, three in

Nathan Stirk, Getty Images

Dane Vilas

September; however, his penetration and control in bagging 20 wickets – plus his more regular white-ball performances – convinced the England selectors to take him on tour.

Several of Lancashire's batsmen performed adequately but, even taking account of the four matches affected by the weather, only Vilas could be completely happy with his return, prompting the decision to sign New Zealand's B-J. Watling for the first nine Championship games of 2020. Rob Jones was the second-highest scorer with 624 runs, thanks to a number of resolute efforts, sometimes when partnering his captain. Vilas aside, Josh Bohannon was the only batsman who averaged over 50; his aggregate included a big century against Derbyshire, which some thought Lancashire's innings of the year.

The heart-warming surprise of the summer came from ex-skipper Steven Croft. Aged 34, he scored 1,235 runs in all formats; his 516 at 73 in the Royal London One-Day Cup helped his side reach the semi-final, where they lost to Hampshire. Croft had not been sure his services would be required in 2019, but at the end of the season he was given a further two-year contract.

Haseeb Hameed's contract talks were apparently much briefer, and had a less happy outcome. A fluent century against Middlesex in April had raised hopes he might be rediscovering the form which had excited team-mates and critics in 2016, but the next 14 first-class innings brought only one fifty. News of his release broke during the Headingley Test, where many had once imagined Hameed would be playing. In November, he signed for Nottinghamshire, and departed with the good wishes of all at Old Trafford.

Two of Lancashire's home venues attracted controversy, although the visit to Cumbrian town Sedbergh for a Championship game won over all but the doctrinaire critics, and the decision to take their Blast quarter-final to Chester-le-Street made the best of a tricky situation when it clashed with the Ashes Test at Old Trafford in early September. Paul Allott, the director of cricket, received plenty of flak for these and other choices. But, when the season was over, he and coach Glen Chapple could look back on a successful year, and be cautiously sanguine about the prospects for the next.

Championship attendance: 23,152.

LANCASHIRE RESULTS

All first-class matches – Played 14: Won 8, Drawn 6.
County Championship matches – Played 14: Won 8, Drawn 6.

Specsavers County Championship, winners of Division 2;
Vitality Blast, quarter-finalists; Royal London One-Day Cup, semi-finalists.

COUNTY CHAMPIONSHIP AVERAGES, BATTING AND FIELDING

Cap		Birthplace	M	I	NO	R	HS	100	Avge	Ct/St
2018	D. J. Vilas††	Johannesburg, SA	14	17	4	1,036	266	2	79.69	47/1
	J. J. Bohannon	Bolton‡	11	12	3	472	174	1	52.44	4
2010	S. J. Croft	Blackpool‡	11	12	2	472	78	0	47.20	4
2017	L. S. Livingstone	Barrow-in-Furness	11	14	1	599	114	1	46.07	7
	R. P. Jones	Warrington	14	19	2	624	122	1	36.70	11
2017	A. L. Davies	Darwen‡	10	14	1	468	147	1	36.00	6
2018	†K. K. Jennings	Johannesburg, SA	14	21	2	588	97	0	30.94	17
2016	H. Hameed	Bolton‡	10	15	3	341	117	1	28.41	5
2018	T. E. Bailey	Preston‡	9	10	0	207	68	0	20.70	5
2019	G. J. Maxwell¶	Melbourne, Aust	4	5	0	96	59	0	19.20	3
	S. Mahmood	Birmingham	9	10	2	136	34	0	17.00	0
	†J. S. Lehmann¶	Melbourne, Aust	3	4	0	35	22	0	8.75	0
	R. J. Gleeson	Blackpool‡	9	8	4	34	11	0	8.50	2
2018	G. Onions	Gateshead	10	10	1	65	18	0	7.22	1
2003	†J. M. Anderson§	Burnley‡	6	6	2	25	9*	0	6.25	4
2019	M. W. Parkinson	Bolton‡	4	4	0	19	14	0	4.75	3

Also batted: J. A. Burns¶ (*Brisbane, Australia*) (1 match) 10; B. D. Guest (*Manchester‡*) (1 match) 17, 11 (5 ct); L. J. Hurt (*Preston‡*) (1 match) 38; D. J. Lamb (*Preston‡*) (1 match) 49; S. D. Parry (*Manchester‡*) (cap 2015) (1 match) 0.

‡ *Born in Lancashire.* § *ECB contract.* ¶ *Official overseas player.* †† *Other non-England-qualified.*

BOWLING

	Style	O	M	R	W	BB	5I	Avge
J. M. Anderson	RFM	159.4	61	281	30	5-18	2	9.36
M. W. Parkinson	LB	143.5	33	381	20	6-23	1	19.05
G. Onions	RFM	306.1	66	881	45	5-38	3	19.57
R. J. Gleeson	RFM	273.1	61	948	47	6-43	5	20.17
G. J. Maxwell	OB	109.5	27	287	14	5-40	1	20.50
T. E. Bailey	RFM	289.2	81	777	37	5-41	3	21.00
L. S. Livingstone	LB	135.1	42	249	10	2-17	0	24.90
S. Mahmood	RFM	196.3	31	660	21	4-48	0	31.42

Also bowled: J. J. Bohannon (RFM) 109.4–20–365–5; S. J. Croft (RFM/OB) 26–6–60–1; A. L. Davies (RM) 1–0–6–0; L. J. Hurt (RFM) 25–6–66–0; K. K. Jennings (RM) 26–3–68–1; R. P. Jones (LB) 5–1–18–0; D. J. Lamb (RFM) 26–5–89–6; S. D. Parry (SLA) 55–5–156–5.

LEADING ROYAL LONDON CUP AVERAGES (150 runs/4 wickets)

Batting	Runs	HS	Avge	SR	Ct/St
S. J. Croft	516	110	73.71	94.67	5
J. S. Lehmann	191	77*	63.66	98.45	1
D. J. Vilas	439	166	62.71	119.61	15/1
K. K. Jennings	416	96	41.60	81.09	9
J. J. Bohannon	156	55*	31.20	96.29	1
R. P. Jones	186	65	31.00	83.40	6
H. Hameed	168	65	24.00	75.00	2

Bowling	W	BB	Avge	ER
S. Mahmood	28	6-37	18.50	5.42
L. J. Hurt	5	2-24	26.80	5.36
M. W. Parkinson	12	5-51	36.33	5.65
G. J. Maxwell	8	3-42	37.12	5.62
J. M. Anderson	6	3-21	37.83	4.31
G. Onions	9	2-39	48.22	6.00

LEADING VITALITY BLAST AVERAGES (100 runs/15 overs)

Batting	Runs	HS	Avge	SR	Ct/St
G. J. Maxwell	305	79	38.12	**150.99**	8
D. J. Vilas	259	46	32.37	**146.32**	4/4
L. S. Livingstone	273	70	27.30	**135.14**	2
A. L. Davies	307	80*	38.37	**127.91**	5
S. J. Croft	247	94	27.44	**126.66**	8
K. K. Jennings	119	35	29.75	**106.25**	2

Bowling	W	BB	Avge	ER
G. J. Maxwell	6	3-23	33.00	**6.60**
M. W. Parkinson	21	4-30	14.61	**7.48**
L. S. Livingstone	14	3-21	15.35	**7.67**
R. J. Gleeson	9	2-13	26.22	**7.86**
J. P. Faulkner	11	3-36	28.54	**7.88**
S. Mahmood	8	3-33	27.50	**8.80**

FIRST-CLASS COUNTY RECORDS

Highest score for	424	A. C. MacLaren v Somerset at Taunton	1895
Highest score against	315*	T. W. Hayward (Surrey) at The Oval	1898
Leading run-scorer	34,222	E. Tyldesley (avge 45.20)	1909–36
Best bowling for	10-46	W. Hickton v Hampshire at Manchester	1870
Best bowling against	10-40	G. O. B. Allen (Middlesex) at Lord's	1929
Leading wicket-taker	1,816	J. B. Statham (avge 15.12)	1950–68
Highest total for	863	v Surrey at The Oval	1990
Highest total against	707-9 dec	by Surrey at The Oval	1990
Lowest total for	25	v Derbyshire at Manchester	1871
Lowest total against	20	by Essex at Chelmsford	2013

LIST A COUNTY RECORDS

Highest score for	**166**	**D. J. Vilas v Nottinghamshire at Nottingham**	**2019**
Highest score against	186*	C. G. Greenidge (West Indians) at Liverpool	1984
Leading run-scorer	11,969	N. H. Fairbrother (avge 41.84)	1982–2002
Best bowling for	6-10	C. E. H. Croft v Scotland at Manchester	1982
Best bowling against	8-26	K. D. Boyce (Essex) at Manchester	1971
Leading wicket-taker	480	J. Simmons (avge 25.75)	1969–89
Highest total for	**406-9**	**v Nottinghamshire at Nottingham**	**2019**
Highest total against	**417-7**	**by Nottinghamshire at Nottingham**	**2019**
Lowest total for	59	v Worcestershire at Worcester	1963
Lowest total against	52	by Minor Counties at Lakenham	1998

TWENTY20 COUNTY RECORDS

Highest score for	103*	A. N. Petersen v Leicestershire at Leicester	2016
Highest score against	108*	I. J. Harvey (Yorkshire) at Leeds	2004
Leading run-scorer	**3,408**	**S. J. Croft (avge 29.12, SR 123.43)**	**2006–19**
Best bowling for	5-13	S. D. Parry v Worcestershire at Manchester	2016
Best bowling against	6-19	T. T. Bresnan (Yorkshire) at Leeds	2017
Leading wicket-taker	117	S. D. Parry (avge 24.94, ER 7.17)	2009–18
Highest total for	231-4	v Yorkshire at Manchester	2015
Highest total against	211-5	by Derbyshire at Derby	2017
Lowest total for	91	v Derbyshire at Manchester	2003
Lowest total against	53	by Worcestershire at Manchester	2016

ADDRESS

Emirates Old Trafford, Talbot Road, Manchester M16 0PX; 0161 282 4000; enquiries@lancashire-cricket.co.uk; www.lancashirecricket.co.uk.

OFFICIALS

Captain D. J. Vilas
Director of cricket P. J. W. Allott
Head coach G. Chapple
Performance director/asst head coach M. J. Chilton
Academy director G. Yates

President Sir Howard Bernstein
Chairman D. M. W. Hodgkiss
Chief executive D. Gidney
Head groundsman M. Merchant
Scorer C. Rimmer

At Loughborough, April 5–7. LANCASHIRE drew with LOUGHBOROUGH MCCU.

At Lord's, April 11–14. LANCASHIRE beat MIDDLESEX by seven wickets.

LANCASHIRE v NORTHAMPTONSHIRE

At Manchester, May 14–17. Lancashire won by ten wickets. Lancashire 21pts, Northamptonshire 3pts. Toss: Lancashire. County debuts: J. A. Burns; T. Bavuma, J. Overton.

Gleeson achieved a maiden ten-wicket haul, against the club to which he owed his county career; he had joined his native Lancashire in September after four seasons at Northamptonshire. He justified Vilas's decision to bowl with five on the opening day, then dismissed four ex-colleagues in 15 balls of a hostile second-innings spell. That left them eight down and 35 behind, so Vilas claimed the extra half-hour in the hope of a three-day win. Northamptonshire were bowled out, but had inched ahead; Lancashire needed 16 on the final morning, and got there in 16 deliveries. They were clearly impressed by Luke Wood, on loan to Northamptonshire from Nottinghamshire; he had made a battling half-century, before his left-arm swing claimed his first five-wicket return in the Championship, and in August he signed a three-year contract bringing him to Old Trafford. But he could not prevent Lancashire building a 185-run lead. Jennings and Vilas scored 97 apiece, Jones hit 67 and Bailey a career-best 68. Burns made his only appearance for Lancashire before returning to Australia because of post-viral fatigue.

Close of play: first day, Lancashire 29-1 (Jennings 16, Burns 6); second day, Lancashire 276-6 (Vilas 30, Bailey 42); third day, Northamptonshire 200.

Northamptonshire

†R. S. Vasconcelos c Vilas b Gleeson	23	– c Croft b Bailey	22
R. I. Newton lbw b Gleeson	32	– (7) b Gleeson	4
*A. G. Wakely c Vilas b Gleeson	2	– c Hameed b Gleeson	14
T. Bavuma lbw b Onions	39	– c Vilas b Bailey	15
R. I. Keogh lbw b Gleeson	3	– c Vilas b Gleeson	42
J. J. Cobb c Jones b Bailey	0	– lbw b Gleeson	30
L. A. Procter c Jennings b Gleeson	48	– (2) c Jennings b Onions	15
L. Wood c Bailey b Onions	66	– b Livingstone	14
J. Overton lbw b Onions	6	– b Gleeson	0
N. L. Buck b Onions	0	– not out	32
B. W. Sanderson not out	6	– c Jones b Livingstone	6
Lb 5	5	B 2, lb 4	6
	230		**200**

1/38 (1) 2/44 (3) 3/87 (2) (78.2 overs) 230
4/101 (5) 5/102 (6) 6/119 (4)
7/189 (7) 8/209 (9) 9/209 (10) 10/230 (8)

1/34 (1) 2/54 (3) (61.4 overs) 200
3/54 (2) 4/87 (4)
5/140 (6) 6/143 (5) 7/150 (7)
8/150 (9) 9/192 (8) 10/200 (11)

Bailey 14–2–46–1; Mahmood 14–1–46–0; Gleeson 19–2–63–5; Onions 16.2–3–45–4; Livingstone 15–3–25–0. *Second innings*—Bailey 19–7–35–2; Mahmood 13–1–64–0; Onions 10–3–28–1; Gleeson 14–4–50–5; Livingstone 5.4–1–17–2.

Lancashire

K. K. Jennings c Vasconcelos b Sanderson	97	– not out	4
H. Hameed c Vasconcelos b Sanderson	7	– not out	13
J. A. Burns c Vasconcelos b Wood	10		
R. P. Jones lbw b Wood	67		
L. S. Livingstone b Wood	0		
*†D. J. Vilas c and b Wood	97		
S. J. Croft c Vasconcelos b Overton	8		
T. E. Bailey b Buck	68		
S. Mahmood not out	27		
G. Onions c Buck b Wood	8		
R. J. Gleeson lbw b Keogh	0		
B 8, lb 14, nb 4	26		

1/19 (2) 2/36 (3) 3/188 (1)   (149.4 overs) 415   (no wkt, 2.4 overs) 17
4/189 (5) 5/198 (4) 6/209 (7)
7/335 (8) 8/400 (6) 9/414 (10)
10/415 (11)   110 overs: 272-6

Sanderson 28–8–56–2; Overton 24–2–86–1; Wood 27–6–72–5; Buck 25–9–49–1; Keogh 27.4–4–79–1; Procter 15–4–40–0; Cobb 3–1–11–0. *Second innings*—Procter 1.4–0–12–0; Cobb 1–0–5–0.

Umpires: P. K. Baldwin and R. T. Robinson.

LANCASHIRE v WORCESTERSHIRE

At Manchester, May 20–22. Lancashire won by six wickets. Lancashire 20pts, Worcestershire 3pts. Toss: Lancashire. Championship debut: C. J. Ferguson.

Again, Vilas chose to field, and his pace attack vindicated him. But Worcestershire's own seamers were on song, and they might have won had a hamstring injury not prevented Parnell from bowling second time round. On the first morning, Anderson and Onions reduced the visitors to 38 for seven, before two fifty partnerships hoisted them towards 172. Parnell featured in both, then struck three times as Lancashire limped to 88 for five. But next day Livingstone and Vilas added 98, helping them to a 29-run advantage that appeared more significant once Worcestershire collapsed again, to 99 for seven. After another useful innings from Parnell, Lancashire's pursuit of 126 was in trouble at 32 for four, until Vilas and the unflappable Jones secured victory. It was the first time since 1995 that Lancashire had won their opening three Championship games; they supplanted Worcestershire as division leaders. Gleeson collected his third five-wicket haul in four innings, and Lehmann became the third Australian to make his first-class debut for Lancashire in three matches, following Glenn Maxwell and Joe Burns.

Close of play: first day, Lancashire 88-5 (Livingstone 17); second day, Worcestershire 149-9 (Leach 5).

Worcestershire

D. K. H. Mitchell c Jennings b Onions	1	– c Jones b Anderson	6
T. C. Fell lbw b Onions	1	– lbw b Gleeson	40
G. H. Rhodes b Anderson	1	– b Bailey	26
C. J. Ferguson lbw b Anderson	8	– c Livingstone b Gleeson	0
M. H. Wessels lbw b Anderson	6	– lbw b Gleeson	0
R. A. Whiteley b Onions	10	– b Anderson	5
†O. B. Cox c Vilas b Gleeson	32	– lbw b Bailey	19
E. G. Barnard c Livingstone b Anderson	0	– b Livingstone	18
W. D. Parnell b Bailey	63	– c Vilas b Gleeson	25
*J. Leach c Vilas b Anderson	36	– c Anderson b Gleeson	9
C. A. J. Morris not out	3	– not out	1
Lb 7, nb 2	9	Lb 5	5

1/3 (1) 2/6 (2) 3/6 (3)   (58.5 overs) 172   1/8 (1) 2/50 (3)   (70.2 overs) 154
4/14 (5) 5/21 (4) 6/37 (6)   3/54 (4) 4/58 (5)
7/38 (8) 8/90 (7) 9/149 (10) 10/172 (9)   5/77 (2) 6/81 (6) 7/99 (7)
    8/141 (8) 9/149 (9) 10/154 (10)

Anderson 17–5–25–5; Onions 16–2–52–3; Gleeson 13–0–56–1; Bailey 12.5–2–32–1. *Second innings*—Anderson 21–6–39–2; Onions 12–6–24–0; Bailey 13.3–4–39–2; Gleeson 17.2–6–37–5; Livingstone 6.3–1–10–1.

Lancashire

K. K. Jennings c Fell b Leach	3	– b Leach		23
H. Hameed lbw b Morris	29	– c Wessels b Morris		4
J. S. Lehmann c Wessels b Parnell	8	– lbw b Barnard		5
R. P. Jones c Mitchell b Parnell	25	– not out		31
L. S. Livingstone b Parnell	69	– c Wessels b Leach		0
J. M. Anderson lbw b Parnell	4			
*†D. J. Vilas b Parnell	39	– (6) not out		60
S. J. Croft c Mitchell b Morris	0			
T. E. Bailey c Barnard b Morris	2			
G. Onions c Leach b Morris	4			
R. J. Gleeson not out	1			
Lb 11, nb 6	17	B 4		4

1/10 (1) 2/21 (3) 3/56 (2)   (65.2 overs) 201   1/8 (2)   (4 wkts, 42.2 overs) 127
4/82 (4) 5/88 (6) 6/186 (7)   2/30 (3) 3/32 (1)
7/187 (8) 8/191 (9) 9/195 (5) 10/201 (10)   4/32 (5)

Leach 17–5–34–1; Morris 16.2–2–52–4; Parnell 22–9–47–5; Barnard 10–0–57–0. *Second innings*—Leach 12–3–29–2; Morris 12–5–30–1; Barnard 12–2–36–1; Whiteley 5–1–18–0; Rhodes 1.2–0–10–0.

Umpires: B. J. Debenham and P. J. Hartley.

At Cheltenham, May 27–30. LANCASHIRE drew with GLOUCESTERSHIRE.

LANCASHIRE v LEICESTERSHIRE

At Liverpool, June 3–6. Drawn. Lancashire 13pts, Leicestershire 9pts. Toss: uncontested. First-class debut: H. J. Swindells.

Aigburth's first four-day match since 2014 saw Lancashire frustrated by rain and obdurate Leicestershire batting, led by Horton, their former opener, who had learned much of his cricket nearby. Livingstone's first Championship century for nearly two years laid the foundations for a substantial total; Bohannon and Bailey added 131 for the eighth wicket, though Bohannon was stranded two short of a maiden century just before lunch on the second day. Rain prevented further play until the following morning, when Leicestershire struggled to 82 for five. Cosgrove and debutant keeper Harry Swindells put on 50, then Klein and Callum Parkinson (twin of Lancashire's Matt) shared their own eighth-wicket century stand. But they could not save the follow-on, and nightwatchman-opener Wright fell to Onions by the close. The final morning was delayed, and Lancashire's attempt to force a win was defied by Horton and Azad, who both defended for around three hours. With Livingstone bowling 63 overs of leg-spin in the match for 85 runs, at one stage the over-rate read +18.

Close of play: first day, Lancashire 347-7 (Bohannon 41, Bailey 29); second day, Lancashire 449; third day, Leicestershire 5-1 (Horton 3, Parkinson 2).

Lancashire

K. K. Jennings run out (Azad)	0	G. Onions c Mohammad Abbas b Wright	2
H. Hameed c Swindells b Klein	30	R. J. Gleeson c Swindells b Klein	11
J. S. Lehmann b Klein	22		
R. P. Jones c Swindells b Mohammad Abbas	11	B 5, lb 8, nb 6	19
L. S. Livingstone c Cosgrove b Dexter	114		
*†D. J. Vilas c Swindells b Mohammad Abbas	34	1/0 (1) 2/46 (3) (119.3 overs) 449
S. J. Croft b Parkinson	51	3/55 (2) 4/84 (4) 5/128 (6)
J. J. Bohannon not out	98	6/264 (5) 7/283 (7) 8/414 (9)
T. E. Bailey c Dexter b Wright	57	9/418 (10) 10/449 (11) 110 overs: 410-7

Mohammad Abbas 27–3–93–2; Wright 30–2–117–2; Klein 26.3–5–89–3; Dexter 22–6–69–1; Parkinson 11–0–51–1; Ackermann 3–0–17–0.

Leicestershire

M. H. Azad lbw b Onions	4	– (4) c Vilas b Croft		39
*P. J. Horton c and b Bailey	11	– b Livingstone		49
N. J. Dexter c Jennings b Bailey	1	– (5) lbw b Onions		27
M. J. Cosgrove lbw b Onions	70	– (6) not out		5
C. N. Ackermann c Vilas b Gleeson	17	– (7) not out		6
H. E. Dearden c Jennings b Livingstone	2			
†H. J. Swindells c Jennings b Livingstone	37			
C. F. Parkinson lbw b Gleeson	37	– (3) c Livingstone b Gleeson		15
D. Klein lbw b Gleeson	87			
C. J. C. Wright not out	9	– (1) b Onions		0
Mohammad Abbas c Vilas b Gleeson	0			
B 1, lb 10, nb 2	13	B 1, lb 3, w 1, p 5		10

1/13 (1) 2/16 (3) 3/17 (2)   (98 overs) 288   1/1 (1)   (5 wkts, 98 overs) 151
4/61 (5) 5/82 (6) 6/132 (4)   2/30 (3) 3/87 (2)
7/150 (7) 8/269 (8) 9/288 (9) 10/288 (11)   4/134 (4) 5/140 (5)

Bailey 24–5–79–2; Onions 18–1–59–2; Gleeson 22–8–58–4; Bohannon 7–0–36–0; Livingstone 27–9–45–2. *Second innings*—Gleeson 15–6–34–1; Onions 21–7–28–2; Bailey 11–3–16–0; Livingstone 36–17–40–1; Bohannon 6–3–7–0; Croft 9–2–17–1.

Umpires: N. L. Bainton and R. J. Warren.

At Worcester, June 10–13. LANCASHIRE drew with WORCESTERSHIRE.

At Derby, June 17–19. LANCASHIRE beat DERBYSHIRE by ten wickets.

LANCASHIRE v DURHAM

At Sedbergh, June 30–July 3. Drawn. Lancashire 11pts, Durham 9pts. Toss: uncontested.

Lancashire's enterprise in visiting the Cumbrian fells (or, as others pointed out, the Yorkshire Dales National Park) was rewarded by a compelling match in handsome surroundings. There were queues outside the gates of the school ground on the first morning, and plenty of support at a venue equidistant from Manchester and Chester-le-Street. Thanks to Vilas and Jones, Lancashire scored a competitive 337 before Bancroft and Lees replied with a stand of 70, Durham's first opening partnership above 14 in a dozen attempts since early April. Bancroft was eventually bowled by Anderson for 77, halting a duel to be resumed, briefly, at the Edgbaston Test. In his next over Anderson took his 950th first-class wicket – Clark, lbw – but on the third morning he suffered the calf injury which would limit him to four overs in the Ashes. Rimmington's uncomplicated hitting reduced Durham's deficit to 56; he then completed career-best match figures of eight for 116, but not before a second half-century from Vilas set up a target of 304 in 79 overs, a task Durham never seriously attempted. Bancroft's unbeaten 92 ensured a deserved draw, though, and may have added to his enthusiasm for Sedbergh: "It's like a postcard wherever you look."

Close of play: first day, Lancashire 275-5 (Vilas 67, Croft 29); second day, Durham 199-5 (Trevaskis 24, Rimmington 1); third day, Lancashire 204-7 (Vilas 74, Mahmood 11).

Lancashire

K. K. Jennings b Rushworth	11	– c Eckersley b Rushworth	0
A. L. Davies c Eckersley b Carse	38	– c Harte b Rimmington	15
H. Hameed c Bancroft b Raine	24	– c Bancroft b Rushworth	0
L. S. Livingstone lbw b Rimmington	35	– c Bancroft b Raine	35
R. P. Jones lbw b Rushworth	52	– run out (Trevaskis)	5
*†D. J. Vilas c Rimmington b Rushworth	72	– c and b Rimmington	85
S. J. Croft c Bancroft b Carse	42	– b Rimmington	35
J. J. Bohannon not out	33	– c Eckersley b Carse	22
S. Mahmood lbw b Rimmington	2	– not out	31
G. Onions c Eckersley b Rimmington	0	– c Eckersley b Raine	0
J. M. Anderson c Clark b Rimmington	4	– b Rimmington	0
B 1, lb 15, nb 8	24	B 4, lb 13, nb 2	19

1/24 (1) 2/72 (2) 3/81 (3) (116.5 overs) 337
4/141 (4) 5/228 (5) 6/293 (7)
7/293 (6) 8/305 (9) 9/313 (10)
10/337 (11)

1/0 (1) 2/0 (3) (78.3 overs) 247
3/51 (2) 4/55 (4)
5/59 (5) 6/146 (7) 7/174 (8)
8/229 (6) 9/236 (10) 10/247 (11)

Rushworth 27–5–61–3; Carse 25–7–82–2; Rimmington 25.5–6–74–4; Raine 24–3–62–1; Harte 11–3–27–0; Trevaskis 3–0–14–0; Burnham 1–0–1–0. *Second innings*—Rushworth 17–5–53–2; Carse 19–1–68–1; Raine 19–4–45–2; Rimmington 16.3–5–42–4; Harte 3–0–13–0; Trevaskis 2–0–2–0; Clark 1–0–6–0; Burnham 1–0–1–0.

Durham

*C. T. Bancroft b Anderson	77	– not out	92
A. Z. Lees c Anderson b Mahmood	16	– b Mahmood	0
G. J. Harte b Onions	14	– b Mahmood	0
J. T. A. Burnham c Anderson b Livingstone	26	– b Mahmood	20
G. Clark lbw b Anderson	0	– b Bohannon	26
L. Trevaskis c Vilas b Onions	38	– c Jones b Onions	3
N. J. Rimmington lbw b Onions	53		
†E. J. H. Eckersley lbw b Onions	3	– (7) b Mahmood	20
B. A. Raine c Croft b Jennings	5	– (8) not out	19
B. A. Carse not out	1		
C. Rushworth c Vilas b Onions	6		
B 4, lb 13, w 5, nb 20	42	Lb 3, w 5, nb 6	14

1/70 (2) 2/136 (3) 3/136 (1) (104.5 overs) 281
4/136 (5) 5/197 (4) 6/263 (6)
7/269 (8) 8/274 (7) 9/274 (10) 10/281 (11)

1/7 (2) 2/11 (3) (6 wkts, 75 overs) 194
3/39 (4) 4/108 (5)
5/117 (1) 6/149 (7)

Anderson 18.2–7–39–2; Onions 31.5–6–93–5; Mahmood 24–2–59–1; Livingstone 11–5–21–1; Jennings 7–2–8–1. *Second innings*—Onions 17–3–38–2; Mahmood 19–2–58–3; Jennings 11–1–34–0; Bohannon 19–3–44–1; Croft 7–2–15–0; Jones 2–1–2–0.

Umpires: S. J. O'Shaughnessy and P. R. Pollard.

At Northampton, July 7–10. LANCASHIRE drew with NORTHAMPTONSHIRE.

LANCASHIRE v SUSSEX

At Manchester, July 13–15. Lancashire won by an innings and 51 runs. Lancashire 23pts, Sussex 1pt. Toss: Sussex.

Lancashire's former captain, Jack Bond, died two days before this game, and was remembered in a minute's silence on the first morning. A one-sided match was all but decided by the close, with Sussex bowled out for 127 on a blameless pitch, before Lancashire ran up a 22-run lead with nine wickets in hand. All the visiting batsmen had fallen to spinners Parkinson and Maxwell, with Parkinson collecting a career-best six for 23 on his way to a maiden ten-wicket haul, in his first Championship appearance of 2019. Yet Sussex had been 77 without loss. Their collapse – ten for 50 in 27 overs – reflected a collective lack of confidence. Five of Lancashire's top six passed 50, but only Vilas reached a century, before declaring on the second evening, 367 ahead. When Sussex slumped to 39 for four next morning another humiliation beckoned, but Rawlins tucked into Parkinson's leg-spin and reached a maiden century off 99 balls, only to hit his 100th back to the bowler. This was Hameed's last match for Lancashire before the club announced he would be released at the end of the season.

Close of play: first day, Lancashire 149-1 (Jennings 53, Hameed 4); second day, Sussex 15-0 (Salt 3, Chopra 10).

Sussex

P. D. Salt c Bohannon b Maxwell	40	– b Parkinson	37
V. Chopra lbw b Parkinson	32	– c Vilas b Gleeson	15
L. W. P. Wells c and b Maxwell	5	– lbw b Onions	0
S. van Zyl c Jones b Parkinson	5	– c Vilas b Gleeson	6
*†B. C. Brown c Vilas b Maxwell	4	– c Hameed b Onions	4
D. M. W. Rawlins c Croft b Maxwell	0	– c and b Parkinson	100
D. Wiese lbw b Parkinson	4	– lbw b Parkinson	77
C. J. Jordan not out	21	– c Vilas b Gleeson	11
W. A. T. Beer lbw b Parkinson	0	– not out	29
A. Sakande c Bohannon b Parkinson	7	– c Vilas b Onions	15
Mir Hamza b Parkinson	0	– lbw b Parkinson	0
B 4, lb 3, nb 2	9	B 8, lb 6, nb 8	22

1/77 (1) 2/77 (2) 3/87 (3)   (46.2 overs) 127   1/20 (2) 2/25 (3)   (69.1 overs) 316
4/87 (4) 5/88 (6) 6/95 (5)   3/34 (4) 4/39 (5)
7/95 (7) 8/95 (9) 9/123 (10) 10/127 (11)   5/117 (1) 6/245 (6) 7/266 (7)
                                      8/284 (8) 9/315 (10) 10/316 (11)

Gleeson 8–2–40–0; Onions 6–2–16–0; Maxwell 17–6–41–4; Parkinson 15.2–5–23–6. *Second innings*—Gleeson 17–2–62–3; Parkinson 27.1–2–142–4; Onions 8–2–18–3; Maxwell 16–2–68–0; Jones 1–0–12–0.

Lancashire

K. K. Jennings c Rawlins b Mir Hamza	65
A. L. Davies c Brown b Rawlins	72
H. Hameed lbw b Wiese	11
G. J. Maxwell c Salt b Sakande	59
R. P. Jones b Beer	88
†D. J. Vilas not out	132
S. J. Croft b Brown b Beer	31
B 16, lb 11, w 1, nb 8	36

1/132 (2)   (6 wkts dec, 136.2 overs) 494
2/166 (1) 3/184 (3) 4/277 (4)
5/371 (5) 6/494 (7)   110 overs: 370-4

J. J. Bohannon, G. Onions, R. J. Gleeson and M. W. Parkinson did not bat.

Mir Hamza 18–6–49–1; Jordan 4–1–16–0; Wiese 16–1–47–1; Sakande 20–3–89–1; Wells 22–1–92–0; Beer 24.2–5–76–2; Rawlins 32–5–98–1.

Umpires: T. Lungley and A. G. Wharf.

At Colwyn Bay, August 18–20. LANCASHIRE beat GLAMORGAN by an innings and 150 runs.

LANCASHIRE v DERBYSHIRE

At Manchester, September 10–12. Lancashire won by an innings and 45 runs. Lancashire 23pts, Derbyshire 3pts. Toss: Derbyshire.

Bohannon's much praised maiden hundred was the highlight of a victory that confirmed Lancashire's promotion. Recently moved up to No. 3, he advanced to 174, and his 199-run stand with Livingstone – compiled mostly on the second day, when Jennings was the only wicket to fall – was the county's biggest of the season. On the first, Godleman had reached his century off 180 balls, a fact relayed with relish by PA announcer John Gwynne, who also commentates on darts. It was Derbyshire's first Championship hundred against Lancashire since Chris Adams, Karl Krikken and Dean Jones all hit one in the same match in 1996. Meanwhile, Gleeson took four in six overs to break the back of the batting. After the alliance between Bohannon and Livingstone, Vilas helped build a match-winning lead, and passed 1,000 Championship runs for the season. Derbyshire were reasonably placed at tea on day three, on 49 for two, but collapsed against the spinners; the game ended deep into a damp evening, when Rampaul skyed a swipe at Parkinson to Vilas.

Close of play: first day, Lancashire 20-1 (Jennings 12, Bohannon 4); second day, Lancashire 269-2 (Bohannon 150, Livingstone 70).

Derbyshire

L. M. Reece c Vilas b Maxwell	20	– b Bailey		6
*B. A. Godleman lbw b Mahmood	111	– lbw b Bailey		10
W. L. Madsen lbw b Gleeson	27	– c Livingstone b Bailey		28
J. L. du Plooy b Gleeson	2	– c Livingstone b Maxwell		15
A. L. Hughes c Vilas b Gleeson	0	– c Gleeson b Maxwell		33
†H. R. Hosein lbw b Gleeson	0	– b Maxwell		12
M. J. J. Critchley lbw b Bailey	22	– b Parkinson		1
F. J. Hudson-Prentice b Gleeson	18	– run out (Davies)		12
A. K. Dal b Mahmood	0	– st Vilas b Parkinson		1
Hamidullah Qadri not out	17	– not out		0
R. Rampaul c Parkinson b Mahmood	14	– c Vilas b Parkinson		0
B 4, lb 7, nb 2	13	B 8, lb 1, nb 2		11

1/66 (1) 2/107 (3) 3/111 (4)   (78.4 overs) 244   1/12 (1) 2/37 (2)   (51 overs) 129
4/121 (5) 5/123 (6) 6/181 (7)   3/53 (3) 4/69 (4)
7/211 (2) 8/211 (9) 9/215 (8) 10/244 (11)   5/110 (6) 6/113 (7) 7/125 (5)
                                                               8/129 (8) 9/129 (9) 10/129 (11)

Bailey 18–6–47–1; Gleeson 22–4–64–5; Mahmood 11.4–2–45–3; Maxwell 19–6–46–1; Parkinson 8–0–31–0. *Second innings*—Bailey 7–2–14–3; Gleeson 6–1–34–0; Mahmood 1–0–4–0; Maxwell 18–5–39–3; Parkinson 18–7–28–3; Livingstone 1–0–1–0.

Lancashire

K. K. Jennings b Hamidullah Qadri	38	M. W. Parkinson lbw b Critchley		1
A. L. Davies c Madsen b Rampaul	4	R. J. Gleeson not out		2
J. J. Bohannon c Madsen b Hudson-Prentice	174			
L. S. Livingstone c Hosein b Rampaul	71	B 4, lb 3		7
G. J. Maxwell b Rampaul	0			
R. P. Jones b Dal	37	1/12 (2) 2/75 (1) (127.4 overs) 418
*†D. J. Vilas c Hosein b Dal	51	3/274 (4) 4/274 (5) 5/298 (3)
T. E. Bailey run out (Dal)	26	6/365 (7) 7/401 (8) 8/411 (6)
S. Mahmood lbw b Dal	7	9/414 (10) 10/418 (9) 110 overs: 378-6

Reece 28–7–70–0; Rampaul 19–7–47–3; Hamidullah Qadri 16–1–70–1; Critchley 23–1–79–1; Hudson-Prentice 18–2–73–1; Dal 17.4–2–60–3; du Plooy 5–1–11–0; Hughes 1–0–1–0.

Umpires: I. D. Blackwell and J. H. Evans.

LANCASHIRE v MIDDLESEX

At Manchester, September 16–19. Lancashire won by 104 runs. Lancashire 21pts, Middlesex 4pts (after 2pt penalty). Toss: uncontested.

Lancashire were confirmed as Division Two champions at 4.30 on the first day, when Northamptonshire earned only one batting point against Durham. But what followed was the prelude to a spirited Middlesex recovery in Old Trafford's finest match of the season. Lancashire's 259 had looked formidable when Bailey took five wickets in 24 deliveries, and the visitors finished the first day on 39 for six. But Middlesex president Mike Selvey took the players out for dinner, and his encouragement and largesse inspired Simpson to oversee a remarkable fightback, including three substantial partnerships with the tail. His career-best 167 not out enabled them to reach 337, and a lead

HIGHEST TOTAL AFTER LOSING FIRST SIX FOR UNDER 40

Total	6th wkt		
337	**34**	**Middlesex v Lancashire at Manchester**	**2019**
308	39	Northamptonshire v Surrey at The Oval	1947
299	35	Somerset v Northamptonshire at Northampton	2001
298	21	Gentlemen of England v Cambridge University at Cambridge.	1886
298	33	Western Province v Border at East London	1966-67
294	16	Nomads v Antonians at Colombo (Vihara Mahadevi)	1994-95
289	36	Somerset v Gloucestershire at Bristol	2003
278	24	Worcestershire v Essex at Clacton-on-Sea	1948
273	29	Leicestershire v Northamptonshire at Leicester	1977
265	31	Surrey v Hampshire at Portsmouth	1978

of 78 after they had begun the day simply hoping to save the follow-on. Despite 97 from Jennings and another half-century from Livingstone, Lancashire were eight down and only 211 ahead before Croft helped them whip up 58 in 59 balls on the final morning. Then Middlesex's top order collapsed again to Bailey and Onions. Though Andersson stood firm for three and a half hours in a maiden fifty, Bailey completed a ten-wicket haul, before Mahmood bowled Andersson – the signal for prolonged celebrations as Bob Dylan's "Hurricane" blared out from the home dressing-room.

Close of play: first day, Middlesex 39-6 (Simpson 4, Harris 5); second day, Lancashire 14-1 (Jennings 7, Mahmood 5); third day, Lancashire 289-8 (Croft 7, Parkinson 1).

Lancashire

K. K. Jennings lbw b Cummins	22 – b Sowter	97
A. L. Davies c Simpson b Harris	16 – c Harris b Cummins	0
J. J. Bohannon c Simpson b Roland-Jones	19 – (4) lbw b Roland-Jones	28
L. S. Livingstone lbw b Bamber	84 – (5) c Simpson b Bamber	68
R. P. Jones b Harris	11 – (6) c Sowter b Cummins	16
†D. J. Vilas b Malan b Cummins	0 – (7) lbw b Bamber	2
S. J. Croft not out	55 – (8) b Harris	40
T. E. Bailey c Cummins b Sowter	9 – (9) c Malan b Cummins	4
S. Mahmood lbw b Harris	6 – (3) c Simpson b Cummins	34
M. W. Parkinson lbw b Sowter	0 – c Simpson b Roland-Jones	14
G. Onions lbw b Sowter	13 – not out	4
B 1, lb 5, w 2, nb 16	24	B 14, lb 8, nb 18	40

1/49 (2) 2/49 (1) 3/88 (3)	(75.2 overs) 259	1/1 (2) 2/75 (3)	(102.5 overs) 347
4/126 (5) 5/129 (6) 6/182 (4)		3/126 (4) 4/253 (1)	
7/203 (8) 8/228 (9) 9/229 (10) 10/259 (11)		5/265 (5) 6/271 (7) 7/276 (6)	
		8/282 (9) 9/325 (10) 10/347 (8)	

Bamber 16–4–49–1; Roland-Jones 16–3–51–1; Harris 15–3–59–3; Cummins 13–3–52–2; Sowter 15.2–3–42–3. *Second innings*—Cummins 21–4–77–4; Roland-Jones 28–5–86–2; Sowter 17–4–58–1; Bamber 20–6–53–2; Harris 12.5–4–31–1; Holden 4–1–20–0.

Middlesex

S. D. Robson c Vilas b Onions	8	– (2) lbw b Onions	14
N. R. T. Gubbins c Vilas b Bailey	5	– (1) b Bailey	1
M. D. E. Holden c and b Bailey	5	– lbw b Bailey	0
*D. J. Malan c Vilas b Bailey	0	– c Bailey b Onions	0
M. K. Andersson lbw b Bailey	4	– b Mahmood	83
M. L. Cummins lbw b Bailey	2	– (10) c Vilas b Bailey	9
†J. A. Simpson not out	167	– (6) lbw b Parkinson	5
J. A. R. Harris b Parkinson	32	– (7) c Vilas b Bailey	38
T. S. Roland-Jones c Onions b Parkinson	32	– (8) lbw b Bailey	5
N. A. Sowter c Livingstone b Mahmood	52	– (9) c Jennings b Parkinson	1
E. R. Bamber b Jennings b Parkinson	7	– not out	1
B 2, lb 9, nb 12	23	B 4, lb 4	8

1/15 (1) 2/15 (2) 3/15 (4)   (103.2 overs) 337   1/2 (1) 2/2 (3)   (61.2 overs) 165
4/23 (5) 5/27 (6) 6/34 (3)   3/3 (4) 4/40 (2)
7/141 (8) 8/217 (9) 9/311 (10) 10/337 (11)   5/55 (6) 6/136 (7) 7/142 (8)
                                                8/143 (9) 9/154 (10) 10/165 (5)

Bailey 32–9–78–5; Onions 24–2–117–1; Mahmood 17–3–63–1; Livingstone 10–3–19–0; Parkinson 20.2–5–49–3. *Second innings*—Bailey 14–2–41–5; Onions 12–4–13–2; Mahmood 6.2–2–23–1; Parkinson 24–4–56–2; Livingstone 5–0–24–0.

Umpires: N. J. Llong and S. J. O'Shaughnessy.

At Leicester, September 23–26. LANCASHIRE drew with LEICESTERSHIRE. *Lancashire end the season unbeaten.*

LEICESTERSHIRE

In the bleak midsummer

R**ICHARD** R**AE**

Leaving Hove on April 8, Leicestershire players and long-suffering supporters were entitled to be cheerful, even optimistic. Sussex, among the pre-season promotion favourites, had been beaten by seven wickets, the promising all-rounder Tom Taylor had taken ten wickets and, on his Championship debut, Hassan Azad had looked a seriously good prospect at No. 3. Mohammad Abbas, who took 50 Championship wickets in 2018, was yet to arrive.

But hope can be cruel. The severe financial constraints under which Leicestershire operate meant head coach Paul Nixon and his staff needed everything to go in their favour. Individual form, injuries and key moments of fortune on the field had to align for the county to have a chance of competing. They did not align – and while spirit was rarely lacking, there was a grim inevitability about finishing bottom of every table.

There were no more wins in the Championship, although in May a first victory at Lord's for 39 years looked assured, until rain and bad light rescued Middlesex. Pressing for victory cost Leicestershire dear: Taylor exacerbated a back condition, and needed an operation, ruling him out for the summer.

Deprived of a wicket-taking seamer, Leicestershire desperately needed Abbas to repeat his feats of the previous season. Unfortunately, the nip and sharp movement that made him so dangerous in 2018 had deserted him. He made the valid points that a reduced seam, the weather and the pitches made life more challenging. Twenty-nine wickets in nine matches was still a reasonable return, but his demeanour suggested fatigue was also a factor. He had been playing without a decent break for two years.

It was just as well that Chris Wright, having moved from Warwickshire because he wanted more bowling, proved as resilient and consistent as his new employers had hoped. He bowled more than 420 Championship overs, taking 47 wickets at 30. The back-up seamers were less reliable, however. Will Davis, formerly of Derbyshire, took 23 wickets in ten matches. At times, he was dangerous; at others, disconcertingly innocuous. Gavin Griffiths, who made great progress in 2018, managed nine in four. Troubled by a long-standing shoulder problem, Neil Dexter rarely looked like beating the bat. In the circumstances, left-armer Dieter Klein was unfortunate to play just six matches. Spin rarely figured in captain Paul Horton's plans. When it did, the part-time off-breaks of Colin Ackermann were deemed good enough, with slow left-armer Callum Parkinson often omitted.

With the wonderful exception of Azad, Leicestershire's batting became alarmingly brittle. Time and again, good starts were wasted. Mark Cosgrove and Ackermann made 13 half-centuries between them, but turned only one into a hundred, Cosgrove's magnificent match-saving innings against

Hassan Azad

Durham at Chester-le-Street in August. Nor did others develop as hoped: Harry Dearden made a single half-century in 19 Championship innings, while wicketkeeper Lewis Hill lost his place to the 20-year-old Harry Swindells.

Azad, who graduated from Loughborough in midsummer with a first-class master's in chemical engineering, was frequently left holding up an end, and did so with admirable sangfroid, accumulating 1,189 runs at 54, the second-highest Championship tally in the country after Warwickshire's Dominic Sibley. Azad made three centuries (all against Gloucestershire) and eight fifties. His technique may not be expansive, but he has the ability to play the ball late, along with limitless determination, concentration and bravery. In some of his earlier innings, he occasionally got into a tangle against the short ball, which resulted in most pace attacks trying to bounce him out. He was not fazed, and appeared to be the ideal red-ball opener.

As might be expected from a team guided by Nixon, Leicestershire's one glimpse of success came in the T20 Blast. Despite not having an overseas player, they were fourth in the North Group with three games to play. But they lost all three, to send them slithering to the bottom of the table, which hardly reflected a gutsy effort. The only consolation came against Warwickshire, when a packed – and astonished – Grace Road saw Ackermann become the first player anywhere to take seven wickets in a T20 match. Qualification was never a possibility in the Royal London One-Day Cup. Just two wins, one in a dead match, meant the competition was euphemistically described as a "learning experience".

Off the field, the end-of-season picture was just as bleak. In August, the club had to ask the ECB for a £300,000 loan to cover repayments due on debts understood to be over £2m. That was followed in December by news that the city council had agreed to loan the county £1.75m. It appears unlikely an overseas player will be affordable in the near future. Departures from the playing staff included Dexter, Ateeq Javid and Aadil Ali. With scope to strengthen the squad severely limited, Nixon can only hope senior players find form, younger ones make rapid progress – and everyone stays fit.

Championship attendance: 8,994.

LEICESTERSHIRE RESULTS

All first-class matches – Played 15: Won 2, Lost 6, Drawn 7.
County Championship matches – Played 14: Won 1, Lost 6, Drawn 7.

Specsavers County Championship, 10th in Division 2;
Vitality Blast, 9th in North Group; Royal London One-Day Cup, 9th in North Group.

COUNTY CHAMPIONSHIP AVERAGES, BATTING AND FIELDING

Cap		Birthplace	M	I	NO	R	HS	100	Avge	Ct/St
	†M. H. Azad	Quetta, Pakistan	14	26	4	1,189	137	3	54.04	7
2019	C. N. Ackermann††	George, SA	14	25	6	675	70*	0	35.52	19
2015	†M. J. Cosgrove††	Elizabeth, Aust.	13	23	3	697	107*	1	34.85	2
	G. H. Rhodes	Birmingham	3	6	2	128	61*	0	32.00	1
	N. J. Dexter	Johannesburg, SA	8	12	0	359	180	1	29.91	1
	P. J. Horton	Sydney, Australia	14	26	1	744	100*	1	29.76	11
	T. A. I. Taylor	Stoke-on-Trent	3	4	0	115	57	0	28.75	1
	C. F. Parkinson	Bolton	4	7	0	158	37	0	22.57	0
	D. Klein††	Lichtenburg, SA	6	6	0	122	87	0	20.33	0
	†H. E. Dearden	Bury	13	19	0	375	61	0	19.73	6
	L. J. Hill	Leicester‡	7	11	1	196	67	0	19.60	23/1
	H. J. Swindells	Leicester‡	7	10	0	168	37	0	16.80	12/1
	C. J. C. Wright	Chipping Norton	14	21	3	295	60	0	16.38	3
	W. S. Davis	Stafford	10	17	8	142	39*	0	15.77	1
	A. Javid	Birmingham	4	8	0	113	69	0	14.12	0
	B. W. M. Mike	Nottingham	5	8	1	73	16	0	10.42	0
	G. T. Griffiths	Ormskirk	4	7	0	41	22	0	5.85	1
2018	Mohammad Abbas¶	Sialkot, Pakistan	9	11	3	22	11	0	2.75	4

Also batted: †H. A. Evans (*Bedford*) (1 match) 0, 5*; S. T. Evans (*Leicester‡*) (1 match) 1.

‡ *Born in Leicestershire.* ¶ *Official overseas player.* †† *Other non-England-qualified.*

BOWLING

	Style	O	M	R	W	BB	5I	Avge
T. A. I. Taylor	RFM	98	16	344	14	6-47	1	24.57
Mohammad Abbas	RFM	281.5	81	747	29	4-52	0	25.75
D. Klein	LFM	112	15	467	16	4-113	0	29.18
C. J. C. Wright	RFM	424.2	78	1,455	47	5-30	2	30.95
W. S. Davis	RFM	264.5	59	871	23	4-73	0	37.86
B. W. M. Mike	RFM	104.3	14	486	11	3-41	0	44.18
C. N. Ackermann	OB	180	22	703	12	5-69	1	58.58

Also bowled: M. J. Cosgrove (RM) 17.1–5–36–0; H. E. Dearden (OB) 2–0–13–0; N. J. Dexter (RM) 120.3–25–426–3; H. A. Evans (RFM) 21–3–79–4; G. T. Griffiths (RFM) 110.3–19–380–9; A. Javid (OB) 3–0–8–0; C. F. Parkinson (SLA) 64.4–9–237–5; G. H. Rhodes (OB) 4.4–0–23–0.

LEADING ROYAL LONDON CUP AVERAGES (100 runs/3 wickets)

Batting	Runs	HS	Avge	SR	Ct
C. N. Ackermann	428	152*	61.14	92.04	2
T. A. I. Taylor	242	98*	48.40	113.61	6
H. E. Dearden	304	91	38.00	95.29	0
L. J. Hill	239	148	29.87	121.93	6
C. F. Parkinson	100	39*	25.00	98.03	1
M. J. Cosgrove	184	59	23.00	80.00	3

Bowling	W	BB	Avge	ER
D. Klein	12	4-72	33.66	6.69
Mohammad Abbas	3	2-55	38.00	5.70
C. N. Ackermann	5	3-55	42.00	6.00
G. T. Griffiths	7	3-92	43.00	7.00
T. A. I. Taylor	8	3-57	47.12	5.89

LEADING VITALITY BLAST AVERAGES (100 runs/15 overs)

Batting	Runs	HS	Avge	SR	Ct
A. M. Lilley . . .	248	66	20.66	167.56	10
M. J. Cosgrove . . .	319	45	29.00	134.03	1
L. J. Hill	207	58	20.70	131.01	5
C. N. Ackermann . .	342	58	28.50	127.61	2
H. J. Swindells . . .	175	63	19.44	110.06	3
H. E. Dearden	158	37	17.55	106.04	5

Bowling	W	BB	Avge	ER
C. N. Ackermann . . .	12	7-18	12.41	6.04
C. F. Parkinson	12	2-17	25.75	7.53
G. T. Griffiths	9	3-14	22.22	7.79
A. M. Lilley	3	1-11	46.66	7.85
W. S. Davis	8	3-24	22.87	8.13
D. Klein	5	1-24	61.80	9.96

FIRST-CLASS COUNTY RECORDS

Highest score for	309*	H. D. Ackerman v Glamorgan at Cardiff	2006
Highest score against	355*	K. P. Pietersen (Surrey) at The Oval	2015
Leading run-scorer	30,143	L. G. Berry (avge 30.32)	1924–51
Best bowling for	10-18	G. Geary v Glamorgan at Pontypridd	1929
Best bowling against	10-32	H. Pickett (Essex) at Leyton	1895
Leading wicket-taker	2,131	W. E. Astill (avge 23.18)	1906–39
Highest total for	701-4 dec	v Worcestershire at Worcester	1906
Highest total against	761-6 dec	by Essex at Chelmsford	1990
Lowest total for	25	v Kent at Leicester	1912
Lowest total against {	24	by Glamorgan at Leicester	1971
	24	by Oxford University at Oxford	1985

LIST A COUNTY RECORDS

Highest score for	201	V. J. Wells v Berkshire at Leicester	1996
Highest score against	201*	R. S. Bopara (Essex) at Leicester	2008
Leading run-scorer	8,216	N. E. Briers (avge 27.66)	1975–95
Best bowling for	6-16	C. M. Willoughby v Somerset at Leicester	2005
Best bowling against	6-21	S. M. Pollock (Warwickshire) at Birmingham	1996
Leading wicket-taker	308	K. Higgs (avge 18.80)	1972–82
Highest total for	406-5	v Berkshire at Leicester	1996
Highest total against	458-4	by India A at Leicester	2018
Lowest total for	36	v Sussex at Leicester	1973
Lowest total against {	62	by Northamptonshire at Leicester	1974
	62	by Middlesex at Leicester	1998

TWENTY20 COUNTY RECORDS

Highest score for	113	B. A. Raine v Warwickshire at Birmingham	2018
Highest score against	103*	A. N. Petersen (Lancashire) at Leicester	2016
Leading run-scorer	1,579	M. J. Cosgrove (avge 27.22, SR 132.24)	2015–19
Best bowling for	7-18	C. N. Ackermann v Warwickshire at Leicester . . .	2019
Best bowling against	5-21	J. A. Brooks (Yorkshire) at Leeds	2013
Leading wicket-taker	69	C. W. Henderson (avge 26.95, ER 6.92)	2004–12
Highest total for	229-5	v Warwickshire at Birmingham	2018
Highest total against	255-2	by Yorkshire at Leicester	2019
Lowest total for	90	v Nottinghamshire at Nottingham	2014
Lowest total against	72	by Derbyshire at Derby	2013

ADDRESS

Fischer County Ground, Grace Road, Leicester LE2 8EB; 0116 283 2128; enquiries@leicester-shireccc.co.uk; www.leicestershireccc.co.uk.

OFFICIALS

Captain P. J. Horton
    (Twenty20) C. N. Ackermann
Head coach P. A. Nixon
Academy director A. J. Maiden
President J. Birkenshaw

Chairman M. Duke
Chief executive K. Rothery
Head groundsman A. B. Ward
Scorer P. J. Rogers

LEICESTERSHIRE v LOUGHBOROUGH MCCU

At Leicester, March 26–28. Leicestershire won by an innings and 220 runs. Toss: Leicestershire. First-class debuts: B. J. Bhabra, H. A. Evans, T. S. Haynes, J. S. Kendall, L. P. J. Kimber, A. E. King. County debuts: M. H. Azad, W. S. Davis, A. M. Lilley, C. J. C. Wright.

In an uncomfortably one-sided match, Javid and Azad established a Leicestershire second-wicket record partnership of 309 in 96 overs, before both retired. It surpassed the unbroken 289 between David Gower and Chris Balderstone against Essex at Grace Road in 1981. (It would in turn be broken in June, with Azad, who was still studying at Loughborough, and would play for them in their next first-class match, involved once more.) Only Nick Welch passed 40 for Loughborough in either innings, while Taylor and Will Davis, a seamer from Stafford making his county debut, collected six wickets each.

Close of play: first day, Leicestershire 100-1 (Javid 45, Azad 39); second day, Leicestershire 463-4 (Dexter 69, Hill 4).

Loughborough MCCU

T. S. Haynes b Taylor	13	– c Azad b Wright 6
N. A. Hammond c Hill b Wright	1	– c Horton b Taylor 9
N. R. Welch b Davis	18	– c Taylor b Lilley 44
L. P. J. Kimber b Taylor	19	– lbw b Griffiths 18
*A. D. Tillcock c Hill b Taylor	20	– c Horton b Lilley 0
J. S. Kendall not out	37	– c Hill b Davis 25
†A. E. King c Hill b Wright	7	– c Dearden b Taylor 33
C. W. G. Sanders b Wright	0	– b Davis 0
B. J. Bhabra c Hill b Davis	10	– b Davis 4
W. J. N. Pereira b Davis	0	– lbw b Taylor 0
H. A. Evans lbw b Griffiths	0	– not out 4
B 16, lb 6, nb 6	28	B 1, lb 3, nb 4 8

1/13 (2) 2/21 (1) 3/49 (3) (54.5 overs) 153
4/81 (4) 5/82 (5) 6/113 (7)
7/113 (8) 8/140 (9) 9/140 (10) 10/153 (11)

1/14 (1) 2/36 (2) (56.2 overs) 151
3/80 (3) 4/81 (4)
5/89 (5) 6/135 (6) 7/135 (8)
8/147 (7) 9/147 (9) 10/151 (10)

Wright 13–7–22–3; Taylor 16·5–5–26–3; Davis 11–1–46–3; Griffiths 10.5–3–35–1; Dexter 4–2–2–0. *Second innings*—Wright 13·5–5–24–1; Taylor 13.2–5–40–3; Davis 13–3–37–3; Griffiths 7–2–24–1; Lilley 10–1–22–2.

Leicestershire

A. Javid retired out	143	T. A. I. Taylor not out	10
*P. J. Horton b Sanders	7	B 9, lb 20, w 2, nb 20	51
M. H. Azad retired out	139		
H. E. Dearden c and b Kimber	56	1/19 (2) (5 wkts dec, 151 overs) 524	
N. J. Dexter c King b Bhabra	82	2/328 (1) 3/328 (3)	
†L. J. Hill not out	36	4/453 (4) 5/505 (5)	

A. M. Lilley, C. J. C. Wright, G. T. Griffiths and W. S. Davis did not bat.

Sanders 31–3–123–1; Pereira 25–6–60–0; Evans 26–3–64–0; Tillcock 29–5–95–0; Bhabra 25–4–101–1; Kimber 15–1–52–1.

Umpires: I. N. Ramage and R. T. Robinson.

At Hove, April 5–8. LEICESTERSHIRE beat SUSSEX by seven wickets.

LEICESTERSHIRE v WORCESTERSHIRE

At Leicester, April 11–14. Worcestershire won by an innings and 18 runs. Worcestershire 24pts, Leicestershire 4pts. Toss: Leicestershire. County debut: H. D. Rutherford.

Horton's decision to put Worcestershire in rebounded horribly. On a firm relaid pitch – rated outstanding by both captains – Mitchell, Rutherford and stand-in skipper Cox made hundreds against an attack missing Pakistan seamer Mohammad Abbas, delayed by visa problems. Mitchell was particularly severe on the back-up bowlers, while Rutherford, the New Zealander making his county debut, prospered after surviving a confident appeal for a catch behind off Taylor on 15. It was the first time since 2007, against Surrey at New Road, that three Worcestershire batsmen had scored centuries in the same innings. Their seam quartet then defied a biting east wind to bowl with relentless accuracy. Javid hung around for 12 minutes short of five hours in making 69, while Cosgrove's belligerent 67 included eight boundaries in nine balls off Parnell. But, armed with a lead of 251, Cox enforced the follow-on, paving the way for Morris to collect a career-best seven for 45.

Close of play: first day, Worcestershire 348-4 (Rutherford 116, Whiteley 18); second day, Leicestershire 180-4 (Javid 55, Wright 8); third day, Leicestershire 132-4 (Ackermann 43, Wright 4).

Worcestershire

D. K. H. Mitchell c Horton b Ackermann	114	E. G. Barnard not out		53
T. C. Fell b Davis	28	B 4, lb 23, nb 16		43
B. L. D'Oliveira c Ackermann b Mike	0			—
H. D. Rutherford c Hill b Taylor	123	1/59 (2)	(6 wkts dec, 138.5 overs)	553
M. H. Wessels lbw b Wright	43	2/64 (3) 3/230 (1)		
R. A. Whiteley lbw b Mike	49	4/316 (5) 5/360 (4)		
*†O. B. Cox not out	100	6/408 (6)	110 overs: 405-5	

W. D. Parnell, J. C. Tongue and C. A. J. Morris did not bat.

Wright 29–4–94–1; Taylor 35–4–122–1; Mike 23.5–2–119–2; Davis 25–5–89–1; Ackermann 22–3–93–1; Cosgrove 1–0–1–0; Javid 3–0–8–0.

Leicestershire

A. Javid c Wessels b Parnell	69	– b Morris	5
*P. J. Horton c Mitchell b Tongue	15	– lbw b Morris	20
M. H. Azad lbw b Morris	1	– c Mitchell b Tongue	54
M. J. Cosgrove c D'Oliveira b Barnard	67	– c Fell b Morris	0
C. N. Ackermann b Tongue	5	– c Cox b Whiteley	69
C. J. C. Wright c Rutherford b Barnard	17	– b Tongue	5
H. E. Dearden lbw b Parnell	13	– b Morris	0
†L. J. Hill c Cox b Tongue	31	– c Cox b Morris	0
T. A. I. Taylor c Fell b Tongue	23	– c Whiteley b Morris	57
B. W. M. Mike c Wessels b Barnard	1	– c Fell b Morris	6
W. S. Davis not out	4	– not out	10
B 17, lb 23, nb 16	56	Lb 3, nb 4	7

1/23 (2) 2/24 (3) 3/135 (4)	(91.3 overs) 302	1/6 (1) 2/31 (2)	(87.3 overs) 233
4/160 (5) 5/190 (6) 6/220 (7)		3/31 (4) 4/124 (3)	
7/249 (1) 8/297 (8) 9/298 (9) 10/302 (10)		5/134 (6) 6/135 (7) 7/135 (8)	
		8/194 (5) 9/206 (10) 10/233 (9)	

Tongue 23–4–46–4; Morris 17–5–48–1; Parnell 19–3–106–2; Barnard 23.3–8–40–3; D'Oliveira 9–2–22–0. *Second innings*—Tongue 19–6–46–2; Barnard 15–5–23–0; Morris 19.3–9–45–7; Parnell 13–1–44–0; D'Oliveira 18–6–66–0; Whiteley 3–0–6–1.

Umpires: J. W. Lloyds and P. R. Pollard.

At Leicester, May 1. LEICESTERSHIRE lost to PAKISTANIS by 58 runs (see Pakistan tour section).

At Lord's, May 14–17. LEICESTERSHIRE drew with MIDDLESEX.

LEICESTERSHIRE v DERBYSHIRE

At Leicester, May 27–30. Derbyshire won by 65 runs. Derbyshire 19pts, Leicestershire 3pts. Toss: Derbyshire.

Asked to make 234, Leicestershire were 82 for two and, as head coach Paul Nixon put it, in "complete control". But Cosgrove could not resist Madsen's occasional off-spin, and picked out long-on. Azad battled hard – he faced 226 balls in the match, and was the only home batsman to reach 30 – but Leicestershire's long tail was exposed. After he was dismissed on the last morning, Derbyshire romped to a win that lifted them to second place. Madsen had hit 47, comfortably the highest score in Derbyshire's first innings, then the only half-century of the match (including 11 fours) in the second. Under cloudy skies, on a slow but blameless pitch, Palladino's five-for had helped them secure a slender first-innings advantage. Leicestershire gave themselves a chance by taking eight wickets in the final session of the second day, but it turned out Derbyshire already had enough.

Close of play: first day, Leicestershire 55-4 (Azad 13, Dearden 4); second day, Derbyshire 160-8 (van Beek 1, Palladino 0); third day, Leicestershire 110-4 (Azad 44, Dearden 0).

Derbyshire

L. M. Reece lbw b Klein	12	– c Hill b Davis	20
*B. A. Godleman c Horton b Wright	7	– c Hill b Mohammad Abbas	23
W. L. Madsen lbw b Mohammad Abbas	47	– c Horton b Mohammad Abbas	51
T. C. Lace c Horton b Davis	5	– c and b Wright	21
A. L. Hughes c Hill b Mohammad Abbas	0	– b Wright	2
†H. R. Hosein lbw b Wright	10	– c Hill b Mohammad Abbas	22
M. J. J. Critchley c Ackermann b Mohammad Abbas	8	– c Hill b Klein	0
A. K. Dal c Dearden b Wright	4	– b Davis	5
L. V. van Beek not out	15	– b Klein	26
A. P. Palladino c Azad b Davis	5	– lbw b Wright	11
R. Rampaul c Wright b Klein	7	– not out	14
Lb 8, w 1, nb 10	19	Lb 9, nb 10	19

1/24 (1) 2/24 (2) 3/52 (4)   (50.4 overs) 139
4/63 (5) 5/90 (6) 6/92 (3)
7/102 (7) 8/114 (8) 9/122 (10) 10/139 (11)

1/37 (1) 2/77 (2)   (72.5 overs) 214
3/106 (3) 4/126 (4)
5/127 (5) 6/130 (7) 7/159 (8)
8/159 (6) 9/190 (10) 10/214 (9)

Mohammad Abbas 17–6–38–3; Wright 16–5–39–3; Klein 8.4–2–30–2; Davis 9–3–24–2. *Second innings*—Mohammad Abbas 22–6–58–3; Wright 23–5–71–3; Klein 14.5–2–36–2; Davis 13–4–40–2.

Leicestershire

A. Javid lbw b Palladino	3	– c Hosein b Palladino	5
*P. J. Horton b Palladino	10	– b Rampaul	18
M. H. Azad not out	46	– b Madsen b Reece	44
M. J. Cosgrove c Madsen b Reece	7	– c van Beek b Madsen	28
C. N. Ackermann lbw b Palladino	18	– b Reece	10
H. E. Dearden lbw b Reece	22	– lbw b Reece	14
‡L. J. Hill c Madsen b van Beek	1	– c Hosein b Rampaul	6
D. Klein c Hosein b van Beek	0	– p Critchley b van Beek	5
C. J. C. Wright c Hosein b Palladino	4	– not out	11
W. S. Davis b van Beek	7	– c Hosein b Rampaul	2
Mohammad Abbas c Madsen b Palladino	1	– b Palladino	11
Lb 1	1	B 1, lb 7, nb 6	14

1/13 (2) 2/14 (1) 3/24 (4)   (56.3 overs) 120
4/50 (5) 5/82 (6) 6/85 (7)
7/85 (8) 8/92 (9) 9/107 (10) 10/120 (11)

1/16 (1) 2/24 (2)   (59 overs) 168
3/82 (4) 4/106 (5)
5/123 (3) 6/128 (6) 7/133 (8)
8/149 (7) 9/151 (10) 10/168 (11)

Palladino 18.3–7–29–5; Rampaul 13–4–39–0; Reece 10–2–31–2; van Beek 15–5–20–3. *Second innings*—Palladino 12–3–30–2; Rampaul 14–3–38–3; Reece 17–4–47–3; Madsen 4–0–12–1; van Beek 12–2–33–1.

Umpires: G. D. Lloyd and M. Newell.

At Liverpool, June 3–6. LEICESTERSHIRE drew with LANCASHIRE.

LEICESTERSHIRE v MIDDLESEX

At Leicester, June 10–13. Drawn. Leicestershire 5pts, Middlesex 6pts. Toss: uncontested.

Paul Nixon suggested it was time for a revision of the regulation on uncontested tosses in matches badly hit by the weather, since bowling points are more quickly achievable than batting. Not until 3.10 on the third afternoon did the umpires decide play could begin. Eleven overs were possible, during which Middlesex took three wickets to earn a bonus point, before the rain returned, wiping out the rest of the match.

Close of play: first day, no play; second day, no play; third day, Leicestershire 36-3 (Azad 17, Ackermann 4).

Leicestershire

M. H. Azad not out	. . . .	17
*P. J. Horton run out (Scott)	. . . .	0
S. T. Evans b Murtagh	. . . .	1
M. J. Cosgrove c Malan b Helm	. . . .	13
C. N. Ackermann not out	. . . .	4
Lb 1	. . . .	1
		—
1/7 (2) 2/12 (3) (3 wkts, 11 overs)		36
3/31 (4)		

N. J. Dexter, H. E. Dearden, †H. J. Swindells, D. Klein, C. J. C. Wright and Mohammad Abbas did not bat.

Murtagh 6–1–26–1; Helm 5–2–9–1.

Middlesex

S. D. Robson, S. S. Eskinazi, N. R. T. Gubbins, *D. J. Malan, P. R. Stirling, G. F. B. Scott, †J. A. Simpson, T. S. Roland-Jones, T. G. Helm, S. T. Finn, T. J. Murtagh.

Umpires: U. V. Gandhe and S. J. O'Shaughnessy.

LEICESTERSHIRE v GLOUCESTERSHIRE

At Leicester, June 17–20. Drawn. Leicestershire 11pts, Gloucestershire 12pts. Toss: uncontested.

Batting records tumbled as a lack of depth in both teams' seam resources was glaringly exposed in a game of 1,269 runs and just 20 wickets. Dent's gamble on putting Leicestershire in backfired when Azad and Dexter added 320 in 85 overs for the second wicket, 11 more than the club record established by Ateeq Javid and Azad himself against Loughborough MCCU in April; Dexter went on to a career-best 180. Mohammad Abbas then reduced Gloucestershire to 16 for three, but rain ended the second day early, and on the third Dent and Higgins put on 318, a sixth-wicket record for the fixture, to ease fears. Dent eventually fell for 176, while Higgins's 199 was the highest score by a Gloucestershire No. 7, beating Jack Crapp's 168 against Sussex at Eastbourne in 1936. The last five wickets had added 440, earning an unlikely lead. With a draw inevitable, and Gloucestershire using ten bowlers, Azad and Horton helped themselves to hundreds, Azad becoming the 11th Leicestershire batsman to hit two in a match.

Close of play: first day, Leicestershire 343-5 (Wright 6, Ackermann 0); second day, Gloucestershire 41-3 (Dent 15, Howell 16); third day, Gloucestershire 503-6 (Higgins 196, van Buuren 20).

Leicestershire

M. H. Azad c Roderick b Payne	137	– not out	100
*P. J. Horton c Roderick b Sayers	0	– not out	100
N. J. Dexter c Roderick b Shaw	180		
C. J. C. Wright c Howell b Sayers	6		
M. J. Cosgrove c Roderick b Shaw	1		
W. S. Davis c Dent b Sayers	2		
C. N. Ackermann not out	56		
H. E. Dearden c Roderick b Shaw	21		
†L. J. Hill c van Buuren b Payne	44		
D. Klein lbw b Shaw	12		
Mohammad Abbas b Dent	0		
B 5, lb 9, nb 14	28	B 4, lb 5, nb 2	11

1/6 (2) 2/326 (1) 3/332 (3)   (139.4 overs) 487   (no wkt dec, 56.4 overs) 211
4/336 (5) 5/339 (6) 6/345 (4)
7/391 (8) 8/454 (9) 9/486 (10)
10/487 (11)   110 overs: 380-6

Payne 32–8–96–2; Sayers 27–4–91–3; Shaw 24–6–85–4; Higgins 19–2–87–0; Howell 3–0–12–0; van Buuren 31–6–87–0; Hammond 3–0–14–0; Dent 0.4–0–1–1. *Second innings*— Payne 4–1–21–0; Sayers 6–3–10–0; Shaw 6–0–15–0; van Buuren 10–1–32–0; Higgins 6–0–9–0; Howell 5–0–17–0; Taylor 8–0–39–0; Bracey 7–0–30–0; Hammond 3–0–12–0; Dent 1.4–0–17–0.

Gloucestershire

M. A. H. Hammond c Hill b Mohammad Abbas	4	D. A. Payne not out	18
*C. D. J. Dent b Klein	176	J. Shaw lbw b Klein	9
J. R. Bracey lbw b Mohammad Abbas	4	C. J. Sayers b Klein	3
†G. H. Roderick c Hill b Mohammad Abbas	0	B 6, lb 20, nb 32	58
B. A. C. Howell c Ackermann b Wright	52		
J. M. R. Taylor b Davis	5	1/8 (1) 2/16 (3) 3/16 (4) (137 overs) 571
R. F. Higgins b Wright	199	4/93 (5) 5/131 (6) 6/449 (2)
G. L. van Buuren b Klein	43	7/513 (7) 8/545 (8) 9/559 (10)
		10/571 (11) 110 overs: 458-6

Mohammad Abbas 30–13–66–3; Wright 30–5–114–2; Klein 23–3–113–4; Davis 21–3–83–1; Dexter 18–1–87–0; Ackermann 13–0–69–0; Dearden 2–0–13–0.

Umpires: B. J. Debenham and P. R. Pollard.

At Northampton, June 24–27. LEICESTERSHIRE drew with NORTHAMPTONSHIRE.

LEICESTERSHIRE v DURHAM

At Leicester, July 7–10. Durham won by 119 runs. Durham 19pts, Leicestershire 4pts. Toss: Durham. County debut: J. O. I. Campbell.

In his first game at Grace Road since returning to his native North-East, Raine had a decisive impact on a fluctuating contest. He collected nine wickets, including a second-innings five-for, to complete Durham's third win in five matches, and lift them into the crowded promotion race. Leicestershire, meanwhile, were consigned to the bottom. Wright's first five-wicket haul for them, including his 400th Championship victim, had ensured they dominated the first day. But Rushworth and Raine kept the deficit to 95, giving Durham's batsmen a chance to make amends. Bancroft and Lees put on 187 for the first wicket, and nightwatchman Rimmington reached the nineties. Needing 393, Leicestershire were 160 for three at lunch on the last day, but Raine's dismissal of Azad, caught by Eckersley – another Grace Road old boy – was the catalyst for a collapse.

Close of play: first day, Leicestershire 124-4 (Ackermann 22, Dearden 14); second day, Durham 191-4 (Lees 70, Rimmington 4); third day, Leicestershire 58-1 (Azad 13, Wright 13).

Durham

*C. T. Bancroft c Hill b Mohammad Abbas	36	– b Davis	109
A. Z. Lees lbw b Mohammad Abbas	5	– c Hill b Griffiths	93
G. J. Harte lbw b Wright	18	– (4) lbw b Mohammad Abbas	33
J. T. A. Burnham c Azad b Davis	4	– (5) b Dexter	1
G. Clark c Ackermann b Wright	4	– (6) run out (Ackermann)	21
L. Trevaskis lbw b Dexter	3	– (7) c Horton b Griffiths	64
†E. J. H. Eckersley c Mohammad Abbas b Wright	25	– (8) not out	47
B. A. Raine b Wright	15		
N. J. Rimmington c Horton b Wright	3	– (3) lbw b Mohammad Abbas	92
C. Rushworth lbw b Davis	2		
J. O. I. Campbell not out	0		
Lb 2	2	B 9, lb 9, w 1, nb 8	27

1/11 (2) 2/45 (3) 3/50 (4)   (47.3 overs) 117   1/187 (1)   (7 wkts dec, 128.2 overs) 487
4/55 (5) 5/64 (6) 6/76 (1)   2/258 (2) 3/349 (3)
7/102 (8) 8/114 (9) 9/115 (8) 10/117 (10)   4/350 (5) 5/350 (4) 6/384 (6) 7/487 (7)

Mohammad Abbas 13–7–24–2; Wright 13–5–30–5; Davis 9.3–2–21–2; Dexter 4–1–15–1; Griffiths 8–2–25–0. *Second innings*—Mohammad Abbas 27–7–79–2; Wright 24–2–112–0; Davis 23–6–62–1; Ackermann 26–5–88–0; Griffiths 17.2–0–84–2; Dexter 11–3–44–1.

Leicestershire

M. H. Azad lbw b Raine	14	– c Eckersley b Raine	62
*P. J. Horton b Rushworth	50	– c Eckersley b Rimmington	30
N. J. Dexter c Bancroft b Raine	2	– (4) lbw b Raine	0
M. J. Cosgrove lbw b Raine	21	– (5) b Rushworth	60
C. N. Ackermann not out	62	– (6) c Bancroft b Rimmington	13
H. E. Dearden c Bancroft b Rushworth	18	– (7) lbw b Raine	24
†L. J. Hill lbw b Raine	8	– (8) lbw b Rimmington	1
G. T. Griffiths c Bancroft b Campbell	8	– (9) c Eckersley b Rushworth	22
C. J. C. Wright lbw b Rushworth	13	– (3) lbw b Raine	34
W. S. Davis c Eckersley b Rushworth	8	– not out	0
Mohammad Abbas b Rushworth	0	– c Clark b Raine	1
B 1, lb 5, nb 2	8	B 13, lb 11, nb 2	26

1/32 (1) 2/62 (3) 3/78 (2)   (84.5 overs) 212   1/42 (2) 2/97 (3)   (82.3 overs) 273
4/97 (4) 5/130 (6) 6/148 (7)   3/97 (4) 4/178 (1)
7/179 (8) 8/200 (9) 9/212 (10) 10/212 (11)   5/210 (6) 6/234 (5) 7/235 (8)
                                           8/272 (7) 9/272 (9) 10/273 (11)

Rushworth 24.5–7–55–5; Campbell 17–3–43–1; Rimmington 17–2–59–0; Raine 25–7–49–4; Burnham 1–1–0–0. *Second innings*—Rushworth 19–2–80–2; Raine 21.3–9–47–5; Campbell 11–0–44–0; Rimmington 16–4–44–3; Trevaskis 15–4–34–0.

Umpires: P. K. Baldwin and I. D. Blackwell.

At Cheltenham, July 15–18. LEICESTERSHIRE lost to GLOUCESTERSHIRE by six wickets.

At Chester-le-Street, August 18–21. LEICESTERSHIRE drew with DURHAM.

LEICESTERSHIRE v NORTHAMPTONSHIRE

At Leicester, September 10–13. Northamptonshire won by seven wickets. Northamptonshire 23pts, Leicestershire 6pts. Toss: uncontested. County debuts: H. A. Evans, G. H. Rhodes; G. K. Berg.

Northamptonshire's third successive victory took them second in the table. But the win was not achieved without anxiety: on the first day Azad, who passed 1,000 runs in his first Championship season, and the in-form Cosgrove added 122 for Leicestershire's third wicket. Their hopes of passing 400 faded, however, when Sanderson trimmed Cosgrove's off bail with a beauty, though a career-best unbeaten 61 from George Rhodes in the first match of a loan spell from Worcestershire

EIGHT LBWs IN A FIRST-CLASS INNINGS

Oxford University v Warwickshire at Oxford	1980
Sussex v Essex at Hove	1992
Bengal v Hyderabad at Secunderabad	1997-98
Rajasthan v Uttar Pradesh at Jaipur	2000-01
Kerala v Goa at Palakkad	2008-09
Gloucestershire v Glamorgan at Cardiff	2010
South Australia v Queensland at Adelaide	2010-11
Yorkshire v Northamptonshire at Leeds	2014
Western Australia v Victoria at Alice Springs	2016-17
Pakistan Television v United Bank at Sialkot	2017-18
Leicestershire v Northamptonshire at Leicester	**2019**

ensured they did not fold meekly. An attractive century from Keogh, who put on 148 with Rossington, edged Northamptonshire in front, before their seamers turned the match decisively in their favour. Sanderson completed a pair for Horton, and took his 50th Championship wicket of the season when he removed Dexter, one of eight lbws in the innings. Procter bowled Wright to end the possibility of a world-record nine.

Close of play: first day, Leicestershire 276-8 (Rhodes 51, Davis 0); second day, Northamptonshire 325-7 (Bracewell 7, Berg 4); third day, Northamptonshire 22-0 (Curran 10, Newton 12).

Leicestershire

M. H. Azad b Procter	86	– c Wakely b Berg	6
*P. J. Horton c Wakely b Hutton	0	– lbw b Sanderson	0
C. N. Ackermann c Newton b Berg	16	– lbw b Hutton	60
M. J. Cosgrove b Sanderson	65	– lbw b Hutton	8
G. H. Rhodes not out	61	– lbw b Sanderson	4
N. J. Dexter lbw b Procter	0	– lbw b Sanderson	42
H. J. Swindells lbw b Berg	17	– lbw b Bracewell	0
C. F. Parkinson lbw b Hutton	16	– lbw b Berg	25
*C. J. C. Wright c Curran b Procter	10	– b Procter	20
W. S. Davis run out (Keogh)	22	– lbw b Bracewell	8
H. A. Evans lbw b Hutton	0	– not out	5
B 8, lb 4, w 1, nb 4	17	B 5, lb 4, nb 2	11

1/4 (2) 2/28 (3) 3/150 (4) (105.3 overs) 308 1/0 (2) 2/20 (1) (72.3 overs) 189
4/183 (1) 5/183 (6) 6/224 (7) 3/36 (4) 4/51 (5)
7/246 (8) 8/275 (9) 9/302 (10) 10/308 (11) 5/103 (3) 6/104 (7) 7/155 (8)
8/155 (6) 9/175 (10) 10/189 (9)

Sanderson 24–6–70–1; Hutton 24.3–8–62–3; Bracewell 15–2–64–0; Berg 18–8–43–2; Procter 22–7–54–3; Keogh 2–0–3–0. *Second innings*—Hutton 20–7–40–2; Sanderson 18–5–37–3; Berg 12–4–33–2; Bracewell 13–2–44–2; Procter 5.3–3–8–1; Keogh 4–0–18–0.

Northamptonshire

B. J. Curran c Swindells b Davis	27	– c Ackermann b Davis	40
R. I. Newton b Evans	17	– lbw b Evans	29
A. G. Wakely c Swindells b Evans	37	– not out	44
R. I. Keogh c Rhodes b Davis	132	– c Ackermann b Parkinson	17
R. E. Levi b Wright	19	– not out	11
*†A. M. Rossington c Wright b Evans	63		
L. A. Procter b Ackermann	2		
D. A. J. Bracewell c Cosgrove b Davis	38		
G. K. Berg lbw b Davis	5		
B. A. Hutton c Swindells b Wright	0		
B. W. Sanderson not out	0		
B 4, lb 9, w 2, nb 2	17	Lb 1	1

1/42 (2) 2/63 (1) 3/118 (3) (92.2 overs) 357 1/68 (2) (3 wkts, 39.4 overs) 142
4/156 (5) 5/304 (6) 6/309 (7) 2/87 (1) 3/116 (4)
7/314 (4) 8/338 (9) 9/357 (10) 10/357 (8)

Wright 24–3–92–2; Evans 19–3–65–3; Davis 20.2–5–73–4; Dexter 9–1–32–0; Parkinson 15–2–66–0; Ackermann 5–2–16–1. *Second innings*—Davis 11–4–31–1; Wright 9–0–30–0; Parkinson 14–1–46–1; Evans 2–0–14–1; Rhodes 3.4–0–20–0.

Umpires: P. R. Pollard and B. V. Taylor.

At Cardiff, September 16–19. LEICESTERSHIRE lost to GLAMORGAN by 291 runs.

LEICESTERSHIRE v LANCASHIRE

At Leicester, September 23–26. Drawn. Leicestershire 8pts, Lancashire 8pts. Toss: uncontested. First-class debut: L. J. Hurt.

The loss of more than 200 overs to the weather – including the entire second day – helped Lancashire, already confirmed as Division Two champions, complete the season unbeaten; Leicestershire finished last, with a solitary victory. But there was a sprinkling of individual milestones. Azad's unbeaten 83 in the second innings took his aggregate to 1,189, the best in Division Two (only

OH BROTHER – DISMISSED BY YOUR TWIN

Batsman	*Bowler*		
D. W. Varey	J. G. Varey	Cambridge U v Oxford U at Lord's	1982
R. S. Tillekeratne	D. S. Tillekeratne	Nondescripts v Badureliya at Maggona	2016-17
C. F. Parkinson	**M. W. Parkinson**	**Leicestershire v Lancashire at Leicester**	**2019**
M. W. Parkinson	**C. F. Parkinson**	**Lancashire v Leicestershire at Leicester**	**2019**

Warwickshire's Dom Sibley, in Division One, had more). After taking nine for 100 in the match, Gleeson finished as Lancashire's leading Championship wicket-taker, with 47. On the first day, Lancashire leg-spinner Matt Parkinson learned of his selection for England's tour of New Zealand when twelfth man Mahmood, who was also included, called down from the dressing-room balcony. He celebrated by trapping twin brother Callum leg-before. Two days later, Callum exacted revenge when he dismissed Matt with his left-arm spin – the first time twins had dismissed each other in a first-class game.

Close of play: first day, Lancashire 2-1 (Davies 0, Bohannon 0); second day, no play; third day, Leicestershire 40-0 (Azad 9, Horton 30).

Leicestershire

M. H. Azad c and b Gleeson	9	– not out		83
*P. J. Horton c Jennings b Gleeson	0	– b Gleeson		30
C. N. Ackermann c Livingstone b Gleeson	0	– c Vilas b Gleeson		49
M. J. Cosgrove b Bailey	17	– c Bailey b Gleeson		2
G. H. Rhodes b Gleeson	43	– not out		16
H. E. Dearden b Parkinson	30			
†H. J. Swindells b Gleeson	0			
C. F. Parkinson lbw b Parkinson	29			
B. W. M. Mike c Parkinson b Livingstone	9			
D. Klein b Gleeson	3			
C. J. C. Wright not out	5			
Lb 10	10	B 3, nb 8		11

1/0 (2) 2/9 (1) 3/16 (3)   (67.1 overs) 155   1/40 (2)   (3 wkts dec, 61 overs) 191
4/58 (4) 5/82 (5) 6/82 (7)   2/146 (3) 3/154 (4)
7/118 (6) 8/147 (9) 9/147 (8) 10/155 (10)

Bailey 19–8–38–1; Gleeson 15.1–3–43–6; Hurt 13–4–32–0; Parkinson 18–6–31–2; Livingstone 2–1–1–1. *Second innings*—Bailey 8–0–41–0; Gleeson 18–5–57–3; Bohannon 9–4–29–0; Hurt 12–2–34–0; Parkinson 13–4–21–0; Davies 1–0–6–0.

Lancashire

K. K. Jennings b Wright	0	L. J. Hurt lbw b Parkinson		38
A. L. Davies c Ackermann b Klein	9	M. W. Parkinson lbw b Parkinson		4
J. J. Bohannon c Horton b Mike	20	R. J. Gleeson not out		0
L. S. Livingstone c Swindells b Mike	10	B 4, lb 6, nb 8		18
R. P. Jones b Mike	4			
*†D. J. Vilas b Klein	18	1/0 (1) 2/20 (2) 3/36 (4) (47.3 overs) 170
S. J. Croft b Horton b Klein	44	4/54 (5) 5/67 (3) 6/77 (6)
T. E. Bailey c sub (A. M. Lilley) b Wright	5	7/94 (8) 8/154 (7) 9/165 (10) 10/170 (9)

Wright 16–1–53–2; Klein 15–2–65–3; Mike 12–2–41–4; Cosgrove 1–0–1–0; Parkinson 3.3–3–0–2.

Umpires: J. D. Middlebrook and S. J. O'Shaughnessy.

MIDDLESEX

Captain abandons ship

KEVIN HAND

It was supposed to be a new era, with the no-nonsense Australian Stuart Law taking over as coach – but familiar failings were on display right from the start. Law's stint began with a desperate batting performance at Northampton, where Middlesex were saved by Dawid Malan's unbeaten 160, and a listless home defeat by Lancashire. Things hardly improved, not helped by old grumbles about benign pitches at Lord's. There were only three Championship victories all summer, and Middlesex never pushed for promotion, even with three spots available. They finished a lowly eighth, a drop of four places from 2018.

By the end of Malan's second year as captain, it was one of county cricket's worst-kept secrets that he was off to pastures new, despite having two years left on his contract. Several teams were mentioned in the rumour mill, but he eventually signed for Yorkshire. "I've been banging my head against a wall for a wee while," he said during England's Twenty20 series in New Zealand. He added, pointedly: "I don't want to finish my career just plodding along in county cricket. I want to be somewhere that really wants to challenge to win stuff."

It was a sad end to a Middlesex career which began in 2006. Malan finished with 9,887 first-class runs for the club at 38, with 23 centuries, as well as more than 6,500 in white-ball games. Helped by a career-best 199 against Derbyshire, he had crept past 1,000 in the 2019 Championship season, with Sam Robson not far behind. Wicketkeeper John Simpson came next, after Nick Gubbins and Stevie Eskinazi both had poor red-ball seasons. Simpson hit 167, his highest score, during a remarkable rearguard against Division Two champions Lancashire, not far from his Bury birthplace: Middlesex recovered from 34 for six to reach 337, a lead of 78. But they still lost.

The bowling was once again headed by Tim Murtagh, whose 43 Championship wickets cost only 17 apiece. Toby Roland-Jones had a reasonable comeback after injury, but Steven Finn struggled with various niggles, and managed only 17 wickets in seven Championship outings. Miguel Cummins, the West Indian Test fast bowler, made an impression at the end of the season, and signed a three-year Kolpak deal. Spin, though, was almost non-existent. Ollie Rayner played only two matches before joining Kent on loan, while Nathan Sowter's leg-breaks were more successful in white-ball games.

To replace Malan as batsman and captain, Law signed Peter Handscomb, who had played 16 Tests for Australia, and last season briefly turned out for Durham. England's World Cup-winning captain Eoin Morgan will lead the T20 side. Murtagh, meanwhile, was forced to choose between club and country after an ECB ruling that Ireland internationals would be classified as overseas players from 2020. Murtagh had sent England crashing to 85 all out on the first day of Ireland's Test at Lord's in July but, mindful that his top-level career was winding down (he turned 38 in August), he accepted a two-year deal with Middlesex. Murtagh went some way towards refuting Malan's claims: "I wouldn't have committed my future to Middlesex unless I felt they shared my ambition to win trophies, and we have a huge amount of young talent here. Under the new coaching regime, we've got a harmonious dressing-room that is excited for the new season."

Miguel Cummins

Paul Stirling – nine years younger than Murtagh – went the other way, and stuck with Ireland; he probably deserved more red-ball opportunities than Middlesex gave him. George Scott joined his former team-mate (and fellow all-rounder) Ryan Higgins at Gloucestershire, while the energetic left-arm seamer Tom Barber moved to Nottinghamshire.

There were signs of an upward curve in the shorter formats, but it was gradual – Middlesex reached the quarter-finals of both the Royal London Cup and the Vitality Blast. The Twenty20 campaign did get off to a rollicking start, helped by the sparkling form of A. B. de Villiers, and at Taunton the highest successful run chase in England sealed qualification, for only the second time since they won the competition in 2008. But another woeful batting effort allowed Nottinghamshire to saunter home.

The 50-over campaign also began encouragingly. Law had rejigged the batting order, and was rewarded with six wins out of eight, as Middlesex finished second in their group. Eskinazi and Gubbins did well down the order, sharing an unbroken fifth-wicket stand of 184 to see off Gloucestershire, while Sowter claimed 25 wickets, second only to Lancashire's Saqib Mahmood. Seamer Tom Helm also prospered, with 19.

Group success meant a home quarter-final – but Lancashire racked up 304, and Middlesex were soon in tatters at 24 for five. James Harris led a stirring comeback with a maiden century, putting on 197 with Simpson, but the tail had too much to do. It was a coming-of-age innings for Harris, who batted as high as No. 6 for some of the season, compensating for his loss of penetration with the ball. Max Holden spanked 166 at Canterbury in the last group game – beating Andrew Strauss's 11-year-old county List A record – but that was a rare highlight in his otherwise disappointing season.

Another summer of discontent led to inevitable criticism of Angus Fraser, Middlesex's long-serving director of cricket. He and Law will need to re-energise the squad, or Malan's parting comments could come back to haunt them.

Championship attendance: 40,933.

MIDDLESEX RESULTS

All first-class matches – Played 15: Won 3, Lost 5, Drawn 7.
County Championship matches – Played 14: Won 3, Lost 5, Drawn 6.

Specsavers County Championship, 8th in Division 2;
Vitality Blast, quarter-finalists; Royal London One-Day Cup, quarter-finalists.

COUNTY CHAMPIONSHIP AVERAGES, BATTING AND FIELDING

Cap		Birthplace	M	I	NO	R	HS	100	Avge	Ct/St
2016	P. R. Stirling††	Belfast, N. Ireland	3	4	1	150	138	1	50.00	2
2010	†D. J. Malan	Roehampton‡	13	22	1	1,005	199	4	47.85	17
2011	†J. A. Simpson	Bury	14	22	3	773	167*	2	40.68	35
2013	S. D. Robson	Paddington, Aust.	14	24	1	858	140*	2	37.30	9
2015	J. A. R. Harris	Morriston	9	16	3	435	80	0	33.46	2
2009	S. T. Finn	Watford	7	9	3	155	56	0	25.83	2
2019	T. G. Helm	Stoke Mandeville	7	9	1	187	46	0	23.37	1
2012	T. S. Roland-Jones	Ashford‡	11	17	3	327	54	0	23.35	3
2008	†E. J. G. Morgan‡	Dublin, Ireland	2	4	1	69	36*	0	23.00	0
2016	†N. R. T. Gubbins	Richmond	14	24	0	530	91	0	22.08	3
	G. F. B. Scott	Hemel Hempstead	7	11	1	204	55	0	20.40	3
2018	S. S. Eskinazi††	Johannesburg, SA	12	21	0	403	75	0	19.19	12
	N. A. Sowter††	Penrith, Australia	7	11	1	184	57*	0	18.40	4
	†M. D. E. Holden	Cambridge	9	16	0	218	54	0	13.62	1
2008	†T. J. Murtagh††	Lambeth	11	15	4	149	33	0	13.54	2
2015	O. P. Rayner	Walsrode, Germany	2	4	1	29	28*	0	9.66	2
	†M. L. Cummins¶	St Michael, Barb.	3	5	1	34	22*	0	8.50	3
	R. G. White	Ealing‡	2	4	0	22	10	0	5.50	0
	E. R. Bamber	Westminster‡	5	8	2	30	8	0	5.00	3

Also batted: M. K. Andersson (*Reading*) (2 matches) 4, 83, 8; T. C. Lace (*Hammersmith‡*) (1 match) 51, 4 (10 ct).

‡ *Born in Middlesex.* § *ECB contract.* ¶ *Official overseas player.* †† *Other non-England-qualified.*

BOWLING

	Style	O	M	R	W	BB	5I	Avge
T. J. Murtagh	RFM	295.3	93	757	43	6-51	4	17.60
T. G. Helm	RFM	208	39	600	24	5-36	2	25.00
T. S. Roland-Jones	RFM	302.5	60	963	33	7-52	3	29.18
S. T. Finn	RFM	149.5	25	548	17	5-75	1	32.23
E. R. Bamber	RFM	125	31	381	11	5-93	1	34.63
J. A. R. Harris	RFM	247	41	876	22	4-98	0	39.81
N. A. Sowter	LB	180.4	23	650	14	3-42	0	46.42

Also bowled: M. L. Cummins (RF) 81–19–266–8; S. S. Eskinazi (OB) 2–0–4–0; M. D. E. Holden (OB) 14–1–66–0; D. J. Malan (LB) 42–3–134–4; E. J. G. Morgan (OB) 3–1–4–0; O. P. Rayner (OB) 72–16–183–5; S. D. Robson (LB/RM) 9.5–0–44–2; G. F. B. Scott (RM) 39–6–123–3; J. A. Simpson (OB) 1–0–2–0; P. R. Stirling (OB) 8–0–29–2.

LEADING ROYAL LONDON CUP AVERAGES (150 runs/4 wickets)

Batting	Runs	HS	Avge	SR	Ct/St
N. R. T. Gubbins	417	98*	59.57	106.64	2
S. D. Robson	196	106	49.00	87.11	3
S. S. Eskinazi	327	107*	46.71	106.16	3
M. D. E. Holden	225	166	45.00	98.68	2
G. F. B. Scott	188	63	37.60	138.23	5
D. J. Malan	173	95	34.60	92.02	4
L. R. P. L. Taylor	177	94	29.50	87.19	2
J. A. Simpson	232	74	29.00	111.53	11/3

Bowling	W	BB	Avge	ER
T. J. Murtagh	7	3-24	20.28	3.64
N. A. Sowter	25	6-62	20.84	5.83
T. G. Helm	19	5-71	28.78	6.43
T. S. Roland-Jones	13	3-46	33.53	5.93
J. A. R. Harris	7	4-65	33.85	6.12

LEADING VITALITY BLAST AVERAGES (120 runs/15 overs)

Batting	Runs	HS	Avge	SR	Ct/St
A. B. de Villiers	348	88*	69.60	**182.19**	6
E. J. G. Morgan	341	83*	42.62	**168.81**	1
D. J. Malan	490	117	40.83	**147.59**	3
J. A. Simpson	202	42*	25.25	137.41	5/3
S. S. Eskinazi	256	57*	32.00	131.95	4
P. R. Stirling	223	33	20.27	129.65	1
T. S. Roland-Jones	121	40	24.20	124.74	7

Bowling	W	BB	Avge	ER
Mujeeb Zadran	7	2-31	40.28	**7.23**
N. A. Sowter	16	4-29	27.93	**8.43**
T. S. Roland-Jones	19	5-21	19.89	**8.55**
S. T. Finn	19	5-16	23.84	**9.43**
T. G. Helm	15	3-27	29.60	**9.48**

FIRST-CLASS COUNTY RECORDS

Highest score for	331*	J. D. B. Robertson v Worcestershire at Worcester	1949
Highest score against	341	C. M. Spearman (Gloucestershire) at Gloucester	2004
Leading run-scorer	40,302	E. H. Hendren (avge 48.81)	1907–37
Best bowling for	10-40	G. O. B. Allen v Lancashire at Lord's	1929
Best bowling against	9-38	R. C. Robertson-Glasgow (Somerset) at Lord's	1924
Leading wicket-taker	2,361	F. J. Titmus (avge 21.27)	1949–82
Highest total for	642-3 dec	v Hampshire at Southampton	1923
Highest total against	850-7 dec	by Somerset at Taunton	2007
Lowest total for	20	v MCC at Lord's	1864
Lowest total against {	31	by Gloucestershire at Bristol	1924
	31	by Glamorgan at Cardiff	1997

LIST A COUNTY RECORDS

Highest score for	166	M. D. E. Holden v Kent at Canterbury	**2019**
Highest score against	166	L. J. Wright (Sussex) at Lord's	**2019**
Leading run-scorer	12,029	M. W. Gatting (avge 34.96)	1975–98
Best bowling for	7-12	W. W. Daniel v Minor Counties East at Ipswich	1978
Best bowling against	6-27	J. C. Tredwell (Kent) at Southgate	2009
Leading wicket-taker	491	J. E. Emburey (avge 24.68)	1975–95
Highest total for	380-5	v Kent at Canterbury	**2019**
Highest total against	368-2	by Nottinghamshire at Lord's	2014
Lowest total for	23	v Yorkshire at Leeds	1974
Lowest total against	41	by Northamptonshire at Northampton	1972

TWENTY20 COUNTY RECORDS

Highest score for	129	D. T. Christian v Kent at Canterbury	2014
Highest score against	123	I. A. Cockbain (Gloucestershire) at Bristol	2018
Leading run-scorer	3,318	D. J. Malan (avge 32.85, SR 128.00)	2006–19
Best bowling for	6-28	J. K. Fuller v Hampshire at Southampton	2018
Best bowling against	6-24	T. J. Murtagh (Surrey) at Lord's	2005
Leading wicket-taker	83	S. T. Finn (avge 22.90, ER 8.14)	2008–19
Highest total for	227-4	v Somerset at Taunton	**2019**
Highest total against	254-3	by Gloucestershire at Uxbridge	2011
Lowest total for	92	v Surrey at Lord's	2013
Lowest total against	74	by Essex at Chelmsford	2013

ADDRESS

Lord's Cricket Ground, London NW8 8QN; 020 7289 1300; enquiries@middlesexccc.com; www.middlesexccc.com.

OFFICIALS

Captain 2019 D. J. Malan
2020 P. S. P. Handscomb
(Twenty20) E. J. G. Morgan
Managing director of cricket A. R. C. Fraser
Head coach S. G. Law
Head of youth cricket R. I. Coutts

President M. W. W. Selvey
Chairman M. I. O'Farrell
Secretary/chief executive R. J. Goatley
Head groundsman K. McDermott
Scorer D. K. Shelley

MIDDLESEX v OXFORD MCCU

At Northwood, March 26–28. Drawn. Toss: Oxford MCCU. First-class debuts: Z. Akhter, C. G. Harrison, C. J. McBride, C. J. Searle, L. J. P. Shaw, M. J. Taylor.

It looked like a mismatch: an almost full-strength Middlesex against a university side containing six debutants. But the students worked hard on the first day, when Middlesex managed only a fraction above four an over on a slow pitch, despite a century from Eskinazi and a late burst from Morgan, whose unbeaten 61 included ten fours and a six. Middlesex's seamers, three with Test caps, knocked Oxford over next day for 131, but Malan waived the follow-on; this time, Gubbins reached three figures before retiring, and Simpson got his eye in. Set a notional 448, Oxford might have crumbled after losing four wickets to Murtagh, three in the space of four balls. But Welshman Matt Taylor and the South African-born Calvin Harrison, two of the debutants, put on an unbeaten 85 in 33 overs to earn an honourable draw. The match was played at the Merchant Taylors' School ground, ringed with trees still leafless after the winter.

Close of play: first day, Oxford MCCU 24-2 (Taylor 6, McBride 12); second day, Middlesex 136-2 (Gubbins 71, Harris 2).

Middlesex

S. D. Robson c Shaw b Searle	42	
N. R. T. Gubbins c Pettman b Heathfield	33	– retired out 105
S. S. Eskinazi retired out	125	
*D. J. Malan c Taylor b Harrison	54	
M. D. E. Holden c Adair b Heathfield	9	– (1) b Pettman 0
E. J. G. Morgan not out	61	
†J. A. Simpson not out	18	– (3) b Harrison 62
J. A. R. Harris (did not bat)		– (4) not out 34
T. S. Roland-Jones (did not bat)		– (5) not out 9
B 1, lb 6, nb 16	23	Lb 1, nb 2 3

1/68 (1) 2/96 (2)　　　　　(5 wkts dec, 88 overs) 365　　1/0 (1)　　　(3 wkts dec, 63 overs) 213
3/222 (4) 4/261 (5) 5/325 (3)　　　　　　　　　　　　2/131 (3) 3/194 (2)

S. T. Finn and T. J. Murtagh did not bat.

Pettman 20–4–71–0; Searle 11–0–73–1; Robertson 18–3–58–0; Akhter 16–1–69–0; Heathfield 14–0–57–2; Harrison 9–4–30–1. *Second innings*—Pettman 9–4–9–1; Robertson 8–1–20–0; Akhter 10–0–43–0; Searle 16–6–56–0; Heathfield 9–0–42–0; Harrison 11–1–42–1.

Oxford MCCU

T. D. Heathfield lbw b Murtagh	0	– lbw b Murtagh 47
†J. C. Seward lbw b Roland-Jones	3	– b Murtagh 19
M. J. Taylor b Harris	25	– not out 61
C. J. McBride c Gubbins b Roland-Jones	28	– lbw b Murtagh 0
H. R. D. Adair b Murtagh	6	– c Simpson b Murtagh 0
C. G. Harrison b Murtagh	26	– not out 37
L. J. P. Shaw c Robson b Finn	11	
*T. H. S. Pettman c Eskinazi b Roland-Jones	2	
Z. Akhter not out	11	
W. J. R. Robertson c Simpson b Finn	0	
C. J. Searle c Morgan b Finn	0	
B 6, lb 8, w 3, nb 2	19	B 5, lb 4, nb 4 13

1/0 (1) 2/6 (2) 3/40 (4)　　　　　(54.5 overs) 131　　1/29 (2)　　　(4 wkts, 64 overs) 177
4/51 (5) 5/82 (3) 6/103 (6)　　　　　　　　　　　　2/92 (1) 3/92 (4)
7/105 (8) 8/125 (7) 9/125 (10) 10/131 (11)　　　　4/92 (5)

Murtagh 15–8–26–2; Roland-Jones 15–2–45–4; Finn 12.5–3–20–3; Harris 12–2–26–1. *Second innings*—Murtagh 11–7–9–4; Finn 9–1–32–0; Roland-Jones 11–2–36–0; Harris 14–2–30–0; Holden 9–0–38–0; Robson 5–0–18–0; Malan 5–2–5–0.

Umpires: B. J. Debenham and R. J. Warren.

At Northampton, April 5–8. MIDDLESEX drew with NORTHAMPTONSHIRE.

MIDDLESEX v LANCASHIRE

At Lord's, April 11–14. Lancashire won by seven wickets. Lancashire 22pts, Middlesex 3pts. Toss: uncontested.

Middlesex had avoided defeat in their first match despite following on, but there was no escape against a side including Anderson, making a rare domestic appearance at one of his favourite grounds. Over two innings, he claimed six for 70 from 38 thrifty overs; his first victim (Robson) was his 300th for Lancashire. Middlesex put up little resistance on the first day once Bailey, who finished with five for 67, ended a partnership of 112 between Gubbins and Eskinazi; six wickets went down after tea. Lancashire's openers responded with a stand of 123 against testing seam bowling and, although Jennings fell for 52, Hameed continued to his first Championship century since August 2016, reaching three figures by pulling Roland-Jones for a cathartic six into the Grand Stand. Rob Jones then dropped anchor, lasting 320 minutes and ending a similar drought: his only previous first-class hundred had come in September 2016, also against Middlesex. Murtagh, at 37 a year older than Anderson, took five for 69 from 35 overs as Lancashire amassed 427. Trailing by 162, Middlesex lost Gubbins in the first over on the third evening. Next day they recovered to 146 for four, before Holden and Morgan fell to successive balls from Maxwell, who picked up a maiden five-for with his off-spin in the first of his two stints with Lancashire. Set 39, they lost three, two to the seldom-seen leg-breaks of Robson, who doubled his career tally. After Davies injured his hand on the first morning, Guest made an appearance behind the stumps, and took five catches.

Close of play: first day, Middlesex 236-9 (Roland-Jones 23); second day, Lancashire 267-4 (Jones 55, Vilas 19); third day, Middlesex 68-2 (Robson 41, Harris 0).

Middlesex

S. D. Robson c Maxwell b Anderson	3	– (2) c †Guest b Anderson	63
N. R. T. Gubbins lbw b Bailey	55	– (1) c Maxwell b Anderson	0
S. S. Eskinazi c †Guest b Bailey	75	– lbw b Onions	25
*D. J. Malan c Jennings b Anderson	24	– (5) c †Guest b Maxwell	51
M. D. E. Holden c Jones b Anderson	34	– (6) c Jennings b Maxwell	7
E. J. G. Morgan c Jones b Bohannon	8	– (7) lbw b Maxwell	0
†J. A. Simpson b Maxwell	2	– (8) b Maxwell	17
J. A. R. Harris c †Guest b Bailey	3	– (4) c †Guest b Bohannon	20
T. S. Roland-Jones c Anderson b Bailey	35	– b Anderson	5
S. T. Finn c Jennings b Bailey	4	– not out	3
T. J. Murtagh not out	16	– lbw b Maxwell	0
B 2, lb 4	6	Lb 7, nb 2	9

1/14 (1) 2/126 (2) 3/151 (3)   (100 overs) 265   1/0 (1) 2/68 (2)   (81.5 overs) 200
4/181 (4) 5/199 (6) 6/206 (7)   3/116 (4) 4/116 (2)
7/206 (5) 8/216 (8) 9/236 (10) 10/265 (9)   5/146 (6) 6/146 (7) 7/187 (5)
     8/192 (9) 9/200 (8) 10/200 (11)

Anderson 21–7–41–3; Onions 21–5–74–0; Bailey 24–6–67–5; Bohannon 14–4–41–1; Maxwell 20–4–36–1. *Second innings*—Anderson 17–9–29–3; Bailey 19–6–48–0; Onions 18–5–45–1; Bohannon 11–2–31–1; Maxwell 16.5–4–40–5.

Lancashire

K. K. Jennings c Simpson b Harris	52	– c sub (L. B. K. Hollman) b Murtagh .	8
H. Hameed c and b Malan	117	– not out	13
B. D. Guest b Murtagh	17	– b Robson	11
G. J. Maxwell b Murtagh	1	– c Harris b Robson	5
R. P. Jones lbw b Murtagh	122	– not out	1
*D. J. Vilas lbw b Malan	68		
J. J. Bohannon c Robson b Malan	5		
T. E. Bailey b Murtagh	1		
†A. L. Davies c Simpson b Murtagh	17		
G. Onions b Harris	12		
J. M. Anderson not out	2		
Lb 11, nb 2	13	B 1	1

1/123 (1) 2/150 (3) 3/152 (4)　　(138 overs) 427　1/12 (1)　　(3 wkts, 15 overs) 39
4/231 (2) 5/374 (6) 6/388 (7)　　　　　　　　　　2/26 (3) 3/34 (4)
7/389 (8) 8/404 (5) 9/417 (9)
10/427 (10)　　　　　　　　110 overs: 332-4

Murtagh 35–16–69–5; Roland-Jones 29–3–92–0; Finn 29–2–90–0; Harris 27–2–105–2; Malan 18–2–60–3. *Second innings*—Murtagh 4–1–9–1; Harris 5–0–11–0; Malan 4–0–14–0; Robson 2–0–4–2.

Umpires: M. Burns and B. V. Taylor.

MIDDLESEX v LEICESTERSHIRE

At Lord's, May 14–17. Drawn. Middlesex 11pts, Leicestershire 10pts. Toss: uncontested. County debut: T. C. Lace.

A seesaw encounter might have gone either way on the last day, which started with Leicestershire – all ten wickets intact – needing 267 more for their first Championship victory at Lord's since 1980. But rain permitted only 61 overs, and the game ended in a draw. Despite losing Robson to the first ball of the match – one of four wickets for Mohammad Abbas – Middlesex had the better of the opening two days, making 349 in a consistent batting display. There were three half-centuries, including Scott's first, and 51 from the debutant Tom Lace, recalled from a loan spell at Derby to replace Dawid Malan, who had a groin strain (Eskinazi captained instead). They bowled Leicestershire out for 268, with Rayner's four wickets including his 300th in first-class cricket. Alarm bells sounded when Middlesex dipped to 114 for eight on the third day, only 195 in front, but Simpson and Helm – both dropped early on – put on 85. Next morning, Middlesex spurned chances themselves: Azad was missed twice in single figures, by Robson at slip and Gubbins at midwicket. Later Dearden hoisted to deep midwicket, and survived after Bamber – yelling for the ball while hurtling from mid-on – failed even to reach the catch when two team-mates seemed better placed.

Close of play: first day, Middlesex 325-8 (Scott 52, Helm 17); second day, Leicestershire 257-9 (Wright 6); third day, Leicestershire 38-0 (Javid 6, Horton 28).

Middlesex

S. D. Robson lbw b Mohammad Abbas	0	– (2) c Hill b Taylor	22
M. D. E. Holden c Hill b Mohammad Abbas	41	– (1) c Ackermann b Taylor	5
N. R. T. Gubbins c Mohammad Abbas b Ackermann	75	– c Hill b Wright	36
T. C. Lace c Hill b Mike	51	– c Horton b Wright	4
*S. S. Eskinazi c Hill b Ackermann	33	– c Ackermann b Mohammad Abbas	20
†J. A. Simpson lbw b Mike	18	– not out	59
G. F. B. Scott c Ackermann b Wright	55	– b Wright	3
J. A. R. Harris lbw b Mohammad Abbas	24	– c Hill b Taylor	12
O. P. Rayner lbw b Mohammad Abbas	0	– c Azad b Ackermann	1
T. G. Helm not out	37	– lbw b Mike	46
E. R. Bamber run out (Wright)	1	– lbw b Mike	8
Lb 8, nb 6	14	B 1, lb 2, nb 4	7

1/0 (1) 2/113 (2) 3/131 (3)   (103.3 overs) 349
4/177 (5) 5/228 (4) 6/229 (6)
7/284 (8) 8/284 (9) 9/346 (7) 10/349 (11)

1/9 (1) 2/32 (2)   (74.4 overs) 223
3/48 (4) 4/91 (3)
5/91 (5) 6/94 (7) 7/113 (8)
8/114 (9) 9/199 (10) 10/223 (11)

Mohammad Abbas 30–9–72–4; Wright 25.3–9–77–1; Taylor 6–0–26–0; Mike 17–2–95–2; Ackermann 15–1–53–2; Cosgrove 10–4–18–0. *Second innings*—Mohammad Abbas 19–8–31–1; Taylor 19–3–74–3; Wright 18–4–51–3; Mike 5.4–1–30–2; Ackermann 13–1–34–1.

Leicestershire

A. Javid lbw b Helm	1	– lbw b Harris	12
*P. J. Horton c Rayner b Bamber	43	– lbw b Bamber	36
M. H. Azad b Harris	21	– lbw b Harris	33
M. J. Cosgrove lbw b Rayner	28	– lbw b Rayner	22
C. N. Ackermann c Simpson b Rayner	63	– not out	70
H. E. Dearden c Eskinazi b Rayner	61	– b Helm	21
†L. J. Hill lbw b Harris	14	– not out	7
T. A. I. Taylor c and b Rayner	2		
B. W. M. Mike c Simpson b Helm	5		
C. J. C. Wright b Helm	12		
Mohammad Abbas not out	1		
B 8, lb 7, nb 2	17	B 6, lb 9, w 8, nb 2	25

1/12 (1) 2/62 (3) 3/80 (2)   (89.3 overs) 268
4/113 (4) 5/223 (6) 6/242 (5)
7/246 (7) 8/246 (8) 9/257 (9) 10/268 (10)

1/51 (1)   (5 wkts, 74 overs) 226
2/66 (2) 3/104 (4)
4/154 (3) 5/206 (6)

Helm 21.3–6–62–3; Bamber 18–5–51–1; Harris 23–7–65–2; Rayner 22–5–58–4; Scott 5–1–17–0. *Second innings*—Helm 17–0–62–1; Bamber 15–7–20–1; Harris 20–4–75–2; Rayner 21–6–52–1; Holden 1–0–2–0.

Umpires: I. D. Blackwell and M. J. Saggers.

At Worcester, May 27–30. MIDDLESEX beat WORCESTERSHIRE by 127 runs.

MIDDLESEX v SUSSEX

At Lord's, June 2–5. Sussex won by an innings and 50 runs. Sussex 24pts, Middlesex 2pts. Toss: Middlesex.

The feel-good factor from Middlesex's win at New Road didn't last long: after choosing to bat they were shot out midway through the first day for 138. Only Harris, promoted to No. 6, passed 18 as Wiese recorded his best figures for Sussex. The reliable Murtagh made early inroads in the reply, but van Zyl was unmovable, making 173 in 455 minutes. He put on 177 for the fifth wicket with captain-keeper Brown, who had already taken five catches, and now hit out against the second new ball, completing his third century in consecutive matches. Beer's 50 inflated the lead to an imposing 343 before a declaration late on the second evening. Middlesex survived until stumps, and next day the weather allowed only 20 overs. But the fourth dawned fine, and Sussex secured an innings victory early in the last hour. Robinson led the way, moving the ball both in and out; he finished with seven for 98, and ten in the match. He also helped account for the tenacious Harris, breaking his thumb shortly before Mir Hamza dismissed him for 80. Sussex's 44-year-old coach Jason Gillespie watched the closing stages from the field, as a substitute after injuries to Evans and Salt. Thanks to the World Cup and two Tests, this was Middlesex's last Championship match at Lord's until September.

Close of play: first day, Sussex 169-4 (van Zyl 46, Brown 5); second day, Middlesex 9-0 (Holden 0, Robson 9); third day, Middlesex 61-4 (Gubbins 11, Harris 10).

Middlesex

S. D. Robson c Brown b Robinson	18	– (2) b Robinson	23
M. D. E. Holden c Evans b Wiese	12	– (1) c Wells b Robinson	5
N. R. T. Gubbins c Brown b Mir Hamza	2	– lbw b Wiese	33
*D. J. Malan c Brown b Wiese	15	– c Jordan b Robinson	2
S. S. Eskinazi c Brown b Wiese	6	– c Salt b Robinson	6
J. A. R. Harris not out	38	– c Brown b Mir Hamza	80
†J. A. Simpson c Finch b Wiese	4	– c Jordan b Robinson	76
T. S. Roland-Jones c Brown b Wiese	14	– b Robinson	17
O. P. Rayner lbw b Robinson	0	– not out	28
E. R. Bamber lbw b Robinson	5	– b Robinson	4
T. J. Murtagh b Mir Hamza	10	– c Wells b Mir Hamza	1
B 1, lb 3, nb 10	14	Lb 6, nb 12	18

1/29 (1) 2/37 (3) 3/41 (2)   (43.4 overs) 138
4/52 (4) 5/63 (5) 6/85 (7)
7/101 (8) 8/102 (9) 9/110 (10) 10/138 (11)

1/22 (1) 2/33 (2)   (107.2 overs) 293
3/35 (4) 4/51 (5)
5/109 (3) 6/212 (6) 7/245 (8)
8/288 (7) 9/292 (10) 10/293 (11)

Mir Hamza 9.4–2–35–2; Robinson 16–1–50–3; Wiese 15–7–26–5; Wells 1–0–2–0; Jordan 2–0–21–0. *Second innings*—Robinson 35–10–98–7; Mir Hamza 24.2–6–71–2; Wiese 21–6–58–1; Jordan 15–3–40–0; Wells 6–2–8–0; Beer 6–0–12–0.

Sussex

P. D. Salt b Murtagh	50	O. E. Robinson b Harris	7
L. W. P. Wells lbw b Murtagh	7		
H. Z. Finch lbw b Murtagh	27	Lb 8, nb 2	10
S. van Zyl lbw b Harris	173		
L. J. Evans lbw b Harris	31	1/23 (2) (9 wkts dec, 136.4 overs) 481	
*†B. C. Brown b Roland-Jones	107	2/79 (3) 3/96 (1)	
D. Wiese c Roland-Jones b Harris	18	4/156 (5) 5/333 (6)	
C. J. Jordan b Bamber	1	6/377 (7) 7/381 (8)	
W. A. T. Beer not out	0	8/469 (4) 9/481 (10) 110 overs: 410-7	

Mir Hamza did not bat.

Murtagh 27–6–69–3; Roland-Jones 25–1–116–1; Harris 24.4–0–98–4; Bamber 27–7–96–1; Rayner 29–5–73–0; Robson 4–0–21–0.

Umpires: J. W. Lloyds and J. D. Middlebrook.

At Leicester, June 10–13. MIDDLESEX drew with LEICESTERSHIRE. *Only 11 overs are possible.*

MIDDLESEX v GLAMORGAN

At Radlett, June 16–19. Drawn. Middlesex 12pts, Glamorgan 9pts. Toss: uncontested.

The maiden Championship match at Cobden Hill, in Hertfordshire, was spoiled by the weather, which allowed only 51 overs on the first day and 36 on the last, when afternoon rain prevented a possible Glamorgan run-chase. Hard-working centuries from Robson and Stirling underpinned Middlesex's first innings on a lively surface which had been under the covers for much of the previous week. It was Stirling's second (and higher) Championship century, in his first first-class innings since Ireland's Test against Afghanistan in March. De Lange, in particular, enjoyed little luck: he beat Eskinazi several times, had him dropped at third slip by Hemphrey, and had two confident lbw appeals rejected. Finn, back to something like his rhythmical best, enjoyed the conditions when Glamorgan batted, taking five wickets; he bowled Root with a peach that flattened off and middle stumps. Some late defiance from Cullen and Wagg helped avert the follow-on, before Middlesex tried to build their lead on the fourth morning.

Close of play: first day, Middlesex 151-3 (Robson 85, Stirling 3); second day, Glamorgan 112-3 (Lloyd 12, Root 16); third day, Glamorgan 274-9 (Wagg 37, van der Gugten 0).

Middlesex

S. D. Robson c Cullen b Labuschagne	107	– (2) c Hemphrey b Labuschagne 36
S. S. Eskinazi lbw b Lloyd	31	– (1) c Labuschagne b van der Gugten . 13
N. R. T. Gubbins lbw b Wagg	5	– lbw b Labuschagne 38
*D. J. Malan c Cullen b de Lange	20	– c Cullen b de Lange 18
P. R. Stirling b Labuschagne	138	– not out 8
G. F. B. Scott b Carey	31	– not out 11
†J. A. Simpson c Cullen b van der Gugten	15	
T. G. Helm lbw b Labuschagne	8	
N. A. Sowter c Cullen b de Lange	28	
S. T. Finn not out	15	
T. J. Murtagh b de Lange	0	
Lb 5, w 1, nb 6	12	Lb 1 1

1/77 (2) 2/92 (3) 3/133 (4)   (117.4 overs) 410   1/42 (1)   (4 wkts, 33 overs) 125
4/222 (5) 5/298 (6) 6/333 (7)   2/81 (2) 3/91 (3)
7/357 (8) 8/382 (5) 9/396 (9)   4/111 (4)
10/410 (11)   110 overs: 366-7

De Lange 26.4–4–94–3; Carey 23–5–76–1; van der Gugten 22–4–61–1; Wagg 22–2–68–1; Lloyd 9–1–37–1; Labuschagne 11–0–52–3; Morgan 4–0–17–0. *Second innings*—de Lange 10–2–30–1; Carey 8–3–25–0; van der Gugten 5–1–22–1; Wagg 4–0–22–0; Labuschagne 6–0–25–2.

Glamorgan

C. R. Hemphrey lbw b Murtagh	27	M. de Lange c Murtagh b Stirling 4
N. J. Selman run out (Gubbins)	0	L. J. Carey c Scott b Finn 12
M. Labuschagne c Stirling b Finn	51	T. van der Gugten not out 2
*D. L. Lloyd c Helm b Finn	59	B 1, lb 13, nb 4 18
W. T. Root b Finn	17	
A. O. Morgan c Simpson b Finn	0	1/0 (2) 2/80 (1) 3/86 (3) (86 overs) 288
†T. N. Cullen c Eskinazi b Stirling	50	4/114 (5) 5/118 (6) 6/204 (4)
G. G. Wagg c Gubbins b Helm	48	7/229 (7) 8/233 (9) 9/266 (10) 10/288 (8)

Murtagh 18–3–57–1; Helm 20–4–62–1; Finn 21–3–75–5; Sowter 21–7–48–0; Stirling 4–0–21–2; Scott 2–0–11–0.

Umpires: N. L. Bainton and G. D. Lloyd.

At Derby, June 30–July 3. MIDDLESEX drew with DERBYSHIRE. *Middlesex end the match bottom of the table.*

MIDDLESEX v GLOUCESTERSHIRE

At Northwood, July 7–9. Middlesex won by 78 runs. Middlesex 19pts, Gloucestershire 4pts. Toss: uncontested.

Middlesex's victory in a low-scoring match, played at Merchant Taylors' School as Lord's was busy with the World Cup, was mainly down to their bowlers – with bat as well as ball. After Roland-Jones took advantage of variable bounce to claim a career-best seven for 52, which restricted Gloucestershire's lead to 29, he was joined by Helm in the second innings at 124 for seven. They added 99 – a Middlesex eighth-wicket record against Gloucestershire – to give themselves something to bowl at. The target was still only 216, but Middlesex unleashed Murtagh (who had flown back from Ireland duty in time for the second day). He removed Dent first ball, and Gloucestershire were soon sunk at 40 for seven. Van Buuren hit nine fours, but Murtagh returned to uproot Payne's leg stump and have Shaw caught behind, then Roland-Jones finished things off with his tenth wicket of the match. Middlesex were lucky to escape after an undistinguished batting display on the first day, not helped by a damp outfield. Malan top-scored with 28, while Shaw claimed four good wickets. Gloucestershire were in trouble themselves, before Higgins, against his former county, made a determined unbeaten 61 to go with seven wickets in the match.

Close of play: first day, Gloucestershire 59-2 (Dent 27, Roderick 10); second day, Middlesex 96-3 (Malan 8, Scott 18).

Middlesex

S. D. Robson c Roderick b Shaw	23	– (2) c Hammond b Higgins	22
S. S. Eskinazi lbw b Sayers	9	– (1) c Roderick b Higgins	37
N. R. T. Gubbins c Roderick b Shaw	26	– b Higgins	10
*D. J. Malan c van Buuren b Shaw	28	– c Roderick b Shaw	8
G. F. B. Scott lbw b Payne	12	– c Howell b Sayers	22
R. G. White c Roderick b Higgins	9	– c Higgins b Higgins	10
†J. A. Simpson c and b Shaw	27	– lbw b Payne	10
T. S. Roland-Jones c Bracey b Sayers	1	– not out	51
T. G. Helm lbw b Higgins	4	– c Hammond b Payne	46
N. A. Sowter b Higgins	3	– c Shaw b Sayers	5
E. R. Bamber not out	4		
T. J. Murtagh (did not bat)		– (11) c Shaw b Sayers	9
B 11, lb 11, nb 4	26	B 5, lb 9	14

1/26 (2) 2/51 (1) 3/98 (4)   (74.2 overs) 172   1/53 (2) 2/68 (1)   (85.3 overs) 244
4/101 (3) 5/117 (5) 6/123 (6)   3/73 (4) 4/96 (4)
7/134 (8) 8/139 (9) 9/151 (10) 10/172 (7)   5/108 (5) 6/118 (6) 7/124 (7)
     8/223 (9) 9/230 (10) 10/244 (11)

Murtagh replaced Bamber after being released from the Ireland squad.

Payne 20–6–31–1; Sayers 19–7–34–2; Higgins 20–6–52–3; Shaw 15.2–4–33–4. *Second innings*— Payne 18–4–53–2; Sayers 24.3–6–60–3; Shaw 20–4–71–1; Higgins 18–4–35–4; van Buuren 5–1–11–0.

Gloucestershire

M. A. H. Hammond c Malan b Roland-Jones	21	– (2) c Eskinazi b Murtagh	16
*C. D. J. Dent b Roland-Jones	38	– (1) c Robson b Murtagh	0
J. R. Bracey c Eskinazi b Roland-Jones	0	– lbw b Murtagh	15
†G. H. Roderick lbw b Murtagh	40	– c Simpson b Helm	5
B. G. Charlesworth c Malan b Roland-Jones	1	– c Robson b Helm	2
B. A. C. Howell c Simpson b Roland-Jones	0	– b Roland-Jones	1
R. F. Higgins not out	61	– c Malan b Roland-Jones	0
G. L. van Buuren c Eskinazi b Roland-Jones	12	– not out	57
D. A. Payne c Malan b Helm	4	– b Murtagh	16
J. Shaw lbw b Roland-Jones	14	– c Simpson b Murtagh	0
C. J. Sayers lbw b Sowter	0	– b Roland-Jones	19
B 4, lb 4, nb 2	10	Lb 6	6

1/36 (1) 2/40 (3) 3/85 (2)   (73.3 overs) 201   1/0 (1) 2/20 (3)   (44.3 overs) 137
4/87 (5) 5/87 (6) 6/118 (4)   3/35 (2) 4/39 (4)
7/140 (8) 8/145 (9) 9/188 (10) 10/201 (11)   5/40 (6) 6/40 (7) 7/40 (5)
     8/91 (9) 9/99 (10) 10/137 (11)

Bamber 7–0–19–0; Helm 21–6–65–1; Roland-Jones 21–7–52–7; Murtagh 12–5–28–1; Scott 10–4–24–0; Sowter 2.3–1–5–1. *Second innings*—Murtagh 12–2–44–5; Helm 13–0–35–2; Roland-Jones 12.3–3–27–3; Scott 2–0–7–0; Sowter 5–0–18–0.

Umpires: M. Burns and J. D. Middlebrook.

At Cardiff, July 13–16. MIDDLESEX beat GLAMORGAN by 256 runs. *Sam Robson carries his bat through Middlesex's second innings.*

At Hove, August 18–20. MIDDLESEX lost to SUSSEX by seven wickets.

MIDDLESEX v DURHAM

At Lord's, September 10–12. Durham won by 44 runs. Durham 19pts, Middlesex 3pts. Toss: Middlesex. First-class debut: S. Steel. County debut: M. L. Cummins.

After his side slipped to a defeat that effectively ended their slim promotion hopes but boosted Durham's, Malan was critical of a sticky Lord's surface, on which neither team reached 200. "It was a really slow wicket that nibbled," he said, "so scoring was extremely tough." Middlesex had looked in charge when Finn and his fellow seamers hustled Durham out for 147, of which Handscomb – later confirmed as Malan's replacement as Middlesex captain for 2020 – made 54. But the hosts struggled in turn, crashing to 87 for seven on a chaotic first day. The tail narrowed the gap next morning, with the last two wickets scrounging 46 valuable runs. Angus Robson, younger brother of Middlesex's Sam, then survived nearly four hours for 64, while 39s from the unrelated Steels – opener Cameron and debutant Scott – dragged Durham 195 in front. Sam Robson followed the family example with a career-best 65, but no one else faced more than 40 balls as the lively Carse bounded to career-best figures, including a post-lunch spell of five for nine to end the match.

Close of play: first day, Middlesex 87-7 (Harris 5, Cummins 0); second day, Middlesex 21-0 (Gubbins 8, Robson 9).

Durham

A. Z. Lees lbw b Harris	26	– run out (Murtagh)	13
C. T. Steel b Finn	29	– c Simpson b Cummins	39
A. J. Robson c Eskinazi b Cummins	0	– c Holden b Finn	64
P. S. P. Handscomb b Murtagh	54	– lbw b Harris	3
G. J. Harte c Simpson b Murtagh	6	– lbw b Finn	0
S. Steel lbw b Murtagh	2	– c Cummins b Murtagh	39
*†E. J. H. Eckersley lbw b Finn	8	– lbw b Harris	2
B. A. Raine c Robson b Harris	2	– c Malan b Scott	11
B. A. Carse c Simpson b Finn	9	– lbw b Harris	0
N. J. Rimmington c Robson b Finn	0	– lbw b Finn	6
C. Rushworth not out	0	– not out	0
Lb 3, nb 8	11	Lb 6, nb 8	14

1/56 (1) 2/56 (2) 3/59 (3)   (54 overs) 147
4/80 (5) 5/86 (6) 6/107 (7)
7/126 (8) 8/147 (9) 9/147 (4) 10/147 (10)

1/51 (1) 2/66 (2)   (69.5 overs) 191
3/79 (4) 4/80 (5)
5/127 (6) 6/141 (7) 7/160 (8)
8/161 (9) 9/182 (10) 10/191 (3)

Murtagh 14–6–32–3; Cummins 15–4–38–1; Finn 12–2–41–4; Harris 13–6–33–2. *Second innings*—Murtagh 20–10–38–1; Cummins 19–8–50–1; Finn 12.5–3–49–3; Harris 15–3–43–3; Scott 3–0–5–1.

Middlesex

S. D. Robson c Eckersley b Rushworth	20	– (2) c Eckersley b Rushworth	65
N. R. T. Gubbins lbw b Carse	0	– c Lees b Carse	17
S. S. Eskinazi b Rimmington	24	– lbw b Rushworth	0
*D. J. Malan b Raine	24	– lbw b Raine	2
M. D. E. Holden c Harte b Rushworth	5	– lbw b Raine	9
G. F. B. Scott b Raine	9	– c Eckersley b Carse	14
†J. A. Simpson lbw b Raine	0	– b Carse	15
J. A. R. Harris b Raine	14	– c Carse	0
M. L. Cummins not out	22	– b Carse	1
S. T. Finn b Raine	11	– not out	9
T. J. Murtagh c S. Steel b Rushworth	14	– b Carse	8
		B 4, lb 7	11

1/0 (2) 2/43 (3) 3/51 (1)   (43.4 overs) 143
4/59 (5) 5/77 (6) 6/77 (7)
7/86 (4) 8/97 (8) 9/121 (10) 10/143 (11)

1/31 (1) 2/34 (3)   (48.4 overs) 151
3/45 (4) 4/99 (5)
5/107 (2) 6/124 (6) 7/124 (8)
8/134 (9) 9/139 (7) 10/151 (11)

Rushworth 14.4–4–46–3; Carse 9–3–37–1; Rimmington 8–1–34–1; Raine 12–5–26–5. *Second innings*—Rushworth 19–4–67–2; Raine 13–3–32–2; Carse 9.4–2–26–6; Rimmington 4–0–13–0; Harte 3–1–2–0.

Umpires: R. A. Kettleborough and R. J. Warren.

At Manchester, September 16–19. MIDDLESEX lost to LANCASHIRE by 104 runs. *In the first innings, Middlesex recover from 34-6 to 337.*

MIDDLESEX v DERBYSHIRE

At Lord's, September 23–26. Drawn. Middlesex 9pts, Derbyshire 11pts. Toss: uncontested.

A drab end-of-season encounter between two sides with no chance of promotion was rendered even more inconsequential by the weather, which affected all four days. There was not even time for two full innings. Robson continued his good form, just missing a third century of the summer, while Malan's 72 took him past 1,000 runs in the Championship. There were four wickets for the lively Reece, while Hudson-Prentice – formerly on the MCC groundstaff – docked the tail with three in eight balls. On the third day, Godleman reached his own 1,000 runs for the summer; on a sleepy fourth, the nippy, accurate Bamber completed a maiden five-for, while du Plooy reached his second hundred of the season, both at Middlesex's expense. Hughes was Murtagh's 700th first-class victim for Middlesex.

Close of play: first day, Middlesex 176-3 (Malan 51, Andersson 4); second day, Middlesex 199-5 (Malan 66, Harris 0); third day, Derbyshire 199-4 (du Plooy 55, Hosein 56).

Middlesex

S. D. Robson c Hosein b Hughes	93		M. L. Cummins b Hudson-Prentice		0
N. R. T. Gubbins c Hosein b Reece	0		E. R. Bamber c Hughes b Hudson-Prentice		0
M. D. E. Holden c Madsen b Conners	19		T. J. Murtagh c Critchley b Hudson-Prentice		3
*D. J. Malan lbw b Reece	72		B 1, lb 4, nb 8		13
M. K. Andersson c Hosein b Reece	8				—
†J. A. Simpson lbw b Dal	4		1/13 (2) 2/65 (3) 3/155 (1)	(89.1 overs)	260
J. A. R. Harris not out	25		4/186 (5) 5/199 (6) 6/213 (4)		
T. S. Roland-Jones lbw b Reece	23		7/251 (8) 8/252 (9) 9/252 (10) 10/260 (11)		

Reece 28–9–61–4; Hudson-Prentice 24.1–5–65–3; Dal 16–4–37–1; Melton 5–0–40–0; Conners 12–1–41–1; Hughes 4–1–11–1.

Derbyshire

L. M. Reece lbw b Bamber	26		F. J. Hudson-Prentice c Simpson b Bamber		28
*B. A. Godleman c Malan b Roland-Jones	27		A. K. Dal not out		13
W. L. Madsen lbw b Bamber	0		B 2, lb 8, w 1, nb 6		17
J. L. du Plooy not out	100				—
A. L. Hughes c Cummins b Murtagh	20		1/49 (1) 2/49 (3)	(7 wkts, 77 overs)	304
†H. R. Hosein c Malan b Bamber	57		3/55 (2) 4/103 (5)		
M. J. J. Critchley c Murtagh b Bamber	16		5/202 (6) 6/228 (7) 7/275 (8)		

S. Conners and D. R. Melton did not bat.

Murtagh 17–2–59–1; Bamber 22–2–93–5; Roland-Jones 5–0–15–1; Cummins 13–0–49–0; Harris 15–1–53–0; Holden 5–0–25–0.

Umpires: I. D. Blackwell and B. V. Taylor.

NORTHAMPTONSHIRE

And now for something completely different

Alex Winter

At lunchtime on a cloudless mid-September day at Wantage Road, the Northamptonshire players sat on the outfield of the deserted ground, and drank champagne. Victory over Durham had all but ensured promotion to Division One of the Championship after an absence of five seasons.

The following week, their elevation confirmed after a sodden final day of the season at Bristol, the team joined their Gloucestershire rivals for a double promotion celebration in the home dressing-room. Among the visiting party was Tony Kingston, Northamptonshire's scorer since 1990, who had missed the season through illness. Success was all the sweeter for the presence of a much-loved club servant.

It had been a remarkable turnaround. In June, Northamptonshire were bottom of the table after seven matches, and Alex Wakely had resigned as captain. His replacement, wicketkeeper Adam Rossington, breathed new life into the team. Unassuming and softly spoken, he applied a ruthless streak to bowling changes, and was inclined to attack for longer than Wakely. He played a number of important innings.

Wakely had led the county with great integrity, first in the fairytale T20 triumph of 2013, then across all formats from 2015. His tenure included a second Blast title, in 2016, and nine Championship wins the following summer, usually enough for promotion. But he stood down a tired man, worn out by a litany of defeats in 2018, and a poor start to the season. Wakely immediately reported an uplift in his wellbeing, and made useful runs, including a hundred against Worcestershire in August, as the promotion race hotted up. While Northamptonshire were recording their third win, to confirm the gathering momentum of their challenge, other results went in their favour.

Their first victory had come away to Sussex at the beginning of July, when Ben Sanderson's ten wickets helped Northamptonshire to a 393-run win, their largest ever. Sanderson, who passed 200 first-class wickets during the game, matched his 2018 total of 60 Championship victims.

Another notable away victory came soon after, against Derbyshire at Chesterfield. Batsmen on both sides appeared to mistrust the pitch, which made Temba Bavuma's hundred one of the performances of the summer. It had taken him nine innings into his mid-season stint as overseas player to register a fifty, but that contribution – and another century, against a high-class Lancashire attack – justified his signing.

After Worcestershire had been thrashed at Wantage Road, victory at Leicester set up the promotion showdown against Durham. The first day was a defining one for Rossington. With his side on the verge of being rolled over, he produced

Adam Rossington

a true captain's innings – slog-sweeping the seamers for seven sixes to change the course of the game. Sanderson and Brett Hutton then ran through their opponents to set up the victory that made promotion all but certain.

Despite struggling with an ankle injury, Hutton not only collected 35 wickets at 20, but complemented Sanderson perfectly, often shouldering the bulk of the workload. The seam attack were strengthened by the arrival of Gareth Berg on loan from Hampshire for the final three matches, ahead of a two-year deal. At 38, his signing raised a few eyebrows, but coach David Ripley insisted his fitness was exemplary, and his top-flight experience crucial. The bowling will also be boosted by Pakistan all-rounder Fahim Ashraf: after an impressive spell in the T20 Blast, he was signed for the first half of the summer.

Ashraf provided an edge to the T20 bowling that was lacking in 2018, and there was enough of an all-round improvement to ensure that hopes of a quarter-final place remained alive deep into the group stage. But it proved impossible to string a run of results together, and four washouts were the most they have suffered in a T20 season. Victories at Edgbaston, and at home against holders Worcestershire, were countered by defeats when not adjusting to different conditions – on Chester-le-Street's huge outfield, or a sticky pitch at Derby. The top order were inconsistent, not helped by Richard Levi missing the first half of matches with a neck injury. Two big hitters have joined for this year's Blast: West Indies' white-ball captain Kieron Pollard and Ireland's Paul Stirling.

Levi, who signed a one-year contract extension, also failed to find form in the Royal London One-Day Cup, in which Northamptonshire were well placed in all but the match at Old Trafford, yet won only twice, despite the recruitment of West Indies Test captain Jason Holder. His early-season stay coincided with just one 50-over victory out of five, and two Championship matches.

Ricardo Vasconcelos's season was ended by an ankle injury suffered playing football before the match at Chesterfield, but some strong performances earned him a five-year contract. If he can flourish against Division One attacks, Northamptonshire have a chance of being competitive. Inevitably, they will need other batsmen to have good seasons, and Rob Keogh will bear some of the burden after signing a two-year deal. The club's first goal is to improve dramatically on their previous season in the top flight, in 2014, when they lost 12 of their 16 games.

Promotion was followed by changes to the coaching staff. The development of Sanderson and many other bowlers had been overseen by the affable Phil Rowe. He stood down as David Ripley's assistant after 15 years at the club, while John Sadler and Chris Liddle joined the backroom team.

Championship attendance: 17,791.

NORTHAMPTONSHIRE RESULTS

All first-class matches – Played 15: Won 5, Lost 2, Drawn 8.
County Championship matches – Played 14: Won 5, Lost 2, Drawn 7.

Specsavers County Championship, 2nd in Division 2;
Vitality Blast, 7th in North Group; Royal London One-Day Cup, 8th in North Group.

COUNTY CHAMPIONSHIP AVERAGES, BATTING AND FIELDING

Cap		Birthplace	M	I	NO	R	HS	100	Avge	Ct/St
	†R. S. Vasconcelos†† .	*Johannesburg, SA* ..	10	18	2	750	184	2	46.87	16
2019	A. M. Rossington....	*Edgware*	13	19	2	787	82	0	46.29	32/2
	T. Bavuma¶........	*Cape Town, SA* ...	8	15	0	566	134	2	37.73	7
2012	A. G. Wakely.....	*Hammersmith*	12	16	1	548	102	1	36.53	12
	†L. A. Procter.......	*Oldham*	14	21	7	510	86*	0	36.42	4
2019	R. I. Keogh.......	*Dunstable*	14	22	0	744	150	2	33.81	4
	†S. A. Zaib........	*High Wycombe* ...	3	5	0	163	54	0	32.60	0
	N. L. Buck	*Leicester*	10	13	4	287	53	0	31.88	2
2018	J. J. Cobb	*Leicester*	6	10	0	314	68	0	31.40	2
2017	R. E. Levi††.......	*Johannesburg, SA* .	4	6	1	144	60	0	28.80	2
	†B. J. Curran......	*Northampton‡*....	7	11	1	273	52	0	27.30	3
	†M. T. Coles	*Maidstone*	4	5	1	98	41*	0	24.50	3
2017	R. I. Newton......	*Taunton*	10	19	2	396	105	1	23.29	1
	†L. Wood	*Sheffield*	4	6	1	116	66	0	23.20	1
	B. A. Hutton	*Doncaster*	10	15	4	203	34*	0	18.45	9
2018	B. W. Sanderson ...	*Sheffield*	14	17	6	162	28	0	14.72	4

Also batted: G. K. Berg (*Cape Town, SA*) (3 matches) 5, 3, 1; D. A. J. Bracewell¶ (*Tauranga, NZ*) (3 matches) 38, 1, 15; †E. N. Gay (*Bedford*) (1 match) did not bat (1 ct); J. O. Holder¶ (*St George, Barbados*) (2 matches) 40, 3 (4 ct); B. Muzarabani†† (*Harare, Zimbabwe*) (2 matches) 1*, 1 (1 ct); J. Overton (*Barnstaple*) (2 matches) 6, 0, 19 (2 ct); D. Pretorius¶ (*Randfontein, SA*) (1 match) 111.

‡ *Born in Northamptonshire.*   ¶ *Official overseas player.*   †† *Other non-England-qualified.*

BOWLING

	Style	O	M	R	W	BB	5I	Avge
B. W. Sanderson....................	RFM	448.2	118	1,179	60	6-37	3	19.65
B. A. Hutton.......................	RFM	263.3	72	700	35	6-57	2	20.00
N. L. Buck	RFM	207.1	38	814	22	5-54	1	37.00
L. A. Procter......................	RM	204.1	43	697	17	4-26	0	41.00
R. I. Keogh........................	OB	225.2	37	804	13	3-43	0	61.84

Also bowled: T. Bavuma (RM) 1–0–2–0; G. K. Berg (RFM) 59.3–18–153–8; D. A. J. Bracewell (RFM) 54.7–212–4; J. J. Cobb (OB) 27–4–91–1; M. T. Coles (RFM) 69–13–268–9; J. O. Holder (RFM) 52–6–199–4; B. Muzarabani (RFM) 31–2–160–4; J. Overton (RFM) 55.2–3–223–6; D. Pretorius (RFM) 20–6–54–2; A. M. Rossington (RM) 5–0–20–0; R. S. Vasconcelos (OB) 1.3–0–9–0; L. Wood (LFM) 110–18–332–9; S. A. Zaib (SLA) 4–0–16–0.

LEADING ROYAL LONDON CUP AVERAGES (100 runs/4 wickets)

Batting	Runs	HS	Avge	SR	Ct
J. O. Holder.....	284	86	71.00	132.09	1
L. A. Procter	175	50*	58.33	99.43	3
R. S. Vasconcelos	255	112	51.00	98.45	3
R. I. Keogh	359	102	44.87	87.34	3
A. M. Rossington	184	68	36.80	129.57	6
A. G. Wakely	288	66	36.00	92.90	2
J. J. Cobb........	227	63	28.37	75.91	3
R. E. Levi	197	58	24.62	90.36	4

Bowling	W	BB	Avge	ER
J. O. Holder	7	3-26	22.85	5.92
B. W. Sanderson ..	14	3-44	26.50	5.75
N. L. Buck	11	3-44	31.27	6.14
B. Muzarabani ...	6	3-28	32.16	5.12
L. A. Procter......	5	2-51	59.20	4.96

ᴠITALITY BLAST AVERAGES (100 runs/15 overs)

		HS	Avge	SR	Ct/St	Bowling	W	BB	Avge	ER
628	156	44	26.00	**144.44**	0	J. J. Cobb	2	1-17	63.50	**5.77**
...ngton	239	54	23.90	**137.35**	4/3	R. I. Keogh	10	3-30	13.00	**6.50**
...Cobb	254	84	25.40	**137.29**	1	G. G. White	10	2-18	27.50	**7.23**
D. Pretorius	225	50*	25.00	**129.31**	1	B. W. Sanderson .	11	4-28	19.18	**7.81**
R. I. Keogh	177	59*	35.40	**105.98**	3	Fahim Ashraf	11	2-26	29.63	**8.11**
A. G. Wakely ...	188	47*	23.50	**105.02**	5	D. Pretorius	6	3-17	29.66	**8.40**
						N. L. Buck	5	1-14	35.80	**9.67**

FIRST-CLASS COUNTY RECORDS

Highest score for	331*	M. E. K. Hussey v Somerset at Taunton	2003
Highest score against	333	K. S. Duleepsinhji (Sussex) at Hove	1930
Leading run-scorer	28,980	D. Brookes (avge 36.13)	1934–59
Best bowling for	10-127	V. W. C. Jupp v Kent at Tunbridge Wells	1932
Best bowling against	10-30	C. Blythe (Kent) at Northampton	1907
Leading wicket-taker	1,102	E. W. Clark (avge 21.26).	1922–47
Highest total for	781-7 dec	v Nottinghamshire at Northampton	1995
Highest total against	701-7 dec	by Kent at Beckenham	2017
Lowest total for	12	v Gloucestershire at Gloucester	1907
Lowest total against	33	by Lancashire at Northampton	1977

LIST A COUNTY RECORDS

Highest score for	172*	W. Larkins v Warwickshire at Luton	1983
Highest score against	184	M. J. Lumb (Nottinghamshire) at Nottingham	2016
Leading run-scorer	11,010	R. J. Bailey (avge 39.46)	1983–99
Best bowling for	7-10	C. Pietersen v Denmark at Brøndby	2005
Best bowling against	7-35	D. E. Malcolm (Derbyshire) at Derby	1997
Leading wicket-taker	251	A. L. Penberthy (avge 30.45).	1989–2003
Highest total for	425	v Nottinghamshire at Nottingham	2016
Highest total against	445-8	by Nottinghamshire at Nottingham	2016
Lowest total for	41	v Middlesex at Northampton	1972
Lowest total against	{ 56	by Leicestershire at Leicester.	1964
	{ 56	by Denmark at Brøndby.	2005

TWENTY20 COUNTY RECORDS

Highest score for	111*	L. Klusener v Worcestershire at Kidderminster	2007
Highest score against	161	A. Lyth (Yorkshire) at Leeds	2017
Leading run-scorer	**2,506**	**A. G. Wakely (avge 26.94, SR 119.39)**	**2009–19**
Best bowling for	6-21	A. J. Hall v Worcestershire at Northampton	2008
Best bowling against	5-6	P. D. Collingwood (Durham) at Chester-le-Street	2011
Leading wicket-taker	73	D. J. Willey (avge 19.45, ER 7.42)	2009–15
Highest total for	231-5	v Warwickshire at Birmingham	2018
Highest total against	260-4	by Yorkshire at Leeds	2017
Lowest total for	47	v Durham at Chester-le-Street	2011
Lowest total against	86	by Worcestershire at Worcester	2006

ADDRESS

County Ground, Abington Avenue, Northampton NN1 4PR; 01604 514455; reception@nccc.co.uk; www.northantscricket.com.

OFFICIALS

Captain 2019 A. G. Wakely/A. M. Rossington
2020 A M Rossington
(ltd overs) J. J. Cobb
Head coach D. Ripley
Academy director K. J. Innes

President Lord Naseby
Chairman G. G. Warren
Chief executive R. Payne
Head groundsman C. Harvey
Scorers A. C. Kingston

NORTHAMPTONSHIRE v DURHAM MCCU

At Northampton, March 31–April 2. Drawn. Toss: Northamptonshire. First-class debuts: W. F. Angus, J. F. Emanuel, N. C. MacDonagh. County debut: B. Muzarabani.

In brilliant sunshine, Northamptonshire made merry on the opening day. Newton took the chance to harvest runs, scoring his 14th first-class hundred, while Cobb made his first for the county, the fourth of his career. Blessing Muzarabani, their Kolpak signing from Zimbabwe, showed promise amid some erratic bowling. Curran, promoted to open, scored a half-century in the second innings, but rain washed out the last day, depriving Northamptonshire of the opportunity of a first first-class win against a university side since 2007.

Close of play: first day, Northamptonshire 481-7 (Curran 31, Buck 0); second day, Northamptonshire 108-3 (Levi 11, Procter 3).

Northamptonshire

R. S. Vasconcelos c MacDonagh b Angus	34	– (2) c Graves b Subramanyan	21
*R. I. Newton b Benjamin b Emanuel	118		
J. J. Cobb retired out	139		
R. E. Levi st MacDonagh b Emanuel	4	– (3) not out	11
R. I. Keogh c Benjamin b Subramanyan	67		
†A. M. Rossington c Bedford b Angus	15	– (4) b Dewes	1
L. A. Procter b Dewes	46	– (5) not out	3
B. J. Curran not out	31	– (1) c sub (X. G. Owen) b Subramanyan	64
N. L. Buck not out	0		
B 5, lb 4, w 4, nb 14	27	Lb 1, w 1, nb 6	8

1/89 (1) 2/241 (2)   (7 wkts dec, 110 overs) 481
3/245 (4) 4/348 (3)
5/379 (6) 6/413 (5) 7/481 (7)

1/59 (2)   (3 wkts, 40 overs) 108
2/100 (1) 3/103 (4)

B. W. Sanderson and B. Muzarabani did not bat.

Campbell 15–4–63–0; Angus 18–0–71–2; Emanuel 20–1–81–2; Subramanyan 32–1–140–1; Graves 16–0–76–0; Dewes 9–0–41–1. *Second innings*—Angus 6–0–31–0; Emanuel 3–0–8–0; Subramanyan 17–4–42–2; Graves 8–4–25–0; Dewes 6–5–1–1.

Durham MCCU

L. Bedford b Buck	2	J. Subramanyan b Buck	11
A. H. J. Dewes lbw b Buck	0	W. F. Angus b Keogh	0
T. B. Powe c Rossington b Muzarabani	26	J. O. I. Campbell not out	0
*B. W. M. Graves c Rossington b Sanderson	31	B 13, lb 8, nb 4	25
C. F. B. Scott b Keogh	4		
C. G. Benjamin c Levi b Keogh	0	1/0 (2) 2/13 (1) 3/57 (3) (56.2 overs) 136
J. F. Emanuel c Cobb b Muzarabani	20	4/64 (5) 5/66 (6) 6/88 (4)
†N. C. MacDonagh b Keogh	17	7/115 (7) 8/126 (8) 9/136 (9) 10/136 (10)

Sanderson 12–4–18–1; Buck 12–3–28–3; Procter 13–6–25–0; Muzarabani 10–1–29–2; Keogh 9.2–2–15–4.

Umpires: R. J. Bailey and I. N. Ramage.

NORTHAMPTONSHIRE v MIDDLESEX

At Northampton, April 5–8. Drawn. Northamptonshire 12pts, Middlesex 9pts. Toss: uncontested. County debuts: J. O. Holder, L. Wood.

For the second year in succession, Harris thwarted Northamptonshire's attempts to turn their dominance into victory. Middlesex were 130 for seven in response to 445 but – with the support of Roland-Jones and Finn – Harris added a determined 61, after being dropped at slip on 25. Even so, Wakely enforced the follow-on, as he had against Middlesex the previous season, when Northamptonshire lost. Middlesex were quickly ten for two, but 22 overs were stolen by bad light on the third evening, and on the final day Malan steered his team to safety. Watched by national selector Ed Smith, he batted over six hours for his unbeaten 160 – his highest since 2015. Earlier, Northamptonshire had been heartened by their solid batting display, despite six wickets for Murtagh,

HIGHEST NORTHAMPTONSHIRE TOTALS WITHOUT A HUNDRED

	HS		
498	87 (A. G. Wakely)......	v Kent at Northampton..............	2016
476	96 (A. J. Swann).......	v Surrey at Northampton	2001
471	93 (K. M. Curran)......	v Lancashire at Northampton.......	1996
469	92 (D. J. Sales).........	v Derbyshire at Chesterfield.........	2010
457	90* (J. V. Murdin†)......	v Glamorgan at Northampton......	1925
453	91* (A. J. Hall)........	v Glamorgan at Northampton......	2013
445	**81* (L. A. Procter).**	**v Middlesex at Northampton.**......	**2019**
444-9 dec	83 (A. J. Lamb).........	v Essex at Chelmsford...........	1992
430	87 (G. J. Thompson).....	v Leicestershire at Northampton ...	1912
430	96 (R. A. Haywood)	v Surrey at Northampton........	1920

† *Batting at No. 11.*

who passed 700 in the Championship. Wakely worked hard for 76, and Procter went on to an unbeaten 81 on the second morning. West Indies captain Holder, their eye-catching new recruit, made 40 and took two wickets. The match ended bizarrely: with Middlesex trying to improve their over-rate, Northamptonshire batted for 6.5 overs from the very occasional bowlers, including Simpson, who wore his cap, while Malan kept wicket without pads.

Close of play: first day, Northamptonshire 310-6 (Holder 36, Procter 9); second day, Middlesex 134-7 (Harris 3, Roland-Jones 1); third day, Middlesex 109-2 (Robson 40, Malan 55).

Northamptonshire

R. S. Vasconcelos c Simpson b Murtagh.........	38 – not out	5
R. I. Newton lbw b Murtagh	7 – not out	5
*A. G. Wakely c Robson b Murtagh	76	
J. J. Cobb c Roland-Jones b Murtagh...........	9	
R. I. Keogh c Eskinazi b Finn	46	
†A. M. Rossington b Roland-Jones	67	
J. O. Holder c Simpson b Murtagh..............	40	
L. A. Procter not out	81	
L. Wood c Robson b Finn	29	
N. L. Buck c Simpson b Finn...................	4	
B. W. Sanderson c Eskinazi b Murtagh	23	
Lb 11, nb 14.....................	25	

1/19 (2) 2/65 (1) 3/83 (4) 4/182 (3) (132 overs) 445 (no wkt, 6.5 overs) 10
5/224 (5) 6/291 (6) 7/317 (7)
8/370 (9) 9/374 (10) 10/445 (11) 110 overs: 355-7

Murtagh 32–5–80–6; Roland-Jones 30–8–89–1; Harris 31–4–110–0; Finn 29–7–119–3; Holder 4–0–19–0; Malan 6–0–17–0. *Second innings*—Morgan 3–1–4–0; Eskinazi 2–0–4–0; Simpson 1–0–2–0; Robson 0.5–0–0–0.

Middlesex

S. D. Robson c Rossington b Holder	26	– (2) c Holder b Buck	41
N. R. T. Gubbins c Wakely b Holder	22	– (1) c Holder b Buck	6
S. S. Eskinazi c Rossington b Buck	4	– c Vasconcelos b Buck	0
*D. J. Malan c Rossington b Wood	19	– not out	160
M. D. E. Holden c Cobb b Wood	10	– c Rossington b Keogh	54
E. J. G. Morgan b Vasconcelos b Buck	25	– not out	36
†J. A. Simpson c Holder b Sanderson	3		
J. A. R. Harris not out	61		
T. S. Roland-Jones lbw b Buck	27		
S. T. Finn c Holder b Buck	34		
T. J. Murtagh c Wood b Buck	2		
B 17, lb 9, w 8, nb 4	38	B 1, lb 6, w 5, nb 8	20

1/39 (2) 2/48 (3) 3/56 (1)   (80.4 overs) 271
4/84 (4) 5/104 (5) 6/130 (6)
7/130 (7) 8/189 (9) 9/263 (10) 10/271 (11)

1/10 (1)   (4 wkts dec, 102.3 overs) 317
2/10 (3) 3/119 (2)
4/224 (5)

Sanderson 22–7–52–1; Wood 19.5–5–53–2; Holder 17–1–62–2; Buck 16.4–3–54–5; Procter 6–1–24–0. *Second innings*—Buck 19–4–53–3; Sanderson 25–5–67–0; Wood 14–1–48–0; Holder 14–3–58–0; Procter 8–2–25–0; Keogh 15–3–44–1; Cobb 7–2–15–0; Vasconcelos 0.3–0–0–0.

Umpires: P. J. Hartley and P. R. Pollard.

At Cardiff, April 11–14. NORTHAMPTONSHIRE drew with GLAMORGAN. *Northampton score 750, their second-highest first-class total.*

At Northampton, April 29. NORTHAMPTONSHIRE lost to PAKISTANIS by eight wickets (see Pakistan tour section).

At Manchester, May 14–17. NORTHAMPTONSHIRE lost to LANCASHIRE by ten wickets.

NORTHAMPTONSHIRE v SUSSEX

At Northampton, May 20–23. Drawn. Northamptonshire 11pts, Sussex 13pts. Toss: Northamptonshire.
At 68 for six on the first morning, Sussex were on the ropes. Then Jordan edged his first ball at catchable height between wicketkeeper and slip. It was a *Sliding Doors* moment: he went on to a career-best 166, while Brown made 156 as the pair added 309, the second-highest for any wicket in the fixture. More setbacks awaited Northamptonshire, who became the first team to use two concussion substitutes. Before play on the second day, Wakely suffered a delayed reaction to walking into a wooden beam at his house the previous night; and, in the final over, Wood was struck on the helmet by Jordan, and did not resume next morning. Before that Vasconcelos and Cobb, Wakely's locum, made fifties in a spirited Northamptonshire response. As Sussex pursued quick runs on the third day, Salt blazed a 90-ball hundred, but Brown did not declare until four overs into the final morning, 393 ahead. Northamptonshire had 90 to survive, and were five down after 37. But Rossington, who had taken over the captaincy, and Hutton, Wood's replacement, offered unyielding defence across 35 overs, and saved the match.
Close of play: first day, Sussex 370-6 (Brown 153, Jordan 158); second day, Northamptonshire 242-6 (Procter 23, Overton 1); third day, Sussex 292-4 (van Zyl 52, Brown 51).

Sussex

P. D. Salt b Sanderson	12	– c Cobb b Overton	122
T. J. Haines c Bavuma b Sanderson	12	– c Overton b Buck	12
L. W. P. Wells c Rossington b Procter	20	– c Procter b Overton	36
S. van Zyl c Keogh b Sanderson	1	– not out	81
H. Z. Finch b Buck	4	– c Bavuma b Sanderson	13
*†B. C. Brown lbw b Wood	156	– not out	60
D. Wiese b Overton	0		
C. J. Jordan c Rossington b Overton	166		
D. R. Briggs not out	19		
A. Sakande c Overton b Buck	8		
Mir Hamza c Vasconcelos b Overton	1		
B 3, lb 18, nb 2	23	B 5, lb 3, w 5, nb 2	15

1/20 (1) 2/25 (2) 3/27 (4)   (118.2 overs) 422   1/64 (2)   (4 wkts dec, 69 overs) 339
4/35 (5) 5/65 (3) 6/68 (7)   2/170 (1) 3/182 (3)
7/377 (6) 8/402 (8) 9/419 (10)   4/210 (5)
10/422 (11)   110 overs: 405-8

Sanderson 28–7–78–3; Wood 24–2–65–1; Overton 20.2–1–79–3; Buck 21–2–89–2; Procter 19–4–71–1; Keogh 6–0–19–0. *Second innings*—Sanderson 12–1–39–1; Buck 10–1–77–1; Overton 11–0–58–2; Hutton 4–1–9–0; Procter 9–1–37–0; Keogh 23–1–111–0.

Northamptonshire

B. J. Curran c Salt b Mir Hamza	3	– c Brown b Mir Hamza	36
R. S. Vasconcelos lbw b Briggs	83	– c Salt b Mir Hamza	10
J. J. Cobb c Mir Hamza b Sakande	62	– b Mir Hamza	68
T. Bavuma c Jordan b Mir Hamza	8	– run out (Wiese).	23
R. I. Keogh c Jordan b Wells	41	– lbw b Jordan	15
†A. M. Rossington c Finch b Jordan	13	– not out	69
L. A. Procter not out.	49	– c Brown b Mir Hamza	25
L. Wood retired hurt.	1		
J. Overton lbw b Wells	19		
B. A. Hutton c Finch b Jordan	2	– (8) not out	25
N. L. Buck c Brown b Sakande	51		
B. W. Sanderson b Briggs	12		
B 11, lb 7, nb 6	24	B 4, lb 5, nb 8	17

1/6 (1) 2/143 (2) 3/159 (4)   (101.3 overs) 368   1/13 (2)   (6 wkts, 89.3 overs) 288
4/165 (3) 5/186 (6) 6/238 (5)   2/112 (1) 3/133 (3)
7/264 (9) 8/267 (10) 9/337 (11) 10/368 (12)   4/161 (5) 5/162 (4) 6/218 (7)

*In the first innings Wood retired hurt at 241-6. Cobb replaced *A. G. Wakely, and Hutton replaced Wood, both as concussion substitutes.*

Mir Hamza 21–6–53–2; Wiese 19–1–84–0; Sakande 15–1–61–2; Jordan 20–2–67–2; Haines 8–2–27–0; Briggs 9.3–1–40–2; Wells 9–1–18–2. *Second innings*—Mir Hamza 19–2–51–4; Wiese 13–1–63–0; Sakande 11.3–2–39–0; Jordan 16–2–42–1; Haines 2–0–3–0; Briggs 16–1–45–0; Wells 12–2–36–0.

Umpires: S. J. O'Shaughnessy and R. J. Warren.

NORTHAMPTONSHIRE v GLAMORGAN

At Northampton, June 2–5. Glamorgan won by an innings and 143 runs. Glamorgan 24pts, Northamptonshire 4pts. Toss: uncontested.

Glamorgan's first innings victory since 2014 briefly took them top of Division Two, and prompted the resignation of Wakely as Northamptonshire captain a day later. The win was set up on the first morning by the pace of de Lange, who took only one top-order wicket, but his hostility brought wickets for others. Glamorgan stumbled to 20 for three in reply, when Vasconcelos dropped Root at second slip before he had scored. He made the most of his fortune, compiling a career-best 229 off

252 balls with 30 fours and a six. It was the highest score for Glamorgan against Northamptonshire, beating Roy Fredericks's 228 not out at Swansea in 1972. Two sessions of the third day were lost to rain, but Northamptonshire began the final morning with ten wickets in hand. Needing to bat all day, they did not get halfway; Hogan and de Lange were irresistible, sharing seven wickets. Wakely had been in charge of the Championship team since 2015, and in white-ball matches since 2013, winning two T20 titles.

Close of play: first day, Glamorgan 5-0 (Selman 4, Hemphrey 1); second day, Glamorgan 452-9 (van der Gugten 0, Hogan 0); third day, Northamptonshire 68-0 (Curran 48, Vasconcelos 18).

Northamptonshire

B. J. Curran c Lloyd b Hogan	1	– c Cullen b de Lange	52
R. S. Vasconcelos c de Lange	13	– c Cullen b Hogan	18
*A. G. Wakely c Hemphrey b Douthwaite	28	– c Cullen b Hogan	3
T. Bavuma c Labuschagne b van der Gugten	8	– lbw b Hogan	34
R. I. Keogh c Lloyd b van der Gugten	4	– lbw b Hogan	43
†A. M. Rossington c Labuschagne b Hogan	77	– not out	23
J. J. Cobb c Cullen b de Lange	31	– c Cullen b de Lange	0
L. A. Procter not out	26	– c Cullen b de Lange	0
L. Wood c Cullen b Hogan	0	– b Labuschagne	6
N. L. Buck c Hemphrey b de Lange	0	– c Carlson b Labuschagne	10
B. W. Sanderson b de Lange	2	– absent hurt	
B 6, lb 3, nb 10	19	Nb 6	6

1/6 (1) 2/36 (2) 3/49 (4) (59 overs) 209
4/57 (5) 5/61 (3) 6/147 (7)
7/196 (6) 8/198 (9) 9/201 (10) 10/209 (11)

1/72 (1) 2/72 (2) (63.5 overs) 195
3/89 (3) 4/146 (4)
5/165 (5) 6/166 (7)
7/172 (8) 8/181 (9) 9/195 (10)

Hogan 17–6–39–3; de Lange 16–3–64–4; van der Gugten 11–1–33–2; Douthwaite 10–0–41–1; Labuschagne 2–0–17–0; Lloyd 3–0–6–0. *Second innings*—Hogan 16–6–32–4; de Lange 18–2–61–3; Douthwaite 9–4–31–0; van der Gugten 12–0–46–0; Labuschagne 7.5–0– 22–2; Lloyd 1–0–3–0.

Glamorgan

N. J. Selman c Rossington b Sanderson	4	T. van der Gugten not out	30
C. R. Hemphrey c Wakely b Sanderson	37	M. G. Hogan c Buck b Keogh	54
M. Labuschagne b Sanderson	6		
*D. L. Lloyd b Sanderson	0	B 8, lb 13, nb 16	37
W. T. Root c Bavuma b Procter	229		
K. S. Carlson c Vasconcelos b Buck	7	1/6 (1) 2/18 (3) (112.3 overs) 547
D. A. Douthwaite c Procter b Keogh	44	3/20 (4) 4/103 (2) 5/120 (6)
†T. N. Cullen c Rossington b Wood	63	6/207 (7) 7/374 (8) 8/448 (5)
M. de Lange c Wood b Procter	36	9/452 (9) 10/547 (11) 110 overs: 524-9

Sanderson 29–4–127–4; Wood 26–4–94–1; Buck 25–4–149–1; Procter 17–2–77–2; Keogh 12.3–0–71–2; Cobb 3–1–8–0.

Umpires: N. G. B. Cook and T. Lungley.

At Chester-le-Street, June 10–13. NORTHAMPTONSHIRE drew with DURHAM.

At Northampton, June 20. NORTHAMPTONSHIRE lost to AUSTRALIA A by six wickets (see Australia A tour section).

NORTHAMPTONSHIRE v LEICESTERSHIRE

At Northampton, June 24–27. Drawn. Northamptonshire 10pts, Leicestershire 10pts. Toss: uncontested.

Still seeking their first win of the season, Northamptonshire slumped to the bottom of the table after this stalemate. Wakely showed application to make 65 against some penetrative bowling, before being brilliantly caught by Ackermann at second slip off Mohammad Abbas. But that was an isolated highlight: on the first day, Leicestershire spilled at least seven catches, and Coles swung merrily at No. 9 to add some weight to the total. After the second day was washed out, Leicestershire's response was dominated by Azad. On 92, to great surprise, he scooped a simple catch to square leg. Northamptonshire had a lead of six, but trouble loomed at 108 for four, before Bavuma helped secure the draw with 68, his first significant score in nine Championship innings since arriving from South Africa.

Close of play: first day, Leicestershire 6-0 (Azad 3, Horton 3); second day, no play; third day, Leicestershire 273-7 (Hill 17, Wright 0).

Northamptonshire

R. S. Vasconcelos c Dearden b Davis	25	– c Azad b Mohammad Abbas	12
R. I. Newton c Ackermann b Wright	5	– c Ackermann b Mohammad Abbas	0
A. G. Wakely c Ackermann b Mohammad Abbas	65	– lbw b Mohammad Abbas	46
T. Bavuma c Hill b Klein	20	– c Azad b Klein	68
R. I. Keogh lbw b Wright	34	– c Horton b Wright	7
*†A. M. Rossington b Davis	45	– st Hill b Ackermann	19
L. A. Procter c Hill b Wright	18	– not out	15
B. A. Hutton lbw b Mohammad Abbas	17	– not out	23
M. T. Coles not out	41		
N. L. Buck c Dearden b Wright	5		
B. W. Sanderson c and b Mohammad Abbas	8		
B 6, lb 6, nb 4	16	Lb 2, nb 14	16

1/10 (2) 2/63 (1) 3/112 (4)   (90.5 overs) 299   1/2 (2)   (6 wkts dec, 58 overs) 206
4/151 (3) 5/187 (5) 6/210 (6)   2/19 (1) 3/88 (3)
7/243 (7) 8/245 (8) 9/250 (10) 10/299 (11)   4/108 (5) 5/165 (6) 6/167 (4)

Mohammad Abbas 21.5–8–49–3; Wright 23–5–78–4; Davis 19–4–47–2; Dexter 11–4–37–0; Klein 14–0–74–1; Ackermann 2–1–2–0. *Second innings*—Wright 15–2–39–1; Mohammad Abbas 12–3–39–3; Dexter 10–3–23–0; Davis 7–2–29–0; Klein 10–1–60–1; Ackermann 4–1–14–1.

Leicestershire

M. H. Azad c Coles b Procter	92	W. S. Davis not out	10
*P. J. Horton c Hutton b Buck	29	Mohammad Abbas c Coles b Sanderson	4
N. J. Dexter lbw b Hutton	27		
M. J. Cosgrove lbw b Sanderson	63	B 5, lb 17, nb 6	28
C. N. Ackermann lbw b Procter	0		
H. E. Dearden c Rossington b Sanderson	7	1/60 (2) 2/107 (3) (103.2 overs) 293
†L. J. Hill c Rossington b Coles	17	3/222 (1) 4/224 (5)
D. Klein lbw b Coles	15	5/234 (6) 6/235 (4) 7/270 (8)
C. J. C. Wright lbw b Coles	1	8/273 (7) 9/276 (9) 10/293 (11)

Sanderson 27.2–6–64–3; Hutton 22–6–52–1; Coles 21–6–51–3; Buck 11–1–44–1; Procter 12–3–37–2; Keogh 10–2–23–0.

Umpires: N. A. Mallender and B. V. Taylor. R. A. White replaced Taylor after the first day.

At Hove, June 30–July 2. NORTHAMPTONSHIRE beat SUSSEX by 393 runs.

NORTHAMPTONSHIRE v LANCASHIRE

At Northampton, July 7–10. Drawn. Northamptonshire 12pts, Lancashire 10pts. Toss: uncontested.

Lancashire's status as promotion favourites cut no ice with a rejuvenated Northamptonshire. Despite the loss of James Anderson, Lancashire fielded a high-class attack – but they were quickly made to look ordinary. Bavuma arrived when Northamptonshire were threatening to waste a promising start, and compiled a brilliant maiden Championship hundred. He had reached 86 when the second new ball was taken and, to general astonishment, twice hit Onions over extra cover for six. Onions removed him next over for 103; later, his fifth wicket was his 600th in the Championship. After Northamptonshire had been bowled out for the highest total Lancashire conceded all season, Sanderson reduced them to two for two. They were indebted to Davies, who showed sound judgment in a career-best 147. Attempting to build on a lead of 127, the home team slumped to 14 for three, before Newton and Keogh made steadying contributions. Rossington's declaration on the final morning gave Lancashire a maximum of 89 overs to survive. With four batsmen making fifties – including Hameed's second of the season – they never looked in danger.

Close of play: first day, Northamptonshire 334-5 (Rossington 76, Procter 9); second day, Lancashire 211-4 (Davies 124, Croft 38); third day, Northamptonshire 214-6 (Procter 25, Hutton 23).

Northamptonshire

R. S. Vasconcelos c Croft b Parry	77	– lbw b Onions 4
R. I. Newton c Vilas b Onions	11	– c Vilas b Gleeson 48
R. E. Levi c Jennings b Gleeson	38	– lbw b Onions 0
T. Bavuma c Vilas b Onions	103	– c Bohannon b Gleeson 1
R. I. Keogh b Onions	6	– run out (Hameed) 74
*†A. M. Rossington c Vilas b Onions	76	– b Parry 33
L. A. Procter not out	48	– b Parry 29
B. A. Hutton b Gleeson	1	– c Jennings b Bohannon 24
M. T. Coles b Onions	5	– b Parry 23
N. L. Buck b Parry	39	– not out 6
B. W. Sanderson b Gleeson	13	– not out 8
B 7, lb 18	25	B 2, lb 4, w 1, nb 6 13

1/36 (2) 2/134 (1) 3/138 (3) (129.4 overs) 442
4/154 (5) 5/303 (4) 6/334 (6)
7/335 (8) 8/352 (9) 9/413 (10)
10/442 (11) 110 overs: 362-8

1/13 (1) (9 wkts dec, 66 overs) 263
2/13 (3) 3/14 (4)
4/110 (2) 5/164 (5) 6/168 (6)
7/220 (8) 8/225 (7) 9/250 (9)

Mahmood 22–5–64–0; Onions 25–7–77–5; Gleeson 29.4–6–118–3; Parry 33–3–97–2; Jones 1–0–2–0; Bohannon 12–3–35–0; Jennings 2–0–14–0; Croft 5–1–10–0. *Second innings*—Gleeson 13–5–62–2; Onions 9–0–42–2; Bohannon 10–0–58–1; Jennings 6–0–12–0; Parry 22–2–59–3; Jones 1–0–2–0; Croft 5–1–18–0.

Lancashire

K. K. Jennings c Levi b Sanderson	0	– lbw b Coles 20
A. L. Davies c Bavuma b Keogh	147	– lbw b Sanderson 53
H. Hameed b Sanderson	0	– b Keogh 55
R. P. Jones c Procter b Keogh	44	– lbw b Hutton 11
J. J. Bohannon c Vasconcelos b Keogh	2	– not out 65
S. J. Croft lbw b Sanderson	78	
*†D. J. Vilas not out	27	– (6) not out 53
S. D. Parry b Hutton	0	
S. Mahmood c Vasconcelos b Hutton	1	
G. Onions c Rossington b Sanderson	4	
R. J. Gleeson c Rossington b Hutton	8	
Lb 4	4	B 1, lb 15, nb 2 18

1/2 (1) 2/2 (3) 3/129 (4) (94 overs) 315
4/131 (5) 5/266 (2) 6/290 (6)
7/295 (8) 8/297 (9) 9/306 (10) 10/315 (11)

1/60 (1) (4 wkts, 82.3 overs) 275
2/80 (2) 3/111 (4)
4/185 (3)

Sanderson 26–7–62–4; Hutton 23–3–77–3; Buck 11–1–53–0; Coles 8–0–40–0; Procter 15–5–36–0; Keogh 11–2–43–3. *Second innings*—Sanderson 21–9–55–1; Hutton 15.3–4–43–1; Buck 10–1–41–0; Coles 8–1–46–1; Keogh 22–10–50–1; Procter 6–1–24–0.

Umpires: D. J. Millns and C. M. Watts.

At Chesterfield, July 14–16. NORTHAMPTONSHIRE beat DERBYSHIRE by 72 runs.

NORTHAMPTONSHIRE v WORCESTERSHIRE

At Northampton, August 18–20. Northamptonshire won by ten wickets. Northamptonshire 22pts, Worcestershire 2pts. Toss: Worcestershire. Championship debuts: J. A. Haynes; D. Pretorius.

Northamptonshire moved back into the promotion places with a comprehensive performance, dictating terms from the moment Leach chose to bat. Within an hour, Hutton had claimed a five-for and twice been on a hat-trick. Ali, returning for Worcestershire after being dropped from England's Ashes squad, made a haphazard 42, before Leach's innings fifty added respectability to the total. But Northamptonshire surged into a commanding lead on the back of contrasting hundreds: Wakely was a model of patience, while Pretorius, an overseas Twenty20 recruit making his sole first-class appearance of the season, bristled with aggression. Ali picked up three late wickets with his off-breaks, but proved costly and resorted to two overs of seam. Any hope Worcestershire had of saving the game was removed by a superb opening burst by Sanderson of four for 13 in nine overs. Wessels counter-attacked against his first county, but Northamptonshire were not to be denied. There were two wickets for Muzarabani, a concussion substitute for Buck, who had been hit on the head as nightwatchman on the first evening. The bowler, Tongue, strained his side, and neither he nor Buck resumed the next morning.

Close of play: first day, Northamptonshire 140-3 (Wakely 63, Buck 2); second day, Worcestershire 42-4 (Ali 10, Leach 4).

Worcestershire

D. K. H. Mitchell c Wakely b Sanderson	2	– c Hutton b Sanderson		4
J. A. Haynes b Hutton	0	– c Rossington b Sanderson		19
M. M. Ali c Procter b Buck	42	– run out (Hutton/Rossington)		40
C. J. Ferguson lbw b Hutton	1	– b Sanderson		0
A. G. Milton c Rossington b Hutton	0	– lbw b Sanderson		0
M. H. Wessels lbw b Hutton	6	– (7) not out		84
†O. B. Cox c Keogh b Hutton	0	– (8) b Pretorius		5
E. G. Barnard b Pretorius	27	– (9) lbw b Muzarabani		18
W. D. Parnell c Keogh b Hutton	30	– (10) b Muzarabani		7
*J. Leach not out	53	– (6) lbw b Keogh		27
J. C. Tongue c Wakely b Buck	20	– c Wakely b Keogh		2
Lb 3, nb 2	5	B 4, lb 8, w 5		17

1/0 (2) 2/14 (1) 3/15 (4)   (46.3 overs) 186   1/22 (1) 2/23 (2)   (61.2 overs) 223
4/15 (5) 5/31 (6) 6/31 (7)   3/23 (4) 4/29 (5)
7/58 (3) 8/108 (9) 9/134 (8) 10/186 (11)   5/95 (6) 6/97 (3) 7/112 (8)
8/166 (9) 9/196 (10) 10/223 (11)

Sanderson 12–2–40–1; Hutton 16–4–57–6; Buck 5.3–1–31–2; Pretorius 11–3–33–1; Procter 2–0–22–0. *Second innings*—Sanderson 13.5–5–33–4; Hutton 10–1–49–0; Pretorius 9–3–21–1; Keogh 20.2–1–61–2; Muzarabani 9–0–47–2.

Northamptonshire

B. J. Curran lbw b Parnell	10	– not out		17
R. I. Newton b Tongue	2	– not out		17
A. G. Wakely b Parnell	102			
R. I. Keogh c Mitchell b Parnell	53			
N. L. Buck retired hurt	2			
D. Pretorius c sub (J. J. Dell) b Barnard	111			
*†A. M. Rossington b Leach	1			
S. A. Zaib c Milton b Leach	32			
B. A. Hutton lbw b Ali	8			
L. A. Procter not out	17			
B. W. Sanderson c Ferguson b Ali	8			
B. Muzarabani b Ali	1			
B 5, lb 11, w 1, nb 12	29	Nb 2		2

1/4 (2) 2/26 (1) 3/128 (4)   (123.1 overs) 376
4/269 (3) 5/290 (7) 6/312 (6)
7/336 (9) 8/356 (8) 9/369 (11)
10/376 (12)

(no wkt, 4.3 overs) 36

110 overs: 336-7

In the first innings Buck retired hurt at 140-3. Muzarabani replaced Buck, as a concussion substitute.

Leach 25–4–67–2; Tongue 8.3–0–27–1; Parnell 25.3–7–65–3; Barnard 19–7–62–1; Ali 39.1–8–126–3; Mitchell 6–1–13–0. *Second innings*—Leach 2.3–0–17–0; Ali 2–0–19–0.

Umpires: M. Burns and M. Newell.

At Leicester, September 10–13. NORTHAMPTONSHIRE beat LEICESTERSHIRE by seven wickets.

NORTHAMPTONSHIRE v DURHAM

At Northampton, September 16–19. Northamptonshire won by 169 runs. Northamptonshire 20pts, Durham 3pts. Toss: uncontested. County debut: B-J. Watling.

The Northamptonshire players sipped champagne on the outfield after a fourth successive victory left them on the cusp of promotion. They needed just four points from their final match against Gloucestershire, nine points from promotion themselves. Durham had seen their own lingering hopes snuffed out by another impressive all-round display. Bowling first beneath heavy cloud and under lights, they had wastefully allowed Northamptonshire to reach 99 for one just after lunch. Then Rushworth tuned his radar – and they slumped to 150 for eight. Rossington led a thrilling counter-thrust, his 82 culminating in a sequence of 60 from 22 balls, including seven sixes, as he skilfully targeted the short Clarke Road boundary. Sanderson then struck three times before the close to confirm Northamptonshire's fightback, and finished with six next morning as Durham were skittled for 131. It was not the end of the contest, however. At 65 for four, Northamptonshire were far from unassailable, and it needed fifties from Levi and Rossington, and an unbeaten 86 from Procter, to re-establish control. Hutton's five-for sealed the deal.

Close of play: first day, Durham 37-4 (Burnham 2, S. Steel 2); second day, Northamptonshire 235-6 (Procter 43, Bracewell 15); third day, Durham 212-8 (Eckersley 54, Salisbury 2).

Northamptonshire

B. J. Curran b Rushworth	36	– c Watling b Raine	19
R. I. Newton c Robson b Raine	26	– c Eckersley b Raine	0
A. G. Wakely b Rushworth	28	– c Robson b Salisbury	30
R. I. Keogh c Eckersley b Rushworth	0	– lbw b Salisbury	4
R. E. Levi c Robson b Carse	16	– c Burnham b Rushworth	60
*†A. M. Rossington c Lees b Salisbury	82	– b Raine	52
L. A. Procter c Eckersley b Raine	8	– not out	86
D. A. J. Bracewell lbw b Rushworth	1	– c Robson b Raine	15
G. K. Berg b Raine	3	– c Robson b Rushworth	1
B. A. Hutton c Lees b Rushworth	4	– c C. T. Steel b Carse	16
B. W. Sanderson not out	0	– lbw b Carse	14
B 5, lb 7, w 1	13	B 10, lb 3, w 1, nb 4	18

1/50 (2) 2/99 (3) 3/99 (4)   (59.1 overs) 217
4/108 (1) 5/119 (5) 6/134 (7)
7/139 (8) 8/150 (9) 9/194 (10) 10/217 (6)

1/0 (2) 2/54 (1)   (87 overs) 315
3/54 (3) 4/65 (4)
5/156 (5) 6/195 (6) 7/235 (8)
8/238 (9) 9/264 (10) 10/315 (11)

Rushworth 21–4–68–5; Carse 12–1–73–1; Raine 17–4–53–3; Salisbury 9.1–6–11–1. *Second innings*—Rushworth 21–6–54–2; Raine 27–6–93–4; Salisbury 17–2–68–2; Carse 15–1–71–2; S. Steel 7–3–16–0.

Durham

A. Z. Lees c Wakely b Sanderson	15	– b Hutton	9
C. T. Steel c Hutton b Sanderson	7	– lbw b Hutton	8
A. J. Robson lbw b Sanderson	9	– c Rossington b Hutton	1
B-J. Watling lbw b Berg	0	– b Procter	35
J. T. A. Burnham lbw b Sanderson	2	– c Rossington b Procter	45
S. Steel b Sanderson	6	– b Sanderson	1
*†E. J. H. Eckersley st Rossington b Hutton	37	– not out	67
B. A. Raine c Rossington b Hutton	18	– b Hutton	5
B. A. Carse b Sanderson	7	– c Levi b Bracewell	30
M. E. T. Salisbury c Rossington b Berg	13	– lbw b Hutton	8
C. Rushworth not out	12	– c Curran b Sanderson	0
Lb 5	5	B 10, lb 6, w 5, nb 2	23

1/14 (2) 2/32 (1) 3/33 (4)   (48.3 overs) 131
4/35 (3) 5/41 (6) 6/42 (5)
7/99 (8) 8/102 (7) 9/106 (9) 10/131 (10)

1/16 (1) 2/18 (3)   (88.2 overs) 232
3/19 (2) 4/85 (4)
5/96 (6) 6/106 (5) 7/134 (8)
8/187 (9) 9/221 (10) 10/232 (11)

Hutton 17–6–29–2; Sanderson 18–3–54–6; Berg 7.3–2–17–2; Bracewell 5–1–22–0; Procter 1–0–4–0. *Second innings*—Hutton 25–6–59–5; Sanderson 21.2–8–43–2; Berg 9–1–25–0; Bracewell 12–2–40–1; Procter 10–1–37–2; Keogh 11–4–12–0.

Umpires: P. J. Hartley and R. J. Warren.

At Bristol, September 23–26. NORTHAMPTONSHIRE drew with GLOUCESTERSHIRE. *The teams hold a joint party after a rain-hit draw secures promotion for both.*

NOTTINGHAMSHIRE

No wins, no excuses, no escape

Jon Culley

After Nottinghamshire's uncomfortable brush with relegation in 2018, they hoped a clutch of new players would lead to better things. Instead, a collapse during the second half of that season turned out to be the precursor of relegation in 2019. For the first time since 1967, Nottinghamshire did not win a first-class match. Their points tally of 67 was the lowest by any county since the introduction of two divisions in 2000, even adjusting for the reduction from 16 matches to 14. They earned 16 batting points, five down on a dismal 21 the previous year.

Their ten defeats were all emphatic: two by an innings, three by 200 runs or more, three by 100-plus, two by eight wickets. Nottinghamshire were relegated with two rounds to go. This was in contrast to their white-ball form: they finished top of their Royal London Cup group, and second in their Vitality Blast group, though they could not reach either final.

In the Championship, the new players – batsmen Ben Slater (from Derbyshire), Ben Duckett (Northamptonshire) and Joe Clarke (Worcestershire), plus all-rounder Zak Chappell (Leicestershire) – were universally disappointing. Opening the batting, Slater made a century against Cambridge and 76 in the first Championship fixture, against Yorkshire, but in 23 subsequent innings reached 30 only four times. Duckett scored a double-hundred and 82 against Cambridge, and was one of only three players to complete a Championship century, but in 15 of his 23 innings he failed to get to 25. Chappell, who had toured India with England Lions in early 2019, suffered injuries but, even when fit, could not hold down a place. In six matches in all formats for Nottinghamshire, he contributed 67 runs; he took a single wicket, while on loan to Gloucestershire in the Blast.

Clarke, who had made 12 first-class centuries in four seasons at Worcester, carried the greatest expectations. But in January 2019 he had to testify in the trial of his former team-mate Alex Hepburn on rape charges. He and Yorkshire's Tom Köhler-Cadmore were dropped from the Lions programme after it emerged that they had formed a WhatsApp group with Hepburn to brag about sexual conquests. The original trial failed to reach a verdict, so a retrial was arranged for April. Clarke scored 112 and 97 not out against Yorkshire before his second court appearance, but once Hepburn was convicted – and in particular after a later hearing saw him jailed for five years – Clarke was deeply affected. The ECB fined him and Köhler-Cadmore £2,000 each for bringing the game into disrepute, though they were deemed to have served a four-match suspension already after their exclusion from the Lions tour. Not until the penultimate round of the Championship did Clarke return to his best. Chastened by being dropped, he hit twin hundreds against Warwickshire (despite making 498 inside four sessions, Nottinghamshire contrived to lose). In between his peaks against Yorkshire and

Luke Fletcher

Warwickshire, he totalled 175 in 17 Championship innings.

Wicketkeeper-batsman Tom Moores averaged only 14, compared with 29 in 2018, and for the second year running Samit Patel failed to record a Championship century. He spent the final rounds on loan to Glamorgan. Steven Mullaney, the captain, was characteristically resilient: despite knee surgery in July, he was the leading Championship run-scorer with 694 (and the team's third centurion).

The bowling was bolstered first by Australia's James Pattinson, and later by India's off-spinner Ravichandran Ashwin, who claimed 34 wickets in five matches – just behind Luke Fletcher's 35 from 12 – and, less predictably, headed the batting averages. Fletcher, who also took 17 in the Royal London One-Day Cup, was named Player of the Season.

Paul Coughlin had another year disrupted by injury, and decided to return to Durham. Jake Ball was again short of his best, and Stuart Broad's longest period of continued availability for the county yielded no match-winning performances. Harry Gurney, who had opted out of first-class cricket after claiming 254 Championship wickets over seven seasons, was missed, while Matt Milnes, who had turned down a new contract, took 55 in his first year with Kent. Luke Wood, who spent four Championship games on loan at Northamptonshire, announced a move to Old Trafford just after his best return of the season.

Alex Hales was another player in a personal crisis, banished by England following two failed tests for recreational drug use. Contracted for white-ball cricket only, he helped Nottinghamshire reach the semi-finals of both limited-overs competitions. The highlight of his season was a 165-run opening stand with Chris Nash to secure a ten-wicket victory over Middlesex in the Blast quarter-final. He also made 52 in the semi against Worcestershire, only for Nottinghamshire to implode when a place in the final was within their grasp.

Doubts over the future of head coach Peter Moores ended when he agreed a new two-year contract, vowing to reverse the decline over which he had presided. Former England bowling coach Kevin Shine arrived as his assistant. They were expected to hand more opportunities to youth in Division Two: contracts were given to two 21-year-old bowlers – left-arm spinner Liam Patterson-White, who had taken 20 wickets in five matches, and fast bowler Jack Blatherwick – plus batsmen Joey Evison, 18, and Ben Compton, 25, a grandson of Denis. Haseeb Hameed joined from Lancashire, and in December Moores was delighted to sign Pakistan seamer Mohammad Abbas, after two seasons with Leicestershire, and all-rounder Peter Trego, who had left Somerset.

Championship attendance: 29,032.

NOTTINGHAMSHIRE RESULTS

All first-class matches - Played 15: Lost 10, Drawn 5.
County Championship matches – Played 14: Lost 10, Drawn 4.

Specsavers County Championship, 8th in Division 1;
Vitality Blast, semi-finalists; Royal London One-Day Cup, semi-finalists.

COUNTY CHAMPIONSHIP AVERAGES, BATTING AND FIELDING

Cap		Birthplace	M	I	NO	R	HS	100	Avge	Ct/St
2019	R. Ashwin¶	Madras, India . . .	5	10	1	339	66*	0	37.66	2
	J. M. Clarke	Shrewsbury . . .	12	21	1	621	125	3	31.05	6
	C. D. Nash	Cuckfield	12	22	1	641	85	0	30.52	4
2013	S. J. Mullaney	Warrington	13	24	0	694	157	2	28.91	13
	†B. M. Duckett	Farnborough, Kent .	13	23	0	630	140	1	27.39	7
	P. Coughlin	Sunderland	5	7	0	167	49	0	23.85	7
	†B. T. Slater	Chesterfield	13	24	1	471	76	0	20.47	6
	J. D. Libby	Plymouth	5	10	0	189	77	0	18.90	3
2017	†J. L. Pattinson¶	Melbourne, Aust . .	3	5	2	55	22	0	18.33	0
2008	S. R. Patel	Leicester	9	16	1	258	52	0	17.20	2
	†L. A. Patterson-White	Sunderland	5	8	2	91	58*	0	15.16	3
2016	J. T. Ball	Mansfield‡	13	20	0	323	48	0	14.04	29/1
2008	S. C. J. Broad§	Nottingham‡	10	16	11	67	15*	0	13.40	3
	Z. J. Chappell	Grantham	7	13	4	109	30	0	12.11	3
	†L. Wood	Sheffield	3	6	1	59	29	0	11.80	1
2014	L. J. Fletcher	Nottingham‡	12	9	1	87	52	0	10.87	0
	M. Carter	Lincoln	12	22	1	209	25*	0	9.95	2
			5	7	0	51	23	0	7.28	5

Also batted: J. M. Blatherwick (*Nottingham‡*) (2 matches) 4*, 2*; †B. G. Compton (*Durban, SA*) (2 matches) 14, 13, 16* (1 ct); J. D. M. Evison (*Peterborough*) (1 match) 45, 12 (1 ct).

‡ *Born in Nottinghamshire.*   § *ECB contract.*   ¶ *Official overseas player.*

BOWLING

	Style	O	M	R	W	BB	5I	Avge
L. A. Patterson-White	SLA	134.5	17	420	20	5-73	1	21.00
R. Ashwin	OB	297.4	73	836	34	6-69	4	24.58
L. J. Fletcher	RFM	326.4	68	926	35	5-50	2	26.45
S. C. J. Broad	RFM	195.4	44	509	17	5-73	1	29.94
L. Wood	LFM	93	12	349	11	5-67	1	31.72
S. J. Mullaney	RM	166	32	536	13	4-48	0	41.23
P. Coughlin	RFM	135.4	19	530	11	3-37	0	48.18
J. T. Ball	RFM	246.5	42	878	15	2-57	0	58.53

Also bowled: J. M. Blatherwick (RFM) 34.4–3–192–2; M. Carter (OB) 137.4–14–529–6; Z. J. Chappell (RFM) 40.4-3–178–0; B. M. Duckett (OB) 4–0–16–0; J. D. M. Evison (RM) 9–0–33–0; J. D. Libby (OB) 4–0–32–0; S. R. Patel (SLA) 117.5–18–391–7; J. L. Pattinson (RFM) 74–12–235–8.

LEADING ROYAL LONDON CUP AVERAGES (120 runs/3 wickets)

Batting	Runs	HS	Avge	SR	Ct/St
B. T. Slater	315	100	78.75	88.23	0
S. J. Mullaney . .	305	81	50.83	114.66	2
J. M. Clarke . . .	340	139	42.50	129.27	1
S. R. Patel . . .	210	136*	42.00	84.00	2
T. J. Moores . . .	281	74	40.14	132.54	8/2
C. D. Nash . . .	157	56	39.25	85.79	0
L. J. Fletcher . .	138	46*	34.50	164.28	2
B. M. Duckett . .	145	86	20.71	115.07	6

Bowling	W	BB	Avge	ER
L. J. Fletcher	17	5-56	21.64	5.82
J. L. Pattinson . .	11	5-61	24.00	5.38
J. T. Ball	14	4-62	25.57	6.62
M. Carter	7	3-60	43.28	5.90
S. R. Patel	8	2-42	45.50	5.76
S. J. Mullaney . . .	3	1-35	81.00	7.14

LEADING VITALITY BLAST AVERAGES (90 runs/15 overs)

Batting	Runs	HS	Avge	SR	Ct/St		Bowling	W	BB	Avge	ER
T. J. Moores....	218	69	31.14	144.37	7/2		M. Carter	14	3-14	19.78	**6.59**
C. D. Nash	98	74*	98.00	142.02	1		Imad Wasim	10	2-21	16.60	**6.64**
D. T. Christian ..	183	41*	36.60	140.76	6		S. R. Patel......	6	2-26	43.83	**6.74**
A. D. Hales	418	83*	38.00	140.26	8		L. Wood	11	3-16	17.54	**7.01**
B. M. Duckett ..	255	64	25.50	128.78	10		D. T. Christian ...	8	3-26	19.00	**8.00**
S. R. Patel	93	34	18.60	127.39	3		H. F. Gurney.....	22	5-30	18.00	**9.00**
J. M. Clarke	248	50	27.55	119.23	1		J. T. Ball........	4	2-21	35.75	**9.53**

FIRST-CLASS COUNTY RECORDS

Highest score for	312*	W. W. Keeton v Middlesex at The Oval	1939
Highest score against	345	C. G. Macartney (Australians) at Nottingham	1921
Leading run-scorer	31,592	G. Gunn (avge 35.69)	1902–32
Best bowling for	10-66	K. Smales v Gloucestershire at Stroud........	1956
Best bowling against	10-10	H. Verity (Yorkshire) at Leeds	1932
Leading wicket-taker	1,653	T. G. Wass (avge 20.34)	1896–1920
Highest total for	791	v Essex at Chelmsford	2007
Highest total against	781-7 dec	by Northamptonshire at Northampton	1995
Lowest total for	13	v Yorkshire at Nottingham.	1901
Lowest total against {	16	by Derbyshire at Nottingham.	1879
	16	by Surrey at The Oval	1880

LIST A COUNTY RECORDS

Highest score for	187*	A. D. Hales v Surrey at Lord's	2017
Highest score against	191	D. S. Lehmann (Yorkshire) at Scarborough........	2001
Leading run-scorer	11,237	R. T. Robinson (avge 35.33)	1978–99
Best bowling for	6-10	K. P. Evans v Northumberland at Jesmond	1994
Best bowling against	7-41	A. N. Jones (Sussex) at Nottingham	1986
Leading wicket-taker	291	C. E. B. Rice (avge 22.60)	1975–87
Highest total for	445-8	v Northamptonshire at Nottingham	2016
Highest total against	425	by Northamptonshire at Nottingham	2016
Lowest total for	57	v Gloucestershire at Nottingham	2009
Lowest total against	43	by Northamptonshire at Northampton	1977

TWENTY20 COUNTY RECORDS

Highest score for	113*	D. T. Christian v Northants at Northampton	2018
Highest score against	111	W. J. Durston (Derbyshire) at Nottingham	2010
Leading run-scorer	**3,558**	**S. R. Patel (avge 27.16, SR 127.16)**	**2003–19**
Best bowling for	5-22	G. G. White v Lancashire at Nottingham	2013
Best bowling against	5-13	A. B. McDonald (Leicestershire) at Nottingham....	2010
Leading wicket-taker	**154**	**S. R. Patel (avge 26.81, ER 7.32)**	**2003–19**
Highest total for	227-3	by Derbyshire at Nottingham........	2017
Highest total against	227-5	by Yorkshire at Leeds	2017
Lowest total for	91	v Lancashire at Manchester	2006
Lowest total against	90	by Leicestershire at Nottingham	2014

ADDRESS

County Cricket Ground, Trent Bridge, Nottingham NG2 6AG; 0115 982 3000; administration@nottsccc.co.uk; www.nottsccc.co.uk.

OFFICIALS

Captain (Ch'ship/one-day) S. J. Mullaney
(Twenty20) D. T. Christian
Director of cricket M. Newell
Head coach P. Moores
President W. Taylor

Chairman R. W. Tennant
Chief executive L. J. Pursehouse
Chairman, cricket committee D. J. Bicknell
Head groundsman S. Birks
Scorer R. Marshall

At Cambridge, March 31–April 2. NOTTINGHAMSHIRE drew with CAMBRIDGE MCCU.

NOTTINGHAMSHIRE v YORKSHIRE

At Nottingham, April 5–8. Drawn. Nottinghamshire 12pts, Yorkshire 9pts. Toss: uncontested.

Each team fielded four Test players, but Nottinghamshire held the upper hand. They led by 446 when they declared ahead of the final day; on a moribund surface, a draw was always likely, but it took a resilient unbroken partnership of 253 between Ballance and Root to see Yorkshire to safety. Their South African Kolpak signing Olivier had picked up seven wickets, while Nottinghamshire were encouraged by a prolific home debut from Clarke. In his previous innings at Trent Bridge, for Worcestershire ten months earlier, he had scored 177 not out; this time, he made a century on the opening day and an unbeaten 97 on the third, but was stranded by the declaration. Broad produced hostile spells in both innings, and on the last day struck Root on the helmet with the first ball he faced. Play halted while he was checked for concussion, but he compiled his first county hundred in almost three years.

Close of play: first day, Nottinghamshire 324-5 (Clarke 109, Moores 11); second day, Yorkshire 206-5 (Root 56, Tattersall 4); third day, Nottinghamshire 329-5 (Clarke 97, Patel 23).

Nottinghamshire

B. T. Slater c Tattersall b Olivier	76	– c Lyth b Coad	2
B. M. Duckett c Waite b Patterson	43	– c Lyth b Olivier	61
C. D. Nash lbw b Waite	21	– c Root b Olivier	75
J. M. Clarke b Olivier	112	– not out	97
*S. J. Mullaney c Lyth b Olivier	31	– b Waite	52
S. R. Patel c Brook b Patterson	11	– (7) not out	23
†T. J. Moores c Ballance b Olivier	27	– (6) c Tattersall b Waite	1
P. Coughlin c Tattersall b Patterson	46		
S. C. J. Broad lbw b Olivier	0		
L. J. Fletcher c Köhler-Cadmore b Patterson	3		
J. T. Ball not out	15		
B 10, lb 10, w 1, nb 2	23	B 6, lb 4, w 2, nb 6	18

1/75 (2) 2/125 (3) 3/172 (1)   (120.3 overs) 408   1/6 (1)   (5 wkts dec, 70 overs) 329
4/226 (5) 5/249 (6) 6/329 (4)   2/94 (2) 3/196 (3)
7/358 (7) 8/358 (9) 9/375 (10)   4/278 (5) 5/300 (6)
10/408 (8)   110 overs: 368-8

Coad 28–4–96–0; Olivier 28–6–96–5; Waite 22–4–91–1; Patterson 30.3–7–78–4; Root 12–1–27–0. *Second innings*—Coad 13–2–57–1; Olivier 14–1–66–2; Patterson 14–2–52–0; Root 11–5–57–0; Waite 16–0–71–2; Lyth 2–0–16–0.

Yorkshire

A. Lyth c Fletcher b Ball	81	– b Ball	21
H. C. Brook lbw b Broad	30	– c Nash b Ball	2
G. S. Ballance b Fletcher	7	– not out	101
J. E. Root c Mullaney b Patel	73	– not out	130
T. Köhler-Cadmore c Coughlin b Broad	22		
J. A. Leaning b Fletcher	0		
J. A. Tattersall b Fletcher	9		
M. J. Waite c Mullaney b Patel	22		
S. A. Patterson c Mullaney b Patel	4		
B. O. Coad not out	26		
D. Olivier c Moores b Broad	7		
B 6, lb 2, nb 2	10	B 9, lb 12, nb 2	23

1/39 (2) 2/70 (3) 3/153 (1)   (82.3 overs) 291   1/19 (2)   (2 wkts, 78.2 overs) 277
4/194 (5) 5/195 (6) 6/215 (7)   2/24 (1)
7/253 (4) 8/256 (8) 9/265 (9) 10/291 (11)

Broad 20.3–4–56–3; Ball 17–3–67–1; Coughlin 13–1–49–0; Fletcher 20–5–64–3; Mullaney 3–0–16–0; Patel 9–2–31–3. *Second innings*—Ball 18–3–73–2; Broad 11–2–20–0; Coughlin 13–1–58–0; Fletcher 8–3–10–0; Patel 25.2–3–81–0; Duckett 3–0–14–0.

Umpires: D. J. Millns and R. J. Warren.

NOTTINGHAMSHIRE v SOMERSET

At Nottingham, April 11–13. Somerset won by an innings and 14 runs. Somerset 24pts, Nottinghamshire 4pts (after 1pt penalty). Toss: uncontested.

Broad caught the eye again, but he was one of the few positives for Nottinghamshire, who were thoroughly outplayed in their seventh successive Championship defeat by Somerset. In the first innings, Gregory had exploited conditions suiting seam and swing to take six for 68, his best figures for five years. In the second, the spin of Leach proved Nottinghamshire's undoing; never before in a seven-year career had he claimed a five-for in early April, but here he collected six for 36. Broad's five-wicket return was his first in county cricket since 2015; as if not Somerset soon recovered from losing their top three for ten apiece on the first evening. A 223-run stand between Abell and 21-year-old Bartlett, who made a near-flawless career-best 133, was a fourth-wicket record for this fixture, and Gregory chipped in with a run-a-ball fifty to ensure a safe batting point. Trailing by 140, Nottinghamshire capitulated, their last eight tumbling for 60. They lost by an innings midway through the third day, and were fined one point for a slow over-rate.

Close of play: first day, Somerset 74-3 (Abell 22, Bartlett 9); second day, Nottinghamshire 25-2 (Slater 13, Fletcher 4).

Nottinghamshire

B. T. Slater c Davies b Davey	24	– st Davies b Leach	34
B. M. Duckett lbw b Brooks	0	– c Abell b Brooks	4
C. D. Nash c Leach b Gregory	58	– c Davies b Brooks	0
J. M. Clarke c Davies b Gregory	2	– (5) b Leach	2
*S. J. Mullaney lbw b Gregory	26	– (6) st Davies b Leach	16
S. R. Patel b Gregory	33	– (7) lbw b Leach	24
†T. J. Moores c Trescothick b Overton	47	– (8) c Trescothick b Leach	8
L. Wood c Abell b Gregory	52	– (9) c Trescothick b Brooks	0
S. C. J. Broad b Overton	5	– (10) c Azhar Ali b Brooks	5
L. J. Fletcher b Gregory	0	– (4) c Overton b Leach	21
J. T. Ball not out	8	– not out	0
Lb 4, nb 4	8	B 9, lb 1, nb 2	12

1/0 (2) 2/51 (1) 3/54 (4)   (66.4 overs) 263   1/8 (2) 2/16 (3)   (59.1 overs) 126
4/106 (5) 5/119 (3) 6/177 (6)   3/66 (1) 4/72 (5)
7/223 (7) 8/237 (9) 9/246 (10) 10/263 (8)   5/81 (4) 6/97 (6) 7/111 (8)
                              8/120 (9) 9/126 (7) 10/126 (10)

Gregory 16.4–3–68–6; Brooks 15–1–77–1; Davey 15–2–55–1; Overton 16–5–48–2; Abell 4–1–11–0. *Second innings*—Gregory 14–4–33–0; Brooks 14.1–7–22–4; Overton 9–1–15–0; Davey 5–3–10–0; Leach 17–6–36–6.

Somerset

M. E. Trescothick c Moores b Broad	10	M. J. Leach b Broad	1
Azhar Ali lbw b Broad	10	J. A. Brooks not out	1
J. C. Hildreth c Moores b Fletcher	10		
*T. B. Abell c Moores b Wood	101	B 15, lb 10, w 1, nb 8	34
G. A. Bartlett b Fletcher	133		
†S. M. Davies c Moores b Ball	22	1/19 (2) 2/36 (1) (108.1 overs) 403
L. Gregory c Duckett b Broad	50	3/36 (3) 4/259 (4)
C. Overton c Patel b Fletcher	4	5/310 (6) 6/316 (5) 7/332 (8)
J. H. Davey c sub (K. S. Leverock) b Broad	25	8/400 (9) 9/400 (7) 10/403 (10)

Ball 25.2–122–1; Broad 25.1–4–73–5; Fletcher 26–6–66–3; Wood 18–2–62–1; Mullaney 7–0–23–0; Patel 7–0–32–0.

Umpires: M. A. Gough and S. J. O'Shaughnessy.

At Chelmsford, May 14–16. NOTTINGHAMSHIRE lost to ESSEX by eight wickets.

At Newclose, May 20–23. NOTTINGHAMSHIRE lost to HAMPSHIRE by 244 runs.

At Birmingham, June 3–6. NOTTINGHAMSHIRE drew with WARWICKSHIRE.

NOTTINGHAMSHIRE v HAMPSHIRE

At Sookholme, June 9–12. Drawn. Nottinghamshire 5pts, Hampshire 8pts. Toss: uncontested.

Poor weather allowed play only on the first day at Welbeck CC, a venue making its first-class debut after hosting several one-day matches. Situated in the north of the county between the hamlets of Sookholme and Nettleworth, the ground had been developed through the philanthropy of John Fretwell, an entrepreneur who played for the club in its earlier incarnation as Welbeck Colliery. Nottinghamshire were denied any batting points for the third time in four games, as overcast conditions and good bounce played into the hands of Abbott; he earned his 12th haul of five-plus in his fourth season with Hampshire. There was time for Ball, a former Welbeck player, to dismiss Rahane before three days of rain.

Close of play: first day, Hampshire 93-2 (Weatherley 47, Crane 5); second day, no play; third day, no play.

Nottinghamshire

B. T. Slater b Barker	0	L. Wood b Abbott		0
B. M. Duckett c Alsop b Fuller	22	L. J. Fletcher c Northeast b Abbott		4
C. D. Nash lbw b Abbott	6	J. T. Ball not out		0
J. M. Clarke c Weatherley b Abbott	6	B 7, lb 3, w 1, nb 16		27
S. R. Patel c Alsop b Abbott	24			
*S. J. Mullaney c Alsop b Fuller	45	1/0 (1) 2/17 (3) 3/41 (4)	(60.2 overs)	162
†T. J. Moores lbw b Barker	6	4/55 (2) 5/85 (5) 6/105 (7)		
J. L. Pattinson b Abbott	22	7/156 (8) 8/158 (9) 9/162 (10) 10/162 (6)		

Barker 16–6–40–2; Abbott 14–3–37–6; Fuller 14.2–5–33–2; Edwards 13–2–37–0; Crane 3–0–5–0.

Hampshire

J. J. Weatherley not out		47
O. C. Soames c Mullaney b Fletcher		2
A. M. Rahane c Mullaney b Ball		34
M. S. Crane not out		5
B 2, lb 1, nb 2		5
1/5 (2) 2/85 (3) (2 wkts, 33 overs)		93

*S. A. Northeast, R. R. Rossouw, †T. P. Alsop, J. K. Fuller, K. H. D. Barker, K. J. Abbott and F. H. Edwards did not bat.

Fletcher 7–3–10–1; Pattinson 10–2–31–0; Wood 6–1–18–0; Ball 7–3–21–1; Mullaney 3–0–10–0.

Umpires: N. G. B. Cook and P. R. Pollard.

At Tunbridge Wells, June 17–20. NOTTINGHAMSHIRE lost to KENT by 285 runs.

NOTTINGHAMSHIRE v ESSEX

At Nottingham, June 30–July 3. Essex won by an innings and 123 runs. Essex 22pts, Nottinghamshire 2pts. Toss: Nottinghamshire. County debut: R. Ashwin.

Nottinghamshire's collapse from 126 for two to 213 after electing to bat set the tone for another dismal performance. Ravichandran Ashwin bowled 60 overs on his county debut – only Patel, at Chester-le-Street in 2009, had sent down as many in an innings for the club in the previous 25 years – but Essex took control through unhurried batting on a slow, flat pitch. Dropped on 81, Browne occupied the crease for seven and a half hours, scoring his first Championship century for two years, while Bopara's stylish hundred steered them to their largest total in 2019; it took Broad's athletic dive on the midwicket boundary to remove him. Needing 306 to make Essex bat again, Nottinghamshire sabotaged their own efforts. Mullaney was bowled shouldering arms, and Slater run out in a mix-up with Clarke, who was caught behind soon afterwards. That ended any realistic prospect of denying Essex their fifth win in six matches, and first away from Chelmsford; it arrived 40 minutes into the fourth afternoon, with Harmer becoming the first to reach 50 first-class wickets in the season.

Close of play: first day, Essex 72-1 (Browne 39, Westley 25); second day, Essex 345-3 (Browne 163, Bopara 62); third day, Nottinghamshire 100-5 (Duckett 32, Fletcher 4).

Nottinghamshire

*S. J. Mullaney c Wheater b Beard	74	– b Porter		0
B. M. Duckett c Cook b Porter	8	– (6) c Wheater b Harmer		39
B. T. Slater c Wheater b Beard	14	– (2) run out (Beard)		10
C. D. Nash c Wheater b Beard	28	– (3) lbw b Siddle		13
J. M. Clarke lbw b Siddle	15	– (4) c Wheater b Beard		21
S. R. Patel lbw b Siddle	39	– (5) c Cook b Harmer		20
R. Ashwin lbw b Porter	5	– (9) c Siddle b Porter		35
†T. J. Moores b Harmer	0	– b Beard		14
L. J. Fletcher lbw b Porter	1	– (7) c Wheater b Harmer		11
S. C. J. Broad not out	19	– lbw b Harmer		6
J. T. Ball c Wheater b Siddle	1	– not out		0
B 1, lb 6, nb 2	9	B 9, w 5		14

1/13 (2) 2/71 (3) 3/126 (4)   (69.1 overs) 213
4/141 (1) 5/151 (5) 6/162 (7)
7/163 (8) 8/168 (9) 9/211 (6) 10/213 (11)

1/0 (1) 2/13 (3)   (89.2 overs) 183
3/40 (2) 4/49 (4)
5/95 (5) 6/110 (6) 7/115 (7)
8/158 (8) 9/175 (10) 10/183 (9)

Porter 18–5–49–3; Siddle 19.1–6–38–3; Beard 13–1–62–3; Harmer 16–2–42–1; Bopara 3–1–15–0. *Second innings*—Porter 15.2–2–42–2; Siddle 21–8–44–1; Harmer 40–24–35–4; Beard 11–2–45–2; Bopara 1–0–5–0; Westley 1–0–3–0.

Essex

N. L. J. Browne lbw b Broad	163	P. M. Siddle c Broad b Ball	33
A. N. Cook c Moores b Broad	2	A. P. Beard not out	0
T. Westley c Mullaney b Ashwin	42	B 3, lb 2, w 4, nb 6	15
D. W. Lawrence b Fletcher	64		
R. S. Bopara c Broad b Ball	135	(9 wkts dec, 167.4 overs)	519
*R. N. ten Doeschate lbw b Ashwin	22		
†A. J. A. Wheater lbw b Ashwin	23		
S. R. Harmer c Moores b Broad	20		

J. A. Porter did not bat.

1/10 (2) 2/95 (3) 3/215 (4) 4/346 (1) 5/384 (6) 6/422 (7) 7/463 (8) 8/519 (9) 9/519 (5)   110 overs: 319-3

Fletcher 25–5–94–1; Broad 33–8–75–3; Ashwin 60–17–162–3; Ball 24.4–3–93–2; Patel 24–2–88–0; Duckett 1–0–2–0.

Umpires: M. Burns and B. V. Taylor.

At Taunton, July 7–9. NOTTINGHAMSHIRE lost to SOMERSET by 132 runs. *Nottinghamshire suffer an eighth successive defeat by Somerset.*

NOTTINGHAMSHIRE v SURREY

At Nottingham, July 13–15. Surrey won by 167 runs. Surrey 20pts, Nottinghamshire 3pts. Toss: Surrey.

Staking their hopes of arresting their slide on Ashwin, Nottinghamshire prepared a turning pitch. He took six wickets in each innings, twice keeping Surrey below 250, and match figures of 12 for 144 were his best outside India. But he was trumped by fellow off-spinner Virdi, who collected 14 for 139 in his first senior game since a back injury in the winter. Showing little sign of rustiness, he took a career-best eight as Nottinghamshire folded on the second day; Ashwin top-scored with 27. Brimming with confidence, Virdi followed up with another six on the third, as Surrey completed only their second win of the season. Ashwin was unbeaten on 66, the game's highest score, but none of his team-mates emerged with much credit – in terms of footwork, Surrey's Smith, who had just turned 19, outshone them all. Of the 39 wickets, only two fell to seam bowling (Slater to Morkel twice); Batty claimed his 600th Championship victim on the third afternoon.

Close of play: first day, Nottinghamshire 20-1 (Libby 8, Moores 8); second day, Surrey 184-7 (Clark 43, Batty 18).

Surrey

*R. J. Burns lbw b Ashwin...............	22	– lbw b Patterson-White	5
R. S. Patel lbw b Ashwin	1	– lbw b Ashwin	0
D. Elgar b Ashwin	59	– c Moores b Ashwin	13
†J. L. Smith c Slater b Ashwin	42	– b Patel...................	57
S. G. Borthwick lbw b Patel.............	29	– b Ashwin	18
W. G. Jacks c and b Patterson-White......	14	– c Clarke b Patterson-White	19
R. Clarke lbw b Patterson-White	34	– c Clarke b Ashwin	10
J. Clark c Patterson-White b Ashwin	17	– lbw b Ashwin	54
G. J. Batty c Libby b Ashwin............	3	– c Libby b Ashwin.............	29
M. Morkel b Patterson-White	3	– not out	16
G. S. Virdi not out	0	– not out	0
B 9, lb 5, nb 2..........	16	B 3	3
	240		224

1/8 (2) 2/45 (1) 3/126 (3) (89.2 overs) 240 1/1 (2) (9 wkts dec, 79.2 overs) 224
4/141 (4) 5/158 (6) 6/193 (5) 2/13 (1) 3/19 (3)
7/224 (8) 8/236 (7) 9/240 (10) 10/240 (9) 4/78 (5) 5/112 (4) 6/114 (6)
7/130 (7) 8/207 (8) 9/216 (9)

Broad 11–3–34–0; Wood 10–1–30–0; Ashwin 33.2–9–69–6; Patterson-White 22–3–62–3; Patel 12–4–25–1; Chappell 1–0–6–0. *Second innings*—Ashwin 31–8–75–6; Patterson-White 30–5–82–2; Patel 15–5–38–1; Chappell 3.2–0–26–0.

Nottinghamshire

B. T. Slater c Jacks b Morkel............	1	– (2) c Smith b Morkel	0
J. D. Libby lbw b Virdi	23	– (1) lbw b Virdi	21
†T. J. Moores b Virdi	12	– lbw b Virdi	6
J. M. Clarke c Jacks b Batty............	1	– b Virdi	19
*S. J. Mullaney lbw b Virdi	0	– c Jacks b Batty	8
S. R. Patel c Burns b Virdi	12	– lbw b Virdi	3
R. Ashwin c Smith b Virdi	27	– not out	66
L. A. Patterson-White c Jacks b Virdi	0	– c Burns b Batty.............	0
L. Wood lbw b Virdi	20	– c Clarke b Virdi	5
S. C. J. Broad not out	7	– st Smith b Virdi	30
Z. J. Chappell b Virdi.................	0	– c Jacks b Batty	8
B 6, lb 5, nb 2..........	13	B 10, lb 4, w 1..........	15
	116		181

1/8 (1) 2/35 (2) 3/40 (4) (52.5 overs) 116 1/21 (2) 2/30 (3) (48.3 overs) 181
4/40 (3) 5/41 (5) 6/66 (6) 3/47 (1) 4/61 (4)
7/66 (8) 8/109 (7) 9/116 (9) 10/116 (11) 5/71 (6) 6/71 (5) 7/73 (8)
8/92 (9) 9/148 (10) 10/181 (11)

Morkel 8–4–8–1; Virdi 25.5–6–61–8; Batty 19–6–36–1. *Second innings*—Morkel 7–0–27–1; Virdi 21–5–78–6; Batty 20.3–6–62–3.

Umpires: D. J. Millns and R. T. Robinson.

At Scarborough, August 18–21. NOTTINGHAMSHIRE lost to YORKSHIRE by 143 runs.

NOTTINGHAMSHIRE v KENT

At Nottingham, September 10–12. Kent won by 227 runs. Kent 22pts, Nottinghamshire 3pts. Toss: Kent. First-class debut: M. K. O'Riordan.

A tour de force from 43-year-old Darren Stevens turned the match, and confirmed Nottinghamshire's relegation. On the first afternoon, Kent had been toiling at 119 for five, with four for Ashwin (back from India's Caribbean tour) on another helpful surface. Then Stevens introduced himself to Ashwin with a six over long-off. Altogether, he hit him for 54 from 40 deliveries, in a 90-ball 88; he was last out at 304, to Coughlin, whose third wickets were his first at Trent Bridge in two seasons bedevilled by injury since he moved from Durham. Next, Stevens took the new ball and seized five for 39, earning Kent a lead of 180; the highest score was 22 from Mullaney, returning after knee surgery. Declining to enforce the follow-on, Billings ran up a fluent hundred, while Ashwin collected five more wickets to reach 32 in four Championship matches. Nottinghamshire's target was 440; only Ashwin and Coughlin resisted as they went down to their fifth three-day thrashing. Stevens stole the spotlight again. Another five victims gave him only the second haul of ten in his 22-year career, and made him the oldest seamer to take ten in a match since Derek Shackleton in 1968. It included his 500th first-class wicket, his 500th for Kent, and his 500th in the Championship. Kent began to rethink their decision to release him at the end of the season.

Close of play: first day, Nottinghamshire 35-2 (Slater 18, Fletcher 1); second day, Kent 236-8 (Podmore 4).

Kent

Z. Crawley lbw b Fletcher	3	– b Fletcher	82
D. J. Bell-Drummond st Moores b Ashwin	45	– c Coughlin b Fletcher	8
J. M. Cox lbw b Ashwin	22	– lbw b Ashwin	20
*S. W. Billings c Mullaney b Ashwin	4	– c and b Patterson-White	100
H. G. Kuhn c Coughlin b Patterson-White	56	– c Moores b Fletcher	5
†O. G. Robinson b Ashwin	6	– lbw b Ashwin	8
D. I. Stevens c Ball b Coughlin	88	– lbw b Ashwin	0
M. K. O'Riordan c Mullaney b Patterson-White	12	– b Patterson-White	9
O. P. Rayner c Moores b Coughlin	26	– b Ashwin	0
H. W. Podmore c Duckett b Coughlin	11	– lbw b Ashwin	16
M. E. Milnes not out	3	– not out	4
B 12, lb 4, nb 12	28	Lb 1, nb 6	7

1/18 (1) 2/72 (3) 3/78 (4) (81.4 overs) 304
4/105 (2) 5/119 (6) 6/188 (5)
7/235 (8) 8/279 (9) 9/299 (10) 10/304 (7)

1/25 (2) 2/165 (1) (56.5 overs) 259
3/175 (5) 4/186 (6)
5/186 (7) 6/227 (8) 7/228 (9)
8/236 (4) 9/252 (10) 10/259 (3)

In the second innings Cox, when 13, retired hurt at 42-1 and resumed at 236-8.

Fletcher 17–2–43–1; Ball 11–3–32–0; Ashwin 32–10–121–4; Coughlin 10.4–3–37–3; Patterson-White 11–0–55–2. *Second innings*—Fletcher 14–5–40–3; Ball 8–0–49–0; Coughlin 10.3–1–49–0; Ashwin 18.5–1–89–5; Patterson-White 5.3–0–31–2.

Nottinghamshire

J. D. Libby lbw b Stevens	1	– (4) b Milnes	17
B. T. Slater c Robinson b Podmore	20	– (5) lbw b Stevens	19
C. D. Nash b Milnes	11	– lbw b Stevens	0
L. J. Fletcher c Crawley b Milnes	17	– (10) c Kuhn b Rayner	10
B. M. Duckett c and b Podmore	8	– (2) b Podmore	20
*S. J. Mullaney lbw b Stevens	22	– (1) b Stevens	10
L. A. Patterson-White c Rayner b Stevens	11	– (9) not out	5
R. Ashwin lbw b Podmore	7	– (6) c Kuhn b Rayner	55
†T. J. Moores lbw b Stevens	1	– c Milnes b Podmore	9
P. Coughlin c Podmore b Stevens	8	– (8) c Robinson b Stevens	39
J. T. Ball not out	4	– c Robinson b Stevens	14
B 4, lb 4, nb 6	14	B 4, lb 2, nb 8	14

1/5 (1) 2/26 (3) 3/41 (2)	(53.1 overs) 124	1/27 (1) 2/27 (3)	(51.2 overs) 212
4/53 (5) 5/77 (4) 6/104 (6)		3/33 (2) 4/64 (5)	
7/111 (7) 8/111 (8) 9/117 (9) 10/124 (10)		5/91 (4) 6/108 (7) 7/183 (8)	
		8/183 (6) 9/195 (10) 10/212 (11)	

Podmore 17–5–27–3; Stevens 17.1–7–39–5; Milnes 8–1–30–2; Rayner 8–3–10–0; O'Riordan 3–0–10–0. *Second innings*—Podmore 13–2–55–2; Stevens 18.2–3–53–5; Milnes 9–2–50–1; Rayner 7–2–25–2; O'Riordan 4–0–23–0.

Umpires: P. J. Hartley and G. D. Lloyd.

NOTTINGHAMSHIRE v WARWICKSHIRE

At Nottingham, September 16–19. Warwickshire won by eight wickets. Warwickshire 23pts, Nottinghamshire 6pts. Toss: uncontested. First-class debuts: J. M. Blatherwick, B. G. Compton, J. D. M. Evison.

Nottinghamshire gave debuts to three players, among them Ben Compton, grandson of Denis and cousin of Nick, and 17-year-old Joey Evison, an England Under-19 all-rounder and the county's first player born after 2000. Already relegated, they batted with a sense of liberation, amassing 498, their highest Championship total of the season. Mullaney's 179, including five sixes, was a career-best; Clarke, who had been dropped for the previous game, made his first century since April; and Evison struck nine fours in his 45. Yet victory eluded them. Sibley carried his bat – for the second time this summer – for 215 across nine hours to ensure Warwickshire finished only ten behind, and Nottinghamshire's batting soon reverted to type – five down for 105 at the end of the third day. Clarke fought back with his second hundred of the match, to leave a target of 271 from 58 overs. Warwickshire made it with a couple to spare, after Sibley emulated Clarke with another century; they were the first pair of opposing batsmen to score twin hundreds in a Championship fixture since Michael Vaughan and Stuart Law at Chelmsford in 1999. A match aggregate of 1,517 was the highest of the season, but Nottinghamshire's seventh consecutive defeat meant they had not won at Trent Bridge since May 2018.

Close of play: first day, Nottinghamshire 425-6 (Ashwin 29, Coughlin 22); second day, Warwickshire 264-2 (Sibley 115, Hain 67); third day, Nottinghamshire 105-5 (Clarke 59, Coughlin 4).

Nottinghamshire

*S. J. Mullaney c Hannon-Dalby b Patel	179	– c Hain b Hannon-Dalby	2
B. G. Compton b Rhodes	14	– c Burgess b Patel	13
C. D. Nash b Brookes	0	– lbw b Hannon-Dalby	4
J. M. Clarke c Sibley b Rhodes	125	– b Hannon-Dalby	112
†B. M. Duckett c Hain b Hannon-Dalby	8	– b Garrett	4
J. D. M. Evison lbw b Brookes	45	– b Hannon-Dalby	12
R. Ashwin c Burgess b Brookes	38	– (8) lbw b Garrett	42
P. Coughlin lbw b Garrett	49	– (7) c Burgess b Brookes	16
L. J. Fletcher c Banks b Hannon-Dalby	10	– c Hain b Patel	5
Z. J. Chappell c Hain b Garrett	20	– c Banks b Patel	29
J. M. Blatherwick not out	4	– not out	2
Lb 2, nb 4	6	B 9, lb 2, nb 8	19

1/54 (2) 2/75 (3) 3/280 (1)   (115.4 overs) 498   1/2 (1) 2/16 (3)   (71 overs) 260
4/301 (5) 5/358 (4) 6/382 (6)   3/46 (2) 4/51 (5)
7/447 (7) 8/464 (9) 9/489 (8)   5/99 (6) 6/122 (7) 7/195 (8)
10/498 (10)   110 overs: 482-8   8/202 (9) 9/256 (10) 10/260 (4)

Hannon-Dalby 28–4–101–2; Garrett 18.4–4–72–2; Brookes 27–5–131–3; Rhodes 16.4–1–89–2; Patel 25–4–103–1; Lamb 0.2–0–0–0. *Second innings*—Hannon-Dalby 22–5–54–4; Brookes 18–2–77–1; Patel 18–3–52–3; Garrett 9.1–2–53–2; Rhodes 3.5–0–13–0.

Warwickshire

W. M. H. Rhodes lbw b Coughlin	36	– c Chappell b Coughlin	65
D. P. Sibley not out	215	– b Coughlin	109
R. M. Yates c Fletcher b Ashwin	23		
S. R. Hain c Evison b Fletcher	76	– retired hurt	16
M. J. Lamb b Blatherwick	5	– not out	1
L. Banks c †Clarke b Coughlin	41		
†M. G. K. Burgess b Mullaney	31	– (3) not out	61
H. J. H. Brookes c Ashwin b Mullaney	8		
*J. S. Patel c Coughlin b Mullaney	9		
O. J. Hannon-Dalby b Mullaney	9		
G. A. Garrett lbw b Ashwin	0		
B 18, lb 7, nb 10	35	B 8, lb 7, nb 4	19

1/77 (1) 2/121 (3) 3/281 (4)   (135 overs) 488   1/146 (1)   (2 wkts, 55.4 overs) 271
4/300 (5) 5/361 (6) 6/437 (7)   2/217 (2)
7/449 (8) 8/467 (9) 9/487 (10)
10/488 (11)   110 overs: 402-5

In the second innings Hain retired hurt at 267-2.

Fletcher 19–1–52–1; Blatherwick 16–1–87–1; Ashwin 40–12–92–2; Coughlin 17–3–75–2; Chappell 18–2–76–0; Mullaney 16–1–48–4; Evison 9–0–33–0. *Second innings*—Blatherwick 7.4–1–23–0; Ashwin 18–2–76–0; Coughlin 17–2–85–2; Chappell 3–0–15–0; Mullaney 10–0–57–0.

Umpires: R. J. Bailey and R. A. Kettleborough.

At The Oval, September 23–26. NOTTINGHAMSHIRE drew with SURREY. *Nottinghamshire conclude the season without a first-class win, for the first time since 1967.*

SOMERSET

The second generation

RICHARD LATHAM

After a summer that marked the end of Marcus Trescothick's 27 seasons as a Somerset player, there were bittersweet emotions in the Taunton dressing-room, and among supporters. In late May, the club ended a 14-year wait for a trophy with a convincing six-wicket victory over Hampshire in the Royal London Cup final at Lord's. But a first Championship title evaporated yet again, after a heavy defeat by Hampshire in the penultimate match was followed by a rain-ruined draw against Essex, who clung on to their lead. It was the third time in four years that Somerset had been runners-up, and the sixth time in the 21st century.

Their barnstorming start had produced a wave of optimism, and encouraged director of cricket Andy Hurry to talk about a possible clean sweep of trophies. They secured a raucously celebrated victory in the last domestic one-day final at Lord's, and won nine of their first 12 Championship matches, apparently in control of the title race. But a big defeat by Essex at Chelmsford had already indicated that the pursuit was on, and Somerset surrendered the leadership after losing by an innings at Leeds in mid-July.

Essex arrived for the showdown needing a draw for the title, but there was still hope of a glorious finale. Groundsman Simon Lee, in his last match before joining Hampshire, produced a turning pitch to aid the home spinners, but the weather meant only 72.4 overs were possible on the first two days, with the third washed out. There was drama on the final afternoon, when Essex collapsed, and Tom Abell forfeited the second innings to pursue the slenderest chance of victory. But it was not to be. Trescothick, on as a substitute fielder, led the team off.

The drama wasn't quite over. In November, Somerset were found guilty of preparing a poor pitch for the Championship decider. They would begin 2020 on minus 12 points, with a further 12-point penalty suspended for two years.

Batting frailties were at the root of the team's near miss. No one surpassed Abell's 756 runs, or his equally modest average of 31, although George Bartlett was not far behind. There were regular signs of promise from Bartlett and the other rising star, Tom Banton, but Trescothick, who averaged ten in eight innings, and James Hildreth, with 553 runs at 23 and a solitary hundred, were unable to rise to former glories. Azhar Ali's second season as overseas player saw him contribute only 344 in 16 innings, while his late-season replacement, Murali Vijay, accumulated just 42 in three matches, when a significant contribution might have tilted the advantage back to Somerset. Often, it was the middle and late order which ensured a decent total.

In contrast, the attack mainly fired. Lewis Gregory led the way with 51 wickets at 15, ably supported by the Overton twins. Jack Brooks's first season

Tom Banton

Andy Kearns, Getty Images

at Taunton was marred by injury, but he still claimed 25. Josh Davey and Tim Groenewald, in his final summer before joining Kent, provided useful back-up. Jack Leach, between Test commitments, again showed his effectiveness on dry pitches, but it was another largely frustrating summer for Dom Bess, who was selected for only half the Championship fixtures, and spent time on loan at Yorkshire. So it came as a pleasant surprise when he was called up as cover for England's tour of South Africa. Steve Davies enjoyed an excellent time behind the stumps, with 50 dismissals, and Somerset's fielding drew widespread praise, particularly for Abell's brilliance in the covers.

Banton's emergence as one of the most exciting white-ball batting talents in the country began with a hundred in the opening Royal London Cup game, against Kent at Taunton. Another century followed in the quarter-final against Worcestershire, and he decorated the final with a superb 69 off 67 balls, demonstrating his range of shots and sweet timing. Overall, the competition brought him 454 runs at 51. Michael Vaughan may have been the first to draw comparisons with Kevin Pietersen, but plenty followed. By the end of the year, he had made his T20 international debut in New Zealand, was playing for Brisbane Heat in the Big Bash League, and had an IPL deal with Kolkata Knight Riders.

Victory at Lord's provided an appropriate end to Peter Trego's distinguished career with Somerset, which had begun in 2000. He had played his part in the triumph, with a stunning 141 in the group win over Essex at Taunton. Hildreth, who marshalled the chase in the final with an unbeaten 69, finished as Somerset's leading run-scorer, with 457, just ahead of Banton and Azhar Ali, whose 451 included a century against Essex. Craig Overton claimed 20 wickets.

In the Vitality Blast, the team failed to recover from losing three of their first four matches. Four wins in five raised hopes of reaching the knockout stages, but defeats by Surrey at The Oval, and Middlesex at Taunton scuppered them. Packed houses, though, were richly entertained by Pakistan's Babar Azam, who played mainly orthodox shots, and was the tournament's leading run-scorer, with 578 at 52. Banton was the only other batsman to pass 500 in the competition, emphasising the strength of Somerset's T20 top order.

The squad have been strengthened for another assault on the title by the signing of South African seamer Vernon Philander on a Kolpak deal. The batting should be boosted by the arrival of Australia's Matthew Wade for the first seven Championship games. Off the field in 2019, there was sadness at the death of chairman Charles Clark, while former ECB executive Gordon Hollins became the club's fourth CEO in three years after the departure of Andrew Cornish.

Championship attendance: 37,671.

SOMERSET RESULTS

All first-class matches – Played 15: Won 10, Lost 3, Drawn 2.
County Championship matches – Played 14: Won 9, Lost 3, Drawn 2.

Specsavers County Championship, 2nd in Division 1;
Vitality Blast, 6th in South Group; Royal London One-Day Cup, winners.

COUNTY CHAMPIONSHIP AVERAGES, BATTING AND FIELDING

Cap		Birthplace	M	I	NO	R	HS	100	Avge	Ct/St
2018	T. B. Abell	Taunton‡	14	25	1	756	101	1	31.50	13
	G. A. Bartlett	Frimley	14	24	1	718	137	2	31.21	1
	T. Banton	Chiltern	10	18	0	533	79	0	29.61	6
2015	L. Gregory	Plymouth	11	18	2	465	129*	1	29.06	10
2017	†S. M. Davies	Bromsgrove	14	24	1	642	109	1	27.91	47/3
2018	R. E. van der Merwe‡‡	Johannesburg, SA . .	4	6	1	132	60	0	26.40	7
2019	Azhar Ali¶	Lahore, Pakistan . . .	9	16	2	344	79	0	24.57	3
	D. M. Bess	Exeter	7	13	3	233	52*	0	23.30	3
2007	J. C. Hildreth	Milton Keynes	14	24	0	553	105	1	23.04	17
2019	J. Overton	Barnstaple	8	14	2	252	52*	0	21.00	16
2016	C. Overton	Barnstaple	10	15	1	230	40	0	16.42	12
	J. H. Davey††	Aberdeen	5	9	1	92	36	0	11.50	1
	J. A. Brooks	Oxford	8	12	6	68	35*	0	11.33	2
1999	†M. E. Trescothick	Keynsham‡	5	8	0	86	23	0	10.75	9
2016	T. D. Groenewald . . .	Pietermaritzburg, SA .	7	13	3	100	17	0	10.00	1
	M. Vijay¶	Madras, India	3	5	0	42	29	0	8.40	5
2017	†M. J. Leach	Taunton‡	9	13	4	53	11*	0	5.88	7

Also batted: Babar Azam¶ (*Lahore, Pakistan*) (1 match) 0, 40; †E. J. Byrom†† (*Harare, Zimbabwe*) (1 match) 6, 14 (2 ct).

‡ *Born in Somerset.*   ¶ *Official overseas player.*   †† *Other non-England-qualified.*

BOWLING

	Style	O	M	R	W	BB	5I	Avge
L. Gregory	RFM	284.1	81	804	51	6-32	4	15.76
M. J. Leach	SLA	250.3	71	596	34	6-36	2	17.52
R. E. van der Merwe	SLA	66.5	21	177	10	4-41	0	17.70
J. H. Davey	RFM	107.5	29	301	17	5-21	1	17.70
J. Overton	RFM	156.5	29	521	28	5-70	1	18.60
C. Overton	RFM	282.3	64	810	37	5-31	2	21.89
D. M. Bess	OB	174.3	44	447	19	5-59	1	23.52
T. B. Abell	RM	103.2	30	313	13	4-39	0	24.07
T. D. Groenewald	RFM	163.3	32	472	18	5-51	1	26.22
J. A. Brooks	RFM	214.1	51	728	25	5-33	1	29.12

Also bowled: Azhar Ali (LB) 2–2–0–0.

LEADING ROYAL LONDON CUP AVERAGES (150 runs/4 wickets)

Batting	Runs	HS	Avge	SR	Ct/St		**Bowling**	W	BB	Avge	ER
C. Overton	213	66*	71.00	131.48	7		Azhar Ali	7	5-34	19.42	7.15
J. C. Hildreth . . .	457	93	45.70	98.49	2		C. Overton	20	5-18	20.10	4.84
T. Banton	454	112	41.27	94.58	11/1		J. H. Davey	14	4-36	27.28	4.86
Azhar Ali	451	110	41.00	79.96	8		J. Overton	8	4-64	28.50	6.00
P. D. Trego	389	141	35.36	96.52	0		R. E. van der Merwe	11	3-29	36.09	5.42
G. A. Bartlett . . .	207	57*	34.50	99.51	4		T. D. Groenewald	7	3-34	36.14	6.57
L. Gregory	287	52	31.88	141.37	4		L. Gregory	10	2-35	43.80	5.94
T. B. Abell	253	44	25.30	86.34	3						

LEADING VITALITY BLAST AVERAGES (100 runs/15 overs)

Batting	Runs	HS	Avge	SR	Ct/St	Bowling	W	BB	Avge	ER
E. J. Byrom ...	185	54*	23.12	196.80	2	M. T. C. Waller .	13	3-19	27.76	7.70
T. B. Abell	354	101*	44.25	177.88	11	R. E. van der Merwe	15	5-32	25.80	8.41
T. Banton	549	100	42.23	161.47	6/1	T. D. Groenewald	8	2-22	21.87	8.75
Babar Azam ...	578	102*	52.54	149.35	5	J. E. Taylor.....	14	2-12	29.64	9.46
P. D. Trego....	116	47*	38.66	124.73	1	C. Overton	11	3-32	33.27	9.63
J. C. Hildreth ..	216	40	19.63	122.72	4	T. A. Lammonby .	8	2-32	27.25	10.90

FIRST-CLASS COUNTY RECORDS

Highest score for	342	J. L. Langer v Surrey at Guildford...............	2006
Highest score against	424	A. C. MacLaren (Lancashire) at Taunton	1895
Leading run-scorer	21,142	H. Gimblett (avge 36.96).......................	1935–54
Best bowling for	10-49	E. J. Tyler v Surrey at Taunton	1895
Best bowling against	10-35	A. Drake (Yorkshire) at Weston-super-Mare......	1914
Leading wicket-taker	2,165	J. C. White (avge 18.03)	1909–37
Highest total for	850-7 dec	v Middlesex at Taunton	2007
Highest total against	811	by Surrey at The Oval	1899
Lowest total for	25	v Gloucestershire at Bristol	1947
Lowest total against	22	by Gloucestershire at Bristol	1920

LIST A COUNTY RECORDS

Highest score for	184	M. E. Trescothick v Gloucestershire at Taunton ..	2008
Highest score against	167*	A. J. Stewart (Surrey) at The Oval..............	1994
Leading run-scorer	7,374	M. E. Trescothick (avge 36.87).................	1993–2014
Best bowling for	8-66	S. R. G. Francis v Derbyshire at Derby	2004
Best bowling against	7-39	A. Hodgson (Northamptonshire) at Northampton .	1976
Leading wicket-taker	309	H. R. Moseley (avge 20.03).....................	1971–82
Highest total for	413-4	v Devon at Torquay	1990
Highest total against	429-9	by Nottinghamshire at Taunton	2017
Lowest total for	{ 58	v Essex at Chelmsford........................	1977
	{ 58	v Middlesex at Southgate......................	2000
Lowest total against	60	by Kent at Taunton...........................	1979

TWENTY20 COUNTY RECORDS

Highest score for	151*	C. H. Gayle v Kent at Taunton	2015
Highest score against	122*	J. J. Roy (Surrey) at The Oval	2015
Leading run-scorer	3,575	J. C. Hildreth (avge 24.15, SR 123.74)	2004–19
Best bowling for	6-5	A. V. Suppiah v Glamorgan at Cardiff	2011
Best bowling against	5-11	A. F. Milne (Kent) at Taunton	2017
Leading wicket-taker	137	A. C. Thomas (avge 20.17, ER 7.67)............	2008–15
Highest total for	250-3	v Gloucestershire at Taunton	2006
Highest total against	231-5	by Kent at Canterbury	2018
Lowest total for	82	v Kent at Taunton............................	2010
Lowest total against	73	by Warwickshire at Taunton	2013

ADDRESS

Cooper Associates County Ground, St James's Street, Taunton TA1 1JT; 01823 425301;
enquiries@somersetcountycc.co.uk; www.somersetcountycc.co.uk.

OFFICIALS

Captain T. B. Abell
    (Twenty20) L. Gregory
Director of cricket A. Hurry
Head coach J. I. D. Kerr
Academy director S. D. Snell
President B. C. Rose
Chairman 2019 C. F. B. Clark/R. D. Brice

Chairman 2020 G. M. Baird
Chief executive 2019 A. Cornish
    2020 G. M. Hollins
Head groundsman 2019 S. Lee
    2020 S. Hawkins
Scorer P. Rhodes

SOMERSET v CARDIFF MCCU

At Taunton, March 26–28. Somerset won by 568 runs. Toss: Somerset. First-class debuts: D. A. Douthwaite, O. M. D. Kolk, Y. J. Odedra, S. J. Reingold. County debut: J. A. Brooks.

The future of these matches as first-class fixtures came under the spotlight again as Cardiff were humiliated. Somerset recorded the biggest win by runs in a first-class match in England, beating Australia's 562-run victory over England at The Oval in 1934, and the eighth-largest overall. It was painful viewing. James Hildreth's 45th first-class hundred helped them race to 387 for four at nearly four and a half an over, before the students slumped to 13 for four by the close. Next day, only Oskar Kolk and Dan Douthwaite, both old boys of Reed's School in Surrey, offered resistance. Gregory preferred batting practice to the follow-on, and Byrom recorded his first Somerset century. Set 615, Cardiff were demolished for 46 in 16 overs, with Craig Overton taking six for 24.

Close of play: first day, Cardiff MCCU 13-4 (Kolk 0, Woodland 5); second day, Somerset 253-6 (Byrom 59, Overton 52).

Somerset

M. E. Trescothick c Ludlow b Evans	22	– run out (Evans)	37
Azhar Ali b Odedra	22	– c Machado b Odedra	33
J. C. Hildreth not out	158	– b Sisodiya	20
G. A. Bartlett b Evans	38	– lbw b Sisodiya	16
†S. M. Davies b Sisodiya	46	– b Sisodiya	0
E. J. Byrom not out	58	– not out	115
*L. Gregory (did not bat)		– c Ludlow b Douthwaite	26
C. Overton (did not bat)		– c Sisodiya b Douthwaite	58
J. H. Davey (did not bat)		– st Machado b Reingold	7
M. J. Leach (did not bat)		– c Ludlow b Sisodiya	3
J. A. Brooks (did not bat)		– not out	11
B 14, lb 4, w 1, nb 24	43	B 9, lb 6, nb 4	19

1/26 (1) 2/81 (2)   (4 wkts dec, 88 overs) 387
3/149 (4) 4/277 (5)

1/51 (2)   (9 wkts dec, 86 overs) 345
2/72 (1) 3/102 (4)
4/102 (5) 5/109 (3) 6/174 (7)
7/268 (8) 8/304 (9) 9/319 (10)

Evans 16–4–76–2; Punja 7.3–2–26–0; Douthwaite 16–1–68–0; Odedra 12–0–41–1; Sisodiya 15.3–1–63–1; Woodland 9–1–53–0; Pearce 1–0–5–0; Reingold 11–1–37–0. *Second innings*—Evans 13–3–49–0; Douthwaite 21–4–97–2; Odedra 9–0–54–1; Reingold 18–3–51–1; Sisodiya 25–3–79–4.

Cardiff MCCU

J. H. Ludlow b Brooks	1	– c Leach b Overton	4
S. J. Reingold lbw b Gregory	7	– b Davey	0
Y. J. Odedra lbw b Gregory	0	– (9) c Byrom b Overton	4
*L. Machado lbw b Brooks	0	– (3) lbw b Davey	6
O. M. D. Kolk c Byrom b Brooks	33	– (4) b Overton	9
*A. J. Woodland b Gregory	11	– (8) b Davey	0
S. J. Pearce c Leach b Gregory	5	– (5) b Overton	11
D. A. Douthwaite c Gregory b Overton	42	– c Byrom b Overton	3
P. Sisodiya c Trescothick b Davey	7	– (7) b Overton	2
B. N. Evans b Overton	0	– not out	3
Y. Punja not out	0	– c Davies b Davey	0
B 4, lb 6, nb 2	12	Lb 1, w 1, nb 2	4

1/8 (2) 2/8 (1) 3/8 (4)   (50.2 overs) 118
4/8 (3) 5/24 (6) 6/38 (7)
7/85 (8) 8/114 (8) 9/114 (9) 10/118 (10)

1/4 (1) 2/6 (2) 3/19 (3)   (16 overs) 46
4/23 (4) 5/35 (6) 6/36 (5)
7/38 (8) 8/38 (7) 9/43 (9) 10/46 (11)

Brooks 14–2–34–3; Gregory 13–5–28–4; Davey 8–1–19–1; Overton 7.2–2–15–2; Leach 3–1–12–0. *Second innings*—Overton 8–0–24–6; Davey 8–0–21–4.

Umpires: I. D. Blackwell and J. H. Evans.

SOMERSET v KENT

At Taunton, April 5–8. Somerset won by 74 runs. Somerset 19pts, Kent 4pts. Toss: uncontested. County debut: M. T. Renshaw.

The tipping point in a seesaw contest came with Somerset seven wickets down in their second innings and only 73 ahead. Bartlett put on 67 with Craig Overton and, on the final morning, 62 for the last wicket with Brooks. It had looked as if Kent would mark their return to the top tier with victory, but a target of 206 against Somerset's powerful seam attack proved too demanding. An inspired Gregory struck four early blows, Brooks – on Championship debut for Somerset – grabbed the wicket of Australian Test batsman Renshaw, and Overton removed Kuhn, both for ducks. At 45 for six, Kent had no way back. After rain had washed out the first four sessions, Kent wasted no time in hustling Somerset out for 171. They lost their last six wickets for 41, with Claydon claiming five for 46. Under Taunton's new floodlights, Kent appeared in control at 71 without loss, but were pegged back by Gregory and Overton. Somerset were four down before they had wiped out a deficit of 38, only for their late-order heroics to prove decisive.

Close of play: first day, no play; second day, Kent 84-2 (Dickson 41, Renshaw 1); third day, Somerset 171-7 (Bartlett 35, Overton 27).

Somerset

M. E. Trescothick b Podmore	10	– lbw b Stevens	5
Azhar Ali c Dickson b Milnes	24	– c Crawley b Podmore	2
J. C. Hildreth c Crawley b Claydon	27	– c Robinson b Stevens	2
*T. B. Abell c Milnes b Claydon	49	– c Robinson b Claydon	30
E. J. Byrom c Stevens b Milnes	6	– c Robinson b Milnes	14
†S. M. Davies c Milnes b Claydon	18	– b Claydon	39
G. A. Bartlett lbw b Claydon	6	– lbw b Claydon	63
L. Gregory c Renshaw b Milnes	4	– b Claydon	7
C. Overton c and b Podmore	14	– c Crawley b Milnes	28
J. H. Davey c Robinson b Claydon	7	– c Robinson b Claydon	2
J. A. Brooks not out	5	– not out	35
Lb 1	1	B 5, lb 3, nb 8	16

1/30 (1) 2/49 (2) 3/63 (3)　　　　(48 overs) 171
4/80 (5) 5/130 (6) 6/140 (7)
7/145 (8) 8/145 (4) 9/165 (10) 10/171 (9)

1/5 (1) 2/7 (3)　　　　(71.3 overs) 243
3/17 (2) 4/32 (5)
5/90 (4) 6/103 (6) 7/111 (8)
8/178 (9) 9/181 (10) 10/243 (7)

Podmore 12–2–36–2; Stevens 11–1–48–0; Milnes 13–2–40–3; Claydon 12–0–46–5. *Second innings*—Podmore 19–2–66–1; Stevens 15.3–4–34–3; Claydon 18–3–66–4; Milnes 11–1–54–2; Bell-Drummond 6–0–13–0; Renshaw 2–0–2–0.

Kent

S. R. Dickson c Hildreth b Davey	43	– c Overton b Gregory	0
Z. Crawley c Trescothick b Overton	37	– c Azhar Ali b Gregory	21
H. W. Podmore c Byrom b Davey	2	– (9) lbw b Brooks	6
M. T. Renshaw c Abell b Gregory	5	– (3) c Gregory b Brooks	0
D. J. Bell-Drummond c Trescothick b Gregory	33	– (4) lbw b Gregory	18
*H. G. Kuhn b Overton	18	– (5) lbw b Overton	0
A. J. Blake b Gregory	6	– c Davies b Overton	20
†O. G. Robinson c Byrom b Brooks	13	– (7) c Overton b Gregory	2
D. I. Stevens c Gregory b Overton	6	– (8) not out	43
M. E. Milnes c Davies b Abell	5	– c Hildreth b Gregory	10
M. E. Claydon not out	13	– c Hildreth b Davey	7
B 4, lb 20, nb 2	26	Lb 4	4

1/71 (2) 2/83 (3) 3/87 (1)　　　　(73.5 overs) 209
4/97 (4) 5/144 (6) 6/160 (7)
7/165 (5) 8/187 (9) 9/193 (8) 10/209 (10)

1/0 (1) 2/1 (3)　　　　(46 overs) 131
3/36 (4) 4/41 (5)
5/41 (2) 6/45 (7) 7/82 (6)
8/93 (9) 9/124 (10) 10/131 (11)

Gregory 17–8–26–3; Brooks 20–6–70–1; Davey 18–4–40–2; Overton 17–2–46–3; Abell 1.5–0– 3–1. *Second innings*—Gregory 13–4–18–5; Brooks 10–1–38–2; Overton 9–3–23–2; Davey 9–2–35–1; Abell 5.0–0–13–0.

Umpires: R. J. Bailey and R. K. Illingworth.

At Nottingham, April 11–13. SOMERSET beat NOTTINGHAMSHIRE by an innings and 14 runs.

SOMERSET v SURREY

At Taunton, May 14–17. Drawn. Somerset 11pts, Surrey 12pts. Toss: Surrey.

Rain on the final morning put paid to a potentially intriguing finish. Surrey had slept uneasily at 152 for five, just 134 ahead, but the pressure eased when the weather allowed just six overs of the first session. Any remaining nerves disappeared when Jacks completed a composed half-century, before more bad weather made the draw inevitable. In bright sunshine on the opening day, Burns and Elgar had hit centuries to put Surrey in a commanding position. Gregory persevered from the River End, and the seamers found more swing when the ball was changed after Elgar had deposited it in the Tone. Fifties from Azhar Ali, Hildreth and Davies kept Somerset in the game, but it was Gregory's impressive third-day hundred, including five sixes, that gave them a slender lead. Only a calming contribution from Burns, meant Surrey weren't in greater peril entering the final day.

Close of play: first day, Surrey 330-6 (Patel 25, Clarke 28); second day, Somerset 243-5 (Davies 54, Gregory 18); third day, Surrey 152-5 (Jacks 31, Morkel 0).

Surrey

*R. J. Burns c Overton b Groenewald	107	– st Davies b Leach	78
M. D. Stoneman c Davies b Brooks	50	– c Trescothick b Gregory	3
S. G. Borthwick c Overton b Gregory	103	– lbw b Overton	15
D. Elgar lbw b Gregory	103	– (8) c Davies b Groenewald	17
†B. T. Foakes c Davies b Abell	3	– lbw b Gregory	9
R. S. Patel b Leach	32	– (4) b Leach	12
W. G. Jacks lbw b Gregory	0	– (6) lbw b Overton	54
R. Clarke not out	59	– (9) not out	15
M. Morkel c Davies b Groenewald	1	– (7) c Overton b Leach	27
G. J. Batty lbw b Leach	0	– not out	15
C. McKerr c Groenewald b Leach	10		
B 5, lb 6, w 1, nb 2	14	B 5, lb 3, nb 2	10

1/96 (2) 2/99 (3) 3/265 (1)   (122 overs) 380
4/268 (5) 5/291 (4) 6/295 (7) 7/350 (6)
8/351 (9) 9/352 (10) 10/380 (11)   110 overs: 351-7

1/4 (2) 2/19 (3)   (8 wkts, 89 overs) 255
3/43 (4) 4/94 (5)
5/148 (1) 6/204 (7) 7/204 (6) 8/235 (8)

Gregory 28–2–82–3; Brooks 21–6–70–1; Overton 23–3–65–0; Groenewald 24–5–62–2; Leach 24–2–85–3; Abell 8–1–35–1. *Second innings*—Overton 20–7–58–2; Gregory 16–1–73–2; Leach 33–11–70–3; Groenewald 16–2–46–1; Abell 2–2–0–0; Azhar Ali 2–2–0–0.

Somerset

M. E. Trescothick c Foakes b McKerr	4	M. J. Leach c Borthwick b Clarke	6
Azhar Ali c Patel b Batty	60	J. A. Brooks b Clarke	0
J. C. Hildreth c and b Clarke	90		
T. B. Abell c Elgar b Morkel	1	B 1, lb 7, w 1, nb 2	11
G. A. Bartlett lbw b McKerr	11		
S. M. Davies lbw b Batty	58	1/10 (1) 2/104 (2) (106.3 overs) 398
L. Gregory not out	129	3/117 (4) 4/141 (5)
C. Overton c Foakes b McKerr	15	5/211 (3) 6/251 (6) 7/302 (8)
T. D. Groenewald c Borthwick b Morkel	13	8/366 (9) 9/398 (10) 10/398 (11)

Morkel 27–4–68–2; Clarke 19.3–2–74–3; McKerr 19–3–94–3; Patel 9–0–52–0; Batty 32–7–102–2.

Umpires: N. G. B. Cook and D. J. Millns.

SOMERSET v WARWICKSHIRE

At Taunton, May 20–22. **Somerset won by 49 runs.** Somerset 20pts, Warwickshire 3pts. Toss: uncontested. County debut: L. C. Norwell.

Somerset earned an extra day to prepare for the Royal London Cup final by completing victory over Warwickshire with five sessions to spare. Seventeen wickets had fallen on a helter-skelter first day, although it was the second that proved decisive. With the exception of Hain in Warwickshire's second innings, neither batting line-up could cope with a green pitch. Somerset's 209 – which would have been even flimsier without 47 extras, 20 in no-balls from Brookes – included a career-

---

BEST BOWLING ON FIRST-CLASS DEBUT FOR WARWICKSHIRE

8-47*	S. J. Whitehead	v Nottinghamshire at Nottingham	1894
7-41	**L. C. Norwell**	**v Somerset at Taunton**	**2019**
7-58†	V. C. Brewster	v Oxford University at Birmingham	1965
7-80	H. H. Streak	v Northamptonshire at Birmingham (first innings)	2004
6-17†	S. A. Piolet	v Durham UCCE at Durham	2009
6-36†	A. B. Crawford	v Indians at Birmingham	1911
6-58*	E. J. Diver	v Nottinghamshire at Nottingham	1894
6-65†	C. L. Metters	v Worcestershire at Birmingham	2011
6-78	H. H. Streak	v Northamptonshire at Birmingham (second innings)	2004
6-89	E. S. H. Giddins	v Durham at Birmingham	1998

* *In Warwickshire's first first-class match.* † *First-class debut.*

---

best five for 18 from Hannon-Dalby. But Craig Overton responded with five for 31 as Somerset gained a lead of 74 on the second morning. Norwell, on his injury-delayed Warwickshire debut, then became the latest seamer to revel in the conditions. He bowled superbly either side of lunch, and finished with seven for 41. Warwickshire never looked like reaching a target of 239, despite Hain's application. "We had the game's outstanding batsman and bowler, but still lost," said coach Jim Troughton.

Close of play: first day, Warwickshire 110-7 (Banks 26); second day, Warwickshire 103-6 (Hain 43, Brookes 1).

Somerset

M. E. Trescothick c Rhodes b Hannon-Dalby	5	– lbw b Norwell	23
Azhar Ali b Norwell	15	– c Rhodes b Norwell	0
J. C. Hildreth c Yates b Brookes	15	– lbw b Norwell	0
*T. B. Abell lbw b Hannon-Dalby	14	– c Ambrose b Norwell	23
G. A. Bartlett b Brookes	15	– c Ambrose b Brookes	14
†S. M. Davies lbw b Patel	23	– c Rhodes b Norwell	10
L. Gregory c Banks b Hannon-Dalby	20	– b Norwell	2
C. Overton b Norwell	15	– not out	36
J. H. Davey c Banks b Hannon-Dalby	36	– c Brookes b Hannon-Dalby	10
T. D. Groenewald not out	4	– c Ambrose b Brookes	17
M. J. Leach c Banks b Hannon-Dalby	0	– c Ambrose b Norwell	9
B 16, lb 9, nb 22	47	B 12, lb 6, nb 2	20

1/13 (1) 2/36 (3) 3/57 (4)		(47.2 overs) 209	1/8 (2) 2/14 (3)	(41.5 overs) 164
4/61 (2) 5/77 (5) 6/123 (7)			3/37 (1) 4/46 (4)	
7/147 (8) 8/205 (6) 9/205 (9) 10/209 (11)			5/68 (5) 6/75 (6) 7/78 (6)	
			8/107 (9) 9/139 (10) 10/164 (11)	

Brookes 11–2–60–2; Hannon-Dalby 11.2–5–18–5; Norwell 10–1–51–2; Rhodes 3–0–20–0; Patel 12–4–35–1. *Second innings*—Hannon-Dalby 11–2–39–1; Norwell 12.5–3–41–7; Brookes 10–2–45–2; Patel 8–3–21–0.

Warwickshire

W. M. H. Rhodes run out (Abell/Overton)	8	– c Davies b Gregory	0
D. P. Sibley c Overton b Groenewald	26	– c Gregory b Leach	24
R. M. Yates c Davies b Overton	8	– c Davies b Gregory	8
S. R. Hain lbw b Overton	18	– not out	92
A. J. Hose lbw b Overton	2	– lbw b Overton	4
L. Banks lbw b Overton	26	– lbw b Abell	11
†T. R. Ambrose b Gregory	9	– run out (Bartlett)	5
H. J. H. Brookes c Gregory b Leach	7	– c Davies b Gregory	2
*J. S. Patel c Abell b Leach	0	– b Overton	4
L. C. Norwell b Overton	9	– c Davies b Groenewald	13
O. J. Hannon-Dalby not out	11	– c Overton b Gregory	13
B 8, lb 2, w 1	11	Lb 11, nb 2	13

1/13 (1) 2/29 (3) 3/51 (4) (54.1 overs) 135
4/53 (5) 5/79 (2) 6/99 (7)
7/110 (8) 8/110 (9) 9/110 (6) 10/135 (10)

1/0 (1) 2/26 (3) (71.4 overs) 189
3/46 (2) 4/55 (5)
5/84 (6) 6/89 (7) 7/109 (8)
8/120 (4) 9/140 (10) 10/189 (11)

Gregory 11–4–24–1; Overton 16.1–8–31–5; Davey 9–0–31–0; Groenewald 6–1–18–1; Abell 5–3–7–0; Leach 7–5–14–2. *Second innings*—Gregory 14.4–3–48–4; Overton 16–4–38–2; Davey 10–3–23–0; Leach 11–2–16–1; Groenewald 11–4–16–1; Abell 9–1–37–1.

Umpires: J. W. Lloyds and N. A. Mallender.

At Guildford, June 3–6. SOMERSET beat SURREY by 102 runs. *Marcus Trescothick makes his final first-class appearance.*

At Canterbury, June 10–13. SOMERSET beat KENT by ten wickets.

At Chelmsford, June 23–25. SOMERSET lost to ESSEX by 151 runs.

SOMERSET v HAMPSHIRE

At Taunton, June 30–July 3. Somerset won by 313 runs. Somerset 24pts, Hampshire 6pts. Toss: Somerset.

Somerset underlined the potency of their attack by demolishing third-placed Hampshire. With Essex thrashing Nottinghamshire, the top two had established daylight between them and the rest. Hildreth hit a lovely first Championship hundred of the season as Somerset earned maximum batting points on the opening day – though from 401 for five they were pegged back by an inspired spell with the second new ball by Abbott, who finished with six for 84. Hampshire's response was dominated by a century from Northeast, who fought a compelling battle with Jamie Overton, confirming his return to form and fitness with five wickets, all caught behind by Davies. Somerset consolidated a lead of 59 with an opening partnership of 128 between Abell and Azhar Ali, before Banton underlined his promise with an attractive 70; Hampshire were set an improbable 418. Soames fell in the first over, and next morning eight tumbled for 86, with Weatherley unable to bat after breaking his right ankle. He was not Hampshire's only concern: when wicketkeeper Alsop tweaked a hamstring on the first day, Aneurin Donald – fielding as a substitute – replaced him behind the stumps until the arrival at the ground of Lewis McManus.

Close of play: first day, Hampshire 15-1 (Weatherley 8, Rahane 5); second day, Hampshire 329-8 (Crane 11, Alsop 6); third day, Hampshire 12-1 (Abbott 0, Rahane 8).

Somerset

*T. B. Abell c Weatherley b Abbott	82	– b Barker	58
Azhar Ali lbw b Abbott	12	– c Fuller b Abbott	79
J. C. Hildreth c Barker b Edwards	105	– c Weatherley b Barker	2
T. Banton lbw b Fuller	79	– c sub (†L. D. McManus) b Crane	70
G. A. Bartlett c sub (†L. D. McManus) b Edwards	68	– c sub (C. G. Harrison) b Crane	33
†S. M. Davies lbw b Fuller	2	– not out	36
L. Gregory c Weatherley b Abbott	25	– c Northeast b Edwards	28
D. M. Bess not out	8	– b Edwards	10
J. Overton lbw b Abbott	0	– st sub (†L. D. McManus) b Crane	0
T. D. Groenewald lbw b Abbott	0	– not out	10
M. J. Leach c sub (†L. D. McManus) b Abbott	5		
B 6, lb 7, w 1, nb 14	28	B 8, lb 6, w 4, nb 14	32

1/18 (2) 2/196 (3) 3/237 (1)　　　(87.5 overs) 408　　1/128 (1)　　(8 wkts dec, 83 overs) 358
4/353 (4) 5/361 (6) 6/401 (7)　　　　　　　　　　　　2/138 (3) 3/165 (2)
7/401 (5) 8/402 (9) 9/402 (10) 10/408 (11)　　　　　4/260 (5) 5/270 (4)
　　　　　　　　　　　　　　　　　　　　　　　　　6/325 (7) 7/344 (8) 8/347 (9)

Barker 17–1–52–0; Abbott 17.5–4–84–6; Edwards 21–4–71–2; Fuller 10–1–51–2; Crane 12–0–88–0; Weatherley 10–0–49–0. *Second innings*—Abbott 14–0–57–1; Edwards 15–1–52–2; Fuller 12–0–61–0; Crane 24–1–122–3; Barker 18–1–52–2.

Hampshire

J. J. Weatherley c Davies b Overton	14	– absent hurt	
O. C. Soames c Davies b Overton	0	– (1) b Gregory	0
A. M. Rahane c Gregory b Leach	55	– c Overton b Gregory	8
*S. A. Northeast c Abell b Bess	101	– c Abell b Leach	23
R. R. Rossouw lbw b Bess	44	– c Banton b Overton	8
J. K. Fuller c Davies b Overton	37	– b Bess	35
K. H. D. Barker c Davies b Overton	38	– c Abell b Leach	4
K. J. Abbott c Davies b Overton	5	– (2) c Davies b Overton	4
M. S. Crane c Hildreth b Gregory	18	– (8) c Leach b Bess	3
†T. P. Alsop c Abell b Gregory	11	– not out	0
F. H. Edwards not out	1	– (9) b Leach	4
B 4, lb 17, nb 4	25	B 4, lb 7, nb 4	15

1/2 (2) 2/37 (1) 3/138 (3)　　　(106.3 overs) 349　　1/0 (1) 2/18 (3)　　(34.2 overs) 104
4/220 (4) 5/225 (5) 6/306 (7)　　　　　　　　　　　3/18 (2) 4/28 (5) 5/85 (4)
7/311 (6) 8/314 (8) 9/339 (10) 10/349 (9)　　　　　6/89 (7) 7/97 (6) 8/104 (9) 9/104 (8)

Gregory 21.3–6–69–2; Overton 23–4–70–5; Leach 32–7–89–1; Groenewald 7–0–34–0; Abell 3–1–8–0; Bess 20–5–58–2. *Second innings*—Gregory 8–3–20–2; Overton 7–3–24–2; Leach 10–4–14–3; Groenewald 5–1–23–0; Bess 4.2–1–12–3.

Umpires: D. J. Millns and R. J. Warren.

SOMERSET v NOTTINGHAMSHIRE

At Taunton, July 7–9. Somerset won by 132 runs. Somerset 22pts, Nottinghamshire 4pts. Toss: Somerset. First-class debut: L. A. Patterson-White.

A three-day win over the bottom team kept Somerset on course for the title, but only after digging themselves out of an awkward situation on the third afternoon. When Indian Test off-spinner Ashwin and 20-year-old debutant Liam Patterson-White, a slow left-armer, reduced their second innings to 115 for eight, their lead was a precarious 200 – only for Jamie Overton to join Azhar Ali in a stand of 51. Set 255, Nottinghamshire collapsed, losing eight wickets after tea; just after six o'clock, Overton bowled Ball to give everyone a day off. On the first, Patterson-White had to leave the field with tonsillitis, and on a spin-friendly surface he was missed. Somerset were in peril at 145 for six, but Davies and Bess added 128 to steer them towards respectability. In reply, Nottinghamshire lost Nash to concussion for 50 when he was hit by an Overton bouncer, but showed resolve to reach 201 for two. The departure of Libby for 77 sparked an implosion, however, and they lost seven for 40 in 21 overs to Leach and Bess. Patterson-White had the consolation of a second innings five-for.

Close of play: first day, Somerset 326; second day, Somerset 7-1 (Abell 3, Azhar Ali 2).

Somerset

*T. B. Abell c Slater b Ashwin	17	– c Slater b Ashwin	24
Azhar Ali c Mullaney b Wood	10	– (3) not out	65
J. C. Hildreth c Mullaney b Ball	44	– (4) c Moores b Ashwin	7
T. Banton hit wkt b Ashwin	25	– (5) lbw b Patterson-White	4
G. A. Bartlett b Wood	18	– b Patterson-White	0
†S. M. Davies lbw b Wood	74	– (7) lbw b Ashwin	2
L. Gregory c Ashwin b Ball	9	– (8) c sub (S. G. Budinger) b Patterson-White	9
D. M. Bess c Mullaney b Wood	51	– (9) lbw b Patterson-White	5
J. Overton c Duckett b Fletcher	34	– (10) c Moores b Ashwin	24
T. D. Groenewald not out	9	– (2) c Moores b Ashwin	0
M. J. Leach lbw b Ashwin	1	– c Slater b Patterson-White	0
B 11, lb 11, nb 12	34	B 20, lb 1, nb 8	29

1/22 (2) 2/52 (1) 3/96 (3) (94.3 overs) 326
4/122 (5) 5/132 (4) 6/145 (7)
7/273 (8) 8/292 (6) 9/325 (9) 10/326 (11)

1/1 (1) 2/56 (1) (59.4 overs) 169
3/70 (4) 4/75 (5)
5/79 (6) 6/94 (7) 7/109 (8)
8/115 (9) 9/166 (10) 10/169 (11)

Fletcher 17–1–50–1; Ball 18–2–64–2; Wood 23–3–85–4; Ashwin 34.3–6–93–3; Libby 2–0–12–0. *Second innings*—Ashwin 30–8–59–5; Wood 6–2–16–0; Patterson-White 23.4–2–73–5.

Nottinghamshire

B. T. Slater c Abell b Overton	15	– c Banton b Leach	2
J. D. Libby c Gregory b Leach	77	– lbw b Leach	0
C. D. Nash retired hurt	50		
B. M. Duckett c Davies b Bess	38	– (7) c Gregory b Overton	13
*S. J. Mullaney c Abell b Bess	24	– c Hildreth b Bess	9
R. Ashwin b Bess	23	– (4) c Bartlett b Leach	41
†T. J. Moores c Banton b Leach	1	– (3) c Hildreth b Overton	22
L. A. Patterson-White b Banton b Leach	0	– (9) b Overton	2
L. J. Fletcher c Hildreth b Bess	3	– (8) c Groenewald b Bess	6
L. Wood c Leach b Bess	0	– not out	4
J. T. Ball not out	1	– b Overton	8
S. R. Patel (did not bat)		– (6) c Hildreth b Leach	1
B 4, lb 3, nb 2	9	B 8, nb 6	14

1/35 (1) 2/169 (4) 3/201 (2) (88.1 overs) 241
4/217 (5) 5/222 (7) 6/226 (8)
7/236 (6) 8/238 (10) 9/241 (9)

1/2 (2) 2/21 (1) (43.5 overs) 122
3/35 (3) 4/67 (5)
5/78 (6) 6/95 (4) 7/102 (7)
8/108 (8) 9/110 (9) 10/122 (11)

In the first innings Nash retired hurt at 121-1. Patel replaced Nash, as a concussion substitute.

Gregory 10–2–28–0; Overton 10–2–39–1; Groenewald 12–2–29–0; Leach 31–11–79–3; Bess 25.1–4–59–5. *Second innings*—Gregory 4–0–14–0; Leach 18–4–42–4; Bess 14–4–34–2; Overton 7.5–3–24–4.

Umpires: N. G. B. Cook and B. J. Debenham.

At Leeds, July 13–16. SOMERSET lost to YORKSHIRE by an innings and 73 runs.

At Birmingham, August 18–21. SOMERSET beat WARWICKSHIRE by five wickets.

SOMERSET v YORKSHIRE

At Taunton, September 10–12. Somerset won by 298 runs. Somerset 19pts, Yorkshire 3pts. Toss: uncontested. County debut: M. Vijay.

Abell's gritty first-innings batting on a testing pitch set up Somerset's fifth home Championship win in six games, and kept the title race alive. They had slumped to 85 for six on the first day, before Jamie Overton hit 40 in a ninth-wicket stand of 51 with Abell. Somerset's mood was lifted further when they took three wickets before the close, including the big one: Ballance, trapped by Bess, not long back from a second loan spell at Yorkshire. The pattern continued on the second morning, as Yorkshire lost six for 17, with Coad absent ill. After a first-innings five-for, left-arm spinner Maharaj was given the new ball. He struck in his second over and picked up four more – taking his total against Somerset to 31 in six innings – but proved expensive. Abell made his second half-century of the match, and this time received staunch support from the middle order. Yorkshire's target of 426 looked out of range, and so it proved: Davey took a career-best five for 21 as they folded meekly.

Close of play: first day, Yorkshire 70-3 (Köhler-Cadmore 6, Patterson 0); second day, Somerset 269-5 (Bartlett 39, Gregory 38).

Somerset

M. Vijay c Tattersall b Olivier	7	lbw b Maharaj	0
†S. M. Davies c Fraine b Patterson	11	c sub (J. A. Leaning) b Patterson	4
*T. B. Abell lbw b Maharaj	66	lbw b Bresnan	62
J. C. Hildreth b Olivier	1	c Brook b Lyth	58
T. Banton c Lyth b Bresnan	2	c Lyth b Maharaj	43
G. A. Bartlett c Lyth b Coad	12	st Tattersall b Maharaj	47
L. Gregory c Tattersall b Coad	12	b Maharaj	39
D. M. Bess c Bresnan b Maharaj	15	b Bresnan	0
R. E. van der Merwe lbw b Maharaj	10	c Köhler-Cadmore b Maharaj	30
J. Overton not out	40	b Patterson	18
J. H. Davey lbw b Maharaj	0	not out	2
B 12, lb 7, nb 4	23	B 16, lb 4, nb 6	26

1/18 (2) 2/31 (1) 3/37 (4)   (72.5 overs) 199   1/4 (1) 2/4 (2)   (83.2 overs) 329
4/46 (5) 5/70 (6) 6/85 (7)   3/121 (4) 4/191 (5)
7/130 (8) 8/148 (9) 9/199 (3) 10/199 (11)   5/191 (3) 6/272 (7) 7/273 (8)
     8/291 (6) 9/310 (9) 10/329 (10)

Coad 13–4–23–1; Patterson 12–4–24–1; Bresnan 10–2–27–1; Olivier 14–2–52–2; Maharaj 23.5–7–54–5. *Second innings*—Maharaj 36–9–122–5; Patterson 13.2–1–65–2; Olivier 8–1–47–0; Lyth 9–0–25–1; Bresnan 17–2–50–2.

Yorkshire

A. Lyth c Davies b Davey	21	c Overton b Davey	1
W. A. R. Fraine c Davies b Gregory	6	(7) c and b Davey	5
G. S. Ballance lbw b Bess	35	c Davies b Overton	23
T. Köhler-Cadmore c Overton b Gregory	14	c Hildreth b Davey	11
*S. A. Patterson b van der Merwe	8	(9) not out	24
H. C. Brook lbw b Davey	–	(5) b van der Merwe	10
†J. A. Tattersall c Hildreth b van der Merwe	0	(2) c Hildreth b Overton	20
T. T. Bresnan c Vijay b Davey	4	(6) run out (Bess)	17
K. A. Maharaj c and b van der Merwe	4	(8) lbw b Davey	0
D. Olivier not out	0	b Bess b Davey	4
B. O. Coad absent ill	–	absent ill	
Lb 1, nb 4	5	B 4, lb 2, nb 6	12

1/27 (2) 2/27 (1) 3/70 (3)   (33.3 overs) 103   1/7 (1) 2/47 (3)   (45.2 overs) 127
4/86 (4) 5/88 (5) 6/92 (7)   3/54 (2) 4/71 (5) 5/94 (6)
7/98 (6) 8/99 (8) 9/103 (9)   6/94 (4) 7/94 (8) 8/103 (7) 9/127 (10)

Gregory 10–0–36–2; Davey 6–2–30–3; Overton 3–1–9–0; Bess 6–2–13–1; van der Merwe 8.3–4–14–3. *Second innings*—Gregory 9–4–22–0; Davey 11.2–4–21–5; Bess 4–0–12–0; Overton 6–1–21–2; van der Merwe 15–3–45–1.

Umpires: M. A. Gough and M. J. Saggers.

At Southampton, September 16–18. SOMERSET lost to HAMPSHIRE by 136 runs. *Somerset surrender pole position to Essex.*

SOMERSET v ESSEX

At Taunton, September 23–26. Drawn. Somerset 9pts, Essex 8pts. Toss: Somerset.

Rain ruined Taunton's title showdown, though there was an unexpectedly gripping denouement when Essex, who needed only to avoid defeat to claim their second Championship in three years, had already turned their thoughts to a glass of bubbly. At 2.45 on the last afternoon, they had reached 102 for one in their first innings in response to Somerset's 203, and were all but safe. Then Alastair Cook fell to Leach after a painstaking fifty on a pitch offering extravagant turn and bounce. Sensing an opening, Leach and van der Merwe took nine for 39 in a frantic spell. Somerset's lead was 62 but, with only one slim chance of snatching a sensational victory and their first Championship, Abell forfeited their second innings. It was the most speculative of long shots: his bowlers had seven minutes plus a minimum of 16 overs in the last hour to bowl Essex out again. With seven men around the bat, Browne was dropped off Leach's third ball, and the tension drained out of the contest. Essex were 18 short of victory when the teams shook hands at 5.20. For home supporters, the disappointment of a third runners-up finish in four years was alleviated slightly by the appearance of Marcus Trescothick kneeling in the cordon as a substitute fielder on his final day before retirement. Harmer had collected his tenth five-for of the season in the Somerset first innings. Two months later, a Cricket Discipline Committee ruled the pitch "poor", citing "excessive unevenness of bounce". Somerset would start the 2020 season on minus 12 points, with the threat of losing 12 more if they transgressed again within two years.

Close of play: first day, Somerset 75-4 (Abell 24, Bartlett 5); second day, Essex 25-0 (Browne 16, A. N. Cook 5); third day, no play.

Somerset

M. Vijay c Wheater b S. J. Cook	6		C. Overton lbw b Harmer		0
*S. M. Davies lbw b S. J. Cook	2		R. E. van der Merwe b Nijjar		60
*T. B. Abell lbw b Harmer	45		M. J. Leach not out		11
J. C. Hildreth lbw b Harmer	32		B 8, lb 3, nb 4		15
T. Banton lbw b Harmer	0				
G. A. Bartlett c Bopara b Harmer	5		1/7 (1) 2/14 (2) 3/61 (4) (61.4 overs)		203
L. Gregory lbw b S. J. Cook	17		4/61 (5) 5/75 (6) 6/96 (7)		
D. M. Bess b S. J. Cook	10		7/126 (3) 8/130 (9) 9/144 (8) 10/203 (10)		

Porter 11–0–43–0; S. J. Cook 19–9–26–4; Harmer 27–5–105–5; Nijjar 4.4–0–18–1.

Somerset forfeited their second innings.

Essex

N. L. J. Browne c Hildreth b Bess	18	– c Vijay b Bess	10
A. N. Cook c Banton b Leach	53	– not out	30
T. Westley c Gregory b van der Merwe	36	– not out	1
D. W. Lawrence c Overton b Leach	0		
R. S. Bopara c Abell b van der Merwe	1		
*R. N. ten Doeschate c Abell b Leach	4		
†A. J. A. Wheater c Davies b van der Merwe	12		
S. R. Harmer c Vijay b van der Merwe	0		
A. S. S. Nijjar lbw b Leach	2		
S. J. Cook b Leach	0		
J. A. Porter not out	0		
B 12, lb 1, nb 2	15	Lb 4	4
	141		45

1/35 (1) 2/102 (2) 3/102 (4)   (68.2 overs) 141   1/38 (1)   (1 wkt, 18 overs) 45
4/111 (5) 5/126 (6) 6/126 (3)
7/126 (8) 8/137 (9) 9/137 (10) 10/141 (7)

Gregory 5–1–14–0; Overton 4–1–7–0; Leach 25–9–32–5; Bess 17–5–34–1; van der Merwe 17.2–7–41–4. *Second innings*—Leach 7–2–13–0; Bess 7–3–8–1; van der Merwe 4–0–20–0.

Umpires: R. J. Bailey and A. G. Wharf.

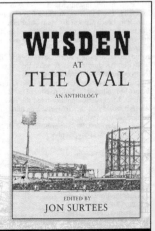

SURREY

A leaky defence

RICHARD SPILLER

After the party, the hangover. Surrey were runaway champions in 2018, but their summer never got off the ground, and they finished sixth. There was no compensation in the white-ball competitions: bottom in their Royal London Cup group, one place higher in the Vitality Blast. Overall, just eight matches were won – no county managed fewer – in a season which started slowly, flickered into life, then conked out.

International calls had always threatened to stretch Surrey, but an even greater challenge came from a stream of injuries. The most keenly felt absences were Sam and Tom Curran, who played six Championship matches between them, because of the IPL, England calls, and injury; and Ollie Pope, who missed nine after dislocating his left shoulder in April. Their youthful vigour had been a key factor 12 months earlier.

Creditable draws against Essex and Somerset were split by the disastrous Royal London campaign, which brought seven defeats and a pyrrhic victory: Pope, Rikki Clarke and Jason Roy sustained injuries. Back in the Championship, possible victory over Kent at Beckenham was stymied by failing to declare, while Sam Curran tweaked a hamstring. Then came heavy losses to Warwickshire and Somerset. Rain allowed Yorkshire to escape at Guildford, and Surrey finally got off the mark when they won the return against Warwickshire. In other seasons, they might have feared becoming the latest champions to be relegated, yet safety was all but assured with four matches remaining, when they despatched a hapless Nottinghamshire at Trent Bridge. A late rally never materialised, with hammerings by Hampshire and Essex alleviated only by a rediscovery of batting form at home.

The T20 Blast was the last fleeting hope of success. Surrey won one of the first eight matches – when Glamorgan were skittled for 44 – and a burst of four victories proved too late. The fact that the seven matches at The Oval were watched by a total of 165,461 spectators was some compensation. With Roy on international duty, the T20 batting was led by Australia's Aaron Finch, but his tally shrank from 589 in nine games the previous year to 398 from 13, and the rest offered little. Spinners Gareth Batty and Imran Tahir shared 32 wickets, while Tom Curran claimed 17.

Pope's injury was a grievous blow, after he had started with a double-century against MCC in Dubai. He made a rapid recovery from surgery to return by late July, and two Championship centuries – including another double – showed how badly he had been missed. He averaged 80, and earned an England tour spot. The form of Pope and captain Rory Burns had camouflaged the retirement of Kumar Sangakkara. And with Burns enjoying a successful Ashes, their absence left gaps: Surrey were bowled out for under 200 nine times.

Rikki Clarke

Mark Stoneman, Scott Borthwick and the South African opener Dean Elgar – who arrived late, suffered from kidney stones, and left early – all fell short of expectation. So did Ben Foakes, who captained when Burns was away, although his keeping remained peerless in a side whose outfielding was brittle. Youngsters Ryan Patel and Will Jacks recorded maiden Championship centuries, before fading. Surrey's youth system produced another exciting talent in wicketkeeper Jamie Smith: he hit a century on debut in Dubai, but was later afflicted by back trouble.

It wasn't just the batsmen. Morne Morkel's second season proved harder than his first, with the spark of 2018 absent. With the Currans often missing, he lacked support, especially as Jade Dernbach was confined to T20 by fitness problems. Conor McKerr endured a long period on the sidelines, while Matt Dunn's impressive start – 13 wickets in three matches – also ended in injury. Jordan Clark, signed from Lancashire, began slowly because of a knee problem, but his bustling seamers claimed 21 wickets, and he was underused in the T20.

It meant an enormous burden fell on 37-year-old Clarke, whose 43 wickets were complemented by 662 runs and generally reliable catching at slip. And an attack already long on experience gained even more with the recall of 41-year-old off-spinner Batty; at Edgbaston, he took a career best eight for 64, including a hat-trick as Warwickshire hit out. Batty, who earned another one-year contract, was playing only because Amar Virdi – half his age – started the season with a back injury, and was then left out because the coaching staff were unhappy with his fitness. A haul of 14 wickets at Trent Bridge on his return was a reminder of his ability.

Two internationals joined for 2020: Hashim Amla, having retired from South African duty, agreed a two-year Kolpak deal, while the former England left-arm seamer Reece Topley signed from Sussex. Other overseas imports were the Australian seamer Michael Neser for the Championship, and his compatriot D'Arcy Short, an attacking batsman, and Pakistan leg-spinning all-rounder Shadab Khan for the T20 Blast. Arun Harinath and Freddie van den Bergh were released.

Off the field, membership hit 13,000, and the latest stage of The Oval's redevelopment began as Surrey ushered in their 175th anniversary year.

Championship attendance: 38,228.

SURREY RESULTS

All first-class matches – Played 15: Won 2, Lost 6, Drawn 7.
County Championship matches – Played 14: Won 2, Lost 6, Drawn 6.

Specsavers County Championship, 6th in Division 1;
Vitality Blast, 8th in South Group; Royal London One-Day Cup, 9th in South Group.

COUNTY CHAMPIONSHIP AVERAGES, BATTING AND FIELDING

Cap		Birthplace	M	I	NO	R	HS	100	Avge	Ct/St
2018	O. J. D. Pope	Chelsea	5	8	1	561	221*	2	80.14	4
2014	†R. J. Burns	Epsom‡	8	16	0	603	107	1	37.68	8
2005	R. Clarke	Orsett	14	25	5	662	88	0	33.10	18
2018	†S. G. Borthwick	Sunderland	13	23	0	705	137	2	30.65	16
2018	†M. D. Stoneman	Newcastle-u-Tyne	13	23	0	685	100	1	29.78	5
2018	†S. M. Curran§	Northampton	5	9	0	265	80	0	29.44	0
	†D. Elgar¶	Welkom, SA	10	19	0	555	103	1	29.21	6
	G. S. Virdi	Chiswick	5	6	5	28	14*	0	28.00	0
	W. G. Jacks	Chertsey‡	10	16	0	427	120	1	26.68	13
2016	B. T. Foakes	Colchester	13	23	1	575	69	0	26.13	39/6
	J. L. Smith	Epsom‡	8	14	1	338	57	0	26.00	4/1
	J. Clark	Whitehaven	9	15	4	268	54	0	24.36	1
	†R. S. Patel	Sutton‡	8	14	1	292	100*	1	22.46	3
2011	G. J. Batty	Bradford	8	15	4	123	29	0	11.18	2
	C. McKerr††	Johannesburg, SA	4	5	1	35	17*	0	8.75	1
2018	†M. Morkel††	Vereeniging, SA	14	22	3	131	27	0	6.89	3
	†M. P. Dunn	Egham‡	3	5	3	2	2*	0	1.50	0

Also batted: T. K. Curran§ (*Cape Town, SA*) (cap 2016) (1 match) 8, 22*; A. J. Finch¶ (*Colac, Australia*) (1 match) 90 (1 ct); L. E. Plunkett§ (*Middlesbrough*) (3 matches) 0, 0, 2; F. O. E. van den Bergh (*Bickley*) (1 match) 16.

‡ *Born in Surrey.* § *ECB contract.* ¶ *Official overseas player.* †† *Other non-England-qualified.*

BOWLING

	Style	O	M	R	W	BB	5I	Avge
G. S. Virdi	OB	140	34	452	23	8-61	2	19.65
M. P. Dunn	RFM	90.2	18	277	13	5-43	1	21.30
R. Clarke	RFM	332	73	1,031	43	7-74	2	23.97
G. J. Batty	OB	234.3	43	678	26	8-64	1	26.07
S. M. Curran	LFM	156.5	28	510	19	3-50	0	26.84
M. Morkel	RF	413	94	1,297	44	4-43	0	29.47
J. Clark	RM	151.4	17	636	21	5-77	1	30.28

Also bowled: S. G. Borthwick (LB) 22–1–113–0; R. J. Burns (RM) 1–1–0–0; T. K. Curran (RFM) 28–6–118–3; D. Elgar (SLA) 15.4–2–57–2; W. G. Jacks (OB) 1–1–0–0; C. McKerr (RFM) 89–11–366–7; R. S. Patel (RM) 56.3–6–213–4; L. E. Plunkett (RFM) 33–5–160–1; M. D. Stoneman (OB) 2–0–15–0; F. O. E. van den Bergh (SLA) 21.4–1–88–1.

LEADING ROYAL LONDON CUP AVERAGES (100 runs/4 wickets)

Batting

	Runs	HS	Avge	SR	Ct/St
B. T. Foakes	328	82	46.85	87.23	8/3
D. Elgar	180	64	45.00	68.96	1
R. J. Burns	198	55	24.75	76.44	4
J. Clark	119	79	23.80	88.14	1
J. L. Smith	110	40	22.00	88.70	2
W. G. Jacks	164	56	20.50	84.10	6
M. D. Stoneman	162	70	20.25	79.02	2

Bowling

	W	BB	Avge	ER
T. K. Curran	6	3-26	10.50	3.31
M. Morkel	13	4-23	18.38	4.52
R. Clarke	4	4-43	29.25	5.05
G. J. Batty	9	4-29	29.66	4.52
W. G. Jacks	5	2-32	30.80	5.43
L. E. Plunkett	7	4-50	32.42	7.13
S. C. Meaker	5	3-58	41.40	6.30
C. McKerr	8	3-56	41.75	6.44

LEADING VITALITY BLAST AVERAGES (100 runs/15 overs)

Batting	Runs	HS	Avge	SR	Ct
A. J. Finch	398	102*	36.18	**167.22**	7
W. G. Jacks	272	63	20.92	**151.95**	4
J. Clark	203	60	25.37	**145.00**	3
S. M. Curran	230	53	32.85	**143.75**	5
O. J. D. Pope	302	48	30.20	**132.45**	8
T. K. Curran	110	31	15.71	**126.43**	3
M. D. Stoneman	144	53	18.00	**97.95**	2

Bowling	W	BB	Avge	ER
G. J. Batty	13	3-7	23.38	**7.26**
Imran Tahir	19	4-25	20.26	**8.19**
J. W. Dernbach	11	2-27	31.09	**8.88**
J. Clark	6	1-15	38.66	**8.92**
T. K. Curran	17	3-3	17.94	**9.19**
S. M. Curran	5	2-23	47.20	**9.63**

FIRST-CLASS COUNTY RECORDS

Highest score for	357*	R. Abel v Somerset at The Oval	1899
Highest score against	366	N. H. Fairbrother (Lancashire) at The Oval	1990
Leading run-scorer	43,554	J. B. Hobbs (avge 49.72)	1905–34
Best bowling for	10-43	T. Rushby v Somerset at Taunton	1921
Best bowling against	10-28	W. P. Howell (Australians) at The Oval	1899
Leading wicket-taker	1,775	T. Richardson (avge 17.87)	1892–1904
Highest total for	811	v Somerset at The Oval	1899
Highest total against	863	by Lancashire at The Oval	1990
Lowest total for	14	v Essex at Chelmsford	1983
Lowest total against	16	by MCC at Lord's	1872

LIST A COUNTY RECORDS

Highest score for	268	A. D. Brown v Glamorgan at The Oval	2002
Highest score against	187*	A. D. Hales (Nottinghamshire) at Lord's	2017
Leading run-scorer	10,358	A. D. Brown (avge 32.16)	1990–2008
Best bowling for	7-30	M. P. Bicknell v Glamorgan at The Oval	1999
Best bowling against	7-15	A. L. Dixon (Kent) at The Oval	1967
Leading wicket-taker	409	M. P. Bicknell (avge 25.21)	1986–2005
Highest total for	496-4	v Gloucestershire at The Oval	2007
Highest total against	429	by Glamorgan at The Oval	2002
Lowest total for	64	v Worcestershire at Worcester	1978
Lowest total against	44	by Glamorgan at The Oval	1999

TWENTY20 COUNTY RECORDS

Highest score for	131*	A. J. Finch v Sussex at Hove	2018
Highest score against	129	C. S. Delport (Essex) at Chelmsford	**2019**
Leading run-scorer	2,977	J. J. Roy (avge 30.37, SR 149.67)	2008–18
Best bowling for	6-24	T. J. Murtagh v Middlesex at Lord's	2005
Best bowling against	5-16	S. T. Finn (Middlesex) at Lord's	**2019**
Leading wicket-taker	114	J. W. Dernbach (avge 26.76, ER 8.37)	2005–19
Highest total for	250-6	v Kent at Canterbury	2018
Highest total against	240-3	by Glamorgan at The Oval	2015
Lowest total for	88	v Kent at The Oval	2012
Lowest total against	44	by Glamorgan at The Oval	**2019**

ADDRESS

The Kia Oval, Kennington, London SE11 5SS; 0844 375 1845; enquiries@surreycricket.com; www.surreycricket.com.

OFFICIALS

Captain R. J. Burns	**Academy director** G. T. J. Townsend
(Twenty20) J. W. Dernbach	**President** K. D. Schofield
Director of cricket A. J. Stewart	**Chairman** R. W. Thompson
Head coach M. J. Di Venuto	**Chief executive** R. A. Gould
Assistant head coach V. S. Solanki	**Head groundsman** L. E. Fortis
Assistant coach R. L. Johnson	**Scorer** P. J. Makepeace

At Dubai, March 24–27. SURREY drew with MCC (see MCC section).

At The Oval, April 4–6 (not first-class). **Drawn. Surrey 586-8 dec** (133.2 overs) (M. D. Stoneman 117, S. G. Borthwick 151, R. S. Patel 103*, T. K. Curran 76); ‡**Durham MCCU 55-1** (25.4 overs). *County debut:* L. E. Plunkett. *Surrey's batsmen feasted on a persevering but toothless attack. Stoneman and Borthwick both retiring with appetites sated. Patel cashed in on the decision to bat past tea on the second day, after only 46.1 overs between showers on the first. Just 22.4 were possible on the last before bad light closed in, spoiling Surrey's hopes of time in the field to prepare for their Championship defence.*

SURREY v ESSEX

At The Oval, April 11–14. Drawn. Surrey 11pts, Essex 13pts. Toss: Surrey. County debut: R. G. White. Championship debut: R. K. Patel.

The familiar obstacle of ten Doeschate, who had ended Surrey's chances of going through the 2018 season undefeated, ensured Essex had marginally the better of a match which long seemed destined for stalemate. Surrey's first innings owed much to two young batsmen who might not have been playing but for injuries to others. The 21-year-old Ryan Patel took 36 balls to get off the mark, then accelerated on the second morning to reach his maiden century, while Jacks – a year younger – started with a six on the way to his highest first-class score. Siddle's control stood out. When Essex batted, Lawrence drove elegantly, and looked set to repeat his century as a 17-year-old in this fixture in 2015. He hit six fours from Plunkett's first 14 balls on his Championship debut for his third county, and reached 93 before falling to the canny Clarke. Rishi Patel stroked six boundaries full of debut promise, while ten Doeschate's belligerence brought his third hundred against Surrey, and Siddle ensured a handy lead. Burns and Pope found their touch in a stand of 127 to snuff out danger, principally from Harmer, then Jacks made another attractive fifty. On the second morning, a spectator collapsed and died from a heart attack.

Close of play: first day, Surrey 342-7 (Patel 70, Plunkett 0); second day, Essex 202-4 (Lawrence 87, ten Doeschate 20); third day, Surrey 68-0 (Burns 34, Stoneman 34).

Surrey

*R. J. Burns c White b Porter	31	– c ten Doeschate b Harmer	98
M. D. Stoneman c White b Siddle	45	– b Siddle	35
R. S. Patel not out	100	– c Browne b Harmer	1
O. J. D. Pope c Lawrence b Siddle	4	– c Porter b Harmer	69
†B. T. Foakes c Cook b Harmer	69	– st White b Harmer	19
W. G. Jacks b Siddle	88	– c Westley b Harmer	54
R. Clarke lbw b Siddle	0	– not out	25
T. K. Curran lbw b Harmer	8	– not out	22
L. E. Plunkett b Siddle	0		
F. O. E. van den Bergh lbw b Siddle	16		
M. Morkel c Siddle b Harmer	7		
Lb 17, nb 10	27	Lb 1	1

1/75 (1) 2/82 (2) 3/86 (4)   (114.1 overs) 395   1/70 (2)   (6 wkts dec, 103 overs) 324
4/181 (5) 5/332 (6) 6/332 (7)   2/71 (3) 3/198 (4)
7/341 (8) 8/346 (9) 9/372 (10)   4/203 (1) 5/251 (5) 6/296 (6)
10/395 (11)   110 overs: 386-9

Porter 24–5–104–1; Siddle 32–8–104–6; Quinn 23–4–89–0; Harmer 32.1–12–72–3; ten Doeschate 0.5–0–1–0; Westley 1.1–0–5–0; Lawrence 1–0–3–0. *Second innings*—Porter 19–3–60–0; Siddle 17–2–67–1; Harmer 36–13–88–5; Quinn 15–1–58–0; Westley 5–1–25–0; Lawrence 11–3–25–0.

Essex

N. L. J. Browne lbw b Morkel	9	
A. N. Cook c Foakes b Curran	11	– not out 0
T. Westley c Pope b Curran	41	
D. W. Lawrence c Burns b Clarke	93	
R. K. Patel c Clarke b Curran.	31	
*R. N. ten Doeschate lbw b Plunkett	130	
†R. G. White c Foakes b Morkel	39	
S. R. Harmer b Clarke	17	
P. M. Siddle not out	41	
J. A. Porter c Jacks b Morkel	8	– (1) not out 0
M. R. Quinn b van den Bergh	10	
B 4, lb 10, w 2, nb 2	18	

1/20 (2) 2/20 (1) 3/116 (3)	(119.4 overs) 448	(no wkt, 1 over) 0
4/168 (5) 5/249 (4) 6/351 (7)		
7/383 (8) 8/385 (6) 9/415 (10)		
10/448 (11)	110 overs: 412-8	

Morkel 27–4–97–3; Curran 28–6–118–3; Clarke 25–9–46–2; Plunkett 18–4–85–1; van den Bergh 21.4–1–88–1. *Second innings*—Burns 1–1–0–0.

Umpires: N. G. B. Cook and R. A. Kettleborough.

At Taunton, May 14–17. SURREY drew with SOMERSET.

At Beckenham, May 20–23. SURREY drew with KENT.

At Birmingham, May 27–30. SURREY lost to WARWICKSHIRE by 130 runs. *Gareth Batty takes 8-64, including a hat-trick.*

SURREY v SOMERSET

At Guildford, June 3–6. Somerset won by 102 runs. Somerset 22pts, Surrey 4pts. Toss: Somerset.

Thrashed here a year earlier, Somerset broke their duck at Woodbridge Road at the fifth time of asking, in style. "This was a massive win for us," said Abell, their captain. "Surrey had eight Test players in their team." A grassy and bouncy pitch, allied to atmospheric assistance, kept the seamers interested throughout, but batting was possible with discretion. Bartlett, born a few miles away in Frimley, made the most of being dropped at slip first ball, which would have made it 35 for four; his fluent drives, during successive partnerships of 95 with Banton and Davies, put Somerset firmly in charge. Bartlett eventually fell for 137, his highest score. Surrey found the going harder, with the Overton twins relishing the conditions; only the classy Foakes, and a solid knock from Patel, prevented the follow-on. Morkel's fierce counterblast was repelled by a silky innings from Hildreth, but Dunn found a full length and reaped career-best figures as Somerset's last seven tumbled for 39. Surrey required 267; Burns and Borthwick offered hope before they were separated near the end of a third day which featured 17 wickets. Brooks was too much for the rest on the final morning, when 168 more were needed. His burst of three wickets in seven balls – including Elgar for a duck, after a single in the first innings – left Surrey teetering, before Groenewald and Craig Overton mopped up in time for an early lunch. This turned out to be Marcus Trescothick's last match for Somerset.

Close of play: first day, Surrey 0-0 (Burns 0, Stoneman 0); second day, Surrey 188-5 (Patel 40, Jacks 13); third day, Surrey 99-2 (Borthwick 35, Batty 4).

Somerset

M. E. Trescothick c Foakes b Clarke	18	– c Foakes b Morkel	11
*T. B. Abell c Elgar b Morkel	5	– c Jacks b Morkel	9
J. C. Hildreth lbw b Dunn	6	– lbw b Patel	64
T. Banton c Jacks b Dunn	44	– lbw b Dunn	12
G. A. Bartlett c Foakes b Morkel	137	– c Foakes b Clarke	16
†S. M. Davies b Dunn	41	– lbw b Dunn	16
C. Overton b Clarke	40	– c and b Morkel	1
J. Overton b Clarke	20	– c Foakes b Dunn	2
T. D. Groenewald c Foakes b Morkel	1	– b Dunn	10
M. J. Leach not out	5	– b Dunn	5
J. A. Brooks c Foakes b Morkel	13	– not out	0
Lb 4, nb 10	14	Lb 7	7

1/21 (2) 2/27 (1) 3/35 (3)   (92 overs) 344   1/21 (2) 2/28 (1)   (49.2 overs) 153
4/130 (4) 5/225 (6) 6/298 (5)   3/50 (4) 4/114 (3)
7/320 (7) 8/321 (9) 9/323 (8) 10/344 (11)   5/116 (5) 6/118 (7) 7/131 (8)
     8/134 (6) 9/152 (10) 10/153 (9)

Morkel 22–8–64–4; Dunn 20–2–85–3; Clarke 20–3–72–3; Patel 12–0–54–0; Batty 18–1–65–0.
Second innings—Morkel 16–3–41–3; Dunn 15.2–3–43–5; Clarke 11–0–49–1; Batty 1–0–1–0;
Patel 6–2–12–1.

Surrey

*R. J. Burns c Trescothick b C. Overton	2	– c Hildreth b Brooks	48
M. D. Stoneman b Brooks	21	– b Brooks	12
S. G. Borthwick c Davies b C. Overton	36	– b Groenewald	45
D. Elgar lbw b J. Overton	1	– (5) b Brooks	0
†B. T. Foakes c Davies b J. Overton	57	– (6) c Trescothick b Brooks	2
R. S. Patel c Groenewald b J. Overton	63	– (7) c J. Overton b C. Overton	27
W. G. Jacks c Trescothick b C. Overton	13	– (8) lbw b Groenewald	0
R. Clarke c J. Overton b C. Overton	20	– (9) c Davies b Groenewald	8
M. Morkel b Leach b C. Overton	0	– (10) c Leach b C. Overton	2
G. J. Batty c Davies b Groenewald	0	– (4) b Brooks	14
M. P. Dunn not out	0	– not out	1
B 4, lb 9, w 1, nb 4	18	Lb 4, w 1	5

1/26 (2) 2/36 (1) 3/38 (4)   (73 overs) 231   1/22 (2) 2/94 (1)   (56.3 overs) 164
4/119 (5) 5/154 (3) 6/190 (7)   3/118 (4) 4/118 (5)
7/218 (8) 8/218 (9) 9/223 (10) 10/231 (6)   5/120 (6) 6/127 (3) 7/131 (8)
     8/153 (9) 9/161 (7) 10/164 (10)

C. Overton 20–9–38–5; Brooks 17–6–57–1; Groenewald 14–4–45–1; J. Overton 14–2–46–3;
Abell 3–0–15–0; Leach 5–1–17–0. *Second innings*—C. Overton 16.3–2–59–2; Brooks
13–4–33–5; Groenewald 11–3–29–3; J. Overton 9–3–13–0; Leach 3–0–21–0; Abell 4–3–5–0.

Umpires: P. K. Baldwin and P. J. Hartley.

SURREY v YORKSHIRE

At Guildford, June 10–13. Drawn. Surrey 11pts, Yorkshire 8pts. Toss: uncontested. First-class debut:
J. A. Thompson. Championship debut: J. L. Smith.

Bad weather removed more than half the playing time from Guildford's 99th first-class match,
including an opening day doused by a month's worth of rain. A porous outfield and outstanding
work by the groundstaff meant the game started promptly next morning, which surprised Yorkshire,
who then lost Olivier, their pace spearhead, to a hip injury after bowling 12 overs. Stoneman
rediscovered his touch, before Foakes (captaining in place of Rory Burns, who had injured his back)
and the 18-year-old Jamie Smith gave Surrey the upper hand on an amiable pitch; some of Smith's
drives in his first Championship innings delighted the crowd. Debutant seamer Jordan Thompson had
claimed two Test players as his first victims, and later the persistent Patterson hauled Yorkshire back
into it with three wickets – all bowled – in the 86th over. With only 27.4 possible on the third day,
the fourth seemed likely to be a battle for bonus points, but Yorkshire wilted under an assault led by

Morkel, with Foakes taking two catches outstanding even by his standards. Thompson hit boldly to delay the follow-on, before more drizzle hastened the stalemate.

Close of play: first day, no play; second day, Surrey 290-8 (Clark 7, Morkel 5); third day, Yorkshire 58-1 (Fraine 17, Ballance 6).

Surrey

M. D. Stoneman c Tattersall b Thompson .	61	M. Morkel c Lyth b Coad	5
D. Elgar c Bess b Patterson	24	M. P. Dunn not out	2
S. G. Borthwick c Lyth b Thompson....	21		
R. S. Patel lbw b Coad...............	19	B 14, lb 2, nb 8	24
*†B. T. Foakes b Patterson..............	62		—
J. L. Smith b Patterson...............	56	1/78 (2) 2/98 (1)	(100.4 overs) 313
W. G. Jacks b Patterson...............	0	3/142 (4) 4/147 (3)	
R. Clarke lbw b Coad	13	5/265 (5) 6/265 (7) 7/266 (6)	
J. Clark c sub (M. D. Fisher) b Patterson..	26	8/285 (8) 9/291 (10) 10/313 (9)	

Coad 25-4-71-3; Olivier 12-3-42-0; Bess 18-1-62-0; Patterson 26.4-4-81-5; Thompson 19-6-41-2.

Yorkshire

A. Lyth c Jacks b Clarke	30	– not out	15
W. A. R. Fraine c Foakes b Morkel	25	– not out	14
G. S. Ballance c Elgar b Morkel	6		
T. Köhler-Cadmore c Foakes b Clarke........	14		
J. A. Leaning c Foakes b Morkel	4		
†J. A. Tattersall c Clarke b Clark.............	7		
D. M. Bess c Clarke b Clark	0		
J. A. Thompson c Morkel b Dunn	34		
*S. A. Patterson c Foakes b Clarke	6		
B. O. Coad b Morkel	0		
D. Olivier not out	13		
Lb 7, nb 2	9	Lb 1	1

1/51 (1) 2/58 (3) 3/75 (2)	(48 overs) 148	(no wkt, 13.3 overs)	30
4/79 (5) 5/93 (6) 6/93 (7)			
7/93 (4) 8/109 (9) 9/114 (10) 10/148 (8)			

Morkel 16-4-43-4; Dunn 11-3-26-1; Clark 8-1-37-2; Clarke 13-4-35-3. *Second innings—* Morkel 3-1-7-0; Dunn 4-2-9-0; Clarke 4-2-8-0; Patel 2.3-1-5-0.

Umpires: J. W. Lloyds and R. T. Robinson.

SURREY v WARWICKSHIRE

At The Oval, June 23–26. Surrey won by 74 runs. Surrey 19pts, Warwickshire 4pts. Toss: uncontested. County debut: T. J. Lester.

Dismissed before tea on a torrid opening day, Surrey responded well enough to win before lunch on the fourth – their first Championship victory of the season. Warwickshire's makeshift attack, led by Hannon-Dalby and supplemented by Lancashire left-armer Toby Lester, made good use of an uncharacteristically green Oval pitch. Rhodes and Sibley then picked off some loose offerings to launch the reply. Warwickshire had to work much harder after that, with Jordan Clark well worth his three wickets, and the lead was confined to 36. Miles gamely fought back from conceding 21 in his first over to earn five wickets with movement and aggression. Surrey were grateful to all-rounders Sam Curran and Rikki Clarke for setting a challenging target, yet Warwickshire had more than four sessions to reach 290. They threatened to do it while Sibley was defying his old county, but Curran – restricted to 30 overs in the match after a hamstring injury by order of the ECB – made a vital double breakthrough, removing Hose and Lamb in four balls. Morkel picked up a smart return catch off his toes to snare Sibley, and 41-year-old Batty exultantly finished the job with another caught and bowled, his fourth wicket.

Close of play: first day, Warwickshire 89-1 (Sibley 22, Yates 10); second day, Surrey 141-3 (Elgar 13, Foakes 5); third day, Warwickshire 148-3 (Sibley 52, Miles 9).

Surrey

*R. J. Burns c Ambrose b Hannon-Dalby	0	– lbw b Patel	34
M. D. Stoneman c sub (L. Banks) b Miles	33	– c Ambrose b Hannon-Dalby	71
S. G. Borthwick lbw b Lester	1	– c Rhodes b Patel	11
D. Elgar lbw b Lester	25	– c Lester b Miles	53
†B. T. Foakes c Yates b Hannon-Dalby	30	– c Yates b Miles	12
S. M. Curran c Ambrose b Lester	0	– c Hannon-Dalby b Miles	52
J. L. Smith b Miles	19	– lbw b Hannon-Dalby	14
R. Clarke b Miles	8	– c Yates b Patel	49
J. Clark c Ambrose b Lester	26	– c Ambrose b Miles	9
M. Morkel c Ambrose b Patel	12	– c Ambrose b Miles	6
G. J. Batty not out	0	– not out	2
B 2, lb 2, w 10, nb 8	40	B 4, lb 5, w 1, nb 2	12

1/8 (1) 2/25 (3) 3/72 (2)   (56.3 overs) 194   1/77 (1) 2/109 (3)   (80 overs) 325
4/110 (4) 5/110 (6) 6/116 (5)   3/135 (2) 4/169 (5)
7/142 (8) 8/166 (7) 9/194 (9) 10/194 (10)   5/222 (4) 6/247 (7) 7/286 (6)
    8/295 (9) 9/311 (10) 10/325 (8)

Hannon-Dalby 17–7–35–2; Lester 15–5–41–4; Miles 11–0–58–3; Lamb 6–1–30–0; Rhodes 4–2–5–0; Patel 3.3–1–3–1. *Second innings*—Hannon-Dalby 21–8–61–2; Lester 17–3–88–0; Patel 22–9–65–3; Miles 18–2–91–5; Rhodes 1–0–2–0; Lamb 1–0–9–0.

Warwickshire

W. M. H. Rhodes c Foakes b Clarke	51	– lbw b Batty	43
D. P. Sibley c Clarke b Morkel	31	– c and b Morkel	73
R. M. Yates c Foakes b Curran	48	– c Foakes b Morkel	4
S. R. Hain lbw b Clark	15	– st Foakes b Batty	26
A. J. Hose c Elgar b Morkel	9	– (6) lbw b Curran	21
M. J. Lamb c Foakes b Curran	5	– (7) b Curran	0
†T. R. Ambrose lbw b Curran	18	– (8) run out (Borthwick)	0
C. N. Miles c Foakes b Clark	20	– (5) lbw b Clarke	9
*J. S. Patel c Burns b Clark	12	– st Foakes b Batty	17
O. J. Hannon-Dalby c Borthwick b Clark	2	– c and b Batty	8
T. J. Lester not out	0	– not out	0
Lb 9, w 2, nb 8	19	B 8, lb 1, w 1, nb 4	14

1/76 (1) 2/99 (2) 3/130 (4)   (76.1 overs) 230   1/70 (1) 2/77 (3)   (74.2 overs) 215
4/158 (5) 5/175 (6) 6/180 (3)   3/137 (4) 4/149 (5)
7/209 (8) 8/217 (7) 9/228 (10) 10/230 (9)   5/190 (6) 6/190 (7) 7/190 (8)
    8/196 (2) 9/208 (9) 10/215 (10)

Morkel 18.1–2–72–3; Curran 17–3–50–3; Clarke 19–4–33–1; Clark 19–4–62–3; Batty 3–1–4–0. *Second innings*—Morkel 19–3–57–2; Curran 13–2–27–2; Clark 10–2–35–0; Clarke 15–3–53–1; Batty 17.2–5–34–4.

Umpires: J. D. Middlebrook and M. J. Saggers.

At Scarborough, June 30–July 3. SURREY lost to YORKSHIRE by 123 runs.

SURREY v KENT

At The Oval, July 7–10. Kent won by five wickets. Kent 23pts, Surrey 5pts. Toss: uncontested.

Kent's first win at The Oval for 11 years owed much to their bowlers, who exploited a seaming pitch and cloudy conditions more skilfully than Surrey's. Podmore and Milnes were consistently testing and, although Elgar and Foakes coped well, only Curran really broke free. Much of the action on an attritional second day came off the field. Surrey had asked if Batty, who had picked up a bug overnight and was yet to play any part, could be replaced by fellow off-spinner Amar Virdi. Kent had no objection, and Steve Davis, the ECB's liaison officer, initially agreed. But Lord's ruled it out, as neither international calls nor concussion were involved. Virdi was padded up when the news came through; Batty returned on the final day. Surrey were further irked that a ball which landed in a noxious puddle near the groundsmen's shed was not immediately replaced. "We had blokes running off the field to wash their hands," said coach Michael Di Venuto, who complained of a "rancid smell". Denly batted for more than five hours (like Clarke, he passed 10,000 Championship runs) and saw off the challenging Morkel. Kent's eventual lead of 98 proved decisive, as Stevens relished the third day's muggy conditions. They needed only 121 and, although Morkel struck twice in the first five balls, Robinson followed up six catches in Surrey's second innings by attacking fiercely. He ended proceedings – and brought up a half-century – with a six off Elgar.

Close of play: first day, Surrey 244-6 (Foakes 57, Clarke 5); second day, Kent 285-4 (Kuhn 50, Robinson 1); third day, Surrey 179-6 (Curran 22, Clarke 19).

Surrey

*R. J. Burns c Robinson b Stewart	30	– c Robinson b Milnes	41
M. D. Stoneman lbw b Podmore	0	– c Robinson b Stevens	14
D. Elgar lbw b Stewart	63	– lbw b Stevens	65
S. G. Borthwick b Podmore	2	– c Robinson b Milnes	0
†B. T. Foakes b Podmore	60	– c Robinson b Stevens	7
S. M. Curran c Kuhn b Milnes	43	– c Robinson b Milnes	29
J. L. Smith lbw b Stewart	14	– lbw b Stevens	4
R. Clarke lbw b Milnes	27	– c Robinson b Stevens	31
J. Clark not out	2	– b Podmore	15
M. Morkel b Milnes	0	– (11) not out	3
G. J. Batty absent ill	–	– (10) lbw b Milnes	2
B 15, lb 7, nb 8	30	Lb 4, w 1, nb 2	7

1/1 (2) 2/73 (1) 3/99 (4) (84.5 overs) 271 1/24 (2) 2/107 (1) (77.1 overs) 218
4/121 (3) 5/191 (6) 6/224 (7) 3/107 (4) 4/124 (5)
7/267 (5) 8/269 (8) 9/271 (10) 5/145 (3) 6/151 (7) 7/187 (6)
8/209 (8) 9/212 (10) 10/218 (9)

Podmore 19-3-42-3; Stevens 17-4-30-0; Stewart 15-0-84-3; Milnes 20.5-4-54-3; Rayner 9-2-26-0; Bell-Drummond 4-1-13-0. *Second innings*—Podmore 16.1-3-45-1; Stevens 22-4-60-5; Stewart 12-1-38-0; Milnes 22-4-61-4; Rayner 5-3-10-0.

Kent

Z. Crawley c Borthwick b Clark	69	– c Foakes b Morkel	0
S. R. Dickson b Curran	1	– lbw b Clarke	18
J. L. Denly c Elgar b Morkel	88	– b Morkel	0
D. J. Bell-Drummond b Clark	64	– c Foakes b Curran	26
*H. G. Kuhn c Stoneman b Curran	54	– c Clarke b Batty	22
†O. G. Robinson lbw b Clarke	36	– not out	51
G. Stewart c Clarke b Curran	0	– not out	3
D. I. Stevens c Stoneman b Elgar	29		
O. P. Rayner b Clarke	6		
H. W. Podmore b Clarke	4		
M. E. Milnes not out	1		
Lb 7, nb 10	17	Lb 2, nb 2	4

1/16 (2) 2/99 (1) 3/209 (4) (107.3 overs) 369 1/0 (1) (5 wkts, 30.4 overs) 124
4/281 (3) 5/299 (5) 6/299 (7) 2/0 (3) 3/40 (2)
7/350 (6) 8/364 (8) 9/364 (9) 10/369 (10) 4/50 (4) 5/97 (5)

Morkel 23-5-70-1; Curran 25-8-56-3; Clarke 21.3-3-64-3; Clark 22-2-95-2; Borthwick 8-0-45-0; Stoneman 2-0-15-0; Elgar 6-0-17-1. *Second innings*—Morkel 8-3-22-2; Curran 9-0-36-1; Batty 7-0-30-1; Clarke 6-0-28-1; Elgar 4-0-6-0.

Umpires: S. J. O'Shaughnessy and B. V. Taylor.

At Nottingham, July 13–15. SURREY beat NOTTINGHAMSHIRE by 167 runs. *Amar Virdi takes 14 wickets in his first match of the season.*

SURREY v HAMPSHIRE

At The Oval, August 18–21. Drawn. Surrey 12pts, Hampshire 10pts. Toss: Hampshire. First-class debut: H. R. C. Came.

Pope marked his first four-day appearance since a shoulder injury in April with a superb maiden Championship double-century, stocked with strokes of sublime quality. He batted for exactly seven hours, hit 22 fours from 337 balls, and shared big stands with Borthwick – who made his first Championship hundred for over two years – and Finch to power Surrey more than 200 in front. The declaration left their bowlers two sessions to bowl Hampshire out again (the first two days had been shortened by rain). Virdi's three wickets gave them a sniff, but the Sydney-born Felix Organ – fluent throughout, after an early let-off by Patel at third slip – and Dawson ensured a draw. On the opening day, Hampshire had been tied down by Clarke, en route to the second seven-for of his long career, before Abbott and Ryan Stevenson, who hit a maiden half-century, cashed in on an easy-paced surface, adding 114 for the ninth wicket. Three players were replaced during the match: Sam Curran batted at No. 3 before joining England's Headingley Test squad, Pope later followed him up the M1 as a standby, and Hampshire's Harry Came made his first-class debut after Donald was concussed at short leg by a shot from Borthwick.

Close of play: first day, Hampshire 222-7 (McManus 5, Abbott 0); second day, Surrey 109-2 (Stoneman 52, Borthwick 26); third day, Surrey 490-5 (Pope 176, Foakes 12).

Hampshire

F. S. Organ c Foakes b Clark	26	– st Foakes b Virdi	77
I. G. Holland lbw b Clarke	51	– c Foakes b Virdi	6
*J. M. Vince c Foakes b Morkel	47	– lbw b Clarke	1
S. A. Northeast lbw b Clarke	6	– c Borthwick b McKerr	32
R. R. Rossouw c Stoneman b Clarke	18	– c Foakes b Virdi	40
L. A. Dawson lbw b Clarke	28	– not out	65
A. H. T. Donald c Foakes b Clarke	32		
†L. D. McManus c Stoneman b Clarke	11		
K. J. Abbott c Finch b Curran	72		
R. A. Stevenson lbw b Clarke	51		
F. H. Edwards not out	3		
H. R. C. Came (did not bat)		– (7) not out	23
Lb 15, w 5, nb 2	22	Lb 3, nb 6	9

1/73 (1) 2/110 (2) 3/116 (4)   (107 overs) 367   1/38 (2)   (5 wkts, 64 overs) 253
4/142 (5) 5/172 (3) 6/212 (6)   2/39 (3) 3/91 (4)
7/217 (7) 8/234 (9) 9/348 (10) 10/367 (9)   4/156 (1) 5/175 (5)

Came replaced Donald, as a concussion substitute.

Morkel 26–5–73–1; Curran 20–1–92–1; Clarke 28–8–74–7; Virdi 14–4–33–0; Clark 15–0–65–1; Patel 4–0–15–0. *Second innings*—Morkel 11–0–55–0; Clarke 8–0–54–1; Virdi 25–9–54–3; McKerr 7–0–31–1; Borthwick 6–1–28–0; Clark 7–1–28–0.

Surrey

M. D. Stoneman c Holland b Edwards	63	J. Clark not out	10
R. S. Patel c McManus b Edwards	2		
S. M. Curran c Stevenson b Edwards	14	B 4, lb 11, w 7, nb 12	34
S. G. Borthwick c Northeast b Edwards	100		
O. J. D. Pope not out	221	1/11 (2) (7 wkts dec, 156 overs) 579	
A. J. Finch c Organ b Stevenson	90	2/40 (3) 3/133 (1)	
†B. T. Foakes b Abbott	17	4/265 (4) 5/453 (6)	
R. Clarke lbw b Edwards	28	6/502 (7) 7/556 (8) 110 overs: 376-4	

M. Morkel, G. S. Virdi, C. McKerr and W. G. Jacks did not bat.

McKerr and Jacks replaced Curran and Pope, who left to join England's Test squad.

Edwards 22–1–125–5; Abbott 26–6–83–1; Holland 28–4–81–0; Dawson 53–8–180–0; Stevenson 25–1–87–1; Organ 2–0–8–0.

Umpires: R. J. Bailey and N. A. Mallender.

At Southampton, September 10–12. SURREY lost to HAMPSHIRE by 272 runs.

At Chelmsford, September 16–18. SURREY lost to ESSEX by an innings and 40 runs.

SURREY v NOTTINGHAMSHIRE

At The Oval, September 23–26. Drawn. Surrey 10pts, Nottinghamshire 7pts. Toss: Surrey.

Despite the rain, which allowed just 127.3 overs – including only two on the second day and none on the last – Surrey gathered enough points to climb back to sixth in the table. They reached 400 for only the third time in 2019, mainly thanks to an attractive third-wicket partnership between Borthwick and Pope that stretched, owing to the interruptions, from the first morning to the third afternoon. They had come together when Coughlin struck twice in his second over, but that was the end of the good news for relegated Nottinghamshire. Pope made the most of two early let-offs – Moores missed a stumping, then Slater dropped him at midwicket – with some lip-smacking strokes: he ended an abbreviated season averaging 80 in 2019, and 58 overall, the highest by any Englishman who had played as many as his 31 first-class matches. He and Borthwick put on 222, taking heavy toll of the wayward Blatherwick, who was unsettled by eight no-balls. Clarke and Clark then ensured full batting points with some forceful hitting. Mullaney and Slater needed early luck against Morkel, whose figures were unflattering. With the clouds massing, Compton hit Borthwick's only delivery – a no-ball – for two, giving him peculiar-looking figures when bad light ended a forgettable season for both sides.

Close of play: first day, Surrey 246-2 (Borthwick 109, Pope 78); second day, Surrey 248-2 (Borthwick 109, Pope 79); third day, Nottinghamshire 77-1 (Slater 29, Compton 16).

Surrey

M. D. Stoneman c Moores b Coughlin	31	J. Clark not out	23
S. G. Borthwick c Ball b Mullaney	137		
J. L. Smith c Moores b Coughlin	0	B 17, lb 11, nb 16	44
O. J. D. Pope c Compton b Ball	106		
*†B. T. Foakes b Blatherwick	8		(6 wkts dec, 107.3 overs) 402
W. G. Jacks lbw b Mullaney	17	1/70 (1) 2/70 (3) 3/292 (4)	
R. Clarke not out	36	4/311 (5) 5/339 (6) 6/350 (2)	

L. E. Plunkett, M. Morkel and G. S. Virdi did not bat.

Ball 20–3–49–1; Blatherwick 11–1–82–1; Mullaney 21–1–73–2; Carter 28–2–77–0; Coughlin 24–3–83–2; Patterson-White 3.3–0–10–0.

Nottinghamshire

*S. J. Mullaney lbw b Clarke	21
B. T. Slater not out	29
B. G. Compton not out	16
B 4, lb 2, w 1, nb 4	11
	—
1/39 (1) (1 wkt, 20 overs)	77

J. M. Clarke, B. M. Duckett, L. A. Patterson-White, †T. J. Moores, P. Coughlin, M. Carter, J. T. Ball and J. M. Blatherwick did not bat.

Morkel 4–0–24–0; Clarke 5–3–11–1; Clark 5–0–18–0; Plunkett 4–1–14–0; Virdi 1–1–0–0; Jacks 1–1–0–0; Borthwick 0–0–4–0.

Umpires: M. J. Saggers and C. M. Watts.

SUSSEX

Feeling the draft

BRUCE TALBOT

There was a case to be made that the highlights of Sussex's summer actually came in the autumn. As the season ended, they snapped up Australian left-hander Travis Head for the whole of 2020, and in October they persuaded popular head coach Jason Gillespie to sign a new contract, as well as securing the experienced all-rounder Ravi Bopara from Essex; Mitch Claydon had already agreed a move from Kent.

All went down well with a restless membership; the loss of 11 players to The Hundred, less so. It could be argued that Sussex had never managed to replace Ed Joyce, so the arrival of Head, who had worked with Gillespie at Adelaide Strikers, was welcome – as was James Kirtley's appointment as pace-bowling coach.

Supporters certainly needed cheering up. With three counties promoted in the Championship, this was supposed to be the year Sussex reclaimed their place in Division One. Instead, they fell from third to sixth. Captain Ben Brown identified a familiar cause – a lack of depth, particularly in batting – for underachievement in a competition that meant much to fans still clinging to memories of the Chris Adams era. "There were times when we put out a side that could compete in Division One," said Brown, "and other times when even on paper the opposition looked stronger than us."

Only he and Stiaan van Zyl passed 700 Championship runs. Worryingly, Phil Salt, hampered in midsummer by a hand injury, Luke Wells and Harry Finch (whose average plummeted to 12) all regressed from 2018, when the paucity of runs had been bailed out by the brilliance of Jofra Archer. Brown lamented that promising batsmen were not guarding their wicket more keenly. "We've got guys who have all the shots," he said. "But they need to learn about the defensive aspects against the moving ball. It requires hard work and dedication."

Too often Brown and the dependable David Wiese – who played every match in all the county competitions – needed to mount a lower-order rearguard. Sometimes they pulled it off, but Sussex could not reliably make big first-innings totals. The management did their best to find a winning blend: 24 players were used in the Championship, with 14 making six appearances or fewer. In their final fixture, Sussex fielded only four frontline batsmen, including Tom Clark, an 18-year-old Academy product. Will Beer, better known for his one-day leg-spin, reinvented himself as a top-three batsman, with mixed success, but in hindsight the decisions to allow Luke Wright to concentrate on white-ball cricket, and Michael Burgess to join Warwickshire, may have been hasty. At the end of the season, seamer Abi Sakande was released, at his own request.

Bryn Lemon, Getty Images

Stiaan van Zyl

While Archer was making headlines on the world stage, Ollie Robinson led the Sussex attack outstandingly. His 63 wickets were more than double anyone else's haul – next came Wiese with 30 – and included eight for 34 against Middlesex, the best return in Division Two. Robinson earned an England Lions call, but the longer Sussex remain out of the top flight, the greater the danger of such a prized asset leaving. Mir Hamza, the Pakistan left-armer, took 21 wickets in six Championship games. And it was heartening to see Reece Topley bowling with the red ball, having apparently overcome back problems, though the news that he turned down a contract offer was a disappointment; in October, he joined Surrey. Injury continued to plague George Garton, who missed most of the season. Sussex spinners had a lean time, claiming 34 wickets between them, at 47.

The county's white-ball form was better. Seven of their eight home matches in the Blast sold out, and the crowd saw some sparkling cricket. Eight wins put them top of the South Group, and brought a home quarter-final against defending champions Worcestershire. Salt steered Sussex to a decent 184, but then they ran into Moeen Ali, who made them pay for dropping him three times with a match-winning hundred. Failing to reach finals day was a huge disappointment let-down for such a talented squad, who had fought on despite losing two key players – Tymal Mills to injury, and Rashid Khan to Afghanistan – in quick succession.

Performances also improved in the Royal London Cup, but from a low base, and they did not reach the knockouts. Their chances of qualifying in 2020 are slim too: the tournament clashes with The Hundred, whose player draft took more cricketers from Sussex than any other team. For supporters in the north of the county, there was a crumb of comfort: after a gap of five years, Horsham is back on the rota for 50-over games.

Off the field, Sussex unveiled ambitious plans to redevelop the Sea End at Hove, on and around the site of the Sussex Cricketer pub. The first phase should see a new restaurant and bar, together with 40 apartments, conference space and offices. Proceeds from the sale of the flats would fund further development inside the ground, which is scheduled to take between five and seven years. The vision is laudable, but supporters will also want to see a more competitive team, particularly in red-ball cricket, much sooner.

Championship attendance: 21,900.

SUSSEX RESULTS

All first-class matches – Played 15: Won 4, Lost 5, Drawn 6.
County Championship matches – Played 14: Won 4, Lost 5, Drawn 5.

Specsavers County Championship, 6th in Division 2;
Vitality Blast, quarter-finalists; Royal London One-Day Cup, 5th in South Group.

COUNTY CHAMPIONSHIP AVERAGES, BATTING AND FIELDING

Cap		Birthplace	M	I	NO	R	HS	100	Avge	Ct/St
	†G. H. S. Garton	*Brighton‡*	3	4	2	112	59*	0	56.00	2
2019	†S. van Zyl††	*Cape Town, SA*	12	20	3	820	173	2	48.23	4
2014	B. C. Brown	*Crawley‡*	14	22	3	812	156	3	42.73	52/1
	†D. M. W. Rawlins	*Bermuda*	6	10	1	328	100	1	36.44	5
	P. D. Salt	*Bodelwyddan*	10	19	1	603	122	2	33.50	13
	W. A. T. Beer	*Crawley‡*	10	15	2	377	97	0	29.00	1
2014	C. J. Jordan	*Lowlands, Barbados*	11	16	1	429	166	1	28.60	17
	D. R. Briggs	*Newport, IoW*	4	5	2	80	24	0	26.66	2
2016	D. Wiese††	*Roodepoort, SA*	14	20	0	527	77	0	26.35	1
	L. J. Evans	*Lambeth*	7	11	0	264	113	1	24.00	6
2016	†L. W. P. Wells	*Eastbourne‡*	14	25	3	527	98*	0	23.95	5
2019	O. E. Robinson	*Margate*	11	16	4	255	59	0	21.25	3
	A. D. Thomason	*Birmingham*	3	6	0	113	90	0	18.83	1
	V. Chopra	*Barking*	2	4	0	74	32	0	18.50	2
	†T. J. Haines	*Crawley‡*	6	11	0	159	39	0	14.45	2
	H. Z. Finch	*Hastings‡*	8	14	1	161	48	0	12.38	12
	A. Sakande	*Chester*	5	7	3	38	15	0	9.50	2
	Mir Hamza¶	*Karachi, Pakistan*	6	7	2	14	8	0	2.80	2

Also batted: M. G. K. Burgess (*Epsom*) (1 match) 9; †A. T. Carey¶ (*Loxton, Australia*) (1 match) 56, 69* (1 ct); †T. G. R. Clark (*Haywards Heath‡*) (1 match) 13; †E. O. Hooper (*Eastbourne‡*) (1 match) 20; R. J. W. Topley (*Ipswich*) (2 matches) 1*, 5; J. D. Warner (*Wakefield*) (2 matches) 1*, 13*.

‡ *Born in Sussex.* ¶ *Official overseas player.* †† *Other non-England-qualified.*

BOWLING

	Style	O	M	R	W	BB	5I	Avge
O. E. Robinson	RFM/OB	380.3	83	1,036	63	8-34	6	16.44
Mir Hamza	LFM	195	48	577	21	4-51	0	27.47
D. M. W. Rawlins	SLA	89	10	330	10	3-19	0	33.00
D. Wiese	RFM	339.3	68	1,048	30	5-26	2	34.93
C. J. Jordan	RFM	297	58	919	26	4-58	0	35.34
L. W. P. Wells	LB	148.4	21	497	11	5-63	1	45.18

Also bowled: W. A. T. Beer (LB) 150.1–24–474–8; D. R. Briggs (SLA) 83.3–11–255–4; B. C. Brown (RM) 2–0–15–0; L. J. Evans (RFM) 2–0–11–0; H. Z. Finch (RFM) 2–0–9–0; G. H. S. Garton (LFM) 30.5–2–107–4; T. J. Haines (RM) 70–17–198–5; E. O. Hooper (SLA) 20.5–5–65–1; A. Sakande (RFM) 111.3–11–458–9; A. D. Thomason (RFM) 52–2–239–2; R. J. W. Topley (LFM) 22.3–4–81–6; J. D. Warner (RFM) 30.2–4–141–4.

LEADING ROYAL LONDON CUP AVERAGES (100 runs/4 wickets)

Batting	Runs	HS	Avge	SR	Ct/St
D. Wiese	395	171	98.75	120.42	2
L. J. Wright	409	166	58.42	97.14	3
L. J. Evans	335	110	41.87	96.82	1
P. D. Salt	241	137*	40.16	114.76	3
B. C. Brown	172	64	28.66	93.47	6/2
H. Z. Finch	164	89	23.42	88.17	4

Bowling	W	BB	Avge	ER
Mir Hamza	18	4-43	26.88	6.46
G. H. S. Garton	9	3-42	29.66	5.93
D. R. Briggs	11	2-11	37.81	5.62
W. A. T. Beer	7	2-49	46.71	5.27
D. Wiese	6	3-54	62.33	6.13
A. Sakande	4	1-32	68.50	6.85

LEADING VITALITY BLAST AVERAGES (100 runs/21 overs)

Batting	Runs	HS	Avge	SR	Ct
P. D. Salt	406	78*	36.90	**161.11**	13
D. M. W. Rawlins . . .	155	69	22.14	**159.79**	8
A. T. Carey.	264	78	37.71	**152.60**	4
D. Wiese.	284	66	40.57	**149.47**	5
L. J. Evans	358	65*	44.75	**139.29**	5
L. J. Wright	388	76*	35.27	**125.97**	1

Bowling	W	BB	Avge	ER
T. S. Mills	7	3-23	21.42	**6.52**
Rashid Khan	7	2-41	33.85	**7.40**
O. E. Robinson . . .	11	4-15	20.27	**7.77**
W. A. T. Beer	9	3-22	18.22	**7.80**
D. R. Briggs	8	3-35	43.75	**8.33**
R. J. W. Topley . . .	17	4-33	17.94	**8.47**
C. J. Jordan	10	2-28	30.40	**9.21**

FIRST-CLASS COUNTY RECORDS

Highest score for	344*	M. W. Goodwin v Somerset at Taunton	2009
Highest score against	322	E. Paynter (Lancashire) at Hove	1937
Leading run-scorer	34,150	J. G. Langridge (avge 37.69)	1928–55
Best bowling for	10-48	C. H. G. Bland v Kent at Tonbridge	1899
Best bowling against	9-11	A. P. Freeman (Kent) at Hove	1922
Leading wicket-taker	2,211	M. W. Tate (avge 17.41)	1912–37
Highest total for	742-5 dec	v Somerset at Taunton	2009
Highest total against	726	by Nottinghamshire at Nottingham	1895
Lowest total for	{ 19	v Surrey at Godalming	1830
	{ 19	v Nottinghamshire at Hove	1873
Lowest total against	18	by Kent at Gravesend	1867

LIST A COUNTY RECORDS

Highest score for	**171**	**D. Wiese v Hampshire at Southampton**	**2019**
Highest score against	198*	G. A. Gooch (Essex) at Hove.	1982
Leading run-scorer	7,969	A. P. Wells (avge 31.62)	1981–96
Best bowling for	7-41	A. N. Jones v Nottinghamshire at Nottingham . . .	1986
Best bowling against	8-21	M. A. Holding (Derbyshire) at Hove	1988
Leading wicket-taker	370	R. J. Kirtley (avge 22.35).	1995–2010
Highest total for	399-4	v Worcestershire at Horsham	2011
Highest total against	377-9	by Somerset at Hove	2003
Lowest total for	49	v Derbyshire at Chesterfield	1969
Lowest total against	36	by Leicestershire at Leicester	1973

TWENTY20 COUNTY RECORDS

Highest score for	153*	L. J. Wright v Essex at Chelmsford	2014
Highest score against	152*	G. R. Napier (Essex) at Chelmsford.	2008
Leading run-scorer	**4,106**	**L. J. Wright (avge 32.58, SR 150.34)**	**2004–19**
Best bowling for	5-11	Mushtaq Ahmed v Essex at Hove	2005
Best bowling against	{ 5-14	A. D. Mascarenhas (Hampshire) at Hove.	2004
	{ 5-14	K. J. Abbott (Middlesex) at Hove	2015
Leading wicket-taker	**93**	**W. A. T. Beer (avge 26.39, ER 7.39)**	**2008–19**
Highest total for	242-5	v Gloucestershire at Bristol	2016
Highest total against	242-3	by Essex at Chelmsford	2008
Lowest total for	67	v Hampshire at Hove	2004
Lowest total against	85	by Hampshire at Southampton	2008

ADDRESS

The 1st Central County Ground, Eaton Road, Hove BN3 3AN; 0844 264 0202; info@sussex-cricket.co.uk; www.sussexcricket.co.uk.

OFFICIALS

Captain B. C. Brown
(Twenty20) L. J. Wright
Director of cricket K. Greenfield
Head coach J. N. Gillespie
Academy director R. G. Halsall
President Sir Rod Aldridge

Chairman R. C. Warren
CEO/chairman cricket committee C. R. Andrew
Head groundsman 2019 A. Mackay
      2020 B. J. Gibson
Scorer 2019 M. J. Charman
      2020 G. J. Irwin

SUSSEX v CARDIFF MCCU

At Hove, March 31–April 2. Drawn. Toss: Cardiff MCCU. First-class debuts: M. T. Foster, J. H. Gibbs.

Despite a scorecard skewed in Sussex's favour, there were eye-catching displays from a few Cardiff students, especially Dan Douthwaite. He bowled Salt in his first over and van Zyl in his 11th, though he would shine brighter with bat in hand. In reply to an imposing first-day total of 480, built mainly around a 121-ball 139 from Wiese, Cardiff lurched from 48 for one to 55 for six against Jordan's pace. But neither Douthwaite nor Prem Sisodiya, whose left-arm spin had done for the remainder of Sussex's top five, was daunted, and they added 77. When the ninth wicket fell at 159, it seemed improbable that Douthwaite, on 57, would reach three figures. Yet with sterling (if scoreless) support from Jack Gibbs, he did, tucking in to Wells and Wiese, and cracking 43 from his last 19 balls. Sussex led by 277, and had doubled that by the time rain intervened ten overs into the final day. Van Zyl reached his own hundred, a gratifying sight for Sussex after he missed most of 2018 with a knee problem.

Close of play: first day, Sussex 480-9 (Jordan 15, Sakande 2); second day, Sussex 220-2 (van Zyl 92, Brown 51).

Sussex

P. D. Salt b Douthwaite	1	– c Carlson b Reingold	65
T. J. Haines lbw b Sisodiya	93		
L. W. P. Wells c Kolk b Sisodiya	66	– (5) not out	7
S. van Zyl b Douthwaite	8	– (2) retired out	103
H. Z. Finch b Sisodiya	15	– (3) c Kolk b Reingold	3
*†B. C. Brown c Ludlow b Gibbs	10	– (4) not out	86
M. G. K. Burgess lbw b Evans	95		
D. Wiese c Carlson b Foster	139		
C. J. Jordan not out	15		
O. E. Robinson b Gibbs	5		
A. Sakande not out	2		
B 5, lb 4, nb 22	31	Lb 7, w 1, nb 2	10

1/5 (1) 2/169 (3) (9 wkts dec, 97 overs) 480
3/186 (4) 4/196 (2) 5/215 (6)
6/223 (5) 7/443 (7) 8/469 (8) 9/476 (10)

1/102 (1) (3 wkts, 50.3 overs) 274
2/110 (3) 3/257 (2)

Evans 14–1–47–1; Douthwaite 16–1–85–2; Gibbs 16–1–54–2; Foster 10–1–59–1; Reingold 16–0–104–0; Sisodiya 18–2–76–3; Carlson 7–0–46–0. *Second innings*—Evans 9–0–36–0; Douthwaite 5–0–40–0; Gibbs 8.3–0–62–0; Reingold 10–0–64–2; Pearce 13–0–53–0; Carlson 5–1–12–0.

Cardiff MCCU

J. H. Ludlow c Jordan b Sakande	4	B. N. Evans b Wells	0
S. J. Reingold c Brown b Haines	22	M. T. Foster b Jordan	6
†L. Machado c Burgess b Jordan	19	J. H. Gibbs c Wells b Wiese	0
K. S. Carlson lbw b Jordan	0	B 7, lb 2, nb 6	15
O. M. D. Kolk c Brown b Jordan	0		
*S. J. Pearce b Jordan	4	1/11 (1) 2/48 (3) 3/50 (4) (56.4 overs) 203
D. A. Douthwaite not out	100	4/50 (2) 5/54 (5) 6/55 (6)
P. Sisodiya b Wells	33	7/132 (8) 8/132 (9) 9/159 (10) 10/203 (11)

Robinson 12–3–36–0; Sakande 11–5–21–1; Wiese 6.4–1–34–1; Jordan 14–3–53–5; Haines 6–2–14–1; Wells 7–1–36–2.

Umpires: M. Newell and B. V. Taylor.

SUSSEX v LEICESTERSHIRE

At Hove, April 5–8. Leicestershire won by seven wickets. Leicestershire 21pts, Sussex 3pts. Toss: uncontested. County debut: Mir Hamza. Championship debut: M. H. Azad.

Leicestershire's first Championship win in Sussex since 1999 at Arundel owed much to their calm approach to a tricky target of 230 on a pitch that did not deteriorate as predicted. Hassan Azad, who faced 173 balls for a gritty half-century on Championship debut, epitomised their efforts, and the victory came an hour after lunch on the final day. Sussex had been up against it after staggering to 36 for five on the first morning. Wiese counter-attacked effectively, before becoming the fifth victim of Taylor's career-best six for 47. His sharp pace and late movement suggested he could have a bright future. Leicestershire were scarcely better placed at 59 for five – Pakistan left-arm seamer Mir Hamza took three on county debut – but Hill oversaw resistance that brought a lead of 79. Even so, Sussex fancied their chances. Openers Salt and Haines wiped out the arrears, and the hosts built a promising position before abruptly losing their last eight for 97, mainly to a combination of Taylor (who completed a maiden ten-for) and Ackermann (whose much-improved off-spin gained him a maiden five-for).

Close of play: first day, Leicestershire 131-5 (Dearden 26, Hill 40); second day, Sussex 211-2 (Wells 41, van Zyl 41); third day, Leicestershire 99-1 (Horton 53, Azad 27).

Sussex

P. D. Salt c Hill b Wright	0	– c and b Ackermann		80
T. J. Haines c and b Taylor	18	– lbw b Ackermann		39
L. W. P. Wells c Dearden b Taylor	0	– b Taylor		48
S. van Zyl b Wright	28	– c Hill b Taylor		41
H. Z. Finch c Hill b Taylor	2	– c Hill b Wright		48
*†B. C. Brown b Taylor	0	– c and b Ackermann		0
D. Wiese b Taylor	51	– lbw b Taylor		0
C. J. Jordan c Horton b Wright	12	– c Azad b Ackermann		18
O. E. Robinson b Taylor	23	– c Hill b Ackermann		0
D. R. Briggs c and b Griffiths	20	– c Hill b Taylor		16
Mir Hamza not out	4	– not out		0
B 2, lb 7, nb 6	15	B 6, lb 10, nb 2		18

1/0 (1) 2/5 (3) 3/28 (2)   (44.2 overs) 173   1/105 (2) 2/136 (1)   (84.1 overs) 308
4/30 (5) 5/36 (6) 6/100 (4)   3/211 (4) 4/234 (3)
7/120 (8) 8/128 (7) 9/163 (9) 10/173 (10)   5/235 (6) 6/236 (7) 7/285 (8)
                                       8/285 (9) 9/308 (10) 10/308 (5)

Wright 15–4–53–3; Taylor 16–2–47–6; Griffiths 7.2–0–34–1; Davis 6–0–30–0. *Second innings—* Wright 16.1–5–54–1; Taylor 22–7–75–4; Griffiths 13–2–50–0; Davis 9–1–44–0; Ackermann 24–3–69–5.

Leicestershire

A. Javid c and b Mir Hamza	7	– lbw b Wiese		11
*P. J. Horton c Brown b Mir Hamza	26	– c Jordan b Robinson		61
M. H. Azad c Jordan b Robinson	6	– c Salt b Robinson		59
M. J. Cosgrove lbw b Mir Hamza	11	– not out		53
C. N. Ackermann c Finch b Robinson	0	– not out		24
H. E. Dearden lbw b Robinson	40			
†L. J. Hill b Briggs	67			
T. A. I. Taylor lbw b Haines	33			
C. J. C. Wright c van Zyl b Robinson	18			
G. T. Griffiths c Brown b Jordan	1			
W. S. Davis not out	18			
B 1, lb 16, nb 8	25	B 1, lb 9, nb 14		24

1/13 (1) 2/30 (3) 3/54 (4)   (79 overs) 252   1/27 (1)   (3 wkts, 73 overs) 232
4/55 (2) 5/59 (5) 6/151 (6)   2/115 (2) 3/176 (3)
7/203 (7) 8/218 (8) 9/221 (10) 10/252 (9)

Robinson 19–6–46–4; Mir Hamza 19–3–71–3; Wiese 17–5–38–0; Jordan 11–3–33–1; Haines 8–3–19–1; Briggs 5–0–28–1. *Second innings—*Robinson 17–6–28–2; Wiese 11–3–31–1; Mir Hamza 12–2–49–0; Haines 5–2–6–0; Jordan 12–0–61–0; Briggs 8–2–21–0; Wells 8–1–26–0.

Umpires: P. K. Baldwin and J. H. Evans.

At Chester-le-Street, April 11–14. SUSSEX beat DURHAM by six wickets.

At Northampton, May 20–23. SUSSEX drew with NORTHAMPTONSHIRE. *From 68 for six, Ben Brown and Chris Jordan add 309.*

SUSSEX v GLAMORGAN

At Hove, May 27–30. Drawn. Sussex 13pts, Glamorgan 8pts. Toss: Glamorgan. First-class debut: J. D. Warner.

Fifteen wickets fell on the first day, but the pitch soon flattened. Despite that, there would probably have been a result if 75 overs had not been lost to the weather on the third. Lloyd had unwisely chosen to bat, and Selman was alone in showing much application, particularly against Mir Hamza; he remained undefeated after 156 balls. Sussex were soon in the ascendancy: by the end of the busy first day, the forthright Salt had made his second successive hundred, and they led by 22. That had become 234 by the time they were dismissed on the second afternoon, thanks to another back-to-

CARRYING THE BAT MOST OFTEN FOR GLAMORGAN

5	A. H. Dyson	. . . . .	v Northants, Middx, Lancs, Sir J. Cahn's XI, Glos	1931 to 1939
4	T. R. Morgan	. . . .	v Yorks, Notts, Lancs, Leics	1922 to 1923
2	N. V. H. Riches	. .	v Leics, Yorks	1921 to 1922
2	W. E. Bates	. . . .	v Worcs, Northants.	1927 to 1928
2	D. E. Davies	. . . .	v South Africans, Somerset	1935 to 1935
2	**N. J. Selman**	. . . . .	**v Northants, Sussex**	**2016 to 2019**

Nine others have achieved the feat once for Glamorgan.

back century, this time from Brown. Sussex looked to have strengthened their grip when Hamza inflicted a pair on Hemphrey, but Labuschagne played superbly for a chanceless career-best 182 in just under five hours. He and Selman added 291, Glamorgan's best for the second wicket (beating 252 by Matthew Maynard and David Hemp against Northamptonshire in 2002). Selman fell for 99, and Wells worked his way through the batting to take his maiden five-for, but not swiftly enough. Sussex, asked to score 233 in 27 overs, called off their chase when Salt was quickly dismissed. For the hosts, Jared Warner, a seamer on loan from Yorkshire, took three wickets on the first day of his first-class debut.

Close of play: first day, Sussex 208-5 (Brown 29); second day, Glamorgan 137-1 (Selman 45, Labuschagne 77); third day, Glamorgan 218-1 (Selman 64, Labuschagne 131).

Glamorgan

N. J. Selman not out.	76	– (2) lbw b Wiese 99
C. R. Hemphrey lbw b Mir Hamza	0	– (1) lbw b Mir Hamza 0
M. Labuschagne c Finch b Wiese	14	– c Brown b Wells. 182
*D. L. Lloyd b Mir Hamza.	6	– c Jordan b Wells. 17
W. T. Root c Brown b Wiese	3	– c Jordan b Mir Hamza 2
K. S. Carlson c Finch b Jordan.	12	– c Brown b Wiese 0
D. A. Douthwaite b Jordan.	6	– c Brown b Wells. 63
G. G. Wagg c Brown b Jordan.	44	– c Evans b Briggs 25
†T. N. Cullen c Jordan b Warner	6	– not out 28
M. de Lange b Warner	0	– lbw b Wells 0
T. van der Gugten c Brown b Warner	1	– lbw b Wells 1
B 8, lb 2, nb 8.	18	B 17, lb 19, w 3, nb 10. 49
	(55.2 overs) 186	(125.1 overs) 466

1/5 (2) 2/30 (3) 3/41 (4)   (55.2 overs) 186   1/0 (1) 2/291 (3)   (125.1 overs) 466
4/44 (5) 5/76 (6) 6/102 (7)   3/327 (2) 4/330 (5)
7/174 (8) 8/180 (9) 9/180 (10) 10/186 (11)   5/331 (6) 6/371 (4) 7/416 (7)
     8/452 (8) 9/460 (10) 10/466 (11)

Mir Hamza 13–1–49–2; Wiese 13–1–42–2; Warner 7.2–3–35–3; Jordan 12–1–31–3; Briggs 10–2–19–0. *Second innings*—Mir Hamza 29–8–94–2; Wiese 23–2–91–2; Jordan 20–2–75–0; Warner 10–0–44–0; Briggs 20–2–63–1; Wells 23.1–4–63–5.

Sussex

P. D. Salt c Cullen b Douthwaite	103	– c van der Gugten b de Lange	5
L. W. P. Wells c Labuschagne b Douthwaite	30	– not out	16
H. Z. Finch b Labuschagne	31	– not out	22
S. van Zyl b Labuschagne	0		
L. J. Evans b van der Gugten	4		
*†B. C. Brown c Root b de Lange	131		
D. Wiese b van der Gugten	34		
C. J. Jordan c Cullen b Labuschagne	35		
D. R. Briggs c Carlson b de Lange	24		
J. D. Warner not out	1		
Mir Hamza b de Lange	1		
B 9, lb 7, nb 10	26	Lb 2, nb 2	4

1/85 (2) 2/121 (3) 3/121 (4)   (93.4 overs)   420   1/12 (1)   (1 wkt, 15 overs)   47
4/126 (5) 5/208 (1) 6/315 (7)
7/370 (8) 8/403 (6) 9/414 (9) 10/420 (11)

De Lange 21.4–2–89–3; van der Gugten 26–2–96–2; Wagg 12–0–52–0; Douthwaite 12–0–78–2; Labuschagne 16–2–61–3; Hemphrey 3–0–13–0; Lloyd 3–0–15–0. *Second innings*—de Lange 7–0–25–1; Douthwaite 4–0–15–0; Labuschagne 3–0–3–0; Hemphrey 1–0–2–0.

Umpires: P. K. Baldwin and D. J. Millns.

At Lord's, June 2–5. SUSSEX beat MIDDLESEX by an innings and 50 runs. *Ben Brown hits his third hundred in three matches.*

SUSSEX v GLOUCESTERSHIRE

At Arundel, June 11–14. Drawn. Sussex 10pts, Gloucestershire 10pts. Toss: uncontested. County debut: C. J. Sayers.

A turgid pitch, a slow outfield, circumspect batting and rain that never stopped for long all condemned the game to a draw. After persistent downpours for two days, simply starting on time – in front of a crowd of 3,000 – was an achievement. Conditions, though, were tailor-made for Beer, playing only his 12th Championship game, 11 years after his debut. Having hit a maiden fifty from No. 9 against Middlesex, he stood in for the injured opener, Phil Salt – and grafted. When he eventually lost his off stump to the persevering Payne, Beer had batted for seven hours 41 minutes and faced 336 balls; he was just three short of a century, and the groans could be heard in Hove. Sussex declared at the start of the third day, which – like the second – was curtailed. The sun did come out on the last, but the captains could not agree a target. Instead, Gloucestershire batted on: Roderick made his first hundred for almost three years, and Higgins his second of the season, both in attractive fashion. With the game drifting, Brown handed the gloves to Briggs and sent down some whimsical left-arm spin.

Close of play: first day, Sussex 257-5 (Beer 76, Wiese 14); second day, Sussex 351-8 (Robinson 10, Briggs 1); third day, Gloucestershire 146-3 (Roderick 51, Howell 5).

Sussex

L. W. P. Wells c Roderick b M. D. Taylor	15	O. E. Robinson not out	10
W. A. T. Beer b Payne	97	D. R. Briggs not out	1
H. Z. Finch c Roderick b Payne	10	B 12, lb 11, nb 10	33
S. van Zyl c Bracey b Payne	54		
L. J. Evans c J. M. R. Taylor b van Buuren	24	1/34 (1) 2/44 (3) (8 wkts dec, 126 overs)	351
*†B. C. Brown b M. D. Taylor	33	3/154 (4) 4/199 (5)	
D. Wiese lbw b van Buuren	67	5/241 (6) 6/332 (7)	
C. J. Jordan b van Buuren	7	7/334 (2) 8/342 (8)	110 overs: 313-5

A. Sakande did not bat.

Payne 29–9–71–3; Sayers 24–8–79–0; Higgins 23–8–49–0; M. D. Taylor 25–3–83–2; van Buuren 25–3–46–3.

Gloucestershire

M. A. H. Hammond c Briggs b Robinson . .	5	G. L. van Buuren not out.	37
*C. D. J. Dent c Brown b Jordan	59	B 1, lb 6	7
J. R. Bracey c Briggs b Wiese	21		
†G. H. Roderick c Brown b Robinson	158	1/12 (1) (6 wkts dec, 127.3 overs)	444
B. A. C. Howell lbw b Beer	29	2/72 (3) 3/132 (2)	
J. M. R. Taylor b Robinson	9	4/206 (5) 5/223 (6)	
R. F. Higgins not out	119	6/359 (4) 110 overs: 369-6	

D. A. Payne, M. D. Taylor and C. J. Sayers did not bat.

Robinson 29–7–88–3; Sakande 18–3–57–0; Jordan 18–3–70–1; Wiese 11–3–25–1; Briggs 15–3–39–0; Wells 14.3–2–59–0; Beer 16–2–64–1; Finch 2–0–9–0; Evans 2–0–11–0; Brown 2–0–15–0.

Umpires: N. L. Bainton and I. D. Blackwell.

At Kidderminster, June 18–21. SUSSEX drew with WORCESTERSHIRE.

SUSSEX v DURHAM

At Hove, June 24–27. Durham won by 196 runs. Durham 23pts, Sussex 3pts. Toss: Durham.

Durham outplayed Sussex, their victory lifting them off the bottom of the table. The *coup de grâce* came from Raine who, after going wicketless in the first innings, bowled gun-barrel straight in the second to take a career-best six for 27, including a burst of four for none in 16 balls either side of lunch on the third day. The most sustained resistance came from van Zyl and nightwatchman Robinson: both batted for more than three and a half hours, but Raine proved too much. On the first day, Durham had stumbled to 90 for five, with Jordan claiming four cheap wickets – including three ducks. But Bancroft and Eckersley (who made his first century since leaving Leicestershire) added 282, a county sixth-wicket record, before Rawlins's left-arm spin helped bring the innings to a rapid close. Sussex, who had donated 52 in extras, then folded for 232 – and could have been asked to follow on, 152 behind. When Lees reached three figures, Durham had three centuries in a game, a luxury they had last enjoyed in 2013. Bancroft's declaration on the third evening set a target of 437. The umpires were kept busy, warning Robinson for an altercation with Lees, and removing Carse – who had taken five for 43 in the first innings – from the attack for running on the pitch in the second.

Close of play: first day, Durham 259-5 (Bancroft 120, Eckersley 70); second day, Sussex 231-9 (Rawlins 56, Robinson 3); third day, Sussex 59-3 (van Zyl 17, Robinson 0).

MOST EXTRAS CONCEDED IN A MATCH BY SUSSEX

b	lb	w	nb		
97	19	26	5	47	v Durham at Chester-le-Street 1999
84	14	29	1	40	v Middlesex at Hove 2015
84	**25**	**26**	**5**	**28**	**v Durham at Hove** **2019**
83	7	22	–	54	v Durham at Chester-le-Street 1997
82	9	9	24	40	v Derbyshire at Derby 1999
82	25	22	2	33	v Essex at Colchester 2016
80	5	37	14	24	v Somerset at Taunton 1999

Durham

*C. T. Bancroft lbw b Rawlins	158	– c Finch b Robinson	5
A. Z. Lees c Finch b Jordan	0	– c Brown b Beer	143
G. J. Harte c van Zyl b Thomason	31	– c Rawlins b Wells	77
J. T. A. Burnham c Brown b Jordan	13	– not out	17
G. Clark c Evans b Jordan	0	– not out	10
L. Trevaskis lbw b Jordan	0		
†E. J. H. Eckersley c and b Wells	118		
B. A. Raine lbw b Rawlins	9		
B. A. Carse c Jordan b Rawlins	2		
W. J. Weighell c Brown b Beer	1		
C. Rushworth not out	0		
B 11, lb 23, nb 18	52	B 14, lb 3, w 5, nb 10	32

1/0 (2) 2/64 (3) 3/88 (4) 4/90 (5) (113.1 overs) 384   1/10 (1)   (3 wkts dec, 68.5 overs) 284
5/90 (6) 6/372 (7) 7/372 (1)   2/230 (3) 3/268 (2)
8/383 (8) 9/384 (9) 10/384 (10)
110 overs: 375-7

Robinson 20–2–64–0; Jordan 26–7–58–4; Wiese 21–3–48–0; Thomason 17–2–87–1; Wells 8–0–45–1; Beer 15.1–2–29–1; Rawlins 6–1–19–3. *Second innings*—Robinson 5–1–17–1; Jordan 9–4–24–0; Wiese 11–0–35–0; Beer 12.5–1–60–1; Wells 14–1–47–1; Rawlins 10–1–47–0; Thomason 7–0–37–0.

Sussex

L. W. P. Wells c Lees b Rushworth	2	– c Burnham b Rushworth	0
W. A. T. Beer lbw b Carse	0	– lbw b Rushworth	36
H. Z. Finch lbw b Rushworth	0	– c and b Rushworth	0
S. van Zyl b Harte	34	– c Eckersley b Raine	48
L. J. Evans c Eckersley b Weighell	20	– (6) c Eckersley b Raine	0
*†B. C. Brown c Rushworth b Carse	26	– (7) lbw b Raine	1
D. Wiese lbw b Trevaskis	56	– (8) lbw b Raine	0
C. J. Jordan c Bancroft b Carse	6	– (9) c Eckersley b Raine	44
D. M. W. Rawlins c Bancroft b Carse	56	– (10) not out	20
A. D. Thomason c Lees b Carse	3	– (11) c Bancroft b Raine	6
O. E. Robinson not out	4	– (5) c Burnham b Rushworth	59
B 9, lb 4, nb 12	25	B 5, lb 9, nb 12	26

1/2 (1) 2/2 (2) 3/2 (3)   (70.2 overs) 232   1/0 (1) 2/4 (3)   (96.3 overs) 240
4/41 (5) 5/89 (4) 6/96 (6)   3/59 (2) 4/141 (4)
7/110 (8) 8/219 (7) 9/223 (10) 10/232 (9)   5/141 (6) 6/143 (7) 7/143 (8)
8/197 (5) 9/220 (9) 10/240 (11)

Rushworth 15–4–38–2; Carse 14.2–3–43–5; Weighell 12–2–44–1; Trevaskis 14–3–41–1; Harte 4–0–23–1. *Second innings*—Rushworth 21–7–44–4; Carse 14.5–1–66–0; Raine 22.3–13–27–6; Weighell 11–6–23–0; Trevaskis 26–10–65–0; Lees 0.1–0–0–0; Clark 1–0–1–0.

Umpires: B. J. Debenham and A. G. Wharf.

SUSSEX v NORTHAMPTONSHIRE

At Hove, June 30–July 2. Northamptonshire won by 393 runs. Northamptonshire 21pts, Sussex 3pts. Toss: Northamptonshire. County debut: V. Chopra.

Ben Sanderson led a remorseless seam attack, finishing with career-best match figures of ten for 55, including his 200th wicket, as winless Northamptonshire crushed Sussex. The margin of 393 runs was a Championship record for both victors and vanquished (though Sussex lost to Cambridge University by 425 at Hove in 1890). The hosts were missing a raft of first-choice players, but there was little excuse for insipid batting that altogether spanned 78.4 overs. In their second innings, theoretically chasing 499, they lost nine for 70 in 19, prompting boos from fed-up members, some of whom called for the return of Chris Adams and Matt Prior in coaching roles. Calamitous defeat had looked unlikely on the first day, when Robinson – who, like Sanderson, also finished with his 200th wicket, in only his 50th first-class game, and also finished with ten in the match – reduced Northamptonshire, bottom of the table, to 99 for six. But the tail wagged, and their bowlers adeptly exploited a pitch that offered gentle seam and swing. Northamptonshire's catching was flawless, unlike Sussex's technique against the moving ball.

Close of play: first day, Sussex 7-2 (Thomason 0, Wells 1); second day, Northamptonshire 212-4 (Keogh 21, Buck 1).

Northamptonshire

R. S. Vasconcelos lbw b Robinson	2	– lbw b Sakande	88
R. I. Newton c Brown b Robinson	14	– c Chopra b Robinson	54
A. G. Wakely c Evans b Wiese	36	– c Brown b Sakande	19
T. Bavuma c Brown b Thomason	14	– c Salt b Rawlins	25
R. I. Keogh lbw b Robinson	21	– b Robinson	21
*†A. M. Rossington c Brown b Robinson	35	– (7) c Chopra b Robinson	14
L. A. Procter c Wells b Robinson	1	– (8) lbw b Robinson	7
S. A. Zaib c Brown b Sakande	54	– (9) c Sakande b Rawlins	29
B. A. Hutton b Sakande	24	– (10) not out	10
N. L. Buck not out	34	– (6) c Brown b Sakande	51
B. W. Sanderson c Thomason b Robinson	28	– c Brown b Rawlins	6
B 4, lb 2, nb 4	10	Lb 4, w 1, nb 2	7

1/2 (1) 2/29 (2) 3/58 (4)   (87 overs) 273   1/108 (2) 2/154 (3)   (77.2 overs) 331
4/76 (3) 5/97 (5) 6/99 (7)   3/169 (1) 4/205 (4)
7/150 (6) 8/204 (9) 9/205 (8) 10/273 (11)   5/217 (5) 6/249 (7) 7/265 (8)
                                     8/304 (6) 9/318 (9) 10/331 (11)

Robinson 24–7–63–6; Wiese 18–3–40–1; Sakande 17–1–64–2; Thomason 7–0–33–1; Beer 16–4–44–0; Rawlins 5–0–23–0. *Second innings*—Robinson 17–1–69–4; Wiese 13–3–58–0; Sakande 16–0–74–3; Thomason 6–0–32–0; Beer 15–1–60–0; Rawlins 10.2–2–34–3.

Sussex

P. D. Salt c Hutton b Sanderson	1	– lbw b Hutton	0
V. Chopra lbw b Hutton	5	– c Rossington b Buck	22
A. D. Thomason c Vasconcelos b Sanderson	4	– (10) b Sanderson	6
L. W. P. Wells c Vasconcelos b Hutton	5	– (3) c Rossington b Hutton	11
L. J. Evans c Wakely b Sanderson	6	– (4) lbw b Hutton	3
D. M. W. Rawlins c Hutton b Sanderson	31	– (5) c Bavuma b Buck	8
*†B. C. Brown c Rossington b Procter	10	– (6) c Keogh b Sanderson	46
D. Wiese c Rossington b Sanderson	28	– (7) c Rossington b Sanderson	1
W. A. T. Beer lbw b Hutton	1	– (8) c Hutton b Sanderson	0
O. E. Robinson not out	11	– (9) c Rossington b Hutton	0
A. Sakande c Wakely b Sanderson	3	– not out	0
Lb 1	1	B 4, lb 2, nb 2	8

1/6 (2) 2/6 (1) 3/15 (4)   (44.1 overs) 106   1/3 (1) 2/35 (3)   (34.3 overs) 105
4/15 (3) 5/26 (5) 6/49 (7)   3/41 (4) 4/41 (2)
7/83 (6) 8/92 (9) 9/94 (8) 10/106 (11)   5/66 (5) 6/92 (7) 7/92 (8)
                                    8/99 (6) 9/101 (9) 10/105 (10)

Sanderson 16.1–5–37–6; Hutton 17–6–47–3; Procter 5–2–16–1; Buck 6–4–5–0. *Second innings*—Sanderson 11.3–4–18–4; Hutton 13–3–32–4; Buck 6–1–21–2; Procter 3–0–15–0; Keogh 1–0–13–0.

Umpires: P. K. Baldwin and J. W. Lloyds.

At Arundel, July 7–10. SUSSEX lost to AUSTRALIA A by ten wickets (see Australia A tour section).

At Manchester, July 13–15. SUSSEX lost to LANCASHIRE by an innings and 51 runs.

SUSSEX v MIDDLESEX

At Hove, August 18–20. Sussex won by seven wickets. Sussex 22pts, Middlesex 3pts. Toss: Sussex. First-class debut: E. O. Hooper. Championship debut: A. T. Carey.

From the moment he had Robson caught behind with his first ball, Robinson was irrepressible. Settling on the perfect length and finding enough seam movement, he took a career-best eight for 34 in the first innings and six for 101 in the second, giving him the best match return for Sussex since 1964. In two games against Middlesex in 2019, he had taken 24 wickets; in six over three seasons, 52. Play did not start until 2.30, but Robinson made up for lost time – and was heading for all ten until Haines dismissed Roland-Jones, the penultimate wicket of an unseemly collapse that ended with Middlesex humbled for 75. They fought back, though, reducing Sussex to 151 for seven – before a forthright counter-attack from Beer helped the last three wickets add 158. Trailing by 234, Middlesex needed at least one major contribution, but instead got four half-centuries, while Malan fell to Elliot Hooper, a 23-year-old slow left-armer from Hastings, for 19. Sussex were delayed by a last-wicket stand of 79, with Finn hitting his first fifty for Middlesex, and were making heavy weather of a ticklish target of 145, with Finch completing a second successive pair, and a fifth duck in six innings. Then Carey, signed after a head-turning World Cup with Australia, struck four sixes in a Sowter over. Sussex, now sixth, bolstered their faint chances of promotion, and Middlesex were not wholly out of the reckoning.

Close of play: first day, Sussex 128-3 (Wells 52, Carey 46); second day, Middlesex 149-4 (Robson 61, Simpson 30).

Middlesex

S. D. Robson c Brown b Robinson	0	– (2) c Finch b Robinson	68
S. S. Eskinazi c Finch b Robinson	24	– (1) b Robinson	4
N. R. T. Gubbins c Haines b Robinson	3	– c Salt b Warner	28
*D. J. Malan c Brown b Robinson	3	– b Hooper	19
P. R. Stirling lbw b Robinson	4	– b Robinson	0
†J. A. Simpson b Robinson	2	– b Robinson	89
J. A. R. Harris c Finch b Robinson	0	– c Brown b Robinson	66
T. S. Roland-Jones c Finch b Haines	9	– st Brown b Haines	11
N. A. Sowter c Brown b Robinson	2	– c Brown b Robinson	0
S. T. Finn lbw b Beer	5	– c Carey b Wiese	56
T. J. Murtagh not out	20	– not out	25
Lb 1, nb 2	3	Lb 8, nb 4	12

1/0 (1) 2/16 (3) 3/26 (4) (21.4 overs) 75
4/32 (5) 5/37 (2) 6/37 (7)
7/42 (6) 8/44 (9) 9/50 (8) 10/75 (10)

1/4 (1) 2/72 (3) (112.2 overs) 378
3/105 (4) 4/110 (5)
5/171 (2) 6/258 (6) 7/277 (8)
8/278 (9) 9/299 (7) 10/378 (10)

Robinson 11–2–34–8; Wiese 4–1–11–0; Haines 6–0–28–1; Beer 0.4–0–1–1. *Second innings—*Robinson 35–6–101–6; Wiese 18.2–3–62–1; Haines 16–6–45–1; Warner 13–1–62–1; Hooper 20.5–5–65–1; Beer 6.1–1–19–0; Wells 3–0–16–0.

Sussex

P. D. Salt c Gubbins b Murtagh	4	– b Murtagh	10
L. W. P. Wells c Gubbins b Roland-Jones	62	– not out	48
T. J. Haines c Stirling b Roland-Jones	5	– b Finn	11
H. Z. Finch lbw b Roland-Jones	0	– c Eskinazi b Murtagh	0
A. T. Carey c Malan b Roland-Jones	56	– not out	69
*†B. C. Brown c Simpson b Murtagh	3		
D. Wiese c Simpson b Roland-Jones	0		
W. A. T. Beer b Murtagh	77		
O. E. Robinson c and b Sowter	37		
E. O. Hooper c Simpson b Finn	20		
J. D. Warner not out	13		
B 1, lb 11, nb 20	32	Lb 5, nb 2	7

1/4 (1) 2/15 (3) 3/15 (4) (84.3 overs) 309
4/140 (2) 5/151 (5) 6/151 (6)
7/151 (7) 8/239 (9) 9/280 (10) 10/309 (8)

1/18 (1) (3 wkts, 37.2 overs) 145
2/39 (3) 3/44 (4)

Murtagh 18.3–8–39–3; Roland-Jones 20–4–70–5; Harris 18–3–86–0; Finn 13–4–51–1; Sowter 13–1–49–1; Malan 2–0–2–0. *Second innings*—Murtagh 11–4–19–2; Roland-Jones 10–0–41–0; Finn 5–1–12–1; Harris 3–0–17–0; Sowter 4.2–0–43–0; Stirling 4–0–8–0.

Umpires: B. J. Debenham and J. H. Evans.

At Bristol, September 10–13. SUSSEX beat GLOUCESTERSHIRE by eight wickets.

At Derby, September 16–18. SUSSEX lost to DERBYSHIRE by 181 runs.

SUSSEX v WORCESTERSHIRE

At Hove, September 23–26. Drawn. Sussex 7pts, Worcestershire 7pts. Toss: uncontested. First-class debut: T. G. R. Clark.

A pair of underachieving teams endured a downbeat game that lost much of the first two days – and all of the last two – to rain. Wiese fulfilled his ambition of playing every match, in all formats, and was part of another Sussex middle-order recovery. Tom Clark, a highly regarded 18-year-old from Ardingly College, shaped up encouragingly in tricky conditions. A couple of days after losing the T20 Blast final, Worcestershire were a little lethargic – perhaps miffed at staying 25 miles away, because the Labour Party conference was on in Brighton. Moeen Ali was absent after asking for a break from red-ball cricket, while Mitchell found time amid the rain to see his beloved Aston Villa win just up the road.

Close of play: first day, Sussex 150-5 (Brown 7, Clark 0); second day, Sussex 299-8 (Garton 59, Robinson 0); third day, no play.

Sussex

L. W. P. Wells c Cox b Barnard	0		G. H. S. Garton not out		59
T. J. Haines c Rutherford b Morris	0		O. E. Robinson not out		0
W. A. T. Beer c Cox b Barnard	7				
S. van Zyl c Rutherford b Morris	56		B 5, lb 7, nb 14		26
D. M. W. Rawlins c Mitchell b Finch	58				
*†B. C. Brown lbw b Barnard	33		1/0 (1) 2/6 (2) (8 wkts, 85 overs)		299
T. G. R. Clark c Wessels b Parnell	13		3/32 (3) 4/126 (4) 5/150 (5)		
D. Wiese b Morris	47		6/193 (7) 7/193 (6) 8/289 (8)		

R. J. W. Topley did not bat.

Barnard 20–4–64–3; Morris 18–3–63–3; Parnell 16.1–8–39–1; Finch 20–1–77–1; D'Oliveira 7.5–0–37–0; Mitchell 3–1–7–0.

Worcestershire

D. K. H. Mitchell, *H. D. Rutherford, T. C. Fell, J. A. Haynes, M. H. Wessels, †O. B. Cox, E. G. Barnard, B. L. D'Oliveira, W. D. Parnell, C. A. J. Morris, A. W. Finch.

Umpires: P. K. Baldwin and J. W. Lloyds.

WARWICKSHIRE

Stretched to breaking

PAUL BOLTON

There could be no disputing who got the better deal when Ashley Giles and Paul Farbrace swapped employers early in 2019. Giles stepped down as Warwickshire's sport director to become the ECB's director of cricket, and arrived at Lord's in time to perform the topping-out ceremony of the World Cup success. Farbrace, a key figure in England's one-day revival, exchanged his role as their assistant coach for Giles's old office at Edgbaston. He could have been forgiven for believing he had inherited little more than a pile of bricks. The rebuilding of Warwickshire's squad had only just started when Giles departed, which meant Farbrace faced a challenging first season back in county cricket.

Just about everything that could go wrong did go wrong – apart from the fact that, as a one-off, only one team were relegated. Having returned early from the Pakistan Super League because of a foot injury, Ian Bell played a couple of second-team matches in July, then hurt his knee. For the first time since 2000, he played no first-team cricket for Warwickshire, a double blow after the retirement of Jonathan Trott in 2018. Worse was to follow, as a succession of seamers broke down. Olly Stone suffered a back injury shortly after his Test debut against Ireland in July, and did not appear again. Ryan Sidebottom managed only two early-season outings, while injuries restricted Liam Norwell and Craig Miles, two winter recruits from Gloucestershire.

Warwickshire used 24 in the Championship, and ten were newcomers. Resources were so stretched there were only two capped players in the side that faced Hampshire at Edgbaston in May. The nadir came in Canterbury at the end of June, when the new ball was taken by two loan signings: Ben Mike from Leicestershire and Toby Lester from Lancashire. The attack also included James Wainman, a former Yorkshire left-armer, who had been recruited on a short-term contract. When the team bus broke down en route to Kent, Jim Troughton called Edgbaston to report they were about to lose a coach; he had to reassure them he wasn't resigning.

But Troughton and Farbrace remained positive, and captain Jeetan Patel refused to use the injuries as an excuse. Instead, Patel – who led by example – preferred to focus on the opportunities offered to the rookies. No one grasped his chance more firmly than Dom Sibley. Having ended 2018 with hundreds in Warwickshire's last three matches, he repeated the feat in his first three games of 2019 – including for MCC against Surrey in Dubai. He added three more, and finished as the Championship's leading run-scorer, winning a place in England's Test squads for New Zealand and South Africa.

Will Rhodes, Sibley's opening partner, found runs harder to come by than he had in Division Two, but his medium-pace added value to a depleted attack, and he was rewarded with his first five-wicket haul, against Essex at Chelmsford. There were maiden centuries for Rob Yates, a left-hander from Warwick School who drew comparisons with, and praise from, Alastair Cook; and Matt Lamb, whose 173 against Essex at Edgbaston set up the draw which secured top-flight survival. With Bell sidelined, Sam Hain assumed the role of senior batsman, and responded by scoring his first Championship centuries in three years, going close to 1,000 runs for the first time.

Michael Bradley, AFP

Dominic Sibley

While the seamers kept the medical staff busy, Patel played in every match across the three competitions. He will continue for Warwickshire beyond his 40th birthday. But Rhodes, a former England Under-19 captain, will lead the side in 2020 – Patel's last season before he moves into full-time coaching.

Injuries also meant unexpected opportunities for Olly Hannon-Dalby, who started the season as sixth-choice seamer, and was in danger of being pigeonholed as a white-ball specialist. But he relished the chance to transfer his skills to the Championship, and took 44 wickets, including nine in the victory over his former county at York. He was rewarded with his county cap, alongside Sibley.

If injuries explained why Warwickshire were at the wrong end of Division One, they could not excuse two flaccid white-ball campaigns. There was sufficient talent to mount a challenge, but they struggled to land a blow. Only Northamptonshire and Leicestershire finished below them in their Royal London Cup group. And in the Vitality Blast, Leicestershire kept Warwickshire off the bottom of the North Group – on net run-rate.

Off the field, Norman Gascoigne stepped down after ten years as chairman, and was succeeded by Mark McCafferty, a former chief executive of Premiership Rugby. Gascoigne, once a banker, had overseen the transformation of Edgbaston with the construction of the £32m pavilion development – and its associated debt. He also drove through corporate governance reforms that led to the traditional committee being replaced by a board of directors packed with business expertise, but short on cricket experience.

By way of balance, chief executive Neil Snowball – who joins the ECB – began his "Bearification" of the club. It included replacing external signage describing Edgbaston as a conference-and-events venue with the more welcoming "Home of Warwickshire County Cricket Club and Birmingham Bears". The club also held a number of events to celebrate the 25th anniversary of the 1994 treble-winning season, and produced commemorative caps for players who had appeared in a first-class match for the county.

Championship attendance: 17,799.

WARWICKSHIRE RESULTS

All first-class matches – Played 14: Won 3, Lost 6, Drawn 5.
County Championship matches – Played 14: Won 3, Lost 6, Drawn 5.

Specsavers County Championship, 7th in Division 1;
Vitality Blast, 8th in North Group; Royal London One-Day Cup, 7th in North Group.

COUNTY CHAMPIONSHIP AVERAGES, BATTING AND FIELDING

Cap		Birthplace	M	I	NO	R	HS	100	Avge	Ct/St
2019	D. P. Sibley	Epsom	13	21	2	1,324	244	5	69.68	5
2018	S. R. Hain	Hong Kong	12	19	3	822	129*	2	51.37	16
	M. G. K. Burgess	Epsom	5	7	1	248	64	0	41.33	4
†W. M. H. Rhodes		Nottingham	14	23	0	770	109	1	33.47	13
†R. M. Yates		Solihull‡	12	19	0	570	141	1	30.00	10
	L. C. Norwell	Bournemouth	4	6	2	120	64	0	30.00	1
	M. J. Lamb	Wolverhampton	5	8	1	208	173	1	29.71	1
2012	J. S. Patel¶	Wellington, NZ	14	22	4	365	70*	0	20.27	8
2007	T. R. Ambrose	Newcastle, Aust	12	20	0	399	107	1	19.95	39/3
	H. J. H. Brookes	Solihull‡	11	17	2	285	84	0	19.00	1
	A. J. Hose	Newport, IoW	11	20	0	340	111	1	17.00	3
	L. Banks	Newcastle-u-Lyme	8	13	0	220	50	0	16.92	14
	G. A. Garrett	Harpenden	3	4	2	32	24	0	16.00	0
	C. N. Miles	Swindon	5	8	1	77	27	0	11.00	2
2019	†O. J. Hannon-Dalby	Halifax	12	15	5	102	17*	0	10.20	2
	O. P. Stone	Norwich	2	4	0	22	21	0	5.50	1

Also batted: E. A. Brookes (*Solihull‡*) (1 match) 0; †T. J. Lester (*Blackpool*) (2 matches) 0*, 0* (1 ct); B. W. M. Mike (*Nottingham*) (2 matches) 45*, 7, 72; T. P. Milnes (*Stourbridge*) (1 match) 12, 1; †D. R. Mousley (*Birmingham‡*) (1 match) 3, 0; R. N. Sidebottom†† (*Shepparton, Australia*) (1 match) 27*, 4*; A. T. Thomson (*Macclesfield*) (2 matches) 9, 18; J. C. Wainman (*Harrogate*) (1 match) did not bat.

‡ *Born in Warwickshire.*   ¶ *Official overseas player.*   †† *Other non-England-qualified.*

BOWLING

	Style	O	M	R	W	BB	5I	Avge
O. J. Hannon-Dalby	RFM	399	108	1,129	44	5-18	2	25.65
L. C. Norwell	RFM	110.5	30	360	14	7-41	1	25.71
J. S. Patel	OB	635.1	183	1,712	64	8-36	4	26.75
W. M. H. Rhodes	RFM	149.1	37	425	15	5-17	1	28.33
C. N. Miles	RFM	118.4	17	542	17	5-91	1	31.88
H. J. H. Brookes	RFM	315.3	52	1,350	32	3-100	0	42.18

Also bowled: L. Banks (OB) 3–0–9–0; E. A. Brookes (RFM) 12–2–41–0; G. A. Garrett (RM) 84.5–19–302–8; M. J. Lamb (RFM) 34.2–3–166–3; T. J. Lester (LFM) 55–11–233–5; B. W. M. Mike (RFM) 36–1–163–1; T. P. Milnes (RFM) 13–2–50–0; R. N. Sidebottom (RFM) 34–6–119–2; O. P. Stone (RF) 66.3–10–270–7; A. T. Thomson (OB) 10–0–54–1; J. C. Wainman (LM) 23–4–112–3.

LEADING ROYAL LONDON CUP AVERAGES (100 runs/4 wickets)

Batting	Runs	HS	Avge	SR	Ct
S. R. Hain	385	161*	77.00	87.50	2
A. T. Thomson	239	68*	47.80	92.99	3
T. R. Ambrose	139	77	34.75	65.87	2
L. Banks	250	61	31.25	85.03	1
E. J. Pollock	188	57	23.50	110.58	2
W. M. H. Rhodes	152	43	19.00	76.38	3
D. P. Sibley	115	29	14.37	65.71	4

Bowling	W	BB	Avge	ER
J. S. Patel	16	5-45	24.00	5.12
O. J. Hannon-Dalby	9	3-81	32.44	6.63
A. T. Thomson	10	3-27	32.60	5.01
H. J. H. Brookes	8	3-50	44.50	7.52
C. R. Woakes	4	3-47	49.75	5.28
G. D. Panayi	5	2-44	74.40	6.41

LEADING VITALITY BLAST AVERAGES (100 runs/20 overs)

Batting	Runs	HS	Avge	SR	Ct/St
E. J. Pollock....	129	77	21.50	157.31	2
A. J. Hose	300	69	33.33	149.25	5
M. J. Lamb....	102	35	34.00	130.76	0
W. M. H. Rhodes	129	45	16.12	126.47	3
D. P. Sibley	257	64	32.12	125.36	2
S. R. Hain	459	85	41.72	118.60	5
M. G. K. Burgess	123	28*	13.66	113.88	6/1

Bowling	W	BB	Avge	ER
C. J. Green	5	1-19	29.00	6.69
J. S. Patel	11	2-21	29.72	7.26
A. T. Thomson ..	6	2-28	40.33	8.06
F. H. Edwards....	9	4-22	22.88	8.24
H. J. H. Brookes..	13	3-26	24.69	8.75
W. M. H. Rhodes .	8	2-25	22.25	8.90

FIRST-CLASS COUNTY RECORDS

Highest score for	501*	B. C. Lara v Durham at Birmingham.............	1994
Highest score against	322	I. V. A. Richards (Somerset) at Taunton	1985
Leading run-scorer	35,146	D. L. Amiss (avge 41.64)......................	1960–87
Best bowling for	10-41	J. D. Bannister v Comb. Services at Birmingham	1959
Best bowling against	10-36	H. Verity (Yorkshire) at Leeds	1931
Leading wicket-taker	2,201	W. E. Hollies (avge 20.45)	1932–57
Highest total for	810-4 dec	v Durham at Birmingham	1994
Highest total against	887	by Yorkshire at Birmingham	1896
Lowest total for	16	v Kent at Tonbridge.........................	1913
Lowest total against	15	by Hampshire at Birmingham	1922

LIST A COUNTY RECORDS

Highest score for	206	A. I. Kallicharran v Oxfordshire at Birmingham....	1984
Highest score against	172*	W. Larkins (Northamptonshire) at Luton	1983
Leading run-scorer	11,254	D. L. Amiss (avge 33.79).....................	1963–87
Best bowling for	7-32	R. G. D. Willis v Yorkshire at Birmingham	1981
Best bowling against	6-27	M. H. Yardy (Sussex) at Birmingham	2005
Leading wicket-taker	396	G. C. Small (avge 25.48).....................	1980–99
Highest total for	392-5	v Oxfordshire at Birmingham	1984
Highest total against	415-5	by Nottinghamshire at Nottingham	2016
Lowest total for	59	v Yorkshire at Leeds	2001
Lowest total against	56	by Yorkshire at Birmingham	1995

TWENTY20 COUNTY RECORDS

Highest score for	158*	B. B. McCullum v Derbyshire at Birmingham	2015
Highest score against	115	M. M. Ali (Worcestershire) at Birmingham.......	2018
Leading run-scorer	2,111	I. R. Bell (avge 31.50, SR 128.56)...............	2003–18
Best bowling for	5-19	N. M. Carter v Worcestershire at Birmingham	2005
Best bowling against	7-18	C. N. Ackermann (Leicestershire) at Leicester ...	2019
Leading wicket-taker	135	J. S. Patel (avge 23.78, ER 6.89)	2009–19
Highest total for	242-2	v Derbyshire at Birmingham	2015
Highest total against	231-5	by Northamptonshire at Birmingham	2018
Lowest total for	73	v Somerset at Taunton	2013
Lowest total against {	96	by Northamptonshire at Northampton	2011
	96	by Gloucestershire at Cheltenham	2013

ADDRESS

Edgbaston Stadium, Birmingham B5 7QU; 0844 635 1902; info@edgbaston.com; www.edgbaston.com.

OFFICIALS

Captain 2019 J. S. Patel	**President** Earl of Aylesford
2020 W. M. H. Rhodes	**Chairman 2019** N. Gascoigne
2020 (Twenty20) C. J. Green	**2020** M. McCafferty
Sport director P. Farbrace	**Chief executive 2019** N. Snowball
First-team coach J. O. Troughton	**Head groundsman** G. Barwell
Elite development manager P. Greetham	**Scorer** M. D. Smith

At Birmingham, April 5–7 (not first-class). **Warwickshire won by 530 runs.** ‡**Warwickshire 246** (64 overs) (A. D. Thomason 62*; J. B. Fallows 3-36, A. J. Neal 3-52) **and 464-9 dec** (105.3 overs) (W. M. H. Rhodes 92, A. J. Hose 200; J. L. Haynes 3-98); **Leeds/Bradford MCCU 78** (28.4 overs) (A. D. Thomason 5-6) **and 102** (36.3 overs) (T. P. Milnes 3-21, J. S. Patel 3-12). *County debut: C. N. Miles. Warwickshire were given a rude awakening on the first day, slipping to 118-7, and needed Aaron Thomason to save them from further embarrassment. He then starred with the ball as Leeds/Bradford folded against his medium pace. Hose's double-hundred in the second innings included nine sixes, before the students were routed again.*

WARWICKSHIRE v KENT

At Birmingham, April 11–14. Kent won by eight wickets. Kent 24pts, Warwickshire 4pts. Toss: Kent.

These teams has last met in September 2018, when they were competing for the Division Two title. Warwickshire had won by an innings, but Kent gained revenge with their first top-flight victory since September 2010. On a pitch rated "Test-match quality" by Kent assistant coach Allan Donald, a former Warwickshire favourite, Crawley and Robinson had made fluent centuries. A depleted home attack included Tom Milnes, released by Warwickshire in 2015 (and by Derbyshire in 2017). In reply, Sibley scored a composed hundred – for the fifth successive match – but Warwickshire narrowly failed to avoid the follow-on, and were 121 for seven, with defeat seemingly inevitable, when Ambrose and Brookes embarked on a gritty stand of 144. Kent, who would eventually spend 213 overs in the field, began to flag, before the second new ball proved decisive, leaving them to score 123 in a minimum of 28 overs; Crawley and Renshaw negotiated a hostile opening burst to ensure Kent's first win at Edgbaston since 2005. Their players wore black armbands in memory of Paul Bell-Drummond – brother of Kent's Daniel – who died on the eve of the match.

Close of play: first day, Kent 367-5 (Robinson 59, Stevens 19); second day, Warwickshire 136-3 (Sibley 60, Hose 29); third day, Warwickshire 79-4 (Hain 34, Ambrose 17).

Kent

S. R. Dickson c Banks b Sidebottom	31	– (2) lbw b Brookes	5
Z. Crawley c Ambrose b Patel	108	– (1) lbw b Patel	45
M. T. Renshaw c Ambrose b Miles	36	– not out	48
D. J. Bell-Drummond c Ambrose b Brookes	6	– not out	18
*H. G. Kuhn lbw b Miles	72		
†O. G. Robinson st Ambrose b Patel	143		
D. I. Stevens lbw b Brookes	23		
H. W. Podmore lbw b Sidebottom	6		
M. E. Milnes c Rhodes b Patel	28		
A. E. N. Riley not out	3		
B 16, lb 11, w 5, nb 16	48	Lb 8	8

1/82 (1) 2/169 (3)   (9 wkts dec, 136.5 overs) 504   1/6 (2)   (2 wkts, 19.4 overs) 124
3/198 (4) 4/204 (2)   2/86 (1)
5/323 (5) 6/382 (7) 7/403 (8)
8/487 (9) 9/504 (6)   110 overs: 416-7

M. E. Claydon did not bat.

Brookes 26–5–80–2; Miles 29–4–127–2; Sidebottom 29–6–90–2; Milnes 13–2–50–0; Patel 35.5–9–113–3; Rhodes 4–1–17–0. *Second innings*—Sidebottom 5–0–29–0; Brookes 6–0–33–1; Patel 5–1–25–1; Miles 3.4–1–29–0.

Warwickshire

W. M. H. Rhodes c Robinson b Stevens	16	– lbw b Podmore	0
D. P. Sibley lbw b Podmore	132	– c Crawley b Stevens	5
L. Banks c Crawley b Milnes	7	– c Riley b Podmore	9
S. R. Hain c Robinson b Milnes	17	– c Robinson b Podmore	38
A. J. Hose c Robinson b Milnes	31	– c Renshaw b Claydon	6
†T. R. Ambrose lbw b Stevens	44	– lbw b Milnes	107
T. P. Milnes c Riley b Podmore	12	– lbw b Stevens	1
C. N. Miles lbw b Podmore	1	– lbw b Podmore	8
H. J. H. Brookes c Crawley b Claydon	0	– lbw b Milnes	84
*J. S. Patel c Kuhn b Stevens	40	– lbw b Podmore	0
R. N. Sidebottom not out	27	– not out	4
B 9, lb 6, w 2, nb 2	19	B 6, lb 12	18

1/26 (1) 2/36 (3) 3/84 (4)   (120 overs) 346   1/0 (1) 2/16 (2)   (93.1 overs) 280
4/154 (5) 5/241 (6) 6/260 (7)   3/30 (3) 4/49 (5)
7/262 (8) 8/273 (2) 9/273 (9)   5/89 (4) 6/106 (7) 7/121 (8)
10/346 (10)   110 overs: 298-9   8/265 (6) 9/266 (10) 10/280 (9)

Podmore 24–4–61–3; Stevens 30–8–56–3; Milnes 22–7–50–3; Claydon 18–5–70–1; Riley 17–3–58–0; Renshaw 2–0–14–0; Bell-Drummond 7–3–22–0. *Second innings*—Podmore 29–9–62–5; Stevens 22–4–60–2; Claydon 14–2–49–1; Milnes 13.1–0–65–2; Riley 14–5–23–0; Renshaw 1–0–3–0.

Umpires: R. K. Illingworth and N. A. Mallender.

WARWICKSHIRE v HAMPSHIRE

At Birmingham, May 14–17. Hampshire won by 314 runs. Hampshire 22pts, Warwickshire 3pts. Toss: Hampshire. First-class debut: R. M. Yates.

Warwickshire fielded only two capped players – Patel and Ambrose – and the disparity in experience and nous was obvious for most of a one-sided match. Hannon-Dalby and Patel worked hard to keep them in the contest on a pitch that was never straightforward, but Alsop's career-best 150 put Hampshire in command. In reply, Sibley showed monumental concentration, carrying his bat for the second time in a row against Hampshire, and extending his run of centuries to six games. But the pace of Abbott and Edwards was too much for his team-mates. Hampshire scored freely – especially Rossouw, with a rapid 76 – before declaring, and a 70-minute rain delay on the last morning could not derail their charge to victory. Warwickshire had probably sensed the inevitable the evening before, when Sibley was caught behind cheaply off Abbott.

Close of play: first day, Hampshire 291-6 (Alsop 131, Berg 7); second day, Warwickshire 184-7 (Sibley 95, Brookes 2); third day, Warwickshire 42-2 (Yates 21, Miles 1).

Hampshire

J. J. Weatherley lbw b Hannon-Dalby	12	– c Ambrose b Brookes	46
O. C. Soames c Ambrose b Patel	12	– c Patel b Miles	62
†T. P. Alsop c Miles b Patel	150	– b Patel	25
*S. A. Northeast lbw b Hannon-Dalby	22	– not out	55
R. R. Rossouw c Miles b Patel	0	– c Brookes b Hannon-Dalby	76
L. A. Dawson c Yates b Hannon-Dalby	19	– lbw b Patel	6
A. H. T. Donald c Banks b Hannon-Dalby	75	– not out	16
G. K. Berg c and b Patel	26		
K. H. D. Barker c Ambrose b Patel	13		
K. J. Abbott b Patel	2		
F. H. Edwards not out	6		
B 1, lb 12, nb 4	17	B 4, lb 8, nb 4	16

1/19 (1) 2/44 (2) 3/117 (4)   (117.3 overs) 354   1/102 (2)   (5 wkts dec, 50 overs) 302
4/122 (5) 5/171 (6) 6/225 (7)   2/137 (1) 3/147 (3)
7/327 (8) 8/336 (3) 9/343 (10)   4/258 (5) 5/264 (6)
10/354 (9)   110 overs: 339-8

Brookes 23–4–84–0; Hannon-Dalby 27–6–69–4; Miles 15–1–77–0; Patel 40.3–12–94–6; Rhodes 10–3–15–0; Thomson 2–0–2–0. *Second innings*—Brookes 9–0–61–1; Hannon-Dalby 12–1–68–1; Patel 21–3–107–2; Miles 4–0–23–1; Thomson 4–0–31–0.

Warwickshire

W. M. H. Rhodes c Weatherley b Abbott	10	– c Rossouw b Dawson	16
D. P. Sibley not out	109	– c Alsop b Abbott	3
R. M. Yates b Dawson	6	– b Edwards	21
A. J. Hose b Edwards	10	– (5) b Abbott	1
L. Banks b Abbott	23	– (6) c Edwards b Dawson	4
A. T. Thomson lbw b Abbott	9	– (7) lbw b Barker	18
†T. R. Ambrose lbw b Abbott	0	– (8) b Berg	10
C. N. Miles c Soames b Edwards	11	– (4) b Edwards	1
H. J. H. Brookes c Dawson b Weatherley	12	– b Barker	0
*J. S. Patel c Alsop b Berg	17	– c Alsop b Edwards	10
O. J. Hannon-Dalby b Berg	8	– not out	17
B 4, lb 2, w 4, nb 8	18	B 5, lb 2, w 1	8

1/34 (1) 2/48 (3) 3/88 (4)   (92.5 overs) 233   1/3 (2) 2/34 (1)   (53.5 overs) 109
4/135 (5) 5/145 (6) 6/145 (7)   3/42 (3) 4/43 (5)
7/171 (8) 8/197 (9) 9/223 (10) 10/233 (11)   5/43 (4) 6/64 (6) 7/75 (7)
     8/75 (8) 9/75 (9) 10/109 (10)

Abbott 21–5–50–4; Edwards 18–3–50–2; Barker 15–6–26–0; Berg 13.5–4–41–2; Dawson 21–5–48–1; Weatherley 4–0–12–1. *Second innings*—Abbott 9–5–11–2; Barker 12–2–23–2; Dawson 13–6–16–2; Edwards 12.5–3–36–3; Berg 7–3–16–1.

Umpires: B. J. Debenham and P. J. Hartley.

At Taunton, May 20–22. WARWICKSHIRE lost to SOMERSET by 49 runs.

WARWICKSHIRE v SURREY

At Birmingham, May 27–30. Warwickshire won by 130 runs. Warwickshire 21pts, Surrey 3pts. Toss: uncontested.

In a match dominated by two grizzled off-spinners, Warwickshire secured their first win of the season to leave Surrey's title defence stuck in second gear. Patel, the Warwickshire captain, was rewarded for setting up a declaration, taking eight for 36 in Surrey's second innings, and 12 for 89 in the match – both career-bests. Earlier on a hectic final day, his fellow off-spinner Batty had finished with eight for 64, including a hat-trick; his innings and match figures were the best of a long career. It was the first time two bowlers aged over 39 had taken eight-fors in the same match since Kent's Tich Freeman and Northamptonshire's Vallance Jupp at Tunbridge Wells in 1932. Warwickshire had made determined progress on the first day, and were given late impetus by a stand of 95 between Brookes and Norwell. Patel then bowled 31 overs unchanged to help his team to a lead of 105. With only 22 overs on the third day, it looked as if Warwickshire might be frustrated, but a dressing-room meeting produced a bold plan for victory, and they sacrificed wickets in pursuit of quick runs on the final morning, setting Surrey 272 in 74 overs. Clarke, returning to Edgbaston for the first time since he rejoined Surrey in 2017, threatened to thwart them, but Patel was not to be denied.

Close of play: first day, Warwickshire 275-8 (Brookes 35, Norwell 58); second day, Warwickshire 26-0 (Rhodes 8, Sibley 16); third day, Warwickshire 76-2 (Rhodes 34, Hain 12).

Warwickshire

W. M. H. Rhodes lbw b Batty	39	–	c Burns b Batty	54
D. P. Sibley lbw b Batty	17	–	lbw b Batty	23
R. M. Yates lbw b Morkel	20	–	b Batty	3
S. R. Hain lbw b Dunn	47	–	c Burns b Batty	41
A. J. Hose b Dunn	38	–	c Borthwick b Batty	9
L. Banks b Patel	1	–	c Burns b Dunn	13
†T. R. Ambrose lbw b Dunn	1	–	c Burns b Batty	6
H. J. H. Brookes not out	41	–	c Borthwick b Batty	5
*J. S. Patel c Clarke b Patel	8	–	c Borthwick b Batty	0
L. C. Norwell b Morkel	64	–	not out	0
O. J. Hannon-Dalby b Morkel	4			
Lb 4, w 1, nb 8	13		B 6, lb 4, nb 2	12

1/58 (2) 2/63 (1) 3/93 (3)   **(91 overs) 293**   1/44 (2)   (9 wkts dec, 53.4 overs) 166
4/165 (4) 5/168 (6) 6/172 (5)   2/50 (3) 3/109 (1)
7/177 (7) 8/186 (9) 9/281 (10) 10/293 (11)   4/137 (5) 5/154 (6) 6/155 (4)
                                                  7/166 (7) 8/166 (9) 9/166 (8)

Morkel 23–8–87–3; Dunn 24–7–65–3; Patel 12–2–35–2; Clarke 13–5–38–0; Batty 18–4–47–2; Elgar 1–0–17–0. *Second innings*—Morkel 12–2–39–0; Dunn 16–1–49–1; Batty 22.4–3–64–8; Clarke 3–1–4–0.

Surrey

*R. J. Burns c Yates b Hannon-Dalby	40	–	lbw b Brookes	38
M. D. Stoneman b Norwell	0	–	lbw b Patel	12
S. G. Borthwick lbw b Norwell	40	–	b Patel	4
D. Elgar c Banks b Patel	4	–	(6) b Patel	4
†B. T. Foakes not out	57	–	(4) c Norwell b Patel	5
R. S. Patel c Sibley b Patel	0	–	(8) lbw b Patel	0
W. G. Jacks c Rhodes b Patel	0	–	(5) lbw b Patel	16
R. Clarke run out (Sibley)	28	–	(7) not out	51
M. Morkel b Patel	1	–	lbw b Patel	1
G. J. Batty lbw b Brookes	13	–	c Hain b Patel	2
M. P. Dunn lbw b Brookes	0	–	b Brookes	0
Lb 3, nb 2	5		B 8	8

1/10 (2) 2/73 (1) 3/88 (3)   **(69.2 overs) 188**   1/30 (2) 2/42 (3)   (63.4 overs) 141
4/92 (4) 5/92 (6) 6/92 (7)   3/50 (4) 4/69 (1)
7/150 (8) 8/151 (9) 9/188 (10) 10/188 (11)   5/82 (6) 6/93 (5) 7/93 (8)
                                                  8/117 (9) 9/123 (10) 10/141 (11)

Hannon-Dalby 16–4–44–1; Norwell 14–2–64–2; Patel 31–14–53–4; Brookes 8.2–3–24–2. *Second innings*—Norwell 8–2–34–0; Patel 31–18–36–8; Hannon-Dalby 10–4–26–0; Brookes 12.4–4–35–2; Rhodes 2–1–2–0.

Umpires: I. D. Blackwell and S. J. O'Shaughnessy.

WARWICKSHIRE v NOTTINGHAMSHIRE

At Birmingham, June 3–6. Drawn. Warwickshire 9pts, Nottinghamshire 6pts. Toss: Warwickshire.

    Duckett's first Championship hundred for Nottinghamshire saved them from defeat in a bad-tempered contest which earned them a Level One warning for their conduct. There were flashpoints when Pattinson had an lbw appeal turned down against Hose, and when a Broad delivery gloved by Banks to Moores was called a no-ball on height. "The game was played hard, very hard, and there were a couple of incidents that would have been borderline," said Mullaney, the Nottinghamshire captain. His opposite number, Jeetan Patel, was spoken to by the umpires after he gave Mullaney a send-off after his first-innings duck. In a Warwickshire innings that had stretched into the third morning because of bad weather, Hose made a hard-working maiden first-class century, and Sibley another impressive contribution to an imposing total. Patel then took six for 16 as Nottinghamshire collapsed miserably, losing their last eight for 28. They rediscovered their resolve in the follow-on, with Duckett and Nash adding 199 for the second wicket. Patel lifted his wicket tally in two matches to 22, but Pattinson blocked for most of the last hour to ensure the draw.

Close of play: first day, Warwickshire 181-3 (Sibley 81, Hose 17); second day, Warwickshire 311-7 (Hose 84, Patel 6); third day, Nottinghamshire 116-1 (Duckett 71, Nash 26).

Warwickshire

W. M. H. Rhodes c Carter b Fletcher	15	*J. S. Patel b Fletcher ... 23
D. P. Sibley c Mullaney b Fletcher	87	L. C. Norwell not out ... 34
R. M. Yates b Broad	24	B 9, lb 7, w 1, nb 10 ... 27
S. R. Hain run out (Nash/Patel)	23	
A. J. Hose c Clarke b Patel	111	1/33 (1) (9 wkts dec, 146.5 overs) 391
L. Banks lbw b Carter	27	2/82 (3) 3/139 (4)
†T. R. Ambrose lbw b Mullaney	20	4/189 (5) 5/237 (6) 6/300 (7) 7/304 (8)
H. J. H. Brookes lbw b Mullaney	0	8/329 (9) 9/391 (5) 110 overs: 237-5

O. J. Hannon-Dalby did not bat.

Fletcher 32–11–65–3; Pattinson 26–4–64–0; Broad 28–9–79–1; Carter 27–6–79–1; Mullaney 24–8–47–2; Patel 9.5–0–41–1.

Nottinghamshire

B. T. Slater c Hain b Hannon-Dalby	12	– c Ambrose b Patel	15
B. M. Duckett c Patel b Brookes	15	– c Hain b Patel	140
C. D. Nash c Patel b Norwell	25	– lbw b Brookes	85
J. M. Clarke c Hain b Patel	7	– c Rhodes b Patel	0
S. R. Patel b Patel	5	– c Hain b Brookes	2
*S. J. Mullaney c Hain b Norwell	0	– c Sibley b Patel	29
†T. J. Moores lbw b Patel	4	– c Ambrose b Norwell	17
J. L. Pattinson not out	6	– not out	19
L. J. Fletcher c Ambrose b Patel	3	– c and b Brookes	9
S. C. J. Broad lbw b Patel	6	– not out	1
M. Carter lbw b Patel	0		
Lb 4, nb 10	14	B 4, lb 9, w 6, nb 18	37

1/12 (1) 2/44 (2) 3/69 (3)	(44.4 overs) 97	1/40 (1) (8 wkts, 124 overs) 354	
4/69 (4) 5/74 (6) 6/74 (5)		2/239 (3) 3/243 (4)	
7/79 (7) 8/83 (9) 9/97 (10) 10/97 (11)		4/250 (5) 5/255 (3)	
		6/315 (6) 7/317 (7) 8/342 (9)	

Hannon-Dalby 11–5–23–1; Norwell 10–8–6–2; Brookes 10–5–48–1; Patel 13.4–7–16–6. *Second innings*—Hannon-Dalby 19–3–57–0; Norwell 29–6–103–1; Patel 47–21–72–4; Brookes 26–8–100–3; Rhodes 2–0–7–0; Banks 1–0–2–0.

Umpires: R. T. Robinson and M. J. Saggers.

At York, June 17–20. WARWICKSHIRE beat YORKSHIRE by three wickets.

At The Oval, June 23–26. WARWICKSHIRE lost to SURREY by 74 runs.

At Canterbury, June 30–July 3. WARWICKSHIRE drew with KENT.

At Southampton, July 6–9. WARWICKSHIRE drew with HAMPSHIRE. *Sam Hain scores a century in each innings.*

At Chelmsford, July 13–16. WARWICKSHIRE lost to ESSEX by 187 runs.

WARWICKSHIRE v SOMERSET

At Birmingham, August 18–21. Somerset won by five wickets. Somerset 21pts, Warwickshire 7pts. Toss: Warwickshire. First-class debut: G. A. Garrett. Championship debut: Babar Azam.

Somerset kept their title challenge on track with a laboured victory over an inexperienced Warwickshire team who, for much of the contest, had looked the likelier victors. The first day belonged to 19-year-old left-hander Yates, who made a stylish maiden hundred at No. 3, putting on 153 with Rhodes and 89 with the patient Hain. After consolidating their advantage with early wickets, Warwickshire could not shift Davies, although Somerset needed a precious unbeaten fifty from Bess and 36 from Craig Overton to avert the follow-on. Yates flourished again, but Somerset seized

YOUNGEST WARWICKSHIRE FIRST-CLASS CENTURIONS

Years	Days			
18	336	S. R. Hain (134)	v Northamptonshire at Northampton	2014
19	56	I. R. Bell (130)	v Oxford UCCE at Oxford	2001
19	69	P. A. Smith (114)	v Oxford University at Birmingham.	1983
19	296	R. Sale (101).	v Sussex at Birmingham.	1939
19	309	P. Cranmer (113)	v Northamptonshire at Birmingham	1934
19	321	J. D. Ratcliffe (127*)	v Cambridge University at Cambridge	1989
19	**333**	**R. M. Yates (141)**	**v Somerset at Birmingham**	**2019**
20	33	A. R. I. Umeed (101)	v Durham at Birmingham.	2016
20	61	K. D. Smith (124).	v Glamorgan at Birmingham	1976
20	143	C. R. Woakes (131*)	v Hampshire at Southampton	2009

Maiden hundreds only. Hain and Bell scored further centuries while under 21.

control as Warwickshire sought to build on their lead of 111: nine wickets tumbled for 98 as Abell and Jamie Overton made decisive inroads. A target of 258 looked tricky, especially when Somerset slipped to 49 for three. Babar Azam, their T20 overseas recruit making his red-ball debut for the club, had been out first ball in the first innings, but now knuckled down. Banton, a product of the Warwickshire Academy, played with calm assurance, before Bartlett and Bess ensured victory with few further alarms.

Close of play: first day, Warwickshire 303-4 (Yates 139, Ambrose 16); second day, Somerset 167-5 (Davies 89, Bess 1); third day, Somerset 8-0 (Abell 8, Davies 0).

Warwickshire

W. M. H. Rhodes c Davies b C. Overton.	82	– c Hildreth b Abell.	30
D. P. Sibley c van der Merwe b Brooks.	0	– lbw b Brooks	9
R. M. Yates c van der Merwe b Brooks.	141	– lbw b J. Overton	53
S. R. Hain c Davies b van der Merwe	25	– lbw b Abell.	0
A. J. Hose lbw b C. Overton.	17	– c Davies b Brooks	7
T. R. Ambrose c Davies b Brooks	18	– lbw b C. Overton	19
M. G. K. Burgess b C. Overton	52	– c van der Merwe b J. Overton	0
H. J. H. Brookes c van der Merwe b J. Overton. . . .	12	– c Davies b J. Overton.	4
J. S. Patel c Hildreth b Abell	25	– lbw b Abell.	8
O. J. Hannon-Dalby c Davies b Abell	13	– c J. Overton b Abell	5
G. A. Garrett not out	2	– not out	6
B 13, lb 13, w 2, nb 4.	32	Lb 5	5

1/0 (2)	2/153 (1)	3/242 (4)		(127 overs) 419	1/26 (2) 2/48 (1) (50.4 overs) 146
4/275 (5)	5/306 (3)	6/313 (6)	7/338 (8)		3/48 (4) 4/65 (5)
8/404 (7)	9/404 (9)	10/419 (10)		110 overs: 379-7	5/107 (3) 6/107 (7) 7/113 (8)
					8/135 (6) 9/135 (9) 10/146 (10)

C. Overton 31–7–98–3; Brooks 25–3–104–3; J. Overton 18–0–86–1; Bess 25–7–62–0; Abell 15–6–31–2; van der Merwe 13–7–12–1. *Second innings*—C. Overton 13–1–40–1; Brooks 14–5–32–2; Abell 13.4–4–39–4; J. Overton 8–1–26–3; Bess 2–1–4–0.

Somerset

*T. B. Abell b Brookes	10	– lbw b Brookes	25
†S. M. Davies c Rhodes b Patel	109	– c Ambrose b Hannon-Dalby	16
J. C. Hildreth lbw b Hannon-Dalby	6	– lbw b Hannon-Dalby	4
Babar Azam c Brookes b Hannon-Dalby	0	– lbw b Garrett	40
T. Banton c Ambrose b Rhodes	23	– c Ambrose b Patel	66
G. A. Bartlett b Garrett	26	– not out	54
D. M. Bess not out	52	– not out	40
R. E. van der Merwe c Ambrose b Rhodes	1		
C. Overton lbw b Hannon-Dalby	36		
J. Overton c Yates b Brookes	22		
J. A. Brooks c Hain b Rhodes	0		
Lb 11, nb 12	23	B 5, lb 6, nb 2	13

1/29 (1) 2/44 (3) 3/44 (4)   (92 overs) 308   1/33 (2)   (5 wkts, 72.4 overs) 258
4/107 (5) 5/166 (6) 6/193 (2)   2/41 (3) 3/49 (1)
7/202 (8) 8/267 (9) 9/307 (10) 10/308 (11)   4/139 (4) 5/170 (5)

Hannon-Dalby 20–3–65–3; Brookes 13–0–69–2; Garrett 20–6–56–1; Patel 26–8–70–1; Rhodes 13–4–37–3. *Second innings*—Hannon-Dalby 18–6–59–2; Brookes 16.4–3–56–1; Rhodes 10–2–33–0; Garrett 14–3–42–1; Patel 14–2–57–1.

Umpires: I. J. Gould and R. J. Warren.

WARWICKSHIRE v ESSEX

At Birmingham, September 10–13. Drawn. Warwickshire 10pts, Essex 9pts. Toss: uncontested. First-class debut: E. A. Brookes.

Essex arrived intent on buffing up their title credentials after six straight wins, but left chastened by Warwickshire's fighting performance. Following Nottinghamshire's three-day defeat by Kent, it secured their top-flight status. They were grateful for ten Doeschate's decision to bowl – he admitted he had misread the pitch – with Sibley passing 1,000 Championship runs for the season, and Hain compiling 82. But the most eye-catching contribution came from Lamb, playing only because four others were injured. His previous five innings in 2019 had produced 29 runs, but he now scored his maiden first-class century, extending it to 173 in seven hours. He was reprieved on 110, when he edged Porter to Alastair Cook at slip and, believing the catch had been taken, began to walk off. But Cook had dropped it, and Harmer – seeing Lamb out of his ground – threw down the stumps. He was initially given out by square-leg umpire Nick Cook, but Harmer agreed to withdraw the appeal. Westley's first hundred of the season dominated the Essex response, before Patel's six-for allowed him to enforce the follow-on. Essex saved the match comfortably, with Westley falling three short of a second century, though Somerset's 19-point haul against Yorkshire saw them return to the top of the table.

Close of play: first day, Warwickshire 269-3 (Hain 77, Lamb 69); second day, Essex 31-1 (Browne 16, S. J. Cook 0); third day, Essex 278-6 (Westley 123, Wheater 1).

Warwickshire

W. M. H. Rhodes c Wheater b Harmer	38	O. J. Hannon-Dalby lbw b Harmer	1
D. P. Sibley c and b Harmer	51	G. A. Garrett st Wheater b Harmer	24
L. Banks c Bopara b Harmer	0		
S. R. Hain c Lawrence b Porter	82	B 8, lb 20, nb 18	46
M. J. Lamb c Harmer b Bopara	173		
†M. G. K. Burgess c Harmer b Porter	5	1/87 (1) 2/91 (3) (175.5 overs) 517
E. A. Brookes c Bopara b Harmer	0	3/140 (2) 4/290 (4) 5/296 (6)
H. J. H. Brookes run out (Harmer)	46	6/297 (7) 7/402 (8) 8/468 (5)
*J. S. Patel not out	51	9/471 (10) 10/517 (11) 110 overs: 320-6

Porter 35–8–105–2; S. J. Cook 31–8–82–0; Harmer 59.5–15–143–6; Beard 22–1–84–0; Bopara 19–6–53–1; Westley 1–0–4–0; ten Doeschate 3–0–7–0; Lawrence 5–0–11–0.

Essex

N. L. J. Browne lbw b Patel	65	– c Banks b Garrett	0
A. N. Cook c Sibley b Patel	7	– not out	57
S. J. Cook c Banks b Hannon-Dalby	4		
T. Westley b H. J. H. Brookes	141	– (3) c Patel b Lamb	97
D. W. Lawrence c Sibley b Garrett	28	– (4) not out	1
R. S. Bopara b Patel	11		
*R. N. ten Doeschate lbw b H. J. H. Brookes	0		
†A. J. A. Wheater c Hain b Patel	4		
S. R. Harmer b Patel	0		
A. P. Beard c Banks b Patel	20		
J. A. Porter not out	2		
B 7, lb 11, nb 24	42	W 1, nb 2	3

1/31 (2) 2/52 (3) 3/158 (1)   (118.3 overs) 324   1/0 (1)   (2 wkts, 55 overs) 158
4/233 (5) 5/264 (6) 6/271 (7)   2/157 (3)
7/288 (8) 8/288 (9) 9/320 (4)
10/324 (10)   110 overs: 299-8

Hannon-Dalby 28–10–68–1; Garrett 14–1–55–1; Patel 45.3–16–73–6; H. J. H. Brookes 18–2–79–2; Rhodes 10–1–21–0; E. A. Brookes 3–0–10–0. *Second innings*—Garrett 9–3–24–1; Hannon-Dalby 7–1–21–0; Patel 17–4–39–0; H. J. H. Brookes 6–0–20–0; Lamb 4–0–15–1; Rhodes 3–1–8–0; E. A. Brookes 9–2–31–0.

Umpires: N. G. B. Cook and D. J. Millns.

At Nottingham, September 16–19. WARWICKSHIRE beat NOTTINGHAMSHIRE by eight wickets. *Dominic Sibley makes 324 runs in the match.*

WARWICKSHIRE v YORKSHIRE

At Birmingham, September 23–26. Drawn. Yorkshire 7pts, Warwickshire 5pts. Toss: Yorkshire. First-class debut: T. W. Loten.

Heavy rain swept in on the first afternoon, ruling out play for the rest of the match. On the pitch used for Twenty20 finals day two days earlier, Köhler-Cadmore marked his 100th first-class innings with a fluent century. He was given good support by Tom Loten, who made a composed fifty on his first-class debut. Sibley's selection for England's Test tour of New Zealand was announced on the first day; on the last, he and Hannon-Dalby were awarded their county caps.

Close of play: first day, Yorkshire 261-2 (Köhler-Cadmore 165); second day, no play; third day, no play.

Yorkshire

A. Lyth c Hain b Miles	26
T. Köhler-Cadmore not out	165
T. W. Loten c Rhodes b Thomson	58
B 5, lb 5, nb 2	12

1/77 (1) 2/261 (3)   (2 wkts, 64 overs) 261

G. S. Ballance, H. C. Brook, †J. A. Tattersall, D. J. Willey, M. D. Fisher, *S. A. Patterson, D. Olivier and A. Y. Patel did not bat.

Hannon-Dalby 12–2–47–0; Brookes 11–1–54–0; Miles 10–2–46–1; Patel 20–5–64–0; Thomson 4–0–21–1; Rhodes 7–1–19–0.

Warwickshire

W. M. H. Rhodes, D. P. Sibley, R. M. Yates, S. R. Hain, †T. R. Ambrose, M. G. K. Burgess, A. T. Thomson, C. N. Miles, H. J. H. Brookes, *J. S. Patel, O. J. Hannon-Dalby.

Umpires: G. D. Lloyd and R. J. Warren.

WORCESTERSHIRE

Out of bounce

JOHN CURTIS

Worcestershire were left to reflect on a season in which they fell lamentably short of expectations in the County Championship, but again demonstrated the full range of their talents in the white-ball formats. After relegation in 2018, they were fancied to make their customary swift return to the top tier, but it never happened.

Convincing victories in the opening matches, against Leicestershire and Durham, appeared to endorse the bookmakers, but from there the four-day season went into sharp decline. They had to wait until September for their only other Championship win, against Glamorgan at New Road, narrowly avoiding a first wooden spoon since 1932.

The problem was straightforward: the frontline batting did not produce enough runs, with the usually reliable Daryl Mitchell and main overseas player Callum Ferguson experiencing lean summers. The fact that Riki Wessels, recruited from Nottinghamshire, finished as leading run-scorer in the Championship with a modest 593 at 28 spoke volumes.

Alex Gidman, in his first season as head coach, was not afraid to make changes, or experiment with the batting order in an effort to find solutions. Wessels was one of five opening partners for Mitchell, and all-rounder Ed Barnard once found himself pushed up to No. 4. But all too often, the first five wickets went down with fewer than 100 on the board, leaving the lower order to strive for respectability.

Recognising the need to bolster the batting for 2020, Gidman recruited the former New Zealand opener Hamish Rutherford, who is available for the whole season after two short stints in 2019. He made a strong impression, becoming only the second Worcestershire player to score hundreds on both his Championship and one-day debuts, after the Australian Phil Jaques. Competition for top-order places has also increased with the arrival of Jake Libby from Nottinghamshire on a three-year contract. And there are high hopes of 19-year-old batsman Jack Haynes, son of the former Worcestershire all-rounder Gavin. He made his first-class debut against the Australians, and went on to play four times in the Championship.

Gidman is putting greater emphasis on red-ball practice and game-management, an area where the bowlers struggled at times in 2019. The home games with Derbyshire and Sussex, and both against Gloucestershire offered examples of the attack failing to capitalise on an advantage at crucial moments. Three of those matches were lost.

The big plus was the return to regular first-team action of seamer Charlie Morris after a three-year battle to remodel his action. He had clearly regained his former potency: in the opening Championship fixture, against Leicestershire, he took a career-best seven for 45. He finished with 44 wickets at 21, a total equalled by Barnard. Leach, who claimed 41, showed no ill effects from an 11-month lay-off with a stress fracture of the back, but injuries prevented Josh Tongue and Dillon Pennington building on the promise of 2018. Ben Twohig missed the entire season with a knee injury, and Moeen Ali's absence – first during the World Cup, and later when he took a break from the game – meant Worcestershire laboured for long periods without a recognised spinner.

Riki Wessels

Midsummer flooding at New Road led to two Championship matches being switched at short notice to Kidderminster, once a regular destination. The pitches provided by the club were more than adequate, and produced two excellent games.

Compensation for the Championship struggles came in the limited-overs competitions. Worcestershire were within an ace of becoming the first team to retain the T20 title, and lost the final of the Vitality Blast to Essex on the last ball. As in 2018, Ali proved an inspiring leader, and played one of the innings of the summer – 121 not out off 60 deliveries in the quarter-final against Sussex at Hove. That day, and on other occasions, Wessels put aside his reputation as a brutal hitter to play an invaluable supporting role. No Worcestershire batsman has scored more T20 runs in a season than his 461.

Pat Brown proved he was no one-season wonder. His array of variations, and another excellent contribution to finals day, earned an England T20 debut in New Zealand, and a contract with Melbourne Stars in the Big Bash. But he was ruled out of that, and the white-ball leg of the South African tour, after he was diagnosed in January with a stress fracture of the back.

Worcestershire's strength was not to rely on one or two individuals. The team ethic was demonstrated in the Blast semi-final against Nottinghamshire, when Wayne Parnell bowled a nerveless last over. The Australian batsman Ashton Turner will join Rutherford as a T20 overseas player.

For the fourth year running, Worcestershire qualified for the knockout stages of the Royal London One-Day Cup. But, having secured a home quarter-final, they were comprehensively outplayed by the eventual winners, Somerset.

A month after the end of the season, Matt Rawnsley, the former Worcestershire spinner, quit as CEO after over 18 months in the role.

Championship attendance: 17,869.

WORCESTERSHIRE RESULTS

All first-class matches – Played 15: Won 3, Lost 7, Drawn 5.
County Championship matches – Played 14: Won 3, Lost 7, Drawn 4.

Specsavers County Championship, 9th in Division 2;
Vitality Blast, finalists; Royal London One-Day Cup, quarter-finalists.

COUNTY CHAMPIONSHIP AVERAGES, BATTING AND FIELDING

Colours		Birthplace	M	I	NO	R	HS	100	Avge	Ct/St
2019	H. D. Rutherford¶	Dunedin, NZ	4	5	0	220	123	1	44.00	3
2012	B. L. D'Oliveira	Worcester‡	7	9	1	298	103	1	37.25	3
2007	†M. M. Ali§	Birmingham	2	4	0	126	42	0	31.50	2
2019	C. J. Ferguson¶	Adelaide, Aust.	9	17	1	503	127	1	31.43	8
2019	M. H. Wessels	Maroochydore, Aust	14	23	2	593	118	1	28.23	21
2009	O. B. Cox	Wordsley‡	14	22	2	531	100*	1	26.55	38/1
2012	J. Leach	Stafford	12	20	4	420	54*	0	26.25	1
2013	†R. A. Whiteley	Sheffield	10	16	1	391	88	0	26.06	4
2018	W. D. Parnell††	Port Elizabeth, SA	7	8	0	205	63	0	25.62	2
2005	D. K. H. Mitchell	Badsey‡	14	24	2	559	139	2	25.40	18
2015	E. G. Barnard	Shrewsbury	14	21	2	429	56	0	22.57	11
2013	T. C. Fell	Hillingdon	5	7	0	136	40	0	19.42	4
2019	J. A. Haynes	Worcester‡	4	6	0	95	31	0	15.83	1
2019	J. J. Dell	Tenbury Wells‡	6	11	0	158	61	0	14.36	5
2014	C. A. J. Morris	Hereford	11	15	8	96	29*	0	13.71	0
2017	J. C. Tongue	Redditch‡	4	5	1	51	20*	0	12.75	0
2016	G. H. Rhodes	Birmingham	3	6	0	59	28	0	9.83	0
2019	A. W. Finch	Wordsley‡	7	9	4	43	17	0	8.60	0
2018	D. Y. Pennington	Shrewsbury	4	8	0	44	18	0	5.50	0
2018	A. G. Milton	Redhill	3	6	0	17	12	0	2.83	4

‡ *Born in Worcestershire.*   § *ECB contract.*   ¶ *Official overseas player.*   †† *Other non-England-qualified.*

BOWLING

	Style	O	M	R	W	BB	5I	Avge
J. C. Tongue	RFM	113.3	23	322	17	5-37	1	18.94
C. A. J. Morris	RFM	293	67	945	44	7-45	3	21.47
E. G. Barnard	RFM	371	100	993	44	6-42	1	22.56
W. D. Parnell	LFM	157.4	42	507	22	5-47	1	23.04
J. Leach	RFM	384.4	83	1,081	41	6-79	1	26.36
B. L. D'Oliveira	LB	170.4	22	556	14	7-92	1	39.71
A. W. Finch	RM	152.2	26	583	11	2-23	0	53.00

Also bowled: M. M. Ali (OB/RM) 55.3–10–210–7; D. K. H. Mitchell (RM) 34–7–79–1; D. Y. Pennington (RFM) 115–29–301–8; G. H. Rhodes (OB) 22.2–2–90–0; R. A. Whiteley (LM) 79.4–5–303–8.

LEADING ROYAL LONDON CUP AVERAGES (150 runs/4 wickets)

Batting	Runs	HS	Avge	SR	Ct/St
H. D. Rutherford	317	126	63.40	105.66	1
C. J. Ferguson	151	103*	50.33	94.37	2
R. A. Whiteley	290	131	36.25	118.85	2
M. H. Wessels	313	130	34.77	137.88	3
O. B. Cox	238	87	34.00	92.24	11/1
T. C. Fell	220	53	27.50	72.60	5
D. K. H. Mitchell	169	101	24.14	96.57	6

Bowling	W	BB	Avge	ER
W. D. Parnell	22	5-24	18.86	5.63
C. A. J. Morris	11	2-17	27.63	5.62
P. R. Brown	5	3-80	39.40	6.15
B. L. D'Oliveira	6	2-20	44.16	5.52
D. K. H. Mitchell	6	2-40	44.66	5.22
J. C. Tongue	6	2-35	50.16	7.05
E. G. Barnard	7	3-26	51.85	5.50

LEADING VITALITY BLAST AVERAGES (150 runs/15 overs)

Batting	Runs	HS	Avge	SR	Ct/St	Bowling	W	BB	Avge	ER
M. M. Ali	365	121*	73.00	171.36	3	D. K. H. Mitchell	7	2-17	33.00	6.41
R. A. Whiteley .	198	89*	22.00	150.00	7	M. M. Ali.	11	4-18	15.81	6.69
M. J. Guptill . .	259	86*	32.37	145.50	3	P. R. Brown. . .	17	2-21	24.76	8.12
W. D. Parnell . .	178	81*	22.25	134.84	2	E. G. Barnard. .	12	2-21	34.66	8.48
M. H. Wessels .	461	91	35.46	129.85	9	W. D. Parnell. . .	13	4-25	29.84	8.62
O. B. Cox	203	44*	25.37	114.68	8/3	D. Y. Pennington	9	2-26	33.00	9.28

FIRST-CLASS COUNTY RECORDS

Highest score for	405*	G. A. Hick v Somerset at Taunton.	1988
Highest score against	331*	J. D. B. Robertson (Middlesex) at Worcester	1949
Leading run-scorer	34,490	D. Kenyon (avge 34.18)	1946–67
Best bowling for	9-23	C. F. Root v Lancashire at Worcester	1931
Best bowling against	10-51	J. Mercer (Glamorgan) at Worcester	1936
Leading wicket-taker	2,143	R. T. D. Perks (avge 23.73).	1930–55
Highest total for	701-6 dec	v Surrey at Worcester	2007
Highest total against	701-4 dec	by Leicestershire at Worcester	1906
Lowest total for	24	v Yorkshire at Huddersfield.	1903
Lowest total against	30	by Hampshire at Worcester	1903

LIST A COUNTY RECORDS

Highest score for	192	C. J. Ferguson v Leicestershire at Worcester	2018
Highest score against	161*	S. R. Hain (Warwickshire) at Worcester.	2019
Leading run-scorer	16,416	G. A. Hick (avge 44.60)	1985–2008
Best bowling for	7-19	N. V. Radford v Bedfordshire at Bedford	1991
Best bowling against	7-15	R. A. Hutton (Yorkshire) at Leeds	1969
Leading wicket-taker	370	S. R. Lampitt (avge 24.52)	1987–2002
Highest total for	404-3	v Devon at Worcester	1987
Highest total against	399-4	by Sussex at Horsham	2011
Lowest total for	58	v Ireland v Worcester	2009
Lowest total against	45	by Hampshire at Worcester	1988

TWENTY20 COUNTY RECORDS

Highest score for	127	T. Köhler-Cadmore v Durham at Worcester	2016
Highest score against	141*	C. L. White (Somerset) at Worcester.	2006
Leading run-scorer	2,589	M. M. Ali (avge 29.08, SR 141.47)	2007–19
Best bowling for	5-24	A. Hepburn v Nottinghamshire at Worcester	2017
Best bowling against	6-21	A. J. Hall (Northamptonshire) at Northampton	2008
Leading wicket-taker {	92	D. K. H. Mitchell (avge 29.06, ER 7.65)	2005–19
	92	J. D. Shantry (avge 28.21, ER 8.07)	2010–17
Highest total for	227-6	v Northamptonshire at Kidderminster	2007
Highest total against	233-6	by Yorkshire at Leeds	2017
Lowest total for	53	v Lancashire at Manchester	2016
Lowest total against	93	by Gloucestershire at Bristol	2008

ADDRESS

Blackfinch New Road, Worcester WR2 4QQ; 01905 748474; info@wccc.co.uk; www.wccc.co.uk.

OFFICIALS

Captain J. Leach	**President** C. Duckworth
(ltd-overs) M. M. Ali	**Chairman** F. Hira
First-team coach A. P. R. Gidman	**Chief executive 2019** M. J. Rawnsley
Assistant/one-day coach A. Richardson	**Head groundsman** T. R. Packwood
Head of player development K. Sharp	**Scorers** S. M. Drinkwater and P. M. Mellish
Academy coach E. J. Wilson	

At Cambridge, April 5–7. WORCESTERSHIRE drew with CAMBRIDGE MCCU.

At Leicester, April 11–14. WORCESTERSHIRE beat LEICESTERSHIRE by an innings and 18 runs.

WORCESTERSHIRE v DURHAM

At Worcester, May 14–17. Worcestershire won by five wickets. Worcestershire 23pts, Durham 4pts.
Toss: Durham. First-class debut: J. J. Dell.

Chasing 81 to win on the last morning, Worcestershire were given a working-over by Rushworth, who single-handedly reduced them to 55 for five, before Whiteley and Cox held firm to ensure successive Championship victories. Worcestershire were led by Leach who, returning after 11 months out with a stress fracture of his back, was straight back in the swing of things, taking two wickets with the new ball. Bancroft and Burnham rebuilt the Durham innings from 14 for three with a stand of 149, but nobody could push on to a substantial score. Morris followed up his seven-for at Leicester with six for 53, before Worcestershire forged ahead, thanks to a resilient 61 on debut from Josh Dell, and a century on his first home Championship appearance for his new county from Wessels. In front of Ashley Giles, England's director of cricket, Tongue took five Durham wickets, and a three-day finish seemed likely until Trevaskis showed the application that proved beyond some of his senior colleagues. But he could not prevent Durham's fifth successive Championship defeat.

Close of play: first day, Worcestershire 1-1 (Fell 1, Morris 0); second day, Worcestershire 321-6 (Whiteley 62, Cox 28); third day, Durham 197.

Durham

C. T. Steel c Wessels b Leach	5	– b Leach	17
A. Z. Lees b Morris	0	– lbw b Morris	2
*C. T. Bancroft lbw b Tongue	70	– b Tongue	25
G. J. Harte lbw b Leach	1	– st Cox b Barnard	25
J. T. A. Burnham c Cox b Morris	76	– c Cox b Tongue	26
†E. J. H. Eckersley c Cox b Morris	22	– b Tongue	12
L. Trevaskis b Leach	5	– lbw b Tongue	47
B. A. Raine c Mitchell b Morris	42	– c Mitchell b Leach	23
M. J. Potts c Mitchell b Morris	20	– not out	7
M. E. T. Salisbury c Mitchell b Morris	8	– b Tongue	0
C. Rushworth not out	4	– c Cox b Leach	2
B 8, lb 10, nb 2	20	B 8, lb 3	11

1/6 (2) 2/10 (1) 3/14 (4)   (92 overs) 273   1/14 (2) 2/20 (1)   (65.5 overs) 197
4/163 (3) 5/167 (5) 6/177 (7)   3/69 (3) 4/77 (4)
7/237 (8) 8/240 (6) 9/268 (10) 10/273 (9)   5/106 (6) 6/129 (5) 7/178 (8)
     8/194 (7) 9/194 (10) 10/197 (11)

Leach 19–4–59–3; Morris 19–4–53–6; Barnard 17–5–32–0; Tongue 17–4–50–1; Whiteley 8–0–24–0; Rhodes 10–1–36–0; Mitchell 2–1–1–0. *Second innings*—Leach 15.5–1–49–3; Morris 15–3–44–1; Barnard 13–2–36–1; Tongue 13–3–37–5; Rhodes 7–1–19–0; Whiteley 2–1–1–0.

Worcestershire

D. K. H. Mitchell lbw b Rushworth	0	– lbw b Rushworth	9
T. C. Fell lbw b Salisbury	6	– lbw b Rushworth	36
C. A. J. Morris c Eckersley b Salisbury	3		
G. H. Rhodes lbw b Raine	28	– (3) b Rushworth	0
J. J. Dell b Harte	61	– (4) b Rushworth	4
M. H. Wessels c Steel b Potts	118	– (5) b Rushworth	0
R. A. Whiteley b Rushworth	72	– (6) not out	8
†O. B. Cox c Potts b Salisbury	38	– (7) not out	15
E. G. Barnard c Rushworth b Trevaskis	25		
*J. Leach b Salisbury	0		
J. C. Tongue not out	20		
B 7, lb 9, w 1, nb 2	19	B 2, lb 8, nb 2	12

1/0 (1) 2/6 (2) 3/17 (3) 4/64 (4)   (123.3 overs) 390   1/26 (1)   (5 wkts, 19.4 overs) 84
5/204 (5) 6/236 (6) 7/337 (7)   2/26 (3) 3/42 (4)
8/354 (8) 9/354 (10) 10/390 (9)   110 overs: 354-7   4/42 (5) 5/55 (2)

Rushworth 27–6–90–2; Salisbury 25–7–67–4; Potts 20–3–73–1; Raine 27–7–56–1; Harte 17–3–57–1; Trevaskis 6.3–0–29–1; Burnham 1–0–2–0. *Second innings*—Rushworth 9–3–28–5; Salisbury 3–0–22–0; Raine 6–1–18–0; Potts 1–0–2–0; Burnham 0.4–0–4–0.

Umpires: J. H. Evans and J. D. Middlebrook.

At Manchester, May 20–22. WORCESTERSHIRE lost to LANCASHIRE by six wickets.

WORCESTERSHIRE v MIDDLESEX

At Worcester, May 27–30. Middlesex won by 127 runs. Middlesex 20pts, Worcestershire 3pts. Toss: Worcestershire.

Murtagh returned from international duty with Ireland to bowl Middlesex to their first victory of the season. As Worcestershire set off in pursuit of 353 on the final morning, he nipped out Fell and Rhodes, then collected three more after lunch; he finished with six for 51. Batting was difficult throughout against uneven bounce and seam movement. In the circumstances, the contributions of Middlesex captain Malan, back after suffering a groin injury in England's ODI victory in Dublin earlier in the month, were priceless. He top-scored with 45 in the first innings, then hit his 23rd first-class hundred in the second, sharing a third-wicket stand of 201 with Gubbins. Murtagh took the plaudits in the second innings, though Helm's career-best five for 36 in the first had established Middlesex's dominance.

Close of play: first day, Worcestershire 64-3 (Fell 18, Tongue 0); second day, Middlesex 195-2 (Gubbins 72, Malan 107); third day, Middlesex 287-6 (Simpson 30, Roland-Jones 11).

Middlesex

S. D. Robson lbw b Tongue	16	– (2) lbw b Leach	9
M. D. E. Holden c Cox b Morris	0	– (1) lbw b Leach	2
N. R. T. Gubbins b Whiteley	27	– c Wessels b Morris	91
*D. J. Malan lbw b Morris	45	– c Whiteley b Barnard	124
S. S. Eskinazi lbw b Whiteley	27	– c Cox b Tongue	1
J. A. R. Harris lbw b Barnard	12	– c Cox b Morris	10
†J. A. Simpson c Whiteley b Morris	35	– not out	30
T. S. Roland-Jones c Wessels b Leach	12	– not out	11
T. G. Helm c Cox b Tongue	1		
N. A. Sowter lbw b Tongue	20		
T. J. Murtagh not out	0		
B 3, lb 9, w 2, nb 12	26	B 1, lb 5, w 1, nb 2	9

1/2 (2) 2/43 (1) 3/66 (3)   (66.2 overs) 221   1/11 (2)   (6 wkts dec, 72 overs) 287
4/128 (5) 5/151 (4) 6/151 (6)   2/20 (1) 3/221 (3)
7/182 (8) 8/191 (9) 9/221 (10) 10/221 (7)   4/222 (5) 5/241 (6) 6/251 (4)

Leach 15–1–58–1; Morris 15.2–2–53–3; Tongue 17–2–49–3; Barnard 10.2–7–14–1; Whiteley 8.4–0–35–2. *Second innings*—Leach 16–2–48–2; Morris 15–0–74–2; Tongue 16–4–67–1; Barnard 12–1–41–1; Whiteley 5–0–19–0; Rhodes 4–0–25–0; Mitchell 4–1–7–0.

Worcestershire

D. K. H. Mitchell c Simpson b Helm	3	– b Murtagh	51
T. C. Fell b Helm	19	– c Robson b Murtagh	4
G. H. Rhodes c Simpson b Helm	4	– lbw b Murtagh	0
C. J. Ferguson lbw b Roland-Jones	37	– c Eskinazi b Murtagh	43
J. C. Tongue c Sowter b Helm	7	– (10) c Eskinazi b Harris	2
M. H. Wessels b Murtagh	7	– (5) c Malan b Murtagh	0
R. A. Whiteley c Eskinazi b Helm	3	– (6) c Robson b Harris	60
†O. B. Cox lbw b Harris	16	– (7) c Simpson b Helm	14
E. G. Barnard lbw b Murtagh	6	– (8) c Simpson b Roland-Jones	11
*J. Leach not out	32	– (9) b Murtagh	11
C. A. J. Morris lbw b Sowter	15	– not out	5
Lb 3, w 2, nb 2	7	B 11, lb 8, w 5	24

1/5 (1) 2/9 (3) 3/62 (4) (63.5 overs) 156 1/5 (2) 2/9 (3) (73.3 overs) 225
4/74 (2) 5/75 (5) 6/85 (6)   3/92 (4) 4/92 (5)
7/85 (7) 8/106 (9) 9/116 (8) 10/156 (11) 5/135 (1) 6/168 (7) 7/188 (8)
              8/207 (9) 9/210 (10) 10/225 (6)

Murtagh 17–9–25–2; Helm 19–5–36–5; Harris 10–2–44–1; Roland-Jones 16–6–46–1; Sowter 1.5–0–2–1. *Second innings*—Murtagh 18–7–51–6; Helm 16–4–35–1; Roland-Jones 12–3–36–1; Harris 14.3–2–46–2; Sowter 12–3–38–0.

Umpires: N. A. Mallender and B. V. Taylor.

WORCESTERSHIRE v LANCASHIRE

At Worcester, June 10–13. Drawn. Worcestershire 6pts, Lancashire 8pts. Toss: uncontested. First-class debut: A. W. Finch.

Lancashire dominated the 71.3 overs possible over four soggy days; the second and fourth were washouts. It was little surprise when Vilas chose to bowl under leaden skies and, for the second time in three weeks, Worcestershire had no answer to the guile and experience of Anderson and Onions; they shared eight wickets as the home team collapsed for 98. After waiting two days to begin their reply, Lancashire lost three quick wickets, but were stabilised by Hameed and Livingstone.

Close of play: first day, Worcestershire 98; second day, no play; third day, Lancashire 110–3 (Hameed 22, Livingstone 53).

Worcestershire

D. K. H. Mitchell c Vilas b Onions	4	*J. Leach b Onions	18
J. J. Dell b Mahmood	18	C. A. J. Morris c Vilas b Anderson	1
C. J. Ferguson lbw b Onions	1	A. W. Finch not out	2
M. H. Wessels lbw b Anderson	3	Lb 9, w 2	11
R. A. Whiteley c Hameed b Anderson	1		
E. G. Barnard c Vilas b Anderson	32	1/13 (1) 2/19 (3) 3/22 (4) (38.1 overs) 98
†O. B. Cox c Vilas b Mahmood	2	4/24 (5) 5/39 (2) 6/57 (7)
W. D. Parnell b Onions	5	7/66 (8) 8/92 (9) 9/95 (10) 10/98 (6)

Anderson 14.1–5–24–4; Onions 14–1–55–4; Mahmood 8–4–8–2; Livingstone 2–1–2–0.

Lancashire

K. K. Jennings lbw b Leach	....	6
A. L. Davies c Cox b Parnell	....	24
H. Hameed not out	....	22
R. P. Jones b Parnell	....	0
L. S. Livingstone not out	....	53
W 1, nb 4	....	5

1/14 (1) 2/32 (2)   (3 wkts, 33.2 overs) 110
3/32 (4)

*†D. J. Vilas, S. J. Croft, J. J. Bohannon, S. Mahmood, G. Onions and J. M. Anderson did not bat.

Leach 10–4–20–1; Morris 7–1–28–0; Parnell 7–1–18–2; Finch 5.2–1–23–0; Barnard 4–0–21–0.

Umpires: R. J. Bailey and M. Newell.

WORCESTERSHIRE v SUSSEX

At Kidderminster, June 18–21. Drawn. Worcestershire 12pts, Sussex 10pts. Toss: Worcestershire. First-class debut: A. D. Thomason.

With New Road under water, this fixture was delayed by a day and moved to Kidderminster, where Worcestershire had not played first-class cricket since 2008. Aaron Thomason, Birmingham-born but newly arrived at Sussex after being released by Warwickshire, produced the game's key innings – 90 at No. 10, having walked out to bat with Sussex leading by just 186. He survived a difficult chance on two, and 110 came while he was at the crease, taking the game beyond Worcestershire. Thomason shielded last man Sakande so successfully that he faced only 26 of the 113 balls they were together; they added 82, a tenth-wicket record for this fixture, though Worcestershire were hampered by injuries to Leach and Parnell. Sussex were also indebted to Brown, whose first-innings 80 had helped turn 102 for six into 255. He then put on 157 in the second with Evans, who completed his first Championship hundred for four years. In Worcestershire's first innings, fifties from Ferguson and Wessels laid a platform, but they did not take control of the game until the last five wickets added 231.

Close of play: first day, Sussex 185-6 (Brown 64, Jordan 44); second day, Worcestershire 262-6 (Cox 53, D'Oliveira 20); third day, Sussex 236-5 (Evans 106, Wiese 27).

Sussex

L. W. P. Wells c Barnard b Parnell	....	29	– lbw b Leach	....	0
W. A. T. Beer c Cox b Finch	....	3	– c and b Barnard	....	9
H. Z. Finch c Dell b Parnell	....	0	– b Finch	....	4
S. van Zyl b Leach	....	28	– c Dell b Parnell	....	18
L. J. Evans b Parnell	....	2	– c Cox b Whiteley	....	113
*†B. C. Brown b Barnard	....	80	– c sub (O. E. Westbury) b Barnard	...	64
D. Wiese lbw b Leach	....	5	– lbw b Leach	....	47
C. J. Jordan c Dell b Finch	....	52	– lbw b Barnard	....	18
O. E. Robinson c Cox b Barnard	....	38	– c Barnard b Whiteley	....	23
A. D. Thomason lbw b Whiteley	....	4	– b D'Oliveira	....	90
A. Sakande not out	....	0	– not out	....	5
B 4, lb 4, nb 6	....	14	B 7, lb 17, w 1, nb 8	....	33

1/12 (2) 2/20 (3) 3/53 (1)	(73.1 overs) 255	1/0 (1) 2/11 (3) (121 overs) 424
4/55 (5) 5/89 (4) 6/102 (7)		3/30 (2) 4/34 (4)
7/194 (8) 8/250 (9) 9/255 (10) 10/255 (6)		5/191 (6) 6/252 (5) 7/280 (7)
		8/314 (8) 9/342 (9) 10/424 (10)

Leach 14–4–32–1; Finch 18–6–41–2; Parnell 19–2–92–4; Barnard 14.1–3–52–2; Whiteley 4–1–12–1; D'Oliveira 4–0–18–0. *Second innings*—Leach 23–4–69–2; Finch 22–4–85–1; Parnell 4–1–12–1; Barnard 28–7–68–3; Whiteley 16–0–73–2; D'Oliveira 22–2–71–1; Mitchell 6–0–22–0.

Worcestershire

D. K. H. Mitchell c Evans b Robinson	0	– not out	34
J. J. Dell lbw b Robinson	8	– lbw b Sakande	15
C. J. Ferguson c van Zyl b Jordan	56	– c Jordan b Beer	13
M. H. Wessels c Robinson b Jordan	55	– not out	4
R. A. Whiteley c Sakande b Jordan	21		
E. G. Barnard lbw b Wells	29		
†O. B. Cox c Brown b Robinson	61		
B. L. D'Oliveira lbw b Robinson	31		
W. D. Parnell b Wells	43		
*J. Leach not out	54		
A. W. Finch b Robinson	0		
Lb 11, nb 14	25	B 6, lb 6, nb 4	16

1/0 (1) 2/11 (2) 3/104 (4) (112.5 overs) 383 1/32 (2) (2 wkts, 24 overs) 82
4/152 (5) 5/152 (3) 6/226 (6) 2/55 (3)
7/281 (7) 8/296 (8) 9/364 (9)
10/383 (11) 110 overs: 364-9

Robinson 29.5–4–84–5; Sakande 10–1–58–0; Wiese 14–4–55–0; Jordan 25–5–76–3; Beer 15–3–49–0; Thomason 11–0–33–0; Wells 8–2–17–2. *Second innings*—Robinson 4–0–8–0; Jordan 4–3–1–0; Wells 4–1–20–0; Sakande 4–0–16–1; Beer 4–1–8–1; Thomason 4–0–17–0.

Umpires: U. V. Gandhe and R. T. Robinson.

At Kidderminster, June 25. WORCESTERSHIRE v AUSTRALIA A. Abandoned (see Australia A tour section).

At Cardiff, June 30–July 3. WORCESTERSHIRE drew with GLAMORGAN. *Brett D'Oliveira takes a career-best 7-92 and scores a century at No. 9.*

WORCESTERSHIRE v DERBYSHIRE

At Kidderminster, July 7–10. Derbyshire won by 82 runs. Derbyshire 19pts, Worcestershire 3pts. Toss: Derbyshire.

Derbyshire recovered from being bowled out for 108 on the first day to register a comfortable third win of the season. They owed much to Lace, on loan from Middlesex, who in the second innings batted eight hours for an unbeaten 132. His fortitude was in stark contrast to a frantic opening day on which 20 wickets fell. There was swing and seam movement, but the procession demonstrated poor technique. After Leach and Morris ripped through Derbyshire, they were quickly matched by Reece and Hudson-Prentice, and the visitors were batting again by stumps. With moisture disappearing from the pitch, the game shifted into a lower gear. Lace and Madsen added 103 in 40 overs, with Lace reaching his hundred in 266 balls. Just as crucial was his stand of 99 for the ninth wicket with Palladino. Set 373, Worcestershire tumbled to 48 for five; Hudson-Prentice at one point had figures of 8–8–0–2. A three-day finish was averted by Ferguson, who hit his first Championship century, and put on 164 with Cox.

Close of play: first day, Derbyshire 19-0 (Reece 12, Godleman 7); second day, Derbyshire 272-6 (Lace 101, Hudson-Prentice 0); third day, Worcestershire 156-5 (Ferguson 71, Cox 44).

Derbyshire

L. M. Reece c Wessels b Leach	31	– lbw b Leach	20
*B. A. Godleman c Ferguson b Pennington	8	– c Wessels b Pennington	26
W. L. Madsen lbw b Barnard	11	– c D'Oliveira b Pennington	60
T. C. Lace c Cox b Morris	1	– not out	132
J. L. du Plooy c Wessels b Morris	14	– c Ferguson b D'Oliveira	8
†H. R. Hosein lbw b Leach	0	– c Dell b Barnard	33
M. J. J. Critchley c Mitchell b Leach	0	– c Mitchell b Barnard	13
F. J. Hudson-Prentice c Cox b Morris	31	– c Cox b Barnard	4
A. K. Dal c Mitchell b Morris	0	– lbw b Leach	0
A. P. Palladino not out	6	– c Ferguson b Leach	58
R. Rampaul c Wessels b Barnard	4	– c Whiteley b Barnard	0
W 2	2	B 12, lb 3, w 6, nb 2	23

1/13 (2) 2/32 (3) 3/33 (4)   (44.2 overs) 108   1/46 (1) 2/46 (2)   (131.4 overs) 377
4/63 (1) 5/63 (6) 6/63 (7)   3/149 (3) 4/168 (5)
7/83 (5) 8/83 (9) 9/101 (8) 10/108 (11)   5/250 (6) 6/264 (7) 7/276 (8)
                                         8/277 (9) 9/376 (10) 10/377 (11)

Leach 14–6–33–3; Pennington 9–3–27–1; Morris 13–5–26–4; Barnard 8.2–3–22–2. *Second innings*—Leach 29–9–73–3; Pennington 25–3–92–2; D'Oliveira 22–3–63–1; Morris 22–5–64–0; Barnard 26.4–12–48–4; Whiteley 6–1–18–0; Mitchell 1–0–4–0.

Worcestershire

D. K. H. Mitchell lbw b Reece	13	– c Hosein b Palladino	7
J. J. Dell c Hosein b Rampaul	0	– lbw b Rampaul	0
C. J. Ferguson c du Plooy b Palladino	0	– lbw b Hudson-Prentice	127
M. H. Wessels lbw b Hudson-Prentice	13	– c du Plooy b Rampaul	4
R. A. Whiteley c Hosein b Reece	5	– b Hudson-Prentice	16
E. G. Barnard c Dal b Reece	17	– b Hudson-Prentice	0
†O. B. Cox lbw b Reece	4	– b Rampaul	62
B. L. D'Oliveira c Madsen b Rampaul	5	– lbw b Palladino	30
*J. Leach c Madsen b Hudson-Prentice	14	– c Reece b Palladino	28
D. Y. Pennington lbw b Hudson-Prentice	18	– lbw b Rampaul	0
C. A. J. Morris not out	0	– not out	0
Lb 9, nb 2	11	B 4, lb 10, nb 2	16

1/0 (2) 2/23 (3) 3/36 (1)   (39.5 overs) 113   1/12 (1) 2/16 (2)   (116.5 overs) 290
4/40 (4) 5/60 (5) 6/70 (7)   3/22 (4) 4/48 (5)
7/77 (8) 8/77 (6) 9/110 (10) 10/113 (9)   5/48 (6) 6/212 (7) 7/249 (3)
                                         8/285 (8) 9/286 (10) 10/290 (9)

Palladino 8–3–11–1; Rampaul 13–2–36–2; Reece 12–4–30–4; Hudson-Prentice 6.5–0–27–3. *Second innings*—Palladino 20.5–9–34–3; Rampaul 24–4–64–4; Reece 18–8–38–0; Hudson-Prentice 20–12–42–3; Critchley 19–5–40–0; Madsen 4–0–19–0; du Plooy 7–1–13–0; Dal 4–0–26–0.

Umpires: J. W. Lloyds and R. J. Warren.

At Chester-le-Street, July 13–16. WORCESTERSHIRE lost to DURHAM by 109 runs.

At Cheltenham, July 21–24. WORCESTERSHIRE lost to GLOUCESTERSHIRE by 13 runs.

At Worcester, August 7–9. WORCESTERSHIRE drew with AUSTRALIANS (see Australian tour section).

At Northampton, August 18–20. WORCESTERSHIRE lost to NORTHAMPTONSHIRE by ten wickets.

WORCESTERSHIRE v GLAMORGAN

At Worcester, September 10–12. Worcestershire won by 155 runs. Worcestershire 20pts, Glamorgan 3pts. Toss: uncontested. County debut: K. C. Brathwaite.

On his 200th first-class appearance for Worcestershire, Mitchell rediscovered form with a second-innings hundred to steer them towards a first win in ten Championship matches. For Glamorgan, a third successive defeat was a further blow to their promotion ambitions. They had initially enjoyed the better of things, with Hogan and the returning van der Gugten hustling Worcestershire out for 205. But Glamorgan lost two wickets before the close, and on the second day Morris completed his third five-wicket haul of the summer to give Worcestershire a narrow lead. Seizing the moment, Mitchell hunkered down nearly six hours for 139, his first century since the season's opening Championship match, and passed 13,000 first-class runs. He looked set to carry his bat, but was run out after a mix-up with No. 11 Finch. Glamorgan were none for two in the first over, Kraigg Brathwaite run out without facing, and Worcestershire wrapped up a three-day win.

Close of play: first day, Glamorgan 44-2 (Brathwaite 15, Lloyd 9); second day, Worcestershire 153-2 (Mitchell 52, Haynes 22).

Worcestershire

D. K. H. Mitchell c Cooke b Hogan	36	– run out (van der Gugten/Cooke)	139
H. D. Rutherford b Hogan	19	– c Brathwaite b Smith	52
M. M. Ali c Selman b van der Gugten	18	– c Hogan b Patel	26
J. A. Haynes lbw b van der Gugten	17	– lbw b Patel	31
A. G. Milton c Cooke b Carey	12	– c Cooke b Patel	5
M. H. Wessels c Patel b Smith	45	– lbw b Hogan	32
†O. B. Cox lbw b van der Gugten	7	– c Cooke b Hogan	0
E. G. Barnard not out	29	– c and b van der Gugten	6
*J. Leach lbw b Smith	7	– c sub (G. G. Wagg) b van der Gugten	4
C. A. J. Morris b Hogan	9	– b Patel	1
A. W. Finch c Lloyd b Hogan	5	– not out	0
Lb 1	1	Lb 3	3
	205		**299**

1/21 (2) 2/57 (3) 3/80 (1) (70 overs) 205
4/101 (5) 5/119 (4) 6/147 (7)
7/163 (6) 8/175 (9) 9/199 (10) 10/205 (11)

1/70 (2) 2/107 (3) (95.2 overs) 299
3/176 (4) 4/190 (5)
5/234 (6) 6/248 (7) 7/281 (8)
8/291 (9) 9/298 (10) 10/299 (1)

Hogan 16–4–53–4; Carey 13–2–37–1; van der Gugten 12–2–44–3; Smith 14–6–39–2; Lloyd 3–1–10–0; Patel 12–2–21–0. *Second innings*—Hogan 21–4–74–2; Carey 15.2–4–44–0; Smith 13–0–45–1; van der Gugten 14–2–68–2; Patel 31–9–59–4; Root 1–0–6–0.

Glamorgan

N. J. Selman c Mitchell b Morris	6	– c Mitchell b Leach	0
K. C. Brathwaite c Cox b Morris	19	– run out (Barnard)	0
T. N. Cullen c Cox b Barnard	10	– b Leach	5
D. L. Lloyd c and b Ali	35	– b Barnard	29
W. T. Root c Barnard b Morris	8	– c Barnard b Morris	26
S. R. Patel c Milton b Finch	5	– lbw b Barnard	7
*†C. B. Cooke c Wessels b Leach	24	– b Ali	45
R. A. J. Smith b Morris	18	– lbw b Morris	4
T. van der Gugten not out	29	– c Ali b Finch	13
L. J. Carey c Milton b Ali	16	– c Barnard b Ali	12
M. G. Hogan c Milton b Morris	15	– not out	10
Lb 6, nb 2	8	B 1, lb 3, w 1	5
	193		**156**

1/19 (1) 2/31 (3) 3/56 (2) (65.5 overs) 193
4/64 (5) 5/75 (6) 6/98 (4)
7/120 (7) 8/137 (8) 9/176 (10) 10/193 (11)

1/0 (1) 2/0 (2) (38.2 overs) 156
3/20 (3) 4/44 (4)
5/54 (6) 6/98 (5) 7/102 (8)
8/128 (9) 9/139 (7) 10/156 (10)

Leach 15–2–37–1; Morris 17.5–3–73–5; Finch 14–3–42–1; Barnard 12–9–7–1; Ali 7–1–28–2. *Second innings*—Leach 10–3–24–2; Morris 9–2–32–2; Barnard 5–0–26–2; Finch 7–1–33–1; Ali 7.2–1–37–2.

Umpires: N. L. Bainton and J. W. Lloyds.

WORCESTERSHIRE v GLOUCESTERSHIRE

At Worcester, September 16–18. Gloucestershire won by six wickets. Gloucestershire 20pts, Worcestershire 4pts. Toss: uncontested.

Gloucestershire overcame an attack of stage fright to complete a three-day victory that took them to the brink of Division One. They needed only 115 to win, but had slumped to 54 for four by the close of the second day of a breakneck contest. Next morning, there was the unusual sight of a pre-play huddle between the not-out batsmen and their team-mates. Less than an hour later, Hammond and nightwatchman Shaw had taken their fifth-wicket stand to 74, and Gloucestershire were home and dry. "Last night got a bit tense," said coach Richard Dawson. "The huddle settled the nerves a bit." On the opening day, the new-ball pair of Payne and Higgins had shared seven wickets as Worcestershire were bowled out for 221. That looked a reasonable total when the visitors tumbled to 155 for seven, before the same pair put on a rapid 62, helped by some indisciplined bowling – though Barnard's six for 42 was a season's best. Worcestershire were soon in dire straits at 33 for five, Higgins collecting his 50th wicket of the summer, and never recovered. On the first afternoon, umpire Nick Cook, troubled by a sore knee sustained while gardening, was replaced by Mike Burns.

Close of play: first day, Gloucestershire 87-4 (Roderick 17, Charlesworth 6); second day, Gloucestershire 54-4 (Hammond 11, Shaw 4).

Worcestershire

D. K. H. Mitchell c Smith b Payne	10	– lbw b Payne 0
H. D. Rutherford lbw b Higgins	7	– run out (Dent) 19
J. A. Haynes lbw b Payne	8	– c †Bracey b Higgins 20
A. G. Milton b Higgins	0	– lbw b Higgins 0
M. H. Wessels c Charlesworth b Shaw	72	– b Payne 5
†O. B. Cox c Smith b Higgins	2	– lbw b Higgins 1
E. G. Barnard c Roderick b Charlesworth	30	– lbw b Shaw 6
*J. Leach c Dent b Shaw	26	– c Hammond b Higgins 10
D. Y. Pennington b Higgins	9	– lbw b Gabriel 6
C. A. J. Morris not out	8	– not out 29
A. W. Finch b Payne	17	– b Gabriel 6
B 5, lb 11, nb 16	32	B 9, lb 9, nb 8 26

1/20 (1) 2/20 (2) 3/24 (4)   (55 overs) 221   1/0 (1) 2/23 (3)   (39.5 overs) 128
4/48 (3) 5/71 (6) 6/153 (7)   3/23 (4) 4/28 (5)
7/187 (5) 8/196 (8) 9/196 (9) 10/221 (11)   5/33 (6) 6/44 (7) 7/55 (2)
                                                              8/85 (9) 9/90 (8) 10/128 (11)

Payne 16–3–57–3; Higgins 18–1–55–4; Gabriel 6–0–39–0; Shaw 12–2–40–2; Charlesworth 3–0–14–1. *Second innings*—Payne 12–2–37–2; Higgins 13–4–34–4; Shaw 8–1–19–1; Gabriel 6.5–0–20–2.

Gloucestershire

J. R. Bracey c Cox b Barnard	23	– c Cox b Leach	2
*C. D. J. Dent c Haynes b Barnard	18	– lbw b Finch	22
T. M. J. Smith lbw b Mitchell	9	– lbw b Morris	5
M. A. H. Hammond c Cox b Barnard	5	– not out	35
†G. H. Roderick lbw b Barnard	40	– c Mitchell b Finch	0
B. G. Charlesworth lbw b Barnard	21		
R. F. Higgins c Cox b Leach	42		
J. M. R. Taylor c Barnard b Pennington	4		
D. A. Payne b Barnard	43		
J. Shaw b Leach	0	– (6) not out	38
S. T. Gabriel not out	2		
B 5, lb 11, w 4, nb 8	28	B 6, lb 1, nb 6	13

1/33 (1)   2/42 (2)   3/56 (3)   (65.2 overs) 235   1/8 (1)   (4 wkts, 42.3 overs) 115
4/56 (4)   5/128 (6)   6/135 (5)   2/19 (3)   3/41 (2)
7/155 (8)   8/217 (7)   9/217 (10)   10/235 (9)   4/41 (5)

Leach 19–2–61–2; Morris 10–2–51–0; Barnard 14.2–3–42–6; Mitchell 9–2–20–1; Finch 5–1–24–0; Pennington 8–3–21–1. *Second innings*—Leach 9–2–27–1; Morris 6–1–13–1; Pennington 10–2–26–0; Barnard 9–2–19–0; Finch 8.3–3–23–2.

Umpires: P. K. Baldwin and N. G. B. Cook. M. Burns replaced Cook from the first day.

At Hove, September 23–26. WORCESTERSHIRE drew with SUSSEX.

YORKSHIRE

Lost in transition

GRAHAM HARDCASTLE

The result of Yorkshire's Championship campaign – fifth in Division One – divided opinion at Headingley. But everybody agreed that their performances in white-ball cricket were not good enough. They failed to qualify in either the Royal London One-Day Cup or the Vitality Blast, nor looked like doing so, and remained without limited-overs silverware since 2002.

At the start of September, with three Championship rounds remaining, Yorkshire were third, 37 points behind Essex and 35 behind Somerset, their next opponents: hopes of a third title in six years were slim, but alive. Instead, they were beaten by Somerset at Taunton, then – humiliatingly – at home by Kent a week later. The 433-run margin in that game was a county record, and the fourth-heaviest in Championship history.

Ever since Yorkshire, under the guidance of coach Jason Gillespie, went close to winning a third successive four-day crown in 2016, his successor Andrew Gale and director of cricket Martyn Moxon have spoken regularly about a period of transition. Gone are experienced heads Ryan Sidebottom, Liam Plunkett and Jack Brooks; coming through are home-grown talents such as Harry Brook, Will Fraine, Jonny Tattersall and Matthew Fisher, who need time to bed in.

In that respect, five victories – which matched 2016 and 2018, and bettered 2017 – could be viewed as progress. Yorkshire brushed aside leaders Somerset by an innings in July, and beat defending champions Surrey and bottom side Nottinghamshire in pulsating encounters at Scarborough, ending a run of four defeats there. But the Kent defeat took off the gloss, and gave ammunition to those supporters who feel their side should be mounting an annual challenge. Fifth was Yorkshire's lowest finish since they were relegated in 2011; another such season will increase the pressure on Gale and Moxon.

The summer had begun with a come-from-behind draw against Nottinghamshire at Trent Bridge, where Gary Ballance and Joe Root averted defeat with fourth-day centuries, after Kolpak signing Duanne Olivier had taken five for 96 in the first innings. He finished as Yorkshire's leading Championship wicket-taker, with 43, but did not manage another five-for until September. He admitted he had hoped for better, after some good Test returns for South Africa during the winter. Back in April, the Nottinghamshire draw looked a good one, against a side who had recruited heavily and been tipped as title challengers. By the time they were relegated without a victory, it looked more like an opportunity missed.

Ballance scored another century in an innings victory over Hampshire at Southampton, where he has amassed over 1,000 runs in eight first-class matches for Yorkshire and England. And he soon made it four hundreds in

Gary Ballance

four games, against Kent and – this time at home – Hampshire. Ballance ended the season with 1,014 first-class runs, and was voted Players' Player and Members' Player of the Year.

He also reached three figures, alongside Brook, to set up victory over Leicestershire in the Royal London One-Day Cup's opening round. But it was one of only two wins in the competition. In the Blast, they were in danger of ending up with the wooden spoon, until three wins in their last four matches lifted them to fifth. Defeats by Derbyshire at Headingley, after Olivier conceded 32 in an over, and Nottinghamshire at Trent Bridge, where they had needed six off the last five balls, were particularly costly. Yorkshire tied three white-ball games, including two against Warwickshire.

There had been frustration in the Championship too: the first two home fixtures, against Hampshire and Essex, were rain-affected draws, though defeat by Warwickshire at York was the one which really got away. Former Yorkshire seamer Oliver Hannon-Dalby claimed nine wickets in the match, before the visitors successfully chased 217 on the final day, despite four late victims for fledgling slow left-armer James Logan. In hindsight, Logan was held back too long, with part-time off-spinner Jack Leaning used first. Leaning later signed for Kent, while seamer Josh Shaw spent most of the season on loan to Gloucestershire, and made the move permanent in August.

Injuries played their part. Adil Rashid never returned after England's World Cup triumph because of a long-term shoulder problem, while fellow leg-spinner Josh Poysden was ruled out for the rest of the season when he fractured his skull in training in July. Fisher, a highly rated seamer, broke both thumbs and dislocated a shoulder.

South African left-arm spinner Keshav Maharaj was Yorkshire's best bowler: he played five Championship games between July and September, and took a fabulous 38 wickets, including ten in each game against Somerset; he agreed to return briefly in 2020, before his wedding in May. Indian off-spinner Ravichandran Ashwin will arrive after the IPL. Captain Steve Patterson had a solid year, with 36 wickets – including his 400th in all first-class cricket. Tom Köhler-Cadmore stood out with the bat and in the field: across all formats, he scored 1,729 runs and held 42 catches, mostly at first slip. His aggregate, including 828 in the Championship, was boosted by an unbeaten 165 as he moved up to open during the rain-soaked final-week draw at Edgbaston. But Yorkshire managed only 24 batting points, and in November strengthened the top order by signing Middlesex captain and England batsman Dawid Malan on a four-year contract.

Championship attendance: 54,861.

YORKSHIRE RESULTS

All first-class matches – Played 15: Won 6, Lost 4, Drawn 5.
County Championship matches – Played 14: Won 5, Lost 4, Drawn 5.

Specsavers County Championship, 5th in Division 1;
Vitality Blast, 5th in North Group; Royal London One-Day Cup, 6th in North Group.

COUNTY CHAMPIONSHIP AVERAGES, BATTING AND FIELDING

Cap		Birthplace	M	I	NO	R	HS	100	Avge	Ct/St
2012	†G. S. Ballance	Harare, Zimbabwe .	14	23	2	975	159	5	46.42	4
2019	T. Köhler-Cadmore . .	Chatham	14	22	1	828	165*	2	39.42	30
	D. M. Bess	Exeter	4	5	1	156	91*	0	39.00	1
2010	†A. Lyth	Whitby‡	14	25	2	804	95	0	34.95	26
	M. D. Fisher	York‡	4	5	1	115	47*	0	28.75	1
2016	†D. J. Willey§	Northampton‡	5	7	1	171	46	0	28.50	3
	W. A. R. Fraine	Huddersfield‡	8	15	1	393	106	1	28.07	8
2016	J. A. Leaning	Bristol	8	12	1	295	77*	0	26.81	3
	K. A. Maharaj¶	Durban, SA	5	9	0	239	85	0	26.55	1
	J. A. Tattersall	Harrogate‡	14	21	1	523	92	0	26.15	32/3
	H. C. Brook	Keighley‡	10	16	0	353	101	1	22.06	7
	D. Olivier††	Groblersdal, SA . . .	13	17	11	130	24	0	21.66	3
2006	T. T. Bresnan	Pontefract‡	4	8	0	143	58	0	17.87	1
2018	B. O. Coad	Harrogate‡	11	14	2	196	48	0	16.33	0
2012	S. A. Patterson	Beverley‡	14	20	2	271	60	0	15.05	6

Also batted: †J. E. G. Logan (*Wakefield*‡) (1 match) 20*, 7; T. W. Loten (*York*‡) (1 match) 58; †A. Y. Patel¶ (*Bombay, India*) (2 matches) 20, 0*; M. L. Revis (*Steeton*‡) (1 match) 9, 0 (1 ct); J. E. Root§ (*Sheffield*‡) (2 matches) 73, 130*, 94 (2 ct); J. Shaw (*Wakefield*‡) (1 match) 6; †J. A. Thompson (*Leeds*‡) (2 matches) 34, 0, 2; M. J. Waite (*Leeds*‡) (2 matches) 22, 5* (1 ct).

‡ *Born in Yorkshire.* § *ECB contract.* ¶ *Official overseas player.* †† *Other non-England-qualified.*

BOWLING

	Style	O	M	R	W	BB	5I	Avge
K. A. Maharaj	SLA	266	76	719	38	7-52	4	18.92
B. O. Coad	RFM	340	82	955	37	6-52	1	25.81
M. D. Fisher	RFM	82	16	288	11	3-59	0	26.18
D. J. Willey	LFM	88.2	21	316	11	3-71	0	28.72
S. A. Patterson	RFM	396.4	111	1,050	36	5-81	1	29.16
D. Olivier	RF	365.5	66	1,390	43	5-96	2	32.32

Also bowled: D. M. Bess (OB) 97–24–234–7; T. T. Bresnan (RFM) 82–17–262–6; J. A. Leaning (OB) 30–8–96–3; J. E. G. Logan (SLA) 21–6–41–4; A. Lyth (OB) 25–3–79–1; A. Y. Patel (SLA) 35–0–231–2; J. E. Root (OB) 43–2–158–0; J. Shaw (RFM) 8–3–24–0; J. A. Thompson (RM) 40–10–105–5; M. J. Waite (RFM) 59–5–235–6.

LEADING ROYAL LONDON CUP AVERAGES (100 runs/4 wickets)

Batting	Runs	HS	Avge	SR	Ct/St	**Bowling**	W	BB	Avge	ER
G. S. Ballance . .	294	156	49.00	108.08	2	M. W. Pillans	16	5-29	21.50	6.57
J. A. Tattersall . .	232	79	46.40	120.83	10/2	D. J. Willey	5	2-26	32.40	6.23
H. C. Brook	275	103	45.83	102.23	1	S. A. Patterson . . .	8	4-45	32.87	6.11
T. Köhler-Cadmore	290	97	41.42	81.92	5	T. T. Bresnan	6	2-27	43.16	5.88
D. J. Willey	121	72*	40.33	96.8	2	J. E. Poysden	6	2-31	50.50	5.50
T. T. Bresnan . . .	117	89	29.25	105.40	1					
A. Lyth	201	78	28.71	109.23	3					

LEADING VITALITY BLAST AVERAGES (100 runs/16 overs)

Batting	Runs	HS	Avge	SR	Ct		Bowling	W	BB	Avge	ER
N. Pooran	122	67	40.66	184.84	2		K. A. Maharaj	2	1-17	63.00	6.30
A. Lyth	379	69	37.90	155.96	4		J. W. Shutt	10	5-11	16.40	6.83
T. Köhler-Cadmore	435	96*	62.14	141.23	4		D. J. Willey	9	4-18	30.33	7.87
H. C. Brook	123	38	20.50	136.66	7		A. Lyth	12	5-31	12.25	8.16
D. J. Willey	136	32	15.11	125.92	3		D. M. Bess	4	2-30	43.50	8.70
J. A. Leaning	113	39	28.25	122.82	3		J. A. Thompson	4	1-19	57.00	9.12
J. A. Tattersall	110	39*	27.50	122.22	6		D. Olivier	6	2-29	31.83	11.23

FIRST-CLASS COUNTY RECORDS

Highest score for	341	G. H. Hirst v Leicestershire at Leicester	1905
Highest score against	318*	W. G. Grace (Gloucestershire) at Cheltenham....	1876
Leading run-scorer	38,558	H. Sutcliffe (avge 50.20)	1919–45
Best bowling for	10-10	H. Verity v Nottinghamshire at Leeds	1932
Best bowling against	10-37	C. V. Grimmett (Australians) at Sheffield	1930
Leading wicket-taker	3,597	W. Rhodes (avge 16.02)	1898–1930
Highest total for	887	v Warwickshire at Birmingham	1896
Highest total against	681-7 dec	by Leicestershire at Bradford..................	1996
Lowest total for	23	v Hampshire at Middlesbrough	1965
Lowest total against	13	by Nottinghamshire at Nottingham	1901

LIST A COUNTY RECORDS

Highest score for	191	D. S. Lehmann v Nottinghamshire at Scarborough ..	2001
Highest score against	177	S. A. Newman (Surrey) at The Oval	2009
Leading run-scorer	8,699	G. Boycott (avge 40.08).	1963–86
Best bowling for	7-15	R. A. Hutton v Worcestershire at Leeds	1969
Best bowling against	7-32	R. G. D. Willis (Warwickshire) at Birmingham ...	1981
Leading wicket-taker	308	C. M. Old (avge 18.96)	1967–82
Highest total for	411-6	v Devon at Exmouth	2004
Highest total against	375-4	by Surrey at Scarborough.	1994
Lowest total for	54	v Essex at Leeds.	2003
Lowest total against	23	by Middlesex at Leeds.........................	1974

TWENTY20 COUNTY RECORDS

Highest score for	161	A. Lyth v Northamptonshire at Leeds	2017
Highest score against	111	D. L. Maddy (Leicestershire) at Leeds...........	2004
Leading run-scorer	**2,619**	**A. Lyth (avge 26.45, SR 143.19)**	**2008–19**
Best bowling for	6-19	T. T. Bresnan v Lancashire at Leeds	2017
Best bowling against	4-9	C. K. Langeveldt (Derbyshire) at Leeds	2008
Leading wicket-taker	**118**	**T. T. Bresnan (avge 24.72, ER 8.09)**	**2003–19**
Highest total for	260-4	v Northamptonshire at Leeds	2017
Highest total against	231-4	by Lancashire at Manchester	2015
Lowest total for	90-9	v Durham at Chester-le-Street	2009
Lowest total against	90	by Glamorgan at Cardiff	2016

ADDRESS

Emerald Headingley, Leeds LS6 3BU; 0843 504 3099; cricket@yorkshireccc.com; www.york-shireccc.com.

OFFICIALS

Captain S. A. Patterson	**President** G. A. Cope
2020 (Twenty20) D. J. Willey	**Chairman** R. Smith
Director of cricket M. D. Moxon	**Chief executive** M. A. Arthur
First-team coach A. W. Gale	**Head groundsman** A. Fogarty
2nd XI coach/Academy director I. M. Dews	**Scorer** J. T. Potter

At Weetwood, Leeds, March 31–April 2. YORKSHIRE beat LEEDS/BRADFORD MCCU by an innings and 151 runs.

At Nottingham, April 5–8. YORKSHIRE drew with NOTTINGHAMSHIRE.

At Southampton, April 11–14. YORKSHIRE beat HAMPSHIRE by an innings and 44 runs.

At Canterbury, May 14–17. YORKSHIRE beat KENT by 172 runs.

YORKSHIRE v HAMPSHIRE

At Leeds, May 27–30. Drawn. Yorkshire 8pts, Hampshire 9pts. Toss: Yorkshire.

Ballance became only the second batsman, after Len Hutton, to score five hundreds in five Championship matches for Yorkshire, though his side were frustrated, with more than 100 overs lost to rain. Hutton achieved the feat twice, going on to hit seven in succession across 1947 and 1948. Ballance's run had started at Worcester in September 2018; this was the only century on home soil. It helped Yorkshire set a target of 279 in 48 overs, despite conceding a lead of 54. They had been in trouble on the opening day, when the fiery Edwards claimed five wickets after rain delayed play until 12.20; there were five further interruptions. Next day Hampshire failed to capitalise, with injudicious strokes from India's Rahane (stumped) and South Africa's Rossouw (caught by first slip off a top edge). Though both Yorkshire openers went cheaply, Ballance led a strong recovery, and Hampshire were 35 for three as the final session began, after Coad removed Rahane and Northeast. Half-centuries from Weatherley and Rossouw prevented further alarm, and Hampshire briefly headed Division One.

Close of play: first day, Hampshire 14-1 (Weatherley 8); second day, Yorkshire 5-0 (Lyth 3, Brook 1); third day, Yorkshire 207-3 (Ballance 83, Leaning 17).

Yorkshire

A. Lyth c Weatherley b Barker	18	– c Weatherley b Barker	9
H. C. Brook b Edwards	17	– c Weatherley b Barker	9
G. S. Ballance c sub (†A. H. T. Donald) b Barker	12	– lbw b Crane	100
T. Köhler-Cadmore b Fuller	45	– lbw b Holland	69
J. A. Leaning c Rahane b Fuller	19	– b Barker	41
†J. A. Tattersall c sub (†A. H. T. Donald) b Edwards	14	– not out	51
D. J. Willey c Barker b Edwards	34	– not out	26
D. M. Bess c Holland b Fuller	6		
*S. A. Patterson b Edwards	0		
B. O. Coad b Edwards	0		
D. Olivier not out	0		
B 9, lb 3, nb 4	16	B 9, lb 10, nb 8	27

1/44 (2) 2/50 (1) 3/65 (3)   (56.2 overs) 181   1/15 (2)   (5 wkts dec, 91 overs) 332
4/116 (5) 5/131 (4) 6/170 (6)   2/20 (1) 3/161 (4)
7/175 (7) 8/175 (9) 9/177 (10) 10/181 (8)   4/239 (3) 5/268 (5)

Barker 16–6–40–2; Edwards 15–4–49–5; Fuller 13.2–4–51–3; Holland 12–2–29–0. *Second innings*—Barker 26–6–64–3; Edwards 16–2–68–0; Fuller 15–1–63–0; Holland 17–6–40–1; Crane 17–2–78–1.

Hampshire

J. J. Weatherley c Lyth b Olivier	14	– c Willey b Bess 66
O. C. Soames lbw b Coad	2	– c and b Olivier 0
A. M. Rahane st Tattersall b Bess	31	– b Coad 0
*S. A. Northeast lbw b Coad	50	– c Willey b Coad 14
R. R. Rossouw c Köhler-Cadmore b Willey	12	– not out 54
†T. P. Alsop c Lyth b Olivier	14	– (7) not out 3
I. G. Holland lbw b Patterson	19	– (6) b Bess 14
J. K. Fuller not out	54	
K. H. D. Barker c Köhler-Cadmore b Willey	14	
M. S. Crane b Coad	5	
F. H. Edwards b Coad	1	
B 9, lb 3, w 1, nb 6	19	Lb 5, nb 2 7

1/14 (2) 2/32 (1) 3/80 (3)   (74.1 overs) 235   1/4 (2) 2/7 (3)   (5 wkts, 46 overs) 158
4/93 (5) 5/133 (6) 6/143 (4)   3/35 (4) 4/137 (1)
7/180 (5) 8/207 (9) 9/225 (10) 10/235 (11)   5/153 (6)

Coad 19.1–7–41–4; Olivier 16–3–54–2; Patterson 18–7–31–1; Willey 9–1–52–2; Bess 11–1–37–1; Leaning 1–0–8–0. *Second innings*—Coad 12–2–43–2; Olivier 9–4–38–1; Willey 6–1–27–0; Patterson 5–1–20–0; Bess 13–5–24–2; Leaning 1–0–1–0.

Umpires: R. J. Bailey and N. L. Bainton.

YORKSHIRE v ESSEX

At Leeds, June 3–6. Drawn. Yorkshire 11pts, Essex 9pts. Toss: Yorkshire. First-class debut: W. E. L. Buttleman.

Rain stymied Yorkshire again, costing almost 100 overs and denying Ballance the chance of a sixth century in consecutive Championship matches; he was 51 when the final session was washed out. Yorkshire had chosen to bat, and three batsmen came close to three figures: Lyth and Köhler-Cadmore were caught behind by teenager Will Buttleman (on his official debut, two months after substituting for Adam Wheater at the start of Essex's wicketkeeper injury crisis), while Bess – in his third game on loan from Somerset – was stranded chasing a maiden Championship century. After a rain-shortened second day, Essex slipped from 190 for three to 223 for seven, 18 short of the follow-on target. The chances of reverse swing had been boosted by the ball being scuffed when a six from Westley hit concrete. But the first of two sixes clubbed by Siddle saved them from batting again, and he extended his tenth-wicket stand with Sam Cook to 86 on the final morning, after a minute's silence for the 75th anniversary of the D-Day landings.

Close of play: first day, Yorkshire 289-6 (Tattersall 20, Bess 30); second day, Essex 18-1 (Browne 10, Westley 3); third day, Essex 252-9 (Siddle 39, S. J. Cook 3).

Yorkshire

A. Lyth c Buttleman b Porter	95	– not out 56
W. A. R. Fraine b S. J. Cook	39	– c A. N. Cook b Porter 0
G. S. Ballance run out (S. J. Cook)	14	– not out 51
T. Köhler-Cadmore c Buttleman b S. J. Cook	83	
J. A. Leaning c Harmer b Siddle	3	
†J. A. Tattersall c Buttleman b Bopara	45	
D. J. Willey lbw b Harmer	3	
D. M. Bess not out	91	
*S. A. Patterson lbw b Porter	8	
B. O. Coad c A. N. Cook b Porter	1	
D. Olivier c Harmer b S. J. Cook	1	
B 1, lb 3, w 1, nb 2	7	

1/77 (2) 2/97 (3) 3/224 (1)   (125.4 overs) 390   1/1 (2)   (1 wkt, 42.5 overs) 107
4/229 (5) 5/247 (4) 6/252 (7)
7/342 (6) 8/379 (9) 9/387 (10)
10/390 (11)   110 overs: 325-6

Porter 28–6–84–3; S. J. Cook 28.4–6–91–3; Siddle 20–3–68–1; Harmer 33–9–90–1; Bopara 16–1–53–1. *Second innings*—Porter 9.5–2–30–1; S. J. Cook 10–3–24–0; Harmer 10–4–22–0; Westley 4.5–1–14–0; Bopara 5–2–7–0; ten Doeschate 1.1–0–5–0; Lawrence 2–0–5–0.

Essex

N. L. J. Browne lbw b Bess	35	J. A. Porter c Köhler-Cadmore b Patterson . 0
A. N. Cook c Köhler-Cadmore b Coad	2	S. J. Cook not out ... 37
T. Westley c Tattersall b Willey	77	
D. W. Lawrence c Fraine b Olivier	21	B 5, lb 4, nb 6 ... 15
R. S. Bopara b Olivier	44	
*R. N. ten Doeschate c Lyth b Bess	0	1/3 (2) 2/97 (1) (116.5 overs) 309
S. R. Harmer c Lyth b Bess	18	3/132 (3) 4/190 (4) 5/191 (6)
†W. E. L. Buttleman c Tattersall b Willey	0	6/191 (5) 7/197 (8) 8/213 (7)
P. M. Siddle lbw b Patterson	60	9/223 (10) 10/309 (9) 110 overs: 295-9

Coad 26–7–73–1; Olivier 28–12–74–2; Patterson 17.5–2–69–2; Willey 19–8–39–2; Bess 26–11–45–3.

Umpires: N. A. Mallender and S. J. O'Shaughnessy.

At Guildford, June 10–13. YORKSHIRE drew with SURREY.

YORKSHIRE v WARWICKSHIRE

At York, June 17–20. Warwickshire won by three wickets. Warwickshire 21pts, Yorkshire 5pts. Toss: uncontested.

York's only previous first-class match had been in 1890, at Wigginton Road, until the World Cup diverted Yorkshire to Clifton Park, home of York CC. The winning runs were struck by one of the club's former players – but he was Warwickshire captain Jeetan Patel, and the visitors' key performers were Yorkshire exiles Hannon-Dalby and Rhodes. On a surface which slowed, Hannon-Dalby celebrated his 30th birthday by completing career-best match figures of nine for 137. Yorkshire had started solidly on the opening day, but after lunch lost five for eight to him and Miles. In reply, Rhodes and Yates were both dropped on one – by Fraine and Lyth – though the bowlers fought back to secure a five-run lead, extended to a defendable 216. Then Rhodes and Sibley shared Warwickshire's first century opening partnership of the summer: Rhodes hit three leg-side sixes in one over from part-time spinner Leaning (another York player). Six wickets fell after tea, including slow left-armer Logan's first four victims, in his second first-class game. But Patel, who had earlier claimed his 700th for Warwickshire across all formats, inflicted Yorkshire's first defeat with ten overs to go.

Close of play: first day, Yorkshire 208-8 (Patterson 36, Logan 0); second day, Warwickshire 192-5 (Hain 23, Ambrose 11); third day, Yorkshire 178-7 (Leaning 47, Patterson 9).

Yorkshire

A. Lyth c Ambrose b Hannon-Dalby		7 – c Ambrose b Miles	37
W. A. R. Fraine c Lamb b Miles	42	lbw b Hannon-Dalby	1
G. S. Ballance lbw b Patel	54	c Rhodes b Hannon-Dalby	18
T. Köhler-Cadmore lbw b Miles	0	c Ambrose b Lamb	20
J. A. Leaning b Miles	0	lbw b Patel	65
†J. A. Tattersall c Hain b Hannon-Dalby	4	c Ambrose b Hannon-Dalby	17
J. A. Thompson lbw b Hannon-Dalby	0	b Patel	2
D. J. Willey b Miles	46	st Ambrose b Patel	0
*S. A. Patterson b Hannon-Dalby	60	b Hannon-Dalby	9
J. E. G. Logan not out	20	b Patel	7
B. O. Coad b Hannon-Dalby	2	not out	5
B 7, lb 16, w 1	24	B 4, lb 10, nb 16	30

1/8 (1) 2/93 (2) 3/93 (4) (92.4 overs) 259   1/3 (2) 2/31 (3) (81 overs) 211
4/93 (5) 5/101 (6) 6/101 (7)   3/68 (4) 4/97 (1)
7/145 (3) 8/205 (8) 9/253 (9) 10/259 (11)   5/127 (6) 6/134 (7) 7/140 (8)
8/179 (9) 9/200 (10) 10/211 (5)

Hannon-Dalby 26.4–9–76–5; Norwell 20–6–51–0; Patel 29–7–65–1; Miles 17–3–44–4. *Second innings*—Hannon-Dalby 25–7–61–4; Norwell 7–2–10–0; Miles 11–1–47–1; Patel 31–8–48–4; Lamb 7–1–31–1.

Warwickshire

W. M. H. Rhodes c Leaning b Coad	28	– b Willey	83
D. P. Sibley b Patterson	67	– c Patterson b Logan	81
R. M. Yates c Köhler-Cadmore b Patterson	49	– c Willey b Logan	9
S. R. Hain c Lyth b Willey	25	– c Tattersall b Patterson	8
A. J. Hose lbw b Patterson	0	– b Logan	24
M. J. Lamb c Lyth b Willey	11	– b Logan	7
†T. R. Ambrose c Köhler-Cadmore b Willey	39	– c Köhler-Cadmore b Thompson	2
C. N. Miles c Patterson b Coad	27	– not out	0
*J. S. Patel c Tattersall b Thompson	5	– not out	4
L. C. Norwell lbw b Thompson	0		
O. J. Hannon-Dalby not out	0		
Lb 3	3	Lb 1	1

1/38 (1) 2/139 (2) 3/148 (3)   (98.2 overs) 254   1/132 (1)   (7 wkts, 66 overs) 219
4/148 (5) 5/166 (6) 6/201 (4)   2/166 (3) 3/181 (2)
7/234 (8) 8/250 (9) 9/250 (10) 10/254 (7)   4/183 (4) 5/202 (6) 6/213 (5) 7/215 (7)

Coad 26–4–83–2; Willey 21.2–3–71–3; Patterson 23–8–33–3; Logan 8–2–19–0; Thompson 12–4–28–2; Leaning 8–2–17–0. *Second innings*—Coad 11–1–33–0; Patterson 17–4–36–1; Willey 13–3–56–1; Thompson 9–0–36–1; Leaning 3–0–35–0; Logan 13–4–22–4.

Umpires: J. H. Evans and D. J. Millns.

YORKSHIRE v SURREY

At Scarborough, June 30–July 3. Yorkshire won by 123 runs. Yorkshire 22pts, Surrey 7pts. Toss: Yorkshire. County debut: K. A. Maharaj.

Yorkshire grabbed five for six either side of tea on the final day to swing what had been a nip-and-tuck contest, which ended their run of four Championship defeats at North Marine Road. Set 318 in 83 overs, Surrey had looked good at 157 for two, but Elgar was run out by Willey, and Coad removed Foakes and Curran for ducks. After tea, Maharaj – the South African slow left-armer making his Yorkshire debut – struck twice. Tensions rose as Jordan Clark supported Smith for an hour, and the last man, Bradford-born Batty, survived 33 minutes. But, with 11 balls to go, Olivier had Batty caught at second slip, sending the crowd into raptures. Earlier, Patterson had won Yorkshire's tenth successive contested toss, a post-war record, and Fraine scored an elegant maiden hundred. Clark checked their progress with his second five-for against them, following one for Lancashire a year earlier, and Stoneman's only first-class century in 2019 helped Surrey to a lead of 35. But Yorkshire had a strong second innings, boosted by Coad's career-best 48 at No. 10; for Surrey, despite a host of starts, only Stoneman and Elgar reached 50.

Close of play: first day, Surrey 48-0 (Stoneman 28, Elgar 14); second day, Surrey 362; third day, Yorkshire 303-9 (Coad 16, Olivier 0).

Yorkshire

A. Lyth c Smith b Clarke	55	c Foakes b Clarke	68
W. A. R. Fraine c Foakes b Morkel	106	c Clark b Patel	43
G. S. Ballance c Borthwick b Clark	23	lbw b Curran	23
T. Köhler-Cadmore b Clark	5	st Foakes b Batty	42
J. A. Leaning c Borthwick b Clark	0	lbw b Clarke	0
†J. A. Tattersall c Foakes b Clark	11	c Clarke b Curran	38
D. J. Willey c Stoneman b Curran	19	c Borthwick b Curran	43
K. A. Maharaj b Curran	0	c Borthwick b Morkel	10
*S. A. Patterson c Clarke b Clark	46	c Patel b Morkel	2
B. O. Coad c Patel b Morkel	25	c Foakes b Batty	48
D. Olivier not out	11	not out	11
Lb 8, nb 18	26	B 8, lb 8, nb 8	24

1/116 (1) 2/187 (3) 3/201 (4)   (79.2 overs) 327
4/205 (2) 5/205 (5) 6/231 (7)
7/231 (8) 8/250 (6) 9/295 (10) 10/327 (9)

1/94 (2) 2/131 (3)   (106.1 overs) 352
3/162 (1) 4/168 (5)
5/225 (4) 6/251 (6) 7/276 (7)
8/286 (9) 9/295 (9) 10/352 (10)

Morkel 21–5–77–2; Curran 18.4–3–84–2; Clarke 16–3–56–1; Clark 17.4–3–77–5; Batty 6–0–25–0. *Second innings*—Morkel 21–7–61–2; Curran 26–4–90–3; Clark 3–0–22–0; Clarke 13–2–36–2; Batty 32.1–5–87–2; Patel 11–1–40–1.

Surrey

M. D. Stoneman c Tattersall b Olivier	100	(2) c Fraine b Maharaj	46
D. Elgar b Coad	24	(1) run out (Willey)	71
S. G. Borthwick c Köhler-Cadmore b Willey	24	b Willey	24
R. S. Patel c Tattersall b Maharaj	26	c Fraine b Maharaj	9
*†B. T. Foakes c Leaning b Coad	40	b Coad	0
S. M. Curran c Leaning b Coad	43	c Tattersall b Coad	0
J. L. Smith c Lyth b Willey	28	not out	24
R. Clarke c Köhler-Cadmore b Maharaj	26	c Tattersall b Maharaj	0
J. Clark c Lyth b Maharaj	25	b Olivier	1
M. Morkel b Olivier	0	run out (Köhler-Cadmore)	0
G. J. Batty not out	9	c Lyth b Olivier	4
Lb 1, nb 16	17	B 10, lb 5	15

1/68 (2) 2/110 (3) 3/182 (4)   (107.4 overs) 362
4/186 (1) 5/267 (6) 6/286 (5)
7/303 (7) 8/334 (8) 9/334 (10) 10/362 (9)

1/93 (2) 2/136 (3)   (81.2 overs) 194
3/157 (1) 4/157 (5)
5/157 (6) 6/163 (4) 7/163 (8)
8/180 (9) 9/180 (10) 10/194 (11)

Coad 21–4–60–3; Olivier 25–3–111–2; Patterson 23–5–58–0; Maharaj 23.4–5–75–3; Willey 14–3–55–2; Leaning 1–0–2–0. *Second innings*—Coad 14–7–30–2; Olivier 13.2–1–32–2; Maharaj 33–11–69–3; Patterson 11–0–32–0; Willey 6–2–16–1; Leaning 4–4–0–0.

Umpires: I. D. Blackwell and A. G. Wharf.

At Chelmsford, July 7–9. YORKSHIRE lost to ESSEX by eight wickets.

YORKSHIRE v SOMERSET

At Leeds, July 13–16. Yorkshire won by an innings and 73 runs. Yorkshire 22pts, Somerset 1pt. Toss: uncontested.

Yorkshire's innings victory was set up by Maharaj, only the third spinner to take ten in a match for them since the turn of the century, after James Middlebrook at Southampton in 2000 and Adil Rashid at Worcester in 2011. He also hit 72, to supplement three centuries – from Ballance, Köhler-Cadmore and Harry Brook, who rediscovered his form after dropping down the order, and reached three figures just before he was last out. Bess, back with Somerset between two spells on loan to

Yorkshire, took four wickets; Jack Brooks, who had left Headingley the previous year, managed two. But Somerset were four down on the second evening, and next day Maharaj claimed the remaining six on a helpful pitch. They were asked to follow on, 324 behind. Though the second innings was tougher work for the home attack, Patterson brought victory before lunch on the fourth day, with four wickets including Banton, the 400th of his first-class career; Groenewald had attained the same landmark by dismissing Ballance on the opening day. Somerset's second defeat of the season knocked them off the top of the table, while Yorkshire's fourth win maintained their slim title hopes.

Close of play: first day, Yorkshire 282-3 (Köhler-Cadmore 77, Shaw 0); second day, Somerset 76-4 (Hildreth 36, Davies 12); third day, Somerset 159-4 (Banton 58, Groenewald 0).

Yorkshire

A. Lyth c Abell b Bess	35	K. A. Maharaj c J. Overton b Bess	72
W. A. R. Fraine c Bess b Brooks	45	*S. A. Patterson c Davies b Bess	1
G. S. Ballance c J. Overton b Groenewald	111	D. Olivier not out	2
T. Köhler-Cadmore c J. Overton		B 8, lb 12, nb 2	22
b C. Overton	102		
J. Shaw b Groenewald	6	1/80 (2) 2/82 (1)	(160.1 overs) 520
H. C. Brook c Azhar Ali b Abell	101	3/281 (3) 4/305 (5) 5/319 (4)	
†J. A. Tattersall c J. Overton b Brooks	5	6/351 (7) 7/398 (8) 8/503 (9)	
M. D. Fisher c Banton b Bess	20	9/506 (10) 10/520 (6)	110 overs: 339-5

C. Overton 28–3–91–1; Brooks 28–2–96–2; Groenewald 26–7–74–2; J. Overton 20–3–71–0; Bess 42–11–130–4; Abell 16.1–7–38–1.

Somerset

*T. B. Abell c Brook b Fisher	6	– c Tattersall b Fisher	53
Azhar Ali c Lyth b Olivier	4	– lbw b Fisher	41
J. C. Hildreth lbw b Maharaj	37	– c Patterson b Maharaj	1
T. Banton c Tattersall b Maharaj	5	– b Patterson	63
G. A. Bartlett c Patterson b Olivier	4	– c Lyth b Maharaj	5
†S. M. Davies c Lyth b Maharaj	37	– (7) c Olivier b Patterson	24
D. M. Bess lbw b Maharaj	7	– (8) b Patterson	4
C. Overton b Maharaj	2	– (9) lbw b Patterson	23
J. Overton not out	52	– (10) lbw b Maharaj	21
T. D. Groenewald lbw b Maharaj	15	– (6) c Fraine b Fisher	8
J. A. Brooks c Köhler-Cadmore b Maharaj	9	– not out	2
B 9, lb 5, nb 4	18	B 1, lb 4, w 1	6

1/8 (1) 2/31 (2) 3/36 (4)	(67.3 overs) 196	1/89 (2) 2/94 (3)	(82.5 overs) 251
4/49 (5) 5/85 (3) 6/101 (7)		3/101 (1) 4/148 (5)	
7/103 (8) 8/138 (6) 9/182 (10) 10/196 (11)		5/167 (6) 6/188 (4) 7/192 (8)	
		8/211 (7) 9/239 (10) 10/251 (9)	

Fisher 11–4–38–1; Patterson 12–6–30–0; Olivier 14–2–56–2; Maharaj 26.3–9–52–7; Shaw 4–3–6–0. *Second innings*—Fisher 15.3–3–61–3; Patterson 20.5–5–54–4; Olivier 8–2–33–0; Maharaj 34–11–75–3; Shaw 4–0–18–0; Lyth 1–0–5–0.

Umpires: M. Burns and P. J. Hartley.

YORKSHIRE v NOTTINGHAMSHIRE

At Scarborough, August 18–21. Yorkshire won by 143 runs. Yorkshire 20pts, Nottinghamshire 3pts. Toss: uncontested.

Not for the first time, Yorkshire bounced back after a first-morning collapse. They were 38 for five by the 14th over, all taken by left-arm seamer Wood, in what proved his only five-wicket Championship haul for Nottinghamshire; the day after the match ended, it was announced he would join Lancashire for 2020. But Tattersall added 121 with Bresnan, and guided Yorkshire past 200, only to fall eight short of a maiden Championship century. Next day, Nottinghamshire lost all ten for 143 in 44 overs – four to the pacy Olivier – though Moores hit three sixes off Maharaj, one out of the ground and another caught in the crowd. Yorkshire were soon extending a lead of 48, with a confident 81 from Lyth at the venue where he played league cricket. Fletcher struck four times in a fabulous 11-over spell on the third afternoon, but winless Nottinghamshire found themselves facing an unlikely target of 387. Maharaj grabbed six to complete their eighth defeat, two overs after lunch on the final day.

Close of play: first day, Nottinghamshire 41-0 (Slater 29, Libby 12); second day, Yorkshire 177-2 (Ballance 52, Patterson 5); third day, Nottinghamshire 135-4 (Duckett 47, Patterson-White 16).

Yorkshire

A. Lyth c Moores b Wood	4	– c Coughlin b Patterson-White	81
W. A. R. Fraine c Nash b Wood	11	– lbw b Fletcher	24
G. S. Ballance c Libby b Wood	0	– c sub (L. R. Bhabra) b Wood	61
T. Köhler-Cadmore b Wood	1	– (5) lbw b Fletcher	59
H. C. Brook c Moores b Wood	6	– (6) c Ball b Patterson-White	18
†J. A. Tattersall c Moores b Patterson-White	92	– (7) c Duckett b Fletcher	7
T. T. Bresnan c Moores b Patterson-White	58	– (8) c Moores b Fletcher	2
K. A. Maharaj b Fletcher	7	– (9) c and b Coughlin	35
*S. A. Patterson not out	16	– (4) c Nash b Coughlin	9
B. O. Coad lbw b Patterson-White	4	– c Coughlin b Fletcher	11
D. Olivier b Patterson-White	14	– not out	4
Lb 5, nb 14	19	B 8, lb 2, w 1, nb 16	27

1/5 (1) 2/5 (3) 3/7 (4) (76.1 overs) 232
4/13 (5) 5/38 (2) 6/159 (7)
7/178 (8) 8/204 (6) 9/212 (10) 10/232 (11)

1/64 (2) 2/172 (1) (101.3 overs) 338
3/185 (4) 4/199 (3)
5/232 (6) 6/273 (7) 7/281 (8)
8/302 (5) 9/320 (10) 10/338 (9)

Fletcher 17–2–46–1; Wood 17–0–67–5; Ball 13–3–44–0; Coughlin 12–1–36–0; Patterson-White 17.1–5–34–4. *Second innings*—Fletcher 27–6–67–5; Wood 13–3–71–1; Ball 21–6–59–0; Coughlin 18.3–4–58–2; Patterson-White 22–2–73–2.

Nottinghamshire

B. T. Slater c Tattersall b Coad	29	– c Köhler-Cadmore b Olivier	18
J. D. Libby b Olivier	18	– c Tattersall b Patterson	11
*C. D. Nash c and b Olivier	33	– lbw b Maharaj	30
J. M. Clarke c Tattersall b Coad	8	– c Tattersall b Maharaj	4
B. M. Duckett b Maharaj	13	– c Fraine b Olivier	75
L. A. Patterson-White c Tattersall b Patterson	15	– not out	58
†T. J. Moores c Tattersall b Olivier	48	– c Fraine b Maharaj	5
P. Coughlin c Brook b Maharaj	0	– c Lyth b Bresnan	9
L. Wood c Lyth b Coad	6	– b Maharaj	0
L. J. Fletcher c Brook b Olivier	4	– lbw b Maharaj	15
J. T. Ball not out	1	– c Lyth b Maharaj	0
B 4, lb 1, nb 4	9	B 9, lb 5, nb 4	18

1/41 (1) 2/65 (2) 3/90 (3) (61 overs) 184
4/94 (5) 5/125 (5) 6/131 (6)
7/132 (8) 8/173 (9) 9/179 (7) 10/184 (10)

1/29 (1) 2/42 (2) (79 overs) 243
3/51 (4) 4/103 (3)
5/181 (5) 6/187 (7) 7/218 (8)
8/219 (9) 9/243 (10) 10/243 (11)

Coad 16–3–58–3; Olivier 17–3–60–4; Maharaj 15–4–49–2; Patterson 13–9–12–1. *Second innings*—Coad 11–2–21–0; Olivier 15–2–54–2; Maharaj 30–7–95–6; Patterson 11–3–25–1; Bresnan 10–3–31–1; Lyth 2–0–3–0.

Umpires: D. J. Millns and M. J. Saggers.

At Taunton, September 10–12. YORKSHIRE lost to SOMERSET by 298 runs.

YORKSHIRE v KENT

At Leeds, September 16–19. Kent won by 433 runs. Kent 24pts, Yorkshire 4pts. Toss: Kent. First-class debut: M. L. Revis. County debut: A. Y. Patel.

Billings became the first to score twin Championship hundreds at Headingley, but even he accepted the game belonged to Darren Stevens. Aged 43 years, he became the second-oldest to combine a double-hundred with a five-for in one match, behind W. G. Grace (46 years) for Gloucestershire against Somerset in 1895. His 237 off 225 balls was a career-best, as well as Kent's best against Yorkshire, and came straight after a ten-wicket haul at Nottingham. A week later, Kent reversed their decision to release him. Stevens's performance set up Kent's biggest win by runs, and Yorkshire's

---

OLDEST FIRST-CLASS DOUBLE-CENTURIONS SINCE 1945

Years	Days			
50	143	C. K. Nayudu (200) . . .	Holkar v Baroda at Indore	1945-46
44	58	W. W. Keeton (210) . . .	Nottinghamshire v Yorkshire at Sheffield	1949
44	68	W. W. Keeton (208) . . .	Nottinghamshire v Glamorgan at Nottingham .	1949
43	3	V. S. Hazare (203) . . .	Baroda v Services at Baroda	1957-58
43	16	W. R. Hammond (211*) . . .	Gloucestershire v Nottinghamshire at Bristol .	1946
43	17	G. A. Gooch (201)	Essex v Somerset at Taunton	1996
43	47	W. R. Hammond (214). . .	Gloucestershire v Somerset at Bristol	1946
43	117	W. R. Hammond (208).	MCC v Western Australia at Perth	1946-47
43	**139**	**D. I. Stevens (237).** . . .	**Kent v Yorkshire at Leeds.**	**2019**
43	355	D. E. Davies (215) . . .	Glamorgan v Essex at Brentwood	1948

---

heaviest defeat. On the opening morning, Olivier had reduced Kent to 39 for five after Yorkshire lost a contested toss for the first time in two years. Billings and Stevens regained control by adding 346, a sixth-wicket record for Kent, against Yorkshire, and at Headingley. Billings declared on the second morning, waived the follow-on when Yorkshire were bowled out 213 behind, and went on to his third century in successive first-class innings; New Zealand left-arm spinner Ajaz Patel conceded 100-plus for the second time in the match, his county debut. Kent eventually set a target of 551, and Stevens was quickly back in action, dismissing debutant Matthew Revis (more than 25 years his junior) in his first over, and claiming four for 11 as Yorkshire crumbled to 43 for six. He added a fifth in his opening over next day, following team-mates Milnes and Podmore to 50 Championship wickets. It was all done by lunch.

Close of play: first day, Kent 482-8 (Rayner 40, Milnes 14); second day, Kent 2-0 (Crawley 0, Bell-Drummond 2); third day, Yorkshire 44-6 (Tattersall 1, Bresnan 0).

Kent

Z. Crawley lbw b Olivier	4 –	lbw b Fisher	15
D. J. Bell-Drummond b Fisher	10 –	b Fisher.	7
†O. G. Robinson c Tattersall b Olivier	4 –	c Tattersall b Olivier	97
F. du Plessis b Olivier	0 –	c Köhler-Cadmore b Patterson	36
*S. W. Billings c Lyth b Olivier	138 –	not out	122
H. G. Kuhn lbw b Olivier.	8 –	run out (Tattersall)	8
D. I. Stevens c Revis b Patel	237 –	c Köhler-Cadmore b Patel	21
O. P. Rayner not out.	40 –	run out (Ballance).	1
H. W. Podmore b Fisher.	0 –	not out	24
M. E. Milnes not out	14		
B 6, lb 15, nb 6.	27	B 1, lb 3, nb 2	6

1/4 (1) 2/8 (3) 3/8 (4)   (8 wkts dec, 96 overs) 482
4/22 (2) 5/39 (6) 6/385 (7)
7/454 (5) 8/455 (9)

1/14 (2)   (7 wkts dec, 74 overs) 337
2/23 (1) 3/101 (4)
4/225 (3) 5/235 (6) 6/297 (7) 7/300 (8)

M. E. Claydon did not bat.

Olivier 24–2–108–5; Fisher 19–2–79–2; Patterson 20–4–90–0; Bresnan 15–2–58–0; Patel 15–0–119–1; Lyth 3–1–7–0. *Second innings*—Olivier 15–2–57–1; Fisher 12–2–38–2; Bresnan 11–1–49–0; Patterson 12–1–59–1; Patel 20–0–112–1; Lyth 4–0–18–0.

Yorkshire

A. Lyth c du Plessis b Stevens	5	– lbw b Stevens	9
M. L. Revis c Robinson b Milnes	9	– lbw b Stevens	0
G. S. Ballance lbw b Stevens	4	– c du Plessis b Stevens	2
T. Köhler-Cadmore b Milnes	36	– c Rayner b Stevens	19
H. C. Brook lbw b Milnes	36	– c Kuhn b Milnes	13
†J. A. Tattersall c Crawley b Podmore	27	– (7) c du Plessis b Bell-Drummond	41
T. T. Bresnan b Milnes	39	– (8) c Robinson b Stevens	0
M. D. Fisher not out	47	– (9) c Robinson b Podmore	7
*S. A. Patterson b Podmore	10	– (6) c Crawley b Milnes	0
D. Olivier lbw b Milnes	10	– b Bell-Drummond	24
A. Y. Patel b Rayner	20	– not out	0
Lb 16, nb 10	26	Lb 2	2

1/9 (1) 2/17 (3) 3/36 (2)   (92 overs) 269   1/4 (2) 2/9 (1)   (55.2 overs) 117
4/95 (5) 5/106 (4) 6/141 (6)   3/16 (3) 4/43 (5)
7/194 (7) 8/220 (9) 9/244 (10) 10/269 (11)   5/43 (4) 6/43 (6) 7/46 (8)
                                                 8/81 (9) 9/116 (10) 10/117 (7)

Podmore 21–5–60–2; Stevens 20–8–50–2; Claydon 13–3–34–0; Milnes 21–1–87–5; Rayner 15–7–21–1; Bell-Drummond 2–1–1–0. *Second innings*—Podmore 12–3–31–1; Stevens 18–7–20–5; Milnes 10–4–24–2; Claydon 6–0–26–0; Rayner 6–2–7–0; Bell-Drummond 3.2–0–7–2.

Umpires: M. A. Gough and D. J. Millns.

At Birmingham, September 23–26. YORKSHIRE drew with WARWICKSHIRE.

VITALITY BLAST IN 2019

Alan Gardner

1 Essex   2 Worcestershire   3= Derbyshire, Nottinghamshire

Modern Twenty20 is a game of planning and data analysis, match-ups and phases. The best teams nail down role-definition, and know their strategy inside-out. Mini-dynasties spring up, from Hampshire via Perth Scorchers to Chennai Super Kings, as the number-crunchers help hammer out the kinks in cricket's most quixotic format. Specialist coaches, targeted recruitment, innovative tactics and a common sense of purpose – those are the markers of success. Alternatively, you can just rock up to finals day on your first run of form in two years and make off with the prize, as Essex did in the Vitality Blast.

Victory in the T20 a few days before sealing another Championship was an unexpected case of double bubble. It all came together with the vim of a Guy Ritchie caper, the destination of the title in the balance until the last ball. Worcestershire's Wayne Parnell was tasked with preventing the single that Essex needed to bring the scores level and claim victory by virtue of fewer wickets lost. He had faced the same scenario in the semi-final against Nottinghamshire, when he responded with a dot ball. Now, though, Simon Harmer – Essex's captain and, it turned out, Player of the Match twice on finals day, emulating Ben Cox's 2018 feat – struck the winning boundary through backward point, and set off on a delirious lap of Edgbaston.

Harmer's reaction contrasted with his downbeat mood a few weeks earlier as Essex prepared for their final group game. "Frustrating and challenging," had been his description of his first season as T20 captain. The Eagles had struggled to get airborne, winning just two of their opening ten matches (including four washouts). Results picked up, yet a quarter-final spot seemed a mathematical fancy. But Kent collapsed, and Hampshire stumbled against Glamorgan – their only win of a miserable season – which allowed Essex to sneak through with five victories, the fewest for a team reaching the knockouts in six years of the 14-game Blast season (in 2018, three teams with seven wins failed to qualify). They proceeded to despatch the North Group winners, Lancashire, in a match shifted to Chester-le-Street because of the Ashes Test at Old Trafford.

HIGHEST AGGREGATES IN A COUNTY T20 MATCH

462	Warwickshire (231-5) tied with Northamptonshire (231-5) at Birmingham	2018
457	Kent (231-5) beat Somerset (226-5) at Canterbury	2018
456	**Yorkshire (255-2) beat Leicestershire (201-4) at Leicester**	**2019**
455	Glamorgan (240-3) beat Surrey (215) at The Oval	2015
453	**Middlesex (227-4) beat Somerset (226-5) at Taunton**	**2019**
451	Sussex (226-3) beat Essex (225-3) at Chelmsford	2014
451	Kent (227-7) beat Somerset (224-7) at Taunton	2015
449	Worcestershire (227-6) beat Northamptonshire (222-3) at Kidderminster	2007
449	Nottinghamshire (227-3) beat Derbyshire (222-5) at Nottingham	2017
448	Nottinghamshire (225-5) beat Yorkshire (223-5) at Nottingham	2017

Babar… Boom! Leading scorer in the Vitality Blast: Somerset's Babar Azam.

While Worcestershire were hoping to become the first county to retain the domestic T20 trophy, and Nottinghamshire were targeting a second triumph in three seasons, Essex's primary aim was to get beyond the semi-finals for the first time. Their opponents were Derbyshire, who had become – under the guidance of Dominic Cork – the 18th and last county to qualify for finals day. But on a tired surface that made chasing difficult, their challenge fell away.

Harmer led by example, his finals-day haul of seven for 35 a record, though Essex's transformation had not been entirely straightforward. Varun Chopra, their leading run-scorer in 2018, was dropped, and Ravi Bopara left out for two games after being given an unfamiliar role at No. 6. He openly chafed against the move, but channelled his frustration into scoring 278 runs at a strike-rate of 175 in the last seven matches (Essex won six and tied the other). It was Bopara looking on nonchalantly from the non-striker's end when Harmer wheeler-dealed his way to a victory that must have felt much like a vindication.

There was something old school about the way Essex threw everything together and came up trumps. Mohammad Amir and Adam Zampa were represented at Edgbaston by cardboard cut-outs; only three of a possible eight overseas players were available for the latest finals day yet. And the squad featured four home-grown bowlers – Jamie Porter, Sam Cook, Aaron Beard and Aron Nijjar – who had made just 32 T20 appearances between them (18 by Porter, who did not play in the final). Slow left-armer Nijjar had not featured at all during the group stage, but delivered in both games; Dan Lawrence, a wristy revelation at No. 4, suddenly found conditions suitable for his part-time spin. The upshot was that Essex cobbled together five successive wins at the sharp end of the competition.

Yet for much of the final, it seemed as if Worcestershire were on course to defend their title. Then again, for much of the first semi, Nottinghamshire had seemed to be cruising towards a similarly modest target – only to suffer a dramatic loss of composure, with 11 needed from 12 balls, and eight wickets in hand. Ben Duckett, unbeaten on 49 from 42, slumped over his bat handle in despair after failing to make contact with Parnell's final ball, which completed a nerveless display in the field from Moeen Ali's side.

That the final was contested by the teams finishing fourth in their groups was further evidence of the importance of peaking at the right time. Sussex had matched Lancashire's eight wins in topping the South Group, only to be blown away in the quarter-finals by Ali's unbeaten 121 from 60. Nottinghamshire alone made the most of home advantage in the last eight, ending Middlesex's foray with a ten-wicket thrashing, before Derbyshire saw off Gloucestershire at Bristol.

From cock of the walk to feather duster? Time will tell

While qualification from the North Group was wrapped up before the final round, the South Group culminated in a five-way showdown for two spots. Kent missed out, despite starting off with six wins out of seven; so did Hampshire and Somerset, who had the Blast's two leading run-scorers in Babar Azam and Tom Banton, but were ambushed by Eoin Morgan in Taunton, as Middlesex squeezed through.

The tournament had begun four days after England's World Cup catharsis, with several counties reporting a bump in interest. The year-on-year trend of rising attendances continued, although an overall figure of 894,000 for the group stage was slightly down, because of an unprecedented number of washouts – 24, with all eight on August 16 abandoned without a ball bowled, another unwanted first. Still, average attendances for games that went ahead increased by 15% on 2018 to 8,550, and the London derby at Lord's set a new record (27,773) for a domestic T20 in England. Lancashire, who three times surpassed their best crowd for non-Roses games, sold 23,000 tickets for the visit of Yorkshire, only for another deluge.

Whether it was down to the wet summer or a packed schedule that steadily drained the life from pitches, scoring-rates fell for the first time in three years: runs came at 8.34 an over, compared with 8.83 in 2018. While Azam and A. B. de Villiers provided overseas stardust with the bat, the most successful bowler was Ravi Rampaul, Derbyshire's 34-year-old Trinidadian Kolpak. There were four ties (though no super overs), equalling the most in a season, and Leicestershire's unheralded off-spinner Colin Ackermann became the first man anywhere to take a T20 seven-for.

In short, it was all rather good fun, which makes it a shame to have to mention The Hundred. The ECB's new white-ball competition was poised to take centre stage in 2020, relegating the Blast to a support act. From cock of the walk to feather duster? Time will tell, but T20 has always done a good job of confounding expectations.

FINAL GROUP TABLES

	North Group	P	W	L	T	NR	Pts	NRR
1	LANCASHIRE........	14	8	2	0	4	20	0.75
2	NOTTINGHAMSHIRE....	14	6	4	0	4	16	0.33
3	DERBYSHIRE.........	14	7	5	0	2	16	0.02
4	WORCESTERSHIRE.....	14	6	5	0	3	15	0.20
5	Yorkshire............	14	4	5	1	4	13	0.33
6	Durham.............	14	5	7	0	2	12	−0.04
7	Northamptonshire.....	14	4	6	0	4	12	−0.54
8	Warwickshire	14	4	7	1	2	11	−0.46
9	Leicestershire	14	4	7	0	3	11	−0.47

	South Group	P	W	L	T	NR	Pts	NRR
1	SUSSEX	14	8	3	1	2	19	0.80
2	GLOUCESTERSHIRE....	14	7	3	1	3	18	0.24
3	MIDDLESEX	14	7	6	0	1	15	0.21
4	ESSEX	14	5	4	1	4	15	−0.46
5	Kent...............	14	6	6	0	2	14	0.00
6	Somerset	14	6	7	0	1	13	0.44
7	Hampshire	14	5	6	1	2	13	0.02
8	Surrey	14	5	7	1	1	12	−0.24
9	Glamorgan...........	14	1	8	1	4	7	−1.38

Prize money

£256,060 for winners: ESSEX.
£123,934 for runners-up: WORCESTERSHIRE.
£30,212 for losing semi-finalists: DERBYSHIRE, NOTTINGHAMSHIRE.
£4,500 for losing quarter-finalists: GLOUCESTERSHIRE, LANCASHIRE, MIDDLESEX, SUSSEX.
Match-award winners received £2,500 in the final, £1,000 in the semi-finals, £500 in the quarter-finals and £225 in the group games. The Most Valuable Player (D'Arcy Short of Durham) received £5,000.

VITALITY BLAST AVERAGES

BATTING (250 runs, strike-rate of 135)

		M	I	NO	R	HS	100	50	Avge	SR	4	6
1	A. B. de Villiers (*Middx*)	8	8	3	348	88*	0	4	69.60	**182.19**	21	20
2	T. B. Abell (*Somerset*)	13	10	2	354	101*	1	2	44.25	**177.88**	38	11
3†	M. M. Ali (*Worcs*)	7	7	2	365	121*	1	2	73.00	**171.36**	25	30
4†	E. J. G. Morgan (*Middx*)	9	9	1	341	83*	0	3	42.62	**168.81**	18	23
5†	C. S. Delport (*Essex*)	14	14	0	409	129	1	3	29.21	**167.62**	40	24
6	A. J. Finch (*Surrey*)	13	13	2	398	102*	1	1	36.18	**167.22**	33	23
7	R. S. Bopara (*Essex*)	12	11	5	291	70*	0	1	48.50	**162.56**	18	14
8	T. Banton (*Somerset*)	13	13	0	549	100	1	4	42.23	**161.47**	67	23
9	P. D. Salt (*Sussex*)	14	13	2	406	78*	0	4	36.90	**161.11**	41	16
10†	A. Lyth (*Yorks*)	10	10	0	379	69	0	3	37.90	**155.96**	45	14
11†	A. T. Carey (*Sussex*)	10	8	1	264	78	0	1	37.71	**152.60**	26	10
12	D. W. Lawrence (*Essex*)	14	13	2	386	69	0	4	35.09	**152.56**	24	21
13	W. G. Jacks (*Surrey*)	13	13	0	272	63	0	1	20.92	**151.95**	23	17
14	G. J. Maxwell (*Lancs*)	11	9	1	305	79	0	3	38.12	**150.99**	27	12
15	D. Wiese (*Sussex*)	14	10	3	284	66	0	1	40.57	**149.47**	22	13
16	Babar Azam (*Somerset*)	13	13	2	578	102*	1	4	52.54	**149.35**	60	14
17	A. J. Hose (*Warwicks*)	10	10	1	300	69	0	2	33.33	**149.25**	24	17
18†	D. J. Malan (*Middx*)	14	14	2	490	117	1	2	40.83	**147.59**	54	16
19	W. L. Madsen (*Derbys*)	14	14	4	464	69	0	4	46.40	**146.83**	52	13
20	D. J. Vilas (*Lancs*)	12	10	2	259	46	0	0	32.37	**146.32**	21	8

		M	I	NO	R	HS	100	50	Avge	SR	4	6
21	M. J. Guptill (*Worcs*) ...	9	9	1	259	86*	0	1	32.37	**145.50**	15	19
22†	C. A. Ingram (*Glam*)	12	11	1	261	50*	0	2	26.10	**145.00**	19	15
23	Z. Crawley (*Kent*)......	12	11	0	307	89	0	2	27.90	**144.81**	28	12
24	T. Köhler-Cadmore (*Yorks*)	10	10	3	435	96*	0	5	62.14	**141.23**	29	19
25†	M. A. H. Hammond (*Glos*)	13	12	0	322	63	0	2	26.83	**140.61**	39	10
26	A. D. Hales (*Notts*).....	12	12	1	418	83*	0	5	38.00	**140.26**	41	18
27	D. L. Lloyd (*Glam*)......	12	11	0	358	63	0	3	32.54	**139.84**	46	7
28†	D. J. M. Short (*Durham*)	12	12	1	483	77*	0	4	43.90	**139.59**	59	14
29	L. J. Evans (*Sussex*)	14	13	5	358	65*	0	2	44.75	**139.29**	37	9
30	J. J. Cobb (*Northants*)...	11	10	0	254	84	0	2	25.40	**137.29**	14	18
31	S. Steel (*Durham*)......	11	11	0	369	70	0	1	33.54	**136.66**	28	15
32	L. S. Livingstone (*Lancs*)	10	10	0	273	70	0	2	27.30	**135.14**	23	14

BOWLING (10 wickets, economy-rate of 7.80)

		Style	O	Dots	R	W	BB	4I	Avge	SR	ER
1	C. N. Ackermann (*Leics*).	OB	24.4	63	149	12	7-18	1	12.41	12.33	**6.04**
2	R. I. Keogh (*Northants*)..	OB	20	36	130	10	3-30	0	13.00	12.00	**6.50**
3	M. Carter (*Notts*)	OB	42	102	277	14	3-14	0	19.78	18.00	**6.59**
4	L. A. Dawson (*Hants*)	SLA	46.3	88	308	10	3-11	0	30.80	27.90	**6.62**
5	Imad Wasim (*Notts*)......	SLA	25	53	166	10	2-21	0	16.60	15.00	**6.64**
6	B. A. C. Howell (*Glos*) ..	RM	26	62	173	10	5-18	1	17.30	15.60	**6.65**
7	M. M. Ali (*Worcs*).......	OB	26	54	174	11	4-18	1	15.81	14.18	**6.69**
8	R. Rampaul (*Derbys*).....	RFM	54	135	362	23	3-17	0	15.73	14.08	**6.70**
9	J. W. Shutt (*Yorks*)......	OB	24	44	164	10	5-11	1	16.40	14.40	**6.83**
10	A. L. Hughes (*Derbys*)...	RM	36	69	249	10	3-13	0	24.90	21.60	**6.91**
11	N. J. Rimmington (*D'ham*)	RFM	43.5	89	305	16	3-15	0	19.06	16.43	**6.95**
12	L. Trevaskis (*Durham*) ..	SLA	40.1	83	281	12	3-16	0	23.41	20.08	**6.99**
13	L. Wood (*Notts*).........	LFM	27.3	65	193	11	3-16	0	17.54	15.00	**7.01**
14	M. S. Crane (*Hants*).....	LB	26	49	183	11	3-22	0	16.63	14.18	**7.03**
15	M. J. J. Critchley (*Derbys*)	LB	44.1	81	315	17	4-36	1	18.52	15.58	**7.13**
16	G. G. White (*Northants*) .	SLA	38	62	275	10	2-18	0	27.50	22.80	**7.23**
17	G. J. Batty (*Surrey*)	OB	41.5	71	304	13	3-7	0	23.38	19.30	**7.26**
18	J. S. Patel (*Warwicks*) ...	OB	45	85	327	11	2-21	0	29.72	24.54	**7.26**
19	D. A. Payne (*Glos*)......	LFM	47	117	347	16	3-32	0	21.68	17.62	**7.38**
20	Mohammad Amir (*Essex*)	LFM	27	70	201	10	4-29	1	20.10	16.20	**7.44**
21	R. S. Bopara (*Essex*)	RM	35	64	261	12	3-18	0	21.75	17.50	**7.45**
22	M. W. Parkinson (*Lancs*).	LB	41	71	307	21	4-30	1	14.61	11.71	**7.48**
23	I. Qayyum (*Kent*)........	SLA	30.1	43	226	12	5-21	1	18.83	15.08	**7.49**
24	C. F. Parkinson (*Leics*) ..	SLA	41	80	309	12	2-17	0	25.75	20.50	**7.53**
25	A. J. Tye (*Glos*)	RFM	49.3	120	376	15	2-23	0	25.06	19.80	**7.59**
26	L. S. Livingstone (*Lancs*)	LB	28	53	215	14	3-21	0	15.35	12.00	**7.67**
27	A. F. Milne (*Kent*)......	RF	31.3	76	242	10	3-21	0	24.20	18.90	**7.68**
28	M. T. C. Waller (*Somerset*)	LB	46.5	76	361	13	3-19	0	27.76	21.61	**7.70**
29	O. E. Robinson (*Sussex*) .	RFM	28.4	75	223	11	4-15	1	20.27	15.63	**7.77**

LEADING WICKETKEEPERS

Dismissals	M			Dismissals	M	
11 (8 ct, 3 st)	14	O. B. Cox (*Worcs*)		9 (5 ct, 4 st)	14	A. J. A. Wheater (*Essex*)
10 (9 ct, 1 st)	12	C. B. Cooke (*Glam*)		8 (6 ct, 2 st)	12	O.G. Robinson (*Kent*)
10 (7 ct, 3 st)	13	J. R. Bracey (*Glos*)		8 (4 ct, 4 st)	13	D. J. Vilas (*Lancs*)
9 (7 ct, 2 st)	12	T. J. Moores (*Notts*)		8 (5 ct, 3 st)	13	L. D. McManus (*Hants*)
9 (9 ct)	14	D. Smit (*Derbys*)		8 (5 ct, 3 st)	14	J. A. Simpson (*Middx*)

LEADING FIELDERS

Ct	M		Ct	M	
13	14	P. D. Salt (*Sussex*)	10	12	B. M. Duckett (*Notts*)
12	13	A. J .Tye (*Glos*)	10	13	M. Klinger (*Glos*)
12	14	S. R. Harmer (*Essex*)	10	13	A. M. Lilley (*Leics*)
12	14	W. L. Madsen (*Derbys*)	10	13	M. T. C. Waller (*Somerset*)
11	13	T. B. Abell (*Somerset*)	10	14	B. A. Godleman (*Derbys*)
10	10	H. G. Kuhn (*Kent*)			

NORTH GROUP

DERBYSHIRE

At Chesterfield, July 20. **Derbyshire won by five wickets.** ‡**Yorkshire 164-8** (20 overs) (J. A. Tattersall 39*, J. A. Thompson 50; M. R. J. Watt 4-19); **Derbyshire 166-5** (19.1 overs) (B. A. Godleman 70*, J. L. du Plooy 30). *PoM:* B. A. Godleman. *Attendance:* 4,331. *County debuts:* D. I. Stevens (Derbyshire); N. Pooran (Yorkshire). *Billy Godleman's 70* anchored a composed Derbyshire display. Jordan Thompson (50 off 27 balls, with five sixes) had given Yorkshire a late lift with a maiden first-team half-century, but it wasn't enough to fully repair the damage done by Scotland slow-left armer Mark Watt, who helped reduce them to 77-6. Darren Stevens, on loan from Kent, became the second-oldest player to make his Derbyshire debut: at 43 years 81 days, he was behind only William Jervis, who was club president when he played his only match, aged 46 years 181 days, in 1873. Stevens bowled one over for 12, and was out for two.*

At Derby, July 26 (floodlit). **Nottinghamshire won by 27 runs. Nottinghamshire 198-5** (20 overs) (A. D. Hales 63, B. M. Duckett 64); ‡**Derbyshire 171-8** (20 overs) (L. M. Reece 61; H. F. Gurney 5-30). *PoM:* H. F. Gurney. *Attendance:* 4,190. *County debut:* Imad Wasim (Nottinghamshire). *A stand of 92 in nine overs for Nottinghamshire's second wicket between Alex Hales (63 off 42) and Ben Duckett (64 off 40) left Derbyshire needing a daunting 199. Thanks to Harry Gurney's first T20 five-for (plus his run-out of Alex Hughes), they fell well short. Luis Reece top-scored with 61 off 42.*

At Derby, July 28. **Derbyshire v Lancashire. Abandoned.**

At Derby, August 9 (floodlit). **Durham won by seven runs.** ‡**Durham 160-5** (20 overs) (D. J. M. Short 68, S. Steel 47); **Derbyshire 153-7** (20 overs) (B. A. Godleman 39, W. L. Madsen 30, F. J. Hudson-Prentice 31*; L. Trevaskis 3-16). *PoM:* L. Trevaskis. *Attendance:* 2,738. *A stand of 114 in 13.3 overs between Durham openers D'Arcy Short, whose 68 included 11 fours and a six, and Scott Steel appeared to pave the way for a high-scoring contest. But the weather worsened and, on a slow pitch, Derbyshire could never quite keep up with the rate. Six reached double figures in the chase, but none made more than Godleman's 39, as slow left-armer Liam Trevaskis produced a thrifty 3-16.*

At Derby, August 13 (floodlit). **Derbyshire won by 20 runs.** ‡**Derbyshire 181-2** (20 overs) (L. M. Reece 51, B. A. Godleman 92); **Worcestershire 161-7** (20 overs) (M. J. Guptill 45, C. J. Ferguson 37; M. J. J. Critchley 4-36). *PoM:* B. A. Godleman. *Attendance:* 1,966. *Leg-spinner Matt Critchley celebrated his 23rd birthday with a T20-best 4-36, to stifle the Worcestershire reply, after overseas duo Martin Guptill and captain Callum Ferguson had taken them to a promising 86-1 in the 11th over. Earlier, Godleman also managed a competition-best, falling in the final over for 92 from 67 balls; he and Reece had shared a county-record opening stand of 135. Derbyshire moved into the top four in a tight group.*

At Derby, August 15 (floodlit). **Leicestershire won by 55 runs.** ‡**Leicestershire 149-7** (20 overs) (M. J. Cosgrove 38); **Derbyshire 94** (18.2 overs) (C. N. Ackermann 3-9, G. T. Griffiths 3-14). *PoM:* C. N. Ackermann. *Attendance:* 2,829. *Derbyshire's batting imploded against the off-spin of Colin Ackermann and the seam of Gavin Griffiths to cast their opponents' own faltering effort with the bat in a more generous light. All Leicestershire's top order had reached double figures (though only two got to 20), while six of Derbyshire's top seven couldn't make ten, as they slumped to 28-6.*

At Derby, August 23 (floodlit). **Derbyshire won by nine wickets.** ‡**Northamptonshire 100** (18 overs) (A. L. Hughes 3-13); **Derbyshire 101-1** (17.1 overs) (W. L. Madsen 51*). *PoM:* W. L. Madsen. *Attendance:* 2,547. *Derbyshire stayed in quarter-final contention after an alarming Northamptonshire collapse, in which their last seven tumbled for 17 in 32 balls. Fynn Hudson-*

Prentice (2–10–2–2) had removed the openers, before Hughes (4–13–13–3) hastened the visitors' demise. Derbyshire strolled home, Wayne Madsen hitting 51* in a second-wicket stand with Godleman (28*) of 67*.

Derbyshire away matches

July 24: lost to Warwickshire by 49 runs.
July 31: lost to Worcestershire by two wickets.
August 2: beat Northamptonshire by six wickets.
August 11: beat Yorkshire by 55 runs.

August 16: no result v Nottinghamshire.
August 25: beat Leicestershire by nine wickets.
August 26: beat Lancashire by 11 runs.

DURHAM

At Chester-le-Street, July 19 (floodlit). **Durham won by seven runs. Durham 148-4** (20 overs) (D. J. M. Short 46, S. Steel 37); ‡**Northamptonshire 141-9** (20 overs) (A. M. Rossington 47, R. I. Keogh 30*). *PoM:* D. J. M. Short. *Attendance:* 6,078. *County debuts:* D. J. M. Short (Durham); Fahim Ashraf, D. Pretorius (Northamptonshire). *Australian D'Arcy Short made an immediate impact on his Durham debut. First he scored 46, as the hosts made a competitive 148 on a grudging surface. Then he took 2-19, including top-scorer Adam Rossington, with his left-arm wrist-spin to help seal a narrow win – despite a late flurry from Rob Keogh.*

At Chester-le-Street, July 31 (floodlit). **Durham won by eight wickets. Leicestershire 142-7** (20 overs) (C. N. Ackermann 52); ‡**Durham 143-2** (14.4 overs) (D. J. M. Short 70, G. Clark 59*). *PoM:* D. J. M. Short. *Attendance:* 4,069. *Five days after hitting Leicestershire's bowlers for 77* off 36 balls at Grace Road, Short repeated the dose – this time 70 off 36 as he shared another century opening stand with Graham Clark (59* off 38). Earlier, Short had claimed another tidy two-for (he later picked up his third match award in five), as Leicestershire were limited to 142, built around a half-century from Colin Ackermann.*

At Chester-le-Street, August 2 (floodlit). **Lancashire won by five wickets.** ‡**Durham 139** (19.5 overs) (G. Clark 30, A. Z. Lees 39; M. W. Parkinson 4-30); **Lancashire 140-5** (18.5 overs) (L. S. Livingstone 70). *PoM:* L. S. Livingstone. *Attendance:* 7,805. *Matt Parkinson's leg-spin tormented the batsmen, notching four wickets as Durham slipped from 103-4 in the 14th over. Liam Livingstone, who took two, then showed off his power, smashing 70 off 48. Dane Vilas ensured a mid-innings wobble would not cost Lancashire, who pulled further away at the top of the group.*

At Chester-le-Street, August 11. **Durham v Nottinghamshire. Abandoned.**

At Chester-le-Street, August 15 (floodlit). **Worcestershire won by three runs. Worcestershire 117-7** (20 overs) (M. J. Potts 3-22); ‡**Durham 114-6** (20 overs) (D. J. M. Short 42, S. Steel 31). *PoM:* P. R. Brown. *Attendance:* 4,062. *Durham squandered a glorious opportunity, after an opening stand of 79 between Short and Scott Steel left them needing 39 off 51 balls. But Ed Barnard removed Steel, and next over Daryl Mitchell got rid of Clark and Short. Durham panicked against tight bowling, and failed to hit another boundary, with Pat Brown easily defending nine off the last. Worcestershire had struggled to make headway, too, with only Tom Fell (28 off 24) and Ross Whiteley (24* off 19) finding any timing; Matty Potts took a career-best 3-22.*

At Chester-le-Street, August 23 (floodlit). **Yorkshire won by 14 runs. Yorkshire 146-6** (20 overs) (T. Köhler-Cadmore 52, J. A. Leaning 39; N. J. Rimmington 3-16); ‡**Durham 132** (19 overs) (S. Steel 49; J. W. Shutt 5-11, A. Lyth 3-19). *PoM:* J. W. Shutt. *Attendance:* 9,130. *County debut:* H. R. D. Adair (Durham). *Another collapse cost Durham dear, after Short and Steel had begun with 70 inside eight overs. The damage was done by off-spinner Jack Shutt, who finished with 4–14–11–5 – figures bettered in the 2019 Blast only by Leicestershire's Colin Ackermann – as the last eight fell for 26. Adam Lyth, another off-spinner, picked up a career-best, with 3-19. Yorkshire's total centred on a half-century from Tom Köhler-Cadmore.*

At Chester-le-Street, August 27 (floodlit). **Warwickshire won by seven wickets** (DLS). **Durham 151-5** (19 overs) (D. J. M. Short 50, H. R. D. Adair 32); ‡**Warwickshire 153-3** (18.5 overs) (E. J. Pollock 77, D. P. Sibley 33). *PoM:* E. J. Pollock. *Attendance:* 3,521. *Ed Pollock put a disappointing competition behind him, hitting 77 off 45 balls to end Durham's hopes of a quarter-final place, and lift Warwickshire off the bottom. Short kickstarted the game with four fours in 19-year-old George Garrett's opening over, going on to his fourth fifty of a prolific tournament. Pollock and*

Dominic Sibley began with 83 in eight overs in reply, before Warwickshire edged home with a ball to spare in a game reduced to 19 a side by rain.

Durham away matches

July 21: lost to Lancashire by 72 runs.
July 26: beat Leicestershire by nine wickets.
July 28: lost to Worcestershire by nine wickets.
August 7: lost to Northamptonshire by 21 runs.

August 9: beat Derbyshire by seven runs.
August 16: no result v Yorkshire.
August 30: beat Nottinghamshire by 47 runs.

LANCASHIRE

At Manchester, July 21. **Lancashire won by 72 runs.** ‡**Lancashire 189-3** (20 overs) (S. J. Croft 65*, G. J. Maxwell 58); **Durham 117** (16.4 overs) (S. Steel 58; M. W. Parkinson 3-30). *PoM:* G. J. Maxwell. *Attendance:* 13,710. *Lancashire became the first county to use a hybrid pitch – natural turf, plus 5% twisted yarn for greater durability – in a competitive match, and marked the occasion with a comfortable win. Alex Davies hit Brydon Carse on to Brian Statham Way, before Glenn Maxwell deposited Ben Raine on to the TV gantry in the pavilion. Maxwell (58 off 33) added 92 with Steven Croft, who batted through the innings for 65*. Durham never came close; only Scott Steel passed 12.*

At Manchester, July 26 (floodlit). **Lancashire won by 21 runs (DLS).** ‡**Worcestershire 130-9** (20 overs) (M. J. Guptill 37; L. S. Livingstone 3-21); **Lancashire 71-1** (9 overs). *PoM:* L. S. Livingstone. *Attendance:* 10,531. *Lancashire's bowlers restricted Worcestershire to an inadequate score, and their batsmen were well ahead of the rate when the rain came. Having dismissed three of the top five, Liam Livingstone then hit two sixes. The visitors' only highlight was provided by his dismissal: Ed Barnard sprinted 15 yards from deep square leg to hold a diving catch.*

At Manchester, August 3 (floodlit). **Lancashire won by three runs.** ‡**Lancashire 151-6** (20 overs) (G. J. Maxwell 73, D. J. Vilas 46); **Nottinghamshire 148-9** (20 overs) (S. R. Patel 34, D. T. Christian 41*; M. W. Parkinson 3-22). *PoM:* G. J. Maxwell. *Attendance:* 9,712. *Luke Wood struck twice in the first over, and Imad Wasim in the fourth, to leave Lancashire 14-3. But Maxwell and Dane Vilas added 107 in 11, a fifth-wicket club record (Maxwell later equalled another, holding four catches as an outfielder). Nottinghamshire's batsmen lacked their shrewdness, although Dan Christian's three leg-side sixes off Saqib Mahmood in the penultimate over meant they needed 12 off James Faulkner's last. He responded with two wickets, and conceded only eight, as Lancashire maintained their unbeaten record.*

At Manchester, August 9 (floodlit). **Lancashire v Yorkshire. Abandoned.**

At Manchester, August 16 (floodlit). **Lancashire v Warwickshire. Abandoned.**

At Manchester, August 26. **Derbyshire won by 11 runs.** ‡**Derbyshire 162-3** (20 overs) (B. A. Godleman 57, W. L. Madsen 69); **Lancashire 151-9** (20 overs) (L. S. Livingstone 58; R. Rampaul 3-19). *PoM:* W. L. Madsen. *Attendance:* 14,752. *Derbyshire earned a quarter-final spot with a third successive victory, seeing off a Lancashire team already assured of a home tie in the last eight. Billy Godleman and Wayne Madsen, whose 69 needed only 39 balls, put on 112 for Derbyshire's second wicket. At 99-3 in the 13th over of the chase, Lancashire were in the hunt. Livingstone, however, was caught behind off Alex Hughes, and two balls later Keaton Jennings fell to Matt Critchley. Ravi Rampaul turned the screw in the final over.*

At Manchester, August 30 (floodlit). **Lancashire won by five wickets.** ‡**Leicestershire 142-9** (20 overs) (M. J. Cosgrove 39); **Lancashire 143-5** (18.4 overs) (A. L. Davies 39). *PoM:* G. J. Maxwell. *Attendance:* 15,196. *Lancashire clinched top place in the North Group with a routine win in front of a record Old Trafford crowd for a non-Roses T20 match. Mark Cosgrove's 39 off 19 balls had given Leicestershire a solid start but, of the rest, only Arron Lilley (28 off 20) threatened to sustain it, and four batsmen were run out. Lancashire openers Davies and Livingstone replied with 54 in five overs, and victory came with eight balls to spare.*

Lancashire away matches

July 19: no result v Leicestershire.
July 25: beat Yorkshire by nine runs.
July 28: no result v Derbyshire.
August 2: beat Durham by five wickets.

August 11: lost to Warwickshire by 15 runs.
August 14: beat Northamptonshire by eight wickets.
August 25: beat Worcestershire by 25 runs.

LEICESTERSHIRE

At Leicester, July 19 (floodlit). **Lancashire v ‡Leicestershire. Abandoned.**

At Leicester, July 23 (floodlit). **Yorkshire won by 54 runs.** Yorkshire 255-2 (20 overs) (A. Lyth 69, T. Köhler-Cadmore 96*, N. Pooran 67); ‡Leicestershire 201-4 (20 overs) (M. J. Cosgrove 31, A. M. Lilley 47, L. J. Hill 49*). *PoM:* T. Köhler-Cadmore. *Attendance:* 2,824. *With the boundaries brought in, Yorkshire smashed their second-highest T20 total. It included 19 sixes, eight by Tom Köhler-Cadmore, who needed only 54 balls for his 96*, and put on 116 in ten overs with fellow opener Adam Lyth (69 in 35, with four sixes). Yorkshire's West Indian recruit Nicholas Pooran was also in explosive form, hitting six sixes in his 28-ball 67. Leicestershire responded with 12 of their own, yet were never on terms; the match total of 31 equalled the domestic record, set the previous week by Essex and Surrey.*

At Leicester, July 26 (floodlit). **Durham won by nine wickets.** ‡Leicestershire 158 (20 overs) (M. J. Cosgrove 36, C. N. Ackermann 58; M. J. Potts 3-28, N. J. Rimmington 3-26); Durham 161-1 (11.1 overs) (D. J. M. Short 77*, S. Steel 70). *PoM:* D. J. M. Short. *Attendance:* 2,834. *Durham inflicted a third successive defeat on Leicestershire with insulting ease. The 20-year-old Scott Steel raced to his second fifty, in his third T20 appearance, in 19 balls. D'Arcy Short was more refined, but scarcely less explosive, hitting 77* from 36, with six sixes. Matty Potts had polished off Leicestershire's stuttering innings with a hat-trick.*

At Leicester, August 7 (floodlit). **Leicestershire won by 55 runs.** ‡Leicestershire 189-6 (20 overs) (H. J. Swindells 63, L. J. Hill 58; H. J. H. Brookes 3-26); Warwickshire 134 (17.4 overs) (S. R. Hain 61, A. J. Hose 34; C. N. Ackermann 7-18). *PoM:* C. N. Ackermann. *Attendance:* 3,193. *Colin Ackermann collected the world's best T20 figures on an extraordinary evening. His 7-18 bettered Arul Suppiah's 6-5 for Somerset against Glamorgan in 2011. Ackermann, who had only twice taken more than two wickets in a T20 innings, found turn, and was assisted by brainless Warwickshire batting: three of his victims were bowled swinging across the line, and four caught. "It was the first time it has turned at Grace Road, so I tried to use my height and get a bit of bounce," he said. Harry Swindells and Lewis Hill had added 62 for Leicestershire's fourth wicket.*

At Leicester, August 9 (floodlit). **No result (DLS).** ‡Leicestershire 137-9 (20 overs) (M. J. Cosgrove 32, H. E. Dearden 37; B. W. Sanderson 4-28, D. Pretorius 3-17); Northamptonshire 16-0 (2.4 overs). *Rain saved Leicestershire from almost certain defeat. Excellent bowling from Ben Sanderson and Dwaine Pretorius had put Northamptonshire in the driving seat, before their target was revised to 133 in 19 overs. Fourteen more balls were needed for a result.*

At Leicester, August 23 (floodlit). **Nottinghamshire won by seven wickets.** ‡Leicestershire 161-8 (20 overs) (H. J. Swindells 61, C. N. Ackermann 42; L. J. Fletcher 3-17); Nottinghamshire 165-3 (18.5 overs) (A. D. Hales 60, B. M. Duckett 47). *PoM:* A. D. Hales. *Attendance:* 4,704. *Nottinghamshire remained on course for the quarter-finals with a comfortable victory. Alex Hales and Ben Duckett put on 96 for the second wicket to ensure they could survive a stumble when they were dismissed in successive overs. Leicestershire had reached 118-2 in the 15th, before fading, as Luke Fletcher celebrated his return to the team with three wickets.*

At Leicester, August 25. **Derbyshire won by nine wickets.** ‡Leicestershire 124-9 (20 overs) (M. J. Cosgrove 45); Derbyshire 128-1 (18.3 overs) (B. A. Godleman 52*, W. L. Madsen 37*). *PoM:* B. A. Godleman. *Attendance:* 3,220. *Derbyshire took a decisive step towards the last eight with an easy win, built on Billy Godleman's third fifty of the tournament. Leicestershire had been placed at 59-2 from the powerplay, but folded after Mark Cosgrove – who had looked in great touch – ran himself out. Godleman and Luis Reece took 24 off the third over to launch the reply.*

Leicestershire away matches

July 21: lost to Warwickshire by seven wickets.
July 27: beat Nottinghamshire by 21 runs.
July 31: lost to Durham by eight wickets.
August 4: beat Worcestershire by 33 runs.

August 15: beat Derbyshire by 55 runs.
August 16: no result v Northamptonshire.
August 30: lost to Lancashire by five wickets.

NORTHAMPTONSHIRE

At Northampton, July 26 (floodlit). **Northamptonshire won by 21 runs** (DLS). **Northamptonshire 155-6** (20 overs) (R. I. Keogh 59*, A. G. Wakely 38); ‡**Warwickshire 111-8** (16 overs). *PoM:* R. I. Keogh. *Attendance: 5,246. Northamptonshire won their first home 20-over game since August 2017, thanks to Rob Keogh's career-best 59*, his first T20 fifty. In front of an excellent crowd, they had been in trouble at 36-3, before Keogh, given a rare chance up the order, and Alex Wakely added 84. Set a revised 133 in 16 overs, Warwickshire looked threatening only when Sam Hain was hitting 29 off 23.*

At Northampton, July 28. **Northamptonshire v Yorkshire. Abandoned.**

At Northampton, August 2 (floodlit). **Derbyshire won by six wickets.** ‡**Northamptonshire 180-5** (20 overs) (A. M. Rossington 50, J. J. Cobb 84; R. Rampaul 3-17); **Derbyshire 184-4** (18 overs) (L. M. Reece 60, W. L. Madsen 59*). *PoM:* W. L. Madsen. *Attendance: 5,340. Derbyshire shrugged off a challenging total to win comfortably with a beautifully paced chase. Luis Reece struck three sixes in his 60 off 37, and Wayne Madsen, bristling with aggression from the start, saw them home with something to spare. Northamptonshire captain Josh Cobb had hit seven sixes in his 50-ball stay, after Adam Rossington began with a 34-ball 50.*

At Northampton, August 7 (floodlit). **Northamptonshire won by 21 runs. Northamptonshire 145-6** (20 overs) (A. G. Wakely 47*, D. Pretorius 37; M. J. Potts 3-31); ‡**Durham 124-8** (20 overs) (P. S. P. Handscomb 65*; R. I. Keogh 3-30). *PoM:* A. G. Wakely. *Attendance: 5,330. On a pitch that encouraged the spinners and made life hard for batsmen, Northamptonshire clinched a victory that looked unlikely when they spluttered to 145-6. Wakely's 47* off 35 proved crucial, then Keogh's off-breaks brought him three key wickets. Peter Handscomb passed 1,000 T20 runs, scoring more than half Durham's meagre total.*

At Northampton, August 14 (floodlit). **Lancashire won by eight wickets. Northamptonshire 157-7** (20 overs) (A. M. Rossington 40, D. Pretorius 38; J. P. Faulkner 3-36); ‡**Lancashire 160-2** (18.3 overs) (A. L. Davies 75*, D. J. Vilas 31*). *PoM:* A. L. Davies. *Attendance: 3,211. Alex Davies illuminated a damp, miserable evening with a match-winning innings that strengthened Lancashire's grip at the top of the North Group. He hit 75* off 58, and received staunch support. In contrast, the Northamptonshire batsmen struggled to find any momentum, Dwaine Pretorius coming closest with three sixes in his 22-ball 38.*

At Northampton, August 16 (floodlit). **Northamptonshire v Leicestershire. Abandoned.**

At Northampton, August 30 (floodlit). **Northamptonshire won by seven wickets.** ‡**Worcestershire 188-5** (20 overs) (M. H. Wessels 45, M. M. Ali 51, O. B. Cox 44*); **Northamptonshire 189-3** (18.5 overs) (A. M. Rossington 54, J. J. Cobb 62, D. Pretorius 50*). *PoM:* J. J. Cobb. *Attendance: 5,244. Worcestershire were denied a home quarter-final by a superb display of hitting by Northamptonshire. Cobb caught the eye with seven sixes in his 32-ball 62; four came in an over from Ed Barnard, one sailing out of the ground. There were also destructive half-centuries from Rossington (54 off 30, with four sixes) and Pretorius (50* off 36, with three). Earlier, Moeen Ali (51 off 31) smashed one of his four sixes on to the roof of the Ken Turner Stand.*

Northamptonshire away matches

July 19: lost to Durham by seven runs.
July 24: lost to Nottinghamshire by seven wickets.
August 9: no result v Leicestershire.
August 11: no result v Worcestershire.

August 23: lost to Derbyshire by nine wickets.
August 25: beat Warwickshire by four wickets.
August 29: lost to Yorkshire by 80 runs.

NOTTINGHAMSHIRE

At Nottingham, July 18 (floodlit). **Worcestershire won by 28 runs.** ‡**Worcestershire 161-6** (20 overs) (M. M. Ali 32, E. G. Barnard 42*); **Nottinghamshire 133-9** (20 overs) (A. D. Hales 52; M. M. Ali 4-18). *PoM:* E. G. Barnard. *Attendance:* 12,613. *Ed Barnard's 42* from 19 balls lifted defending champions Worcestershire from 107-6 with four overs left to a total that proved beyond Nottinghamshire on a slow pitch. Alex Hales, in his first competitive match for over nine weeks, hit 52 from 34 balls, following limp dismissals for Joe Clarke and Ben Duckett. But, after Moeen Ali – who had earlier hit 32 – tore out the middle order with 4-4 in 11 balls, Nottinghamshire's fate was sealed.*

At Nottingham, July 24 (floodlit). **Nottinghamshire won by seven wickets.** ‡**Northamptonshire 152-8** (20 overs) (J. J. Cobb 36, D. Pretorius 34; D. T. Christian 3-32); **Nottinghamshire 155-3** (18.1 overs) (J. M. Clarke 45, A. D. Hales 33). *PoM:* D. T. Christian. *Attendance:* 13,961. *Watched by a record crowd for a midweek domestic match at Trent Bridge, Northamptonshire recovered from 82-6 to set a stiffer challenge than had seemed likely, with Graeme White hitting 17 off the 19th over, bowled by Dan Christian. However, Clarke and Hales established a winning platform, putting on 79 in 8.5 overs, and the target was passed with 11 balls to spare, when Tom Moores heaved Nathan Buck over the rope. Nottinghamshire's victory, their first in the competition, maintained their unbeaten group-stage record in ten matches against Northamptonshire.*

At Nottingham, July 27. **Leicestershire won by 21 runs.** **Leicestershire 125-3** (11 overs) (M. J. Cosgrove 37*, A. M. Lilley 66); ‡**Nottinghamshire 104-6** (11 overs) (T. J. Moores 44*). *PoM:* A. M. Lilley. *Attendance:* 7,828. *In a match reduced to 11 overs a side, Arron Lilley's 30-ball 66, his maiden T20 century, inspired Leicestershire to their first win. He put on 86 in seven overs with Mark Cosgrove, who batted through the innings for 37*, facing only 23 of its 66 deliveries. Nottinghamshire fell behind the rate after losing Hales and Duckett in quick succession and, despite five sixes from Moores (44* off 19), finished well short.*

At Nottingham, August 2 (floodlit). **Nottinghamshire won by 71 runs.** ‡**Nottinghamshire 184-4** (20 overs) (J. M. Clarke 50, T. J. Moores 69); **Warwickshire 113** (17.3 overs) (L. Wood 3-16, M. Carter 3-14). *PoM:* M. Carter. *Attendance:* 12,060. *Moores made Warwickshire suffer after Liam Banks at long-off dropped him off Will Rhodes on 16, smashing six sixes in a 38-ball 69. He added 55 in 27 with Christian to help Nottinghamshire set an imposing total, before the visitors lost their last nine for 63 in ten overs. Nottinghamshire's three slow bowlers offered few scoring opportunities, off-spinner Matt Carter taking a competition-best 3-14.*

At Nottingham, August 16 (floodlit). **Nottinghamshire v Derbyshire. Abandoned.**

At Nottingham, August 25. **Nottinghamshire won by three runs.** ‡**Nottinghamshire 148-7** (20 overs) (J. M. Clarke 50, J. D. Libby 35, D. T. Christian 31*; A. Lyth 5-31); **Yorkshire 145-7** (20 overs) (A. Lyth 48). *PoM:* M. Carter. *Attendance:* 13,737. *Adam Lyth shone with ball and bat, but couldn't prevent Yorkshire's exit from the competition, as Nottinghamshire advanced to the last eight. Two days after taking 3-19 with his off-breaks against Durham, he claimed 5-31, equalling in two matches his career haul from his previous 109. And Yorkshire needed only 50 off 39 with eight wickets in hand when he fell to Harry Gurney for 48. The equation boiled down to six off five balls, but Gurney removed Will Fraine, then limited Jordan Thompson to two from the last four. Nottinghamshire's own innings was built on a scratchy 50 by Clarke, and needed late impetus from Christian.*

At Nottingham, August 30 (floodlit). **Durham won by 47 runs.** ‡**Durham 171-8** (20 overs) (S. Steel 45, D. J. M. Short 36, G. Clark 41; D. T. Christian 3-26); **Nottinghamshire 124** (17.2 overs) (T. J. Moores 33; N. J. Rimmington 3-15). *PoM:* N. J. Rimmington. *Attendance:* 13,078. *Scott Steel and D'Arcy Short hit 70 off the first 37 balls as Durham took control while Graham Clark (41 off 24) provided a strong finish. Needing victory to secure a home quarter-final, Nottinghamshire lost Clarke in the first over, and never recovered.*

Nottinghamshire away matches

July 19: no result v Yorkshire.
July 26: beat Derbyshire by 27 runs.
August 3: lost to Lancashire by three runs.
August 9: beat Warwickshire by 28 runs (DLS).

August 11: no result v Durham.
August 23: beat Leicestershire by seven wickets.
August 28: no result v Worcestershire.

WARWICKSHIRE

At Birmingham, July 21. **Warwickshire won by seven wickets. Leicestershire 115-9** (20 overs) (F. H. Edwards 4-22); ‡**Warwickshire 117-3** (14.5 overs) (S. R. Hain 31, A. C. Agar 41*). *PoM:* F. H. Edwards. *Attendance:* 11,255. *County debuts:* A. C. Agar, F. H. Edwards (Warwickshire). *Signed on loan from Hampshire before the washed-out match against Worcestershire two days earlier, Fidel Edwards made a spectacular start, claiming three wickets in his first over – including Neil Dexter, bowled by the first ball of the match. After Harry Dearden and Colin Ackermann rebuilt, Edwards returned to grab a fourth. Australia's Ashton Agar, Warwickshire's other debutant, top-scored as they cantered home.*

At Birmingham, July 24 (floodlit). **Warwickshire won by 49 runs. Warwickshire 205-5** (20 overs) (S. R. Hain 85, A. J. Hose 69; R. Rampaul 3-21); ‡**Derbyshire 156-9** (20 overs) (J. L. du Plooy 70). *PoM:* S. R. Hain. *Attendance:* 7,230. *Sam Hain and Adam Hose (69 from 35 balls) shared 113 from 65 to lay the foundations for Warwickshire's highest total of the season. Edwards again struck an early blow, while Leus du Plooy fought a lone hand, with 70 from 43. Derbyshire were choked by the miserly spin of Jeetan Patel (1-17) and Agar (1-22).*

At Birmingham, August 9 (floodlit). **Nottinghamshire won by 28 runs (DLS). Warwickshire 119-9** (20 overs) (S. R. Hain 48; L. Wood 3-24); ‡**Nottinghamshire 86-2** (11 overs) (J. M. Clarke 47*). *PoM:* J. M. Clarke. *Attendance:* 7,046. *County debut:* C. J. Green (Warwickshire). *Just 18 hours after concluding a match for Toronto Nationals across the Atlantic, the Australian off-spinner Chris Green made his Warwickshire debut. But he went wicketless from two overs and scored only six as Nottinghamshire easily won a rain-affected match. The Warwickshire innings had contained no sixes and just eight fours; with three wickets, Luke Wood was the pick of the bowlers. Joe Clarke made sure Nottinghamshire were ahead before the drizzle got heavier.*

At Birmingham, August 11. **Warwickshire won by 15 runs.** ‡**Warwickshire 179-6** (20 overs) (D. P. Sibley 51, A. J. Hose 65; M. W. Parkinson 3-23, L. S. Livingstone 3-38); **Lancashire 164-7** (20 overs) (K. K. Jennings 35, G. J. Maxwell 79). *PoM:* A. J. Hose. *Attendance:* 7,675. *Dom Sibley, solidly, and Hose, spectacularly, with seven sixes, pushed Warwickshire to an above-par total on a used pitch, and helped inflict a first defeat on group leaders. Needing 180, the visitors slumped to 28-3 in the sixth, but Keaton Jennings and Glenn Maxwell put on 107, and they were in the game until Will Rhodes bowled Maxwell for a 39-ball 79.*

At Birmingham, August 23 (floodlit). **Worcestershire won by nine wickets.** ‡**Warwickshire 184-5** (20 overs) (S. R. Hain 46, A. J. Hose 48, M. J. Lamb 35); **Worcestershire 188-1** (18.4 overs) (M. H. Wessels 65*, M. M. Ali 85*). *PoM:* M. M. Ali. *Attendance:* 16,194. *Moeen Ali, dropped from England's Ashes squad, took out his frustrations on the Warwickshire attack. After scoring hundreds in both white-ball competitions at Edgbaston in 2018, he hit an imperious 85* off 46 balls, with six sixes, in a partnership of 138* – a record for the fixture – with Riki Wessels.*

At Birmingham, August 25. **Northamptonshire won by four wickets.** ‡**Warwickshire 150-6** (20 overs) (W. M. H. Rhodes 45); **Northamptonshire 153-6** (19.4 overs) (R. E. Levi 44, J. J. Cobb 42). *PoM:* J. J. Cobb. *Attendance:* 6,201. *Fahim Ashraf steered Northamptonshire over the line with two balls to spare after they briefly looked like messing up their chase. Richard Levi had made his highest score of the competition to launch the pursuit of 151, and Josh Cobb pushed them into a strong position, before they lost four for 18. Warwickshire had struggled on a pitch that helped the spinners, but Rhodes gave them something to bowl at.*

At Birmingham, August 30 (floodlit). **Yorkshire won by 19 runs. Yorkshire 200-3** (20 overs) (T. Köhler-Cadmore 94*, A. Lyth 42); ‡**Warwickshire 181-5** (20 overs) (D. P. Sibley 37, S. R. Hain 64*). *PoM:* T. Köhler-Cadmore. *Attendance:* 11,272. *Yorkshire's Tom Köhler-Cadmore lit up a dead rubber with 94* off 63, and shared a record opening partnership for this fixture of 102 with Adam Lyth. David Willey hit three sixes. Hain's 64* completed his most productive T20 season (459), but he lacked support.*

Warwickshire away matches

July 19: no result v Worcestershire.
July 26: lost to Northamptonshire by 21 runs (DLS).
August 2: lost to Nottinghamshire by 71 runs.
August 4: tied with Yorkshire.

August 7: lost to Leicestershire by 55 runs.
August 16: no result v Lancashire.
August 27: beat Durham by seven wickets (DLS).

WORCESTERSHIRE

At Worcester, July 19. **Worcestershire v Warwickshire. Abandoned.**

At Worcester, July 28. **Worcestershire won by nine wickets. Durham 181-8** (20 overs) (A. Z. Lees 44, P. S. P. Handscomb 37); ‡**Worcestershire 184-1** (12.1 overs) (M. H. Wessels 74, M. J. Guptill 86*). *PoM:* M. J. Guptill. *Attendance:* 3,515. *County debut:* P. S. P. Handscomb (Durham). *After a six-week absence because of flooding, Worcestershire returned to New Road in style. A fortnight after his World Cup final disappointment, Martin Guptill hit 86* off 35 balls, including ten sixes, and put on 148 in 53 with Riki Wessels, a record for any wicket in this fixture. Seamer Matty Potts conceded 50 in three overs. Durham had started well, but stuttered after D'Arcy Short was brilliantly run out by Brett D'Oliveira's direct hit.*

At Worcester, July 31. **Worcestershire won by two wickets. Derbyshire 156-4** (20 overs) (J. L. du Ploy 52*); ‡**Worcestershire 159-8** (19 overs) (W. D. Parnell 81*). *PoM:* W. D. Parnell. *Attendance:* 2,921. *Wayne Parnell's 81* from 46, his first T20 half-century for Worcestershire, proved decisive as the hosts survived a rocky start and a nervy finish. Their powerful top three had gone for 35; then, with victory in sight, they lost four for seven, before limping home with an over to spare. Leus du Ploy top-scored for Derbyshire, and removed D'Oliveira from the attack with a stinging return drive that broke his thumb.*

At Worcester, August 4. **Leicestershire won by 33 runs. Leicestershire 152** (20 overs) (A. M. Lilley 31, C. N. Ackermann 37; W. D. Parnell 4-25); ‡**Worcestershire 119** (19.2 overs) (O. B. Cox 30; G. T. Griffiths 3-23, W. S. Davis 3-24). *PoM:* C. N. Ackermann. *Attendance:* 3,662. *Leicestershire's shock win, based around disciplined bowling and sharp catching moved them off the bottom of the table. Earlier, Parnell had taken four wickets, but the outstanding moment of the Leicestershire innings was Callum Ferguson's stunning catch at mid-on to remove Mark Cosgrove. After the visitors lost their last five for 15 in 16 balls, Worcestershire's task seemed routine. But, with three wickets apiece, Gavin Griffiths and Will Davis had other ideas.*

At Worcester, August 11. **Worcestershire v Northamptonshire. Abandoned.**

At Worcester, August 25. **Lancashire won by 25 runs. Lancashire 218-5** (20 overs) (L. S. Livingstone 32, S. J. Croft 94, J. P. Faulkner 34*); ‡**Worcestershire 193-7** (20 overs) (R. A. Whiteley 89*; G. J. Maxwell 3-23). *PoM:* S. J. Croft. *Attendance:* 4,853. *Steven Croft equalled his career-best to help Lancashire confirm top spot in the North Group, and a home quarter-final. Only Daryl Mitchell, whose four overs cost 26, stemmed the flow. Saqib Mahmood struck two early blows, and Glenn Maxwell's three wickets included Moeen Ali in his first over. Ross Whiteley offered late defiance, his 89* off 40 including his 100th T20 six for Worcestershire.*

At Worcester, August 28. **Worcestershire v Nottinghamshire. Abandoned.**

Worcestershire away matches

July 18: beat Nottinghamshire by 28 runs.
July 26: lost to Lancashire by 21 runs (DLS).
August 2: beat Yorkshire by five wickets.
August 13: lost to Derbyshire by 20 runs.

August 15: beat Durham by three runs.
August 23: beat Warwickshire by nine wickets.
August 30: lost to Northamptonshire by seven wickets.

YORKSHIRE

At Leeds, July 19 (floodlit). **Yorkshire v Nottinghamshire. Abandoned.**

At Leeds, July 25 (floodlit). **Lancashire won by nine runs.** ‡**Lancashire 170-6** (20 overs) (D. J. Vilas 43); **Yorkshire 161-9** (20 overs) (D. J. Willey 32, H. C. Brook 30, N. Pooran 43; S. Mahmood 3-33). *PoM:* S. Mahmood. *Attendance:* 16,647. *County debut:* J. W. Shutt. *A sell-out crowd saw Yorkshire fall short of a challenging target. Jack Shutt, a debutant off-spinner from Barnsley, had removed Steven Croft and Liam Livingstone, only to be collared by Dane Vilas, who hit 43 off 24. Shutt was playing because leg-spinner Josh Poysden had been hit on the head while bowling in the nets three days earlier, suffering a fractured skull and internal bleeding; he was ruled out for the rest of the season. At 131-4 with 23 balls to go, Yorkshire had a chance, but five fell for 20 – including the West Indian Nicholas Pooran for a lively 43 off 31, including three sixes off Matt Parkinson's leg-breaks – as Lancashire closed things out.*

At Leeds, August 2 (floodlit). **Worcestershire won by five wickets.** ‡**Yorkshire 177-7** (20 overs) (A. Lyth 68, T. Köhler-Cadmore 40); **Worcestershire 179-5** (17.3 overs) (M. H. Wessels 91). PoM: M. H. Wessels. *Attendance:* 10,198. *Yorkshire lost seven for 73 after openers Adam Lyth (68 off 48) and Tom Köhler-Cadmore (40 off 27) put on 104 in 11.2 overs; both fell to the off-breaks of George Rhodes. Riki Wessels took control of the chase, blasting 91 in 51 balls, with ten fours and five sixes, before Worcestershire romped home.*

At Leeds, August 4. **Tied. Warwickshire 177-4** (20 overs) (D. P. Sibley 64, S. R. Hain 31); ‡**Yorkshire 177-4** (20 overs) (A. Lyth 40, T. Köhler-Cadmore 76*, D. J. Willey 30). PoM: T. Köhler-Cadmore. *Attendance:* 6,448. *Yorkshire had to settle for their third limited-overs tie of 2019 after requiring a straightforward 47 from 40 balls with nine wickets in hand. Stand-in captain Köhler-Cadmore (Steven Patterson had left himself out to accommodate the spin of Shutt) batted through the innings, after another punchy opening stand with Lyth, this time 88 in 9.2. Needing seven off the last five balls, from Fidel Edwards (on loan from Hampshire) and Jonny Tattersall could manage only six. Earlier, Dominic Sibley (64 off 43) underpinned Warwickshire's innings in his first T20 game of the summer.*

At Leeds, August 11. **Derbyshire won by 55 runs. Derbyshire 207-5** (20 overs) (W. L. Madsen 66, J. L. du Plooy 51); ‡**Yorkshire 152** (17.1 overs) (J. A. Leaning 36; L. V. van Beek 4-17). PoM: W. L. Madsen. *Attendance:* 8,869. *Derbyshire completed a third successive T20 double against Yorkshire, and overhauled them at the bottom of the table. Wayne Madsen and Leus du Plooy shared an explosive 87 in seven overs for the third wicket, with du Plooy hitting 29 of 32 that came from the 12th, bowled by Duanne Olivier. Logan van Beek then claimed two wickets at both ends of a routine defence, finishing with a career-best 4-17.*

At Leeds, August 16 (floodlit). **Yorkshire v Durham. Abandoned.**

At Leeds, August 29 (floodlit). **Yorkshire won by 80 runs.** ‡**Yorkshire 187-7** (20 overs) (T. Köhler-Cadmore 51, A. Lyth 50, H. C. Brook 38); **Northamptonshire 107** (18 overs) (T. B. Sole 41*; D. J. Willey 4-18). PoM: D. J. Willey. *Attendance:* 8,366. *Yorkshire's first home win was too little, too late. Köhler-Cadmore (51 off 41) and Lyth (50 off 28) both fell the ball after reaching a half-century, while Harry Brook thrashed 38 off 17, as Northamptonshire used eight bowlers. David Willey then struck four times with the new ball against his former county, and it needed Tom Sole's format-best 41* to bring up three figures. Brook held four outfield catches, equalling Yorkshire's T20 record.*

Yorkshire away matches

July 20: lost to Derbyshire by five wickets.
July 23: beat Leicestershire by 54 runs.
July 28: no result v Northamptonshire.
August 9: no result v Lancashire.

August 23: beat Durham by 14 runs.
August 25: lost to Nottinghamshire by three runs.
August 30: beat Warwickshire by 19 runs.

SOUTH GROUP

ESSEX

At Chelmsford, July 19 (floodlit). **Essex won by 52 runs. Essex 226-4** (15 overs) (C. S. Delport 129, D. W. Lawrence 57*); ‡**Surrey 174-7** (15 overs) (A. J. Finch 40, J. Clark 45, R. J. Burns 47*; M. R. Quinn 3-34). PoM: C. S. Delport. *Attendance:* 4,507. *County debut:* Imran Tahir (Surrey). *In a match reduced to 15 overs a side, Cameron Delport marked his home debut with Essex's quickest T20 hundred – from 38 balls, six faster than Graham Napier against Sussex at Chelmsford in 2008. He hit 14 sixes and seven fours, and piled on 135 in less than seven overs for the fourth wicket with Dan Lawrence, who reached his own half-century in 18 balls, another Essex record. Tom Curran's three overs disappeared for 63, while two from leg-spinner Imran Tahir – making his debut for an unprecedented eighth county – cost 39. Will Jacks (29 from eight) shot out of the blocks in the chase, hitting four consecutive fours in Shane Snater's first over, then successive sixes off Matt Quinn. But Quinn took three wickets in four balls, and Rikki Clarke also fell for a duck, to leave Surrey sunk at 32-4. A partial recovery meant the game finished with 400 runs from 30 overs.*

At Chelmsford, July 27 (floodlit). **Essex v Gloucestershire. Abandoned.** *Gloucestershire's visit was washed out for the third year running.*

MOST SIXES IN AN ENGLISH DOMESTIC T20 INNINGS

16	G. R. Napier (152*)........	Essex v Sussex at Chelmsford	2008
15	C. H. Gayle (151*)	Somerset v Kent at Taunton	2015
14	**C. S. Delport (129)**........	**Essex v Surrey at Chelmsford**	**2019**
11	K. J. O'Brien (119)	Gloucestershire v Middlesex at Uxbridge...	2011
11	L. J. Wright (153*)	Sussex v Essex at Chelmsford	2014
11	B. B. McCullum (158*)	Warwickshire v Derbyshire at Birmingham .	2015
11	R. A. Whiteley (91*)........	Worcestershire v Yorkshire at Leeds	2015
11	**M. M. Ali (121*)**	**Worcestershire v Sussex at Hove**	**2019**

At Chelmsford, August 1 (floodlit). **Hampshire won by seven wickets. Essex 133** (16.4 overs) (T. Westley 44, A. J. A. Wheater 39; M. S. Crane 3-24); ‡**Hampshire 134-3** (15.4 overs) (J. M. Vince 87*). *PoM:* J. M. Vince. *Attendance:* 4,810. *Essex shrugged off the first-ball departure of Delport to reach 81-1 in the ninth – but then lost nine for 52 on a decent track, with spinners Liam Dawson (2-31) and Mason Crane sharing four. James Vince replied with 87* from 54 balls to take Hampshire to a comfortable victory, their first at Chelmsford in any format for five years.*

At Chelmsford, August 7 (floodlit). **Somerset won by 114 runs.** ‡**Somerset 225-6** (20 overs) (T. Banton 39, Babar Azam 56, T. B. Abell 45, E. J. Byrom 44; R. S. Bopara 3-18); **Essex 111** (12.5 overs) (M. T. C. Waller 3-26, R. E. van der Merwe 5-32). *PoM:* R. E. van der Merwe. *Attendance:* 4,728. *Tom Banton and Babar Azam had 50 on the board after 3.5 overs, and Ed Byrom hit four sixes as 69 came from the last four. Essex collapsed again, losing their last eight for 36 in 5.1 overs, and slid to their second-biggest T20 defeat by runs – behind 143, also at Somerset's hands, at Chelmsford in 2011. Slow left-armer Roelof van der Merwe took three wickets in four balls on the way to a maiden five-for in his 201st T20 match.*

At Chelmsford, August 14 (floodlit). **Essex v Middlesex. Abandoned.**

At Chelmsford, August 16 (floodlit). **Essex v Glamorgan. Abandoned.**

At Chelmsford, August 30 (floodlit). **Essex won by ten runs.** ‡**Essex 189-6** (20 overs) (C. S. Delport 64, R. S. Bopara 47*); **Kent 179** (20 overs) (Z. Crawley 89, F. du Plessis 32; J. A. Porter 3-28). *PoM:* R. S. Bopara. *Attendance:* 5,025. *Essex extended their unbeaten run to seven to sneak into the quarter-finals at the expense of Kent (for whom this was a fifth defeat in seven, plus two no-results) and Hampshire (who lost to previously winless Glamorgan at Cardiff). Delport provided the early fireworks, with 64 from 29 balls, then Ravi Bopara showcased his new role as finisher with 47* from 27 down at No. 6. Zak Crawley cracked a format-best 89 from 55 in the chase, but Kent's last seven wickets tumbled for 29.*

Essex away matches

July 18: lost to Middlesex by seven wickets.
July 26: lost to Kent by 22 runs.
August 2: beat Gloucestershire by 25 runs.
August 9: no result v Glamorgan.

August 22: beat Sussex by nine runs.
August 25: tied with Hampshire.
August 29: beat Surrey by 19 runs.

GLAMORGAN

At Cardiff, July 18 (floodlit). **Somerset won by eight wickets. Glamorgan 180-5** (20 overs) (J. L. Lawlor 43, D. L. Lloyd 57, C. A. Ingram 50*); ‡**Somerset 181-2** (18 overs) (T. Banton 64, Babar Azam 35, P. D. Trego 47*). *PoM:* T. Banton. *Attendance:* 6,224. *County debut:* Babar Azam (Somerset). *After Glamorgan's openers Jeremy Lawlor and David Lloyd put on 88 in 8.5 overs, Colin Ingram thrashed 26 (64466) from the last five balls of the innings, from Craig Overton, to set a challenging target. But Somerset made an even better start: Tom Banton, who hit five sixes, added 98 in nine overs with Babar Azam, and Peter Trego muscled them home with 47* from 31.*

At Cardiff, July 26 (floodlit). **Middlesex won by eight wickets. Glamorgan 136** (19.3 overs) (T. S. Roland-Jones 5-21); ‡**Middlesex 137-2** (17.2 overs) (S. S. Eskinazi 51, D. J. Malan 45*, M. D. E. Holden 30*). *PoM:* T. S. Roland-Jones. *Attendance:* 7,215. *Glamorgan had been humbled for 44 by Surrey the night before, and lost heavily again. For the second day running, they fell foul of a hat-*

trick, Toby Roland-Jones polishing off the innings with the first three balls of the 20th over. Stevie Eskinazi shrugged off a head injury received while trying to prevent a boundary in the field, and hit 51 from 29 in an opening stand of 75 with Dawid Malan, who was still there when Middlesex completed a routine victory.

At Cardiff, August 1 (floodlit). **Tied. Glamorgan 172-5** (20 overs) (D. L. Lloyd 35, Fakhar Zaman 58, C. B. Cooke 42*); **‡Gloucestershire 172-7** (20 overs) (I. A. Cockbain 40, R. F. Higgins 37, A. J. Tye 38*; A. G. Salter 4-12). *PoM:* A. J. Tye. *Attendance:* 4,129. *With two overs to go, and Gloucestershire needing 33, Glamorgan looked on course for their first win. But Benny Howell (15) and Andrew Tye took 19 from Marchant de Lange's over, with Tye badly dropped by Ingram at mid-off. Then, after Howell hoisted Lukas Carey for six (and falling next ball), it boiled down to three from the last delivery: two for Tye meant a tie. Earlier, Fakhar Zaman had made his first half-century for Glamorgan, while Andrew Salter improved his best T20 figures for the second time in a week.*

At Cardiff, August 9 (floodlit). **No result. Essex 30-1** (4 overs) v **‡Glamorgan.** *County debut:* C. Z. Taylor (Glamorgan).

At Cardiff, August 11. **Surrey won by seven wickets. Glamorgan 152-6** (20 overs) (C. A. Ingram 41, G. G. Wagg 36*); **‡Surrey 155-3** (19 overs) (M. D. Stoneman 53, W. G. Jacks 32; R. A. J. Smith 3-21). *PoM:* M. D. Stoneman. *Attendance:* 3,307. *Surrey completed the double over Glamorgan. Ingram top-scored again, but Shaun Marsh bagged a third-ball duck in his first game of the season after breaking his arm. Ruaidhri Smith then dismissed Aaron Finch for nought, and added two more wickets, but Mark Stoneman made sure of victory with an unhurried 53. Ollie Pope (28*) ended the match with his second six of a de Lange over that cost 21.*

At Cardiff, August 26. **Sussex won by seven wickets. ‡Glamorgan 174-4** (20 overs) (S. E. Marsh 52, N. J. Selman 40, C. A. Ingram 50); **Sussex 176-3** (16.5 overs) (A. T. Carey 61, L. J. Evans 45*; A. G. Salter 3-37). *PoM:* A. T. Carey. *Attendance:* 3,922. *In their 13th match, winless Glamorgan rarely looked like breaking their duck, despite a welcome return to form for Marsh. Another Australian, Alex Carey, opened for Sussex (Luke Wright had injured his wrist in the field), and clobbered 61 from 30 balls, with ten fours and a six, as he and Phil Salt (27 from 18) hurried to 83 in the eighth over. There was no let-up: David Wiese (25* from 16) hammered a huge six off Smith that smacked into the Sophia Gardens media centre, and Laurie Evans finished things off.*

At Cardiff, August 30 (floodlit). **Glamorgan won by 28 runs. ‡Glamorgan 216-5** (20 overs) (S. E. Marsh 32, N. J. Selman 33, C. A. Ingram 44, D. L. Lloyd 40, C. B. Cooke 45); **Hampshire 188-8** (20 overs) (J. M. Vince 43, S. A. Northeast 60; R. I. Walker 3-39). *PoM:* C. B. Cooke. *Attendance:* 4,158. *At the last gasp, Glamorgan finally won – and ended Hampshire's quarter-final hopes. Glamorgan's highest total of the season (and their highest at Cardiff) included 13 sixes – four apiece for Ingram and Lloyd – with Chris Wood taking 2-67. James Vince gave the chase a quick start, slamming nine fours in his 26-ball 43, but Hampshire fell behind the rate, despite Sam Northeast's sprightly 60. Seamer Roman Walker, just 19, made up for a mauling by Sussex in the previous match with three wickets, two in the 19th over.*

Glamorgan away matches

July 19: no result v Gloucestershire.
July 25: lost to Surrey by 97 runs.
August 2: lost to Hampshire by 41 runs.
August 6: lost to Sussex by nine wickets.

August 14: no result v Kent.
August 16: no result v Essex.
August 24: lost to Somerset by 25 runs.

MOST EXPENSIVE FIGURES IN THE T20 CUP

0-77	B. W. Sanderson ...	Northamptonshire v Yorkshire at Leeds ..	2017
0-67	R. J. Kirtley.......	Sussex v Essex at Chelmsford..........	2008
2-67	**C. P. Wood**......	**Hampshire v Glamorgan at Cardiff**....	**2019**
1-65	P. I. Walter	Essex v Kent at Chelmsford	2017
2-65	M. J. Hoggard	Yorkshire v Lancashire at Leeds	2005
0-64	Abdul Razzaq	Hampshire v Somerset at Taunton.......	2010

GLOUCESTERSHIRE

At Cheltenham, July 19. **No result**. Glamorgan 96-8 (15.3 overs) (B. A. C. Howell 5-18) v ‡**Gloucestershire**. *Benny Howell returned career-best figures to help reduce Glamorgan to 96-8. But rain brought a premature end, to the frustration of a sell-out Festival crowd.*

At Cheltenham, July 25. **Gloucestershire won by two wickets.** ‡**Middlesex** 148-9 (20 overs) (S. S. Eskinazi 40, D. J. Lincoln 30, J. A. Simpson 42*; D. A. Payne 3-32); **Gloucestershire** 151-8 (19.2 overs) (M. A. H. Hammond 63, B. A. C. Howell 33; S. T. Finn 3-30). *PoM:* M. A. H. Hammond. *Attendance: 4,763. County debut: D. J. Lincoln (Middlesex). Cheltenham-born Miles Hammond top-scored with a sparkling 63 from 35 balls, but Gloucestershire, chasing 149, were in trouble when he departed at 84-5. A stand of 45 between Howell and Jack Taylor (24) steadied the ship and, although both fell, the innings had enough impetus to bring victory. Middlesex had earlier declined from 73-1 to 91-5, before John Simpson shored things up. They gave a debut to Dan Lincoln, a former goalkeeper at Reading FC, because A. B. de Villiers was nursing a hand injury.*

At Bristol, August 2 (floodlit). **Essex won by 25 runs.** ‡**Essex** 206-3 (20 overs) (T. Westley 86*, C. S. Delport 51, D. W. Lawrence 56); **Gloucestershire** 181-5 (20 overs) (R. F. Higgins 77*, J. M. R. Taylor 42). *PoM:* T. Westley. *Attendance: 4,394. Essex ran up their highest total against Gloucestershire thanks to a superbly judged 86* from Tom Westley, plus fifties from Cameron Delport and Dan Lawrence; three wicketless overs of Tom Smith's left-arm spin cost 55. After 11, the Gloucestershire reply was floundering at 68-4. Ryan Higgins took the fight to Essex with a 43-ball 77*, putting on 93 with Taylor in seven overs, but the task was too great.*

At Bristol, August 4. **Sussex won by three wickets.** Gloucestershire 159-6 (20 overs) (J. R. Bracey 30, I. A. Cockbain 61*); ‡**Sussex** 163-7 (19.4 overs) (D. Wiese 37, D. M. W. Rawlins 35*; D. A. Payne 3-35). *PoM:* D. M. W. Rawlins. *Attendance: 2,903. At the end of the 19th over, Sussex needed another 14. But a penalty for a slow over-rate reduced the target to eight, and Delray Rawlins did the rest, finishing with 35* from 17 balls. Ian Cockbain had glued the Gloucestershire innings with 61*, his only fifty of the tournament.*

At Bristol, August 7 (floodlit). **Gloucestershire won by five wickets.** Kent 125-8 (20 overs) (D. J. Bell-Drummond 62); ‡**Gloucestershire** 131-5 (18.5 overs). *PoM:* B. A. C. Howell. *Attendance: 2,270. A stand of 35* between Taylor and Howell guided Gloucestershire to victory on a sticky pitch. Of the Kent batsmen, only opener Daniel Bell-Drummond managed any fluency: he batted until the last over for a 56-ball 62. A target of 126 seemed modest, but it was almost impossible for batsmen to settle. Howell eventually grabbed the game by the scruff, and struck 25* from 14 balls. He had earlier taken 1-20; all told, five bowlers took two wickets.*

At Bristol, August 13 (floodlit). **Gloucestershire won by seven wickets.** ‡**Hampshire** 139-6 (20 overs) (A. H. T. Donald 44; C. J. Liddle 3-25); **Gloucestershire** 144-3 (17.5 overs) (M. Klinger 40, J. R. Bracey 64). *PoM:* J. R. Bracey. *Attendance: 5,047. County debut: Z. J. Chappell (Gloucestershire). James Bracey hit his maiden T20 fifty, and shared a crucial second-wicket stand of 102 with captain Michael Klinger, as Gloucestershire overhauled a modest target with time to spare. On another grudging pitch, left-arm seamer Chris Liddle claimed 3-25 to peg Hampshire back, after Aneurin Donald (44 from 23 balls) had given them a turbocharged start.*

At Bristol, August 23 (floodlit). **Gloucestershire won by 25 runs.** Gloucestershire 189-4 (20 overs) (M. A. H. Hammond 56, M. Klinger 74); ‡**Somerset** 164 (19.3 overs) (Babar Azam 44, J. C. Hildreth 40, T. A. Lammonby 31; T. M. J. Smith 3-19). *PoM:* T. M. J. Smith. *Attendance: 7,725. On what many in the capacity crowd assumed would be his last appearance at Nevil Road, Klinger scored a match-winning 74 from 52 balls, and departed to a standing ovation. (In the event, Gloucestershire secured a home quarter-final, and Klinger would return for another farewell.) He formed the bedrock of an imposing 189-4, and gained useful support from Hammond. Somerset reached 90-1 in the tenth over, but struggled to combat spinners Smith and Graeme van Buuren, who claimed a combined 5-46.*

Gloucestershire away matches

July 27: no result v Essex.
August 1: tied with Glamorgan.
August 9: beat Surrey by nine runs (DLS).
August 11: lost to Middlesex by nine runs (DLS).

August 16: no result v Somerset.
August 29: beat Kent by five runs.
August 30: beat Sussex by three wickets.

HAMPSHIRE

At Southampton, July 19 (floodlit). **Hampshire v ‡Sussex. Abandoned.** *County debuts:* C. H. Morris (Hampshire); R. J. W. Topley (Sussex).

At Southampton, July 21. **Kent won by two wickets. ‡Hampshire 145-5** (20 overs) (J. M. Vince 51, S. A. Northeast 35); **Kent 146-8** (19.5 overs) (A. J. Blake 57*; K. J. Abbott 3-22). *PoM:* A. J. Blake. *Attendance:* 10,021. *Kent required 16 off the final over, from Chris Wood, then 12 from the last three deliveries. Alex Blake, who had arrived at 41-4, did it in two; Imran Qayyum contributed a single to a ninth-wicket stand of 24*. James Vince and Sam Northeast had earlier given the Hampshire innings some backbone, though scoring was never straightforward.*

At Southampton, August 2 (floodlit). **Hampshire won by 41 runs. ‡Hampshire 128-7** (20 overs); **Glamorgan 87** (15.3 overs) (L. A. Dawson 3-11, M. S. Crane 3-22). *PoM:* L. A. Dawson. *Attendance:* 10,020. *A third successive win put Hampshire back on course after they began with a washout and two defeats. Glamorgan had now lost four, to go with a tie and a no-result. Spinners Mason Crane and Liam Dawson took a combined 6-33 as the visitors crumbled: their last eight wickets fell for 45. On a slow pitch, Hampshire's Lewis McManus (23*) hit the only six of the match, while Glamorgan opener David Lloyd was the game's highest scorer, with 26.*

At Southampton, August 9 (floodlit). **Somerset won by 63 runs (DLS). Somerset 202-4** (20 overs) (Babar Azam 102*, T. B. Abell 57); **‡Hampshire 69-6** (12.1 overs). *PoM:* Babar Azam. *Attendance:* 6,438. *Off the last ball of the Somerset innings, Babar Azam brought up his hundred with his sixth six – to finish on a career-best 102*. He faced 55 balls and shared a stand of 113 in 11 overs for the third wicket with Tom Abell, who reached a maiden T20 fifty. Hampshire made a botch of their reply, and it was a mercy when rain, which had twice interrupted the Somerset innings, returned.*

At Southampton, August 16 (floodlit). **Hampshire v Surrey. Abandoned.**

At Southampton, August 25. **Tied. Essex 139-7** (20 overs) (A. J. A. Wheater 34, D. W. Lawrence 69; K. J. Abbott 3-15); **‡Hampshire 139-6** (20 overs) (S. A. Northeast 73, L. A. Dawson 31). *PoM:* D. W. Lawrence. *Attendance:* 8,069. *For the second year running, these teams fought out a tie. When McManus joined Northeast at the fall of the fifth wicket, Hampshire needed 32 from 13 balls; it came down to 11 from the last over, bowled by Mohammad Amir, then two from the final ball. Northeast was run out by Adam Zampa going for a second. The match had begun with Wood dismissing Tom Westley – the fifth time in ten matches he had taken a wicket in the first over of the innings.*

At Southampton, August 29 (floodlit). **Hampshire won by eight wickets. ‡Middlesex 153-5** (20 overs) (A. B. de Villiers 52*); **Hampshire 155-2** (18.3 overs) (J. M. Vince 66*, A. H. T. Donald 51). *PoM:* J. M. Vince. *Attendance:* 10,116. *Vince and Aneurin Donald broke the back of Hampshire's chase with an opening stand of 96 in 11 overs. Donald's half-century was his first in Twenty20 cricket for Hampshire, Vince his 30th. A. B. de Villiers had buttressed Middlesex's total, but it soon looked insufficient. Both teams still had the chance of making the quarters if they won their last match; on paper, it looked as though Hampshire, facing winless Glamorgan, had the easier task.*

Hampshire away matches

July 24: lost to Sussex by 14 runs.
July 26: beat Somerset by four wickets.
August 1: beat Essex by seven wickets.
August 4: lost to Kent by four wickets.

August 13: lost to Gloucestershire by seven wickets.
August 22: beat Middlesex by seven wickets.
August 30: lost to Glamorgan by 28 runs.

KENT

At Canterbury, July 20 (floodlit). **Kent won by 41 runs. ‡Kent 165-9** (20 overs) (O. G. Robinson 53, Mohammad Nabi 34; R. E. van der Merwe 3-19); **Somerset 124** (18.3 overs) (I. Qayyum 5-21). *PoM:* I. Qayyum. *Attendance:* 4,671. *County debuts:* Mohammad Nabi (Kent); T. A. Lammonby (Somerset). *Left-armer Imran Qayyum became the first Kent spinner to take a Twenty20 five-for, and helped deliver a convincing victory. That was perhaps no surprise: Kent had now won their 11 most recent games with Somerset, equalling the record in T20 cricket. After Daniel Bell-Drummond chose to bat, T20 debutant Ollie Robinson and the experienced Mohammad Nabi put on 61 to oversee a recovery from 7-2. Robinson hit the game's only fifty, though Nabi's 20-ball 34 gave greater oomph.*

Somerset were well placed at 54-1, but not at 74-7, after Qayyum – with five wickets and a run-out – had caused havoc. There was a comic moment when the Overton twins, unsure of a boundary catch, ran three, only to discover that Nabi had held on fairly, and none would count.

At Canterbury, July 26 (floodlit). **Kent won by 22 runs. ‡Kent 175-6** (20 overs) (D. J. Bell-Drummond 43, Z. Crawley 32, H. G. Kuhn 55*); **Essex 153-7** (20 overs) (R. N. ten Doeschate 58*). *PoM:* H. G. Kuhn. *Attendance:* 6,018. *Kent welcomed back Heino Kuhn, unavailable for the previous two games because of concussion, and he promptly struck 55* from 31 balls, building on an opening stand of 51. Set a demanding 176, Essex lost Cameron Delport – run out by Adam Milne with a direct hit from cover – before Ryan ten Doeschate did his best to up the rate. He made 58*, but not fast enough, and Kent cemented their place at the top of the group with a third straight win.*

FIVE WICKETS IN A TWENTY20 INNINGS FOR KENT

5-11	A. F. Milne	v Somerset at Taunton	2017
5-17	Wahab Riaz	v Gloucestershire at Beckenham	2011
5-21	**I. Qayyum**	**v Somerset at Canterbury**	**2019**
5-31	M. E. Claydon	v New Zealanders at Canterbury	2013

At Beckenham, August 4. **Kent won by four wickets. Hampshire 135** (19.2 overs) (J. M. Vince 44; A. F. Milne 3-21, G. C. Viljoen 3-15); **‡Kent 138-6** (19.5 overs) (H. G. Kuhn 41; K. J. Abbott 3-31). *PoM:* A. F. Milne. *Attendance:* 4,398. *Another win made it six from seven for high-flying Kent. A well-timed chase brought victory from the penultimate ball when Milne edged a boundary. On a grudging pitch, he and Hardus Viljoen had shared six wickets as Hampshire were downed for 135. James Vince laboured to 44 from 47 and, had 24 runs not come from the 15th – completed by Bell-Drummond after Fred Klaassen bowled two beamers – Hampshire would have been deeper in trouble. Bell-Drummond and Zak Crawley then made starts, but it was Kuhn's 41 from 33 that made the difference in a tense chase.*

At Canterbury, August 14 (floodlit). **Kent v Glamorgan. Abandoned.**

At Canterbury, August 16 (floodlit). **Kent v Sussex. Abandoned.**

At Canterbury, August 23 (floodlit). **Surrey won by one run. ‡Surrey 171-7** (20 overs) (W. G. Jacks 63; I. Qayyum 3-22); **Kent 170-3** (20 overs) (D. J. Bell-Drummond 64, Z. Crawley 59, H. G. Kuhn 32*). *PoM:* W. G. Jacks. *Attendance:* 6,032. *County debut:* M. K. O'Riordan (Kent). *Without Milne and Nabi, Kent slid to unexpected defeat by Surrey. Twenties from Mark Stoneman, Aaron Finch and Sam Curran were eclipsed by a 27-ball 63 from Will Jacks, who clobbered six sixes off his last 11 balls, as 42 gushed from 13, undoing the good work of Qayyum. Kent scored merrily in reply, and after 12 overs were 112-0 (Surrey had been 82-4); Crawley hit his first T20 fifty. With 15 required off nine, Alex Blake holed out, and neither Sam Billings nor Kuhn – who hit the last ball, from Curran, for four when six were needed – could match Jacks.*

At Canterbury, August 29 (floodlit). **Gloucestershire won by five runs. Gloucestershire 180-3** (20 overs) (M. Klinger 102*); **‡Kent 175-8** (20 overs) (F. du Plessis 60, S. W. Billings 55; R. F. Higgins 3-36). *PoM:* M. Klinger. *Attendance:* 5,417. *County debut:* F. du Plessis (Kent). *Kent suffered another blow: five straight wins had now given way to one in their last eight. Gloucestershire, meanwhile, confirmed their progress with a sixth successive victory over them. Michael Klinger dominated a weakened attack with a chanceless 65-ball 102*, reaching his century – his seventh and last for Gloucestershire – from the final ball of the innings. Kent were on track after Billings and South African captain Faf du Plessis both made fifties. But, in a similar scenario to their last game, Blake was caught at long-off with 12 needed from nine, and du Plessis followed next ball in identical fashion; Ryan Higgins ended with 3-36. David Payne conceded only six from the last.*

Kent away matches

July 21: beat Hampshire by two wickets.	August 7: lost to Gloucestershire by five wickets
July 30: beat Surrey by nine wickets (DLS).	August 10: lost to Somerset by 55 runs
August 1: beat Middlesex by 28 runs.	August 30: lost to Essex by ten runs.
August 2: lost to Sussex by nine wickets.	

MIDDLESEX

At Lord's, July 18 (floodlit). **Middlesex won by seven wickets. Essex 164-6** (20 overs) (T. Westley 40, R. N. ten Doeschate 74*; T. G. Helm 3-27); ‡**Middlesex 166-3** (17 overs) (D. J. Malan 43, A. B. de Villiers 88*). *PoM*: A. B. de Villiers. *Attendance*: 27,450. County debuts: A. B. de Villiers, Mujeeb Zadran (Middlesex); C. S. Delport (Essex). *Making his debut in English domestic cricket, and batting on the pitch used four days previously for the World Cup final, A. B. de Villiers entranced a sell-out crowd with 88* from 43 balls, including six sixes, one (off Dan Lawrence) soaring into the top tier of the Grand Stand. De Villiers put on 105 in ten overs with Dawid Malan, as Middlesex made short work of a competitive target. Earlier, Essex were indebted to a rapid 74* from former T20 captain Ryan ten Doeschate; Simon Harmer, who had taken the reins for the Blast, fared less well, conceding 38 in his three overs.*

At Lord's, August 1 (floodlit). **Kent won by 28 runs. Kent 204-4** (20 overs) (Z. Crawley 30, H. G. Kuhn 54*, A. J. Blake 66*); ‡**Middlesex 176-7** (20 overs) (J. A. Simpson 37, T. S. Roland-Jones 31*; G. C. Viljoen 3-32). *PoM*: A. J. Blake. *Attendance*: 26,919. *Alex Blake bludgeoned five sixes – four in an over from Steven Finn – in his 29-ball 66*. He put on 114* in eight with Heino Kuhn, to propel Kent to a score that always looked beyond Middlesex. They were never on terms once de Villiers departed for ten, one of three early victims for Hardus Viljoen.*

At Richmond, August 4. **Middlesex won by 35 runs. Middlesex 215-4** (20 overs) (P. R. Stirling 31, D. J. Malan 56, A. B. de Villiers 88*); ‡**Somerset 180** (17.2 overs) (T. Banton 41, T. B. Abell 41; N. A. Sowter 4-29). *PoM*: A. B. de Villiers. *Attendance*: 3,814. *Spectators at one of the smaller out-grounds had to be on their guard as de Villiers launched nine sixes (and a four) in his 35-ball 88*. Tom Banton gave the chase a good start, but from 79-1 Somerset lost six for 28, four to Nathan Sowter's leg-breaks.*

At Lord's, August 8 (floodlit). **Middlesex won by 64 runs. Middlesex 210-8** (20 overs) (A. B. de Villiers 64, E. J. G. Morgan 70; T. K. Curran 3-36); ‡**Surrey 146** (18.4 overs) (A. J. Finch 47, S. M. Curran 39; S. T. Finn 5-16). *PoM*: S. T. Finn. *Attendance*: 27,773. *A fourth-wicket stand of 115 between de Villiers (in his last match for three weeks) and Eoin Morgan, whose 37-ball 70 included five sixes in his first substantial innings since lifting the World Cup, took Middlesex to an imposing total. Morgan was cheered to and from the crease by a record crowd for a domestic T20 match in England. The chase always looked beyond Surrey once Sowter had Aaron Finch stumped; Finn accounted for the middle order, finishing with a maiden five-for in his 95th T20 match.*

At Radlett, August 11. **Middlesex won by nine runs** (DLS). ‡**Gloucestershire 168-8** (20 overs) (M. A. H. Hammond 42, J. R. Bracey 32; S. T. Finn 3-18); **Middlesex 156-3** (18.1 overs) (D. J. Malan 91*, P. R. Stirling 33). *PoM*: D. J. Malan. *Attendance*: 2,307. *Malan was on course for his second century of the tournament when rain swept in to end the first T20 match at Cobden Hill, but his side had their noses in front. Finn had earlier bowled with fire to restrict Gloucestershire.*

At Lord's, August 22 (floodlit). **Hampshire won by seven wickets. Middlesex 128** (20 overs) (Mohammad Hafeez 34; K. J. Abbott 3-25, C. H. Morris 3-22); ‡**Hampshire 131-3** (14.5 overs) (J. M. Vince 69, L. A. Dawson 35*). *PoM*: J. M. Vince. *Attendance*: 26,002. County debuts: Mohammad Hafeez (Middlesex); T. Shamsi (Hampshire). *The South African pace pair of Kyle Abbott and Chris Morris derailed Middlesex, who lost six for seven at the end of their innings. Pakistan's Mohammad Hafeez top-scored on his debut as a temporary replacement for de Villiers. James Vince ensured Hampshire would win with ease, his 42-ball 69 containing 11 fours.*

At Uxbridge, August 24. **Sussex won by eight wickets.** ‡**Middlesex 171-5** (20 overs) (P. R. Stirling 30, D. J. Malan 31, E. J. G. Morgan 47, Mohammad Hafeez 48); **Sussex 172-2** (16 overs) (L. J. Wright 48, L. J. Evans 52*, A. T. Carey 41*). *PoM*: L. J. Evans. *Attendance*: 2,653. *With two away matches to come, Middlesex had to wait for confirmation of a quarter-final place after an emphatic Sussex victory, set up by Luke Wright (48 from 27 balls) and rubber-stamped by Laurie Evans and Alex Carey, who put on 81* in seven overs. Evans won the match – and completed a 25-ball half-century – with a six off Sowter. Middlesex's innings had fizzled out with four dot balls, including the run-out of Hafeez, top-scorer again.*

Middlesex away matches

July 23: beat Surrey by 37 runs.

July 25: lost to Gloucestershire by two wickets.

July 26: beat Glamorgan by eight wickets.

August 9: lost to Sussex by four wickets.

August 14: no result v Essex.

August 29: lost to Hampshire by eight wickets.

August 30: beat Somerset by six wickets.

SOMERSET

At Taunton, July 26 (floodlit). **Hampshire won by four wickets.** Somerset 172-3 (20 overs) (Babar Azam 95*, P. D. Trego 35); ‡**Hampshire 174-6** (19.3 overs) (A. H. T. Donald 48, L. A. Dawson 47*). *PoM:* J. K. Fuller. *Attendance:* 7,400. *Hampshire staged a smash-and-grab raid under the floodlights to stun Taunton. At 96-4 off 14, they had looked out of it, but Liam Dawson and James Fuller (28 off 12) added a rapid 44 and, when 24 was plundered off the 17th, bowled by Jerome Taylor, they suddenly became favourites. Earlier, Babar Azam had made a sparkling home debut, hitting nine fours and three sixes in his 95*.*

At Taunton, July 28. **Sussex won by 13 runs.** Sussex 184-8 (20 overs) (L. J. Evans 33, A. T. Carey 78; L. Gregory 3-30); ‡**Somerset 171-5** (20 overs) (T. Banton 51, Babar Azam 83). *PoM:* A. T. Carey. *Attendance:* 7,325. *County debut:* A. T. Carey (Sussex). *After flying to Geneva the previous day to get his visa stamped, and so ensure he could stay on with Sussex, Australia's Alex Carey played a starring role. He hit seven fours and four sixes in his 46-ball 78, and put on 61 for the fourth wicket with David Wiese. Despite an opening stand of 96 in 11.5 overs between Tom Banton and Babar, Somerset fell short.*

At Taunton, August 2 (floodlit). **Somerset won by eight wickets.** Surrey 203-4 (20 overs) (A. J. Finch 72, S. M. Curran 53, O. J. D. Pope 37); ‡**Somerset 207-2** (18.4 overs) (T. Banton 71, Babar Azam 43, J. C. Hildreth 31*, E. J. Byrom 54*). *PoM:* E. J. Byrom. *Attendance:* 7,497. *Home supporters acclaimed two stars of the future, as Somerset recorded their first home win in a high-scoring tussle. The 20-year-old Banton smashed 71 off 37 balls, reducing Babar to the supporting cast, while Ed Byrom, two years older, hit 54* off 19. Only once before, when they knocked off Hampshire's 216-5 at Taunton in 2010, had Somerset chased more to win. Surrey thought they had established a winning position after captain Aaron Finch blasted four sixes in his 72.*

At Taunton, August 10 (floodlit). **Somerset won by 55 runs.** ‡**Somerset 206-8** (20 overs) (T. Banton 100, T. B. Abell 63); **Kent 151** (18.4 overs) (D. J. Bell-Drummond 36, Z. Crawley 35; C. Overton 3-32). *PoM:* T. Banton. *Attendance:* 6,942. *Banton made a dazzling first T20 century, from 51 balls, to help Somerset end a run of 11 T20 defeats by Kent, adding 102 with captain Tom Abell for the third wicket. Led by Daniel Bell-Drummond and Zak Crawley, Kent made a bright start, but their hopes were wrecked by three wickets for Craig Overton in the 13th over.*

At Taunton, August 16 (floodlit). **Somerset v Gloucestershire. Abandoned.**

At Taunton, August 24 (floodlit). **Somerset won by 25 runs.** Somerset 177-8 (20 overs) (T. Banton 34, Babar Azam 63; M. de Lange 3-36); ‡**Glamorgan 152** (20 overs) (D. L. Lloyd 63, A. G. Salter 39*; M. T. C. Waller 3-19). *PoM:* Babar Azam. *Attendance:* 6,886. *Somerset handed leg-spinner Max Waller the new ball again, and he took three cheap wickets as Glamorgan slumped to another defeat. Babar had once more shown what a shrewd signing he was, and anchored the innings.*

At Taunton, August 30 (floodlit). **Middlesex won by six wickets.** ‡**Somerset 226-5** (20 overs) (T. Banton 62, T. B. Abell 101*, E. J. Byrom 44); **Middlesex 227-4** (17 overs) (D. J. Malan 41, A. B. de Villiers 32, E. J. G. Morgan 83*). *PoM:* E. J. G. Morgan. *Attendance:* 7,498. *Eoin Morgan played an innings of dazzling brilliance to secure a quarter-final place for Middlesex, at Somerset's expense. His 83* off 29 balls (including eight sixes) helped the visiting team complete the highest successful chase in county T20 history. Taking advantage of short boundaries and a nervy attack Morgan plundered 23 off an over from Tom Lammonby, as Middlesex cruised home. The prospect had looked bright for Somerset when Abell hit his first T20 hundred, off 46 balls.*

HIGHEST SUCCESSFUL T20 CHASES

245-5	Australia (set 244) v New Zealand at Auckland	2017-18
242-6	**St Kitts and Nevis Patriots (242) v Jamaica Tallawahs at Basseterre**	**2019**
236-6	West Indies (232) v South Africa at Johannesburg	2014-15
230-8	England (230) v South Africa at Mumbai	2015-16
227-4	**Middlesex (227) v Somerset at Taunton**	**2019**
226-3	Sussex (226) v Essex at Chelmsford	2014
226-6	**Central Punjab (223) v Northern Areas at Faisalabad**	**2019-20**
225-5	Nottinghamshire (224) v Yorkshire at Nottingham	2017
225-6	Jamaica Tallawahs (224) v Trinbago Knight Riders at Port-of-Spain	2018
224-5	Cape Cobras (223) v Titans at Centurion	2010-11
223-8	Hobart Hurricanes (223) v Melbourne Renegades at Melbourne (Docklands) . . .	2016-17

Somerset away matches

July 18: beat Glamorgan by eight wickets.
July 20: lost to Kent by 41 runs.
August 4: lost to Middlesex by 35 runs.
August 7: beat Essex by 114 runs.

August 9: beat Hampshire by 63 runs (DLS).
August 23: lost to Gloucestershire by 25 runs.
August 27: lost to Surrey by six wickets.

SURREY

At The Oval, July 23 (floodlit). **Middlesex won by 37 runs. ‡Middlesex 209-3** (20 overs) (S. S. Eskinazi 42, D. J. Malan 117, G. F. B. Scott 35*); **Surrey 172-9** (20 overs) (O. J. D. Pope 47, T. K. Curran 31; T. S. Roland-Jones 4-35). *PoM:* D. J. Malan. *Attendance:* 23,768. *Middlesex took charge from the start: after an opening stand of 131 with Stevie Eskinazi, Dawid Malan sprinted to 117 from 57 balls, with seven sixes and 11 fours. Surrey lost their first wicket to Mujeeb Zadran's fifth ball of the innings, and never found their feet. Toby Roland-Jones finished with four, including top-scorers Ollie Pope and Tom Curran.*

At The Oval, July 25 (floodlit). **Surrey won by 97 runs. Surrey 141** (20 overs) (W. G. Jacks 40; M de Lange 4-26, A. G. Salter 4-23); **‡Glamorgan 44** (12.5 overs) (T. K. Curran 3-3, Imran Tahir 3-8, G. J. Batty 3-7). *PoM:* T. K. Curran. *Attendance:* 22,338. *County debut:* Fakhar Zaman (Glamorgan). *Glamorgan had not lost any of their seven previous T20 matches at The Oval, but now came unstuck, slumping to the lowest all-out total in the competition's history, undercutting Northamptonshire's 47 in Durham in 2011. They were stunned by Tom Curran's hat-trick in the second over, and fortysomething spinners Gareth Batty and Imran Tahir mopped up. Surrey had earlier slipped from 73-1 to 99-6, as Andrew Salter claimed a career-best. The start was delayed 40 minutes by a thunderstorm, and there were brief hold-ups for unscheduled visits by a fox and a seagull.*

At The Oval, July 30 (floodlit). **Kent won by nine wickets** (DLS). **Surrey 54-4** (7 overs) (A. J. Finch 36*); **‡Kent 55-1** (4 overs) (Mohammad Nabi 43*). *PoM:* Mohammad Nabi. *Attendance:* 20,212. *After a late start, Surrey's innings was interrupted after one delivery; initially reduced to 13 overs, the match eventually became a seven-over thrash. Aaron Finch made 36* from 20, but the rest never got going. Adam Milnes even managed a maiden, and finished with 1-8 from his two overs. Kent's target was unchanged, and Mohammad Nabi made sure of victory in spectacular style: his 43* came from 12 balls, with five sixes.*

At The Oval, August 9 (floodlit). **Gloucestershire won by nine runs** (DLS). **‡Gloucestershire 165-8** (20 overs) (M. A. H. Hammond 30, J. R. Bracey 33, I. A. Cockbain 40); **Surrey 94-2** (12 overs) (S. M. Curran 51*). *PoM:* D. A. Payne. *Attendance:* 23,173. *Led by Ian Cockbain's sprightly 40, Gloucestershire posted a competitive total on a reused pitch. Surrey had 52-2 from 7.5 overs when rain arrived, then needed another 52 from 4.1 to reach a revised target of 104. They fell short, despite Sam Curran's 35-ball 51*, including two sixes off Andrew Tye in the final over, which started with 25 wanted. Left-arm seamer David Payne had figures of 3–9–9–0.*

At The Oval, August 15 (floodlit). **Surrey won by 26 runs. Surrey 163-8** (20 overs) (S. M. Curran 47, O. J. D. Pope 48; W. A. T. Beer 3-22); **‡Sussex 137-8** (20 overs) (L. J. Evans 34, D. Wiese 31*;

Imran Tahir 3-24, T. K. Curran 3-20). *PoM*: O. J. D. Pope. *Attendance*: 23,657. *Contrasting innings by Sam Curran (47 from 24 balls) and Pope (48 from 44) set up Sussex's first defeat, even though leg-spinner Will Beer (4–5–22–3) did not concede a boundary. One of Curran's three sixes, off David Wiese, was caught by a spectator, who won £1,000. Sussex faltered after reaching 60-1, in the face of some testing slower balls from Jordan Clark (3–8–19–1) and three wickets apiece for Tahir and Tom Curran.*

At The Oval, August 27 (floodlit). **Surrey won by six wickets. ‡Somerset 157-9** (20 overs) (T. Banton 47, Babar Azam 37; Imran Tahir 4-25); **Surrey 158-4** (16.3 overs) (A. J. Finch 102*). *PoM*: A. J. Finch. *Attendance*: 22,810. *Tom Banton and Babar Azam gave Somerset a speedy start with 80 from 8.2 overs, but they declined sharply against Tahir and Batty (2-24). Surrey scooted home: Finch engaged beast mode with a 52-ball century that included nine sixes.*

At The Oval, August 29 (floodlit). **Essex won by 19 runs. ‡Essex 186-4** (20 overs) (T. Westley 30, R. N. ten Doeschate 55*, R. S. Bopara 70*); **Surrey 167** (19.5 overs) (O. J. D. Pope 35, J. Clark 60; J. A. Porter 4-38). *PoM*: R. S. Bopara. *Attendance*: 24,124. *Essex, in the late run of form that would take them all the way to the title, ended Surrey's involvement. After a ponderous start – Batty's four overs cost 15 – Essex were 69-4 in the tenth, but Ravi Bopara hammered 70* from 35 balls, and put on 117* with Ryan ten Doeschate. In his first T20 match of the summer, Jamie Porter reduced Surrey to 29-3, and returned to account for top-scorer Clark, whose 60 came from 32.*

Surrey away matches

July 19: lost to Essex by 52 runs.
July 26: tied with Sussex.
August 2: lost to Somerset by eight wickets.
August 8: lost to Middlesex by 64 runs.

August 11: beat Glamorgan by seven wickets.
August 16: no result v Hampshire.
August 23: beat Kent by one run.

SUSSEX

At Hove, July 24 (floodlit). **Sussex won by 14 runs. Sussex 188-6** (20 overs) (P. D. Salt 73, D. Wiese 44*); **‡Hampshire 174** (19 overs) (R. R. Rossouw 60, L. D. McManus 32; R. J. W. Topley 4-33, D. R. Briggs 3-35). *PoM*: R. J. W. Topley. *Attendance*: 5,719. *Against the county he played for 21 times in three stop–start seasons, Reece Topley took four wickets, including three in the third over of Hampshire's chase. His hostile left-arm pace showed signs of the fire that had brought 16 England appearances before a series of back injuries. Phil Salt's bludgeoning had been as impressive as his placement and, once Topley filleted Hampshire's top order, Sussex were in control.*

At Hove, July 26 (floodlit). **Tied. Sussex 144-8** (20 overs) (L. J. Wright 76*; G. J. Batty 3-20); **‡Surrey 144-8** (20 overs) (W. G. Jacks 35, O. J. D. Pope 43). *PoM*: L. J. Wright. *Attendance*: 6,076. *Less than a fortnight since that super over, Jofra Archer helped engineer another tie. After Luke Wright had held the Sussex innings together with 76*, Archer dismissed Aaron Finch and Ollie Pope, and looked to have overcome his side injury (though he might have developed a sore hand after so many autographs). Needing 29 off five, Surrey were favourites. But Tymal Mills bowled Tom Curran and Ryan Patel in the 18th; Gareth Batty scurried two off the last ball.*

At Hove, August 2 (floodlit). **Sussex won by nine wickets. Kent 154-8** (20 overs) (D. J. Bell-Drummond 40, Mohammad Nabi 43; T. S. Mills 3-23); **‡Sussex 158-1** (16 overs) (P. D. Salt 63*, L. J. Evans 65*). *PoM*: L. J. Evans. *Attendance*: 6,014. *Two undefeated teams met in front of another capacity crowd, who saw Kent's five-match winning streak come to an abrupt halt. A clinical Sussex bowled with great control – especially Mills and Rashid Khan in the middle overs – and on a good pitch Kent's score looked 20 or 30 light. An unbroken stand between Salt and Laurie Evans turned into a contest to see who could clear the Cow Corner hospitality boxes more often, and Sussex cruised home; Evans edged the sixes contest 3–2.*

At Hove, August 6 (floodlit). **Sussex won by nine wickets. ‡Glamorgan 146-9** (20 overs) (D. L. Lloyd 50; R. J. W. Topley 3-20); **Sussex 150-1** (13.5 overs) (P. D. Salt 78*, L. J. Wright 56). *PoM*: P. D. Salt. *Attendance*: 5,435. *Once again, Sussex enjoyed a nine-wicket victory, though against the* *bottom team, not the top. David Lloyd fell immediately after reaching 50, and Glamorgan couldn't regain momentum; Topley led the way with 3-20. On a flat pitch, the Sussex chase quickly became a stroll for Salt and Wright, whose opening stand of 130 equalled the all-wicket record for this fixture (made by Glamorgan's Jacques Rudolph and Chris Cooke at Arundel in 2017, the visitors' only T20 victory in Sussex).*

At Hove, August 9 (floodlit). **Sussex won by four wickets. Middlesex 127-6** (20 overs) (S. S. Eskinazi 57*, T. S. Roland-Jones 40; O. E. Robinson 4-15); ‡**Sussex 130-6** (16.2 overs) (A. T. Carey 32; N. A. Sowter 3-20). *PoM:* O. E. Robinson. *Attendance:* 5,912. *Sussex consolidated their position at the top with a fifth successive win, after Middlesex looked a batsman light – in fact, they were without Eoin Morgan and A. B. de Villiers. Three wickets for Ollie Robinson, who cannily exploited early seam movement, left them 28-4 after the powerplay; he ended with a career-best 4-15. Sussex lost wickets regularly as they attacked the chase, but Australian wicketkeeper Alex Carey, batting at Hove for the first time, helped see them home.*

At Hove, August 22 (floodlit). **Essex won by nine runs. Essex 168-5** (20 overs) (T. Westley 34, D. W. Lawrence 59*, R. S. Bopara 45); ‡**Sussex 159-9** (20 overs) (L. J. Evans 35, D. Wiese 66; Mohammad Amir 4-29). *PoM:* D. W. Lawrence. *Attendance:* 6,027. *County debut:* J. P. Behrendorff (Sussex). *Essex's late and unlikely charge towards finals day began when they inflicted a first home defeat on Sussex, who needed 39 from 29 balls with five wickets left. Then Simon Harmer ended David Wiese's typically swashbuckling 66; Sussex retained a chance until Mohammad Amir took two wickets and conceded just three runs in the 19th. Earlier, Dan Lawrence and the explosive Ravi Bopara added 82 in eight overs on a flat pitch.*

At Hove, August 30 (floodlit). **Gloucestershire won by three wickets. Sussex 163-8** (20 overs) (L. J. Wright 41, D. M. W. Rawlins 69; D. A. Payne 3-36); ‡**Gloucestershire 168-7** (20 overs) (M. Klinger 48, I. A. Cockbain 37, G. L. van Buuren 37*). *PoM:* D. M. W. Rawlins. *Attendance:* 6,039. *Needing six off the last, Gloucestershire looked likely to join Sussex in gaining a home quarter-final. Topley yielded four from the first five balls, so it came down to the last – which Graeme van Buuren despatched over midwicket for six. Both sides fought well in the field. Sussex were on course for 200 when Wright and Delray Rawlins – who later picked up 2-19 with his left-arm spin – were in full flow, but came up short. Despite Michael Klinger's departure triggering a Gloucestershire slowdown, van Buuren kept his nerve.*

Sussex away matches

July 19: no result v Sussex.
July 28: beat Somerset by 13 runs.
August 4: beat Gloucestershire by three wickets.
August 15: lost to Surrey by 26 runs.

August 16: no result v Kent.
August 24: beat Middlesex by eight wickets.
August 26: beat Glamorgan by seven wickets.

QUARTER-FINALS

At Chester-le-Street, September 4 (floodlit). **Essex won by six wickets. Lancashire 159-5** (20 overs) (A. L. Davies 80*, D. J. Vilas 41); ‡**Essex 165-4** (19.2 overs) (C. S. Delport 44, R. N. ten Doeschate 45*, R. S. Bopara 39*). *PoM:* R. S. Bopara. *Attendance:* 1,007. *With Old Trafford hosting an Ashes Test, Lancashire had to choose another venue for their home quarter-final. The players selected Riverside, where they had won their seven previous T20 games; in cheerless weather, barely a thousand spectators turned up – the lowest attendance in this year's tournament. None of that worried Essex, who secured a place in their fifth finals day thanks to a stand of 60* in five overs between Ryan ten Doeschate and Ravi Bopara. Essex had needed 23 off two, but Dane Vilas's decision to hand the 19th over to Liam Livingstone – even though Saqib Mahmood's two had cost just ten – proved crucial. Livingstone conceded 22, including three sixes. Two balls later, Bopara – who had claimed the important wickets of Steven Croft and Glenn Maxwell – finished things off with his fourth six, off Matt Parkinson. Lancashire's total had relied on opener Alex Davies's 80* from 55, and a steady 41 from Vilas.*

At Nottingham, September 5 (floodlit). **Nottinghamshire won by ten wickets. Middlesex 160-8** (20 overs) (E. J. G. Morgan 53); ‡**Nottinghamshire 165-0** (16.2 overs) (C. D. Nash 74*, A. D. Hales 83*). *PoM:* C. D. Nash. *Attendance:* 8,752. *Alex Hales hit seven sixes, including the winning blow, as Nottinghamshire's openers treated a Middlesex total built around Eoin Morgan's 31-ball 53 with contempt. Hales finished with 83* off 47 (having been dropped on 47 and 56), while Chris Nash – playing his first T20 game of the season after replacing Joe Clarke – thrashed 74* off 53 (having been dropped on 31). Their stand of 165* was Nottinghamshire's highest in the format. Morgan, who had been instrumental in dropping Hales from England's World Cup squad earlier in the summer following two failed drugs tests, had rescued Middlesex from 43-4, before their eventual 160 was exposed as hopelessly inadequate. Dan Christian, Nottinghamshire's captain, described his side's performance as "just about perfect".*

At Hove, September 6 (floodlit). **Worcestershire won by eight wickets. Sussex 184-6** (20 overs) (P. D. Salt 72, L. J. Evans 43*); ‡**Worcestershire 187-2** (17.4 overs) (M. H. Wessels 47, M. M. Ali 121*). *PoM:* M. M. Ali. *Attendance:* 5,779. *This was a repeat of the 2018 final, and again Sussex lost. They had no answer to Moeen Ali, whose career-best 60-ball 121* included 11 sixes, one of which should have brought his downfall on 78. But it slipped through David Wiese's hands at deep square, and Worcestershire advanced to 128-1 in the 13th; Alex Carey had been guilty of a more calamitous error when he dropped Ali on five. Wessels proved the perfect foil for Ali's aggression, and they added 177, a Worcestershire all-wicket record. At 108-1 in the 11th, Sussex had been heading for 200. Although Daryl Mitchell proved expensive – his two overs cost 38 – he picked up the free-scoring openers, and the innings tailed off.*

At Bristol, September 7 (floodlit). **Derbyshire won by seven wickets. Gloucestershire 135-7** (20 overs) (M. A. H. Hammond 31, I. A. Cockbain 45*); ‡**Derbyshire 137-3** (17.1 overs) (W. L. Madsen 47). *PoM:* W. L. Madsen. *Attendance:* 6,830. *Derbyshire became the last of the 18 counties to reach finals day, thanks to an unexpected victory – even if it was Gloucestershire's third quarter-final defeat in four seasons. Leading the way was Wayne Madsen, whose assured 47 helped speed them to Edgbaston, with 17 balls to spare. Gloucestershire had gained a decent start, but Michael Klinger's last innings before retirement ended when he was run out for 15. All the Derbyshire bowlers were incisive, economical, or both, and a target of 136 was clearly inadequate.*

Finals Day Reports by Graham Hardcastle

SEMI-FINALS

NOTTINGHAMSHIRE v WORCESTERSHIRE

At Birmingham, September 21. Worcestershire won by one run. Toss: Nottinghamshire.

If Nottinghamshire's season, which had already seen them relegated in the Championship, were made into a horror movie, their implosion here would be the gory, improbable ending. Hales's crisp 52 off 42 balls had helped leave them needing only 11 from two overs, with eight wickets in hand and Duckett going well. Worcestershire's hopes of becoming the first side to defend the domestic T20 title looked over. But Brown, the 21-year-old seamer who two days later earned his maiden England T20 call-up for the tour of New Zealand, conceded only four runs in an over that produced three wickets (including a run-out). That meant Parnell was defending seven off the last – or realistically, six, given the separator for a tie was fewer wickets lost. But Patel and Duckett were unable to find the boundary, leaving Duckett needing a single off the last for the tie that would have been enough for Nottinghamshire. Amid high drama, Parnell pulled out of his run-up to warn Patel for backing up too far. Then, with Cox standing up to the stumps, Duckett swung and missed – and immediately slumped to his knees. Coach Peter Moores said: "It's as gutting a loss as I can remember." Earlier, Worcestershire captain Ali struck three sixes in nine balls, before Whiteley muscled three more to lift them to a serviceable 147 for nine. Ali also had Hales caught behind, having opened the bowling with his off-breaks, and picked up one for 13.

Player of the Match: M. M. Ali. *Attendance (for all three matches on finals day):* 24,500.

Worcestershire

		B	4/6
1 H. D. Rutherford *c 2 b 10*	5	7	0
2 M. H. Wessels *b 6*	34	38	3
3 *M. M. Ali *b 10*	21	9	0/3
4 W. D. Parnell *c 4 b 6*	15	14	0/1
5 †O. B. Cox *c 5 b 4*	1	2	0
6 B. L. D'Oliveira *b 10*	7	8	0
7 R. A. Whiteley *c 9 b 11*	36	24	1/3
8 E. G. Barnard *run out (8)*	4	6	0
9 D. K. H. Mitchell *c 4 b 11*	13	12	0/1
10 P. R. Brown *not out*	0	1	0
11 C. A. J. Morris *not out*	0	0	0
B 1, lb 1, w 7, nb 2	11		

6 overs: 54-2   (20 overs) 147-9

1/10 2/40 3/76 4/78 5/89 6/91 7/97 8/140 9/146

Wood 4–6–33–0; Carter 4–10–32–3; Gurney 4–11–27–2; Patel 3–7–17–0; Mullaney 4–10–32–2; Christian 1–2–4–1.

Nottinghamshire

		B	4/6
1 C. D. Nash *c 9 b 8*	24	16	3/1
2 A. D. Hales *c 5 b 3*	52	42	4/2
3 B. M. Duckett *not out*	49	42	5
4 *D. T. Christian *c 3 b 10*	15	13	0/1
5 †T. J. Moores *c 2 b 10*	1	2	0
6 S. J. Mullaney *run out (2/5)*	0	0	0
7 S. R. Patel *not out*	5	5	0

6 overs: 52-1   (20 overs) 146-5

1/51 2/100 3/137 4/139 5/140

8 J. M. Clarke, 9 L. Wood, 10 M. Carter and 11 H. F. Gurney did not bat.

Ali 4–11–13–1; Parnell 4–6–42–0; Morris 2–4–19–0; Brown 4–7–21–2; Barnard 3–3–32–1; Mitchell 2–4–11–0; D'Oliveira 1–2–8–0.

Umpires: R. J. Bailey and A. G. Wharf.   Third umpire: D. J. Millns.

DERBYSHIRE v ESSEX

At Birmingham, September 21. Essex won by 34 runs. Toss: Essex.

Derbyshire were overpowered by a buoyant Essex side chasing a historic double – and Harmer was not about to let the opportunity slide. Prolific with the red ball, he had taken only ten wickets in his maiden campaign as T20 captain. But now he exploited a pitch of "excessive turn", according to Derbyshire captain Godleman, to return career-best figures of four for 19, as Derbyshire slipped from 30 for one to 126. Left-arm spinner Nijjar, playing his first T20 game of the season, and second ever, chipped in with three for 26, including the key wicket of Madsen, bowled round his legs on the sweep. Earlier, after Essex chose to bat, Delport (55 off 31) dominated an opening stand of 78 in eight overs with Westley. Reece helped drag things back with his left-arm seam, before Bopara and Wheater added late impetus. Reece then began the chase with two fours and a six off Porter's first three balls, but things unravelled quickly in front of a crowd still catching their breath after the hectic morning semi-final.

Player of the Match: S. R. Harmer.

Essex

		B	4/6
1 T. Westley *c 4 b 1*	39	34	3
2 C. S. Delport *c 1 b 5*	55	31	9
3 D. W. Lawrence *c 7 b 5*	3	5	0
4 R. N. ten Doeschate *lbw b 1*	1	3	0
5 R. S. Bopara *c 1 b 11*	27	23	2
6 †A. J. A. Wheater *not out*	20	17	1
7 P. I. Walter *not out*	8	8	0
B 3, lb 1, w 1, nb 2	7		

6 overs: 56-0   (20 overs) 160-5

1/78 2/93 3/96 4/107 5/141

8 *S. R. Harmer, 9 A. S. S. Nijjar, 10 A. P. Beard and 11 J. A. Porter did not bat.

Rampaul 4–5–30–1; van Beek 2–3–17–0; Hudson-Prentice 2–2–25–0; Hughes 4–7–24–2; Critchley 4–4–36–0; Reece 4–6–24–2.

Derbyshire

		B	4/6
1 L. M. Reece *c 6 b 10*	19	7	3/1
2 *B. A. Godleman *b 8*	9	6	2
3 W. L. Madsen *b 9*	17	12	2/1
4 J. L. du Plooy *b 8*	9	11	0
5 A. L. Hughes *st 6 b 9*	23	27	3
6 A. K. Dal *b 8*	0	1	0
7 M. J. J. Critchley *b 9*	5	8	0
8 †D. Smit *c 2 b 8*	19	18	1
9 F. J. Hudson-Prentice *b 3*	1	2	0
10 L. V. van Beek *not out*	16	12	1/1
11 R. Rampaul *c 9 b 2*	6	8	0/1
Lb 1, w 1	2		

6 overs: 59-3   (18.4 overs) 126

1/19 2/30 3/48 4/66 5/66 6/81 7/86 8/91 9/118

Porter 2–5–24–0; Beard 1–4–6–1; Harmer 4–14–19–4; Nijjar 4–10–26–3; Bopara 3–6–19–0; Lawrence 3–7–20–1; Delport 1.4–3–11–1.

Umpires: D. J. Millns and M. J. Saggers.   Third umpire: R. J. Bailey.

Sarah Ansell, Getty Images

When the chips are down: Simon Harmer catches Moeen Ali, and Worcestershire are on the back foot.

FINAL

ESSEX v WORCESTERSHIRE

At Birmingham, September 21 (floodlit). Essex won by four wickets. Toss: Essex.

This was Simon Harmer's day. Fresh from a four-wicket haul in the afternoon win over Derbyshire, he shone again, claiming three for 16, before hitting the runs that secured Essex's first T20 title in a thrilling final. Harmer's combined figures of seven for 35 from eight overs was a finals-day record, and he won the match award in both games. Top of the Championship with a round to go, Essex were halfway towards a historic double, completed at Taunton five days later.

Harmer had made the clever call to bat second after winning the toss, despite a wearing pitch. His theory was that a late September evening was likely to bring dew, and help the ball skid on to the bat. The most help for spinners, he felt, would be in the first innings. And so it proved, although Essex's pursuit of 146 still went to the wire.

For Worcestershire, Wessels and Ali had made thirties in a measured second-wicket stand of 56 inside eight overs, advancing from five for one after three balls following the dismissal of New Zealand batsman Rutherford, bowled by Lawrence's part-time off-spin. But Ali chipped a low return catch to Harmer, who trapped Cox – star of the previous year's finals day – next ball. No one else reached 20 as Essex took pace off the ball, and Harmer also bowled Parnell. Lawrence struck again, as did the medium-pace duo of Delport and Bopara, who finished with two for 30 – the start of his role as best supporting actor to his captain.

In pursuit, Essex slipped to 82 for five in the 14th over against Ali and Parnell. But Bopara hit two sixes and two fours in an unbeaten 36 off 22 balls to keep them in touch, and dominated a sixth-wicket stand of 47 in 5.3 overs with Walter. But it was Harmer's contribution which proved the difference. He came to the crease with 17 needed off eight balls, and crashed 14 off his first six. Parnell was left defending two off the last, as he was earlier in the day against Nottinghamshire. This time he was unsuccessful, as Harmer squeezed a boundary beyond a diving point, and galloped off on a jubilant lap of honour.

Player of the Match: S. R. Harmer.

Worcestershire

		B	4/6
1 H. D. Rutherford *b 4*	4	3	1
2 M. H. Wessels *run out (7/9)*	31	34	2/1
3 *M. M. Ali *c and b 8*	32	26	3/2
4 †O. B. Cox *lbw b 8*	0	1	0
5 W. D. Parnell *b 8*	19	19	1/1
6 D. K. H. Mitchell *c 2 b 4*	19	15	3
7 R. A. Whiteley *c 8 b 2*	7	6	0/1
8 B. L. D'Oliveira *c 4 b 6*	10	9	1
9 E. G. Barnard *c 1 b 6*	5	5	0
10 P. R. Brown *not out*	1	2	0
B 4, lb 2, w 11	17		

6 overs: 47-1   (20 overs) 145-9

1/5 2/61 3/61 4/90 5/112 6/119 7/127 8/136 9/145

11 C. A. J. Morris did not bat.

Lawrence 4–11–26–2; Cook 2–7–19–0; Beard 1–2–7–0; Bopara 4–7–30–2; Harmer 4–17–16–3; Nijjar 4–9–31–0; Delport 1–2–10–1.

Essex

		B	4/6
1 T. Westley *c 10 b 5*	36	31	4
2 C. S. Delport *c 2 b 5*	1	7	0
3 †A. J. A. Wheater *b 6*	15	15	1
4 D. W. Lawrence *c 2 b 3*	23	18	1/1
5 R. N. ten Doeschate *c 6 b 3*	1	4	0
6 R. S. Bopara *not out*	36	22	2/2
7 P. I. Walter *b 10*	14	16	1
8 *S. R. Harmer *not out*	18	7	3
Lb 3, w 1	4		

6 overs: 36-1   (20 overs) 148-6

1/9 2/47 3/65 4/75 5/82 6/129

9 A. S. S. Nijjar, 10 A. P. Beard and 11 S. J. Cook did not bat.

Ali 4–11–22–2; Morris 2–2–17–0; Parnell 4–4–34–2; Brown 4–8–28–1; Barnard 2–4–17–0; D'Oliveira 2–3–15–0; Mitchell 2–4–12–1.

Umpires: D. J. Millns and A. G. Wharf.   Third umpire: M. J. Saggers.

ROYAL LONDON ONE-DAY CUP IN 2019

REVIEW BY SAM MORSHEAD

1 Somerset   2 Hampshire   3= Lancashire, Nottinghamshire

Backed into a corner by the ECB, the 50-over competition came out fighting. From 2020, the tournament was to become "developmental", with star players taking part in The Hundred instead, and overseas imports barred. The one-day cup – for decades the showpiece of the county season – has become a casualty of the ECB's search for a new audience. The Lord's final was collateral damage: the climax would now be at Trent Bridge.

In the circumstances, the Royal London Cup could have been forgiven for moping around during its five-and-a-half-week window between mid-April and late May. Instead, it basked in glorious spring sunshine – only three games were ruined by the weather – and demanded attention.

The curtain did not come down with a vintage Lord's final, but Somerset were popular winners. Desperate to see them end a 14-year wait for a trophy, their supporters lined up for buses in Taunton before sunrise, sang their "Blackbird" song in boisterous clusters around the ground, and tried to drain the bars of cider. Their opponents, Hampshire, had to do without captain James Vince, South African batsman Aiden Markram – both had been prolific in the group stages – and all-rounder Liam Dawson, because they had joined World Cup squads. To their credit, the ECB made an unsuccessful approach to the ICC to get the England pair special dispensation to play.

Hampshire were also lacking in the stands. Before they had reached the final, many of their followers had bought tickets for the World Cup warm-up between England and Australia at the Rose Bowl. The Somerset fans, meanwhile, more vocal as well as more ubiquitous, revelled in their team's performance. Jamie Overton grabbed three key wickets, while James Hildreth, a veteran of so many near misses, steered them to victory with time and wickets to spare.

The scheduling of the tournament, with the final before June, handed ammunition to those grumbling about its downgrading. The three-day turnaround between the end of the group matches and the first knockouts left many supporters unhappy, particularly those from Lancashire, who had to plan a trip to Lord's for a day/night clash with Middlesex at the last minute. At least Lancashire softened the blow with a 20-run victory, defending 304 despite an outstanding maiden hundred by James Harris.

In the other eliminator, at New Road, Somerset cantered past Worcestershire to set up a semi-final with Nottinghamshire. Tom Banton, who crouches at the crease like Kevin Pietersen and has the 360-degree range of Jos Buttler, hit a fluent hundred. Banton underlined his promise with 59 in another comfortable win in the semi-final at Trent Bridge, and caught the eye again at Lord's. In the other semi, Gareth Berg's five wickets helped Hampshire defeat Lancashire and reach back-to-back finals.

Alex Davidson, Getty Images

Knockout punch: Player of the Match Jamie Overton removes Hampshire's Rilee Rossouw, winner of the award in 2018.

Earlier, there had been an abundance of runs, often at an accelerated rate: 43 totals over 300 in the group stages, with 400 breached three times, twice by Nottinghamshire. At Trent Bridge on Good Friday, their North Group match against Lancashire produced 823 runs. Nottinghamshire's 417 for seven was their fourth-highest List A total, and the most conceded by Lancashire, who still came within 12 of a successful chase, after captain Dane Vilas hit 166 from 100 balls, their highest one-day score.

Nottinghamshire head coach Peter Moores suggested 50-over cricket had become "an extended version of Twenty20", and there were 11 scores of more than 150, all bar one at better than a run a ball. The art of building an innings on the foundations of a steady 40- or 50-ball start is something the shortest format will never be able to teach. David Wiese nearly dragged Sussex to what would have been a remarkable victory over Hampshire at Hove with 171 off 125 balls, despite having taken 57 to get to his half-century. Glamorgan captain Chris Cooke cracked 161 from 127 against Gloucestershire, though his first 50 occupied 66. The Gloucestershire attack also conceded the tournament's highest individual score, 190 off 154, by Vince (also Hampshire's highest). Vince had needed 63 balls to reach 50.

There was no early caution from Worcestershire's Riki Wessels. At Derby, he showed disdain for anything short, anything full, anything wide – and anything on his stumps. He blasted 130 off 62, including 11 sixes. It was a devastating assault. Thanks to The Hundred's head-hunters, it looked as if it was perfectly possible none of these batsmen would feature in the 50-over competition in 2020.

However, the bat was not always king. Saqib Mahmood, a fiery 22-year-old seamer from Birmingham, was outstanding. He collected 28 wickets at 18, three more than the next best; he bowled 95.3 overs, six more than anyone else; and he troubled batsmen everywhere with pace and accuracy. Mahmood became the first Lancashire bowler to take five-fors in consecutive List A games, following six for 37 against Northamptonshire with five for 14 against Leicestershire. Nathan Sowter, an Australian-born leg-spinner, claimed 25 wickets at 20 for Middlesex, while Dawson's 18 at 20 for Hampshire, with an economy-rate of 4.11, earned him his World Cup call-up.

There was no shortage of excitement if you were watching Yorkshire. In successive matches, they tied with Warwickshire, lost by one run against Lancashire and were involved in a DLS tie with Derbyshire.

Attendances were understandably mixed, so early in the season, but Nottinghamshire illustrated the potential of target marketing for the match against Yorkshire in late April. It was promoted as a family fun day, and good weather, sensible scheduling and an admission price of £1 produced a full house.

Prize money

£154,000 for winners: SOMERSET.
£72,000 for runners-up: HAMPSHIRE.
£23,150 for losing semi-finalists: LANCASHIRE, NOTTINGHAMSHIRE.
There was no financial reward for winning individual matches.

FINAL GROUP TABLES

North Group

	North Group	P	W	L	T	NR	Pts	NRR
1	NOTTINGHAMSHIRE	8	6	1	0	1	13	0.61
2	WORCESTERSHIRE	8	6	2	0	0	12	1.08
3	LANCASHIRE	8	5	3	0	0	10	0.34
4	Durham	8	4	2	0	2	10	0.47
5	Derbyshire	8	3	4	1	0	7	−0.07
6	Yorkshire	8	2	3	2	1	7	−0.09
7	Warwickshire	8	2	5	1	0	5	−0.09
8	Northamptonshire	8	2	6	0	0	4	0.06
9	Leicestershire	8	2	6	0	0	4	−1.31

South Group

	South Group	P	W	L	T	NR	Pts	NRR
1	HAMPSHIRE	8	7	1	0	0	14	1.02
2	MIDDLESEX	8	6	2	0	0	12	0.13
3	SOMERSET	8	5	3	0	0	10	0.50
4	Gloucestershire	8	5	3	0	0	10	0.27
5	Sussex	8	4	4	0	0	8	0.01
6	Glamorgan	8	3	4	0	1	7	−0.29
7	Kent	8	2	5	0	1	5	−0.96
8	Essex	8	2	6	0	0	4	0.32
9	Surrey	8	1	7	0	0	2	−0.10

Where counties finished tied on points, positions were decided by (a) most wins, (b) net run-rate. Group winners were awarded a home semi-final, while second and third contested quarter-finals.

ROYAL LONDON ONE-DAY CUP AVERAGES

BATTING (350 runs at 35)

		M	I	NO	Runs	HS	100	50	Avge	SR	4	6
1	D. Wiese (*Sussex*)	8	7	3	395	171	1	3	98.75	120.42	41	13
2	C. T. Bancroft (*Durham*) . . .	8	7	3	377	151*	2	0	94.25	95.44	26	9
3	†A. Z. Lees (*Durham*)	8	7	3	361	115	1	4	90.25	83.37	25	5
4	V. Chopra (*Essex*)	5	5	0	421	156	3	0	84.20	88.25	37	5
5	S. R. Hain (*Warwicks*)	7	7	2	385	161*	1	2	77.00	87.50	23	7
6	†B. A. Godleman (*Derbys*) . . .	8	8	1	521	116	3	1	74.42	88.30	40	10
7	S. J. Croft (*Lancs*)	10	9	2	516	110	1	3	73.71	94.67	46	13
8	J. M. Vince (*Hants*)	7	7	0	509	190	1	3	72.71	110.89	52	8
9	†W. T. Root (*Glam*)	8	7	1	386	113*	1	2	64.33	95.30	35	4
10	D. J. Vilas (*Lancs*)	10	9	2	439	166	1	2	62.71	119.61	30	16
11	C. N. Ackermann (*Leics*) . . .	8	8	1	428	152*	2	1	61.14	92.04	43	7
12	†N. R. T. Gubbins (*Middx*) . . .	8	8	1	417	98*	0	4	59.57	106.64	57	0
13	L. J. Wright (*Sussex*)	7	7	0	409	166	1	2	58.42	97.14	39	12
14	A. K. Markram (*Hants*)	8	8	0	466	130	1	3	58.25	101.96	57	5
15	W. L. Madsen (*Derbys*)	8	8	1	406	119*	1	2	58.00	106.84	42	11
16	Z. Crawley (*Kent*)	8	7	0	394	120	1	2	56.28	87.55	45	0
17	†R. R. Rossouw (*Hants*)	10	9	1	388	93	0	4	48.50	111.17	42	2
18	T. Westley (*Essex*)	8	8	0	373	77	0	4	46.62	99.20	36	4
19	J. C. Hildreth (*Somerset*) . . .	11	11	1	457	93	0	4	45.70	98.49	36	8
20	R. I. Keogh (*Northants*)	8	8	0	359	102	1	3	44.87	87.34	30	0
21	†K. K. Jennings (*Lancs*)	10	10	0	416	96	0	5	41.60	81.09	49	0
22	T. Banton (*Somerset*)	11	11	0	454	112	2	3	41.27	94.58	50	13
23	Azhar Ali (*Somerset*)	11	11	0	451	110	1	2	41.00	79.96	36	4
24	†T. P. Alsop (*Hants*)	10	10	1	351	130*	2	0	39.00	90.00	42	4
25	P. D. Trego (*Somerset*)	11	11	0	389	141	1	1	35.36	96.52	36	8

BOWLING (12 wickets)

		Style	O	M	R	W	BB	4I	Avge	SR	ER
1	M. Morkel (*Surrey*)	RFM	52.5	3	239	13	4-23	1	18.38	24.38	4.52
2	S. Mahmood (*Lancs*)	RFM	95.3	7	518	28	6-37	3	18.50	20.46	5.42
3	W. D. Parnell (*Worcs*)	LFM	73.4	2	415	22	5-24	2	18.86	20.09	5.63
4	C. Overton (*Somerset*)	RFM	83	3	402	20	5-18	1	20.10	24.90	4.84
5	L. A. Dawson (*Hants*)	SLA	89	2	366	18	3-37	0	20.33	29.66	4.11
6	N. A. Sowter (*Middx*)	LB	89.2	0	521	25	6-62	4	20.84	21.44	5.83
7	M. W. Pillans (*Yorks*)	RFM	52.2	0	344	16	5-29	1	21.50	19.62	6.57
8	L. J. Fletcher (*Notts*)	RFM	63.1	2	368	17	5-56	1	21.64	22.29	5.82
9	P. M. Siddle (*Essex*)	RFM	49	1	265	12	4-60	1	22.08	24.50	5.40
10	K. J. Abbott (*Hants*)	RFM	81.5	1	471	20	3-36	0	23.55	24.55	5.75
11	J. S. Patel (*Warwicks*)	OB	75	6	384	16	5-45	1	24.00	28.12	5.12
12	J. T. Ball (*Notts*)	RFM	54	0	358	14	4-62	1	25.57	23.14	6.62
13	M. de Lange (*Glam*)	RF	62.5	2	421	16	4-63	1	26.31	23.56	6.70
14	B. W. Sanderson (*Northants*) . .	RFM	64.3	5	371	14	3-44	0	26.50	27.64	5.75
15	B. A. C. Howell (*Gloucs*)	RM	52.4	1	319	12	3-45	0	26.58	26.33	6.05
16	Mir Hamza (*Sussex*)	LFM	74.5	0	484	18	4-43	1	26.88	24.94	6.46
17	J. H. Davey (*Somerset*)	RFM	78.3	6	382	14	4-36	1	27.28	33.64	4.86
18	T. G. Helm (*Middx*)	RFM	85	0	547	19	5-71	2	28.78	26.84	6.43
19	M. E. Milnes (*Kent*)	RFM	71.5	1	494	16	5-79	1	30.87	26.93	6.87
20	M. S. Crane (*Hants*)	LB	74.1	1	446	14	3-42	0	31.85	31.78	6.01
21	T. S. Roland-Jones (*Middx*) .	RFM	73.3	1	436	13	3-46	0	33.53	33.92	5.93
22	D. Klein (*Leics*)	LFM	60.2	5	404	12	4-72	1	33.66	30.16	6.69
23	M. W. Parkinson (*Lancs*) . . .	LB	77.1	0	436	12	5-51	1	36.33	38.58	5.65

LEADING WICKETKEEPERS

Dismissals	M			Dismissals	M		
19 (14 ct, 5 st)	10	T. P. Alsop (Hants)		12 (11 ct, 1 st)	8	O. B. Cox (Worcs)	
16 (14 ct, 2 st)	8	R. G. White (Essex)		12 (11 ct, 1 st)	11	T. Banton (Somerset)	
14 (11 ct, 3 st)	9	J. A. Simpson (Middx)		11 (8 ct, 3 st)	7	B. T. Foakes (Surrey)	
14 (13 ct, 1 st)	10	D. J. Vilas (Lancs)		10 (8 ct, 2 st)	9	T. J. Moores (Notts)	
12 (10 ct, 2 st)	7	J. A. Tattersall (Yorks)					

LEADING FIELDERS

Ct	M			Ct	M		
12	11	R. E. van der Merwe (Somerset)		8	11	Azhar Ali (Somerset)	
9	9	N. A. Sowter (Middx)		7	11	C. Overton (Somerset)	
9	10	K. K. Jennings (Lancs)					

NORTH GROUP

DERBYSHIRE

At Derby, April 19. **Derbyshire won by 53 runs.** ‡Derbyshire 268-6 (50 overs) (B. A. Godleman 87, J. L. du Plooy 30, M. J. J. Critchley 64*); **Northamptonshire 215** (43.5 overs) (J. O. Holder 30, L. A. Procter 50*, B. W. Sanderson 31; L. V. van Beek 3-50, A. L. Hughes 4-44). *County debuts: J. L. du Plooy, M. R. J. Watt (Derbyshire). Attendance: 665. Despite the vigilance of Billy Godleman, Derbyshire slipped to 137-5. But Matt Critchley equalled his best one-day score, and they ended up with too many for Northamptonshire. Their reply began poorly, and needed Luke Procter's 50* from No. 8 to gain respectability. Seamer Alex Hughes took his best one-day figures.*

At Derby, April 21. **Nottinghamshire won by six wickets.** ‡Derbyshire 297-8 (50 overs) (L. M. Reece 88, B. A. Godleman 116, W. L. Madsen 38; L. J. Fletcher 5-56); **Nottinghamshire 299-4** (45.1 overs) (B. T. Slater 83, J. M. Clarke 37, J. D. Libby 41, T. J. Moores 52*, S. J. Mullaney 68*; A. F. Gleadall 3-43). *Attendance: 860. Luke Fletcher's first one-day five-for proved decisive after Derbyshire had made a superb start. Luis Reece and Godleman put on 153 in 30.1 overs, then Wayne Madsen lifted the tempo with 38 off 28. But the innings lost its way, with Fletcher bowling three batsmen in the final over. On his first return to Derby since his move down the A52, Ben Slater made a solid 83, and Nottinghamshire were only briefly discomforted, when 18-year-old seamer Alfie Gleadall took three top-order wickets. Tom Moores and Steven Mullaney hit eight sixes between them in a stand of 126*.*

At Derby, April 30. **Derbyshire won by five wickets.** Warwickshire 288-7 (50 overs) (S. R. Hain 34, A. T. Thomson 68*, A. J. Mellor 58; L. V. van Beek 3-69); ‡Derbyshire 289-5 (46.3 overs) (L. M. Reece 37, B. A. Godleman 40, W. L. Madsen 119*, A. L. Hughes 69; A. T. Thomson 3-57). *Attendance: 599. Madsen's fifth one-day hundred kept alive Derbyshire's hopes of reaching the quarter-finals, but ended Warwickshire's. The visitors had survived a mid-innings collapse to post a competitive total, thanks to Alex Thomson, but Madsen was business-like, and a stand of 134 with Hughes turned the match in Derbyshire's direction. Thomson completed a solid all-round performance with 3-57.*

At Derby, May 6. **Worcestershire won by four wickets.** ‡Derbyshire 351-9 (50 overs) (L. M. Reece 128, W. L. Madsen 113, A. L. Hughes 43); **Worcestershire 353-6** (48.2 overs) (M. H. Wessels 130, T. C. Fell 49, C. J. Ferguson 103*; M. J. J. Critchley 3-73). *Attendance: 585. In a match of four hundreds, the most telling came from Riki Wessels, who raced to three figures in 47 balls, and in all hit 11 sixes. Callum Ferguson's century was more measured, but he steered Worcestershire to a home quarter-final, and ended Derbyshire's remote chance of progressing. Reece and Madsen, with his second century in a row, added 222 for the second wicket, a record for the fixture.*

Derbyshire away matches

April 24: beat Leicestershire by seven wickets.
April 26: tied with Yorkshire.

April 28: lost to Durham by three wickets.
May 2: lost to Lancashire by 30 runs.

DURHAM

At Chester-le-Street, April 17. **Durham won by 72 runs. Durham 342-5** (50 overs) (S. Steel 68, C. T. Bancroft 151*, M. J. Richardson 101); ‡**Northamptonshire 270** (43.5 overs) (A. G. Wakely 66, A. M. Rossington 43, J. O. Holder 86; M. E. T. Salisbury 3-51, M. J. Potts 4-62). *County debut:* S. Steel (Durham). *Attendance:* 1,194. *Cameron Bancroft hit a superb 151* on his white-ball debut for Durham to lift them to their third-highest one-day total. Ben Sanderson had reduced them to 7-2, but Bancroft put on 119 with Scott Steel (three days short of his 20th birthday), then 208 with Michael Richardson – a fourth-wicket record for Durham, and their second-highest for any wicket. Jason Holder's 86 off 68 offered dogged resistance for Northamptonshire, but they lost their last four for three.*

At Chester-le-Street, April 19. **Durham won by six wickets.** ‡**Leicestershire 233-9** (50 overs) (L. J. Hill 33, T. A. I. Taylor 59, D. Klein 46; B. A. Carse 3-58, M. J. Potts 3-45); **Durham 234-4** (45.3 overs) (S. Steel 35, C. T. Bancroft 118*, M. J. Richardson 39). *Attendance:* 1,417. *Bancroft made his second successive hundred to steer Durham home. They again lost early wickets, but Bancroft renewed his alliance with Richardson to add 101. With victory in sight, he became more expansive, and his eventual 118* came off 117 balls. Leicestershire had been 112-7, before Tom Taylor and Dieter Klein added 81.*

At Chester-le-Street, April 28. **Durham won by three wickets. Derbyshire 255-8** (50 overs) (W. L. Madsen 38, J. L. du Plooy 32, T. C. Lace 48, M. J. J. Critchley 49*); ‡**Durham 260-7** (46.4 overs) (S. Steel 32, A. Z. Lees 55, C. T. Bancroft 45, M. J. Richardson 72*, J. T. A. Burnham 45). *Attendance:* 1,389. *Durham's win was more comfortable than the margin suggested, after Derbyshire paid the price for a tame effort with the bat. Several batsmen struggled to read the pace of the pitch; only Tom Lace and Matt Critchley found fluency. Durham's reply was unhurried, until Richardson hit out. Derbyshire tried nine bowlers.*

At Gosforth, April 30. **Lancashire won by three wickets. Durham 229** (48.2 overs) (A. Z. Lees 115; G. J. Maxwell 3-42); ‡**Lancashire 230-7** (49.2 overs) (S. J. Croft 99, R. P. Jones 33*). *Attendance:* 1,694. *Graham Onions struck Ben Raine for two sixes in a row to calm Lancashire nerves and seal the fate of his former employers. The visitors had looked in control, until the dismissal of Steven Croft caused a wobble. In the scenic surroundings of South Northumberland CC, Alex Lees had scored his first one-day hundred for Durham, and went on to a career-best 115.*

Durham away matches

April 24: lost to Worcestershire by four wickets (DLS). May 3: no result v Nottinghamshire.
April 26: beat Warwickshire by seven wickets (DLS). May 6: no result v Yorkshire.

LANCASHIRE

At Manchester, April 17. **Worcestershire won by 125 runs.** ‡**Worcestershire 367** (49.1 overs) (H. D. Rutherford 108, M. H. Wessels 72, D. K. H. Mitchell 101, R. A. Whiteley 36; M. W. Parkinson 5-51); **Lancashire 242** (40.4 overs) (K. K. Jennings 54, B. D. Guest 36, G. J. Maxwell 35, S. J. Croft 32*). *Attendance:* 2,191. *Hamish Rutherford cracked a hundred on his white-ball debut for Worcestershire, and Daryl Mitchell compiled his fourth in seven innings against Lancashire, to tee up an emphatic win. Worcestershire had raced to 106 off 13 overs, thanks to Rutherford and Riki Wessels, before Mitchell ensured their work was not wasted. Matt Parkinson's best one-day figures could not stem the flow. The visitors made shrewd use of a seven-man attack; Lancashire were never in the running.*

At Manchester, April 24. **Lancashire won by 45 runs** (DLS). **Northamptonshire 269** (50 overs) (R. S. Vasconcelos 50, R. I. Keogh 66, J. O. Holder 72, L. A. Procter 36; S. Mahmood 6-37); ‡**Lancashire 164-2** (28.4 overs) (K. K. Jennings 63, H. Hameed 65). *Attendance:* 1,482. *Saqib Mahmood became the first Lancashire bowler to take a one-day six-for in 21 years. He struck three* *times in his first four overs, although Northamptonshire fought back with a stand of 89 for the sixth wicket between Rob Keogh, whose 66 did not include a boundary, and Jason Holder. Keaton Jennings and Haseeb Hameed put on 130 in 23.2 overs to ensure Lancashire were well ahead of the rate when rain arrived.*

At Manchester, April 28. **Lancashire won by nine wickets. Leicestershire 80** (37 overs) (S. Mahmood 5-14); ‡**Lancashire 83-1** (19 overs) (S. J. Croft 37*). *Attendance: 1,308. Bowling fast and straight, Mahmood took his second five-wicket haul in a row, a Lancashire record, as Leicestershire slumped to their lowest total against them. Steven Croft, who passed 4,000 List A runs, marshalled an unhurried chase. Chelsea footballers Eden Hazard, Gonzalo Higuaín and Pedro Rodríguez, staying at the hotel on the ground before their match against Manchester United that afternoon, watched the first innings from their balcony.*

BEST ONE-DAY BOWLING FOR LANCASHIRE

6-10	C. E. H. Croft	v Scotland at Manchester	1982
6-18	G. Chapple	v Essex at Lord's	1996
6-25	G. Chapple	v Yorkshire at Leeds	1998
6-29	D. P. Hughes	v Somerset at Manchester	1977
6-37	**S. Mahmood**	**v Northamptonshire at Manchester**	**2019**
5-7	G. Chapple	v Minor Counties at Lakenham	1998
5-10	Wasim Akram	v Leicestershire at Leicester	1993
5-12	B. Wood	v Derbyshire at Southport	1976
5-13	K. Shuttleworth	v Nottinghamshire at Nottingham	1972
5-13	D. P. Hughes	v Glamorgan at Manchester	1976
5-13	P. A. J. DeFreitas	v Cumberland at Kendal	1989
5-14	**S. Mahmood**	**v Leicestershire at Manchester**	**2019**

At Manchester, May 2. **Lancashire won by 30 runs. Lancashire 239-6** (38 overs) (K. K. Jennings 84, J. S. Lehmann 77*); ‡**Derbyshire 209-7** (38 overs) (B. A. Godleman 42, A. K. Dal 52, H. R. Hosein 41*). *County debut: J. S. Lehmann (Lancashire). Attendance: 1,084. Lancashire notched a fifth successive win after rain reduced the match to 38 overs a side. Jake Lehmann, son of the former Australia coach Darren, hit 77* on Lancashire debut, and added 86 for the fourth wicket with Jennings. Derbyshire struggled until a seventh-wicket stand of 76 in ten overs between Anuj Dal and Harvey Hosein briefly revived their hopes. Lancashire's three spinners held their nerve.*

Lancashire away matches

April 19: lost to Nottinghamshire by 11 runs.   April 30: beat Durham by three wickets.
April 21: beat Yorkshire by one run.   May 4: lost to Warwickshire by five wickets (DLS).

LEICESTERSHIRE

At Leicester, April 21. **Leicestershire won by 38 runs.** ‡**Leicestershire 377-4** (50 overs) (H. E. Dearden 91, C. N. Ackermann 152*, L. J. Hill 118); **Worcestershire 339** (46.2 overs) (B. L. D'Oliveira 57, R. A. Whiteley 131, E. G. Barnard 61, Extras 34; D. Klein 4-72, C. N. Ackermann 3-55). *Attendance: 645. Three batsmen made a maiden one-day hundred as Leicestershire won a high-scoring encounter, but Lewis Hill hogged the spotlight. In a hyperactive innings packed with innovative shots, his 118 came off 62 balls. Colin Ackermann's more conventional hundred glued the innings together after two wickets in the first over. He added 170 with Harry Dearden, a Leicestershire fourth-wicket record. Worcestershire slumped to 24-4, but Ross Whiteley's 131 off 100 kept them in the hunt. Ed Barnard maintained the charge, and Leicestershire could not relax until he fell. Ackermann finished with three wickets.*

At Leicester, April 24. **Derbyshire won by seven wickets** (DLS). **Leicestershire 312-8** (50 overs) (H. E. Dearden 36, C. N. Ackermann 119); ‡**Derbyshire 266-3** (39 overs) (B. A. Godleman 106, W. L. Madsen 60, J. L. du Plooy 73*). *Attendance: 425. In a frenetic final over, Derbyshire needed six off two balls after century-maker Billy Godleman had been run out. Leus du Plooy swung a Dieter Klein long hop for four, then scrambled two to long-on. Godleman, making his second successive century, had put Derbyshire in control of a revised target of 266 in 39 overs before their late alarms. For Leicestershire, Ackermann also made a second consecutive hundred, but no one else passed 36.*

LEICESTERSHIRE'S HIGHEST ONE-DAY TOTALS

406-5	v Berkshire at Leicester (60-over match)	1996
382-6	v Minor Counties at Leicester (50)	1998
377-4	**v Worcestershire at Leicester (50)**	**2019**
376-4	v Worcestershire at Worcester (50)	2018
371-6	v Scotland at Leicester (50)	1997
363-7	v Warwickshire at Leicester (50)	2017
354-7	v Wiltshire at Swindon (60)	1984
344-4	v Durham at Chester-le-Street (40)	1996
341-6	v Hampshire at Leicester (60)	1987
340	**v Warwickshire at Leicester (50)**	**2019**

At Leicester, May 4. **Northamptonshire won by 29 runs.** ‡**Northamptonshire 290-6** (50 overs) (J. J. Cobb 43, A. G. Wakely 36, R. I. Keogh 102, B. J. Curran 69); **Leicestershire 261-9** (50 overs) (C. N. Ackermann 40, T. A. I. Taylor 39, B. W. M. Mike 41, C. F. Parkinson 39*; N. L. Buck 3-44). *Attendance: 1,036. Northamptonshire recovered from 104-4 thanks to a stand of 156 between Rob Keogh and Ben Curran. Keogh's second one-day hundred came off 85 balls. Leicestershire crashed to 95-5 before the lower order worked hard to bring a sliver of respectability.*

At Leicester, May 6. **Leicestershire won by 36 runs.** ‡**Leicestershire 340** (49.3 overs) (H. E. Dearden 69, C. N. Ackermann 74, T. A. I. Taylor 98*; O. J. Hannon-Dalby 3-81); **Warwickshire 304** (47.1 overs) (E. J. Pollock 57, R. M. Yates 66, L. Banks 38, C. N. Miles 31; D. Klein 3-66, T. A. I. Taylor 3-58). *County debut:* R. M. Yates (Warwickshire). *Attendance: 490. Tom Taylor produced a stellar all-round performance to ensure Leicestershire ended a disappointing competition on a high. First, he hit a career-best 98* off 56 balls to build on solid contributions from Dearden and Ackermann. Then, he then took three wickets, held two smart catches and ran out 19-year-old Rob Yates, who top-scored on debut.*

Leicestershire away matches

April 17: lost to Yorkshire by 213 runs.
April 19: lost to Durham by six wickets.
April 26: lost to Nottinghamshire by 87 runs (DLS).
April 28: lost to Lancashire by nine wickets.

NORTHAMPTONSHIRE

At Northampton, April 21. **Northamptonshire won by 194 runs. Northamptonshire 358-6** (50 overs) (R. E. Levi 48, A. G. Wakely 50, R. I. Keogh 69, A. M. Rossington 68, J. O. Holder 60*; H. J. H. Brookes 3-80); ‡**Warwickshire 164** (34.4 overs) (E. J. Pollock 36, W. M. H. Rhodes 30, A. T. Thomson 36; B. Muzarabani 3-28, B. W. Sanderson 3-44, J. O. Holder 3-26). *Attendance: 1,402. After two away defeats, Northamptonshire inflicted a shellacking on a lacklustre Warwickshire. Alex Wakely, Rob Keogh and Adam Rossington all made half-centuries to establish firm foundations for Jason Holder, whose 60* off 31 catapulted Northamptonshire to their third-highest one-day total. He then contributed three wickets to a slick bowling performance that sent the visitors tumbling to their heaviest one-day defeat, beating 184 by Leicestershire at Coventry in 1972. It was Northamptonshire's fourth-biggest win.*

NORTHAMPTONSHIRE'S HIGHEST ONE-DAY TOTALS

425	v Nottinghamshire at Nottingham (40-over match)	2016
360-2	v Staffordshire at Northampton (60)	1990
358-6	**v Warwickshire at Northampton (50)**	**2019**
355-6	v Durham at Northampton (50)	2016
352-8	v Nottinghamshire at Nottingham (60)	1995
351	**v Yorkshire at Northampton (50)**	**2019**
339-7	v Yorkshire at Northampton (50)	2006
339-9	v Nottinghamshire at Sookholme (50)	2018
326-4	v Lancashire at Liverpool (50)	2017
325-7	v Yorkshire at Northampton (60)	1992
325-7	**v Nottinghamshire at Northampton (50)**	**2019**

At Northampton, April 26. **Worcestershire won by 20 runs.** Worcestershire 254-9 (50 overs) (H. D. Rutherford 126); ‡**Northamptonshire 234** (48.4 overs) (J. J. Cobb 44, A. G. Wakely 46, L. A. Procter 35*; W. D. Parnell 3-45). *County debut:* I. G. Holland (Northamptonshire). *Attendance:* 1,079. *Hamish Rutherford's third century in five appearances sent Northamptonshire tumbling to a fourth defeat and almost certain elimination. Richard Levi's stunning slip catch to dismiss Tom Fell provided a highlight as Northamptonshire picked up early wickets, but they could not dislodge Rutherford, who found support from Brett D'Oliveira in a stand of 84. At 126-3 after 30 overs, the home team were well placed, but they were strangled by Daryl Mitchell's canny medium-pace and D'Oliveira's leg-spin.*

At Northampton, May 1. **Yorkshire won by five wickets (DLS).** ‡**Northamptonshire 351** (49.3 overs) (R. E. Levi 58, R. S. Vasconcelos 112, J. J. Cobb 58, J. O. Holder 36, A. M. Rossington 45*; M. W. Pillans 3-65); **Yorkshire 175-5** (24.4 overs) (T. Köhler-Cadmore 67, H. C. Brook 47). *Attendance:* 1,054. *Yorkshire's latest nerve-jangling finish saw them sneak home with two balls to spare, and keep their qualifying hopes alive. Northamptonshire had nothing to show for their sixth-highest one-day total. Ricardo Vasconcelos hit a maiden one-day hundred but the total still felt inadequate. After a rain break, Yorkshire needed 47 off 25. Three successive sixes for Gary Ballance off Keogh put them in the driving seat, and Jonny Tattersall calmly finished the job.*

At Northampton, May 6. **Nottinghamshire won by one wicket.** ‡**Northamptonshire 325-7** (50 overs) (R. S. Vasconcelos 74, J. J. Cobb 63, R. I. Keogh 71, A. G. Wakely 53); **Nottinghamshire 328-9** (49.3 overs) (A. D. Hales 36, S. R. Patel 136*, T. J. Moores 69; N. L. Buck 3-60, B. W. Sanderson 3-66). *Attendance:* 1,923. *Nottinghamshire clinched top spot in the North Group – and a home semi-final – thanks to a magnificent one-day career-best from Samit Patel. With 12 needed off the final over, and No. 11 Jake Ball fresh to the middle, the 34-year-old Patel hit Ben Sanderson for a six and two fours. "A few people were thinking I might have been past it," he said. Northamptonshire had looked in charge until Tom Moores's 69 off 55 tipped the scales.*

Northamptonshire away matches

April 17: lost to Durham by 72 runs.   April 24: lost to Lancashire by 45 runs (DLS).
April 19: lost to Derbyshire by 53 runs.   May 4: beat Leicestershire by 29 runs.

NOTTINGHAMSHIRE

At Nottingham, April 19. **Nottinghamshire won by 11 runs.** ‡**Nottinghamshire 417-7** (50 overs) (B. T. Slater 74, J. M. Clarke 139, B. M. Duckett 30, T. J. Moores 74, L. J. Fletcher 46*); **Lancashire 406-9** (50 overs) (H. Hameed 30, S. J. Croft 110, D. J. Vilas 166, J. J. Bohannon 35; J. L. Pattinson 5-61). *County debut:* Z. J. Chappell. *Attendance:* 4,085. *Records tumbled on a dizzying day, as Nottinghamshire squeezed home. They owed much to James Pattinson, whose previous deed for the county had been to hit the winning runs in the 2017 final; his five-for included both Lancashire's centurions, Steven Croft and Dane Vilas. Earlier, Joe Clarke made a brilliant career-best 139 off 99, becoming the first Nottinghamshire player to score a hundred on his one-day debut since Brian Bolus in 1963. Their total was their third-highest (for seven days), and the highest conceded by*

Lancashire, who then made their own record total. The match aggregate of 823 was the ninth-highest globally, while Vilas's 166 off 100 was Lancashire's highest one-day score.

At Nottingham, April 26. **Nottinghamshire won by 87 runs** (DLS). **Nottinghamshire 433-7** (50 overs) (C. D. Nash 56, J. M. Clarke 55, B. M. Duckett 86, J. D. Libby 66, T. J. Moores 50, S. J. Mullaney 81; G. T. Griffiths 3-92); ‡**Leicestershire 259** (33.2 overs) (H. E. Dearden 74, M. J. Cosgrove 59, P. J. Horton 36; L. J. Fletcher 3-53). *Attendance:* 2,433. *Trent Bridge was treated to another explosive display from Nottinghamshire, who passed 400 for the second time in a week. All the top six hit fifties, with Tom Moores (50 off 32) and Steven Mullaney (81 off 41) adding a brutal 91 in 7.3 overs. Leicestershire's chase was interrupted by rain, and their target reduced to 347 in 37. A mid-innings collapse saw them lose five for 15 in 16 balls.*

NOTTINGHAMSHIRE'S HIGHEST ONE-DAY TOTALS

445-8	v Northamptonshire at Nottingham (50-over match) ..	2016
433-7	**v Leicestershire at Nottingham (50)**	**2019**
429-9	v Somerset at Taunton (50)	2017
417-7	**v Lancashire at Nottingham (50)**.................	**2019**
415-5	v Warwickshire at Nottingham (50)	2016
409-7	v Leicestershire at Leicester (50)	2018
373-5	v Essex at Chelmsford (50)	2017
368-2	v Middlesex at Lord's (50)........................	2014
346-9	v Ireland at Nottingham (50)	2009
344-6	v Northumberland at Jesmond (60)	1994

At Nottingham, April 28. **Nottinghamshire won by four wickets.** ‡**Yorkshire 213** (42.2 overs) (A. Lyth 63, H. C. Brook 39, M. J. Waite 32; J. T. Ball 3-32); **Nottinghamshire 214-6** (34.3 overs) (C. D. Nash 35, J. M. Clarke 40, S. R. Patel 36, S. J. Mullaney 54*; M. W. Pillans 3-57). *Attendance:* 13,961. *When Yorkshire reached 112-1 in the 16th, the scene was set for another day of record-breaking. But Jake Ball took 3-32, and they folded swiftly. Mullaney's 54* off 58 saw Nottinghamshire to a fifth successive win. Cut-price admission for a Family Fun Day drew a bumper crowd for the second year in a row.*

At Grantham, May 3. ‡**Nottinghamshire v Durham. Abandoned.**

Nottinghamshire away matches

April 21: beat Derbyshire by six wickets.

April 23: beat Warwickshire by 118 runs.

May 1: lost to Worcestershire by five wickets.

May 6: beat Northamptonshire by one wicket.

WARWICKSHIRE

At Birmingham, April 19. **Tied. Warwickshire 270-8** (50 overs) (S. R. Hain 40, T. R. Ambrose 77, W. M. H. Rhodes 43, L. Banks 31; M. W. Pillans 3-56); ‡**Yorkshire 270-9** (50 overs) (D. J. Willey 40, J. A. Tattersall 79, T. T. Bresnan 89; C. R. Woakes 3-47, H. J. H. Brookes 3-50). *Attendance:* 2,420. *Both sides rued missed chances: the hosts had Yorkshire on the ropes at 33-4, but Jonny Tattersall and Tim Bresnan put on 138 for the sixth wicket to shift the balance. Tim Ambrose's patient 77, meanwhile, had been crucial to Warwickshire's challenging total.*

At Birmingham, April 23. **Nottinghamshire won by 118 runs.** ‡**Nottinghamshire 301-9** (50 overs) (B. T. Slater 100, J. M. Clarke 39, S. J. Mullaney 40, L. J. Fletcher 32, J. L. Pattinson 33; J. S. Patel 5-45); **Warwickshire 183** (37.5 overs) (A. T. Thomson 55; L. J. Fletcher 3-21, M. Carter 3-60). *Attendance:* 1,755. *Ben Slater's first one-day hundred for Nottinghamshire laid the foundations, but they were indebted to Luke Fletcher and James Pattinson for an eighth-wicket partnership of 50 that nudged them towards 300. The pair then joined forces with off-spinner Matt Carter, who took the new ball, to reduce Warwickshire's challenging total.*

At Birmingham, April 26. **Durham won by seven wickets** (DLS). **Warwickshire 244-8** (50 overs) (S. R. Hain 50, T. R. Ambrose 62, C. R. Woakes 50; B. A. Carse 3-52); ‡**Durham 211-3** (33.4 overs)

(G. Clark 66, A. Z. Lees 78*, G. J. Harte 51*). *Attendance: 757. Half-centuries from Graham Clark, Alex Lees and Gareth Harte – his first in one-day cricket – guided Durham past a revised target with 14 balls to spare. Sam Hain and Ambrose had made half-centuries for Warwickshire but they lacked momentum until Chris Woakes hit a 44-ball 50.*

At Birmingham, May 4. **Warwickshire won by five wickets** (DLS). **Lancashire 277-7** (50 overs) (K. K. Jennings 31, S. J. Croft 45, D. J. Vilas 83, J. J. Bohannon 37*, S. Mahmood 45; A. T. Thomson 3-27); ‡**Warwickshire 256-5** (44.3 overs) (E. J. Pollock 38, S. R. Hain 84*, L. Banks 61, A. J. Mellor 30*; J. M. Anderson 3-21). *Attendance: 3,947. Defeat left Lancashire sweating on results elsewhere for their quarter-final place. Their innings had been sprinkled with cameos, but there was no defining contribution. James Anderson's high-class opening spell had Warwickshire struggling in pursuit of a revised target of 255 in 45, until Hain and Liam Banks put on 111 for the fourth wicket.*

Warwickshire away matches

April 21: lost to Northamptonshire by 194 runs.   April 30: lost to Derbyshire by five wickets.
April 28: beat Worcestershire by 34 runs.   May 6: lost to Leicestershire by 36 runs.

WORCESTERSHIRE

At Worcester, April 24. **Worcestershire won by four wickets** (DLS). **Durham 114-4** (27.2 overs) (A. Z. Lees 52*); ‡**Worcestershire 152-6** (22.2 overs) (H. D. Rutherford 33, O. B. Cox 31*). *Attendance: 1,111. After a four-hour rain break, Worcestershire were set 152 in 24 overs. Hamish Rutherford and Riki Wessels raced to 50 inside five, but it needed a soothing stand of 51 between Ben Cox and Ross Whiteley to seal the win. For Durham, Cameron Bancroft was dismissed for the first time in the competition after back-to-back unbeaten hundreds.*

At Worcester, April 28. **Warwickshire won by 34 runs.** ‡**Warwickshire 315-5** (50 overs) (S. R. Hain 161*, L. Banks 44, A. T. Thomson 33); **Worcestershire 281** (47.2 overs) (H. D. Rutherford 42, M. H. Wessels 37, T. C. Fell 53, W. D. Parnell 76, J. C. Tongue 34; J. S. Patel 3-37). *Attendance: 1,515. Sam Hain batted with growing authority to guide Warwickshire to their highest one-day total against Worcestershire. On a tricky pitch, Hain proceeded cautiously: he went 19 overs without a boundary. But, after reaching his hundred in 110 balls, he gambolled to his highest one-day score, in 141. Rutherford and Wessels were again quick out of the blocks, and Wayne Parnell hit 76 off 57, but Jeetan Patel's miserly spell strangled the chase.*

At Worcester, May 1. **Worcestershire won by five wickets.** ‡**Nottinghamshire 121** (32 overs) (C. D. Nash 51; W. D. Parnell 5-24); **Worcestershire 124-5** (25.1 overs) (T. C. Fell 48*). *Attendance: 1,325. Nottinghamshire never recovered from the havoc wreaked by the home seamers, and lost their unbeaten record. Charlie Morris and Pat Brown reduced them to 31-3, before Parnell registered his best one-day figures in England. Worcestershire also found batting tricky, but Tom Fell dug in.*

At Worcester, May 4. **Worcestershire won by 150 runs.** ‡**Worcestershire 293-7** (50 overs) (T. C. Fell 31, G. H. Rhodes 106, O. B. Cox 87; S. A. Patterson 4-45); **Yorkshire 143** (33 overs) (T. Köhler-Cadmore 31, M. W. Pillans 31; W. D. Parnell 5-25, E. G. Barnard 3-26). *Attendance: 1,398. Seizing his chance after Daryl Mitchell was ruled out by a back injury, George Rhodes hit his maiden century to end Yorkshire's hopes of qualifying. Steven Patterson had Worcestershire in peril at 62-4, before Rhodes and Cox added 169, a county fifth-wicket record. Parnell then collected his second five-wicket haul of the week. Worcestershire needed to win at Derby to reach the knockouts.*

Worcestershire away matches

April 17: beat Lancashire by 125 runs.   April 26: beat Northamptonshire by 20 runs.
April 21: lost to Leicestershire by 38 runs.   May 6: beat Derbyshire by four wickets.

YORKSHIRE

At Leeds, April 17. **Yorkshire won by 213 runs.** **Yorkshire 379-7** (50 overs) (H. C. Brook 103, G. S. Ballance 156, J. A. Tattersall 58; T. A. I. Taylor 3-57); ‡**Leicestershire 166** (29.3 overs) (M. J. Cosgrove 42; M. W. Pillans 5-29). *Attendance: 2,877. Yorkshire recovered from 17-3 to record the highest one-day total at Headingley, and their joint-highest against first-class opposition. Gary*

Ballance hit a career-best 156, and put on 211 with Harry Brook, a county fourth-wicket record. At 20 years 54 days, Brook became Yorkshire's third-youngest one-day centurion, behind Sachin Tendulkar (19 years 101 days) in 1992, and Anthony McGrath (19 years 332 days) in 1995. Mark Cosgrove was the only Leicestershire batsman to detain the home team; Mat Pillans collected his first one-day five-for.

At Leeds, April 21. **Lancashire won by one run.** ‡Lancashire **311-6** (50 overs) (S. J. Croft 97, R. P. Jones 65, J. J. Bohannon 55*); **Yorkshire 310** (50 overs) (T. Köhler-Cadmore 97, G. S. Ballance 72, J. A. Tattersall 49; S. Mahmood 3-76). *County debut:* L. J. Hurt (Lancashire). *Attendance:* 4,683. *Lancashire ended an 11-year wait for a one-day win over Yorkshire when, with three needed off two balls, and Saqib Mahmood holding his nerve, Jonny Tattersall and Josh Poysden (attempting a second) were both run out. Steven Croft had fallen three short of consecutive centuries, and Lancashire were grateful to Josh Bohannon, who raced to a maiden one-day fifty after taking 41 off Tim Bresnan's final two overs.*

At Leeds, April 26. **Tied (DLS).** ‡**Yorkshire 308-2** (40 overs) (T. Köhler-Cadmore 79, A. Lyth 78, D. J. Willey 72*, H. C. Brook 59*); **Derbyshire 224-3** (22 overs) (B. A. Godleman 107*, J. L. du Plooy 75, M. J. J. Critchley 33*). *Attendance:* 1,847. *Billy Godleman became the first Derbyshire player to hit three successive one-day centuries, reaching a 59-ball hundred in the final over, with eight fours and five sixes. But, with two needed off the last delivery, he and Matt Critchley could only scramble a bye. It was Yorkshire's second tie in three games. A rain break of nearly three and a half hours had given Derbyshire a revised target of 225 in 22 overs.*

At Leeds, May 6. **No result. Durham 182-2** (34.2 overs) (B. A. Raine 32, S. Steel 68, A. Z. Lees 51*) v ‡**Yorkshire.** *County debuts:* B. D. Birkhead, W. A. R. Fraine, T. W. Loten, J. D. Warner (Yorkshire). *Attendance:* 1,932. *Successive no-results ended Durham's qualification hopes. They had been going well against an experimental Yorkshire line-up, Alex Lees marking his return to his former county with a fifth successive fifty.*

Yorkshire away matches

April 19: tied with Warwickshire.
April 28: lost to Nottinghamshire by four wickets.
May 1: beat Northamptonshire by five wickets (DLS)
May 4: lost to Worcestershire by 150 runs.

SOUTH GROUP

ESSEX

At Chelmsford, April 19. **Middlesex won by 38 runs. Middlesex 366-8** (50 overs) (D. J. Malan 95, N. R. T. Gubbins 56, G. F. B. Scott 63; P. M. Siddle 3-71); ‡**Essex 328** (49.2 overs) (V. Chopra 127, T. Westley 77, R. N. ten Doeschate 32; N. A. Sowter 6-62). *Attendance:* 3,190. *After Dawid Malan's even-paced 95, No. 7 George Scott thumped 63 from 30 balls, with five sixes, to propel Middlesex to their highest List A total against Essex. Robbie White, on loan against Hampshire, took four catches and a stumping. Two days after making a century against Glamorgan, Varun Chopra kept his side in the hunt with 127, putting on 158 with Tom Westley, but Essex's chase fizzled out after Chopra and Ravi Bopara (20) fell in the same over from Toby Roland-Jones (2-74). Leg-spinner Nathan Sowter, who had never managed more than three wickets before, kicked off a successful personal campaign with Middlesex's best one-day return since Chad Keegan took 6-33 at Trent Bridge in 2005.*

At Chelmsford, April 28. **Essex won by 111 runs.** ‡**Essex 341-6** (50 overs) (R. K. Patel 35, T. Westley 48, R. S. Bopara 89, R. N. ten Doeschate 89); **Hampshire 230** (40.5 overs) (J. M. Vince 47, R. R. Rossouw 93, G. K. Berg 41; M. T. Coles 4-48, R. S. Bopara 3-39). *Attendance:* 2,039. *A fifth-wicket stand of 150 – a List A record for Essex against Hampshire – between Bopara and Ryan ten Doeschate (who faced only 53 balls) set up a big total. Bopara hit Kyle Abbott into the River Can. Hampshire were soon in trouble at 37-3, and only Rilee Rossouw made much impression, with 93 from 72. Matt Coles recorded his best one-day figures for Essex, while Peter Siddle finished with 2-18 from eight overs. Jamie Porter took four outfield catches, equalling the Essex record held by five others, including Allan Border and Mark Waugh.*

At Chelmsford, April 30. **Sussex won by one wicket.** ‡Essex 283-7 (50 overs) (A. N. Cook 36, T. Westley 61, D. W. Lawrence 54, R. N. ten Doeschate 35; D. Wiese 3-54); **Sussex 287-9** (49.5 overs) (L. J. Wright 30, G. H. S. Garton 38, L. J. Evans 68, W. A. T. Beer 75, D. R. Briggs 37*; M. T. Coles 3-72). *Attendance: 2,148. Essex's chances of progressing disappeared when Sussex's last pair, Danny Briggs – on his 28th birthday – and Mir Hamza (9*), pilfered 27* in 23 balls. Sussex had seemed out of it when they lost four wickets in 15 balls to slip to 94-6, but Laurie Evans and Will Beer (who hit a maiden List A half-century) rescued them with a stand of 121, a county record for the seventh wicket. Essex had not made the most of a good start: the openers put on 73, then Westley and Dan Lawrence added 104.*

At Chelmsford, May 7 (day/night). **Gloucestershire won by four wickets.** ‡Essex 293 (49.5 overs) (V. Chopra 156); **Gloucestershire 294-6** (48.5 overs) (C. D. J. Dent 89, J. R. Bracey 113*, B. A. C. Howell 30*; A. P. Beard 3-51). *Attendance: 1,569. Chopra flowed to his third hundred of the competition – but ended up on the losing side for the second time. In reply, James Bracey purred to a maiden List A century, sharing stands of 117 with Chris Dent and 86* in 8.4 overs with Benny Howell, batting with a runner after injuring a hamstring. Results elsewhere meant Gloucestershire failed to make the quarter-finals.*

Essex away matches

April 17: beat Glamorgan by 180 runs.
April 23: lost to Surrey by 65 runs.

April 26: lost to Somerset by 36 runs (DLS).
May 5: lost to Kent by six wickets.

GLAMORGAN

At Cardiff, April 17. **Essex won by 180 runs.** Essex 326-7 (50 overs) (V. Chopra 111, A. N. Cook 40, T. Westley 69, D. W. Lawrence 56); ‡**Glamorgan 146** (31 overs) (M. de Lange 36; R. S. Bopara 3-26). *Attendance: 873. Glamorgan offered little, losing with 19 overs to spare after dipping to 82-7; five were caught behind by Robbie White. Varun Chopra underpinned Essex's sizeable score with a well-paced century, sharing successive stands of 67, 116 and 78.*

At Cardiff, April 21. **Somerset won by two runs.** ‡Somerset 261-9 (50 overs) (J. C. Hildreth 67, C. Overton 41*; M. de Lange 3-37, M. Labuschagne 3-46); **Glamorgan 259** (48.1 overs) (D. L. Lloyd 84, G. G. Wagg 62, L. J. Carey 39; J. H. Davey 4-36, C. Overton 3-51). *Attendance: 882. Another embarrassing defeat looked odds-on when Glamorgan nosedived to 21-5 – and 41-6 – in reply to a Somerset total boosted by 83 for the last two wickets. But David Lloyd and Graham Wagg put on 99, then Lukas Carey and Timm van der Gugten (18*) added 57, before Carey was caught at the second attempt by Azhar Ali at mid-off with just three required.*

At Cardiff, April 25. **No result.** ‡Glamorgan 68-2 (15 overs) v Kent. *The match was reduced to 49 overs before the start, then 40 after a shower – but only 15 were possible. Kent captain Sam Billings dislocated his shoulder in the field at the end of the first, the day after returning from the IPL, and was ruled out of contention for a World Cup place.*

At Cardiff, April 28. **Glamorgan won by 64 runs.** Glamorgan 323-7 (50 overs) (D. L. Lloyd 31, W. T. Root 113*, C. R. Hemphrey 31, G. G. Wagg 30, M. de Lange 58*; M. Morkel 3-47); ‡**Surrey 259** (46.4 overs) (B. T. Foakes 35, J. L. Smith 34, J. Clark 79, S. C. Meaker 50; M. de Lange 4-63, G. G. Wagg 3-46). *Attendance: 607. Glamorgan shrugged off another indifferent start – 69-4 after a superb opening spell by Morne Morkel – to record their first win of the tournament. It was set up by Billy Root and Marchant de Lange, who both improved their List A career-bests during a rollicking eighth-wicket stand of 113* in 63 balls. De Lange then claimed three quick wickets; Surrey were soon 28-4, and never on terms, despite a seventh-wicket rearguard of 107 between Jordan Clark, who equalled his one-day best, and Stuart Meaker, who obliterated his previous-highest of 21.*

Glamorgan away matches

April 19: lost to Hampshire by seven wickets.
April 30: beat Gloucestershire by 74 runs.

May 5: lost to Middlesex by five wickets.
May 7: beat Sussex by two wickets.

GLOUCESTERSHIRE

At Bristol, April 17. **Gloucestershire won by 147 runs.** ‡Gloucestershire 235 (47.5 overs) (C. D. J. Dent 75, G. H. Roderick 74; R. Clarke 4-43, T. K. Curran 3-26); Surrey 88 (24 overs) (C. J. Liddle 3-17, T. M. J. Smith 3-7). *Attendance: 1,362. Chris Dent and Gareth Roderick put on 152 for Gloucestershire's second wicket, but no one else got to grips with the surface. Once their partnership was broken, eight fell for 79 to present Surrey with a modest target. Instead, they folded in the face of probing seam from Dan Worrall and Chris Liddle. Slow left-armer Tom Smith took three late wickets.*

At Bristol, April 23. **Gloucestershire won by six wickets. Kent** 282-8 (50 overs) (Z. Crawley 85, J. L. Denly 56, A. P. Rouse 45*); ‡Gloucestershire 283-4 (46.5 overs) (C. D. J. Dent 41, G. T. Hankins 33, G. H. Roderick 100*; J. R. Bracey 67). *Attendance: 1,204. Roderick's first one-day hundred for four years, from 80 balls, propelled Gloucestershire to a comprehensive victory over injury-hit Kent. Joe Denly, returning from the IPL, and Zak Crawley hit fifties to set up a decent total. But Roderick and James Bracey put on 138 to break the back of the chase.*

At Bristol, April 28. **Gloucestershire won by four wickets.** ‡Somerset 242-9 (50 overs) (Azhar Ali 43, T. B. Abell 42, L. Gregory 52; B. A. C. Howell 3-45); Gloucestershire 246-6 (49.2 overs) (M. A. H. Hammond 48, G. L. van Buuren 61, J. M. R. Taylor 43*, R. F. Higgins 30*). *Attendance: 1,791. Somerset surrendered their 100% record in a tight contest. They had looked on course to sneak a fifth victory as Gloucestershire's reply stuttered, before Jack Taylor and Ryan Higgins put on 49* for the seventh wicket. Graeme van Buuren had hit an aggressive 61, but a used pitch proved too tricky for most.*

At Bristol, April 30. **Glamorgan won by 74 runs.** ‡Glamorgan 331-7 (50 overs) (C. B. Cooke 161, W. T. Root 98; B. A. C. Howell 3-83); Gloucestershire 257 (48.3 overs) (C. D. J. Dent 30, G. L. van Buuren 41, J. M. R. Taylor 75, R. F. Higgins 38, D. A. Payne 36*; M. de Lange 3-41, G. G. Wagg 3-57). *County debut: D. A. Douthwaite (Glamorgan). Attendance: 1,107. A fourth-wicket partnership of 234 – a record for any wicket in this fixture – between Glamorgan captain Chris Cooke and Billy Root powered the visitors to a formidable total. Cooke's career-best 161 came off 127 balls, and included eight sixes. Three quick wickets for Marchant de Lange undermined Gloucestershire's response, although Taylor made a defiant 75.*

Gloucestershire away matches

April 21: lost to Middlesex by six wickets.
April 26: lost to Hampshire by 71 runs (DLS).

May 5: beat Sussex by 116 runs.
May 7: beat Essex by four wickets.

HAMPSHIRE

At Southampton, April 19. **Hampshire won by seven wickets.** ‡Glamorgan 292-9 (50 overs) (D. L. Lloyd 68, W. T. Root 39, G. G. Wagg 68; K. J. Abbott 3-47); Hampshire 293-3 (41.5 overs) (T. P. Alsop 130*, A. K. Markram 31, J. M. Vince 95). *Attendance: 2,656. Glamorgan had no answer to the silky combination of Tom Alsop and James Vince, who put on 161 in 22 overs for the second wicket. Alsop's 130* off 115 was a career-best, as Hampshire sauntered home. After winning the toss, Glamorgan had been 140-6 in the 27th, until Wagg clattered a career-best 68.*

At Southampton, April 23. **Hampshire won by 119 runs.** Hampshire 301-9 (50 overs) (A. K. Markram 88, R. R. Rossouw 64, L. A. Dawson 43; T. G. Helm 5-71); ‡Middlesex 182 (35.4 overs) (J. A. Simpson 36, E. J. G. Morgan 41, S. S. Eskinazi 33, S. T. Finn 30*; K. J. Abbott 3-36, A. K. Markram 3-39, L. A. Dawson 3-37). *Attendance: 1,621. Aiden Markram hit 88 off 90 in a commanding Hampshire total, then removed three Middlesex batsmen with his part-time off-breaks. Earlier, Tom Helm's expensive five-for included four wickets in eight balls.*

At Southampton, April 26. **Hampshire won by 71 runs** (DLS). Hampshire 331-8 (50 overs) (J. M. Vince 190, L. A. Dawson 73; C. J. Liddle 4-66); ‡Gloucestershire 246 (43.5 overs) (J. R. Bracey 40, B. A. C. Howell 32, J. M. R. Taylor 32, R. F. Higgins 45; M. S. Crane 3-64). *Attendance: 1,357. Vince hit a county record one-day score – surpassing his own best – after Hampshire fought back from 65-4. He made 190 off 154, and added 186 with Liam Dawson to bring up a formidable total. Gloucestershire's target was revised to 318 in 47 overs, but it was academic.*

HIGHEST ONE-DAY SCORES FOR HAMPSHIRE

190	J. M. Vince	v Gloucestershire at Southampton	2019
178	J. M. Vince	v Glamorgan at Southampton	2017
177	C. G. Greenidge	v Glamorgan at Southampton (Northlands Road)	1975
173*	C. G. Greenidge	v Minor Counties South at Amersham	1973
172	C. G. Greenidge	v Surrey at Southampton (Northlands Road)	1987
171	J. M. Vince	v Yorkshire at Southampton	2018
167*	S. M. Ervine	v Ireland at Southampton	2009
166*	T. E. Jesty	v Surrey at Portsmouth	1983
165*	V. P. Terry	v Berkshire at Southampton (Northlands Road)	1985
163*	C. G. Greenidge	v Warwickshire at Birmingham	1979
162*	C. G. Greenidge	v Lancashire at Manchester	1983

At Southampton, May 2. **Hampshire won by nine runs. ‡Hampshire 355-5** (50 overs) (T. P. Alsop 124, A. H. T. Donald 41, A. K. Markram 130); **Sussex 346** (49.3 overs) (P. D. Salt 31, D. Wiese 171, B. C. Brown 64; K. J. Abbott 3-64, M. S. Crane 3-55). *Attendance:* 2,129. *A thrilling contest was settled in the final over, when Mason Crane had Mir Hamza stumped, bringing to an end Sussex's valiant pursuit. Things had looked routine for Hampshire after hundreds for Alsop and Markram took them to their fifth-highest one-day total, and Sussex stumbled to 103-5. But David Wiese and Ben Brown put on 232, a sixth-wicket record for the fixture, with Wiese's eventual 171, off 126 balls and including nine sixes. With three overs to go, they were 335-5, but Crane removed Brown, before Kyle Abbott got rid of Wiese and Danny Briggs. When Crane struck twice in the last over, Sussex had lost five for 11 – and the game.*

HIGHEST ONE-DAY SCORES FOR SUSSEX

171	D. Wiese	v Hampshire at Southampton	2019
166	L. J. Wright	v Middlesex at Lord's	2019
163	C. J. Adams	v Middlesex at Arundel	1999
158	R. K. Rao	v Derbyshire at Derby	1997
158*	M. W. Goodwin	v Essex at Chelmsford	2006
157*	M. G. Bevan	v Essex at Chelmsford	2000
146	E. C. Joyce	v Gloucestershire at Hove	2009
144	M. J. Prior	v Warwickshire at Hove	2005
144	M. W. Goodwin	v Surrey at Hove	2009
141*	G. D. Mendis	v Warwickshire at Hove	1980

Hampshire away matches

April 17: beat Kent by 90 runs.
April 28: lost to Essex by 111 runs.

April 30: beat Surrey by 53 runs.
May 5: beat Somerset by seven wickets.

KENT

At Canterbury, April 17 (day/night). **Hampshire won by 90 runs. Hampshire 310-9** (50 overs) (J. M. Vince 56, S. A. Northeast 105*, R. R. Rossouw 55; M. E. Milnes 5-79); **‡Kent 220** (40 overs) (Z. Crawley 49, D. I. Stevens 30, H. W. Podmore 40). *County debuts:* A. H. T. Donald, J. K. Fuller (Hampshire). *Attendance:* 1,750. *In his first game at Canterbury since leaving for Hampshire in 2017, Sam Northeast hit an imperious 105* to ensure they won a rerun of the 2018 final. Hampshire had been 224-6 when Northeast pressed the accelerator, and their total was always too many for a Kent side without captain Sam Billings and his deputy Joe Denly. Matt Milnes picked up a five-for on his one-day debut.*

At Beckenham, April 21. **Sussex won by seven wickets.** ‡Kent 298 (49.4 overs) (Z. Crawley 30, S. R. Dickson 30, M. T. Renshaw 109, O. G. Robinson 46, H. W. Podmore 32; G. H. S. Garton 3-42); **Sussex 302-3** (40 overs) (P. D. Salt 137*, L. J. Evans 46, H. Z. Finch 89). *Attendance:* 1,412. *Matt Renshaw's first one-day hundred made no difference to the outcome as Sussex strolled home. He reached three figures in 105 balls, and put on 121 with Ollie Robinson, but Kent lost their last eight for 96. Phil Salt's 137*, also his maiden one-day century, came off 106.*

At Beckenham, May 5. **Kent won by six wickets. Essex 271-9** (50 overs) (A. N. Cook 53, T. Westley 58, M. T. Coles 34; M. E. Milnes 3-60); ‡Kent 272-4 (46.4 overs) (D. J. Bell-Drummond 120*, Z. Crawley 94). *Attendance:* 1,186. *Daniel Bell-Drummond's 120*, and opening stand with Zak Crawley of 188, a Kent record against Essex, ensured a comfortable victory. In contrast to the visitors' cautious start, Bell-Drummond and Crawley reached three figures in the 16th over. Alastair Cook and Tom Westley had made fifties, but the Essex batting lacked depth.*

At Canterbury, May 7 (day/night). **Middlesex won by 33 runs.** ‡**Middlesex 380-5** (50 overs) (M. D. E. Holden 166, N. R. T. Gubbins 47, L. R. P. L. Taylor 94); **Kent 347** (48.5 overs) (Z. Crawley 120, M. T. Renshaw 49, H. G. Kuhn 36, A. J. Blake 43; J. A. R. Harris 4-65). *Attendance:* 1,101. *Max Holden hit Middlesex's highest one-day score, surpassing 163 by Andrew Strauss against Surrey at The Oval in 2008, to ensure a place in the quarter-finals. Holden faced 139 balls for his 166, which included only one six, and added a Middlesex record 191 for the third wicket with Ross Taylor. After conceding their highest total, Kent put up a spirited response, including a first one-day hundred for Crawley. His 120 was Kent's best one-day score against Middlesex, surpassing Colin Cowdrey's 107 in 1972.*

MIDDLESEX'S HIGHEST ONE-DAY TOTALS

380-5	**v Kent at Canterbury (50-over match)**	**2019**
367-6	v Sussex at Hove (50)	2015
366-8	**v Essex at Chelmsford (50)**	**2019**
364-6	**v Somerset at Radlett (50)**	**2019**
350-6	v Lancashire at Lord's (40)	2012
341-5	v Sussex at Lord's (50)	2017
341-7	v Somerset at Lord's (50)	2009
337-5	v Somerset at Southgate (45)	2003
333-4	v Gloucestershire at Southgate (45)	2005
325-5	v Leicestershire at Leicester (55)	1992

Kent away matches

April 19: lost to Somerset by 264 runs.
April 23: lost to Gloucestershire by six wickets.

April 25: no result v Glamorgan.
May 2: beat Surrey by eight wickets.

MIDDLESEX

At Lord's, April 21. **Middlesex won by six wickets. Gloucestershire 283-7** (50 overs) (C. D. J. Dent 47, G. H. Roderick 38, J. R. Bracey 83, B. A. C. Howell 55); ‡**Middlesex 287-4** (42.2 overs) (E. J. G. Morgan 38, S. S. Eskinazi 107*, N. R. T. Gubbins 98*). *Attendance:* 3,142. *Middlesex's new coach Stuart Law revamped the batting order in an attempt to instil a more attacking approach – but after an indifferent start to the chase it was the usual opening pair of Stevie Eskinazi and Nick Gubbins who brought victory, with a fifth-wicket stand of 184* in 25 overs. Gloucestershire's star was James Bracey, whose 61-ball 83 included four sixes over the short Tavern boundary; he shared a fourth-wicket stand of 111 with Benny Howell.*

At Lord's, April 27. **Sussex won by 122 runs. Sussex 298** (48 overs) (L. J. Wright 166, B. C. Brown 55; T. J. Murtagh 3-24, N. A. Sowter 4-48); ‡**Middlesex 176** (33.3 overs) (S. S. Eskinazi 42; Mir Hamza 3-43). *Attendance:* 2,200. *In a match reduced to 48 overs, Luke Wright hit 166, Sussex's highest List A score, eclipsing Chris Adams's 163 in 1999, also against Middlesex (David Wiese claimed the record five days later). Wright clattered ten fours and nine sixes, but of the others only*

Ben Brown reached 20. After he and Wright put on 174, the last five wickets added 22. But it was enough: Middlesex could not manage even a fifty partnership.

At Radlett, May 1. **Middlesex won by 118 runs. Middlesex 364-6** (50 overs) (S. D. Robson 106, M. D. E. Holden 45, N. R. T. Gubbins 90, S. S. Eskinazi 30, J. A. Simpson 32); ‡**Somerset 246** (43.4 overs) (Azhar Ali 46, R. E. van der Merwe 38; N. A. Sowter 3-50). *Attendance: 1,380. Sam Robson, recalled to an injury-hit side, struck his maiden white-ball hundred as Middlesex piled up a lofty total – the second-highest on the Cobden Hill ground, after Lancashire's 381-3 in the NatWest Trophy against Hertfordshire in 1999. Somerset were sunk at 124-6 in the 25th over, although the tail narrowed the margin of defeat.*

At Lord's, May 5. **Middlesex won by five wickets. Glamorgan 285** (49.4 overs) (J. L. Lawlor 38, C. B. Cooke 46, W. T. Root 37, C. R. Hemphrey 87; T. S. Roland-Jones 3-46, N. A. Sowter 4-58); ‡**Middlesex 289-5** (47.3 overs) (S. D. Robson 79, N. R. T. Gubbins 92, S. S. Eskinazi 71*). *Attendance: 2,258. Charlie Hemphrey's 81-ball 87 lifted Glamorgan to a competitive total, but Robson and Gubbins put Middlesex in control with a second-wicket stand of 147, then Eskinazi kept them on course for the quarter-finals with another win. Robson had earlier aired his leg-breaks for the first time in white-ball cricket, and took a wicket third ball, when Marnus Labuschagne played on.*

Middlesex away matches

April 19: beat Essex by 38 runs.
April 23: lost to Hampshire by 119 runs.

April 25: beat Surrey by 37 runs.
May 7: beat Kent by 33 runs.

SOMERSET

At Taunton, April 19. **Somerset won by 264 runs. Somerset 358-9** (50 overs) (T. Banton 107, L. Gregory 51, C. Overton 66*); ‡**Kent 94** (27 overs) (C. Overton 5-18). *Attendance: 5,038. Somerset hammered their white-ball bogey team to record their biggest one-day win against a first-class county. Tom Banton hit a sparkling first hundred for Somerset, reaching three figures in 76 balls. Craig Overton maintained the charge with his highest one-day score – 66* off 36 – then produced career-best bowling figures. An understrength Kent were overwhelmed.*

At Taunton, April 26 (day/night). **Somerset won by 36 runs (DLS). Somerset 353-5** (39 overs) (Azhar Ali 110, P. D. Trego 141, J. C. Hildreth 40; P. M. Siddle 4-60); ‡**Essex 154-6** (17 overs) (T. Westley 32, D. W. Lawrence 51, R. N. ten Doeschate 35; T. D. Groenewald 3-34). *Attendance: 3,068. Somerset made it four from four in the first fixture under Taunton's new permanent floodlights. Rain meant a 39-over match started two hours late, then forced another lengthy break during the Essex innings. When they resumed, the revised target was 191 from 17, and 21 an over. Azhar Ali hit his first century at Taunton, and Peter Trego went on to 141 from 101 balls. A presentation was made to James Hildreth in recognition of his most appearances across all formats for Somerset.*

At Taunton, May 5. **Hampshire won by seven wickets.** ‡**Somerset 216** (40.3 overs) (T. B. Abell 36, G. A. Bartlett 40, R. E. van der Merwe 38; K. J. Abbott 3-36); **Hampshire 221-3** (31.3 overs) (A. H. T. Donald 57, A. K. Markram 61, S. A. Northeast 51*). *Attendance: 4,900. Hampshire secured top spot in the South Group, and a home semi-final. Somerset, their form in freefall, had to win their last game against Surrey. On a used pitch, all their top six got a start, but none passed George Bartlett's 40. Aiden Markram, in his final game before joining South Africa's World Cup preparations, made a measured 61 for Hampshire.*

At Taunton, May 7 (day/night). **Somerset won by five wickets. Surrey 289-9** (50 overs) (D. Elgar 64, B. T. Foakes 46, J. L. Smith 40, R. S. Patel 41*; C. Overton 3-48, J. Overton 4-64); ‡**Somerset 292-5** (45.4 overs) (T. Banton 53, J. C. Hildreth 93, G. A. Bartlett 57*, L. Gregory 36*; C. McKerr 3-56). *Attendance: 3,204. Somerset booked their place in the knockouts thanks to Hildreth's perfectly paced 93 off 89. Surrey, left with only two points, were confirmed as the weakest team in the competition. Asked to bat, they had struggled against the combined muscle of the Overton twins, though Dean Elgar top-scored against his former county.*

Somerset away matches

April 21: beat Glamorgan by two runs.
April 24: beat Sussex by 68 runs (DLS).

April 28: lost to Gloucestershire by four wickets.
May 1: lost to Middlesex by 118 runs.

SURREY

At The Oval, April 23. **Surrey won by 65 runs. Surrey 278-8** (50 overs) (J. J. Roy 35*, R. J. Burns 55, B. T. Foakes 82, O. J. D. Pope 39; S. J. Cook 3-37); ‡**Essex 213** (42.5 overs) (D. W. Lawrence 50, R. S. Bopara 47; M. Morkel 4-23, L. E. Plunkett 4-50). *Attendance: 3,349. Surrey paid a cruel price for victory – their only one – as Jason Roy (thigh), Ollie Pope (shoulder) and Rikki Clarke (finger) all suffered injuries. Ben Foakes provided resilience in a beautifully judged 82. Dan Lawrence and Ravi Bopara added 90 for Essex's fourth wicket, but the last four fell for nine: Liam Plunkett despatched Simon Harmer and Ryan ten Doeschate with successive deliveries after a stand of 46, then Peter Siddle became Gareth Batty's 250th one-day victim.*

At The Oval, April 25. **Middlesex won by 37 runs.** ‡**Middlesex 277** (49.2 overs) (L. R. P. L. Taylor 64, N. R. T. Gubbins 33, T. S. Roland-Jones 45, N. A. Sowter 31; G. J. Batty 4-29); **Surrey 240** (48 overs) (D. Elgar 43, R. J. Burns 49, B. T. Foakes 71; T. G. Helm 4-40, N. A. Sowter 4-37). *County debuts: L. R. P. L. Taylor (Middlesex); J. Clark (Surrey). Attendance: 2,379. A stand of 66 between Toby Roland-Jones and Nathan Sowter transformed the match after Middlesex limped to 185-8, despite Ross Taylor's debut half-century. Batty's tight ten overs included three for one in six balls. But, with Sowter and Tom Helm bowling well, Foakes could not gain sufficient support from a depleted Surrey line-up. Their innings was briefly interrupted by a fox, which trotted in front of the OCS Stand.*

At The Oval, April 30. **Hampshire won by 53 runs. Hampshire 307** (49.2 overs) (A. K. Markram 88, L. A. Dawson 108; C. McKerr 3-59, S. C. Meaker 3-58); ‡**Surrey 254** (46.2 overs) (M. D. Stoneman 70, R. J. Burns 38; K. J. Abbott 3-58). *Attendance: 5,993. Liam Dawson's superb 93-ball 108 – his first senior century for three years – gave Hampshire the upper hand in front of 6,000 children on Schools Day. Stuart Meaker was banned from bowling after two high full tosses; Conor McKerr completed his over with a ball Dawson hoisted for six. Surrey also started well – Mark Stoneman and Will Jacks opened with 66 from 13 overs – but subsided again, with Dawson taking 2-39 as Hampshire made it five wins out of six.*

At The Oval, May 2. **Kent won by eight wickets.** ‡**Surrey 127** (35.2 overs) (D. Elgar 62*; M. E. Milnes 3-37); **Kent 131-2** (28 overs) (D. J. Bell-Drummond 41, M. T. Renshaw 32*, H. G. Kuhn 36*). *Attendance: 3,023. Dean Elgar stood almost alone in resisting Kent's bowlers, led by Matt Milnes: only two others reached double figures in a sorry display. Kent had an hour to bat before lunch, and completed their first win of the tournament – and Surrey's seventh defeat out of eight – at 4.15, just before the onset of steady rain.*

Surrey away matches

April 17: lost to Gloucestershire by 147 runs.
April 19: lost to Sussex by two wickets.
April 28: lost to Glamorgan by 64 runs.
May 7: lost to Somerset by five wickets.

SUSSEX

At Hove, April 19. **Sussex won by two wickets.** ‡**Surrey 274-9** (50 overs) (M. D. Stoneman 38, W. G. Jacks 56, B. T. Foakes 64, O. J. D. Pope 33; Mir Hamza 4-43); **Sussex 278-8** (48.1 overs) (P. D. Salt 32, L. J. Wright 69, D. Wiese 92*; T. K. Curran 3-37). *Attendance: 3,782. David Wiese thrilled a big Good Friday crowd with his then highest one-day score for Sussex, calmly steering them home with 11 balls to spare, after the outcome had been in the balance at 255-8. There were contrasting fortunes for two Surrey bowlers vying for a place in England's World Cup squad: Liam Plunkett's six overs went for 57, while Tom Curran bowled beautifully for 3-37. A slow pitch inhibited the strokemakers, although Will Jacks and Ben Foakes made attractive fifties for Surrey.*

At Hove, April 24. **Somerset won by 68 runs** (DLS). **Somerset 283-8** (50 overs) (Azhar Ali 68, J. C. Hildreth 81, T. B. Abell 44, L. Gregory 50; Mir Hamza 3-54); ‡**Sussex 62-4** (16.3 overs). *Attendance: 1,216. Somerset seemed to have overperformed on a slow pitch after several useful contributions. James Hildreth top-scored, but the fireworks came from Lewis Gregory, who raced to 50 in 25 balls. With Wright absent ill, Sussex lacked top-order oomph, and were well behind when rain arrived.*

At Eastbourne, May 5. **Gloucestershire won by 116 runs.** ‡**Gloucestershire 335-6** (50 overs) (C. D. J. Dent 46, M. A. H. Hammond 95, G. H. Roderick 53, B. A. C. Howell 41, J. M. R. Taylor 69*); **Sussex 219** (43.2 overs) (L. J. Evans 44, D. Wiese 55; M. D. Taylor 3-39, B. A. C. Howell

3-48). Attendance: 2,357. Sussex lost for the third successive year since returning to The Saffrons. The decisive innings was played by Jack Taylor, whose 69* came off 26 balls, with eight sixes; Gloucestershire plundered 135 off the final ten overs. Sussex were one run better off after 40, but lost their last five for 14. Benny Howell finished the match with a hat-trick.

At Hove, May 7 (day/night). **Glamorgan won by two wickets.** ‡Sussex 347-7 (50 overs) (L. J. Wright 97, L. J. Evans 110, D. Wiese 57*; M. de Lange 3-74); Glamorgan 348-8 (48.4 overs) (J. L. Lawlor 48, C. B. Cooke 41, M. Labuschagne 54, W. T. Root 78, D. A. Douthwaite 52*). *County debut: R. I. Walker (Glamorgan). Attendance: 2,715. Glamorgan completed their highest successful chase, and the highest at Hove. Playing in an unnamed shirt because his was still on order, Dan Douthwaite made sure everyone knew who he was with 52* off 35 to ease them home. Earlier, he had taken 2-46. The Sussex innings had been built on an 87-ball 110 by Laurie Evans, and 97 from Luke Wright, who broke a bulb on the scoreboard with a six.*

Sussex away matches

April 21: beat Kent by seven wickets.　　　　April 30: beat Essex by one wicket.
April 27: beat Middlesex by 122 runs.　　　　May 2: lost to Hampshire by nine runs.

QUARTER-FINALS

At Worcester, May 10. **Somerset won by 147 runs. Somerset 337-8** (50 overs) (T. Banton 112, P. D. Trego 37, J. C. Hildreth 38; P. R. Brown 3-80, W. D. Parnell 3-50); ‡**Worcestershire 190** (38 overs) (D. K. H. Mitchell 34, R. A. Whiteley 33; Azhar Ali 5-34). *Attendance: 1,049. A superb hundred by Tom Banton, his second of the competition, took Somerset to a total Worcestershire never threatened. Banton, who shared an opening stand of 66 with Azhar Ali, and 115 for the second wicket with Peter Trego, hit 112 off 103 balls. Craig and Jamie Overton added 32 from the last 16 to lift Somerset to a challenging total. Wayne Parnell took his tally to 22 wickets in the tournament. Worcestershire's top seven all reached double figures, but none hung around. Azhar's leg-spin bamboozled the lower-middle order and tail.*

At Lord's, May 10 (day/night). **Lancashire won by 20 runs. Lancashire 304-4** (50 overs) (K. K. Jennings 96, S. J. Croft 68, D. J. Vilas 70*); ‡**Middlesex 284** (48.5 overs) (J. A. R. Harris 117, J. A. Simpson 74; S. Mahmood 4-38). *PoM: S. Mahmood. Attendance: 2,258. Middlesex slumped to 24-5 after ten overs, but were revived by a stand of 197 between James Harris, who hit his maiden county century, and John Simpson. They enjoyed the short Tavern boundary, but both departed in the 41st over, and the tail had too much to do. The early damage had been inflicted by the pacy Saqib Mahmood, who ended the match tied with Middlesex leg-spinner Nathan Sowter as the competition's leading wicket-taker with 25 (Mahmood added three more in the semi-final). Lancashire's innings had been anchored by Keaton Jennings. He put on 159 with Steven Croft, before Dane Vilas cracked 70* from 67 balls.*

SEMI-FINALS

HAMPSHIRE v LANCASHIRE

At Southampton, May 12. Hampshire won by four wickets. Toss: Lancashire.
　　Berg, who had previously taken four wickets in six matches in the tournament, recorded his first one-day five-for as Hampshire booked a return ticket to Lord's. He removed Lancashire's last four in nine balls as they struggled to impose themselves on the pitch used for the 734-run bonanza between England and Pakistan the previous day. Mahmood then reduced Hampshire to 23 for three, before Vince and Rossouw, hero of the 2018 final, put on 122. Fittingly, Berg was at the crease when the match was won with an over to spare. Anderson hobbled off during his seventh over after being hit on the knee by a rasping return drive from Fuller.
　　Attendance: 2,051.

Lancashire

K. K. Jennings b Crane	63	J. M. Anderson b Berg		1
L. S. Livingstone c Crane b Edwards	22	M. W. Parkinson not out		1
S. J. Croft c Alsop b Berg	10			
J. S. Lehmann c Fuller b Dawson	62	B 1, lb 2, w 3, nb 4		10
*†D. J. Vilas c Vince b Crane	15			—
R. P. Jones c Dawson b Crane	38	1/37 (2) 2/62 (3)	(47.4 overs)	241
J. J. Bohannon b Berg	14	3/129 (1) 4/151 (5) 5/199 (4)		
S. Mahmood c Vince b Berg	3	6/231 (6) 7/232 (7) 8/234 (9)		
G. Onions c Vince b Berg	2	9/240 (10) 10/241 (8)	10 overs: 55-1	

Abbott 7–0–50–0; Edwards 9–0–45–1; Berg 6.4–0–26–5; Dawson 10–0–49–1; Fuller 5–0–26–0; Crane 10–1–42–3.

Hampshire

†T. P. Alsop c Vilas b Mahmood	0	J. K. Fuller not out		20
A. H. T. Donald c Croft b Mahmood	3			
*J. M. Vince run out (Jones)	79	B 2, w 7, nb 2		11
S. A. Northeast b Mahmood	1			—
R. R. Rossouw b Livingstone	85	(6 wkts, 49 overs)		245
L. A. Dawson c Jennings b Parkinson	28	1/0 (1) 2/17 (2)		
G. K. Berg not out	18	3/23 (4) 4/145 (3)		
		5/204 (6) 6/221 (5)	10 overs: 39-3	

K. J. Abbott, M. S. Crane and F. H. Edwards did not bat.

Mahmood 10–2–46–3; Anderson 6.4–0–34–0; Onions 7–0–41–0; Parkinson 10–0–39–1; Livingstone 10–0–49–1; Jones 2.2–0–21–0; Croft 3–0–13–0.

Umpires: D. J. Millns and M. J. Saggers.   Third umpire: P. K. Baldwin.

NOTTINGHAMSHIRE v SOMERSET

At Nottingham, May 12. Somerset won by 115 runs. Toss: Nottinghamshire.

Somerset concluded a hectic week by winning their third must-win game in six days. Given the high scores on the ground earlier in the competition, their 337 looked vulnerable, but Nottinghamshire stumbled against van der Merwe, and came up well short. Somerset had been given a terrific start by a stand of 93 in 14 overs between Banton and Azhar Ali, and Trego made sure the pace did not slacken. But Ball made effective use of his slower delivery, and the visitors needed some late-order biffing from the Overton twins to reach a challenging total. The pair then combined to take the key wickets of Clarke, Slater and Hales. Nottinghamshire lost four for 25 in nine overs: there was no way back.

Attendance: 4,706.

Somerset

†T. Banton c Moores b Gurney	59	J. Overton run out (Moores)		27
Azhar Ali b Ball	72	J. H. Davey run out (Duckett)		1
P. D. Trego run out (Mullaney)	73			
J. C. Hildreth c and b Ball	1	B 4, lb 11, w 3		18
*T. B. Abell c Moores b Fletcher	18			—
G. A. Bartlett b Mullaney	0	1/93 (1) 2/183 (2)	(50 overs)	337
L. Gregory c Duckett b Ball	37	3/185 (4) 4/227 (5) 5/228 (6)		
R. E. van der Merwe c Mullaney b Ball	11	6/252 (3) 7/287 (7) 8/289 (8)		
C. Overton not out	20	9/336 (10) 10/337 (11)	10 overs: 69-0	

Fletcher 9–0–44–1; Ball 10–0–62–4; Carter 2–0–30–0; Patel 9–0–48–0; Gurney 10–0–86–1; Mullaney 10–0–52–1.

Nottinghamshire

B. T. Slater c van der Merwe b J. Overton .	58	J. T. Ball c Abell b Davey		0
J. M. Clarke c Azhar Ali b C. Overton	14	H. F. Gurney not out		1
A. D. Hales c Banton b C. Overton.......	54			
B. M. Duckett c C. Overton b van der Merwe	1	W 3		3
S. R. Patel lbw b van der Merwe........	3			
*S. J. Mullaney b Davey	29	1/38 (2) 2/110 (1)	(38.2 overs)	222
†T. J. Moores c J. Overton b van der Merwe	16	3/125 (4) 4/131 (3) 5/135 (5)		
L. J. Fletcher c Azhar Ali b Gregory......	43	6/156 (7) 7/186 (6) 8/197 (9)		
M. Carter c Bartlett b Azhar Ali	0	9/203 (10) 10/222 (8)	10 overs: 66-1	

C. Overton 7–0–44–2; Davey 8–0–56–2; Gregory 5.2–0–31–1; J. Overton 6–0–30–1; van der Merwe 9–0–29–3; Azhar Ali 3–0–32–1.

Umpires: M. Burns and N. G. B. Cook.

FINAL

HAMPSHIRE v SOMERSET

RICHARD WHITEHEAD

At Lord's, May 25. Somerset won by six wickets. Toss: Hampshire.

No longer will James Hildreth have to feel wistful during pre-match meetings in the Taunton Long Room. He confessed that his eyes would sometimes roam over the honours boards, and come to rest on the occasions during his long career when Somerset had come up short. Between lifting the Twenty20 Cup in 2005 and this emphatic triumph, they had trailed up the aisle as bridesmaids ten times. Just as he had 14 years earlier, Hildreth hit the winning runs. "It's a relief," he said. "Normally we're head in hands."

In the last one-day final at Lord's (at least until the next ECB rethink), Somerset were utterly dominant, and won with more than six overs unused. After a minor alarm, in which they lost four wickets, Hildreth stroked them serenely to victory. As the target grew closer, and their fans livelier, he paused to savour the occasion. "It's why you play, isn't it – for these moments."

Holders Hampshire had lost James Vince, Liam Dawson and Aiden Markram to World Cup calls, as well as the backing of those supporters who were otherwise engaged at the Rose Bowl watching Steve Smith score a hundred in a warm-up game for Australia against England. Even so, their performance was unusually tepid. Wickets fell regularly in the face of a cohesive effort by the Somerset seamers, matched by the swarming intensity of their fielders. Northeast, captain in Vince's absence, mounted a partial recovery, but after moving past 50 he decided it was time to accelerate, and was bowled playing an awful heave against his opposite number, Abell. There were three wickets en route to the match award for Jamie Overton – back from a red-ball loan to Northamptonshire – although an unbroken ninth-wicket stand of 64 between Fuller and Crane raised Hampshire morale.

An enduring legend around the old September one-day final was that a decent performance could earn a winter tour. It is less easy to deliver a selectorial nudge in late May, but Somerset's 20-year-old opener Banton must have made an impression on the watching Ed Smith. He seemed unburdened by comparisons with Kevin Pietersen, and – in the most memorable passage of the day – launched a thrilling counter-attack at Edwards's slingy thunderbolts. A flamingo whip through the leg side was followed next ball by a nonchalant flick over square leg for six. By the time he fell for a 67-ball 69, he and Azhar Ali had put on 112 for the first wicket inside 20 overs, and broken the back of the chase. Other Somerset sides might have reached for the panic button when three more wickets fell, but they were not bothered by history. "This is a new team – we want to create our own dynasty," said Abell, happily engaging with talk of a treble.

Although Hampshire's appearance in the final could not necessarily have been foreseen, the scheduling smacked of contempt for a competition that was being banished to the margins. Hildreth reflected on the end of an era of Lord's finals that began with Ted Dexter decorously raising the Gillette Cup in 1963. "It's great that we got the opportunity to play in it," he said. "But it's sad in a way, because you want other guys to experience it in the future."

Player of the Match: J. Overton. *Attendance:* 15,756.

Hampshire

†T. P. Alsop c Hildreth b Davey	16	K. J. Abbott b Abell		2
A. H. T. Donald c van der Merwe b Davey	11	M. S. Crane not out		28
J. J. Weatherley b Gregory	12	Lb 3, w 6		9
*S. A. Northeast b Abell	56			—
R. R. Rossouw b J. Overton	28	1/16 (2) 2/31 (1)	(8 wkts, 50 overs)	244
G. K. Berg c Bartlett b J. Overton	27	3/50 (3) 4/96 (5)		
J. K. Fuller not out	55	5/145 (6) 6/164 (4)		
C. P. Wood c Bartlett b J. Overton	0	7/165 (8) 8/180 (9)	10 overs: 43-2	

F. H. Edwards did not bat.

C. Overton 10–0–52–0; Davey 8–0–28–2; Gregory 8–0–42–1; J. Overton 10–1–48–3; van der Merwe 9–0–52–0; Abell 5–0–19–2.

Somerset

†T. Banton c Alsop b Edwards	69	G. A. Bartlett not out		14
Azhar Ali c Rossouw b Edwards	45	Lb 4, w 1		5
P. D. Trego c Wood b Fuller	29			—
J. C. Hildreth not out	69	1/112 (1) 2/121 (2)	(4 wkts, 43.3 overs)	245
*T. B. Abell c Donald b Edwards	14	3/170 (3) 4/203 (5)	10 overs: 64-0	

L. Gregory, R. E. van der Merwe, C. Overton, J. Overton and J. H. Davey did not bat.

Edwards 9.3–0–69–3; Abbott 9–0–43–0; Wood 6–1–28–0; Berg 4–0–13–0; Crane 10–0–62–0; Fuller 5–0–26–1.

Umpires: R. J. Bailey and M. J. Saggers.   Third umpire: A. G. Wharf.

AUSTRALIA A IN ENGLAND IN 2019

STEVEN LYNCH

This was an A-team with a bigger A than usual. The Australians were going to be pitched into the Ashes little more than a fortnight after the World Cup, and so their shadow side included several players who had missed out on the 50-over team but were destined for the Tests, including captain Tim Paine. In the end, half the players from the first-class leg of the tour appeared in the Ashes.

Five limited-overs games kicked off the trip – four won, the other washed out. Matthew Wade hammered 117 against Northamptonshire, then 155 at Derby, and finished with 355 runs and a strike-rate of 182. Against Gloucestershire, Will Pucovski and Travis Head put on 267. But thoughts really turned to the Ashes once Paine took charge for the first-class games. Sussex were despatched at Arundel, after Joe Burns and Marcus Harris shared an opening stand of 214, then Head and Wade added hundreds as the Australians had the better of the match against England Lions at Canterbury.

The original itinerary included a four-day game between the A-team and the full Australian line-up at Southampton, but this was changed to a 12-a-side practice match, and used as a final trial before Ashes squad were selected. The canny selectors had allowed Cameron Bancroft and Marnus Labuschagne to continue scoring runs in county cricket, before roping them in at the Rose Bowl, where they clinched Ashes spots; Burns missed out.

AUSTRALIA A SQUAD

*T. D. Paine (FC), S. A. Abbott (50), A. C. Agar (50), J. M. Bird (FC), J. A. Burns (FC), P. S. P. Handscomb (FC/50), M. S. Harris (FC), J. R. Hazlewood (FC/50), T. M. Head (FC/50), J. M. Holland (FC), M. R. Marsh (FC/50), M. G. Neser (FC/50), K. R. Patterson (FC/50), J. L. Pattinson (FC/50), W. J. Pucovski (FC/50), D. J. M. Short (50), C. P Tremain (FC), A. J. Turner (50), A. J. Tye (50), M. S. Wade (FC/50). *Coach:* G. A. Hick. *Assistant coaches:* R. J. Harris and A. C. Voges. *Manager:* T. J. Cooley. *Selector:* T. V. Hohns.

Head captained in the 50-over matches. K. W. Richardson was originally selected for the 50-over leg, but was drafted into the World Cup squad, and replaced by Tye. Burns was a late addition to the squad for the first-class games.

At Northampton, June 20 (day/night). **Australia A won by six wickets.** ‡Northamptonshire 262-9 (50 overs) (R. I. Newton 53, A. G. Wakely 53; A. C. Agar 3-55); **Australia A 265-4** (36 overs) (M. S. Wade 117, P. S. P. Handscomb 64). *County debut:* J. M. Blatherwick. *Northamptonshire's total, which included half-centuries for Rob Newton and Alex Wakely, and 49 for skipper Josh Cobb, looked decent – until Matthew Wade got going. Not long after learning that another Australian left-hander, David Warner, had hammered 166 against Bangladesh in the World Cup not far away at Trent Bridge, Wade hit 18 fours and three sixes in his 67-ball 117. Peter Handscomb ensured there would be no hiccups, and Australia A won with 14 overs to spare.*

At Derby, June 23. **Australia A won by seven wickets.** Derbyshire 283-9 (50 overs) (J. L. du Plooy 115; A. J. Tye 6-65); ‡Australia A 287-3 (35.2 overs) (M. S. Wade 155, T. M. Head 68). *County debut:* F. J. Hudson-Prentice. *Wade led the way again as the Australians made quicker work of an even higher target. This time, he clattered 155 from 71 balls, with 14 fours and 11 sixes; Travis Head helped him add 205 for the second wicket in 21 overs. Wade reached 100 from 45 balls (the fastest by an Australian in List A cricket, beating David Hussey by four) and 150 in 68, behind only A. B. de Villiers, who got there in 64 for South Africa v West Indies at Sydney during the 2015 World Cup. Earlier, Leus du Plooy had made his first century for Derbyshire, who were hampered by six batsmen making scores between ten and 19. Andrew Tye finished with six wickets.*

At Kidderminster, June 25. **Worcestershire v Australia A. Abandoned**. *This match was originally scheduled for Worcester, but flooding caused it to be switched to Kidderminster – where it rained.*

At Bristol, June 30. **Australia A won by five wickets. Gloucestershire 246-8** (50 overs) (G. T. Hankins 74, J. R. Bracey 83; M. R. Marsh 3-43); ‡**Australia A 247-5** (42.1 overs) (W. J. Pucovski 51, P. S. P. Handscomb 57, M. R. Marsh 53*; C. J. Liddle 3-59). *County debuts*: T. J. Price, G. P. Willows. *Gloucestershire were riding high at 169-1 in the 32nd over, but three wickets for Mitchell Marsh pegged them back, while Josh Hazlewood had figures of 10–4–24–1. Wade made another lightning start, before departing for 41 from 20, with four sixes. Will Pucovski scored a more sedate half-century during a third-wicket stand of 101 with Handscomb, then Marsh made sure of victory with a rapid 53*, with five sixes.*

At Bristol, July 2. **Australia A won by nine runs.** ‡**Australia A 353-3** (50 overs) (W. J. Pucovski 137, T. M. Head 138); **Gloucestershire 344-7** (50 overs) (J. R. Bracey 71, I. A. Cockbain 53, R. F. Higgins 55*, B. A. C. Howell 64; S. A. Abbott 4-52). *Australia A batted first for a change and, after Wade made 42 from 37, Pucovski and Head put on 267, before both departed in the 49th over. Gloucestershire made a valiant effort, falling only ten short of a lofty target, not helped when Sean Abbott removed Benny Howell (64 from 37) and Tom Smith in three deliveries near the end. The Australian new-ball pair proved expensive: Hazlewood finished with 0-66, Michael Neser 1-76.*

SUSSEX v AUSTRALIA A

At Arundel, July 7–10. Australia A won by ten wickets. Toss: Sussex.

Sussex made stuttering progress against the fiery Pattinson on a first day limited to 33 overs, but next morning Rawlins, the Bermuda-born left-hander, added 58 with wicketkeeper Rouse, before Beer and the tail spirited the total to 263. With Ashes places on the line, Burns and Harris – in his maiden first-class match in England – took few chances, and put on 214, both hitting 18 fours, but it would not be enough to get Burns an Ashes gig. Two wickets in four balls for Mir Hamza slowed the scoring on the third morning, and the eventual lead was 110. Sussex's second innings disintegrated, with Bird snatching three in ten balls; from 30 without loss, they were all out on the stroke of stumps for 120. Pattinson finished with seven in the match, but Hazlewood – bowling with a red ball for the first time since a back stress fracture in January – failed to strike. The formalities were concluded next morning, when Harris smacked three fours in the first over.

Close of play: first day, Sussex 118-5 (Rawlins 5, Sakande 0); second day, Australia A 203-0 (Burns 88, Harris 100); third day, Sussex 120.

Sussex

P. D. Salt c Hazlewood b Bird	37	– b Pattinson	21
V. Chopra lbw b Pattinson	30	– lbw b Neser	17
*L. W. P. Wells b Pattinson	16	– c Paine b Bird	4
L. J. Evans b Neser	18	– lbw b Bird	0
D. M. W. Rawlins lbw b Holland	69	– c Paine b Bird	0
A. Kapil c Harris b Pattinson	0	– not out	33
A. Sakande b Neser	0	– (10) lbw b Pattinson	7
†A. P. Rouse c Burns b Pattinson	20	– (7) c Patterson b Holland	13
W. A. T. Beer not out	28	– (8) c Patterson b Holland	12
A. D. Thomason b Holland	12	– (9) b Holland	4
Mir Hamza c Bird b Holland	10	– b Pattinson	0
B 8, lb 11, nb 4	23	Lb 9	9

1/69 (1) 2/73 (2) 3/112 (4)   (70.5 overs) 263   1/30 (2) 2/40 (3)   (40.4 overs) 120
4/116 (5) 5/118 (6) 6/135 (7)   3/40 (4) 4/44 (5)
7/193 (8) 8/223 (5) 9/251 (10) 10/263 (11)   5/44 (1) 6/73 (7) 7/95 (8)
                                          8/101 (9) 9/120 (10) 10/120 (11)

Hazlewood 19–6–46–0; Pattinson 20–6–60–4; Bird 9–0–44–1; Neser 11–3–45–2; Holland 11.5–5–49–3. *Second innings*—Hazlewood 6–3–7–0; Neser 11–1–39–1; Pattinson 6.4–0–17–3; Bird 7–1–18–3; Holland 10–3–30–3.

Australia A

J. A. Burns c Chopra b Mir Hamza	133	– (2) not out	0
M. S. Harris c Rouse b Sakande	109	– (1) not out	12
K. R. Patterson c Rouse b Mir Hamza	4		
T. M. Head lbw b Wells	34		
W. J. Pucovski c Rouse b Mir Hamza	13		
*†T. D. Paine c Rouse b Thomason	20		
M. G. Neser b Sakande	1		
J. L. Pattinson lbw b Sakande	13		
J. M. Bird lbw b Wells	17		
J. R. Hazlewood b Thomason	5		
J. M. Holland not out	2		
B 5, lb 8, w 1, nb 8	22		

1/214 (2) 2/224 (3) 3/285 (4)	(96.1 overs) 373	(no wkt, 1 over)	12
4/313 (1) 5/322 (5) 6/323 (7)			
7/339 (8) 8/365 (6) 9/371 (9) 10/373 (10)			

Mir Hamza 17–3–56–3; Sakande 24–5–89–3; Thomason 22.1–0–107–2; Beer 1–0–4–0; Rawlins 20–2–66–0; Wells 12–3–38–2. *Second innings*—Thomason 1–0–12–0.

Umpires: Hassan Adnan and P. J. Hartley.

ENGLAND LIONS v AUSTRALIAN XI

At Canterbury, July 14–17. Drawn. Toss: England Lions.

A superb all-round performance by Sam Curran kept England Lions in the game, culminating in a tenacious unbroken sixth-wicket stand with Hain, which spanned 31 overs on the final afternoon. The Australians had looked unstoppable while Head, who stroked 20 fours, and Wade were putting on 219, but the last six wickets added only 17, with Curran taking five in 18 balls. The in-form Sibley anchored the reply with a four-hour 74, before Curran provided late impetus with 50. The Australians might have hoped for quick runs to build on a lead of 130 but, with Leach finding turn, the Lions bowlers kept a brake on the scoring, which hovered around three an over throughout the third day. Wade went to hospital for an X-ray after he was hit on the elbow by Gregory, the Lions captain, who had taken his 50th wicket of the season earlier in the match. Paine declared on the fourth morning, but three wickets for Neser after an opening stand of 80 dented the Lions' slim chances of chasing 383. When Northeast fell, after completing 10,000 first-class runs, the Australians smelt blood at 154 for five – but Hain and Curran settled in for the next two hours.

Close of play: first day, Australian XI 362-4 (Head 130, Marsh 24); second day, England Lions 232-6 (Curran 32); third day, Australian XI 223-6 (Neser 20, Tremain 9).

Australian XI

J. A. Burns lbw b Gregory	19	– (2) c Hain b Porter	9
M. S. Harris c Robinson b Gregory	34	– (1) c Sibley b Leach	50
K. R. Patterson b Porter	32	– c Robinson b Leach	38
T. M. Head not out	139	– c Northeast b Gregory	12
M. S. Wade lbw b Curran	114	– retired hurt	2
M. R. Marsh c Foakes b Curran	38	– lbw b Robinson	26
*†T. D. Paine c Foakes b Curran	0	– c Leach b Leach	38
M. G. Neser c Foakes b Curran	0	– c Curran b Leach	32
C. P. Tremain b Curran	0	– not out	18
J. M. Bird b Curran	11	– c sub (J. A. Gordon) b Leach	4
J. M. Holland b Gregory	0		
B 1, lb 5, nb 4	10	B 16, lb 6, nb 1	23

1/23 (1) 2/76 (2) 3/101 (3)	(99.5 overs) 397	1/33 (2) (8 wkts dec, 77.5 overs)	252
4/320 (5) 5/380 (6) 6/380 (7)		2/106 (1) 3/109 (3)	
7/382 (8) 8/382 (9) 9/396 (10) 10/397 (11)		4/121 (4) 5/176 (6)	
		6/196 (7) 7/248 (8) 8/252 (10)	

In the second innings Wade retired hurt at 117-3.

Porter 19–4–68–1; Gregory 22.5–5–65–3; Robinson 18–2–88–0; Curran 23–3–95–6; Leach 17–0–75–0. *Second innings*—Gregory 12–6–30–1; Curran 11–2–26–0; Porter 9–3–14–1; Robinson 17–4–51–1; Leach 28.5–5–109–5.

England Lions

Z. Crawley b Bird	15	– c Paine b Neser	43
D. P. Sibley lbw b Marsh	74	– c Paine b Neser	30
†B. T. Foakes c Paine b Tremain	8	– c Paine b Neser	7
S. A. Northeast c Harris b Tremain	2	– b Marsh	34
J. R. Bracey c Patterson b Bird	37	– c Paine b Bird	31
S. R. Hain c Paine b Holland	39	– not out	53
S. M. Curran st Paine b Holland	50	– not out	56
*L. Gregory b Bird	0		
O. E. Robinson not out	15		
M. J. Leach c Paine b Tremain	0		
J. A. Porter lbw b Tremain	1		
B 1, lb 15, nb 10	26	B 6, lb 6, nb 1	13

1/26 (1) 2/49 (3) 3/51 (4) (90.1 overs) 267   1/80 (1) (5 wkts, 84 overs) 267
4/140 (5) 5/159 (2) 6/232 (6)   2/87 (2) 3/98 (3)
7/233 (8) 8/260 (7) 9/261 (10) 10/267 (11)   4/143 (5) 5/154 (4)

Bird 23–8–51–3; Tremain 17.1–2–70–4; Neser 7–3–19–0; Marsh 13–3–38–1; Holland 28–9–56–2; Head 2–0–17–0. *Second innings*—Bird 19–4–65–1; Neser 16–3–38–3; Tremain 13–4–31–0; Holland 24–2–81–0; Head 7–1–25–0; Marsh 5–1–15–1.

Umpires: J. H. Evans and C. M. Watts.

For the trial match at Southampton (July 23–25), see Australian tour section.

THE UNIVERSITIES IN 2019

CAMBRIDGE MCCU v ESSEX

At Cambridge, March 26–28. Essex won by 286 runs. Toss: Essex. First-class debuts: V. Bajaj, J. J. Cantrell, J. C. H. Park-Johnson, R. K. Patel, M. J. E. Smith.

The earliest start to any English season – two days earlier than 2017 – meant cricket was played on Greenwich Mean Time for the first time since 1914. On the opening day, Cook eased to an unbeaten 150, his 64th first-class century, in the first match since his knighthood was announced. He tried to play it down, but the Fenner's scorecard billed him as Sir Alastair anyway. He and Wheater put on 217 as Essex made hay after a wobbly start, but Browne fell just short of a hundred in the second innings as the lead reached 443. The students resisted gamely, twice lasting more than 50 overs, but found scoring difficult against a strong attack: the highest of their 13 double-figure scores was Ben Seabrook's unbeaten 44. Chopra reached 10,000 first-class runs during the first innings, while Bopara claimed his 250th wicket in the second: Akil Greenidge, son of the former West Indian Test opener Alvin. All six MCCU games were belatedly made 10.30am starts when it was realised that evening light was at a premium before the clocks went back.

Close of play: first day, Cambridge MCCU 36-1 (Park-Johnson 12, Greenidge 4); second day, Essex 119-1 (Browne 58, Bopara 20).

Essex

N. L. J. Browne c Hyde b Rippington	8	– c Hyde b Guest	98
A. N. Cook not out	150		
V. Chopra c Patel b Guest	29	– (2) c Hyde b Guest	27
R. S. Bopara c Greenidge b Park-Johnson	1	– (3) c Patel b Cantrell	55
†A. J. A. Wheater c Patel b Chapman	130		
*S. R. Harmer c Hyde b Smith	26	– (4) not out	16
M. T. Coles not out	3	– (5) not out	15
B 9, lb 4, w 1, nb 26	40	B 4, lb 5, nb 12	21

1/12 (1) 2/67 (3)   (5 wkts dec, 89.3 overs) 387   1/73 (2)   (3 wkts dec, 69 overs) 232
3/92 (4) 4/309 (5) 5/378 (6)   2/182 (3) 3/209 (1)

A. S. S. Nijjar, A. P. Beard, J. A. Porter and M. R. Quinn did not bat.

Rippington 19–2–108–1; Smith 9.3–2–34–1; Park-Johnson 14–2–69–1; Guest 14–4–33–1; Chapman 19–2–58–1; Cantrell 9–0–54–0; Seabrook 5–0–18–0. *Second innings*—Rippington 15–1–62–0; Smith 6–1–20–0; Guest 18–4–47–2; Park-Johnson 7–1–28–0; Cantrell 14–2–40–1; Chapman 9–3–26–0.

Cambridge MCCU

V. B. Bajaj c Harmer b Beard	20	– c Coles b Quinn	17
J. C. H. Park-Johnson run out (Harmer)	12	– c Nijjar b Porter	4
A. D. Greenidge c Wheater b Beard	24	– c Wheater b Bopara	21
R. K. Patel c Quinn b Coles	33	– c Browne b Beard	3
*C. J. Guest c Wheater b Beard	0	– b Harmer	13
B. M. A. Seabrook not out	44	– c Bopara b Harmer	15
J. J. Cantrell c Nijjar b Bopara	19	– c Cook b Bopara	17
†E. R. B. Hyde b Porter	8	– c Browne b Harmer	19
L. J. Chapman c Cook b Quinn	4	– b Nijjar	5
S. E. Rippington c Chopra b Porter	2	– not out	8
M. J. E. Smith run out (Beard)	0	– c Quinn b Nijjar	17
B 2, lb 4, nb 4	10	B 9, lb 4, w 1, nb 4	18

1/32 (1) 2/36 (2) 3/93 (3)   (61.5 overs) 176   1/25 (2) 2/25 (1)   (52.4 overs) 157
4/93 (5) 5/93 (4) 6/129 (7)   3/40 (4) 4/58 (3)
7/147 (8) 8/160 (9)   5/62 (5) 6/103 (7)
9/175 (10) 10/176 (11)   7/103 (6) 8/128 (9)
                                      9/128 (8) 10/157 (11)

Porter 17.5–5–47–2; Quinn 15–4–50–1; Beard 10–3–24–3; Coles 7–1–17–1; Harmer 8–0–15–0; Bopara 4–0–17–1. *Second innings*—Porter 6–2–13–1; Coles 6–2–13–0; Quinn 5–1–7–1; Beard 5–1–20–1; Bopara 11–1–35–2; Harmer 14–6–28–3; Nijjar 5.4–0–28–2.

Umpires: P. K. Baldwin and P. R. Pollard.

At Derby, March 26–28. LEEDS/BRADFORD MCCU lost to DERBYSHIRE by 336 runs.

At Chester-le-Street, March 26–28. DURHAM MCCU lost to DURHAM by 296 runs.

At Leicester, March 26–28. LOUGHBOROUGH MCCU lost to LEICESTERSHIRE by an innings and 220 runs.

At Northwood, March 26–28. OXFORD MCCU drew with MIDDLESEX.

At Taunton, March 26–28. CARDIFF MCCU lost to SOMERSET by 568 runs. *Cardiff suffer the biggest defeat by runs in English first-class cricket.*

CAMBRIDGE MCCU v NOTTINGHAMSHIRE

At Cambridge, March 31–April 2. Drawn. Toss: Nottinghamshire. County debut: J. M. Clarke.

Rain washed out the final day, and spared Cambridge another hammering: Nottinghamshire were 648 ahead – and still batting – by the end of the second. They had sprinted away on the first with an opening stand of 325 in 58 overs between Slater and Duckett, who hit 34 fours and four sixes. He extended his first century for his new county to 216, the highest individual score in this fixture, beating Walter Keeton's 200 for Nottinghamshire in 1932. The student bowlers stuck to their task: when not being dictated to by Duckett, the captain Callum Guest delivered ten maidens (and 137 dot balls) and finished with three for 100 with his off-breaks. Cambridge battened down the hatches for 53 overs, with Guest surviving for nearly two hours and Ben Seabrook top-scoring again, but they still conceded a lead of 417. Duckett uncharitably returned for a second helping from the buffet, clattering 82 from 52 balls as the lead spiralled.

Close of play: first day, Nottinghamshire 527-7 (Coughlin 5, Wood 5); second day, Nottinghamshire 231-5 (Patel 15, Coughlin 4).

Nottinghamshire

B. T. Slater c Bajaj b Guest 130		
B. M. Duckett b Guest 216	– (4) c Chapman b Keeping	82
C. D. Nash b Rippington 25	– b Rippington.	1
J. M. Clarke lbw b Rippington. 2	– (1) b Guest	20
*S. J. Mullaney c Patel b Chapman 51	– c Patel b Chapman	79
S. R. Patel c Guest b Cantrell 46	– not out	15
†T. J. Moores c Greenidge b Chapman 5	– (2) c Seabrook b Rippington	19
P. Coughlin c Guest b Rippington 29	– (7) not out.	4
L. Wood not out 19		
J. T. Ball c Park-Johnson b Guest 0		
L. J. Fletcher absent		
B 21, lb 4, w 9, nb 8 42	B 5, lb 4, nb 2.	11

1/325 (2) 2/393 (1) 3/396 (4)   (117.3 overs) 565   1/45 (1)   (5 wkts, 34 overs) 231
4/414 (3) 5/498 (5) 6/517 (6)   2/45 (2) 3/50 (3)
7/517 (7) 8/565 (8) 9/565 (10)   4/186 (4) 5/218 (5)

Rippington 26–1–120–3; Park-Johnson 14–1–69–0; Guest 30.3–10–100–3; Chapman 25–1–133–2; Seabrook 5–0–35–0; Cantrell 17–1–83–1. *Second innings*—Rippington 8–1–46–2; Park-Johnson 8–0–70–0; Guest 8–0–37–1; Keeping 6–0–23–1; Chapman 4–0–46–1.

Cambridge MCCU

V. B. Bajaj c Patel b Ball	2	†E. R. B. Hyde not out	8
J. C. H. Park-Johnson c Duckett b Ball	12	L. J. Chapman b Patel	0
A. D. Greenidge c Mullaney b Wood	4	S. E. Rippington b Wood	1
R. K. Patel lbw b Mullaney	23	Lb 9	9
*C. J. Guest lbw b Patel	34		
B. M. A. Seabrook c Moores b Ball	35	1/10 (1) 2/23 (2) 3/37 (3) (53.1 overs) 148
J. J. Cantrell lbw b Patel	10	4/56 (4) 5/108 (6) 6/129 (7)
J. B. R. Keeping c Moores b Wood	10	7/134 (5) 8/144 (8) 9/145 (10) 10/148 (11)

Ball 13–4–26–3; Wood 13.1–6–31–3; Coughlin 9–0–52–0; Mullaney 7–4–9–1; Patel 11–4–21–3.

Umpires: N. L. Bainton and J. D. Middlebrook.

At Canterbury, March 31–April 2. LOUGHBOROUGH MCCU drew with KENT.

LEEDS/BRADFORD MCCU v YORKSHIRE

At Weetwood, Leeds, March 31–April 2. Yorkshire won by an innings and 151 runs. Toss: Leeds/Bradford MCCU. County debut: D. Olivier.

This fixture returned to the Weetwood campus after six years at Headingley, but the students could not make home advantage count, sliding to 119 on the first day after bravely choosing to bat. Olivier, Yorkshire's new Kolpak signing, took two wickets, including his 400th in first-class cricket, and Coad claimed the last three in four balls; in between, Matthew Waite, a Leeds-born seamer, picked up a cheap maiden five-for. Yorkshire dwarfed the students' total, mainly thanks to a fifth-wicket stand of 213 between Köhler-Cadmore – his highest score ended with a four, six and a skyed catch, all off Darren Ironside's leg-spin – and wicketkeeper Jonny Tattersall, whose unbeaten 135 was his maiden first-class century. Armed with a lead of 370, Yorkshire's attack worked their way through some determined batting: Saad Ashraf's 62 used up 200 minutes, while skipper Angus Dahl lasted 100.

Close of play: first day, Yorkshire 164-3 (Kohler-Cadmore 64, Leaning 20); second day, Leeds/Bradford MCCU 91-3 (Dahl 31, Ashraf 30).

Leeds/Bradford MCCU

J. L. Haynes lbw b Waite	20	– lbw b Coad	18
T. R. Cornall b Olivier	10	– lbw b Olivier	9
O. R. Batchelor c Tattersall b Waite	2	– c Tattersall b Coad	0
*A. E. C. Dahl b Lyth b Coad	46	– b Olivier	36
S. T. Ashraf b Waite	24	– st Tattersall b Leaning	62
D. A. Ironside lbw b Waite	0	– c Köhler-Cadmore b Patterson	18
†J. Read c Leaning b Olivier	5	– c Köhler-Cadmore b Pillans	15
A. J. Neal c Tattersall b Waite	0	– b Pillans	15
J. B. Fallows c Tattersall b Coad	1	– absent hurt	
J. B. R. Holling b Coad	0	– (9) c Köhler-Cadmore b Waite	13
S. Cantwell not out	1	– (10) not out	21
B 1, lb 1, nb 8	10	B 5, lb 3, nb 4	12

1/36 (2) 2/40 (3) 3/49 (1)   (49.5 overs) 119   1/30 (1) 2/30 (3)   (74 overs) 219
4/88 (5) 5/88 (6) 6/93 (7)   3/30 (2) 4/99 (4) 5/134 (6)
7/102 (8) 8/118 (4) 9/118 (10) 10/119 (9)   6/163 (5) 7/177 (7) 8/180 (8) 9/219 (9)

Coad 10.5–4–21–3; Olivier 14–4–38–2; Patterson 9–4–17–0; Waite 12.5–5–16–5; Pillans 4–1–25–0. *Second innings*—Coad 16–5–37–2; Olivier 10.4–5–30–2; Patterson 10–3–28–1; Waite 13–5–41–1; Leaning 11–0–32–1; Lyth 3.2–1–9–0; Pillans 10–1–34–2.

Yorkshire

A. Lyth lbw b Cantwell	12	*S. A. Patterson c Neal b Haynes	39
H. C. Brook c Read b Holling	17	M. W. Pillans c Fallows b Ironside	3
G. S. Ballance c sub (S. F. G. Bullen) b Neal	39	B. O. Coad not out	10
T. Köhler-Cadmore c sub (S. F. G. Bullen)		B 8, lb 7, nb 8	23
b Ironside.	176		
J. A. Leaning b Neal	20	1/31 (2) 2/31 (1) (8 wkts dec, 112 overs)	489
†J. A. Tattersall not out	135	3/119 (3) 4/165 (5)	
M. J. Waite c Read b Neal	15	5/378 (4) 6/406 (7) 7/475 (8) 8/478 (9)	

D. Olivier did not bat.

Fallows 17–5–43–0; Cantwell 24–4–88–1; Holling 18–3–98–1; Neal 22–3–77–3; Haynes 20–0–94–1; Dahl 8–0–54–0; Ironside 3–0–20–2.

Umpires: P. J. Hartley and N. Pratt.

At Northampton, March 31–April 2. DURHAM MCCU drew with NORTHAMPTONSHIRE.

OXFORD MCCU v HAMPSHIRE

At Oxford, March 31–April 2. Drawn. Toss: Oxford MCCU. First-class debut: M. S. Rizvi. County debut: K. H. D. Barker.

Oxford escaped with a draw after the last day was washed out: they were already 430 behind, having lurched from 85 for two to 95 for nine after Tom Heathfield and wicketkeeper James Seward shared an opening stand of 53. They ran aground against Berg and Dawson, who had combined figures of six for 15 from 25 overs, while Barker, in his first match since joining from Warwickshire, claimed one for 17 in 14. Hampshire had jogged along at four and a half an over on the first day, with Vince and Northeast making untroubled centuries.

Close of play: first day, Hampshire 448-8 (Barker 23, Abbott 10); second day, Hampshire 66-4 (Berg 13, Abbott 4).

Hampshire

J. J. Weatherley b Pettman	5	– lbw b Robertson	14
*J. M. Vince c Rizvi b Harrison	139		
O. C. Soames c Seward b Robertson	21	– (2) lbw b Pettman	3
S. A. Northeast b Pettman	118		
R. R. Rossouw c Harrison b McBride	3	– (4) b Robertson	22
L. A. Dawson c Pettman b Searle	82		
†T. P. Alsop lbw b Pettman	0	– (3) lbw b Robertson	6
G. K. Berg lbw b Pettman	2	– (5) not out	13
K. H. D. Barker c Pettman b Robertson	44		
K. J. Abbott not out	18	– (6) not out	4
B 2, lb 11, w 9, nb 24	46	Nb 4	4

1/30 (1) 2/121 (3)	(9 wkts dec, 105.2 overs)	478
3/266 (2) 4/269 (5)		
5/366 (4) 6/366 (7) 7/375 (8) 8/424 (6) 9/478 (9)		

1/17 (1)	(4 wkts, 14 overs)	66
2/27 (2) 3/27 (3)		
4/54 (4)		

F. H. Edwards did not bat.

Pettman 24–6–82–4; Robertson 22.2–1–102–2; Heathfield 16–0–90–0; Searle 21–1–81–1; Harrison 7–0–41–1; McBride 5–0–15–1; Rizvi 9–1–46–0; Scott 1–0–8–0. *Second innings*—Pettman 5–1–22–1; Robertson 7–2–32–3; Searle 2–0–12–0.

Oxford MCCU

T. D. Heathfield b Dawson	29	*T. H. S. Pettman c Alsop b Abbott	1
†J. C. Seward lbw b Berg	28	W. J. R. Robertson not out	8
M. J. Taylor lbw b Dawson	15	C. J. Searle lbw b Edwards	8
C. J. McBride lbw b Dawson	7	B 5, lb 5, nb 4	14
C. G. Harrison c Vince b Edwards	2		—
D. N. C. Scott c Alsop b Berg	0	1/53 (2) 2/71 (1) 3/85 (4) (67 overs) 114
L. J. P. Shaw c Alsop b Dawson	0	4/88 (5) 5/88 (6) 6/88 (3)
M. S. Rizvi lbw b Barker	2	7/89 (7) 8/91 (8) 9/95 (9) 10/114 (11)

Edwards 13–2–26–2; Abbott 14–1–46–1; Barker 14–7–17–1; Berg 11–8–4–2; Dawson 14–9–11–4; Weatherley 1–1–0–0.

Umpires: N. G. B. Cook and T. Lungley.

At Hove, March 31–April 2. CARDIFF MCCU drew with SUSSEX.

At The Oval, April 4–6 (not first-class). DURHAM MCCU drew with SURREY.

At Cambridge, April 4–6 (not first-class). **Drawn. ‡Worcestershire 215** (62.3 overs) (K. Suresh 5–44) **and 272-4 dec** (74 overs) (D. K. H. Mitchell 74, J. J. Dell 63*, R. A. Whiteley 55*); **Cambridge MCCU 154** (55 overs) (J. B. R. Keeping 86; C. A. J. Morris 3-50) **and 19-0** (8 overs). *County debut:* M. H. Wessels. *Rain, which allowed only 30 overs on the final day after an abbreviated second, ruled out a result. Cambridge's bowlers had reduced Worcestershire to 40-6 on the first morning, Karthik Suresh finishing with 5-44. The tail, led by Ed Barnard (40), spared the county's blushes, and Cambridge struggled in turn; they stayed afloat thanks to Jack Keeping's forthright 86, including 16 fours. Worcestershire did better second time round, before the weather closed in.*

At Cardiff, April 5–7 (not first-class). CARDIFF MCCU drew with GLAMORGAN.

At Bristol, April 5–7 (not first-class). OXFORD MCCU drew with GLOUCESTERSHIRE.

At Loughborough, April 5–7 (not first-class). **Drawn. ‡Lancashire 468-7 dec** (126 overs) (H. Hameed 218, R. P. Jones 103*) **and 314-3 dec** (56 overs) (K. K. Jennings 69, G. J. Maxwell 82, D. J. Vilas 71*); **Loughborough MCCU 152** (66.2 overs) (J. A. Clifford 65; J. M. Anderson 3-21, M. H. A. Footitt 3-26) **and 95-2** (30 overs). *County debuts:* M. H. A. Footitt, G. J. Maxwell. *Haseeb Hameed showed a welcome return to form, although it was not reflected in the averages as this match, being the students' third of the season, did not have first-class status. He hit 32 fours and two sixes in 387 minutes, and put on 212 for the sixth wicket with Richard Jones after Lancashire were in a spot of bother at 198-5. Loughborough laboured in reply, only James Clifford making more than 27, and – after Lancashire went in again, despite a lead of 316 – were set the little matter of 631 in what became 30 overs.*

At Birmingham, April 5–7 (not first-class). LEEDS/BRADFORD MCCU lost to WARWICKSHIRE by 530 runs.

THE UNIVERSITY MATCHES IN 2018

At Cambridge, May 17. **Cambridge University won by five wickets. ‡Oxford University 131-7** (20 overs) (G. T. Hargrave 48; J. C. Vitali 3-17); **Cambridge University 132-5** (20 overs) (A. J. Moen 35*, A. R. Amin 36). *James Vitali was the last-over specialist as Cambridge took the overall lead in the Varsity T20 match, 5–4 since the first in 2008 (two were abandoned and one a no-result). First he claimed two wickets in the final over as Oxford were restricted to 131, then he scrambled the winning run from the last delivery.*

At Lord's, May 28. **Oxford University won by 56 runs. ‡Oxford University 227-9** (50 overs) (G. T. Hargrave 59, J. Diwakar 52; K. Suresh 4-40); **Cambridge University 171** (43.4 overs) (A. J. Moen 34, S. R. Collings-Wells 37, K. Suresh 38; M. J. Fanning 3-30, F. J. H. Foster 3-31). *Oxford won the one-day Varsity Match for the seventh time running, giving them a 16-9 lead. They were rescued from 28-3 in the sixth over by a stand of 91 between George Hargrave and Jei Diwakar, before the tenth-wicket pair Freddie Foster (26*) and Matt Fanning (29*) added a crucial 53* in the last 9.1 overs; they later shared six wickets. Nick Taylor, who had been on the victorious Oxford side in this fixture in 2017, and Alex Moen put on 54 for Cambridge's first wicket, but they then slid to 74-5, and fell short, despite defiant knocks from Sam Collings-Wells and Karthik Suresh.*

CAMBRIDGE UNIVERSITY v OXFORD UNIVERSITY

At Cambridge, July 2–4. Oxford University won by eight wickets. Toss: Cambridge University. First-class debuts: A. R. Amin, N. R. Johns, A. J. Moen, J. C. Vitali; J. M. M. Bevin, J. Diwakar, F. J. H. Foster, G. T. Hargrave.

A superb innings from George Hargrave, who cracked 146 before departing at 256, set Oxford up for victory, their first at Fenner's since 2013. Hargrave put on 104 with his captain, Alex Rackow, but his eventual dismissal started a collapse of seven for 40, with Aaron Amin taking four wickets to confine the lead to 68. Amin had earlier helped Cambridge recover from 87 for six, putting on 64 with Karthik Suresh, who then added a further 50 with James Vitali. Toby Pettman then reprised his five-for in the previous year's Varsity Match as Cambridge subsided, the one sizeable contribution coming from opener Nick Taylor, whose only other first-class match had been for Oxford in this fixture in 2017. Oxford needed just 90 to win, and Rackow led them home on the third afternoon. Later in the year came reports that the Varsity Match (and other MCCU games) would lose first-class status after the 2020 season.

Close of play: first day, Cambridge University 228; second day, Oxford University 285-7 (Pettman 11, Swanson 1).

Cambridge University

N. P. Taylor c Swanson b Pettman	0	– c Rogers b Foster	59
S. A. Turner run out (Hargrave)	38	– c Claughton b Pettman	5
N. R. Johns lbw b Foster	14	– c Claughton b Searle	10
A. J. Moen c Swanson b Fanning	0	– lbw b Swanson	6
*A. C. H. Dewhurst c Claughton b Pettman	16	– lbw b Pettman	28
†E. R. B. Hyde c Claughton b Pettman	2	– st Claughton b Foster	11
A. R. Amin b Fanning	24	– b Pettman	0
K. Suresh c Claughton b Searle	54	– c Rackow b Pettman	0
J. C. Vitali not out	46	– c Foster b Pettman	15
T. W. Balderson c Rogers b Searle	10	– lbw b Searle	7
J. O. Cross-Zamirski c Claughton b Fanning	0	– not out	6
B 9, lb 2, w 1, nb 12	24	B 5, lb 5	10

1/0 (1) 2/44 (3) 3/49 (4)　　(101.5 overs) 228　　1/5 (2) 2/22 (3)　　(62.2 overs) 157
4/82 (2) 5/86 (5) 6/87 (6)　　　　　　　　　　　　3/44 (4) 4/115 (1)
7/151 (7) 8/201 (8)　　　　　　　　　　　　　　　5/115 (5) 6/115 (7)
9/227 (10) 10/228 (11)　　　　　　　　　　　　　7/115 (8) 8/141 (9)
　　　　　　　　　　　　　　　　　　　　　　　9/143 (6) 10/157 (10)

Pettman 26–8–61–3; Searle 16–5–49–2; Fanning 22.5–7–47–3; Foster 23–10–44–1; Swanson 13–8–16–0; Rogers 1–1–0–0. *Second innings*—Pettman 13–6–19–5; Searle 12.2–4–31–2; Fanning 11–2–35–0; Swanson 11–4–26–1; Foster 15–7–36–2.

Oxford University

O. J. W. Rogers c Hyde b Suresh	0		
G. T. Hargrave c Amin b Balderson	146	– b Amin	5
J. Diwakar c Amin b Vitali	24	– (1) c Taylor b Amin	21
*A. J. W. Rackow b Suresh	52	– (3) not out	32
J. M. M. Bevin c Hyde b Vitali	29	– (4) not out	18
†T. H. Claughton b Amin	8		
F. J. H. Foster run out (Vitali)	1		
T. H. S. Pettman c Hyde b Amin	13		
B. Swanson b Amin	3		
C. J. Searle not out	6		
M. J. Fanning c and b Amin	1		
B 6, lb 4, w 1, nb 2	13	B 14, lb 1, nb 2	17

1/18 (1) 2/73 (3) 3/177 (4)　　(101.1 overs) 296　　1/21 (2)　　(2 wkts, 14.4 overs) 93
4/256 (2) 5/260 (5) 6/265 (7)　　　　　　　　　　2/28 (1)
7/279 (6) 8/287 (9) 9/290 (8) 10/296 (11)

Suresh 18–5–59–2; Cross-Zamirski 12–0–50–0; Vitali 19–4–50–2; Amin 22.1–6–56–4; Balderson 27–9–55–1; Moen 3–0–16–0. *Second innings*—Suresh 2–0–17–0; Cross-Zamirski 5–0–17–0; Amin 5–1–26–2; Vitali 1–0–8–0; Balderson 1.4–0–10–0.

Umpires: J. D. Middlebrook and N. Pratt.

Cambridge University *A. C. H. Dewhurst *(St Paul's School and Robinson)*, A. R. Amin *(Merchant Taylors' School, Northwood, and Emmanuel)*, T. W. Balderson *(Cheadle Hulme High School and Downing)*, J. O. Cross-Zamirski *(The Perse School and Downing)*, E. R. B. Hyde *(Tonbridge School and Jesus)*, N. R. Johns *(Sandford Park School, Dublin, and Homerton)*, A. J. Moen *(Tonbridge School and Magdalene)*, K. Suresh *(Cranleigh School and Wolfson)*, N. P. Taylor *(The Perse School, St Catherine's College, Oxford, and Clare)*, S. A. Turner *(St Paul's School and Christ's)*, J. C. Vitali *(Sherborne School, University College, London, and Christ's)*.

S. P. Shankar *(Oakridge International School, Hyderabad, Edinburgh University and Sidney Sussex)*, O. B. Taylor *(West Bridgford Academy and Fitzwilliam)* and N. J. Winder *(Tonbridge School and Robinson)* played in the 50- and 20-over matches, and S. R. Collings-Wells *(Portsmouth Grammar School and Corpus Christi)* in the 50-over game. Johns and Turner missed both, while Balderson and Hyde sat out the 50-over match, and Cross-Zamirski the T20.

Oxford University *A. J. W. Rackow *(Dulwich College and St Hilda's)*, J. M. M. Bevin *(King's College, Auckland, Otago University and Exeter)*, T. H. Claughton *(King Edward's School, Birmingham, and Kellogg)*, J. Diwakar *(King Edward VI School, Camp Hill, and Hertford)*, M. J. Fanning *(St Joseph's Roman Catholic High School, Horwich, and St Anne's)*, F. J. H. Foster *(Eltham College and St Cross)*, G. T. Hargrave *(Shrewsbury School and Hertford)*, T. H. S. Pettman *(Tonbridge School and Jesus)*, O. J. W. Rogers *(Eton College and St Edmund Hall)*, C. J. Searle *(Hampton School and Worcester)*, B. Swanson *(Alleyn's School and St Peter's)*.

J. Duxbury *(Bedford School and Queen's)* and M. A. Naylor *(Finham Park School, Coventry, and St Cross)* played in the 50- and 20-over matches, and C. Mingard *(The Judd School and Hertford)* in the 50-over game. Rogers sat out both, while Rackow and Swanson missed the 50-over match, and Diwakar the T20. Pettman captained in the 50-over game.

This was the 174th University Match, a first-class fixture dating back to 1827. Cambridge have won 60 and Oxford 58, with 56 drawn. It was played at Lord's until 2000.

MCC UNIVERSITIES CHAMPIONSHIP

The format of the MCC Universities Championship was changed in 2019 to a composite points system similar to the one used in the women's Ashes. Each of the six MCCUs played three three-day matches (earning 16 points for a win, plus bonus points), five 50-over matches in the existing BUCS Championship (ten points for a win), and four Twenty20 matches (five points for a win). Leeds/Bradford, who went through the season undefeated, finished top of the table, just ahead of Loughborough: the match in the last round of fixtures between the top two, which had shaped up as a title shoot-out, was abandoned.

With Lord's unavailable because of the World Cup, there was no one-day MCC Universities Challenge final in 2019.

Leeds/Bradford 92pts, Loughborough 87, Durham 58, Oxford 49, Cardiff South Wales 45, Cambridge 36.

WINNERS

2001	Loughborough	2008	Loughborough	2015	Cardiff
2002	Loughborough	2009	Leeds/Bradford	2016	Loughborough
2003	Loughborough	2010	Durham	2017	Loughborough
2004	Oxford	2011	Cardiff	2018	Loughborough
2005	Loughborough	2012	Cambridge	2019	Leeds/Bradford
2006	Oxford	2013	Leeds/Bradford		
2007	Cardiff/Glamorgan	2014	Loughborough		

MCC IN 2019

STEVEN LYNCH

The busiest international year yet at Lord's featured five matches in the World Cup, culminating in the breathless final. That was followed by Ireland's maiden Test appearance on a ground where they had first played in 1858: a familiar face, Middlesex's Tim Murtagh, embarrassed England on the opening day, but they prevailed in the end. Then came the Test against Australia, which ended in an exciting draw, despite the loss of the first day to rain. Before all this, Somerset had won what could be the last county one-day final at Lord's. It amounted to a challenging first season for Karl McDermott, the new head groundsman, who had taken over from Mick Hunt.

There was little time for staff to relax: soon after the Ashes Test, construction started to replace the Compton and Edrich Stands at the Nursery End. The project, estimated to cost £52m, will provide 2,600 extra seats, and improved facilities.

MCC's world cricket committee, chaired by Mike Gatting, continued to make informed suggestions about the international game. In 2019, they proposed that the ball be standardised, and that the free-hit rule after a no-ball used in one-day games be adopted in Tests; they also came up with ways of speeding up over-rates. Shakib Al Hasan stepped down from the committee after receiving a ban from international cricket; Alastair Cook and the West Indies board president, Ricky Skerritt, joined early in 2020.

Notable deaths during the year included the former MCC presidents Lord Bramall (1988–89) and Dennis Silk (1992–94), and the former England all-rounder Edna Barker, one of the first group of women given honorary membership in 1999.

In all, MCC teams played more than 550 matches in the British Isles in 2018. Of 521 men's games, 210 were won, 87 drawn, three tied, 107 lost, and 114 abandoned or cancelled. There were 34 women's matches, of which 16 were won, one drawn and 12 lost, with five abandoned. Tommy Hodson, the former Cheshire wicketkeeper, hung up his gloves (and the helmet he wore behind the stumps for many years) after a record 764 matches for MCC. He celebrated his 80th birthday in December.

MCC teams also toured Mexico and Costa Rica, Nepal and Sierra Leone. In Nepal, a strong side captained by Essex's Tom Westley won a first-class match against the national side by 208 runs.

In March 2020, the team for the traditional season curtain-raiser against the county champions was due to be led by Kumar Sangakkara, who was announced as MCC's first non-British president at the AGM in May. At 41, he was the youngest president since the Duke of Edinburgh in 1949, and would become the first sitting president to captain the club in a first-class game for almost 200 years. The match was scheduled to be played in Galle, in his native Sri Lanka.

MCC v SURREY

At Dubai (ICC Academy), March 24–27, 2019. Drawn. Toss: MCC. First-class debut: J. L. Smith.

After being played in Barbados in 2018, the traditional pipe-opener between MCC and the county champions returned to the Gulf (it took place in Abu Dhabi from 2010 to 2017). But the March weather was more Derby than Dubai: rain restricted the fourth day to 19 overs, sparing MCC a tricky rearguard after they conceded a lead of 255. Surrey's young guns did most of the damage. Tall seamer Conor McKerr, in his tenth first-class match, and slow left-armer Freddie van den Bergh, in his eighth, took three wickets apiece as MCC struggled to 265. Surrey started indifferently, when Jacks – who had just smashed a 25-ball century against Lancashire in a T10 warm-up – popped a return catch to Trego, honours were roughly even at 144 for four. The ball was seaming a little under cloudy skies, which followed a sandstorm. But 21-year-old Pope and Jamie Smith, making his debut at 18, accelerated, eventually adding 266. Pope extended his maiden double-century to 251 from just 297 balls, with 23 fours and six sixes, while Smith – chosen as wicketkeeper because Ben Foakes was ill – was almost as impressive; he reached three figures with successive fours off the expensive Bess, and went on to the highest score for Surrey on first-class debut. "It could have been his 101st game," said Surrey coach Michael Di Venuto. "It looked like two 35-year-olds out there at times." Faced with a big deficit, MCC's openers dug in, putting on 190 before Rhodes was bowled by a Borthwick leg-break, but Sibley reached a satisfying century against his former county. He and Abell fell to successive balls from Clarke on the last day, before the rain set in.

Close of play: first day, Surrey 20-0 (Burns 7, Stoneman 8); second day, Surrey 389-4 (Pope 183, Smith 123); third day, MCC 221-1 (Sibley 102, Westley 13).

MCC

W. M. H. Rhodes st Smith b van den Bergh	46	– b Borthwick	88
D. P. Sibley c Jacks b McKerr	19	– b Clarke	128
T. Westley b McKerr	0	– b Borthwick	28
D. W. Lawrence c Smith b van den Bergh	58	– not out	2
T. B. Abell lbw b Borthwick	41	– lbw b Clarke	0
P. D. Trego c McKerr b van den Bergh	18	– not out	0
†O. B. Cox lbw b Borthwick	27		
D. M. Bess run out (Smith)	4		
*S. C. J. Broad b McKerr	15		
S. D. Parry b Patel	4		
S. J. Cook not out	0		
B 5, lb 14, nb 14	33	B 4, lb 7, w 6, nb 2	19

1/41 (2) 2/45 (3) 3/107 (1)   (90.5 overs) 265   1/190 (1)   (4 wkts, 85 overs) 265
4/193 (5) 5/209 (4) 6/216 (6)   2/256 (3) 3/264 (2)
7/240 (8) 8/254 (7) 9/263 (9) 10/265 (10)   4/264 (5)

Morkel 10–1–29–0; Clarke 11–4–23–0; McKerr 14–4–40–3; van den Bergh 24–4–54–3; Patel 11.5–1–36–1; Borthwick 15–1–55–2; Jacks 5–1–9–0. *Second innings*—Morkel 16–4–34–0; van den Bergh 26–3–87–0; Clarke 9–6–11–2; Jacks 10–1–33–0; McKerr 3–1–10–0; Patel 3–0–15–0; Borthwick 18–1–64–2.

Surrey

*R. J. Burns c Lawrence b Cook	12	C. McKerr c Broad b Parry	0
M. D. Stoneman c Lawrence b Cook	21	M. Morkel c Trego b Bess	3
S. G. Borthwick c and b Broad	16		
O. J. D. Pope c Sibley b Rhodes	251	B 9, lb 4, w 5	18
W. G. Jacks c and b Trego	20		
†J. L. Smith c Rhodes b Broad	127	1/29 (1) 2/38 (2) (128.1 overs) 520
R. S. Patel c Sibley b Parry	36	3/80 (3) 4/144 (5)
R. Clarke not out	16	5/410 (6) 6/489 (4) 7/505 (7)
F. O. E. van den Bergh b Parry	0	8/505 (9) 9/509 (10) 10/520 (11)

Cook 23–4–75–2; Broad 20–7–83–2; Trego 15.4–4–44–1; Rhodes 16–1–64–1; Bess 29.1–1–159–1; Parry 18–3–54–3; Lawrence 7–0–28–0.

Umpires: R. J. Bailey and M. Burns.

THE MINOR COUNTIES IN 2019

PHILIP AUGUST

Nearly everything will be different in Minor Counties cricket in 2020 but, in one important respect, nothing changes – **Berkshire** are still the team to beat. They won a fourth consecutive Championship title, after a desperately close contest with Staffordshire in the final. Since finishing 2014 without a victory, and bottom of the Western Division, Berkshire have played 30 Championship matches, winning 23 and drawing seven. Last summer, they achieved their main aim of matching Devon's four titles in the mid-1990s. For good measure, they also picked up the 50-over trophy.

They had wrapped up their division before the last round of games, and their response to tight finishes in both finals underlined their self-belief. As in previous summers, left-arm spinner Chris Peploe was crucial. It is not just his wickets (34 at 12 in 2019), but his economy-rate (1.66). Berkshire could call on another slow left-armer, Luke Beaven, who in four matches took 13 wickets at nine, and also conceded under two an over. Off-spinning all-rounder Euan Woods was ever-present, and his runs and wickets were significant too.

Berkshire did not just beat their Western Division opponents – they smashed them. Cornwall escaped with a draw in a rain-affected game, but Wales, Shropshire and Dorset all lost by more than 200 runs, and Herefordshire by an innings. Cheshire, eventual runners-up, ran them closest, losing by a mere 148.

Cheshire finished 35 points behind Berkshire, with three wins; spinners David Wainwright and Simon Normanton took 28 wickets each. **Wiltshire** and **Oxfordshire**, unbeaten for the second season running, also won three. Wiltshire's elevated position was mainly thanks to left-arm spinner Jake Lintott, whose 33 wickets at under ten brought him the Frank Edwards Trophy for best bowler, and off-spinner Joe King, who managed 29 at 18. Their batsmen, by contrast, could muster only nine bonus points.

Devon benefited from having Somerset's Peter Trego for three games, which produced 435 runs at 108, and two hundreds. Alex Barrow, formerly of Somerset himself, also made three appearances, and contributed 394 at 78, with three centuries. But big totals were rare. **Herefordshire** managed just four batting bonus points – comfortably the fewest in the country – while **Shropshire**, with just one win, against Cornwall, finished bottom for the first time since three-day cricket was introduced in 2002.

In the Eastern Division, **Staffordshire** so nearly had an outstanding season. Poor batting cost them dearly in the Championship final at Banbury, and they lost their rain-ruined Trophy semi-final to Cumberland in a bowl-out. The divisional title had been settled by a showdown between the two leading teams in the last round. **Norfolk** travelled to Staffordshire with a slender points advantage, but appeared to play for the draw they needed to be champions. Instead, Staffordshire took their last wicket with five overs remaining, to sneak the title by five points. For Staffordshire, seamer Tim Maxfield and slow left-armer Paul Byrne each took 26 wickets, while Michael Hill (697 runs), Matthew Morris (514) and Peter Wilshaw (436) all scored heavily. How they could have done with some of those runs in the final.

Despite their late stumble, Norfolk enjoyed a strong season. Ashley Watson, yet another left-arm spinner, was the leading wicket-taker in the two divisions, with 39 at 15. Just behind was seamer Andy Hanby, with 37 at 16. As with other counties, high scoring proved hard, but Sam Arthurton and Tom New both totalled just under 400. **Cambridgeshire** finished third, and unbeaten; in their final match, against Hertfordshire, Waqas Hussain and Josh Smith put on 243 for the second wicket, beating a record that had stood since 1904.

After three seasons as divisional champions, **Lincolnshire** slipped to fourth. This was in no small part down to the suspension of fast bowler Alex Willerton after he was reported for a suspect action. Louis Kimber appeared in only two games, but racked up 452 runs, including 246 against Hertfordshire, the county's highest score (beating Raymond Frearson's 232 against Cambridgeshire in 1925). He followed that with 177 against Bedfordshire.

Bedfordshire recorded their first win at home for nine years when slow left-armer Tom Brett took 12 for 108 against Hertfordshire. Dominic Chatfield, of **Hertfordshire**, won the Wilfred Rhodes batting award with 627 runs at 69, a good effort in a disappointing Championship season for the club; winning the T20 Final in the Wormsley sunshine provided some consolation. **Cumberland** were hit by the weather, with three games severely disrupted. The only win for **Buckinghamshire** came against the bottom side, **Northumberland**.

Meanwhile at the end of 2019, 124 years of history disappeared when the Minor Counties Cricket Association were dissolved, and replaced by the National Counties Cricket Association, to which all 20 clubs will belong. Each will now be run on a template set out by the ECB, and payments from the governing body will depend on the clubs meeting governance and selection criteria – teams must have eight under-25s, and eight who can demonstrate strong local connections. The fixture list has had a makeover, too: there will be just four three-day matches, and more 50-over cricket. The Eastern and Western Divisions will each be divided into two tiers of five, based on 2019 finishing positions.

Minor Counties cricket has always adapted, and will do so again, but it is hoped these sweeping changes are for the good of those who play and run the game at this level.

> " At Lord's, New Zealand lost the boundary countback 27–17, but gained in dignity. Ironically, the ICC's Player of the Tournament was Williamson, a connoisseur of the crafty single."
> New Zealand Cricket in 2019, page 980

MINOR COUNTIES CHAMPIONSHIP 2019

	Eastern Division	P	W	L	D	Bonus points Batting	Bowling	Pts	NRPW
1	STAFFORDSHIRE (3)	6	4	0	2	19	21	112	11.72
2	Norfolk (5).	6	4	1	1	15	24	107	6.83
3	Cambridgeshire (6)	6	3	0	3	17	21	98	−3.81
4	Lincolnshire (1)	6	3	2	1	14	21	87	3.13
5	Suffolk (2)	6	2	1	3	17	22	83	5.32
6	Cumberland (7)	6	1	2	3	15	23	66	1.41
7	Buckinghamshire (4).	6	1	3	2	11	23	58	−6.12
8	Bedfordshire (9).	6	1	3	2	10	17	51	−7.11
9	Hertfordshire (8)	6	0	3	3	17	19	48	−0.93
10	Northumberland (10).	6	0	4	2	13	20	41	−11.64

	Western Division	P	W	L	D	Bonus points Batting	Bowling	Pts	NRPW
1	BERKSHIRE (1)	6	5	0	1	18	24	126	16.98
2	Cheshire (6).	6	3	2	1	15	24	91	3.38
3	Wiltshire (5).	6	3	2	1	9	23	82	2.21
4	Oxfordshire (2)	6	3	3	0	12	21	81	1.05
5	Dorset (9).	6	2	1	3	14	21	79	2.98
6	Cornwall (4).	6	2	2	2	11	23	74	−2.03
7	Devon (8).	6	2	4	0	16	23	69	4.20
8	Wales Minor Counties (10). .	6	2	3	1	11	20	65	−9.32
9	Herefordshire (7)	6	2	4	0	4	23	59	−8.70
10	Shropshire (3)	6	1	4	1	8	20	48	−12.09

Win = 16pts; draw = 4pts. NRPW is net runs per wicket (runs per wicket for, less runs per wicket against). Devon, Wales Minor Counties and Wiltshire all had two points deducted for a slow over-rate.

LEADING AVERAGES IN 2019

BATTING (300 runs at 40.00)

		M	I	NO	R	HS	100	50	Avge	Ct/St
1	L. P. J. Kimber (*Lincolnshire*).	2	4	0	452	246	2	0	113.00	1
2	P. D. Trego (*Devon*)	3	6	2	435	159	2	2	108.75	6
3	A. W. R. Barrow (*Devon*)	3	6	1	394	141	3	0	78.80	5
4	D. Chatfield (*Hertfordshire*)	6	11	2	627	174*	1	5	69.66	2
5	J. du Toit (*Cumbria*)	4	7	1	390	101*	1	4	65.00	2
6	H. S. Fisher (*Dorset*).	5	9	2	415	101*	1	3	59.28	1
7	†M. J. Hill (*Staffordshire*).	7	13	1	697	153	2	4	58.08	1
8	R. T. Sehmi (*Cheshire*).	6	10	1	515	145	2	2	57.22	12/4
9	J. J. Smith (*Cambridgeshire*).	3	6	0	331	130	2	1	55.16	4
10	Z. A. Malik (*Staffordshire*)	3	6	0	329	164	2	0	54.83	2
11	M. J. Richardson (*Northumberland*) .	4	8	1	381	155	1	3	54.42	9/2
12	†A. J. Woodland (*Buckinghamshire*) .	5	9	2	373	89	0	3	53.28	6
13	J. C. Mickleburgh (*Suffolk*).	5	9	1	426	155	1	3	53.25	2
14	†M. W. Thompson (*Devon*)	4	8	2	302	132	1	2	50.33	16
15	Waqas Hussain (*Cambridgeshire*) . .	6	12	0	602	161	2	2	50.16	4
16	D. J. Lincoln (*Berkshire*).	4	7	0	346	82	0	4	49.42	7
17	H. R. C. Ellison (*Berkshire*)	5	9	1	388	102	1	3	48.50	6
18	L. A. Webb (*Dorset*)	6	10	0	469	161	1	3	46.90	5
19	A. G. Oxley (*Suffolk*).	4	7	0	317	124	1	1	45.28	3
20	J. M. Kettleborough (*Bedfordshire*) .	4	7	0	314	154	1	1	44.85	9
21	L. J. Thomason (*Cambridgeshire*) . .	5	10	1	397	109	2	2	44.11	7
22	S. S. Arthurton (*Norfolk*).	6	11	2	395	68*	0	4	43.88	2
23	†T. J. New (*Norfolk*)	6	10	1	385	79	0	4	42.77	15/1
24	S. M. Dutton (*Cumbria*)	5	9	1	325	84	0	2	40.62	1

BOWLING (19 wickets at 24.00)

		Style	O	M	R	W	BB	5I	Avge
1	J. B. Lintott (*Wiltshire*)	SLA	133.5	29	329	33	5-21	3	9.96
2	T. M. Nugent (*Berkshire*)	RFM	91.1	26	239	19	5-40	3	12.57
3	C. T. Peploe (*Berkshire*)	SLA	261.1	89	433	34	7-14	2	12.73
4	A. M. Watson (*Norfolk*)	SLA	237.3	51	619	39	7-58	4	15.87
5	D. O. Conway (*Herefordshire*)	RFM	96.1	24	304	19	6-51	1	16.00
6	A. J. Hanby (*Norfolk*)	RFM	186.1	38	615	37	6-70	3	16.62
7	T. Maxfield (*Staffordshire*)	RFM	141.2	24	455	26	7-48	2	17.50
8	J. A. J. Rishton (*Berkshire*)	RFM	160	35	503	28	5-46	1	17.96
9	J. M. King (*Wiltshire*)	OB	181	43	526	29	6-56	2	18.13
10	G. M. Andrew (*Oxfordshire*)	RFM	195	41	483	26	5-38	1	18.57
11	Tahir Afridi (*Wiltshire*)	LM	147.1	40	378	20	5-63	1	18.90
12	B. J. Currie (*Dorset*)	LFM	174.3	37	530	28	5-51	2	18.92
13	D. J. Wainwright (*Cheshire*)	SLA	200.2	52	550	28	6-94	2	19.64
14	G. M. Smith (*Cornwall*)	RFM/OB	142.2	23	399	20	5-35	2	19.95
15	A. C. Libby (*Cornwall*)	SLA	202	58	484	24	5-46	1	20.16
16	S. Normanton (*Cheshire*)	OB	143.1	22	572	28	4-28	0	20.42
17	H. M. Whitlock (*Devon*)	RFM	168.4	38	505	24	4-23	0	21.04
18	T. W. W. Rash (*Suffolk*)	RFM	126.3	18	413	19	5-50	1	21.73
19	T. Brett (*Bedfordshire*)	SLA	214.2	39	601	27	7-46	2	22.25
20	J. K. H. Naik (*Dorset*)	OB	258.1	70	616	27	4-47	0	22.81
21	T. Bulcock (*Cumbria*)	SLA	198.1	57	597	26	6-96	1	22.96
22	L. J. Chapman (*Hertfordshire*)	OB	199.5	36	662	28	6-54	3	23.64

CHAMPIONSHIP FINAL

At Bodicote, September 15–17. **Berkshire won by one wicket.** Staffordshire 150 (48.4 overs) **and 110** (38.5 overs) (T. M. Nugent 5-40; J. A. J. Rishton 4-21); ‡**Berkshire 164** (45.2 overs) (R. K. Morris 89; M. A. Johal 3-32, R. P. Hemmings 4-21) **and 97-9** (40.2 overs) (J. L. B. Davies 42*; T. Maxfield 7-48). *Jack Davies showed immense resolve to steer Berkshire to their fourth consecutive title, by the slimmest of margins. He batted throughout the fourth innings for 42*, and hit the winning boundary off his 103rd ball, after last man Mungo Russell had joined him with ten needed. Staffordshire seamer Tim Maxfield took 7-48 in a valiant 20-over spell. The pitch was hard and tinged with green, which helped the seamers take 34 of the 38 wickets to fall to bowlers, but it was not to blame for the three-day finish. Richard Morris's 89 had given Berkshire a narrow first-innings lead.*

T20 FINAL

At Wormsley, August 25. **Hertfordshire won by nine wickets.** ‡Dorset 104-9 (20 overs) (F. S. Organ 48*; B. J. Frazer 3-23); **Hertfordshire 109-1** (12.5 overs) (H. R. C. Ellison 62*, R. K. Patel 38*). *A disciplined Hertfordshire bowling display allowed Dorset just five boundaries, and paved the way for a comfortable victory. In contrast, Harry Ellison and Rishi Patel hit 11 fours and five sixes.*

TROPHY FINAL

At Wormsley, August 28. **Berkshire won by one run.** Berkshire 144 (46.4 overs) (J. L. B. Davies 31, C. T. Peploe 31; T. Bulcock 3-25); ‡Cumberland 143-9 (50 overs) (L. E. Beaven 3-31, E. D. Woods 3-23). *Last pair Toby Bulcock and Adam Syddall came desperately close to winning the Trophy for Cumberland. They put on 22*, but could not scramble the three needed off the final ball to tie the scores, and earn victory on fewer wickets lost. Both sides had struggled against high-class spin, and it took a stand of 40 for the eighth wicket between Chris Peploe and Tom Nugent to give Berkshire something to bowl at.*

SECOND ELEVEN CHAMPIONSHIP IN 2019

North Division	P	W	L	D	Bat	Bowl	Total points
1 LEICESTERSHIRE (6)..	8	2	0	6	19	24	105
2 Yorkshire (5)	8	3	1	4	10	25	103
3 Nottinghamshire (4).....	8	2	0	6	15	26	103
4 Lancashire (3)	8	1	0	7	19	30	100
5 Northamptonshire (8)....	8	1	2	5	18	21	80
6 Warwickshire (2).......	8	1	3	4	21	22	79
7 Durham (1)...........	8	0	1	7	22	22	79
8 Worcestershire (9)......	8	1	2	5	14	22	77
9 Derbyshire (10)	8	0	2	6	20	16	66

South Division	P	W	L	D	Bat	Bowl	Total points
1 HAMPSHIRE (2).......	9	5	0	4	24	25	149
2 Kent (5)	9	4	1	4	31	27	142
3 Sussex (5)	9	3	1	5	23	20	116
4 Somerset (7)...........	9	1	1	7	25	32	108
5 MCCYC (7)...........	9	2	1	6	23	20	103.5*
6 Essex (1)	9	2	3	4	23	28	103
7 Glamorgan (3)	9	1	0	8	19	23	98
8 Surrey (4).............	9	1	3	5	21	28	90
9 Middlesex (9)..........	9	1	3	5	22	25	88
10 Gloucestershire (6)......	9	0	7	2	14	23	47

Win = 16pts; draw = 5pts.
* *Docked 1.5pts for a slow over-rate. MCCYC played in the North Division in 2018.*

LEADING AVERAGES IN 2019

BATTING (380 runs)

		M	I	NO	R	HS	100	50	Avge	Ct/St
1	B. J. Taylor (*Hants*)	5	7	2	495	141	2	2	99.00	1
2	T. A. R. Scriven (*Hants*)	8	11	6	420	116*	1	2	84.00	4
3	H. Z. Finch (*Sussex*)	4	7	2	388	115*	2	1	77.60	6
4	L. A. Patterson-White (*Notts*)	8	11	2	670	153	3	1	74.44	1
5	W. A. R. Fraine (*Yorks*)	5	8	2	420	157*	2	1	70.00	4
6	A. Javid (*Leics*)	8	12	3	608	207*	1	2	67.55	2
7	S. A. Zaib (*Northants*)	8	12	5	461	136	1	3	65.85	4
8	B. G. Compton (*Kent, Notts*)	9	14	3	694	144	4	1	63.09	4
9	F. J. Hudson-Prentice (*Derbys, MCCYC*)	7	10	3	425	137*	1	2	60.71	2
10	E. J. Byrom (*Somerset*)	8	14	2	725	170	3	3	60.41	2
11	S. J. D. Burgess (*Kent*)...........	7	10	1	529	119*	2	3	58.77	4
12	E. N. Gay (*Northants*)	8	13	1	672	186*	2	3	56.00	1
13	T. D. Rouse (*Kent, Somerset*).......	9	13	3	525	106*	2	2	52.50	7
14	F. S. Organ (*Hants*)	9	13	1	602	127	3	1	50.16	8
15	F. I. N. Khushi (*Essex*)..........	9	13	1	567	156	1	3	47.25	8
16	H. R. C. Came (*Hants*)...........	10	15	3	558	89*	0	4	46.50	6
17	B. G. F. Green (*Somerset*)	9	14	4	462	101*	2	2	46.20	3
18	A. G. Milton (*Worcs*)............	8	13	3	444	138	2	1	44.40	19/1
19	S. T. Evans (*Leics*).............	8	11	2	393	146	1	2	43.66	3
20	A. Harinath (*Hants, Surrey*)........	7	10	1	383	78	0	3	42.55	0
21	M. E. Trescothick (*Somerset*).......	6	10	0	384	93	0	5	38.40	4
22	G. P. Willows (*Glos*)	9	16	2	484	164	1	1	34.57	3
23	J. M. Cooke (*Glam, Sussex*)........	12	18	1	580	131	1	4	34.11	1
24	O. C. Soames (*Hants*)	7	12	0	388	117	1	2	32.33	4
25	C. R. Brown (*Glam*).............	9	15	2	408	162*	2	1	31.38	5

BOWLING (15 wickets)

		Style	O	M	R	W	BB	5I	Avge
1	E. A. Brookes (*Warwicks*)	RFM	88	17	273	18	6-18	1	15.16
2	B. M. J. Allison (*Essex*)	RFM	167.1	43	445	29	5-23	2	15.34
3	J. H. Davey (*Somerset*)	RFM	94.5	20	274	17	6-52	2	16.11
4	T. J. Haines (*Sussex*)	RM	136.2	46	307	19	5-29	1	16.15
5	A. S. S. Nijjar (*Essex*)	SLA	238.5	71	630	32	5-52	1	19.68
6	E. R. Bamber (*Middlesex*)	RFM	124.3	28	331	16	3-33	0	20.68
7	J. Watson (*Kent*)	RFM	97	11	353	17	5-60	1	20.76
8	J. M. Lysaught (*Kent*)	RM	177.2	41	541	26	5-38	2	20.80
9	R. A. Stevenson (*Hants*)	RFM	123.5	23	397	19	5-39	2	20.89
10	K. H. D. Barker (*Hants*)	LFM	90.3	18	322	15	4-57	0	21.46
11	M. H. A. Footitt (*Notts*)	LFM	138.5	32	387	18	5-51	1	21.50
12	A. Sakande (*Sussex*)	RFM	138	28	371	17	4-30	0	21.82
13	T. A. R. Scriven (*Hants*)	RFM	144	31	383	16	5-14	1	23.93
14	A. Neill (*Glos*)	RFM	154.4	36	456	19	5-74	1	24.00
15	H. A. Evans (*Leics*)	RFM	155.4	42	440	18	5-50	2	24.44
16	L. A. Patterson-White (*Notts*)	SLA	148	29	489	20	5-90	1	24.45
17	J. M. Blatherwick (*Notts*)	RFM	148.3	25	534	21	4-80	0	25.42
18	G. S. Virdi (*Surrey*)	OB	151	28	506	19	5-31	2	26.63
19	A. Karvelas (*Derbys, Kent, Worcs*)	RFM	135.3	29	433	16	5-62	1	27.06
20	M. K. O'Riordan (*Kent*)	OB	181.3	29	608	21	5-83	1	28.95
21	P. Sisodiya (*Glam*)	SLA	179.4	24	613	20	5-48	1	30.65
22	R. I. Walker (*Glam*)	RFM	150	30	486	15	2-21	0	32.40
23	D. T. Moriarty (*Essex, MCCYC, Surrey*)	SLA	307.2	62	987	30	4-61	0	32.90
24	T. N. Walallawita (*Middlesex*)	SLA	262.1	60	739	22	4-78	0	33.59
25	I. S. Sohi (*Kent, MCCYC, Sussex, Surrey*)	RFM	166	11	711	21	3-36	0	33.85
26	N. N. Gilchrist (*Somerset*)	RM	203.2	36	767	20	4-111	0	38.35

SECOND ELEVEN CHAMPIONSHIP FINAL

At Southampton, September 3–6. **Hampshire won by 143 runs.** ‡Hampshire 343 (113.5 overs) (H. R. Came 41, F. S. Middleton 132*, S. W. Currie 54, Extras 30; H. A. Evans 5-65) and 278 (109 overs) (F. S. Organ 39, H. R. C. Came 42, J. K. Fuller 31, K. H. D. Barker 60, Extras 30; A. M. Lilley 4-58, C. F. Parkinson 3-66); Leicestershire 187 (57.2 overs) (L. J. Hill 69; K. H. D. Barker 4-57, J. K. Fuller 4-29) and 291 (73.3 overs) (A. Javid 86, A. M. Ali 35, L. J. Hill 33, C. F. Parkinson 30, B. W. M. Mike 37; R. A. Stevenson 5-65). *Hampshire relied on a six-hour century from the 17-year-old Fletcha Middleton in the first innings of the match, and a five-for from Ryan Stevenson in the last, when Ateeq Javed held them up for over four hours.*

SECOND ELEVEN TROPHY FINAL

At Beckenham, June 27. **Kent won by 16 runs.** Kent 276 (47.5 overs) (C. J. Haggett 40, A. J. Blake 110, A. P. Rouse 32; G. H. I. Harding 3-39); ‡Durham 260 (49.3 overs) (M. A. Jones 60, M. J. Richardson 49, S. J. D. Bell 30, S. W. Poynter 37; F. J. Klaassen 3-60, A. Karvelas 3-49, M. K. O'Riordan 4-43). *At 203-4 in the 35th, Kent might have expected a more commanding total; Durham, 210-4 in the 44th, had a chance if they put their foot down. They did, but wickets fell too fast.*

SECOND ELEVEN TWENTY20 FINAL

At Arundel, August 15. **Glamorgan won by one run.** ‡Glamorgan 122-7 (20 overs) (W. T. Root 49*; J. K. Fuller 3-23); Hampshire 121-8 (20 overs) (I. G. Holland 58; R. I. Walker 3-17). *Glamorgan, at the start of finals day, had hit 204-4 against Nottinghamshire, but none of the other teams found runs easy to come by, not even Glamorgan in the final; their 122 proved enough – by a whisker.*

LEAGUE CRICKET IN 2019

Sheriff win shoot-out

GEOFFREY DEAN

The quest to become Yorkshire's champion club went down to the last ball of the season on a sunlit September afternoon at Headingley. Sheriff Hutton Bridge, Yorkshire Premier League North winners, and Woodlands, champions of the Bradford League, met in a showpiece final to decide who would be the county's top dog. Woodlands began the last over, bowled by Dave Henstock, needing seven, which came down to three off the final delivery. But Kez Ahmed holed out to deep point, giving Henstock a fourth wicket, and Sheriff Hutton Bridge the trophy.

Eddie Barnes was named Player of the Match for his 54 and two cheap wickets, but he was adamant the award had gone to the wrong man. "Dave was magnificent in that last over," he said. "For him to be as calm as that was incredible." Sheriff Hutton Bridge had earned their day out after beating Richmondshire, winners of the North Yorkshire & South Durham League, while Woodlands defeated Doncaster Town, the Premier League South winners.

There was a remarkable transformation in Surrey, where perennial strugglers East Molesey were crowned champions for the first time since 1980. "We've just about stayed up on the last day in the last three seasons," said left-arm spinner Jonathan Fawcett. "In 2018, we didn't actually win a game until July, and we all thought we'd go down. There's been no real change of personnel, but I think we took confidence from our wins at the end of that season, and from winning nearly every week this time." East Molesey won 16 out of 18, with Fawcett claiming 48 wickets, and seamer Andrew Westphal 47.

In Devon, Heathcoat had been waiting a little longer for a league title – their entire 128-year existence – and won three more games than their nearest challengers, Paignton. Captain Jackson Thompson admitted emotions ran high on the day they secured the championship. "There was incredible euphoria," he said. "Like Ben Stokes, we believe we can win from any position."

In their 13th season in the Lincolnshire Premier League, Woodhall Spa won for the first time, after being runners-up twice. They clinched the title in style, when Alex King crashed a six to give them a two-wicket victory at Sleaford. "I don't think we could believe we'd done it," said all-rounder Ross Dixon. "It's been such a hard slog. Of all our wins, maybe one or two were comfortable. The rest have been pulling through tight situations."

Spondon lifted their first Derbyshire Premier League title for 12 years. Joe Ashdown and Chris Windmill were the only survivors from that triumph, and earned tributes from captain Adam Finlay: "Joe and Windy have been a massive part of our success over the years, and hugely deserve another winners' medal." In the Home Counties Premier League, Henley clinched their seventh title in 11 years, and their third in succession. Although they finished unbeaten, local rivals High Wycombe gave them a fright on the day they were crowned champions, losing by two runs after being set 337. "We've got a core of players who have played together for a long time, and know how to win," said captain Michael Richards.

Bangor's mix of experience and youth helped them win the North Wales League under the leadership of club stalwart Gareth Edwards, who had not captained the side for 20 years. "It's a huge achievement for us – I'm about three times older than some of the guys," he said, referring to Owen Reilly and Tomos Davies, two Wales Under-17 players who were part of the squad. "In the past, we relied on one or two, but now we've got real strength in depth."

The drama was not confined to the leading clubs and, in the Northern League, Kendal staged a great escape. Needing to win their last two games to avoid relegation, they looked doomed in the penultimate match when they were dismissed for 79 by title challengers Garstang. But captain Chris Miller then took four for 23 as Garstang were shot out for 70. In the final round, Kendal were still reliant on bottom club Barrow overcoming Penrith. Against all expectations, Barrow won for only the second time all season, while Kendal trounced Netherfield, sending Penrith down instead.

In another seesaw battle at the bottom of the North Yorkshire & South Durham Premier Division, relegation came down to the final over of the final round in the match between Darlington and Middlesbrough. Requiring 11 to stay up, Darlington's last-wicket pair could manage only six.

Chris Aspin writes: There was an unwanted milestone in the Lancashire League, when Milnrow became the first club to step down from the league since Bury in 1894. Their summer had begun ominously, when they could not raise a Second XI, and conceded their opening match. In June, they were unable to field a T20 side at Rawtenstall. A week later, Milnrow – one of the founders of the Central Lancashire League in 1892 – resigned. They agreed to fulfil their fixtures until the end of the season, though even that proved difficult: against Haslingden, their groundsman had to make up the numbers. Haslingden then made 273 for five, the season's highest score in the second tier, and dismissed Milnrow for 91.

This was the first season of two divisions, each with 12 clubs, and Burnley secured their 16th title on the last day, finishing 12 points ahead of defending champions Walsden. Accrington and Church were relegated, Colne and Middleton promoted. Once again, most clubs had to hire substitute professionals, because their contracted players arrived late, or left early. Haslingden's Ryan Burl, called up for Zimbabwe's tours of the Netherlands and Ireland, appeared in just 14 of their 22 matches.

The huge totals of recent years were not repeated. Darwen's 302 for five against Crompton was the highest; Rochdale's 36 against Walsden the lowest. In the sweltering summer of 2018, there had been 51 centuries; last season, 28. Three were scored by Crompton's Denis Louis, an amateur wicketkeeper-batsman who learned his cricket in the Caribbean. He hit 140 against Church,

134 against Walsden and an unbeaten 119 against Norden. He was the first division's leading run-scorer, with 775 at 48, while team-mate Mohammad Jamal managed 669 at 37.

Walsden's professional Umesh Karunaratne claimed 56 wickets at 11, and Jonathan Fielding of Ramsbottom led the amateurs with 49 at 13. Jack Wynn, who joined Ramsbottom from Milnrow, took the season's best figures, eight for 26, including a hat-trick, to shoot out Lowerhouse for 86. Former county all-rounder Jim Allenby, stand-in professional for Burnley, took the summer's other hat-trick, removing Church's top order, before scoring an unbeaten 47.

Colne, the second division champions, won 15 games, thanks largely to their South African professional James Price, who scored 1,019 runs at 78, and took 50 wickets at 13. Especially memorable was his 128 against Rishton, including ten sixes; his team-mates contributed 36, and Extras 22, to a total of 186. Price then took three for 23 to help dismiss Rishton for 133. Rishton's Mansoor Amjad, with 1,001 at 71, was the only other player to reach four figures.

Sachithra Serasinghe, Bacup's Sri Lankan professional, had a prolific summer, with 798 runs at 44, and 59 wickets at 11. Dale Highton, the Middleton captain, also took 59 at 11. Clinton Perren, the former Queensland all-rounder, hit 569 runs for Littleborough, and against Rishton shared a second-wicket stand of 119 with his son, Zac. There were notable milestones for Andrew Payne of Rawtenstall, who collected his 10,000th run and 400th wicket.

In the Worsley Cup game against Great Harwood, Clitheroe's Charlie Dewhurst (146) and Peter Dibb (123) put on an unbroken 270 for the third wicket. It was a club record, and the second-highest stand in the competition's long history. Another notable innings was played by Church captain Levi Wolfenden. Against Ramsbottom, he smashed 100 off 56 balls, with nine sixes. Seven balls sailed out of the ground, and were never seen again. Wolfenden completed a remarkable afternoon by opening the bowling and taking four for 53. Keith Roscoe, the 58-year-old Rawtenstall captain, collected 37 wickets, to take his total to 1,799 since his debut in 1979.

Darwen won their second Worsley Cup in three seasons, beating Todmorden in the final by six wickets. Ramsbottom became Twenty20 champions for the fourth time, with a 46-run victory over Bacup. Norden beat Darwen to win the Lancashire Cricket Federation knockout cup.

ECB PREMIER LEAGUE TABLES IN 2019

An asterisk denotes one tie.

Birmingham and District Premier League

		P	W	L	Pts
1	**Berkswell**	22	15	1	389
2	Shrewsbury	22	11	6	313
3	Barnt Green	22	9	8	267
4	Shifnal	22	10	8	266
5	Knowle & Dorridge	22	10	8	256
6	Walsall	22	8	8	252
7	Kidderminster	22	9	9	245
8	Smethwick	22	7	10	225
9	West Bromwich Dartmouth	22	7	10	224
10	Moseley	22	6	8	221
11	Dorridge	22	6	12	210
12	Kenilworth Wardens	22	3	13	153

Bradford Premier League

		P	W	L	Pts
1	**Woodlands**	22	14	3	301
2	Townville	22	12	5	259
3	Hanging Heaton	22	8*	9	239
4	Pudsey St Lawrence	22	10	7	236
5	New Farnley	22	8*	7	227
6	Bradford & Bingley	22	8	9	224
7	Farsley	22	9	8	217
8	Methley	22	7*	10	209
9	Cleckheaton	22	8	9	207
10	Wrenthorpe	22	7	11	190
11	Undercliffe	22	6	11	184
12	Lightcliffe	22	4*	12	161

Cheshire County League Premier Division

		P	W	L	Pts
1	**Chester Boughton Hall**	22	15	3	432
2	Neston	22	10*	5	355
3	Timperley	22	11	4	338
4	Nantwich	22	10	6	330
5	Alderley Edge	22	9*	4	327
6	Hyde	22	10	6	315
7	Widnes	22	6	7	273
8	Cheadle	22	7	9	242
9	Oulton Park	22	6	11	232
10	Toft	22	6	10	226
11	Marple	22	2	14	161
12	Grappenhall	22	1	14	131

Cornwall Premier Division

		P	W	L	Pts
1	**Penzance**	18	17	1	343
2	Redruth	18	14	3	294
3	Werrington	18	11	7	257
4	St Just	18	12	6	254
5	St Austell	18	11	7	249
6	Wadebridge	18	7	11	199
7	Truro	18	7	11	182
8	Grampound Road	18	5	13	173
9	Callington	18	3	14	131
10	Falmouth	18	2	16	124

Derbyshire Premier League

		P	W	L	Pts
1	**Spondon**	22	14	5	360
2	Ticknall	22	14	7	353
3	Ockbrook & Borrowash	22	14	6	344
4	Chesterfield	22	11	7	323
5	Sandiacre Town	22	12	6	322
6	Denby	22	11	7	312
7	Elvaston	22	9	11	266
8	Alvaston & Boulton	22	8	10	251
9	Swarkestone	22	9	10	243
10	Eckington	22	5	13	195
11	Clifton	22	3	15	156
12	Dunstall	22	2	15	135

Devon Premier League

		P	W	L	Pts
1	**Heathcoat**	18	15	3	304
2	Paignton	18	12	5	267
3	Sidmouth	18	12	6	257
4	Plymouth	18	10	8	245
5	Exeter	18	8	10	211
6	Exmouth	18	8	10	209
7	Sandford	18	7	11	200
8	Bovey Tracey	18	8	10	199
9	North Devon	18	6	11	184
10	Torquay	18	3	15	155

East Anglian Premier League

		P	W	L	Pts
1	**Frinton-on-Sea**	22	15	1	443*
2	Swardeston	22	13	3	417
3	Sudbury	22	12	4	400
4	Horsford	22	11	8	340
5	Great Witchingham	22	8	7	305
6	Cambridge	22	8	9	286
	Copdock & Old Ipswich	22	8	9	286
8	Bury St Edmunds	22	7	8	274
9	Saffron Walden	22	6	12	244
10	Mildenhall	22	6	13	234
11	Burwell & Exning	22	4	13	225
12	Vauxhall Mallards	22	3	14	123

† *Frinton awarded 18pts, and Vauxhall Mallards deducted 32pts, after Mallards unable to produce a team.*

Essex League Premier Division

		P	W	L	Pts
1	**Brentwood**	**18**	**14**	**3**	**316**
2	Wanstead & Snaresbrook	18	11	4	286
3	Chelmsford	18	10	6	264
4	Hadleigh & Thundersley	18	9	5	256
5	Hornchurch	18	11	5	252
6	Billericay	18	7	9	195
7 {	Belhus	18	5	10	183
	Chingford	18	5	11	183
9	Buckhurst Hill	18	5	11	175
10	Ilford	18	2	15	110

Hertfordshire League Premier Division

		P	W	L	Pts
1	**Radlett**	**18**	**13**	**4**	**388**
2	Welwyn Garden City	18	11	2	379
3	Potters Bar	18	11	4	363
4	North Mymms	18	8	6	303
5	Totteridge Millhillians	18	9	7	295
6	Harpenden	18	6	10	253
7	Hertford	18	6	9	230
8	West Herts	18	4	11	210
9	Luton Town & Indians	18	5	10	206
10	Bishop's Stortford	18	2	12	146

Home Counties Premier League

		P	W	L	Pts
1	**Henley**	**18**	**14**	**0**	**346**
2	Banbury	18	11	4	290
3	Datchet	18	10	4	260
4	Aston Rowant	18	8	9	259
5	High Wycombe	18	8	5	255
6	Finchampstead	18	5*	7	213
7	Buckingham Town	18	5	9	206
8	Tring Park	18	6	7	202
9	Horspath	18	1*	13	149
10	Slough	18	2	12	147

Kent League Premier Division

		P	W	L	Pts
1	**Beckenham**	**18**	**13**	**3**	**267**
2	Bexley	18	12	4	252
3	Tunbridge Wells	18	10	6	225
4	Sevenoaks Vine	18	9	7	213
5	Sandwich Town	18	8	9	193
6	Bickley Park	18	8	8	192
7	Lordswood	18	8	8	189
8	Blackheath	18	5	12	150
9	Canterbury	18	5	12	144
10	HSBC	18	4	13	117

Leics and Rutland League Premier Division

		P	W	L	Pts
1	**Rothley Park**	**22**	**18**	**3**	**488**
2	Barrow Town	22	13*	7	411
3	Sileby Town	22	13	7	404
4	Langtons	22	12	7	376
5	Loughborough Town	22	10	9	322
6	Kibworth	22	9	10	319
7	Leicester Ivanhoe	22	9	10	308
8	Syston Town	22	9	9	300
9	Kegworth Town	22	7	11	289
10	Cropston	22	7	12	287
11	Lutterworth	22	6*	13	279
12	Barkby United	22	2	17	187

Lincolnshire Cricket Board Premier League

		P	W	L	Pts
1	**Woodhall Spa**	**18**	**12**	**4**	**272**
2	Bracebridge Heath	18	11	5	243
3	Bourne	18	10	6	231
4	Sleaford	18	9	6	227
5	Grantham	18	9	8	225
6	Lindum	18	8	8	212
7	Market Deeping	18	7	8	188
8	Scunthorpe Town	18	4	12	144
9	Louth	18	4	10	143
10	Boston	18	4	11	126

Liverpool and District Competition

		P	W	L	Pts
1	**Bootle**	**22**	**16**	**2**	**399**
2	Ormskirk	22	14	3	381
3	Northern	22	10	5	308
4	New Brighton	22	9	6	259
5	Formby	22	8	7	259
6	Wallasey	22	8	7	245
7	Orrell Red Triangle	21	7	9	230
8	Rainhill	22	8	10	226
9	Leigh	22	5	9	207
10	Southport & Birkdale	22	4	14	168
11	Colwyn Bay	22	3	10	159
12	Lytham	22	3	13	158

Middlesex County League Division One

		P	W	L	Pts
1	**North Middlesex**	**18**	**11**	**3**	**135**
2 {	Ealing	18	10	3	118
	Hampstead	18	11	6	118
4	Shepherds Bush	18	8*	6	92
5	Teddington	18	7*	7	84
6	Richmond	18	7	10	82
7	Finchley	18	7	8	80
8 {	Stanmore	18	6	8	79
	Twickenham	18	7	10	79
10	Harrow St Mary's	18	1	14	27

Northamptonshire League Premier Division

		P	W	L	Pts
1	Peterborough Town....	22	17	2	373
2	Finedon Dolben	22	15	4	358
3	Old Northamptonians ..	22	14	6	328
4	Oundle Town	22	13	7	299
5	Northampton Saints.....	22	10	8	286
6	Rushden & Higham Town	22	11	6	284
7	Brigstock	22	9	10	250
8	Geddington	22	9	10	243
9	Brixworth............	22	5	12	178
10	Horton House	22	4	16	158
11	Desborough Town......	22	4	15	152
12	Wollaston	22	2	17	116

North East Premier Division

		P	W	L	Pts
1	Burnmoor............	22	12	3	377
2	South Northumberland...	22	10	3	354
3	Chester-le-Street	22	10	3	329
4	Eppleton	22	8	5	275
5	Hetton Lyons	22	7	7	265
6	Tynemouth...........	22	6	7	246
7	Benwell Hill	22	5	6	237
8	Burnopfield	22	5	7	230
9	Sacriston	22	5	6	226
10	Whitburn	22	4	7	194
11	Felling	22	3	10	171
12	Newcastle	22	2	13	124

N Staffs & S Cheshire League Premier Division

		P	W	L	Pts
1	Porthill Park	22	13	3	376
2	J & G Meakin.........	22	13	6	372
3	Cheadle	22	10	5	291
4	Stone...............	22	7*	9	270
5	Moddershall & Oulton ..	22	9*	6	269
6	Checkley	22	9	7	259
7	Ashcombe Park.......	22	8	8	254
	Whitmore............	22	7	11	254
9	Longton	22	7	9	241
10	Leek	22	7	9	237
11	Hem Heath	22	5	12	192
12	Blythe	22	3	13	188

North Wales League Premier Division

		P	W	L	Pts
1	Bangor	22	17	2	234
2	Menai Bridge	22	14	4	210
3	Mochdre	22	13	6	185
4	Denbigh.............	22	11	7	170
5	Llandudno	22	11	9	165
6	Northop	22	11	7	155
7	Gresford	22	9	9	152
	St Asaph	22	9	9	152
9	Pwllheli	22	10	11	146
10	Brymbo	22	5	14	106
11	Pontblyddyn.........	22	4	15	89
12	Connah's Quay	22	0	21	16

N Yorks & S Durham League Premier Division

		P	W	L	Pts
1	Richmondshire	22	15	1	374
2	Marton..............	22	12	2	359
3	Barnard Castle	22	8	6	298
4	Marske	22	7	7	280
5	Thornaby	22	8	7	264
6	Billingham Synthonia ..	22	6*	7	249
7	Stokesley	22	5	8	232
8	Hartlepool	22	5	10	231
9	Great Ayton	22	9	6	218†
10	Middlesbrough	22	3	10	209
11	Darlington	22	3*	9	198
12	Seaton Carew	22	4	12	186

† *Deducted 60pts (including 50pts for disciplinary reasons).*

Northern Premier League

		P	W	L	Pts
1	Leyland.............	22	14	2	249
2	Garstang	22	12*	4	234
3	Blackpool...........	22	9	5	216
4	Fleetwood	22	11*	8	209
5	Fulwood & Broughton ..	22	10	7	207
6	Longridge	22	7	7	171
7	Chorley	22	7	8	159
8	Netherfield	22	7	9	157
9	St Annes	22	5	9	134
10	Kendal.............	22	7	9	123
11	Penrith.............	22	4	12	114
12	Barrow	22	2	15	76

Nottinghamshire Cricket Board Premier League

		P	W	L	Pts
1	Kimberley Institute ..	22	10	3	316
2	Cavaliers & Carrington ..	22	7	5	289
3	Wollaton	22	7	4	277
4	Cuckney	22	5	4	275
5	Caythorpe	22	7	5	253
6	Papplewick & Linby ...	22	7	6	252
7	Radcliffe-on-Trent....	22	5	6	233
8	Plumtree	22	6	6	230
9	Attenborough	22	7	8	229
10	Hucknall	22	5	6	222
11	Farnsfield...........	22	3	6	199
12	Gedling Colliery	22	1	12	133

South Wales Premier League Division One

		P	W	L	Pts
1	St Fagans	18	12	4	25
2	Neath..............	18	9	9	22
3	Cardiff.............	18	9	7	22
4	Newport............	18	9	8	21
	Port Talbot Town	18	9	9	21
6	Pontarddulais	18	8	8	20
7	Ammanford	18	7	10	19
8	Bridgend Town.	18	8	8	19
9	Mumbles	18	7	10	18
10	Clydach	18	6	11	16

Southern Premier League

		P	W	L	Avge
1	**Bashley (Rydal)**	17	14	3	19.11
2	St Cross Symondians	14	10	3	18.14
3	South Wilts	16	10	6	16.18
4	Lymington	17	9	6	14.82
5	Hants CCC Academy	16	7	6	13.37
6	Burridge	17	5	8	11.81
7	Havant	17	6	9	11.52
8	Alton	16	5	9	11.43
9	Bournemouth	16	5	10	10.68
10	Basingstoke & North Hants	15	2	13	7.06

Surrey Championship Premier Division

		P	W	L	Pts
1	**East Molesey**	18	16	2	358
2	Reigate Priory	18	14	3	323
3	Banstead	18	9	5	230
4	Wimbledon	18	9	8	226
5	Weybridge	18	7	7	199
6	Ashtead	18	6	9	184
7	Sunbury	18	6	7	164
8	Esher	18	6	11	158
9	Sutton	18	2	11	90
10	Guildford	18	2	14	89

Sussex League Premier Division

		P	W	L	Pts
1	**Roffey**	18	14	0	449
2	Brighton & Hove	18	9	8	346
3	Three Bridges	18	9	6	345
4	Middleton-on-Sea	18	7*	7	332
5	East Grinstead	18	7	7	327
6	Preston Nomads	18	8	8	318
7	Eastbourne	18	8	7	317
8	Cuckfield	18	6*	8	283
9	Horsham	18	5	12	258
10	Mayfield	18	4	13	244

West of England Premier League

		P	W	L	Pts
1	**Potterne**	18	13*	4	301
2	Bath	18	11*	5	270
3	Bedminster	18	11	6	243
4	Cheltenham	18	8*	9	223
5	Bridgwater	18	8	10	217
6	Clevedon	18	9	9	213
7	Lansdown	18	7	10	208
8	Downend	18	8*	7	207
9	Taunton St Andrews	18	5	13	165
10	Bristol	18	5	12	159

Yorkshire North Premier League

		P	W	L	Pts
1	**Sheriff Hutton Bridge**	22	10	3	148
2	Stamford Bridge	22	7	4	127
2	Woodhouse Grange	22	10	6	127
4	York	22	7	5	119
4	Yorkshire Academy	22	5	4	119
6	Castleford	22	7	3	113
6	Dunnington	22	9	8	113
8	Clifton Alliance	22	7	6	101
9	Scarborough	22	4	10	88
10	Harrogate	22	7	9	84
11	Sessay	22	3	9	66
12	Beverley Town	22	2	11	49

Yorkshire South Premier League

		P	W	L	Pts
1	**Doncaster Town**	22	15	4	184
2	Wakefield Thornes	22	11	7	162
3	Treeton	22	12	7	160
4	Sheffield Collegiate	22	10	6	156
5	Tickhill	22	10	7	148
6	Whitley Hall	22	9	9	144
7	Barnsley Woolley Miners	22	10	9	142
8	Elsecar	22	8	12	120
8	Wickersley Old Village	22	8	9	120
10	Hallam	22	7	10	114
11	Cleethorpes	22	6	12	110
12	Aston Hall	22	4	16	82

LANCASHIRE LEAGUE TABLES IN 2019

Division One

		P	W	L	Pts
1	**Burnley**	22	15	5	186
2	Walsden	22	13	5	174
3	Lowerhouse	22	13	7	170
4	Ramsbottom	22	13*	6	170
5	Norden	22	10	9	146
6	Todmorden	22	11	9	141
7	Crompton	22	9	10	127
8	Clitheroe	22	9	11	126
9	Darwen	22	8	10	124
10	Rochdale	22	5*	14	99
11	Church	22	5	15	98
12	Accrington	22	5	15	79

Division Two

		P	W	L	Pts
1	**Colne**	22	15	4	191
2	Middleton	22	14*	4	186
3	Enfield	22	12	7	166
4	Littleborough	22	11	9	158
5	Haslingden	22	10	8	158
6	Rishton	22	9	11	139
7	Rawtenstall	22	9	11	135
8	East Lancashire	22	9*	10	134
9	Nelson	22	8	12	134
10	Bacup	22	9	11	123
11	Great Harwood	22	8	11	106
12	Milnrow	22	2	18	47

OTHER LEAGUE WINNERS IN 2019

Airedale & Wharfedale	Otley
Bolton	Walkden
Cambs & Hunts	Sawston & Babraham
Cumbria	Carlisle
Greater Manchester	Egerton
Huddersfield	Hoylandswaine
Norfolk Alliance	North Runcton
North Essex	Clacton
Northumberland & Tyneside Senior	Alnmouth & Lesbury
Pembrokeshire	Neyland
Quaid-e-Azam	Keighley RZM
Ribblesdale	Settle
Shropshire	Wem
South Wales Association	Cowbridge
Thames Valley	Wargrave
Two Counties	Witham
Warwickshire	Walmley
Worcestershire	Astwood Bank

ECB CITY CUP IN 2019

RICHARD WHITEHEAD

In its 11th year, the ECB City Cup – brainchild of former *Wisden* editor Scyld Berry – was given a makeover. Most significant was a reduction in the age of the participants. Previously, teams had been made up of 19–21-year-olds. But Mo Bobat, in his former job as player identification lead for the ECB (he later became performance director), felt that was too old, and unlikely to throw up any unpolished diamonds that county youth set-ups had overlooked.

In 2019, teams featured players aged 15 to 18 – young enough, in Bobat's view, to have plenty of scope for development. The competition remained part of the ECB's South Asian Action Plan, but was not limited to those communities.

Sixteen cities took part and, in another change, four teams qualified for a finals day at Loughborough, rather than a one-off decider at Grace Road. South London, run by the Surrey Cricket Foundation, proved strongest. Their squad were selected after a T20 round robin involving teams from the boroughs of Croydon, Lambeth, Southwark and Wandsworth, and they had a powerful combination for the finals on August 25.

Bradford, the holders, took on South London in the first semi-final and, after picking up an early wicket, might have had visions of retaining their crown. They were soon forced to think again. Abhay Gonella, the South London captain, bludgeoned 140 off 66 balls, with 20 fours and six sixes. He put on 152 for the second wicket with Esmatullah Zadran, as South London posted a formidable 210 for six. In reply, Bradford were bowled out for 109.

In the second semi-final, Wolverhampton could muster only 103 against East London, with Bilaal Anwar taking three for 21. Opening the batting, he then hit 58 off 54 balls, as East London won by five wickets with three overs in hand.

The final, a London derby, was another one-sided affair, with South London's batting power again proving decisive. Finlay Milton's breakneck century trumped another excellent innings from Anwar.

Final　At Loughborough, August 25. **South London won by 70 runs. South London 215-5** (20 overs) (F. Milton 103*, Esmatullah Zadran 49; Haris Latif 3-18). **East London 145-7** (20 overs) (Bilaal Anwar 69*; W. Heaver 3-31, Aaryan Pillai 3-18). *Finlay Milton's explosive hundred paved the way for an emphatic South London victory. Batting at No. 5, he came in at 44-3, and smashed 103* off just 41 balls, with seven fours and nine sixes. He added 97 with Esmatullah Zadran in a daunting total; Haris Latif took an impressive 3-18. Bilaal Anwar hit a defiant 69*, but East London were never in the hunt. William Heaver and Aaryan Pillai each took three wickets.*

ROYAL LONDON CLUB CHAMPIONSHIP AND VITALITY CLUB T20 IN 2019

The prizes just kept coming for Swardeston in 2019. The end of a year that saw them scoop a unique double by winning the Royal London Club Championship at Lord's and the Vitality Club T20 did not mean an end to the awards. In November, they were voted best sports team in Norfolk. Then, in the New Year's Honours list, their stalwart club captain Peter Thomas received a British Empire Medal for services to club cricket. "I am humbled," Thomas said. "But it isn't all about me – so many other people have worked tirelessly."

Hard work was one of the qualities underlined by Swardeston captain Joe Gatting, the former Sussex and Hampshire all-rounder. They established a template that served them well throughout the 40-over competition: bat first, post a formidable total, then let the bowlers apply pressure. Most of their wins were by thumping margins. Just once in their triumphal progress did they chase, beating Chelmsford by eight wickets in the group stages. And only Cambridge seriously threatened their dominance. Their Group 13 match at Clare College was won by just six runs, after an outstanding all-round performance by Gatting – 81 and four for 38.

In the knockouts, they won at Finchley and, in the last eight, at Bexley, before sweeping aside Ealing by 32 runs in a home semi-final. There were plenty of notable performances on the march to Lord's. Gatting hit an unbeaten century against Bourne, scored 79 and took four wickets against Finchley, and made 72 against Bexley. Callum Taylor, who opens the batting with his brother Jordan, scored 97 against Cambridge, and took four for 29 in the semi-final. Peter Lambert hit 71 in the quarter-final, and 81 in the semi.

In the Vitality T20, Swardeston had pedigree: they had won the competition in 2010 and 2016, and lost to Hanging Heaton in the 2018 final. On finals day at Derby, they thrashed Cranleigh in the semi – Gatting and Lambert put on 99 for the fourth wicket – before defeating Toft in the final. Seamer Callum Taylor took five for 18.

ROYAL LONDON CLUB CHAMPIONSHIP FINAL

NANTWICH v SWARDESTON

At Lord's, September 16. Swardeston won by 59 runs (DLS). Toss: Nantwich.

As they celebrated their first victory in the national club competition in front of the Pavilion, there was only one piece of history that concerned the Swardeston players: they had slain the ghosts of their 2016 final meltdown against South Northumberland. But for those with longer memories, there was a deeper significance. In its 50th year, the final had returned to Lord's for the first time since 2008. "To have a chance to play here with your good mates is amazing," said captain Joe Gatting, whose uncle, Mike, played there rather more often. "To win the game makes it extra special." At 25 for two after Nantwich had gambled by putting them in, Swardeston must have feared a repeat of 2016. But 19-year-old Alfie Cooper led the revival with 61, Gatting contributed 49, and Peter Lambert took the game away from Nantwich with a belligerent 60 from 37. The new-ball pair of James Warrington and Mitchell Spencer each took three wickets. Nantwich also made a poor start, but Luke Robinson and Ryan Brown were mounting a strong recovery when they were interrupted by rain. Chasing a revised 253 from 35, they lost wickets regularly.

Player of the Match: P. A. Lambert.

Swardeston

J. G. Taylor b Spencer	5	R. W. Sims not out	10
C. J. Taylor c Johnston b Warrington	4	M. J. G. Taylor not out	11
†S. K. Gray c Cook-Sievewright b Stockton	21		
A. J. H. Cooper c Cook-Sievewright b Spencer	61	B 2, l-b 5, w 16, n-b 2	25
*J. S. Gatting b Warrington	49		
P. A. Lambert b Spencer	60	1/12 (2) 2/25 (1) (7 wkts, 40 overs)	280
L. R. K. Denmark lbw Warrington	34	3/76 (3) 4/137 (4)	

M. W. Thomas and T. R. S. Oxley did not bat.

5/173 (5) 6/219 (7) 7/263 (6)   8 overs: 55-2

Warrington 8–0–60–3; Spencer 7–0–62–3; Stockton 8–0–35–1; Griffiths 8–0–35–0; Doyle 8–1–63–0; Robinson 1–0–18–0.

Nantwich

S. D. Rimmer c Lambert b Oxley	13	M. T. Spencer b Thomas	1
H. J. Dobson c Thomas b Gatting	9	J. E. Warrington b Oxley	16
T. L. Robinson c Cooper b Gatting	54		
R. K. Brown c Denmark b C. J. Taylor	59	L-b 9, w 6, n-b 1	16
O. M. Griffiths c Gatting b Sims	3		
*R. M. Doyle b Thomas	0	1/17 (1) 2/41 (2) 3/122 (3) (32.4 overs)	193
B. J. Johnston c Cooper b Sims	7	4/147 (5) 5/147 (6) 6/150 (4)	
†R. A. Cook-Sievewright b C. J. Taylor	3	7/157 (7) 8/158 (8) 9/161 (10)	
P. E. Stockton not out	12	10/193 (11)	

8 overs: 33-1

Oxley 5.4–0–20–2; Sims 7–0–43–2; C. J. Taylor 7–0–22–2; Gatting 7–0–37–2; Thomas 6–0–62–2.

Umpires: N. Davies and J. P. Flatley.   Third umpire: H. Cohen.

VITALITY CLUB T20

First semi-final At Derby, September 22. **Swardeston won by 47 runs. Swardeston 200-6** (20 overs) (J. S. Gatting 61, P. A. Lambert 70; J. Hamblin 3-42); ‡**Cranleigh 153-8** (20 overs) (M. Crump 33*).

Second semi-final At Derby, September 22. **Toft won by six wickets.** ‡**Sheffield Collegiate 118-6** (20 overs) (S. Hunt 40; J. H. Lomas 3-19); **Toft 119-4** (12 overs).

Final At Derby, September 22. **Swardeston won by 21 runs. Swardeston 178-7** (20 overs) (J. G. Taylor 45, P. A. Lambert 33, L. R. K. Denmark 39). ‡**Toft 157** (19.2 overs) (J. Scott 41; C. J. Taylor 5-18).

THE CRICKETER VILLAGE CUP IN 2019

Benj Moorehead

A small village in north Hertfordshire, perched on a chalk ridge three miles south of Royston, and with fewer than 500 inhabitants, is preventing a Yorkshire stranglehold on the Village Cup. Reed, who still play on the village green, won their third Lord's final in eight years, all against teams from the Broad Acres. Indeed, seven of the past eight finals have included a Yorkshire club, and the county would have claimed them all but for Reed.

Club captain Tom Greaves attributed the success to team unity. Most have been together for the past decade – six have appeared in all three finals – and nine of the XI at Lord's in 2019 came through the colts. "We play in a league where there's a lot of paid players, whereas we're just 11 mates," said Sean Tidey, whose 347 runs and 16 wickets made him Reed's most effective all-rounder. Greaves was the heartbeat of the side, unerring with his off-spin (17 wickets at 11), and a feisty hitter in the lower order. He relishes Lord's: a match-winning fifty in 2012, three wickets and a six to seal victory in 2017, and now a stunning 67 not out.

Reed repeatedly won by emphatic margins, never losing more than five wickets, and taking 76 out of a possible 80. The only wobble occurred in a low-scoring semi-final against Sarisbury Athletic (Hampshire), when a sixth-wicket partnership of 93 between Stuart Smith and Mitchell Cooper saw them home. Sarisbury's fine debut season had drawn hundreds to the later rounds. "Most of the boys have never played in front of that many people," said Jon Floyd, the chairman of selectors.

Houghton Main, from Barnsley, scrapped their way to Lord's, regularly forced to defend scores below 200, notably in their sixth-round win over the holders, Folkton & Flixton. But they had the best new-ball bowlers in the competition: Zimbabwe-born Biswick Kapala and his Afghan team-mate Imran Khan, who shared 44 wickets. The 22-year-old Imran, who left Afghanistan in 2015, was recommended to Houghton Main by Kapala in 2018, and took 132 wickets in his first two seasons. He bagged 24 at an average of six in eight Village Cup matches last summer, along with 310 runs. Neither Imran nor Kapala is likely to be village cricketers for much longer.

Still, it was hard to look past Houghton's bespectacled keeper-batsman Simon Ward. His two centuries included a crushing 103 in the narrow semi-final defeat of Astwood Bank (Worcestershire), while his lightning hands made up for what he lacked in agility. Ward has a self-deprecating Twitter account, @DatFatCricketer, which has a cult following in club circles. "When I'm batting, there are no quick singles," he said. "People say: 'Why don't you try to lose weight?' But I enjoy eating. When I diet, I'm miserable."

Earlier in the tournament, Craig Estlea looked set to become the highest run-scorer since digital records began, after blazing 513 in four innings for West Suffolk club Worlington. But he managed just nine in the defeat by Foxton, falling 15 short of Joe Adams's 537 for Glynde & Beddingham in 2009.

For the second season running, the Village Cup was without a headline sponsor. Houghton Main, like Folkton & Flixton the previous year, had to raise funds to travel to London. The dream of a Lord's final still drives this competition, but it comes at a price.

FINAL

HOUGHTON MAIN v REED

At Lord's, September 15. Reed won by seven wickets. Toss: Reed.

Houghton Main's 160 may have looked vulnerable, but none of their seven previous opponents had managed even 150, most blown away by the new-ball pair of Biswick Kapala and Imran Khan. Each took a wicket in his first over, but they were seen off by Robert Lankester and Tom Greaves, whose partnership of 123 turned the match. Greaves was busy and aggressive, scampering to his fifty off 42 balls, while Lankester mixed resolute defence with dashing strokeplay, before he was stumped down the leg side by Simon Ward, standing up to Imran. Even so, Reed coasted to their target with nearly 14 overs to spare. Houghton Main were a bowler light after a disturbing injury to opening batsman Ian Simon, who was stretchered off after top-edging a delivery from Toby Fynn into his face when not wearing a helmet. He was taken to St Mary's Hospital in Paddington, and released five days later with a shattered cheekbone and three fractures of his eye socket. The players left the field for 20 minutes while Simon received treatment; the medics included team-mate Yousuf Rehman, a neurosurgeon, who had just been dismissed for a duck – one of three quick wickets that wrecked Houghton Main's steady start. Imran and Kapala counter-attacked gamely after the break, both sharing fifty stands with the dogged Callum Honeyman, but another mini-collapse prevented a late charge.

Player of the Match: T. D. Greaves.

Houghton Main

†S. A. Ward c Cooper b Fynn		18	L. C. Salisbury st Wharton b Cooper		0
I. D. Simon retired hurt		8	M. P. Bates lbw b Cooper		1
*M. T. Brown c Wharton b J. P. Tidey		1	S. Honeyman not out		3
Yousuf Rehman b J. P. Tidey		0	Lb 3, w 16		19
C. J. Honeyman not out		40			—
Imran Khan c Greaves b S. W. Tidey		37	1/30 (1) 2/35 (3) (8 wkts, 40 overs)		160
B. Kapala c Martin b S. W. Tidey		33	3/35 (4) 4/89 (6) 5/141 (7)		
J. K. Allinson b S. W. Tidey		0	6/141 (8) 7/143 (9) 8/146 (10)		

Simon retired hurt at 35-3.

Fynn 8–3–25–1; J. P. Tidey 8–2–19–2; Greaves 8–0–36–0; Cooper 8–1–37–2; S. W. Tidey 8–0–40–3.

Reed

†R. J. T. Wharton lbw b Imran Khan		1
S. W. Tidey c Ward b Kapala		9
R. A. Lankester st Ward b Imran Khan		59
*T. D. Greaves not out		67
J. A. Heslam not out		10
Lb 4, w 9, nb 2		15

1/3 (1) 2/15 (2)   (3 wkts, 26.1 overs) 161
3/138 (3)

S. G. Smith, M. G. Martin, M. D. Cooper, J. L. Caine, J. P. Tidey and T. G. Fynn did not bat.

Imran Khan 7–1–32–2; Kapala 6–0–40–1; Bates 6–0–25–0; C. J. Honeyman 3–0–27–0; Yousuf Rehman 3–0–23–0; Brown 1–0–8–0; S. Honeyman 0.1–0–2–0.

Umpires: C. R. Bryant and G. C. Hall.

DISABILITY CRICKET IN 2019

Worcestershire force

HUGH CHEVALLIER

Last summer, while England's men turned their attention from their storming Bastille Day triumph at Lord's to the Ashes, so the Physical Disability team faced a new challenge of their own. Back in 2015, Iain Nairn had captained them to victory in the first PD T20 World Series in Bangladesh, and his task was to defend their title over a few August days. Four teams from Asia – Afghanistan, Bangladesh, India and Pakistan – joined the hosts in a round-robin tournament that used several venues in Worcestershire.

It soon became clear that India and Afghanistan had some mighty hitters and, after an unbeaten 69 from Callum Flynn had guided England to a tight victory over Pakistan at Kidderminster, they lost to both: by seven wickets to the Afghans, and by 25 runs to India in a rain-affected game. Top spot in the league brought an automatic place in the final at New Road, and India secured that by reaching the last round of group games unbeaten. For England to make the second v third semi-final, they had to beat Bangladesh, and hope that India carried on in the same vein and defeated Pakistan.

India obliged, but Bangladesh proved stern opposition. Batting first, England relied on 45s from Angus Brown and Flynn who, as well as going unbeaten once again, held a last-over catch in the deep that brought a five-run win and a semi-final rematch with Afghanistan.

England lost early wickets, but recovered to make 147 for seven, thanks to Jamie Goodwin (49) and Liam O'Brien (53 not out). Halfway through their reply, the Afghans seemed better placed: four down, they were exactly halfway to their target. Then off-spinner Fred Bridges turned the tide with a spell of three for five in 12 balls. England were home by ten, and into the New Road final later the same day.

Ravindra Sante gave India a healthy base, with 53 from 34 balls, then Suganesh Mahendran increased the momentum with 33 from 11. Their 180 for seven was the second-highest total of the tournament but, at 90 for two in the 11th, Nairn's team were on track. Not for long: England, perhaps exhausted at playing four games in three days, subsided to 144 for nine, and the second PD T20 World Series went to a fabulous, undefeated, India. For Nairn, who in December decided to call it a day at the age of 39, it was a disappointing end to five successful years as England captain (see Cricket People, page 160).

Back in March, the England Deaf team took part in a T20 competition at La Manga in south-eastern Spain. Also there were teams from Barking (east London), Barnes (west London) and Düsseldorf (nowhere near London), as well as the Spanish national side. The smaller clubs fell by the wayside, with England's Deaf team edging aside the Spanish by virtue of losing fewer wickets, after both teams finished on 114.

Final approach: captains Iain Nairn of England and Vikrant Keni of India before the Worcester decider.

In October, the ECB Learning Disabilities side played three ODIs and five T20Is against Australia at Brisbane. Head and shoulders the Player of the Series was Dan Bowser, from Devon, who hit 60 or more in five of his seven innings, collecting 499 runs for the trip, and a familiar(ish) average of 99.80. Ian Martin, ECB's Head of Disability Cricket, said: "I couldn't be prouder of all the players and staff who've achieved this fantastic result. Australia is a tough place to play cricket as a touring England side, and these boys have excelled in challenging conditions to win all eight matches." Indeed, the Learning Disabilities team have been dominant, losing just once in international cricket in a decade.

The going was tougher for the England Blind team in November, when they journeyed to the UAE to face Pakistan in a T20 series. All six games went to their opponents, who had much the upper hand throughout. On one occasion, Pakistan made 312 from their 20 overs. By way of consolation, Sam Murray did complete an unbeaten century.

SENIOR CRICKET IN 2019

To win one Ashes series in a year is a notable achievement. To win two is special. That was the feat pulled off by the England Over-60s in 2019, with wins in three-match one-day series at home and in Australia.

Both finished 2–1, the tight away series going to a decider. For much of the final match at the Peter Burge Oval in Brisbane in December, it seemed as if the "grey Ashes" trophy was heading back to Australia. Batting first after winning the toss, England had made 226 for eight, with Neil Calvert defying the heat to hit 74 off 90 balls.

The total was at least 15 short of what John Foster, the England captain, had wanted, and his worst fears were confirmed by Australia's response. Scoring briskly from the start, they kept comfortably up with the rate, until the dismissal of Mark Gaskell, bowled by John Courtney for 82. Australia needed 12 with the last pair at the crease, and Rex Bennett batting with a runner. The pressure proved too much: all three batsmen ended up at the same end, and England completed an unlikely ten-run victory.

England had taken a series lead after a nervy opening encounter at the Bradman Oval, Bowral. Kent's Jim Phillips hit 25 from 28 balls to guide them home, after they were struggling in pursuit of Australia's 152 for seven. England had been 37 for three, then 107 for five in the 40th over. Richard Harris, despite being hampered by injury, top-scored with 40 from 86 balls, to add to earlier figures of three for 19. But any hopes England had of closing out the series in the second match at Lake Macquarie were ended by a 22-run Australia victory.

In the home series, in June, England had taken an early grip with an 11-run win at Maldon. In a match marred by a number of players having to leave the field injured, a lush outfield hampered scoring. Batting first, England did not hit a boundary until the 19th over, and were indebted to late acceleration from Simon Clements (56 not out) and Murphy Walwyn (32). In contrast, Australia got off to a flyer, but England reeled them back in and, by the start of the last over, they needed 13, with one wicket in hand. A run-out gave England the lead.

The Ashes were retained in the second match at Kidderminster, where England won by four wickets, but only after Rupert Staple – their Player of the Series – hit his first ball for the winning boundary with two to spare. Staple had earlier taken four for 20 in an Australia innings that featured a century, completed off the final delivery, by Glenn Richardson.

Australia gained a consolation victory at Hove, skittling England for 95, before themselves losing their seventh, eighth and ninth wickets on 93. A boundary did the trick; Courtney took four for 25.

In between the first and second Ashes matches, England played Pakistan at Oswestry, winning a one-sided game. John Punchard hit 76 from 91 balls, the top score in a whopping 344 for three. Pakistan were bowled out for 77.

Winners of age-group competitions – Over-50 Championship **Essex**. Over-60 Championship **Lancashire**. Over-70 Championship **Essex**.

UNDER-19 TRI-SERIES IN 2019

STEVEN LYNCH

1 India   2 Bangladesh   3 England

Bangladesh seemed in control of this 50-over tri-series: they finished top of the qualifying table, had the leading wicket-taker (Tanzim Hasan Sakib, with 12), and three of the competition's six centuries, including one in the final by Mahmudul Hasan, who thus lived up to his nickname, "Joy". But, as so often at the crunch, they lost out to India.

The Indian batting, as might be expected from a side coached by Rahul Dravid, was impressive. Divyaansh Saxena, a correct opener, led the run-scorers with 321, one more than Bangladesh's Towhid Hridoy, who averaged 80. India's performance was all the more noteworthy for their inexperience: of the team in the first match, only captain Priyam Garg and 17-year-old Yashashvi Jaiswal – a tall, stylish left-hander who later in the year picked up a lucrative IPL contract – had played at this level before. "This tournament is about giving people the opportunity," said a proud Dravid. "It's really creditable, since most of the boys are playing Under-19 cricket for the first time, compared with Bangladesh, who have been preparing for a really long time."

England failed to make the most of home advantage, never recovering from losing their first two matches by comfortable margins. They perked up a little, enjoying an exciting tie against Bangladesh, before signing off with victory over India. Jon Lewis, their coach, was not too disheartened: "We were up against two countries who are very strong at this level."

NATIONAL SQUADS

England   *G. P. Balderson (Lancashire), K. L. Aldridge (Somerset), F. J. Bean (Yorkshire), B. G. Charlesworth (Gloucestershire), T. G. R. Clark (Sussex), J. M. Cox (Kent), B. C. Cullen (Middlesex), L. Doneathy (Durham), J. D. M. Evison (Nottinghamshire), L. P. Goldsworthy (Somerset), Hamidullah Qadri (Derbyshire), J. A. Haynes (Worcestershire), G. C. H. Hill (Yorkshire), N. J. H. Kimber (Nottinghamshire), D. J. Leech (Yorkshire), E. O. Leonard (Somerset), J. P. Morley (Lancashire), D. R. Mousley (Warwickshire), J. P. A. Taylor (Derbyshire). *Coach:* J. Lewis.

Bangladesh   *Akbar Ali, Avishek Das, Mahmudul Hasan, Mrittunjoy Chowdhury, Parvez Hossain, Prantik Nawroz, Rakibul Hasan, Rishad Hossain, Sahin Alam, Shahadat Hossain, Shamim Hossain, Shoriful Islam, Tanzid Hasan, Tanzim Hasan Sakib, Towhid Hridoy. *Coach:* M. N. Nawaz.

India   *P. K. Garg, R. Bishnoi, S. Hegde, Y. B. K. Jaiswal, D. C. Jurel, P. D. Kanpillewar, Karan Lal, P. Maurya, S. S. Mishra, P. Patel, V. Patil, Qamran Iqbal, S. G. Rawat, S. Rizvi, D. A. Saxena, K. Tyagi, P. Tyagi, N. T. T. Varma. *Coach:* R. Dravid.
   R. Salam was originally selected, but was withdrawn over doubts about his birth certificate; Maurya replaced him.

At Worcester, July 21. **India won by five wickets.** ‡**England 204** (46.3 overs) (L. P. Goldsworthy 58; K. Tyagi 3-35, R. Bishnoi 3-40); **India 205-5** (39.2 overs) (Y. B. Jaiswal 78). *England struggled past 200, with seamer Kartik Tyagi and off-spinner Ravi Bishnoi claiming three apiece. Left-hander Yashashvi Jaiswal anchored the chase, completed with more than ten overs in hand.*

At Worcester, July 22. **Bangladesh won by six wickets.** ‡**England 200-7** (50 overs) (L. P. Goldsworthy 69*, K. L. Aldridge 58; Tanzim Hasan Sakib 4-49); **Bangladesh 204-4** (38.1 overs) (Towhid Hridoy 70*, Shahadat Hossain 57). *England went down to their second heavy defeat in two days, despite a seventh-wicket stand of 111 between Lewis Goldsworthy and Kasey Aldridge, which rescued them from 87-6. Medium-pacer Tanzim Hasan Sakib took four wickets, and ran out wicketkeeper Finlay Bean. Bangladesh breezed home, with Towhid Hridoy and Shahadat Hossain putting on 114 for the fourth wicket.*

At Worcester, July 24. **India won by 35 runs.** ‡**India 264-5** (50 overs) (Y. B. Jaiswal 63, P. K. Garg 100*); **Bangladesh 229** (47.1 overs) (Akbar Ali 56; K. Tyagi 4-16, S. Hegde 3-59). *India's captain Priyam Garg eased to his first century in youth ODIs, to underpin a total that proved beyond Bangladesh. They slipped to 79-5, before skipper Akbar Ali and Shamim Hossain (46) added 98.*

At Cheltenham, July 26. **England won by five wickets. India 256-6** (50 overs) (D. A. Saxena 51); ‡**England 257-5** (48.4 overs) (B. G. Charlesworth 52, J. A. Haynes 89; S. Hegde 3-60). *England finally got off the mark. India had looked in trouble at 193-6 in the 44th over, but Shubhang Hegde and Karan Lal slammed 63* from 27 balls. In front of his home crowd, Gloucestershire's Ben Charlesworth stroked a neat half-century, and Jack Haynes scored 89. After he fell, making it 198-5 in the 43rd, George Hill hit a run-a-ball 41*, and put on 59* with Aldridge (29* off 16).*

At Cheltenham, July 27. **Bangladesh v India. Abandoned.**

At Cheltenham, July 28. **Bangladesh won by seven wickets. England 242-9** (50 overs) (B. G. Charlesworth 68; Mrittunjoy Chowdhury 4-52); ‡**Bangladesh 245-3** (48.3 overs) (Mahmudul Hasan 81, Towhid Hridoy 75*). *At 211-5 after 45, with Charlesworth banking another fifty, a decent total was on the cards – but England added only 31, and Bangladesh won again, after a well-paced chase. It was supervised by Mahmudul Hasan and Towhid, who shared a third-wicket stand of 136. Left-arm seamer Mrittunjoy Chowdhury had been the pick of the bowlers.*

At Billericay, July 30. **Bangladesh won by two wickets** (DLS). **India 221-5** (36 overs) (P. D. Kanpillewar 53, D. C. Jurel 70); ‡**Bangladesh 219-8** (31.3 overs) (Parvez Hossain 51; S. S. Mishra 3-47). *Bangladesh pulled off a rare victory over India, in a match shortened by rain: their target was revised to 218 in 32 overs.*

At Billericay, August 1. **Bangladesh won by 72 runs. Bangladesh 224** (47.1 overs) (Tanzid Hasan 117; N. J. H. Kimber 5-38); ‡**England 152** (39 overs) (Tanzim Hasan Sakib 3-28, Rakibul Hasan 3-19). *Tanzid Hasan's century lifted Bangladesh to 204-2 in the 40th over, but from there eight tumbled for 20, Nottinghamshire seamer Nick Kimber finishing with five wickets. England made a hash of the chase, however, and there was no comeback from 102-7. Slow left-armer Rakibul Hasan took 3-19, including top-scorer Haynes for 40.*

At Chelmsford, August 3. **India won by one wicket. England 204** (49.5 overs) (S. S. Mishra 3-38, P. Tyagi 5-33); ‡**India 205-9** (36.3 overs) (Y. B. Jaiswal 78; H. Qadri 5-61). *India's narrow victory eliminated England, who again paid for patchy batting. They were 113-7 before Hill, who top-scored with 40, put on 76 with Kimber, before both fell to seamer Purnank Tyagi. Jaiswal had little trouble in waltzing to 78 from 83 balls but, after his demise, India dipped to 186-9. Kartik Tyagi (no relation to Purnank) looked on while No. 11 Sushank Mishra (18*) belted two sixes to break English hearts.*

At Beckenham, August 5. **Tied. England 256-7** (50 overs) (J. M. Cox 122*, G. P. Balderson 56; Rakibul Hasan 3-33); ‡**Bangladesh 256-6** (50 overs) (Towhid Hridoy 104*, Shahadat Hossain 76; L. Doneathy 3-60). *An exciting match boiled down to the final over, bowled by medium-pacer Hill. Towhid needed seven from the last three balls, and connected with all of them – but he could run only two each time, so the match was tied. Wicketkeeper Jordan Cox, in his only match of the tournament, batted through England's innings for 122*, and put on 108 for the seventh wicket with his captain, George Balderson. It looked enough when Bangladesh slipped to 61-3, but Towhid, who completed his own century in that last over, and Shahadat put on 160 in 34.*

At Beckenham, August 7. **No result.** ‡**India 244** (49.3 overs) (S. Hegde 69; Shoriful Islam 3-43, Avishek Das 3-59, Shamim Hossain 3-38); **Bangladesh 19-2** (5.5 overs). *A downpour meant Bangladesh escaped with a point, which ensured they would top the qualifying table.*

At Beckenham, August 9. **England won by eight wickets** (DLS). ‡**India 278-8** (50 overs) (D. A. Saxena 102, P. K. Garg 51, N. T. T. Varma 52; G. P. Balderson 3-60, J. D. M. Evison 3-46); **England 214-2** (41.3 overs) (T. G. R. Clark 66, D. R. Mousley 74*). *England at least ended the tournament in good heart, after a close-run victory. Opener Tom Clark shared stands of 72 with*

Charlesworth (46) and Dan Mousley, who made sure a revised target of 214 in 42 overs was reached with three balls to spare. It was tough on India's opener Divyaansh Saxena, who compiled his first century in youth ODIs, and Tilak Varma, only 16, who thumped 52 from 25 balls.

BANGLADESH 11pts, INDIA 8pts, England 5pts.

Final At Hove, August 11. **India won by six wickets.** ‡**Bangladesh 261** (50 overs) (Parvez Hossain 60, Mahmudul Hasan 109); **India 264-4** (48.4 overs) (Y. B. Jaiswal 50, D. A. Saxena 55, P. K. Garg 73, D. C. Jurel 59*). *Bangladesh seemed set for riches at 123-1, but kept losing wickets in pairs, undoing Mahmudul's good work. Apart from the top three, only Shamim – with 32 from No. 7 – made more than six. India were always in control of the chase. Openers Jaiswal and Saxena put on 104; after they both fell to Rakibul, Garg and wicketkeeper Dhruv Jurel added 109. Varma finished things off with a boundary in the penultimate over.*

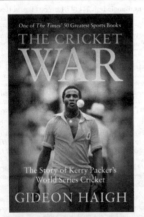

YOUTH CRICKET IN 2019

Richard Whitehead

It is a long way from the war-torn cities of Afghanistan, via a refugee camp in northern France, to the bucolic surroundings of Southill Park CC in Bedfordshire. But it was a journey made by Luton Blue Tigers, a team of Afghan teenagers assembled by Amran Malik, a development officer with Wicketz, the Lord's Taverners scheme to help young people in deprived communities.

There are about 30 Blue Tigers, aged between 16 and 19, who were housed in Luton after their arrival in the UK; some have been here for nearly ten years, others just a few months. "I heard there had been some antisocial behaviour among the Afghan boys," said Malik. Their energies needed to be channelled constructively. "People had tried to get them playing sport, but they didn't want to play football. They wanted to play cricket."

Their tales were frequently traumatic. Many had walked from their homeland to escape the Taliban, often taking nearly a year to reach the notorious Jungle camp in Calais. "Some of their stories are shocking," said Malik. "They witnessed terrible things in the camp – things we can't even imagine."

They instantly relished the cricket sessions, and began to show their skills. "They tend to be better bowlers than batsmen, because you can chalk a set of stumps on a wall and practise bowling," said Malik. Wicketz is a 48-week programme designed so that the charity's intervention can be genuinely beneficial, not just a brief respite. Links are established with further education colleges, allowing the teenagers to develop skills that may help them find work.

There are Wicketz hubs in 19 UK towns and cities, each in a deprived area. The scheme is open to 8–19-year-olds, and its principal aim is to use cricket to tackle the social issues often experienced by young people trapped in poverty. In Luton, Malik set up pairs competitions with teenagers from other communities, in a bid to help the Afghans integrate.

The Luton Blue Tigers name was chosen to give them an identity, and an association with the Afghan national team. Last summer, they played their first proper match, against an XI from Southill Park. Overlooked by the 18th-century Southill Park House, their beautiful ground with its thatched pavilion offered a stark contrast to the environments experienced by the Afghan players.

To their delight, they won. "It was our first game against a typical English village team, and we beat them," said Malik. One of the players, Zilal Mohmand, added: "I'm really happy and amazed by what we have achieved. All we did before was roam the streets. Now Amran has given us the opportunity to play cricket and come together as a team. Cricket has changed my life."

Winners of age-group competitions
Under-17 County Championship **Surrey**. Under-17 County Cup **Leicestershire & Rutland**. Under-17 Women's County Championship **Warwickshire**. Under-17 Women's T20 **Kent** Under-15 County Cup **Surrey**. Under-15 Bunbury Festival **South & South West**. Under-15 Women's County Championship **Kent**.

THE 2019 ECB DAVID ENGLISH BUNBURY FESTIVAL

In 2017, the South & South West team failed to win a 50-over match at the Bunbury Festival at Stowe School. How times have changed. After winning the tournament the following year – albeit with one defeat – they stormed through the 2019 competition unbeaten. To add icing to the cake, they also completed a hat-trick of Twenty20 titles. "South & South West have raised the bar," said ECB national performance manager and festival director David Graveney. "It's now for the others to respond."

This was the second year the ECB have run the festival as part of their player pathway programme. One tweak was the introduction of a midweek rest day to enable coaches to assess performances, and help the players with recovery. But the presence of the ebullient David English, founder of the competition 33 years ago, was a reminder that the week is about fun and life experience, as much as developing the skills of the best Under-15 players in the country. Felsted School in Essex proved an excellent venue.

South & South West flexed their muscles on the opening day of 50-over matches. Opting to bowl, they dismissed the Midlands for 179, with Will Gilderson and Charlie Brennan each taking four wickets. They made the chase look routine, captain James Coles hitting a hundred, as they eased home by seven wickets with 14 overs in hand. In the other match, the North – powered by a century from Matthew Weston – defeated London & East by 68 runs.

But the North found life tougher on the second day, bowled out for 88 by South & South West. Ryan Kilminster took four wickets, and the target was knocked off without loss. The other game was a thriller: boosted by fifties from Ben Wilcox, Danial Ibrahim and Jamal Richards, London & East squeezed home by two wickets off the first ball of the final over against the Midlands.

As the only unbeaten team, South & South West held the trump cards going into the final round, and made it three out of three, beating London & East by three wickets after being set 172. Opener Charlie Sharland hit 50 and, despite losing wickets regularly, they clinched the 50-over title in the 35th.

In the T20 semi-final on the opening day of the Festival, South & South West had defeated the North by six wickets with an over in hand; Coles made 66 not out off 48 balls. In the final, against London & East, they mounted another composed chase, passing a target of 117 with eight balls to spare. Sharland hit fifty again, and put on 79 for the first wicket with Zach Lion-Cachet. Nathan Fernandes's 68 not out was the highlight of London & East's eight-wicket win over the Midlands in the other semi. Coles was named Player of the Tournament, to complete a grand slam for South & South West.

SCHOOLS CRICKET IN 2019

Review by Douglas Henderson

Two pieces of academic research were published during 2019 that were of interest to followers of schools cricket. They considered whether a student's performance is affected by playing sport in the run-up to exams, and both determined that participation either had no impact or was, more commonly, beneficial. In other words, keeping up your other interests – especially sporting – meant you were likely to get the same, or better, grades.

The first study was commissioned by the Headmasters' and Headmistresses' Conference, and carried out by Peter Clough, professor of psychology at Huddersfield University; the second by the University of Cambridge Sports Service. Both can be read in full at www.schoolscricketonline.co.uk.

Schools have adopted a range of stratagems to counter a belief that it is best to revise, revise and revise again – to the exclusion of all else. Perhaps the most effective has been a simple rule: if you don't have an exam the next day, then play sport as usual. That at least should allow full availability for Saturday matches. However, some schools in these pages say the pressure of exams prevented their strongest team from ever taking the field.

One more option is to write to parents with the evidence, explaining the policy of maintaining a programme of activities, including sport, during the exam season. Such a ploy depends on school authorities being supportive of the value of exercise, which most are.

Another headache for those who organise cricket is the ever-decreasing length of the summer term. Boarding schools should in theory have greater access to students' time, but many report an endless stream of exeats, revision weeks and even breaks for post-exam stress.

In the circumstances, it's a wonder any cricket is played at all, but there is good news. Over half the schools featured here completed at least 14 matches, even if many were short-format games, such as in the National Schools Twenty20 competition. Several played more than 20, and Winchester, noted for academic prowess, played 27. Perhaps there's a moral somewhere.

It has become difficult, even for long-established cricket schools, to maintain fixtures and coaching programme for boys. Yet there has been remarkable progress in the girls' game. This year sees two new competitions for Under-18 girls: one, run by *School Sport* magazine, is a Twenty20 format, while the other follows the new 100-ball structure, and will run alongside the Under-17 (boys') tournament, promoted by *The Cricket Paper* and run by Andy Barnard, Gwen Davies and Rob Morris of Shrewsbury School.

The weather seemed unusually capricious: some schools were apparently unaffected by rain, while two – Wellington School in Somerset, and Worth in Sussex – lamented that nine matches were washed out. There was also the strange phenomenon of a run of wet Fridays and Saturdays in an otherwise dry spell, as well as a period of about ten days in June – just as exam pressure was easing – when the heavens opened. Sevenoaks, who suffered five abandon-

WISDEN SCHOOLS CRICKETERS OF THE YEAR

2007	Jonny Bairstow	St Peter's School, York
2008	James Taylor	Shrewsbury School
2009	Jos Buttler	King's College, Taunton
2010	Will Vanderspar	Eton College
2011	Daniel Bell-Drummond	Millfield School
2012	Tom Abell	Taunton School
2013	Tom Köhler-Cadmore	Malvern College
2014	Dylan Budge	Woodhouse Grove
2015	Ben Waring	Felsted School
2016	A. J. Woodland	St Edward's School, Oxford
2017	Teddie Casterton	RGS, High Wycombe
2018	Nathan Tilley	Reed's School
2019	**Tawanda Muyeye**	**Eastbourne College**

ments, had the most impressive record, winning all but one of the 14 games that survived; eight more schools reported a win-rate of 80% or more.

Two batsmen pushed their averages into three figures: Joe Gordon of St Edmund's, Canterbury, took his to an outstanding 106, while the remarkable ability of The Oratory's Michael Williams to defend his wicket gave him a figure of 290; only once in four innings did his opponents prise him out. Reaching 1,000 runs was a marginally less exclusive club, made up of Johnny Figy of Winchester, Joe Burslem at Felsted, and Eastbourne's Tawanda Muyeye. Gordon and Muyeye were the only two to make a double-hundred. In the era of one-day declaration games, a double was almost impossible, but once 50-over cricket grew widespread around 15 years ago, they became a little more common. The number seems to have diminished because so many fixtures have become either 35-over afternoon affairs or Twenty20 games.

Of the bowlers, 28 took at least ten wickets at under ten apiece – including an incisive trio from Dollar – but only three managed 40 or more: Alex Rennie at Bedford, Haileybury's Tom Newby, and James Flatt from Winchester.

The vast majority of cricketing schools entered the National Twenty20 competition, now seen as the pinnacle of the game at this level. There is concern that a handful of strong establishments are dominant, and in some areas, such as the South West, it is an achievement in itself to progress beyond the first round. There are several ideas for circumventing the issue, such as introducing a plate competition, or perhaps two divisions.

Once again, finals day benefited from glorious weather at the lovely Arundel ground. The winners were Malvern, who produced two superb displays of all-round strength. In the first semi, Sedbergh inserted Millfield, limited them to 121 for nine, and comfortably knocked off the runs. In the second, Malvern chose to bat, and built a formidable 195 for five; Merchant Taylors', Northwood, after nailbiting finishes in their two previous rounds, fell gallantly short. The final was an unexpected thriller: Sedbergh inserted Malvern, but this time could not make quick inroads. A target of 156 was steep rather than insuperable, though it looked as much when Sedbergh were 57 for seven. But an astonishing fightback meant they needed 14 from 15 balls, with the last pair together. Then Malvern broke through, and the trophy was theirs.

Tawanda Muyeye of Eastbourne College: Wisden Schools Cricketer of the Year for 2019.

It is not unusual these days for a school cricket career to peak in Year 12 (lower sixth); those in their final summer may be released to play at a higher level, perhaps for a top club, a county Second XI – or sometimes the firsts. There were several highly talented cricketers who, though still in full-time education, played little for their school. The clearest instance of this had come in 2016, when Sam Curran took many more wickets for Surrey in the Championship than for Wellington College on the schools circuit. In 2019, gifted cricketers such as Ben Charlesworth (St Edward's, Oxford), Joey Evison (Stamford), Jack Haynes (Malvern) and Matthew Revis (Sedbergh) turned their attention further afield; all four played first-class cricket.

However, the annual Wisden award is in recognition of exceptional first-team performances for a school from within these pages – and the 2019 winner is Tawanda Muyeye. He is a player of immense presence, a batsman destined to empty bars. People in the know at Eastbourne have learned to ask when he will next be playing, so they can feast on his style, which shows the aggressive influence of Viv Richards and Kevin Pietersen, two of his idols. Like them, he intimidates the attack, turning respectable bowlers into fodder for his swinging bat.

Muyeye, a popular, hard-working, self-effacing student who hails from just outside Harare, is on a sports scholarship; he has family in the UK, and hopes to qualify for England rather than his native Zimbabwe. Rob Ferley, his coach at Eastbourne, says he is also the best off-spinner of his age group in the county, as well as an electric fielder with exceptional hand–eye co-ordination. But it is the reliability of his fast, wristy run-scoring that has given Sussex cause to be interested in his development, and makes him such an exciting prospect.

MCC Schools v ESCA

At Lord's, September 3. **MCC Schools won by eight runs.** ‡MCC Schools 296-6 (50 overs) (B. B. A. Geddes 73, J. G. Timms 53, G. S. Ealham 90, A. S. Kopparambil 30*, Extras 31; J. M. Coles 3-47); ESCA 288 (49.4 overs) (J. J. Fielding 46, J. M. Coles 42, A. Horton 95; G. S. Ealham 5-60, M. L. Revis 3-47).

MCC *B. B. A. Geddes (*St John's, Leatherhead*), G. S. Ealham (*Cranleigh School*), W. A. Hobson (*Repton School*), G. F. Horbury (*St Aidan's High School, Harrogate*), A. S. Kopparambil (*Mount Kelly School*), T. S. Mackintosh Sabater (*Merchiston Castle School*), T. S. Muyeye (*Eastbourne College*), C. D. Peet (*Stewart's Melville College*), M. L. Revis (*Sedbergh School*), H. J. R. Startin (*Magdalen College School*), J. C. Timms (*Haileybury*).

ESCA *W. L. Naish (*Wycliffe College*), R. B. S. V. Balaji (*King Edward VI Aston School*), N. A. Barnwell (*Caterham School*), A. S. Chima (*Repton School*), J. M. Coles (*Magdalen College School*), J. J. Fielding (*Shrewsbury School*), A. J. Horton (*St Edward's School, Oxford*), N. Khelawon (*New Hall School*), P. Odedra (*Judgemeadow Community College, Leicester*), A. Prasad (*City of London School*), M. H. N. Saleem (*Clifton College*), H. A. Sullivan (*Temple Moor High School*).

SCHOOLS AVERAGES

BEST BATTING AVERAGE (5 completed innings)

		I	NO	Runs	HS	100	Avge
1	J. A. Gordon (*St Edmund's, Canterbury*)	8	3	530	226	1	106.00
2	J. D. M. Evison (*Stamford School*)	7	2	442	124	2	88.40
3	S. J. Young (*Millfield School*)	7	2	430	134*	3	86.00
4	R. Hanley (*Royal Grammar School, Newcastle*)	12	5	592	110*	1	84.57
5	I. V. A. Dilkes (*St Lawrence College*)	14	3	911	163*	4	82.81
6	H. C. Procter (*Sevenoaks School*)	13	4	723	152*	1	80.33
7	T. R. Carter (*King's School, Macclesfield*)	10	5	398	118*	1	79.60
8	J. A. D. Lawrenson (*Victoria College, Jersey*)	6	1	397	116	2	79.40
9	J. H. Burslem (*Felsted School*)	19	3	1,215	143*	3	75.93
10	O. R. Welch (*Ratcliffe College*)	9	2	522	129	1	74.57
11	A. Bassingthwaighte (*Bishop's Stortford College*)	13	3	742	145*	1	74.20
12	G. H. Politis (*Merchant Taylors', Crosby*)	16	5	776	93*	0	70.54
13	T. S. Muyeye (*Eastbourne College*)	19	3	1,112	209	3	69.50
14	M. L. Levitt (*Haileybury*)	17	3	963	175*	4	68.78
15	N. J. L. Morgan (*Reed's School*)	13	4	605	177*	2	67.22
16	A. H. Makin (*Manchester Grammar School*)	12	5	469	117*	1	67.00
16	D. Long-Martinez (*Norwich School*)	7	1	402	158*	1	67.00
18	J. C. Timms (*Haileybury*)	17	6	728	100*	1	66.18
19	S. J. Lister (*Gordonstoun School*)	8	2	397	101*	1	66.16
20	J. J. Figy (*Winchester College*)	25	5	1,307	120	1	65.35
21	T. D. Prest (*Canford School*)	6	1	320	105*	1	64.00
22	J. M. de Caires (*St Albans School*)	17	4	825	138*	3	63.46
23	A. J. Horton (*St Edward's School, Oxford*)	12	2	631	144	1	63.10
24	Y. Machani (*King Edward's School, Birmingham*)	9	4	311	139	1	62.20
25	B. B. A. Geddes (*St John's School, Leatherhead*)	15	3	737	135	1	61.41
26	R. N. Bell (*Oakham School*)	13	4	549	140*	1	61.00
27	F. J. R. Horler (*Radley College*)	15	2	784	130	2	60.30
28	J. S. Hawkins (*Bishop's Stortford College*)	12	4	482	135*	1	60.25
29	J. L. Haynes (*Malvern College*)	13	2	662	124	1	60.18

M. Williams (Oratory) hit 290 runs from four innings, three not out, at 290.00.

MOST RUNS

		I	NO	R	HS	100	Avge
1	J. J. Figy (*Winchester College*)	25	5	1,307	120	3	65.35
2	J. H. Burslem (*Felsted School*)	19	3	1,215	143*	3	75.93
3	T. S. Muyeye (*Eastbourne College*)	19	3	1,112	209	3	69.50
4	M. L. Levitt (*Haileybury*)	17	3	963	175*	4	68.78
5	I. V. A. Dilkes (*St Lawrence College*)	14	3	911	163*	4	82.81
6	A. L. Ayers (*Dauntsey's School*)	20	4	884	101	1	55.25
7	A. R. Carter (*Wellington College*)	20	4	869	148	3	54.31
8	J. M. de Caires (*St Albans School*)	17	4	825	138*	3	63.46
9	B. J. E. Robinson (*Tonbridge School*)	19	1	809	110*	1	44.94
10	D. J. Humes (*Shrewsbury School*)	22	0	798	108	1	36.27
11	F. J. R. Horler (*Radley College*)	15	2	784	130	2	60.30
12	G. H. Politis (*Merchant Taylors', Crosby*)	16	5	776	93*	0	70.54
13	D. W. Oldreive (*Gresham's School*)	20	3	762	94*	0	44.82
14	A. Bassingthwaighte (*Bishop's Stortford College*)	13	3	742	145*	1	74.20
15	B. B. A. Geddes (*St John's School, Leatherhead*)	15	3	737	135	1	61.41
16	H. A. de Lucchi (*Gresham's School*)	21	4	730	127*	1	42.94
17	J. C. Timms (*Haileybury*)	17	6	728	100*	1	66.18
18	H. C. Procter (*Sevenoaks School*)	13	4	723	152*	1	80.33
19	N. Khelawon (*New Hall School*)	22	0	720	137	1	32.72
20	H. Gouldstone (*Bedford School*)	16	1	719	103	1	47.92
21	D. N. Holland (*Malvern College*)	21	6	717	176*	2	47.80
22	W. A. Hobson (*Repton School*)	18	4	685	188*	1	48.93
23	M. R. Wells (*Bedford School*)	16	2	675	99	0	48.21
24	M. T. Roberts (*St Peter's School, York*)	18	4	673	150*	2	48.07
25	I. A. Rahman (*King's School, Canterbury*)	17	1	669	105	1	41.81
26	V. A. Gandhi (*New Hall School*)	23	4	664	72	0	34.94
27	J. L. Haynes (*Malvern College*)	13	2	662	124	1	60.18
28	J. J. O'Riordan (*Tonbridge School*)	19	5	652	89*	0	46.57
29	M. A. C. Keast (*Wellington College*)	20	1	644	107	1	33.89
30	M. L. Revis (*Sedbergh School*)	17	6	642	86	0	58.36

BEST BOWLING AVERAGE (10 wickets)

		O	M	R	W	BB	Avge
1	J. M. W. Bathurst (*Manchester Grammar School*)	15.2	0	59	10	6-17	5.90
2	M. W. G. Knowles (*Hampton School*)	48	4	150	19	6-7	7.89
3	T. B. Douglas (*Dollar Academy*)	61	16	168	21	4-20	8.00
	L. C. Haworth (*Rossall School*)	35	8	104	13	5-9	8.00
5	E. C. Watson (*St Peter's School, York*)	33	9	121	15	5-13	8.06
6	B. L. Matthew (*Bede's School*)	21.3	1	90	11	3-7	8.18
7	C. J. Creighton (*Shiplake College*)	80	14	289	35	5-29	8.25
8	J. S. Cairns (*Birkenhead School*)	35	9	83	10	3-13	8.30
9	J. W. J. Corran (*Birkenhead School*)	73	18	209	25	5-16	8.36
10	E. P. Marshall (*Alleyn's School*)	24	3	85	10	4-12	8.50
11	S. Graham (*Solihull School*)	59	4	129	15	3-11	8.60
12	L. O. R. Snookes (*Berkhamsted School*)	54.1	10	174	20	4-10	8.70
13	R. S. Disborough (*Dollar Academy*)	25	4	88	10	5-11	8.80
14	J. A. Grabinar (*University College School*)	82.3	22	264	29	6-19	9.10
15	J. A. Wills (*Lancaster Royal Grammar School*)	35	1	165	18	4-16	9.16
16	R. N. Bell (*Oakham School*)	30	3	129	14	5-23	9.21
17	F. Fallows (*Bromsgrove School*)	44	7	120	13	4-13	9.23
18	O. W. Anderson (*Dr Challoner's Grammar School*)	50	7	148	16	4-26	9.25
19	C. D. Furmidge (*Wilson's School*)	27.5	1	167	18	3-19	9.27
20	A. V. Holmes (*St Benedict's School, Ealing*)	33.4	1	161	17	5-17	9.47
21	O. T. B. Bingham (*Skinners' School*)	22	3	114	12	4-9	9.50
	B. Haworth (*Kirkham Grammar School*)	30.3	1	95	10	2-8	9.50
23	R. Kingham (*Forest School*)	88	15	305	32	4-12	9.53

		O	M	R	W	BB	Avge
24	Y. Machani (*King Edward's School, Birmingham*)...	24	1	115	12	4-15	9.58
25	M. J. T. Haynes (*Shiplake College*)................	24	2	96	10	5-17	9.60
26	I. Faisal (*The High School of Glasgow*)...........	28	4	126	13	4-24	9.69
27	W. Gair (*Rossall School*).......................	28	1	98	10	3-17	9.80
28	O. T. J. Robertson (*George Watson's College*)......	35	6	129	13	4-20	9.92

W. Robbins (Stonyhurst College) took seven wickets at an average of 4.00.

MOST WICKETS

		O	M	R	W	BB	Avge
1	A. I. Rennie (*Bedford School*).................	188	32	655	43	6-8	15.23
2	T. S. C. Newby (*Haileybury*).................	179.2	28	672	41	7-56	16.39
3	J. T. F. Flatt (*Winchester College*)	142	15	654	40	6-10	16.35
4 {	D. C. Goodman (*Clifton College*).............	137.1	28	416	38	4-37	10.94
	S. Hunt (*St John's School, Leatherhead*)..........	111	10	465	38	5-16	12.23
6	D. W. Oldreive (*Gresham's School*).............	121.3	9	496	36	5-59	13.77
7 {	C. J. Creighton (*Shiplake College*)	80	14	289	35	5-29	8.25
	W. R. Halliday (*Berkhamsted School*)	99.1	15	375	35	7-10	10.71
9 {	W. Lucas (*Eastbourne College*)	122	10	488	34	4-35	14.35
	A. W. Garrett (*Shrewsbury School*)	159.1	20	505	34	6-35	14.85
	V. A. Gandhi (*New Hall School*)	122.5	14	523	34	4-21	15.38
	J. L. Butler (*Dauntsey's School*)	150.4	19	565	34	6-82	16.61
13 {	R. V. Parekh (*Lancaster Royal Grammar School*)...	109	17	351	33	5-11	10.63
	B. W. Warren (*St Albans School*)	122	21	447	33	4-92	13.54
	F. J. Linzee Gordon (*Eton College*).............	196.4	40	591	33	6-66	17.90
16 {	R. Kingham (*Forest School*).................	88	15	305	32	4-12	9.53
	H. J. R. Chambers (*Abingdon School*)	112.3	4	533	32	5-14	16.65
	J. Pocklington (*Eastbourne College*)	122	15	451	31	4-29	14.54
18 {	B. P. Withers (*Gresham's School*)	125.5	20	488	31	3-17	15.74
	W. J. East (*Langley Park School*)	105	7	501	31	4-13	16.16
	J. B. Grant (*Dauntsey's School*)	150	19	547	31	3-11	17.64
22 {	J. A. Chohan (*Harrow School*)	122.4	19	476	30	5-16	15.86
	S. S. Shah (*Merchant Taylors', Northwood*).......	111	9	478	30	4-14	15.93
	J. D. Porter (*Worksop College*)	108	11	483	30	6-30	16.10
	J. A. Grabinar (*University College School*)	82.3	22	264	29	6-19	9.10
	A. G. Tomson (*Malvern College*).............	90.2	3	388	29	5-18	13.37
	L. G. Evans (*Shrewsbury School*)	128.1	15	471	29	3-7	16.24
25 {	J. W. Dickenson (*Malvern College*).............	112.1	7	478	29	4-19	16.48
	G. A. M. Freeman (*Christ's Hospital*)	96.1	9	481	29	4-21	16.58
	H. C. Bevan-Thomas (*Tonbridge School*)	127.3	18	501	29	5-22	17.27
	J. E. Bridge (*Haileybury*).................	98.2	6	541	29	5-31	18.65
	S. T. Young (*Felsted School*)	128.3	13	545	29	6-11	18.79
	J. M. de Caires (*St Albans School*)	135	12	545	29	4-28	18.79

OUTSTANDING SEASONS (minimum 7 matches)

	P	W	L	T	D	A	%W
Sevenoaks School.............	14	13	1	0	0	5	92.85
Malvern College.............	19	17	2	0	0	3	89.47
St John's School, Leatherhead	19	17	2	0	0	0	89.47
Shiplake College.............	16	14	2	0	0	2	87.50
Magdalen College School.............	13	11	2	0	0	0	84.61
Sedbergh School.............	18	15	3	0	0	0	83.33
Harrow School.............	23	19	3	0	1	1	82.60
Ratcliffe College.............	11	9	2	0	0	3	81.81
Eastbourne College.............	20	16	4	0	0	1	80.00
Shrewsbury School.............	24	19	4	0	1	0	79.16
Felsted School.............	19	15	4	0	0	1	78.94
Berkhamsted School.............	18	14	3	0	1	1	77.77

	P	W	L	T	D	A	%W
Manchester Grammar School	13	10	2	0	1	4	76.92
Tonbridge School	21	16	2	1	2	2	76.19
Dauntsey's School	20	15	5	0	0	1	75.00
Gresham's School.	24	18	4	0	2	0	75.00
Whitgift School.	15	11	3	0	1	0	73.33
Dollar Academy	11	8	2	0	1	6	72.72
Solihull School	11	8	3	0	0	3	72.72
Rossall School	7	5	1	0	1	3	71.42
Clifton College	17	12	3	1	1	2	70.58
Haileybury	17	12	3	0	2	0	70.58
Dean Close School	10	7	2	0	1	1	70.00
King's College, Taunton	20	14	5	1	0	1	70.00

Stonyhurst College won three of their four matches.

SCHOOLS A–Z

In the results line, A = abandoned without a ball bowled. An asterisk indicates captain. The qualification for the averages (which now include Twenty20 games, but not overseas tour games) is 150 runs or ten wickets. Counties have been included for all schools. Since cricket does not follow the current complex system of administrative division, *Wisden* adheres to the county boundaries in existence before the dissolution of Middlesex in 1965. Schools affected by those and subsequent boundary changes – such as Eton College, which was removed from Buckinghamshire and handed to Berkshire – are listed under their former county.

Abingdon School *Berkshire*   P19 W10 L9
Master i/c J. M. Golding   **Coach** Dr C. J. Burnand
The first team played some excellent cricket, with Freddie Smith and Harvey Jupp passing 500 runs – giving the side a batting depth lacking in recent years. With runs on the board, the bowling was dominated by the wrist-spin of Jupp and Hector Chambers; both enjoyed superb all-round summers. The highlight was a four-wicket victory against a strong MCC side.
Batting *H. A. Jupp 553 at 50.27; F. E. H. Smith 570 at 40.71; H. J. R. Chambers 487 at 30.43; J. A. T. Lawson 204 at 15.69; J. H. Coombs 234 at 15.60; L. M. Hilditch 154 at 14.00.
Bowling H. A. Jupp 25 at 14.52; H. J. R. Chambers 32 at 16.65; E. G. Hyman 12 at 32.58.

Aldenham School *Hertfordshire*   P14 W4 L10 A3
Master i/c L. J. Kirsten   **Coach** D. J. Goodchild
Despite plenty of rain, the XI showed genuine promise. Dan Travers, Viren Patel, Sam Harvey and Charlee Eve-Raw were the leading batsmen; Harvey, Prithvi Nakrani and Joel Clarke were the backbone of the attack. Patel is an exciting prospect.
Batting T. Francis 165 at 55.00; V. Patel 190 at 38.00; *D. Travers 216 at 30.85; S. A. Harvey 268 at 22.33; C. J. G. Eve-Raw 194 at 19.40.
Bowling T. Francis 12 at 12.50; S. A. Harvey 20 at 15.10; P. Nakrani 14 at 16.50; K. Thakrar 10 at 18.20; J. T. Clarke 18 at 20.16.

Alleyn's School *Surrey*   P10 W4 L4 D2 A2
Master i/c R. N. Ody   **Coach** P. E. Edwards
It was another enjoyable season for the first team, superbly captained by Zach Wood, who has made a significant contribution to Alleyn's cricket. Younger talents suggest it should be a successful 2020.
Batting N. F. A. Baker 164 at 41.00; *Z. B. Wood 248 at 31.00.
Bowling E. P. Marshall 10 at 8.50; L. M. Stylianou 12 at 17.00.

Ampleforth College *Yorkshire*   P9 W4 L4 D1 A5
Master i/c C. M. Booth
Thomas Wade and Kit MacLellan were the outstanding cricketers of a disappointingly damp summer. Highlights included victories against MCC, Emeriti CC and the Yorkshire Gentlemen, and a longer fixture list for the girls' side.
Batting T. W. Wade 243 at 34.71; F. G. H. Brooksbank 178 at 29.66; C. B. Kerr-Dineen 172 at 28.66; K. D. MacLellan 185 at 23.12.
Bowling K. D. MacLellan 21 at 13.04; E. J. Gibson 10 at 20.70.

Alex Rennie of Bedford School took 43 wickets with his left-arm spin.

Bancroft's School *Essex* P12 W6 L4 D2

Master i/c C. G. Greenidge

The school had a reasonable season, though the prioritising of exams caused the cancellation of four matches. Much depended on captain Deven Solanki; he was well supported by wicketkeeper-batsman Nibras Zamir.

Batting A. K. Agedah 337 at 48.14; N. A. Zamir 314 at 34.88; D. V. Solanki 188 at 31.33; K. Mangaleswaran 227 at 20.63.

Bowling *D. V. Solanki 17 at 19.29; B. J. Bagley 10 at 26.60.

Bede's School *Sussex* P12 W8 L3 D1

Master i/c A. P. Wells **Coaches** N. J. Lenham and R. J. Kirtley

A great year saw Bede's girls becoming Under-15 national T20 outdoor and indoor champions. The boys' first team won the county cup for the third year running, making it nine years out of 12. The boys' Under-14s won the county cup, while the Under-17s were finalists in the national cup.

Batting S. H. Lenham 268 at 53.60; R. A. Worrell 418 at 52.25; *A. G. H. Orr 437 at 43.70; J. R. McCammon 187 at 37.40; B. L. Matthew 180 at 22.50; T. Gordon 216 at 21.60.

Bowling B. L. Matthew 11 at 8.18; J. P. Sarro 22 at 13.77; H. Crocombe 21 at 14.47; S. H. Lenham 13 at 22.53; F. S. Sheppard 11 at 27.36.

Bedford School *Bedfordshire* P17 W11 L3 D3 A1

Master i/c I. G. S. Steer **Coach** T. Brett

Under the captaincy of classy batsman-keeper Harry Gouldstone, Bedford had an excellent season. Michael Wells recorded eight scores of 50 or more, while Tom O'Toole shone with bat and ball later in the term. Rahul Sheemar had another good all-round year, though it was slow left-armer Alex Rennie who led the bowling: he claimed 43 wickets, more than anyone in these pages, taking his first-team total to 109, a school record.

Batting T. O'Toole 417 at 59.57; M. R. Wells 675 at 48.21; *H. Gouldstone 719 at 47.93; M. R. Catt 316 at 35.11; R. Sheemar 234 at 33.42; T. G. L. Blythman 262 at 21.83; R. G. Bascetta-Pollitt 212 at 17.66.

Bowling A. I. Rennie 43 at 15.23; C. Melly 11 at 18.54; T. O'Toole 21 at 22.14; H. J. Warren 13 at 24.92; R. Sheemar 13 at 27.92; P. W. Barrington 10 at 40.40.

Bedford Modern School *Bedfordshire*
P12 W2 L10 A4

Master i/c J. Mousley **Coach** P. J. Woodroffe

A disappointing summer was not improved by poor weather. There were good all-round contributions from Ryan Lammin and Robert Bassin; Tom Saunders was an excellent captain. The introduction of some talented younger players gave cause for optimism.

Batting R. J. Lammin 168 at 28.00; R. G. S. Bassin 163 at 23.28.

Bowling R. G. S. Bassin 11 at 12.09; R. J. Lammin 10 at 19.90.

Berkhamsted School *Hertfordshire*
P18 W14 L3 D1 A1

Master i/c G. R. A. Campbell **Coach** N. Kirwan

Berkhamsted won 14 of their 18 matches. The major contributors to a superb year were Will Halliday, whose debut season brought 35 wickets, and captain Scott Rolfe, who struck two centuries.

Batting *S. J. T. Rolfe 616 at 47.38; T. D. Lazeris 165 at 27.50; B. A. M. Harris 286 at 23.83; D. J. H. Young 349 at 23.26; N. Cunnold 328 at 20.50; L. A. K. Golding 152 at 15.20.

Bowling L. O. R. Snookes 20 at 8.70; N. Cunnold 18 at 10.55; W. R. Halliday 35 at 10.71; J. Abbott 26 at 18.46; B. A. M. Harris 17 at 20.64; J. J. P. Baron 19 at 22.31.

Birkenhead School *Cheshire*
P15 W10 L4 D1

Master i/c P. N. Lindberg **Coach** N. R. Walker

A strong squad, made up of players from Years 10–13, fared superbly. Astute captaincy by Toby Brown and a talented bowling attack led by Jack Corran compensated for inconsistent batting.

Batting S. J. Botes 473 at 36.38; *T. A. Brown 359 at 29.91; A. A. L. Rutherford 291 at 29.10; J. D. Breheny 315 at 24.23; H. P. T. Wild 208 at 23.11.

Bowling J. W. J. Corran 25 at 8.36; S. J. Botes 15 at 11.46; R. A. Shenoy 10 at 12.80; T. A. Brown 13 at 13.46; J. D. Breheny 10 at 17.30; H. P. T. Wild 12 at 22.25.

Bishop's Stortford College *Hertfordshire*
P13 W9 L2 D2

Master i/c M. Drury **Coach** N. D. Hughes

The team enjoyed an outstanding season, their success based on the runs of Adam Bassingthwaighte and Joseph Hawkins, who shared the captaincy.

Batting *A. Bassingthwaighte 742 at 74.20; *J. S. Hawkins 482 at 60.25; T. H. Snelling 393 at 35.72.

Bowling T. A. Williams 12 at 22.41; J. M. Radley 21 at 22.80; J. D. Woollerson 15 at 23.20; J. H. J. Pilcher 15 at 23.86.

Bloxham School *Oxfordshire*
P13 W6 L6 D1

Master i/c G. N. Webber

A youthful first XI had an excellent season, with strong showings against Stowe, MCC, Warwick and Abingdon. The school regularly fielded 11 teams, which is encouraging.

Batting *T. S. Parker 500 at 45.45; B. Sinton 204 at 20.40; H. Hopkins 173 at 14.41.

Bowling J. Marshall 10 at 19.60; B. S. Parker 14 at 23.21.

Blundell's School *Devon*
P12 W4 L7 D1 A3

Master i/c L. J. Lewis

A young team enjoyed mixed fortunes. There were fine wins against Queen's Taunton, King's Bruton, Mount Kelly and Downside in the first half of term, but availability issues meant it was difficult to field the strongest team, and results tailed off.

Batting J. J. du'Gay 324 at 54.00; T. C. A. Reynolds 322 at 35.77; J. W. Burnand 230 at 23.00; I. A. Khan 176 at 22.00; W. J. Bucknell 158 at 17.55.

Bowling J. R. H. Hancock 17 at 14.29; W. Kennaugh 15 at 16.33; W. J. Bucknell 21 at 17.04.

Bradfield College *Berkshire*
P18 W5 L10 D3 A3

Master i/c M. S. Hill **Coach** J. R. Wood

The summer was much better than the results might suggest. A young team grew in confidence, and by the end of term were playing competitive cricket. Huge credit must go to the leadership of Tom Ettridge.

Batting D. R. A. McMurray 268 at 44.66; *T. A. W. Ettridge 420 at 26.25; Z. B. Lion-Cachet 334 at 25.69; J. R. J. Nichols 375 at 25.00; S. S. E. Gumbs 346 at 24.71; S. A. J. Kendall 247 at 24.70; H. E. King 367 at 24.46; L. G. J. Pincus 166 at 23.71; K. K. Khanna 235 at 19.58.

Bowling K. R. Naha 14 at 15.07; H. E. King 12 at 23.66; F. M. Simpson 10 at 24.60; J. R. J. Nichols 11 at 31.63; T. A. W. Ettridge 10 at 33.40; K. K. Khanna 20 at 33.80.

Brentwood School *Essex* P15 W7 L7 D1

Master i/c O. C. Prior **Coach** J. C. Mickleburgh

Brentwood won the Under-19 Essex Cup, with captain Robin Das scoring an excellent 88 on finals day; the team were genuinely strong in Twenty20 cricket. Jack Levy may become a top all-rounder.

Batting *R. Das 566 at 47.16; J. S. Levy 264 at 33.00; C. B. Balsom 204 at 20.40; H. J. Deacon 253 at 19.46.

Bowling S. James 16 at 16.50; J. S. Levy 12 at 18.25; T. G. Ridgwell 15 at 19.13; H. N. Bajwa 19 at 21.63.

Brighton College *Sussex* P9 W5 L3 D1 A1

Master i/c M. P. Smethurst **Coach** M. W. Machan

Brighton College reached the County Cup final, played at Hove. And against Portsmouth Grammar School, Jono Conolly hit 138 and claimed five for 24. This was also a breakout season for youngster Ravi Jadav, who took 13 wickets.

Batting *J. M. Conolly 312 at 44.57; H. M. E. Moorat 328 at 41.00; A. J. Bushell 211 at 35.16; F. R. Davis 155 at 31.00; T. J. Green 160 at 20.00.

Bowling J. M. Conolly 14 at 17.14; W. J. Pearce 11 at 19.00; A. J. Bushell 13 at 22.00; R. J. Jadav 13 at 28.46.

Bristol Grammar School *Gloucestershire* P12 W4 L8 A5

Master i/c T. M. Lacey

Thomas Quinlan broke the school record when he hit 196 not out against Monmouth, while Adam Hares took six for 21 against King Edward's, Bath – the best figures this century. Matthew Brewer finished his first-team career with 1,790 runs.

Batting M. J. M. Brewer 237 at 59.25; T. H. J. Quinlan 480 at 43.63; *H. S. Canagarajah 186 at 31.00; A. A. Hares 187 at 23.37.

Bowling A. A. Hares 16 at 12.37.

Bromsgrove School *Worcestershire* P10 W6 L3 D1 A5

Master i/c D. J. Fallows

There were notable wins against Shrewsbury and Stowe; Jasper Davidson was the mainstay of the batting, and Henry Marshall of the attack. The school reached the national semi-final in September and once again reached the regional T20 finals day at New Road. Davidson represented Scotland Under-19s, and helped them qualify for their World Cup.

Batting J. J. Davidson 274 at 39.14; A. J. Hinkley 228 at 25.33; D. E. Meredith 154 at 22.00.

Bowling F. Fallows 13 at 9.23; H. J. Marshall 17 at 15.05; D. E. Meredith 13 at 16.69; *G. O. Marshall 10 at 22.00.

Bryanston School *Dorset* P9 W4 L5

Master i/c S. D. Morris **Coaches** P. J. Norton and J. E. Morris

Bryanston enjoyed an instructive season that contained several highly competitive fixtures: five of nine matches were decided in the last three balls.

Batting T. Saunders 296 at 37.00; *C. W. Robertson 160 at 17.77.

Bowling The leading bowler was T. Saunders, who took eight wickets at 21.62.

Canford School *Dorset* P12 W7 L5

Master i/c M. Keech **Coaches** J. H. Shackleton and S. L. Ives

A disappointing season ended positively when Tom Prest and Freddie Peters hit centuries. Despite superb captaincy from Matthew Daubeney, the team failed to make the most of their natural talent.

Batting T. D. Prest 320 at 64.00; F. J. Peters 225 at 45.00; *M. J. Daubeney 233 at 38.83.

Bowling T. D. O. Sykes 11 at 20.54.

Caterham School *Surrey* P15 W4 L11 A3

Master i/c J. N. Batty

Caterham had a mixed summer, but did record victories against Reigate Grammar School, John Fisher, The Judd and Eltham College. Simon Dickson was a good leader, and had useful support from Joseph Haynes, Ankush Patel and Tom Williamson.

Batting J. J. Haynes 213 at 21.30; A. Patel 287 at 20.50; T. B. Williamson 197 at 19.70; *S. E. Dickson 204 at 13.60.

Bowling A. Patel 12 at 20.41; M. Santana 10 at 23.80; J. J. Haynes 13 at 24.53; T. B. Williamson 11 at 26.27.

Charterhouse *Surrey*   P16 W11 L4 D1 A2
Master i/c M. P. Bicknell
Charterhouse had another excellent year. Captain Ross Richardson scored 553 runs, and was well supported by Ayush Patel, who made 400. Ollie Sheen, Jonny Miles and Freddie Clinton were the backbone of the bowling.
Batting *R. A. J. Richardson 553 at 42.53; A. A. Patel 400 at 33.33; F. Clinton 157 at 26.16; A. R. R. Wilman 350 at 23.33; T. C. P. Rawlings 319 at 21.26; D. W. F. Campbell 160 at 17.77; W. G. Briggs 208 at 17.33.
Bowling F. Clinton 24 at 13.95; J. B. Miles 21 at 16.80; O. B. G. Sheen 21 at 18.85; J. A. Burns 14 at 24.14; A. A. Patel 11 at 24.18; A. R. R. Wilman 11 at 30.72.

Cheadle Hulme School *Cheshire*   P15 W2 L12 D1 A2
Master i/c G. Clinton   **Coach** K. R. Brown
Though results were modest, the team developed strongly over the term. Oliver Latter proved an excellent captain, and Archie Tittle contributed several good all-round performances.
Batting *O. Latter 326 at 29.63; B. J. Staniforth 207 at 20.70; A. J. Tittle 174 at 19.33; L. J. Newton 231 at 19.25; M. Fisher 173 at 15.72.
Bowling A. J. Tittle 13 at 21.92; O. Latter 10 at 25.80.

Cheltenham College *Gloucestershire*   P17 W5 L9 D3 A1
Master i/c M. K. Coley   **Coach** M. P. Briers
A season of highs and lows included good wins over Radley, Abingdon, MCC and Winchester, as well as a one-run defeat by Marlborough. James Boyle, in Year 12, shone all summer, scoring 637 runs and taking 12 wickets.
Batting J. A. S. Boyle 637 at 39.81; J. R. J. Gunn 484 at 37.23; O. C. D. Butcher 406 at 31.23; T. A. McCormick 236 at 29.50; J. A. Clement 218 at 27.25; S. Blake 345 at 26.53; A. J. Pearce 201 at 22.33.
Bowling F. S. Milton 12 at 26.50; F. G. E. Watson-Smyth 19 at 26.84; J. R. J. Gunn 13 at 27.53; J. A. S. Boyle 12 at 28.66; *A. J. Sharam 13 at 30.38.

Chigwell School *Essex*   P11 W4 L6 D1 A3
Master i/c F. A. Griffith   **Coach** V. Chopra
A loyal, enthusiastic and talented team came on in leaps and bounds. Haaris Usman topped the batting, and finished just behind Shayan Pithiyan in the bowling. Ben Kearin, Ben Chillingworth and Gaurav Nair also hit valuable runs.
Batting H. Usman 503 at 50.30; B. H. P. Kearin 364 at 36.40; *B. D. Chillingworth 174 at 17.40; G. Nair 152 at 16.88.
Bowling S. Pithiyan 10 at 17.50; H. Usman 11 at 19.45.

Chislehurst & Sidcup Grammar School *Kent*   P7 W2 L5 A4
Master i/c R. A. Wallbridge   **Coach** B. Stock
A young and enthusiastic squad learned a great deal. Captain Robert Woods spearheaded the early-season attack, while Oliver Smith was the main all-rounder. Most players should return richer for the experience.
Batting The leading batsman was S. R. G. Naylor, who hit 140 runs at 70.00.
Bowling O. V. C. Smith 11 at 12.90.

Christ's Hospital *Sussex*   P17 W10 L5 D2 A3
Master i/c D. H. Messenger   **Coach** T. E. Jesty
Captain Ben Kinnear led a young XI, who surpassed expectation by equalling the post-1945 record of ten wins. Sussex Academy player Gus Freeman hit most runs and took most wickets. Several victories were set up by the new-ball pair of Nathan Cooper and Arthur Pinkney, who shared 49 wickets. Solly Woodall also showed maturity with the bat.
Batting G. A. M. Freeman 593 at 42.35; S. J. Woodall 357 at 27.46; *B. E. Kinnear 315 at 26.25; A. P. Heath 283 at 25.72; G. L. Cooper 273 at 24.81; N. S. Cooper 153 at 19.12.
Bowling A. R. Pinkney 24 at 14.75; N. S. Cooper 25 at 16.00; G. A. M. Freeman 29 at 16.58; F. J. R. Bond 10 at 18.40; I. B. T. Lordon 18 at 18.72.

Churcher's College *Hampshire*   P10 W4 L6
Master i/c R. Maier
Results were less impressive than of late, but the team played some good cricket. With a young squad full of potential, there is optimism for the future.
Batting M. Crane 268 at 33.50; H. I. McMillan 153 at 21.85.
Bowling M. Crane 14 at 15.00; H. I. McMillan 12 at 16.00.

Clayesmore School *Dorset*   P17 W7 L8 D2 A2
Master i/c D. O. Conway
Harry Morgan led a youthful, ever-improving team, including four Year 10 boys. A successful cricket week culminated in an exciting draw against MCC.
Batting J. J. Gordon 425 at 38.63; J. Berry 227 at 18.91; *H. B. Morgan 231 at 15.40; T. Berry 159 at 14.45.
Bowling A. Raj Iyer 22 at 13.45; T. Berry 13 at 15.00; J. Cazalet 15 at 16.33; J. J. Gordon 17 at 19.11; W. Betts 10 at 28.50.

Clifton College *Gloucestershire*   P17 W12 L3 T1 D1 A2
Master i/c J. C. Bobby   **Coach** J. R. A. Williams
Clifton were better with the ball than the bat. Opener Ollie Meadows scored three centuries, and captain Dom Goodman bowled superbly, finishing with 38 wickets. The game of the season was a tie with King's College, Taunton. Notable wins came against Cheltenham, Sherborne and MCC.
Batting O. J. Meadows 617 at 41.13; *D. C. Goodman 532 at 33.25; H. R. Ascherl 219 at 24.33; J. H. Millard 247 at 22.45; F. A. Yates 247 at 20.58; J. Lloyd 161 at 17.88.
Bowling D. C. Goodman 38 at 10.94; R. Kilmister 27 at 16.33; T. C. Hurle 15 at 17.86; H. R. Ascherl 24 at 19.75; O. J. Meadows 18 at 22.77.

Colston's School *Gloucestershire*   P12 W3 L7 D2 A2
Master i/c L. M. Evans   **Coach** P. B. Muchall
Sam Manning led a youthful team stronger at bowling than batting. Runs were difficult to come by, until a superb victory at Monkton Combe.
Batting J. W. Waite 165 at 55.00; J. M. Peterson 281 at 31.22; H. J. Wheeler 164 at 20.50; Z. Hamid 151 at 16.77.
Bowling J. W. Waite 20 at 14.95; *S. J. Manning 16 at 26.56; M. J. Hunkin 10 at 28.70; M. I. Waite 12 at 30.08.

Cranleigh School *Surrey*   P15 W6 L7 D2
Master i/c A. P. Forsdike   **Coach** S. D. Welch
An inexperienced side had a mixed year, but with more than half the players returning, there are the makings of a strong team. Chris Pyle, Jonte Marshall and Max Bell all celebrated three years in the XI.
Batting G. S. Ealham 517 at 43.08; T. E. Lawes 340 at 24.28; J. A. Green 322 at 23.00; C. T. Pyle 299 at 23.00; J. H. Marshall 201 at 20.10; *W. R. J. Dahl 253 at 19.46; M. A. Bell 250 at 19.23; S. S. D. Shanmugavel 151 at 16.77.
Bowling H. B. W. Stiles 26 at 15.76; J. H. Marshall 14 at 18.64; M. A. Bell 19 at 19.21; Y. Majid 17 at 24.35; T. E. Lawes 15 at 25.26; T. M. Ealham 14 at 38.64.

Dauntsey's School *Wiltshire*   P20 W15 L5 A1
Master i/c A. J. Palmer   **Coach** J. R. Ayling
An excellent season, the last for Andy Palmer after 21 years at Dauntsey's, was rounded off by retaining the Monkhouse Intersport League and reaching the quarter-finals of the National T20 Cup. Wicketkeeper Alex Ayers passed 1,100 runs (including our tour), and made 20 stumpings. Leg-spinner Jack Grant and off-spinner Jack Butler were a constant threat, while seamers Tom Swanton and George Lishman were reliable. Grant and captain Archie Ayling hit maiden centuries.
Batting A. L. Ayers 884 at 55.25; T. J. Swanton 340 at 42.50; J. B. Grant 558 at 39.85; *A. J. Ayling 371 at 30.91.
Bowling J. L. Butler 34 at 16.61; J. B. Grant 31 at 17.64; G. M. E. Lishman 27 at 18.29; T. J. Swanton 26 at 19.69; A. J. Ayling 10 at 20.90.

Dean Close School *Gloucestershire*
P10 W7 L2 D1 A1

Master i/c A. G. A. Milne
Coach M. J. Powell

This was Dean Close's best season for some years; the team were well led by all-rounders Oliver Horne and James Boden. The emergence of young talent such as Nicholas Schubach, Jack Logan and Kameel Shabedeen bodes well.

Batting N. J. Schubach 351 at 35.10; J. W. Hunt 266 at 33.25; *O. P. Horne 201 at 22.33.

Bowling J. D. Boden 13 at 18.76; J. M. Schubach 11 at 19.18.

Denstone College *Staffordshire*
P13 W7 L3 T1 D2 A4

Master i/c S. M. Guy
Coach G. R. Dipple

The weather was a cause of frustration, but in better conditions in the last fortnight the school enjoyed a fine two-day victory against Langley Park and a tie against Derbyshire Academy. During the final week, an astonishing 2,371 runs were scored.

Batting J. R. Redman 468 at 52.00; D. M. Afford 519 at 51.90; *M. A. Webber 469 at 36.07; A. W. O'Hara 426 at 32.76; A. I. Cooper 252 at 28.00.

Bowling J. R. Redman 13 at 18.53; R. B. Hughes 11 at 20.63; A. I. Cooper 11 at 20.81; A. D. Billington 20 at 22.25; E. A. Gaffney 13 at 29.46; R. C. Owens 12 at 40.16.

Dr Challoner's Grammar School *Buckinghamshire*
P9 W4 L5 A4

Master i/c N. J. S. Buchanan

Dr Challoner's performed well in patches, registering wins against a number of local rivals. A core of Year 13 players performed strongly, and will be tough to replace. Captain Ollie Anderson was superb with the ball throughout.

Batting M. J. Weatherall 213 at 30.42; S. Dey 220 at 27.50.

Bowling *O. W. Anderson 16 at 9.25; R. J. Walsh 14 at 13.21.

Dollar Academy *Clackmannanshire*
P11 W8 L2 D1 A6

Master i/c P. A. Ross
Coach E. T. N. Pollock

After a slow start, Dollar Academy played some outstanding cricket, and ended the season Scottish National T20 Champions for the second year in a row. All-rounder Toby Douglas led from the front, while Jamie Cairns was selected for Scotland Under-19s.

Batting J. S. Cairns 177 at 88.50; *J. R. Jordan 266 at 38.00; T. B. Douglas 303 at 33.66; E. C. Smith 184 at 30.66.

Bowling T. B. Douglas 21 at 8.00; J. S. Cairns 10 at 8.30; R. S. Disborough 10 at 8.80.

Dover College *Kent*
P5 W1 L3 D1

Master i/c G. R. Hill

Exams and poor weather made it a short season. There is much potential, though, and prospects are better for 2020, when Ryan Sewell returns as captain.

Batting The leading batsman was *R. P. Sewell, who hit 106 runs at 53.00.

Bowling The leading bowler was H. C. Mashiter-Yates, who took nine wickets at 19.11.

Downside School *Somerset*
P6 W1 L5 A3

Master i/c A. G. Longshaw

Downside endured a tough season, their one win coming against Downside Wanderers. Bede Kemp scored 100 against Blundell's, and Charlie Hobbs 78 against Downside Wanderers.

Batting The leading batsman was B. Kemp, who hit 138 runs at 34.50.

Bowling The leading bowler was S. Norris, who took six wickets at 33.33.

Dulwich College *Surrey*
P18 W10 L4 T1 D3

Master i/c P. C. Greenaway
Coaches C. W. J. Athey and S. C. J. Middleton

On a challenging circuit, the first team had a season full of progress, and recorded ten wins. Three batsmen made 400 runs or more, while three bowlers collected at least 20 wickets. The summer ended on a high with two wins from three at the Framlingham festival. Bill Athey retired as the pro after 18 wonderful years.

Batting J. E. Crowfoot 576 at 36.00; A. D. Kenningham 506 at 31.62; F. H. Cox 405 at 25.31; *L. B. Wilson 387 at 21.50; H. D. B. Loynes 179 at 17.90; O. J. Creasey 170 at 17.00; L. J. Cunningham 231 at 14.43.

Bowling J. E. Crowfoot 24 at 18.04; L. G. McGuiness-Smith 21 at 24.76; B. H. Kemp 20 at 29.60; H. D. B. Loynes 17 at 30.94.

Durham School *County Durham*   P14 W7 L6 D1 A2

Master i/c M. B. Fishwick

The team improved during an enjoyable season, and achieved some excellent results. The Mike Hirsch Award for outstanding cricketer went to Jonny Bushnell; the Maurice Bell Award for most improved player to Niall Butler.

Batting *J. Bushnell 288 at 41.14; S. M. E. North 311 at 38.87; R. C. Fyfe 198 at 28.28; N. J. Butler 237 at 21.54.

Bowling S. M. E. North 11 at 30.27; L. Giacomelli 10 at 38.70.

Eastbourne College *Sussex*   P20 W16 L4 A1

Master i/c R. S. Ferley   Coach J. C. Tredwell

Tawanda Muyeye's school-record 1,112 runs included a magnificent double-hundred against Brighton College, when Eastbourne passed 400 for the first time in a 50-over game. In his debut season, Will Lucas took 34 wickets; Joe Pocklington signed off after three years in the first team with 31.

Batting T. S. Muyeye 1,112 at 69.50; F. J. Logan 485 at 44.09; O. H. Streets 332 at 41.50; J. Pocklington 372 at 33.81; D. K. Ibrahim 425 at 32.69; O. J. Carter 366 at 30.50; B. E. Hounsell 173 at 28.83; W. Lucas 301 at 25.08; *H. A. Tagg 250 at 16.66.

Bowling W. Lucas 34 at 14.35; J. Pocklington 31 at 14.54; T. S. Muyeye 23 at 16.73; B. E. Hounsell 15 at 25.46; J. Pratt 11 at 28.63.

Edinburgh Academy *Midlothian*   P13 W5 L7 T1 A5

Master i/c R. W. Sales

The first XI had an up-and-down season with several matches – especially Saturday fixtures – lost to rain. They also lost tight games they might have won. The team were well led by Robert Simpson, with Campbell Swanson hitting most runs.

Batting C. N. Turner 180 at 45.00; C. F. Swanson 322 at 29.27; H. Ali 164 at 20.50.

Bowling *D. R. C. Simpson 13 at 13.30; A. T. B. Stirling 14 at 20.07; J. Binsted 12 at 24.41; T. J. Peel 14 at 29.75; H. Ali 12 at 29.75.

Elizabeth College, Guernsey *Channel Islands*   P16 W9 L7

Master i/c T. P. Eisenhuth   Coach M. R. Stokes

The team worked tirelessly in training sessions before and after school, and made great progress. It was most satisfying to win games against quality opposition. Highlights included a first victory in five years against MCC, and posting 199 in a T20 against a strong Melbourne Grammar School side.

Batting N. M. Le Tissier 580 at 52.72; M. P. Philp 311 at 44.42; C. G. Clapham 300 at 30.00.

Bowling K. P. Le Gallez 14 at 23.35.

Ellesmere College *Shropshire*   P9 W6 L3

Master i/c G. Owen   Coach R. Jones

Results would have had an even better look had the first XI won their last two games, against adult sides. It was a positive season, though a shame the school were never able to field their best team.

Batting C. A. Davies 318 at 79.50; J. W. Carter 162 at 23.14.

Bowling H. Newton 18 at 10.38.

Eltham College *Kent*   P11 W1 L10 A2

Master i/c J. L. D. Baldwin   Coach Yasir Arafat

After a superb 2018 and a successful winter tour, the summer of 2019 was a struggle. But a young side showed promise in several close matches, Ken Dixson leading admirably in difficult circumstances: 29 players were used in 11 games. Dixson hit most runs, while Connor Fuller was the outstanding bowler.

Batting A. Garimella 159 at 26.50; *K. M. Dixson 210 at 21.00; B. M. N. Mirchandani 159 at 19.87.

Bowling The leading bowler was C. D. J. Fuller, who took eight at 29.75.

Emanuel School *Surrey*   P18 W7 L9 D2 A2

Master i/c T. Gwynne   Coach M. G. Stear

A team largely comprising Year 13s won early-season Saturday games against Tiffin and Alleyn's, but reliable runs proved elusive. Sinan Mahmud was an outstanding captain, and made 600, while Will Ellis hit 485; Billy Hughes and Sacha Banks were the pick of the bowlers. The strongest performances came in draws against Reed's and MCC.

Joe Burslem of Felsted hit 1,215 runs; Cranleigh's George Ealham played for MCC Schools.

Batting W. A. Ellis 485 at 53.88; *S. K. Mahmud 600 at 37.50; I. P. Barker 276 at 18.40; E. C. R. Pretzlik 251 at 17.92; B. I. Thesiger 155 at 14.09; N. C. Hughes 212 at 12.47.
Bowling G. J. C. Wilson 11 at 17.63; J. H. Ash Vie 14 at 22.57; A. G. E. Banks 18 at 25.38; B. W. Hughes 19 at 28.05; I. P. Barker 15 at 33.40.

Epsom College *Surrey*   P15 W4 L10 D1
Master i/c D. C. Shirazi   **Coach** S. A. Whatling
This was a tough season for a very young team, but eight regulars return for 2020. Ben Garrett and Makeen Alikhan headed the batting averages, Tom Allen and Anish Patel the bowling.
Batting B. G. G. Garrett 251 at 31.37; M. R. Alikhan 326 at 23.28; *T. Allen 218 at 21.80; W. M. D. Hodgson 281 at 20.07; T. Lynagh 210 at 19.09; A. Koep 175 at 15.90; J. A. Webster 252 at 15.75.
Bowling T. Allen 15 at 22.60; A. Patel 16 at 24.50; K. Jain 13 at 27.38; O. H. King 10 at 32.30; W. M. D. Hodgson 12 at 36.91.

Eton College *Buckinghamshire*   P17 W7 L7 T1 D2 A2
Master i/c R. R. Montgomerie   **Coach** T. W. Roberts
Eton lost wickets in clusters too often. A strong seam and effective off-spin attack put pressure on opponents, and the team defended some low totals, as well as losing other exciting finishes. Freddy Linzee Gordon kept working on his off-spin and took 33 wickets, while Billy Lowther, captain and wicketkeeper, was the outstanding batsman.
Batting *W. G. D. Lowther-Pinkerton 564 at 40.28; M. D. D. Ritchie 342 at 22.80; L. D. Rhys Williams 291 at 22.38; M. O. Anscomb 246 at 22.36; B. C. W. Porter 336 at 21.00; J. W. Gammell 183 at 16.63.
Bowling F. J. Linzee Gordon 33 at 17.90; B. C. W. Porter 19 at 19.68; A. C. Beagles 19 at 22.26; J. W. Gammell 12 at 28.25; X. J. Watt 12 at 28.50.

Felsted School *Essex*   P19 W15 L4
Master i/c J. E. R. Gallian   **Coaches** C. S. Knightley, A. Mohindru and N. J. Lockhart
The first XI had an excellent season, showing a great team ethos under the captaincy of Joe Burslem, whose 1,215 runs broke the school record. It was a pleasure to watch the side develop and grow in confidence during the summer.

Batting *J. H. Burslem 1,215 at 75.93; H. G. R. Gallian 538 at 41.38; D. T. Karr 414 at 37.63; A. Akbar 433 at 36.08; C. S. Horton 260 at 32.50; D. M. Townsend 161 at 23.00; J. D. Bird 194 at 16.16.
Bowling S. T. Young 29 at 18.79; J. P. W. O'Connor 22 at 20.90; K. A. Morley-Jacob 20 at 21.50; E. J. Snooks 20 at 24.85; J. P. A. V. Hoile 15 at 29.53; J. K. Woodmore 11 at 32.54; C. S. Horton 11 at 33.54.

Fettes College *Midlothian*   P12 W5 L6 D1 A4
Master i/c A. B. Russell

Rain marred the programme, but an experienced and talented group, led by outstanding batsman Robert Edwards, performed well; there was strong support from fast bowler Ben MacLeod. Exam demands meant many younger players made debuts.
Batting R. A. Edwards 202 at 50.50; D. C. Hood 331 at 41.37; O. J. Norton 227 at 25.22.
Bowling B. M. MacLeod 11 at 12.18; N. H. D. Stanic 13 at 15.84; O. J. Norton 12 at 16.25.

Forest School *Essex*   P21 W13 L7 D1
Master i/c J. F. Perham   Coach J. S. Foster

Cricket has become a major sport for Forest's girls: 140 have been able to learn, train and compete. The boys' teams continued to do well, with every age-group side reaching their County Cup final.
Batting T. Dixon 157 at 31.40; H. Sewell 286 at 26.00; Z. Aspery 177 at 25.28; F. Britt 289 at 24.08; J. Coughlan 315 at 21.00; *C. Allen 335 at 20.93; J. Hendericks 193 at 17.54; L. Dolden 184 at 15.33.
Bowling R. Kingham 32 at 9.53; J. Greatorex 11 at 12.90; J. Coughlan 13 at 14.46; F. Britt 14 at 14.85; J. O'Callaghan 16 at 17.00; K. Arawwawala 17 at 17.05.

Framlingham College *Suffolk*   P21 W14 L6 D1 A1
Master i/c C. D. Gange   Coach N. R. Gandy

After a great tour to the UAE, the team had a successful season, especially given their youth. There were notable performances against MCC, Cambridge University and Suffolk Under-17s. Harry Bureau, the captain, and Henry Bevan were the main contributors with bat and ball.
Batting *H. G. Bureau 560 at 32.94; H. T. J. Bevan 554 at 30.77; H. R. N. Williams 448 at 28.00; J. Lecompte 326 at 27.16; C. A. Kent 323 at 23.07; B. P. Chapman 329 at 21.93; J. Mermagen 157 at 15.70; B. C. Farrant 242 at 15.12; M. M. Dehlvi 170 at 13.07.
Bowling F. J. Heldreich 17 at 11.47; B. G. A. Smart 10 at 16.00; W. H. White 21 at 18.85; H. T. J. Bevan 21 at 20.00; H. R. N. Williams 19 at 20.42; H. G. Bureau 17 at 20.88; E. W. Fox 16 at 24.50; E. G. Darley 19 at 25.89.

George Watson's College *Midlothian*   P11 W7 L4 A6
Master i/c M. J. Leonard   Coach A. D. W. Patterson

Rain was an unwelcome companion. However, when the first team played, they showed their strength in depth, and enjoyed big wins over rival schools. Olly Snodgrass led from the front, with Oliver Robertson proving a capable all-rounder. The best result was a cup defeat of Merchiston Castle.
Batting O. T. J. Robertson 276 at 46.00; E. P. Rhodes 171 at 34.20; F. Kinloch 202 at 22.44.
Bowling O. T. J. Robertson 13 at 9.92; S. Ali 10 at 11.50; *O. J. Snodgrass 11 at 15.00; G. W. R. Carr 10 at 16.70; J. A. Reid 10 at 11.50.

The Glasgow Academy *Lanarkshire*   P5 W3 L2 A5
Master i/c P. J. W. Smith   Coach V. Hariharan

An encouraging season contained exciting wins against The High School of Glasgow and Kelvinside Academy, en route to the semi-finals of the Scottish Schools Cup. But with five matches abandoned, progress of our budding cricketers was curtailed.
Batting The leading batsman was *R. S. Heginbottom, who hit 139 runs at 46.33.
Bowling The leading bowler was J. M. D. Olney, who took six wickets at 9.00.

The High School of Glasgow *Lanarkshire*   P8 W2 L4 D2 A4
Master i/c S. C. Leggat   Coach K. J. A. Robertson

A difficult, damp season allowed only eight completed fixtures, five in the last week. Highlights included centuries for John Greene (against XL Club and Gordonstoun) and Jai Tyagi (Gordonstoun). Ibrahim Faisal (Year 9) is a prospect for the future.
Batting J. A. Greene 295 at 59.00; J. Tyagi 213 at 30.42.
Bowling I. Faisal 13 at 9.69; J. A. Greene 12 at 15.00; G. H. Shafar 10 at 18.60.

Gordonstoun School *Morayshire*   P8 W3 L4 D1
Master i/c R. Denyer

A young team, with eight new students all playing an active role, had a good season. It started well against tough opposition, and finished brilliantly with the visit of teams from the UK and abroad.

Batting *S. J. Lister 397 at 66.16; H. F. C. Thorpe 252 at 50.40.

Bowling O. R. A. Ayere 7 at 27.71; S. J. Lister 8 at 41.87; R. A. Spencer-Nairn 7 at 59.71.

Gresham's School *Norfolk*   P24 W18 L4 D2
Master i/c D. J. Atkinson   **Coach** C. Brown

It was an outstanding summer, and the team won three-quarters of their fixtures. The captaincy was shared between Hudson de Lucchi and Declan Oldreive; both topped 700 runs. Ben Wilcox (Year 10) scored 632, and was selected for the Bunbury Festival. Oldreive and Bennett Withers finished with more than 30 wickets each.

Batting B. A. Wilcox 632 at 48.61; *D. W. Oldreive 762 at 44.82; *H. A. de Lucchi 730 at 42.94; F. C. Wilcox 388 at 24.25; N. G. Laws 308 at 20.53; S. Ndlela 244 at 20.33.

Bowling D. W. Oldreive 36 at 13.77; B. P. Withers 31 at 15.74; H. J. Adams 12 at 15.75; F. C. Wilcox 11 at 16.18; S. Ndlela 26 at 18.03; C. O. Adams 25 at 19.56; L. D. Hart 12 at 22.50; H. A. de Lucchi 14 at 24.57.

Haberdashers' Aske's Boys' School *Hertfordshire*   P17 W5 L10 D2 A2
Master i/c S. D. Charlwood   **Coaches** D. H. Kerry and J. P. Hewitt

There were good wins against Bancroft's and Exeter CC, among others, but results were largely disappointing, with both injury and exam pressures to contend with. Youngsters Niyam Shah and Ashish Padki showed promise and, with junior sides winning three of the four Hertfordshire Schools competitions, the future looks rosier.

Batting *V. Jegatheesan 493 at 29.00; H. J. J. Cobb 380 at 25.33; N. Shah 206 at 22.88; E. A. Cleaver 223 at 22.30; S. Singh 226 at 20.54; J. E. J. Cobb 249 at 19.15; A. Pindoria 158 at 14.36; T. A. Choudhury 167 at 13.91.

Bowling C. Mullapudi 16 at 24.56; T. A. Choudhury 15 at 26.73; H. J. J. Cobb 13 at 29.84; A. Padki 10 at 40.30.

Haileybury *Hertfordshire*   P17 W12 L3 D2
Master i/c R. C. Kitzinger   **Coach** C. E. Igolen-Robinson

An outstanding season was built around strong batting: Michael Levitt hit four centuries and shared two unbroken double-century stands with Jack Timms. Tom Newby took 12 wickets in the match against Cheltenham, while Jake Ratcliffe's excellent captaincy hastened victories against MCC, Uppingham and Felsted.

Batting M. L. Levitt 963 at 68.78; J. C. Timms 728 at 66.18; T. S. C. Newby 189 at 47.25; K. O. Roomans 338 at 33.80; W. G. Meacock 330 at 25.38; *J. A. D. Ratcliffe 310 at 23.84; H. C. Willgoss 236 at 19.66.

Bowling T. S. C. Newby 41 at 16.39; M. L. Levitt 22 at 17.45; J. E. Bridge 29 at 18.65; H. C. Willgoss 16 at 24.43; H. P. C. Flint Cahan 21 at 26.09.

Hampton School *Middlesex*   P16 W11 L3 T1 D1
Master i/c A. M. Banerjee   **Coach** C. P. Harrison

Hampton enjoyed another busy season, which contained many outstanding performances. A young side, led by Joe Wheeler, showed real promise and gained valuable experience for 2020.

Batting D. L. Manuel 214 at 42.80; B. C. Cullen 352 at 35.20; M. Avant-Smith 310 at 34.44; *J. F. D. Wheeler 364 at 33.09; T. J. H. Berg 257 at 25.70; R. P. Desai 224 at 24.88; W. F. Greenall 262 at 21.83; T. J. A. Chandler 150 at 21.42; T. H. Wallace 152 at 16.88.

Bowling M. W. G. Knowles 19 at 7.89; B. C. Cullen 10 at 14.10; M. M. Cooper 15 at 17.00; J. F. D. Wheeler 19 at 20.73; T. J. Miller 10 at 21.20; A. D. Bhasin 10 at 36.40.

Harrow School *Middlesex*   P23 W19 L3 D1 A1
Master i/c M. J. G. Davis

Harrow had an outstanding year. Of their 23 fixtures, they drew one and won 19, including a superb victory over a strong Eton at Lord's. Musa Iqbal led the team brilliantly, and bowled with great control and skill. He was supported by Christian Boland and Jafer Chohan, while reliable batting came from Luke Harrington-Myers and Charlie Witter.

Batting C. Witter 501 at 41.75; R. S. Wijeratne 335 at 30.45; L. H. Harrington-Myers 392 at 30.15; T. N. Sheopuri 328 at 29.81; H. H. Dicketts 409 at 29.21; P. Patel 273 at 24.81.
Bowling J. E. Langston 15 at 14.73; J. A. Chohan 30 at 15.86; C. S. Boland 22 at 16.40; *M. Ali 22 at 16.45; M. Akhtar 17 at 18.11.

The Harvey Grammar School *Kent*
P7 W2 L4 D1 A1

Master i/c G. Meers
Coach P. M. Castle

A keen and committed team, mostly from Years 10–12, gained valuable experience, and showed real promise. Jamie McVittie's 84 against the XL Club was the batting highlight.
Batting J. McVittie 186 at 37.20.
Bowling The leading bowler was J. A. Brierly, who took eight wickets at 17.25.

Highgate School *Middlesex*
P6 W2 L3 D1 A1

Master i/c A. S. Iga

A side including many up-and-coming players had a modestly successful summer under the astute captaincy of Henry Everitt
Batting *O. G. H. Everitt 204 at 51.00; W. R. R. Bliss 174 at 43.50.
Bowling The leading bowler was O. G. H. Everitt, who took eight wickets at 14.37.

Hurstpierpoint College *Sussex*
P17 W8 L9

Master i/c N. J. K. Creed
Coaches J. E. Anyon and P. G. Hudson

Many of the 2018 team returned, and fared well. Bertie Foreman was leading wicket-taker, Mason Robinson the highest run-scorer. Jack Carson toured Cape Town with Sussex in March, and played Second XI cricket for them over the summer. Seven of the side return for 2020.
Batting *J. J. Carson 545 at 49.54; T. J. Shepperson 500 at 41.66; M. L. Robinson 563 at 37.53; F. C. Longley 218 at 27.25; B. J. Caidan 247 at 20.58.
Bowling A. M. Foreman 19 at 13.84; R. L. Liebers 14 at 21.14; F. C. Longley 10 at 24.70; J. J. Carson 11 at 28.36.

Hymers College *Yorkshire*
P12 W5 L5 D2 A1

Master i/c G. Tipping

Hymers College had a promising season, given the age and experience of the side. They won as many as they lost, and showed determination and character all term.
Batting S. J. Elstone 462 at 46.20; C. J. Rawlins 270 at 38.57; T. W. Douglas 181 at 30.16; B. L. Renwick 200 at 25.00.
Bowling G. Balaji 12 at 16.25; C. H. Phillips 11 at 17.09; A. Chawla 14 at 20.07.

John Hampden Grammar School *Buckinghamshire*
P17 W6 L10 D1 A3

Master i/c S. K. Parbery

Victory at the Bablake T20 tournament was followed by an inaugural fixture against MCC. Solid contributions from Harvey Hewson, Taran Sohi and Will Midwinter ensured competitive scores in most matches. All-rounder Daniel Broughton produced probing spells of fast bowling in his final season, including four for 98 against MCC.
Batting H. J. E. Hewson 322 at 40.25; W. C. S. Midwinter 341 at 28.42; T. S. Sohi 356 at 27.38; *K. P. Devereux 214 at 16.46; D. J. Broughton 169 at 15.36; F. G. Fayers 167 at 13.92.
Bowling J. P. Child 11 at 11.00; R. J. Woodhead 12 at 20.33; K. P. Devereux 13 at 22.00; D. J. Broughton 14 at 29.07; F. G. Fayers 11 at 29.09.

John Lyon School *Middlesex*
P19 W10 L6 D3 A4

Master i/c A. S. Ling
Coach S. H. Cloete

The school's most successful season for several years included victory in the Middlesex Cup. Dhanesh Jegatheesan batted impressively, and was again supported by Rahil Thapar, who took 26 wickets. The captain, Abhay Hirani, passed 1,000 first-team runs.
Batting D. Jegatheesan 463 at 46.30; *A. D. Hirani 435 at 39.54; A. Sundaram 255 at 23.18; R. S. Thapar 246 at 22.36; K. Jariwala 208 at 17.33.
Bowling A. Patel 19 at 13.63; R. S. Thapar 26 at 16.38; A. D. Hirani 18 at 21.22; A. Sutaria 11 at 22.00; D. Deu 10 at 25.20; C. A. O. Rashid 14 at 27.50.

The Judd School *Kent* P10 W2 L7 D1 A4

Master i/c R. M. Richardson

The team was intelligently led by Rory Easton, and most return for 2020. Bowlers Sam Wheatley and Wilf Rutter were well supported by batsman Sam Jones and all-rounder Sam Ward.

Batting *R. A. Easton 198 at 28.28.

Bowling R. A. Easton 12 at 14.50.

Kimbolton School *Huntingdonshire* P14 W5 L7 D2

Master i/c M. S. Gilbert **Coach** A. J. Tudor

Kimbolton were strong in bowling: seamers Charlie Evans, Archie Carroll and Oliver Greenhow, and spinners Ben Szczepanski and Chris Oliver all took ten wickets or more. The XI proved a good fielding unit and held many smart catches. George Jessop and Oliver Greenhow will aim to develop their batting talent.

Batting O. J. Greenhow 332 at 27.66; G. H. Jessop 373 at 26.64; B. D. Szczepanski 155 at 15.50.

Bowling T. W. Felix 10 at 15.90; O. J. Greenhow 18 at 18.61; B. D. Szczepanski 19 at 18.63; C. W. Evans 19 at 23.68; A. R. Carroll 11 at 32.54; C. M. Oliver 14 at 37.85.

King Edward's School, Birmingham *Warwickshire* P15 W9 L5 D1 A7

Master i/c L. M. Roll **Coach** N. W. Round

A team made up mainly of Year 12s acquitted themselves well against all opposition, with captain Arnav Kulkarni keeping wicket to a high standard. Most fixtures were shorter-format matches.

Batting Y. Machani 311 at 62.20; S. Poshakwale 231 at 25.66; *A. R. Kulkarni 176 at 25.14; M. S. Dogra 245 at 24.50; V. M. Sinha 223 at 18.58.

Bowling Y. Machani 12 at 9.58; R. S. Sandhu 13 at 12.69; P. S. Gajula 10 at 12.70; E. M. Ali 15 at 17.13; G. H. Sohail 12 at 17.41.

King Edward VI School, Southampton *Hampshire* P12 W5 L7 A3

Master i/c A. D. Penn **Coach** D. Kent

There were excellent performances against Canford and Dauntsey's; the school also won the Altham Trophy for the third year running. Jovan Dhariwal, who finished with 94 in the final match, was the driving force behind the team.

Batting *J. Dhariwal 399 at 49.88.

Bowling J. Dhariwal 13 at 15.92; N. Damley-Jones 11 at 21.63.

King's College, Taunton *Somerset* P20 W14 L5 T1 A1

Master i/c R. J. Woodman **Coach** A. W. R. Barrow

Another successful summer contained some outstanding team and individual performances: captain Sam Wyatt scored a magnificent 122 against Gloucestershire Under-19s, and Luke Oldknow made a destructive century against St Thomas College, Sri Lanka. Jacques Banton took two five-wicket hauls, and Ed Middleton and Max Mejzner managed one each.

Batting J. Banton 509 at 39.15; C. M. Sharland 219 at 36.50; *S. G. Wyatt 553 at 32.52; M. Mejzner 154 at 30.80; L. D. Oldknow 321 at 26.75; E. W. O. Middleton 257 at 25.70; W. T. Smale 258 at 21.50; W. J. Chesterman 169 at 21.12.

Bowling J. Banton 20 at 12.70; L. D. Oldknow 12 at 13.58; T. Hall 28 at 14.75; E. W. O. Middleton 17 at 16.82; S. Baker 20 at 17.50; M. Mejzner 26 at 17.61.

King's College School, Wimbledon *Surrey* P20 W10 L9 D1 A2

Master i/c B. T. Hudson **Coach** J. N. Thornley

Injuries prevented several Year 13s from assuming a big role, but younger players made the most of the opportunities. Pranav Khera's 141 not out against RGS Guildford was a highlight – perhaps a hint of things to come from a promising squad.

Batting *S. H. Patel 234 at 78.00; P. Khera 327 at 46.71; F. B. Lamy 332 at 30.18; A. R. Pillai 365 at 28.07; C. A. King 240 at 26.66; D. Harish 243 at 22.09.

Bowling D. Harish 15 at 17.80; D. Patel 12 at 19.50; A. Ramesh 15 at 27.26; A. R. Pillai 13 at 30.30.

King's School, Bruton *Somerset* P16 W9 L6 T1

Master i/c L. R. Corbin O'Grady

King's School Bruton had a longer fixture list than for many seasons. The year-round dedication led to some fantastic performances.

Batting T. A. G. Rogers 363 at 25.92; R. W. Tudhope 347 at 21.68; M. J. Harvey 354 at 20.82; *H. H. Macleod-Ash 166 at 13.83.
Bowling P. T. Jenkins 28 at 15.53; L. W. Haywood 11 at 15.81; R. W. Tudhope 18 at 19.50; J. A. Gartell 11 at 20.63; S. H. Houldsworth 18 at 21.27.

The King's School, Canterbury *Kent*

P17 W7 L9 D1 A1

Master i/c R. A. L. Singfield   **Coach** M. A. Ealham

It proved a good yet challenging season. Isaac Rahman topped both averages; he and Fred Sharp scored maiden first XI centuries. Zach Barker and Charles Brooker collected five-wicket hauls, and Dhiren Gidoomal, the captain, was a most useful all-rounder.

Batting I. A. Rahman 669 at 41.81; F. H. A. Sharp 496 at 41.33; *D. V. Gidoomal 344 at 26.46; F. D. Miller 284 at 17.75; Z. C. Barker 157 at 14.27.
Bowling I. A. Rahman 21 at 16.76; C. P. M. Brooker 16 at 23.43; D. V. Gidoomal 16 at 24.00; Z. C. Barker 20 at 26.80; M. S. C. L. Barton 13 at 28.69.

King's School, Chester *Cheshire*

P13 W2 L9 D2

Master i/c S. Neal   **Coach** J. Potts

Max Dunbavand skippered a young side with aplomb, and was the mainstay of the team with bat and ball. Henry Goodfellow and Jake Liddle hit invaluable runs, while Rishi Muthuvelu was also among the wickets.

Batting *M. J. Dunbavand 347 at 31.54; J. A. Liddle 198 at 24.75; H. T. E. Goodfellow 254 at 23.09.
Bowling R. Muthuvelu 12 at 25.75; *M. J. Dunbavand 12 at 27.25.

The King's School in Macclesfield *Cheshire*

P16 W10 L5 D1 A5

Master i/c S. Moores   **Coach** A. J. Harris

A strong finish to the season brought five consecutive wins under the excellent leadership of all-rounder Angus Thomson. The team lose several key players, but not Joey Chong or Adam Kenyon – leading run-scorer and chief wicket-taker.

Batting T. R. Carter 398 at 79.60; J. W. Chong 551 at 45.91; *A. J. Thomson 475 at 36.53; G. J. C. Holden 232 at 25.77; S. J. Buckingham 202 at 25.25; S. S. Crosby 170 at 18.88.
Bowling A. S. Kenyon 18 at 17.66; S. H. Cheetham 10 at 19.20; W. Fosbrook 11 at 21.72; H. H. S. Elms 10 at 24.70.

King's School, Rochester *Kent*

P18 W5 L10 D3 A2

Master i/c C. H. Page   **Coach** D. A. Saunders

A young team gave proof of their development by collecting more runs and more wickets, despite the number of wins remaining unchanged. Had the rain held off a little longer, and a few tight finishes gone the other way, the picture would have been much brighter; there is good reason for optimism.

Batting T. D. J. Castle 422 at 28.13; M. E. Butler 181 at 25.85; G. J. Taylor 331 at 23.64; H. T. Fermor 289 at 22.23; R. J. Butler 175 at 19.44; M. D. W. Castle 165 at 18.33; *T. J. Miles 173 at 15.72.
Bowling M. E. Butler 11 at 23.00; H. T. Fermor 21 at 23.52; T. D. J. Castle 12 at 26.58; R. J. Butler 11 at 32.57; J. P. R. Watkins 13 at 33.92.

The King's School, Worcester *Worcestershire*

P13 W5 L8 A1

Master i/c S. D. Greenall   **Coach** A. A. D. Gillgrass

Once again, the first team benefited from a strong bowling attack, who proved a handful in all formats. Run-scoring was more of a challenge, in part because of the weather. The highlight was reaching the regional final of the National Schools T20 competition.

Batting A. J. Robb 226 at 32.28; C. W. A. Francis 251 at 25.10; O. K. Tsiquaye 283 at 23.58; M. D. M. Richardson 176 at 22.00; O. W. G. Preston 170 at 14.16.
Bowling T. C. A. Otley 20 at 11.45; *E. R. Burgoyne 10 at 15.70; Z. Z. Hussain 14 at 20.28; O. K. Tsiquaye 15 at 24.40.

Kingswood School, Bath *Somerset*

P15 W10 L4 D1

Master i/c J. O. Brown

Kingswood had one of their best seasons of recent years. The Year 13 quartet of Hamish Walker, Will Jeffery, Oscar Kenyon and captain Nathan Gregg were key contributors; Year 9 Somerset player Noah Davis had an encouraging debut season.

Batting O. P. Kenyon 234 at 39.00; H. J. Walker 373 at 31.08; M. J. Kershaw 338 at 26.00; W. J. Jeffery 253 at 21.08; N. J. Davis 213 at 19.36; *N. J. W. Gregg 251 at 17.92.
Bowling S. M. King 16 at 15.25; M. W. R. Hooper 19 at 17.10; M. J. Kershaw 15 at 19.46; O. P. Kenyon 14 at 20.57.

Kirkham Grammar School *Lancashire* P7 L6 D1
Master i/c J. R. Lyon
A short summer term was curtailed further by rain. There was time for seven games, but none produced a win. Nathan Wood, captain for a second year, was one of five playing a fourth season in the first team. Some young talent bodes well for the next few seasons.
Batting J. van der Ryst 151 at 30.20.
Bowling B. Haworth 10 at 9.50.

Lancaster Royal Grammar School *Lancashire* P19 W12 L6 D1 A3
Master i/c G. A. J. Mason   **Coach** B. Swarbrick
Lancaster retained the prestigious RGS Festival trophy for the first time, beating Newcastle, Worcester, Colchester and High Wycombe. Rohan Parekh bowled superbly to claim 33 wickets, and was a thoughtful leader. There were centuries from Yuvraj Chhabra and Joe Wills, though the side were all capable of runs. Team spirit was an extra weapon in their armoury.
Batting J. A. Wills 385 at 38.50; T. E. J. Anderton 414 at 31.84; Y. Chhabra 250 at 31.25; B. D. Rosbottom 267 at 24.27; J. Raju 288 at 22.15; H. Malik 198 at 15.23.
Bowling J. A. Wills 18 at 9.16; *R. V. Parekh 33 at 10.63; J. A. Derham 20 at 16.75; J. A. Eccles 19 at 17.00; T. E. J. Anderton 19 at 18.52; C. W. Wilkinson 19 at 21.57.

Lancing College *Sussex* P12 W1 L10 D1 A1
Master i/c R. J. Maru
Well led by Matthew Lee, Lancing fielded a young side – seniors were often unavailable because of exams – and it proved a difficult term. However, the future looks more promising, with some talented youngsters making their first-team debuts, including 13-year-old George Hannington-Hodge.
Batting O. J. Devaux 178 at 14.83.
Bowling A. R. Capsey 10 at 16.50; *M. G. E. Lee 22 at 18.27.

Langley Park School for Boys *Kent* P17 W10 L7 A3
Master i/c J. M. A. Batten
Sydney Sherlock captained the first team through a successful summer, which included an excellent T20 run and a 100% record in the Kent League and Cup. James McGruer struck the ball beautifully, and William East held his nerve at crucial moments to bowl superbly.
Batting J. C. McGruer 503 at 45.72; S. A. J. De Vaux 308 at 44.00; O. H. Jasper 240 at 40.00; J. B. East 344 at 34.40; *S. A. Sherlock 297 at 27.00; D. G. Murrell 265 at 24.09; T. Mills 171 at 21.37.
Bowling O. H. Jasper 18 at 13.38; A. G. Pomering 11 at 14.63; W. J. East 31 at 16.16; W. Black 15 at 22.46; J. B. East 12 at 37.25.

Leicester Grammar School *Leicestershire* P5 W2 L2 D1 A2
Master i/c L. Potter
This was the shortest summer term for many years, amounting to just seven weeks of cricket. With rain affecting two, it was a frustrating season, and only five first XI games were played. The best moments were a good draw against MCC and a win over Wyggeston & Queen Elizabeth I College.
Batting *H. Pounds 121 at 30.25.
Bowling The leading bowler was H. Pounds, who took six wickets at 19.83.

The Leys School *Cambridgeshire* P18 W10 L7 D1 A2
Master i/c R. I. Kaufman   **Coach** W. J. Earl
It was another excellent year for the first team: they reached the last eight of the National Schools T20 Cup and became regional champions. Other highlights were the defeats of Oakham, Oundle and MCC. The future looks rosy for this very young team.
Batting T. D. P. Aubrey 510 at 34.00; J. R. H. Davies 408 at 34.00; *O. P. L. Howell 443 at 29.53; J. S. Howlett 317 at 28.81; W. M. P. Routledge 337 at 28.08; H. S. McKenzie 341 at 24.35.
Bowling R. C. B. Bramley 23 at 20.21; J. R. H. Davies 13 at 23.30; F. J. C. Tucker 13 at 38.30.

Jack Haynes helps Malvern to victory over Sedbergh in the National T20 Cup final at Arundel.

The Cathedral School, Llandaff *Glamorgan*
P11 W4 L7 A2
Master i/c M. G. Barrington   **Coach** D. E. Lewis-Williams
The school owes thanks to the departing Year 13s for their efforts in the first XI, and especially to Will Youngs, who led magnificently. It was interesting to try out the new 100-ball format at Sophia Gardens, and to host the South Africa and Bangladesh World Cup squads while they were in Wales.
Batting P. K. Jha 193 at 27.57.
Bowling E. L. C. Griffith 13 at 10.23.

Lord Wandsworth College *Hampshire*
P14 W9 L4 D1
Master i/c D. M. Beven   **Coach** R. S. Pyper
The first team had a good season, scoring some notable victories on the way. Retaining most of the squad from 2018 and adding strong young players allowed the team to play some competitive and exciting cricket.
Batting *A. J. Brown 466 at 38.83; J. O. Wheeler 405 at 36.81; H. C. Trussler 388 at 35.27; J. A. Young 170 at 15.45.
Bowling J. O. Wheeler 17 at 20.05; N. G. Hindle 12 at 21.16; A. J. Campbell 16 at 22.06; S. M. Gilley 13 at 25.76.

Loughborough Grammar School *Leicestershire*
P13 W5 L7 D1 A4
Master i/c M. I. Gidley
The weather made it a stop–start season. Captain Dylan Church and Year 10 Aryan Patel were the leading run-scorers, but the bowling was not so reliable. The two-day game against Manchester Grammar School ended in defeat from the last ball.
Batting *D. T. P. Church 502 at 45.63; A. Patel 417 at 34.75; L. Wales 229 at 28.62.
Bowling A. J. Thompson 13 at 22.23; A. Bates 10 at 22.80; C. G. Crowson 12 at 34.58.

Magdalen College School *Oxfordshire*
P13 W11 L2
Master i/c C. J. W. Boyle   **Coach** A. A. Duncan
The first team enjoyed another successful year, winning all but one of their 50-over matches in the regular season. Louis Mase and Sammy Lion-Cachet were the leading batsmen, while captain Ollie Price and Tom Chesser were very effective in the middle overs with the ball.

Batting S. J. Lion-Cachet 358 at 35.80; *O. J. Price 303 at 30.30; L. W. Mase 296 at 29.60; J. W. D. Jelfs 255 at 25.50; J. M. Coles 221 at 24.55; A. E. L. Eisner 195 at 19.50.
Bowling H. J. R. Startin 16 at 13.31; O. J. Price 15 at 13.40; T. A. Winn 11 at 14.72; T. N. S. Chesser 15 at 14.80.

Malvern College *Worcestershire*   P19 W17 L2 A3
Master i/c M. A. Hardinges   **Coach** N. A. Brett
The highlight of a hugely successful summer was winning the National T20 competition. Jack Haynes proved an adept leader, and played for England Under-19s. The innings of the season was Dan Holland's 176 not out to help bring victory in the two-day game against Wellington College.
Batting *J. L. Haynes 662 at 60.18; D. N. Holland 717 at 47.80; G. W. White 168 at 42.00; L. A. Tulacz 374 at 37.40; R. H. Hardwick 398 at 26.53; R. M. Edavalath 156 at 26.00.
Bowling A. G. Tomson 29 at 13.37; D. N. Holland 22 at 16.40; J. W. Dickenson 29 at 16.48; J. S. G. Catto 13 at 17.46; J. O. Baker 24 at 17.50; R. M. Edavalath 15 at 21.13; L. A. Tulacz 15 at 27.13.

The Manchester Grammar School *Lancashire*   P13 W10 L2 D1 A4
Master i/c M. Watkinson
There were many excellent team and individual performances in a magnificent season. The progress made by some youngsters was especially pleasing. The outstanding players were Alec Makin, George Bell, Aaryaman Roy and George Poyser.
Batting *A. H. Makin 469 at 67.00; A. Roy 269 at 53.80; G. J. Bell 431 at 43.10; D. Adams 209 at 41.80; A. Dooler 187 at 20.77.
Bowling J. M. W. Bathurst 10 at 5.90; A. H. Makin 21 at 12.85; L. K. Anson 17 at 15.23; G. W. Poyser 17 at 18.47.

Marlborough College *Wiltshire*   P14 W8 L3 D3 A1
Master i/c M. P. L. Bush   **Coach** M. W. Alleyne
A maturing team played some impressive cricket, claiming notable scalps on a competitive circuit. In a cracking season that included three thrilling last-over finishes, Will Cook scored six half-centuries and led with distinction.
Batting *W. E. B. Cook 449 at 49.88; B. R. L. Spink 363 at 33.00; W. J. Hammersley 394 at 32.83; F. J. A. Kottler 247 at 22.45; W. J. Pembroke 211 at 21.10.
Bowling A. A. G. Del Mar 18 at 16.94; F. S. G. Hazlitt 17 at 20.52; H. G. W. Mayne 12 at 21.25; O. C. J. Mace 14 at 26.71; J. A. Cleverly 14 at 26.85.

Merchant Taylors' School, Crosby *Lancashire*   P17 W8 L7 D2 A4
Master i/c S. P. Sutcliffe
Merchant Taylors' had a mixed summer, with one more win than defeat. The high points were a third consecutive victory against MCC, wins against King's Macclesfield and Myerscough College on the local circuit, and St Patrick's College from Australia. George Politis batted beautifully, and the spinners fared well with the ball. Jackson Darkes-Sutcliffe and Harvey Rankin took the most wickets, while Robert Rankin is a talented all-rounder.
Batting *G. H. Politis 776 at 70.54; R. F. Rankin 374 at 37.40; H. J. Rankin 305 at 30.50; *K. T. Mahambrey 195 at 16.25; J. Darkes-Sutcliffe 192 at 16.00.
Bowling K. T. Mahambrey 12 at 16.66; H. J. Rankin 15 at 17.93; R. F. Rankin 13 at 20.23; C. G. Snaylam 11 at 26.27; J. Darkes-Sutcliffe 16 at 30.06.

Merchant Taylors' School, Northwood *Hertfordshire* P21 W13 L8
Master i/c I. McGowan
An exciting season featured some wonderful games, especially in the National T20 competition. The side were South of England champions for the second year running, thanks to some excellent individual performances; the school also prospered on a competitive North London circuit.
Batting *D. J. Burnell 570 at 40.71; R. K. Randev 383 at 31.91; J. J. Leathem 185 at 26.42; R. Day 272 at 22.66; M. A. John 201 at 15.46; S. R. Sardana 211 at 15.07; A. Sandhu 205 at 14.64; J. T. Baxter 192 at 12.80.
Bowling S. S. Shah 30 at 15.93; S. R. Sardana 23 at 17.34; M. A. John 21 at 21.28; S. V. A. Patel 10 at 22.30; R. Day 16 at 23.00; D. J. Burnell 12 at 29.25.

Tom Mackintosh Sabater, from Merchiston Castle, and Millfield's Kasey Aldridge.

Merchiston Castle School *Midlothian*   P12 W7 L4 T1 A1
Master i/c R. D. McCann
The team took real momentum into July, after some early-season T20. Tom Mackintosh Sabater was selected for MCC Schools at Lord's, recognition of a fantastic summer with bat and gloves.
Batting *T. S. Mackintosh Sabater 423 at 47.00.
Bowling O. Ashley 13 at 19.07.

Millfield School *Somerset*   P20 W13 L7 A2
Master i/c M. A. Garaway   **Coach** G. D. Hook
Millfield lost in the semi-final of the National T20 Cup but registered impressive victories against MCC, Gloucestershire Academy, OMCC, Grey College and a strong King's Taunton (twice). Sam Young hit three centuries in just seven innings. He and Ned Leonard, Kasey Aldridge and Lewis Goldsworthy represented England Under-19s.
Batting *S. J. Young 430 at 86.00; A. W. McCallum 166 at 41.50; L. P. Goldsworthy 286 at 40.85; J. W. Baird 334 at 33.40; C. S. Dhindsa 347 at 31.54; K. L. Aldridge 185 at 20.55; M. Critchley 237 at 14.81.
Bowling N. O. Leonard 11 at 20.72; C. J. J. Mason 11 at 23.81; M. W. Hancock 20 at 24.05; A. W. McCallum 16 at 31.12.

Mill Hill School *Middlesex*   P12 W3 L6 D3 A1
Master i/c S. Patel
Mill Hill endured another season of rebuilding and transition, with three wins. Even so, there were many positives, with many young players gaining invaluable experience.
Batting J. L. Taylor 284 at 35.50.
Bowling J. L. Taylor 13 at 16.69; R. Bhoja 12 at 18.58.

Monkton Combe *Somerset*   P15 W3 L9 D3 A1
Master i/c M. B. Abington   **Coach** J. C. A. Leggett
Luke Walker led a limited but enthusiastic side with a real feel for the tactics of the game. Outstanding fielding was a memorable feature, with some fantastic catches.
Batting L. J. Walker 477 at 31.80; M. J. Garrod 175 at 19.44; J. B. Abington 198 at 15.23; K. Gurung 173 at 14.41; E. A. Walker 162 at 11.57.
Bowling O. Adeleye 14 at 23.50; L. J. Walker 17 at 23.64.

Monmouth School *Monmouthshire*
P14 W9 L5 A3

Master i/c A. J. Jones   **Coaches** G. I. Burgess and S. P. James

The highlight was a school-record chase against Bristol Grammar School. Centuries from Nathan Lee (127) and Harry Friend (140 not out) meant Monmouth reached 354 for two with an over to spare.

Batting H. Friend 344 at 49.14; *N. J. Lee 504 at 38.76; M. Burger 287 at 35.87; S. Swingwood 339 at 30.81.

Bowling N. J. Lee 23 at 13.34; S. Swingwood 25 at 15.00; M. Burger 17 at 22.29; B. W. Skailes 12 at 26.00.

Mount Kelly School *Devon*
P13 W4 L9 A1

Master i/c J. R. H. Carr

An early-season win over Eton College Thirds offered encouragement. Several close matches could have gone either way, though the experience gained can only be a plus. With just three players leaving, next season promises much.

Batting K. Burns 510 at 42.50; *O. Allsop 226 at 25.11; A. S. Kopparambil 250 at 25.00.

Bowling J. Kopparambil 17 at 14.47.

New Hall School *Essex*
P24 W14 L7 D3 A1

Master i/c P. M. Davidge

This was a record-breaking season for the first XI: most wins, highest total (333 for four against Kimbolton), regional champions and winners of the Castle Festival (both for the first time). The team continued to play a mixture of formats, from T20 to two days.

Batting M. Cook 347 at 38.55; *V. A. Gandhi 664 at 34.94; N. Khelawon 720 at 32.72; S. C. Sullivan 389 at 32.41; R. J. McKenna 215 at 26.87; C. M. Limrick 355 at 25.35; T. F. Debenham 310 at 20.66; E. M. Pickering 150 at 16.66; J. Hussain 260 at 13.68.

Bowling V. A. Gandhi 34 at 15.38; C. M. Limrick 22 at 17.36; J. W. Murphy 14 at 18.21; A. D. Berry 16 at 18.68; S. C. Sullivan 11 at 21.09; E. M. Pickering 14 at 22.14; T. F. Debenham 17 at 25.41; N. Khelawon 14 at 29.50.

Newcastle under Lyme School *Staffordshire*
P17 W6 L11 A3

Master i/c G. M. Breen   **Coach** J. F. Brown

The side won two matches, but were outclassed by boarding schools. In his sixth and final season in the team, captain Peter Vickers averaged 91, but played only nine games.

Batting *P. J. Vickers 274 at 91.33; R. G. Hesketh 223 at 24.77; P. E. Heiskanen 215 at 17.91.

Bowling P. M. Clarke 12 at 17.00; R. G. Hesketh 15 at 20.13; W. D. Clarke 10 at 23.10; P. E. Heiskanen 10 at 33.30.

Norwich School *Norfolk*
P13 W8 L4 D1 A2

Master i/c J. L. O. Cawkwell   **Coach** R. W. Sims

The team struggled for early-season momentum because of the weather, but finished strongly, winning several competitive matches in a busy period. The most notable performances were a brilliant unbeaten 158 by Dani Long-Martinez that helped bring a comfortable victory over MCC, and six for 16 by James Hardy against The Perse.

Batting D. Long-Martinez 402 at 67.00; Z. P. T. Taylor 255 at 36.42; *C. Nunn 229 at 32.71; W. R. Hollis 246 at 27.33; G. F. Harrad 238 at 26.44.

Bowling J. P. Hardy 17 at 19.58; J. Cherry 12 at 21.41; D. G. Hastings 13 at 27.84; S. Grisewood 13 at 28.53.

Nottingham High School *Nottinghamshire*
P20 W13 L6 D1

Master i/c M. Baker   **Coach** P. M. Borrington

Sacheth Menon fostered an excellent team spirit, and his side enjoyed a successful season. Key performances came from a range of players, many of whom return for 2020.

Batting B. R. Martindale 262 at 32.75; *S. R. Menon 341 at 31.00; J. A. Croasdale 260 at 26.00; E. M. Martin 176 at 25.14; M. H. Loveridge 185 at 20.55; S. I. M. King 163 at 18.11; J. M. Williams 175 at 13.46.

Bowling E. M. Martin 13 at 22.30; D. Das 10 at 25.80; S. R. Menon 13 at 26.23.

Oakham School *Rutland*
P16 W10 L5 D1 A2

Master i/c N. C. Johnson

Despite exam pressure fuelling the drive towards afternoon-only T20 games, there were nine traditional all-day matches (three after term had ended), as well as seven short-format fixtures. Richard Bell topped both averages, even though he played over half the matches in his preferred position of wicketkeeper.

Batting R. N. Bell 549 at 61.00; *N. J. H. Kimber 313 at 34.77; H. J. S. Tattersall 342 at 28.50; B. M. Lewin 197 at 19.70.

Bowling R. N. Bell 14 at 9.21; G. A. Axtel 14 at 11.57; H. J. S. Tattersall 17 at 15.35; C. F. Morley 17 at 19.23; J. A. M. Tattersall 13 at 24.53.

The Oratory School *Oxfordshire*
P11 W4 L6 D1 A2

Master i/c S. C. B. Tomlinson   **Coach** C. T. Peploe

A young team performed maturely, and there were fine collective and individual performances, especially later in the summer. Nine regulars return, encouraging optimism for 2020.

Batting M. Williams 290 at 290.00; J. K. Wallace 180 at 20.00; W. Cassar 185 at 18.50.

Bowling J. K. Wallace 24 at 11.66; A. Baxter 15 at 14.33; T. Winterbottom 12 at 15.00.

Oundle School *Northamptonshire*
P16 W6 L8 D2 A1

Master i/c D. W. Foster   **Coach** M. J. Roberts

Oundle performed valiantly through a tough fixture list. James Esler, the captain, was player of the year, hitting most runs and taking most wickets. Fellow all-rounder Tommy Simeons was one of a core group who gave strong support.

Batting *J. I. Esler 395 at 35.90; T. J. Simeons 347 at 31.54; T. M. R. Stanton 167 at 20.87; O. R. R. Thain 194 at 19.40; W. G. De Capell Brooke 197 at 16.41.

Bowling H. J. Woodrow 17 at 18.17; T. J. Simeons 17 at 21.64; J. I. Esler 20 at 22.70; J. O. C. Howard 14 at 24.14; C. Preece 15 at 24.53.

The Perse School *Cambridgeshire*
P16 W6 L10 A1

Master i/c S. M. Park

A promising year saw younger cricketers excel. Alex Maynard (Under-15) hit a magnificent 140 in the school festival, while Nikhil Gorantla, Charles Bell and Henry Howarth, all Under-16, made significant contributions.

Batting A. J. Maynard 327 at 40.87; B. M. Cross 253 at 31.62; N. V. Gorantla 215 at 26.87; G. W. H. Doel 162 at 20.25; D. F. Shaw 171 at 15.54.

Bowling C. D. Bell 11 at 21.90; H. J. S. Howarth 11 at 30.18; G. Means 11 at 38.18.

Pocklington School *Yorkshire*
P12 W3 L8 D1 A6

Master i/c D. Byas

A summer badly disrupted by weather prevented the batsmen from discovering the good form shown in previous seasons.

Batting W. D. Watts 318 at 24.46; R. N. Boddy 262 at 17.46.

Bowling J. G. S. Matthews 14 at 14.64; T. P. P. Kirby 18 at 16.66; *J. D. Goddard 19 at 20.15.

The Portsmouth Grammar School *Hampshire*
P14 W8 L6

Master i/c S. J. Curwood   **Coach** P. C. Bew

Joe Kooner-Evans, the captain, and Max Beckett both prospered in their last season. Many younger players also did their bit, and the school won a thrilling game against MCC. Prospects for 2020 look bright.

Batting T. Wallis 608 at 50.66; *J. F. Kooner-Evans 379 at 37.90; E. R. L. Moger 243 at 30.37; C. M. Pratt 226 at 20.54.

Bowling T. Sambles 15 at 16.66; J. F. Kooner-Evans 13 at 17.07; M. Beckett 14 at 17.28; J. F. Peacre 11 at 23.90; W. A. Doyle 18 at 24.44.

Prior Park College *Somerset*
P10 W4 L5 D1 A1

Master i/c R. J. Pandya   **Coach** M. D. Bond

Prior Park won four of their ten matches, but it might have been better: after a strong start, the team struggled to close out games. Will South, the top run-scorer and leading wicket-taker, hit his maiden century; he had useful support from vice-captain Greg Harden.

Batting *W. A. South 250 at 41.66; A. C. J. Wortelhock 196 at 32.66; D. Aspray 180 at 25.71.

Bowling W. A. South 13 at 17.76; G. C. H. Harden 10 at 24.50.

Queen Elizabeth Grammar School, Wakefield *Yorkshire* P9 W3 L4 D2
Master i/c S. A. Wood
A positive season produced victories against Old Savilians, Ashville and Bradford GS, as well as a last-ball defeat by St Peter's York in the National T20. Amai Ganjam batted well all summer, and his 57 against MCC took the school within five runs of victory.
Batting A. Ganjam 184 at 61.33.
Bowling The leading bowler was M. J. Flathers, who took nine wickets at 16.66.

Queen Elizabeth's Hospital, Bristol *Gloucestershire* P10 W4 L6
Master i/c P. E. Joslin **Coach** D. Forder
Ben Jarman captained the side and was well supported by two more Bens, Yuen and Harding. Early defeats did not dampen enthusiasm, and there were four wins in one week. Spinner Hector Newton topped the bowling.
Batting F. G. D. Vaughan 176 at 35.20; B. J. Yuen 239 at 26.55; *B. W. Jarman 160 at 17.77.
Bowling H. T. Newton 15 at 15.20.

Queen Mary's Grammar School, Walsall *Staffordshire* P6 W4 L1 D1 A3
Master i/c B. T. Gibbons **Coach** J. O. Hawkins
In a summer marred by poor weather, the team won more games than they lost, and were runners-up in the Stratford six-a-side. Anusha Chauhan became the first girl to play in the first team, and Rohit Suglani the first to captain the side for three seasons.
Batting M. J. Curtiss 168 at 42.00.
Bowling The leading bowler was A. Sharma, who took eight wickets at 8.25.

Queen's College, Taunton *Somerset* P14 W5 L9
Master i/c J. B. Lintott **Coach** P. J. Mann
The season started brilliantly, with five straight wins against strong opposition, but it was downhill thereafter. Batsmen Tom Hazell-Evans and Charlie Kassapian were real positives, while James Duckering, who captained superbly all term, bowled consistently.
Batting T. Hazell-Evans 372 at 37.20; C. M. Kassapian 286 at 28.60; *J. P. Duckering 153 at 19.12.
Bowling J. P. Duckering 11 at 25.36.

Radley College *Oxfordshire* P14 W7 L7 A2
Master i/c S. H. Dalrymple **Coach** A. R. Wagner
A mixed summer saw dominant performances… and some off days. The John Harvey Trophy was a fitting achievement for a talented group, whose victories included St Edward's, Eton and Marlborough.
Batting P. R. Barnett 262 at 65.50; F. J. R. Horler 784 at 60.30; H. J. A. W. Chapman 497 at 49.70; *H. W. Purton 393 at 30.23; J. S. Sharp 150 at 16.66.
Bowling A. J. G. Haynes 19 at 20.52; W. G. Barker 12 at 29.66; H. W. Purton 11 at 30.54; H. J. A. W. Chapman 12 at 34.25; F. J. R. Horler 10 at 36.00.

Ratcliffe College *Leicestershire* P11 W9 L2 A3
Master i/c E. O. Woodcock
The run of recent success continued with a pleasing return of nine wins from 11. Captain Toby Snell finished his career with 2,047 runs and 61 wickets, and was well backed up by Oliver Welch, George Morgan-Jones and Aled King.
Batting O. R. Welch 522 at 74.57; *T. Snell 522 at 58.00; T. M. C. Page 192 at 32.00.
Bowling G. W. A. Morgan-Jones 25 at 11.84; T. Snell 11 at 14.54; A. D. King 10 at 20.60.

Reed's School *Surrey* P14 W7 L3 D4 A1
Master i/c M. R. Dunn **Coach** K. T. Medlycott
An inexperienced side, well captained by Harry Williams, produced some excellent cricket. Jack Fletcher was a talented all-rounder, while Nick Morgan, Max Newbold and Williams led the batting. Marcus Jones, Tom Hancock and Maxwell Dunn shone with the ball.
Batting N. J. L. Morgan 605 at 67.22; M. J. Newbold 444 at 55.50; *H. P. R. Williams 343 at 34.30; J. W. Fletcher 315 at 31.50; A. C. Lewis 238 at 26.44.
Bowling M. O. Jones 15 at 22.80; T. E. A. Hancock 13 at 25.53; M. M. Dunn 10 at 28.40; N. J. L. Morgan 16 at 35.93; J. W. Fletcher 12 at 36.41.

Reigate Grammar School *Surrey*
P10 W4 L5 D1 A2

Master i/c J. M. C. Leck   **Coach** J. E. Benjamin

A young first XI showed good determination on a relatively strong circuit. Performances reflected fight and character, and there were a number of positive results against local opponents.

Batting W. Timmons 157 at 19.62; *J. M. V. Flanders 174 at 19.33; D. Grant 169 at 18.77.

Bowling E. Russ 12 at 16.16; J. M. V. Flanders 13 at 17.23; T. Wilbraham 11 at 18.72.

Repton School *Derbyshire*
P19 W10 L6 D3 A2

Master i/c C. M. W. Read   **Coach** I. M. Pollock

After defeats at Malvern and Shrewsbury, Repton found their tempo as the term progressed and played some exciting, positive cricket. Wins against MCC in a timed encounter, and Trent College in the National Schools T20, were highlights. Will Hobson caught the eye: he hit an unbeaten 188, and his left-arm spin raked in 25 wickets.

Batting Z. P. Wenham 204 at 51.00; W. A. Hobson 685 at 48.93; A. S. Chima 492 at 44.73; E. A. Berlusconi 515 at 36.79; S. F. J. Sayer 280 at 21.54.

Bowling *T. A. Buffin 20 at 16.70; W. A. Hobson 25 at 22.20; S. F. J. Sayer 16 at 27.81; T. S. Jones 13 at 32.30; E. A. Berlusconi 10 at 38.20.

Rossall School *Lancashire*
P7 W5 L1 D1 A3

Master i/c M. J. Kelly

Rossall gained encouraging results, with notable victories over Giggleswick, Stonyhurst and Barnard Castle. Owing to the weather and exams, fixtures were limited. In the final game of the season, Rossall defeated Edinburgh Academy by one run – with Will Gair taking the final wicket in his last game for the school.

Batting *C. Ardron 178 at 59.33; C. Clark 167 at 33.40.

Bowling L. C. Haworth 13 at 8.00; W. Gair 10 at 9.80; C. Clark 11 at 16.63.

Royal Grammar School, Guildford *Surrey*
P15 W9 L6 A1

Master i/c R. C. Black   **Coach** M. W. Barnes

Abhay Gonella ended his school career with a century against Reed's, 70 not out against MCC, four for 23 against Trinity and four for 26 against Cranleigh. Tom Eves hit unbeaten scores of 69 and 108 in his last two innings.

Batting T. Eves 216 at 72.00; *A. P. Gonella 574 at 44.15; W. J. Perceval 406 at 25.37; T. M. Humphreys 300 at 25.00; T. Perceval 150 at 16.66; H. J. A. Relph 211 at 16.23; H. M. C. Turrell 162 at 16.20; A. Gandhi 154 at 15.40; A. Ashfaque 175 at 14.58.

Bowling A. P. Gonella 18 at 20.44; T. M. Humphreys 17 at 21.94; H. M. C. Turrell 10 at 34.10; T. Eves 16 at 34.50.

Royal Grammar School, High Wycombe *Bucks*
P15 W6 L7 D2 A3

Master i/c B. T. R. Berryman

A youthful side, weak in batting, had a varied season. James Baldwin, the captain, and keeper Oli Shaw did both pass 300 runs, while spinners Zain Khan and James Dalby shared 37 wickets.

Batting *J. F. Baldwin 326 at 32.60; O. R. W. Shaw 325 at 27.08; G. F. Lasseter 280 at 23.33; Z. A. Khan 172 at 15.63; M. N. Arabi 161 at 14.63.

Bowling J. C. T. D. Dalby 20 at 19.20; Z. A. Khan 17 at 22.17; M. N. Arabi 14 at 22.64; G. F. Lasseter 12 at 25.16.

Royal Grammar School, Newcastle *Northumberland*
P12 W8 L4 A5

Master i/c M. J. Smalley   **Coach** D. Shurben

A pleasing, if wet, summer included reaching the northern final of the National T20, victories over Durham Academy, Durham School and Ashville, and second place in the RGS Festival. Rory Hanley led the side well, and scored heavily.

Batting *R. Hanley 592 at 84.57; R. J. Green 261 at 29.00.

Bowling R. Hanley 10 at 16.00; S. Kanakala 17 at 17.23; J. A. Boaden 13 at 19.53; C. J. Fletcher 10 at 27.20.

Ben Charlesworth – from St Edward's, Oxford, to Gloucestershire.

Royal Grammar School, Worcester *Worcestershire*   P17 W6 L10 D1 A3

Master i/c P. J. Newport   **Coach** P. J. Scott

RGS Worcester hosted a successful festival, finishing runners-up to Lancaster. Captain Ben Sutton played for the England Physical Disabilities senior side in the World Series.

Batting A. E. P. Rees 447 at 27.93; J. M. Morgan-Iqbal 158 at 22.57; J. E. J. Rees 302 at 18.87; J. M. Corlett 257 at 18.35; J. I. Mann 213 at 17.75; *B. R. Sutton 154 at 15.40; L. R. Allen 151 at 15.10; T. R. Bonham 177 at 13.61.

Bowling B. R. Sutton 21 at 17.61; B. J. Hallam 18 at 19.61; N. D. Southwick 13 at 21.00; O. J. N. Sankey 14 at 27.92; L. R. Allen 19 at 28.36; S. A. Ford 13 at 28.46.

Rugby School *Warwickshire*   P11 W3 L5 D3 A1

Master i/c M. J. Powell   **Coaches** N. J. Tester, A. E. L. Thomson and S. P. Robinson

Several young players made their first-team debuts in 2019. Jacob Bethell, an all-rounder of talent, was well supported by fellow Year 10 Eddie King, who made 57 not out against Shrewsbury. The highlights of a short, wet season were an unbeaten hundred by Bethell against Cheltenham, and victory over Bedford in the National T20.

Batting J. G. Bethell 414 at 46.00; A. F. H. Gibbs 386 at 35.09; J. S. Z. Montfort Bebb 210 at 16.15; W. R. Gardener 159 at 14.45; H. L. Ogle 178 at 12.71.

Bowling J. G. Bethell 21 at 16.57; W. R. Gardener 12 at 25.41; M. W. Richards 10 at 32.70.

Rydal Penrhos *Denbighshire*   P10 W4 L6

Master i/c A. Boyd   **Coach** M. T. Leach

This was a pleasing summer for the Rydal Penrhos team, a group with bags of enthusiasm and potential. Fine solo efforts came from captain Owen Reilly and the youngster Aaron Senn.

Batting *O. Reilly 372 at 53.14; S. Bixby 151 at 21.57.

Bowling A. Senn 18 at 13.38; O. Reilly 12 at 17.33.

St Albans School *Hertfordshire*   P17 W10 L5 D2

Master i/c M. C. Ilott

St Albans enjoyed their best start to a season, with seven straight wins, before a midsummer blip brought heavy defeats by local opposition. Excellent performances against MCC, New Hall and at the King's (Bruton) Festival ensured a strong finish.

Batting *J. M. de Caires 825 at 63.46; H. J. I. Craig 371 at 26.50; S. T. Perrin 370 at 26.42; T. C. E. Platts 187 at 20.77; B. W. Warren 279 at 19.92; J. Deane 256 at 17.06; B. E. Yurkwich 162 at 10.80.
Bowling B. W. Warren 33 at 13.54; J. Deane 10 at 16.70; J. M. de Caires 29 at 18.79; B. M. Griggs 17 at 24.88; C. O. Appleyard 13 at 25.15.

St Benedict's School, Ealing *Middlesex*   P15 W8 L6 D1
Master i/c K. Newell
Despite tailing off towards the end, it was a productive year. Captain Tomek Tsang was in fine form before his season was cut short, Alex Holmes shone as an all-rounder, and two exciting prospects emerged in off-spinner George Curtis-Raleigh and 14-year-old batsman Jared Braddock.
Batting *T. J. L. Tsang 288 at 48.00; A. V. Holmes 347 at 31.54; J. H. Braddock 342 at 28.50; C. Gray 175 at 21.87; T. J. Knight 277 at 18.46.
Bowling A. V. Holmes 17 at 9.47; H. J. Ritchie 12 at 16.75; G. C. Curtis-Raleigh 13 at 17.23; B. Morris 17 at 19.70; R. P. Pilgrim 14 at 23.00.

St Edmund's School, Canterbury *Kent*   P10 W5 L3 D2 A1
Master i/c D. G. Stubbings   **Coaches** C. W. Bodle, H. L. Alleyne and C. Penn
St Edmund's had a winning summer, thanks to the efforts of Joe Gordon, Matty Nordin and Harry Sherwin. The young team have great promise.
Batting *J. A. Gordon 530 at 106.00; M. A. Nordin 217 at 36.16.
Bowling H. J. Sherwin 10 at 21.40.

St Edward's School, Oxford *Oxfordshire*   P16 W10 L4 D2
Master i/c P. O. B. Swainson   **Coach** D. P. Simpkins
The first XI were a young, talented side, which was reflected in their results. Excellent victories against the two toughest opponents, Malvern and Harrow, were bookended by disappointing defeats by Radley and Marlborough.
Batting A. J. Horton 631 at 63.10; *B. G. Charlesworth 466 at 51.77; P. A. Ades 511 at 46.45; J. E. Marsh 168 at 28.00; J. O. Regan 330 at 27.50.
Bowling L. A. Charlesworth 22 at 14.22; B. Jacobs 19 at 18.47; J. O. Regan 22 at 19.50; J. E. Marsh 23 at 19.78; K. Barman 17 at 21.64.

St George's College, Weybridge *Surrey*   P10 W5 L3 D2
Master i/c O. J. Clayson   **Coach** R. Hall
A new, young side led by Charlie Brennen competed with passion and enthusiasm. There was much cause for optimism for 2020.
Batting O. Rousham 395 at 56.42; J. Furness 210 at 26.25.
Bowling *C. Brennen 15 at 19.86; A. Behl 13 at 20.76.

St John's School, Leatherhead *Surrey*   P19 W17 L2
Master i/c D. J. Hammond
The summer of 2019 was one of the best in the school's history, with 17 wins from 19 games. Going unbeaten in Saturday fixtures, and retaining the annual end-of-season festival, were highlights.
Batting *B. B. A. Geddes 737 at 61.41; L. C. Trimming 522 at 37.28; H. Mead 514 at 36.71; J. Moss 266 at 33.25; J. Potter 273 at 27.30; W. Farnsworth 285 at 23.75; F. Dudson 226 at 22.60; S. Hunt 155 at 22.14.
Bowling S. Hunt 38 at 12.23; F. Dudson 13 at 16.69; A. Tubman 15 at 19.20; J. Potter 17 at 19.41; W. Farnsworth 18 at 19.55; M. Simpson 13 at 21.00.

St Joseph's College *Surrey*   P11 W2 L7 D2
Master i/c E. M. Tyler
A young, energetic side showed character throughout the summer. While results didn't always go their way, St Joseph's gained plenty of invaluable experience.
Batting *J. Marston 314 at 52.33; H. D. Skinner 232 at 38.67.
Bowling The leading bowler was L. J. Millions, who took nine wickets at 19.00.

St Lawrence College *Kent*   P16 W10 L4 D2 A3
Master i/c S. M. Simmons   **Coach** T. Moultor
Isaac Dilkes, whose given names match those of Viv Richards, hit four centuries in his last year broke the school batting record and played for Kent Seconds. Joe Mitchell also scored consistently while Lewis Wain was the first to take 20 wickets since 2002.

Sedbergh bowlers George Hill and Matthew Revis.

Batting *I. V. A. Dilkes 911 at 82.81; J. A. Mitchell 500 at 38.46; H. R. M. Collins 251 at 27.88; T. Marshall 221 at 27.62; A. E. Ralph Harding 231 at 19.25.
Bowling C. I. T. French 14 at 10.50; L. P. Wain 23 at 14.78; J. R. P. McCaffrey 15 at 15.00; G. C. T. Kidd 12 at 16.66; I. V. A. Dilkes 12 at 20.16.

St Paul's School *Surrey*   P15 W8 L6 D1
Master i/c N. E. Briers
St Paul's enjoyed significant wins against Bradfield, Epsom, Reed's, The Leys and MCC. This very young team, with only one leaver, finished the season with six victories in a row, with 16-year-old Middlesex Academy player Anosh Malik striking four centuries in succession.
Batting A. Malik 538 at 41.38; A. Sofat 384 at 32.00; Z. J. L. Campbell 150 at 30.00; *R. P. N. Tegner 379 at 27.07; F. P. Eltringham 360 at 25.71; F. W. J. Harrison 176 at 25.14; F. A. Bell 216 at 19.63.
Bowling D. B. Whiley 21 at 20.23; F. W. J. Harrison 28 at 22.03; M. E. L. Fumagalli 14 at 30.00; Z. J. L. Campbell 16 at 30.06; A. Sofat 12 at 39.41.

St Peter's School, York *Yorkshire*   P22 W15 L5 D2
Master i/c G. J. Sharp
There were gratifying wins against Sedbergh, Trent, Repton, and Worksop, while the XI reached the northern final of the National T20 Cup for the third year running. All but two of the squad return, including the captain, Christopher Wood.
Batting M. T. Roberts 673 at 48.07; M. Lodge 554 at 46.16; B. T. Lodge 531 at 35.40; *C. D. S. Wood 417 at 27.80; H. Gration 388 at 27.71; I. N. Giannini 275 at 27.50.
Bowling E. C. Watson 15 at 8.06; M. T. Roberts 24 at 13.54; O. J. Tomalin 27 at 15.25; F. H. Southgate 22 at 16.18; C. D. S. Wood 25 at 19.88; J. R. Bramley 21 at 23.47; I. N. Gianinni 15 at 25.73.

Sedbergh School *Yorkshire*   P18 W15 L3 A7
Master i/c M. P. Speight
George Hill led a team blessed with depth in batting and bowling through an excellent season – despite the wet weather: Sedbergh won the BOWS festival for a second consecutive year, and narrowly lost to Malvern in the National Schools T20 final. Hill, an astute captain who played for England Under-19s, was well supported by Matthew Revis, Leo Johnson and Ben Davidson.
Batting M. L. Revis 642 at 58.36; *G. C. H. Hill 569 at 51.72; B. J. Davidson 336 at 28.00; L. S. Johnson 249 at 27.66.
Bowling G. C. H. Hill 27 at 13.66; L. S. Johnson 12 at 14.08; B. J. Davidson 21 at 15.33; C. Aspinwall 12 at 20.25; O. Green 25 at 20.64; A. Little 16 at 24.50; M. Revis 13 at 26.23.

Sevenoaks School *Kent*
P14 W13 L1 A5

Master i/c D. T. Smith **Coach** P. J. Hulston

The first XI had a magnificent summer – as proven by 13 wins in 14 matches. Henry Procter had a phenomenal season with the bat, while wickets were shared around. Highlights were winning the local league and T20 tournament, as well as beating MCC.

Batting H. C. Procter 723 at 80.33; *H. F. Houillon 330 at 36.66.

Bowling M. Procter 16 at 12.12; H. C. Procter 14 at 14.35.

Sherborne School *Dorset*
P13 W5 L8

Master i/c A. D. Nurton **Coach** M. G. Pardoe

Batting fragility was always likely to be a concern in 2019, and so it proved. Sometimes, though, there were significant contributions down the order, and the slow bowlers did their bit to ensure several good wins.

Batting J. J. E. Meaker 245 at 35.00; O. R. Dixon 162 at 27.00; S. F. Carty 287 at 26.09; *J. E. B. Walliker 200 at 25.00; R. P. W. O'Brien 216 at 24.00; L. H. McLaughlin 241 at 20.08.

Bowling T. F. C. Clark 23 at 12.00; L. H. McLaughlin 13 at 30.53.

Shiplake College *Oxfordshire*
P16 W14 L2 A2

Master i/c M. Griffiths **Coach** P. M. McCraw

Shiplake enjoyed a superb season, with 14 wins from 16 games. Callum Creighton was outstanding with the ball all term, and captain Matthew Dalrymple's two centuries at the Reading Blue Coat T20 tournament was a wonderful end to his school career.

Batting *M. R. Dalrymple 524 at 32.75; E. W. Lee 295 at 24.58; J. Angell 255 at 15.93.

Bowling C. J. Creighton 35 at 8.25; M. J. T. Haynes 10 at 9.60; C. Theodorou 14 at 30.92.

Shrewsbury School *Shropshire*
P24 W19 L4 D1

Master i/c A. S. Barnard **Coach** A. J. Shantry

A convincing and skilful first team outplayed the vast majority of opponents and finished with 19 wins. But they found the most important matches a stretch too far – until they beat Eton on the last day of the season to win the Silk Trophy for the sixth time in 12 years.

Batting W. B. S. Sissons 505 at 38.84; L. G. Evans 367 at 36.70; *D. J. Humes 798 at 36.27; P. J. H. Clark 244 at 34.85; M. J. Bevans 551 at 34.43; L. H. J. Litchfield 274 at 34.25; R. X. Clarke 530 at 29.44; A. W. Garrett 159 at 22.71; H. R. Cooke 203 at 20.30.

Bowling P. J. H. Clark 12 at 12.83; A. W. Garrett 34 at 14.85; L. G. Evans 29 at 16.24; W. B. S. Sissons 19 at 20.31; J. P. Pattenden 17 at 24.29; A. B. Mobbs 14 at 24.78.

Simon Langton Grammar School for Boys *Kent*
P15 W6 L7 D2

Master i/c J. K. R. Whitnell **Coach** D. Carter

After a fantastic tour of Barbados, it was a season of what-ifs – exiting the Kent Cup and the Kent T20 competition in the semis. A wonderful showing in the Tonbridge Festival, and a hard-fought draw against MCC, ended the season on a high.

Batting J. Goldbacher 205 at 29.28; A. Beck 204 at 22.66; T. Williams 203 at 20.30.

Bowling A. Di Biase 9 at 28.00.

The Skinners' School *Kent*
P14 W8 L5 D1 A1

Master i/c W. G. Burrows

The Skinners' School had a pleasing summer, with early wins against Eltham College and King's Rochester, as well as a thrilling draw with MCC. Despite narrow defeats by Sevenoaks and Sutton Valence, the school reached the Kent County League final for the second year running. Charles MacDonald-Gay made two unbeaten centuries.

Batting *O. J. E. Daniels 375 at 37.50; C. O. F. MacDonald-Gay 365 at 33.18; E. B. Shepherdson 178 at 19.77; J. C. Poulsom 170 at 17.00.

Bowling O. T. B. Bingham 12 at 9.50; T. J. D. Ponsford 12 at 22.75.

Solihull School *Warwickshire*
P11 W8 L3 A3

Master i/c D. L. Maddy **Coach** D. Smith

With a short term and poor weather, the young team did well to play 11 matches, winning all but three. Ashish Chakrapani, who hit two hundreds, and Samuel Graham are exciting prospects.

Batting B. J. Griffin 266 at 53.20; A. M. Chakrapani 367 at 45.87.

Bowling S. Graham 15 at 8.60; F. A. H. Roll 16 at 15.62.

Joey Evison, from Stamford School, made his Nottinghamshire debut in September.

Stamford School *Lincolnshire* P11 W7 L2 D2 A3

Master i/c D. W. Headley

After a spring deluge, the weather relented, and allowed excellent cricket: Joey Evison hit two centuries, while captain Patrick Harrington and Hamish Bell scored maiden hundreds. Mark Saunders and Caius Headley returned five-wicket hauls; George Hooper provided sterling support.

Batting J. D. M. Evison 442 at 88.40; *P. J. Harrington 392 at 43.55; K. J. Calnan 221 at 36.83; H. P. R. Bell 223 at 27.87; M. S. Saleem 176 at 25.14.

Bowling C. K. Headley 19 at 15.10; M. C. Saunders 17 at 15.76; G. J. Hooper 14 at 18.00.

Stewart's Melville College, Edinburgh *Midlothian* P16 W6 L8 D2

Master i/c J. A. Beharrell **Coach** A. Ranson

A young team won six matches, and improved as the term progressed. With many changes to the side each week, Finley Campbell proved an adept captain.

Batting C. D. Peet 196 at 32.66; F. T. Peet 164 at 23.42; *F. Campbell 215 at 17.91; S. L. Tait 171 at 17.10; O. J. Rees 175 at 13.46.

Bowling B. Z. Ali 15 at 13.20; F. T. Peet 18 at 15.16; A. Aniruddhan 15 at 15.20; S. L. Tait 22 at 17.27.

Stonyhurst College *Lancashire* P4 W3 L1 A4

Master i/c D. F. Haasbroek

The first XI had a slow start against Rossall, but bounced back against Kirkham Grammar School. There were comfortable wins in the next two games, before bad weather washed out all four remaining fixtures.

Batting The leading batsman was M. Diamond, who hit 102 runs at 34.00.

Bowling The leading bowler was W. Robbins, who took seven wickets at 4.00.

Stowe School *Buckinghamshire* P14 W5 L6 T1 D2 A3

Master i/c J. A. Knott **Coach** H. J. L. Swayne

A young side had mixed results, though since all but one of the final XI return, there is confidence for 2020. Year 11 James Cronie was the leading run-scorer and wicket-taker, and he played for Northamptonshire Seconds. (He also scored heavily for the county Under-17 side, who won the ECB 50-over competition.) Captain Rufus Easdale was a real threat with the new ball, and turned out for Suffolk.

Batting J. P. Cronie 530 at 37.85; G. S. Holmes 249 at 24.90; J. A. L. Mercer 286 at 20.42; E. W. Snushall 195 at 19.50; R. J. Noble 163 at 16.30.

Bowling O. N. J. Taylor 12 at 20.33; J. P. Cronie 17 at 23.23; *R. E. A. Easdale 14 at 28.50.

Sutton Valence School *Kent*   P11 W4 L4 D3

Master i/c V. J. Wells

A young team performed reasonably, with four victories – and draws against MCC and the Band of Brothers. Arthur Genders was the top wicket-taker, and Ben Watkins top run-scorer. With just three leavers, the team should fare better still in 2020.

Batting O. J. Payne-Cook 255 at 42.50; B. P. W. Watkins 285 at 31.66; J. J. Stanton-Gleaves 205 at 20.50.

Bowling A. C. Genders 14 at 21.35; G. A. U. Baker 10 at 24.70; M. D. Savage 12 at 25.33.

Taunton School *Somerset*   P14 W7 L6 D1

Master i/c P. N. Sanderson   **Coach** M. E. Trescothick

Results were good: the first XI were unbeaten on Saturdays until after half-term, and there were block wins against Blundell's, Colston's and Bristol Grammar School. The school squeezed past Millfield courtesy of a bowl-out after the teams tied in the National T20. Harry Ledger led the batting, and Thomas Walsh the bowling.

Batting C. J. Harding 261 at 43.50; H. F. M. Ledger 239 at 26.55.

Bowling The leading bowler was T. R. Walsh, who took eight wickets at 19.00.

Tiffin School *Surrey*   P12 W3 L7 D2 A2

Masters i/c K. Balasubramaniam and M. J. Williams

Such a short and interrupted season did not produce an outstanding set of results. Exams again played havoc with senior sides, but the school are working to find solutions to this desperate problem.

Batting S. Patel 205 at 34.16; *S. Shori 248 at 31.00; T. E. S. Jones 151 at 18.87.

Bowling R. Ikram 11 at 10.27; P. Sivagnanasundaram 11 at 16.18; T. E. S. Jones 11 at 21.72.

Tonbridge School *Kent*   P21 W16 L2 T1 D2 A2

Master i/c C. D. Morgan   **Coach** I. Baldock

The first XI went unbeaten in the Cowdrey Cup (retaining the trophy) and Saturday fixtures, and in the National T20, though their run ended after tying a quarter-final: they had lost nine wickets to Merchant Taylors' eight. The outstanding batsman was Ben Robinson, who hit over 800 runs, while the bowling had a balance of seam and spin; slow left-armer Harry Bevan-Thomas took 29 wickets.

Batting *J. J. O'Riordan 652 at 46.57; H. C. Bevan-Thomas 507 at 46.09; B. J. E. Robinson 809 at 44.94; M. D. Purves 396 at 36.00; F. E. H. Geffen 459 at 32.78; S. O. Gilliland 220 at 22.00; T. J. J. Tribe 229 at 20.81; S. M. Hadfield 244 at 17.42; T. S. A. Geffen 154 at 17.11.

Bowling A. A. Ramanathan 10 at 17.10; H. C. Bevan-Thomas 29 at 17.27; S. O. Gilliland 18 at 23.77; S. M. Hadfield 13 at 25.23; J. A. S. Dare 12 at 25.23; E. A. J. Surguy 26 at 26.00; F. E. H. Geffen 26 at 27.80; T. J. Masding 12 at 29.33.

Trent College *Derbyshire*   P9 W4 L5 A6

Master i/c S. A. J. Boswell   **Coach** P. Johnson

It proved a challenging summer for a young first team, not helped by the weather stealing six games. The highlight was an end-of-season victory over a good Norwich side.

Batting N. J. Gillingham 160 at 22.85; *A. D. Moore 161 at 17.88; F. S. Landa 156 at 17.33.

Bowling S. G. Westbrook 12 at 13.91; F. S. Landa 10 at 15.60; S. Q. Haider 11 at 17.18.

Trinity School *Surrey*   P15 W8 L7

Master i/c S. D. Schofield   **Coach** A. D. Brown

The school enjoyed a year of steady progress; a young squad, intelligently captained by Fin Baker, were a pleasure to coach.

Batting F. R. G. Harris 294 at 36.75; *F. S. Baker 276 at 25.09; A. J. Burcombe 164 at 23.42; N. M. Johnsen 151 at 18.87; A. M. Zaborniak 254 at 18.14; A. M. Connaghton 158 at 15.80; A. Sabesan 167 at 15.18.

Bowling M. L. Cadiz 25 at 16.88; M. A. Lilley 19 at 18.00; F. S. Baker 13 at 23.07; A. Sabesan 14 at 23.35.

University College School, Hampstead *Middlesex* P16 W7 L8 D1 A1
Master i/c D. J. Brown   **Coaches** A. P. van der Looy and A. R. Wilkes
After the departure of key players the year before, 2019 was a time of rebuilding. The side had an adroit captain in Henry Raschke, and his batting proved crucial. Joel Grabinar's pace was also a potent weapon. Late-season successes augur well.
Batting *H. L. Raschke 417 at 46.33; J. A. Grabinar 245 at 20.41; A. J. Pemberton 255 at 18.21; S. Giacopazzi 184 at 15.33.
Bowling J. A. Grabinar 29 at 9.10; M. A. Charles 13 at 13.00; D. E. L. Rendell 13 at 15.46; S. Giacopazzi 15 at 26.53.

Victoria College, Jersey *Channel Islands* P10 W4 L6
Master i/c M. D. Smith   **Coach** E. C. Corbel
Openers Josh Lawrenson and Patrick Gouge created history by both hitting back-to-back hundreds; Gouge's 172 against Elizabeth College was Victoria's second-highest score. Dylan Kotedia and Ben Le Gallais led the bowling.
Batting P. B. Gouge 370 at 92.50; J. A. D. Lawrenson 397 at 79.40; T. E. R. Heelis 213 at 26.62.
Bowling B. C. Le Gallais 14 at 17.50; D. M. Kotedia 14 at 18.14; *E. J. W. Giles 13 at 18.53; R. G. Forrest 10 at 30.40.

Warwick School *Warwickshire* P16 W3 L13 A3
Master i/c S. R. G. Francis
It was a tough year. A team effort was required on all fronts, and sadly the school could manage only three victories. Ibrahim Afzal was the pick of the squad with bat and ball.
Batting I. I. Afzal 479 at 36.84; J. A. Treasure 213 at 23.66; *H. W. Mortimer 233 at 17.92; R. S. Mohan 168 at 15.27.
Bowling I. I. Afzal 22 at 21.95; H. J. Chambers 17 at 27.17.

Watford Grammar School for Boys *Hertfordshire* P13 W9 L3 D1 A2
Master i/c L. Samarasinghe   **Coach** A. Needham
This was a brilliant season. Watford, a state-funded school, are fortunate to have four pitches, allowing up to 17 sides to play block fixtures every Saturday against many of the independent schools in the area.
Batting E. J. Stock 372 at 41.33; K. S. Patel 229 at 32.71; H. W. A. Kendal 242 at 30.25; Y. Malhotra 205 at 15.76; S. K. Manzoor 170 at 15.45.
Bowling Y. Malhotra 26 at 10.69; B. C. Beesley 16 at 15.31; S. K. Manzoor 12 at 20.41.

Wellingborough School *Northamptonshire* P12 W6 L4 D2 A1
Master i/c G. E. Houghton   **Coach** L. M. Sharples
A quieter season than usual included notable victories over Stamford, Bloxham and the XL Club. Against Leicester GS, James Sales – son of Northamptonshire stalwart David – hit a century *and* took a hat-trick; Joshua Griffiths claimed six for four against Kimbolton.
Batting N. J. Piper 328 at 54.66; J. J. G. Sales 331 at 47.28; *J. R. Clarke 152 at 21.71; M. W. Mills 170 at 18.88.
Bowling J. H. Griffiths 21 at 10.71; J. J. G. Sales 16 at 12.81; O. J. Bevan 10 at 16.10; J. R. Clarke 12 at 19.33; C. T. Blake 13 at 26.15.

Wellington College *Berkshire* P21 W9 L7 T1 D4
Master i/c D. M. Pratt   **Coach** H. Grice
When the side played as a group, they recorded excellent wins, including Radley and a strong Oakham. The captain, Archie Carter, dominated the batting; although Harry Petrie opened the bowling with real pace, the attack was largely based around spin.
Batting *A. R. Carter 869 at 54.31; M. A. C. Keast 644 at 33.89; M. S. Bradbury 494 at 30.87; J. A. D. Lewis 212 at 26.50; C. R. Bradbury 262 at 26.20; R. S. Hanekom 163 at 23.28; M. P. O'Donoghue 278 at 21.38; M. J. Watson 223 at 13.11.
Bowling H. W. Petrie 27 at 16.74; J. N. Masih 18 at 24.44; M. S. Bradbury 20 at 25.00; M. P. O'Donoghue 21 at 26.14; S. F. Daniel 15 at 26.86; M. N. D. Thomas 15 at 29.33.

Wellington School *Somerset*   P14 W7 L6 D1 A9
Master i/c P. S. Lawrence
With nine fixtures abandoned and a tenth rained off after play had started, this was a damp, disappointing summer. Even so, Harry Donelan claimed 20 wickets, and Liam Naylor hit 517 runs.
Batting L. Naylor 517 at 51.70; A. Joshi 316 at 26.33; T. Brooks 364 at 24.26; *O. O'Livey 165 at 20.62.
Bowling C. Dourado 14 at 15.00; H. Donelan 20 at 15.15; N. Pickering 13 at 18.84.

Wells Cathedral School *Somerset*   P11 W6 L4 D1 A3
Master i/c J. A. Boot   **Coach** D. M. J. Peck
Fine wins over Queen's Taunton and Queen Elizabeth Hospital School, plus a battling draw against MCC, were highlights. Jacob Potts was denied a first hundred for the school by a superb caught and bowled; Sahil Jadhav, though, batted outstandingly to reach three figures against MCC.
Batting S. Jadhav 165 at 55.00; J. J. D. Potts 403 at 44.77; B. Ake 161 at 20.12.
Bowling J. J. D. Potts 15 at 17.86; A. J. Padgett 10 at 19.10.

Wellsway School *Somerset*   P9 W4 L4 D1
Master i/c R. May
The season turned out better than expected, given the youth of the team, and there is optimism for 2020. Sam Lowe hit a century against Beechen Cliff, and 85 against the XL Club a few days later.
Batting S. Lowe 268 at 44.66; M. Saleem 200 at 40.00; S. Parsons 89 at 29.66; B. Clarke 164 at 27.33.
Bowling B. Clarke 10 at 14.30; *W. Burston 11 at 15.54.

Westminster School *Middlesex*   P10 W5 L5 A4
Master i/c J. D. Kershen   **Coach** S. K. Ranasinghe
The 1st XI were unpredictable – and much stronger at home than away. Captain Lucas McConnell set the example with bat and ball, while Angus Mackay and Junaid Ahmed played a few impressive innings. Bowlers Alex Gardiner, Arun Ghai, Gaurav Kocher and Will Whiu all showed promise, and over half the side should be available in 2020.
Batting A. R. Mackay 190 at 38.00; *L. F. McConnell 240 at 26.66; J. F. Ahmed 239 at 26.55.
Bowling G. Kocher 13 at 11.84; W. J. M. Whiu 10 at 13.00; A. A. K. Ghai 14 at 14.14; A. N. W. Gardiner 10 at 18.90; *L. F. McConnell 15 at 20.00.

Whitgift School *Surrey*   P15 W11 L3 D1
Master i/c D. M. Ward   **Coach** P. R. Hindmarch
The school played plenty of outstanding cricket in an enjoyable summer. The T20 campaign looked promising, but for the third year running ended in defeat by Merchant Taylors'. Nine of the first XI have departed, so some rebuilding is necessary.
Batting N. M. J. Reifer 255 at 85.00; J. A. Cleaver 311 at 38.87; J. A. G. Rodnight 292 at 32.44; N. Young 307 at 30.70; B. P. M. Sewell 419 at 26.18; G. W. M. Roberts 353 at 23.53; J. J. Baxter 160 at 20.00; R. L. A. Low 259 at 19.92.
Bowling *W. G. Heaver 26 at 14.23; M. Rana 11 at 15.09; H. J. Cutmore 10 at 15.40; N. Young 24 at 16.70; B. P. M. Sewell 20 at 19.45; S. J. Eyre 19 at 21.68; T. Patel 13 at 22.53.

Wilson's School *Surrey*   P16 W8 L6 T1 D1
Master i/c A. K. Parkinson   **Coach** C. K. Bullen
It was a busy term either side of the exam break; Pranav Madan hit a superb century against the XL Club, while Callum Furmidge, the 2020 captain, topped both averages. The outgoing skipper, Riley Jarrold, took 16 wickets.
Batting C. D. Furmidge 350 at 38.88; R. Gamage 241 at 34.42; P. Madan 431 at 33.15; A. C. Dutta 180 at 25.71; F. H. R. Michael 231 at 19.25.
Bowling C. D. Furmidge 18 at 9.27; *R. D. Jarrold 16 at 15.75; L. B. Tomas 10 at 22.90; R. Gamage 12 at 25.41; D. A. Read 10 at 34.40.

Winchester College *Hampshire*   P27 W14 L10 T1 D2
Master i/c G. E. Munn   **Coach** P. N. Gover
The first team had an excellent year, reaching the regional semi-final of the National Schools T20 (beating St Edward's on the way) and defeating Eton. Johnny Figy was the outstanding batsman, hitting 1,307 runs, while James Flatt took 40 wickets.

Batting J. J. Figy 1,307 at 65.35; H. C. Davis 375 at 31.25; F. J. Egleston 530 at 29.44; *S. A. Lee 437 at 27.31; C. A. S. Byers 389 at 24.31; J. T. F. Flatt 239 at 21.72; W. J. La Fontaine Jackson 189 at 21.00; J. S. Scull 194 at 16.16; H. E. A. Axtell 399 at 15.96.
Bowling J. T. F. Flatt 40 at 16.35; S. C. Tall 13 at 17.23; F. J. Egleston 25 at 25.60; W. E. H. Richards 12 at 31.83; J. J. Figy 18 at 32.66; J. S. Scull 21 at 33.23.

Woodbridge School *Suffolk*
P10 W6 L2 D2 A6

Master i/c I. J. Simpson   **Coach** D. Brous

Six wins and two draws from ten starts – six fixtures were abandoned – made it a successful year. Left-arm seamers Daniel Davies and Toby Stowe were superb, while Thomas Harper's off-spin gave good support. The batting was strong, too, especially the young opening pair of Daniel Norman and Thomas Harper, who shared a stand of 166. Benjamin Harper captained superbly.
Batting D. I. S. Norman 294 at 58.80; *B. E. Harper 266 at 53.20; T. A. Harper 371 at 41.22; D. R. Davies 171 at 28.50.
Bowling T. B. Stowe 14 at 12.35; D. R. Davies 14 at 16.21; T. A. Harper 10 at 30.80.

Woodhouse Grove School *Yorkshire*
P12 W6 L4 D2 A7

Master i/c R. I. Frost   **Coach** A. Sidebottom

Woodhouse Grove enjoyed a good term after a successful 12-day tour to Barbados and St Lucia in April. Owen Tennant shone with the bat, and was selected for Yorkshire Under-19s. Ian Frost retired as cricket master after 26 years.
Batting O. T. Tennant 527 at 47.90; J. O. Stephenson 274 at 39.14; R. Newman 295 at 26.81; H. Hart 223 at 24.77; S. Sola 215 at 17.91.
Bowling R. Newman 16 at 16.37; S. Sola 11 at 29.81.

Worksop College *Nottinghamshire*
P15 W10 L4 T1 A5

Master i/c N. J. Longhurst   **Coach** I. C. Parkin

A superb season culminated in victory at the Woodard Festival. There were outstanding wins against King's Taunton, Hurstpierpoint, Sedbergh and Repton, where Ruben Senekal smashed 186 runs. Seven bowlers took more than ten wickets.
Batting R. Senekal 570 at 47.50; *A. R. Shannon 432 at 36.00; O. M. Blackburn 436 at 31.14; P. K. Delahunty 365 at 30.41; J. D. Porter 295 at 24.58; J. du Toit 235 at 23.50; A. S. Winiarski 216 at 15.42.
Bowling A. R. Shannon 12 at 11.00; J. D. Porter 30 at 16.10; J. Blackburn 11 at 17.63; J. du Toit 17 at 17.76; O. M. Blackburn 18 at 19.22; I. Harris 14 at 19.35; C. Beaumont 13 at 25.46.

Worth School *Sussex*
P14 W5 L3 D6 A9

Master i/c R. Chaudhuri

The summer was split into two, the first part marred by weather and exam pressure, the second marked by the team hitting their stride. Akshay Ramani, Anish Padalkar, Krishan Nayee and Mali Lewis all passed 250 runs; Ramani and Nayee led the bowling.
Batting A. Padalkar 531 at 48.27; A. M. Ramani 568 at 47.33; *K. J. Nayee 313 at 44.71; J. M. Mcloughlin 206 at 25.75; M. B. Lewis 277 at 21.30.
Bowling K. J. Nayee 18 at 14.83; A. M. Ramani 20 at 21.30; M. B. Lewis 12 at 26.91.

Wrekin College *Shropshire*
P13 W3 L8 T1 D1 A2

Master i/c J. R. Mather   **Coach** J. Shaw

A young team who did their best to punch above their weight relied on a group of talented Year 11s. Luke Thornton was a real threat with the new ball, while Matthew Lamb, a Year 9, made useful runs at No. 3, as well as chipping in with his off-spin.
Batting P. J. Ward-Clayton 244 at 24.40; M. J. Lamb 217 at 24.11; L. Thornton 168 at 18.66; *O. G. Davies 119 at 11.90.
Bowling L. Thornton 12 at 14.66; M. J. Lamb 12 at 25.25.

Wycliffe College *Gloucestershire*
P10 W5 L4 D1 A4

Master i/c M. J. Kimber

The weather played havoc with the fixtures, but the highlight for an enthusiastic squad was reaching the regional semi-final of the National Twenty20. Will Naish, Will Salter and Matthew Cole dominated the batting, spinners Cole and Charlie Lister the bowling. Naish and Oliver Wood played for Gloucestershire Under-17s, Naish also turning out for the county Seconds.
Batting *W. L. Naish 179 at 59.66; W. Salter 175 at 58.33; M. C. Cole 236 at 33.71.
Bowling M. C. Cole 15 at 17.33; C. Lister 12 at 18.66.

STREET CHILD CRICKET WORLD CUP IN 2019

Isabelle Westbury

It is likely that, in years to come, the dramatic cricket that defined 2019 will enshroud everything else. Yet before the World Cup and Headingley, Lord's hosted a game which was always meant to transcend what happened on the pitch.

On a blustery day in early May, the Street Child Cricket World Cup reached its climax. Each team were given the opportunity to play on the sport's most famous surface and, by the evening, the summer's first world champions had been crowned. The accolade fell to India South, who eased to victory over England.

Organised by the British charity Street Child United, the tape-ball tournament was contested, in all, by eight teams; the others were Bangladesh, India North, Mauritius, Nepal, Tanzania and West Indies. Each consisted of children aged 14 to 17, who were either living on the streets, or at risk of doing so. After ten years of organising football tournaments and mini-Olympics, the charity were making their first foray into cricket. It was also the first time they had staged a mixed-gender event.

"When we were in Brazil [for the 2018 football tournament], an MCC member emailed me about this phenomenal impact we were having in places like India and Pakistan," said John Wroe, the charity's founder and CEO. "Seven thousand people met our Pakistan football team in Karachi on their return. But, they said, cricket is so much bigger than football in these countries. Why on earth are you not doing a cricket World Cup? I was then in India recently, and one of the young people said to me: 'Cricket is our religion, but Lord's is our temple.' And so it happened: the Street Child Cricket World Cup was born."

Street Child United aim to harness the power of sport to campaign against the widespread stigma and negative treatment faced by street-connected children. For the lucky few, this was a life-changing experience, a chance to swap stories and discuss how best to improve their plight.

But the impact is not confined to those attending: it is also a platform. There was a visit to the Houses of Parliament, and a general assembly, where young leaders delivered messages on behalf of street-connected children from each country. And there was widespread coverage; England's captain, Jasmin Akter, was included in the BBC's list of 100 inspiring and influential women from around the world. When the spotlight fades, then comes the behind-the-scenes political lobbying, the pro bono legal work, the day-to-day running of the charities.

The event itself was special. As one member recalled in MCC's magazine: "When the senior steward in the Long Room said that the day of the Street Child Cricket World Cup final was, as far as he was concerned, the most important of the year, in a year that would later see a World Cup final and an Ashes Test, that was a memorable moment."

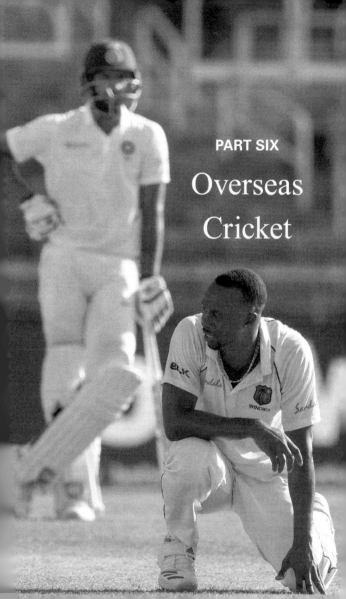

PART SIX

Overseas
Cricket

WORLD TEST CHAMPIONSHIP, 2019–2021

The 2019 Ashes was the first series to count towards the ICC's new World Test Championship. Aimed at giving context to all Tests, the Championship awards points for qualifying series, and culminates in a final, expected to be played at Lord's in 2021.

The first iteration, which runs from 2019 to early 2021, features the nine teams who led the Test rankings table in March 2018. They will play six qualifying series, three home and three away, each containing at least two games. Some series will not count towards the Championship: matches involving Afghanistan, Ireland and Zimbabwe, who were not included in the first cycle, and some others, including England's trip to New Zealand late in 2019, which had been arranged before the Championship schedule was drawn up.

A maximum of 120 points are available for each series, with the number on offer for individual matches varying according to how many games are played (see table below).

The early pace-setters were India, who won all seven matches in their three series that counted towards the Championship, beating South Africa 3–0, and West Indies and Bangladesh 2–0. That gave them the maximum of 360 points for the three whitewashes. Australia were second, after a drawn Ashes – both sides collected 56 points – was followed by full-points victories at home against Pakistan and New Zealand. England moved up to third after winning 3–1 in South Africa in early 2020.

CHAMPIONSHIP TABLE

		Series	Tests	W	L	D	Pen	Series wins	Pts
1	India	3	7	7	0	0	0	3	360
2	Australia	3	10	7	2	1	0	2	296
3	England	2	9	5	3	1	0	1	146
4	Pakistan	2	4	1	2	1	0	1	80
5	Sri Lanka	2	4	1	2	1	0	0	80
6	New Zealand	2	5	1	4	0	0	0	60
7	South Africa	2	7	1	6	0	6	0	24
8	West Indies	1	2	0	2	0	0	0	0
9	Bangladesh	1	2	0	2	0	0	0	0

Penalties are deducted for slow over-rates.
To January 28, 2020. Teams tied on points are separated first by the number of series won, and then by runs-per-wicket ratio (runs scored per wicket lost, divided by runs conceded per wicket taken).

HOW THE POINTS WORK

Up to 120 points are available for each series. How they are awarded for each match depends on the number of individual Tests played:

	Win	Draw	Tie
Five-Test series	24	8	12
Four-Test series	30	10	15
Three-Test series	40	13	20
Two-Test series	60	20	30

AFGHANISTAN CRICKET IN 2019

A crisis of leadership

Shahid Hashmi

A cute video of children celebrating Afghanistan's emphatic Test victory over Bangladesh at Chittagong in September went viral, demonstrating the interest of the country's younger population in cricket. To nurture them, however, it is vital that more matches are held in Afghanistan, as soon as possible. Fortunately, the Afghanistan Cricket Board, now under the chairmanship of Farhan Yusufzai, intend to make it happen.

"We are planning to construct an international-standard cricket ground in Kabul in the next three to five years to host international teams in the best possible way," the board announced in 2019. During the year, the Pakistan domestic team Habib Bank played matches in different formats in Kabul. A team from Tajikistan, and India's disability side, also toured. The board's plans need to come to fruition – home matches would lift the standard of

AFGHANISTAN IN 2019

	Played	Won	Lost	Drawn/No result
Tests	3	2	1	–
One-day internationals	20	4	15	1
Twenty20 internationals	10	7	3	–

JANUARY		
FEBRUARY	1 Test, 5 ODIs and 3 T20Is (in India) v Ireland	(page 862)
MARCH		
APRIL		
MAY	2 ODIs (a) v Scotland	(page 1104)
	2 ODIs (a) v Ireland	(page 972)
JUNE	World Cup (in England)	(page 237)
JULY		
AUGUST		
SEPTEMBER	1 Test (a) v Bangladesh	(page 914)
	T20I tri-series (in Bangladesh) v Bangladesh and Zimbabwe	(page 917)
OCTOBER		
NOVEMBER	1 Test, 3 ODIs and 3 T20Is (in India) v West Indies	(page 869)
DECEMBER		

For a review of Afghanistan domestic cricket in 2019, see page 873.

Trading places: Gulbadeen Naib and the man he controversially supplanted, Asghar Afghan, during the World Cup match against India.

Afghanistan's cricket, which has already made great strides, and build on the burgeoning interest.

So would more Tests: Afghanistan played just three in 2019. The win over Bangladesh was the highlight, though in March they easily defeated fellow newcomers Ireland at Dehradun in India. They switched to Lucknow for an end-of-year match against West Indies, but suffered a three-day thumping. Soberingly, they were outperformed in spin bowling, an area that is usually their strongest suit.

A dismal World Cup was at the centre of an ODI year that was an unmitigated disaster. There was evidence of muddled thinking in April, when Asghar Afghan was replaced as captain by Gulbadeen Naib. The move was criticised by leading players Rashid Khan and Mohammad Nabi, an early indicator that the squad were far from unified. "With just months to go for such a mega event like World Cup, changing the captain will cause uncertainty, and team morale will be affected," said Rashid, presciently. Once the tournament began, there was controversy when wicketkeeper Mohammad Shahzad was sent home with what was reported as a knee injury. Once he got there, he posted a tearful video insisting he was fit. Fast bowler Aftab Alam was also back home before his team-mates, after a disciplinary infringement.

Late in the competition, they came close to beating India and Pakistan, only to lose their nerve in tight finishes. The match against Pakistan at Headingley seemed within their grasp, until Gulbadeen brought himself back on, and conceded 18 off the over. Nine matches brought nine defeats and the wooden spoon – a crushing disappointment after all the progress, not least for the ex-pat fans who turned out in large numbers.

Regular leadership changes suggested confusion over future direction – or maybe the involvement of politics at board level. When Asghar was sacked, Rahmat Shah was named as Test captain, while Rashid got the T20 job. But after the World Cup shambles, Rashid was appointed leader across all formats. He began triumphantly with the Test win in Bangladesh but, after the defeat by West Indies, it was recognised that taking on the leadership, as well as being the main strike weapon, was too much of a burden. Asghar was reinstated, with Rashid his deputy. Fans were left to ponder how differently the World Cup might have panned out without the turbulence. A forgettable year in 50-over cricket ended with a 3–0 whitewash by West Indies.

The story was a lot brighter in T20 cricket, the format the Afghans regard as their best. They beat the Irish 3–0 in the spring, shared a tri-series with the hosts in Bangladesh, and – most impressively – defeated West Indies 2–1 at the end of the year. They can approach the Twenty20 World Cup in Australia later this year with realistic hopes of causing an upset or two.

Yusufzai took office soon after the World Cup. His plans include making the board financially viable. Further ahead, he wants to develop facilities that will help turn the enthusiasm for the game into a regular supply of talent. "Although the ACB is not getting enough funds from ICC in comparison to other Full Member nations, we manage to avoid a financial crisis while having such busy domestic and international competitions, as well running administration, development and infrastructure," said a board statement.

There were encouraging signs from the Under-19s, who reached the semi-finals of two Asia Cup tournaments. And domestic cricket appears to be thriving, with a wide range of competitions in all formats. Matches in the Shpageeza T20 competition were shown live on Afghan television, creating huge interest.

AFGHANISTAN v IRELAND IN INDIA IN 2018-19

IAN CALLENDER

Twenty20 internationals (3): Afghanistan 3, Ireland 0
One-day internationals (5): Afghanistan 2, Ireland 2
Test match (1): Afghanistan 1, Ireland 0

Ireland's first Test tour was always going to be tough: they were facing Afghanistan, who had one of the best spin attacks in world cricket, on turning tracks. A share of the 50-over series – one of the five games fell victim to the weather – was for the Irish the highlight of the four-week trip. For the Afghans, though, there was a predictable 3–0 sweep in the T20s, when their opponents' lack of big hitters was exposed. After the ODIs came the Test which, played on a used surface, brought Afghanistan their first victory.

Three pitches were prepared at Dehradun but early on match referee Javagal Srinath ruled the proposed Test wicket out of bounds, so all nine games were played on just two strips. That prompted Ireland to leave Boyd Rankin, their attack leader, out of the white-ball games despite having struck every 25 deliveries in the white-ball games; he still finished as their leading wicket-taker, with 13. In the Test, Ireland fielded four slow bowlers – five, if Paul Stirling was included. George Dockrell's left-arm spin improved as the trip wore on, and he claimed 11 victims in all.

Not that he could match the success of his Afghan counterparts. They dictated many of the nine games, and the fortunes of leg-spinner Rashid Khan often determined the result. In the Twenty20s, he took 11 of the 19 Irish wickets to fall to bowlers, while in the Test he had figures of seven for 102. In the ODIs, he was limited to five wickets, if at a healthy economy-rate of 3.9.

Rashid proved he was more than a world-class bowler when he made his fourth international fifty – his third against Ireland – to help swing the fourth ODI. The captain, Asghar Afghan, was the most consistent batsman, hitting 226 runs in the 50-over games, and a half-century in the Test. With the World Cup looming, Afghanistan rang the changes, using 19 players in the one-dayers (and 30 across the three formats). Ireland looked enviously at their strength in depth. One player to make a splash was the 20-year-old Hazratullah Zazai, who ransacked the Irish attack en route to an unbeaten 162, the joint-third-highest score in all Twenty20 cricket. The Afghan total was an outright record 278 for three.

Andrew Balbirnie and Stirling were the only Irishmen to top 300 runs at Dehradun, though Dockrell's batting offered encouragement: he contributed 215. The old guard, on whom Ireland had long depended, had mixed fortunes. Kevin O'Brien's bat was more productive than William Porterfield's – 274 runs rather than 51 – while Tim Murtagh (five wickets at 52) did not rival Rankin's returns. Still, there were signs of the next generation. All-rounder Shane Getkate played throughout the T20 series, while batsman James McCollum and slow left-armer James Cameron-Dow won debuts during the

ODIs. They were the first new caps awarded by Graham Ford since he was appointed coach in December 2017. All three were well into their twenties.

It was a shame DRS proved too expensive. Though Porterfield insisted it was the same for both sides, Ireland suffered more: Stirling was given lbw in the Test despite an inside edge.

IRELAND TOURING PARTY

*W. T. S. Porterfield (T/50), A. Balbirnie (T/50/20), J. Cameron-Dow (T/50), P. K. D. Chase (50/20), G. H. Dockrell (T/50/20), S. C. Getkate (20), J. B. Little (20), A. R. McBrine (T/50/20), B. J. McCarthy (T/50), J. A. McCollum (T/50), T. J. Murtagh (T/50), K. J. O'Brien (T/50/20), S. W. Poynter (T/50/20), W. B. Rankin (T/50/20), J. N. K. Shannon (20), S. Singh (T/50/20), P. R. Stirling (T/50/20), H. T. Tector (20), S. R. Thompson (T/20), L. J. Tucker (T/50/20). *Coach:* G. X. Ford.

Stirling captained in the Twenty20 matches.

First Twenty20 international   At Dehradun, February 21, 2019 (floodlit). **Afghanistan won by five wickets.** ‡Ireland 132-6 (20 overs) (G. H. Dockrell 34*, S. W. Poynter 31*); **Afghanistan 136-5** (19.2 overs) (Mohammad Nabi 49*, Najibullah Zadran 40*). *PoM:* Mohammad Nabi. *A stand of 86* between Mohammad Nabi and Najibullah Zadran steered Afghanistan to victory from a precarious 50-5, and left Paul Stirling ruing his decision to bat. Evening dew made it tricky for the bowlers and, though Afghanistan needed 41 from five overs, a flurry of boundaries hurried them home. Ireland had slumped to 65-6 after Rashid Khan took two wickets in his first four balls. But fears he would run through the lower order were unfounded: George Dockrell and Stuart Poynter doubled the total in eight overs. Afghanistan made far greater use of spin. Rashid, Nabi and Mujeeb Zadran took a combined 5-57 from 12 overs, while Ireland's slow bowlers sent down only nine deliveries, three when a hamstring problem forced Stuart Thompson to hobble from the field.*

AFGHANISTAN v IRELAND

Second Twenty20 international

At Dehradun, February 23, 2019 (floodlit). Afghanistan won by 84 runs. Toss: Afghanistan.

In a match dominated by the bat, the left-handed Hazratullah Zazai scorched a breathtaking unbeaten 162 from 62 balls. If that was not quite the record for Twenty20 internationals – Aaron Finch hit 172 for Australia against Zimbabwe at Harare in 2018 – this game did set several new marks. Between them, the Afghans pinged 22 sixes, of which Hazratullah contributed 16; both were unparalleled in T20Is. The superlatives went on: Afghanistan's total of 278, and the 236 put on by the openers, were records in all T20s. Hazratullah reached his first fifty from 25 balls, his second from 17 and his third from 16, and his overall strike-rate was 261. He gave two chances, on 72 and 113. Usman Ghani was no slouch and, when he brought up his fifty, from 31 balls, Afghanistan were 146-0 in the 12th over. The pace never slackened, and they crashed 72 off the last four. The mayhem continued at the start of Ireland's reply and, after eight overs, Stirling and O'Brien had put them fractionally ahead: 90 against 89. But they were slowed by Rashid Khan, and the pressure told. O'Brien fell at 126 – an all-wicket Irish record – while Stirling made 91, another national record, from 50 balls. After his dismissal, though, they managed only 60 from 41. Rashid emerged with figures of four for 25; the Irish bowlers had no wish to revisit the scorecard.

Player of the Match: Hazratullah Zazai.

Afghanistan

		B	4/6
1 Hazratullah Zazai *not out*	162	62	11/16
2 Usman Ghani *c 9 b 10*	73	48	7/3
3 †Shafiqullah Shafaq *c 4 b 11* .	7	3	0/1
4 Mohammad Nabi *b 9*	17	5	1/1
5 Najibullah Zadran *not out* . . .	1	2	0
Lb 4, w 14	18		

6 overs: 64-0 (20 overs) 278-3

1/236 2/256 3/273

6 *Asghar Afghan, 7 Samiullah Shenwari, 8 Karim Janat, 9 Rashid Khan, 10 Mujeeb Zadran and 11 Fareed Ahmad did not bat.

12th man Najeeb Tarakai.

Little 4–10–49–1; Rankin 4–10–35–1; Chase 3–5–43–1; Dockrell 2–1–24–0; Getkate 3–2–48–0; Singh 1–0–16–0; Stirling 1–1–24–0; O'Brien 2–1–35–0.

Ireland

		B	4/6
1 *P. R. Stirling *c 12 b 10* . . .	91	50	12/2
2 K. J. O'Brien *c 8 b 11*	37	25	2/2
3 A. Balbirnie *b 9*	2	4	0
4 L. J. Tucker *c 4 b 9*	2	5	0
5 S. C. Getkate *lbw b 9*	24	16	1/2
6 G. H. Dockrell *b 9*	0	1	0
7 S. Singh *not out*	17	12	1/1
8 †S. W. Poynter *not out*	15	7	1/1
W 6	6		

6 overs: 69-0 (20 overs) 194-6

1/126 2/134 3/134 4/143 5/150 6/165

9 J. B. Little, 10 W. B. Rankin and 11 P. K. D. Chase did not bat.

Mujeeb Zadran 4–10–30–1; Fareed Ahmad 3–5–45–1; Mohammad Nabi 3–2–36–0; Karim Janat 4–8–30–0; Samiullah Shenwari 2–0–28–0; Rashid Khan 4–7–25–4.

Umpires: Ahmed Shah Durrani and Bismillah Shinwari. Third umpire: Ahmed Shah Pakteen.
Referee: J. Srinath.

Third Twenty20 international At Dehradun, February 24, 2019 (floodlit). **Afghanistan won by 32 runs.** Afghanistan 210-7 (20 overs) (Hazratullah Zazai 31, Mohammad Nabi 81; W. B. Rankin 3-53); ‡Ireland 178-8 (20 overs) (K. J. O'Brien 74, A. Balbirnie 47; Rashid Khan 5-27). *PoM:* Mohammad Nabi. *PoS:* Mohammad Nabi. *T20I debut:* Ziaur Rahman (Afghanistan). *Rashid became the first player in over 700 Twenty20 internationals to claim four wickets in four balls as Afghanistan sailed to a tenth successive victory over Ireland in the format. No one at the ground realised Rashid's third wicket had brought a hat-trick, because his first – snuffing out O'Brien's highest T20I innings – ended the 16th over. When Rashid dismissed Dockrell and Shane Getkate, there was no mass celebration. That came when a googly trapped Simi Singh, to leave Ireland, needing 211, shipwrecked on 158-7. Rashid added a fifth to give him his second T20I five-for, both against Ireland. Until his intervention, Ireland had been in the reckoning, thanks to a second-wicket stand of 96 between O'Brien and Andrew Balbirnie. Debutant seamer Ziaur Rahman broke the partnership, and Ireland managed only 50 from the remaining 38 balls. By contrast, Afghanistan had made 99 from the last 42, with Mohammad Nabi (81 from 36) running amok.*

First one-day international At Dehradun, February 28, 2019 (day/night). **Afghanistan won by five wickets.** ‡Ireland 161 (49.2 overs) (P. R. Stirling 89, G. H. Dockrell 37; Dawlat Zadran 3-35, Mujeeb Zadran 3-14); Afghanistan 165-5 (41.5 overs) (Mohammad Shahzad 43, Gulbadeen Naib 46). *PoM:* Gulbadeen Naib. *ODI debut:* J. A. McCollum (Ireland). *Mujeeb Zadran, opening the bowling on a slow pitch, did not concede a run until his fourth over – and by its end he had figures of 4–3–2–3. His victims included Ireland captain William Porterfield and James McCollum, out first ball on debut. Ireland's cautious approach meant they were 91-6 after 38 overs; without Stirling, who brought up his half-century from 105 deliveries, comfortably his slowest in ODIs, things would have been far worse. He was last out for 89, having gained support from Dockrell – they put on 76 for the seventh wicket – but no one else. In all, there were six lbws, with Dawlat Zadran claiming three. Mohammad Shahzad, omitted from the T20 squad, set Afghanistan on course for an undemanding target of 162. Two wickets in four balls from Boyd Rankin proved an inconvenience, but no more, and Gulbadeen Naib steered them to within touching distance of victory.*

Second one-day international At Dehradun, March 2, 2019 (day/night). **No result.** ‡Afghanistan 250-7 (48.3 overs) (Hazratullah Zazai 67, Rahmat Shah 54, Hashmatullah Shahidi 52; G. H. Dockrell 3-51) v Ireland. *ODI debuts:* Ikram Alikhil, Sayed Shirzad (Afghanistan); J. Cameron-Dow (Ireland). *Rain drove the players off nine balls before the end of the first innings, never to return. Ireland felt they had the momentum after Afghanistan slipped from 226-4 in the 43rd; three batsmen scored half-centuries, but none went on. A debut for James Cameron-Dow, a 28-year-old slow left-armer* *from South Africa with an Irish passport, meant the visitors fielded four specialist spinners. His first over cost 18, with Hazratullah helping himself to two sixes and a four.*

Third one-day international At Dehradun, March 5, 2019 (day/night). **Ireland won by four wickets.** ‡**Afghanistan 256-8** (50 overs) (Hazratullah Zazai 34, Asghar Afghan 75, Najibullah Zadran 104*); **Ireland 260-6** (49 overs) (A. Balbirnie 145*, G. H. Dockrell 54). PoM: A. Balbirnie. *Balbirnie's 145* guided Ireland to their first victory of the tour. It was their highest score against a Full Member (though Ed Joyce had a higher score against Afghanistan as an Associate). In 49*

HIGHEST ODI SCORES FOR IRELAND

177	P. R. Stirling	v Canada at Toronto		2010
160*	E. C. Joyce	v Afghanistan at Belfast		2016
145*	**A. Balbirnie**	**v Afghanistan at Dehradun**		**2018-19**
142	K. J. O'Brien	v Kenya at Nairobi (Ruaraka)		2006-07
139	W. T. S. Porterfield	v UAE at Dubai (ICC Academy)		2017-18
135	**A. Balbirnie**	**v West Indies at Malahide**		**2019**
130	**P. R. Stirling**	**v Bangladesh at Clontarf**		**2019**
126	P. R. Stirling	v UAE at Harare		2017-18

previous ODI innings, he had managed eight sixes; now he hit eight in one sitting. His century, made on a turning pitch against a world-class spin attack, was the best innings in the Ireland colours since Kevin O'Brien scored 113 against England at the 2011 World Cup. His stand of 143 with Dockrell rescued Ireland from 73-4. Balbirnie reached his third ODI century from 111 balls, then scorched 45 from his next 25. Afghanistan had seemed out of sight after walloping 93 off the final ten overs, with Najibullah – whose second fifty came from 22 deliveries – bringing up his maiden century in the last, two balls after being dropped on 97. The costliest miss, though, happened in the 20th, when Asghar Afghan, on 18, survived a stumping chance that would have left them 74-6; his eventual 75 helped set a testing target.

Fourth one-day international At Dehradun, March 8, 2019 (day/night). **Afghanistan won by 109 runs. Afghanistan 223** (49.1 overs) (Asghar Afghan 54, Mohammad Nabi 64, Rashid Khan 52; J. Cameron-Dow 3-32); ‡**Ireland 114** (35.3 overs) (Aftab Alam 4-25). PoM: Rashid Khan. *With the World Cup in mind, Afghanistan made several changes – and still proved too good for Ireland, who slumped to their eighth-lowest ODI total. In his only game of the series, opening bowler Aftab Alam took four wickets, including three in nine balls as Ireland collapsed from 90-5 to 114 all out. O'Brien was top scorer with a boundaryless 26 from 57, while Balbirnie followed a century with a duck. Afghanistan had earlier staggered to 81-6, but recovered thanks first to the efforts of Asghar, then Nabi and Rashid, who put on 86.*

Fifth one-day international At Dehradun, March 10, 2019 (day/night). **Ireland won by five wickets. Afghanistan 216-6** (50 overs) (Asghar Afghan 82*, Mohammad Nabi 40, Rashid Khan 35*); ‡**Ireland 219-5** (47.2 overs) (P. R. Stirling 70, A. Balbirnie 68, K. J. O'Brien 33*). PoM: Asghar Afghan. PoS: A. Balbirnie. ODI debut: Zahir Khan (Afghanistan). *Ireland, fielding the same team for the fourth game running, pulled off a series-levelling victory. They relied heavily on their spinners, who bowled all but 11 overs and produced their best display of the tour, limiting Afghanistan to 216-6 – though they dropped at least three chances and conceded 50 off the last four overs. Porterfield and Stirling managed their only half-century opening stand of the series, ended when debutant left-arm wrist-spinner Zahir Khan bowled Porterfield with a wrong'un. Stirling had made 70 when he fell lbw, despite replays showing he was hit outside the line; with no DRS, it proved Rashid's 200th international wicket. Ten short of the target, Balbirnie, to his evident disgust, was bowled by the economical Mujeeb Zadran (10–2–26–1); O'Brien's unbeaten 33 helped settle matters. The Afghanistan innings had followed a familiar pattern: early wickets followed by middle-order recovery. From 50-4, Asghar added 76 with Nabi and 65 with Rashid, before retiring hurt in the last over. He did not retake the field, yet surprisingly won the match award.*

AFGHANISTAN v IRELAND

Only Test

At Dehradun, March 15–18, 2019. Afghanistan won by seven wickets. Toss: Ireland. Test debuts: Ihsanullah Janat, Ikram Alikhil, Waqar Salamkheil; J. Cameron-Dow, G. H. Dockrell, A. R. McBrine, J. A. McCollum, S. W. Poynter.

On the stroke of lunch on the fourth day, Afghanistan became the fourth of Test cricket's 12 teams to win one of their first two matches. Only Australia and England (in the first series of all, back in 1876-77) and Pakistan (in 1952-53) had broken their duck so quickly.

The result was effectively decided on the first morning, when Ireland slumped to 69 for eight; despite a last-wicket stand of 87 more than doubling the score, they were always playing catch-up. There were similarities between this and Ireland's maiden Test at Malahide the previous May, when they hit 130 and 339, and set Pakistan a target of 160. Here they scored 172 and 288, which challenged Afghanistan to make 147. They managed it more easily than did Pakistan, thanks partly to Rahmat Shah's second half-century of the game.

Afghanistan made three changes from their first Test, when they lost to India inside two days, giving debuts to 18-year-old wicketkeeper Ikram Alikhil, opening batsman Ihsanullah Janat and 17-year-old left-arm wrist-spinner Waqar Salamkheil. Meanwhile, Cricket Ireland president Aideen Rice handed caps to batsman James McCollum, playing only his

OLDEST No. 11s TO HIT A TEST FIFTY

Years	Days			
37	292	P. L. Symcox (54). . . .	South Africa v Australia at Adelaide	1997-98
37	**225**	**T. J. Murtagh (54*). .**	**Ireland v Afghanistan at Dehradun.**	**2018-19**
34	284	G. D. McGrath (61). .	Australia v New Zealand at Brisbane	2004-05
32	364	R. M. Hogg (52)	Australia v West Indies at Georgetown.	1983-84
31	347	J. M. Anderson (81) . .	England v India at Nottingham	2014
31	193	F. R. Spofforth (50). .	Australia v England at Melbourne	1884-85
31	109	S. Shillingford (53*) . .	West Indies v New Zealand at Kingston.	2014
30	289	T. L. Best (95).	West Indies v England at Birmingham	2012
30	105	Ghulam Ahmed (50). .	India v Pakistan at Delhi	1952-53

second international, Durham wicketkeeper Stuart Poynter, and three slow bowlers: Andy McBrine, James Cameron-Dow and George Dockrell. On a slow surface which had already staged three internationals (two Twenty20s and a one-dayer), they also preferred all-rounder Thompson to the extra pace of Boyd Rankin.

Porterfield chose to bat but, after Ireland reached 37 for none, nine wickets tumbled for 48, with spinners Mohammad Nabi, Rashid Khan and Salamkheil all grabbing at least two. With the score 85, out strode Murtagh. During the one-day series, he had faced three balls and made two ducks, and he had not reached 50 in any cricket since 2011, the year before his Ireland debut. But now he outscored Dockrell to reach a counter-attacking half-century from 72 balls.

In the reply, Rahmat moved to Afghanistan's first Test fifty, from a steady 121 balls. And with Hashmatullah Shahidi following suit, from 140, they were in control at 198 for two, the third-wicket pair having added 130. But then Hashmatullah missed an attempted sweep against an off-break from McBrine, and the momentum slipped. Despite another fifty, from Asghar Afghan, the Irish began to inch their way back. The last eight fell for 116, including Rahmat, nervously deflecting the ball on to his stumps on 98. The wickets were spread around, with Thompson claiming three, to add to the four he had taken at Malahide.

Ireland, trailing by 142, lost Porterfield before the end of the second day – and Stirling next morning when umpire Ravi failed to see a thick inside edge. There was no DRS. Balbirnie, after a pair on Test debut and a single scoring shot on the first day, made a classy 82 to lead a recovery. But he and McCollum had both gone by the time the deficit was erased. Rashid took his fifth five-for against Ireland, who again benefited from Murtagh's bat. This time the tenth wicket added 58, pushing the lead into three figures. For only the third time in Tests, a team had added 50 or more for the last wicket in both innings; Murtagh also became the first Test No. 11 to reach 25 in both innings.

TOP-SCORING FROM No. 11 IN TESTS

F. R. Spofforth (50/163)	Australia v England at Melbourne	1884-85
T. R. McKibbin (16/44)	Australia v England at The Oval	1896
A. E. E. Vogler (62*/333)	South Africa v England at Cape Town	1905-06
Asif Masood (9*/199)	Pakistan v West Indies at Lahore	1974-75
A. M. J. G. Amerasinghe (34/215)	Sri Lanka v New Zealand at Kandy	1983-84
Talha Jubair (31/124)	Bangladesh v India at Chittagong	2004-05
S. J. Harmison (42/304)	England v South Africa at Cape Town	2004-05
N. M. Lyon (14/47)	Australia v South Africa at Cape Town	2011-12
A. C. Agar (98/280)	Australia v England at Nottingham	2013
S. Shillingford (53*/216)	West Indies v New Zealand at Kingston	2014
T. J. Murtagh (54*/172)	**Ireland v Afghanistan at Dehradun**	**2018-19**

These were no more than crumbs of comfort. Ireland needed early breakthroughs on the fourth morning, and one should have come in the third over, when Thompson dropped Ihsanullah. Afghanistan had no serious alarms – though with just three needed they did lose two wickets. It fell to Hashmatullah to hit the winning boundary.

Player of the Match: Rahmat Shah.

Close of play: first day, Afghanistan 90-2 (Rahmat Shah 22, Hashmatullah Shahidi 13); second day, Ireland 22-1 (Stirling 8, Balbirnie 14); third day, Afghanistan 29-1 (Ihsanullah Janat 16, Rahmat Shah 11).

Ireland

*W. T. S. Porterfield lbw b Mohammad Nabi	9	– c Ikram Alikhil b Yamin Ahmadzai	0
P. R. Stirling c Ikram Alikhil b Yamin Ahmadzai	26	– lbw b Yamin Ahmadzai	14
A. Balbirnie b Yamin Ahmadzai	4	– c Ikram Alikhil b Waqar Salamkheil	82
J. A. McCollum b Rashid Khan	4	– lbw b Rashid Khan	39
K. J. O'Brien lbw b Mohammad Nabi	12	– lbw b Rashid Khan	56
†S. W. Poynter lbw b Rashid Khan	0	– c Ihsanullah Janat b Waqar Salamkheil	1
S. R. Thompson c Hashmatullah Shahidi b Mohammad Nabi	3	– c Ihsanullah Janat b Rashid Khan	1
G. H. Dockrell c Ikram Alikhil b Yamin Ahmadzai	39	– lbw b Rashid Khan	25
A. R. McBrine b Waqar Salamkheil	3	– st Ikram Alikhil b Rashid Khan	4
J. Cameron-Dow lbw b Waqar Salamkheil	9	– not out	32
T. J. Murtagh not out	54	– c Rahmat Shah b Yamin Ahmadzai	27
B 4, lb 5	9	B 4, lb 2, w 1	7

1/37 (2) 2/41 (1) 3/41 (3)	(60 overs) 172	1/0 (1) 2/33 (2) (93 overs) 288
4/55 (4) 5/55 (6) 6/59 (5)		3/137 (3) 4/141 (4)
7/62 (7) 8/69 (9) 9/85 (10) 10/172 (8)		5/150 (6) 6/157 (7) 7/220 (8)
		8/229 (5) 9/230 (9) 10/288 (11)

Yamin Ahmadzai 12–2–41–3; Wafadar Momand 8–3–31–0; Mohammad Nabi 14–5–36–3; Rashid Khan 12–5–20–2; Waqar Salamkheil 14–4–35–2. *Second innings*—Yamin Ahmadzai 14–1–52–3; Mohammad Nabi 20–1–58–0; Rashid Khan 34–7–82–5; Waqar Salamkheil 17–2–66–2; Wafadar Momand 8–0–24–0.

Afghanistan

Mohammad Shahzad c and b Cameron-Dow	40	– c Poynter b McBrine	2
Ihsanullah Janat lbw b Cameron-Dow	7	– not out	65
Rahmat Shah b Murtagh	98	– st Poynter b Cameron-Dow	76
Hashmatullah Shahidi lbw b McBrine	61	– (5) not out	4
*Asghar Afghan c Poynter b Thompson	67		
Mohammad Nabi c Cameron-Dow b Thompson	0	– (4) run out (Murtagh/Poynter)	1
†Ikram Alikhil b McBrine	7		
Rashid Khan lbw b Dockrell	10		
Yamin Ahmadzai lbw b Dockrell	2		
Wafadar Momand c Balbirnie b Thompson	6		
Waqar Salamkheil not out	1		
B 5, lb 3, w 4, nb 3	15	W 1	1

1/27 (2) 2/68 (1) 3/198 (4)   (106.3 overs) 314   1/5 (1)   (3 wkts, 47.5 overs) 149
4/226 (3) 5/227 (6) 6/255 (7)   2/144 (3) 3/145 (4)
7/272 (8) 8/280 (9) 9/311 (5) 10/314 (10)

Murtagh 22–9–33–1; McBrine 27–4–77–2; Cameron-Dow 18–0–94–2; Thompson 17.3–5–28–3; Dockrell 18–4–63–2; O'Brien 4–1–11–0. *Second innings*—Dockrell 22–7–58–0; McBrine 13–5–35–1; Cameron-Dow 5.5–0–24–1; Murtagh 5–3–15–0; Thompson 1–0–9–0; Balbirnie 1–0–8–0.

Umpires: R. K. Illingworth and S. Ravi.   Third umpire: Ahmed Shah Pakteen.
Referee: J. Srinath.

AFGHANISTAN v WEST INDIES IN INDIA IN 2019-20

SANTOSH SURI

One-day internationals (3): Afghanistan 0, West Indies 3
Twenty20 internationals (3): Afghanistan 2, West Indies 1
Test match (1): Afghanistan 0, West Indies 1

If Afghanistan's players didn't know it before, this tour proved that, the longer the format, the harder the challenge. They won the T20 series, and the 50-over games were all reasonably close – but they fell in a heap in the solitary Test. West Indies were helped by the fact that Afghanistan's home base in India had shifted from Dehradun – which had no five-star hotel – to Lucknow, so their spinners were less familiar with the pitches. In the event, they were outperformed by the tourists' slow men, in particular Rahkeem Cornwall, who in his second Test took ten wickets.

Afghanistan's batsmen seemed unable to adapt to the waiting game required in Tests, hamstrung by their lack of experience. "If you don't score big runs against top teams, you will struggle," said Rashid Khan. Even though he had won his first Test in charge, in Bangladesh two months earlier, it began to look as if saddling him with the captaincy might not have been wise: he was only 21, and also expected to be the main wicket-taker. It was no surprise when Asghar Afghan was reappointed a few weeks later.

If Cornwall was the big red-ball plus for West Indies, they had concerns about the form of regular opener Kraigg Brathwaite. Two failures in the Test meant he had not made a half-century for ten matches, stretching back to October 2018. There was a change at the helm in the white-ball matches, with Kieron Pollard taking over as captain from Jason Holder. He had a good start, winning all three of the 50-over games, before narrowly losing the T20s. An interesting addition was leg-spinner Hayden Walsh, born in the Virgin Islands, who not long before had been representing the United States; he took three wickets as West Indies won the second ODI. Holder remained in the white-ball side; of the other Test players, only Shimron Hetmyer and Shai Hope appeared in the T20s. Those three didn't get much rest, as the West Indians went straight into two limited-overs series against India.

WEST INDIES TOURING PARTY

*J. O. Holder (T/50/20), F. A. Allen (20), S. W. Ambris (T/50), K. C. Brathwaite (T), S. S. J. Brooks (T), J. D. Campbell (T), R. L. Chase (T/50), R. R. S. Cornwall (T), S. S. Cottrell (50/20), S. O. Dowrich (T), S. O. Hetmyer (T/50/20), S. D. Hope (T/50), A. S. Joseph (T/50/20), B. A. King (50/20), E. Lewis (50/20), K. M. A. Paul (T/50), K. A. Pierre (50/20), K. A. Pollard (50/20), N. Pooran (50/20), D. Ramdin (20), K. A. J. Roach (T), S. E. Rutherford (20), R. Shepherd (50), L. M. P. Simmons (20), H. R. Walsh (50/20), J. A. Warrican (T), K. O. K. Williams (20). *Coach:* P. V. Simmons.
Pollard captained in the white-ball matches.

First one-day international At Lucknow, November 6, 2019 (day/night). **West Indies won by seven wickets. Afghanistan 194** (45.2 overs) (Rahmat Shah 61, Ikram Alikhil 58, Asghar Afghan 35); ‡**West Indies 197-3** (46.3 overs) (S. D. Hope 77*, R. L. Chase 94). *PoM:* R. L. Chase.

ODI debut: R. Shepherd (West Indies). *Rahmat Shah and wicketkeeper Ikram Alikhil dominated a disappointing Afghanistan innings with a third-wicket stand of 111. It ended when Alikhil wandered out of his ground to congratulate Rahmat on his half-century, without realising the ball was not dead: Shai Hope gleefully removed the bails. Of the rest, only Asghar Afghan and Gulbadeen Naib (17) reached double figures. Jason Holder, who had been supplanted as white-ball captain by Kieron Pollard, sent down 47 dot balls on the way to 2-21. West Indies lost two early wickets, but the Afghan spinners struggled to control the ball as dew fell. Hope, whose 77* occupied 133 deliveries, and the more adventurous Roston Chase put on 163. Leg-spinner Hayden Walsh, who little more than two months previously had played the last of his nine white-ball internationals for the USA, made his debut for West Indies, and dismissed Gulbadeen.*

Second one-day international At Lucknow, November 9, 2019 (day/night). **West Indies won by 47 runs. West Indies 247-9** (50 overs) (S. D. Hope 43, E. Lewis 54, S. O. Hetmyer 34, N. Pooran 67; Naveen-ul-Haq 3-60); ‡**Afghanistan 200** (45.4 overs) (Rahmat Shah 33, Najibullah Zadran 56, Mohammad Nabi 32; S. S. Cottrell 3-29, R. L. Chase 3-30, H. R. Walsh 3-36). *PoM:* N. Pooran. *Another convincing West Indian batting display set up a series-clinching victory. Hope and Evin Lewis put on 98 before being parted in the 25th over, and Nicholas Pooran added 67 from 50 balls to take the total close to 250. Afghanistan's batsmen kept trying big shots, and struggled to 109-5 after 27. Najibullah Zadran and Mohammad Nabi shared a stand of 68, but three quick wickets for Walsh hastened the end. The West Indians were more taxed by flying insects than by batsmen: several wore face masks in the field.*

Third one-day international At Lucknow, November 11, 2019 (day/night). **West Indies won by five wickets. Afghanistan 249-7** (50 overs) (Hazratullah Zazai 50, Asghar Afghan 86, Najibullah Zadran 30, Mohammad Nabi 50*; K. M. A. Paul 3-44); ‡**West Indies 253-5** (48.4 overs) (S. D. Hope 109*, B. A. King 39, K. A. Pollard 32, R. L. Chase 42*). *PoM:* S. D. Hope. *PoS:* R. L. Chase. *ODI debuts:* Ibrahim Zadran (Afghanistan); B. A. King (West Indies). *Hope's superb century – his seventh in ODIs – took West Indies to a clean sweep, which had looked unlikely when Lewis and Shimron Hetmyer both fell in the third over, from Mujeeb Zadran. That made it 4-2, but Hope shared four successive fifty partnerships – the first with debutant Brandon King – as West Indies sailed home, helped again by the dew, which hindered the spinners. Afghanistan's innings had been rescued from 118-5 in the 29th by a stand of 127 between Asghar, who clubbed six sixes, and Mohammad Nabi. Pooran was caught on TV scratching the ball with his thumbnail, and banned for four T20 internationals by referee Chris Broad.*

First Twenty20 international At Lucknow, November 14, 2019 (floodlit). **West Indies won by 30 runs. West Indies 164-5** (20 overs) (E. Lewis 68, K. A. Pollard 32*); ‡**Afghanistan 134-9** (20 overs) (K. O. K. Williams 3-17). *PoM:* K. A. Pollard. *T20I debuts:* Ibrahim Zadran (Afghanistan); B. A. King (West Indies). *Lewis cracked 68 from 41 balls, but only 64 more runs came after he top-edged an attempted pull to long-off in the 12th over. Afghanistan were 69-3 at halfway, before injudicious strokes sparked a collapse: 94-4 became 111-9, and Pollard had started his term as West Indies' official white-ball captain with four wins out of four.*

Second Twenty20 international At Lucknow, November 16, 2019 (floodlit). **Afghanistan won by 41 runs. ‡Afghanistan 147-7** (20 overs) (K. O. K. Williams 3-23); **West Indies 106-8** (20 overs) (Karim Janat 5-11). *PoM:* Karim Janat. *Rashid Khan changed the script by opting to bat first, and Afghanistan squared the series in a low-scoring game. Hazratullah Zazai hit the first ball of the match, from Holder, for six – but the eventual 147, with Hazratullah and Karim Janat both making 26, was hardly imposing. West Indies, however, fared even worse: five fell between 11 and 14. Afghanistan's bowling hero was not one of their vaunted spinners, but the unsung medium-pacer Janat, who took four wickets in 16 balls on his way to a maiden international five-for.*

Third Twenty20 international At Lucknow, November 17, 2019 (floodlit). **Afghanistan won by 29 runs. ‡Afghanistan 156-8** (20 overs) (Rahmanullah Gurbaz 79); **West Indies 127-7** (20 overs) (S. D. Hope 52; Naveen-ul-Haq 3-24). *PoM:* Rahmanullah Gurbaz. *PoS:* Karim Janat. *To the delight of a decent-sized crowd, Afghanistan took the series after another good bowling performance, led by seamer Naveen-ul-Haq, in only his fourth T20I. The spinners clamped down, too: Mujeeb returned 3–13–9–2, and Rashid 4–9–18–1. It meant West Indies never threatened a target of 157, despite Hope's 52 from 46. Afghanistan's innings had been dominated by 17-year-old Rahmanullah Gurbaz, who spanked 79 from 52, with five sixes.*

AFGHANISTAN v WEST INDIES

Test Match

At Lucknow, November 27–29, 2019. West Indies won by nine wickets. Toss: West Indies. Test debuts: Hamza Hotak, Nasir Ahmadzai.

Afghanistan went into their fourth Test – the first against West Indies – with high hopes of a third victory. Their spinners had recently embarrassed Bangladesh at Chittagong, and were expected to do well again on what passes for home turf in India. But they were beaten at their own game, with West Indies' Rahkeem Cornwall hauling in ten wickets, and the match was done and dusted early on the third day.

Cornwall was an unlikely destroyer, propelling his huge frame to the crease from five dainty steps to send down innocuous-looking off-breaks. But his size produced nip and bounce, which proved fatal to Afghanistan's batsmen. The key passage came on the first afternoon, when they slipped from 84 for one to 111 for seven: Cornwall claimed four for eight in 21 balls, and scooped up a low slip catch to account for Rashid Khan. Only opener Javed Ahmadi, with 39 (followed by 62 in the second innings) made more than 34. Cornwall, meanwhile, joined rarefied company: his final figures had been bettered away from home among West Indian spinners only by Lance Gibbs (twice, both in Manchester), Sonny Ramadhin and Alf Valentine (also Manchester). "It's a dream to do it in only my second Test," he said. "The pitches back home are similar, which helped."

West Indies' other hero was the Barbadian Shamarh Brooks, a late bloomer at 31, who battled to a maiden century in his third Test, after channelling some old advice from Everton Weekes: "When I was 13, he told me that when you're batting against spin, you have to get very close to it, or very far from it. On a pitch like this, against their quality

---

TEN WICKETS IN A TEST BY A WEST INDIAN SPINNER

11-152	S. Ramadhin (5-66 and 6-86)	v England at Lord's.	1950
11-157	L. R. Gibbs (5-59 and 6-98)	v England at Manchester.	1963
11-204†	A. L. Valentine (8-104 and 3-100)	v England at Manchester.	1950
11-229	W. Ferguson (5-137 and 6-92)	v England at Port-of-Spain	1947-48
10-93	S. Shillingford (5-59 and 5-34).	v Zimbabwe at Roseau	2012-13
10-106	L. R. Gibbs (5-37 and 5-69)	v England at Manchester.	1966
10-121	**R. R. S. Cornwall (7-75 and 3-46)**	**v Afghanistan at Lucknow**	**2019-20**
10-160	A. L. Valentine (4-121 and 6-39).	v England at The Oval	1950
10-174	D. Bishoo (2-125 and 8-49)	v Pakistan at Dubai	2016-17
10-219	S. Shillingford (6-119 and 4-100)	v Australia at Roseau	2011-12

† *On debut.*

---

bowlers, it was just about trusting your defence." Brooks finally fell, after more than four hours, to slow left-armer Hamza Hotak, one of his five wickets on debut after replacing Mohammad Nabi, who had retired from Tests. Brooks's 111, and important partnerships with Campbell and Dowrich, set up a lead of 90. Cornwall was helped by a parsimonious spell from Holder, who conceded only 22 from his 17 overs, and took two wickets. He added three more as Afghanistan's second innings was wrapped up in 43 balls on the third morning.

Given that his side included three spinners, it was a surprise Holder had chosen to bowl, but he was more than justified by the result. "It was a gut feeling," he explained. "We didn't get the new-ball wickets we wanted, but the spinners delivered. Warrican was also key – his control helped Cornwall."

The success of the amiable Cornwall gave Holder and his side a huge boost, with sterner challenges looming. Rashid, though, was left to reflect on a comprehensive defeat:

"We are not batting long – people are getting out for thirties and forties. We need to work on that. But it's still early days, only our fourth game, against an experienced side. We want more Tests – just one per year isn't good enough."

The Ekana Stadium was the third venue in Lucknow to stage a Test. India met Pakistan at the University ground in 1952-53, and Sri Lanka at the K. D. Singh Babu Stadium in 1993-94.

Player of the Match: R. R. S. Cornwall.

Close of play: first day, West Indies 68-2 (Campbell 30, Brooks 19); second day, Afghanistan 109-7 (Afsar Zazai 2).

Afghanistan

Ibrahim Zadran c Holder b Cornwall	17	– lbw b Cornwall	23
Javed Ahmadi c Brooks b Warrican	39	– c Cornwall b Chase	62
Ihsanullah Janat c Hope b Cornwall	24	– run out (Hope/Dowrich)	1
Rahmat Shah c Holder b Cornwall	4	– b Brooks b Cornwall	0
Asghar Afghan c Dowrich b Cornwall	4	– c Brooks b Cornwall	0
Nasir Ahmadzai c Hope b Cornwall	2	– b Chase	15
†Afsar Zazai lbw b Cornwall	32	– (8) c Dowrich b Holder	7
*Rashid Khan c Cornwall b Holder	1	– (9) c Dowrich b Holder	1
Hamza Hotak c Dowrich b Holder	34	– (7) c Cornwall b Chase	1
Yamin Ahmadzai c Warrican b Cornwall	18	– b Holder	1
Zahir Khan not out	0	– not out	0
B 7, lb 5	12	B 4, lb 4, nb 1	9

1/28 (1) 2/84 (2) 3/90 (3)   (68.3 overs) 187   1/53 (1) 2/55 (3)   (43.1 overs) 120
4/91 (4) 5/95 (6) 6/98 (5)   3/55 (4) 4/59 (5)
7/111 (8) 8/165 (7) 9/187 (9) 10/187 (10)   5/96 (6) 6/98 (7) 7/109 (2)
    8/111 (9) 9/119 (10) 10/120 (8)

Roach 8-1-33-0; Holder 17-10-22-2; Cornwall 25.3-5-75-7; Warrican 13-1-35-1; Chase 5-0-10-0. *Second innings*—Roach 4-2-5-0; Holder 6.1-2-20-3; Warrican 12-3-31-0; Cornwall 18-3-46-3; Chase 3-1-10-3.

West Indies

K. C. Brathwaite lbw b Hamza Hotak	11	– c Afsar Zazai b Hamza Hotak	8
J. D. Campbell c Ihsanullah Janat b Hamza Hotak	55	– not out	19
S. D. Hope c Ihsanullah Janat b Rashid Khan	7	– not out	6
S. S. J. Brooks b Hamza Hotak	111		
S. O. Hetmyer lbw b Rashid Khan	13		
R. L. Chase c Ibrahim Zadran b Zahir Khan	2		
†S. O. Dowrich lbw b Zahir Khan	42		
*J. O. Holder st Afsar Zazai b Hamza Hotak	11		
R. R. S. Cornwall lbw b Rashid Khan	5		
K. A. J. Roach lbw b Hamza Hotak	3		
J. A. Warrican not out	4		
Lb 12, nb 1	13		

1/27 (1) 2/34 (2) 3/116 (2)   (83.3 overs) 277   1/22 (1)   (1 wkt, 6.2 overs) 33
4/137 (5) 5/150 (6) 6/224 (7)
7/243 (8) 8/260 (9) 9/270 (4) 10/277 (10)

Yamin Ahmadzai 10-3-24-0; Hamza Hotak 28.3-4-74-5; Rashid Khan 32-5-114-3; Zahir Khan 13-2-53-2. *Second innings*—Yamin Ahmadzai 1-0-8-0; Javed Ahmadi 1-0-9-0; Hamza Hotak 2.2-1-5-1; Rashid Khan 2-0-11-0.

Umpires: N. N. Menon and P. R. Reiffel.   Third umpire: Ahmed Shah Pakteen.
Referee: B. C. Broad.

DOMESTIC CRICKET IN AFGHANISTAN IN 2019

The second season of first-class cricket in Afghanistan introduced a new competition – the Mirwais Nika provincial three-day tournament, which took place in February and March, ahead of the previously established four-day Ahmad Shah Abdali tournament (both were named after 18th-century emirs).

The Mirwais Nika was contested by five regional teams, all beginning with K, and all representing the zones competing for the Ahmad Shah Abdali – Kunduz from Amo, Kandahar from Boost, Kunar from Speen Ghar, Khost from Mis-e-Ainak and Kabul from Band-e-Amir. Each included three players from the zonal first-class sides, one fast bowler selected by the Afghanistan Cricket Board's development department, and the top performers from a preceding two-day tournament. All matches (ten group games and a four-day final) were staged on two grounds, at Ghazi Amanullah Khan Town and Asadabad. Only one reached an outright result – Khost defeated Kandahar by 104 runs – but **Kunduz** and **Kabul** reached the final, where Kabul amassed 531 and took a huge first-innings lead. It ensured they would claim the inaugural trophy, despite not having time to bowl out Kunduz again.

Kabul's Nisar Wahdat dominated the tournament with 653 runs – almost twice the next-best aggregate – at 93; he scored three centuries, including 262 against Khost and 137 in the final. They also possessed the two leading wicket-takers, leg-spinner Parviz Amin, with 24, and seamer Mohammadullah Hamkar, who struck with his first ball on first-class debut, and finished with 17 after claiming eight in the final. Hayatullah of Kunduz was named Player of the Tournament, for his 297 runs and eight wickets in four games. In the first round, two debutants, Hanif Kunrai and Ijaz Ul Haq, shared an unbroken stand of 318 for Kunar's seventh wicket against Kandahar.

The Ahmad Shah Abdali competition began with five rounds in April and May, but was then put on hold for six months, citing "other domestic tournaments and the unavailability of the national cricketers". Though it began with six teams, Kabul dropped out when they resumed in November. **Speen Ghar** held a narrow lead at the break, and finished as runaway champions after winning their last three games, in December. Band-e-Amir, who had won the first two competitions, were bottom, without a win until the final round.

Speen Ghar's Najeeb Tarakai was the tournament's leading run-scorer with 828, including centuries in four successive matches – but after scoring 651 at 93 in those games, he was elevated to the captaincy and managed only 177 at 22 in the remaining five. His team-mate Bahir Shah could not quite rise to the record-breaking heights of his debut season, but passed 2,000 first-class runs in his 21st match, and headed the Ahmad Shah Abdali averages with 533 at 88. Munir Ahmad scored 809 runs for Boost, including centuries in his last three matches, and had 23 dismissals, mostly as wicketkeeper. Hayatullah's batting form carried over from the Mirwais Nika: he scored another 638 runs, giving him 935 at 58 over the year.

Zohaib Ahmadzai, a 17-year-old left-arm spinner, bowled **Amo** into second place with 46 wickets, including nine for 37, the best first-class return in Afghanistan, to complete an innings victory over Mis Ainak; he deprived himself of all ten by running out the other batsman. Dastagir Khan, a medium-pacer, recorded the first hat-trick in Afghanistan, for Boost; he dismissed three top-order Band-e-Amir batsmen for ducks in the fourth over of their encounter in April.

In August, eight teams competed in a Provincial Challenge Cup. It was won by **Nangarhar Province**, who won all their group games, plus the semi and the final, where Tarakai scored 121 against Kabul. **Mis Ainak** won the Ghazi Amanullah Khan regional one-day tournament in September; despite being third in the table, they beat leaders Amo in a play-off and Boost in the final. A few weeks later, their Twenty20 side, **Mis Ainak Knights**, won the Shpageeza T20 tournament, dominating the group stage and defeating Band-e-Amir Dragons in the final.

FIRST-CLASS AVERAGES IN 2019

BATTING (300 runs)

		M	I	NO	R	HS	100	Avge	Ct/St
1	Ihsanullah Janat (*Mis Ainak*)	4	6	0	524	248	2	87.33	2
2	Bahir Shah (*Kunar/Speen Ghar*)	9	14	5	733	156*	2	81.44	5
3	Farhan Zakhil (*Kabul*)	4	6	0	422	108	2	70.33	1
4	†Shahidullah (*Mis Ainak*)	7	12	1	772	189	3	70.18	9
5	Nasir Ahmadzai (*Boost*)	6	10	2	516	172	2	64.50	5
6	Sadam Mangal (*Khost/Mis Ainak*)	7	12	3	561	167	2	62.33	4
7	Darwish Rasooli (*Speen Ghar*)	4	7	1	368	124	2	61.33	7
8	Hayatullah (*Kunduz/Amo*)	12	19	3	935	130	4	58.43	18
9	Abdul Malik (*Amo*)	8	13	0	730	179	2	56.15	6
10	Nisar Wahdat (*Kabul/Band-e-Amir*)	10	17	1	891	262	3	55.68	7
11	Najeeb Tarakai (*Speen Ghar*)	9	15	0	828	200	4	55.20	5
12	†Zahid Zakhail (*Kunduz/Amo*)	9	15	2	712	215*	1	54.76	5
13	Rahmanullah Gurbaz (*Kabul*)	4	6	0	328	153	1	54.66	4
14	Munir Ahmad (*Boost*)	9	16	1	809	209	3	53.93	22/1
15	Fazal Niazai (*Mis Ainak*)	7	13	2	588	132	3	53.45	0
16	Abdul Wasi (*Amo*)	8	13	4	455	87	0	50.55	2
17	Amanullah Rafiqi (*Kabul/Band-e-Amir*)	9	15	1	679	111*	1	48.50	10
18	Nasir Khan (*Speen Ghar*)	6	9	1	341	121	1	42.62	4
19	Zia-ul-Haq (*Band-e-Amir*)	8	16	1	616	102	1	41.06	6
20	Waqarullah Ishaq (*Kandahar/Boost*)	11	18	3	615	156*	1	41.00	11
21	Shabir Noori (*Speen Ghar*)	6	10	0	376	93	0	37.60	2
22	Younas Ahmadzai (*Mis Ainak*)	6	12	0	451	170	2	37.58	10
23	Suliman Safi (*Kabul/Band-e-Amir*)	7	11	1	375	101*	1	37.50	3
24	†Abdul Hadi (*Kunduz/Amo*)	7	11	2	336	115*	1	37.33	12
25	Ihsan Mangal (*Amo*)	5	10	1	331	107	1	36.77	5
26	Nasibullah Sherdali (*Kandahar/Boost*)	7	13	1	438	109	1	36.50	4
27	Imran Janat (*Band-e-Amir*)	7	14	0	350	72	0	25.00	4
28	Mohammad Sardar (*Kabul/Band-e-Amir*)	10	17	0	398	85	0	24.87	20/3

BOWLING (15 wickets)

		Style	O	M	R	W	BB	5I	Avge
1	Zia-ur-Rehman (*Mis Ainak*)	SLA	219.2	81	505	35	6-46	3	14.42
2	Zohaib Ahmadzai (*Amo*)	SLA	216.2	55	673	46	9-37	4	14.63
3	Azmatullah Omarzai (*Speen Ghar*)	RFM	95	20	307	15	4-73	0	20.46
4	Rokhan Barakzai (*Boost*)	SLA	116.4	23	334	16	5-44	1	20.87
5	Parviz Amin (*Kabul/Band-e-Amir*)	LB	189.4	37	731	32	6-58	4	22.84
6	Sharafuddin Ashraf (*Amo*)	SLA	122	25	416	18	7-86	1	23.11
7	Nasratullah (*Band-e-Amir*)	SLA	119.1	26	396	16	5-64	1	24.75
8	Tariq Stanikzai (*Kunar/Speen Ghar*)	SLA	164.5	45	478	19	5-66	1	25.15
9	Mohammadullah Hamkar (*Kabul/B-e-A*)	RFM	121.3	21	488	19	7-77	1	25.68
10	Yousuf Zazai (*Amo*)	RFM	138.1	30	516	20	6-85	2	25.80
11	Waqarullah Ishaq (*Kandahar/Boost*)	LM	165.5	37	546	21	3-29	0	26.00
12	Samiullah (*Kunduz*)		116.1	20	421	16	5-93	1	26.31
13	Yamin Ahmadzai (*Boost*)	RFM	186	34	608	23	5-37	1	26.43
14	Zahir Khan (*Mis Ainak*)	SLW	172.3	28	813	30	6-52	2	27.10
15	Fareed Ahmad (*Speen Ghar*)	LFM	249.3	45	874	31	6-27	1	28.19
16	Nijat Masood (*Band-e-Amir*)	RM	126	23	490	17	5-45	1	28.82
17	Mohammad Alam (*Boost*)	SLA	205.2	33	585	20	4-64	0	29.25
18	Salim (*Kunduz/Amo*)		225.3	31	819	26	5-52	1	31.50
19	M. Hashum (*Khost/Boost*)	RM	124.5	20	480	15	5-59	1	32.00
20	Abdullah Adil (*Band-e-Amir*)	RM	126.3	22	504	15	5-75	1	33.60
21	Abdul Wasi (*Amo*)	LB	262.3	35	974	26	5-74	1	37.46
22	Dastagir Khan (*Kandahar/Boost*)	RM	282.1	38	1102	29	5-75	1	38.00
23	Abdul Baqi (*Boost*)	LB	185.3	17	809	20	4-87	0	40.45

MIRWAIS NIKA PROVINCIAL THREE-DAY TOURNAMENT IN 2019

	P	W	L	D	A	1st-inns pts	Pts
KUNDUZ...	4	0	0	3	1	18	49
KABUL	4	0	0	4	0	18	46
Khost	4	1	0	2	1	6	44
Kunar	4	0	0	3	1	6	37
Kandahar ...	4	0	1	2	1	0	24

Win = 14pts; draw = 7pts; first-innings lead = 6pts; abandoned = 10pts.

Final At Ghazi Amanullah Khan Town, March 12–15, 2019. **Drawn. Kabul won by virtue of their first-innings lead. Kabul 531** (Mirwais Zazai 159) **and 346-4 dec** (Suliman Safi 101*, Nisar Wahdat 137); ‡**Kunduz 222** (Mohammadullah Hamkar 7-77) **and 188-3.** *Mirwais Zazai struck ten sixes in a brisk 159, sharing century stands with Amanullah Rafiqi (67) and Mohammad Sardar (85), before 44* from No. 10 Kashmir Khan lifted Kabul past 500. Then seamer Mohammadullah Hamkar swept Kunduz aside with a career-best seven. Kabul led by 309 but, knowing that was probably enough to guarantee the trophy, chose to bat again: Suliman Safi and Nisar Wahdat made up for first-innings ducks with a 217-run partnership, and the 15-year-old Suliman (out for 99 when these teams met three weeks earlier) reached a maiden hundred, before Kunduz were set a notional target of 656.*

AHMAD SHAH ABDALI FOUR-DAY TOURNAMENT IN 2019

	P	W	L	D	A	1st-inns pts	Pts
Speen Ghar..	9	4	0	5	0	45	136
Amo	9	3	2	4	0	24	94
Mis Ainak...	9	2	3	4	0	27	83
Boost	9	2	3	4	0	18	74
Kabul	5	1	0	3	1	12	57
Band-e-Amir	9	1	5	2	1	18	56

Outright win = 14pts; draw = 7pts; first-innings lead = 6pts; no decision on first innings = 3pts; abandoned = 10pts.

CHAMPIONS

2017	Band-e-Amir		2018	Band-e-Amir		2019	Speen Ghar

PROVINCIAL CHALLENGE CUP GRADE ONE IN 2019

50-over league plus knockout

Group A	P	W	L	Pts	NRR	**Group B**	P	W	L	Pts	NRR
KHOST............	3	2	1	4	1.06	NANGARHAR....	3	3	0	6	1.39
KANDAHAR......	3	2	1	4	0.95	KABUL	3	2	1	4	−0.01
Paktia	3	1	2	2	−0.72	Logar............	3	1	2	2	0.18
Balkh............	3	1	2	2	−1.34	Herat	3	0	3	0	−1.60

Semi-finals Kabul beat Khost by ten wickets; Nangarhar beat Kandahar by six wickets.

Final At Kabul, August 9, 2019. **Nangarhar won by six wickets. Kabul 273-8** (50 overs); ‡**Nangarhar 274-4** (47.4 overs) (Najeeb Tarakai 121). *Nangarhar secured the trophy with their fifth straight win, after a maiden one-day hundred from their captain, Najeeb Tarakai. He scored 121 in 90 balls, with nine sixes, and added 83 with Shawkat Zaman (81*). Put in, Kabul had limped to 66-4, before Zia-ul-Haq (84) and Amanullah Rafiqi (52) started a fightback with a stand of 97.*

GHAZI AMANULLAH KHAN REGIONAL TOURNAMENT IN 2019

50-over league plus knockout

	P	W	L	Pts	NRR
AMO	4	3	1	6	0.54
BOOST	4	3	1	6	0.04
MIS AINAK.	4	2	2	4	0.61
Speen Ghar.	4	2	2	4	0.44
Band-e-Amir	4	0	4	0	−1.63

Preliminary finals   1st v 2nd: Boost beat Amo by 56 runs. **Final play-off:** Mis Ainak beat Amo by 36 runs.

Final   At Kabul, September 24, 2019. Mis Ainak won by 88 runs. Mis Ainak 199 (44.5 overs); ‡**Boost 111** (23.1 overs). *Mis Ainak won their first title in a low-scoring final. There was only one half-century stand – Ibrahim Zadran and Imran Mir put on 70 for their third wicket – as Samiullah Shenwari's leg-spin claimed a career-best 4-24. Needing 200, Boost survived less than half their 50 overs. Ihsanullah Janat scored 60, the game's only half-century, but no one else passed ten, and slow left-armer Zia-ur-Rehman finished them off with 3-18.*

SHPAGEEZA T20 TOURNAMENT IN 2019

20-over league plus knockout

	P	W	L	Pts	NRR
MIS AINAK KNIGHTS	5	4	1	12	0.31
BAND-E-AMIR DRAGONS .	5	3	2	9	1.07
KABUL EAGLES	5	3	2	9	0.54
SPEEN GHAR TIGERS	5	2	3	6	0.21
Amo Sharks.	5	2	3	6	−0.23
Boost Defenders	5	1	4	3	−1.98

Preliminary finals   1st v 2nd: Mis Ainak Knights beat Band-e-Amir Dragons by seven wickets. **3rd v 4th:** Kabul Eagles beat Speen Ghar Tigers by 16 runs. **Final play-off:** Band-e-Amir Dragons beat Kabul Eagles by three runs.

Final   At Kabul, October 18, 2019. Mis Ainak Knights won by four wickets. Band-e-Amir Dragons 154-7 (20 overs); ‡**Mis Ainak Knights 155-6** (19.5 overs). *Mis Ainak collected their second trophy in four weeks. Band-e-Amir captain Rashid Khan raced to 18, before falling to international team-mate Mohammad Nabi in the second over, and Naveen-ul-Haq later grabbed three in five deliveries, though Batin Shah's 15-ball 23 got them past 150. Mis Ainak's top order built a solid platform and, though four wickets fell in the game's last three overs, they got home with a ball to spare.*

The Afghanistan Premier League, held in the United Arab Emirates, can be found on page 1154.

AUSTRALIAN CRICKET IN 2019

Resolutely Roundhead

DANIEL BRETTIG

Cultural renewal, redemption, rejuvenation, rediscovery. All these terms were bandied around as Australian cricket got back on its feet after the sandpaper scandal of 2018. Yet for all the buzzwords, the equation was straightforward. While Steve Smith and David Warner were suspended, Test captain Tim Paine and his one-day counterpart Aaron Finch presided over, at best, a pair of mid-tier teams. When Smith and Warner returned, to accompany a fully fit battery of fast bowlers and the wiles of Nathan Lyon, perhaps only India could reasonably be expected to beat such an assembly of runs and wickets.

AUSTRALIA IN 2019

	Played	Won	Lost	Drawn/No result
Tests	12	8	2	2
One-day internationals	23	16	7	–
Twenty20 internationals	8	7	–	1

NOVEMBER		
DECEMBER	4 Tests, 3 ODIs and 3 T20Is (h) v India	(see *Wisden 2019*, page 820)
JANUARY	2 Tests (h) v Sri Lanka	(page 881)
FEBRUARY	5 ODIs and 2 T20Is (a) v India	(page 931)
MARCH	5 ODIs (in the UAE) v Pakistan	(page 999)
APRIL		
MAY		
JUNE	World Cup (in England)	(page 237)
JULY		
AUGUST	5 Tests (a) v England	(page 381)
SEPTEMBER		
OCTOBER	3 T20Is (h) v Sri Lanka	(page 886)
NOVEMBER	2 Tests and 3 T20Is (h) v Pakistan	(page 888)
DECEMBER		
JANUARY	3 Tests (h) v New Zealand	(page 896)
FEBRUARY		

For a review of Australian domestic cricket from the 2018-19 season, see page 906.

High command: team captain Tim Paine and head coach Justin Langer at Old Trafford.

This is not to say all was smooth from the moment the pair began their reintegration by visiting a pre-World Cup camp in the UAE in March. The team had begun to function without them, atomising Sri Lanka at Brisbane and Canberra (hosting its first Test), and winning a one-day series in India for the first time in almost ten years. Then there was the matter of the sustained hostility they would undoubtedly face in England, for a two-legged World Cup and Ashes challenge that would stretch even the most united of squads.

No expense was spared. The coach, Justin Langer, got his wish to have two former captains by his side: Ricky Ponting for the World Cup, and Steve Waugh for four of the five Ashes Tests (significantly, perhaps, he missed only Headingley, where Ben Stokes pulled off his miracle). The brains trust sculpted a game plan with English conditions in mind, favouring containment and discipline in the field, and preservation of wickets with the bat. It was more Roundhead than the Cavalier approach favoured by England, but the World Cup master plan served Australia well until they fell foul of Chris Woakes and Jofra Archer on a fresh Edgbaston pitch. The semi-final was a creditable result after mediocre performances over the previous four years, but it didn't satisfy Langer.

As England squeaked past New Zealand on that glorious Lord's evening, most of Australia's Ashes side were engaged in a low-key game against England Lions at Canterbury. A preliminary squad of 25 convened in Southampton a few days later, and the group was pared down to 17 via an internal trial match that saw some of the northern summer's most competitive – if least watched – cricket: Marnus Labuschagne and Cameron Bancroft, after stints at Glamorgan and Durham, emerged from a scrap on a borderline dangerous pitch to edge out Joe Burns and Kurtis Patterson. Australia's pacemen, meanwhile, were encouraged to bowl a tight line, and a length targeting the top of off stump, having erred too full and wide in England four years earlier.

The short turnaround between World Cup and Ashes arguably offered the more settled Australians an early advantage, even if a typically raucous Birmingham crowd tried to even up the ledger. But after an early tumble of wickets, Smith asserted himself with a breathtaking century on the opening day, then added another in the second innings to seal a commanding victory. Australia were also rewarded for choosing Peter Siddle and James Pattinson over Josh Hazlewood and Mitchell Starc: Siddle's suffocating spell on the final day earned rare praise from Langer. Hazlewood returned for the Second Test, and harried England's top order, while Starc's sole contribution, in the Fourth at Old Trafford, was still significant.

In between, at Lord's and Headingley, were fits and starts from a team that looked capable of becoming great, but were not there yet. Smith's horrifying blow on the neck from Archer forced him out of the closing stages at Lord's – but gave Labuschagne an unexpected chance to demonstrate the coolness and technical aptitude for local climes he had already shown for Glamorgan. When he added two more sure-footed half-centuries at Headingley, the Australians looked to have secured the urn with two matches to spare, before being shattered by Stokes. Lyon fumbled one simple chance to win the game, then was denied an lbw shout for another, leaving him and the team to be ridiculed on their way to Old Trafford.

However, the events of 2018 had bred resilience, and in Langer the Australians had a methodical man who, next day, ensured they sifted over the mistakes of the final hour at Headingley. When Paine walked out with Joe Root for a crucial toss in Manchester, fate smiled on him for once: Australia had first, and best, use of the pitch. Enter the fit-again Smith, who carved out two more innings of impish majesty, defying every plan England tried. The bowlers finished the job with less than an hour to spare, sparking scenes of unrestrained jubilation: Australia had not only retained the Ashes in England for the first time since 2001, but done so with an approach that never threatened to cross the behavioural line. No one epitomised this better than Pat Cummins, who was at once a snarling fast bowler and a friendly salesman for the game, without any hint of contradiction.

An emotionally flat display at The Oval, where Paine unaccountably chose to bowl, deprived the Australians of an outright win. But it did give Langer a handy message to drive home: more ruthlessness and consistency were required. This was music to the ears of Labuschagne, in particular: he took the chance to feast on Pakistan and New Zealand, and finished as the only man to score more than 1,000 Test runs in 2019, despite not starting until August. Meanwhile, after a nightmare Ashes, Warner filled his boots, soaring to an unbeaten 335 against Pakistan at Adelaide. After Starc's sidelining in England, he returned a vastly improved bowler. And if Smith was not the run machine he had been a few months earlier, he was still the glue in each of Australia's first innings against New Zealand, especially during an MCG Test that drew over 200,000 spectators. Paine's men won all five home Tests by huge margins, and vaulted to second in the new World Test Championship table – the likely reward a showdown with India at Lord's in 2021.

If there were problems in the Australian game, they came at other levels. Pattinson and Marcus Stoinis both stooped to homophobic slurs during domestic matches, showing that improved behaviour by the national team was yet to filter down. And the six-month suspension of Hobart Hurricanes' Emily Smith for a seemingly minor infraction – posting a team line-up to her Instagram account before it had been officially announced – opened fault lines in a relationship that had been healing between the board and the Australian Cricketers' Association. Most incongruous of all was the national team's co-option by the prime minister, Scott Morrison, as a source of distraction during a bushfire season the government waited far too long to address. Even the cricketers' improved reputation, it seemed, brought unexpected problems.

AUSTRALIA v SRI LANKA IN 2018-19

Peter Lalor

Test matches (2): Australia 2, Sri Lanka 0

Sri Lanka's administrators had landed their embattled team with an arduous few months, since trips to New Zealand and South Africa sandwiched this brief stopover in Australia. Sri Lanka had lost five of the six internationals across the Tasman, and that disappointing form continued with crushing defeats in both Tests, costing Dinesh Chandimal the captaincy.

Few visiting sides can have arrived in such a sorry state. Corruption in the game at home, administrative infighting, injuries and poor discipline hardly added up to a recipe for improved results. "It's always tough as players, so many things happening," said Chandimal before the First Test.

It may have been the tail end of the home summer, but the Australians were in no mood to take it easy after their own horror stretch. The fallout from the sandpaper saga had overshadowed much of the season, and the struggle to find a convincing line-up in the absence of Steve Smith and David Warner had been shown up when India won a Test series in Australia for the first time. The hiccups continued. In an attempt to display faith and conviction, the selectors named their squad well before the Tests – only for New South Wales batsman Kurtis Patterson to be drafted in at the last moment, thanks to twin unbeaten hundreds for a Cricket Australia XI in a warm-up. He made his debut at Brisbane, edging out the talented 20-year-old Will Pucovski. Then, when Josh Hazlewood broke down, Jhye Richardson was called up, and won his first Baggy Green amid reports that experienced seamer Peter Siddle had been assured he was playing.

It didn't matter. Sri Lanka had lost 11 and drawn two of their previous Tests in Australia, and slumped badly again, surrendering the Warne–Muralitharan Trophy they had won, for the first time, with a 3–0 whitewash at home in 2016. They were without Angelo Mathews, who twanged a hamstring in New Zealand, but had high hopes of Lahiru Kumara, after his pace ruffled Kiwi feathers. He and the experienced Suranga Lakmal were expected to enjoy conditions at the Gabba's first day/night Test.

Lakmal did take five wickets but, by then, his batsmen had already been blown away; Pat Cummins ended up with ten for 62 in an innings victory. Sri Lanka's woes were compounded when Kumara and Dushmantha Chameera went down with injuries, and they were forced to field an entirely new pace attack when Lakmal failed a fitness test on the morning of the Second Test, the first played in Canberra. Australia's tall total included their first individual centuries of the home summer: Joe Burns made 180, while Travis Head and Patterson helped themselves to maiden hundreds. Tim Paine's decision to waive the follow-on prevented another innings defeat, but Australia still ran out easy winners. Mitchell Starc was the main destroyer this time, a slight tweak to his delivery stride paying dividends with a pair of five-fors. Sri Lanka's

Clutch control: Pat Cummins holds on to a return catch from Lahiru Thirimanne at Canberra.

batsmen finished with just two half-centuries between them in the Tests, with only the entertaining Niroshan Dickwella averaging over 30.

Sri Lanka's upheaval continued when Chandika Hathurusinghe, their coach, was relieved of selection duties before the Second Test. Shortly after it, Chandimal was dumped as captain and player; he had done himself few favours by insisting on batting at No. 3, scoring just 24 runs in four attempts. Opener Dimuth Karunaratne took charge for the South African tour that followed, which was shaping up as Sri Lanka's darkest hour. As it turned out, dawn was not far away.

SRI LANKAN TOURING PARTY

*L. D. Chandimal, P. V. D. Chameera, D. M. de Silva, D. P. D. N. Dickwella, A. N. P. R. Fernando, M. V. T. Fernando, C. Karunaratne, F. D. M. Karunaratne, C. B. R. L. S. Kumara, R. A. S. Lakmal, B. K. G. Mendis, M. D. K. Perera, M. D. K. J. Perera, C. A. K. Rajitha, W. S. R. Samarawickrama, P. A. D. L. R. Sandakan, A. R. S. Silva, H. D. R. L. Thirimanne. *Coach:* U. C. Hathurusinghe.

A. N. P. R. Fernando was ruled out with a damaged hamstring before the Tests, while Chameera and Kumara were injured during the First Test, and were replaced by M. V. T. Fernando and C. Karunaratne.

AUSTRALIA v SRI LANKA

First Test

At Brisbane, January 24–26, 2019 (day/night). Australia won by an innings and 40 runs. Toss: Sri Lanka. Test debuts: K. R. Patterson, J. A. Richardson.

In recent years, the Australian season has begun with the humiliation of opponents at the Gabba, where the humidity is draining and the bounce frightening. The last touring side to win here were West Indies, in 1988-89, since when Australia had won 22 and drawn seven. India avoided the ritual flogging by insisting their four-match series, which started in December 2018, should be arranged differently, with Adelaide staging the First Test; they also declined to play a day/night game. And so Sri Lanka, whose board have rather less financial leverage, found themselves playing under lights in Queensland. It did not end well.

Chandimal took the option – crazy or brave, depending on your point of view – of batting first on a pitch renowned for being at its most testing at the start. The openers held on for ten overs, but then came a collapse. Thirimanne and Chandimal fell in successive overs, Karunaratne was undone by Lyon – the only wicket in the innings to fall to spin – and soon Sri Lanka were floundering at 66 for five. Dickwella, who later proved a lively commentator when keeping wicket, made a freewheeling 64 that included an audacious scoop off the pacy Starc. It was by far the biggest contribution of an innings that lasted just 56.4 overs.

Australia had included two debutants. Compact seamer Jhye Richardson stood in for the injured Josh Hazlewood, while Kurtis Patterson barged his way into the squad courtesy of two undefeated centuries in the tourists' only warm-up game. The hosts had 25 testing overs to face under lights on the first evening, losing Burns and the out-of-touch Khawaja – but Harris battled through to the close, before falling in the first over next day. Sri Lanka had a sniff at 82 for four, but Labuschagne – who hit only three fours – and Head shared a patient stand of 166, spanning almost 50 overs; both made career-bests. The Sri Lankan bowlers got a little carried away by the pitch's reputation and overdid the short stuff – although Lakmal dismissed Head and Paine with successive balls, and finished with five for 75, his third five-for in 55 Tests, though second in two. He kept the total within bounds, but Australia still finished 179 in front.

It proved enough. Cummins had gone wicketless in the final Test against India at Sydney, but now filled his boots: after four for 39 in the first innings, he pocketed six more – his best in all cricket – slicing through some flimsy batting to finish with ten for 62, Australia's best at home against Sri Lanka, beating Peter Siddle's nine for 104 at Hobart in 2012-13.

Australia's win was only their second in eight Tests since the sandpaper shenanigans; their struggles were exemplified by the fact that Head's 84 was their highest score since Khawaja's century against Pakistan in Dubai in October 2018. Justin Langer, the coach, admitted to sleepless nights worrying about the ramifications of defeat by Sri Lanka. But that never looked likely: he could rest a little better knowing he would not go down as the first Australian coach to lose a series to them at home.

Player of the Match: P. J. Cummins.

Close of play: first day, Australia 72-2 (Harris 40, Lyon 0); second day, Sri Lanka 17-1 (Thirimanne 6).

Sri Lanka

F. D. M. Karunaratne c Paine b Lyon	24	– c Paine b Cummins	3
H. D. R. L. Thirimanne c Labuschagne b Cummins	12	– c Paine b Cummins	32
*L. D. Chandimal c Burns b Richardson	5	– c Patterson b Cummins	0
B. K. G. Mendis b Richardson	14	– c Burns b Cummins	1
A. R. S. Silva c Paine b Cummins	9	– c Burns b Cummins	3
D. M. de Silva c Paine b Richardson	5	– b Richardson	14
†D. P. D. N. Dickwella c Patterson b Cummins	64	– c Harris b Richardson	24
M. D. K. Perera c Labuschagne b Starc	1	– c Patterson b Cummins	8
R. A. S. Lakmal c Labuschagne b Starc	7	– st Paine b Lyon	24
P. V. D. Chameera c Patterson b Cummins	0	– not out	5
C. B. R. L. S. Kumara not out	0	– absent hurt	
W 1, nb 2	3	B 9, lb 15, nb 1	25

1/26 (2) 2/31 (3) 3/54 (1)   (56.4 overs) 144
4/58 (4) 5/66 (6) 6/91 (5)
7/102 (9) 8/106 (8) 9/144 (7) 10/144 (10)

1/17 (1) 2/17 (3)   (50.5 overs) 139
3/19 (4) 4/35 (5) 5/69 (6)
6/79 (2) 7/109 (7) 8/110 (8) 9/139 (9)

In the first innings Perera, when 1, retired hurt at 93-6 and resumed at 102-7.

Starc 12–2–41–2; Richardson 14–5–26–3; Cummins 14.4–3–39–4; Lyon 16–3–38–1. *Second innings*—Starc 14–1–56–0; Richardson 13.5–5–19–2; Lyon 8.5–3–17–1; Cummins 15–8–23–6.

Australia

M. S. Harris c Thirimanne b Kumara	.....	44	P. J. Cummins c Dickwella b Chameera ...	0
J. A. Burns c Mendis b Lakmal	....	15	M. A. Starc not out	 26
U. T. Khawaja b Perera	....	11	J. A. Richardson c Karunaratne b Perera...	1
N. M. Lyon c Mendis b Lakmal	....	1	B 6, lb 17, w 2, nb 5	 30
M. Labuschagne c Thirimanne b de Silva..		81		
T. M. Head lbw b Lakmal	....	84	1/37 (2) 2/72 (3) 3/76 (1) (106.2 overs)	323
K. R. Patterson lbw b Lakmal	....	30	4/82 (4) 5/248 (5) 6/272 (6)	
*†T. D. Paine c Mendis b Lakmal	....	0	7/272 (8) 8/278 (9) 9/304 (7) 10/323 (11)	

Lakmal 27–9–75–5; Kumara 15–5–37–1; Chameera 21–3–68–1; Perera 32.2–9–84–2; de Silva 8–3–22–1; Karunaratne 3–0–14–0.

Umpires: M. Erasmus and R. K. Illingworth.   Third umpire: M. A. Gough.
Referee: J. Srinath.

AUSTRALIA v SRI LANKA

Second Test

At Canberra, February 1–4, 2019. Australia won by 366 runs. Toss: Australia. Test debut: C. Karunaratne.

Almost 92 years after Canberra became Australia's capital, it finally staged a Test match. The Manuka Oval was the country's 11th Test ground (Perth Stadium had been the tenth, seven weeks earlier). But if the venue was new, the story was familiar: Sri Lanka sank to a whopping defeat well inside the distance. They were not helped by injuries, which wiped out their pace attack: Dushmantha Chameera and Lahiru Kumara had broken down in Brisbane, while Suranga Lakmal failed a fitness test on his back just before the start here. As well as replacing the seamers – all-rounder Chamika Karunaratne won his first cap – the selectors (now excluding Sri Lanka's coach Chandika Hathurusinghe) recalled Kusal Perera in place of Roshen Silva.

The Australians were having a much better time of it. After no centuries in six Tests, three batsmen tucked in: Burns, Head and Patterson made the most of gentle conditions and the second-choice attack. Test hundreds are rarely insignificant, but all three had special value, with an Ashes tour looming. Burns had been ignored against India, but forced his way back thanks to good first-class form. This was a bid to open in England – and a timely one, as Harris's form was tailing off.

Head delivered on the promise he had shown in his first seven matches, and finished the Australian summer with a Test average of 51. Patterson's hundred, meanwhile, came in just his second appearance at this level. Paine declared at a towering 534 for five, with four Sri Lankan bowlers chalking up centuries of their own. Only Vishwa Fernando, with three wickets, made much impression on the venerable scoreboard, which had seen service at the MCG before being carefully rebuilt in Canberra in the 1980s.

After the bowlers' suffering came misery for the batsmen, at the hands of Australia's quicks. The openers shared another useful stand, but Dimuth Karunaratne was hit on the back of the neck by a Cummins bouncer, which delayed the game before he was taken to hospital. There was no lasting damage, and he courageously returned next day to top-score with 59. Kusal Perera was also hit, by Richardson, and eventually retired hurt as well – although not before waving away two offers of medical help. The Sri Lankans did not have a team doctor, and the sight of a batsman twice insisting to the physiotherapist that he was all right, before doubling over in distress, was a warning that cricket's concussion protocols are out of step with best practice.

Starc made the most of the batsmen's discomfort, with five for 54. He had been out of sorts throughout the home summer, and under pressure going into this match. But adjustments to his delivery stride seemed to do the trick: Sri Lanka were bundled out for 215, with Thirimanne's deception by Lyon starting the slide. Paine's decision to bat again despite a lead of 319 was good news for Khawaja, who had passed 50 only once in 11 innings since his century in Dubai four months earlier. Recapturing his easy, languid style, he reached three figures before a declaration set Sri Lanka a notional 516.

The chase never started. Starc took another five-for against a side who appeared demoralised. Thirimanne ground his way to 30, and Mendis top-scored with 42, but no one else lasted more than an hour and a quarter. Cummins took three cheap wickets to finish with 14 for 109 in the series, and soon went top of the ICC's Test bowling rankings.

Player of the Match: M. A. Starc.   *Player of the Series*: P. J. Cummins.

Close of play: first day, Australia 384-4 (Burns 172, Patterson 25); second day, Sri Lanka 123-3 (M. D. K. J. Perera 11, de Silva 1); third day, Sri Lanka 17-0 (F. D. M. Karunaratne 8, Thirimanne 8).

Australia

M. S. Harris c C. Karunaratne b Fernando	11	– c Mendis b Rajitha	14
J. A. Burns b Rajitha	180	– c Mendis b Fernando	9
U. T. Khawaja c Mendis b Fernando	0	– not out	101
M. Labuschagne c Dickwella b C. Karunaratne	6	– c Dickwella b Rajitha	4
T. M. Head lbw b Fernando	161	– not out	59
K. R. Patterson not out	114		
*†T. D. Paine not out	45		
Lb 3, w 4, nb 10	17	W 3, nb 6	9

1/11 (1) 2/15 (3)   (5 wkts dec, 132 overs) 534   1/16 (1)   (3 wkts dec, 47 overs) 196
3/28 (4) 4/336 (5) 5/404 (2)   2/25 (2) 3/37 (4)

P. J. Cummins, M. A. Starc, J. A. Richardson and N. M. Lyon did not bat.

Rajitha 28–5–103–1; Fernando 30–3–126–3; C. Karunaratne 22–0–130–1; M. D. K. Perera 32–4–112–0; de Silva 20–2–60–0. *Second innings*—Fernando 11–1–43–1; Rajitha 13–2–64–2; M. D. K. Perera 15–3–52–0; C. Karunaratne 4–1–18–0; de Silva 4–0–19–0.

Sri Lanka

F. D. M. Karunaratne c Patterson b Starc	59	– b Starc	8
H. D. R. L. Thirimanne c Khawaja b Lyon	41	– c and b Cummins	30
*L. D. Chandimal c Paine b Starc	15	– c Labuschagne b Starc	4
B. K. G. Mendis b Cummins	6	– (5) c Patterson b Labuschagne	42
M. D. K. J. Perera retired hurt	29	– (6) c Paine b Starc	0
D. M. de Silva hit wkt b Starc	25	– (7) c Head b Richardson	6
†D. P. D. N. Dickwella lbw b Labuschagne	25	– (4) b Starc	27
C. Karunaratne c Starc b Lyon	0	– c Paine b Cummins	22
M. D. K. Perera c Paine b Starc	10	– c Paine b Cummins	4
C. A. K. Rajitha not out	0	– not out	2
M. V. T. Fernando b Starc	0	– b Starc	0
B 1, lb 4	5	B 1, lb 1, w 2	4

1/90 (2) 2/101 (4) 3/120 (3)   (68.3 overs) 215   1/18 (1) 2/28 (3)   (51 overs) 149
4/180 (6) 5/181 (1) 6/182 (8)   3/58 (2) 4/83 (4)
7/215 (7) 8/215 (9) 9/215 (11)   5/83 (6) 6/97 (7) 7/143 (5)
                                                               8/143 (8) 9/148 (9) 10/149 (11)

In the first innings F. D. M. Karunaratne, when 46, retired hurt at 82-0 and resumed at 157-3, when M. D. K. J. Perera retired hurt.

Starc 13.3–2–54–5; Richardson 15–4–49–0; Cummins 14–3–32–1; Lyon 24–6–70–2; Labuschagne 2–1–5–1. *Second innings*—Starc 18–2–46–5; Richardson 9–1–29–1; Lyon 13–1–51–0; Cummins 8–2–15–3; Labuschagne 3–1–6–1.

Umpires: M. A. Gough and R. K. Illingworth.   Third umpire: M. Erasmus.
Referee: J. Srinath.

AUSTRALIA v SRI LANKA IN 2019-20

Andrew Wu

Twenty20 internationals (3): Australia 3, Sri Lanka 0

The previous Australian season had ended with Sri Lanka being walloped in a couple of Tests, and the new one started in similar fashion, with a shellacking in three Twenty20s. It was a mark of the low regard in which Australia had held the shortest format that this was their first series victory over Sri Lanka at home. In their previous 20-over series here, in February 2017, the Sri Lankans had faced a makeshift side, as the main Australian team were in India preparing for a Test series. The board had to appoint stand-ins as captain and coach. They chose well: this time, Justin Langer and Aaron Finch were in permanent charge.

Those who believe T20 is a better spectacle at franchise level gathered plenty of ammunition during this one-sided series. The fact that the next Twenty20 World Cup was due to be played in Australia 12 months later should have provided some context – but there was little interest in the three games. Although Lasith Malinga returned as captain, along with some senior players who had opted out of Sri Lanka's tour of Pakistan, his side were otherwise relatively inexperienced, and had just one warm-up game. That was against the Prime Minister's XI in Canberra, a gentle affair in which the PM himself, Scott Morrison, ran the drinks. Predictably, the Sri Lankans struggled when the real thing came around. Only Kusal Perera scored more than 21, while the bowlers claimed just six wickets between them.

Even though it was the first time locals could see Steve Smith and David Warner in action after their ball-tampering bans, the turnstiles were hardly spinning. It was the earliest start to a home summer since 2005-06, and TV coverage was behind a paywall, which reduced awareness. A few weeks after being made to look a novice by Stuart Broad in the Ashes, Warner clobbered 100, 60 and 57 without being dismissed.

The subject of mental health among elite sportsmen resurfaced with the news that Glenn Maxwell, one of the format's most popular players, needed time out to deal with issues. At Adelaide, Maxwell clouted 62, though it transpired that he had opened up about his turmoil to Langer only the day before.

SRI LANKA TOURING PARTY

*S. L. Malinga, P. W. H. de Silva, D. P. D. N. Dickwella, A. N. P. R. Fernando, B. O. P. Fernando, W. I. A. Fernando, M. D. Gunathilleke, G. S. F. N. G. Jayasuriya, C. B. R. L. S. Kumara, B. K. G. Mendis, M. D. K. J. Perera, P. B. B. Rajapaksa, C. A. K. Rajitha, P. A. D. L. R. Sandakan, M. D. Shanaka, I. Udana. *Interim coach:* R. J. Ratnayake.

First Twenty20 international At Adelaide, October 27, 2019. **Australia won by 134 runs. Australia 233-2** (20 overs) (A. J. Finch 64, D. A. Warner 100*, G. J. Maxwell 62); ‡**Sri Lanka 99-9** (20 overs) (A. Zampa 3-14). PoM: D. A. Warner. *In his first home international since Sandpapergate, David Warner delighted a modest crowd of 16,268 by smashing his maiden T20I century, from 56* *balls, after Lasith Malinga had inserted Australia on a good track. Warner put on 122 with Aaron Finch and 107 with Glenn Maxwell, who clattered 62 off 28. Seamer Kasun Rajitha's four wicketless overs cost 75, the most expensive in the format. The entire Sri Lankan team couldn't match Warner's tally; the top score was Dasun Shanaka's 17, and the margin of defeat the fourth-highest by runs in T20Is between Test-playing nations.*

BIGGEST VICTORIES BY RUNS IN A T20 INTERNATIONAL

257	**Czech Republic (278-4) beat Turkey (21)**	. . . .	Ilfov (Romania)	. . . . . .	**2019**
173	**Romania (226-6) beat Turkey (53)**	. . . .	Ilfov (Romania)	. . . . . .	**2019**
172	Sri Lanka (260-6) beat Kenya (88)	. . . .	Johannesburg	. . . .	2007-08
143	Pakistan (203-5) beat West Indies (60)	. . . .	Karachi	. . . .	2017-18
143	India (213-4) beat Ireland (70)	. . . .	Malahide	. . . .	2018
141	**Nepal (236-3) beat Bhutan (95-6)**	. . . .	Kirtipur	. . . .	**2019-20**
137	**England (182-6) beat West Indies (45)**	. . . .	Basseterre	. . . .	**2018-19**
135	**Austria (239-3) beat Luxembourg (104-8)**	. . . .	Ilfov (Romania)	. . . . . .	**2019**
134	**Australia (233-2) beat Sri Lanka (99-9)**	. . . .	Adelaide	. . . .	**2019-20**
133	**Papua New Guinea (216-4) beat Philippines (83-8)**	. .	Port Moresby	. . . .	**2018-19**
130	South Africa (211-5) beat Scotland (81)	. . . .	The Oval	. . . .	2009

Second Twenty20 international   At Brisbane, October 30, 2019 (floodlit). **Australia won by nine wickets.** ‡**Sri Lanka 117** (19 overs); **Australia 118-1** (13 overs) (D. A. Warner 60*, S. P. D. Smith 53*). *PoM:* D. A. Warner. *Malinga opted to bat first this time, but his side only just made it into three figures. Kusal Perera's 27 was the top score against some disciplined bowling – Pat Cummins (2-29) was the most expensive. Finch departed first ball, but Warner and Steve Smith coasted home with a stand of 117*. Mitchell Starc missed the match to attend the wedding of his brother Brandon, the Commonwealth Games high-jump champion.*

Third Twenty20 international   At Melbourne, November 1, 2019 (floodlit). **Australia won by seven wickets. Sri Lanka 142-6** (20 overs) (M. D. K. J. Perera 57); ‡**Australia 145-3** (17.4 overs) (A. J. Finch 37, D. A. Warner 57*). *PoM:* D. A. Warner. *PoS:* D. A. Warner. *Another day, another drubbing for the Sri Lankans. Home fans were heavily outnumbered by Sri Lankan supporters, who left disappointed after Australia eased to a whitewash. Perera, with 57 from 45 balls, led an improved batting performance, although a target of 143 was never a problem once openers Finch and Warner knocked up 69 inside nine overs. Warner saw the chase through, finishing the series with 217 runs without dismissal, at a strike-rate of 147, while Cummins claimed 6-79 from 12 overs.*

AUSTRALIA v PAKISTAN IN 2019-20

Adam Collins

Twenty20 internationals (3): Australia 2, Pakistan 0
Test matches (2): Australia 2 (120pts), Pakistan 0 (0pts)

A nostalgic lament accompanied Azhar Ali's hapless team. With Waqar Younis on the coaching staff, and Wasim Akram in the commentary box, Pakistan's winless tour was routinely compared with better times in Australia. Just as in every visit since 1999-2000, they were swept in the Tests, having fared little better in the T20s. Pakistan's losing streak Down Under now stretched to 14 Tests. The only difference from the previous four series – all lost 3–0 – was that this contained only two matches. Even so, it was probably the least competitive of the lot.

The disparity was best highlighted by the fact that Australia batted only once in each Test. David Warner piled up 489 runs, including 335 not out at Adelaide, the second-highest score by an Australian; it helped atone for his horror Ashes. That he didn't clear the ropes until he had passed 300 was a reminder of his evolution as a Test opener in home conditions. Only England's Wally Hammond, with 563 in New Zealand in 1932-33, had scored more in a series from just two innings.

Just as telling were the contributions of Joe Burns, Warner's recalled opening partner, and Marnus Labuschagne, who rattled off consecutive centuries – his first for Australia – while barely giving a chance. The middle order had a quiet time: in both matches, Steve Smith entered with the score past 350; at Adelaide, Travis Head became only the third Australian to take part in a Test win without batting, bowling or taking a catch, after Bill Johnston (twice) and Craig McDermott.

The two men most in need of wickets both tucked in. Overlooked for all but one Ashes Test, Mitchell Starc reclaimed the new ball, and made it count. He started in top gear in the forgettable T20 hors d'oeuvre – which might also have been a clean sweep but for rain in Sydney – and romped through the

---

MOST CONSECUTIVE TEST DEFEATS IN ONE COUNTRY

14*	Pakistan in Australia............	**1999-2000 to 2019-20**
13	Bangladesh in Bangladesh........	2001-02 to 2004-05
9	India in Australia..............	1947-48 to 1977-78
9	West Indies in Australia..........	2000-01 to 2009-10
9*	**Bangladesh in New Zealand**......	**2001-02 to 2018-19**
8	South Africa in South Africa.......	1888-89 to 1898-99
8	South Africa in Australia..........	1911-12 to 1952-53
8	England in Australia.............	1920-21 to 1924-25
8	India in England	1959 to 1967
8*	Zimbabwe in Sri Lanka...........	1996-97 to 2017
8	Bangladesh in Sri Lanka.........	2001-02 to 2007
8	England in Australia.............	2013-14 to 2017-18

* *Sequence unbroken.*

Daniel Kalisz, Cricket Australia/Getty Images

Bound to succeed: David Warner celebrates his triple-hundred at Adelaide with a trademark leap.

Tests, taking 14 wickets, six in the first innings at Adelaide. Nathan Lyon had not previously shone against Pakistan, but rounded off the series with a welcome five-for. Pat Cummins and Josh Hazlewood shared 18.

Sean Abbott made the most of his return to the T20 team, claiming the match award in Perth, while fellow seamer Kane Richardson also pressed his claims. Only Babar Azam, who made two half-centuries, and Iftikhar Ahmed were able to lay a glove on the Australians, who made it seven straight 20-over wins a year before their home World Cup. They were also reminded that Smith was still a vital member of the short-form team, after a dazzling unbeaten 51-ball 80 in Canberra.

Babar took his good form into the Tests, making a superb rearguard century at Brisbane, before falling three short of another at Adelaide. Mohammad Rizwan prospered too, silencing those critical of Sarfraz Ahmed's sacking. Asad Shafiq and Shan Masood had their moments, but collectively Pakistan were overawed. Yasir Shah's leg-spin was savaged. He had averaged 84 with the ball on his previous visit, and now fared even worse: four wickets at 100.50, while leaking around five an over. However, a defiant century from No. 8 in Adelaide showed his spirit.

Pakistan's pace attack had started by blowing away Australia A in a warm-up, but after that only Shaheen Shah Afridi delivered the goods. As he was still only 19, it was asking a lot for him to lead an attack shorn of Mohammad Amir and Wahab Riaz – both retired from Tests, to the chagrin of selector/coach Misbah-ul-Haq – but he did his best. Fellow teenagers Naseem Shah and Musa

Khan fought well, but were not ready for Test cricket, while Imran Khan and Mohammad Abbas were reduced versions of their former selves. Abbas was left out at Brisbane, and failed to strike at Adelaide. It summed up Pakistan's miserable tour.

PAKISTAN TOURING PARTY

*Azhar Ali (T), Abid Ali (T), Asad Shafiq (T), Asif Ali (20), Babar Azam (T/20), Fakhar Zaman (20), Haris Sohail (T/20), Iftikhar Ahmed (T/20), Imad Wasim (20), Imam-ul-Haq (T/20), Imran Khan (T), Kashif Bhatti (T), Khushdil Shah (20), Mohammad Abbas (T), Mohammad Amir (20), Mohammad Hasnain (20), Mohammad Irfan (20), Mohammad Rizwan (T/20), Musa Khan (T/20), Naseem Shah (T), Shadab Khan (20), Shaheen Shah Afridi (T), Shan Masood (T), Usman Qadir (20), Wahab Riaz (20), Yasir Shah (T). *Coach:* Misbah-ul-Haq.
   Babar Azam captained in the T20s.

First Twenty20 international   At Sydney, November 3, 2019. **No result. Pakistan 107-5** (15 overs) (Babar Azam 59*, Mohammad Rizwan 31); ‡**Australia 41-0** (3.1 overs) (A. J. Finch 37*). *With Australia chasing a revised 119 in 15 overs, Aaron Finch had just clobbered 25 from the third (which also included a no-ball) when a storm scuppered the contest. Finch grumbled that, despite an earlier lengthy interruption, 20 minutes were still allocated to the break at change of innings: another 11 deliveries would have meant a result. Pakistan's own momentum was halted at 88-3 in the 13th. They had made a decent recovery after losing Fakhar Zaman and Haris Sohail in the first two overs. Babar Azam hit a classy half-century, and Mohammad Rizwan batted promisingly, but Pakistan could add only 19 from 14 balls after the restart.*

Second Twenty20 international   At Canberra, November 5, 2019 (floodlit). **Australia won by seven wickets. ‡Pakistan 150-6** (20 overs) (Babar Azam 50, Iftikhar Ahmed 62*); **Australia 151-3** (18.3 overs) (S. P. D. Smith 80*). *PoM:* S. P. D. Smith. *Critics who suggested Steve Smith shouldn't be part of Australia's T20 World Cup calculations were silenced by his brilliant 80* from 51 balls. After losing Finch and David Warner in the powerplay, Australia had work to do, which suited Smith. He unveiled precise strokeplay and a deep bag of tricks, including one ostentatious cross-court forehand, and collected exactly 50 in boundaries. For once, Warner's major contribution was not with the bat, although he did spank 20 from 11 balls: earlier he had run out Pakistan's top-scorer Babar with a direct hit from deep midwicket. Iftikhar Ahmed made the most of the final four overs, clearing the ropes three times – but 150 never looked enough on a belter.*

Third Twenty20 international   At Perth, November 8, 2019 (floodlit). **Australia won by ten wickets. Pakistan 106-8** (20 overs) (Iftikhar Ahmed 45; K. W. Richardson 3-18); ‡**Australia 109-0** (11.5 overs) (D. A. Warner 48*, A. J. Finch 52*). *PoM:* S. A. Abbott. *PoS:* S. P. D. Smith. *T20I debuts: Khushdil Shah, Musa Khan (Pakistan). Australia finished their run of six T20 internationals in 13 days with five wins (plus a no-result). Sent in on a brisk and bouncy track, Pakistan soon lost Babar to Mitchell Starc's inswinger, the first of three wickets in the powerplay. With Pat Cummins given a rest, Sean Abbott had figures of 4–16–14–2 in his first international for five years. Iftikhar played another punchy innings – 45 from 37 – but Imam-ul-Haq was the only other to reach double figures. Warner and Finch then cruised to victory with 49 balls to spare. The only negative was how few Australians had the chance to bat in the series, though it was hardly a bad problem to have.*

At Perth Stadium, November 11–13, 2019 (day/night). Drawn. ‡**Pakistanis 428** (118 overs) (Asad Shafiq 119, Babar Azam 157, Yasir Shah 53; J. A. Richardson 3-79) **and 152-3 dec** (40.5 overs) (Shan Masood 65, Iftikhar Ahmed 79*); **Australia A 122** (56.4 overs) (Imran Khan 5-32) **and 91-2** (35 overs). *The Pakistanis dominated this floodlit first-class warm-up, although they put batting practice ahead of a probable victory by waiving the follow-on, despite a lead of 306. From 60-3, Asad Shafiq and Babar (who hit 24 fours) added 276, before both retired at the end of the 90th over. Australia A lost Test opener Joe Burns first ball, and were soon 57-9. Cameron Bancroft (49) added 65 for the last wicket with Riley Meredith, whose 19* was only his second double-figure score in 15 first-class matches. A brisk spell from 16-year-old Naseem Shah (8–3–21–1) secured him a Test debut; he had missed the second day's play after news of his mother's death reached him from Pakistan.*

AUSTRALIA v PAKISTAN

First Test

At Brisbane, November 21–24, 2019. Australia won by an innings and five runs. Australia 60pts. Toss: Pakistan. Test debut: Naseem Shah.

Pakistan had been regular Gabba victims over the 30 summers since Australia last lost a Test there, and so it proved once more. For the hosts, as important as the victory were the batsmen who set it up: Warner brilliant after his catastrophic Ashes, Burns back with him at the top after too long away, and Labuschagne making the next step with a maiden century, to follow a memorable northern summer. Then the first-choice fast-bowling trio – who had turned out together only once in England – took 18 wickets between them.

By contrast, Pakistan were outmatched with the bat – with the honourable exceptions of Babar Azam and Mohammad Rizwan – and largely impotent with the ball. A fifth away defeat in a row was a formality well before the end of the second day, which was all the more frustrating after Shan Masood and Azhar Ali had reached lunch unscathed on the first. But they didn't last much longer, and five wickets tumbled for 19, including Babar, who drove expansively at his fourth ball, from Hazlewood.

Asad Shafiq, who made a century here in 2016-17, watched the chaos from the non-striker's end. But punchy cameos from Rizwan and Yasir Shah gave him time to accumulate 76. Rizwan made 37 before he was caught behind, although extensive replays were needed before Michael Gough, the third umpire, somehow ruled that part of Cummins's foot was behind the line. The controversy took some of the gloss off a good bowling display, led by Starc, who was on a hat-trick after striking twice with the second new ball.

Australia's tidy work continued on a hot second morning, with Warner and Burns skating to an even 100 by lunch. Their stand called into question the decisions which had led to 13 changes of opening partnership since these two were split up in 2016. Imran Khan suffered stage fright after being picked ahead of Mohammad Abbas, and 16-year-old debutant Naseem Shah lacked the consistency to go with his pace. Shortly after lunch, Naseem found Warner's edge, only for replays to reveal a big no-ball. Warner was nearly run out by Yasir Shah on 93, but his 22nd Test century – and 16th at home – was otherwise seldom in doubt. At his home ground, Burns eventually swept Yasir on to his leg stump on 97. His expression spoke volumes, but a 222-run stand meant more than the milestone. Warner said he wanted Burns to stay as his opening partner.

Enter Labuschagne. Already displaying several affectations learned from watching Smith, he quickly began accumulating like him. On the third morning, when Warner was able to add only three to his overnight 151 in the first hour, Labuschagne was soon into the nineties. After drinks, Warner fell to a brutish Naseem bouncer: a high-class first Test victim, however belated. At 296 balls, it was also – for a week – Warner's longest innings.

But this was Labuschagne's day, more so when Smith quickly lost his off stump to Yasir. After four consecutive half-centuries in England, Labuschagne was now able to celebrate properly, when a thick edge delivered his first Test hundred, in front of his family. He still wasn't done, adding a brisk 110 with Wade, before Head helped the total past 500. Finally, on 185, Labuschagne departed, after 279 balls and 20 fours. The tail did not last long, which massaged some battered bowling figures – not least Yasir's, whose four wickets cost 205.

Pakistan had 17 overs to survive that night, but were three down inside half an hour. Starc accounted for Azhar and Haris Sohail – via another timid waft – before Shafiq nicked a beauty from Cummins. Masood and Babar avoid further disasters, and continued an hour into the fourth day, before Masood lost a battle with Cummins's bouncer. Six balls later, Iftikhar completed a miserable comeback by edging Hazlewood: 94 for five.

Unfazed, Babar shifted into his most elegant gear. Helped by Rizwan, he reached 50 before lunch, and reduced the deficit under 100 shortly before tea. A year earlier, he had fallen for 99 against Australia in Abu Dhabi, but this time two fours off Cummins completed a quality century. He celebrated ecstatically, then fell to Lyon shortly afterwards.

Rizwan, in his second Test, three years after his debut, and replacing the deposed captain Sarfraz Ahmed, saw a similar opportunity. After his stand of 132 with Babar, he wielded a horizontal bat in the best traditions of punchy wicketkeepers. But, after putting on 79 with Yasir, he slashed at Hazlewood, and was caught at deep backward point. The match was done and dusted five overs later, though Babar and Rizwan left Brisbane as Pakistan's big pluses. Not many touring players can say that after a Gabba hiding.

Player of the Match: M. Labuschagne.   *Attendance:* 45,991.

Close of play: first day, Pakistan 240; second day, Australia 312-1 (Warner 151, Labuschagne 55); third day, Pakistan 64-3 (Shan Masood 27, Babar Azam 20).

Pakistan

Shan Masood c Smith b Cummins	27	– c Paine b Cummins 42
*Azhar Ali c Burns b Hazlewood	39	– lbw b Starc 5
Haris Sohail c Paine b Starc	1	– c Paine b Starc 8
Asad Shafiq b Cummins	76	– c Smith b Cummins 0
Babar Azam c Burns b Hazlewood	1	– c Paine b Lyon 104
Iftikhar Ahmed c Labuschagne b Lyon	7	– c Paine b Hazlewood 0
†Mohammad Rizwan c Paine b Cummins	37	– c Lyon b Hazlewood 95
Yasir Shah b Starc	26	– c Wade b Hazlewood 42
Shaheen Shah Afridi c Paine b Starc	0	– c Cummins b Hazlewood 10
Naseem Shah c and b Starc	7	– (11) not out. 0
Imran Khan not out	5	– (10) c Wade b Starc 5
B 4, lb 8, w 1, nb 1	14	B 9, lb 9, w 5, nb 1 24

1/75 (1) 2/75 (2) 3/77 (3)   (86.2 overs) 240   1/13 (2) 2/25 (3)   (84.2 overs) 335
4/78 (5) 5/94 (6) 6/143 (7)   3/25 (4) 4/93 (1)
7/227 (8) 8/227 (9) 9/227 (4) 10/240 (10)   5/94 (6) 6/226 (5) 7/305 (7)
                                                     8/324 (8) 9/331 (9) 10/335 (10)

Starc 18.2–5–52–4; Hazlewood 20–6–46–2; Cummins 22–7–60–3; Lyon 17–3–40–1; Labuschagne 8–0–24–0; Smith 1–0–6–0. *Second innings*—Starc 16.2–1–73–3; Cummins 21–6–69–2; Hazlewood 21–3–63–4; Lyon 21–3–74–1; Labuschagne 5–0–38–0.

Australia

D. A. Warner c Mohammad Rizwan b Naseem Shah	154	P. J. Cummins c Mohammad Rizwan b Imran Khan . 7
J. A. Burns b Yasir Shah	97	M. A. Starc lbw b Yasir Shah 5
M. Labuschagne c Babar Azam b Shaheen Shah Afridi	185	N. M. Lyon not out 13
S. P. D. Smith b Yasir Shah	4	J. R. Hazlewood lbw b Yasir Shah 5
M. S. Wade c Mohammad Rizwan b Haris Sohail	60	B 6, lb 4, nb 3 13
T. M. Head c Mohammad Rizwan b Haris Sohail	24	
*†T. D. Paine c Asad Shafiq b Shaheen Shah Afridi	13	

1/222 (2) 2/351 (1)   (157.4 overs) 580
3/358 (4) 4/468 (5)
5/506 (6) 6/545 (7) 7/546 (3)
8/559 (9) 9/567 (8) 10/580 (11)

Shaheen Shah Afridi 34–7–96–2; Imran Khan 24–3–73–1; Naseem Shah 20–1–68–1; Iftikhar Ahmed 12–0–53–0; Yasir Shah 48.4–1–205–4; Haris Sohail 19–1–75–2.

Umpires: R. K. Illingworth and R. A. Kettleborough.   Third umpire: M. A. Gough.
Referee: J. J. Crowe.

" The left-handed batsman is a thorough nuisance and a cause of waste of time."
A History of Left-Handed Batting, page 85

AUSTRALIA v PAKISTAN

Second Test

At Adelaide, November 29–December 2, 2019 (day/night). Australia won by an innings and 48 runs. Australia 60pts. Toss: Australia. Test debut: Musa Khan.

This game will be long remembered for David Warner amassing the tenth-highest score in Test cricket. And his relentless unbeaten 335 might have gone to the top of the list but for Paine's declaration, timed to get Pakistan batting under the lights. Alongside Labuschagne, Warner overwhelmed an attack in which Shaheen Shah Afridi was a lone beacon. Australia's bowlers did the rest, Starc snaring six wickets in the first innings, and Lyon five in the second, after Paine enforced the follow-on. Babar Azam fell just short of another hundred, before Yasir Shah's unlikely century provided a moment for celebration after he had returned his country's second-worst Test figures.

With rain forecast, Paine had made an obvious decision to bat, though Burns was quickly sorted out by Afridi. But Pakistan's next success was more than a day away: the recalled Mohammad Abbas lacked his customary nip, while Musa Khan experienced a similar ride to fellow teenager Naseem Shah in the First Test. The attack quickly wilted. Warner reached 50, shortly before the century stand, and after dinner pushed a single to

HIGHEST TEST SCORES IN AUSTRALIA

380	M. L. Hayden	Australia v Zimbabwe at Perth (WACA)	2003-04
335*	**D. A. Warner**	**Australia v Pakistan at Adelaide**	**2019-20**
329*	M. J. Clarke	Australia v India at Sydney	2011-12
307	R. M. Cowper	Australia v England at Melbourne	1965-66
299*	D. G. Bradman	Australia v South Africa at Adelaide	1931-32
290	L. R. P. L. Taylor	New Zealand v Australia at Perth (WACA)	2015-16
287†	R. E. Foster	England v Australia at Sydney	1903-04
277	B. C. Lara	West Indies v Australia at Sydney	1992-93
270	D. G. Bradman	Australia v England at Melbourne	1936-37
269*	A. C. Voges	Australia v West Indies at Hobart	2015-16
268	G. N. Yallop	Australia v Pakistan at Melbourne	1983-84

† *On Test debut.*

point, and leapt for joy; his 23rd Test century was his first against a pink ball. Labuschagne soon followed him to three figures. There was no let-up: by stumps Australia had 302 for one, and the stand was already worth 294, the highest for the second wicket at Adelaide, beating 275 by Colin McDonald and Lindsay Hassett against South Africa in 1952-53.

Next morning, Warner's whirring legs between the wickets signalled a desire for many more. At 330, the partnership became the highest for the second wicket in Australia, beating the unbeaten 329 of Alastair Cook and Jonathan Trott for England at Brisbane in 2010-11. Labuschagne, flawless throughout, was eventually castled for 162 by Afridi with the second new ball, ending a stand of 361, the highest for any Australian wicket against Pakistan. Four deliveries later, Warner reached his second double.

Thoughts of just how far he could go were briefly put aside as Smith – batting with Warner for the first time since their sandpaper bans – pulled level with Don Bradman on 6,996 Test runs, before cruising to 7,000 in his 126th innings, five fewer than Wally Hammond, the previous-fastest to the mark (Bradman had only 80 innings).

On 226, Warner was again reprieved by a wayward front foot, Musa following Naseem in missing out on a notable first Test wicket. He motored past his previous-best (253) to reach 262 by tea. Smith became Afridi's third victim, but Wade proved the perfect co-pilot with some equally determined running. All told, Warner zipped between the wickets 295 times.

Soon, he was pulling Abbas for four to complete the 31st Test triple-century, witnessed by his tearful wife, Candice. Each over seemed to bring another notch on the all-time table. He knew Paine was going to declare at 5.40, though Warner was given another over to pass Bradman's (and Mark Taylor's) 334, which he did from his 418th and final ball; he finished with 39 fours and a six. The decision to frustrate those who wanted him to go for Brian Lara's 400 – and others who thought 334 was the place to pause – but Paine wanted to bowl under the lights, and was mindful of the forecast.

Pakistan quickly lost Imam-ul-Haq before the dinner break, caught in the gully, inevitably by Warner, and five more in the evening session, four to Starc. The last required a spectacular Paine dive to dispose of Brisbane hero Mohammad Rizwan for a duck. Resuming a hefty 294 short of the follow-on target, Babar Azam and Yasir spent the third morning frustrating the Australians. Babar moved past 50, and Yasir played his shots. When Starc's awayswing eventually sorted out Babar, he left to a rousing ovation.

FEWEST INNINGS TO REACH 7,000 TEST RUNS

		T	HS	100	50	Avge
126	S. P. D. Smith (Australia)	**70**	239	**26**	27	63.75
131	W. R. Hammond (England)	80	336*	22	23	60.88
134	V. Sehwag (India/World)	79	319	21	22	54.56
136	S. R. Tendulkar (India)	85	217	28	57.98
138	G. S. Sobers (West Indies)	79	365*	22	27	58.78
138	V. Kohli (India)	**81**	254*	**26**	22	55.10
138	K. C. Sangakkara (Sri Lanka)	83	287	19	31	55.42
139	Mohammad Yousuf (Pakistan)	82	223	24	29	55.11
140	S. M. Gavaskar (India)	80	221	25	31	54.10
140	I. V. A. Richards (West Indies)	94	291	22	31	53.48

Average shown at the end of the innings in which 7,000 was reached.
D. G. Bradman (Australia) scored 6,996 runs in 80 Test innings.

Starc trapped Afridi next ball, and came close to a hat-trick when he found Abbas's leading edge. But Yasir kept swinging, reaching a maiden half-century, then careering into the nineties. His 100th run was predictably madcap and euphoric, just clearing Cummins at mid-on. Having seen Warner leap three times, he did so himself. No one had played more than Yasir's 56 Test innings before a maiden century without already passing 50 (his previous-best of 42 had come at Brisbane).

An entertaining stand of 87 with Abbas ended when Cummins took his 50th Test wicket of the year, and Yasir finally fell for 113, having dragged Pakistan from 89 for six to 302 – still 88 short of the follow-on. Despite being in the field for nearly 95 overs, Paine popped Pakistan in again, and three more tumbled before stumps. Next day, a flurry of wickets gave Lyon a five-for, and 50 at Adelaide, where he once worked as a groundsman. Rizwan was bowled by Hazlewood, and the *coup de grâce* came when Cummins threw the stumps down to run out Abbas. But this was Warner's match.

Player of the Match: D. A. Warner *Attendance:* 91,879.
Player of the Series: D. A. Warner.
Close of play: first day, Australia 302-1 (Warner 166, Labuschagne 126); second day, Pakistan 96-6 (Babar Azam 43, Yasir Shah 4); third day, Pakistan 39-3 (Shan Masood 14, Asad Shafiq 8).

Australia

D. A. Warner not out 335		M. S. Wade not out 38		
J. A. Burns c Mohammad Rizwan				
b Shaheen Shah Afridi . 4		Lb 6, w 1, nb 7. 14		
M. Labuschagne b Shaheen Shah Afridi . . . 162				
S. P. D. Smith c Mohammad Rizwan		1/8 (2) (3 wkts dec, 127 overs) 589		
b Shaheen Shah Afridi . 36		2/369 (3) 3/490 (4)		

T. M. Head, *†T. D. Paine, P. J. Cummins, M. A. Starc, N. M. Lyon and J. R. Hazlewood did not bat.

Mohammad Abbas 29–7–100–0; Shaheen Shah Afridi 30–5–88–3; Musa Khan 20–1–114–0; Yasir Shah 32–1–197–0; Iftikhar Ahmed 15–0–75–0; Azhar Ali 1–0–9–0.

Pakistan

Shan Masood c Paine b Hazlewood	19	– c Starc b Lyon	68
Imam-ul-Haq c Warner b Starc	2	– lbw b Hazlewood	0
*Azhar Ali c Smith b Cummins	9	– c Smith b Starc	9
Babar Azam c Paine b Starc	97	– c Paine b Hazlewood	8
Asad Shafiq c Paine b Starc	9	– c Warner b Lyon	57
Iftikhar Ahmed c Paine b Starc	10	– c Labuschagne b Lyon	27
†Mohammad Rizwan c Paine b Starc	0	– b Hazlewood	45
Yasir Shah c Lyon b Cummins	113	– lbw b Lyon	13
Shaheen Shah Afridi lbw b Starc	0	– c Hazlewood b Lyon	1
Mohammad Abbas c Warner b Cummins	29	– run out (Cummins)	1
Musa Khan not out	12	– not out	4
Lb 2	2	Lb 6	6

1/3 (2) 2/22 (3) 3/38 (1)   (94.4 overs) 302
4/69 (5) 5/89 (6) 6/89 (7)
7/194 (4) 8/194 (9) 9/281 (10) 10/302 (8)

1/2 (2) 2/11 (3)   (82 overs) 239
3/20 (4) 4/123 (1)
5/154 (5) 6/201 (6) 7/221 (8)
8/229 (9) 9/235 (7) 10/239 (10)

Starc 25–6–66–6; Cummins 22.4–2–83–3; Hazlewood 14–2–48–1; Lyon 22–3–65–0; Labuschagne 10–2–32–0; Smith 1–0–6–0. *Second innings*—Starc 16–3–47–1; Hazlewood 23–4–63–3; Cummins 15–4–45–0; Lyon 25–7–69–5; Labuschagne 3–0–9–0.

Umpires: M. A. Gough and R. K. Illingworth.   Third umpire: R. A. Kettleborough.
Referee: J. J. Crowe.

AUSTRALIA v NEW ZEALAND IN 2019-20

Gideon Haigh

Test matches (3): Australia 3 (120pts), New Zealand 0 (0pts)

A series that appeared to brim with promise turned into another home walkover, as Australia streeted New Zealand in three consecutive Tests, each with a day to spare, to retain the Trans-Tasman Trophy. Even if Australia have usually had the edge over their neighbours, New Zealand have resisted defiantly and resourcefully. Not this time. They played well below their No. 2 ranking, and managed only five innings over 50. With the exception of the indefatigable Neil Wagner, who bowled no fewer than 157.3 overs for 17 wickets at 22, and to a lesser extent Tim Southee, their bowlers were barely more than steady.

For Australia, the clean sweep concluded a home summer powerfully restating their ownership of their conditions – even as bushfires burned across the land, leading to concerns (unfounded, it turned out) that the Sydney Test would be affected. It also featured an unfamiliar accent. Steve Smith and David Warner contributed usefully, but the outstanding batsman on either side was South African-born Marnus Labuschagne, whose double-century in Sydney was his first, not only in Tests but in first-class cricket, and unlikely to be his last.

The acquisitive Labuschagne faced 940 deliveries across the three Tests, 49 of which he hit for four, three for six. Equally impressive was his defence, which in its patience and technical purity confirmed the good notices he had attracted in England and against Pakistan. By the end of the series, he had become the world's third-ranked Test batsman, having started 2019 at 110. At Melbourne, where New Zealand were playing their first Test in 32 years (and only their fourth in all), the decisive partnership was shared by Travis Head and Tim Paine. Warner contributed a breezy hundred under little pressure at Sydney. Of the rest, little else was required.

Australia's high-class pace attack, with Nathan Lyon in reserve, proved impossible to resist. Josh Hazlewood's injury at Perth Stadium, whose hard surfaces left everyone footsore, placed an additional onus on Pat Cummins and Mitchell Starc, but they were more than equal to the responsibility, especially when augmented by James Pattinson. In the last Test, Lyon remedied an indifferent record at the SCG with ten wickets for 118. None of the frontline bowlers gave away more than three an over.

New Zealand's tour was blighted by injuries from the moment Lockie Ferguson, on Test debut, suffered a calf strain on the opening day of the series

---

CLEAN SWEEPS

Summers in which Australia won all their home Tests (minimum five matches):

1920-21	v England (5)	2004-05	v New Zealand (2), Pakistan (3)
1931-32	v South Africa (5)	2006-07	v England (5)
1999-2000	v Pakistan (3), India (3)	2013-14	v England (5)
2000-01	v West Indies (5)	**2019-20**	**v Pakistan (2), New Zealand (3)**

at Perth. Trent Boult, who arrived unfit, broke his hand while batting at Melbourne; Matt Henry and Tom Latham both broke fingers in the field at Sydney, where influenza had already ruled out Kane Williamson, Mitchell Santner and Henry Nicholls, while "workload management" scrubbed Southee.

But, really, the damage was done by the visitors' desultory approach to the series, their two home Tests against England preventing the most rudimentary match practice in Australian conditions. New Zealand were expected to go from misty rain on a pudding pitch with a red ball to – ten days later and three time zones west – 40-degree temperatures on a bouncy surface with a pink ball, with just two training sessions to acclimatise. Five sessions in the field knocked the stuffing from them; the sixth, which involved batting under lights as the day faded, left them 109 for five in reply to 416. From there, things got worse. Excessive temperatures persuaded the New Zealanders to cancel the first day of their two-day practice match against a Victoria XI, and the tourists were voluntarily undermined when Williamson sent Australia in on a flat track at the MCG, deceived by some cloud cover which promptly blew away.

MOST TEST RUNS IN AN AUSTRALIAN SUMMER

		T	*I*	*NO*	*HS*	*100*	*50*	*Avge*	
965	R. T. Ponting (Australia)	6	11	2	257	3	3	107.22	2003-04
952	M. L. Hayden (Australia)	6	11	2	380	3	3	105.77	2003-04
949	M. L. Hayden (Australia)	7	14	1	137	4	4	73.00	2005-06
944	R. T. Ponting (Australia)	7	14	3	149	5	4	85.81	2005-06
905	W. R. Hammond (England) . . .	5	9	1	251	4	0	113.12	1928-29
896	**M. Labuschagne (Australia)** .	**5**	**8**	**0**	**215**	**4**	**3**	**112.00**	**2019-20**
892	M. J. Clarke (Australia)	6	10	2	259*	3	3	111.50	2012-13
834	R. N. Harvey (Australia)	5	9	0	205	4	3	92.66	1952-53
818	D. A. Warner (Australia)	6	10	1	253	4	1	90.88	2015-16
810	D. G. Bradman (Australia)	5	9	0	270	3	1	90.00	1936-37
806	D. G. Bradman (Australia)	5	5	1	299*	4	0	201.50	1931-32
787	M. J. Clarke (Australia)	6	9	1	329*	3	0	98.37	2011-12
786	**D. A. Warner (Australia)**	**5**	**8**	**2**	**335***	**3**	**0**	**131.00**	**2019-20**
769	S. P. D. Smith (Australia)	4	8	2	192	4	2	128.16	2018-19
766	A. N. Cook (England)	5	7	1	235*	3	2	127.66	2010-11

Williamson was perhaps the gravest disappointment, restricted to 57 runs in four hits. In the last, he was unlucky, speculatively dismissed lbw; otherwise, New Zealand's numero uno was uncharacteristically hesitant. Ross Taylor became his country's highest Test scorer, but otherwise had little impact. The best batting performance came from Tom Blundell, whose 121 in the second innings at Melbourne came in the first game in which he had opened in his first-class career. Solid in defence behind a low crouch, and a crisp timer of the ball, he looked made for a task that was well beyond his team-mates.

NEW ZEALAND TOURING PARTY

*K. S. Williamson, T. D. Astle, T. A. Blundell, T. A. Boult, C. de Grandhomme, L. H. Ferguson, M. J. Henry, T. W. M. Latham, H. M. Nicholls, G. D. Phillips, J. A. Raval, M. J. Santner, W. E. R. Somerville, T. G. Southee, L. R. P. L. Taylor, N. Wagner, B-J. Watling. *Coach:* G. R. Stead.

Ferguson sustained a calf injury in the First Test and returned home. Boult fractured his right hand while batting in the Second, and was replaced by Somerville. Phillips was called up for the Third after illness hit the squad.

TEST MATCH AVERAGES

AUSTRALIA – BATTING AND FIELDING

	T	I	NO	R	HS	100	50	Avge	Ct/St
M. Labuschagne	3	6	0	549	215	2	3	91.50	0
†D. A. Warner	3	6	1	297	111*	1	0	59.40	3
S. P. D. Smith	3	5	0	214	85	0	2	42.80	5
†T. M. Head	3	5	0	213	114	1	1	42.60	2
T. D. Paine	3	4	0	153	79	0	1	38.25	13/2
†M. S. Wade	3	5	1	119	38	0	0	29.75	1
J. A. Burns	3	6	0	155	53	0	1	25.83	3
†M. A. Starc	3	4	0	76	30	0	0	19.00	2
P. J. Cummins	3	4	0	41	20	0	0	10.25	1
N. M. Lyon	3	4	2	15	8	0	0	7.50	3

Played in two Tests: †J. L. Pattinson 14*, 2 (1 ct). Played in one Test: †J. R. Hazlewood 0*.

BOWLING

	Style	O	M	R	W	BB	5I	Avge
N. M. Lyon	OB	116.2	24	345	20	5-50	2	17.25
M. A. Starc	LF	89.5	18	268	15	5-52	1	17.86
P. J. Cummins	RF	101.4	27	225	12	5-28	1	18.75
J. L. Pattinson	RFM	49	11	135	6	3-34	0	22.50

Also bowled: J. R. Hazlewood (RFM) 1.2–1–0–1; T. M. Head (OB) 7–1–24–0; M. Labuschagne (LB) 22–2–61–2; M. S. Wade (RM) 3–0–21–0.

NEW ZEALAND – BATTING AND FIELDING

	T	I	NO	R	HS	100	50	Avge	Ct
T. A. Blundell	2	4	0	172	121	1	0	43.00	1
L. R. P. L. Taylor	3	6	0	152	80	0	1	25.33	3
C. de Grandhomme	3	6	0	148	52	0	1	24.66	3
†T. W. M. Latham	3	6	0	126	50	0	1	21.00	2
B-J. Watling	3	6	0	105	40	0	0	17.50	5
†H. M. Nicholls	2	4	0	61	33	0	0	15.25	2
K. S. Williamson	2	4	0	57	34	0	0	14.25	2
†J. A. Raval	2	4	0	45	31	0	0	11.25	2
†N. Wagner	3	6	3	32	18*	0	0	10.66	2
†M. J. Santner	2	4	0	32	27	0	0	8.00	3
T. G. Southee	2	4	0	24	10	0	0	6.00	1

Played in one Test: T. D. Astle 25*, 17 (1 ct); T. A. Boult 8; L. H. Ferguson 0*, 1*; M. J. Henry 3; G. D. Phillips 52, 0 (1 ct); W. E. R. Somerville 0, 7.

BOWLING

	Style	O	M	R	W	BB	5I	Avge
N. Wagner	LFM	157.3	33	387	17	4-83	0	22.76
T. G. Southee	RFM	99.4	22	309	12	5-69	1	25.75
C. de Grandhomme	RFM	111	17	287	7	3-78	0	41.00
T. D. Astle	LB	40	1	152	3	2-111	0	50.66

Also bowled: T. A. Blundell (OB) 3–0–13–0; T. A. Boult (LFM) 40–3–121–1; L. H. Ferguson (RF) 11–1–47–0; M. J. Henry (RFM) 44–5–148–2; J. A. Raval (LB) 13–1–33–1; M. J. Santner (SLA) 69–6–250–1; W. E. R. Somerville (OB) 39–2–135–1.

AUSTRALIA v NEW ZEALAND

First Test

At Perth Stadium, December 12–15, 2019 (day/night). Australia won by 296 runs. Australia 40pts. Toss: Australia. Test debut: L. H. Ferguson.

Test cricket involves an ability to compete in all conditions and climes. This game set New Zealand an extreme task. Nine days after their previous Test, against England at Hamilton, had been ended by rain, having featured a red ball, grassy banks and mild temperatures, this match unfolded with a pink ball in a huge and largely empty stadium with the mercury over 40°C throughout – tough even for the umpires, including Aleem Dar, overseeing a record 129th Test.

Not surprisingly, the New Zealanders failed, never recovering from five sessions in the field after losing the toss and going a man down, when Lockie Ferguson's debut Test fell foul of a calf injury. For the bulk of that time – 369 minutes and 240 balls – Labuschagne was in possession, if not the ascendant, applying himself patiently to drawing the sting of New Zealand's attack. He drove handsomely and turned the strike over deftly, and continued his precocious adaptation to the pace of Test cricket. His second Test century might well have been his 20th; the innings vaulted him to fifth in the ICC rankings, with a total of barely 1,000 runs.

New Zealand played a waiting game, which proved disarmingly effective against Smith, who never looked comfortable in an innings of 43 from 164 deliveries, the bulk of them short from Wagner and Southee, with five or six fielders on the leg side. The Australians also lost Wade before the close, letting the ball go, and were grateful for Head's ten boundaries in his 56. On the second day, it was the Australians who decelerated, so that the reply was postponed until the floodlights came on: Paine was last out, having taken three hours over his 39, while Southee and Wagner collected four wickets apiece. In the first two overs after tea, when the surface was partially shadowed by the huge stands, New Zealand lost both openers, seemingly slow to pick the ball up.

Hazlewood, clutching a hamstring, then joined Ferguson on the sidelines, leaving both teams to regroup – Paine even threw the ball to Wade for a couple of overs. But after putting on 76 with Taylor, Williamson fended at one he should have left, and was caught at slip by Smith, who timed his dive superbly. Starc struck twice more before the close: Nicholls caught behind down leg, nightwatchman Wagner yorked first ball. Taylor never retrieved his fluency on the third day, Smith catching him smartly, and the rest offered little resistance. Labuschagne bowled Santner through the gate with a perfect leg-break. Australia led by 250.

The pitch had quickened under the harsh sun, and now offered the pace bowlers good bounce and carry, with cracks opening to introduce uncertainties. With liberal amounts of short stuff, Southee and Wagner kept Australia from running away with the match, Wagner again confounding Smith, whose heedless hook flew straight to backward square leg. Not for four years had a seamer got through as many overs in a Test as Wagner's 60.

The Australian advantage, however, was irreducible. Burns made a painstaking half-century, and Labuschagne a fluent one, while Wade got into a virility contest with Wagner, allowing himself to be hit on the upper body, and staring back stonily. New Zealand kept reining in their hosts, except for the disappointing Santner, who lacked rhythm and accuracy. But when Australia finally declared an hour into the fourth day, it was with a lead of 467. The end came quickly. Before the first break, Lyon caught Raval off Starc, and had Williamson taken at short leg. After it, he took his record at Perth Stadium to 14 wickets in two outings, only Watling and de Grandhomme detaining the Australians for long.

Paine welcomed the clinical victory, and the role of Labuschagne: "Granted, we have some players back, which is helping, but there's been improvement in the guys who were given a chance 18 months ago, and the experienced players have put some icing on the top. We are moving in the right direction." New Zealand coach Gary Stead thought that, despite the defeat, his team were doing the same. "There's no excuses,' he said. "We know we can be better."

Player of the Match: M. A. Starc.   *Attendance:* 65,540.

Close of play: first day, Australia 248-4 (Labuschagne 110, Head 20); second day, New Zealand 109-5 (Taylor 66, Watling 0); third day, Australia 167-6 (Wade 8, Cummins 1).

Australia

D. A. Warner c and b Wagner	43	– c sub (T. A. Blundell) b Southee	19
J. A. Burns lbw b de Grandhomme	9	– c Nicholls b Southee	53
M. Labuschagne b Wagner	143	– c Santner b Wagner	50
S. P. D. Smith c Southee b Wagner	43	– c Raval b Wagner	16
M. S. Wade b Southee	12	– c Raval b de Grandhomme	17
T. M. Head c Santner b Southee	56	– c de Grandhomme b Southee	5
*†T. D. Paine c Watling b Southee	39	– b Southee	0
P. J. Cummins b Raval	20	– c Watling b Wagner	13
M. A. Starc c Williamson b Southee	30	– c Taylor b Southee	23
N. M. Lyon c de Grandhomme b Wagner	8	– not out	0
J. R. Hazlewood not out	0		
B 2, lb 1, w 8, nb 2	13	Lb 7, w 8, nb 6	21

1/40 (2) 2/75 (1) 3/207 (4) (146.2 overs) 416   1/44 (1) (9 wkts dec, 69.1 overs) 217
4/225 (5) 5/301 (3) 6/325 (6)   2/131 (3) 3/148 (2)
7/363 (8) 8/408 (9) 9/416 (10) 10/416 (7)   4/154 (4) 5/160 (6) 6/160 (7)
7/180 (8) 8/189 (5) 9/217 (9)

Southee 30.2–7–93–4; Ferguson 11–1–47–0; Wagner 37–7–92–4; de Grandhomme 22–8–37–1; Santner 33–5–111–0; Raval 13–1–33–1. *Second innings*—Southee 21.1–6–69–5; de Grandhomme 17–2–47–1; Wagner 23–4–59–3; Santner 8–0–35–0.

New Zealand

J. A. Raval b Hazlewood	1	– c Lyon b Starc	1
T. W. M. Latham c and b Starc	0	– lbw b Lyon	18
*K. S. Williamson c Smith b Starc	34	– c Wade b Lyon	14
L. R. P. L. Taylor c Smith b Lyon	80	– c Paine b Starc	22
H. M. Nicholls c Paine b Starc	7	– c Head b Lyon	21
N. Wagner b Starc	0	– (10) c Paine b Starc	8
†B-J. Watling b Cummins	8	– (6) c Paine b Starc	40
C. de Grandhomme c Smith b Starc	23	– (7) c Smith b Cummins	33
M. J. Santner b Labuschagne	2	– (8) c Head b Cummins	0
T. G. Southee c sub (M. G. Neser) b Lyon	8	– (9) c Smith b Lyon	4
L. H. Ferguson not out	0	– not out	1
B 1, lb 2	3	Lb 6, w 2, nb 1	9

1/1 (2) 2/1 (1) 3/77 (3) (55.2 overs) 166   1/6 (1) 2/21 (3) (65.3 overs) 171
4/97 (5) 5/97 (6) 6/120 (7)   3/57 (4) 4/57 (2)
7/147 (4) 8/155 (8) 9/166 (9) 10/166 (10)   5/98 (6) 6/154 (7) 7/154 (6)
8/154 (8) 9/163 (10) 10/171 (9)

Starc 18–2–52–5; Hazlewood 1.2–1–0–1; Cummins 14.4–3–46–1; Wade 2–0–8–0; Lyon 14.2–2–48–2; Labuschagne 5–1–9–1. *Second innings*—Starc 14–5–45–4; Cummins 19–6–31–2; Lyon 22.3–3–63–4; Head 5–1–13–0; Labuschagne 5–0–13–0.

Umpires: Aleem Dar and N. J. Llong.   Third umpire: M. Erasmus.
Referee: R. B. Richardson.

> **"**'I just blocked and blocked,' remembered last man Jim Higgs, 'and he was trying to hit Colin Croft over cover.'"
> Obituaries, page 233

AUSTRALIA v NEW ZEALAND

Second Test

At Melbourne, December 26–29, 2019. Australia won by 247 runs. Australia 40pts. Toss: New Zealand.

Offered first innings by Williamson, Australia lapped New Zealand in the Boxing Day Test, retaining the Trans-Tasman Trophy. Local fans experienced more competition than local players, a sizeable contingent of hardy New Zealanders making their presence heard and seen throughout what was otherwise a setback for their highly ranked team.

Matt Page's MCG pitch had been the subject of heavy scrutiny in the pre-match coverage, after the abandonment of Victoria's Sheffield Shield game against Western Australia earlier in December because conditions were deemed unsafe. Perth patriots made opportunistic noises about taking the Boxing Day Test off Melbourne's hands. Events, however, left Melburnians feeling more secure about their annual institution. Never have so many spectators watched New Zealand play a Test: 80,473 on the first day, and 203,472 in all. And not since 1975 has a team other than England drawn so many to the MCG. The pitch, meanwhile, played consistently, while also encouraging pace bowlers, especially Australia's quicker threesome, which featured Pattinson in support of Cummins and Starc. It was adjudged "very good" by match referee Richie Richardson.

Williamson's decision to bowl was based around the return from injury of Boult, who duly struck in the match's first over, castling Burns with one that swung in, then jagged through the gate. It turned out to be his only wicket, in addition to sustaining a broken hand while batting. Warner played with discipline, Smith settled in for a long, therapeutic innings, avoiding the bouncers of Wagner, mindful of the leg gullies and forward square legs in which Williamson invested. Labuschagne kept him company for a while before dragging on via his elbow, Wade for almost as long before driving over-ambitiously; Head, without ever looking completely secure, then settled in. A Smith century seemed almost foreordained, until a steepling bouncer from Wagner took the shoulder of the bat and looped towards gully, where Nicholls took an athletic catch in his fingertips. Smith's introverted 85 had lasted six minutes short of six hours.

The match's crucial partnership ensued, with Paine compiling a scintillating 79, perhaps his best innings as Australian captain, while Head cut and cuffed his way on. With their work worth 150 in 43 overs, Paine was given lbw on review to what the naked eye had taken for a contact point outside off stump. Head reached a second Test hundred in the next over, and Australia's last five fell for 33, leaving them with an hour to make inroads. Cummins removed Blundell and, with the end in sight, Pattinson claimed the crucial wicket of Williamson, whose attempt to pull from wide of off stump was an aberration.

The third morning brought a superb spell from Cummins, who nicked off Taylor (from over the wicket), and trapped Nicholls (from round) with consecutive deliveries – ending his run of 70 Test wickets without an lbw. After lunch, Cummins so confined Latham that he aimed a wild drive at a wide tempter. His fifth five-wicket haul brought his 2019 total to 59, comfortably leading the world. New Zealand's paltry total might have been worse, but for the review of a catch to leg gully offered by Santner off Starc, which third umpire Aleem Dar turned down, despite replays indicating ball had hit wristband.

Deciding against the follow-on, despite a lead of 319, Australia spent an unhurried four hours over their second innings, in which Smith fell to Wagner again, caught at leg gully. This was Wagner's 200th wicket in his 46th Test – only two more than Richard Hadlee. Even the Australians were in awe of his fitness: Head called him "an absolute machine".

In nominal pursuit of 488, New Zealand disintegrated in a pre-lunch burst from Pattinson of 2–0–5–3. Ball-tracking cut both ways. Blundell had nought when the Australians did not review an lbw reprieve granted by Nigel Llong, which would have been overturned;

Williamson had nought when he reviewed an lbw given by Marais Erasmus, which was intersecting leg stump so lightly it should arguably have been overturned.

New Zealand had nowhere to go after that, although Blundell – having shaved the beard he had worn in the first innings – surged towards a second Test century. Picked in place of the struggling Jeet Raval, he seemed to grow in confidence in line with the support from New Zealand supporters in Bays M21 and M22. "It's pretty hard not to notice them," Blundell said. "And it was pretty special hearing your name getting chanted." Nicholls played some meaty strokes, until stumped the ball after hitting a six; the rest made little impact, and Blundell missed the chance to carry his bat when he was last out, dragging Labuschagne to mid-on. He was the 75th man to open in a Test without previously having done so in first-class cricket – but the first to make a hundred.

Head won the match award, although there were cases for Paine, whose innings was reinforced by eight dismissals and a run-out, and for the crowd, whose number exceeded the combined totals for the summer's earlier Tests at Brisbane, Adelaide and Perth.

Player of the Match: T. M. Head.   *Attendance:* 203,472.

Close of play: first day, Australia 257-4 (Smith 77, Head 25); second day, New Zealand 44-2 (Latham 9, Taylor 2); third day, Australia 137-4 (Wade 15, Head 12).

Australia

D. A. Warner c Southee b Wagner	41	– c Blundell b Wagner	38
J. A. Burns b Boult	0	– c Watling b Santner	35
M. Labuschagne b de Grandhomme	63	– run out (Latham/Santner)	19
S. P. D. Smith c Nicholls b Wagner	85	– c Southee b Wagner	7
M. S. Wade c Watling b de Grandhomme	38	– not out	30
T. M. Head c Santner b Wagner	114	– b Wagner	28
*†T. D. Paine lbw b Wagner	79		
M. A. Starc c Williamson b Southee	1		
J. L. Pattinson not out	14		
P. J. Cummins c Latham b Southee	0		
N. M. Lyon c Wagner b Southee	1		
B 5, lb 22, w 4	31	B 4, lb 4, w 2, nb 1	11

1/1 (2)   2/61 (1)   3/144 (3)   (155.1 overs) 467   1/62 (1)   (5 wkts dec, 54.2 overs) 168
4/216 (5)   5/284 (4)   6/434 (7)   2/100 (3)   3/110 (2)
7/435 (8)   8/458 (6)   9/463 (10)   10/467 (11)   4/110 (4)   5/168 (6)

Boult 31–9–91–1; Southee 33.1–6–103–3; de Grandhomme 30–5–68–2; Wagner 38–11–83–4; Santner 20–1–82–0; Blundell 3–0–13–0. *Second innings*—Boult 9–0–30–0; Southee 15–3–44–0; de Grandhomme 5–0–14–0; Wagner 17.2–1–50–3; Santner 8–0–22–1.

New Zealand

T. W. M. Latham c Paine b Cummins	50	– c Paine b Pattinson	8
T. A. Blundell c Paine b Cummins	15	– c Lyon b Labuschagne	121
*K. S. Williamson c Paine b Pattinson	9	– lbw b Pattinson	0
L. R. P. L. Taylor c Burns b Cummins	4	– b Pattinson	2
H. M. Nicholls lbw b Cummins	0	– st Paine b Lyon	33
†B-J. Watling c Burns b Pattinson	7	– c Warner b Lyon	22
C. de Grandhomme c Warner b Starc	11	– c Warner b Lyon	9
M. J. Santner c Paine b Pattinson	3	– c Paine b Lyon	27
T. G. Southee c Paine b Cummins	10	– run out (Pattinson/Paine)	2
N. Wagner not out	18	– not out	6
T. A. Boult b Starc	8	– absent hurt	
B 4, lb 4, w 2, nb 3	13	Lb 7, w 2, nb 1	10

1/23 (2)   2/39 (3)   3/46 (4)   (54.5 overs) 148   1/32 (1)   2/33 (3)   (71 overs) 240
4/46 (5)   5/58 (6)   6/97 (7)   3/35 (4)   4/89 (5)   5/161 (6)
7/112 (1)   8/116 (8)   9/124 (9)   10/148 (11)   6/172 (7)   7/212 (8)   8/214 (9)   9/240 (2)

Starc 12.5–4–30–2; Cummins 17–5–28–5; Pattinson 15–2–34–3; Lyon 9–1–35–0; Wade 1–0–13–0. *Second innings*—Starc 15–3–59–0; Cummins 18–4–47–0; Pattinson 12–3–35–3; Lyon 23–4–81–4; Labuschagne 3–1–11–1.

Umpires: M. Erasmus and N. J. Llong.   Third umpire: Aleem Dar.
Referee: R. B. Richardson.

AUSTRALIA v NEW ZEALAND

Third Test

At Sydney, January 3–6, 2020. Australia won by 279 runs. Australia 40pts. Toss: Australia. Test debut: G. D. Phillips.

With Cricket Australia aligning themselves with the push for four-day Tests, the team fell in step, completing their fifth consecutive four-day victory. New Zealand, having waited over three decades to be the drawcard of an Australian summer, suffered a third consecutive overpowering defeat.

There were some mitigations. While Australia enjoyed the luxury of an unchanged team, a flu virus knocked the stuffing from New Zealand's squad, ruling out Kane Williamson, Henry Nicholls and Mitchell Santner; Tim Southee was also rested, surprisingly given the injury to Trent Boult. Their misfortune provided an opening for fast bowler Matt Henry and Auckland's South African-born batsman Glenn Phillips, who arrived on the eve of the match for his Test debut. Also called up for a pitch tipped to deteriorate were slow bowlers Todd Astle and Will Somerville. The New Zealand infirmary was further swelled during the game by the spread of the virus to Raval (recalled to bat at No. 3), a broken thumb for Henry, and a broken finger for Latham – both sustained in the field.

Latham, who as Williamson's proxy was leading New Zealand for the first time, called incorrectly, condemning his team to another five sessions in the field, most of the time spent trying to get the better of Labuschagne. His maiden first-class double-century spanned more than eight and a half hours, and 363 deliveries, 19 stroked for four, one slogged for six. He was light on his feet, fluent through the covers, productive off the pads: his fourth Test hundred of the year was perhaps his best. Wagner slowed him; no bowler troubled him; his 215 came from 377 while he was at the wicket. This was partly because of another introspective innings by Smith, who contributed only 63 of the 156 they added for the third.

New Zealand worked around Labuschagne as though navigating a traffic hazard, and did well to remove the last five for 44 on the second day, then get through to stumps unscathed in the persons of Latham and Blundell. Raval then defied his sickness to guide them to the relative security of 117 for one, before it started to go wrong, again.

As ever, there were curious interludes with the DRS. With lunch in sight on the third day, Raval was given out lbw to Lyon by Aleem Dar. He strolled down the pitch for a casual consultation with Latham and, just as the 15-second timer expired, requested a review with a gesture that looked as if he was trying to attract the attention of a barman. Dar indulged him, but his decision was upheld: it seemed as if the New Zealanders had lost a review they should never have been granted. Just after lunch, Taylor was also given out lbw by Dar, again correctly, but elected to review, having taken several steps towards the dressing-room – another one squandered.

It was a match for some substandard cricket. Blundell got in an ugly tangle, Latham chipped softly to mid-on, Watling chopped on meekly, de Grandhomme was run out going for a second after jogging the first, Wagner had a pointless slog, and Henry held his pose as Paine stumped him. Only Phillips could claim to have forced Australia to get him out, bowled by a superb nip-backer from Cummins after a three-hour half-century in which he was favoured, deservedly, by luck.

The Australians again took a third-innings canter, in which Warner helped himself to an unbeaten 111 – his 24th Test hundred, and 18th at home. He was also penalised five runs by Dar, who was having an eventful match, for running on the pitch, to which he responded with wounded innocence. The runs were retrospectively incorporated in New Zealand's first innings. Labuschagne added another fifty to his relentless progress, hitting out at the end, and thereby missing the chance to overtake Wally Hammond's ancient marker for runs in a five-Test Australian summer: 905 at 113, in 1928-29. Labuschagne finished with 896 at 112, at which point New Zealand's second innings abruptly slipped to 22 for four.

One record came their way, rather mutedly: Taylor became New Zealand's highest Test scorer with a drive down the ground off Lyon for three that took him past Stephen Fleming's 7,172. The Australians applauded warmly. Taylor waved his bat perfunctorily,

AUSTRALIA'S BEST MATCH FIGURES AGAINST NEW ZEALAND

11-123	D. K. Lillee (5-51 and 6-72)	Auckland	1976-77
10-118	**N. M. Lyon (5-68 and 5-50)**	**Sydney**	**2019-20**
10-132	M. G. Johnson (4-59 and 6-73)	Hamilton	2009-10
10-174	R. G. Holland (6-106 and 4-68)	Sydney	1985-86
9-67	S. K. Warne (3-36 and 6-31)	Hobart	1993-94
9-69	M. G. Johnson (4-30 and 5-39)	Brisbane	2008-09
9-97	**M. A. Starc (5-52 and 4-45)**	**Perth**	**2019-20**
9-136	J. R. Hazlewood (3-66 and 6-70)	Adelaide	2015-16
9-171	B. Lee (4-66 and 5-105)	Adelaide	2008-09

and was bowled next over by Cummins comprehensively. De Grandhomme struck a few muscular blows, but there was no stopping Lyon: his ten for 118 from almost 48 overs, compared with the four for 287 from 79 taken by the visiting spinners, was another index of the teams' disparity.

Pre-match forebodings about smoke from Australia's bushfires proved unfounded: early hazes on the first and fourth days blew away, returning after the match to show how lucky this was. CA had committed to pulling the players off in the event of a perceived threat to health, as had happened in a Big Bash League match in Canberra in late December. In the event, the greatest health threat was Paine's team.

Player of the Match: M. Labuschagne. *Attendance:* 114,068.

Player of the Series: M. Labuschagne.

Close of play: first day, Australia 283-3 (Labuschagne 130, Wade 22); second day, New Zealand 63-0 (Latham 26, Blundell 34); third day, Australia 40-0 (Warner 23, Burns 16).

Australia

D. A. Warner c de Grandhomme b Wagner	45	– not out	111
J. A. Burns c Taylor b de Grandhomme	18	– lbw b Astle	40
M. Labuschagne c and b Astle	215	– c Latham b Henry	59
S. P. D. Smith c Taylor b de Grandhomme	63		
M. S. Wade b Somerville	22		
T. M. Head c Watling b Henry	10		
*†T. D. Paine b de Grandhomme	35		
J. L. Pattinson b Wagner	2		
P. J. Cummins c Phillips b Astle	8		
M. A. Starc b Wagner	22		
N. M. Lyon not out	6		
Lb 6, w 1, nb 1	8	B 3, lb 3, w 1	7

1/39 (2) 2/95 (1) 3/251 (4)   (150.1 overs) 454   1/107 (2)   (2 wkts dec, 52 overs) 217
4/288 (5) 5/331 (6) 6/410 (7)   2/217 (3)
7/416 (3) 8/426 (8) 9/430 (9) 10/454 (10)

Henry 32–3–94–1; de Grandhomme 24–1–78–3; Wagner 33.1–9–66–3; Somerville 29–2–99–1; Astle 32–0–111–2. *Second innings*—Henry 12–2–54–1; de Grandhomme 13–1–43–0; Wagner 9–1–37–0; Somerville 10–0–36–0; Astle 8–1–41–1.

New Zealand

*T. W. M. Latham c Starc b Cummins	49	– lbw b Starc	1
T. A. Blundell b Lyon	34	– c Lyon b Starc	2
J. A. Raval lbw b Lyon	31	– c Paine b Lyon	12
L. R. P. L. Taylor lbw b Cummins	22	– b Cummins	22
G. D. Phillips b Cummins	52	– c Paine b Lyon	0
†B-J. Watling b Starc	9	– c Cummins b Lyon	19
C. de Grandhomme run out (Wade/Paine)	20	– c Burns b Lyon	52
T. D. Astle not out	25	– c Pattinson b Lyon	17
W. E. R. Somerville b Lyon	0	– b Starc	7
N. Wagner b Lyon	0	– not out	0
M. J. Henry st Paine b Lyon	3	– absent hurt	
B 1, lb 4, nb 1, p 5	11	B 3, lb 1	4

1/68 (2) 2/117 (3) 3/117 (1)   (95.4 overs) 256   1/3 (2) 2/4 (1)   (47.5 overs) 136
4/145 (4) 5/163 (6) 6/195 (7)   3/22 (3) 4/22 (5) 5/38 (4)
7/235 (5) 8/237 (9) 9/237 (10) 10/251 (11)   6/107 (7) 7/128 (8) 8/136 (9) 9/136 (6)

Starc 21–1–57–1; Cummins 22–6–44–3; Pattinson 16–3–58–0; Lyon 30.4–10–68–5; Labuschagne 4–0–8–0; Head 2–0–11–0. *Second innings*—Starc 9–3–25–3; Cummins 11–3–29–1; Pattinson 6–3–8–0; Lyon 16.5–4–50–5; Labuschagne 5–0–20–0.

Umpires: Aleem Dar and M. Erasmus. Third umpire: N. J. Llong.
Referee: R. B. Richardson.

The Strangers Who Came Home is a compelling social history, bringing to life the first Australian cricket tour of England in 1878. Against all odds these 'strangers' beat MCC (including WG Grace) at Lord's. It was a tour which helped to pioneer international sport, and provided the stimulus for Australian nationhood.

To order at discount visit wisdenalmanack.com

DOMESTIC CRICKET IN AUSTRALIA IN 2018-19

Peter English

There has been a feeling in Australian cricket in recent years that New South Wales produce Test players, while Victoria win titles. Those trophy-winning skills were on show as **Victoria** captured their 32nd Sheffield Shield. They already had the one-day JLT Cup, while the BBL final was played by the two Melbourne teams, and won by state coach Andrew McDonald's Renegades.

The Dukes ball replaced the home-grown Kookaburra over the second half of the Shield season, as part of preparation for the Ashes, but nothing could stop the Victorians. The 1,000-run barrier had not been broken in the competition since 2014-15, but Marcus Harris, the assured opener navigating his first Test summer, led the list with 1,188, including a century in a low-scoring final against New South Wales.

Young strokemaker Will Pucovski collected 649. He started with 243 against Western Australia, before missing four games to deal with mental health issues, then made the Test squad against Sri Lanka, all before his 21st birthday. Nic Maddinson had an eventful season after arriving from Sydney without a contract – he scored hundreds in his first three Shield games for Victoria, interrupted by a broken arm, then sat out the final with a fractured thumb. Seamer Scott Boland was the Shield Player of the Year for his 48 wickets at 19, despite an MCG surface generally showing less life than a week-old scone. He was backed up by Chris Tremain, with 45, while Jon Holland's 26 made him the leading spinner in a competition controlled by pace.

In the one-day tournament, completed by October, a new quirk meant all six teams qualified for the knockouts, with the bottom four contesting quarter-finals. A year earlier, Victoria's fourth place wouldn't have got them into the play-off; this time, they reached the final, and swept past Tasmania – despite seven wickets and a last-over hat-trick for seamer Gurinder Sandhu. Cameron White's 88 was the game's other highlight, but he was released at the end of the season, aged 35, after an 18-year career. White first led Victoria aged 20, was the official captain a year later, and won a record 38 of his 77 Shield games in charge. He featured in seven Shield-winning campaigns, and lifted the trophy three times.

As so often, runners-up **New South Wales** had to perform without their international stars. Trent Copeland was an unfashionable seamer in a state of fast-bowling resources, but when Mitchell Starc, Josh Hazlewood and Pat Cummins were away – and he wasn't commentating for Channel 7 – Copeland could be unplayable. He was the season's leading wicket-taker with 52 at 18, more than half after Christmas, when the Dukes balls were weaving around. Kurtis Patterson piled up 724 runs and earned a Test debut, while openers Daniel Hughes and Nick Larkin made hefty contributions.

Third in the Shield, **Western Australia** lost a one-day semi-final to Victoria after a perfect five wins in the group stage. Fireworks came from D'Arcy Short, who blasted 257 against Queensland, the third-highest score in List A cricket, from 148 balls, with 23 sixes, a world record by six. After his ball-tampering ban, Cameron Bancroft carried his bat for 138 on his return to first-class cricket in February.

Queensland's defence of the Shield sputtered as their specialist batsmen lacked consistency. Michael Neser, looking to establish himself as an all-rounder, led the state averages with 481 at 43, combined with 33 wickets, while Mark Steketee took an eye-catching 42; more will be needed, after Luke Feldman decided to rejoin the Queensland Police full-time.

In **Tasmania**, the story was usually about Matthew Wade, sidelined from the Test squad since the re-emergence of state team-mate Tim Paine. Wade's batting brought him 1,021 runs, earning much respect but no recognition from the selectors – until the tour of England. Bellerive Oval always suits swing bowlers, and Jackson Bird ruled the roost on his way to 50 victims. But it was another season to forget for **South Australia**, who did not win a Shield game, and finished last for the second year running.

FIRST-CLASS AVERAGES IN 2018-19

BATTING (450 runs)

		M	I	NO	R	HS	100	Avge	Ct
1	†N. J. Maddinson (*Victoria*)	5	8	1	563	162	3	80.42	2
2	C. A. Pujara (*India*)	4	7	0	521	193	3	74.42	3
3	†M. S. Wade (*Tasmania*)	10	20	3	1,021	137	2	60.05	15
4	†M. S. Harris (*Victoria/Australia*)	16	29	2	1,515	250*	3	56.11	13
5	W. J. Pucovski (*Victoria*)	7	13	1	649	243	2	54.08	2
6	†S. E. Marsh (*West Australia/Australia*)	7	13	1	626	163*	1	52.16	6
7	†T. M. Head (*South Australia/Australia*)	13	23	1	1,024	161	1	46.54	5
8	†K. R. Patterson (*NSW/Australia*)	13	22	3	868	134	3	45.68	16
9	M. G. Neser (*Queensland*)	9	16	5	481	76*	0	43.72	2
10	J. A. Burns (*Queensland/Australia*)	12	23	2	889	180	1	42.33	17
11	†D. P. Hughes (*New South Wales*)	11	20	1	742	134	2	39.05	11
12	A. J. Doolan (*Tasmania*)	10	20	0	761	115	1	38.05	9
13	M. W. Short (*Victoria*)	10	16	2	510	80	0	36.42	7
14	N. C. R. Larkin (*Victoria*)	11	20	1	687	175*	2	36.15	11
15	P. S. P. Handscomb (*Victoria/Australia*)	8	13	0	466	123	1	35.84	13
16	T. L. W. Cooper (*South Australia*)	8	15	0	517	178	2	34.46	9
17	M. C. Henriques (*New South Wales*)	11	19	0	654	152	1	34.42	7
18	M. R. Marsh (*West Australia/Australia*)	8	15	0	486	151	2	32.40	3
19	J. C. Silk (*Tasmania*)	10	20	0	645	113	1	32.25	10
20	C. L. White (*Victoria*)	9	16	2	450	119	1	32.14	18
21	†J. S. Lehmann (*South Australia*)	10	19	1	572	126	1	31.77	3
22	C. R. Hemphrey (*Queensland*)	10	20	2	487	93	0	27.05	7
23	M. Labuschagne (*Queensland/Australia*)	12	21	0	545	81	0	25.95	18
24	†J. B. Weatherald (*South Australia*)	10	19	0	488	150	1	25.68	8

BOWLING (20 wickets)

		Style	O	M	R	W	BB	5I	Avge
1	J. J. Bumrah (*India*)	RFM	157.1	48	357	21	6-33	1	17.00
2	T. A. Copeland (*New South Wales*)	RFM	408.2	112	947	52	6-86	3	18.21
3	D. J. Worrall (*South Australia*)	RFM	126	32	365	20	7-64	1	18.25
4	P. J. Cummins (*NSW/Australia*)	RF	225.4	50	580	31	6-23	2	18.70
5	J. L. Pattinson (*Victoria*)	RFM	151	26	492	26	5-25	1	18.92
6	J. A. Richardson (*W Aust/Australia*)	RFM	241.4	67	637	33	8-47	2	19.30
7	S. M. Boland (*Victoria*)	RFM	332.1	64	944	48	7-54	2	19.66
8	J. M. Mennie (*South Australia*)	RFM	302.4	79	730	37	5-39	1	19.72
9	H. N. A. Conway (*New South Wales*)	RFM	197.5	60	443	22	5-14	1	20.13
10	M. T. Steketee (*Queensland*)	RFM	288.2	64	872	42	4-29	0	20.76
11	J. M. Bird (*Tasmania*)	RFM	397.4	108	1,110	50	7-59	4	22.20
12	S. A. Abbott (*New South Wales*)	RFM	320	75	825	37	7-45	2	22.29
13	C. P. Tremain (*Victoria*)	RFM	326	70	1,009	45	5-13	3	22.42
14	M. G. Neser (*Queensland*)	RFM	291.1	86	760	33	5-15	1	23.03
15	L. W. Feldman (*Queensland*)	RFM	271.3	88	710	30	5-20	1	23.66
16	P. M. Siddle (*Victoria*)	RFM	226.2	46	638	26	5-28	1	24.53
17	M. A. Starc (*NSW/Australia*)	LF	228.2	40	744	27	5-46	2	27.55
18	N. M. Lyon (*NSW/Australia*)	OB	450.5	76	1,244	45	6-122	3	27.64
19	S. N. J. O'Keefe (*New South Wales*)	SLA	270.5	72	559	20	5-52	1	27.95
20	J. M. Holland (*Victoria*)	SLA	298	70	732	26	5-31	3	28.15
21	G. T. Bell (*Tasmania*)	RM	305.1	75	903	32	4-17	0	28.21
22	M. L. Kelly (*Western Australia*)	RFM	313.1	87	856	30	6-67	2	28.53
23	R. P. Meredith (*Tasmania*)	RFM	250.4	54	783	27	4-61	0	29.00
24	N. P. Winter (*South Australia*)	LFM	338.3	73	913	25	4-23	0	36.52
25	M. J. Swepson (*Queensland*)	LB	242	26	916	24	4-76	0	38.16

SHEFFIELD SHIELD IN 2018-19

	P	W	L	D	*Bat*	*Bowl*	*Pts*
VICTORIA	10	6	1	3	9.78	9.2	57.98
NEW SOUTH WALES .	10	5	2	3	5.62	8.1	46.72
Western Australia	10	5	3	2	3.80	8.1	43.90
Queensland	10	3	5	2	3.72	8.1	31.82
Tasmania	10	3	5	2	2.69	8.9	30.59*
South Australia	10	0	6	4	5.01	7.5	16.51

Bonus pts (column header over *Bat*, *Bowl*)

*   *One point deducted for slow over-rate.*

Outright win = 6pts; draw = 1pt. Bonus points awarded for the first 100 overs of each team's first innings: 0.01 batting points for every run over the first 200; 0.1 bowling points for each wicket taken.

FINAL

VICTORIA v NEW SOUTH WALES

At St Kilda, March 28–31, 2019. Victoria won by 177 runs. Toss: Victoria.

Harris's third century in a Sheffield Shield final helped Victoria win the trophy for the fourth time in five seasons. He batted most of the first day for 141, in a match which produced only two other scores above 50. Seven wickets fell before lunch in overcast conditions next day, as Copeland wound up the home innings, and New South Wales's top three disappeared with only 38 on the board. Siddle's fifth wicket – his 200th in Shield cricket – ensured a first-innings lead of 168, which Victoria set about extending on a rain-shortened third day, when Pucovski hit 51, and Copeland took his 50th wicket of the season. New South Wales found themselves with nearly two days to chase 388, and their hopes rose while Patterson was scoring 76 out of a stand of 120 with Hughes. But they lost their last eight for 48. When Boland trapped Nevill, it was the game's 14th lbw, equalling the Shield record; when Abbott was caught a few minutes later, Victoria had beaten New South Wales for the third time in this tournament. Cricket Australia had introduced a trial whereby, if the final was drawn, bonus points would be awarded for the first 100 overs of each first innings (as in the qualifying stage) to decide the Shield winners, rather than the team heading the league automatically becoming champions. The aim was to discourage table leaders, who have home advantage, from preparing pitches favouring a draw.

Player of the Match: M. S. Harris.

Close of play: first day, Victoria 266-6 (Pattinson 11, Tremain 13); second day, Victoria 48-1 (Dean 24); third day, Victoria 207-7 (Pattinson 9, Siddle 2).

Victoria

*T. J. Dean c Copeland b Conway	23	– lbw b Abbott	25
M. S. Harris c Copeland b Abbott	141	– b Abbott	23
W. J. Pucovski lbw b Copeland	17	– lbw b Abbott	51
†S. E. Gotch c Edwards b Copeland	2	– lbw b Conway	20
C. L. White c Hughes b Abbott	7	– lbw b O'Keefe	36
M. W. Short c Nevill b Henriques	34	– lbw b Conway	26
J. L. Pattinson not out	23	– c Conway b Abbott	15
C. P. Tremain c Abbott b Copeland	13	– c Nevill b Copeland	9
P. M. Siddle lbw b Copeland	8	– c Nevill b Copeland	2
S. M. Boland lbw b Copeland	1	– b Copeland	0
J. M. Holland c and b Conway	0	– not out	4
B 8, lb 4, w 6, nb 2	20	B 1, lb 2, w 2, nb 3	8

1/63 (1) 2/103 (3) 3/113 (4)	(100.5 overs) 289	1/48 (2) 2/53 (1) (89.2 overs) 219
4/124 (5) 5/204 (6) 6/251 (2)		3/121 (4) 4/127 (3)
7/266 (8) 8/280 (9) 9/288 (10) 10/289 (11)		5/183 (5) 6/187 (6) 7/205 (8)
		8/207 (9) 9/213 (7) 10/219 (10)

Copeland 31–6–74–5; Abbott 23–3–77–2; O'Keefe 14–3–28–0; Conway 22.5–5–58–2; Henriques 4–0–22–1; Edwards 4–0–14–0; Sangha 2–1–4–0. *Second innings*—Copeland 22.2–8–52–3; Abbott 23–4–82–4; Conway 16–7–31–2; O'Keefe 23–11–32–1; Sangha 3–0–18–0; Henriques 2–1–1–0.

New South Wales

D. P. Hughes lbw b Siddle	2	– c White b Pattinson	41
N. C. R. Larkin lbw b Pattinson	2	– b Pattinson	4
K. R. Patterson c Gotch b Tremain	19	– c and b Siddle	76
M. C. Henriques lbw b Siddle	35	– c Gotch b Pattinson	23
J. J. S. Sangha lbw b Pattinson	21	– run out (Siddle)	4
*†P. M. Nevill b Pattinson	4	– lbw b Boland	18
J. R. Edwards c Gotch b Siddle	20	– c Gotch b Pattinson	6
S. N. J. O'Keefe lbw b Siddle	1	– b Tremain	1
T. A. Copeland c White b Siddle	0	– b Boland	6
S. A. Abbott c and b Tremain	1	– c Pattinson b Boland	6
H. N. A. Conway not out	2	– not out	0
B 4, lb 9, nb 1	14	B 9, lb 14, nb 2	25

1/8 (1) 2/8 (2) 3/38 (3)   (39 overs) 121   1/12 (2) 2/132 (3)   (63.3 overs) 210
4/88 (5) 5/94 (6) 6/96 (4)   3/162 (1) 4/166 (5)
7/110 (8) 8/110 (9) 9/111 (10) 10/121 (7)   5/169 (4) 6/175 (7) 7/182 (8)
                                                          8/190 (9) 9/207 (6) 10/210 (10)

Siddle 14–4–28–5; Pattinson 10–1–30–3; Tremain 9–4–27–2; Boland 6–0–23–0. *Second innings*—Siddle 15–2–54–1; Pattinson 16–4–41–4; Tremain 10–2–32–1; Boland 11.3–2–30–3; Holland 11–1–30–0.

Umpires: S. J. Nogajski and P. Wilson.   Third umpire: G. A. Abood.
Referee: D. J. Harper.

SHEFFIELD SHIELD WINNERS

1892-93	Victoria	1923-24	Victoria	1956-57	New South Wales
1893-94	South Australia	1924-25	Victoria	1957-58	New South Wales
1894-95	Victoria	1925-26	New South Wales	1958-59	New South Wales
1895-96	New South Wales	1926-27	South Australia	1959-60	New South Wales
1896-97	New South Wales	1927-28	Victoria	1960-61	New South Wales
1897-98	Victoria	1928-29	New South Wales	1961-62	New South Wales
1898-99	Victoria	1929-30	Victoria	1962-63	Victoria
1899-1900	New South Wales	1930-31	Victoria	1963-64	South Australia
1900-01	Victoria	1931-32	New South Wales	1964-65	New South Wales
1901-02	New South Wales	1932-33	New South Wales	1965-66	New South Wales
1902-03	New South Wales	1933-34	Victoria	1966-67	Victoria
1903-04	New South Wales	1934-35	Victoria	1967-68	Western Australia
1904-05	New South Wales	1935-36	South Australia	1968-69	South Australia
1905-06	New South Wales	1936-37	Victoria	1969-70	Victoria
1906-07	New South Wales	1937-38	New South Wales	1970-71	South Australia
1907-08	Victoria	1938-39	South Australia	1971-72	Western Australia
1908-09	New South Wales	1939-40	New South Wales	1972-73	Western Australia
1909-10	South Australia	1940–46	*No competition*	1973-74	Victoria
1910-11	New South Wales	1946-47	Victoria	1974-75	Western Australia
1911-12	New South Wales	1947-48	Western Australia	1975-76	South Australia
1912-13	South Australia	1948-49	New South Wales	1976-77	Western Australia
1913-14	New South Wales	1949-50	New South Wales	1977-78	Western Australia
1914-15	Victoria	1950-51	Victoria	1978-79	Victoria
1915–19	*No competition*	1951-52	New South Wales	1979-80	Victoria
1919-20	New South Wales	1952-53	South Australia	1980-81	Western Australia
1920-21	New South Wales	1953-54	New South Wales	1981-82	South Australia
1921-22	Victoria	1954-55	New South Wales	1982-83	New South Wales*
1922-23	New South Wales	1955-56	New South Wales	1983-84	Western Australia

1984-85	New South Wales	1996-97	Queensland*	2008-09	Victoria
1985-86	New South Wales	1997-98	Western Australia	2009-10	Victoria
1986-87	Western Australia	1998-99	Western Australia*	2010-11	Tasmania
1987-88	Western Australia	1999-2000	Queensland	2011-12	Queensland
1988-89	Western Australia	2000-01	Queensland	2012-13	Tasmania
1989-90	New South Wales	2001-02	Queensland	2013-14	New South Wales
1990-91	Victoria	2002-03	New South Wales*	2014-15	Victoria
1991-92	Western Australia	2003-04	Victoria	2015-16	Victoria*
1992-93	New South Wales	2004-05	New South Wales*	2016-17	Victoria
1993-94	New South Wales	2005-06	Queensland	2017-18	Queensland
1994-95	Queensland	2006-07	Tasmania	2018-19	Victoria
1995-96	South Australia	2007-08	New South Wales		

New South Wales have won the title 46 times, Victoria 32, Western Australia 15, South Australia 13, Queensland 8, Tasmania 3.

The tournament was the Pura Milk Cup in 1999-2000, and the Pura Cup from 2000-01 to 2007-08.

*   *Second in table but won final. Finals were introduced in 1982-83.*

JLT ONE-DAY CUP IN 2018-19

50-over league plus knockout

	P	W	L	Bonus	Pts	NRR
Western Australia......	5	5	0	3	23	1.94
Tasmania	5	3	2	1	13	−0.25
South Australia	5	2	3	1	9	−0.17
Victoria	5	2	3	1	9	−0.46
New South Wales......	5	2	3	1	9	−0.48
Queensland...........	5	1	4	1	5	−0.32

Win = 4pts; 1 bonus point awarded for achieving victory with a run-rate 1.25 times that of the opposition, and 2 bonus points for victory with a run-rate twice that of the opposition.

Quarter-finals   Queensland beat South Australia by 24 runs (DLS); Victoria advanced on their better net run-rate in the qualifying rounds after their match with New South Wales was abandoned.

Semi-finals   Tasmania beat Queensland by six wickets; Victoria beat Western Australia by 63 runs.

Final   At St Kilda, October 10, 2018. **Victoria won by 110 runs.** ‡**Victoria 274** (50 overs) (G. S. Sandhu 7-56); **Tasmania 164** (40.4 overs). *Victoria claimed a decisive win despite falling away after Cameron White (88) had led them to 171-2 in 33 overs. Gurinder Sandhu collected four wickets in the innings' last five deliveries, concluding with a hat-trick, to finish with a career-best seven. Victoria's captain and keeper Peter Handscomb followed a brisk 49 with four catches, and Tasmania's chase never got going.*

The KFC T20 Big Bash League has its own section (page 1130).

BANGLADESH CRICKET IN 2019

Shakib shocks a nation

Utpal Shuvro

In a tumultuous year for Bangladesh cricket, most of the news was bad. The national team suffered some humiliating defeats, but everything was overshadowed by events off the field. In New Zealand in March, the Test squad were minutes away from being caught in a mass shooting at a mosque near Hagley Park in Christchurch. The Third Test had been due to start next day, but it was called off, and the party immediately flew home.

In October, the country's cricketers staged an all-out revolt against the governing body – a big story quickly overshadowed when Shakib Al Hasan, Bangladesh's greatest player, was banned for two years (one suspended) by the ICC for failing to report approaches by a bookmaker. The news sent the country into shock. At first, there was disbelief, but the details were quickly confirmed. With teary eyes, and flanked by board officials, Shakib read a statement: "I am extremely sad to have been banned from the game I love, but

BANGLADESH IN 2019

	Played	Won	Lost	Drawn/No result
Tests	5	–	5	–
One-day internationals	18	7	11	–
Twenty20 internationals	7	4	3	–

JANUARY		
FEBRUARY	2 Tests and 3 ODIs (a) v New Zealand	(page 985)
MARCH		
APRIL		
MAY	ODI tri-series (in Ireland) v Ireland and West Indies	(page 969)
JUNE	World Cup (in England)	(page 237)
JULY	3 ODIs (a) v Sri Lanka	(page 1032)
AUGUST		
SEPTEMBER	1 Test (h) v Afghanistan	(page 914)
	T20I tri-series (h) v Afghanistan and Zimbabwe	(page 917)
OCTOBER		
NOVEMBER	2 Tests and 3 T20Is (a) v India	(page 949)
DECEMBER		

For a review of Bangladesh domestic cricket from the 2018-19 season, see page 924.

Allison Joyce, Getty Images

Safely home: Mahmudullah is reflective after the team's early return from New Zealand.

I completely accept my sanction for not reporting the approaches. I didn't do my duty in this instance."

It transpired that he had failed to report three approaches, all made on WhatsApp by bookmaker Deepak Aggarwal. The first two came during a home ODI tri-series involving Sri Lanka and Zimbabwe in January 2018; the third before an IPL match later in the year. Shakib told the ICC anti-corruption unit he had not provided any information, or received any money, after the contact with Aggarwal.

The news threw Bangladesh cricket into a tailspin. Shakib had been captain of the Test and T20 teams that were due to fly to India next day. The Test job was given to Mominul Haque, the T20 to Mahmudullah; after losing the 20-over matches 2–1, Bangladesh were thrashed in the Tests. It was not the first time Shakib had been in trouble: only a few days earlier, he had failed to attend a pre-tour training camp. But no one had doubted his integrity. He had taken a strong stand during Mohammad Ashraful's match-fixing trial in 2014, and reported an earlier approach from a bookmaker to the ICC.

This all followed within days of the stand-off between the players and the Bangladesh Cricket Board. In Mirpur, a group of 50 cricketers, including the big names from the national team, used a press conference to present 11 demands to the administrators. These included improvements to facilities, a return to franchises in the Bangladesh Premier League, pay rises for groundsmen and umpires, and more money for all first-class players. With Shakib at the forefront of the protest, they threatened to strike if the conditions were not met.

To many, they appeared reasonable, but the board's response was furious. President Nazmul Hassan attacked the players, making comments that bordered on personal insults. The players responded with two more demands, including revenue sharing. There was a real danger of the India tour being called off. But it all calmed down quickly. After a two-hour meeting in Mirpur, the board agreed to adopt nine of the 13 demands, and a truce was declared.

Amid the scandal and acrimony, there was some cricket, too. Events in Christchurch put sport's importance into perspective but, before the tour was abandoned, Bangladesh had been whitewashed in the one-day series, and demolished in the first two Tests. Things improved when they arrived in the British Isles for the World Cup. They won a warm-up tri-series in Ireland, then started the tournament by posting what was briefly their highest ODI total, in a barnstorming victory over South Africa at The Oval. Although they lost to New Zealand and England, victory over West Indies, while completing the second-highest run-chase in the competition's history, made them contenders for the semi-finals.

From there, it all went wrong, and Bangladesh slipped to eighth in the table. The wretched form of captain Mashrafe bin Mortaza, who took one for 361, hardly helped. He had been elected to parliament a few months earlier, and the distraction appeared to have affected his fitness. But it was coach Steve Rhodes who paid the price. Despite being in post for barely a year, he was sacked immediately after the tournament. In August, South African Russell Domingo was named as his replacement, on a two-year contract.

The World Cup was a personal triumph for Shakib. He worked hard on his fitness after a disappointing IPL, and was rewarded with 606 runs at 86, including two hundreds and five fifties, and 11 wickets. No one had scored 500 and taken ten in the same competition. He was named in the ICC's Team of the Tournament, despite his side's failure to reach the last four, and was a contender to be voted the leading player.

Domingo took charge for the one-off home Test against Afghanistan. He walked into the public spat between Shakib and Hassan, then saw his new charges humbled by the Afghans. Bangladesh perked up in the Twenty20 tri-series that followed, but there was frustration when the final was washed out. The tour of India then proved a disaster after the early optimism of the T20 win. Domingo must have wondered what he had let himself in for.

BANGLADESH v AFGHANISTAN IN 2019-20

Mohammad Isam

Test match (1): Bangladesh 0, Afghanistan 1

Since October 2016, Bangladesh had beaten England, Australia and West Indies in Tests at home, and Sri Lanka away – but their first meeting with Afghanistan ended in embarrassing defeat, after the newcomers outclassed them throughout. Bangladesh almost escaped with a draw thanks to the Chittagong weather, which halved the fourth day and allowed only 13 balls before tea on the fifth, but the Afghans grabbed the four wickets they needed once play restarted, completing victory with 20 balls to spare. Having beaten Ireland in March, they became only the second country, after Australia in the 1870s, to win two of their first three Tests.

Bangladesh looked short of ideas against Afghanistan's accomplished spinners, while their own slow bowlers were one-dimensional. They fielded poorly, too, which said a lot about their state of mind: all the country's players would soon mount a strike in protest at their treatment by the Bangladesh board. Shakib Al Hasan said before and after the match that he did not want to captain the side, and was criticised by the board's outspoken president, Nazmul Hassan, who suggested Shakib didn't actually want to play Test cricket at all. It was a lot to take in for the new coach, the South African Russell Domingo, who had been appointed a fortnight before the match, following Steve Rhodes's post-World Cup sacking.

Afghanistan had made changes since their own underwhelming World Cup. Rahmat Shah, installed as Test captain in April, was replaced before he had even led the team on to the field. If he was disappointed, he did not show it, completing his country's first Test century to set up a challenging total, helped by 92 from Asghar Afghan, Rahmat's predecessor.

Rashid Khan was appointed instead, becoming – at 20 – the youngest Test captain. Fears he would be overburdened were allayed by a sensational performance: he followed a fighting 51 with 11 wickets, including the last three in quick succession as Afghanistan grabbed victory in the nick of time.

FIRST-TEST BLUES

Bangladesh's inaugural Test against each opponent:

India	Lost by nine wickets	Dhaka	2000-01
Zimbabwe	Lost by an innings and 32 runs	Bulawayo	2000-01
Pakistan	Lost by an innings and 264 runs	Multan	2001-02
Sri Lanka	Lost by an innings and 137 runs	Colombo (SSC)	2001-02
New Zealand	Lost by an innings and 52 runs	Hamilton	2001-02
South Africa	Lost by an innings and 107 runs	East London	2002-03
West Indies	Lost by an innings and 310 runs	Dhaka	2002-03
Australia	Lost by an innings and 132 runs	Darwin	2003
England	Lost by seven wickets	Dhaka	2003-04
Afghanistan	**Lost by 224 runs**	**Chittagong**	**2019-20**

Bangladesh have not yet met Ireland in a Test.

AFGHANISTAN TOURING PARTY

*Rashid Khan, Afsar Zazai, Asghar Afghan, Hashmatullah Shahidi, Ibrahim Zadran, Ihsanullah Janat, Ikram Alikhil, Javed Ahmadi, Mohammad Nabi, Qais Ahmad, Rahmat Shah, Sayed Shirzad, Shapoor Zadran, Yamin Ahmadzai, Zahir Khan. *Interim coach:* A. J. Moles.

BANGLADESH v AFGHANISTAN

Only Test

At Chittagong, September 5–9, 2019. Afghanistan won by 224 runs. Toss: Afghanistan. Test debuts: Ibrahim Zadran, Qais Ahmad, Zahir Khan.

Afghanistan pulled off a superb victory in their first Test against Bangladesh, although they were nearly thwarted by the weather. After setting the hosts 398, and reducing them to 136 for six before rain ended the fourth day, they sat around for hours on the fifth. The weather relented briefly, allowing 13 balls just after lunch before another shower. When play resumed after tea, they had little more than an hour to take four wickets. Left-arm wrist-spinner Zahir Khan, one of three debutants, claimed the vital scalp of Shakib Al Hasan, then Rashid Khan rounded off a superb captaincy debut by claiming the last three in quick succession, to take his side home with 20 balls to spare.

At 20 years 350 days, Rashid had become the youngest Test captain of all, undercutting Zimbabwe's Tatenda Taibu by eight days. (The South African Graeme Smith was the previous-youngest to win a Test, aged 22 in 2002-03.) Rashid was hardly awed by the armband, following a half-century with 11 wickets for his mesmerising leg-spin variations. He also won the toss, allowing Afghanistan first use of a pitch expected to take increasing turn. Bangladesh did not select a recognised seamer, but their spinners never exerted the grip they had managed in their recent victories over England and Australia.

Rahmat Shah had just missed becoming Afghanistan's first Test centurion six months earlier, when he was out for 98 against Ireland. He made no mistake this time, hitting 102 in three and a half hours; the ball after reaching three figures, he lazily edged the 18-year-old off-spinner Nayeem Hasan to slip. Rahmat put on 120 with Asghar Afghan, who missed a century of his own when he miscued a wild slog off slow left-armer Taijul Islam (whose first wicket, Ihsanullah Janat, had been his 100th in Tests). Measured innings from Afsar Zazai and Rashid – his first Test half-century – lifted the total to an imposing 342, which looked even better when Shadman Islam fell in the first over. He was playing instead of Tamim Iqbal, who had asked for a break from cricket.

Bangladesh reached 88 for three on the second afternoon, but wobbled when the experienced pair of Shakib and Mushfiqur Rahim fell in three balls from Rashid. Mominul Haque grafted to 52 before holing out to mid-on. The bowler, Mohammad Nabi, surprised many that evening by announcing this would be his last Test. He was 34, and had been almost ever-present in Afghanistan's rise from the lower reaches of world cricket.

Boosted by a sensible knock from Mosaddek Hossain, Bangladesh reached 205 next morning, and reduced Afghanistan to 28 for three as they sought to build on a lead of 137. But they were rescued by the debutant opener Ibrahim Zadran, who showed maturity beyond his 17 years in surviving 208 balls. He occasionally threw off the shackles, hitting four sixes in his 87. Afghan and Zazai chipped in again as the lead swelled close to 400 early on the fourth day.

Given the forecast, Rashid might have declared earlier. But his varied spin attack made regular incisions, and an early finish was on the cards when Mahmudullah pushed a Rashid googly to short leg. That made it 125 for six, but the weather was closing in. Concern in the Afghanistan camp grew when the final day started wet: play did get under way after lunch, but only 13 balls were possible before another downpour. Just when Bangladesh might have thought they had escaped, the clouds cleared, and the match resumed after tea. Afghanistan needed four wickets in 18.3 overs – and got them, amid ecstatic celebrations. Rashid administered the *coup de grâce* when Soumya Sarkar nudged one off his hip to short leg,

Rashid's 11th wicket of a superb match. He joined Imran Khan (1982-83) and Allan Border (1988-89) as the only captains to score a half-century and take ten or more wickets in a Test.

Player of the Match: Rashid Khan.

Close of play: first day, Afghanistan 271-5 (Asghar Afghan 88, Afsar Zazai 35); second day, Bangladesh 194-8 (Mosaddek Hossain 44, Taijul Islam 14); third day, Afghanistan 237-8 (Afsar Zazai 34, Yamin Ahmadzai 0); fourth day, Bangladesh 136-6 (Shakib Al Hasan 39, Soumya Sarkar 0).

Afghanistan

Ibrahim Zadran c Mahmudullah b Taijul Islam	21 – (2) c Mominul Haque b Nayeem Hasan .	87
Ihsanullah Janat b Taijul Islam	9 – (1) lbw b Shakib Al Hasan	4
Rahmat Shah c Soumya Sarkar b Nayeem Hasan .	102 – c and b Shakib Al Hasan	0
Hashmatullah Shahidi c Soumya Sarkar b Mahmudullah .	14 – c Soumya Sarkar b Nayeem Hasan ..	12
Asghar Afghan c Mushfiqur Rahim b Taijul Islam .	92 – c Shakib Al Hasan b Taijul Islam ...	50
Mohammad Nabi b Nayeem Hasan	0 – (7) c Mominul Haque b Mehedi Hasan	8
†Afsar Zazai b Taijul Islam	41 – (6) not out	48
*Rashid Khan c and b Mehedi Hasan	51 – b Taijul Islam	24
Qais Ahmad c Mominul Haque b Shakib Al Hasan	9 – lbw b Shakib Al Hasan............	14
Yamin Ahmadzai c Soumya Sarkar b Shakib Al Hasan.	0 – run out (Shadman Islam/ Mushfiqur Rahim).	9
Zahir Khan not out	0 – c Mominul Haque b Mehedi Hasan ..	0
Lb 1, nb 2	3 B 4	4

1/19 (2) 2/48 (1) 3/77 (4)	**(117 overs) 342**	1/4 (1) 2/4 (3)	**(90.1 overs) 260**
4/197 (3) 5/197 (6) 6/278 (5)		3/28 (4) 4/136 (5)	
7/299 (7) 8/322 (9) 9/327 (10) 10/342 (8)		5/171 (2) 6/180 (7) 7/210 (8)	
		8/235 (9) 9/260 (10) 10/260 (11)	

Taijul Islam 41–5–116–4; Shakib Al Hasan 22–1–64–2; Mehedi Hasan 28–5–73–1; Nayeem Hasan 13–0–43–2; Mahmudullah 4–0–9–1; Soumya Sarkar 4–0–26–0; Mominul Haque 4–0–9–0; Mosaddek Hossain 1–0–1–0. *Second innings*—Shakib Al Hasan 19–3–58–3; Mehedi Hasan 12.1–3–35–2; Taijul Islam 28–6–86–2; Nayeem Hasan 17–2–61–2; Mominul Haque 10–6–13–0; Mosaddek Hossain 4–1–3–0.

Bangladesh

Shadman Islam c Afsar Zazai b Yamin Ahmadzai .	0 – (2) lbw b Mohammad Nabi	41
Soumya Sarkar lbw b Mohammad Nabi	17 – (8) c Ibrahim Zadran b Rashid Khan .	15
Liton Das b Rashid Khan	33 – (1) lbw b Zahir Khan	9
Mominul Haque c Asghar Afghan b Mohammad Nabi.	52 – (5) lbw b Rashid Khan............	3
*Shakib Al Hasan lbw b Rashid Khan...........	11 – (6) c Afsar Zazai b Zahir Khan	44
†Mushfiqur Rahim c Ibrahim Zadran b Rashid Khan	0 – (4) lbw b Rashid Khan............	23
Mahmudullah b Rashid Khan	7 – c Ibrahim Zadran b Rashid Khan...	7
Mosaddek Hossain not out	48 – (3) c Asghar Afghan b Zahir Khan..	12
Mehedi Hasan b Qais Ahmad	11 – lbw b Rashid Khan..............	12
Taijul Islam b Mohammad Nabi	14 – lbw b Rashid Khan..............	0
Nayeem Hasan lbw b Rashid Khan	7 – not out	1
B 4, lb 1	5 B 4, lb 2	6

1/0 (1) 2/38 (2) 3/54 (3)	**(70.5 overs) 205**	1/30 (1) 2/52 (3)	**(61.4 overs) 173**
4/88 (5) 5/88 (6) 6/104 (7)		3/78 (4) 4/82 (5)	
7/130 (4) 8/146 (9) 9/194 (10) 10/205 (11)		5/106 (2) 6/125 (7) 7/143 (6)	
		8/166 (9) 9/166 (10) 10/173 (8)	

Yamin Ahmadzai 10–2–21–1; Mohammad Nabi 24–6–56–3; Zahir Khan 9–1–46–0; Rashid Khan 19.5–3–55–5; Qais Ahmad 8–2–22–1. *Second innings*—Yamin Ahmadzai 4–1–14–0; Mohammad Nabi 20–5–39–1; Rashid Khan 21.4–6–49–6; Zahir Khan 15–0–59–3; Qais Ahmad 1–0–6–0.

Umpires: N. J. Llong and P. Wilson. Third umpire: N. N. Menon.
Referee: B. C. Broad.

BANGLADESH T20 TRI-SERIES IN 2019-20

Mohammad Isam

1= Bangladesh, Afghanistan   3 Zimbabwe

This Twenty20 tri-series looked intriguing. Despite a disappointing World Cup, Afghanistan were favourites, especially as the tournament followed their stunning victory in a one-off Test at Chittagong, arguably Bangladesh's most embarrassing defeat. Zimbabwe were in disarray at home after their board were suspended by the ICC, while Bangladesh had rarely relished the shortest format. But the hosts did collect most wins in the league stage, and shared the trophy with Afghanistan when the final was washed out.

Bangladesh had made several changes after their Test defeat, but of several rookies only Afif Hossain – a left-hander who turned 20 just before the final – made much impression, with a rapid half-century in the first match. There were more runs overall for old hands Mahmudullah (126) and Shakib Al Hasan (96), while medium-pacer Mohammad Saifuddin was joint-leading wicket-taker, on seven, with Afghan spinner Mujeeb Zadran.

Afghanistan's newcomers had a better time. Rahmanullah Gurbaz, just 17, was voted Player of the Series after three important innings, while the opening attack of Fareed Ahmad and Naveen-ul-Haq looked promising. There were also important contributions from Mujeeb, Hazratullah Zazai and Najibullah Zadran: Afghanistan's ambitious T20 plans aimed to entrust responsibility to new players, rather than rely on the likes of Rashid Khan and Mohammad Nabi, and were starting to bear fruit.

Zimbabwe struggled in their first international assignment since the ICC suspension (reversed not long after this tour). They were also lacking their influential all-rounder Sikandar Raza, after a separate dispute with the board. And they cited "disciplinary issues raised by the captain", Hamilton Masakadza, who then announced he would retire after the tournament. He had a fitting send-off, when his 71 set up victory over Afghanistan in the last match, and he finished level with Rahmanullah as the leading scorer, with 133. There were also useful knocks from Ryan Burl, Regis Chakabva and Richmond Mutumbami, but the bowling was too dependent on Kyle Jarvis.

NATIONAL SQUADS

Bangladesh *Shakib Al Hasan, Abu Haider, Afif Hossain, Aminul Islam, Liton Das, Mahmudullah, Mehedi Hasan, Mohammad Naim, Mohammad Saifuddin, Mosaddek Hossain, Mushfiqur Rahim, Mustafizur Rahman, Nazmul Hossain, Rubel Hossain, Sabbir Rahman, Shafiul Islam, Soumya Sarkar, Taijul Islam, Yeasin Arafat. *Coach:* R. C. Domingo.

Afghanistan *Rashid Khan, Asghar Afghan, Dawlat Zadran, Fareed Ahmad, Fazal Niazai, Gulbadeen Naib, Hazratullah Zazai, Karim Janat, Mohammad Nabi, Mujeeb Zadran, Najeeb Tarakai, Najibullah Zadran, Naveen-ul-Haq, Rahmanullah Gurbaz, Shafiqullah Shinwari, Shahidullah Kamal, Sharafuddin Ashraf. *Interim coach:* A. J. Moles.

Zimbabwe *H. Masakadza, R. P. Burl, R. W. Chakabva, T. L. Chatara, C. R. Ervine, K. M. Jarvis, N. Madziva, T. Maruma, C. B. Mpofu, T. T. Munyonga, C. T. Mutombodzi, R. Mutumbami, A. Ndlovu, B. R. M. Taylor, S. C. Williams. Coach: L. S. Rajput.*

At Mirpur, September 13, 2019 (floodlit). **Bangladesh won by three wickets. Zimbabwe 144-5** (18 overs) (H. Masakadza 34, R. P. Burl 57*); ‡**Bangladesh 148-7** (17.4 overs) (Mosaddek Hossain 30*, Afif Hossain 52). *PoM:* Afif Hossain. *T20I debuts:* Taijul Islam (Bangladesh); T. T. Munyonga (Zimbabwe). *Zimbabwe were reeling at 63-5 in the tenth over, before Ryan Burl and Tino Mutombodzi (27*) put on 81* in a match reduced to 18 a side. Burl's 57* came from 32 balls, and included 30 off Shakib Al Hasan's final over (644646). Bangladesh were in an even worse state in their tenth: 60-6, after fiery spells from Kyle Jarvis and Tendai Chatara, and a superb catch in the deep by Burl. But they were rescued by a stand of 82 between Mosaddek Hossain and Afif Hossain, who fell with only three required after making 52 from 26 balls in his second T20I, 18 months after a two-ball duck in his first. Bangladesh's first victory since the World Cup earned them a congratulatory call from the prime minister.*

At Mirpur, September 14, 2019 (floodlit). **Afghanistan won by 28 runs. Afghanistan 197-5** (20 overs) (Rahmanullah Gurbaz 43, Najibullah Zadran 69*, Mohammad Nabi 38); ‡**Zimbabwe 169-7** (20 overs) (R. W. Chakabva 42*). *PoM:* Najibullah Zadran. *T20I debuts:* Rahmanullah Gurbaz (Afghanistan); A. Ndlovu (Zimbabwe). *Despite the 17-year-old debutant Rahmanullah Gurbaz blasting 43 from 24 balls, Afghanistan looked to be heading for a middling score, before Najibullah Zadran and Mohammad Nabi butchered seven sixes from consecutive deliveries by Chatara and Neville Madziva. Their stand of 107 in 40 balls lifted the total to 197, which Zimbabwe never threatened after slipping to 44-4.*

At Mirpur, September 15, 2019 (floodlit). **Afghanistan won by 25 runs. ‡Afghanistan 164-6** (20 overs) (Asghar Afghan 40, Mohammad Nabi 84*; Mohammad Saifuddin 4-33); **Bangladesh 139** (19.5 overs) (Mahmudullah 44; Mujeeb Zadran 4-15). *PoM:* Mohammad Nabi. *Nabi's superb 54-ball 84*, with seven sixes, rescued Afghanistan from a precarious 40-4 in the sixth over; they made 55 in the last five, of which Nabi contributed 47. Mujeeb Zadran soon had Bangladesh in trouble at 32-4, including Liton Das and Soumya Sarkar for ducks.*

At Chittagong, September 18, 2019 (floodlit). **Bangladesh won by 39 runs. Bangladesh 175-7** (20 overs) (Liton Das 38, Mushfiqur Rahim 32, Mahmudullah 62; K. M. Jarvis 3-32); ‡**Bangladesh 136** (20 overs) (R. Mutumbami 54; Shafiul Islam 3-36). *PoM:* Mahmudullah. *T20I debuts:* Aminul Islam, Nazmul Hossain (Bangladesh). *An improved batting display, spearheaded by Mahmudullah's 41-ball 62, with five sixes and a solitary four, lifted Bangladesh to an imposing total. Zimbabwe were 2-2 after nine balls, and 44-6 in the ninth over. An eighth-wicket stand of 58 between Richmond Mutumbami and Jarvis (27) narrowed the margin, but it was still a thumping defeat.*

At Chittagong, September 20, 2019 (floodlit). **Zimbabwe won by seven wickets. ‡Afghanistan 155-8** (20 overs) (Rahmanullah Gurbaz 61, Hazratullah Zazai 31; C. B. Mpofu 4-30); **Zimbabwe 156-3** (19.3 overs) (H. Masakadza 71, R. W. Chakabva 39). *PoM:* C. B. Mpofu. *T20I debut:* Fazal Niazai (Afghanistan). *Hamilton Masakadza rounded off his long international career in perfect style with 71 from 42 balls, which helped Zimbabwe to their first T20I win over Afghanistan, after eight defeats. Afghanistan's 155-8 was underwhelming, after Rahmanullah shot out of the blocks with 61 from 47 during an opening stand of 83 with Hazratullah Zazai; a format-best 4-30 from Chris Mpofu slowed them down. After the match, both sides gave Masakadza – draped in the Zimbabwe flag – a guard of honour, while a sparse crowd made enough noise for a memorable farewell.*

At Chittagong, September 21, 2019 (floodlit). **Bangladesh won by four wickets. Afghanistan 138-7** (20 overs) (Hazratullah Zazai 47); ‡**Bangladesh 139-6** (19 overs) (Shakib Al Hasan 70*). *PoM:* Shakib Al Hasan. *T20I debut:* Naveen-ul-Haq (Afghanistan). *Bangladesh had not beaten Afghanistan in T20Is since March 2014, the first of their five previous meetings. But now, after his bowlers had restricted Afghanistan to 138 (from 75-0 in the ninth, they lost seven for 39), Shakib scored more than half the runs to anchor the chase, finishing with 70* from 45 balls. The result was still in doubt at 104-6 after 15.5 overs, but Shakib settled it in the 18th, from Rashid Khan, which cost 18.*

BANGLADESH 6pts, AFGHANISTAN 4pts, Zimbabwe 2pts.

Final At Mirpur, September 24, 2019 (floodlit). **Bangladesh v Afghanistan. Abandoned.** *PoS:* Rahmanullah Gurbaz (Afghanistan). *After three hours of steady rain, the umpires called the match off, and the teams shared the trophy. Both bemoaned the absence of a reserve day, but it rained the following evening too.*

BANGLADESH U19 v ENGLAND U19 IN 2018-19

Under-19 Twenty20 international (1): Bangladesh 1, England 0
Under-19 one-day internationals (3): Bangladesh 3, England 0
Under-19 Tests (2): Bangladesh 2, England 0

It was not until the final day of a demanding tour that the England Under-19 players were forced to give up on their attempts to register a victory. Beaten in the single Twenty20 and whitewashed in the ODIs, they still had a chance of squaring the Test series. But Bangladesh squeezed home by three wickets, extending the period since England's last Test win on the subcontinent to 23 years.

As head coach Jon Lewis pointed out, though, these tours are not measured solely by results. "To run the Bangladesh team so close was a great effort," he said. "We have shown we have the courage to fight all the way to the last session of the last day of this tour." An inexperienced squad had battled hard in alien conditions, but often struggled to score at a decent rate across the formats. Then there was the question of spin: Bangladesh's slower bowlers took 28 wickets in the Tests, England's ten.

The tour was staged in the middle of the two-year cycle for the Under-19 World Cup, and featured a mix of newcomers and those who had played in the tournament in New Zealand a year earlier. Tom Lammonby and Jamie Smith, the two captains, and Adam Finch would be too old for the 2020 World Cup in South Africa, but gained precious experience of Asian conditions.

There were some outstanding individual performances. Gloucestershire's Ben Charlesworth was Player of the Series in the ODIs after totalling 180 runs, including a century; Lewis Goldsworthy managed 155. Charlesworth carried his form into the Tests, but he was shaded by Smith, who scored 90 and 104 in the second game. Hamidullah Qadri, an off-spinner, finished with nine wickets across the 50-over and Test matches, while Finch took eight. George Hill collected seven in difficult conditions for seamers, and also contributed 250 runs. "I believe these types of experiences, win or lose, are invaluable to our best young players," said Lewis. "You might only see the direct benefit of that in 2025 or 2028."

Bangladesh had several players who underlined their potential. Mahmudul Hasan was the dominant batsman, with 148 runs at 74 in the ODIs and 188 at 94 in the Tests. Slow left-armer Minhazur Rahman took 16 wickets at 15 in the Tests.

> **"**December's BBC Sports Personality of the Year award became not so much about who would win, but about who would finish second and third."
> The Leading Cricketer in the World in 2019, page 63

ENGLAND TOURING PARTY

*T. A. Lammonby (Somerset), K. L. Aldridge (Somerset), G. P. Balderson (Lancashire), B. G. Charlesworth (Gloucestershire), J. M. Cox (Kent), A. W. Finch (Worcestershire), L. P. Goldsworthy (Somerset), Hamidullah Qadri (Derbyshire), G. C. H. Hill (Yorkshire), L. B. K. Hollman (Middlesex), D. J. Leech (Yorkshire), J. P. Morley (Lancashire), D. R. Mousley (Warwickshire), W. C. F. Smeed (Somerset). J. L. Smith (Surrey). *Coach:* J. Lewis.

Smith captained in the white-ball matches.

Under-19 Twenty20 international At Cox's Bazar, January 27, 2019. **Bangladesh won by seven wickets. ‡England** 120-8 (20 overs) (G. C. H. Hill 34; Tanzim Hasan Sakib 4-30); **Bangladesh** 123-3 (18.5 overs) (Mahmudul Hasan 44, Parvez Hossain 33). *PoM:* Tanzim Hasan Sakib. *Three early strikes from 16-year-old seamer Tanzim Hasan Sakib put England on the ropes at 37-4. George Hill and Lewis Goldsworthy stopped the rot, but they were never able to press the accelerator. Bangladesh's response was calm and unhurried: Mahmudul Hasan took 54 balls over his 44, and they completed the job with seven to spare.*

First Under-19 one-day international At Cox's Bazar, January 29, 2019. **Bangladesh won by five wickets. ‡England** 209-7 (50 overs) (L. P. Goldsworthy 61; Tanzim Hasan Sakib 3-47); **Bangladesh** 210-5 (45.4 overs) (Parvez Hossain 80). *PoM:* Parvez Hossain. *The format changed, but not the storyline. England opted to bat, Tanzim took three early wickets, and the recovery failed to trouble the Bangladeshis. Goldsworthy top-scored with 61, but took 99 balls and managed just three boundaries. Parvez Hossain added 82 for the second and third wickets with Prantik Nawroz and Mahmudul; by the time Adam Finch removed Parvez, Bangladesh were almost home.*

Second Under-19 one-day international At Cox's Bazar, January 31, 2019. **Bangladesh won by five wickets. ‡England** 256-7 (50 overs) (L. P. Goldsworthy 73; Mrittunjoy Chowdhury 4-50); **Bangladesh** 258-5 (47.5 overs) (Tanzid Hasan 70, Mahmudul Hasan 58*, Akbar Ali 57; Hamidullah Qadri 3-48). *PoM:* Tanzid Hasan. *Goldsworthy continued to make a strong impression in a much-improved England batting performance. After Jamie Smith had again decided to bat, Ben Charlesworth and Will Smeed put on 87 for the first wicket in 18 overs, before Goldsworthy contributed 73. Bangladesh were unfazed: Tanzid Hasan hit a rapid 70 and, despite three wickets for Hamidullah Qadri's off-breaks, the outcome was settled by a fifth-wicket stand of 106 between Mahmudul and Akbar Ali.*

Third Under-19 one-day international At Cox's Bazar, February 2, 2019. **Bangladesh won by 63 runs. ‡Bangladesh** 266-9 (50 overs) (Mahmudul Hasan 57, Shamim Hossain 72, Shahadat Hossain jnr 51*; G. C. H. Hill 3-37); **England** 203 (46.3 overs) (B. G. Charlesworth 115; Asadullah Galib 4-17). *PoM:* Shamim Hossain. *PoS:* B. G. Charlesworth. *A battling hundred from Charlesworth earned him the series award, but could not prevent a whitewash. Bangladesh batted first this time, and made the highest total of the series, Shamim Hossain top-scoring with 72; Hill took three wickets with his economical seamers. Charlesworth batted 45 overs for his 115, but of the rest only Goldsworthy (21) and Luke Hollman (30) made any impression.*

BANGLADESH v ENGLAND

First Under-19 Test

At Chittagong (ZAC), February 7–10, 2019. Bangladesh won by eight wickets. Toss: England.

A promising start for England gave way to a humbling defeat. The problem they had experienced in the white-ball matches – an inability to score quickly on unfamiliar surfaces – was again at the heart of their troubles. They looked solid enough after winning the toss: openers George Balderson and Ben Charlesworth put on 124. But they were undone by a steady trickle of departures to slow left-armer Ruhel Ahmed, including Charlesworth, caught behind for 99. Parvez Hossain and Towhid Hridoy both hit sixties but, when the Bangladeshis were 262 for five, England still had a slender lead. From that point, however, the hosts accelerated away, with captain Akbar Ali and Shahadat Hossain passing 80; they declared 118 in front. The England spin trio of Hamidullah Qadri, Luke Hollman and Jack Morley had just three wickets to show for 69 overs of toil. Bangladesh rammed home their advantage when England batted again. This time they were tormented by another slow left-armer, Minhazur Rahman, who had figures of six for 28 from 25 overs. George Hill and Hollman dug in for nearly two hours to delay the inevitable, but Bangladesh needed just 35 to win, and Parvez Hossain hit his second ball for six to finish the contest with a flourish.

Close of play: first day, England 261-8 (Mousley 7, Finch 4); second day, Bangladesh 266-5 (Akbar Ali 56, Shahadat Hossain 0); third day, England 89-6 (Hill 12, Hollman 0).

England

G. P. Balderson c and b Ruhel Ahmed.	65	– c Akbar Ali b Minhazur Rahman	10
B. G. Charlesworth c Akbar Ali b Ruhel Ahmed. . .	99	– c Minhazur Rahman	
		b Asadullah Galib.	20
L. P. Goldsworthy b Ruhel Ahmed	4	– c Akbar Ali b Asadullah Galib.	17
*T. A. Lammonby c Akbar Ali b Ruhel Ahmed	7	– lbw b Minhazur Rahman	12
†J. L. Smith lbw b Minhazur Rahman	14	– c Akbar Ali b Asadullah Galib.	0
G. C. H. Hill c Towhid Hridoy b Asadullah Galib	26	– b Minhazur Rahman	32
D. R. Mousley not out	26	– b Shahadat Hossain	4
L. B. K. Hollman b Asadullah Galib	0	– lbw b Minhazur Rahman	29
Hamidullah Qadri lbw b Minhazur Rahman	10	– b Minhazur Rahman.	5
A. W. Finch b Minhazur Rahman	4	– lbw b Minhazur Rahman	4
J. P. Morley run out (Rakibul Hasan)	0	– not out	0
B 6, lb 7, nb 7, p 5	25	B 6, lb 8, nb 5	19

1/124 (1) 2/128 (3) 3/144 (4)	(94.2 overs)	280	1/20 (1) 2/52 (2) (84.3 overs) 152
4/174 (5) 5/230 (2) 6/240 (6)			3/58 (3) 4/58 (5)
7/240 (8) 8/257 (9) 9/265 (10) 10/280 (11)			5/73 (4) 6/89 (7) 7/134 (6)
			8/141 (8) 9/151 (9) 10/152 (10)

Ruhel Ahmed 20.2–5–71–4; Asadullah Galib 19–1–68–2; Towhid Hridoy 16–5–29–0; Rakibul Hasan 17–3–34–0; Shamim Hossain 3–0–16–0; Minhazur Rahman 16–3–37–3; Shahadat Hossain 3–0–7–0. *Second innings*—Asadullah Galib 15–2–30–3; Shamim Hossain 5–3–7–0; Ruhel Ahmed 10–8–8–0; Minhazur Rahman 25.3–16–28–6; Rakibul Hasan 23–5–48–0; Towhid Hridoy 3–1–11–0; Shahadat Hossain 3–2–6–1.

Bangladesh

Tanzid Hasan c Hill b Finch.	4	– b Finch	0
Amite Hasan run out (Morley)	49	– st Smith b Hollman	10
Parvez Hossain c Hamidullah Qadri b Balderson . .	62	– (4) not out.	6
Towhid Hridoy c Hollman b Goldsworthy	61		
Shamim Hossain lbw b Hamidullah Qadri.	12	– (3) not out.	20
*†Akbar Ali c Hill b Lammonby	82		
Shahadat Hossain jnr c Charlesworth b Hill	84		
Rakibul Hasan c Hill b Hamidullah Qadri	14		
Minhazur Rahman c Smith b Hollman.	5		
Ruhel Ahmed not out	1		
B 9, lb 12, nb 3	24	B 4	4

1/12 (1) 2/105 (2)	(9 wkts dec, 121.5 overs)	398	1/4 (1) 2/34 (2) (2 wkts, 10 overs) 40
3/146 (3) 4/173 (5)			
5/262 (4) 6/313 (6) 7/337 (8) 8/372 (9) 9/398 (7)			

Asadullah Galib did not bat.

Finch 20.3–5–57–1; Balderson 13.3–5–44–1; Hamidullah Qadri 28–3–105–2; Hollman 19–2–67–1; Morley 22–0–69–0; Hill 10.5–3–14–1; Goldsworthy 4–0–13–1; Lammonby 4–2–8–1. *Second innings*—Finch 2–1–6–1; Hollman 5–0–19–1; Hamidullah Qadri 3–0–11–0.

Umpires: Gazi Sohel and Moniruzzaman.
Referee: Debabrata Paul.

BANGLADESH v ENGLAND

Second Under-19 Test

At Chittagong (MAA), February 15–18, 2019. Bangladesh won by three wickets. Toss: Bangladesh.

Stellar batting performances from Jamie Smith and George Hill were not quite enough to guide England to their first Under-19 Test victory on the subcontinent since 1996-97, when a team led by Andrew Flintoff beat Pakistan in Faisalabad. Smith scored 194 runs in the match – including a second-innings century – and Hill 91 in the first innings, but Bangladesh overturned a deficit of 109, and England flew home with six defeats out of six. After they had been put in, Charlesworth and Smith added 152 for the second wicket. Later, after three wickets in four balls, Hill helped shore things up, though the last four fell for 11. England looked in control when they reduced Bangladesh to 84 for five, but Mahmudul Hasan and Shahadat Hossain kept them in the game. Seamer Kasey Aldridge finished with four for 44. Smith batted aggressively as England sought to extend their lead, making 104 in 106 balls, but lacked support. Minhazur Rahman picked up another four wickets to take his tally to 16. When Bangladesh set off in pursuit of 333 before the close of the third day, England sensed an opportunity to level the series. But Mahmudul's five-hour century – and partnership of 142 with Towrid Hridoy – ensured Bangladesh completed a well-judged chase.

Close of play: first day, England 295-6 (Hill 79, Hollman 6); second day, Bangladesh 194-6 (Mahmudul Hasan 62, Ruhel Ahmed 0); third day, Bangladesh 34-1 (Tanzid Hasan 28).

England

G. P. Balderson c Tanzid Hasan b Asadullah Galib	9	– c Amite Hasan b Asadullah Galib ...	9
B. G. Charlesworth c Mahmudul Hasan b Mujakkir Hussain .	63	– lbw b Asadullah Galib	6
J. L. Smith c Akbar Ali b Ruhel Ahmed	90	– c and b Minhazur Rahman	104
*T. A. Lammonby c Parvez Hossain b Minhazur Rahman .	24	– lbw b Mujakkir Hussain	12
L. P. Goldsworthy c Akbar Ali b Ruhel Ahmed ...	0	– c Mahmudul Hasan b Minhazur Rahman .	13
G. C. H. Hill c Towhid Hridoy b Asadullah Galib .	91	– b Minhazur Rahman..............	20
†J. M. Cox b Minhazur Rahman	13	– b Mujakkir Hussain	30
L. B. K. Hollman lbw b Mujakkir Hussain	24	– c Shahadat Hossain b Minhazur Rahman .	7
K. L. Aldridge lbw b Minhazur Rahman	10	– not out	9
Hamidullah Qadri c Tanzid Hasan b Mujakkir Hussain .	0	– not out	4
A. W. Finch not out	0		
Lb 1, w 4, nb 8	13	B 1, lb 1, w 6, nb 1........	9

1/16 (1) 2/168 (2) 3/168 (3)   (102.5 overs) 337   1/10 (2)   (8 wkts dec, 54 overs) 223
4/168 (5) 5/238 (4) 6/275 (7)   2/36 (1) 3/80 (4)
7/326 (6) 8/327 (8) 9/327 (10) 10/337 (9)   4/109 (5) 5/168 (3)
                                                   6/182 (6) 7/192 (8) 8/217 (7)

Ruhel Ahmed 19–5–77–2; Asadullah Galib 21–4–70–2; Minhazur Rahman 32.5–6–106–3; Mujakkir Hussain 29–6–74–3; Shahadat Hossain 1–0–9–0. *Second innings*—Mujakkir Hussain 13–2–50–2; Asadullah Galib 15–1–58–2; Minhazur Rahman 18–2–74–4; Ruhel Ahmed 7–0–37–0; Mahmudul Hasan 1–0–2–0.

Bangladesh

Tanzid Hasan b Balderson	36	– c Hamidullah Qadri b Finch	51
Amite Hasan c Cox b Finch	4	– lbw b Aldridge	6
Parvez Hossain c Smith b Aldridge	18	– st Cox b Hamidullah Qadri	37
Mahmudul Hasan c Cox b Balderson	74	– c sub (D. R. Mousley) b Hollman	114
Towhid Hridoy b Aldridge	0	– b Finch	76
*†Akbar Ali c Finch b Hollman	7	– c and b Aldridge	5
Shahadat Hossain jnr c Smith b Hamidullah Qadri	56	– c Smith b Hamidullah Qadri	20
Ruhel Ahmed c Lammonby b Balderson	4	– not out	4
Minhazur Rahman not out	11	– not out	3
Mujakkir Hussain c Cox b Aldridge	0		
Asadullah Galib b Aldridge	4		
B 2, lb 9, nb 3	14	B 1, lb 1, w 13, nb 2	17

1/9 (2) 2/55 (1) 3/67 (3)   (88 overs) 228   1/34 (2)   (7 wkts, 93.5 overs) 333
4/67 (5) 5/84 (4) 6/194 (7)   2/67 (1) 3/121 (3)
7/210 (8) 8/217 (4) 9/224 (10) 10/228 (11)   4/263 (5) 5/282 (6) 6/326 (4) 7/330 (7)

Finch 18.4–3–61–1; Aldridge 17.2–3–44–4; Balderson 17–6–40–3; Hollman 16–2–39–1; Hamidullah Qadri 12–3–19–1; Hill 7–2–14–0. *Second innings*—Finch 18–1–60–2; Aldridge 17–2–79–2; Hamidullah Qadri 17.5–1–61–2; Balderson 4–0–19–0; Hollman 12–2–47–1; Hill 11–2–34–0; Goldsworthy 14–2–31–0.

Umpires: Mahfuzur Rahman and Tanvir Ahmed.
Referee: Akhtar Ahmad.

DOMESTIC CRICKET IN BANGLADESH IN 2018-19

Utpal Shuvro

There was a romantic element to **Rajshahi** regaining the crown in the National Cricket League in November 2018. Though it was their sixth first-class title, equalling Khulna's record, they had spent the three seasons since the competition was divided into two tiers languishing in the lower. But, a year after finally securing promotion, they became champions again.

With only three of 12 first-tier matches reaching an outright result, Rajshahi clinched the title in the final round with their second victory, when they beat Barisal after skittling them for 97 on the opening day. Their previous win had come in the season's most intriguing game, against defending champions Khulna. After three days, with Rajshahi's first innings still in progress, it seemed to be heading for a tame draw. With that in mind, the selectors called up Khulna's Soumya Sarkar for a one-day international against Zimbabwe. Soumya took two domestic flights to reach Chittagong, where he won the match award for a stroke-filled century – but meanwhile Khulna had lost. After taking a 122-run first-innings lead, Rajshahi bundled them out for 158 and knocked off a target of 37 in 4.4 overs. This ended an unbeaten run of 25 matches for Khulna (18 drawn) since February 2015. Meanwhile, Dhaka were promoted after topping the second tier – also on two wins – while Barisal were relegated.

Rajshahi's leading run-scorer was Junaid Siddique, with 404, though he was only seventh in the list of the tournament's top aggregates. Not far behind was opener Mizanur Rahman, who etched his name in the record book with five successive NCL hundreds – three in Rajshahi's last three matches of 2017-18, two in the first two rounds this time (he batted only once in each game). Two team-mates, seamer Farhad Reza and slow left-armer Sanjamul Islam, were among the top four wicket-takers, with 42 between them.

But the bowlers' top spot went to Chittagong's Nayeem Hasan, a lanky off-spinner who took 28 wickets at 25. He also recorded the season's best performance, eight for 106 against Dhaka, when still 17 – the youngest to take eight in an innings in the competition. A month later, he became the youngest to take a five-for on Test debut, against West Indies on his home ground. Shadman Islam of Dhaka Metropolis was the highest scorer with 648 in ten innings. An opener in the classical mould, he too was rewarded with a cap against West Indies, and scored 76 in Bangladesh's first innings victory in any Test.

A more seasoned campaigner, Tushar Imran of Khulna, continued his domestic run-spree by scoring three hundreds, the most in this tournament. In the first round, against Rajshahi, he became the first Bangladeshi to score centuries in both innings twice (he had done it in the Bangladesh Cricket League six months earlier). In his third game, while making a hundred against Rangpur, he became the first Bangladeshi to score 11,000 first-class runs.

In the franchise-based Bangladesh Cricket League, all four teams were in contention until the final round, when **South Zone** beat North Zone to retain the title, their fourth in seven editions of the competition. Left-arm spinner Abdur Razzak took seven wickets in the first innings of that match, and five in the second, to finish the first-class season with 43 – giving him 91 in the calendar year, a Bangladesh record for a bowler.

The one-day Dhaka Premier League was closely contested, with the title eventually decided on net run-rate. Legends of Rupganj led the tournament until the penultimate round, but **Abahani** came back strongly to retain the title. Needing to win their last game, they did it in style, thanks to Soumya, who became the first Bangladeshi to score a double-century in List A cricket: an unbeaten 208 with 16 sixes, the most by any batsman on Bangladeshi soil.

FIRST-CLASS AVERAGES IN 2018-19

BATTING (500 runs)

		M	I	NO	R	HS	100	Avge	Ct/St
1	Yasir Ali (*Chittagong/East Zone*)......	9	11	2	677	112	2	75.22	9
2	†Shadman Islam (*Dhaka Met/Bang/CZ*)	8	13	0	807	189	2	62.07	7
3	Rony Talukdar (*Dhaka/East Zone*).....	10	16	1	886	228*	2	59.06	4
4	†Junaid Siddique (*Rajshahi/North Zone*) .	12	19	3	904	120*	3	56.50	12
5	†Mominul Haque (*Chittagong/Bang/EZ*)	11	20	1	1,052	194	5	55.36	7
6	Naeem Islam (*Rangpur/North Zone*) ...	12	20	1	966	137	3	50.84	3
7	†Soumya Sarkar (*Khulna/Bangladesh*)...	7	11	1	501	103*	1	50.10	3
8	Anamul Haque (*Khulna/South Zone*) ...	11	21	2	936	180	3	49.26	9/4
9	Farhad Hossain (*Rajshahi/North Zone*) .	12	19	4	733	103*	1	48.86	13
10	Mahmudul Hasan (*Rangpur/East Zone*) .	11	19	3	781	135	1	48.81	6
11	Shamsur Rahman (*Dhaka Met/E Zone*) .	9	14	1	621	153	2	47.76	2
12	Jahurul Islam (*Rajshahi/North Zone*) ..	12	17	3	667	163*	2	47.64	22/2
13	Mehedi Hasan (*Khulna/South Zone*) ...	11	18	5	598	86	0	46.00	12
14	Tushar Imran (*Khulna/South Zone*)	11	20	1	821	159	3	43.21	2
15	Mizanur Rahman (*Rajshahi/North Zone*)	9	15	0	643	165	2	42.86	6
16	Abdul Mazid (*Dhaka/Central Zone*)....	12	20	1	807	141*	3	42.47	8
17	†Fazle Mahmud (*Barisal/South Zone*) ...	9	16	1	619	195	1	41.26	4
18	Ziaur Rahman (*Khulna/North Zone*) ...	11	17	1	658	112	1	41.12	6
19	Al-Amin (*Barisal/South Zone*)	9	15	1	519	128	1	37.07	5
20	Mohammad Ashraful (*Dhaka Met/EZ*)..	10	17	1	576	136	1	36.00	4
21	Shuvagata Hom (*Dhaka/Central Zone*) .	11	16	1	503	106	1	33.53	10

BOWLING (20 wickets)

		Style	O	M	R	W	BB	5I	Avge
1	Mehedi Hasan (*Bangladesh*)	OB	143.1	27	403	26	7-58	3	15.50
2	Nayeem Hasan (*Chittagong/Ban/EZ*)	OB	322.2	71	925	44	8-47	4	21.02
3	Shahidul Islam (*Dhaka Met/C Zone*).	RM	243.5	54	673	29	6-64	2	23.20
4	Farhad Reza (*Rajshahi/East Zone*)..	RFM	269.3	53	843	34	7-32	1	24.79
5	Arafat Sunny (*Dhaka Met/C Zone*) ..	SLA	268	54	801	31	7-57	1	25.83
6	Shahadat Hossain (*Dhaka Met/C Zone*)..	RFM	158.2	25	555	21	4-46	0	26.42
7	Abu Haider (*Dhaka Met/C Zone*) ...	LFM	143.2	10	584	22	6-86	1	26.54
8	Shuvagata Hom (*Dhaka/C Zone*)....	OB	248.1	60	665	25	5-53	1	26.60
9	Taijul Islam (*Rajshahi/Bang/E Zone*)	SLA	405.2	80	1,291	48	6-33	5	26.89
10	Al-Amin Hossain (*Khulna/S Zone*) ..	RFM	238.4	49	698	25	4-67	0	27.92
11	Ebadat Hossain (*Sylhet/North Zone*) .	RFM	211.5	34	727	26	6-51	1	27.96
12	Sanjamul Islam (*Rajshahi/N Zone*) ..	SLA	477.4	69	1,495	49	7-69	5	30.51
13	Abdur Razzak (*Khulna/South Zone*) .	SLA	442.3	70	1,314	43	7-69	4	30.55
14	Mehedi Hasan snr (*Khulna/S Zone*) .	OB	303	63	904	29	5-72	1	31.17
15	Enamul Haque (*Sylhet/East Zone*)...	SLA	267.5	42	885	28	6-165	2	31.60
16	Abu Jayed (*E Zone/Bang/Sylhet*) ...	RFM	234.2	37	851	25	6-74	1	34.04
17	Sohag Gazi (*Barisal/North Zone*) ...	OB	269.5	45	870	23	5-40	1	37.82
18	Mosharraf Hossain (*Dhaka/C Zone*) .	SLA	331.4	62	1,017	22	4-53	0	46.22

WALTON LED TV NATIONAL CRICKET LEAGUE IN 2018-19

Tier One	P	W	L	D	Pts	**Tier Two**	P	W	L	D	Pts
Rajshahi	6	2	0	4	34.81	Dhaka	6	2	1	3	29.35
Rangpur	6	1	0	5	24.59						
Khulna	6	0	1	4*	16.15	Dhaka Metropolis ...	6	1	2	3	25.13
						Chittagong	6	1	1	4	21.11
Barisal............	6	0	2	3*	14.61	Sylhet	6	1	1	4	20.12

* *Plus one abandoned match.*

Outright win = 8pts; draw = 2pts; abandoned = 2pts. Bonus points awarded for the first 100 overs of each team's first innings, when each team have had the chance to face 100 overs or been bowled out: 0.01 batting points for every run over the first 250; 0.5 bowling points for the fifth, seventh and ninth wicket taken.

Dhaka were promoted to Tier One, and Barisal relegated.

NATIONAL CRICKET LEAGUE WINNERS

†1999-2000	Chittagong	2005-06	Rajshahi	2012-13	Khulna
2000-01	Biman Bangladesh	2006-07	Dhaka	2013-14	Dhaka
	Airlines	2007-08	Khulna	2014-15	Rangpur
2001-02	Dhaka	2008-09	Rajshahi	2015-16	Khulna
2002-03	Khulna	2009-10	Rajshahi	2016-17	Khulna
2003-04	Dhaka	2010-11	Rajshahi	2017-18	Khulna
2004-05	Dhaka	2011-12	Rajshahi	2018-19	Rajshahi

† *The National Cricket League was not first-class in 1999-2000.*

Khulna and Rajshahi have won the title 6 times, Dhaka 5, Biman Bangladesh Airlines, Chittagong and Rangpur 1.

BANGLADESH CRICKET LEAGUE IN 2018-19

				Bonus pts		
	P	W	L	D	Bat	Bowl	Pts
South Zone	6	2	1	3	3.88	6.0	31.88
East Zone	6	1	0	5	5.14	6.0	29.14
Central Zone	6	1	2	3	0.87	8.5	23.37
North Zone	6	0	1	5	2.61	6.0	18.61

Outright win = 8pts; draw = 2pts. Bonus points awarded for the first 100 overs of each team's first innings, when each team have had the chance to face 100 overs or been bowled out: 0.01 batting points for every run over the first 250; 0.5 bowling points for the fifth, seventh and ninth wicket taken.

DHAKA PREMIER LEAGUE IN 2018-19

50-over league plus Super League and Relegation League

Preliminary League

	P	W	L	Pts
LEGENDS OF RUPGANJ	11	10	1	20
PRIME BANK..........	11	8	3	16
ABAHANI	11	8	3	16
PRIME DOLESHWAR...	11	7	4	14
SH. JAM. DHANMONDI	11	6	5	12
MOHAMMEDAN	11	6	5	12
Shinepukur	11	5*	5	11
Gazi Grp Cricketers	11	5	6	10
Khelaghar Samaj Kalyan ..	11	3	8	6
Brothers Union	11	3	8	6
Krira Shikkha Protisthan...	11	2*	8	5
Uttara	11	2	9	4

Super League

	P	W	L	Pts
Abahani	16	13	3	26
Legends of Rupganj	16	13	3	26
Prime Doleshwar	16	10	6	20
Sheikh Jamal Dhanmondi .	16	9	7	18
Prime Bank	16	8	8	16
Mohammedan	16	7	9	14

Relegation League

	P	W	L	Pts
Brothers Union	13	4	9	8
Uttara	13	4	9	8
Krira Shikkha Protisthan ..	13	2*	10	5

* *Plus one tie.*

The top six teams advanced to the Super League, carrying forward all their results from the Preliminary League, and then playing the other five qualifiers again. Teams tied on points were separated on head-to-head results.

The Bangladesh Premier League has its own section (page 1133).

INDIAN CRICKET IN 2019

Almost perfect

S H A R D A   U G R A

In a year bookended by two landmarks – a series victory in Australia, and a first home day/night Test – the midterm wasn't too bad either. Apart from the World Cup semi-final, that is. The tournament is often, perhaps unfairly, taken as a measure of Indian cricket's health, and while their exit at the hands of New Zealand carried an emotional sting, it did not come as a huge shock.

India love their World Cups, and have three to their name in the two formats. The first, in 1983, triggered the spark which led to a revolution. The second, the inaugural World T20 in 2007, changed cricket for ever. The third, in 2011, seemed to confirm India's status as the modern game's giants. Their intensely committed fans now expect their team to win every big event, but it is seven years since India claimed a global title – the 2013 Champions Trophy. Once the disappointment of the World Cup faded, however, a new challenge presented itself: the World Test Championship.

INDIA IN 2019

	Played	Won	Lost	Drawn/No result
Tests	8	7	–	1
One-day internationals	28	19	8	1
Twenty20 internationals	16	9	7	–

DECEMBER	4 Tests and 3 ODIs (a) v Australia	(see *Wisden 2019*, page 820)
JANUARY	5 ODIs and 3 T20Is (a) v New Zealand	(page 982)
FEBRUARY		
MARCH	5 ODIs and 2 T20Is (h) v Australia	(page 931)
APRIL		
MAY		
JUNE	World Cup (in England)	(page 237)
JULY		
AUGUST	2 Tests, 3 ODIs and 3 T20Is (a) v West Indies	(page 1047)
SEPTEMBER		
OCTOBER	3 Tests and 2 T20Is (h) v South Africa	(page 939)
NOVEMBER	2 Tests and 3 T20Is (h) v Bangladesh	(page 949)
DECEMBER	3 ODIs and 3 T20Is (h) v West Indies	(page 955)

For a review of Indian domestic cricket from the 2018-19 season, see page 961.

Smiles ahead of the rest: Mayank Agarwal, Mohammed Shami, Ravindra Jadeja and Virat Kohli have reasons to be cheerful.

Virat Kohli's team gave themselves an excellent start to shoot for the final, to be held in June 2021, winning seven Championship Tests out of seven. They churned out clinical performances, regardless of opposition, venue or conditions – whether it was the New Year's Test in Sydney, where a draw sealed the Border–Gavaskar Trophy, the cleanout of West Indies in the Caribbean, the innings wins at home against South Africa, or the pink-ball drubbing of Bangladesh. After a draining 2018, which included three high-pressure away series, a trimmer programme was welcome, but still left India with plenty of Championship points, plus a stat to treasure: the first team to win four consecutive Tests by an innings.

In a break from history, their efficiency stemmed from the skill and experience of their quick bowlers, who continued to rewrite Indian cricket's playbook. In the first decade of the 21st century, the bat-once-bat-big formula had depended on scoreboard pressure created by a *galactico* line-up. But the growth and variety of India's fast-bowling resources: the menacing accuracy of Mohammed Shami, the hardy Umesh Yadav, the lethal endurance of Ishant Sharma. It meant they did not need to resort to underprepared turners as a response to whoppings abroad.

Instead, the whoppings could now be meted out. For the first time, a clutch of quicks spearheaded Test wins at home. In the day/nighter against Bangladesh at Kolkata, a five-man attack featured two spinners, Ravichandran Ashwin and Ravindra Jadeja, who bowled only seven (wicketless) overs between them. The sharp, searing spells of Ishant and Yadav didn't give Bangladesh a look-in – and this with Bhuvneshwar Kumar on standby, and Jasprit Bumrah absent injured. Across the year, Shami picked up 33 wickets at 16, Ishant 25 at 15, Yadav 23 at 13, and Bumrah 14 at 13. These were numbers to conjure with.

At the top of the batting line-up, Mayank Agarwal emerged as a calm natural, following 215 against South Africa at Visakhapatnam with 108 at Pune, and 243 against Bangladesh at Indore. With him was Rohit Sharma, flourishing in his new role as Test opener: twin hundreds at Visakhapatnam, then a double-century of his own, also against the South Africans, at Ranchi. The fact that Kohli, too, ticked off a double (254 not out at Pune) could almost be forgotten amid a wealth of runs: only K. L. Rahul averaged below 46, and was dropped after the August series in the Caribbean.

India's ODI year, which brought 19 wins in 27 completed matches, ended in Cuttack, with a tense finish to a competitive series against West Indies. But any diagnosis returned, like a single-minded moth, to the World Cup combustion. India's prime weak links had been clearly identified in advance: an over-dependence on the top three, a weak middle order, and the absence of a big hitter at the death. None of this was adequately addressed, however, and twice it cost them: a failed chase against England in the group stage, with five wickets – and M. S. Dhoni – still standing. New Zealand then defended 239 in the semi-final, with the swing of Matt Henry and the pace of Trent Boult reducing India to 24 for four; a late surge was in vain. Victory in four bilateral series out of five was little consolation.

Meanwhile, India have now gone five editions without winning the Twenty20 World Cup. That hot potato will once again present itself in October to a team whose players grew up in the world's most coveted T20 league. In 2019, India played more T20s (16) than any other Full Member bar Ireland, winning nine and losing seven – a ratio that placed them eighth out of the 12 Test teams, even if the ICC rankings had them fifth at the end of the year.

Yet removed from Kohli's on-field juggernaut was a parallel universe, in which the BCCI's old geezers and young Turks were involved in a six-year tussle to regain control from the Indian Supreme Court. The Court had ordered the administrative overhaul of the BCCI, as laid down in the Lodha Committee recommendations, and in 2016 instituted a Committee of Administrators to oversee it. Headed by a retired career bureaucrat, Vinod Rai, the COA became their own centre of power, and leaker of stories. During their three-year existence, they filed 11 status reports with the Court regarding the intransigence of either the BCCI or their state associations. News reports calculated the BCCI's legal fees to be between Rs119 and 350 crores (£13m and £37m), with the board taking care of expenses for both litigant and defendant.

In October, the BCCI and the state associations were led kicking and screaming to their first general assembly elections for three years, bringing an end to their mud-wrestle with the COA. Only once their constitutions were amended to fit in with a diluted template of Lodha reforms did the eager mandarins get back the keys to their office.

From the scrum of political juggling, a smorgasbord of characters stepped into different roles – someone's brother, someone else's son. Yet all this was blurred by one appointment: the elevation of former captain Sourav Ganguly to the BCCI presidency. "Unanimously" elected (which means there were no rival candidates), Ganguly – as head of the Cricket Association of Bengal, and a public figure with a cult following like no other cricket official on the planet

– was both eminently qualified and instantly acceptable. His appointment has been seen as a piece of political manoeuvring, but many have been lulled into believing they can control Ganguly. He is his own man, and may try to wriggle out of a straitjacket imposed by the Lodha guidelines – that his tenure be limited to ten months.

Eventually, Ganguly will be judged on his empathy with cricketers, and his loyalty to the Indian game, but that is the least of it. His nose for sniffing out palace intrigues, and his nous for handling them, will undergo its most strenuous examination. To follow Indian cricket in the year that lies ahead will require senses to be on high alert, and eyesight at 2020.

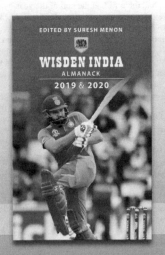

INDIA v AUSTRALIA IN 2018-19

Chetan Narula

Twenty20 internationals (2): India 0, Australia 2
One-day internationals (5): India 2, Australia 3

With an unexpected twist, Australia's first one-day series win since January 2017 had its roots in the ball-tampering saga of 2018: forced to trial different players because of the bans for David Warner and Steve Smith, they stunned India on their home turf.

For India, whose players would soon embark on the IPL, it was a final one-day outing before their World Cup fixture against South Africa at Southampton on June 5; perhaps they felt victory did not matter as much as trying out fringe players. After establishing a 2–1 lead in the 50-over series with an unchanged – if slightly unfamiliar – side, India kept experimenting. Bhuvneshwar Kumar had missed the first three matches, and M. S. Dhoni would miss the last two. Left-arm wrist-spinner Kuldeep Yadav played all five, but leg-spinner Yuzvendra Chahal appeared only once; Kuldeep was usually paired with slow left-armer Ravindra Jadeja instead. In hindsight, it was misguided, leading to India's first defeat in a home one-day series for more than three years, and only their second anywhere since losing the 2017 Champions Trophy final.

Australia experimented too, but their selections had more to do with necessity while Smith and Warner completed their 12-month bans for ball-tampering. A few weeks earlier, they had lost a one-day series at home to India 2–1, despite putting up a tough fight, but the foundation for their victory here was laid during a 2–0 win in the Twenty20 internationals, in which Glenn Maxwell scored 169 runs at a strike-rate of 172; India never fully recovered.

Another factor in India's defeat was a lack of runs from the top order. Since the Champions Trophy, Shikhar Dhawan, Rohit Sharma and Virat Kohli had scored 56% of their one-day runs, but Dhawan and Sharma shared only one opening partnership above 15 – a stand of 193 in a losing cause at Mohali. That left Kohli desperately short of support, though he shone as usual, notching up 310 in five games, including two more hundreds, to move within eight of Sachin Tendulkar's ODI record of 49 (and from 235 fewer innings).

But Usman Khawaja outdid even Kohli, scoring 383 at 76, including two hundreds and two fifties. Australia built on this to complete their first one-day series win on Indian soil for nearly ten years. Peter Handscomb and Ashton Turner helped them chase a mammoth 359 at Mohali, and captain Aaron Finch managed 93 in the win at Ranchi after a poor summer at home.

Among the bowlers, Pat Cummins and Adam Zampa stood out. Cummins was as tireless as he had been in the home Tests against India and Sri Lanka; despite conditions unfavourable to pace, he was effective with the old ball and the new, picking up 14 wickets at 15. Including the T20 games, Zampa dismissed Kohli three times with his leg-spin, and picked up 11 wickets in the ODI series, outbowling Kuldeep, Jadeja and Nathan Lyon.

The result ended a dreadful run for Australia, which had produced only four 50-over wins in 24 completed matches. But questions remained for India, leaving Kohli to state that the contest had come down to "desire".

AUSTRALIAN TOURING PARTY

*A. J. Finch (50/20), J. P. Behrendorff (50/20), A. T. Carey (50/20), N. M. Coulter-Nile (50/20), P. J. Cummins (50/20), P. S. P. Handscomb (50/20), U. T. Khawaja (50/20), N. M. Lyon (50/20), S. E. Marsh (50/20), G. J. Maxwell (50/20), J. A. Richardson (50/20), K. W. Richardson (50/20), D. J. M. Short (50/20), M. P. Stoinis (50/20), A. J. Turner (50/20), A. J. Tye (50/20), A. Zampa (50/20). *Coach:* J. L. Langer.

K. W. Richardson flew home after injuring his side before the T20Is; Tye replaced him for the ODI series. During the first part of the tour, Short acted as cover for Marsh, on paternity leave.

INDIA v AUSTRALIA

First Twenty20 International

At Visakhapatnam, February 24, 2019 (floodlit). Australia won by three wickets. Toss: Australia. Twenty20 international debuts: M. Markande; P. S. P. Handscomb.

A spin-friendly, two-paced pitch set the tone for the tour. In a low-scoring game, Maxwell and Bumrah prospered, and Australia pulled through in a close finish. Out of form and favour, Indian opener Rahul had returned to smack a 36-ball 50, his first international half-century in 14 innings, before Coulter-Nile had him caught at mid-off, and followed up with two more momentum-stealing wickets. With Cummins and Zampa, he restricted India to an inadequate 126. Australia didn't make the best start either, as Finch fell first ball; but Short and Maxwell were in fine fettle after the Big Bash League. Short anchored the innings, while Maxwell swung the game, despite a flurry of five wickets for 24. Bumrah took two in the penultimate over, leaving a target of 14 off six balls, but Cummins, who hit the last two deliveries for four and two, and Richardson held their nerve against a wayward Umesh Yadav.

Player of the Match: N. M. Coulter-Nile.

India		B	4/6
1 R. G. Sharma c 10 b 11		5	8 0
2 K. L. Rahul c 3 b 7		50	36 6/1
3 *V. Kohli c 7 b 10		24	17 3
4 R. R. Pant run out (11/5)		3	5 0
5 †M. S. Dhoni not out		29	37 0/1
6 K. D. Karthik b 7		1	3 0
7 K. H. Pandya c 4 b 7		1	6 0
8 U. T. Yadav lbw b 8		2	4 0
9 Y. S. Chahal not out		0	4 0
Lb 2, w 9		11	

6 overs: 49-1   (20 overs) 126-7

1/14 2/69 3/80 4/92 5/94 6/100 7/109

10 J. J. Bumrah and 11 M. Markande did not bat.

Behrendorff 3–9–16–1; Richardson 4–11–31–0; Coulter-Nile 4–11–26–3; Zampa 3–7–22–1; Cummins 4–9–19–1; Short 2–3–10–0.

Australia		B	4/6
1 D. J. M. Short run out (7/5)		37	37 5
2 M. P. Stoinis run out (8/9)		1	5 0
3 *A. J. Finch lbw b 10		0	1 0
4 G. J. Maxwell c 2 b 9		56	43 6/2
5 †P. S. P. Handscomb c 5 b 10		13	15 0
6 A. J. Turner b 7		0	5 0
7 N. M. Coulter-Nile b 10		4	8 0
8 P. J. Cummins not out		7	3 1
9 J. A. Richardson not out		7	3 1
W 2		2	

6 overs: 41-2   (20 overs) 127-7

1/5 2/5 3/89 4/101 5/102 6/113 7/113

10 A. Zampa and 11 J. P. Behrendorff did not bat.

Bumrah 4–18–16–3; Chahal 4–11–28–1; Yadav 4–8–35–0; Pandya 4–8–17–1; Markande 4–6–31–0.

Umpires: N. N. Menon and C. Shamshuddin.   Third umpire: A. K. Chaudhary.
Referee: C. K. Nandan.

INDIA v AUSTRALIA

Second Twenty20 International

At Bangalore, February 27, 2019 (floodlit). Australia won by seven wickets. Toss: Australia.

This game had Maxwell's stamp all over it: he hit nine sixes in his third Twenty20 international hundred, the last of them back over Kaul's head to hasten victory. With Rohit Sharma rested, Dhawan had opened with Rahul, who regaled his home crowd with 47 in 26 deliveries, before Kohli and Dhoni added 100 off 50. It was only Kohli's second T20I half-century since November 2017 – though he had played just 12 of India's 27 fixtures in that time, often skipping this format to rest. A vintage 40 continued Dhoni's free-flowing start to 2019, and 190 seemed a defendable total, especially when Australia were 22 for two. But Maxwell and Short repeated their double act from Visakhapatnam, putting on 73. By the time Short was dismissed, the dew had arrived, and Maxwell obliterated the spinners, picking boundaries at will as he raced to his hundred off 50 balls. This was India's first home T20 bilateral series defeat since October 2015.

Player of the Match: G. J. Maxwell. Player of the Series: G. J. Maxwell.

India

		B	4/6
1 K. L. Rahul c 9 b 7	47	26	3/4
2 S. Dhawan c 2 b 11	14	24	1
3 *V. Kohli not out	72	38	2/6
4 R. R. Pant c 9 b 1	1	6	0
5 †M. S. Dhoni c 3 b 8	40	23	3/3
6 K. D. Karthik not out	8	3	2
Lb 3, w 5	8		

6 overs: 53-0 (20 overs) **190-4**

1/61 2/70 3/74 4/174

7 V. Shankar, 8 K. H. Pandya, 9 Y. S. Chahal, 10 J. J. Bumrah and 11 S. Kaul did not bat.

Behrendorff 3–7–17–1; Richardson 4–8–45–0; Coulter-Nile 3–6–33–1; Cummins 3–5–40–1; Zampa 3–5–40–1; Short 3–7–29–1.

Australia

		B	4/6
1 D. J. M. Short c 1 b 7	40	28	6
2 M. P. Stoinis b 11	7	11	1
3 *A. J. Finch c 2 b 7	8	7	1
4 G. J. Maxwell not out	113	55	7/9
5 †P. S. P. Handscomb not out	20	18	1
Lb 1, w 4, nb 1	6		

6 overs: 42-2 (19.4 overs) **194-3**

1/13 2/22 3/95

6 A. J. Turner, 7 N. M. Coulter-Nile, 8 P. J. Cummins, 9 J. A. Richardson, 10 A. Zampa and 11 J. P. Behrendorff did not bat.

Shankar 4–10–38–2; Bumrah 4–6–30–0; Kaul 3.4–6–45–1; Chahal 4–2–47–0; Pandya 4–6–33–0.

Umpires: A. K. Chaudhary and C. K. Nandan. Third umpire: N. N. Menon.
Referee: R. S. Madugalle.

INDIA v AUSTRALIA

First One-Day International

At Hyderabad, March 2, 2019 (day/night). India won by six wickets. Toss: Australia. One-day international debut: A. J. Turner.

A change in format, and a spinners' pitch, lifted India – with Dhoni and Jadhav sharing a match-winning century stand, just as they had to clinch their one-day series in Australia in January. At 99 for four, India had looked vulnerable. But Dhoni scored his fourth successive one-day half-century against these opponents, adding an unbroken 141 in 25 overs with Jadhav, who followed up seven economical overs of off-breaks, and the wicket of Stoinis, with his seventh ODI score of 50-plus. Australia had made another poor start, with Finch's second duck in three innings; his highest score in six matches against India in 2019 was 14. Despite 50 from Khawaja, the bowlers made regular strikes and never allowed the scoring-rate to get away; even Maxwell, batting alongside one-day debutant Ashton Turner, could not accelerate, and Australia finished with a below-par 236. Sharma and Dhawan were briefly reunited at the top, though Coulter-Nile removed Dhawan first ball, and Zampa got rid of Kohli and Rayudu. No one could stop Dhoni, however, as he and Jadhav steered India into the lead.

Player of the Match: K. M. Jadhav.

Australia

U. T. Khawaja c Shankar b Yadav		50
*A. J. Finch c Dhoni b Bumrah		0
M. P. Stoinis c Kohli b Jadhav		37
P. S. P. Handscomb st Dhoni b Yadav		19
G. J. Maxwell b Mohammed Shami		40
A. J. Turner b Mohammed Shami		21
†A. T. Carey not out		36

N. M. Coulter-Nile c Kohli b Bumrah		28
P. J. Cummins not out		0
W 5		5
		—
1/0 (1) 2/87 (3) (7 wkts, 50 overs)		236
3/97 (1) 4/133 (4)		
5/169 (6) 6/173 (5) 7/235 (8) 10 overs: 38-1		

A. Zampa and J. P. Behrendorff did not bat.

Mohammed Shami 10–2–44–2; Bumrah 10–0–60–2; Shankar 3–0–22–0; Yadav 10–0–46–2; Jadeja 10–0–33–0; Jadhav 7–0–31–1.

India

R. G. Sharma c Finch b Coulter-Nile		37
S. Dhawan c Maxwell b Coulter-Nile		0
*V. Kohli lbw b Zampa		44
A. T. Rayudu c Carey b Zampa		13
†M. S. Dhoni not out		59

K. M. Jadhav not out		81
Lb 1, w 5		6
		—
1/4 (2) 2/80 (3) (4 wkts, 48.2 overs)		240
3/95 (1) 4/99 (4) 10 overs: 42-1		

V. Shankar, R. A. Jadeja, K. Yadav, Mohammed Shami and J. J. Bumrah did not bat.

Behrendorff 10–0–46–0; Coulter-Nile 9–2–46–2; Cummins 10–0–46–0; Zampa 10–0–49–2; Stoinis 9.2–0–52–0.

Umpires: N. N. Menon and J. S. Wilson.   Third umpire: H. D. P. K. Dharmasena.
Referee: R. S. Madugalle.

INDIA v AUSTRALIA

Second One-Day International

At Nagpur, March 5, 2019 (day/night). India won by eight runs. Toss: Australia.
Kohli scored his 40th ODI hundred, and India edged Australia in a thriller. He was a class apart, taking India from a shaky 75 for three to a competitive total on a searing afternoon. Only one of his team-mates passed 21: Shankar's 41-ball 46 broke Australia's shackles, though as in Wellington a month earlier he was run out in sight of a maiden international fifty. Cummins claimed four for 29, and Zampa dismissed Jadhav and Dhoni with successive deliveries. When Australia replied, Finch rediscovered some form during an opening stand of 83 with Khawaja, but Kohli deployed his options cleverly, using spin for most of the middle overs in helpful conditions; Kuldeep Yadav grabbed three wickets. Handscomb scored 48, and Stoinis kept the tourists in the hunt with a half-century. Kohli then bet on his strike bowlers: Australia needed 33 from 34 balls with five wickets in hand, but Kuldeep bowled Carey, before Bumrah struck twice in three deliveries. With 11 required from six, Kohli turned to the off-spin of Shankar, who had previously bowled a single expensive over. In three balls, he trapped Stoinis and bowled Zampa, to complete India's 500th one-day win.
    Player of the Match: V. Kohli.

India

R. G. Sharma c Zampa b Cummins		0
S. Dhawan lbw b Maxwell		21
*V. Kohli c Stoinis b Cummins		116
A. T. Rayudu lbw b Lyon		18
V. Shankar run out (Zampa)		46
K. M. Jadhav c Finch b Zampa		11
†M. S. Dhoni c Khawaja b Zampa		0
R. A. Jadeja c Khawaja b Cummins		21
K. Yadav b Cummins		3

Mohammed Shami not out		2
J. J. Bumrah b Coulter-Nile		0
B 1, lb 7, w 4		12
		—
1/0 (1) 2/38 (2) 3/75 (4) (48.2 overs)		250
4/156 (5) 5/171 (6) 6/171 (7)		
7/238 (8) 8/248 (3) 9/249 (9)		
10/250 (11) 10 overs: 39-2		

Cummins 9–2–29–4; Coulter-Nile 8.2–0–52–1; Maxwell 10–0–45–1; Zampa 10–0–62–2; Lyon 10–0–42–1; Stoinis 1–0–12–0.

Australia

*A. J. Finch lbw b Yadav	37	N. M. Lyon not out 6
U. T. Khawaja c Kohli b Jadhav	38	A. Zampa b Shankar 2
S. E. Marsh c Dhoni b Jadeja	16	
P. S. P. Handscomb run out (Jadeja)	48	Lb 3, w 10 13
G. J. Maxwell b Yadav	4	
M. P. Stoinis lbw b Shankar	52	1/83 (1) 2/83 (2) (49.3 overs) 242
†A. T. Carey b Yadav	22	3/122 (3) 4/132 (5) 5/171 (4)
N. M. Coulter-Nile b Bumrah	4	6/218 (7) 7/223 (8) 8/223 (9)
P. J. Cummins c Dhoni b Bumrah	0	9/240 (6) 10/242 (11) 10 overs: 60-0

Mohammed Shami 10–0–60–0; Bumrah 10–0–29–2; Jadeja 10–0–48–1; Shankar 1.3–0–15–2; Yadav 10–0–54–3; Jadhav 8–0–33–1.

Umpires: H. D. P. K. Dharmasena and N. N. Menon. Third umpire: J. S. Wilson.
Referee: R. S. Madugalle.

INDIA v AUSTRALIA

Third One-Day International

At Ranchi, March 8, 2019 (day/night). Australia won by 32 runs. Toss: India.

With the news that Dhoni would be rested for the last two games, it seemed this might be his final international on Indian soil, and he walked off his home ground waving at a boisterous crowd. On his initiative, India wore military camouflage caps to honour security forces killed in a terror attack in Kashmir three weeks before. Australia pulled one back after Kohli opted to bowl on the best batting pitch so far. Khawaja and Finch opened with 193; Finch broke loose at last, exploiting short boundaries to hit his first half-century in ten ODI innings, while Khawaja reached a maiden hundred. Kuldeep Yadav took three wickets but went for runs as Australia passed 300. India had misread conditions, anticipating dew that never arrived, and Cummins and Richardson reduced them to 27 for three. Kohli's 123 was another masterful display; if Nagpur had been about accumulation, he batted here in fifth gear, reaching three figures in 85 balls. But it wasn't enough, as he became one of three key wickets for Zampa.

Player of the Match: U. T. Khawaja.

Australia

*A. J. Finch lbw b Yadav	93	†A. T. Carey not out 21
U. T. Khawaja c Bumrah b Mohammed Shami	104	Lb 4, w 6 10
G. J. Maxwell run out (Jadeja/Dhoni)	47	
S. E. Marsh c Shankar b Yadav	7	1/193 (1) 2/239 (2) (5 wkts, 50 overs) 313
M. P. Stoinis not out	31	3/258 (3) 4/263 (4)
P. S. P. Handscomb lbw b Yadav	0	5/263 (6) 10 overs: 52-0

J. A. Richardson, P. J. Cummins, N. M. Lyon and A. Zampa did not bat.

Mohammed Shami 10–0–52–1; Bumrah 10–0–53–0; Jadeja 10–0–64–0; Yadav 10–0–64–3; Shankar 8–0–44–0; Jadhav 2–0–32–0.

India

S. Dhawan c Maxwell b Richardson	1	Mohammed Shami c Cummins b Richardson	8
R. G. Sharma lbw b Cummins	14	J. J. Bumrah not out 0
*V. Kohli b Zampa	123	B 1, lb 10, w 4 15
A. T. Rayudu b Cummins	2	
†M. S. Dhoni b Zampa	26	1/11 (1) 2/15 (2) 3/27 (4) (48.2 overs) 281
K. M. Jadhav lbw b Zampa	26	4/86 (5) 5/174 (6) 6/219 (3)
V. Shankar c Richardson b Lyon	32	7/251 (7) 8/273 (8) 9/281 (10)
R. A. Jadeja c Maxwell b Richardson	24	10/281 (9) 10 overs: 40-3
K. Yadav c Finch b Cummins	10	

Cummins 8.2–1–37–3; Richardson 9–2–37–3; Stoinis 6–0–39–0; Lyon 10–0–57–1; Zampa 10–0–70–3; Maxwell 5–0–30–0.

Umpires: C. Shamshuddin and J. S. Wilson.　　　Third umpire: H. D. P. K. Dharmasena.
Referee: R. S. Madugalle.

INDIA v AUSTRALIA

Fourth One-Day International

At Mohali, March 10, 2019 (day/night). Australia won by four wickets. Toss: India.

Ashton Turner smacked a sensational unbeaten 84 off 43 balls to level the series. He raced to his first international fifty in 33, and his ferocity helped Australia record their highest one-day run-chase with 13 deliveries to spare. On a placid surface, India's openers finally stood up, Dhawan and Sharma amassing 193 in 31 overs, a record for the first wicket against Australia (beating their own 178 at Nagpur in October 2013). Dhawan stroked a fluent hundred, and Sharma 95 – but once he fell the innings lost momentum. In Dhoni's absence, Kohli batted at No. 4, but the experiment failed, and Rahul was too slow at No. 3, though cameos from Pant and Shankar pushed India past 350; Cummins

---

AUSTRALIA'S HIGHEST SUCCESSFUL ODI CHASES

359-6	**(47.5 overs)**	**v India at Mohali (set 359)**	**2018-19**
334-8	(49.2 overs)	v England at Sydney (334)	2010-11
330-7	(49.1 overs)	v South Africa at Port Elizabeth (327)	2001-02
316-4	(48.5 overs)	v Pakistan at Lahore (316)	1998-99
310-5	(49.2 overs)	v India at Perth (310)	2015-16
309-3	(49 overs)	v India at Brisbane (309)	2015-16
304-6	(49.3 overs)	v India at Mohali (304)	2013-14
304-7	(49.5 overs)	v England at Hobart (304)	2014-15
302-6	(48.2 overs)	v England at Nottingham (300)	2009
301-9	(49.3 overs)	v England at Brisbane (301)	2013-14

Australia have twice scored 300-plus batting second to lose.

---

equalled Australia's most expensive five-for. They lost Finch and Marsh early, but that enabled Handscomb and Khawaja to set their own pace. Khawaja dropped anchor, while Handscomb skilfully manoeuvred the spin attack in a maiden ODI century. Their 192-run partnership in 30 overs never let the asking-rate swell out of reach. India didn't just miss Dhoni with the bat: the spinners lacked his guidance, and Kohli could have used his counsel. The crowd missed him too, chanting his name, and turning on Pant when he fumbled two stumpings. The first was off Handscomb, but it was a life for Turner, on 38, that cost India most dearly. He was later dropped twice in an over from Bhuvneshwar Kumar; India's fielding was disastrous, and it was not all down to the dew.

Player of the Match: A. J. Turner.

India

R. G. Sharma c Handscomb b Richardson	95	Y. S. Chahal c and b Cummins	0
S. Dhawan b Cummins	143	J. J. Bumrah not out	6
K. L. Rahul c Carey b Zampa	26		
*V. Kohli c Carey b Richardson	7	B 1, lb 1, w 5	7
†R. R. Pant c Finch b Cummins	36		
K. M. Jadhav c Richardson b Cummins	10	1/193 (1) 2/254 (2)　(9 wkts, 50 overs)	358
V. Shankar c Maxwell b Cummins	26	3/266 (4) 4/296 (3)	
Bhuvneshwar Kumar c Carey b Richardson	14	5/314 (5) 6/331 (6) 7/344 (8)	
K. Yadav not out	1	8/351 (7) 9/352 (10)　　　　10 overs: 58-0	

Cummins 10–0–70–5; Behrendorff 10–1–61–0; Richardson 9–0–85–3; Maxwell 8–1–61–0; Zampa 10–0–57–1; Finch 3–0–22–0.

Australia

*A. J. Finch b Bhuvneshwar Kumar	0	J. A. Richardson not out	0
U. T. Khawaja c Yadav b Bumrah	91		
S. E. Marsh b Bumrah	6	B 4, lb 8, w 5	17
P. S. P. Handscomb c Rahul b Chahal	117		
G. J. Maxwell lbw b Yadav	23	1/3 (1) 2/12 (3) (6 wkts, 47.5 overs)	359
A. J. Turner not out	84	3/204 (2) 4/229 (5)	
†A. T. Carey c Dhawan b Bumrah	21	5/271 (4) 6/357 (7) 10 overs: 47-2	

P. J. Cummins, A. Zampa and J. P. Behrendorff did not bat.

Bhuvneshwar Kumar 9–0–67–1; Bumrah 8.5–0–63–3; Shankar 5–0–29–0; Yadav 10–0–64–1; Jadhav 5–0–44–0; Chahal 10–0–80–1.

Umpires: A. K. Chaudhary and H. D. P. K. Dharmasena.   Third umpire: J. S. Wilson.
Referee: R. S. Madugalle.

INDIA v AUSTRALIA

Fifth One-Day International

At Delhi, March 13, 2019 (day/night). Australia won by 35 runs. Toss: Australia.
There was little surprise that the Feroz Shah Kotla reverted to a two-paced strip for the decider, but the selection of three seamers and two spinners unbalanced India. It seemed a desperate ploy to counter the pitch, the dew and the Australians, but left the batting short. More sensibly, Australia brought back Lyon as an extra spinner, and Finch chose to bat. Khawaja maintained his remarkable run with a second hundred in three matches, adding 99 for the second wicket with Handscomb before the surface began to deteriorate. Bhuvneshwar Kumar and the spinners chipped away, but Richardson's 29 took Australia to 272. India needed the tallest chase at Delhi this millennium to win the series, but were soon 91 for three, with all three local boys – Dhawan, Kohli and Pant – back in the hut. Again, Zampa was the pick of the bowlers; the writing was on the wall when he had Sharma and Jadeja stumped in the same over. Despite a fighting seventh-wicket partnership of 91 from Jadhav and Bhuvneshwar, India were never in the hunt. After taking a 2–0 lead, they had lost a one-day series at home for the first time since South Africa's visit in October 2015.
Player of the Match: U. T. Khawaja.   *Player of the Series:* U. T. Khawaja.

Australia

U. T. Khawaja c Kohli b Bhuvneshwar Kumar	100	J. A. Richardson run out (Kohli/Pant)	29
*A. J. Finch b Jadeja	27	P. J. Cummins c and b Bhuvneshwar Kumar	15
P. S. P. Handscomb c Pant b Mohammed Shami	52	N. M. Lyon not out	1
		B 1, w 3	4
G. J. Maxwell c Kohli b Jadeja	1	1/76 (2) 2/175 (1) (9 wkts, 50 overs)	272
M. P. Stoinis b Bhuvneshwar Kumar	20	3/178 (4) 4/182 (3)	
A. J. Turner c Jadeja b Yadav	20	5/210 (6) 6/225 (5) 7/229 (7)	
*A. T. Carey c Pant b Mohammed Shami	3	8/263 (9) 9/272 (8) 10 overs: 52-0	

A. Zampa did not bat.

Bhuvneshwar Kumar 10–0–48–3; Mohammed Shami 9–0–57–2; Bumrah 10–0–39–0; Yadav 10–0–74–1; Jadeja 10–0–45–2; Jadhav 1–0–8–0.

India

R. G. Sharma st Carey b Zampa 56
S. Dhawan c Carey b Cummins. 12
*V. Kohli c Carey b Stoinis. 20
†R. R. Pant c Turner b Lyon 16
V. Shankar c Khawaja b Zampa 16
K. M. Jadhav c Maxwell b Richardson 44
R. A. Jadeja st Carey b Zampa 0
Bhuvneshwar Kumar c Finch b Cummins . 46
Mohammed Shami c and b Richardson. . . . 3

K. Yadav b Stoinis 8
J. J. Bumrah not out. 1

Lb 7, w 8 15
                                              —
1/15 (2) 2/68 (3) 3/91 (4)   (50 overs) 237
4/120 (5) 5/132 (1) 6/132 (7)
7/223 (8) 8/223 (6) 9/230 (9)
10/237 (10)   10 overs: 43-1

Cummins 10–1–38–2; Richardson 10–0–47–2; Stoinis 4–0–31–2; Lyon 10–1–34–1; Zampa 10–1–46–3; Maxwell 6–0–34–0.

Umpires: C. K. Nandan and J. S. Wilson.   Third umpire: H. D. P. K. Dharmasena.
Referee: R. S. Madugalle.

INDIA v SOUTH AFRICA IN 2019-20

CHETAN NARULA

Twenty20 internationals (3): India 1, South Africa 1
Test matches (3): India 3, South Africa 0

If South Africa had hoped for redemption after the World Cup, they did not find it in India, where they lost all three Tests by wide margins. "It was like copy-and-paste in every Test," said their glum captain, Faf du Plessis. "They bat first, they score 500, they declare when it's dark, they get three wickets when it's dark – and when day three starts, you're under pressure." After their first innings of the series, in which they made 431, South Africa passed 200 only once. India, meanwhile, were never bowled out at all.

Virat Kohli's team continued their turbocharged start to the World Test Championship, and cantered to their 11th successive series victory at home – a record, beating two runs of ten by Australia. The batsmen led the way: Kohli's career-best unbeaten 254 at Pune was one of three double-centuries, each by a different man, a unique feat in a Test series. Rohit Sharma made a triumphant return. He followed his record-breaking World Cup with 529 runs at 132, his opening partner, Mayank Agarwal, was not far behind. India's bowling attack were full of aces: Ravichandran Ashwin returned to form with 15 wickets, while his spin partner Ravindra Jadeja claimed 13. Seamers Mohammed Shami and Umesh Yadav were also in double figures, which meant Jasprit Bumrah – out with a minor stress fracture in his back – was hardly missed. "Normally in India, you have two players who hog the limelight," said Ravi Shastri, their coach. "Here, we've had six or seven."

In contrast, South Africa's batsmen failed miserably – save for the first innings of the series – their spinners proved ineffective, and the pacemen did not adjust to the SG ball: Kagiso Rabada was their leading wicket-taker, with seven (at 40). The only hint of good news came in the T20 series, which preceded the Tests: victory in Bangalore meant the spoils were shared. (South Africa were due to return in March 2020 for three 50-over internationals). With du Plessis rested, Quinton de Kock was given a trial run as captain, and played two stroke-filled innings. He carried his good form into the First Test, making a superb 111, while Temba Bavuma and Aiden Markram both had poor trips.

WHO NEEDS ELEVEN?

Teams not bowled out in any innings of a three-Test series:

Pakistan	v India in Pakistan	1978-79
Pakistan	v Australia in Pakistan	1982-83
Australia	v Sri Lanka in Australia	1995-96
South Africa	v New Zealand in New Zealand	1998-99
New Zealand	v Australia in Australia	2001-02
Sri Lanka	v Bangladesh in Sri Lanka	2007
Australia	v West Indies in Australia	2015-16
India	**v South Africa in India**	**2019-20**

SOUTH AFRICAN TOURING PARTY

F. du Plessis (T), T. Bavuma (T/20), C. J. Dala (20), T. B. de Bruyn (T), Q. de Kock (T/20), D. Elgar (T), B. C. Fortuin (20), M. Z. Hamza (T), B. E. Hendricks (20), R. R. Hendricks (20), H. Klaasen (T), G. F. Linde (T/20), K. A. Maharaj (T), A. K. Markram (T), D. A. Miller (20), S. Muthusamy (T), L. T. Ngidi (T), A. A. Nortje (T/20), A. M. Phehlukwayo (20), V. D. Philander (T), D. L. Piedt (T), D. Pretorius (20), K. Rabada (T/20), T. Shamsi (20), H. E. van der Dussen (20). Interim team director: T. E. Nkwe.

De Kock captained in the T20s. J. J. Smuts was originally named in the T20 squad, but was withdrawn over fitness doubts and replaced by Linde, who was also added to the Test squad when Maharaj injured his shoulder during the Second Test. R. S. Second was originally selected for the Tests, but injured his ankle and was replaced by Klaasen.

TEST MATCH AVERAGES

INDIA – BATTING AND FIELDING

	T	I	NO	R	HS	100	50	Avge	Ct/St
V. Kohli	3	4	2	317	254*	1	0	158.50	1
R. G. Sharma	3	4	0	529	212	3	0	132.25	4
M. A. Agarwal	3	4	0	340	215	2	0	85.00	1
A. M. Rahane	3	4	1	216	115	1	1	72.00	2
†R. A. Jadeja	3	4	1	212	91	0	2	70.66	2
C. A. Pujara	3	4	0	145	81	0	2	36.25	2

Played in three Tests: R. Ashwin 1*, 14; Mohammed Shami 10*; W. P. Saha 21, 24 (11 ct, 1 st). Played in two Tests: I. Sharma did not bat; U. T. Yadav 31 (1 ct). Played in one Test: S. Nadeem 1* (1 ct); G. H. Vihari 10.

BOWLING

	Style	O	M	R	W	BB	5I	Avge
S. Nadeem	SLA	17.2	5	40	4	2-18	0	10.00
U. T. Yadav	RF	39	7	134	11	3-22	0	12.18
Mohammed Shami	RFM	74.5	21	192	13	5-35	1	14.76
R. Ashwin	OB	138	35	379	15	7-145	1	25.26
R. A. Jadeja	SLA	149.2	38	399	13	4-87	0	30.69

Also bowled: V. Kohli (RM) 1–0–4–0; I. Sharma (RFM) 38–7–125–2; R. G. Sharma (OB) 6–2–14–0; G. H. Vihari (OB) 9–1–38–0.

SOUTH AFRICA – BATTING AND FIELDING

	T	I	NO	R	HS	100	50	Avge	Ct/St
†S. Muthusamy	2	4	0	98	49*	0	0	49.00	2
†D. Elgar	3	6	1	232	160	1	0	46.40	2
V. D. Philander	2	4	1	81	44*	0	0	27.00	0
†Q. de Kock	3	6	0	156	111	1	0	26.00	2/2
K. A. Maharaj	2	4	0	103	72	0	1	25.75	0
F. du Plessis	3	6	0	142	64	0	2	23.66	3
D. L. Piedt	2	4	0	83	56	0	1	20.75	1
T. B. de Bruyn	3	5	0	82	30	0	0	16.40	1
T. Bavuma	3	6	0	96	38	0	0	16.00	1
A. K. Markram	2	4	0	44	39	0	0	11.00	0
†K. Rabada	3	6	0	51	18	0	0	8.50	0
A. A. Nortje	2	4	2	12	5*	0	0	6.00	1

Played in one Test: M. Z. Hamza 62, 0; H. Klaasen 6, 5 (3 ct, 1 st); †G. F. Linde 37, 27; L. T. Ngidi 0*, 0 (1 ct).

BOWLING

	Style	O	M	R	W	BB	5I	Avge
G. F. Linde	SLA	31	2	133	4	4-133	0	33.25
K. Rabada.	RF	90	20	285	7	3-85	0	40.71
K. A. Maharaj	SLA	127	16	514	6	3-189	0	85.66

Also bowled: D. Elgar (SLA) 5–0–30–1; A. K. Markram (OB) 2–0–17–0; S. Muthusamy (SLA) 37.3–2–180–2; L. T. Ngidi (RFM) 20–5–83–0; A. A. Nortje (RF) 49.3–10–179–1; V. D. Philander (RFM) 60–15–155–2; D. L. Piedt (OB) 54–7–310–2.

INDIA v SOUTH AFRICA

First Twenty20 International

At Dharamsala, September 15, 2019 (floodlit). Abandoned.
    The start of India's home season was delayed after persistent rain led to an early abandonment at the picturesque ground in the foothills of the Himalayas.

INDIA v SOUTH AFRICA

Second Twenty20 International

At Mohali, September 18, 2019 (floodlit). India won by seven wickets. Toss: India. Twenty20 international debuts: T. Bavuma, B. C. Fortuin, A. A. Nortje.

Kohli smacked an unbeaten 72 from 52 balls as India coasted to victory with an over to spare. They were never in much danger, with Dhawan helping Kohli put on 61 after Sharma had departed for 12, made up of two sixes. Bjorn Fortuin, a slow left-armer from Paarl, marked his T20 international debut with the wicket of Pant, who had been preferred as India's wicketkeeper to M. S. Dhoni. South Africa's innings was given a good start by de Kock, who slapped a 35-ball fifty in his first T20 match as captain, but only 61 more were added after he fell in the 12th over. Bavuma, who made 49, was also making his debut in the format, nearly five years after his first Test.

Player of the Match: V. Kohli.

South Africa

		B	4/6
1 R. R. Hendricks c 9 b 10	6	11	1
2 *†Q. de Kock c 3 b 11	52	37	8
3 T. Bavuma c 8 b 10	49	43	3/1
4 H. E. van der Dussen c and b 8 . .	1	2	0
5 D. A. Miller b 6	18	15	0/1
6 D. Pretorius not out	10	7	0/1
7 A. L. Phehlukwayo not out	8	5	0/1
Lb 5	5		

6 overs: 39-1   (20 overs) 149-5

1/31 2/88 3/90 4/126 5/129

8 B. C. Fortuin, 9 K. Rabada, 10 A. A. Nortje and 11 T. Shamsi did not bat.

Washington Sundar 3–8–19–0; Chahar 4–12–22–2; Saini 4–11–34–1; Jadeja 4–2–31–1; H. H. Pandya 4–6–31–1; K. H. Pandya 1–1–7–0.

India

		B	4/6
1 R. G. Sharma lbw b 7	12	12	0/2
2 S. Dhawan c 5 b 11	40	31	4/1
3 *V. Kohli not out	72	52	4/3
4 †R. R. Pant c 11 b 8	4	5	0
5 S. S. Iyer not out	16	14	2
Lb 2, w 5	7		

6 overs: 47-1   (19 overs) 151-3

1/33 2/94 3/104

6 H. H. Pandya, 7 K. H. Pandya, 8 R. A. Jadeja, 9 M. S. Washington Sundar, 10 D. L. Chahar and 11 N. Saini did not bat.

Rabada 3–11–24–0; Nortje 3–6–27–0; Phehlukwayo 3–9–20–1; Pretorius 3–4–27–0; Shamsi 3–2–19–1; Fortuin 4–6–32–1.

Umpires: A. K. Chaudhary and C. Shamshuddin.   Third umpire: N. N. Menon.
Referee: R. B. Richardson.

INDIA v SOUTH AFRICA

Third Twenty20 International

At Bangalore, September 22, 2019 (floodlit). South Africa won by nine wickets. Toss: India.

Kohli put aside his preference for chasing, and decided to bat first – but a superb innings by his opposite number squared the series. Only Dhawan got going for India, who lost three wickets in the last over, and ended up with a disappointing 134. Fortuin (who shared the new ball with Rabada) and Beuran Hendricks finished with four for 33 from seven overs. South Africa's openers had 76 on the board by halfway and, although Reeza Hendricks fell to the first ball of the 11th over, de Kock – who hit five sixes – finished the job with Bavuma.

Player of the Match: B. E. Hendricks.   *Player of the Series:* Q. de Kock.

India		B	4/6
1 S. Dhawan c 3 b 11	36	25	4/2
2 R. G. Sharma c 1 b 10	9	8	2
3 *V. Kohli c 7 b 9	9	15	0
4 †R. R. Pant c 7 b 8	19	20	1/1
5 S. S. Iyer st 2 b 8	5	8	0
6 H. H. Pandya c 5 b 9	14	18	1
7 K. H. Pandya c 2 b 10	4	7	0
8 R. A. Jadeja c and b 9	19	17	1/1
9 M. S. Washington Sundar	4	1	1
run out (2/9)			
10 D. L. Chahar not out	0	0	0
11 N. Saini not out	0	1	0
B 1, lb 2, w 12	15		

6 overs: 54-1   (20 overs) 134-9

1/22 2/63 3/68 4/90 5/92 6/98 7/127 8/133 9/133

Fortuin 3–6–19–2; Rabada 4–10–39–3; B. E. Hendricks 4–13–14–2; Phehlukwayo 4–9–28–0; Shamsi 4–12–23–1; Pretorius 1–3–8–0.

South Africa		B	4/6
1 R. R. Hendricks c 3 b 6	28	26	4
2 *†Q. de Kock not out	79	52	6/5
3 T. Bavuma not out	27	23	2/1
Lb 2, w 4	6		

6 overs: 43-0   (16.5 overs) 140-1

1/76

4 H. E. van der Dussen, 5 D. A. Miller, 6 D. Pretorius, 7 A. L. Phehlukwayo, 8 B. C. Fortuin, 9 K. Rabada, 10 B. E. Hendricks and 11 T. Shamsi did not bat.

Washington Sundar 4–11–27–0; Chahar 3–10–15–0; Saini 2–4–25–0; K. H. Pandya 3.5–2–40–0; H. H. Pandya 2–5–23–1; Jadeja 2–5–8–0.

Umpires: N. N. Menon and C. K. Nandan.   Third umpire: A. K. Chaudhary.
Referee: R. B. Richardson.

INDIA v SOUTH AFRICA

First Test

At Visakhapatnam, October 2–6, 2019. India won by 203 runs. India 40pts. Toss: India. Test debut: S. Muthusamy.

India continued their dominant home Test form, wrapping up a convincing victory midway through the fifth day. The batting star was Rohit Sharma: recalled after a stellar World Cup, and opening for the first time, he became the first Indian to score twin centuries from the top of the order since Sunil Gavaskar against West Indies at Calcutta in 1978-79. Not far behind was Agarwal – in his first home Test, and fifth overall – who extended his maiden century to 215, and shared an opening stand of 317, India's highest for any wicket against South Africa. The visitors began well, with fighting centuries from Elgar and de Kock, but then fell apart – for the rest of the series, as it turned out.

Agarwal and Sharma were India's ninth different opening pair since July 2017, but looked comfortable from the start. By the end of a truncated first day, they had motored past 200, and were not separated until Maharaj enticed Sharma down the pitch to end the third-highest opening stand for India, behind 413 by Vinoo Mankad and Pankaj Roy against New Zealand at Madras in 1955-56, and 410 by Virender Sehwag and Rahul Dravid against Pakistan at Lahore in 2005-06. Both openers hit 23 fours and six sixes.

MOST SIXES IN A TEST MATCH

13	R. G. Sharma (176 and 127)...	India v South Africa at Visakhapatnam	2019-20
12	Wasim Akram (257*).........	Pakistan v Zimbabwe at Sheikhupura	1996-97
11	N. J. Astle (10 and 222)	NZ v England at Christchurch (Lancaster Park) .	2001-02
11	M. L. Hayden (380)	Australia v Zimbabwe at Perth (WACA)	2003-04
11	B. B. McCullum (202)	New Zealand v Pakistan at Sharjah	2014-15
11	B. B. McCullum (195)	NZ v Sri Lanka at Christchurch (Hagley Park)..	2014-15
11	B. A. Stokes (258 and 26)......	England v South Africa at Cape Town	2015-16
10	W. R. Hammond (336*).......	England v New Zealand at Auckland	1932-33
10	K. C. Sangakkara (319 and 105).	Sri Lanka v Bangladesh at Chittagong (ZAC)...	2013-14
10	S. O. Hetmyer (39 and 93)	West Indies v Bangladesh at Mirpur	2018-19

The middle order failed to convert starts, but Kohli was still able to declare on passing 500. He fell himself for 20, a distinguished maiden scalp for South Africa's debutant slow left-armer Senuran Muthusamy, who said: "My forefathers are from the south of India, in Tamil Nadu, so it's been really special."

Ashwin, in his first Test for nearly a year, made two quick breakthroughs and, with Jadeja removing the nightwatchman, South Africa were three down by the end of the second day. When Bavuma fell next morning, it was 63 for four, but Elgar and du Plessis rebuilt in a stand of 115, attacking the spinners on a pitch offering slow turn. Elgar pushed on to his 12th Test century, now aided by de Kock, who helped add 164, South Africa's highest for the sixth wicket against India, and dragged their side close to 400 before both fell in the third day's final session. Muthusamy resisted for more than two hours, but Ashwin mopped up on the fourth to finish with seven wickets.

Led again by Sharma, India were almost in one-day mode as they built on a lead of 71. He thumped seven more sixes on his way to 127, which raised his Test average in India to 98. Pujara was circumspect at first, crawling to eight from 62, but then opened out, finishing with 81 from 148 balls, 64 in boundaries. He helped Sharma put on 169, and then Jadeja spanked 40 from 32 to allow Kohli to set a target of 395 in a day plus nine overs. In all, there were 37 sixes in the match, 27 by India, 13 by Sharma – all Test records.

Elgar, the first-innings hero, perished on the fourth evening when Kohli was eventually persuaded by Jadeja to review an lbw appeal that was skidding into middle, and before lunch on the final day South Africa were sunk at 70 for eight. Ashwin bowled de Bruyn, his 350th wicket in his 66th Test, equal-fastest to the mark with Muttiah Muralitharan. Mohammed Shami ripped out three, including Bavuma and de Kock for ducks, and Jadeja struck three times in an over. Muthusamy and Piedt hung around for 32 overs, more than doubling the score, but just as South Africa dared to dream of a great escape, Shami returned. Piedt edged his first ball into the stumps, and Rabada a big drive to the wicketkeeper, giving Shami the first five-for by an Indian fast bowler in the fourth innings of a home Test since Javagal Srinath, also against South Africa, at Ahmedabad in 1996-97.

Player of the Match: R. G. Sharma.

Close of play: first day, India 202-0 (Agarwal 84, R. G. Sharma 115); second day, South Africa 39-3 (Elgar 27, Bavuma 2); third day, South Africa 385-8 (Muthusamy 12, Maharaj 3); fourth day, South Africa 11-1 (Markram 3, de Bruyn 5).

India

M. A. Agarwal c Piedt b Elgar	215	– c du Plessis b Maharaj	7
R. G. Sharma st de Kock b Maharaj	176	– st de Kock b Maharaj	127
C. A. Pujara b Philander	6	– lbw b Philander	81
*V. Kohli c and b Muthusamy	20	– (5) not out	31
A. M. Rahane c Bavuma b Maharaj	15	– (6) not out	27
R. A. Jadeja not out	30	– (4) b Rabada	40
G. H. Vihari b Elgar b Maharaj	10		
†W. P. Saha c Muthusamy b Piedt	21		
R. Ashwin not out	1		
B 4, lb 1, w 1, nb 2	8	B 8, lb 2	10

1/317 (2) 2/324 (3) (7 wkts dec, 136 overs) 502   1/21 (1) (4 wkts dec, 67 overs) 323
3/377 (4) 4/431 (5)   2/190 (3) 3/239 (2)
5/436 (1) 6/457 (7) 7/494 (8)   4/286 (4)

I. Sharma and Mohammed Shami did not bat.

Philander 22–4–68–1; Rabada 24–7–66–0; Maharaj 55–6–189–3; Piedt 19–1–107–1; Muthusamy 15–1–63–1; Elgar 1–0–4–1. *Second innings*—Philander 12–5–21–1; Maharaj 22–0–129–2; Rabada 13–3–41–1; Piedt 17–3–102–0; Muthusamy 3–0–20–0.

South Africa

D. Elgar c Pujara b Jadeja	160	– (2) lbw b Jadeja	2
A. K. Markram b Ashwin	5	– (1) c and b Jadeja	39
T. B. de Bruyn c Saha b Ashwin	4	– b Ashwin	10
D. L. Piedt b Jadeja	18	– (10) b Mohammed Shami	56
T. Bavuma lbw b I. Sharma	18	– (4) b Mohammed Shami	0
*F. du Plessis c Pujara b Ashwin	55	– (5) b Mohammed Shami	13
†Q. de Kock b Ashwin	111	– (6) b Mohammed Shami	0
S. Muthusamy not out	33	– (7) not out	49
V. D. Philander b Ashwin	0	– (8) lbw b Jadeja	0
K. A. Maharaj c Agarwal b Ashwin	9	– (9) lbw b Jadeja	0
K. Rabada lbw b Ashwin	15	– c Saha b Mohammed Shami	18
B 12, lb 4, nb 5	21	B 2, lb 2	4

1/14 (2) 2/31 (3) 3/34 (4)   (131.2 overs) 431   1/4 (2) 2/19 (3)   (63.5 overs) 191
4/63 (5) 5/178 (6) 6/342 (1)   3/20 (4) 4/52 (5)
7/370 (7) 8/376 (9) 9/396 (10) 10/431 (11)   5/60 (6) 6/70 (1) 7/70 (8)
                                                    8/70 (9) 9/161 (10) 10/191 (11)

I. Sharma 16–2–54–1; Mohammed Shami 18–4–47–0; Ashwin 46.2–11–145–7; Jadeja 40–5–124–2; Vihari 9–1–38–0; R. G. Sharma 2–1–7–0. *Second innings*—Ashwin 20–5–44–1; Jadeja 25–6–87–4; Mohammed Shami 10.5–2–35–5; I. Sharma 7–2–18–0; R. G. Sharma 1–0–3–0.

Umpires: C. B. Gaffaney and R. K. Illingworth. Third umpire: N. J. Llong.
Referee: R. B. Richardson.

INDIA v SOUTH AFRICA

Second Test

At Pune, October 10–13, 2019. India won by an innings and 137 runs. India 40pts. Toss: India. Test debut: A. A. Nortje.

With Kohli roaring to his highest Test score, India were rarely troubled as they clinched a record 11th successive home series victory. South Africa collapsed twice after conceding 601: their top five managed only three double-figure scores in the match, with Markram bagging a pair.

On a pitch that offered early movement, Sharma failed for once, his dismissal for 14 by Rabada ending a run of seven 50-plus scores at home. But that was the last of the good

IMPROVING HIGHEST TEST SCORE MOST OFTEN

15	V. Kohli (I)	4	15	27	30	52	63	75	116	119	141	169	200	211	235	243	254*		
11	D. B. Vengsarkar (I) .		7	16	30	39	48	49	78	83	157*	159	164*	166				
10	J. H. Kallis (SA)		1	7	39	61	101	132	148*	160	189*	201*	224					
10	D. R. Martyn (A)	36	67*	74	78	89*	105	118	124*	133	161	165						
10	Mushtaq Ahmed (P) . .		0	4	5*	6	11	12*	18	20*	27	42	59					
10	K. C. Sangakkara (SL)		23	24	25	74	98	105*	140	230	270	287	319					

news for a South African attack reshaped to include the rapid debutant Anrich Nortje. Agarwal tucked in again, his eventual 108 including 76 in boundaries. He put on 138 with Pujara, before South Africa glimpsed an opening when both fell in the space of ten overs, with the new ball not far off. But Kohli slammed the door shut, and was soon in total command. He had 63 by the end of the first day, and opened up on the second, dominating stands of 178 with Rahane and 225 with Jadeja, no slouch himself, with 91 from 104 balls.

Kohli turned his 26th Test century into his seventh (and highest) double, the most for India, exceeding the six of Virender Sehwag and Sachin Tendulkar. Faced by innocuous spin bowling and substandard fielding, Kohli looked more than capable of pressing on to 300, but instead – leading India for the 50th time, and seeking his 30th win – he declared to give South Africa around an hour's batting on the second evening. It paid off: as in the First Test, three wickets went down before the close, with the recalled Yadav sharing the spoils with Mohammed Shami. Du Plessis and de Kock resisted for a time next day, but even a surprising ninth-wicket stand of 109 between Philander and Maharaj – a South African record against India, beating the mark set by Muthusamy and Piedt in the previous match – could not get South Africa even halfway to India's total. Maharaj's 72, which contained a dozen defiant fours, was his highest Test score.

South Africa were all out at the end of the third day, with Ashwin claiming four more victims, and the fourth was a similar story: following on against a rested attack, they lost wickets in clumps, before more late resistance from Philander and Maharaj, who faced 461 deliveries between them in the match. This time they put on 56 for the eighth wicket – but it couldn't last. Yadav broke through, and India soon completed their second innings victory over South Africa, after Kolkata in 2009-10.

Kohli and the bowlers shared the headlines, but there was also appreciation for the unsung wicketkeeper, Saha, whose diving catches to dismiss de Bruyn in both innings off the slippery Yadav were the highlights of a silky display.

Player of the Match: V. Kohli.
Close of play: first day, India 273-3 (Kohli 63, Rahane 18); second day, South Africa 36-3 (de Bruyn 20, Nortje 2); third day, South Africa 275.

India

M. A. Agarwal c du Plessis b Rabada	108
R. G. Sharma c de Kock b Rabada	14
C. A. Pujara c du Plessis b Rabada	58
V. Kohli not out	254
A. M. Rahane c de Kock b Maharaj	59
R. A. Jadeja c de Bruyn b Muthusamy	91
Lb 6, nb 11	17

1/25 (2)   (5 wkts dec, 156.3 overs) 601
2/163 (3) 3/198 (1)
4/376 (5) 5/601 (6)

†W. P. Saha, R. Ashwin, U. T. Yadav, I. Sharma and Mohammed Shami did not bat.

Philander 26-6-66-0; Rabada 30-3-93-3; Nortje 25-5-100-0; Maharaj 50-10-196-1; Muthusamy 19.3-1-97-1; Elgar 4-0-26-0; Markram 2-0-17-0.

South Africa

D. Elgar b Yadav	6	– (2) c Yadav b Ashwin	48
A. K. Markram lbw b Yadav	0	– (1) lbw b I. Sharma	0
T. B. de Bruyn c Saha b Yadav	30	– c Saha b Yadav	8
T. Bavuma c Saha b Mohammed Shami	8	– (5) c Rahane b Jadeja	38
A. A. Nortje c Kohli b Mohammed Shami	3	– (11) not out	0
*F. du Plessis c Rahane b Ashwin	64	– (4) c Saha b Ashwin	5
†Q. de Kock b Ashwin	31	– (6) b Jadeja	5
S. Muthusamy lbw b Jadeja	7	– (7) c R. G. Sharma b Mohammed Shami	9
V. D. Philander not out	44	– (8) c Saha b Yadav	37
K. A. Maharaj c R. G. Sharma b Ashwin	72	– (9) lbw b Jadeja	22
K. Rabada lbw b Ashwin	2	– (10) c R. G. Sharma b Yadav	4
Lb 8	8	B 8, lb 3, w 2	13

1/2 (2) 2/13 (1) 3/33 (4) (105.4 overs) 275
4/41 (5) 5/53 (3) 6/128 (7)
7/139 (8) 8/162 (6) 9/271 (10) 10/275 (11)

1/0 (1) 2/21 (3) (67.2 overs) 189
3/70 (4) 4/71 (2)
5/79 (6) 6/125 (5) 7/129 (7)
8/185 (8) 9/189 (10) 10/189 (9)

I. Sharma 10–1–36–0; Yadav 13–2–37–3; Jadeja 36–15–81–1; Mohammed Shami 17–3–44–2; Ashwin 28.4–9–69–4; R. G. Sharma 1–1–0–0. *Second innings*—I. Sharma 5–2–17–1; Yadav 8–3–22–3; Mohammed Shami 9–2–34–1; Ashwin 21–6–45–2; Jadeja 21.2–4–52–3; R. G. Sharma 2–0–4–0; Kohli 1–0–4–0.

Umpires: C. B. Gaffaney and N. J. Llong.   Third umpire: R. K. Illingworth.
Referee: R. B. Richardson.

INDIA v SOUTH AFRICA

Third Test

At Ranchi, October 19–22, 2019. India won by an innings and 202 runs. India 40pts. Toss: India. Test debuts: S. Nadeem; H. Klaasen, G. F. Linde.

India wrapped up the series 3–0 with another thumping victory, their fifth out of five in the fledgling ICC World Championship. South Africa shook up their side, moving de Kock up to open, handing the gloves to Heinrich Klaasen, and introducing a second debutant in off-spinner George Linde, as Keshav Maharaj had injured his shoulder. There were five changes in all, but nothing worked for du Plessis, not even taking vice-captain Bavuma out with him for the toss: Kohli won it for the third time running, and a familiar tale unfolded.

India did lose two quick wickets to Rabada, and Kohli fell cheaply to Nortje, who had endured an expensive wicketless debut at Pune. But Sharma and Rahane survived for the rest of an abbreviated day, and took their stand to 267 on the second. Rahane eventually fell after completing his 11th century, but Sharma was unstoppable, rumbling to his maiden Test double, surpassing the 177 he made on debut, against West Indies at Kolkata six years previously. It was India's third double-century of the series, all by different batsmen, and took Sharma's series aggregate to 529, the most for either side in this fixture, beating Jacques Kallis's 498 in South Africa in 2010-11 (no Indian had previously exceeded Mohammad Azharuddin's 388 in 1996-97). Sharma reached 100 and 200 with sixes, a double achieved previously only by Wasim Akram (for Pakistan against Zimbabwe at Sheikhupura in 1996-97) and Sanath Jayasuriya (Sri Lanka v Pakistan at Faisalabad in 2004-05). He hit four other sixes, making 19 in the series, to go with 62 fours.

Umesh Yadav joined in, clouting five sixes – and a single – in his ten-ball 31, which lifted India towards 500, and allowed Kohli to declare again shortly before the second-day close, despite more indifferent weather. Once again, India's bowlers made immediate

ALL CHANGE!

Most changes from previous Test by a touring team in mid-series:

5	South Africa v England at Leeds	1929
5	India v England at Leeds	1959
5	England v Australia at Perth (WACA).	1974-75
5	West Indies v South Africa at Durban	1998-99
5	Bangladesh v Sri Lanka at Colombo (SSC)	2002
5	Australia v India at Delhi	2012-13
5†	**South Africa v India at Ranchi**	**2019-20**
5	**New Zealand v Australia at Sydney**	**2019-20**

† *T. B. de Bruyn, dropped after the previous match, returned as a concussion substitute.*

inroads: Elgar fell second ball, gloving Mohammed Shami to Saha after the first had scooted away for four byes, and the promoted de Kock fell in the second over.

Hamza made a composed maiden half-century on the third day, but the tourists had little else to cheer. Only Bavuma and Linde scored more than six, although Nortje did face 55 balls in making four, as South Africa crashed to 162, trailing by 335. The wickets were shared: Umesh Yadav claimed three, plus a run-out, while there were two for the seasoned local debutant, 30-year-old slow left-armer Shahbaz Nadeem. India had intended to play three spinners and, when Kuldeep Yadav reported a shoulder injury, Nadeem was whistled up for his maiden cap, after taking 424 wickets in 110 first-class matches spread over 15 years. His first scalp was a classic spinner's dismissal: Bavuma was beaten in the flight after skipping down the track, and Saha completed the stumping.

South Africa were following on halfway through the day, and fared even worse. In a twinkling it was 36 for five, with Elgar also out of the match after being hit on the helmet by Yadav (in his previous over, another snorter had smacked him on the shoulder). The lower order again put their seniors to shame: Linde hung around for 55 balls, Piedt for 73. De Bruyn entered the fray as a concussion substitute for Elgar, and top-scored with 30, which at least pushed the match into a fourth day. On the third, South Africa had lost 16 wickets, a number they had exceeded only twice, with 19 against England at Cape Town in 1888-89, in their second official Test, and at Old Trafford in 1912, on the day the Australian leg-spinner Jimmy Matthews took two hat-tricks.

The optimistic souls who turned up on the fourth morning saw just 12 deliveries, as the match was finished off by Nadeem. First de Bruyn under-edged a cut, and was well caught by Saha. Next ball, No. 12 Ngidi flapped a drive back down the pitch. It hit non-striker Nortje on the left wrist, and bounced up for a return catch. It was a strange way to end – but almost a relief for the beleaguered South Africans, who could finally fly home.

Player of the Match: R. G. Sharma. *Player of the Series:* R. G. Sharma.
Close of play: first day, India 224-3 (Sharma 117, Rahane 83); second day, South Africa 9-2 (Hamza 0, du Plessis 1); third day, South Africa 132-8 (de Bruyn 30, Nortje 5).

India

M. A. Agarwal c Elgar b Rabada	10	S. Nadeem not out.	1
R. G. Sharma c Ngidi b Rabada	212	Mohammed Shami not out	10
C. A. Pujara lbw b Rabada	0		
*V. Kohli lbw b Nortje	12	B 10, lb 6, nb 1	17
A. M. Rahane c Klaasen b Linde.	115		
R. A. Jadeja c Klaasen b Linde	51	1/12 (1) (9 wkts dec, 116.3 overs) 497
*W. P. Saha b Linde	24	2/16 (3) 3/39 (4)
R. Ashwin st Klaasen b Piedt	14	4/306 (5) 5/370 (2) 6/417 (7)
U. T. Yadav c Klaasen b Linde	31	7/450 (6) 8/464 (8) 9/482 (9)

Rabada 23–7–85–3; Ngidi 20–5–83–0; Nortje 24.3–5–79–1; Linde 31–2–133–4; Piedt 18–3–101–1.

South Africa

D. Elgar c Saha b Mohammed Shami	0	– (2) retired hurt 16
Q. de Kock c Saha b Yadav	4	– (1) b Yadav................ 5
M. Z. Hamza b Jadeja	62	– b Mohammed Shami 0
*F. du Plessis b Yadav	1	– lbw b Mohammed Shami 4
T. Bavuma st Saha b Nadeem	32	– c Saha b Mohammed Shami...... 0
†H. Klaasen b Jadeja	6	– lbw b Yadav.............. 5
G. F. Linde c Sharma b Yadav	37	– run out (Nadeem) 27
D. L. Piedt lbw b Mohammed Shami	4	– b Jadeja................ 23
K. Rabada run out (Yadav)	0	– (10) c Jadeja b Ashwin 12
A. A. Nortje lbw b Nadeem	4	– (11) not out............. 5
L. T. Ngidi not out	0	– (12) c and b Nadeem 0
T. B. de Bruyn (did not bat)	–	(9) c Saha b Nadeem 30
B 8, lb 3, nb 1	12	B 5, lb 1 6

1/4 (1) 2/8 (2) 3/16 (4)   (56.2 overs) 162
4/107 (3) 5/107 (5) 6/119 (6)
7/129 (8) 8/130 (9) 9/162 (7) 10/162 (10)

1/5 (1) 2/10 (3)   (48 overs) 133
3/18 (4) 4/22 (5)
5/36 (6) 6/67 (7) 7/98 (8)
8/121 (10) 9/133 (9) 10/133 (12)

In the second innings Elgar retired hurt at 26-4. De Bruyn replaced him, as a concussion substitute.

Mohammed Shami 10–4–22–2; Yadav 9–1–40–3; Nadeem 11.2–4–22–2; Jadeja 14–3–19–2; Ashwin 12–1–48–0. *Second innings*—Mohammed Shami 10–6–10–3; Yadav 9–1–35–2; Jadeja 13–5–36–1; Nadeem 6–1–18–2; Ashwin 10–3–28–1.

Umpires: R. K. Illingworth and N. J. Llong.   Third umpire: C. B. Gaffaney.
Referee: R. B. Richardson.

INDIA v BANGLADESH IN 2019-20

Mohammad Isam

Twenty20 internationals (3): India 2, Bangladesh 1
Test matches (2): India 2 (120pts), Bangladesh 0 (0pts)

For Bangladesh, there were no illusions that a tour of India risked being overwhelming. And, after beginning with the unexpected fillip of a Twenty20 win, so it proved. The Bangladeshis went on to lose the 20-over series, as well as the Tests at Indore and Kolkata, where India's bowlers ran riot, and their batsmen were remorseless. Ishant Sharma, Umesh Yadav and Mohammed Shami – who between them took 33 wickets at 13 – looked like the best seam attack in world cricket.

Bangladesh were a mess off the field, too. Two weeks before the tour began, the players threatened to go on strike unless the board met their demands, which included higher wages, better facilities and improvements to the domestic structure. Nazmul Hassan, board president, retaliated during a bizarre hour-long press conference next day, calling the players' behaviour a "conspiracy", and leaving little room for negotiation. But after lengthy discussions, the strike was called off.

More instability was to follow. Shakib Al Hasan, the country's greatest cricketer and the leader of the rebellion, failed to show up at a pre-tour training camp, instead making headlines by signing a deal with a telecom company – breaking the board's rules. On October 29, three days after he had finally appeared at the camp (for a few hours), and a day before the players were due to fly to India, it was announced that Shakib had been banned by the ICC for two years (one suspended) for failing to report three corrupt approaches in 2018. Bangladeshi cricket went into mourning, with many fans refusing to accept what had happened. Several hundred took to the streets in Shakib's home town of Magura to demand the ICC revoke the suspension. But the evidence was damning. As the experienced opening batsman Tamim Iqbal had already opted out of the tour because his wife was about to give birth, Bangladesh were in chaos even before they landed in India.

The Bangladesh Cricket Board accepted their Indian counterparts' proposal to play a pink-ball Test, both countries' first. They had refused a similar request by New Zealand, but when Sourav Ganguly – the new BCCI president – came calling, they couldn't say no. That, though, was for the end of the tour. First, Bangladesh surprised everyone with a hard-fought T20 win in Delhi, their first over India in the format. Virat Kohli had been rested, but the Indians still had enough batting talent to hit back in the remaining two matches, under the leadership of Rohit Sharma. Deepak Chahar, a medium-pacer from Rajasthan, starred with the ball, taking world-record figures of six for seven in the Nagpur decider, including a hat-trick.

The First Test at Indore was an annihilation, as India's opener Mayank Agarwal and their fast bowlers decimated Bangladesh, who – under new captain Mominul Haque – had boldly chosen to bat. But the day/night Test was always going to be the jewel in the crown, and Ganguly – a favourite in Bangladesh because of his Bengali roots – made sure his home city laid on a memorable show. Kolkata was properly dressed up, and a full house on all three days was testament to the novelty value.

Ganguly invited Bangladesh's prime minister Sheikh Hasina to the match, along with the Bangladesh squad from their inaugural Test, at Dhaka in November 2000, when he had been India's captain. He also invited Bengal's chief minister Mamata Banerjee, plus the great and good of Indian cricket and sport. The ceremonies were prolonged, but no one could fault Ganguly's attention to detail. The cricket, though, didn't match the occasion, as Bangladesh crumbled twice. Kohli lit up the second day with a century, though the cricket-loving Eden Gardens crowd would have preferred a bit more fight from their next-door neighbours.

BANGLADESH TOURING PARTY

*Mominul Haque (T), Abu Haider (20), Abu Jayed (T), Afif Hossain (20), Al-Amin Hossain (T/20), Aminul Islam (20), Arafat Sunny (20), Ebadat Hossain (T), Imrul Kayes (T), Liton Das (T/20), Mahmudullah (T/20), Mehedi Hasan (T/20), Mithun Ali (T/20), Mohammad Naim (20), Mosaddek Hossain (T/20), Mushfiqur Rahim (T/20), Mustafizur Rahman (T/20), Nayeem Hasan (T), Saif Hasan (T), Shadman Islam (T), Shafiul Islam (20), Soumya Sarkar (20), Taijul Islam (T). *Coach:* R. C. Domingo.

Shakib Al Hasan was initially named as captain, but was then banned by the ICC. Mominul Haque took over as Test captain, and Mahmudullah for the T20s. Shakib was replaced in the T20 squad by Mithun Ali. Mohammad Saifuddin was originally chosen for the T20s, but injured his back and was replaced by Abu Haider; Taijul Islam was also added. Tamim Iqbal was selected in both squads, but withdrew for family reasons; Imrul Kayes replaced him for the Tests.

First Twenty20 international   At Delhi, November 3, 2019 (floodlit). **Bangladesh won by seven wickets. India 148-6** (20 overs) (S. Dhawan 41); ‡**Bangladesh 154-3** (19.3 overs) (Soumya Sarkar 39, Mushfiqur Rahim 60*). *PoM:* Mushfiqur Rahim. *T20I debuts:* S. R. Dube (India); Mohammad Naim (Bangladesh). *Mushfiqur Rahim's splendid 43-ball 60* helped Bangladesh to their maiden T20 win over India, at the ninth attempt, boosting morale after a chaotic build-up. They had needed 20 from ten balls when Mushfiqur took four successive fours off left-arm seamer Khaleel Ahmed, before Mahmudullah, the captain, pulled the debutant medium-pacer Shivam Dube for six. Earlier, Bangladesh took advantage of India's off-colour batting. Shafiul Islam and Aminul Islam, a leg-spinner playing his second international, shared four wickets, while Mahmudullah ran out Shikhar Dhawan. The game took place in thick smog, as debate raged about whether it should have been called off. Two Bangladeshis vomited on the field, and BCCI president Sourav Ganguly later tweeted to thank both sides for playing "under tuff [sic] conditions".*

Second Twenty20 international   At Rajkot, November 7, 2019 (floodlit). **India won by eight wickets. Bangladesh 153-6** (20 overs) (Mohammad Naim 36, Soumya Sarkar 30, Mahmudullah 30); ‡**India 154-2** (15.4 overs) (R. G. Sharma 85, S. Dhawan 31). *PoM:* R. G. Sharma. *Bangladesh threw away their best start in more than a year, before Rohit Sharma gunned down a target of 154. In his 100th T20 international, he blasted six fours and six sixes – including three pulls in a row off Mosaddek Hossain – in his 43-ball 85, after an opening stand of 118 with Dhawan. India cruised home in the 16th over, making Bangladesh pay for wasting a 60-run opening stand between Liton Das and Mohammad Naim. Liton enjoyed a reprieve on 17, when he was lured out of his ground by Yuzvendra Chahal, only for Rishabh Pant's stumping to be ruled illegal because he had taken the ball a fraction in front of the stumps; Liton thrashed the free hit for four. But he and Naim were two of four batsmen to fall between 29 and 36, and Mahmudullah admitted his side had finished 25–30 short of par.*

Third Twenty20 international   At Nagpur, November 10, 2019 (floodlit). **India won by 30 runs. India 174-5** (20 overs) (K. L. Rahul 52, S. S. Iyer 62); ‡**Bangladesh 144** (19.2 overs) (Mohammad Naim 81; D. L. Chahar 6-7, S. R. Dube 3-30). *PoM:* D. L. Chahar. *PoS:* D. L. Chahar. *Seamer Deepak Chahar upended a possible Bangladesh comeback with perhaps the most stunning spell in T20 history. He finished with six wickets for seven runs – but, as much as the numbers, it was the timing of his wickets that helped India clinch the series. He claimed two early victims, before 20-year-old left-hander Naim counter-attacked with a 48-ball 81, adding 98 in ten overs with Mithun Ali. But Chahar returned to have Mithun caught in the deep, then Dube dismissed Naim and Afif Hossain with successive deliveries. And a collapse of eight for 34 was complete when Chahar closed out the game with a hat-trick, spanning two overs, removing Shafiul Islam, Mustafizur Rahman and Aminul Islam. His analysis was the best in T20 internationals, beating 6-8 by the Sri Lankan spinner Ajantha Mendis against Zimbabwe at Hambantota in 2012-13.*

INDIA v BANGLADESH

First Test

At Indore, November 14–16, 2019. India won by an innings and 130 runs. India 60pts. Toss: Bangladesh.

Mayank Agarwal reached his second double-hundred, six weeks after his first, to power India to a thumping win. Along the way, Bangladesh were given a harsh lesson by India's pace attack, and knocked over twice in the equivalent of little more than four sessions.

India were over halfway to a first-innings lead by the end of the opening day. Bangladesh had chosen to bat – a decision Mominul Haque, captaining in his first Test because of the corruption ban imposed on Shakib Al Hasan, later admitted was "bad" – and were rolled for 150. After Yadav and Ishant Sharma ripped out the openers, Mohammed Shami and Ashwin undid the middle order: Mominul was bowled leaving a delivery from Ashwin that drifted on to off stump. The last five fell for just ten. It was a sorry procession.

Abu Jayed removed Rohit Sharma cheaply on the first evening, and created a bit of a flutter next morning. He had Pujara brilliantly caught at gully by the substitute Saif Hasan, and in his next over trapped Kohli for his tenth Test duck – and first against Bangladesh. But these were momentary lapses. Agarwal set about reasserting India's dominance during a fourth-wicket stand of 190 with Rahane, who contributed 86. He became a fourth victim for Jayed, who finished with four for 108, compared with four team-mates' combined analysis of two for 384.

First, though, Jadeja helped add a further 123 with Agarwal, who finally fell for 243 from 330 balls, including 28 fours and eight sixes, which equalled the Indian record for a Test innings (Navjot Sidhu also hit eight against Sri Lanka at Lucknow in 1993-94). Agarwal's second Test double had come in his 12th innings; only compatriot Vinod Kambli (five innings) had made two more quickly, while even Bradman had to wait until his 13th. To rub it in, Yadav blasted three more sixes in ten balls to hasten an overnight declaration after a day in which India cracked 407 runs in 88 overs.

Trailing by 343, Bangladesh were already down and out, and the formalities were completed on the third day. What little fight there was came from Mushfiqur Rahim, who top-scored with 64, their only half-century of the match. Shami once again troubled the middle order, finishing with match figures of seven for 58, while Ishant and Yadav at times looked unplayable. Ashwin rounded things off with his fifth wicket of the game.

Mominul could say little in defence of his team, but perhaps inadvertently criticised Shadman Islam and Imrul Kayes, who became the first pair of openers in Test history to fall twice for the same score (six) in both innings – Shadman twice to Ishant, Imrul twice to Yadav. "It would be easier for the rest of the batting line-up if the openers played out the first 15 to 20 overs," said Mominul. "India have a threatening attack, but we also failed as a batting unit."

Player of the Match: M. A. Agarwal.

Close of play: first day, India 86-1 (Agarwal 37, Pujara 43); second day, India 493-6 (Jadeja 60, Yadav 25).

Bangladesh

Shadman Islam c Saha b I. Sharma	6	– b I. Sharma	6
Imrul Kayes c Rahane b Yadav	6	– b Yadav	6
*Mominul Haque b Ashwin	37	– lbw b Mohammed Shami	7
Mithun Ali lbw b Mohammed Shami	13	– c Agarwal b Mohammed Shami	18
Mushfiqur Rahim b Mohammed Shami	43	– c Pujara b Ashwin	64
Mahmudullah b Ashwin	10	– c R. G. Sharma b Mohammed Shami	15
†Liton Das c Kohli b I. Sharma	21	– c and b Ashwin	35
Mehedi Hasan lbw b Mohammed Shami	0	– b Yadav	38
Taijul Islam run out (Jadeja/Saha)	1	– c Saha b Mohammed Shami	6
Abu Jayed not out	7	– not out	4
Ebadat Hossain b Yadav	2	– c Yadav b Ashwin	1
Lb 3, w 1	4	B 2, lb 9, w 1, nb 1	13

1/12 (2) 2/12 (1) 3/31 (4)	(58.3 overs) 150	1/10 (2) 2/16 (1)	(69.2 overs) 213
4/99 (3) 5/115 (6) 6/140 (5)		3/37 (3) 4/44 (4)	
7/140 (8) 8/140 (7) 9/148 (9) 10/150 (11)		5/72 (6) 6/135 (7) 7/194 (8)	
		8/208 (9) 9/208 (5) 10/213 (11)	

I. Sharma 12–6–20–2; Yadav 14.3–3–47–2; Mohammed Shami 13–5–27–3; Ashwin 16–1–43–2; Jadeja 3–0–10–0. *Second innings*—I. Sharma 11–3–31–1; Yadav 14–1–51–2; Mohammed Shami 16–7–31–4; Jadeja 14–2–47–0; Ashwin 14.2–6–42–3.

India

M. A. Agarwal c Abu Jayed b Mehedi Hasan	243
R. G. Sharma c Liton Das b Abu Jayed	6
C. A. Pujara c sub (Saif Hasan) b Abu Jayed	54
*V. Kohli lbw b Abu Jayed	0
A. M. Rahane c Taijul Islam b Abu Jayed	86
R. A. Jadeja not out	60
†W. P. Saha b Ebadat Hossain	12

U. T. Yadav not out	25
Lb 1, w 3, nb 3	7
1/14 (2)	(6 wkts dec, 114 overs) 493
2/105 (3) 3/119 (4)	
4/309 (5) 5/432 (1) 6/454 (7)	

R. Ashwin, I. Sharma and Mohammed Shami did not bat.

Ebadat Hossain 31–5–115–1; Abu Jayed 25–3–108–4; Taijul Islam 28–4–120–0; Mehedi Hasan 27–0–125–1; Mahmudullah 3–0–24–0.

Umpires: M. Erasmus and R. J. Tucker. Third umpire: N. N. Menon.
Referee: R. S. Madugalle.

INDIA v BANGLADESH

Second Test

At Kolkata, November 22–24, 2019 (day/night). India won by an innings and 46 runs. India 60pts. Toss: Bangladesh.

After endless handshakes with the Bangladesh prime minister, Sheikh Hasina, and other dignitaries, the ringing of the Eden Gardens bell, selfies by the dressing-room, and general grandstanding, India's first pink-ball Test, finally got under way. It was a crushing disappointment: in front of a crowd of around 60,000 – Kolkata's largest for the first day of a Test in many years – Bangladesh's batsmen dished up a performance that fell well short of the occasion.

In the best light of the day, they were six down in the first session after winning another toss, with Mominul Haque, Mithun Ali and Mushfiqur Rahim all gone for ducks. To make matters worse, Liton Das – one of only two to reach 20 – retired hurt at the interval after a blow on the head from Mohammed Shami. Later, Mehedi Hasan emerged at No. 10 as a concussion substitute, but not before Shami had struck 18-year-old Nayeem Hasan on the helmet with his first ball after the break. Nayeem continued until his dismissal, but didn't bat again in the match, with Taijul Islam becoming his side's second concussion replacement. And while Taijul was allowed to bowl his slow left-armers because he had replaced off-spinner Nayeem, Mehedi was not allowed to bowl his off-breaks, because Liton was the wicketkeeper.

It was chaos, and Ishant Sharma cashed in, hoovering up the cheapest of his ten Test five-fors, though only his second at home, 12 years after his first (in his first home Test). Yadav and Shami chipped in as Bangladesh were blown away in 30.3 overs. Abu Jayed became the third man to bat at No. 12 in a Test – and, like the other two (West Indies' Shannon Gabriel and South Africa's Lungi Ngidi, both earlier in 2019), failed to score.

India lost Agarwal and Rohit Sharma early, but India's middle order took charge. Kohli put on 94 with Pujara, then 99 with Rahane, and made up for his duck in the previous match with his 27th Test century. It was another exercise in watchable strokeplay – four of the 18 fours in his eventual 136 came in succession off Jayed – interspersed with doses of patience. There were loose balls on offer from a below-par attack, but Kohli rarely loses concentration in such circumstances. His innings ended only when Taijul pulled off a superb catch at deep fine leg.

Al-Amin Hossain, in his first Test for five years, and Ebadat Hossain took three wickets apiece, but India declared 241 ahead on the second evening, the time of day both sides had nominated in advance as the trickiest for batting. So it proved: Ishant picked up three more as Bangladesh slipped to 13 for four, including Mominul for a pair. After a barrage of short bowling, Mushfiqur and Mahmudullah counter-attacked – only for Mahmudullah's hamstring to give way, leading to another retirement.

A two-day finish had looked on the cards, but Bangladesh got to stumps on 152 for six, having recovered a modicum of self-respect. However, Mahmudullah did not bat again next day, when Mushfiqur's response to a desperate situation was to hit out. He finally fell for 74, which included 13 fours, but there was only 47 minutes' play; it was the shortest completed Test in India by balls bowled (968), edging out the two-day thrashing of Afghanistan (1,028) in June 2018. Yadav finished with five wickets, and Ishant with match figures of nine for 78.

In completing an national-record seventh consecutive win (they had won six in a row in 2013), India became the first side to win four successive Tests by an innings. And, in a sign of the times, their fast bowlers had accounted for all 19 wickets to fall, another national record for home Tests; never before had an Indian spinner failed to take a wicket in a home win. Their cricket was changing fast – and Bangladesh had no means of keeping up.

Player of the Match: I. Sharma.   *Player of the Series:* I. Sharma.

Close of play: first day, India 174-3 (Kohli 59, Rahane 23); second day, Bangladesh 152-6 (Mushfiqur Rahim 59).

❝ Against Lancashire, he put on 173 with his captain, Colin Cowdrey, the highest partnership in first-class cricket between two future members of the House of Lords.**"**

Obituaries, page 228

Bangladesh

Shadman Islam c Saha b Yadav	29	– lbw b I. Sharma	0
Imrul Kayes lbw b I. Sharma	4	– c Kohli b I. Sharma	5
*Mominul Haque c R. G. Sharma b Yadav	0	– c Saha b I. Sharma	0
Mithun Ali b Yadav	0	– c Mohammed Shami b Yadav	6
Mushfiqur Rahim b Mohammed Shami	0	– c Jadeja b Yadav	74
Mahmudullah c Saha b I. Sharma	6	– retired hurt	39
†Liton Das retired hurt	24		
Nayeem Hasan b I. Sharma	19		
Ebadat Hossain b I. Sharma	1	– c Kohli b Yadav	0
Mehedi Hasan c Pujara b I. Sharma	8	– (7) c Kohli b I. Sharma	15
Al-Amin Hossain not out	1	– (10) c Saha b Yadav	21
Abu Jayed c Pujara b Mohammed Shami	0	– (11) not out	2
Taijul Islam (did not bat)		– (8) c Rahane b Yadav	11
B 8, lb 6	14	B 8, lb 9, w 5	22

1/15 (2) 2/17 (3) 3/17 (4)	(30.3 overs) 106	1/0 (1) 2/2 (3) (41.1 overs) 195
4/26 (5) 5/38 (1) 6/60 (6)		3/9 (4) 4/13 (2)
7/82 (9) 8/98 (10) 9/105 (8) 10/106 (12)		5/133 (7) 6/152 (8)
		7/152 (9) 8/184 (5) 9/195 (10)

In the first innings, Liton Das retired hurt at 73-6; Mehedi Hasan replaced him, as a concussion substitute. In the second, Mahmudullah retired hurt at 82-4. During India's innings, Taijul Islam replaced Nayeem Hasan, as a concussion substitute.

I. Sharma 12–4–22–5; Yadav 7–2–29–3; Mohammed Shami 10.3–2–36–2; Jadeja 1–0–5–0. *Second innings*—I. Sharma 13–2–56–4; Yadav 14.1–1–53–5; Mohammed Shami 8–0–42–0; Ashwin 5–0–19–0; Jadeja 1–0–8–0.

India

M. A. Agarwal c Mehedi Hasan b Al-Amin Hossain	14	R. Ashwin lbw b Al-Amin Hossain	9
R. G. Sharma lbw b Ebadat Hossain	21	U. T. Yadav c Shadman Islam b Abu Jayed	0
C. A. Pujara c Shadman Islam b Ebadat Hossain	55	I. Sharma lbw b Al-Amin Hossain	0
*V. Kohli c Taijul Islam b Ebadat Hossain	136	Mohammed Shami not out	10
A. M. Rahane c Ebadat Hossain b Taijul Islam	51	B 12, lb 2, w 8	22
R. A. Jadeja b Abu Jayed	12		
†W. P. Saha not out	17		

1/26 (1)	(9 wkts dec, 89.4 overs) 347
2/43 (2) 3/137 (3)	
4/236 (5) 5/289 (6) 6/308 (4)	
7/329 (8) 8/330 (9) 9/331 (10)	

Al-Amin Hossain 22.4–3–85–3; Abu Jayed 21–6–77–2; Ebadat Hossain 21–3–91–3; Taijul Islam 25–2–80–1.

Umpires: M. Erasmus and J. S. Wilson.   Third umpire: R. J. Tucker.

Referee: R. S. Madugalle.

INDIA v WEST INDIES IN 2019-20

Debasish Datta

Twenty20 internationals (3): India 2, West Indies 1
One-day internationals (3): India 2, West Indies 1

For once in their recent encounters with West Indies, India did not have things all their own way. In the Caribbean in August, there had been only one team in it; this time, West Indies earned a big win in each series to ensure both went to a decider. It made for eminently more watchable cricket.

The starring roles were mostly filled by familiar names. Virat Kohli bookended the six matches with Player of the Match performances, and was Player of the Series in the Twenty20 games, while Rohit Sharma concluded an extraordinarily prolific year in 50-over cricket with 258 runs at 86. But others prospered, too. K. L. Rahul opened the batting in the absence of the injured Shikhar Dhawan, and was India's second-highest run-scorer in each series. Shreyas Iyer continued the favourable impression he had made in the West Indies with 130 runs from No. 4 in the ODIs.

For the tourists, the games followed on from those against Afghanistan in Lucknow. Kieron Pollard, the new white-ball captain, had enjoyed mixed fortunes there, but against India he put his IPL experience to good effect, showing shrewd judgment of pitches. He was effective with the bat, but had a poor time with the ball. Shimron Hetmyer was occasionally brilliant.

In an ICC experiment, these were the first series in which TV umpires called front-foot no-balls. West Indies seamer Kesrick Williams was the first to transgress, and the governing body later judged the trial a success. The technology was later used at the women's T20 World Cup in Australia, with on-field umpires instructed not to call any front-foot no-balls.

But the major umpiring controversy came in the first ODI, in Chennai, after Shaun George decided Ravindra Jadeja had made his ground while attempting a quick single, despite a direct hit from Roston Chase. George did not call for a replay but, when it was shown, Jadeja was clearly out. West Indies' fielders urged George to consult the TV umpire, and he changed his decision. Kohli was unimpressed: "The fielder asked how was that, and the umpire said not out. The dismissal ends there."

WEST INDIES TOURING PARTY

*K. A. Pollard (50/20), F. A. Allen (20), S. W. Ambris (50), R. L. Chase (50), S. S. Cottrell (50/20), S. O. Hetmyer (50/20), J. O. Holder (50), S. D. Hope (50), A. S. Joseph (50), B. A. King (50/20), E. Lewis (50/20), K. M. A. Paul (50), K. A. Pierre (50/20), N. Pooran (20), D. Ramdin (20), S. E. Rutherford (20), R. Shepherd (50), L. M. P. Simmons (20), H. R. Walsh (50/20), K. O. K. Williams (20). *Coach*: P. V. Simmons.

First Twenty20 international At Hyderabad, December 6, 2019 (floodlit). **India won by six wickets. West Indies 207-5** (20 overs) (E. Lewis 40, B. A. King 31, S. O. Hetmyer 56, K. A. Pollard 37); ‡**India 209-4** (18.4 overs) (K. L. Rahul 62, V. Kohli 94*). PoM: V. Kohli. *Virat Kohli hit his highest T20I score, as India eased home with eight balls to spare, despite a challenging West Indies* *total based around Shimron Hetmyer's 56 off 41. K. L. Rahul, opening in place of the injured Shikhar Dhawan, hit 62 off 40, and put on 100 with Kohli, who – in front of a capacity crowd – had remonstrated with himself as he struggled to 26 off 25 balls. He later said he had been trying to hit the ball too hard. But his fluency returned, and he scored 68 off the next 25. He even found time to mock Kesrick Williams's notebook celebration, after hitting him for a four and a six. It was India's second-highest successful chase at home.*

Second Twenty20 international   At Thiruvananthapuram, December 8, 2019 (floodlit). **West Indies won by eight wickets. India 170-7** (20 overs) (S. R. Dube 54, R. R. Pant 33*); ‡**West Indies 173-2** (18.3 overs) (L. M. P. Simmons 67*, E. Lewis 40, N. Pooran 38*). *PoM:* L. M. P. Simmons. *At 93-2 at the halfway point, India look set for a series-clinching total, after pinch-hitter Shivam Dube crashed 54 off 30. Instead, Williams and leg-spinner Hayden Walsh dragged West Indies back into it, conceding just 58 off their eight overs. When the tourists replied to an underpowered total, India dropped catches, and were unable to apply the brakes. Lendl Simmons batted sensibly for 67* off 45, and the three left-handers after him negated the threat of spinners Yuzvendra Chahal and Ravindra Jadeja.*

Third Twenty20 international   At Mumbai, December 11, 2019 (floodlit). **India won by 67 runs. India 240-3** (20 overs) (R. G. Sharma 71, K. L. Rahul 91, V. Kohli 70*); ‡**West Indies 173-8** (20 overs) (S. O. Hetmyer 41, K. A. Pollard 68). *PoM:* K. L. Rahul. *PoS:* V. Kohli. *Talk that India might let the series slip appeared ridiculous as they piled up a huge total, then defended it with ease. Rohit Sharma and Rahul went on the offensive from the start, and put on 135 in 11.4 overs. That set the stage for Kohli to smash 70* off 29, including seven sixes; he had reached 50 in 21 balls, his fastest T20I half-century. India's total was their third-highest, and the highest at this venue. At 17-3, West Indies were soon in trouble. Hetmyer launched a partial recovery, and captain Kieron Pollard added some respectability with 68 off 39, but it was nowhere near enough.*

First one-day international   At Chennai, December 15, 2019. **West Indies won by eight wickets. India 287-8** (50 overs) (R. G. Sharma 36, S. S. Iyer 70, R. R. Pant 71, K. M. Jadhav 40); ‡**West Indies 291-2** (47.5 overs) (S. D. Hope 102*, S. O. Hetmyer 139). *PoM:* S. O. Hetmyer. *ODI debut:* S. R. Dube (India). *Contrasting hundreds from Shai Hope and Hetmyer paved the way for West Indies to seize the initiative in the ODI series. Hope compiled a careful 102* off 151, giving Hetmyer the freedom to blast 139 from 106, with 11 fours and seven sixes. Kohli had had no hesitation in batting first, but the departure of Sharma left India 80-3 in the 19th; Sheldon Cottrell had removed Rahul and Kohli in the seventh. Shreyas Iyer and Rishabh Pant regrouped with a stand of 114, and India needed one well-set batsman to be there for the closing efforts.*

Second one-day international   At Visakhapatnam, December 18, 2019. **India won by 107 runs. India 387-5** (50 overs) (R. G. Sharma 159, K. L. Rahul 102, S. S. Iyer 53, R. R. Pant 39); ‡**West Indies 280** (43.3 overs) (E. Lewis 30, S. D. Hope 78, N. Pooran 75, K. M. A. Paul 46; Mohammed Shami 3-39, K. Yadav 3-52). *PoM:* R. G. Sharma. *ODI debut:* K. A. Pierre (West Indies). *Sharma scored his seventh ODI century of 2019 – only Sachin Tendulkar, with nine in 1998, had made more in a calendar year – and his 28th in all, as India produced a powerful all-round display. He and Rahul put on 227 in 37 overs, accelerating effortlessly after a measured first 20. Sharma's 159 came off 138 balls, while Rahul hit 102 off 104. Kohli fell for a first-ball duck, but the crowd's disappointment was alleviated by an electrifying stand of 73 in four overs between Iyer (53 off 32) and Pant (39 off 16); Iyer crashed 31 off an over from Roston Chase. West Indies blazed away from the start, and a fourth-wicket partnership of 106 between Hope and Pooran gave India cause for concern. Mohammed Shami's pace upset West Indies' momentum, before Kuldeep Yadav's second ODI hat-trick settled the issue. Jadeja was given run out after West Indies' fielders persuaded umpire George to consult his TV colleague.*

Third one-day international   At Cuttack, December 22, 2019. **India won by four wickets. West Indies 315-5** (50 overs) (S. D. Hope 42, R. L. Chase 38, S. O. Hetmyer 37, N. Pooran 89, K. A. Pollard 74*); ‡**India 316-6** (48.4 overs) (R. G. Sharma 63, K. L. Rahul 77, V. Kohli 85, R. A. Jadeja 39*; K. M. A. Paul 3-59). *PoM:* V. Kohli. *PoS:* R. G. Sharma. *ODI debut:* N. Saini (India). *Kohli's magnificent innings took India close to a series-sealing victory, but they needed nerveless No. 8 Shardul Thakur's six-ball 17* to get them over the line. West Indies had risen to the challenge in the decider by posting 315 after being put in: Pooran and Pollard added 135 for the fifth wicket, and 105 came in the last eight overs. They might have had more, but for a cautious start by Evin Lewis. Sharma, Rahul and Kohli all passed 50, but a middle-order wobble put India under pressure, until Jadeja joined his captain.*

INDIA A v ENGLAND LIONS IN 2018-19

A-Team one-day internationals (5): India A 4, England Lions 1
A-Team Test matches (2): India A 1, England Lions 0

England Lions had a chastening time in India early in 2019, surrendering the one-day series 4–1, and losing the Second A-team Test after saving the First in gritty fashion. India A had too much firepower, even though they rotated their side extensively: 23 different players appeared in the one-dayers, with none appearing in all five games.

It was a similar story in the Tests, with the home side making four changes between the two matches. There were promising centuries for Abhimanyu Easwaran and Srikar Bharat, and a superb 206 for Priyank Panchal. The full Test side were encouraged by a return to form for K. L. Rahul, who ground out eighties in both four-day games, and there were one-day runs for Ajinkya Rahane and fringe Test players Hanuma Vihari and Rishabh Pant. Seamer Navdeep Saini collected nine wickets in the red-ball games.

The Lions' leading scorer overall was Ben Duckett, with 147 runs in the one-dayers and 175 in the Tests; Sam Billings, the captain, just shaded him in the ODIs, with 156, including the only international century of the tour. The Lions found it hard to score quickly enough: none of their batsmen managed a run a ball in the ODIs, and Jonathan Trott, the batting coach, said the four-day series was "a typical case of them not doing the basics well for longer".

The bowlers also struggled in Indian conditions. Seamer Zak Chappell took seven wickets in both series, and slow left-armer Danny Briggs five. Andy Flower, the Lions' head coach, was still upbeat. "Briggs has been very steady all the way through, and Lewis Gregory has been solid as a rock and taken some important wickets with the new ball. One thing we found particularly tough was scoring runs out here – but that's the purpose of coming, to learn about Indian conditions."

ENGLAND LIONS SQUAD

*S. W. Billings (Kent; FC/50), T. E. Bailey (Lancashire; FC/50), D. M. Bess (Somerset; FC/50), D. R. Briggs (Hampshire; FC/50), M. Carter (Nottinghamshire; 50), Z. J. Chappell (Nottinghamshire; FC/50), A. L. Davies (Lancashire; 50), B. M. Duckett (Nottinghamshire; FC/50), L. Gregory (Somerset; FC/50), S. R. Hain (Warwickshire; FC/50), M. D. E. Holden (Middlesex; FC), W. G. Jacks (Surrey; FC/50), S. Mahmood (Lancashire; 50), T. J. Moores (Nottinghamshire; FC/50), S. J. Mullaney (Nottinghamshire; FC/50), J. Overton (Somerset; FC/50), O. J. D. Pope (Surrey; FC/50), J. A. Porter (Essex; FC/50), G. S. Virdi (Surrey; FC). *Coach:* A. Flower. *Batting coach:* J. L. Trott. *Fast-bowling coach:* K. J. Shine. *Spin-bowling coach:* P. M. Such. *Fielding coach:* C. D. Hopkinson.
   J. M. Clarke (Nottinghamshire) and T. Köhler-Cadmore (Yorkshire) were originally selected, but withdrawn by the ECB after revelations in the rape trial of their former Worcestershire team-mate Alex Hepburn; Jacks and Moores were named as replacements. Mullaney was added to the 50-over squad after Moores injured his leg. Visa complications meant Mahmood was late arriving in India, and Bailey was added to the 50-over squad as cover.

At Thumba, January 18, 2019. **Indian Board President's XI won by four wickets.** ‡England Lions **255-6** (50 overs) (A. L. Davies 100; M. Markande 3-41); **Indian Board President's XI 256-6** (49.2 overs) (R. D. Gaikwad 110, R. K. Bhui 93*; Z. J. Chappell 3-53). *Alex Davies made a steady* *century, but Ruturaj Gaikwad put on 94 with Ishan Kishan (36), and 124 with Ricky Bhui. The President's XI lost five for 26 after Gaikwad was out, though had enough in hand.*

At Thumba, January 20, 2019. **Indian Board President's XI won by five wickets. England Lions 104** (22.3 overs) (S. W. Billings 52; P. Jaswal 4-16, N. Saini 4-32); ‡**Indian Board President's XI 105-5** (21.2 overs) (J. A. Porter 5-36). *Apart from captain Sam Billings, only opener Will Jacks (14) reached double figures in a miserable Lions batting display. The President's XI also made an uncertain start, but Deepak Hooda (36*) and Kishan (34) put on 52 from 36-3. Jamie Porter took all five wickets that eventually fell, including Kishan and Himmat Singh with successive balls. The President's XI chose from 14 players.*

First A-Team one-day international   At Thiruvananthapuram, January 23, 2019. **India A won by three wickets. England Lions 285-7** (50 overs) (A. L. Davies 54, S. W. Billings 108*); ‡**India A 288-7** (49.1 overs) (A. M. Rahane 59, I. P. Kishan 57*; Z. J. Chappell 3-84). *PoM: I. P. Kishan. This was a tale of two captains: Billings underpinned a competitive Lions total with a busy century, finishing with 108* from 104 balls, then Ajinkya Rahane made sure India A got off to a good start with 59 from 87. When Rahane and Hanuma Vihari fell to Danny Briggs to make it 166-4 in the 34th over, the match was in the balance, but Kishan (57* off 48) and Krunal Pandya (29) kept their side on course with a stand of 60, and the winning boundary came in the final over.*

Second A-Team one-day international   At Thiruvananthapuram, January 25, 2019. **India A won by 138 runs. India A 303-6** (50 overs) (A. M. Rahane 91, G. H. Vihari 92, S. S. Iyer 65); ‡**England Lions 165** (37.4 overs) (M. Markande 3-32). *PoM: G. H. Vihari. Billings decided to bowl first, and was rewarded with an early wicket, but then the attack perspired for 30 overs while Rahane and Vihari put on 181. Both were out in the nineties, but Shreyas Iyer cracked 65 from 47 to lift the total past 300. The Lions were never in touch, not helped by losing Sam Hain and Ollie Pope for second-ball ducks.*

Third A-Team one-day international   At Thiruvananthapuram, January 27, 2019. **India A won by 60 runs. ‡India A 172** (47.1 overs) (J. Overton 3-34); **England Lions 112** (30.5 overs) (K. H. Pandya 4-21). *PoM: K. H. Pandya. India clinched the series with another comfortable victory, their bowlers to the fore this time. Their batsmen had struggled after Lewis Gregory pinned Rahane with the first ball of the match, and the Lions looked well on top at 111-7. But Deepak Chahar thrashed 39 from No. 9, with four sixes, to give his fellow bowlers something to defend. Openers Alex Davies and Will Jacks managed a single between them, and when slow left-armer Pandya – who finished with four wickets – trapped Ben Duckett (39), it was game over at 78-7.*

Fourth A-Team one-day international   At Thiruvananthapuram, January 29, 2019. **India A won by six wickets. ‡England Lions 221-8** (50 overs) (O. J. D. Pope 65, S. J. Mullaney 58*; S. N. Thakur 4-49); **India A 222-4** (46.3 overs) (R. R. Pant 73*). *PoM: R. R. Pant. The Lions made another indifferent start, slipping to 55-4, before Billings (24) put on 58 with Pope, who then added 63 with Steven Mullaney. Seamer Shardul Thakur took four wickets. An upset looked possible with India A 102-4 in the 28th, but Rishabh Pant and Hooda (47*) – like Thakur, playing their first match of the series – scorched to a 4–0 lead by piling on 120* in 19 overs. There was a brief interruption when a swarm of bees flew over the ground, bothering some spectators.*

Fifth A-Team one-day international   At Thiruvananthapuram, January 31, 2019. **England Lions won by one wicket. ‡India A 121** (35 overs) (J. Overton 3-24); **England Lions 125-9** (30.3 overs) (B. M. Duckett 70*; D. L. Chahar 3-25, R. D. Chahar 3-43). *PoM: B. M. Duckett. The Lions picked up a consolation victory, although they made a meal of it. Gregory again took a wicket with the first ball of the match – K. L. Rahul this time – and India A could not recover from 72-7. The Lions sprinted to 87-4 in the 17th over but, with only 35 needed, lost five for 27. The Chahar cousins, Deepak and Rahul, shared six wickets. Duckett was still there, and he and last man Tim Bailey collected the 11 required. It took six overs before Duckett – who hit ten fours – swung Rahul Chahar away for the winning six.*

At Thumba, February 3–4 (not first-class). **Drawn. England Lions 145-6 dec** (60 overs) (A. Rajpoot 4-20) **and 83-2 dec** (30 overs); ‡**Indian Board President's XI 134-5 dec** (30 overs) **and 246-6 dec** (59.3 overs) (R. K. Bhui 51, I. P. Kishan 55*). *It was decided beforehand that the Lions (who chose from all 16 tourists) would bat for 60 overs and the President's XI (who chose from 13) for 30 on the first day, and vice versa on the second. The Lions found it hard going in the first innings, Hain top-scored with 40*, from 118 balls. Kishan made 40* from 49 in the President's XI first innings, and 55 from 55 in the second, hitting six sixes in all.*

INDIA A v ENGLAND LIONS

First A-Team Test

At Wayanad, February 7–10, 2019. Drawn. Toss: India A.

England Lions tenaciously batted through the final day with few alarms: Pope shared a third-wicket stand of 105 in 40 overs with Hain, who faced 178 balls in all, and did not fall until the draw was assured. They were helped by a docile pitch, on which India A had run up 540, although off-spinner Jalaj Saxena and the experienced slow left-armer Shahbaz Nadeem found slow turn on the fourth day. On the first, Duckett had punched 15 fours in an aggressive 80, and there were more sedate sixties for Hain and Jacks. After Navdeep Saini polished off the innings in an hour on the second day, Rahul played himself back to form with a patient 89, which took 69 overs, although he missed out on his first century since the Oval Test in September 2018. The Lions sniffed an opening next day at 262 for four – India A captain Ankit Bawne fell for a duck – but Priyank Panchal and wicketkeeper Srikar Bharat slammed the door shut with a stand of 196. Panchal went on to 206, his third first-class double-century, and the declaration came with the lead exactly 200. Openers Holden and Duckett survived five overs on the third evening and, though both fell next morning – Holden to a catch at silly point he was convinced he had touched the ground – the Lions hung on, helped by two brief stoppages for bad light.

Close of play: first day, England Lions 303-5 (Mullaney 39, Jacks 40); second day, India A 219-1 (Rahul 88, Panchal 89); third day, England Lions 20-0 (Holden 9, Duckett 9).

England Lions

M. D. E. Holden c Srikar Bharat b Saini	26	– c Easwaran b Saxena	29
B. M. Duckett b Thakur	80	– c Rahul b Aavesh Khan	30
S. R. Hain c Srikar Bharat b Saxena	61	– lbw b Saxena	57
O. J. D. Pope b Aavesh Khan	8	– c Srikar Bharat b Nadeem	63
*†S. W. Billings c Srikar Bharat b Saini	9	– c Easwaran b Nadeem	5
S. J. Mullaney b Saini	42	– not out	3
W. G. Jacks lbw b Nadeem	63	– not out	13
L. Gregory b Thakur	3		
D. R. Briggs lbw b Saini	1		
Z. J. Chappell b Saini	6		
J. A. Porter not out	1		
B 12, lb 21, w 3, nb 4	40	B 5, lb 8, nb 1	14

1/82 (1) 2/130 (3) 3/162 (4)   (104.3 overs) 340   1/63 (2)   (5 wkts, 82 overs) 214
4/201 (5) 5/238 (3) 6/310 (6)   2/81 (1) 3/186 (4)
7/321 (8) 8/322 (9) 9/338 (7) 10/340 (10)   4/198 (5) 5/198 (3)

Thakur 24–1–77–2; Saini 23.3–5–79–5; Aavesh Khan 12–3–35–1; Saxena 17–3–49–1; Nadeem 26–6–59–1; Panchal 2–0–8–0. *Second innings*—Saini 8–0–27–0; Aavesh Khan 11–1–30–1; Saxena 25–11–41–2; Nadeem 27–11–56–2; Thakur 10–0–44–0; Easwaran 1–0–3–0.

India A

K. L. Rahul c sub (J. Overton) b Briggs	89	S. N. Thakur not out	12
A. R. Easwaran b Chappell	31		
P. K. Panchal c Billings b Chappell	206	B 12, lb 4	16
*A. R. Bawne c Billings b Chappell	0		
R. K. Bhui c Hain b Porter	16	1/48 (2) (6 wkts dec, 134.5 overs) 540
†K. Srikar Bharat c sub (J. Overton) b Briggs	142	2/222 (1) 3/223 (4)
J. S. Saxena not out	28	4/262 (5) 5/458 (3) 6/524 (6)

S. Nadeem, Aavesh Khan and N. A. Saini did not bat.

Porter 23–4–83–1; Gregory 26–7–86–0; Mullaney 25–5–61–0; Chappell 24–2–105–3; Briggs 30.5–2–144–2; Jacks 6–0–45–0.

Umpires: Y. C. Barde and V. A. Kulkarni.
Referee: D. S. Manohar.

INDIA A v ENGLAND LIONS

Second A-Team Test

At Mysore, February 13–15, 2019. India A won by an innings and 68 runs. Toss: India A.

Another batting marathon proved beyond the Lions, who slumped to defeat inside three days, and surrendered the series. In all, their two innings lasted little more than 100 overs, after India A had knocked the stuffing out of them with another big total. Rahul and Abhimanyu Easwaran led off with an opening stand of 179, before fifties from Panchal and Srikar Bharat helped push the score close to 400. The bowlers stuck to their task: seamers Bailey and Mullaney were economical, and Chappell took four wickets; slow left-armer Briggs claimed three, but was expensive. The Indian attack, spearheaded by the pacy pair of Saini and Varun Aaron, made regular inroads: no Lions batsman lasted longer than 40 balls, although seven made it into double figures. They were following on before the end of the second day, and although Duckett made a defiant 50, it was leg-spinner Mayank Markande who did most of the damage on the third, his five wickets including Gregory for 44.

Close of play: first day, India A 282-3 (Nair 14); second day, England Lions 24-0 (Holden 5, Duckett 13).

India A

*K. L. Rahul c Pope b Chappell	81	V. R. Aaron c Pope b Briggs	16
A. R. Easwaran c Pope b Bess	117	N. A. Saini not out	7
P. K. Panchal b Bailey	50		
K. K. Nair c Pope b Chappell	14	B 16, lb 11, w 2	29
S. D. Lad b Chappell	9		
†K. Srikar Bharat lbw b Briggs	46	1/179 (1) 2/252 (2) (114.4 overs)	392
J. S. Saxena c Gregory b Chappell	1	3/282 (3) 4/282 (4)	
S. Nadeem c Mullaney b Gregory	11	5/295 (5) 6/297 (7) 7/335 (8)	
M. Markande c Gregory b Briggs	11	8/354 (9) 9/368 (6) 10/392 (10)	

Gregory 20–1–75–1; Bailey 27–10–57–1; Briggs 13.4–1–71–3; Chappell 22–6–60–4; Mullaney 14–6–31–0; Bess 18–3–71–1.

England Lions

M. D. E. Holden lbw b Saini	19	– lbw b Saxena	7
B. M. Duckett c Srikar Bharat b Nadeem	15	– lbw b Saxena	50
S. R. Hain c Srikar Bharat b Aaron	5	– lbw b Nadeem	15
†O. J. D. Pope b Saini	25	– lbw b Markande	7
*S. W. Billings b Saini	5	– c Srikar Bharat b Saini	20
S. J. Mullaney b Nadeem	19	– c Lad b Markande	2
L. Gregory c Saxena b Aaron	11	– c Nair b Markande	44
D. M. Bess c Panchal b Saxena	16	– c Nair b Markande	6
T. E. Bailey not out	13	– c Srikar Bharat b Aaron	4
Z. J. Chappell c Lad b Saxena	0	– c Nair b Markande	0
D. R. Briggs b Nadeem	6	– not out	2
B 8, lb 2	10	B 14, lb 6, nb 3	23

1/23 (1) 2/33 (3) 3/46 (2)	(48.4 overs)	144	1/40 (1) 2/67 (2)	(53.3 overs) 180
4/59 (5) 5/76 (4) 6/96 (7)			3/83 (4) 4/114 (3)	
7/107 (6) 8/125 (9) 9/127 (10) 10/144 (11)			5/118 (5) 6/140 (6) 7/148 (8)	
			8/154 (9) 9/155 (10) 10/180 (7)	

Aaron 12–4–47–2; Saini 10–5–30–3; Saxena 10–4–10–2; Nadeem 9.4–1–32–3; Markande 7–1–15–0. *Second innings*—Saini 11–3–25–1; Nadeem 11–6–25–1; Saxena 12–3–40–2; Aaron 9–1–39–1; Markande 10.3–1–31–5.

Umpires: K. N. Ananthapadmanabhan and N. Pandit.
Referee: P. R. Mohapatra.

DOMESTIC CRICKET IN INDIA IN 2018-19

R. MOHAN

It was a record-breaking season in more ways than one. The number of teams in the Ranji Trophy rose from 28 to 37 after India's Supreme Court ruled that Bihar, who were supplanted by newly independent Jharkhand early in the century, should regain first-class status. The BCCI also added seven north-eastern states plus the union of Puducherry, putting the nine new teams in a Plate division from which one side qualified for the quarter-finals. It meant that, including age-group sides, there were 2,024 matches played by 4,600 cricketers across 105 cities.

Some felt the quality of cricket in the Plate Group diluted standards, but statisticians were kept busy: slow left-armer Ashutosh Aman took 68 wickets for Bihar at an astonishing average of 6.48 – beating Bishan Bedi's Ranji record of 64 at 8.53 in 1974-75 – with nine five-fors and five hauls of ten in a match. Milind Kumar of Sikkim scored 1,331 runs at 121, briefly threatening V. V. S. Laxman's all-time tournament record of 1,415 in 1999-2000. Back in the Elite groups, Madhya Pradesh opener Ajay Rohera broke the world record for the highest score on first-class debut, with an unbeaten 267 against Hyderabad, beating Amol Muzumdar's 260 for Mumbai in 1993-94.

Vidarbha became only the third team to defend the double of the Ranji Trophy and the Irani Cup, following Mumbai and Karnataka. They won a hard-fought Ranji final against Saurashtra on a sluggish home pitch in Nagpur, and were 11 short of an outright victory over the Rest of India in the Irani game, but retained the cup on first-innings lead. Their future looked bright too: after a pre-season resident programme for young players in Nagpur, their Under-19 and Under-23 sides won 50-over competitions, and the Under-19s were runners-up in the four-day final.

But it was 40-year-old Wasim Jaffer who led Vidarbha's batting. He was the only man in the Elite groups to reach 1,000 runs, including four centuries, extending his Ranji record to 40 (he had made 35 for Mumbai). He set another tournament record when he clocked up 149 appearances. Aditya Sarwate was their most successful bowler with 55 wickets, just behind fellow left-arm spinner Dharmendrasinh Jadeja, who took 59 for Saurashtra. In the Irani Cup, Akshay Karnewar surprised umpires and batsmen by switching from slow left-arm to right-arm off-spin, for the first time at this level, and followed up with a maiden century; he had also played a key role in the Ranji final, shoring up Vidarbha's first innings with 73 not out in the company of the tail.

> ## Shahbaz Nadeem took eight for ten, the best return in List A cricket

In the 50-over Vijay Hazare Trophy, yet another left-arm spinner, Shahbaz Nadeem, collected the best return in all List A cricket, 10–4–10–8 for Jharkhand against Rajasthan, beating eight for 15 by Delhi's Rahul Sanghvi in 1997-98. **Mumbai** beat Delhi in the tournament final, though when it came to four-day cricket neither qualified for the Ranji knockout – the first time Mumbai had gone out at the group stage in 11 seasons. **Karnataka** won the Syed Mushtaq Ali T20 competition with a 100% record in their 12 games. The Duleep Trophy, now contested by three representative teams, was played with pink balls at a new first-class venue, Dindigul in southern India; **India Blue** won the final by an innings when their spinners routed the Red team. A high-scoring Deodhar Trophy final was won by **India C**, who had two centuries to India B's one.

The BCCI continued their experiment of sending out neutral groundsmen to counter the problem of clubs preparing dust bowls for home advantage; the balance swung towards harder and greener pitches before a call went out ahead of the Ranji knockouts to provide more assistance to spinners. Meanwhile, the recurrent problem of poor umpiring was exacerbated by the number of matches, and there was an allegation that exams for aspiring domestic umpires were being leaked to some candidates.

FIRST-CLASS AVERAGES IN 2018-19

BATTING (750 runs)

		M	I	NO	R	HS	100	Avge	Ct/St
1	Milind Kumar (*Sikkim*)	8	14	3	1,331	261	6	121.00	8
2	†R. K. Singh (*Uttar Pradesh*)	10	13	4	953	163*	4	105.88	5
3	P. Bisht (*Meghalaya*)	8	12	2	892	343	2	89.20	16/2
4	S. Gill (*Punjab/India A*)	6	11	2	782	268	2	86.88	5
5	Y. Nagar (*Meghalaya*)	8	12	2	865	166	4	86.50	7
6	A. R. Easwaran (*Bengal/India A*) . . .	10	16	2	1,131	201*	4	80.78	6
7	P. Akshath Reddy (*Hyderabad*)	8	12	2	797	250	2	79.70	4
8	Yashpal Singh (*Manipur*)	8	15	4	860	156*	4	78.18	7
9	†A. A. Kazi (*Nagaland*)	8	14	3	814	200*	3	74.00	3
10	Wasim Jaffer (*Vidarbha*)	11	15	0	1,037	206	4	69.13	10
11	T. S. Kohli (*Mizoram*)	8	16	4	826	156	2	68.83	6
12	P. K. Garg (*Uttar Pradesh*)	10	15	3	814	206	2	67.83	9
13	R. N. B. Indrajith (*Tamil Nadu/Ind Grn*)	10	15	2	790	109	3	60.76	19
14	P. K. Panchal (*Gujarat/Ind A/Ind Grn*)	13	22	2	1,164	206	5	58.20	11
15	R. Jonathan (*Nagaland*)	8	14	0	809	131	3	57.78	5
16	A. V. Wadkar (*Vidarbha/India Red*) . .	14	21	5	899	144*	3	56.18	23/7
17	R. K. Bhui (*Andhra/India A/India Blue*)	12	19	0	949	187	4	49.94	9
18	S. P. Jackson (*Saurashtra*)	11	21	3	853	147	2	47.38	10
19	†A. Mukund (*Tamil Nadu/India A*)	11	18	0	790	178	3	43.88	5
20	K. Srikar Bharat (*Andhra/Ind A/Ind Bl*)	13	21	2	829	178*	3	43.63	48/4
21	S. D. Lad (*Mumbai/India A/India Red*)	10	19	0	825	130	2	43.42	4
22	†F. Y. Fazal (*Vidarbha/India Blue*)	15	23	1	942	151	3	42.81	17
23	H. M. Desai (*Saurashtra*)	11	21	0	781	116	1	37.19	21
24	S. S. Patel (*Saurashtra*)	11	21	0	760	102	1	36.19	28/1

BOWLING (35 wickets, average 25.00)

		Style	O	M	R	W	BB	5I	Avge
1	A. Aman (*Bihar*)	SLA	231.3	76	441	68	8-51	9	6.48
2	Pankaj Singh (*Puducherry*)	RFM	172.5	56	412	45	7-21	3	9.15
3	B. C. Mohanty (*Odisha*)	RFM	281.2	100	515	44	6-20	4	11.70
4	A. V. Choudhary (*Rajasthan*)	LM	281.3	66	721	49	5-11	7	14.71
5	D. Dhapola (*Uttarakhand*)	RM	268.2	60	698	45	7-50	6	15.51
6	S. S. Quadri (*Bihar*)	LB	182.3	33	544	35	6-19	3	15.54
7	Gurender Singh (*Meghalaya*)	SLA	354.1	88	897	53	6-41	5	16.92
8	Aavesh Khan (*Madhya Prad/Ind A*) . .	RM	204.2	41	638	37	7-24	3	17.24
9	S. Sandeep Warrier (*Kerala*)	RFM	316	87	772	44	5-33	4	17.54
10	J. D. Unadkat (*Ind Blue/Saurashtra*) .	LFM	307	78	816	46	7-86	3	17.73
11	Saurabh Kumar (*Ind Bl/Uttar Pradesh*)	SLA	499	140	1,271	70	7-32	7	18.15
12	R. G. More (*Karnataka*)	RM	231.4	47	696	37	6-60	4	18.81
13	R. Mohanty (*Odisha*)	RFM	240.5	44	777	40	6-55	3	19.42
14	Tanveer-ul-Hak (*Rajasthan/Rest*)	LFM	376.2	105	1,019	51	6-42	2	19.98
15	I. H. Chaudhary (*Sikkim*)	RM	268.2	46	1,050	51	7-51	5	20.58
16	A. K. Das (*Assam*)	RM	256.2	60	765	36	6-67	3	21.25
17	A. A. Sarwate (*Ind Green/Vidarbha*) .	SLA	514	112	1,412	66	6-43	7	21.39
18	D. Pathania (*Services*)	RM	348	83	863	39	5-56	2	22.12
19	B. Thampi (*India Blue/Kerala*)	RFM	245.4	45	823	36	5-27	1	22.86
20	Parvez Rasool (*Ind Red/Jam & Kash*)	OB	402.5	88	1,063	46	8-85	2	23.10
21	A. Rajpoot (*Ind A/Ind Gr/UP/Rest*) . .	RM	416.3	97	1,225	52	6-25	3	23.55
22	M. K. Hussain (*Assam*)	RFM	300.5	49	966	40	5-39	3	24.15
23	S. Nadeem (*Ind Red/Ind A/Jharkhand*)	SLA	374.2	111	895	37	7-62	2	24.18
24	J. S. Saxena (*Ind Gr/Kerala/Ind A*) . .	OB	362.3	75	877	36	8-45	2	24.36
25	V. Mishra (*India Green/Delhi*)	SLA	396.3	82	952	39	6-30	3	24.41

DULEEP TROPHY IN 2018-19

	P	W	L	D	1st-inns pts	Pts	Quotient
INDIA RED	2	0	0	2	4	6	1.44
INDIA BLUE	2	0	0	2	2	4	0.87
India Green	2	0	0	2	0	2	0.78

Outright win = 6pts; lead on first innings in a drawn match = 3pts; deficit on first innings in a drawn match = 1pt; no decision on first innings = 1pt.

Final At Dindigul, September 4–7, 2018 (day/night). **India Blue won by an innings and 187 runs. ‡India Blue 541** (N. Gangta 130); **India Red 182** (Swapnil Singh 5-58) **and 172** (D. Hooda 5-56, Saurabh Kumar 5-51). *India Blue piled up 541 over two days, thanks to big partnerships between Ricky Bhui and Anmolpreet Singh, who added 144, and Nikhil Gangta and Swapnil Singh, who put on 153. Then their spinners bowled out Red twice by the penultimate morning, with five-wicket hauls for slow left-armers Swapnil and Saurabh Kumar, and off-spinner Deepak Hooda.*

RANJI TROPHY IN 2018-19

Elite A	P	W	L	D	1st-inns pts	Bonus	Pts	Quotient
VIDARBHA	8	3	0	5	4	2	29	1.34
SAURASHTRA	8	3	0	5	6	0	29	1.10
KARNATAKA	8	3	2	3	6	0	27	1.31
GUJARAT	8	3	0	5	2	1	26	1.30
Baroda	8	3	1	4	4	0	26	1.05
Mumbai	8	1	2	5	6	0	17	0.92
Railways	8	1	4	3	4	1	14	0.86
Maharashtra	8	0	4	4	4	0	8	0.69
Chhattisgarh	8	0	4	4	2	0	6	0.63

Elite B	P	W	L	D	1st-inns pts	Bonus	Pts	Quotient
KERALA	8	4	3	1	0	1	26	1.15
Madhya Pradesh	8	3	2	3	2	1	24	1.13
Bengal	8	2	1	5	6	0	23	1.07
Punjab	8	2	1	5	4	2	23	1.01
Himachal Pradesh	8	3	3	2	0	2	22	1.04
Andhra	8	1	2	5	6	0	17	0.90
Hyderabad	8	1	1	6	4	1	17	0.84
Tamil Nadu	8	1	2	5	4	0	15	1.01
Delhi	8	1	3	4	4	0	14	0.82

Elite C	P	W	L	D	1st-inns pts	Bonus	Pts	Quotient
RAJASTHAN	9	7	0	2	4	3	51	1.55
UTTAR PRADESH	9	5	0	4	4	3	41	1.98
Jharkhand	9	5	1	3	6	1	40	1.27
Odisha	9	4	3	2	0	0	26	1.10
Haryana	9	3	4	2	2	0	22	0.84
Assam	9	3	4	2	0	1	21	0.84
Jammu & Kashmir	9	3	5	1	0	0	19	0.82
Services	9	2	3	4	2	1	19	0.93
Tripura	9	1	6	2	2	1	11	0.71
Goa	9	0	7	2	4	0	6	0.63

					1st-inns			
Plate	P	W	L	D	pts	Bonus	Pts	Quotient
UTTARAKHAND............	8	6	0	2	2	4	44	2.43
Bihar	8	6	1	1*	0	3	40	2.30
Puducherry	8	4	0	4*	2	3	33	1.83
Meghalaya	8	4	2	2	2	1	29	1.34
Sikkim	8	4	3	1	0	2	27	0.75
Manipur	8	4	5	0	0	0	18	0.85
Nagaland	8	2	4	2	2	2	18	1.03
Arunachal Pradesh	8	0	7	1	2	0	3	0.43
Mizoram	8	0	7	1	0	0	1	0.38

*   *Includes one abandoned match.*

Outright win = 6pts; bonus for winning by an innings or ten wickets = 1pt; lead on first innings in a drawn match = 3pts; deficit on first innings in a drawn match = 1pt; no decision on first innings = 1pt; abandoned = 1pt. Teams tied on points were ranked on most wins, and then on quotient.

The five teams with most points across Elite A and B, the top two from Elite C and the top Plate team advanced to the quarter-finals.

Quarter-finals   Karnataka beat Rajasthan by six wickets; Kerala beat Gujarat by 113 runs; Saurashtra beat Uttar Pradesh by six wickets; Vidarbha beat Uttarakhand by an innings and 115 runs.

Semi-finals   Saurashtra beat Karnataka by five wickets; Vidarbha beat Kerala by an innings and 11 runs.

Final   At Nagpur (VCA Academy), February 3–7, 2019. **Vidarbha won by 78 runs.** ‡**Vidarbha 312 and 200** (D. A. Jadeja 6-96); **Saurashtra 307** (S. S. Patel 102; A. A. Sarwate 5-98) **and 127** (A. A. Sarwate 6-59). *Vidarbha retained the Ranji Trophy after left-arm spinner Aditya Sarwate collected 11-157 to finish with 55 in the tournament. Their crown seemed to be slipping on the opening day, when they were 139-6, but Akshay Karnewar batted four hours for 73* and led them to 312. Snell Patel's five-hour century, and a last-wicket stand of 60 between captain Jaydev Unadkat (46) and Chetan Sakariya (28*), kept Saurashtra's deficit down to five runs. Another slow left-armer, Dharmendrasinh Jadeja, ensured Vidarbha's top order stumbled again, but Sarwate's 49 took them from 105-6 to 200 before he skittled Saurashtra in their pursuit of 206.*

RANJI TROPHY WINNERS

1934-35	Bombay	1957-58	Baroda	1980-81	Bombay
1935-36	Bombay	1958-59	Bombay	1981-82	Delhi
1936-37	Nawanagar	1959-60	Bombay	1982-83	Karnataka
1937-38	Hyderabad	1960-61	Bombay	1983-84	Bombay
1938-39	Bengal	1961-62	Bombay	1984-85	Bombay
1939-40	Maharashtra	1962-63	Bombay	1985-86	Delhi
1940-41	Maharashtra	1963-64	Bombay	1986-87	Hyderabad
1941-42	Bombay	1964-65	Bombay	1987-88	Tamil Nadu
1942-43	Baroda	1965-66	Bombay	1988-89	Delhi
1943-44	Western India	1966-67	Bombay	1989-90	Bengal
1944-45	Bombay	1967-68	Bombay	1990-91	Haryana
1945-46	Holkar	1968-69	Bombay	1991-92	Delhi
1946-47	Baroda	1969-70	Bombay	1992-93	Punjab
1947-48	Holkar	1970-71	Bombay	1993-94	Bombay
1948-49	Bombay	1971-72	Bombay	1994-95	Bombay
1949-50	Baroda	1972-73	Bombay	1995-96	Karnataka
1950-51	Holkar	1973-74	Karnataka	1996-97	Mumbai
1951-52	Bombay	1974-75	Bombay	1997-98	Karnataka
1952-53	Holkar	1975-76	Bombay	1998-99	Karnataka
1953-54	Bombay	1976-77	Bombay	1999-2000	Mumbai
1954-55	Madras	1977-78	Karnataka	2000-01	Baroda
1955-56	Bombay	1978-79	Delhi	2001-02	Railways
1956-57	Bombay	1979-80	Delhi	2002-03	Mumbai

2003-04	Mumbai		2009-10	Mumbai		2015-16	Mumbai
2004-05	Railways		2010-11	Rajasthan		2016-17	Gujarat
2005-06	Uttar Pradesh		2011-12	Rajasthan		2017-18	Vidarbha
2006-07	Mumbai		2012-13	Mumbai		2018-19	Vidarbha
2007-08	Delhi		2013-14	Karnataka			
2008-09	Mumbai		2014-15	Karnataka			

Bombay/Mumbai have won the Ranji Trophy 41 times, Karnataka 8, Delhi 7, Baroda 5, Holkar 4, Bengal, Hyderabad, Madras/Tamil Nadu, Maharashtra, Railways, Rajasthan and Vidarbha 2, Gujarat, Haryana, Nawanagar, Punjab, Uttar Pradesh and Western India 1.

IRANI CUP IN 2018-19

Ranji Trophy Champions (Vidarbha) v Rest of India

At Nagpur (VCA Academy), February 12–16, 2019. **Drawn. Vidarbha won by virtue of their first-innings lead. ‡Rest of India 330** (G. H. Vihari 114) **and 374-3 dec** (G. H. Vihari 180*); **Vidarbha 425** (A. K. Karnewar 102) **and 269-5.** *For the second year running, Hanuma Vihari scored a century for the Rest, and he later made it three in three innings during a 229-run partnership with his captain, Ajinkya Rahane (87), who set a target of 280. Vidarbha finished 11 short with five down, but retained the Irani Cup on their first-innings lead, established by No. 8 Akshay Karnewar's maiden hundred.*

VIJAY HAZARE TROPHY IN 2018-19

Four 50-over leagues plus knockout

Quarter-finals   Delhi beat Haryana by five wickets; Mumbai beat Bihar by nine wickets; Hyderabad beat Andhra by 14 runs; Jharkhand beat Maharashtra by eight wickets (VJD).

Semi-finals   Mumbai beat Hyderabad by 60 runs (VJD); Delhi beat Jharkhand by two wickets.

Final   At Bangalore, October 20, 2018. **Mumbai won by four wickets. Delhi 177** (45.4 overs); **‡Mumbai 180-6** (35 overs). *Mumbai coasted to victory with 15 overs to spare, despite Navdeep Saini reducing them to 25-3 in the first five; Siddhesh Lad (48) and wicketkeeper Aditya Tare (71) put them back on course, adding 105 for the fifth wicket. Earlier, Tare had made three catches and a stumping, as Delhi also had a shaky start – 21-3 in six – and a less convincing fightback.*

DEODHAR TROPHY IN 2018-19

50-over knockout for India A, India B and India C

Final   At Delhi (Feroz Shah Kotla), October 27, 2018. **India C won by 29 runs. ‡India C 352-7** (50 overs) (A. M. Rahane 144*, I. P. Kishan 114); **India B 323** (46.1 overs) (S. S. Iyer 148). *After winning the toss, Ajinkya Rahane batted throughout his side's innings, surging to a stand of 210 in 31 overs with fellow opener Ishan Kishan – though there was an embarrassing moment when he celebrated his century, only to find that the scoreboard had made an error, and he was still 97. India B were just ahead of the asking-rate as Shreyas Iyer steered them to 309-6, striking eight sixes in a one-day-best 148, but they fell away once he was dismissed by leg-spinner Rahul Chahar.*

SYED MUSHTAQ ALI TROPHY IN 2018-19

Five 20-over leagues, two super leagues plus final

Final   At Indore (Holkar), March 14, 2019 (floodlit). **Karnataka won by eight wickets. Maharashtra 155-4** (20 overs); **‡Karnataka 159-2** (18.3 overs). *Karnataka, who had won 14 consecutive Twenty20 games since January 2018, clinched their first T20 title. Naushad Shaikh dominated Maharashtra's innings, with 69* in 41 balls, but Mayank Agarwal smashed 85* in 57, adding 92 in ten overs for Karnataka's second wicket with the tournament's leading scorer, Rohan Kadam (60 in 39).*

The Vivo Indian Premier League has its own section (page 1135).

IRISH CRICKET IN 2019

Reality bites

IAN CALLENDER

If the Lord's Test was Irish cricket's highlight, then qualification for this year's T20 World Cup in Australia was the most important achievement. It offered some compensation for the huge disappointment of missing the one-day World Cup in England. Yet as one storm cleared, others formed. In December came a series of blows: financial constraints at Cricket Ireland meant their second home Test, against Bangladesh and scheduled for May 2020, was downgraded to a Twenty20 international, while a T20 series against Afghanistan, planned for August, was cancelled. A couple of days later, it transpired that February's Test in Sri Lanka was off too, because the hosts had been unable to find a broadcaster. The hope was that it could be scheduled for later in the year.

In 2019, Ireland played 39 games – only in 2010 had that total been higher – winning 19 and losing 19, with one, against Afghanistan at Dehradun in

IRELAND IN 2019

	Played	Won	Lost	Drawn/No result
Tests	2	–	2	–
One-day internationals	14	6	7	1
Twenty20 internationals	23	13	10	–

JANUARY		
FEBRUARY ⎫	T20I series (in Oman) v Oman, Netherlands and Scotland	(page 1098)
MARCH ⎭	1 Test, 5 ODIs and 3 T20Is (in India) v Afghanistan	(page 862)
APRIL		
MAY	1 ODI (h) v England	(page 364)
	ODI tri-series (h) v Bangladesh and West Indies	(page 969)
	2 ODIs (h) v Afghanistan	(page 972)
JUNE		
JULY	3 ODIs and 2 T20Is (h) v Zimbabwe	(page 973)
	1 Test (a) v England	(page 374)
AUGUST		
SEPTEMBER	T20I tri-series (h) v Netherlands and Scotland	(page 975)
OCTOBER ⎫	T20I series (in Oman) v Oman, Hong Kong, Nepal and Netherlands	(page 1100)
NOVEMBER ⎭	Twenty20 World Cup Qualifier (in the UAE)	(page 1086)
DECEMBER		

For a review of Irish domestic cricket from the 2019 season, see page 977.

Packing a punch: Andrew Balbirnie, later named captain in all formats, celebrates a wicket at Lord's.

India, rained off. Most encouragement came in the shortest format, where Ireland won 13 out of 23, although only one, against Zimbabwe at Bready, of their five against fellow Full Members. Whether that form is good enough to make much impact in Australia must be doubtful, but at least Ireland have risen to 14th in the world rankings. And, in January 2020, they defeated West Indies by four runs in Grenada, on the back of a 47-ball 95 from Paul Stirling.

Andrew Balbirnie was captain for that T20 victory, after he was asked to lead in all formats in November. His predecessor, William Porterfield, had been in charge of the Test and ODI teams only, and Gary Wilson was replaced as T20 captain. Porterfield had been at the helm since April 2008, for a staggering 253 matches (including 172 internationals). He won 129 and lost 106 – only Jason Molins has a better win percentage, though from just 41 games.

Graham Ford gave seven new caps – after none in the previous 21 months – with five in the squad for the T20 World Cup Qualifier in the UAE. Topping their group guaranteed them a place in Australia, though they lost their semi-final to the Netherlands, before overcoming Namibia in the third-place play-off.

The find of the year was Mark Adair, a 23-year-old former Warwickshire pace bowler who won a surprise debut in the ODI against England in May, after an injury to Stuart Thompson. Adair, who was there as a net bowler, took his chance and, though he had to wait until his second match to claim a wicket, he hit 32 off 30 balls against England. He played all 27 games to the end of 2019, and picked up 48 wickets – only three bowlers have taken more in a calendar year for Ireland. In August, he was given a central contract.

Other additions to the T20 squad included 21-year-old David Delany, who offered raw pace, his 22-year-old cousin, Gareth Delany, who provided power hitting, and Harry Tector, a middle-order batsman. South Africa-born Shane

Getkate, a seam-bowling all-rounder, made his debut in a quadrangular T20 series in Oman at the start of the year, but had more success against Zimbabwe in July, when Ireland enjoyed their first clean sweep against a Full Member.

By the end of 2019, Gareth Delany had a T20 strike-rate of 152, the highest of any Ireland player, and was threatening to disrupt the experienced top order of Stirling, Kevin O'Brien and Balbirnie. Until last year, O'Brien had not opened in T20 internationals, but his elevation to bat alongside Stirling in Oman was an instant success. In their second match, against Scotland, they put on 115, an Irish T20 all-wicket record; eight days later, against Afghanistan in Dehradun, they managed 126. Neither could avert defeat.

Registration changes resulting from Ireland becoming a Full Member meant that Stirling would be counted as an overseas player if he stayed at Middlesex. To Ford's relief, if not his county's, he chose to follow the international path (and then joined Northamptonshire for the T20 Blast – as an overseas player). Stirling was the year's outstanding batsman across the formats, finishing with 1,516 runs at an average of 43; Balbirnie (1,314 at 38) and O'Brien (1,147 at 31) were not far behind. In one-day internationals, Balbirnie enjoyed a purple patch that began with an unbeaten 145 against Afghanistan, and contained two more centuries and a fifty in his next nine innings.

James McCollum, a top-order batsman, and James Cameron-Dow, a slow left-armer born in Cape Town, were capped during the one-day series against Afghanistan in March; Ireland won the last by five wickets, and shared the series 2–2. Later on the tour, the pair were two of five Test debutants, along with George Dockrell, Andy McBrine and, in his farewell Ireland match after committing to Durham, Stuart Poynter. Afghanistan won by seven wickets.

By lunch on the first day of the Test against England, Ireland were in dreamland. Tim Murtagh had put his name on the honours board after taking five for 13 – the cheapest Test five-for at Lord's – and England were humbled for 85. Ireland gained a lead of 122, thanks mainly to a second Test half-century from Balbirnie, but that was nullified by 92 from nightwatchman Jack Leach. On an overcast third morning, a target of 182 was never likely. But a total of 38 (another Lord's Test record) was more living nightmare than dreamland. In another unwelcome development, Murtagh, who turned 38 a week later, chose to see out his career with Middlesex.

In a one-day tri-series involving Bangladesh and West Indies, and shared between Clontarf and Malahide, Ireland lost three games; a fourth fell victim to rain. They were not wholly outclassed, setting West Indies 328, and Bangladesh 293, before losing both. Ireland split a two-match ODI series against Afghanistan in Belfast, and a two-match T20 series against Zimbabwe in Bready. And they won a T20 tri-series in Malahide against the Netherlands and Scotland in September. The following month, they flew to Oman for a short T20 pentangular, coming second to the hosts.

Ireland's women failed to reach the T20 World Cup when they lost to Bangladesh in the semi-final of the qualifying tournament in Dundee in September. Despite the disappointment, Ed Joyce – in interim charge at the time – was appointed head coach a fortnight later.

IRELAND TRI-NATION SERIES IN 2019

Ian Callender

1 Bangladesh   2 West Indies   3 Ireland

Bangladesh, with their full World Cup squad available, won the Dublin tri-series with something to spare. Their first game, against Ireland, was washed out, but they easily topped the table. Then, in the rain-interrupted final, they had to score 58 more runs than West Indies had in 24 overs, yet won with seven balls to spare.

No Bangladeshi reached 200 runs overall – left-hander Soumya Sarkar made 193 – but they had four of the leading nine batsmen, plus four of the top seven wicket-takers. And, in a high-scoring series, the economy-rates were particularly impressive: of those who bowled at least ten overs, only Mosaddek Hossain, Mehedi Hasan, Shakib Al Hasan and Mohammad Saifuddin went for less than five.

The pitches were slow but true. Every match was won by the side that batted second, apart from the opening game, when West Indies racked up 381 for three against Ireland, including a world-record first-wicket stand of 365 between John Campbell and Shai Hope.

West Indies were without seven of their World Cup squad, still at the IPL, although there was no excuse for lethargic fielding. Hope was the outstanding batsman, with 470 runs, almost 200 more than his team-mate Sunil Ambris. Campbell cracked 179 in that huge opening stand, but missed the rest of the tournament with a back injury. As they had shown not long before against England, West Indies had a formidable one-day batting line-up. But, of the bowlers, only Shannon Gabriel averaged under 31; five others exceeded 66.

Hosts Ireland had a similar problem. Their main batsmen all contributed, but the bowlers leaked more than 1,000 runs over three games. Andrew Balbirnie proved himself the natural successor to Ed Joyce at No. 3 with a superb 135 against West Indies – his fourth ODI century since January 2018 – although he received a demerit point for his reaction to an umpiring howler against Bangladesh. William Porterfield dropped to No. 4 where, at the second attempt, he hit a half-century, his first for 23 international innings. But the bowlers managed only 12 wickets; Tim Murtagh and George Dockrell sent down 44 fruitless overs between them.

NATIONAL SQUADS

Ireland   *W. T. S. Porterfield, M. R. Adair, A. Balbirnie, G. H. Dockrell, J. B. Little, A. R. McBrine, B. J. McCarthy, J. A. McCollum, T. J. Murtagh, K. J. O'Brien, W. B. Rankin, P. R. Stirling, L. J. Tucker, G. C. Wilson. *Coach:* G. X. Ford.
    S. R. Thompson was originally selected, but injured his shoulder and was replaced by Adair.

Bangladesh   *Mashrafe bin Mortaza, Abu Jayed, Farhad Reza, Liton Das, Mahmudullah, Mehedi Hasan, Mithun Ali, Mohammad Saifuddin, Mosaddek Hossain, Mushfiqur Rahim, Mustafizur Rahman, Nayeem Hasan, Rubel Hossain, Sabbir Rahman, Shakib Al Hasan, Soumya Sarkar, Tamim Iqbal, Taskin Ahmed, Yasir Ali. *Coach:* S. J. Rhodes.

West Indies *J. O. Holder, F. A. Allen, S. W. Ambris, D. M. Bravo, J. D. Campbell, J. L. Carter, R. L. Chase, S. S. Cottrell, S. O. Dowrich, S. T. Gabriel, S. D. Hope, A. R. Nurse, A. R. Reifer, K. A. J. Roach. *Coach:* F. L. Reifer.

At Clontarf, May 5. **West Indies won by 196 runs.** West Indies 381-3 (50 overs) (J. D. Campbell 179, S. D. Hope 170); ‡**Ireland 185** (34.4 overs) (K. J. O'Brien 68, G. C. Wilson 30; S. T. Gabriel 3-44, A. R. Nurse 4-51). *PoM:* J. D. Campbell. *West Indies announced their arrival in Dublin with a record-smashing display against an Ireland attack that had given England a scare at Malahide two days earlier. Openers John Campbell and Shai Hope piled on a chanceless 365 in 47.2 overs.*

HIGHEST PARTNERSHIPS IN ODIs

Runs	Wkt				
372	2nd	C. H. Gayle/M. N. Samuels	WI v Z	Canberra	2014-15
365	**1st**	**J. D. Campbell/S. D. Hope.**	**WI v Ire**	**Malahide.**	**2019**
331	2nd	S. R. Tendulkar/R. Dravid	I v NZ	Hyderabad	1999-2000
318	2nd	S. C. Ganguly/R. Dravid	I v SL	Taunton	1999
304	1st	Imam-ul-Haq/Fakhar Zaman	P v Z	Bulawayo.	2018
286	1st	W. U. Tharanga/S. T. Jayasuriya.	SL v E	Leeds	2006
284	1st	D. A. Warner/T. M. Head	A v P	Adelaide.	2016-17
282*	1st	Q. de Kock/H. M. Amla.	SA v B	Kimberley	2017-18
282	1st	W. U. Tharanga/T. M. Dilshan . .	SL v Z	Pallekele	2010-11
275*	4th	M. Azharuddin/A. Jadeja.	I v Z	Cuttack	1997-98
274	1st	J. A. H. Marshall/B. B. McCullum	NZ v Ire	Aberdeen	2008

Campbell, whose five previous ODIs had produced just 69 runs, clattered 179 from 137 balls, while Hope's career-best 170 came from 152. The total was the highest in a men's ODI in Ireland; left-arm seamer Josh Little, who had taken four wickets on debut against England, came down to earth with 0-72. On a good batting surface, Ireland reached 152-3 in the 27th over, but the last seven tumbled for 33, and West Indies picked up a bonus point.

At Clontarf, May 7. **Bangladesh won by eight wickets.** ‡**West Indies 261-9** (50 overs) (S. D. Hope 109, S. W. Ambris 38, R. L. Chase 51; Mashrafe bin Mortaza 3-49); **Bangladesh 264-2** (45 overs) (Tamim Iqbal 80, Soumya Sarkar 73, Shakib Al Hasan 61*, Mushfiqur Rahim 32*). *PoM:* S. D. Hope. *ODI debut:* S. O. Dowrich (West Indies). *Hope, now partnered by Sunil Ambris as Campbell had injured his back, continued where he had left off against Ireland, purring to a sixth ODI hundred. But after reaching 205-2 in the 41st over, West Indies lost seven for 56, and Bangladesh were in charge once Tamim Iqbal and Soumya Sarkar put on 144, their country's highest opening stand against West Indies. Sarkar was out to a superb boundary catch by Darren Bravo, but some of the other fielding was undistinguished – Tamim was dropped on one – and Shakib Al Hasan gambolled to a run-a-ball 61*.*

At Malahide, May 9. **Ireland v Bangladesh. Abandoned.**

At Malahide, May 11. **West Indies won by five wickets.** ‡**Ireland 327-5** (50 overs) (P. R. Stirling 77, A. Balbirnie 135, K. J. O'Brien 63); **West Indies 331-5** (47.5 overs) (S. D. Hope 50, S. W. Ambris 148, R. L. Chase 46, J. L. Carter 43*, J. O. Holder 36; W. B. Rankin 3-65). *PoM:* S. W. Ambris. *Led by Andrew Balbirnie, who put on 146 for the second wicket with Paul Stirling and 84 for the fourth with Kevin O'Brien (63 from 40 balls), Ireland reached their second-highest ODI total at home. But it wasn't enough: with Ambris extending his maiden ODI century to 148, from 126 balls, West Indies kept abreast of the asking-rate. Although Ambris fell to the last ball of the 40th over with 76 still needed, Jonathan Carter and Jason Holder steered their side to the brink. The match aggregate of 658 was a record for an ODI in Ireland.*

At Malahide, May 13. **Bangladesh won by five wickets.** ‡**West Indies 247-9** (50 overs) (S. D. Hope 87, J. O. Holder 62; Mashrafe bin Mortaza 3-60, Mustafizur Rahman 4-43); **Bangladesh 248-5** (47.2 overs) (Soumya Sarkar 54, Mushfiqur Rahim 63, Mithun Ali 43, Mahmudullah 30*; A. R. Nurse 3-53). *PoM:* Mustafizur Rahman. *ODI debuts:* Abu Jayed (Bangladesh); R. A. Reifer (West Indies). *Bangladesh booked their place in the final, and eliminated Ireland. The West Indians produced another sloppy display in the field: Sarkar and Mushfiqur Rahim took advantage during sensible half-centuries, while Mithun Ali was dropped twice and Mahmudullah once. Hope had*

IRELAND'S HIGHEST ODI TOTALS

	Overs		
331-6	50	v Scotland (307-9) at Dubai (ICC)............................	2017-18
331-8	50	v Zimbabwe (326) at Hobart†	2014-15
329-7	49.1	v England (327-8) at Bangalore†.............................	2010-11
328-6	50	v Canada (195) at Clontarf................................	2011
327-5	**50**	**v West Indies (331-5) at Malahide**	**2019**
325-8	50	v Canada (233) at Toronto	2010
320-8	50	v Scotland (323-5) at Edinburgh	2011
313-6	44	v United Arab Emirates (91) at Harare (Old Hararians)	2017-18
308-7	50	v Canada (312-4) at Nairobi (Jaffery)	2006-07

† *World Cup.*

---

earlier continued his prolific form, holding the innings together and sharing a fifth-wicket stand of 100 with Holder. But only 48 came from the last eight overs, and the total looked insignificant when Bangladesh's openers cracked 54 inside nine.

At Clontarf, May 15. **Bangladesh won by six wickets.** ‡Ireland 292-8 (50 overs) (P. R. Stirling 130, W. T. S. Porterfield 94; Abu Jayed 5-58); **Bangladesh 294-4** (43 overs) (Tamim Iqbal 57, Liton Das 76, Shakib Al Hasan 50*, Mushfiqur Rahim 35, Mahmudullah 35*). *PoM:* Abu Jayed. Ireland's bowlers struggled again, and Bangladesh raced past their target of 293. Tamim and Liton Das, in his first match of the tournament, put on 117 in 16.4 overs, then Shakib added another brisk half-century before retiring with a side strain. The only highlight for the home side was Boyd Rankin's 200th wicket in all matches for Ireland – Mushfiqur, caught behind by Gary Wilson. It had been a different story earlier in the day, when Stirling underpinned another strong Irish batting performance with his eighth ODI century. He was unusually restrained, facing 141 balls in all, although he did take 21 off a Shakib over. Stirling put on 174 – a third-wicket record for Ireland in ODIs – with William Porterfield, who made his highest international score for 14 months.

BANGLADESH 14pts, WEST INDIES 9pts, Ireland 2pts.

Final   At Malahide, May 17. **Bangladesh won by five wickets** (DLS). **West Indies 152-1** (24 overs) (S. D. Hope 74, S. W. Ambris 69*); ‡**Bangladesh 213-5** (22.5 overs) (Soumya Sarkar 66, Mushfiqur Rahim 36, Mosaddek Hossain 52*). *PoM:* Mosaddek Hossain. *PoT:* S. D. Hope. *Bangladesh clinched the trophy in style, with the seventh win in their last nine ODIs against West Indies. Set 210 in 24 overs after a five-hour rain interruption, they charged to victory with an over to spare. The match was in the balance at 143-5 in the 16th, but No. 7 Mosaddek Hossain thrashed 52* from 27 deliveries, with five sixes. West Indies had been satisfied with their start, and were 131-0 when the rain arrived in the 21st. They had 23 balls left after the restart, but managed just 21 runs, despite losing only one wicket.*

IRELAND v AFGHANISTAN IN 2019

IAN CALLENDER

One-day internationals (2): Ireland 1, Afghanistan 1

Without a match for nine days, and forced for financial reasons to prepare in Scotland rather than in Ireland, Afghanistan were skittled in the first game of this short series. But days later, they hit 305, to draw level. Afghanistan's most dangerous batsmen, Mohammad Shahzad and Rahmat Shah, put on 150. The bowlers departed for England in less good heart. On two new pitches, the first tinged with green, the Afghan spinners were nullified: Mujeeb Zadran, Rashid Khan and Mohammad Nabi collected two for 155 in 38 overs. The medium-pace of Gulbadeen Naib, the new captain, was more successful, taking six for 43 in the second match. Ireland's bowlers recovered from their pummelling in the preceding tri-series, with seamer Mark Adair collecting four for 19 in the first game. That allowed William Porterfield to sniff back-to-back wins for the first time in any format for 14 months. He might have missed a trick: off-spinner Andy McBrine shimmied through ten overs for 17 after opening in the first game, but did not come on in the second until the 16th. Adair took three more wickets, but they cost 71. Player of the Series Paul Stirling made 71 and 50 – giving him four successive ODI half-centuries – and Porterfield 53 in the victory, but the rest of the batting was disappointing.

AFGHANISTAN TOURING PARTY

*Gulbadeen Naib, Aftab Alam, Asghar Afghan, Dawlat Zadran, Hamid Hassan, Hashmatullah Shahidi, Hazratullah Zazai, Mohammad Nabi, Mohammad Shahzad, Mujeeb Zadran, Najibullah Zadran, Noor Ali Zadran, Rahmat Shah, Rashid Khan, Samiullah Shenwari. *Coach*: P. V. Simmons.

First one-day international At Belfast, May 19. **Ireland won by 72 runs. Ireland 210** (48.5 overs) (P. R. Stirling 71, W. T. S. Porterfield 53, K. J. O'Brien 32; Dawlat Zadran 3-35, Aftab Alam 3-28); ‡**Afghanistan 138** (35.4 overs) (M. R. Adair 4-19, W. B. Rankin 3-40). *For the first time in their six one-day series against Afghanistan, Ireland won the opening match, despite an under-par total on a green Stormont pitch. Paul Stirling and William Porterfield put on 99 for the third wicket – but the last five tumbled for 18. Afghanistan started uncharacteristically slowly, making only 21-2 in the ten-over powerplay. With his second ball, Mark Adair soon took the first of four wickets. Asghar Afghan (29) and Mohammad Nabi (27) tonked 54 in nine overs, but Kevin O'Brien ended the fightback; Boyd Rankin then took three wickets in nine balls, the last his 100th in ODIs (ten were for England). Afghanistan's only lower total against Ireland was 104 at Clontarf in 2012.*

Second one-day international At Belfast, May 21. **Afghanistan won by 126 runs. Afghanistan 305-7** (50 overs) (Mohammad Shahzad 101, Rahmat Shah 62, Hashmatullah Shahidi 47, Najibullah Zadran 60*; M. R. Adair 3-71); ‡**Ireland 179** (41.2 overs) (P. R. Stirling 50, G. C. Wilson 34; Gulbadeen Naib 6-43). *PoS*: P. R. Stirling. *This was more like the aggressive Afghanistan who had qualified for the World Cup. It took them just 15 deliveries to match their ten-over score from the previous game, and there were ten fours in the first nine overs. Mohammad Shahzad, whose 88-ball 101 was his sixth ODI century, and Rahmat Shah added 150 for the second wicket, and Najibullah Zadran crashed 60* from 33 to raise the highest ODI total at Stormont (England's 301-7 in 2006). Ireland were never in touch once the in-form Stirling became the first of six wickets for Gulbadeen Naib; only Rashid Khan had better figures (7-18 against West Indies in St Lucia in 2018; he also took 6-43 v Ireland in 2016-17). This was Rashid's 59th ODI, but the first his side had won without his taking a wicket.*

IRELAND v ZIMBABWE IN 2019

IAN CALLENDER

One-day internationals (3): Ireland 3, Zimbabwe 0
Twenty20 internationals (3): Ireland 1, Zimbabwe 1

Ireland completed a clean sweep over a fellow Full Member for the first time, but after a 3–0 win in the one-day series and victory in the second Twenty20 match – the first was rained off – the Zimbabweans broke their duck in the final game of a tour overshadowed by political turmoil in Harare.

Days after the squad returned home, Zimbabwe Cricket were suspended from the ICC because of government interference in their affairs. Zimbabwe were barred from ICC global events with immediate effect, and their funding was withdrawn. While the men's team were in Ireland, it was reported that they had not been paid; a women's tour, meant to be taking place alongside this one, was cancelled for financial reasons.

Ireland took full advantage of the turmoil, especially in the 50-over matches. Tim Murtagh defied the years to take nine wickets, including his first five-for in 20 seasons of List A cricket, and was well supported by the new generation: Mark Adair backed up the good impression he had made in the tri-series against Bangladesh and West Indies, while Shane Getkate made his ODI debut and took two wickets in each of the three games.

James McCollum, after just 17 runs in his first five ODIs, justified the selectors' faith: he made two half-centuries, and finished with 148 runs. That was seven more than Paul Stirling, whose run of six successive one-day fifties ended when he was out for 32 in the third match.

Craig Ervine, who had formerly been a professional with Lisburn in Northern Ireland, was Zimbabwe's leading scorer, just ahead of Sean Williams. They were the visitors' only consistent batsmen – their unbroken stand of 111 clinched the final T20 game – although there were two promising innings from Ryan Burl down the order.

Stirling rattled up 83 in 10.5 overs to win the first of the T20 games to survive the weather. When he was out to the first ball of the last match, it gave a chance to Ireland's new middle order, mainly young talent from the interprovincial T20 tournament. Adair hit 38 off 15, while Getkate and Gareth Delany caught the eye. They were helped by Greg Thompson, who returned to Ireland colours for a third spell, 15 years after his debut, aged 16, against MCC.

ZIMBABWE TOURING PARTY

*H. Masakadza, R. P. Burl, T. L. Chatara, E. Chigumbura, C. R. Ervine, K. M. Jarvis, T. S. Kamunhukamwe, S. F. Mire, P. J. Moor, C. B. Mpofu, R. Mutumbami, A. Ndlovu, Sikandar Raza, B. R. M. Taylor, D. T. Tiripano, S. C. Williams. *Coach:* L. S. Rajput.

First one-day international At Bready, July 1. **Ireland won by four wickets. Zimbabwe 254-9** (50 overs) (C. R. Ervine 105, R. P. Burl 49*; M. R. Adair 4-73); ‡**Ireland 258-6** (48.3 overs) (P. R. Stirling 57, A. Balbirnie 101; T. L. Chatara 3-36). *ODI debut:* S. C. Getkate (Ireland). *After Tendai*

Chatara held Ireland up with wickets in three successive overs, Andrew Balbirnie's fifth ODI century took them to the brink of victory; when he was run out, thinking the ball had eluded mid-on, Mark Adair and Shane Getkate finished things off. Adair had earlier removed opener Tinashe Kamunhukamwe with his first delivery. Craig Ervine's century underpinned Zimbabwe's innings, but he received little support until Ryan Burl thrashed four late sixes.

Second one-day international At Belfast, July 4. **Ireland won by five runs. Ireland 242-9** (50 overs) (P. R. Stirling 52, J. A. McCollum 73, L. J. Tucker 56; S. F. Mire 4-43); ‡**Zimbabwe 237-9** (50 overs) (C. R. Ervine 43, S. C. Williams 58, Sikandar Raza 31, R. P. Burl 53, D. T. Tiripano 33; T. J. Murtagh 5-21). *Tim Murtagh's first five-for in 210 List A matches, dating back to 2000, gave Ireland an unbeatable 2–0 lead. He reduced Zimbabwe to 14-3, and later conceded only a single off the 49th, which started with Zimbabwe needing 15. They fell just short of Ireland's 242, a disappointing total after an opening stand of 111 between Paul Stirling (with his sixth successive ODI fifty) and James McCollum, whose 73 was his maiden half-century.*

MOST SUCCESSIVE HALF-CENTURIES IN ODIs

9	Javed Miandad (Pakistan)...............	1986-87 to 1987-88
6	C. G. Greenidge (West Indies)..........	1979-80 to 1980
6	A. H. Jones (New Zealand).............	1988-89
6	M. E. Waugh (Australia)...............	1998-99
6	Mohammad Yousuf (Pakistan)..........	2003-04
6	K. S. Williamson (New Zealand)	2015
6	**L. R. P. L. Taylor (New Zealand)**	**2017-18 to 2018-19**
6	**C. H. Gayle (West Indies)**..............	**2018 to 2019**
6	**P. R. Stirling (Ireland)**	**2019**

Third one-day international At Belfast, July 7. **Ireland won by six wickets.** ‡**Zimbabwe 190** (46.5 overs) (S. C. Williams 67; T. J. Murtagh 3-39); **Ireland 191-4** (41.2 overs) (P. R. Stirling 32, J. A. McCollum 54, W. T. S. Porterfield 49, K. J. O'Brien 35*). *PoS:* T. J. Murtagh. *Ireland eased to a 3–0 clean sweep, helped by some sloppy fielding – three catches were dropped. Murtagh took two wickets in his first five overs, and Zimbabwe never really recovered, despite a gritty 67 from Sean Williams. Stirling and McCollum kicked off the chase with 60 in 12.5 overs, and Ireland were rarely troubled. William Porterfield, presiding over his 50th ODI victory as captain, passed 4,000 runs.*

First Twenty20 international At Belfast, July 10 (floodlit). **Ireland v Zimbabwe. Abandoned.**

Second Twenty20 international At Bready, July 12 (floodlit). **Ireland won by nine wickets** (DLS). **Zimbabwe 132-8** (13 overs) (C. R. Ervine 55, S. C. Williams 34; M. R. Adair 4-40); ‡**Ireland 134-1** (10.5 overs) (P. R. Stirling 83*). *T20I debuts:* M. R. Adair, G. J. Delany (Ireland). *Stirling's whirlwind 83*, from 36 balls with seven sixes and six fours, powered Ireland to their first T20 victory over a Full Member since March 2014, when they beat Zimbabwe in the World Twenty20 in Bangladesh. After two early interruptions, the match was reduced to 13 overs, and Ireland's target revised to 134.*

Third Twenty20 international At Bready, July 14. **Zimbabwe won by eight wickets. Ireland 171-9** (20 overs) (G. C. Wilson 47, G. J. Thompson 32, M. R. Adair 38; K. M. Jarvis 3-38); ‡**Zimbabwe 172-2** (16.4 overs) (B. R. M. Taylor 39, C. R. Ervine 68*, S. C. Williams 58*). *What a difference two days made: Stirling was out first ball, and Zimbabwe had little difficulty chasing down 172, even though skipper Hamilton Masakadza made a duck. Ervine and Williams finished things off with a stand of 111* from 62 balls as Ireland's inexperienced attack struggled.*

IRELAND TWENTY20 TRI-SERIES IN 2019

IAN CALLENDER

1 Ireland 2 Scotland 3 Netherlands

When the Euro T20 Slam was postponed for a year in August, the three countries who would have been providing teams moved swiftly to organise an international tri-series. With the T20 World Cup Qualifier taking place in October, there was concern their players would be left short of match practice.

Ireland won the tournament, but there was little to choose between the teams. Scotland also won two games, and the Netherlands, though under-strength, might also have picked up the trophy if the opening match, against the hosts, hadn't been abandoned. After the damp start, the sun shone on Malahide for five successive days.

With the Qualifier so near, Ireland decided not to risk Paul Stirling, who had a calf strain. It deprived them of their best batsman, although Gareth Delany proved a capable stand-in opener, while Andrew Balbirnie was Ireland's most prolific batsman, with 129 at 43; the pair had the best strike-rates of the series.

Scotland had the outstanding batsman in George Munsey, who was named Player of the Series for his 194 runs. In the first match against the Netherlands, he hit the only hundred of the series, in 41 balls, the fifth-fastest in T20 internationals. The Scots also had the leading wicket-taker: slow left-armer Hamza Tahir collected seven at 15.

The Netherlands left out four of their probable squad for the qualifiers, including Ryan ten Doeschate and Roelof van der Merwe. Captain Pieter Seelaar was their best batsman, with 104 runs at 52, and seamer Shane Snater took five wickets at 16.

At Malahide, September 15. **Ireland v Netherlands. Abandoned.**

At Malahide, September 16. **Scotland won by 58 runs. Scotland 252-3** (20 overs) (H. G. Munsey 127*, K. J. Coetzer 89; S. Snater 3-42); ‡**Netherlands 194-7** (20 overs) (P. M. Seelaar 96*, S. A. Edwards 37). *T20I debuts:* C. Floyd (Netherlands); O. J. Hairs (Scotland). *Scotland blitzed the sixth-highest T20I total thanks to a turbocharged opening partnership of 200 off 91 balls between George Munsey and captain Kyle Coetzer; it was the third-highest partnership for any wicket in T20 internationals. At the end of the powerplay, Scotland were 72-0, and by halfway they had reached 116; Munsey then took 32 off the 13th, bowled by Max O'Dowd. The rate slowed once the partnership was broken, but Munsey's eventual 127* off 56 balls included 14 sixes. The Netherlands lost two wickets in the second over, but captain Pieter Seelaar made a defiant 96*.*

At Malahide, September 17. **Ireland won by four wickets.** ‡**Scotland 193-7** (20 overs) (H. G. Munsey 34, C. S. MacLeod 72; W. B. Rankin 3-29); **Ireland 194-6** (17.4 overs) (G. J. Delany 52, A. Balbirnie 64; M. R. J. Watt 3-38). *T20I debuts:* D. C. A. Delany, H. T. Tector (Ireland). *Scotland were brought back to earth by a solid all-round Ireland performance. Rankin broke the opening partnership for 167 fewer than the previous day, which left Calum MacLeod to make the major contribution. Gareth Delany, replacing the injured Paul Stirling, hit a 25-ball fifty, but was outshone by Andrew Balbirnie's 64 from 32.*

At Malahide, September 18. **Netherlands won by six wickets.** ‡**Ireland 181-7** (20 overs) (K. J. O'Brien 30, A. Balbirnie 45, H. T. Tector 60); **Netherlands 183-4** (19.1 overs) (M. P. O'Dowd 69, B. N. Cooper 91*; G. H. Dockrell 3-23). *Ben Cooper's highest T20 score, plus a record Dutch partnership for any wicket, steered the Netherlands to their only win of the tournament. After Tobias*

Visée was bowled by the first ball of the innings, from Mark Adair, O'Dowd and Cooper put on 144. George Dockrell took three quick wickets, but Scott Edwards hit three fours off Stuart Thompson in the 19th, and Cooper's seventh six won the game. Ireland had been well placed at 128-2 in the 12th, before Balbirnie's dismissal slowed them down.

At Malahide, September 19. **Scotland won by six wickets. ‡Netherlands 123** (20 overs) (B. F. W. de Leede 30; H. Tahir 4-30); **Scotland 126-4** (13.2 overs). *T20I debuts:* Vikramjit Singh (Netherlands); T. B. Sole (Scotland). *A comfortable win, achieved with 40 balls to spare, set Scotland up for a decider against the hosts. Seelaar's decision to bat backfired, as Hamza Tahir took his first T20I four-for. Bas de Leede and Clayton Floyd fought back with a stand of 43, a Dutch seventh-wicket record, but they had nowhere near enough. Scotland were helped by regular wides from an ill-disciplined Netherlands attack.*

At Malahide, September 20. **Ireland won by one run. Ireland 186-9** (20 overs) (K. J. O'Brien 63, G. C. Wilson 31); **‡Scotland 185-6** (20 overs) (M. H. Cross 66*, R. D. Berrington 76). *PoT:* H. G. Munsey. *Ireland squeaked home to take the series after a thrilling finale. Scotland began the last over needing 15, but fell agonisingly short, leaving Matt Cross, who batted through the innings, stuck on 66*. It was also tough on Richie Berrington, who had hit seven fours and five sixes in his 76. Ireland's total was set up by Kevin O'Brien's 63 off 45.*

Ireland 5pts, Scotland 4pts, Netherlands 3pts.

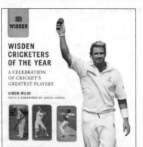

DOMESTIC CRICKET IN IRELAND IN 2019

Ian Callender

Rain ruined the interprovincial season. Of 39 days scheduled across the three formats, only 11 were uninterrupted, while 17 were washed out. In the three-day Championship, five of the six games were drawn, and the other abandoned.

Leinster Lightning, who regained the Championship title, lost less play than their two rivals, and had more opportunity to accrue bonus points. They led by 11 when **Northern Knights** and **North West Warriors** arrived at the final round; the 16 points for a win would have given either the title. Instead, they suffered only the second complete washout in seven seasons of the three-day Championship, both at Bready.

In the one game to get as far as a third innings, Leinster met Northern at Malahide, which witnessed the tournament's only centuries. Harry Tector hit 146 for Northern, and Simi Singh replied with an unbeaten 100, allowing Leinster captain George Dockrell to declare, eight behind, with nearly two sessions to go. By the time Northern were 114 for six, they were in full defensive mode, playing out 52 consecutive dot balls. Singh dismissed them for 131, collecting five for 38, but with just eight overs left the teams shook hands. A fortnight later, Test captain William Porterfield was stranded on 95 when the last day of North West's game with Leinster was wiped out.

Singh, yet to make his Test debut, finished top of the batting and bowling averages. With so little play, only he and Tector reached 150 runs, and his 13 wickets, at less than nine apiece, put him well ahead of anyone else. Craig Young – who bowled 25 overs to Singh's 74 – managed to take seven at ten for North West.

The opening three fixtures of the 50-over Interprovincial Cup were played in La Manga in April, but it rained in Spain too: the first game was abandoned, the second truncated (that week, it was dry in Dublin). Leinster claimed the Cup for the sixth successive season. Like runners-up Northern, they won three matches, but both their games against North West Warriors were abandoned, whereas – in a further weather-related twist – Northern were the only team to complete all six matches, but lost half of them.

Leinster's Andrew Balbirnie dominated the one-day cup, scoring 350 in just four innings – the next-best was 208 in six by Northern opener Marc Ellison. Balbirnie scored a match-winning 125 against Northern, and was involved in three century partnerships, two with Lorcan Tucker and one with Jack Tector, who made the only other hundred, against North West. The Ulster sides were involved in two nailbiters: North West won by three runs when Northern lost six for eight chasing a revised target, and Northern won by two when Shane Getkate trapped North West's No. 11 with one ball to go.

FIRST-CLASS AVERAGES IN 2019

BATTING (70 runs)

		M	I	NO	R	HS	100	Avge	Ct
1	S. Singh (*Leinster*)	4	4	2	204	100*	1	102.00	1
2	H. T. Tector (*Northern*)	3	3	1	189	146	1	94.50	0
3	†G. R. J. Kennedy (*North West*)	3	3	2	85	73*	0	85.00	0
4	†W. T. S. Porterfield (*North West*)	3	3	1	123	95*	0	61.50	1
5	A. Balbirnie (*Leinster*)	3	3	0	133	81	0	44.33	4
6	†G. I. Hume (*North West*)	3	3	1	74	54*	0	37.00	1
7	C. M. J. McLoughlin-Gavin (*Leinster*)	4	4	0	121	86	0	30.25	2
8	M. P. Ellison (*Northern*)	3	3	0	81	36	0	27.00	2
9	J. A. McCollum (*Northern*)	3	3	0	76	44	0	25.33	0
10	G. C. Wilson (*Northern*)	3	3	0	73	36	0	24.33	2
11	J. B. Tector (*Leinster*)	4	4	0	75	34	0	18.75	2

BOWLING (4 wickets)

		Style	O	M	R	W	BB	5I	Avge
1	S. Singh (*Leinster*)	OB	74.1	25	113	13	5-38	1	8.69
2	C. A. Young (*North West*)	RFM	25	6	71	7	4-26	0	10.14
3	D. C. A. Delany (*Northern*)	RFM	25	2	111	6	3-48	0	18.50
4	B. J. McCarthy (*Leinster*)	RFM	61	17	169	8	5-51	1	21.12
5	M. T. Foster (*Northern*)	RFM	26	6	88	4	2-38	0	22.00
6	H. T. Tector (*Northern*).	OB	39.1	9	112	5	3-48	0	22.40
7	G. H. Dockrell (*Leinster*)	SLA	54.2	14	143	6	2-32	0	23.83
8	T. E. Kane (*Leinster*).	RFM	55	11	139	4	2-25	0	34.75
9	P. K. D. Chase (*Leinster*)	RFM	38.3	4	178	4	2-24	0	44.50

TEST TRIANGLE INTERPROVINCIAL CHAMPIONSHIP IN 2019

						Bonus pts		
	P	W	L	D	A	Bat	Bowl	Pts
Leinster	4	0	0	4†	0	7	12	40
Northern.	4	0	0	3*	1	5	9	35
North West.	4	0	0	3†	1	3	6	33

    *   *Two with at least six hours lost.*   †   *Three with at least six hours lost.*

Win = 16pts; draw with less than six hours' play lost = 3pts; draw with at least six hours' play lost = 6pts; abandoned = 6pts. Bonus points awarded for the first 100 overs of each team's first innings: one batting point for the first 150 runs and then for 200, 250 and 300; one bowling point for the third wicket taken and for every subsequent two.

INTERPROVINCIAL CHAMPIONS

2013	Leinster	2016	Leinster	2019	Leinster
2014	Leinster	2017	Leinster		
2015	Leinster	2018	North West		

The Interprovincial Championship was not first-class until 2017.

Leinster have won the title 6 times, North West 1.

TEST TRIANGLE INTERPROVINCIAL CUP IN 2019

50-over league

	P	W	L	A	Bonus	Pts	NRR
Leinster	6	3	1	2	2	18	0.27
Northern	6	3	3	0	2	14	0.63
North West	6	1	3	2	0	8	−1.24

Winners of Irish Leagues and Cups
Irish Senior Cup **Pembroke**. Leinster League **Pembroke**. Leinster League Cup **The Hills**. Munster Senior League **Cork County**. Munster Senior Cup **Cork County**. Northern League **CIYMS**. Northern Challenge Cup **CIYMS**. North West League **Brigade**. North West Senior Cup **Brigade**.

The Test Triangle Interprovincial Trophy appears on page 1155.

NEW ZEALAND CRICKET IN 2019

Overshadowed by tragedy

ANDREW ALDERSON

The year revolved around an imperceptible defeat, a question mark beside the national team's performance and – towering over all else – a terrorism tragedy.

The Lord's World Cup final loss, by zero runs, marked the zenith of New Zealand's playing achievements, the phrase "boundary countback" entering the national vernacular after the tie with England across the two innings and two super overs. In contrast, the 3–0 Test trouncing in Australia, completed early in 2020, represented the nadir. Any hopes this generation would be crowned the country's greatest team were shelved, for now. The series had lost relevance once it reached a hazy Sydney for a dead-rubber match distracted by the bushfire crisis.

NEW ZEALAND IN 2019

	Played	Won	Lost	Drawn/No result
Tests	8	4	3	1
One-day internationals	21	13	7	1
Twenty20 internationals	12	7	4	1

DECEMBER	2 Tests, 3 ODIs and 1 T20I (h) v Sri Lanka	(see *Wisden 2019*, page 917)
JANUARY	5 ODIs and 3 T20Is (h) v India	(page 982)
FEBRUARY		
MARCH	2 Tests and 3 ODIs (h) v Bangladesh	(page 985)
APRIL		
MAY		
JUNE	World Cup (in England)	(page 237)
JULY		
AUGUST	2 Tests and 3 T20Is (a) v Sri Lanka	(page 1034)
SEPTEMBER		
OCTOBER		
NOVEMBER	2 Tests and 5 T20Is (h) v England	(page 420)
DECEMBER		
JANUARY	3 Tests (a) v Australia	(page 896)

For a review of New Zealand domestic cricket from the 2018-19 season, see page 906.

However, any cricketing success or failure had been put in perspective by an attack in Christchurch on March 15, during the visit of Bangladesh. The tourists had arrived to worship at the Al Noor mosque moments after a heavily armed gunman opened fire; 51 people died. A white supremacist – prime minister Jacinda Ardern vowed never to mention the man by name – stood accused, with the trial set for June 2020. The players fled on foot to Hagley Oval, then flew home as soon as they could, with the Third Test cancelled.

Four months later, New Zealand reached their second consecutive World Cup final. Fans were treated to a catalogue of momentous feats on the way: Kane Williamson's clinical century against South Africa at Edgbaston; Trent Boult's tightrope catch at long-on to dismiss West Indian Carlos Brathwaite at Old Trafford; and, at the same venue, Martin Guptill's laser-beam run-out of M. S. Dhoni in the two-day semi-final against India.

At Lord's, New Zealand lost the boundary countback 27–17, but gained in dignity. Ironically, the ICC's Player of the Tournament was Williamson, a connoisseur of the crafty single. At the press conference, he mustered more smiles than self-pity, speaking of "a tough pill to swallow", "small margins" and "uncontrollables" – but never of excuses. His final answer precipitated a rare act: an ovation from the media pack. England deserved their victory after a four-year white-ball revolution, but the New Zealanders' reactions offered a glimpse of cricket at its most uplifting.

In Tests, their reputation initially grew, and they rose to second in the world behind India. A 2–0 triumph over Bangladesh had extended a record run of series victories to five, and was followed by a 1–1 draw from behind in Sri Lanka, and a 1–0 home win over England. But the aura dimmed in Australia, despite much-anticipated Test returns to Melbourne and Sydney for the first time in over 30 years. Conditions were furnace-like, and opponents flinty-eyed, as the Australians reasserted a dominance derailed by the ball-tampering scandal.

The absence at various points through the series of Williamson, Boult, Henry Nicholls, Mitchell Santner and Lockie Ferguson inflicted further blows. Déjà vu reigned: New Zealand conceded over 400 in each first innings, and were in the field for at least part of every day of the series, though no match reached a fifth; the margins of defeat were 296, 247 and 279.

For the tourists – highlights were few. Novice opener Tom Blundell became the first New Zealander to score a Test century at the MCG, while Neil Wagner's relentless but successful short-pitched attack saw the terms "leg theory" and "Bodyline" bandied about; he dismissed Steve Smith four times out of five. Wagner's world-class status as a first- or second-change seamer was evident throughout 2019, when he claimed 43 wickets at 17. He took at least three wickets in every innings bar one (when he took two), and moved to 200 in his 46th Test, a record for a left-arm quick; for New Zealand, only Richard Hadlee (44) had got there faster.

B-J. Watling also shone. His middle-order pluck brought him 105 not out against Sri Lanka, then – in his next innings – 205 against England during Mount Maunganui's debut Test. Both helped secure innings victories. He became the country's most successful Test wicketkeeper too, overtaking Adam

Philip Brown, Popperfoto/Getty Images

Brothers in arms: Neil Wagner, Tom Latham, Kane Williamson, Tim Southee, B-J. Watling, and Henry Nicholls.

Parore's 201 dismissals in March. Ross Taylor underlined his enduring excellence, becoming the top run-scorer in both Tests and one-day internationals. Ferguson's World Cup performance was also notable, immobilising batsmen with pace on his way to 21 wickets at 19, second only to Mitchell Starc's 27.

At home, Wellington's Luke Woodcock retired after a national-record 143 first-class matches for one province. In a further tribute to longevity, Ewen Chatfield – who had played the last of his 43 Tests in 1989 – received the Bert Sutcliffe Medal for service, after retiring from club cricket, aged 68, because he was not playing to his "standards". In his final innings, he fell just 100 short of a maiden century.

New Zealand Cricket's budgeted $NZ1m operating profit actually turned into a $1.3m loss. Operating revenue was up $6.3m, but cash reserves dropped $5.8m to $14.2m. A couple of factors suggested this would not be a long-term problem: payouts from two World Cups (the 20-over version in 2021, and its 50-over equivalent in 2023) and a new six-year domestic broadcast deal with telecommunications giant Spark. Martin Stewart, chief executive of Sky, the previous rights-holders, hinted at the scale of the deal when he said they had been "outbid by miles".

NZC and the Players' Association agreed a new three-year plan to help safeguard the women's game. A payment pool of $4.1m was created, and the number of contracts rose from 15 to 79, as domestic players featured for the first time. Meanwhile, White Ferns captain Amy Satterthwaite benefited from new maternity-leave provisions, as she prepared for parenthood with team-mate and partner Lea Tahuhu. New life had been breathed into an old game.

NEW ZEALAND v INDIA IN 2018-19

Mark Geenty

One-day internationals (5): New Zealand 1, India 4
Twenty20 internationals (3): New Zealand 2, India 1

The last time India toured New Zealand, early in 2014, they lost the one-dayers 4–0. The rematch was one of the most eagerly awaited series since, with the sides ranked second and third in the world locking horns. But it wasn't even close: fresh from Test and one-day series wins across the Tasman, India ruled the roost, a shock for New Zealand fans accustomed to their side being hard to beat at home.

Virat Kohli had squeezed in a visit to Melbourne to chat with tennis great (and cricket fan) Roger Federer at the Australian Open, before his team boarded the plane to Auckland in search of another tick on their World Cup checklist. They got it, in bold print. The 4–1 margin in the 50-over matches looked comprehensive on paper, and in reality it was even more convincing. Their only defeat came at Hamilton, with the series already sealed. Kane Williamson won a crucial toss, then swing and seam from Trent Boult and Colin de Grandhomme skittled India for 92. But Kohli's men took everything else in their stride, including a peculiar delay in the opening match at Napier, where the setting sun caused a 40-minute hold-up.

Five years previously, New Zealand's lowest total in five ODIs was 271; now their highest was 243, demonstrating the excellence of the Indian attack, with Mohammed Shami and Bhuvneshwar Kumar sharing the new ball, before wrist-spinners Yuzvendra Chahal and Kuldeep Yadav took up the cudgels. The seamers were so effective that Colin Munro was briefly dropped, and Henry Nicholls pushed up the order. Williamson never really got going, a modest 64 his highest score of the series.

After Kohli piloted his team to victory at Napier, it was announced he would return home after the third match to rest: and he signed off in style; his 60 at Mount Maunganui sealed the series. India were already without one of their standout performers in Australia, Jasprit Bumrah, who was rested, but all-rounder Hardik Pandya returned to the fold after the second match, having been suspended, along with K. L. Rahul, for inappropriate comments on an Australian TV chat show. But even with some of the big names absent, India's fans flocked in. Just under 37,000 people crammed Eden Park for the second Twenty20 international. The decibel level was much louder for the tourists, and helped them to victory.

But the home fans got to cheer as well, as New Zealand pinched the T20 series. Munro was more effective in the shorter format, and formed a dynamic opening partnership with Tim Seifert. They set up two totals in excess of 200, which Mitchell Santner's canny spin helped defend.

INDIAN TOURING PARTY

*V. Kohli (50), K. K. Ahmed (50/20), Bhuvneshwar Kumar (50/20), Y. S. Chahal (50/20), S. Dhawan (50/20), M. S. Dhoni (50/20), S. Gill (50/20), R. A. Jadeja (50), K. M. Jadhav (50/20), K. D. Karthik (50/20), S. Kaul (20), Mohammed Shami (50/20), H. H. Pandya (50), K. H. Pandya (20), R. R. Pant (20), A. T. Rayudu (50), V. Shankar (50/20), R. G. Sharma (50/20), M. Siraj (50), K. Yadav (50/20). *Coach:* R. J. Shastri.

Kohli was rested after the third ODI and returned home; Sharma took over as captain.

First one-day international At Napier, January 23, 2019 (day/night). **India won by eight wickets** (DLS). ‡**New Zealand 157** (38 overs) (K. S. Williamson 64; Mohammed Shami 3-19, K. Yadav 4-39); **India 156-2** (34.5 overs) (S. Dhawan 75*, V. Kohli 45). *PoM:* Mohammed Shami. *McLean Park, returfed and boasting a new drainage system, got some play in an ODI for the first time since the 2015 World Cup – two intervening matches had been washed out – but India dominated. New Zealand's openers both fell in single figures to Mohammed Shami (Martin Guptill was his 100th ODI wicket), then spinners Kuldeep Yadav and Yuzvendra Chahal shared 6-82, which included top-scorer Kane Williamson, who holed out to long-on as the last five wickets tumbled for 24. The only thing to delay India's victory charge was the sun – ironically, for a ground often cursed by rain. There was a 40-minute hold-up as it set behind the bowler's arm at one end. Either side of the interruption, which cost one over (India's target was amended slightly to 156), Shikhar Dhawan – who passed 5,000 runs in ODIs – and Virat Kohli put on 91 in unhurried fashion before, in a rare moment of joy for the hosts, Kohli feathered Lockie Ferguson's bouncer to Tom Latham.*

Second one-day international At Mount Maunganui, January 26, 2019 (day/night). **India won by 90 runs.** ‡**India 324-4** (50 overs) (R. G. Sharma 87, S. Dhawan 66, V. Kohli 43, A. T. Rayudu 47, M. S. Dhoni 48*); **New Zealand 234** (40.2 overs) (C. Munro 31, T. W. M. Latham 34, D. A. J. Bracewell 57; K. Yadav 4-45). *PoM:* R. G. Sharma. *After a powerful batting display, iced by Kedar Jadhav (22* from ten balls) and M. S. Dhoni taking 21 from Ferguson's final over, India's bowlers dismantled New Zealand again. Williamson chopped Shami on, Ross Taylor was lured out of his crease by Jadhav, and Latham flummoxed by a quicker one – the first of four more wickets for Yadav. Embarrassment loomed at 166-8 in the 31st over, but Doug Bracewell's muscular maiden ODI half-century added some respectability.*

Third one-day international At Mount Maunganui, January 28, 2019 (day/night). **India won by seven wickets.** ‡**New Zealand 243** (49 overs) (L. R. P. L. Taylor 93, T. W. M. Latham 51; Mohammed Shami 3-41); **India 245-3** (43 overs) (R. G. Sharma 62, V. Kohli 60, A. T. Rayudu 40*, K. D. Karthik 38*). *PoM:* Mohammed Shami. *India clinched the series in familiar style, sailing to victory after restricting New Zealand with the ball. There was a good return for Hardik Pandya, back from suspension: after taking a superb catch diving to his left at midwicket to send back Williamson for 28, he had Henry Nicholls and Mitchell Santner nicking behind in successive overs. Although Taylor made 93, New Zealand's 243 was never enough – as proved by Rohit Sharma and Kohli in a second-wicket stand of 113 in 20 overs. Kohli's series ended when he drove uppishly to the leaping Nicholls at extra cover, but Ambati Rayudu and Dinesh Karthik (who had taken four catches deputising for Dhoni behind the stumps) knocked off the rest. Both Taylor and Sharma passed 10,000 runs in List A cricket.*

Fourth one-day international At Hamilton, January 31, 2019 (day/night). **New Zealand won by eight wickets. India 92** (30.5 overs) (T. A. Boult 5-21, C. de Grandhomme 3-26); ‡**New Zealand 93-2** (14.4 overs) (H. M. Nicholls 30*, L. R. P. L. Taylor 37*). *PoM:* T. A. Boult. *ODI debut:* S. Gill (India). *Trent Boult took advantage of helpful conditions, finding springy bounce and lavish swing. He bowled his ten overs off the reel, and finished with 5-21; when he came off, India were in shreds at 55-8, though they had passed their lowest ODI total (54 against Sri Lanka at Sharjah in 2000-01). They staggered to 92 – No. 10 Chahal top-scored with 18* – but New Zealand completed victory before the floodlights kicked in, Taylor collecting successive sixes off Chahal near the end. Nicholls made a composed start as opener, after Colin Munro was dropped. Kohli's replacement, 19-year-old Shubman Gill, had a torrid introduction to international cricket: he was clanged on the helmet by Boult, and gave a return catch in his next over after making nine from 21 balls.*

Fifth one-day international At Wellington (Westpac), February 3, 2019 (day/night). **India won by 35 runs.** ‡**India 252** (49.5 overs) (A. T. Rayudu 90, V. Shankar 45, K. M. Jadhav 34, H. H. Pandya 45; M. J. Henry 4-35, T. A. Boult 3-39); **New Zealand 217** (44.1 overs) (K. S. Williamson 39, T. W. M. Latham 37, J. D. S. Neesham 44; Y. S. Chahal 3-41). *PoM:* A. T. Rayudu. *PoS:* Mohammed Shami. *When India slumped to 18-4 in the tenth over, a repeat of the fourth match* *looked on the cards. But while Boult and Matt Henry ended up with 7-74 between them, the other five bowlers managed only 1-166, as Rayudu rebuilt the innings in style. Pandya belted 45 from 22 balls, including three successive sixes off leg-spinner Todd Astle, and the total stretched to 252. It was more than enough, as India made it 4–1. Shami again removed the openers, Williamson got bogged down – his 39 used up 73 balls – and three wickets for Chahal kept the middle order quiet. Jimmy Neesham threatened briefly but, after swinging hard for 44 from 32, he wandered from his crease after an lbw appeal, and Dhoni underarmed the ball into the stumps to run him out.*

First Twenty20 international   At Wellington (Westpac), February 6, 2019 (floodlit). **New Zealand won by 80 runs. New Zealand 219-6** (20 overs) (T. L. Seifert 84, C. Munro 34, K. S. Williamson 34); ‡**India 139** (19.2 overs) (M. S. Dhoni 39; T. G. Southee 3-17). *PoM:* T. L. Seifert. *T20I debut:* D. J. Mitchell (New Zealand). *What a difference three days – and a change of format – made: on Waitangi Day (New Zealand's national day), Tim Seifert lit the blue touchpaper with 84 from 43 balls, including six of his side's 14 sixes, to set up an imposing total. His previous-highest score in 11 white-ball internationals was 22. Tim Southee, left out of the final ODI three days earlier on his favourite ground, returned to take three wickets, including top-scorer Dhoni, as India fell well short. The debutant Daryl Mitchell was one of eight Northern Districts players in New Zealand's team.*

Second Twenty20 international   At Auckland, February 8, 2019 (floodlit). **India won by seven wickets.** ‡**New Zealand 158-8** (20 overs) (L. R. P. L. Taylor 42, C. de Grandhomme 50; K. H. Pandya 3-28); **India 162-3** (18.5 overs) (R. G. Sharma 50, S. Dhawan 30, R. R. Pant 40*). *PoM:* K. H. Pandya. *India squared the series chiefly thanks to slow left-armer Krunal Pandya, who took three wickets as New Zealand failed to exploit Eden Park's short straight boundaries. His second victim, the unfortunate Mitchell, was given out lbw second ball: he reviewed, but the decision stood, despite Hot Spot showing an inside edge, which was not enough to convince third umpire Shaun Haig. The usually placid Williamson, the non-striker, queried the decision vehemently – and fell to Pandya himself next over. Four sixes from Colin de Grandhomme swelled the total, but India had few problems once openers Sharma and Dhawan put on 79.*

Third Twenty20 international   At Hamilton, February 10, 2019 (floodlit). **New Zealand won by four runs. New Zealand 212-4** (20 overs) (T. L. Seifert 43, C. Munro 72, C. de Grandhomme 30); ‡**India 208-6** (20 overs) (R. G. Sharma 38, V. Shankar 43, K. D. Karthik 33*). *PoM:* C. Munro. *PoS:* T. L. Seifert. *T20I debut:* B. M. Tickner (New Zealand). *New Zealand took the T20 series 2–1 after the closest match on the tour. Southee started the last over with 16 wanted, and kept things tight, although Karthik did smash the final ball for six. Santner had done the damage earlier, removing the dangerous Dhawan in the first over, then snaring top-scorer Vijay Shankar for a 28-ball 43. New Zealand looked home and hosed when Dhoni's departure made it 145-6 in the 16th, but Karthik and Krunal Pandya (26*) got India close with a stand of 63*. Seifert had given the home side's innings another rapid start, putting on 80 with Munro, who went on to 72 from 40, with five sixes. Yadav took 2-26 in his four overs, but eight from the Pandya brothers yielded 0-98.*

NEW ZEALAND v BANGLADESH IN 2018-19

Andrew Alderson

One-day internationals (3): New Zealand 3, Bangladesh 0
Test matches (2): New Zealand 2, Bangladesh 0

Life in New Zealand lurched into numb horror at 1.40pm on March 15, 2019. An Australian white-supremacist gunman entered the Al Noor mosque near Hagley Park in Christchurch and murdered 42 people, before killing seven more at the Linwood Islamic Centre across town. Two more died later, taking the death toll to 51. A further 50 were injured.

The atrocity occurred about half a mile from Hagley Oval, where the Third Test against Bangladesh was due to start next day. A press conference with Mahmudullah, the tourists' captain, had overrun, and the team headed for Al Noor later than expected. Their bus arrived seconds after the gunman had run out. Death was everywhere, panic reigned, and the players made hasty calls to the journalists they had just left. They decided to abandon the bus and ran back to the haven of Hagley Oval, encountering the press, who were rushing to help.

Within three hours, the New Zealand board had abandoned the Test. "I've spoken to my counterpart at Bangladesh Cricket," said their chief executive David White. "We agree it's inappropriate to play cricket at this time. Both teams are deeply affected." The tourists flew home immediately. Any perception of New Zealand as immune from terrorism had disappeared.

There were many questions – about racism, security intelligence and gun laws. Prime minister Jacinda Ardern mourned "one of New Zealand's darkest days", vowed never to mention the terrorist's name, and wore a hijab out of solidarity with the Muslim community. She gave assurances that inclusivity would help the healing, and offered a pledge: "They are us." As the country reeled, New Zealanders' tolerance and compassion provided at least some balm.

The tragedy, in a city recovering from a devastating earthquake, reduced New Zealand's Test and one-day international wins to insignificance. For what little it mattered, Bangladesh had now gone 15 Tests without defeating New Zealand, who justified their No. 2 ranking with a fifth consecutive series victory, extending their best sequence.

Both Tests followed a similar formula. Bangladesh were sent in, and offered resistance that would have struggled to heat a light-bulb filament. New Zealand countered with two crushing first innings. Batting had proved Bangladesh's downfall during the one-day internationals as well, twice losing four wickets inside the ten powerplay overs. Only a few of the tourists shone. Mahmudullah's crisis leadership in the absence of Shakib Al Hasan and Mushfiqur Rahim was strong in the Tests, as was the follow-me approach of Tamim Iqbal, with 278 runs at an average of nearly 70.

For New Zealand, format-specialists thrived. Neil Wagner took 16 cheap wickets in the Tests, with 14 coming from balls directed at armpits. Some questioned his ethics, but not his accuracy or tenacity. Few maiden centuries,

THE CHRISTCHURCH TERRORIST ATTACK
"This can't happen here"

M OHAMMAD I SAM

Not in New Zealand. This was my overriding thought as I sped towards Dean Avenue, from where Tamim Iqbal, Bangladesh's opening batsman, had phoned me for help. I thought he was joking when he explained what was going on inside the Al Noor mosque. This was New Zealand, I kept thinking. This can't happen here.

Along with 16 other members of the Bangladesh squad who had been heading to the mosque for prayers, Tamim was inside the team bus when they saw people running out of the building covered in blood. When the gunman's own footage of the massacre was analysed by the players in the hours after their brush with death, one thing became clear: had they arrived on the scene even a minute earlier, they would almost certainly have been caught up in the carnage. The sight of their bus in his video was a reminder of how close they came. Quite probably they were saved by Mahmudullah's pre-match press conference dragging on longer than usual.

The Bangladesh players remained under their seats for several minutes. Some believed staying put was best, but the majority thought fleeing the bus could save their lives, in case the gunman came in their direction. The decision was left to Tamim, Mushfiqur Rahim, captain Mahmudullah and computer analyst Shrinivas Chandrasekaran, who promptly asked two of the younger players, Mehedi Hasan and Khaled Ahmed, to cover their traditional *namaaz* clothing.

I met them after they had got off the bus, and were running towards Hagley Park. Someone suddenly said we shouldn't run, in case it confused the police. My heart sank when I stared at the empty park, thinking there may be multiple gunmen. At that stage, my mind was flashing between the dead body I had just seen, and the Mumbai attacks in 2008, when shooters ran amok.

But there were no gunmen around, and we safely reached Hagley Oval, where confusion gave way to a grim clarity. In the next few hours, a clearer picture (and the awful details) of what had gone on emerged. Many of the players, who had already broken down in tears as we walked briskly from the scene, were slumped in dressing-room chairs, faces full of horror. Within an hour, the team were whisked away to a hotel in midtown Christchurch, where the city had been preparing for a night of revelry: it was the start of the St Patrick's Day weekend.

The Bangladesh team still didn't feel safe in their hotel, where they were advised by staff not to go near the windows. After team manager Khaled Mashud's press conference, where he described exactly how they escaped, he hosted the seven touring journalists for a sombre meal. We all sat quietly, some talking about what had happened, as a TV blared out every detail. It was hard to believe that only a few hours earlier we had all been chatting about cricket.

Mohammad Isam is ESPNcricinfo's Bangladesh correspondent.

meanwhile, had been harder earned than opener Jeet Raval's: he got there in his 28th innings, after regularly and stoically taking the shine off the ball. B-J. Watling overtook Adam Parore's wicketkeeping dismissals record, and Martin Guptill returned to his one-day pomp with consecutive centuries.

One disappointment was the DRS. On the third day of the First Test, New Zealand reviewed a first-ball caught-behind decision against Mahmudullah. A noise was heard on the audio track one frame after the ball passed the bat. That lag between sound and vision was understood to have been discussed between television bosses and match officials before the game, but conveyed to few others, including the fans. The only way to reduce the time difference was apparently by moving from a 25-frame-a-second camera to a more expensive super slo-mo device. Mahmudullah was given not out.

Soon after the abrupt end of the tour, Mustafizur Rahman and Mehedi Hasan were both married: two shafts of light after a passage of darkness.

BANGLADESH TOURING PARTY

*Mahmudullah (T/50), Abu Jayed (T), Ebadat Hossain (T), Khaled Ahmed (T), Liton Das (T/50), Mashrafe bin Mortaza (50), Mehedi Hasan (T/50), Mithun Ali (T/50), Mohammad Saifuddin (50), Mominul Haque (T), Mushfiqur Rahim (T/50), Mustafizur Rahman (T/50), Nayeem Hasan (T/50), Rubel Hossain (50), Sabbir Rahman (50), Shadman Islam (T), Shafiul Islam (50), Shakib Al Hasan (T), Soumya Sarkar (T/50), Taijul Islam (T), Tamim Iqbal (T/50). Coach: S. J. Rhodes.

Shakib Al Hasan was named as captain for the Tests, but broke a finger beforehand. Taskin Ahmed was named in both squads, but injured his left ankle, and was replaced by Shafiul Islam for the ODIs, and Ebadat Hossain for the Tests. Mashrafe bin Mortaza captained in the ODIs.

First one-day international At Napier, February 13, 2019 (day/night). **New Zealand won by eight wickets.** ‡**Bangladesh 232** (48.5 overs) (Soumya Sarkar 30, Mithun Ali 62, Mohammad Saifuddin 41; T. A. Boult 3-40, M. J. Santner 3-45); **New Zealand 233-2** (44.3 overs) (M. J. Guptill 117*, H. M. Nicholls 53, L. R. P. L. Taylor 45*). PoM: M. J. Guptill. *Searing pace bowling from Matt Henry and Trent Boult had Bangladesh flailing at 42-4, before they limped to 232, mainly thanks to Mithun Ali and Mohammad Saifuddin, whose stand of 84 was a national record for the eighth wicket. The circumstances provided a perfect Petri dish from which Martin Guptill, returning from a back injury, cultivated a 15th ODI hundred, having been dropped on 47 down the leg side by Mushfiqur Rahim off Mehedi Hasan. Henry Nicholls continued to adapt as an opener, cobbling together 53 from 80 balls under minimal pressure. Their partnership of 103 was New Zealand's first century opening stand in ODIs for 24 matches, and victory came with 33 balls to spare.*

Second one-day international At Christchurch (Hagley Oval), February 16, 2019. **New Zealand won by eight wickets. Bangladesh 226** (49.4 overs) (Mithun Ali 57, Sabbir Rahman 43; L. H. Ferguson 3-43); ‡**New Zealand 229-2** (36.1 overs) (M. J. Guptill 118, K. S. Williamson 65*). PoM: M. J. Guptill. *"Ditto Napier" best summed up the second match, though this one was over even more quickly. The key protagonist was again Guptill, with a different supporting cast. This time, New Zealand won the toss, but Bangladesh's run-flow was cauterised by Boult and Henry, who restricted them to 32-2 in the powerplay. Lockie Ferguson and Todd Astle caused middle-order damage, and Jimmy Neesham polished off the tail. Mithun survived a chance in the slips on five to Ross Taylor, who had just put down Mushfiqur (both misses were off Ferguson), and went on to make 57, with some sparkling off-side strokes; his sixth-wicket partnership of 75 with Sabbir Rahman gave spine to the innings. Guptill resumed his Napier antics with 118 off 88 balls, punishing bowlers to all parts, and putting on 143 for the second wicket with Kane Williamson.*

Third one-day international At Dunedin (University Oval), February 20, 2019. **New Zealand won by 88 runs. New Zealand 330-6** (50 overs) (H. M. Nicholls 64, L. R. P. L. Taylor 69, T. W. M. Latham 59, J. D. S. Neesham 37, C. de Grandhomme 37*); ‡**Bangladesh 242** (47.2 overs) (Sabbir Rahman 102, Mohammad Saifuddin 44, Mehedi Hasan 37; T. G. Southee 6-65). PoM: T. G. Southee. *PoS: M. J. Guptill. This resembled an open-wicket practice for New Zealand in their last official ODI before the World Cup. Sabbir's maiden international century produced a late flurry, but that*

BEST ODI FIGURES IN NEW ZEALAND

7-33	T. G. Southee	New Zealand v England at Wellington	2014-15
7-34	T. A. Boult	New Zealand v West Indies at Christchurch .	2017-18
6-28	M. A. Starc	Australia v New Zealand at Auckland	2014-15
6-30	Waqar Younis	Pakistan v New Zealand at Auckland.......	1994-95
6-33	T. A. Boult	New Zealand v Australia at Hamilton	2016-17
6-65	**T. G. Southee........**	**New Zealand v Bangladesh at Dunedin ...**	**2018-19**

proved a sideshow to the Tim Southee circus. He bookended the innings: three at the start, as Bangladesh staggered to 2-3, and three at the end, including Sabbir for 102. He had bettered his eventual 6-65 only once in 139 ODIs. After the early loss of Colin Munro, the cogs in New Zealand's innings had turned smoothly. Nicholls, Taylor and Tom Latham – captaining in Williamson's planned absence – each worked through the gears; when Taylor reached 51, he passed Stephen Fleming's New Zealand-record 8,007 ODI runs. Carefree cameos from Neesham and Colin de Grandhomme paved the way for a 3–0 whitewash.

NEW ZEALAND v BANGLADESH

First Test

At Hamilton, February 28–March 3, 2019. New Zealand won by an innings and 52 runs. Toss: New Zealand. Test debut: Ebadat Hossain.

A lack of pace-bowling experience and top-order application cost Bangladesh dear, as New Zealand ground them into the Patumahoe clay. Tamim Iqbal set a tone his team could not match, blazing 126 off 128 balls on the opening day, including 86 before lunch – but no one else reached 30. Wagner's short-pitched expertise brought reward against opponents allergic to risk-free pulling and hooking, securing five for 47 as Bangladesh lost their last nine for 113.

Enter Raval and Latham, under a Waikato sun baking a banquet of runs into the pitch. Their 254-run partnership was New Zealand's highest for the first wicket for 47 years (and their third-highest ever), and 20 more than Bangladesh had managed in total; Raval's hundred was his first in Tests.

Williamson and Nicholls maintained the momentum in a fourth-wicket stand of 100 in 25 overs, before Williamson moved to his 20th Test century. It was only the second time New Zealand's top three had all reached three figures in one Test innings, after Mark Richardson, Lou Vincent and Scott Styris against India at Mohali in October 2003. With the help of nightwatchman Wagner, then de Grandhomme, Williamson propelled them to a national-record 715 for six, beating 690 against Pakistan at Sharjah in 2014-15. (Only Sri Lanka, with 730 for six at Mirpur in January 2014, had scored more against Bangladesh.) After pulling Abu Jayed to long leg for his 19th four, and bringing up his second Test double-century from just 257 balls, Williamson declared. The innings had been a brick-by-brick deconstruction of the tourists' morale, rather than a wrecking-ball demolition.

Bangladesh's three-man seam attack – boasting four Test caps between them – struggled to hit a good length, while the logic of resting Mustafizur Rahman, who offered left-arm variety and had played a dozen Tests, seemed questionable. Off-spinner Mehedi Hasan battled, too: figures of two for 246 from 49 overs were Bangladesh's most expensive (surpassing Taijul Islam's four for 219 against Sri Lanka at Chittagong in January 2018) and the sixth-most expensive overall. New Zealand's lead of 481 – their biggest in Tests – towered over Bangladesh as they took guard again a refreshed attack.

Tamim prospered again, making 74 from 86 balls, but humiliation beckoned at 126 for four. Instead, Soumya Sarkar and Mahmudullah ducked and dived against a barrage of short-pitched bowling, and constructed a rearguard fifth-wicket stand of 235 in 54 overs. Soumya completed a maiden Test hundred, from just 94 balls, equalling Bangladesh's fastest (Tamim at Lord's in 2010), and Mahmudullah registered a career-best, as the pair pulled and hooked with aplomb. Their resistance was perhaps best illustrated by Sky TV's decision to turn off the stump mikes as fielders began to grumble.

But when Boult finally bowled Soumya for 149 from 171 balls, with 21 fours and five sixes, the rest followed meekly: six fell for 68, and Boult finished with five. Watling also deserved a sliver of the limelight: when he caught last man Ebadat Hossain, it was his 202nd Test dismissal as a wicketkeeper, breaking the New Zealand record held by Adam Parore since 2002. It was testament to Watling's skill, and the strength of New Zealand's modern-day pace bowling, that he needed only 52 matches to get there, compared with Parore's 67.

Player of the Match: K. S. Williamson.

Close of play: first day, New Zealand 86-0 (Raval 51, Latham 35); second day, New Zealand 451-4 (Williamson 93, Wagner 1); third day, Bangladesh 174-4 (Soumya Sarkar 39, Mahmudullah 15).

Bangladesh

Tamim Iqbal c Williamson b de Grandhomme	126	– c Watling b Southee	74
Shadman Islam b Boult	24	– c Boult b Wagner	37
Mominul Haque c Watling b Wagner	12	– c Taylor b Boult	8
Mithun Ali c Latham b Wagner	8	– c Williamson b Boult	0
Soumya Sarkar c Watling b Southee	1	– b Boult	149
*Mahmudullah c Boult b Wagner	22	– c Boult b Southee	146
†Liton Das c Boult b Wagner	29	– b Boult	1
Mehedi Hasan c Nicholls b Wagner	10	– c Raval b Wagner	1
Abu Jayed c Watling b Southee	2	– b Boult	3
Khaled Ahmed b Southee	0	– not out	4
Ebadat Hossain not out	0	– c Watling b Southee	0
W 6		W 6	6

1/57 (2) 2/121 (3) 3/147 (4)   (59.2 overs) 234   1/88 (2) 2/100 (3)   (103 overs) 429
4/149 (5) 5/180 (1) 6/207 (6)   3/110 (4) 4/126 (1)
7/217 (8) 8/226 (9) 9/234 (10) 10/234 (7)   5/361 (5) 6/379 (7) 7/380 (8)
                                       8/413 (9) 9/429 (6) 10/429 (11)

Boult 13–1–62–1; Southee 14–2–76–3; de Grandhomme 11–0–39–1; Wagner 16.2–4–47–5; Astle 5–1–10–0. *Second innings*—Boult 28–3–123–5; Southee 24–4–98–3; de Grandhomme 10–1–33–0; Wagner 24–4–104–2; Astle 15–3–58–0; Williamson 2–0–13–0.

New Zealand

J. A. Raval c Khaled Ahmed b Mahmudullah	132	†B-J. Watling c Liton Das b Mehedi Hasan	31
T. W. M. Latham c Mithun Ali b Soumya Sarkar	161	C. de Grandhomme not out	76
*K. S. Williamson not out	200	Lb 7, w 2, nb 2	11
L. R. P. L. Taylor lbw b Soumya Sarkar	4		
H. M. Nicholls b Mehedi Hasan	53	1/254 (1) (6 wkts dec, 163 overs) 715	
N. Wagner c Liton Das b Ebadat Hossain	47	2/333 (2) 3/349 (4)	

T. D. Astle, T. G. Southee and T. A. Boult did not bat.

4/449 (5) 5/509 (6) 6/605 (7)

Abu Jayed 30–5–103–0; Ebadat Hossain 27–4–107–1; Khaled Ahmed 30–6–149–0; Soumya Sarkar 21–1–68–2; Mehedi Hasan 49–2–246–2; Mahmudullah 1–0–3–1; Mominul Haque 5–0–32–0.

Umpires: N. J. Llong and P. R. Reiffel. Third umpire: R. S. A. Palliyaguruge.
Referee: D. C. Boon.

NEW ZEALAND v BANGLADESH

Second Test

At Wellington, March 8–12, 2019. New Zealand won by an innings and 12 runs. Toss: New Zealand.

The first two days were lost to rain, but New Zealand were not going to let that worry them, especially when the coin landed in their favour. As so often, the Basin Reserve pitch was touted as a green mamba, yet offered minimal venom. Once it was unveiled – and forensic analysis conducted to differentiate the strip from the outfield – both sides had to judge the best tempo for the abridged timeframe. The chances of the surface deteriorating into a spinners' den were minimal.

As a result, Matt Henry replaced Todd Astle in the New Zealand side for his first Test since December 2017. Bangladesh persevered with spin, opting for Taijul Islam's left-armers over Mehedi Hasan's off-breaks. First, though, their openers' decisiveness in attack and defence provided an early antidote to any movement, as New Zealand's five-man pace battery looked off-colour. That glitch was rectified by tea: in the middle session alone, seven wickets tumbled for 77. Wagner led the way with four for 28, despite splitting the webbing on his non-bowling (right) hand in the field. Bangladesh were all out for 211.

A tidy opening spell from Abu Jayed removed the New Zealand openers, but that proved a false dawn. A stand of 172 in just 31 overs between Williamson and Taylor (dropped twice on 20 in three balls off Jayed) was followed by 216 in 40 between Taylor and Nicholls – a fourth-wicket record in this fixture. A mini-replica of the First Test loomed. New Zealand declared at 432 for six, with Taylor finally falling for 200, his third Test double and his 18th hundred, passing his late mentor Martin Crowe. He also eclipsed Crowe's mark of 1,123 for most runs at the Basin Reserve. Nicholls's unbeaten 107 was his fifth Test century.

Trailing by 221, a demoralised Bangladesh then lost Tamim Iqbal, their batting talisman, second ball, after he hit the first for four. However, New Zealand suffered their own loss when Williamson departed for scans on his left shoulder after falling awkwardly in the gully. He was scheduled to miss the final Test, with Southee set to take charge.

Bangladesh began the final day at 80 for three, but were dismissed by lunch for 209, losing their last seven for 97 as Boult and Wagner scythed through the batting. Reserve fielder Peter Bocock assumed the wicketkeeping duties after Watling strained a hamstring in the warm-ups; Latham, New Zealand's preferred one-day keeper, stayed in the slip cordon. Bocock crouched in Latham's gloves and Watling's pads and shirt, with the Test number taped out over out of respect. His joy at spending 33 overs behind the stumps was a memory to cherish, before the tour was enveloped by tragedy.

Player of the Match: L. R. P. L. Taylor.

Close of play: first day, no play; second day, no play; third day, New Zealand 38-2 (Williamson 10, Taylor 19); fourth day, Bangladesh 80-3 (Mithun Ali 25, Soumya Sarkar 12).

Bangladesh

Tamim Iqbal c Southee b Wagner	74	– b Boult	4
Shadman Islam c Taylor b de Grandhomme	27	– c Watling b Henry	29
Mominul Haque c Watling b Wagner	15	– c Southee b Boult	10
Mithun Ali c Watling b Wagner	3	– c Southee b Wagner	47
Soumya Sarkar c Watling b Henry	20	– c Taylor b Boult	28
*Mahmudullah c de Grandhomme b Wagner	13	– c Boult b Wagner	67
†Liton Das c Williamson b Southee	33	– c Boult b Wagner	1
Taijul Islam lbw b Boult	8	– c Latham b Wagner	0
Mustafizur Rahman b Boult	0	– b Boult	16
Abu Jayed b Boult	4	– not out	0
Ebadat Hossain not out	0	– b Wagner	0
B 4, lb 7, w 2, nb 1	14	Lb 4, w 3	7

1/75 (2) 2/119 (3) 3/127 (4)   (61 overs) 211   1/4 (1) 2/20 (3)   (56 overs) 209
4/134 (1) 5/152 (5) 6/168 (6)   3/55 (2) 4/112 (5)
7/206 (8) 8/206 (9) 9/207 (7) 10/211 (10)   5/152 (4) 6/158 (7) 7/170 (8)
                                                   8/203 (9) 9/209 (6) 10/209 (11)

Boult 11–3–38–3; Southee 15–2–52–1; de Grandhomme 7–0–15–1; Henry 15–0–67–1; Wagner 13–4–28–4. *Second innings*—Boult 16–5–52–4; Southee 12–1–57–0; Henry 9–3–40–1; de Grandhomme 5–0–11–0; Wagner 14–4–45–5.

New Zealand

J. A. Raval c Soumya Sarkar b Abu Jayed .	3	†B-J. Watling c Soumya Sarkar b Abu Jayed	8
T. W. M. Latham c Liton Das b Abu Jayed	4		
*K. S. Williamson c and b Taijul Islam	74	Lb 5, w 7, nb 1................	13
L. R. P. L. Taylor c Liton Das			
b Mustafizur Rahman .	200	1/5 (2) 2/8 (1) (6 wkts dec, 84.5 overs)	432
H. M. Nicholls b Taijul Islam	107	3/180 (3) 4/396 (5)	
C. de Grandhomme not out	23	5/421 (4) 6/432 (7)	

T. G. Southee, M. J. Henry, N. Wagner and T. A. Boult did not bat.

Abu Jayed 18.5–2–94–3; Ebadat Hossain 16–2–84–0; Mustafizur Rahman 14–2–74–1; Soumya Sarkar 6–0–35–0; Taijul Islam 21–0–99–2; Mominul Haque 9–0–41–0.

Umpires: R. S. A. Palliyaguruge and P. R. Reiffel.   Third umpire: N. J. Llong.
Referee: D. C. Boon.

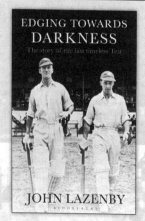

DOMESTIC CRICKET IN NEW ZEALAND IN 2018-19

Mark Geenty

A few days before the end of the New Zealand season, a gunman opened fire at a Christchurch mosque around half a mile from Hagley Oval, killing 51 people. The Third Test against Bangladesh – whose players were heading for the mosque when the attack began – was cancelled, while Wellington and Canterbury called off their last Plunket Shield game. The other two final-round matches went ahead.

It was a tough call for Central Districts spinner Ajaz Patel, a devout Muslim; he had made a memorable debut for New Zealand four months earlier, though hadn't been picked to play Bangladesh. After some reflection, he took the field with his team-mates. "I didn't know how to cope with those emotions," he said. "I felt completely hollow." But he emphasised the need to show love and move forward. Northern Districts won the match, but **Central Districts** finished 13 points clear of Canterbury to claim back-to-back first-class titles for the first time since 1967-68. Celebrations were subdued, as a mark of respect, but it remained a fitting farewell for their South African coach Heinrich Malan. Over six seasons, he had moulded Central Districts into a force in all formats – they had also won the Twenty20 Super Smash a month earlier. Malan moved to Auckland for 2019-20.

In a reduced Plunket Shield, down from ten rounds to eight, Central Districts won their first three matches and were never headed, finishing with five victories in all. The first came against Canterbury, at Nelson, after both captains forfeited an innings in a rain-hit match; Ryan McCone, in his final season, secured the winning wicket with six balls to go, after Canterbury's last pair Will Williams and Andrew Hazeldine had survived almost 26 overs.

Central Districts had a new captain: 34-year-old opener Greg Hay took over from Will Young, who stepped aside after hoisting the trophy in 2017-18 to focus on his batting. Hay continued his prolific form with 633 Plunket Shield runs at 48, second only to Wellington's Devon Conway, on 659. Conway had arrived from South Africa in 2017, signalling his intention to qualify for New Zealand; his run-fest across the formats earned him the Domestic Player of the Year award.

Fourth-placed **Northern Districts'** leg-spinner Ish Sodhi was the tournament's leading wicket-taker with 36, ahead of Wellington's bustling Hamish Bennett, on 32. Either side of international duty, seamer Matt Henry snared 23 victims in four matches to help **Canterbury** move up the ladder into the runners-up spot, while **Auckland** finished third, thanks to 610 runs from Glenn Phillips, plus 49 wickets shared by spinner Will Somerville and seamer Matt McEwan.

Wellington and **Otago** filled the bottom two places in the Plunket Shield, though a few months earlier they had set the pace in 50-over cricket, contesting the Ford Trophy final. Wellington gave up home advantage for their play-off against third-placed Auckland, because of a craft-beer festival at the Basin Reserve. No bother: they won at Eden Park's Outer Oval, then made the long trip south to beat table-topping Otago by three wickets, with one-day captain Bennett taking four wickets – each rapturously celebrated – to finish the competition with 28 at 14.

The Ford Trophy lost players to concurrent series for New Zealand's senior and A-teams, but Hamish Rutherford averaged 65 in the seven innings he played for Otago. The run-charts were led by Wellington opener Andrew Fletcher, with 618; next came team-mate Jimmy Neesham with 503, plus 13 wickets. Neesham made an instant impact after shifting from Otago to Wellington, and was recalled to the one-day international squad.

Popular all-rounder Luke Woodcock retired after 143 first-class appearances for Wellington, a record for a single major association, over 18 seasons. Across all three formats, he played 384 games (seven for New Zealand), scoring 10,594 runs and taking 339 wickets. Coach Bruce Edgar also bade Wellington farewell after four seasons.

FIRST-CLASS AVERAGES IN 2018-19

BATTING (350 runs)

		M	I	NO	R	HS	100	Avge	Ct/St
1	C. de Grandhomme (*Northern Districts / NZ*)	6	8	4	370	115	1	92.50	5
2	†T. W. M. Latham (*Canterbury / NZ*)	6	8	1	641	264*	3	91.57	7
3	K. S. Williamson (*Northern Districts / NZ*) .	5	7	1	499	200*	1	83.16	5
4	†D. P. Conway (*Wellington*)	7	12	4	659	203*	2	82.37	6
5	S. J. Murdoch (*Canterbury*)	5	9	3	443	130*	1	73.83	3
6	†H. M. Nicholls (*Canterbury / NZ*)	6	8	1	511	162*	1	73.00	3
7	L. R. P. L. Taylor (*Central Districts / NZ*)	5	6	0	396	200	1	66.00	4
8	G. D. Phillips (*Auckland / NZ A*)	9	13	2	660	138*	1	60.00	10
9	W. A. Young (*Central Districts / NZ A*)	6	7	0	382	150	1	54.57	7
10	G. R. Hay (*Central Districts*)	8	13	0	633	226	2	48.69	2
11	†J. A. Raval (*Auckland / New Zealand*)	7	9	0	429	132	1	47.66	4
12	†M. G. Bracewell (*Wellington*)	7	12	2	475	98	0	47.50	5
13	†H. D. Rutherford (*Otago / NZ A*)	9	15	1	658	115	2	47.00	5
14	C. D. Fletcher (*Canterbury / NZ A*)	9	12	1	517	108	1	47.00	30
15	D. Cleaver (*Central Districts / NZ A*)	9	14	1	580	117	1	44.61	29
16	†K. Noema-Barnett (*Central Districts*)	5	8	0	350	108	2	43.75	2
17	J. F. Carter (*Northern Districts*)	6	10	0	423	109	1	42.30	8
18	†H. R. Cooper (*Northern Districts*)	8	15	2	471	78	0	36.23	6
19	R. R. O'Donnell (*Auckland*)	8	11	0	390	73	0	35.45	12
20	T. L. Seifert (*Northern Districts / NZ A*)	8	12	1	381	86	0	34.63	15/2
21	C. T. Hawkins (*Otago*)	6	11	0	377	76	0	34.27	5
22	M. Renwick (*Otago*)	8	15	0	499	131	1	33.26	6
23	†S. M. Solia (*Auckland*)	8	13	0	415	81	0	31.92	3
24	G. K. Beghin (*Auckland*)	8	13	1	370	140	1	30.83	4

BOWLING (13 wickets)

		Style	O	M	R	W	BB	5I	Avge
1	H. K. Bennett (*Wellington*)	RFM	192.2	42	572	32	5-39	3	17.87
2	N. Wagner (*Northern Districts / NZ*)	LFM	222.3	49	681	34	5-45	2	20.02
3	J. A. Brown (*Auckland*)	RFM	91.3	19	305	15	3-17	0	20.33
4	T. A. Boult (*Northern Districts / NZ*)	LFM	192	52	582	28	6-30	2	20.78
5	M. B. McEwan (*Auckland*)	RFM	210.1	68	515	24	5-23	1	21.45
6	R. J. McCone (*Central Districts*)	LM	193.1	54	538	24	5-47	1	22.41
7	M. J. Henry (*Canterbury / NZ*)	RFM	187.5	44	594	25	5-46	2	23.76
8	M. B. Bacon (*Otago*)	RFM	200.2	29	763	31	6-73	1	24.61
9	T. G. Southee (*New Zealand*)	RFM	159	42	499	20	6-68	1	24.95
10	I. S. Sodhi (*Northern Districts*)	LB	314.4	67	899	36	6-127	2	24.97
11	D. A. J. Bracewell (*C Districts / NZ A*)	RFM	265.5	64	757	30	5-78	1	25.23
12	S. H. A. Rance (*C Districts / NZ A*)	RFM	172.2	28	589	23	5-53	1	25.60
13	W. E. R. Somerville (*Auckland*)	OB	249.5	82	649	25	4-141	0	25.96
14	B. G. Lister (*Auckland*)	LM	152	44	396	15	3-39	0	26.40
15	J. D. Baker (*Northern Districts*)	RFM	188.5	59	566	20	4-68	0	28.30
16	S. C. Kuggeleijn (*Northern Districts*)	RFM	175.1	34	625	22	5-68	1	28.40
17	S. M. Solia (*Auckland*)	RFM	151	27	461	16	3-23	0	28.81
18	B. M. Tickner (*C Districts / NZ A*)	RFM	206.1	44	618	21	4-25	0	29.42
19	O. R. Newton (*Wellington*)	RM	152.3	37	475	15	4-58	0	31.66
20	I. G. McPeake (*Wellington*)	RFM	168	39	569	17	3-44	0	33.47
21	W. S. A. Williams (*Canterbury*)	RM	163.3	39	573	17	3-60	0	33.69
22	A. T. E. Hazeldine (*Canterbury*)	LF	137.2	17	589	15	5-33	1	39.26
23	A. Y. Patel (*Central Districts / NZ A*)	SLA	249	81	594	14	4-84	0	42.42
24	J. A. Duffy (*Otago*)	RFM	259.5	57	796	17	3-63	0	46.82
25	J. S. Patel (*Wellington*)	OB	253.1	66	729	15	4-88	0	48.60

PLUNKET SHIELD IN 2018-19

	P	W	L	D	Bat	Bowl	Pts	NARPW
					Bonus pts			
Central Districts.....	8	5	2	1	20	26	106	7.36
Canterbury.........	8	4	2	1*	15	22	93†	0.71
Auckland..........	8	3	2	3	14	27	77	6.94
Northern Districts ...	8	3	2	3	8	28	72	1.36
Wellington.........	8	1	3	3*	19	23	62†	3.31
Otago.............	8	1	6	1	8	21	41	−21.91

* *Plus one abandoned.* † *6pts added after match cancelled because of a terrorist attack.*

Outright win = 12pts; abandoned = 2pts. Bonus points were awarded as follows for the first 110 overs of each team's first innings: one batting point for the first 200 runs, then for 250, 300 and 350; one bowling point for the third wicket taken, then for the fifth, seventh and ninth. Net average runs per wicket is calculated by subtracting average runs conceded per wicket from average runs scored per wicket.

PLUNKET SHIELD WINNERS

1921-22	Auckland	1957-58	Otago	1989-90	Wellington
1922-23	Canterbury	1958-59	Auckland	1990-91	Auckland
1923-24	Wellington	1959-60	Canterbury	1991-92	{ Central Districts
1924-25	Otago	1960-61	Wellington		{ Northern Districts
1925-26	Wellington	1961-62	Wellington	1992-93	Northern Districts
1926-27	Auckland	1962-63	Northern Districts	1993-94	Canterbury
1927-28	Wellington	1963-64	Auckland	1994-95	Auckland
1928-29	Auckland	1964-65	Canterbury	1995-96	Auckland
1929-30	Wellington	1965-66	Wellington	1996-97	Canterbury
1930-31	Canterbury	1966-67	Central Districts	1997-98	Canterbury
1931-32	Wellington	1967-68	Central Districts	1998-99	Central Districts
1932-33	Otago	1968-69	Auckland	1999-2000	Northern Districts
1933-34	Auckland	1969-70	Otago	2000-01	Wellington
1934-35	Canterbury	1970-71	Central Districts	2001-02	Auckland
1935-36	Wellington	1971-72	Otago	2002-03	Auckland
1936-37	Auckland	1972-73	Wellington	2003-04	Wellington
1937-38	Auckland	1973-74	Wellington	2004-05	Auckland
1938-39	Auckland	1974-75	Otago	2005-06	Central Districts
1939-40	Auckland	1975-76	Canterbury	2006-07	Northern Districts
1940–45	No competition	1976-77	Otago	2007-08	Canterbury
1945-46	Canterbury	1977-78	Auckland	2008-09	Auckland
1946-47	Auckland	1978-79	Otago	2009-10	Northern Districts
1947-48	Otago	1979-80	Northern Districts	2010-11	Canterbury
1948-49	Canterbury	1980-81	Auckland	2011-12	Northern Districts
1949-50	Wellington	1981-82	Wellington	2012-13	Central Districts
1950-51	Otago	1982-83	Wellington	2013-14	Canterbury
1951-52	Canterbury	1983-84	Canterbury	2014-15	Canterbury
1952-53	Otago	1984-85	Wellington	2015-16	Auckland
1953-54	Central Districts	1985-86	Otago	2016-17	Canterbury
1954-55	Wellington	1986-87	Central Districts	2017-18	Central Districts
1955-56	Canterbury	1987-88	Otago	2018-19	Central Districts
1956-57	Wellington	1988-89	Auckland		

Auckland have won the title outright 23 times, Wellington 20, Canterbury 19, Otago 13, Central Districts 10, Northern Districts 7. Central Districts and Northern Districts also shared the title once.

The tournament was known as the Shell Trophy from 1975-76 to 2000-01, and the State Championship from 2001-02 to 2008-09.

THE FORD TROPHY IN 2018-19

50-over league plus knockout

	P	W	L	NR/A	Bonus	Pts	NRR
OTAGO	10	7	3	0	2	30	−0.17
WELLINGTON	10	6	3	1	3	29	0.96
AUCKLAND	10	5	5	0	1	21	−0.41
Northern Districts	10	4	4	2	0	20	−0.28
Central Districts	10	3	5	2	1	17	0.03
Canterbury	10	2	7	1	1	11	−0.10

2nd v 3rd   Wellington beat Auckland by three wickets.

Final   At Dunedin (University Oval), December 1, 2018. **Wellington won by three wickets.** ‡**Otago 234-8** (50 overs); **Wellington 235-7** (48.4 overs). *Otago chose to bat, but slumped to 57-7 by the 16th over, with Hamish Bennett (4-46) grabbing three in four balls, before Michael Rippon (82) and Christi Viljoen (87*) came to the rescue by adding 146. Wellington's reply began almost as rockily – 75-5 in 17 overs – but they too were rescued by a lower-order partnership, 118 from Malcolm Nofal (73) and Peter Younghusband (49), and got home with eight balls to spare.*

The Burger King Super Smash has its own section (page 1146).

PAKISTAN CRICKET IN 2019

Misbah of all trades

OSMAN SAMIUDDIN

Little happened in Pakistan cricket which didn't bear the distinctive authorship of Misbah-ul-Haq. In a year of great change, it was Misbah who emerged – as he had a decade earlier, while still a player – as the man in almost total control.

By the end of 2019, he was the national team's coach. He was the chief selector. He was head coach of the Pakistan Super League's most successful franchise, Islamabad United. He was involved in the squad selection of all six teams in the Quaid-e-Azam Trophy. And he was on the board cricket committee which grilled coach Mickey Arthur after the World Cup. The same panel then recommended Arthur's removal as coach, paving the way for… Misbah. Short of attending ICC meetings and doing the team's laundry, Misbah was everywhere.

This was too much power, even if Misbah was the man least likely to abuse it, with plenty of potential (and actual) conflicts of interest. But, two years after his retirement, his return to the game – and rapid rise – was only a significant

PAKISTAN IN 2019

	Played	Won	Lost	Drawn/No result
Tests	6	1	4	1
One-day internationals	25	9	15	1
Twenty20 internationals	10	1	8	1

DECEMBER		
JANUARY	3 Tests, 5 ODIs and 3 T20Is (a) v South Africa	(see *Wisden 2019*, page 1007)
FEBRUARY		
MARCH	5 ODIs (in the UAE) v Australia	(page 999)
APRIL		
MAY	5 ODIs and 1 T20I (a) v England	(page 366)
JUNE	World Cup (in England)	(page 237)
JULY		
AUGUST		
SEPTEMBER	3 ODIs and 3 T20Is (h) v Sri Lanka	(page 1002)
OCTOBER		
NOVEMBER	2 Tests and 3 T20Is (a) v Australia	(page 888
DECEMBER	2 Tests (h) v Sri Lanka	(page 1002

For a review of Pakistan domestic cricket from the 2018-19 season, see page 1013.

Arif Ali, AFP/Getty Images

Coachload: one of Misbah-ul-Haq's many roles at the PCB was head coach.

subplot in a transformative, maybe even regenerative, year. It ended with great hope. In December, Rawalpindi and Karachi hosted the first Tests in Pakistan for over ten years. And, for the first time, the entire PSL was set to be played at home – across four cities – early in 2020.

The Pakistan Cricket Board were emboldened enough to demand that all their home series should now be played in Pakistan, and it was difficult to argue. From the time Zimbabwe broke the drought in 2015, the PCB had played this gradual return almost pitch-perfect: they were not inert, opting for a drip-drip approach, in which each incident-free tour was a small win, building towards a bigger one. A T20 here, some ODIs there, a few PSL games, a PSL final, a Full Member visit, a World XI tour, and now two Tests.

Other developments were more precipitous. The Quaid-e-Azam Trophy is no stranger to overhauls, but the 2019-20 season saw arguably its biggest. At the insistence of Imran Khan – prime minister, patron of the board, former captain and all-round legend (and almost as busy as Misbah) – the departmental teams were removed from the domestic scene.

Banks, airlines and gas companies had been part of the landscape in one way or another from the beginning. From the 1970s, their importance had grown considerably, because they offered players financial rewards otherwise beyond them. It was these departments that effectively enabled the profession-alisation of the game in Pakistan. Imran, however, had long been an opponent, believing the only way for domestic cricket to thrive was on a model similar to Australia's Sheffield Shield: fewer teams, all region-based, with – in theory – greater competition for places.

At a stroke, the number of Quaid-e-Azam teams was reduced from 16 to six and a bloated 25 in 2013-14), and the number of first-class cricketers from

353 to 114. But with that went a loss of financial stability for the players. The domestic central contracts offered by the PCB paid significantly less than most had earned as employees for the various departments, where they were also given health cover and other benefits. Stories of first-class players working for Uber to make up for lost income were common. It was not easy to find a cricketer happy with the change.

This cut in earnings – Pakistan's top players were already among the lowest-paid internationally – offset the positives. Kookaburra balls were used, a no-toss rule trialled, and pitches given greater attention. The aim was clear: to nullify medium-pacers who had feasted for years on poor surfaces. It worked, though perhaps the balance tipped too far in favour of batsmen.

These were only the most pressing challenges faced by Wasim Khan, who had arrived from England in February 2019 as the board's new CEO. His recruitment, by chairman Ehsan Mani, was seen as a coup – though by the end of the year the scale of the work ahead was uncomfortably clear. Khan has to convince more teams to tour, find a way to better remunerate disgruntled cricketers, and uncover new revenue streams.

The story on the field was less complicated: Pakistan were poor across the formats. They succumbed to painfully familiar Test whitewashes in South Africa and Australia. They hung on by the skin of their teeth to the top T20 ranking, despite winning just one of their ten matches, and losing eight. They lost 15 of their 25 one-day internationals, although they might have made it to the World Cup semi-finals but for a heavy defeat by West Indies in their opening game.

Somebody had to pay, and it turned out to be both Arthur and Sarfraz Ahmed, who was not only relieved of the captaincy, but dumped from all three teams as well. The T20 removal felt harsh, given the exemplary record he had overseen, but Pakistan were in a mess under his leadership, his own form was patchy, and some racially tinged remarks in South Africa – for which he was briefly banned – had eroded any credit.

The one ray of light was Babar Azam, who joined the company of the game's most elite batsmen with a flurry of Test runs in South Africa and Australia, then finally in front of adoring home crowds. Backing this up were his usual white-ball feats: a magnificent World Cup hundred against New Zealand at Edgbaston, an extraordinary 90 in a T20 in Johannesburg, and an exceptional season for Somerset in the Vitality Blast.

Given how long it had been since Pakistan had a batsman like Babar to celebrate, perhaps the year was actually a good one.

"The match burst into life like the opening scene of a Hollywood blockbuster, when Mohammad Amir's first ball induced a drag-on by Guptill, prompting a volcanic eruption of noise."
New Zealand v Pakistan, World Cup 2019, page 292

PAKISTAN v AUSTRALIA IN THE UAE IN 2018-19

Paul Radley

One-day internationals (5): Pakistan 0, Australia 5

A series shoehorned awkwardly into the schedule as a World Cup tune-up worked perfectly for Australia. But it was a disaster for Pakistan: by the end, their coach Mickey Arthur was batting away fierce criticism of the decision to rest a raft of senior players. Australia, however, looked chipper two months ahead of their World Cup defence.

The teams had met for Test and Twenty20 series the previous October (see *Wisden 2019*, page 933), with Pakistan winning both. At the time it had seemed sensible to split the tour, to give both sides extra 50-over practice ahead of the big event. But that overlooked the workload demanded of the Pakistan players. Since Australia's visit, they had hosted New Zealand and toured South Africa, with matches in all three formats, then slogged through the Pakistan Super League. As all but the last nine days of the PSL were abroad, Arthur reasoned it was important to give some of his key men a break.

Six were given time off, including the captain Sarfraz Ahmed, while Fahim Ashraf became the seventh midway through the series. Shoaib Malik, seemingly the last senior player standing, retained the captaincy he had inherited when Sarfraz was suspended in South Africa, but picked up a rib injury and missed the last two games. One of the replacements, Umar Akmal, returned after two years on the sidelines – but maintained a history of disciplinary issues by being fined for breaching a team curfew.

It was hardly surprising that a resurgent Australia swept the series. "In terms of morale, we are all incredibly disappointed," said Arthur. "We are a very proud cricket nation, and we represent 210 million people. But I think there is a bigger picture – we have a World Cup to win."

The Australians had arrived fresh from a come-from-behind 3–2 win in India. The transformation from the tour five months earlier was enormous. Back then, they were falling apart; now, the pieces seemed to be falling into place. Aaron Finch embodied the change. In October, he had been entirely out of form in the white-ball games. But, having come to terms with his promotion to the captaincy after Tim Paine was jettisoned, he reached new levels of excellence, with 451 runs at 112. "A lot of people were slamming us," he said. "They were writing us off – not just for one-day cricket, but for all forms of

APPLYING THE WHITEWASH

Bilateral one-day series won 5–0 by Australia:

New Zealand (a)	2004-05		West Indies (h)	2012-13
West Indies (a)	2007-08		**Pakistan (in the UAE)**	**2018-19**
Pakistan (h)	2009-10			

Australia have twice lost series 5–0: in South Africa (2016-17), and in England (2018).

cricket." Another Australian to hit the heights was Glenn Maxwell, who hammered 258 runs at a strike-rate of 139. "He can be Virat Kohli," enthused coach Justin Langer.

AUSTRALIAN TOURING PARTY

*A. J. Finch, J. P. Behrendorff, A. T. Carey, N. M. Coulter-Nile, P. J. Cummins, P. S. P. Handscomb, U. T. Khawaja, N. M. Lyon, S. E. Marsh, G. J. Maxwell, J. A. Richardson, K. W. Richardson, M. P. Stoinis, A. J. Turner, A. Zampa. *Coach:* J. L. Langer.

First one-day international   At Sharjah, March 22, 2019 (day/night). **Australia won by eight wickets.** ‡**Pakistan 280-5** (50 overs) (Shan Masood 40, Haris Sohail 101*, Umar Akmal 48); **Australia 281-2** (49 overs) (A. J. Finch 116, S. E. Marsh 91*, P. S. P. Handscomb 30*). *PoM:* A. J. Finch. *ODI debuts:* Mohammad Abbas, Shan Masood (Pakistan). *Pakistan's batsmen were rarely troubled on a typical Sharjah featherbed; Haris Sohail helped himself to his first ODI century. But a target of 281 never felt like a challenge for an Australian side full of confidence. Aaron Finch set the tone: having ended an indifferent run with 93 to kickstart the comeback in India, he now made 116, his 12th ODI century, and put on 172 for the second wicket with Shaun Marsh.*

Second one-day international   At Sharjah, March 24, 2019 (day/night). **Australia won by eight wickets.** ‡**Pakistan 284-7** (50 overs) (Haris Sohail 34, Mohammad Rizwan 115, Shoaib Malik 60); **Australia 285-2** (47.5 overs) (U. T. Khawaja 88, A. J. Finch 153*). *PoM:* A. J. Finch. *ODI debut:* Mohammad Hasnain (Pakistan). *A paltry crowd might have wondered whether they were watching a rerun of the first game. Pakistan chose to bat, went at a similar tempo, and barely exceeded their total of two days earlier; this time there was a hundred from wicketkeeper Mohammad Rizwan. Australia again reeled in the target with ease, winning by an identical margin, with another century from Finch. He finished the job this time, but had to work hard against Pakistan's debutant fast bowler Mohammad Hasnain, just 18 and a standout in the PSL, where he often exceeded 90mph. A bouncer broke Finch's helmet when he had 19, but there were no ill effects: he went on to a career-best 153* after an opening stand of 209 with Usman Khawaja.*

Third one-day international   At Abu Dhabi, March 27, 2019 (day/night). **Australia won by 80 runs.** ‡**Australia 266-6** (50 overs) (A. J. Finch 90, P. S. P. Handscomb 47, G. J. Maxwell 71); **Pakistan 186** (44.4 overs) (Imam-ul-Haq 46, Shoaib Malik 31, Umar Akmal 36, Imad Wasim 43; P. J. Cummins 3-23, A. Zampa 4-43). *PoM:* P. J. Cummins. *Finch fell ten short of a third successive century, but his effort still underpinned another comfortable win for Australia, who clinched the series. He had won the toss on an unsettled day, but somehow the stadium avoided the worst of the electrical storms buzzing around the Gulf: there were two brief interruptions, though no overs were lost. Khawaja fell for a duck in the first over but, after Finch holed out on the long-on boundary, Glenn Maxwell took over, slamming 71 from 55 balls. Pat Cummins soon had Pakistan reeling at 16-3, and leg-spinner Adam Zampa lopped off the tail with four wickets in ten balls.*

Fourth one-day international   At Dubai, March 29, 2019 (day/night). **Australia won by six runs.** **Australia 277-7** (50 overs) (A. J. Finch 39, U. T. Khawaja 62, G. J. Maxwell 98, A. T. Carey 55); ‡**Pakistan 271-8** (50 overs) (Abid Ali 112, Mohammad Rizwan 104; N. M. Coulter-Nile 3-53). *PoM:* G. J. Maxwell. *ODI debuts:* Abid Ali, Saad Ali (Pakistan). *Australia won again, but their opponents had reason to cheer. Abid Ali, a 31-year-old opener from Lahore, became the third Pakistani to make a century in his first ODI, after Salim Elahi (1995-96) and Imam-ul-Haq (2017-18). He put on 144 for the third wicket with Rizwan, who made his second hundred of the series – but from 253-4 at the start of the 48th over, needing just 25 more, Pakistan still managed to lose. Earlier, Australia had been lifted from a middling 140-5 by Maxwell, who hit 98 from 82 balls, during a stand of 134 with wicketkeeper Alex Carey, whose half-century was his first in ODIs. Imad Wasim captained Pakistan for the first time, as Shoaib Malik was injured.*

WHEN TWO IS NOT ENOUGH

Losing an ODI despite two batsmen making hundreds in the run-chase:

India (M. Azharuddin 111*, A. Jadeja 119) v Sri Lanka at Colombo (RPS) 1997-98
Zimbabwe (S. V. Carlisle 109, S. M. Ervine 100) v India at Adelaide 2003-04
India (S. Dhawan 126, V. Kohli 106) v Australia at Canberra 2015-16
Pakistan (Abid Ali 112, Mohammad Rizwan 104) v Australia at Dubai **2018-19**
England (J. E. Root 107, J. C. Buttler 103) v Pakistan at Nottingham **2019**

There have been 24 instances of a team losing after hitting two centuries when batting first.

Fifth one-day international At Dubai, March 31, 2019 (day/night). **Australia won by 20 runs.**
Australia 327-7 (50 overs) (U. T. Khawaja 98, A. J. Finch 53, S. E. Marsh 61, G. J. Maxwell 70;
Junaid Khan 3-73, Usman Shinwari 4-49); ‡**Pakistan 307-7** (50 overs) (Shan Masood 50, Haris
Sohail 130, Umar Akmal 43, Imad Wasim 50*; J. P. Behrendorff 3-63). *PoM:* G. J. Maxwell. *PoS:*
A. J. Finch. *Australia completed a 5–0 whitewash in a high-scoring encounter. For the second match
running, one of their batsmen scored 98 – Khawaja this time – but Maxwell was at it again,
hammering 70 from 33 balls. Seamer Usman Shinwari took four wickets, despite needing treatment
for heat exhaustion, as did Khawaja. In Dubai's ten years as an ODI ground – this was the 34th
official match – no side had chased more than 300 to win. Led by Sohail, who struck his second
century of the series, Pakistan gave it a good shot, but still fell short against disciplined bowling.
After a century in his first ODI, Abid Ali came down to earth with a golden duck in his second.*

PAKISTAN v SRI LANKA IN 2019-20

Shahid Hashmi and Fidel Fernando

One-day internationals (3): Pakistan 2, Sri Lanka 0
Twenty20 internationals (3): Pakistan 0, Sri Lanka 3
Test matches (2): Pakistan 1 (80pts), Sri Lanka 0 (20pts)

Test cricket returned to Pakistan for the first time since the attack on the Sri Lankan team coach in Lahore in March 2009. Sri Lanka were the opposition again, having been satisfied by the security, and general atmosphere, during their white-ball series in September and October. Rumesh Ratnayake, the interim coach who had taken charge for that leg, before the appointment of South African Mickey Arthur for the Tests, said he felt it was safe to play more international matches in Pakistan. Two Tests were arranged, although in the meantime Pakistan toured Australia, where they lost heavily.

Concerns remained that security arrangements would be overwhelming, and the players forced to spend their downtime in hotels. Ten Sri Lankans had turned down the white-ball tour, but now everyone made themselves available, including seamer Suranga Lakmal, who had been on the bus in 2009. Shortly before departure, however, he wents down with dengue fever, and withdrew.

When the teams reconvened in December, the First Test – played in Rawalpindi because Lahore was expected to be shrouded in smog – was a disappointing damp draw. But Karachi stayed fine for the Second, which Pakistan won. By then, it felt almost like a normal tour. Security remained tight: troops lined the route from hotel to ground, while spectators endured long queues and multiple inspections. But still they flocked to the cordoned-off Rawalpindi stadium, despite the frigid weather. When the sun finally shone, on the fifth day, they were in resounding voice, spurring opener Abid Ali towards a debut hundred, but reserving their biggest cheers for Babar Azam, who had become their new favourite.

By the Second Test, things were so normal that locals even started barracking Pakistan's captain Azhar Ali (who hails from Lahore) for failing to include local hero Fawad Alam in the team. The Sri Lankans had also begun to relax: on one of Rawalpindi's rainy days, they went shopping, and in Karachi left their hotel for meals in the evenings. Test captain Dimuth Karunaratne had been among those unwilling to travel in September, but admitted: "I do regret not coming for the shorter formats. I can say that Pakistan is now safe for cricket."

The return was a feather in the cap of Pakistan's board, who had been desperate to avoid the huge costs of continually relocating home series to the UAE. Representatives from England, Australia and Ireland were invited to watch the one-day matches and assess the security arrangements.

The white-ball games had initially been in doubt after renewed terrorist fears, but went ahead, amid security arrangements usually reserved for visiting heads of state. Pakistan took the 50-over series, but were shocked in the T20s

Taking guard: the Pindi Cricket Stadium is well protected for the arrival of the Sri Lankan team.

despite Sri Lanka fielding a weakened line-up against the world's top-ranked team, they pulled off a 3–0 whitewash. All three matches were sell-outs, despite even tighter security in Lahore. The result cost Sarfraz Ahmed the captaincy in all formats.

The spirit shown by Sri Lanka's young guns was a welcome boost after their underwhelming World Cup. "How can you say this is a B-team?" said opener Danushka Gunathilleke. "We beat the No. 1 team in the world!" Newcomers Bhanuka Rajapaksa and Oshada Fernando – at 27, both older than the archetypal Asian debutant – did well in the T20s, with Nuwan Pradeep Fernando and Isuru Udana sharing 12 wickets in the first two games. They helped inflict some poor starts on Pakistan, for whom Babar did little after a magnificent century in the first ODI. The lively 19-year-old Mohammad Hasnain took a hat-trick in the first T20.

SRI LANKA TOURING PARTY

*F. D. M. Karunaratne (T), L. D. Chandimal (T), D. M. de Silva (T), P. W. H. de Silva (50/20), D. P. D. N. Dickwella (T), L. Embuldeniya (T), A. M. Fernando (T), A. N. P. R. Fernando (50/20), B. O. P. Fernando (T/50/20), M. V. T. Fernando (T), W. I. A. Fernando (50/20), M. D. Gunathilleke (50/20), G. S. N. F. G. Jayasuriya (50/20), C. B. R. L. S. Kumara (T/50/20), L. D. Madushanka (20), A. D. Mathews (T), B. K. G. Mendis (T), A. K. Perera (50/20), M. D. K. Perera (T), M. D. K. J. Perera (T), P. B. B. Rajapaksa (20), C. A. K. Rajitha (T/50/20), M. B. Ranasinghe (50/20), W. S. R. Samarawickrama (50/20), P. A. D. L. R. Sandakan (T/50/20), M. D. Shanaka (50/20), H. D. R. L. Thirimanne (T/50), I. Udana (50/20). *Coach:* R. J. Ratnayake (50/20), J. M. Arthur (T).

Thirimanne captained in the 50-over matches, and Shanaka in the T20s. R. A. S. Lakmal was originally selected for the Test party, but went down with dengue fever and was replaced by A. M. Fernando.

LIMITED-OVERS INTERNATIONAL REPORTS BY SHAHID HASHMI

First one-day international   At Karachi, September 27, 2019 (day/night). **Pakistan v Sri Lanka. Abandoned.**

Second one-day international   At Karachi, September 30, 2019 (day/night). **Pakistan won by 67 runs.** ‡**Pakistan 305-7** (50 overs) (Fakhar Zaman 54, Imam-ul-Haq 31, Babar Azam 115, Haris Sohail 40, Iftikhar Ahmed 32*); **Sri Lanka 238** (46.5 overs) (G. S. N. F. G. Jayasuriya 96, M. D. Shanaka 68, P. W. H. de Silva 30; Usman Shinwari 5-51). *PoM:* Usman Shinwari. *One-day international cricket returned to Pakistan for the first time in more than four years, and to Karachi for more than a decade. The match was pushed back 24 hours to allow the outfield to dry after recent rain. Pakistan won, mainly thanks to a sparkling century from Babar Azam, who put on 111 with Haris Sohail. Later, Iftikhar Ahmed – in his first ODI for almost four years – spanked 32* from 20 balls to lift the total over 300. Sri Lanka nosedived to 28-5 in the 11th, before Shehan Jayasuriya and Dasun Shanaka gave them an outside chance by putting on 177, a national sixth-wicket record, beating 159 by Chamara Kapugedera and Chamara Silva against West Indies at Port-of-Spain in April 2008. But Usman Shinwari, who had taken three early wickets, returned to break the partnership, and finished with five.*

Third one-day international   At Karachi, October 2, 2019 (day/night). **Pakistan won by five wickets.** ‡**Sri Lanka 297-9** (50 overs) (M. D. Gunathilleke 133, H. D. R. L. Thirimanne 36, M. B. Ranasinghe 36, M. D. Shanaka 43; Mohammad Amir 3-50); **Pakistan 299-5** (48.2 overs) (Fakhar Zaman 76, Abid Ali 74, Babar Azam 31, Haris Sohail 56). *PoM:* Abid Ali. *PoS:* Babar Azam. *ODI debut:* M. B. Ranasinghe (Sri Lanka). *A masterly run-a-ball century from Danushka Gunathilleke set the platform for a useful total, inflated by some late biffing from Shanaka (43 from 24 balls). But Pakistan clinched the series with relative ease. Openers Fakhar Zaman and Abid Ali put on 123. Then Haris shared stands of 55 with Sarfraz Ahmed (23) and 43 with Iftikhar (28*), before falling in sight of victory.*

First Twenty20 international   At Lahore, October 5, 2019 (floodlit). **Sri Lanka won by 64 runs. Sri Lanka 165-5** (20 overs) (M. D. Gunathilleke 57, W. I. A. Fernando 33, P. B. B. Rajapaksa 32; Mohammad Hasnain 3-37); ‡**Pakistan 101** (17.4 overs) (A. N. P. R. Fernando 3-21, I. Udana 3-11). *PoM:* M. D. Gunathilleke. *T20I debuts:* P. B. B. Rajapaksa, M. B. Ranasinghe (Sri Lanka). *Sri Lanka shocked top-ranked Pakistan, bowling them out for 101. Sri Lanka's own 165 might have been bigger: openers Gunathilleke and Avishka Fernando started with 84 in 9.4 overs, but the innings stalled, with seamer Mohammad Hasnain becoming the youngest (at 19 years 183 days) to take a hat-trick in a T20 international, a record previously held by Afghanistan's Rashid Khan. Pakistan struggled to 68-3 in the 12th, then lost seven for 33; Nuwan Pradeep Fernando and Isuru Udana returned format-best figures.*

Second Twenty20 international   At Lahore, October 7, 2019 (floodlit). **Sri Lanka won by 35 runs.** ‡**Sri Lanka 182-6** (20 overs) (P. B. B. Rajapaksa 77, G. S. N. F. G. Jayasuriya 34); **Pakistan 147** (19 overs) (Imad Wasim 47; A. N. P. R. Fernando 4-25, P. W. H. de Silva 3-38). *PoM:* P. B. B. Rajapaksa. *Left-hander Bhanuka Rajapaksa claimed to have modelled his batting style on Adam Gilchrist, and now did a passable impression, despatching the bowlers to all parts of the Gaddafi Stadium during a 48-ball 77. It included six sixes, three off Hasnain (0-39), the hat-trick hero of the previous game. Rajapaksa dominated a stand of 94 with Jayasuriya, no slouch himself, with 34 from 28. Pakistan again lost Babar Azam cheaply and, with the recalled Umar Akmal falling first ball for the second match running, were 52-5 after eight. Asif Ali (29) and Imad Wasim added 75 but, after they were parted in the 16th, the rest fell away. Pradeep Fernando improved his best figures again, as Sri Lanka beat Pakistan in a T20 series at the seventh attempt.*

Third Twenty20 international   At Lahore, October 9, 2019 (floodlit). **Sri Lanka won by 13 runs.** ‡**Sri Lanka 147-7** (20 overs) (B. O. P. Fernando 78*; Mohammad Amir 3-27); **Pakistan 134-6** (20 overs) (Haris Sohail 52; P. W. H. de Silva 3-21). *PoM:* P. W. H. de Silva. *PoS:* P. W. H. de Silva. *T20I debut:* B. O. P. Fernando (Sri Lanka). *Sri Lanka completed the whitewash with a hard-earned win, despite resting five players, including Udana and Pradeep Fernando. One of the replacements, the debutant Oshada Fernando, rescued his side from 30-3 with a composed 48-ball 78*; no one else passed 13. Pakistan lost Fakhar first ball and, although Babar and Haris added 76, it took 12 overs. That left the rest too much to do, with leg-spinner Wanindu Hasaranga de Silva claiming three important wickets.*

T EST REPORTS BY F IDEL F ERNANDO

PAKISTAN v SRI LANKA

First Test

At Rawalpindi, December 11–15, 2019. Drawn. Pakistan 20pts, Sri Lanka 20pts. Toss: Sri Lanka. Test debuts: Abid Ali, Usman Shinwari.

Pakistan's first home Test for a decade was a let-down. The board had decided to stage the match in Rawalpindi because of smog in Lahore, fog in Multan and building work in Faisalabad – but it meant playing in winter in the country's far north. Temperatures in the mornings and evenings were frequently in single figures and, with the sun setting around 5.30, it was always going to be difficult to fit in 90 overs. And it rained.

The weather interfered to such an extent that a draw was inevitable from early on. There were 68.1 overs on the first day, helped by the floodlights being on for hours, but only a total of 23.4 over the next two; the fourth was a washout. But the novelty of Test cricket in Pakistan meant big crowds kept showing up, and they were rewarded with three excellent centuries.

The first and, given the conditions, probably the best, was by Dhananjaya de Silva. He entered on the first afternoon, with the floodlights glaring and his team having lost four for 31 after an opening score of 96. Despite some testing spells from Pakistan's seamers, he was confident from the start, and shared three useful partnerships. Thanks to the weather, his century spanned all five days, and was compiled almost completely under lights; despite many interruptions, de Silva rarely looked in trouble. De Silva reached three figures on the final morning, from 165 balls, with a typically languid cover-drive, and Karunaratne declared shortly afterwards.

Pakistan batted in much friendlier conditions. The pitch had settled, and the sun was shining. To the delight of a raucous crowd, the third-wicket pair picked up the rate after a cautious beginning, and eventually added 162 in 38 overs. Abid Ali concentrated on the leg side, but Babar Azam was imperious all around the wicket, pulling Kumara's bouncers and driving the other seamers in style. Abid was the 13th Pakistani to score a century in his first Test – and the oldest, at 32 – and the first man to make a century on Test and one-day international debut, having hit 112 against Australia at Dubai earlier in the year (England's Enid Bakewell had achieved the double in the women's game). Abid's hundred came from 183 balls, but Babar needed only 118, prompting the loudest cheer of the match.

Player of the Match: Abid Ali.

Close of play: first day, Sri Lanka 202-5 (de Silva 38, Dickwella 11); second day, Sri Lanka 263-6 (de Silva 72, Perera 2); third day, Sri Lanka 282-6 (de Silva 87, Perera 6); fourth day, no play.

Sri Lanka

F. D. M. Karunaratne lbw b Shaheen Shah Afridi	59	D. M. de Silva not out 102
B. O. P. Fernando c Haris Sohail b Naseem Shah	40	†D. P. D. N. Dickwella c Babar Azam b Shaheen Shah Afridi . 33
B. K. G. Mendis c Mohammad Rizwan b Usman Shinwari	10	M. D. K. Perera not out 16
A. D. Mathews c Asad Shafiq b Naseem Shah	31	B 5, lb 7, nb 3 15
L. D. Chandimal b Mohammad Abbas	2	1/96 (1) (6 wkts dec, 97 overs) 308

2/109 (2) 3/120 (3)
4/127 (5) 5/189 (4) 6/256 (7)

C. A. K. Rajitha, M. V. T. Fernando and C. B. R. L. S. Kumara did not bat.

Mohammad Abbas 27–9–72–1; Shaheen Shah Afridi 22–7–58–2; Usman Shinwari 15–4–54–1; Naseem Shah 27–5–92–2; Haris Sohail 3–0–12–0; Shan Masood 1–1–0–0; Asad Shafiq 2–0–8–0.

Pakistan

Shan Masood c Chandimal b Rajitha	. . . .	0
Abid Ali not out.	. . . .	109
*Azhar Ali c Karunaratne b Kumara	. . . .	36
Babar Azam not out.	. . . .	102
B 2, w 1, nb 2	. . . .	5

1/3 (1) 2/90 (3)   (2 wkts, 70 overs) 252

Asad Shafiq, Haris Sohail, †Mohammad Rizwan, Usman Shinwari, Mohammad Abbas, Shaheen
   Shah Afridi and Naseem Shah did not bat.

Rajitha 6–2–5–1; M. V. T. Fernando 13–1–49–0; Kumara 14–4–46–1; Perera 24–0–85–0; de
   Silva 11–0–48–0; B. O. P. Fernando 1–0–3–0; Mendis 1–0–14–0.

Umpires: M. A. Gough and R. A. Kettleborough.   Third umpire: R. K. Illingworth.
Referee: A. J. Pycroft.

PAKISTAN v SRI LANKA

Second Test

At Karachi, December 19–23, 2019. Pakistan won by 263 runs. Pakistan 60pts. Toss:
Pakistan.

The Rawalpindi rain gave way to dry Karachi, and Pakistan romped home on the final
morning after overturning a first-innings deficit with a monumental batting effort. The last
time the National Stadium had hosted a Test, back in 2009, Younis Khan amassed a triple-
century, while Mahela Jayawardene and Thilan Samaraweera countered with doubles;
many recent domestic games had also been run-fests. Initially, at least, this surface was
not quite as bland.

There was a green tinge on the first morning, although Pakistan made reasonable
progress to 127 for three after winning the toss, with Babar Azam and Asad Shafiq going
well. Then seven tumbled for 64, with Kumara – who occasionally nudged the speed gun
over 150kph – and slow left-armer Embuldeniya each claiming four. With the pitch
flattening out, Sri Lanka had a chance to make the game safe, but on the second morning
stumbled to 80 for five. Several batsman wasted starts – only Oshada Fernando, the first to
go, failed to reach double figures – and it was left to Chandimal to ensure a lead, which
some late thumps by Perera extended to 80. The new-ball pair shared nine wickets:
Shaheen Shah Afridi took five, while Mohammad Abbas, who had looked short of a gallop
in Australia, captured four.

Pakistan emphatically turned the tables on the third day. Abid Ali was rarely troubled
in adding another century in his second Test and, although Shan Masood was not quite so
assured in defence, he was soon skipping along on a dead pitch, and reached his own
second hundred, more than four years after the first (also against Sri Lanka, at Pallekele).
The openers put on 278, easily Pakistan's best against Sri Lanka, but Abid was not
finished: he took the aggregate for his first three Test innings to 321, exceeded only by
Reginald "Tip" Foster of England (355 against Australia in 1903-04) and the West Indian
Lawrence Rowe (336 v New Zealand in 1971-72). The attack were anaemic, apart from
occasional flashes of pace from Kumara.

Now Azhar Ali batted himself back into form, reaching his first Test fifty of the year at the
last opportunity, then going on to the third century of the innings. Babar Azam joined in
as well, pulling and cutting the tiring bowlers as he zipped to a hundred in 131 balls,
narrowly the quickest of the four. It was only the second time the top four had all made
centuries in the same innings, after India (Dinesh Karthik, Wasim Jaffer, Rahul Dravid
and Sachin Tendulkar) against Bangladesh at Mirpur in 2007.

Sri Lanka needed 476 but, perhaps worn out by 131 overs in the field, they offered
meagre resistance. Not long after tea on the fourth day, when Chandimal and de Silva

YOUNGEST TO TAKE FIVE WICKETS IN A TEST INNINGS

Yrs	Days			
16	307	Nasim-ul-Ghani (5-116)	Pakistan v West Indies at Georgetown	1957-58
16	**311**	**Naseem Shah (5-31)**	**Pakistan v Sri Lanka at Karachi**	**2019-20**
17	260	Mohammad Amir (5-79)	Pakistan v Australia at Melbourne	2009-10
17	356	Nayeem Hasan (5-61)	Bangladesh v West Indies at Chittagong	2018-19
18	36	Enamul Haque jnr (6-45)	Bangladesh v Zimbabwe at Chittagong	2004-05
18	48	D. L. Vettori (5-84)	New Zealand v Sri Lanka at Hamilton	1996-97
18	196	P. J. Cummins (6-79)	Australia v South Africa at Johannesburg	2011-12
18	236	Shahid Afridi (5-52)	Pakistan v Australia at Karachi	1998-99
18	253	Wasim Akram (5-56)	Pakistan v New Zealand at Dunedin	1984-85
18	294	R. J. Shastri (5-125)	India v New Zealand at Auckland	1980-81
18	301	E. Chigumbura (5-54)	Zimbabwe v Bangladesh at Chittagong	2004-05
18	319	Shahid Nazir (5-53)	Pakistan v Zimbabwe at Sheikhupura	1996-97
18	334	L. Sivaramakrishnan (6-64)	India v England at Bombay	1984-85
18	341	Waqar Younis (7-86)	Pakistan v New Zealand at Lahore	1990-91
18	361	Mehedi Hasan (6-80)	Bangladesh v England at Chittagong	2016-17

Only the first instance in mentioned for each player. See note in Records section (in Youngest Test Players) about birthdates.

departed in successive overs, they were 97 for five. But opener Oshada Fernando and Dickwella counter-attacked, putting on 104, before Dickwella tried one reverse-sweep too many. Fernando's 13th four brought up a breezy maiden Test hundred, but Perera swished at what became the last ball of the day, from the teenage fast bowler Naseem Shah.

Naseem's first ball of the final morning accounted for Embuldeniya and, although Vishwa Fernando avoided the hat-trick, the end was not long delayed. Oshada fell without addition, to Yasir Shah, and Naseem became the second-youngest to take a five-for in a Test when he finished the match by trapping Vishwa in front. The last four had fallen for none.

"It has been a tough year for us, so it was an emotional moment returning home to play," said Azhar. "It was a big advantage to be playing at home. Special thanks to Sri Lanka from the bottom of our hearts: they have given us immense happiness by playing in Pakistan."

Player of the Match: Abid Ali.   *Player of the Series:* Abid Ali.

Close of play: first day, Sri Lanka 64-3 (Mathews 8, Embuldeniya 3); second day, Pakistan 57-0 (Shan Masood 21, Abid Ali 32); third day, Pakistan 395-2 (Azhar Ali 57, Babar Azam 22); fourth day, Sri Lanka 212-7 (B. O. P. Fernando 102).

Pakistan

Shan Masood b M. V. T. Fernando	5	– c B. O. P. Fernando b Kumara	135
Abid Ali lbw b Kumara	38	– lbw b Kumara	174
*Azhar Ali b M. V. T. Fernando	0	– st Dickwella b Embuldeniya	118
Babar Azam st Dickwella b Embuldeniya	60	– not out	100
Asad Shafiq c M. V. T. Fernando b Kumara	63		
Haris Sohail lbw b Embuldeniya	9		
Mohammad Rizwan b Kumara	4	– (5) not out	21
Yasir Shah lbw b Kumara	0		
Mohammad Abbas c de Silva b Embuldeniya	0		
Shaheen Shah Afridi c Mathews b Embuldeniya	5		
Naseem Shah not out	1		
B 4, lb 2	6	Lb 5, w 2	7

1/10 (1) 2/10 (3) 3/65 (2)   (59.3 overs) 191
4/127 (4) 5/167 (6) 6/172 (7)
7/172 (8) 8/179 (9) 9/185 (5) 10/191 (10)

1/278 (1)   (3 wkts dec, 131 overs) 555
2/355 (2) 3/503 (3)

M. V. T. Fernando 13–3–31–2; Kumara 18–5–49–4; Karunaratne 1–0–11–0; Embuldeniya 20.3–3–71–4; Perera 7–0–23–0. *Second innings*—M. V. T. Fernando 24–2–105–0; Kumara 29–5–139–2; Embuldeniya 50–4–193–1; Perera 21–1–94–0; de Silva 7–0–19–0.

Sri Lanka

B. O. P. Fernando c Mohammad Rizwan b Shaheen Shah Afridi.	4	– (2) c Asad Shafiq b Yasir Shah	102
*F. D. M. Karunaratne b Mohammad Abbas	25	– (1) c Mohammad Rizwan b Mohammad Abbas.	16
B. K. G. Mendis c Haris Sohail b Mohammad Abbas	13	– c Babar Azam b Naseem Shah	0
A. D. Mathews c Mohammad Rizwan b Shaheen Shah Afridi.	13	– c Mohammad Rizwan b Shaheen Shah Afridi.	19
L. Embuldeniya c Asad Shafiq b Mohammad Abbas	13	– (9) c Mohammad Rizwan b Naseem Shah.	0
L. D. Chandimal c Shan Masood b Haris Sohail	74	– (5) lbw b Naseem Shah	2
D. M. de Silva c Mohammad Abbas b Shaheen Shah Afridi.	32	– (6) b Yasir Shah	0
†D. P. D. N. Dickwella b Mohammad Abbas	21	– (7) b Haris Sohail	65
M. D. K. Perera lbw b Shaheen Shah Afridi	48	– (8) c Mohammad Rizwan b Naseem Shah.	5
M. V. T. Fernando not out	5	– lbw b Naseem Shah	0
C. B. R. L. S. Kumara b Shaheen Shah Afridi	0	– not out	0
B 4, lb 10, w 6, nb 3	23	Lb 3	3

1/28 (1) 2/39 (2) 3/61 (3)   (85.5 overs) 271
4/78 (5) 5/80 (4) 6/147 (7)
7/184 (8) 8/235 (6) 9/271 (9) 10/271 (11)

1/39 (1) 2/40 (3)   (62.5 overs) 212
3/70 (4) 4/96 (5)
5/97 (6) 6/201 (7) 7/212 (8)
8/212 (9) 9/212 (2) 10/212 (10)

Shaheen Shah Afridi 26.5–5–77–5; Mohammad Abbas 27–9–55–4; Naseem Shah 16–1–71–0; Yasir Shah 13–0–43–0; Haris Sohail 3–0–11–1. *Second innings*—Shaheen Shah Afridi 14–3–51–1; Mohammad Abbas 12–2–33–1; Naseem Shah 12.5–4–31–5; Yasir Shah 20–3–84–2; Haris Sohail 4–0–10–1.

Umpires: B. N. J. Oxenford and J. S. Wilson.   Third umpire: G. O. Brathwaite.
Referee: J. J. Crowe.

DOMESTIC CRICKET IN PAKISTAN IN 2018-19

ABID ALI KAZI

The election of Imran Khan as prime minister in 2018 heralded change at the Pakistan Cricket Board. He automatically became Patron of the PCB; the chairman, Najam Sethi, promptly submitted his resignation, writing that, as Imran had his own vision for Pakistan cricket, he should assemble his own management team. Ehsan Mani, the former ICC president, came in as chairman, while Wasim Khan, the Birmingham-born county cricketer who had served four years as Leicestershire's chief executive, was appointed managing director.

Although the structure of the domestic programme remained unchanged in 2018-19 for the fourth consecutive season, an unusual period of stability, a dramatically streamlined format was unveiled in March 2019 to fulfil Imran's vision. The first-class Quaid-e-Azam Trophy's 16 teams – eight departmental sides and eight regional – would be replaced in 2019-20 by six provincial teams, similar to the line-up that had sometimes contested the Pentangular Cup, though Punjab, the largest province, was divided into two regions, Central and Southern.

The changes were controversial, but their proponents hoped to raise playing standards. The 2018-19 season had been another difficult one for batsmen, with the quality of first-class pitches coming under scrutiny again. There were ten Quaid-e-Azam totals below 100 (down from 25 in the previous tournament). Four were at Faisalabad, where **Sui Northern Gas**, who had dominated the competition in recent years, were skittled for 35 as Habib Bank's Junaid Khan collected seven for 17. The collapse led to their only defeat; they headed their qualifying pool, then their Super Eight group, to reach their fourth final in five seasons.

It pitted them against **Habib Bank** again, but they were frustrated by a draw. Sui Northern, led by former Test captain Misbah-ul-Haq, declared on the last day, setting a target of 263, and their opponents were 183 for six when the umpires took the players off because of bad light. Habib Bank had enjoyed a first-innings lead of 168, so became national champions for the first time since 2010-11 – though Misbah declined to attend the presentation ceremony in protest at the umpires' decision. A month earlier, Habib Bank had also won the Quaid-e-Azam One-Day Cup, beating WAPDA by 62 runs in the final at Lahore.

Both Quaid-e-Azam tournaments were dominated by the departmental teams, but they were excluded from the National T20 Cup and the one-day Pakistan Cup. The final of the National T20 Cup, restricted to eight regional teams, saw **Lahore Whites** beat Rawalpindi by two wickets. The Pakistan Cup was contested by the five provincial sides (with only one from Punjab), and the final won by **Khyber Pakhtunkhwa**, who beat Baluchistan by nine runs.

No batsman reached 1,000 first-class runs; the highest aggregate was 886 by Khurram Manzoor of Karachi Whites. Three more reached 700 – Imran Farhat and Umar Akmal (both Habib Bank), and Umar Amin (Sui Southern Gas), with Amin's team-mate Fawad Alam only one run short. The batting averages were headed by Iftikhar Ahmed of finalists Sui Northern Gas, who scored 660 at 73. The season's highest innings was 265 by Shehzar Mohammad, the son of Shoaib Mohammad and grandson of Hanif; he featured in successive stands of 332 and 238 when Karachi Whites played Multan.

For the second season running, seamer Aizaz Cheema of Lahore Blues was the leading wicket-taker (with 59) and had the best average (13). No one else reached 50. Cheema took a hat-trick against Pakistan Television, only to finish on the losing side after Tabish Khan demolished the Blues with eight for 41, the best innings return of the season. The best match figures were 14 for 120, which also included a hat-trick, by Habib Bank's slow left-armer Abdur Rehman against Karachi Whites.

FIRST-CLASS AVERAGES IN 2018-19

BATTING (400 runs, average 25.00)

		M	I	NO	R	HS	100	Avge	Ct/St
1	Iftikhar Ahmed (*Sui Northern Gas*)	7	10	1	660	145	3	73.33	9
2	†Fawad Alam (*Sui Southern Gas*)	10	13	3	699	170*	3	69.90	4
3	Khurram Manzoor (*Karachi Whites*)	8	13	0	886	199	3	68.15	5
4	Adil Amin (*Sui Southern Gas*)	9	12	1	654	211*	3	59.45	3
5	†Umar Amin (*Sui Southern Gas*)	9	13	0	728	172	3	56.00	12
6	†Ali Sarfraz (*Islamabad*)	5	9	0	487	185	2	54.11	0
7	Zohaib Khan (*Habib Bank*)	8	14	4	536	101*	1	53.60	5
8	†Imran Rafiq (*Multan*)	7	13	1	610	148	2	50.83	2
9	Shehzar Mohammad (*Karachi Whites*)	5	10	1	436	265	1	48.44	1
10	Abid Ali (*Habib Bank*)	5	10	0	472	134	2	47.20	2
11	†Ali Rafiq (*Lahore Whites*)	6	10	1	421	121	1	46.77	2
12	†Saud Shakil (*Pakistan Television*)	5	10	1	414	108*	1	46.00	2
13	Nabi Gul (*Peshawar*)	5	10	0	442	138	2	44.20	9
14	Mohammad Hasan (*Karachi Whites*)	9	16	2	616	125	2	44.00	33/3
15	†Imran Farhat (*Habib Bank*)	11	19	2	744	128	1	43.76	7
16	Asad Afridi (*FATA*)	5	10	0	437	97	0	43.70	4
17	Omair Bin Yousuf (*Karachi Whites*)	8	15	1	582	163	2	41.57	6
18	Umar Akmal (*Habib Bank*)	10	19	1	736	129	2	40.88	5
19	†Salman Butt (*WAPDA*)	10	16	1	610	129	1	40.66	4
20	Misbah-ul-Haq (*Sui Northern Gas*)	8	13	1	423	91	0	35.25	6
21	†Israrullah (*Peshawar*)	10	20	1	624	133*	1	32.84	15
22	Akbar Badshah (*Peshawar*)	10	19	2	512	114*	1	30.11	4
23	Jahid Ali (*KRL*)	10	20	3	484	124*	1	28.47	6
24	†Rizwan Hussain (*Lahore Blues*)	8	16	1	421	97	0	28.06	6
25	Imran Butt (*Sui Northern Gas*)	11	18	0	473	111	1	26.27	18
26	Saad Nasim (*Lahore Blues*)	10	19	1	469	67*	0	26.05	9
27	†Rameez Aziz (*Habib Bank*)	11	19	1	467	87	0	25.94	15
28	Usman Arshad (*KRL*)	10	18	1	434	65	0	25.52	17

BOWLING (25 wickets, average 25.00)

		Style	O	M	R	W	BB	5I	Avge
1	Aizaz Cheema (*Lahore Blues*)	RFM	273.3	76	779	59	6-40	5	13.20
2	Kashif Bhatti (*Sui Southern Gas*)	SLA	283	82	691	49	6-59	3	14.10
3	Nauman Ali (*KRL*)	SLA	322	99	611	43	6-52	4	14.20
4	Ali Shafiq (*KRL*)	RFM	162.5	37	433	29	8-70	2	14.93
5	Haseeb Azam (*Rawalpindi*)	RFM	180.5	58	486	32	6-29	2	15.18
6	Taj Wali (*Peshawar*)	LFM	192.4	39	557	36	5-24	2	15.47
7	Mohammad Ilyas (*Peshawar*)	RFM	155.3	29	525	33	5-44	3	15.90
8	Mohammad Ali (*ZTBL*)	RFM	160.5	36	473	25	6-102	2	18.92
9	Tabish Khan (*Pakistan Television*)	RFM	190.3	44	561	28	8-41	2	20.03
10	Waqas Ahmed (*Lahore Whites*)	RF	163.5	29	583	29	5-142	1	20.10
11	Touseeq Shah (*Rawalpindi*)	RFM	220.4	60	651	32	5-30	2	20.34
12	Sadaf Hussain (*KRL*)	LFM	283.3	78	755	36	5-44	1	20.97
13	Abdur Rehman (*Habib Bank*)	SLA	291.2	49	971	46	8-70	2	21.10
14	Khalid Usman (*WAPDA*)	SLA	244.3	56	587	27	6-47	3	21.74
15	Zulfiqar Babar (*WAPDA*)	SLA	286.5	74	692	31	6-58	2	22.32
16	Asif Afridi (*FATA*)	LFM	258.1	70	686	30	6-36	2	22.86
17	Adeel Malik (*Karachi Whites*)	RFM	227.1	66	599	26	5-32	1	23.03
18	Sajid Khan (*Peshawar*)	OB	280.5	61	789	34	6-35	1	23.20
19	Bilawal Bhatti (*Sui Northern Gas*)	RFM	234.5	28	851	36	6-38	1	23.63
20	Nasir Ahmed (*Peshawar*)	LFM	156.2	24	609	25	5-24	1	24.36
21	Umar Gul (*Habib Bank*)	RFM	243.1	56	781	32	5-34	1	24.40
22	Mohammad Irfan (*Lahore Whites*)	SLA	364	104	838	34	5-47	3	24.64
23	Khurram Shehzad (*Habib Bank*)	RFM	238.5	56	842	34	6-37	3	24.76
24	Imran Khalid (*Sui Northern Gas*)	SLA	221.5	47	624	25	5-25	1	24.96

QUAID-E-AZAM TROPHY IN 2018-19

PRELIMINARY GROUPS

Pool A	P	W	L	D	Pts	Pool B	P	W	L	D	Pts
SUI NORTHERN GAS .	7	5	1	1	45	SUI SOUTHERN GAS .	7	4	1	2	45
PESHAWAR	7	5	2	0	39	WAPDA	7	4	2	1	34
KRL	7	4	2	1	33	KARACHI WHITES . .	7	3	1	3	34
HABIB BANK	7	2	3	2	24	LAHORE BLUES.	7	3	4	0	27
National Bank	7	2	3	2	24	Rawalpindi	7	3	3	1	21
FATA	7	2	5	0	18	Pakistan Television . .	7	2	4	1	18
Lahore Whites	7	1	1	5	15	Multan	7	2	3	2	16
Islamabad	7	1	5	1	10	ZTBL	7	2	5	0	15

SUPER EIGHT

Group 1	P	W	L	D	Pts	Group 2	P	W	L	D	Pts
SUI NORTHERN GAS .	3	2	0	1	19	HABIB BANK	3	2	0	1	21
WAPDA	3	2	1	0	19	Sui Southern Gas	3	2	0	1	19
KRL	3	1	1	1	12	Peshawar	3	1	2	0	6
Lahore Blues	3	0	3	0	0	Karachi Whites	3	0	3	0	0

FATA = Federally Administered Tribal Areas; KRL = Khan Research Laboratories; WAPDA = Water and Power Development Authority; ZTBL = Zarai Taraqiati Bank Limited.

Outright win = 6pts; win by an innings = 1pt extra; lead on first innings in a won or drawn game = 3pts; draw after following on = 1pt; no result on first innings = 1pt. Teams tied on points were ranked on most wins, then fewest losses, then net run-rate.

The top four teams from the preliminary groups advanced to the Super Eight groups, but did not carry forward their earlier results.

Final At Karachi (UBL), December 4–8, 2018. **Drawn. Habib Bank won by virtue of their first-innings lead. ‡Sui Northern Gas 304 and 430-7 dec; Habib Bank 472** (Abid Ali 134, Umar Akmal 113) **and 183-6.** *Misbah-ul-Haq made a four-hour 91 after choosing to bat, but was one of three top-order victims for Khurram Shehzad, before Abdur Rehman mopped up Sui Northern's tail. In reply, Abid Ali put on 150 with Agha Salman (56) and 122 with Umar Akmal, who steered Habib Bank into the lead. Sui Northern openers Imran Butt (95) and Ali Waqas (65) wiped out the deficit in a 170-run stand, then Abdur Rehman took his match haul to eight. The declaration set Habib Bank 263 on the final day; Bilawal Bhatti took 3-46, and they were six down when bad light ended play, ensuring they took the title.*

QUAID-E-AZAM TROPHY WINNERS

1953-54	Bahawalpur	1974-75	Punjab A	1990-91	Karachi Whites
1954-55	Karachi	1975-76	National Bank	1991-92	Karachi Whites
1956-57	Punjab	1976-77	United Bank	1992-93	Karachi Whites
1957-58	Bahawalpur	1977-78	Habib Bank	1993-94	Lahore City
1958-59	Karachi	1978-79	National Bank	1994-95	Karachi Blues
1959-60	Karachi	1979-80	PIA	1995-96	Karachi Blues
1961-62	Karachi Blues	1980-81	United Bank	1996-97	Lahore City
1962-63	Karachi A	1981-82	National Bank	1997-98	Karachi Blues
1963-64	Karachi Blues	1982-83	United Bank	1998-99	Peshawar
1964-65	Karachi Blues	1983-84	National Bank	1999-2000	PIA
1966-67	Karachi	1984-85	United Bank	2000-01	Lahore City Blues
1968-69	Lahore	1985-86	Karachi	2001-02	Karachi Whites
1969-70	PIA	1986-87	National Bank	2002-03	PIA
1970-71	Karachi Blues	1987-88	PIA	2003-04	Faisalabad
1972-73	Railways	1988-89	ADBP	2004-05	Peshawar
1973-74	Railways	1989-90	PIA	2005-06	Sialkot

2006-07	Karachi Urban	2011-12	PIA	2016-17	WAPDA
2007-08	Sui Northern Gas	2012-13	Karachi Blues	2017-18	Sui Northern Gas
2008-09	Sialkot	2013-14	Rawalpindi	2018-19	Habib Bank
2009-10	Karachi Blues	2014-15	Sui Northern Gas		
2010-11	Habib Bank	2015-16	Sui Northern Gas		

The competition has been contested sometimes by regional teams, sometimes by departments, and sometimes by a mixture of the two. Karachi teams have won the Quaid-e-Azam Trophy 20 times, Pakistan International Airlines 7, National Bank 5, Lahore teams, Sui Northern Gas and United Bank 4, Habib Bank 3, Bahawalpur, Peshawar, Punjab, Railways and Sialkot 2, Agricultural Development Bank of Pakistan, Faisalabad, Rawalpindi and Water And Power Development Authority 1.

QUAID-E-AZAM ONE-DAY CUP IN 2018-19

Two 50-over leagues plus knockout

Quarter-finals WAPDA beat National Bank by eight wickets; Habib Bank beat Sui Southern Gas by 166 runs; KRL beat Multan by six wickets; Pakistan Television beat Islamabad by nine runs.

Semi-finals WAPDA beat KRL by five wickets; Habib Bank beat Pakistan Television by seven runs.

Final At Lahore (Gaddafi), November 4, 2018. **Habib Bank won by 62 runs. Habib Bank 291-7** (50 overs); ‡**WAPDA 229** (44.4 overs). *Coming in at 169-5, Zohaib Khan scored 68* in 57 balls as Habib Bank finished just short of 300. Amad Butt's 3-49 triggered a WAPDA collapse, with their last five wickets falling for 22 in six overs.*

PAKISTAN CUP IN 2018-19

50-over league plus final

Final At Rawalpindi (Cricket), April 12, 2019 (day/night). **Khyber Pakhtunkhwa won by nine runs.** ‡**Khyber Pakhtunkhwa 307-7** (50 overs) (Abid Ali 132); **Baluchistan 298-9** (50 overs). *Abid Ali hit 132 in 119 balls, and added 136 with Mohammad Saeed (51). No. 9 Sohail Khan pushed Khyber Pakhtunkhwa past 300 with 45* in 20, before claiming 3-75 in Baluchistan's run-chase.*

NATIONAL T20 CUP IN 2018-19

20-over league plus knockout

Semi-finals Rawalpindi beat Karachi Whites by six runs; Lahore Whites beat Islamabad by 88 runs.

Final At Multan, December 25, 2018. **Lahore Whites won by two wickets.** ‡**Rawalpindi 162-8** (20 overs); **Lahore Whites 165-8** (19.2 overs). *Saif Badar arrived at 95-4 in the 12th over, and hit 35* in 23 balls, holding firm as Lahore Whites struggled to 129-8. He saw them home by adding 36* in 15 with No. 10 Amad Butt.*

The HBL Pakistan Super League has its own section (page 1148).

SOUTH AFRICAN CRICKET IN 2019

Change and decay

COLIN BRYDEN

South African cricket sank to its lowest ebb in 28 years of unity, before – in a dramatic conclusion to the year – a team under new management defeated England in the First Test at Centurion. It proved a false dawn, and in the remainder of the series South Africa were heavily beaten, including an innings defeat at Port Elizabeth, their first at home in ten years.

"Things had to get real bad before they could get better," said captain Faf du Plessis of the sweeping changes that resulted in the temporary appointment of former captain Graeme Smith as Cricket South Africa's director of cricket, and of Mark Boucher as head coach; his contract was due to run until after the 2023 World Cup. "Real bad" was no exaggeration, and went some way to explaining

SOUTH AFRICA IN 2019

Tests	Played	Won	Lost	Drawn/No result
Tests	8	3	5	–
One-day internationals	19	11	7	1
Twenty20 internationals	8	5	2	1

DECEMBER		
JANUARY	3 Tests, 5 ODIs and 3 T20Is (h) v Pakistan	(see *Wisden 2019*, page 1007)
FEBRUARY		
MARCH	2 Tests, 5 ODIs and 3 T20Is (h) v Sri Lanka	(page 1016)
APRIL		
MAY		
JUNE	World Cup (in England)	(page 237)
JULY		
AUGUST		
SEPTEMBER	3 Tests and 2 T20Is (a) v India	(page 939)
OCTOBER		
NOVEMBER		
DECEMBER		
JANUARY	4 Tests, 3 ODIs and 3 T20Is (h) v England	(page 440)
FEBRUARY		

For a review of South African domestic cricket from the 2018-19 season, see page 1029.

Brenton Geach, AFP/Getty Images

Protean Proteas: Graeme Smith, Enoch Nkwe, Mark Boucher and convenor of selectors Linda Zondi.

– perhaps mitigating – the shocking performance of the national team. The year's first disappointment followed a comfortable home Test series win against Pakistan, and was a bolt from the blue: Sri Lanka became the first side other than England or Australia to win a Test series on South African soil.

It would be stretching a point to place the blame for the two Sri Lankan defeats on much more than poor play by the losers, or the strengths of the victors. But it did not help that the board had given Thabang Moroe, CSA chief executive, the power to sign off all team selections, apparently because of concern that racial transformation targets were being missed. When Ottis Gibson, then head coach, objected, the decision was rescinded.

Serious meddling was revealed when a report on a disastrous World Cup – South Africa finished seventh – was leaked. Moroe and the board were blamed for not securing the early release of South African players from the Indian Premier League – unlike Australia and England. Du Plessis, Quinton de Kock and Imran Tahir played in the final, on May 12, and were said to be exhausted on their return home. They had little chance for rest: on May 24, all three were playing a World Cup warm-up.

Kagiso Rabada, the spearhead of the attack, had left the IPL early – because of injury. The report highlighted inflexibility when it came to managing the workloads of star black players, such as Rabada and Lungi Ngidi. Transformation targets were being put ahead of the team. Rabada played in all eight Tests and 18 of 19 ODIs, as well as 12 IPL matches. It was hardly surprising he was not at his sharpest at the World Cup. Ngidi spent much of the time injured.

One of the criticisms of Moroe was the disdain with which he treated the South African Cricketers' Association. Shortly before the World Cup, SACA launched a court action against CSA, seeking to overturn a decision that changed the domestic system into one tier, of 12 teams, rather than two (six franchise teams and a subsidiary provincial competition). This was taken without the consultation required by a memorandum of understanding between the two bodies. SACA also sought access to detailed financial statements after the board cited a projected loss of R654m over four years. The World Cup report, which CSA chose not to make public, said the dispute was "untimely and unfortunate", and affected the players. Another unfortunate incident occurred on the day of departure for the World Cup, when Gibson was told his contract would not be extended, despite a verbal understanding to the contrary.

But Moroe announced that a team director would be appointed, who would report to a director of cricket, who in turn would report to him. Enoch Nkwe, a former first-class cricketer with a single, successful, season in charge of the Lions franchise, was appointed interim team director, in preference to Boucher and Ashwell Prince. Nkwe took the team to India, where they lost the three Tests by 203 runs, an innings and 137, and an innings and 202.

After another dispute with SACA, over unpaid fees relating to the 2018 Mzansi Super League, three CSA employees were suspended, including former international player Corrie van Zyl, who had been appointed interim director of cricket. SACA claimed Moroe was responsible for the payment issue.

Media criticism of Moroe and CSA came to a head when five journalists had their accreditation withdrawn. This unleashed a storm. Standard Bank, the national team sponsor, said they would not renew their agreement with the board because an association with cricket was damaging. Another sponsor, financial services company Momentum, said they would continue, but only if the board resigned. Two former chief executives, Ali Bacher and Haroon Lorgat, made the same call. The accreditations were quickly restored.

Three independent board members and one non-independent member did resign – but president Chris Nenzani, vice-president Beresford Williams and six others remained, citing their endorsement by the Members' Council, the ultimate controlling body. Moroe was suspended on full pay on unspecified charges of misconduct; Jacques Faul, the chief executive of the Northerns union, was made acting-CEO on a six-month contract. In December, Faul signed Smith, initially for three months, and Boucher as head coach (and Nkwe as assistant). Drafted in as batting consultant was Jacques Kallis, so reuniting three giants of the South African game.

The year saw a string of retirements. Hashim Amla, South Africa's second-highest Test run-scorer (behind Kallis) picked up a two-year Kolpak deal with Surrey. Meanwhile, Dale Steyn, the nation's leading Test wicket-taker, with 439, gave up the longest format in a bid to prolong his white-ball career. J.-P. Duminy stepped down from all internationals. The depredation caused by Kolpak contracts with British counties continued to affect the standard of domestic cricket, with seam bowlers highest on the shopping list. As if to prove the point, Vernon Philander headed to Somerset for the 2020 season after retiring from internationals at the end of the England series.

Smith and Boucher also face political challenges. A pressure group, apparently reflecting the view of black African clubs in Gauteng, objected to Smith's appointment, while there was criticism that the team for the First Test against England included seven white players. CSA policy remained that national teams should average at least six players of colour – including two black Africans – over the course of a season. But with Ngidi injured, the burden fell on Rabada.

SOUTH AFRICA v SRI LANKA IN 2018-19

Lungani Zama

Test matches (2): South Africa 0, Sri Lanka 2
One-day internationals (5): South Africa 5, Sri Lanka 0
Twenty20 internationals (3): South Africa 3, Sri Lanka 0

Two Tests against Sri Lanka seemed an inconsequential final act of the season as South Africa considered their challenge for the World Cup. All the talk was of who would make the cut for the squad in England. It's true that Sri Lanka had won both Tests when South Africa toured there in July 2018, but since then they had staggered from bad to worse, losing at home to England, before being pummelled in New Zealand and pulverised in Australia. Dinesh Chandimal had lost the captaincy and his place, and coach Chandika Hathurusinghe – no longer involved in selection – much of his power.

But the focus on the World Cup caused the South Africans to take their eye off the (red) ball. Sri Lanka had lost 11 of their previous 13 Tests in the Republic – but the two non-defeats (a draw in 2000-01, and a victory in 2011-12) had both been in Durban. And this time at Kingsmead an incredible unbeaten 153 from Kusal Perera spirited them to a one-wicket victory.

Against shell-shocked opponents, Dimuth Karunaratne's side completed the heist with victory in the Second Test. South Africa's first-innings lead of 68 looked crucial on a seaming surface at Port Elizabeth, but Suranga Lakmal grabbed four for 39 as the hosts were bundled out for 128. Newcomer Oshada Fernando and the experienced Kusal Mendis sailed serenely home as Sri Lanka became the first Asian team to win a Test series in South Africa in 21 attempts.

It was a superb start to Karunaratne's tenure. "The tours of New Zealand and Australia were tough," he said. "We learned a lot. The players realised what to do and what not to do, and that's why we're here. It's a great feeling."

For South Africa the feelings were less good. Their frustrated captain Faf du Plessis admitted to a "massive dent" in his side's confidence, which he found hard to explain: "Maybe mentally the boys were off the boil at the end of a long season, but that's not an excuse. It's probably up there with the most disappointing series loss."

HIGHEST FOURTH-INNINGS SCORES IN TEST VICTORIES

214*	C. G. Greenidge	West Indies v England at Lord's	1984
182	A. R. Morris	Australia v England at Leeds	1948
173*	D. G. Bradman	Australia v England at Leeds	1948
173*	M. A. Butcher	England v Australia at Leeds	2001
171*	Younis Khan	Pakistan v Sri Lanka at Pallekele	2015
168	S. M. Nurse	West Indies v New Zealand at Auckland	1968-69
160	J. Darling	Australia v England at Sydney	1897-98
154*	G. C. Smith	South Africa v England at Birmingham	2008
153*	B. C. Lara	West Indies v Australia at Bridgetown	1998-99
153*	**M. D. K. J. Perera**	**Sri Lanka v South Africa at Durban**	**2018-19**
151*	R. N. Harvey	Australia v South Africa at Durban	1949-50

As things turned out, it was a sad farewell for home fans to two South African greats, who announced their Test retirements later in the year. Dale Steyn ended up with 439 Test wickets – 18 more than Shaun Pollock – although he aimed to continue in the white-ball formats. Hashim Amla, meanwhile, amassed 9,282 runs in 124 Tests (only Jacques Kallis made more for South Africa) and averaged nearly 50 in ODIs.

Sri Lanka did not win another match on the tour, as the seething South Africans won all eight limited-overs games. Another captain paid the price: Lasith Malinga was jettisoned, and replaced by Karunaratne for the World Cup, even though he had not played a one-day international since the previous tournament, in 2015.

South Africa's World Cup squad, meanwhile, finally took shape – although Duanne Olivier, the fast bowler who might have been a part of it, shocked his country by signing a Kolpak deal with Yorkshire. J-P. Duminy made a welcome return after a shoulder injury, while Amla, Reeza Hendricks and Aiden Markram were locked in a race for two spots. Amla took time away, as his father was seriously ill, but in the end it was Hendricks who missed out. Leg-spinner Imran Tahir picked up nine wickets in the ODIs, while pacemen Kagiso Rabada, Lungi Ngidi and the rapid newcomer Anrich Nortje all collected eight. Another seamer, Andile Phehlukwayo, claimed seven in the three T20 games.

SRI LANKAN TOURING PARTY

*F. D. M. Karunaratne (T), A. Dananjaya (50/20), D. M. de Silva (T/50/20), D. P. D. N. Dickwella (T/50/20), L. Embuldeniya (T), A. M. Fernando (20), B. O. P. Fernando (T/50), M. V. T. Fernando (T/50), W. I. A. Fernando (50/20), C. Karunaratne (T), R. A. S. Lakmal (T/20), S. L. Malinga (50/20), B. K. G. Mendis (T/50/20), P. H. K. D. Mendis (50/20), A. K. Perera (T/50/20), M. D. K. J. Perera (T/50), N. L. T. C. Perera (50/20), P. A. R. P. Perera (50/20), C. A. K. Rajitha (T/50), W. S. R. Samarawickrama (20), P. A. D. L. R. Sandakan (T/50/20), M. Shiraz (T), J. K. Silva (T), T. A. M. Siriwardene (T), H. D. R. L. Thirimanne (T), W. U. Tharanga (50), I. Udana (50/20), J. D. F. Vandersay (20). *Coach:* U. C. Hathurusinghe.

Malinga captained in the white-ball matches. M. D. K. J. Perera injured his hamstring in the third ODI, but was not replaced.

SOUTH AFRICA v SRI LANKA

First Test

At Durban, February 13–16, 2019. Sri Lanka won by one wicket. Toss: Sri Lanka. Test debuts: L. Embuldeniya, B. O. P. Fernando.

No one saw it coming. Not South Africa, after a summer in which they had outbatted Pakistan. Not the media, who had seen the same side dispose of India, Australia and then Pakistan over the course of two home seasons. And certainly not Sri Lanka, who were short of experience and confidence. How wrong they all were.

The hero was the attacking left-hander Kusal Perera, who produced arguably the greatest fourth-innings display in any Test, less than a fortnight after he had been concussed by a bouncer from the Australian seamer Jhye Richardson in Canberra. Sri Lanka had begun their unlikely chase of 304 on the third afternoon and, when Mendis fell for a duck to a poor shot, looked dead in the water at 52 for three. Everyone expected South Africa to cruise home some time on the fourth day – but Perera had other ideas, responding to blows to the body with blows to the fence.

The one that didn't get away... Vishwa Fernando and Kusal Perera at the moment of victory.

Still, the counter-attack surely couldn't be sustained for long. The debutant Oshada Fernando helped Perera add 58, but then Dickwella went without scoring, Steyn's sixth wicket of the match. Although de Silva played pleasantly for 48, the fat lady started her warm-up routine when he and Lakmal fell to successive balls from Maharaj. Soon Sri Lanka were on the brink at 226 for nine. Perera was hitting out, but another 78 were needed, and he had only the No. 11, Vishwa Fernando, for company. No first-class match, let alone a Test, had ever been won from such a position.

Even without Philander, who had tweaked a hamstring, South Africa had Steyn, Rabada, Olivier and Maharaj – and, soon enough, the second new ball. But Perera kept swinging, and connecting. He launched Steyn majestically, ridiculously, over square leg for six; he bullied Olivier, and didn't let Rabada settle, on the way to only his second Test century (his first had come as long ago as October 2016, against Zimbabwe at Harare). At the other end, Fernando kept playing at the ball, which kept missing his edge. Still South Africa were favourites; one good delivery was all they needed.

The first cracks started to appear with 34 wanted. Fernando, exposed to Steyn, scurried through for a cheeky single off the second ball of an over, and du Plessis had a belated shy at the stumps. There was nobody backing up: one turned into five. Steyn shot his captain a look; it seemed to dawn on the South Africans that this might go the wrong way. Perera, having done so much, didn't stutter over his closing lines. He top-edged Rabada for six, then late-cut him for four to complete an unbelievable victory.

Hints of an upset had been visible on the opening morning, when the left-arm swing of the unheralded Vishwa Fernando helped reduce South Africa to 17 for three. Bavuma played well for 47, but was unlucky to be run out at the non-striker's end, when Fernando fingertipped a piercing de Kock straight-drive. Du Plessis departed just as he looked set to

HIGHEST LAST-WICKET STANDS TO WIN A FIRST-CLASS MATCH

78	M. D. K. J. Perera/M. V. T. Fernando	**Sri Lanka v South Africa at Durban** ...	**2018-19**
77	T. W. Leather/R. K. Oxenham	Australian XI v Madras at Madras.......	1935-36
76	**B. A. Stokes/M. J. Leach**	**England v Australia at Leeds**	**2019**
72	**W. K. I. Fernando/S. P. Udeshi**	**Chilaw M v Ports Auth. at Katunayake..**	**2018-19**
68	A. C. Agar/M. G. Hogan...........	W Australia v S Australia at Adelaide ...	2012-13
66	P. I. Bedford/M. O. C. Sturt	Middlesex v Gloucestershire at Gloucester	1961
64	G. W. Humpage/R. G. D. Willis.....	Warwickshire v Yorkshire at Birmingham	1983
58	C. R. Swan/L. W. Feldman........	Queensland v Victoria at Brisbane.......	2009-10
57	J. B. Mortimore/J. Davey	Gloucestershire v Glamorgan at Bristol...	1973
57	Inzamam-ul-Haq/Mushtaq Ahmed	Pakistan v Australia at Karachi	1994-95
54	J. M. Gregory/E. J. Long	Aust Imperial Forces v Yorks at Sheffield .	1919

take flight, and de Kock had to bail his side out with an attacking 80. A total of 235 was not as many as South Africa had wanted, but they were heartened by the scalp of Thirimanne before stumps.

Perera's 51 took Sri Lanka close to parity, but he watched his team-mates struggle: the seamers took all nine wickets to fall to bowlers, with Steyn's swing proving particularly troublesome. South Africa had a lead of 44, and looked ready to stretch it over the horizon while du Plessis and de Kock were putting on 96. But from 251 for five, the last five wickets went down for eight. The star was the debutant Lasith Embuldeniya, a left-arm spinner auditioning for the spot vacated by the retired Rangana Herath. He bowled beautifully to claim five for 66, while Vishwa Fernando collected four more. Except, as it turned out, he hadn't quite finished.

Fernando made six of the tenth-wicket stand, facing just 27 balls in 73 minutes, and had the best view in the house as Perera carved his way to 153, matching Brian Lara's fourth-innings masterpiece to down Australia at Bridgetown in March 1999. That was the quality of Perera: a once-in-a-lifetime knock that shocked South Africa, and shook the rest of the cricket world.

Player of the Match: M. D. K. J. Perera.

Close of play: first day, Sri Lanka 49-1 (Karunaratne 28, B. O. P. Fernando 17); second day, South Africa 126-4 (du Plessis 25, de Kock 15); third day, Sri Lanka 83-3 (B. O. P. Fernando 28, Perera 12).

South Africa

A. K. Markram b M. V. T. Fernando............	11	– (2) c Mendis b Rajitha	28
D. Elgar c Dickwella b M. V. T. Fernando	0	– (1) c and b Embuldeniya	35
H. M. Amla c Mendis b Lakmal	3	– c Thirimanne b M. V. T. Fernando ...	16
T. Bavuma run out (M. V. T. Fernando)	47	– lbw b Embuldeniya	3
*F. du Plessis c Dickwella b Rajitha	35	– lbw b M. V. T. Fernando	90
†Q. de Kock c M. V. T. Fernando b Rajitha	80	– lbw b Embuldeniya	55
V. D. Philander c and b Rajitha	4	– b Embuldeniya	18
K. A. Maharaj c Dickwella b M. V. T. Fernando...	2	– lbw b M. V. T. Fernando	4
K. Rabada c B. O. P. Fernando b M. V. T. Fernando	3	– c Dickwella b Embuldeniya	0
D. W. Steyn b Embuldeniya	15	– b M. V. T. Fernando.............	1
D. Olivier not out	0	– not out	2
Lb 6, nb 2	8	Lb 2, w 2, nb 3	7

1/0 (2) 2/9 (3) 3/17 (1)   (59.4 overs) 235   1/36 (2) 2/70 (3)   (79.1 overs) 259
4/89 (5) 5/110 (4) 6/131 (7)   3/77 (4) 4/95 (1)
7/178 (8) 8/186 (9) 9/219 (10) 10/235 (6)   5/191 (6) 6/251 (7) 7/255 (5)
                                     8/256 (9) 9/256 (8) 10/259 (10)

Lakmal 14–3–29–1; M. V. T. Fernando 17–1–62–4; Rajitha 14.4–0–68–3; Karunaratne 3–0–9–0; Embuldeniya 10–1–51–1; B. O. P. Fernando 1–0–10–0. *Second innings*—Lakmal 20–5–52–0; M. V. T. Fernando 17.1–2–71–4; Rajitha 13–1–54–1; Embuldeniya 26–3–66–5; de Silva 2–0–8–0; B. O. P. Fernando 1–0–6–0.

Sri Lanka

*F. D. M. Karunaratne lbw b Philander	30	lbw b Philander	20
H. D. R. L. Thirimanne c de Kock b Steyn	0	c du Plessis b Rabada	21
B. O. P. Fernando lbw b Steyn	19	c du Plessis b Steyn	37
B. K. G. Mendis c du Plessis b Philander	12	c de Kock b Olivier	0
M. D. K. J. Perera c sub (M. Z. Hamza) b Steyn	51	not out	153
†D. P. D. N. Dickwella c Steyn b Olivier	8	c and b Steyn	0
D. M. de Silva c Olivier b Rabada	23	lbw b Maharaj	48
R. A. S. Lakmal c Markram b Steyn	4	c du Plessis b Maharaj	0
L. Embuldeniya c Steyn b Rabada	24	c Markram b Olivier	4
C. A. K. Rajitha run out (Markram)	12	lbw b Maharaj	1
M. V. T. Fernando not out	1	not out	6
B 3, lb 3, w 1	7	Lb 13, w 1	14

1/19 (2) 2/51 (3) 3/53 (1)   (59.2 overs) 191   1/42 (2)   (9 wkts, 85.3 overs) 304
4/76 (4) 5/90 (6) 6/133 (7)   2/42 (1) 3/52 (4)
7/142 (8) 8/152 (5) 9/184 (10) 10/191 (9)   4/110 (3) 5/110 (6) 6/206 (7)
                                                              7/206 (8) 8/215 (9) 9/226 (10)

Steyn 20-7-48-4; Philander 10-2-32-2; Rabada 12.2-2-48-2; Olivier 13-3-22-36-1; Maharaj 3-0-16-0; Elgar 1-0-5-0. *Second innings*—Steyn 18-1-71-2; Philander 8-3-13-1; Maharaj 20-1-71-3; Rabada 22.3-3-97-1; Olivier 16-3-35-2; Markram 1-0-4-0.

Umpires: Aleem Dar and R. A. Kettleborough.   Third umpire: I. J. Gould.
Referee: R. B. Richardson.

SOUTH AFRICA v SRI LANKA

Second Test

At Port Elizabeth, February 21–23, 2019. Sri Lanka won by eight wickets. Toss: South Africa. Test debut: P. W. A. Mulder.

Stung by their Durban defeat, South Africa were desperate to get level, and looked on course when they claimed a first-innings lead of 68. But a miserable batting display left Sri Lanka requiring fewer than 200 to complete the first series win by an Asian side in South Africa – and they sailed home, without First Test hero Kusal Perera needing to bat.

The hosts were initially undone by their other Durban nemesis, Vishwa Fernando, who dismissed Elgar and Amla with successive balls, before Rajitha's direct hit from mid-on ran out Bavuma to make it 15 for three. Markram repaired some of the damage with the aid of de Kock, who again looked a class apart, making a defiant 86 from 87 balls. Rabada helped him add 59, but a total of 222 – with Fernando and Rajitha both taking three wickets – was another disappointing effort. De Silva took two cheap wickets with his off-breaks, including the vital scalp of de Kock, after Embuldeniya dislocated his left thumb attempting a return catch off Rabada.

South Africa's bowlers, led by Rabada and Olivier (in his last Test before joining Yorkshire on a Kolpak deal), knocked Sri Lanka over for 154, which owed much to a sparky 42 from Dickwella. Another fast-moving Test was half-done before lunch on the second day.

Elgar was out to the last ball before the interval, but Amla and du Plessis steered South Africa to the relative calm of 90 for three, a lead of 158. Then the wheels fell off. Amla edged a non-turner from de Silva to slip, and de Kock – unable to pull off his usual rescue act – lobbed a return catch to Lakmal just before tea. The rest subsided around du Plessis. The last six batsmen managed just 18 between them, as South Africa lost seven for 38; Lakmal seized the moment to claim four for 39. From contemplating a massive rearguard, Sri Lanka now needed only 197 to march into the history books.

The pitch was starting to play lower and take turn, and the openers departed in the space of six balls to make it a nervy 34 for two. However, Oshada Fernando and Mendis hurried along at more than four and a half an over. Mendis cracked 13 fours, three in the first over he faced from Steyn, who ended up wicketless in what transpired to be his final Test. Fernando helped himself to two sixes off Maharaj, and ten fours, the pick a sumptuous pull off Rabada. They eventually put on an unbroken 163 as Sri Lanka – bruised and heavily beaten in Australia just a few weeks before – strolled home on the stroke of lunch on the third day, to complete perhaps the most stunning 2–0 Test whitewash of all.

There were heroes all around for the tourists, who had outplayed South Africa in all departments. "We never expected to do it," admitted Karunaratne. "But when we started winning, we had the faith."

Player of the Match: B. K. G. Mendis.   *Player of the Series:* M. D. K. J. Perera.

Close of play: first day, Sri Lanka 60-3 (Thirimanne 25, Rajitha 0); second day, Sri Lanka 60-2 (B. O. P. Fernando 17, Mendis 10).

South Africa

D. Elgar b M. V. T. Fernando	6	– (2) c Dickwella b M. V. T. Fernando	2
A. K. Markram lbw b Rajitha	60	– (1) c B. O. P. Fernando b Rajitha	18
H. M. Amla b M. V. T. Fernando	0	– c Mendis b de Silva	32
T. Bavuma run out (Rajitha)	0	– c Dickwella b Rajitha	6
*F. du Plessis b Karunaratne	25	– not out	50
†Q. de Kock b de Silva	86	– c and b Lakmal	1
P. W. A. Mulder lbw b Rajitha	9	– c Mendis b de Silva	5
K. A. Maharaj c Dickwella b Rajitha	6	– lbw b Lakmal	6
K. Rabada c Dickwella b de Silva	22	– c Mendis b Lakmal	0
D. W. Steyn not out	3	– c Thirimanne b de Silva	0
D. Olivier c Dickwella b M. V. T. Fernando	0	– lbw b Lakmal	6
B 1, lb 6, nb 4	11	Lb 1, nb 1	2

1/15 (1) 2/15 (3) 3/15 (4) (61.2 overs) 222
4/73 (5) 5/130 (2) 6/145 (7)
7/157 (8) 8/216 (6) 9/221 (9) 10/222 (11)

1/10 (2) 2/31 (1) (44.3 overs) 128
3/51 (4) 4/90 (3)
5/91 (6) 6/100 (7) 7/113 (8)
8/115 (9) 9/116 (10) 10/128 (11)

Lakmal 13–2–33–0; M. V. T. Fernando 18.2–2–62–3; Rajitha 15–2–67–3; Embuldeniya 5.3–0–26–0; Karunaratne 4.3–1–12–1; de Silva 5–0–15–2. *Second innings*—Lakmal 16.3–3–39–4; M. V. T. Fernando 10–1–32–1; Rajitha 7–1–20–2; de Silva 11–1–36–3.

Sri Lanka

*F. D. M. Karunaratne c de Kock b Rabada	17	– c de Kock b Olivier	19
H. D. R. L. Thirimanne c and b Olivier	29	– c de Kock b Rabada	10
B. O. P. Fernando b Olivier	0	– not out	75
B. K. G. Mendis c de Kock b Olivier	16	– not out	84
C. A. K. Rajitha b Rabada	1		
M. D. K. J. Perera c de Kock b Rabada	20		
D. M. de Silva c de Kock b Mulder	19		
†D. P. D. N. Dickwella c Elgar b Rabada	42		
R. A. S. Lakmal lbw b Maharaj	7		
M. V. T. Fernando not out	0		
L. Embuldeniya absent hurt			
Lb 1, nb 2	3	B 4, lb 5	9

1/25 (1) 2/34 (3) 3/59 (4) (37.4 overs) 154
4/64 (2) 5/66 (5) 6/97 (6)
7/128 (7) 8/154 (9) 9/154 (8)

1/32 (2) (2 wkts, 45.4 overs) 197
2/34 (1)

Steyn 10–2–39–0; Rabada 12.4–3–38–4; Olivier 10–1–61–3; Mulder 3–2–6–1; Maharaj 2–0–9–1. *Second innings*—Steyn 8–0–38–0; Rabada 15–2–53–1; Olivier 12–2–46–1; Mulder 4–1–6–0; Maharaj 4–1–60–0.

Umpires: Aleem Dar and I. J. Gould.   Third umpire: R. A. Kettleborough.
Referee: R. B. Richardson.

First one-day international   At Johannesburg, March 3, 2019. **South Africa won by eight wickets. Sri Lanka 231** (47 overs) (M. D. K. J. Perera 33, B. O. P. Fernando 49, B. K. G. Mendis 60, D. M. de Silva 39; L. T. Ngidi 3-60, Imran Tahir 3-26); ‡**South Africa 232-2** (38.5 overs) (Q. de Kock 81, F. du Plessis 112*, H. E. van der Dussen 32*). PoM: F. du Plessis. ODI debuts: A. A. Nortje (South Africa); B. O. P. Fernando (Sri Lanka). *South Africa went into their final one-day series ahead of the World Cup intent on finalising their squad for England. A call-up was handed to tearaway Anrich Nortje, while Aiden Markram was released to play for his domestic side, the Titans. Sri Lanka, still in dreamland after the Test series, welcomed back the experience and expertise of Lasith Malinga, their white-ball captain. But the South Africans gained revenge: Lungi Ngidi started with real menace, while Imran Tahir sent down ten exemplary overs, taking 3-26; the only real resistance came from Kusal Mendis. Quinton de Kock's relentless form continued with a 72-ball 81, and Faf du Plessis sealed the deal with a superb century.*

Second one-day international   At Centurion, March 6, 2019 (day/night). **South Africa won by 113 runs. South Africa 251** (45.1 overs) (Q. de Kock 94, F. du Plessis 57; N. L. T. C. Perera 3-26); ‡**Sri Lanka 138** (32.2 overs) (B. O. P. Fernando 31; K. Rabada 3-43). PoM: Q. de Kock. *For the umpteenth time in the home summer, de Kock stole the show, with 94 from 70 balls, demoralising Vishwa Fernando (1-47 in five overs) with some vicious drives. Du Plessis chipped in with a determined 57, but a total of 251 was a let down after de Kock's fireworks. However, it didn't matter much: a revitalised Kagiso Rabada produced a lightning new-ball spell, and Ngidi (2-14) was miserly at the other end. Sri Lanka spiralled to a disappointing 138.*

Third one-day international   At Durban, March 10, 2019. **South Africa won by 71 runs** (DLS). **South Africa 331-5** (50 overs) (Q. de Kock 121, F. du Plessis 36, H. E. van der Dussen 50, D. A. Miller 41*, D. Pretorius 31, A. L. Phehlukwayo 38*); ‡**Sri Lanka 121-5** (24 overs) (B. K. G. Mendis 41). PoM: Q. de Kock. ODI debut: P. H. K. D. Mendis (Sri Lanka). *De Kock had missed out on a century at Centurion, but made no mistake here, with another majestic performance. His 121 from 108 balls left fans wanting more, as he departed with 19 overs left. The other batsmen continued the assault, and a big total was rounded off by Andile Phehlukwayo's 38* from 15 balls. The only thing that stood between South Africa and a series victory was the weather. Rain intervened with Sri Lanka 75-2 after 16, and the playing time was extended by an hour in order to get at least the four more overs required to constitute a game, despite concerns about the soggy outfield. With the target amended to 193 off 24, the spinners rushed through the last few overs to secure a winning 3–0 lead.*

Fourth one-day international   At Port Elizabeth, March 13, 2019 (day/night). **South Africa won by six wickets. Sri Lanka 189** (39.2 overs) (I. Udana 78; A. A. Nortje 3-57); ‡**South Africa 190-4** (32.5 overs) (Q. de Kock 51, F. du Plessis 43, J-P. Duminy 31*; D. M. de Silva 3-41). PoM: I. Udana. ODI debut: P. A. R. P. Perera (Sri Lanka). *With the series won, South Africa shuffled the pack again. J-P. Duminy had recovered from a long-term shoulder injury, while Markram was recalled after an avalanche of domestic runs. South Africa bowled first in brilliant coastal sunshine, and Nortje delighted his home crowd with an opening spell of 6–0–19–3. But he later ran into Isuru Udana, who clattered him for three straight sixes en route to 78 from 57 balls: Nortje's last two overs cost 38. Even that lifted Sri Lanka to only 189, which South Africa polished off with more than 17 overs to spare, almost before the floodlights were needed. De Kock led off with another attractive half-century.*

Fifth one-day international   At Cape Town, March 16, 2019 (day/night). **South Africa won by 41 runs** (DLS). ‡**Sri Lanka 225** (49.3 overs) (B. K. G. Mendis 56, A. K. Perera 31, P. A. R. P. Perera 33, I. Udana 32; K. Rabada 3-50); **South Africa 135-2** (28 overs) (A. K. Markram 67*). PoM: A. K. Markram. PoS: Q. de Kock. *This game was all about what didn't happen: a broken floodlight meant play had to stop once the late-summer light faded. Although a DLS victory confirmed a 5–0 win, it was embarrassing for the hosts. The Sri Lankans might have wished the lights had gone off even sooner: only Mendis made much impression as they reached 225. With Markram giving a timely reminder of his class with 67* after a rare failure from de Kock, South Africa were well ahead at the premature end.*

First Twenty20 international   At Cape Town, March 19, 2019 (floodlit). **South Africa won after a super over, following a tie. Sri Lanka 134-7** (20 overs) (P. H. K. D. Mendis 41; A. L. Phehlukwayo 3-25); ‡**South Africa 134-8** (20 overs) (H. E. van der Dussen 34, D. A. Miller 41). PoM: D. A. Miller. T20I debut: W. I. A. Fernando (Sri Lanka). *South Africa needed a super over to prevail in a match they couldn't finish off, and raised questions about their ability to soak up pressure. Tahir helped them out, conceding only five in the eliminator after South Africa had accrued 14, but it shouldn't have got that far: Sri Lanka's 134-7, of which 23 came in the last two overs,* *looked under par, despite Kamindu Mendis's feisty 29-ball 41. South Africa seemed comfortable while Rassie van der Dussen and David Miller were putting on 66 in seven overs, but the loss of five for 15 left Tahir to scramble a single from the last ball to force the tie.*

Second Twenty20 international At Centurion, March 22, 2019 (floodlit). **South Africa won by 16 runs. South Africa 180-3** (20 overs) (R. R. Hendricks 65, H. E. van der Dussen 64, J-P. Duminy 33*); ‡**Sri Lanka 164-9** (20 overs) (I. Udana 84*; C. H. Morris 3-32). *PoM:* H. E. van der Dussen. *T20I debuts:* A. K. Markram, S. Qeshile (South Africa). *South Africa rang the changes: du Plessis, de Kock and Rabada were all rested, 20-year-old Warriors wicketkeeper Sinethemba Qeshile made his debut, and Duminy took over the captaincy. Reeza Hendricks (65 from 46 balls) and van der Dussen (64 from 44) put on 116 for the second wicket, before Duminy added a breezy 33* from 17. Sri Lanka were soon in the mire at 62-6 from ten overs, with Dale Steyn (2-34) and Chris Morris proving too hot to handle. Tabraiz Shamsi then showed great control, finishing with 4–14–16–2. Not for the first time, Udana gave Sri Lanka something to cheer, blazing 84* from 48 deliveries, with six sixes and eight fours. He took his side close, but South Africa still clinched the series.*

Third Twenty20 international At Johannesburg, March 24, 2019. **South Africa won by 45 runs** (DLS). **South Africa 198-2** (20 overs) (R. R. Hendricks 66, D. Pretorius 77*, J-P. Duminy 34*); ‡**Sri Lanka 137** (15.4 overs) (D. P. D. N. Dickwella 38, I. Udana 36; A. L. Phehlukwayo 4-24). *PoM:* D. Pretorius. *PoS:* R. R. Hendricks. *In the final international of the summer, the South Africans found inspiration from two locals as they completed an 8–0 whitewash in the white-ball formats. Hendricks continued his good form with 66, but it was Dwaine Pretorius who stood out, hammering 77* from 42 deliveries. Thanks to their stand of 90 – and a 14-ball 34* from Duminy – South Africa reached 198. A high-veld storm meant Sri Lanka's target was amended to 183 from 17 overs, but Phehlukwayo befuddled the batsmen with his selection of slower balls, and they showed few signs of making a game of it. Another Udana blast – 36 from 23, with four sixes – at least narrowed the margin.*

DOMESTIC CRICKET IN SOUTH AFRICA IN 2018-19

COLIN BRYDEN

The **Lions** bounced back to win two franchise titles under a new management team. In 2017-18, they had finished bottom of the first-class table, and failed to reach the knockout stages of either limited-overs tournament. But under Enoch Nkwe and Temba Bavuma, South Africa's first black African coach–captain combination at franchise level, they won the Four-Day Franchise Series and the CSA T20 Challenge. In difficult economic times, neither competition found a sponsor.

Nkwe, who succeeded Geoffrey Toyana, had enjoyed a respectable first-class career after a century on debut in 2002, but it was cut short after he gashed his wrist on broken glass, paralysing two of his fingers. He moved into coaching, running the Gauteng provincial side who feed the Lions, and had stints as assistant coach of the Netherlands men's team and South Africa's women. He was also at the helm of Jozi Stars, who won the inaugural Mzansi Super League in December 2018, and the following August was appointed South Africa's interim team director.

In contrast to 2017-18, when there were only seven outright results in the four-day competition's 30 fixtures, there were 20 this time, and the Lions alone won seven. For most of the season they played catch-up with **Cape Cobras**, who beat them by an innings in their second match, and led the table until the final round. Needing to win, the Lions were 96 for six on the opening day against the **Warriors** (in third place, but too far behind to mount a challenge). They recovered when Bjorn Fortuin and Delano Potgieter added 301, a South African seventh-wicket record. While the Cobras were heading for a draw against the Dolphins, the Lions claimed the crown in the tournament's dying moments, bowling the Warriors' last man with nine balls to go. By then, they had lost Rassie van der Dussen, who averaged 55 in six matches, to international duty; Kagiso Rapulana stepped up, and averaged 84 in four. Left-arm seamer Beuran Hendricks led the bowling with 32 wickets.

Three months later, the Lions defeated the Warriors again, in the climax of the T20 Challenge, displaced to April and May after the MSL occupied the prime November–December slot. Autumnal chill and floodlit cricket did not make a happy marriage, but the final, a day game in early May, turned into another nailbiter. A century from Bavuma helped the Lions reach 203, but Warriors captain Jon-Jon Smuts responded in kind, and they needed 12 off five balls when he was caught going for his eighth six.

The **Cobras** won six four-day games, before falling at the last hurdle. The two Danes – off-spinner Piedt, the season's leading wicket-taker with 54, and fast bowler Paterson – carried their attack. Pieter Malan formed a powerful opening partnership with his younger brother, Janneman, both averaging more than 50; so did Zubayr Hamza, who was rewarded with a Test debut. The four-day tournament's leading run-scorer was Keegan Petersen of the **Knights**, whose 923 put him two ahead of the Warriors' Edward Moore.

The **Titans**, regularly losing their best players to national calls, finished last in the four-day series and fifth in the T20, both of which they had won in 2017-18, but triumphed in the Momentum One-Day Cup (the only senior competition still attracting a sponsor). Aiden Markram hit 127 against the **Dolphins** in the final, his third century in five matches, which brought him 542 runs; the next-best total was 453 in ten.

In the provincial competitions, **Northerns** reached two finals; they lost the 50-Over Challenge to **Easterns**, but shared the Three-Day Cup after drawing a week later with **Eastern Province**. Namibia, three-day runners-up in 2017-18, pulled out of both tournaments at short notice, citing the time and cost of travelling to South Africa. They had already competed in September's Africa T20 Cup, which had expanded to include Uganda and Nigeria, but was won by **Gauteng**.

FIRST-CLASS AVERAGES IN 2018-19

BATTING (650 runs)

		M	I	NO	R	HS	100	Avge	Ct/St
1	A. J. Pienaar (*South Western Districts*) ..	10	15	3	957	150*	4	79.75	6
2	†T. Koekemoer (*Eastern Province*)......	10	15	5	697	130	2	69.70	3
3	†M. J. Ackerman (*KZ-Natal/Dolphins*)...	10	17	4	887	137	3	68.23	8
4	†J. L. du Plooy (*Northerns/Titans*)	12	15	3	744	119	4	62.00	7
5	K. D. Petersen (*Knights/Northern Cape*)	13	25	3	1,263	165*	4	57.40	11/2
6	†E. M. Moore (*Warriors/E Province*)....	16	30	2	1,590	227*	4	56.78	12
7	R. van Tonder (*Free State/Knights*)	8	15	3	674	250*	1	56.16	2
8	N. J. van den Bergh (*Lions/North West*) .	11	18	3	797	217*	2	53.13	34/2
9	S. Qeshile (*Warriors*).................	10	18	4	735	99	0	52.50	18
10	J. M. Richards (*Gauteng*).............	9	17	1	828	145	4	51.75	5
11	P. J. Malan (*Cape Cobras*)	10	16	0	821	153	3	51.31	5
12	†N. Brand (*Northerns/Titans*).........	12	17	2	755	159	1	50.33	5
13	W. B. Marshall (*Easterns*)...........	10	19	3	797	201*	4	49.81	6
14	†V. B. van Jaarsveld (*Dolphins*)	8	14	0	673	138	3	48.07	5
15	P. J. van Biljon (*Knights*).............	9	18	2	766	177*	3	47.87	11
16	†W. Coulentianos (*Easterns*)..........	10	18	3	712	172	1	47.46	5
17	D. G. Bedingham (*Cape Cobras/Boland*)	10	16	2	663	112	2	47.35	13
18	A. P. Agathangelou (*Titans/Northerns*) .	11	18	1	783	182	2	46.05	11
19	†J. D. Vandiar (*Northerns/Titans*)......	11	17	1	721	139	2	45.06	6
20	†D. A. Hendricks (*Lions/Gauteng*)....	12	21	2	784	197	1	41.26	12
21	G. Roelofsen (*Dolphins/KZN Inland*)..	15	24	4	753	125*	2	37.65	40/2
22	S. C. Cook (*Lions/Gauteng*)..........	16	29	1	993	188	4	35.46	4
23	M. Y. Vallie (*Warriors/Border*)	11	21	1	703	110	1	35.15	2
24	T. G. Mokoena (*Knights/Northern Cape*)	13	25	0	767	113	1	30.68	4

BOWLING (25 wickets, average 30.00)

		Style	O	M	R	W	BB	5I	Avge
1	S. H. Jamison (*Gauteng*)	RFM	196.4	53	544	37	5-16	3	14.70
2	P. Fojela (*Border*)	RFM	165	31	462	31	5-39	2	14.90
3	D. Olivier (*Knights/South Africa*)	RF	326.5	74	1,041	58	6-37	3	17.94
4	G. A. Stuurman (*E Prov/Warriors*)..	RM	350.4	90	1,025	56	5-16	5	18.30
5	M. N. Piedt (*South Western Districts*) .	RFM	246.2	60	650	35	6-35	3	18.57
6	K. J. Dudgeon (*KZ-Natal/Dolphins*)..	RFM	312.5	67	973	52	7-43	5	18.71
7	D. M. Dupavillon (*KwaZulu-Natal*)..	RF	166.1	30	510	26	7-24	2	19.61
8	D. Potgieter (*Gauteng/Lions*)	RFM	208.1	50	631	31	4-63	0	20.35
9	T. Koekemoer (*Eastern Province*)	OB	179.2	29	602	29	6-48	2	20.75
10	J. F. Smith (*Cape Cobras/W Prov*) ...	RFM	179.3	45	535	25	5-26	2	21.40
11	J. G. Dill (*Western Province*).........	RM	278.2	83	730	34	5-43	2	21.47
12	M. B. Njoloza (*Western Province*).....	LFM	225.3	66	605	28	5-28	1	21.60
13	L. B. Adam (*Eastern Province*)	SLA	292.4	73	814	37	5-38	2	22.00
14	N. Burger (*Gauteng/Lions*)	LFM	215.5	53	616	28	5-36	1	22.00
15	K. Rabada (*South Africa*)	RF	148.5	24	554	25	4-38	0	22.16
16	E. Bosch (*Dolphins*)................	RFM	214.1	41	724	31	6-38	1	23.35
17	B. E. Hendricks (*Lions*)	LFM	231.5	58	761	32	5-45	2	23.78
18	C. J. Alexander (*North West/Lions*) ..	RF	166.2	29	604	25	6-71	1	24.16
19	K. I. Simmonds (*Boland*)...........	SLA	246.5	46	798	32	7-87	1	24.93
20	R. A. Cartwright (*Easterns*).........	RF	168	32	656	26	5-49	1	25.23
21	D. Paterson (*Cape Cobras*)	RFM	270.2	62	862	34	6-63	2	25.35
22	T. Mnyaka (*Free State/Knights*)	RFM	232.4	36	763	29	4-16	0	26.31
23	M. P. Siboto (*Lions*)................	RFM	225.3	40	711	26	5-54	1	27.34
24	D. L. Piedt (*Cape Cobras*)...........	OB	511.5	112	1,498	54	8-130	5	27.74
25	R. R. Richards (*Easterns*)	LFM	218.1	50	709	25	5-40	1	28.36
26	B. D. Walters (*Border/Warriors*)	RF	348.5	73	1,197	42	6-94	2	28.50
27	S. A. Mothoa (*Titans/Northerns*)	RFM	269.4	49	919	32	7-115	2	28.71

FOUR-DAY FRANCHISE SERIES IN 2018-19

	P	W	L	D	A	Bat	Bowl	Pts
						Bonus pts		
Lions	10	7	2	1	0	44.22	33	195.22
Cape Cobras .	10	6	2	2	0	38.00	40	186.00
Warriors......	10	3	4	3	0	39.84	38	143.84
Knights	10	2	4	3	1	31.04	27	113.04
Dolphins	10	1	4	5	0	33.16	31	110.16
Titans.......	10	1	4	4	1	30.66	29	104.66

Outright win = 16pts; draw = 6pts; abandoned = 5pts. Bonus points awarded for the first 100 overs of each team's first innings: one batting point for the first 150 runs and 0.02 of a point for every subsequent run; one bowling point for the third wicket taken and for every subsequent two.

CHAMPIONS

1889-90	Transvaal	1954-55	Natal	1989-90	{ Eastern Province
1890-91	Kimberley	1955-56	Western Province		{ Western Province
1892-93	Western Province	1958-59	Transvaal	1990-91	Western Province
1893-94	Western Province	1959-60	Natal	1991-92	Eastern Province
1894-95	Transvaal	1960-61	Natal	1992-93	Orange Free State
1896-97	Western Province	1962-63	Natal	1993-94	Orange Free State
1897-98	Western Province	1963-64	Natal	1994-95	Natal
1902-03	Transvaal	1965-66	{ Natal	1995-96	Western Province
1903-04	Transvaal		{ Transvaal	1996-97	Natal
1904-05	Transvaal	1966-67	Natal	1997-98	Free State
1906-07	Transvaal	1967-68	Natal	1998-99	Western Province
1908-09	Western Province	1968-69	Transvaal	1999-2000	Gauteng
1910-11	Natal	1969-70	{ Transvaal	2000-01	Western Province
1912-13	Natal		{ Western Province	2001-02	KwaZulu-Natal
1920-21	Western Province	1970-71	Transvaal	2002-03	Easterns
1921-22	{ Transvaal	1971-72	Transvaal	2003-04	Western Province
	{ Natal	1972-73	Transvaal	2004-05	{ Dolphins
	{ Western Province	1973-74	Natal		{ Eagles
1923-24	Transvaal	1974-75	Western Province	2005-06	{ Dolphins
1925-26	Transvaal	1975-76	Natal		{ Titans
1926-27	Transvaal	1976-77	Natal	2006-07	Titans
1929-30	Transvaal	1977-78	Western Province	2007-08	Eagles
1931-32	Western Province	1978-79	Transvaal	2008-09	Titans
1933-34	Natal	1979-80	Transvaal	2009-10	Cape Cobras
1934-35	Transvaal	1980-81	Natal	2010-11	Cape Cobras
1936-37	Natal	1981-82	Western Province	2011-12	Titans
1937-38	{ Natal	1982-83	Transvaal	2012-13	Cape Cobras
	{ Transvaal	1983-84	Transvaal	2013-14	Cape Cobras
1946-47	Natal	1984-85	Transvaal	2014-15	Lions
1947-48	Natal	1985-86	Western Province	2015-16	Titans
1950-51	Natal	1986-87	Transvaal	2016-17	Knights
1951-52	Natal	1987-88	Transvaal	2017-18	Titans
1952-53	Western Province	1988-89	Eastern Province	2018-19	Lions

Transvaal/Gauteng have won the title outright 25 times, Natal/KwaZulu-Natal 21, Western Province 18, Titans 5, Cape Cobras 4, Orange Free State/Free State 3, Eagles/Knights, Eastern Province and Lions 2, Easterns and Kimberley 1. The title has been shared seven times as follows: Transvaal 4, Natal and Western Province 3, Dolphins 2, Eagles, Eastern Province and Titans 1.

The tournament was the Currie Cup from 1889-90 to 1989-90, the Castle Cup from 1990-91 to 1995-96, the SuperSport Series from 1996-97 to 2011-12, and the Sunfoil Series from 2012-13 to 2017-18. There was no sponsor in 2018-19.

From 1971-72 to 1990-91, the non-white South African Cricket Board of Control (later the South African Cricket Board) organised their own three-day tournaments. These are now recognised as first-class (see *Wisden 2006*, pages 79–80). A list of winners appears in *Wisden 2007*, page 1346.

CSA PROVINCIAL THREE-DAY CUP IN 2018-19

Pool A	P	W	L	D	Pts	Pool B	P	W	L	D	Pts
EASTERN PROV .	10	4	0	6	178.68	NORTHERNS . . .	10	3	1	6	164.84
Gauteng	10	5	1	4	172.94	Western Province .	10	3	3	4	141.52
Free State	10	2	2	6	131.62	SW Districts	10	2	2	6	124.04†
Easterns	10	2	2	6	124.48	KwaZulu-Natal . . .	10	2	2	6	123.04
Boland	10	2	3	5*	119.28†	North West	10	3	5	2‡	101.10‡
KZN Inland.	10	1	1	8*	113.42	Border.	10	1	4	5	94.86†
						Northern Cape. . . .	10	1	5	4‡	83.92†

* *Includes one abandoned match.*   † *Points deducted for slow over-rates.*

‡ *The drawn match between Northern Cape and North West lost first-class status after North West breached the regulations on substitutes. North West lost 14.12pts earned during the game, while Northern Cape retained their 10.1pts.*

Outright win = 16pts; draw = 6pts; abandoned = 5pts. Bonus points awarded for the first 100 overs of each team's first innings: one batting point for the first 150 runs and 0.02 of a point for every subsequent run; one bowling point for the third wicket taken and for every subsequent two.

The teams were divided into two pools, one of six and one of seven (Namibia had dropped out since 2017-18). Those in Pool A played the other five teams, plus five from the other pool; those in Pool B played the other six plus four from the other pool; all results counted towards the final table. The pool leaders met in a four-day final.

Final   At Port Elizabeth, April 11–14, 2019. **Drawn. ‡Eastern Province 477** (T. Koekemoer 130; S. A. Mothoa 7-115) **and 85-5 dec; Northerns 272** (J. L. du Plooy 119) **and 147-2.** *Bad light hindered Eastern Province's attempt to convert a massive first-innings advantage into victory, and the teams shared the title. Tian Koekemoer batted six and a half hours for a career-best 130, sharing two century stands before he became one of seven victims for Alfred Mothoa. Northerns were bowled out 205 behind, despite Leus du Plooy's century, but survived after being set 291.*

MOMENTUM ONE-DAY CUP IN 2018-19

50-over league plus knockout

	P	W	L	NR/A	Bonus	Pts	NRR
TITANS	10	6	4	0	4	28	0.94
DOLPHINS	10	5	4	1	1	23	0.01
WARRIORS.	10	5	4	1	0	22	–0.50
CAPE COBRAS. . . .	10	5	5	0	0	20	–0.48
Knights	10	3	5	2	2	18	0.11
Lions	10	2	4	4	0	16	–0.07

Semi-finals   Titans beat Cape Cobras by five wickets; Dolphins beat Warriors by seven wickets.

Final   At Centurion, March 31, 2019. **Titans won by 135 runs. Titans 356-5** (50 overs) (A. K. Markram 127); **‡Dolphins 221** (39.4 overs). *The Titans won the 50-over title for the third time in five seasons. Aiden Markram set up their huge total by smashing 127 in 88 balls, including eight sixes, his third century of the tournament. Needing more than seven an over, the Dolphins were always struggling after two early wickets for Dale Steyn, who finished with 8–1–36–3.*

CSA T20 CHALLENGE IN 2018-19

20-over league plus knockout

	P	W	L	NR/A	Bonus	Pts	NRR
LIONS	10	5	2	3	2	28	0.52
WARRIORS.	10	4	2	4	1	25	0.36
CAPE COBRAS. . . .	10	5	4	1	1	23	–0.35
DOLPHINS	10	3	3	4	1	21	0.22
Titans	10	3	4	3	1	19	0.15
Knights	10	0	5	5	0	10	–0.86

Semi-finals Lions beat Dolphins by eight wickets; Warriors beat Cape Cobras by 15 runs.

Final At Johannesburg, May 5, 2019. **Lions won by 11 runs. Lions 203-4** (20 overs) (T. Bavuma 104); ‡**Warriors 192** (19.2 overs) (J. T. Smuts 121). *Temba Bavuma's 63-ball 104 was his maiden T20 century; he added 165 for the Lions' third wicket with Rassie van der Dussen (73). In reply, Bavuma's fellow captain Jon-Jon Smuts hit 121 in 60 deliveries, with seven sixes – almost a lone hand as the Warriors subsided to the left-arm spin of Bjorn Fortuin (4-27) and the pace of Migael Pretorius (3-35). When Smuts fell in the final over, the Lions lifted their second trophy of the season.*

CSA PROVINCIAL 50-OVER CHALLENGE IN 2018-19

50-over league plus final

Pool A	P	W	L	NR	Pts	Pool B	P	W	L	NR	Pts
EASTERNS.	10	7	3	0	30	NORTHERNS.	10	9	1	0	38
Gauteng.	10	6	4	0	30	SW Districts.	10	6	3	1	28
Free State.	10	6	4	0	26	North West.	10	5	3	2	25
Eastern Province	10	5	4	1	25	Western Province.	10	4	6	0	19
KwaZulu-Natal Inland .	10	4	6	0	18	Northern Cape	10	3	5	2	17
Boland.	10	3	7	0	13	KwaZulu-Natal	10	3	7	0	13
						Border	10	0	8	2	4

Final At Centurion, April 7, 2019. **Easterns won by two wickets. Northerns 276-8** (50 overs); ‡**Easterns 277-8** (46.5 overs). *Leus du Plooy dominated Northerns' innings, with 85*. But solid batting from Easterns' top order ensured their victory, despite three late wickets.*

AFRICA T20 CUP IN 2018-19

20-over league plus semi-finals and final

Pool A	P	W	L	Pts	Pool B	P	W	L	Pts
EASTERNS	4	3	1	14	GAUTENG.	4	3	1	15
KwaZulu-Natal.	4	3	1	12	Zimbabwe.	4	3	1	13
Uganda.	4	2	2	9	Northerns	4	3	1	13
Western Province . . .	4	1	3	5	Free State	4	1	3	4
KZN Inland	4	1	3	5	SW Districts	4	0	4	0

Pool C	P	W	L	Pts	Pool D	P	W	L	Pts
BORDER	4	3	1	13	NORTH WEST	4	3	1	14
Eastern Province . . .	4	3	1	13	Boland.	4	3	1	14
Namibia	4	3	1	13	Northern Cape	4	3	1	14
Kenya	4	1	3	4	Limpopo	4	1	3	5
Mpumalanga.	4	0	4	0	Nigeria	4	0	4	0

Semi-finals Gauteng beat North West by 27 runs; Border beat Easterns by seven wickets.

Final At East London, September 24, 2018. **Gauteng won by three wickets. Border 130** (20 overs); ‡**Gauteng 131-7** (19.2 overs). *Border made a disastrous start – 3-3 in the second over, with both openers out first ball – and only 51* from No. 8 Bamanye Xenxe got them to three figures. Gauteng were 79-6, but Zanzima Pongolo followed up 3-20 with 30* to see them home.*

The Mzansi Super League has its own section (page 1150).

SRI LANKAN CRICKET IN 2019

Clean up or clear out

Sa'adi Thawfeeq

In a potentially defining moment in the history of the country's cricket, a bill was passed in parliament in November that made Sri Lanka the first South Asian nation to criminalise offences relating to match-fixing. The maximum term for anyone found guilty was ten years. The bill was the work of sports minister Harin Fernando, who has been closely involved with the Sri Lanka team, but won important backing from World Cup-winning captain Arjuna Ranatunga, now a cabinet minister.

Fernando worked with the ICC's anti-corruption unit in drafting the bill, which covers all sport in Sri Lanka, but is clearly aimed at cleaning up cricket. It includes provision to punish groundsmen who prepare pitches to suit gambling interests, and former players who introduce corrupt individuals to current cricketers. It is also now a criminal offence for players to fail to report

SRI LANKA IN 2019

	Played	Won	Lost	Drawn/No result
Tests	8	3	4	1
One-day internationals	21	7	14	–
Twenty20 internationals	13	4	8	1

DECEMBER	2 Tests, 3 ODIs and 1 T20I (a) v New Zealand	(see *Wisden 2019*, page 917)
JANUARY	2 Tests (a) v Australia	(page 881)
FEBRUARY		
MARCH	2 Tests, 5 ODIs and 3 T20Is (a) v South Africa	(page 1016)
APRIL		
MAY	2 ODIs (a) v Scotland	(page 1104)
JUNE	World Cup (in England)	(page 237)
JULY	3 ODIs (h) v Bangladesh	(page 1032)
AUGUST	2 Tests and 3 T20Is (h) v New Zealand	(page 1034)
SEPTEMBER	2 ODIs and 3 T20Is (a) v Pakistan	(page 1002)
OCTOBER		
NOVEMBER	3 T20Is (a) v Australia	(page 886)
DECEMBER	2 Tests (a) v Pakistan	(page 1002)

For a review of Sri Lankan domestic cricket from the 2018-19 season, see page 1044.

Thanaka Basnayaka/NurPhoto, Getty Images

Waved away: Lasith Malinga acknowledges the packed house that came to see his final ODI.

approaches by possible corrupters. The hope of everyone desperate to see Sri Lanka restored to their former standing is that this legislation will help rid the country of the corruption that has overshadowed all else in recent times.

In February, Sanath Jayasuriya, one of Sri Lanka's greatest players, and recently chairman of selectors, was handed a two-year ban by the ICC after admitting two breaches of the anti-corruption code. The ICC also announced that a 15-day amnesty had resulted in 11 players coming forward with evidence to assist their inquiry.

In October, Fernando banned former Sri Lanka Cricket president Thilanga Sumathipala from holding any position in cricket administration, following an investigation into his links with the gambling industry. A court case was launched by Nishantha Ranatunga, a former SLC presidential candidate, questioning Sumathipala's fitness to stand for the presidency again. The elections had been postponed while a group of sports ministry officials ran SLC. But when they were eventually held, Shammi Silva, a close associate of Sumathipala, was elected: the board remained under the control of a familiar coterie.

Understandably, politics overshadowed cricket; often, that was just as well. The year began with the tame surrender of the Warne–Muralitharan Trophy in a two-match series in Australia, after which Dinesh Chandimal was sacked as captain. What happened next defied logic. Under Dimuth Karunaratne, Sri Lanka became the first Asian team to win a Test series in South Africa. The

First Test win in Durban was among the greatest in their history, Kusal Perera's stunning 153 not out carrying them to a one-wicket victory. South Africa came back hard in Port Elizabeth, but Sri Lanka stayed calm to wrap up a 2–0 win.

The eight white-ball matches that followed were all won by South Africa, leading to the axing of Lasith Malinga as one-day captain, and the appointment of Karunaratne for the World Cup, where little went right. Sri Lanka were hampered by two washouts, but grumbled about pitches, scheduling and hotels. An unexpected victory over England at Headingley raised hopes of qualifying for the semi-finals, but it was not to be.

With SLC under pressure to act from the sports ministry, that spelled the end of the brief and stormy tenure of head coach Chandika Hathurusinghe, with a year and a half to run on his contract. The board cited the ball-tampering incident during a Test against West Indies in St Lucia in 2018, and his failure to provide reports on the work he was doing with individual players.

Hathurusinghe responded by suing for wrongful dismissal, and claiming $5m in compensation. A clause in his contract meant the dispute would be settled in Geneva rather than Colombo. It was all in stark contrast to his appointment at the end of 2017, when the board were desperate to lure him away from Bangladesh. Fast-bowling coach Rumesh Ratnayake stood in as interim coach until the arrival of the vastly experienced South African Mickey Arthur at the end of the year.

Arthur's first assignment came in December, in Pakistan, where Sri Lanka became the first team to play a Test series since the terrorist attack on their team bus in Lahore ten years earlier. But it was a curious tour. The white-ball matches took place in September, and ten Sri Lanka players refused to tour, citing security concerns. But when their stand-ins whitewashed Pakistan in the Twenty20 matches, they all made themselves available for the Tests, which did not take place until December. After a rain-ruined First Test, Arthur's debut ended in a 1–0 defeat.

There was not much cricket for home fans, but two visits did at least go ahead, despite security worries following the Easter Sunday terrorist attacks on churches and hotels. Soon after the World Cup, Bangladesh arrived for a three-match one-day series that included Malinga's farewell appearance in the format. He was given a grand send-off by a 35,000 crowd at the R. Premadasa Stadium that included the country's president, Maithripala Sirisena. Sri Lanka won 3–0. In August and September, New Zealand shared a Test series 1–1, followed by three T20 internationals. In between the two legs of the Pakistan tour, Sri Lanka visited to Australia for three T20s in preparation for the World Cup later in 2020. All three were lost heavily.

Amid the gloom, Sri Lanka's cricket community were cheered when former captain Kumar Sangakkara became the first non-British president of MCC.

SRI LANKA v BANGLADESH IN 2019

Rex Clementine

One-day internationals (3): Sri Lanka 3, Bangladesh 0

This was the first series Sri Lanka had hosted since the Easter Sunday terrorist attacks, which had killed more than 250 people three months earlier. A decade after the end of their long civil war, it felt as if the country was back to square one. Initially, the tour – already brought forward from December to avoid a clash with the Bangladesh Premier League – was in jeopardy, but the authorities were determined to put safety concerns to rest. The Bangladesh squad were guarded by the police's Special Task Force, with heavy security imposed on their hotel. All three one-day internationals were played at the R. Premadasa Stadium in Colombo, a disappointment for the outposts of Kandy and Dambulla, and fans were checked thoroughly as they entered.

The teams should have met at the World Cup in England a few weeks earlier, but their match at Bristol was washed out, and both ended up in the bottom half of the table. Back at home, Sri Lanka controlled the series from start to finish, with three big victories. The first match was overshadowed by Lasith Malinga's announcement that this would be his farewell to one-day international cricket. But, while they experimented with the bowling attack, a strong Sri Lankan batting line-up led by Angelo Mathews and Kusal Perera kept them on top throughout.

Bangladesh had arrived in some disarray. Their coach, Steve Rhodes, had departed after the World Cup; their best player, all-rounder Shakib Al Hasan, was given leave to go on a pilgrimage to Mecca after an outstanding tournament in England; batsman-keeper Liton Das was getting married; and captain Mashrafe bin Mortaza was ruled unfit. Tamim Iqbal, Bangladesh's leading run-scorer in all three formats, took over the captaincy, but the role did not suit him. He had a disastrous series, managing only 21 runs; Mushfiqur Rahim played well for 175, just behind Mathews and Perera.

BANGLADESH TOURING PARTY

Tamim Iqbal, Anamul Haque, Farhad Reza, Mahmudullah, Mehedi Hasan, Mithun Ali, Mosaddek Hossain, Mushfiqur Rahim, Mustafizur Rahman, Rubel Hossain, Sabbir Rahman, Shafiul Islam, Soumya Sarkar, Taijul Islam, Taskin Ahmed. Coach: Khaled Mahmud.

Shakib Al Hasan, Liton Das, Mashrafe bin Mortaza and Mohammad Saifuddin were originally selected. Shakib and Liton withdrew for personal reasons and were replaced by Anamul Haque and Taijul Islam. Mortaza pulled out with a hamstring injury, and Saifuddin with a bad back, and were replaced by Taskin Ahmed and Farhad Reza; Tamim Iqbal took over the captaincy from Mortaza.

First one-day international At Colombo (RPS), July 26 (day/night). **Sri Lanka won by 91 runs.** ‡**Sri Lanka 314-8** (50 overs) (F. D. M. Karunaratne 36, M. D. K. J. Perera 111, B. K. G. Mendis 43, A. D. Mathews 48; Shafiul Islam 3-62); **Bangladesh 223** (41.4 overs) (Mushfiqur Rahim 67, Sabbir Rahman 60; S. L. Malinga 3-38, A. N. P. R. Fernando 3-51). *PoM:* M. D. K. J. Perera. *Tickets sold out once Lasith Malinga announced this would be his final one-day international; a crowd of 35,000 included the president and the leader of the opposition. They saw Malinga bowl both Bangladesh openers with yorkers, then return to end the game with his 338th ODI victim – Mustafizur Rahman,* *who skyed a slower ball to mid-off. Lahiru Kumara took only one wicket in his first international for six months, but his pace suggested he might help fill the gap left by Malinga. Sri Lanka's comprehensive victory had been set up by Kusal Perera, who reached his fifth ODI century, in 82 balls; his team-mates did not make the most of a platform of 207-3, but did pass 300, with Malinga scoring the last runs of the innings.*

Second one-day international   At Colombo (RPS), July 28 (day/night). **Sri Lanka won by seven wickets.** ‡**Bangladesh 238-8** (50 overs) (Mushfiqur Rahim 98*, Mehedi Hasan 43); **Sri Lanka 242-3** (44.4 overs) (W. I. A. Fernando 82, M. D. K. J. Perera 30, B. K. G. Mendis 41*, A. D. Mathews 52*). *PoM:* W. I. A. Fernando. *Avishka Fernando, whose match-winning hundred against West Indies had been one of Sri Lanka's few World Cup highlights, delighted the home fans as he hooked and pulled his way to 82 off 75 balls. On leaving the field, he learned that his father, Colin, a diabetic, had been rushed to hospital after fainting while watching him, though he was discharged. Kusal Mendis and Angelo Mathews had completed the victory which sealed Sri Lanka's first one-day series win at home for nearly four years. Mushfiqur Rahim had rescued Bangladesh from 88-5, after Tamim Iqbal was bowled for the sixth successive innings, and unorthodox off-spinner Akila Dananjaya (2-39) provided the control Sri Lanka had lacked in the World Cup.*

Third one-day international   At Colombo (RPS), July 31 (day/night). **Sri Lanka won by 122 runs.** ‡**Sri Lanka 294-8** (50 overs) (F. D. M. Karunaratne 46, M. D. K. J. Perera 42, B. K. G. Mendis 54, A. D. Mathews 87, M. D. Shanaka 30; Shafiul Islam 3-68, Soumya Sarkar 3-56); **Bangladesh 172** (36 overs) (Soumya Sarkar 69, Taijul Islam 39*; M. D. Shanaka 3-27). *PoM:* A. D. Mathews. *PoS:* A. D. Mathews. *Mathews, carrying injuries to his calf, ankle and hamstring, answered critics who felt he should restrict himself to Test cricket by finishing as the leading scorer in this series, with 187 runs – though he never bowled. His 87 helped Sri Lanka complete a 3–0 whitewash. A decent start, middle-overs consolidation and late power-hitting meant another big total. With the series already won, they made four changes, including Dasun Shanaka, who smashed 30 off 14 balls and took 3-27, and Kasun Rajitha, who bowled with fire for figures of 5–0–17–2. For Bangladesh, Soumya Sarkar followed up three wickets with a steady half-century.*

SRI LANKA v NEW ZEALAND IN 2019

Fidel Fernando

Test matches (2): Sri Lanka 1 (60pts), New Zealand 1 (60pts)
Twenty20 internationals (3): Sri Lanka 1, New Zealand 2

Batting collapses, turning pitches, torrential downpours, hard-fought centuries and even a spin bowler reported for throwing: this two-Test series featured all Sri Lanka's most familiar tropes. What's more, their five-year drawless streak at home continued, despite the rain, with both teams taking 60 World Test Championship points. This was particularly remarkable in Colombo, where the second innings of the match did not end until early on the fifth day; a skilled New Zealand bowling performance, and some brainless batting, sent things hurtling to a conclusion. That made it 27 Tests since Sri Lanka had hosted a draw.

That this tour took place at all was a relief, following the Easter Sunday suicide bomb attacks on April 21, which had claimed more than 250 lives. Just two months before the trip was set to begin, there had been nervousness at Sri Lanka Cricket that New Zealand would withdraw over safety concerns. But a successful ODI series in Colombo in late July against Bangladesh helped quell fears, while security assessments conducted by both boards suggested it remained feasible to stage a long tour at a range of venues. Perhaps New Zealand Cricket were sympathetic to SLC's plight: in March, they had cancelled a Test in Christchurch after the Bangladesh tourists were almost caught up in a horrific attack on a nearby mosque.

In the event, the tour could not have begun in more heart-warming fashion. The first day of New Zealand's three-day practice match, just north of Colombo, was enlivened by a group of local spectators producing a cake to celebrate Kane Williamson's 29th birthday. Williamson, whose global fandom had skyrocketed during New Zealand's run to the World Cup final the previous month, headed over in a drinks break to take a bite of the cake, then fed some back to the spectator holding it, as per South Asian tradition. A video of the fun went viral, and Williamson further endeared himself to the Sri Lankan public.

He went on to have an unusually quiet series, scoring nought, four and 20, but Ross Taylor, B-J. Watling and Tom Latham helped propel New Zealand to a reasonable position in the First Test, and a commanding one in the Second. By losing at Galle, then winning at the P. Sara Oval, they replicated their previous visit, in 2012-13.

The Twenty20 series was used by both teams as a proving ground for fringe players, with a view to the T20 World Cup in 2020. New Zealand rested Williamson and spearhead Trent Boult, but outstanding performances from stand-in captain Tim Southee helped them to a 2–0 lead. In the dead rubber, Lasith Malinga took four wickets in four balls to send a packed Pallekele stadium into raptures.

NEW ZEALAND TOURING PARTY

*K. S. Williamson (T), T. D. Astle (T/20), T. A. Blundell (T), T. A. Boult (T), T. C. Bruce (20), C. de Grandhomme (T/20), L. H. Ferguson (20), M. J. Guptill (20), S. C. Kuggeleijn (20), T. W. M. Latham (T), D. J. Mitchell (20), C. Munro (20), H. M. Nicholls (T), A. Y. Patel (T), S. H. A. Rance (20), J. A. Raval (T), H. D. Rutherford (20), M. J. Santner (T/20), T. L. Seifert (20), I. S. Sodhi (20), W. E. R. Somerville (T), T. G. Southee (T/20), L. R. P. L. Taylor (T/20), N. Wagner (T), B-J. Watling (T). *Coach:* G. R. Stead.

Southee captained in the T20 series. Ferguson missed it after breaking a thumb in practice. Rutherford was called up as cover after various injuries, and played in the last match after Guptill returned home with a torn stomach muscle.

SRI LANKA v NEW ZEALAND

First Test

At Galle, August 14–18, 2019. Sri Lanka won by six wickets. Sri Lanka 60pts. Toss: New Zealand.

Galle's bowler-friendly surface produced another gripping Test, ultimately decided by an outstanding hundred from Karunaratne. Set 268 to win at a venue where the previous-highest successful pursuit had been 99, Sri Lanka were set on course by his partnership of 161 with Thirimanne – the highest opening stand in the fourth innings of a Test in Sri Lanka – and never looked back.

How expertly they dismantled the chase. The new ball, which at Galle has often yielded seam movement, as well as exaggerated turn, was negotiated without major incident. Early on, there were plays, misses and plenty of thick edges, but these were inevitable on a worn surface; vitally, the openers did not allow the blemishes to disturb their concentration. No four was hit until the 22nd over, when Karunaratne latched on to a wide delivery from off-spinner Somerville. Until then, only 37 runs had accrued, but the batsmen were nicely positioned to take advantage of a softer ball.

The rate eventually quickened, and it wasn't until the 61st over that New Zealand broke through, Somerville trapping Thirimanne for 64. They had, however, missed two chances when Karunaratne had 58: Latham dropped a bat–pad catch at short leg off Patel, before Watling missed a stumping off Somerville. Karunaratne went on to his ninth Test hundred (and the first of his captaincy), before edging a drive off Southee. Only two other Sri Lankan openers (Kusal Mendis and Sanath Jayasuriya, twice) had scored fourth-innings centuries, though only Karunaratne's was in a winning cause. Mathews and de Silva ensured victory.

Taylor had hit 86 on the first day, before Mendis, Mathews and Dickwella – who put on 81 for the eighth wicket with Lakmal – replied with fifties to help earn Sri Lanka an 18-run lead. But Watling's second-innings 77 was the most impressive half-century of the lot. He arrived with New Zealand 81 for four, just 63 ahead; soon, it was 124 for six. But he

SRI LANKA'S HIGHEST SUCCESSFUL TEST RUN-CHASES

391-6	v Zimbabwe at Colombo (RPS)	2017
352-9	v South Africa at Colombo (PSO)..................	2006
326-5	v Zimbabwe at Colombo (SSC)	1997-98
304-9	**v South Africa at Durban**........................	**2018-19**
268-4	**v New Zealand at Galle**.........................	**2019**
220-8	v Pakistan at Rawalpindi..........................	1999-2000
197-2	**v South Africa at Port Elizabeth**	**2018-19**
172-4	v West Indies at Colombo (SSC)	2005
171-3	v Pakistan at Colombo (PSO)	2009

hauled them out of danger in the company of the lower order, adding 54 with Southee, then 46 with Somerville, who supervised another 61 for the last two wickets to extend Sri Lanka's chase.

As so often at Galle, spinners took most of the wickets – though in one case a rich haul was followed by career-threatening news. Dananjaya had taken five for 80 with his off-breaks in the first innings, in his first Test since returning from suspension for failing a biomechanical test in November 2018. Despite having cleared a re-assessment in February, he was now reported again for throwing. He would go on to fail another test, and be suspended from international cricket for a year. Williamson's action was also reported, but he was later exonerated.

New Zealand's left-arm spinner Ajaz Patel also claimed a five-wicket haul in the first innings, while fellow left-armer Embuldeniya, and off-spinners de Silva and Somerville, produced penetrative spells. In the end, though, the laurels went to an opening batsman.

Player of the Match: F. D. M. Karunaratne.

Close of play: first day, New Zealand 203-5 (Taylor 86, Santner 8); second day, Sri Lanka 227-7 (Dickwella 39, Lakmal 28); third day, New Zealand 195-7 (Watling 63, Somerville 5); fourth day, Sri Lanka 133-0 (Karunaratne 71, Thirimanne 57).

New Zealand

J. A. Raval c de Silva b Dananjaya	33	– c Karunaratne b de Silva	4
T. W. M. Latham c Dickwella b Dananjaya	30	– c Thirimanne b Dananjaya	45
*K. S. Williamson c Karunaratne b Dananjaya	0	– c Perera b Embuldeniya	4
L. R. P. L. Taylor c Dickwella b Lakmal	86	– c de Silva b Embuldeniya	3
H. M. Nicholls lbw b Dananjaya	42	– c Mendis b de Silva	26
†B-J. Watling lbw b Dananjaya	1	– c Dickwella b Kumara	77
M. J. Santner lbw b Lakmal	13	– c Lakmal b Embuldeniya	12
T. G. Southee run out (de Silva/Dickwella)	14	– st Dickwella b Embuldeniya	23
W. E. R. Somerville not out	9	– not out	40
T. A. Boult c Perera b Lakmal	18	– c de Silva b Kumara	26
A. Y. Patel lbw b Lakmal	0	– lbw b de Silva	14
Lb 2, nb 1	3	B 4, lb 5, nb 2	11

1/64 (2) 2/64 (3) 3/71 (1)   (83.2 overs) 249   1/8 (1) 2/20 (3)   (106 overs) 285
4/171 (5) 5/179 (6) 6/205 (4)   3/25 (4) 4/81 (2)
7/216 (7) 8/222 (8) 9/249 (10) 10/249 (11)   5/98 (5) 6/124 (7) 7/178 (8)
    8/224 (6) 9/260 (10) 10/285 (11)

Lakmal 15.2–5–29–4; Kumara 10–1–37–0; Dananjaya 30–3–80–5; de Silva 6–0–20–0; Embuldeniya 22–1–81–0. *Second innings*—Lakmal 15–2–37–0; Dananjaya 32–4–84–1; de Silva 12–3–25–3; Embuldeniya 37–4–99–4; Kumara 10–0–31–2.

Sri Lanka

*F. D. M. Karunaratne lbw b Patel	39	– c Watling b Southee	122
H. D. R. L. Thirimanne st Watling b Patel	10	– lbw b Somerville	64
B. K. G. Mendis c Taylor b Patel	53	– c Raval b Patel	10
A. D. Mathews c Taylor b Patel	50	– not out	28
M. D. K. J. Perera c Santner b Boult	1	– c Santner b Boult	23
D. M. de Silva c and b Patel	5	– not out	14
†D. P. D. N. Dickwella c Williamson b Somerville	61		
A. Dananjaya c Taylor b Somerville	0		
R. A. S. Lakmal b Boult	40		
L. Embuldeniya lbw b Somerville	5		
C. B. R. L. S. Kumara not out	0		
B 1, lb 1, w 1	3	B 6, lb 1	7

1/27 (2) 2/66 (1) 3/143 (3)   (93.2 overs) 267   1/161 (2)   (4 wkts, 86.1 overs) 268
4/144 (5) 5/155 (6) 6/158 (4)   2/174 (3) 3/218 (1)
7/161 (8) 8/242 (9) 9/262 (7) 10/267 (10)   4/250 (5)

Boult 20–4–45–2; Southee 7–3–17–0; Somerville 22.2–3–83–3; Patel 33–6–89–5; Santner 11–0–31–0. *Second innings*—Boult 9.1–1–34–1; Southee 12–2–33–1; Somerville 31–6–73–1; Patel 18–0–74–1; Santner 13–2–38–0; Williamson 3–0–9–0.

Umpires: M. A. Gough and R. K. Illingworth.   Third umpire: B. N. J. Oxenford.
Referee: A. J. Pycroft.

SRI LANKA v NEW ZEALAND

Second Test

At Colombo (PSO), August 22–26, 2019. New Zealand won by an innings and 65 runs. New Zealand 60pts. Toss: Sri Lanka.

For much of this Test, it seemed unseasonal downpours in Colombo would make a draw inevitable. Only 66 overs were bowled on the first two days, as afternoon thunderstorms lashed the ground; the fourth was also significantly shortened by bad light and bad weather. But Sri Lanka Cricket's practice of covering the entire ground allowed the surface to remain in reasonable condition, and the groundstaff were able to give the Test a slim chance of yielding a result. On the last day, New Zealand emphatically seized it – and squared the series.

In theory, Sri Lanka had to bat out 91 overs after a final-morning declaration, but in reality – with bad light often settling in after 4.30 – that figure was closer to 80. Sri Lanka had bowled and fielded poorly to give up a 187-run first-innings lead, but their situation was far from dire. In fact, they had saved a match from a worse position against the same opposition eight months earlier at Wellington, where – despite a deficit of 296 – Mendis and Mathews had batted unscathed from the third evening to the fifth morning.

On this occasion, though, the Sri Lankans showed no fight. Thirimanne ran himself out in the first over, before Perera – opening in place of the injured Karunaratne, who had torn a quad muscle – played the worst shot of the day in the third, nicking a wide one from Boult. Mathews was caught off de Grandhomme, and de Silva off Patel. It was 32 for five, before Karunaratne – down at No. 7 – put on 41 with Dickwella who, despite being his team's most impetuous batsman, gave them at least some hope of securing the draw that would have earned them a 1–0 win. But he was finally ninth out for 51 off 161 deliveries, when he was caught at short leg by Latham, who cleverly intercepted, then athletically deflected, a paddle sweep. Five balls later, Boult removed Embuldeniya, and New Zealand had only their second Test win in Sri Lanka since 1997-98.

> Boult and Southee joined Richard Hadlee and Daniel Vettori with 250 Test wickets

Although their path to victory was eased by some loose batting, New Zealand's attack were relentless. Quicks often play a role at the P. Sara Oval, which is more conducive to bounce than most South Asian surfaces, and their three seamers took five wickets on the final day to the spinners' four. During the game, both Boult and Southee moved past 250 Test wickets, joining Richard Hadlee and Daniel Vettori as the only New Zealanders to reach the mark.

Before the bowlers sewed things up, however, the batsmen made Sri Lanka toil in the field. Having lost his opening partner Raval for a duck, Latham scored his tenth Test hundred – and fourth against Sri Lanka – to help transform a scoreboard reading 126 for four into a healthy 431 for six. Watling produced another outstanding innings, making an unbeaten 105 while adding 143 with Latham and 113 with de Grandhomme, who substantially advanced the timing of the declaration by thumping 83 off 77 balls.

Sri Lanka's attack were listless, though the injured Karunaratne was not captaining the side through the course of a poor fourth day. The baton passed instead to Mathews, under whose leadership Sri Lanka had previously shown a tendency to allow middle- and lower-order partnerships to flourish. Karunaratne later stopped short of criticising him, but did suggest he would have done things differently.

In any case, it was Sri Lanka's errors with the bat that had allowed New Zealand into this match. Even in the first innings, they had underperformed, with only Karunaratne and de Silva passing 50. But de Silva's 109 was by a distance the most pleasing knock of the series, his languid pulls, effortless cuts and elegant cover-drives lighting up a gloomy innings.

Player of the Match: T. W. M. Latham.	*Player of the Series:* B-J. Watling.

Close of play: first day, Sri Lanka 85-2 (Karunaratne 49, Mathews 0); second day, Sri Lanka 144-6 (de Silva 32, M. D. K. Perera 5); third day, New Zealand 196-4 (Latham 111, Watling 25); fourth day, New Zealand 382-5 (Watling 81, de Grandhomme 83).

Sri Lanka

*F. D. M. Karunaratne c Watling b Southee	65	– (7) lbw b Southee	21
H. D. R. L. Thirimanne c Williamson b Somerville	2	– (1) run out (Patel)	0
B. K. G. Mendis c Watling b de Grandhomme	32	– b Somerville	20
A. D. Mathews c Watling b Boult	2	– c Taylor b de Grandhomme	7
M. D. K. J. Perera lbw b Boult	0	– (2) c Watling b Boult	0
D. M. de Silva b Boult	109	– (5) c Southee b Patel	1
†D. P. D. N. Dickwella c Watling b Southee	0	– (6) c Latham b Patel	51
M. D. K. Perera lbw b Patel	13	– c Taylor b Southee	0
R. A. S. Lakmal c Watling b Southee	10	– c Latham b Somerville	14
L. Embuldeniya b Boult	0	– c Williamson b Boult	5
C. B. R. L. S. Kumara not out	5	– not out	0
B 1, lb 2, nb 3	6	Lb 2, w 1	3

1/29 (2) 2/79 (3) 3/93 (4)	(90.2 overs) 244	1/0 (1) 2/4 (2)	(70.2 overs) 122
4/93 (5) 5/130 (1) 6/130 (7)			3/11 (4) 4/22 (5)
7/171 (8) 8/214 (9) 9/224 (10) 10/244 (6)			5/32 (3) 6/73 (7) 7/75 (8)
			8/115 (9) 9/118 (6) 10/122 (10)

Boult 22.2–6–75–3; Southee 29–7–63–4; de Grandhomme 17–3–35–1; Somerville 6–3–20–1; Patel 16–4–48–1. *Second innings*—Boult 14.2–8–17–2; Southee 12–6–15–2; Patel 19–3–31–2; de Grandhomme 4–1–8–1; Somerville 21–6–49–2.

New Zealand

J. A. Raval c de Silva b M. D. K. Perera	0	T. G. Southee not out	24
T. W. M. Latham lbw b M. D. K. Perera	154		
*K. S. Williamson c Mendis b Kumara	20		
L. R. P. L. Taylor c de Silva b Embuldeniya	23	Lb 4, w 3	7
H. M. Nicholls c de Silva b M. D. K. Perera	15		
†B-J. Watling not out	105	1/1 (1) 2/34 (3) (6 wkts dec, 115 overs) 431
C. de Grandhomme c Kumara		3/84 (4) 4/126 (5)
b Embuldeniya	83	5/269 (2) 6/382 (7)

W. E. R. Somerville, T. A. Boult and A. Y. Patel did not bat.

M. D. K. Perera 37–4–114–3; de Silva 5–1–10–0; Lakmal 11–2–32–0; Kumara 25–0–115–1; Embuldeniya 37–4–156–2.

Umpires: M. A. Gough and B. N. J. Oxenford.	Third umpire: R. K. Illingworth.
Referee: A. J. Pycroft.

First Twenty20 international At Pallekele, September 1 (floodlit). **New Zealand won by five wickets.** ‡**Sri Lanka 174-4** (20 overs) (B. K. G. Mendis 79, D. P. D. N. Dickwella 33); **New Zealand 175-5** (19.3 overs) (C. de Grandhomme 44, L. R. P. L. Taylor 48). *PoM:* L. R. P. L. Taylor. *T20I debut:* P. W. H. de Silva (Sri Lanka). *Colin de Grandhomme and Ross Taylor thrashed 79 in 37 balls for New Zealand's fourth wicket to set up a last-over victory. Coming together at a perilous 39-3 in the eighth, they quickly moved ahead of the required rate. And though Taylor fell with 31 still required off 19 balls, New Zealand had enough firepower to secure victory. Daryl Mitchell and Mitchell Santner completed the job with three to spare. Earlier, Kusal Mendis had* *produced the innings of the game – a 53-ball 79 – to give Sri Lanka a fast start. Tim Southee conceded only 20 in his four overs, though his new-ball partner Seth Rance was smashed for 58, including four of Sri Lanka's five sixes.*

Second Twenty20 international At Pallekele, September 3 (floodlit). **New Zealand won by four wickets.** ‡**Sri Lanka 161-9** (20 overs) (W. I. A. Fernando 37, D. P. D. N. Dickwella 39; S. H. A. Rance 3-33); **New Zealand 165-6** (19.4 overs) (C. de Grandhomme 59, T. C. Bruce 53; A. Dananjaya 3-36). *PoM:* T. G. Southee. *The second match followed a similar pattern to the first. New Zealand again lost three early wickets, before a 109-run fourth-wicket stand – this time between de Grandhomme and Tom Bruce (Ross Taylor was out with a niggle) – secured another last-over victory. De Grandhomme hit 59 off 46, and Bruce 53 off 46, after joining forces at 38-3. There was, though, late drama. De Grandhomme fell to the second ball of the penultimate over, with 15 wanted. Then Bruce and Mitchell were out off the first two deliveries of the last, with the requirement now seven. Sri Lanka would probably have won if, next ball, Shehan Jayasuriya had not collided with Mendis on the wide long-on boundary after catching Santner, causing both fielders to tumble over the rope. Six runs were awarded, and Santner pulled the next for four to seal the series. Southee had again led New Zealand's bowling effort, taking 2-18, as four Sri Lankans reached 20, but none 40.*

Third Twenty20 international At Pallekele, September 6 (floodlit). **Sri Lanka won by 37 runs.** ‡**Sri Lanka 125-8** (20 overs) (M. D. Gunathilleke 30; M. J. Santner 3-12, T. D. Astle 3-28); **New Zealand 88** (16 overs) (S. L. Malinga 5-6). *PoM:* S. L. Malinga. *PoS:* T. G. Southee. *T20I debut:* L. D. Madushanka (Sri Lanka). *The Pallekele stadium had been full for all three games, despite the threat of rain, and in the final match the crowd were rewarded by a Lasith Malinga performance for the ages. In his second over, he single-handedly derailed New Zealand's chase, removing Colin Munro (bowled), Hamish Rutherford (lbw), de Grandhomme (bowled) and Taylor (lbw) in successive deliveries with a string of wickedly late, full-length swingers. All four balls either*

FOUR WICKETS IN FOUR BALLS IN INTERNATIONAL CRICKET

S. L. Malinga	Sri Lanka v South Africa at Providence (ODI World Cup) . . .	2006-07
Rashid Khan	**Afghanistan v Ireland at Dehradun (T20)**	**2018-19**
S. L. Malinga	Sri Lanka v New Zealand at Pallekele (T20)	2019

---

hit, or would have hit, the base of the stumps. It was his fifth international hat-trick (Pakistan's Wasim Akram took four; no one else had more than two). Munro's wicket meant Malinga became the first to claim 100 in T20Is. Later he removed Tim Seifert, taking the sequence to five for one (a wide) in nine deliveries. He finished with 4–20–6–5. Three wickets (including a run-out) then fell in the ninth over, bowled by Akila Dananjaya, and it needed three sixes from Southee, and a last-wicket stand of 36, to lift New Zealand to as many as 88. Earlier, Santner's 3-12 had helped restrict Sri Lanka to 125-8. Thanks to Malinga, it was more than enough.

DOMESTIC CRICKET IN SRI LANKA IN 2018-19

Sa'adi Thawfeeq

Sri Lanka's oldest club, **Colombo**, formed in 1832, won only their third first-class title in February 2019, and their first for 12 years (they also won three before the competition had first-class status). They headed their preliminary group in Premier League Tier A, and finished on top of the Super Eight table, with four wins in seven matches. They entered the final round just over one point ahead of Sinhalese; to seal the title, they needed 290 on the last day to beat Nondescripts, and got there with five wickets to spare.

Colombo's eventual lead was 13 points, but the next four teams were clustered with less than one point between them. Their nearest challengers, Sinhalese, had high hopes after reducing previous champions Chilaw Marians to 92 for five chasing 366, but suffered a shock defeat after a stand of 206 between Risith Upamal Dias, unbeaten on 112, and Nimesh Vimukthi, whose 120 was his maiden first-class hundred. Their efforts meant Chilaw Marians rose to third, while Sinhalese dropped to fifth. But Saracens squeezed into the runners-up position on first-innings points; they piled up 574 for nine in reply to Tamil Union's 330, despite missing their captain, Milinda Siriwardene, and Kasun Rajitha, both touring South Africa with the national team.

Burgher won the Plate section of Tier A, jumping into first place when they beat Ports Authority by an innings in the final round. **Lankan** were champions of Tier B, despite having only one outright victory to runners-up Navy's three.

Colombo could field eight international players, including their capable captain Ashan Priyanjan, who had often led Sri Lanka A. The outstanding performer was left-arm spinner Malinda Pushpakumara, who joined Colombo from Chilaw Marians. He was the tournament's leading wicket-taker with 63 at 20, including ten for 37 in Saracens' second innings to set up a 235-run victory at Moratuwa in January. He became only the second Sri Lankan to pick up all ten in first-class cricket, after seamer Pramodya Wickremasinghe, who had claimed ten for 41 for Sinhalese against Kalutara in 1991-92 – though another slow left-armer, Saracens' Chamikara Edirisinghe, almost beat Pushpakumara to it in the same match. He dismissed the first nine Colombo batsmen, before the tenth fell to occasional bowler Ashen Bandara, his maiden first-class wicket. Pushpakumara also collected most victims in all first-class cricket in Sri Lanka for the third successive season; all but one of the top 15 wicket-takers were spinners.

The season's outstanding batting performance came in Tier A's penultimate round, when Nondescripts captain Angelo Perera scored 201 and 231 against Sinhalese. The only other cricketer to score two double-hundreds in a first-class match had been Arthur Fagg, with 244 and 202 not out for Kent against Essex in 1938. Perera earned an international recall for the South African tour.

The season featured 17 double-centuries – 15 in Tier A – with Kaushal Silva's 273 for Sinhalese against the Army the highest. Five batsmen passed 1,000 first-class runs. In his ninth season, Oshada Fernando rose from obscurity to amass 1,181 at 73, including six centuries, for Chilaw Marians; he earned a Test debut in South Africa, and helped secure Sri Lanka's historic 2–0 whitewash with an unbeaten 75 at Port Elizabeth. Pathum Nissanka of Nondescripts was the leading first-class run-scorer, and headed the averages with 1,346 at 89, bolstered by a double-hundred against Ireland Wolves.

Colombo also reached the final of the 50-over Premier Limited-Overs tournament, but lost to holders **Sinhalese**. In the Super Four Provincial Limited-Overs competition, for four district teams, **Galle District** and **Colombo District** met in the final for the third year running – and, after winning a trophy apiece in the previous two, shared this one when rain ended the game. The Super Four first-class and Twenty20 tournaments, introduced in 2017-18, were dropped.

FIRST-CLASS AVERAGES IN 2018-19

BATTING (650 runs, average 40.00)

		M	I	NO	R	HS	100	Avge	Ct/St
1	P. Nissanka (*Nondescripts/Sri Lanka A*)	9	17	2	1,346	217	5	89.73	5
2	†N. T. Paranavitana (*Tamil Union*)	10	14	3	931	215*	4	84.63	11
3	S. C. Serasinghe (*Tamil Union*)	10	14	2	1,001	204	5	83.41	3
4	P. A. R. P. Perera (*Colts*)	10	17	5	1,001	206*	4	83.41	7
5	†H. L. P. Maduwantha (*Saracens*)	8	10	1	729	217	3	81.00	11
6	A. K. Perera (*Nondescripts/Sri Lanka A*)	8	15	2	1,032	231	5	79.38	3
7	B. O. P. Fernando (*Chilaw Marians*)	9	16	0	1,181	234	6	73.81	16
8	†M. M. M. S. Cooray (*Colts*)	10	19	5	931	142	4	66.50	8
9	†P. C. de Silva (*Nondescripts*)	8	16	4	784	114	4	65.33	2
10	J. K. Silva (*Sri Lanka/Sinhalese*)	10	16	0	991	273	3	61.93	14
11	†P. B. B. Rajapaksa (*Burgher*)	9	13	1	742	268	2	61.83	7
12	S. M. D. Jayawardene (*Bloomfield*)	6	12	1	661	165	3	60.09	11
13	†M. L. R. Buddika (*Burgher*)	9	14	1	781	119	2	60.07	3
14	P. W. H. de Silva (*Colombo*)	9	16	3	765	106	1	58.84	16
15	K. N. A. Bandara (*Saracens*)	10	14	2	698	106	1	58.16	15
16	†D. L. Perera (*Kurunegala Youth*)	8	15	1	792	116	3	56.57	14/3
17	M. R. P. U. Dias (*Chilaw Marians*)	8	14	2	677	112*	2	56.41	0
18	S. M. A. Priyanjan (*Colombo/SL A*)	10	15	2	709	180	2	54.53	6
19	†K. P. N. M. Karunanayake (*Saracens*)	10	14	1	686	149	2	52.76	7
20	K. D. V. Wimalasekara (*Army*)	10	17	0	889	178	3	52.29	2
21	†M. B. Ranasinghe (*Colombo*)	8	13	0	669	180	2	51.46	16/9
22	D. D. de Soysa (*Army*)	10	17	3	686	139	2	49.00	13
23	A. N. Nanayakkara (*Ports Authority*)	9	17	3	650	137	2	46.42	8
24	†M. L. Udawatte (*Nondescripts*)	10	20	3	770	162	2	45.29	10
25	N. H. G. Cooray (*Chilaw Marians*)	10	17	1	666	162*	1	41.62	4
26	L. U. Igalagamage (*Nondescripts*)	10	20	0	831	127	1	41.55	22/7
27	†S. Ridma (*Army*)	10	16	0	657	119	1	41.06	6

BOWLING (30 wickets, average 30.00)

		Style	O	M	R	W	BB	5I	Avge
1	S. S. Peiris (*Navy*)	OB	172.4	17	630	38	6-51	3	16.57
2	R. M. G. K. Sirisoma (*Galle*)	SLA	241	57	640	38	8-50	3	16.84
3	S. P. Udeshi (*Chilaw Marians*)	SLA	420.4	100	1,186	57	6-70	6	20.80
4	H. G. K. Dilshan (*Navy*)	SLA	254.5	38	870	41	6-109	2	21.21
5	P. M. Pushpakumara (*SL/Colombo*)	SLA	531.3	92	1,604	72	10-37	7	22.27
6	H. M. Jayawardene (*Police*)	OB	283	58	892	40	6-38	1	22.30
7	P. W. H. de Silva (*Colombo*)	LB	222.4	33	740	33	6-80	2	22.42
8	P. C. de Silva (*Nondescripts*)	SLA	259.1	46	839	36	6-32	3	23.30
9	D. S. Hettiarachchi (*Police*)	SLA	426.5	77	1,304	54	6-51	5	24.14
10	K. N. Peiris (*Ragama/Sri Lanka A*)	OB	207.2	19	781	32	8-94	2	24.40
11	L. Embuldeniya (*Nondescripts/SL A*)	SLA	299.2	53	905	36	6-96	2	25.13
12	M. N. V. Silva (*Chilaw Marians*)	SLA	264.4	37	794	31	6-46	2	25.61
13	R. T. M. Wanigamuni (*Moors*)	OB	238	32	795	30	5-124	1	26.50
14	S. M. S. M. Senanayake (*Sinhalese*)	OB	343.1	47	1,088	41	7-88	4	26.53
15	R. S. D. Jayaratne (*Kurunegala Yth*)	OB	214.1	25	871	32	5-58	1	27.21
16	J. U. Chaturanga (*Air Force*)	SLA	304	67	831	30	6-100	1	27.70
17	M. A. Aponso (*Ragama*)	SLA	423.3	86	1,308	47	8-148	3	27.82
18	D. S. Tillakaratne (*Burgher*)	LFM	310.4	46	955	34	5-56	2	28.08
19	M. A. P. Madushan (*Kalutara Town*)	OB	262.5	33	892	31	6-102	4	28.77
20	S. N. Peiris (*Sinhalese*)	OB	335.4	58	1,067	37	6-45	3	28.83
21	K. T. H. Ratnayake (*Sinhalese*)	OB	437	56	1,540	53	7-50	4	29.05
22	E. M. C. D. Edirisinghe (*Saracens*)	SLA	447	59	1,516	52	9-87	1	29.15
23	S. A. D. U. Indrasiri (*Negombo*)	SLA	381.1	41	1,120	38	6-68	3	29.47
24	B. M. A. J. Mendis (*Tamil Union*)	LB	246.4	32	889	30	9-53	2	29.63

PREMIER LEAGUE TOURNAMENT TIER A IN 2018-19

Group A	P	W	L	D	Pts	Group B	P	W	L	D	Pts
NONDESCRIPTS	6	2	0	4	78.935	COLOMBO	6	3	1	2	85.900
CHILAW MARIANS .	6	2	0	4	69.575	SINHALESE.......	6	3	0	3	82.430
TAMIL UNION......	6	0	0	6	65.270	SARACENS	6	1	1	4	51.675
ARMY............	6	1	0	5	50.655	COLTS	6	0	1	5	48.930
Ragama	6	0	0	6	40.440	Badureliya........	6	0	0	6	38.055
Ports Authority	6	0	2	4	32.165	Burgher...........	6	0	2	4	32.720
Moors............	6	0	3	3	31.540	Negombo..........	6	0	2	4	30.630

Super Eight	P	W	L	D	Pts	Plate	P	W	L	D	Pts
Colombo	7	4	2	1	88.305	Burgher...........	5	1	0	4	53.095
Saracens..........	7	1	1	5	75.195	Ragama	5	0	0	5	45.230
Chilaw Marians	7	2	0	5	74.515	Badureliya	5	0	0	5	44.460
Colts..............	7	2	1	4	74.430	Moors	5	0	0	5	36.540
Sinhalese	7	2	2	3	74.350	Negombo..........	5	0	0	5	35.825
Tamil Union........	7	1	0	6	70.410	Ports Authority	5	0	1	4	27.115
Nondescripts	7	0	3	4	61.285						
Army	7	0	3	4	28.595						

The top four teams from each group advanced to the Super Eight, carrying forward their results against fellow qualifiers, then played the other four qualifiers. The bottom three from each group entered the Plate competition, run on the same principles. The bottom-placed Plate team, Ports Authority, were relegated and replaced by Lankan, the winners of Tier B.

Outright win = 12pts; win by an innings = 2pts extra; lead on first innings in a drawn game = 8pts. Bonus points were awarded as follows: 0.15pts for each wicket taken and 0.005pts for each run scored, up to 400 runs per innings.

CHAMPIONS

1988-89	{ Nondescripts { Sinhalese	1997-98	Sinhalese	2008-09	Colts
1989-90	Sinhalese	1998-99	Bloomfield	2009-10	Chilaw Marians
1990-91	Sinhalese	1999-2000	Colts	2010-11	Bloomfield
1991-92	Colts	2000-01	Nondescripts	2011-12	Colts
1992-93	Sinhalese	2001-02	Colts	2012-13	Sinhalese
1993-94	Nondescripts	2002-03	Moors	2013-14	Nondescripts
1994-95	{ Bloomfield { Sinhalese	2003-04	Bloomfield	2014-15	Ports Authority
		2004-05	Colts	2015-16	Tamil Union
1995-96	Colombo	2005-06	Sinhalese	2016-17	Sinhalese
1996-97	Bloomfield	2006-07	Colombo	2017-18	Chilaw Marians
		2007-08	Sinhalese	2018-19	Colombo

Sinhalese have won the title outright 8 times, Colts 6, Bloomfield 4, Colombo and Nondescripts 3, Chilaw Marians 2, Moors, Ports Authority and Tamil Union 1. Sinhalese have shared it twice, Bloomfield and Nondescripts once each.

The tournament was known as the Lakspray Trophy from 1988-89 to 1989-90, the P. Saravanamuttu Trophy from 1990-91 to 1997-98, and the Premier League from 1998-99.

PREMIER LEAGUE TOURNAMENT TIER B IN 2018-19

	P	W	L	D	Pts
Lankan	8	1	0	7	87.770
Navy	8	3	0	5	82.250
Bloomfield	8	2	0	6	77.545
Galle	8	2	1	5	70.185
Panadura	8	1	3	4	69.495
Police	8	0	1	7	67.305
Air Force	8	0	0	8	66.620
Kurunegala Youth .	8	0	3	5	60.630
Kalutara Town	8	1	2	5	50.655

Outright win = 12pts; win by an innings = 2pts extra; lead on first innings in a drawn game = 8pts. Bonus points were awarded as follows: 0.15pts for each wicket taken and 0.005pts for each run scored, up to 400 runs per innings.

PREMIER LIMITED-OVERS TOURNAMENT IN 2018-19

Four 50-over mini-leagues plus knockout

Quarter-finals   Colombo beat Nondescripts by 46 runs; Moors beat Army by five wickets; Saracens beat Panadura by seven wickets; Sinhalese beat Ragama by five wickets.

Semi-finals   Colombo beat Moors by five wickets; Sinhalese beat Saracens by 36 runs (DLS).

Final   At Colombo (RPS), March 19, 2019. **Sinhalese won by seven wickets. ‡Colombo 250-8** (50 overs); **Sinhalese 254-3** (44.2 overs) (M. D. Gunathilleke 116, D. S. Weerakkody 101). *As in the previous season's final, Dhanushka Gunathilleke scored a century; this time he shared an opening stand of 212 in 35 overs with fellow left-hander Sandun Weerakkody, who reached a maiden one-day hundred. Together, they all but ensured Sinhalese retained their title.*

SUPER FOUR PROVINCIAL LIMITED-OVERS TOURNAMENT IN 2018-19

50-over league plus final and third-place play-off

Third-place play-off   Dambulla District beat Kandy District by 94 runs.

Final   At Dambulla, April 11, 2019. **No result. ‡Galle District 337-7** (50 overs) (H. D. R. L. Thirimanne 115) **v Colombo District.** *Galle and Colombo District contested their third successive one-day final, and shared the title when Colombo's innings was washed out. Before the rain, Lahiru Thirimanne hit 115 and added 144 in 15.3 overs with Wanindu Hasaranga de Silva, whose 87 came in 53 balls.*

The SLC Twenty20 tournament in 2018-19 can be found on page 1154.

WEST INDIES CRICKET IN 2019

Tackling the in-tray

Vaneisa Baksh

In the first few months of the year came two surprising events, both of which turned out to be markers for what was to follow. The first took shape in January, when England arrived for a full tour. There was depressingly little interest in the Caribbean, and few were paying attention when the Tests began. West Indies ran away with the First, in Barbados, to triumph by 381 runs, suggesting something unusual was at play. But they did it again in Antigua, where the margin was ten wickets, allowing captain Jason Holder to enjoy the almost forgotten pleasure of holding the Wisden Trophy.

England recovered their composure and took the last Test, before the one-dayers were shared 2–2. The dominant 50-over force was Chris Gayle who, having announced he would retire after the World Cup, hit 424 runs at 106, and passed 10,000 in ODIs. Despite England waltzing to victory in the T20s, the overall impression was of a newly competitive West Indies.

WEST INDIES IN 2019

	Played	Won	Lost	Drawn/No result
Tests	6	3	3	–
One-day internationals	28	10	15	3
Twenty20 internationals	12	2	10	–

For a review of West Indian domestic cricket from the 2018-19 season, see page 1059.

Will he? Won't he? The on–off retirement of Chris Gayle, one of several issues with which Jason Holder had to grapple.

The second surprise came on March 24, when Cricket West Indies booted out their long-standing president, Dave Cameron, and brought in Ricky Skerritt, a politician from St Kitts and Nevis, and once West Indies team manager. Change began quickly: he worked to instil a philosophy of inclusion and respect for players, while an early priority was an apology to former head coach Phil Simmons for the manner of his sacking in 2016. In October, he came back for a second spell in charge, replacing interim coach Floyd Reifer, who had himself taken over from Richard Pybus in April. Other changes included a new selection panel, the appointment of Kieron Pollard as white-ball captain in September, and the recruitment of additional support staff, including Trevor Penney, who would concentrate on the limited-overs teams.

In May, by way of a World Cup warm-up, West Indies competed in a triangular one-day tournament in Ireland. The highlight was a monumental stand of 365 – the largest opening partnership in ODIs, and the second-largest for any wicket – by John Campbell and Shai Hope, as West Indies crushed the hosts. However, they lost the rain-affected final against Bangladesh. It proved a decent indication of how the team would fare on the biggest stage: flashes of brilliance, but ultimately disappointing. It was hard to criticise Carlos Braithwaite, and yet… Against New Zealand, West Indies were going down for the third time, at 164 for seven, chasing 292. Somehow, he carved out a battling hundred. But, with six needed from seven balls, and the No. 11 for company, he biffed another down the ground – only for Trent Boult to hold a stunning catch at long-on. And that was the end of that. Early on, West Indies had demolished Pakistan, but they finished ninth, above Afghanistan, the only other team they beat.

Then, in August, India were the opposition for two T20Is in Lauderhill, Florida, and another in Guyana, which also staged the first of the ODIs. From there, it was a flight to Port-of-Spain for two more. Neither the venue, nor Gayle's decision to rescind his international retirement, made much difference: India won all five completed games. Nor did switching the colour of the ball change their fortunes: West Indies lost the Tests by 318 and 257 runs. There was plenty in Skerritt's in-tray.

By November, he had worked through some of the backlog. In India to play Afghanistan, West Indies came out on top in two of the three formats. Next came the sterner test of India on their own patch. Once again, with Pollard captaining in the limited-overs games, West Indies put up a better show, winning one each of the three T20s and ODIs.

Though there was no definite proof of a corner being turned – and in January 2020 Ireland shared a T20 series – something did seem to have happened within the team psyche, starting with that England series. And it did feel as though the removal of the high-handed Cameron had fostered a new atmosphere. Even Pollard, known for a brusque manner, was called a mentor, a nurturing figure among his charges. There is a changing of the guard, and an optimism that younger batsmen (including Shimron Hetmyer, Nicholas Pooran and Evin Lewis) and bowlers (Keemo Paul, Oshane Thomas and Alzarri Joseph) are growing in confidence, ready to take the mantle from their olders.

The women's team, led by Stafanie Taylor, endured some difficult times. In February, they shared a T20 series courageously staged in Karachi, then lost 2–1 to Pakistan in a one-day series in Dubai. They won their three T20 games against Ireland in May, but lost all six – three 20- and three 50-over – matches when they hosted Australia in September. Next, they beat India by one run in the first ODI, thanks to 94 from Taylor, but lost the remaining two. Taylor was included in the ICC's Women's ODI Team of the Year.

There was cause for celebration in the 2020 New Year's Honours list, when two greats were given knighthoods: arise, Sir Clive Lloyd and Sir Gordon Greenidge. And cause for sadness at the death of stalwarts from longer ago: Seymour Nurse at the age of 85, and Basil Butcher a year older. Two distinguished Jamaicans, former president of the WICB Pat Rousseau, and cricket commentator Tony Becca, also died during the year.

If 2019 was, like much of the past two decades, a year of upheaval in West Indies cricket, there was a sense that some changes were for the better; the spirit of the game seemed to have come alive again; and there was something to look forward to in Caribbean cricket.

WEST INDIES v INDIA IN 2019

Barry Wilkinson

Twenty20 internationals (3): West Indies 0, India 3
One-day internationals (3): West Indies 0, India 2
Test matches (2): West Indies 0 (0pts), India 2 (120pts)

Less than a year earlier, West Indies had been brushed aside on the subcontinent; back on home soil, they were on the receiving end of another drubbing. India were in cruise control, while West Indies hardly landed a blow – victory over England at the start of the year felt like a distant memory. For India there was a long list of pluses: they shot to the top of the World Test Championship, Virat Kohli became their most successful captain, Jasprit Bumrah bowled magnificently, and they seemed to have found a new batting star in Hanuma Vihari, who averaged 93 in the Tests. While Kohli celebrated, his opposite number Jason Holder called for wholesale reform of West Indies' domestic structure. "It's not one or two individuals that need to find solutions," he said. "It's the collective Cricket West Indies."

West Indies had not won a Test series against India since 2002, and at no point did they look like improving on that record: both matches were in the top ten of India's biggest away wins by runs. With victory in the First Test, Kohli eased past Sourav Ganguly as India's most successful captain overseas; in the Second, he went beyond M. S. Dhoni's overall record of 27 Test wins. "It's a by-product of a quality team," he said. "If we didn't have these bowlers, I don't think the results would have been possible."

Before the First Test, Sunil Gavaskar questioned the wisdom of leaving out Ravichandran Ashwin, but such was the potency of the pace attack he was not missed. Bumrah took 13 wickets at nine – including India's third Test hat-trick – and had complete mastery over the batsmen. He now had five-wicket hauls in Australia, England, South Africa and the West Indies, a unique feat among Indian bowlers.

The hosts struggled to find any crumbs of comfort. Their batting returns were pitifully low: Holder was their leading run-scorer, with 104 at 26. He also bowled well – eight wickets at 22 – but the stand-out performer was Kemar Roach, who took nine at 22, troubled the best batsmen, and was singled out by Holder for his hostility and commitment.

The white-ball matches at the start of the tour had offered both teams the chance to shake off disappointing World Cups. In the Twenty20 series, India gave a debut to Navdeep Saini and a second outing to Deepak Chahar, both of whom had shone in the IPL, and they produced encouraging performances. The ODIs were dominated by Kohli, who collected his 42nd and 43rd centuries, and overhauled Sourav Ganguly to become India's second-highest one-day run-scorer, behind Sachin Tendulkar. Chris Gayle, meanwhile, moved past Brian Lara to go top of the West Indian list, though his future remained in doubt. Evin Lewis was comfortably West Indies' top-scorer, with 148.

INDIA TOURING PARTY

*V. Kohli (T/50/20), M. A. Agarwal (T), K. K. Ahmed (50/20), R. Ashwin (T), Bhuvneshwar Kumar (50/20), J. J. Bumrah (T), Y. S. Chahal (50), D. L. Chahar (20), R. D. Chahar (20), S. Dhawan (50/20), S. S. Iyer (50/20), R. A. Jadeja (T/50/20), K. M. Jadhav (50), Mohammed Shami (T/50), M. K. Pandey (50/20), K. H. Pandya (20), R. R. Pant (T/50/20), C. A. Pujara (T), A. M. Rahane (T), K. L. Rahul (T/50/20), W. P. Saha (T), N. Saini (50/20), R. G. Sharma (T/50/20), G. H. Vihari (T), M. S. Washington Sundar (20), K. Yadav (T/50), U. T. Yadav (T). *Coach:* R. J. Shastri.

First Twenty20 international   At Lauderhill, Florida, August 3. **India won by four wickets. West Indies 95-9** (20 overs) (K. A. Pollard 49; N. Saini 3-17); ‡**India 98-6** (17.2 overs). *PoM:* N. Saini. *T20I debut:* N. Saini (India). *On a tricky pitch that never allowed batsmen to go for their shots, India did just enough. Navdeep Saini, on his international debut, made an instant impact. In his first over, he snared Nicholas Pooran with a well-aimed bouncer, then bowled Shimron Hetmyer first ball. In the 20th, he removed Kieron Pollard, whose careful 49 had rebuilt West Indies' innings from 33-5. The only blot on Saini's day was a demerit point for a send-off aimed at Pooran. With no need to hurry, India began watchfully, but were briefly wrong-footed when Virat Kohli's departure left them 69-5.*

Second Twenty20 international   At Lauderhill, Florida, August 4. **India won by 22 runs** (DLS). ‡**India 167-5** (20 overs) (R. G. Sharma 67); **West Indies 98-4** (15.3 overs) (R. Powell 54). *PoM:* K. H. Pandya. *The brief Florida excursion ended prematurely when the players left the field to the flash of lightning. It soon began to rain heavily, with West Indies well behind the rate. Before the damp conclusion, the game had at least been more entertaining than the previous day's torpid affair. Rohit Sharma recaptured his World Cup form, hitting 67 in 51 balls; the second of his three sixes took him past Chris Gayle's T20I record tally of 105. West Indies made a poor start, but Rovman Powell dragged them back into contention with a career-best 54 off 34. They lost momentum when Krunal Pandya removed Pooran and Powell in the 14th and, soon after, the skies lit up.*

Third Twenty20 international   At Providence, Guyana, August 6. **India won by seven wickets. West Indies 146-6** (20 overs) (K. A. Pollard 58, R. Powell 32*; D. L. Chahar 3-4); ‡**India 150-3** (19.1 overs) (V. Kohli 59, R. R. Pant 65*). *PoM:* D. L. Chahar. *PoS:* K. H. Pandya. *T20I debut:* R. D. Chahar (India). *An outstanding opening spell of swing bowling from Deepak Chahar set up India's whitewash. Chahar, whose leg-spinning cousin Rahul took 1-27 on debut, reduced West Indies to 14-3 by the end of his third over. Pollard, with six sixes in his 58, and Pooran rebuilt with 66 for the fourth wicket. But any hopes of a consolation victory disappeared in a brilliant stand of 106 in 12.5 overs between Kohli and Rishabh Pant.*

First one-day international   At Providence, Guyana, August 8. **No result.** Reduced to 34 overs a side. **West Indies 54-1** (13 overs) (E. Lewis 40*) v ‡**India.** *All eyes were on Chris Gayle, as he chased the 13 he needed to become West Indies' all-time leading ODI run-scorer. But he was dismissed for four off 31 balls, and looked horribly out of touch. A delayed start and regular rain interruptions meant the 13 overs possible were spread across five and a half hours.*

Second one-day international   At Port-of-Spain, Trinidad, August 11. **India won by 59 runs** (DLS). ‡**India 279-7** (50 overs) (V. Kohli 120, S. S. Iyer 71; C. R. Brathwaite 3-53); **West Indies 210** (42 overs) (E. Lewis 65, N. Pooran 42; Bhuvneshwar Kumar 4-31). *PoM:* V. Kohli. *Gayle made 11 to creep past Brian Lara's tally of 10,405, and become West Indies' most prolific ODI batsman, but was comfortably outshone by Kohli. After failing to turn any of his five fifties at the World Cup into hundreds, he was at his imperious best, stroking his 42nd ODI century. He moved second on India's all-time run-scoring list. His fourth-wicket stand of 125 with the recalled Shreyas Iyer formed the bedrock of his side's total. After a second rain interruption, West Indies's target became 270 in 46 overs. Evin Lewis and Pooran kept them in the hunt, but a three-wicket burst by Bhuvneshwar Kumar gave India an unassailable lead.*

Third one-day international   At Port-of-Spain, Trinidad, August 14. **India won by six wickets** (DLS). ‡**West Indies 240-7** (35 overs) (C. H. Gayle 72, E. Lewis 43, N. Pooran 30; K. K. Ahmed 3-68); **India 256-4** (32.3 overs) (S. Dhawan 36, V. Kohli 114*, S. S. Iyer 65). *PoM:* V. Kohli. *PoS:* V. Kohli. *Another day, another century for Kohli, who batted with growing authority after being dropped behind on 11 by Shai Hope off Keemo Paul. On his way to steering India past a revised target of 255 in 35 overs, he became the first to score 20,000 international runs in a single decade. Again, his main alliance was with the silky Iyer, who had batted in such command that it was a surprise when he fell to Kemar Roach. Gayle's 301st ODI had all the trappings of a farewell, although he later announced he was available "until further notice".*

WEST INDIES v INDIA

First Test

At North Sound, Antigua, August 22–25. India won by 318 runs. India 60pts. Toss: West Indies. Debut: S. S. J. Brooks.

In a devastating burst that must have been an uncomfortable reminder for older spectators of the glory days of Caribbean fast bowling, Bumrah blew West Indies away to earn India an emphatic four-day victory. Assisted by new-ball partner Ishant Sharma, he reaped the rewards of a rapid outswinger that was too good for several frontline West Indies batsmen.

At 15 for five, then 37 for seven, they had looked like falling short of their lowest Test total: 47 against England at Kingston in 2003-04, when Steve Harmison ran amok. But they scraped their way to 50 for nine, before Roach and Cummins doubled the score in

INDIA'S BIGGEST AWAY WINS BY RUNS

318	**v West Indies at North Sound**	**2019**
304	v Sri Lanka at Galle	2017
279	v England at Leeds	1986
278	v Sri Lanka at Colombo (PSO).	2015
272	v New Zealand at Auckland	1967-68
257	**v West Indies at Kingston**	**2019**
237	v West Indies at Gros Islet	2016
235	v Sri Lanka at Colombo (SSC).	1993
222	v Australia at Melbourne	1976-77
203	v England at Nottingham	2018

less than seven overs, with Roach launching five sixes. Even so, a total of 100 was their lowest against India, undercutting 103 at Kingston more than 13 years earlier. Bumrah ended up with figures of 8–4–7–5, the cheapest five-for in India's history, beating slow left-armer Venkatapathy Raju's six for 12 against Sri Lanka at Chandigarh in 1990-91. West Indies captain Holder admitted Bumrah had bowled some "magic balls", but added: "Our batsmen need to look at themselves seriously in the mirror."

It had all been very different in the first hour of the opening day. Encouraged by a damp atmosphere and a green-looking pitch, Holder put India in, and was rewarded by two wickets for the hostile Roach, followed by the early departure of Kohli, who was worked over by Gabriel before being well caught in the gully for nine by debutant Shamarh Brooks, a 30-year-old batsman from Barbados. Rahul and Rahane began the rebuilding operation carefully, only driving when the ball had stopped swinging.

CHEAPEST TEST FIVE-FORS

5-2	E. R. H. Toshack . . .	Australia v India at Brisbane.	1947-48
6-3	J. J. C. Lawson	West Indies v Bangladesh at Dhaka	2002-03
5-6	H. Ironmonger	Australia v South Africa at Melbourne.	1931-32
8-7	G. A. Lohmann.	England v South Africa at Port Elizabeth.	1895-96
6-7	A. E. R. Gilligan . . .	England v South Africa at Birmingham	1924
5-7	V. D. Philander.	South Africa v New Zealand at Cape Town.	1912-13
5-7	**J. J. Bumrah**	**India v West Indies at North Sound**	**2019**
6-8	D. W. Steyn	South Africa v Pakistan at Johannesburg	2012-13
6-8	K. A. J. Roach	West Indies v Bangladesh at North Sound	2018
6-9	M. J. Clarke	Australia v India at Mumbai.	2004-05
5-9	T. B. A. May.	Australia v West Indies at Adelaide	1992-93

Rahane's departure at 189 for six, chopping on against Gabriel, gave West Indies another opening. But, with the help of the stubborn Sharma, Jadeja compiled a restrained 58 in almost three hours to steer India towards a more respectable total. West Indies battled hard on the second day, with all their top eight reaching double figures. Crucially, though, none made more than Chase's 48. And from 174 for five shortly before the close, they were fatally undermined by a burst from Sharma, who claimed the big wickets of Hope and Hetmyer, then added Roach for a duck, all in seven balls. Holder squeezed 41 in 17 overs out of the ninth wicket – with Cummins contributing a 45-ball duck – that ate up more than an hour and a half. But West Indies had blown their chance.

Building on a lead of 75, India took complete control. Rahane made his first Test hundred for two years, extending his time in the middle during the game to more than nine hours, and his average against West Indies to 91. He added 106 for the fourth wicket with Kohli and 135 for the fifth with Vihari, before Kohli felt comfortable setting West Indies a target of 419. Bumrah made sure India got a day off.

Player of the Match: A. M. Rahane.

Close of play: first day, India 203-6 (Pant 20, Jadeja 3); second day, West Indies 189-8 (Holder 10, Cummins 0); third day, India 185-3 (Kohli 51, Rahane 53).

India

K. L. Rahul c Hope b Chase	44	– b Chase	38
M. A. Agarwal c Hope b Roach	5	– lbw b Chase	16
C. A. Pujara c Hope b Roach	2	– b Roach	25
*V. Kohli c Brooks b Gabriel	9	– c Campbell b Chase	51
A. M. Rahane b Gabriel	81	– c Holder b Gabriel	102
G. H. Vihari c Hope b Roach	32	– c Hope b Holder	93
†R. R. Pant c Holder b Roach	24	– c sub (K. M. A. Paul) b Chase	7
R. A. Jadeja c Hope b Holder	58	– not out	1
I. Sharma b Gabriel	19		
Mohammed Shami c and b Chase	0		
J. J. Bumrah not out	4		
B 9, lb 8, nb 2	19	B 6, lb 4	10

1/5 (2) 2/7 (3) 3/25 (4)   (96.4 overs) 297   1/30 (2)   (7 wkts dec, 112.3 overs) 343
4/93 (1) 5/175 (6) 6/189 (5)   2/73 (1) 3/81 (3)
7/207 (7) 8/267 (9) 9/268 (10) 10/297 (8)   4/187 (4) 5/322 (5) 6/336 (7) 7/343 (6)

Roach 25–6–66–4; Gabriel 22–5–71–3; Holder 20.4–11–36–1; Cummins 13–1–49–0; Chase 16–3–58–2. *Second innings*—Roach 20–8–29–1; Gabriel 16–3–63–1; Chase 38–5–132–4; Holder 18.3–4–45–1; Cummins 7–1–20–0; Campbell 6–0–20–0; Brathwaite 7–0–24–0.

West Indies

K. C. Brathwaite c and b Sharma	14	– c Pant b Bumrah	1
J. D. Campbell b Mohammed Shami	23	– b Bumrah	7
S. S. J. Brooks c Rahane b Jadeja	11	– lbw b Sharma	2
D. M. Bravo lbw b Bumrah	18	– b Bumrah	2
R. L. Chase c Rahul b Sharma	48	– (6) b Mohammed Shami	12
†S. D. Hope c Pant b Sharma	24	– (7) b Bumrah	2
S. O. Hetmyer c and b Sharma	35	– (5) c Rahane b Sharma	1
*J. O. Holder c Pant b Mohammed Shami	39	– b Bumrah	8
K. A. J. Roach c Kohli b Sharma	0	– c Pant b Sharma	38
M. L. Cummins b Jadeja	0	– (11) not out	19
S. T. Gabriel not out	2	– (10) c Pant b Mohammed Shami	0
B 4, lb 1, w 1, nb 2	8	Lb 7, nb 1	8

1/36 (2) 2/48 (1) 3/50 (3)   (74.2 overs) 222   1/7 (1) 2/10 (2)   (26.5 overs) 100
4/88 (4) 5/130 (5) 6/174 (6)   3/10 (3) 4/13 (5)
7/179 (7) 8/179 (9) 9/220 (8) 10/222 (10)   5/15 (4) 6/27 (7) 7/37 (8)
                                              8/50 (6) 9/50 (10) 10/100 (9)

Sharma 17–5–43–5; Bumrah 18–4–55–1; Mohammed Shami 17–3–48–2; Jadeja 20.2–4–64–2; Vihari 2–0–7–0. *Second innings*—Sharma 9.5–1–31–3; Bumrah 8–4–7–5; Jadeja 4–0–42–0; Mohammed Shami 5–3–13–2.

Umpires: R. A. Kettleborough and R. J. Tucker.   Third umpire: P. R. Reiffel.
Referee: D. C. Boon.

WEST INDIES v INDIA

Second Test

At Kingston, Jamaica, August 30–September 2. India won by 257 runs. India 60pts. Toss: West Indies. Test debuts: R. R. S. Cornwall, J. N. Hamilton.

The margin may have been slightly less emphatic, but that was no comfort to West Indies, as India strolled to another easy win. There were a few tweaks to the script, but the starring roles went to roughly the same characters. Kohli, Rahane and Vihari scored the bulk of the runs; Bumrah claimed a hat-trick.

The match marked a milestone for Kohli: his 28th Test victory as captain took him past M. S. Dhoni as India's most successful leader. He shrugged off the compliments. "Captaincy is just a 'c' in front of your name," he said. "It's the collective effort that matters." Holder opted to put India in again, and he did most to exert control after they had raced away in the early overs. The debutant off-spinner Rahkeem Cornwall – thought to be the heaviest Test player of all time, at around 22 stone – had a busy start to his Test career. He took two slip catches and a wicket, when Pujara lobbed to point.

Agarwal was made to work hard for his 55 but, with Holder bowling a consistently challenging line, India were far from secure at 115 for three. Kohli began the fightback, though Vihari played the major hand, his first Test hundred. The total was enhanced by Sharma, who helped Vihari add 112 for the eighth wicket and compiled a maiden Test fifty, at the 126th attempt (only England's James Anderson, from 131, had needed more innings).

Holder finished with his sixth Test five-for, but his team were soon in trouble against the irrepressible Bumrah. Campbell had already gone in his third over, caught behind by Pant. In his fourth, he removed Bravo (held low down at second slip), Brooks (leg-before aiming across the line) and Chase (another lbw, on review) in successive balls. It was India's third Test hat-trick – following Harbhajan Singh against Australia at Kolkata in 2000-01, and Irfan Pathan against Pakistan at Karachi in 2005-06. Chase would have escaped, but Kohli was certain there had been no inside edge, and asked for DRS. When Bumrah had Brathwaite caught behind for ten, he had five for ten, and his figures across two innings stretching back to the First Test were a remarkable ten for 17. He later added Holder, giving him six of the first seven wickets to fall, but in the end had to settle for a Test-best six for 27. India had a towering lead of 299.

Their attempts to build on it were undermined by Roach, who took three quick wickets, including Kohli for a first-ball duck, but Rahane and Vihari ended any hopes of a fightback with an unbroken stand of 111. Bumrah took a back seat when West Indies batted again, Mohammed Shami and Jadeja collecting three wickets apiece. Bravo was hit on the helmet by Bumrah early on the fourth day, and West Indies used Jermaine Blackwood as a concussion substitute. Gabriel became Test cricket's first No. 12.

Player of the Match: G. H. Vihari.

Close of play: first day, India 264-5 (Vihari 42, Pant 27); second day, West Indies 87-7 (Hamilton 2, Cornwall 4); third day, West Indies 45-2 (Bravo 18, Brooks 4).

India

K. L. Rahul c Cornwall b Holder	13	– c Hamilton b Roach	6
M. A. Agarwal c Cornwall b Holder	55	– lbw b Roach	4
C. A. Pujara c Brooks b Cornwall	6	– c Brooks b Holder	27
*V. Kohli c Hamilton b Holder	76	– c Hamilton b Roach	0
A. M. Rahane c Hamilton b Roach	24	– not out	64
G. H. Vihari b Roach b Holder	111	– not out	53
†R. R. Pant b Holder	27		
R. A. Jadeja c Bravo b Cornwall	16		
I. Sharma c Hetmyer b Brathwaite	57		
Mohammed Shami c Hamilton b Cornwall	0		
J. J. Bumrah not out	0		
B 11, lb 19, w 1	31	B 8, lb 4, nb 2	14

1/32 (1) 2/46 (3) 3/115 (2)   (140.1 overs) 416   1/9 (2)   (4 wkts dec, 54.4 overs) 168
4/164 (5) 5/202 (4) 6/264 (7)   2/36 (1) 3/36 (4)
7/302 (8) 8/414 (9) 9/416 (10) 10/416 (6)   4/57 (3)

Roach 30–9–77–1; Gabriel 21–4–74–0; Holder 32.1–9–77–5; Cornwall 41–10–105–3; Chase
14–4–45–0; Brathwaite 2–0–8–1. *Second innings*—Roach 10–3–28–3; Holder 11.4–5–20–1;
Cornwall 23–7–68–0; Gabriel 7–3–18–0; Chase 3–0–22–0.

West Indies

K. C. Brathwaite c Pant b Bumrah	10	– (2) c Pant b Sharma	3
J. D. Campbell c Pant b Bumrah	2	– (1) c Kohli b Mohammed Shami	16
D. M. Bravo c Rahul b Bumrah	4	– retired hurt	23
S. S. J. Brooks lbw b Bumrah	0	– run out (Kohli)	50
R. L. Chase lbw b Bumrah	0	– lbw b Jadeja	12
S. O. Hetmyer b Mohammed Shami	34	– c Agarwal b Sharma	1
*J. O. Holder c sub (R. G. Sharma) b Bumrah	18	– (8) b Jadeja	39
†J. N. Hamilton c Kohli b Sharma	5	– (9) c Rahul b Jadeja	0
R. R. S. Cornwall c Rahane b Mohammed Shami	14	– (10) c Pant b Mohammed Shami	1
K. A. J. Roach c Agarwal b Jadeja	17	– (11) c Pant b Mohammed Shami	5
S. T. Gabriel not out	0	– (12) not out	0
J. Blackwood (did not bat)		– (7) c Pant b Bumrah	38
B 8, lb 5	13	B 14, lb 2, w 5, nb 1	22

1/9 (2) 2/13 (3) 3/13 (4)   (47.1 overs) 117   1/9 (2) 2/37 (1)   (59.5 overs) 210
4/13 (5) 5/22 (1) 6/67 (6)   3/97 (5) 4/98 (6)
7/78 (7) 8/97 (9) 9/117 (8) 10/117 (10)   5/159 (7) 6/177 (4) 7/177 (9)
                                                     8/180 (10) 9/206 (11) 10/210 (8)

In the second innings Bravo retired hurt at 55-2. Blackwood replaced him, as a concussion substitute.

Sharma 10.5–3–24–1; Bumrah 12.1–3–27–6; Mohammed Shami 13–3–34–2; Jadeja 11.1–7–19–1.
Second innings—Sharma 12–3–37–2; Bumrah 11–4–31–1; Mohammed Shami 16–2–65–3; Jadeja
19.5–4–58–3; Vihari 1–0–3–0.

Umpires: R. A. Kettleborough and P. R. Reiffel.   Third umpire: R. J. Tucker.
Referee: D. C. Boon.

UNDER-19 TRI-SERIES IN 2019-20

1 Sri Lanka   2 England   3 West Indies

A three-way warm-up for the Under-19 World Cup gave most satisfaction to Sri Lanka, who defeated England easily in the final. But there was plenty for head coach Jon Lewis to be optimistic about as England flew home for Christmas, before heading to South Africa. "I'm proud of the performances the boys have put in over the last four weeks," he said. "We've shown we can beat two strong opponents in unfamiliar and challenging conditions, and employed a good, aggressive brand of cricket." There was precious little encouragement for West Indies, however. Despite the advantage of home soil, they won just twice.

Although the matches were all in Antigua, it felt like two different tournaments. In the early games, at the Sir Vivian Richards Stadium, run-scoring was difficult on unresponsive surfaces. So batsmen rejoiced once the action switched to the Coolidge ground, where totals rose significantly.

Kent's Jordan Cox was the second-highest run-scorer, with 228 runs at 45, which included one of two hundreds in the tournament. Nottinghamshire's Joey Evison led the averages, with 127 at 63 and a strike-rate of 114. In the last group game, against Sri Lanka, he slammed an unbeaten 50 off 18 balls, matching the fastest Under-19 half-century, made by India's Rishabh Pant. England's seamers also prospered: captain George Balderson was the second-highest wicket-taker with 15 at 10, and Kasey third, with 13 at 11.

But the Sri Lankans dominated. Kamil Mishara, who opened in most games, topped the run-charts with 230 at 32, and Navod Paranavithana made the competition's highest score – 108 against England in the final. Leg-spinner Kavindu Nadeeshan was the leading wicket-taker, with 18 at ten.

ENGLAND UNDER-19 TOURING PARTY

England *G. P. Balderson (Lancashire), K. L. Aldridge (Somerset), B. G. Charlesworth (Gloucestershire), T. G. R. Clark (Sussex), J. M. Cox (Kent), B. C. Cullen (Middlesex), S. W. Currie (Hampshire), H. G. Duke (Yorkshire), J. D. M. Evison (Nottinghamshire), L. P. Goldsworthy (Somerset), J. A. Haynes (Worcestershire), G. C. H. Hill (Yorkshire), L. B. K. Hollman (Middlesex), D. R. Mousley (Warwickshire), Hamidullah Qadri (Kent), S. J. Young (Somerset). *Coach:* J. Lewis.

At North Sound, Antigua, December 6, 2019. **West Indies won by 36 runs. West Indies 164** (46 overs) (L. J. A. Julien 69; K. L. Aldridge 4-38); ‡**England 128** (30.4 overs) (A. R. Nedd 5-27). *PoM:* A. R. Nedd. *Ashmead Nedd, a slow left-armer from Guyana, sent England tumbling to defeat in the tournament opener. Four victims in his first international five-for were in the lower order, but he stubbed out any hope of an England recovery after a poor start to their chase. George Balderson had put West Indies in, but was frustrated by a partnership of 90 for the second wicket between Mbecki Joseph and Leonardo Julien, who toughed it out for 25 overs. West Indies lost eight for 42 – Kasey Aldridge taking 4-38 – but England also found batting difficult, Aldridge top-scoring with 28 from No. 9.*

At North Sound, Antigua, December 8, 2019. **England won by 29 runs. ‡England 169** (49.4 overs) (N. R. J. Young 3-16, M. J. S. Patrick 3-27); **West Indies 140** (36.4 overs) (G. P. Balderson 4-47, K. L. Aldridge 3-32). *PoM:* G. P. Balderson. *With ten and a half overs to go, England had slumped to 114-8, and were in danger of a below-par total. But Dan Mousley (48) and Scott Currie (22) put* *on 55 to give the attack something to work with. Balderson then removed Joseph and Julien in the fifth over, and returned to add two more victims. Aldridge impressed again, with three wickets.*

At North Sound, Antigua, December 10, 2019. **Sri Lanka won by one wicket. West Indies 137-9** (50 overs) (D. A. O. de Silva 3-18; K. Nadeeshan 4-20); ‡**Sri Lanka 138-9** (40.1 overs) (R. R. Simmonds 3-31). *PoM: K. Nadeeshan. In another low-scoring encounter, Sri Lanka scrambled home thanks to a last-wicket stand of 37* between Sonal Dinusha (46*) and Demuni de Silva (10*). De Silva had earlier taken three wickets, but was beaten to the match award by leg-spinner Kavindu Nadeeshan's 4-20. For West Indies, only Kevlon Anderson had got beyond 30.*

At North Sound, Antigua, December 11, 2019. **Sri Lanka won by 27 runs** (DLS). ‡**England 149-4** (45 overs); **Sri Lanka 143-4** (37 overs) (W. A. A. Sachintha 70*). *Sri Lanka were ahead of schedule chasing a revised target of 163 in 45 overs when rain returned, thanks to 70* from Wickramasinghe Sachintha. England's frontline batsmen again struggled; they were 83-4 in the 32nd, before Lewis Goldsworthy and Joey Evison added 66*.*

At North Sound, Antigua, December 12, 2019. **England won by five wickets. West Indies 116** (40.1 overs) (K. L. Aldridge 5-18); ‡**England 117-5** (38.1 overs). *PoM: K. L. Aldridge. England stayed in the hunt for a place in the final after Aldridge's 5-18 set up a second victory over the hosts. He struck two early blows, and received excellent support – off-spinner Hamidullah Qadri removed top-scorer Kimani Melius, West Indies' captain, for 35. England took their time, but were always in control after openers Ben Charlesworth and Jordan Cox put on 46.*

At Coolidge, Antigua, December 14, 2019. **Sri Lanka won by 130 runs.** ‡**Sri Lanka 234-9** (50 overs) (N. D. Perera 91*; M. W. Forde 4-31); **West Indies 104** (34.4 overs) (D. S. Thilakaratne 3-10, K. Nadeeshan 4-17). *PoM: N. D. Perera. A change of venue did nothing for West Indies' fortunes. After all the stodgy scoring, Nipun Perera hit 91* off 98 with six sixes, and powered Sri Lanka to the highest score of the tournament so far. Their spinners also surprised the surface, Nadeeshan taking his second four-for, while slow left-armer Sudeera Thilakaratne picked up 3-10.*

At Coolidge, Antigua, December 15, 2019. **England won by four wickets. Sri Lanka 113** (42.4 overs) (G. P. Balderson 3-18; S. W. Currie 3-18); ‡**England 115-6** (33 overs) (K. Nadeeshan 3-33). *PoM: G. P. Balderson. A disciplined display from the England bowlers earned them a place in the final. Balderson struck twice in his first two overs, and shared six wickets with his new-ball partner, Currie. When Charlesworth and Mousley added 52 for the second wicket, it looked as if England would stroll home, but they lost five for 36 to set nerves jangling. Balderson and Luke Hollman provided the cool heads.*

At Coolidge, Antigua, December 17, 2019. **West Indies won by seven runs. West Indies 207-9** (50 overs) (M. J. S. Patrick 57, N. R. J. Young 55; D. A. O. de Silva 5-44); ‡**Sri Lanka 200-8** (50 overs) (R. V. P. K. Mishara 50, N. D. Perera 74; M. W. Forde 3-29, N. R. J. Young 3-48). *It came too late to revive their interest in the tournament, but West Indies regained some pride. They were in peril again at 84-5, before Matthew Patrick and Nyeem Young put on 85. Demuni de Silva collected a five-for, but Sri Lanka's batsmen struggled to score quickly; Perera's 74 took 128 balls, and included just two fours.*

At Coolidge, Antigua, December 19, 2019. **England won by 44 runs. England 292-4** (50 overs) (J. M. Cox 105*, J. D. M. Evison 50*); ‡**Sri Lanka 248-9** (50 overs) (N. D. Paranavithana 73, W. R. R. de Silva 52, G. S. Dinusha 51*). *PoM: J. M. Cox. Cox hit the tournament's first hundred, and Evison six sixes in an 18-ball 50*, as England comfortably won the dress rehearsal for the final. The pair hit 43 off the last two overs. Sri Lanka responded with a century opening stand, but England took regular wickets.*

England 8pts, **Sri Lanka** 6pts, West Indies 4pts.

Final At Coolidge, Antigua, December 21, 2019. **Sri Lanka won by 77 runs.** ‡**Sri Lanka 265-9** (50 overs) (N. D. Paranavithana 108, R. V. P. K. Mishara 69; G. P. Balderson 4-55, B. C. Cullen 3-43); **England 188** (43.1 overs) (J. M. Cox 77; K. Nadeeshan 3-43). *PoM: N. D. Paranavithana. Sri Lanka's spin attack proved too canny for England, after their openers Navod Paranavithana and Kamil Mishara had put on 124. England fought back with eight for 76 in the final 12 overs, but Sri Lanka still had a formidable total. Cox starred again, with 77, although England needed more than one significant contribution. Nine of the wickets fell to spin.*

DOMESTIC CRICKET IN THE WEST INDIES IN 2018-19

HAYDN GILL

A packed international calendar, and the growing number of Twenty20 tournaments around the world, have hit first-class cricket in the Caribbean hard. The absence of the leading players has created opportunities for others, but also led to a decline in the quality of the competition, a lack of spectator interest and the authorities' inability to attract corporate sponsors.

The fifth season of the franchise system produced the same champions as the first four. **Guyana's** fifth consecutive first-class title emulated Jamaica (2007-08 to 2011-12) and Barbados (1975-76 to 1979-80) – though Barbados shared one.

As usual, Guyana relied on a team effort, though wicketkeeper Anthony Bramble was their best batsman, with two hundreds and 580 runs at 52. Left-arm spinner Veerasammy Permaul was the tournament's joint-second-highest wicket-taker, with 42, and Romario Shepherd the most successful seamer, with 37, in another season dominated by slow bowlers. Three more of their seamers collected 20-plus, ensuring that, in the third year of so-called pace points – awarded for every wicket taken by pace rather than spin – Guyana continued to beat their rivals in that field too.

They were well ahead after completing their slate of matches with a round to go, but **Leeward Islands** had a slim chance if they could claim maximum points in their last game, against **Barbados**, and take at least 16 wickets with seam. Their title hopes ended once they were dismissed for 90 on the first day, and on the second afternoon they made a bizarre declaration, to surrender the game by an innings. The intention was to prevent Barbados from usurping their second place, by denying them any further pace points. Leewards miscalculated, however: Barbados, fielding an all-pace attack, had just taken the wicket they needed to pull 0.2 points ahead, and finished as runners-up.

Shepherd, who combined his wickets with a handy 315 runs, was one of the players who caught the eye of the West Indies selectors: he made his international debut against Afghanistan in November. So did Jamaica's No. 3, Brandon King, a model of consistency; he hit a century and six fifties in seven matches, averaged 48, and followed up with more success in the Caribbean Premier League. Before then, Rahkeem Cornwall, a heavy-set all-rounder who had been knocking on the door for the previous few years, was finally rewarded after another outstanding season for Leewards. His off-spin earned 54 wickets at 17, the most in the tournament, to go with 419 runs, and won him a Test debut against India in August.

It was encouraging that the four-day competition's top ten run-scorers featured six players (including King) with no previous international experience, while the corresponding bowlers' list had seven (including Cornwall and Shepherd). There were still some familiar names: Windward Islands' opening batsman Devon Smith, aged 37, was the leading scorer for the second successive tournament, with 745 at 43, while Trinidadian leg-spinner Imran Khan claimed 42 scalps.

But the stark reality was that standards remained poor. Marginal improvements in the 2017-18 tournament – 35 centuries, nine totals of 400-plus – had offered some cause for optimism, but in 2018-19 the number of hundreds dropped back to 21, and there were only four totals over 400, two by Guyana. Meanwhile, there were 17 under 150; four did not even reach three figures. The shortage of runs led to 29 outright results in the 30 matches; eight ended inside three days, and another two in two.

There were first-time champions in the Super50 tournament, where Guyana were beaten in the final by **Combined Campuses & Colleges**, led by Carlos Brathwaite. The team – who played at first-class level for seven seasons, but have been restricted to limited-overs games since the franchise system was introduced in 2014-15 – headed their group, overwhelmed Trinidad & Tobago in the semi-final, and upstaged Guyana thanks to tight bowling plus Kyle Corbin's forceful half-century.

FIRST-CLASS AVERAGES IN 2018-19

BATTING (375 runs, average 20.00)

		M	I	NO	R	HS	100	Avge	Ct/St
1	S. O. Dowrich (*Barbados/West Indies*) ...	5	8	1	378	116*	1	54.00	11/1
2	A. Bramble (*Guyana*)	10	14	3	580	168	2	52.72	42/1
3	S. W. Ambris (*Windward Islands*)	6	11	1	490	102*	1	49.00	10
4	B. A. King (*Jamaica*)	7	14	1	630	133	1	48.46	9
5	†D. S. Smith (*Windward Islands*)	9	18	1	745	199	2	43.82	18
6	†J. L. Carter (*Barbados*)	10	19	2	689	149*	1	40.52	21
7	D. C. Thomas (*Leeward Islands*)	9	18	1	685	117*	1	40.29	24/1
8	M. V. Hodge (*Leeward Islands*)	10	20	2	711	158	2	39.50	10
9	J. N. Mohammed (*Trinidad & Tobago*) ..	10	20	2	634	121	2	35.22	8
10	K. A. Edwards (*Windward Islands*)	7	13	1	418	139	1	34.83	5
11	†T. Chanderpaul (*Guyana*)	10	20	4	542	117*	1	33.87	6
12	C. A. K. Walton (*Jamaica*)	7	14	0	453	125	1	32.35	9
13	†L. R. Johnson (*Guyana*)	10	20	5	480	76	0	32.00	12
14	J. Blackwood (*Jamaica*)	8	16	1	465	72*	0	31.00	15
15	T. Warde (*Leeward Islands*)	9	17	3	415	83	0	29.64	3
16	J. N. Hamilton (*Leeward Islands*)	7	13	0	385	77	0	29.61	12/1
17	T. T. Walcott (*Barbados*)	9	16	2	409	66	0	29.21	27/2
18	†A. S. Athanaze (*Windward Islands*) ..	9	18	2	460	66	0	28.75	7
19	†J. L. Solozano (*Trinidad & Tobago*) ...	10	20	0	572	104	1	28.60	3
20	R. R. S. Cornwall (*Leeward Islands*) ..	9	16	1	419	65	0	27.93	12
21	K. A. R. Hodge (*Windward Islands*) ...	10	19	1	481	66	0	26.72	9
22	K. U. Carty (*Leeward Islands*)	10	20	0	519	114	1	25.95	5
23	I. Khan (*Trinidad & Tobago*)	10	19	2	438	86	0	25.76	4
24	R. O. Cato (*Windward Islands*)	8	16	0	403	103	1	25.18	6
25	†S. A. R. Moseley (*Barbados*)	10	19	0	441	64	0	23.21	1
26	D. D. H. Smith (*Barbados*)	10	17	0	393	67	0	23.11	19/2

BOWLING (20 wickets)

		Style	O	M	R	W	BB	5I	Avge
1	J. E. Taylor (*Jamaica*)	RFM	119.4	31	320	26	5-28	1	12.30
2	N. O. Miller (*Jamaica*)	SLA	291.5	68	643	41	7-50	4	15.68
3	R. A. Reifer (*Guyana*)	LFM	146	37	408	26	5-20	1	15.69
4	J. A. Warrican (*Barbados*)	SLA	149.1	39	406	25	8-45	2	16.24
5	K. A. J. Roach (*Barbados/West Indies*) .	RFM	122.5	38	337	20	5-17	1	16.85
6	R. R. S. Cornwall (*Leeward Islands*) ..	OB	346.2	93	955	54	6-57	3	17.68
7	A. S. Joseph (*Leeward Is/West Indies*) ..	RFM	237.1	57	740	41	5-66	1	18.04
8	K. M. A. Paul (*Guyana/West Indies*) ...	RFM	128	29	417	23	6-57	1	18.13
9	M. J. Mindley (*Barbados*)	RFM	141	33	377	20	5-78	1	18.85
10	R. Shepherd (*Guyana*)	RFM	257.3	67	745	37	5-24	1	20.13
11	V. Permaul (*Guyana*)	SLA	334.2	76	896	42	5-57	1	21.33
12	I. Khan (*Trinidad & Tobago*)	LB	313.5	65	944	42	7-47	4	22.47
13	M. L. Cummins (*Barbados*)	RFM	203	42	603	26	4-19	0	23.19
14	S. H. Lewis (*Windward Islands*)	RFM	183.3	35	541	23	7-76	1	23.52
15	S. Berridge (*Leeward Islands*)	RFM	185	38	594	25	4-34	0	23.76
16	C. Pestano (*Guyana*)	RFM	158.2	34	536	22	4-31	0	24.36
17	A. Phillip (*Trinidad & Tobago*)	RFM	190.4	34	688	28	5-74	1	24.57
18	D. K. Jacobs (*Leeward Islands*)	LB	201.2	28	625	24	6-62	2	26.04
19	K. A. R. Hodge (*Windward Islands*) ...	SLA	340.4	81	793	30	6-68	1	26.43
20	J. Thomas (*Windward Islands*)	RFM	225.4	37	766	28	4-44	0	27.35
21	A. Frazer (*Jamaica*)	OB	181	42	566	20	4-65	0	28.30
22	R. O. O. Jordan (*Windward Islands*) ..	RFM	226.1	36	741	25	4-47	0	29.64
23	B. N. L. Charles (*Trinidad & Tobago*)..	OB	218.2	56	610	20	5-72	2	30.50
24	L. M. Edward (*Windward Islands*)	SLA	342.5	74	846	27	5-67	1	31.33

Averages do not include tours by India A and India in July–September 2019.

WICB PROFESSIONAL CRICKET LEAGUE IN 2018-19

	P	W	L	D	Bonus points			
					Bat	Bowl	Pace	Pts
Guyana	10	7	3	0	16	30	24.2	154.2
Barbados	10	6	4	0	14	27	21.2	134.2
Leeward Islands	10	6	3	1	15	28	16.0	134.0
Trinidad & Tobago	10	4	5	1	18	27	16.4	112.4
Jamaica	10	3	7	0	15	29	17.2	97.2
Windward Islands	10	3	7	0	11	29	16.0	92.0

Win = 12pts; draw = 3pts. Bonus points were awarded as follows for the first 110 overs of each team's first innings: one batting point for the first 200 runs and then for 250, 300, 350 and 400; one bowling point for the third wicket taken and then for the sixth and ninth. In addition, 0.2pts awarded for every wicket taken by a pace bowler, across both innings.

REGIONAL CHAMPIONS

1965-66	Barbados	1983-84	Barbados	2001-02	Jamaica
1966-67	Barbados	1984-85	Trinidad & Tobago	2002-03	Barbados
1967-68	*No competition*	1985-86	Barbados	2003-04	Barbados
1968-69	Jamaica	1986-87	Guyana	2004-05	Jamaica
1969-70	Trinidad	1987-88	Jamaica	2005-06	Trinidad & Tobago
1970-71	Trinidad	1988-89	Jamaica	2006-07	Barbados
1971-72	Barbados	1989-90	Leeward Islands	2007-08	Jamaica
1972-73	Guyana	1990-91	Barbados	2008-09	Jamaica
1973-74	Barbados	1991-92	Jamaica	2009-10	Jamaica
1974-75	Guyana	1992-93	Guyana	2010-11	Jamaica
1975-76 {	Trinidad	1993-94	Leeward Islands	2011-12	Jamaica
	Barbados	1994-95	Barbados	2012-13	Barbados
1976-77	Barbados	1995-96	Leeward Islands	2013-14	Barbados
1977-78	Barbados	1996-97	Barbados	2014-15	Guyana
1978-79	Barbados	1997-98 {	Leeward Islands	2015-16	Guyana
1979-80	Barbados		Guyana	2016-17	Guyana
1980-81	Combined Islands	1998-99	Barbados	2017-18	Guyana
1981-82	Barbados	1999-2000	Jamaica	2018-19	Guyana
1982-83	Guyana	2000-01	Barbados		

Barbados have won the title outright 21 times, Jamaica 12, Guyana 10, Trinidad/Trinidad & Tobago 4, Leeward Islands 3, Combined Islands 1. Barbados, Guyana, Leeward Islands and Trinidad have also shared the title.

The tournament was known as the Shell Shield from 1965-66 to 1986-87, the Red Stripe Cup from 1987-88 to 1996-97, the President's Cup in 1997-98, the Busta Cup from 1998-99 to 2001-02, the Carib Beer Cup from 2002-03 to 2007-08, the Headley–Weekes Trophy from 2008-09 to 2012-13, the President's Trophy in 2013-14, and the WICB Professional Cricket League from 2014-15, though it was sponsored by Digicel in 2016-17.

REGIONAL SUPER50 IN 2018-19

50-over league plus knockout

Zone A	P	W	L	BP	Pts	Zone B	P	W	L	BP	Pts
GUYANA	8	5	1†	5	29	CAMPUSES/COLLEGES	8	5	2*	4	26
TRINIDAD & TOBAGO	8	5	1†	3	27	JAMAICA	8	4	3*	3	21
West Indies B	8	2	2‡	0	16	Barbados	8	4	3*	1	19
Windward Islands	8	1	5†	1	9	Leeward Islands	8	2	4†	1	13
Canada	8	1	5†	0	8	USA	8	2	5*	2	12

*   Plus one no-result.   †   Plus two no-results.   ‡   Plus four no-results.

eat Jamaica by one wicket; Combined Campuses & Colleges beat Trinidad
wickets.

1058 dgetown, October 28, 2018 (day/night). **Combined Campuses & Colleges won by**
Se ts. **Guyana 204** (49.1 overs); ‡**Combined Campuses & Colleges 205-4** (37.4 overs).
apuses & Colleges won their first regional title, with more than 12 overs to spare. Carlos
Brathwaite put *Guyana* in and took three wickets, including opener Tagenarine Chanderpaul for a
steady 56, while *Jermaine* Levy grabbed four. Kyle Corbin hit 72 in 53 balls – at more than twice
Chanderpaul's strike-rate – and shared an opening stand of 109 with Kjorn Ottley, before Brathwaite
saw them home with a rapid 30*.

The Caribbean Premier League has its own section (page 1152).

ZIMBABWE CRICKET IN 2019

Falling off a precipice

LIAM BRICKHILL

Zimbabwe's year was defined by boardroom, not sporting, dramas. Their cricket is no stranger to tumult, but the brouhaha in 2019 far exceeded anything that had come before – and the mid-year suspension of Zimbabwe's ICC membership rocked the game to its core. Key to the saga were two powerful men: Tavengwa Mukuhlani, who was re-elected Zimbabwe Cricket chairman in June, and Gerald Mlotshwa, the new chairman of the Sports and Recreation Commission, the umbrella body of all sporting organisations in the country.

A lawyer, Mlotshwa represented several cricketers, and former coach Heath Streak, in lawsuits against ZC, and was part of an attempt to set up a players' union in 2018. His father-in-law is Zimbabwe president, Emmerson Mnangagwa. And so ZC came under considerable pressure when the new SRC board involved themselves in their affairs at the end of May.

The row escalated when the board held elections in June, contravening an SRC directive that the vote be delayed. Four days later, the SRC announced

ZIMBABWE IN 2019

	Played	Won	Lost	Drawn/No result
Tests	–	–	–	–
One-day internationals	9	4	5	–
Twenty20 internationals	12	5	6	1

JANUARY		
FEBRUARY		
MARCH		
APRIL	4 ODIs (h) v United Arab Emirates	(page 1061)
MAY		
JUNE	2 ODIs and 2 T20Is (a) v Netherlands	(page 1094)
JULY	3 ODIs and 3 T20Is (a) v Ireland	(page 973)
AUGUST		
SEPTEMBER	T20I tri-series (in Bangladesh) v Afghanistan and Bangladesh	(page 917)
OCTOBER	T20I tri-series (in Singapore) v Nepal and Singapore	(page 1105)
NOVEMBER		
DECEMBER		

For a review of Zimbabwe domestic cricket from the 2018-19 season, see page 1066.

the suspension of the entire ZC board, setting in motion a chaotic period leading up to the ICC's annual conference in mid-July. Mlotshwa's clout in Zimbabwe held no sway with the ICC, who saw the move as a clear breach of their constitution, which forbids government interference in the game's administration. A ban was swiftly imposed – an unprecedented move against a Full Member – and it pushed Zimbabwean cricket over the precipice.

The collateral damage was immense. Zimbabwe's men did not play a Test in 2019, and lost more than half their 21 white-ball internationals, even though the only Test nations they met were Afghanistan, Bangladesh and Ireland. The players returned from a miserable European tour to uncertainty; within weeks, all-rounder Solomon Mire announced his international retirement. "I don't know what we have to do right now," said a downcast Sikandar Raza, one of the seniors. "Do we just burn our kits and apply for jobs?"

Suspension meant Zimbabwe could not participate in ICC events, so they missed out on the chance of reaching the Twenty20 World Cup in Australia late in 2020; their place at the qualifying event in the UAE went to Nigeria. Meanwhile, series against India, Afghanistan and West Indies were deferred or cancelled. The women's team were hit even harder. After storming to a 50-run win in the final of the T20 World Cup Africa Region Qualifier in May, they did not play for the rest of the year, and also missed their T20 World Cup.

It wasn't just the players who suffered. Langton Rusere, who had made history in 2018 by becoming the first Zimbabwean to umpire in the final of a global tournament, at the women's World T20 in Antigua, was prevented from standing in West Indies' one-day series in India. Cricket in Zimbabwe, from the national sides down to local clubs, ground to a halt.

The year had started in reasonable shape. A deal was brokered to restructure crippling debts of around $18m. The ICC offered a further lifeline with a revised funding package. In March, Vintcent van der Bijl – a consultant to ZC, and a member of MCC's world cricket committee – insisted there was a "viable game" in Zimbabwe. The following month, the United Arab Emirates were thumped 4–0, which helped make up for the dramatic defeat that had ended Zimbabwe's World Cup qualification dreams. Only a few weeks later, this tentative progress was completely shattered. The players were inexorably drawn into the argument, and forced to pick sides, compromising fragile team unity as the mood soured. The death of former ZC chairman Peter Chingoka in August added to the sombre mood.

The feeling of change was reinforced by Hamilton Masakadza's tearful announcement of his retirement in September. The guard of honour he received in Bangladesh was one of the most poignant images of the year, and he signed off with a vintage blast, 71 from 42 balls. He had made his debut, and scored a Test century against West Indies, aged 17 in 2001.

However, Masakadza was not lost to the game, and almost immediately moved into administration: in October, he was appointed ZC's director of cricket. After assurances from Zimbabwe's sports minister, the former Olympic swimming gold medallist Kirsty Coventry, the ICC suspension was lifted, allowing the Under-19s to take part in their World Cup early in 2020 – but discussions about funding continued. Masakadza may yet find cricket administration more taxing than any bowler he faced in his long career.

ZIMBABWE v UNITED ARAB EMIRATES IN 2018-19

Neil Manthorp

One-day internationals (4): Zimbabwe 4, United Arab Emirates 0

This series had a double significance for Zimbabwe. They were desperately in need of international cricket, having not played for five months, and were seeking revenge for a devastating three-run defeat by the United Arab Emirates in the World Cup Qualifier just over a year earlier.

Zimbabwe could field a strong side, despite missing their most experienced batsmen – the injured Brendan Taylor and Hamilton Masakadza – and had recently completed their domestic season. But the UAE, whose players were all born in Pakistan or India, arrived for their first bilateral series against a Full Member with an ageing squad (only one was below 29), because their Under-19 team were engaged in their own World Cup qualifier, which they won.

"Four or five of them, including some born in the UAE, would have been in contention for the senior squad, but we decided to let them be at full strength for the Under-19 tournament," said their coach, Scotsman Dougie Brown. With inaugural first-class and 50-over domestic leagues starting in September 2019, Brown was bullish about the UAE's future.

Zimbabwe Cricket, whose finances were now strictly supervised by the ICC, felt as if they were still coming to terms with their own tumble out of the mainstream. But the players applied themselves with discipline and conviction, and looked organised and well coached.

Only the most basic, five-camera television coverage was possible, with no third-umpire decisions, even for line calls; when the Dubai-based sponsor Surya Pumps failed to pay the balance, the final two games were not televised at all. The tourists beat a ZC Chairman's XI in their only warm-up match, with opener Ashfaq Ahmed making an unbeaten 131, but were barely competitive in the one-day series. They were hampered by the unfamiliarity of rainy conditions, which made them look worse than perhaps they were.

In Masakadza's absence, Peter Moor captained Zimbabwe with efficient simplicity, and they were good value for the 4–0 scoreline, their first whitewash for ten years. But it could not come close to compensating for the World Cup elimination inflicted by the UAE a year earlier, which had left the country's professional cricketers grasping for meaning or motivation.

UNITED ARAB EMIRATES TOURING PARTY

*Mohammad Naveed, Amir Hayat, Ashfaq Ahmed, Ghulam Shabbir, Imran Haider, Mohammad Boota, Mohammad Usman, Qadeer Ahmed, C. P. Rizwan, Rohan Mustafa, Shaiman Anwar, Sultan Ahmed, C. Suri, Zahoor Khan. *Coach:* D. R. Brown.

First one-day international At Harare, April 10. **Zimbabwe won by seven wickets. United Arab Emirates 110** (44.5 overs) (Mohammad Boota 36; T. L. Chatara 3-25); ‡**Zimbabwe 111-3** (23.1 overs) (R. W. Chakabva 38, C. R. Ervine 51). *PoM:* T. L. Chatara. *ODI debut:* Sultan Ahmed (UAE). *The UAE had to bat on a pitch spiced up by torrential rain – it seamed, bounced and even spun prodigiously – while Zimbabwe's bowlers produced one of their most disciplined performances* *in a decade. Kyle Jarvis and Tendai Chatara didn't bowl a loose delivery during the ten-over powerplay – which yielded 19-3 – and Donald Tiripano maintained the stranglehold. Though conditions never eased, the tourists refused to give their wickets away, and were so determined to survive that they neglected scoring opportunities, especially singles. For Zimbabwe, Regis Chakabva nudged and pushed, while Craig Ervine was more clinical, hitting a couple of straight-driven sixes, and falling only just short of victory.*

Second one-day international   At Harare, April 12. **Zimbabwe won by four runs** (DLS). **United Arab Emirates 169-9** (35 overs) (Ghulam Shabbir 56, Shaiman Anwar 72; K. M. Jarvis 4-17, D. T. Tiripano 3-34); ‡**Zimbabwe 185-4** (32 overs) (R. W. Chakabva 78*, P. J. Moor 45*). *PoM:* P. J. Moor. *Jarvis reduced the UAE to 12-3, but Ghulam Shabbir and Shaiman Anwar would not be rushed, adding 131 in 24 overs. The 40-year-old Anwar showed a strong leg-side game at the end, with seven fours and two sixes; leg-spinner Brandon Mavuta's single over cost 16. But a rain break left just six overs for a slog. And when Shabbir was caught at cover and Anwar at fine leg, the innings folded. The chase produced the tour's most dramatic moments. The match officials had made a hash of the recalculation, and it was obvious daylight would be gone before the new scheduled close. Initially chasing 210 in 35, Zimbabwe wobbled slowly to 92-4 before Moor, who had signalled for a DLS sheet as the sun was setting, crashed three sixes, doing just enough to put his team ahead before night descended.*

Third one-day international   At Harare, April 14. **Zimbabwe won by 131 runs. Zimbabwe 307-4** (50 overs) (S. F. Mire 40, C. R. Ervine 64, S. C. Williams 109*, P. J. Moor 58*); ‡**United Arab Emirates 176** (46.2 overs) (C. P. Rizwan 47, Mohammad Usman 49; R. P. Burl 4-32). *PoM:* S. C. Williams. *Finally winning first use of the pitch, the UAE bowlers hoped to exploit it as Zimbabwe had done, but soon realised these would be no easy wickets. Barrel-chested Solomon Mire and an aggressive Ervine added 104 – Mire blocked or whacked, until he holed out to deep midwicket, while Ervine flourished against the spinners. The wispy left-hander Sean Williams cut, swept and ran hard as he completed his third ODI century; he and Moor put on 145, including 131 in the last 13 overs. Jarvis and Christopher Mpofu reduced the chase to 15-3, and Rizwan then scored 47 in 102 balls, showing how low a priority victory was for the UAE.*

Fourth one-day international   At Harare, April 16. **Zimbabwe won by three wickets** (DLS). ‡**United Arab Emirates 175** (47.1 overs) (C. Suri 46, C. P. Rizwan 45); **Zimbabwe 129-7** (24.5 overs) (T. Maruma 35). *PoM:* K. M. Jarvis. *PoS:* R. W. Chakabva. *Afternoon rain disrupted play again, reducing Zimbabwe's target to 128 in 30 overs. The UAE's best bowling performance, and some sloppy home batting, gave them a chance of a consolation win, until Timycen Maruma snatched it away. At 79-5, with 49 required from 12.3, Zimbabwe needed a calm head – or so it seemed. But, after being dropped on nought, Maruma counter-attacked, walloping three fours and a couple of leg-side sixes in a breezy 22-ball 35. Earlier, UAE opener Chirag Suri's organised 46 anchored the top order, while Rizwan continued his whimsical disregard for the fact that overs were limited, inching to 45 from 87 deliveries.*

DOMESTIC CRICKET IN ZIMBABWE IN 2018-19

John Ward

It was a season of austerity in Zimbabwe, because of stringent financial conditions imposed by the ICC to resolve the long-standing crisis of mismanagement. The domestic competitions were reduced to four provincial teams; sadly, the youthful Rising Stars had to drop out after a single season, in which they had won the Pro50 trophy. The remaining sides played six matches apiece in each of the three competitions; because of a lack of funds, the programme did not start until December, often a wet month. One round of the Logan Cup, in January, was abandoned after a single (rainy) day because of civil unrest. For once, most of the international players were available, which meant higher standards, but made it more difficult for promising youngsters, including the former Rising Stars, to find places.

Team names mutated yet again. With the so-called franchise system dropped, the provincial sides were simply called Eagles (based in Harare), Tuskers (Bulawayo), Mountaineers (Mutare) and Rhinos (Kwekwe).

Mountaineers remained the team with the greatest depth and experience. Following a defeat by Rhinos, and the match called off after one day, they won the last four by huge margins, to claim their third successive Logan Cup. They rotated their squad to involve as many players as possible; only Donald Tiripano appeared in all six games. He was the leading wicket-taker, with 25, and also scored 215 runs, to be named the tournament's best all-rounder. The batting award went to the rejuvenated Timycen Maruma, the leading scorer with 409 at 81. Seamer Victor Nyauchi made significant progress, and Tafadzwa Tsiga, formerly of Rising Stars, broke through as a wicketkeeper-batsman.

Eagles had a useful side but few high performers; no one scored a first-class century, though Elton Chigumbura and Richmond Mutumbami came close. The surprise bowling package was Chamu Chibhabha, better known as a batsman: his nippy medium-pacers collected 16 wickets at 18. The team re-established themselves as Pro50 experts, winning all their completed fixtures to take the trophy.

Tuskers never won a first-class match. A Bulawayo-residents-only policy told against them, while Sikandar Raza was plying his trade in the franchise T20 leagues, and Sean Williams missed the Logan Cup. Chris Mpofu bowled well, while Brian Chari found hitherto unknown consistency with five fifties in nine innings, but they had little support. In limited-overs cricket, though, it was a different story, thanks to Craig Ervine. A batsman of moods, at his best Ervine looks world-class, and he found the form of his life in the two white-ball tournaments, with 750 runs for five dismissals. In the Pro50, he scored 422 in five innings, with two centuries including 168 not out, helping Tuskers finish as runners-up; 328 in the T20 tournament, reinstated after two years' absence, secured the title.

This should have been **Rhinos'** season, not least because they had 15 internationals in their squad. But, despite good captaincy by P. J. Moor, also their leading batsman, they fired only fitfully. They opened with a fine victory over Mountaineers – thanks to a maiden century from Tarisai Musakanda, and figures of six for seven from Carl Mumba – but lost the next match to Eagles by an innings, after scoring 352, and blew hot and cold after that. Musakanda lapsed into indiscipline, and the team were too inconsistent to exploit their great talent.

The ICC's decision in July 2019 to suspend Zimbabwe Cricket's membership and freeze their funding, citing the government's suspension of the elected board, caused great hardship to the players and other ZC employees. Even after reinstatement in October, the annual grant on which ZC depend was slashed from $9m to $5m, and by January 2020 they had not been paid for over six months. The Logan Cup, which could not start until mid-December, was suspended within a month as the money ran out. The game's future in Zimbabwe looked more bleak and uncertain than ever, and the ICC shared much of the responsibility.

FIRST-CLASS AVERAGES IN 2018-19

BATTING (150 runs)

		M	I	NO	R	HS	100	Avge	Ct/St
1	T. Maruma (*Mountaineers*)	5	5	0	409	165	2	81.80	7
2	R. Mutumbami (*Eagles*)	4	6	1	291	99	0	58.20	11
3	H. Masakadza (*Mountaineers*)	2	3	0	163	126	1	54.33	4
4	P. J. Moor (*Rhinos*)	6	10	1	392	139	1	43.55	4
5	†P. S. Masvaure (*Rhinos*)	5	9	1	324	127	1	40.50	3
6	T. E. Tsiga (*Mountaineers*)	5	5	0	200	124	1	40.00	16
7	B. B. Chari (*Tuskers*)	6	9	0	356	85	0	39.55	4
8	†B. M. Chapungu (*Rhinos*)	4	7	0	252	62	0	36.00	4
9	†C. R. Ervine (*Tuskers*)	5	9	0	296	141	1	32.88	9
10	T. K. Musakanda (*Rhinos*)	6	9	0	359	119	1	32.63	6
11	R. W. Chakabva (*Eagles*)	6	9	0	289	64	0	32.11	17/1
12	D. T. Tiripano (*Mountaineers*)	6	7	0	215	71	0	30.71	0
13	C. Ncube (*Tuskers*)	6	9	0	269	119	1	29.88	4
14	E. Chigumbura (*Eagles*)	6	8	1	205	98	0	29.28	3
15	I. Kaia (*Mountaineers*)	5	8	1	192	56	0	27.42	4
16	†C. Zhuwao (*Eagles*)	5	7	0	181	60	0	25.85	3
17	N. P. Mayavo (*Rhinos*)	6	10	2	199	73	0	24.87	7/2
18	C. T. Mutombodzi (*Eagles*)	5	9	2	170	49	0	24.28	2
19	T. R. Mupariwa (*Tuskers*)	6	9	0	218	69	0	24.22	4
20	T. S. Kamunhukamwe (*Eagles*)	5	7	0	164	59	0	23.42	2
21	N. Madziva (*Rhinos*)	6	9	1	160	68	0	20.00	3

BOWLING (10 wickets)

		Style	O	M	R	W	BB	5I	Avge
1	T. L. Chatara (*Mountaineers*)	RFM	52.4	17	109	12	3-15	0	9.08
2	D. T. Tiripano (*Mountaineers*)	RFM	131.4	33	381	25	5-42	2	15.24
3	W. T. Mashinge (*Mountaineers*)	RFM	73	14	238	15	5-38	1	15.86
4	V. M. Nyauchi (*Mountaineers*)	RFM	111.3	22	361	20	4-27	0	18.05
5	C. J. Chibhabha (*Eagles*)	RM	95.3	22	290	16	4-19	0	18.12
6	C. T. Mumba (*Rhinos*)	RFM	78.4	11	233	12	6-7	1	19.41
7	N. M'shangwe (*Mountaineers*)	LB	59	12	219	11	4-36	0	19.90
8	N. Madziva (*Rhinos*)	RFM	80	17	245	11	3-20	0	22.27
9	H. K. Ziwira (*Eagles*)	RFM	74	17	248	11	5-62	1	22.54
10	T. S. Chisoro (*Rhinos*)	LFM	104	20	306	13	4-22	0	23.53
11	C. B. Mpofu (*Tuskers*)	RFM	154.1	29	477	20	6-60	2	23.85
12	R. Ngarava (*Tuskers*)	LFM	80.5	15	265	11	4-26	0	24.09
13	B. A. Mavuta (*Rhinos*)	LB	112.1	12	461	19	7-157	1	24.26
14	T. N. Garwe (*Eagles*)	RFM	136.4	44	340	13	5-34	1	26.15
15	A. Ndlovu (*Tuskers*)	SLA	97.2	19	339	10	5-109	1	33.90
16	E. Masuku (*Tuskers*)	RM	113.5	13	527	15	4-70	0	35.13

LOGAN CUP IN 2018-19

					1st-inns	Bonus pts		
	P	W	L	D	pts	Bat	Bowl	Pts
Mountaineers	6	4	1	1	4	5	10	45
Rhinos	6	2	2	2	2	5	6	29
Eagles	6	2	2	2	2	2	6	26
Tuskers	6	0	3	3	1	3	6	16

Win = 6pts; draw = 2pts; lead on first innings = 1pt. Bonus points were awarded as follows in either innings: one batting point for a team reaching 300 and for each subsequent 100, one batting point for a batsman scoring 150, and one bowling point for a team taking ten wickets.

LOGAN CUP WINNERS

1993-94	Mashonaland U24	2006-07	Easterns
1994-95	Mashonaland	2007-08	Northerns
1995-96	Mashonaland	2008-09	Easterns
1996-97	Mashonaland	2009-10	Mashonaland Eagles
1997-98	Mashonaland	2010-11	Matabeleland Tuskers
1998-99	Mashonaland	2011-12	Matabeleland Tuskers
1999-2000	Mashonaland	2012-13	Matabeleland Tuskers
2000-01	Mashonaland	2013-14	Mountaineers
2001-02	Mashonaland	2014-15	Matabeleland Tuskers
2002-03	Mashonaland	2015-16	Mashonaland Eagles
2003-04	Mashonaland	2016-17	Manicaland Mountaineers
2004-05	Mashonaland	2017-18	Manicaland Mountaineers
2005-06	*No competition*	2018-19	Mountaineers

Mashonaland/Northerns/Mashonaland Eagles have won the title 12 times, Easterns/Mountaineers and Matabeleland/Matabeleland Tuskers 6, Mashonaland Under-24 1.

PRO50 CHAMPIONSHIP IN 2018-19

50-over league

	P	W	L	A	Bonus	Pts	NRR
EAGLES..........	6	5	0	1	2	24	1.27
TUSKERS	6	3	2	1	1	15	0.23
Mountaineers	6	2	4	0	2	10	−0.04
Rhinos	6	1	5	0	0	4	−1.18

Final   At Harare, March 9, 2019. **Eagles won by two wickets. Tuskers 202** (45.2 overs); ‡**Eagles 203-8** (46.1 overs). *Tuskers started badly when Richard Ngarava bowled Brian Chari in the opening over, and were 91-5 before Ernest Masuku hit a maiden one-day fifty that helped them reach 200. In reply, Tinashe Kamunhukamwe brought up a 30-ball half-century with his third six, as Eagles reached 80-2 in the powerplay, but then stalled, and became one of three victims in eight deliveries for slow left-armer Ainsley Ndlovu. Regis Chakabva dug in, however, and his 38* saw Eagles home with nearly four overs to spare.*

The Domestic Twenty20 Championship can be found on page 1154.

INTERNATIONAL RESULTS IN 2019

TEST MATCHES

	P	W	L	D	% won	% lost	% drawn
India.............	8	7	0	1	**87.50**	0.00	12.50
Australia........	12	8	2	2	**66.66**	16.66	16.66
Afghanistan......	3	2	1	0	**66.66**	33.33	0.00
New Zealand......	8	4	3	1	**50.00**	37.50	12.50
West Indies......	6	3	3	0	**50.00**	50.00	0.00
Sri Lanka........	8	3	4	1	**37.50**	50.00	12.50
South Africa.....	8	3	5	0	**37.50**	62.50	0.00
England..........	12	4	6	2	**33.33**	50.00	16.66
Pakistan.........	6	1	4	1	**16.66**	66.66	16.66
Ireland..........	2	0	2	0	**0.00**	100.00	0.00
Bangladesh.......	5	0	5	0	**0.00**	100.00	0.00
Totals...........	39	35	35	4	**89.74**	89.74	10.25

Zimbabwe played no Tests in 2019.

ONE-DAY INTERNATIONALS (Full Members only)

	P	W	L	NR	% won	% lost
England..........	22	15	5	2	**75.00**	25.00
India............	28	19	8	1	**70.37**	29.62
Australia.........	23	16	7	0	**69.56**	30.43
New Zealand......	21	13	8	0	**61.90**	38.09
South Africa......	19	11	7	1	**61.11**	38.88
Ireland..........	14	6	7	1	**46.15**	53.84
West Indies.......	28	10	15	3	**40.00**	60.00
Bangladesh........	18	7	11	0	**38.88**	61.11
Pakistan.........	25	9	15	1	**37.50**	62.50
Sri Lanka........	20	6	14	0	**30.00**	70.00
Afghanistan......	19	3	15	1	**16.66**	83.33
Zimbabwe........	3	0	3	0	**0.00**	100.00
Totals...........	120	115	115	5		

The following teams also played official ODIs in 2019, some against Full Members (not included above): Netherlands (P2 W2); Namibia (P5 W4 L1); USA (P9 W6 L3); Nepal (P3 W2 L1); Oman (P5 W3 L2); Scotland (P9 W4 L5); UAE (P10 W2 L8); Papua New Guinea (P9 W1 L8).

TWENTY20 INTERNATIONALS (Full Members only)

	P	W	L	NR	% won	% lost
Australia..........	8	7	0	1	**100.00**	0.00
England..........	9	7	2	0	**77.77**	22.22
South Africa......	8	6	2	0	**75.00**	25.00
Afghanistan......	10	7	3	0	**70.00**	30.00
New Zealand......	12	7	5	0	**58.33**	41.66
Bangladesh.......	7	4	3	0	**57.14**	42.85
India............	16	9	7	0	**56.25**	43.75
Zimbabwe........	6	2	4	0	**33.33**	66.66
Sri Lanka........	13	4	9	0	**30.76**	69.23
Ireland..........	5	1	4	0	**20.00**	80.00
West Indies.......	12	2	10	0	**16.66**	83.33
Pakistan.........	10	1	8	1	**11.11**	88.88
Totals...........	58	57	57	1		

All white-ball matches between Full Members only. The % won/lost excludes no-results. With the extension of Twenty20 international status to all Associate Members of the ICC, a further 59 teams also played official T20Is in 2019.

MRF TYRES ICC TEAM RANKINGS

TEST CHAMPIONSHIP (As at January 31, 2020)

		Matches	Points	Rating
1	India	42	5,046	120
2	Australia	40	4,320	108
3	England	50	5,253	105
4	New Zealand	33	3,449	105
5	South Africa	36	3,537	98
6	Sri Lanka	46	4,191	91
7	Pakistan	33	2,795	85
8	West Indies	33	2,675	81
9	Bangladesh	26	1,566	60
10	Zimbabwe	12	208	17

Afghanistan had a rating of 49 and Ireland 0, but neither had played sufficient Tests to achieve a ranking.

ONE-DAY CHAMPIONSHIP (As at December 31, 2019)

		Matches	Points	Rating
1	England	54	6,745	125
2	India	61	7,364	121
3	New Zealand	43	4,837	112
4	Australia	50	5,543	111
5	South Africa	47	5,193	110
6	Pakistan	51	5,019	98
7	Bangladesh	46	3,963	86
8	Sri Lanka	56	4,520	81
9	West Indies	55	4,372	79
10	Afghanistan	43	2,440	57
11	Ireland	29	1,466	51
12	Zimbabwe	35	1,538	44

Remaining rankings: 13 Netherlands (37), 14 Scotland (30), 15 USA (25), 16 Namibia (23), 17 Oman (22), 18 Nepal (19), 19 UAE (9), 20 Papua New Guinea (0).

TWENTY20 CHAMPIONSHIP (As at December 31, 2019)

		Matches	Points	Rating
1	Pakistan	31	8,366	270
2	Australia	26	6,986	269
3	England	21	5,568	265
4	South Africa	18	4,720	262
5	India	39	10,071	258
6	New Zealand	24	6,056	252
7	Sri Lanka	27	6,413	238
8	Afghanistan	23	5,422	236
9	Bangladesh	23	5,212	227
10	West Indies	30	6,757	225
11	Zimbabwe	21	4,082	194
12	Nepal	24	4,602	192
13	Scotland	23	4,310	187
14	Ireland	36	6,630	184
15	United Arab Emirates	26	4,781	184
16	Netherlands	31	5,547	179
17	Oman	18	3,187	177
18	Papua New Guinea	30	5,277	176

Remaining rankings: 19 Namibia (153), 20 Hong Kong (143), 21 Singapore (134), 22 Qatar (131), 23 Canada (126), 24 Saudi Arabia (121), 25 Jersey (114), 26 Italy (111), 27 Kenya (108), 28 Kuwait (104), 29 Denmark (103), 30 Bermuda (92), 31 Germany (85), 32 USA (81), 33 Botswana (79), 34 Ghana (77), 35 Uganda (76), 36 Norway (71), 37 Guernsey (70), 38 Austria (70), 39 Malaysia (68), 40 Nigeria (66), 41 Romania (62), 42 Sweden (58), 43 Tanzania (56), 44 Spain (55), 45 Cayman Islands (54), 46 Philippines (48), 47 Argentina (45), 48 France (45), 49 Vanuatu (43), 50 Belize (42), 51 Luxembourg (39), 52 Bahrain (37), 53 Peru (35), 54 Fiji (35), 55 Malawi (35), 56 Panama (32), 57 Belgium (32), 58 Samoa (32), 59 Japan (32), 60 Costa Rica (32), 61 Mexico (31), 62 Hungary (30), 63 Bulgaria (29), 64 Czech Republic (28), 65 Thailand (26), 66 Israel (25), 67 Portugal (24), 68 Finland (23), 69 South Korea (22), 70 Isle of Man (21), 71 Mozambique (19), 72 Chile (19), 73 Bhutan (15), 74 Maldives (14), 75 Sierra Leone (12), 76 Brazil (11), 77 St Helena (9), 78 Malta (8), 79 Myanmar (3), 80 Indonesia (0), 81= China (0), Gambia (0), Gibraltar (0), Lesotho (0), Rwanda (0), Swaziland (0), Turkey (0).

The ratings are based on all Test series, one-day and Twenty20 internationals completed since May 1, 2016.

The Shorter Wisden

book and audio book

It includes the Notes by the Editor, the obituaries, all the front-of-book articles and reviews, plus reports of all England's Test matches in the previous year.

To order at discount visit
wisdenalmanack.com

MRF TYRES ICC PLAYER RANKINGS

Introduced in 1987, the rankings have been backed by various sponsors, but were taken over by the ICC in January 2005. They rank cricketers on a scale up to 1,000 on their performances in Tests. The rankings take into account playing conditions, the quality of the opposition and the result of the matches. In August 1998, a similar set of rankings for one-day internationals was launched, and Twenty20 rankings were added in October 2011.

The leading players in the Test rankings on January 31, 2020, were:

	Batsmen	Points		Bowlers	Points
1	V. Kohli (I)	928	1	P. J. Cummins (A)	904
2	S. P. D. Smith (A)	911	2	N. Wagner (NZ)	852
3	M. Labuschagne (A)	827	3	J. O. Holder (WI)	830
4	K. S. Williamson (NZ)	814	4	K. Rabada (SA)	802
5	D. A. Warner (A)	793	5	M. A. Starc (A)	796
6	C. A. Pujara (I)	791	6	J. J. Bumrah (I)	794
7	Babar Azam (P)	767	7	J. M. Anderson (E)	775
8	J. E. Root (E)	764	8	R. Ashwin (I)	772
9	A. M. Rahane (I)	759	9	Mohammed Shami (I)	771
10	B. A. Stokes (E)	718	10	J. R. Hazlewood (A)	769

The leading players in the one-day international rankings on December 31, 2019, were:

	Batsmen	Points		Bowlers	Points
1	V. Kohli (I)	887	1	J. J. Bumrah (I)	785
2	R. G. Sharma (I)	873	2	T. A. Boult (NZ)	740
3	Babar Azam (P)	834	3	Mujeeb Zadran (Afg)	707
4	F. du Plessis (SA)	820	4	K. Rabada (SA)	694
5	L. R. P. L. Taylor (NZ)	817	5	P. J. Cummins (A)	693
6	K. S. Williamson (NZ)	796	6	C. R. Woakes (E)	676
7	D. A. Warner (A)	794	7 {	M. A. Starc (A)	663
			{	Mohammad Amir (P)	663
8	J. E. Root (E)	787	9	M. J. Henry (NZ)	656
9	S. D. Hope (WI)	782	10	L. H. Ferguson (NZ)	649
10	Q. de Kock (SA)	781			

The leading players in the Twenty20 international rankings on December 31, 2019, were:

	Batsmen	Points		Bowlers	Points
1	Babar Azam (P)	879	1	Rashid Khan (Afg)	749
2	A. J. Finch (A)	810	2	Mujeeb Zadran (Afg)	742
3	D. J. Malan (E)	782	3	M. J. Santner (NZ)	698
4	C. Munro (NZ)	780	4	Imad Wasim (P)	681
5	G. J. Maxwell (A)	766	5	A. Zampa (A)	674
6	K. L. Rahul (I)	734	6	A. L. Phehlukwayo (SA)	665
7	E. Lewis (WI)	699	7	A. U. Rashid (E)	660
8	Hazratullah Zazai (Afg)	692	8	Shadab Khan (P)	657
9	R. G. Sharma (I)	686	9	A. C. Agar (A)	649
10	V. Kohli (I)	685	10	C. J. Jordan (E)	640

TEST AVERAGES IN CALENDAR YEAR 2019

BATTING (250 runs, average 20.00)

		T	I	NO	R	HS	100	50	Avge	SR	Ct/St
1	Abid Ali (P)	2	3	1	321	174	1	1	160.50	58.57	0
2	R. G. Sharma (I)	5	6	0	556	212	3	0	92.66	75.95	6
3	S. P. D. Smith (A)	8	13	0	965	211	3	4	74.23	56.26	21
4	A. M. Rahane (I)	8	11	2	642	115	2	5	71.33	49.96	9
5	†Tamim Iqbal (B)	2	4	0	278	126	1	2	69.50	84.24	0
6	M. A. Agarwal (I)	8	11	0	754	243	3	2	68.54	59.04	4
7	Babar Azam (P)	6	11	2	616	104	3	3	68.44	72.30	4
8	G. H. Vihari (I)	4	6	1	341	111	1	2	68.20	56.36	0
9	V. Kohli (I)	8	11	2	612	254*	2	2	68.00	63.28	8
10	M. Labuschagne (A)	11	17	0	1,104	185	3	7	64.94	55.44	10
11	†R. A. Jadeja (I)	8	10	3	440	91	0	5	62.85	61.62	3
12	B-J. Watling (NZ)	8	11	1	559	205	2	2	55.90	41.22	28/1
13	L. R. P. L. Taylor (NZ)	8	12	1	607	200	2	3	55.18	64.23	12
14	C. de Grandhomme (NZ)	6	8	2	323	83	0	3	53.83	83.24	4
15	K. S. Williamson (NZ)	8	12	2	514	200*	2	2	51.40	59.90	8
16	†T. W. M. Latham (NZ)	8	12	0	601	161	3	1	50.08	52.67	7
17	†T. M. Head (A)	11	17	2	742	161	2	4	49.46	54.35	5
18	J. O. Holder (WI)	5	8	1	344	202*	1	0	49.14	70.20	8
19	†D. A. Warner (A)	9	16	1	725	335*	2	1	48.33	62.28	14
20	†Q. de Kock (SA)	8	15	0	713	129	2	5	47.53	78.95	32/2
21	Rahmat Shah (Afg)	3	6	0	280	102	1	2	46.66	51.85	1
22	B. O. P. Fernando (SL)	4	7	1	277	102	1	1	46.16	53.99	3
23	C. A. Pujara (I)	8	11	0	507	193	1	4	46.09	51.52	6
24	†B. A. Stokes (E)	11	21	3	821	135*	2	4	45.61	52.66	13
25	J. A. Burns (A)	6	9	0	402	180	1	2	44.66	53.45	7
26	Asad Shafiq (P)	6	9	0	378	88	0	5	42.00	61.96	7
27	F. du Plessis (SA)	7	14	2	497	103	1	4	41.41	48.48	9
28	†Shan Masood (P)	6	11	0	440	135	1	2	40.00	52.75	1
29	†M. D. K. J. Perera (SL)	5	9	2	277	153*	1	1	39.57	75.68	2
30	†M. S. Wade (A)	9	16	2	532	117	2	1	38.00	57.51	6
31	J. E. Root (E)	12	23	0	851	226	2	4	37.00	46.32	25
32	Mahmudullah (B)	5	10	1	332	146	1	1	36.88	61.82	1
33	†R. J. Burns (E)	12	23	0	824	133	2	5	35.82	43.78	11
34	†F. D. M. Karunaratne (SL) . . .	8	15	0	527	122	1	3	35.13	47.30	4
35	D. M. de Silva (SL)	8	14	2	403	109	2	0	33.58	57.24	7
36	†H. M. Nicholls (NZ)	8	11	0	361	107	1	1	32.81	51.35	4
37	†D. P. D. N. Dickwella (SL) . . .	8	13	0	421	65	0	4	32.38	62.09	15/3
38	J. L. Denly (E)	11	21	0	651	94	0	6	31.00	41.54	5
39	†J. D. Campbell (WI)	6	12	2	298	55	0	1	29.80	61.69	4
40	†U. T. Khawaja (A)	6	11	2	265	101*	1	0	29.44	60.36	4
41	A. K. Markram (SA)	7	13	0	372	90	0	3	28.61	64.92	4
42	J. C. Buttler (E)	10	20	0	502	70	0	3	25.10	48.45	16
43	†D. Elgar (SA)	8	16	2	351	160	1	0	25.07	55.10	8
44	T. D. Paine (A)	12	17	2	361	79	0	2	24.06	47.18	56/2
45	B. K. G. Mendis (SL)	8	15	1	313	84*	0	2	22.35	53.32	13
46	†H. D. R. L. Thirimanne (SL) . .	6	12	0	251	64	0	1	20.91	35.40	5

BOWLING (10 wickets)

		Style	O	M	R	W	BB	5I	Avge	SR
1	J. J. Bumrah (I)	RF	72.1	21	184	14	6-27	2	13.14	30.92
2	U. T. Yadav (I)	RF	88.4	14	314	23	5-53	1	13.65	23.13
3	I. Sharma (I)	RFM	135.4	34	389	25	5-22	2	15.56	32.56
4	Rashid Khan (Afg)	LB	121.3	26	331	21	6-49	3	15.76	34.71

		Style	O	M	R	W	BB	5I	Avge	SR
5	Mohammed Shami (I)	RFM	194.2	49	550	33	5-35	1	16.66	35.33
6	J. O. Holder (WI)	RFM	151.2	57	345	20	5-77	1	17.25	45.40
7	N. Wagner (NZ)	LFM	269.5	55	766	43	5-44	4	17.81	37.65
8	K. A. J. Roach (WI)	RFM	193.5	63	488	27	5-17	1	18.07	43.07
9	P. J. Cummins (A)	RF	440	119	1,188	59	6-23	2	20.13	44.74
10	M. A. Starc (A)	LF	257	45	870	42	6-66	4	20.71	36.71
11	J. L. Pattinson (A)	RFM	92	20	236	11	3-34	0	21.45	50.18
12	D. Olivier (SA)	RF	110	18	435	20	5-51	1	21.75	33.00
13	R. R. S. Cornwall (WI)	OB	107.3	25	294	13	7-75	1	22.61	49.61
14	J. R. Hazlewood (A)	RFM	275.4	70	762	33	5-30	1	23.09	50.12
15	R. A. S. Lakmal (SL)	RFM	131.5	31	326	14	5-75	1	23.28	56.50
16	A. S. Joseph (WI)	RFM	66.2	16	238	10	2-12	0	23.80	39.80
17	C. R. Woakes (E)	RFM	154.4	31	477	20	6-17	1	23.85	46.40
18	R. Ashwin (I)	OB	173.2	42	483	20	7-145	1	24.15	52.00
19	S. C. J. Broad (E)	RFM	367.4	89	1,080	43	5-86	1	25.11	51.30
20	K. Rabada (SA)	RF	245.5	40	904	33	4-38	0	27.39	44.69
21	J. C. Archer (E)	RF	274	63	822	30	6-45	3	27.40	54.80
22	V. D. Philander (SA)	RFM	169.2	53	422	15	4-16	0	28.13	67.73
23	M. M. Ali (E)	OB	139.2	18	520	18	4-36	0	28.88	46.44
24	Shaheen Shah Afridi (P)	LFM	154	30	493	17	5-77	1	29.00	54.35
25	T. G. Southee (NZ)	RFM	313.4	64	958	33	5-69	1	29.03	57.03
26	T. A. Boult (NZ)	LFM	210.5	44	670	23	5-123	1	29.13	55.00
27	C. A. K. Rajitha (SL)	RFM	96.4	13	381	13	3-67	0	29.30	44.61
28	R. L. Chase (WI)	OB	149.4	17	500	17	8-60	1	29.41	52.82
29	D. W. Steyn (SA)	RFM	122.1	21	444	15	4-48	0	29.60	48.86
30	J. M. Anderson (E)	RFM	135.1	35	362	12	5-46	1	30.16	67.58
31	M. V. T. Fernando (SL)	LFM	153.3	16	581	18	4-62	0	32.27	51.16
32	C. de Grandhomme (NZ)	RFM	161	28	363	11	2-41	0	33.00	87.81
33	N. M. Lyon (A)	OB	515.3	91	1,497	45	6-49	2	33.26	68.73
34	S. M. Curran (E)	LFM	183.5	40	604	18	4-58	0	33.55	61.27
35	R. A. Jadeja (I)	SLA	255.4	66	725	21	4-87	0	34.52	73.04
36	M. J. Leach (E)	SLA	151.4	27	489	14	4-49	0	34.92	65.00
37	B. A. Stokes (E)	RFM	242.3	42	780	22	4-59	0	35.45	66.13
38	S. T. Gabriel (WI)	RF	162.1	34	507	13	3-45	0	39.00	74.84
39	C. B. R. L. S. Kumara (SL) . .	RFM	121	20	454	11	4-49	0	41.27	66.00
40	L. Embuldeniya (SL)	SLA	208	20	743	17	5-66	1	43.70	73.41
41	Mohammad Abbas (P)	RFM	169	44	491	11	4-55	0	44.63	92.18
42	K. A. Maharaj (SA)	SLA	178.4	21	710	12	3-71	0	59.16	89.33

MOST DISMISSALS BY A WICKETKEEPER

Dis		T			Dis		T		
58	(56ct, 2st)	12	T. D. Paine (A)		29	(28ct, 1st)	8	B-J. Watling (NZ)	
34	(32ct, 2st)	7	Q. de Kock (SA)		18	(17ct, 1st)	5	W. P. Saha (I)	
30	(26ct, 4st)	7	J. M. Bairstow (E)		18	(15ct, 3st)	8	D. P. D. N. Dickwella (SL)	

Bairstow played three further Tests when not keeping wicket, taking one catch, and de Kock played one, but took no catches.

MOST CATCHES IN THE FIELD

Ct	T			Ct	T		
25	12	J. E. Root (E)		13	8	B. K. G. Mendis (SL)	
21	8	S. P. D. Smith (A)		13	11	B. A. Stokes (E)	
14	9	D. A. Warner (A)		12	8	L. R. P. L. Taylor (NZ)	

ONE-DAY INTERNATIONAL AVERAGES
IN CALENDAR YEAR 2019

BATTING (500 runs, average 30.00)

		M	I	NO	R	HS	100	50	Avge	SR	4	6
1	†Shakib Al Hasan (B) ...	11	11	3	746	124*	2	7	93.25	95.88	70	4
2	H. E. van der Dussen (SA).	18	14	5	664	95	0	7	73.77	81.87	37	16
3	†D. A. Warner (A)	10	10	1	647	166	3	3	71.88	89.36	66	8
4	J. J. Roy (E)	14	12	0	845	153	3	6	70.41	118.18	91	26
5	F. du Plessis (SA).	19	17	5	814	112*	2	6	67.83	88.76	84	8
6	S. D. Hope (WI).	28	26	4	1,345	170	4	8	61.13	77.92	117	21
7	Babar Azam (P)	20	20	2	1,092	115	3	6	60.66	92.30	109	9
8	M. S. Dhoni (I).	18	16	6	600	87*	0	6	60.00	82.30	42	11
9	†B. A. Stokes (E)	20	17	5	719	89	0	7	59.91	92.53	59	18
10	V. Kohli (I).	26	25	2	1,377	123	5	7	59.86	96.36	133	8
11	K. S. Williamson (NZ). .	20	19	3	948	148	2	6	59.25	75.35	83	6
12	R. G. Sharma (I).	28	27	1	1,490	159	7	6	57.30	89.92	146	36
13	L. R. P. L. Taylor (NZ)	21	20	3	943	137	1	7	55.47	86.51	80	12
14	P. R. Stirling (Ire).	14	13	0	692	130	1	7	53.23	76.29	69	15
15	†E. J. G. Morgan (E)	21	18	3	791	148	2	5	52.73	112.19	57	41
16	†N. Pooran (WI).	19	17	3	728	118	1	5	52.00	110.13	67	27
17	A. J. Finch (A)	23	23	1	1,141	153*	4	6	51.86	89.42	98	36
18	J. E. Root (E)	22	20	2	910	107	3	4	50.55	92.85	83	3
19	†Haris Sohail (P)	15	15	2	654	130	2	3	50.30	90.83	54	10
20	Mushfiqur Rahim (B). . .	18	18	3	754	102*	1	5	50.26	90.08	62	8
21	†C. H. Gayle (WI)	17	15	0	753	162	2	5	50.20	109.76	55	56
22	†U. T. Khawaja (A)	22	22	0	1,085	104	2	8	49.31	84.89	107	5
23	†Q. de Kock (SA).	17	17	1	774	121	1	7	48.37	100.12	100	10
24	K. L. Rahul (I)	13	13	1	572	111	2	3	47.66	81.13	49	9
25	J. C. Buttler (E)	20	16	2	667	150	1	4	47.64	135.56	49	32
26	†Imam-ul-Haq (P)	21	21	2	904	151	3	3	47.57	79.29	79	8
27	A. Balbirnie (Ire)	14	13	1	567	145*	3	1	47.25	87.63	45	16
28	J. M. Bairstow (E)	20	18	0	844	128	3	4	46.88	102.92	106	20
29	†T. A. Carey (A)	23	20	6	605	85	0	4	43.21	97.42	69	3
30	†M. D. K. J. Perera (SL) .	16	15	0	646	111	2	3	43.06	99.84	79	4
31	Asghar Afghan (Afg) . . .	17	17	3	569	86	0	4	40.64	78.91	36	20
32	†Najibullah Zadran (Afg) .	17	16	3	509	104*	1	2	39.15	97.32	51	15
33	†S. O. Hetmyer (WI)	23	20	3	658	139	2	2	38.70	107.16	54	22
34	†S. Dhawan (I)	18	17	1	583	143	2	2	36.43	91.81	74	4
35	M. J. Guptill (NZ)	20	20	2	650	138	3	1	36.11	97.30	65	20
36	†Fakhar Zaman (P).	20	20	0	683	138	1	5	34.15	90.94	77	12
37	G. J. Maxwell (A)	23	22	3	635	98	0	3	33.42	132.29	67	21
38	B. K. G. Mendis (SL). . .	19	19	1	587	66	0	4	32.61	77.13	44	9
39	Rahmat Shah (Afg)	20	20	0	646	113	1	4	32.30	68.57	73	7

BOWLING (15 wickets, average 35.00)

		Style	O	M	R	W	BB	4I	Avge	SR	ER
1	N. Pokana (PNG).	LFM	76.3	7	292	20	3-25	0	14.60	22.95	3.81
2	M. A. Starc (A)	LF	92.2	5	502	27	5-26	4	18.59	20.51	5.43
3	J. D. S. Neesham (NZ). .	RFM	97	2	521	25	5-31	1	20.84	23.28	5.37
4	J. A. Richardson (A) . . .	RFM	71	8	361	17	4-26	1	21.23	25.05	5.08
5	P. J. Cummins (A)	RF	141.3	11	670	31	5-70	2	21.61	27.38	4.73
6	Usman Shinwari (P).	LFM	69	4	358	16	5-51	3	22.37	25.87	5.18
7	Mohammed Shami (I) . .	RFM	177.2	10	951	42	5-69	3	22.64	25.33	5.36
8	Shaheen Shah Afridi (P).	LFM	107.1	4	618	27	6-35	3	22.88	23.81	5.76
9	L. T. Ngidi (SA).	RFM	63.2	4	348	15	3-60	0	23.20	25.33	5.49
10	L. H. Ferguson (NZ) . . .	RF	159.4	5	830	35	4-37	2	23.71	27.37	5.19

		Style	O	M	R	W	BB	4I	Avge	SR	ER
11	Bhuvneshwar Kumar (I) .	RFM	149.5	7	784	33	4-31	2	23.75	27.24	5.23
12	T. A. Boult (NZ)	LFM	193.4	16	911	38	5-21	3	23.97	30.57	4.70
13	J. J. Bumrah (I).	RF	132.5	9	615	25	4-55	1	24.60	31.88	4.62
14	J. C. Archer (E)	RF	122.5	10	569	23	3-27	0	24.73	32.04	4.63
15	Mohammad Amir (P). . .	LFM	121	7	590	23	5-30	1	25.65	31.56	4.87
16	M. A. Wood (E).	RF	132.4	2	736	27	4-60	1	27.25	29.48	5.54
17	A. L. Phehlukwayo (SA)	RFM	115.3	4	611	22	4-22	1	27.77	31.50	5.29
18	Y. S. Chahal (I)	LB	142	0	815	29	6-42	2	28.10	29.37	5.73
19	Mustafizur Rahman (B) .	LFM	141.1	3	957	34	5-59	3	28.14	24.91	6.77
20	Imran Tahir (SA)	LB	140	4	622	22	4-29	1	28.27	38.18	4.44
21	W. B. Rankin (Ire)	RFM	110.5	5	585	20	3-40	0	29.25	33.25	5.27
22	L. E. Plunkett (E).	RFM	106	0	586	20	4-35	1	29.30	31.80	5.52
23	Gulbadeen Naib (Afg) . .	RFM	113.2	2	649	22	6-43	1	29.50	30.90	5.72
24	C. R. Woakes (E)	RFM	145	8	864	29	5-54	2	29.79	30.00	5.95
25	Dawlat Zadran (Afg) . . .	RFM	83	4	509	17	3-35	0	29.94	29.29	6.13
26	Mujeeb Zadran (Afg) . .	OB	140.5	10	575	19	3-14	0	30.26	44.47	4.08
27	M. J. Henry (NZ)	RFM	144.4	12	736	24	4-35	2	30.66	36.16	5.08
28	S. L. Malinga (SL)	RFM	140.2	7	831	27	4-43	1	30.77	31.18	5.92
29	K. Rabada (SA)	RF	155.1	11	771	24	3-43	0	32.12	38.79	4.96
30	J. P. Behrendorff (A) . . .	LFM	98.3	7	517	16	5-44	1	32.31	36.93	5.24
31	A. N. P. R. Fernando (SL) .	RFM	99.2	5	615	19	4-31	2	32.36	31.36	6.19
32	S. S. Cottrell (WI)	LFM	176.2	8	1,024	31	5-46	2	33.03	34.12	5.80
33	M. R. Adair (Ire)	RFM	80.4	3	509	15	4-19	2	33.93	32.26	6.30
34	O. R. Thomas (WI)	RFM	91.2	1	621	18	5-21	2	34.50	30.44	6.79
35	K. Yadav (I)	SLW	208	3	1,110	32	4-39	2	34.68	39.00	5.33

MOST DISMISSALS BY A WICKETKEEPER

Dis		M			Dis		M	
34	(29ct, 5st)	23	A. T. Carey (A)		24	(18ct, 6st)	20	J. C. Buttler (E)
32	(31ct, 1st)	27	S. D. Hope (WI)		21	(20ct, 1st)	18	Sarfraz Ahmed (P)
30	(28ct, 2st)	18	T. W. M. Latham (NZ)		20	(19ct, 1st)	17	Q. de Kock (SA)

Hope played one further one-day international when not keeping wicket, but took no catches.

MOST CATCHES IN THE FIELD

Ct	M			Ct	M	
21	26	V. Kohli (I)		17	24	S. S. Cottrell (WI)
18	22	J. E. Root (E)		16	19	F. du Plessis (SA)
18	27	J. O. Holder (WI)		15	23	G. J. Maxwell (A)

TWENTY20 INTERNATIONAL AVERAGES IN CALENDAR YEAR 2019

BATTING (350 runs, strike-rate 120.00)

		M	I	NO	R	HS	100	50	Avge	SR	4	6
1	†H. G. Munsey (Scot)	15	15	1	526	127*	1	3	37.57	**166.45**	47	34
2	B. R. S. de Silva (Kuwait)	10	10	1	358	103	1	2	39.77	165.74	29	24
3	T. P. Visée (Neth)	18	18	0	376	78	0	3	20.88	**156.01**	47	16
4	K. J. O'Brien (Ire)	23	23	0	729	124	1	3	31.69	155.43	67	36
5	T. H. David (Sing)	12	12	1	408	77	0	3	37.09	148.90	36	17
6	V. Kohli (I)	10	10	4	466	94*	0	5	77.66	**147.93**	29	23
7	T. P. Ura (PNG)	17	17	5	572	107*	1	4	47.66	147.04	41	30
8	P. Khadka (Nepal)	18	18	2	541	106*	1	3	33.81	145.82	60	25
9	A. Balbirnie (Ire)	21	20	2	601	83	0	3	33.38	**143.77**	71	11
10	K. L. Rahul (I)	9	9	1	356	91	0	4	44.50	142.40	35	14
11	P. R. Stirling (Ire)	20	20	2	748	91	0	8	41.55	140.60	90	23

		M	I	NO	R	HS	100	50	Avge	SR	4	6
12	R. D. Berrington (Scot)	15	15	3	380	76	0	1	31.66	**140.22**	31	17
13	†Syed Aziz (Malaysia)	14	14	2	415	87	0	4	34.58	**139.73**	43	16
14	M. G. Erasmus (Namibia)	16	14	3	407	72	0	4	37.00	**138.90**	33	20
15	R. G. Sharma (I).	14	14	0	396	85	0	4	28.28	**138.46**	33	22
16	Babar Azam (P)	10	10	1	374	90	0	4	41.55	**136.99**	41	7
17	Muhammad Tanveer (Qatar) . . .	15	15	4	428	57*	0	4	38.90	**129.30**	36	22
18	C. S. MacLeod (Scot).	15	14	2	440	74	0	3	36.66	**128.27**	46	8
19	†B. N. Cooper (Neth)	21	21	4	637	91*	0	5	37.47	**127.91**	56	20
20	Jatinder Singh (Oman).	14	14	2	399	68*	0	3	33.25	**127.07**	47	5
21	S. J. Baard (Namibia)	13	13	2	387	92	0	4	35.18	**126.88**	32	13
22	K. J. Coetzer (Scot)	13	13	0	351	89	0	3	27.00	**125.35**	38	13
23	N. S. Dhaliwal (Canada)	12	11	2	361	69	0	3	40.11	**124.05**	22	16
24	J. W. Jenner (Jersey)	17	17	2	365	71	0	3	24.33	**122.07**	24	14
25	M. P. O'Dowd (Neth)	24	24	0	702	69	0	6	29.25	**120.82**	69	16

BOWLING (15 wickets, economy-rate 7.00)

		Style	O	M	R	W	BB	4I	Avge	SR	ER
1	D. Ravu (PNG).	RFM	42.1	94	221	24	5-15	2	9.20	10.54	**5.24**
2	B. M. Scholtz (Namibia)	SLA	53	136	285	22	4-12	1	12.95	14.45	**5.37**
3	R. E. van der Merwe (Neth). . .	SLA	65.1	177	368	23	4-35	1	16.00	17.00	**5.64**
4	N. Vanua (PNG).	RM	50.2	97	286	21	5-17	2	13.61	14.38	**5.68**
5	J. N. Frylinck (Namibia)	LFM	42.1	127	240	21	4-21	1	11.42	12.04	**5.69**
6	N. Pokana (PNG).	LFM	51.5	101	298	17	3-21	0	17.52	18.29	**5.74**
7	C. W. Perchard (Jersey)	RM	46.5	83	275	20	5-17	2	13.75	14.05	**5.87**
8	Khawar Ali (Oman)	LB	47.3	111	289	21	4-16	1	13.76	13.57	**6.08**
9	Mohammad Nadeem (Oman) . .	RFM	51	141	318	18	4-23	1	17.66	17.00	**6.23**
10	J. J. Smit (Namibia)	LFM	37.1	100	234	16	3-19	0	14.62	13.93	**6.29**
11	Rohan Mustafa (UAE)	OB	50	117	315	20	4-18	1	15.75	15.00	**6.30**
12	C. Viljoen (Namibia)	RM	37.1	95	236	20	5-9	2	11.80	11.15	**6.34**
13	D. G. Blampied (Jersey).	LB	61.4	82	395	24	4-20	1	16.45	15.41	**6.40**
14	Aamer Kaleem (Oman)	SLA	36	102	231	17	5-15	2	13.58	12.70	**6.41**
15	A. Bohara (Nepal)	RM	54	122	350	16	4-35	1	21.87	20.25	**6.48**
16	S. Lamichhane (Nepal)	LB	59	172	384	28	4-20	1	13.71	12.64	**6.50**
17	D. L. Chahar (I).	RFM	31.5	93	208	16	6-7	1	13.00	11.93	**6.53**
18	M. R. Adair (Ire)	RFM	62.5	173	413	27	4-40	1	15.29	13.96	**6.57**
19	Rashid Khan (Afg)	LB	39	84	258	20	5-27	2	12.90	11.70	**6.61**
20	Saad Bin Zafar (Canada)	SLA	43	125	285	17	3-8	0	16.76	15.17	**6.62**
21	E. J. B. Miles (Jersey)	SLA	40	50	266	17	3-10	0	15.64	14.11	**6.65**
22	M. R. J. Watt (Scot)	SLA	48	113	323	23	3-18	0	14.04	12.52	**6.72**
23	Bilal Khan (Oman).	LFM	56	175	378	24	4-19	2	15.75	14.00	**6.75**
24	B. D. Glover (Neth)	RFM	65	188	448	28	4-12	2	16.00	13.92	**6.89**

Details of dot balls bowled are incomplete for Vanua, Pokana, Perchard, Blampied and Miles.

MOST DISMISSALS BY A WICKETKEEPER

Dis		M			Dis		M	
26	(23ct, 3st)	23	S. A. Edwards (Neth)		14	(10ct, 4st)	14	J. Vira (Vanuatu)
16	(15ct, 1st)	17	K. Doriga (PNG)		13	(9ct, 4st)	14	Hamza Tariq (Canada)
15	(10ct, 5st)	15	Z. E. Green (Namibia)		12	(8ct, 4st)	13	M. H. Cross (Scot)

Edwards, Green and Cross each played one further T20I when not keeping wicket, but took no catches.

MOST CATCHES IN THE FIELD

Ct		M			Ct		M	
17		17	B. D. H. Stevens (Jersey)		14		23	K. J. O'Brien (Ire)
16		17	J. W. Jenner (Jersey)		13		21	B. N. Cooper (Neth)
14		17	L. Siaka (PNG)					

OTHER FIRST-CLASS TOURS IN 2019

SRI LANKA A v IRELAND WOLVES IN 2018-19

A-Team Test matches (2): Sri Lanka A 1, Ireland Wolves 0
A-Team one-day internationals (5): Sri Lanka A 5, Ireland Wolves 0

Ireland's A-Team, known as the Wolves, undertook a month-long tour of Sri Lanka early in 2019, captained by 19-year-old Harry Tector, whose older brother, Jack, was also part of a youthful squad. Sri Lanka A, who included several with Test experience, won the first four-day game easily, but were surprised in the second, where the Wolves amassed 508 and made them follow on; they escaped thanks to Pathum Nissanka's double-century. Slow left-armers ruled the roost in the two Tests: Lasith Embuldeniya took 14 wickets, and Ireland's James Cameron-Dow 13. But the Irish bowlers were exposed in the 50-over series, with the Sri Lankans winning all five games by wide margins. Avishka Fernando piled up 523 runs, with three centuries, while the experienced Upul Tharanga hit two. Lorcan Tucker and Harry Tector replied with hundreds for Ireland Wolves.

Touring party *H. T. Tector (FC/50), M. R. Adair (FC/50), J. Cameron-Dow (FC/50), G. J. Delany (50), S. T. Doheny (FC), J. J. Garth (FC/50), S. C. Getkate (50), A. P. Gillespie (FC), J. B. Little (FC/50), B. J. McCarthy (FC/50), J. A. McCollum (FC/50), N. A. Rock (FC/50), J. N. K. Shannon (FC/50), J. B. Tector (FC/50), S. R. Thompson (50), L. J. Tucker (FC), C. A. Young (FC/50). *Coach:* P. Johnston.

First Test At Colombo (SSC), January 5–7, 2019. **Sri Lanka A won by ten wickets. ‡Ireland Wolves 153** (45.2 overs) (J. A. McCollum 76; A. M. S. Sahabh 4-47, L. Embuldeniya 4-46) **and 196** (54.3 overs) (J. N. K. Shannon 32; L. Embuldeniya 5-73); **Sri Lanka A 308** (77.1 overs) (T. A. M. Siriwardene 104, P. H. K. D. Mendis 91; J. Cameron-Dow 7-77, M. R. Adair 3-43) **and 44-0** (6.5 overs). *Ireland Wolves slumped to 62-6 on the first morning, and never recovered, as Sri Lanka A took a 1–0 lead with a day to spare. Left-arm spinner James Cameron-Dow took seven for 77.*

Second Test At Hambantota, January 13–16, 2019. **Drawn. Ireland Wolves 508-8 dec** (138 overs) (J. A. McCollum 72, S. T. Doheny 58, L. J. Tucker 80, N. A. Rock 85, M. R. Adair 32, J. J. Garth 45, J. Cameron-Dow 76*; C. Karunaratne 3-99, L. Embuldeniya 3-142) **and 89-3** (24 overs) (J. A. McCollum 45*); **‡Sri Lanka A 303** (73.2 overs) (A. K. Perera 127, S. Ashan 72; C. A. Young 3-76, J. Cameron-Dow 5-99) **and 468-7 dec** (105.1 overs) (P. Nissanka 217, P. H. K. D. Mendis 53, C. Karunaratne 100*; J. J. Garth 3-140). *A superb collective batting effort, then five more wickets for Cameron-Dow, enabled Ireland Wolves to enforce the follow-on. Pathum Nissanka's second double-century, and a maiden first-class hundred for Chamika Karunaratne, ensured a draw.*

First one-day international At Hambantota, January 19, 2019. **Sri Lanka A won by 60 runs. Sri Lanka A 365-5** (50 overs) (W. I. A. Fernando 128, W. U. Tharanga 66, T. A. M. Siriwardene 111*); **‡Ireland Wolves 305** (48.2 overs) (J. N. K. Shannon 67, L. J. Tucker 109, H. T. Tector 31, S. C. Getkate 37; H. I. A. Jayaratne 3-39). *Avishka Fernando, who hit five of Sri Lanka A's 13 sixes, put on 161 for the first wicket with Upul Tharanga, then 91 for the second with Milinda Siriwardene, who sprinted to 111* from 75 balls. The Wolves made a noble effort: wicketkeeper Lorcan Tucker hit his maiden List A century, finishing with 109 from 86, but the loss of Tucker and Harry Tector in four balls cooked the Irish goose.*

Second one-day international At Hambantota, January 21, 2019. **Sri Lanka A won by 175 runs. ‡Sri Lanka A 337-5** (50 overs) (W. I. A. Fernando 55, W. U. Tharanga 103, A. K. Perera 72*, P. H. K. D. Mendis 76); **Ireland Wolves 162** (35.5 overs) (M. R. Adair 43, S. C. Getkate 56; T. A. M. Siriwardene 4-26). *After Tharanga anchored another big total, there was less of a fight from the Wolves, who lost two wickets in Isuru Udana's opening over, and were soon 53-6.*

Third one-day international At Colombo (SSC), January 24, 2019. **Sri Lanka A won by eight wickets. ‡Ireland Wolves 268-6** (50 overs) (L. J. Tucker 36, H. T. Tector 103, S. C. Getkate 86; I. Udana 3-45); **Sri Lanka A 272-2** (31.1 overs) (W. I. A. Fernando 89, M. B. Ranasinghe 113*, A. K. Perera 35*). *A fifth-wicket stand of 178 between Harry Tector, who cracked a maiden List A* *century, and Shane Getkate set up a decent Irish total. But Sri Lanka A steamed past it, with Fernando and Minod Bhanuka Ranasinghe piling on 155 for the second wicket in 20 overs.*

Fourth one-day international At Colombo (SSC), January 26, 2019. **Sri Lanka A won by 202 runs.** ‡Sri Lanka A 353-6 (50 overs) (W. I. A. Fernando 139, M. B. Ranasinghe 34, A. K. Perera 56*, P. H. K. D. Mendis 50*); **Ireland Wolves** 151 (30.4 overs) (S. Singh 31; I. Udana 3-33, P. H. K. D. Mendis 3-34). *Fernando thrashed another century, hitting ten fours and seven sixes. After he was out in the 40th over, Angelo Perera and Kamindu Mendis added 102*. Mendis took three wickets as the Wolves subsided to another huge defeat.*

Fifth one-day international At Colombo (RPS), January 29, 2019. **Sri Lanka A won by 101 runs.** ‡Sri Lanka A 403-7 (50 overs) (W. I. A. Fernando 112, W. U. Tharanga 120, M. D. Shanaka 39, P. C. de Silva 50; G. J. Delany 3-58); **Ireland Wolves** 302 (50 overs) (S. R. Thompson 30, J. A. McCollum 43, S. Singh 41, L. J. Tucker 53, N. A. Rock 78; D. A. S. Gunaratne 4-51). *Fernando rounded off a superb series with his third century, and an opening stand of 206 in 29 overs with Tharanga. Josh Little's nine overs cost 89, as Sri Lanka A roared past 400. Ireland Wolves were never going to avoid the whitewash, but they did have the satisfaction of passing 300, with 18-year-old left-hander Neil Rock posting a maiden List A half-century.*

INDIA A v SRI LANKA A IN 2019

A-Team Test matches (2): India A 2, Sri Lanka A 0
A-Team one-day internationals (6): India A 2, Sri Lanka A 2

Sri Lanka A, captained by Ashan Priyanjan, bounced back well from thumping defeats in the two four-day games, to share the one-day series. India A had steamrollered the first red-ball match, Priyank Panchal and Abhimanyu Easwaran opening with a stand of 352. Niroshan Dickwella, temporarily out of favour with the full Sri Lankan team, hit a century in reply, but it was not enough. Shehan Jayasuriya made 320 runs for once out in the one-dayers, with two centuries. But he was outgunned by India A's opener Ruturaj Gaikwad, whose 470 included 187 not out in a rain-reduced first game, and an undefeated 125 in the second; his other innings were 84 and 74.

Touring party *S. M. A. Priyanjan (FC/50), M. M. M. S. Cooray (FC/50), A. Dananjaya (FC/50), D. P. D. N. Dickwella (FC/50), A. M. Fernando (FC/50), M. V. T. Fernando (FC), M. D. Gunathilleke (50), H. I. A. Jayaratne (50), G. S. N. F. G. Jayasuriya (50), C. Karunaratne (FC/50), C. B. R. L. S. Kumara (FC/50), P. H. K. D. Mendis (FC/50), P. Nissanka (50), P. A. R. P. Perera (FC), P. M. Pushpakumara (FC), P. B. B. Rajapaksa (FC/50), W. S. R. Samarawickrama (FC/50), P. A. D. L. R. Sandakan (FC/50), M. D. Shanaka (50). *Coach:* R. L. Dias.

D. V. T. Chameera and L. Embuldeniya were originally selected, but withdrew injured, and were replaced by A. M. Fernando and Pushpakumara.

First Test At Belgaum, May 25–27. **India A won by an innings and 205 runs.** ‡India A 622-5 dec (142 overs) (P. K. Panchal 160, A. R. Easwaran 233, Anmolpreet Singh 116*, S. D. Lad 76); **Sri Lanka A** 232 (63.4 overs) (W. S. R. Samarawickrama 31, S. M. A. Priyanjan 49, D. P. D. N. Dickwella 103; R. D. Chahar 4-78) **and** 185 (52.3 overs) (W. S. R. Samarawickrama 48, S. M. A. Priyanjan 39; R. D. Chahar 4-45). *PoM:* A. R. Easwaran. *Priyank Panchal and Abhimanyu Easwaran batted almost throughout the first day against an attack containing five Test bowlers, putting on 352. Easwaran continued next morning to his highest score, then Anmolpreet Singh added another century, putting on 153 in 31 overs with Siddhesh Lad, as the total crested 600. Sri Lanka A couldn't match that in two attempts, despite Niroshan Dickwella's feisty hundred.*

Second Test At Hubli, May 31–June 3. **India A won by 152 runs.** ‡India A 269 (69.1 overs) (Anmolpreet Singh 65, S. D. Lad 32, K. Srikar Bharat 117; C. B. R. L. S. Kumara 4-53, P. A. D. L. R. Sandakan 4-64) **and** 372 (82.2 overs) (Anmolpreet Singh 60, S. D. Lad 58, K. Srikar Bharat 60, R. D. Chahar 84, J. Yadav 53; M. V. T. Fernando 3-68, P. A. D. L. R. Sandakan 3-87); **Sri Lanka A** 212 (60 overs) (D. P. D. N. Dickwella 39, P. A. R. P. Perera 36, P. H. K. D. Mendis 68; J. Yadav 3-24) **and** 277 (66.4 overs) (P. B. B. Rajapaksa 110, P. H. K. D. Mendis 46, M. V. T. Fernando 32; R. D. Chahar 5-112). *PoM:* K. Srikar Bharat. *After their first-match heroics, Panchal and Easwaran both fell for ducks, but India A regrouped well. Sri Lanka A never threatened a target of 430, despite Bhanuka Rajapaksa's first representative century since Under-19 days.*

First one-day international   At Belgaum, June 6. **India A won by 48 runs. India A 317-4** (42 overs) (R. D. Gaikwad 187*, Anmolpreet Singh 65, I. P. Kishan 45; C. B. R. L. S. Kumara 3-62); ‡**Sri Lanka A 269-6** (42 overs) (G. S. N. F. G. Jayasuriya 108*, M. D. Shanaka 44). *PoM:* R. D. Gaikwad. *In an innings shortened to 42 overs, opener Ruturaj Gaikwad thrashed 187* from 136 balls. Sri Lanka A fell short, despite Shehan Jayasuriya's workmanlike century.*

Second one-day international   At Belgaum, June 8. **India A won by ten wickets. Sri Lanka A 242-7** (50 overs) (G. S. N. F. G. Jayasuriya 101, H. I. A. Jayaratne 79*); ‡**India A 243-0** (33.3 overs) (R. D. Gaikwad 125*, S. Gill 109 retired hurt). *PoM:* S. Gill. *Jayasuriya and Gaikwad again traded hundreds – and India A again came out on top. Gaikwad and Shubman Gill shared an opening stand of 226*, before Gill went down with cramp, and retired after 30 overs.*

Third one-day international   At Belgaum, June 10. **Sri Lanka A won by six wickets** (DLS). ‡**India A 291-8** (50 overs) (P. Chopra 129, D. Hooda 53; C. Karunaratne 5-36); **Sri Lanka A 266-4** (43.5 overs) (D. P. D. N. Dickwella 62, M. M. M. S. Cooray 88, G. S. N. F. G. Jayasuriya 66*, M. D. Shanaka 36*). *PoM:* C. Karunaratne. *Sri Lanka A's target was revised to 266 in 46 overs.*

Fourth one-day international   At Hubli, June 13. **No result. India A 208-4** (22 overs) (R. D. Gaikwad 84, Anmolpreet Singh 85*); ‡**Sri Lanka A 10-1** (1.5 overs). *Gaikwad, rested for the previous game, was at it again: he hit 84 from 59, and put on 125 with Anmolpreet, in a match reduced to 22 overs. The weather intervened again early in the Sri Lankan chase.*

Fifth one-day international   At Hubli, June 14. **No result.** ‡**Sri Lanka A 22-1** (3.3 overs) **v India A.** *An attempt to replay the previous day's washout was scuppered by yet more rain.*

Sixth one-day international   At Hubli, June 15. **Sri Lanka A won by seven wickets. India A 259** (50 overs) (R. D. Gaikwad 74, R. K. Bhui 38, D. Hooda 37; M. K. P. A. D. Perera 3-51); ‡**Sri Lanka A 260-3** (47.4 overs) (D. P. D. N. Dickwella 111, M. M. M. S. Cooray 61, G. S. N. F. G. Jayasuriya 45*, S. M. A. Priyanjan 33*; R. Shreyas Gopal 3-49). *PoM:* D. P. D. N. Dickwella. *Gaikwad rounded off a remarkable series with 74 from 73 balls: he finished with 470 runs at 235, and a strike-rate of 129. However, Dickwella's century spirited Sri Lanka A to a share of the spoils.*

BANGLADESH A v AFGHANISTAN A IN 2019

A-Team Test matches (2): Bangladesh A 0, Afghanistan A 1
A-Team one-day internationals (5): Bangladesh A 2, Afghanistan A 2

Afghanistan gave notice of their growing depth at international level when their A-team, captained by Nasir Ahmadzai, won the first four-day game, before the second was spoiled by rain. The one-dayers were shared, with some young talent coming to the fore: Ibrahim Zadran made 273 runs, and Rahmanullah Gurbaz 201. Both made centuries – and both were only 17. For Bangladesh A, left-hand opener Mohammad Naim – a veteran of 19 – scored consistently, and hit 126 in the final one-dayer, where his side squared the series after losing the first two.

Touring party   *Nasir Ahmadzai (FC/50), Afsar Zazai (FC), Bahir Shah (FC), Darwish Rasooli (FC/50), Fareed Ahmad (50), Fazal Niazai (FC/50), Ibrahim Zadran (FC/50), Karim Janat (50), Mirwais Ashraf (50), Munir Ahmad (50), Naveen-ul-Haq (FC), Qais Ahmad (FC/50), Rahmanullah Gurbaz (FC/50), Sayed Shirzad (FC/50), Shahidullah (FC/50), Sharafuddin Ashraf (FC/50), Usman Ghani (FC/50), Waqarullah Ishaq (FC), Yamin Ahmadzai (FC), Zia-ur-Rehman (FC/50).

First Test   At Khulna, July 5–8. **Afghanistan A won by seven wickets. Bangladesh A 253** (78.3 overs) (Mohammad Naim 49, Anamul Haque 121*, Afif Hossain 50; Yamin Ahmadzai 3-57, Qais Ahmad 3-80) **and 175** (58.4 overs) (Imrul Kayes 34, Afif Hossain 41; Qais Ahmad 7-65); ‡**Afghanistan A 257** (78.2 overs) (Usman Ghani 39, Ibrahim Zadran 37, Afsar Zazai 45, Sharafuddin Ashraf 31, Qais Ahmad 46*; Sanjamul Islam 3-81, Kamrul Islam 3-47, Tanveer Haider 3-31) **and 173-3** (58.2 overs) (Ibrahim Zadran 76*, Nasir Ahmadzai 59*). *PoM:* Qais Ahmad. *Wicketkeeper Anamul Haque's 121*, which spanned 342 minutes, gave the Bangladeshis a chance. But 18-year-old leg-spinner Qais Ahmad demolished their second effort, and Afghanistan A steamed home on the fourth day.*

Second Test   At Chittagong (ZAC), July 12–15. **Drawn. Bangladesh A 200** (77.3 overs) (Mohammad Naim 65, Raqibul Hasan 61; Yamin Ahmadzai 3-42, Sharafuddin Ashraf 3-49, Qais Ahmad 3-57); ‡**Afghanistan A 163-2** (44 overs) (Ibrahim Zadran 96, Bahir Shah 52*). *PoM:* Ibrahim Zadran. *Only 41 overs were possible across the first three days, with none on the second.*

First one-day international   At Chittagong (ZAC), July 19. **Afghanistan A won by ten wickets.** ‡**Bangladesh A 201-8** (50 overs) (Afif Hossain 59, Farhad Reza 30); **Afghanistan A 202-0** (43.5 overs) (Rahmanullah Gurbaz 105*, Ibrahim Zadran 86*). *PoM:* Rahmanullah Gurbaz. *Afghanistan A's talented openers, both 17, sprinted home with 37 balls to spare.*

Second one-day international   At Chittagong (ZAC), July 21. **Afghanistan A won by four wickets. Bangladesh A 278-9** (50 overs) (Imrul Kayes 40, Mithun Ali 85, Mohammad Naim 49, Sabbir Rahman 35; Karim Janat 3-43, Fazal Niazai 3-48); ‡**Afghanistan A 281-6** (49.1 overs) (Ibrahim Zadran 127, Sharafuddin Ashraf 36*). *PoM:* Ibrahim Zadran. *Another mature innings from Ibrahim Zadran, who clouted seven sixes, helped Afghanistan A go 2–0 up. There was still a lot to do when he was out at 244-6 in the 47th, but Sharafuddin Ashraf (36* off 17) and Fazal Niazai (15*) clouted 37* in 18 balls.*

Third one-day international   At Chittagong (ZAC), July 24. **Bangladesh A won by seven wickets. Afghanistan A 122** (32.4 overs) (Abu Jayed 4-28, Mehedi Hasan 3-24); ‡**Bangladesh A 123-3** (30.3 overs) (Fazle Mahmud 57*). *PoM:* Abu Jayed. *Rahmanullah fell for a duck this time, the first of four wickets for seamer Abu Jayed, and Afghanistan A were soon 50-5.*

Fourth one-day international   At Savar, July 27. **No result** (DLS). **Bangladesh A 176** (40 overs) (Imrul Kayes 33, Afif Hossain 45; Naveen-ul-Haq 5-40); ‡**Afghanistan A 57-0** (8.2 overs) (Ibrahim Zadran 30*). *After seamer Naveen-ul-Haq's first List A five-for, Afghanistan A's target was revised to 187 in 40 overs. They seemed set for a series-clinching victory when the weather closed in.*

Fifth one-day international   At Savar, July 29. **Bangladesh A won by 62 runs. Bangladesh A 262-9** (50 overs) (Mohammad Naim 126, Afif Hossain 53; Karim Janat 3-73); ‡**Afghanistan A 200** (45.1 overs) (Rahmanullah Gurbaz 54, Nasir Ahmadzai 47, Sharafuddin Ashraf 35; Yeasin Arafat 3-40). *PoM:* Mohammad Naim. *Bangladesh A squared the series after Mohammad Naim's 126 set up a winning total.*

WEST INDIES A v INDIA A IN 2019

A-Team one-day internationals (5): West Indies A 1, India A 4
A-Team Test matches (3): West Indies A 0, India A 2

India A emphasised their bench strength with a dominant display, winning six of the eight international matches. Much of the drama came before the trip, when opener Prithvi Shaw was withdrawn after an inadvertent doping violation – he had bought over-the-counter cough syrup which turned out to contain a banned ingredient. Shaw's replacement, Ruturaj Gaikwad, collected 207 runs in the one-dayers, although he was pipped by the 19-year-old left-hander Shubman Gill (218). Gill also topped the charts in the four-day games, 204 of his 244 runs coming in one innings, at the Brian Lara Stadium in Trinidad. Slow left-armer Shahbaz Nadeem winkled out 15 wickets in the red-ball matches, and off-spinner Krishnappa Gowtham 12. For West Indies A, the leading performer was Sunil Ambris from St Vincent, with 161 against the white ball, and 195 against the red. Barbados fast bowler Chemar Holder claimed 15 wickets in the four-day games.

Touring party   *G. H. Vihari (FC/50), Aavesh Khan (FC/50), M. A. Agarwal (FC), K. K. Ahmed (50), Anmolpreet Singh (FC/50), D. L. Chahar (50), R. D. Chahar (50), S. R. Dube (FC), A. R. Easwaran (FC), R. D. Gaikwad (50), S. Gill (FC/50), K. Gowtham (FC), S. S. Iyer (50), I. P. Kishan (50), M. Markande (FC), S. Nadeem (FC), P. K. Panchal (FC), M. K. Pandey (50), K. H. Pandya (50), A. R. Patel (50), W. P. Saha (FC), N. Saini (50), S. Sandeep Warrier (FC), M. Siraj (FC), K. Srikar Bharat (FC), M. S. Washington Sundar (50), U. T. Yadav (FC). *Coach:* R. Dravid.
    Pandey captained in the 50-over matches. P. P. Shaw was originally selected, but was banned after failing a drugs test; he was replaced by Gaikwad.

First one-day international   At Coolidge, Antigua, July 11. **India A won by 65 runs.** ‡**India A 190** (48.5 overs) (S. S. Iyer 77, G. H. Vihari 34; A. Jordan 3-43, R. L. Chase 4-19); **West Indies A 125** (35.5 overs) (J. L. Carter 41*, R. Powell 41; K. K. Ahmed 3-16). *PoM:* S. S. Iyer. *Four wickets* *for captain Roston Chase's off-breaks – and three for his Barbados team-mate, fast bowler Akeem Jordan – appeared to have put West Indies A on top. But they were soon 30-4, with left-arm seamer Khaleel Ahmed taking three, and slipped to a heavy defeat.*

Second one-day international   At North Sound, Antigua, July 14. **India A won by 65 runs. India A 255-8** (50 overs) (R. D. Gaikwad 85, S. Gill 62; R. Shepherd 4-36); ‡**West Indies A 190** (43.5 overs) (R. A. Reifer 71, R. Shepherd 34*; N. Saini 5-46). *PoM:* R. D. Gaikwad. *Four wickets for Guyana seamer Romario Shepherd meant India A failed to build on an opening stand of 151 between Ruturaj Gaikwad and Shubman Gill. But West Indies A nosedived from 47-1 to 84-6, en route to a second 65-run defeat in four days.*

Third one-day international   At North Sound, Antigua, July 16. **India A won by 148 runs.** ‡**India A 295-6** (50 overs) (S. Gill 77, S. S. Iyer 47, M. K. Pandey 100); **West Indies A 147** (34.2 overs) (S. W. Ambris 30, K. M. A. Paul 34; K. H. Pandya 5-25). *PoM:* M. K. Pandey. *India A captain Manish Pandey spanked 100 from 87 balls, with five sixes, to clinch the series. West Indies A were 89-2, before slow left-armer Krunal Pandya took the first of his five wickets.*

Fourth one-day international   At Coolidge, Antigua, July 19. **West Indies A won by five runs. West Indies A 298-9** (50 overs) (S. W. Ambris 46, D. C. Thomas 70, R. L. Chase 84, J. L. Carter 50; K. K. Ahmed 4-67, Aavesh Khan 3-62); ‡**India A 293-9** (50 overs) (K. H. Pandya 45, M. S. Washington Sundar 45, A. R. Patel 81*). *PoM:* R. L. Chase. *West Indies A finally pulled off a victory – just. After solid innings from Devon Thomas and Chase, Jonathan Carter hit 50 from 43 to lift the total close to 300. When India A were 160-6, it looked more than enough, but Akshar Patel gave the home side a scare, clattering 81* from 63 balls, and sharing stands of 60 with Washington Sundar and 69 with Ahmed, who followed his four wickets with 15 runs. India A started the last over needing eight but, after Navdeep Saini was run out, could manage only two singles.*

Fifth one-day international   At Coolidge, Antigua, July 21. **India A won by eight wickets.** ‡**West Indies A 236** (47.4 overs) (S. W. Ambris 61, S. E. Rutherford 65, K. A. Pierre 35*); **India A 237-2** (33 overs) (R. D. Gaikwad 99, S. Gill 69, S. S. Iyer 61*). *PoM:* R. D. Gaikwad. *India A made it 4–1 with another comfortable victory, set up by Gaikwad's successive stands of 110 with Gill (69 off 40 balls) and Shreyas Iyer (61* off 64).*

First Test   At North Sound, Antigua, July 24–27. **India A won by six wickets.** ‡**West Indies A 228** (66.5 overs) (J. Blackwood 53, R. R. S. Cornwall 59; S. Nadeem 5-62) **and 180** (77 overs) (M. V. Hodge 36, S. S. J. Brooks 53, R. L. Chase 32; M. Siraj 3-38, S. Nadeem 5-47); **India A 312** (104.3 overs) (P. K. Panchal 49, S. Gill 40, G. H. Vihari 31, W. P. Saha 66, S. R. Dube 71; M. L. Cummins 4-40) **and 97-4** (30 overs). *This match hinged on a sixth-wicket partnership of 124 between Wriddhaman Saha and Shivam Dube, which turned a probable deficit into a lead of 84. Slow left-armer Shahbaz Nadeem then took his match haul to 10-109 as the home batsmen underperformed again, and India A strolled home on the fourth morning.*

Second Test   At Port-of-Spain, Trinidad, July 31–August 3. **India A won by seven wickets.** ‡**West Indies A 318** (113 overs) (K. C. Brathwaite 36, M. V. Hodge 65, S. S. J. Brooks 53, S. O. Dowrich 36, R. R. S. Cornwall 56*; M. Siraj 3-63, M. Markande 3-79) **and 149** (39.5 overs) (S. W. Ambris 71, J. Blackwood 31; S. Sandeep Warrier 3-43, K. Gowtham 5-17); **India A 190** (47 overs) (P. K. Panchal 58, S. R. Dube 79; C. K. Holder 5-54, R. Shepherd 3-29) **and 278-3** (79.1 overs) (P. K. Panchal 68, M. A. Agarwal 81, A. R. Easwaran 59*, Anmolpreet Singh 51*). *PoM:* P. K. Panchal. *India A took the series with another come-from-behind victory, this time conceding a first-innings lead of 128 after Chemar Holder reduced them to 20-5. There were no such alarms in the second innings, as a target of 278 was chased down with ease. Priyank Panchal and Mayank Agarwal supplied an opening stand of 150 and, after three quick wickets, Abhimanyu Easwaran and Anmolpreet Singh put on 100*.*

Third Test   At Tarouba, Trinidad, August 6–9. **Drawn. India A 201** (67.5 overs) (M. A. Agarwal 33, G. H. Vihari 55, W. P. Saha 62; C. K. Holder 3-47, A. Frazer 3-53) **and 365-4 dec** (90 overs) (S. Gill 204*, G. H. Vihari 118*); ‡**West Indies A 194** (72.4 overs) (J. L. Solozano 69*, S. W. Ambris 43; K. Gowtham 6-67) **and 314-6** (109 overs) (J. L. Solozano 92, B. A. King 77, S. W. Ambris 69; S. Nadeem 5-103). *Gill became the youngest to score a double-century for an Indian representative side, aged 19 years 334 days; Gautham Gambhir was 20 when he hit 218 for the Indian Board President's XI against the Zimbabwean tourists at Vijayawada in 2001-02. It looked likely to bring a 3–0 sweep, but the West Indies A batting came together at last, and they survived the final day. Local left-hander Jeremy Solozano made 92 from 251 balls, Brandon King contributed a sparky 77, and Sunil Ambris hung on until the draw was all but assured.*

INDIA A v SOUTH AFRICA A IN 2019

A-Team one-day internationals (5): India A 4, South Africa A 1
A-Team Test matches (2): India A 1, South Africa A 0

Just before the full South African side arrived in India, their A-Team paid a fact-finding visit. Several of the players stayed on to join up with the main party, including Aiden Markram, who captained in the red-ball matches, and white-ball skipper Temba Bavuma. India A proved too strong in the 50-over games, all affected by the weather. The Indians shuffled their side: no one played in all five matches, although Shivam Dube made 155 runs for once out in four. South Africa A opener Reeza Hendricks hit the only limited-overs century, in a valiant rearguard in the opening game, but undistinguished batting in the first four-day match cost his side that series. The jury remained out on the value of the preparation: Markram hit 161 in the second unofficial Test, but in the real thing a few weeks later bagged a pair in Pune, and was dropped.

Touring party *A. K. Markram (FC), T. Bavuma (50), M. P. Breetzke (50), T. B. de Bruyn (FC), C. J. Dala (50), B. C. Fortuin (50), M. Z. Hamza (FC), B. E. Hendricks (50), R. R. Hendricks (FC), M. Jansen (FC/50), H. Klaasen (FC/50), G. F. Linde (FC/50), J. N. Malan (50), P. J. Malan (FC), E. M. Moore (FC), P. W. A. Mulder (FC), S. Muthusamy (FC), L. T. Ngidi (FC), A. A. Nortje (50), V. D. Philander (FC), D. L. Piedt (FC), S. Qeshile (50), L. L. Sipamla (FC/50), K. Verreynne (50), K. Zondo (FC/50). *Coach:* M. Maketa.

Bavuma captained in the 50-over matches.

First one-day international At Thiruvananthapuram, August 29. **India A won by 69 runs. India A 327-6** (47 overs) (S. Gill 46, M. K. Pandey 39, I. P. Kishan 37, S. R. Dube 79*, A. R. Patel 60*); ‡**South Africa A 258** (45 overs) (R. R. Hendricks 110, K. Zondo 30, H. Klaasen 58; Y. S. Chahal 5-47). *PoM:* A. R. Patel. *When Anrich Nortje removed Krunal Pandya in the 36th over, India A were 206-6. But Shivam Dube (79* from 60 balls, with six sixes) and Akshar Patel (60* from 36) piled on 121* in the last 11 – it had become a 47-over match after a delayed start – and the total proved beyond the tourists, despite Reeza Hendricks's 13th List A century.*

Second one-day international At Thiruvananthapuram, August 31. **India A won by two wickets. South Africa A 162-5** (21 overs) (T. Bavuma 40, H. Klaasen 31, G. F. Linde 52*); ‡**India A 163-8** (20 overs) (Anmolpreet Singh 30, I. P. Kishan 55). *PoM:* I. P. Kishan. *Another rain reduced this to a 21-over match. George Linde blasted 52* from 25 balls, with five sixes, at the end of South Africa A's innings, but was matched by Ishan Kishan (55 from 24).*

Third one-day international At Thiruvananthapuram, September 2. **India A won by four wickets.** ‡**South Africa A 207-8** (30 overs) (J. N. Malan 37, M. P. Breetzke 36, H. Klaasen 44); **India A 208-6** (27.5 overs) (I. P. Kishan 40, M. K. Pandey 81, S. R. Dube 45*). *PoM:* M. K. Pandey. *The weather forced a 30-over match this time.*

Fourth one-day international At Thiruvananthapuram, September 4–5. **South Africa A won by four runs** (DLS). **South Africa A 137-1** (25 overs) (R. R. Hendricks 60*); ‡**India A 188-9** (25 overs) (S. Dhawan 52, S. R. Dube 31; A. A. Nortje 3-36, M. Jansen 3-25, L. L. Sipamla 3-55). *India A's target was revised to 193 in 25; they declined from 161-3 to 178-9 inside four overs.*

Fifth one-day international At Thiruvananthapuram, September 6. **India A won by 36 runs.** ‡**India A 204-4** (20 overs) (S. Dhawan 51, S. V. Samson 91, S. S. Iyer 36); **South Africa A 168** (20 overs) (R. R. Hendricks 59, K. Verreynne 44; S. N. Thakur 3-9). *PoM:* S. V. Samson. *Reduced to 20 overs a side. Sanju Samson strong-armed 91 from 48 balls, with seven sixes, and put on 135 in 12.3 overs for the second wicket with opener Shikhar Dhawan.*

First Test At Thiruvananthapuram, September 9. **India A won by seven wickets. South Africa A 164** (51.5 overs) (D. L. Piedt 33, M. Jansen 45*; S. N. Thakur 3-29, K. Gowtham 3-64) **and 186** (58.5 overs) (M. Z. Hamza 44, H. Klaasen 48, P. W. A. Mulder 46; S. Nadeem 3-21); ‡**India A 303** (87.5 overs) (R. D. Gaikwad 30, S. Gill 90, K. Srikar Bharat 33, J. S. Saxena 61*, S. N. Thakur 34; L. T. Ngidi 3-50, D. L. Piedt 3-84) **and 49-3** (9.4 overs). *PoM:* J. S. Saxena. *Both South Africa A openers fell for ducks on the first morning, and they were soon 22-5.*

Second Test At Mysore, September 17–20. **Drawn. India A 417** (123 overs) (S. Gill 92, K. K. Nair 78, W. P. Saha 60, S. R. Dube 68, J. S. Saxena 48*; P. W. A. Mulder 3-47, D. L. Piedt 3-78) **and 202-3 dec** (70 overs) (P. K. Panchal 109, A. R. Easwaran 37, K. K. Nair 51*); ‡**South Africa A**

400 (109.3 overs) (A. K. Markram 161, T. B. de Bruyn 41, P. W. A. Mulder 131*; S. Nadeem 3-76, K. Yadav 4-121). *PoM:* A. K. Markram. *Aiden Markram led a disciplined reply to India A's big total: he faced 253 balls, and put on 155 with Wiaan Mulder in a sixth-wicket partnership that spanned 48 overs. Priyank Panchal enlivened the final day with a classy century.*

SRI LANKA A v BANGLADESH A IN 2019-20

A-Team Test matches (3): Sri Lanka A 0, Bangladesh A 0
A-Team one-day internationals (3): Sri Lanka A 1, Bangladesh A 2

Bangladesh showed their representative teams were no longer pushovers away from home, sharing a run-filled four-day series, before emerging victorious in the one-dayers. Mominul Haque, the captain, led a strong batting display with 117 in the third Test. For the home side, Kamindu Mendis was in fine form, adding one-day runs to a first-class 169, while Pathum Nissanka and Sangeeth Cooray also caught the eye with centuries.

Touring party *Mominul Haque (FC), Abu Haider (50), Abu Jayed (FC/50), Afif Hossain (50), Anamul Haque (FC/50), Ariful Haque (50), Ebadat Hossain (FC/50), Jahurul Islam (FC), Mehedi Hasan Miraz (FC), Mehedi Hasan Rana (FC/50), Mithun Ali (FC/50), Mohammad Naim (50), Nazmul Hossain (FC/50), Nurul Hasan (FC/50), Rishad Hossain (FC), Saif Hasan (50), Salauddin Sakil (FC), Sanjamul Islam (50), Shadman Islam (FC), Soumya Sarkar (FC). *Coach:* S. G. Helmot.
Mithun Ali captained in the 50-over matches.

First Test   At Katunayake, September 23–26, 2019. **Sri Lanka A v Bangladesh A. Abandoned.**

Second Test   At Hambantota, September 29–October 1, 2019. **Drawn.** ‡**Bangladesh A 360** (120.1 overs) (Jahurul Islam 90, Shadman Islam 53, Mithun Ali 92, Mehedi Hasan Miraz 57; A. M. Fernando 3-59, R. T. M. Wanigamuni 3-57) **and 1-0** (1 over); **Sri Lanka A 450** (121.1 overs) (M. M. M. S. Cooray 104, P. H. K. D. Mendis 169, S. M. A. Priyanjan 37, P. A. R. P. Perera 61; Mehedi Hasan Miraz 5-150). *This match was shifted from Galle after bad weather, and reduced to a three-day game, which left little scope for a result. Sangeeth Cooray and Kamindu Mendis put on 165 for the second wicket.*

Third Test   At Hambantota, October 4–7, 2019. **Drawn.** ‡**Sri Lanka A 268** (90.2 overs) (P. Nissanka 85, P. H. K. D. Mendis 62, K. I. C. Asalanka 44; Mehedi Hasan Miraz 7-84) **and 357-2** (107 overs) (P. Nissanka 192, M. M. M. S. Cooray 89, P. H. K. D. Mendis 67*); **Bangladesh A 330** (83.1 overs) (Shadman Islam 77, Mominul Haque 117, Nurul Hasan 36, Mehedi Hasan Miraz 38*; A. M. S. Sahahab 5-63, N. G. R. P. Jayasuriya 3-114). *Pathum Nissanka's 192 ensured another draw, after Mehedi Hasan's off-breaks, followed by a solid batting display, had brought the Bangladeshis a first-innings lead of 62.*

First one-day international   At Colombo (RPS), October 9, 2019. **Sri Lanka A won by seven wickets.** ‡**Bangladesh A 116** (33.3 overs) (Saif Hasan 32; S. M. A. Priyanjan 4-10); **Sri Lanka A 120-3** (25.5 overs) (S. M. A. Priyanjan 50*). *Sri Lanka A's captain Ashan Priyanjan dominated this low-scoring encounter, following four wickets for his seamers with a well-paced 50* after his side dipped to 51-3.*

Second one-day international   At Colombo (RPS), October 10, 2019. **Bangladesh A won by one wicket. Sri Lanka A 226-9** (50 overs) (P. H. K. D. Mendis 61, P. A. R. P. Perera 52); ‡**Bangladesh A 227-9** (50 overs) (Mohammad Naim 68, Mithun Ali 52; R. T. M. Wanigamuni 3-40). *Bangladesh A squared the series in a last-ball thriller: with the No. 11 at the other end, Sanjamul Islam (11*) squeezed Ramesh Mendis Wanigamuni for the winning run.*

Third one-day international   At Colombo (RPS), October 12, 2019. **Bangladesh A won by 98 runs** (DLS). **Bangladesh A 322-9** (50 overs) (Saif Hasan 117, Mohammad Naim 66, Mithun Ali 32, Extras 32; M. V. T. Fernando 3-69, S. A. Fernando 4-50); ‡**Sri Lanka A 130-6** (24.4 overs) (P. H. K. D. Mendis 55, S. M. A. Priyanjan 34). *Bangladesh A claimed the series when rain stopped play with Sri Lanka A hopelessly adrift of a target of 229. The tourists' openers, Saif Hasan and Mohammad Naim, had put on 120 to set a platform for an imposing total.*

For England Lions in India in 2018-19, see page 957. For Australia A in England in 2019, see page 778.

OTHER INTERNATIONAL MATCHES IN 2019

ICC WORLD CRICKET LEAGUE DIVISION TWO IN 2019

1 Namibia   2 Oman   3 Papua New Guinea   4 USA

The fifth and final instalment of the World Cricket League's second division was played in Namibia early in 2019. The prize on offer for the top four teams was official one-day international status, plus a place in the revamped World Cup League Two, effectively a new second tier for ODI cricket. Surprise packets Oman topped the table, but lost to the hosts in the final, while three wins proved enough for the United States to finish third in the group stage, and claim the prize of their first official 50-over internationals since the 2004 Champions Trophy. The vital fourth place, though, boiled down to hundredths and thousandths on net run-rate: Papua New Guinea retained ODI status by the narrowest of margins, pipping Canada who, along with Hong Kong, were consigned to the third tier.

Although Hong Kong finished bottom, they had the leading scorer in Anshuman Rath, their 22-year-old captain, whose 290 runs included an unbeaten century in the opening game, against Canada. Sadly for Hong Kong, this was likely to be the last they would see of the prolific Rath, who moved to India with the aim of qualifying to play for Vidarbha in the Ranji Trophy. The leading wicket-taker was Pakistan-born Ali Khan – a fast bowler with a wicked yorker – who took 17 at 12 for the United States, including five for 46 in an exciting two-run victory over Namibia. But Khan was also missing later in the year, after declining a central contract with the new American board.

FINAL TABLE

50-over league plus play-offs

	P	W	L	Pts	NRR
OMAN	5	4	1	8	−0.04
NAMIBIA	5	3	2	6	1.39
UNITED STATES OF AMERICA	5	3	2	6	0.70
PAPUA NEW GUINEA	5	2	3	4	−0.40
Canada	5	2	3	4	−0.41
Hong Kong	5	1	4	2	−1.44

Fifth place play-off   At Windhoek (United), April 27. **Canada won by five wickets.** ‡Hong Kong **113** (36.1 overs) (Babar Hayat 32; Saad Bin Zafar 4-30); **Canada 114-5** (16.5 overs) (H. Patel 50, Ravinderpal Singh 41*). *PoM:* H. Patel.

Third place play-off   At Windhoek (Wanderers), April 27. **Papua New Guinea won by five wickets. USA 164** (43.4 overs) (M. D. Patel 39, T. K. Patel 50*; N. Pokana 3-28, N. Vanua 4-37); ‡**Papua New Guinea 165-5** (33 overs) (L. Siaka 62). *PoM:* N. Vanua. *ODI debuts:* S. K. Atai (PNG); Ali Khan, K. I. Gore, Jasdeep Singh, A. Jones, J. S. Malhotra, S. N. Netravalkar, M. D. Patel, T. K. Patel, S. R. Taylor, H. R. Walsh (USA). *This match (and the final) were given one-day international status by the ICC. The USA's only other official ODIs were two thumping defeats (by Australia and New Zealand) in the 2004 Champions Trophy: all the team were making their debuts, apart from 33-year-old Xavier Marshall, who played 24 ODIs (and seven Tests) for West Indies between 2004-05 and 2008-09. Timil Patel made their first ODI half-century.*

Final At Windhoek (Wanderers), April 27. **Namibia won by 145 runs.** ‡**Namibia 226-7** (50 overs) (K. J. Birkenstock 61, Z. E. Green 38); **Oman 81** (29 overs) (J. J. Smit 3-21, J. N. Frylinck 5-13). *PoM:* J. N. Frylinck. *ODI debuts:* S. J. Baard, K. J. Birkenstock, M. G. Erasmus, J. N. Frylinck, Z. E. Green, J. P. Kotze, B. N. Scholtz, J. J. Smit, C. Viljoen, C. G. Williams, H. N. Ya France (Namibia); Aaqib Ilyas, Bilal Khan, Fayyaz Butt, Jatinder Singh, Kaleemullah, Khawar Ali, Khurram Nawaz, Mohammad Nadeem, Sandeep Goud, Suraj Kumar, Zeeshan Maqsood (Oman). *Namibia had previously contested only six official ODIs (all defeats, in the 2003 World Cup), Oman none; all 22 players were making their debuts. Oman had won their first four group games (including against Namibia) to top the table, but lost the last, to PNG, by 145 runs. Now, a day later, they went down by an identical margin, to hand Namibia the title. Only Kagiso Rabada (6-16 in 2015) and Fidel Edwards (6-22 in 2003-04) had better bowling figures on ODI debut than left-arm seamer Jan Frylinck's 5-13. Eight of the Oman team were born in Pakistan, the other three in India.*

ICC WORLD CUP LEAGUE TWO, 2019–22

The first cycle of the ICC's restructured competition to provide a clearer pathway to World Cup qualification began in August 2019. By the end of the year, the United States were top of the table, with Scotland second, although Namibia, Oman and the UAE had played half as many games, and Nepal none. By January 2022, all seven sides are scheduled to have had 18 matches, all official one-day internationals. The top three in the table will go straight into the 2022 Qualifier for the following year's World Cup, while the other four will face further play-offs, with the leading sides from the World Cup Challenge League's two groups.

WORLD CUP LEAGUE TWO TABLE

	P	W	L	A	Pts	NRR
United States of America	8	6	2	0	12	0.41
Scotland	8	4	3	1	9	0.13
Namibia	4	3	1	0	6	0.51
Oman	4	3	1	0	6	−0.23
United Arab Emirates	4	1	2	1	3	−0.55
Nepal	0	0	0	0	0	0.00
Papua New Guinea	8	0	8	0	0	−0.45

As at December 31, 2019.

At Aberdeen, August 14. **Oman won by four wickets.** Papua New Guinea 229-8 (50 overs) (T. P. Ura 54, L. Siaka 41; Zeeshan Maqsood 3-35); ‡Oman 234-6 (49.1 overs) (Aaqib Ilyas 41, Sandeep Goud 67*, Fayyaz Butt 32*). *PoM:* Sandeep Goud. *ODI debuts:* J. A. Odedra (Oman); G. Toka (Papua New Guinea). *Oman won an official ODI for the first time, at the second attempt.*

At Aberdeen, August 15. **Oman won by eight wickets.** ‡Scotland 168 (44.4 overs) (M. H. Cross 33, K. J. Coetzer 56, C. D. Wallace 36; Khawar Ali 4-23); Oman 169-2 (45.1 overs) (Khawar Ali 79*, Aaqib Ilyas 61). *PoM:* Khawar Ali. *ODI debuts:* A. Neill (Scotland); Aamer Kaleem (Oman). *Scotland made 54-0 in the ten-over powerplay, but lost all ten for 97. Oman had only 27-0 after ten, but Khawar Ali followed his four wickets with 79* from 140 balls, and put on 123 in 30 overs for the second wicket with Aaqib Ilyas (61 from 92).*

At Aberdeen, August 17. **Scotland won by three wickets.** Papua New Guinea 205-9 (50 overs) (T. P. Ura 46, A. Vala 36, C. J. A. Amini 32, K. Doriga 39*; M. A. Leask 3-38, H. Tahir 4-37); ‡Scotland 207-7 (48.5 overs) (K. J. Coetzer 96, C. S. MacLeod 36; N. Pokana 3-25, A. Vala 3-37). *PoM:* K. J. Coetzer. *ODI debuts:* G. T. Main, H. Tahir (Scotland). *Slow left-armer Hamza Tahir, from Paisley, marked his first ODI with four wickets.*

At Aberdeen, August 18. **Scotland won by 85 runs.** Scotland 223-7 (50 overs) (M. H. Cross 59, R. D. Berrington 68, C. D. Wallace 53*); ‡Oman 138 (38.2 overs) (Sandeep Goud 32; S. M. Sharif 3-23, H. Tahir 5-38). *PoM:* H. Tahir. *ODI debut:* A. V. Lalcheta (Oman). *Calum MacLeod became the second Scotland batsman (after Kyle Coetzer) to score 2,000 runs in ODIs* *when he reached 7*; Matt Cross was the seventh to 1,000 at 8*. Debutant slow left-armer Ajay Lalcheta took his first two wickets (Cross and Michael Leask) with successive balls in his sixth over.*

At Aberdeen, August 20. **Scotland won by 38 runs. Scotland 242-7** (50 overs) (K. J. Coetzer 62, H. G. Munsey 34, R. D. Berrington 81); ‡**Papua New Guinea 204-9** (50 overs) (A. Vala 48, L. Siaka 33, D. Ravu 38*). *PoM:* R. D. Berrington. *Richie Berrington's 64-ball 81 included six sixes, and one four.*

At Aberdeen, August 21. **Oman won by four wickets. Papua New Guinea 206-9** (50 overs) (T. P. Ura 34, H. Hiri 31*; J. A. Odedra 4-34); ‡**Oman 207-6** (47.4 overs) (Khawar Ali 32, Aaqib Ilyas 63, Suraj Kumar 35*; C. J. A. Amini 3-39). *PoM:* Aaqib Ilyas.

At Lauderhill, September 13. **USA won by five runs** (DLS). ‡**USA 251-9** (50 overs) (M. D. Patel 35, A. Jones 77, K. I. Gore 31, E. H. Hutchinson 42*; N. Pokana 3-40, J. Kila 3-40); **Papua New Guinea 159-6** (23 overs) (A. Vala 48, C. J. A. Amini 53; K. I. Gore 3-25). *PoM:* A. Jones. *ODI debuts:* E. H. Hutchinson, N. K. Patel (USA). *The USA's last pair, Elmore Hutchinson and Saurabh Netravalkar, put on 49*, which proved vital. After a mid-innings downpour, Papua New Guinea's target was revised to 165 in 23 overs, and they fell just short, despite Chris Amini's 53 from 34 balls. This was the USA's first win in an official ODI, after three defeats.*

At Lauderhill, September 17. **USA won by five wickets.** ‡**Namibia 121** (46 overs) (K. J. Birkenstock 32, Z. E. Green 36; S. R. Taylor 4-23); **USA 122-5** (31.2 overs) (S. R. Taylor 43, M. D. Patel 30*; Z. Groenewald 3-28). *PoM:* S. R. Taylor. *ODI debut:* Z. Groenewald (Namibia).

At Lauderhill, September 19. **USA won by 62 runs.** ‡**USA 177** (48.1 overs) (M. D. Patel 66; N. Pokana 3-44, J. Kila 3-27); **Papua New Guinea 115** (38.1 overs) (A. Vala 38; K. I. Gore 4-20). *PoM:* K. I. Gore. *Monank Patel anchored a modest USA total. PNG were favourites at 87-3, but then lost seven for 28, with the Bronx-born slow left-armer Karima Gore taking four wickets, the first three in the same over.*

At Lauderhill, September 20. **Namibia won by 139 runs** (DLS). **Namibia 287-8** (49 overs) (J. P. Kotze 136, J. N. Frylinck 60; Jasdeep Singh 4-51); ‡**USA 142** (37 overs) (A. Jones 44; Z. Groenewald 5-20). *PoM:* J. P. Kotze. *Jean-Pierre "JP" Kotze, who blasted 11 fours and eight sixes in all from 108 balls, made Namibia's first ODI century. Jan Frylinck later added 60 from 43. The USA's target was revised to 282 in 47 overs, but they were demolished by Zhivago Groenewald's five-for.*

At Lauderhill, September 22. **Namibia won by four wickets.** ‡**Papua New Guinea 219-8** (50 overs) (A. Vala 38, L. Siaka 33, C. J. A. Amini 44, N. Vanua 30; Z. Groenewald 3-46); **Namibia 222-6** (48.2 overs) (J. P. Kotze 43, M. G. Erasmus 88, C. G. Williams 36*). *PoM:* M. G. Erasmus. *A measured 88 from Namibia's captain, Gerhard Erasmus, set up victory.*

At Lauderhill, September 23. **Namibia won by 27 runs.** ‡**Namibia 260-9** (50 overs) (S. J. Baard 73, C. G. Williams 32, Z. E. Green 41, J. J. Smit 33; N. Pokana 3-32); **Papua New Guinea 233** (47.3 overs) (A. Vala 104; B. M. Scholtz 4-27). *PoM:* A. Vala. *ODI debut:* R. Hekure (Papua New Guinea). *PNG slipped to their eighth defeat out of eight in this competition in 2019, despite Asad Vala's maiden ODI century.*

At Sharjah, December 8. **USA won by three wickets.** Reduced to 47 overs a side. ‡**United Arab Emirates 202** (45.2 overs) (C. Suri 46, Mohammad Usman 59*; S. N. Netravalkar 5-32); **USA 206-7** (45.2 overs) (X. M. Marshall 34, A. Jones 95; Junaid Siddique 3-37). *PoM:* A. Jones. *ODI debuts:* V. Aravind, Basil Hameed, D. D. P. D'Silva, Junaid Siddique, K. P. Meiyappan, Waheed Ahmed (UAE); I. G. Holland, A. Homraj, N. P. Kenjige, C. A. H. Stevenson (USA). *The UAE side included six debutants, mainly as a result of an anti-corruption enquiry which had seen four players suspended. Juan "Rusty" Theron made his ODI debut for the USA, after 13 white-ball internationals for South Africa between October 2010 and March 2012; he had moved to America in 2015. Left-arm seamer Netravalkar (8*), the USA's Mumbai-born captain, claimed their first ODI five-for; Aaron Jones, born in Queens in New York, later added their highest score.*

At Sharjah, December 9. **USA won by 35 runs.** ‡**USA 282-8** (50 overs) (M. D. Patel 82, A. Jones 74, I. G. Holland 44; S. M. Sharif 3-55, M. R. J. Watt 4-42); **Scotland 247** (47.2 overs) (M. A. Jones 52, C. S. MacLeod 86, R. D. Berrington 34; J. Theron 3-46, C. A. H. Stevenson 3-43). *PoM:* M. D. Patel. *The USA ran up a reasonable total, despite losing Xavier Marshall to the first ball of the match, from Safyaan Sharif. Patel and Jones added 140 for the third wicket in 28 overs. Ian Holland, born in Wisconsin but raised in Australia (he had played for Victoria, Hampshire and Northamptonshire), scored 44 from 29 balls, and added 2-43. Scotland were 238-5 in the 45th, then lost five for nine.*

At Sharjah, December 11. **United Arab Emirates v Scotland. Abandoned.**

At Dubai (ICC Academy), December 12. **USA won by 98 runs.** USA 213 (49.5 overs) (X. M. Marshall 31, A. Jones 46, A. Homraj 34, N. K. Patel 40); ‡**United Arab Emirates 115** (33 overs) (Basil Hameed 38; S. N. Netravalkar 3-11, C. A. H. Stevenson 3-22, I. G. Holland 3-11). *PoM:* S. N. Netravalkar. *The UAE struggled after slipping from 29-1 to 32-5.*

At Dubai (ICC Academy), December 14. **Scotland won by four wickets.** USA 245-9 (50 overs) (X. M. Marshall 50, S. R. Taylor 56, N. K. Patel 38, C. A. H. Stevenson 34*; M. R. J. Watt 3-33); ‡**Scotland 246-6** (48.5 overs) (C. S. MacLeod 62, R. D. Berrington 36; C. A. H. Stevenson 3-67). *PoM:* J. H. Davey.

At Dubai (ICC Academy), December 15. **United Arab Emirates won by seven wickets.** Scotland 220 (48.3 overs) (M. H. Cross 53, K. J. Coetzer 95; Junaid Siddique 3-49, Rohan Mustafa 3-35); ‡**United Arab Emirates 224-3** (43.5 overs) (C. Suri 67, Basil Hameed 63*, Mohammad Usman 36*). *PoM:* Basil Hameed. *ODI debut:* J. F. John (UAE). *Scotland wasted an opening stand of 138 between Cross and Coetzer, adding only 82. After Chirag Suri made 67, Basil Hameed and Mohammad Usman eased the UAE home with a stand of 86*.*

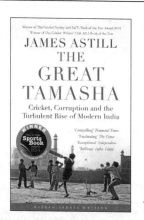

ICC TWENTY20 WORLD CUP QUALIFIER IN 2019-20

PETER DELLA PENNA

1 Netherlands   2 Papua New Guinea   3 Ireland   4 Namibia   5 Scotland   6 Oman

The T20 World Cup Qualifier showcased a new era of Associate cricket, highlighting how much the sport's collective depth has grown below the top flight of Full Member nations. That depth was evident not only in the results, but in the absentees: Nepal and the USA, who had secured ODI status in March 2018 and April 2019 respectively, had not even made it out of the regional qualifying rounds. It was a harbinger of what would follow in Dubai and Abu Dhabi.

Singapore, appearing at the tournament for the first time after dumping out Nepal in the Asia regional qualifier, stunned reigning co-champions Scotland on the opening day of the tournament, defending seven off the final over, even with Associate Player of the Year Calum MacLeod at the crease. Meanwhile, Papua New Guinea, who entered the competition on the back of eight straight defeats, won two of their first three matches, before dominating the Netherlands (the other co-champions). They rode the momentum all the way to the final.

Ireland, the only Test nation at the event, and winners on the previous two occasions the Qualifier had been held in the UAE, in 2012 and 2013, were rocked both by an understrength host team – several players, including captain Mohammad Naveed, had been suspended on the eve of the tournament on anti-corruption charges – and Canada. Like PNG, the Irish qualified automatically for this year's World Cup in Australia by topping one of two groups of seven, though only two points separated them from sixth-placed Jersey in an impossibly tight Group B (where Nigeria alone were off the pace, after coming in as late replacements when Zimbabwe's ICC suspension meant they were ineligible; the ban was eventually lifted, but too late for the gutted Zimbabweans). Oman, who seven years earlier had been regularly humiliated, clinched a trip to Australia via an elimination play-off win over Hong Kong.

Namibia, so often a bridesmaid, finally progressed, with a group of players mostly unscarred by past failures. Led by their dynamic 24-year-old captain, Player of the Tournament Gerhard Erasmus, they bounced back from lopsided defeats by the Netherlands and PNG, embarking on a five-match winning streak halted only in the semi-finals.

Despite this wave of new talent putting their stamp on the event, there was still room for the Associate bluebloods to demonstrate they were capable of keeping up with the times. Nowhere was that more evident than with the eventual champions, the Netherlands. The 39-year-old Ryan ten Doeschate won the match award against Namibia, and earning a place in the ICC's Tournament XI. He was joined there by left-arm-spinning all-rounder Roelof van der Merwe, whose experience was instrumental in several victories. Meanwhile, the Dutch pace attack of Paul van Meekeren, Brandon Glover, Fred Klaassen and Timm van der Gugten embodied raw pace, skill and variety that may make some Full Member nations envious, not to mention worried, come the tournament proper in October. There was less good news for Kenya, semi-finalists in the 50-over World Cup proper in 2003: they failed to escape the group stage here.

Scotland were not able to match their 2015 high, yet captain Kyle Coetzer said that securing a spot in Australia through an elimination play-off win over the UAE was a prouder accomplishment than finishing as co-champions on home soil four years earlier: they had struggled on their previous three visits to the UAE, in 2010, 2012 and 2013. This time, with the help of the reverse-sweeping theatrics of George Munsey, and the disciplined slow left-armers Hamza Tahir and Mark Watt, Scotland righted the wrongs of the past.

Even the tournament's two winless teams had their memorable moments. Nigeria's Sulaimon Runsewe became a social-media star after he sprinted off the field mid-innings against Canada to use the toilet. It was hard to judge who laughed harder: opponents or team-mates. Sussex's Delray Rawlins, meanwhile, saved his best performance for the TV cameras, rampaging to 46 off 21 balls for Bermuda against Scotland, four days after he fetched a £50,000 tag from Southern Brave in The Hundred draft. Kamau Leverock, nephew of Dwayne – whose slip catch against India lit up the 2007 World Cup – made a belligerent unbeaten 43 off 24. Earlier, he had taken a sensational one-handed leaping catch at backward point in a non-televised match against Singapore. Had the cameras been rolling, it would have brought an instantaneous split-screen comparison to his uncle.

The tournament took on a bittersweet mood when it was reported that it might fall victim to cost-cutting measures – although the ICC insisted that was not the case, even if fitting in a full global qualifying programme ahead of the next T20 World Cup in 2021 (when the tournament replaces the Champions Trophy) was going to prove difficult.

Regardless of its future, PNG's run to the final ensured a heart-warming conclusion to this event, as a team made up of fully indigenous talent qualified for their first major ICC competition. Their adventurous batting, canny bowling and electric fielding showed why the Qualifier, built on so many successful years of investment and development work in emerging nations, remains so compelling and important.

NATIONAL SQUADS

Bermuda *D. C. Stovell, O. Bascome, O. G. L. Bascome, O. O. Bascome, D. L. Brangman, J. T. Darrell, A. C. Douglas, T. S. Fray, M. O. Jones, K. S. Leverock, G. H. O'Brien, D. M. W. Rawlins, S. Smith, R. J. Trott, J. J. Tucker. *Coach:* H. Bascome.

Canada *N. S. Dhaliwal, Abraash Khan, N. Dutta, G. D. R. Eranga, J. O. A. Gordon, Hamza Tariq, D. A. Heyliger, Junaid Siddiqui, N. R. Kirton, N. R. Kumar, Ravinderpal Singh, Rizwan Cheema, Saad Bin Zafar, R. A. Thomas, S. A. Wijeratne. *Coach:* M. Desai.

Hong Kong *Aizaz Khan, Ahsan Abbasi, A. Bhagwat, K. M. Christie, Ehsan Khan, Haroon Arshad, R. Kapur, S. S. McKechnie, Mohammad Ghazanfar, Nizakat Khan, N. Rana, K. D. Shah, Shahid Wasif, Simandeep Singh, Waqas Barkat. *Coach:* D. T. Johnston.
  Babar Hayat, Ehsan Nawaz and Tanveer Ahmed were originally selected, but pulled out, apparently in protest at the omission of former captain Tanvir Afzal; they were replaced by Haroon Arshad, Kapur and Shahid Wasif. Waqas Khan was also chosen, but withdrew to attend the birth of his first child, and was replaced by Simandeep Singh.

Ireland *G. C. Wilson, M. R. Adair, A. Balbirnie, D. C. A. Delany, G. J. Delany, G. H. Dockrell, S. C. Getkate, B. J. McCarthy, K. J. O'Brien, W. B. Rankin, S. Singh, P. R. Stirling, H. T. Tector, S. R. Thompson, L. J. Tucker, C. A. Young. *Coach:* G. X. Ford.

D. C. A. Delany injured his knee during the tournament and was replaced by McCarthy.

Jersey *C. W. Perchard, C. P. F. Bisson, D. G. Blampied, H. L. Carlyon, J. S. E. Dunford, N. J. Ferraby, N. A. Greenwood, A. W. Hawkins-Kay, J. W. Jenner, E. J. B. Miles, R. J. G. Palmer, W. J. R. Robertson, B. D. H. Stevens, J. T. S. Sumerauer, B. Ward. *Coach:* N. J. MacRae.

Kenya *S. O. Ngoche, S. R. Bhudia, E. R. Bundi, A. R. Gandhi, D. M. Gondaria, I. A. Karim, P. Kerai, J. S. Kundi, A. A. Obanda, C. O. Obuya, N. M. Odhiambo, L. N. Oluoch, E. A. Otieno, R. N. Patel, R. R. Patel. *Coach:* M. O. Odumbe.

Namibia *M. G. Erasmus, S. J. Baard, K. J. Birkenstock, N. Davin, J. N. Frylinck, Z. E. Green, Z. Groenewald, J. P. Kotze, T. Lungameni, B. M. Scholtz, B. Shikongo, J. J. Smit, C. Viljoen, C. G. Williams, H. N. Ya France. *Coach:* P. de Bruyn.

Netherlands *P. M. Seelaar, C. N. Ackermann, P. R. P. Boissevain, B. N. Cooper, S. A. Edwards, B. D. Glover, F. J. Klaassen, M. P. O'Dowd, S. Snater, A. J. Staal, R. N. ten Doeschate, T. van der Gugten, R. E. van der Merwe, P. A. van Meekeren, T. P. Visée. *Coach:* R. J. Campbell.

Nigeria *A. A. Onikoyi, A. S. Abioye, A. Adedeji, V. D. Adewoye, D. Ajekun, C. M. Akachukwu, D. Gim, S. Ogundipe, I. O. Okpe, S. A. Okpe, C. N. Onwuzulike, A. M. Oyede, S. Runsewe, M. Taiwo. *Coach:* U. Ogbemi.

Oman *Zeeshan Maqsood, Aamer Kaleem, Aaqib Ilyas, Bilal Khan, Fayyaz Butt, Jatinder Singh, Kaleemullah, Khawar Ali, Khurram Nawaz, Mehran Khan, Mohammad Nadeem, Naseem Khushi, J. A. Odedra, Sandeep Goud, Suraj Kumar. *Coach:* L. R. D. Mendis.

Papua New Guinea *A. Vala, C. J. A. Amini, S. K. Atai, S. Bau, K. Doriga, R. Hekure, H. Hiri, J. Kila, A. Nao, N. Pokana, D. Ravu, J. B. Reva, L. Siaka, T. P. Ura, N. Vanua. *Coach:* J. H. Dawes.

Scotland *K. J. Coetzer, R. D. Berrington, D. E. Budge, M. H. Cross, J. H. Davey, A. C. Evans, O. J. Hairs, M. A. Leask, C. S. MacLeod, H. G. Munsey, A. Neill, S. M. Sharif, T. B. Sole, H. Tahir, C. D. Wallace, M. R. J. Watt. *Coach:* S. Burger.

Hairs injured his foot during the tournament and was replaced by Budge.

Singapore *Amjad Mahboob, A. G. Achar, U. Aryaman Sunil, V. Baskaran, S. Chandramohan, T. H. David, A. Dixit, A. Dutta, R. Gaznavi, A. Krishna, Manpreet Singh, N. M. S. Param, J. Prakash, R. Rangarajan, Sidhant Singh, S. Vijayakumar. *Coach:* Bilal Asad.

Krishna injured a hamstring during the tournament and was replaced by Achar.

United Arab Emirates *Ahmed Raza, V. Aravind, Ashfaq Ahmed, D. D. P. D'Silva, Faizan Asif, Ghulam Shabbir, Imran Haider, Junaid Siddique, Mohammad Boota, Mohammad Usman, Rameez Shahzad, Rohan Mustafa, Sultan Ahmed, C. Suri, Waheed Ahmed, Zahoor Khan, Zawar Farid. *Coach:* D. R. Brown.

Mohammad Naveed was originally named as captain, but he, Qadeer Ahmed and Shaiman Anwar were withdrawn while the UAE board investigated corruption allegations; they were replaced by D'Silva, Junaid Siddique and Waheed Ahmed. Ashfaq Ahmed was suspended in mid-tournament, and a few days later Ghulam Shabbir walked out; they were replaced by Aravind and Faizan Asif.

QUALIFYING TABLES

Group A	P	W	L	Pts	NRR
PAPUA NEW GUINEA	6	5	1	10	2.08
NETHERLANDS	6	5	1	10	1.77
NAMIBIA	6	4	2	8	1.08
SCOTLAND	6	3	3	6	0.25
Kenya	6	2	4	4	−1.14
Singapore	6	2	4	4	−1.37
Bermuda	6	0	6	0	−2.84

Group B

	P	W	L	Pts	NRR
IRELAND	6	4	2	8	1.59
OMAN	6	4	2	8	0.99
UNITED ARAB EMIRATES . . .	6	4	2	8	0.68
HONG KONG	6	3	3	6	0.48
Canada	6	3	3	6	0.24
Jersey	6	3	3	6	0.08
Nigeria	6	0	6	0	−4.67

The top team in each group qualified automatically for the T20 World Cup in Australia; the other teams in capitals entered the play-offs for the remaining four places.

Play-offs

Group A 2nd v Group B 3rd At Dubai (Sports City), October 29, 2019. **Netherlands won by eight wickets.** ‡**United Arab Emirates 80-9** (20 overs) (B. D. Glover 4-12); **Netherlands 81-2** (15.1 overs) (B. N. Cooper 41*). *PoM:* B. D. Glover. *The Netherlands sealed their spot in the T20 World Cup for the third time. The UAE were 9-5 in the fifth over, and stumbled to 80-9, all the wickets going to the Dutch pacemen. Ben Cooper then calmly anchored the simple chase. The UAE faced a further play-off with Scotland for a place in Australia.*

Group B 2nd v Group A 3rd At Dubai (Sports City), October 29, 2019 (floodlit). **Namibia won by 54 runs.** ‡**Namibia 161-7** (20 overs) (C. G. Williams 45, J. J. Smit 59; Bilal Khan 4-19); **Oman 107** (19.1 overs) (Khawar Ali 41; B. M. Scholtz 3-14, M. G. Erasmus 3-19). *PoM:* J. J. Smit. *Namibia reached the final stages of a global competition for the first time since the 2003 World Cup, with spinners Bernard Scholtz (slow left-arm) and captain Gerhard Erasmus (leg-breaks) throttling the Oman batsmen, taking 6-33 in their eight overs. Namibia's innings had been given late impetus by Johannes Smit, who crashed 59 from 25 balls, with five sixes. "I'm lost for words," he said. Oman had another chance to reach the big event, in a play-off against Hong Kong.*

Qualifying play-off At Dubai (Sports City), October 30, 2019. **Scotland won by 90 runs.** ‡**Scotland 198-6** (20 overs) (H. G. Munsey 65, K. J. Coetzer 34, R. D. Berrington 48); **United Arab Emirates 108** (18.3 overs) (Rameez Shahzad 34; S. M. Sharif 3-21, M. R. J. Watt 3-21). *PoM:* H. G. Munsey. *Scotland ensured their place in Australia with a thumping victory. George Munsey, whose 43-ball 65 included five sixes, laid a good platform in an opening stand of 87 with Kyle Coetzer. After Kyle Coetzer fell to a superb one-handed boundary catch by Rameez Shahzad, Richie Berrington slammed 48 from 18 to push his side close to 200. The UAE were 12-2 after 13 balls, and never threatened: from 81-3 in the 12th, they lost seven for 27.*

Qualifying play-off At Dubai (Sports City), October 30, 2019. **Oman won by 12 runs.** ‡**Oman 134-7** (20 overs) (Jatinder Singh 67*); **Hong Kong 122-9** (20 overs) (S. S. McKechnie 44; Bilal Khan 4-23). *PoM:* Jatinder Singh. *Oman began their must-win match disastrously, slipping to 42-6 after nine overs. But Jatinder Singh, who batted throughout the innings, doubled the score with Aamer Kaleem (17), then put on 50* in 19 balls with Naseem Khushi, who crunched 26* from nine. It was enough to take Oman to the main event; Hong Kong also started abjectly, against left-arm seamer Bilal Khan, and were soon 18-5. Manchester-born Scott McKechnie repaired some of the damage with 44 from 46, but was lbw in the 17th, with 33 still needed, and the tail fell short. "We showed great fight after losing six wickets," said Zeeshan Mahmood, Oman's delighted captain. "Jatinder played a fighting innings – and Bilal was unplayable today."*

Fifth-place play-off At Dubai (ICC Academy), October 31, 2019. **Scotland won by five wickets.** ‡**Oman 167-7** (20 overs) (Khawar Ali 43; A. C. Evans 3-36); **Scotland 168-5** (19 overs) (M. H. Cross 61*, M. A. Leask 38). *PoM:* M. H. Cross. *With qualification guaranteed, this was a more relaxed affair. Oman did well to reach 167 – Josh Davey's four overs cost 41 – but Matt Cross made up for Coetzer's first-over departure with 61* from 45.*

Semi-final At Dubai (Sports City), November 1, 2019. **Netherlands won by 21 runs.** Netherlands **158-4** (20 overs) (B. N. Cooper 37, R. N. ten Doeschate 43*); ‡**Ireland 137-9** (20 overs) (P. M. Seelaar 3-17). *PoM:* R. E. van der Merwe. *A disciplined Irish bowling display restricted the Netherlands to 102-4 after 15 overs – but Ryan ten Doeschate (43 from 25 balls) and Roelof van der Merwe (25**

from 16) smacked 56 from the last five. Paul Stirling and Kevin O'Brien began the chase with 52 in seven overs, but a comfortable 80-2 became 108-9, and Ireland missed out on the final.

Semi-final At Dubai (Sports City), November 1, 2019. **Papua New Guinea won by 18 runs.** ‡**Papua New Guinea 130-5** (20 overs) (C. J. A. Amini 31, S. Bau 40*); **Namibia 112-5** (20 overs) (S. J. Baard 34, J. P. Kotze 30). *PoM:* N. Vanua. *PNG recovered from 31-3 thanks to Chris Amini and Sese Bau, and the chase proved beyond Namibia. Seamer Norman Vanua finished with 4–14–16–2.*

Third-place play-off At Dubai (Sports City), November 2, 2019. **Ireland won by 27 runs.** ‡**Ireland 135** (19.1 overs) (A. Balbirnie 46; J. J. Smit 3-19, C. G. Williams 3-34); **Namibia 108** (18.2 overs) (M. G. Erasmus 51; S. Singh 3-25). *PoM:* S. Singh. *Another disappointing performance with the bat sentenced Namibia to their second defeat in two days. Ireland managed only a dozen boundaries – five from top-scorer Andrew Balbirnie – in what looked an underwhelming total. But Erasmus fell for a fighting 34-ball 51 as Namibia's last five wickets added only 16. Stirling, who made 25, finished as the tournament's leading run-scorer, with 291.*

Final At Dubai (Sports City), November 2, 2019. **Netherlands won by seven wickets.** ‡**Papua New Guinea 128-8** (20 overs) (L. Siaka 39; B. D. Glover 3-24); **Netherlands 134-3** (19 overs) (B. N. Cooper 41, R. N. ten Doeschate 34*). *PoM:* B. D. Glover. *PoT:* M. G. Erasmus (Namibia). *The Netherlands claimed the trophy, after their potent attack made regular inroads to limit PNG to a sub-par total. Glover took three more wickets, finishing with 16 at ten in the tournament (only Oman's Bilal Khan, with 18, had more). The Dutch made steady progress, and ten Doeschate finished the match with his third six.*

Final placings 1 Netherlands. 2 Papua New Guinea. 3 Ireland. 4 Namibia. 5 Scotland. 6 Oman. 7 United Arab Emirates. 8 Hong Kong. 9 Canada. 10 Jersey. 11 Kenya. 12 Singapore. 13 Bermuda. 14 Nigeria.

The top six teams qualified for the Twenty20 World Cup in Australia in October 2020.

CRICKET IN NAMIBIA IN 2019

Back in the big time

HELGE SCHUTZ

After a barren 17 years, Namibia finally reached a global tournament again when they finished fourth at the T20 World Cup Qualifier, held in the UAE in October and November. That was the icing on the cake of a year of tremendous progress, in which they regained their one-day international status.

A catalyst for the dramatic upturn had been the appointment as president of Cricket Namibia in July 2018 of Rudi van Vuuren, a member of the team that competed in the nation's last big event, the 2003 World Cup. Also significant was the decision to install Pierre de Bruyn as national coach in early 2019. Former South Africa all-rounder Albie Morkel joined the coaching staff too.

Financial constraints forced a withdrawal from the South African provincial competitions at the start of the 2018-19 season. Namibia had competed against their neighbours for more than 20 years, so this felt like a backward step. But a renewed focus on the clubs, and thorough preparation for World Cricket League Division Two, held in the capital, Windhoek, laid the foundations of success. After two wins and two defeats, their hopes of reaching the final were hanging by a thread when they met Hong Kong. A brilliant batting performance, featuring hundreds from Stephen Baard and Jean-Pierre Kotze, set up a 151-run win. That secured a final against Oman and, more importantly, the return of ODI status, and qualification for the World Cup League Two. Buoyed by this double, Namibia thrashed Oman by 145 runs. Left-arm seamer Jan Frylinck was Player of the Match, with five for 13, but the tournament award went to all-rounder Johannes Smit, who scored 221 runs at 55, and took 13 wickets at 14. Two months later, Smit became the first Namibian to be signed by a T20 franchise, joining Vancouver Knights in Canada's Global T20.

Namibia also performed well in the World Cup League Two, held in Florida in September. They won four of their eight matches – one was abandoned – and finished fourth, behind Scotland on run-rate. But the highlight came in the T20 World Cup Qualifier, where they overcame a poor start to secure a place in the main event in Australia. After defeats by the Netherlands and Papua New Guinea, they beat Scotland, Bermuda, Kenya and Singapore. In the last two, captain Gerhard Erasmus scored 52 not out and 72. Victory over Oman in the play-off – Smit blasted 59 off 25 balls – earned qualification. The third-place match was lost to Ireland, despite another fifty from Erasmus, whose leadership had played a key part in Namibia's rejuvenation.

It will be important to ensure the game has healthy roots at home. With that in mind, Cricket Namibia took a roadshow around the country in November, to try to enthuse far-flung parts of the population. There are barely 500 senior players, so they need to unearth new talent.

CRICKET IN NEPAL IN 2019

Khadka quits at the summit

Ujjwal Acharya

It was a year of mixed fortunes on the field – including the departure of a highly regarded leader – and a significant development off it. In October, the ICC conditionally lifted their suspension of Nepal, imposed in 2016 after a breach of regulations relating to government interference. This has cleared the way for Nepali cricket to expand, and opened up new funding opportunities.

The day after the announcement, Paras Khadka surprised everyone by stepping down as national captain shortly before his 32nd birthday. He had led Nepal since 2009, and enjoyed a tremendous year with the bat, but clearly felt the lifting of the suspension marked the right moment to move on. He handed over to his long-time deputy, Gyanendra Malla.

In January, Khadka had become Nepal's first ODI centurion – 115 in a decider against the UAE. He followed that by leading the team to another 2–1 win, in the T20 series, again making a key contribution in the decisive game. And in September, he completed a notable double by scoring Nepal's first T20 international hundred, against Singapore in a triangular series. After his resignation, he became just the second Nepali, after Sandeep Lamichhane, to play franchise cricket, making three appearances in the Abu Dhabi T10 League.

But he could not prevent the year's biggest disappointment: the failure to reach the T20 World Cup Qualifier, which would have given Nepal a shot at reaching the main event in Australia. After defeats by hosts Singapore and Qatar in the Asia Regional Finals in July, they finished third in their group. However, after 12 wins in 19 matches in the format in 2019, they finished the year placed 12th in the ICC rankings.

Nepal took part in three other events. In July, they toured Malaysia, winning 2–0. In the Singapore T20 Tri-Series in September, they beat the hosts, but lost twice to Zimbabwe. The following month, they defeated the Netherlands and Hong Kong in the Oman Pentangular, but lost to Ireland and Oman. Nepal hosted the 13th South Asian Games in December, with both men and women winning bronze. In the women's tournament, off-spinner Anjali Chand made headlines with figures of 2.1–2–0–6, including a hat-trick, against the Maldives. In their first international, the Maldives, who were bowled out for 16 in their first international. Chand's figures were the best in men's or women's T20 internationals.

ICC's decision to provisionally lift their ban came after the Cricket Association of Nepal had voted in a 17-member central working committee in a closely supervised election. But the new committee, chaired by CAN's president, Chatur Bahadur Chand, did nothing noteworthy in their early months, frustrating cricket lovers, who have long demanded proper plans and a strong domestic structure.

CRICKET IN THE NETHERLANDS IN 2019

All roads lead to Australia

DAVE HARDY

Twenty20 is taking over the world, and the Netherlands is no exception. The four-day Intercontinental Cup has been consigned to history, and the Dutch team played just two official ODIs in 2019, both against Zimbabwe, both won. That left the landscape dominated by the 20-over format, but at least there was some tangible reward when they won the T20 World Cup Qualifier in the UAE in the autumn, to earn a place in the main event in Australia.

The Netherlands won five of their six group matches, losing only to Papua New Guinea, and secured the main goal of qualification by thumping the hosts in the play-off. In the final, they exacted revenge for that earlier defeat, beating PNG by seven wickets. Ben Cooper was the most prolific batsman, with 246 runs at 30; Ryan ten Doeschate not far behind, with 233 at 46. But it was the bowlers who were the architects of the triumph: seamer Brandon Glover, a new name in the attack, took 16 wickets at ten, Paul van Meekeren 15 at 14, and Roelof van der Merwe 14 at 12.

Over the course of the year, there was a wide variation in the Netherlands' results, often explained by the availability of the best players. All the leading names were in attendance in the UAE, and they were expertly guided by head coach Ryan Campbell and his staff. One new face was Leicestershire all-rounder Colin Ackermann, who had made his debut in the preceding series in Oman. Six of the party had county contracts – the most in a Netherlands squad – but only three were Dutch-born.

The emphasis on the national team led to a lively club-versus-country debate. Oddly, an international was held on the day of a full league programme, and – more controversially – Netherlands players were prevented from turning out for their clubs, or restricted in the number of overs they could bowl. It was perhaps no coincidence that Excelsior '20, of Schiedam, the only team not to supply players to the national team, won the 50-over *Topklasse* for the third time in five years. The competition was played with a white ball for the first time, and with no limit on foreign players. Six of their bowlers took at least 20 wickets at under 20, but their highest-ranked batsman was 24th in the national averages. Quick, of The Hague, champions as recently as 2014, were relegated for the first time since 1991. VOC, of Rotterdam, were Twenty20 champions for the first time, and also won a European ten-over tournament in La Manga.

Dutch players featured in the Global T20 tournament in Canada, with opening batsman Tobias Visée making a good impression. The Dutch season was due to conclude with a similar tournament featuring six franchises, two each from the Netherlands, Scotland and Ireland, plus some global stars, but it was cancelled two weeks before the start.

NETHERLANDS v ZIMBABWE IN 2019

Bertus de Jong

One-day internationals (2): Netherlands 2, Zimbabwe 0
Twenty20 internationals (2): Netherlands 1, Zimbabwe 1

The start of Zimbabwe's European tour saw a number of firsts: the Netherlands' first internationals against Full Member opposition since regaining official status, the first staged at Deventer, the first played while a World Cup was going on elsewhere – and, as it turned out, the first whitewash of a Full Member by an Associate. Zimbabwe had come out on top on their previous visit, taking an unofficial series 2–1 in 2017, but this time they did not win a game until the second Twenty20 match – and only after the Dutch had dramatically forced a super over.

Neither side was at full strength. Zimbabwe had lost Graeme Cremer to early retirement and Blessing Muzarabani to Kolpak, while the Dutch were missing some of their overseas brigade, notably Ryan ten Doeschate, Michael Rippon and Logan van Beek. But faith in a largely Netherlands-based squad paid off: ODI debutants Max O'Dowd (their top-scorer in three of the four games) and Toby Visée maintained their domestic form. Roelof van der Merwe was the star of the T20s.

The series marked the Netherlands' return to the official ODI table after almost five years, but more importantly demonstrated the growing depth of the squad. Victory provided a boost for the battles ahead: the T20 World Cup Qualifier in October, and the start of the ODI Super League in May 2020.

For Zimbabwe, the results confirmed an over-reliance on the old guard, particularly Brendan Taylor and Craig Ervine. During the tour, news also emerged that the Sports and Recreation Commission had suspended the entire Zimbabwe Cricket board, along with acting managing director Givemore Makoni – actions which would soon lead to Zimbabwe's suspension from the ICC on grounds of government interference. The men's team flew on to Ireland as planned, but the women's tour, scheduled for July, was cancelled.

ZIMBABWE TOURING PARTY

*H. Masakadza, R. P. Burl, T. L. Chatara, E. Chigumbura, C. R. Ervine, K. M. Jarvis, T. S. Khamunhukamwe, S. F. Mire, P. J. Moor, C. B. Mpofu, R. Mutumbami, A. Ndlovu, Sikandar Raza, B. R. M. Taylor, D. T. Tiripano, S. C. Williams. *Coach:* L. S. Rajput.

First one-day international At Deventer, June 19. **Netherlands won by seven wickets** (DLS). ‡**Zimbabwe 205-8** (47 overs) (B. R. M. Taylor 71, K. M. Jarvis 32*); **Netherlands 208-3** (42.4 overs) (M. P. O'Dowd 86*, B. N. Cooper 35, W. Barresi 39*). *ODI debuts:* M. P. O'Dowd, T. P. Visée (Netherlands); A. Ndlovu (Zimbabwe). *In sweltering weather more typical of their homeland, Zimbabwe struggled in the first ODI at the Sportpark Het Schootsveld. An early rain break trimmed six overs off the match, although the DLS target remained unchanged. A disciplined bowling display kept Zimbabwe's batsmen quiet, Brendan Taylor top-scoring with 71. Seamer Ainsley Ndlovu trapped Toby Visée lbw with the first ball of his ODI career, but Max O'Dowd, a third debutant, anchored the chase with 86*. Roelof van der Merwe was playing his first ODI for the Netherlands, after 13 for South Africa a decade earlier.*

Second one-day international   At Deventer, June 21. **Netherlands won by three wickets.** ‡**Zimbabwe 290-6** (50 overs) (C. R. Ervine 84, B. R. M. Taylor 51, Sikandar Raza 85*); **Netherlands 291-7** (49.2 overs) (T. P. Visée 41, M. P. O'Dowd 59, R. E. van der Merwe 57, S. A. Edwards 44*, P. M. Seelaar 32; S. C. Williams 4-43). *ODI debuts*: B. D. Glover, Saqib Zulfiqar (Netherlands). *Zimbabwe were unchanged, but looked a different side as they racked up 290. Ervine – who spent 18 balls on nought – made 84 from 107, while Taylor hit a rather quicker half-century; finally, Sikandar Raza hammered five sixes in his 85* from 68. But it wasn't enough: the Netherlands completed their highest ODI chase with four balls to spare, and took the series 2–0. Visée started with 41 from 33, then O'Dowd and van der Merwe made important contributions, and captain Pieter Seelaar thrashed 32 from 15 near the end. Slow left-armer Sean Williams ensured a tense finish with four wickets.*

First Twenty20 international   At Rotterdam, June 23. **Netherlands won by 49 runs. Netherlands 199-6** (20 overs) (M. P. O'Dowd 30, B. N. Cooper 54, R. E. van der Merwe 75*); ‡**Zimbabwe 150** (19.5 overs) (C. R. Ervine 59; B. D. Glover 3-20, F. J. Klaassen 3-36, P. M. Seelaar 3-28). *T20I debut*: B. D. Glover (Netherlands). *Two days after their record 50-over chase, the Netherlands made their highest T20 total, with van der Merwe's 75* from 39 balls – his highest score in internationals – powering them past their 193-4 against Ireland at Sylhet in March 2014. Ervine's enterprising 37-ball 59 kept Zimbabwe in the hunt, but no one else reached 20. Seamer Brandon Glover, who played an Under-19 Test for South Africa in 2014, took 3-20 in his first T20 match of any kind.*

Second Twenty20 international   At Rotterdam, June 25. **Zimbabwe won a super over, following a tie.** ‡**Netherlands 152-8** (20 overs) (M. P. O'Dowd 56); **Zimbabwe 152** (20 overs) (B. R. M. Taylor 40; R. E. van der Merwe 4-35, P. A. van Meekeren 3-25). *Zimbabwe sneaked a consolation win in the super over, after van der Merwe had denied them a more conventional victory. With three balls remaining, Zimbabwe needed one to win after the first two deliveries of the over disappeared for sixes – but van der Merwe bowled Elton Chigumbura and Chris Mpofu, then Tendai Chatara was run out. The super over was less tense: Zimbabwe collected 18-0 off Fred Klaassen, but the Netherlands had only 3-1 before O'Dowd swatted Chatara for a consolation six. O'Dowd had been the batting star in the match proper, with 56 from 40 balls. Zimbabwe's chase stalled after Paul van Meekeren dismissed Williams and Ervine in the 11th over, and they were 97-6 after 14. But Chigumbura (29 off 18, with three sixes) and Ryan Burl (23 off 14) muscled them close.*

NETHERLANDS v UNITED ARAB EMIRATES IN 2019

Twenty20 internationals (4): Netherlands 0, United Arab Emirates 4

All four matches were close – but the UAE came out on the right end each time. The Netherlands were without any of their English county players, which didn't help. UAE opener Ashfaq Ahmed smacked 210 runs – he had three half-centuries and a 25, and a strike-rate of 140 – while team-mate Rohan Mustafa was the leading wicket-taker, with eight for his off-breaks. Max O'Dowd led the way for the Dutch, with 148 runs.

First Twenty20 international   At Amstelveen, August 3. **United Arab Emirates won by 13 runs.** United Arab Emirates 181-5 (20 overs) (Ashfaq Ahmed 54, Mohammad Usman 52); ‡Netherlands 168-4 (20 overs) (M. P. O'Dowd 51, B. N. Cooper 31, S. A. Edwards 34). *T20I debuts:* A. J. Staal (Netherlands); D. D. P. D'Silva (UAE). *Ashfaq Ahmed led the way with 54 from 35 balls, including 11 fours, and Mohammad Usman rounded the UAE innings off with 52 from 34. Max O'Dowd hit 51 from 35 in reply, but the Netherlands were holed below the waterline by the dismissals of Ben Cooper and Scott Edwards.*

Second Twenty20 international   At Amstelveen, August 5. **United Arab Emirates won by five wickets.** Netherlands 136-9 (20 overs) (B. N. Cooper 46, P. M. Seelaar 34; Rohan Mustafa 3-27); ‡United Arab Emirates 140-5 (19.3 overs) (Rameez Shahzad 49, Mohammad Usman 34). *T20I debuts:* P. R. P. Boissevain, T. S. Braat (Netherlands); Waheed Ahmed (UAE). *The Netherlands were 80-3 in the 12th, but added only 56 more and lost six wickets. Seamers Mohammad Naveed (1-21) and Zahoor Khan (2-20) applied the brakes. Rameez Shahzad and Mohammad Usman added 59 for the UAE's fourth wicket and, although both fell in sight of victory, Mohammad Boota (11*) hit the winning boundary in the final over.*

Third Twenty20 international   At Voorburg, August 6. **United Arab Emirates won by 14 runs.** United Arab Emirates 152-8 (20 overs) (Ashfaq Ahmed 56; T. S. Braat 3-26); ‡Netherlands 138-9 (20 overs) (M. P. O'Dowd 65; Rohan Mustafa 3-30). *T20I debut:* Zawar Farid (UAE). *The UAE clinched the series, their total proving too much for the Dutch, despite O'Dowd's battling 65.*

Fourth Twenty20 international   At Voorburg, August 8. **United Arab Emirates won by seven wickets.** ‡Netherlands 150-6 (20 overs); **United Arab Emirates 153-3** (19.4 overs) (Ashfaq Ahmed 75, Ghulam Shabbir 58*). *The UAE seemed to be cruising to victory while Ashfaq (a career-best 75 off 53) and Ghulam Shabbir (a maiden T20I half-century) were putting on 111 for the second wicket. But two wickets in four balls meant the match went down to the final over. Dilip D'Silva (9*) crashed the winning four off seamer Vivian Kingma to seal the whitewash.*

CRICKET IN OMAN IN 2019

Mission accomplished

PAUL BIRD

Oman achieved their main aim in 2019 by securing their place in the T20 World Cup in Australia. They went to the qualifying tournament in the UAE with high expectations, and as less of a surprise package than in 2015, when they provided one of the stories of the year by battling through to the finals in India. This time, there was a different sort of pressure.

They defeated the UAE, Hong Kong, Nigeria and Canada comfortably, but lost to Ireland, which gave added significance to their final group match, against Jersey. A win would have ensured automatic qualification. But they lost by 14 runs, and faced a play-off against Namibia. That match appeared within their grasp, when they were 55 for one after five overs, chasing 162, with Khawar Ali going well. Then six fell for 32, and they lost by 54.

Fortunately, they had a final chance, in a qualifier against Hong Kong – and, despite a nervy performance, they made it. Jatinder Singh made 67 from 50 balls, but only two others got into double figures, and a total of 134 looked meagre. However, a new-ball burst by Bilal Khan and Fayyaz Butt reduced Hong Kong to 18 for five; they rallied, and the eventual margin was only 12 runs, but Oman were through. Jatinder enjoyed a marvellous tournament, with 267 runs – the third-highest – at 38. And left-arm seamer Bilal was the highest wicket-taker, with 18 at 12, including two four-fors.

Their self-belief had been boosted considerably by success in a warm-up tournament on home soil. Oman came out on top in a competition that involved Ireland, Nepal, the Netherlands and Hong Kong, thanks to some superb performances from their bowlers, notably leg-spinner Khawar and slow left-armer Aamer Kaleem. They had fared less well in a home quadrangular competition in February, finishing behind Scotland, the Netherlands and Ireland.

The quality of the country's international facility at Al Amerat, outside the capital, Muscat, was recognised at the end of the year, when a World Cup Challenge League tournament was held there, after being switched from Hong Kong. Oman now has some of the best turf wickets in the Gulf, only a few years after having none at all.

But it is not all good news. Oman's progress still seems to have gone unnoticed among the indigenous population. Only two Omani-born players made international appearances in 2019: Sufyan Mehmood, who made his debut in 2015, played in just his third game against Scotland in February, and was joined by Wasim Ali, former captain of the Under-19s. Neither was selected for the T20 World Cup Qualifier. The team continue to be made up of players born in India and Pakistan. There is a youth scheme, but it is concentrated on primary schools, so the benefits are a long way from being felt by the national team.

OMAN T20 QUADRANGULAR IN 2018-19

1 Scotland   2 Netherlands   3 Ireland   4 Oman

This short tournament, comprising six matches in five days, allowed Oman to see how they measured up against three of Europe's bigger cricketing powers. The answer was mixed: they lost all three games, but enjoyed decent passages in each. It also served as a warm-up for Scotland, who stayed on for a seesaw ODI series against the hosts, and Ireland, who left the Gulf bound for Dehradun in northern India, where they would take on Afghanistan.

With Oman unable to land a telling blow, the competition boiled down to how the matches between the other three panned out. The Netherlands beat Scotland, who beat Ireland, who beat the Netherlands... so they had to be separated on net run-rate. Comfortably ahead were Scotland, thanks to their hard-hitting opener George Munsey, who faced only 47 balls for his 98 runs, and to left-arm spinner Mark Watt, whose seven victims at 11 (and an economy-rate of under seven) made him the leading bowler. The Scots also benefited from the reliable Calum MacLeod, dismissed only once in accumulating 117.

The games, played on a placid surface, tended to follow a pattern: the openers prospered, while the middle order didn't. All three European teams set records for their first wicket. The heaviest run-scorer, with 193 from 103 balls, was Tobias Visée, from The Hague, and a strike-rate of 187 made him almost as fast as Munsey. He added consistency to speed, with innings of 71, 44 and 78. That last innings, from 36 deliveries, came against Ireland, who had lost their previous five Twenty20 internationals to the Netherlands. At the end of a phenomenal final over that contained two wickets and a last-ball six, Ireland had halted an unwelcome sequence.

NATIONAL SQUADS

Oman   *A. V. Lalcheta, Aamer Kaleem, Bilal Khan, Fayyaz Butt, S. Goud, Jatinder Singh, Kaleemullah, Khawar Ali, Khurram Nawaz, Mehran Khan, Mohammad Nadeem, Naseem Khushi, J. V. Odedra, Sufyan Mehmood, Wasim Ali. *Coach:* L. R. D. Mendis.

Ireland   *P. R. Stirling, A. Balbirnie, P. K. D. Chase, G. H. Dockrell, S. C. Getkate, J. B. Little, A. R. McBrine, K. J. O'Brien, S. W. Poynter, W. B. Rankin, S. Singh, H. T. Tector, S. R. Thompson, L. J. Tucker. *Coach:* G. X. Ford.

Netherlands   *P. M. Seelaar, W. Barresi, B. N. Cooper, S. A. Edwards, F. J. Klaassen, S. J. Myburgh, M. P. O'Dowd, Sikander Zulfiqar, S. Snater, R. N. ten Doeschate, T. van der Gugten, R. E. van der Merwe, P. A. van Meekeren, T. P. Visée. *Coach:* R. J. Campbell.

Scotland   *K. J. Coetzer, R. D. Berrington, M. H. Cross, A. C. Evans, C. N. Greaves, M. A. Leask, C. S. MacLeod, H. G. Munsey, A. Neill, S. M. Sharif, R. A. J. Smith, H. Tahir, C. D. Wallace, M. R. J. Watt. *Interim head coach:* T. M. B. Bailey.

At Al Amerat, Oman, February 13, 2019. **Netherlands won by seven wickets. Scotland 153-7** (20 overs) (H. G. Munsey 32, C. S. MacLeod 53); ‡**Netherlands 154-3** (19.5 overs) (T. P. Visée 71). *PoM:* T. P. Visée. *T20I debut:* R. A. J. Smith (Scotland). *George Munsey gave Scotland an electrifying start but, once he fell for an 11-ball 32 (with five fours and two sixes), the innings tailed off. Max O'Dowd held a superb catch at deep square leg to despatch Richie Berrington, Calum MacLeod hung around for 45 deliveries without cutting loose, and a total of 153 felt gettable. When Stephan Myburgh and Tobias Visée put on 100 inside 12 overs – the first century opening stand by the Dutch, and only their second for any wicket – it seemed a breeze. The Netherlands had no cause to hurry, and victory came with a ball to spare.*

At Al Amerat, Oman, February 13, 2019. **Ireland won by 15 runs. Ireland 159-5** (20 overs) (P. R. Stirling 71, A. Balbirnie 34); ‡**Oman 144-9** (20 overs) (S. Singh 3-15). *PoM:* P. R. Stirling. *T20I debuts:* Fayyaz Butt, J. V. Odedra (Oman); S. C. Getkate (Ireland). *At 70-2 in the ninth, Oman needed another 90 at around 7.5 an over, and Ireland seemed set to lose a fifth successive T20I. The spinners, though, struck back: four wickets fell in 11 balls, and the complexion of the contest changed. The Irish had also squandered a position of strength, lurching from 122-1 to 128-4. But thanks to the captain, Paul Stirling, they had enough.*

At Al Amerat, Oman, February 15, 2019. **Netherlands won by eight wickets. Oman 166-4** (20 overs) (Jatinder Singh 63, Khurram Nawaz 58); ‡**Netherlands 167-2** (18.5 overs) (S. J. Myburgh 34, T. P. Visée 44, B. N. Cooper 50*, R, N. ten Doeschate 32*). *PoM:* R. E. van der Merwe. *T20I debut:* S. Goud (Oman). *Oman raised the tempo of their innings, adding 120 runs in the last ten overs. The third-wicket stand between an initially cautious Jatinder Singh and a more explosive Khurram Nawaz put on 89, though the fireworks came in Naseem Khushi's 28 from 11. Without the calming left-arm spin of Roelof van der Merwe, who gave away just 14 singles in four overs, Oman might have been out of sight. Instead, the Dutch took advantage of a true pitch and shoddy fielding to make it two wins from two.*

At Al Amerat, Oman, February 15, 2019. **Scotland won by six wickets. Ireland 180-7** (20 overs) (P. R. Stirling 56, K. J. O'Brien 65; M. R. J. Watt 3-26); ‡**Scotland 181-4** (18.3 overs) (H. G. Munsey 50, K. J. Coetzer 74, C. S. MacLeod 35*). *PoM:* K. J. Coetzer. *Both sides set record opening stands. For Ireland, Stirling and Kevin O'Brien put on 115 from 70 balls, before an inspired spell from slow left-armer Mark Watt removed the top three. There was modest support down the order, and on a flat pitch the Scots were set 181. Their openers put on 109 from just 52 – George Munsey smashed 50 from 27 and Kyle Coetzer an even faster 74 from 38 – allowing the middle order to absorb a pair of ducks, from Berrington and Matthew Cross, then coast home.*

At Al Amerat, Oman, February 17, 2019. **Ireland won by one wicket. Netherlands 182-9** (20 overs) (T. P. Visée 78, M. P. O'Dowd 38; S. R. Thompson 4-18); ‡**Ireland 183-9** (20 overs) (K. J. O'Brien 46, A. Balbirnie 83; F. J. Klaassen 3-31, P. A. van Meekeren 4-38). *PoM:* A. Balbirnie. *Finishes don't get much tighter. Ireland, seven down, needed 12 from the last over, bowled by Paul van Meekeren. Stuart Poynter took a single from the first, and Josh Little a boundary from the second; but Little was run out from the third trying to turn one into two. Boyd Rankin skyed the next and was caught, though did get Poynter back on strike. He declined a single from the fifth, then clonked a last-gasp leg-side six, ending the Netherlands' run of five T20I victories over Ireland. Earlier, Visée, dropped on ten, went on to a 36-ball 78, and his stand of 116 with the more sober O'Dowd was – as had become traditional in Oman – a national first-wicket record. Almost as predictable was a subsequent collapse, the damage now inflicted by Stuart Thompson, the eighth bowler used by Stirling; his 4-18 was a career-best in all cricket. At 99-1 in the 11th over, with Andy Balbirnie heading for his highest T20 score, Ireland were in control, but Fred Klaassen and van Meekeren came within a whisker of swinging it for the Dutch.*

At Al Amerat, Oman, February 17, 2019. **Scotland won by seven wickets. Oman 111** (19.3 overs) (Sandeep Goud 31*; A. Neill 3-21, M. R. J. Watt 3-20); ‡**Scotland 115-3** (15.3 overs) (R. D. Berrington 47*). *PoM:* A. Neill. *T20I debuts:* Wasim Ali (Oman); A. Neill (Scotland). *After dismissing Oman for comfortably the lowest total of the tournament, Scotland won with sufficient speed to finish top on net run-rate. The performance of debutant Adrian Neill – a 6ft 8in seamer born in South Africa – was instrumental in dismantling Oman. He struck twice in his first two overs as they limped to 17-4 after six, and past three figures thanks only to Sandeep Goud, who walloped 31* from No. 8. Mohammad Nadeem bowled the Scottish openers and, when Cross was third out at 42, the game was evenly poised. Berrington and MacLeod saw Scotland home – and to the title.*

Scotland 4pts (NRR 0.87), Netherlands 4pts (0.20), Ireland 4pts (0.03), Oman 0pt (–1.10).

OMAN PENTANGULAR T20 SERIES IN 2019-20

1 Oman   2 Ireland   3 Nepal

As final preparation for the T20 World Cup Qualifier in the UAE, which started a week later, four of the combatants – plus Nepal, who had failed to reach the eliminator – assembled in Oman to acclimatise. Ireland were the favourites, but it was the home side that came out on top, winning all four of their matches with some ease. Their bowlers made the difference: only Ireland scored more than 100 against them (and still lost by 43 runs). Leg-spinner Khawar Ali finished with nine wickets for 60, slow left-armer Aamer Kaleem nine for 70, and seamer Mohammad Nadeem seven for 68. Ireland's Kevin O'Brien hit the only century of the tournament, against Hong Kong, whose inexperienced side were outclassed.

NATIONAL SQUADS

Oman   *Zeeshan Maqsood, Aamer Kaleem, Aaqib Ilyas, Bilal Khan, Fayyaz Butt, Jatinder Singh, Kaleemullah, Khawar Ali, Khurram Nawaz, Mehran Khan, Mohammad Nadeem, Naseem Khushi, J. A. Odedra, Sandeep Goud, Sufyan Mehmood, Suraj Kumar. *Coach:* L. R. D. Mendis.

Hong Kong   *Aizaz Khan, Ahsan Abbasi, A. Bhagwat, K. M. Christie, Ehsan Khan, Haroon Arshad, R. Kapur, S. S. McKechnie, Mohammad Ghazanfar, Nizakat Khan, N. Rana, K. D. Shah, Shahid Wasif, Waqas Barkat, Waqas Khan. *Coach:* D. T. Johnston.

Ireland   *G. C. Wilson, M. R. Adair, A. Balbirnie, G. J. Delany, G. H. Dockrell, S. C. Getkate, B. J. McCarthy, K. J. O'Brien, W. B. Rankin, S. Singh, P. R. Stirling, H. T. Tector, S. R. Thompson, L. J. Tucker, C. A. Young. *Coach:* G. X. Ford.

Nepal   *P. Khadka, D. S. Airee, B. Bhandari, S. Bhari, A. Bohara, S. Jora, S. Kami, K. C. Karan, S. Lamichhane, K. Malla, I. Pandey, R. K. Paudel, L. N. Rajbanshi, P. Sarraf, A. Sheikh. *Coach:* U. Patwal.

Netherlands   *P. M. Seelaar, C. N. Ackermann, P. R. P. Boissevain, B. N. Cooper, S. A. Edwards, B. D. Glover, F. J. Klaassen, M. P. O'Dowd, S. Snater, A. J. Staal, T. van der Gugten, R. E. van der Merwe, P. A. van Meekeren, T. P. Visée. *Coach:* R. J. Campbell.

At Al Amerat, October 5, 2019. **Ireland won by six wickets. Netherlands 167-7** (20 overs) (M. P. O'Dowd 38, B. N. Cooper 65); ‡**Ireland 169-4** (18.2 overs) (A. Balbirnie 32, H. T. Tector 47*). *T20I debut:* C. N. Ackermann (Netherlands). *All six Irish batsmen reached double figures as they chased down a Dutch total which owed much to Ben Cooper's 45-ball 65. Harry Tector finished the job for Ireland with 47* from 26. The South African-born all-rounder Colin Ackermann, who had taken 7-18 – the best figures in T20 matches – for Leicestershire two months previously, made his international debut for the Netherlands, but failed to strike.*

At Al Amerat, October 5, 2019. **Oman won by seven wickets.** ‡**Hong Kong 96-9** (20 overs); **Oman 97-3** (13.5 overs) (Khawar Ali 32, Zeeshan Maqsood 39*). *T20I debuts:* Suraj Kumar (Oman); Ahsan Abbasi, A. Bhagwat, K. M. Christie, Haroon Arshad, S. S. McKechnie, N. Rana (Hong Kong). *After restricting Hong Kong to under 100 – none of their bowlers went for more than a run a ball – Oman breezed past the modest target with 37 to spare.*

At Al Amerat, October 6, 2019. **Nepal won by four wickets. Hong Kong 125-6** (20 overs) (K. D. Shah 31, Waqas Barkat 37; K. C. Karan 4-36); ‡**Nepal 126-6** (19 overs) (B. Bhandari 58*). *T20I debuts:* R. Kapur, Mohammad Ghazanfar (Hong Kong). *Nepal made a meal of what looked a straightforward chase, dipping to 36-4 in the seventh after their captain Paras Khadka fell first ball to Kinchit Shah. But wicketkeeper Binod Bhandari saved the day.*

At Al Amerat, October 6, 2019. **Oman won by 43 runs. Oman 173-9** (20 overs) (Jatinder Singh 40, Aamer Kaleem 46); ‡**Ireland 130** (16.2 overs) (K. J. O'Brien 39; Mohammad Nadeem 3-14, Khawar Ali 3-28). *Jatinder Singh held the Oman innings together, lasting until the 16th over, and then the bowlers stepped in. After Kevin O'Brien fell for 39 from 16, with four sixes, no one else could reach 20 for Ireland.*

At Al Amerat, October 7, 2019. **Ireland won by 66 runs.** ‡**Ireland 208-5** (20 overs) (P. R. Stirling 36, K. J. O'Brien 124; Ehsan Khan 3-32); **Hong Kong 142-9** (20 overs) (Haroon Arshad 45). *O'Brien's blitz – he hit 12 fours and seven sixes – and opening stand of 80 with Paul Stirling put the match well beyond Hong Kong. It was Ireland's first century in T20 internationals; O'Brien had also scored their first in Tests (and fourth in ODIs, after Jeremy Bray and two by William Porterfield).*

At Al Amerat, October 7, 2019. **Nepal won by four wickets. Netherlands 133** (19.3 overs) (M. P. O'Dowd 43; S. Lamichhane 4-20, K. C. Karan 4-17); ‡**Nepal 134-6** (19.5 overs) (P. Khadka 33, K. C. Karan 31*). *Nepal pulled off another narrow victory, thanks to K. C. Karan, who slapped 17 off the first five balls of the final over. The Netherlands had earlier fallen away from 97-2 in the 13th, losing eight for 36. Karan took four wickets, and ran out Fred Klaassen.*

At Al Amerat, October 9, 2019. **Ireland won by 13 runs.** ‡**Ireland 145-8** (20 overs) (P. R. Stirling 59, A. Balbirnie 38); **Nepal 132** (19.5 overs) (M. R. Adair 3-22, G. H. Dockrell 3-23). *A second-wicket stand of 88 between Stirling and Andrew Balbirnie set up a good Irish total, swelled by two late sixes from Stuart Thompson (21* from 11). It proved just beyond Nepal, who declined from 100-2 in the 15th to 116-8, with slow left-armer George Dockrell striking three times in seven balls.*

At Al Amerat, October 9, 2019. **Oman won by seven wickets.** ‡**Netherlands 94** (15.3 overs) (Khawar Ali 4-16, Zeeshan Maqsood 4-7); **Oman 95-3** (15.1 overs) (Aaqib Ilyas 44). *The Netherlands were bundled out for 94, with leg-spinner Khawar Ali taking a hat-trick, before Zeeshan Maqsood grabbed four wickets in 11 balls.*

At Al Amerat, October 10, 2019. **Netherlands won by 37 runs. Netherlands 185-4** (20 overs) (T. P. Visée 68, R. E. van der Merwe 50*, S. A. Edwards 42*); ‡**Hong Kong 148-7** (20 overs) (Haroon Arshad 68; B. D. Glover 4-26). *In the wooden-spoon match, Roelof van der Merwe (50* from 34) and Scott Edwards (42* from 21) biffed 64* from the last 31 balls. That set up a target too steep for Hong Kong, despite their best batting performance of the tournament, led by Haroon Arshad's 68 from 40.*

At Al Amerat, October 10, 2019. **Oman won by six wickets. Nepal 64** (11 overs) (Aamer Kaleem 5-15); ‡**Oman 65-4** (11.5 overs) (Suraj Kumar 42*). *Oman made sure of the title with another clinical bowling display, despatching Nepal for their second-lowest T20I total, after 53 against Ireland in Belfast in July 2015. Only Aarif Sheikh (20) and Dipendra Airee (11) reached double figures, as left-arm spinner Aamer Kaleem picked up Oman's first international five-for.*

Oman 8pts, Ireland 6pts, Nepal 4pts, Netherlands 2pts, Hong Kong 0pts.

CRICKET IN PAPUA NEW GUINEA IN 2019

Arrested development

ANDREW NIXON

To call 2019 a year of contrasts for Papua New Guinea would be an understatement. They were almost unbeatable in Twenty20, but had a wretched time in ODIs. The seniors qualified triumphantly for the T20 World Cup, while the Under-19s were knocked out of their 50-over tournament. It was a rollercoaster 12 months.

The T20 World Cup Qualifier in the UAE in October and November provided a tremendous demonstration of PNG's emerging stature. At the group stage, they notched impressive victories over Namibia – featuring a national record first-wicket stand of 125 between Tony Ura and captain Asad Vala – and the Netherlands, and lost narrowly to Scotland. But they almost made a hash of completing the job on the final day of qualification, when Kenya reduced them to 19 for six. Norman Vanua led a recovery with 54, and they bowled out Kenya for 73 to win comfortably. Even so, they had to await the result of the game between the Netherlands and Scotland. There were celebrations from the watching PNG players when the Dutch failed to chase their target quickly enough: they knew they had won the group – and secured automatic qualification – on net run-rate.

PNG beat Namibia again to secure a place in the final against the Netherlands, which they lost by seven wickets. That defeat, and the one by Scotland, were their only T20 reversals all year. During a tournament in which a number of players struggled with the heat, PNG were unchanged in all eight matches. Earlier in the year, they marched through the East Asia–Pacific qualifier, and won gold at the Pacific Games, beating Vanuatu in the final.

It was a different story in 50-over cricket, though it began well in April, when they regained ODI status at the World Cricket League Division Two tournament in Namibia. On the final day of the round-robin stage, they needed a huge turnaround in net run-rate to overtake Canada. They beat Oman by 145 runs, then saw the Canadians fail to restrict the USA, enabling PNG to sneak above them. They celebrated by winning the third-place play-off against the USA, but it was downhill from there. Eight successive games were lost in two World Cup League Two events, in Scotland and the USA.

The PNG women also won their regional T20 World Cup Qualifier, but missed out on the main event after losing to Thailand. In the Pacific Games, they lost the gold medal match to Samoa. The Under-19s were also attempting to reach the World Cup, but missed out in extraordinary circumstances. On the day they were due to play the decisive game against hosts Japan, it was announced that ten PNG players had been suspended for disciplinary reasons, and the match forfeited. It emerged that they were in a police cell, after being arrested the previous night for shoplifting. All were asked to undertake community service at home.

CRICKET IN SCOTLAND IN 2019

It never rains…

WILLIAM DICK

After the fireworks of their historic ODI victory over England the previous year, it may be harsh to describe 2019 as a damp squib for Scottish cricket. But there was certainly nothing to match the euphoria. The national side were unable to add to their haul of big-name victims, losing to Afghanistan and Sri Lanka when they visited Edinburgh as part of their World Cup warm-ups.

After the first match against the Afghans was washed out, Scotland appeared to be in good shape in the second, following a Calum MacLeod century. However, in an echo of their misfortune against West Indies in the World Cup Qualifier in 2018, the Scots came out on the wrong side of the DLS calculations, two runs adrift when the rain arrived. Bad weather also put paid to the first match against Sri Lanka, who won the second comfortably.

The rest of the year's 50-over fixtures were in the World Cup League Two, starting in Aberdeen in August. After a humbling eight-wicket defeat by Oman in the opener, Scotland bounced back to beat Papua New Guinea twice and the Omanis in the return fixture. Slow left-armer Hamza Tahir took four for 37 on his ODI debut, in the first game against PNG, and five for 38 in the win over Oman. Scotland fared less well when the action switched to the UAE in December. They had one win and one defeat from two games against the USA, but contrived to lose to the hosts. It was a disappointing conclusion to Shane Burger's first ten months as national coach.

The UAE was also the venue for the year's most significant action – the T20 World Cup Qualifier. Scotland secured their place at the global showpiece in Australia later this year, but not with the expected style or comfort. Having gone into the tournament as one of the favourites, they were quickly playing catch-up, following a shock opening defeat by Singapore. They had to settle for fifth place, clinched with a rousing chase against Oman.

Oman had been the victims of one of Scotland's most eye-catching performances at the start of the year, when Adrian Neill and Ruaidhri Smith each claimed four for seven to dismiss their hosts for 24 in the first match of a 50-over series; the Scots won 2–1.

The best individual performance was George Munsey's unbeaten 127 from 56 balls in the T20 win over the Netherlands at Malahide in September, the highest score in the format by a Scotland batsman. Their total of 252 for three, and Munsey's opening partnership of 200 with Kyle Coetzer, were also national records.

The Under-19s were unbeaten in winning the Europe Region Qualifier, and took their place at the World Cup in South Africa at the beginning of 2020. The women's team finished a disappointing third in Group A of the T20 World Cup Qualifier, held in Tayside. Scotland defeated the USA, but came up short against Bangladesh and Papua New Guinea. Their most noteworthy performance saw them defeat Ireland for the first time in eight years, during a T20 quadrangular in the Netherlands. They went on to finish a creditable second, behind Thailand.

Malcolm Cannon left his role as chief executive of Cricket Scotland after four years. He was replaced by Gus Mackay, a former Zimbabwe international, who had previously been managing director of Worcester Warriors rugby union club. Mackay intends to continue the pursuit of Full Member status: "This will help us achieve our vision to make cricket mainstream in Scotland, and ensure the long-term sustainability of the game here."

Domestically, Forfarshire were the team of the year, winning the Eastern Premier, the National Grand Final and the Murgitroyd T20 Cup. Eastern Knights won the 50-over and T20 titles.

Winners of Scottish Leagues and Cups
Eastern Premier Division **Forfarshire**. Western Premier Division **Uddingston**. National Champions **Forfarshire**. Citylets Scottish Cup **Heriot's**. Murgitroyd T20 Cup **Forfarshire**. Tilney Pro50 Cup **Eastern Knights**. Tilney T20 Blitz **Eastern Knights**. Women's Premier League **Edinburgh South/ Stewart's Melville**. Beyond Boundaries Women's T20 Cup **Carlton**.

SCOTLAND v AFGHANISTAN IN 2019

First one-day international   At Edinburgh, May 8. **Scotland v Afghanistan. Abandoned.**

Second one-day international   At Edinburgh, May 10. **Afghanistan won by two runs** (DLS). ‡**Scotland 325-7** (50 overs) (M. H. Cross 32, K. J. Coetzer 79, C. S. MacLeod 100, R. D. Berrington 33; Gulbadeen Naib 3-72); **Afghanistan 269-3** (44.5 overs) (Mohammad Shahzad 55, Rahmat Shah 113, Hashmatullah Shahidi 59*). *PoM:* Rahmat Shah. *With Kyle Coetzer making 79, and Calum MacLeod hitting his eighth century, Scotland were hopeful of reprising their shock victory over England 11 months earlier, in their previous official one-day international (when MacLeod also made a hundred). Captaining Afghanistan for the first time, Gulbadeen Naib took three wickets, but had his figures spoiled by George Munsey, who clubbed 20 from the first four balls of his tenth over en route to 28 from 13. A patient century from Rahmat Shah kept Afghanistan in touch as the clouds gathered, and they had their noses in front when the rain intensified. They were without Mohammad Nabi and Rashid Khan, still at the IPL; Mujeeb Zadran arrived on the eve of the match, but did not play. This was Afghanistan's 112th ODI, and Asghar Afghan's 100th, but the first without Nabi; the previous record holder was Steve Tikolo, who played in Kenya's first 49.*

SCOTLAND v SRI LANKA IN 2019

First one-day international   At Edinburgh, May 18. **Scotland v Sri Lanka. Abandoned.**

Second one-day international   At Edinburgh, May 21. **Sri Lanka won by 35 runs** (DLS). **Sri Lanka 322-8** (50 overs) (W. I. A. Fernando 74, F. D. M. Karunaratne 77, B. K. G. Mendis 66, H. D. R. L. Thirimanne 44*; B. T. J. Wheal 3-49); ‡**Scotland 199** (33.2 overs) (M. H. Cross 55, K. J. Coetzer 34, H. G. Munsey 61; A. N. P. R. Fernando 4-34). *PoM:* A. N. P. R. Fernando. *Scotland were left regretting dropped catches as their summer programme ended in defeat. The forecast of rain influenced Coetzer's decision to bowl, but he watched as Avishka Fernando and Dimuth Karunaratne, leading the side in his first ODI since the 2015 World Cup, put on 123, though both were dropped off seamer Brad Wheal. Kusal Mendis and Lahiru Thirimanne kept the scoreboard moving, before Wheal produced an impressive second spell. Chasing a revised 235 in 34 overs, Scotland were well behind the rate when a downpour looked to have brought an early conclusion. But the rain stopped, and there was time for Munsey to threaten an upset with 61 from 42 balls.*

SINGAPORE TWENTY20 TRI-SERIES IN 2019-20

1 Zimbabwe   2 Nepal   3 Singapore

The Indian Association ground at Balestier Road hosted Singapore's first international tri-series, as part of the build-up to the T20 World Cup Qualifier in the UAE. And Singapore, ranked 21st in the world, pulled off a shock by beating a Test-playing nation for the first time, when Zimbabwe went down by four runs in the third match. Singapore's captain, Amjad Mahboob, took two important wickets, and said: "We believed in ourselves. Pre-game, I told the boys to play to our potential, to not be scared." Sean Williams was leading Zimbabwe for the first time after Hamilton Masakadza's retirement, and his side regrouped to win the trophy. Nepal and Singapore both collected three points, although Nepal's net run-rate was slightly better. Their captain, Paras Khadka, slammed the only century of the tournament, but Singapore-born Tim David, who has played for Perth Scorchers in Australia's Big Bash, topped the run-charts with 152.

NATIONAL SQUADS

Singapore   *Amjad Mahboob, A. G. Achar, U. Aryaman Sunil, V. Baskaran, S. Chandramohan, T. H. David, A. Dixit, A. Dutta, R. Gaznavi, A. Krishna, Manpreet Singh, A. Mutreja, N. M. S. Param, J. Prakash, U. Rakshit, R. Rangarajan, Sidhant Singh, S. Vijayakumar. *Coach:* Bilal Asad.

Nepal   *P. Khadka, D. S. Airee, B. Bhandari, S. Bhari, A. Bohara, S. Jora, S. Kami, K. C. Karan, S. Lamichhane, K. Malla, I. Pandey, R. K. Paudel, L. Rajbanshi, P. Sarraf, A. Sheikh. *Coach:* U. Patwal.

Zimbabwe   *S. C. Williams, R. P. Burl, R. W. Chakabva, B. B. Chari, T. L. Chatara, C. R. Ervine, D. Jakiel, N. Madziva, T. Maruma, W. P. Masakadza, W. T. Mashinge, P. J. Moor, C. T. Mutombodzi, R. Mutumbami, T. T. Munyonga, R. Ngarava. *Coach:* L. S. Rajput.

At Singapore, September 27, 2019 (floodlit). **Zimbabwe won by five wickets.** ‡Nepal 132-6 (20 overs) (D. S. Airee 40); **Zimbabwe 133-5** (18.1 overs) (R. P. Burl 41*, R. Mutumbami 40*; S. Lamichhane 3-15). PoM: R. Mutumbami. *T20I debuts:* K. Malla, I. Pandey (Nepal); B. B. Chari (Zimbabwe). *What looked a regulation chase for Zimbabwe had a chaotic start, as leg-spinner Sandeep Lamichhane took three wickets in nine balls, before a run-out made it 37-4 in the fifth over. But from 64-5 at halfway, Ryan Burl and Richmond Mutumbami made the game safe with a stand of 69*.*

At Singapore, September 28, 2019 (floodlit). **Nepal won by nine wickets.** ‡Singapore 151-3 (20 overs) (S. Chandramohan 35, T. H. David 64*); **Nepal 154-1** (16 overs) (P. Khadka 106*, A. Sheikh 39*). PoM: P. Khadka. *T20I debuts:* U. Aryaman Sunil, N. M. S. Param, Sidhant Singh (Singapore); S. Bhari (Nepal). *Tim David thumped four sixes in his 44-ball 64*, which took Singapore past 150. But Paras Khadka trumped him, clattering nine in Nepal's first T20I century; his stand of 145* with Aarif Sheikh hastened victory.*

At Singapore, September 29, 2019 (floodlit). **Singapore won by four runs.** ‡Singapore 181-9 (18 overs) (R. Rangarajan 39, T. H. David 41, Manpreet Singh 41; R. P. Burl 3-24); **Zimbabwe 177-7** (18 overs) (R. W. Chakabva 48, S. C. Williams 66, C. T. Mutombodzi 32). PoM: S. C. Williams. *T20I debuts:* A. G. Achar, A. Dutta (Singapore); R. Ngarava (Zimbabwe). *Singapore pulled off their greatest triumph, beating a Test nation for the first time in an official international. They made 62-0 in the powerplay, before Rohan Rangarajan fell for 39 off 22, with eight fours; David then cracked four sixes, and wicketkeeper Manpreet Singh 41 from 23, in a match reduced to 18 overs a side. At 142-2 in the 14th, Zimbabwe were favourites, but Singapore's captain Amjad Mahboob nabbed opposite number Sean Williams for 66, and in the next over medium-pacer Janak*

Prakash removed Burl and Mutumbami, the finishers in the first match. Zimbabwe needed six from the last two balls, but Timycen Maruma was run out, and Tony Munyonga could manage only a single. "These things happen," said a downcast Williams.

At Singapore, October 1, 2019 (floodlit). **Zimbabwe won by 40 runs. Zimbabwe 160-6** (20 overs) (S. C. Williams 53); ‡**Nepal 120-9** (20 overs) (B. Bhandari 33; S. C. Williams 3-21). *PoM:* S. C. Williams. *T20I debuts:* D. Jakiel, W. T. Mashinge (Zimbabwe). *Zimbabwe bounced back with a comfortable victory that rarely looked in doubt after Khadka fell for 12 in the sixth over of the Nepal chase. That was one of three wickets for slow left-armer Williams, who took the new ball after top-scoring.*

At Singapore, October 2, 2019 (floodlit). **Singapore v Nepal. Abandoned.**

At Singapore, October 3, 2019 (floodlit). **Zimbabwe won by eight wickets. Singapore 167-7** (20 overs) (S. Chandramohan 66, T. H. David 47); ‡**Zimbabwe 168-2** (18.4 overs) (P. J. Moor 92*, T. T. Munyonga 44). *PoM:* P. J. Moor. *A stand of 90 between Surendran Chandramohan and the consistent David set up another competitive Singapore total, but P. J. Moor prevented more embarrassment for Zimbabwe. He made 92*, his highest international score, from 60 balls with nine fours and six sixes, and put on 84 in ten overs with Munyonga.*

Zimbabwe 6pts (NRR 0.83), Nepal 3pts (−0.38), Singapore 3pts (−0.87).

CRICKET IN THE UAE IN 2019

Timeline of a scandal

PAUL RADLEY

For the UAE's first assignment of 2019, the national team had an average age of 32 years six months, typical of a side who have always relied on ready-made expatriate players qualifying by residency. But in the last match of the year, the average age was down to 25. The dramatic shift was not a sudden commitment to youth, but the result of a corruption scandal in which several senior cricketers were banned.

There had been problems at the start of the year, too, with Rohan Mustafa (who lost the captaincy), Ahmed Raza and Rameez Shahzad slapped with eight-week suspensions for critical social-media posts about facilities at a tournament in Pakistan. But this minor embarrassment was overshadowed in October, when six players were embroiled in a spot-fixing scandal.

The timing could not have been worse: ICC's anti-corruption officials entered the players' area in Dubai during the UAE's last warm-up match before the T20 World Cup Qualifier, and led away Mohammed Naveed (the new captain), experienced batsman Shaiman Anwar and seamer Qadeer Ahmed. They were soon charged with breaches of the ICC's code of conduct.

Worse was to come. After two matches of the Qualifier, opening batsman Ashfaq Ahmed was suspended as part of the investigation, then wicketkeeper Ghulam Shabbir went missing. He failed to turn up for a team meeting, and did not board the bus to the ground. Worried officials checked local hospitals, but it turned out he had flown to his home in Pakistan without warning, leaving his kit at the hotel. Despite initial denials, he was also implicated in the inquest. It later emerged that Amir Hayat, a seamer who had been omitted from the Qualifier, had also left without explanation.

Given these seismic shocks, it was no surprise that the UAE – who had gone into the tournament ranked second of the 14 teams – failed to qualify for the big event in Australia. This was hard luck on Mohammad Usman, whose unbeaten 89 against Canada was one of the country's best innings.

By the time of the UAE's next matches – against the USA and Scotland in the World Cup League Two in December – the investigation was ongoing, and the Emirates board had disbanded the selection committee. Dougie Brown, the coach, was given responsibility for picking the team, and went for youth: there were three university students and a schoolboy in the new squad, which included three players bound for the Under-19 World Cup in South Africa.

And the kids were all right. After struggling against the Americans, who led the fledgling table, the UAE finished the year with a morale-boosting win, beating their coach's native Scotland by seven wickets. But it did not save him: Brown was replaced by the former Indian all-rounder Robin Singh early in 2020.

T10 LEAGUE IN 2018-19

PAUL RADLEY

1 Northern Warriors   2 Pakhtoons

When the T10 League was launched in late 2017, the idea that a batsman might score a century seemed risible. But in the tournament's second year, it began to look a matter of when, not if. Shaji Ul Mulk, the UAE property magnate who founded the competition, offered an apartment in one of his developments to the first to get there. Soon, he may be handing over the keys.

Just to prove it was possible, Sherfane Rutherford, a 20-year-old Guyanese left-hander, hit a hundred for Bengal Tigers in a warm-up match. When the action began, Alex Hales – one of those who had laughed off the idea – went closest, with an unbeaten 87 off 32 balls for Maratha Arabians in the semi-final against the Tigers. Not far behind was his England team-mate Jonny Bairstow, who stopped off on his way home from a tour of Sri Lanka to play two games for Kerala Kings, and hit 84 not out off 24 balls, also against the Tigers.

There was no lack of fireworks elsewhere. The opening match included a stunning display by Afghanistan's Mohammad Shahzad, who crashed 74 from 16 balls for Rajputs against Sindhis. With opening partner Brendon McCullum, he chased 95 in four overs. "I would have said there was no chance of someone hitting a century," said Sindhis coach Tom Moody. "But looking at the wicket, the size of the ground, and the striking by Shahzad, there is no reason a batsman couldn't."

The competition was expanded from six teams to eight, and played over 12 days, with a mix of two and three matches a day, all at Sharjah. Amid the orgy of boundaries, the bowlers had their moments. Sindhis leg-spinner Pravin Tambe – en route to the first T10 five-wicket haul – and the Tigers' Aamer Yamin took hat-tricks, around 40 minutes apart in different matches. But the Player of the Tournament was Hardus Viljoen, who took 18 wickets at seven for the champions, Northern Warriors. The Warriors, who beat Pakhtoons in the final, also had the leading run-scorer: Trinidadian Nicolas Pooran hit 324 runs at 54. Defending champions Punjabi Legends did not qualify for the play-offs.

T10 LEAGUE IN 2018-19

	P	W	L	NR	Pts	NRR
NORTHERN WARRIORS	6	5	1	0	10	3.07
PAKHTOONS	6	4	2	0	8	0.26
MARATHA ARABIANS	6	3	3	0	6	0.63
BENGAL TIGERS	6	3	3	0	6	0.37
Punjabi Legends	6	3	3	0	6	–1.12
Rajputs	6	2	3	1	5	–0.78
Kerala Kings	6	2	3	1	5	–1.18
Sindhis	6	1	5	0	2	–1.72

Perhaps the most positive sign was that the post-tournament discussion was about cricket. This time, the sport spoke for itself, rather than in the inaugural year, when sponsored dot balls and incessant boundary interviews with celebrities flown in from the subcontinent suggested a gaudy vanity project. "Proof of concept was achieved last year and consolidated this year," said Ul Mulk. The final was held on the UAE's national day and, with free entry to the north stand, there was a raucous atmosphere. Thousands gathered outside to view the action on the stadium's big screens.

Play-offs **1st v 2nd** Pakhtoons beat Northern Warriors by 13 runs; **3rd v 4th** Maratha Arabians beat Bengal Tigers by seven wickets; **Final eliminator** Northern Warriors beat Maratha Arabians by ten wickets; **Third-place play-off** Bengal Tigers beat Maratha Arabians by six wickets.

Final At Sharjah, December 2, 2018 (floodlit). **Northern Warriors won by 22 runs. Northern Warriors 140-3** (10 overs) (R. Powell 61*, A. D. Russell 38); ‡**Pakhtoons 118-7** (10 overs) (A. D. S. Fletcher 37; C. J. Green 2-11, G. C. Viljoen 2-24). *PoM:* R. Powell. *PoT:* G. C. Viljoen. *Northern Warriors' Caribbean contingent powered them to a comfortable victory – and spoiled the day for Shahid Afridi's UAE fan club. The Warriors' total was set up by third-wicket pair Rovman Powell and Andre Russell, who slammed 62 in 3.2 overs. Powell hit eight fours and four sixes in his 61*. In what proved a pivotal moment, Russell crashed 27 off the sixth over, bowled by Liam Dawson. Pakhtoons looked well placed at 62-1 at halfway but, when Hardus Viljoen bowled Afridi, their hopes departed – along with most of the crowd.*

UNITED ARAB EMIRATES v NEPAL IN 2018-19

One-day internationals (3): UAE 1, Nepal 2
Twenty20 internationals (3): UAE 1, Nepal 2

To the delight of their army of expatriate fans, Nepal came from behind in both the one-day and Twenty20 matches to win two series. It was a triumph for their captain, Paras Khadka, who scored Nepal's first ODI hundred in the decider, and for a group of talented youngsters. Sandeep Lamichhane, the 18-year-old leg-spinner, took seven wickets at 16 in the ODIs, and five at 13 in the T20s. Sundeep Jora, 17, totalled 81 runs in the T20 games, and Rohit Paudel, a year younger, 71 in two ODIs. The numbers were not spectacular but, in only Nepal's second one-day series, they revealed potential. "They field unbelievably well, and at critical moments they don't get flustered," said the UAE coach, Dougie Brown. The 39-year-old Shaiman Anwar was a beacon, scoring 98 runs at 32 in the ODIs, and 103 at 34 in the T20s. Nepal's large and vocal following gathered in a section of the ICC Academy ground dubbed "Kathmandu Corner". For the second T20 match, several hundred were locked out, leading to calls for bigger venues for their next tour. In Nepal, there were photographs of children watching footage on their phones during lessons; rocketing demand caused the live stream to crash.

NEPAL TOURING TEAM

*P. Khadka (50/20), D. S. Airee (50/20), P. S. Airee (50/20), B. Bhandari (50/20), A. Bohara (20), S. Jora (20), S. Kami (50/20), K. C. Karan (50/20), S. Lamichhane (50/20), G. Malla (50/20), R. K. Paudel (50/20), L. N. Rajbanshi (50/20), B. Regmi (50/20), P. Sarraf (50/20), A. Sheikh (50/20). Coach: J. Tamata.

First one-day international At Dubai (ICC Academy), January 25, 2019. **United Arab Emirates won by three wickets. Nepal 113** (33.5 overs) (S. Kami 30; Mohammad Naveed 3-31, Amir Hayat 3-19); ‡**United Arab Emirates 116-7** (32.1 overs) (Ghulam Shabbir 30). PoM: Amir Hayat. *ODI debuts: Fahad Nawaz (UAE); B. Bhandari, L. N. Rajbanshi, P. Sarraf (Nepal). Such was the level of support for Nepal that UAE captain Mohammad Naveed said it felt like an away match. But his team were not cowed, and squeezed home in a low-scoring contest, thanks to an eighth-wicket partnership of 43* between Amir Hayat and Imran Haider, who had earlier shared five wickets. On a green pitch, Nepal's batsmen had struggled – only Sompal Kami reached 30 – but their bowlers fought back tenaciously. The UAE were in peril at 73-7, before Hayat and Haider saved the day.*

Second one-day international At Dubai (ICC Academy), January 26, 2019. **Nepal won by 145 runs.** ‡**Nepal 242-9** (50 overs) (G. Malla 44, R. K. Paudel 55; Amir Hayat 3-41, Imran Haider 3-54); **United Arab Emirates 97** (19.3 overs) (S. Kami 5-33, S. Lamichhane 4-24). PoM: S. Kami. *ODI debut: C. P. Rizwan (UAE). After top-scoring for Nepal in the first match, Kami returned to his stronger suit, taking his country's first ODI five-for. Sandeep Lamichhane also collected four cheap wickets. At 16 years 146 days, Nepal's Rohit Paudel had become the youngest scorer of an ODI half-century, taking a record held by Pakistan's Shahid Afridi since October 1996.*

Third one-day international At Dubai (ICC Academy), January 28, 2019. **Nepal won by four wickets. United Arab Emirates 254-6** (50 overs) (C. P. Rizwan 45, Shaiman Anwar 87, Mohammad Boota 59*); ‡**Nepal 255-6** (44.4 overs) (G. Malla 31, P. Khadka 115). PoM: P. Khadka. *ODI debut: S. Jora (Nepal). When Kami hit C. P. Rizwan for six to complete Nepal's chase, his team-mates sprinted into the middle to celebrate their first ODI series win. They shared it with their boisterous supporters, who had turned up in numbers, despite it being the first day of the working week. Nepal captain Paras Khadka was the principal architect, hitting his country's first ODI hundred. His side had been wobbling at 129-4 in the 26th, but he ensured they got home with plenty to spare.*

First Twenty20 international At Dubai (ICC Academy), January 31, 2019. **United Arab Emirates won by 21 runs. United Arab Emirates 153-6** (20 overs) (Shaiman Anwar 59, Mohammad Usman 30); ‡**Nepal 132-7** (20 overs) (S. Jora 53*). *PoM:* Shaiman Anwar. *T20I debuts:* Mohammad Boota, C. P. Rizwan (UAE); A. Bohara, S. Jora, R. K. Paudel (Nepal). *Naveed spearheaded the UAE attack with 2-19 to earn a 1–0 lead. They were tidy at the start, and shrewd at the death, snuffing out Nepal's winning hopes. Sundeep Jora, on debut, had kept Nepal interested with 53*; at 17 years 103 days, he took the record for the youngest scorer of a T20I half-century from Hiral Patel of Canada. The UAE had begun poorly after being put in, but a stand of 61 for the fourth wicket between Shaiman Anwar and Mohammad Usman proved decisive.*

Second Twenty20 international At Dubai (ICC Academy), February 1, 2019. **Nepal won by four wickets.** ‡**United Arab Emirates 107** (19.2 overs) (C. P. Rizwan 44; A. Bohara 3-20); **Nepal 111-6** (19.3 overs) (D. S. Airee 47*). *PoM:* D. S. Airee. *T20I debut:* P. Sarraf (Nepal). *Dipendra Airee steered Nepal to a series-levelling victory. At 46-5 in the 11th, they were teetering but, supported by Pawan Sarraf, Airee regrouped, and finished the final over with a six and a four. Nepal's bowlers had done the spadework. Kami struck twice in the first three overs, and Abinash Bohara's three wickets included top-scorer Rizwan.*

Third Twenty20 international At Dubai (ICC Academy), February 3, 2019. **Nepal won by 14 runs. Nepal 104-8** (10 overs); ‡**United Arab Emirates 90-8** (10 overs) (Shaiman Anwar 30). *PoM:* K. C. Karan. *PoS:* A. Bohara. *A rain delay of more than two hours reduced the contest to a ten-over shoot-out, but Nepal were not fazed. After being put in, they recovered from a poor start to post a challenging total, built around Khadka's 29 off 14. In contrast, the UAE reached 29 at the end of the second over. But K. C. Karan removed top-scorer Anwar, then Naveed for a duck, and Nepal's fielding stood up under pressure as they completed their second come-from-behind series win in six days.*

UNITED ARAB EMIRATES v USA IN 2018-19

Twenty20 internationals (2): UAE 1, USA 0

The UAE were relieved to secure a narrow series win against the USA, who were on their first official T20 tour. A rain-ruined first match had been heading in the American's direction, before an excellent all-round performance from the hosts in the second, including a stunning diving catch at deep midwicket by Ahmed Raza. The USA stayed on to play seven 50-over matches, winning six. They beat the UAE five times, and also defeated Lancashire, who were in Dubai to warm up for the county season. Pubudu Dassanayake, the USA coach, said: "It is not easy, especially when you have to put Caribbean players together with Asians, because they have learned the game in different ways."

First Twenty20 international At Dubai (ICC Academy), March 15, 2019. **No result. USA 152-7** (15 overs) (S. R. Taylor 72); ‡**United Arab Emirates 29-2** (3.3 overs). *T20I debuts:* E. H. Hutchinson, Jasdeep Singh, A. Jones, J. S. Malhotra, S. N. Netravalkar, M. D. Patel, T. K. Patel, K. R. P. Silva, S. R. Taylor, H. R. Walsh (USA). *The USA had looked well set to win their first official T20 international, when the last of several rain interruptions ended the match, with nine more balls needed to trigger DLS. The UAE target was 143 in 13. Steven Taylor hit a commanding 72 off 39. Former West Indies Test batsman Xavier Marshall was the only USA player not making his international debut.*

Second Twenty20 international At Dubai (ICC Academy), March 16, 2019. **United Arab Emirates won by 24 runs.** ‡**United Arab Emirates 182-7** (20 overs) (Rohan Mustafa 45, Shaiman Anwar 62); **USA 158-6** (20 overs) (S. R. Taylor 49, X. M. Marshall 31; Sultan Ahmed 3-33). *PoM:* Shaiman Anwar. *Helped by a strong cross-wind, the UAE bowlers made it hard for the USA to clear the short boundary on the west side by aiming outside off stump. Slow left-armer Sultan Ahmed took the new ball and picked up three wickets, including Taylor, who top-scored again. In the UAE innings, Shaiman Anwar hit six sixes in his 62.*

CRICKET IN THE USA IN 2019

Forward, then back

PETER DELLA PENNA

American cricket always seems to be in a state of flux. The year started well, with USA Cricket readmitted to the ICC. The United States were one of the first three Associate Members in 1965, but were expelled in 2017 after a series of administrative dogfights. The men recaptured official ODI status, thanks to a top-four finish at the World Cricket League Division Two in April. And USAC's new board signed a commercial-rights deal with American Cricket Enterprises, promising $1bn of investment. But the second half of the year was grimly familiar to those who had endured the troubled era of the USA Cricket Association.

In Namibia for WCL Division Two, the USA defeated the hosts by two runs, thanks to a five-for by fast bowler Ali Khan, the tournament's leading wicket-taker, with 17. A century from former West Indies batsman Xavier Marshall helped defeat Hong Kong, and secured the prize of 36 official ODIs through to 2022. The success energised ACE, who pledged a T20 franchise league by 2021. Their investment also helped put most of the players on central contracts. But, as The Notorious B. I. G. once sang, "The more money we come across, the more problems we see."

And the problems mounted up. Pubudu Dassanayake, the national side's head coach for three years, jumped in July before he was pushed, under pressure from ACE. The new board's elections, due in August, had not taken place by the end of the year. And the men's, Under-19 and women's teams all failed in World Cup qualifying events. Two of the most influential players, Khan and Hayden Walsh, rejected central contracts, with Walsh joining West Indies after a successful Caribbean Premier League. Two of the replacements – Ian Holland and Cameron Stevenson – were Australian-raised holders of US passports, which highlighted a long-term neglect of domestic development. The USA still ended 2019 top of the Cricket World Cup League Two table, with six wins out of eight. If they are in the top three by January 2022, they will go straight to the qualifying tournament for the 2023 World Cup.

Meanwhile, USAC's membership base plummeted by 87% from a year earlier. More than 5,500 had signed up ahead of the inaugural elections in 2018, but only 713 renewed their membership. The elections were repeatedly delayed – one of the governance violations that had led to three suspensions of the previous board, before their eventual expulsion.

Iain Higgins, a lawyer and former ICC chief operations officer, took over as USAC's chief executive in September. All eyes will be on him in 2020: can he right a ship perpetually on the brink of capsizing?

OTHER TWENTY20 INTERNATIONALS

Turkish non-delight

STEVEN LYNCH

The ICC's decision to award full Twenty20 international status to men's matches between all their member countries, from the start of 2019, always promised to shake up the record books. A similar decision for the women's game, implemented midway through 2018, had resulted in some weird and wonderful tables. There is undoubtedly charm and a whiff of romance about lists featuring exotic venues and improbable teams – but statisticians chuntered about the lowering of standards, and the problems of cataloguing a format which had suddenly mushroomed: 71 countries played official T20 internationals in 2019, with more in the pipeline. These matches could, thought some, be given second-tier status.

Several new landmarks came in the Romania Cup, a five-way tournament played in Ilfov, the home of the Transylvanian Cricket League. It was cut-throat stuff at the top: Austria pinched the title on net run-rate from the Czech Republic and Romania. But the records mainly involved Turkey, who were bowled out for 21, 28 and 32, the three lowest totals in men's T20 internationals (they spanked 53 in their other game). The 21, which included a record eight ducks, represented a comeback from seven for five, but since the Czech Republic had run up 278 for four – equalling the highest T20I total – there was little dancing in the streets of Istanbul. Thrashings by 279 runs (by the Czechs) and 173 (by Romania) knocked Sri Lanka–Kenya and Pakistan–West Indies off the top of the heaviest-defeats list. Turkey's squad included four men over 54, who became the oldest male international cricketers: Osman Goker, 59, was the senior.

Salman Ali, a spokesman for Cricket Turkey, explained: "Seven of our regular players were not issued visas due to various issues, and we had to field a makeshift team because we love our cricket. We were the only side that used only the pool of local talent. All of our players were from Turkish heritage."

It was not just about pratfalls. Botswana also fielded a 53-year-old – the sprightly Antiguan-born seamer James Moses – but were not disgraced after challenging neighbours Namibia, who gained official ODI status during 2019. And tournaments such as the Central American Championships, played in Mexico and won by Belize, featured some close matches with sensible scores.

Elsewhere, match-ups were more redolent of football. Belgium and Germany did battle at Waterloo: Germany won 3–0, but soon lost 2–0 to Italy. Finland had a tough time, losing 2–0 to Denmark in Brøndby, then going down 2–1 to Spain at home in Kerava, just north of Helsinki. Jersey tied the first match of a series with old rivals Guernsey, before winning the last two games; they went on to perform creditably at the T20 World Cup Qualifier. Even more exotic encounters found Malaysia entertaining Vanuatu, and Malawi taking on Mozambique.

CRICKET ROUND THE WORLD IN 2019

COMPILED BY JAMES COYNE AND TIMOTHY ABRAHAM

ICC CRICKET WORLD CUP CHALLENGE LEAGUE AND WORLD CRICKET LEAGUE

In a global pyramid structure with a ten-team World Cup at its apex, reaching the 2023 finals in India was more a motivational speech than sensible aspiration for the 12 nations who embarked on the Cricket World Cup Challenge League – the third tier of qualification. Its unforgiving predecessor, the World Cricket League, ended in Windhoek in a fashion in keeping with its 12-year history. The top four in WCL Division Two took their place in CWC League 2, and secured ODI status; the bottom two joined the teams from Divisions Three and below in the Challenge League. Yet again, a WCL host nation – in this case Namibia – were promoted. They lost two group games, yet stormed to the title, with Jan Frylinck taking five for 18 in the final against Oman.

Papua New Guinea – who later in the year qualified for the T20 World Cup – were going down when Oman reduced them to 32 for five. But their fortunes turned in a stand of 129 between Sese Bau and Kiplin Doriga. Oman then collapsed so spectacularly to left-arm seamer Nosaina Pokana that opener Khawar Ali carried his bat for 29, and PNG won by 145 runs.

That meant Canada were relegated by 0.012 of a run. Despite beating the USA in their last game, they failed to take the tenth wicket, or keep the last pair down to two runs from the final over. Hong Kong's Anshuman Rath headed the run-scoring charts with 290, but could not keep his side – beleaguered by a corruption scandal – off bottom.

Instead of the WCL's promotion and relegation – which caused stress to member boards – the Challenge League comprised 12 teams in two pools, each playing three round robins between 2019 and 2021. The winners would play off with League 2 sides to reach the 2023 World Cup Qualifier.

The first League A was held in Kuala Lumpur, with half the games at Kinrara Oval, now saved from commercial development. Canada racked up 408, 379 and 302 batting first, but lost to Singapore, who then made the short trip home to beat Zimbabwe in a T20 international. Vanuatu somehow defended 65, dismissing Malaysia for 52, with Patrick Matautaava taking five for 19, but they lost their four other games.

The ICC moved the first League B to Oman because of unrest in Hong Kong. It was no surprise that Bermuda – who had to cope without vice-captain Rodney Trott, after his embattled board failed to update his passport – were bottom. It was more of a jolt that Uganda went unbeaten and were so far ahead of Kenya, whose slump continued with just one win from five, their travails signposted by the recall of 46-year-old seamer Lameck Onyango. Italy, who would normally have been relegated from the WCL, survived the restructure, as the 32nd-ranked team in 50-over cricket; they made early headway by beating Kenya, thanks to a century from their South African import Nikolai Smith. JAMES COYNE

QUALIFYING FOR THE T20 WORLD CUP IN 2020

In the first full year since the ICC liberalised the T20 international format, there were almost 600 played across the world by both genders. Most important to the Associates were the final rounds of regional heats, feeding into the global Qualifiers for the men's and women's T20 World Cups in 2020.

Uganda were left cursing the rain in Kampala, where the last four matches in the African Qualifier were washed out, denying them the probability of overhauling Nigeria in third spot. In theory, only the top two qualified. But Zimbabwe were banned from global competition following their board's suspension from the ICC, so Nigeria were added to the T20 World Cup Qualifier instead.

The carrot of appearing in a globally televised T20 World Cup Qualifier prompted several professionals to dig out their EU passports. Germany were fancied to top the European stage, with Craig Meschede and Michael Richardson forming a high-class opening pair. But the late withdrawal of bowlers Dieter Klein and Ollie Rayner on county duty cost Germany in the crunch match: Jersey's Ben Ward smashed 58 not out, and took two wickets in one over of leg-spin to help send his side through.

UAE, as hosts of the T20 World Cup Qualifier, were given a belated bye in Asia, where Nepal were outmuscled in the decisive game by Singapore's Perth Scorchers batsman Tim David, who hit 77 off 43 balls. The USA missed a prime opportunity, beaten twice by hosts Bermuda in the Americas. Delray Rawlins, in his first competitive game since representing England Under-19s, spearheaded the first of those wins with 63.

Germany failed to pass 63 on their debut in the European women's qualifier in La Manga, though the women's regional tournament had few shocks. Namibia were added to the women's global qualifier because of Zimbabwe's enforced absence.　　JAMES COYNE

Reports of both T20 World Cup Qualifiers are on pages 1086 and 1186.

ANTARCTICA

It's a far-flung take on a familiar domestic tale: the unexpected discovery of a hidden treasure in a corner of home. During renovations at the Casey Research Station in the Australian Antarctic Division, an employee found a dusty cricket bat. Covering the well-oiled face were the signatures of the Australia and Sri Lanka teams from the 1987-88 Test at the WACA. Underneath the scrawls of Allan Border, Steve Waugh and Arjuna Ranatunga was an inscription in fine calligraphy: "To the past and future Antartic (*sic*) expeditioners on the opening of the new Casey Station 1988." The most popular theory as to how it ended up in Antarctica, nearly 2,500 miles from its origin, concerns former station leader and sled-dog handler Tom Maggs, who died in 2017. Maggs, whose daughter Bonnie is married to Australia's Test captain Tim Paine, was said to have asked Peter Cummings, the Casey carpenter at the time, to bring back a piece of memorabilia from a secondment at the MCG. Cummings returned with the bat, which was admired, displayed, then forgotten. It's a plausible account, but if Cummings was working in Melbourne, why a signed bat from Perth? Shaun Gillies, Casey's building services supervisor, believes expeditioners used to tune in to a high-frequency audio feed of Channel Nine commentary, and were able to talk during the advert breaks directly to the commentators, who may have arranged for the signed bat to be shipped out to their most isolated listeners. The mystery remains unsolved, but Casey's current crop have put it to good use in the annual Australia Day match on ice. Not that they would allow such a cherished piece of willow to make contact with a ball. "We flip the bat to decide who bats or bowls," said Gillies. "We try to make sure it doesn't hit the deck, because we don't want to put any dents in it." SAM SHERINGHAM

ARGENTINA

The Street Child World Cup finals (see page 856), held at Lord's in 2019, have an echo in some of the most disadvantaged *barrios* of Buenos Aires. The Cricket Sin Fronteras (Cricket Without Borders) initiative began ten years ago in the impoverished south-eastern Villa 21–24 in Barracas. Daniel Juarez and Silvina Román, then auditors for the Archdiocese of Buenos Aires, noticed the possibilities offered by cricket for the social inclusion and personal development of local youngsters. Support was readily given by inspirational local priest Padre José María Di Paola, known to all as Padre Pepe: Caacupé CC were born, named after a shrine in Paraguay, from where many of the inhabitants trace their roots. Significantly, endorsement came from the city's sports-loving Archbishop, Jorge Mario Bergoglio, later Pope Francis. But, after Padre Pepe was chased off his patch by drug dealers, he moved north in 2013 to a parish where many of the residents eke out an existence scavenging from the municipal recycling dump. Pepe took Sin Fronteras with him, and before long another club were created, extending to the local Penal Unit 46, where the prisoners formed their own side, Los Leones de Judah. In 2017, Sin Fronteras travelled to Rome, where Pope Francis blessed bats handmade by the prisoners, and a match was played at Capannelle against St Peter's CC, the Vatican's team. This was reciprocated in early 2019, when St Peter's visited Buenos Aires on one of their Light of Faith tours. Some of the junior cricketers underwent a coaching session with the touring Hurlingham Club (founded on the banks of the Thames in 1869 to shoot pigeons). The club celebrated their 150th anniversary with a short tour that included matches and a dinner at their namesake Hurlingham Club in the northern suburbs of Buenos Aires – a bastion of the Anglo-Argentine community since their foundation in 1888. Sin Fronteras currently extend across seven schools, and involve 1,500 boys and girls, some progressing to junior Argentine sides. It is the Latinisation programme Argentine cricket desperately needed, after centuries as a sport played in members' clubs. CHARLES FELLOWS-SMITH

THE EUROPEAN CRICKET LEAGUE
Club Med, with Pavel

JAMES COYNE

For Daniel Weston, the light-bulb moment came when he attended an ICC Europe conference armed with data showing there were 23m cricket fans in Europe. "An ICC figure got up and said, independently: 'Research suggests there are 22m cricket fans in Europe…' I thought: 'I'm on to something here.'"

Weston, 36, a hedge-fund manager who has settled in Munich, came through the Western Australia youth system as a wicketkeeper-batsman. His dapper glovework stood out for Munich CC and Germany, and he watched the number of cricket clubs spiral from 50 to 370 on the back of Afghan and Pakistani migration.

Across much of Europe, cricket is a haphazard, self-funded, immigrant game, given little mainstream coverage. And yet the standard of fast bowling or ball-striking can be phenomenal. One day, Weston bought 18 GoPro cameras, and broadcast these audacious skills on smartphones via his app, German Cricket TV. He had his eye on a cricketing Champions League, and took the idea to Roger Feiner, former director of broadcasting at FIFA, arguing that cricket was the summertime bat-and-ball team sport Europe was missing. Though sceptical, Feiner gave him invaluable connections. Soon, New Balance, Kookaburra and Red Bull were commercial partners or suppliers, and Weston had struck a deal for an eight-team European Cricket League with 43 broadcast partners across 120 countries. Heading to La Manga in July were VOC Rotterdam (Netherlands), Svanholm (Denmark), SG Findorff (Germany), Ville de Dreux (France), JCC Brescia (Italy), Catalunya (Spain), Cluj (Romania) and St Petersburg (Russia) – with €20,000 for the winners.

The ICC sanctioned the ten-overs-a-side ECL on the proviso that no more than four ODI players took part. In the event, there were three, all with Dutch champions VOC, and their refined hitting was telling: Scott Edwards smoked 137 not out off 39 balls as VOC easily defeated Findorff in the final. The 50-yard boundaries led to fast scoring, and 45-minute innings appealed to football-conditioned Europeans. The Dutch, German and Danish clubs fared best, with flashes of brilliance and ineptitude from most.

The first hundred, off just 28 balls, had come from Dreux's Ahmed Nabi, against Cluj. He was out when Cluj's president, Pavel Florin, shuffled in to bowl, despite not having recovered from a broken leg. A broad-shouldered, greying, 40-year-old bodybuilder and nightclub manager, Florin was one of few native European players, and his old-style lob bowling was about to catapult him to fame. His over, which cost a respectable 13, with no sixes, went viral. Twitter was predictably judgmental, with Florin ridiculed, then feted; both seemed wide of the mark. "My bowling isn't beautiful," he said. "But I'm a slow bowler. Is it a problem? I think not."

Australian broadcasters Fox Cricket rushed to poke fun, tweeting: "Ladies and gentlemen… welcome to the European Cricket League", followed by three shoulder-shrugging emojis. "My reaction," says Weston, "was 'who are these arrogant pricks?'" Then he found out that viewership had tripled, and soon the ECL were trumpeting a supposed worldwide audience of 140m households. Florin milked his fame: he appeared in the MCC president's box during the Lord's Ashes Test, was interviewed on *TMS*, and played for Surrey Hills fifth XI in Melbourne league cricket. His Australian visa application was initially rejected, but another backlash brought an abrupt U-turn.

Ahead of the 2020 event, Weston was selling €50 shares in the ECL, and looking to double the teams to 16, competing over a week. And Florin could be back, since Cluj retained their Romanian title. When this Champions League introduces a second group stage to capitalise on the global TV bounty, cricket will truly have conquered Europe.

ECUADOR

Julian Assange's removal from the Ecuadorian embassy in London got rid of a "stone in the shoe", according to the country's president, Lenín Moreno. The decision, however, caused minor consternation among Ecuador's cricketers. Some had written to Assange, the Australian founder of WikiLeaks, offering honorary membership of the Quito CC, shortly before Moreno ended his near seven-year asylum. In Belmarsh Prison since April 2019, and reportedly in poor health, Assange had yet to reply. He does, however, have a connection with the game. Born in Townsville, Queensland, he boasted of his family's cricket pedigree: "My paternal great-grandfather, James Greer Kelly, had four sons who were brilliant sportsmen, well known for their prowess at cricket." Should Assange ever make it to Quito, he will find a vertiginous backdrop for breathless games of high-altitude cricket at 2,765m above sea level. Matches take place on a bumpy field inside Parque Carolina, in front of shirtless bodybuilders, a large portrait of Pope John Paul II, and two active volcanoes. The bustling green space is open to the public, and breaks in play have been caused by everything from vagabonds clutching bottles of hooch to teenage dance troupes waving pom-poms. During anti-government protests last year, an army helicopter landed on the dusty cricket strip one Saturday afternoon, although a military curfew meant that day's match had already been cancelled. Quito's cricketers have been joined by enthusiastic Venezuelans. More than a million entered Ecuador following the crisis in their own country, and some are eager to adapt their baseball skills. Quito CC have struck up relations with tapeball cricketers in the port city of Guayaquil, where the sport was first played in 1873. The Ecuador Cricket Federation are set to be established in early 2020, to put the game on a firmer footing and spread it among nationals, with the intention of participating in the next South American Championships.   TIMOTHY ABRAHAM

GUAM

The world's largest per capita consumers of tinned Spam are found on this US island territory in the Pacific Ocean, 4,000 miles from Hawaii on the other side of the International Date Line. The processed pork was introduced by US soldiers during the Second World War, and the average Guamanian consumes 16 tins a year; Guam CC's players usually request a different filling for their teatime sandwiches. The club comprise 25 diehards who gather every Sunday, all year round, either in the shadow of American Football goalposts at the University of Guam, or at the tranquil palm-tree-lined Ypao Park in Tamuning. With matting too expensive to ship, the wicket is uncut grass. A net has been built next to a local gym, and attempts made to encourage locals, who are all US citizens, to participate. "We have done demonstrations for the local rotary club, US Navy, and university students," says Jetan Sahni, the driving force of cricket on the island since 1996. A lack of fresh opposition proves a little frustrating – the nearest country is Palau, 800 miles to the south-west. In the Pacific, there are no easy away trips.   OWEN AMOS

ICELAND

After 17 years of jaunty social games, Icelandic cricket's merry ship had been foundering at the start of 2018, having hit the twin icebergs of player politics and bankruptcy. In desperation, Krikketsamband Íslands took to Twitter, and put the whole team up for sale. A global community of cricket bloggers came to the rescue, and a crowdfunding campaign raised $10,000 in six months. A high-profile social media presence – risqué and iconoclastic, frequently at the expense of other cricketing nations – became Iceland's shtick, with replica jerseys bought by fans in every continent. The team travelled to London, beating a Rest of the World XI captained by former New Zealand seamer Iain O'Brien, and won their first international, against Switzerland, by 115 runs. The country's first cricket ground – and the world's northernmost – was created at the aptly named Vidistadatun (Meadow of the Willow) in Hafnarfjörður. At the opening ceremony in May 2019, the first ball was bowled by the British ambassador, and struck by Katrin Jakobsdóttir, Iceland's prime minister. The guest opponents were the Captain Scott XI, stars of the books *Rain Men* and *Penguins Stopped Play*, who urged the Icelanders to commit their own saga to print.   KIT HARRIS

LATVIA

Latvia's cricketing pretensions rest on claims – long enshrined in *Wisden* (see page 1358) – that Jānis Lūsis, the great Soviet javelin thrower of the 1960s and '70s, once hurled the cricket ball 150 yards (137 metres). That's a world record if true, though the competition, a staple of Victorian sports days, is rather less celebrated in Latvia than Lūsis's haul of Olympic medals. "It's possible I did it," says Lūsis, now 80. "I've thrown stones further than 137 metres!" So, for now, Robert Percival clings to the verified record of 140 yards and two feet, set at Durham Sands Racecourse in 1882. Still, Latvia can just about claim a 1987 World Cup winner in the Adelaide-born Andris Kārlis Zesers, son of a Latvian construction worker, who played against India and New Zealand in that tournament; Evan Gulbis has won two Sheffield Shields for Victoria. They would all be surprised to know Latvia has just marked a kind of centenary. After the country's hard-won independence from the Russian Empire in 1918, the United Baltic Corporation of London began passenger and cargo services, bringing a small British community to Riga. The Riga Cricket Club took out English-language notices in local newspapers ahead of matches against visiting Royal Navy ships. In a period of their national life that many Latvians look back on fondly, the sight of Riga CC playing in Peters Park was part of a weekend stroll on the west bank of the Daugava – until a policeman insisted on inspecting the game from short midwicket, and was struck on the head. The municipality banned the game on safety grounds. Riga CC relocated to Mežaparks, a lakeside forest suburb, where they rented from the Baltic German club SV Kaiserwald. Most foreigners left Latvia under ratcheting tension in the 1930s, and the two fields where Riga CC had pitched stumps became haunting memorials of two brutal occupations: the Nazis turned Kaiserwald into a Jewish concentration camp; and, in 1985, the Soviet occupiers erected a statue in Peters Park (renamed Victory Park) to symbolise their triumph. The monument's continuing presence offends many Latvians; ultra-nationalists attempted to blow it up in 1997. Latvia's second independence brought cricket back via Indian and Sri Lankan medical students, who revived the name of Riga CC at a ground out by Tukums Airport. And with a matting wicket recently laid in full view of faculty buildings and residential tower blocks at Turība University – midwicket is again occupied, this time by a cluster of birch trees – cricket is starting to get visibility once more… as long as local bobbies accept the ball is hard.   JAMES COYNE

LEBANON

To call Shatila, a district of Beirut, a refugee camp suggests rows of temporary structures. But in its square kilometre there are as many as 25,000 refugees from Palestine and, more recently, Syria – and an unlikely cricket team. Labyrinthine, ramshackle Shatila, set up in 1949, has precious little space, and is a no-go area for most Beirutians; even the police do not venture in, as drugs, weapons and violence are rife. And yet Richard Verity, a member of North Middlesex CC who works for management consultants McKinsey, decided he would start a team, with help from local educational charity Basmeh & Zeitooneh, London-based charity Capital Kids Cricket, and volunteer language students from Durham University. "On the first day, about 20 curious children turned up," he says. "On the second, we had 120. We were working through Arabic interpreters, and had to teach everything twice – to the facilitators, then the children – but we did a week of coaching, and it was a good fit. There seemed to be some kind of benefit in teaching a game that had no colonial echoes for the Syrian refugees, who had never heard of it. It could stand on its own two feet." At Brummana High School in Mount Lebanon, they have a keen ally in David Gray, a cricket-loving Scottish headmaster. Away games for Shatila are the first time many children had left the camp. "It's a bit counter-cultural in this world, but we're teaching these children to win cricket matches," Verity added. "There is no condescension." He has taken the game to the Beqaa Valley too, two hours closer to the Syrian border, where most refugees farm the land in exchange for being allowed to live there. "Many things did not come naturally to the children: concentration, obeying rules, not fighting each other. But they always turn up: in storms, in heatwaves, in Ramadan." Political unrest has shut schools, and the banks will not dispense cash, but cricket goes on.   JAMES GRAY

LIBERIA

Michael Nyannah had to walk before he could make runs. In 1992, Liberia's civil war forced him to flee his homeland as a child, on foot, to neighbouring Côte d'Ivoire. He stayed for four years while the conflict raged, and became hooked on cricket at a refugee school, vowing to pursue it on his return home. Africa's oldest republic – created for freed African-American slaves – Liberia has had the odd brush with cricket. In March 1882, during a territorial dispute with Sierra Leone, it made its first recorded appearance when the *Monrovia Observer* mentioned a "cricket match between eleven gentlemen from the Man-of-War *Briton* and eleven gentlemen of this city, with victory for the latter". In 1963, Britons and West Indians laid a matting wicket on top of hard laterite soil in an army garrison, but the up-and-down track caused too many injuries, and cricket retreated. So Nyannah was starting from scratch with the Liberia National Cricket Federation in 2003: the kit comprised one cricket bat donated by an Indian expat. A drive to recruit more Liberians began in 2010 at the William Gabriel Kpoleh Memorial High School. On Fridays, Nyannah taught the history and Laws of cricket, with Saturdays for practice. Eventually, the school laid a permanent cement wicket. A decade later, many of the original boys represent an all-Liberian side who compete in the mainly expat Liberian Premier League. The 12 other teams have chipped in to cover the costs of transport and kit. LPL matches take place in the shadow of Monrovia's SKD Stadium, though Ebola stopped play in 2014, when the football ground was commandeered as a treatment clinic. The Ministry of Youth and Sport now recognise the game, and have allotted space for a dedicated ground. In 2018, former World Footballer of the Year George Weah was sworn in as Liberia's president. It is hoped his Jamaican wife, Clar, will fill him in on cricket's nuances. TIM OSCROFT

MALI

After almost 18 years of cricket, Mali entered the record books for their eye-watering six all out – Extras top-scored with five – against Rwanda. Their subsequent totals on debut in the Kwibuka Women's T20 tournament in Kigali were 11, 10, 30 for nine, 17 and 14. Yet there was more to the story than the scorecards. In 2001, few Malians knew anything about cricket. In those days of handmade local equipment, a small band in one school in Bamako caught the bug. Led by the courageous Kawory Berthe, a group of slightly bemused Malians and an amateur enthusiast – me – formed La Fédération Malienne de Cricket, or FeMaCrik, recognised by national government, and admitted as an ICC Affiliate Member. In a country of many cultures, limited resources and multiple languages, FeMaCrik have taken the love of cricket and its values through Bamako's suburbs and deep into the interior. Despite the enthusiast's permanent return to the UK in 2011, a coup in 2012, civil unrest and continuing insecurity, the sport is still spreading. The cricket programme in the desert city of Tombouctou (Timbuktu) even survived a 2012 jihadist occupation. There are many adult men's, youth and junior sides, all with regular competitions. For young women, the picture is more complicated, with expectations or imperatives that they should find a job or get married; the youngest member of an inexperienced squad taken to Rwanda was 14-year-old Balkissa Coulibaly. Some years ago, the ICC and others invested in training Malian coaches and umpires. A pack of kit arrived recently, but the carton contained T-shirts. The real need is for bats, balls and stumps, especially plastic sets. The second priority is a ground: Malians currently play on hard basketball courts, football pitches, desert or rocky patches. Plastic Flicx pitches were unrolled, but are now unusable. Another essential is to break the chicken-and-egg cycle of conditional aid: people have offered equipment or grounds if FeMaCrik can increase the number of players. But without equipment you cannot play! The Malians, though, are inspirational. Given encouragement and investment, they will enter the record books for better reasons. PHIL WATSON

MEXICO

From its home at the Reforma Athletic Club, Mexican cricket is on the up and up. The club, on the outskirts of Mexico City, lay claim to the second-highest grass wicket in the world and, at 2,300 metres above sea level, the ball travels further. Reforma's position, and a distinctive triangular-roofed clubhouse, has long been a draw for touring sides. MCC came in 2017, and again in April 2019, this time as guests for the men's Central American Championships. MCC were beaten in the final by Belize, for whom Glenford Banner rained sixes into Reforma's tennis courts. Also in April, Mexico's women won a series against Costa Rica, and were crowned the first champions of Central America. Ana Laura Montenegro was selected in the ICC Americas Women's XI who travelled to Florida to provide warm-up opposition in the T20 World Cup Americas Qualifier: they beat Canada, and might have shocked the USA if not for rain. In recognition of the Asociación Mexicana de Cricket's development drive, Mexico's women won the 2019 ICC Best Mother and Daughter Programme award. Men's league cricket is now established in Mexico City, Guadalajara, Monterrey and Queretaro, with the first national championship won by Guadalajara, who triumphed again in 2019 on their home carpet at the city's university. The men's national team, boosted by expansion beyond the historic heartland of Mexico City, won the 2018 South American Championships in Bogotá, and were runners-up in Lima a year later. There was, perhaps, some latitude in allowing a Central American team to compete south of the Darién Gap. CRAIG WHITE (*secretary of the Asociación Mexicana de Cricket*)

MOROCCO

In the mid-1990s, Mohamed Drissi was outside Rabat's Hilton Hotel with the rest of Morocco's tiny band of cricketers, when they had a chance encounter with a fellow Arab. Intrigued, he promised to provide some kit: Abdul Rahman Bukhatir had grown to love cricket during trips to Lord's in the 1970s, and built a stadium in Sharjah, his home town. The sport's biggest names flocked there, but Sharjah was shrouded in match-fixing allegations, and Bukhatir shifted focus to Tangier, where he built a $28m sports complex. In 2002, Pakistan, Sri Lanka and South Africa were tempted for a triangular tournament: Sanath Jayasuriya's side won the $250,000 bounty – and the inaugural Morocco Cup. Bukhatir discovered more Moroccan cricketers playing with a tennis ball on scrubland in Casablanca; he provided equipment, as well as Mohinder and Surinder Amarnath as coaches. Locals began to play too, and in 1999 the Fédération Royale Marocaine de Cricket joined the ICC. However, plans for another Morocco Cup, featuring Australia, New Zealand and West Indies, foundered after suicide bombings in Casablanca in May 2003 killed 45. Tangier never hosted another major series, but Bukhatir was still ploughing $100,000 a year into the domestic game, and a second ground was built at Salé. Morocco's national team, now coached by Australia's Gary Cosier, were keen, if not as keen as their administrators were on Bukhatir's largesse. Cosier returned home, and Bukhatir pulled the plug. The government stepped in with $90,000 a year, but greed and feckless administration stymied progress. In 2009, Morocco were in Qatar en route to ICC Africa Division Three in Malawi, when the players discovered no one had arranged visas, and they had to fly home. Officials ignored repeated requests for accounts and an updated constitution, and the federation fell apart; a digger was abandoned on the outfield at Tangier, sheep grazed in the nets. Morocco were expelled from the ICC in 2018, the cricketers knowing nothing about an ultimatum ICC Africa claimed to have issued. After two decades and more than $5m investment, Bukhatir's international ground lies derelict. The game in the Maghreb looks finished.   STEVE MENARY

ZANZIBAR

Who is Zanzibar's most famous cricketer? A clue: he is also the most famous person to have come from the archipelago, and his real name was Farrokh Bulsara. Before he became Queen frontman Freddie Mercury, Farrokh was sent from Zanzibar to St Peter's boarding school in Panchgani, India. Depending on which of his former classmates or biographers you believe, he either "loathed" cricket, or was "especially good" at it. In later years, Mercury was renowned for his white outfits on stage, but school photos show he sported cricket whites too. His prowess, however, seemingly went no further than house matches. He went back to Zanzibar in 1963 and, if he played any cricket there, it would have been among the last in any official structure. In January 1964, a month after Zanzibar gained independence from the British, members of the African majority overthrew the ruling sultan and his mainly Arab government in a bloody revolution that claimed 17,000 lives. Zanzibar joined with Tanganyika to form modern-day Tanzania. Along with thousands of other South Asians and Arabs, the Bulsara family – who were Parsis – fled; they settled in Harrow. The revolution led to the game's decline, with the Cricket Association of Zanzibar lying dormant for more than two decades – a far cry from its heyday, when employees of the British-based Eastern Telegraph Company introduced cricket in the late 1870s. The first recorded match took place in 1890 – 23 years before mainland Tanganyika. Almost all clubs had been organised along ethnic lines, and many were repurposed after independence, while pitches at the Mnazi Mmoja grounds in Stone Town were lost to flooding. There was an attempt to revive cricket in 2007, when MCC popped over during a tour of Tanzania and Malawi. MCC were comfortable 57-run winners over the Zanzibar Stars in a 15-over-a-side thrash at the Amaan Football Stadium. A smattering of Indian expats continue to play tapeball on concrete pitches, and they recently captured the interest of a local television channel, but a return to the glory days appears a way off.   JACK SKELTON

GLOBAL TOURNAMENTS

ICC WORLD CRICKET LEAGUE

	Date	Promoted	Relegated
Division Two	Apr	Namibia, Oman, Papua New Guinea, USA	Canada, Hong Kong

CRICKET WORLD CUP CHALLENGE LEAGUE

	Date	Points after first round
League A	Sep	Canada 8, Singapore 8, Qatar 6, Denmark 4, Malaysia 2, Vanuatu 2
League B	Dec	Uganda 10, Hong Kong 7, Italy 5, Jersey 4, Kenya 3, Bermuda 1

ICC T20 WORLD CUP REGIONAL QUALIFIERS

	Date	Promoted	Others
Africa	May	Namibia, Kenya, Nigeria	Uganda, Botswana, Ghana
Americas	Aug	Canada, Bermuda	USA, Cayman Islands
Asia	Jul	Singapore	Qatar, Nepal, Kuwait, Malaysia
East Asia–Pacific	Mar	PNG	Philippines, Vanuatu
Europe	Jun	Jersey	Germany, Italy, Denmark, Guernsey, Norway

OTHER TOURNAMENTS

	Date	Winners	Runners-up	Others
Asian W Region T20	Jan	Saudi Arabia	Qatar	Bahrain, Kuwait, Maldives
Spain T20 tri-series	Mar	Spain	Malta	Estonia XI
C American Champ	Apr	Belize	MCC	Panama, Mexico, Costa Rica
Malaysia T20 tri-series	Jun	Malaysia	Maldives	Thailand
Pacific Games	Jul	PNG	Vanuatu	Samoa
Romania Cup T20	Aug	Austria	Czech Rep	Romania, Luxembourg, Turkey
S American Champ	Oct	Argentina	Mexico	Peru, Colombia, Uruguay, Brazil, Chile
Hellenic Premier Lge	Oct	Bulgaria	Greece	Serbia
Iberia Cup T20	Oct	Spain	Portugal	Gibraltar
South Asian Games	Dec	Bangladesh U23	Sri Lanka U23	Nepal, Maldives, Bhutan

ICC T20 WOMEN'S WORLD CUP REGIONAL QUALIFIERS

	Date	Promoted	Others
Africa	May	Zimbabwe, *Namibia	Tanzania, Uganda, Rwanda, Kenya, Nigeria, Mozambique, Sierra Leone
Americas	May	USA	Canada
Asia	Feb	Thailand	Nepal, UAE, China, Hong Kong, Malaysia, Kuwait
East Asia–Pacific	May	PNG	Samoa, Vanuatu, Indonesia, Japan, Fiji
Europe Qualifier	Jun	Netherlands, Scotland	Germany

* *Namibia qualified after Zimbabwe were suspended from international competition.*

OTHER WOMEN'S TOURNAMENTS

	Date	Winners	Runners-up	Others
C American Champ	Apr	Mexico	Costa Rica	–
East Asia T20 Cup	Sep	China	Hong Kong	Japan, South Korea
Pacific Games	Jul	Samoa	PNG	Vanuatu, Fiji
S American Champ	Oct	Brazil	Argentina	Chile, Mexico, Peru
South Asian Games	Dec	Bangladesh U23	Sri Lanka U23	Nepal, Maldives
Thailand T20 Smash	Jan	Thailand	Nepal	UAE, Indonesia, Hong Kong, Myanmar, Malaysia, Thailand A, Bhutan, China

Overseas Twenty20 Franchise Cricket

OVERSEAS TWENTY20 FRANCHISE CRICKET IN 2018-19

Freddie Wilde

Since the birth of Twenty20, it has been easy to be swept along by hyperbole: everything is apparently bigger, better and faster. In some respects, this is a consequence of the way the franchise leagues have been presented on television, but it should not mask the fact that we have essentially been watching the evolution of an entirely new sport. Maybe everything seems bigger, better and faster, because it is.

Never has this point been more relevant than during the 2019 Indian Premier League, when West Indian Andre Russell enjoyed a season that in years to come may be regarded as seminal in the development of T20 batting. Russell's performances for Kolkata Knight Riders represented a quantum leap. In 13 innings, he hit 510 runs off 249 balls at a strike-rate of 204. He hammered 31 fours and 52 sixes, and maintained the pace with absurd consistency. For six breathless weeks across India, Russell bent matches to his will. It felt like the future of batting.

His whirlwind season was the highlight of a typically competitive IPL that ended with Mumbai Indians, who had topped the group table, sealing a record fourth title by beating their great rivals Chennai Super Kings by one run in the final. The match-up between two sides who have won seven titles between them is perhaps the greatest rivalry the 20-over game has seen. Chennai have been dominant against every other IPL team using a strategy heavily dependent on spin, but Mumbai's pace battery, led by Lasith Malinga and Jasprit Bumrah, and expertly marshalled by Rohit Sharma, have been able to defeat them regularly. Mumbai now lead 18–12.

In the Pakistan Super League, Quetta Gladiators and Peshawar Zalmi are developing a similarly fascinating rivalry. They met in the final this year, and Quetta were victorious in an unusually one-sided encounter. Eight of their previous 13 matches had been decided in the last over, or by a margin of one run. This time, Quetta – twice runners-up – were deserving winners of a league that is now seeing more fixtures played in Pakistan, and not just the UAE: in 2018-19, it was eight matches; the plan for 2019-20 was that it should be all of them. The PSL continued to produce wonderful domestic bowlers, but an emphasis on overseas batsmen seems to have blocked home-grown talent.

ROLL OF HONOUR

	Winner	
Mzansi Super League (SA)	Jozi Stars	November–December 2018
Big Bash League (Australia)	Melbourne Renegades	December–February 2018-19
Super Smash (New Zealand)	Central Stags	December–February 2018-19
Bangladesh Premier League	Comilla Victorians	January–February 2019
Pakistan Super League	Quetta Gladiators	February–March 2019
Indian Premier League	Mumbai Indians	March–May 2019
Global T20 Canada	Winnipeg Hawks	July–August 2019
T20 Blast (England)	Essex	July–September 2019
Caribbean Premier League	Barbados Tridents	September–October 2019

The most remarkable match of the year was the final of Australia's Big Bash League between the Melbourne teams, the Renegades and the Stars. Needing 53 off 43 balls with all their wickets in hand, the Stars were cruising towards their first title. But the Renegades took pace off the ball, and the Stars imploded, falling 13 short in an astonishing choke. The Renegades, led by Aaron Finch, scored just three fifties in the competition, but consistently strangled opposing sides with their intelligently deployed bowling.

Despite the epic final, the BBL's first season with a full home-and-away programme ran into difficulties. Tired pitches and a lack of big-name overseas players made it difficult to maintain interest. It was a reminder that even the established competitions face challenges.

In South Africa, the Mzansi Super League – a scaled-back version of the scrapped T20 Global League – was finally launched, but also encountered problems, and Cricket South Africa were unable to strike a broadcast deal with long-time partner SuperSport. The silver lining was that cricket was on free-to-air television in South Africa for the first time in years.

The second season of the Global T20 Canada was completed, but not without incident: players from Montreal Tigers and Toronto Nationals refused to board the bus for one match, in protest at missing payments. Administrative issues continue to plague some of the smaller leagues, and the Euro T20 Slam, involving teams from Ireland, Scotland and the Netherlands, and proposed for early autumn, was cancelled a fortnight before it was due to start.

The year proved that knockout cricket means the best teams do not necessarily win tournaments. The Renegades won the BBL, but the strongest team were arguably Hobart Hurricanes, who lost just four times in the round-robin stage, but were eliminated in the semi-finals. Cricket Australia amended the finals structure for 2019-20 to give more opportunities to teams finishing higher in the table.

No side were more dominant than Guyana Amazon Warriors in the Caribbean Premier League, yet they still ended up without the trophy. They won 11 matches – ten group games plus a qualifier – but were beaten in the final by Barbados Tridents. Well led by Shoaib Malik, Guyana relied heavily on a slow-bowling attack featuring Imran Tahir and the Australian off-spinner Chris Green. They also provided a heart-warming moment: coach Johan Botha was reduced to tears in a pitchside interview when emerging star Brandon King scored a hundred.

The vagaries of knockout cricket were also demonstrated in the T20 Blast, when Sussex and Lancashire, who had dominated the regional groups, lost in the quarter-finals. Essex, meanwhile, sneaked into the knockout stage after an extraordinary run of results fell in their favour, and ended up winning the competition off the last ball. The travails of Hobart, Guyana, Sussex and Lancashire – and the triumph of Essex – offer a cautionary tale of not judging T20 teams by their trophy cabinets.

THE LEADING TWENTY20 CRICKETER IN 2019

Andre Russell

ALAN GARDNER

There was a period in 2019 when, to adapt a phrase, T20 was Andre Russell's game, and everyone else was just trying to play it. He had long been one of the most coveted picks on the circuit, with his brutally clean hitting, 90mph bowling, and athleticism in the field. But, for a few weeks at the IPL, Russell was like a console player who had suddenly levelled up.

His exploits with Kolkata Knight Riders – 510 runs and 11 wickets – won him the Most Valuable Player award. His tally of 52 sixes was 18 clear of the next (Chris Gayle), and not far off Gayle's IPL record 59, in 2012. Yet it was Russell's ability to overhaul seemingly impossible targets that set him apart.

To continue with the gaming theme, it was as if he had switched into Beast Mode. In the second match of the tournament, with Kolkata chasing 182 to beat Sunrisers Hyderabad in front of their home crowd, Russell smashed 49 not out off 19 balls; they had needed 53 from 18, but walked off victorious, with two to spare. The IPL had never seen anything like it.

This was no one-off. In Bangalore 12 days later, Kolkata were in the same position: 53 needed from 18. Russell had made one off two, then hit seven of his next 11 for six, bringing the scores level with an over to spare. He finished unbeaten on 48 off 13, at a vertiginous strike-rate of 369.

His season was studded with such contributions: 48 off 17 against Kings XI Punjab; 62 off 28 against Delhi Capitals; 65 off 25 in the rematch with Royal Challengers Bangalore (this time in defeat); 80 not out off 40 against Mumbai Indians. The old-fashioned notion of getting your eye in was jettisoned. Russell came out of the blocks as if the blocks didn't exist, a 100m sprinter materialising at full speed halfway down the track. It was enough to win him a part in West Indies' 50-over World Cup plans, although knee problems scotched his chances of making an impact.

In part, Russell credited his rise to the lessons learned while serving a one-year anti-doping ban between 2017 and 2018, the suspension triggered after he missed three tests. "I changed my mentality since I got banned," he said. "I was slacking off. I was big. I was lazy. I wasn't practising hard. I came back stronger, leaner, more muscular. I'm hitting the ball effortlessly for six."

That was certainly how it seemed. Overall in 2019, Russell played 46 times across five major leagues, scoring 1,080 runs, with 101 sixes and a strike-rate of 182 (in successful chases, that rose to 222). The next best for anyone with even 750 runs was 156, by A. B. de Villiers. There were 43 wickets and 23 catches as well. No wonder the rest were left in his wake.

THE LEADING TWENTY20 CRICKETER IN THE WORLD

2018 Rashid Khan (Afg) | 2019 Rashid Khan (Afg) | **2020 Andre Russell (WI)**

KFC TWENTY20 BIG BASH LEAGUE IN 2018-19

Daniel Cherny

1 Melbourne Renegades   2 Melbourne Stars

A jaw-dropping finish to the final and an exciting conclusion to the league stage provided a reminder of what Twenty20 cricket can deliver. But they were isolated highlights in the eighth edition of the Big Bash. Much of the rest was eminently forgettable.

When Cricket Australia decided to expand the competition to a full home-and-away schedule lasting two months, they risked creating too much of a good thing. So it proved. The quality of the cricket dropped, while ratings plateaued for the new broadcast pairing of Channel Seven and Fox. Average attendances fell below 6,000, although the increase in matches – teams played 14 league games rather than ten – meant the aggregate attendance grew.

The length of the tournament and the comparatively low sums on offer meant that some big-name overseas players opted instead for the Bangladesh Premier League. Despite eye-catching performances from Tom Curran of Sydney Sixers and the Nepali leg-spinner Sandeep Lamichhane of Melbourne Stars, most of the stand-out names were Australian. There were too many one-sided matches, while sluggish pitches at Melbourne's Docklands Stadium and the Sydney Showground hampered big hitting. At the Gabba, the lights failed during the Brisbane Heat–Sydney Thunder match, delivering a blow to the Thunder's semi-final hopes. Problems with the outfield at Alice Springs meant the fixture between Adelaide Strikers and Perth Scorchers had to be switched to Adelaide Oval. To complete the charge sheet, umpiring was poor throughout.

None of this troubled **Melbourne Renegades**, who won their first Big Bash title. Captained by Aaron Finch, they had the leading wicket-taker in Kane Richardson, who took 24 – with the help of the extra games, a BBL record – at 17, and made shrewd use of leg-spinner Cameron Boyce, who had been discarded by Hobart. The English seamer Harry Gurney gained no marks for artistic impression, but bowled impressively at the death and earned the nickname "the left-arm Mr Bean" from commentator Mark Waugh. The Renegades had no one in the top 12 run-scorers: their success was built on team values.

Their cross-city rivals **Melbourne Stars** had a patchy tournament, sneaking into the semis on the back of a 43-ball 82 from captain Glenn Maxwell against the Sixers. They leaned on Marcus Stoinis, who led the batting averages with 533 at 53, and took 14 wickets at 16. Lamichhane collected 11 at 17.

Led by their explosive opening pair, D'Arcy Short and Matthew Wade, **Hobart Hurricanes** were the outstanding side of the regular season. Short blasted past his own BBL aggregate record, set a year earlier, to hit 637 runs at a strike-rate of 140, while Wade also surpassed the previous record, with 592 (strike-rate 146). But they could not prevent Hobart from becoming the sixth team to lose a semi-final after topping the table.

Sydney Sixers had looked a good bet until they lost a tight semi-final to the Renegades. Josh Philippe, snatched from under the noses of Perth just before the start of the competition, batted superbly, scoring 304 runs at a strike-rate of 158, the highest of anyone to make more than 200. Holders **Adelaide Strikers** were unable to recapture their sparkle. Leg-spinner Rashid Khan, who remained in Australia when his father died in Afghanistan, took 19 wickets – one more than in 2017-18 – but his average and his strike-rate both increased. Victory over **Perth Scorchers** in a wooden-spoon shoot-out kept them off bottom place. Perth struggled after the departure of coach Justin Langer to the national side, but they gave Cameron Bancroft the opportunity to return after his sandpaper ban; he responded with 298 runs at 33.

At their best, **Brisbane Heat** looked unstoppable, but they were inconsistent and missed out on the semi-finals by a point. In their last match, against the Stars, openers Max Bryant and Ben Cutting chased 157 in ten overs to keep their hopes alive, but other results did not go in their favour. Brendon McCullum announced he would not be returning, and Daniel Vettori left the coaching set-up. The England pair of Jos Buttler and Joe Root had contrasting fortunes for **Sydney Thunder**. When they left for England's tour of the Caribbean in early January, Buttler was the competition's leading run-scorer, with 273 at 39, while Root had managed just 93 at 15. The Thunder also fell just short of the top four.

KFC T20 BIG BASH LEAGUE IN 2018-19

	P	W	L	NR	Pts	NRR
HOBART HURRICANES	14	10	4	0	20	0.60
MELBOURNE RENEGADES	14	8	6	0	16	0.17
SYDNEY SIXERS	14	8	6	0	16	0.04
MELBOURNE STARS	14	7	7	0	14	−0.06
Brisbane Heat	14	6	7	1	13	0.24
Sydney Thunder	14	6	7	1	13	0.00
Adelaide Strikers	14	6	8	0	12	−0.47
Perth Scorchers	14	4	10	0	8	−0.50

Semi-final At Hobart, February 14, 2019 (floodlit). **Melbourne Stars won by six wickets. Hobart Hurricanes 153-7** (20 overs) (D. J. M. Short 35, B. R. McDermott 53, G. J. Bailey 37; D. J. Worrall 4-23); ‡**Melbourne Stars 157-4** (18.5 overs) (P. S. P. Handscomb 35, G. J. Maxwell 43*, S. E. Gotch 33*; Qais Ahmad 3-33). *PoM:* D. J. Worrall. *A destructive opening spell from seamer Dan Worrall ambushed Hobart. Worrall's smart variations accounted for Matthew Wade and Caleb Jewell in the second over and, when Adam Zampa removed D'Arcy Short, the Hurricanes were 42-3 in the powerplay. Ben McDermott and George Bailey put on 76, but boundaries proved elusive. The Stars made a hesitant start, until captain Glenn Maxwell and Seb Gotch soothed nerves.*

Semi-final At Melbourne (Docklands), February 15, 2019 (floodlit). **Melbourne Renegades won by three wickets. Sydney Sixers 180-3** (20 overs) (J. R. Philippe 52, D. P. Hughes 52); ‡**Melbourne Renegades 184-7** (19.5 overs) (A. J. Finch 44, S. B. Harper 36, D. T. Christian 31*). *PoM:* D. T. Christian. *A much-improved surface at the Docklands Stadium led to a good contest – and a win for the hosts that ensured Melbourne would have its first BBL winner. The outcome was in the balance when Renegades captain Aaron Finch was bowled trying to switch-hit Steve O'Keefe, but Dan Christian and Cameron Boyce added 41 in 3.3 overs to ensure victory. The Sixers' total was built on an opening stand of 87 from Josh Philippe and Daniel Hughes. Umpire Gerard Abood called a no-ball from square leg during the Sixers' innings when he adjudged that Renegades wicketkeeper Sam Harper had moved his gloves in front of the stumps prior to delivery.*

FINAL

MELBOURNE RENEGADES v MELBOURNE STARS

At Melbourne (Docklands), February 17, 2019. Melbourne Renegades won by 13 runs. Toss: Melbourne Stars.

When the Stars whittled their target down to 53 from 43 balls with ten wickets in hand, it looked as if the BBL crown was heading across town to the MCG. Instead, they lost seven for 19 in five calamitous overs, with Boyce, Tremain and Christian each taking two. "They were probably one over away from breaking our heart," said Finch. Asked to bat, the Renegades had looked ponderous on a sluggish pitch. They were 65 for five in the 11th over, before Cooper and Christian launched a patient rescue mission, and added an unbeaten 80. The Stars opening pair, Dunk and Stoinis, lopped a substantial chunk off the target by putting on 93, but it took them until the end of the 13th over, giving the Renegades an outside chance. "We probably needed to kill the game earlier, go a bit harder while the ball was hard and just get ahead of the rate," said Maxwell. Finch was officially reprimanded for swinging his bat at a chair in the players' tunnel; he had been run out at the non-striker's end, when White's straight-drive deflected off the foot of Bird, the bowler.

Player of the Match: D. T. Christian.   *Attendance:* 40,816.

Player of the Tournament: D. J. M. Short (Hobart Hurricanes).

Melbourne Renegades

		B	4/6
1 M. S. Harris *c 3 b 9*	12	10	2
2 *A. J. Finch *run out (9)*	13	10	2
3 †S. B. Harper *c and b 9*	6	7	1
4 C. L. White *lbw b 8*	12	12	1
5 M. W. G. Harvey *b 8*	14	16	2
6 T. L. W. Cooper *not out*	43	35	2/1
7 D. T. Christian *not out*	38	30	2/1
Lb 3, w 4	7		

6 overs: 47-3   (20 overs) 145-5

1/16 2/25 3/47 4/49 5/65

8 C. J. Boyce, 9 K. W. Richardson, 10 C. P. Tremain and 11 H. F. Gurney did not bat.

Worrall 4–10–37–0; Bird 3–10–25–2; Zampa 4–11–21–2; Lamichhane 4–12–16–0; Stoinis 2–2–19–0; Bravo 3–5–24–0.

Melbourne Stars

		B	4/6
1 B. R. Dunk *c 7 b 8*	57	45	4/1
2 M. P. Stoinis *b 8*	39	38	2/1
3 †P. S. P. Handscomb *c 7 b 10*	0	2	0
4 *G. J. Maxwell *c 5 b 10*	1	6	0
5 N. J. Maddinson *c 2 b 11*	6	7	0
6 S. E. Gotch *c 5 b 7*	2	5	0
7 D. J. Bravo *c 4 b 7*	3	3	0
8 A. Zampa *not out*	17	10	1/1
9 J. M. Bird *not out*	4	4	0
Lb 1, w 2	3		

6 overs: 36-0   (20 overs) 132-7

1/93 2/94 3/99 4/99 5/108 6/108 7/112

10 D. J. Worrall and 11 S. Lamichhane did not bat.

Richardson 4–8–27–0; Tremain 4–13–21–2; Gurney 4–9–20–1; Boyce 4–5–30–2; Christian 4–7–33–2.

Umpires: G. A. Abood and S. J. Nogajski.   Third umpire: S. D. Fry.
Referee: R. W. Stratford.

BIG BASH FINALS

2011-12	SYDNEY SIXERS beat Perth Scorchers by seven wickets at Perth.
2012-13	BRISBANE HEAT beat Perth Scorchers by 34 runs at Perth.
2013-14	PERTH SCORCHERS beat Hobart Hurricanes by 39 runs at Perth.
2014-15	PERTH SCORCHERS beat Sydney Sixers by four wickets at Canberra.
2015-16	SYDNEY THUNDER beat Melbourne Stars by three wickets at Melbourne (MCG).
2016-17	PERTH SCORCHERS beat Sydney Sixers by nine wickets at Perth.
2017-18	ADELAIDE STRIKERS beat Hobart Hurricanes by 25 runs at Adelaide.
2018-19	MELBOURNE RENEGADES beat Melbourne Stars by 13 runs at Melbourne (Docklands).

UCB BANGLADESH PREMIER LEAGUE IN 2018-19

MOHAMMAD ISAM

1 Comilla Victorians   2 Dhaka Dynamites

By the time the 2018-19 Bangladesh Premier League reached its climax, it had become a tournament of redemption. Players needing to prove a point, whether old hands or new, did so in style. The competition was arguably more watchable than Australia's Big Bash League, which lasted 61 days to the BPL's 35 and had fewer international stars. It even included Steve Smith and David Warner, still suspended from Australian domestic cricket, though both had their stints cut short by elbow injuries.

But it was Bangladesh's most prolific batsman, Tamim Iqbal, who grabbed the limelight in the final. He took calculated risks to score 141 not out and lead **Comilla Victorians** to the title against favourites **Dhaka Dynamites**, who boasted a bowling line-up of Andre Russell, Rubel Hossain, Shakib Al Hasan and Sunil Narine.

The tournament was also a triumph for Rilee Rossouw, who at first seemed only to be holding down a place at **Rangpur Riders** until the arrival of A. B. de Villiers. By the midway stage his quick runs at the top and stability in the middle overs had made him the most valuable asset in their star-studded batting, and he finished as the highest run-scorer, with 558 at 69.

BANGLADESH PREMIER LEAGUE IN 2018-19

	P	W	L	Pts	NRR
RANGPUR RIDERS	12	8	4	16	1.01
COMILLA VICTORIANS	12	8	4	16	0.06
CHITTAGONG VIKINGS	12	7	5	14	−0.29
DHAKA DYNAMITES	12	6	6	12	0.97
Rajshahi Kings	12	6	6	12	−0.51
Sylhet Sixers	12	5	7	10	0.06
Khulna Titans	12	2	10	4	−1.25

Dhaka qualified ahead of Rajshahi on net run-rate.

Among the bowlers, seamers Taskin Ahmed, of **Sylhet Sixers**, and Rubel stood out, with 22 wickets apiece. Taskin's success followed a horrid run of injury and poor form, so it was unfortunate that he tore an ankle ligament in the last group game; it ruled him out of Bangladesh's tour of New Zealand, which would have been his international comeback after nearly a year away.

Though the BPL tends to be dominated by established names, Aliss Al Islam, an off-spinner with an iffy action, stole the headlines with a hat-trick on debut for Dhaka. He started badly, dropping two easy chances off Mithun Ali, but made amends when he sparked Rangpur's collapse from 146 for two chasing 184; Dhaka won by two runs.

Robbie Frylinck, a journeyman cricketer from South Africa, had a tournament to remember: his all-round prowess lifted unfancied **Chittagong Vikings** into the knockouts. He was most effective in the early rounds, when the pitches at Mirpur offered a bit of movement, and he regularly delivered when the team needed late runs. Another overseas player who made his mark was Surrey's Jason Roy; he played only four games for Sylhet, but took a couple of catches on the boundary which made the highlights reel at the end of the tournament.

3rd v 4th   At Mirpur, February 4, 2019. **Dhaka Dynamites won by six wickets. ‡Chittagong Vikings 135-8** (20 overs) (C. S. Delport 36, Mosaddek Hossain 40; S. P. Narine 4-15); **Dhaka Dynamites 136-4** (16.4 overs) (W. U. Tharanga 51, S. P. Narine 31; Khaled Ahmed 3-20). PoM: S. P. Narine. *Dhaka had scraped into the play-offs on net run-rate, but leapfrogged Chittagong after Trinidadian off-spinner Sunil Narine followed up four wickets with a 16-ball 31 opening the batting. Though Dhaka captain Shakib Al Hasan fell first ball to Khaled Ahmed, Upul Tharanga saw them most of the way to a straightforward target of 136.*

1st v 2nd   At Mirpur, February 4, 2019 (floodlit). **Comilla Victorians won by eight wickets. ‡Rangpur Riders 165-5** (20 overs) (C. H. Gayle 46, R. R. Rossouw 44, B. A. C. Howell 53*); **Comilla Victorians 166-2** (18.5 overs) (E. Lewis 71*, Anamul Haque 39, Shamsur Rahman 34*). PoM: E. Lewis. *Rangpur had won their previous two encounters with Comilla by nine wickets, but were weakened by the departure of A. B. de Villiers and the injured Alex Hales. Despite Chris Gayle's efforts, and a 70-run stand between Rilee Rossouw and Benny Howell, Comilla reached the final with seven deliveries to spare, as Evin Lewis batted throughout their innings for 71* in 53 balls.*

Final play-off   At Mirpur, February 6, 2019 (floodlit). **Dhaka Dynamites won by five wickets. Rangpur Riders 142** (19.4 overs) (Mithun Ali 38, R. S. Bopara 49; Rubel Hossain 4-23); **‡Dhaka Dynamites 147-5** (16.4 overs) (Rony Talukdar 35, A. D. Russell 40*). PoM: Rubel Hossain. *Dhaka completed their comeback from fourth place in the league to their fifth final by beating table leaders Rangpur with more than three overs in hand. Rangpur suffered a severe blow when Rubel Hossain dismissed Gayle and Rossouw with successive deliveries in the fifth over; they fought back to reach 106-3, but lost their last seven for 36. Any doubts Dhaka felt at 97-5 were resolved by Andre Russell, who hit 40* in 19 balls, and won the game with three successive sixes.*

Final   At Mirpur, February 8, 2019 (floodlit). **Comilla Victorians won by 17 runs. Comilla Victorians 199-3** (20 overs) (Tamim Iqbal 141*); **‡Dhaka Dynamites 182-9** (20 overs) (W. U. Tharanga 48, Rony Talukdar 66; Wahab Riaz 3-28). PoM: Tamim Iqbal. PoS: Shakib Al Hasan. *Just as he had done in the previous final, against Rangpur, Shakib asked the opposition to bat – and once again a left-handed opener blasted a big hundred to sink Dhaka. Tamim Iqbal emulated Gayle in the earlier game by slamming a career-best 141* off 61 balls, with 11 sixes – a well-judged effort against a tough attack, with 24 the next-best score. Comilla's bowlers ensured Tamim's work wasn't wasted, though a 38-ball 66 from Rony Talukdar gave them a scare. Wahab Riaz took three wickets, and Mohammad Saifuddin and Tissara Perera two each, but it was Tamim they chaired off the ground for his mammoth century.*

BPL FINALS

2011-12	DHAKA GLADIATORS beat Barisal Burners by eight wickets at Mirpur.
2012-13	DHAKA GLADIATORS beat Chittagong Kings by 43 runs at Mirpur.
2015-16	COMILLA VICTORIANS beat Barisal Bulls by three wickets at Mirpur.
2016-17	DHAKA DYNAMITES beat Rajshahi Kings by 56 runs at Mirpur.
2017-18	RANGPUR RIDERS beat Dhaka Dynamites by 57 runs at Mirpur.
2018-19	COMILLA VICTORIANS beat Dhaka Dynamites by 17 runs at Mirpur.

There was no tournament in 2013-14 or 2014-15, following a match-fixing scandal and pay disputes.

VIVO INDIAN PREMIER LEAGUE IN 2018-19

Kritika Naidu

1 Mumbai Indians   2 Chennai Super Kings

For the first time in its 12 editions, the Indian Premier League was served as an entrée. In 2011 and 2015, it had begun a few days after the World Cup final; in 2019, it finished less than three weeks before the World Cup started. Briefly, it claimed the spotlight, but the real focus was elsewhere.

There was concern about managing the workload for international players, though some used the opportunity to strengthen their claims for selection. It proved useful match practice for the likes of Steve Smith and David Warner, whose year-long ban from Australian cricket (they also missed the previous IPL) was about to expire. But many overseas players left early for national training camps and warm-up series. The franchises best prepared for these departures went furthest, and **Mumbai Indians**, one of the teams least affected, picked up their fourth IPL title.

It was a strange competition in other ways, too. Though it was the second tournament since the IPL had finally breached the English fortress, and ten of their players appeared, franchises were not so reliant on imports: there were 13 instances of teams not fielding their full quota of four overseas cricketers. Twelve teenagers got a game, the most since 2008, the inaugural season. The spinners reaped most rewards with 263 wickets, 62 for Chennai Super Kings – whose pitches at the Chepauk came under scrutiny.

Mumbai Indians had a reputation as slow starters, but belied that in a near-perfect season. Quinton de Kock, a transfer from Royal Challengers Bangalore, scored 529 runs, Hardik Pandya smashed 402 at a strike-rate of 191, Jasprit Bumrah did what he does best, and young leg-spinner Rahul Chahar choked opponents in the middle.

They snatched the trophy from right under **Chennai Super Kings'** noses, winning the final by a single run. A stone's throw from victory, Chennai were trumped by the mastery of Sri Lanka's warhorse Lasith Malinga: six perfect yorkers meant CSK scored only seven off the last over – and lost two wickets.

Chennai trampled most sides, winning seven of their first eight games and powering into the play-offs. Yet they lost four out of four against Mumbai. There were occasional glimpses of vintage M. S. Dhoni, but he had to bear much of the load in an otherwise fragile batting line-up of fading stars. As a result, he depended largely on his spinners, led by Imran Tahir, the tournament's leading wicket-taker, with 26. Seamer Deepak Chahar was a breath of fresh air; his efficiency in the powerplays and at the death brought him 22, the most by an Indian.

Delhi Capitals changed their name from the Daredevils, and transformed their fortunes. Bottom the previous year, they charged into the play-offs for the first time since 2012. Despite disappointing returns from their overseas batsmen, a dynamic Indian line-up – Shikhar Dhawan (back home after stints with three other IPL sides), Shreyas Iyer, Rishabh Pant and Prithvi Shaw – infused a new fearlessness, supervised by the robust thinktank of Ricky Ponting and Sourav Ganguly. With the spinners failing to meet expectations, Kagiso Rabada carried the attack alongside Ishant Sharma. Rabada spurred Delhi on in the early stages, knocking over Andre Russell's stumps with a lethal yorker in a super over against Kolkata, and grabbed 25 wickets in 12 games before returning to South Africa ahead of the play-offs. Delhi finished level on points with Mumbai and Chennai, but without Rabada they bowed out in the final qualifier.

Dhawan's previous team, **Sunrisers Hyderabad**, did not miss him while their formidable opening pair, Ashes rivals Warner and Jonny Bairstow, were sharing four century stands and scoring over half the team's runs. Warner had returned with an insatiable thirst to prove himself, and did so vehemently, with 692 runs – 99 more than anyone else – while Bairstow plundered 445. But once they departed for their national sides, their team-mates felt the pinch. The Sunrisers slid through to the play-offs – the first team to qualify on just 12 points. A wonky middle order and an attack punching below their weight meant they soon slid out again.

Kolkata Knight Riders failed to reach the play-offs for the first time since 2015. A promising start was derailed by a string of losses and poor decision-making, which caused discord within their camp. Russell was the sole standout: he struck 52 sixes, scored 510 runs at a strike-rate of 204, and picked up 11 wickets. Kolkata missed a trick by not promoting him and Shubman Gill sooner, as their top order failed to fire. Their spinners were ineffective, especially on Eden Gardens' unhelpful pitches; Kuldeep Yadav was dropped after just four wickets in nine games. The pace attack lacked sting, and Kolkata finished with only 56, the fewest by any side in the IPL's 12 seasons.

Chris Gayle, in his 40th year, forged a successful opening partnership with K. L. Rahul, but that was one of the few bright spots for **Kings XI Punjab**. As in 2018, they succumbed to second-half syndrome, losing six of their last eight games after a good start, with the middle order inspiring little confidence. Off-spinner Mujeeb Zadran and seamer Andrew Tye learned that success one season doesn't guarantee any the next, and Kings XI conceded more runs in the powerplay than any other side. Ravichandran Ashwin's run-out of Jos Buttler at the non-striker's end, on the third day of the tournament, kept his team in the news longer than their performances did, triggering a worldwide debate on the spirit of cricket.

There was disharmony elswhere, too. Even the usually composed Dhoni stormed out to the middle during one match to argue with the umpires over a no-ball decision; the authorities let him off with a 50% fine. In the final week, umpire Nigel Llong had an outburst himself, kicking a door after an on-field spat with Virat Kohli over another no-ball.

Rajasthan Royals changed captains halfway through a shambolic season, replacing Ajinkya Rahane with Steve Smith. Buttler, leg-spinner Shreyas Gopal and fast bowler Jofra Archer gave them something to celebrate, but Ben Stokes underperformed. They avoided the wooden spoon on net run-rate; instead, it went to **Royal Challengers Bangalore**, though 11 points was a record for the bottom-placed side, and only one behind the Sunrisers, who qualified. In hindsight, two shoddy no-ball calls may have cost Bangalore a top-four finish. Their over-reliance on the batting of Kohli and A. B. de Villiers, poor death bowling and an inability to seize key moments meant they had begun with six defeats. Dale Steyn arrived in April as a replacement and injected some spunk into their attack for two games until he suffered a shoulder inflammation, and the ever-reliable Yuzvendra Chahal's spin earned 18 wickets. But that couldn't massage a surprising statistic: of his 110 games as RCB captain, Kohli had now lost 56.

VIVO INDIAN PREMIER LEAGUE IN 2018-19

	P	W	L	NR	Pts	NRR
MUMBAI INDIANS	14	9	5	0	18	0.42
CHENNAI SUPER KINGS	14	9	5	0	18	0.13
DELHI CAPITALS	14	9	5	0	18	0.04
SUNRISERS HYDERABAD	14	6	8	0	12	0.57
Kolkata Knight Riders	14	6	8	0	12	0.02
Kings XI Punjab	14	6	8	0	12	−0.25
Rajasthan Royals	14	5	8	1	11	−0.44
Royal Challengers Bangalore	14	5	8	1	11	−0.60

INDIAN PREMIER LEAGUE

At Chennai, March 23 (floodlit). **Chennai Super Kings won by seven wickets. Royal Challengers Bangalore 70** (17.1 overs) (Harbhajan Singh 3-20, Imran Tahir 3-9); ‡**Chennai Super Kings 71-3** (17.4 overs). *PoM:* Harbhajan Singh. *Chennai's spinners dismissed Bangalore for the joint-sixth-lowest total in IPL history, as Harbhajan Singh, Imran Tahir and Ravindra Jadeja took a combined 12–46–44–8. On a pitch later described by M. S. Dhoni as "too slow", only opener Parthiv Patel made double figures; he was last out for 29. Leg-spinner Yuzvendra Chahal then conceded only six singles from his four overs, but Chennai were in no rush. Suresh Raina became the first to reach 5,000 IPL runs before he became the game's tenth victim of spin.*

At Kolkata, March 24 (floodlit). **Kolkata Knight Riders won by six wickets. Sunrisers Hyderabad 181-3** (20 overs) (D. A. Warner 85, J. M. Bairstow 39, V. Shankar 40*); ‡**Kolkata Knight Riders 183-4** (19.4 overs) (N. Rana 68, R. V. Uthappa 35, A. D. Russell 49*). *PoM:* A. D. Russell. *David Warner returned to Sunrisers Hyderabad exactly a year after the Cape Town sandpaper imbroglio that had brought him a 12-month ban. He made an assured 85 from 53 balls, and put on 118 for the first wicket with Jonny Bairstow, yet was still eclipsed. With three overs left, Kolkata needed a mountainous 53; Andre Russell clobbered four sixes and three fours from his next ten balls, to bring the summit in sight. Shubman Gill reached the peak with two sixes.*

At Mumbai, March 24 (floodlit). **Delhi Capitals won by 37 runs. Delhi Capitals 213-6** (20 overs) (S. Dhawan 43, C. A. Ingram 47, R. R. Pant 78*; M. J. McClenaghan 3-40); ‡**Mumbai Indians 176** (19.2 overs) (Yuvraj Singh 53, K. H. Pandya 32). *PoM:* R. R. Pant. *Rishabh Pant blasted 78* from 27 balls to fire Delhi to a winning total in their first match under a new name. They had previously been called the Daredevils, but co-owner Parth Jindal explained: "Delhi is the power centre of the country, it is the capital, therefore the name." A rapid half-century from 37-year-old Yuvraj Singh could not get Mumbai Indians close.*

At Jaipur, March 25 (floodlit). **Kings XI Punjab won by 14 runs. Kings XI Punjab 184-4** (20 overs) (C. H. Gayle 79, S. N. Khan 46*); ‡**Rajasthan Royals 170-9** (20 overs) (J. C. Buttler 69, S. V. Samson 30). *PoM:* C. H. Gayle. *Rajasthan were 108-2 when Ravichandran Ashwin ran out Jos Buttler backing up at the non-striker's end. Third umpire Bruce Oxenford ruled it was out, but the arguments continued for days. MCC initially said it was within the spirit of cricket, then decided it probably wasn't, because Ashwin had paused in his delivery stride and waited for Buttler to move before flicking off the bails. Law 41.16 stated that a batsman could be run out if he left the crease before "the instant when the bowler would normally have been expected to release the ball"; there were doubts about whether this moment passed once Ashwin aborted the delivery. Earlier, Chris Gayle had accelerated from a characteristically slow start to reach a 33-ball fifty. In reply, Buttler's* *half-century needed just 29, but Sam Curran's dismissal of Steve Smith triggered a collapse of seven in 17 legal balls.*

At Delhi, March 26 (floodlit). **Chennai Super Kings won by six wickets. ‡Delhi Capitals 147-6** (20 overs) (S. Dhawan 51; D. J. Bravo 3-33); **Chennai Super Kings 150-4** (19.4 overs) (S. R. Watson 44, S. K. Raina 30, M. S. Dhoni 32*). *PoM:* S. R. Watson. *Chennai proved too canny for Delhi. Dwayne Bravo (aged 35) was kept on the leash until the final overs and – despite an expensive start – stopped the Capitals accelerating. Shane Watson (37) then coolly directed the chase after shading a duel with Kagiso Rabada.*

At Kolkata, March 27 (floodlit). **Kolkata Knight Riders won by 28 runs. Kolkata Knight Riders 218-4** (20 overs) (R. V. Uthappa 67*, N. Rana 63, A. D. Russell 48); **‡Kings XI Punjab 190-4** (20 overs) (M. A. Agarwal 58, D. A. Miller 59*, Mandeep Singh 33*). *PoM:* A. D. Russell. *Punjab were left to regret a careless no-ball, when Mohammed Shami bowled Russell on three – only to discover there were just three fielders inside the circle. Russell thrashed 45 from his next 12 deliveries, building on the flair of Nitish Rana (63 off 34) and the diligence of Robin Uthappa (67* off 50). K. L. Rahul and Gayle fell cheaply in reply, and not even fifties from Mayank Agarwal and David Miller could get the Kings XI close. Their total had been boosted by four when Russell was blinded by the floodlights at mid-off, allowing the ball – which was being passed around the field, and apparently dead – to run away to the boundary. An intervention from Ashwin, the Kings XI captain, persuaded the officials to award overthrows.*

At Bangalore, March 28 (floodlit). **Mumbai Indians won by six runs. Mumbai Indians 187-8** (20 overs) (R. G. Sharma 48, S. A. Yadav 38, H. H. Pandya 32*; Y. S. Chahal 4-38); **‡Royal Challengers Bangalore 181-5** (20 overs) (P. A. Patel 31, V. Kohli 46, A. B. de Villiers 70*; J. J. Bumrah 3-20). *PoM:* J. J. Bumrah. *Had the umpires seen Lasith Malinga overstepping as he delivered the final ball, and had the resulting free hit gone for six, Bangalore would have won. But they didn't, and Mumbai celebrated their first victory. Jasprit Bumrah, bowling the 17th and 19th overs, was their hero: he restricted the Challengers to six runs, and struck twice.*

At Hyderabad, March 29 (floodlit). **Sunrisers Hyderabad won by five wickets. ‡Rajasthan Royals 198-2** (20 overs) (A. M. Rahane 70, S. V. Samson 102*); **Sunrisers Hyderabad 201-5** (19 overs) (D. A. Warner 69, J. M. Bairstow 45, V. Shankar 35; R. Shreyas Gopal 3-27). *PoM:* Rashid Khan. *Sanju Samson hit a 54-ball century, and put on 119 for the second wicket with Ajinkya Rahane, but they were trumped by the Sunrisers' feisty opening pair: Warner (who hit eight of his 11 boundaries before his partner managed one) and Bairstow piled on 110 in 9.4 overs, then Vijay Shankar (35 from 15) made sure of a comfortable win.*

At Mohali, March 30 (floodlit). **Kings XI Punjab won by eight wickets. Mumbai Indians 176-7** (20 overs) (R. G. Sharma 32, Q. de Kock 60, H. H. Pandya 31); **‡Kings XI Punjab 177-2** (18.4 overs) (K. L. Rahul 71*, C. H. Gayle 40, M. A. Agarwal 43). *PoM:* M. A. Agarwal. *Quinton de Kock's 60 off 39 deliveries led Mumbai Indians to 120-2, but their run-rate dropped after he was out. Agarwal might have been run out backing up, like Buttler a few days earlier, but Krunal Pandya chose not to break the wicket; Agarwal advanced to 43 in 21, and Rahul batted throughout the innings to finish the job.*

At Delhi, March 30 (floodlit). **Delhi Capitals won a super over, following a tie. Kolkata Knight Riders 185-8** (20 overs) (K. D. Karthik 50, A. D. Russell 62); **‡Delhi Capitals 185-6** (20 overs) (P. P. Shaw 99, S. S. Iyer 43). *PoM:* P. P. Shaw. *Delhi flirted with disaster after Prithvi Shaw's classy 99 had put them in charge, but Rabada rescued them with a nerveless super over. They had needed 12 off nine with six wickets in hand, but Kuldeep Yadav's wrist-spin contrived a tie. Earlier, Russell launched six sixes in Kolkata's late assault.*

At Hyderabad, March 31 (floodlit). **Sunrisers Hyderabad won by 118 runs. Sunrisers Hyderabad 231-2** (20 overs) (J. M. Bairstow 114, D. A. Warner 100*); **‡Royal Challengers Bangalore 113** (19.5 overs) (C. de Grandhomme 37; Mohammad Nabi 4-11, S. Sharma 3-19). *PoM:* J. M. Bairstow. *An IPL record opening partnership of 185 in 16.2 overs between Bairstow (114 off 56) and Warner (100* off 55) hurried Hyderabad to their highest score and biggest win. It was the pair's third successive century stand, another IPL record. Bangalore then slipped from 13-0 to 35-6, as Afghanistan off-spinner Mohammad Nabi took four for 11.*

TWO HUNDREDS IN A TWENTY20 INNINGS

K. J. O'Brien (119)/H. J. H. Marshall (102)　Glos v Middx at Uxbridge . . . .　2011
V. Kohli (109)/A. B. de Villiers (129*) . . .　RCB v Gujarat Lions at Bangalore. . . . .　2015-16
A. D. Hales (100)/R. R. Rossouw (100*) .　Rangpur Rdrs v Chit Vkgs at Chittagong　**2018-19**
J. M. Bairstow (114)/D. A. Warner (100*)　Sunrisers Hyd'bad v RCB at Hyderabad .　**2018-19**

At Chennai, March 31 (floodlit). **Chennai Super Kings won by eight runs. Chennai Super Kings 175-5** (20 overs) (S. K. Raina 36, M. S. Dhoni 75*); ‡**Rajasthan Royals 167-8** (20 overs) (R. A. Tripathi 39, B. A. Stokes 46). PoM: M. S. Dhoni. *Dhoni hit Jaydev Unadkat for four sixes in the last over, including the final three balls, to propel Chennai to a total that proved narrowly beyond Rajasthan, despite a 26-ball 46 from Ben Stokes.*

At Mohali, April 1 (floodlit). **Kings XI Punjab won by 14 runs. Kings XI Punjab 166-9** (20 overs) (S. N. Khan 39, D. A. Miller 43; C. H. Morris 3-30); ‡**Delhi Capitals 152** (19.2 overs) (S. Dhawan 30, R. R. Pant 39, C. A. Ingram 38; S. M. Curran 4-11). PoM: S. M. Curran. *The Capitals looked set for victory at 144-3 in the 17th over – but, needing only 23, they lost seven for eight in a sensational collapse, finished off by a hat-trick from Curran, playing his second IPL match. The slide was started by Shami (2-27), who uprooted Pant's middle stump; next over, he knocked back two of Hanuma Vihari's.*

At Jaipur, April 2 (floodlit). **Rajasthan Royals won by seven wickets. Royal Challengers Bangalore 158-4** (20 overs) (P. A. Patel 67, M. P. Stoinis 31*; R. Shreyas Gopal 3-12); ‡**Rajasthan Royals 164-3** (19.5 overs) (J. C. Buttler 59, S. P. D. Smith 38, R. A. Tripathi 34*). PoM: R. Shreyas Gopal. *Of the two winless teams, it was Rajasthan who broke their duck. Shreyas Gopal removed Virat Kohli, A. B. de Villiers and Shimron Hetmyer in successive overs. The Challengers added to their problems by dropping several catches. When Smith fell, the target was five off the final over, and Rahul Tripathi smashed the penultimate ball for six.*

At Mumbai, April 3 (floodlit). **Mumbai Indians won by 37 runs. Mumbai Indians 170-5** (20 overs) (S. A. Yadav 59, K. H. Pandya 42); ‡**Chennai Super Kings 133-8** (20 overs) (K. M. Jadhav 58; S. L. Malinga 3-34, H. H. Pandya 3-20). PoM: H. H. Pandya. *Hardik Pandya starred as Mumbai ended Chennai's unbeaten run, hitting 25 off eight in a match-changing partnership of 45 off two overs with Kieron Pollard. Then he collected three cheap wickets.*

At Delhi, April 4 (floodlit). **Sunrisers Hyderabad won by five wickets. Delhi Capitals 129-8** (20 overs) (S. S. Iyer 43); ‡**Sunrisers Hyderabad 131-5** (18.3 overs) (J. M. Bairstow 48). PoM: J. M. Bairstow. *Bairstow's 28-ball 48 broke the back of a tricky chase on a sluggish Feroz Shah Kotla pitch, though he was dropped on five when left-arm spinner Akshar Patel failed to hold on to a return catch. The win took Hyderabad top.*

At Bangalore, April 5 (floodlit). **Kolkata Knight Riders won by five wickets. Royal Challengers Bangalore 205-3** (20 overs) (V. Kohli 84, A. B. de Villiers 63); ‡**Kolkata Knight Riders 206-5** (19.1 overs) (C. A. Lynn 43, R. V. Uthappa 33, N. Rana 37, A. D. Russell 48*). PoM: A. D. Russell. *Kohli and de Villiers added 108 for the second wicket in nine overs as Bangalore racked up a commanding 205-3. Yet it could not prevent a fifth successive defeat. The Challengers' nemesis was Russell who, undaunted by needing 53 from three overs, crashed seven sixes and a four to reach 48* from 13 balls, and spirited Kolkata across the line with five to spare. Tim Southee's last over cost 29.*

At Chennai, April 6 (floodlit). **Chennai Super Kings won by 22 runs.** ‡**Chennai Super Kings 160-3** (20 overs) (F. du Plessis 54, M. S. Dhoni 37*; R. Ashwin 3-23); **Kings XI Punjab 138-5** (20 overs) (K. L. Rahul 55, S. N. Khan 67). PoM: Harbhajan Singh. *Chennai's spinners rescued them after a seemingly modest total. Harbhajan (4–10–17–2) removed Gayle and Agarwal in his first over, then Jadeja and Imran Tahir kept it tight, finishing with 0-44 from their eight. Rahul and Sarfaraz Khan put on 110 for the third wicket, but used up more than 15 overs and, when Miller fell for six, Kings XI were done for.*

At Hyderabad, April 6 (floodlit). **Mumbai Indians won by 40 runs. Mumbai Indians 136-7** (20 overs) (K. A. Pollard 46*; A. S. Joseph 6-12). PoM: A. S. Joseph. *On his IPL debut, Alzarri Joseph bowled Warner with his first delivery (he began with a wicket-maiden), and finished with 6-12, the best return in the tournament's history, beating Sohail*

Tanvir's 6-14 in the inaugural season. The Sunrisers could not even reach three figures. On an awkward pitch, only Mumbai's Pollard passed 20.

At Bangalore, April 7 (floodlit). **Delhi Capitals won by four wickets. Royal Challengers Bangalore 149-8** (20 overs) (V. Kohli 41, M. M. Ali 32; K. Rabada 4-21); ‡**Delhi Capitals 152-6** (18.5 overs) (S. S. Iyer 67). *PoM: K. Rabada. Bangalore paid for dropping Shreyas Iyer in the first over of Delhi's reply. He marched on to 67, condemning RCB to a sixth successive defeat. Rabada returned his best T20 figures.*

At Jaipur, April 7 (floodlit). **Kolkata Knight Riders won by eight wickets. Rajasthan Royals 139-3** (20 overs) (J. C. Buttler 37, S. P. D. Smith 73*); ‡**Kolkata Knight Riders 140-2** (13.5 overs) (C. A. Lynn 50, S. P. Narine 47). *PoM: H. F. Gurney. A curious innings from Rajasthan was put into perspective by Kolkata's opening stand of 91 in 8.3 overs between Chris Lynn and Sunil Narine. When Lynn had 13 he inside-edged Dhawal Kulkarni on to his leg stump: the Zing bail lit up, but wasn't dislodged, and the ball ran away for four. For the Royals, Smith had eaten up 59 balls for his 73*, while Stokes managed just 7* off 14. On his IPL debut, Nottinghamshire left-arm seamer Harry Gurney had figures of 4–9–25–2.*

At Mohali, April 8 (floodlit). **Kings XI Punjab won by six wickets. Sunrisers Hyderabad 150-4** (20 overs) (D. A. Warner 70*); ‡**Kings XI Punjab 151-4** (19.5 overs) (K. L. Rahul 71*, M. A. Agarwal 55). *PoM: K. L. Rahul. Rahul steered Punjab to a victory that had seemed straightforward until seamer Sandeep Sharma removed Agarwal and Miller in the 18th over. Rahul maintained his cool, and his hard work did not go to waste.*

At Chennai, April 9 (floodlit). **Chennai Super Kings won by seven wickets. Kolkata Knight Riders 108-9** (20 overs) (A. D. Russell 50*; D. L. Chahar 3-20); ‡**Chennai Super Kings 111-3** (17.2 overs) (F. du Plessis 43*). *PoM: D. L. Chahar. The Knight Riders never recovered from slipping to 29-4 in the powerplay, with Deepak Chahar taking three as batsmen swished across the line. Russell at least got them into three figures, with 50* from No. 7, but CSK maintained their unbeaten home record with ease.*

At Mumbai, April 10 (floodlit). **Mumbai Indians won by three wickets. Kings XI Punjab 197-4** (20 overs) (K. L. Rahul 100*, C. H. Gayle 63); ‡**Mumbai Indians 198-7** (20 overs) (K. A. Pollard 83; Mohammed Shami 3-31). *PoM: K. A. Pollard. Pollard set up an unexpected victory for Mumbai, who were only 65-3 after ten overs. He crashed ten sixes in a 31-ball 83, six off Curran. Kings XI Punjab had made a dazzling start, with Gayle hitting 63 in 36 balls as he and Rahul raised 116; Rahul completed his first IPL century, but no one else passed eight.*

At Jaipur, April 11 (floodlit). **Chennai Super Kings won by four wickets. Rajasthan Royals 151-7** (20 overs); ‡**Chennai Super Kings 155-6** (20 overs) (A. T. Rayudu 57, M. S. Dhoni 58). *PoM: M. S. Dhoni. Mitchell Santner slapped the final ball of the match, from Stokes, for six to settle an enthralling encounter. Eighteen were needed off the last over, then four off one ball, only for Stokes to bowl a wide. Chennai had been 24 for four before Dhoni and Ambati Rayudu added 95 in 11.5 overs. Dhoni was later fined for returning to the middle in the last over to argue with the umpires after a no-ball was first given, then revoked.*

At Kolkata, April 12 (floodlit). **Delhi Capitals won by seven wickets. Kolkata Knight Riders 178-7** (20 overs) (S. Gill 65, A. D. Russell 45); ‡**Delhi Capitals 180-3** (18.5 overs) (S. Dhawan 97*, R. R. Pant 46). *PoM: S. Dhawan. Shikhar Dhawan's 97* off 63 propelled Delhi to victory, after he added 105 in 11.3 overs with Pant (46 off 31). Kolkata had lost Joe Denly first ball, his only delivery all tournament. Aggression from Gill (65 off 39) and the inevitable Russell (45 off 21) were not enough.*

At Mumbai, April 13 (floodlit). **Rajasthan Royals won by four wickets. Mumbai Indians 187-5** (20 overs) (R. G. Sharma 47, Q. de Kock 81; J. C. Archer 3-39); ‡**Rajasthan Royals 188-6** (19.3 overs) (A. M. Rahane 37, J. C. Buttler 89, S. V. Samson 31; K. H. Pandya 3-34). *PoM: J. C. Buttler. Stationed at either long-on or long-off after handing the gloves to Samson, Buttler held three smart catches to help rein in Mumbai's lightning start. Openers Rohit Sharma and de Kock put on 96, before both were c Buttler b Archer. Buttler then tore into Joseph, whose third – and last – over cost 28 (644446), to speed Rajasthan towards victory.*

At Mohali, April 13 (floodlit). **Royal Challengers Bangalore won by eight wickets. Kings XI Punjab 173-4** (20 overs) (C. H. Gayle 99*); ‡**Royal Challengers Bangalore 174-2** (19.2 overs) (V. Kohli 67, A. B. de Villiers 59*). *PoM: A. B. de Villiers. RCB won a game at the seventh attempt, with de Villiers (59* from 38) and Marcus Stoinis (28*) backing up Kohli's well-paced 67. They* *trumped Gayle, who hit five sixes (and ten fours) from 64 balls, and became the second to be stranded on 99* in the IPL, after Suresh Raina for CSK against Sunrisers in 2013. Gayle biffed 48 in the powerplay, slowed down against the spinners – Moeen Ali returned 4–10–19–1 – then clouted 30 from his final 13 deliveries. On 95 with one to go, he squirted a Mohammed Siraj yorker for four.*

At Kolkata, April 14 (floodlit). **Chennai Super Kings won by five wickets. Kolkata Knight Riders 161-8** (20 overs) (C. A. Lynn 82; Imran Tahir 4-27); ‡**Chennai Super Kings 162-5** (19.4 overs) (S. K. Raina 58*, R. A. Jadeja 31*). *PoM:* Imran Tahir. *Table leaders Chennai secured their seventh win in eight. Imran Tahir's leg-spin collected four wickets, with some spectacular catches in the deep; one removed Lynn, on his return from flu, for 82 from 51. Raina, reprieved after being given lbw second ball, steadied CSK from 81-4, and shared a match-clinching stand of 40* in 4.3 overs with Jadeja.*

At Hyderabad, April 14 (floodlit). **Delhi Capitals won by 39 runs. Delhi Capitals 155-7** (20 overs) (C. Munro 40, S. S. Iyer 45; K. K. Ahmed 3-30); ‡**Sunrisers Hyderabad 116** (18.5 overs) (D. A. Warner 51, J. M. Bairstow 41; K. Rabada 4-22, C. H. Morris 3-22, K. M. A. Paul 3-17). *PoM:* K. M. A. Paul. *Warner and Bairstow put on 72 inside ten overs to lay solid foundations for Hyderabad, but they then lost ten for 44. Rabada, Chris Morris and Keemo Paul did the damage.*

At Mumbai, April 15 (floodlit). **Mumbai Indians won by five wickets. Royal Challengers Bangalore 171-7** (20 overs) (A. B. de Villiers 75, M. M. Ali 50; S. L. Malinga 4-31); ‡**Mumbai Indians 172-5** (19 overs) (Q. de Kock 40, H. H. Pandya 37*). *PoM:* S. L. Malinga. *Bangalore slumped to their seventh defeat, despite blistering innings from de Villiers (75 off 51) and Ali (50 off 32, with five sixes). But three wickets in the 20th over, from Malinga – one a run-out – ended their charge, before de Kock and Sharma thrashed 70 for Mumbai's first wicket. The rest was a stroll.*

At Mohali, April 16 (floodlit). **Kings XI Punjab won by 14 runs. Kings XI Punjab 182-6** (20 overs) (K. L. Rahul 52, C. H. Gayle 30, D. A. Miller 40; J. C. Archer 3-15); ‡**Rajasthan Royals 168-7** (20 overs) (R. A. Tripathi 50, S. T. R. Binny 31*). *PoM:* R. Ashwin. *The match award went to Ashwin for a four-ball 17, canny bowling (2-24, without a boundary) and captaining Punjab to a win. But the outstanding bowler came from the losers: Archer, excellent throughout, conceded just 15, and grabbed three wickets, Gayle among them.*

At Hyderabad, April 17 (floodlit). **Sunrisers Hyderabad won by six wickets. ‡Chennai Super Kings 132-5** (20 overs) (S. R. Watson 31, F. du Plessis 45); **Sunrisers Hyderabad 137-4** (16.5 overs) (D. A. Warner 50, J. M. Bairstow 61*). *PoM:* D. A. Warner. *A superb containing performance by the Sunrisers bowlers – Rashid Khan had figures of 4–13–17–2, with only three runs in the last two overs – restricted CSK, who had won their previous four games, but were without Dhoni because of back trouble. Warner then scorched to a 24-ball fifty, including ten fours, before Bairstow took over: he ended a run of three defeats with a six off Karn Sharma.*

At Delhi, April 18 (floodlit). **Mumbai Indians won by 40 runs. ‡Mumbai Indians 168-5** (20 overs) (R. G. Sharma 30, Q. de Kock 35, K. H. Pandya 37*, H. H. Pandya 32); **Delhi Capitals 128-9** (20 overs) (S. Dhawan 35; R. D. Chahar 3-19). *PoM:* H. H. Pandya. *Hardik Pandya joined his brother Krunal at 104-4 and slogged 32 in 15 balls, with 50 coming off Mumbai's last three overs. Delhi's reply reached 49-0, before leg-spinner Rahul Chahar struck three times in 12 deliveries; another mini-collapse at 107, when three wickets fell in successive balls – to Malinga, a run-out and Bumrah – meant they finished well short.*

At Kolkata, April 19 (floodlit). **Royal Challengers Bangalore won by ten runs. Royal Challengers Bangalore 213-4** (20 overs) (V. Kohli 100, M. M. Ali 66); ‡**Kolkata Knight Riders 203-5** (20 overs) (N. Rana 85*, A. D. Russell 65). *PoM:* V. Kohli. *Kohli hit his first IPL hundred since 2016, before Bangalore weathered a late assault from Russell – who smashed nine sixes as he added 118 with Nitish Rana – to secure their second win. Kohli had scratched his way to 50 in 40 but, rediscovering his timing, took just 17 more to reach three figures; Ali made a sparkling 66 off 28.*

At Jaipur, April 20 (floodlit). **Rajasthan Royals won by five wickets. Mumbai Indians 161-5** (20 overs) (Q. de Kock 65, S. A. Yadav 34); ‡**Rajasthan Royals 162-5** (19.1 overs) (S. V. Samson 35, S. P. D. Smith 59*, R. Parag 43; R. D. Chahar 3-29). *PoM:* S. P. D. Smith. *A change of captaincy – Smith replacing Rahane – coincided with Rajastan's third win in nine games. Smith responded to his new role with 59* off 48 balls, and was aided by 43 off 29 by 17-year-old Riyan Parag Das. De Kock (65 off 47) had given Mumbai a swift start, but Archer (who dropped three catches) conceded only 16 from three overs at the death.*

At Delhi, April 20 (floodlit). **Delhi Capitals won by five wickets. Kings XI Punjab 163-7** (20 overs) (C. H. Gayle 69, Mandeep Singh 30; S. Lamichhane 3-40); ‡**Delhi Capitals 166-5** (19.4 overs) (S. Dhawan 56, S. S. Iyer 58*). PoM: S. S. Iyer. *The loss of Gayle, who mistimed a googly from Sandeep Lamichhane and was caught on the midwicket boundary for a 37-ball 69, took the wind from Punjab's sails. A target of 164 gave Delhi few problems, thanks largely to fifties from Dhawan and Iyer.*

At Hyderabad, April 21 (floodlit). **Sunrisers Hyderabad won by nine wickets. Kolkata Knight Riders 159-8** (20 overs) (C. A. Lynn 51, R. K. Singh 30; K. K. Ahmed 3-33); ‡**Sunrisers Hyderabad 161-1** (15 overs) (D. A. Warner 67, J. M. Bairstow 80*). PoM: K. K. Ahmed. *Warner and Bairstow continued their rollicking form, putting on 131 in 12.2 overs, their fourth century opening stand of the tournament. Bairstow finished the match with five overs to spare by slamming Piyush Chawla for four, six and six. The Sunrisers' bowlers had shone earlier, seamers Bhuvneshwar Kumar and left-armer Khaleel Ahmed sharing 5-68.*

At Bangalore, April 21 (floodlit). **Royal Challengers Bangalore won by one run. Royal Challengers Bangalore 161-7** (20 overs) (P. A. Patel 53); ‡**Chennai Super Kings 160-8** (20 overs) (M. S. Dhoni 84*). PoM: P. A. Patel. *Bottom-placed Bangalore narrowly defeated leaders Chennai, who needed 26 off the last over, from Umesh Yadav. Dhoni hit 24 off the first five deliveries before Umesh bowled the sixth outside off stump; Dhoni missed an attempted steer behind point, then set off for a bye to tie the scores and earn a super over. But Patel, pulling off his right wicketkeeping glove, threw down the stumps as Shardul Thakur dived for the line. Dhoni finished on a career-best 48-ball 84*.*

At Jaipur, April 22 (floodlit). **Delhi Capitals won by six wickets. Rajasthan Royals 191-6** (20 overs) (A. M. Rahane 105*, S. P. D. Smith 50); ‡**Delhi Capitals 193-4** (19.2 overs) (P. P. Shaw 42, S. Dhawan 54, R. R. Pant 78*). PoM: R. R. Pant. *Delhi moved top of the table on net run-rate after a well-paced chase, Pant hitting 78* off 36. Earlier, Rahane made a shimmering century for Rajasthan after being dropped on 16. Team-mate Ashton Turner recorded a T20-record fifth successive duck (for three teams).*

At Chennai, April 23 (floodlit). **Chennai Super Kings won by six wickets. Sunrisers Hyderabad 175-3** (20 overs) (D. A. Warner 57, M. K. Pandey 83*); ‡**Chennai Super Kings 176-4** (19.5 overs) (S. R. Watson 96, S. K. Raina 38). PoM: S. R. Watson. *Watson scored his first half-century of this IPL, in his 11th innings, to break the back of Chennai's pursuit of 176. After playing out a maiden from Bhuvneshwar, he finished with a match-winning 96 off 53. Hyderabad had lost Bairstow for nought, but Warner notched another fifty, and Manish Pandey opened his shoulders for 83* off 49.*

At Bangalore, April 24 (floodlit). **Royal Challengers Bangalore won by 17 runs. Royal Challengers Bangalore 202-4** (20 overs) (P. A. Patel 43, A. B. de Villiers 82*, M. P. Stoinis 46*); ‡**Kings XI Punjab 185-7** (20 overs) (K. L. Rahul 42, M. A. Agarwal 35, N. Pooran 46; U. T. Yadav 3-36). PoM: A. B. de Villiers. *When Ashwin completed the 17th over to end his stint with a boundaryless 1-15, Bangalore were an uncertain 138-4. Then de Villiers and Stoinis turned the taps on full: 16, 21 and 27 gushed from the final three as Punjab lost control. Even so, they reached the start of the 18th in better shape, but could not translate 167-3 into victory. During the first innings, the game was held up for two minutes when no one could find the ball after a strategic timeout at the end of the 14th over. The fourth official brought out a box of replacements before umpire Shamshuddin remembered he had put it in his pocket.*

At Kolkata, April 25 (floodlit). **Rajasthan Royals won by three wickets. Kolkata Knight Riders 175-6** (20 overs) (K. D. Karthik 97*); ‡**Rajasthan Royals 177-7** (19.2 overs) (A. M. Rahane 34, R. P. Das 47; P. P. Chawla 3-20). PoM: V. R. Aaron. *Figures of 4–17–20–2 from the rapid Varun Aaron, whose only previous over of the season had cost 16, set KKR back, but Dinesh Karthik dragged them to a respectable total with 97* from 50, including nine sixes. It wasn't enough, however, to prevent a sixth straight defeat: the Royals were in trouble at 98-5 in the 13th, before Parag Das hit 47 from 31, then Archer (27* from 12 in his last match of the tournament) crashed the first two balls of the final over for four and six.*

At Chennai, April 26 (floodlit). **Mumbai Indians won by 46 runs. Mumbai Indians 155-4** (20 overs) (R. G. Sharma 67, E. Lewis 32); ‡**Chennai Super Kings 109** (17.4 overs) (M. Vijay 38; S. L. Malinga 4-37). PoM: R. G. Sharma. *Mumbai conclusively ended Chennai's unbeaten home run in their sixth game at Chepauk. Dhoni was missing with a fever; acting-captain Raina chose to bowl on a pitch at its best early on, when Sharma made the most of it, and stand-in keeper*

Rayudu failed to appeal when Evin Lewis nicked Harbhajan. Chasing 156 to book their place in the play-offs, CSK lost five of their top six in single figures.

At Jaipur, April 27 (floodlit). **Rajasthan Royals won by seven wickets. Sunrisers Hyderabad 160-8** (20 overs) (D. A. Warner 37, M. K. Pandey 61); ‡**Rajasthan Royals 161-3** (19.1 overs) (A. M. Rahane 39, L. S. Livingstone 44, S. V. Samson 48*). *PoM:* J. D. Unadkat. *Rajasthan stayed in contention for the play-offs with a comprehensive win (and incidentally confirmed Chennai's qualification). They owed much to Unadkat's bowling and fielding (2-26 and three catches), and a 78-run opening stand between Rahane and Liam Livingstone.*

At Delhi, April 28 (floodlit). **Delhi Capitals won by 16 runs.** ‡**Delhi Capitals 187-5** (20 overs) (S. Dhawan 50, S. S. Iyer 52); **Royal Challengers Bangalore 171-7** (20 overs) (P. A. Patel 39, M. P. Stoinis 32*). *PoM:* S. Dhawan. *Delhi regained top spot with a hard-fought win, and guaranteed a play-off place for the first time in seven years. Fifties for Dhawan and Iyer proved too much for struggling Bangalore.*

At Kolkata, April 28 (floodlit). **Kolkata Knight Riders won by 34 runs. Kolkata Knight Riders 232-2** (20 overs) (S. Gill 76, C. A. Lynn 54, A. D. Russell 80*); ‡**Mumbai Indians 198-7** (20 overs) (H. H. Pandya 91). *PoM:* A. D. Russell. *Kolkata made the highest total of the tournament thanks to half-centuries from their top three. Most serene was Gill; most destructive was Russell, who hit 80* from 40 balls, including eight sixes. But for sheer power, no one could match the 34-ball 91 from Pandya, who pillaged nine.*

At Hyderabad, April 29 (floodlit). **Sunrisers Hyderabad won by 45 runs. Sunrisers Hyderabad 212-6** (20 overs) (D. A. Warner 81, M. K. Pandey 36); ‡**Kings XI Punjab 167-8** (20 overs) (K. L. Rahul 79; K. K. Ahmed 3-40, Rashid Khan 3-21). *PoM:* D. A. Warner. *Warner didn't seem to miss Bairstow, who had returned to England, as he dominated an opening onslaught of 78 in 6.2 overs with stand-in Wriddhaman Saha (28). Afghan spinner Mujeeb felt the heat, with 0-66, as Warner's 81 from 56 set up an imposing total; only Basil Thampi, with 0-70 for the Sunrisers v RCB in 2018, had conceded more in an IPL match. It was all too much for the Kings XI, despite Rahul's 79.*

At Bangalore, April 30 (floodlit). **No result. Royal Challengers Bangalore 62-7** (5 overs) (R. Shreyas Gopal 3-12); ‡**Rajasthan Royals 41-1** (3.2 overs). *Play was reduced to five overs a side after heavy rain. Kohli and de Villiers battered 35 off nine balls, before a hat-trick from Gopal – Kohli caught at long-on, de Villiers at cover and Stoinis at mid-off. Rajasthan were on course when the rain returned.*

At Chennai, May 1 (floodlit). **Chennai Super Kings won by 80 runs. Chennai Super Kings 179-4** (20 overs) (F. du Plessis 39, S. K. Raina 59, M. S. Dhoni 44*); ‡**Delhi Capitals 99** (16.2 overs) (S. S. Iyer 49; Imran Tahir 4-12, R. A. Jadeja 3-9). *PoM:* M. S. Dhoni. *More than half Chennai's runs came in the final six overs as a late blitz set up a thumping win. Delhi succumbed to spin – Imran Tahir's figures were his best at the IPL.*

At Mumbai, May 2 (floodlit). **Mumbai won a super over, following a tie.** ‡**Mumbai Indians 162-5** (20 overs) (Q. de Kock 69*; K. K. Ahmed 3-42); **Sunrisers Hyderabad 162-6** (20 overs) (M. K. Pandey 71*, Mohammad Nabi 31). *PoM:* J. J. Bumrah. *Mumbai were made to sweat over a play-off place after a last-ball six from Pandey earned Hyderabad a super over. But two wickets, including the run-out of Pandey, meant they lasted only four deliveries, and Mumbai needed just three to reach a target of nine, and join Chennai and Delhi in the qualifiers. During the game proper, de Kock's 69* from 58 was balanced out by Pandey's 71* from 47.*

At Mohali, May 3 (floodlit). **Kolkata Knight Riders won by seven wickets. Kings XI Punjab 183-6** (20 overs) (M. A. Agarwal 36, N. Pooran 48, S. M. Curran 55*); ‡**Kolkata Knight Riders 185-3** (18 overs) (S. Gill 65*, C. A. Lynn 46). *PoM:* S. Gill. *A Kolkata victory meant they retained a chance of reaching the next stage, but not Punjab. The game's two half-centuries came from precocious talents: Gill, just 19, hit a mature 65* from 49 balls, to negate the flourish with which Curran – one year his senior – had ended the Kings XI innings. His format-best 55* came from 24.*

At Delhi, May 4 (floodlit). **Delhi Capitals won by five wickets.** ‡**Rajasthan Royals 115-9** (20 overs) (R. P. Das 50; I. Sharma 3-38, A. Mishra 3-17); **Delhi Capitals 121-5** (16.1 overs) (R. R. Pant 53*; I. S. Sodhi 3-26). *PoM:* A. Mishra. *Defeat, set up by Ishant Sharma's three wickets in the powerplay, ensured the Royals missed out on the play-offs; the Capitals were already through, but needed to knock off their target inside ten overs to go top of the table on net run-rate. Three wickets for leg-spinner Ish Sodhi scuppered that, but Pant's 53* from 38, studded with five sixes, ensured a comfortable victory.*

At Bangalore, May 4 (floodlit). **Royal Challengers Bangalore won by four wickets. Sunrisers Hyderabad 175-7** (20 overs) (M. J. Guptill 30, K. S. Williamson 70*; M. S. Washington Sundar 3-24); ‡**Royal Challengers Bangalore 178-6** (19.2 overs) (S. O. Hetmyer 75, Gurkeerat Singh 65; K. K. Ahmed 3-37). PoM: S. O. Hetmyer. *Bangalore won their final game, which meant Hyderabad's hopes of qualifying depended on Kolkata losing next day. Patel, Kohli and de Villiers were all out inside three overs of RCB's chase, but Hetmyer and Gurkeerat Singh added 144, a fourth-wicket IPL record, and Umesh Yadav completed victory with successive fours. Umpire Nigel Llong later paid Rs5,000 (about £56) for repairs to a door which he had kicked in the interval, after giant-screen replays showed he had been wrong to call a no-ball in Yadav's final over.*

At Mohali, May 5 (floodlit). **Kings XI Punjab won by six wickets. Chennai Super Kings 170-5** (20 overs) (F. du Plessis 96, S. K. Raina 53; S. M. Curran 3-35); ‡**Kings XI Punjab 173-4** (18 overs) (K. L. Rahul 71, N. Pooran 36; Harbhajan Singh 3-57). PoM: K. L. Rahul. *Rahul's savage 19-ball fifty earned Kings XI a consolation victory, but Chennai secured second place and a spot in the first qualifier by making sure it took them more than 14.3 overs to reach their target. They were indebted to Harbhajan and Jadeja, who applied the brakes when it looked as if Punjab might embarrass them.*

At Mumbai, May 5 (floodlit). **Mumbai Indians won by nine wickets. Kolkata Knight Riders 133-7** (20 overs) (C. A. Lynn 41, R. V. Uthappa 40; S. L. Malinga 3-35); ‡**Mumbai Indians 134-1** (16.1 overs) (Q. de Kock 30, R. G. Sharma 55*, S. A. Yadav 46*). PoM: H. H. Pandya. *Three wickets for Malinga, including Russell first ball, knocked the stuffing out of Kolkata, who needed a win to stand a chance of progressing. Sharma and Suryakumar Yadav then added 88* in ten overs to confirm their elimination and give fourth place to Hyderabad, while Mumbai's victory ensured they finished top.*

Play-offs

1st v 2nd At Chennai, May 7 (floodlit). **Mumbai Indians won by six wickets.** ‡**Chennai Super Kings 131-4** (20 overs) (A. T. Rayudu 42*, M. S. Dhoni 37*); **Mumbai Indians 132-4** (18.3 overs) (S. A. Yadav 71*). PoM: S. A. Yadav. *On a turning pitch, Chennai struggled to make the progress Dhoni had expected after opting to bat. None of the top four managed better than a run a ball and, though Rayudu and Dhoni raised the tempo, there was no explosion. Teenager Rahul Chahar returned 2-14. Yadav sailed Mumbai into the final after they had slipped to 21-2. Chennai had another chance three days later.*

3rd v 4th At Visakhapatnam, May 8 (floodlit). **Delhi Capitals won by two wickets. Sunrisers Hyderabad 162-8** (20 overs) (M. J. Guptill 36, M. K. Pandey 30; K. M. A. Paul 3-32); ‡**Delhi Capitals 165-8** (19.5 overs) (P. P. Shaw 56, R. R. Pant 49). PoM: R. R. Pant. *The power of Delhi's young blades Shaw and Pant took them to 158-7, needing just five off the last over. Even though Khaleel Ahmed donated a wide, they almost blew it. After two singles, Amit Mishra and Paul were running a bye as the Sunrisers appealed for caught behind, then attempted a run-out; when the review for the catch was turned down, Mishra was given out for obstructing the field, as he had changed course. Paul hit the penultimate delivery for four.*

Final play-off At Visakhapatnam, May 10 (floodlit). **Chennai Super Kings won by six wickets. Delhi Capitals 147-9** (20 overs) (R. R. Pant 38); ‡**Chennai Super Kings 151-4** (19 overs) (F. du Plessis 50, S. R. Watson 50). PoM: F. du Plessis. *Chennai Super Kings forced their way into their second successive final. Even Pant couldn't secure a big total after Delhi were put in and reduced to 80-5, whereas du Plessis and Watson recovered from a first-over muddle that nearly resulted in a run-out to reach 81-0 by the halfway mark. Rayudu (20*) took Chennai home with an over to spare.*

FINAL

CHENNAI SUPER KINGS v MUMBAI INDIANS

At Hyderabad, May 12, 2019 (floodlit). Mumbai Indians won by one run. Toss: Mumbai Indians.

Mumbai Indians' fourth win of the season over Chennai Super Kings secured a record fourth IPL title – just. Chennai needed nine off the final over, from Malinga, with Watson going strong on 76. He had got it down to five off three before he was run out, pushing for a second: four off two. The new batsman, Thakur, managed two off the fifth delivery, so had to score two more off the sixth to win; Malinga trapped him with a slower ball. Watson had survived a run-out attempt and three dropped catches, but the Super Kings would never have got close without him. Bumrah and Rahul

Falling short: Shane Watson is run out by Quinton de Kock, and Mumbai are two balls from victory.

Chahar conceded only 14 apiece; earlier, Rahul's cousin and opponent Deepak had survived being hit for three sixes by de Kock in his second over, yielding just six runs in his other three. Pollard lashed out for 41 to lift the target to 150. Mumbai's fourth title in seven years was their second in a row secured by one run, after pipping Rising Pune Supergiant in 2016-17, also at Hyderabad.

Player of the Match: J. J. Bumrah.
Player of the Tournament: A. D. Russell (Kolkata Knight Riders).

Mumbai Indians

		B	4/6
1 †Q. de Kock *c 5 b 8*	29	17	0/4
2 *R. G. Sharma *c 5 b 9*	15	14	1/1
3 S. A. Yadav *b 11*	15	17	1
4 I. P. Kishan *c 3 b 11*	23	26	3
5 K. H. Pandya *c and b 8*	7	7	0
6 K. A. Pollard *not out*	41	25	3/3
7 H. H. Pandya *lbw b 9*	16	10	1/1
8 R. D. Chahar *c 1 b 9*	0	2	0
9 M. J. McClenaghan *run out (1/6)*	0	2	0
10 J. J. Bumrah *not out*	0	0	0
W 3	3		

6 overs: 45-2   (20 overs) 149-8

1/45 2/45 3/82 4/89 5/101 6/140 7/140 8/141

11 S. L. Malinga did not bat.

Chahar 4–17–26–3; Thakur 4–10–37–2; Harbhajan Singh 4–7–27–0; Bravo 3–7–24–0; Imran Tahir 3–7–23–2; Jadeja 2–3–12–0.

Chennai Super Kings

		B	4/6
1 F. du Plessis *st 1 b 5*	26	13	3/1
2 S. R. Watson *run out (5/11)*	80	59	8/4
3 S. K. Raina *lbw b 8*	8	14	0
4 A. T. Rayudu *c 1 b 10*	1	4	0
5 *†M. S. Dhoni *run out (4)*	2	8	0
6 D. J. Bravo *c 1 b 10*	15	15	0/1
7 R. A. Jadeja *not out*	5	5	0
8 S. N. Thakur *lbw b 11*	2	2	0
B 5, w 4	9		

6 overs: 53-1   (20 overs) 148-7

1/33 2/70 3/73 4/82 5/133 6/146 7/148

9 D. L. Chahar, 10 Harbhajan Singh and 11 Imran Tahir did not bat.

McClenaghan 4–12–24–0; K. H. Pandya 3–8–39–1; Malinga 4–7–49–1; Bumrah 4–13–14–2; Chahar 4–13–14–1; H. H. Pandya 1–4–3–0.

Umpires: I. J. Gould and N. N. Menon.   Third umpire: N. J. Llong.
Referee: J. Srinath.

BURGER KING SUPER SMASH IN 2018-19

Mark Geenty

1 Central Stags   2 Knights

After a nine-year wait for a title, **Central Stags** showed their determination to make amends, and thrashed Knights in the final. With a bowling attack full of internationals, and an explosive batting line-up, they have often had the credentials. And this time they made the potential count, even if they took a roundabout route. After losing four of their nine completed matches in the league stage, they finished third and needed to defeat **Auckland Aces** in the eliminator. An emphatic victory in that match was a useful warm-up for the final.

A change of captain was key to their success. Inspired by his new responsibilities, Tom Bruce was Player of the Tournament after scoring 353 runs at 39, with a strike-rate of 158. His predecessor, Will Young, looked liberated, and in the eliminator made a vital 83 off 54 balls. Their leading bowler was tall seamer Blair Tickner, newly capped at T20 level by New Zealand, who took 16 wickets at 15. He had to sit out the 2nd v 3rd match after injuring an ankle during a game of football in training, but returned for the final to play a full part.

Kyle Jamieson took six for seven, the best T20 figures in New Zealand

Knights had seemed likely to retain their title. They won seven matches to finish top of the league ahead of Auckland by virtue of more victories, and earned a home final at Seddon Park in Hamilton. They had plenty of big-match experience, and were also able to whistle up Tim Southee and Mitchell Santner, who were released from New Zealand's series against Bangladesh. Daryl Mitchell (not the Worcestershire player) was their stand-out batsman, with 323 runs, the third-highest in the competition, while Scott Kuggeleijn took 13 wickets at 19. And, in the South African Kyle Abbott, they had one of the most successful imports.

With the Big Bash going on at the same time across the Tasman, there were few overseas players, but the Aces gained good value from Kent's Daniel Bell-Drummond, who scored 223 runs at 74 in five appearances. He became something of a talisman as they stormed into the eliminator.

Otago Volts, having lost in the final of the 50-over Ford Trophy, kicked off with two wins, but faded to fourth. They, along with the two teams who finished below them, each won three matches, and benefited from some notable individual performances. **Wellington Firebirds** had the leading run-scorer in Devon Conway, South African-born but qualifying for New Zealand, who hit 363 at 45. **Canterbury Kings** may have finished bottom, but they were responsible for two of the most eye-catching displays. Against the Aces, Kyle Jamieson took six for seven, the best T20 figures in New Zealand, and Tom Latham smashed 110 off 60 balls in a losing cause against the Stags at Napier.

BURGER KING SUPER SMASH IN 2018-19

	P	W	L	NR/A	Pts	NRR
KNIGHTS	10	7	3	0	28	1.03
AUCKLAND ACES	10	6	2	2	28	0.57
CENTRAL STAGS	10	5	4	1	22	−0.63
Otago Volts	10	3	5	2	16	−0.63
Wellington Firebirds	10	3	6	1	14	−0.01
Canterbury Kings	10	3	7	0	12	−0.41

Teams level on points were separated by most wins.

2nd v 3rd   At Auckland (Eden Park Outer Oval), February 15, 2019. **Central Stags won by 44 runs. Central Stags 219-4** (20 overs) (W. A. Young 83, T. C. Bruce 35, D. Cleaver 77*); ‡**Auckland Aces 175-5** (20 overs) (C. Munro 33, D. J. Bell-Drummond 64, G. D. Phillips 30). *At 76-3 in the eighth over, there was still a chance that Craig Cachopa's gamble of inserting the Stags would come off. Then Will Young and wicketkeeper Dane Cleaver – who blasted five sixes in his 77* off 37 – put on 143, and left the Aces a formidable task. They were quick out of the blocks, but Adam Milne (1/24) and Seth Rance (2-31) skilfully applied the brakes.*

Final   At Hamilton, February 17, 2019. **Central Stags won by 67 runs.** ‡**Central Stags 147-8** (20 overs) (D. Foxcroft 63); **Knights 80** (14.4 overs) (A. F. Milne 3-12, A. Y. Patel 3-24). *After losing their previous three finals, the Stags finally remembered their lines and won with plenty to spare. It didn't look like they had enough in the bank when Kyle Abbott and spinners Ish Sodhi and Mitchell Santner restricted them to 147-8, which was reliant on Dean Foxcroft's 63 off 50 balls. Then the Knights collapsed in a heap, losing nine for 48, with many batsmen appearing to be giving catching practice. Doug Bracewell collected the key scalps of Tim Seifert and Dean Brownlie, before Adam Milne and Ajaz Patel cleaned up.*

SUPER SMASH FINALS

2005-06	CANTERBURY WIZARDS beat Auckland Aces by six wickets at Auckland.
2006-07	AUCKLAND ACES beat Otago Volts by 60 runs at Auckland.
2007-08	CENTRAL STAGS beat Northern Knights by five wickets at New Plymouth.
2008-09	OTAGO VOLTS headed the table; the final against Canterbury Wizards at Dunedin was washed out.
2009-10	CENTRAL STAGS beat Auckland Aces by 78 runs at New Plymouth.
2010-11	AUCKLAND ACES beat Central Stags by four runs at Auckland.
2011-12	AUCKLAND ACES beat Canterbury Wizards by 44 runs at Auckland.
2012-13	OTAGO VOLTS beat Wellington Firebirds by four wickets at Dunedin.
2013-14	NORTHERN KNIGHTS beat Otago Volts by five wickets at Hamilton.
2014-15	WELLINGTON FIREBIRDS beat Auckland Aces by six wickets at Hamilton.
2015-16	AUCKLAND ACES beat Otago Volts by 20 runs at New Plymouth.
2016-17	WELLINGTON FIREBIRDS beat Central Stags by 14 runs at New Plymouth.
2017-18	KNIGHTS beat Central Stags by nine wickets at Hamilton.
2018-19	CENTRAL STAGS beat Knights by 67 runs at Hamilton.

> **❝** I saw Martin Guptill still lying on the ground. I've always felt that the only thing worse than a sore loser is a sore winner. I'm sure people could understand why we were all running around like headless chickens, but going over to commiserate seemed the right thing to do."
> Memories of the super over, page 34

THE HBL PAKISTAN SUPER LEAGUE IN 2018-19

Charles Reynolds

1 Quetta Gladiators   2 Peshawar Zalmi

The fourth edition of the Pakistan Super League saw a successful continuation of the board's attempts to reintroduce high-profile cricket to the nation. The 2018-19 season featured more matches on home soil, with many of the overseas stars who had steered clear of the later stages agreeing to play in Pakistan after the early games in the UAE.

In 2017-18, only the last three matches were played in Pakistan, but this time it was eight. An escalation in tensions with India meant some were shifted from Lahore, just across the border, to Karachi, but in the end things ran smoothly enough to allow the Pakistan Cricket Board to contemplate staging the whole of the 2019-20 tournament at home.

It was a case of third time lucky for **Quetta Gladiators**, who won at last after losing the first two finals. They had been hamstrung by the reluctance of overseas players to visit Pakistan, but this time fielded a first-choice side throughout. Their star performer was Shane Watson, voted Player of the Tournament after topping the run-charts with 430, at a thumping strike-rate of 143. Umar Akmal's move to Quetta from Lahore brought a welcome return to form, while the 18-year-old fast bowler Mohammad Hasnain announced himself with three wickets in the final.

Peshawar Zalmi topped the table, but had to settle for runners-up medals for the second year in a row after a one-sided final. Kamran Akmal was again their key man: he became the PSL's leading scorer overall, and only Watson bettered his 357 runs. Kamran's opening partner, Imam-ul-Haq, made 341 runs, while Kieron Pollard contributed 284 at a strike-rate of 173. Peshawar also had two of the top three wicket-takers in what remained a bowler-friendly competition: Hasan Ali claimed 25, and Wahab Riaz 17.

The appearance of **Multan Sultans** was something of a surprise, since their franchise agreement had apparently been terminated over what the PCB called an "inability to meet its financial obligations". But new owners stepped in, and decided to keep alive arguably T20's finest team name. However, they were not able to improve their on-field performance, and finished fifth, as they had in 2017-18.

Also unable to qualify were **Lahore Qalandars**, though they were at least consistent: they had now finished last in every season. Lahore had hoped the acquisition of A. B. de Villiers would improve their fortunes, and he did score 218 runs in seven matches. But they still could not avoid the wooden spoon, sealed after a horror run of four defeats at the end of the group stage.

Defending champions **Islamabad United** could not quite recapture the previous season's magic, although new signing Cameron Delport proved a hit with the bat (355 runs), and Fahim Ashraf did well with the ball. His 21 wickets included the tournament's best return, six for 19 against the Qalandars.

Karachi Kings again failed to make the final. They reached the knockouts despite three defeats in their first four games, but recovered thanks to the batting of Colin Ingram (344 runs), Babar Azam (335) and Lancashire's Liam Livingstone (321). The surprise packet in their bowling was 19-year-old slow left-armer Umar Khan, who had been signed as an "emerging player". Going for a respectable 7.1 an over, he took 15 wickets.

PAKISTAN SUPER LEAGUE IN 2018-19

	P	W	L	Pts	NRR
PESHAWAR ZALMI	10	7	3	14	0.82
QUETTA GLADIATORS	10	7	3	14	0.37
ISLAMABAD UNITED	10	5	5	10	0.12
KARACHI KINGS	10	5	5	10	−0.67
Multan Sultans	10	3	7	6	0.17
Lahore Qalandars	10	3	7	6	−0.83

1st v 2nd At Karachi, March 13, 2019 (floodlit). **Quetta Gladiators won by ten runs. Quetta Gladiators 186-6** (20 overs) (S. R. Watson 71, Ahsan Ali 46); ‡**Peshawar Zalmi 176-7** (20 overs) (K. A. Pollard 44, D. J. G. Sammy 46). PoM: S. R. Watson. *Quetta made sure of a place in the final, their total of 186 proving just too much. Shane Watson set it up with 71 from 43 balls, including six sixes; he put on 111 for the second wicket with Ahsan Ali in 10.4 overs. Peshawar Zalmi struggled to 90-5, with the pacy Mohammad Hasnain taking 2-14 from his first three, before their West Indian contingent muscled them close: Kieron Pollard clubbed 44 from 22 balls, and skipper Darren Sammy 46 from 21, with five sixes. They put on 83 in six overs, but both fell in the 20th, from Watson. He might not have bowled, but Quetta's Australian leg-spinner Fawad Ahmed was in hospital after being hit in the face by an Imam-ul-Haq straight-drive during his second over – it was completed by Rilee Rossouw, who dismissed Imam (23) with his first delivery.*

3rd v 4th At Karachi, March 14, 2019 (floodlit). **Islamabad United won by four wickets.** ‡**Karachi Kings 161-9** (20 overs) (Babar Azam 42, C. Munro 32, L. S. Livingstone 30; Musa Khan 3-42); **Islamabad United 164-6** (19.3 overs) (C. S. Delport 38, A. D. Hales 41, Hussain Talat 32). PoM: A. D. Hales. *Holders Islamabad lived to fight another day, getting home in the final over when Asif Ali (24* from ten balls) hit Mohammad Amir for four. Karachi had rocketed away at the start, Colin Munro biffing 32 from 11 as the six-over powerplay produced 78. But from 102-1 in the 11th, they lost momentum, and managed only 11 in the last three. Islamabad stacked their four overseas players at the top of the order, and were indebted to Alex Hales's patient 41. At 129-5 after 17, they needed 33 more – and scooted home.*

Final play-off At Karachi, March 15, 2019 (floodlit). **Peshawar Zalmi won by 48 runs. Peshawar Zalmi 214-5** (40 overs) (Kamran Akmal 74, Imam-ul-Haq 58, K. A. Pollard 37, D. J. G. Sammy 30*); ‡**Islamabad United 166-9** (20 overs) (C. A. K. Walton 48, Fahim Ashraf 31; Hasan Ali 3-29, C. J. Jordan 3-26). PoM: Kamran Akmal. *Put in, Peshawar Zalmi ran up the second-highest total of the tournament, which proved too much for Islamabad. Kamran Akmal (74 from 43 balls) and Imam (58 from 33) gave them a great start with an opening stand of 135. Then Pollard took over, hitting 37 from 21 before being given out obstructing the field after kneeing the ball away to avoid being run out. Needing a record PSL chase, Islamabad were up against it once Chris Jordan nabbed Hales for a single, to make it 26-2 in the fourth over.*

Final At Karachi, March 17, 2019 (floodlit). **Quetta Gladiators won by eight wickets. Peshawar Zalmi 138-8** (20 overs) (Umar Amin 38; Mohammad Hasnain 3-30); ‡**Quetta Gladiators 139-2** (17.5 overs) (Ahmed Shehzad 58*, R. R. Rossouw 39*). PoM: Mohammad Hasnain. PoT: S. R. Watson (Quetta Gladiators). *Twice defeated in previous finals, Quetta Gladiators pulled off a thumping victory, chasing down their modest target with 13 balls to spare. Peshawar Zalmi never really got going against some tight bowling: Mohammad Nawaz, who conceded 31, was the most expensive of the Gladiators' attack, while Hasnain removed three international batsmen in Imam, Umar Amin and Pollard. Although Watson was run out in the third over, Ahmed Shehzad made sure of the title, sharing stands of 47 with Ahsan Ali (25) and 73* with Rossouw. The presentation ceremony was a muted affair, out of respect for the victims of a terrorist attack on two mosques in Christchurch, New Zealand, two days earlier.*

MZANSI SUPER LEAGUE IN 2018-19

Colin Bryden

1 Jozi Stars   2 Cape Town Blitz

South Africa's first city-based franchise T20 competition was a curate's egg. There was a boost to the pay packets of home players, and free-to-air television exposure for domestic cricket, where audiences were encouraging. But it drew only moderate crowds, and failed to secure a title sponsor; some star names found the T10 League in the UAE a more attractive proposition. Organised on the hoof in three months, the Mzansi Super League (*mzansi* is Xhosa for "south", and an informal name for the country) was a far cry from the grand designs of the ill-fated Global League project. But Cricket South Africa's chief executive Thabang Moroe was upbeat: "It's a plane that took off without wings. It managed to fly, and now it's landed safely."

Jozi Stars – Jozi is a nickname for Johannesburg – lost three of their first four matches, but recovered to finish second, which was enough for them to reach the final when their semi was rained off. On home turf, they then outplayed **Cape Town Blitz**, who had started the tournament in ominous form. Clever recruitment proved key to the Stars' success. Captain Dane Vilas, picked up in the first round of the draft, proved an able leader, and was fifth in the batting averages. In the second round, they nabbed Rassie van der Dussen, who finished as leading run-scorer, with 469 at 58. Reeza Hendricks was the only batsman to score two hundreds. Australian all-rounder Dan Christian, signed in the third round, was arguably the leading import, and the Stars secured a bargain in the ninth: Duanne Olivier, who ended as the leading wicket-taker, with 20 at 13. Kagiso Rabada, their local marquee player, took 13 wickets at 18, and often struck when it mattered most. In the closing stages, they had to do without Chris Gayle, who returned to the Caribbean after the death of his mother.

The Blitz had looked unstoppable. Quinton de Kock finished joint-top of the averages with Hendricks (both hit 412 at 58, although de Kock's strike-rate was higher), and batted with his customary flair; he was well supported by Janneman Malan, getting his first taste of franchise cricket. Dale Steyn took 12 wickets and had one of the best economy-rates, but an injury after three matches to paceman Anrich Nortje, whose fiery start earned him an IPL contract, reduced their potency.

Durban Heat had been installed as favourites by some, but they underperformed, and Rashid Khan arrived too late to turn the tide. Hashim Amla, their star player, was dropped midway through the competition, returning for their last two matches. A. B. de Villiers made his only home appearances of the summer, for **Tshwane Spartans** of Pretoria, but his best innings, an unbeaten 93 off 52 against Durban, came in a losing cause in a dead rubber. **Paarl Rocks**, led by Faf du Plessis, finished third in the table and attracted a loyal following to Boland Park. But they were denied the chance of making the final when the semi was abandoned. **Nelson Mandela Bay Giants**, based at Port Elizabeth, had Nottinghamshire's Ben Duckett and Surrey's Jason Roy, but narrowly missed the cut.

Two British men – described by CSA as "known match-fixers – were arrested on suspicion of involvement in illegal gambling at the Durban v Jozi match at Kingsmead, and there were two similar arrests at the start of the tournament at the Paarl–Tshwane fixture.

MZANSI SUPER LEAGUE IN 2018-19

	P	W	L	NR	Bonus pts	Pts	NRR
CAPE TOWN BLITZ	10	6	3	1	4	30	0.94
JOZI STARS	10	6	4	0	5	29	1.29
PAARL ROCKS	10	5	5	0	2	22	−0.29
Nelson Mandela Bay Giants	10	4	4	2	1	21	−0.44
Tshwane Spartans	10	4	6	0	0	16	−1.04
Durban Heat	10	3	6	1	0	14	−0.71

2nd v 3rd At Johannesburg, December 14, 2018 (floodlit). **Jozi Stars v Paarl Rocks. Abandoned.** Jozi Stars advanced to the final thanks to finishing above Paarl Rocks.

Final At Cape Town, December 16, 2018 (floodlit). **Jozi Stars won by eight wickets.** ‡Cape **Town Blitz 113-7** (20 overs); **Jozi Stars 115-2** (17.3 overs) (R. R. Hendricks 33, H. E. van der Dussen 59*). *PoM:* B. E. Hendricks. *PoT:* Q. de Kock. *Cape Town's success had been built on their batting, but in front of their home fans – the Blitz Brigade – it let them down. With Janneman Malan absent ill, more pressure fell on Quinton de Kock; when he was dismissed by Beuran Hendricks in the second over, it already felt like a pivotal moment. Then Jozi's Reeza Hendricks and Rassie van der Dussen continued their prolific form by adding 86 for the second wicket, before captain Dane Vilas hit the winning runs.*

THE HERO CARIBBEAN PREMIER LEAGUE IN 2019

Peter Miller

1 Barbados Tridents   2 Guyana Amazon Warriors

For much of the seventh instalment of the Caribbean Premier League, the Amazon Warriors were on course to end a sequence of near misses. They won all ten of their group games, and the first qualifier, to go straight to their fifth final. But Barbados Tridents peaked at the right moment, dominating the match and claiming their second CPL title.

Guyana Amazon Warriors had several eye-catching performers. The 40-year-old Imran Tahir took 16 wickets with his leg-breaks, while Chris Green, an Australian off-spinner entrusted with the new ball, managed 13. Brandon King, a Jamaican, was the leading scorer, his 496 runs including 132 not out – a tournament record – in the qualifying play-off, as well as 32 sixes.

Barbados Tridents, led by West Indies Test captain Jason Holder, put aside an up-and-down season to produce a glorious ending. For the first half of the competition, it looked as if they would struggle to reach the knockouts, with only two wins from their first six matches. But three out of four at the end saw them safely through, in second spot. That meant they had another chance after losing the first qualifier to the Warriors, and they reached the final by restricting Trinbago Knight Riders to below 150, before doing the same to the Warriors. The Tridents' bowling star was leg-spinner Hayden Walsh, who had played nine white-ball internationals for the United States. He was the official ICC Americas representative in the Tridents squad (each team had one), and ended Player of the Tournament, with 22 wickets. Walsh was rewarded with a call-up to the West Indies ODI and T20 squads.

St Kitts & Nevis Patriots reached the knockouts after a series of tight matches, including a super-over victory against the Knight Riders. Their success was achieved thanks to Carlos Brathwaite's belief in himself and his young side.

Holders **Trinbago Knight Riders** won their first four matches, but a run of five defeats and a no-result meant they scraped into the knockouts. Dwayne Bravo missed the tournament, and Sunil Narine was briefly sidelined – both with finger injuries. Kieron Pollard stepped up, and clattered 349 runs at a strike-rate of 159. Soon after, he was restored to the West Indies set-up as the white-ball captain.

St Lucia Zouks would have reached the knockouts for the first time since 2016 if they had beaten the Tridents in their final game, but they went down by 24 runs. Their leading performer was the larger-than-life Rahkeem Cornwall, who belted 254 runs at a strike-rate of 190 after being promoted to open.

For the first time, **Jamaica Tallawahs** failed to qualify from the group stage, and finished last. Chris Gayle hit 116 – his 22nd T20 hundred – against the Patriots. But that was the high spot: they won only once more, with poor bowling and shoddy fielding contributing to an early exit.

CARIBBEAN PREMIER LEAGUE IN 2019

	P	W	L	NR/A	Pts	NRR
GUYANA AMAZON WARRIORS	10	10	0	0	20	1.72
BARBADOS TRIDENTS.............	10	5	5	0	10	0.51
ST KITTS & NEVIS PATRIOTS	10	5	5	0	10	–0.10
TRINBAGO KNIGHT RIDERS	10	4	5	1	9	–0.02
St Lucia Zouks.......................	10	3	6	1	7	–0.74
Jamaica Tallawahs	10	2	8	0	4	–1.37

3rd v 4th At Providence, Guyana, October 6, 2019. **Trinbago Knight Riders won by six wickets.**
St Kitts & Nevis Patriots 125-7 (20 overs) (L. J. Evans 55; C. J. Jordan 3-30); ‡**Trinbago Knight**
Riders 128-4 (18.4 overs) (L. M. P. Simmons 51, D. Ramdin 32*). PoM: S. P. Narine. *Laurie Evans*
made 55 from 47 balls, with eight fours – but the rest could manage only seven boundaries between
them as the Patriots limped to 125, with Evans's Sussex team-mate Chris Jordan taking three
wickets. Sunil Narine claimed figures of 4–19–10–2, despite having barely recovered from breaking
his right index finger. The Knight Riders were 31-3 in the sixth, but Lendl Simmons hit a stop–start
half-century, before Denesh Ramdin and skipper Kieron Pollard (26) blasted them home with a*
stand of 50 in 19 balls.*

1st v 2nd At Providence, Guyana, October 6, 2019 (floodlit). **Guyana Amazon Warriors won by**
30 runs. ‡**Guyana Amazon Warriors 218-3** (20 overs) (B. A. King 132*, Shoaib Malik 32);
Barbados Tridents 188-8 (20 overs) (A. D. Hales 36, J. L. Carter 49; R. Shepherd 3-50). PoM:
B. A. King. *The Warriors eased to their 11th successive victory – a West Indian T20 record – after*
a blitz from opener Brandon King, whose 132 (more than the Patriots had managed in total on the*
same pitch earlier in the day) came from 72 balls, and contained 11 sixes and ten fours. It was the
highest score in the CPL, beating Andre Russell's 121 for Jamaica Tallawahs against Trinbago*
Knight Riders in 2018. The Tridents reached 50 in 5.3 overs, but could not maintain the rate; Imran
Tahir finished with 4–13–13–2.

Final play-off At Tarouba, Trinidad, October 10, 2019 (floodlit). **Barbados Tridents won by 12**
runs. Barbados Tridents 160-6 (20 overs) (J. Charles 35); ‡**Trinbago Knight Riders 148**
(19.3 overs) (S. Prasanna 51). PoM: A. R. Nurse. *The Tridents grabbed their second chance of a*
place in the final thanks to tight bowling, especially from captain Jason Holder (4–10–24–1) and
off-spinner Ashley Nurse (4–12–14–2), which kept the Knight Riders behind the rate. In all, there
were 51 dot balls. Down at No. 7, the Sri Lankan Seekkuge Prasanna gave them a chance with 51
from 27, but with 14 wanted he fell to the first delivery of the 20th over, entrusted to left-arm seamer
Raymon Reifer, who then dismissed Khary Pierre to finish with 2-13. Earlier, the Tridents had also
struggled, until Reifer and Nurse clubbed 48 – including five sixes – from the last 14 balls.*

Final At Tarouba, Trinidad, October 12, 2019 (floodlit). **Barbados Tridents won by 27 runs.**
‡**Barbados Tridents 171-6** (20 overs) (J. Charles 39, J. L. Carter 50*); **Guyana Amazon Warriors**
144-9 (20 overs) (B. A. King 43; R. A. Reifer 4-24). PoM: J. L. Carter. PoT: H. R. Walsh (Barbados
Tridents). *With the Tridents 108-6 in the 15th over, Holder might have been regretting his decision*
to bat – but they collected 63 from the last 31 deliveries, with Jonathan Carter smacking four sixes
in his 27-ball 50. King made another useful start for the Warriors, but regular wickets – including*
four for Reifer, who completed the best figures in a CPL final – led to their first defeat of the
tournament. It meant a second title for the Tridents, whose overseas players in the final were the
English trio of Harry Gurney, Alex Hales and Phil Salt, and Shakib Al Hasan from Bangladesh.

CPL FINALS

2013 JAMAICA TALLAWAHS beat Guyana Amazon Warriors by seven wickets.
2014 BARBADOS TRIDENTS beat Guyana Amazon Warriors by eight runs (DLS).
2015 TRINIDAD & TOBAGO RED STEEL beat Barbados Tridents by 20 runs.
2016 JAMAICA TALLAWAHS beat Guyana Amazon Warriors by nine wickets.
2017 TRINBAGO KNIGHT RIDERS beat St Kitts & Nevis Patriots by three wickets.
2018 TRINBAGO KNIGHT RIDERS beat Guyana Amazon Warriors by eight wickets.
2019 BARBADOS TRIDENTS beat Guyana Amazon Warriors by 27 runs.

OTHER DOMESTIC T20 COMPETITIONS IN 2018-19

AFGHANISTAN PREMIER LEAGUE IN 2018-19

There was a sprinkling of stardust in Afghanistan's revamped T20 competition, which was played in Sharjah in October 2018, after around 40 overseas players had thrown their names in the hat for the IPL-style auction held in March. Chris Gayle and Ravi Bopara did most of the heavy lifting in the final, as **Balkh Legends**, who had topped the qualifying table, took the trophy with something to spare. Gayle finished with 315 runs, behind only the Afghan pair of Mohammad Shahzad (344) and Hazratullah Zazai, whose 322 included the tournament's only century, 124 from 55 balls for Kabul Zwanan against Nangarhar Leopards. And against Balkh, Hazratullah smashed six sixes in an over; the unfortunate bowler was slow left-armer Abdullah Mazari, who also sent down a wide. Sri Lankan left-arm seamer Isuru Udana was the leading wicket-taker, with 15.

	P	W	L	Pts	NRR
BALKH LEGENDS	8	6	2	12	0.78
PAKTIA ROYALS	8	5	3	10	0.14
KABUL ZWANAN	8	4	4	8	−0.07
NANGARHAR LEOPARDS	8	3	5	6	−0.58
Kandahar Kings	8	2	6	4	−0.22

Semi-finals Balkh Legends beat Nangarhar Leopards by 171 runs; Kabul Zwanan beat Paktia Royals by 90 runs.

Final At Sharjah, October 21, 2018 (floodlit). **Balkh Legends won by four wickets.** ‡Kabul Zwanan 132-9 (20 overs) (Javed Ahmadi 32; Qais Ahmad 5-18); Balkh Legends 138-6 (18.1 overs) (C. H. Gayle 56, R. S. Bopara 32*; W. D. Parnell 3-35). *PoM:* Qais Ahmad. *Despite losing two partners in Balkh's first over, Chris Gayle bulldozed on to 56 out of 87-4, then Ravi Bopara took over. Gulbadeen Naib completed victory with a six off his third ball. Earlier, 18-year-old leg-spinner Qais Ahmad had strangled Kabul's innings with 5-18, the best return of the tournament.*

SRI LANKA CRICKET TWENTY20 TOURNAMENT IN 2018-19

Four 20-over mini-leagues plus knockout

With Sri Lanka's long-promised franchise league again failing to materialise, the country's traditional teams fought out the domestic T20 competition over a fortnight in February 2019. Nondescripts were the holders, but narrowly lost the final, with **Moors** squeezing home by one wicket in a fluctuating game at the P. Sara Oval. Moors had already beaten Nondescripts in the group phase. Dinesh Chandimal, free to play for Nondescripts as he had been dropped from the national side for the tour of South Africa, was the leading batsman, with 261 runs; he made one of the competition's three centuries. Seekkuge Prasanna, another looking for an international recall, hammered 202 runs for the Army at a strike-rate of 208. Slow left-armer Malinda Pushpakumara had a remarkable tournament, taking 20 wickets at an average of seven, and conceding only 5.6 runs per over.

Quarter-finals Army beat Chilaw Marians by 51 runs; Colombo tied with Ragama, and won a super over; Moors beat Galle by four wickets; Nondescripts beat Tamil Union by 45 runs.

Semi-finals Nondescripts beat Colombo by one run; Moors beat Army by six wickets.

Final At Colombo (PSO), February 27, 2019. **Moors won by one wicket. Nondescripts 173-7** (20 overs) (M. L. Udawatte 31, P. Nissanka 52; A. Thilanchana 3-30; ‡**Moors 174-9** (20 overs) (R. T. M. Wanigamuni 37, N. M. Subasinghe 47; G. K. D. B. Gunaratne 3-18). *Pathum Nissanka made the only half-century of the final, before becoming one of medium-pacer Adeesha Thilanchana's three victims. Moors slipped to 39-4, but Ramesh Mendis Wanigamuni added 49 with Thilanchana (26) and 60 with Nimanda Madushanka Subasinghe (47 from 23). Four wickets tumbled in the last three overs, but No. 10 Shiran Fernando finished the job with 16* from six.*

ZIMBABWE DOMESTIC TWENTY20 CHAMPIONSHIP IN 2018-19

For the first time in three years, Zimbabwe managed to organise a T20 competition. Things had changed since the previous event, in 2015-16, which was won by Mashonaland Eagles, with Matabeleland Tuskers bottom of the table. This time **Tuskers** came out on top, although the final was a disappointment, thanks to Cyclone Idai, which had already affected several of the group games. Rain stopped play towards the end of the first innings, and Tuskers won by virtue of their better qualifying record. They possessed the outstanding batsman of the competition in Craig Ervine, who made 328 runs in six innings, three not-out. Only team-mate Brian Chari, with 238, came within 100 of Ervine's total. Tendai Chatara led the way for the bowlers with seven wickets, although there was a remarkable spell – his only one of the tournament – by the Tuskers' 18-year-old slow left-armer Milton Shumba, who wrapped up Mountaineers' innings in a qualifying game with four for four in 14 balls.

	P	W	L	A	Bonus	Pts	NRR
TUSKERS	6	3	2	1	2	16	1.86
MOUNTAINEERS	6	2	2	2	1	13	−0.66
Eagles	6	2	2	0	0	12	−0.64
Rhinos	6	2	3	1	0	10	−0.92

Third-place play-off At Harare, March 17, 2019. **Rhinos won by seven runs** (DLS). **Eagles 115-7** (20 overs) (C. Zhuwao 48; M. Chikowero 3-10); ‡**Rhinos 47-2** (7.3 overs). *Rain interrupted the Rhinos' chase, then ended the game when they were ahead of the target.*

Final At Harare, March 17, 2019. **No result. Tuskers won by virtue of heading the table. Tuskers 113-5** (17.2 overs) (C. R. Ervine 55*; R. Kaia 3-8) v ‡**Mountaineers**. *Cyclone Idai spoiled the final too. Craig Ervine hit 55* off 46 balls, but had little support once opener Brian Chari fell for 27, as Roy Kaia returned figures of 2–6–8–3.*

TEST TRIANGLE INTERPROVINCIAL CUP IN 2019

Leinster Lightning had won five of the six previous T20 competitions in Ireland, but had to settle for second place, as **Northern Knights** took their first title. The tournament was split between Dublin in the south (six matches in June) and Bready in the north (six in mid-August), but the weather was atrocious, washing out two of the first batch and all six at Bready; Leinster completed only two of their scheduled six matches. The last Dublin game turned out to be the decider, as the Knights pipped Leinster by eight runs. Greg Thompson's unbeaten 65 was the highest score of a soggy tournament.

	P	W	L	A	Bonus	Pts	NRR
Northern Knights.......	6	3	0	3	1	19	2.45
Leinster Lightning......	6	1	1	4	0	12	-0.18
North West Warriors....	6	0	1	5	0	10	-4.03
Munster Reds..........	6	0	2	4	0	8	-0.85

Elsewhere, **Lalitpur Patriots** beat Bhairahawa Gladiators by 14 runs in the final of Nepal's Everest Premier League in December 2018, even though the Gladiators boasted Ryan ten Doeschate of Essex and the Netherlands. The overseas contingent also included Scotland's captain Kyle Coetzer, the South African batsman Richard Levi, and the big-hitting Irish pair of Kevin O'Brien and Paul Stirling. Nepal had two other T20 competitions, the Pokhara Premier League (won by Pokhara Paltan) and the Dhangadhi Premier League (won by CYC Attariya). Sunny Patel, who formerly played for Gujarat in India's Ranji Trophy, was Player of the Tournament in both.

The second edition of the Global T20 Canada was won by **Winnipeg Hawks**, after a super over in the final against Vancouver Knights, the previous champions. Winnipeg's J–P. Duminy topped the run-lists with 326, although Chris Gayle smashed the highest score, an unbeaten 122 for Vancouver against Montreal Tigers. The competition had its share of financial problems, with one match delayed while the players demanded payment.

Hong Kong's T20 Blitz, which had attracted some big-name players in the past, was cancelled after three seasons for financial reasons. But the purely domestic Hong Kong Premier League boiled down to the last match, between two teams with 100% records: **Pakistan Association** beat Kowloon by one wicket.

PART EIGHT

Women's Cricket

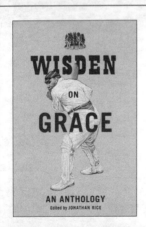

WOMEN'S CRICKET IN 2019

Melinda Farrell

Australia's overwhelming dominance of the women's Ashes bolstered the view that they are pulling so far ahead of the rest of the world – on the back of superior investment in domestic competitions – that it may be years before other countries can bridge the gap. Still, there were encouraging signs of growth elsewhere, sometimes in surprising areas.

England's build-up to Australia's visit largely went to plan. Although they lost their first one-day series of the year, in India, they won the last game, beat India in the Twenty20 leg of the tour, and went on to whitewash Sri Lanka in both formats. The home summer started equally well: they defeated West Indies comfortably in the one-day series, plus the only T20 to survive the rain.

Their batting guns were in form under Heather Knight's steady leadership: the likes of Tammy Beaumont, Danni Wyatt and Nat Sciver all produced significant scores, Amy Jones blossomed as an opening bat, and Sophie Ecclestone's left-arm spin was an exciting prospect. The stage was set for the actors to reclaim the Ashes on home soil.

But Australia's superiority in all facets was evident as they won the three ODIs that opened the multi-format series. If one senior batter missed out, others took up the mantle, with captain Meg Lanning, Alyssa Healy and Ellyse Perry sharing much of the run-scoring. Though Beaumont made the only century of the series, for the most part England's batting faltered. Australia's attack was led superbly by Perry, who netted a magnificent seven for 22 at Canterbury – arguably the international bowling performance of the year.

The sole Test offered Perry a rare opportunity to display her talents with the red ball: she elegantly compiled 116 and 76 not out. At a time when cricket is debating the merits of four-day Tests for men, the scarcity of the format for women perhaps told in some cautious tactics: Australia spent more than two days batting, before declaring their first innings, at which point the draw – which guaranteed they would retain the Ashes – was a foregone conclusion. There was scant consolation for England when they won the third T20, following thumpings in the first two. That would remain Australia's only defeat in 2019, a year when they also swept aside New Zealand, West Indies and Sri Lanka.

There are often casualties for a losing Ashes side, particularly at home. In this case, it was the coach, Mark Robinson, who had revamped England after his appointment in 2015, bringing through several new players and overseeing the 2017 World Cup victory. The ECB turned to Australia for his replacement, signing former international opener Lisa Keightley to take the reins in good time for the women's T20 World Cup in early 2020. She inherited a team that had finished 2019 on a more positive note, convincingly defeating Pakistan in Malaysia.

Another departure from the England side was Sarah Taylor, for different reasons. Taylor, only 30, was widely regarded as the best female wicketkeeper in the world – some high-profile players suggested she was the best, full stop. On top of her glovework, she had been one of England's most stylish and proficient batters since her debut in 2006. But her well-known struggles with mental health issues made touring, in particular, difficult. After several extended breaks from the game, she retired from international cricket at the end of the English summer.

That summer also saw the final Kia Super League, after four seasons in which the English T20 tournament had grown in popularity. Born out of an awareness that the Women's Big Bash League in Australia had created a depth of talent and intensity of competition that dwarfed England's unwieldy amateur county competitions, the KSL became a victim when the ECB decided to reboot men's domestic cricket; they wanted their new tournament, The Hundred, to run in parallel for women and men.

But as 2019 drew to a close, there were no concrete details on domestic T20 and 50-over cricket in 2020. There were murmurs of massive financial investment and restructuring, along with claims that the ECB's deals with the BBC and Sky, to broadcast both the men's and women's Hundred, would increase the popularity of the women's game. But the demise of the KSL after such a short life suggests that, rather than forging a path in its own best interests, women's cricket in England is still a hostage to men's.

As one Super League expired, another emerged: Cricket South Africa launched their inaugural Women's Super League in September. The four-team T20 competition was designed to widen the talent pool ahead of the T20 World Cup, with promising domestic players lining up alongside internationals.

Cricket New Zealand announced significant investment in their women players in August, increasing the number of central contracts from 15 to 17, and raising the base retainer. They also offered 54 domestic, and eight development, contracts. While the value of the domestic contracts ($3,250 per season) was modest, it was a promising start, and mirrors the route Cricket Australia took towards professionalism. In a historic advance, New Zealand also became the first board to offer maternity leave, quickly followed by CA. New Zealand captain Amy Satterthwaite and Australia's Jess Duffin were the first to benefit from a policy that could extend women's professional careers.

Among these developments, the absence of a women's IPL in the calendar remains glaring, although the BCCI experimented with four exhibition matches in May, and the in-form national team looked the side most likely to challenge Australia's domination of the game.

Elsewhere in Asia, the women's game is burgeoning at an exciting rate, nowhere more than in Thailand. In September, they defied expectations by defeating Papua New Guinea in the semi-final of the T20 World Cup Qualifier in Scotland, to book their place in Australia – the first Thai cricketers to play in any World Cup.

And 2020 started with further encouraging news, when the Brazil Cricket Association announced they were awarding 14 central contracts to the national T20 squad – a benefit not yet available to Brazil's male cricketers. After Thailand's World Cup qualification, it hinted at the exciting prospect of international expansion far beyond what had seemed possible ten years earlier.

WOMEN'S INTERNATIONAL SERIES IN 2019

NEW ZEALAND v INDIA IN 2018-19

One-day internationals (3): New Zealand 1, India 2
Twenty20 internationals (3): New Zealand 3 India 0

India put to one side the infighting which dominated the build-up to their first assignment of the year to win the ODI series comfortably. New Zealand turned the tables in the T20s, but the games were close. Despite unfamiliarity with the conditions, Smriti Mandhana was dominant, and finished the 50-over series with 196 runs at 98. Amy Satterthwaite could not match that, but was also in excellent form with 168 at 56. Mandhana was equally impressive in the T20s – 180 at 60 – but the more influential was Sophie Devine, with 153 at 51 and four wickets. The teams welcomed the chance to play their matches before the men's T20 fixtures. "The opportunity to play in front of impressive crowds is experience in the bank," said Devine.

First one-day international   At Napier, January 24, 2019 (day/night). **India won by nine wickets.** **New Zealand 192** (48.4 overs) (S. W. Bates 36, A. E. Satterthwaite 31; E. K. Bisht 3-32, P. Yadav 3-42); ‡**India 193-1** (33 overs) (J. I. Rodrigues 81*, S. S. Mandhana 105). *PoM:* S. S. Mandhana. *A classy run-a-ball 105 from Smriti Mandhana – her fourth ODI century – eased India to only their second 50-over away win against New Zealand in their last ten matches. She put on 190 for the first wicket with Jemimah Rodrigues, before falling with three needed; victory was wrapped up with 17 overs to spare. New Zealand had begun with 61 for the first wicket, then India's spinners took over. All ten fell for 131, as five batsmen passed 20 without reaching 40.*

Second one-day international   At Mount Maunganui, January 29, 2019 (day/night). **India won by eight wickets. New Zealand 161** (44.2 overs) (A. E. Satterthwaite 71; J. N. Goswami 3-23); ‡**India 166-2** (35.2 overs) (S. S. Mandhana 90*, M. D. Raj 63*). *PoM:* S. S. Mandhana. *India claimed the series without breaking sweat, as Mandhana and Mithali Raj put on 151* for the third wicket to brush aside New Zealand's paltry total. Only Amy Satterthwaite – captaining her country for just the fifth time in ODIs – had made headway against India's spinners, with left-armer Ekta Bisht taking 2-14 from eight overs. The tourists quickly found themselves 15-2 in reply, before Mandhana took over, hitting 90* off 83 balls – her eighth score of 50-plus in ten ODI innings.*

Third one-day international   At Hamilton, February 1, 2019 (day/night). **New Zealand won by eight wickets. India 149** (44 overs) (D. B. Sharma 52; L. M. Tahuhu 3-26, A. M. Peterson 4-28); ‡**New Zealand 153-2** (29.2 overs) (S. W. Bates 57, A. E. Satterthwaite 66*). *PoM:* A. M. Peterson. *New Zealand's consolation win lifted them back above India into second place in the ICC Championship. The damage was done by opening bowlers Lea Tahuhu and Anna Peterson, who shared 7-56 as India slumped to 149. Half-centuries from Suzie Bates and Satterthwaite wrapped up the chase with more than 20 overs in hand. Raj became the first woman to play 200 ODIs, but made only nine.*

Women's Championship: India 4pts, New Zealand 2pts.

First Twenty20 international   At Wellington (Westpac), February 6, 2019. **New Zealand won by 23 runs. New Zealand 159-4** (20 overs) (S. F. M. Devine 62, A. E. Satterthwaite 33); ‡**India 136** (19.1 overs) (S. S. Mandhana 58, J. I. Rodrigues 39; L. M. Tahuhu 3-20). *PoM:* L. M. Tahuhu. *T20I debuts:* C. A. Gurrey, R. A. Mair (New Zealand); P. S. Punia (India). *A dizzying collapse of nine for 34 cost India victory in the T20 series opener, after the in-form Mandhana and Rodrigues had lifted them to 102-1 in pursuit of 160. The slide was triggered by a superb one-handed catch at deep extra cover by Hannah Rowe to see off Mandhana, who had just broken her own record – by one ball – for India's fastest T20I fifty (24 deliveries). Tahuhu removed Rodrigues four balls later, before producing a double wicket-maiden as India panicked. New Zealand's 159 was built around Sophie Devine's 62 off 48.*

Second Twenty20 international   At Auckland, February 8, 2019. **New Zealand won by four wickets. India 135-6** (20 overs) (S. S. Mandhana 36, J. I. Rodrigues 72); ‡**New Zealand 136-6** (20 overs) (S. W. Bates 62). *PoM:* S. W. Bates. *Rowe's last-ball single gave New Zealand the series, after they had threatened to make a mess of their chase. At 101-2 in the 15th over, they were well on course, but three wickets – including Bates, for 62 off 52 – left them needing nine off the last over, from Mansi Joshi. Katey Martin hit the first ball for four, before falling to the second, and it needed Rowe's cool head to see her side home. Earlier, India had collapsed again, after another strong stand between Mandhana (36 off 27) and Rodrigues (a career-best 72 off 53). From 71-1 in the tenth, they could manage only 135-6.* In her second T20I, seamer Rosemary Mair had figures of 4–8–17–2.

Third Twenty20 international   At Hamilton, February 10, 2019. **New Zealand won by two runs.** ‡**New Zealand 161-7** (20 overs) (S. F. M. Devine 72, A. E. Satterthwaite 31); **India 159-4** (20 overs) (S. S. Mandhana 86). *PoM:* S. F. M. Devine. *Devine's all-round class proved the difference as New Zealand completed a 3–0 whitewash. First she struck 72 off 52 to set up a testing total, then she took the key wickets of Rodrigues and Mandhana, who thrashed 86 from 62. When she fell, India needed 39 from 27 balls, which became 16 off the last over, bowled by Leigh Kasperek. Nine came from the first three deliveries, but Raj – in her first game of the series – had to hit the last for four, and could manage only a single to midwicket.*

PAKISTAN v WEST INDIES IN 2018-19

Twenty20 internationals (3): Pakistan 1, West Indies 2
One-day internationals (3): Pakistan 2, West Indies 1

For a time, it looked as if it was going to be a case of Deandra Dottin – and 21 others. She dominated the early matches to the extent that West Indies must have sensed a whitewash. Then there was a shift in momentum: Pakistan won the third Twenty20 international, and became a cohesive force, coming from behind in the ODIs to record their first series win against West Indies. It also lifted them above their opponents to fourth in the World Championship. The T20 matches were held in Karachi, before the teams relocated to Dubai.

First Twenty20 international   At Karachi (Southend), January 31, 2019. **West Indies won by 71 runs.** ‡**West Indies 160-2** (20 overs) (D. J. S. Dottin 90*, C. N. Nation 50*); **Pakistan 89** (18 overs) (Bismah Maroof 38; S. S. Connell 3-29). *PoM:* D. J. S. Dottin. *Pakistan's 100th Twenty20 international – their first on home soil – ended in overwhelming defeat. Deandra Dottin (90* from 60 balls) got West Indies off to a flyer, and added 109 for the third wicket with Chedean Nation, who reached 50 in the final over. Pakistan needed a quick start themselves, but were bogged down by suffocating bowling: Shakera Selman had figures of 3–12–8–2, and her new-ball partner, Shamilia Connell, collected three wickets. Apart from captain Bismah Maroof, only Javeria Khan (19) passed seven.* "We have worked hard," said Pakistan's head coach Mark Coles, "but maybe it was the nerves of playing a big game at home."

Second Twenty20 international   At Karachi (Southend), February 1, 2019. **West Indies won an eliminator over, following a tie. ‡Pakistan 132-4** (20 overs) (Bismah Maroof 31); **West Indies 132-6** (20 overs) (Kycia A. Knight 32, S. A. Campbelle 41). *PoM:* S. A. Campbelle. *West Indies secured the series, but only after being pushed to a tie-breaker by a battling Pakistan. Needing 13 off the final over, bowled by 21-year-old slow left-armer Nashra Sandhu, West Indies scored nine off the first three, but Merissa Aguilleira was stumped off the fourth, and they made a hash of finishing the job. Dottin strode to their rescue, smashing Sana Mir for 18 in the super over; in a hapless response, Pakistan managed only 1–2. After deciding to bat, they had posted a competitive total without breaking the shackles. Kycia Knight and Dottin (22) launched the reply in style, but West Indies slumped with victory in sight.*

Third Twenty20 international   At Karachi (Southend), February 3, 2019. **Pakistan won by 12 runs. ‡Pakistan 150-6** (20 overs) (Nida Dar 53); **West Indies 138-8** (20 overs) (D. J. S. Dottin 46; Anam Amin 3-34). *PoM:* Nida Dar. *PoS:* D. J. S. Dottin and Nida Dar. *T20I debut:* K. Ramharack (West Indies). *Mir celebrated becoming the first Asian woman to play 100 T20Is by taking two* *wickets in a consolation victory. Nida Dar had hit a career-best 53 off 40, and put on 67 for the fifth wicket with Aliya Riaz (24*) to ensure a solid start was not wasted. Then slow left-armer Anam Amin took 3-34, including the prize wicket of Dottin for 46, as West Indies' chase faltered.*

First one-day international At Dubai (Sports City), February 7, 2019. **West Indies won by 146 runs. ‡West Indies 216-5** (50 overs) (D. J. S. Dottin 96, S. R. Taylor 58; Kainat Imtiaz 3-49); **Pakistan 70** (29.5 overs) (D. J. S. Dottin 3-14, A. S. S. Fletcher 3-17). PoM: D. J. S. Dottin. *Dottin was once more the architect of a thumping victory, scoring 96, then taking three wickets as Pakistan were hustled out for 70. "There are days when I feel like I can do anything," she said. Dottin put on 143 with captain Stafanie Taylor, who had sat out the T20 series. Their total was always likely to be too much for Pakistan, who lost nine for 24 in a calamitous collapse.*

Second one-day international At Dubai (ICC Academy), February 9, 2019. **Pakistan won by 34 runs. ‡Pakistan 240** (49.4 overs) (Sidra Ameen 96, Nida Dar 81); **West Indies 206** (49.4 overs) (S. R. Taylor 48, N. Y. McLean 82; Diana Baig 4-34, Sana Mir 3-21). PoM: Sidra Ameen. *Two days after being humbled, Pakistan were transformed. A vastly improved batting performance was followed by a magnificent display from their bowlers. After a stuttering start, a fourth-wicket stand of 102 between Sidra Ameen and Dar set them on course. Ameen was run out four short of a maiden international hundred, but Dar powered on to 81. Pakistan scented victory when Diana Baig bowled Dottin for five; she added three more victims, and there were also three for Mir in a miserly spell. Natasha McLean delayed the celebrations with a career-best 82 off 76.*

Third one-day international At Dubai (ICC Academy), February 11, 2019. **Pakistan won by four wickets. ‡West Indies 159** (47.3 overs) (S. R. Taylor 52; Diana Baig 3-42, Nashra Sandhu 3-21); **Pakistan 163-6** (47.2 overs) (Sidra Ameen 52). PoM: Sidra Ameen. PoS: Sidra Ameen. *ODI debut: K. Ramharack (West Indies). Pakistan clinched their first series victory over West Indies in any format after an impressive all-round effort. Again led by Baig, their bowlers exerted control from the start. Her 3-42 was well backed up by Sandhu's 3-21. Dottin was run out for 28, and only Taylor's measured 52 steered West Indies to respectability. Ameen carried her form from the second match into the run-chase; Pakistan wobbled after she was fourth out, but regrouped to ease home with 16 balls to spare.*

Women's Championship: Pakistan 4pts, West Indies 2pts.

SOUTH AFRICA v SRI LANKA IN 2018-19

Twenty20 internationals (3): South Africa 3, Sri Lanka 0
One-day internationals (3): South Africa 3, Sri Lanka 0

For South Africa, it was mission accomplished. Before their first assignments of the year, captain Dane van Niekerk spoke of the need for a new start after failing to reach the last four at the 2018 World Twenty20. "We've had to rethink our strategies," she said. "We want to play an attacking brand of cricket." Sri Lanka felt the full impact of South Africa's intent, losing all six matches, although they came close to pulling off a win in each series. Before she was ruled out by injury after the first ODI, van Niekerk was inspirational with bat and ball. Fellow leg-spinning all-rounder Sune Luus also produced some outstanding performances, collecting 11 wickets in four appearances.

First Twenty20 international At Cape Town, February 1, 2019. **South Africa won by seven wickets. ‡Sri Lanka 90-8** (20 overs) (D. van Niekerk 3-12); **South Africa 94-3** (14.2 overs) (D. van Niekerk 71*). PoM: D. van Niekerk. *T20I debut: U. N. Thimashini (Sri Lanka). Dane van Niekerk all but won the match on her own. At 44-1 after the powerplay, Sri Lanka had a platform, but they subsided against her leg-spin. She then raced to 71* from 55, making short work of a feeble target.*

Second Twenty20 international At Johannesburg, February 3, 2019. **South Africa won by two wickets. Sri Lanka 105** (19.4 overs) (H. A. S. D. Siriwardene 38; M. Kapp 3-17, S. E. Luus 5-14); **‡South Africa 107-8** (19.5 overs) (D. van Niekerk 33). PoM: S. E. Luus. *Sri Lanka's fielding collapsed under pressure, allowing South Africa to secure the series off the penultimate ball – despite sliding to 97-8 after van Niekerk's departure. They had needed eight off the last over, but a fumble* *by wicketkeeper Anushka Sanjeewani allowed the well-set Nadine de Klerk to grab the strike and retake the initiative. Sri Lanka's 105 looked underweight, after the recalled Sune Luus took her second T20I five-for.*

Third Twenty20 international At Centurion, February 6, 2019. **South Africa won by 39 runs. South Africa 163-5** (20 overs) (D. van Niekerk 38, T. Brits 36, L. Goodall 35); ‡**Sri Lanka 124-8** (20 overs) (A. M. C. Jayangani 43; N. de Klerk 3-27). *PoM:* S. E. Luus. *PoS:* D. van Niekerk. *South Africa flexed their muscles to compile a total that Sri Lanka never looked like matching. Their first five all got into double figures, with van Niekerk top-scoring again, despite retiring briefly on 35 with stomach trouble. Chamari Atapattu Jayangani made a defiant 43 off 36, but lacked support.*

First one-day international At Potchefstroom, February 11, 2019. **South Africa won by seven runs. South Africa 225-7** (48 overs) (A. Steyn 75, D. van Niekerk 102; O. U. Ranasinghe 3-40); ‡**Sri Lanka 218-9** (48 overs) (W. P. M. Weerakkodi 47, H. A. S. D. Siriwardene 49, N. N. D. de Silva 39*; M. M. Klaas 3-46). *PoM:* D. van Niekerk. *ODI debuts:* F. Tunnicliffe (South Africa); U. N. Thimashini (Sri Lanka). *Van Niekerk's first international hundred elevated her into elite company, but Sri Lanka had victory in sight before choking. In a match reduced to 48 overs, they were 29-2 in the tenth, when van Niekerk joined Andrie Steyn in a calming stand of 117. She accelerated after Steyn's dismissal, and reached three figures off 114 balls, with her wife, Marizanne Kapp, at the other end. Van Niekerk joined Lisa Sthalekar, Stafanie Taylor and Ellyse Perry as the only women to score 2,000 runs and take 100 wickets in ODIs. Sri Lanka's pursuit was launched by Prasadini Weerakkodi's fluent 47, backed up by Shashikala Siriwardene's 49. Needing 31 from 30, they lost three quick wickets – two to run-outs – before an ice-cool final over from Kapp saw South Africa home.*

Second one-day international At Potchefstroom, February 14, 2019. **South Africa won by 30 runs** (DLS). **South Africa 268-7** (50 overs) (L. Wolvaardt 64, L. Goodall 52, M. Kapp 69*); ‡**Sri Lanka 231** (46.2 overs) (A. M. C. Jayangani 94, M. A. A. Sanjeewani 46, H. M. D. Samarawickrama 30). *PoM:* M. Kapp. *Unfazed by the absence of van Niekerk – ruled out for three months with a stress fracture of her right femur – South Africa produced a powerful batting display. Coming in at No. 7 in the 41st, Kapp slammed 69* off 34 balls. Sri Lanka's target became 262 off 47, and they took up the challenge, Jayangani and Sanjeewani putting on 110 for the second wicket. But slick fielding meant the rest were unable to maintain the momentum.*

Third one-day international At Potchefstroom, February 17, 2019. **South Africa won by six wickets.** ‡**Sri Lanka 139** (44.2 overs) (S. E. Luus 4-30); **South Africa 141-4** (38.2 overs) (M. du Preez 61*; I. Ranaweera 3-23). *PoM:* M. du Preez. *PoS:* A. Steyn. *ODI debut:* M. T. Sewwandi (Sri Lanka). *Stand-in captain Luus took four wickets as South Africa took their winning streak at home to 14 games in all formats. After competing strongly in the first two matches, Sri Lanka folded. Jayangani fell for a duck off the fifth ball, and there was no recovery. Mignon du Preez became the first South African woman to pass 3,000 ODI runs.*

Women's Championship: South Africa 6pts, Sri Lanka 0pts.

AUSTRALIA v NEW ZEALAND IN 2018-19

One-day internationals (3): Australia 3, New Zealand 0

Australia's iron grip on the Rose Bowl trophy continued with a whitewash. The first match was close, but they won the other two with something to spare. Since New Zealand's last victory, in 1998-99, Australia had won 16 of the 17 series, with a draw in 2008-09. Meg Lanning's team proved too strong in all departments: Ellyse Perry hit a maiden one-day century, while slow left-armer Jess Jonassen took nine for 70 in the first two matches. New Zealand's batting was too dependent on captain Amy Satterthwaite and Sophie Devine, while their bowling at times looked innocuous.

First one-day international At Perth (WACA), February 22, 2019. **Australia won by five runs. Australia 241** (49.4 overs) (R. L. Haynes 67, A. K. Gardner 34, J. L. Jonassen 36; S. F. M. Devine 3-32); ‡**New Zealand 236-9** (50 overs) (A. E. Satterthwaite 92, K. T. Perkins 48; J. L. Jonassen

4-43). *PoM*: J. L. Jonassen. *ODI debut*: R. A. Mair (New Zealand). *New Zealand looked likely winners at 188-4 in the 42nd over, needing another 54 – but Katie Perkins popped a return catch to the nagging Jess Jonassen, who later removed Amelia Kerr and Leigh Kasperek with successive deliveries. Amy Satterthwaite was left with too much to do, and became Jonassen's fourth victim, in the 49th over. New Zealand required seven off the final two balls, but Megan Schutt removed Lea Tahuhu, and Hayley Jensen could manage only a single off the last. Earlier, 20-year-old debutant seamer Rosemary Mair had claimed a distinguished maiden scalp – Australia's captain Meg Lanning, for six, to a superb slip catch by Satterthwaite. She added top-scorer Rachael Haynes. Australia were indebted to late runs from Ashleigh Gardner and Jonassen.*

Second one-day international At Adelaide (Karen Rolton Oval), February 24, 2019. **Australia won by 95 runs. Australia 247-7** (50 overs) (A. J. Healy 46, E. A. Perry 107*, B. L. Mooney 42; A. C. Kerr 3-30); ‡**New Zealand 152** (38 overs) (S. F. M. Devine 47, A. E. Satterthwaite 37; J. L. Jonassen 5-27). *PoM*: E. A. Perry. *Before this match, Ellyse Perry had made 25 half-centuries in 79 ODI innings without reaching three figures – but she finally got there, hitting the penultimate ball of the innings, from Jensen, for four through the despairing grasp of Anna Peterson at deep midwicket. Perry celebrated by hammering the final delivery for six. Her innings – and fourth-wicket stand of 98 with Beth Mooney – set up a total high enough to withstand the loss of three in four balls to Kerr's leg-breaks. New Zealand were soon 26-2, with Perry removing Suzie Bates; although Sophie Devine and Satterthwaite added 67, Jonassen claimed a career-best as Australia retained the Rose Bowl.*

Third one-day international At St Kilda, March 3, 2019. **Australia won by seven wickets. ‡New Zealand 231-8** (50 overs) (S. W. Bates 35, S. F. M. Devine 58, A. E. Satterthwaite 49, K. T. Perkins 41; A. K. Gardner 3-49); **Australia 233-3** (47.5 overs) (R. L. Haynes 46, A. J. Healy 46, M. M. Lanning 48, E. A. Perry 54*, B. L. Mooney 52*). *PoM*: A. K. Gardner. *PoS*: J. L. Jonassen. *Australia eased to a 3–0 whitewash on a sweltering day in Victoria. New Zealand started well, the openers putting on 70, before Bates and No. 3 Lauren Down were both caught by Perry at midwicket off successive deliveries from leg-spinner Georgia Wareham. Satterthwaite and Perkins rebuilt as New Zealand reached 231, but the confident Australians never faltered in the chase. After an opening stand of 84, Lanning atoned for two failures with a patient 48, then Perry – with another half-century – and Mooney did the rest.*

Women's Championship: Australia 6pts, New Zealand 0pts.

INDIA v ENGLAND IN 2018-19

One-day internationals (3): India 2, England 1
Twenty20 internationals (3): India 0, England 3

England's sixth ODI series in India resulted in defeat, like the previous five, before they recovered to sweep the T20 matches in Guwahati. In the 50-over games, all at Mumbai's Wankhede Stadium, their bowlers had little answer to Smriti Mandhana, who hit two fifties (followed by another in the T20s), or new-ball bowlers Shikha Pandey (eight wickets at nine, with an economy-rate of 2.60) and Jhulan Goswami (eight at 11, and 3.52). But Danielle Wyatt built on her half-century in the third ODI to lead England's assault in the T20s, thrashing 123 runs for twice out. Katherine Brunt took five wickets in each series.

ENGLAND TOURING PARTY

*H. C. Knight (Berkshire), T. T. Beaumont (Kent), K. H. Brunt (Yorkshire), K. L. Cross (Lancashire), F. R. Davies (Sussex), S. I. R. Dunkley (Middlesex), S. Ecclestone (Lancashire), G. A. Elwiss (Sussex), A. Hartley (Lancashire), A. E. Jones (Warwickshire), L. A. Marsh (Kent), N. R. Sciver (Surrey), A. Shrubsole (Somerset), L. C. N. Smith (Sussex), S. J. Taylor (Sussex), L. Winfield (Yorkshire), D. N. Wyatt (Sussex). *Coach*: M. A. Robinson.

Taylor was selected only for the ODIs in India. F. C. Wilson (Middlesex) joined the party for the tour of Sri Lanka which followed.

First one-day international At Mumbai, February 22, 2019. **India won by 66 runs. India 202** (49.4 overs) (J. I. Rodrigues 48, M. D. Raj 44, J. N. Goswami 30); ‡**England 136** (41 overs) (H. C. Knight 39*, N. R. Sciver 44; E. K. Bisht 4-25). *PoM*: E. K. Bisht. *ODI debut*: H. Deol (India). *Left-arm spinner Ekta Bisht was central to a startling England collapse as India breezed to victory. At 111-3 in the 31st over, the tourists were on course. But Bisht ran out Nat Sciver, who had backed up too far, with a cute backhand flick, then took four cheap wickets – including the last three in five balls – as England lost seven for 25. It left Heather Knight, batting at No. 4, stranded on 39*. India's batsmen had suffered a stumble of their own: 69-0 became 95-5, and it needed the experience of captain Mithali Raj and Jhulan Goswami to post a defendable total.*

Second one-day international At Mumbai, February 25, 2019. **India won by seven wickets.** ‡**England 161** (43.3 overs) (N. R. Sciver 85; J. N. Goswami 4-30, S. S. Pandey 4-18); **India 162-3** (41.1 overs) (S. S. Mandhana 63, P. G. Raut 32, M. D. Raj 47*). *PoM*: J. N. Goswami. *The new-ball pair of Goswami and Shikha Pandey took four wickets each as another shaky England batting display gifted India the series. After choosing to bat, they slipped from 93-4 to 119-9, and it needed a national record tenth-wicket stand of 42 between Sciver (last out, for 85) and Alex Hartley (0* in 17 balls) to avert total meltdown. Pandey, a squadron leader in the Indian Air Force, finished with a career-best 10–1–18–4. Anya Shrubsole then removed Jemimah Rodrigues for a duck, but Smriti Mandhana put on 73 with Punam Raut and 66 with Raj. Sarah Taylor became the second female wicketkeeper, after India's Anju Jain, to complete 50 ODI stumpings when she removed Raut.*

Third one-day international At Mumbai, February 28, 2019. **England won by two wickets.** ‡**India 205-8** (50 overs) (S. S. Mandhana 66, P. G. Raut 56; K. H. Brunt 5-28); **England 208-8** (48.5 overs) (H. C. Knight 47, D. N. Wyatt 56, G. A. Elwiss 33*; J. N. Goswami 3-41). *PoM*: K. H. Brunt. *PoS*: S. S. Mandhana. *A day after it was announced that Katherine Brunt would finally appear on a Lord's honours board, she starred as England picked up two consolation points in the World Championship. MCC had agreed to give ODI performances the same treatment as Tests, bringing into play Brunt's 5-25 against South Africa in 2008. Now, she managed 5-28 (the first five to fall), as India lost six for 21; they were her best international figures since July 2011. Even so, at 49-5 in pursuit of 206, England seemed set to lose 3–0. But Danielle Wyatt added 69 with Knight, then 56 with Georgia Elwiss, before Brunt helped apply the finishing touches. India had recovered from the loss of Rodrigues for another duck, thanks to a second-wicket stand of 129 between Mandhana and Raut. Then Brunt took over.*

Women's Championship: India 4pts, England 2pts.

First Twenty20 international At Guwahati, March 4, 2019. **England won by 41 runs. England 160-4** (20 overs) (D. N. Wyatt 35, T. T. Beaumont 62, H. C. Knight 40); ‡**India 119-6** (20 overs). *PoM*: T. T. Beaumont. *T20I debut*: H. Deol (India). *India never came close to chasing 161 after slow left-armer Linsey Smith removed Mandhana and Rodrigues with successive balls to leave them 23-3. After ten overs, it was 46-5 – and game over. England had been boosted by an opening stand of 89 in 11.3 overs between Wyatt and Tammy Beaumont, before Smith smashed 40 off 20, including five fours in a row off seamer Arundhati Reddy.*

Second Twenty20 international At Guwahati, March 7, 2019. **England won by five wickets. India 111-8** (20 overs) (K. H. Brunt 3-17); ‡**England 114-5** (19.1 overs) (D. N. Wyatt 64*). *PoM*: D. N. Wyatt. *T20I debut*: B. S. Fulmali (India). *England secured the series thanks to a suffocating display with the ball, and the nervelessness of Wyatt. India managed only six fours and two sixes, both by Mandhana (12) off Shrubsole in the second over; Brunt and Smith (2-11 off three) kept things especially tight. But Wyatt, whose 64* came from 55 balls, had to wait until the arrival of Lauren Winfield (29 off 23) at No. 6 before she found a reliable partner. Victory came with five to spare.*

Third Twenty20 international At Guwahati, March 9, 2019. **England won by one run.** ‡**England 119-6** (20 overs); **India 118-6** (20 overs) (S. S. Mandhana 58, M. D. Raj 30*). *PoM*: K. L. Cross. *PoS*: D. N. Wyatt. *A remarkable final over from Kate Cross earned England a 3–0 whitewash. With India, four down, needing just three, Cross bowled three dots, before dismissing Bharti Fulmali, playing only her second international, and Anuja Patil (stumped). With Raj looking on aghast from the non-striker's end, Pandey managed only a single off the last. It meant Mandhana's swashbuckling 58 off 39 went to waste. Wyatt and Beaumont had put on 51 for England's first wicket in 7.2 overs, before India's quintet of spinners – led by the thrifty Patil (2-13) – slowed the scoring.*

SRI LANKA v ENGLAND IN 2018-19

Martin Davies

One-day internationals (3): Sri Lanka 0, England 3
Twenty20 internationals (3): Sri Lanka 0, England 3

England travelled straight from their tour of India to Sri Lanka, where the only thing they lost was the toss – Heather Knight called it wrong in all six internationals. But her team won each game to finish their subcontinental tour with ten consecutive victories. Six points in the Championship lifted them from fifth to second, and closer to automatic qualification for the 2021 World Cup. The winning margins showed the chasm between the sides, even with England missing Sarah Taylor, and nursing Katherine Brunt, while Sophie Ecclestone and Georgia Elwiss soon joined the injury list. Their absences cleared the way for others, and no one seized the opportunity more than Amy Jones. Opening the batting in the one-day series, she hit three fifties, finishing with 209 runs from 168 balls, with 25 fours and seven sixes, then forced her way past Tammy Beaumont to open in the second and third T20 internationals. Kate Cross and Alex Hartley picked up useful wickets in the one-day series. Pace bowler Freya Davies made an accomplished debut, playing all three Twenty20 games, as did leg-spinner Sophia Dunkley. The six defeats left Sri Lanka in the doldrums: they had won only one of their last 15 ODIs, which meant they were stuck to the bottom of the Championship, and only one of their last 16 completed T20Is.

For England squad list, see India series above.

First one-day international   At Hambantota, March 16, 2019. **England won by 154 runs** (DLS). **England 331-7** (50 overs) (A. E. Jones 79, T. T. Beaumont 35, H. C. Knight 61, N. R. Sciver 93, D. N. Wyatt 47); ‡**Sri Lanka 159-8** (40 overs) (A. M. C. Jayangani 30, N. N. D. de Silva 45, O. U. Ranasinghe 51*; K. H. Brunt 3-24). *Inserted on a good track with a fast outfield, England racked up 331-7, their highest one-day total against Sri Lanka (and their joint-sixth-highest overall), thanks to half-centuries from Amy Jones, Heather Knight and Nat Sciver, plus a 26-ball 47 from Danni Wyatt. England plundered 91 from the last seven overs. Sri Lanka came out guns blazing, but three wickets from Katherine Brunt, and some calamitous running, left them 46-7. Nilakshi de Silva and Oshadi Ranasinghe carefully added 88 – an eighth-wicket record in women's ODIs – and there was time for Ranasinghe to reach a maiden fifty on her 33rd birthday, taking the hosts halfway to a rain-revised target of 314 from 40 overs.*

Second one-day international   At Hambantota, March 18, 2019. **England won by six wickets.** ‡**Sri Lanka 187-9** (50 overs) (H. M. D. Samarawickrama 42; A. Hartley 3-36); **England 188-4** (33.3 overs) (A. E. Jones 54, T. T. Beaumont 43, L. Winfield 44; S. I. P. Fernando 3-45). *This time Sri Lanka elected to bat, and their openers scored a cautious 41 in 13 overs before Laura Marsh dismissed both in four deliveries, including a stunning reaction catch by Lauren Winfield at slip to see off Chamari Atapattu Jayangani. Sri Lanka struggled to keep the scoreboard ticking over, although young left-hander Harshitha Madavi Samarawickrama and Hansima Karunaratne added 72, before a bizarre run-out: Karunaratne had got home before the wicket was broken, but wandered out of her crease again, and Jones removed a stump with ball in hand. Boundary catches off the last two deliveries of the innings, bowled by Alex Hartley, ensured Sri Lanka finished on 187. Jones rattled to 54 out of 69 before holing out, then Tammy Beaumont and Winfield fell either side of a brief rain break, but England cruised home.*

Third one-day international At Katunayake, March 21, 2019. **England won by eight wickets.** ‡Sri Lanka 174 (50 overs) (H. M. D. Samarawickrama 42); **England 177-2** (26.1 overs) (A. E. Jones 76, T. T. Beaumont 63). *The third ODI followed a similar pattern to the second, with Sri Lanka choosing to bat, and Samarawickrama top-scoring; they were dismissed for an uncompetitive 174, with two wickets apiece for Kate Cross, Anya Shrubsole and Hartley. Jones and Beaumont began with 127 in 18 overs, before both were bowled by Shashikala Siriwardene, but Winfield emphatically wrapped up victory with six over wide long-on.*

Women's Championship: England 6pts, Sri Lanka 0pts.

First Twenty20 international At Colombo (PSO), March 24, 2019. **England won by eight wickets.** ‡Sri Lanka 94 (19 overs) (L. C. N. Smith 3-18); **England 95-2** (14.2 overs) (T. T. Beaumont 50*). *T20I debut:* F. R. Davies (England). *England's bowlers restricted the Sri Lankans to 94: Shrubsole dismissed both openers to overtake Danielle Hazell's England record of 85 T20I wickets, seamer Freya Davies claimed 2-28 on international debut, and slow left-armer Linsey Smith finished with three. England made 41-1 in the powerplay, and needed only 50 more balls to finish the job. Jones was run out at the non-striker's end for the second time in four innings, but Beaumont batted throughout and hit the winning single, diving home to complete her fifty.*

Second Twenty20 international At Colombo (PSO), March 26, 2019. **England won by eight wickets.** ‡Sri Lanka 108-6 (20 overs); **England 109-2** (13.5 overs) (D. N. Wyatt 37, A. E. Jones 36). *Sri Lanka raised a circumspect 45 for the first wicket in seven overs, but failed to accelerate against disciplined line and length. Only 48 came from the last ten. But England knocked off a meagre 109 inside 14, with only two wickets down. A new opening partnership – Wyatt and the in-form Jones – broke the back of the chase, putting on 79 before Wyatt was stumped. Though Jones followed, it was too little too late for Sri Lanka.*

Third Twenty20 international At Colombo (PSO), March 28, 2019. **England won by 96 runs.** England 204-2 (20 overs) (D. N. Wyatt 51, A. E. Jones 57, T. T. Beaumont 42*, N. R. Sciver 49*); ‡Sri Lanka 108-6 (20 overs) (H. I. H. Karunaratne 44*). *T20I debut:* A. R. G. M. L. Methtananda (Sri Lanka). *England finally got to bat first again, and made hay while the sun shone, reaching their second-highest T20 total, and a record by any side in Sri Lanka. Wyatt and Jones put on 96 in ten overs, while Sciver and Beaumont smashed 88 off the last seven to lift them beyond 200. Early wickets took the wind out of Sri Lanka's reply; they mustered barely half their target in another thumping defeat, England's tenth win on the bounce since the final ODI in India four weeks earlier.*

SOUTH AFRICA v PAKISTAN IN 2019

One-day internationals (3): South Africa 1, Pakistan 1
Twenty20 internationals (5): South Africa 3, Pakistan 2

Pakistan fared better than expected on only their second bilateral tour of South Africa (their first had been more than 12 years earlier). A tie in the deciding one-day international at Benoni took them above New Zealand into fifth place in the ICC Championship, and they also pushed the hosts all the way in the Twenty20 matches, eventually losing after being 2–1 up. Sana Mir took ten wickets across the eight games with her off-breaks, while South African opener Lizelle Lee crashed three half-centuries in the T20s.

First one-day international At Potchefstroom, May 6. **Pakistan won by eight wickets.** South Africa 63 (22.5 overs) (Sana Mir 4-11); ‡Pakistan 66-2 (14.4 overs) (Javeria Khan 34*). *PoM:* Sana Mir. *ODI debut:* Fatima Sana (Pakistan). *Sana Mir helped skittle South Africa for their second-lowest total, behind 51 against New Zealand at Bowral in 2008-09; their last seven tumbled for 33. Shabnim Ismail struck with her third ball, and Marizanne Kapp followed up with a wicket in her 100th ODI, but Pakistan cruised home with 212 deliveries to spare – a national record. It was their first away win against South Africa in seven completed attempts.*

Second one-day international At Potchefstroom, May 9. **South Africa won by eight wickets.** Pakistan 147 (42 overs) (Nahida Khan 37, Bismah Maroof 32; M. M. Klaas 3-27); ‡South Africa 148-2 (36.4 overs) (L. Lee 40, L. Wolvaardt 74*). *PoM:* M. M. Klaas. *Seamer Masabata Klaas* *claimed the tenth hat-trick in women's one-day internationals, and the second by a South African – after Dane van Niekerk against West Indies at Basseterre in 2012-13 – as the hosts drew level in style. Pakistan lost their last six for six, before Laura Wolvaardt took control with 74*.*

Third one-day international   At Benoni, May 12. **Tied. South Africa** 265-6 (50 overs) (L. Lee 57, L. Wolvaardt 56, S. E. Luus 80); ‡**Pakistan 265-9** (50 overs) (Javeria Khan 74, Aliya Riaz 71; M. M. Klaas 3-55). *PoM:* Aliya Riaz. *PoS:* L. Wolvaardt. *Pakistan No. 11 Nashra Sandhu hit her first ball for six, and her second for a single, to secure a tie. The tourists had looked dead and buried when Javeria Khan was fifth out for 74, with 101 needed. But Aliya Riaz – armed with an ODI average of 12 – added 71 to the two wickets she managed earlier, setting up the tense finale. South Africa were grateful for fifties from Lizelle Lee and Wolvaardt, plus 80 off 84 by captain Sune Luus.*

Women's Championship: South Africa 3pts, Pakistan 3pts.

First Twenty20 international   At Pretoria (L. C. de Villiers), May 15. **Pakistan won by seven wickets. South Africa** 119-7 (20 overs) (C. L. Tryon 43; Sana Mir 3-14); ‡**Pakistan 120-3** (18 overs) (Bismah Maroof 53*, Nida Dar 53). *PoM:* Nida Dar. *T20I debuts:* S. Jafta (South Africa); Fatima Sana (Pakistan). *South Africa were always struggling after Mir removed both openers for ducks, despite Chloe Tryon's hard-hit 43. Javeria Rauf then became the third opener to fall for nought, but half-centuries from Pakistan captain Bismah Maroof and Nida Dar settled matters.*

Second Twenty20 international   At Pietermaritzburg, May 18. **South Africa won by eight wickets.** ‡**Pakistan 128-5** (20 overs) (Bismah Maroof 63*); **South Africa 129-2** (19.5 overs) (L. Lee 56, M. Kapp 56*). *PoM:* L. Lee. *T20I debut:* Rameen Shamim (Pakistan). *Kapp's maiden T20I half-century, from her 62nd innings, helped South Africa square the series with a ball to spare. She added 96 for the second wicket with Lee, who fell with two needed from three. Earlier, Maroof scored another fifty, but lacked support.*

Third Twenty20 international   At Pietermaritzburg, May 19. **Pakistan won by four wickets. South Africa 138-3** (20 overs) (T. Brits 70*, N. de Klerk 36); ‡**Pakistan 139-6** (19.4 overs) (Nida Dar 32, Iram Javed 55, Aliya Riaz 30; M. R. Daniels 3-13). *PoM:* Iram Javed. *T20I debut:* N. Shangase (South Africa). *Pakistan recovered from 3-3 after 16 balls to secure a last-over victory, thanks to a maiden T20I fifty for Iram Javed. Opening bowlers Shabnim Ismail and Moseline Daniels had combined figures of 5-25 from eight overs, but five other South Africans managed 1-113. Their curate's egg 138-3 had been based on 70* from Tazmin Brits – another maiden half-century in the format – though she ate up 61 balls.*

Fourth Twenty20 international   At Benoni, May 22. **South Africa won by four wickets. Pakistan 172-5** (20 overs) (Bismah Maroof 37, Nida Dar 75, Aliya Riaz 35*); ‡**South Africa 174-6** (19.1 overs) (L. Lee 60; Fatima Sana 3-27). *PoM:* L. Lee. *Lee battered 60 off 31 to help level the series again after Dar threatened to steal the show. Her 75 off 37 had made up for a slow start by Pakistan, while Aliya Riaz cracked 35* off 17. Dar then got through four tight overs, taking one for 21, but Lee gave South Africa the breathing space they needed.*

Fifth Twenty20 international   At Benoni, May 23. **South Africa won by nine wickets. Pakistan 125-5** (20 overs); ‡**South Africa 127-1** (15.1 overs) (L. Lee 75*, N. de Klerk 37*). *PoM:* L. Lee. *PoS:* Nida Dar. *The decider turned into an anticlimax after South Africa's bowlers, led by the economical Ismail (1-16), prevented any Pakistani reaching 30. Lee took care of the chase, hammering 75* from 48, and adding 100* in 11.2 overs with 19-year-old Nadine de Klerk. A 3–2 win came with nearly five overs to spare.*

IRELAND v WEST INDIES IN 2019

Twenty20 internationals (3): Ireland 0, West Indies 3

Ireland were outclassed, despite the efforts of Kim Garth, a 23-year-old Dubliner who made 142 of her side's 303 runs, and was dismissed only twice (she also took over the captaincy after Laura Delany was injured). West Indies, by contrast, racked up 484 runs across 60 overs after batting first on each occasion, with Hayley Matthews's whitewash-clinching century the highlight.

First Twenty20 international At Dublin (YMCA), May 26. **West Indies won by 64 runs.** ‡**West Indies 139-4** (20 overs) (S. R. Taylor 75); **Ireland 75** (18.4 overs) (K. J. Garth 46; A. S. S. Fletcher 4-14). *T20I debuts:* L. Little, S. MacMahon, U. Raymond-Hoey, R. Stokell (Ireland). *An inexperienced Ireland side including four newcomers in the format were dismantled by the leg-breaks of Afy Fletcher. Only No. 3 Kim Garth reached double figures, before she was ninth and last out, with captain Laura Delany unable to bat after being hit on the ankle in the field. West Indies' innings was dominated by their captain, Stafanie Taylor, whose 75 off 53 balls was as many as Ireland made in total.*

Second Twenty20 international At Dublin (Sydney Parade), May 28. **West Indies won by 45 runs.** ‡**West Indies 157-6** (20 overs) (H. K. Matthews 33, S. C. King 34; K. J. Garth 3-22); **Ireland 112-6** (20 overs) (K. J. Garth 51*). *T20I debut:* A. L. Kerrison (Ireland). *West Indies clinched the series with another easy win, despite all-round resistance from stand-in captain Garth, in place of the injured Delany. She followed three cheap wickets for her seamers with an unbeaten half-century, adding respectability to an Ireland score that at one point read 67-6.*

Third Twenty20 international At Dublin (Sydney Parade), May 29. **West Indies won by 72 runs.** **West Indies 188-1** (20 overs) (H. K. Matthews 107*, C. N. Nation 63*); ‡**Ireland 116-3** (20 overs) (M. V. Waldron 55*, K. J. Garth 45). *PoS:* H. K. Matthews. *A maiden T20I century for Hayley Matthews ensured a West Indies whitewash. Her 62-ball 107* included nine sixes, equalling the T20I record, set by compatriot Deandra Dottin against South Africa at Basseterre in 2010. Matthews helped set another: a stand of 162* in 15 overs with Chedean Nation (63* off 46) was the best for the second wicket, and an all-wicket record for West Indies. Ireland were not in contention, despite a maiden international half-century from 35-year-old Mary Waldron, and more runs for Garth.*

ENGLAND v WEST INDIES IN 2019

Raf Nicholson

One-day internationals (3): England 3, West Indies 0
Twenty20 internationals (3): England 1, West Indies 0

Rain rivalled England as the winner of West Indies' tour: four of the six matches were weather-affected, and two of the Twenty20 games abandoned. It meant a dejected West Indies barely got to stretch their legs in their strongest format, after they had demonstrated little positive intent with the bat in the 50-over games. Before the tour, their captain, Stafanie Taylor, had lamented the health of women's cricket in the Caribbean, expressing her frustration that it always lagged behind the men's game in the financial queue, and concluded that winning the World T20 in 2015-16 had changed almost nothing. It showed on the field: West Indies never really looked able to compete with England. The absence of Deandra Dottin, who needed shoulder surgery, and the international retirement of long-serving keeper Merissa Aguilleira were keenly felt. For England, it was not the best preparation for the Ashes, but there was a chance for Amy Jones, the Player of the ODI Series, to continue her international renaissance, with 189 runs across the three matches. In the one T20 to survive the rain, Danni Wyatt enjoyed the opportunity to bat herself into form. A couple of younger players also performed well: off-spinning all-rounder Bryony Smith made her one-day debut at Chelmsford, while Linsey Smith, a slow left-armer, bowled tidily in her first T20 at home.

WEST INDIES TOURING PARTY

S. R. Taylor, S. A. Campbelle, S. S. Connell, B. Cooper, A. S. S. Fletcher, C. A. Henry, S. C. King, Kycia A. Knight, Kyshona A. Knight, N. Y. McLean, H. K. Matthews, C. N. Nation, K. Ramharack, S. C. Selman. Coach: H. W. D. Springer.

D. J. S. Dottin was originally selected but withdrew with a shoulder injury and was replaced by Cooper.

First one-day international   At Leicester, June 6 (day/night). **England won by 208 runs.** ‡**England 318-9** (50 overs) (A. E. Jones 91, T. T. Beaumont 32, H. C. Knight 94, N. R. Sciver 32; H. K. Matthews 4-57); **West Indies 110** (36 overs) (C. N. Nation 42*; S. Ecclestone 3-30, L. A. Marsh 3-30). *PoM:* A. E. Jones. *England's first total of 300-plus against West Indies in any format led to the biggest ODI win by runs in this fixture. The innings' first and last deliveries went for six, struck by opener Amy Jones and No. 11 Sophie Ecclestone. Jones and captain Heather Knight added a solid 146 for the third wicket, though both fell in the 90s; a maiden international hundred eluded Jones again when she holed out to mid-off. West Indies were 27-3 by the 11th over, after Katherine Brunt struck with successive balls – she finished with 5–2–6–2 – and the pace of a resurgent Kate Cross did for the dangerous Stafanie Taylor. Most of the tourists got out through half-hearted prods and pokes, showing little interest in the target; the only one to offer resistance was Chedean Nation, unbeaten across more than 25 overs.*

Second one-day international   At Worcester, June 9. **England won by 121 runs** (DLS). ‡**England 233-7** (41 overs) (T. T. Beaumont 61, N. R. Sciver 35, A. Shrubsole 32*; A. S. S. Fletcher 3-48); **West Indies 87-6** (28 overs). *PoM:* A. Shrubsole. *England were 73-1 when a 90-minute rain break cut their innings to 41 overs; leg-spinner Afy Fletcher picked up three quick wickets on the resumption, including Tammy Beaumont for 61. But a gutsy run-a-ball 35 from Nat Sciver, and sixes from Anya Shrubsole and Ecclestone, helped add 88 in the last ten overs, and swung the momentum in their favour. Shrubsole followed up 32* off 16 balls – her highest score for England – by removing openers Britney Cooper and Hayley Matthews in her first spell. As West Indies retreated into themselves again, two wickets from Cross reduced them to 32-4 from 13 overs, before further rain, which might have saved them. But it stopped in time for play to continue; now chasing a notional 209 in 28, they went down to another thrashing.*

Third one-day international   At Chelmsford, June 13 (day/night). **England won by 135 runs** (DLS). **England 258-4** (39 overs) (A. E. Jones 80, T. T. Beaumont 46, S. J. Taylor 70, H. C. Knight 40*); ‡**West Indies 131** (37.4 overs) (Kycia A. Knight 38). *PoM:* A. E. Jones. *PoS:* A. E. Jones. *ODI debut:* B. F. Smith (England). *England whitewashed West Indies, who managed less than half a revised target of 267. Rain had halted the match in its 11th over, reducing it to 39 a side, but England seemed invigorated by the break, as openers Jones and Beaumont launched a barrage of boundaries; on her 26th birthday, Jones brought up her fifth half-century in six ODI innings. Sarah Taylor resolved questions over her place with a 61-ball 70, before Heather Knight's 40* off 19 took them past 250. West Indies had to bat without Stafanie Taylor, who had gone for an X-ray after injuring her hand. Matthews struck Cross for six in the second over, but was stopped in her tracks next ball by a breathtaking, full-stretch diving catch from Fran Wilson at cover, which went viral on social media. From there it was all downhill, only Kycia Knight lasting long.*

Women's Championship: England 6pts, West Indies 0pts.

First Twenty20 international   At Northampton, June 18 (floodlit). **England v West Indies. Abandoned.**

Second Twenty20 international   At Northampton, June 21 (floodlit). **England won by 42 runs.** ‡**England 180-6** (20 overs) (A. E. Jones 37, D. N. Wyatt 81, N. R. Sciver 31); **West Indies 138-9** (20 overs) (S. C. King 43, C. N. Nation 32). *PoM:* D. N. Wyatt. *England ran up their highest T20 total against West Indies, helped by squandered chances as Jones and Danni Wyatt opened with 67 in nine overs. Chinelle Henry grassed a sitter at mid-off when Wyatt was 17*; she went on to 81 from 55 balls, before falling in the penultimate over. Knight strained a hamstring scoring 22 in 11, so Shrubsole led in the field. Set an imposing 181, West Indies showed some fight at last: Stacy-Ann King and Nation, who lifted two huge leg-side sixes, added 38 for the fourth wicket in 27 balls. But both fell in the 13th over – King caught by Wyatt in the deep, Nation run out by Wilson's swift return to bowler Linsey Smith – and West Indies finished well short.*

Third Twenty20 international   At Derby, June 25 (floodlit). **England v West Indies. Abandoned.**

ENGLAND v AUSTRALIA IN 2019

Kalika Mehta

One-day internationals (3): England 0, Australia 3
Test match (1): England 0, Australia 0
Twenty20 internationals (3): England 1, Australia 2
Overall Ashes points: England 4, Australia 12

Australia arrived intent not just on retaining the women's Ashes, but on correcting their slip-up at home in 2017-18, when a resurgent England came from behind to draw the multi-format series. Meg Lanning's message to her side was clear: they were here to be ruthless. And that was exactly what they were, in a series effortlessly dominated by the all-round feats of Ellyse Perry, surely among the greatest female players of all time.

In the World Twenty20 final in the Caribbean in November 2018, the Australians had shown that ruthless streak as they bowled out England for 105, before cantering to an eight-wicket win. That match, though a one-off many months before the Ashes, offered some insight into the gulf opening up between the sides.

England had won their previous 14 completed games, but it was obvious they had not faced stiff enough competition. Australia's preparation against England A, meanwhile, did little more than allow some of their batters to make morale-boosting runs. Both teams, though, showed signs of rust in the first two one-day internationals, at Leicester – but Australia had the nous and mettle to come out on top in the crunch moments. England's fielding left much to be desired. Though an off-colour Anya Shrubsole picked up three wickets in the second game, she lacked accuracy throughout the series, especially to Perry and Alyssa Healy, and was picked off with ease.

It was England's batting that cost them the Ashes, however. They consistently collapsed against the pace of Perry, the seam of Delissa Kimmince and the spin of Sophie Molineux. Occasionally, someone would show application: Nat Sciver made 64 in the first 50-over match, and Tammy Beaumont a hundred in the second, while Amy Jones grafted to a half-century on Test debut. But when patience and a solid defence were required, England generally crumbled, unable to keep out the consistent line and length of Perry, Megan Schutt et al, or to resist deliveries dangled wide of off.

Heeding the instruction not to take their foot off the pedal, Australia romped to five victories either side of the drawn Test – in which they looked the only possible winners – before losing the final Twenty20 international. Three weeks later, it was announced that England coach Mark Robinson, who had presided over the World Cup triumph in 2017, was moving on.

Perry was the leading run-scorer and wicket-taker across the seven games, with 378 runs at 94, including a Test century, and 15 wickets at 12, including seven for 22 when she skittled England for 75 in the final one-day international. She won four match awards, as well as Player of the Series. Lanning amassed

Harry Trump, Getty Images

Jump for cover… Amy Jones takes evasive action as Ellyse Perry marches remorselessly on during her second-innings 76 at Taunton.

359 runs at nearly 60; only Sciver reached 200 for England, though slow left-armer Sophie Ecclestone managed 13 wickets.

The gap between the two top women's teams was growing, and it seemed likely England would need time to close it. While Australia had long been investing in grassroots cricket, and could boast over 80 professional players and a highly competitive domestic set-up, England would begin that process only in 2020, with the ECB investing £20m over two years.

"We know we have significantly underperformed," said Clare Connor, the ECB managing director of women's cricket. "We will have a look at our preparation, selection and where our players are at – some haven't developed as well as we thought. While our Kia Super League has helped us bridge the gap between the domestic and the international game, we've still got a huge amount more we need to do."

AUSTRALIA TOURING PARTY

*M. M. Lanning, N. E. Bolton, N. J. Carey, A. K. Gardner, R. L. Haynes, A. J. Healy, J. L. Jonassen, D. M. Kimmince, S. G. Molineux, B. L. Mooney, E. A. Perry, M. Schutt, E. J. Villani, T. J. Vlaeminck, G. L. Wareham. *Coach:* M. P. Mott.

Molineux missed the ODI series while recovering from shoulder surgery, but joined the squad for the Test and T20Is.

First one-day international At Leicester, July 2 (day/night). **Australia won by two wickets. England 177** (46.5 overs) (N. R. Sciver 64; E. A. Perry 3-43); ‡**Australia 178-8** (42.3 overs) (A. J. Healy 66; S. Ecclestone 3-34). Australia 2pts. *PoM:* E. A. Perry. *England's campaign to reclaim the Ashes began with a narrow defeat, thanks to poor batting. Put in, their top order disintegrated against Ellyse Perry's pace; they were 19-4 after she removed Amy Jones, Tammy Beaumont and Heather Knight in her first three overs. Nat Sciver reached 50 for the 15th time in ODIs to help drag England to 177, but they were all out with 19 deliveries remaining. Australia's own top order had problems, despite a punchy 71-ball 66 from opener Alyssa Healy, who struck two sixes. The match* *was in the balance when she holed out off Laura Marsh to make it 105-5 in the 26th over, and left-arm spinner Sophie Ecclestone's 3-34 almost helped England pull off victory. But Delissa Kimmince's 14*, followed by five wides when Katherine Brunt slipped down leg, saw Australia over the line.*

Second one-day international   At Leicester, July 4 (day/night). **Australia won by four wickets.** ‡**England 217** (47.4 overs) (T. T. Beaumont 114; D. M. Kimmince 5-26); **Australia 218-6** (45.2 overs) (E. A. Perry 62, R. L. Haynes 30, B. L. Mooney 43*, J. L. Jonassen 31*; A. Shrubsole 3-47). Australia 2pts. *PoM:* D. M. Kimmince. *Beaumont's maiden Ashes century was not enough to stop Australia securing their 14th successive series win in bilateral ODIs. On the same surface used two days earlier, she reached three figures from 99 balls, with little support; Danni Wyatt's 25 was the next-best score. Kimmince claimed the last four wickets in nine deliveries to complete her first five-wicket haul. Chasing 218 – more than they had ever made to beat England in England – Australia wobbled to 17-2, but Perry added 46 with Meg Lanning and 53 with Rachael Haynes, before being caught behind by Jones, keeping wicket as Sarah Taylor was injured. Brunt went off after twisting her ankle celebrating Lanning's dismissal, though she managed to resume bowling. But from 158-6, Beth Mooney and Jess Jonassen eased Australia to victory.*

Third one-day international   At Canterbury, July 7. **Australia won by 194 runs. Australia 269-7** (50 overs) (A. J. Healy 68, M. M. Lanning 69; N. R. Sciver 3-51); ‡**England 75** (32.5 overs) (E. A. Perry 7-22). Australia 2pts. *PoM:* E. A. Perry. *Perry's sensational 7-22 routed England for 75, their third-lowest one-day total, and worst against Australia. Her figures were the best for Australia in any limited-overs international, and the fourth-best in all women's ODIs. Perry removed Jones for the third time running, for a three-ball duck, then had Beaumont lbw and Taylor caught behind with successive deliveries. Megan Schutt interrupted her rampage by trapping Sciver, before Perry added Knight and Wyatt in her fifth over, reducing England to 21-6. In her second spell, she bowled Shrubsole, and had Ecclestone caught at mid-off. Earlier, Healy and Lanning had put on 109 for the second wicket as Australia exploited sloppy fielding. A total of 269-7 was their best against England in England; 194 runs was England's second-heaviest defeat, and they had not been whitewashed in an ODI series since losing 5–0 in India in January 2002.*

Women's Championship: Australia 6pts, England 0pts.

ENGLAND v AUSTRALIA

Only Test

At Taunton, July 18–21. Drawn. England 2pts, Australia 2pts. Toss: Australia. Test debuts: K. L. Gordon, A. E. Jones; A. K. Gardner, S. G. Molineux, T. J. Vlaeminck.

After suffering an ODI whitewash, England went into the sole Test knowing that anything other than victory would end their hopes of reclaiming the Ashes. Unsurprisingly, they requested a used surface in Taunton, a pitch played on during the men's World Cup a month earlier, and picked three spinners – Ecclestone, Marsh and debutant Kirstie Gordon.

The scars of a dismal showing in their previous home Test, in 2015, when Australia beat them by 161 runs at Canterbury, looked fresh on a ragged opening day, as four of the tourists' top five reached half-centuries. England's best moment came when Gordon bowled Healy, to claim her first Test wicket. But on a gloomy second day, Perry created more history, becoming only the fourth woman to score centuries in successive Test innings, following her unbeaten 213 against England at North

HUNDREDS IN CONSECUTIVE INNINGS IN WOMEN'S TESTS

E. R. Wilson (Aus)	100 v Eng at Melbourne; 127 v Eng at Adelaide.	1957-58
E. Bakewell (Eng)	124 v NZ at Wellington; 114 v NZ at Christchurch	1968-69
S. C. Taylor (Eng)	177 v SA at Shenley; 131 v SA at Taunton.	2003
E. A. Perry (Aus)	**213* v Eng at North Sydney; 116 v Eng at Taunton**	**2017-18 to 2019**

Sydney in November 2017. She played carefully, showing off a perfect defence in between finding the boundary. In a rare hint of nerves, she was almost run out twice on 99, but on the second occasion she brought up her hundred off 246 balls, courtesy of an overthrow; her fourth-wicket stand with Haynes eventually grew to 162. Rain wiped out the next two sessions, but Mooney returned next day to craft a maiden Test fifty, before Lanning declared at 420 for eight.

It was disappointing but not surprising that England were unable to show the same application. Perry bowled Beaumont for a duck with her seventh delivery, and left-arm spinner Sophie Molineux later dismissed Knight, Jones and Taylor to force England into their shells: they scored just 14 in the final 15 overs of the third day.

Knight declared 145 behind on the final morning, in the hope of getting a target to chase, and Marsh dismissed both openers cheaply. But the poise of Perry ruled out any risk of a collapse; she was still there, on 76, when the players shook hands. Splitting the four points available ensured Australia retained the Ashes, and meant England could only draw the series.

Player of the Match: E. A. Perry.

Close of play: first day, Australia 265-3 (Perry 84, Haynes 54); second day, Australia 341-5 (Mooney 7, Jonassen 4); third day, England 199-6 (Sciver 62, Shrubsole 1).

Australia

†A. J. Healy b Gordon	58	– (2) b Marsh	13
N. E. Bolton b Brunt	6		
*M. M. Lanning b Ecclestone	57	– c Elwiss b Gordon	21
E. A. Perry c Knight b Marsh	116	– not out	76
R. L. Haynes lbw b Marsh	87	– (1) lbw b Marsh	1
B. L. Mooney c Jones b Sciver	51	– (5) c Beaumont b Ecclestone	25
J. L. Jonassen c Sciver b Brunt	8	– (6) lbw b Knight	37
S. G. Molineux b Ecclestone	21	– (7) b Gordon	41
A. K. Gardner not out	5	– (8) c Beaumont b Knight	7
B 8, lb 3	11	B 7, lb 2	9

1/25 (2) 2/91 (1) (8 wkts dec, 154.4 overs) 420
3/160 (3) 4/322 (4)
5/335 (5) 6/356 (7) 7/408 (8) 8/420 (6)

1/14 (2) (7 wkts, 64 overs) 230
2/15 (1) 3/67 (3)
4/105 (5) 5/168 (6) 6/221 (7) 7/230 (8)

M. L. Schutt and T. J. Vlaeminck did not bat.

Brunt 22–5–48–2; Shrubsole 21–6–63–0; Ecclestone 34.2–8–90–2; Sciver 13.4–2–44–1; Gordon 26.4–7–69–1; Marsh 34–5–90–2; Elwiss 3–2–5–0. *Second innings*—Ecclestone 16–6–37–1; Brunt 4–0–23–0; Marsh 13–2–42–2; Gordon 10–1–50–2; Elwiss 7–0–27–0; Shrubsole 6–0–17–0; Knight 8–0–25–2.

England

A. E. Jones c Haynes b Molineux	64	L. A. Marsh lbw b Jonassen	28
T. T. Beaumont b Perry	0	S. Ecclestone not out	9
*H. C. Knight lbw b Molineux	28	B 1, lb 6, w 6, nb 5	18
G. A. Elwiss run out (Bolton)	9		
N. R. Sciver b Jonassen	88	1/1 (2) (9 wkts dec, 107.1 overs) 275
†S. J. Taylor lbw b Molineux	5	2/80 (3) 3/111 (4)
K. H. Brunt b Gardner	15	4/119 (1) 5/132 (6) 6/189 (7)
A. Shrubsole st Healy b Molineux	11	7/210 (8) 8/252 (5) 9/275 (9)

K. L. Gordon did not bat.

Perry 13–3–44–1; Schutt 7–4–6–0; Molineux 37–6–95–4; Vlaeminck 11–2–37–0; Jonassen 21.1–5–50–2; Gardner 18–5–36–1.

Umpires: M. J. Saggers and A. G. Wharf. Third umpire: P. K. Baldwin.
Referee: W. M. Noon.

First Twenty20 international At Chelmsford, July 26 (floodlit). **Australia won by 93 runs. Australia 226-3** (20 overs) (B. L. Mooney 54, M. M. Lanning 133*); ‡**England 133-9** (20 overs) (L. Winfield 33; M. Schutt 3-25). Australia 2pts. PoM: M. M. Lanning. *Lanning made the highest individual score in women's T20Is, beating her own 126 (a month earlier, Sterre Kalis also made*

126*, *for the Netherlands against Germany). Australia reached 226, their highest T20 total, and took an unbeatable 10–2 lead in the series. Lanning added 134 with Mooney for the second wicket, launching 17 fours and seven sixes in a 63-ball 133* – as many as England managed in total. Perry picked up 2-11 from three overs, and Schutt, ranked No. 1 bowler in T20Is as well as ODIs, 3-25. Only Lauren Winfield reached 30 as England suffered their biggest T20 defeat, and their first in any format at Chelmsford – which was sold out – following six wins in ODIs and eight in T20Is.*

Second Twenty20 international At Hove, July 28. **Australia won by seven wickets. ‡England 121-8** (20 overs) (T. T. Beaumont 43); **Australia 122-3** (17.5 overs) (M. M. Lanning 43*, E. A. Perry 47*). Australia 2pts. *PoM:* E. A. Perry. *When she moved to 45, Perry became the first cricketer, male or female, to combine 1,000 runs with 100 wickets in T20 internationals. Her 103rd victim had been Jones, when she dismissed her (for a second-ball duck) for the fourth time on tour. England's batting was below par again: Beaumont managed 43, but no one else passed 17. Although Australia slipped to 35-3, Lanning and Perry put on 87* to secure a clinical fifth win. With only one match left, they had hopes of becoming the first team to finish undefeated in a multi-format Ashes series; before the Ashes expanded to cover limited-overs cricket, Belinda Clark's Australians had been unbeaten throughout their tours in 1998 and 2001.*

Third Twenty20 international At Bristol, July 31 (floodlit). **England won by 17 runs. England 139-5** (20 overs); **‡Australia 122-8** (20 overs) (E. A. Perry 60*; K. H. Brunt 3-21, S. Ecclestone 3-22). England 2pts. *PoM:* K. H. Brunt. *PoS:* E. A. Perry. *T20I debut:* M. K. Villiers (England). *England finally tasted victory, with the help of debutant Mady Villiers, a 20-year-old off-spinner from Essex. From 84-5, Winfield and Brunt shared a battling stand of 55* to raise England's first competitive total of the series. Healy made a brisk start to Australia's reply, though Mooney and Lanning managed only two apiece, but became Villiers's first international scalp when she launched a full toss to Ecclestone at mid-off; four balls later, Villiers had Ashleigh Gardner stumped for a golden duck. Ecclestone and Brunt claimed three apiece as Australia collapsed around Perry – whose 60* meant that, as in 2015, she finished the series as the leading run-scorer and wicket-taker.*

NETHERLANDS QUADRANGULAR TOURNAMENT IN 2019

1 Thailand   2 Scotland   3 Ireland   4 Netherlands

Surprise packets Thailand emerged from a hectic week in Deventer at the top of the table, to start an exciting run which took them all the way to the Twenty20 World Cup in Australia in February 2020. They won five of their six matches, all against better-established teams, and did the double over Ireland and hosts Netherlands, losing only to Scotland. It was a team effort: Nattakam Chantam (144) and Nannapat Koncharoenkai (136) were two of the five to pass 100 runs (Ireland's Gaby Lewis topped the list with 180). Seamer Nattaya Boochatham and off-spinner Onnicha Kamchomphu took nine wickets, as did 14-year-old Katherine Fraser, still a pupil at the Mary Erskine School in Edinburgh. In the last match, the Netherlands were skittled for 40 – a significant figure for Thailand's captain, Sornnarin Tippoch, who was part of the side humbled for exactly that score in each of their first three international matches, against Nepal, Hong Kong and Malaysia a dozen years previously.

At Deventer, August 8. **Ireland won by 79 runs. Ireland 169-5** (20 overs) (E. A. J. Richardson 63*); **‡Netherlands 90-7** (20 overs) (B. J. A. de Leede 50). *ODI debuts:* F. C. J. Overdijk, A. H. Thomson, F. E. M. van Arkel (Netherlands); H. Little, L. Paul, O. Prendergast (Ireland). *Eimear*

Richardson's 63* from 41 balls, with 11 fours, propelled Ireland to a score the Netherlands never threatened, despite Babette de Leede's maiden international half-century. Of the rest, only captain Juliet Post (18) passed five.

At Deventer, August 8. **Thailand won by 74 runs. ‡Thailand 129-3** (20 overs) (N. Chantam 60*, N. Koncharoenkai 33); **Scotland 55** (15.4 overs) (O. Kamchomphu 4-8). *Off-spinner Onnicha Kamchomphu had 4-8 from three overs, including three wickets in four balls, as Scotland were bundled out for 55; only Lorna Jack (12) reached double figures.*

At Deventer, August 9. **Scotland won by five runs** (DLS). **‡Netherlands 86-6** (16 overs) (R. Rijke 39; K. J. G. Fraser 3-17); **Scotland 41-0** (7 overs). *ODI debut: M. M. H. Zwilling (Netherlands); E. L. Watson (Scotland). Rain reduced this to a 16-over match, then returned to end play early, with Scotland narrowly ahead of their seven-over target of 37.*

At Deventer, August 9. **Thailand won by four runs. Thailand 54-4** (10 overs); **‡Ireland 50-7** (10 overs) (N. Boochatham 3-18). *Thailand's bowlers again allowed only one opponent – Shauna Kavanagh, who made 12 – to reach double figures in a game reduced to ten overs a side.*

At Deventer, August 10. **Thailand won by eight wickets. ‡Netherlands 54** (17.5 overs) (N. Boochatham 3-3); **Thailand 55-2** (8 overs) (N. Chantam 42*). *ODI debut: G. Bloemen (Netherlands). The Netherlands stumbled to 30-6 by halfway as Thailand's bowlers put in another impressive display.*

At Deventer, August 10. **Scotland won by 11 runs. ‡Scotland 105-6** (20 overs) (L. Jack 32; E. A. J. Richardson 3-14); **Ireland 94-7** (20 overs) (K. J. Garth 30). *Ireland started the last over on 84-4, but lost three wickets – including Richardson, their batting star from the first match, who had earlier taken three with her off-breaks.*

At Deventer, August 12. **Scotland won by five wickets. Thailand 123-7** (20 overs) (C. Sutthiruang 35; K. J. G. Fraser 3-14); **‡Scotland 126-5** (20 overs) (S. J. Bryce 63*). *Scotland's captain Sarah Bryce anchored her side with 63* from 57 balls to inflict Thailand's only defeat of the tournament. Katherine Fraser, only 14, took the first three wickets.*

At Deventer, August 12. **No result. ‡Ireland 213-4** (20 overs) (G. H. Lewis 71, O. Prendergast 38, M. V. Waldron 31*, R. Stokell 36; L. K. Bennett 3-22); **Netherlands 18-1** (2.4 overs). *Ireland were unlucky that rain intervened after 18-year-old Gaby Lewis, who hit four sixes, and Orla Prendergast, just 17, had set up the highest score of the tournament with an opening stand of 112.*

At Deventer, August 13. **Thailand won by seven wickets** (DLS). **‡Ireland 87-8** (16.5 overs) (S. Tippoch 3-10, O. Kamchomphu 3-12); **Thailand 67-3** (10.2 overs). *Ireland were held up when Kamchomphu took a hat-trick; rain interrupted play next over. Thailand needed 64 in 11.*

At Deventer, August 13. **Scotland won by 62 runs** (DLS). **Scotland 148-4** (20 overs) (S. J. Bryce 41, L. Jack 54*); **‡Netherlands 60-8** (13.3 overs) (M. J. McColl 3-22). *Bryce made 41 of an opening stand of 50 with Jack, who batted through Scotland's innings. The Netherlands collapsed again – Sterre Kalis (12) alone reached double figures – and were way adrift of a target of 123 when the weather closed in.*

At Deventer, August 14. **Ireland won by nine wickets. ‡Scotland 126-7** (20 overs) (S. J. Bryce 49; L. Maritz 3-4); **Ireland 130-1** (13.1 overs) (G. H. Lewis 65*, K. J. Garth 47*). *ODI debut: A. Hogg (Scotland). Three wickets in three overs from seamer Lara Maritz sent Scotland spinning from 86-3 to 91-6. Lewis, who cracked a dozen fours, and Kim Garth sped Ireland home with a stand of 113*.*

At Deventer, August 14. **Thailand won by 93 runs. Thailand 133-8** (20 overs) (N. Koncharoenkai 57; M. M. H. Zwilling 3-8); **‡Netherlands 40** (12 overs) (S. Laomi 3-11, R. Padunglerd 3-5). *After wicketkeeper Nannapat Koncharoenkai's 43-ball 57, Thailand rounded off a triumphant tournament with a dominant bowling display: after reaching 24-0 in five overs, the Netherlands lost all ten for 16. Leg-spinner Suleeporn Laomi and seamer Ratanaporn Padunglerd both took three wickets, and there were three run-outs.*

Thailand 10pts, Scotland 8pts, Ireland 5pts, Netherlands 1pt.

WEST INDIES v AUSTRALIA IN 2019-20

One-day internationals (3): West Indies 0, Australia 3
Twenty20 internationals (3): West Indies 0, Australia 3

Australia continued their relentless march through 2019, sweeping West Indies aside with almost embarrassing ease: only one of the six internationals was remotely close. It took their record for the year to nine ODI wins out of nine, and five out of six T20s. Alyssa Healy and Meg Lanning shared a stand of 225 in the first ODI, in which Australia amassed 308 – a total they matched in the second, with Ellyse Perry adding another century. Healy finished a series in which only six Australians got to the crease with 241 runs at a strike-rate of 133. She added 108 at 154 in the T20s, while slow left-armer Jess Jonassen took seven for 37 in her 12 overs. Stafanie Taylor's defiant unbeaten 70 in the first ODI was a rare highlight for West Indies, who were without Hayley Matthews following a disciplinary breach.

First one-day international At Coolidge, Antigua, September 5, 2019 (day/night). **Australia won by 178 runs. Australia 308-4** (50 overs) (A. J. Healy 122, M. M. Lanning 121, E. A. Perry 33*); ‡**West Indies 130** (37.3 overs) (S. R. Taylor 70*; E. A. Perry 3-17). *PoM:* A. J. Healy. *ODI debut:* S. Gajnabi (West Indies). *Rachael Haynes fell to the first ball of the match, from Shamilia Connell, but from there Australian dominated. Alyssa Healy and Meg Lanning put on 225, the second-highest partnership for Australia in ODIs, behind 244 for the third wicket by Karen Rolton and Lisa Sthalekar against Ireland in Dublin in 2005. Lanning reached three figures with the third of her four sixes, one landing in the swimming pool at the old Stanford ground at Coolidge. It was Lanning's 13th ODI hundred, in her 76th innings (Hashim Amla was the fastest man to get to 13, in 83). West Indies also lost a wicket first ball, and were soon 8-3, with three ducks. Stafanie Taylor was unmovable, with 70* from 115, but of the rest only Chinelle Henry (14) reached double figures.*

Second one-day international At North Sound, Antigua, September 8, 2019. **Australia won by 151 runs.** ‡**Australia 308-2** (50 overs) (A. J. Healy 58, E. A. Perry 112*, B. L. Mooney 56*, A. K. Gardner 57*); **West Indies 157-8** (50 overs) (Kyshona Knight 32, S. S. Grimmond 31). *PoM:* E. A. Perry. *ODI debuts:* S. S. Grimmond (West Indies); E. A. Burns (Australia). *Australia again made 308, inspired this time by a century from Ellyse Perry. After Healy punched 58 from 43, with 46 in boundaries, Perry helped add 215* for the third wicket, with Beth Mooney retiring from heat exhaustion, and Ashleigh Gardner slamming 57* from 25. West Indies struggled to score – Kyshona Knight's 32 ate up 81 balls – and slipped to another hefty defeat.*

Third one-day international At North Sound, Antigua, September 11, 2019. **Australia won by eight wickets.** ‡**West Indies 180** (50 overs) (Kyshona Knight 40, C. A. Henry 39, S. S. Grimmond 34; M. Schutt 3-24); **Australia 182-2** (31.1 overs) (A. J. Healy 61, M. M. Lanning 58*, E. A. Perry 33*). *PoM:* A. J. Healy. *PoS:* E. A. Perry. *Australia's bowlers again proved difficult to get away: West Indies crept to 104-6 in the 36th, before Henry and Sheneta Grimmond added 64 in ten. Megan Schutt, parsimonious throughout the series, ended the innings with a hat-trick. Australia strolled past the target, with Healy's 61 from 32, including 11 fours and a six, lighting the touchpaper.*

Women's Championship: Australia 6pts, West Indies 0pts.

First Twenty20 international At Bridgetown, Barbados, September 14, 2019 (floodlit). **Australia won by six wickets.** ‡**West Indies 106-8** (20 overs) (S. R. Taylor 44*; M. Schutt 3-31); **Australia 108-4** (18.5 overs) (M. M. Lanning 54*). *PoM:* M. M. Lanning. *T20I debuts:* S. Gajnabi, S. S. Grimmond (West Indies); E. A. Burns (Australia). *Schutt took three more wickets as West Indies were restricted to 106, then Lanning's run-a-ball 54* guided Australia home. They won with seven balls to spare, the narrowest margin of the tour.*

Second Twenty20 international At Bridgetown, Barbados, September 16, 2019 (floodlit). **Australia won by nine wickets. West Indies 97-9** (20 overs) (B. Cooper 39); ‡**Australia 98-1** (14.3 overs) (A. J. Healy 58*). *PoM:* A. J. Healy. *At 55-2 at halfway, West Indies seemed on course to set a testing target – but five tumbled for nine in 19 balls. Healy crashed 58* from 43 as Australia sauntered to victory.*

Third Twenty20 international   At Bridgetown, Barbados, September 18, 2019 (floodlit). **Australia won by nine wickets.** ‡**West Indies 81** (20 overs) (G. L. Wareham 3-14, J. L. Jonassen 4-7); **Australia 83-1** (7.3 overs) (A. J. Healy 38). *PoM:* J. L. Jonassen. *PoS:* A. J. Healy. *Australia clinched a double clean sweep as West Indies imploded again, this time losing six for six after being 75-4. Slow left-armer Jess Jonassen took three wickets in an over, and conceded only seven singles in all, while Georgia Wareham grabbed three with her leg-breaks. Healy clattered 38 from 16 balls, with six fours and two sixes, and Australia had no trouble in completing the 19th win in their past 21 T20 internationals.*

INDIA v SOUTH AFRICA IN 2019-20

Twenty20 internationals (6): India 3, South Africa 1
One-day internationals (3): India 3, South Africa 0

India won all but one of the seven games played on South Africa's visit, with another two washed out. The tour took place outside the framework of the Women's Championship, as the teams had already played their three matches in South Africa in February 2018. With Dane van Niekerk ruled out by a foot injury, Sune Luus led the tourists, and Marizanne Kapp was available only for the one-day fixtures (where she won the series award). They generally struggled to score against the spinners, especially Deepti Sharma, Poonam Yadav and Ekta Bisht, except in a glorious 105-run victory in the final Twenty20 game, and the second one-day international, where India needed a record chase to beat them. Free admission led to huge crowds, estimated at 12,000 to 20,000 in Surat, which hosted all the T20 matches.

First Twenty20 international   At Surat, September 24, 2019 (floodlit). **India won by 11 runs. India 130-8** (20 overs) (H. Kaur 43; S. Ismail 3-26); ‡**South Africa 119** (19.5 overs) (M. du Preez 59; D. B. Sharma 3-8). *PoM:* D. B. Sharma. *T20I debuts:* S. Verma (India); N. Mlaba (South Africa). *An enthusiastic crowd saw India end a run of seven T20I defeats since the World T20 in November 2018. Shafali Verma, their 15-year-old opener, fell in Shabnim Ismail's first over, but Harmanpreet Kaur's 34-ball 43 led her team to 104-3, before they lost five in 21 deliveries. South Africa smashed 18 off their opening over, from Pooja Vastrakar, then ran aground against the off-breaks of Deepti Sharma, who did not concede a run until her fourth over. Mignon du Preez hit 59 in 43 balls, and her third six brought the target down to 12 off five; but leg-spinner Poonam Yadav did not concede another run, and had du Preez and debutante Nonkululeko Mlaba stumped.*

Second Twenty20 international   At Surat, September 26, 2019 (floodlit). **India v South Africa. Abandoned.**

Third Twenty20 international   At Surat, September 29, 2019 (floodlit). **India v South Africa. Abandoned.**

Fourth Twenty20 international   At Surat, October 1, 2019 (floodlit). **India won by 51 runs. India 140-4** (17 overs) (S. Verma 46, J. I. Rodrigues 33); ‡**South Africa 89-7** (17 overs) (P. Yadav 3-13). *PoM:* P. Yadav. *The rain which had wiped out the previous two games relented to allow 17 overs a side, and India ran up a bigger total than they had managed in 20 a week earlier. They were helped by sloppy fielding: Smriti Mandhana was dropped three times on her way to 13. Verma had a happier outing than on her debut, striking 46 out of 65 in by the ninth over, when fellow teenager Jemimah Rodrigues took over. Again, South Africa were bogged down by the spin of Sharma and Yadav; only Tazmin Brits (20) and Laura Wolvaardt (23) reached double figures.*

Fifth Twenty20 international   At Surat, October 3, 2019 (floodlit). **India won by five wickets. South Africa 98-8** (20 overs) (R. P. Yadav 3-23); ‡**India 99-5** (17.1 overs) (H. Kaur 34*). *PoM:* H. Kaur. *T20I debut:* A. E. Bosch (South Africa). *This was an extra match to compensate for the two washouts; India went 3–0 up to secure the series (again). Slow left-armer Radha Yadav returned a career-best 3-23, and reinforced the spinners' stranglehold over South Africa, who managed only*

25 in the powerplay. Their highest score was Wolvaardt's 17, and they failed to reach 100 after losing three in three deliveries across the last two overs; Sharma collected two wickets to follow her two catches. India in turn struggled to 29-3, but Kaur, who passed 2,000 T20I runs, steered them home.

Sixth Twenty20 international At Surat, October 4, 2019 (floodlit). **South Africa won by 105 runs. ‡South Africa 175-3** (20 overs) (L. Lee 84, S. E. Luus 62); **India 70** (17.3 overs) (N. de Klerk 3-18). *PoM:* L. Lee. *PoS:* D. B. Sharma. *In a complete turnaround, South Africa inflicted India's heaviest defeat in T20Is, to the disappointment of a crowd estimated at 20,000. An opening stand of 144 from Lizelle Lee, whose 84 was her highest score, and Sune Luus helped them pile up 175, their second-highest total in the format, after 205-1 against the Netherlands at Potchefstroom in 2010-11. Their seamers then ran through India's top order, reducing them to 13-6, before Veda Krishnamurthy and Arundhati Reddy added 49 to reach their lowest T20I total, 62 against Australia at Billericay in 2011; Reddy and the tail saw them safely past that mark, before Nadine de Klerk returned to complete a career-best 3-18.*

First one-day international At Vadodara (Reliance), October 9, 2019. **India won by eight wickets. ‡South Africa 164** (45.1 overs) (L. Wolvaardt 39, M. Kapp 54; J. N. Goswami 3-33); **India 165-2** (41.4 overs) (P. S. Punia 75*, J. I. Rodrigues 55). *PoM:* P. S. Punia. *ODI debuts:* P. S. Punia (India); N. Shangase (South Africa). *India regained control, winning with more than eight overs to spare. Their captain, Mithali Raj, was at the crease; earlier, she had become the first woman to play ODIs for more than 20 years (she made her debut, aged 16, against Ireland at Milton Keynes in 1999). Jhulan Goswami, eight days older, dismissed Lee with the first ball of the match, and South Africa's total would have been paltry without a fifty from the recently arrived Marizanne Kapp, who was last out, Goswami's third victim. Debutante Priya Punia (replacing the injured Mandhana) batted throughout India's reply, sharing an opening stand of 83 with Rodrigues before hitting the winning run.*

Second one-day international At Vadodara (Reliance), October 11, 2019. **India won by five wickets. South Africa 247-6** (50 overs) (L. Lee 40, L. Wolvaardt 69, M. du Preez 44, L. Goodall 38); **‡India 248-5** (48 overs) (P. G. Raut 65, M. D. Raj 66, H. Kaur 39*, Extras 30; A. Khaka 3-69). *PoM:* P. G. Raut. *India completed their fifth successive ODI series victory with their highest winning chase, beating 245-9 (also against South Africa) in the final of the World Cup Qualifier in Colombo in 2016-17. South Africa had raised their game, with three top-order half-century stands, including 76 from openers Lee and Wolvaardt. But Raj, whose 66 was her 60th ODI score of 50-plus, and Punam Raut added 129 for India's third wicket, their sixth century partnership. They fell in consecutive overs, before Kaur hit 39* of the 52 still required.*

Third one-day international At Vadodara (Reliance), October 14, 2019. **India won by six runs. ‡India 146** (45.5 overs) (H. Kaur 38, S. S. Pandey 35; M. Kapp 3-20); **South Africa 140** (48 overs) (E. K. Bisht 3-32). *PoM:* E. K. Bisht. *PoS:* M. Kapp. *India whitewashed South Africa for the first time in ODIs after successfully defending a low total. Kaur – the game's top scorer with 38 – and Shikha Pandey joined forces at 71-6, and added 49 before Kaur became Kapp's third victim; the tail scraped together another 26, which would prove crucial. South Africa's top order also stumbled, before Luus and Kapp put on 40 for the sixth wicket. Though both fell to the spinners, the target from the last seven overs was 13, with three wickets left: India extracted all three while conceding only six, with a wicket-maiden for Ekta Bisht.*

AUSTRALIA v SRI LANKA IN 2019-20

Twenty20 internationals (3): Australia 3, Sri Lanka 0
One-day internationals (3): Australia 3, Sri Lanka 0

The results were not unexpected, but Australia's dominance was still ominous for their rivals. Sri Lanka had not played for six months, and had only one warm-up. It showed: they were crushed in all six matches. But there was plenty to enjoy. In the first Twenty20, Beth Mooney and Sri Lanka captain Chamari Atapattu Jayangani made rapid hundreds. In the third, Alyssa Healy slammed an unbeaten 148, the highest score in the format. In the ODIs, Australia's bowlers flexed their muscles. Slow left-armer Jess Jonassen took six wickets at 11, and leg-spinner Georgia Wareham, also outstanding in the T20s, five at 16; Rachael Haynes hit 237 runs at 79. Atapattu was a beacon for Sri Lanka across the six matches, totalling 289, with two hundreds.

First Twenty20 international At North Sydney, September 29, 2019. **Australia won by 41 runs.** ‡**Australia 217-4** (20 overs) (A. J. Healy 43, B. L. Mooney 113, A. K. Gardner 49); **Sri Lanka 176-7** (20 overs) (A. M. C. Jayangani 113). *PoM:* B. L. Mooney. *The statisticians were working overtime, after Beth Mooney's 54-ball hundred was followed by a century in 60 from Sri Lanka's undaunted captain, Chamari Atapattu Jayangani. An aggregate of 393 was the second-highest in women's T20 internationals, and Australia's 217 their second-highest total.*

Second Twenty20 international At North Sydney, September 30, 2019 (floodlit). **Australia won by nine wickets.** ‡**Sri Lanka 84-8** (20 overs); **Australia 87-1** (9.4 overs) (E. A. Burns 30*). *PoM:* B. L. Mooney. *After the fireworks of the first match, the second was a non-event. Australia clinched the series easily, after Sri Lanka folded in the face of concerted bowling and outstanding fielding. The hosts galloped home with more than half their overs in hand, though Nilakshi Silva's brilliant catch to remove Alyssa Healy warmed a chilly crowd.*

Third Twenty20 international At North Sydney, October 2, 2019. **Australia won by 132 runs.** ‡**Australia 226-2** (20 overs) (A. J. Healy 148*, R. L. Haynes 41); **Sri Lanka 94-7** (20 overs) (A. M. C. Jayangani 30; N. J. Carey 3-15). *PoM:* A. J. Healy. *In a series stuffed with stats, Healy hit the highest score in a women's T20 international. Her 148* off 61 balls, with 19 fours and seven sixes, surpassed 133* from Meg Lanning, at the other end when her record fell, against England at Taunton in July. "When it came up on the big screen, I said: 'I'm coming to get you Meg,'" Healy said. She reached three figures in 46 balls. Sri Lanka had no answer, although Atapattu hung around defiantly. It was Australia's biggest win by runs.*

FASTEST WOMEN'S T20 INTERNATIONAL HUNDREDS

Balls			
38	D. J. S. Dottin (112)	West Indies v South Africa at Basseterre	2010
46	**A. J. Healy (148*)**	**Australia v Sri Lanka at North Sydney**	**2018-19**
47	T. T. Beaumont (116)	England v South Africa at Taunton	2018
49	H. Kaur (103)	India v New Zealand at Providence	2018-19
52	D. N. Wyatt (124)	England v India at Mumbai (Brabourne)	2017-18
53	M. M. Lanning (126)	Australia v Ireland at Sylhet	2013-14
54	**B. L. Mooney (113)**	**Australia v Sri Lanka at North Sydney**	**2018-19**
56	D. N. Wyatt (100)	England v Australia at Canberra	2017-18
60	**A. M. C. Jayangani (113)**	**Sri Lanka v Australia at North Sydney**	**2018-19**
63	S. A. Fritz (116*)	South Africa v Netherlands at Potchefstroom	2010-11
63	D. J. S. Dottin (112)	West Indies v Sri Lanka at Coolidge	2017-18
65	B. L. Mooney (117*)	Australia v England at Canberra	2017-18

First one-day international At Brisbane (Allan Border Field), October 5, 2019. **Australia won by 157 runs.** ‡**Australia 281-8** (50 overs) (R. L. Haynes 56, M. M. Lanning 73, B. L. Mooney 66); **Sri Lanka 124** (41.3 overs) (H. A. S. D. Siriwardene 30). *PoM:* M. M. Lanning. *A performance of all-round authority from Australia was far too good for Sri Lanka in the first of the ODIs. Showing nimble footwork against the spinners, three of their top order made half-centuries, with Lanning's 73 off 66 the pick. Shashikala Siriwardene, having taken over the captaincy from Atapattu, dug in for 30, but received little support, as the pace of Tayla Vlaeminck proved especially troubling.*

Second one-day international At Brisbane (Allan Border Field), October 7, 2019. **Australia won by 110 runs.** ‡**Australia 282-8** (50 overs) (A. J. Healy 69, R. L. Haynes 118, M. M. Lanning 45; W. G. A. K. K. Kulasuriya 3-50); **Sri Lanka 172-9** (50 overs) (M. A. A. Sanjeewani 36, H. M. D. Samarawickrama 39; J. L. Jonassen 4-31). *PoM:* R. L. Haynes. *ODI debut: H. L. Graham (Australia).* *Rachael Haynes stole the thunder of her more illustrious team-mates with her first international hundred. Putting on 116 for the first wicket with Healy, and 103 for the second with Lanning, she* *made 118 off 132, with just eight fours. Australia had looked set for a huge total, but Sri Lanka fought back, taking six for 63 in the last ten. Their reply started solidly, but they struggled to keep up with the rate. Jess Jonassen's 4-31 included her 100th ODI wicket.*

Third one-day international At Brisbane (Allan Border Field), October 9, 2019. **Australia won by nine wickets. ‡Sri Lanka 195-8** (50 overs) (A. M. C. Jayangani 103); **Australia 196-1** (26.5 overs) (R. L. Haynes 63, A. J. Healy 112*). PoM: A. J. Healy. *Sri Lanka batted first, but it made no difference. Australia recorded their 18th successive win, beating the record set by Belinda Clark's team between 1997 and 1999. Healy hit her third ODI hundred, putting on 159 for the first wicket with Haynes, and completed the chase with a six. Atapattu batted into the penultimate over for her fifth ODI century, but fought a lone hand.*

Women's Championship: Australia 6pts, Sri Lanka 0pts.

PAKISTAN v BANGLADESH IN 2019-20

Twenty20 internationals (3): Pakistan 3, Bangladesh 0
One-day internationals (2): Pakistan 1, Bangladesh 1

Bangladesh's women ventured to Pakistan for the second time, following a series in Karachi in late 2015. They were whitewashed in the T20s, despite Jahanara Alam's nine wickets at six, but shared the 50-over series – which did not count towards the World Championship, as these teams had already played – with a last-gasp victory. Bismah Maroof and Nahida Khan scored well for Pakistan, who were without their experienced off-spinner Nida Dar, playing for Sydney Thunder in the Big Bash.

First Twenty20 international At Lahore, October 26, 2019. **Pakistan won by 14 runs. ‡Pakistan 126-7** (20 overs) (Bismah Maroof 34, Umaima Sohail 33; Jahanara Alam 4-17); **Bangladesh 112-7** (20 overs) (Rumana Ahmed 50). PoM: Bismah Maroof. *T20I debut: Sadia Iqbal (Pakistan). Bismah Maroof's 34th and last run made her the tenth woman – but the first from Pakistan – to score 2,000 in T20 internationals. Jahanara Alam took four wickets to restrict Pakistan to 126 in their first T20I at the Gaddafi Stadium, but Bangladesh fell short, despite Rumana Ahmed's 30-ball 50, a maiden half-century in her 59th match.*

Second Twenty20 international At Lahore, October 28, 2019. **Pakistan won by 15 runs. Pakistan 167-3** (20 overs) (Javeria Khan 52, Bismah Maroof 70*); **‡Bangladesh 152-7** (20 overs) (Sanjida Islam 45, Farzana Haque 30; Sadia Iqbal 3-19). PoM: Bismah Maroof. *Javeria Khan and Maroof – whose 70* was her highest score in T20Is – put on 95 for the second wicket to lift Pakistan to a total that again proved beyond Bangladesh. Slow left-armer Sadia Iqbal, in her second international, took three wickets in six balls.*

Third Twenty20 international At Lahore, October 30, 2019. **Pakistan won by 28 runs. ‡Pakistan 117-7** (20 overs) (Javeria Khan 54, Umaima Sohail 31; Jahanara Alam 3-12); **Bangladesh 89-8** (20 overs) (Nigar Sultana 30). PoM: Javeria Khan. PoS: Bismah Maroof and Jahanara Alam. *T20I debuts: Saba Nazir (Pakistan); Sanjida Akther (Bangladesh). Javeria and Umaima Sohail put on 67, but a Pakistan clean sweep looked unlikely when no one else managed double figures. Instead, Bangladesh limped to 12-4 after seven overs, and were never on terms.*

First one-day international At Lahore, November 2, 2019. **Pakistan won by 29 runs. ‡Pakistan 215** (48.5 overs) (Nahida Khan 68, Bismah Maroof 39, Aliya Riaz 37; Jahanara Alam 3-44); **Bangladesh 186** (47.4 overs) (Nigar Sultana 58; Sana Mir 3-49). PoM: Nahida Khan. *ODI debut: Sadia Iqbal (Pakistan). Pakistan were 131-2, but Maroof and Nahida fell in four balls, before Aliya Riaz dragged them past 200. Bangladesh were 90-2, but regular wickets kept them adrift of the rate. Off-spinner Sana Mir's third wicket – top-scorer Nigar Sultana – was her 150th in ODIs.*

Second one-day international At Lahore, November 4, 2019. **Bangladesh won by one wicket. ‡Pakistan 210** (48.4 overs) (Nahida Khan 63, Bismah Maroof 34, Aliya Riaz 36; Rumana Ahmed 3-35); **Bangladesh 211-9** (49.5 overs) (Murshida Khatun 44, Farzana Haque 67, Rumana Ahmed 31). PoM: Farzana Haque. PoS: Nahida Khan and Farzana Haque. *ODI debut: Syeda Aroob Shah (Pakistan). Bangladesh finally recorded a win, squaring the 50-over series with a wicket and a ball to spare. They looked home and dry at 168-3 in the 39th, but the demise of top-scorer Farzana Haque set nerves jangling.*

WEST INDIES v INDIA IN 2019-20

One-day internationals (3): West Indies 1, India 2
Twenty20 internationals (5): West Indies 0, India 5

India completed a triumphant tour of the Caribbean, coming from behind to win the 50-over series, then sweeping all five T20 games. Teenage opening batsman Shafali Verma shone in the first two 20-over wins, in St Lucia, scoring 73 and 69 not out from a total of 84 balls; she hit all eight of India's sixes in the series. Their spinners proved unplayable during the T20s: Deepti Sharma took eight wickets at 5.62, Radha Yadav seven at 7.71, and Anuja Patil five at 4.80. For West Indies, no one averaged 20 with the bat, while only Afy Fletcher conceded less than a run a ball. They badly missed their injured captain, Stafanie Taylor, who had shone during the one-day series, with 193 runs.

First one-day international   At North Sound, Antigua, November 1, 2019 (day/night). **West Indies won by one run.** ‡**West Indies 225-7** (50 overs) (N. Y. McLean 51, S. R. Taylor 94, C. N. Nation 43); **India 224** (50 overs) (P. S. Punia 75, J. I. Rodrigues 41; A. Mohammed 5-46). *PoM:* S. R. Taylor. *ODI debuts:* A. A. Alleyne, S. Hector (West Indies). *Anisa Mohammed's off-breaks bowled West Indies to the narrowest of wins, only their fifth in 23 ODIs against India, and their first in seven years. At 170-2 in the 40th over needing a further 56, India were comfortable, only to lose eight for 54, including three in their final eight balls. With two wanted off the last, No. 11 Poonam Yadav was caught by Stacy-Ann King, giving Mohammed – who had taken only one ODI wicket since October 2017 – her sixth five-for, and lifting her past 150 in the format. There were also two thrifty wickets for captain Stafanie Taylor, who had earlier hit 94 from 91 – the backbone of West Indies' 225-7. Priya Punia replied with 75, but her dismissal triggered India's collapse.*

Second one-day international   At North Sound, Antigua, November 3, 2019 (day/night). **India won by 53 runs.** ‡**India 191-6** (50 overs) (P. G. Raut 77, M. D. Raj 40, H. Kaur 46); **West Indies 138** (47.2 overs) (S. A. Campbelle 39). *PoM:* P. G. Raut. *West Indies suffered a collapse of their own – eight for 60 – as India drew level. Though they had lost both openers cheaply, Punam Raut steadily rebuilt the Indian innings, before Harmanpreet Kaur upped the tempo. In reply, West Indian opener Natasha McLean was stretchered off after tweaking a hamstring but, at 78-1 in the 25th, the hosts were in control. Poonam Yadav removed Taylor and Chedean Nation with her economical leg-breaks, however, and West Indies' composure deserted them.*

Third one-day international   At North Sound, Antigua, November 6, 2019. **India won by six wickets.** ‡**West Indies 194** (50 overs) (S. R. Taylor 79, S. C. King 38); **India 195-4** (42.1 overs) (J. I. Rodrigues 69, S. S. Mandhana 74; H. K. Matthews 3-27). *PoM:* S. R. Taylor. *PoS:* S. R. Taylor. *India sealed the series after a powerful opening stand of 141 in 25 overs between Jemimah Rodrigues and Smriti Mandhana (74 off 63 on her return from a foot injury). Mandhana reached 2,000 ODI runs in her 51st innings; only the Australian duo of Belinda Clark (38 innings) and Meg Lanning (45) had got there more quickly. Later, Raut also passed 2,000 (in her 67th). West Indies had been 84-5, before Taylor and King put on 96, but the last five tumbled for 14.*

Women's Championship: India 4pts, West Indies 2pts.

First Twenty20 international   At Gros Islet, St Lucia, November 9, 2019 (floodlit). **India won by 84 runs. India 185-4** (20 overs) (S. Verma 73, S. S. Mandhana 67); ‡**West Indies 101-9** (20 overs) (S. A. Campbelle 33). *PoM:* S. Verma. *T20I debut:* A. A. Alleyne (West Indies).. *Fifteen-year-old Shafali Verma bludgeoned West Indies with 73 off 49 balls, including four sixes, in an opening stand of 143 in 15.3 overs with Mandhana – an Indian all-wicket record. Seamer Chinelle Henry's only over cost 26 (Verma 24, plus two wides). Mandhana chipped in with 11 fours in her 46-ball 67, but was missed four times in a sloppy fielding display. India's 185-4 equalled the most West Indies had conceded in a T20I (New Zealand made 185-3 at Mount Maunganui in March 2018). The chase was a non-event: Shemaine Campbelle made 33, but no one else passed 13. Radha Yadav, a 19-year-old slow left-armer, took 2-10 from her four overs.*

Second Twenty20 international   At Gros Islet, St Lucia, November 10, 2019. **India won by ten wickets.** ‡**West Indies 103-7** (20 overs) (C. N. Nation 32; D. B. Sharma 4-10); **India 104-0**

(10.3 overs) (S. Verma 69*, S. S. Mandhana 30*). *PoM:* D. B. Sharma. *Verma flourished for the second time in two days, battering 69* off 35, with ten fours and two sixes, in another decisive opening stand with Mandhana – 104* in 10.3 overs. Henry's lone over this time cost 18. Earlier, Deepti Sharma had claimed a career-best 4-10 with her off-spin as West Indies stuttered to 103-7. India's second ten-wicket T20 win was West Indies' first such defeat.*

Third Twenty20 international At Providence, Guyana, November 14, 2019 (floodlit). **India won by seven wickets.** ‡**West Indies 59-9** (20 overs); **India 60-3** (16.4 overs) (J. I. Rodrigues 40*). *PoM:* J. I. Rodrigues. *India clinched the series with ease after limiting West Indies to 59-9, their lowest 20-over score, undercutting 70-8 against England at Hove in 2012. Only Nation and Henry, both with 11, reached double figures, while the spin-bowling Yadavs, Radha and Poonam, took 3-14 in eight overs. The previously prolific Verma then fell third ball, and Mandhana for three, before Rodrigues completed the formalities.*

Fourth Twenty20 international At Providence, Guyana, November 17, 2019. **India won by five runs. India 50-7** (9 overs) (H. K. Matthews 3-13); ‡**West Indies 45-5** (9 overs). *PoM:* H. K. Matthews. *Rain meant a nine-over scrap, but nothing could stop India. Hayley Matthews did her best, claiming three wickets in six balls with her off-breaks after India opted to bowl. Leg-spinner Fletcher took 2-2 from her two overs. But, chasing a modest 51, the hosts got in a tangle against India's slow bowlers, and 13 off the last, from off-spinner Anuja Patil, proved beyond them.*

Fifth Twenty20 international At Providence, Guyana, November 20, 2019 (floodlit). **India won by 61 runs.** ‡**India 134-3** (20 overs) (J. I. Rodrigues 50, V. Krishnamurthy 57*); **West Indies 73-7** (20 overs). *PoM:* V. Krishnamurthy. *PoS:* S. Verma. *India completed a 5–0 hammering after Veda Krishnamurthy, whose 57* was the higher of her two T20I half-centuries (from 56 innings), and Rodrigues added 117 for their third wicket. West Indies, by now demoralised, barely put up a fight with the bat, Patil claiming 3-2 from three overs after opening the bowling.*

PAKISTAN v ENGLAND IN MALAYSIA IN 2019-20

One-day internationals (3): Pakistan 0, England 2
Twenty20 internationals (3): Pakistan 0, England 3

England wrapped up their ICC Championship programme with a trip to Kuala Lumpur to face a Pakistan side who were battling for a place in the top four, and automatic qualification for the 2021 World Cup. Rain robbed Heather Knight's team of a 3–0 win, though they still ensured no one could overtake their second place in the table. They then managed a whitewash in the 20-over games, batting first each time, with Amy Jones totalling 179 runs from 126 balls. Leg-spinner Sarah Glenn performed well in her debut series, which was overseen by assistant coach Ali Maiden ahead of the full-time appointment of Australian Lisa Keightley, in Malaysia from the second ODI on a watching brief. For Pakistan, captain Bismah Maroof battled hard to make three sixties.

ENGLAND TOURING PARTY

*H. C. Knight (Berkshire), T. T. Beaumont (Kent), K. H. Brunt (Yorkshire), K. L. Cross (Lancashire), F. R. Davies (Sussex), S. Ecclestone (Lancashire), S. Glenn (Worcestershire), K. L. Gordon (Nottinghamshire), A. E. Jones (Warwickshire), N. R. Sciver (Surrey), A. Shrubsole (Berkshire), M. K. Villiers (Essex), F. C. Wilson (Kent), L. Winfield (Yorkshire), D. N. Wyatt (Sussex). *Coach:* A. J. Maiden.

First one-day international At Kuala Lumpur, December 9, 2019. **England won by 75 runs.** ‡**England 284-6** (50 overs) (T. T. Beaumont 107, D. N. Wyatt 110, H. C. Knight 41; Rameen Shamim 3-61); **Pakistan 209** (44.4 overs) (Bismah Maroof 69, Aliya Riaz 39; K. L. Cross 4-32). *PoM:* D. N. Wyatt. *ODI debuts:* Rameen Shamim (Pakistan); S. Glenn (England). *England's victory was based on their highest opening partnership for more than three years – 188 in 34 overs between Tammy Beaumont, who scored her seventh ODI century, and Danielle Wyatt, who scored her first,* *from just 86 balls. They were England's first overseas one-day hundreds for six years. Only 96 followed from the remaining 16 overs, but Pakistan lost both openers cheaply, and Bismah Maroof alone hung around after that, helping her side to their first total of 200 against England (they would do it again three days later). Kate Cross finished with four wickets, and 20-year-old debutante leg-spinner Sarah Glenn two, while Katherine Brunt became the first England bowler – and the sixth in all – to reach 150 in ODIs when she trapped Nida Dar.*

Second one-day international   At Kuala Lumpur, December 12, 2019. **England won by 127 runs. ‡England 327-4** (50 overs) (H. C. Knight 86, N. R. Sciver 100*, F. C. Wilson 85*); **Pakistan 200** (44.5 overs) (Nahida Khan 40, Bismah Maroof 64). *PoM:* H. C. Knight. *Nat Sciver became England's third centurion of the series to set up their tenth win in ten ODIs against Pakistan, and clinch the series. She finished with 100* from 85 balls, and added 146* in 14.1 overs with Fran Wilson, who hit a career-best 85* from 49. Earlier, captain Heather Knight made 86. Pakistan reached a steady 101-2 in reply, only to lose eight for 99 – including Maroof, who top-scored again, with 64.*

Third one-day international   At Kuala Lumpur, December 14, 2019. **No result. Pakistan 145-8** (37.4 overs) (Nahida Khan 55, Javeria Khan 37; A. Shrubsole 3-32, S. Glenn 4-18) **v ‡England.** *PoS:* H. C. Knight. *ODI debuts:* Kaynat Hafeez (Pakistan); F. R. Davies (England). *Rain spared Pakistan a likely 3–0 whitewash, earning them a point that lifted them to fourth in the ICC Women's Championship. They had been well placed at 96-0 off 20 overs – a record for Pakistan's first wicket – only to slip to 145-8 off 37.4 before the weather intervened. Glenn and Anya Shrubsole shared seven wickets, while Freya Davies conceded only 19 in seven overs on her ODI debut.*

Women's Championship: England 5pts, Pakistan 1pt.

First Twenty20 international   At Kuala Lumpur, December 17, 2019. **England won by 29 runs. England 154-4** (20 overs) (A. E. Jones 53, T. T. Beaumont 30, N. R. Sciver 34*); **‡Pakistan 125** (18.4 overs) (Bismah Maroof 60; S. Ecclestone 3-21). *PoM:* A. E. Jones. *T20I debuts:* Syeda Aroob Shah (Pakistan); S. Glenn (England). *England carried on their dominance from the 50-over series, with Amy Jones biffing ten fours in a 39-ball 53, and Davies removing both Pakistan openers for ducks. Maroof made another sixty, but only two others reached double figures as Sophie Ecclestone collected three wickets.*

Second Twenty20 international   At Kuala Lumpur, December 19, 2019. **England won by 84 runs. ‡England 185-5** (20 overs) (A. E. Jones 89, D. N. Wyatt 55); **Pakistan 101-9** (20 overs) (Iram Javed 38). *PoM:* A. E. Jones. *Another big opening stand set up another big England win, as Jones (89 off 52) and Wyatt (55 off 36, in her 100th T20I) began with 120 in 11.2 overs. From there, England should have made more than 185-5, but Pakistan's reply was a non-event, handing the tourists another unassailable lead.*

Third Twenty20 international   At Kuala Lumpur, December 20, 2019. **England won by 26 runs. ‡England 170-3** (20 overs) (A. E. Jones 37, H. C. Knight 43); **Pakistan 144-5** (20 overs) (Javeria Khan 57*). *PoM:* A. E. Jones. *This time, there was no rain around to deprive England of a 3–0 win. Their innings was a model of consistency, all five who batted scoring between 23 and 43. Javeria Khan resisted to the tune of 57* from 46 balls, but Pakistan were never up with the rate, despite managing their highest T20 total against England. Glenn and Ecclestone had combined figures of 6–19–24–3.*

WOMEN'S T20 WORLD CUP QUALIFIER IN 2019

1 Bangladesh   2 Thailand

Eight teams assembled in soggy Scotland in August, to fight it out over two places in the T20 World Cup, to be played in Australia in February and March 2020. Bangladesh, who won the final, were hardly surprise qualifiers – but the other big winners were Thailand, who had never reached a global tournament in any sport before, men's or women's.

Thailand's success was based on a strong attack, led by seamer Chanida Sutthiruang, who took most wickets (12), and went for just above four an over. Fielding an unchanged side throughout, Thailand did not concede a three-figure total until the final, with qualification assured. They bowled Namibia out for 61, then – to top the group – restricted Ireland to 90 for nine after making only 92 for seven themselves in a rain-affected match in Dundee. In the vital semi-final, Papua New Guinea cobbled together only 67 in their 20 overs, and the gleeful Thais were Australia-bound. "We have worked hard all year, and planned well," said their captain, Sornnarin Tippoch. Her side would face rather sterner tests against England, Pakistan, South Africa and West Indies in the tournament proper.

Bangladesh had the best all-round side: slow left-armer Nahida Akter took ten wickets at six apiece, while Sanjida Islam scored 156 runs. Their captain, Salma Khatun, was delighted to take the trophy, but admitted: "Our mission next time is to avoid having to qualify."

Sanjida's aggregate was exceeded only by Scotland's captain Kathryn Bryce, with 168 (her younger sister, Sarah, was next, with 121). Unfortunately for the hosts, the sisters were doing it mainly by themselves, and Scotland finished fifth: no one else made 50 runs, and Bryce senior led the bowling with eight wickets, although 14-year-old Katherine Fraser managed six.

Arguably the most disappointed to miss out were Ireland, whose narrow defeat by Thailand condemned them to a semi against Bangladesh. A young side performed well in their first tournament for many years without either of the Joyce twins, Cecelia or Isobel. But there was still a reassuring Joyce presence: brother Ed was the coach.

For the first time, the ICC appointed an all-female panel of umpires. It included the former England Test player Sue Redfern, and the South African Lauren Agenbag – who was, at 23, younger than many of the players.

NATIONAL SQUADS

Bangladesh   *Salma Khatun, Avasha Rahman, Fahima Khatun, Farzana Haque, Jahanara Alam, Khadija Tul Kubra, Murshida Khatun, Nahida Akter, Nigar Sultana, Ritu Moni, Sanjida Islam, Shaila Sharmin, Shamima Sultana, Sobhana Mostary. *Coach:* A. Jain.

Ireland   *L. K. Delany, K. J. Garth, S. M. Kavanagh, G. H. Lewis, L. Little, S. MacMahon, L. Maritz, L. Paul, O. Prendergast, C. Raack, U. Raymond-Huey, E. A. J. Richardson, R. Stokell, M. V. Waldron. *Coach:* E. C. Joyce.

Namibia *Y. Khan, J. A. Diergaardt, M. P. Enright, D. Foerster, M. Gorases, K. Green, V. H. Hamunyela, E. Kejarukua, R. Khan, W. N. Mwatile, S. N. Shihepo, A. van der Merwe, I. van Zyl, S. A. Wittmann. *Coach:* L. Nhamburo.

Netherlands *J. Post, L. K. Bennett, C. A. de Lange, B. J. A. de Leede, S. L. Kalis, H. W. A. Landheer, E. N. Lynch, F. Overdijk, R. Rijke, H. D. J. Siegers, S. N. L. Siegers, D. van Deventer, M. Veringmeier, I. J. R. Zwilling. *Coach:* S. Trouw.

Papua New Guinea *K. Arua, N. M. Ambo, V. Araa, G. Buruka, V. K. Frank, N. Ila, S. L. Jimmy, R. Oa, K. H. Oala, T. Ruma, B. H. Tau, M. Tom, I. Toua, N. N. Vare. *Coach:* R. Dikana.

Scotland *K. E. Bryce, A. Aitken, S. J. Bryce, P. A. Chatterji, K. J. G. Fraser, R. S. Glen, R. V. Hawkins, L. Jack, M. J. McColl, K. McGill, A. M. Maqsood, H. R. A. Rainey, E. L. Watson, R. K. Willis. *Coach:* S. T. Knox.

Thailand *S. Tippoch, N. Boochatham, N. Chaiwai, N. Chantham, O. Kamchomphu, R. Kanoh, N. Koncharoenkai, S. Laomi, S. Lateh, W. Liengprasert, P. Maya, R. Padunglerd, C. Sutthiruang, A. Yenyueak. *Coach:* J. C. Gamage.

United States of America *S. Sriharsha, C. Beckford, S. M. Bhaskar, S. K. Chandhrasekar, S. Farooq, N. T. Gruny, U. Iftikhar, M. Kandanala, G. Kodali, S. Ramautar, L. Ramjit, A. G. Rao, E. H. Rendler, O. T. Wallerson. *Coach:* J. C. Price.

WOMEN'S T20 WORLD CUP QUALIFIER TABLES

Group A	P	W	L	Pts	NRR	Group B	P	W	L	Pts	NRR
BANGLADESH	3	3	0	6	2.82	THAILAND	3	3	0	6	1.52
PAPUA NEW GUINEA	3	2	1	4	0.44	IRELAND	3	2	1	4	0.90
Scotland	3	1	2	2	0.37	Netherlands	3	1	2	2	−0.61
USA	3	0	3	0	−3.06	Namibia	3	0	3	0	−1.50

Semi-final At Dundee, September 5. **Bangladesh won by four wickets.** ‡**Ireland 85** (20 overs) (Fahima Khatun 3-18); **Bangladesh 86-6** (18.3 overs) (Sanjida Islam 32*). *PoM:* Sanjida Islam. *Bangladesh clinched a place at the T20 World Cup with a nervy victory. Ireland looked out of it at 44-5 in the 14th over, but captain Laura Delany (25) and Eimear Richardson (25) gave them something to bowl at. Bangladesh also made a poor start, and were 30-4 in the ninth – but Sanjida Islam hauled them back into it with 32*, putting on 38 with Ritu Moni, and clinched qualification with nine to spare.*

Semi-final At Dundee, September 5. **Thailand won by eight wickets.** ‡**Papua New Guinea 67-7** (20 overs); **Thailand 68-2** (17.3 overs) (N. Chaiwai 32). *PoM:* S. Laomi (Thailand). *Disciplined bowling, Thailand's stock-in-trade, set up the chance to qualify for Australia. PNG found it almost impossible to score: they managed just three boundaries, and Kaia Arua's 16* was one of only three double-figure contributions. Leg-spinner Suleeporn Laomi took 1-5 in her four overs, while captain Sornnarin Tippoch's off-breaks yielded 0-12; the new-ball pair of Chanida Sutthiruang (2-15) and Nattaya Boochatham (0-18) were also miserly. Thailand's batters went steadily towards their modest target, Naruemol Chaiwai falling only when her team were in touching distance of the big prize.*

Final At Dundee, September 7. **Bangladesh won by 70 runs.** ‡**Bangladesh 130-5** (20 overs) (Sanjida Islam 71*, Murshida Khatun 33); **Thailand 60-7** (20 overs). *PoM:* Sanjida Islam. *PoT:* C. Sutthiruang (Thailand). *Bangladesh took the title with a convincing all-round display. Openers Sanjida Islam and Murshida Khatun started with 68 in ten overs; Sanjida's 71* from 60 balls was the highest score of the tournament outside the lower play-offs. Now it was Thailand's turn to have difficulty getting the ball off the square: in the 15th over they were 41-4, at which point three wickets went down without addition.*

Final standings

1 Bangladesh. 2 Thailand. 3 Ireland. 4 Papua New Guinea. 5 Scotland. 6 Netherlands. 7 USA. 8 Namibia.

Bangladesh and Thailand qualified for the 2019-20 T20 World Cup.

OTHER WOMEN'S TWENTY20 INTERNATIONALS

Mali and Co

STEVEN LYNCH

Parts of *Wisden's* Records section took one helluva beating in 2019, thanks to the ICC's decision to give official status to all T20 international matches between member countries. Particularly hit was the list of the lowest women's scores: the ten smallest were all made last year, five by Mali. They were all out for six against Rwanda in June, a new low equalled by the Maldives against Bangladesh during the South Asian Games in December. Two days later, the Maldives managed eight – including seven wides – against Nepal.

Mali made it to ten against Uganda, but still ended up on top of other tables. They were replying to 314 for two, the highest in men's or women's T20Is; the victory margin of 304 runs was another dizzying best (or worst).

It's easy to be sniffy about Mali's presence, and plenty were – but there is an uplifting backstory to their international appearances, teased out by *The Cricketer's* Sam Morshead. He discovered that, in 2001, an English teacher had suggested cricket as a way to encourage Malian children to learn the language. By chance, his school included four English pupils, who passed on their knowledge of the game. Before long, it was being played in outposts up the River Niger, and a federation was recognised by the ICC in 2005. But there are no proper grounds, which is an obstacle to funding, as well as improving playing standards. Ten of the team in the Rwanda tournament had played their first competitive matches only two months previously. The federation president thought of withdrawing the team after the early shellackings, but the captain, Youma Sangare, talked him out of it: "Mr President, we came for this game. Even if we have to die, we play."

No one died. And Sangare collected the fair-play award on behalf of her team, which meant they returned home with some silverware.

At a slightly more exalted level, there was a surprise at the T20 World Cup Qualifier, when Thailand joined Bangladesh at the main event, edging out Ireland, Papua New Guinea and hosts Scotland. A few weeks earlier in August, Thailand had warmed up by winning a four-way tournament in the Netherlands, again featuring Ireland and Scotland.

Elsewhere, Brazil upset old rivals Argentina in the final of the South American Championships, played in Peru. They were celebrating even more when the board managed to fund central contracts.

Nepal's Anjali Chand, an off-spinner, started her international career with six for none – a new T20I best – against the Maldives. She came up against them two matches later in a South Asian Games play-off: this time she took four for one. In between, a wicketless over against Bangladesh meant Chand's figures after the tournament were ten for four, at an average of 0.40.

ICC WOMEN'S CHAMPIONSHIP IN 2017–2020

In 2014, the ICC introduced a women's Championship as a qualifying tournament for the World Cup, and to create a more meaningful programme for the leading teams. Australia won the first edition, which ended in November 2016, and by the start of 2020 were assured of winning the second.

Each of the eight sides from the previous World Cup play each other in three one-day internationals over two and a half years (they can arrange more games if they choose, but only the designated three carry points). New Zealand, the hosts of the next World Cup, in early 2021, and the other top four in the final table will advance directly to the tournament, while the remaining three will contest a further qualifier with seven others. At the end of January 2020, three series remained: South Africa v Australia, Sri Lanka v New Zealand, and India v Pakistan.

As in the previous cycle, India declined to play Pakistan; then, the ICC awarded the six points for the series to Pakistan, but this time India argued that, as their government would not permit them to play, the points should be split. This decision would settle which of the two would claim the fifth guaranteed World Cup place, alongside Australia, England, South Africa and New Zealand.

QUALIFYING TABLE

	P	W	L	T	NR	Pts	NRR
AUSTRALIA	18	17	1	0	0	34	1.83
ENGLAND	21	14	6	0	1	29	1.26
SOUTH AFRICA..	18	10	6	1	1	22	−0.30
India.............	18	10	8	0	0	20	0.46
Pakistan..........	18	7	9	1	1	16	−0.46
NEW ZEALAND..	18	7	11	0	0	14	−0.20
West Indies	21	6	14	0	1	13	−1.03
Sri Lanka.........	18	1	17	0	0	2	−1.61

As at March 1, 2020.

MRF TYRES ICC WOMEN'S RANKINGS

In 2015, the ICC introduced a table of women's international rankings, which combined results from Tests, one-day internationals and Twenty20 internationals. In 2018, after Twenty20 international status was extended to all Associate women's teams, this was replaced by separate rankings for one-day and Twenty20 cricket. All rankings are at December 31, 2019.

ONE-DAY INTERNATIONAL TEAM RANKINGS

		Matches	Points	Rating
1	Australia	26	3,945	152
2	India............	30	3,747	125
3	England	29	3,568	123
4	New Zealand	23	2,533	110
5	South Africa	33	3,154	96
6	West Indies	24	1,979	82
7	Pakistan.........	25	1,835	73
8	Sri Lanka	22	1,208	55
9	Bangladesh	10	542	54
10	Ireland	6	110	18

TWENTY20 INTERNATIONAL TEAM RANKINGS

		Matches	*Points*	*Rating*
1	Australia	25	7,331	293
2	England	25	7,010	280
3	New Zealand	18	4,963	276
4	India	33	8,566	260
5	West Indies	27	6,708	248
6	South Africa	24	5,776	241
7	Pakistan	31	7,080	228
8	Sri Lanka	22	4,420	201
9	Bangladesh	29	5,641	195
10	Ireland	22	3,622	165
11	Thailand	41	6,582	161
12	Zimbabwe	20	3,153	158

Remaining rankings: 13 Scotland (145), 14 Nepal (129), 15 Papua New Guinea (126), 16 United Arab Emirates (122), 17 Uganda (121), 18 Samoa (121), 19 Tanzania (101), 20 Kenya (92), 21 Netherlands (86), 22 Indonesia (82), 23 Hong Kong (74), 24 Namibia (70), 25 China (68), 26 Japan (54), 27 Vanuatu (49), 28 Belize (45), 29 Malaysia (44), 30 Rwanda (43), 31 Myanmar (42), 32 Argentina (42), 33 USA (41), 34 Botswana (41), 35 Jersey (40), 36 Brazil (39), 37 Kuwait (39), 38 Sierra Leone (39), 39 France (37), 40 Germany (33), 41 Nigeria (30), 42 Denmark (28), 43 South Korea (18), 44 Bhutan (17), 45 Malawi (16), 46 Chile (12), 47 Mexico (10), 48 Austria (9), 49 Costa Rica (9), 50 Mozambique (8), 51 Belgium (7), 52 Singapore (1), 53= Fiji (0), Lesotho (0), Mali (0), Norway (0), Peru (0).

PLAYER RANKINGS

In October 2008, the ICC launched a set of rankings for women cricketers, on the same principles as those for men, based on one-day international performances. Twenty20 rankings were added in September 2012. There are no Test rankings.

The leading players in the women's one-day international rankings on December 31, 2019, were:

	Batsmen	*Points*		*Bowlers*	*Points*
1	A. E. Satterthwaite (NZ)	759	1	J. L. Jonassen (A.)	755
2	S. R. Taylor (WI)	748	2	M. Schutt (A.)	731
3	A. J. Healy (A.)	738	3	E. A. Perry (A.)	710
4	E. A. Perry (A.)	737	4	M. Kapp (SA)	708
5	S. S. Mandhana (I.)	735	5	J. N. Goswami (I.)	692
6	M. M. Lanning (A.)	719	6	S. Ismail (SA)	688
7	T. T. Beaumont (E)	718	7	P. Yadav (I.)	680
8	M. D. Raj (I.)	689	8	S. S. Pandey (I.)	676
9	L. Wolvaardt (SA)	685	9	Sana Mir (P.)	663
10	S. F. M. Devine (NZ)	683	10	A. Shrubsole (E)	645
	S. W. Bates (NZ)	683			

The leading players in the women's Twenty20 international rankings on December 31, 2019, were:

	Batsmen	*Points*		*Bowlers*	*Points*
1	S. W. Bates (NZ)	768	1	M. Schutt (A.)	773
2	M. M. Lanning (A.)	740	2	R. P. Yadav (I.)	769
3	A. J. Healy (A.)	717	3	S. Ismail (SA)	751
4	J. I. Rodrigues (I.)	699	4	S. Ecclestone (E)	727
5	B. L. Mooney (A.)	692	5	D. B. Sharma (I.)	726
6	S. F. M. Devine (NZ)	670	6	P. Yadav (I.)	716
7	S. S. Mandhana (I.)	669	7	L. M. Kasperek (NZ)	696
8	S. R. Taylor (WI)	649	8	J. L. Jonassen (A.)	678
9	L. Lee (SA)	636	9	A. S. S. Fletcher (WI)	677
	H. Kaur (I.)	636	10	A. C. Kerr (NZ)	674

WOMEN'S ONE-DAY INTERNATIONAL AVERAGES IN CALENDAR YEAR 2019

BATTING (200 runs)

		M	I	NO	R	HS	100	50	Avge	SR	4	6
1	E. A. Perry (A)	12	11	5	441	112*	2	2	73.50	81.06	36	3
2	S. S. Mandhana (I)	7	7	1	423	105	1	4	70.50	94.63	49	9
3	†A. E. Satterthwaite (NZ). .	6	6	1	346	92	0	3	69.20	80.27	34	1
4	A. J. Healy (A)	12	12	1	669	122	2	5	60.81	110.03	95	9
5	M. M. Lanning (A)	11	11	2	477	121	1	3	53.00	85.33	58	5
6	†B. L. Mooney (A)	12	10	3	332	66	0	2	47.42	81.17	31	1
7	S. R. Taylor (WI)	12	11	1	472	94	0	5	47.20	64.21	37	6
8	H. C. Knight (E)	15	14	4	469	94	0	3	46.90	81.00	54	2
9	N. R. Sciver (E)	14	12	1	479	100*	1	3	43.54	89.53	55	2
10	T. T. Beaumont (E).	15	14	0	601	114	2	2	42.92	78.66	73	2
11	M. D. Raj (I)	12	11	3	338	66	0	2	42.25	58.27	34	2
12	L. Wolvaardt (SA)	9	9	1	335	74*	0	4	41.87	71.88	38	0
13	P. G. Raut (I)	8	8	0	307	77	0	3	38.37	56.64	29	1
14	†R. L. Haynes (A)	12	12	0	450	118	1	3	37.50	73.52	46	3
15	Nahida Khan (P)	11	11	1	331	68	0	3	33.10	78.80	41	0
16	†A. M. C. Jayangani (SL). .	9	9	0	297	103	1	1	33.00	73.51	41	3
17	A. E. Jones (E)	15	14	0	444	91	0	5	31.71	96.73	47	10
18	†Bismah Maroof (P)	10	10	1	273	69	0	2	30.33	76.90	32	0
19	J. I. Rodrigues (I)	12	12	1	327	81*	0	3	29.72	72.66	42	1
20	Javeria Khan (P)	11	11	1	286	74	0	1	28.60	59.45	38	0
21	D. N. Wyatt (E)	13	11	1	282	110	1	1	28.20	95.59	27	4
22	H. M. D. Samarawickrama (SL)	9	9	0	240	42	0	0	26.66	66.29	25	1
23	Sidra Ameen (P)	9	9	0	221	96	0	2	24.55	52.61	25	0
24	Aliya Riaz (P)	11	10	0	220	71	0	1	22.00	70.73	24	5

BOWLING (10 wickets)

		Style	O	M	R	W	BB	4I	Avge	SR	ER
1	J. L. Jonassen (A)	SLA	92.5	11	290	23	5-27	3	12.60	24.21	3.12
2	E. A. Perry (A)	RFM	75	13	284	21	7-22	1	13.52	21.42	3.78
3	E. K. Bisht (I)	SLA	74	3	286	17	4-25	1	16.82	26.11	3.86
4	K. L. Cross (E)	RFM	75	10	291	17	4-32	1	17.11	26.47	3.88
5	Sana Mir (P)	OB	73.3	9	262	15	4-11	1	17.46	29.40	3.56
6	M. M. Klaas (SA)	RFM	39.2	1	192	10	3-27	0	19.20	23.60	4.88
7	H. K. Matthews (WI)	OB	33.1	1	193	10	4-57	1	19.30	19.90	5.81
8	K. H. Brunt (E)	RFM	75.3	7	273	14	5-28	1	19.50	32.35	3.61
9	A. Shrubsole (E)	RFM	114.2	16	431	22	3-32	0	19.59	31.18	3.76
10	M. Schutt (A)	RFM	87.5	12	315	16	3-24	0	19.68	32.93	3.58
11	S. S. Pandey (I)	RM	95.4	8	359	18	4-18	1	19.94	31.88	3.75
12	P. Yadav (I)	LB	101.5	9	380	19	3-42	0	20.00	32.15	3.73
13	J. N. Goswami (I)	RFM	95.2	7	362	18	4-30	1	20.11	31.77	3.79
14	M. Kapp (SA)	RFM	72	10	271	12	3-20	0	22.58	36.00	3.76
15	Diana Baig (P)	RFM	51	5	246	10	4-34	1	24.60	30.60	4.82
16	A. K. Gardner (A)	OB	83	7	304	12	3-49	0	25.33	41.50	3.66
17	L. A. Marsh (E)	OB	69	2	279	11	3-30	0	25.36	37.63	4.04
18	G. L. Wareham (A)	LB	94	5	385	15	2-18	0	25.66	37.60	4.09
19	S. Ecclestone (E)	SLA	94.1	6	376	14	3-30	0	26.85	40.35	3.99
20	A. S. S. Fletcher (WI)	LB	92.5	3	421	15	3-17	0	28.06	37.13	4.53
21	D. B. Sharma (I)	OB	107.2	8	422	15	2-24	0	28.13	42.93	3.93
22	Nashra Sandhu (P)	SLA	92.3	6	361	12	3-21	0	30.08	46.25	3.90

WOMEN'S TWENTY20 INTERNATIONAL AVERAGES IN CALENDAR YEAR 2019

BATTING (275 runs)

		M	I	NO	R	HS	100	50	Avge	SR	4	6
1	A. J. Healy (A)	9	9	2	372	148*	1	1	53.14	173.02	54	11
2	L. Lee (SA)	9	9	1	318	84	0	4	39.75	139.47	50	4
3	A. E. Jones (E)	12	12	0	377	89	0	3	31.41	130.90	50	6
4	D. N. Wyatt (E)	13	13	1	422	81	0	4	35.16	129.05	45	10
5	†S. S. Mandhana (I)	14	14	1	405	86	0	4	31.15	124.61	54	8
6	S. J. Bryce (Scot)	15	15	4	349	65	0	2	31.72	116.72	40	3
7	F. O. Kibasu (Tanzania)	10	10	4	324	108*	1	2	54.00	110.58	35	0
8	Y. Angraeni (Indonesia)	17	15	1	373	112	1	1	26.64	110.02	53	0
9	T. T. Beaumont (E)	13	13	5	318	62	0	2	39.75	109.27	32	3
10	†Bismah Maroof (P)	14	14	3	459	70*	0	4	41.72	108.00	52	1
11	E. R. Oza (UAE)	11	11	1	296	82	0	2	29.60	106.47	37	1
12	Nigar Sultana (B)	13	12	5	309	113*	1	0	44.14	101.31	30	4
13	J. I. Rodrigues (I)	15	13	1	302	72	0	2	25.16	98.05	31	1
14	S. L. Kalis (Neth)	12	12	1	325	126*	1	0	29.54	94.47	32	5
15	R. Musamali (Uganda)	14	13	5	276	103*	1	0	34.50	93.87	27	0
16	K. J. Garth (Ire)	11	11	3	335	51*	0	1	41.87	93.83	31	2
17	N. Chantham (Thai)	24	24	7	498	69*	0	2	29.29	90.38	56	1
18	†B. H. Tau (PNG)	17	15	5	320	62*	0	1	32.00	90.14	35	2
19	M. Mupachikwa (Z)	13	13	1	355	75*	0	2	29.58	83.13	39	0
20	N. Chaiwai (Thai)	25	25	9	517	64*	0	2	25.85	80.78	39	0
21	R. S. M. Lili'i (Samoa)	12	12	5	323	51	0	1	46.14	77.83	31	2
22	A. van der Merwe (Nam)	19	19	3	345	53*	0	1	21.56	76.83	23	0

BOWLING (17 wickets)

		Style	O	M	R	W	BB	4I	Avge	SR	ER
1	A. C. Mushangwe (Z)	LB	54.5	6	143	23	3-6	0	6.21	14.30	2.60
2	T. S. Granger (Z)	OB	29	4	83	17	3-11	0	4.88	10.23	2.86
3	N. M. P. Suwandewi (Indonesia)	RM	58	9	181	18	5-8	1	10.05	19.33	3.12
4	S. Tippoch (Thai)	OB	76	6	243	31	4-4	2	7.83	14.70	3.19
5	N. Boochatham (Thai)	RFM	76.2	7	247	40	4-3	2	6.17	11.45	3.23
6	N. Thapa (Nepal)	LFM	32.3	2	105	17	6-8	2	6.17	11.47	3.23
7	S. Laomi (Thai)	LB	83.2	8	270	37	4-9	1	7.29	13.51	3.24
8	K. Y. Chan (HK)	LM	49.3	7	167	22	5-7	1	7.59	13.50	3.37
9	Nahida Akter (B)	SLA	30.1	4	102	19	4-11	1	5.36	9.52	3.38
10	Chan Ka Man (HK)	OB	48.5	6	166	21	3-13	0	7.90	13.95	3.39
11	C. Sutthiruang (Thai)	RM	74.1	7	254	34	5-4	2	7.47	13.08	3.42
12	S. L. Jimmy (PNG)	OB	56	1	210	19	4-13	1	11.05	17.68	3.75
13	L. S. Mulivai (Samoa)	RM	45.1	2	170	17	4-18	1	10.00	15.94	3.76
14	N. K. F. Rada Rani (Indonesia)	RM	52.1	5	201	21	4-11	1	9.57	14.90	3.85
15	K. Arua (PNG)	SLW	51.3	2	199	20	5-7	1	9.95	15.45	3.86
16	O. Kamchomphu (Thai)	OB	47.4	0	185	23	4-6	2	8.04	12.43	3.88
17	Han Lili (China)	LB	47.3	1	196	17	2-11	0	11.52	16.76	4.12
18	L. O. Telea (Samoa)	RM	41.4	4	176	22	3-8	0	8.00	11.36	4.22
19	R. Oa (PNG)	RM	59	3	257	24	5-13	3	10.70	14.75	4.35
20	T. Iosefo (Samoa)	RM	42.1	0	207	21	3-15	0	9.85	12.04	4.90
21	D. B. Sharma (I)	OB	51.1	4	263	19	4-10	1	13.84	16.15	5.14
22	R. P. Yadav (I)	SLA	48.5	3	277	21	3-23	0	13.19	13.95	5.67

WOMEN'S BIG BASH LEAGUE IN 2018-19

Adam Collins

1 Brisbane Heat   2 Sydney Sixers

The climax of the inaugural Women's Big Bash League in 2015-16 had been defined by dire catching. Fast-forward three years, and fielding was again a talking point – this time for all the right reasons. The semi-finals will be remembered for superb outfielding under pressure in the closing stages. And the final was a gem, with **Brisbane Heat** becoming the first non-Sydney team to win the title, in the process denying the Sixers a hat-trick.

Credit was also due to the organisers. Instead of the semi-finals and final being curtain-raisers to men's BBL games, they were standalone matches. The idyllic (and sold-out) Drummoyne Oval in the Sydney suburbs proved a perfect venue.

The Heat reached their first final after a dramatic conclusion to their game against **Sydney Thunder**, who needed five from the final ball. It looked as if Nicola Carey's slog-sweep had done the job, but Haidee Birkett sprinted around the rope to complete a stunning grab. The second semi-final, between **Sydney Sixers** and **Melbourne Renegades**, produced another thrilling climax. With the Renegades needing three off the last, Sophie Molineux slashed towards deep point, only for Erin Burns's outstretched hand to stop the ball just short of the rope. Sarah Aley threw in to wicketkeeper Alyssa Healy, whose dead-eye relay to the bowler's end ran out Molineux, and forced a tie. Ellyse Perry – who had a remarkable season – hit a six to settle the super over in the Sixers' favour.

But they could not repeat that escape in the final. Defying illness, Beth Mooney hit 65 off 46 balls for the Heat, and Laura Harris started the celebrations with the winning hit in the last over. Several players had made key contributions throughout the season. All-rounder Sammy-Jo Johnson took 20 wickets at 17, made 260 runs at a strike-rate of 139, and was the find of the summer. The Heat also leaned on the experience of Delissa Kimmince, joint-highest wicket-taker with 22 at 17, and Jess Jonassen, who took 15 with her slow left-armers.

Powered along by the extraordinary consistency of Perry, the Sixers had looked unstoppable. She amassed 778 runs – 222 more than Sophie Devine of Adelaide Strikers, the second-highest run-scorer – including two hundreds. Perry had attracted criticism for batting too conservatively in the World T20 in November, but there were no such gripes now. It was not all about one player, though: Healy also scored heavily, and Marizanne Kapp collected 20 wickets at 17, with an economy-rate of five.

There were 39 totals in excess of 150 – which was up 22 on the previous year – and six centuries, up by three. In addition to Perry and Healy, Mooney, Lizelle Lee and Grace Harris reached three figures. Harris's 42-ball hundred for the Heat against Melbourne Stars was the fastest in the competition's history, and the second-fastest in all women's T20 matches. There was a dramatic increase in the number of sixes, 270: up from 207 in 2017-18.

Perth Scorchers missed the finals again, even with Australian captain Meg Lanning in a line-up sprinkled with big names. **Adelaide Strikers** also failed to make the top four, despite a magnificent all-round season for Devine; apart from her runs, she claimed the competition's only five-for. Her fellow New Zealander Suzie Bates passed 400 runs, too. But, like the Scorchers, the Strikers' bowling was too leaky.

The bottom two positions were unchanged. **Melbourne Stars'** troubles were easy to diagnose: no one totalled 300, despite Lee's 55-ball hundred in their opening-day win over the Sixers. They beat them again, but there was little to cheer in between. **Hobart Hurricanes** got good returns from their overseas recruits Heather Knight and Smriti Mandhana, but not much else.

The new broadcasters Seven and Fox Sports got behind the tournament, and their average audience was 212,000. The aggregate match attendance was 135,861. Those figures were down on the previous season, but viewing of online clips rose to 3.8m.

WOMEN'S BIG BASH LEAGUE IN 2018-19

	P	W	L	NR	Pts	NRR
SYDNEY SIXERS	14	10	4	0	20	0.50
SYDNEY THUNDER	14	9	4	1	19	0.47
BRISBANE HEAT	14	9	5	0	18	1.11
MELBOURNE RENEGADES	14	7	6	1	15	−0.07
Perth Scorchers	14	7	7	0	14	−0.47
Adelaide Strikers	14	5	8	1	11	−0.33
Melbourne Stars	14	5	8	1	11	−0.90
Hobart Hurricanes	14	2	12	0	4	−0.36

Semi-final At Sydney (Drummoyne Oval), January 19, 2019. **Brisbane Heat won by four runs. Brisbane Heat 140-7** (20 overs) (S. J. Johnson 33, L. M. Harris 32*); ‡**Sydney Thunder 136-7** (20 overs) (R. H. Priest 44; J. L. Barsby 3-23). PoM: S. J. Johnson. *When Brisbane Heat slumped to 38-3 in the seventh over, a first WBBL final looked uncertain. But a magnificent performance from Sammy-Jo Johnson dragged them back into it, before an athletic boundary catch by Haidee Birkett denied Sydney Thunder the five they needed off the last ball. Johnson's 33 off 26 had led Brisbane's recovery, and Laura Harris's 32* off 25 gave them something to defend. Johnson then conceded just 12 off her four overs, and her team-mates exploited a stodgy surface to stifle the chase. Nicola Carey (19 off ten balls) hit back, but perished aiming for a match-winning slog-sweep.*

Semi-final At Sydney (Drummoyne Oval), January 19, 2019. **Sydney Sixers won a super over following a tie. ‡Sydney Sixers 131-4** (20 overs) (E. A. Perry 54*, D. van Niekerk 51*); **Melbourne Renegades 131-6** (20 overs) (S. G. Molineux 55, J. E. Duffin 41). PoM: E. A. Perry. *Ellyse Perry crashed the fourth ball of the super over for six to take the Sixers through after another gripping contest. She had batted through the Sixers' innings for 54*, taken the wicket of Emma Inglis, and run out Renegades captain Amy Satterthwaite. The Sixers also owed much to Dane van Niekerk's rapid 51*. Sophie Molineux watched from the other end as the Renegades slumped to 19-3 but, after support from Jess Duffin, she seemed set to complete a remarkable chase. But Molineux was run out off the last ball as she pushed for a third, following excellent work on the boundary by Erin Burns.*

FINAL

BRISBANE HEAT v SYDNEY SIXERS

At Sydney (Drummoyne Oval), January 26, 2019. Brisbane Heat won by three wickets. Toss: Sydney Sixers.

Beth Mooney may have played the innings that secured Brisbane Heat's first title, but she was not watching when they clinched victory. Having conquered illness and heat exhaustion, with the help of an inhaler and anti-nausea tablets, to hit 65, she returned to the dressing-room, had an ice bath, and nervously awaited the outcome. "They were pretty oppressive conditions," she said, "and I haven't been well the past couple of weeks, but I had a job to do." The Heat needed 30 off 31 balls when she was fourth out, and a flurry of three wickets did not help. But Laura Harris hammered a four through midwicket off the second ball of the final over to complete a well-paced chase. Earlier, Delissa Kimmince bowled Sixers opener Alyssa Healy with a beauty, and Ellyse Perry, stymied by a slow pitch, skyed Jess Jonassen to Mooney for 33. Dane van Niekerk's 32 off 15 at least set a challenging total.

Player of the Match: B. L. Mooney.   *Player of the Tournament*: E. A. Perry.

Sydney Sixers		*B*	*4/6*
1 †A. J. Healy *b 9*	18	13	2/1
2 *E. A. Perry *c 2 b 5*	33	37	1
3 A. K. Gardner *c 9 b 1*	23	28	2
4 E. A. Burns *c 2 b 9*	12	12	1
5 S. J. McGlashan *c 1 b 3*	2	5	0
6 D. van Niekerk *not out*	32	15	2/2
7 M. Kapp *c 4 b 1*	7	9	0
8 L. G. Smith *st 2 b 1*	0	1	0
Lb 4	4		

6 overs: 28-1   (20 overs) 131-7

1/26 2/69 3/83 4/89 5/97 6/120 7/131

9 S. E. Aley, 10 H. I. Silver-Holmes and 11 L. R. Cheatle did not bat.

Brisbane Heat		*B*	*4/6*
1 G. M. Harris *run out (4/3)*	1	4	0
2 †B. L. Mooney *c 2 b 6*	65	46	9
3 S. J. Johnson *b 7*	4	4	1
4 *K. L. H. Short *c 4 b 6*	29	35	2
5 J. L. Jonassen *lbw b 4*	2	3	0
6 J. E. Dooley *lbw b 4*	9	8	0
7 L. M. Harris *not out*	9	10	1
8 L. Wolvaardt *run out (7/11)*	9	5	1
9 D. M. Kimmince *not out*	2	2	0
W 1, nb 1	2		

6 overs: 26-2   (19.2 overs) 132-7

1/6 2/14 3/98 4/102 5/103 6/116 7/126

10 J. L. Barsby and 11 H. P. Birkett did not bat.

Johnson 4–12–22–1; Jonassen 4–8–28–1; Kimmince 4–10–25–2; G. M. Harris 4–9–23–3; Birkett 2–1–15–0; Barsby 2–2–14–0.

Kapp 3.2–9–16–1; Gardner 1–4–8–0; Perry 4–11–20–0; van Niekerk 4–4–34–2; Aley 1–2–7–0; Smith 1–3–15–0; Cheatle 1–3–7–0; Burns 4–7–25–2.

Umpires: D. M. Koch and D. J. Shepard.   Third umpire: C. A. Polosak.
Referee: D. Talalla.

WOMEN'S BIG BASH FINALS

2015-16   SYDNEY THUNDER beat Sydney Sixers by three wickets at Melbourne.
2016-17   SYDNEY SIXERS beat Perth Scorchers by seven runs at Perth.
2017-18   SYDNEY SIXERS beat Perth Scorchers by nine wickets at Adelaide.
2018-19   BRISBANE HEAT beat Sydney Sixers by three wickets at Sydney (Drummoyne Oval).

KIA SUPER LEAGUE IN 2019

Syd Egan

1 Western Storm   2 Southern Vipers   3 Loughborough Lightning

The fourth season of the Kia Super League was also the last, with the six-team Twenty20 tournament due to be superseded by the eight-team Hundred. **Western Storm** reached their fourth final, and became the only side to lift the trophy twice when they beat the inaugural winners, **Southern Vipers**.

Western Storm had won nine of their ten league games, thanks to a batting line-up so long that Indian all-rounder Deepti Sharma came in at No. 6. After a slow start – three defeats from four – **Loughborough Lightning** won their last six, starting at Guildford, where South Africa's Mignon du Preez hit a sparkling 70 not out off 41 balls to beat Surrey Stars with five overs to spare. Along with England's Amy Jones, du Preez drove Lightning to a comfortable second in the league, and a berth in the play-off.

The other play-off spot was hotly contested between **Southern Vipers** and **Yorkshire Diamonds**. After early wins, the Vipers were always in pole position, but the brilliance of the Diamonds' Indian star, 18-year-old Jemimah Rodrigues, made them sweat. She took time to acclimatise to English conditions, but found her feet with 58 at Loughborough, followed by a cool match-winning 42 not out in a tight game with Surrey Stars. But, against the Vipers at York, she hit the jackpot – an unbeaten 112 off 58. Sadly for the Diamonds, it wasn't quite enough – they finished two points adrift, despite winning one more game than the Vipers, who went on to the final.

Defending champions **Surrey Stars** won their first two games, but no more until the final round, and finished fifth. **Lancashire Thunder's** only points came in a tie; they propped up the table for the third year out of four.

Danni Wyatt became the first English Player of the Tournament, scoring 466 for the Vipers at 42, including a century strewn with seven sixes against the Stars at Arundel. Western Storm's captain, Heather Knight, was the leading run-scorer across all four tournaments, with 1,062. Her team-mate, seamer Freya Davies, took 19 wickets at 13, a Super League record, and was also the second-leading wicket-taker in all four seasons, her total of 37 topped only by Thunder's left-arm spinner, Sophie Ecclestone, who had 39.

Over its four seasons, the Super League achieved many of its goals. Given the chance to watch some of the world's biggest stars, the crowds came out in numbers unprecedented for domestic women's cricket, and the standard of play was generally excellent. For the domestic players, the opportunity to be professionals, albeit for two months a year, helped them build their skills and fitness, as well as their bank balances. But with six or more internationals per team, including three overseas stars, the younger English players (particularly batsmen) were often limited to bit parts.

The challenge for The Hundred, and the Centres of Excellence which will underpin it, is to address this imbalance without undermining the positives.

KIA SUPER LEAGUE IN 2019

20-over league plus play-off and final

	P	W	L	T	A	Bonus	Pts	NRR
WESTERN STORM...............	10	9	1	0	0	3	39	1.10
LOUGHBOROUGH LIGHTNING	10	7	3	0	0	4	32	0.79
SOUTHERN VIPERS	10	4	4	1	1	2	22	0.42
Yorkshire Diamonds	10	5	5	0	0	0	20	−0.45
Surrey Stars	10	3	6	0	1	2	16	−0.85
Lancashire Thunder	10	0	9	1	0	0	2	−1.19

Play-off At Hove, September 1. **Southern Vipers won by five wickets. ‡Loughborough Lightning 143** (19.5 overs) (S. W. Bates 3-22); **Southern Vipers 145-5** (19 overs) (S. W. Bates 37, D. N. Wyatt 31). *PoM:* S. W. Bates. *Bidding for their first final, Loughborough Lightning elected to bat, but never quite got going: Lauren Bell dismissed their openers cheaply, and Suzie Bates struck three times in the final over. Chasing 144, Bates and Danni Wyatt raced to 71-0 in the six-over powerplay – then both fell within six balls. The middle order limped to 123-5, before regaining their nerve to see the Vipers through.*

FINAL

SOUTHERN VIPERS v WESTERN STORM

At Hove, September 1. Western Storm won by six wickets. Toss: Southern Vipers.

In front of a thinner crowd than for previous finals, the Vipers made another rapid start, with Susie Bates and Danni Wyatt plundering 62 off the powerplay, before Bates fell to a sensational return catch from Sonia Odedra – chasing a leading edge halfway to extra cover. Wyatt swept onwards to 73 in 42 balls, and she and captain Tammy Beaumont got to 134 for one. But, once they were dismissed in successive overs, the Vipers slowed down, and closed on 172 for seven. Though Western Storm lost Smriti Mandhana for a first-ball duck, this brought in Heather Knight, who marshalled a perfectly paced chase, with late support from Deepti Sharma. They added 71 in 6.3 overs; Knight hit the winning four shortly after becoming the only player to score 1,000 runs in the Super League, and lifted the trophy for the second time in three years.

Player of the Match: H. C. Knight. *Player of the Tournament:* D. N. Wyatt.

Southern Vipers

		B	4/6
1 S. W. Bates *c and b 9*	26	19	5
2 D. N. Wyatt *c 8 b 6*	73	42	10/2
3 *T. T. Beaumont *c 11 b 8*	33	28	3/1
4 M. E. Bouchier *run out (4)*....	0	0	0
5 A. Wellington *lbw b 11*	13	10	2
6 F. M. K. Morris *b 8*	12	14	1
7 P. J. Scholfield *c 5 b 10*	2	3	0
8 M. Kelly *not out*	3	3	0
9 †C. E. Rudd *not out*	4	1	1
Lb 2, w 4..................	6		

6 overs: 62-0   (20 overs)   172-7

1/65 2/134 3/136 4/138 5/158 6/161 7/168

10 N. E. Farrant and 11 L. K. Bell did not bat.

Nicholas 4–11–28–1; Davies 4–7–40–1; Sharma 4–4–40–1; Shrubsole 4–10–26–2; Odedra 2–4–16–1; Knight 2–2–20–0.

Western Storm

		B	4/6
1 †R. H. Priest *st 9 b 5*	27	22	5
2 S. S. Mandhana *c 8 b 10*	0	1	0
3 *H. C. Knight *not out*	78	53	9/3
4 F. C. Wilson *c 2 b 10*........	18	17	3
5 S. N. Luff *c 9 b 5*...........	0	1	0
6 D. B. Sharma *not out*	39	22	7
Lb 3, w 7, nb 2	12		

6 overs: 50-1   (19 overs)   174-4

1/2 2/50 3/90 4/103

7 N. D. Dattani, 8 A. Shrubsole, 9 S. B. Odedra, 10 F. R. Davies and 11 C. L. Nicholas did not bat.

Farrant 3–10–19–2; Bell 4–8–44–0; Bates 4–8–39–0; Wyatt 2–4–23–0; Wellington 4–9–31–2; Morris 2–3–15–0.

Umpires: M. Newell and R. White.   Third umpire: M. Burns.

WINNERS

2016 Southern Vipers | 2017 Western Storm | 2018 Surrey Stars | 2019 Western Storm

ENGLISH DOMESTIC CRICKET IN 2019

The advent of the women's Hundred meant 2019 was likely to be the final outing of the 50-over women's County Championship, and **Kent** reasserted their dominance at the last. Captain Tammy Beaumont led them to six wins out of seven in the Royal London Women's One-Day Cup, to secure their eighth title since 2006 – though their great rivals, Sussex, who had six titles, had the satisfaction of being the only team to beat them, by 160 runs in their last game. Yorkshire, who had won the County Championship and its predecessor, the Area Championship, every year but one from 1992 to 2002, were second for the third season running, with Sussex and the two most recent champions, Lancashire and Hampshire, close behind. Beaumont and England team-mate Fran Wilson contributed 500 runs between them for Kent, while Surrey's Bryony Smith was the division's leading scorer, with 347 at 57. Left-arm wrist-spinner Katie Thompson and seamer Beth Langston picked up 15 wickets apiece for Yorkshire.

Middlesex, relegated the previous season, beat Berkshire in the final round of Division Two, to pip them to the title. By then, both sides' star batsmen had left to play the West Indians – Sophia Dunkley, who scored 451 runs in her six games for Middlesex, and England captain Heather Knight, who made 403 in four for Berkshire.

In 2020, the only 50-over competition was expected to be for the eight regional Centres of Excellence, which were being formed to feed the Hundred franchise teams, leaving the Vitality Twenty20 Cup as the one remaining senior county competition. **Warwickshire**, bottom of Division One in the Royal London Cup, claimed the T20 title when they beat Lancashire in the last round, to finish one point ahead of them and two ahead of Kent. **Somerset** won the second division.

Warwickshire also won the Under-17 County Cup final, by five runs, with Staffordshire runners-up for the second successive season, despite the all-round efforts of their captain, Ilenia Sims, who followed five for 23 with 46 runs. In the inaugural Under-17 County T20, Kent won the final against Lancashire; the same counties met in the Under-15 Cup final, which Kent also won, thanks to a century from captain Grace Scrivens.

In club cricket, the second year of the Vitality Women's Club T20 Cup (which replaced the National Knockout Cup in 2018) saw **Bishop's Stortford**, the Midlands regional winners, defeat Ansty from Sussex in the final of the Cup section. Kent's **St Lawrence & Highland Court** beat Five Ways Old Edwardians from Birmingham in the Plate.

WOMEN'S COUNTY CHAMPIONSHIP WINNERS

1997	Yorkshire	2003	Sussex	2009	Kent	2015	Yorkshire
1998	Yorkshire	2004	Sussex	2010	Sussex	2016	Kent
1999	East Midlands	2005	Sussex	2011	Kent	2017	Lancashire
2000	Yorkshire	2006	Kent	2012	Kent	2018	Hampshire
2001	Yorkshire	2007	Kent	2013	Sussex	2019	Kent
2002	Yorkshire	2008	Sussex	2014	Kent		

Kent won the County Championship 8 times, Sussex and Yorkshire 6, East Midlands, Hampshire and Lancashire 1.

Not all of the winners of the Area Championship which ran from 1980 to 1996 are known. Yorkshire won at least 6 titles, East Midlands and Middlesex 3, West and West Midlands 1.

ROYAL LONDON WOMEN'S ONE-DAY CUP IN 2019

50-over league

Division One

	P	W	L	T	NR	Bat	Bowl	Pts
						Bonus pts		
Kent	7	6	1	0	0	23	23	106
Yorkshire	7	5	2	0	0	20	23	93
Sussex	7	4	3	0	0	19	26	85
Lancashire	7	4	3	0	0	24	18	82
Hampshire	7	3	4	0	0	23	27	80
Nottinghamshire. . .	7	3	4	0	0	23	22	75
Surrey	7	2	5	0	0	20	19	59
Warwickshire	7	1	6	0	0	22	18	50

Division Two

	P	W	L	T	NR	Bat	Bowl	Pts
						Bonus pts		
Middlesex	7	5	1	1	0	24	23	102
Berkshire	7	5	1	0	1	19	24	98
Essex	7	5	2	0	0	19	25	94
Devon.	7	4	2	0	1	19	20	84
Wales	7	3	3	1	0	23	20	78
Worcestershire	7	2	5	0	0	14	19	53
Somerset.	7	1	6	0	0	19	24	53
Durham	7	1	6	0	0	19	17	46

Division Three

Group A: STAFFORDSHIRE 106pts, Derbyshire 90, Leicestershire 82, Lincolnshire 51, Cumbria 43, Scotland 37, Northumberland 8.

Group B: NORTHAMPTONSHIRE 86, Netherlands 62, Norfolk 57, Hertfordshire 47, Suffolk 45, Cambridgeshire & Huntingdonshire 14.

Group C: OXFORDSHIRE 90, Buckinghamshire 70, Cornwall 50, Gloucestershire 50, Dorset 30, Wiltshire 14.

Win = 10pts; tie = 5pts; no result = 5pts; match conceded = –5pts, with 18pts awarded to team conceded against. Up to four batting and four bowling points available to each team in each match.

DIVISION ONE AVERAGES

BATTING (160 runs)

		M	I	NO	R	HS	100	50	Avge	SR	Ct/St
1	S. W. Bates (*Hants*)	4	3	1	160	63*	0	2	80.00	80.40	0
2	F. C. Wilson (*Kent*)	6	5	1	257	83	0	3	64.25	78.11	2
3	A. E. Jones (*Warwicks*)	6	6	1	302	101*	1	2	60.40	89.34	5/2
4	B. F. Smith (*Surrey*)	6	6	0	347	106	1	2	57.83	88.52	2
5	T. T. Beaumont (*Kent*)	6	6	1	243	87	0	2	48.60	76.65	11
6	G. E. B. Boyce (*Lancs*)	7	7	1	262	83	0	1	43.66	66.66	2
7	J. L. Gunn (*Notts*)	6	6	1	187	62*	0	1	37.40	66.54	2
8	S. B. Odedra (*Notts*)	7	7	0	236	72	0	2	33.71	52.09	2
9	M. Blythin (*Kent*)	7	7	2	165	51*	0	1	33.00	60.21	7
10	S. J. Bryce (*Notts*)	6	6	0	175	60	0	3	29.16	63.63	7/3
11	H. J. Armitage (*Yorks*)	7	7	0	165	59	0	1	23.57	57.29	2
12	E. L. Lamb (*Lancs*)	7	7	0	160	33	0	0	22.85	61.77	3
13	F. Morris (*Hants*)	7	7	0	160	68	0	1	22.85	74.76	6

BOWLING (11 wickets)

		Style	O	M	R	W	BB	4I	Avge	SR	ER
1	K. C. Thompson (*Yorks*)....	SLW	54.5	10	126	15	3-15	0	8.40	21.93	2.29
2	P. A. C. Cowdrill (*Hants*)....	LB	40.5	2	137	12	4-19	1	11.41	20.41	3.35
3	B. A. Langston (*Yorks*).....	RM	58	8	195	15	5-8	1	13.00	23.20	3.36
4	N. Harman (*Sussex*)......	LB	45.3	6	188	14	6-40	2	13.42	19.50	4.13
5	C. E. Dean (*Hants*)........	OB	50.5	5	175	12	3-34	0	14.58	25.41	3.44
6	F. M. K. Morris (*Hants*)....	OB	54	4	179	12	4-24	1	14.91	27.00	3.31
7	G. K. Davis (*Warwicks*) ...	OB	58.4	8	193	12	4-18	2	16.08	29.33	3.28
8	M. S. Belt (*Kent*).........	OB	60.3	7	213	12	3-20	0	17.75	30.25	3.52
9	S. Munro (*Notts*).........	RM	57.3	7	250	14	4-48	1	17.85	24.64	4.34
10	T. G. Norris (*Sussex*)......	LM	63	7	207	11	3-32	0	18.81	34.36	3.28
11	H. V. Jones (*Surrey*)	RM	56	1	263	11	2-15	0	23.90	30.54	4.69

VITALITY WOMEN'S TWENTY20 CUP IN 2019

Division One: Warwickshire 20pts, Lancashire 19, Kent 18, Hampshire 17, Surrey 17, Sussex 13, Wales 10, Middlesex 10, Nottinghamshire 6.
Division Two: Somerset 24, Durham 20, Scotland 18, Yorkshire 18, Essex 18, Worcestershire 14, Devon 14, Cheshire 4, Derbyshire 2.
Division Three: *Group A:* Berkshire 28, Oxfordshire 24, Cornwall 16, Gloucestershire 14, Dorset 6, Wiltshire 2; *Group B:* Northamptonshire 32, Buckinghamshire 20, Hertfordshire 16, Norfolk 12, Lincolnshire 12, Cambridgeshire 12, Suffolk 8; *Group C:* Staffordshire 26, Cumbria 14, Leicestershire 12, Shropshire 4.

VITALITY WOMEN'S CLUB T20 FINALS IN 2019

Cup final At Newport, June 30. **Bishop's Stortford won by seven wickets. Ansty** 125-3 (20 overs) (L. B. Western 73*, N. Sole 31); ‡**Bishop's Stortford** 127-3 (18.1 overs) (N. A. Little 59*, E. M. Vasey 36). *Both teams had coasted through their semi-finals – Bishop's Stortford overwhelmed Bridgwater by ten wickets, while Ansty beat Sessay by nine. In the final, each team's innings followed the same outline: Lucy Western and Natasha Sole put on 90 for Ansty after two cheap wickets, then Stortford lost their openers early, before Nikki Little and Ella Vasey added 100 to take them most of the way to victory.*

Plate final At Newport, June 30. **St Lawrence & Highland Court won by seven wickets. ‡Five Ways Old Edwardians** 140-6 (20 overs) (L. Hill 49, G. A. Cant 58*); **St Lawrence & Highland Court** 141-3 (13.5 overs) (E. J. Marsh 30, A. C. Richards 38, M. Sturge 35*). *For Five Ways, Laura Hill and Georgia Cant opened with 87, but no one else reached double figures, and there were three run-outs. St Lawrence made a solid start, and 14-year-old Megan Sturge steered them home with six overs in hand.*

THE UNIVERSITY MATCHES IN 2019

At Cambridge, May 17. **Oxford University won by five wickets. ‡Cambridge University** 80-6 (20 overs) (C. N. Allison 37*); ‡**Oxford University** 81-5 (15.2 overs) (C. E. Reeves 4-12). *Only captain Chloe Allison and Coral Reeves reached double figures as Cambridge struggled against tight bowling. Reeves later collected four wickets, three bowled – but with only 81 required, Vanessa Picker (24) got her team most of the way, and Oxford won with 28 balls to spare.*

At Oxford, June 22. **Oxford University won by 200 runs. ‡Oxford University** 266-2 (50 overs) (V. M. Picker 135*, O. Lee-Smith 40, S. E. G. Taylor 50, Extras 41); **Cambridge University** 66 (25 overs) (S. L. Bennett 5-18). *Oxford recorded their sixth successive victory in the 50-over Varsity Match, held in the Parks because the men's World Cup had displaced the Lord's date on offer to the exam period. Picker batted through the innings for 135*, sharing century stands with Liv Lee-Smith and Sophie Taylor. Then Sam Bennett reduced Cambridge to 52-6 almost single-handed: in ten overs off the reel, she trapped one and bowled four, interrupted by a wicket for Amy Hearn. Her colleagues completed the job by the halfway mark.*

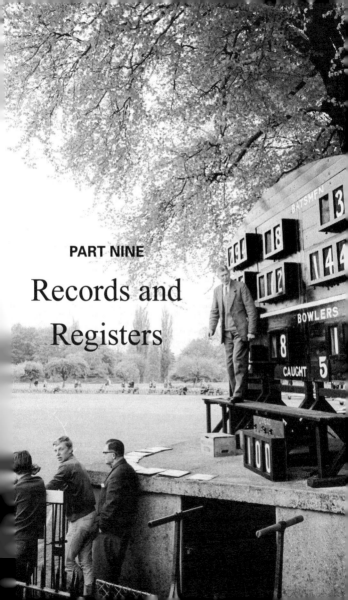

PART NINE

Records and
Registers

FEATURES OF 2019

This section covers the calendar year. Some of the features listed occurred in series and seasons reported in *Wisden 2019*, and some in series and seasons that will be reported in *Wisden 2021*; these items are indicated by [W19] or [W21].

Double-Hundreds (79)

	Mins	Balls	4	6		
335*	554	418	39	1	D. A. Warner........	Australia v Pakistan (2nd Test) at Adelaide.
327*	485	352	48	5	D. P. Conway	Wellington v Canterbury at Wellington.[W21]
307*		408	26	0	T. Kohli...........	Mizoram v Arunachal P at Puducherry.[W21]
273		345	29	1	J. K. Silva	Sinhalese v Army at Colombo (CCC).
271*	522	347	27	7	T. L. W. Cooper	S Australia v Victoria at Melbourne.[W21]
268		173	22	19	P. B. B. Rajapaksa ...	Burgher v Ports Au at Colombo (Moors).
266	302	240	35	6	D. J. Vilas.........	Lancashire v Glamorgan at Colwyn Bay.
262	335	299	31	8	Nisar Wahdat	Kabul v Khost at Ghazi Am Khan Town.
256*	527	333	29	3	A. G. S. Gous	Free State v KZN Inld at Bloemfontein.[W21]
254*	435	336	33	2	V. Kohli	India v South Africa (2nd Test) at Pune.
251		297	23	6	‡O. J. D. Pope......	Surrey v MCC at Dubai.
249*	712	512	26	0	Abid Ali	Sindh v Baluchistan at Karachi.[W21]
248	341	239	30	9	Ihsanullah Janat.....	Mis Ainak v Boost at Asadabad.
244	640	491	34	0	‡D. P. Sibley	Warwickshire v Kent at Canterbury.
243*	601	410	29	1	Sami Aslam..........	S Punjab v C Punjab at Lahore.[W21]
243	467	330	28	8	‡M. A. Agarwal	India v Bangladesh (1st Test) at Indore.
241*		301	35	2	A. J. Mandal	Chhattisgarh v Uttar at Naya Raipur.[W21]
237	549	376	35	0	Salman Butt.........	C Punjab v Baluchistan at Quetta.[W21]
237		397	25	5	G. Satish	Vidarbha v Andhra at Mulapadu.[W21]
237	263	225	28	9	D. I. Stevens	Kent v Yorkshire at Leeds.
234		209	11	17	B. O. P. Fernando ...	Chilaw Mar v Colts at Colombo (NCC).
233*		236	33	4	Arslan Khan	Chandigarh v Arun P at Chandigarh.[W21]
233		321	22	3	‡A. R. Easwaran	India A v Sri Lanka A at Belgaum.
231		268	20	3	‡A. K. Perera........	Nondescripts v Sinhalese at Col (PSO).
229	359	252	30	1	W. T. Root	Glamorgan v Northants at Northampton.
228	545	341	15	6	‡E. M. Moore	Warriors v Dolphins at Durban.[W21]
227*	467	298	21	4	‡E. M. Moore	E Province v Gauteng at Johannesburg.
227	487	327	25	0	B. A. Godleman	Derbyshire v Glamorgan at Swansea.
226	636	441	22	1	J. E. Root..........	England v NZ (2nd Test) at Hamilton.
224	498	381	31	1	T. W. M. Latham	Canterbury v Wellington at Wellington.[W21]
224	405	328	23	5	N. J. Maddinson	Victoria v S Australia at Melbourne.[W21]
223		212	30	6	W. I. A. Fernando ...	Colts v Tamil Union at Colombo (SSC).
222*		332	25	2	T. L. Jayasinghe	Panadura v Kurunegala Y at Colombo (Pol).
222	356	253	27	5	H. J. Kotze	Boland v Easterns at Paarl.
221*	420	337	22	0	‡O. J. D. Pope	Surrey v Hampshire at The Oval.
220*	488	329	19	4	Saif Hasan..........	Dhaka v Rangpur at Chittagong.[W21]
218		265	20	8	Umar Akmal	C Punjab v Northern Areas at Karachi.[W21]
218	528	347	23	3	P. J. van Biljon	Knights v Dolphins at Bloemfontein.[W21]
217*	370	227	29	2	N. J. van den Bergh...	Lions v Titans at Benoni.
217		367	27	0	‡H. L. P. Maduwantha .	Saracens v Chilaw M at Colombo (SSC).
217		274	28	0	P. Nissanka	SL A v Ireland Wolves at Hambantota.
216	204	180	34	4	B. M. Duckett	Notts v Cambridge MCCU at Cambridge.
216	362	266	29	5	Zeeshan Malik	Northern Areas v S Punjab at Sialkot.[W21]
215*		372	22	2	N. T. Paranavitana....	Tamil Union v Colombo at Katunayake.
215*	531	420	30	0	‡D. P. Sibley	Warwickshire v Notts at Nottingham.
215*	420	316	25	2	Zahid Zakhail	Amo v Mis Ainak at Khost.
215	485	371	23	6	‡M. A. Agarwal	India v SA (1st Test) at Visakhapatnam.
215		393	14	4	R. S. S. S. de Zoysa...	Ragama v Burgher at Colombo (Bloomfd).
214	522	387	18	3	Imran Butt..........	Baluchistan v Khyber Pakh at Quetta.[W21]
214		436	29	0	S. E. Marsh	Western Australia v Victoria at Perth.[W21]

	Mins	Balls	4	6		
212		483	18	0	‡H. L. P. Maduwantha .	Saracens v Tamil U at Colombo (NCC).
212	403	255	28	6	R. G. Sharma.	India v South Africa (3rd Test) at Ranchi.
211	284	200	27	3	Faizan Riaz	Northern Areas v Sindh at Karachi.W21
211	444	309	25	0	Fawad Alam	Sindh v Southern Punjab at Karachi.W21
211	513	319	24	2	S. P. D. Smith	Australia v Eng (4th Test) at Manchester.
209	316	282	27	2	Munir Ahmad	Boost v Amo at Ghazi A Khan Town.W21
206	441	296	26	0	Wasim Jaffer.	Vidarbha v Uttarakhand at Nagpur.
206		313	26	3	P. K. Panchal.	India A v England Lions at Wayanad.
205*		272	18	2	R. Dalal.	Arunachal P v Mizoram at Puducherry.W21
205	667	473	24	1	B-J. Watling	NZ v England (1st Test) at Mt Maunganui.
204*	326	248	19	2	S. Gill	India A v West Indies A at Tarouba.
204*	450	351	21	0	W. L. Madsen	Derbyshire v Gloucestershire at Bristol.
204*		301	22	3	Mandeep Singh	Punjab v Hyderabad at Patiala.W21
204		261	21	1	S. C. Serasinghe	Tamil U v Sinhalese at Colombo (NCC).
204	479	360	21	1	R. van Tonder	Knights v Titans at Bloemfontein.
202*	284	229	23	8	J. O. Holder.	WI v England (1st Test) at Bridgetown.
202*	406	319	19	6	Imrul Kayes	Khulna v Rangpur at Khulna.W21
202*	498	345	24	1	R. D. Rickelton	Gauteng v Free State at Johannesburg.W21
202		179	19	7	P. P. Shaw	Mumbai v Baroda at Vadodara.W21
201*		373	16	0	‡A. R. Easwaran	Bengal v Punjab at Kolkata.
201*	312	199	23	0	W. B. Marshall	Easterns v Border at East London.
201	435	342	20	1	M. Z. Hamza	Cape Cob v Dolphins at Pietermaritzburg.
201		203	20	1	‡A. K. Perera.	Nondescripts v Sinhalese at Col (PSO).
200*	235	189	31	4	Hanif Kunrai	Kunar v Kandahar at Asadabad.
200*		388	22	1	P. A. R. P. Perera	Colts v Burgher at Colombo (BRC).
200*	382	257	19	0	K. S. Williamson	NZ v Bangladesh (1st Test) at Hamilton.
200		220	20	2	P. Dogra	Puducherry v Mizoram at Kolkata.W21
200	188	135	11	19	Najeeb Tarakai	Speen Ghar v Mis Ainak at Asadabad.
200	321	212	19	4	L. R. P. L. Taylor	NZ v Bangladesh (2nd Test) at Wellington.

‡   *M. A. Agarwal, A. R. Easwaran, H. L. P. Maduwantha, E. M. Moore, A. K. Perera, O. J. D. Pope and D. P. Sibley each scored two double-hundreds; Perera did so in one match.*

Hundred on First-Class Debut

133	Abdullah Shafiq	Central Punjab v Southern Punjab at Karachi.W21
125	Amite Hasan	Sylhet v Dhaka Metropolis at Cox's Bazar.W21
124	V. D. Amugoda	Kalutara Town v Panadura at Panadura.
233*	Arslan Khan	Chandigarh v Arunachal Pradesh at Chandigarh.W21
105	S. Bhambri.	Chandigarh v Arunachal Pradesh at Chandigarh.W21
200*	Hanif Kunrai	Kunar v Kandahar at Asadabad.
146	G. T. Hargrave.	Oxford University v Cambridge University at Cambridge.
100*	Hayatullah	Kunduz v Kabul at Ghazi Amanullah Khan Town.
153*	Ijaz Ul Haq	Kunar v Kandahar at Asadabad.
103*	K. Karan Shinde	Andhra v Madhya Pradesh at Indore.
102	D. Mor.	Railways v Uttar Pradesh at Meerut.W21
110	G. Panditharatne	Bloomfield v Air Force at Colombo (Bloomfield).
163	D. Ranatunga.	Kurunegala Youth v Air Force at Kurunegala.
153	N. F. Smit	North West v Border at Potchefstroom.W21
127	J. L. Smith	Surrey v MCC at Dubai.
133*	D. L. Solway	New South Wales v South Australia at Adelaide.W21
160	C. A. Wakim	Tasmania v South Australia at Adelaide.

Three Hundreds in Successive Innings

S. W. Billings (Kent)	100	v Nottinghamshire at Nottingham.
	138 and 122*	v Yorkshire at Leeds.
B. O. P. Fernando (Chilaw Marians) .	105	v Saracens at Colombo (SSC).
	109 and 234	v Colts at Colombo (NCC).

A. A. Inham (Kalutara Town)	142		v Panadura at Panadura.
	165 and 103		v Bloomfield at Colombo (Bloomfield).
R. Jonathan (Nagaland)	100		v Bihar at Patna (*Dec 2018*).
	131		v Arunachal Prad at Dimapur (*Dec 2018*).
	123		v Puducherry at Dimapur.
M. Labuschagne (Australia)	185		v Pakistan (1st Test) at Brisbane.
	162		v Pakistan (2nd Test) at Adelaide.
	143		v New Zealand (1st Test) at Perth.
S. C. Serasinghe (Tamil Union)	152		v Ragama at Colombo (NCC).
	160		v Moors at Colombo (Moors).
	204		v Sinhalese at Colombo (NCC).
T. A. M. Siriwardene (Saracens)	175		v Badureliya at Maggona.
	102		v Burgher at Colombo (Burgher).
	104		SL A v Ireland Wolves at Colombo (SSC).

Double-Hundred in Each Innings of a Match

A. K. Perera	201	231	Nondescripts v Sinhalese at Colombo (PSO).

Hundred in Each Innings of a Match

Ahmed Shehzad	100	100*	Central Punjab v Southern Punjab at Karachi.[W21]
Anamul Haque	126	151*	Khulna v Dhaka at Cox's Bazar.[W21]
M. H. Azad	137	100*	Leicestershire v Gloucestershire at Leicester.
S. W. Billings	138	122*	Kent v Yorkshire at Leeds.
J. M. Clarke	125	112	Nottinghamshire v Warwickshire at Nottingham.
R. Dalal	178	205*	Arunachal Pradesh v Mizoram at Puducherry.[W21]
A. J. Doolan	170*	116	Tasmania v South Australia at Adelaide.[W21]
Farhan Zakhil	104	108	Kabul v Boost at Kabul.
B. O. P. Fernando	109	234	Chilaw Marians v Colts at Colombo (NCC).
S. R. Hain	129*	104	Warwickshire v Hampshire at Southampton.
A. A. Inham	165	103	Kalutara Town v Bloomfield at Colombo (Bloomfield).
M. Labuschagne	106	100	Glamorgan v Worcestershire at Cardiff.
A. K. Perera	201	231	Nondescripts v Sinhalese at Colombo (PSO).
K. D. Petersen	161	165*	Knights v Cape Cobras at Bloemfontein.
Shahidullah	122	189	Mis Ainak v Amo at Asadabad.
R. G. Sharma	176	127	India v South Africa (1st Test) at Visakhapatnam.
D. P. Sibley	215*	109	Warwickshire v Nottinghamshire at Nottingham.
A. A. S. Silva	144*	151	Badureliya v Moors at Colombo (Burgher).
S. P. D. Smith	144	142	Australia v England (1st Test) at Birmingham.
K. Verreynne	155	115	Cape Cobras v Titans at Benoni.[W21]
G. H. Vihari	114	180*	Rest of India v Vidarbha at Nagpur.

Carrying Bat through Completed Innings

Almas Shaukat	92*	Uttar Pradesh (175) v Railways at Meerut.[W21]
C. T. Bancroft	138*	Western Australia (279) v New South Wales at Sydney.
K. H. Devdhar	160*	Baroda (307) v Mumbai at Vadodara.[W21]
C. R. Gnaneshwar	74*	Andhra (181) v Bengal at Kolkata.[W21]
A. Z. Lees	107*	Durham (242) v Derbyshire at Chester-le-Street.
P. S. Masvaure	67*	Rhinos (156) v Eagles at Harare.[W21]
S. D. Robson	140*	Middlesex (342) v Glamorgan at Cardiff.
Sami Aslam	243*	Southern Punjab (467) v Central Punjab at Lahore.[W21]
N. J. Selman	76*	Glamorgan (186) v Sussex at Hove.
D. P. Sibley	109*	Warwickshire (233) v Hampshire at Birmingham.
D. P. Sibley	215*	Warwickshire (488) v Nottinghamshire at Nottingham.
A. A. S. Silva	144*	Badureliya (383) v Moors at Colombo (Burgher).
J. L. Solozano	69*	West Indies A (194) v India A at Tarouba.
J. J. Weatherley	29*	Hampshire (88) v Essex at Chelmsford.

Hundred before Lunch

B. M. Duckett . . . . 148* Nottinghamshire v Camb MCCU at Cambridge on day 1.
N. J. van den Bergh . . . . 40* to 146* Lions v Titans at Benoni on day 3.

Fast Double-Hundreds

P. B. B. Rajapaksa . . . . . 129 balls Burgher v Ports Authority at Colombo (Moors).
Najeeb Tarakai . . . . 134 balls Speen Ghar v Mis Ainak at Asadabad.

Most Sixes in an Innings

19	Najeeb Tarakai (200)	Speen Ghar v Mis Ainak at Asadabad.
19	P. B. B. Rajapaksa (268)	Burgher v Ports Authority at Colombo (Moors).
17	B. O. P. Fernando (234)	Chilaw Marians v Colts at Colombo (NCC).
15	Rahimullah Sahak (151)	Kandahar v Kabul at Asadabad.
10	S. Jayathilake (140)	Kalutara Town v Bloomfield at Colombo (Bloomfield).
10	Mirwais Zazai (159)	Kabul v Kunduz at Ghazi Amanullah Khan Town.
10	R. L. B. Rambukwella (124)	Tamil Union v Sinhalese at Colombo (NCC).
9	Ihsanullah Janat (248)	Mis Ainak v Boost at Asadabad.
9	Ijaz Ul Haq (153*)	Kunar v Kandahar at Asadabad.
9	D. I. Stevens (237)	Kent v Yorkshire at Leeds.
9	Usama Mir (77*)	Lankan v Panadura at Panagoda.
9	H. S. M. Zoysa (117)	Lankan v Galle at Katugastota.

Most Runs in Boundaries

	4	6		
222	48	5	D. P. Conway (327*) . .	Wellington v Canterbury at Wellington.[W21]
202	22	19	P. B. B. Rajapaksa (268)	Burgher v Ports Authority at Colombo (Moors).

Long Innings

Mins

712	Abid Ali (249*)	Sindh v Baluchistan at Karachi.[W21]
667	B-J. Watling (205)	New Zealand v England (1st Test) at Mount Maunganui.
640	D. P. Sibley (244)	Warwickshire v Kent at Canterbury.
636	J. E. Root (226)	England v New Zealand (2nd Test) at Hamilton.
630	D. A. Hendricks (197)	Lions v Titans at Benoni.
601	Sami Aslam (243*)	Southern Punjab v Central Punjab at Lahore.[W21]

Unusual Dismissals

Obstructing the Field
K. Cotani (7) . . . . North West v Free State at Bloemfontein.

First-Wicket Partnership of 100 in Each Innings

111	169	M. N. Erlank/V. B. van Jaarsveld, Dolphins v Cape Cobras at Pietermaritzburg.
162	171	E. M. Moore/J. van Heerden, Eastern Province v South Western Districts at Oudtshoorn.

Highest Wicket Partnerships

First Wicket

352　P. K. Panchal/A. R. Easwaran, India A v Sri Lanka A at Belgaum.
325　B. T. Slater/B. M. Duckett, Nottinghamshire v Cambridge MCCU at Cambridge.
317　W. I. A. Fernando/M. M. M. S. Cooray, Colts v Tamil Union at Colombo (SSC).
317　M. A. Agarwal/R. G. Sharma, India v South Africa (1st Test) at Visakhapatnam.
303　R. S. Vasconcelos/R. I. Newton, Northamptonshire v Glamorgan at Cardiff.
293　H. J. Hunt/J. B. Weatherald, South Australia v Tasmania at Adelaide.[W21]
283　Sami Aslam/Umar Siddiq, Southern Punjab v Baluchistan at Quetta.[W21]
278　Shan Masood/Abid Ali, Pakistan v Sri Lanka (2nd Test) at Karachi.
274　L. M. Reece/B. A. Godleman, Derbyshire v Sussex at Derby.

Second Wicket

361　D. A. Warner/M. Labuschagne, Australia v Pakistan (2nd Test) at Adelaide.
358　Zeeshan Malik/Umar Amin, Northern Areas v Southern Punjab at Sialkot.[W21]
320　M. H. Azad/N. J. Dexter, Leicestershire v Gloucestershire at Leicester.
309　A. Javid/M. H. Azad, Leicestershire v Loughborough MCCU at Leicester.
304　S. R. Ramaswamy/Wasim Jaffer, Vidarbha v Uttarakhand at Nagpur.
291　L. Senokwane/R. H. Frenz, North West v South Western Districts at Potchefstroom.
291　N. J. Selman/M. Labuschagne, Glamorgan v Sussex at Hove.

Third Wicket

307　P. B. B. Rajapaksa/M. L. R. Buddika, Burgher v Ports Authority at Colombo (Moors).
291　B. A. Godleman/T. C. Lace, Derbyshire v Glamorgan at Swansea.
289　P. S. Masvaure/P. J. Moor, Rhinos v Tuskers at Harare.
283　N. T. Paranavitana/S. C. Serasinghe, Tamil Union v Saracens at Colombo (NCC).
270　N. T. Paranavitana/S. C. Serasinghe, Tamil Union v Ragama at Colombo (NCC).
263　Akbar-ur-Rehman/Imran Farhat, Baluchistan v Sindh at Karachi.[W21]

Fourth Wicket

308　J. A. Burns/T. M. Head, Australia v Sri Lanka (2nd Test) at Canberra.
291　P. J. van Biljon/R. van Tonder, Knights v Dolphins at Bloemfontein.[W21]
278*　W. L. Madsen/A. L. Hughes, Derbyshire v Gloucestershire at Bristol.
276　Asad Shafiq/Babar Azam, Pakistanis v Australia A at Perth.[W21]
268　P. J. Malan/K. Verreynne, Cape Cobras v Titans at Benoni.[W21]
267　P. Nissanka/A. K. Perera, Nondescripts v Sinhalese at Colombo (PSO).
267　R. G. Sharma/A. M. Rahane, India v South Africa (3rd Test) at Ranchi.

Fifth Wicket

390　D. A. Hendricks/N. J. van den Bergh, Lions v Titans at Benoni.
315*　S. Gill/G. H. Vihari, India A v West Indies A at Tarouba.
278　Fawad Alam/Sarfraz Ahmed, Sindh v Southern Punjab at Karachi.[W21]
266　O. J. D. Pope/J. L. Smith, Surrey v MCC at Dubai.
262　I. G. Holland/A. H. T. Donald, Hampshire v Warwickshire at Southampton.

Sixth Wicket

346　S. W. Billings/D. I. Stevens, Kent v Yorkshire at Leeds.
318　C. D. J. Dent/R. F. Higgins, Gloucestershire v Leicestershire at Leicester.
282　C. T. Bancroft/E. J. H. Eckersley, Durham v Sussex at Hove.
276　H. L. P. Maduwantha/K. P. N. M. Karunanayake, Saracens v Tamil U at Colombo (NCC).
227　Umar Akmal/Kamran Akmal, Central Punjab v Sindh at Karachi.[W21]
221　C. D. J. Dent/R. F. Higgins, Gloucestershire v Derbyshire at Derby.

252 runs were added for Jharkhand's sixth wicket v Tripura by S. S. Tiwary, I. R. Jaggi and A. S. Roy; Jaggi retired hurt when over 200 runs had been added.

Seventh Wicket

399　A. N. Khare/A. J. Mandal, Chhattisgarh v Uttarakhand at Naya Raipur.[W21]
318*　Hanif Kunrai/Ijaz Ul Haq, Kunar v Kandahar at Asadabad.
309　B. C. Brown/C. J. Jordan, Sussex v Northamptonshire at Northampton.
301　B. C. Fortuin/D. Potgieter, Lions v Warriors at Potchefstroom.

295*   S. O. Dowrich/J. O. Holder, West Indies v England (1st Test) at Bridgetown.
261   B-J. Watling/M. J. Santner, New Zealand v England (1st Test) at Mount Maunganui.

Eighth Wicket

206   Aamer Yamin/Mohammad Irfan, Southern Punjab v Sindh at Karachi.[W21]
154   B. A. Raine/B. A. Carse, Durham v Northamptonshire at Chester-le-Street.
151   Zabid Hossain/Shahidul Islam, Dhaka Metropolis v Chittagong at Mirpur.[W21]
151   Yashpal Singh/Iqbal Abdulla, Sikkim v Goa at Porvorim.[W21]

Ninth Wicket

167   G. G. Wagg/L. J. Carey, Glamorgan v Derbyshire at Swansea.
164   A. M. E. M. Amarasinghe/K. A. S. N. Rajaguru, Nondescripts v Colts at Colombo (CCC).
162   R. S. S. S. de Zoysa/D. T. Hewathantri, Ragama v Burgher at Colombo (Bloomfield).
153   M. Marais/P. Fojela, Border v Easterns at East London.

Tenth Wicket

183   B. Swanepoel/L. B. Adam, Northern Cape v KwaZulu-Natal at Kimberley.[W21]
132   P. A. R. P. Perera/P. A. K. P. Jayawickrama, Colts v Burgher at Colombo (Burgher).
108*   Fawad Alam/Mir Hamza, Sindh v Khyber Pakhtunkhwa at Karachi.[W21]

Most Wickets in an Innings

10-37	P. M. Pushpakumara	Colombo v Saracens at Moratuwa.
9-14	E. L. Hawken	North West v Easterns at Potchefstroom.[W21]
9-37	Zohaib Ahmadzai	Amo v Mis Ainak at Khost.[W21]
9-40	K. J. Abbott	Hampshire v Somerset at Southampton.
9-52	R. Sanjay Yadav	Meghalaya v Nagaland at Dimapur.[W21]
9-87	E. M. C. D. Edirisinghe	Saracens v Colombo at Moratuwa.
8-22	R. R. Singh	Manipur v Mizoram at Kolkata.[W21]
8-26	Ruyel Miah	Sylhet v Chittagong at Bogra.[W21]
8-34	O. E. Robinson	Sussex v Middlesex at Hove.
8-35	Naveen-ul-Haq	Kabul v Mis Ainak at Kabul.
8-36	J. S. Patel	Warwickshire v Surrey at Birmingham.
8-45	J. A. Warrican	Barbados v Windward Islands at Arnos Vale.
8-46	K. J. Abbott	Hampshire v Somerset at Southampton.
8-50	R. M. G. K. Sirisoma	Galle v Panadura at Panadura.
8-60	R. L. Chase	West Indies v England (1st Test) at Bridgetown.
8-60	K. Gowtham	Karnataka v Tamil Nadu at Dindigul.[W21]
8-61	G. S. Virdi	Surrey v Nottinghamshire at Nottingham.
8-64	G. J. Batty	Surrey v Warwickshire at Birmingham.
8-64	C. J. Sayers	South Australia v New South Wales at Adelaide.[W21]
8-71	Nauman Ali	Northern Areas v Central Punjab at Faisalabad.[W21]
8-80	S. Randiv	Galle v Bloomfield at Colombo (Bloomfield).
8-94	K. N. Peiris	Ragama v Badureliya at Colombo (Bloomfield).
8-98	S. R. Harmer	Essex v Kent at Chelmsford.
8-108	S. S. Bachhav	Maharashtra v Railways at Delhi.
8-112	Bilal Asif	Central Punjab v Northern Areas at Karachi.[W21]

Most Wickets in a Match

17-86	K. J. Abbott	Hampshire v Somerset at Southampton.
16-110	P. M. Pushpakumara	Colombo v Saracens at Moratuwa.
14-135	O. E. Robinson	Sussex v Middlesex at Hove.
14-139	G. S. Virdi	Surrey v Nottinghamshire at Nottingham.
14-170	K. Gowtham	Karnataka v Tamil Nadu at Dindigul.[W21]
14-182	K. N. Peiris	Ragama v Badureliya at Colombo (Bloomfield).
13-65	Ruyel Miah	Sylhet v Chittagong at Bogra.[W21]
13-73	E. L. Hawken	North West v Easterns at Potchefstroom.[W21]
13-107	I. M. Lemtur	Nagaland v Meghalaya at Dimapur.[W21]
13-112	R. Sanjay Yadav	Meghalaya v Nagaland at Dimapur.[W21]

13-127	Qais Ahmad	Speen Ghar v Band-e-Amir at Ghazi Amanullah Khan Town.
13-131	C. J. Sayers.	South Australia v New South Wales at Adelaide.[W21]
13-141	D. L. Piedt	Cape Cobras v Titans at Oudtshoorn.
12-53	H. V. Patel	Haryana v Tripura at Lahli.[W21]
12-61	S. R. Harmer	Essex v Hampshire at Chelmsford.
12-65	S. J. Cook	Essex v Kent at Canterbury.
12-68	D. R. F. Weerasinghe	Galle v Navy at Welisara.
12-79	U. T. Yadav	Vidarbha v Kerala at Wayanad.
12-89	J. S. Patel	Warwickshire v Surrey at Birmingham.
12-93	R. M. G. K. Sirisoma	Galle v Panadura at Panadura.
12-101	K. J. Dudgeon	KwaZulu-Natal v Gauteng at Johannesburg.
12-105	Zohaib Ahmadzai.	Amo v Mis Ainak at Khost.[W21]
12-140	Abdur Razzak.	Khulna v Rangpur at Mirpur.[W21]
12-144	R. Ashwin	Nottinghamshire v Surrey at Nottingham.
12-149	N. O. Miller	Jamaica v Trinidad & Tobago at Kingston.

Hat-Tricks (12)

A. Aman	Bihar v Manipur at Patna.
G. J. Batty	Surrey v Warwickshire at Birmingham.
J. J. Bumrah	India v West Indies (2nd Test) at Kingston.
M. A. R. Cohen	Western Province v Gauteng at Johannesburg.
Dastagir Khan	Boost v Band-e-Amir at Ghazi Amanullah Khan Town.
K. Gowtham	India A v West Indies A at Tarouba.
R. B. Kalaria	Gujarat v Kerala at Wayanad.
B. G. Lister	Auckland v Otago at Auckland.
S. W. Masakadza	Mountaineers v Eagles at Harare.
T. L. Moreki	Titans v Dolphins at Centurion.[W21]
A. Phillip.	Trinidad & Tobago v Jamaica at Kingston.
J. F. Smith.	Western Province v Border at Cape Town.

Wicket with First Ball in First-Class Career

U. L. D. A. Kaushalya	Panadura v Navy at Welisara.
B. Mauer.	Border v Northern Cape at East London.
Mohammadullah Hamkar. .	Kabul v Khost at Ghazi Amanullah Khan Town.

Match Double (100 runs and 10 wickets)

| I. Khan . . . . | 71, 39; 5-54, 5-65 | Trinidad & Tobago v Windward Islands at Arnos Vale. |

Most Wicketkeeping Dismissals in an Innings

6 (6ct)	Adnan Akmal	Southern Punjab v Baluchistan at Quetta.[W21]
6 (6ct)	Q. de Kock.	South Africa v England (1st Test) at Centurion.
6 (3ct, 3st)	P. D. Dias	Burgher v Ports Authority at Colombo (Moors).
6 (5ct, 1st)	C. Fortuin.	Eastern Province v Boland at Port Elizabeth.
6 (6ct)	B. J. H. Holt.	New South Wales v Tasmania at Hobart.
6 (6ct)	Jamal Anwar	Northern Areas v Baluchistan at Karachi.[W21]
6 (5ct, 1st)	H. Klaasen.	Titans v Warriors at East London.
6 (6ct)	K. C. Koyana	Western Province v Gauteng at Johannesburg.
6 (6ct)	S. W. Poynter	Durham v Durham MCCU at Chester-le-Street.
6 (5ct, 1st)	Qasim Oryakhail	Speen Ghar v Boost at Khost.[W21]
6 (6ct)	O. G. Robinson	Kent v Surrey at The Oval.
6 (6ct)	B. R. Sharath	Karnataka v Himachal Pradesh at Mysore.[W21]
6 (6ct)	S. Sharath.	Karnataka v Saurashtra at Bangalore.
6 (6ct)	K. Srikar Bharat.	Andhra v Bengal at Kolkata.[W21]

Most Wicketkeeping Dismissals in a Match

11 (11ct)	Adnan Akmal	Southern Punjab v Baluchistan at Quetta.W21
10 (10ct)	J. R. Doran.	Tasmania v Victoria at Hobart.W21
10 (10ct)	Sarfraz Ahmed.	Pakistan v South Africa (3rd Test) at Johannesburg. W19
9 (8ct, 1st)	C. Fortuin.	Eastern Province v Boland at Port Elizabeth.
9 (9ct)	B. J. H. Holt.	New South Wales v Tasmania at Hobart.
9 (8ct, 1st)	Jamal Anwar	Northern Areas v Baluchistan at Karachi.W21
9 (9ct)	S. W. Poynter	Durham v Durham MCCU at Chester-le-Street.
9 (7ct, 2st)	A. O. Thomas	Jamaica v Guyana at Kingston.
9 (7ct, 2st)	Zabid Hossain	Dhaka Metropolis v Barisal at Barisal.W21

Most Catches in an Innings in the Field

6	T. Köhler-Cadmore	Yorkshire v Kent at Canterbury.
5	I. R. Jaggi.	Jharkhand v Jammu & Kashmir at Jammu.
5	D. S. Smith.	Windward Islands v Barbados at Bridgetown.
5	H. E. Vithana	Galle v Kalutara Town at Galle.

Most Catches in a Match in the Field

7	T. Köhler-Cadmore	Yorkshire v Hampshire at Southampton.
7	H. E. Vithana	Galle v Kalutara Town at Galle.
6	T. Köhler-Cadmore	Yorkshire v Kent at Canterbury.
6	S. S. B. Magala	Warriors v Dolphins at Durban.W21
6	J. N. Malan.	Cape Cobras v Lions at Potchefstroom.W21
6	K. Mukunth	Tamil Nadu v Himachal Pradesh at Dindigul.W21
6	S. S. Pundir	Jammu & Kashmir v Maharashtra at Pune.W21
6	S. P. D. Smith	Australia v England (5th Test) at The Oval.
6	D. A. Warner	Australia v England (3rd Test) at Leeds.

No Byes Conceded in Total of 500 or More

Adnan Akmal	Southern Punjab v Baluchistan (500-9 dec) at Quetta.W21
Adnan Akmal	Southern Punjab v Northern Areas (550-6 dec) at Sialkot.W21
Q. de Kock	South Africa v India (601-5 dec) (2nd Test) at Pune.
P. V. R. de Silva	Colts v Chilaw Marians (560) at Colombo (NCC).
D. P. D. N. Dickwella	Sri Lanka v Australia (534-5 dec) (2nd Test) at Canberra.
D. P. D. N. Dickwella	Sri Lanka v Pakistan (555-3 dec) (2nd Test) at Karachi.
Liton Das	Bangladesh v New Zealand (715-6 dec) (1st Test) at Hamilton.
Mohammad Rizwan	Pakistan v Australia (589-3 dec) (2nd Test) at Adelaide.
Munir Ahmad	Boost v Speen Ghar (536) at Asadabad.
Munir Ahmad	Boost v Mis Ainak (508) at Asadabad.
D. L. Perera.	Kurunegala Youth v Panadura (579-8 dec) at Colombo (Police).
Rehan Afridi	Khyber Pakhtunkhwa v Baluchistan (553-8 dec) at Quetta.W21
Rohail Nazir	Northern Areas v Central Punjab (675-8 dec) at Karachi.W21
D. M. Sarathchandra	Tamil Union v Colts (615) at Colombo (SSC).
K. L. Yangfo.	Arunachal Pradesh v Chandigarh (503-2 dec) at Chandigarh.W21

Highest Innings Totals

750	Northamptonshire v Glamorgan at Cardiff.
715-6 dec	New Zealand v Bangladesh (1st Test) at Hamilton.
675-8 dec	Central Punjab v Northern Areas at Karachi.W21
671-6	South Australia v Victoria at Melbourne.W21
629	Vidarbha v Uttarakhand at Nagpur.
629	Burgher v Ports Authority at Colombo (Moors).
622-7 dec	India v Australia (4th Test) at Sydney. W19

622-5 dec	India A v Sri Lanka A at Belgaum.
620-9 dec	Mizoram v Arunachal Pradesh at Puducherry.[W21]
619	Uttar Pradesh v Assam at Kanpur.
616-6 dec	Victoria v South Australia at Melbourne.[W21]
615	Colts v Tamil Union at Colombo (SSC).
615-9 dec	New Zealand v England (1st Test) at Mount Maunganui.
601-5 dec	India v South Africa (2nd Test) at Pune.

Lowest Innings Totals

35†	Madhya Pradesh v Andhra at Indore.
35†	Tripura v Rajasthan at Agartala.
38	Ireland v England (only Test) at Lord's.
40	Kent v Essex at Canterbury.
46	Cardiff MCCU v Somerset at Taunton.
49	Tripura v Haryana at Lahli.[W21]
50	Gauteng v Eastern Province at Johannesburg.
57	Galle v Navy at Welisara.
59	Kent v Somerset at Canterbury.
61	Boost v Speen Ghar at Khost.[W21]
65	Mizoram v Manipur at Kolkata.[W21]
65	Sikkim v Puducherry at Puducherry.[W21]
67	England v Australia (3rd Test) at Leeds.
68	Tripura v Haryana at Lahli.[W21]
69	Hyderabad v Delhi at Delhi.[W21]

† *One man absent.*

Highest Fourth-Innings Totals

402	Tasmania v Western Australia at Hobart (set 454).
402	Band-e-Amir v Amo at Ghazi Amanullah Khan Town (set 410).

Match Aggregate of 1,500 Runs

1,560 for 30	Chilaw Marians (560 and 423-5 dec) v Colts (308 and 269-5) at Colombo (NCC).
1,517 for 32	Nottinghamshire (498 and 260) v Warwickshire (488 and 271-2) at Nottingham.
1,512 for 36	Colts (615 and 251-8 dec) v Tamil Union (315 and 331-8) at Colombo (SSC).
1,503 for 26	Nondescripts (444 and 579-6) v Sinhalese (480) at Colombo (PSO).
1,500 for 32	Wellington (525-7 dec and 247-6 dec) v Canterbury (415-9 dec and 313) at Wellington.[W21]

Matches Dominated by Batting (1,200 runs at 80 runs per wicket)

1,287 for 12 (107.25)	Victoria (616-6 dec) v South Australia (671-6) at Melbourne.[W21]

Four Individual Hundreds in an Innings

Central Punjab (597-9 dec) v Southern Punjab at Karachi.[W21]
Pakistan (555-3 dec) v Sri Lanka (2nd Test) at Karachi.

Six Individual Fifties in an Innings

Northamptonshire (750) v Glamorgan at Cardiff.

Large Margin of Victory

Somerset (387-4 dec and 345-9 dec) beat Cardiff MCCU (118 and 46) at Taunton by 568 runs.
Kent (482-8 dec and 337-7 dec) beat Yorkshire (269 and 117) at Leeds by 433 runs.

Win after Following On

Tripura (289 and 211) lost to Jharkhand (136 and 418-8 dec) at Agartala by 54 runs.[W21]

Most Extras in an Innings

	b	lb	w	nb	
61	18	25	2	16	Northamptonshire (750) v Glamorgan at Cardiff.
60	7	7	0	46	Sussex (370) v Gloucestershire at Bristol.
58	6	20	0	32	Gloucestershire (571) v Leicestershire at Leicester.
56	17	23	0	16	Leicestershire (302) v Worcestershire at Leicester.
54	22	9	21	2	New Zealand (615-9 dec) v England (1st Test) at Mount Maunganui.
52	16	18	8	10	Lions (593-5 dec) v Titans at Benoni.
52	11	23	0	18	Durham (384) v Sussex at Hove.
51	9	20	2	20	Leicestershire (524-5 dec) v Loughborough MCCU at Leicester.

Career Aggregate Milestones

15,000 runs	S. C. Cook, Imran Farhat, C. A. Pujara.
10,000 runs	G. J. Bailey, V. Chopra, A. Lyth, P. J. Malan, S. A. Northeast, A. M. Rahane, T. Westley.
1,000 wickets.	D. S. Hettiarachchi.
500 wickets	R. Clarke, D. I. Stevens, S. van Zyl, C. L. White, K. S. Williamson.

RECORDS

COMPILED BY PHILIP BAILEY

This section covers
- first-class records to December 31, 2019 (page 1220).
- List A one-day records to December 31, 2019 (page 1248).
- List A Twenty20 records to December 31, 2019 (page 1251).
- All-format career records to December 31, 2019 (page 1253).
- Test records to January 31, 2020, the end of the Zimbabwe v Sri Lanka series (page 1254).
- Test records series by series (page 1288).
- one-day international records to December 31, 2019 (page 1333).
- World Cup records (page 1334).
- Twenty20 international records to December 31, 2019 (page 1350).
- miscellaneous other records to December 31, 2019 (page 1356).
- women's Test records, one-day international and Twenty20 international records to December 31, 2019 (page 1360).

The sequence
- Test series records begin with those involving England, arranged in the order their opponents entered Test cricket (Australia, South Africa, West Indies, New Zealand, India, Pakistan, Sri Lanka, Zimbabwe, Bangladesh, Ireland, Afghanistan). Next come all remaining series involving Australia, then South Africa – and so on until Ireland v Afghanistan records appear on page 1329.

Notes
- Unless otherwise stated, all records apply only to first-class cricket. This is considered to have started in 1815, after the Napoleonic War.
- mid-year seasons taking place outside England are given simply as 2018, 2019, etc.
- (E), (A), (SA), (WI), (NZ), (I), (P), (SL), (Z), (B), (Ire), (Afg) indicates the nationality of a player or the country in which a record was made.
- in career records, dates in italic indicate seasons embracing two different years (i.e. non-English seasons). In these cases, only the first year is given, e.g. *2019* for 2019-20.

See also
- up-to-date records on www.wisdenrecords.com.
- Features of 2019 (page 1202).

CONTENTS

FIRST-CLASS RECORDS

BATTING RECORDS

BOWLING RECORDS

ALL-ROUND RECORDS

WICKETKEEPING RECORDS

FIELDING RECORDS

TEAM RECORDS

LIST A ONE-DAY RECORDS

LIST A TWENTY20 RECORDS

ALL-FORMAT CAREER RECORDS

TEST RECORDS

BATTING RECORDS

BOWLING RECORDS

TEST SERIES

ONE-DAY INTERNATIONAL RECORDS

TWENTY20 INTERNATIONAL RECORDS

MISCELLANEOUS RECORDS

WOMEN'S TEST AND OTHER INTERNATIONAL RECORDS

NOTES ON RECORDS

The Don drops off

STEVEN LYNCH

For 80 years, Arthur Fagg stood alone: the only man to score two double-centuries in the same first-class match, for Kent against Essex at Colchester in 1938. But early in 2019 he was joined by Angelo Perera, who made 201 and 231 in a domestic match in Sri Lanka.

Others elbowed their way into long-standing lists. Hampshire's Kyle Abbott collected the best match figures in first-class cricket since Jim Laker demolished Australia in 1956; Leicestershire's Colin Ackermann became the first to claim seven wickets in a senior Twenty20 game; and Jimmy Anderson's 30 wickets in the 2019 English season cost 9.40 each, the lowest average since Imran Khan in 1983. Some tables proved particularly popular: between 1846 – when Tom Marsden made 227 for Sheffield & Leicester – and 2010, only a dozen batsmen marked their first-class debut with a double-century. But nine have done so since, most recently the Indian left-hander Arslan Khan, for Chandigarh in December 2019.

Stuart Broad is making progress up a couple of lists. By the end of the South African tour, he had 485 Test wickets, seventh overall and eyeing Courtney Walsh's 519. He had also collected 35 Test ducks, eight fewer than Walsh (and level with Glenn McGrath).

The proliferation of international cricket means that, to keep the Records section within bounds, *Wisden* occasionally has to prune the tables. For the last few years, the list of Most Test Runs had been quietly expanded to retain Don Bradman's tally of 6,996. But, with five batsmen reaching 7,000 in 2019 – leaving Bradman in 53rd – pressure of space meant the bar had to be raised (the equivalent table for bowlers includes 33 names). Bradmaniacs should be reassured his name still appears 24 times in 13 general tables in the Test records, and dominates the Ashes section. And he may never be elbowed out of the list of highest Test averages, as his 99.94 still leads the way by a country mile – although second and third places are currently occupied by two other acquisitive Australians, Marnus Labuschagne (63.43) and Steve Smith (62.84).

ROLL OF DISHONOUR

The following players have either been banned after being found guilty of breaching anti-corruption codes, or have admitted to some form of on-field corruption:

Amit Singh (I), Ata-ur-Rehman (P), M. Azharuddin (I), A. Bali (I), G. H. Bodi (SA), A. Chandila (I), A. A. Chavan (I), P. Cleary (A), W. J. Cronje (SA), Danish Kaneria (P), H. H. Gibbs (SA), C. L. Hall (A), Haseeb Amjad (HK), Irfan Ahmed (HK), Irfan Ansari (UAE), A. Jadeja (I), S. T. Jayasuriya (SL), H. N. K. Jensen (NZ), Khalid Latif (P), J. Logan (A), K. S. Lokuarachchi (SL), P. Matshikwe (SA), N. E. Mbhalati (SA), M. D. Mishra (I), Mohammad Amir (P), Mohammad Ashraful (B), Mohammad Asif (P), Mohammad Irfan (P), Mohammad Nawaz (P), Nadeem Ahmed (HK), Nasir Jamshed (P), Naved Arif (P), M. O. Odumbe (Ken), A. N. Petersen (SA), M. Prabhakar (I), Salim Malik (P), Salman Butt (P), M. N. Samuels (WI), H. N. Shah (I), Shakib Al Hasan (B), Shariful Haque (B), Sharjeel Khan (P), Ajay Sharma (I), S. Sreesanth (I), S. J. Srivastava (I), T. P. Sudhindra (I), J. Symes (SA), S. K. Trivedi (I), T. L. Tsolekile (SA), L. L. Tsotsobe (SA), L. Vincent (NZ), M. S. Westfield (E), H. S. Williams (SA), A. R. Yadav (I), Yousuf Mahmood (Oman).

FIRST-CLASS RECORDS

This section covers first-class cricket to December 31, 2019. Bold type denotes performances in the calendar year 2019 or, in career figures, players who appeared in first-class cricket in that year.

BATTING RECORDS

HIGHEST INDIVIDUAL INNINGS

In all first-class cricket, there have been **224** individual scores of 300 or more. The highest are:

501*	B. C. Lara	Warwickshire v Durham at Birmingham	1994
499	Hanif Mohammad	Karachi v Bahawalpur at Karachi	1958-59
452*	D. G. Bradman	NSW v Queensland at Sydney	1929-30
443*	B. B. Nimbalkar	Maharashtra v Kathiawar at Poona	1948-49
437	W. H. Ponsford	Victoria v Queensland at Melbourne	1927-28
429	W. H. Ponsford	Victoria v Tasmania at Melbourne	1922-23
428	Aftab Baloch	Sind v Baluchistan at Karachi	1973-74
424	A. C. MacLaren	Lancashire v Somerset at Taunton	1895
405*	G. A. Hick	Worcestershire v Somerset at Taunton.	1988
400*	B. C. Lara	West Indies v England at St John's	2003-04
394	Naved Latif	Sargodha v Gujranwala at Gujranwala	2000-01
390	S. C. Cook	Lions v Warriors at East London	2009-10
385	B. Sutcliffe	Otago v Canterbury at Christchurch.	1952-53
383	C. W. Gregory	NSW v Queensland at Brisbane	1906-07
380	M. L. Hayden	Australia v Zimbabwe at Perth	2003-04
377	S. V. Manjrekar	Bombay v Hyderabad at Bombay	1990-91
375	B. C. Lara	West Indies v England at St John's	1993-94
374	D. P. M. D. Jayawardene	Sri Lanka v South Africa at Colombo (SSC)	2006
369	D. G. Bradman	South Australia v Tasmania at Adelaide	1935-36
366	N. H. Fairbrother	Lancashire v Surrey at The Oval	1990
366	M. V. Sridhar	Hyderabad v Andhra at Secunderabad	1993-94
365*	C. Hill	South Australia v NSW at Adelaide.	1900-01
365*	G. S. Sobers	West Indies v Pakistan at Kingston	1957-58
364	L. Hutton	England v Australia at The Oval	1938
359*	V. M. Merchant	Bombay v Maharashtra at Bombay	1943-44
359*	S. B. Gohel	Gujarat v Orissa at Jaipur.	2016-17
359	R. B. Simpson	NSW v Queensland at Brisbane	1963-64
357*	R. Abel	Surrey v Somerset at The Oval.	1899
357	D. G. Bradman	South Australia v Victoria at Melbourne	1935-36
356	B. A. Richards	South Australia v Western Australia at Perth	1970-71
355*	G. R. Marsh	Western Australia v South Australia at Perth.	1989-90
355*	K. P. Pietersen	Surrey v Leicestershire at The Oval	2015
355	B. Sutcliffe	Otago v Auckland at Dunedin	1949-50
353	V. V. S. Laxman	Hyderabad v Karnataka at Bangalore	1999-2000
352	W. H. Ponsford	Victoria v NSW at Melbourne	1926-27
352	C. A. Pujara	Saurashtra v Karnataka at Rajkot.	2012-13
351*	S. M. Gugale	Maharashtra v Delhi at Mumbai.	2016-17
351	K. D. K. Vithanage	Tamil Union v Air Force at Katunayake	2014-15
350	Rashid Israr	Habib Bank v National Bank at Lahore	1976-77

A fuller list can be found in Wisdens up to 2011.

DOUBLE-HUNDRED ON DEBUT

227	T. Marsden	Sheffield & Leicester v Nottingham at Sheffield.	1826
207	N. F. Callaway	New South Wales v Queensland at Sydney	1914-15
		In his only first-class innings. He was killed in action in France in 1917.	
240	W. F. E. Marx	Transvaal v Griqualand West at Johannesburg	1920-21
200*	A. Maynard	Trinidad v MCC at Port-of-Spain	1934-35
232*	S. J. E. Loxton	Victoria v Queensland at Melbourne.	1946-47

215*	G. H. G. Doggart	Cambridge University v Lancashire at Cambridge . . .	1948
202	J. Hallebone	Victoria v Tasmania at Melbourne	1951-52
230	G. R. Viswanath	Mysore v Andhra at Vijayawada.	1967-68
260	A. A. Muzumdar	Bombay v Haryana at Faridabad.	1993-94
209*	A. Pandey	Madhya Pradesh v Uttar Pradesh at Bhilai	1995-96
210*	D. J. Sales	Northamptonshire v Worcestershire at Kidderminster	1996
200*	M. J. Powell	Glamorgan v Oxford University at Oxford	1997
201*	M. C. Juneja	Gujarat v Tamil Nadu at Ahmedabad	2011-12
213	Jiwanjot Singh	Punjab v Hyderabad at Mohali	2012-13
202	A. Gupta	Punjab v Himachal Pradesh at Dharamsala.	2017-18
256*	Bahir Shah	Speen Ghar v Amo at Ghazi Amanullah Town.	2017-18
203	B. D. Schmulian	C. Districts v N. Districts at Mount Maunganui	2017-18
228	M. Raghav	Manipur v Nagaland at Dimapur.	2018-19
267*	A. R. Rohera	Madhya Pradesh v Hyderabad at Indore	2018-19
200*	**Hanif Kunrai**	**Kunar v Kandahar at Asadabad**	**2018-19**
233*	**Arslan Khan**	**Chandigarh v Arunachal Pradesh at Chandigarh** .	**2019-20**

TWO SEPARATE HUNDREDS ON DEBUT

148	and 111	A. R. Morris	New South Wales v Queensland at Sydney	1940-41
152	and 102*	N. J. Contractor	Gujarat v Baroda at Baroda	1952-53
132*	and 110	Aamer Malik	Lahore A v Railways at Lahore	1979-80
130	and 100*	Noor Ali	Afghanistan v Zimbabwe XI at Mutare	2009
158	and 103*	K. H. T. Indika	Police v Seeduwa Raddoluwa at Colombo (Police)	2010-11
126	and 112	V. S. Awate	Maharashtra v Vidarbha at Nagpur.	2012-13
154*	and 109*	T. J. Dean	Victoria v Queensland at Melbourne	2015-16
102	and 142	Haji Murad	Amo v Speen Ghar at Ghazi Amanullah Town . .	2017-18

TWO DOUBLE-HUNDREDS IN A MATCH

A. E. Fagg	244	202*	Kent v Essex at Colchester.	1938
A. K. Perera	**201**	**231**	**Nondescripts v Sinhalese at Colombo (PSO)**	**2018-19**

TRIPLE-HUNDRED AND HUNDRED IN A MATCH

G. A. Gooch.	333	123	England v India at Lord's.	1990
K. C. Sangakkara	319	105	Sri Lanka v Bangladesh at Chittagong	2013-14

DOUBLE-HUNDRED AND HUNDRED IN A MATCH

In addition to Fagg, Perera, Gooch and Sangakkara, there have been **65** further instances of a batsman scoring a double-hundred and a hundred in the same first-class match. The most recent are:

N. V. Ojha.	219*	101*	India A v Australia A at Brisbane	2014
S. D. Robson	231	106	Middlesex v Warwickshire at Lord's	2016
G. S. Ballance	108	203*	Yorkshire v Hampshire at Southampton	2017
B. O. P. Fernando . .	**109**	**234**	**Chilaw Marians v Colts at Colombo (NCC)**	**2018-19**
D. P. Sibley.	**215***	**109**	**Warwickshire v Notts at Nottingham**	**2019**
R. Dalal.	**178**	**205***	**Arunachal Pradesh v Mizoram at Puducherry** .	**2019-20**

Zaheer Abbas achieved the feat four times, for Gloucestershire between 1976 and 1981, and was not out in all eight innings. M. R. Hallam did it twice for Leicestershire, in 1959 and 1961; N. R. Taylor twice for Kent, in 1990 and 1991; G. A. Gooch for England in 1990 (see above) and Essex in 1994; M. W. Goodwin twice for Sussex, in 2001 and 2007; and C. J. L. Rogers for Northamptonshire in 2006 and for Derbyshire in 2010.

TWO SEPARATE HUNDREDS IN A MATCH MOST TIMES

R. T. Ponting	8	J. B. Hobbs.	6	M. L. Hayden	5
Zaheer Abbas	8	G. M. Turner	6	G. A. Hick	5
W. R. Hammond	7	C. B. Fry.	5	C. J. L. Rogers	5
M. R. Ramprakash	7	G. A. Gooch	5		

W. Lambert scored 107 and 157 for Sussex v Epsom at Lord's in 1817, a feat not repeated until W. G. Grace's 130 and 102* for South of the Thames v North of the Thames at Canterbury in 1868.

FIVE HUNDREDS OR MORE IN SUCCESSION

D. G. Bradman (1938-39)	6	B. C. Lara (1993-94–1994)	5
C. B. Fry (1901)	6	P. A. Patel (2007–2007-08)	5
M. J. Procter (1970-71)	6	K. C. Sangakkara (2017)	5
M. E. K. Hussey (2003)	5	E. D. Weekes (1955-56)	5

Bradman also scored four hundreds in succession twice, in 1931-32 and 1948–1948-49; W. R. Hammond did it in 1936-37 and 1945–1946, and H. Sutcliffe in 1931 and 1939.

T. W. Hayward (Surrey v Nottinghamshire and Leicestershire), D. W. Hookes (South Australia v Queensland and New South Wales) and V. Sibanda (Zimbabwe XI v Kenya and Mid West v Southern Rocks) are the only players to score two hundreds in each of two successive matches. Hayward scored his in six days, June 4–9, 1906.

The most fifties in consecutive innings is ten – by E. Tyldesley in 1926, by D. G. Bradman in the 1947-48 and 1948 seasons and by R. S. Kaluwitharana in 1994-95.

MOST HUNDREDS IN A SEASON

D. C. S. Compton (1947)	18	W. R. Hammond (1937)	13
J. B. Hobbs (1925)	16	T. W. Hayward (1906)	13
W. R. Hammond (1938)	15	E. H. Hendren (1923)	13
H. Sutcliffe (1932)	14	E. H. Hendren (1927)	13
G. Boycott (1971)	13	E. H. Hendren (1928)	13
D. G. Bradman (1938)	13	C. P. Mead (1928)	13
C. B. Fry (1901)	13	H. Sutcliffe (1928)	13
W. R. Hammond (1933)	13	H. Sutcliffe (1931)	13

Since 1969 (excluding G. Boycott – above)

G. A. Gooch (1990)	12	M. R. Ramprakash (1995)	10
S. J. Cook (1991)	11	M. R. Ramprakash (2007)	10
Zaheer Abbas (1976)	11	G. M. Turner (1970)	10
G. A. Hick (1988)	10	Zaheer Abbas (1981)	10
H. Morris (1990)	10		

The most outside England is nine by V. Sibanda in Zimbabwe (2009-10), followed by eight by D. G. Bradman in Australia (1947-48), D. C. S. Compton (1948-49), R. N. Harvey and A. R. Morris (both 1949-50) all three in South Africa, M. D. Crowe in New Zealand (1986-87), Asif Mujtaba in Pakistan (1995-96), V. V. S. Laxman in India (1999-2000), M. G. Bevan in Australia (2004-05) and Zia-ul-Haq in Afghanistan (2017-18).

The most double-hundreds in a season is six by D. G. Bradman (1930), five by K. S. Ranjitsinhji (1900) and E. D. Weekes (1950), and four by Arun Lal (1986-87), C. B. Fry (1901), W. R. Hammond (1933 and 1934), E. H. Hendren (1929-30), V. M. Merchant (1944-45), C. A. Pujara (2012-13) and G. M. Turner (1971-72).

MOST DOUBLE-HUNDREDS IN A CAREER

D. G. Bradman	37	W. G. Grace	13	Younis Khan	12
W. R. Hammond	36	B. C. Lara	13	J. W. Hearne	11
E. H. Hendren	22	C. P. Mead	13	L. Hutton	11
M. R. Ramprakash	17	W. H. Ponsford	13	D. S. Lehmann	11
H. Sutcliffe	17	K. C. Sangakkara	13	V. M. Merchant	11
C. B. Fry	16	J. T. Tyldesley	13	C. J. L. Rogers	11
G. A. Hick	16	P. Holmes	12	A. Sandham	11
J. B. Hobbs	16	Javed Miandad	12	G. Boycott	10
C. G. Greenidge	14	J. L. Langer	12	R. Dravid	10
K. S. Ranjitsinhji	14	**C. A. Pujara**	**12**	M. W. Gatting	10
G. A. Gooch	13	R. B. Simpson	12	S. M. Gavaskar	10

J. Hardstaff jnr.	10	D. P. M. D. Jayawardene	10	R. T. Simpson	10
V. S. Hazare	10	I. V. A. Richards	10	G. M. Turner	10
B. J. Hodge	10	A. Shrewsbury	10	Zaheer Abbas	10

MOST HUNDREDS IN A CAREER

(100 or more)

		Total	Total Inns	100th 100 Season	Inns	400+	300+	200+
1	J. B. Hobbs	197	1,315	1923	821	0	1	16
2	E. H. Hendren	170	1,300	1928-29	740	0	1	22
3	W. R. Hammond	167	1,005	1935	680	0	4	36
4	C. P. Mead	153	1,340	1927	892	0	0	13
5	G. Boycott	151	1,014	1977	645	0	0	10
6	J. H. Sutcliffe	149	1,088	1932	700	0	1	17
7	F. E. Woolley	145	1,532	1929	1,031	0	1	9
8	G. A. Hick	136	871	1998	574	1	3	16
9	L. Hutton	129	814	1951	619	0	1	11
10	G. A. Gooch	128	990	1992-93	820	0	1	13
11	W. G. Grace	126	1,493	1895	1,113	0	3	13
12	D. C. S. Compton	123	839	1952	552	0	1	9
13	T. W. Graveney	122	1,223	1964	940	0	0	7
14	D. G. Bradman	117	338	1947-48	295	1	6	37
15	I. V. A. Richards	114	796	1988-89	658	0	1	10
	M. R. Ramprakash	114	764	2008	676	0	1	17
17	Zaheer Abbas	108	768	1982-83	658	0	0	10
18	A. Sandham	107	1,000	1935	871	0	1	11
	M. C. Cowdrey	107	1,130	1973	1,035	0	1	3
20	T. W. Hayward	104	1,138	1913	1,076	0	1	8
21	G. M. Turner	103	792	1982	779	0	1	10
	J. H. Edrich	103	979	1977	945	0	1	4
23	L. E. G. Ames	102	951	1950	916	0	0	9
	E. Tyldesley	102	961	1934	919	0	0	7
	D. L. Amiss	102	1,139	1986	1,081	0	0	3

In the above table, 200+, 300+ and 400+ include all scores above those figures.
G. A. Gooch's record includes his century in South Africa in 1981-82, which is no longer accepted by the ICC. G. Boycott and Zaheer Abbas scored their 100th hundreds in Test matches.

Current Players

The following who played in 2019 have scored 40 or more hundreds.

M. E. Trescothick	66	C. A. Pujara	49	D. Elgar	41
A. N. Cook	65	S. C. Cook	48	J. K. Silva	41
Wasim Jaffer	57	J. C. Hildreth	46	G. S. Ballance	40
H. M. Amla	52	S. P. D. Smith	42	N. T. Paranavitana	40

MOST RUNS IN A SEASON

	Season	I	NO	R	HS	100	Avge
D. C. S. Compton	1947	50	8	3,816	246	18	90.85
W. J. Edrich	1947	52	8	3,539	267*	12	80.43
T. W. Hayward	1906	61	8	3,518	219	13	66.37
L. Hutton	1949	56	6	3,429	269*	12	68.58
F. E. Woolley	1928	59	4	3,352	198	12	60.94
H. Sutcliffe	1932	52	7	3,336	313	14	74.13
W. R. Hammond	1933	54	5	3,323	264	13	67.81
E. H. Hendren	1928	54	7	3,311	209*	13	70.44
R. Abel	1901	68	8	3,309	247	7	55.15

3,000 in a season has been surpassed on 19 other occasions (a full list can be found in Wisden 1999 and earlier editions). W. R. Hammond, E. H. Hendren and H. Sutcliffe are the only players to achieve the feat three times. K. S. Ranjitsinhji was the first batsman to reach 3,000 in a season, with 3,159 in 1899. M. J. K. Smith (3,245 in 1959) and W. E. Alley (3,019 in 1961) are the only players except those listed above to have reached 3,000 since World War II.

W. G. Grace scored 2,739 runs in 1871 – the first batsman to reach 2,000 in a season. He made ten hundreds including two double-hundreds, with an average of 78.25 in all first-class matches.

The highest aggregate in a season since the reduction of County Championship matches in 1969 was 2,755 by S. J. Cook (42 innings) in 1991, and the last batsman to achieve 2,000 in England was M. R. Ramprakash (2,026 in 2007); C. A. Pujara scored 2,064 in India in 2016-17.

2,000 RUNS IN A SEASON MOST TIMES

J. B. Hobbs 17	F. E. Woolley 13	C. P. Mead 11
E. H. Hendren 15	W. R. Hammond 12	T. W. Hayward 10
H. Sutcliffe 15	J. G. Langridge 11	

Since the reduction of County Championship matches in 1969, G. A. Gooch is the only batsman to have reached 2,000 runs in a season five times.

1,000 RUNS IN A SEASON MOST TIMES

Includes overseas tours and seasons

W. G. Grace 28	A. Jones 23	G. Gunn 20
F. E. Woolley 28	T. W. Graveney 22	T. W. Hayward 20
M. C. Cowdrey 27	W. R. Hammond 22	G. A. Hick 20
C. P. Mead 27	D. Denton 21	James Langridge 20
G. Boycott 26	J. H. Edrich 21	J. M. Parks 20
J. B. Hobbs 26	G. A. Gooch 21	M. R. Ramprakash 20
E. H. Hendren 25	R. Rhodes 21	A. Sandham 20
D. L. Amiss 24	D. B. Close 20	M. J. K. Smith 20
W. G. Quaife 24	K. W. R. Fletcher 20	C. Washbrook 20
H. Sutcliffe 24	M. W. Gatting 20	

F. E. Woolley reached 1,000 runs in 28 consecutive seasons (1907–1938), C. P. Mead in 27 (1906–1936).

Outside England, 1,000 runs in a season has been reached most times by D. G. Bradman (in 12 seasons in Australia).

Three batsmen have scored 1,000 runs in a season in each of four different countries: G. S. Sobers in West Indies, England, India and Australia; M. C. Cowdrey and G. Boycott in England, South Africa, West Indies and Australia.

HIGHEST AGGREGATES OUTSIDE ENGLAND

	Season	I	NO	R	HS	100	Avge
In Australia							
D. G. Bradman	1928-29	24	6	1,690	340*	7	93.88
In South Africa							
J. R. Reid	1961-62	30	2	1,915	203	7	68.39
In West Indies							
E. H. Hendren	1929-30	18	5	1,765	254*	6	135.76
In New Zealand							
M. D. Crowe	1986-87	21	3	1,676	175*	8	93.11
In India							
C. A. Pujara	2016-17	29	4	2,064	256*	7	82.56
In Pakistan							
Saadat Ali	1983-84	27	1	1,649	208	4	63.42

	Season	I	NO	R	HS	100	Avge
In Sri Lanka							
R. P. Arnold..............	1995-96	24	3	1,475	217*	5	70.23
In Zimbabwe							
V. Sibanda...............	2009-10	26	4	1,612	215	9	73.27
In Bangladesh							
Tushar Imran.............	2016-17	16	2	1,249	220	5	89.21
In Afghanistan							
Zia-ul-Haq...............	2017-18	31	4	1,616	148	8	59.85

Excluding Pujara in India (above), the following aggregates of over 2,000 runs have been recorded in more than one country:

M. Amarnath (P/I/WI)......	1982-83	34	6	2,234	207	9	79.78
J. R. Reid (SA/A/NZ)	1961-62	40	2	2,188	203	7	57.57
S. M. Gavaskar (I/P)	1978-79	30	6	2,121	205	10	88.37
R. B. Simpson (I/P/A/WI) ...	1964-65	34	4	2,063	201	8	68.76
M. H. Richardson (Z/SA/NZ) .	2000-01	34	3	2,030	306	4	65.48

The only other player to hit ten hundreds in an overseas season was V. V. S. Laxman in India and Australia in 1999-2000.

LEADING BATSMEN IN AN ENGLISH SEASON

(Qualification: 8 completed innings)

Season	Leading scorer	Runs	Avge	Top of averages	Runs	Avge
1946	D. C. S. Compton	2,403	61.61	W. R. Hammond......	1,783	84.90
1947	D. C. S. Compton	3,816	90.85	D. C. S. Compton	3,816	90.85
1948	L. Hutton...........	2,654	64.73	D. G. Bradman	2,428	89.92
1949	L. Hutton...........	3,429	68.58	J. Hardstaff	2,251	72.61
1950	R. T. Simpson	2,576	62.82	E. D. Weekes	2,310	79.65
1951	J. D. Robertson	2,917	56.09	P. B. H. May	2,339	68.79
1952	L. Hutton...........	2,567	61.11	D. S. Sheppard	2,262	64.62
1953	W. J. Edrich	2,557	47.35	R. N. Harvey........	2,040	65.80
1954	D. Kenyon..........	2,636	51.68	D. C. S. Compton	1,524	58.61
1955	D. J. Insole	2,427	42.57	D. J. McGlew	1,871	58.46
1956	T. W. Graveney......	2,397	49.93	K. Mackay	1,103	52.52
1957	T. W. Graveney......	2,361	49.18	P. B. H. May	2,347	61.76
1958	P. B. H. May	2,231	63.74	P. B. H. May	2,231	63.74
1959	M. J. K. Smith	3,245	57.94	V. L. Manjrekar	755	68.63
1960	M. J. K. Smith	2,551	45.55	R. Subba Row.......	1,503	55.66
1961	W. E. Alley	3,019	56.96	W. M. Lawry	2,019	61.18
1962	J. H. Edrich	2,482	51.70	R. T. Simpson........	867	54.18
1963	J. B. Bolus..........	2,190	41.32	G. S. Sobers	1,333	47.60
1964	T. W. Graveney......	2,385	54.20	K. F. Barrington	1,872	62.40
1965	J. H. Edrich	2,319	62.67	M. C. Cowdrey	2,093	63.42
1966	A. R. Lewis	2,198	41.47	G. S. Sobers	1,349	61.31
1967	C. A. Milton	2,089	46.42	K. F. Barrington	2,059	68.63
1968	B. A. Richards.......	2,395	47.90	G. Boycott	1,487	64.65
1969	J. H. Edrich	2,238	69.93	J. H. Edrich	2,238	69.93
1970	G. M. Turner........	2,379	61.00	G. S. Sobers	1,742	75.73
1971	G. Boycott..........	2,503	100.12	G. Boycott	2,503	100.12
1972	Majid Khan..........	2,074	61.00	G. Boycott	1,230	72.35
1973	G. M. Turner........	2,416	67.11	G. M. Turner........	2,416	67.11
1974	R. T. Virgin.........	1,936	56.94	C. H. Lloyd.........	1,458	63.39
1975	G. Boycott..........	1,915	73.65	R. B. Kanhai	1,073	82.53
1976	Zaheer Abbas	2,554	75.11	Zaheer Abbas	2,554	75.11
1977	I. V. A. Richards.....	2,161	65.48	G. Boycott	1,701	68.04
1978	D. L. Amiss.........	2,030	53.42	C. E. B. Rice........	1,871	66.82

Season	Leading scorer	Runs	Avge	Top of averages	Runs	Avge
1979	K. C. Wessels	1,800	52.94	G. Boycott	1,538	102.53
1980	P. N. Kirsten	1,895	63.16	A. J. Lamb	1,797	66.55
1981	Zaheer Abbas	2,306	88.69	Zaheer Abbas	2,306	88.69
1982	A. I. Kallicharran	2,120	66.25	G. M. Turner	1,171	90.07
1983	K. S. McEwan	2,176	64.00	I. V. A. Richards	1,204	75.25
1984	G. A. Gooch	2,559	67.34	C. G. Greenidge	1,069	82.23
1985	G. A. Gooch	2,208	71.22	I. V. A. Richards	1,836	76.50
1986	C. G. Greenidge	2,035	67.83	C. G. Greenidge	2,035	67.83
1987	G. A. Hick	1,879	52.19	M. D. Crowe	1,627	67.79
1988	G. A. Hick	2,713	77.51	R. A. Harper	622	77.75
1989	S. J. Cook	2,241	60.56	D. M. Jones	1,510	88.82
1990	G. A. Gooch	2,746	101.70	G. A. Gooch	2,746	101.70
1991	S. J. Cook	2,755	81.02	C. L. Hooper	1,501	93.81
1992	P. D. Bowler	2,044	65.93	Salim Malik	1,184	78.93
	M. A. Roseberry	2,044	56.77			
1993	P. D. Bowler	2,023	63.21	D. C. Boon	1,437	75.63
1994	B. C. Lara	2,066	89.82	J. D. Carr	1,543	90.76
1995	M. R. Ramprakash	2,258	77.86	M. R. Ramprakash	2,258	77.86
1996	G. A. Gooch	1,944	67.03	S. C. Ganguly	762	95.25
1997	S. P. James	1,775	68.26	G. A. Hick	1,524	69.27
1998	J. P. Crawley	1,851	74.04	J. P. Crawley	1,851	74.04
1999	S. G. Law	1,833	73.32	S. G. Law	1,833	73.32
2000	D. S. Lehmann	1,477	67.13	M. G. Bevan	1,124	74.93
2001	M. E. K. Hussey	2,055	79.03	D. R. Martyn	942	104.66
2002	I. J. Ward	1,759	62.82	R. Dravid	773	96.62
2003	S. G. Law	1,820	91.00	S. G. Law	1,820	91.00
2004	R. W. T. Key	1,896	79.00	R. W. T. Key	1,896	79.00
2005	O. A. Shah	1,728	66.46	M. E. K. Hussey	1,074	76.71
2006	M. R. Ramprakash	2,278	103.54	M. R. Ramprakash	2,278	103.54
2007	M. R. Ramprakash	2,026	101.30	M. R. Ramprakash	2,026	101.30
2008	S. C. Moore	1,451	55.80	T. Frost	1,003	83.58
2009	M. E. Trescothick	1,817	75.70	M. R. Ramprakash	1,350	90.00
2010	M. R. Ramprakash	1,595	61.34	J. C. Hildreth	1,440	65.45
2011	M. E. Trescothick	1,673	79.66	I. R. Bell	1,091	90.91
2012	N. R. D. Compton	1,494	99.60	N. R. D. Compton	1,494	99.60
2013	C. J. L. Rogers	1,536	51.20	S. M. Katich	1,097	73.13
2014	A. Lyth	1,619	70.39	J. E. Root	1,052	75.14
2015	J. C. Hildreth	1,758	56.70	J. M. Bairstow	1,226	72.11
2016	K. K. Jennings	1,602	64.08	S. A. Northeast	1,402	82.47
2017	K. C. Sangakkara	1,491	106.50	K. C. Sangakkara	1,491	106.50
2018	R. J. Burns	1,402	60.95	O. J. D. Pope	1,098	61.00
2019	**D. P. Sibley**	**1,575**	**68.47**	**S. P. D. Smith**	**797**	**99.62**

The highest average recorded in an English season was 115.66 (2,429 runs, 26 innings) by D. G. Bradman in 1938.

In 1953, W. A. Johnston averaged 102.00 from 17 innings, 16 not out.

MOST RUNS

Dates in italics denote the first half of an overseas season; i.e. *1945* denotes the 1945-46 season.

		Career	R	I	NO	HS	100	Avge
1	J. B. Hobbs	1905–1934	61,237	1,315	106	316*	197	50.65
2	F. E. Woolley	1906–1938	58,969	1,532	85	305*	145	40.75
3	E. H. Hendren	1907–1938	57,611	1,300	166	301*	170	50.80
4	C. P. Mead	1905–1936	55,061	1,340	185	280*	153	47.67
5	W. G. Grace	1865–1908	54,896	1,493	105	344	126	39.55
6	W. R. Hammond	1920–1951	50,551	1,005	104	336*	167	56.10
7	H. Sutcliffe	1919–1945	50,138	1,088	123	313	149	51.95
8	G. Boycott	1962–1986	48,426	1,014	162	261*	151	56.83
9	T. W. Graveney	1948–*1971*	47,793	1,223	159	258	122	44.91

		Career	R	I	NO	HS	100	Avge
10	G. A. Gooch	1973–2000	44,846	990	75	333	128	49.01
11	T. W. Hayward	1893–1914	43,551	1,138	96	315*	104	41.79
12	D. L. Amiss	1960–1987	43,423	1,139	126	262*	102	42.86
13	M. C. Cowdrey	1950–1976	42,719	1,130	134	307	107	42.89
14	A. Sandham	1911–1937	41,284	1,000	79	325	107	44.82
15	G. A. Hick	1983–2008	41,112	871	84	405*	136	52.23
16	L. Hutton	1934–1960	40,140	814	91	364	129	55.51
17	M. J. K. Smith	1951–1975	39,832	1,091	139	204	69	41.84
18	W. Rhodes	1898–1930	39,802	1,528	237	267*	58	30.83
19	J. H. Edrich	1956–1978	39,790	979	104	310*	103	45.47
20	R. E. S. Wyatt	1923–1957	39,405	1,141	157	232	85	40.04
21	D. C. S. Compton	1936–1964	38,942	839	88	300	123	51.85
22	E. Tyldesley	1909–1936	38,874	961	106	256*	102	45.46
23	J. T. Tyldesley	1895–1923	37,897	994	62	295*	86	40.66
24	K. W. R. Fletcher	1962–1988	37,665	1,167	170	228*	63	37.77
25	C. G. Greenidge	1970–1992	37,354	889	75	273*	92	45.88
26	J. W. Hearne	1909–1936	37,252	1,025	116	285*	96	40.98
27	L. E. G. Ames	1926–1951	37,248	951	95	295	102	43.51
28	D. Kenyon	1946–1967	37,002	1,159	59	259	74	33.63
29	W. J. Edrich	1934–1958	36,965	964	92	267*	86	42.39
30	J. M. Parks	1949–1976	36,673	1,227	172	205*	51	34.76
31	M. W. Gatting	1975–1998	36,549	861	123	258	94	49.52
32	D. Denton	1894–1920	36,479	1,163	70	221	69	33.37
33	G. H. Hirst	1891–1929	36,323	1,215	151	341	60	34.13
34	I. V. A. Richards	1971–1993	36,212	796	63	322	114	49.40
35	A. Jones	1957–1983	36,049	1,168	72	204*	56	32.89
36	W. G. Quaife	1894–1928	36,012	1,203	185	255*	72	35.37
37	R. E. Marshall . . .	1945–1972	35,725	1,053	59	228*	68	35.94
38	M. R. Ramprakash . . .	1987–2012	35,659	764	93	301*	114	53.14
39	G. Gunn	1902–1932	35,208	1,061	82	220	62	35.96

Some works of reference provide career figures which differ from those in this list, owing to the exclusion or inclusion of matches recognised or not recognised as first-class by Wisden. A fuller list can be found in Wisdens up to 2011.

Current Players with 20,000 Runs

	Career	R	I	NO	HS	100	Avge
M. E. Trescothick	1993–2019	26,234	675	36	284	66	41.05
A. N. Cook	2003–2019	23,667	538	41	294	65	47.61
I. R. Bell	1999–2018	20,256	516	55	262*	57	43.93

HIGHEST CAREER AVERAGE

(Qualification: 10,000 runs)

Avge		Career	I	NO	R	HS	100
95.14	D. G. Bradman	1927–1948	338	43	28,067	452*	117
71.22	V. M. Merchant	1929–1951	229	43	13,248	359*	44
67.46	Ajay Sharma	1984–2000	166	16	10,120	259*	38
65.18	W. H. Ponsford	1920–1934	235	23	13,819	437	47
64.99	W. M. Woodfull	1921–1934	245	39	13,388	284	49
58.24	A. L. Hassett	1932–1953	322	32	16,890	232	59
58.19	V. S. Hazare	1934–1966	365	45	18,621	316*	60
57.93	**S. P. D. Smith**	**2007–2019**	**227**	**26**	**11,644**	**239**	**42**
57.84	S. R. Tendulkar	1988–2013	490	51	25,396	248*	81
57.83	D. S. Lehmann	1987–2007	479	33	25,795	339	82
57.32	M. G. Bevan	1989–2006	400	66	19,147	216	68
57.22	A. F. Kippax	1918–1935	256	33	12,762	315*	43
56.84	**Fawad Alam**	**2003–2019**	**258**	**43**	**12,222**	**296***	**34**
56.83	G. Boycott	1962–1986	1,014	162	48,426	261*	151

Avge		*Career*	*I*	*NO*	*R*	*HS*	*100*
56.55	C. L. Walcott	*1941–1963*	238	29	11,820	314*	40
56.37	K. S. Ranjitsinhji	*1893–1920*	500	62	24,692	285*	72
56.22	R. B. Simpson	*1952–1977*	436	62	21,029	359	60
56.10	W. R. Hammond	*1920–1951*	1,005	104	50,551	336*	167
56.02	M. D. Crowe	*1979–1995*	412	62	19,608	299	71
55.90	R. T. Ponting	*1992–2013*	494	62	24,150	257	82
55.51	L. Hutton	*1934–1960*	814	91	40,140	364	129
55.34	E. D. Weekes	*1944–1964*	241	24	12,010	304*	36
55.33	R. Dravid	*1990–2011*	497	67	23,794	270	68
55.11	S. V. Manjrekar	*1984–1997*	217	31	10,252	377	31

G. A. Headley scored 9,921 runs, average 69.86, between 1927-28 and 1954.

FASTEST FIFTIES

Minutes

11	C. I. J. Smith (66)	Middlesex v Gloucestershire at Bristol	1938
13	Khalid Mahmood (56)	Gujranwala v Sargodha at Gujranwala.	2000-01
14	S. J. Pegler (50)	South Africans v Tasmania at Launceston	1910-11
14	F. T. Mann (53)	Middlesex v Nottinghamshire at Lord's	1921
14	H. B. Cameron (56)	Transvaal v Orange Free State at Johannesburg	1934-35
14	C. I. J. Smith (52)	Middlesex v Kent at Maidstone	1935

The number of balls taken to achieve fifties was rarely recorded until recently. C. I. J. Smith's two fifties (above) may have taken only 12 balls each. Khalid Mahmood reached his fifty in 15 balls.

Fifties scored in contrived circumstances and with the bowlers' compliance are excluded from the above list, including the fastest of them all, in 8 minutes (13 balls) by C. C. Inman, Leicestershire v Nottinghamshire at Nottingham, 1965, and 10 minutes by G. Chapple, Lancashire v Glamorgan at Manchester, 1993.

FASTEST HUNDREDS

Minutes

35	P. G. H. Fender (113*)	Surrey v Northamptonshire at Northampton	1920
40	G. L. Jessop (101)	Gloucestershire v Yorkshire at Harrogate	1897
40	Ahsan-ul-Haq (100*)	Muslims v Sikhs at Lahore	1923-24
42	G. L. Jessop (191)	Gentlemen of South v Players of South at Hastings .	1907
43	A. H. Hornby (106)	Lancashire v Somerset at Manchester	1905
43	D. W. Hookes (107)	South Australia v Victoria at Adelaide	1982-83
44	R. N. S. Hobbs (100)	Essex v Australians at Chelmsford	1975

The fastest recorded authentic hundred in terms of balls received was scored off 34 balls by D. W. Hookes (above). Research of the scorebook has shown that P. G. H. Fender scored his hundred from between 40 and 46 balls. He contributed 113 to an unfinished sixth-wicket partnership of 171 in 42 minutes with H. A. Peach.

E. B. Alletson (Nottinghamshire) scored 189 out of 227 runs in 90 minutes against Sussex at Hove in 1911. It has been estimated that his last 139 runs took 37 minutes.

Hundreds scored in contrived circumstances and with the bowlers' compliance are excluded, including the fastest of them all, in 21 minutes (27 balls) by G. Chapple, Lancashire v Glamorgan at Manchester, 1993, 24 minutes (27 balls) by M. L. Pettini, Essex v Leicestershire at Leicester, 2006, and 26 minutes (36 balls) by T. M. Moody, Warwickshire v Glamorgan at Swansea, 1990.

FASTEST DOUBLE-HUNDREDS

Minutes

103	Shafiqullah Shinwari (200*)	Kabul v Boost at Asadabad	2017-18
113	R. J. Shastri (200*)	Bombay v Baroda at Bombay	1984-85
120	G. L. Jessop (286)	Gloucestershire v Sussex at Hove	1903
120	C. H. Lloyd (201*)	West Indians v Glamorgan at Swansea	1976
130	G. L. Jessop (234)	Gloucestershire v Somerset at Bristol	1905
131	V. T. Trumper (293)	Australians v Canterbury at Christchurch	1913-14

Shafiqullah faced 89 balls, which was also a record.

FASTEST TRIPLE-HUNDREDS

Minutes

181	D. C. S. Compton (300)	MCC v North Eastern Transvaal at Benoni	1948-49
205	F. E. Woolley (305*)	MCC v Tasmania at Hobart	1911-12
205	C. G. Macartney (345)	Australians v Nottinghamshire at Nottingham	1921
213	D. G. Bradman (369)	South Australia v Tasmania at Adelaide	1935-36

The fastest triple-hundred in terms of balls received was scored off 191 balls by M. Marais for Border v Eastern Province at East London in 2017-18.

MOST RUNS IN A DAY BY ONE BATSMAN

390*	B. C. Lara	Warwickshire v Durham at Birmingham	1994
345	C. G. Macartney	Australians v Nottinghamshire at Nottingham	1921
334	W. H. Ponsford	Victoria v New South Wales at Melbourne	1926-27
333	K. S. Duleepsinhji	Sussex v Northamptonshire at Hove	1930
331*	J. D. B. Robertson	Middlesex v Worcestershire at Worcester	1949
325*	B. A. Richards	South Australia v Western Australia at Perth	1970-71

These scores do not necessarily represent the complete innings. See page 1220.

*There have been another **14** instances of a batsman scoring 300 in a day, most recently 319 by R. R. Rossouw, Eagles v Titans at Centurion in 2009-10 (see Wisden 2003, page 278, for full list).*

LONGEST INNINGS

Hrs	Mins			
16	55	R. Nayyar (271)	Himachal Pradesh v Jammu & Kashmir at Chamba	1999-2000
16	10	Hanif Mohammad (337)	Pakistan v West Indies at Bridgetown	1957-58
		Hanif believed he batted 16 hours 39 minutes.		
16	4	S. B. Gohel (359*)	Gujarat v Orissa at Jaipur.	2016-17
15	7	V. A. Saxena (257)	Rajasthan v Tamil Nadu at Chennai	2011-12
14	38	G. Kirsten (275)	South Africa v England at Durban.	1999-2000
14	32	K. K. Nair (328)	Karnataka v Tamil Nadu at Mumbai	2014-15
13	58	S. C. Cook (390)	Lions v Warriors at East London	2009-10
13	56	A. N. Cook (263)	England v Pakistan at Abu Dhabi	2015-16
13	43	T. Kohli (300*)	Punjab v Jharkhand at Jamshedpur	2012-13
13	41	S. S. Shukla (178*)	Uttar Pradesh v Tamil Nadu at Nagpur	2008-09
13	32	A. Chopra (301*)	Rajasthan v Maharashtra at Nasik	2010-11

1,000 RUNS IN MAY

	Runs	*Avge*
W. G. Grace, May 9 to May 30, 1895 (22 days)	1,016	112.88
Grace was 46 years old.		
W. R. Hammond, May 7 to May 31, 1927 (25 days)	1,042	74.42
Hammond scored his 1,000th run on May 28, thus equalling		
Grace's record of 22 days.		
C. Hallows, May 5 to May 31, 1928 (27 days)	1,000	125.00

1,000 RUNS IN APRIL AND MAY

	Runs	*Avge*
T. W. Hayward, April 16 to May 31, 1900	1,074	97.63
D. G. Bradman, April 30 to May 31, 1930	1,001	143.00
On April 30 Bradman was 75 not out.		

		Runs	Avge
D. G. Bradman, April 30 to May 31, 1938		1,056	150.85

Bradman scored 258 on April 30, and his 1,000th run on May 27.

		Runs	Avge
W. J. Edrich, April 30 to May 31, 1938		1,010	84.16

Edrich was 21 not out on April 30. All his runs were scored at Lord's.

		Runs	Avge
G. M. Turner, April 24 to May 31, 1973		1,018	78.30
G. A. Hick, April 17 to May 29, 1988		1,019	101.90

Hick scored a record 410 runs in April, and his 1,000th run on May 28.

MOST RUNS SCORED OFF AN OVER

(All instances refer to six-ball overs)

36	G. S. Sobers	off M. A. Nash, Nottinghamshire v Glam at Swansea (six sixes)....	1968
36	R. J. Shastri	off Tilak Raj, Bombay v Baroda at Bombay (six sixes).........	1984-85
34	E. B. Alletson	off E. H. Killick, Notts v Sussex at Hove (46604446 inc 2 nb).....	1911
34	F. C. Hayes	off M. A. Nash, Lancashire v Glamorgan at Swansea (646666)	1977
34†	A. Flintoff	off A. J. Tudor, Lancs v Surrey at Manchester (64444660 inc 2 nb) .	1998
34	C. M. Spearman	off S. J. P. Moreton, Gloucestershire v Oxford UCCE at Oxford	
		(666466) *Moreton's first over in first-class cricket.*............	2005
32	C. C. Smart	off G. Hill, Glamorgan v Hampshire at Cardiff (664664)	1935
32	I. R. Redpath	off N. Rosendorff, Australians v OFS at Bloemfontein (666644) ...	1969-70
32	P. W. G. Parker	off A. I. Kallicharran, Sussex v Warwicks at Birmingham (466664).	1982
32	I. T. Botham	off I. R. Snook, England XI v C Dists at Palmerston North (466466)	1983-84
32	Khalid Mahmood	off Naved Latif, Gujranwala v Sargodha at Gujranwala (666662)...	2000-01

† *Altogether 38 runs were scored off this over, the two no-balls counting for two extra runs each under ECB regulations.*

The following instances have been excluded because of the bowlers' compliance: 34 – M. P. Maynard off S. A. Marsh, Glamorgan v Kent at Swansea, 1992; 34 – G. Chapple off P. A. Cottey, Lancashire v Glamorgan at Manchester, 1993; 34 – F. B. Touzel off F. J. J. Viljoen, Western Province B v Griqualand West at Kimberley, 1993-94. Chapple scored a further 32 off Cottey's next over.

There were 35 runs off an over received by A. T. Reinholds off H. T. Davis, Auckland v Wellington at Auckland 1995-96, but this included 16 extras and only 19 off the bat.

In a match against KwaZulu-Natal at Stellenbosch in 2006-07, W. E. September (Boland) conceded 34 in an over: 27 to M. Bekker, six to K. Smit, plus one no-ball.

In a match against Canterbury at Christchurch in 1989-90, R. H. Vance (Wellington) deliberately conceded 77 runs in an over of full tosses which contained 17 no-balls and, owing to the umpire's understandable miscalculation, only five legitimate deliveries.

The greatest number of runs scored off an eight-ball over is 34 (40446664) by R. M. Edwards off M. C. Carew, Governor-General's XI v West Indians at Auckland, 1968-69.

MOST SIXES IN AN INNINGS

23	C. Munro (281)	Auckland v Central Districts at Napier............	2014-15
22	Shafiqullah Shinwari (200*)	Kabul v Boost at Asadabad......................	2017-18
19	**P. B. B. Rajapaksa (268)**	**Burgher v Ports Authority at Colombo (Moors)...**	**2018-19**
19	**Najeeb Tarakai (200)**	**Speen Ghar v Mis Ainak at Asadabad........**	**2018-19**
17	**B. O. P. Fernando (234)**	**Chilaw Marians v Colts at Colombo (NCC)....**	**2018-19**
16	A. Symonds (254*)	Gloucestershire v Glamorgan at Abergavenny.......	1995
16	G. R. Napier (196)	Essex v Surrey at Croydon........................	2011
16	J. D. Ryder (175)	New Zealanders v Australia A at Brisbane.........	2011-12
16	Mukhtar Ali (168)	Rajshahi v Chittagong at Savar...................	2013-14

There have been six further instances of 15 sixes in an innings.

MOST SIXES IN A MATCH

24	Shafiqullah Shinwari (22, 200*)	Kabul v Boost at Asadabad	2017-18
23	C. Munro (281)	Auckland v Central Districts at Napier	2014-15
21	R. R. Pant (117, 131)	Delhi v Jharkhand at Thumba	2016-17
20	A. Symonds (254*, 76)	Gloucestershire v Glam at Abergavenny	1995
19	**B. O. P. Fernando (109, 234)**	**Chilaw Marians v Colts at Colombo (NCC) . .**	**2018-19**
19	**P. B. B. Rajapaksa (268)**	**Burgher v Ports Authority at Colombo (Moors)**	**2018-19**
19	**Najeeb Tarakai (200)**	**Speen Ghar v Mis Ainak at Asadabad . . . . . .**	**2018-19**

MOST SIXES IN A SEASON

80	I. T. Botham	1985		51	A. W. Wellard	1933
66	A. W. Wellard	1935		49	I. V. A. Richards	1985
65	Najeeb Tarakai	2017-18		48	A. W. Carr	1925
57	A. W. Wellard	1936		48	J. H. Edrich	1965
57	A. W. Wellard	1938		48	A. Symonds	1995

MOST BOUNDARIES IN AN INNINGS

	4/6			
72	62/10	B. C. Lara (501*)	Warwickshire v Durham at Birmingham . . .	1994
68	68/–	P. A. Perrin (343*)	Essex v Derbyshire at Chesterfield.	1904
65	64/1	A. C. MacLaren (424)	Lancashire v Somerset at Taunton	1895
64	64/–	Hanif Mohammad (499)	Karachi v Bahawalpur at Karachi	1958-59
57	52/5	J. H. Edrich (310*)	England v New Zealand at Leeds.	1965
57	52/5	Naved Latif (394)	Sargodha v Gujranwala at Gujranwala.	2000-01
56	54/2	K. M. Jadhav (327)	Maharashtra v Uttar Pradesh at Pune	2012-13
55	55/–	C. W. Gregory (383)	NSW v Queensland at Brisbane.	1906-07
55	53/2	G. R. Marsh (355*)	W. Australia v S. Australia at Perth	1989-90
55	51/3†	S. V. Manjrekar (377)	Bombay v Hyderabad at Bombay	1990-91
55	52/3	D. S. Lehmann (339)	Yorkshire v Durham at Leeds	2006
55	54/1	D. K. H. Mitchell (298)	Worcestershire v Somerset at Taunton.	2009
55	54/1	S. C. Cook (390)	Lions v Warriors at East London	2009-10
55	47/8	R. R. Rossouw (319)	Eagles v Titans at Centurion	2009-10

† *Plus one five.*

PARTNERSHIPS OVER 500

624	for 3rd	K. C. Sangakkara (287)/D. P. M. D. Jayawardene (374), Sri Lanka v South Africa at Colombo (SSC)	2006
594*	for 3rd	S. M. Gugale (351*)/A. R. Bawne (258*), Maharashtra v Delhi at Mumbai.	2016-17
580	for 2nd	Rafatullah Mohmand (302*)/Aamer Sajjad (289), WAPDA v Sui Southern Gas at Sheikhupura	2009-10
577	for 4th	V. S. Hazare (288)/Gul Mahomed (319), Baroda v Holkar at Baroda.	1946-47
576	for 2nd	S. T. Jayasuriya (340)/R. S. Mahanama (225), Sri Lanka v India at Colombo (RPS)	1997-98
574*	for 4th	F. M. M. Worrell (255*)/C. L. Walcott (314*), Barbados v Trinidad at Port-of-Spain	1945-46
561	for 1st	Waheed Mirza (324)/Mansoor Akhtar (224*), Karachi Whites v Quetta at Karachi	1976-77
555	for 1st	P. Holmes (224*)/H. Sutcliffe (313), Yorkshire v Essex at Leyton	1932
554	for 1st	J. T. Brown (300)/J. Tunnicliffe (243), Yorks v Derbys at Chesterfield . . .	1898
539	for 3rd	S. D. Jogiyani (282)/R. A. Jadeja (303*), Saurashtra v Gujarat at Surat . .	2012-13
523	for 3rd	M. A. Carberry (300*)/N. D. McKenzie (237), Hants v Yorks at Southampton	2011
520*	for 5th	C. A. Pujara (302*)/R. A. Jadeja (232*), Saurashtra v Orissa at Rajkot . . .	2008-09
503	for 1st	R. G. L. Carters (209)/A. J. Finch (288*), Cricket Australia XI v New Zealanders at Sydney	2015-16
502*	for 4th	F. M. M. Worrell (308*)/J. D. C. Goddard (218*), Barbados v Trinidad at Bridgetown	1943-44
501	for 3rd	A. N. Petersen (286)/A. G. Prince (261), Lancs v Glam at Colwyn Bay . . .	2015

HIGHEST PARTNERSHIPS FOR EACH WICKET

First Wicket

561	Waheed Mirza/Mansoor Akhtar, Karachi Whites v Quetta at Karachi.	1976-77
555	P. Holmes/H. Sutcliffe, Yorkshire v Essex at Leyton.	1932
554	J. T. Brown/J. Tunnicliffe, Yorkshire v Derbyshire at Chesterfield	1898
503	R. G. L. Carters/A. J. Finch, Cricket Australia XI v New Zealanders at Sydney .	2015-16
490	E. H. Bowley/J. G. Langridge, Sussex v Middlesex at Hove	1933

Second Wicket

580	Rafatullah Mohmand/Aamer Sajjad, WAPDA v Sui S. Gas at Sheikhupura	2009-10
576	S. T. Jayasuriya/R. S. Mahanama, Sri Lanka v India at Colombo (RPS).	1997-98
480	D. Elgar/R. R. Rossouw, Eagles v Titans at Centurion.	2009-10
475	Zahir Alam/L. S. Rajput, Assam v Tripura at Gauhati.	1991-92
465*	J. A. Jameson/R. B. Kanhai, Warwickshire v Gloucestershire at Birmingham. . .	1974

Third Wicket

624	K. C. Sangakkara/D. P. M. D. Jayawardene, Sri Lanka v SA at Colombo (SSC)	2006
594*	S. M. Gugale/A. R. Bawne, Maharashtra v Delhi at Mumbai	2016-17
539	S. D. Jogiyani/R. A. Jadeja, Saurashtra v Gujarat at Surat	2012-13
523	M. A. Carberry/N. D. McKenzie, Hampshire v Yorkshire at Southampton	2011
501	A. N. Petersen/A. G. Prince, Lancashire v Glamorgan at Colwyn Bay	2015

Fourth Wicket

577	V. S. Hazare/Gul Mahomed, Baroda v Holkar at Baroda.	1946-47
574*	C. L. Walcott/F. M. M. Worrell, Barbados v Trinidad at Port-of-Spain.	1945-46
502*	F. M. M. Worrell/J. D. C. Goddard, Barbados v Trinidad at Bridgetown	1943-44
470	A. I. Kallicharran/G. W. Humpage, Warwickshire v Lancashire at Southport. . .	1982
462*	D. W. Hookes/W. B. Phillips, South Australia v Tasmania at Adelaide	1986-87

Fifth Wicket

520*	C. A. Pujara/R. A. Jadeja, Saurashtra v Orissa at Rajkot	2008-09
494	Marshall Ayub/Mehrab Hossain, Central Zone v East Zone at Bogra	2012-13
479	Misbah-ul-Haq/Usman Arshad, Sui N. Gas v Lahore Shalimar at Lahore	2009-10
464*	M. E. Waugh/S. R. Waugh, New South Wales v Western Australia at Perth. . . .	1990-91
428*	B. C. Williams/M. Marais, Border v Eastern Province at East London	2017-18

Sixth Wicket

487*	G. A. Headley/C. C. Passailaigue, Jamaica v Lord Tennyson's XI at Kingston. .	1931-32
428	W. W. Armstrong/M. A. Noble, Australians v Sussex at Hove	1902
417	W. P. Saha/L. R. Shukla, Bengal v Assam at Kolkata	2010-11
411	R. M. Poore/E. G. Wynyard, Hampshire v Somerset at Taunton	1899
399	B. A. Stokes/J. M. Bairstow, England v South Africa at Cape Town.	2015-16

Seventh Wicket

460	Bhupinder Singh jnr/P. Dharmani, Punjab v Delhi at Delhi.	1994-95
399	**A. N. Khare/A. J. Mandal, Chhattisgarh v Uttarakhand at Naya Raipur.** . .	**2019-20**
371	M. R. Marsh/S. M. Whiteman, Australia A v India A at Brisbane.	2014
366*	J. M. Bairstow/T. T. Bresnan, Yorkshire v Durham at Chester-le-Street	2015
347	D St E. Atkinson/C. C. Depeiza, West Indies v Australia at Bridgetown	1954-55
347	Farhad Reza/Sanjamul Islam, Rajshahi v Chittagong at Savar.	2013-14

Eighth Wicket

433	A. Sims and V. T. Trumper, A. Sims' Aust. XI v Canterbury at Christchurch...	1913-14
392	J. Mishra/J. Yadav, Haryana v Karnataka at Hubli	2012-13
332	I. J. L. Trott/S. C. J. Broad, England v Pakistan at Lord's	2010
313	Wasim Akram/Saqlain Mushtaq, Pakistan v Zimbabwe at Sheikhupura	1996-97
292	R. Peel/Lord Hawke, Yorkshire v Warwickshire at Birmingham	1896

Ninth Wicket

283	A. Warren/J. Chapman, Derbyshire v Warwickshire at Blackwell	1910
268	J. B. Commins/N. Boje, South Africa A v Mashonaland at Harare	1994-95
261	W. L. Madsen/T. Poynton, Derbyshire v Northamptonshire at Northampton	2012
251	J. W. H. T. Douglas/S. N. Hare, Essex v Derbyshire at Leyton	1921
249*†	A. S. Srivastava/K. Seth, Madhya Pradesh v Vidarbha at Indore	2000-01

† *276 unbeaten runs were scored for this wicket in two separate partnerships; after Srivastava retired hurt, Seth and N. D. Hirwani added 27.*

Tenth Wicket

307	A. F. Kippax/J. E. H. Hooker, New South Wales v Victoria at Melbourne	1928-29
249	C. T. Sarwate/S. N. Banerjee, Indians v Surrey at The Oval	1946
239	Aqeel Arshad/Ali Raza, Lahore Whites v Hyderabad at Lahore	2004-05
235	F. E. Woolley/A. Fielder, Kent v Worcestershire at Stourbridge	1909
233	Ajay Sharma/Maninder Singh, Delhi v Bombay at Bombay	1991-92

There have been only 13 last-wicket stands of 200 or more.

UNUSUAL DISMISSALS

Handled the Ball

There have been **63** instances in first-class cricket. The most recent are:

W. S. A. Williams	Canterbury v Otago at Dunedin	2012-13
E. Lewis	Trinidad & Tobago v Leeward Islands at Port-of-Spain	2013-14
C. A. Pujara	Derbyshire v Leicestershire at Derby	2014
I. Khan	Dolphins v Lions at Johannesburg	2014-15
K. Lesporis	Windward Islands v Barbados at Bridgetown	2015-16
S. R. Dickson	Kent v Leicestershire at Leicester	2016
M. Z. Hamza	Cape Cobras v Knights at Bloemfontein	2016-17

Under the 2017 revision of the Laws, Handled the Ball was subsumed under Obstructing the Field.

Obstructing the Field

There have been **31** instances in first-class cricket. T. Straw of Worcestershire was given out for obstruction v Warwickshire in both 1899 and 1901. The most recent are:

W. E. Bell	Northern Cape v Border at Kimberley	2015-16
Jahid Ali	Pakistan A v Zimbabwe A at Bulawayo	2016-17
Ghamai Zadran	Mis Ainak v Boost at Ghazi Amanullah Town	2017-18
Rashid Zadran	Mis Ainak v Band-e-Amir at Kabul	2017-18
Zia-ur-Rehman	Mis Ainak v Amo at Khost	2017-18
R. P. Burl	Rising Stars v Harare Metropolitan Eagles at Harare	2017-18
K. Cotani	**North West v Free State at Bloemfontein**	**2018-19**

Hit the Ball Twice

There have been **21** instances in first-class cricket. The last occurrence in England involved J. H. King of Leicestershire v Surrey at The Oval in 1906. The most recent are:

Aziz Malik	Lahore Division v Faisalabad at Sialkot.............................	1984-85
Javed Mohammad	Multan v Karachi Whites at Sahiwal................................	1986-87
Shahid Pervez	Jammu & Kashmir v Punjab at Srinagar...........................	1986-87
Ali Naqvi	PNSC v National Bank at Faisalabad..............................	1998-99
A. George	Tamil Nadu v Maharashtra at Pune................................	1998-99
Maqsood Raza	Lahore Division v PNSC at Sheikhupura...........................	1999-2000
D. Mahajan	Jammu & Kashmir v Bihar at Jammu	2005-06

Timed Out

There have been **six** instances in first-class cricket:

A. Jordaan	Eastern Province v Transvaal at Port Elizabeth (SACB match)....	1987-88
H. Yadav	Tripura v Orissa at Cuttack.....................................	1997-98
V. C. Drakes	Border v Free State at East London..............................	2002-03
A. J. Harris	Nottinghamshire v Durham UCCE at Nottingham.................	2003
R. A. Austin	Combined Campuses & Colleges v Windward Is at Arnos Vale ...	2013-14
C. Kunje	Bulawayo Met Tuskers v Manica Mountaineers at Bulawayo.....	2017-18

BOWLING RECORDS

TEN WICKETS IN AN INNINGS

In the history of first-class cricket, there have been **81** instances of a bowler taking all ten wickets in an innings, plus a further three instances of ten wickets in 12-a-side matches. Occurrences since the Second World War:

	O	M	R		
*W. E. Hollies (Warwickshire)	20.4	4	49	v Notts at Birmingham..........	1946
J. M. Sims (East)	18.4	2	90	v West at Kingston..............	1948
T. E. Bailey (Essex)	39.4	9	90	v Lancashire at Clacton.........	1949
J. K. Graveney (Glos.)	18.4	2	66	v Derbyshire at Chesterfield......	1949
R. Berry (Lancashire)	36.2	9	102	v Worcestershire at Blackpool.....	1953
S. P. Gupte (President's XI)	24.2	7	78	v Combined XI at Bombay	1954-55
J. C. Laker (Surrey)	46	18	88	v Australians at The Oval........	1956
J. C. Laker (England)	51.2	23	53	v Australia at Manchester........	1956
G. A. R. Lock (Surrey)	29.1	18	54	v Kent at Blackheath............	1956
K. Smales (Nottinghamshire)	41.3	20	66	v Gloucestershire at Stroud.......	1956
P. M. Chatterjee (Bengal)	19	11	20	v Assam at Jorhat...............	1956-57
J. D. Bannister (Warwickshire)	23.3	11	41	v Comb. Services at Birmingham† .	1959
A. J. G. Pearson (Cambridge U.)	30.3	8	78	v Leics at Loughborough.........	1961
N. I. Thomson (Sussex)	34.2	19	49	v Warwickshire at Worthing	1964
P. J. Allan (Queensland)	15.6	3	61	v Victoria at Melbourne..........	1965-66
I. J. Brayshaw (W. Australia)	17.6	4	44	v Victoria at Perth..............	1967-68
Shahid Mahmood (Karachi Whites)	25	5	58	v Khairpur at Karachi...........	1969-70
E. E. Hemmings (International XI)	49.3	14	175	v West Indies XI at Kingston	1982-83
P. Sunderam (Rajasthan)	22	5	78	v Vidarbha at Jodhpur..........	1985-86
S. T. Jefferies (W. Province)	22.5	7	59	v Orange Free State at Cape Town ..	1987-88
Imran Adil (Bahawalpur)	22.5	3	92	v Faisalabad at Faisalabad........	1989-90
G. P. Wickremasinghe (Sinhalese)	19.2	5	41	v Kalutara PCC at Colombo (SSC) .	1991-92
R. L. Johnson (Middlesex)	18.5	6	45	v Derbyshire at Derby	1994
Naeem Akhtar (Rawalpindi B.)	21.3	10	28	v Peshawar at Peshawar.........	1995-96
A. Kumble (India)	26.3	9	74	v Pakistan at Delhi.............	1998-99
D. S. Mohanty (East Zone)	19	5	46	v South Zone at Agartala	2000-01

	O	M	R		
O. D. Gibson (Durham)	17.3	1	47	v Hampshire at Chester-le-Street . . .	2007
M. W. Olivier (Warriors)	26.3	4	65	v Eagles at Bloemfontein	2007-08
Zulfiqar Babar (Multan)	39.4	3	143	v Islamabad at Multan	2009-10
P. M. Pushpakumara (Colombo)	**18.4**	**5**	**37**	**v Saracens at Moratuwa**	**2018-19**

* *W. E. Hollies bowled seven and had three lbw. The only other instance of a bowler achieving the feat without the direct assistance of a fielder came in 1850 when J. Wisden bowled all ten, for North v South at Lord's.*

† *Mitchells & Butlers Ground.*

OUTSTANDING BOWLING ANALYSES

	O	M	R	W		
H. Verity (Yorkshire).	19.4	16	10	10	v Nottinghamshire at Leeds . . .	1932
G. Elliott (Victoria)	19	17	2	9	v Tasmania at Launceston	1857-58
Ahad Khan (Railways).	6.3	4	7	9	v Dera Ismail Khan at Lahore . .	1964-65
J. C. Laker (England).	14	12	2	8	v The Rest at Bradford	1950
D. Shackleton (Hampshire) . .	11.1	7	4	8	v Somerset at Weston-s-Mare .	1955
E. Peate (Yorkshire).	16	11	5	8	v Surrey at Holbeck	1883
K. M. Dabengwa (Westerns) .	4.4	3	1	7	v Northerns at Harare.	2006-07
F. R. Spofforth (Australians) .	8.3	6	3	7	v England XI at Birmingham . .	1884
W. A. Henderson (NE Transvaal)	9.3	7	4	7	v OFS at Bloemfontein	1937-38
Rajinder Goel (Haryana)	7	4	4	7	v Jammu & Kashmir at Chandigarh.	1977-78
N. W. Bracken (NSW)	7	5	4	7	v South Australia at Sydney. . .	2004-05
V. I. Smith (South Africans) . .	4.5	3	1	6	v Derbyshire at Derby	1947
S. Cosstick (Victoria).	21.1	20	1	6	v Tasmania at Melbourne	1868-69
Israr Ali (Bahawalpur)	11	10	1	6	v Dacca U. at Bahawalpur	1957-58
A. D. Pougher (MCC)	3	3	0	5	v Australians at Lord's.	1896
G. R. Cox (Sussex)	6	6	0	5	v Somerset at Weston-s-Mare .	1921
R. K. Tyldesley (Lancashire). .	5	5	0	5	v Leicestershire at Manchester	1924
P. T. Mills (Gloucestershire) . .	6.4	6	0	5	v Somerset at Bristol	1928

MOST WICKETS IN A MATCH

19-90	J. C. Laker	England v Australia at Manchester	1956
17-48†	C. Blythe	Kent v Northamptonshire at Northampton.	1907
17-50	C. T. B. Turner	Australians v England XI at Hastings	1888
17-54	W. P. Howell	Australians v Western Province at Cape Town	1902-03
17-56	C. W. L. Parker	Gloucestershire v Essex at Gloucester.	1925
17-67	A. P. Freeman	Kent v Sussex at Hove.	1922
17-86	**K. J. Abbott**	**Hampshire v Somerset at Southampton.**	**2019**
17-89	W. G. Grace	Gloucestershire v Nottinghamshire at Cheltenham . .	1877
17-89	F. C. L. Matthews	Nottinghamshire v Northants at Nottingham	1923
17-91	H. Dean	Lancashire v Yorkshire at Liverpool	1913
17-91†	H. Verity	Yorkshire v Essex at Leyton	1933
17-92	A. P. Freeman	Kent v Warwickshire at Folkestone	1932
17-103	W. Mycroft	Derbyshire v Hampshire at Southampton	1876
17-106	G. R. Cox	Sussex v Warwickshire at Horsham.	1926
17-106†	T. W. J. Goddard	Gloucestershire v Kent at Bristol	1939
17-119	W. Mead	Essex v Hampshire at Southampton.	1895
17-137	W. Brearley	Lancashire v Somerset at Manchester	1905
17-137	J. M. Davison	Canada v USA at Fort Lauderdale	2004
17-159	S. F. Barnes	England v South Africa at Johannesburg.	1913-14
17-201	G. Giffen	South Australia v Victoria at Adelaide	1885-86
17-212	J. C. Clay	Glamorgan v Worcestershire at Swansea.	1937

† *Achieved in a single day.*

H. Arkwright took 18-96 for MCC v Gentlemen of Kent in a 12-a-side match at Canterbury in 1861.
    *There have been **60** instances of a bowler taking 16 wickets in an 11-a-side match, the most recent being **16-110 by P. M. Pushpakumara for Colombo v Saracens at Moratuwa, 2018-19**.*

FOUR WICKETS WITH CONSECUTIVE BALLS

There have been **44** instances in first-class cricket. R. J. Crisp achieved the feat twice, for Western Province in 1931-32 and 1933-34. A. E. Trott took four in four balls and another hat-trick in the same innings for Middlesex v Somerset in 1907, his benefit match. Occurrences since 2007:

Tabish Khan	Karachi Whites v ZTBL at Karachi............................	2009-10
Kamran Hussain	Habib Bank v Lahore Shalimar at Lahore...................	2009-10
N. Wagner	Otago v Wellington at Queenstown..........................	2010-11
Khalid Usman	Abbottabad v Karachi Blues at Karachi	2011-12
Mahmudullah	Central Zone v North Zone at Savar	2013-14
A. C. Thomas	Somerset v Sussex at Taunton...............................	2014
Taj Wali	Peshawar v Port Qasim Authority at Peshawar...........	2015-16
N. G. R. P. Jayasuriya	Colts v Badureliya at Maggona	2015-16
K. R. Smuts	Eastern Province v Boland at Paarl.........................	2015-16

In their match with England at The Oval in 1863, Surrey lost four wickets in the course of a four-ball over from G. Bennett.

Sussex lost five wickets in the course of the final (six-ball) over of their match with Surrey at Eastbourne in 1972. P. I. Pocock, who had taken three wickets in his previous over, captured four more, taking in all seven wickets with 11 balls, a feat unique in first-class matches. (The eighth wicket fell to a run-out.)

In 1996, K. D. James took four in four balls for Hampshire against Indians at Southampton and scored a century, a feat later emulated by Mahmudullah and Smuts.

HAT-TRICKS

Double Hat-Trick

Besides Trott's performance, which is mentioned in the preceding section, the following instances are recorded of players having performed the hat-trick twice in the same match, Rao doing so in the same innings.

A. Shaw	Nottinghamshire v Gloucestershire at Nottingham	1884
T. J. Matthews	Australia v South Africa at Manchester.....................	1912
C. W. L. Parker	Gloucestershire v Middlesex at Bristol	1924
R. O. Jenkins	Worcestershire v Surrey at Worcester.......................	1949
J. S. Rao	Services v Northern Punjab at Amritsar	1963-64
Amin Lakhani	Combined XI v Indians at Multan	1978-79
M. A. Starc	New South Wales v Western Australia at Sydney (Hurstville)..	2017-18

Five Wickets in Six Balls

W. H. Copson	Derbyshire v Warwickshire at Derby	1937
W. A. Henderson	NE Transvaal v Orange Free State at Bloemfontein	1937-38
P. I. Pocock	Surrey v Sussex at Eastbourne	1972
Yasir Arafat	Rawalpindi v Faisalabad at Rawalpindi	2004-05
N. Wagner	Otago v Wellington at Queenstown	2010-11

Yasir Arafat's five wickets were spread across two innings and interrupted only by a no-ball. Wagner was the first to take five wickets in a single over.

Most Hat-Tricks

D. V. P. Wright	7	R. G. Barlow	4	T. G. Matthews	4
T. W. J. Goddard	6	Fazl-e-Akbar	4	M. J. Procter	4
C. W. L. Parker	6	A. P. Freeman	4	T. Richardson	4
S. Haigh.............	5	J. T. Hearne	4	F. R. Spofforth	4
V. W. C. Jupp	5	J. C. Laker	4	F. S. Trueman	4
A. E. G. Rhodes.......	5	G. A. R. Lock	4		
F. A. Tarrant	5	G. G. Macaulay	4		

Hat-Trick on Debut

There have been **18** instances in first-class cricket. Occurrences since 2000:

S. M. Harwood	Victoria v Tasmania at Melbourne	2002-03
P. Connell	Ireland v Netherlands at Rotterdam	2008
A. Mithun	Karnataka v Uttar Pradesh at Meerut	2009-10
Zohaib Shera	Karachi Whites v National Bank at Karachi	2009-10

R. R. Phillips (Border) took a hat-trick in his first over in first-class cricket (v Eastern Province at Port Elizabeth, 1939-40) having previously played in four matches without bowling.

250 WICKETS IN A SEASON

	Season	O	M	R	W	Avge
A. P. Freeman	1928	1,976.1	423	5,489	304	18.05
A. P. Freeman	1933	2,039	651	4,549	298	15.26
T. Richardson	1895‡	1,690.1	463	4,170	290	14.37
C. T. B. Turner	1888†	2,427.2	1,127	3,307	283	11.68
A. P. Freeman	1931	1,618	360	4,307	276	15.60
A. P. Freeman	1930	1,914.3	472	4,632	275	16.84
T. Richardson	1897‡	1,603.4	495	3,945	273	14.45
A. P. Freeman	1929	1,670.5	381	4,879	267	18.27
W. Rhodes	1900	1,553	455	3,606	261	13.81
J. T. Hearne	1896‡	2,003.1	818	3,670	257	14.28
A. P. Freeman	1932	1,565.5	404	4,149	253	16.39
W. Rhodes	1901	1,565	505	3,797	251	15.12

† *Indicates 4-ball overs.* ‡ *5-ball overs.*

In four consecutive seasons (1928–1931), A. P. Freeman took 1,122 wickets, and in eight consecutive seasons (1928–1935), 2,090 wickets. In each of these eight seasons he took over 200 wickets.

T. Richardson took 1,005 wickets in four consecutive seasons (1894–1897).

The earliest date by which any bowler has taken 100 in an English season is June 12, achieved by J. T. Hearne in 1896 and C. W. L. Parker in 1931, when A. P. Freeman did it on June 13.

100 WICKETS IN A SEASON MOST TIMES

(Includes overseas tours and seasons)

W. Rhodes	23	C. W. L. Parker	16	G. H. Hirst	15
D. Shackleton	20	R. T. D. Perks	16	A. S. Kennedy	15
A. P. Freeman	17	F. J. Titmus	16		
T. W. J. Goddard	16	J. T. Hearne	15		

D. Shackleton reached 100 wickets in 20 successive seasons – 1949-1968.

Since the reduction of County Championship matches in 1969, D. L. Underwood (five times) and J. K. Lever (four times) are the only bowlers to have reached 100 wickets in a season more than twice. The highest aggregate in a season since 1969 is 134 by M. D. Marshall in 1982.

The most instances of 200 wickets in a season is eight by A. P. Freeman, who did it in eight successive seasons – 1928 to 1935 – including 304 in 1928. C. W. L. Parker did it five times, T. W. J. Goddard four times, and J. T. Hearne, G. A. Lohmann, W. Rhodes, T. Richardson, M. W. Tate and H. Verity three times each.

The last bowler to reach 200 wickets in a season was G. A. R. Lock (212 in 1957).

An expanded and regularly updated online version of the Records can be found at
www.wisdenrecords.com

100 WICKETS IN A SEASON OUTSIDE ENGLAND

W		Season	Country	R	Avge
116	M. W. Tate	1926-27	India/Ceylon	1,599	13.78
113	Kabir Khan	1998-99	Pakistan	1,706	15.09
107	Ijaz Faqih	1985-86	Pakistan	1,719	16.06
106	C. T. B. Turner	1887-88	Australia	1,441	13.59
106	R. Benaud	1957-58	South Africa	2,056	19.39
105	Murtaza Hussain	1995-96	Pakistan	1,882	17.92
104	S. F. Barnes	1913-14	South Africa	1,117	10.74
104	Sajjad Akbar	1989-90	Pakistan	2,328	22.38
103	Abdul Qadir	1982-83	Pakistan	2,367	22.98
101	Zia-ur-Rehman	2017-18	Afghanistan	1,995	19.75

LEADING BOWLERS IN AN ENGLISH SEASON

(Qualification: 10 wickets in 10 innings)

Season	Leading wicket-taker	Wkts	Avge	Top of averages	Wkts	Avge
1946	W. E. Hollies	184	15.60	A. Booth	111	11.61
1947	T. W. J. Goddard	238	17.30	J. C. Clay	65	16.44
1948	J. E. Walsh	174	19.56	J. C. Clay	41	14.17
1949	R. O. Jenkins	183	21.19	T. W. J. Goddard	160	19.18
1950	R. Tattersall	193	13.59	R. Tattersall	193	13.59
1951	R. Appleyard	200	14.14	R. Appleyard	200	14.14
1952	J. H. Wardle	177	19.54	F. S. Trueman	61	13.78
1953	B. Dooland	172	16.58	C. J. Knott	38	13.71
1954	B. Dooland	196	15.48	J. B. Statham	92	14.13
1955	G. A. R. Lock	216	14.49	R. Appleyard	85	13.01
1956	D. J. Shepherd	177	15.36	G. A. R. Lock	155	12.46
1957	G. A. R. Lock	212	12.02	G. A. R. Lock	212	12.02
1958	G. A. R. Lock	170	12.08	H. L. Jackson	143	10.99
1959	D. Shackleton	148	21.55	J. B. Statham	139	15.01
1960	F. S. Trueman	175	13.98	J. B. Statham	135	12.31
1961	J. A. Flavell	171	17.79	J. A. Flavell	171	17.79
1962	D. Shackleton	172	20.15	C. Cook	58	17.13
1963	D. Shackleton	146	16.75	C. C. Griffith	119	12.83
1964	D. Shackleton	142	20.40	J. A. Standen	64	13.00
1965	D. Shackleton	144	16.08	H. J. Rhodes	119	11.04
1966	D. L. Underwood	157	13.80	D. L. Underwood	157	13.80
1967	T. W. Cartwright	147	15.52	D. L. Underwood	136	12.39
1968	R. Illingworth	131	14.36	O. S. Wheatley	82	12.95
1969	R. M. H. Cottam	109	21.04	A. Ward	69	14.82
1970	D. J. Shepherd	106	19.16	Majid Khan	11	18.81
1971	L. R. Gibbs	131	18.89	G. G. Arnold	83	17.12
1972	T. W. Cartwright	98	18.64	I. M. Chappell	10	10.60
	B. Stead	98	20.38			
1973	B. S. Bedi	105	17.94	T. W. Cartwright	89	15.84
1974	A. M. E. Roberts	119	13.62	A. M. E. Roberts	119	13.62
1975	P. G. Lee	112	18.45	A. M. E. Roberts	57	15.80
1976	G. A. Cope	93	24.13	M. A. Holding	55	14.38
1977	M. J. Procter	109	18.04	R. A. Woolmer	19	15.21
1978	D. L. Underwood	110	14.49	D. L. Underwood	110	14.49
1979	D. L. Underwood	106	14.85	J. Garner	55	13.83
	J. K. Lever	106	17.30			
1980	R. D. Jackman	121	15.40	J. Garner	49	13.93
1981	R. J. Hadlee	105	14.89	R. J. Hadlee	105	14.89
1982	M. D. Marshall	134	15.73	R. J. Hadlee	61	14.57
1983	J. K. Lever	106	16.28	Imran Khan	12	7.16
	D. L. Underwood	106	19.28			

Season	Leading wicket-taker	Wkts	Avge	Top of averages	Wkts	Avge
1984	R. J. Hadlee	117	14.05	R. J. Hadlee	117	14.05
1985	N. V. Radford........	101	24.68	R. M. Ellison	65	17.20
1986	C. A. Walsh	118	18.17	M. D. Marshall........	100	15.08
1987	N. V. Radford........	109	20.81	R. J. Hadlee	97	12.64
1988	F. D. Stephenson	125	18.31	M. D. Marshall........	42	13.16
1989	D. R. Pringle	94	18.64	T. M. Alderman	70	15.64
	S. L. Watkin	94	25.09			
1990	N. A. Foster	94	26.61	I. R. Bishop	59	19.05
1991	Waqar Younis	113	14.65	Waqar Younis	113	14.65
1992	C. A. Walsh	92	15.96	C. A. Walsh	92	15.96
1993	S. L. Watkin	92	22.80	Wasim Akram	59	19.27
1994	M. M. Patel	90	22.86	C. E. L. Ambrose	77	14.45
1995	A. Kumble	105	20.40	A. A. Donald	89	16.07
1996	C. A. Walsh	85	16.84	C. E. L. Ambrose	43	16.67
1997	A. M. Smith	83	17.63	A. A. Donald	60	15.63
1998	C. A. Walsh	106	17.31	V. J. Wells	36	14.27
1999	A. Sheriyar	92	24.70	Saqlain Mushtaq	58	11.37
2000	G. D. McGrath	80	13.21	C. A. Walsh	40	11.42
2001	R. J. Kirtley	75	23.32	G. D. McGrath	40	15.60
2002	M. J. Saggers	83	21.51	C. P. Schofield	18	18.38
	K. J. Dean...........	83	23.50			
2003	Mushtaq Ahmed.......	103	24.65	Shoaib Akhtar	34	17.05
2004	Mushtaq Ahmed.......	84	27.59	D. S. Lehmann.......	15	17.40
2005	S. K. Warne	87	22.50	M. Muralitharan......	36	15.00
2006	Mushtaq Ahmed.......	102	19.91	Naved-ul-Hasan	35	16.71
2007	Mushtaq Ahmed.......	90	25.66	Harbhajan Singh	37	18.54
2008	J. A. Tomlinson	67	24.76	M. Davies...........	41	14.63
2009	Danish Kaneria	75	23.69	G. Onions...........	69	19.95
2010	A. R. Adams	68	22.17	J. K. H. Naik	35	17.68
2011	D. D. Masters	93	18.13	T. T. Bresnan.......	27	17.68
2012	G. Onions...........	72	14.73	G. Onions...........	72	14.73
2013	G. Onions...........	73	18.92	T. A. Copeland.......	45	18.26
2014	M. H. A. Footitt	84	19.19	G. R. Napier........	52	15.63
2015	C. Rushworth	90	20.54	R. J. Sidebottom.....	43	18.09
2016	G. R. Napier........	69	22.30	J. M. Anderson.......	45	17.00
	J. S. Patel	69	24.02			
2017	J. A. Porter	85	16.74	J. L. Pattinson.........	32	12.06
2018	O. E. Robinson.......	81	17.43	O. P. Stone...........	43	12.30
2019	**S. R. Harmer**.........	**86**	**18.15**	**J. M. Anderson**.......	**30**	**9.40**

MOST WICKETS

Dates in italics denote the first half of an overseas season; i.e. *1970* denotes the 1970-71 season.

		Career	W	R	Avge
1	W. Rhodes	1898–1930	4,187	69,993	16.71
2	A. P. Freeman	1914–1936	3,776	69,577	18.42
3	C. W. L. Parker	1903–1935	3,278	63,817	19.46
4	J. T. Hearne	1888–1923	3,061	54,352	17.75
5	T. W. J. Goddard	1922–1952	2,979	59,116	19.84
6	W. G. Grace	1865–1908	2,876	51,545	17.92
7	A. S. Kennedy	1907–1936	2,874	61,034	21.23
8	D. Shackleton.............	1948–1969	2,857	53,303	18.65
9	G. A. R. Lock	1946–*1970*	2,844	54,709	19.23
10	F. J. Titmus	1949–1982	2,830	63,313	22.37
11	M. W. Tate	1912–1937	2,784	50,571	18.16
12	G. H. Hirst	1891–1929	2,739	51,282	18.72
13	C. Blythe	1899–1914	2,506	42,136	16.81

Some works of reference provide career figures which differ from those in this list, owing to the exclusion or inclusion of matches recognised or not recognised as first-class by Wisden. A fuller list can be found in Wisdens up to 2011.

Current Players with 750 Wickets

	Career	W	R	Avge
H. M. R. K. B. Herath	*1996–2018*	1,080	27,163	25.15
D. S. Hettiarachchi	*1994–2018*	1,001	23,542	23.51
J. M. Anderson	*2002–2019*	952	23,844	25.04
J. S. Patel	*1999–2019*	892	29,239	32.77
T. J. Murtagh	*2000–2019*	816	20,518	25.14
Yasir Arafat	*1997–2019*	790	18,958	23.99
S. C. J. Broad	*2005–2019*	770	21,247	27.59
M. D. K. Perera	*2000–2019*	761	20,400	26.80

ALL-ROUND RECORDS

REMARKABLE ALL-ROUND MATCHES

V. E. Walker	20*	108	10-74	4-17	England v Surrey at The Oval	1859
W. G. Grace	104		2-60	10-49	MCC v Oxford University at Oxford . .	1886
G. Giffen	271		9-96	7-70	South Australia v Victoria at Adelaide	1891-92
B. J. T. Bosanquet	103	100*	3-75	8-53	Middlesex v Sussex at Lord's	1905
G. H. Hirst	111	117*	6-70	5-45	Yorkshire v Somerset at Bath	1906
F. D. Stephenson	111	117	4-105	7-117	Notts v Yorkshire at Nottingham	1988

E. M. Grace, for MCC v Gentlemen of Kent in a 12-a-side match at Canterbury in 1862, scored 192* and took 5-77 and 10-69.

HUNDRED AND HAT-TRICK

G. Giffen, Australians v Lancashire at Manchester	1884
*W. E. Roller, Surrey v Sussex at The Oval	1885
W. B. Burns, Worcestershire v Gloucestershire at Worcester	1913
V. W. C. Jupp, Sussex v Essex at Colchester	1921
R. E. S. Wyatt, MCC v Ceylonese at Colombo (Victoria Park)	1926-27
L. N. Constantine, West Indians v Northamptonshire at Northampton	1928
D. E. Davies, Glamorgan v Leicestershire at Leicester	1937
V. M. Merchant, Dr C. R. Pereira's XI v Sir Homi Mehta's XI at Bombay	1946-47
M. J. Procter, Gloucestershire v Essex at Westcliff-on-Sea	1972
M. J. Procter, Gloucestershire v Leicestershire at Bristol	1979
†K. D. James, Hampshire v Indians at Southampton	1996
J. E. C. Franklin, Gloucestershire v Derbyshire at Cheltenham.	2009
Sohag Gazi, Barisal v Khulna at Khulna	2012-13
Sohag Gazi, Bangladesh v New Zealand at Chittagong	2013-14
†Mahmudullah, Central Zone v North Zone at Savar	2013-14
†K. R. Smuts, Eastern Province v Boland at Paarl	2015-16

* W. E. Roller is the only player to combine 200 with a hat-trick.

† K. D. James, Mahmudullah and K. R. Smuts all combined 100 with four wickets in four balls (Mahmudullah's split between two innings).

THE DOUBLE

The double was traditionally regarded as 1,000 runs and 100 wickets in an English season. The feat became exceptionally rare after the reduction of County Championship matches in 1969.

Remarkable Seasons

	Season	R	W		Season	R	W
G. H. Hirst	1906	2,385	208	J. H. Parks	1937	3,003	101

1,000 Runs and 100 Wickets

W. Rhodes	16	W. G. Grace	8	F. J. Titmus	8
G. H. Hirst	14	M. S. Nichols	8	F. E. Woolley	7
V. W. C. Jupp	10	A. E. Relf	8	G. E. Tribe	7
W. E. Astill	9	F. A. Tarrant	8		
T. E. Bailey	8	M. W. Tate	8†		

† *M. W. Tate also scored 1,193 runs and took 116 wickets on the 1926-27 MCC tour of India and Ceylon.*

R. J. Hadlee (1984) and F. D. Stephenson (1988) are the only players to perform the feat since the reduction of County Championship matches in 1969. A complete list of those performing the feat before then may be found on page 202 of the 1982 Wisden. T. E. Bailey (1959) was the last player to achieve 2,000 runs and 100 wickets in a season; M. W. Tate (1925) the last to reach 1,000 runs and 200 wickets. Full lists may be found in Wisdens up to 2003.

Wicketkeeper's Double

The only wicketkeepers to achieve 1,000 runs and 100 dismissals in a season were L. E. G. Ames (1928, 1929 and 1932, when he scored 2,482 runs) and J. T. Murray (1957).

WICKETKEEPING RECORDS

MOST DISMISSALS IN AN INNINGS

9 (8ct, 1st)	Tahir Rashid	Habib Bank v PACO at Gujranwala	1992-93
9 (7ct, 2st)	W. R. James*	Matabeleland v Mashonaland CD at Bulawayo	1995-96
8 (8ct)	A. T. W. Grout	Queensland v Western Australia at Brisbane	1959-60
8 (8ct)†	D. E. East	Essex v Somerset at Taunton	1985
8 (8ct)	S. A. Marsh‡	Kent v Middlesex at Lord's	1991
8 (6ct, 2st)	T. J. Zoehrer	Australians v Surrey at The Oval	1993
8 (7ct, 1st)	D. S. Berry	Victoria v South Australia at Melbourne	1996-97
8 (7ct, 1st)	Y. S. S. Mendis	Bloomfield v Kurunegala Y at Colombo (Bloomfield)	2000-01
8 (7ct, 1st)	S. Nath§	Assam v Tripura at Guwahati	2001-02
8 (8ct)	J. N. Batty¶	Surrey v Kent at The Oval	2004
8 (8ct)	Golam Mabud	Sylhet v Dhaka at Dhaka	2005-06
8 (8ct)	A. Z. M. Dyili	Eastern Province v Free State at Port Elizabeth	2009-10
8 (8ct)	D. C. de Boorder	Otago v Wellington at Wellington	2009-10
8 (8ct)	R. S. Second	Free State v North West at Bloemfontein	2011-12
8 (8ct)	T. L. Tsolekile	South Africa A v Sri Lanka A at Durban	2012
8 (7ct, 1st)	M. A. R. S. Fernando	Chilaw Marians v Colts at Colombo (SSC)	2017-18

There have been 110 further instances of seven dismissals in an innings. R. W. Taylor achieved the feat three times, and G. J. Hopkins, Kamran Akmal, I. Khaleel, S. A. Marsh, K. J. Piper, Shahin Hossain, T. L. Tsolekile and Wasim Bari twice. Khaleel did it twice in the same match. Marsh's and Tsolekile's two instances both included one of eight dismissals – see above. H. Yarnold made six stumpings and one catch in an innings for Worcestershire v Scotland at Dundee in 1951. A fuller list can be found in Wisdens before 2004.

*	*W. R. James also scored 99 and 99 not out.*	†	*The first eight wickets to fall.*
‡	*S. A. Marsh also scored 108 not out.*	§	*On his only first-class appearance.*
¶	*J. N. Batty also scored 129.*		

WICKETKEEPERS' HAT-TRICKS

W. H. Brain, Gloucestershire v Somerset at Cheltenham, 1893 – three stumpings off successive balls from C. L. Townsend.

K. R. Meherhomji, Freelooters v Nizam's State Railway A at Secunderabad, 1931-32 – three catches off successive balls from L. Ramji.

G. O. Dawkes, Derbyshire v Worcestershire at Kidderminster, 1958 – three catches off successive balls from H. L. Jackson.

R. C. Russell, Gloucestershire v Surrey at The Oval, 1986 – three catches off successive balls from C. A. Walsh and D. V. Lawrence (2).

T. Frost, Warwickshire v Surrey at Birmingham, 2003 – three catches off successive balls from G. G. Wagg and N. M. Carter (2).

MOST DISMISSALS IN A MATCH

14 (11ct, 3st)	I. Khaleel	Hyderabad v Assam at Guwahati	2011-12
13 (11ct, 2st)	W. R. James*	Matabeleland v Mashonaland CD at Bulawayo	1995-96
12 (8ct, 4st)	E. Pooley	Surrey v Sussex at The Oval	1868
12 (9ct, 3st)	D. Tallon	Queensland v New South Wales at Sydney	1938-39
12 (9ct, 3st)	H. B. Taber	New South Wales v South Australia at Adelaide	1968-69
12 (12ct)	P. D. McGlashan	Northern Districts v Central Districts at Whangarei .	2009-10
12 (11ct, 1st)	T. L. Tsolekile	Lions v Dolphins at Johannesburg	2010-11
12 (12ct)	Kashif Mahmood	Lahore Shalimar v Abbottabad at Abbottabad	2010-11
12 (12ct)	R. S. Second	Free State v North West at Bloemfontein	2011-12

* *W. R. James also scored 99 and 99 not out.*

100 DISMISSALS IN A SEASON

128 (79ct, 49st)	L. E. G. Ames	1929	104 (82ct, 22st)	J. T. Murray	1957
122 (70ct, 52st)	L. E. G. Ames	1928	102 (69ct, 33st)	F. H. Huish	1913
110 (63ct, 47st)	H. Yarnold	1949	102 (95ct, 7st)	J. T. Murray	1960
107 (77ct, 30st)	G. Duckworth	1928	101 (62ct, 39st)	F. H. Huish	1911
107 (96ct, 11st)	J. G. Binks	1960	101 (85ct, 16st)	R. Booth	1960
104 (40ct, 64st)	L. E. G. Ames	1932	100 (91ct, 9st)	R. Booth	1964

L. E. G. Ames achieved the two highest stumping totals in a season: 64 in 1932, and 52 in 1928.

MOST DISMISSALS

Dates in italics denote the first half of an overseas season; i.e. *1997* denotes the 1997-98 season.

			Career	*M*	*Ct*	*St*
1	R. W. Taylor	1,649	1960–1988	639	1,473	176
2	J. T. Murray	1,527	1952–1975	635	1,270	257
3	H. Strudwick	1,497	1902–1927	675	1,242	255
4	A. P. E. Knott	1,344	1964–1985	511	1,211	133
5	R. C. Russell	1,320	1981–2004	465	1,192	128
6	F. H. Huish	1,310	1895–1914	497	933	377
7	B. Taylor	1,294	1949–1973	572	1,083	211
8	S. J. Rhodes	1,263	1981–2004	440	1,139	124
9	D. Hunter	1,253	1888–1909	548	906	347

Current Players with 500 Dismissals

			Career	*M*	*Ct*	*St*
925	Kamran Akmal	1997–2019	244	858	67
721	T. R. Ambrose	2001–2019	251	678	43
571	Adnan Akmal	2003–2019	168	537	34
565	S. M. Davies	2005–2019	225	532	33
546	Sarfraz Ahmed	2005–2019	156	493	53
540	P. A. Patel	2001–2019	187	464	76

Some of these figures include catches taken in the field.

FIELDING RECORDS

excluding wicketkeepers

MOST CATCHES IN AN INNINGS

7	M. J. Stewart	Surrey v Northamptonshire at Northampton	1957
7	A. S. Brown	Gloucestershire v Nottinghamshire at Nottingham	1966
7	R. Clarke	Warwickshire v Lancashire at Liverpool.	2011

MOST CATCHES IN A MATCH

10	W. R. Hammond†	Gloucestershire v Surrey at Cheltenham	1928
9	R. Clarke	Warwickshire v Lancashire at Liverpool.	2011
8	W. B. Burns	Worcestershire v Yorkshire at Bradford	1907
8	F. G. Travers	Europeans v Parsees at Bombay	1923-24
8	A. H. Bakewell	Northamptonshire v Essex at Leyton.	1928
8	W. R. Hammond	Gloucestershire v Worcestershire at Cheltenham	1932
8	K. J. Grieves	Lancashire v Sussex at Manchester.	1951
8	C. A. Milton	Gloucestershire v Sussex at Hove	1952
8	G. A. R. Lock	Surrey v Warwickshire at The Oval	1957
8	J. M. Prodger	Kent v Gloucestershire at Cheltenham	1961
8	P. M. Walker	Glamorgan v Derbyshire at Swansea	1970
8	Masood Anwar	Rawalpindi v Lahore Division at Rawalpindi	1983-84
8	M. C. J. Ball	Gloucestershire v Yorkshire at Cheltenham	1994
8	J. D. Carr	Middlesex v Warwickshire at Birmingham.	1995
8	G. A. Hick	Worcestershire v Essex at Chelmsford	2005
8	Naved Yasin	State Bank v Bahawalpur Stags at Bahawalpur.	2014-15
8	A. M. Rahane	India v Sri Lanka at Galle	2015-16

† *Hammond also scored a hundred in each innings.*

MOST CATCHES IN A SEASON

78	W. R. Hammond	1928	71	P. J. Sharpe	1962
77	M. J. Stewart	1957	70	J. Tunnicliffe	1901
73	P. M. Walker	1961			

The most catches by a fielder since the reduction of County Championship matches in 1969 is 59 by G. R. J. Roope in 1971.

MOST CATCHES

Dates in italics denote the first half of an overseas season; i.e. *1970* denotes the 1970-71 season.

		Career	M			Career	M
1,018	F. E. Woolley	1906–1938	979	784	J. G. Langridge	1928–1955	574
887	W. G. Grace	1865–1908	879	764	W. Rhodes	1898–1930	1,107
830	G. A. R. Lock	1946–*1970*	654	758	C. A. Milton	1948–1974	620
819	W. R. Hammond .	1920–1951	634	754	E. H. Hendren	1907–1938	833
813	D. B. Close	1949–1986	786				

The most catches by a current player is 560 by M. E. Trescothick between 1993 and 2019 (including two taken while deputising as wicketkeeper).

TEAM RECORDS

HIGHEST INNINGS TOTALS

1,107	Victoria v New South Wales at Melbourne	1926-27
1,059	Victoria v Tasmania at Melbourne	1922-23
952-6 dec	Sri Lanka v India at Colombo (RPS)	1997-98
951-7 dec	Sind v Baluchistan at Karachi	1973-74
944-6 dec	Hyderabad v Andhra at Secunderabad	1993-94
918	New South Wales v South Australia at Sydney	1900-01
912-8 dec	Holkar v Mysore at Indore	1945-46
912-6 dec†	Tamil Nadu v Goa at Panjim	1988-89
910-6 dec	Railways v Dera Ismail Khan at Lahore	1964-65
903-7 dec	England v Australia at The Oval	1938
900-6 dec	Queensland v Victoria at Brisbane	2005-06

† *Tamil Nadu's total of 912-6 dec included 52 penalty runs from their opponents' failure to meet the required bowling rate.*

The highest total in a team's second innings is 770 by New South Wales v South Australia at Adelaide in 1920-21.

HIGHEST FOURTH-INNINGS TOTALS

654-5	England v South Africa at Durban	1938-39
	After being set 696 to win. The match was left drawn on the tenth day.	
604	Maharashtra (*set 959 to win*) v Bombay at Poona	1948-49
576-8	Trinidad (*set 672 to win*) v Barbados at Port-of-Spain	1945-46
572	New South Wales (*set 593 to win*) v South Australia at Sydney	1907-08
541-7	West Zone (*won*) v South Zone at Hyderabad	2009-10
529-9	Combined XI (*set 579 to win*) v South Africans at Perth	1963-64
518	Victoria (*set 753 to win*) v Queensland at Brisbane	1926-27
513-9	Central Province (*won*) v Southern Province at Kandy	2003-04
507-7	Cambridge University (*won*) v MCC and Ground at Lord's	1896
506-6	South Australia (*won*) v Queensland at Adelaide	1991-92
503-4	South Zone (*won*) v England A at Gurgaon	2003-04
502-6	Middlesex (*won*) v Nottinghamshire at Nottingham	1925
502-8	Players (*won*) v Gentlemen at Lord's	1900
500-7	South African Universities (*won*) v Western Province at Stellenbosch	1978-79

MOST RUNS IN A DAY (ONE SIDE)

721	Australians (721) v Essex at Southend (1st day)	1948
651	West Indians (651-2) v Leicestershire at Leicester (1st day)	1950
649	New South Wales (649-7) v Otago at Dunedin (2nd day)	1923-24
645	Surrey (645-4) v Hampshire at The Oval (1st day)	1909
644	Oxford U. (644-8) v H. D. G. Leveson Gower's XI at Eastbourne (1st day) . . .	1921
640	Lancashire (640-8) v Sussex at Hove (1st day)	1937
636	Free Foresters (636-7) v Cambridge U. at Cambridge (1st day)	1938
625	Gloucestershire (625-6) v Worcestershire at Dudley (2nd day)	1934

MOST RUNS IN A DAY (BOTH SIDES)

(excluding the above)

685	North (169-8 and 255-7), South (261-8 dec) at Blackpool (2nd day)	1961
666	Surrey (607-4), Northamptonshire (59-2) at Northampton (2nd day)	1920
665	Rest of South Africa (339), Transvaal (326) at Johannesburg (1st day)	1911-12
663	Middlesex (503-4), Leicestershire (160-2) at Leicester (1st day)	1947
661	Border (201), Griqualand West (460) at Kimberley (1st day)	1920-21
649	Hampshire (570-8), Somerset (79-3) at Taunton (2nd day)	1901

HIGHEST AGGREGATES IN A MATCH

Runs	Wkts		
2,376	37	Maharashtra v Bombay at Poona	1948-49
2,078	40	Bombay v Holkar at Bombay	1944-45
1,981	35	South Africa v England at Durban	1938-39
1,945	18	Canterbury v Wellington at Christchurch	1994-95
1,929	39	New South Wales v South Australia at Sydney	1925-26
1,911	34	New South Wales v Victoria at Sydney	1908-09
1,905	40	Otago v Wellington at Dunedin	1923-24

In Britain

Runs	Wkts		
1,815	28	Somerset v Surrey at Taunton..............................	2002
1,808	20	Sussex v Essex at Hove...................................	1993
1,795	34	Somerset v Northamptonshire at Taunton.	2001
1,723	31	England v Australia at Leeds	1948
1,706	23	Hampshire v Warwickshire at Southampton...................	1997

LOWEST INNINGS TOTALS

12†	Oxford University v MCC and Ground at Oxford	1877
12	Northamptonshire v Gloucestershire at Gloucester.	1907
13	Auckland v Canterbury at Auckland................................	1877-78
13	Nottinghamshire v Yorkshire at Nottingham	1901
14	Surrey v Essex at Chelmsford	1983
15	MCC v Surrey at Lord's	1839
15†	Victoria v MCC at Melbourne.....................................	1903-04
15†	Northamptonshire v Yorkshire at Northampton	1908
15	Hampshire v Warwickshire at Birmingham	1922
	Following on, Hampshire scored 521 and won by 155 runs.	
16	MCC and Ground v Surrey at Lord's...............................	1872
16	Derbyshire v Nottinghamshire at Nottingham.	1879
16	Surrey v Nottinghamshire at The Oval	1880
16	Warwickshire v Kent at Tonbridge	1913
16	Trinidad v Barbados at Bridgetown	1942-43
16	Border v Natal at East London (first innings)	1959-60
17	Gentlemen of Kent v Gentlemen of England at Lord's..................	1850
17	Gloucestershire v Australians at Cheltenham	1896
18	The Bs v England at Lord's.	1831
18†	Kent v Sussex at Gravesend	1867
18	Tasmania v Victoria at Melbourne	1868-69
18†	Australians v MCC and Ground at Lord's............................	1896
18	Border v Natal at East London (second innings).	1959-60
18†	Durham MCCU v Durham at Chester-le-Street	2012

† *One man absent.*

At Lord's in 1810, The Bs, with one man absent, were dismissed by England for 6.

LOWEST TOTALS IN A MATCH

34	(16 and 18) Border v Natal at East London............................	1959-60
42	(27† and 15†) Northamptonshire v Yorkshire at Northampton..............	1908

† *Northamptonshire batted one man short in each innings.*

LOWEST AGGREGATE IN A COMPLETED MATCH

Runs	Wkts		
85	11†	Quetta v Rawalpindi at Islamabad............................	2008-09
105	31	MCC v Australians at Lord's............................	1878

† Both teams forfeited their first innings.

The lowest aggregate in a match in which the losing team was bowled out twice since 1900 is 157 for 22 wickets, Surrey v Worcestershire at The Oval, 1954.

LARGEST VICTORIES

Largest Innings Victories

Inns and 851 runs	Railways (910-6 dec) v Dera Ismail Khan at Lahore............	1964-65
Inns and 666 runs	Victoria (1,059) v Tasmania at Melbourne..................	1922-23
Inns and 656 runs	Victoria (1,107) v New South Wales at Melbourne............	1926-27
Inns and 605 runs	New South Wales (918) v South Australia at Sydney..........	1900-01
Inns and 579 runs	England (903-7 dec) v Australia at The Oval................	1938
Inns and 575 runs	Sind (951-7 dec) v Baluchistan at Karachi.................	1973-74
Inns and 527 runs	New South Wales (713) v South Australia at Adelaide..........	1908-09
Inns and 517 runs	Australians (675) v Nottinghamshire at Nottingham............	1921

Largest Victories by Runs Margin

685 runs	New South Wales (235 and 761-8 dec) v Queensland at Sydney ..	1929-30
675 runs	England (521 and 342-8 dec) v Australia at Brisbane.........	1928-29
638 runs	New South Wales (304 and 770) v South Australia at Adelaide ...	1920-21
609 runs	Muslim Comm. Bank (575 and 282-0 dec) v WAPDA at Lahore ..	1977-78

Victory Without Losing a Wicket

Lancashire (166-0 dec and 66-0) beat Leicestershire by ten wickets at Manchester......		1956
Karachi A (277-0 dec) beat Sind B by an innings and 77 runs at Karachi		1957-58
Railways (236-0 dec and 16-0) beat Jammu & Kashmir by ten wickets at Srinagar.....		1960-61
Karnataka (451-0 dec) beat Kerala by an innings and 186 runs at Chikmagalur........		1977-78

There have been 30 wins by an innings and 400 runs or more, the most recent being an innings and 413 runs by Dhaka v Barisal at Mirpur in 2014-15.

There have been 25 wins by 500 runs or more, the most recent being 568 runs by Somerset v Cardiff MCCU at Taunton in 2019.

There have been 33 wins by a team losing only one wicket, the most recent being by KwaZulu-Natal Inland v Namibia at Pietermaritzburg in 2015-16.

TIED MATCHES

Since 1948, a tie has been recognised only when the scores are level with all the wickets down in the fourth innings. There have been **40** instances since then, including two Tests (see Test record section); Sussex have featured in five of those, Essex and Kent in four each.

The most recent instances are:

Kalutara PCC v Police at Colombo (Burgher)..........................	2016-17
Guyana v Windward Islands at Providence..........................	2017-18
Chilaw Marians v Burgher at Katunayake..........................	2017-18
Negombo v Kalutara Town at Gampaha..........................	2017-18
Bloomfield v Army at Colombo (Moors)	2017-18
Somerset v Lancashire at Taunton..........................	2018

MATCHES COMPLETED ON FIRST DAY

(Since 1946)

Derbyshire v Somerset at Chesterfield, June 11	1947
Lancashire v Sussex at Manchester, July 12	1950
Surrey v Warwickshire at The Oval, May 16	1953
Somerset v Lancashire at Bath, June 6 (H. F. T. Buse's benefit)	1953
Kent v Worcestershire at Tunbridge Wells, June 15	1960
Griqualand West v Easterns at Kimberley, March 10	2010-11

SHORTEST COMPLETED MATCHES

Balls

121	Quetta (forfeit and 41) v Rawalpindi (forfeit and 44-1) at Islamabad	2008-09
350	Somerset (35 and 44) v Middlesex (86) at Lord's	1899
352	Victoria (82 and 57) v Tasmania (104 and 37-7) at Launceston	1850-51
372	Victoria (80 and 50) v Tasmania (97 and 35-2) at Launceston	1853-54

LIST A ONE-DAY RECORDS

List A is a concept intended to provide an approximate equivalent in one-day cricket of first-class status. It was introduced by the Association of Cricket Statisticians and Historians and is now recognised by the ICC, with a separate category for Twenty20 cricket. Further details are available at stats.acscricket.com/ListA/Description.html. List A games comprise:

(a) One-day internationals.
(b) Other international matches (e.g. A-team internationals).
(c) Premier domestic one-day tournaments in Test-playing countries.
(d) Official tourist matches against the main first-class teams (e.g. counties, states and Board XIs).

The following matches are excluded:

(a) Matches originally scheduled as less than 40 overs per side (e.g. Twenty20 games).
(b) World Cup warm-up games.
(c) Tourist matches against teams outside the major domestic competitions (e.g. universities).
(d) Festival games and pre-season friendlies.

This section covers one-day cricket to December 31, 2019. Bold type denotes performances in the calendar year 2019 or, in career figures, players who appeared in List A cricket in that year.

BATTING RECORDS

HIGHEST INDIVIDUAL INNINGS

268	A. D. Brown	Surrey v Glamorgan at The Oval	2002
264	R. G. Sharma	India v Sri Lanka at Kolkata	2014-15
257	D. J. M. Short	Western Australia v Queensland at Sydney	2018-19
248	S. Dhawan	India A v South Africa at Pretoria	2013
237*	M. J. Guptill	New Zealand v West Indies at Wellington.	2014-15
229*	B. R. Dunk	Tasmania v Queensland at Sydney.	2014-15
222*	R. G. Pollock	Eastern Province v Border at East London	1974-75
222	J. M. How	Central Districts v Northern Districts at Hamilton.	2012-13
220*	B. M. Duckett	England Lions v Sri Lanka A at Canterbury	2016
219	V. Sehwag	India v West Indies at Indore	2011-12
215	C. H. Gayle	West Indies v Zimbabwe at Canberra	2014-15
212*	**S. V. Samson**	**Kerala v Goa at Alur**	**2019-20**
210*	Fakhar Zaman	Pakistan v Zimbabwe at Bulawayo	2018
209*	Abid Ali	Islamabad v Peshawar at Peshawar	2017-18
209	R. G. Sharma	India v Australia at Bangalore	2013-14
208*	R. G. Sharma	India v Sri Lanka at Mohali	2017-18
208*	**Soumya Sarkar**	**Abahani v Sheikh Jamal Dhanmondi at Savar**	**2018-19**
207	Mohammad Ali	Pakistan Customs v DHA at Sialkot	2004-05
206	A. I. Kallicharran	Warwickshire v Oxfordshire at Birmingham	1984
204*	Khalid Latif	Karachi Dolphins v Quetta Bears at Karachi	2008-09
203	A. D. Brown	Surrey v Hampshire at Guildford.	1997
203	**Y. B. Jaiswal**	**Mumbai v Jharkhand at Alur**	**2019-20**
202*	A. Barrow	Natal v SA African XI at Durban.	1975-76
202*	P. J. Hughes	Australia A v South Africa A at Darwin	2014
202	T. M. Head	South Australia v Western Australia at Sydney	2015-16
202	K. V. Kaushal	Uttarakhand v Sikkim at Nadiad	2018-19
201*	R. S. Bopara	Essex v Leicestershire at Leicester.	2008
201	V. J. Wells	Leicestershire v Berkshire at Leicester	1996
200*	S. R. Tendulkar	India v South Africa at Gwalior	2009-10
200	Kamran Akmal	WAPDA v Habib Bank at Hyderabad	2017-18
200	**M. B. van Buuren**	**Gauteng v Western Province at Johannesburg**	**2018-19**

MOST RUNS

	Career	M	I	NO	R	HS	100	Avge
G. A. Gooch	*1973–1997*	614	601	48	22,211	198*	44	40.16
G. A. Hick	*1983–2008*	651	630	96	22,059	172*	40	41.30
S. R. Tendulkar	*1989–2011*	551	538	55	21,999	200*	60	45.54
K. C. Sangakkara	*1997–2017*	528	500	54	19,453	169	39	43.61
I. V. A. Richards	*1973–1993*	500	466	61	16,995	189*	26	41.96
R. T. Ponting	*1992–2013*	456	445	53	16,363	164	34	41.74
C. G. Greenidge	*1970–1992*	440	436	33	16,349	186*	33	40.56
S. T. Jayasuriya	*1989–2011*	557	542	25	16,128	189	31	31.19
A. J. Lamb	*1972–1995*	484	463	63	15,658	132*	19	39.14
D. L. Haynes	*1976–1996*	419	416	44	15,651	152*	28	42.07
S. C. Ganguly	*1989–2011*	437	421	43	15,622	183	31	41.32
K. J. Barnett	*1979–2005*	527	500	54	15,564	136	17	34.89
D. P. M. D. Jayawardene . .	*1995–2016*	546	509	51	15,364	163*	21	33.54
R. Dravid	*1992–2011*	449	416	55	15,271	153	21	42.30
M. G. Bevan	*1989–2006*	427	385	124	15,103	157*	13	57.86

HIGHEST PARTNERSHIP FOR EACH WICKET

367*	for 1st	M. N. van Wyk/C. S. Delport, Dolphins v Knights at Bloemfontein	2014-15
372	for 2nd	C. H. Gayle/M. N. Samuels, West Indies v Zimbabwe at Canberra	2014-15
338	**for 3rd**	**S. V. Samson/S. Baby, Kerala v Goa at Alur**	**2019-20**
276	for 4th	Mominul Haque/A. R. S. Silva, Prime Doleshwar v Abahani at Bogra . .	2013-14
267*	for 5th	Minhazul Abedin/Khaled Mahmud, Bangladeshis v Bahawalpur at Karachi	1997-98
272	**for 6th**	**A. K. Markram/F. Behardien, Titans v Cape Cobras at Cape Town** .	**2018-19**
215*	for 7th	S. Singh/G. H. Dockrell, Leinster v Northern at Dublin	2018
203	for 8th	Shahid Iqbal/Haaris Ayaz, Karachi Whites v Hyderabad at Karachi . . .	1998-99
155	for 9th	C. M. W. Read/A. J. Harris, Nottinghamshire v Durham at Nottingham . . .	2006
128	for 10th	A. Ashish Reddy/M. Ravi Kiran, Hyderabad v Kerala at Secunderabad .	2014-15

BOWLING RECORDS

BEST BOWLING ANALYSES

8-10	S. Nadeem	Jharkhand v Rajasthan at Chennai	2018-19
8-15	R. L. Sanghvi	Delhi v Himachal Pradesh at Una	1997-98
8-19	W. P. U. J. C. Vaas	Sri Lanka v Zimbabwe at Colombo (SSC)	2001-02
8-20*	D. T. Kottehewa	Nondescripts v Ragama at Colombo (Moors)	2007-08
8-21	M. A. Holding	Derbyshire v Sussex at Hove	1988
8-26	K. D. Boyce	Essex v Lancashire at Manchester	1971
8-30	G. D. R. Eranga	Burgher v Army at Colombo (Colts)	2007-08
8-31	D. L. Underwood	Kent v Scotland at Edinburgh	1987
8-38	B. A. Mavuta	Rising Stars v Manicaland Mountaineers at Harare	2017-18
8-40	Yeasin Arafat	Gazi Group Cricketers v Abahani at Fatullah	2017-18
8-43	S. W. Tait	South Australia v Tasmania at Adelaide	2003-04
8-52	K. A. Stoute	West Indies A v Lancashire at Manchester	2010
8-66	S. R. G. Francis	Somerset v Derbyshire at Derby	2004

* *Including two hat-tricks.*

MOST WICKETS

	Career	M	B	R	W	BB	4I	Avge
Wasim Akram	*1984–2003*	594	29,719	19,303	881	5-10	46	21.91
A. A. Donald	*1985–2003*	458	22,856	14,942	684	6-15	38	21.84
M. Muralitharan	*1991–2010*	453	23,734	15,270	682	7-30	29	22.39
Waqar Younis	*1988–2003*	412	19,841	15,098	675	7-36	44	22.36
J. K. Lever	*1968–1990*	481	23,208	13,278	674	5-8	34	19.70
J. E. Emburey	*1975–2000*	536	26,399	16,811	647	5-23	26	25.98
I. T. Botham	*1973–1993*	470	22,899	15,264	612	5-27	18	24.94

WICKETKEEPING AND FIELDING RECORDS

MOST DISMISSALS IN AN INNINGS

8	(8 ct)	D. J. S. Taylor	Somerset v Combined Universities at Taunton ...	1982
8	(5ct, 3st)	S. J. Palframan	Boland v Easterns at Paarl	1997-98
8	(8ct)	D. J. Pipe	Worcestershire v Hertfordshire at Hertford	2001
8	(6ct, 2st)	P. M. Nevill	New South Wales v Cricket Aus XI at Sydney ...	2017-18

*There have been **15** instances of seven dismissals in an innings, the most recent being L. U. Igalagamage (6ct, 1st) for Nondescripts v Army at Colombo (SSC) in 2019-20.*

MOST CATCHES IN AN INNINGS IN THE FIELD

There have been **16** instances of a fielder taking five catches in an innings. The most recent are:

5	A. R. McBrine	Ireland v Sri Lanka A at Belfast	2014
5	Farhad Hossain	Prime Doleshwar v Sheikh Jamal Dhanmondi at Fatullah ...	2017-18
5	Zahid Zakhail	Amo v Boost at Kabul..................	2018
5	**Mominul Haque**	**Legends of Rupganj v Abahani at Savar**..............	**2018-19**

TEAM RECORDS

HIGHEST INNINGS TOTALS

496-4	(50 overs)	Surrey v Gloucestershire at The Oval	2007
445-8	(50 overs)	Nottinghamshire v Northamptonshire at Nottingham	2016
444-3	(50 overs)	England v Pakistan at Nottingham	2016
443-9	(50 overs)	Sri Lanka v Netherlands at Amstelveen	2006
439-2	(50 overs)	South Africa v West Indies at Johannesburg.............	2014-15
438-4	(50 overs)	South Africa v India at Mumbai	2014-15
438-5	(50 overs)	Surrey v Glamorgan at The Oval	2002
438-9	(49.5 overs)	South Africa v Australia at Johannesburg..........	2005-06
434-4	(50 overs)	Australia v South Africa at Johannesburg..........	2005-06
434-4	(50 overs)	Jamaica v Trinidad & Tobago at Coolidge	2016-17
433-3	(50 overs)	India A v South Africa A at Pretoria..........	2013
433-7	**(50 overs)**	**Nottinghamshire v Leicestershire at Nottingham**..........	**2019**

LOWEST INNINGS TOTALS

18	(14.3 overs)	West Indies Under-19 v Barbados at Blairmont	2007-08
19	(10.5 overs)	Saracens v Colts at Colombo (Colts)	2012-13
23	(19.4 overs)	Middlesex v Yorkshire at Leeds	1974
24	**(17.1 overs)**	**Oman v Scotland at Al Amerat**	**2018-19**
30	(20.4 overs)	Chittagong v Sylhet at Dhaka	2002-03
31	(13.5 overs)	Border v South Western Districts at East London.	2007-08
34	(21.1 overs)	Saurashtra v Mumbai at Mumbai	1999-2000
35	(18 overs)	Zimbabwe v Sri Lanka at Harare	2003-04
35	(20.2 overs)	Cricket Coaching School v Abahani at Fatullah	2013-14
35	(15.3 overs)	Rajasthan v Railways at Nagpur.......................	2014-15
36	(25.4 overs)	Leicestershire v Sussex at Leicester	1973
36	(18.4 overs)	Canada v Sri Lanka at Paarl	2002-03

> **❝**
> In sport, you can't get away with lies – at least not for long. It's more important
> than it's ever been that the national side epitomise the culture we live in.**"**
> England's multicultural World Cup winners, page 77

LIST A TWENTY20 RECORDS

This section covers Twenty20 cricket to December 31, 2019. Bold type denotes performances in the calendar year 2019 or, in career figures, players who appeared in Twenty20 cricket in that year.

BATTING RECORDS

HIGHEST INDIVIDUAL INNINGS

175*	C. H. Gayle	RC Bangalore v Pune Warriors at Bangalore	2012-13
172	A. J. Finch	Australia v Zimbabwe at Harare	2018
162*	H. Masakadza	Mountaineers v Mashonaland Eagles at Bulawayo . . .	2015-16
162*	**Hazratullah Zazai**	**Afghanistan v Ireland at Dehradun**	**2018-19**
161	A. Lyth	Yorkshire v Northamptonshire at Leeds	2017
158*	B. B. McCullum	Kolkata Knight Riders v RC Bangalore at Bangalore .	2007-08
158*	B. B. McCullum	Warwickshire v Derbyshire at Birmingham.	2015
156	A. J. Finch	Australia v England at Southampton	2013
153*	L. J. Wright	Sussex v Essex at Chelmsford	2014
152*	G. R. Napier	Essex v Sussex at Chelmsford	2008
151*	C. H. Gayle	Somerset v Kent at Taunton.	2015
150*	Kamran Akmal	Lahore Whites v Islamabad at Rawalpindi	2017-18

MOST RUNS

	Career	M	I	NO	R	HS	100	Avge	SR
C. H. Gayle.	2005–2019	400	392	48	13,152	175*	22	38.23	147.04
K. A. Pollard	2006–2019	496	448	126	9,936	104	1	30.85	150.24
B. B. McCullum.	2004–2018	370	364	33	9,922	158*	7	29.97	136.49
Shoaib Malik	2004–2019	369	348	97	9,357	95*	0	37.27	125.22
D. A. Warner	2006–2019	277	276	35	9,090	135*	8	37.71	142.29
V. Kohli	2006–2019	274	260	49	8,739	113	5	41.41	134.44
A. J. Finch	2008–2019	276	271	31	8,597	172	7	35.82	143.88
A. B. de Villiers	2003–2019	304	286	59	8,511	133*	4	37.49	149.94
R. G. Sharma	2006–2019	324	311	46	8,502	118	6	32.08	133.49
S. K. Raina	2006–2018	319	303	46	8,391	126*	4	32.64	138.00
S. R. Watson	2004–2019	319	311	33	8,196	124*	6	29.48	138.44
D. R. Smith.	2005–2019	337	327	27	7,870	110*	5	26.23	127.44
L. J. Wright	2004–2019	314	291	27	7,588	153*	7	28.74	143.11

HIGHEST PARTNERSHIP FOR EACH WICKET

236	**for 1st**	**Hazratullah Zazai/Usman Ghani, Afghanistan v Ireland at Dehradun .**	**2018-19**
229	for 2nd	V. Kohli/A. B. de Villiers, RC Bangalore v Gujarat Lions at Bangalore . . .	2015-16
213	**for 3rd**	**S. S. Iyer/S. A. Yadav, Mumbai v Sikkim at Indore**	**2018-19**
202*	for 4th	M. C. Juneja/A. Malik, Gujarat v Kerala at Indore	2012-13
150	for 5th	H. M. Amla/D. J. Bravo, Trinbago KR v Barbados Tridents at Port-of-Spain .	2016
161	for 6th	K. Lewis/A. D. Russell, Jamaica Tallawahs v Trinbago KR at Port-of-Spain .	2018
107*	for 7th	L. Abeyratne/P. S. R. Anurudhha, Colombo v Chilaw Marians at Colombo	2015-16
120	for 8th	Azhar Mahmood/I. Udana, Wayamba v Uva at Colombo (RPS)	2012
69	for 9th	C. J. Anderson/J. H. Davey, Somerset v Surrey at The Oval.	2017
63	for 10th	G. D. Elliott/Zulfiqar Babar, Quetta Glad. v Peshawar Zalmi at Sharjah . . .	2015-16

BOWLING RECORDS

BEST BOWLING ANALYSES

7-18	**C. N. Ackermann**	**Leicestershire v Warwickshire at Leicester**	**2019**
6-5	A. V. Suppiah	Somerset v Glamorgan at Cardiff.	2011
6-6	Shakib Al Hasan	Barbados v Trinidad & Tobago at Bridgetown	2013
6-7	S. L. Malinga	Melbourne Stars v Perth Scorchers at Perth	2012-13

6-7	K. A. Jamieson	Canterbury v Auckland at Auckland	2018-19
6-7	D. L. Chahar	India v Bangladesh at Nagpur	2019-20
6-8	B. A. W. Mendis	Sri Lanka v Zimbabwe at Hambantota	2012-13
6-9	P. Fojela	Border v Easterns at East London	2014-15
6-11	I. S. Sodhi	Adelaide Strikers v Sydney Thunder at Sydney	2016-17
6-12	**A. S. Joseph**	**Mumbai Indians v Sunrisers Hyderabad at Hyderabad**	**2018-19**

MOST WICKETS

	Career	M	B	R	W	BB	4I	Avge	ER
D. J. Bravo	*2005–2018*	450	8,760	12,061	490	5-23	11	24.61	8.26
S. L. Malinga	*2004–2019*	288	6,370	7,458	386	6-7	15	19.32	7.02
S. P. Narine	*2010–2019*	336	7,682	7,720	379	5-19	12	20.36	6.02
Imran Tahir	*2005–2019*	282	6,053	7,054	355	5-23	12	19.87	6.99
Shakib Al Hasan	*2006–2019*	308	6,487	7,459	354	6-6	12	21.07	6.89
Sohail Tanvir	*2004–2019*	329	6,926	8,448	340	6-14	8	24.84	7.31
Shahid Afridi	*2004–2019*	309	6,622	7,387	335	5-7	11	22.05	6.69
A. D. Russell	*2009–2019*	314	5,322	7,339	287	4-11	8	25.57	8.27
Wahab Riaz	*2004–2019*	243	5,156	6,123	285	5-8	2	21.48	7.12
Yasir Arafat	2005–2016	226	4,702	6,344	281	4-5	10	22.57	8.09
Rashid Khan	*2015–2019*	198	4,547	4,760	279	5-3	7	17.06	6.28
K. A. Pollard	*2006–2019*	496	4,902	6,709	272	4-15	5	24.66	8.21
Saeed Ajmal	2004–2017	195	4,338	4,706	271	4-14	8	17.36	6.50

WICKETKEEPING AND FIELDING RECORDS

MOST DISMISSALS IN AN INNINGS

7 (7ct)	E. F. M. U. Fernando	Lankan v Moors at Colombo (Bloomfield)	2005-06

MOST CATCHES IN AN INNINGS IN THE FIELD

5	Manzoor Ilahi	Jammu & Kashmir v Delhi at Delhi	2010-11
5	J. M. Vince	Hampshire v Leeward Islands at North Sound	2010-11
5	J. L. Ontong	Cape Cobras v Knights at Cape Town	2014-15
5	A. K. V. Adikari	Chilaw Marians v Bloomfield at Colombo (SSC)	2014-15
5	P. G. Fulton	Canterbury v Northern Districts at Hamilton	2015-16
5	M. W. Machan	Sussex v Glamorgan at Hove	2016

TEAM RECORDS

HIGHEST INNINGS TOTALS

278-3	(20 overs)	Afghanistan v Ireland at Dehradun	2018-19
278-4	(20 overs)	Czech Republic v Turkey at Ilfov	2019
267-2	(20 overs)	Trinbago Knight Riders v Jamaica Tallawahs at Kingston . . .	2019
263-3	(20 overs)	Australia v Sri Lanka at Pallekele	2016
263-5	(20 overs)	RC Bangalore v Pune Warriors at Bangalore	2012-13
262-4	(20 overs)	North West v Limpopo at Paarl	2018-19
260-4	(20 overs)	Yorkshire v Northamptonshire at Leeds	2017
260-5	(20 overs)	India v Sri Lanka at Indore	2017-18
260-6	(20 overs)	Sri Lanka v Kenya at Johannesburg	2007-08

LOWEST INNINGS TOTALS

21	(8.3 overs)	Turkey v Czech Republic at Ilfov	2019
28	(11.3 overs)	Turkey v Luxembourg at Ilfov	2019
30	(11.1 overs)	Tripura v Jharkhand at Dhanbad	2009-10
32	(8.5 overs)	Turkey v Austria at Ilfov	2019
39	(10.3 overs)	Netherlands v Sri Lanka at Chittagong	2013-14

ALL-FORMAT CAREER RECORDS

This section covers combined records in first-class, List A and Twenty20 cricket to December 31, 2019. Bold type denotes a player who appeared in 2019. Daggers denote players who appeared in first-class and List A formats, and double daggers players who appeared in all three; all other players appeared only in first-class cricket.

MOST RUNS

	Career	M	I	NO	R	HS	100	Avge
G. A. Gooch†	1973–2000	1,195	1,591	123	67,057	333	172	45.67
G. A. Hick‡	1983–2008	1,214	1,537	183	64,372	405*	178	47.54
J. B. Hobbs	1905–1934	826	1,315	106	61,237	316*	197	50.65
F. E. Woolley..........	1906–1938	979	1,532	85	58,969	305*	145	40.75
G. Boycott†	1962–1986	922	1,316	206	58,521	261*	159	52.72
E. H. Hendren	1907–1938	833	1,300	166	57,611	301*	170	50.80
D. L. Amiss†	1960–1987	1,062	1,530	160	55,942	262*	117	40.83
C. P. Mead..........	1905–1936	814	1,340	185	55,061	280*	153	47.67
W. G. Grace..........	1865–1908	880	1,493	105	54,896	344	126	39.55
C. G. Greenidge†	1970–1992	963	1,325	108	53,703	273*	125	44.12

MOST WICKETS

	Career	M	B	R	W	BB	5I	Avge
W. Rhodes	1898–1930	1,107	184,940	69,993	4,187	9-24	287	16.71
A. P. Freeman......	1914–1936	592	154,658	69,577	3,776	10-53	386	18.42
C. W. L. Parker.....	1903–1935	635	157,328	63,819	3,278	10-79	277	19.46
J. T. Hearne.......	1888–1923	639	144,470	54,352	3,061	9-32	255	17.75
D. L. Underwood† ...	1963–1987	1,089	159,571	61,111	3,037	9-28	161	20.12
F. J. Titmus†	1949–1982	941	180,576	67,396	2,989	9-52	171	22.54
T. W. J. Goddard....	1922–1952	593	142,186	59,116	2,979	10-113	251	19.84
D. Shackleton†	1948–1973	684	161,071	54,175	2,898	9-30	194	18.69
W. G. Grace........	1865–1908	880	126,056	51,545	2,876	10-49	246	17.92
A. S. Kennedy.......	1907–1936	677	150,917	61,034	2,874	10-37	225	21.23

The figure for balls bowled by Grace is uncertain.

MOST DISMISSALS

	Career	M	Dis	Ct	St
R. W. Taylor†	1960–1988	972	2,070	1,819	251
S. J. Rhodes‡	1981–2004	920	1,929	1,671	258
R. C. Russell‡	1981–2004	946	1,885	1,658	227
A. P. E. Knott†	1964–1985	829	1,741	1,553	188
J. T. Murray†	1952–1975	784	1,724	1,432	292
C. M. W. Read‡	1995–2017	801	1,583	1,430	153
Kamran Akmal‡	*1997–2019*	**830**	**1,615**	**1,358**	**257**
P. A. Nixon‡.................	1989–2011	862	1,549	1,360	189
D. L. Bairstow†	1970–1990	888	1,545	1,372	173
A. C. Gilchrist‡.................	1992–2013	648	1,498	1,356	142

Total dismissals include catches taken when not keeping wicket.

MOST CATCHES IN THE FIELD

	Career	M	Ct		Career	M	Ct
F. E. Woolley....	1906–1938	979	1,018	G. A. Hick‡	1983–2008	1,214	1,008

TEST RECORDS

This section covers all Tests up to January 31, 2020. Bold type denotes performances since January 1, 2019, or, in career figures, players who have appeared in Test cricket since that date.

BATTING RECORDS

HIGHEST INDIVIDUAL INNINGS

400*	B. C. Lara	West Indies v England at St John's	2003-04
380	M. L. Hayden.	Australia v Zimbabwe at Perth.	2003-04
375	B. C. Lara	West Indies v England at St John's	1993-94
374	D. P. M. D. Jayawardene . .	Sri Lanka v South Africa at Colombo (SSC)	2006
365*	G. S. Sobers	West Indies v Pakistan at Kingston	1957-58
364	L. Hutton	England v Australia at The Oval	1938
340	S. T. Jayasuriya	Sri Lanka v India at Colombo (RPS)	1997-98
337	Hanif Mohammad	Pakistan v West Indies at Bridgetown	1957-58
336*	W. R. Hammond	England v New Zealand at Auckland.	1932-33
335*	**D. A. Warner**	**Australia v Pakistan at Adelaide.**	**2019-20**
334*	M. A. Taylor.	Australia v Pakistan at Peshawar	1998-99
334	D. G. Bradman.	Australia v England at Leeds	1930
333	G. A. Gooch.	England v India at Lord's	1990
333	C. H. Gayle	West Indies v Sri Lanka at Galle	2010-11
329*	M. J. Clarke	Australia v India at Sydney	2011-12
329	Inzamam-ul-Haq	Pakistan v New Zealand at Lahore	2002
325	A. Sandham	England v West Indies at Kingston	1929-30
319	V. Sehwag	India v South Africa at Chennai	2007-08
319	K. C. Sangakkara	Sri Lanka v Bangladesh at Chittagong	2013-14
317	C. H. Gayle	West Indies v South Africa at St John's	2004-05
313	Younis Khan	Pakistan v Sri Lanka at Karachi	2008-09
311*	H. M. Amla	South Africa v England at The Oval	2012
311	R. B. Simpson	Australia v England at Manchester	1964
310*	J. H. Edrich	England v New Zealand at Leeds.	1965
309	V. Sehwag	India v Pakistan at Multan	2003-04
307	R. M. Cowper	Australia v England at Melbourne	1965-66
304	D. G. Bradman.	Australia v England at Leeds	1934
303*	K. K. Nair	India v England at Chennai	2016-17
302*	Azhar Ali	Pakistan v West Indies at Dubai.	2016-17
302	L. G. Rowe	West Indies v England at Bridgetown	1973-74
302	B. B. McCullum	New Zealand v India at Wellington	2013-14

*There have been **65** further instances of 250 or more runs in a Test innings.*

The highest innings for the countries not mentioned above are:

266	D. L. Houghton	Zimbabwe v Sri Lanka at Bulawayo	1994-95
219*	Mushfiqur Rahim.	Bangladesh v Zimbabwe at Mirpur	2018-19
118	K. J. O'Brien	Ireland v Pakistan at Malahide.	2018
102	**Rahmat Shah**	**Afghanistan v Bangladesh at Chittagong**	**2019-20**

HUNDRED ON TEST DEBUT

C. Bannerman (165*)	Australia v England at Melbourne	1876-77
W. G. Grace (152)	England v Australia at The Oval	1880
H. Graham (107)	Australia v England at Lord's.	1893
†K. S. Ranjitsinhji (154*)	England v Australia at Manchester.	1896
†P. F. Warner (132*).	England v South Africa at Johannesburg	1898-99
†R. A. Duff (104).	Australia v England at Melbourne	1901-02
§R. E. Foster (287).	England v Australia at Sydney	1903-04
G. Gunn (119)	Australia v England at Sydney	1907-08
†R. J. Hartigan (116)	Australia v England at Adelaide.	1907-08

†H. L. Collins (104)	Australia v England at Sydney	1920-21
W. H. Ponsford (110)	Australia v England at Sydney	1924-25
A. A. Jackson (164)	Australia v England at Adelaide	1928-29
†G. A. Headley (176)	West Indies v England at Bridgetown	1929-30
J. E. Mills (117)	New Zealand v England at Wellington	1929-30
Nawab of Pataudi snr (102)	England v Australia at Sydney	1932-33
B. H. Valentine (136)	England v India at Bombay	1933-34
†L. Amarnath (118)	India v England at Bombay	1933-34
†P. A. Gibb (106)	England v South Africa at Johannesburg	1938-39
S. C. Griffith (140)	England v West Indies at Port-of-Spain	1947-48
A. G. Ganteaume (112)	West Indies v England at Port-of-Spain	1947-48
†J. W. Burke (101*)	Australia v England at Adelaide	1950-51
P. B. H. May (138)	England v South Africa at Leeds	1951
R. H. Shodhan (110)	India v Pakistan at Calcutta	1952-53
B. H. Pairaudeau (115)	West Indies v India at Port-of-Spain	1952-53
†O. G. Smith (104)	West Indies v Australia at Kingston	1954-55
A. G. Kripal Singh (100*)	India v New Zealand at Hyderabad	1955-56
C. C. Hunte (142)	West Indies v Pakistan at Bridgetown	1957-58
C. A. Milton (104*)	England v New Zealand at Leeds	1958
†A. A. Baig (112)	India v England at Manchester	1959
Hanumant Singh (105)	India v England at Delhi	1963-64
Khalid Ibadulla (166)	Pakistan v Australia at Karachi	1964-65
B. R. Taylor (105)	New Zealand v India at Calcutta	1964-65
K. D. Walters (155)	Australia v England at Brisbane	1965-66
J. H. Hampshire (107)	England v West Indies at Lord's	1969
†G. R. Viswanath (137)	India v Australia at Kanpur	1969-70
G. S. Chappell (108)	Australia v England at Perth	1970-71
‡§L. G. Rowe (214, 100*)	West Indies v New Zealand at Kingston	1971-72
A. I. Kallicharran (100*)	West Indies v New Zealand at Georgetown	1971-72
R. E. Redmond (107)	New Zealand v Pakistan at Auckland	1972-73
†F. C. Hayes (106*)	England v West Indies at The Oval	1973
†C. G. Greenidge (107)	West Indies v India at Bangalore	1974-75
†L. Baichan (105*)	West Indies v Pakistan at Lahore	1974-75
G. J. Cosier (109)	Australia v West Indies at Melbourne	1975-76
S. Amarnath (124)	India v New Zealand at Auckland	1975-76
Javed Miandad (163)	Pakistan v New Zealand at Lahore	1976-77
†A. B. Williams (100)	West Indies v Australia at Georgetown	1977-78
†D. M. Wellham (103)	Australia v England at The Oval	1981
†Salim Malik (100*)	Pakistan v Sri Lanka at Karachi	1981-82
K. C. Wessels (162)	Australia v England at Brisbane	1982-83
W. B. Phillips (159)	Australia v Pakistan at Perth	1983-84
¶M. Azharuddin (110)	India v England at Calcutta	1984-85
D. S. B. P. Kuruppu (201*)	Sri Lanka v New Zealand at Colombo (CCC)	1986-87
†M. J. Greatbatch (107*)	New Zealand v England at Auckland	1987-88
M. E. Waugh (138)	Australia v England at Adelaide	1990-91
A. C. Hudson (163)	South Africa v West Indies at Bridgetown	1991-92
R. S. Kaluwitharana (132*)	Sri Lanka v Australia at Colombo (SSC)	1992-93
D. L. Houghton (121)	Zimbabwe v India at Harare	1992-93
P. K. Amre (103)	India v South Africa at Durban	1992-93
†G. P. Thorpe (114*)	England v Australia at Nottingham	1993
G. S. Blewett (102*)	Australia v England at Adelaide	1994-95
S. C. Ganguly (131)	India v England at Lord's	1996
†Mohammad Wasim (109*)	Pakistan v New Zealand at Lahore	1996-97
Ali Naqvi (115)	Pakistan v South Africa at Rawalpindi	1997-98
Azhar Mahmood (128*)	Pakistan v South Africa at Rawalpindi	1997-98
M. S. Sinclair (214)	New Zealand v West Indies at Wellington	1999-2000
†Younis Khan (107)	Pakistan v Sri Lanka at Rawalpindi	1999-2000
Aminul Islam (145)	Bangladesh v India at Dhaka	2000-01
†H. Masakadza (119)	Zimbabwe v West Indies at Harare	2001
T. T. Samaraweera (103*)	Sri Lanka v India at Colombo (SSC)	2001
Taufeeq Umar (104)	Pakistan v Bangladesh at Multan	2001-02

†Mohammad Ashraful (114)	Bangladesh v Sri Lanka at Colombo (SSC)	2001-02
V. Sehwag (105)	India v South Africa at Bloemfontein	2001-02
L. Vincent (104)	New Zealand v Australia at Perth	2001-02
S. B. Styris (107)	New Zealand v West Indies at St George's	2002
J. A. Rudolph (222*)	South Africa v Bangladesh at Chittagong	2003
‡Yasir Hameed (170, 105)	Pakistan v Bangladesh at Karachi	2003
†D. R. Smith (105*)	West Indies v South Africa at Cape Town	2003-04
A. J. Strauss (112)	England v New Zealand at Lord's	2004
M. J. Clarke (151)	Australia v India at Bangalore	2004-05
†A. N. Cook (104*)	England v India at Nagpur	2005-06
M. J. Prior (126*)	England v West Indies at Lord's	2007
M. J. North (117)	Australia v South Africa at Johannesburg	2008-09
†Fawad Alam (168)	Pakistan v Sri Lanka at Colombo (PSS)	2009
†I. J. L. Trott (119)	England v Australia at The Oval	2009
Umar Akmal (129)	Pakistan v New Zealand at Dunedin	2009-10
†A. B. Barath (104)	West Indies v Australia at Brisbane	2009-10
A. N. Petersen (100)	South Africa v India at Kolkata	2009-10
S. K. Raina (120)	India v Sri Lanka at Colombo (SSC)	2010
K. S. Williamson (131)	New Zealand v India at Ahmedabad	2010-11
†K. A. Edwards (110)	West Indies v India at Roseau	2011
S. E. Marsh (141)	Australia v Sri Lanka at Pallekele	2011-12
Abul Hasan (113)	Bangladesh v West Indies at Khulna	2012-13
†F. du Plessis (110*)	South Africa v Australia at Adelaide	2012-13
H. D. Rutherford (171)	New Zealand v England at Dunedin	2012-13
S. Dhawan (187)	India v Australia at Mohali	2012-13
R. G. Sharma (177)	India v West Indies at Kolkata	2013-14
†J. D. S. Neesham (137*)	New Zealand v India at Wellington	2013-14
S. van Zyl (101*)	South Africa v West Indies at Centurion	2014-15
A. C. Voges (130*)	Australia v West Indies at Roseau	2015
S. C. Cook (115)	South Africa v England at Centurion	2015-16
K. K. Jennings (112)	England v India at Mumbai	2016-17
T. A. Blundell (107*)	New Zealand v West Indies at Wellington	2017-18
†K. J. O'Brien (118)	Ireland v Pakistan at Malahide	2018
P. P. Shaw (134)	India v West Indies at Rajkot	2018-19
B. T. Foakes (107)	England v Sri Lanka at Galle	2018-19
Abid Ali (109*)	**Pakistan v Sri Lanka at Rawalpindi**	**2019-20**

† *In his second innings of the match.*

‡ *L. G. Rowe and Yasir Hameed are the only batsmen to score a hundred in each innings on debut.*

§ *R. E. Foster (287, 19) and L. G. Rowe (214, 100*) are the only batsmen to score 300 on debut.*

¶ *M. Azharuddin is the only batsman to score hundreds in each of his first three Tests.*

L. Amarnath and S. Amarnath were father and son.

Ali Naqvi and Azhar Mahmood achieved the feat in the same innings.

Only Bannerman, Houghton, Aminul Islam and O'Brien scored hundreds in their country's first Test.

TWO SEPARATE HUNDREDS IN A TEST

Triple-Hundred and Hundred in a Test

G. A. Gooch (England)	333 and 123 v India at Lord's	1990
K. C. Sangakkara (Sri Lanka)	319 and 105 v Bangladesh at Chittagong	2013-14

The only instances in first-class cricket. M. A. Taylor (Australia) scored 334 and 92 v Pakistan at Peshawar in 1998-99.*

Double-Hundred and Hundred in a Test

K. D. Walters (Australia)	242 and 103 v West Indies at Sydney	1968-69
S. M. Gavaskar (India)	124 and 220 v West Indies at Port-of-Spain	1970-71
†L. G. Rowe (West Indies)	214 and 100* v New Zealand at Kingston	1971-72
G. S. Chappell (Australia)	247* and 133 v New Zealand at Wellington	1973-74
B. C. Lara (West Indies)	221 and 130 v Sri Lanka at Colombo (SSC)	2001-02

† *On Test debut.*

Two Hundreds in a Test

There have been **86** instances of a batsman scoring two separate hundreds in a Test, including the seven listed above. The most recent was by **R. G. Sharma for India v South Africa at Visakhapatnam in 2019-20.**

S. M. Gavaskar (India), R. T. Ponting (Australia) and D. A. Warner (Australia) all achieved the feat three times. C. L. Walcott scored twin hundreds twice in one series, for West Indies v Australia in 1954-55. L. G. Rowe and Yasir Hameed both did it on Test debut.

MOST DOUBLE-HUNDREDS

D. G. Bradman (A.) 12	**V. Kohli (I)** 7	S. R. Tendulkar (I) 6
K. C. Sangakkara (SL) . . 11	M. S. Atapattu (SL) 6	Younis Khan (P.) 6
B. C. Lara (WI) 9	Javed Miandad (P) 6	A. N. Cook (E) 5
W. R. Hammond (E) 7	R. T. Ponting (A) 6	R. Dravid (I) 5
D. P. M. D. Jayawardene (SL) 7	V. Sehwag (I) 6	G. C. Smith (SA) 5

M. J. Clarke (Australia) scored four double-hundreds in the calendar year 2012.

MOST HUNDREDS

S. R. Tendulkar (I) 51	M. J. Clarke (A.) 28	M. Azharuddin (I) 22
J. H. Kallis (SA) 45	A. R. Border (A) 27	I. R. Bell (E) 22
R. T. Ponting (A) 41	**V. Kohli (I)** 27	G. Boycott (E) 22
K. C. Sangakkara (SL) . . 38	G. C. Smith (SA) 27	M. C. Cowdrey (E) 22
R. Dravid (I) 36	**S. P. D. Smith (A).** 26	A. B. de Villiers (SA) . . 22
S. M. Gavaskar (I) 34	G. S. Sobers (WI) 26	W. R. Hammond (E) 22
D. P. M. D. Jayawardene (SL) 34	Inzamam-ul-Haq (P) . . . 25	D. C. Boon (A) 21
B. C. Lara (WI) 34	G. S. Chappell (A) 24	R. N. Harvey (A) 21
Younis Khan (P) 34	Mohammad Yousuf (P) . . 24	G. Kirsten (SA) 21
A. N. Cook (E) 33	I. V. A. Richards (WI). . . 24	A. J. Strauss (E). 21
S. R. Waugh (A) 32	**D. A. Warner (A).** 24	**K. S. Williamson (NZ).** . 21
S. Chanderpaul (WI) . . . 30	Javed Miandad (P). 23	K. F. Barrington (E) 20
M. L. Hayden (A) 30	J. L. Langer (A) 23	P. A. de Silva (SL). 20
D. G. Bradman (A) 29	K. P. Pietersen (E). 23	G. A. Gooch (E) 20
H. M. Amla (SA) **28**	V. Sehwag (I) 23	M. E. Waugh (A). 20

The most hundreds for Zimbabwe is 12 by A. Flower, the most for Bangladesh is 9 by Tamim Iqbal, the most for Ireland is 1 by K. J. O'Brien, and the most for Afghanistan is 1 by Rahmat Shah.

MOST HUNDREDS AGAINST ONE TEAM

D. G. Bradman . . 19 Australia v England		S. R. Tendulkar. . . 11 India v Australia
S. M. Gavaskar . . 13 India v West Indies		K. C. Sangakkara 10 Sri Lanka v Pakistan
J. B. Hobbs . . . . 12 England v Australia		G. S. Sobers . . . . 10 West Indies v England
S. P. D. Smith . . . 11 Australia v England		S. R. Waugh. . . . . 10 Australia v England

MOST DUCKS

	0s	*Inns*		*0s*	*Inns*
C. A. Walsh (WI)	43	185	C. E. L. Ambrose (WI)	26	145
C. S. Martin (NZ)	36	104	**J. M. Anderson (E)**	**26**	**212**
G. D. McGrath (A)	35	138	Danish Kaneria (P)	25	84
S. C. J. Broad (E)	**35**	**203**	D. K. Morrison (NZ)	24	71
S. K. Warne (A)	34	199	B. S. Chandrasekhar (I)	23	80
M. Muralitharan (SL/World)	33	164	H. M. R. K. B. Herath (SL)	23	144
I. Sharma (I)	**31**	**127**	M. Morkel (SA)	22	104
Zaheer Khan (I)	29	127	M. S. Atapattu (SL)	22	156
M. Dillon (WI)	26	68	S. R. Waugh (A)	22	260

	0s	Inns		0s	Inns
S. J. Harmison (E/World)	21	86	B. S. Bedi (I)	20	101
M. Ntini (SA)	21	116	D. L. Vettori (NZ/World)	20	174
Waqar Younis (P)	21	120	M. A. Atherton (E)	20	212
M. S. Panesar (E)	20	68			

CARRYING BAT THROUGH TEST INNINGS

(Figures in brackets show team's total)

A. B. Tancred	26*	(47)	South Africa v England at Cape Town	1888-89
J. E. Barrett	67*	(176)†	Australia v England at Lord's	1890
R. Abel	132*	(307)	England v Australia at Sydney	1891-92
P. F. Warner	132*	(237)†	England v South Africa at Johannesburg	1898-99
W. W. Armstrong	159*	(309)	Australia v South Africa at Johannesburg	1902-03
J. W. Zulch	43*	(103)	South Africa v England at Cape Town	1909-10
W. Bardsley	193*	(383)	Australia v England at Lord's	1926
W. M. Woodfull	30*	(66)§	Australia v England at Brisbane	1928-29
W. M. Woodfull	73*	(193)‡	Australia v England at Adelaide	1932-33
W. A. Brown	206*	(422)	Australia v England at Lord's	1938
L. Hutton	202*	(344)	England v West Indies at The Oval	1950
L. Hutton	156*	(272)	England v Australia at Adelaide	1950-51
Nazar Mohammad¶	124*	(331)	Pakistan v India at Lucknow	1952-53
F. M. M. Worrell	191*	(372)	West Indies v England at Nottingham	1957
T. L. Goddard	56*	(99)	South Africa v Australia at Cape Town	1957-58
D. J. McGlew	127*	(292)	South Africa v New Zealand at Durban	1961-62
C. C. Hunte	60*	(131)	West Indies v Australia at Port-of-Spain	1964-65
G. M. Turner	43*	(131)	New Zealand v England at Lord's	1969
W. M. Lawry	49*	(107)	Australia v India at Delhi	1969-70
W. M. Lawry	60*	(116)‡	Australia v England at Sydney	1970-71
G. M. Turner	223*	(386)	New Zealand v West Indies at Kingston	1971-72
I. R. Redpath	159*	(346)	Australia v New Zealand at Auckland	1973-74
G. Boycott	99*	(215)	England v Australia at Perth	1979-80
S. M. Gavaskar	127*	(286)	India v Pakistan at Faisalabad	1982-83
Mudassar Nazar¶	152*	(323)	Pakistan v India at Lahore	1982-83
S. Wettimuny	63*	(144)	Sri Lanka v New Zealand at Christchurch	1982-83
D. C. Boon	58*	(103)	Australia v New Zealand at Auckland	1985-86
D. L. Haynes	88*	(211)	West Indies v Pakistan at Karachi	1986-87
G. A. Gooch	154*	(252)	England v West Indies at Leeds	1991
D. L. Haynes	75*	(176)	West Indies v England at The Oval	1991
A. J. Stewart	69*	(175)	England v Pakistan at Lord's	1992
D. L. Haynes	143*	(382)	West Indies v Pakistan at Port-of-Spain	1992-93
M. H. Dekker	68*	(187)	Zimbabwe v Pakistan at Rawalpindi	1993-94
M. A. Atherton	94*	(228)	England v New Zealand at Christchurch	1996-97
G. Kirsten	100*	(239)	South Africa v Pakistan at Faisalabad	1997-98
M. A. Taylor	169*	(350)	Australia v South Africa at Adelaide	1997-98
G. W. Flower	156*	(321)	Zimbabwe v Pakistan at Bulawayo	1997-98
Saeed Anwar	188*	(316)	Pakistan v India at Calcutta	1998-99
M. S. Atapattu	216*	(428)	Sri Lanka v Zimbabwe at Bulawayo	1999-2000
R. P. Arnold	104*	(231)	Sri Lanka v Zimbabwe at Harare	1999-2000
Javed Omar	85*	(168)†‡	Bangladesh v Zimbabwe at Bulawayo	2000-01
V. Sehwag	201*	(329)	India v Sri Lanka at Galle	2008
S. M. Katich	131*	(268)	Australia v New Zealand at Brisbane	2008-09
C. H. Gayle	165*	(317)	West Indies v Australia at Adelaide	2009-10
Imran Farhat	117*	(223)	Pakistan v New Zealand at Napier	2009-10
R. Dravid	146*	(300)	India v England at The Oval	2011
T. M. K. Mawoyo	163*	(412)	Zimbabwe v Pakistan at Bulawayo	2011-12
D. A. Warner	123*	(233)	Australia v New Zealand at Hobart	2011-12
C. A. Pujara	145*	(312)	India v Sri Lanka at Colombo (SSC)	2015-16
D. Elgar	118*	(214)	South Africa v England at Durban	2015-16
K. C. Brathwaite	142*	(337)	West Indies v Pakistan at Sharjah	2016-17

A. N. Cook	244*	(491)	England v Australia at Melbourne	2017-18
D. Elgar	86*	(177)	South Africa v India at Johannesburg	2017-18
D. Elgar	141*	(311)	South Africa v Australia at Cape Town	2017-18
F. D. M. Karunaratne	158*	(287)	Sri Lanka v South Africa at Galle	2018
T. W. M. Latham	264*	(578)	New Zealand v Sri Lanka at Wellington	2018-19

† *On debut.* ‡ *One man absent.* § *Two men absent.* ¶ *Father and son.*

T. W. M. Latham (264) holds the record for the highest score by a player carrying his bat in a Test.*
D. L. Haynes and D. Elgar have achieved the feat on three occasions; Haynes also opened the batting and was last man out in each innings for West Indies v New Zealand at Dunedin, 1979-80.
G. M. Turner was the youngest at 22 years 63 days old when he first did it in 1969.

MOST RUNS IN A SERIES

	T	I	NO	R	HS	100	Avge		
D. G. Bradman	5	7	0	974	334	4	139.14	A v E	1930
W. R. Hammond	5	9	1	905	251	4	113.12	E v A	1928-29
M. A. Taylor	6	11	1	839	219	2	83.90	A v E	1989
R. N. Harvey	5	9	0	834	205	4	92.66	A v SA	1952-53
I. V. A. Richards	4	7	0	829	291	3	118.42	WI v E	1976
C. L. Walcott	5	10	0	827	155	5	82.70	WI v A	1954-55
G. S. Sobers	5	8	2	824	365*	3	137.33	WI v P	1957-58
D. G. Bradman	5	9	0	810	270	2	90.00	A v E	1936-37
D. G. Bradman	5	5	1	806	299*	4	201.50	A v SA	1931-32

MOST RUNS IN A CALENDAR YEAR

	T	I	NO	R	HS	100	Avge	Year
Mohammad Yousuf (P)	11	19	1	1,788	202	9	99.33	2006
I. V. A. Richards (WI)	11	19	0	1,710	291	7	90.00	1976
G. C. Smith (SA)	15	25	2	1,656	232	6	72.00	2008
M. J. Clarke (A)	11	18	3	1,595	329*	5	106.33	2012
S. R. Tendulkar (I)	14	23	3	1,562	214	7	78.10	2010
S. M. Gavaskar (I)	18	27	1	1,555	221	5	59.80	1979
R. T. Ponting (A)	15	28	5	1,544	207	6	67.13	2005
R. T. Ponting (A)	11	18	3	1,503	257	6	100.20	2003

M. Amarnath reached 1,000 runs in 1983 on May 3, in his ninth Test of the year.
The only case of 1,000 in a year before World War II was C. Hill of Australia: 1,060 in 1902.
M. L. Hayden (Australia) scored 1,000 runs in each year from 2001 to 2005.

MOST RUNS

		T	I	NO	R	HS	100	Avge
1	S. R. Tendulkar (India)	200	329	33	15,921	248*	51	53.78
2	R. T. Ponting (Australia)	168	287	29	13,378	257	41	51.85
3	J. H. Kallis (South Africa/World)	166	280	40	13,289	224	45	55.37
4	R. Dravid (India/World)	164	286	32	13,288	270	36	52.31
5	A. N. Cook (England)	161	291	16	12,472	294	33	45.35
6	K. C. Sangakkara (Sri Lanka)	134	233	17	12,400	319	38	57.40
7	B. C. Lara (West Indies/World)	131	232	6	11,953	400*	34	52.88
8	S. Chanderpaul (West Indies)	164	280	49	11,867	203*	30	51.37
9	D. P. M. D. Jayawardene (SL)	149	252	15	11,814	374	34	49.84
10	A. R. Border (Australia)	156	265	44	11,174	205	27	50.56
11	S. R. Waugh (Australia)	168	260	46	10,927	200	32	51.06
12	S. M. Gavaskar (India)	125	214	16	10,122	236*	34	51.12
13	Younis Khan (Pakistan)	118	213	19	10,099	313	34	52.05
14	**H. M. Amla (South Africa)**	**124**	**215**	**16**	**9,282**	**311***	**28**	**46.64**
15	G. C. Smith (South Africa/Wld)	117	205	13	9,265	277	27	48.25
16	G. A. Gooch (England)	118	215	6	8,900	333	20	42.58
17	Javed Miandad (Pakistan)	124	189	21	8,832	280*	23	52.57

		T	I	NO	R	HS	100	Avge
18	Inzamam-ul-Haq (Pakistan/World)	120	200	22	8,830	329	25	49.60
19	V. V. S. Laxman (India)	134	225	34	8,781	281	17	45.97
20	A. B. de Villiers (South Africa). . .	114	191	18	8,765	278*	22	50.66
21	M. J. Clarke (Australia).	115	198	22	8,643	329*	28	49.10
22	M. L. Hayden (Australia)	103	184	14	8,625	380	30	50.73
23	V. Sehwag (India/World)	104	180	6	8,586	319	23	49.34
24	I. V. A. Richards (West Indies). . .	121	182	12	8,540	291	24	50.23
25	A. J. Stewart (England)	133	235	21	8,463	190	15	39.54
26	D. I. Gower (England).	117	204	18	8,231	215	18	44.25
27	K. P. Pietersen (England)	104	181	8	8,181	227	23	47.28
28	G. Boycott (England)	108	193	23	8,114	246*	22	47.72
29	G. S. Sobers (West Indies)	93	160	21	8,032	365*	26	57.78
30	M. E. Waugh (Australia).	128	209	17	8,029	153*	20	41.81
31	M. A. Atherton (England)	115	212	7	7,728	185*	16	37.69
32	I. R. Bell (England)	118	205	24	7,727	235	22	42.69
33	J. L. Langer (Australia)	105	182	12	7,696	250	23	45.27
34	M. C. Cowdrey (England)	114	188	15	7,624	182	22	44.06
35	**J. E. Root (England)**	**92**	**169**	**12**	**7,599**	**254**	**17**	**48.40**
36	C. G. Greenidge (West Indies) . . .	108	185	16	7,558	226	19	44.72
37	Mohammad Yousuf (Pakistan) . . .	90	156	12	7,530	223	24	52.29
38	M. A. Taylor (Australia)	104	186	13	7,525	334*	19	43.49
39	C. H. Lloyd (West Indies)	110	175	14	7,515	242*	19	46.67

MOST RUNS FOR EACH COUNTRY

ENGLAND

A. N. Cook 12,472	A. J. Stewart 8,463	K. P. Pietersen 8,181
G. A. Gooch 8,900	D. I. Gower 8,231	G. Boycott 8,114

AUSTRALIA

R. T. Ponting 13,378	S. R. Waugh 10,927	M. L. Hayden 8,625
A. R. Border 11,174	M. J. Clarke 8,643	M. E. Waugh 8,029

SOUTH AFRICA

J. H. Kallis† 13,206	G. C. Smith† 9,253	G. Kirsten 7,289
H. M. Amla **9,282**	A. B. de Villiers 8,765	H. H. Gibbs 6,167

† J. H. Kallis also scored 44 and 39* and G. C. Smith 12 and 0 for the World XI v Australia (2005-06 Super Series Test).

WEST INDIES

B. C. Lara† 11,912	I. V. A. Richards 8,540	C. G. Greenidge 7,558
S. Chanderpaul 11,867	G. S. Sobers 8,032	C. H. Lloyd 7,515

† B. C. Lara also scored 5 and 36 for the World XI v Australia (2005-06 Super Series Test).

NEW ZEALAND

L. R. P. L. Taylor **7,174**	B. B. McCullum 6,453	M. D. Crowe 5,444
S. P. Fleming 7,172	**K. S. Williamson** **6,379**	J. G. Wright 5,334

INDIA

S. R. Tendulkar 15,921	S. M. Gavaskar 10,122	V. Sehwag† 8,503
R. Dravid† 13,265	V. V. S. Laxman 8,781	S. C. Ganguly 7,212

† *R. Dravid also scored 0 and 23 and V. Sehwag 76 and 7 for the World XI v Australia (2005-06 Super Series Test).*

PAKISTAN

Younis Khan 10,099	Inzamam-ul-Haq† 8,829	**Azhar Ali** **5,885**
Javed Miandad. 8,832	Mohammad Yousuf. . . 7,530	Salim Malik. 5,768

† *Inzamam-ul-Haq also scored 1 and 0 for the World XI v Australia (2005-06 Super Series Test).*

SRI LANKA

K. C. Sangakkara. 12,400	S. T. Jayasuriya 6,973	**A. D. Mathews** **5,981**
D. P. M. D. Jayawardene .11,814	P. A. de Silva. 6,361	M. S. Atapattu 5,502

ZIMBABWE

A. Flower. 4,794	A. D. R. Campbell. 2,858	G. J. Whittall 2,207
G. W. Flower. 3,457	H. Masakadza 2,223	**B. R. M. Taylor** **2,028**

BANGLADESH

Tamim Iqbal **4,327**	**Shakib Al Hasan** **3,862**	**Mahmudullah**. **2,739**
Mushfiqur Rahim . . . **4,210**	Habibul Bashar 3,026	Mohammad Ashraful . 2,737

IRELAND

No player has scored 1,000 Test runs for Ireland. The highest total is 258, by **K. J. O'Brien**.

AFGHANISTAN

No player has scored 1,000 Test runs for Afghanistan. The highest total is 298, by **Rahmat Shah**.

HIGHEST CAREER AVERAGE

(Qualification: 20 innings)

Avge		*T*	*I*	*NO*	*R*	*HS*	*100*
99.94	D. G. Bradman (A)	52	80	10	6,996	334	29
63.43	**M. Labuschagne (A)**	**14**	**23**	**0**	**1,459**	**215**	**4**
62.84	**S. P. D. Smith (A)**	**73**	**131**	**16**	**7,227**	**239**	**26**
61.87	A. C. Voges (A)	20	31	7	1,485	269*	5
60.97	R. G. Pollock (SA)	23	41	4	2,256	274	7
60.83	G. A. Headley (WI)	22	40	4	2,190	270*	10
60.73	H. Sutcliffe (E)	54	84	9	4,555	194	16
59.23	E. Paynter (E)	20	31	5	1,540	243	4
58.67	K. F. Barrington (E)	82	131	15	6,806	256	20
58.61	E. D. Weekes (WI)	48	81	5	4,455	207	15
58.45	W. R. Hammond (E).	85	140	16	7,249	336*	22
57.78	G. S. Sobers (WI)	93	160	21	8,032	365*	26
57.40	K. C. Sangakkara (SL)	134	233	17	12,400	319	38
56.94	J. B. Hobbs (E)	61	102	7	5,410	211	15
56.68	C. L. Walcott (WI)	44	74	7	3,798	220	15

Avge		T	I	NO	R	HS	100
56.67	L. Hutton (E).................	79	138	15	6,971	364	19
55.37	J. H. Kallis (SA/World).........	166	280	40	13,289	224	45
55.00	E. Tyldesley (E).................	14	20	2	990	122	3

S. G. Barnes (A) scored 1,072 runs at 63.05 from 19 innings.

BEST CAREER STRIKE-RATES

(Runs per 100 balls. Qualification: 1,000 runs)

SR		T	I	NO	R	100	Avge
86.97	Shahid Afridi (P)..............	27	48	1	1,716	5	36.51
86.20	**T. G. Southee (NZ)............**	**71**	**104**	**10**	**1,662**	**0**	**17.68**
83.78	C. de Grandhomme (NZ)	22	34	4	1,116	1	37.20
82.22	V. Sehwag (I).................	104	180	6	8,586	23	49.34
81.98	A. C. Gilchrist (A)............	96	137	20	5,570	17	47.60
76.49	G. P. Swann (E)...............	60	76	14	1,370	0	22.09
72.85	**D. A. Warner (A).............**	**84**	**155**	**7**	**7,244**	**24**	**48.94**
70.98	**Sarfraz Ahmed (P)............**	**49**	**86**	**13**	**2,657**	**3**	**36.39**
70.95	Q. de Kock (SA)...............	47	80	5	2,934	5	39.12
70.28	M. Muralitharan (SL)	133	164	56	1,261	0	11.67
68.58	**M. A. Starc (A)...............**	**57**	**85**	**17**	**1,515**	**0**	**22.27**
67.88	D. J. G. Sammy (WI).........	38	63	2	1,323	1	21.68
67.28	**D. P. D. N. Dickwella (SL).....**	**37**	**66**	**4**	**1,921**	**0**	**30.98**
66.94	S. Dhawan (I).................	34	58	1	2,315	7	40.61

Comprehensive data on balls faced has been available only in recent decades, and its introduction varied from country to country. Among earlier players for whom partial data is available, Kapil Dev (India) had a strike-rate of 80.91 and I. V. A. Richards (West Indies) 70.19 in those innings which were fully recorded.

HIGHEST PERCENTAGE OF TEAM'S RUNS OVER TEST CAREER

(Qualification: 20 Tests)

	Tests	Runs	Team Runs	% of Team Runs
D. G. Bradman (Australia)........	52	6,996	28,810	24.28
G. A. Headley (West Indies)	22	2,190	10,239	21.38
B. C. Lara (West Indies).........	131	11,953	63,328	18.87
L. Hutton (England).............	79	6,971	38,440	18.13
J. B. Hobbs (England)...........	61	5,410	30,211	17.90
A. D. Nourse (South Africa)	34	2,960	16,659	17.76
S. P. D. Smith (Australia)......	**73**	**7,227**	**41,298**	**17.49**
E. D. Weekes (West Indies).......	48	4,455	25,667	17.35
B. Mitchell (South Africa).......	42	3,471	20,175	17.20
H. Sutcliffe (England)..........	54	4,555	26,604	17.12
K. C. Sangakkara (Sri Lanka)	134	12,400	72,779	17.03
B. Sutcliffe (New Zealand)	42	2,727	16,158	16.87

The percentage shows the proportion of a team's runs scored by that player in all Tests in which he played, including team runs in innings in which he did not bat.

FASTEST FIFTIES

Minutes

24	Misbah-ul-Haq	Pakistan v Australia at Abu Dhabi	2014-15
27	Mohammad Ashraful	Bangladesh v India at Mirpur	2007
28	J. T. Brown	England v Australia at Melbourne	1894-95
29	S. A. Durani	India v England at Kanpur	1963-64
30	E. A. V. Williams	West Indies v England at Bridgetown......	1947-48
30	B. R. Taylor	New Zealand v West Indies at Auckland	1968-69

The fastest fifties in terms of balls received (where recorded) are:

Balls
21	Misbah-ul-Haq	Pakistan v Australia at Abu Dhabi	2014-15
23	D. A. Warner.	Australia v Pakistan at Sydney	2016-17
24	J. H. Kallis	South Africa v Zimbabwe at Cape Town	2004-05
25	S. Shillingford.	West Indies v New Zealand at Kingston.	2014
26	Shahid Afridi.	Pakistan v India at Bangalore	2004-05
26	Mohammad Ashraful	Bangladesh v India at Mirpur	2007
26	D. W. Steyn.	South Africa v West Indies at Port Elizabeth .	2014-15

FASTEST HUNDREDS

Minutes
70	J. M. Gregory	Australia v South Africa at Johannesburg. . . .	1921-22
74	Misbah-ul-Haq	Pakistan v Australia at Abu Dhabi	2014-15
75	G. L. Jessop.	England v Australia at The Oval	1902
78	R. Benaud	Australia v West Indies at Kingston	1954-55
80	J. H. Sinclair	South Africa v Australia at Cape Town	1902-03
81	I. V. A. Richards	West Indies v England at St John's	1985-86
86	B. R. Taylor	New Zealand v West Indies at Auckland	1968-69

The fastest hundreds in terms of balls received (where recorded) are:

Balls
54	B. B. McCullum	New Zealand v Australia at Christchurch. . . .	2015-16
56	I. V. A. Richards	West Indies v England at St John's.	1985-86
56	Misbah-ul-Haq	Pakistan v Australia at Abu Dhabi	2014-15
57	A. C. Gilchrist.	Australia v England at Perth	2006-07
67	J. M. Gregory	Australia v South Africa at Johannesburg. . . .	1921-22
69	S. Chanderpaul	West Indies v Australia at Georgetown.	2002-03
69	D. A. Warner.	Australia v India at Perth.	2011-12
70	C. H. Gayle	West Indies v Australia at Perth	2009-10

FASTEST DOUBLE-HUNDREDS

Minutes
214	D. G. Bradman	Australia v England at Leeds	1930
217	N. J. Astle	New Zealand v England at Christchurch.	2001-02
223	S. J. McCabe	Australia v England at Nottingham.	1938
226	V. T. Trumper.	Australia v South Africa at Adelaide.	1910-11
234	D. G. Bradman	Australia v England at Lord's	1930
240	W. R. Hammond	England v New Zealand at Auckland	1932-33

The fastest double-hundreds in terms of balls received (where recorded) are:

Balls
153	N. J. Astle	New Zealand v England at Christchurch.	2001-02
163	B. A. Stokes	England v South Africa at Cape Town	2015-16
168	V. Sehwag.	India v Sri Lanka at Mumbai (BS)	2009-10
182	V. Sehwag.	India v Pakistan at Lahore.	2005-06
186	B. B. McCullum	New Zealand v Pakistan at Sharjah.	2014-15
194	V. Sehwag.	India v South Africa at Chennai	2007-08

FASTEST TRIPLE-HUNDREDS

Minutes
288	W. R. Hammond	England v New Zealand at Auckland	1932-33
336	D. G. Bradman	Australia v England at Leeds	1930

The fastest triple-hundred in terms of balls received (where recorded) is:

Balls
278	V. Sehwag.	India v South Africa at Chennai	2007-08

MOST RUNS SCORED OFF AN OVER

28	B. C. Lara (466444).......	off R. J. Peterson	WI v SA at Johannesburg .	2003-04
28	G. J. Bailey (462466)......	off J. M. Anderson	A v E at Perth	2013-14
28	**K. A. Maharaj (444660)....**	**off J. E. Root**	**SA v E at Port Elizabeth**	**2019-20**

The sixth ball produced four byes.

27	Shahid Afridi (666621)	off Harbhajan Singh	P v I at Lahore........	2005-06
26	C. D. McMillan (444464) ...	off Younis Khan	NZ v P at Hamilton......	2000-01
26	B. C. Lara (406664)........	off Danish Kaneria	WI v P at Multan........	2006-07
26	M. G. Johnson (446066)	off P. L. Harris	A v SA at Johannesburg ..	2009-10
26	B. B. McCullum (466046)...	off R. A. S. Lakmal	NZ v SL at Christchurch ..	2014-15
26	H. H. Pandya (446660)	off P. M. Pushpakumara	I v SL at Pallekele.......	2017

MOST RUNS IN A DAY

309	D. G. Bradman........	Australia v England at Leeds	1930
295	W. R. Hammond	England v New Zealand at Auckland	1932-33
284	V. Sehwag	India v Sri Lanka at Mumbai	2009-10
273	D. C. S. Compton	England v Pakistan at Nottingham	1954
271	D. G. Bradman........	Australia v England at Leeds	1934

MOST SIXES IN A CAREER

B. B. McCullum (NZ).................	107		M. L. Hayden (A).................	82
A. C. Gilchrist (A)	100		Misbah-ul-Haq (P).................	81
C. H. Gayle (WI)	98		K. P. Pietersen (E)	81
J. H. Kallis (SA/World)	97		M. S. Dhoni (I).................	78
V. Sehwag (I/World)	91		R. T. Ponting (A).................	73
B. C. Lara (WI)	88		**T. G. Southee (NZ)............**	**72**
C. L. Cairns (NZ).................	87		C. H. Lloyd (WI)	70
I. V. A. Richards (WI)	84		Younis Khan (P).................	70
A. Flintoff (E/World).................	82			

SLOWEST INDIVIDUAL BATTING

0	in 101 minutes	G. I. Allott, New Zealand v South Africa at Auckland	1998-99
4*	in 110 minutes	Abdul Razzaq, Pakistan v Australia at Melbourne	2004-05
6	in 137 minutes	S. C. J. Broad, England v New Zealand at Auckland	2012-13
9*	in 184 minutes	Arshad Khan, Pakistan v Sri Lanka at Colombo (SSC)	2000
18	in 194 minutes	W. R. Playle, New Zealand v England at Leeds	1958
19*	in 217 minutes	M. D. Crowe, New Zealand v Sri Lanka at Colombo (SSC)....	1983-84
25	in 289 minutes	H. M. Amla, South Africa v India at Delhi	2015-16
35	in 332 minutes	C. J. Tavaré, England v India at Madras	1981-82
43	in 354 minutes	A. B. de Villiers, South Africa v India at Delhi...........	2015-16
60	in 390 minutes	D. N. Sardesai, India v West Indies at Bridgetown	1961-62
62	in 408 minutes	Ramiz Raja, Pakistan v West Indies at Karachi	1986-87
68	in 458 minutes	T. E. Bailey, England v Australia at Brisbane............	1958-59
86	in 474 minutes	Shoaib Mohammad, Pakistan v West Indies at Karachi	1990-91
99	in 505 minutes	M. L. Jaisimha, India v Pakistan at Kanpur..............	1960-61
104	in 529 minutes	S. V. Manjrekar, India v Zimbabwe at Harare............	1992-93
105	in 575 minutes	D. J. McGlew, South Africa v Australia at Durban.........	1957-58
114	in 591 minutes	Mudassar Nazar, Pakistan v England at Lahore	1977-78
120*	in 609 minutes	J. J. Crowe, New Zealand v Sri Lanka at Colombo (CCC)....	1986-87
136*	in 675 minutes	S. Chanderpaul, West Indies v India at St John's	2001-02
163	in 720 minutes	Shoaib Mohammad, Pakistan v New Zealand at Wellington ...	1988-89
201*	in 777 minutes	D. S. B. P. Kuruppu, Sri Lanka v NZ at Colombo (CCC)	1986-87
275	in 878 minutes	G. Kirsten, South Africa v England at Durban	1999-2000
337	in 970 minutes	Hanif Mohammad, Pakistan v West Indies at Bridgetown	1957-58

SLOWEST HUNDREDS

557 minutes	Mudassar Nazar, Pakistan v England at Lahore	....	1977-78
545 minutes	D. J. McGlew, South Africa v Australia at Durban	....	1957-58
535 minutes	A. P. Gurusinha, Sri Lanka v Zimbabwe at Harare	....	1994-95
516 minutes	J. J. Crowe, New Zealand v Sri Lanka at Colombo (CCC)	....	1986-87
500 minutes	S. V. Manjrekar, India v Zimbabwe at Harare	....	1992-93
488 minutes	P. E. Richardson, England v South Africa at Johannesburg	....	1956-57

The slowest hundred for any Test in England is 458 minutes (329 balls) by K. W. R. Fletcher, England v Pakistan, The Oval, 1974.

The slowest double-hundred in a Test was scored in 777 minutes (548 balls) by D. S. B. P. Kuruppu for Sri Lanka v New Zealand at Colombo (CCC), 1986-87, on his debut.

PARTNERSHIPS OVER 400

624	for 3rd	K. C. Sangakkara (287)/ D. P. M. D. Jayawardene (374)	SL v SA	Colombo (SSC)	2006
576	for 2nd	S. T. Jayasuriya (340)/R. S. Mahanama (225)	SL v I	Colombo (RPS)	1997-98
467	for 3rd	A. H. Jones (186)/M. D. Crowe (299)	NZ v SL	Wellington	1990-91
451	for 2nd	W. H. Ponsford (266)/D. G. Bradman (244) .	A v E	The Oval	1934
451	for 3rd	Mudassar Nazar (231)/Javed Miandad (280*)	P v I	Hyderabad	1982-83
449	for 4th	A. C. Voges (269*)/S. E. Marsh (182)......	A v WI	Hobart	2015-16
446	for 2nd	C. C. Hunte (260)/G. S. Sobers (365*)	WI v P	Kingston	1957-58
438	for 2nd	M. S. Atapattu (249)/K. C. Sangakkara (270)	SL v Z	Bulawayo	2003-04
437	for 4th	D. P. M. D. Jayawardene (240)/ T. T. Samaraweera (231)	SL v P	Karachi	2008-09
429*	for 3rd	J. A. Rudolph (222*)/H. H. Dippenaar (177*)	SA v B	Chittagong	2003
415	for 1st	N. D. McKenzie (226)/G. C. Smith (232) ...	SA v B	Chittagong	2007-08
413	for 1st	M. H. Mankad (231)/Pankaj Roy (173).....	I v NZ	Madras	1955-56
411	for 4th	P. B. H. May (285*)/M. C. Cowdrey (154)..	E v WI	Birmingham	1957
410	for 1st	V. Sehwag (254)/R. Dravid (128*)	I v P	Lahore	2005-06
405	for 5th	S. G. Barnes (234)/D. G. Bradman (234)....	A v E	Sydney	1946-47

415 runs were added for the third wicket for India v England at Madras in 1981-82 by D. B. Vengsarkar (retired hurt), G. R. Viswanath and Yashpal Sharma. 408 runs were added for the first wicket for India v Bangladesh at Mirpur in 2007 by K. D. Karthik (retired hurt), Wasim Jaffer (retired hurt), R. Dravid and S. R. Tendulkar.

HIGHEST PARTNERSHIPS FOR EACH WICKET

First Wicket

415	N. D. McKenzie (226)/G. C. Smith (232)	SA v B	Chittagong	2007-08
413	M. H. Mankad (231)/Pankaj Roy (173)	I v NZ	Madras	1955-56
410	V. Sehwag (254)/R. Dravid (128*)	I v P	Lahore	2005-06
387	G. M. Turner (259)/T. W. Jarvis (182)	NZ v WI	Georgetown	1971-72
382	W. M. Lawry (210)/R. B. Simpson (201)	A v WI	Bridgetown	1964-65

Second Wicket

576	S. T. Jayasuriya (340)/R. S. Mahanama (225)	SL v I	Colombo (RPS)	1997-98
451	W. H. Ponsford (266)/D. G. Bradman (244).......	A v E	The Oval	1934
446	C. C. Hunte (260)/G. S. Sobers (365*)...........	WI v P	Kingston	1957-58
438	M. S. Atapattu (249)/K. C. Sangakkara (270)......	SL v Z	Bulawayo	2003-04
382	L. Hutton (364)/M. Leyland (187)	E v A	The Oval	1938

Third Wicket

624	K. C. Sangakkara (287)/D. P. M. D. Jayawardene (374)	SL v SA	Colombo (SSC)	2006
467	A. H. Jones (186)/M. D. Crowe (299)	NZ v SL	Wellington	1990-91
451	Mudassar Nazar (231)/Javed Miandad (280*)	P v I	Hyderabad	1982-83
429*	J. A. Rudolph (222*)/H. H. Dippenaar (177*)	SA v B	Chittagong	2003
397	Qasim Omar (206)/Javed Miandad (203*)	P v SL	Faisalabad	1985-86

Fourth Wicket

449	A. C. Voges (269*)/S. E. Marsh (182)	A v WI	Hobart	2015-16
437	D. P. M. D. Jayawardene(240)/T. T. Samaraweera (231)	SL v P	Karachi	2008-09
411	P. B. H. May (285*)/M. C. Cowdrey (154)	E v WI	Birmingham	1957
399	G. S. Sobers (226)/F. M. M. Worrell (197*)	WI v E	Bridgetown	1959-60
388	W. H. Ponsford (181)/D. G. Bradman (304)	A v E	Leeds	1934

Fifth Wicket

405	S. G. Barnes (234)/D. G. Bradman (234)	A v E	Sydney	1946-47
385	S. R. Waugh (160)/G. S. Blewett (214)	A v SA	Johannesburg	1996-97
376	V. V. S. Laxman (281)/R. Dravid (180)	I v A	Kolkata	2000-01
359	Shakib Al Hasan (217)/Mushfiqur Rahim (159)	B v NZ	Wellington	2016-17
338	G. C. Smith (234)/A. B. de Villiers (164)	SA v P	Dubai	2013-14

Sixth Wicket

399	B. A. Stokes (258)/J. M. Bairstow (150*)	E v SA	Cape Town	2015-16
365*	K. S. Williamson (242*)/B-J. Watling (142*)	NZ v SL	Wellington	2014-15
352	B. B. McCullum (302)/B-J. Watling (124)	NZ v I	Wellington	2013-14
351	D. P. M. D. Jayawardene (275)/ H. A. P. W. Jayawardene (154*)	SL v I	Ahmedabad	2009-10
346	J. H. Fingleton (136)/D. G. Bradman (270)	A v E	Melbourne	1936-37

Seventh Wicket

347	D. St E. Atkinson (219)/C. C. Depeiza (122)	WI v A	Bridgetown	1954-55
308	Waqar Hassan (189)/Imtiaz Ahmed (209)	P v NZ	Lahore	1955-56
295*	**S. O. Dowrich (116*)/J. O. Holder (202*)**	**WI v E**	**Bridgetown**	**2018-19**
280	R. G. Sharma (177)/R. Ashwin (124)	I v WI	Kolkata	2013-14
261	**B-J. Watling (205)/M. J. Santner (126)**	**NZ v E**	**Mt Maunganui**	**2019-20**

Eighth Wicket

332	I. J. L. Trott (184)/S. C. J. Broad (169)	E v P	Lord's	2010
313	Wasim Akram (257*)/Saqlain Mushtaq (79)	P v Z	Sheikhupura	1996-97
256	S. P. Fleming (262)/J. E. C. Franklin (122*)	NZ v SA	Cape Town	2005-06
253	N. J. Astle (156*)/A. C. Parore (110)	NZ v A	Perth	2001-02
246	L. E. G. Ames (137)/G. O. B. Allen (122)	E v NZ	Lord's	1931

Ninth Wicket

195	M. V. Boucher (78)/P. L. Symcox (108)	SA v P	Johannesburg	1997-98
190	Asif Iqbal (146)/Intikhab Alam (51)	P v E	The Oval	1967
184	Mahmudullah (76)/Abul Hasan (113)	B v WI	Khulna	2012-13
180	J-P. Duminy (166)/D. W. Steyn (76)	SA v A	Melbourne	2008-09
163*	M. C. Cowdrey (128*)/A. C. Smith (69*)	E v NZ	Wellington	1962-63

Tenth Wicket

198	J. E. Root (154*)/J. M. Anderson (81)	E v I	Nottingham	2014
163	P. J. Hughes (81*)/A. C. Agar (98).	A v E	Nottingham	2013
151	B. F. Hastings (110)/R. O. Collinge (68*)	NZ v P	Auckland	1972-73
151	Azhar Mahmood (128*)/Mushtaq Ahmed (59)	P v SA	Rawalpindi	1997-98
143	D. Ramdin (107*)/T. L. Best (95).	WI v E	Birmingham	2012

HIGHEST PARTNERSHIPS FOR EACH COUNTRY

ENGLAND

359	for 1st	L. Hutton (158)/C. Washbrook (195)	v SA	Johannesburg	1948-49
382	for 2nd	L. Hutton (364)/M. Leyland (187)	v A	The Oval	1938
370	for 3rd	W. J. Edrich (189)/D. C. S. Compton (208) . . .	v SA	Lord's	1947
411	for 4th	P. B. H. May (285*)/M. C. Cowdrey (154) . . .	v WI	Birmingham	1957
254	for 5th	K. W. R. Fletcher (113)/A. W. Greig (148) . . .	v I	Bombay	1972-73
399	for 6th	B. A. Stokes (258)/J. M. Bairstow (150*)	v SA	Cape Town	2015-16
197	for 7th	M. J. K. Smith (96)/J. M. Parks (101*).	v WI	Port-of-Spain	1959-60
332	for 8th	I. J. L. Trott (184)/S. C. J. Broad (169).	v P	Lord's	2010
163*	for 9th	M. C. Cowdrey (128*)/A. C. Smith (69*)	v NZ	Wellington	1962-63
198	for 10th	J. E. Root (154*)/J. M. Anderson (81)	v I	Nottingham	2014

AUSTRALIA

382	for 1st	W. M. Lawry (210)/R. B. Simpson (201).	v WI	Bridgetown	1964-65
451	for 2nd	W. H. Ponsford (266)/D. G. Bradman (244). . .	v E	The Oval	1934
315	for 3rd	R. T. Ponting (206)/D. S. Lehmann (160)	v WI	Port-of-Spain	2002-03
449	for 4th	A. C. Voges (269*)/S. E. Marsh (182)	v WI	Hobart	2015-16
405	for 5th	S. G. Barnes (234)/D. G. Bradman (234)	v E	Sydney	1946-47
346	for 6th	J. H. Fingleton (136)/D. G. Bradman (270) . . .	v E	Melbourne	1936-37
217	for 7th	K. D. Walters (250)/G. J. Gilmour (101)	v NZ	Christchurch	1976-77
243	for 8th	R. J. Hartigan (116)/C. Hill (160).	v E	Adelaide	1907-08
154	for 9th	S. E. Gregory (201)/J. McC. Blackham (74) . .	v E	Sydney	1894-95
163	for 10th	P. J. Hughes (81*)/A. C. Agar (98).	v E	Nottingham	2013

SOUTH AFRICA

415	for 1st	N. D. McKenzie (226)/G. C. Smith (232).	v B	Chittagong	2007-08
315*	for 2nd	H. H. Gibbs (211*)/J. H. Kallis (148*).	v NZ	Christchurch	1998-99
429*	for 3rd	J. A. Rudolph (222*)/H. H. Dippenaar (177*) .	v B	Chittagong	2003
308	for 4th	H. M. Amla (208)/A. B. de Villiers (152).	v WI	Centurion	2014-15
338	for 5th	G. C. Smith (234)/A. B. de Villiers (164).	v P	Dubai	2013-14
271	for 6th	A. G. Prince (162*)/M. V. Boucher (117)	v E	Centurion	2008-09
246	for 7th	D. J. McGlew (255*)/A. R. A. Murray (109) . .	v NZ	Wellington	1952-53
150	for 8th {	N. D. McKenzie (103)/S. M. Pollock (111) . . .	v SL	Centurion	2000-01
		G. Kirsten (130)/M. Zondeki (59).	v E	Leeds	2003
195	for 9th	M. V. Boucher (78)/P. L. Symcox (108)	v P	Johannesburg	1997-98
107*	for 10th	A. B. de Villiers (278*)/M. Morkel (35*).	v P	Abu Dhabi	2010-11

WEST INDIES

298	for 1st	C. G. Greenidge (149)/D. L. Haynes (167). . . .	v E	St John's	1989-90
446	for 2nd	C. C. Hunte (260)/G. S. Sobers (365*).	v P	Kingston	1957-58
338	for 3rd	E. D. Weekes (206)/F. M. M. Worrell (167). . .	v E	Port-of-Spain	1953-54
399	for 4th	G. S. Sobers (226)/F. M. M. Worrell (197*). . .	v E	Bridgetown	1959-60
322	for 5th†	B. C. Lara (213)/J. C. Adams (94)	v A	Kingston	1998-99
282*	for 6th	B. C. Lara (400*)/R. D. Jacobs (107*)	v E	St John's	2003-04
347	for 7th	D. St E. Atkinson (219)/C. C. Depeiza (122) . .	v A	Bridgetown	1954-55
212	for 8th	S. O. Dowrich (103)/J. O. Holder (110)	v Z	Bulawayo	2017-18
161	for 9th	C. H. Lloyd (161*)/A. M. E. Roberts (68) . . .	v I	Calcutta	1983-84
143	for 10th	D. Ramdin (107*)/T. L. Best (95).	v E	Birmingham	2012

† *344 runs were added between the fall of the 4th and 5th wickets: P. T. Collins retired hurt when he and Lara had added 22 runs.*

NEW ZEALAND

387	for 1st	G. M. Turner (259)/T. W. Jarvis (182)	v WI	Georgetown	1971-72
297	for 2nd	B. B. McCullum (202)/K. S. Williamson (192)	v P	Sharjah	2014-15
467	for 3rd	A. H. Jones (186)/M. D. Crowe (299)	v SL	Wellington	1990-91
271	for 4th	L. R. P. L. Taylor (151)/J. D. Ryder (201)	v I	Napier	2008-09
222	for 5th	N. J. Astle (141)/C. D. McMillan (142)	v Z	Wellington	2000-01
365*	for 6th	K. S. Williamson (242*)/B-J. Watling (142*) . .	v SL	Wellington	2014-15
261	**for 7th**	**B-J. Watling (205)/M. J. Santner (126)**	**v E**	**Mt Maunganui**	**2019-20**
256	for 8th	S. P. Fleming (262)/J. E. C. Franklin (122*) . .	v SA	Cape Town	2005-06
136	for 9th	I. D. S. Smith (173)/M. C. Snedden (58)	v I	Auckland	1989-90
151	for 10th	B. F. Hastings (110)/R. O. Collinge (68*)	v P	Auckland	1972-73

INDIA

413	for 1st	M. H. Mankad (231)/Pankaj Roy (173)	v NZ	Madras	1955-56
370	for 2nd	M. Vijay (167)/C. A. Pujara (204)	v A	Hyderabad	2012-13
336	for 3rd†	V. Sehwag (309)/S. R. Tendulkar (194*)	v P	Multan	2003-04
365	for 4th	V. Kohli (211)/A. M. Rahane (188)	v NZ	Indore	2016-17
376	for 5th	V. V. S. Laxman (281)/R. Dravid (180)	v A	Kolkata	2000-01
298*	for 6th	D. B. Vengsarkar (164*)/R. J. Shastri (121*). .	v A	Bombay	1986-87
280	for 7th	R. G. Sharma (177)/R. Ashwin (124)	v WI	Kolkata	2013-14
241	for 8th	V. Kohli (235)/J. Yadav (104)	v E	Mumbai	2016-17
149	for 9th	P. G. Joshi (52*)/R. B. Desai (85)	v P	Bombay	1960-61
133	for 10th	S. R. Tendulkar (248*)/Zaheer Khan (75)	v B	Dhaka	2004-05

† *415 runs were scored for India's 3rd wicket v England at Madras in 1981-82, in two partnerships: D. B. Vengsarkar and G. R. Viswanath put on 99 before Vengsarkar retired hurt, then Viswanath and Yashpal Sharma added a further 316.*

PAKISTAN

298	for 1st	Aamir Sohail (160)/Ijaz Ahmed snr (151)	v WI	Karachi	1997-98
291	for 2nd	Zaheer Abbas (274)/Mushtaq Mohammad (100)	v E	Birmingham	1971
451	for 3rd	Mudassar Nazar (231)/Javed Miandad (280*) .	v I	Hyderabad	1982-83
350	for 4th	Mushtaq Mohammad (201)/Asif Iqbal (175) . .	v NZ	Dunedin	1972-73
281	for 5th	Javed Miandad (163)/Asif Iqbal (166)	v NZ	Lahore	1976-77
269	for 6th	Mohammad Yousuf (223)/Kamran Akmal (154)	v E	Lahore	2005-06
308	for 7th	Waqar Hassan (189)/Imtiaz Ahmed (209)	v NZ	Lahore	1955-56
313	for 8th	Wasim Akram (257*)/Saqlain Mushtaq (79) . .	v Z	Sheikhupura	1996-97
190	for 9th	Asif Iqbal (146)/Intikhab Alam (51).	v E	The Oval	1967
151	for 10th	Azhar Mahmood (128*)/Mushtaq Ahmed (59) .	v SA	Rawalpindi	1997-98

SRI LANKA

335	for 1st	M. S. Atapattu (207*)/S. T. Jayasuriya (188) ..	v P	Kandy	2000
576	for 2nd	S. T. Jayasuriya (340)/R. S. Mahanama (225) .	v I	Colombo (RPS)	1997-98
624	for 3rd	K. C. Sangakkara (287)/			
		D. P. M. D. Jayawardene (374).	v SA	Colombo (SSC)	2006
437	for 4th	D. P. M. D. Jayawardene (240)/			
		T. T. Samaraweera (231)	v P	Karachi	2008-09
280	for 5th	T. T. Samaraweera (138)/T. M. Dilshan (168) .	v B	Colombo (PSS)	2005-06
351	for 6th	D. P. M. D. Jayawardene (275)/			
		H. A. P. W. Jayawardene (154*)	v I	Ahmedabad	2009-10
223*	for 7th	H. A. P. W. Jayawardene (120*)/			
		W. P. U. J. C. Vaas (100*)	v B	Colombo (SSC)	2007
170	for 8th	D. P. M. D. Jayawardene (237)/			
		W. P. U. J. C. Vaas (69)	v SA	Galle	2004
118	for 9th	T. T. Samaraweera (83)/B. A. W. Mendis (78) .	v I	Colombo (PSS)	2010
79	for 10th	W. P. U. J. C. Vaas (68*)/M. Muralitharan (43)	v A	Kandy	2003-04

ZIMBABWE

164	for 1st	D. D. Ebrahim (71)/A. D. R. Campbell (103) .	v WI	Bulawayo	2001
160	for 2nd	Sikandar Raza (82)/H. Masakadza (81)	v B	Chittagong	2014-15
194	for 3rd	A. D. R. Campbell (99)/D. L. Houghton (142).	v SL	Harare	1994-95
269	for 4th	G. W. Flower (201*)/A. Flower (156)	v P	Harare	1994-95
277*	for 5th	M. W. Goodwin (166*)/A. Flower (100*)	v P	Bulawayo	1997-98
165	for 6th	D. L. Houghton (121)/A. Flower (59).	v I	Harare	1992-93
154	for 7th	H. H. Streak (83*)/A. M. Blignaut (92)	v WI	Harare	2001
168	for 8th	H. H. Streak (127*)/A. M. Blignaut (91)	v WI	Harare	2003-04
87	for 9th	P. A. Strang (106*)/B. C. Strang (42).	v P	Sheikhupura	1996-97
97*	for 10th	A. Flower (183*)/H. K. Olonga (11*)	v I	Delhi	2000-01

BANGLADESH

312	for 1st	Tamim Iqbal (206)/Imrul Kayes (150)	v P	Khulna	2014-15
232	for 2nd	Shamsur Rahman (106)/Imrul Kayes (115) . . .	v SL	Chittagong	2013-14
236	for 3rd	Mominul Haque (176)/Mushfiqur Rahim (92)..	v SL	Chittagong	2017-18
266	for 4th	Mominul Haque (161)/Mushfiqur Rahim (219*)	v Z	Mirpur	2018-19
359	for 5th	Shakib Al Hasan (217)/Mushfiqur Rahim (159)	v NZ	Wellington	2016-17
191	for 6th	Mohammad Ashraful (129*)/			
		Mushfiqur Rahim (80).	v SL	Colombo (PSS)	2007
145	for 7th	Shakib Al Hasan (87)/Mahmudullah (115). . . .	v NZ	Hamilton	2009-10
144*	for 8th	Mushfiqur Rahim (219*)/Mehedi Hasan (68*) .	v Z	Mirpur	2018-19
184	for 9th	Mahmudullah (76)/Abul Hasan (113).	v WI	Khulna	2012-13
69	for 10th	Mohammad Rafique (65)/Shahadat Hossain (3*)	v A	Chittagong	2005-06

IRELAND

69	for 1st	E. C. Joyce (43)/W. T. S. Porterfield (32).	v P	Malahide	2018
33	**for 2nd**	**P. R. Stirling (14)/A. Balbirnie (82)**	**v Afg**	**Dehradun**	**2018-19**
104	**for 3rd**	**A. Balbirnie (82)/J. A. McCollum (39)**	**v Afg**	**Dehradun**	**2018-19**
14	**for 4th**	**J. A. McCollum (4)/K. J. O'Brien (12)**	**v Afg**	**Dehradun**	**2018-19**
32	for 5th	P. R. Stirling (11)/K. J. O'Brien (118)	v P	Malahide	2018
30	for 6th	K. J. O'Brien (118)/G. C. Wilson (12)	v P	Malahide	2018
114	for 7th	K. J. O'Brien (118)/S. R. Thompson (53).	v P	Malahide	2018
50	for 8th	K. J. O'Brien (118)/T. E. Kane (14)	v P	Malahide	2018
34	for 9th	G. C. Wilson (33*)/W. B. Rankin (17).	v P	Malahide	2018
87	**for 10th**	**G. H. Dockrell (39)/T. J. Murtagh (54*)**	**v Afg**	**Dehradun**	**2018-19**

AFGHANISTAN

53	for 1st	Ibrahim Zadran (23)/Javed Ahmadi (62) . . .	v WI	Lucknow	2019-20
139	for 2nd	Ihsanullah Janat (65*)/Rahmat Shah (76) . .	v Ire	Dehradun	2018-19
130	for 3rd	Rahmat Shah (98)/Hashmatullah Shahidi (61)	v Ire	Dehradun	2018-19
120	for 4th	Rahmat Shah (102)/Asghar Afghan (92)	v B	Chittagong	2019-20
37	for 5th {	Hashmatullah Shahidi (36*)/Asghar Afghan (25) . .	v I	Bangalore	2018
		Javed Ahmadi (62)/Nasir Ahmadzai (15) . .	v WI	Lucknow	2019-20
81	for 6th	Asghar Afghan (92)/Afsar Zazai (41)	v B	Chittagong	2019-20
30	for 7th	Afsar Zazai (48*)/Rashid Khan (24)	v B	Chittagong	2019-20
54	for 8th	Afsar Zazai (32)/Hamza Hotak (34)	v WI	Lucknow	2019-20
31	for 9th	Asghar Afghan (67)/Wafadar Momand (6) . .	v Ire	Dehradun	2018-19
21	for 10th	Mujeeb Zadran (15)/Wafadar Momand (6*). . .	v I	Bangalore	2018

UNUSUAL DISMISSALS

Handled the Ball

W. R. Endean	South Africa v England at Cape Town	1956-57
A. M. J. Hilditch	Australia v Pakistan at Perth	1978-79
Mohsin Khan	Pakistan v Australia at Karachi.	1982-83
D. L. Haynes	West Indies v India at Bombay.	1983-84
G. A. Gooch	England v Australia at Manchester	1993
S. R. Waugh	Australia v India at Chennai	2000-01
M. P. Vaughan	England v India at Bangalore	2001-02

Obstructing the Field

L. Hutton	England v South Africa at The Oval	1951

There have been no cases of Hit the Ball Twice or Timed Out in Test cricket.

BOWLING RECORDS

MOST WICKETS IN AN INNINGS

10-53	J. C. Laker	England v Australia at Manchester.	1956
10-74	A. Kumble	India v Pakistan at Delhi.	1998-99
9-28	G. A. Lohmann	England v South Africa at Johannesburg	1895-96
9-37	J. C. Laker	England v Australia at Manchester.	1956
9-51	M. Muralitharan.	Sri Lanka v Zimbabwe at Kandy	2001-02
9-52	R. J. Hadlee.	New Zealand v Australia at Brisbane	1985-86
9-56	Abdul Qadir.	Pakistan v England at Lahore	1987-88
9-57	D. E. Malcolm.	England v South Africa at The Oval.	1994
9-65	M. Muralitharan.	Sri Lanka v England at The Oval	1998
9-69	J. M. Patel	India v Australia at Kanpur.	1959-60
9-83	Kapil Dev	India v West Indies at Ahmedabad	1983-84
9-86	Sarfraz Nawaz	Pakistan v Australia at Melbourne	1978-79
9-95	J. M. Noreiga.	West Indies v India at Port-of-Spain.	1970-71
9-102	S. P. Gupte.	India v West Indies at Kanpur	1958-59
9-103	S. F. Barnes	England v South Africa at Johannesburg	1913-14
9-113	H. J. Tayfield	South Africa v England at Johannesburg	1956-57
9-121	A. A. Mailey	Australia v England at Melbourne	1920-21
9-127	H. M. R. K. B. Herath . . .	Sri Lanka v Pakistan at Colombo (SSC).	2014
9-129	K. A. Maharaj	South Africa v Sri Lanka at Colombo (SSC)	2018

There have been 79 instances of eight wickets in a Test innings.

The best bowling figures for the countries not mentioned above are:

8-39	Taijul Islam	Bangladesh v Zimbabwe at Mirpur	2014-15
8-109	P. A. Strang	Zimbabwe v New Zealand at Bulawayo.	2000-01
6-49	**Rashid Khan**	**Afghanistan v Bangladesh at Chittagong**	**2019-20**
5-13	**T. J. Murtagh**.	**Ireland v England at Lord's**	**2019**

OUTSTANDING BOWLING ANALYSES

	O	*M*	*R*	*W*		
J. C. Laker (E)	51.2	23	53	10	v Australia at Manchester	1956
A. Kumble (I)	26.3	9	74	10	v Pakistan at Delhi	1998-99
G. A. Lohmann (E)	14.2	6	28	9	v South Africa at Johannesburg	1895-96
J. C. Laker (E)	16.4	4	37	9	v Australia at Manchester	1956
G. A. Lohmann (E)	9.4	5	7	8	v South Africa at Port Elizabeth	1895-96
J. Briggs (E)	14.2	5	11	8	v South Africa at Cape Town	1888-89
S. C. J. Broad (E)	9.3	5	15	8	v Australia at Nottingham.	2015
S. J. Harmison (E)	12.3	8	12	7	v West Indies at Kingston.	2003-04
J. Briggs (E)	19.1	11	17	7	v South Africa at Cape Town	1888-89
M. A. Noble (A)	7.4	2	17	7	v England at Melbourne	1901-02
W. Rhodes (E)	11	3	17	7	v Australia at Birmingham	1902

WICKET WITH FIRST BALL IN TEST CRICKET

	Batsman dismissed			
T. P. Horan	W. W. Read	A v E	Sydney	1882-83
A. Coningham	A. C. MacLaren	A v E	Melbourne	1894-95
W. M. Bradley	F. Laver	E v A	Manchester	1899
E. G. Arnold	V. T. Trumper	E v A	Sydney	1903-04
A. E. E. Vogler	E. G. Hayes	SA v E	Johannesburg	1905-06
J. N. Crawford	A. E. E. Vogler	E v SA	Johannesburg	1905-06
G. G. Macaulay	G. A. L. Hearne	E v SA	Cape Town	1922-23
M. W. Tate	M. J. Susskind	E v SA	Birmingham	1924
M. Henderson	E. W. Dawson	NZ v E	Christchurch	1929-30
H. D. Smith	E. Paynter	NZ v E	Christchurch	1932-33
T. F. Johnson	W. W. Keeton	WI v E	The Oval.	1939
R. Howorth	D. V. Dyer	E v SA	The Oval.	1947
Intikhab Alam	C. C. McDonald	P v A	Karachi	1959-60
R. K. Illingworth	P. V. Simmons	E v WI	Nottingham.	1991
N. M. Kulkarni	M. S. Atapattu	I v SL	Colombo (RPS)	1997-98
M. K. G. C. P. Lakshitha	Mohammad Ashraful	SL v B	Colombo (SSC)	2002
N. M. Lyon	K. C. Sangakkara	A v SL	Galle	2011-12
R. M. S. Eranga	S. R. Watson	SL v A	Colombo (SSC)	2011-12
D. L. Piedt	M. A. Vermeulen	SA v Z	Harare	2014-15
G. C. Viljoen	A. N. Cook	SA v E	Johannesburg	2015-16

HAT-TRICKS

Most Hat-Tricks

S. C. J. Broad	**2**	H. Trumble.	2
T. J. Matthews†	2	Wasim Akram‡	2

† *T. J. Matthews did the hat-trick in each innings of the same match.*

‡ *Wasim Akram did the hat-trick in successive matches.*

Hat-Tricks

There have been **44** hat-tricks in Tests, including the above. Occurrences since 2007:

R. J. Sidebottom	England v New Zealand at Hamilton.	2007-08
P. M. Siddle.	Australia v England at Brisbane	2010-11
S. C. J. Broad.	England v India at Nottingham	2011
Sohag Gazi†	Bangladesh v New Zealand at Chittagong.	2013-14
S. C. J. Broad.	England v Sri Lanka at Leeds	2014
H. M. R. K. B. Herath . . .	Sri Lanka v Australia at Galle	2016
M. M. Ali.	England v South Africa at The Oval	2017
J. J. Bumrah.	**India v West Indies at North Sound.**	**2019**

† *Sohag Gazi also scored 101 not out.*

M. J. C. Allom, P. J. Petherick and D. W. Fleming did the hat-trick on Test debut. D. N. T. Zoysa took one in the second over of a Test (his first three balls); I. K. Pathan in the first over of a Test.

FOUR WICKETS IN FIVE BALLS

M. J. C. Allom.	England v New Zealand at Christchurch.	1929-30
	On debut, in his eighth over: W-WWW	
C. M. Old.	England v Pakistan at Birmingham.	1978
	Sequence interrupted by a no-ball: WW-WW	
Wasim Akram	Pakistan v West Indies at Lahore (*WW-WW*)	1990-91

MOST WICKETS IN A TEST

19-90	J. C. Laker	England v Australia at Manchester.	1956
17-159	S. F. Barnes	England v South Africa at Johannesburg	1913-14
16-136†	N. D. Hirwani.	India v West Indies at Madras.	1987-88
16-137†	R. A. L. Massie	Australia v England at Lord's.	1972
16-220	M. Muralitharan	Sri Lanka v England at The Oval	1998

† *On Test debut.*

There have been 18 further instances of 14 or more wickets in a Test match.

The best bowling figures for the countries not mentioned above are:

15-123	R. J. Hadlee	New Zealand v Australia at Brisbane	1985-86
14-116	Imran Khan	Pakistan v Sri Lanka at Lahore	1981-82
14-149	M. A. Holding	West Indies v England at The Oval	1976
13-132	M. Ntini	South Africa v West Indies at Port-of-Spain.	2004-05
12-117	Mehedi Hasan.	Bangladesh v West Indies at Mirpur.	2018-19
11-104	**Rashid Khan.**	**Afghanistan v Bangladesh at Chittagong**	**2019-20**
11-255	A. G. Huckle	Zimbabwe v New Zealand at Bulawayo.	1997-98
6-65	**T. J. Murtagh**	**Ireland v England at Lord's.**	**2019**

MOST BALLS BOWLED IN A TEST

S. Ramadhin (West Indies) sent down 774 balls in 129 overs against England at Birmingham, 1957, the most delivered by any bowler in a Test, beating H. Verity's 766 for England against South Africa at Durban, 1938-39. In this match Ramadhin also bowled the most balls (588) in any first-class innings, since equalled by Arshad Ayub, Hyderabad v Madhya Pradesh at Secunderabad, 1991-92.

MOST WICKETS IN A SERIES

	T	R	W	Avge		
S. F. Barnes	4	536	49	10.93	England v South Africa	1913-14
J. C. Laker	5	442	46	9.60	England v Australia	1956
C. V. Grimmett	5	642	44	14.59	Australia v South Africa	1935-36
T. M. Alderman	6	893	42	21.26	Australia v England	1981
R. M. Hogg	6	527	41	12.85	Australia v England	1978-79
T. M. Alderman	6	712	41	17.36	Australia v England	1989
Imran Khan	6	558	40	13.95	Pakistan v India	1982-83
S. K. Warne	5	797	40	19.92	Australia v England	2005

The most for South Africa is 37 by H. J. Tayfield against England in 1956-57, for West Indies 35 by M. D. Marshall against England in 1988, for India 35 by B. S. Chandrasekhar against England in 1972-73 (all in five Tests), for New Zealand 33 by R. J. Hadlee against Australia in 1985-86, for Sri Lanka 30 by M. Muralitharan against Zimbabwe in 2001-02, for Zimbabwe 22 by H. H. Streak against Pakistan in 1994-95 (all in three Tests), and for Bangladesh 19 by Mehedi Hasan against England in 2016-17 (two Tests).

MOST WICKETS IN A CALENDAR YEAR

	T	R	W	5I	10M	Avge	Year
S. K. Warne (Australia)	15	2,114	96	6	2	22.02	2005
M. Muralitharan (Sri Lanka)	11	1,521	90	9	5	16.89	2006
D. K. Lillee (Australia).	13	1,781	85	5	2	20.95	1981
A. A. Donald (South Africa)	14	1,571	80	7	–	19.63	1998
M. Muralitharan (Sri Lanka)	12	1,699	80	7	4	21.23	2001
J. Garner (West Indies).	15	1,604	77	4	–	20.83	1984
Kapil Dev (India)	18	1,739	75	5	1	23.18	1983
M. Muralitharan (Sri Lanka)	10	1,463	75	7	3	19.50	2000

MOST WICKETS

		T	Balls	R	W	5I	10M	Avge	SR
1	M. Muralitharan (SL/World).	133	44,039	18,180	800	67	22	22.72	55.04
2	S. K. Warne (Australia).	145	40,704	17,995	708	37	10	25.41	57.49
3	A. Kumble (India).........	132	40,850	18,355	619	35	8	29.65	65.99
4	**J. M. Anderson (England) .**	**151**	**32,779**	**15,670**	**584**	**28**	**3**	**26.83**	**56.12**
5	G. D. McGrath (Australia) .	124	29,248	12,186	563	29	3	21.64	51.95
6	C. A. Walsh (West Indies) ..	132	30,019	12,688	519	22	3	24.44	57.84
7	**S. C. J. Broad (England).**	**138**	**28,079**	**13,827**	**485**	**17**	**2**	**28.50**	**57.89**
8	**D. W. Steyn (South Africa).**	**93**	**18,608**	**10,077**	**439**	**26**	**5**	**22.95**	**42.38**
9	Kapil Dev (India)	131	27,740	12,867	434	23	2	29.64	63.91
10	H. M. R. K. B. Herath (SL)..	93	25,993	12,157	433	34	9	28.07	60.03
11	R. J. Hadlee (New Zealand).	86	21,918	9,611	431	36	9	22.29	50.85
12	S. M. Pollock (South Africa)	108	24,353	9,733	421	16	1	23.11	57.84
13	Harbhajan Singh (India) ...	103	28,580	13,537	417	25	5	32.46	68.53
14	Wasim Akram (Pakistan) ...	104	22,627	9,779	414	25	5	23.62	54.65
15	C. E. L. Ambrose (WI)	98	22,103	8,501	405	22	3	20.99	54.57
16 {	M. Ntini (South Africa).....	101	20,834	11,242	390	18	4	28.82	53.42
{	**N. M. Lyon (Australia) ....**	**96**	**24,568**	**12,320**	**390**	**18**	**3**	**31.58**	**62.99**
18	I. T. Botham (England)	102	21,815	10,878	383	27	4	28.40	56.95
19	M. D. Marshall (West Indies)	81	17,584	7,876	376	22	4	20.94	46.76
20	Waqar Younis (Pakistan) ...	87	16,224	8,788	373	22	5	23.56	43.49
21 {	Imran Khan (Pakistan)	88	19,458	8,258	362	23	6	22.81	53.75
{	**R. Ashwin (India) ....**	**70**	**19,412**	**9,183**	**362**	**27**	**7**	**25.36**	**53.62**
24 {	D. L. Vettori (NZ/World)....	113	28,814	12,441	362	20	3	34.36	79.59
{	D. K. Lillee (Australia)	70	18,467	8,493	355	23	7	23.92	52.01
{	W. P. U. J. C. Vaas (SL)	111	23,438	10,501	355	12	2	29.58	66.02

		T	Balls	R	W	5I	10M	Avge	SR
26	A. A. Donald (South Africa).	72	15,519	7,344	330	20	3	22.25	47.02
27	R. G. D. Willis (England) ...	90	17,357	8,190	325	16	–	25.20	53.40
28	M. G. Johnson (Australia)...	73	16,001	8,891	313	12	3	28.40	51.12
29	Zaheer Khan (India)	92	18,785	10,247	311	11	1	32.94	60.40
30	B. Lee (Australia)	76	16,531	9,554	310	10	–	30.81	53.32
31 {	M. Morkel (South Africa) ...	86	16,498	8,550	309	8	0	27.66	53.39
	L. R. Gibbs (West Indies) ...	79	27,115	8,989	309	18	2	29.09	87.75
33	F. S. Trueman (England)....	67	15,178	6,625	307	17	3	21.57	49.43

MOST WICKETS FOR EACH COUNTRY

ENGLAND

J. M. Anderson **584**	I. T. Botham............383	F. S. Trueman..........307
S. C. J. Broad **485**	R. G. D. Willis 325	D. L. Underwood 297

AUSTRALIA

S. K. Warne 708	**N. M. Lyon** **390**	M. G. Johnson 313
G. D. McGrath 563	D. K. Lillee 355	B. Lee................310

SOUTH AFRICA

D. W. Steyn..........**439**	M. Ntini 390	M. Morkel 309
S. M. Pollock 421	A. A. Donald 330	J. H. Kallis† 291

† *J. H. Kallis also took 0-35 and 1-3 for the World XI v Australia (2005-06 Super Series Test).*

WEST INDIES

C. A. Walsh 519	M. D. Marshall.........376	J. Garner..............259
C. E. L. Ambrose 405	L. R. Gibbs............309	M. A. Holding 249

NEW ZEALAND

R. J. Hadlee 431	**T. G. Southee** **270**	C. S. Martin 233
D. L. Vettori† 361	**T. A. Boult**...........**256**	C. L. Cairns 218

† *D. L. Vettori also took 1-73 and 0-38 for the World XI v Australia (2005-06 Super Series Test).*

INDIA

A. Kumble 619	Harbhajan Singh.......417	Zaheer Khan...........311
Kapil Dev.............434	**R. Ashwin** **362**	**I. Sharma**.............**292**

PAKISTAN

Wasim Akram 414	Imran Khan 362	Abdul Qadir 236
Waqar Younis 373	Danish Kaneria.........261	**Yasir Shah**............**209**

SRI LANKA

M. Muralitharan† **795**
H. M. R. K. B. Herath . . .**433**

W. P. U. J. C. Vaas 355
M. D. K. Perera **156**

R. A. S. Lakmal **151**
S. L. Malinga 101

† *M. Muralitharan also took 2-102 and 3-55 for the World XI v Australia (2005-06 Super Series Test).*

ZIMBABWE

H. H. Streak 216
R. W. Price 80

P. A. Strang 70
H. K. Olonga 68

A. G. Cremer 57
B. C. Strang 56

BANGLADESH

Shakib Al Hasan **210**
Taijul Islam **106**

Mohammad Rafique 100
Mehedi Hasan **90**

Mashrafe bin Mortaza . . . 78
Shahadat Hossain 72

IRELAND

T. J. Murtagh 13

S. R. Thompson 10

AFGHANISTAN

Rashid Khan 23

Yamin Ahmadzai 10

BEST CAREER AVERAGES

(Qualification: 75 wickets)

Avge		T	W	Avge		T	W
10.75	G. A. Lohmann (E)	18	112	18.63	C. Blythe (E)	19	100
16.43	S. F. Barnes (E)	27	189	20.39	J. H. Wardle (E)	28	102
16.53	C. T. B. Turner (A)	17	101	20.53	A. K. Davidson (A)	44	186
16.98	R. Peel (E)	20	101	20.94	M. D. Marshall (WI)	81	376
17.75	J. Briggs (E)	33	118	20.97	J. Garner (WI)	58	259
18.41	F. R. Spofforth (A)	18	94	20.99	C. E. L. Ambrose (WI)	98	405
18.56	F. H. Tyson (E)	17	76				

BEST CAREER STRIKE-RATES

(Balls per wicket. Qualification: 75 wickets)

SR		T	W	SR		T	W
34.19	G. A. Lohmann (E)	18	112	45.74	Shoaib Akhtar (P)	46	178
38.75	S. E. Bond (NZ)	18	87	46.76	M. D. Marshall (WI)	81	376
40.66	**K. Rabada (SA)**	**43**	**197**	47.02	A. A. Donald (SA)	72	330
41.65	S. F. Barnes (E)	27	189	**47.27**	**P. J. Cummins (A)**	**30**	**143**
42.38	**D. W. Steyn (SA)**	**93**	**439**	48.16	**M. A. Starc (A)**	**57**	**244**
43.49	Waqar Younis (P)	87	373	48.78	Mohammad Asif (P)	23	106
44.52	F. R. Spofforth (A)	18	94	**48.92**	**J. L. Pattinson (A)**	**21**	**81**
45.12	J. V. Saunders (A)	14	79	**49.15**	**Mohammed Shami (I)**	**47**	**175**
45.18	J. Briggs (E)	33	118	49.32	C. E. H. Croft (WI)	27	125
45.42	F. H. Tyson (E)	17	76	49.43	F. S. Trueman (E)	67	307
45.46	C. Blythe (E)	19	100				

BEST CAREER ECONOMY-RATES

(Runs per six balls. Qualification: 75 wickets)

ER		T	W	ER		T	W
1.64	T. L. Goddard (SA)	41	123	1.94	W. J. O'Reilly (A)	27	144
1.67	R. G. Nadkarni (I)	41	88	1.94	H. J. Tayfield (SA)	37	170
1.88	H. Verity (E)	40	144	1.95	A. L. Valentine (WI)	36	139
1.88	G. A. Lohmann (E)	18	112	1.95	F. J. Titmus (E)	53	153
1.89	J. H. Wardle (E)	28	102	1.97	S. Ramadhin (WI)	43	158
1.91	R. Illingworth (E)	61	122	1.97	R. Peel (E)	20	101
1.93	C. T. B. Turner (A)	17	101	1.97	A. K. Davidson (A)	44	186
1.94	M. W. Tate (E)	39	155	1.98	L. R. Gibbs (WI)	79	309

HIGHEST PERCENTAGE OF TEAM'S WICKETS OVER TEST CAREER

(Qualification: 20 Tests)

	Tests	Wkts	Team Wkts	% of Team Wkts
M. Muralitharan (Sri Lanka/World)	133	800	2,070	38.64
S. F. Barnes (England)	27	189	494	38.25
R. J. Hadlee (New Zealand)	86	431	1,255	34.34
C. V. Grimmett (Australia)	37	216	636	33.96
Fazal Mahmood (Pakistan)	34	139	410	33.90
Yasir Shah (Pakistan)	**38**	**209**	**633**	**33.01**
W. J. O'Reilly (Australia)	27	144	446	32.28
S. P. Gupte (India)	36	149	470	31.70
Saeed Ajmal (Pakistan)	35	178	575	30.95
Mohammad Rafique (Bangladesh)	33	100	328	30.48
A. V. Bedser (England)	51	236	777	30.37

Excluding the Super Series Test, Muralitharan took 795 out of 2,050 wickets in his 132 Tests for Sri Lanka, a percentage of 38.78.

The percentage shows the proportion of a team's wickets taken by that player in all Tests in which he played, including team wickets in innings in which he did not bowl.

ALL-ROUND RECORDS

HUNDRED AND FIVE WICKETS IN AN INNINGS

England

A. W. Greig	148	6-164	v West Indies	Bridgetown	1973-74
I. T. Botham	103	5-73	v New Zealand	Christchurch	1977-78
I. T. Botham	108	8-34	v Pakistan	Lord's	1978
I. T. Botham	114	6-58, 7-48	v India	Bombay	1979-80
I. T. Botham	149*	6-95	v Australia	Leeds	1981
I. T. Botham	138	5-59	v New Zealand	Wellington	1983-84

Australia

C. Kelleway	114	5-33	v South Africa	Manchester	1912
J. M. Gregory	100	7-69	v England	Melbourne	1920-21
K. R. Miller	109	6-107	v West Indies	Kingston	1954-55
R. Benaud	100	5-84	v South Africa	Johannesburg	1957-58

South Africa

J. H. Sinclair	106	6-26	v England	Cape Town	1898-99
G. A. Faulkner	123	5-120	v England	Johannesburg	1909-10
J. H. Kallis	110	5-90	v West Indies	Cape Town	1998-99
J. H. Kallis	139*	5-21	v Bangladesh	Potchefstroom	2002-03

West Indies

D. St E. Atkinson	219	5-56	v Australia	Bridgetown	1954-55
O. G. Smith	100	5-90	v India	Delhi	1958-59
G. S. Sobers	104	5-63	v India	Kingston	1961-62
G. S. Sobers	174	5-41	v England	Leeds	1966
R. L. Chase	137*	5-121	v India	Kingston	2016

New Zealand

B. R. Taylor†	105	5-86	v India	Calcutta	1964-65

India

M. H. Mankad	184	5-196	v England	Lord's	1952
P. R. Umrigar	172*	5-107	v West Indies	Port-of-Spain . . .	1961-62
R. Ashwin	103	5-156	v West Indies	Mumbai	2011-12
R. Ashwin	113	7-83	v West Indies	North Sound	2016

Pakistan

Mushtaq Mohammad	201	5-49	v New Zealand	Dunedin	1972-73
Mushtaq Mohammad	121	5-28	v West Indies	Port-of-Spain . . .	1976-77
Imran Khan	117	6-98, 5-82	v India	Faisalabad	1982-83
Wasim Akram	123	5-100	v Australia	Adelaide	1989-90

Zimbabwe

P. A. Strang	106*	5-212	v Pakistan	Sheikhupura	1996-97

Bangladesh

Shakib Al Hasan	144	6-82	v Pakistan	Mirpur	2011-12
Sohag Gazi	101*	6-77‡	v New Zealand	Chittagong	2013-14
Shakib Al Hasan	137	5-80, 5-44	v Zimbabwe	Khulna	2014-15

† *On debut.* ‡ *Including a hat-trick; Sohag Gazi is the only player to score a hundred and take a hat-trick in the same Test.*

HUNDRED AND FIVE DISMISSALS IN AN INNINGS

D. T. Lindsay	182	6ct	SA v A	Johannesburg	1966-67
I. D. S. Smith	113*	4ct, 1st	NZ v E	Auckland	1983-84
S. A. R. Silva	111	5ct	SL v I	Colombo (PSS)	1985-86
A. C. Gilchrist	133	4ct, 1st	A v E	Sydney	2002-03
M. J. Prior	118	5ct	E v A	Sydney	2010-11
A. B. de Villiers	103*	6ct and 5ct	SA v P	Johannesburg	2012-13
M. J. Prior	110*	5ct	E v NZ	Auckland	2012-13
B-J. Watling	124	5ct	NZ v I	Wellington	2013-14
B-J. Watling	142*	4ct, 1st	NZ v SL	Wellington	2014-15
J. M. Bairstow	140	5ct	E v SL	Leeds	2016
J. M. Bairstow	101	5ct	E v NZ	Christchurch	2017-18
B-J. Watling	**105***	**5ct**	**NZ v SL**	**Colombo (PSO)**	**2019**

100 RUNS AND TEN WICKETS IN A TEST

A. K. Davidson	44 80	5-135 6-87	} A v WI	Brisbane	1960-61
I. T. Botham	114	6-58 7-48	} E v I	Bombay	1979-80
Imran Khan	117	6-98 5-82	} P v I	Faisalabad	1982-83
Shakib Al Hasan	137 6	5-80 5-44	} B v Z	Khulna	2014-15

Wicketkeeper A. B. de Villiers scored 103 and held 11 catches for South Africa against Pakistan at Johannesburg in 2012-13.*

2,000 RUNS AND 200 WICKETS

	Tests	Runs	Wkts	Tests for 1,000/100 Double
R. Ashwin (India)	**70**	**2,385**	**362**	**24**
R. Benaud (Australia)	63	2,201	248	32
†I. T. Botham (England)	102	5,200	383	21
S. C. J. Broad (England)	**138**	**3,211**	**485**	**35**
C. L. Cairns (New Zealand)	62	3,320	218	33
A. Flintoff (England/World)	79	3,845	226	43
R. J. Hadlee (New Zealand)	86	3,124	431	28
Harbhajan Singh (India)	103	2,224	417	62
Imran Khan (Pakistan)	88	3,807	362	30
M. J. Johnson (Australia)	73	2,065	313	37
†J. H. Kallis (South Africa/World)	166	13,289	292	53
Kapil Dev (India)	131	5,248	434	25
A. Kumble (India)	132	2,506	619	56
S. M. Pollock (South Africa)	108	3,781	421	26
Shakib Al Hasan (Bangladesh)	**56**	**3,862**	**210**	**54**
†G. S. Sobers (West Indies)	93	8,032	235	48
W. P. U. J. C. Vaas (Sri Lanka)	111	3,089	355	47
D. L. Vettori (New Zealand/World)	113	4,531	362	47
†S. K. Warne (Australia)	145	3,154	708	58
Wasim Akram (Pakistan)	104	2,898	414	45

H. H. Streak scored 1,990 runs and took 216 wickets in 65 Tests for Zimbabwe.

† *J. H. Kallis also took 200 catches, S. K. Warne 125, I. T. Botham 120 and G. S. Sobers 109. These four and C. L. Hooper (5,762 runs, 114 wickets and 115 catches for West Indies) are the only players to have achieved the treble of 1,000 runs, 100 wickets and 100 catches in Test cricket.*

WICKETKEEPING RECORDS

MOST DISMISSALS IN AN INNINGS

7 (7ct)	Wasim Bari	Pakistan v New Zealand at Auckland	1978-79
7 (7ct)	R. W. Taylor	England v India at Bombay	1979-80
7 (7ct)	I. D. S. Smith	New Zealand v Sri Lanka at Hamilton	1990-91
7 (7ct)	R. D. Jacobs	West Indies v Australia at Melbourne	2000-01

The first instance of seven wicketkeeping dismissals in a Test innings was a joint effort for Pakistan v West Indies at Kingston in 1976-77. Majid Khan made four catches, deputising for the injured wicketkeeper Wasim Bari, who made three more catches on his return.

There have been 32 instances of players making six dismissals in a Test innings, the most recent being Q. de Kock (6ct) for South Africa v England at Centurion in 2019-20.

MOST STUMPINGS IN AN INNINGS

5	K. S. More	India v West Indies at Madras	1987-88

MOST DISMISSALS IN A TEST

11 (11ct)	R. C. Russell	England v South Africa at Johannesburg . . .	1995-96
11 (11ct)	A. B. de Villiers	South Africa v Pakistan at Johannesburg . . .	2012-13
11 (11ct)	R. R. Pant	India v Australia at Adelaide	2018-19
10 (10ct)	R. W. Taylor	England v India at Bombay	1979-80
10 (10ct)	A. C. Gilchrist	Australia v New Zealand at Hamilton . . .	1999-2000
10 (10ct)	W. P. Saha	India v South Africa at Cape Town	2017-18
10 (10ct)	**Sarfraz Ahmed**	**Pakistan v South Africa at Johannesburg.**	**2018-19**

*There have been **26** instances of players making nine dismissals in a Test, the most recent being J. M. Bairstow (9 ct) for England v Sri Lanka at Leeds in 2016. S. A. R. Silva made 18 in two successive Tests for Sri Lanka against India in 1985-86.*

The most stumpings in a match is 6 by K. S. More for India v West Indies at Madras in 1987-88.

J. J. Kelly (8ct) for Australia v England in 1901-02 and L. E. G. Ames (6ct, 2st) for England v West Indies in 1933 were the only keepers to make eight dismissals in a Test before World War II.

MOST DISMISSALS IN A SERIES

(Played in 5 Tests unless otherwise stated)

29 (29ct)	B. J. Haddin	Australia v England	2013
28 (28ct)	R. W. Marsh	Australia v England	1982-83
27 (25ct, 2st)	R. C. Russell	England v South Africa	1995-96
27 (25ct, 2st)	I. A. Healy	Australia v England (6 Tests)	1997

S. A. R. Silva made 22 dismissals (21ct, 1st) in three Tests for Sri Lanka v India in 1985-86.

H. Strudwick, with 21 (15ct, 6st) for England v South Africa in 1913-14, was the only wicketkeeper to make as many as 20 dismissals in a series before World War II.

MOST DISMISSALS

			T	*Ct*	*St*
1	M. V. Boucher (South Africa/World)	555	147	532	23
2	A. C. Gilchrist (Australia)	416	96	379	37
3	I. A. Healy (Australia)	395	119	366	29
4	R. W. Marsh (Australia)	355	96	343	12
5	M. S. Dhoni (India)	294	90	256	38
6 {	B. J. Haddin (Australia)	270	66	262	8
	P. J. L. Dujon (West Indies)	270	79	265	5
8	A. P. E. Knott (England)	269	95	250	19
9	M. J. Prior (England)	256	79	243	13
10	A. J. Stewart (England)	241	82	227	14
11	Wasim Bari (Pakistan)	228	81	201	27
12	**B-J. Watling (New Zealand)**	**227**	**60**	**219**	**8**
13 {	R. D. Jacobs (West Indies)	219	65	207	12
	T. G. Evans (England)	219	91	173	46
15	D. Ramdin (West Indies)	217	74	205	12
16	Kamran Akmal (Pakistan)	206	53	184	22
17	**Q. de Kock (South Africa)**	**202**	**45**	**191**	**11**
18	A. C. Parore (New Zealand)	201	67	194	7

The record for P. J. L. Dujon excludes two catches taken in two Tests when not keeping wicket; A. J. Stewart's record likewise excludes 36 catches taken in 51 Tests; B-J. Watling's ten in eight Tests and A. C. Parore's three in 11 Tests; Q. de Kock played a further two Tests when not keeping wicket but took no catches.

Excluding the Super Series Test, M. V. Boucher made 553 dismissals (530ct, 23st in 146 Tests) for South Africa, a national record.

W. A. Oldfield made 52 stumpings, a Test record, in 54 Tests for Australia; he also took 78 catches.

The most dismissals by a wicketkeeper playing for the countries not mentioned above are:

		T	*Ct*	*St*
K. C. Sangakkara (Sri Lanka)	151	48	131	20
A. Flower (Zimbabwe)	151	55	142	9
Mushfiqur Rahim (Bangladesh)	**113**	**55**	**98**	**15**
G. C. Wilson (Ireland)	6	1	6	0
Afsar Zazai (Afghanistan)	6	3	5	1

K. C. Sangakkara's record excludes 51 catches taken in 86 matches when not keeping wicket but includes two catches taken as wicketkeeper in a match where he took over when the designated keeper was injured; A. Flower's record excludes nine catches in eight Tests when not keeping wicket, Mushfiqur Rahim's record excludes five catches in 12 Tests when not keeping wicket; G. C. Wilson played a further Test in which he did not keep wicket and took no catches.

FIELDING RECORDS

(Excluding wicketkeepers)

MOST CATCHES IN AN INNINGS

5	V. Y. Richardson	Australia v South Africa at Durban	1935-36
5	Yajurvindra Singh	India v England at Bangalore	1976-77
5	M. Azharuddin	India v Pakistan at Karachi	1989-90
5	K. Srikkanth	India v Australia at Perth	1991-92
5	S. P. Fleming	New Zealand v Zimbabwe at Harare	1997-98
5	G. C. Smith	South Africa v Australia at Perth	2012-13
5	D. J. G. Sammy	West Indies v India at Mumbai	2013-14
5	D. M. Bravo	West Indies v Bangladesh at Arnos Vale	2014-15
5	A. M. Rahane	India v Sri Lanka at Galle	2015-16
5	J. Blackwood	West Indies v Sri Lanka at Colombo (PSO)	2015-16
5	S. P. D. Smith	Australia v South Africa at Cape Town	2017-18
5	**B. A. Stokes**	**England v South Africa at Cape Town**	**2019-20**

MOST CATCHES IN A TEST

8	A. M. Rahane	India v Sri Lanka at Galle	2015-16
7	G. S. Chappell	Australia v England at Perth	1974-75
7	Yajurvindra Singh	India v England at Bangalore	1976-77
7	H. P. Tillekeratne	Sri Lanka v New Zealand at Colombo (SSC)	1992-93
7	S. P. Fleming	New Zealand v Zimbabwe at Harare	1997-98
7	M. L. Hayden	Australia v Sri Lanka at Galle	2003-04
7	K. L. Rahul	India v England at Nottingham	2018

There have been 35 instances of players taking six catches in a Test, the most recent being O. J. D. Pope for England v South Africa at Port Elizabeth in 2019-20.

MOST CATCHES IN A SERIES

(Played in 5 Tests unless otherwise stated)

15	J. M. Gregory	Australia v England	1920-21
14	G. S. Chappell	Australia v England (6 Tests)	1974-75
13	R. B. Simpson	Australia v South Africa	1957-58
13	R. B. Simpson	Australia v West Indies	1960-61
13	B. C. Lara	West Indies v England (6 Tests)	1997-98
13	R. Dravid	India v Australia (4 Tests)	2004-05
13	B. C. Lara	West Indies v India (4 Tests)	2005-06

MOST CATCHES

Ct	T		Ct	T	
210	164†	R. Dravid (India/World)	157	104	M. A. Taylor (Australia)
205	149	D. P. M. D. Jayawardene (SL)	156	156	A. R. Border (Australia)
200	166†	J. H. Kallis (SA/World)	**145**	**99**	**L. R. P. L. Taylor (New Zealand)**
196	168	R. T. Ponting (Australia)	139	118	Younis Khan (Pakistan)
181	128	M. E. Waugh (Australia)	135	134	V. V. S. Laxman (India)
175	161	A. N. Cook (England)	134	115	M. J. Clarke (Australia)
171	111	S. P. Fleming (New Zealand)	128	103	M. L. Hayden (Australia)
169	117†	G. C. Smith (SA/World)	125	145	S. K. Warne (Australia)
164	131†	B. C. Lara (West Indies/World)			

† *Excluding the Super Series Test, Dravid made 209 catches in 163 Tests for India, Kallis 196 in 165 Tests for South Africa, and Lara 164 in 130 Tests for West Indies, all national records. G. C. Smith made 166 catches in 116 Tests for South Africa.*

*The most catches in the field for other countries are Zimbabwe 60 in 60 Tests (A. D. R. Campbell); Bangladesh 37 in 48 Tests (**Mahmudullah**); Ireland 4 in 3 Tests (**P. R. Stirling**); Afghanistan 4 in 2 Tests (**Ibrahim Zadran**) and in 3 Tests (**Ihsanullah Janat**).*

TEAM RECORDS

HIGHEST INNINGS TOTALS

952-6 dec	Sri Lanka v India at Colombo (RPS)	1997-98
903-7 dec	England v Australia at The Oval	1938
849	England v West Indies at Kingston	1929-30
790-3 dec	West Indies v Pakistan at Kingston	1957-58
765-6 dec	Pakistan v Sri Lanka at Karachi	2008-09
760-7 dec	Sri Lanka v India at Ahmedabad	2009-10
759-7 dec	India v England at Chennai	2016-17
758-8 dec	Australia v West Indies at Kingston	1954-55
756-5 dec	Sri Lanka v South Africa at Colombo (SSC)	2006
751-5 dec	West Indies v England at St John's	2003-04

The highest innings totals for the countries not mentioned above are:

715-6 dec	**New Zealand v Bangladesh at Hamilton**	**2018-19**
682-6 dec	South Africa v England at Lord's	2003
638	Bangladesh v Sri Lanka at Galle	2012-13
563-9 dec	Zimbabwe v West Indies at Harare	2001
342	**Afghanistan v Bangladesh at Chittagong**	**2019-20**
339	Ireland v Pakistan at Malahide	2018

HIGHEST FOURTH-INNINGS TOTALS

To win

418-7	West Indies (needing 418) v Australia at St John's	2002-03
414-4	South Africa (needing 414) v Australia at Perth	2008-09
406-4	India (needing 403) v West Indies at Port-of-Spain	1975-76
404-3	Australia (needing 404) v England at Leeds	1948

To tie

347	India v Australia at Madras	1986-87

To draw

654-5	England (needing 696 to win) v South Africa at Durban	1938-39
450-7	South Africa (needing 458 to win) v India at Johannesburg	2013-14
429-8	India (needing 438 to win) v England at The Oval	1979
423-7	South Africa (needing 451 to win) v England at The Oval	1947

To lose

451	New Zealand (lost by 98 runs) v England at Christchurch	2001-02
450	Pakistan (lost by 39 runs) v Australia at Brisbane	2016-17
445	India (lost by 47 runs) v Australia at Adelaide	1977-78
440	New Zealand (lost by 38 runs) v England at Nottingham	1973
431	New Zealand (lost by 121 runs) v England at Napier	2007-08

MOST RUNS IN A DAY (BOTH SIDES)

588	England (398-6), India (190-0) at Manchester (2nd day)	1936
522	England (503-2), South Africa (19-0) at Lord's (2nd day)	1924
509	Sri Lanka (509-9) v Bangladesh at Colombo (PSS) (2nd day)	2002
508	England (221-2), South Africa (287-6) at The Oval (3rd day)	1935

MOST RUNS IN A DAY (ONE SIDE)

509	Sri Lanka (509-9) v Bangladesh at Colombo (PSS) (2nd day)	2002
503	England (503-2) v South Africa at Lord's (2nd day)	1924
494	Australia (494-6) v South Africa at Sydney (1st day)	1910-11
482	Australia (482-5) v South Africa at Adelaide (1st day)	2012-13
475	Australia (475-2) v England at The Oval (1st day)	1934

MOST WICKETS IN A DAY

27	England (18-3 to 53 all out and 62) v Australia (60) at Lord's (2nd day)	1888
25	Australia (112 and 48-5) v England (61) at Melbourne (1st day)	1901-02
24	England (69-1 to 145 and 60-5) v Australia (119) at The Oval (2nd day)	1896
24	India (347-6 to 474) v Afghanistan (109 and 103) at Bangalore (2nd day)	2018

HIGHEST AGGREGATES IN A TEST

Runs	Wkts			Days played
1,981	35	South Africa v England at Durban	1938-39	10†
1,815	34	West Indies v England at Kingston	1929-30	9‡
1,764	39	Australia v West Indies at Adelaide	1968-69	5
1,753	40	Australia v England at Adelaide	1920-21	6
1,747	25	Australia v India at Sydney	2003-04	5
1,723	31	England v Australia at Leeds	1948	5
1,702	28	Pakistan v India at Faisalabad	2005-06	5

† *No play on one day.* ‡ *No play on two days.*

LOWEST INNINGS TOTALS

26	New Zealand v England at Auckland	1954-55
30	South Africa v England at Port Elizabeth	1895-96
30	South Africa v England at Birmingham	1924
35	South Africa v England at Cape Town	1898-99
36	Australia v England at Birmingham	1902
36	South Africa v Australia at Melbourne	1931-32
38	**Ireland v England at Lord's**	**2019**
42	Australia v England at Sydney	1887-88
42	New Zealand v Australia at Wellington	1945-46
42†	India v England at Lord's	1974
43	South Africa v England at Cape Town	1888-89
43	Bangladesh v West Indies at North Sound	2018
44	Australia v England at The Oval	1896
45	England v Australia at Sydney	1886-87
45	South Africa v Australia at Melbourne	1931-32
45	New Zealand v South Africa at Cape Town	2012-13

The lowest innings totals for the countries not mentioned above are:

47	West Indies v England at Kingston	2003-04
49	Pakistan v South Africa at Johannesburg	2012-13
51	Zimbabwe v New Zealand at Napier	2011-12
71	Sri Lanka v Pakistan at Kandy	1994-95
103	Afghanistan v India at Bangalore	2018

FEWEST RUNS IN A FULL DAY'S PLAY

95	Australia (80), Pakistan (15-2) at Karachi (1st day, 5½ hrs)	1956-57
104	Pakistan (0-0 to 104-5) v Australia at Karachi (4th day, 5½ hrs).	1959-60
106	England (92-2 to 198) v Australia at Brisbane (4th day, 5 hrs).	1958-59
	England were dismissed five minutes before the close of play, leaving no	
	time for Australia to start their second innings.	
111	S. Africa (48-2 to 130-6 dec), India (29-1) at Cape Town (5th day, 5½ hrs) . . .	1992-93
112	Australia (138-6 to 187), Pakistan (63-1) at Karachi (4th day, 5½ hrs)	1956-57
115	Australia (116-7 to 165 and 66-5 after following on) v Pakistan at Karachi (4th	
	day, 5½ hrs)	1988-89
117	India (117-5) v Australia at Madras (1st day, 5½ hrs)	1956-57
117	New Zealand (6-0 to 123-4) v Sri Lanka at Colombo (SSC) (5th day, 5¾ hrs) .	1983-84

In England

151	England (175-2 to 289), New Zealand (37-7) at Lord's (3rd day, 6 hrs)	1978
158	England (211-2 to 369-9) v South Africa at Manchester (5th day, 6 hrs).	1998
159	Pakistan (208-4 to 350), England (17-1) at Leeds (3rd day, 6 hrs).	1971

LOWEST AGGREGATES IN A COMPLETED TEST

Runs	Wkts			Days played
234	29	Australia v South Africa at Melbourne	1931-32	3†
291	40	England v Australia at Lord's	1888	2
295	28	New Zealand v Australia at Wellington	1945-46	2
309	29	West Indies v England at Bridgetown	1934-35	3
323	30	England v Australia at Manchester	1888	2

† *No play on one day.*

LARGEST VICTORIES

Largest Innings Victories

Inns & 579 runs	England (903-7 dec) v Australia (201 & 123†) at The Oval	1938
Inns & 360 runs	Australia (652-7 dec) v South Africa (159 & 133) at Johannesburg . .	2001-02
Inns & 336 runs	West Indies (614-5 dec) v India (124 & 154) at Calcutta.	1958-59
Inns & 332 runs	Australia (645) v England (141 & 172) at Brisbane.	1946-47
Inns & 324 runs	Pakistan (643) v New Zealand (73 & 246) at Lahore.	2002
Inns & 322 runs	West Indies (660-5 dec) v New Zealand (216 & 122) at Wellington . .	1994-95
Inns & 310 runs	West Indies (536) v Bangladesh (139 & 87) at Dhaka.	2002-03
Inns & 301 runs	New Zealand (495-7 dec) v Zimbabwe (51 & 143) at Napier	2011-12

† *Two men absent in both Australian innings.*

Largest Victories by Runs Margin

675 runs	England (521 & 342-8 dec) v Australia (122 & 66†) at Brisbane.	1928-29
562 runs	Australia (701 & 327) v England (321 & 145‡) at The Oval	1934
530 runs	Australia (328 & 578) v South Africa (205 & 171§) at Melbourne	1910-11
492 runs	South Africa (488 & 344-6 dec) v Australia (221 and 119) at Johannesburg . .	2017-18
491 runs	Australia (381 & 361-5 dec) v Pakistan (179 & 72) at Perth.	2004-05
465 runs	Sri Lanka (384 and 447-6 dec) v Bangladesh (208 and 158) at Chittagong . . .	2008-09
425 runs	West Indies (211 & 411-5 dec) v England (71 & 126) at Manchester	1976
423 runs	New Zealand (178 & 585-4 dec) v Sri Lanka (104 & 236) at Christchurch . . .	2018-19
409 runs	Australia (350 & 460-7 dec) v England (215 & 186) at Lord's.	1948
408 runs	West Indies (328 & 448) v Australia (203 & 165) at Adelaide.	1979-80
405 runs	Australia (566-8 dec & 254-2 dec) v England (312 & 103) at Lord's.	2015

† *One man absent in Australia's first innings; two men absent in their second.*
‡ *Two men absent in England's first innings; one man absent in their second.*
§ *One man absent in South Africa's second innings.*

TIED TESTS

West Indies (453 & 284) v Australia (505 & 232) at Brisbane 1960-61
Australia (574-7 dec & 170-5 dec) v India (397 & 347) at Madras. 1986-87

MOST CONSECUTIVE TEST VICTORIES

16	Australia	1999-2000 to 2000-01		9	South Africa	2001-02 to 2003
16	Australia	2005-06 to 2007-08		8	Australia	1920-21 to 1921
11	West Indies	1983-84 to 1984-85		8	England	2004 to 2004-05
9	Sri Lanka	2001 to 2001-02				

MOST CONSECUTIVE TESTS WITHOUT VICTORY

44	New Zealand	1929-30 to 1955-56		23	New Zealand	1962-63 to 1967-68
34	Bangladesh	2000-01 to 2004-05		22	Pakistan	1958-59 to 1964-65
31	India	1981-82 to 1984-85		21	Sri Lanka	1985-86 to 1992-93
28	South Africa	1935 to 1949-50		20	West Indies	1968-69 to 1972-73
24	India	1932 to 1951-52		20	West Indies	2004-05 to 2007
24	Bangladesh	2004-05 to 2008-09				

WHITEWASHES

Teams winning every game in a series of four Tests or more:

Five-Test Series

Australia beat England	1920-21		West Indies beat England	1985-86
Australia beat South Africa	1931-32		South Africa beat West Indies	1998-99
England beat India	1959		Australia beat West Indies	2000-01
West Indies beat India	1949-50		Australia beat England	2006-07
West Indies beat England	1984		Australia beat England	2013-14

Four-Test Series

Australia beat India	1967-68		England beat India	2011
South Africa beat Australia	1969-70		Australia beat India	2011-12
England beat West Indies	2004		India beat Australia	2012-13

The winning team in each instance was at home, except for West Indies in England, 1984.

PLAYERS

YOUNGEST TEST PLAYERS

Years	Days			
15	124	Mushtaq Mohammad	Pakistan v West Indies at Lahore	1958-59
16	189	Aqib Javed	Pakistan v New Zealand at Wellington	1988-89
16	205	S. R. Tendulkar	India v Pakistan at Karachi	1989-90

The above table should be treated with caution. All birthdates for Bangladesh and Pakistan (after Partition) must be regarded as questionable because of deficiencies in record-keeping. Hasan Raza was claimed to be 14 years 227 days old when he played for Pakistan against Zimbabwe at Faisalabad in 1996-97; this age was rejected by the Pakistan Cricket Board, although no alternative has been offered. Suggestions that Enamul Haque jnr was 16 years 230 days old when he played for Bangladesh against England in Dhaka in 2003-04 have been discounted by well-informed local observers, who believe he was 18.

The youngest Test players for countries not mentioned above are:

17	78	Mujeeb Zadran	Afghanistan v India at Bangalore	2018
17	122	J. E. D. Sealy	West Indies v England at Bridgetown	1929-30
17	128	Mohammad Sharif	Bangladesh v Zimbabwe at Bulawayo	2000-01
17	189	C. D. U. S. Weerasinghe .	Sri Lanka v India at Colombo (PSS)	1985-86
17	239	I. D. Craig	Australia v South Africa at Melbourne	1952-53
17	352	H. Masakadza	Zimbabwe v West Indies at Harare	2001
18	10	D. L. Vettori	New Zealand v England at Wellington	1996-97
18	149	D. B. Close	England v New Zealand at Manchester	1949
18	340	P. R. Adams	South Africa v England at Port Elizabeth	1995-96
23	**119**	**M. R. Adair**	**Ireland v England at Lord's.**	**2019**

OLDEST PLAYERS ON TEST DEBUT

Years	Days			
49	119	J. Southerton	England v Australia at Melbourne	1876-77
47	284	Miran Bux	Pakistan v India at Lahore	1954-55
46	253	D. D. Blackie	Australia v England at Sydney	1928-29
46	237	H. Ironmonger	Australia v England at Brisbane	1928-29
42	242	N. Betancourt	West Indies v England at Port-of-Spain	1929-30
41	337	E. R. Wilson	England v Australia at Sydney	1920-21
41	27	R. J. D. Jamshedji	India v England at Bombay	1933-34
40	345	C. A. Wiles	West Indies v England at Manchester	1933
40	295	O. Henry	South Africa v India at Durban	1992-93
40	216	S. P. Kinneir	England v Australia at Sydney	1911-12
40	110	H. W. Lee	England v South Africa at Johannesburg	1930-31
40	56	G. W. A. Chubb	South Africa v England at Nottingham	1951
40	37	C. Ramaswami	India v England at Manchester	1936

The oldest Test player on debut for Ireland was E. C. Joyce, 39 years 231 days, v Pakistan at Malahide, 2018; for New Zealand, H. M. McGirr, 38 years 101 days, v England at Auckland, 1929-30; for Sri Lanka, D. S. de Silva, 39 years 251 days, v England at Colombo (PSS), 1981-82; for Zimbabwe, A. C. Waller, 37 years 84 days, v England at Bulawayo, 1996-97; for Bangladesh, Enamul Haque snr, 35 years 58 days, v Zimbabwe at Harare, 2000-01; for Afghanistan, Mohammad Nabi, 33 years 99 days, v India at Bangalore, 2018. A. J. Traicos was 45 years 154 days old when he made his debut for Zimbabwe (v India at Harare, 1992-93), having played three Tests for South Africa in 1969-70.

OLDEST TEST PLAYERS

(Age on final day of their last Test match)

Years	Days			
52	165	W. Rhodes	England v West Indies at Kingston	1929-30
50	327	H. Ironmonger	Australia v England at Sydney	1932-33
50	320	W. G. Grace	England v Australia at Nottingham	1899
50	303	G. Gunn	England v West Indies at Kingston	1929-30
49	139	J. Southerton	England v Australia at Melbourne	1876-77
47	302	Miran Bux	Pakistan v India at Peshawar	1954-55
47	249	J. B. Hobbs	England v Australia at The Oval	1930
47	87	F. E. Woolley	England v Australia at The Oval	1934
46	309	D. D. Blackie	Australia v England at Adelaide	1928-29
46	206	A. W. Nourse	South Africa v England at The Oval	1924
46	202	H. Strudwick	England v Australia at The Oval	1926
46	41	E. H. Hendren	England v West Indies at Kingston	1934-35
45	304	A. J. Traicos	Zimbabwe v India at Delhi	1992-93
45	245	G. O. B. Allen	England v West Indies at Kingston	1947-48
45	215	P. Holmes	England v India at Lord's	1932
45	140	D. B. Close	England v West Indies at Manchester	1976

MOST TEST APPEARANCES

200	S. R. Tendulkar (India)	134	K. C. Sangakkara (Sri Lanka)
168	R. T. Ponting (Australia)	133	M. Muralitharan (Sri Lanka/World)
168	S. R. Waugh (Australia)	133	A. J. Stewart (England)
166	J. H. Kallis (South Africa/World)	132	A. Kumble (India)
164	S. Chanderpaul (West Indies)	132	C. A. Walsh (West Indies)
164	R. Dravid (India/World)	131	Kapil Dev (India)
161	A. N. Cook (England)	131	B. C. Lara (West Indies/World)
156	A. R. Border (Australia)	128	M. E. Waugh (Australia)
151	**J. M. Anderson (England)**	125	S. M. Gavaskar (India)
149	D. P. M. D. Jayawardene (Sri Lanka)	**124**	**H. M. Amla (South Africa)**
147	M. V. Boucher (South Africa/World)	124	Javed Miandad (Pakistan)
145	S. K. Warne (Australia)	124	G. D. McGrath (Australia)
138	**S. C. J. Broad (England)**	121	I. V. A. Richards (West Indies)
134	V. V. S. Laxman (India)	120	Inzamam-ul-Haq (Pakistan/World)

Excluding the Super Series Test, J. H. Kallis has made 165 appearances for South Africa, a national record. The most appearances for New Zealand is 112 by D. L. Vettori; for Bangladesh, 69 by Mushfiqur Rahim; for Zimbabwe, 67 by G. W. Flower; for Afghanistan, 4 by Asghar Afghan, Rahmat Shah, Rashid Khan and Yamin Ahmadzai; and for Ireland, 3 by A. Balbirnie, T. J. Murtagh, K. J. O'Brien, W. T. S. Porterfield, P. R. Stirling and S. R. Thompson.

MOST CONSECUTIVE TEST APPEARANCES FOR A COUNTRY

159	A. N. Cook (England)	May 2006 to September 2018
153	A. R. Border (Australia)	March 1979 to March 1994
107	M. E. Waugh (Australia)	June 1993 to October 2002
106	S. M. Gavaskar (India)	January 1975 to February 1987
101†	B. B. McCullum (New Zealand)	March 2004 to February 2016
98	A. B. de Villiers (South Africa)	December 2004 to January 2015
96†	A. C. Gilchrist (Australia)	November 1999 to January 2008
93	R. Dravid (India)	June 1996 to December 2005
93	D. P. M. D. Jayawardene (Sri Lanka)	November 2002 to January 2013

The most consecutive Test appearances for the countries not mentioned above (excluding Afghanistan and Ireland) are:

85	G. S. Sobers (West Indies)	April 1955 to April 1972
68	**Asad Shafiq (Pakistan)**	**October 2011 to December 2019**
56	A. D. R. Campbell (Zimbabwe)	October 1992 to September 2001
49	Mushfiqur Rahim (Bangladesh)	July 2007 to January 2017

† *Complete Test career.*

Bold type denotes sequence which was still in progress after January 1, 2019.

MOST TESTS AS CAPTAIN

	P	W	L	D		P	W	L	D
G. C. Smith (SA/World)	109	53	29*	27	A. Ranatunga (SL)	56	12	19	25
A. R. Border (A)	93	32	22	38†	M. A. Atherton (E)	54	13	21	20
S. P. Fleming (NZ)	80	28	27	25	**V. Kohli (I)**	**53**	**33**	**10**	**10**
R. T. Ponting (A)	77	48	16	13	W. J. Cronje (SA)	53	27	11	15
C. H. Lloyd (WI)	74	36	12	26	M. P. Vaughan (E)	51	26	11	14
M. S. Dhoni (I)	60	27	18	15	I. V. A. Richards (WI)	50	27	8	15
A. N. Cook (E)	59	24	22	13	M. A. Taylor (A)	50	26	13	11
S. R. Waugh (A)	57	41	9	7	A. J. Strauss (E)	50	24	11	15
Misbah-ul-Haq (P)	56	26	19	11					

* *Includes defeat as World XI captain in Super Series Test against Australia.* † *One tie.*

Most Tests as captain of other countries:

	P	W	L	D
Mushfiqur Rahim (B)	34	7	18	9
A. D. R. Campbell (Z)	21	2	12	7
W. T. S. Porterfield (Ire)	**3**	**0**	**3**	**0**
Asghar Afghan (Afg)	**2**	**0**	**2**	**0**
Rashid Khan (Afg)	**2**	**1**	**1**	**0**

A. R. Border captained Australia in 93 consecutive Tests.

W. W. Armstrong (Australia) captained his country in the most Tests without being defeated: ten matches with eight wins and two draws.

Mohammad Ashraful (Bangladesh) captained his country in the most Tests without ever winning: 12 defeats and one draw.

UMPIRES

MOST TESTS

		First Test	Last Test
131	**Aleem Dar (Pakistan)**	**2003-04**	**2019-20**
128	S. A. Bucknor (West Indies)	1988-89	2008-09
108	R. E. Koertzen (South Africa)	1992-93	2010
95	D. J. Harper (Australia)	1998-99	2011
92	D. R. Shepherd (England)	1985	2004-05
84	B. F. Bowden (New Zealand)	1999-2000	2014-15
78	D. B. Hair (Australia)	1991-92	2008
74	S. J. A. Taufel (Australia)	2000-01	2012
74	**I. J. Gould (England)**	**2008-09**	**2018-19**
73	S. Venkataraghavan (India)	1992-93	2003-04
71	**R. J. Tucker (Australia)**	**2009-10**	**2019-20**
66	H. D. Bird (England)	1973	1996
65	**H. D. P. K. Dharmasena (Sri Lanka)**	**2010-11**	**2019-20**
62	**M. Erasmus (South Africa)**	**2009-10**	**2019-20**
62	**R. A. Kettleborough (England)**	**2010-11**	**2019-20**
61	**N. J. Llong (England)**	**2007-08**	**2019-20**
59	**B. N. Oxenford (Australia)**	**2010-11**	**2019-20**
57	S. J. Davis (Australia)	1997-98	2014-15

SUMMARY OF TESTS

1876-77 to January 31, 2020

	Opponents	Tests	E	A	SA	WI	NZ	I	P	SL	Z	B	Ire	Afg	Wld	Tied	Drawn
England	Australia	351	110	146	–	–	–	–	–	–	–	–	–	–	–	–	95
	South Africa	153	64	–	34	–	–	–	–	–	–	–	–	–	–	–	55
	West Indies	157	49	–	–	57	–	–	–	–	–	–	–	–	–	–	51
	New Zealand	105	48	–	–	–	11	–	–	–	–	–	–	–	–	–	46
	India	122	47	–	–	–	–	26	–	–	–	–	–	–	–	–	49
	Pakistan	83	25	–	–	–	–	–	21	–	–	–	–	–	–	–	37
	Sri Lanka	34	15	–	–	–	–	–	–	8	–	–	–	–	–	–	11
	Zimbabwe	6	3	–	–	–	–	–	–	–	0	–	–	–	–	–	3
	Bangladesh	10	9	–	–	–	–	–	–	–	–	1	–	–	–	–	0
	Ireland	1	1	–	–	–	–	–	–	–	–	–	0	–	–	–	0
Australia	South Africa	98	–	52	26	–	–	–	–	–	–	–	–	–	–	–	20
	West Indies	116	–	58	–	32	–	–	–	–	–	–	–	–	–	1	25
	New Zealand	60	–	34	–	–	8	–	–	–	–	–	–	–	–	–	18
	India	98	–	42	–	–	–	28	–	–	–	–	–	–	–	1	27
	Pakistan	66	–	33	–	–	–	–	15	–	–	–	–	–	–	–	18
	Sri Lanka	31	–	19	–	–	–	–	–	4	–	–	–	–	–	–	8
	Zimbabwe	3	–	3	–	–	–	–	–	–	0	–	–	–	–	–	0
	Bangladesh	6	–	5	–	–	–	–	–	–	–	1	–	–	–	–	0
	ICC World XI	1	–	1	–	–	–	–	–	–	–	–	–	–	0	–	0
South Africa	West Indies	28	–	–	18	3	–	–	–	–	–	–	–	–	–	–	7
	New Zealand	45	–	–	25	–	4	–	–	–	–	–	–	–	–	–	16
	India	39	–	–	15	–	–	14	–	–	–	–	–	–	–	–	10
	Pakistan	26	–	–	15	–	–	–	4	–	–	–	–	–	–	–	7
	Sri Lanka	29	–	–	14	–	–	–	–	9	–	–	–	–	–	–	6
	Zimbabwe	9	–	–	8	–	–	–	–	–	0	–	–	–	–	–	1
	Bangladesh	12	–	–	10	–	–	–	–	–	–	0	–	–	–	–	2
West Indies	New Zealand	47	–	–	–	13	15	–	–	–	–	–	–	–	–	–	19
	India	98	–	–	–	30	–	22	–	–	–	–	–	–	–	–	46
	Pakistan	52	–	–	–	17	–	–	20	–	–	–	–	–	–	–	15
	Sri Lanka	20	–	–	–	4	–	–	–	9	–	–	–	–	–	–	7
	Zimbabwe	10	–	–	–	7	–	–	–	–	0	–	–	–	–	–	3
	Bangladesh	16	–	–	–	10	–	–	–	–	–	4	–	–	–	–	2
	Afghanistan	1	–	–	–	1	–	–	–	–	–	–	–	0	–	–	0
New Zealand	India	57	–	–	–	–	10	21	–	–	–	–	–	–	–	–	26
	Pakistan	58	–	–	–	–	12	–	25	–	–	–	–	–	–	–	21
	Sri Lanka	36	–	–	–	–	16	–	–	9	–	–	–	–	–	–	11
	Zimbabwe	17	–	–	–	–	11	–	–	–	0	–	–	–	–	–	6
	Bangladesh	15	–	–	–	–	12	–	–	–	–	0	–	–	–	–	3
India	Pakistan	59	–	–	–	–	–	9	12	–	–	–	–	–	–	–	38
	Sri Lanka	44	–	–	–	–	–	20	–	7	–	–	–	–	–	–	17
	Zimbabwe	11	–	–	–	–	–	7	–	–	2	–	–	–	–	–	2
	Bangladesh	11	–	–	–	–	–	9	–	–	–	0	–	–	–	–	2
	Afghanistan	1	–	–	–	–	–	1	–	–	–	–	–	0	–	–	0
Pakistan	Sri Lanka	55	–	–	–	–	–	–	20	16	–	–	–	–	–	–	19
	Zimbabwe	17	–	–	–	–	–	–	10	–	3	–	–	–	–	–	4
	Bangladesh	10	–	–	–	–	–	–	9	–	–	0	–	–	–	–	1
	Ireland	1	–	–	–	–	–	–	1	–	–	–	0	–	–	–	0
Sri Lanka	Zimbabwe	20	–	–	–	–	–	–	–	14	0	–	–	–	–	–	6
	Bangladesh	20	–	–	–	–	–	–	–	16	–	1	–	–	–	–	3
Zimbabwe	Bangladesh	16	–	–	–	–	–	–	–	–	7	6	–	–	–	–	3
Bangladesh	Afghanistan	1	–	–	–	–	–	–	–	–	–	0	–	1	–	–	0
Ireland	Afghanistan	1	–	–	–	–	–	–	–	–	–	–	0	1	–	–	0
		2,383	371	393	165	174	99	157	137	92	12	13	0	2	0	2	766

RESULTS SUMMARY OF TESTS

1876-77 to January 31, 2020 (2,383 matches)

	Tests	Won	Lost	Drawn	Tied	% Won	Toss Won
England	1,022	371	304	347	–	36.30	501
Australia	830†	393†	224	211	2	47.34	417
South Africa	439	165	150	124	–	37.58	210
West Indies	545	174	195	175	1	31.92	282
New Zealand	440	99	175	166	–	22.50	219

	Tests	Won	Lost	Drawn	Tied	% Won	Toss Won
India	540	157	165	217	1	29.07	270
Pakistan	427	137	130	160	–	32.08	203
Sri Lanka	289	92	109	88	–	31.83	155
Zimbabwe	109	12	69	28	–	11.00	63
Bangladesh	117	13	88	16	–	11.11	60
Ireland	3	0	3	0	–	0.00	2
Afghanistan	4	2	2	0	–	50.00	1
ICC World XI	1	0	1	0	–	0.00	0

† Includes Super Series Test between Australia and ICC World XI.

ENGLAND v AUSTRALIA

Captains

Season	England	Australia	T	E	A	D
1876-77	James Lillywhite	D. W. Gregory	2	1	1	0
1878-79	Lord Harris	D. W. Gregory	1	0	1	0
1880	Lord Harris	W. L. Murdoch	1	1	0	0
1881-82	A. Shaw	W. L. Murdoch	4	0	2	2
1882	A. N. Hornby	W. L. Murdoch	1	0	1	0

THE ASHES

Captains

Season	England	Australia	T	E	A	D	Held by
1882-83	Hon. Ivo Bligh	W. L. Murdoch	4*	2	2	0	E
1884	Lord Harris[1]	W. L. Murdoch	3	1	0	2	E
1884-85	A. Shrewsbury	T. P. Horan[2]	5	3	2	0	E
1886	A. G. Steel	H. J. H. Scott	3	3	0	0	E
1886-87	A. Shrewsbury	P. S. McDonnell	2	2	0	0	E
1887-88	W. W. Read	P. S. McDonnell	1	1	0	0	E
1888	W. G. Grace[3]	P. S. McDonnell	3	2	1	0	E
1890†	W. G. Grace	W. L. Murdoch	2	2	0	0	E
1891-92	W. G. Grace	J. McC. Blackham	3	1	2	0	A
1893	W. G. Grace[4]	J. McC. Blackham	3	1	0	2	E
1894-95	A. E. Stoddart	G. Giffen[5]	5	3	2	0	E
1896	W. G. Grace	G. H. S. Trott	3	2	1	0	E
1897-98	A. E. Stoddart[6]	G. H. S. Trott	5	1	4	0	A
1899	A. C. MacLaren[7]	J. Darling	5	0	1	4	A
1901-02	A. C. MacLaren	J. Darling[8]	5	1	4	0	A
1902	A. C. MacLaren	J. Darling	5	1	2	2	A
1903-04	P. F. Warner	M. A. Noble	5	3	2	0	E
1905	Hon. F. S. Jackson	J. Darling	5	2	0	3	E
1907-08	A. O. Jones[9]	M. A. Noble	5	1	4	0	A
1909	A. C. MacLaren	M. A. Noble	5	1	2	2	A
1911-12	J. W. H. T. Douglas	C. Hill	5	4	1	0	E
1912	C. B. Fry	S. E. Gregory	3	1	0	2	E
1920-21	J. W. H. T. Douglas	W. W. Armstrong	5	0	5	0	A
1921	Hon. L. H. Tennyson[10]	W. W. Armstrong	5	0	3	2	A
1924-25	A. E. R. Gilligan	H. L. Collins	5	1	4	0	A
1926	A. W. Carr[11]	H. L. Collins[12]	5	1	0	4	E
1928-29	A. P. F. Chapman[13]	J. Ryder	5	4	1	0	E
1930	A. P. F. Chapman[14]	W. M. Woodfull	5	1	2	2	A
1932-33	D. R. Jardine	W. M. Woodfull	5	4	1	0	E
1934	R. E. S. Wyatt[15]	W. M. Woodfull	5	1	2	2	A
1936-37	G. O. B. Allen	D. G. Bradman	5	2	3	0	A
1938†	W. R. Hammond	D. G. Bradman	4	1	1	2	A
1946-47	W. R. Hammond[16]	D. G. Bradman	5	0	3	2	A
1948	N. W. D. Yardley	D. G. Bradman	5	0	4	1	A
1950-51	F. R. Brown	A. L. Hassett	5	1	4	0	A
1953	L. Hutton	A. L. Hassett	5	1	0	4	E
1954-55	L. Hutton	I. W. Johnson[17]	5	3	1	1	E

Captains

Season	England	Australia	T	E	A	D	Held by
1956	P. B. H. May	I. W. Johnson	5	2	1	2	E
1958-59	P. B. H. May	R. Benaud	5	0	4	1	A
1961	P. B. H. May[18]	R. Benaud[19]	5	1	2	2	A
1962-63	E. R. Dexter	R. Benaud	5	1	1	3	A
1964	E. R. Dexter	R. B. Simpson	5	0	1	4	A
1965-66	M. J. K. Smith	R. B. Simpson[20]	5	1	1	3	A
1968	M. C. Cowdrey[21]	W. M. Lawry[22]	5	1	1	3	A
1970-71†	R. Illingworth	W. M. Lawry[23]	6	2	0	4	E
1972	R. Illingworth	I. M. Chappell	5	2	2	1	E
1974-75	M. H. Denness[24]	I. M. Chappell	6	1	4	1	A
1975	A. W. Greig[25]	I. M. Chappell	4	0	1	3	A
1976-77‡	A. W. Greig	G. S. Chappell	1	0	1	0	—
1977	J. M. Brearley	G. S. Chappell	5	3	0	2	E
1978-79	J. M. Brearley	G. N. Yallop	6	5	1	0	E
1979-80‡	J. M. Brearley	G. S. Chappell	3	0	3	0	—
1980‡	I. T. Botham	G. S. Chappell	1	0	0	1	—
1981	J. M. Brearley[26]	K. J. Hughes	6	3	1	2	E
1982-83	R. G. D. Willis	G. S. Chappell	5	1	2	2	A
1985	D. I. Gower	A. R. Border	6	3	1	2	E
1986-87	M. W. Gatting	A. R. Border	5	2	1	2	E
1987-88‡	M. W. Gatting	A. R. Border	1	0	0	1	—
1989	D. I. Gower	A. R. Border	6	0	4	2	A
1990-91	G. A. Gooch[27]	A. R. Border	5	0	3	2	A
1993	G. A. Gooch[28]	A. R. Border	6	1	4	1	A
1994-95	M. A. Atherton	M. A. Taylor	5	1	3	1	A
1997	M. A. Atherton	M. A. Taylor	6	2	3	1	A
1998-99	A. J. Stewart	M. A. Taylor	5	1	3	1	A
2001	N. Hussain[29]	S. R. Waugh[30]	5	1	4	0	A
2002-03	N. Hussain	S. R. Waugh	5	1	4	0	A
2005	M. P. Vaughan	R. T. Ponting	5	2	1	2	E
2006-07	A. Flintoff	R. T. Ponting	5	0	5	0	A
2009	A. J. Strauss	R. T. Ponting	5	2	1	2	E
2010-11	A. J. Strauss	R. T. Ponting[31]	5	3	1	1	E
2013	A. N. Cook	M. J. Clarke	5	3	0	2	E
2013-14	A. N. Cook	M. J. Clarke	5	0	5	0	A
2015	A. N. Cook	M. J. Clarke	5	3	2	0	E
2017-18	J. E. Root	S. P. D. Smith	5	0	4	1	A
2019	**J. E. Root**	**T. D. Paine**	5	2	2	1	A

	T	E	A	D
In Australia	180	57	95	28
In England	171	53	51	67
Totals	**351**	**110**	**146**	**95**

* *The Ashes were awarded in 1882-83 after a series of three matches which England won 2–1. A fourth match was played and this was won by Australia.*
† *The matches at Manchester in 1890 and 1938 and at Melbourne (Third Test) in 1970-71 were abandoned without a ball being bowled and are excluded.*
‡ *The Ashes were not at stake in these series.*

The following deputised for the official touring captain or were appointed by the home authority for only a minor proportion of the series:

[1]A. N. Hornby (First). [2]W. L. Murdoch (First), H. H. Massie (Third), J. McC. Blackham (Fourth). [3]A. G. Steel (First). [4]A. E. Stoddart (First). [5]J. McC. Blackham (First). [6]A. C. MacLaren (First, Second and Fifth). [7]W. G. Grace (First). [8]H. Trumble (Fourth and Fifth). [9]F. L. Fane (First, Second and Third). [10]J. W. H. T. Douglas (First and Second). [11]A. P. F. Chapman (Fifth). [12]W. Bardsley (Third and Fourth). [13]J. C. White (Fifth). [14]R. E. S. Wyatt (Fifth). [15]C. F. Walters (First). [16]N. W. D. Yardley (Fifth). [17]A. R. Morris (Second). [18]M. C. Cowdrey (First and Second). [19]R. N. Harvey (Second). [20]B. C. Booth (First and Third). [21]T. W. Graveney (Fourth). [22]B. N. Jarman (Fourth) [23]I. M. Chappell (Seventh). [24]J. H. Edrich (Fourth). [25]M. H. Denness (First). [26]I. T. Botham (First and Second). [27]A. J. Lamb (First). [28]M. A. Atherton (Fifth and Sixth). [29]M. A. Atherton (Second and Third). [30]A. C. Gilchrist (Fourth). [31]M. J. Clarke (Fifth).

HIGHEST INNINGS TOTALS

For England in England: 903-7 dec at The Oval 1938
       in Australia: 644 at Sydney 2010-11

For Australia in England: 729-6 dec at Lord's 1930
       in Australia: 662-9 dec at Perth 2017-18

LOWEST INNINGS TOTALS

For England in England: 52 at The Oval 1948
       in Australia: 45 at Sydney 1886-87

For Australia in England: 36 at Birmingham 1902
       in Australia: 42 at Sydney 1887-88

DOUBLE-HUNDREDS

For England (14)

364	L. Hutton at The Oval	1938	231*	W. R. Hammond at Sydney	. . .	1936-37
287	R. E. Foster at Sydney	1903-04	227	K. P. Pietersen at Adelaide	. . . . .	2010-11
256	K. F. Barrington at Manchester . . .	1964	216*	E. Paynter at Nottingham	. . . . . .	1938
251	W. R. Hammond at Sydney	1928-29	215	D. I. Gower at Birmingham	. . . . .	1985
244*	A. N. Cook at Melbourne	2017-18	207	N. Hussain at Birmingham	. . . . .	1997
240	W. R. Hammond at Lord's	1938	206	P. D. Collingwood at Adelaide	. .	2006-07
235*	A. N. Cook at Brisbane	2010-11	200	W. R. Hammond at Melbourne	.	1928-29

For Australia (26)

334	D. G. Bradman at Leeds	1930	232	S. J. McCabe at Nottingham	. . . .	1938
311	R. B. Simpson at Manchester . . .	1964	225	R. B. Simpson at Adelaide	. . . . .	1965-66
307	R. M. Cowper at Melbourne	1965-66	219	M. A. Taylor at Nottingham	. . . .	1989
304	D. G. Bradman at Leeds	1934	215	S. P. D. Smith at Lord's	. . . .	2015
270	D. G. Bradman at Melbourne . . .	1936-37	212	D. G. Bradman at Adelaide	. . . . .	1936-37
266	W. H. Ponsford at The Oval	1934	211	W. L. Murdoch at The Oval	. . . .	1884
254	D. G. Bradman at Lord's	1930	**211**	**S. P. D. Smith at Manchester**	. .	**2019**
250	J. L. Langer at Melbourne	2002-03	207	K. R. Stackpole at Brisbane	. . . .	1970-71
244	D. G. Bradman at The Oval	1934	206*	W. A. Brown at Lord's	. . . .	1938
239	S. P. D. Smith at Perth	2017-18	206	A. R. Morris at Adelaide	. . . .	1950-51
234	S. G. Barnes at Sydney	1946-47	201*	J. Ryder at Adelaide	. . . .	1924-25
234	D. G. Bradman at Sydney	1946-47	201	S. E. Gregory at Sydney	. . . .	1894-95
232	D. G. Bradman at The Oval	1930	200*	A. R. Border at Leeds	. . . .	1993

INDIVIDUAL HUNDREDS

In total, England have scored **245** hundreds against Australia, and Australia scored **318** against England. The players with at least five hundreds are as follows:

For England

12: J. B. Hobbs.
 9: D. I. Gower, W. R. Hammond.
 8: H. Sutcliffe.
 7: G. Boycott, J. H. Edrich, M. Leyland.
 5: K. F. Barrington, D. C. S. Compton, A. N. Cook, M. C. Cowdrey, L. Hutton, F. S. Jackson, A. C. MacLaren.

For Australia

19: D. G. Bradman.
11: S. P. D. Smith.
10: S. R. Waugh.
9: G. S. Chappell.
8: A. R. Border, A. R. Morris, R. T. Ponting.
7: D. C. Boon, M. J. Clarke, W. M. Lawry, M. J. Slater.
6: R. N. Harvey, M. A. Taylor, V. T. Trumper, M. E. Waugh, W. M. Woodfull.
5: M. L. Hayden, J. L. Langer, C. G. Macartney, W. H. Ponsford.

RECORD PARTNERSHIPS FOR EACH WICKET

For England

323 for 1st	J. B. Hobbs and W. Rhodes at Melbourne	1911-12
382 for 2nd†	L. Hutton and M. Leyland at The Oval	1938
262 for 3rd	W. R. Hammond and D. R. Jardine at Adelaide	1928-29
310 for 4th	P. D. Collingwood and K. P. Pietersen at Adelaide	2006-07
237 for 5th	D. J. Malan and J. M. Bairstow at Perth	2017-18
215 for 6th {	L. Hutton and J. Hardstaff jnr at The Oval	1938
	G. Boycott and A. P. E. Knott at Nottingham	1977
143 for 7th	F. E. Woolley and J. Vine at Sydney	1911-12
124 for 8th	E. H. Hendren and H. Larwood at Brisbane	1928-29
151 for 9th	W. H. Scotton and W. W. Read at The Oval	1884
130 for 10th	R. E. Foster and W. Rhodes at Sydney	1903-04

For Australia

329 for 1st	G. R. Marsh and M. A. Taylor at Nottingham	1989
451 for 2nd†	W. H. Ponsford and D. G. Bradman at The Oval	1934
276 for 3rd	D. G. Bradman and A. L. Hassett at Brisbane	1946-47
388 for 4th	W. H. Ponsford and D. G. Bradman at Leeds	1934
405 for 5th‡	S. G. Barnes and D. G. Bradman at Sydney	1946-47
346 for 6th†	J. H. Fingleton and D. G. Bradman at Melbourne	1936-37
165 for 7th	C. Hill and H. Trumble at Melbourne	1897-98
243 for 8th†	R. J. Hartigan and C. Hill at Adelaide	1907-08
154 for 9th†	S. E. Gregory and J. McC. Blackham at Sydney	1894-95
163 for 10th†	P. J. Hughes and A. C. Agar at Nottingham	2013

† *Record partnership against all countries.*   ‡ *World record.*

MOST RUNS IN A SERIES

England in England	732 (average 81.33)	D. I. Gower	1985
England in Australia	905 (average 113.12)	W. R. Hammond	1928-29
Australia in England	974 (average 139.14)	D. G. Bradman	1930
Australia in Australia	810 (average 90.00)	D. G. Bradman	1936-37

MOST WICKETS IN A MATCH

In total, England bowlers have taken ten or more wickets in a match **40** times against Australia, and Australian bowlers have done it **43** times against England. The players with at least 12 in a match are as follows:

For England

19-90 (9-37, 10-53)	J. C. Laker at Manchester	1956
15-104 (7-61, 8-43)	H. Verity at Lord's	1934
15-124 (7-56, 8-68)	W. Rhodes at Melbourne	1903-04
14-99 (7-55, 7-44)	A. V. Bedser at Nottingham	1953
14-102 (7-28, 7-74)	W. Bates at Melbourne	1882-83
13-163 (6-42, 7-121)	S. F. Barnes at Melbourne	1901-02
13-244 (7-168, 6-76)	T. Richardson at Manchester	1896

13-256 (5-130, 8-126)	J. C. White at Adelaide	1928-29
12-102 (6-50, 6-52)†	F. Martin at The Oval	1890
12-104 (7-36, 5-68)	G. A. Lohmann at The Oval	1886
12-136 (6-49, 6-87)	J. Briggs at Adelaide	1891-92

There are a further 12 instances of 11 wickets in a match, and 17 instances of ten.

For Australia

16-137 (8-84, 8-53)†	R. A. L. Massie at Lord's	1972
14-90 (7-46, 7-44)	F. R. Spofforth at The Oval	1882
13-77 (7-17, 6-60)	M. A. Noble at Melbourne.	1901-02
13-110 (6-48, 7-62)	F. R. Spofforth at Melbourne.	1878-79
13-148 (6-97, 7-51)	B. A. Reid at Melbourne	1990-91
13-236 (4-115, 9-121)	A. A. Mailey at Melbourne	1920-21
12-87 (5-44, 7-43)	C. T. B. Turner at Sydney	1887-88
12-89 (6-59, 6-30)	H. Trumble at The Oval.	1896
12-107 (5-57, 7-50)	S. C. G. MacGill at Sydney	1998-99
12-173 (8-65, 4-108)	H. Trumble at The Oval.	1902
12-175 (5-85, 7-90)†	H. V. Hordern at Sydney	1911-12
12-246 (6-122, 6-124)	S. K. Warne at The Oval	2005

There are a further 13 instances of 11 wickets in a match, and 18 instances of ten.

† *On first appearance in England–Australia Tests.*

A. V. Bedser, J. Briggs, J. C. Laker, T. Richardson, R. M. Hogg, A. A. Mailey, H. Trumble and C. T. B. Turner took ten wickets or more in successive Tests.

MOST WICKETS IN A SERIES

England in England . . . . 46 (average 9.60)	J. C. Laker.	1956
England in Australia . . . . . . 38 (average 23.18)	M. W. Tate	1924-25
Australia in England . . . . . . 42 (average 21.26)	T. M. Alderman (6 Tests)	1981
Australia in Australia . . . . . . 41 (average 12.85)	R. M. Hogg (6 Tests)	1978-79

WICKETKEEPING – MOST DISMISSALS

	M	Ct	St	Total
†R. W. Marsh (Australia)	42	141	7	148
I. A. Healy (Australia)	33	123	12	135
A. P. E. Knott (England)	34	97	8	105
A. C. Gilchrist (Australia)	20	89	7	96
†W. A. Oldfield (Australia)	38	59	31	90
A. A. Lilley (England)	32	65	19	84
B. J. Haddin (Australia)	20	79	1	80
A. J. Stewart (England)	26	76	2	78
A. T. W. Grout (Australia)	22	69	7	76
T. G. Evans (England)	31	64	12	76

† *The number of catches by R. W. Marsh (141) and stumpings by W. A. Oldfield (31) are respective records in England–Australia Tests.*

Stewart held a further six catches in seven matches when not keeping wicket.

SCORERS OF OVER 2,500 RUNS

	T	I	NO	R	HS	100	Avge
D. G. Bradman (Australia) .	37	63	7	5,028	334	19	89.78
J. B. Hobbs (England)	41	71	4	3,636	187	12	54.26
A. R. Border (Australia) . . .	47	82	19	3,548	200*	8	56.31
D. I. Gower (England)	42	77	4	3,269	215	9	44.78
S. R. Waugh (Australia) . . .	46	73	18	3,200	177*	10	58.18
G. Boycott (England)	38	71	9	2,945	191	7	47.50

	T	I	NO	R	HS	100	Avge
W. R. Hammond (England).	33	58	3	2,852	251	9	51.85
S. P. D. Smith (Australia) .	27	48	5	**2,800**	239	11	**65.11**
H. Sutcliffe (England)	27	46	5	2,741	194	8	66.85
C. Hill (Australia)	41	76	1	2,660	188	4	35.46
J. H. Edrich (England).	32	57	3	2,644	175	7	48.96
G. A. Gooch (England)	42	79	0	2,632	196	4	33.31
G. S. Chappell (Australia) . .	35	65	8	2,619	144	9	45.94

BOWLERS WITH 100 WICKETS

	T	Balls	R	W	5I	10M	Avge
S. K. Warne (Australia)	36	10,757	4,535	195	11	4	23.25
D. K. Lillee (Australia).	29	8,516	3,507	167	11	4	21.00
G. D. McGrath (Australia)	30	7,280	3,286	157	10	0	20.92
I. T. Botham (England)	36	8,479	4,093	148	9	2	27.65
H. Trumble (Australia)	31	7,895	2,945	141	9	3	20.88
R. G. D. Willis (England).	35	7,294	3,346	128	7	0	26.14
S. C. J. Broad (England)	**32**	**6,512**	**3,464**	**118**	**7**	**1**	**29.35**
M. A. Noble (Australia)	39	6,895	2,860	115	9	2	24.86
R. R. Lindwall (Australia)	29	6,728	2,559	114	6	0	22.44
W. Rhodes (England)	41	5,790	2,616	109	6	1	24.00
S. F. Barnes (England)	20	5,749	2,288	106	12	1	21.58
C. V. Grimmett (Australia). . . .	22	9,224	3,439	106	11	2	32.44
D. L. Underwood (England). . .	29	8,000	2,770	105	4	2	26.38
A. V. Bedser (England)	21	7,065	2,859	104	7	2	27.49
J. M. Anderson (England)	**32**	**7,051**	**3,595**	**104**	**5**	**1**	**34.56**
G. Giffen (Australia)	31	6,391	2,791	103	7	1	27.09
W. J. O'Reilly (Australia)	19	7,864	2,587	102	8	3	25.36
C. T. B. Turner (Australia)	17	5,179	1,670	101	11	2	16.53
R. Peel (England)	20	5,216	1,715	101	5	1	16.98
T. M. Alderman (Australia)	17	4,717	2,117	100	11	1	21.17
J. R. Thomson (Australia)	21	4,951	2,418	100	5	0	24.18

RESULTS ON EACH GROUND

In England

	Matches	England wins	Australia wins	Drawn
The Oval.	38	17	7	14
Manchester.	30	7	8	15†
Lord's.	37	7	15	15
Nottingham	22	6	7	9
Leeds	25	8	9	8
Birmingham	15	6	4	5
Sheffield.	1	0	1	0
Cardiff	2	1	0	1
Chester-le-Street.	1	1	0	0

† *Excludes two matches abandoned without a ball bowled.*

In Australia

	Matches	England wins	Australia wins	Drawn
Melbourne	56	20	28	8†
Sydney	56	22	27	7
Adelaide	32	9	18	5
Brisbane				
Exhibition Ground	1	1	0	0
Woolloongabba	21	4	12	5
Perth.	14	1	10	3

† *Excludes one match abandoned without a ball bowled.*

ENGLAND v SOUTH AFRICA

Captains

Season	England	South Africa	T	E	SA	D
1888-89	C. A. Smith[1]	O. R. Dunell[2]	2	2	0	0
1891-92	W. W. Read	W. H. Milton	1	1	0	0
1895-96	Lord Hawke[3]	E. A. Halliwell[4]	3	3	0	0
1898-99	Lord Hawke	M. Bisset	2	2	0	0
1905-06	P. F. Warner	P. W. Sherwell	5	1	4	0
1907	R. E. Foster	P. W. Sherwell	3	1	0	2
1909-10	H. D. G. Leveson Gower[5]	S. J. Snooke	5	2	3	0
1912	C. B. Fry	F. Mitchell[6]	3	3	0	0
1913-14	J. W. H. T. Douglas	H. W. Taylor	5	4	0	1
1922-23	F. T. Mann	H. W. Taylor	5	2	1	2
1924	A. E. R. Gilligan[7]	H. W. Taylor	5	3	0	2
1927-28	R. T. Stanyforth[8]	H. G. Deane	5	2	2	1
1929	J. C. White[9]	H. G. Deane	5	2	0	3
1930-31	A. P. F. Chapman	H. G. Deane[10]	5	0	1	4
1935	R. E. S. Wyatt	H. F. Wade	5	0	1	4
1938-39	W. R. Hammond	A. Melville	5	1	0	4
1947	N. W. D. Yardley	A. Melville	5	3	0	2
1948-49	F. G. Mann	A. D. Nourse	5	2	0	3
1951	F. R. Brown	A. D. Nourse	5	3	1	1
1955	P. B. H. May	J. E. Cheetham[11]	5	3	2	0
1956-57	P. B. H. May	C. B. van Ryneveld[12]	5	2	2	1
1960	M. C. Cowdrey	D. J. McGlew	5	3	0	2
1964-65	M. J. K. Smith	T. L. Goddard	5	1	0	4
1965	M. J. K. Smith	P. L. van der Merwe	3	0	1	2
1994	M. A. Atherton	K. C. Wessels	3	1	1	1
1995-96	M. A. Atherton	W. J. Cronje	5	0	1	4
1998	A. J. Stewart	W. J. Cronje	5	2	1	2
1999-2000	N. Hussain	W. J. Cronje	5	1	2	2
2003	M. P. Vaughan[13]	G. C. Smith	5	2	2	1

THE BASIL D'OLIVEIRA TROPHY

Captains

Season	England	South Africa	T	E	SA	D	Held by
2004-05	M. P. Vaughan	G. C. Smith	5	2	1	2	E
2008	M. P. Vaughan[14]	G. C. Smith	4	1	2	1	SA
2009-10	A. J. Strauss	G. C. Smith	4	1	1	2	SA
2012	A. J. Strauss	G. C. Smith	3	0	2	1	SA
2015-16	A. N. Cook	H. M. Amla[15]	4	2	1	1	E
2017	J. E. Root	F. du Plessis[16]	4	3	1	0	E
2019-20	**J. E. Root**	**F. du Plessis**	**4**	**3**	**1**	**0**	**E**
	In South Africa		85	34	20	31	
	In England		68	30	14	24	
	Totals		**153**	**64**	**34**	**55**	

The following deputised for the official touring captain or were appointed by the home authority for only a minor proportion of the series:

[1]M. P. Bowden (Second). [2]W. H. Milton (Second). [3]Sir Timothy O'Brien (First). [4]A. R. Richards (Third). [5]F. L. Fane (Fourth and Fifth). [6]L. J. Tancred (Second and Third). [7]J. W. H. T. Douglas (Fourth). [8]G. T. S. Stevens (Fifth). [9]A. W. Carr (Fourth and Fifth). [10]E. P. Nupen (First), H. B. Cameron (Fourth and Fifth). [11]D. J. McGlew (Third and Fourth). [12]D. J. McGlew (Second). [13]N. Hussain (First). [14]K. P. Pietersen (Fourth). [15]A. B. de Villiers (Third and Fourth). [16]D. Elgar (First).

SERIES RECORDS

Highest score	E	258	B. A. Stokes at Cape Town..................	2015-16
	SA	311*	H. M. Amla at The Oval..................	2012
Best bowling	E	9-28	G. A. Lohmann at Johannesburg.............	1895-96
	SA	9-113	H. J. Tayfield at Johannesburg.............	1956-57
Highest total	E	654-5	at Durban..................................	1938-39
	SA	682-6 dec	at Lord's.................................	2003
Lowest total	E	76	at Leeds..................................	1907
	SA	30	at Port Elizabeth..........................	1895-96
	SA	30	at Birmingham............................	1924

ENGLAND v WEST INDIES

Captains

Season	England	West Indies	T	E	WI	D
1928	A. P. F. Chapman	R. K. Nunes	3	3	0	0
1929-30	Hon. F. S. G. Calthorpe	E. L. G. Hoad¹	4	1	1	2
1933	D. R. Jardine²	G. C. Grant	3	2	0	1
1934-35	R. E. S. Wyatt	G. C. Grant	4	1	2	1
1939	W. R. Hammond	R. S. Grant	3	1	0	2
1947-48	G. O. B. Allen³	J. D. C. Goddard⁴	4	0	2	2
1950	N. W. D. Yardley⁵	J. D. C. Goddard	4	1	3	0
1953-54	L. Hutton	J. B. Stollmeyer	5	2	2	1
1957	P. B. H. May	J. D. C. Goddard	5	3	0	2
1959-60	P. B. H. May⁶	F. C. M. Alexander	5	1	0	4

THE WISDEN TROPHY

Captains

Season	England	West Indies	T	E	WI	D	Held by
1963	E. R. Dexter	F. M. M. Worrell	5	1	3	1	WI
1966	M. C. Cowdrey⁷	G. S. Sobers	5	1	3	1	WI
1967-68	M. C. Cowdrey	G. S. Sobers	5	1	0	4	E
1969	R. Illingworth	G. S. Sobers	3	2	0	1	E
1973	R. Illingworth	R. B. Kanhai	3	0	2	1	WI
1973-74	M. H. Denness	R. B. Kanhai	5	1	1	3	WI
1976	A. W. Greig	C. H. Lloyd	5	0	3	2	WI
1980	I. T. Botham	C. H. Lloyd⁸	5	0	1	4	WI
1980-81†	I. T. Botham	C. H. Lloyd	4	0	2	2	WI
1984	D. I. Gower	C. H. Lloyd	5	0	5	0	WI
1985-86	D. I. Gower	I. V. A. Richards	5	0	5	0	WI
1988	J. E. Emburey⁹	I. V. A. Richards	5	0	4	1	WI
1989-90‡	G. A. Gooch¹⁰	I. V. A. Richards¹¹	4	1	2	1	WI
1991	G. A. Gooch	I. V. A. Richards	5	2	2	1	WI
1993-94	M. A. Atherton	R. B. Richardson¹²	5	1	3	1	WI
1995	M. A. Atherton	R. B. Richardson	6	2	2	2	WI
1997-98§	M. A. Atherton	B. C. Lara	6	1	3	2	WI
2000	N. Hussain¹³	J. C. Adams	5	3	1	1	E
2003-04	M. P. Vaughan	B. C. Lara	4	3	0	1	E
2004	M. P. Vaughan	B. C. Lara	4	4	0	0	E
2007	M. P. Vaughan¹⁴	R. R. Sarwan¹⁵	4	3	0	1	E
2008-09§	A. J. Strauss	C. H. Gayle	5	0	1	4	WI
2009	A. J. Strauss	C. H. Gayle	2	2	0	0	E
2012	A. J. Strauss	D. J. G. Sammy	3	2	0	1	E

		Captains					
Season	England	West Indies	T	E	WI	D	Held by
2014-15	A. N. Cook	D. Ramdin	3	1	1	1	E
2017	J. E. Root	J. O. Holder	3	2	1	0	E
2018-19	**J. E. Root**	**J. O. Holder**[16]	**3**	**1**	**2**	**0**	**WI**

In England			86	34	30	22	
In West Indies			**71**	**15**	**27**	**29**	
Totals			**157**	**49**	**57**	**51**	

† *The Second Test, at Georgetown, was cancelled owing to political pressure and is excluded.*
‡ *The Second Test, at Georgetown, was abandoned without a ball being bowled and is excluded.*
§ *The First Test at Kingston in 1997-98 and the Second Test at North Sound in 2008-09 were called off on their opening days because of unfit pitches and are shown as draws.*

The following deputised for the official touring captain or were appointed by the home authority for only a minor proportion of the series:
[1]N. Betancourt (Second), M. P. Fernandes (Third), R. K. Nunes (Fourth). [2]R. E. S. Wyatt (Third). [3]K. Cranston (First). [4]G. A. Headley (First), G. E. Gomez (Second). [5]F. R. Brown (Fourth). [6]M. C. Cowdrey (Fourth and Fifth). [7]M. J. K. Smith (First), D. B. Close (Fifth). [8]I. V. A. Richards (Fifth). [9]M. W. Gatting (First), C. S. Cowdrey (Fourth), G. A. Gooch (Fifth). [10]A. J. Lamb (Fourth and Fifth). [11]D. L. Haynes (Third). [12]C. A. Walsh (Fifth). [13]A. J. Stewart (Second). [14]A. J. Strauss (First). [15]D. Ganga (Third and Fourth). [16]K. C. Brathwaite (Third).

SERIES RECORDS

Highest score	E	325	A. Sandham at Kingston	1929-30
	WI	400*	B. C. Lara at St John's	2003-04
Best bowling	E	8-53	A. R. C. Fraser at Port-of-Spain	1997-98
	WI	8-45	C. E. L. Ambrose at Bridgetown	1989-90
Highest total	E	849	at Kingston	1929-30
	WI	751-5 dec	at St John's	2003-04
Lowest total	E	46	at Port-of-Spain	1993-94
	WI	47	at Kingston	2003-04

ENGLAND v NEW ZEALAND

		Captains				
Season	England	New Zealand	T	E	NZ	D
1929-30	A. H. H. Gilligan	T. C. Lowry	4	1	0	3
1931	D. R. Jardine	T. C. Lowry	3	1	0	2
1932-33	D. R. Jardine[1]	M. L. Page	2	0	0	2
1937	R. W. V. Robins	M. L. Page	3	1	0	2
1946-47	W. R. Hammond	W. A. Hadlee	1	0	0	1
1949	F. G. Mann[2]	W. A. Hadlee	4	0	0	4
1950-51	F. R. Brown	W. A. Hadlee	2	1	0	1
1954-55	L. Hutton	G. O. Rabone	2	2	0	0
1958	P. B. H. May	J. R. Reid	5	4	0	1
1958-59	P. B. H. May	J. R. Reid	2	1	0	1
1962-63	E. R. Dexter	J. R. Reid	3	3	0	0
1965	M. J. K. Smith	J. R. Reid	3	3	0	0
1965-66	M. J. K. Smith	B. W. Sinclair[3]	3	0	0	3
1969	R. Illingworth	G. T. Dowling	3	2	0	1
1970-71	R. Illingworth	G. T. Dowling	2	1	0	1
1973	R. Illingworth	B. E. Congdon	3	2	0	1
1974-75	M. H. Denness	B. E. Congdon	2	1	0	1
1977-78	G. Boycott	M. G. Burgess	3	1	1	1
1978	J. M. Brearley	M. G. Burgess	3	3	0	0
1983	R. G. D. Willis	G. P. Howarth	4	3	1	0
1983-84	R. G. D. Willis	G. P. Howarth	3	0	1	2
1986	M. W. Gatting	J. V. Coney	3	0	1	2
1987-88	M. W. Gatting	J. J. Crowe[4]	3	0	0	3

Records and Registers

	Captains					
Season	England	New Zealand	T	E	NZ	D
1990	G. A. Gooch	J. G. Wright	3	1	0	2
1991-92	G. A. Gooch	M. D. Crowe	3	2	0	1
1994	M. A. Atherton	K. R. Rutherford	3	1	0	2
1996-97	M. A. Atherton	L. K. Germon[5]	3	2	0	1
1999	N. Hussain[6]	S. P. Fleming	4	1	2	1
2001-02	N. Hussain	S. P. Fleming	3	1	1	1
2004	M. P. Vaughan[7]	S. P. Fleming	3	3	0	0
2007-08	M. P. Vaughan	D. L. Vettori	3	2	1	0
2008	M. P. Vaughan	D. L. Vettori	3	2	0	1
2012-13	A. N. Cook	B. B. McCullum	3	0	0	3
2013	A. N. Cook	B. B. McCullum	2	2	0	0
2015	A. N. Cook	B. B. McCullum	2	1	1	0
2017-18	J. E. Root	K. S. Williamson	2	0	1	1
2019-20	**J. E. Root**	**K. S. Williamson**	**2**	**0**	**1**	**1**
	In New Zealand		51	18	6	27
	In England		54	30	5	19
	Totals		**105**	**48**	**11**	**46**

The following deputised for the official touring captain or were appointed by the home authority for only a minor proportion of the series:
[1]R. E. S. Wyatt (Second). [2]F. R. Brown (Third and Fourth). [3]M. E. Chapple (First). [4]J. G. Wright (Third). [5]S. P. Fleming (Third). [6]M. A. Butcher (Third). [7]M. E. Trescothick (First).

SERIES RECORDS

Highest score	E	336*	W. R. Hammond at Auckland	1932-33
	NZ	222	N. J. Astle at Christchurch	2001-02
Best bowling	E	7-32	D. L. Underwood at Lord's	1969
	NZ	7-74	B. L. Cairns at Leeds	1983
Highest total	E	593-6 dec	at Auckland	1974-75
	NZ	**615-9 dec**	**at Mount Maunganui**	**2019-20**
Lowest total	E	58	at Auckland	2017-18
	NZ	26	at Auckland	1954-55

ENGLAND v INDIA

	Captains					
Season	England	India	T	E	I	D
1932	D. R. Jardine	C. K. Nayudu	1	1	0	0
1933-34	D. R. Jardine	C. K. Nayudu	3	2	0	1
1936	G. O. B. Allen	Maharajkumar of Vizianagram	3	2	0	1
1946	W. R. Hammond	Nawab of Pataudi snr	3	1	0	2
1951-52	N. D. Howard[1]	V. S. Hazare	5	1	1	3
1952	L. Hutton	V. S. Hazare	4	3	0	1
1959	P. B. H. May[2]	D. K. Gaekwad[3]	5	5	0	0
1961-62	E. R. Dexter	N. J. Contractor	5	0	2	3
1963-64	M. J. K. Smith	Nawab of Pataudi jnr	5	0	0	5
1967	D. B. Close	Nawab of Pataudi jnr	3	3	0	0
1971	R. Illingworth	A. L. Wadekar	3	0	1	2
1972-73	A. R. Lewis	A. L. Wadekar	5	1	2	2
1974	M. H. Denness	A. L. Wadekar	3	3	0	0
1976-77	A. W. Greig	B. S. Bedi	5	3	1	1
1979	J. M. Brearley	S. Venkataraghavan	4	1	0	3
1979-80	J. M. Brearley	G. R. Viswanath	1	1	0	0
1981-82	K. W. R. Fletcher	S. M. Gavaskar	6	0	1	5
1982	R. G. D. Willis	S. M. Gavaskar	3	1	0	2
1984-85	D. I. Gower	S. M. Gavaskar	5	2	1	2
1986	M. W. Gatting[4]	Kapil Dev	3	0	2	1
1990	G. A. Gooch	M. Azharuddin	3	1	0	2

Season	England	India	T	E	I	D
		Captains				
1992-93	G. A. Gooch[5]	M. Azharuddin	3	0	3	0
1996	M. A. Atherton	M. Azharuddin	3	1	0	2
2001-02	N. Hussain	S. C. Ganguly	3	0	1	2
2002	N. Hussain	S. C. Ganguly	4	1	1	2
2005-06	A. Flintoff	R. Dravid	3	1	1	1
2007	M. P. Vaughan	R. Dravid	3	0	1	2
2008-09	K. P. Pietersen	M. S. Dhoni	2	0	1	1
2011	A. J. Strauss	M. S. Dhoni	4	4	0	0
2012-13	A. N. Cook	M. S. Dhoni	4	2	1	1
2014	A. N. Cook	M. S. Dhoni	5	3	1	1
2016-17	A. N. Cook	V. Kohli	5	0	4	1
2018	J. E. Root	V. Kohli	5	4	1	0
	In England		62	34	7	21
	In India		60	13	19	28
	Totals		122	47	26	49

* *Since 1951-52, series in India have been for the De Mello Trophy. Since 2007, series in England have been for the Pataudi Trophy.*

The following deputised for the official touring captain or were appointed by the home authority for only a minor proportion of the series:
[1]D. B. Carr (Fifth). [2]M. C. Cowdrey (Fourth and Fifth). [3]Pankaj Roy (Second). [4]D. I. Gower (First). [5]A. J. Stewart (Second).

The 1932 Indian touring team was led by the Maharaj of Porbandar but he did not play in the Test.

SERIES RECORDS

Highest score	E	333	G. A. Gooch at Lord's	1990
	I	303*	K. K. Nair at Chennai	2016-17
Best bowling	E	8-31	F. S. Trueman at Manchester.	1952
	I	8-55	M. H. Mankad at Madras.	1951-52
Highest total	E	710-7 dec	at Birmingham.	2011
	I	759-7 dec	at Chennai	2016-17
Lowest total	E	101	at The Oval	1971
	I	42	at Lord's	1974

ENGLAND v PAKISTAN

Season	England	Pakistan	T	E	P	D
		Captains				
1954	L. Hutton[1]	A. H. Kardar	4	1	1	2
1961-62	E. R. Dexter	Imtiaz Ahmed	3	1	0	2
1962	E. R. Dexter[2]	Javed Burki	5	4	0	1
1967	D. B. Close	Hanif Mohammad	3	2	0	1
1968-69	M. C. Cowdrey	Saeed Ahmed	3	0	0	3
1971	R. Illingworth	Intikhab Alam	3	1	0	2
1972-73	A. R. Lewis	Majid Khan	3	0	0	3
1974	M. H. Denness	Intikhab Alam	3	0	0	3
1977-78	J. M. Brearley[3]	Wasim Bari	3	0	0	3
1978	J. M. Brearley	Wasim Bari	3	2	0	1
1982	R. G. D. Willis[4]	Imran Khan	3	2	1	0
1983-84	R. G. D. Willis[5]	Zaheer Abbas	3	0	1	2
1987	M. W. Gatting	Imran Khan	5	0	1	4
1987-88	M. W. Gatting	Javed Miandad	3	0	1	2
1992	G. A. Gooch	Javed Miandad	5	1	2	2
1996	M. A. Atherton	Wasim Akram	3	0	2	1
2000-01	N. Hussain	Moin Khan	3	1	0	2
2001	N. Hussain[6]	Waqar Younis	2	1	1	0
2005-06	M. P. Vaughan[7]	Inzamam-ul-Haq	3	0	2	1

Captains

Season	England	Pakistan	T	E	P	D
2006†	A. J. Strauss	Inzamam-ul-Haq	4	3	0	1
2010	A. J. Strauss	Salman Butt	4	3	1	0
2011-12U	A. J. Strauss	Misbah-ul-Haq	3	0	3	0
2015-16U	A. N. Cook	Misbah-ul-Haq	3	0	2	1
2016	A. N. Cook	Misbah-ul-Haq	4	2	2	0
2018	J. E. Root	Sarfraz Ahmed	2	1	1	0
	In England		53	23	12	18
	In Pakistan		24	2	4	18
	In United Arab Emirates		6	0	5	1
	Totals		83	25	21	37

† *In 2008, the ICC changed the result of the forfeited Oval Test of 2006 from an England win to a draw, in contravention of the Laws of Cricket, only to rescind their decision in January 2009.*

U *Played in United Arab Emirates.*

The following deputised for the official touring captain or were appointed by the home authority for only a minor proportion of the series:
[1]D. S. Sheppard (Second and Third). [2]M. C. Cowdrey (Third). [3]G. Boycott (Third). [4]D. I. Gower (Second). [5]D. I. Gower (Second and Third). [6]A. J. Stewart (Second). [7]M. E. Trescothick (First).

SERIES RECORDS

Highest score	E	278	D. C. S. Compton at Nottingham.	1954
	P	274	Zaheer Abbas at Birmingham	1971
Best bowling	E	8-34	I. T. Botham at Lord's.	1978
	P	9-56	Abdul Qadir at Lahore.	1987-88
Highest total	E	598-9 dec	at Abu Dhabi	2015-16
	P	708	at The Oval	1987
Lowest total	E	72	at Abu Dhabi	2011-12
	P	72	at Birmingham.	2010

ENGLAND v SRI LANKA

Captains

Season	England	Sri Lanka	T	E	SL	D
1981-82	K. W. R. Fletcher	B. Warnapura	1	1	0	0
1984	D. I. Gower	L. R. D. Mendis	1	0	0	1
1988	G. A. Gooch	R. S. Madugalle	1	1	0	0
1991	G. A. Gooch	P. A. de Silva	1	1	0	0
1992-93	A. J. Stewart	A. Ranatunga	1	0	1	0
1998	A. J. Stewart	A. Ranatunga	1	0	1	0
2000-01	N. Hussain	S. T. Jayasuriya	3	2	1	0
2002	N. Hussain	S. T. Jayasuriya	3	2	0	1
2003-04	M. P. Vaughan	H. P. Tillekeratne	3	0	1	2
2006	A. Flintoff	D. P. M. D. Jayawardene	3	1	1	1
2007-08	M. P. Vaughan	D. P. M. D. Jayawardene	3	0	1	2
2011	A. J. Strauss	T. M. Dilshan[1]	3	1	0	2
2011-12	A. J. Strauss	D. P. M. D. Jayawardene	2	1	1	0
2014	A. N. Cook	A. D. Mathews	2	0	1	1
2016	A. N. Cook	A. D. Mathews	3	2	0	1
2018-19	J. E. Root	R. A. S. Lakmal[2]	3	3	0	0
	In England		18	8	3	7
	In Sri Lanka		16	7	5	4
	Totals		34	15	8	11

The following deputised for the official touring captain or was appointed by the home authority for only a minor proportion of the series:
[1]K. C. Sangakkara (Third). [2]L. D. Chandimal (First).

SERIES RECORDS

Highest score	E	203	I. J. L. Trott at Cardiff	2011
	SL	213*	D. P. M. D. Jayawardene at Galle	2007-08
Best bowling	E	7-70	P. A. J. DeFreitas at Lord's	1991
	SL	9-65	M. Muralitharan at The Oval	1998
Highest total	E	575-9 dec	at Lord's	2014
	SL	628-8 dec	at Colombo (SSC)	2003-04
Lowest total	E	81	at Galle	2007-08
	SL	81	at Colombo (SSC)	2000-01

ENGLAND v ZIMBABWE

		Captains				
Season	England		Zimbabwe	T	E	Z	D
1996-97	M. A. Atherton		A. D. R. Campbell	2	0	0	2
2000	N. Hussain		A. Flower	2	1	0	1
2003	N. Hussain		H. H. Streak	2	2	0	0
	In England			4	3	0	1
	In Zimbabwe			2	0	0	2
	Totals			6	3	0	3

SERIES RECORDS

Highest score	E	137	M. A. Butcher at Lord's	2003
	Z	148*	M. W. Goodwin at Nottingham.	2000
Best bowling	E	6-33	R. L. Johnson at Chester-le-Street.	2003
	Z	6-87	H. H. Streak at Lord's	2000
Highest total	E	472	at Lord's	2003
	Z	376	at Bulawayo.	1996-97
Lowest total	E	147	at Nottingham	2000
	Z	83	at Lord's	2000

ENGLAND v BANGLADESH

		Captains				
Season	England		Bangladesh	T	E	B	D
2003-04	M. P. Vaughan		Khaled Mahmud	2	2	0	0
2005	M. P. Vaughan		Habibul Bashar	2	2	0	0
2009-10	A. N. Cook		Shakib Al Hasan	2	2	0	0
2010	A. J. Strauss		Shakib Al Hasan	2	2	0	0
2016-17	A. N. Cook		Mushfiqur Rahim	2	1	1	0
	In England			4	4	0	0
	In Bangladesh.			6	5	1	0
	Totals			10	9	1	0

SERIES RECORDS

Highest score	E	226	I. J. L. Trott at Lord's	2010
	B	108	Tamim Iqbal at Manchester.	2010
Best bowling	E	5-35	S. J. Harmison at Dhaka	2003-04
	B	6-77	Mehedi Hasan at Mirpur	2016-17
Highest total	E	599-6 dec	at Chittagong	2009-10
	B	419	at Mirpur	2009-10
Lowest total	E	164	at Mirpur	2016-17
	B	104	at Chester-le-Street	2005

ENGLAND v IRELAND

			Captains				
Season	*England*		*Ireland*	*T*	*E*	*Ire*	*D*
2019E	J. E. Root		W. T. S. Porterfield	1	1	0	0
	In England			1	1	0	0
	Totals...........................			1	1	0	0

E Played in England.

SERIES RECORDS

Highest score	E	92	M. J. Leach at Lord's..........................	2019
	Ire	55	A. Balbirnie at Lord's.........................	2019
Best bowling	E	6-17	C. R. Woakes at Lord's........................	2019
	Ire	5-13	T. J. Murtagh at Lord's	2019
Highest total	E	303	at Lord's.....................................	2019
	Ire	207	at Lord's.....................................	2019
Lowest total	E	85	at Lord's.....................................	2019
	Ire	38	at Lord's.....................................	2019

AUSTRALIA v SOUTH AFRICA

		Captains					
Season	*Australia*		*South Africa*	*T*	*A*	*SA*	*D*
1902-03S	J. Darling		H. M. Taberer[1]	3	2	0	1
1910-11A	C. Hill		P. W. Sherwell	5	4	1	0
1912E	S. E. Gregory		F. Mitchell[2]	3	2	0	1
1921-22S	H. L. Collins		H. W. Taylor	3	1	0	2
1931-32A	W. M. Woodfull		H. B. Cameron	5	5	0	0
1935-36S	V. Y. Richardson		H. F. Wade	5	4	0	1
1949-50S	A. L. Hassett		A. D. Nourse	5	4	0	1
1952-53A	A. L. Hassett		J. E. Cheetham	5	2	2	1
1957-58S	I. D. Craig		C. B. van Ryneveld[3]	5	3	0	2
1963-64A	R. B. Simpson[4]		T. L. Goddard	5	1	1	3
1966-67S	R. B. Simpson		P. L. van der Merwe	5	1	3	1
1969-70S	W. M. Lawry		A. Bacher	4	0	4	0
1993-94A	A. R. Border		K. C. Wessels[5]	3	1	1	1
1993-94S	A. R. Border		K. C. Wessels	3	1	1	1
1996-97S	M. A. Taylor		W. J. Cronje	3	2	1	0
1997-98A	M. A. Taylor		W. J. Cronje	3	1	0	2
2001-02A	S. R. Waugh		S. M. Pollock	3	3	0	0
2001-02S	S. R. Waugh		M. V. Boucher	3	2	1	0
2005-06A	R. T. Ponting		G. C. Smith	3	2	0	1
2005-06S	R. T. Ponting		G. C. Smith[6]	3	3	0	0
2008-09A	R. T. Ponting		G. C. Smith	3	1	2	0
2008-09S	R. T. Ponting		G. C. Smith[7]	3	2	1	0
2011-12S	M. J. Clarke		G. C. Smith	2	1	1	0
2012-13A	M. J. Clarke		G. C. Smith	3	0	1	2
2013-14S	M. J. Clarke		G. C. Smith	3	2	1	0
2016-17A	S. P. D. Smith		F. du Plessis	3	1	2	0
2017-18S	S. P. D. Smith[8]		F. du Plessis	4	1	3	0
	In South Africa........................			54	29	16	9
	In Australia...........................			41	21	10	10
	In England			3	2	0	1
	Totals			98	52	26	20

S Played in South Africa.   A Played in Australia.   E Played in England.

The following deputised for the official touring captain or were appointed by the home authority for only a minor proportion of the series:

[1]J. H. Anderson (Second), E. A. Halliwell (Third). [2]L. J. Tancred (Third). [3]D. J. McGlew (First). [4]R. Benaud (First). [5]W. J. Cronje (Third). [6]J. H. Kallis (Third). [7]J. H. Kallis (Third). [8]T. D. Paine (Fourth).

SERIES RECORDS

Highest score	*A*	299*	D. G. Bradman at Adelaide	1931-32
	SA	274	R. G. Pollock at Durban	1969-70
Best bowling	*A*	8-61	M. G. Johnson at Perth	2008-09
	SA	7-23	H. J. Tayfield at Durban	1949-50
Highest total	*A*	652-7 dec	at Johannesburg	2001-02
	SA	651	at Cape Town	2008-09
Lowest total	*A*	47	at Cape Town	2011-12
	SA	36	at Melbourne	1931-32

AUSTRALIA v WEST INDIES

			Captains					
Season	*Australia*		*West Indies*	*T*	*A*	*WI*	*T*	*D*
1930-31A	W. M. Woodfull		G. C. Grant	5	4	1	0	0
1951-52A	A. L. Hassett[1]		J. D. C. Goddard[2]	5	4	1	0	0
1954-55W	I. W. Johnson		D. St E. Atkinson[3]	5	3	0	0	2

THE FRANK WORRELL TROPHY

		Captains						
Season	*Australia*	*West Indies*	*T*	*A*	*WI*	*T*	*D*	*Held by*
1960-61A	R. Benaud	F. M. M. Worrell	5	2	1	1	1	A
1964-65W	R. B. Simpson	G. S. Sobers	5	1	2	0	2	WI
1968-69A	W. M. Lawry	G. S. Sobers	5	3	1	0	1	A
1972-73W	I. M. Chappell	R. B. Kanhai	5	2	0	0	3	A
1975-76A	G. S. Chappell	C. H. Lloyd	6	5	1	0	0	A
1977-78W	R. B. Simpson	A. I. Kallicharran[4]	5	1	3	0	1	WI
1979-80A	G. S. Chappell	C. H. Lloyd[5]	3	0	2	0	1	WI
1981-82A	G. S. Chappell	C. H. Lloyd	3	1	1	0	1	WI
1983-84W	K. J. Hughes	C. H. Lloyd[6]	5	0	3	0	2	WI
1984-85A	A. R. Border[7]	C. H. Lloyd	5	1	3	0	1	WI
1988-89A	A. R. Border	I. V. A. Richards	5	1	3	0	1	WI
1990-91W	A. R. Border	I. V. A. Richards	5	1	2	0	2	WI
1992-93A	A. R. Border	R. B. Richardson	5	1	2	0	2	WI
1994-95W	M. A. Taylor	R. B. Richardson	4	2	1	0	1	A
1996-97A	M. A. Taylor	C. A. Walsh	5	3	2	0	0	A
1998-99W	S. R. Waugh	B. C. Lara	4	2	2	0	0	A
2000-01A	S. R. Waugh[8]	J. C. Adams	5	5	0	0	0	A
2002-03W	S. R. Waugh	B. C. Lara	4	3	1	0	0	A
2005-06A	R. T. Ponting	S. Chanderpaul	3	3	0	0	0	A
2007-08W	R. T. Ponting	R. R. Sarwan[9]	3	2	0	0	1	A
2009-10A	R. T. Ponting	C. H. Gayle	3	2	0	0	1	A
2011-12W	M. J. Clarke	D. J. G. Sammy	3	2	0	0	1	A
2015W	M. J. Clarke	D. Ramdin	2	2	0	0	0	A
2015-16A	S. P. D. Smith	J. O. Holder	3	2	0	0	1	A
In Australia			66	37	18	1	10	
In West Indies			50	21	14	0	15	
Totals			116	58	32	1	25	

A Played in Australia.   *W Played in West Indies.*

The following deputised for the official touring captain or were appointed by the home authority for only a minor proportion of the series:

[1]A. R. Morris (Third). [2]J. B. Stollmeyer (Fifth). [3]J. B. Stollmeyer (Second and Third). [4]C. H. Lloyd (First and Second). [5]D. L. Murray (First). [6]I. V. A. Richards (Second). [7]K. J. Hughes (First and Second). [8]A. C. Gilchrist (Third). [9]C. H. Gayle (Third).

SERIES RECORDS

Highest score	A	269*	A. C. Voges at Hobart....................	2015-16
	WI	277	B. C. Lara at Sydney.....................	1992-93
Best bowling	A	8-71	G. D. McKenzie at Melbourne	1968-69
	WI	7-25	C. E. L. Ambrose at Perth	1992-93
Highest total	A	758-8 dec	at Kingston	1954-55
	WI	616	at Adelaide............................	1968-69
Lowest total	A	76	at Perth..............................	1984-85
	WI	51	at Port-of-Spain	1998-99

AUSTRALIA v NEW ZEALAND

		Captains				
Season	Australia	New Zealand	T	A	NZ	D
1945-46N	W. A. Brown	W. A. Hadlee	1	1	0	0
1973-74A	I. M. Chappell	B. E. Congdon	3	2	0	1
1973-74N	I. M. Chappell	B. E. Congdon	3	1	1	1
1976-77N	G. S. Chappell	G. M. Turner	2	1	0	1
1980-81A	G. S. Chappell	G. P. Howarth[1]	3	2	0	1
1981-82N	G. S. Chappell	G. P. Howarth	3	1	1	1

TRANS-TASMAN TROPHY

		Captains					
Season	Australia	New Zealand	T	A	NZ	D	Held by
1985-86A	A. R. Border	J. V. Coney	3	1	2	0	NZ
1985-86N	A. R. Border	J. V. Coney	3	0	1	2	NZ
1987-88A	A. R. Border	J. J. Crowe	3	1	0	2	A
1989-90A	A. R. Border	J. G. Wright	1	0	0	1	A
1989-90N	A. R. Border	J. G. Wright	1	0	1	0	NZ
1992-93N	A. R. Border	M. D. Crowe	3	1	1	1	NZ
1993-94A	A. R. Border	M. D. Crowe[2]	3	2	0	1	A
1997-98A	M. A. Taylor	S. P. Fleming	3	2	0	1	A
1999-2000N	S. R. Waugh	S. P. Fleming	3	3	0	0	A
2001-02A	S. R. Waugh	S. P. Fleming	3	0	0	3	A
2004-05A	R. T. Ponting	S. P. Fleming	2	2	0	0	A
2004-05N	R. T. Ponting	S. P. Fleming	3	2	0	1	A
2008-09A	R. T. Ponting	D. L. Vettori	2	2	0	0	A
2009-10N	R. T. Ponting	D. L. Vettori	2	2	0	0	A
2011-12A	M. J. Clarke	L. R. P. L. Taylor	2	1	1	0	A
2015-16A	S. P. D. Smith	B. B. McCullum	3	2	0	1	A
2015-16N	S. P. D. Smith	B. B. McCullum	2	2	0	0	A
2019-20A	**T. D. Paine**	**K. S. Williamson[3]**	**3**	**3**	**0**	**0**	**A**
	In Australia....................		34	20	3	11	
	In New Zealand		26	14	5	7	
	Totals....................		**60**	**34**	**8**	**18**	

A   Played in Australia.   N   Played in New Zealand.

The following deputised for the official touring captain: [1]M. G. Burgess (Second). [2]K. R. Rutherford (Second and Third). [3]T. W. M. Latham (Third).

SERIES RECORDS

Highest score	A	253	D. A. Warner at Perth	2015-16
	NZ	290	L. R. P. L. Taylor at Perth.	2015-16
Best bowling	A	6-31	S. K. Warne at Hobart.	1993-94
	NZ	9-52	R. J. Hadlee at Brisbane	1985-86
Highest total	A	607-6 dec	at Brisbane.	1993-94
	NZ	624	at Perth	2015-16
Lowest total	A	103	at Auckland	1985-86
	NZ	42	at Wellington.	1945-46

AUSTRALIA v INDIA

		Captains					
Season	*Australia*		*India*	*T*	*A*	*I*	*T*	*D*
1947-48A	D. G. Bradman		L. Amarnath	5	4	0	0	1
1956-57I	I. W. Johnson[1]		P. R. Umrigar	3	2	0	0	1
1959-60I	R. Benaud		G. S. Ramchand	5	2	1	0	2
1964-65I	R. B. Simpson		Nawab of Pataudi jnr	3	1	1	0	1
1967-68A	R. B. Simpson[2]		Nawab of Pataudi jnr	4	4	0	0	0
1969-70I	W. M. Lawry		Nawab of Pataudi jnr	5	3	1	0	1
1977-78A	R. B. Simpson		B. S. Bedi	5	3	2	0	0
1979-80I	K. J. Hughes		S. M. Gavaskar	6	0	2	0	4
1980-81A	G. S. Chappell		S. M. Gavaskar	3	1	1	0	1
1985-86A	A. R. Border		Kapil Dev	3	0	0	0	3
1986-87I	A. R. Border		Kapil Dev	3	0	0	1	2
1991-92A	A. R. Border		M. Azharuddin	5	4	0	0	1

THE BORDER–GAVASKAR TROPHY

		Captains						
Season	*Australia*		*India*	*T*	*A*	*I*	*T*	*D*	*Held by*
1996-97I	M. A. Taylor		S. R. Tendulkar	1	0	1	0	0	I
1997-98I	M. A. Taylor		M. Azharuddin	3	1	2	0	0	I
1999-2000A	S. R. Waugh		S. R. Tendulkar	3	3	0	0	0	A
2000-01I	S. R. Waugh		S. C. Ganguly	3	1	2	0	0	I
2003-04A	S. R. Waugh		S. C. Ganguly	4	1	1	0	2	I
2004-05I	R. T. Ponting[4]		S. C. Ganguly[5]	4	2	1	0	1	A
2007-08A	R. T. Ponting		A. Kumble	4	2	1	0	1	A
2008-09I	R. T. Ponting		A. Kumble[6]	4	0	2	0	2	I
2010-11I	R. T. Ponting		M. S. Dhoni	2	0	2	0	0	I
2011-12A	M. J. Clarke		M. S. Dhoni[7]	4	4	0	0	0	A
2012-13I	M. J. Clarke[8]		M. S. Dhoni	4	0	4	0	0	I
2014-15A	M. J. Clarke[9]		M. S. Dhoni[10]	4	2	0	0	2	A
2016-17I	S. P. D. Smith		V. Kohli[11]	4	1	2	0	1	I
2018-19A	**T. D. Paine**		**V. Kohli**	**4**	**1**	**2**	**0**	**1**	**I**
	In Australia			**48**	**29**	**7**	**0**	**12**	
	In India			50	13	21	1	15	
	Totals			**98**	**42**	**28**	**1**	**27**	

A   Played in Australia.   I   Played in India.

The following deputised for the official touring captain or were appointed by the home authority for only a minor proportion of the series:
[1]R. R. Lindwall (Second). [2]W. M. Lawry (Third and Fourth). [3]C. G. Borde (First). [4]A. C. Gilchrist (First, Second and Third). [5]R. Dravid (Third and Fourth). [6]M. S. Dhoni (Second and Fourth). [7]V. Sehwag (Fourth). [8]S. R. Watson (Fourth). [9]S. P. D. Smith (Second, Third and Fourth). [10]V. Kohli (First and Fourth). [11]A. M. Rahane (Fourth).

SERIES RECORDS

Highest score	A	329*	M. J. Clarke at Sydney	2011-12
	I	281	V. V. S. Laxman at Kolkata	2000-01
Best bowling	A	8-50	N. M. Lyon at Bangalore	2016-17
	I	9-69	J. M. Patel at Kanpur	1959-60
Highest total	A	674	at Adelaide	1947-48
	I	705-7 dec	at Sydney	2003-04
Lowest total	A	83	at Melbourne	1980-81
	I	58	at Brisbane	1947-48

AUSTRALIA v PAKISTAN

Captains

Season	Australia	Pakistan	T	A	P	D
1956-57P	I. W. Johnson	A. H. Kardar	1	0	1	0
1959-60P	R. Benaud	Fazal Mahmood[1]	3	2	0	1
1964-65P	R. B. Simpson	Hanif Mohammad	1	0	0	1
1964-65A	R. B. Simpson	Hanif Mohammad	1	0	0	1
1972-73A	I. M. Chappell	Intikhab Alam	3	3	0	0
1976-77A	G. S. Chappell	Mushtaq Mohammad	3	1	1	1
1978-79A	G. N. Yallop[2]	Mushtaq Mohammad	2	1	1	0
1979-80P	G. S. Chappell	Javed Miandad	3	0	1	2
1981-82A	G. S. Chappell	Javed Miandad	3	2	1	0
1982-83P	K. J. Hughes	Imran Khan	3	0	3	0
1983-84A	K. J. Hughes	Imran Khan[3]	5	2	0	3
1988-89P	A. R. Border	Javed Miandad	3	0	1	2
1989-90A	A. R. Border	Imran Khan	3	1	0	2
1994-95P	M. A. Taylor	Salim Malik	3	0	1	2
1995-96A	M. A. Taylor	Wasim Akram	3	2	1	0
1998-99P	M. A. Taylor	Aamir Sohail	3	1	0	2
1999-2000A	S. R. Waugh	Wasim Akram	3	3	0	0
2002-03S/U	S. R. Waugh	Waqar Younis	3	3	0	0
2004-05A	R. T. Ponting	Inzamam-ul-Haq[4]	3	3	0	0
2009-10A	R. T. Ponting	Mohammad Yousuf	3	3	0	0
2010E	R. T. Ponting	Shahid Afridi[5]	2	1	1	0
2014-15U	M. J. Clarke	Misbah-ul-Haq	2	0	2	0
2016-17A	S. P. D. Smith	Misbah-ul-Haq	3	3	0	0
2018-19U	T. D. Paine	Sarfraz Ahmed	2	0	1	1
2019-20A	**T. D. Paine**	**Azhar Ali**	**2**	**2**	**0**	**0**
	In Pakistan		20	3	7	10
	In Australia		37	26	4	7
	In Sri Lanka		1	1	0	0
	In United Arab Emirates		6	2	3	1
	In England		2	1	1	0
	Totals		**66**	**33**	**15**	**18**

P   Played in Pakistan.   A   Played in Australia.
S/U   First Test played in Sri Lanka, Second and Third Tests in United Arab Emirates.
U   Played in United Arab Emirates.   E   Played in England.

The following deputised for the official touring captain or were appointed by the home authority for only a minor proportion of the series:
[1]Imtiaz Ahmed (Second). [2]K. J. Hughes (Second). [3]Zaheer Abbas (First, Second and Third). [4]Yousuf Youhana *later known as Mohammad Yousuf* (Second and Third). [5]Salman Butt (Second).

SERIES RECORDS

Highest score	A	**335***	**D. A. Warner at Adelaide**	**2019-20**
	P	237	Salim Malik at Rawalpindi	1994-95
Best bowling	A	8-24	G. D. McGrath at Perth	2004-05
	P	9-86	Sarfraz Nawaz at Melbourne	1978-79
Highest total	A	624-8 dec	at Melbourne	2016-17
	P	624	at Adelaide	1983-84
Lowest total	A	80	at Karachi	1956-57
	P	53	at Sharjah	2002-03

AUSTRALIA v SRI LANKA

		Captains				
Season	*Australia*		*Sri Lanka*	*T*	*A*	*SL*	*D*
1982-83*S*	G. S. Chappell		L. R. D. Mendis	1	1	0	0
1987-88*A*	A. R. Border		R. S. Madugalle	1	1	0	0
1989-90*A*	A. R. Border		A. Ranatunga	1	1	0	1
1992-93*S*	A. R. Border		A. Ranatunga	3	1	0	2
1995-96*A*	M. A. Taylor		A. Ranatunga[1]	3	3	0	0
1999-2000*S*	S. R. Waugh		S. T. Jayasuriya	3	0	1	2
2003-04*S*	R. T. Ponting		H. P. Tillekeratne	3	3	0	0
2004*A*	R. T. Ponting[2]		M. S. Atapattu	2	1	0	1

THE WARNE–MURALITHARAN TROPHY

		Captains					
Season	*Australia*		*Sri Lanka*	*T*	*A*	*SL*	*D*	*Held by*
2007-08*A*	R. T. Ponting		D. P. M. D. Jayawardene	2	2	0	0	A
2011-12*S*	M. J. Clarke		T. M. Dilshan	3	1	0	2	A
2012-13*A*	M. J. Clarke		D. P. M. D. Jayawardene	3	3	0	0	A
2016*S*	S. P. D. Smith		A. D. Mathews	3	0	3	0	SL
2018-19*A*	**T. D. Paine**		**L. D. Chandimal**	**2**	**2**	**0**	**0**	**A**
	In Australia			15	13	0	2
	In Sri Lanka			16	6	4	6
	Totals			31	19	4	8

A   Played in Australia.   *S   Played in Sri Lanka.*

The following deputised for the official touring captain or was appointed by the home authority for only a minor proportion of the series:
[1]P. A. de Silva (Third). [2]A. C. Gilchrist (First).

SERIES RECORDS

Highest score	A	219	M. J. Slater at Perth	1995-96
	SL	192	K. C. Sangakkara at Hobart	2007-08
Best bowling	A	7-39	M. S. Kasprowicz at Darwin	2004
	SL	7-64	H. M. R. K. B. Herath at Colombo (SSC)	2016
Highest total	A	617-5 dec	at Perth	1995-96
	SL	547-8 dec	at Colombo (SSC)	1992-93
Lowest total	A	106	at Galle	2016
	SL	97	at Darwin	2004

AUSTRALIA v ZIMBABWE

		Captains				
Season	Australia	Zimbabwe	T	A	Z	D
1999-2000Z	S. R. Waugh	A. D. R. Campbell	1	1	0	0
2003-04A	S. R. Waugh	H. H. Streak	2	2	0	0
	In Australia................		2	2	0	0
	In Zimbabwe..............		1	1	0	0
	Totals......................		3	3	0	0

A Played in Australia.   Z Played in Zimbabwe.

SERIES RECORDS

Highest score	A	380	M. L. Hayden at Perth....................	2003-04
	Z	118	S. V. Carlisle at Sydney................	2003-04
Best bowling	A	6-65	S. M. Katich at Sydney................	2003-04
	Z	6-121	R. W. Price at Sydney................	2003-04
Highest total	A	735-6 dec	at Perth................................	2003-04
	Z	321	at Perth................................	2003-04
Lowest total	A	403	at Sydney..............................	2003-04
	Z	194	at Harare	1999-2000

AUSTRALIA v BANGLADESH

		Captains				
Season	Australia	Bangladesh	T	A	B	D
2003A	S. R. Waugh	Khaled Mahmud	2	2	0	0
2005-06B	R. T. Ponting	Habibul Bashar	2	2	0	0
2017-18B	S. P. D. Smith	Mushfiqur Rahim	2	1	1	0
	In Australia................		2	2	0	0
	In Bangladesh.............		4	3	1	0
	Totals......................		6	5	1	0

A Played in Australia.   B Played in Bangladesh.

SERIES RECORDS

Highest score	A	201*	J. N. Gillespie at Chittagong	2005-06
	B	138	Shahriar Nafees at Fatullah	2005-06
Best bowling	A	8-108	S. C. G. MacGill at Fatullah	2005-06
	B	5-62	Mohammad Rafique at Fatullah...........	2005-06
Highest total	A	581-4 dec	at Chittagong	2005-06
	A	427	at Fatullah	2005-06
Lowest total	A	217	at Mirpur	2017-18
	B	97	at Darwin..............................	2003

AUSTRALIA v ICC WORLD XI

Season	Australia	ICC World XI	T	A	ICC	D
2005-06A	R. T. Ponting	G. C. Smith	1	1	0	0

A Played in Australia.

SERIES RECORDS

Highest score	A	111	M. L. Hayden at Sydney		2005-06
	Wld	76	V. Sehwag at Sydney		2005-06
Best bowling	A	5-43	S. C. G. MacGill at Sydney		2005-06
	Wld	4-59	A. Flintoff at Sydney		2005-06
Highest total	A	345	at Sydney		2005-06
	Wld	190	at Sydney		2005-06
Lowest total	A	199	at Sydney		2005-06
	Wld	144	at Sydney		2005-06

SOUTH AFRICA v WEST INDIES

		Captains				
Season	South Africa		West Indies	T	SA	WI	D
1991-92W	K. C. Wessels		R. B. Richardson	1	0	1	0
1998-99S	W. J. Cronje		B. C. Lara	5	5	0	0

SIR VIVIAN RICHARDS TROPHY

		Captains						
Season	South Africa		West Indies	T	SA	WI	D	Held by
2000-01W	S. M. Pollock		C. L. Hooper	5	2	1	2	SA
2003-04S	G. C. Smith		B. C. Lara	4	3	0	1	SA
2004-05W	G. C. Smith		S. Chanderpaul	4	2	0	2	SA
2007-08 S	G. C. Smith		C. H. Gayle[1]	3	2	1	0	SA
2010W	G. C. Smith		C. H. Gayle	3	2	0	1	SA
2014-15S	H. M. Amla		D. Ramdin	3	2	0	1	SA
	In South Africa			15	12	1	2	
	In West Indies			13	6	2	5	
	Totals........................			28	18	3	7	

S Played in South Africa.   W Played in West Indies.

The following deputised for the official touring captain:
  [1]D. J. Bravo (Third).

SERIES RECORDS

Highest score	SA	208	H. M. Amla at Centurion..................		2014-15
	WI	317	C. H. Gayle at St John's		2004-05
Best bowling	SA	7-37	M. Ntini at Port-of-Spain.................		2004-05
	WI	7-84	F. A. Rose at Durban.....................		1998-99
Highest total	SA	658-9 dec	at Durban..............................		2003-04
	WI	747	at St John's		2004-05
Lowest total	SA	141	at Kingston		2000-01
	WI	102	at Port-of-Spain........................		2010

SOUTH AFRICA v NEW ZEALAND

		Captains				
Season	South Africa		New Zealand	T	SA	NZ	D
1931-32N	H. B. Cameron		M. L. Page	2	2	0	0
1952-53N	J. E. Cheetham		W. M. Wallace	2	1	0	1
1953-54S	J. E. Cheetham		G. O. Rabone[1]	5	4	0	1
1961-62S	D. J. McGlew		J. R. Reid	5	2	0	1
1963-64N	T. L. Goddard		J. R. Reid	3	0	0	3
1994-95S	W. J. Cronje		K. R. Rutherford	3	2	1	0
1994-95N	W. J. Cronje		K. R. Rutherford	1	1	0	0
1998-99N	W. J. Cronje		D. J. Nash	3	1	0	2
2000-01S	S. M. Pollock		S. P. Fleming	3	2	0	1

		Captains				
Season	*South Africa*	*New Zealand*	*T*	*SA*	*NZ*	*D*
2003-04N	G. C. Smith	S. P. Fleming	3	1	1	1
2005-06S	G. C. Smith	S. P. Fleming	3	2	0	1
2007-08S	G. C. Smith	D. L. Vettori	2	2	0	0
2011-12N	G. C. Smith	L. R. P. L. Taylor	3	1	0	2
2012-13S	G. C. Smith	B. B. McCullum	2	2	0	0
2016S	F. du Plessis	K. S. Williamson	2	1	0	1
2016-17N	F. du Plessis	K. S. Williamson	3	1	0	2
	In New Zealand		20	8	1	11
	In South Africa.		25	17	3	5
	Totals		45	25	4	16

N Played in New Zealand.   S Played in South Africa.

The following deputised for the official touring captain:
¹B. Sutcliffe (Fourth and Fifth).

SERIES RECORDS

Highest score	SA	275*	D. J. Cullinan at Auckland	1998-99
	NZ	262	S. P. Fleming at Cape Town	2005-06
Best bowling	SA	8-53	G. B. Lawrence at Johannesburg.	1961-62
	NZ	6-60	J. R. Reid at Dunedin	1963-64
Highest total	SA	621-5 dec	at Auckland	1998-99
	NZ	595	at Auckland	2003-04
Lowest total	SA	148	at Johannesburg.	1953-54
	NZ	45	at Cape Town	2012-13

SOUTH AFRICA v INDIA

		Captains				
Season	*South Africa*	*India*	*T*	*SA*	*I*	*D*
1992-93S	K. C. Wessels	M. Azharuddin	4	1	0	3
1996-97I	W. J. Cronje	S. R. Tendulkar	3	1	2	0
1996-97S	W. J. Cronje	S. R. Tendulkar	3	2	0	1
1999-2000I	W. J. Cronje	S. R. Tendulkar	2	2	0	0
2001-02S	S. M. Pollock	S. C. Ganguly	2	1	0	1
2004-05I	G. C. Smith	S. C. Ganguly	2	0	1	1
2006-07S	G. C. Smith	R. Dravid	3	2	1	0
2007-08I	G. C. Smith	A. Kumble¹	3	1	1	1
2009-10I	G. C. Smith	M. S. Dhoni	2	1	1	0
2010-11S	G. C. Smith	M. S. Dhoni	3	1	1	1
2013-14S	G. C. Smith	M. S. Dhoni	2	1	0	1

THE FREEDOM TROPHY

		Captains					
Season	*South Africa*	*India*	*T*	*SA*	*I*	*D*	*Held by*
2015-16I	H. M. Amla	V. Kohli	4	0	3	1	I
2017-18S	F. du Plessis	V. Kohli	3	2	1	0	SA
2019-20I	**F. du Plessis**	**V. Kohli**	**3**	**0**	**3**	**0**	**I**
	In South Africa		20	10	3	7	
	In India		**19**	**5**	**11**	**3**	
	Totals		39	15	14	10	

S Played in South Africa.   I Played in India.

†   *The Third Test at Centurion was stripped of its official status by the ICC after a disciplinary dispute and is excluded.*

The following was appointed by the home authority for only a minor proportion of the series:
¹M. S. Dhoni (Third).

SERIES RECORDS

Highest score	SA	253*	H. M. Amla at Nagpur.....................		2009-10
	I	319	V. Sehwag at Chennai.................		2007-08
Best bowling	SA	8-64	L. Klusener at Calcutta................		1996-97
	I	7-66	R. Ashwin at Nagpur.....................		2015-16
Highest total	SA	620-4 dec	at Centurion............................		2010-11
	I	643-6 dec	at Kolkata.............................		2009-10
Lowest total	SA	79	at Nagpur..............................		2015-16
	I	66	at Durban..............................		1996-97

SOUTH AFRICA v PAKISTAN

		Captains				
Season	South Africa	Pakistan	T	SA	P	D
1994-95S	W. J. Cronje	Salim Malik	1	1	0	0
1997-98P	W. J. Cronje	Saeed Anwar	3	1	0	2
1997-98S	W. J. Cronje[1]	Rashid Latif[2]	3	1	1	1
2002-03S	S. M. Pollock	Waqar Younis	2	2	0	0
2003-04P	G. C. Smith	Inzamam-ul-Haq[3]	2	0	1	1
2006-07S	G. C. Smith	Inzamam-ul-Haq	3	2	1	0
2007-08P	G. C. Smith	Shoaib Malik	2	1	0	1
2010-11U	G. C. Smith	Misbah-ul-Haq	2	0	0	2
2012-13S	G. C. Smith	Misbah-ul-Haq	3	3	0	0
2013-14U	G. C. Smith	Misbah-ul-Haq	2	1	1	0
2018-19S	**F. du Plessis[4]**	**Sarfraz Ahmed**	**3**	**3**	**0**	**0**
	In South Africa...................		**15**	**12**	**2**	**1**
	In Pakistan.....................		7	2	1	4
	In United Arab Emirates............		4	1	1	2
	Totals..........................		**26**	**15**	**4**	**7**

S Played in South Africa.   P Played in Pakistan.   U Played in United Arab Emirates.

The following deputised for the official touring captain or were appointed by the home authority for only a minor proportion of the series:
[1]G. Kirsten (First). [2]Aamir Sohail (First and Second). [3]Yousuf Youhana *later known as Mohammad Yousuf* (First). [4]D. Elgar (Third).

SERIES RECORDS

Highest score	SA	278*	A. B. de Villiers at Abu Dhabi..............		2010-11
	P	146	Khurram Manzoor at Abu Dhabi...........		2013-14
Best bowling	SA	7-29	K. J. Abbott at Centurion		2012-13
	P	6-78	Mushtaq Ahmed at Durban...............		1997-98
		6-78	Waqar Younis at Port Elizabeth		1997-98
Highest total	SA	620-7 dec	at Cape Town		2002-03
	P	456	at Rawalpindi		1997-98
Lowest total	SA	124	at Port Elizabeth		2006-07
	P	49	at Johannesburg.....................		2012-13

SOUTH AFRICA v SRI LANKA

		Captains				
Season	South Africa	Sri Lanka	T	SA	SL	D
1993-94SL	K. C. Wessels	A. Ranatunga	3	1	0	2
1997-98SA	W. J. Cronje	A. Ranatunga	2	2	0	0
2000SL	S. M. Pollock	S. T. Jayasuriya	3	1	1	1
2000-01SA	S. M. Pollock	S. T. Jayasuriya	3	2	0	1

Captains

Season	South Africa	Sri Lanka	T	SA	SL	D
2002-03*SA*	S. M. Pollock	S. T. Jayasuriya[1]	2	2	0	0
2004*SL*	G. C. Smith	M. S. Atapattu	2	0	1	1
2006*SL*	A. G. Prince	D. P. M. D. Jayawardene	2	0	2	0
2011-12*SA*	G. C. Smith	T. M. Dilshan	3	2	1	0
2014*SL*	H. M. Amla	A. D. Mathews	2	1	0	1
2016-17*SA*	F. du Plessis	A. D. Mathews	3	3	0	0
2018*SL*	F. du Plessis	R. A. S. Lakmal	2	0	2	0
2018-19*SA*	**F. du Plessis**	**F. D. M. Karunaratne**	**2**	**0**	**2**	**0**
	In South Africa		15	11	3	1
	In Sri Lanka		14	3	6	5
	Totals		29	14	9	6

SA   Played in South Africa.   SL   Played in Sri Lanka.

The following deputised for the official captain:
  [1]M. S. Atapattu (Second).

SERIES RECORDS

Highest score	SA	224	J. H. Kallis at Cape Town		2011-12
	SL	374	D. P. M. D. Jayawardene at Colombo (SSC)		2006
Best bowling	SA	9-129	K. A. Maharaj at Colombo (SSC)		2018
	SL	7-84	M. Muralitharan at Galle		2000
Highest total	SA	580-4 dec	at Cape Town		2011-12
	SL	756-5 dec	at Colombo (SSC)		2006
Lowest total	SA	73	at Galle		2018
	SL	95	at Cape Town		2000-01

SOUTH AFRICA v ZIMBABWE

Captains

Season	South Africa	Zimbabwe	T	SA	Z	D
1995-96*Z*	W. J. Cronje	A. Flower	1	1	0	0
1999-2000*S*	W. J. Cronje	A. D. R. Campbell	1	1	0	0
1999-2000*Z*	W. J. Cronje	A. Flower	1	1	0	0
2001-02*Z*	S. M. Pollock	H. H. Streak	2	1	0	1
2004-05*S*	G. C. Smith	T. Taibu	2	2	0	0
2014-15*Z*	H. M. Amla	B. R. M. Taylor	1	1	0	0
2017-18*S*	A. B. de Villiers	A. G. Cremer	1	1	0	0
	In Zimbabwe		5	4	0	0
	In South Africa		4	4	0	0
	Totals		9	8	0	1

S   Played in South Africa.   Z   Played in Zimbabwe.

SERIES RECORDS

Highest score	SA	220	G. Kirsten at Harare		2001-02
	Z	199*	A. Flower at Harare		2001-02
Best bowling	SA	8-71	A. A. Donald at Harare		1995-96
	Z	5-101	B. C. Strang at Harare		1995-96
Highest total	SA	600-3 dec	at Harare		2001-02
	Z	419-9 dec	at Bulawayo		2001-02
Lowest total	SA	346	at Harare		1995-96
	Z	54	at Cape Town		2004-05

SOUTH AFRICA v BANGLADESH

		Captains				
Season	South Africa	Bangladesh	T	SA	B	D
2002-03S	S. M. Pollock[1]	Khaled Mashud	2	2	0	0
2003B	G. C. Smith	Khaled Mahmud	2	2	0	0
2007-08B	G. C. Smith	Mohammad Ashraful	2	2	0	0
2008-09S	G. C. Smith	Mohammad Ashraful	2	2	0	0
2015B	H. M. Amla	Mushfiqur Rahim	2	0	0	2
2017-18S	F. du Plessis	Mushfiqur Rahim	2	2	0	0
	In South Africa		6	6	0	0
	In Bangladesh		6	4	0	2
	Totals		12	10	0	2

S Played in South Africa.   B Played in Bangladesh.

The following deputised for the official captain:
[1]M. V. Boucher (First).

SERIES RECORDS

Highest score	SA	232	G. C. Smith at Chittagong	2007-08
	B	77	Mominul Haque at Potchefstroom	2017-18
Best bowling	SA	5-19	M. Ntini at East London	2002-03
	B	6-27	Shahadat Hossain at Mirpur	2007-08
Highest total	SA	583-7 dec	at Chittagong	2007-08
	B	326	at Chittagong	2015
Lowest total	SA	170	at Mirpur	2007-08
	B	90	at Potchefstroom	2017-18

WEST INDIES v NEW ZEALAND

		Captains				
Season	West Indies	New Zealand	T	WI	NZ	D
1951-52N	J. D. C. Goddard	B. Sutcliffe	2	1	0	1
1955-56N	D. St E. Atkinson	J. R. Reid[1]	4	3	1	0
1968-69N	G. S. Sobers	G. T. Dowling	3	1	1	1
1971-72W	G. S. Sobers	G. T. Dowling[2]	5	0	0	5
1979-80N	C. H. Lloyd	G. P. Howarth	3	0	1	2
1984-85W	I. V. A. Richards	G. P. Howarth	4	2	0	2
1986-87N	I. V. A. Richards	J. V. Coney	3	1	1	1
1994-95N	C. A. Walsh	K. R. Rutherford	2	1	0	1
1995-96W	C. A. Walsh	L. K. Germon	2	1	0	1
1999-2000N	B. C. Lara	S. P. Fleming	2	0	2	0
2002W	C. L. Hooper	S. P. Fleming	2	0	1	1
2005-06N	S. Chanderpaul	S. P. Fleming	3	0	2	1
2008-09N	C. H. Gayle	D. L. Vettori	2	0	0	2
2012W	D. J. G. Sammy	L. R. P. L. Taylor	2	2	0	0
2013-14N	D. J. G. Sammy	B. B. McCullum	3	0	2	1
2014W	D. Ramdin	B. B. McCullum	3	1	2	0
2017-18N	J. O. Holder[3]	K. S. Williamson	2	0	2	0
	In New Zealand		29	7	12	10
	In West Indies		18	6	3	9
	Totals		47	13	15	19

N Played in New Zealand.   W Played in West Indies.

The following deputised for the official touring captain or were appointed by the home authority for only a minor proportion of the series:
[1]H. B. Cave (First). [2]B. E. Congdon (Third, Fourth and Fifth). [3]K. C. Brathwaite (Second).

SERIES RECORDS

Highest score	WI	258	S. M. Nurse at Christchurch	1968-69
	NZ	259	G. M. Turner at Georgetown.	1971-72
Best bowling	WI	7-37	C. A. Walsh at Wellington	1994-95
	NZ	7-27	C. L. Cairns at Hamilton	1999-2000
Highest total	WI	660-5 dec	at Wellington	1994-95
	NZ	609-9 dec	at Dunedin (University).	2013-14
Lowest total	WI	77	at Auckland	1955-56
	NZ	74	at Dunedin	1955-56

WEST INDIES v INDIA

			Captains				
Season	*West Indies*		*India*	*T*	*WI*	*I*	*D*
1948-49*I*	J. D. C. Goddard		L. Amarnath	5	1	0	4
1952-53*W*	J. B. Stollmeyer		V. S. Hazare	5	1	0	4
1958-59*I*	F. C. M. Alexander		Ghulam Ahmed[1]	5	3	0	2
1961-62*W*	F. M. M. Worrell		N. J. Contractor[2]	5	5	0	0
1966-67*I*	G. S. Sobers		Nawab of Pataudi jnr	3	2	0	1
1970-71*W*	G. S. Sobers		A. L. Wadekar	5	0	1	4
1974-75*I*	C. H. Lloyd		Nawab of Pataudi jnr[3]	5	3	2	0
1975-76*W*	C. H. Lloyd		B. S. Bedi	4	2	1	1
1978-79*I*	A. I. Kallicharran		S. M. Gavaskar	6	0	1	5
1982-83*W*	C. H. Lloyd		Kapil Dev	5	2	0	3
1983-84*I*	C. H. Lloyd		Kapil Dev	6	3	0	3
1987-88*I*	I. V. A. Richards		D. B. Vengsarkar[4]	4	1	1	2
1988-89*W*	I. V. A. Richards		D. B. Vengsarkar	4	3	0	1
1994-95*I*	C. A. Walsh		M. Azharuddin	3	1	1	1
1996-97*W*	C. A. Walsh[5]		S. R. Tendulkar	5	1	0	4
2001-02*W*	C. L. Hooper		S. C. Ganguly	5	2	1	2
2002-03*I*	C. L. Hooper		S. C. Ganguly	3	0	2	1
2005-06*W*	B. C. Lara		R. Dravid	4	0	1	3
2011*W*	D. J. G. Sammy		M. S. Dhoni	3	0	1	2
2011-12*I*	D. J. G. Sammy		M. S. Dhoni	3	0	2	1
2013-14*I*	D. J. G. Sammy		M. S. Dhoni	2	0	2	0
2016*W*	J. O. Holder		V. Kohli	4	0	2	2
2018-19*I*	J. O. Holder[6]		V. Kohli	2	0	2	0
2019*W*	**J. O. Holder**		**V. Kohli**	**2**	**0**	**2**	**0**
	In India.			47	14	13	20
	In West Indies.			**51**	**16**	**9**	**26**
	Totals.			98	30	22	46

I   Played in India.   W   Played in West Indies.

The following deputised for the official touring captain or were appointed by the home authority for only a minor proportion of the series:

[1]P. R. Umrigar (First), M. H. Mankad (Fourth), H. R. Adhikari (Fifth). [2]Nawab of Pataudi jnr (Third, Fourth and Fifth). [3]S. Venkataraghavan (Second). [4]R. J. Shastri (Fourth). [5]B. C. Lara (Third). [6]K. C. Brathwaite (First).

SERIES RECORDS

Highest score	WI	256	R. B. Kanhai at Calcutta	1958-59
	I	236*	S. M. Gavaskar at Madras	1983-84
Best bowling	WI	9-95	J. M. Noreiga at Port-of-Spain	1970-71
	I	9-83	Kapil Dev at Ahmedabad	1983-84
Highest total	WI	644-8 dec	at Delhi	1958-59
	I	649-9 dec	at Rajkot	2018-19
Lowest total	**WI**	**100**	**at North Sound**	**2019**
	I	75	at Delhi	1987-88

WEST INDIES v PAKISTAN

Captains

Season	West Indies	Pakistan	T	WI	P	D
1957-58*W*	F. C. M. Alexander	A. H. Kardar	5	3	1	1
1958-59*P*	F. C. M. Alexander	Fazal Mahmood	3	1	2	0
1974-75*P*	C. H. Lloyd	Intikhab Alam	2	0	0	2
1976-77*W*	C. H. Lloyd	Mushtaq Mohammad	5	2	1	2
1980-81*P*	C. H. Lloyd	Javed Miandad	4	1	0	3
1986-87*P*	I. V. A. Richards	Imran Khan	3	1	1	1
1987-88*W*	I. V. A. Richards[1]	Imran Khan	3	1	1	1
1990-91*P*	D. L. Haynes	Imran Khan	3	1	1	1
1992-93*W*	R. B. Richardson	Wasim Akram	3	2	0	1
1997-98*P*	C. A. Walsh	Wasim Akram	3	0	3	0
1999-2000*W*	J. C. Adams	Moin Khan	3	1	0	2
2001-02*U*	C. L. Hooper	Waqar Younis	2	0	2	0
2004-05*W*	S. Chanderpaul	Inzamam-ul-Haq[2]	2	1	1	0
2006-07*W*	B. C. Lara	Inzamam-ul-Haq	3	0	2	1
2010-11*W*	D. J. G. Sammy	Misbah-ul-Haq	2	1	1	0
2016-17*U*	J. O. Holder	Misbah-ul-Haq	3	1	2	0
2016-17*W*	J. O. Holder	Misbah-ul-Haq	3	1	2	0
	In West Indies		26	12	7	7
	In Pakistan		21	4	9	8
	In United Arab Emirates		5	1	4	0
	Totals		52	17	20	15

P Played in Pakistan.   *W Played in West Indies.*   *U Played in United Arab Emirates.*

The following were appointed by the home authority or deputised for the official touring captain for a minor proportion of the series:
[1]C. G. Greenidge (First). [2]Younis Khan (First).

SERIES RECORDS

Highest score	WI	365*	G. S. Sobers at Kingston	1957-58
	P	337	Hanif Mohammad at Bridgetown	1957-58
Best bowling	WI	8-29	C. E. H. Croft at Port-of-Spain	1976-77
	P	7-80	Imran Khan at Georgetown	1987-88
Highest total	WI	790-3 dec	at Kingston	1957-58
	P	657-8 dec	at Bridgetown	1957-58
Lowest total	WI	53	at Faisalabad	1986-87
	P	77	at Lahore	1986-87

WEST INDIES v SRI LANKA

Captains

Season	West Indies	Sri Lanka	T	WI	SL	D
1993-94*S*	R. B. Richardson	A. Ranatunga	1	0	0	1
1996-97*W*	C. A. Walsh	A. Ranatunga	2	1	0	1
2001-02*S*	C. L. Hooper	S. T. Jayasuriya	3	0	3	0
2003*W*	B. C. Lara	H. P. Tillekeratne	2	1	0	1
2005*S*	S. Chanderpaul	M. S. Atapattu	2	0	2	0
2007-08*W*	C. H. Gayle	D. P. M. D. Jayawardene	2	1	1	0
2010-11*S*	D. J. G. Sammy	K. C. Sangakkara	3	0	0	3

THE SOBERS–TISSERA TROPHY

		Captains						
Season	*West Indies*		*Sri Lanka*	*T*	*WI*	*SL*	*D*	*Held by*
2015-16S	J. O. Holder		A. D. Mathews	2	0	2	0	SL
2018W	J. O. Holder		L. D. Chandimal[1]	3	1	1	1	SL
	In West Indies			9	4	2	3	
	In Sri Lanka			11	0	7	4	
	Totals			20	4	9	7	

W   Played in West Indies.   S   Played in Sri Lanka.

The following deputised for the official touring captain:
   [1]R. A. S. Lakmal (Third).

SERIES RECORDS

Highest score	WI	333	C. H. Gayle at Galle	2010-11
	SL	204*	H. P. Tillekeratne at Colombo (SSC)	2001-02
Best bowling	WI	8-62	S. T. Gabriel at Gros Islet	2018
	SL	8-46	M. Muralitharan at Kandy	2005
Highest total	WI	580-9 dec	at Galle	2010-11
	SL	627-9 dec	at Colombo (SSC)	2001-02
Lowest total	WI	93	at Bridgetown	2018
	SL	150	at Kandy	2005

WEST INDIES v ZIMBABWE

		Captains					
Season	*West Indies*		*Zimbabwe*	*T*	*WI*	*Z*	*D*
1999-2000W	J. C. Adams		A. Flower	2	2	0	0

THE CLIVE LLOYD TROPHY

		Captains						
Season	*West Indies*		*Zimbabwe*	*T*	*WI*	*Z*	*D*	*Held by*
2001Z	C. L. Hooper		H. H. Streak	2	1	0	1	WI
2003-04Z	B. C. Lara		H. H. Streak	2	1	0	1	WI
2012-13W	D. J. G. Sammy		B. R. M. Taylor	2	2	0	0	WI
2017-18Z	J. O. Holder		A. G. Cremer	2	1	0	1	WI
	In West Indies			4	4	0	0	
	In Zimbabwe			6	3	0	3	
	Totals			10	7	0	3	

W   Played in West Indies.   Z   Played in Zimbabwe.

SERIES RECORDS

Highest score	WI	191	B. C. Lara at Bulawayo	2003-04
	Z	147	H. Masakadza at Bulawayo	2017-18
Best bowling	WI	6-49	S. Shillingford at Bridgetown	2012-13
	Z	6-73	R. W. Price at Harare.	2003-04
Highest total	WI	559-6 dec	at Bulawayo	2001
	Z	563-9 dec	at Harare	2001
Lowest total	WI	128	at Bulawayo	2003-04
	Z	63	at Port-of-Spain	1999-2000

WEST INDIES v BANGLADESH

		Captains				
Season	*West Indies*	*Bangladesh*	*T*	*WI*	*B*	*D*
2002-03*B*	R. D. Jacobs	Khaled Mashud	2	2	0	0
2003-04*W*	B. C. Lara	Habibul Bashar	2	1	0	1
2009*W*	F. L. Reifer	Mashrafe bin Mortaza[1]	2	0	2	0
2011-12*B*	D. J. G. Sammy	Mushfiqur Rahim	2	1	0	1
2012-13*B*	D. J. G. Sammy	Mushfiqur Rahim	2	2	0	0
2014-15*W*	D. Ramdin	Mushfiqur Rahim	2	2	0	0
2018*W*	J. O. Holder	Shakib Al Hasan	2	2	0	0
2018-19*B*	K. C. Brathwaite	Shakib Al Hasan	2	0	2	0
	In West Indies		8	5	2	1
	In Bangladesh		8	5	2	1
	Totals		16	10	4	2

B   Played in Bangladesh.   W   Played in West Indies.

The following deputised for the official touring captain for a minor proportion of the series:
[1]Shakib Al Hasan (Second).

SERIES RECORDS

Highest score	WI	261*	R. R. Sarwan at Kingston	2003-04
	B	136	Mahmudullah at Mirpur	2018-19
Best bowling	WI	6-3	J. J. C. Lawson at Dhaka	2002-03
	B	7-58	Mehedi Hasan at Mirpur	2018-19
Highest total	WI	648-9 dec	at Khulna	2012-13
	B	556	at Mirpur	2012-13
Lowest total	WI	111	at Mirpur	2018-19
	B	43	at North Sound	2018

WEST INDIES v AFGHANISTAN

		Captains				
Season	*West Indies*	*Afghanistan*	*T*	*WI*	*Afg*	*D*
2019-20*I*	**J. O. Holder**	**Rashid Khan**	**1**	**1**	**0**	**0**
	In India		**1**	**1**	**0**	**0**
	Totals		**1**	**1**	**0**	**0**

I   Played in India.

SERIES RECORDS

Highest score	WI	111	**S. S. J. Brooks at Lucknow**	2019-20
	Afg	62	**Javed Ahmadi at Lucknow**	2019-20
Best bowling	WI	7-75	**R. R. S. Cornwall at Lucknow**	2019-20
	Afg	5-74	**Hamza Hotak at Lucknow**	2019-20
Highest total	WI	277	**at Lucknow**	2019-20
	Afg	187	**at Lucknow**	2019-20
Lowest total	WI	277	**at Lucknow**	2019-20
	Afg	120	**at Lucknow**	2019-20

NEW ZEALAND v INDIA

		Captains					
Season	New Zealand	India	T	NZ	I	D
1955-56I	H. B. Cave	P. R. Umrigar[1]	5	0	2	3
1964-65I	J. R. Reid	Nawab of Pataudi jnr	4	0	1	3
1967-68N	G. T. Dowling[2]	Nawab of Pataudi jnr	4	1	3	0
1969-70I	G. T. Dowling	Nawab of Pataudi jnr	3	1	1	1
1975-76N	G. M. Turner	B. S. Bedi[3]	3	1	1	1
1976-77I	G. M. Turner	B. S. Bedi	3	0	2	1
1980-81N	G. P. Howarth	S. M. Gavaskar	3	1	0	2
1988-89I	J. G. Wright	D. B. Vengsarkar	3	1	2	0
1989-90N	J. G. Wright	M. Azharuddin	3	1	0	2
1993-94N	K. R. Rutherford	M. Azharuddin	1	0	0	1
1995-96I	L. K. Germon	M. Azharuddin	3	0	1	2
1998-99N†	S. P. Fleming	M. Azharuddin	2	1	0	1
1999-2000I	S. P. Fleming	S. R. Tendulkar	3	0	1	2
2002-03N	S. P. Fleming	S. C. Ganguly	2	2	0	0
2003-04I	S. P. Fleming	S. C. Ganguly[4]	2	0	0	2
2008-09N	D. L. Vettori	M. S. Dhoni[5]	3	0	1	2
2010-11I	D. L. Vettori	M. S. Dhoni	3	0	1	2
2012-13I	L. R. P. L. Taylor	M. S. Dhoni	2	0	2	0
2013-14N	B. B. McCullum	M. S. Dhoni	2	1	0	1
2016-17I	K. S. Williamson[6]	V. Kohli	3	0	3	0
		In India...........................	34	2	16	16
		In New Zealand	23	8	5	10
		Totals	57	10	21	26

I   Played in India.   N   Played in New Zealand.

† *The First Test at Dunedin was abandoned without a ball being bowled and is excluded.*

The following deputised for the official touring captain or were appointed by the home authority for a minor proportion of the series:
[1]Ghulam Ahmed (First). [2]B. W. Sinclair (First). [3]S. M. Gavaskar (First). [4]R. Dravid (Second). [5]V. Sehwag (Second). [6]L. R. P. L. Taylor (Second).

SERIES RECORDS

Highest score	NZ	302	B. B. McCullum at Wellington............	2013-14
	I	231	M. H. Mankad at Madras	1955-56
Best bowling	NZ	7-23	R. J. Hadlee at Wellington	1975-76
	I	8-72	S. Venkataraghavan at Delhi.............	1964-65
Highest total	NZ	680-8 dec	at Wellington.........................	2013-14
	I	583-7 dec	at Ahmedabad	1999-2000
Lowest total	NZ	94	at Hamilton..........................	2002-03
	I	81	at Wellington.........................	1975-76

NEW ZEALAND v PAKISTAN

		Captains					
Season	New Zealand	Pakistan	T	NZ	P	D
1955-56P	H. B. Cave	A. H. Kardar	3	0	2	1
1964-65N	J. R. Reid	Hanif Mohammad	3	0	0	3
1964-65P	J. R. Reid	Hanif Mohammad	3	0	2	1
1969-70P	G. T. Dowling	Intikhab Alam	3	1	0	2
1972-73N	B. E. Congdon	Intikhab Alam	3	0	1	2
1976-77P	G. M. Turner[1]	Mushtaq Mohammad	3	0	2	1
1978-79N	M. G. Burgess	Mushtaq Mohammad	3	0	1	2

Season	New Zealand	*Captains*	*Pakistan*	T	NZ	P	D
1984-85P	J. V. Coney		Zaheer Abbas	3	0	2	1
1984-85N	G. P. Howarth		Javed Miandad	3	2	0	1
1988-89N†	J. G. Wright		Imran Khan	2	0	0	2
1990-91P	M. D. Crowe		Javed Miandad	3	0	3	0
1992-93N	K. R. Rutherford		Javed Miandad	1	0	1	0
1993-94N	K. R. Rutherford		Salim Malik	3	1	2	0
1995-96N	L. K. Germon		Wasim Akram	1	0	1	0
1996-97P	L. K. Germon		Saeed Anwar	2	1	1	0
2000-01N	S. P. Fleming		Moin Khan[2]	3	1	1	1
2002P‡	S. P. Fleming		Waqar Younis	1	0	1	0
2003-04N	S. P. Fleming		Inzamam-ul-Haq	2	0	1	1
2009-10N	D. L. Vettori		Mohammad Yousuf	3	1	1	1
2010-11N	D. L. Vettori		Misbah-ul-Haq	2	0	1	1
2014-15U	B. B. McCullum		Misbah-ul-Haq	3	1	1	1
2016-17N	K. S. Williamson		Misbah-ul-Haq[3]	2	2	0	0
2018-19U	K. S. Williamson		Sarfraz Ahmed	3	2	1	0
	In Pakistan			21	2	13	6
	In New Zealand			31	7	10	14
	In United Arab Emirates			6	3	2	1
	Totals			58	12	25	21

N   Played in New Zealand.   P   Played in Pakistan.   U   Played in United Arab Emirates.

† *The First Test at Dunedin was abandoned without a ball being bowled and is excluded.*
‡ *The Second Test at Karachi was cancelled owing to civil disturbances.*

The following were appointed by the home authority for only a minor proportion of the series or deputised for the official touring captain:
[1]J. M. Parker (Third).   [2]Inzamam-ul-Haq (Third).   [3]Azhar Ali (Second).

SERIES RECORDS

Highest score	NZ	204*	M. S. Sinclair at Christchurch	2000-01
	P	329	Inzamam-ul-Haq at Lahore	2002
Best bowling	NZ	7-52	C. Pringle at Faisalabad	1990-91
	P	8-41	Yasir Shah at Dubai	2018-19
Highest total	NZ	690	at Sharjah	2014-15
	P	643	at Lahore	2002
Lowest total	NZ	70	at Dacca	1955-56
	P	102	at Faisalabad	1990-91

NEW ZEALAND v SRI LANKA

Season	New Zealand	*Captains*	Sri Lanka	T	NZ	SL	D
1982-83N	G. P. Howarth		D. S. de Silva	2	2	0	0
1983-84S	G. P. Howarth		L. R. D. Mendis	3	2	0	1
1986-87S†	J. J. Crowe		L. R. D. Mendis	1	0	0	1
1990-91N	M. D. Crowe[1]		A. Ranatunga	3	0	0	3
1992-93S	M. D. Crowe		A. Ranatunga	2	0	1	1
1994-95N	K. R. Rutherford		A. Ranatunga	2	0	1	1
1996-97N	S. P. Fleming		A. Ranatunga	2	2	0	0
1997-98S	S. P. Fleming		A. Ranatunga	3	1	2	0
2003S	S. P. Fleming		H. P. Tillekeratne	2	0	0	2
2004-05N	S. P. Fleming		M. S. Atapattu	2	1	0	1
2006-07N	S. P. Fleming		D. P. M. D. Jayawardene	2	1	1	0
2009S	D. L. Vettori		K. C. Sangakkara	2	0	2	0
2012-13S	L. R. P. L. Taylor		D. P. M. D. Jayawardene	2	1	1	0

		Captains				
Season	*New Zealand*	*Sri Lanka*	*T*	*NZ*	*SL*	*D*
2014-15*N*	B. B. McCullum	A. D. Mathews	2	2	0	0
2015-16*N*	B. B. McCullum	A. D. Mathews	2	2	0	0
2018-19*N*	K. S. Williamson	L. D. Chandimal	2	1	0	1
2019*S*	**K. S. Williamson**	**F. D. M. Karunaratne**	**2**	**1**	**1**	**0**
	In New Zealand		19	11	2	6
	In Sri Lanka		17	5	7	5
	Totals.		36	16	9	11

N   Played in New Zealand.   S   Played in Sri Lanka.

† *The Second and Third Tests were cancelled owing to civil disturbances.*

The following was appointed by the home authority for only a minor proportion of the series:
[1]I. D. S. Smith (Third).

SERIES RECORDS

Highest score	NZ	299	M. D. Crowe at Wellington	1990-91
	SL	267	P. A. de Silva at Wellington	1990-91
Best bowling	NZ	7-130	D. L. Vettori at Wellington	2006-07
	SL	6-43	H. M. R. K. B. Herath at Galle	2012-13
Highest total	NZ	671-4	at Wellington	1990-91
	SL	498	at Napier	2004-05
Lowest total	NZ	102	at Colombo (SSC)	1992-93
	SL	93	at Wellington	1982-83

NEW ZEALAND v ZIMBABWE

		Captains				
Season	*New Zealand*	*Zimbabwe*	*T*	*NZ*	*Z*	*D*
1992-93*Z*	M. D. Crowe	D. L. Houghton	2	1	0	1
1995-96*N*	L. K. Germon	A. Flower	2	0	0	2
1997-98*Z*	S. P. Fleming	A. D. R. Campbell	2	0	0	2
1997-98*N*	S. P. Fleming	A. D. R. Campbell	2	2	0	0
2000-01*Z*	S. P. Fleming	H. H. Streak	2	2	0	0
2000-01*N*	S. P. Fleming	H. H. Streak	1	0	0	1
2005-06*Z*	S. P. Fleming	T. Taibu	2	2	0	0
2011-12*Z*	L. R. P. L. Taylor	B. R. M. Taylor	1	1	0	0
2011-12*N*	L. R. P. L. Taylor	B. R. M. Taylor	1	1	0	0
2016*Z*	K. S. Williamson	A. G. Cremer	2	2	0	0
	In New Zealand		6	3	0	3
	In Zimbabwe		11	8	0	3
	Totals		17	11	0	6

N   Played in New Zealand.   Z   Played in Zimbabwe.

SERIES RECORDS

Highest score	NZ	173*	L. R. P. L. Taylor at Bulawayo	2016
	Z	203*	G. J. Whittall at Bulawayo	1997-98
Best bowling	NZ	6-26	C. S. Martin at Napier	2011-12
	Z	8-109	P. A. Strang at Bulawayo	2000-01
Highest total	NZ	582-4 dec	at Bulawayo.	2016
	Z	461	at Bulawayo.	1997-98
Lowest total	NZ	207	at Harare	1997-98
	Z	51	at Napier	2011-12

NEW ZEALAND v BANGLADESH

		Captains				
Season	*New Zealand*	*Bangladesh*	*T*	*NZ*	*B*	*D*
2001-02*N*	S. P. Fleming	Khaled Mashud	2	2	0	0
2004-05*B*	S. P. Fleming	Khaled Mashud	2	2	0	0
2007-08*N*	D. L. Vettori	Mohammad Ashraful	2	2	0	0
2008-09*B*	D. L. Vettori	Mohammad Ashraful	2	1	0	1
2009-10*N*	D. L. Vettori	Shakib Al Hasan	1	1	0	0
2013-14*B*	B. B. McCullum	Mushfiqur Rahim	2	0	0	2
2016-17*N*	K. S. Williamson	Mushfiqur Rahim[1]	2	2	0	0
2018-19*N*†	**K. S. Williamson**	**Mahmudullah**	**2**	**2**	**0**	**0**
	In New Zealand		**9**	**9**	**0**	**0**
	In Bangladesh.		6	3	0	3
	Totals.		**15**	**12**	**0**	**3**

B   Played in Bangladesh.   N   Played in New Zealand.

†   *The Third Test was cancelled owing to a terrorist attack on a nearby mosque.*

The following deputised for the official touring captain for only a minor proportion of the series:
[1]Tamim Iqbal (Second).

SERIES RECORDS

Highest score	NZ	202	S. P. Fleming at Chittagong	2004-05
	B	217	Shakib Al Hasan at Wellington.	2016-17
Best bowling	NZ	7-53	C. L. Cairns at Hamilton.	2001-02
	B	7-36	Shakib Al Hasan at Chittagong.	2008-09
Highest total	NZ	**715-6 dec**	**at Hamilton . . . .**	**2018-19**
	B	595-8 dec	at Wellington.	2016-17
Lowest total	NZ	171	at Chittagong.	2008-09
	B	108	at Hamilton	2001-02

INDIA v PAKISTAN

		Captains				
Season	*India*	*Pakistan*	*T*	*I*	*P*	*D*
1952-53*I*	L. Amarnath	A. H. Kardar	5	2	1	2
1954-55*P*	M. H. Mankad	A. H. Kardar	5	0	0	5
1960-61*I*	N. J. Contractor	Fazal Mahmood	5	0	0	5
1978-79*P*	B. S. Bedi	Mushtaq Mohammad	3	0	2	1
1979-80*I*	S. M. Gavaskar[1]	Asif Iqbal	6	2	0	4
1982-83*P*	S. M. Gavaskar	Imran Khan	6	0	3	3
1983-84*I*	Kapil Dev	Zaheer Abbas	3	0	0	3
1984-85*P*	S. M. Gavaskar	Zaheer Abbas	2	0	0	2
1986-87*I*	Kapil Dev	Imran Khan	5	0	1	4
1989-90*P*	K. Srikkanth	Imran Khan	4	0	0	4
1998-99*I*	M. Azharuddin	Wasim Akram	2	1	1	0
1998-99*I*†	M. Azharuddin	Wasim Akram	1	0	1	0
2003-04*P*	S. C. Ganguly[2]	Inzamam-ul-Haq	3	2	1	0
2004-05*I*	S. C. Ganguly	Inzamam-ul-Haq	3	1	1	1
2005-06*P*	R. Dravid	Inzamam-ul-Haq[3]	3	0	1	2

			Captains				
Season	*India*		*Pakistan*	*T*	*I*	*P*	*D*
2007-08*I*	A. Kumble		Shoaib Malik[4]	3	1	0	2
	In India			33	7	5	21
	In Pakistan			26	2	7	17
	Totals			59	9	12	38

I   Played in India.   P   Played in Pakistan.

† *This Test was part of the Asian Test Championship and was not counted as part of the preceding bilateral series.*

The following were appointed by the home authority for only a minor proportion of the series or deputised for the official touring captain:
[1]G. R. Viswanath (Sixth). [2]R. Dravid (First and Second). [3]Younus Khan (Third). [4]Younis Khan (Second and Third).

SERIES RECORDS

Highest score	*I*	309	V. Sehwag at Multan		2003-04
	P	280*	Javed Miandad at Hyderabad		1982-83
Best bowling	*I*	10-74	A. Kumble at Delhi		1998-99
	P	8-60	Imran Khan at Karachi		1982-83
Highest total	*I*	675-5 dec	at Multan		2003-04
	P	699-5	at Lahore		1989-90
Lowest total	*I*	106	at Lucknow		1952-53
	P	116	at Bangalore		1986-87

INDIA v SRI LANKA

		Captains				
Season	*India*	*Sri Lanka*	*T*	*I*	*SL*	*D*
1982-83*I*	S. M. Gavaskar	B. Warnapura	1	0	0	1
1985-86*S*	Kapil Dev	L. R. D. Mendis	3	0	1	2
1986-87*I*	Kapil Dev	L. R. D. Mendis	3	2	0	1
1990-91*I*	M. Azharuddin	A. Ranatunga	1	1	0	0
1993-94*S*	M. Azharuddin	A. Ranatunga	3	1	0	2
1993-94*I*	M. Azharuddin	A. Ranatunga	3	3	0	0
1997-98*S*	S. R. Tendulkar	A. Ranatunga	2	0	0	2
1997-98*I*	S. R. Tendulkar	A. Ranatunga	3	0	0	3
1998-99*S*†	M. Azharuddin	A. Ranatunga	1	0	0	1
2001*S*	S. C. Ganguly	S. T. Jayasuriya	3	1	2	0
2005-06*I*	R. Dravid[1]	M. S. Atapattu	3	2	0	1
2008*S*	A. Kumble	D. P. M. D. Jayawardene	3	1	2	0
2009-10*I*	M. S. Dhoni	K. C. Sangakkara	3	2	0	1
2010*S*	M. S. Dhoni	K. C. Sangakkara	3	1	1	1
2015-16*S*	V. Kohli	A. D. Mathews	3	2	1	0
2017*S*	V. Kohli	L. D. Chandimal[2]	3	3	0	0
2017-18*I*	V. Kohli	L. D. Chandimal	3	1	0	2
	In India		20	11	0	9
	In Sri Lanka		24	9	7	8
	Totals		44	20	7	17

I   Played in India.   S   Played in Sri Lanka.

† *This Test was part of the Asian Test Championship.*

The following were appointed by the home authority for only a minor proportion of the series:
[1]V. Sehwag (Third). [2]H. M. R. K. B. Herath (First).

SERIES RECORDS

Highest score	I	293	V. Sehwag at Mumbai (BS).	2009-10
	SL	340	S. T. Jayasuriya at Colombo (RPS).	1997-98
Best bowling	I	7-51	Maninder Singh at Nagpur	1986-87
	SL	8-87	M. Muralitharan at Colombo (SSC)	2001
Highest total	I	726-9 dec	at Mumbai (BS).	2009-10
	SL	952-6 dec	at Colombo (RPS)	1997-98
Lowest total	I	112	at Galle.	2015-16
	SL	82	at Chandigarh.	1990-91

INDIA v ZIMBABWE

		Captains					
Season	India		Zimbabwe	T	I	Z	D
1992-93Z	M. Azharuddin		D. L. Houghton	1	0	0	1
1992-93I	M. Azharuddin		D. L. Houghton	1	1	0	0
1998-99Z	M. Azharuddin		A. D. R. Campbell	1	0	1	0
2000-01I	S. C. Ganguly		H. H. Streak	2	1	0	1
2001Z	S. C. Ganguly		H. H. Streak	2	1	1	0
2001-02I	S. C. Ganguly		S. V. Carlisle	2	2	0	0
2005-06Z	S. C. Ganguly		T. Taibu	2	2	0	0
	In India.			5	4	0	1
	In Zimbabwe			6	3	2	1
	Totals			11	7	2	2

I   Played in India.   Z   Played in Zimbabwe.

SERIES RECORDS

Highest score	I	227	V. G. Kambli at Delhi	1992-93
	Z	232*	A. Flower at Nagpur	2000-01
Best bowling	I	7-59	I. K. Pathan at Harare.	2005-06
	Z	6-73	H. H. Streak at Harare	2005-06
Highest total	I	609-6 dec	at Nagpur	2000-01
	Z	503-6	at Nagpur	2000-01
Lowest total	I	173	at Harare.	1998-99
	Z	146	at Delhi.	2001-02

INDIA v BANGLADESH

		Captains					
Season	India		Bangladesh	T	I	B	D
2000-01B	S. C. Ganguly		Naimur Rahman	1	1	0	0
2004-05B	S. C. Ganguly		Habibul Bashar	2	2	0	0
2007B	R. Dravid		Habibul Bashar	2	1	0	1
2009-10B	M. S. Dhoni[1]		Shakib Al Hasan	2	2	0	0
2015B	V. Kohli		Mushfiqur Rahim	1	0	0	1
2016-17I	V. Kohli		Mushfiqur Rahim	1	1	0	0
2019-20I	**V. Kohli**		**Mominul Haque**	**2**	**2**	**0**	**0**
	In Bangladesh.			8	6	0	2
	In India			**3**	**3**	**0**	**0**
	Totals.			11	9	0	2

B   Played in Bangladesh.   I   Played in India.

The following deputised for the official touring captain for a minor proportion of the series:
[1]V. Sehwag (First).

SERIES RECORDS

Highest score	I	248*	S. R. Tendulkar at Dhaka		2004-05
	B	158*	Mohammad Ashraful at Chittagong		2004-05
Best bowling	I	7-87	Zaheer Khan at Mirpur		2009-10
	B	6-132	Naimur Rahman at Dhaka		2000-01
Highest total	I	687-6 dec	at Hyderabad		2016-17
	B	400	at Dhaka.................................		2000-01
Lowest total	I	243	at Chittagong		2009-10
	B	91	at Dhaka.................................		2000-01

INDIA v AFGHANISTAN

		Captains				
Season	*India*	*Afghanistan*	*T*	*I*	*Afg*	*D*
2018*I*	A. M. Rahane	Asghar Stanikzai†	1	1	0	0
	In India........		1	1	0	0
	Totals		1	1	0	0

I Played in India.

† *Later known as Asghar Afghan.*

SERIES RECORDS

Highest score	I	107	S. Dhawan at Bangalore		2018
	Afg	36*	Hashmatullah Shahidi at Bangalore...........		2018
Best bowling	I	4-17	R. A. Jadeja at Bangalore		2018
	Afg	3-51	Yamin Ahmadzai at Bangalore		2018
Highest total	I	474	at Bangalore..............................		2018
	Afg	109	at Bangalore..............................		2018
Lowest total	I	474	at Bangalore..............................		2018
	Afg	103	at Bangalore..............................		2018

PAKISTAN v SRI LANKA

		Captains				
Season	*Pakistan*	*Sri Lanka*	*T*	*P*	*SL*	*D*
1981-82*P*	Javed Miandad	B. Warnapura[1]	3	2	0	1
1985-86*P*	Javed Miandad	L. R. D. Mendis	3	2	0	1
1985-86*S*	Imran Khan	L. R. D. Mendis	3	1	1	1
1991-92*P*	Imran Khan	P. A. de Silva	3	1	0	2
1994-95*S*†	Salim Malik	A. Ranatunga	2	2	0	0
1995-96*P*	Ramiz Raja	A. Ranatunga	3	1	2	0
1996-97*S*	Ramiz Raja	A. Ranatunga	2	0	0	2
1998-99*P*‡	Wasim Akram	H. P. Tillekeratne	1	0	0	1
1998-99*B*‡	Wasim Akram	P. A. de Silva	1	1	0	0
1999-2000*P*	Saeed Anwar[2]	S. T. Jayasuriya	3	1	2	0
2000*S*	Moin Khan	S. T. Jayasuriya	3	2	0	1
2001-02*P*‡	Waqar Younis	S. T. Jayasuriya	1	0	1	0
2004-05*P*	Inzamam-ul-Haq	M. S. Atapattu	2	1	1	0
2005-06*S*	Inzamam-ul-Haq	D. P. M. D. Jayawardene	2	1	0	1
2008-09*P*§	Younis Khan	D. P. M. D. Jayawardene	2	0	0	2
2009*S*	Younis Khan	K. C. Sangakkara	3	0	2	1
2011-12*U*	Misbah-ul-Haq	T. M. Dilshan	3	1	0	2
2012*S*	Misbah-ul-Haq[3]	D. P. M. D. Jayawardene	3	0	1	2

Captains

Season	Pakistan	Sri Lanka	T	P	SL	D
2013-14*U*	Misbah-ul-Haq	A. D. Mathews	3	1	1	1
2014*S*	Misbah-ul-Haq	A. D. Mathews	2	0	2	0
2015*S*	Misbah-ul-Haq	A. D. Mathews	3	2	1	0
2017-18*U*	Sarfraz Ahmed	L. D. Chandimal	2	0	2	0
2019-20*P*	**Azhar Ali**	**F. D. M. Karunaratne**	**2**	**1**	**0**	**1**
	In Pakistan		23	9	6	8
	In Sri Lanka		23	8	7	8
	In Bangladesh		1	1	0	0
	In United Arab Emirates		8	2	3	3
	Totals		55	20	16	19

P *Played in Pakistan.* *S* *Played in Sri Lanka.* *B* *Played in Bangladesh.*
U *Played in United Arab Emirates.*

† *One Test was cancelled owing to the threat of civil disturbances following a general election.*
‡ *These Tests were part of the Asian Test Championship.*
§ *The Second Test ended after a terrorist attack on the Sri Lankan team bus on the third day.*

The following deputised for the official touring captain or were appointed by the home authority for only a minor proportion of the series:
[1]L. R. D. Mendis (Second). [2]Moin Khan (Third). [3]Mohammad Hafeez (First).

SERIES RECORDS

Highest score	P	313	Younis Khan at Karachi	2008-09
	SL	253	S. T. Jayasuriya at Faisalabad	2004-05
Best bowling	P	8-58	Imran Khan at Lahore	1981-82
	SL	9-127	H. M. R. K. B. Herath at Colombo (SSC)	2014
Highest total	P	765-6 dec	at Karachi	2008-09
	SL	644-7 dec	at Karachi	2008-09
Lowest total	P	90	at Colombo (PSS)	2009
	SL	71	at Kandy	1994-95

PAKISTAN v ZIMBABWE

Captains

Season	Pakistan	Zimbabwe	T	P	Z	D
1993-94*P*	Wasim Akram[1]	A. Flower	3	2	0	1
1994-95*Z*	Salim Malik	A. Flower	3	2	1	0
1996-97*P*	Wasim Akram	A. D. R. Campbell	2	1	0	1
1997-98*Z*	Rashid Latif	A. D. R. Campbell	2	1	0	1
1998-99*P*†	Aamir Sohail[2]	A. D. R. Campbell	2	0	1	1
2002-03*Z*	Waqar Younis	A. D. R. Campbell	2	2	0	0
2011-12*Z*	Misbah-ul-Haq	B. R. M. Taylor	1	1	0	0
2013-14*Z*	Misbah-ul-Haq	B. R. M. Taylor[3]	2	1	1	0
	In Pakistan		7	3	1	3
	In Zimbabwe		10	7	2	1
	Totals		17	10	3	4

P *Played in Pakistan.* *Z* *Played in Zimbabwe.*

† *The Third Test at Faisalabad was abandoned without a ball being bowled and is excluded.*

The following were appointed by the home authority for only a minor proportion of the series:
[1]Waqar Younis (First). [2]Moin Khan (Second). [3]H. Masakadza (First).

SERIES RECORDS

Highest score	P	257*	Wasim Akram at Sheikhupura	1996-97
	Z	201*	G. W. Flower at Harare	1994-95
Best bowling	Z	7-66	Saqlain Mushtaq at Bulawayo	2002-03
	Z	6-90	H. H. Streak at Harare	1994-95
Highest total	P	553	at Sheikhupura	1996-97
	Z	544-4 dec	at Harare	1994-95
Lowest total	P	103	at Peshawar	1998-99
	Z	120	at Harare	2013-14

PAKISTAN v BANGLADESH

		Captains				
Season	*Pakistan*	*Bangladesh*	*T*	*P*	*B*	*D*
2001-02P†	Waqar Younis	Naimur Rahman	1	1	0	0
2001-02B	Waqar Younis	Khaled Mashud	2	2	0	0
2003-04P	Rashid Latif	Khaled Mahmud	3	3	0	0
2011-12B	Misbah-ul-Haq	Mushfiqur Rahim	2	2	0	0
2014-15B	Misbah-ul-Haq	Mushfiqur Rahim	2	1	0	1
	In Pakistan		4	4	0	0
	In Bangladesh		6	5	0	1
	Totals		10	9	0	1

P   Played in Pakistan.   B   Played in Bangladesh.

†   *This Test was part of the Asian Test Championship.*

SERIES RECORDS

Highest score	P	226	Azhar Ali at Mirpur	2014-15
	B	206	Tamim Iqbal at Khulna	2014-15
Best bowling	P	7-77	Danish Kaneria at Dhaka	2001-02
	B	6-82	Shakib Al Hasan at Mirpur	2011-12
Highest total	P	628	at Khulna	2014-15
	B	555-6	at Khulna	2014-15
Lowest total	P	175	at Multan	2003-04
	B	96	at Peshawar	2003-04

PAKISTAN v IRELAND

		Captains				
Season	*Pakistan*	*Ireland*	*T*	*P*	*Ire*	*D*
2018Ire	Sarfraz Ahmed	W. T. S. Porterfield	1	1	0	0
	In Ireland		1	1	0	0
	Totals		1	1	0	0

Ire   Played in Ireland.

SERIES RECORDS

Highest score	P	83	Fahim Ashraf at Malahide	2018
	Ire	118	K. J. O'Brien at Malahide	2018
Best bowling	P	5-66	Mohammad Abbas at Malahide	2018
	Ire	4-45	T. J. Murtagh at Malahide	2018
Highest total	P	310-9 dec	at Malahide	2018
	Ire	339	at Malahide	2018
Lowest total	Ire	130	at Malahide	2018

SRI LANKA v ZIMBABWE

		Captains				
Season	*Sri Lanka*	*Zimbabwe*	*T*	*SL*	*Z*	*D*
1994-95Z	A. Ranatunga	A. Flower	3	0	0	3
1996-97S	A. Ranatunga	A. D. R. Campbell	2	2	0	0
1997-98S	A. Ranatunga	A. D. R. Campbell	2	2	0	0
1999-2000Z	S. T. Jayasuriya	A. Flower	3	1	0	2
2001-02S	S. T. Jayasuriya	S. V. Carlisle	3	3	0	0
2003-04Z	M. S. Atapattu	T. Taibu	2	2	0	0
2016-17Z	H. M. R. K. B. Herath	A. G. Cremer	2	2	0	0
2017S	L. D. Chandimal	A. G. Cremer	1	1	0	0
2019-20Z	**F. D. M. Karunaratne**	**S. C. Williams**	**2**	**1**	**0**	**1**
	In Sri Lanka..............................		8	8	0	0
	In Zimbabwe..........................		**12**	**6**	**0**	**6**
	Totals..................................		20	14	0	6

S   Played in Sri Lanka.   Z   Played in Zimbabwe.

SERIES RECORDS

Highest score	SL	270	K. C. Sangakkara at Bulawayo	2003-04
	Z	266	D. L. Houghton at Bulawayo..............	1994-95
Best bowling	SL	9-51	M. Muralitharan at Kandy	2001-02
	Z	**7-113**	**Sikandar Raza at Harare**	**2019-20**
Highest total	SL	713-3 dec	at Bulawayo............................	2003-04
	Z	462-9 dec	at Bulawayo...........................	1994-95
Lowest total	SL	218	at Bulawayo...........................	1994-95
	Z	79	at Galle...............................	2001-02

SRI LANKA v BANGLADESH

		Captains				
Season	*Sri Lanka*	*Bangladesh*	*T*	*SL*	*B*	*D*
2001-02S†	S. T. Jayasuriya	Naimur Rahman	1	1	0	0
2002S	S. T. Jayasuriya	Khaled Mashud	2	2	0	0
2005-06S	M. S. Atapattu	Habibul Bashar	2	2	0	0
2005-06B	D. P. M. D. Jayawardene	Habibul Bashar	2	2	0	0
2007S	D. P. M. D. Jayawardene	Mohammad Ashraful	3	3	0	0
2008-09B	D. P. M. D. Jayawardene	Mohammad Ashraful	2	2	0	0
2012-13S	A. D. Mathews	Mushfiqur Rahim	2	1	0	1
2013-14B	A. D. Mathews	Mushfiqur Rahim	2	1	0	1
2016-17S	H. M. R. K. B. Herath	Mushfiqur Rahim	2	1	1	0
2017-18B	L. D. Chandimal	Mahmudullah	2	1	0	1
	In Sri Lanka................................		12	10	1	1
	In Bangladesh		8	6	0	2
	Totals...................................		20	16	1	3

S   Played in Sri Lanka.   B   Played in Bangladesh.

†   *This Test was part of the Asian Test Championship.*

SERIES RECORDS

Highest score	SL	319	K. C. Sangakkara at Chittagong..............	2013-14
	B	200	Mushfiqur Rahim at Galle	2012-13
Best bowling	SL	7-89	H. M. R. K. B. Herath at Colombo (RPS)....	2012-13
	B	5-70	Shakib Al Hasan at Mirpur	2008-09
Highest total	SL	730-6 dec	at Mirpur	2013-14
	B	638	at Galle................................	2012-13
Lowest total	SL	222	at Mirpur	2017-18
	B	62	at Colombo (PSS)	2007

ZIMBABWE v BANGLADESH

		Captains					
Season	Zimbabwe	Bangladesh	T	Z	B	D	
2000-01Z	H. H. Streak	Naimur Rahman	2	2	0	0	
2001-02B	B. A. Murphy[1]	Naimur Rahman	2	1	0	1	
2003-04Z	H. H. Streak	Habibul Bashar	2	1	0	1	
2004-05B	T. Taibu	Habibul Bashar	2	0	1	1	
2011-12Z	B. R. M. Taylor	Shakib Al Hasan	1	1	0	0	
2012-13Z	B. R. M. Taylor	Mushfiqur Rahim	2	1	1	0	
2014-15B	B. R. M. Taylor	Mushfiqur Rahim	3	0	3	0	
2018-19B	H. Masakadza	Mahmudullah	2	1	1	1	
	In Zimbabwe		7	5	1	1	
	In Bangladesh..................		9	2	5	2	
	Totals		16	7	6	3	

Z   Played in Zimbabwe.   B   Played in Bangladesh.

The following deputised for the official touring captain:

[1]S. V. Carlisle (Second).

SERIES RECORDS

Highest score	Z	171	B. R. M. Taylor at Harare	2012-13
	B	219*	Mushfiqur Rahim at Mirpur................	2018-19
Best bowling	Z	6-59	D. T. Hondo at Dhaka	2004-05
	B	8-39	Taijul Islam at Mirpur	2014-15
Highest total	Z	542-7 dec	at Chittagong	2001-02
	B	522-7 dec	at Mirpur	2018-19
Lowest total	Z	114	at Mirpur	2014-15
	B	107	at Dhaka................................	2001-02

BANGLADESH v AFGHANISTAN

	Captains					
Season	Bangladesh	Afghanistan	T	B	Afg	D
2019-20B	Shakib Al Hasan	Rashid Khan	1	0	1	0
	In Bangladesh ..		1	0	1	0
	Totals		1	0	1	0

B   Played in Bangladesh.

SERIES RECORDS

Highest score	B	52	Mominul Haque at Chittagong	2019-20
	Afg	102	Rahmat Shah at Chittagong.	2019-20
Best bowling	B	4-116	Taijul Islam at Chittagong	2019-20
	Afg	6-49	Rashid Khan at Chittagong	2019-20
Highest total	B	205	at Chittagong	2019-20
	Afg	342	at Chittagong	2019-20
Lowest total	B	173	at Chittagong	2019-20
	Afg	260	at Chittagong	2019-20

IRELAND v AFGHANISTAN

		Captains					
Season	Ireland		Afghanistan	T	Ire	Afg	D
2018-19*I*	W. T. S. Porterfield		Asghar Afghan	1	0	1	0
	In India			1	0	1	0
	Totals.			1	0	1	0

I   Played in India.

SERIES RECORDS

Highest score	Ire	82	A. Balbirnie at Dehradun	2018-19
	Afg	98	Rahmat Shah at Dehradun	2018-19
Best bowling	Ire	3-28	S. R. Thompson at Dehradun	2018-19
	Afg	5-82	Rashid Khan at Dehradun	2018-19
Highest total	Ire	288	at Dehradun	2018-19
	Afg	314	at Dehradun	2018-19
Lowest total	Ire	172	at Dehradun	2018-19
	Afg	314	at Dehradun	2018-19

TEST GROUNDS

in chronological order

	City and Ground	*First Test Match*		*Tests*
1	Melbourne, Melbourne Cricket Ground	March 15, 1877	A v E	112
2	London, Kennington Oval	September 6, 1880	E v A	102
3	Sydney, Sydney Cricket Ground (No. 1)	February 17, 1882	A v E	108
4	Manchester, Old Trafford	July 11, 1884	E v A	79
5	London, Lord's	July 21, 1884	E v A	139
6	Adelaide, Adelaide Oval	December 12, 1884	A v E	78
7	Port Elizabeth, St George's Park	March 12, 1889	SA v E	31
8	Cape Town, Newlands	March 25, 1889	SA v E	58
9	Johannesburg, Old Wanderers	March 2, 1896	SA v E	22
	Now the site of Johannesburg Railway Station.			
10	Nottingham, Trent Bridge	June 1, 1899	E v A	63
11	Leeds, Headingley	June 29, 1899	E v A	78
12	Birmingham, Edgbaston	May 29, 1902	E v A	52
13	Sheffield, Bramall Lane	July 3, 1902	E v A	1
	Sheffield United Football Club have built a stand over the cricket pitch.			
14	Durban, Lord's	January 21, 1910	SA v E	4
	Ground destroyed and built on.			
15	Durban, Kingsmead	January 18, 1923	SA v E	44

	City and Ground	First Test Match		Tests
16	Brisbane, Exhibition Ground	November 30, 1928	A v E	2
	No longer used for cricket.			
17	Christchurch, Lancaster Park	January 10, 1930	NZ v E	40
	Also known under sponsors' names.			
18	**Bridgetown, Kensington Oval**	**January 11, 1930**	**WI v E**	**54**
19	**Wellington, Basin Reserve**	**January 24, 1930**	**NZ v E**	**63**
20	Port-of-Spain, Queen's Park Oval	February 1, 1930	WI v E	61
21	Auckland, Eden Park	February 14, 1930	NZ v E	50
22	Georgetown, Bourda	February 21, 1930	WI v E	30
23	**Kingston, Sabina Park**	**April 3, 1930**	**WI v E**	**52**
24	**Brisbane, Woolloongabba**	**November 27, 1931**	**A v SA**	**62**
25	Bombay, Gymkhana Ground	December 15, 1933	I v E	1
	No longer used for first-class cricket.			
26	**Calcutta** (now **Kolkata**), **Eden Gardens**	**January 5, 1934**	**I v E**	**42**
27	Madras (now *Chennai*),	February 10, 1934	I v E	32
	Chepauk (Chidambaram Stadium)			
28	Delhi, Feroz Shah Kotla	November 10, 1948	I v WI	34
29	Bombay (now *Mumbai*), Brabourne Stadium	December 9, 1948	I v WI	18
	Rarely used for first-class cricket.			
30	Johannesburg, Ellis Park	December 27, 1948	SA v E	6
	Mainly a football and rugby stadium, no longer used for cricket.			
31	Kanpur, Green Park (Modi Stadium)	January 12, 1952	I v E	22
32	Lucknow, University Ground	October 25, 1952	I v P	1
	Ground destroyed, now partly under a river bed.			
33	Dacca (now *Dhaka*),	January 1, 1955	P v I	17
	Dacca (now *Bangabandhu*) Stadium			
	Originally in East Pakistan, now Bangladesh, no longer used for cricket.			
34	Bahawalpur, Dring (now *Bahawal*) Stadium	January 15, 1955	P v I	1
	Still used for first-class cricket.			
35	Lahore, Lawrence Gardens (Bagh-e-Jinnah)	January 29, 1955	P v I	3
	Still used for club and occasional first-class matches.			
36	Peshawar, Services Ground	February 13, 1955	P v I	1
	Superseded by new stadium.			
37	**Karachi, National Stadium**	**February 26, 1955**	**P v I**	**42**
38	Dunedin, Carisbrook	March 11, 1955	NZ v E	10
39	Hyderabad, Fateh Maidan (Lal Bahadur Stadium)	November 19, 1955	I v NZ	3
40	Madras, Corporation Stadium	January 6, 1956	I v NZ	9
	Superseded by rebuilt Chepauk Stadium.			
41	**Johannesburg, Wanderers**	**December 24, 1956**	**SA v E**	**41**
42	Lahore, Gaddafi Stadium	November 21, 1959	P v A	40
43	Rawalpindi, Pindi Club Ground	March 27, 1965	P v NZ	1
	Superseded by new stadium.			
44	Nagpur, Vidarbha CA Ground	October 3, 1969	I v NZ	9
	Superseded by new stadium.			
45	Perth, Western Australian CA Ground	December 11, 1970	A v E	44
	Superseded by new stadium.			
46	Hyderabad, Niaz Stadium	March 16, 1973	P v E	5
47	Bangalore, Karnataka State CA Ground	November 22, 1974	I v WI	23
	(Chinnaswamy Stadium)			
48	Bombay (now *Mumbai*), Wankhede Stadium	January 23, 1975	I v WI	25
49	Faisalabad, Iqbal Stadium	October 16, 1978	P v I	24
50	Napier, McLean Park	February 16, 1979	NZ v P	10
51	Multan, Ibn-e-Qasim Bagh Stadium	December 30, 1980	P v WI	1
	Superseded by new stadium.			
52	St John's (Antigua), Recreation Ground	March 27, 1981	WI v E	22
53	**Colombo, P. Saravanamuttu Stadium/**	**February 17, 1982**	**SL v E**	**22**
	P. Sara Oval			
54	Kandy, Asgiriya Stadium	April 22, 1983	SL v A	21
	Superseded by new stadium at Pallekele.			
55	Jullundur, Burlton Park	September 24, 1983	I v P	1

	City and Ground	First Test Match		Tests
56	Ahmedabad, Sardar Patel (Gujarat) Stadium	November 12, 1983	I v WI	12
57	Colombo, Sinhalese Sports Club Ground	March 16, 1984	SL v NZ	43
58	Colombo, Colombo Cricket Club Ground	March 24, 1984	SL v NZ	3
59	Sialkot, Jinnah Stadium	October 27, 1985	P v SL	4
60	Cuttack, Barabati Stadium	January 4, 1987	I v SL	2
61	Jaipur, Sawai Mansingh Stadium	February 21, 1987	I v P	1
62	Hobart, Bellerive Oval	December 16, 1989	A v SL	13
63	Chandigarh, Sector 16 Stadium	November 23, 1990	I v SL	1
	Superseded by Mohali ground.			
64	**Hamilton, Seddon Park**	**February 22, 1991**	**NZ v SL**	**26**
	Also known under various sponsors' names.			
65	Gujranwala, Municipal Stadium	December 20, 1991	P v SL	1
66	Colombo, R. Premadasa (Khettarama) Stadium	August 28, 1992	SL v A	9
67	Moratuwa, Tyronne Fernando Stadium	September 8, 1992	SL v A	4
68	**Harare, Harare Sports Club**	**October 18, 1992**	**Z v I**	**36**
69	Bulawayo, Bulawayo Athletic Club	November 1, 1992	Z v NZ	1
	Superseded by Queens Sports Club ground.			
70	Karachi, Defence Stadium	December 1, 1993	P v Z	1
71	**Rawalpindi, Rawalpindi Cricket Stadium**	**December 9, 1993**	**P v Z**	**9**
72	Lucknow, K. D. "Babu" Singh Stadium	January 18, 1994	I v SL	1
73	Bulawayo, Queens Sports Club	October 20, 1994	Z v SL	23
74	Mohali, Punjab Cricket Association Stadium	December 10, 1994	I v WI	13
75	Peshawar, Arbab Niaz Stadium	September 8, 1995	P v SL	6
76	**Centurion (*ex Verwoerdburg*), Centurion Park**	**November 16, 1995**	**SA v E**	**25**
77	Sheikhupura, Municipal Stadium	October 17, 1996	P v Z	2
78	St Vincent, Arnos Vale	June 20, 1997	WI v SL	3
79	**Galle, International Stadium**	**June 3, 1998**	**SL v NZ**	**33**
80	Bloemfontein, Springbok Park	October 29, 1999	SA v Z	5
	Also known under various sponsors' names.			
81	Multan, Multan Cricket Stadium	August 29, 2001	P v B	5
82	Chittagong, Chittagong Stadium	November 15, 2001	B v Z	8
	Also known as M. A. Aziz Stadium.			
83	Sharjah, Sharjah Cricket Association Stadium	January 31, 2002	P v WI	9
84	St George's, Grenada, Queen's Park New Stadium	June 28, 2002	WI v NZ	3
85	East London, Buffalo Park	October 18, 2002	SA v B	1
86	Potchefstroom, North West Cricket Stadium	October 25, 2002	SA v B	2
	Now known under sponsor's name.			
87	Chester-le-Street, Riverside Ground	June 5, 2003	E v Z	6
	Also known under sponsor's name.			
88	**Gros Islet, St Lucia, Beausejour Stadium**	**June 20, 2003**	**WI v SL**	**7**
	Now known as Darren Sammy Stadium.			
89	Darwin, Marrara Cricket Ground	July 18, 2003	A v B	2
90	Cairns, Cazaly's Football Park	July 25, 2003	A v B	2
	Also known under sponsor's name.			
91	**Chittagong, Chittagong Divisional Stadium**	**February 28, 2006**	**B v SL**	**19**
	Also known as Bir Shrestha Shahid Ruhul Amin Stadium/Zohur Ahmed Chowdhury Stadium.			
92	Bogra, Shaheed Chandu Stadium	March 8, 2006	B v SL	1
93	Fatullah, Narayanganj Osmani Stadium	April 9, 2006	B v A	2
94	Basseterre, St Kitts, Warner Park	June 22, 2006	WI v I	3
95	Mirpur (Dhaka), Shere Bangla Natl Stadium	May 25, 2007	B v I	19
96	Dunedin, University Oval	January 4, 2008	NZ v B	8
97	Providence Stadium, Guyana	March 22, 2008	WI v SL	2
98	**North Sound, Antigua, Sir Vivian Richards Stadium**	**May 30, 2008**	**WI v A**	**8**
99	Nagpur, Vidarbha CA Stadium, Jamtha	November 6, 2008	I v A	6
100	Cardiff, Sophia Gardens	July 8, 2009	E v A	3
	Now known under sponsor's name.			
101	Hyderabad, Rajiv Gandhi Intl Stadium	November 12, 2010	I v NZ	5
102	Dubai, Dubai Sports City Stadium	November 12, 2010	P v SA	13
103	Abu Dhabi, Sheikh Zayed Stadium	November 20, 2010	P v SA	13

	City and Ground	First Test Match		Tests
104	Pallekele, Muttiah Muralitharan Stadium	December 1, 2010	SL v WI	7
105	Southampton, Rose Bowl	June 16, 2011	E v SL	3
	Now known under sponsor's name.			
106	Roseau, Dominica, Windsor Park	July 6, 2011	WI v I	5
107	Khulna, Khulna Division Stadium	November 21, 2012	B v WI	3
	Also known as Bir Shrestha Shahid Flight Lt Motiur Rahman/Shaikh Abu Naser Stadium.			
108	Christchurch, Hagley Oval	December 26, 2014	NZ v SL	6
109	**Indore, Maharani Usharaje Trust Ground**	**October 8, 2016**	**I v NZ**	**2**
110	Rajkot, Saurashtra CA Stadium	November 9, 2016	I v E	2
111	**Visakhapatnam, Andhra CA-Visakhapatnam DCA Stadium**	**November 17, 2016**	**I v E**	**2**
112	**Pune (Gahunje), Subrata Roy Sahara Stadium**	**February 23, 2017**	**I v A**	**2**
113	**Ranchi, Jharkhand State CA Oval Ground**	**March 16, 2017**	**I v A**	**2**
114	Dharamsala, Himachal Pradesh CA Stadium	March 25, 2017	I v A	1
115	Malahide (Dublin), The Village	May 11, 2018	Ire v P	1
116	Sylhet, Sylhet Stadium	November 3, 2018	B v Z	1
117	**Perth, Optus Stadium**	**December 14, 2018**	**A v I**	**2**
118	Canberra, Manuka Oval	February 1, 2019	A v SL	1
119	**Dehradun, Rajiv Gandhi Cricket Stadium**	**March 15, 2019**	**Afg v Ire**	**1**
120	**Mount Maunganui, Bay Oval**	**November 21, 2019**	**NZ v E**	**1**
121	**Lucknow, Ekana Cricket Stadium**	**November 27, 2019**	**Afg v WI**	**1**
	Also known as Bharat Ratna Shri Atal Bihari Vajpayee Ekana Cricket Stadium.			

Bold type denotes grounds used for Test cricket since January 1, 2019.

ONE-DAY INTERNATIONAL RECORDS

Matches in this section do not have first-class status.

This section covers one-day international cricket to December 31, 2019. Bold type denotes performances since January 1, 2019, or, in career figures, players who have appeared in one-day internationals since that date.

SUMMARY OF ONE-DAY INTERNATIONALS

1970-71 to December 31, 2019

	Opponents	Matches	Won by														Tied	NR
			E	A	SA	WI	NZ	I	P	SL	Z	B	Ire	Afg	Ass	Oth		
England	Australia	149	62	82	–	–	–	–	–	–	–	–	–	–	–	–	2	3
	South Africa	60	27	–	29	–	–	–	–	–	–	–	–	–	–	–	1	3
	West Indies	102	52	–	–	44	–	–	–	–	–	–	–	–	–	–	–	6
	New Zealand	91	42	–	–	–	43	–	–	–	–	–	–	–	–	–	2	4
	India	100	42	–	–	–	–	53	–	–	–	–	–	–	–	–	2	3
	Pakistan	88	53	–	–	–	–	–	32	–	–	–	–	–	–	–	–	3
	Sri Lanka	75	36	–	–	–	–	–	–	36	–	–	–	–	–	–	1	2
	Zimbabwe	30	21	–	–	–	–	–	–	–	8	–	–	–	–	–	–	1
	Bangladesh	21	17	–	–	–	–	–	–	–	–	4	–	–	–	–	–	–
	Ireland	10	8	–	–	–	–	–	–	–	–	–	1	–	–	–	–	1
	Afghanistan	2	2	–	–	–	–	–	–	–	–	–	–	0	–	–	–	–
	Associates	15	13	–	–	–	–	–	–	–	–	–	–	–	1	–	–	1
Australia	South Africa	100	–	48	48	–	–	–	–	–	–	–	–	–	–	–	3	1
	West Indies	140	–	74	–	60	–	–	–	–	–	–	–	–	–	–	3	3
	New Zealand	137	–	91	–	–	39	–	–	–	–	–	–	–	–	–	–	7
	India	137	–	77	–	–	–	50	–	–	–	–	–	–	–	–	–	10
	Pakistan	104	–	68	–	–	–	–	32	–	–	–	–	–	–	–	1	3
	Sri Lanka	97	–	61	–	–	–	–	–	32	–	–	–	–	–	–	–	4
	Zimbabwe	30	–	27	–	–	–	–	–	–	2	–	–	–	–	–	–	1
	Bangladesh	21	–	19	–	–	–	–	–	–	–	1	–	–	–	–	–	1
	Ireland	5	–	4	–	–	–	–	–	–	–	–	0	–	–	–	–	1
	Afghanistan	3	–	3	–	–	–	–	–	–	–	–	–	0	–	–	–	–
	Associates	16	–	16	–	–	–	–	–	–	–	–	–	–	–	–	–	–
	ICC World XI	3	–	3	–	–	–	–	–	–	–	–	–	–	–	0	–	–
South Africa	West Indies	62	–	–	44	15	–	–	–	–	–	–	–	–	–	–	1	2
	New Zealand	71	–	–	41	–	25	–	–	–	–	–	–	–	–	–	–	5
	India	84	–	–	46	–	–	35	–	–	–	–	–	–	–	–	–	3
	Pakistan	79	–	–	50	–	–	–	28	–	–	–	–	–	–	–	–	1
	Sri Lanka	77	–	–	44	–	–	–	–	31	–	–	–	–	–	–	1	1
	Zimbabwe	41	–	–	38	–	–	–	–	–	2	–	–	–	–	–	–	1
	Bangladesh	21	–	–	17	–	–	–	–	–	–	4	–	–	–	–	–	–
	Ireland	5	–	–	5	–	–	–	–	–	–	–	0	–	–	–	–	–
	Afghanistan	1	–	–	1	–	–	–	–	–	–	–	–	0	–	–	–	–
	Associates	18	–	–	18	–	–	–	–	–	–	–	–	–	0	–	–	–
West Indies	New Zealand	65	–	–	–	30	28	–	–	–	–	–	–	–	–	–	–	7
	India	133	–	–	–	63	–	64	–	–	–	–	–	–	–	–	2	4
	Pakistan	134	–	–	–	71	–	–	60	–	–	–	–	–	–	–	3	–
	Sri Lanka	57	–	–	–	28	–	–	–	26	–	–	–	–	–	–	–	3
	Zimbabwe	48	–	–	–	36	–	–	–	–	10	–	–	–	–	–	1	1
	Bangladesh	38	–	–	–	21	–	–	–	–	–	15	–	–	–	–	–	2
	Ireland	9	–	–	–	7	–	–	–	–	–	–	1	–	–	–	–	1
	Afghanistan	9	–	–	–	5	–	–	–	–	–	–	–	3	–	–	–	1
	Associates	19	–	–	–	18	–	–	–	–	–	–	–	–	1	–	–	–
New Zealand	India	107	–	–	–	–	46	55	–	–	–	–	–	–	–	–	1	5
	Pakistan	107	–	–	–	–	48	–	55	–	–	–	–	–	–	–	1	3
	Sri Lanka	99	–	–	–	–	49	–	–	41	–	–	–	–	–	–	1	8
	Zimbabwe	38	–	–	–	–	27	–	–	–	9	–	–	–	–	–	1	1
	Bangladesh	35	–	–	–	–	25	–	–	–	–	10	–	–	–	–	–	–
	Ireland	4	–	–	–	–	4	–	–	–	–	–	0	–	–	–	–	–
	Afghanistan	2	–	–	–	–	2	–	–	–	–	–	–	0	–	–	–	–
	Associates	12	–	–	–	–	12	–	–	–	–	–	–	–	0	–	–	–

	Opponents	Matches	E	A	SA	WI	NZ	I	P	SL	Z	B	Ire	Afg	Ass	Oth	Tied	NR
India	Pakistan	132	–	–	–	–	55		73	–	–	–	–	–	–	–	–	4
	Sri Lanka	159	–	–	–	–	91	–	56	–	–	–	–	–	–	–	1	11
	Zimbabwe	63	–	–	–	–	51	–	–	10	–	–	–	–	–	–	2	–
	Bangladesh	36	–	–	–	–	30	–	–	–	5	–	–	–	–	–	–	1
	Ireland	3	–	–	–	–	3	–	–	–	–	0	–	–	–	–	–	–
	Afghanistan	3	–	–	–	–	2	–	–	–	–	–	0	–	–	–	1	–
	Associates	24	–	–	–	–	22	–	–	–	–	–	–	2	–	–	–	–
Pakistan	Sri Lanka	155	–	–	–	–	–	92	58	–	–	–	–	–	–	–	1	4
	Zimbabwe	59	–	–	–	–	–	52	–	4	–	–	–	–	–	–	1	2
	Bangladesh	37	–	–	–	–	–	32	–	–	5	–	–	–	–	–	–	–
	Ireland	7	–	–	–	–	–	5	–	–	–	1	–	–	–	–	1	–
	Afghanistan	4	–	–	–	–	–	4	–	–	–	–	0	–	–	–	–	–
	Associates	21	–	–	–	–	–	21	–	–	–	–	–	0	–	–	–	–
Sri Lanka	Zimbabwe	57	–	–	–	–	–	–	44	11	–	–	–	–	–	–	–	2
	Bangladesh	48	–	–	–	–	–	–	39	–	7	–	–	–	–	–	–	2
	Ireland	4	–	–	–	–	–	–	4	–	–	0	–	–	–	–	–	–
	Afghanistan	4	–	–	–	–	–	–	3	–	–	–	1	–	–	–	–	–
	Associates	17	–	–	–	–	–	–	16	–	–	–	–	1	–	–	–	–
Zimbabwe	Bangladesh	72	–	–	–	–	–	–	–	28	44	–	–	–	–	–	–	–
	Ireland	13	–	–	–	–	–	–	–	6	–	6	–	–	–	–	1	–
	Afghanistan	25	–	–	–	–	–	–	–	10	–	–	15	–	–	–	–	–
	Associates	50	–	–	–	–	–	–	–	38	–	–	–	9	–	–	1	2
Bangladesh	Ireland	10	–	–	–	–	–	–	–	–	7	2	–	–	–	–	–	1
	Afghanistan	8	–	–	–	–	–	–	–	–	5	–	3	–	–	–	–	–
	Associates	26	–	–	–	–	–	–	–	–	18	–	–	8	–	–	–	–
Ireland	Afghanistan	27	–	–	–	–	–	–	–	–	–	13	13	–	–	–	–	1
	Associates	56	–	–	–	–	–	–	–	–	–	43	–	9	–	–	1	3
Afghanistan	Associates	38	–	–	–	–	–	–	–	–	–	–	24	13	–	–	–	1
Associates	Associates	147	–	–	–	–	–	–	–	–	–	–	–	–	142	–	–	5
Asian CC XI	ICC World XI	1	–	–	–	–	–	–	–	–	–	–	–	–	–	1	–	–
	African XI	6	–	–	–	–	–	–	–	–	–	–	–	–	–	5	–	1
		4,223	375	573	381	398	348	511	486	386	138	125	67	59	186	6	37	147

Associate and Affiliate Members of ICC who have played one-day internationals are Bermuda, Canada, East Africa, Hong Kong, Kenya, Namibia, Nepal, Netherlands, Oman, Papua New Guinea, Scotland, United Arab Emirates and USA. Sri Lanka, Zimbabwe, Bangladesh, Afghanistan and Ireland played one-day internationals before gaining Test status; these are not counted as Associate results.

RESULTS SUMMARY OF ONE-DAY INTERNATIONALS

1970-71 to December 31, 2019 (4,223 matches)

	Matches	Won	Lost	Tied	No Result	% Won (excl. NR)
South Africa	619	381	215	6	17	63.78
Australia	942	573	326	9	34	63.60
India	981	511	420	9	41	54.84
Pakistan	927	486	413	8	20	54.02
England	743	375	333	8	27	52.93
West Indies	816	398	378	10	30	51.27
Afghanistan	126	59	63	1	3	48.37
New Zealand	768	348	374	6	40	48.21
Sri Lanka	849	386	421	5	37	47.84
Ireland	153	67	75	3	8	47.24
Bangladesh	373	125	241	–	7	34.15
Zimbabwe	526	138	370	7	11	27.47
Asian Cricket Council XI	7	4	2	–	1	66.66
Oman	5	3	2	–	–	60.00
USA	11	6	5	–	–	54.54
Nepal	6	3	3	–	–	50.00

	Matches	Won	Lost	Tied	No Result	% Won (excl. NR)
Netherlands	80	31	45	1	3	40.90
Scotland	115	42	66	1	6	38.99
Namibia.	11	4	7	–	–	36.36
Hong Kong	26	9	16	–	1	36.00
Kenya	154	42	107	–	5	28.18
United Arab Emirates	56	15	41	–	–	26.78
Papua New Guinea	27	7	20	–	–	25.92
ICC World XI	4	1	3	–	–	25.00
Canada	77	17	58	–	2	22.66
Bermuda	35	7	28	–	–	20.00
African XI	6	1	4	–	1	20.00
East Africa	3	–	3	–	–	0.00

Matches abandoned without a ball bowled are not included except (from 2004) where the toss took place, in accordance with an ICC ruling. Such matches, like those called off after play began, are now counted as official internationals in their own right, even when replayed on another day. In the percentages of matches won, ties are counted as half a win.

BATTING RECORDS

HIGHEST INDIVIDUAL INNINGS

264	R. G. Sharma	India v Sri Lanka at Kolkata.	2014-15
237*	M. J. Guptill	New Zealand v West Indies at Wellington.	2014-15
219	V. Sehwag	India v West Indies at Indore	2011-12
215	C. H. Gayle	West Indies v Zimbabwe at Canberra.	2014-15
210*	Fakhar Zaman	Pakistan v Zimbabwe at Bulawayo	2018
209	R. G. Sharma	India v Australia at Bangalore	2013-14
208*	R. G. Sharma	India v Sri Lanka at Mohali	2017-18
200*	S. R. Tendulkar	India v South Africa at Gwalior	2009-10
194*	C. K. Coventry	Zimbabwe v Bangladesh at Bulawayo	2009
194	Saeed Anwar	Pakistan v India at Chennai	1997-98
189*	I. V. A. Richards	West Indies v England at Manchester	1984
189*	M. J. Guptill	New Zealand v England at Southampton	2013
189	S. T. Jayasuriya	Sri Lanka v India at Sharjah	2000-01
188*	G. Kirsten	South Africa v UAE at Rawalpindi	1995-96
186*	S. R. Tendulkar	India v New Zealand at Hyderabad	1999-2000
185*	S. R. Watson	Australia v Bangladesh at Mirpur.	2010-11
185	F. du Plessis	South Africa v Sri Lanka at Cape Town.	2016-17
183*	M. S. Dhoni	India v Sri Lanka at Jaipur	2005-06
183	S. C. Ganguly	India v Sri Lanka at Taunton	1999
183	V. Kohli	India v Pakistan at Mirpur	2011-12
181*	M. L. Hayden	Australia v New Zealand at Hamilton	2006-07
181*	L. R. P. L. Taylor	New Zealand v England at Dunedin (University)	2017-18
181	I. V. A. Richards	West Indies v Sri Lanka at Karachi	1987-88
180*	M. J. Guptill	New Zealand v South Africa at Hamilton	2016-17
180	J. J. Roy	England v Australia at Melbourne	2017-18

The highest individual scores for other Test countries are:

177	P. R. Stirling	Ireland v Canada at Toronto.	2010
154	Tamim Iqbal	Bangladesh v Zimbabwe at Bulawayo	2009
131*	Mohammad Shahzad	Afghanistan v Zimbabwe at Sharjah.	2015-16

MOST HUNDREDS

S. R. Tendulkar (I)	49	**L. R. P. L. Taylor (NZ)** .	**20**	**A. J. Finch (A)**	**15**
V. Kohli (I)	**43**	D. P. M. D. Jayawardene		Mohammad Yousuf (P/As)	15
R. T. Ponting (A/World)	30	(SL/Asia)	19	V. Sehwag (I/Wld/Asia)	15
S. T. Jayasuriya (SL/Asia)	28	B. C. Lara (WI/World)	19	**W. U. Tharanga (SL)**	**15**
R. G. Sharma (I)	**28**	M. E. Waugh (A)	18		
H. M. Amla (SA)	**27**	**S. Dhawan (I)**	**17**	*Most hundreds for other*	
A. B. de Villiers (SA)	25	D. L. Haynes (WI)	17	*Test countries:*	
C. H. Gayle (WI/World)	**25**	J. H. Kallis (SA/Wld/Af)	17	**W. T. S. Porterfield (Ire)**	**11**
K. C. Sangakkara (SL)	25	**D. A. Warner (A)**	**17**	**Tamim Iqbal (B)**	**11**
T. M. Dilshan (SL)	22	N. J. Astle (NZ)	16	**B. R. M. Taylor (Z)**	**10**
S. C. Ganguly (I/Asia)	22	A. C. Gilchrist (A/World)	16	Mohammad Shahzad (Afg)	6
H. H. Gibbs (SA)	21	**M. J. Guptill (NZ)**	**16**		
Saeed Anwar (P)	20	**J. E. Root (E)**	**16**		

Ponting's total includes one for the World XI, the only hundred for a combined team.

MOST RUNS

		M	I	NO	R	HS	100	Avge
1	S. R. Tendulkar (India)	463	452	41	18,426	200*	49	44.83
2	K. C. Sangakkara (SL/Asia/World)	404	380	41	14,234	169	25	41.98
3	R. T. Ponting (Australia/World)	375	365	39	13,704	164	30	42.03
4	S. T. Jayasuriya (Sri Lanka/Asia)	445	433	18	13,430	189	28	32.36
5	D. P. M. D. Jayawardene (SL/Asia)	448	418	39	12,650	144	19	33.37
6	Inzamam-ul-Haq (Pakistan/Asia)	378	350	53	11,739	137*	10	39.52
7	**V. Kohli (India)**	**242**	**233**	**39**	**11,609**	**183**	**43**	**59.84**
8	J. H. Kallis (S. Africa/World/Africa)	328	314	53	11,579	139	17	44.36
9	S. C. Ganguly (India/Asia)	311	300	23	11,363	183	22	41.02
10	R. Dravid (India/World/Asia)	344	318	40	10,889	153	12	39.16
11	**M. S. Dhoni (India/Asia)**	**350**	**298**	**85**	**10,773**	**183***	**10**	**50.57**
12	**C. H. Gayle (West Indies/World)**	**301**	**294**	**17**	**10,480**	**215**	**25**	**37.83**
13	B. C. Lara (West Indies/World)	299	289	32	10,405	169	19	40.48
14	T. M. Dilshan (Sri Lanka)	330	303	41	10,290	161*	22	39.27

The leading aggregates for players who have appeared for other Test countries are:

	M	I	NO	R	HS	100	Avge
L. R. P. L. Taylor (New Zealand)	**228**	**212**	**37**	**8,376**	**181***	**20**	**47.86**
E. J. G. Morgan (Ireland/England)	**233**	**217**	**32**	**7,348**	**148**	**13**	**39.71**
Tamim Iqbal (Bangladesh)	202	202	8	6,892	154	11	35.52
A. Flower (Zimbabwe)	213	208	16	6,786	145	4	35.34
Mohammad Nabi (Afghanistan)	**124**	**112**	**12**	**2,782**	**116**	**1**	**27.82**

Excluding runs for combined teams, the record aggregate for Sri Lanka is 13,975 in 397 matches by K. C. Sangakkara; for Australia, 13,589 in 374 matches by R. T. Ponting; for Pakistan, 11,701 in 375 matches by Inzamam-ul-Haq; for South Africa, 11,550 in 323 matches by J. H. Kallis; for West Indies, 10,425 in 298 matches by C. H. Gayle; for England, 6,604 in 210 matches by E. J. G. Morgan; and for Ireland, 4,038 in 114 matches by P. R. Stirling.

BEST CAREER STRIKE-RATES BY BATSMEN

(Runs per 100 balls. Qualification: 1,000 runs)

SR		Position	M	I	R	Avge
130.22	A. D. Russell (WI)	7/8	56	47	1,034	27.21
123.37	G. J. Maxwell (A)	5/6	110	100	2,877	32.32
119.83	J. C. Buttler (E)	6/7	142	117	3,843	40.88
117.00	Shahid Afridi (P/World/Asia)	2/7	398	369	8,064	23.57
114.50	L. Ronchi (A/NZ)	7	85	68	1,397	23.67
111.67	N. L. T. C. Perera (SL)	7/8	161	128	2,210	19.73
108.72	C. J. Anderson (NZ)	6	49	44	1,109	27.72

SR		Position	M	I	R	Avge
107.40	**J. J. Roy (E)**	**1**	**84**	**81**	**3,381**	**42.79**
107.02	**S. O. Hetmyer (WI)**	**4/5**	**43**	**40**	**1,416**	**38.27**
104.69	**C. Munro (NZ).**	**2/6**	**57**	**53**	**1,271**	**24.92**
104.33	V. Sehwag (I/World/Asia)	1/2	251	245	8,273	35.05
104.24	J. P. Faulkner (A)	7/8	69	52	1,032	34.40
104.07	**J. M. Bairstow (E).**	**2/6**	**74**	**68**	**2,861**	**47.68**
104.06	**M. M. Ali (E)**	**2/7**	**101**	**82**	**1,766**	**25.59**
102.18	**K. M. Jadhav (I)**	**6/7**	**71**	**50**	**1,354**	**42.31**
101.09	A. B. de Villiers (SA/Africa)	4/5	228	218	9,577	53.50
100.13	**D. A. Miller (SA)**	**5/6**	**126**	**110**	**3,058**	**38.70**
100.05	D. J. G. Sammy (WI)	7/8	126	105	1,871	24.94

Position means a batsman's most usual position(s) in the batting order.

FASTEST ONE-DAY INTERNATIONAL FIFTIES

Balls

16	A. B. de Villiers.......	South Africa v West Indies at Johannesburg	2014-15
17	S. T. Jayasuriya	Sri Lanka v Pakistan at Singapore	1995-96
17	M. D. K. J. Perera ...	Sri Lanka v Pakistan at Pallekele	2015
17	M. J. Guptill	New Zealand v Sri Lanka at Christchurch	2015-16
18	S. P. O'Donnell	Australia v Sri Lanka at Sharjah...................	1989-90
18	Shahid Afridi	Pakistan v Sri Lanka at Nairobi	1996-97
18	Shahid Afridi	Pakistan v Netherlands at Colombo (SSC)	2002
18	G. J. Maxwell	Australia v India at Bangalore	2013-14
18	Shahid Afridi	Pakistan v Bangladesh at Mirpur	2013-14
18	B. B. McCullum	New Zealand v England at Wellington..............	2014-15
18	A. J. Finch	Australia v Sri Lanka at Dambulla	2016

FASTEST ONE-DAY INTERNATIONAL HUNDREDS

Balls

31	A. B. de Villiers	South Africa v West Indies at Johannesburg	2014-15
36	C. J. Anderson.......	New Zealand v West Indies at Queenstown.	2013-14
37	Shahid Afridi	Pakistan v Sri Lanka at Nairobi	1996-97
44	M. V. Boucher.......	South Africa v Zimbabwe at Potchefstroom	2006-07
45	B. C. Lara	West Indies v Bangladesh at Dhaka................	1999-2000
45	Shahid Afridi	Pakistan v India at Kanpur......................	2004-05
46	J. D. Ryder	New Zealand v West Indies at Queenstown.	2013-14
46	J. C. Buttler	England v Pakistan at Dubai	2015-16
48	S. T. Jayasuriya	Sri Lanka v Pakistan at Singapore	1995-96

HIGHEST PARTNERSHIP FOR EACH WICKET

365	**for 1st**	**J. D. Campbell/S. D. Hope**	**WI v Ire**	**Clontarf**	**2019**
372	for 2nd	C. H. Gayle/M. N. Samuels	WI v Z	Canberra	2014-15
258	for 3rd	D. M. Bravo/D. Ramdin	WI v B	Basseterre	2014-15
275*	for 4th	M. Azharuddin/A. Jadeja	I v Z	Cuttack	1997-98
256*	for 5th	D. A. Miller/J-P. Duminy	SA v Z	Hamilton	2014-15
267*	for 6th	G. D. Elliott/L. Ronchi	NZ v SL	Dunedin	2014-15
177	for 7th	J. C. Buttler/A. U. Rashid	E v NZ	Birmingham	2015
138*	for 8th	J. M. Kemp/A. J. Hall	SA v I	Cape Town	2006-07
132	for 9th	A. D. Mathews/S. L. Malinga	SL v A	Melbourne	2010-11
106*	for 10th	I. V. A. Richards/M. A. Holding	WI v E	Manchester	1984

BOWLING RECORDS

BEST BOWLING ANALYSES

8-19	W. P. U. J. C. Vaas	Sri Lanka v Zimbabwe at Colombo (SSC)	2001-02
7-12	Shahid Afridi	Pakistan v West Indies at Providence	2013
7-15	G. D. McGrath	Australia v Namibia at Potchefstroom...........	2002-03

7-18	Rashid Khan	Afghanistan v West Indies at Gros Islet	2017
7-20	A. J. Bichel	Australia v England at Port Elizabeth	2002-03
7-30	M. Muralitharan	Sri Lanka v India at Sharjah	2000-01
7-33	T. G. Southee	New Zealand v England at Wellington	2014-15
7-34	T. A. Boult	New Zealand v West Indies at Christchurch	2017-18
7-36	Waqar Younis	Pakistan v England at Leeds	2001
7-37	Aqib Javed	Pakistan v India at Sharjah.	1991-92
7-45	Imran Tahir	South Africa v West Indies at Basseterre........	2016
7-51	W. W. Davis	West Indies v Australia at Leeds	1983

The best analyses for other Test countries are:

6-4	S. T. R. Binny	India v Bangladesh at Mirpur	2014
6-19	H. K. Olonga	Zimbabwe v England at Cape Town	1999-2000
6-26	Mashrafe bin Mortaza	Bangladesh v Kenya at Nairobi	2006
6-26	Rubel Hossain	Bangladesh v New Zealand at Mirpur	2013-14
6-31	P. D. Collingwood	England v Bangladesh at Nottingham	2005
6-55	P. R. Stirling	Ireland v Afghanistan at Greater Noida.........	2016-17

HAT-TRICKS

Four Wickets in Four Balls

| S. L. Malinga | Sri Lanka v South Africa at Providence...................... | 2006-07 |

Four Wickets in Five Balls

| Saqlain Mushtaq | Pakistan v Zimbabwe at Peshawar....................... | 1996-97 |
| **A. U. Rashid** | **England v West Indies at St George's** .... | **2018-19** |

Most Hat-Tricks

| S. L. Malinga (SL) ...... | 3 | Saqlain Mushtaq (P)..... | 2 | Wasim Akram (P) ...... | 2 |
| **T. A. Boult (NZ)** .... | **2** | W. P. U. J. C. Vaas† (SL) | 2 | **K. Yadav (I)** .... | **2** |

† *W. P. U. J. C. Vaas took the second of his two hat-tricks, for Sri Lanka v Bangladesh at Pietermaritzburg in 2002-03, with the first three balls of the match.*

Hat-Tricks

There have been **49** hat-tricks in one-day internationals, including the above. Those since 2017-18:

K. Yadav	India v Australia at Kolkata	2017-18
D. S. M. Kumara	Sri Lanka v Bangladesh at Mirpur	2017-18
Imran Tahir	South Africa v Zimbabwe at Bloemfontein	2018-19
T. A. Boult	New Zealand v Pakistan at Abu Dhabi...................	2018-19
Mohammed Shami	**India v Afghanistan at Southampton**	**2019**
T. A. Boult	**New Zealand v Australia at Lord's**......................	**2019**
K. Yadav	**India v West Indies at Visakhapatnam**...................	**2019-20**

MOST WICKETS

		M	Balls	R	W	BB	4I	Avge
1	M. Muralitharan (SL/World/Asia)......	350	18,811	12,326	534	7-30	25	23.08
2	Wasim Akram (Pakistan).............	356	18,186	11,812	502	5-15	23	23.52
3	Waqar Younis (Pakistan).............	262	12,698	9,919	416	7-36	27	23.84
4	W. P. U. J. C. Vaas (SL/Asia)........	322	15,775	11,014	400	8-19	13	27.53
5	Shahid Afridi (Pakistan/World/Asia) ...	398	17,670	13,635	395	7-12	13	34.51
6	S. M. Pollock (SA/World/Africa)	303	15,712	9,631	393	6-35	17	24.50
7	G. D. McGrath (Australia/World)......	250	12,970	8,391	381	7-15	16	22.02
8	B. Lee (Australia)	221	11,185	8,877	380	5-22	23	23.36
9	**S. L. Malinga (Sri Lanka)**............	**226**	**10,936**	**9,760**	**338**	**6-38**	**19**	**28.87**

		M	Balls	R	W	BB	4I	Avge
10	A. Kumble (India/Asia)	271	14,496	10,412	337	6-12	10	30.89
11	S. T. Jayasuriya (Sri Lanka/Asia)	445	14,874	11,871	323	6-29	12	36.75
12	J. Srinath (India)	229	11,935	8,847	315	5-23	10	28.08
13	D. L. Vettori (New Zealand/World)	295	14,060	9,674	305	5-7	10	31.71
14	S. K. Warne (Australia/World)	194	10,642	7,541	293	5-33	13	25.73
15	Saqlain Mushtaq (Pakistan)	169	8,770	6,275	288	5-20	17	21.78
	A. B. Agarkar (India)	191	9,484	8,021	288	6-42	12	27.85
17	Zaheer Khan (India/Asia)	200	10,097	8,301	282	5-42	8	29.43
18	J. H. Kallis (S. Africa/World/Africa)	328	10,750	8,680	273	5-30	4	31.79
19	A. A. Donald (South Africa)	164	8,561	5,926	272	6-23	13	21.78
	J. M. Anderson (England)	194	9,584	7,861	269	5-23	13	29.22
20	Abdul Razzaq (Pakistan/Asia)	265	10,941	8,564	269	6-35	11	31.83
	Harbhajan Singh (India/Asia)	236	12,479	8,973	269	5-31	5	33.35
23	M. Ntini (South Africa/World)	173	8,687	6,559	266	6-22	12	24.65
	Mashrafe bin Mortaza (Bang/Asia)	**217**	**10,789**	**8,759**	**266**	**6-26**	**8**	**32.92**
25	**Shakib Al Hasan (Bangladesh)**	**206**	**10,517**	**7,857**	**260**	**5-29**	**10**	**30.21**
26	Kapil Dev (India)	225	11,202	6,945	253	5-43	4	27.45

The leading aggregates for players who have appeared for other Test countries are:

		M	Balls	R	W	BB	4I	Avge
	H. H. Streak (Zimbabwe)	189	9,468	7,129	239	5-32	8	29.82
	C. A. Walsh (West Indies)	205	10,882	6,918	227	5-1	7	30.47
	Rashid Khan (Afghanistan)	**71**	**3,558**	**2,467**	**133**	**7-18**	**8**	**18.54**
	K. J. O'Brien (Ireland)	142	4,224	3,673	113	4-13	5	32.50

Excluding wickets taken for combined teams, the record for Sri Lanka is 523 in 343 matches by M. Muralitharan; for South Africa, 387 in 294 matches by S. M. Pollock; for Australia, 380 in 249 matches by G. D. McGrath; for India, 334 in 269 matches by A. Kumble; for New Zealand, 297 in 291 matches by D. L. Vettori; for Bangladesh, 265 in 215 matches by Mashrafe bin Mortaza; and for Zimbabwe, 237 in 187 matches by H. H. Streak.

BEST CAREER STRIKE-RATES BY BOWLERS

(Balls per wicket. Qualification: 1,500 balls)

SR		M	W
25.08	**M. A. Starc (A)**	**85**	**172**
26.28	**Mustafizur Rahman (B)**	**56**	**107**
26.75	**Rashid Khan (Afg)**	**71**	**133**
26.95	Mohammed Shami (I)	47	87
27.10	Hamid Hassan (Afg)	32	56
27.22	S. W. Tait (A)	35	62
27.27	**Mohammed Shami (I)**	**73**	**136**
27.32	B. A. W. Mendis (SL)	87	152
28.38	**L. H. Ferguson (NZ)**	**36**	**67**
28.48	M. J. McClenaghan (NZ)	48	82
28.72	R. N. ten Doeschate (Netherlands)	33	55

BEST CAREER ECONOMY-RATES

(Runs conceded per six balls. Qualification: 50 wickets)

ER		M	W
3.09	J. Garner (WI)	98	146
3.28	R. G. D. Willis (E)	64	80
3.30	R. J. Hadlee (NZ)	115	158
3.32	M. A. Holding (WI)	102	142
3.40	A. M. E. Roberts (WI)	56	87
3.48	C. E. L. Ambrose (WI)	176	225

WICKETKEEPING AND FIELDING RECORDS

MOST DISMISSALS IN AN INNINGS

6 (6ct)	A. C. Gilchrist	Australia v South Africa at Cape Town	1999-2000
6 (6ct)	A. J. Stewart	England v Zimbabwe at Manchester	2000
6 (5ct, 1st)	R. D. Jacobs	West Indies v Sri Lanka at Colombo (RPS)	2001-02
6 (6ct)	A. C. Gilchrist	Australia v England at Sydney	2002-03
6 (6ct)	A. C. Gilchrist	Australia v Namibia at Potchefstroom	2002-03
6 (6ct)	A. C. Gilchrist	Australia v Sri Lanka at Colombo (RPS)	2003-04
6 (6ct)	M. V. Boucher	South Africa v Pakistan at Cape Town	2006-07
6 (5ct, 1st)	M. S. Dhoni	India v England at Leeds	2007
6 (6ct)	A. C. Gilchrist	Australia v India at Vadodara	2007-08
6 (5ct, 1st)	A. C. Gilchrist	Australia v India at Sydney	2007-08
6 (6ct)	M. J. Prior	England v South Africa at Nottingham	2008
6 (6ct)	J. C. Buttler	England v South Africa at The Oval	2013
6 (6ct)	M. H. Cross	Scotland v Canada at Christchurch	2013-14
6 (5ct, 1st)	Q. de Kock	S. Africa v N. Zealand at Mount Maunganui	2014-15
6 (6ct)	Sarfraz Ahmed	Pakistan v South Africa at Auckland	2014-15

MOST DISMISSALS

			M	*Ct*	*St*
1	482	K. C. Sangakkara (Sri Lanka/World/Asia)	360	384	98
2	472	A. C. Gilchrist (Australia/World)	282	417	55
3	**444**	**M. S. Dhoni (India/Asia)**	**350**	**321**	**123**
4	424	M. V. Boucher (South Africa/Africa)	294	402	22
5	287	Moin Khan (Pakistan)	219	214	73
6	242	B. B. McCullum (New Zealand)	185	227	15
7	234	I. A. Healy (Australia)	168	195	39
8	**223**	**Mushfiqur Rahim (Bangladesh)**	**203**	**179**	**44**
9	220	Rashid Latif (Pakistan)	166	182	38
10	206	R. S. Kaluwitharana (Sri Lanka)	186	131	75
11	204	P. J. L. Dujon (West Indies)	169	183	21
12	**202**	**J. C. Buttler (England)**	**141**	**171**	**31**

The leading aggregates for players who have appeared for other Test countries are:

	165	A. Flower (Zimbabwe)	186	133	32
	96	N. J. O'Brien (Ireland)	80	82	14
	88	**Mohammad Shahzad (Afghanistan)**	**83**	**63**	**25**

Excluding dismissals for combined teams, the most for Sri Lanka is 473 (378ct, 95st) in 353 matches by K. C. Sangakkara; for Australia, 470 (416ct, 54st) in 281 matches by A. C. Gilchrist; for India, 438 (318ct, 120st) in 347 matches by M. S. Dhoni; and for South Africa, 415 (394ct, 21st) in 289 matches by M. V. Boucher.

K. C. Sangakkara's list excludes 19 catches taken in 44 one-day internationals when not keeping wicket; M. V. Boucher's record excludes one in one; B. B. McCullum's excludes 35 in 75; Mushfiqur Rahim's two in 13; R. S. Kaluwitharana's one in three; A. Flower's eight in 27; N. J. O'Brien's eight in 23; and Mohammad Shahzad's one in one. A. C. Gilchrist played five one-day internationals and J. C. Buttler one without keeping wicket, but they made no catches in those games. R. Dravid (India) made 210 dismissals (196ct, 14st) in 344 one-day internationals but only 86 (72ct, 14st) in 74 as wicketkeeper (including one where he took over during the match).

MOST CATCHES IN AN INNINGS IN THE FIELD

5	J. N. Rhodes	South Africa v West Indies at Bombay	1993-94

*There have been **40** instances of four catches in an innings.*

MOST CATCHES

Ct	M		Ct	M	
218	448	D. P. M. D. Jayawardene (SL/Asia)	127	398	Shahid Afridi (Pak/World/Asia)
160	375	R. T. Ponting (Australia/World)			*Most catches for other Test countries:*
156	334	M. Azharuddin (India)	**124**	**301**	**C. H. Gayle (WI/World)**
140	463	S. R. Tendulkar (India)	108	197	P. D. Collingwood (England)
137	**228**	**L. R. P. L. Taylor (New Zealand)**	86	221	G. W. Flower (Zimbabwe)
133	280	S. P. Fleming (New Zealand/World)	**63**	**136**	**W. T. S. Porterfield (Ireland)**
131	328	J. H. Kallis (SA/World/Africa)	**63**	**142**	**K. J. O'Brien (Ireland)**
130	262	Younis Khan (Pakistan)	**61**	**185**	**Mahmudullah (Bangladesh)**
130	350	M. Muralitharan (SL/World/Asia)	**61**	**217**	**Mashrafe bin Mortaza (Ban/As)**
127	273	A. R. Border (Australia)	**55**	**124**	**Mohammad Nabi (Afghanistan)**

Excluding catches taken for combined teams, the record aggregate for Sri Lanka is 213 in 442 matches by D. P. M. D. Jayawardene; for Australia, 158 in 374 by R. T. Ponting; for New Zealand, 132 in 279 by S. P. Fleming; for South Africa, 131 in 323 by J. H. Kallis; and for West Indies, 123 in 298 by C. H. Gayle.

Younis Khan's record excludes five catches made in three one-day internationals as wicketkeeper.

TEAM RECORDS

HIGHEST INNINGS TOTALS

481-6	(50 overs)	England v Australia at Nottingham.................	2018
444-3	(50 overs)	England v Pakistan at Nottingham	2016
443-9	(50 overs)	Sri Lanka v Netherlands at Amstelveen	2006
439-2	(50 overs)	South Africa v West Indies at Johannesburg...........	2014-15
438-4	(50 overs)	South Africa v India at Mumbai	2015-16
438-9	(49.5 overs)	South Africa v Australia at Johannesburg............	2005-06
434-4	(50 overs)	Australia v South Africa at Johannesburg.............	2005-06
418-5	(50 overs)	South Africa v Zimbabwe at Potchefstroom	2006-07
418-5	(50 overs)	India v West Indies at Indore.......................	2011-12
418-6	**(50 overs)**	**England v West Indies at St George's**	**2018-19**
417-6	(50 overs)	Australia v Afghanistan at Perth	2014-15
414-7	(50 overs)	India v Sri Lanka at Rajkot	2009-10
413-5	(50 overs)	India v Bermuda at Port-of-Spain	2006-07
411-4	(50 overs)	South Africa v Ireland at Canberra	2014-15
411-8	(50 overs)	Sri Lanka v India at Rajkot	2009-10
408-5	(50 overs)	South Africa v West Indies at Sydney	2014-15
408-9	(50 overs)	England v New Zealand at Birmingham	2015
404-5	(50 overs)	India v Sri Lanka at Kolkata	2014-15
402-2	(50 overs)	New Zealand v Ireland at Aberdeen	2008
401-3	(50 overs)	India v South Africa at Gwalior	2009-10

The highest totals by other Test countries are:

399-1	(50 overs)	Pakistan v Zimbabwe at Bulawayo	2018
389	**(48 overs)**	**West Indies v England at St George's**	**2018-19**
351-7	(50 overs)	Zimbabwe v Kenya at Mombasa......................	2008-09
338	(50 overs)	Afghanistan v Ireland at Greater Noida...............	2016-17
333-8	**(50 overs)**	**Bangladesh v Australia at Nottingham**	**2019**
331-6	(50 overs)	Ireland v Scotland at Dubai	2017-18
331-8	(50 overs)	Ireland v Zimbabwe at Hobart.......................	2014-15

HIGHEST TOTALS BATTING SECOND

438-9	(49.5 overs)	South Africa v Australia at Johannesburg (*Won by 1 wicket*) ..	2005-06
411-8	(50 overs)	Sri Lanka v India at Rajkot (*Lost by 3 runs*)	2009-10
389	**(48 overs)**	**West Indies v England at St George's** (*Lost by 29 runs*)	**2018-19**
372-6	(49.2 overs)	South Africa v Durban (*Won by 4 wickets*)	2016-17
366-8	(50 overs)	England v India at Cuttack (*Lost by 15 runs*)	2016-17
365-9	(45 overs)	England v New Zealand at The Oval (*Lost by 13 runs DLS*)...	2015

365	(48.5 overs)	England v Scotland at Edinburgh (*Lost by 6 runs*)	2018
364-4	**(48.4 overs)**	**England v West Indies at Bridgetown** (*Won by 6 wickets*). . .	**2018-19**
362-1	(43.3 overs)	India v Australia at Jaipur (*Won by 9 wickets*).	2013-14
361-7	**(50 overs)**	**Pakistan v England at Southampton** (*Lost by 12 runs*)	**2019**

HIGHEST MATCH AGGREGATES

872-13	(99.5 overs)	South Africa v Australia at Johannesburg	2005-06
825-15	(100 overs)	India v Sri Lanka at Rajkot.	2009-10
807-16	**(98 overs)**	**West Indies v England at St George's**	**2018-19**
763-14	(96 overs)	England v New Zealand at The Oval	2015
747-14	(100 overs)	India v England at Cuttack.	2016-17
743-12	(99.2 overs)	South Australia v Australia at Durban	2016-17
736-15	(98.5 overs)	Scotland v England at Edinburgh.	2018
734-10	**(100 overs)**	**England v Pakistan at Southampton**	**2019**
730-9	(100 overs)	South Africa v West Indies at Johannesburg	2014-15
726-14	(95.1 overs)	New Zealand v India at Christchurch.	2008-09
724-12	**(98.4 overs)**	**West Indies v England at Bridgetown**	**2018-19**

LOWEST INNINGS TOTALS

35	(18 overs)	Zimbabwe v Sri Lanka at Harare	2003-04
36	(18.4 overs)	Canada v Sri Lanka at Paarl	2002-03
38	(15.4 overs)	Zimbabwe v Sri Lanka at Colombo (SSC).	2001-02
43	(19.5 overs)	Pakistan v West Indies at Cape Town	1992-93
43	(20.1 overs)	Sri Lanka v South Africa at Paarl.	2011-12
44	(24.5 overs)	Zimbabwe v Bangladesh at Chittagong	2009-10
45	(40.3 overs)	Canada v England at Manchester	1979
45	(14 overs)	Namibia v Australia at Potchefstroom	2002-03

The lowest totals by other Test countries are:

54	(26.3 overs)	India v Sri Lanka at Sharjah.	2000-01
54	(23.2 overs)	West Indies v South Africa at Cape Town	2003-04
58	(18.5 overs)	Bangladesh v West Indies at Mirpur	2010-11
58	(17.4 overs)	Bangladesh v India at Mirpur.	2014
58	(16.1 overs)	Afghanistan v Zimbabwe at Sharjah	2015-16
64	(35.5 overs)	New Zealand v Pakistan at Sharjah	1985-86
69	(28 overs)	South Africa v Australia at Sydney	1993-94
70	(25.2 overs)	Australia v England at Birmingham	1977
70	(26.3 overs)	Australia v New Zealand at Adelaide.	1985-86
77	(27.4 overs)	Ireland v Sri Lanka at St George's.	2006-07
86	(32.4 overs)	England v Australia at Manchester.	2001

LARGEST VICTORIES

290 runs	New Zealand (402-2 in 50 overs) v Ireland (112 in 28.4 ov) at Aberdeen	2008
275 runs	Australia (417-6 in 50 overs) v Afghanistan (142 in 37.3 overs) at Perth	2014-15
272 runs	South Africa (399-6 in 50 overs) v Zimbabwe (127 in 29 overs) at Benoni. . . .	2010-11
258 runs	South Africa (301-8 in 50 overs) v Sri Lanka (43 in 20.1 overs) at Paarl.	2011-12
257 runs	India (413-5 in 50 overs) v Bermuda (156 in 43.1 overs) at Port-of-Spain	2006-07
257 runs	South Africa (408-5 in 50 overs) v West Indies (151 in 33.1 overs) at Sydney .	2014-15
256 runs	Australia (301-6 in 50 overs) v Namibia (45 in 14 overs) at Potchefstroom . . .	2002-03
256 runs	India (374-4 in 50 overs) v Hong Kong (118 in 36.5 overs) at Karachi	2008
255 runs	Pakistan (337-6 in 47 overs) v Ireland (82 in 23.4 overs) at Dublin	2016

*There have been **54** instances of victory by ten wickets.*

TIED MATCHES

There have been **37** tied one-day internationals. West Indies have tied ten matches; Bangladesh are the only Test country never to have tied. The most recent ties are:

South Africa (230-6 in 31 overs) v West Indies (190-6 in 26.1 overs) at Cardiff (D/L) 2013
Ireland (268-5 in 50 overs) v Netherlands (268-9 in 50 overs) at Amstelveen 2013
Pakistan (229-6 in 50 overs) v West Indies (229-9 in 50 overs) at Gros Islet 2013
Pakistan (266-5 in 47 overs) v Ireland (275-5 in 47 overs) at Dublin (D/L) 2013
New Zealand (314 in 50 overs) v India (314-9 in 50 overs) at Auckland 2013-14
Sri Lanka (286-9 in 50 overs) v England (286-8 in 50 overs) at Nottingham 2016
Zimbabwe (257 in 50 overs) v West Indies (257-8 in 50 overs) at Bulawayo........... 2016-17
Zimbabwe (210 in 46.4 overs) v Scotland (210 in 49.1 overs) at Bulawayo........... 2017-18
Afghanistan (252-8 in 50 overs) v India (252 in 49.5 overs) at Dubai 2018-19
India (321-6 in 50 overs) v West Indies (321-7 in 50 overs) at Visakhapatnam 2018-19

In the 2019 World Cup final at Lord's, New Zealand scored 241-8 and England 241, but England won the match on boundary count after a super over was also tied.

OTHER RECORDS

MOST APPEARANCES

463	S. R. Tendulkar (I)	334	M. Azharuddin (I)
448	D. P. M. D. Jayawardene (SL/Asia)	330	T. M. Dilshan (SL)
445	S. T. Jayasuriya (SL/Asia)	328	J. H. Kallis (SA/World/Africa)
404	K. C. Sangakkara (SL/World/Asia)	325	S. R. Waugh (A)
398	Shahid Afridi (P/World/Asia)	322	W. P. U. J. C. Vaas (SL/Asia)
378	Inzamam-ul-Haq (P/Asia)	311	S. C. Ganguly (I/Asia)
375	R. T. Ponting (A/World)	308	P. A. de Silva (SL)
356	Wasim Akram (P)	304	Yuvraj Singh (I/Asia)
350	**M. S. Dhoni (I/Asia)**	303	S. M. Pollock (SA/World/Africa)
350	M. Muralitharan (SL/World/Asia)	**301**	**C. H. Gayle (WI/World)**
344	R. Dravid (I/World/Asia)	300	T. M. Dilshan (SL)

Excluding appearances for combined teams, the record for Sri Lanka is 441 by S. T. Jayasuriya; for Pakistan, 393 by Shahid Afridi; for Australia, 374 by R. T. Ponting; for South Africa, 323 by J. H. Kallis; for West Indies, 295 by B. C. Lara; for New Zealand, 291 by D. L. Vettori; for Zimbabwe, 221 by G. W. Flower; for Bangladesh, 215 by Mashrafe bin Mortaza; for England, 197 by P. D. Collingwood; for Ireland, 142 by K. J. O'Brien; and for Afghanistan, 124 by Mohammad Nabi.

MOST MATCHES AS CAPTAIN

	P	W	L	T	NR		P	W	L	T	NR
R. T. Ponting (A/World)	230	165	51	2	12	S. C. Ganguly (I/Asia) .	147	76	66	0	5
S. P. Fleming (NZ)	218	98	106	1	13	Imran Khan (P).......	139	75	59	1	4
M. S. Dhoni (I)........	200	110	74	5	11	W. J. Cronje (SA)	138	99	35	1	3
A. Ranatunga (SL)....	193	89	95	1	8	D. P. M. D.					
A. R. Border (A)	178	107	67	1	3	Jayawardene (SL/As)..	129	71	49	1	8
M. Azharuddin (I)	174	90	76	2	6	B. C. Lara (WI)	125	59	59	1	7
G. C. Smith (SA/Af) ..	150	92	51	1	6						

❝His second ball was right on the money, and hit me on the grille. I remember thinking it was one of the fastest I'd faced: it hit me before I could move.**"**
Marnus Labuschagne, Five Cricketers of the Year, page 73

WORLD CUP RECORDS

Bold type denotes performances in the World Cup of 2019, or, in career figures, players who appeared in that tournament.

WORLD CUP FINALS

1975	WEST INDIES (291-8) beat Australia (274) by 17 runs	Lord's
1979	WEST INDIES (286-9) beat England (194) by 92 runs	Lord's
1983	INDIA (183) beat West Indies (140) by 43 runs...................	Lord's
1987	AUSTRALIA (253-5) beat England (246-8) by seven runs	Calcutta
1992	PAKISTAN (249-6) beat England (227) by 22 runs................	Melbourne
1996	SRI LANKA (245-3) beat Australia (241-7) by seven wickets	Lahore
1999	AUSTRALIA (133-2) beat Pakistan (132) by eight wickets.............	Lord's
2003	AUSTRALIA (359-2) beat India (234) by 125 runs	Johannesburg
2007	AUSTRALIA (281-4) beat Sri Lanka (215-8) by 53 runs (D/L method)	Bridgetown
2011	INDIA (277-4) beat Sri Lanka (274-6) by six wickets	Mumbai
2015	AUSTRALIA (186-3) beat New Zealand (183) by seven wickets	Melbourne
2019	**ENGLAND (241) beat New Zealand (241-8) on boundary count after a super over**	Lord's

TEAM RESULTS

	Rounds reached			Matches				
	W	F	SF	P	W	L	T	NR
Australia (12).............	5	7	8	94	69	23	1	1
New Zealand (12)	–	2	8	89	54	34	–	1
India (12).................	2	3	7	84	53	29	1	1
England (12)...............	1	4	6	83	49	32	1	1
Pakistan (12).............	1	2	6	79	45	32	–	2
West Indies (12)............	2	3	4	80	43	35	–	2
South Africa (8)...........	–	–	4	64	38	23	2	1
Sri Lanka (12)	1	3	4	80	38	39	1	2
Bangladesh (6).............	–	–	–	40	14	25	–	1
Zimbabwe (9)	–	–	–	57	11	42	1	3
Ireland (3)	–	–	–	21	7	13	1	–
Kenya (5).................	–	–	1	29	6	22	–	1
Canada (4)................	–	–	–	18	2	16	–	–
Netherlands (4)............	–	–	–	20	2	18	–	–
United Arab Emirates (2).....	–	–	–	11	1	10	–	–
Afghanistan (2)	–	–	–	15	1	14	–	–
Bermuda (1)...............	–	–	–	3	–	3	–	–
East Africa (1)	–	–	–	3	–	3	–	–
Namibia (1)	–	–	–	6	–	6	–	–
Scotland (3)	–	–	–	14	–	14	–	–

The number of tournaments each team has played in is shown in brackets. Matches abandoned or cancelled without a ball bowled are not included.

BATTING RECORDS

Highest Scores

237*	M. J. Guptill	New Zealand v West Indies at Wellington	2014-15
215	C. H. Gayle	West Indies v Zimbabwe at Canberra	2014-15
188*	G. Kirsten	South Africa v United Arab Emirates at Rawalpindi ...	1995-96
183	S. C. Ganguly	India v Sri Lanka at Taunton......................	1999
181	I. V. A. Richards	West Indies v Sri Lanka at Karachi.................	1987-88
178	D. A. Warner	Australia v Afghanistan at Perth	2014-15
175*	Kapil Dev	India v Zimbabwe at Tunbridge Wells	1983

175	V. Sehwag	India v Bangladesh at Mirpur	2010-11
172*	C. B. Wishart	Zimbabwe v Namibia at Harare	2002-03
171*	G. M. Turner†	New Zealand v East Africa at Birmingham	1975
166	**D. A. Warner**	**Australia v Bangladesh at Nottingham**	**2019**
162*	A. B. de Villiers	South Africa v West Indies at Sydney	2014-15
161*	T. M. Dilshan	Sri Lanka v Bangladesh at Melbourne	2014-15
161	A. C. Hudson	South Africa v Netherlands at Rawalpindi	1995-96
160	Imran Nazir	Pakistan v Zimbabwe at Kingston	2006-07

Highest scores for other Test-playing countries:

158	A. J. Strauss	England v India at Bangalore	2010-11
128*	Mahmudullah	Bangladesh v New Zealand at Hamilton	2014-15
115*	J. P. Bray	Ireland v Zimbabwe at Kingston	2006-07
96	Samiullah Shenwari	Afghanistan v Scotland at Dunedin (University Oval) . .	2014-15

† *Turner scored 171* on the opening day of the inaugural World Cup in 1975.*

Most Hundreds

6, R. G. Sharma (I) and S. R. Tendulkar (I); 5, R. T. Ponting (A) and K. C. Sangakkara (SL); **4,** A. B. de Villiers (SA), T. M. Dilshan (SL), S. C. Ganguly (I), D. P. M. D. Jayawardene (SL), **D. A. Warner (A)** and M. E. Waugh (A); **3, S. Dhawan (I), A. J. Finch (A),** M. L. Hayden (A), S. T. Jayasuriya (SL), Ramiz Raja (P), I. V. A. Richards (WI), **J. E. Root (E)** and Saeed Anwar (P).

Most Runs in a Tournament

673, S. R. Tendulkar (I) 2002-03; 659, M. L. Hayden (A) 2006-07; **648, R. G. Sharma (I) 2019**; **647, D. A. Warner (A) 2019**; **606, Shakib Al Hasan (B) 2019**; **578, K. S. Williamson (NZ) 2019**; **556, J. E. Root (E) 2019**; 548, D. P. M. D. Jayawardene (SL) 2006-07; 547, M. J. Guptill (NZ) 2014-15; 541, K. C. Sangakkara (SL) 2014-15; 539, R. T. Ponting (A) 2006-07; **532, J. M. Bairstow (E) 2019**; 523, S. R. Tendulkar (I) 1995-96; **507, A. J. Finch (A) 2019**; 500, T. M. Dilshan (SL) 2010-11.

Most Runs

	M	I	NO	R	HS	100	Avge
S. R. Tendulkar (India)	45	44	4	2,278	152	6	56.95
R. T. Ponting (Australia)	46	42	4	1,743	140*	5	45.86
K. C. Sangakkara (Sri Lanka) . . .	37	35	8	1,532	124	5	56.74
B. C. Lara (West Indies)	34	33	4	1,225	116	2	42.24
A. B. de Villiers (South Africa) . .	23	22	3	1,207	162*	4	63.52
C. H. Gayle (West Indies)	**35**	**34**	**1**	**1,186**	**215**	**2**	**35.93**
S. T. Jayasuriya (Sri Lanka)	38	37	3	1,165	120	3	34.26
J. H. Kallis (South Africa)	36	32	7	1,148	128*	1	45.92
Shakib Al Hasan (Bangladesh) .	**29**	**29**	**4**	**1,146**	**124***	**2**	**45.84**
T. M. Dilshan (Sri Lanka)	27	25	4	1,112	161*	4	52.95
D. P. M. D. Jayawardene (SL) . . .	40	34	3	1,100	115*	4	35.48
A. C. Gilchrist (Australia)	31	31	1	1,085	149	1	36.16
Javed Miandad (Pakistan)	33	30	5	1,083	103*	1	43.32
S. P. Fleming (New Zealand)	33	33	3	1,075	134*	2	35.83
H. H. Gibbs (South Africa)	25	23	4	1,067	143	2	56.15
P. A. de Silva (Sri Lanka)	35	32	3	1,064	145	2	36.68
V. Kohli (India)	**26**	**26**	**4**	**1,030**	**107**	**2**	**46.81**
I. V. A. Richards (West Indies) . .	23	21	5	1,013	181	3	63.31
S. C. Ganguly (India)	21	21	3	1,006	183	4	55.88
M. E. Waugh (Australia)	22	22	3	1,004	130	4	52.84
L. R. P. L. Taylor (New Zealand)	**33**	**30**	**3**	**1,002**	**131***	**1**	**37.11**

Highest Partnership for Each Wicket

282	for 1st	W. U. Tharanga/T. M. Dilshan	SL v Z	Pallekele	2010-11
372	for 2nd	C. H. Gayle/M. N. Samuels	WI v Z	Canberra	2014-15
237*	for 3rd	R. Dravid/S. R. Tendulkar	I v K	Bristol	1999
204	for 4th	M. J. Clarke/B. J. Hodge	A v Neth	Basseterre	2006-07
256*	for 5th	D. A. Miller/J-P. Duminy	SA v Z	Hamilton	2014-15
162	for 6th	K. J. O'Brien/A. R. Cusack	Ire v E	Bangalore	2010-11
116	**for 7th**	**M. S. Dhoni/R. A. Jadeja**	**I v NZ**	**Manchester**	**2019**
117	for 8th	D. L. Houghton/I. P. Butchart	Z v NZ	Hyderabad (India)	1987-88
126*	for 9th	Kapil Dev/S. M. H. Kirmani	I v Z	Tunbridge Wells	1983
71	for 10th	A. M. E. Roberts/J. Garner	WI v I	Manchester	1983

BOWLING RECORDS

Best Bowling

7-15	G. D. McGrath	Australia v Namibia at Potchefstroom	2002-03
7-20	A. J. Bichel	Australia v England at Port Elizabeth	2002-03
7-33	T. G. Southee	New Zealand v England at Wellington	2014-15
7-51	W. W. Davis	West Indies v Australia at Leeds	1983
6-14	G. J. Gilmour	Australia v England at Leeds	1975
6-23	A. Nehra	India v England at Durban	2002-03
6-23	S. E. Bond	New Zealand v Australia at Port Elizabeth	2002-03
6-25	W. P. U. J. C. Vaas	Sri Lanka v Bangladesh at Pietermaritzburg	2002-03
6-27	K. A. J. Roach	West Indies v Netherlands at Delhi	2010-11
6-28	M. A. Starc	Australia v New Zealand at Auckland	2014-15
6-35	**Shaheen Shah Afridi**	**Pakistan v Bangladesh at Lord's**	**2019**
6-38	S. L. Malinga	Sri Lanka v Kenya at Colombo (RPS)	2010-11
6-39	K. H. MacLeay	Australia v India at Nottingham	1983

Best analyses for other Test-playing countries:

5-18	A. J. Hall	South Africa v England at Bridgetown	2006-07
5-21	P. A. Strang	Zimbabwe v Kenya at Patna	1995-96
5-29	**Shakib Al Hasan**	**Bangladesh v Afghanistan at Southampton**	**2019**
5-39	V. J. Marks	England v Sri Lanka at Taunton	1983
4-30	**Mohammad Nabi**	**Afghanistan v Sri Lanka at Cardiff**	**2019**
4-32	A. R. Cusack	Ireland v Zimbabwe at Hobart	2014-15

Other Bowling Records

Hat-tricks: Chetan Sharma, India v New Zealand at Nagpur, 1987-88; Saqlain Mushtaq, Pakistan v Zimbabwe at The Oval, 1999; W. P. U. J. C. Vaas, Sri Lanka v Bangladesh at Pietermaritzburg, 2002-03 (the first three balls of the match); B. Lee, Australia v Kenya at Durban, 2002-03; S. L. Malinga, Sri Lanka v South Africa at Providence, 2006-07 (four wickets in four balls); K. A. J. Roach, West Indies v Netherlands at Delhi, 2010-11; S. L. Malinga, Sri Lanka v Kenya at Colombo (RPS), 2010-11; S. T. Finn, England v Australia at Melbourne, 2014-15; J-P. Duminy, South Africa v Sri Lanka at Sydney, 2014-15; **Mohammed Shami, India v Afghanistan at Southampton, 2019**; **T. A. Boult, New Zealand v Australia at Lord's, 2019**.

Most economical bowling (minimum 10 overs): 12–8–6–1, B. S. Bedi, India v East Africa at Leeds, 1975.

Most expensive bowling: 9–0–110–0, Rashid Khan, Afghanistan v England at Manchester, 2019; 12–1–105–2, M. C. Snedden, New Zealand v England at The Oval, 1983; 10–2–104–1, J. O. Holder, West Indies v South Africa at Sydney, 2014-15; 10–1–101–2, Dawlat Zadran, Afghanistan v Australia at Perth, 2014-15.

Most Wickets in a Tournament

27, M. A. Starc (A) 2019; 26, G. D. McGrath (A) 2006-07; 23, M. Muralitharan (SL) 2006-07, S. W. Tait (A) 2006-07 and W. P. U. J. C. Vaas (SL) 2002-03; 22, T. A. Boult (NZ) 2014-15, B. Lee (A) 2002-03, M. A. Starc (A) 2014-15; **21, L. H. Ferguson (NZ) 2019**, G. B. Hogg (A) 2006-07, G. D. McGrath (A) 2002-03, Shahid Afridi (P) 2010-11 and Zaheer Khan (I) 2010-11; **20,** G. I. Allott (NZ) 1999, **J. C. Archer (E) 2019, Mustafizur Rahman (B) 2019**, S. K. Warne (A) 1999.

Most Wickets

	M	B	R	W	BB	4I	Avge
G. D. McGrath (Australia)....	39	1,955	1,292	71	7-15	2	18.19
M. Muralitharan (Sri Lanka) ..	40	2,061	1,335	68	4-19	4	19.63
S. L. Malinga (Sri Lanka) ...	**29**	**1,394**	**1,281**	**56**	**6-38**	**3**	**22.87**
Wasim Akram (Pakistan).....	38	1,947	1,311	55	5-28	3	23.83
M. A. Starc (Australia)	**18**	**937**	**726**	**49**	**6-28**	**6**	**14.81**
W. P. U. J. C. Vaas (Sri Lanka)	31	1,570	1,040	49	6-25	2	21.22
Zaheer Khan (India).........	23	1,193	890	44	4-42	1	20.22
J. Srinath (India)	34	1,700	1,224	44	4-30	2	27.81
Imran Tahir (South Africa) .	**22**	**1,151**	**847**	**40**	**5-45**	**5**	**21.17**
T. A. Boult (New Zealand) ..	**19**	**1,104**	**850**	**39**	**5-27**	**4**	**21.79**
A. A. Donald (South Africa) ..	25	1,313	913	38	4-17	2	24.02
J. D. P. Oram (New Zealand) ..	23	1,094	768	36	4-39	2	21.33
D. L. Vettori (New Zealand) ..	32	1,689	1,168	36	4-18	2	32.44
B. Lee (Australia)	17	825	629	35	5-42	3	17.97
Wahab Riaz (Pakistan)	**20**	**1,000**	**926**	**35**	**5-46**	**2**	**26.45**
G. B. Hogg (Australia).......	21	951	654	34	4-27	2	19.23
Imran Khan (Pakistan).......	28	1,017	655	34	4-37	2	19.26
S. W. Tait (Australia)........	18	819	731	34	4-39	1	21.50
T. G. Southee (New Zealand)	**18**	**974**	**854**	**34**	**7-33**	**1**	**25.11**
Shakib Al Hasan (Bangladesh)	**29**	**1,433**	**1,222**	**34**	**5-29**	**2**	**35.94**
S. K. Warne (Australia)	28	1,166	624	32	4-29	4	19.50
C. Z. Harris (New Zealand) ...	17	977	861	32	4-7	1	26.90

WICKETKEEPING RECORDS

Most Dismissals in an Innings

6 (6ct)	A. C. Gilchrist	Australia v Namibia at Potchefstroom	2002-03
6 (6ct)	Sarfraz Ahmed	Pakistan v South Africa at Auckland	2014-15
5 (5ct)	S. M. H. Kirmani	India v Zimbabwe at Leicester	1983
5 (4ct, 1st)	J. C. Adams	West Indies v Kenya at Pune	1995-96
5 (4ct, 1st)	Rashid Latif	Pakistan v New Zealand at Lahore	1995-96
5 (5ct)	R. D. Jacobs	West Indies v New Zealand at Southampton	1999
5 (4ct, 1st)	N. R. Mongia	India v Zimbabwe at Leicester	1999
5 (5ct)	Umar Akmal........	Pakistan v Zimbabwe at Brisbane	2014-15
5 (4ct, 1st)	**A. T. Carey ....**	**Australia v Afghanistan at Bristol**	**2019**
5 (5ct)	**T. W. M. Latham ...**	**New Zealand v Afghanistan at Taunton**	**2019**

Most Dismissals in a Tournament

21, A. C. Gilchrist (A) 2002-03 and **T. W. M. Latham (NZ) 2019**; **20, A. T. Carey (A) 2019**; 17, A. C. Gilchrist (A) 2006-07 and K. C. Sangakkara (SL) 2002-03; **16,** R. Dravid (I) 2002-03, P. J. L. Dujon (WI) 1983, B. J. Haddin (A) 2014-15, **S. D. Hope (WI) 2019** and Moin Khan (P) 1999; 15, M. S. Dhoni (I) 2014-15, D. J. Richardson (SA) 1991-92, K. C. Sangakkara (SL) 2006-07.

Most Dismissals

K. C. Sangakkara (SL)	54 (41ct, 13st)	**Mushfiqur Rahim (B)**	28 (21ct, 7st)	
A. C. Gilchrist (A)	52 (45ct, 7st)	D. Ramdin (WI)	26 (26ct)	
M. S. Dhoni (I)	**42 (34ct, 8st)**	A. J. Stewart (E)	23 (21ct, 2st)	
B. B. McCullum (NZ)	32 (30ct, 2st)	**J. C. Buttler (E).**	**22 (20ct, 2st)**	
M. V. Boucher (SA)	31 (31ct)	R. D. Jacobs (WI)	22 (21ct, 1st)	
Moin Khan (P)	30 (23ct, 7st)	Wasim Bari (P)	22 (18ct, 4st)	
B. J. Haddin (A)	29 (29ct)			

B. B. McCullum took a further two catches in nine matches when not keeping wicket.

FIELDING RECORDS

Most Catches

28, R. T. Ponting (A); **20, J. E. Root (E)**; 18, S. T. Jayasuriya (SL); **17, C. H. Gayle (WI)**; **16**, C. L. Cairns (NZ), **F. du Plessis (SA)**, Inzamam-ul-Haq (P), D. P. M D. Jayawardene (SL), B. C. Lara (WI) and **E. J. G. Morgan (Ire/E)**; 15, G. C. Smith (SA).

MOST APPEARANCES

46, R. T. Ponting (A); 45, S. R. Tendulkar (I); 40, D. P. M D. Jayawardene (SL) and M. Muralitharan (SL); 39, G. D. McGrath (A); 38, S. T. Jayasuriya (SL) and Wasim Akram (P); 37, K. C. Sangakkara (SL); 36, J. H. Kallis (SA); **35, P. A. de Silva (SL), C. H. Gayle (WI)** and Inzamam-ul-Haq (P); 34, B. C. Lara (WI), B. B. McCullum (NZ) and J. Srinath (I); **33**, S. P. Fleming (NZ), Javed Miandad (P), **L. R. P. L. Taylor (NZ)** and S. R. Waugh (A); 32, D. L. Vettori (NZ).

TEAM RECORDS

Highest Totals

417-6	(50 overs)	Australia v Afghanistan at Perth	2014-15
413-5	(50 overs)	India v Bermuda at Port-of-Spain	2006-07
411-4	(50 overs)	South Africa v Ireland at Canberra	2014-15
408-5	(50 overs)	South Africa v West Indies at Sydney	2014-15
398-5	(50 overs)	Sri Lanka v Kenya at Kandy	1995-96
397-6	**(50 overs)**	**England v Afghanistan at Manchester.**	**2019**
393-6	(50 overs)	New Zealand v West Indies at Wellington	2014-15
386-6	**(50 overs)**	**England v Bangladesh at Cardiff**	**2019**
381-5	**(50 overs)**	**Australia v Bangladesh at Nottingham**	**2019**
377-6	(50 overs)	Australia v South Africa at Basseterre	2006-07
376-9	(50 overs)	Australia v Sri Lanka at Sydney	2014-15

Highest totals for other Test-playing countries:

372-2	(50 overs)	West Indies v Zimbabwe at Canberra	2014-15
349	(49.5 overs)	Pakistan v Zimbabwe at Kingston	2006-07
340-2	(50 overs)	Zimbabwe v Namibia at Harare	2002-03
333-8	**(50 overs)**	**Bangladesh v Australia at Nottingham**	**2019**
331-8	(50 overs)	Ireland v Zimbabwe at Hobart	2014-15
288	**(50 overs)**	**Afghanistan v West Indies at Leeds**	**2019**

Highest total batting second:

338-8	(50 overs)	England v India at Bangalore	2010-11

Lowest Totals

36	(18.4 overs)	Canada v Sri Lanka at Paarl	2002-03
45	(40.3 overs)	Canada v England at Manchester	1979
45	(14 overs)	Namibia v Australia at Potchefstroom.	2002-03
58	(18.5 overs)	Bangladesh v West Indies at Mirpur.	2010-11
68	(31.3 overs)	Scotland v West Indies at Leicester.	1999
69	(23.5 overs)	Kenya v New Zealand at Chennai.	2010-11
74	(40.2 overs)	Pakistan v England at Adelaide.	1991-92
77	(27.4 overs)	Ireland v Sri Lanka at St George's	2006-07
78	(24.4 overs)	Bermuda v Sri Lanka at Port-of-Spain	2006-07
78	(28 overs)	Bangladesh v South Africa at Mirpur	2010-11

Highest Aggregate

714-13	**(100 overs)**	**Australia v Bangladesh at Nottingham**	**2019**

RESULTS

Largest Victories

10 wkts	India beat East Africa at Leeds	1975
10 wkts	West Indies beat Zimbabwe at Birmingham.	1983
10 wkts	West Indies beat Pakistan at Melbourne	1991-92
10 wkts	South Africa beat Kenya at Potchefstroom	2002-03
10 wkts	Sri Lanka beat Bangladesh at Pietermaritzburg	2002-03
10 wkts	South Africa beat Bangladesh at Bloemfontein	2002-03
10 wkts	Australia beat Bangladesh at North Sound	2006-07
10 wkts	New Zealand beat Kenya at Chennai	2010-11
10 wkts	New Zealand beat Zimbabwe at Ahmedabad	2010-11
10 wkts	Pakistan beat West Indies at Mirpur	2010-11
10 wkts	Sri Lanka beat England at Colombo (RPS).	2010-11
10 wkts	**New Zealand beat Sri Lanka at Cardiff**	**2019**
275 runs	Australia beat Afghanistan at Perth	2014-15
257 runs	India beat Bermuda at Port-of-Spain	2006-07
257 runs	South Africa beat West Indies at Sydney	2014-15
256 runs	Australia beat Namibia at Potchefstroom	2002-03

Narrowest Victories

1 wkt	West Indies beat Pakistan at Birmingham	1975
1 wkt	Pakistan beat West Indies at Lahore.	1987-88
1 wkt	South Africa beat Sri Lanka at Providence.	2006-07
1 wkt	England beat West Indies at Bridgetown	2006-07
1 wkt	Afghanistan beat Scotland at Dunedin	2014-15
1 wkt	New Zealand beat Australia at Auckland	2014-15
1 run	Australia beat India at Madras	1987-88
1 run	Australia beat India at Brisbane	1991-92
2 runs	Sri Lanka beat England at North Sound	2006-07

Ties

Australia v South Africa at Birmingham	1999
South Africa v Sri Lanka (D/L) at Durban.	2002-03
Ireland v Zimbabwe at Kingston	2006-07
India v England at Bangalore.	2010-11

In the 2019 final at Lord's, New Zealand scored 241-8 and England 241, but England won the match on boundary count after a super over was also tied.

TWENTY20 INTERNATIONAL RECORDS

Matches in this section do not have first-class status.

This section covers Twenty20 international cricket to December 31, 2019. Bold type denotes performances since January 1, 2019, or, in career figures, players who have appeared in Twenty20 internationals since that date. The ICC extended official international status to Associate Twenty20 matches from the start of 2019.

RESULTS SUMMARY OF TWENTY20 INTERNATIONALS

2004-05 to December 31, 2019 (1,024 matches)

	Matches	Won	Lost	No Result	% Won (excl. NR)
Afghanistan..................	78	53	25	–	67.94
India.......................	126	79*	44	3	64.22
Pakistan....................	149	91*	57†	1	61.48
South Africa................	115	69*	45	1	60.52
Australia...................	122	65	54†	3	54.62
England.....................	114	58†	52	4	52.72
New Zealand.................	126	63†	60§	3	51.21
Sri Lanka...................	123	60*	62*	1	49.18
Ireland.....................	92	40¶	45	6	47.09
West Indies.................	119	53†	62*	4	46.08
Bangladesh..................	92	30	60	2	33.33
Zimbabwe....................	74	20†	54	–	27.02
Papua New Guinea............	26	17	8	1	68.00
Netherlands.................	75	39	33*	3	54.16
Nepal.......................	31	15	15	1	50.00
Scotland....................	65	29¶	32	3	47.58
United Arab Emirates........	44	19	24	1	44.18
Oman.......................	33	14	18	1	43.75
Canada.....................	31	12	18*	1	40.00
Kenya......................	38	15	23	0	39.47
Hong Kong..................	35	13	22	–	37.14

* *Includes one game settled by a tie-break.*   † *Includes two games settled by a tie-break.*
‡ *Includes three settled by a tie-break.*   § *Includes four settled by a tie-break.*
¶ *Plus one tie.*
Apart from Ireland v Scotland, ties were decided by bowling contests or one-over eliminators.

Matches abandoned without a ball bowled are not included except where the toss took place, when they are shown as no result. In the percentages of matches won, ties are counted as half a win.

A further 51 teams have played Twenty20 internationals, as follows: Argentina (P5 W5); Belize (P3 W3); Spain (P9 W8 L1); Malawi (P7 W5 L1 NR1); Austria (P5 W4 L1); Namibia (P16 W12 L4); Romania (P4 W3 L1); Qatar (P15 W11 L4); Czech Republic (P7 W5 L2); Italy (P8 W5 L2 NR1); Germany (P10 W7 L3); Bulgaria (P3 W2 L1); Greece (P3 W2 L1); Panama (P3 W2 L1); Saudi Arabia (P5 W3 L2); Jersey (P17 W10 L7); Denmark (P9 W4 L3 NR2); Singapore (P12 W6 L6); Bahrain (P4 W2 L2); Peru (P4 W2 L2); Portugal (P4 W2 L2); Uganda (P4 W2 L2); Malaysia (P15 W6 L8 NR1); Kuwait (P10 W4 L6); Mexico (P8 W3 L5); Vanuatu (P14 W5 L9); Philippines (P4 W1 L2 NR1); Bermuda (P15 W4 L10 NR1); USA (P8 W2 L5 NR1); Guernsey (P9 W2 L6 NR1); Brazil (P4 W1 L3); Chile (P4 W1 L3); Luxembourg (P4 W1 L3); Samoa (P4 W1 L3); Thailand (P4 W1 L3); World XI (P4 W1 L3); Nigeria (P9 W2 L7); Maldives (P11 W2 L8 NR1); Finland (P5 W1 L4); Mozambique (P7 W1 L5 NR1); Botswana (P7 L7); Cayman Islands (P6 L6); Norway (P5 L5); Ghana (P4 L4); Gibraltar (P4 L4); Malta (P4 L4); Turkey (P4 L4); Belgium (P3 L3); Costa Rica (P3 L3); Bhutan (P2 L2); Serbia (P2 L2).

BATTING RECORDS

HIGHEST INDIVIDUAL INNINGS

172	A. J. Finch	Australia v Zimbabwe at Harare........................	2018
162*	**Hazratullah Zazai**	**Afghanistan v Ireland at Dehradun................**	**2018-19**
156	A. J. Finch	Australia v England at Southampton.................	2013
145*	G. J. Maxwell	Australia v Sri Lanka at Pallekele..................	2016
127*	**H. G. Munsey**	**Scotland v Netherlands at Malahide...............**	**2019**
125*	E. Lewis	West Indies v India at Kingston.....................	2017
124*	S. R. Watson	Australia v India at Sydney........................	2015-16
124	**K. J. O'BRIEN**	**Ireland v Hong Kong at Al Amerat...............**	**2019-20**
123	B. B. McCullum	New Zealand v Bangladesh at Pallekele.............	2012-13
122	Babar Hayat	Hong Kong v Oman at Fatullah......................	2015-16
119	F. du Plessis	South Africa v West Indies at Johannesburg........	2014-15
118*	Mohammad Shahzad	Afghanistan v Zimbabwe at Sharjah.................	2015-16
118	R. G. Sharma	India v Sri Lanka at Indore.......................	2017-18
117*	R. E. Levi	South Africa v New Zealand at Hamilton............	2011-12
117*	Shaiman Anwar	United Arab Emirates v Papua New Guinea at Abu Dhabi	2016-17
117	C. H. Gayle	West Indies v South Africa at Johannesburg........	2007-08
116*	B. B. McCullum	New Zealand v Australia at Christchurch...........	2009-10
116*	A. D. Hales	England v Sri Lanka at Chittagong.................	2013-14
114*	M. N. van Wyk	South Africa v West Indies at Durban..............	2014-15
113*	**G. J. Maxwell**	**Australia v India at Bangalore..................**	**2018-19**
111*	Ahmed Shehzad	Pakistan v Bangladesh at Mirpur..................	2013-14
111*	R. G. Sharma	India v West Indies at Lucknow...................	2018-19
111*	**Bilal Zalmai**	**Austria v Czech Republic at Ilfov...............**	**2019**
110*	K. L. Rahul	India v West Indies at Lauderhill.................	2016

MOST RUNS

		M	I	NO	R	HS	100	Avge	SR
1 {	**V. Kohli (India)**.................	75	70	20	2,633	94*	0	52.66	138.07
	R. G. Sharma (India)...........	104	96	14	2,633	118	4	32.10	138.21
3	**M. J. Guptill (New Zealand)**......	83	80	7	2,436	105	2	33.36	134.58
4	**Shoaib Malik (Pakistan/World)**...	111	104	30	2,263	75	0	30.58	123.79
5	B. B. McCullum (New Zealand)...	71	70	10	2,140	123	2	35.66	136.21
6	**D. A. Warner (Australia)**.........	76	76	8	2,079	100*	1	30.57	140.85
7	**E. J. G. Morgan (England)**.......	86	83	16	2,002	91	0	29.88	135.72
8	Mohammad Shahzad (Afghanistan)..	65	65	3	1,936	118*	1	31.22	134.81
9	**J-P. Duminy (South Africa)**......	81	75	25	1,934	96*	0	38.68	126.24
10	**P. R. Stirling (Ireland)**..........	72	71	6	1,929	91	0	29.67	137.68
11	Mohammad Hafeez (Pakistan).....	89	86	8	1,908	86	0	24.46	116.12
12	T. M. Dilshan (Sri Lanka).......	80	79	12	1,889	104*	1	28.19	120.47
13	**A. J. Finch (Australia)**..........	58	58	9	1,878	172	2	38.32	156.50
14	**L. R. P. L. Taylor (New Zealand)**..	95	87	19	1,743	63	0	25.63	121.88
15	**Umar Akmal (Pakistan)**.........	84	79	14	1,690	94	0	26.00	122.73
16	A. B. de Villiers (South Africa)..	78	75	11	1,672	79*	0	26.12	135.16
17	**H. Masakadza (Zimbabwe)**......	66	66	2	1,662	93*	0	25.96	117.20
18	**A. D. Hales (England)**..........	60	60	7	1,644	116*	1	31.01	136.65
19	**C. H. Gayle (West Indies)**.......	58	54	4	1,627	117	2	32.54	142.84
20	**M. S. Dhoni (India)**............	98	85	42	1,617	56	0	37.60	126.13
21	Tamim Iqbal (Bangladesh/World)...	75	75	5	1,613	103*	1	23.04	116.63
22	M. N. Samuels (West Indies)......	67	65	10	1,611	89*	0	29.29	116.23
23	S. K. Raina (India).............	78	66	11	1,605	101	1	29.18	134.87
24	**G. J. Maxwell (Australia)**.......	61	54	9	1,576	145*	3	35.02	160.00
25	Shakib Al Hasan (Bangladesh)....	76	76	10	1,567	84	0	23.74	123.77

Excluding runs for the World XI, the record aggregate for Pakistan is **2,251** *in 110 matches by* **Shoaib Malik**, *and for Bangladesh 1,556 in 71 matches by Tamim Iqbal.*

FASTEST TWENTY20 INTERNATIONAL FIFTIES

Balls
12	Yuvraj Singh	India v England at Durban	2007-08
14	C. Munro	New Zealand v Sri Lanka at Auckland	2015-16
16	S. D. Hope	West Indies v Bangladesh at Sylhet	2018-19
17	P. R. Stirling	Ireland v Afghanistan at Dubai	2011-12
17	S. J. Myburgh	Netherlands v Ireland at Sylhet	2013-14
17	C. H. Gayle	West Indies v South Africa at Cape Town	2014-15
18	D. A. Warner	Australia v West Indies at Sydney	2009-10
18	G. J. Maxwell	Australia v Pakistan at Mirpur	2013-14
18	G. J. Maxwell	Australia v Sri Lanka at Pallekele	2016
18	C. Munro	New Zealand v West Indies at Mount Maunganui	2017-18
18	C. Munro	New Zealand v England at Hamilton	2017-18
18	E. Lewis	West Indies v Bangladesh at Mirpur	2018-19

FASTEST TWENTY20 INTERNATIONAL HUNDREDS

Balls
35	D. A. Miller	South Africa v Bangladesh at Potchefstroom	2017-18
35	R. G. Sharma	India v Sri Lanka at Indore	2017-18
41	**H. G. Munsey**	**Scotland v Netherlands at Malahide**	**2019**
42	**Hazratullah Zazai**	**Afghanistan v Ireland at Dehradun**	**2018-19**
45	R. E. Levi	South Africa v New Zealand at Hamilton	2011-12
46	F. du Plessis	South Africa v West Indies at Johannesburg	2014-15
46	K. L. Rahul	India v West Indies at Lauderhill	2016
47	A. J. Finch	Australia v England at Southampton	2013
47	C. H. Gayle	West Indies v England at Mumbai	2015-16
47	C. Munro	New Zealand v West Indies at Mount Maunganui	2017-18
48	E. Lewis	West Indies v India at Lauderhill	2016
48	**D. J. Malan**	**England v New Zealand at Napier**	**2019-20**
49	G. J. Maxwell	Australia v Sri Lanka at Pallekele	2016
49	M. J. Guptill	New Zealand v Australia at Auckland	2017-18
49	**P. Khadka**	**Nepal v Singapore at Singapore**	**2019-20**

HIGHEST PARTNERSHIP FOR EACH WICKET

236	**for 1st**	**Hazratullah Zazai/Usman Ghani**	**Afg v Ire**	**Dehradun**	**2018-19**
166	for 2nd	D. P. M. D. Jayawardene/K. C. Sangakkara	SL v WI	Bridgetown	2010
182	**for 3rd**	**D. J. Malan/E. J. G. Morgan**	**E v NZ**	**Napier**	**2019-20**
161	for 4th	D. A. Warner/G. J. Maxwell	A v SA	Johannesburg	2015-16
119*	for 5th	Shoaib Malik/Misbah-ul-Haq	P v A	Johannesburg	2007-08
101*	for 6th	C. L. White/M. E. K. Hussey	A v SL	Bridgetown	2010
91	for 7th	P. D. Collingwood/M. H. Yardy	E v WI	The Oval	2007
80	for 8th	P. L. Mommsen/S. M. Sharif	Scot v Neth	Edinburgh	2015
66	for 9th	D. J. Bravo/J. E. Taylor	WI v P	Dubai	2016-17
31*	for 10th	Wahab Riaz/Shoaib Akhtar	P v NZ	Auckland	2010-11

BOWLING RECORDS

BEST BOWLING ANALYSES

6-7	**D. L. Chahar**	**India v Bangladesh at Nagpur**	**2019-20**
6-8	B. A. W. Mendis	Sri Lanka v Zimbabwe at Hambantota	2012-13
6-16	B. A. W. Mendis	Sri Lanka v Australia at Pallekele	2011-12
6-25	Y. S. Chahal	India v England at Bangalore	2016-17
5-3	H. M. R. K. B. Herath	Sri Lanka v New Zealand at Chittagong	2013-14
5-3	Rashid Khan	Afghanistan v Ireland at Greater Noida	2016-17
5-4	**P. Arrighi**	**Argentina v Brazil at Lima**	**2019-20**
5-6	Umar Gul	Pakistan v New Zealand at The Oval	2009
5-6	Umar Gul	Pakistan v South Africa at Centurion	2012-13

5-6	S. L. Malinga	Sri Lanka v New Zealand at Pallekele	2019
5-6	A. Nanda	Luxembourg v Turkey at Ilfov	2019
5-9	C. Viljoen	Namibia v Botswana at Kampala	2019
5-11	**Karim Janat**	Afghanistan v West Indies at Lucknow	2019-20
5-13	Elias Sunny	Bangladesh v Ireland at Belfast	2012
5-13	Samiullah Shenwari	Afghanistan v Kenya at Sharjah	2013-14
5-14	Imad Wasim	Pakistan v West Indies at Dubai	2016-17

HAT-TRICKS

Four Wickets in Four Balls

| Rashid Khan | Afghanistan v Ireland at Dehradun | 2018-19 |
| S. L. Malinga | Sri Lanka v New Zealand at Pallekele | 2019 |

Four Wickets in Five Balls

| T. G. Southee | New Zealand v Pakistan at Auckland | 2010-11 |

Hat-Tricks

There have been **12** hat-tricks in Twenty20 internationals, including the above; S. L. Malinga has taken two. The most recent are:

Mohammad Hasnain	Pakistan v Sri Lanka at Lahore	2019-20
Khawar Ali	Oman v Netherlands at Al Amerat	2019-20
N. Vanua	Papua New Guinea v Bermuda at Dubai	2019-20
D. L. Chahar	India v Bangladesh at Nagpur	2019-20

MOST WICKETS

		M	B	R	W	BB	4I	Avge	ER
1	**S. L. Malinga (Sri Lanka)**	79	1,709	2,061	106	5-6	3	19.44	7.23
2	Shahid Afridi (Pakistan/World)	99	2,168	2,396	98	4-11	3	24.44	6.63
3	**Shakib Al Hasan (Bangladesh)**	76	1,667	1,894	92	5-20	4	20.58	6.81
4	Umar Gul (Pakistan)	60	1,203	1,443	85	5-6	6	16.97	7.19
	Saeed Ajmal (Pakistan)	64	1,430	1,516	85	4-19	4	17.83	6.36
6	**Rashid Khan (Afghanistan/World)**	45	1,026	1,052	84	5-3	5	12.52	6.15
7	**G. H. Dockrell (Ireland)**	73	1,328	1,539	75	4-20	1	20.52	6.95
	T. G. Southee (New Zealand)	66	1,401	1,954	75	5-18	1	26.05	8.36
9	**Mohammad Nabi (Afghanistan)**	75	1,540	1,839	69	4-10	3	26.65	7.16
10	B. A. W. Mendis (Sri Lanka)	39	885	952	66	6-8	5	14.42	6.45
	K. M. D. N. Kulasekara (Sri Lanka)	58	1,231	1,530	66	4-31	2	23.18	7.45
12	S. C. J. Broad (England)	56	1,173	1,491	65	4-24	1	22.93	7.62
13	Imran Tahir (South Africa/World)	38	845	948	63	5-23	4	15.04	6.73
14	D. W. Steyn (South Africa)	44	943	1,068	61	4-9	2	17.50	6.79
15	Mohammad Amir (Pakistan)	48	1,054	1,224	59	4-13	1	20.74	6.96
16	**K. J. O'Brien (Ireland)**	90	903	1,134	58	4-45	1	19.55	7.53
	N. L. McCullum (New Zealand)	63	1,123	1,278	58	4-16	2	22.03	6.82
18	S. Badree (West Indies/World)	52	1,146	1,180	56	4-15	1	21.07	6.17
19	**R. E. van der Merwe (SA/Neth)**	43	895	938	54	4-35	1	17.37	6.28
	Mohammad Hafeez (Pakistan)	89	1,117	1,226	54	4-10	1	22.70	6.58
	C. J. Jordan (England)	43	909	1,300	54	4-6	2	24.07	8.58
	Sohail Tanvir (Pakistan)	57	1,214	1,454	54	3-12	0	26.92	7.18
23	**W. B. Rankin (Ireland/England)**	48	1,020	1,138	53	3-16	0	21.47	6.69
	P. M. Seelaar (Netherlands)	49	1,035	1,190	53	4-19	1	22.45	6.89

The leading aggregates for other Test countries are:

	M	B	R	W	BB	4I	Avge	ER
Y. S. Chahal (India)	36	843	1,139	52	6-25	3	21.90	8.10
R. Ashwin (India)	46	1,026	1,193	52	4-8	2	22.94	6.97
S. R. Watson (Australia)	58	930	1,187	48	4-15	1	24.72	7.65
S. C. Williams (Zimbabwe)	38	738	890	32	3-15	0	27.81	7.23

*Excluding the World XI, the record aggregate for Pakistan is 97 in 98 matches by Shahid Afridi; for Afghanistan 82 in 44 matches by **Rashid Khan**; for South Africa 61 in 35 by **Imran Tahir** and by **D. W. Steyn** (see above); and for West Indies 54 in 50 matches by S. Badree.*

WICKETKEEPING AND FIELDING RECORDS

MOST DISMISSALS IN AN INNINGS

5 (3ct, 2st)	Mohammad Shahzad	Afghanistan v Oman at Abu Dhabi	2015-16
5 (5ct)	M. S. Dhoni	India v England at Bristol.	2018
5 (2ct, 3st)	I. A. Karim	**Kenya v Ghana at Kampala**	**2019**
5 (5ct)	K. Doriga	**Papua New Guinea v Vanuata at Apia**	**2019**

*There have been **24** instances of four dismissals in an innings.*

MOST DISMISSALS

			M	Ct	St
1	91	M. S. Dhoni (India)	98	57	34
2	63	D. Ramdin (West Indies)	71	43	20
3	60	Kamran Akmal (Pakistan)	53	28	32
4	58	**Mushfiqur Rahim (Bangladesh)**	80	30	28
5	54	Mohammad Shahzad (Afghanistan)	64	26	28
6	46	Q. de Kock (South Africa)	37	36	10
7 {	45	K. C. Sangakkara (Sri Lanka)	56	25	20
	45	**Sarfraz Ahmed (Pakistan)**	58	35	10

Mushfiqur Rahim's record excludes one catch in four matches when not keeping wicket. Kamran Akmal played five matches and Mohammad Shahzad and Q. de Kock one each in which they did not keep wicket or take a catch.

MOST CATCHES IN AN INNINGS IN THE FIELD

There have been **12** instances of four catches in an innings. The most recent are:

4	A. M. Rahane	India v England at Birmingham.	2014
4	Babar Hayat	Hong Kong v Afghanistan at Mirpur	2015-16
4	**D. A. Miller**	**South Africa v Pakistan at Cape Town**	**2018-19**
4	**J. W. Jenner**	**Jersey v Guernsey at Castel**	**2019**
4	**L. Siaka**	**Papua New Guinea v Vanuatu at Apia**	**2019**
4	**C. S. MacLeod**	**Scotland v Ireland at Malahide**	**2019**
4	**T. H. David**	**Singapore v Scotland at Dubai**	**2019-20**
4	**C. de Grandhomme**	**New Zealand v England at Wellington**	**2019-20**

MOST CATCHES

Ct	M		Ct	M	
50	71	D. A. Miller (South Africa/World)	39	64	Umar Akmal (Pakistan)
50	111	Shoaib Malik (Pakistan/World)	38	104	R. G. Sharma (India)
46	83	M. J. Guptill (New Zealand)	37	73	G. H. Dockrell (Ireland)
44	52	A. B. de Villiers (South Africa)	37	75	V. Kohli (India)
44	95	L. R. P. L. Taylor (New Zealand)	37	86	E. J. G. Morgan (England)
43	76	D. A. Warner (Australia)	35	66	D. J. Bravo (West Indies)
42	78	S. K. Raina (India)	35	81	J-P. Duminy (South Africa)
41	75	Mohammad Nabi (Afghanistan)			

D. A. Miller's record excludes 2 dismissals (1ct, 1st) in one match when keeping wicket; A. B. de Villiers's excludes 28 (21ct, 7st) in 26 matches and Umar Akmal's 13 (11ct, 2st) in 20 matches.

TEAM RECORDS

HIGHEST INNINGS TOTALS

278-3	**(20 overs)**	**Afghanistan v Ireland at Dehradun**	**2018-19**
278-4	**(20 overs)**	**Czech Republic v Turkey at Ilfov**	**2019**
263-3	(20 overs)	Australia v Sri Lanka at Pallekele	2016
260-5	(20 overs)	India v Sri Lanka at Indore	2017-18
260-6	(20 overs)	Sri Lanka v Kenya at Johannesburg	2007-08
252-3	**(20 overs)**	**Scotland v Netherlands at Malahide**	**2019**
248-6	(20 overs)	Australia v England at Southampton	2013
245-5	(18.5 overs)	Australia v New Zealand at Auckland	2017-18
245-6	(20 overs)	West Indies v India at Lauderhill	2016
244-4	(20 overs)	India v West Indies at Lauderhill	2016
243-5	(20 overs)	New Zealand v West Indies at Mount Maunganui	2017-18
243-6	(20 overs)	New Zealand v Australia at Auckland	2017-18
241-3	**(20 overs)**	**England v New Zealand at Napier**	**2019-20**
241-6	(20 overs)	South Africa v England at Centurion	2009-10
240-3	**(20 overs)**	**Namibia v Botswana at Windhoek**	**2019**
240-3	**(20 overs)**	**India v West Indies at Mumbai**	**2019-20**

LOWEST INNINGS TOTALS

21	**(8.3 overs)**	**Turkey v Czech Republic at Ilfov**	**2019**
28	**(11.3 overs)**	**Turkey v Luxembourg at Ilfov**	**2019**
32	**(8.5 overs)**	**Turkey v Austria at Ilfov**	**2019**
39	(10.3 overs)	Netherlands v Sri Lanka at Chittagong	2013-14
45	**(11.5 overs)**	**West Indies v England at Basseterre**	**2018-19**
46	**(12.1 overs)**	**Botswana v Namibia at Windhoek**	**2019**
52	**(15.2 overs)**	**Serbia v Greece at Corfu**	**2019-20**
53	(14.3 overs)	Nepal v Ireland at Belfast	2015
53	**(16 overs)**	**Germany v Italy at Utrecht**	**2019**
53	**(13 overs)**	**Turkey v Romania at Ilfov**	**2019**
56	(18.4 overs)	Kenya v Afghanistan at Sharjah	2013-14
60†	(15.3 overs)	New Zealand v Sri Lanka at Chittagong	2013-14
60†	(13.4 overs)	West Indies v Pakistan at Karachi	2017-18

† *One man absent.*

OTHER RECORDS

MOST APPEARANCES

111	Shoaib Malik (Pakistan/World)		86	E. J. G. Morgan (England)
104	R. G. Sharma (India)		84	Mushfiqur Rahim (Bangladesh)
99	Shahid Afridi (Pakistan/World)		84	Umar Akmal (Pakistan)
98	M. S. Dhoni (India)		83	M. J. Guptill (New Zealand)
95	L. R. P. L. Taylor (New Zealand)		83	Mahmudullah (Bangladesh)
90	K. J. O'Brien (Ireland)		81	J-P. Duminy (South Africa)
89	Mohammad Hafeez (Pakistan)		80	T. M. Dilshan (Sri Lanka)

WORLD TWENTY20 FINALS

2007-08	INDIA (157-5) beat Pakistan (152) by five runs	Johannesburg
2009	PAKISTAN (139-2) beat Sri Lanka (138-6) by eight wickets	Lord's
2010	ENGLAND (148-3) beat Australia (147-6) by seven wickets	Bridgetown
2012-13	WEST INDIES (137-6) beat Sri Lanka (101) by 36 runs	Colombo (RPS)
2013-14	SRI LANKA (134-4) beat India (130-4) by six wickets	Mirpur
2015-16	WEST INDIES (161-6) beat England (155-9) by four wickets	Kolkata

MISCELLANEOUS RECORDS

LARGE ATTENDANCES

Test Series

943,000	Australia v England (5 Tests)	1936-37

In England

549,650	England v Australia (5 Tests)	1953

Test Matches

†‡465,000	India v Pakistan, Calcutta	1998-99
350,534	Australia v England, Melbourne (Third Test)	1936-37

Attendance at India v England at Calcutta in 1981-82 may have exceeded 350,000.

In England

158,000+	England v Australia, Leeds	1948
140,111	England v India, Lord's	2011
137,915	England v Australia, Lord's	1953

Test Match Day

‡100,000	India v Pakistan, Calcutta (first four days)	1998-99
91,112	Australia v England, Melbourne (Fourth Test, first day)	2013-14
90,800	Australia v West Indies, Melbourne (Fifth Test, second day)	1960-61
89,155	Australia v England, Melbourne (Fourth Test, first day)	2006-07

Other First-Class Matches in England

93,000	England v Australia, Lord's (Fourth Victory Match, 3 days)	1945
80,000+	Surrey v Yorkshire, The Oval (3 days)	1906
78,792	Yorkshire v Lancashire, Leeds (3 days)	1904
76,617	Lancashire v Yorkshire, Manchester (3 days)	1926

One-Day Internationals

‡100,000	India v South Africa, Calcutta	1993-94
‡100,000	India v West Indies, Calcutta	1993-94
‡100,000	India v West Indies, Calcutta	1994-95
‡100,000	India v Sri Lanka, Calcutta (World Cup semi-final)	1995-96
‡100,000	India v Australia, Kolkata	2003-04
93,013	Australia v New Zealand, Melbourne (World Cup final)	2014-15
‡90,000	India v Pakistan, Calcutta	1986-87
‡90,000	India v South Africa, Calcutta	1991-92
87,182	England v Pakistan, Melbourne (World Cup final)	1991-92
86,133	Australia v West Indies, Melbourne	1983-84

Twenty20 International

84,041	Australia v India, Melbourne	2007-08

† *Estimated.*
‡ *No official attendance figures were issued for these games, but capacity at Calcutta (now Kolkata) is believed to have reached 100,000 following rebuilding in 1993.*

LORD'S CRICKET GROUND

Lord's and the Marylebone Cricket Club were founded in London in 1787. The Club has enjoyed an uninterrupted career since that date, but there have been three grounds known as Lord's. The first (1787–1810) was situated where Dorset Square now is; the second (1809–13), at North Bank, had to be abandoned owing to the cutting of the Regent's Canal; and the third, opened in 1814, is the present one at St John's Wood. It was not until 1866 that the freehold of Lord's was secured by MCC. The present pavilion was erected in 1890 at a cost of £21,000.

MINOR CRICKET

HIGHEST INDIVIDUAL SCORES

1,009*	P. P. Dhanawade, K. C. Gandhi English School v Arya Gurukul at Kalyan	2015-16
	Dhanawade faced 327 balls in 6 hours 36 minutes and hit 129 fours and 59 sixes	
628*	A. E. J. Collins, Clark's House v North Town at Clifton College	1899
	Junior house match. He batted 6 hours 50 minutes spread over four afternoons	
566	C. J. Eady, Break-o'-Day v Wellington at Hobart	1901-02
556*	P. Moliya, Mohinder Lal Amarnath C Ac U14 v Yogi C Ac U14 at Vadodara . . .	2018-19
546	P. P. Shaw, Rizvi Springfield School v St Francis D'Assisi School at Mumbai . . .	2013-14
515	D. R. Havewalla, B. B. and C. I. Railways v St Xavier's at Bombay	1933-34
506*	J. C. Sharp, Melbourne GS v Geelong College at Melbourne	1914-15
502*	Chaman Lal, Mohindra Coll., Patiala v Government Coll., Rupar at Patiala	1956-57
498	Arman Jaffer, Rizvi Springfield School v IES Raja Shivaji School at Mumbai . . .	2010-11
490	S. Dadswell, North West University v Potchefstroom at Potchefstroom	2017-18
486*	S. Sankruth Sriram, JSS Intl School U16 v Hebron School U16 at Ootacamund .	2014-15
485	A. E. Stoddart, Hampstead v Stoics at Hampstead	1886
475*	Mohammad Iqbal, Muslim Model HS v Government HS, Sialkot at Gujranwala . .	1958-59
473	Arman Jaffer, Rizvi Springfield School v IES VN Sule School at Mumbai	2012-13
466*	G. T. S. Stevens, Beta v Lambda (Univ Coll School house match) at Neasden . .	1919
	Stevens scored his 466 and took 14 wickets on one day	
461*	Ali Zorain Khan, Nagpur Cricket Academy v Reshimbagh Gymkhana at Nagpur	2010-11
459	J. A. Prout, Wesley College v Geelong College at Geelong	1908-09
451*	V. H. Mol, Maharashtra Under-19 v Assam Under-19 at Nasik	2011-12

The highest score in a Minor County match is 323* by F. E. Lacey for Hampshire v Norfolk at Southampton in 1887; the highest in the Minor Counties Championship is 282 by E. Garnett for Berkshire v Wiltshire at Reading in 1908.

HIGHEST PARTNERSHIPS

721* for 1st	B. Manoj Kumar and M. S. Tumbi, St Peter's High School v St Philip's High School at Secunderabad	2006-07
664* for 3rd	V. G. Kambli and S. R. Tendulkar, Sharadashram Vidyamandir School v St Xavier's High School at Bombay	1987-88

Manoj Kumar and Tumbi reportedly scored 721 in 40 overs in an Under-13 inter-school match; they hit 103 fours between them, but no sixes. Their opponents were all out for 21 in seven overs.
Kambli was 16 years old, Tendulkar 14. Tendulkar made his Test debut 21 months later.

MOST WICKETS WITH CONSECUTIVE BALLS

There are **two** recorded instances of a bowler taking nine wickets with consecutive balls. Both came in school games: Paul Hugo, for Smithfield School v Aliwal North at Smithfield, South Africa, in 1930-31, and Stephen Fleming (not the future Test captain), for Marlborough College A v Bohally School at Blenheim, New Zealand, in 1967-68. There are five further verified instances of eight wickets in eight balls, the most recent by Mike Walters for the Royal Army Educational Corps v Joint Air Transport Establishment at Beaconsfield in 1979.

TEN WICKETS FOR NO RUNS

There are **26** recorded instances of a bowler taking all ten wickets in an innings for no runs, the most recent **Akash Choudhary**, for Disha Cricket Academy v Pearl Academy in the Late Bahwer Singh T20 Tournament in Jaipur 2017-18. When Jennings Tune did it, for the Yorkshire club Cliffe v Eastrington at Cliffe in 1923, all ten of his victims were bowled.

NOUGHT ALL OUT

In minor matches, this is more common than might be imagined. The historian Peter Wynne-Thomas says the first recorded example was in Norfolk, where an Eleven of Fakenham, Walsingham and Hempton were dismissed for nought by an Eleven of Licham, Dunham and Brisley in July 1815.

MOST DISMISSALS IN AN INNINGS

The only recorded instance of a wicketkeeper being involved in all ten dismissals in an innings was by Welihinda Badalge Bennett, for Mahinda College against Richmond College in Ceylon (now Sri Lanka) in 1952-53. His feat comprised six catches and four stumpings. There are three other known instances of nine dismissals in the same innings, one of which – by H. W. P. Middleton for Priory v Mitre in a Repton School house match in 1930 – included eight stumpings. Young Rangers' innings against Bohran Gymkhana in Karachi in 1969-70 included nine run-outs.

The widespread nature – and differing levels of supervision – of minor cricket matches mean that record claims have to be treated with caution. Additions and corrections to the above records for minor cricket will only be considered for inclusion in Wisden *if they are corroborated by independent evidence of the achievement.*

Research: Steven Lynch

RECORD HIT

The Rev. W. Fellows, while at practice on the Christ Church ground at Oxford in 1856, reportedly drove a ball bowled by Charles Rogers 175 yards from hit to pitch; it is claimed that the feat was matched by J. W. Erskine in a match at Galle in 1902.

BIGGEST HIT AT LORD'S

The only known instance of a batsman hitting a ball over the present pavilion at Lord's occurred when A. E. Trott, appearing for MCC against Australians on July 31, August 1, 2, 1899, drove M. A. Noble so far and high that the ball struck a chimney pot and fell behind the building.

THROWING THE CRICKET BALL

140 yards 2 feet	Robert Percival, on the Durham Sands racecourse, Co. Durham .	c1882
140 yards 9 inches . . .	Ross Mackenzie, at Toronto	1872
140 yards	"King Billy" the Aborigine, at Clermont, Queensland	1872

Extensive research by David Rayvern Allen has shown that these traditional records are probably authentic, if not necessarily wholly accurate. Modern competitions have failed to produce similar distances although Ian Pont, the Essex all-rounder who also played baseball, was reported to have thrown 138 yards in Cape Town in 1981. There have been speculative reports attributing throws of 150 yards or more to figures as diverse as the South African Test player Colin Bland, the Latvian javelin thrower Jānis Lūsis, who won a gold medal for the Soviet Union in the 1968 Olympics, and the British sprinter Charley Ransome. The definitive record is still awaited.

COUNTY CHAMPIONSHIP

MOST APPEARANCES

762	W. Rhodes	Yorkshire	1898–1930
707	F. E. Woolley	Kent	1906–1938
668	C. P. Mead	Hampshire	1906–1936
617	N. Gifford	Worcestershire (484), Warwickshire (133)	1960–1988
611	W. G. Quaife	Warwickshire	1895–1928
601	G. H. Hirst	Yorkshire	1891–1921

MOST CONSECUTIVE APPEARANCES

423	K. G. Suttle	Sussex	1954–1969
412	J. G. Binks	Yorkshire	1955–1969

J. Vine made 417 consecutive appearances for Sussex in all first-class matches (399 of them in the Championship) between July 1900 and September 1914.

J. G. Binks did not miss a Championship match for Yorkshire between making his debut in June 1955 and retiring at the end of the 1969 season.

UMPIRES

MOST COUNTY CHAMPIONSHIP APPEARANCES

570	T. W. Spencer	1950–1980	517	H. G. Baldwin	1932–1962
531	F. Chester	1922–1955	511	A. G. T. Whitehead	1970–2005
523	D. J. Constant	1969–2006			

MOST SEASONS ON ENGLISH FIRST-CLASS LIST

38	D. J. Constant	1969–2006	27	B. Dudleston	1984–2010
36	A. G. T. Whitehead	1970–2005	27	J. W. Holder	1983–2009
31	K. E. Palmer	1972–2002	27	J. Moss	1899–1929
31	T. W. Spencer	1950–1980	26	W. A. J. West	1896–1925
30	R. Julian	1972–2001	25	H. G. Baldwin	1932–1962
30	P. B. Wight	1966–1995	25	A. Jepson	1960–1984
29	H. D. Bird	1970–1998	25	J. G. Langridge	1956–1980
28	F. Chester	1922–1955	25	B. J. Meyer	1973–1997
28	B. Leadbeater	1981–2008	25	D. R. Shepherd	1981–2005
28	R. Palmer	1980–2007			

> ❝ When a much-anticipated Cricket Council meeting took place in the Long Room on a cold, dark February evening, it was possible to look through the windows and see, not the run stealers flicker to and fro, but the barbed wire silhouetted against the snow-covered turf.❞
> Stop the Seventy Tour, page 112

WOMEN'S TEST RECORDS

This section covers all women's Tests to December 31, 2019.

BATTING RECORDS

HIGHEST INDIVIDUAL INNINGS

242	Kiran Baluch	Pakistan v West Indies at Karachi	2003-04
214	M. D. Raj	India v England at Taunton	2002
213*	E. A. Perry	Australia v England at North Sydney	2017-18
209*	K. L. Rolton	Australia v England at Leeds	2001
204	K. E. Flavell	New Zealand v England at Scarborough	1996
204	M. A. J. Goszko	Australia v England at Shenley	2001
200	J. Broadbent	Australia v England at Guildford	1998

1,000 RUNS IN A CAREER

R	T		R	T	
1,935	27	J. A. Brittin (England)	1,110	13	S. Agarwal (India)
1,676	23	C. M. Edwards (England)	1,078	12	E. Bakewell (England)
1,594	22	R. Heyhoe-Flint (England)	1,030	15	S. C. Taylor (England)
1,301	19	D. A. Hockley (New Zealand)	1,007	14	M. E. Maclagan (England)
1,164	18	C. A. Hodges (England)	1,002	14	K. L. Rolton (Australia)

BOWLING RECORDS

BEST BOWLING ANALYSES

8-53	N. David	India v England at Jamshedpur	1995-96
7-6	M. B. Duggan	England v Australia at Melbourne	1957-58
7-7	E. R. Wilson	Australia v England at Melbourne	1957-58
7-10	M. E. Maclagan	England v Australia at Brisbane	1934-35
7-18	A. Palmer	Australia v England at Brisbane	1934-35
7-24	L. Johnston	Australia v New Zealand at Melbourne	1971-72
7-34	G. E. McConway	England v India at Worcester	1986
7-41	J. A. Burley	New Zealand v England at The Oval	1966

MOST WICKETS IN A MATCH

13-226	Shaiza Khan	Pakistan v West Indies at Karachi	2003-04

50 WICKETS IN A CAREER

W	T		W	T	
77	17	M. B. Duggan (England)	60	19	S. Kulkarni (India)
68	11	E. R. Wilson (Australia)	57	16	R. H. Thompson (Australia)
63	20	D. F. Edulji (India)	55	15	J. Lord (New Zealand)
60	13	C. L. Fitzpatrick (Australia)	50	12	E. Bakewell (England)
60	14	M. E. Maclagan (England)			

WICKETKEEPING RECORDS

SIX DISMISSALS IN AN INNINGS

8 (6ct, 2st)	L. Nye	England v New Zealand at New Plymouth	1991-92
6 (2ct, 4st)	B. A. Brentnall	New Zealand v South Africa at Johannesburg	1971-72

25 DISMISSALS IN A CAREER

		T	Ct	St
58	C. Matthews (Australia)	20	46	12
43	J. Smit (England).	21	39	4
36	S. A. Hodges (England).	11	19	17
28	B. A. Brentnall (New Zealand)	10	16	12

TEAM RECORDS

HIGHEST INNINGS TOTALS

569-6 dec	Australia v England at Guildford	1998
525	Australia v India at Ahmedabad.	1983-84
517-8	New Zealand v England at Scarborough	1996
503-5 dec	England v New Zealand at Christchurch	1934-35

LOWEST INNINGS TOTALS

35	England v Australia at Melbourne	1957-58
38	Australia v England at Melbourne	1957-58
44	New Zealand v England at Christchurch	1934-35
47	Australia v England at Brisbane	1934-35

WOMEN'S ONE-DAY INTERNATIONAL RECORDS

This section covers women's one-day international cricket to December 31, 2019. Bold type denotes performances in the calendar year 2019 or, in career figures, players who appeared in that year.

BATTING RECORDS

HIGHEST INDIVIDUAL INNINGS

232*	A. C. Kerr	New Zealand v Ireland at Dublin	2018
229*	B. J. Clark	Australia v Denmark at Mumbai	1997-98
188	D. B. Sharma	India v Ireland at Potchefstroom	2017
178*	A. M. C. Jayangani . .	Sri Lanka v Australia at Bristol	2017
173*	C. M. Edwards.	England v Ireland at Pune	1997-98
171*	H. Kaur	India v Australia at Derby	2017
171	S. R. Taylor	West Indies v Sri Lanka at Mumbai	2012-13
168*	T. T. Beaumont	England v Pakistan at Taunton	2016
168	S. W. Bates	New Zealand v Sydney	2008-09
157	R. H. Priest	New Zealand v Sri Lanka at Lincoln.	2015-16
156*	L. M. Keightley	Australia v Pakistan at Melbourne.	1996-97
156*	S. C. Taylor	England v India at Lord's	2006
154*	K. L. Rolton.	Australia v Sri Lanka at Christchurch	2000-01
153*	J. Logtenberg	South Africa v Netherlands at Deventer	2007
152*	M. M. Lanning.	Australia v Sri Lanka at Bristol	2017
151	K. L. Rolton.	Australia v Ireland at Dublin	2005
151	S. W. Bates	New Zealand v Ireland at Dublin	2018

MOST RUNS IN A CAREER

R	M		R	M	
6,888	**209**	**M. D. Raj (India)**	4,392	121	S. W. Bates (New Zealand)
5,992	191	C. M. Edwards (England)	4,101	126	S. C. Taylor (England)
4,844	118	B. J. Clark (Australia)	4,064	118	D. A. Hockley (New Zealand)
4,814	141	K. L. Rolton (Australia)	**4,056**	**126**	**S. J. Taylor (England)**
4,756	**126**	**S. R. Taylor (West Indies)**			

BOWLING RECORDS

BEST BOWLING ANALYSES

7-4	Sajjida Shah............	Pakistan v Japan at Amsterdam..................	2003
7-8	J. M. Chamberlain.......	England v Denmark at Haarlem	1991
7-14	A. Mohammed..........	West Indies v Pakistan at Mirpur	2011-12
7-22	**E. A. Perry**..........	**Australia v England at Canterbury**..........	**2019**
7-24	S. Nitschke.............	Australia v England at Kidderminster..........	2005
6-10	J. Lord	New Zealand v India at Auckland..............	1981-82
6-10	M. Maben	India v Sri Lanka at Kandy	2003-04
6-10	S. Ismail...............	South Africa v Netherlands at Savar	2011-12

MOST WICKETS IN A CAREER

W	M		W	M	
225	182	**J. N. Goswami (India)**	142	126	S. R. Taylor (West Indies)
180	109	C. L. Fitzpatrick (Australia)	141	97	N. David (India)
152	112	**E. A. Perry (Australia)**	136	144	J. L. Gunn (England)
151	120	**Sana Mir (Pakistan)**	133	95	S. Ismail (South Africa)
151	122	**A. Mohammed (W. Indies)**	129	103	L. A. Marsh (England)
150	123	**K. H. Brunt (England)**	128	99	D. van Niekerk (S Africa)
146	125	L. C. Sthalekar (Australia)	124	118	H. A. S. D. Siriwardene (SL)

WICKETKEEPING RECORDS

MOST DISMISSALS IN AN INNINGS

6 (4ct, 2st)	S. L. Illingworth	New Zealand v Australia at Beckenham	1993
6 (1ct, 5st)	V. Kalpana..........	India v Denmark at Slough	1993
6 (2ct, 4st)	Batool Fatima	Pakistan v West Indies at Karachi.............	2003-04
6 (4ct, 2st)	Batool Fatima	Pakistan v Sri Lanka at Colombo (PSO)	2010-11

MOST DISMISSALS IN A CAREER

		M	Ct	St
152	**T. Chetty (South Africa)**	106	**107**	**45**
136	**S. J. Taylor (England)**	118	85	51
133	R. J. Rolls (New Zealand)	101	90	43
114	J. Smit (England)	108	69	45
103	M. R. Aguilleira (West Indies).......	104	76	27
99	J. C. Price (Australia)..............	84	69	30
97	Batool Fatima (Pakistan)...........	68	51	46

Chetty's total excludes two catches in two matches, Taylor's and Aguilleira's each exclude two in eight matches and Batool Fatima's three in 15 while not keeping wicket; Price's excludes one taken in the field after giving up the gloves mid-game. Rolls did not keep wicket in three matches and Smit in one; neither took any catches in these games.

TEAM RECORDS

HIGHEST INNINGS TOTALS

491-4	New Zealand v Ireland at Dublin	2018
455-5	New Zealand v Pakistan at Christchurch	1996-97
440-3	New Zealand v Ireland at Dublin	2018
418	New Zealand v Ireland at Dublin	2018
412-3	Australia v Denmark at Mumbai	1997-98
397-4	Australia v Pakistan at Melbourne	1996-97
378-5	England v Pakistan at Worcester	2016
377-7	England v Pakistan at Leicester	2017
376-2	England v Pakistan at Vijayawada	1997-98
375-5	Netherlands v Japan at Schiedam......................	2003

LOWEST INNINGS TOTALS

22	Netherlands v West Indies at Deventer	2008
23	Pakistan v Australia at Melbourne.	1996-97
24	Scotland v England at Reading	2001
26	India v New Zealand at St Saviour	2002
27	Pakistan v Australia at Hyderabad (India).	1997-98
28	Japan v Pakistan at Amsterdam	2003
29	Netherlands v Australia at Perth	1988-89

WOMEN'S WORLD CUP WINNERS

1973	England	1993	England	2008-09	England
1977-78	Australia	1997-98	Australia	2012-13	Australia
1981-82	Australia	2000-01	New Zealand	2017	England
1988-89	Australia	2004-05	Australia		

WOMEN'S TWENTY20 INTERNATIONAL RECORDS

This section covers women's Twenty20 international cricket to December 31, 2019. Bold type denotes performances in the calendar year 2019 or, in career figures, players who appeared in that year. The ICC extended official international status to Associate Twenty20 matches from June 2018.

BATTING RECORDS

HIGHEST INDIVIDUAL INNINGS

148*	**A. J. Healy**	**Australia v Sri Lanka at Sydney**	**2019-20**
133*	**M. M. Lanning**.	**Australia v England at Chelmsford**	**2019**
126*	**S. L. Kalis**.	**Netherlands v Germany at La Manga**	**2019**
126	M. M. Lanning.	Australia v Ireland at Sylhet	2013-14
124*	S. W. Bates	New Zealand v South Africa at Taunton	2018
124	D. N. Wyatt	England v India at Mumbai (BS).	2017-18
117*	B. L. Mooney.	Australia v England at Canberra	2017-18
116*	S. A. Fritz	South Africa v Netherlands at Potchefstroom	2010-11
116	T. T. Beaumont	England v South Africa at Taunton	2018
116	**P. Alako**	**Uganda v Mali at Kigali**	**2019**

MOST RUNS IN A CAREER

R	M		R	M	
3,100	**111**	**S. W. Bates (New Zealand)**	2,177	90	S. J. Taylor (England)
2,900	**100**	**S. R. Taylor (West Indies)**	2,160	106	Bismah Maroof (Pakistan)
2,605	95	C. M. Edwards (England)	2,038	104	H. Kaur (India)
2,580	**94**	**M. M. Lanning (Australia)**	**1,955**	**83**	**S. F. M. Devine (New Zealand)**
2,368	**110**	**D. J. S. Dottin (West Indies)**	**1,809**	**101**	**A. J. Healy (Australia)**
2,364	89	M. D. Raj (India)	1,744	97	Javeria Khan (Pakistan)

BOWLING RECORDS

BEST BOWLING ANALYSES

6-0	A. Chand	Nepal v Maldives at Pokhara	2019
6-3	Mas Elysa	Malaysia v China at Bangkok	2018-19
6-8	B. Mpedi	Botswana v Lesotho at Gaborone	2018
6-8	N. Thapa	Nepal v Hong Kong at Bangkok.	2018-19
6-10	Zon Lin	Myanmar v Indonesia at Bangkok.	2018-19
6-17	A. E. Satterthwaite.	New Zealand v England at Taunton	2007
5-0	N. N. Saidi.	Tanzania v Mali at Kigali	2019
5-3	C. R. Seneviratne.	United Arab Emirates v Kuwait at Bangkok	2018-19
5-4	C. Sutthiruang	Thailand v Indonesia at Bangkok	2018-19

5-5	D. J. S. Dottin	West Indies v Bangladesh at Providence.	2018-19
5-5	**I. D. A. D. A. Laksmi. . . .**	**Indonesia v Philippines at Dasmarinas**	**2019-20**
5-7	**K. Arua. . . . .**	**Papua New Guinea v Japan at Port Vila**	**2019**
5-7	**K. Y. Chan. . . . .**	**Hong Kong v China at Incheon**	**2019**
5-8	S. E. Luus	South Africa v Ireland at Chennai.	2015-16
5-8	**M. M. P. Suwandewi. . . .**	**Indonesia v Philippines at Dasmarinas**	**2019-20**

MOST WICKETS IN A CAREER

W	M		W	M	
118	108	A. Mohammed (West Indies)	85	62	P. Yadav (India)
106	111	E. A. Perry (Australia)	85	85	D. Hazell (England)
92	84	S. Ismail (South Africa)	84	100	S. R. Taylor (West Indies)
92	98	Nida Dar (Pakistan)	80	83	S. F. M. Devine (New Zealand)
90	68	A. Shrubsole (England)	76	74	K. H. Brunt (England)
89	106	Sana Mir (Pakistan)	75	104	J. L. Gunn (England)

WICKETKEEPING RECORDS

MOST DISMISSALS IN AN INNINGS

5 (1ct, 4st)	Kycia A. Knight.	West Indies v Sri Lanka at Colombo (RPS)	2012-13
5 (1ct, 4st)	Batool Fatima	Pakistan v Ireland at Dublin	2013
5 (1ct, 4st)	Batool Fatima	Pakistan v Ireland at Dublin (semi-final).	2013
5 (3ct, 2st)	B. M. Bezuidenhout. . .	New Zealand v Ireland at Dublin	2018
5 (1ct, 4st)	**S. J. Bryce. . . . .**	**Scotland v Netherlands at Arbroath**	**2019**

MOST DISMISSALS IN A CAREER

		M	Ct	St
77	**A. J. Healy (Australia)**	**101†**	**35**	**42**
74	**S. J. Taylor (England)**	**90†**	**23**	**51**
72	**M. R. Aguilleira (West Indies). . . . . .**	**95†**	**38**	**34**
68	R. H. Priest (New Zealand)	68†	38	30
58*	J. L. Gunn (England)	104	58	
57	T. Chetty (South Africa).	68	34	23
54*	L. S. Greenway (England)	85	54	
54*	**S. W. Bates (New Zealand)**	**111**	**54**	
53	**T. Bhatia (India)**	**40**	**16**	**37**
50	Batool Fatima (Pakistan)	45	11	39

* *Catches made by non-wicketkeeper in the field.*

† *Healy's total includes 15 matches in the field where she made two catches, and Aguilleira's ten in the field where she made two catches; Taylor's total includes two matches and Priest's one in the field where they made no catches.*

TEAM RECORDS

HIGHEST INNINGS TOTALS

314-2	**Uganda v Mali at Kigali**.	**2019**
285-1	**Tanzania v Mali at Kigali**	**2019**
260-1	**Indonesia v Philippines at Dasmarinas**	**2019-20**
255-2	**Bangladesh v Maldives at Pokhara**.	**2019-20**
250-3	England v South Africa at Taunton	2018
246-1	**Rwanda v Mali at Kigali**	**2019**
226-2	**Australia v Sri Lanka at Sydney**	**2019-20**
226-3	**Australia v England at Chelmsford**	**2019**
217-2	**Indonesia v Philippines at Dasmarinas**.	**2019-20**
217-4	**Australia v Sri Lanka at Sydney**	**2019-20**
216-1	New Zealand v South Africa at Taunton	2018
213-4	**Ireland v Netherlands at Deventer**	**2019**
210-5	Namibia v Lesotho at Gaborone.	2018

LOWEST INNINGS TOTALS

6	**Mali v Rwanda at Kigali**.................................	**2019**
6	**Maldives v Bangladesh at Pokhara**	**2019-20**
8	**Maldives v Nepal at Pokhara**	**2019-20**
10	**Mali v Uganda at Kigali**	**2019**
11	**Mali v Tanzania at Kigali**	**2019**
14	**China v United Arab Emirates at Bangkok**...................	**2018-19**
14	**Mali v Uganda at Kigali**	**2019**
15	**Philippines v Indonesia at Dasmarinas**	**2019-20**
16	**Maldives v Nepal at Pokhara**	**2019-20**
17†	**Mali v Tanzania at Kigali**	**2019**

† *One woman absent.*

WOMEN'S WORLD TWENTY20 WINNERS

2009	England	2012-13	Australia	2015-16	West Indies
2010	Australia	2013-14	Australia	2018-19	Australia

BIRTHS AND DEATHS

TEST CRICKETERS

Full list from 1876-77 to January 31, 2020

In the Test career column, dates in italics indicate seasons embracing two different years (i.e. non-English seasons). In these cases, only the first year is given, e.g. 1876 for 1876-77. Some non-English series taking place outside the host country's normal season are dated by a single year.

The Test career figures are complete up to January 31, 2020; the one-day international and Twenty20 international totals up to December 31, 2019. Career figures are for one international team only; those players who have appeared for more than one Test team are listed on page 1455, and for more than one one-day international or Twenty20 international team on page 1458.

The forename by which a player is known is underlined if it is not his first name.

Family relationships are indicated by superscript numbers; where the relationship is not immediately apparent from a shared name, see the notes at the end of this section. (CY 1889) signifies that the player was a Wisden Cricketer of the Year in the 1889 Almanack. The 5/10 column indicates instances of a player taking five wickets in a Test innings and ten wickets in a match. OT signifies number of one-day and Twenty20 internationals played.

[1] Father and son(s).	[2] Brothers.	[3] Grandfather, father and son.	[4] Grandfather and grandson.	[5] Great-grandfather and great-grandson.
† Excludes matches for another Test team.	‡ Excludes matches for another ODI or T20I team.			

ENGLAND (695 players)

	Born	Died	Tests	Test Career	Runs	HS	100s	Avge	Wkts	BB	5/10	Avge	Cl/St	O/T
Abel Robert (CY 1890).	30.11.1857	10.12.1936	13	1888–1902	744	132*	2	37.20	–	–	–/–	–	13	–
Absolom Charles Alfred.	7.6.1846	30.7.1889	1	1878	58	52	0	29.00	–	–	–/–	–	0	–
Adams Christopher John (CY 2004). . .	6.5.1970		5	1999	104	31	0	13.00	1	1-42	0/0	59.00	6	5
Afzaal Usman.	9.6.1977		3	2001	83	54	0	16.60	1	1-49	0/0	49.00	0	–
Agnew Jonathan Philip MBE (CY 1988)	4.4.1960		3	1984–1985	10	5	0	10.00	4	2-51	0/0	93.25	0	3
Ali Kabir.	24.11.1980		1	2003	10	9	0	5.00	5	3-80	0/0	27.20	0	14
Ali Moeen Munir (CY 2015).	18.6.1987		60	2014–2019	2,782	155*	5	28.97	181	6-53	5/1	36.59	32	101/25
Allen David Arthur.	29.10.1935	24.5.2014	39	1959–1966	918	88	0	25.50	122	5-30	4/0	30.97	10	–
Allen Sir George Oswald Browning ("Gubby").	31.7.1902	29.11.1989	25	1930–1947	750	122	1	24.19	81	7-80	5/1	29.37	20	–
Allom Maurice James Carrick. . . .	23.3.1906	8.4.1995	5	1929–1930	14	8*	0	14.00	14	5-38	1/0	18.92	4	–
Allott Paul John Walter.	14.9.1956		13	1981–1985	213	52*	0	14.20	26	6-61	1/0	41.69	4	13
Ambrose Timothy Raymond.	1.12.1982		11	2007–2008	447	102	1	29.80	–	–	–/–	–	31	5/1
Ames Leslie Ethelbert George CBE (CY 1929).	3.12.1905	27.2.1990	47	1929–1938	2,434	149	8	40.56	–	–	–/–	–	74/23	–

Name	Born	Died	Tests	Test Career	Runs	HS	100s	Avge	Wkts	BB	5/10	Avge	Ct/St	O/T
Amiss Dennis Leslie MBE OBE (CY 1975)	7.4.1943		50	1966–1977	3,612	262*	11	46.30	–	–	–/–	–	24	18
Anderson James Michael OBE (CY 2009)	30.7.1982		151	2003–2019	1,185	81	0	9.63	584	7-42	28/3	26.83	93	194/19
Andrew Keith Vincent	15.12.1929	27.12.2010	2	1954–1956	29	15	0	9.66	–	–	–/–	–	1	
Ansari Zafar Shahaan	10.12.1991		3	2016	49	32	0	9.80	5	2-76	0/0	55.00	1	
Appleyard Robert MBE (CY 1952)	27.6.1924	17.3.2015	9	1954–1956	51	19*	0	17.00	31	5-51	1/0	17.87	4	1
Archer Alfred German	6.12.1871	15.7.1935	1	1898	31	24*	0	31.00	0	0-15	0/0	–	1	
Archer Jofra Chioke (CY 2020)	1.4.1995		7	2019–2019	97	30	0	8.08	30	6-45	2/0	27.40	0	14/1
Armitage Thomas	25.4.1848	21.9.1922	2	1876	33	21	0	11.00	0	–	–/–	–	0	
Arnold Edward George	7.11.1876	25.10.1942	10	1903–1907	160	40	0	13.33	31	5-37	1/0	25.41	8	
Arnold Geoffrey Graham (CY 1972)	3.9.1944		34	1967–1975	421	59	0	12.02	115	6-45	6/0	28.29	9	14
Arnold John	30.11.1907	4.4.1984	1	1931	34	34	0	17.00	0	–	–/–	–	0	
Astill William Ewart (CY 1933)	1.3.1888	10.2.1948	9	1927–1929	190	40	0	12.66	25	4-58	0/0	34.24	7	
Atherton Michael Andrew OBE (CY 1991)	23.3.1968		115	1989–2001	7,728	185*	16	37.69	2	1-20	0/0	151.00	83	54
Athey Charles William Jeffrey	27.9.1957		23	1980–1988	919	123	1	22.97	0	0-8	–/–	–	13	31
Attewell William (CY 1892)	12.6.1861	11.6.1927	10	1884–1891	150	43*	0	16.66	28	4-42	0/0	22.35	9	
Bailey Robert John	28.10.1963		4	1988–1989	119	43	0	14.87	0	–	–/–	–	0	4
Bailey Trevor Edward CBE (CY 1950)	3.12.1923	10.2.2011	61	1949–1958	2,290	134*	1	29.74	132	7-34	5/1	29.21	32	21
Bairstow David Leslie	1.9.1951	5.1.1998	4	1979–1980	125	59	0	20.83	–	–	–/–	–	12/1	
Bairstow Jonathan Marc (CY 2016)	26.9.1989		70	2012–2019	4,030	167*	6	34.74	0	–	–/–	–	184/13	74/34
Bakewell Alfred Harry (CY 1934)	2.11.1908	23.1.1983	6	1931–1935	409	107	1	45.44	0	–	–/–	–	3	
Balderstone John Christopher	16.11.1940	6.3.2000	2	1976	39	35	0	9.75	1	1-80	0/0	80.00	1	
Ball Jacob Timothy	14.3.1991		4	2016–2017	67	31	0	8.37	3	1-47	0/0	114.33	1	18/2
Ballance Gary Simon (CY 2015)	22.11.1989		23	2013–2017	1,498	156	1	37.45	0	0-0	–/–	–	22	16
Barber Robert William (1967)	26.9.1935		28	1960–1968	1,495	185	1	35.59	42	4-132	0/0	43.00	21	
Barber Wilfred	18.4.1901	10.9.1968	2	1935	83	44	0	20.75	0	–	–/–	–	0	
Barlow Graham Derek	26.3.1950		3	1976–1977	17	7*	0	4.25	0	–	–/–	–	2	6
Barlow Richard Gorton	28.5.1851	31.7.1919	17	1881–1886	591	62	0	22.73	34	7-40	3/0	22.55	14	
Barnes Sydney Francis (CY 1910)	19.4.1873	26.12.1967	27	1901–1913	242	38*	0	8.06	189	9-103	24/7	16.43	12	
Barnes William (CY 1890)	27.5.1852	24.3.1899	21	1880–1890	725	134	1	23.38	51	6-28	3/0	15.54	19	
Barnett Charles John (CY 1937)	3.7.1910	28.5.1993	20	1933–1948	1,098	129	2	35.41	0	0-1	–/–	–	14	
Barnett Kim John (CY 1989)	17.7.1960		4	1988–1989	207	80	0	29.57	0	0-32	–/–	–	2	
Barratt Fred	12.4.1894	29.1.1947	5	1929–1929	28	17	0	9.33	5		0/0	47.00	5	
Barrington Kenneth Frank (CY 1960)	24.11.1930	14.3.1981	82	1955–1968	6,806	256	20	58.67	29	3-4	0/0	44.82	58	
Barton Victor Alexander	6.10.1867	23.1.1906	1	1891	23	23	0	23.00	0	–	–/–	–	1	
Bates Willie	19.11.1855	8.1.1900	15	1881–1886	656	64	0	27.33	50	7-28	4/1	16.42	9	
Batty Gareth Jon	13.10.1977		9	2003–2016	149	38	0	14.90	15	3-55	0/0	60.93	3	10/1

	Born	Died	Tests	Test Career	Runs	HS	100s	Avge	Wkts	BB	5/10	Avge	Ct/St	O/T
Bean George	7.3.1864	16.3.1923	3	1891	92	50	0	18.40	–	–	–/–	–	4	
Bedser Sir Alec Victor CBE (CY 1947)	4.7.1918	4.4.2010	51	1946–1955	714	79	0	12.75	236	7-44	15/5	24.89	26	
Bell Ian Ronald MBE (CY 2008) ..	11.4.1982		118	2004–2015	7,727	235	22	42.69	1	1-33	0/0	76.00	100	161/8
Benjamin Joseph Emmanuel	2.2.1961		1	1994	0	0	0	0.00	4	4-42	0/0	20.00	0	2
Benson Mark Richard	6.7.1958		1	1986	51	30	0	25.50	–	–	–/–	–	0	1
Berry Robert	29.1.1926	2.12.2006	2	1950	6	4*	0	3.00	9	5-63	1/0	25.33	2	
Bess Dominic Mark	22.7.1997		4	2018–2019	112	57	0	18.66	11	5-51	1/0	29.72	2	
Bicknell Martin Paul (CY 2001) ..	14.1.1969		4	1993–2003	45	15	0	6.42	14	4-84	0/0	38.78	2	7
Binks James Graham (CY 1969) ..	5.10.1935		2	1963	91	55	0	22.75	–	–	–/–	–	8	
Bird Morice Carlos	25.3.1888	9.12.1933	10	1909–1913	280	61	0	18.66	8	3-11	0/0	15.00	5	
Birkenshaw Jack MBE	13.11.1940		5	1972–1973	148	64	0	21.14	13	5-57	1/0	36.07	3	
Blackwell Ian David	10.6.1978		1	2005	4	4	0	4.00	0	0-28	0/0	–	0	34
Blakey Richard John	15.1.1967		2	1992	7	6	0	1.75	–	–	–/–	–	2	3
Bligh Hon. Ivo Francis Walter ..	13.3.1859	10.4.1927	4	1882	62	19	0	10.33	–	–	–/–	–	7	
Blythe Colin (CY 1904)	30.5.1879	8.11.1917	19	1901–1909	183	27	0	9.63	100	8-59	9/4	18.63	6	
Board John Henry	23.2.1867	15.4.1924	6	1898–1905	108	29	0	10.80	–	–	–/–	–	8/3	
Bolus John Brian	31.1.1934		7	1963–1963	496	88	0	41.33	0	0-16	0/0	–	2	
Booth Major William (CY 1914) ..	10.12.1886	1.7.1916	2	1913	46	32	0	23.00	7	4-49	0/0	18.57	0	
Bopara Ravinder Singh	4.5.1985		13	2007–2012	575	143	3	31.94	1	1-39	0/0	290.00	6	120/38
Borthwick Scott George	19.4.1990		1	2013	5	4	0	2.50	4	3-33	0/0	20.50	2	2/1
Bosanquet Bernard James Tindal (CY 1905)	13.10.1877	12.10.1936	7	1903–1905	147	27	0	13.36	25	8-107	2/0	24.16	9	
Botham Sir Ian Terence OBE (CY 1978)	24.11.1955		102	1977–1992	5,200	208	14	33.54	383	8-34	27/4	28.40	120	116
Bowden Montague Parker	1.11.1865	19.2.1892	2	1888	25	25	0	12.50	–	–	–/–	–	1	
Bowes William Eric (CY 1932) ..	25.7.1908	4.9.1987	15	1932–1946	28	10*	0	4.66	68	6-33	6/0	22.33	2	
Bowley Edward Henry (CY 1930) ..	6.6.1890	9.7.1974	5	1929–1930	252	109	1	36.00	0	0-7	0/0	–	2	
Boycott Sir Geoffrey OBE (CY 1965)	21.10.1940		108	1964–1981	8,114	246*	22	47.72	7	3-47	0/0	54.57	33	36
Bradley Walter Morris	2.1.1875	19.6.1944	2	1899	23	23*	0	23.00	6	5-67	1/0	38.83	0	
Braund Leonard Charles (CY 1902)	18.10.1875	23.12.1955	23	1901–1907	987	104	3	25.97	47	8-81	3/0	38.51	39	
Brearley John Michael OBE (CY 1977)	28.4.1942		39	1976–1981	1,442	91	0	22.88	–	–	–/–	–	52	25
Brearley Walter (CY 1909)	11.3.1876	30.1.1937	4	1905–1912	21	11*	0	7.00	17	5-110	1/0	21.11	0	
Brennan Donald Vincent	10.2.1920	9.1.1985	2	1951	16	16	0	8.00	–	–	–/–	–	0/1	
Bresnan Timothy Thomas (CY 2012)	28.2.1985		23	2009–2013	575	91	0	26.13	72	5-48	1/0	32.73	8	85/34
Briggs John (CY 1889)	3.10.1862	11.1.1902	33	1884–1899	815	121	0	18.11	118	8-11	9/4	17.75	12	
Broad Brian Christopher	29.9.1957		25	1984–1989	1,661	162	6	39.54	0	0-4	0/0	–	10	34
Broad Stuart Christopher John MBE (CY 2010)	24.6.1986		138	2007–2019	3,211	169	1	18.66	485	8-15	17/2	28.50	46	121/56
Brockwell William (CY 1895) ..	21.11.1865	30.6.1935	7	1893–1899	202	49	0	16.83	5	3-33	0/0	61.80	6	

Name	Born	Died	Tests	Test Career	Runs	HS	100s	Avge	Wkts	BB	5/10	Avge	Ct/St	O/T
Bromley-Davenport Hugh Richard	18.8.1870	23.5.1954	4	1895–1898	128	84	0	21.33	4	2-46	0/0	24.50	1	–
Brookes Dennis (CY 1957)	29.10.1915	9.3.2006	1	1947	17	10	0	8.50	–	–	–/–	–	1	
Brown Alan	17.10.1935		2	1961	–	3*	–	–	3	3-27	0/0	50.00	1	
Brown David John	30.1.1942		26	1965–1969	342	44*	0	11.79	79	5-42	2/0	28.31	7	
Brown Frederick Richard MBE (CY 1933)	16.12.1910	24.7.1991	22	1931–1953	734	79	0	25.31	45	5-49	1/0	31.06	22	
Brown George	6.10.1887	3.12.1964	7	1921–1922	299	84	0	29.90	–	–	–/–	–	9/3	
Brown John Thomas (CY 1895)	20.8.1869	4.11.1904	8	1894–1899	470	140	1	36.15	0	0-22	0/0	–	7	
Brown Simon John Emmerson	29.6.1969		1	1996	11	10*	0	11.00	2	1-60	0/0	69.00	1	
Buckenham Claude Percival	16.1.1876	23.2.1937	4	1909	43	17	0	6.14	21	5-115	1/0	28.23	2	
Burns Rory Joseph (CY 2019)	26.8.1990		15	2018–2019	979	133	2	33.75	–	–	–/–	–	12	
Butcher Alan Raymond (CY 1991)	7.1.1954		1	1979	34	20	0	17.00	0	0-9	0/0	–	0	
[1] **Butcher Mark Alan**	23.8.1972		71	1997–2004	4,288	173*	8	34.58	15	4-42	0/0	36.06	61	1
Butcher Roland Orlando	14.10.1953		3	1980	71	32	0	14.20	–	–	–/–	–	3	
Butler Harold James	12.3.1913	17.7.1991	2	1947–1947	15	15*	0	15.00	12	4-34	0/0	17.91	1	3
Butt Henry Rigden	27.12.1865	21.12.1928	3	1895	22	13	0	7.33	–	–	–/–	–	1/1	
Buttler Joseph Charles MBE (CY 2019)	8.9.1990		41	2014–2019	2,127	106	1	31.74	–	–	–/–	–	88	142/66
Caddick Andrew Richard (CY 2001)	21.11.1968		62	1993–2003	861	49*	0	10.37	234	7-46	13/1	29.91	21	54
Calthorpe *Hon.* Frederick Somerset Gough-	27.5.1892	19.11.1935	4	1929	129	49	0	18.42	1	1-38	0/0	91.00	3	
Capel David John	6.2.1963		15	1987–1989	374	98	0	15.58	21	3-88	0/0	50.66	6	23
Carberry Michael Alexander	29.9.1980		6	2009–2013	345	60	0	28.75	–	–	–/–	–	1	6/1
Carr Arthur William (CY 1923)	21.5.1893	7.2.1963	11	1922–1929	237	63	0	19.75	–	–	–/–	–	3	
Carr Donald Bryce OBE (CY 1960)	28.12.1926	12.6.2016	2	1951	135	76	0	33.75	2	2-84	0/0	70.00	0	
Carr Douglas Ward (CY 1910)	17.3.1872	23.3.1950	1	1909	0	0	0	0.00	7	5-146	1/0	40.28	0	
Cartwright Thomas William MBE.	22.7.1935	30.4.2007	5	1964–1965	26	9	0	5.20	15	6-94	1/0	36.26	2	
Chapman Arthur Percy Frank (CY 1919)	3.9.1900	16.9.1961	26	1924–1930	925	121	1	28.90	–	–	–/–	–	32	
Charlwood Henry Rupert James	19.12.1846	6.6.1888	2	1876	63	36	0	15.75	–	–	–/–	–	1	
Chatterton William	27.12.1861	19.3.1913	1	1891	48	48	0	48.00	–	–	–/–	–	0	
Childs John Henry (CY 1987)	15.8.1951		2	1988	2	2*	0	–	3	1-13	0/0	61.00	1	
Christopherson Stanley	11.11.1861	6.4.1949	1	1884	17	17	0	17.00	1	1-52	0/0	69.00	0	
Clark Edward Winchester	9.8.1902	28.4.1982	8	1929–1934	36	10	0	9.00	32	5-98	1/0	28.09	0	
Clarke Rikki	29.9.1981		2	2003	96	55	0	32.00	4	2-7	0/0	15.00	1	20
Clay John Charles	18.3.1898	11.8.1973	1	1935	–	–	–	–	0	0-30	0/0	–	0	
Close Dennis Brian CBE (CY 1964)	24.2.1931	14.9.2015	22	1949–1976	887	70	0	25.34	18	4-35	0/0	29.55	24	3
Coldwell Leonard John	10.1.1933	6.8.1996	7	1962–1964	9	6*	0	4.50	22	6-85	1/0	27.72	1	
Collingwood Paul David MBE (CY 2007)	26.5.1976		68	2003–2010	4,259	206	10	40.56	17	3-23	0/0	59.88	96	197/35‡
[4] **Compton Denis Charles Scott** CBE (CY 1939)	23.5.1918	23.4.1997	78	1937–1956	5,807	278	17	50.06	25	5-70	1/0	56.40	49	

	Born	Died	Tests	Test Career	Runs	HS	100s	Avge	Wkts	BB	5/10	Avge	Ct/St	O/T
[4]Compton Nicholas Richard Denis (CY 2013)	26.6.1983		16	2012–2016	775	117	2	28.70	—	—	—	—	7	92/4
Cook Sir Alastair Nathan CBE (CY 2012)	25.12.1984		161	2005–2018	12,472	294	33	45.35	1	1-6	0/0	7.00	175	
Cook Cecil ("Sam")	23.8.1921	5.9.1996	1	1947	4	4	0	2.00	0	0-40	0/0	—	0	
Cook Geoffrey	9.10.1951		7	1981–1982	203	66	0	15.61	0	0-4	0/0	—	9	6
Cook Nicholas Grant Billson	17.6.1956		15	1983–1989	179	31	0	8.52	52	6-65	4/1	32.48	5	3
Cope Geoffrey Alan	23.2.1947		3	1977	40	22	0	13.33	8	3-102	0/0	34.62	1	2
Copson William Henry (CY 1937)	27.4.1908	13.9.1971	3	1939–1947	6	6	0	6.00	15	5-85	1/0	19.80	1	
Cork Dominic Gerald (CY 1996)	7.8.1971		37	1995–2002	864	59	0	18.00	131	7-43	5/0	29.81	18	32
Cornford Walter Latter	25.12.1900	6.2.1964	4	1929	36	18	0	9.00	—	—	—/—	—	5/3	
Cottam Robert Michael Henry	16.10.1944		4	1968–1972	27	13	0	6.75	14	4-50	0/0	23.35	2	
Coventry *Hon.* Charles John	26.2.1867	2.6.1929	2	1888	13	12	0	13.00	—	—	—/—	—	1	
Cowans Norman George	17.4.1961		19	1982–1985	175	36	0	7.95	51	6-77	2/0	39.27	9	23
[1]Cowdrey Christopher Stuart	20.10.1957		6	1984–1988	101	38	0	14.42	4	2-65	0/0	77.25	5	3
[1]Cowdrey *Lord* [Michael (Colin)] CBE (CY 1956)	24.12.1932	4.12.2000	114	1954–1974	7,624	182	22	44.06	0	0-1	0/0	—	120	
Coxon Alexander	18.1.1916	22.1.2006	1	1948	19	19	0	9.50	3	2-90	0/0	57.33	0	
Crane Mason Sidney	18.02.1997		1	2017	4	4	0	3.00	1	1-193	0/0	193.00	0	0/2
Cranston James	9.1.1859	10.12.1904	1	1890	31	16	0	15.50	—	—	—/—	—	0	
Cranston Kenneth	20.10.1917	8.1.2007	8	1947–1948	209	45	0	14.92	18	4-12	0/0	25.61	3	
Crapp John Frederick	14.10.1912	13.2.1981	7	1948–1949	319	56	0	29.00	—	—	—/—	—	7	
Crawford John Neville (CY 1907)	1.12.1886	2.5.1963	12	1905–1907	469	74	0	22.33	39	5-48	3/0	29.48	13	
Crawley John Paul	21.9.1971		37	1994–2002	1,800	156*	4	34.61	—	—	—/—	—	29	13
Crawley Zak	3.2.1998		3	2019	164	66	0	27.33	—	—	—/—	—	3	
Croft Robert Damien Bale MBE.	25.5.1970		21	1996–2001	421	37*	0	16.19	49	5-95	1/0	37.24	10	50
[2]Curran Samuel Matthew (CY 2019)	3.6.1998		17	2018–2019	711	78	0	27.34	37	4-58	0/0	31.70	3	2/5
[2]Curran Thomas Kevin	12.03.1995		2	2017	66	39	0	33.00	2	1-65	0/0	100.00	0	17/15
Curtis Timothy Stephen	15.1.1960		5	1988–1989	140	41	0	15.55	0	0-7	0/0	—	3	
Cuttell Willis Robert (CY 1898)	13.9.1863	9.12.1929	2	1898	65	21	0	16.25	6	3-17	0/0	12.16	2	
Dawson Edward William	13.2.1904	4.6.1979	5	1927–1929	175	55	0	19.44	0	0-4	—/—	—	0	
Dawson Liam Andrew	1.3.1990		3	2016–2017	84	66*	0	21.00	7	2-34	0/0	42.57	3	3/6
Dawson Richard Kevin James.	4.8.1980		7	2001–2002	114	19*	0	11.40	11	4-134	0/0	61.54	3	
Dean Harry	13.8.1884	12.3.1957	3	1912	10	8	0	5.00	11	4-19	1/0	13.90	2	
DeFreitas Phillip Anthony Jason (CY 1992)	18.2.1966		44	1986–1995	934	88	0	14.82	140	7-70	4/0	33.57	14	103
Denly Joseph Liam	16.3.1986		14	2018–2019	780	94	0	30.00	2	2-42	0/0	109.50	7	13/10
Denness Michael Henry OBE (CY 1975)	1.12.1940	19.4.2013	28	1969–1975	1,667	188	4	39.69	0	—	—/—	—	28	12
Denton David (CY 1906)	4.7.1874	16.2.1950	11	1905–1909	424	104	1	20.19	—	—	—/—	—	8	
Dewes John Gordon	11.10.1926	12.5.2015	5	1948–1950	121	67	0	12.10	—	—	—/—	—	0	

	Born	Died	Tests	Test Career	Runs	HS	100s	Avge	Wkts	BB	5/10	Avge	Ct/St	O/T
Dexter Edward Ralph CBE (CY 1961)	15.5.1935		62	1958–1968	4,502	205	9	47.89	66	4-10	0/0	34.93	29	
Dilley Graham Roy	18.5.1959	5.10.2011	41	1979–1989	521	56	0	13.35	138	6-38	6/0	29.76	10	36
Dipper Alfred Ernest	9.11.1885	7.11.1945	1	1921	51	40	0	25.50	—	—	—/—	—	0	
Doggart George Hubert Graham OBE	18.7.1925	16.2.2018	2	1950	76	29	0	19.00	—	—	—/—	—	3	
D'Oliveira Basil Lewis CBE (CY 1967)	4.10.1931	18.11.2011	44	1966–1972	2,484	158	5	40.06	47	3-46	0/0	39.55	29	4
Dollery Horace Edgar ("Tom") (CY 1952)	14.10.1914	20.1.1987	4	1947–1950	72	37	0	10.28	—	—	—/—	—	1	
Dolphin Arthur	24.12.1885	23.10.1942	1	1920	1	1	0	0.50	—	—	—/—	—	1	
Douglas John William Henry Tyler (CY 1915)	3.9.1882	19.12.1930	23	1911–1924	962	119	1	29.15	45	5-46	1/0	33.02	9	
Downton Paul Rupert	4.4.1957		30	1980–1988	785	74	0	19.62	—	—	—/—	—	70/5	28
Druce Norman Frank (CY 1898)	1.1.1875	27.10.1954	5	1897	252	64	0	28.00	—	—	—/—	—	5	
Ducat Andrew (CY 1920)	16.2.1886	23.7.1942	1	1921	5	3	0	2.50	—	—	—/—	—	1	
Duckett Ben Matthew (CY 2017)	17.10.1994		4	2016	110	56	0	15.71	—	—	—/—	—	1	3/1
Duckworth George (CY 1929)	9.5.1901	5.1.1966	24	1924–1936	234	39*	0	14.62	0	0-7	0/0	—	45/15	
Duleepsinhji Kumar Shri (CY 1930)	13.6.1905	5.12.1959	12	1929–1931	995	173	3	58.52	0	0-7	0/0	—	10	
Durston Frederick John	11.7.1893	8.4.1965	1	1921	8	6*	0	8.00	5	4-102	0/0	27.20	0	
Ealham Mark Alan	27.8.1969		8	1996–1998	210	53*	0	21.00	17	4-21	0/0	28.70	4	64
Edmonds Philippe-Henri	8.3.1951		51	1975–1987	875	64	0	17.50	125	7-66	2/0	34.18	42	29
Edrich John Hugh MBE (CY 1966)	21.6.1937		77	1963–1976	5,138	310*	12	43.54	0	0-6	0/0	—	43	7
Edrich William John (CY 1940)	26.3.1916	24.4.1986	39	1938–1954	2,440	219	6	40.00	41	4-68	0/0	41.29	39	
Elliott Harry	2.11.1891	2.2.1976	4	1927–1933	61	37*	0	15.25	—	—	—/—	—	8/3	
Ellison Richard Mark (CY 1986)	21.9.1959		11	1984–1986	202	41	0	13.46	35	6-77	3/1	29.94	2	14
Emburey John Ernest (CY 1984)	20.8.1952		64	1978–1995	1,713	75	0	22.53	147	7-78	6/0	38.40	34	61
Emmett George Malcolm	2.12.1912	18.12.1976	1	1948	10	10	0	5.00	—	—	—/—	—	0	
Emmett Thomas	3.9.1841	29.6.1904	7	1876–1881	160	48	0	13.33	9	7-68	1/0	31.55	9	
Evans Alfred John	1.5.1889	18.9.1960	1	1921	18	14	0	9.00	—	—	—/—	—	0	
Evans Thomas Godfrey CBE (CY 1951)	18.8.1920	3.5.1999	91	1946–1959	2,439	104	2	20.49	—	—	—/—	—	173/46	
Fagg Arthur Edward	18.6.1915	13.9.1977	5	1936–1939	150	39	0	18.75	—	—	—/—	—	5	
Fairbrother Neil Harvey	9.9.1963		10	1987–1992	219	83	0	15.64	0	0-9	0/0	—	4	75
Fane Frederick Luther	27.4.1875	27.11.1960	14	1905–1909	682	143	1	26.23	—	—	—/—	—	6	
Farnes Kenneth (CY 1939)	8.7.1911	20.10.1941	15	1934–1938	58	20	0	4.83	60	6-96	3/1	28.65	1	
Farrimond William	23.5.1903	15.11.1979	4	1930–1935	116	35	0	16.57	—	—	—/—	—	5/2	
Fender Percy George Herbert (CY 1915)	22.8.1892	15.6.1985	13	1920–1929	380	60	0	19.00	29	5-90	2/0	40.86	14	
Ferris John James	21.5.1867	17.11.1900	1†	1891	16	16	0	16.00	13	7-37	2/1	7.00	0	
Fielder Arthur (CY 1907)	19.7.1877	30.8.1949	6	1903–1907	78	20	0	11.14	26	6-82	1/0	27.34	4	
Finn Steven Thomas	4.4.1989		36	2009–2016	279	56	0	11.16	125	6-79	5/0	30.40	8	69/21
Fishlock Laurence Barnard (CY 1947)	2.1.1907	25.6.1986	4	1936–1946	47	19*	0	11.75	—	—	—/—	—	1	

Name	Born	Died	Tests	Test Career	Runs	HS	100s	Avge	Wkts	BB	5/10	Avge	Ct/St	O/T
Flavell John Alfred (CY 1965)	15.5.1929	25.2.2004	4	1961-1964	31	14	0	7.75	7	2-65	000	52.42	0	
Fletcher Keith William Robert OBE (CY 1974)	20.5.1944		59	1968-1981	3,272	216	7	39.90	2	1-6	000	96.50	54	24
Flintoff Andrew MBE (CY 2004)	6.12.1977		78§	1998-2009	3,795	167	5	31.89	219	5-58	3/0	33.34	52	138‡7
Flowers Wilfred	7.12.1856	1.11.1926	8	1884-1893	254	56	0	18.14	14	5-46	1/0	21.14	2	
Foakes Benjamin Thomas	15.2.1993		5	2018	332	107	0	41.50	-	-	-	-	10/2	1/1
Ford Francis Gilbertson Justice	14.12.1866	7.2.1940	5	1894	168	48	0	18.66	1	1-47	000	129.00	5	
Foster Frank Rowbotham (CY 1912)	31.1.1889	3.5.1958	11	1911-1912	330	71	0	23.57	45	6-91	4/0	20.57	11	
Foster James Savin	15.4.1980		7	2001-2002	226	48	0	25.11	-	-	-	-	17/1	11/5
Foster Neil Alan (CY 1988)	6.5.1962		29	1983-1993	446	39	0	11.73	88	8-107	5/1	32.85	7	48
Foster Reginald Erskine ("Tip") (CY 1900)	16.4.1878	13.5.1914	8	1903-1907	602	287	1	46.30	-	-	-	-	13	
Fothergill Arnold James	26.8.1854	1.8.1932	2	1888	33	32	0	16.50	8	4-19	000	11.25		
Fowler Graeme	20.4.1957		21	1982-1984	1,307	201	3	35.32	0	0-3	000	-	10	26
Fraser Angus Robert Charles MBE (CY 1996)	8.8.1965		46	1989-1998	388	32	0	7.46	177	8-53	13/2	27.32	9	42
Freeman Alfred Percy ("Tich") (CY 1923)	17.5.1888	28.1.1965	12	1924-1929	154	50*	0	14.00	66	7-71	5/3	25.86	4	
French Bruce Nicholas	13.8.1959		16	1986-1987	308	59	0	18.11	-	-	-	-	38/1	13
Fry Charles Burgess (CY 1895)	25.4.1872	7.9.1956	26	1895-1912	1,223	144	2	32.18	0	0-6	000	-	17	
Gallian Jason Edward Riche	25.6.1971		3	1995-1995	74	28	0	12.33	-	-	-	-	1	
Gatting Michael William OBE (CY 1984)	6.6.1957		79	1977-1994	4,409	207	10	35.55	4	1-14	000	79.25	59	92
Gay Leslie Hewitt	24.3.1871	1.11.1949	1	1894	37	33	0	18.50	-	-	-	-	3/1	
[2] Geary George (CY 1927)	9.7.1893	6.3.1981	14	1924-1934	249	66	0	15.56	46	7-70	4/1	29.41	13	
Gibb Paul Antony	11.7.1913	7.12.1977	8	1938-1946	581	120	2	44.69	-	-	-	-	3/1	
Giddins Edward Simon Hunter	20.7.1971		4	1999-2000	10	7	0	2.50	12	5-15	1/0	20.00	0	
Gifford Norman MBE (CY 1975)	30.3.1940		15	1964-1973	179	25*	0	16.27	33	5-55	1/0	31.09	8	2
Giles Ashley Fraser MBE (CY 2005)	19.3.1973		54	1998-2006	1,421	59	0	20.89	143	5-57	5/0	40.60	33	62
[2] Gilligan Alfred Herbert Harold	29.6.1896	5.5.1978	4	1929	71	32	0	17.75	-	-	-	-	0	
[2] Gilligan Arthur Edward Robert (CY 1924)	23.12.1894	5.9.1976	11	1922-1924	209	39*	0	16.07	36	6-7	2/1	29.05		
Gimblett Harold (CY 1953)	19.10.1914	30.3.1978	3	1936-1939	129	67*	0	32.25	-	-	-	-	2	
Gladwin Clifford	3.4.1916	9.4.1988	8	1947-1949	170	51*	0	28.33	15	3-21	000	38.06	3	
Goddard Thomas William John (CY 1938)	1.10.1900	22.5.1966	8	1930-1939	13	8	0	6.50	22	6-29	1/0	26.72		
Gooch Graham Alan OBE (CY 1980)	23.7.1953		118	1975-1994	8,900	333	20	42.58	23	3-39	000	46.47	103	125
Gough Darren (CY 1999)	18.9.1970		58	1994-2003	855	65	0	12.57	229	6-42	9/0	28.39	13	158‡2
Gover Alfred Richard MBE (CY 1937)	29.2.1908	7.10.2001	4	1936-1946	2	2*	0	-	8	3-85	000	44.87		
Gower David Ivon OBE (CY 1979)	1.4.1957		117	1978-1992	8,231	215	18	44.25	1	1-1	000	20.00	74	114
[2] Grace Edward Mills	28.11.1841	20.5.1911	1	1880	36	36	0	18.00	-	-	-	-	1	
[2] Grace George Frederick	13.12.1850	22.9.1880	1	1880	0	0	0	0.00	-	-	-	-	2	

§ Flintoff's figures exclude 50 runs and seven wickets for the ICC World XI v Australia in the Super Series Test in 2005-06.

	Born	Died	Tests	Test Career	Runs	HS	100s	Avge	Wkts	BB	5/10	Avge	Ct/St	O/T
[2]Grace William Gilbert (CY 1896)	18.7.1848	23.10.1915	22	1880–1899	1,098	170	2	32.29	9	2-12	0/0	26.22	39	
Graveney Thomas William OBE (CY 1953)	16.6.1927	3.11.2015	79	1951–1960	4,882	258	11	44.38		–	–/–	167.00	80	
Greenhough Thomas	9.11.1931	15.9.2009	4	1959–1960	4	2	0	1.33	16	5-35	1/0	22.31	1	
Greenwood Andrew	20.8.1847	12.2.1889	2	1876	77	49	0	19.25					2	
[2]Greig Anthony William (CY 1975)	6.10.1946	29.12.2012	58	1972–1977	3,599	148	8	40.43	141	8-86	6/2	32.20	87	22
Greig Ian Alexander	8.12.1955		2	1982	26	14	0	6.50	4	4-53	0/0	28.50	0	
Grieve Basil Arthur Firebrace	28.5.1864	19.11.1917	2	1888	40	14*	0	40.00					0	
Griffith Stewart Cathie CBE ("Billy")	16.6.1914	7.4.1993	3	1947–1948	157	140	1	31.40					5	
Gunn George (CY 1914)	13.6.1879	29.6.1958	15	1907–1929	1,120	122*	2	40.00					15	
[2]Gunn John Richmond (CY 1904)	19.7.1876	21.8.1963	6	1901–1905	85	24	0	10.62	18	5-76	1/0	21.50	3	
[2]Gunn William (CY 1890)	4.12.1858	29.1.1921	11	1886–1899	392	102*	1	21.77					5	
Habib Aftab	7.2.1972		2	1999	26	19	0	8.66					0	
Haig Nigel Esmé	12.12.1887	27.10.1966	5	1921–1929	126	47	0	14.00	13	3-73	0/0	34.46	4	
Haigh Schofield (CY 1901)	19.3.1871	27.2.1921	11	1898–1912	113	25	0	7.53	24	6-11	1/0	25.91	8	
Hales Alexander Daniel	3.1.1989		11	2015–2016	573	94	0	27.28	0	0-2	0/0	–	8	
Hallows Charles (CY 1928)	4.4.1895	10.11.1972	2	1921–1928	42	26	0	42.00		–	–/–	–	0	
Hameed Haseeb	17.1.1997		3	2016	219	82	0	43.80					4	
Hamilton Gavin Mark	16.9.1974		1	1999	0	0	0	0.00	0	0-63	0/0	–	0	0‡
Hammond Walter Reginald (CY 1928)	19.6.1903	1.7.1965	85	1927–1946	7,249	336*	22	58.45	83	5-36	2/0	37.80	110	3
Hampshire John Harry	10.2.1941	1.3.2017	8	1969–1975	403	107	1	26.86		–	–/–	–	9	
Harding Harold Thomas William ("Wally") (CY 1915)	25.2.1886	8.5.1965	1	1921	30	25	0	15.00					2	
[1]Hardstaff Joseph snr	9.11.1882	2.4.1947	5	1907	311	72	0	31.10					1	
[1]Hardstaff Joseph jnr (CY 1938)	3.7.1911	1.1.1990	23	1935–1948	1,636	205*	4	46.74		–	–/–	–	9	
Harmison Stephen James MBE (CY 2005)	23.10.1978		62§	2002–2009	742	49*	0	12.16	222	7-12	8/1	31.94	7	58/2
Harris Lord [George Robert Canning]	3.2.1851	24.3.1932	4	1878–1884	145	52	0	29.00	1	0-14	0/0	115.00	2	
Hartley John Cabourn	15.11.1874	8.3.1963	2	1905	15	9	0	3.75	1	1-62	0/0	–	2	
Hawke Lord [Martin Bladen] (CY 1909)	16.8.1860	10.10.1938	5	1895–1898	55	30	0	7.85					3	
Hayes Ernest George (CY 1907)	6.11.1876	2.12.1953	5	1905–1912	86	35	0	10.75	1	1-28	0/0	52.00	2	
Hayes Frank Charles	6.12.1946		9	1973–1976	244	106*	1	15.25					7	6
Hayward Thomas Walter (CY 1895)	29.3.1871	19.7.1939	35	1895–1909	1,999	137	3	34.46	14	4-22	0/0	36.71	19	13
[3]Headley Dean Warren	27.1.1970		15	1997–1999	186	31	0	8.45	60	6-60	1/0	27.85	7	
[1,2]Hearne Alec (CY 1894)	22.7.1863	16.5.1952	1	1891	9	9	0	9.00	0	0-2		–	0	
[1,2]Hearne Frank	23.11.1858	14.7.1949	2†	1888	47	27	0	23.50					1	
[1]Hearne George Gibbons	7.1.1856	13.2.1932	1	1891	0	0	0	0.00					0	

§ *Harmison's figures exclude one run and four wickets for the ICC World XI v Australia in the Super Series Test in 2005-06.*

	Born	Died	Tests	Test Career	Runs	HS	100s	Avge	Wkts	BB	5/10	Avge	Ct/St	OIT
Hearne John Thomas (CY 1892)	3.5.1867	17.4.1944	12	1891–1899	126	40	0	9.00	49	6-41	4/1	22.08	4	
Hearne John William (CY 1912)	11.2.1891	14.9.1965	24	1911–1926	806	114	1	26.00	30	5-49	1/0	48.73	13	
Hegg Warren Kevin	23.2.1968		2	1998	30	15	0	7.50				–	8	33
Hemmings Edward Ernest	20.2.1949		16	1982–1990	383	95	0	22.52	43	6-58	1/0	42.44	5	
Hendren Elias Henry ("Patsy") (CY 1920)	5.2.1889	4.10.1962	51	1920–1934	3,525	205*	7	47.63	1	1-27	0/0	31.00	33	
Hendrick Michael (CY 1978)	22.10.1948		30	1974–1981	128	15	0	6.40	87	4-28	0/0	25.83	25	22
Heseltine Christopher	26.11.1869	13.6.1944	2	1895	18	18	0	9.00	5	5-38	1/0	16.80	2	
Hick Graeme Ashley MBE (CY 1987)	23.5.1966		65	1991–2000	3,383	178	6	31.32	23	4-126	0/0	56.78	90	120
Higgs Kenneth (CY 1968)	14.1.1937	7.9.2016	15	1965–1968	185	63	0	11.56	71	6-91	2/0	20.74	4	
Hill Allen	14.11.1843	28.8.1910	2	1876	101	49	0	50.50	7	4-27	0/0	18.57	1	
Hill Arthur James Ledger	26.7.1871		3	1895	251	124	1	62.75	4	4-8	0/0	2.00	1	
Hilton Malcolm Jameson (CY 1957)	2.8.1928	8.7.1990	4	1950–1951	37	15	0	34.07	14	5-61	3/0	30.00	1	
Hirst George Herbert (CY 1901)	7.9.1871	10.5.1954	24	1897–1909	790	85	0	22.57	59	5-48	3/0	30.00	18	
Hitch John William (CY 1914)	7.5.1886	7.7.1965	7	1911–1921	103	51*	0	14.71	7	2-31	0/0	46.42	4	
Hobbs Sir John Berry (CY 1909)	16.12.1882	21.12.1963	61	1907–1930	5,410	211	15	56.94	1	1-19	0/0	165.00	17	
Hobbs Robin Nicholas Stuart	8.5.1942		7	1967–1971	34	15*	0	6.80	12	3-25	0/0	40.08	8	26
Hoggard Matthew James MBE (CY 2006)	31.12.1976		67	2000–2007	473	38	0	7.27	248	7-61	7/1	30.50	24	
Hollies William Eric (CY 1955)	5.6.1912	16.4.1981	13	1934–1950	37	18*	0	5.28	44	7-50	5/0	30.27	2	
[2] Holliake Adam John (CY 2003)	5.9.1971		4	1997–1997	65	45	0	10.83	4	2-31	0/0	33.50	4	35
[2] Holliake Benjamin Caine	11.11.1977	23.3.2002	2	1997–1998	44	28	0	11.00	4	2-105	0/0	49.75	2	20
Holmes Errol Reginald Thorold (CY 1936)	21.8.1905	16.8.1960	5	1934–1935	114	85*	0	16.28	2	1-10	0/0	38.00	4	
Holmes Percy (CY 1920)	25.11.1886	3.9.1971	7	1921–1932	357	88	0	27.46	–		–	–	3	
Hone Leland	30.11.1853	31.12.1896	1	1878	13	7	0	6.50	–		–/–	–	2/1	
Hopwood John Leonard	30.10.1903	15.6.1985	2	1934	12	8	0	6.00	0	0-16	0/0	–	0	
Hornby Albert Neilson ("Monkey")	10.2.1847	17.12.1925	3	1878–1884	21	9	0	3.50	1	1-0	0/0	0.00	0	
Horton Martin John	21.4.1934	3.4.2011	2	1959	60	58	0	30.00	2	2-24	0/0	29.50	0	
Howard Nigel David	18.5.1925	31.5.1979	4	1951	86	23	0	17.20	–		–	–	4	
Howell Henry	29.11.1890	9.7.1932	5	1920–1924	15	5	0	7.50	7	4-115	0/0	79.85	2	
Howorth Richard	26.4.1909	2.4.1980	5	1947–1947	145	45*	0	18.12	19	6-124	1/0	33.42	2	
Humphries Joseph	19.5.1876	7.5.1946	3	1907	44	16	0	8.80	–		–	–	7	
Hunter Joseph	3.8.1855	4.1.1891	5	1884	93	39*	0	18.60	–		–	–	8/3	
Hussain Nasser OBE (CY 2003)	28.3.1968		96	1989–2004	5,764	207	14	37.18	0	0-15	0/0	–	67	88
Hutchings Kenneth Lotherington (CY 1907)	7.12.1882	3.9.1916	7	1907–1909	341	126	1	28.41	1	1-5	0/0	81.00	9	
[1] Hutton Sir Leonard (CY 1938)	23.6.1916	6.9.1990	79	1937–1954	6,971	364	19	56.67	3	1-2	0/0	77.33	57	
[1] Hutton Richard Anthony	6.9.1942		5	1971	219	81	0	36.50	9	3-72	0/0	28.55	9	
Iddon John	8.1.1902	17.4.1946	5	1934–1935	170	73	0	28.33	0	0-3	0/0	–	0	

Name	Born	Died	Tests	Test Career	Runs	HS	100s	Avge	Wkts	BB	5/10	Avge	Ct/St	O/T
Igglesden Alan Paul	8.10.1964		3	1989–1993	6	3*	0	3.00	6	2-91	0/0	54.83	–	4
Ikin John Thomas	7.3.1918	15.9.1984	18	1946–1955	606	60	0	20.89	3	1-38	0/0	118.00	31	–
Illingworth Raymond CBE (CY 1960)	8.6.1932		61	1958–1973	1,836	113	2	23.24	122	6-29	3/0	31.20	45	3
Illingworth Richard Keith	23.8.1963		9	1991–1995	128	28	0	18.28	19	4-96	0/0	32.36	5	25
Ilott Mark Christopher	27.8.1970		5	1993–1995	28	15	0	7.00	12	3-48	0/0	45.16	0	–
Insole Douglas John CBE (CY 1956)	18.4.1926	5.8.2017	9	1950–1957	408	110*	1	27.20	–	–	–/–	–	8	–
Irani Ronald Charles	26.10.1971		3	1996–1999	86	41	0	17.20	3	1-22	0/0	37.33	0	31
Jackman Robin David (CY 1981)	13.8.1945		4	1980–1982	42	17	0	7.00	14	4-110	0/0	31.78	0	15
Jackson Sir Francis Stanley (CY 1894)	21.11.1870	9.3.1947	20	1893–1905	1,415	144*	5	48.79	24	5-52	1/0	33.29	10	–
Jackson Herbert Leslie (CY 1959)	5.4.1921	25.4.2007	2	1949–1961	15	8	0	15.00	7	2-26	0/0	22.14	1	–
James Stephen Peter	7.9.1967		2	1998	71	36	0	17.75	–	–	–/–	–	1	–
Jameson John Alexander	30.6.1941		4	1971–1973	214	82	0	26.75	1	1-17	0/0	17.00	0	3
Jardine Douglas Robert (CY 1928)	23.10.1900	18.6.1958	22	1928–1933	1,296	127	1	48.00	–	0-10	0/0	–	26	–
Jarvis Paul William	29.6.1965		9	1987–1992	132	29*	0	10.15	21	4-107	0/0	45.95	2	16
Jenkins Roland Oliver (CY 1950)	24.11.1918	22.7.1995	9	1948–1952	198	39	0	18.00	32	5-116	1/0	34.31	4	–
Jennings Keaton Kent	19.6.1992		17	2016–2018	781	146*	2	25.19	0	0-2	0/0	–	17	–
Jessop Gilbert Laird (CY 1898)	19.5.1874	11.5.1955	18	1899–1912	569	104	1	21.88	10	4-68	0/0	35.40	11	–
Johnson Richard Leonard	29.12.1974		3	2003–2003	59	26	0	14.75	16	6-33	2/0	17.18	0	10
Jones Arthur Owen	16.8.1872	21.12.1914	12	1899–1909	291	34	0	13.85	3	3-73	0/0	44.33	15	–
Jones Geraint Owen MBE	14.7.1976		34	2003–2006	1,172	100	1	23.91	–	–	–/–	–	128/5	49/2
Jones Ivor Jeffrey	10.12.1941		15	1963–1967	38	16	0	4.75	44	6-118	1/0	40.20	4	–
Jones Simon Philip MBE (CY 2006)	25.12.1978		18	2002–2005	205	44	0	15.76	59	6-53	0/0	28.23	4	8
Jordan Christopher James	4.10.1988		8	2014–2014	180	35	0	18.00	21	4-18	0/0	35.80	14	31/43
Jupp Henry	19.11.1841	8.4.1889	2	1876	68	63	0	17.00	–	–	–/–	–	2	–
Jupp Vallance William Crisp (CY 1928)	27.3.1891	9.7.1960	8	1921–1928	208	38	0	17.33	28	4-37	0/0	22.00	5	–
Keeton William Walter (CY 1940)	30.4.1905	10.10.1980	2	1934–1939	57	25	0	14.25	–	–	–/–	–	0	–
Kennedy Alexander Stuart (CY 1933)	24.1.1891	15.11.1959	5	1922	93	41*	0	15.50	31	5-76	2/0	19.32	5	–
Kenyon Donald	15.5.1924	12.11.1996	8	1951–1955	192	87	0	12.80	–	–	–/–	–	5	–
Kerrigan Simon Christopher	10.5.1989		1	2013	1	1*	0	–	0	0-53	0/0	–	0	–
Key Robert William Trevor (CY 2005)	12.5.1979		15	2002–2004	775	221	1	31.00	–	–	–/–	–	11	5/1
Khan Amjad	14.10.1980		1	2008	–	–	–	–	1	1-111	0/0	122.00	0	0/1
Killick *Rev.* Edgar Thomas	9.5.1907	18.5.1953	2	1929	81	31	0	20.25	–	–	–/–	–	2	–
Kilner Roy (CY 1924)	17.10.1890	5.4.1928	9	1924–1926	233	74	0	33.28	24	4-51	0/0	30.58	6	–
King John Herbert	16.4.1871	18.11.1946	1	1909	64	60	0	32.00	1	1-99	0/0	99.00	0	–
Kinnear Septimus Paul (CY 1912)	13.5.1871	16.10.1928	1	1911	52	30	0	26.00	–	–	–/–	–	2	–
Kirtley Robert James	10.1.1975		4	2003–2003	32	12	0	5.33	19	6-34	1/0	29.52	3	11/1

	Born	Died	Tests	Test Career	Runs	HS	100s	Avge	Wkts	BB	5/10	Avge	Ct/St	OT
Knight Albert Ernest (CY 1904)	8.10.1872	25.4.1946	3	1903	81	70*	0	16.20	–	–	–/–	–	1	–
Knight Barry Rolfe	18.2.1938		29	1961–1969	812	127	2	26.19	70	4-38	0/0	31.75	14	–
Knight Donald John (CY 1915)	12.5.1894	5.1.1960	2	1921	54	38	0	13.50	–	–	–/–	–	1	–
Knight Nicholas Verity	28.11.1969		17	1995–2001	719	113	1	23.96	–	–	–/–	–	26	100
Knott Alan Philip Eric MBE (CY 1970)	9.4.1946		95	1967–1981	4,389	135	5	32.75	–	–	–/–	–	250/19	20
Knox Neville Alexander (CY 1907)	10.10.1884	3.3.1935	2	1907	24	8*	0	8.00	3	2-39	0/0	35.00	–	–
Laker James Charles (CY 1952)	9.2.1922	23.4.1986	46	1947–1958	676	63	0	14.08	193	10-53	9/3	21.24	12	–
Lamb Allan Joseph (CY 1981)	20.6.1954		79	1982–1992	4,656	142	14	36.09	1	1-56	0/0	23.00	75	122
Langridge James (CY 1932)	10.7.1906	10.9.1966	8	1933–1946	242	70	0	26.88	19	7-56	2/0	21.73	6	–
Larkins Wayne	22.11.1953		13	1979–1990	493	64	0	20.54	–	–	–/–	–	8	25
Larter John David Frederick	24.4.1940		10	1962–1965	16	10	0	3.20	37	5-57	2/0	25.43	5	–
Larwood Harold MBE (CY 1927)	14.11.1904	22.7.1995	21	1926–1932	485	98	0	19.40	78	6-32	4/1	28.35	15	–
Lathwell Mark Nicholas	26.12.1971		2	1993	78	33	0	19.50	–	–	–/–	–	0	–
Lawrence David Valentine ("Syd")	28.1.1964		5	1988–1991	60	34	0	10.00	18	5-106	1/0	37.55	0	1
Leach Matthew Jack	22.6.1991		10	2017–2019	220	92	0	18.33	34	5-83	1/0	29.02	5	–
Leadbeater Edric	15.8.1927	17.4.2011	2	1951	40	38	0	20.00	2	1-38	0/0	109.00	3	–
Lee Henry William	26.10.1890	21.4.1981	1	1930	19	18	0	9.50	–	–	–/–	–	0	–
Lees Walter Scott (CY 1906)	25.12.1875	10.9.1924	5	1905	66	25*	0	11.00	26	6-78	2/0	17.96	2	–
Legge Geoffrey Bevington	26.1.1903	21.11.1940	5	1927–1929	299	196	1	49.83	0	0-34	0/0	–	1	–
Leslie Charles Frederick Henry	8.12.1861	12.2.1921	4	1882	106	54	0	15.14	4	3-31	0/0	11.00	1	–
Lever John Kenneth MBE (CY 1979)	24.2.1949		21	1976–1986	306	53	0	11.76	73	7-46	3/1	26.72	11	22
Lever Peter	17.9.1940		17	1970–1975	350	88*	0	21.87	41	6-38	2/0	36.80	11	10
Leveson Gower *Sir* Henry Dudley Gresham	8.5.1873	1.2.1954	3	1909	95	31	0	23.75	–	–	–/–	–	1	–
Levett William Howard Vincent ("Hopper")	25.1.1908	1.12.1995	1	1933	7	5	0	7.00	–	–	–/–	–	3	–
Lewis Anthony Robert CBE	6.7.1938		9	1972–1973	457	125	1	32.64	–	–	–/–	–	0	–
Lewis Clairmonte Christopher	14.2.1968		32	1990–1996	1,105	117	1	23.02	93	6-111	3/0	37.52	25	53
Lewis Jonathan	26.8.1975		1	2006	27	20	0	13.50	3	3-68	0/0	40.66	0	13/2
Leyland Maurice (CY 1929)	20.7.1900	1.1.1967	41	1928–1938	2,764	187	9	46.06	6	3-91	0/0	97.50	13	–
Lilley Arthur Frederick Augustus ("Dick") (CY 1897)	28.11.1866	17.11.1929	35	1896–1909	903	84	0	20.52	1	1-23	0/0	23.00	70/22	–
Lillywhite James	23.2.1842	25.10.1929	2	1876	16	10	0	8.00	8	4-70	0/0	15.75	1	–
Lloyd David	18.3.1947		9	1974–1974	552	214*	1	42.46	0	0-4	0/0	–	11	8
Lloyd Timothy Andrew	5.11.1956		1	1984	10	10*	0	–	–	–	–/–	–	0	3
Loader Peter James (CY 1958)	25.10.1929	15.3.2011	13	1954–1958	76	17	0	5.84	39	6-36	1/0	22.51	2	–
Lock Graham Anthony Richard (CY 1954)	5.7.1929	30.3.1995	49	1952–1967	742	89	0	13.74	174	7-35	9/3	25.58	59	–
Lockwood William Henry (CY 1899)	25.3.1868	26.4.1932	12	1893–1902	231	52*	0	17.76	43	7-71	5/1	20.53	4	–

Name	Born	Died	Tests	Test Career	Runs	HS	100s	Avge	Wkts	BB	5/10	Avge	Ct/St	O/T
Lohmann George Alfred (CY 1889)	2.6.1865	1.12.1901	18	*1886–1896*	213	62*	0	8.87	112	9-28	9/5	10.75	28	–
Lowson Frank Anderson	1.7.1925	8.9.1984	7	*1951–1955*	245	68	0	18.84	–	–	–	–	5	–
Lucas Alfred Perry	20.2.1857	12.10.1923	5	*1878–1884*	157	55	0	19.62	0	0-23	0/0	–	1	–
Luckhurst Brian William (CY 1971)	5.2.1939	1.3.2005	21	*1970–1974*	1,298	131	4	36.05	1	1-9	0/0	32.00	14	3
Lyth Adam (CY 2015)	25.9.1987		7	*2015*	265	107	1	20.38	0	0-0	0/0	–	8	–
Lyttleton Hon. Alfred	7.2.1857	5.7.1913	4	*1880–1884*	94	31	0	15.66	4	4-19	0/0	4.75	2	–
Macaulay George Gibson (CY 1924)	7.12.1897	13.12.1940	8	*1922–1933*	112	76	0	18.66	24	5-64	1/0	27.58	5	–
MacBryan John Crawford William (CY 1925)	22.7.1892	14.7.1983	1	*1924*	–	–	–	–	–	–	–	–	–	–
McCague Martin John	24.5.1969		3	*1993–1994*	21	11	0	4.20	6	4-121	0/0	65.00	1	–
McConnon James Edward	21.6.1922	26.1.2003	2	*1954*	18	11	0	9.00	4	3-19	0/0	18.50	4	–
McGahey Charles Percy (CY 1902)	12.2.1871	10.1.1935	2	*1901*	38	18	0	9.50	–	–	–	–	1	–
McGrath Anthony	6.10.1975		4	*2003*	201	81	0	40.20	4	3-16	0/0	14.00	3	14
MacGregor Gregor (CY 1891)	31.8.1869	20.8.1919	8	*1890–1893*	96	31	0	12.00	–	–	–	–	14/3	–
McIntyre Arthur John William (CY 1958)	14.5.1918	26.12.2009	3	*1950–1955*	19	7	0	3.16	–	–	–	–	8	–
MacKinnon Francis Alexander	9.4.1848	27.2.1947	1	*1878*	5	5	0	2.50	–	–	–	–	0	–
MacLaren Archibald Campbell (CY 1895)	1.12.1871	17.11.1944	35	*1894–1909*	1,931	140	5	33.87	–	–	–	–	29	–
McMaster Joseph Emile Patrick	16.3.1861	7.6.1929	1	*1888*	0	0	0	0.00	–	–	–	–	0	–
Maddy Darren Lee	23.5.1974		3	*1999–1999*	46	24	0	11.50	0	0-40	0/0	–	4	8/4
Mahmood Sajid Iqbal	21.12.1981		8	*2006–2006*	81	34	0	8.10	20	4-22	0/0	38.10	0	26/4
Makepeace Joseph William Henry	22.8.1881	19.12.1952	4	*1920*	279	117	1	34.87	–	–	–	–	0	–
Malan Dawid Johannes	03.09.1987		15	*2017–2018*	724	140	1	27.84	0	0-7	0/0	–	11	1/9
Malcolm Devon Eugene (CY 1995)	22.2.1963		40	*1989–1997*	236	29	0	6.05	128	9-57	5/0	37.09	7	10
Mallender Neil Alan	13.8.1961		2	*1992*	8	4	0	2.66	10	5-50	1/0	21.50	3	–
Mann Francis George CBE	6.9.1917	8.8.2001	7	*1948–1949*	376	136*	1	37.60	–	–	–	–	3	–
Mann Francis Thomas	3.3.1888	6.10.1964	5	*1922*	281	84	0	35.12	–	–	–	–	4	–
Marks Victor James	25.6.1955		6	*1982–1983*	249	83	0	27.66	11	3-78	0/0	44.00	0	34
Marriott Charles Stowell ("Father")	14.9.1895	13.10.1966	1	*1933*	0	0	0	0.00	11	6-59	2/1	8.72	0	–
Martin Frederick (CY 1892)	12.10.1861	13.12.1921	2	*1890–1891*	14	13	0	7.00	14	6-50	2/1	10.07	2	–
Martin John William	16.2.1917	4.1.1987	1	*1947*	26	26	0	13.00	1	1-111	0/0	129.00	0	–
Martin Peter James	15.11.1968		8	*1995–1997*	115	29	0	8.84	17	4-60	0/0	34.11	6	20
Mason John Richard (CY 1898)	26.3.1874	15.10.1958	5	*1897*	129	32	0	12.90	2	1-8	0/0	74.50	3	–
Matthews Austin David George	3.5.1904	29.7.1977	1	*1937*	2	2*	0	2.00	2	1-13	0/0	32.50	1	–
May Peter Barker Howard CBE (CY 1952)	31.12.1929	27.12.1994	66	*1951–1961*	4,537	285*	13	46.77	–	–	–	–	42	–
Maynard Matthew Peter (CY 1998)	21.3.1966		4	*1988–1993*	87	35	0	10.87	–	–	–	–	3	14
Mead Charles Philip (CY 1912)	9.3.1887	26.3.1958	17	*1911–1928*	1,185	182*	4	49.37	–	–	–	–	4	–
Mead Walter (CY 1904)	1.4.1868	18.3.1954	1	*1899*	7	7	0	3.50	1	1-91	0/0	91.00	1	–

	Born	Died	Tests	Test Career	Runs	HS	100s	Avge	Wkts	BB	5/10	Avge	Ct/St	O/T
Midwinter William Evans	19.6.1851	3.12.1890	4†	1881	95	36	0	13.57	10	4-81	0/0	27.20	5	5
Milburn Colin ("Ollie") (CY 1967)	23.10.1941	28.2.1990	9	1966–1968	654	139	2	46.71	–	–	–/–	–	7	–
Miller Audley Montague	8.3.1869	26.6.1959	1	1895	24	20*	0	–	–	–	–/–	–	0	–
Miller Geoffrey OBE	8.9.1952	–	34	1976–1984	1,213	98*	0	25.80	60	5-44	1/0	30.98	17	25
Milligan Frank William	19.3.1870	31.3.1900	2	1898	58	38	0	14.50	0	0-0	0/0	–	1	–
Milligan Geoffrey	2.10.1934	6.4.2005	6	1961–1962	60	32*	0	12.00	–	–	–/–	–	13/2	–
Milton Clement Arthur (CY 1959)	10.3.1928	25.4.2007	6	1958–1959	204	104*	1	25.50	0	0-12	0/0	–	5	–
Mitchell Arthur	13.9.1902	25.12.1976	6	1933–1936	298	72	0	29.80	0	0-4	0/0	–	9	–
Mitchell Frank (CY 1902)	13.8.1872	11.10.1935	2†	1898	88	41	0	22.00	–	–	–/–	–	2	–
Mitchell Thomas Bignall	4.9.1902	27.1.1996	5	1932–1935	20	9	0	5.00	8	2-49	0/0	62.25	1	–
Mitchell-Innes Norman Stewart ("Mandy")	7.9.1914	28.12.2006	1	1935	5	5	0	5.00	–	–	–/–	–	0	–
Mold Arthur Webb (CY 1892)	27.5.1863	29.4.1921	3	1893	0	0*	0	0.00	7	3-44	0/0	33.42	1	–
Moon Leonard James	9.2.1878	23.11.1916	4	1905	182	36	0	22.75	–	–	–/–	–	4	–
Morgan Eoin Joseph Gerard CBE (CY 2011)	10.9.1986	–	16	2010–2011	700	130	2	30.43	–	–	–/–	–	11	210†/86
Morley Frederick	16.12.1850	28.9.1884	4	1880–1882	6	2*	0	1.50	16	5-56	1/0	18.50	4	–
Morris Hugh	5.10.1963	–	3	1991	115	44	0	19.16	–	–	–/–	–	3	–
Morris John Edward	1.4.1964	–	3	1990	71	32	0	23.66	–	–	–/–	–	3	8
Mortimore John Brian	14.5.1933	13.2.2014	9	1958–1964	243	73*	0	24.30	13	3-36	0/0	56.38	3	–
Moss Alan Edward	14.11.1930	12.3.2019	9	1953–1960	61	26	0	10.16	21	4-35	0/0	29.80	1	–
Moxon Martyn Douglas (CY 1993)	4.5.1960	–	10	1986–1989	455	99	0	28.43	0	0-3	0/0	–	10	8
Mullally Alan David (CY 1995)	12.7.1969	–	19	1996–2001	127	24	0	5.52	58	5-105	1/0	31.24	6	50
Munton Timothy Alan (CY 1995)	30.7.1965	–	2	1992	25	25*	0	25.00	4	2-22	0/0	50.00	2	–
Murdoch William Lloyd	18.10.1854	18.2.1911	1†	1891	12	12	0	12.00	–	–	–/–	–	0/1	–
Murray John Thomas MBE (CY 1967)	1.4.1935	24.7.2018	21	1961–1967	506	112	0	22.00	–	–	–/–	–	52/3	–
Newham William	12.12.1860	26.6.1944	1	1887	26	17	0	13.00	–	–	–/–	–	0	–
Newport Philip John	11.10.1962	–	3	1988–1990	110	40*	0	27.50	10	4-87	0/0	41.70	0	–
Nichols Morris Stanley (CY 1934)	6.10.1900	26.1.1961	14	1929–1939	355	78*	0	29.58	41	6-35	2/0	28.09	11	–
Oakman Alan Stanley Myles	20.4.1930	6.9.2018	2	1956	14	10	0	7.00	0	0-21	0/0	–	7	–
O'Brien Sir Timothy Carew	5.11.1861	9.12.1948	5	1884–1895	59	20	0	7.37	–	–	–/–	–	4	–
O'Connor Jack	6.11.1897	22.1.1977	4	1929–1929	153	51	0	21.85	1	1-31	0/0	72.00	2	–
Old Christopher Middleton (CY 1979)	22.12.1948	–	46	1972–1981	845	65	0	14.82	143	7-50	4/0	28.11	22	32
Oldfield Norman	5.5.1911	19.4.1996	1	1939	99	80	0	49.50	–	–	–/–	–	0	–
Onions Graham (CY 2010)	9.9.1982	–	9	2009–2012	30	17*	0	10.00	32	5-38	1/0	29.90	0	4
Ormond James	20.8.1977	–	2	2001–2001	38	18	0	12.66	9	2-70	0/0	92.50	0	–
Overton Craig	10.04.1994	–	4	2017–2019	124	41*	0	20.66	9	3-105	0/0	44.77	1	1
Padgett Douglas Ernest Vernon	20.7.1934	–	2	1960	51	31	0	12.75	0	0-8	0/0	–	0	–

	Born	Died	Tests	Test Career	Runs	HS	100s	Avge	Wkts	BB	5/10	Avge	Ct/St	O/T
Paine George Alfred Edward (CY 1935). . . .	11.6.1908	30.3.1978	4	1934	97	49	0	16.16	17	5-168	1/0	27.47	5	
Palairet Lionel Charles Hamilton (CY 1893).	27.5.1870	27.3.1933	2	1902	49	20	0	12.25	–	–	–	–	2	
Palmer Charles Henry CBE.	15.5.1919	31.3.2005	1	1953	22	22	0	11.00	0	0-15	0/0	–	5	
Palmer Kenneth Ernest MBE.	22.4.1937		1	1964	10	10	0	10.00	1	1-113	0/0	189.00	–	
Panesar Mudhsuden Singh ("Monty") (CY2007)	25.4.1982		50	2005-2013	220	26	0	4.88	167	6-37	12/2	34.71	10	26/1
Parfitt Peter Howard (CY 1963)	8.12.1936		37	1961-1972	1,882	131*	7	40.91	12	2-5	0/0	47.83	42	
Parker Charles Warrington Leonard (CY 1923)	14.10.1882	11.7.1959	1	1921	3	3*	0	–	2	2-32	–	16.00	–	
Parker Paul William Giles	15.1.1956		1	1981	13	13	0	6.50	–	–	–	–	3	
Parkhouse William Gilbert Anthony . . .	12.10.1925	10.8.2000	7	1950-1959	373	78	0	28.69	–	–	–/–	–	3	
Parkin Cecil Harry (CY 1924)	18.2.1886	15.6.1943	10	1920-1924	160	36	0	12.30	32	5-38	2/0	35.25	3	
Parks James Horace (CY 1938).	12.5.1903	21.11.1980	1	1937	29	22	0	14.50	3	2-26	0/0	12.00	–	
Parks James Michael (CY 1968). . . .	21.10.1931		46	1954-1967	1,962	108*	2	32.16	1	1-43	0/0	51.00	103/11	
Pataudi Iftikhar Ali Khan, Nawab of (CY 1932)	16.3.1910	5.1.1952	3†	1932-1934	144	102	1	28.80	–	–	–/–	–		
Patel Minal Mahesh	7.7.1970		2	1996	45	27	0	22.50	1	1-101	0/0	180.00	2	
Patel Samit Rohit	30.11.1984		6	2011-2015	151	42	0	16.77	7	2-27	0/0	60.14	3	36/18
Pattinson Darren John	2.8.1979		1	2008	21	13	0	10.50	2	2-95	0/0	48.00	–	
Peate Edmund	2.3.1855	11.3.1900	9	1881-1886	70	13	0	11.66	31	6-85	3/0	22.03	2	
Peebles Ian Alexander Ross (CY 1931)	20.1.1908	27.2.1980	13	1927-1931	98	26	0	10.88	45	6-63	3/0	30.91	5	
Peel Robert (CY 1889)	12.2.1857	12.8.1941	20	1884-1896	427	83	0	14.72	101	7-31	5/1	16.98	17	
Penn Frank.	7.3.1851	26.12.1916	1	1880	50	27*	0	50.00	–	0-2	–/–	–	2	
Perks Reginald Thomas David	4.10.1911	22.11.1977	2	1938-1939	3	2*	0	9.00	11	5-100	2/0	32.27	1	
Phillipson Hylton.	8.6.1866	4.12.1935	1	1891-1894	63	30	0	47.28	–	–	–/–	–	8/3	
Pietersen Kevin Peter MBE (CY 2006)	27.6.1980		104	2005-2013	8,181	227	23	47.28	10	3-52	0/0	88.60	62	134‡/37
Pigott Anthony Charles Shackleton . . .	4.6.1958		1	1983	12	8*	0	12.00	2	2-75	0/0	37.50	–	
Pilling Richard (CY 1891)	11.8.1855	28.3.1891	8	1881-1888	91	23	0	7.58	–	–	–/–	–	10/4	
Place Winston	7.12.1914	25.1.2002	3	1947	144	107	1	28.80	–	–	–/–	–	0	
Plunkett Liam Edward	6.4.1985		13	2005-2014	238	55*	0	15.86	41	5-64	1/0	37.46	3	89/22
Pocock Patrick Ian	24.9.1946		25	1967-1984	206	33	0	6.24	67	6-79	3/0	44.41	15	1
Pollard Richard	19.6.1912	16.12.1985	4	1946-1948	13	10*	0	13.00	15	5-24	1/0	25.20	3	
Poole Cyril John.	13.3.1921	11.2.1996	3	1951	161	69*	0	40.25	–	0-9	–/–	–	–	
Pope George Henry	27.11.1911	29.10.1993	1	1947	8	8*	0	–	1	1-49	0/0	85.00	–	
Pope Oliver John Douglas	2.1.1998		7	2018-2019	430	135*	1	47.77	–	–	–/–	–	12	
Pougher Arthur Dick.	19.4.1865	20.5.1926	1	1891	17	17	0	17.00	3	3-26	0/0	8.66	2	
Price John Sidney Ernest	22.7.1937		15	1963-1972	66	32	0	7.33	40	5-73	1/0	35.02	7	
Price Wilfred Frederick Frank . . .	25.4.1902	13.1.1969	1	1938	6	6	0	3.00	–	–	–/–	–	2	

	Born	Died	Tests	Test Career	Runs	HS	100s	Avge	Wkts	BB	5/10	Avge	Ct/St	O/T
Prideaux Roger Malcolm	31.7.1939		3	1968–1968	102	64	0	20.40	0	0-0	–/–	–	0	44
Pringle Derek Raymond	18.9.1958		30	1982–1992	695	63	0	15.10	70	5-95	3/0	35.97	0	68/10
Prior Matthew James (CY 2010)	26.2.1982		79	2007–2014	4,099	131*	7	40.18	–	–	–/–	–	243/13	–
Pullar Geoffrey (CY 1960)	1.8.1935	26.12.2014	28	1959–1962	1,974	175	4	43.86	1	1-1	0/0	37.00	2	–
Quaife William George (CY 1902)	17.3.1872	13.10.1951	7	1899–1901	228	68	0	19.00	0	0-6	0/0	–	4	–
Radford Neal Victor (CY 1986)	7.6.1957		3	1986–1987	21	12*	0	7.00	4	2-131	0/0	87.75	2	6
Radley Clive Thornton MBE (CY 1979)	13.5.1944		8	1977–1978	481	158	2	48.10	–	–/–	–/–	–	4	–
Ramprakash Mark Ravin MBE (CY 2007)	5.9.1969		52	1991–2002	2,350	154	2	27.32	4	1-2	0/0	119.25	39	18
Randall Derek William (CY 1980)	24.2.1951		47	1976–1984	2,470	174	7	33.37	0	0-1	0/0	–	31	49
Ranjitsinhji Kumar Shri (CY 1897)	10.9.1872	2.4.1933	15	1896–1902	989	175	2	44.95	1	1-23	0/0	39.00	13	–
Rankin William Boyd	5.7.1984		1†	2013	13	13	0	6.50	1	1-47	0/0	81.00	0	7¼/2‡
Rashid Adil Usman	17.2.1988		19	2015–2018	540	61	0	19.28	60	5-49	2/0	39.83	4	99/40
Read Christopher Mark Wells (CY 2011)	10.8.1978		15	1999–2006	360	55	0	18.94	–	–/–	–/–	–	48/6	36/1
Read Holcombe Douglas ("Hopper")	28.1.1910	5.1.2000	1	1935	–	–	–	–	6	4-136	0/0	33.33	0	–
Read John Maurice (CY 1890)	9.2.1859	17.2.1929	17	1882–1893	461	57	0	17.07	–	–	–/–	–	8	–
Read Walter William (CY 1893)	23.11.1855	6.1.1907	18	1882–1893	720	117	1	27.69	0	0-27	0/0	–	16	–
Reeve Dermot Alexander OBE (CY 1996)	2.4.1963		3	1991	124	59	0	24.80	2	1-4	0/0	30.00	1	29
Relf Albert Edward (CY 1913)	26.6.1874	26.3.1937	13	1903–1913	416	63	0	23.11	25	5-85	1/0	24.96	14	–
Rhodes Harold James	22.7.1936		2	1959	–	0*	–	–	9	4-50	0/0	27.11	0	–
Rhodes Steven John (CY 1995)	17.6.1964		11	1994–1994	294	65*	0	24.50	–	–/–	–/–	–	46/3	9
Rhodes Wilfred (CY 1899)	29.10.1877	8.7.1973	58	1899–1929	2,325	179	2	30.19	127	8-68	6/1	26.96	60	–
Richards Clifton James ("Jack")	10.8.1958		8	1986–1988	285	133	0	21.92	–	–/–	–/–	–	20/1	22
² Richardson Derek Walter ("Dick")	3.11.1934		1	1957	33	33	0	33.00	0	0-2	0/0	–	1	–
² Richardson Peter Edward (CY 1957)	4.7.1931	16.2.2017	34	1956–1963	2,061	126	5	37.47	3	2-10	0/0	16.00	6	–
Richardson Thomas (CY 1897)	11.8.1870	2.7.1912	14	1893–1897	177	25*	0	11.06	88	8-94	11/4	25.22	5	–
Richmond Thomas Leonard	23.6.1890	29.12.1957	1	1921	6	4	0	3.00	2	2-69	0/0	43.00	0	–
Ridgway Frederick	10.8.1923	26.9.2015	5	1951	49	24	0	8.16	7	4-83	0/0	54.14	3	–
Robertson John David Benbow (CY 1948)	22.2.1917	12.10.1996	11	1947–1951	881	133	2	46.36	2	2-17	0/0	29.00	6	–
Robins Robert Walter Vivian (CY 1930)	3.6.1906	12.12.1968	19	1929–1937	612	108	1	26.60	64	6-32	1/0	27.46	12	–
Robinson Robert Timothy (CY 1986)	21.11.1958		29	1984–1989	1,601	175	4	36.38	0	0-0	0/0	–	8	26
Robson Samuel David	1.7.1989		7	2014	336	127	1	30.54	–	–/–	–/–	–	5	–
Roland-Jones Tobias Skelton	29.01.1988		4	2017	82	25	0	20.50	17	5-57	1/0	19.64	0	1
Roope Graham Richard James	12.7.1946	26.11.2006	21	1972–1978	860	77	0	30.71	0	0-2	0/0	–	35	8
Root Charles Frederick	16.4.1890	20.1.1954	3	1926	–	–	–	–	8	4-84	0/0	24.25	1	–
Root Joseph Edward MBE (CY 2014)	30.12.1990		92	2012–2019	7,599	254	17	48.40	28	4-87	0/0	50.07	114	143/32
Rose Brian Charles (CY 1980)	4.6.1950		9	1977–1980	358	70	0	25.57	–	–/–	–/–	–	4	2

	Born	Died	Tests	Test Career	Runs	HS	100s	Avge	Wkts	BB	5/10	Avge	Ct/St	O/T
Roy Jason Jonathan	21.7.1990		5	2019	187	72	0	18.70	0	0-6	–/–	–	1	84/32
Royle Vernon Peter Fanshawe Archer	29.1.1854	21.5.1929	2	1878	21	18	0	10.50	0	0-6	0/0	–	2	
Rumsey Frederick Edward	4.12.1935		5	1964–1965	30	21*	0	15.00	17	4-25	0/0	27.11	0	
Russell Albert Charles ("Jack") (*CY 1923*)	7.10.1887	23.3.1961	10	1920–1922	910	140	5	56.87	–	–	–/–	–	8	40
Russell Robert Charles ("Jack") (*CY 1990*)	15.8.1963		54	1988–1997	1,897	128*	2	27.10	–	–	–/–	–	153/12	
Russell William Eric	3.7.1936		10	1961–1967	362	70	0	21.29	0	0-19	0/0	–	4	
Saggers Martin John	23.5.1972		3	2003–2004	1	1	0	0.33	7	2-29	0/0	35.28	0	
Salisbury Ian David Kenneth (*CY 1993*)	21.1.1970		15	1992–2000	368	50	0	16.72	20	4-163	0/0	76.95	5	4
Sandham Andrew (*CY 1923*)	6.7.1890	20.4.1982	14	1921–1929	879	325	2	38.21	0	–	–/–	–	4	
Schofield Christopher Paul	6.10.1978		2	2000	67	57	0	22.33	0	0-73	0/0	–	0	0/4
Schultz Sandford Spence	29.8.1857	18.12.1937	1	1878	20	20	0	20.00	1	1-16	0/0	26.00	0	
Scotton William Henry	15.1.1856	9.7.1893	15	1881–1886	510	90	0	22.17	0	0-20	0/0	–	4	
Selby John	1.7.1849	11.3.1894	6	1876–1881	256	70	0	23.27	–	–	–/–	–	2	
Selvey Michael Walter William	25.4.1948		3	1976–1976	15	5*	0	7.50	6	4-41	0/0	57.16	1	
Shackleton Derek (*CY 1959*)	12.8.1924	28.9.2007	7	1950–1963	113	42	0	18.83	18	4-72	0/0	42.66	1	
Shah Owais Alam	22.10.1978		6	2005–2008	269	88	0	26.90	0	0-12	0/0	–	2	71/17
Shahzad Ajmal	27.7.1985		1	2010	5	5	0	5.00	4	3-45	0/0	15.75	1	11/3
Sharp John	15.2.1878	28.1.1938	3	1909	188	105	1	47.00	3	3-67	0/0	37.00	1	
Sharpe John William (*CY 1892*)	9.12.1866	19.6.1936	3	1890–1891	44	26	0	22.00	11	6-84	1/0	27.72	2	
Sharpe Philip John (*CY 1963*)	27.12.1936	19.5.2014	12	1963–1969	786	111	1	46.23	–	–	–/–	–	17	
Shaw Alfred	29.8.1842	16.1.1907	7	1876–1881	111	40	0	10.09	12	5-38	1/0	23.75	4	
Sheppard Rt Rev. Lord [David Stuart] (*CY 1953*)	6.3.1929	5.3.2005	22	1950–1962	1,172	119	3	37.80	–	–	–/–	–	12	
Sherwin Mordecai (*CY 1891*)	26.2.1851	3.7.1910	3	1886–1888	30	21*	0	15.00	0	0-2	0/0	–	5/2	
Shrewsbury Arthur (*CY 1890*)	11.4.1856	19.5.1903	23	1881–1893	1,277	164	3	35.47	0	–	–/–	–	29	
Shuter John	9.2.1855	5.7.1920	1	1888	28	28	0	28.00	–	–	–/–	–	0	
Shuttleworth Kenneth	13.11.1944		5	1970–1971	46	21	0	7.66	12	5-47	1/0	35.58	1	
Sibley Dominic Peter	5.9.1995		6	2019	362	133*	1	40.22	0	–	–/–	–	5	
Sidebottom Arnold	1.4.1954		1	1985	2	2	0	2.00	1	1-65	0/0	65.00	0	
Sidebottom Ryan Jay (*CY 2008*)	15.1.1978		22	2001–2009	313	31	0	15.65	79	7-47	5/1	28.24	5	25/18
Silverwood Christopher Eric Wilfred	5.3.1975		6	1996–2002	29	10	0	7.25	11	5-91	1/0	40.36	2	7
Simpson Reginald Thomas (*CY 1950*)	27.2.1920	24.11.2013	27	1948–1954	1,401	156*	4	33.35	2	2-4	0/0	11.00	5	
Simpson-Hayward George Hayward Thomas	7.6.1875	2.10.1936	5	1909	105	29*	0	15.00	23	6-43	2/0	18.26	1	
Sims James Morton	13.5.1903	27.4.1973	4	1935–1936	16	12	0	4.00	11	5-73	1/0	43.63	6	
Sinfield Reginald Albert	24.12.1900	17.3.1988	1	1938	6	6	0	6.00	2	1-51	0/0	61.50	0	
Slack Wilfred Norris	12.12.1954	15.1.1989	3	1985–1986	81	52	0	13.50	0	–	–/–	–	3	2
Smailes Thomas Francis	27.3.1910	1.12.1970	1	1946	25	25	0	25.00	3	3-44	0/0	20.66	0	

	Born	Died	Tests	Test Career	Runs	HS	100s	Avge	Wkts	BB	5/10	Avge	Ct/St	O/T
Small Gladstone Cleophas	18.10.1961		17	1986–1990	263	59	0	15.47	55	5-48	2/0	34.01	9	53
Smith Alan Christopher CBE	25.10.1936		6	1962	118	69*	0	29.50					20	
Smith Andrew Michael	1.10.1967		1	1997	4	4*	0	4.00	0	0-89	0/0		0	
Smith Cedric Ivan James (CY 1935)	25.8.1906	8.2.1979	5	1934–1937	102	27	0	10.20	15	5-16	1/0	26.20	1	
Smith Sir Charles Aubrey	21.7.1863	20.12.1948	1	1888	3	3	0	3.00	7	5-19	1/0	8.71	0	
[2] Smith Christopher Lyall (CY 1984)	15.10.1958		8	1983–1986	392	91	0	30.15	3	2-31	0/0	13.00	5	4
Smith David Mark	9.1.1956		2	1985	80	47	0	20.00					0	2
Smith David Robert	5.10.1934	17.12.2003	5	1961	38	34	0	9.50	6	2-60	0/0	59.83	2	
Smith Denis (CY 1935)	24.1.1907	12.9.1979	2	1935	128	57	0	32.00					2	
Smith Donald Victor	14.6.1923		2	1957	25	16*	0	8.33	1	1-12	0/0	97.00	0	
Smith Edward	19.7.1977		3	2003	87	64	0	17.40					5	
Smith Ernest James ("Tiger")	6.2.1886	31.8.1979	11	1911–1913	113	22	0	8.69					17/3	
Smith Harry	21.5.1891	12.11.1937	1	1928	7	7	0	7.00					1	
Smith Michael John Knight OBE (CY 1960)	30.6.1933		50	1958–1972	2,278	121	3	31.63	1	1-10	0/0	128.00	53	
[2] Smith Robin Arnold (CY 1990)	13.9.1963		62	1988–1995	4,236	175	3	43.67	0	0-6	0/0		39	71
Smith Thomas Peter Bromley (CY 1947)	30.10.1908	4.8.1967	4	1946	33	24	0	6.60	3	2-172	0/0	106.33	1	
Smithson Gerald Arthur	1.11.1926	6.9.1970	2	1947	70	35	0	23.33					2	
Snow John Augustine (CY 1973)	13.10.1941		49	1965–1976	772	73	0	13.54	202	7-40	8/1	26.66	16	9
Southerton James	16.11.1827	16.6.1880	2	1876	7	6	0	3.50	7	4-46	0/0	15.28	2	
Spooner Reginald Herbert (CY 1905)	21.10.1880	2.10.1961	10	1905–1912	481	119	1	32.06					4	
Spooner Richard Thompson	30.12.1919	20.12.1997	7	1951–1955	354	92	0	27.23					10/2	
Stanyforth Ronald Thomas	30.5.1892	20.2.1964	4	1927	13	6*	0	2.60					7/2	
Staples Samuel James (CY 1929)	18.9.1892	4.6.1950	3	1927	65	39	0	13.00	15	3-50	0/0	29.00	5	
Statham John Brian CBE (CY 1955)	17.6.1930	10.6.2000	70	1950–1965	675	38	0	11.44	252	7-39	9/1	24.84	28	
Steel Allan Gibson	24.9.1858	15.6.1914	13	1880–1888	600	148	2	35.29	29	3-27	0/0	20.86	5	
Steele David Stanley OBE (CY 1976)	29.9.1941		8	1975–1976	673	106	1	42.06	2	1-1	0/0	19.50	7	1
Stephenson John Patrick	14.3.1965		1	1989	36	25	0	18.00					0	
Stevens Greville Thomas Scott (CY 1918)	7.1.1901	19.9.1970	10	1922–1929	263	69	0	15.47	20	5-90	2/1	32.40	9	
Stevenson Graham Barry	16.12.1955	21.1.2014	2	1979–1980	28	27*	0	28.00	5	3-111	0/0	36.60	0	4
[1] Stewart Alec James OBE (CY 1993)	8.4.1963		133	1989–2003	8,463	190	15	39.54	0	0-5	0/0		263/14	170
Stewart Michael James OBE (CY 1958)	16.9.1932		8	1962–1963	385	87	0	35.00					6	
Stoddart Andrew Ernest (CY 1893)	11.3.1863	3.4.1915	16	1887–1897	996	173	2	35.57	2	1-10	0/0	47.00	6	
Stokes Benjamin Andrew OBE (CY 2016)	4.6.1991		63	2013–2019	4,056	258	13	36.54	147	6-22	4/0	32.68	72	95/23
Stone Oliver Peter	9.10.1993		1	2019	19	19	0	9.50	5	3-29	0/0	9.66	0	4
Stoneman Mark Daniel	26.06.1987		11	2017–2018	526	60	0	27.68					0	
[1] Storer William (CY 1899)	25.1.1867	28.2.1912	6	1897–1899	215	51	0	19.54	2	1-24	0/0	54.00	11	

	Born	Died	Tests	Test Career	Runs	HS	100s	Avge	Wkts	BB	5/10	Avge	Ct/St	OTT
Strauss Sir Andrew John OBE (CY 2005)	2.3.1977		100	2004-2012	7,037	177	21	40.91			-/-		121	127/4
Street George Benjamin	6.12.1889	24.4.1924	1	1922	11	7*	0	11.00			-/-		0/1	
Strudwick Herbert (CY 1912)	28.1.1880	14.2.1970	28	1909-1926	230	24	0	7.93			-/-		61/12	
[2]Studd Charles Thomas	2.12.1860	16.7.1931	5	1882-1882	160	48	0	20.00	3	2-35	0/0	32.66	5	
[2]Studd George Brown	20.10.1859	13.2.1945	4	1882	31	9	0	4.42			-/-		8	
Subba Row Raman CBE (CY 1961)	29.1.1932		13	1958-1961	984	137	3	46.85	0	0-2	0/0		5	
Such Peter Mark	12.6.1964		11	1993-1999	67	14*	0	6.09	37	6-67	2/0	33.56	4	
Sugg Frank Howe (CY 1890)	11.1.1862	29.5.1933	2	1888	55	31	0	27.50			-/-		0	
Sutcliffe Herbert (CY 1920)	24.11.1894	22.1.1978	54	1924-1935	4,555	194	16	60.73			-/-		23	
Swann Graeme Peter (CY 2010)	24.3.1979		60	2008-2013	1,370	85	0	22.09	255	6-65	17/3	29.96	54	79/39
Swetman Roy	25.10.1933		11	1958-1959	254	65	0	16.93			-/-		24/2	
[1]Tate Frederick William	24.7.1867	24.2.1943	1	1902	9	5*	0	9.00	2	2-7	0/0	25.50	2	
[1]Tate Maurice William (CY 1924)	30.5.1895	18.5.1956	39	1924-1935	1,198	100*	1	25.48	155	6-42	7/1	26.16	11	2
Tattersall Roy	17.8.1922	9.12.2011	16	1950-1954	50	10*	0	5.00	58	7-52	4/1	26.08	8	27
Tavaré Christopher James	27.10.1954		31	1980-1989	1,755	149	2	32.50	0	0-0	0/0		20	29
Taylor James William Arthur	6.1.1990		7	2012-2015	312	76	0	26.00			-/-		7	27
Taylor Jonathan Paul	8.8.1964		2	1992-1994	34	17*	0	17.00	3	1-18	0/0	52.00	0	1
Taylor Kenneth	21.8.1935		3	1959-1964	57	24	0	11.40	0	0-6	0/0		1	
Taylor Leslie Brian	25.10.1953		2	1985	1	1*	0		4	2-34	0/0	44.50	0	2
Taylor Robert William MBE (CY 1977)	17.7.1941		57	1970-1983	1,156	97	0	16.28			-/-		1677	27
Tennyson Lord Lionel Hallam (CY 1914)	7.11.1889	6.6.1951	9	1913-1921	345	74*	0	31.36			-/-		6	
Terry Vivian Paul	14.1.1959		2	1984	16	8	0	5.33			-/-		2	
Thomas John Gregory	12.8.1960		5	1985-1986	83	31*	0	13.83	10	4-70	0/0	50.40	5	3
Thompson George Joseph (CY 1906)	27.10.1877	3.3.1943	6	1909-1909	273	63	0	30.33	23	4-50	0/0	27.73	3	
Thomson Norman Ian	23.1.1929		5	1964	69	39	0	23.00	9	2-55	0/0	63.11	3	
Thorpe Graham Paul MBE (CY 1998)	1.8.1969		100	1993-2005	6,744	200*	16	44.66	0	0-0	0/0		105	82
Titmus Frederick John MBE (CY 1963)	24.11.1932	23.3.2011	53	1955-1974	1,449	84*	0	22.29	153	7-79	7/0	32.22	35	2
Tolchard Roger William	15.6.1946		4	1976	129	67	0	25.80			-/-		2	1
[1]Townsend Charles Lucas (CY 1899)	7.11.1876	17.10.1958	2	1899	51	38	0	17.00	6	3-50	0/0	25.00	2	
[1]Townsend David Charles Humphery	20.4.1912	27.1.1997	3	1934	77	36	0	12.83	0	0-9	0/0		4	
[4]Townsend Leslie Fletcher (CY 1934)	8.6.1903	17.2.1993	4	1929-1933	97	40	0	16.16	6	2-22	0/0	34.16	4	
Tredwell James Cullum	27.2.1982		2	2009-2014	37	25*	0	22.50	11	4-47	0/0	29.18	0	45/17
[4]Tremlett Christopher Timothy	2.9.1981		12	2007-2013	113	25*	0	10.27	53	6-48	2/0	27.00	2	15/1
[4]Tremlett Maurice Fletcher	5.7.1923	30.7.1984	3	1947	20	18*	0	6.66	4	2-98	0/0	56.50	4	
Trescothick Marcus Edward MBE (CY 2005)	25.12.1975		76	2000-2006	5,825	219	14	43.79	1	1-34	0/0	155.00	95	123/3
[2]Trott Albert Edwin (CY 1899)	6.2.1873	30.7.1914	2+	1898	23	16	0	5.75	17	5-49	1/0	11.64	0	

	Born	Died	Tests	Test Career	Runs	HS	100s	Avge	Wkts	BB	5/10	Avge	Ct/St	O/T
Trott Ian Jonathan Leonard (CY 2011)	22.4.1981		52	2009–2014	3,835	226	9	44.08	5	1-5	0/0	80.00	29	68/7
Trueman Frederick Sewards OBE (CY 1953)	6.2.1931	1.7.2006	67	1952–1965	981	39*	0	13.81	307	8-31	17/3	21.57	64	
Tudor Alex Jeremy	23.10.1977		10	1998–2002	229	99*	0	19.08	28	5-44	1/0	34.39	3	3
Tufnell Neville Charsley	13.6.1887	3.8.1951	1	1909	14	14	0	14.00	–	–	–/–	–	0/1	
Tufnell Philip Clive Roderick	29.4.1966		42	1990–2001	153	22*	0	5.10	121	7-47	5/2	37.68	12	20
Turnbull Maurice Joseph Lawson (CY 1931)	16.3.1906	5.8.1944	9	1929–1936	224	61	0	20.36	–	–	–/–	–	1	
2 Tyldesley [George] Ernest (CY 1920)	5.2.1889	5.5.1962	14	1921–1928	990	122	3	55.00	0	0-2	0/0	–	2	
2 Tyldesley John Thomas (CY 1902)	22.11.1873	27.11.1930	31	1898–1909	1,661	138	4	30.75	–	–	–/–	–	16	
Tyldesley Richard Knowles (CY 1925)	11.3.1897	17.9.1943	7	1924–1930	47	29	0	7.83	19	3-50	0/0	32.57	1	
Tylecote Edward Ferdinando Sutton	23.6.1849	15.3.1938	6	1882–1886	152	66	0	19.00	–	–	–/–	–	5/5	
Tyler Edwin James	13.10.1864	25.1.1917	1	1895	0	0	0	0.00	4	3-49	0/0	18.56	–	
Tyson Frank Holmes (CY 1956)	6.6.1930	27.9.2015	17	1954–1958	230	37*	0	10.95	76	7-27	4/1	18.56	4	
Udal Shaun David	18.3.1969		4	2005	109	33*	0	18.16	8	4-14	0/0	43.00	1	11
Ulyett George	21.10.1851	18.6.1898	25	1876–1890	949	149	1	24.33	50	7-36	1/0	20.40	19	
Underwood Derek Leslie MBE (CY 1969)	8.6.1945		86	1966–1981	937	45*	0	11.56	297	8-51	17/6	25.83	44	26
Valentine Bryan Herbert	17.1.1908	2.2.1983	7	1933–1938	454	136	2	64.85	–	–	–/–	–	2	
Vaughan Michael Paul OBE (CY 2003)	29.10.1974		82	1999–2008	5,719	197	18	41.44	6	2-71	0/0	93.50	44	86/2
Verity Hedley (CY 1932)	18.5.1905	31.7.1943	40	1931–1939	669	66*	0	20.90	144	8-43	5/2	24.37	30	
Vernon George Frederick	20.6.1856	10.8.1902	1	1882	14	11*	0	14.00	–	–	–/–	–	–	
Vince James Michael	14.3.1991		13	2016–2017	548	83	0	24.90	0	0-0	0/0	–	8	13/12
Vine Joseph (CY 1906)	15.5.1875	25.4.1946	2	1911	46	36	0	46.00	–	–	–/–	–	–	
Voce William (CY 1933)	8.8.1909	6.6.1984	27	1929–1946	308	66	0	13.39	98	7-70	3/2	27.88	15	
Waddington Abraham	4.2.1893	28.10.1959	2	1920	16	7	0	4.00	1	1-35	0/0	119.00	1	
Wainwright Edward (CY 1894)	8.4.1865	28.10.1919	5	1893–1897	132	49	0	14.66	0	0-11	0/0	–	2	
Walker Peter Michael	17.2.1936		3	1960	128	52	0	32.00	0	0-8	0/0	–	5	
Walters Cyril Frederick (CY 1934)	28.8.1905	23.12.1992	11	1933–1934	784	102	1	52.26	–	–	–/–	–	6	
Ward Alan	10.8.1947		5	1969–1976	40	21	0	8.00	14	4-61	0/0	32.35	3	
Ward Albert (CY 1890)	21.11.1865	6.1.1939	7	1893–1894	487	117	1	37.46	–	–	–/–	–	1	
Ward Ian James	30.9.1972		5	2001	129	39	0	16.12	–	–	–/–	–	2	
Wardle John Henry (CY 1954)	8.1.1923	23.7.1985	28	1947–1957	653	66	0	19.78	102	7-36	5/1	20.39	12	
Warner Sir Pelham Francis (CY 1904)	2.10.1873	30.1.1963	15	1898–1912	622	132*	1	23.92	–	–	–/–	–	3	
Warr John James	16.7.1927	9.5.2016	2	1950	4	4	0	1.00	1	1-76	0/0	281.00	0	
Warren Arnold	2.4.1875	3.9.1951	1	1905	7	7	0	7.00	6	5-57	1/0	18.83	1	
Washbrook Cyril CBE (CY 1947)	6.12.1914	27.4.1999	37	1937–1956	2,569	195	6	42.81	1	1-25	0/0	33.00	12	1
Watkin Steven Llewellyn (CY 1994)	15.9.1964		3	1991–1993	25	13	0	5.00	11	4-65	0/0	27.72	4	
Watkins Albert John ("Allan")	21.4.1922	3.8.2011	15	1948–1952	810	137*	2	40.50	11	3-20	0/0	50.36	17	4

	Born	Died	Tests	Test Career	Runs	HS	100s	Avge	Wkts	BB	5/10	Avge	Ct/St	O/T
Watkinson Michael	1.8.1961		4	1995-1995	167	82*	0	33.40	10	3-64	0/0	34.80	1	—
Watson Willie (CY 1954)	7.3.1920	24.4.2004	23	1951-1958	879	116	2	25.85	—	—	-/-	—	8	—
Webbe Alexander Josiah	16.1.1855	19.2.1941	1	*1878*	4	4	0	2.00	—	—	-/-	—	2	—
Wellard Arthur William (CY 1936)	8.4.1902	31.12.1980	2	1937-1938	47	38	0	11.75	7	4-81	0/0	33.85	2	—
Wells Alan Peter	2.10.1961		1	1995	3	3*	0	3.00	—	—	-/-	—	—	—
Westley Thomas	13.03.1989		5	2017	193	59	0	24.12	0	0-12	0/0	—	1	—
Wharton Alan	30.4.1923	26.8.1993	1	1949	20	13	0	10.00	—	—	-/-	—	—	—
Whitaker John James (CY 1987)	5.5.1962		1	1986	11	11	0	11.00	—	—	-/-	—	0	—
White Craig	16.12.1969		30	1994-2002	1,052	121	1	24.46	59	5-32	3/0	37.62	14	2
White David William ("Butch")	14.12.1935	1.8.2008	2	1961	0	0	0	0.00	4	3-65	0/0	29.75	0	51
White John Cornish (CY 1929)	19.2.1891	2.5.1961	15	1921-1930	239	29	0	18.38	49	8-126	3/1	32.26	6	—
Whysall William Wilfrid (CY 1925)	31.10.1887	11.11.1930	4	1924-1930	209	76	0	29.85	0	—	0/0	—	7	—
Wilkinson Leonard Litton	5.11.1916	3.9.2002	3	*1938*	3	2	0	3.00	7	2-12	0/0	38.71	0	—
Willey Peter	6.12.1949		26	1976-1986	1,184	102*	2	26.90	7	2-73	0/0	65.14	3	26
Williams Neil FitzGerald	2.7.1962	27.3.2006	1	1990	38	38	0	38.00	2	2-148	0/0	74.00	0	—
Willis Robert George Dylan MBE (CY 1978)	30.5.1949	4.12.2019	90	1970-1984	840	28*	0	11.50	325	8-43	16/0	25.20	39	64
Wilson Clement Eustace Macro (CY 1978)	15.5.1875	8.2.1944	2	*1898*	42	18	0	14.00	0	—	0/0	—	0	—
Wilson Donald	7.8.1937	21.7.2012	6	1963-1970	75	42	0	12.50	11	2-17	0/0	42.36	1	—
Wilson Evelyn Rockley	25.3.1879	21.7.1957	1	*1920*	10	5	0	5.00	3	2-28	0/0	12.00	0	—
Woakes Christopher Roger (CY 2017)	2.3.1989		33	2013-2019	1,177	137*	1	26.75	95	6-17	3/1	30.88	15	99/8
Wood Arthur (CY 1939)	25.8.1898	1.4.1973	4	1938-1939	80	53	0	20.00	—	—	-/-	—	10/1	—
Wood Barry	26.12.1942		12	1972-1978	454	90	0	21.61	0	0-2	0/0	—	6	13
Wood George Edward Charles	22.8.1893	18.3.1971	3	*1924*	7	6	0	3.50	—	—	-/-	—	5/1	—
Wood Henry (CY 1891)	14.12.1853	30.4.1919	4	1888-1891	204	134*	1	68.00	—	—	-/-	—	2/1	—
Wood Mark Andrew	11.1.1990		15	2015-2019	392	52	0	19.60	48	5-41	2/0	31.41	7	51/5
Wood Reginald	7.3.1860	6.1.1915	1	*1886*	6	6	0	3.00	—	—	-/-	—	0	—
Woods Samuel Moses James (CY 1889)	13.4.1867	30.4.1931	3†	*1895*	122	53	0	30.50	5	3-28	0/0	25.80	4	—
Woolley Frank Edward (CY 1911)	27.5.1887	18.10.1978	64	1909-1934	3,283	154	5	36.07	83	7-76	4/1	33.91	64	—
Woolmer Robert Andrew (CY 1976)	14.5.1948	18.3.2007	19	1975-1981	1,059	149	3	33.09	4	1-8	0/0	74.75	10	—
Worthington Thomas Stanley (CY 1937)	21.8.1905	31.8.1973	9	1929-1936	321	128	1	29.18	8	2-19	0/0	39.50	8	6
Wright Charles William	27.5.1863	10.1.1936	3	*1895*	125	71	0	31.25	—	—	-/-	—	0	—
Wright Douglas Vivian Parson (CY 1940)	21.8.1914	13.11.1998	34	1938-1950	289	45	0	11.11	108	7-105	6/1	39.11	10	—
Wyatt Robert Elliott Storey (CY 1930)	2.5.1901	20.4.1995	40	1927-1936	1,839	149	2	31.70	18	3-4	0/0	35.66	16	—
Wynyard Edward George	1.4.1861	30.10.1936	3	1896-1905	72	30	0	12.00	0	—	0/0	—	0	—
Yardley Norman Walter Dransfield (CY 1948)	19.3.1915	3.10.1989	20	1938-1950	812	99	0	25.37	21	3-67	0/0	33.66	14	—
Young Harding Isaac ("Sailor")	5.2.1876	12.12.1964	2	1899	43	43	0	21.50	12	4-30	0/0	21.83	1	—

	Born	Died	Tests	Test Career	Runs	HS	Avge	Wkts	BB	5/10	Avge	Ct/St	OIT
Young John Albert	14.10.1912	5.2.1993	8	1947–1949	28	10*	5.60	17	3-65	0/0	44.52	5	
Young Richard Alfred	16.9.1885	1.7.1968	2	1907	27	13	6.75	–	–	–/–	–	6	

AUSTRALIA (458 players)

	Born	Died	Tests	Test Career	Runs	HS	100s	Avge	Wkts	BB	5/10	Avge	Ct/St	OIT
a'Beckett Edward Lambert	11.8.1907	2.6.1989	4	1928–1931	143	41	0	20.42	3	1-41	0/0	105.66	4	
Agar Ashton Charles	14.10.1993		4	2013–2017	195	98	0	32.50	9	3-46	0/0	45.55	4	9/21
Alderman Terence Michael (CY 1982)	12.6.1956		41	1981–1990	203	26*	0	6.54	170	6-47	14/1	27.15	27	65
Alexander George	22.4.1851	6.11.1930	2	1880–1884	52	33	0	13.00	2	2-69	0/0	46.50	2	
Alexander Harry Houston	9.6.1905	15.4.1993	1	1932	17	17*	0	17.00	1	1-129	0/0	154.00	0	
Allan Francis Erskine	2.12.1849	9.2.1917	1	1878	5	5	0	5.00	4	2-30	0/0	20.00	0	
Allan Peter John	31.12.1935		1	1965	–	–	–	–	2	2-58	0/0	41.50	0	
Allen Reginald Charles	2.7.1858	2.5.1952	1	1886	44	30	0	22.00	–	–	–/–	–	2	
Andrews Thomas James Edwin	26.8.1890	28.1.1970	16	1921–1926	592	94	0	26.90	1	1-23	0/0	116.00	12	
Angel Jo	22.4.1968		4	1992–1994	35	11	0	5.83	10	3-54	0/0	46.30	1	3
² Archer Kenneth Alan	17.1.1928		5	1950–1951	234	48	0	26.00	–	–	–/–	–	0	
² Archer Ronald Graham	25.10.1933	27.5.2007	19	1952–1956	713	128	1	24.58	48	5-53	1/0	27.45	20	
Armstrong Warwick Windridge (CY 1903)	22.5.1879	13.7.1947	50	1901–1921	2,863	159*	6	38.68	87	6-35	3/0	33.59	44	
Badcock Clayvel Lindsay ("Jack")	10.4.1914	13.12.1982	7	1936–1938	160	118	1	14.54	–	–	–/–	–	3	
Bailey George John	7.9.1982		5	2013	183	53	0	26.14	–	–	–/–	–	10	90/29‡
Bancroft Cameron Timothy	19.11.1992		10	2017–2019	446	82*	0	26.23	–	–	–/–	–	16	0/1
² Bannerman Alexander Chalmers	21.3.1854	19.9.1924	28	1878–1893	1,108	94	0	23.08	4	3-111	0/0	40.75	21	
² Bannerman Charles	23.7.1851	20.8.1930	3	1876–1878	239	165*	1	59.75	–	–	–/–	–	0	
Bardsley Warren (CY 1910)	6.12.1882	20.1.1954	41	1909–1926	2,469	193*	6	40.47	–	–	–/–	–	12	
Barnes Sidney George	5.6.1916	16.12.1973	13	1938–1948	1,072	234	3	63.05	4	2-25	0/0	54.50	14	
Barnett Benjamin Arthur	23.3.1908	29.6.1979	4	1938	195	57	0	27.85	–	–	–/–	–	3/2	
Barrett John Edward	15.10.1866	6.2.1916	2	1890	80	67*	0	26.66	–	–	–/–	–	1	
Beard Graeme Robert	19.8.1950		3	1979	114	49	0	22.80	1	1-26	0/0	109.00	0	
Beer Michael Anthony	9.6.1984		2	2010–2011	6	2*	0	3.00	3	2-56	0/0	59.33	1	2
² Benaud John	11.5.1944		3	1972	223	142	1	44.60	–	–	–/–	–	0	
² Benaud Richard OBE (CY 1962)	6.10.1930	10.4.2015	63	1951–1963	2,201	122	3	24.45	248	7-72	16/1	27.03	65	
Bennett Murray John	6.10.1956		3	1984–1985	71	23	0	23.66	6	3-79	0/0	54.16	5	8
Bevan Michael Gwyl	8.5.1970		18	1994–1997	785	91	0	29.07	29	6-82	1/1	24.24	8	232

	Born	Died	Tests	Test Career	Runs	HS	100s	Avge	Wkts	BB	5/10	Avge	Ct/St	O/T
Bichel Andrew John	27.8.1970		19	1996-2003	355	71	0	16.90	58	5-60	1/0	32.24	16	67
Bird Jackson John	11.12.1986		9	2012-2017	43	19*	0	14.33	34	5-59	1/0	30.64	2	
Blackham John McCarthy (CY 1891)	11.5.1854	28.12.1932	35	1876-1894	800	74	0	15.68					37/24	
Blackie Donald Dearnes	5.4.1882	18.4.1955	3	1928	24	11*	0	8.00	14	6-94	1/0	31.71	2	
Blewett Gregory Scott	28.10.1971		46	1994-1999	2,552	214	4	34.02	14	2-9	0/0	51.42	45	32
Bollinger Douglas Erwin	24.7.1981		12	2008-2010	54	21	0	7.71	50	5-28	2/0	25.92	2	39/9
Bonnor George John	25.2.1855	27.6.1912	17	1880-1888	512	128	1	17.06	2	1-5	0/0	42.00	16	
Boon David Clarence MBE (CY 1994)	29.12.1960		107	1984-1995	7,422	200	21	43.65	0	0-0	0/0		99	181
Booth Brian Charles MBE	19.10.1933		29	1961-1965	1,773	169	5	42.21	3	2-33	0/0	48.66	17	
Border Allan Robert (CY 1982)	27.7.1955		156	1978-1993	11,174	205	27	50.56	39	7-46	2/1	39.10	156	273
Boyle Henry Frederick	10.12.1847	21.11.1907	12	1878-1884	153	36*	0	12.75	32	6-42	1/0	20.03	10	
Bracken Nathan Wade	12.9.1977		5	2003-2005	70	37	0	17.50	12	4-48	0/0	42.08	2	116/19
Bradman Sir Donald George AC (CY 1931)	27.8.1908	25.2.2001	52	1928-1948	6,996	334	29	99.94	2	1-8	0/0	36.00	32	
Bright Raymond James	13.7.1954		25	1977-1986	445	33	0	14.35	53	7-87	4/1	41.13	13	11
Bromley Ernest Harvey	2.9.1912	1.2.1967	2	1932-1934	38	26	0	9.50	0	0-19	0/0		2	
Brown William Alfred (CY 1939)	31.7.1912	16.3.2008	22	1934-1948	1,592	206*	4	46.82			—/—		14	
Bruce William	22.5.1864	3.8.1925	14	1884-1894	702	80	0	29.25	12	3-88	0/0	36.66	12	
Burge Peter John Parnell (CY 1965)	17.5.1932	5.10.2001	42	1954-1965	2,290	181	4	38.16			—/—		23	
Burke James Wallace (CY 1957)	12.6.1930	2.2.1979	24	1950-1958	1,280	189	3	34.59	8	4-37	0/0	28.75	18	
Burn Edwin James Kenneth (K. E.)	17.9.1862	20.7.1956	2	1890	41	19	0	10.25			—/—		1	
Burns Joseph Antony	6.9.1989		21	2014-2019	1,379	180	4	38.30			—/—		23	6
Burton Frederick John	2.11.1865	25.8.1929	2	1886-1887	4	2*	0	2.00			—/—		1/1	
Callaway Sydney Thomas	6.2.1868	25.11.1923	3	1891-1894	87	41	0	17.40	6	5-37	1/0	23.66	1	
Callen Ian Wayne	2.5.1955		1	1977	26	22*	0		6	3-83	0/0	31.83	1	5
Campbell Gregory Dale	10.3.1964		4	1989-1989	16	6*	0	2.50	13	3-79	0/0	38.69	1	12
Carkeek William ("Barlow")	17.10.1878	20.2.1937	6	1912	16	6*	0	5.33			—/—		6	
Carlson Phillip Henry	8.8.1951		2	1978	23	21	0	5.75	2	2-41	0/0	49.50	2	4
Carter Hanson	15.3.1878	8.6.1948	28	1907-1921	873	72	0	22.97			—/—		44/21	
Cartwright Hilton William Raymond	14.2.1992		2	2016-2017	55	37	0	27.50	0	0-15	0/0		0	2
Casson Beau	7.12.1982		1	2007	10	10	0	10.00	3	3-86	0/0	43.00	2	
[2,4] Chappell Gregory Stephen MBE (CY 1973)	7.8.1948		87	1970-1983	7,110	247*	24	53.86	47	5-61	1/0	40.70	122	74
[2,4] Chappell Ian Michael (CY 1976)	26.9.1943		75	1964-1979	5,345	196	14	42.42	20	2-21	0/0	65.80	105	16
[2,4] Chappell Trevor Martin	21.10.1952		3	1981	79	27	0	15.80			—/—		2	20
Charlton Percie Chater	9.4.1867	30.9.1954	2	1890	29	11	0	7.25	3	3-18	0/0	8.00	0	
Chipperfield Arthur Gordon	17.11.1905	29.7.1987	14	1934-1938	552	109	1	32.47	5	3-91	0/0	87.40	15	
Clark Stuart Rupert	28.9.1975		24	2005-2009	248	39	0	13.05	94	5-32	2/0	23.86	4	39/9

	Born	Died	Tests	Test Career	Runs	HS	100s	Avge	Wkts	BB	5/10	Avge	Ct/St	O/T
Clark Wayne Maxwell	19.9.1953		10	1977–1978	98	33	0	5.76	44	4-46	0/0	28.75	6	2
Clarke Michael John (CY 2010)	2.4.1981		115§	2004–2015	8,643	329*	28	49.10	31	6-9	2/0	38.19	134	245/34
Colley David John	15.3.1947		3	1972	84	54	0	21.00	6	3-83	0/0	52.00	1	1
Collins Herbert Leslie	21.11.1888	28.5.1959	19	1920–1926	1,352	203	4	45.06	4	2-47	0/0	63.00	13	
Coningham Arthur	14.7.1863	13.6.1939	1	1894	13	10	0	6.50	2	2-17	0/0	38.00	0	
Connolly Alan Norman	29.6.1939		29	1963–1970	260	37	0	10.40	102	6-47	4/0	29.22	17	1
Cook Simon Hewitt	29.1.1972		2	1997	–	3*	0	–	7	5-39	1/0	20.28	0	
Cooper Bransby Beauchamp	15.3.1844	7.8.1914	1	1876	18	15	0	9.00	–		–/–	–	2	
§Cooper William Henry	11.9.1849	5.4.1939	2	1881–1884	13	7	0	6.50	9	6-120	1/0	25.11	1	
Copeland Trent Aaron	14.3.1986		3	2011	39	23*	0	13.00	6	2-24	0/0	37.83	2	
Corling Grahame Edward	13.7.1941		5	1964	5	3	0	1.66	12	4-60	0/0	37.25	1	
Cosier Gary John	25.4.1953		18	1975–1978	897	168	2	28.93	5	2-26	0/0	68.20	14	9
Cottam John Thomas	5.9.1867	30.1.1897	1	1886	4	3	0	2.00	–		–/–	–	1	
Cotter Albert ("Tibby")	3.12.1883	31.10.1917	21	1903–1911	457	45	0	13.05	89	7-148	7/0	28.64	8	
Coulthard George	1.8.1856	22.10.1883	1	1881	6	6*	0	–	–		–/–	–	0	
Cowan Edward James McKenzie	16.6.1982		18	2011–2013	1,001	136	1	31.28	–		–/–	–	24	
Cowper Robert Maskew	5.10.1940		27	1964–1968	2,061	307	5	46.84	36	4-48	1/0	31.63	21	
Craig Ian David	12.6.1935	16.11.2014	11	1952–1957	358	53	0	19.88	–		–/–	–	2	
Crawford William Patrick Anthony	3.8.1933	21.1.2009	4	1956–1956	53	34	0	17.66	7	3-28	0/0	15.28	1	
Cullen Daniel James	10.4.1984		1	2005	–	–	–	–	1	1-25	0/0	54.00	0	5
Cummins Patrick James (CY 2020)	8.5.1993		30	2011–2019	647	63	0	17.02	143	6-23	5/1	21.82	13	58/25
Dale Adam Craig	30.12.1968		2	1997–1998	6	5	0	2.00	6	3-71	0/0	31.16	0	30
Darling Joseph (CY 1900)	21.11.1870	2.1.1946	34	1894–1905	1,657	178	3	28.56	–		–/–	–	27	
Darling Leonard Stuart	14.8.1909	24.6.1992	12	1932–1936	474	85	0	27.88	0	0-3	0/0	–	8	
Davidson Warrick Maxwell	1.5.1957		14	1977–1979	697	91	0	26.80	–		–/–	–	5	18
Davidson Alan Keith MBE (CY 1962)	14.6.1929		44	1953–1962	1,328	80	0	24.59	186	7-93	14/2	20.53	42	
Davis Ian Charles	25.6.1953		15	1973–1977	692	105	1	26.61	–		–/–	–	9	3
Davis Simon Peter	8.11.1959		1	1985	0	0	0	0.00	0	0-70	0/0	–	0	39
De Courcy James Harry	18.4.1927	20.6.2000	3	1953	81	41	0	16.20	–		–/–	–	3	
Dell Anthony Ross	6.8.1947		2	1970–1973	6	3*	0	–	6	3-65	0/0	26.66	0	
Dodemaide Anthony Ian Christopher	5.10.1963		10	1987–1992	202	50	0	22.44	34	6-58	1/0	28.02	6	24
Doherty Xavier John	22.12.1982		4	2010–2012	51	18*	0	12.75	7	3-131	0/0	78.28	2	60/11
Donnan Henry	12.11.1864	13.8.1956	5	1891–1896	75	15	0	8.33	0	0-22	0/0	–	4	
Dooland Alexander James	29.11.1985		4	2013–2014	191	89	0	23.87	–		–/–	–	2	
Dooland Bruce (CY 1955)	1.11.1923	8.9.1980	3	1946–1947	76	29	0	19.00	9	4-69	0/0	46.55	3	

§ Clarke's figures include 44 runs and one catch for Australia v the ICC World XI in the Super Series Test in 2005-06.

Name	Born	Died	Tests	Test Career	Runs	HS	100s	Avge	Wkts	BB	5/10	Avge	Ct/St	O/T
Duff Reginald Alexander	17.8.1878	13.12.1911	22	1901–1905	1,317	146	2	35.59	4	2-43	0/0	21.25	14	–
Duncan John Ross Frederick	25.3.1944		1	1970	3	3	0	3.00	0	0-30	0/0	–	0	–
Dyer Gregory Charles	16.3.1959		6	1986–1987	131	60	0	21.83					22/2	23
Dymock Geoffrey	21.7.1945		21	1973–1979	236	31*	0	9.44	78	7-67	5/1	27.12	1	15
Dyson John	11.6.1954		30	1977–1984	1,359	127*	2	26.64					10	29
Eady Charles John	29.10.1870	20.12.1945	2	1896–1901	20	10*	0	6.66	7	3-30	0/0	16.00	2	
Eastwood Kenneth Humphrey	23.11.1935		1	1970	5	5	0	2.50	1	1-21	0/0	21.00	1	
Ebeling Hans Irvine	1.1.1905	12.1.1980	1	1934	43	41	0	21.50	3	3-74	0/0	29.66	0	
Edwards John Dunlop	12.6.1860	31.7.1911	3	1888	48	26	0	9.60					1	
Edwards Ross	1.12.1942		20	1972–1975	1,171	170*	2	40.37	0	0-20	–/–	–	7	9
Edwards Walter John	23.12.1949		3	1974	68	30	0	11.33					1	
Elliott Matthew Thomas Gray (CY 1998)	28.9.1971		21	1996–2004	1,172	199	3	33.48					14	1
Emery Philip Allen	25.6.1964		1	1994	8	8*	0	–					5/1	–
Emery Sidney Hand	15.10.1885	7.1.1967	4	1912	6	5	0	3.00	5	2-46	0/0	49.80	2	
Evans Edwin	26.3.1849	2.7.1921	6	1881–1886	82	33	0	10.25	7	3-64	0/0	47.42	5	
Fairfax Alan George	16.6.1906	17.5.1955	10	1928–1930	410	65	0	51.25	21	4-31	0/0	30.71	15	
Faulkner James Peter	29.4.1990		–	2013	45	23	0	22.50	6	4-51	0/0	16.33	0	69/24
Favell Leslie Ernest MBE	6.10.1929	14.6.1987	19	1954–1960	757	101	1	27.03					9	
Ferguson Callum James	21.11.1984		–	2016	4	3	0	2.00					–	30/3
Ferris John James (CY 1889)	21.5.1867	17.11.1900	8†	1886–1890	98	20*	0	8.16	48	5-26	4/0	14.25	4	
Finch Aaron James	17.11.1986		–	2018	278	62	0	27.80	0	0-8	–/–	–	7	119/58
Fingleton John Henry Webb OBE	28.4.1908	22.11.1981	18	1931–1938	1,189	136	5	42.46					13	
Fleetwood-Smith Leslie O'Brien ("Chuck")	30.3.1908	16.3.1971	10	1935–1938	54	16*	0	9.00	42	6-110	2/1	37.38	0	
Fleming Damien William	24.4.1970		20	1994–2000	305	71*	0	19.06	75	5-30	2/0	25.89	9	88
Francis Bruce Colin	18.2.1948		3	1972	52	27	0	10.40					–	
Freeman Eric Walter	13.7.1944		11	1967–1969	345	76	0	19.16	34	4-52	0/0	33.17	5	
Freer Frederick Alfred William	4.12.1915	2.11.1998	1	1946	28	28*	0	–	3	2-49	0/0	24.66	0	
Gannon John Bryant ("Sam")	8.2.1947		3	1977	3	3*	0	3.00	11	4-77	0/0	32.81	3	
Garrett Thomas William	26.7.1858	6.8.1943	19	1876–1887	339	51*	0	12.55	36	6-78	2/0	26.94	7	
Gaunt Ronald Arthur	26.2.1934	30.3.2012	3	1957–1963	6	3	0	3.00	7	3-53	0/0	44.28	1	
Gehrs Donald Raeburn Algernon	29.11.1880	25.6.1953	6	1903–1910	221	67	0	20.09	0	0-4	0/0	–	6	
George Peter Robert	16.10.1986		–	2010	2	2	0	1.00	1	2-48	0/0	38.50	0	
² **Giffen George (CY 1894)**	27.3.1859	29.11.1927	31	1881–1896	1,238	161	1	23.35	103	7-117	7/1	27.09	24	
² **Giffen Walter Frank**	20.9.1861	28.6.1949	3	1886–1891	11	3	0	1.83					0	
Gilbert David Robert	29.12.1960		9	1985–1986	57	15	0	7.12	16	3-48	0/0	52.68	2	14
Gilchrist Adam Craig (CY 2002)	14.11.1971		96§	1999–2007	5,570	204*	17	47.60					379/37	286/13

§ *Gilchrist's figures include 95 runs, five catches and two stumpings for Australia v the ICC World XI in the Super Series Test in 2005-06.*

	Born	Died	Tests	Test Career	Runs	HS	100s	Avge	Wkts	BB	5/10	Avge	Ct/St	O/T
Gillespie Jason Neil (CY 2002) ...	19.4.1975		71	1996–2005	1,218	201*	1	18.73	259	7-37	8/0	26.13	27	97/1
Gilmour Gary John ...	26.6.1951	10.6.2014	15	1973–1976	483	101	1	23.00	54	6-85	3/0	26.03	8	5
Gleeson John William ...	14.3.1938	8.10.2016	29	1967–1972	395	45	0	10.39	93	5-61	3/0	36.20	17	
Graham Henry ...	22.11.1870	7.2.1911	6	1893–1896	301	107	2	30.10		0-9	-/-		3	
2 Gregory David William ...	15.4.1845	4.8.1919	3	1876–1878	60	43	0	20.00	0	0-9	0/0		0	
1,2 Gregory Edward James ...	29.5.1839	22.4.1899	1	1876	11	11	0	5.50			-/-		0	
Gregory Jack Morrison (CY 1922) ...	14.8.1895	7.8.1973	24	1920–1928	1,146	119	2	36.96	85	7-69	4/0	31.15	37	
Gregory Ross Gerald ...	28.2.1916	10.6.1942	2	1936	153	80	0	51.00	0	0-14	0/0		1	
1 Gregory Sydney Edward (CY 1897) ...	14.4.1870	31.7.1929	58	1890–1912	2,282	201	4	24.53	0	0-4	0/0		25	
Grimmett Clarence Victor (CY 1931) ...	25.12.1891	2.5.1980	37	1924–1935	557	50	0	13.92	216	7-40	21/7	24.21	17	1
Groube Thomas Underwood ...	2.9.1857	5.8.1927	1	1880	11	11	0	5.50			-/-		0	
Grout Arthur Theodore Wallace ...	30.3.1927	9.11.1968	51	1957–1965	890	74	0	15.08			-/-		163/24	
Guest Colin Ernest John ...	7.10.1937	8.12.2018	1	1962	11	11	0	11.00	0	0-8	0/0		0	
Haddin Bradley James ...	23.10.1977		66	2007–2015	3,265	169	4	32.97			-/-		262/8	126/34
Hamence Ronald Arthur ...	25.11.1915	24.3.2010	3	1946–1947	81	30*	0	27.00			-/-		1	
Hammond Jeffrey Roy ...	19.4.1950		5	1972	28	19	0	9.33	15	4-38	0/0	32.53	2	1
Handscomb Peter Stephen Patrick ...	26.4.1991		16	2016–2018	934	110	2	38.91			-/-		28	22/2
Harris Marcus Sinclair ...	21.7.1992		9	2018–2019	385	79	0	24.06			-/-		7	
Harris Ryan James (CY 2014) ...	11.10.1979		27	2009–2014	603	74	0	21.53	113	7-117	5/0	23.52	13	21/3
Harry John ...	1.8.1857	27.10.1919	1	1894	8	6	0	4.00			-/-		1	
Hartigan Roger Joseph ...	12.12.1879	7.6.1958	2	1907	170	116	1	42.50	0	0-7	0/0		1	
Hartkopf Albert Ernst Victor ...	28.12.1889	20.5.1968	1	1924	80	80	0	40.00	1	1-120	0/0	134.00	0	
Harvey Mervyn Roye ...	29.4.1918	18.3.1995	1	1946	43	31	0	21.50			-/-		0	
2 Harvey Robert Neil MBE (CY 1954) ...	8.10.1928		79	1947–1962	6,149	205	21	48.41	3	1-8	0/0	40.00	64	
Hassett Arthur Lindsay MBE (CY 1949) ...	28.8.1913	16.6.1993	43	1938–1953	3,073	198*	10	46.56	0	0-1	0/0		30	
Hastings John Wayne ...	4.11.1985		1	2012	52	32	0	26.00	1	1-51	0/0	153.00	1	29/9
Hauritz Nathan Michael ...	18.10.1981		17	2004–2010	426	75	0	25.05	63	5-53	2/0	34.98	3	58/3
Hawke Neil James Napier ...	27.6.1939	25.12.2000	27	1962–1968	365	45*	0	16.59	91	7-105	6/1	29.41	9	
Hayden Matthew Lawrence (CY 2003) ...	29.10.1971		103§	1993–2008	8,625	380	30	50.73	0	0-7	0/0		128	160/9
Hazlewood Josh Reginald ...	8.1.1991		51	2014–2019	402	39	0	12.18	195	6-67	7/0	26.20	18	44/7
Hazlitt Gervys Rignold ...	4.9.1888	30.10.1915	9	1907–1912	89	34*	0	11.12	23	7-25	1/0	27.08	4	
Head Travis Michael ...	29.12.1993		17	2018–2019	1,091	161	2	41.96	0	0-0	0/0		10	42/16
Healy Ian Andrew (CY 1994) ...	30.4.1964		119	1988–1999	4,356	161*	4	27.39			-/-		366/29	168
Hendry Hunter Scott Thomas Laurie ("Stork") ...	24.5.1895	16.12.1988	11	1921–1928	335	112	1	20.93	16	3-36	0/0	40.00	10	
Henriques Moises Constantino ...	1.2.1987		4	2012–2016	164	81*	0	23.42	2	1-48	0/0	82.00	1	11/11

§ *Hayden's figures include 188 runs and three catches, for Australia v the ICC World XI in the Super Series Test in 2005-06.*

	Born	Died	Tests	Test Career	Runs	HS	100s	Avge	Wks	BB	5/10	Avge	Ct/St	O/T
Hibbert Paul Anthony	23.7.1952	27.11.2008	1	1977	15	13	0	7.50	–	–	–/–	–	1	–
Higgs James Donald	11.7.1950		22	1977–1980	111	16	0	5.55	66	7-143	2/0	31.16	3	–
Hilditch Andrew Mark Jefferson	20.5.1956		18	1978–1985	1,073	119	2	31.55	–	–	–/–	–	13	8
Hilfenhaus Benjamin William	15.3.1983		27	2008–2012	355	56*	0	13.65	99	5-75	2/0	28.50	7	25/7
Hill Clement (CY 1900)	18.3.1877	5.9.1945	49	1896–1911	3,412	191	7	39.21	–	–	–/–	–	33	–
Hill John Charles	25.6.1923	11.8.1974	3	1953–1954	21	8*	0	7.00	8	3-35	0/0	34.12	2	–
Hoare Desmond Edward	19.10.1934		1	1960	35	35	0	17.50	2	2-68	0/0	78.00	0	–
Hodge Bradley John	29.12.1974		6	2005–2007	503	203*	1	55.88	0	0-8	0/0	–	9	25/15
Hodges John Robart	11.8.1855	d unknown	2	1876	10	8	0	3.33	6	2-7	0/0	14.00	0	–
Hogan Tom George	23.9.1956		7	1982–1983	205	42*	0	18.63	15	5-66	1/0	47.06	1	16
Hogg George Bradley	6.2.1971		7	1996–2007	186	79	0	26.57	17	2-40	0/0	54.88	7	123/15
Hogg Rodney Malcolm	5.3.1951		38	1978–1984	439	52	0	9.75	123	6-74	6/2	28.47	1	71
Hohns Trevor Victor	23.1.1954		7	1988–1989	136	40	0	22.66	17	3-59	0/0	34.11	3	–
Hole Graeme Blake	6.1.1931	14.2.1990	18	1950–1954	789	66	0	25.45	3	1-9	0/0	42.00	21	–
Holland Jonathan Mark	29.5.1987		6	2016–2018	6	3	0	3.00	9	3-83	0/0	63.77	1	–
Holland Robert George	19.10.1946	17.9.2017	11	1984–1985	35	10	0	3.18	34	6-54	3/2	39.76	5	2
Hookes David William	3.5.1955	19.1.2004	23	1976–1985	1,306	143*	1	34.36	1	1-4	0/0	41.00	12	39
Hopkins Albert John Young	3.5.1874	25.4.1931	20	1901–1909	509	43	0	16.41	26	4-81	0/0	26.76	11	–
Horan Thomas Patrick	8.3.1854	16.4.1916	15	1876–1884	471	124	1	18.84	11	6-40	1/0	13.00	6	–
Hordern Herbert Vivian MBE	10.2.1883	17.6.1938	7	1910–1911	254	50	0	23.09	46	7-90	5/2	23.36	6	–
Hornibrook Percival Mitchell	27.7.1899	25.8.1976	6	1928–1930	60	26	0	10.00	17	7-92	1/0	39.05	7	–
Howell William Peter	29.12.1869	14.7.1940	18	1897–1903	158	35	0	7.52	49	5-81	1/0	28.71	12	–
Hughes Kimberley John (CY 1981)	26.1.1954		70	1977–1984	4,415	213	9	37.41	0	0-0	0/0	–	50	97
Hughes Mervyn Gregory (CY 1994)	23.11.1961		53	1985–1993	1,032	72*	0	16.64	212	8-87	7/1	28.38	23	33
Hughes Phillip Joel	30.11.1988	27.11.2014	26	2008–2013	1,535	160	3	32.65	–	–	–/–	–	15	25/1
Hunt William Alfred	26.8.1908	30.12.1983	1	1931	0	0	0	0.00	0	0-14	0/0	–	0	–
Hurst Alan George	15.7.1950		12	1973–1979	102	26	0	6.00	43	5-28	2/0	27.90	3	8
Hurwood Alexander	17.6.1902	26.9.1982	2	1930	5	5	0	2.50	11	4-22	0/0	15.45	1	–
Hussey Michael Edward Killeen	27.5.1975		79	2005–2012	6,235	195	19	51.52	7	1-0	0/0	43.71	85	185/38
Inverarity Robert John	31.1.1944		6	1968–1972	174	56	0	17.40	4	3-26	0/0	23.25	4	–
Iredale Francis Adams	19.6.1867	15.4.1926	14	1894–1899	807	140	2	36.68	0	0-3	0/0	–	16	–
Ironmonger Herbert	7.4.1882	31.5.1971	14	1928–1932	42	12	0	2.62	74	7-23	4/2	17.97	3	–
Iverson John Brian	27.7.1915	24.10.1973	5	1950	3	1*	0	0.75	21	6-27	1/0	15.23	2	–
Jackson Archibald Alexander	5.9.1909	16.2.1933	8	1928–1930	474	164	1	47.40	–	–	–/–	–	7	–
Jaques Philip Anthony	3.5.1979		11	2005–2007	902	150	3	47.47	–	–	–/–	–	7	6
Jarman Barrington Noel	17.2.1936		19	1959–1968	400	78	0	14.81	–	–	–/–	–	50/4	–

	Born	Died	Tests	Test Career	Runs	HS	100s	Avge	Wkts	BB	5/10	Avge	Ct/St	O/T
Jarvis Arthur Harwood	19.11.1860	15.11.1933	11	1884–1894	303	82	0	16.83	–	–	–/–	–	9/9	1
Jenner Terrence James	8.9.1944	24.5.2011	9	1970–1975	208	74	0	23.11	24	5-90	1/0	31.20	5	5
Jennings Claude Burrows	5.6.1884	20.6.1950	6	1912	107	32	0	17.83	–	–	–/–	–	5	
Johnson Ian William Geddes CBE	8.12.1917	9.10.1998	45	1945–1956	1,000	77	0	18.51	109	7-44	3/0	29.19	30	
Johnson Leonard Joseph	18.3.1919	2.4.1977	1	1947	25	25*	0	12.33	6	3-8	0/0	12.33	2	
Johnson Mitchell Guy	2.11.1981		73	2007–2015	2,065	123*	1	22.20	313	8-61	12/3	28.40	27	153/30
Johnston William Arras (CY 1949)	26.2.1922	25.5.2007	40	1947–1954	273	29	0	11.37	160	6-44	7/0	23.91	16	
Jones Dean Mervyn (CY 1990)	24.3.1961		52	1983–1992	3,631	216	11	46.55	1	1-5	0/0	64.00	34	164
Jones Ernest	30.9.1869	23.11.1943	19	1894–1902	126	20	0	5.04	64	7-88	3/1	29.01	21	
Jones Samuel Percy	1.8.1861	14.7.1951	12	1881–1887	428	87	0	21.40	6	4-47	0/0	18.66	12	
Joslin Leslie Ronald	13.12.1947		1	1967	9	7	0	4.50	–	–	–/–	–	0	
Julian Brendon Paul	10.8.1970		7	1993–1995	128	56*	0	16.00	15	4-36	0/0	39.93	4	25
Kasprowicz Michael Scott	10.2.1972		38	1996–2005	445	25	0	10.59	113	7-36	4/0	32.88	16	43/2
Katich Simon Mathew	21.8.1975		56§	2001–2010	4,188	157	10	45.03	21	6-65	1/0	30.23	39	45/3
Kelleway Charles	25.4.1886	16.11.1944	26	1910–1928	1,422	147	3	37.42	52	5-33	1/0	32.36	24	
Kelly James Joseph (CY 1903)	10.5.1867	14.8.1938	36	1896–1905	664	46*	0	17.02	–	–	–/–	–	43/20	
Kelly Thomas Joseph Dart	3.5.1844	20.7.1893	2	1876–1878	64	35	0	21.33	–	–	–/–	–	1	
Kendall Thomas Kingston	24.8.1851	17.8.1924	2	1876	39	17*	0	13.00	14	7-55	1/0	15.35	2	
Kent Martin Francis	23.11.1953		3	1981	171	54	0	28.50	–	–	–/–	–	6	5
Kerr Robert Byers	16.6.1961		2	1985	31	17	0	7.75	–	–	–/–	–	1	4
Khawaja Usman Tariq	18.12.1986		44	2010–2019	2,887	174	8	40.66	0	0-1	0/0	–	35	40/9
Kippax Alan Falconer	25.5.1897	5.9.1972	22	1924–1934	1,192	146	2	36.12	0	0-2	0/0	–	13	
Kline Lindsay Francis	29.9.1934	2.10.2015	13	1957–1960	58	15*	0	8.28	34	7-75	1/0	22.82	9	
Krejza Jason John	14.1.1983		2	2008	71	32	0	23.66	13	8-215	1/1	43.23	4	8
Labuschagne Marnus (CY 2020)	22.6.1994		14	2018–2019	1,459	215	4	63.43	12	3-45	0/0	38.66	13	
Laird Bruce Malcolm	21.11.1950		21	1979–1982	1,341	92	0	35.28	0	0-3	0/0	–	16	23
Langer Justin Lee (CY 2001)	21.11.1970		105§	1992–2006	7,696	250	23	45.27	0	0-0	0/0	–	73	8
Langley Gilbert Roche Andrews (CY 1957)	14.9.1919	14.5.2001	26	1951–1956	374	53	0	14.96	–	–	–/–	–	83/15	
Laughlin Trevor John	30.1.1951		3	1977–1978	87	35	0	17.40	6	5-101	1/0	43.66	3	6
Laver Frank Jonas	7.12.1869	24.9.1919	15	1899–1909	196	45	0	11.52	37	8-31	2/0	26.05	8	
Law Stuart Grant (CY 1998)	18.10.1968		1	1995	54	54*	0	54.00	0	0-9	0/0	–	1	54
Lawry William Morris (CY 1962)	11.2.1937		67	1961–1970	5,234	210	13	47.15	0	0-0	0/0	–	30	1
Lawson Geoffrey Francis	7.12.1957		46	1980–1989	894	74	0	15.96	180	8-112	11/2	30.56	10	79
Lee Brett (CY 2006)	8.11.1976		76§	1999–2008	1,451	64	0	20.15	310	5-30	10/0	30.81	23	221/25

§ *Katich's figures include two runs and one catch, Langer's 22 runs and one catch, and Lee's four runs, two wickets and one catch for Australia v the ICC World XI in the Super Series Test in 2005-06.*

	Born	Died	Tests	Test Career	Runs	HS	100s	Avge	Wkts	BB	5/10	Avge	Ct/St	O/T
Lee Philip Keith (CY 2001) ..	15.9.1904	9.8.1980	2	1931-1932	57	42	0	19.00	5	4-111	0/0	42.40	11	117
Lehmann Darren Scott (CY 2001)	5.2.1970		27	1997-2004	1,798	177	5	44.95	15	3-42	0/0	27.46	11	63
Lillee Dennis Keith MBE (CY 1973)	18.7.1949		70	1970-1983	905	73*	0	13.71	355	7-83	23/7	23.92	23	
Lindwall Raymond Russell MBE (CY 1949)	3.10.1921	23.6.1996	61	1945-1959	1,502	118	2	21.15	228	7-38	12/0	23.03	26	
Love Hampden Stanley Bray	10.8.1895	22.7.1969	1	1932	8	5	0	4.00	–	–	–/–	–	3	
Love Martin Lloyd	30.3.1974		5	2002-2003	233	100*	1	46.60	–	–	–	–	7	
Loxton Samuel John Everett OBE	29.3.1921	3.12.2011	12	1947-1950	554	101	1	36.93	8	3-55	0/0	43.62	7	
Lyon Nathan Michael	20.11.1987		96	2011-2019	1,031	47	0	12.27	390	8-50	18/3	31.58	48	29/2
Lyons John James	21.5.1863	21.7.1927	14	1886-1897	731	134	1	27.07	6	5-30	1/0	24.83	3	
McAlister Peter Alexander	11.7.1869	10.5.1938	8	1903-1909	252	41	0	16.80	–	–	–/–	–	10	
Macartney Charles George (CY 1922)	27.6.1886	9.9.1958	35	1907-1926	2,131	170	7	41.78	45	7-58	2/1	27.55	17	
McCabe Stanley Joseph (CY 1935)	16.7.1910	25.8.1968	39	1930-1938	2,748	232	6	48.21	36	4-13	0/0	42.86	41	
McCool Colin Leslie	9.12.1916	5.4.1986	14	1945-1949	459	104*	1	35.30	36	5-41	3/0	26.61	14	
McCormick Ernest Leslie	16.5.1906	28.6.1991	12	1935-1938	54	17*	0	6.00	36	4-101	0/0	29.97	8	
McCosker Richard Bede (CY 1976)	11.12.1946		25	1974-1979	1,622	127	4	39.56	–	–	–/–	–	21	14
McDermott Craig John (CY 1986)	14.4.1965		71	1984-1995	940	42*	0	12.20	291	8-97	14/2	28.63	19	138
McDonald Andrew Barry	15.6.1981		4	2008	107	68	0	21.40	9	3-25	0/0	33.33	2	
McDonald Colin Campbell	17.11.1928		47	1951-1961	3,107	170	5	39.32	0	0-3	0/0	–	14	
McDonnell Edgar Arthur (CY 1922)	6.1.1891	22.7.1937	11	1920-1921	116	36	0	16.57	43	5-32	2/0	33.27	3	
McDonnell Percy Stanislaus	13.11.1858	24.9.1896	19	1880-1888	955	147	3	28.93	0	0-11	0/0	–	6	
McGain Bryce Edward	25.3.1972		1	2008	2	2	0	1.00	0	0-149	0/0	–	–	
MacGill Stuart Charles Glyndwr	25.2.1971		44§	1997-2007	349	43	0	9.69	208	8-108	12/2	29.02	16	3
McGrath Glenn Donald (CY 1998)	9.2.1970		124§	1993-2006	641	61	0	7.36	563	8-24	29/3	21.64	38	249±2
McIlwraith John	7.9.1857	5.7.1938	1	1886	9	7	0	4.50	–	–	–	–	1	
McIntyre Peter Edward	27.4.1966		2	1994-1996	22	16	0	7.33	5	3-103	0/0	38.80	0	
McKay Clinton James	22.2.1983		1	2009	10	10	0	10.00	1	1-56	0/0	101.00	1	59/6
Mackay Kenneth Donald MBE	24.10.1925	13.6.1982	37	1956-1962	1,507	89	0	33.48	50	6-42	2/0	34.42	16	
McKenzie Graham Douglas (CY 1965)	24.6.1941		60	1961-1970	945	76	0	12.27	246	8-71	16/3	29.78	34	1
McKibbin Thomas Robert	10.12.1870	15.12.1939	5	1894-1897	88	28*	0	14.66	17	3-35	0/0	29.17	4	
McLaren John William	22.12.1886	17.11.1921	1	1911	0	0*	0	–	1	1-23	0/0	70.00	0	
Maclean John Alexander	27.4.1946		4	1978	79	33*	0	11.28	–	–	–	–	18	2
[2] McLeod Charles Edward	24.10.1869	26.11.1918	17	1894-1905	573	112	1	23.87	33	5-65	2/0	40.15	9	
[2] McLeod Robert William	19.1.1868	14.6.1907	6	1891-1893	146	31	0	13.27	12	5-53	1/0	31.83	3	
McShane Patrick George	18.4.1858	11.12.1903	3	1884-1887	26	12*	0	5.20	1	1-39	0/0	48.00	2	
Maddinson Nicolas James	21.12.1991		3	2016	27	22	0	6.75	0	0-9	0/0	–	2	0/6

§ MacGill's figures include no runs and nine wickets and McGrath's two runs and three wickets for Australia v the ICC World XI in the Super Series Test in 2005-06.

	Born	Died	Tests	Test Career	Runs	HS	100s	Avge	Wkts	BB	Avge	5/10	Ct/St	O/T
Maddocks Leonard Victor	24.5.1926	27.8.2016	7	1954–1956	177	69	0	17.70	–	–	–	–/–	19/1	
Maguire John Norman	15.9.1956		3	1983	28	15*	0	7.00	10	4-57	32.30	0/0		23
Mailey Arthur Alfred	3.1.1886	31.12.1967	21	1920–1926	222	46*	0	11.10	99	9-121	33.91	6/2	14	
Mallett Ashley Alexander	13.7.1945		38	1968–1980	430	43*	0	11.62	132	8-59	29.84	6/1	30	9
Malone Michael Francis	9.10.1950		1	1977	46	46	0	46.00	6	5-63	12.83	0/0		10
Mann Anthony Longford	8.11.1945	15.11.2019	4	1977	189	105	1	21.00	4	3-12	79.00	0/0	3	4
Manou Graham Allan	23.4.1979		1	2009	21	13*	0	21.00	–	–	–	–/–		
Marr Alfred Percy	28.3.1862	15.3.1940	1	1884	5	5	0	2.50	0	0-3	–	0/0	0	
[1] **Marsh Geoffrey Robert**	31.12.1958		50	1985–1991	2,854	138	4	33.18	–	–	–	–/–	38	117
[1,2] **Marsh Mitchell Ross**	20.10.1991		32	2014–2019	1,260	181	2	25.20	42	5-46	38.64	1/0	16	53/11
Marsh Rodney William MBE (CY 1982)	4.11.1947		96	1970–1983	3,633	132	3	26.51	0	0-3	–	0/0	343/12	92
[1,2] **Marsh Shaun Edward**	9.7.1983		38	2011–2018	2,265	182	6	34.31	–	–	–	–/–	23	73/15
Martin John Wesley	28.7.1931	16.7.1992	8	1960–1966	214	55	0	17.83	17	3-56	48.94	0/0	5	
Martyn Damien Richard (CY 2002)	21.10.1971		67	1992–2006	4,406	165	13	46.37	2	1-0	84.00	0/0	36	208/4
Massie Hugh Hamon	11.4.1854	12.10.1938	9	1881–1884	249	55	0	15.56	–	–	–	–/–	5	
Massie Robert Arnold Lockyer (CY 1973)	14.4.1947		6	1972–1972	78	42	0	11.14	31	8-53	20.87	2/1	1	3
Matthews Christopher Darrell	22.9.1962		3	1986–1988	54	32	0	10.80	6	3-95	52.16	0/0	1	
Matthews Gregory Richard John	15.12.1959		33	1983–1992	1,849	130	4	41.08	61	5-103	48.22	2/1	17	59
Matthews Thomas James	3.4.1884	14.10.1943	8	1911–1912	153	53	0	17.00	16	4-29	26.18	0/0	7	
Maxwell Glenn James	14.10.1988		7	2012–2017	339	104	1	26.07	8	4-127	42.62	0/0	7	110/61
May Timothy Brian Alexander	26.1.1962		24	1987–1994	225	42*	0	14.06	75	5-9	34.74	3/0	6	47
Mayne Edgar Richard	2.7.1882	26.10.1961	4	1912–1921	64	25*	0	21.33	0	0-1	–	0/0	3	
Mayne Lawrence Charles	23.1.1942		6	1964–1969	76	13	0	9.50	19	4-43	33.05	0/0	2	
Meckiff Ian	6.1.1935		18	1957–1963	154	45*	0	11.84	45	6-38	31.62	2/0	9	
Mennie Joe Matthew	24.12.1988		1	2016	10	10	0	5.00	1	1-85	85.00	0/0		2
Meuleman Kenneth Douglas	5.9.1923	10.9.2004	1	1945	0	0	0	0.00	–	–	–	–/–		
Midwinter William Evans	19.6.1851	3.12.1890	8†	1876–1886	174	37	0	13.38	14	5-78	23.78	1/0	5	
Miller Colin Reid	6.2.1964		18	1998–2000	174	43	0	8.28	69	5-32	26.15	3/1	6	
Miller Keith Ross MBE (CY 1954)	28.11.1919	11.10.2004	55	1945–1956	2,958	147	7	36.97	170	7-60	22.97	7/1	38	
Minnett Roy Baldwin	13.6.1888	21.10.1955	9	1911–1912	391	90	0	26.06	11	4-34	26.36	0/0	6	
Misson Francis Michael	19.11.1938		5	1960–1961	38	25*	0	19.00	16	4-58	38.50	0/0	6	
Moody Thomas Masson (CY 2000)	2.10.1965		8	1989–1992	456	106	2	32.57	2	1-17	73.50	0/0	9	76
Moroney John	24.7.1917	1.7.1999	7	1949–1951	383	118	2	34.81	–	–	–	–/–	0	
Morris Arthur Robert MBE (CY 1949)	19.1.1922	22.8.2015	46	1946–1954	3,533	206	12	46.48	2	1-5	25.00	0/0	15	
Morris Samuel	22.6.1855	20.9.1931	1	1884	14	10*	0	14.00	2	2-73	36.50	0/0		
Moses Henry	13.2.1858	7.12.1938	6	1886–1894	198	33	0	19.80	–	–	–	–/–		

	Born	Died	Tests	Test Career	Runs	HS	100s	Avge	Wkts	BB	5/10	Avge	Ct/St	O/T
Moss Jeffrey Kenneth	29.6.1947		1	1978	60	38*	0	60.00	–	–	-/-	–	0	1
Moule William Henry	31.1.1858	24.8.1939	1	1880	40	34	0	20.00	3	3-23	0/0	7.66	0	
Muller Scott Andrew	11.7.1971		2	1999	6	6*	0	–	7	3-68	0/0	36.85	1	
Murdoch William Lloyd	18.10.1854	18.2.1911	18†	1876–1890	896	211	2	32.00	–	–	-/-	–	14	
Musgrove Henry Alfred	27.11.1858	2.11.1931	1	1884	13	9	0	6.50	–	–	-/-	–	0	
Nagel Lisle Ernest	6.3.1905	23.11.1971	1	1932	21	21*	0	21.00	2	2-110	0/0	55.00	0	
Nash Laurence John	2.5.1910	24.7.1986	2	1931–1936	30	17	0	15.00	10	4-18	0/0	12.60	6	
Nevill Peter Michael	13.10.1985		17	2015–2016	468	66	0	22.28	–	–	-/-	–	61/2	0/9
Nicholson Matthew James	2.10.1974		1	1998	14	9	0	7.00	4	3-56	0/0	28.75	0	
Nitschke Holmesdale Carl ("Jack")	14.4.1905	29.9.1982	2	1931	53	47	0	26.50	–	–	-/-	–	3	
Noble Montague Alfred (CY 1900)	28.1.1873	22.6.1940	42	1897–1909	1,997	133	1	30.25	121	7-17	9/2	25.00	26	
Noblet Geffery	14.9.1916	16.8.2006	3	1949–1952	22	13*	0	7.33	7	3-21	0/0	26.14	1	
North Marcus James	28.7.1979		21	2008–2010	1,171	128	5	35.48	14	6-55	2/1	42.21	17	2/1
Nothling Otto Ernest	1.8.1900	26.9.1965	1	1928	52	44	0	26.00	0	0-12	0/0	–	0	
O'Brien Leo Patrick Joseph	2.7.1907	13.3.1997	5	1932–1936	211	61	0	26.37	–	–	-/-	–	3	
O'Connor John Denis Alphonsus	9.9.1875	23.8.1941	4	1907–1909	86	20	0	12.28	13	5-40	1/0	26.15	3	
O'Donnell Simon Patrick	26.1.1963		6	1985–1985	206	48	0	29.42	6	3-37	0/0	84.00	4	87
Ogilvie Alan David	3.6.1951		5	1977	178	47	0	17.80	–	–	-/-	–	5	
O'Keefe Stephen Norman John	9.12.1984		9	2014–2017	86	25	0	9.55	35	6-35	2/1	29.40	0	0/7
O'Keeffe Kerry James	25.11.1949		24	1970–1977	644	85	0	25.76	53	5-101	1/0	38.07	15	2
Oldfield William Albert Stanley MBE (CY 1927)	9.9.1894	10.8.1976	54	1920–1936	1,427	65*	0	22.65	–	–	-/-	–	78/52	
O'Neill Norman Clifford Louis (CY 1962)	19.2.1937		42	1958–1964	2,779	181	6	45.55	17	4-41	0/0	39.23	21	
O'Reilly William Joseph OBE (CY 1935)	20.12.1905	6.10.1992	27	1931–1945	410	56*	0	12.81	144	7-54	11/3	22.59	7	
Oxenham Ronald Keven	28.7.1891	16.8.1939	7	1928–1931	151	48	0	15.10	14	4-39	0/0	37.28	4	
Paine Timothy David	8.12.1984		31	2010–2019	1,330	92	0	31.66	–	–	-/-	–	133/7	35/10‡
Palmer George Eugene	22.2.1859	22.8.1910	17	1880–1886	296	48	0	14.09	78	7-65	6/2	21.51	13	
Park Roy Lindsay	30.7.1892	23.1.1947	1	1920	0	0	0	0.00	0	0-9	0/0	–	0	
Pascoe Leonard Stephen	13.2.1950		14	1977–1981	106	30*	0	10.60	64	5-59	1/0	26.06	2	29
Patterson Kurtis Robert	5.4.1993		2	2018	144	114*	1	144.00	–	–	-/-	–	6	
²Pattinson James Lee	3.5.1990		21	2011–2019	417	47*	0	26.06	81	5-27	4/0	26.33	6	15/4
Pellew Clarence Everard ("Nip")	21.9.1893	9.5.1981	10	1920–1921	484	116	2	37.23	0	0-3	0/0	–	4	
Phillips Wayne Bentley	1.3.1958		27	1983–1985	1,485	159	2	32.28	–	–	-/-	–	52	48
Phillips Wayne Norman	7.11.1962		1	1991	22	14	0	11.00	–	–	-/-	–	0	
Philpott Peter Ian	21.11.1934		8	1964–1965	93	22	0	10.33	26	5-90	1/0	38.46	5	

	Born	Died	Tests	Test Career	Runs	HS	100s	Avge	Wkts	BB	5/10	Avge	Ct/St	O/T
Ponsford William Harold MBE (CY 1935)	19.10.1900	6.4.1991	29	1924–1934	2,122	266	7	48.22	–	–	–	–	21	374‡/17
Ponting Ricky Thomas (CY 2006)	19.12.1974		168§	1995–2012	13,378	257	41	51.85	5	1-0	0/0	55.20	196	
Pope Roland James	18.2.1864	27.7.1952	1	1884	3	3	0	1.50	–	–	–	–	1	
Quiney Robert John	20.8.1982		2	2012	9	9	0	3.00	0	0-3	0/0	–	0	
Rackemann Carl Gray	3.6.1960		12	1982–1990	53	15*	0	5.30	39	6-86	3/1	29.15	5	52
Ransford Vernon Seymour (CY 1910)	20.3.1885	19.3.1958	20	1907–1911	1,211	143*	1	37.84	1	1-9	0/0	28.00	10	
Redpath Ian Ritchie MBE	11.5.1941		66	1963–1975	4,737	171	8	43.45	0	0-0	0/0	–	83	5
Reedman John Cole	9.10.1865	25.3.1924	1	1894	21	17	0	10.50	1	1-12	0/0	24.00	1	
Reid Bruce Anthony	14.3.1963		27	1985–1992	93	13	0	4.65	113	7-51	5/2	24.63	5	61
Reiffel Paul Ronald	19.4.1966		35	1991–1997	955	79*	0	26.52	104	6-71	5/0	26.96	15	92
Renneberg David Alexander	23.9.1942		8	1966–1967	22	9	0	3.66	23	5-39	2/0	36.08	2	
Renshaw Matthew Thomas	28.3.1996		11	2016–2017	636	184	2	33.47	0	0-4	0/0	–	8	
Richardson Arthur John	24.7.1888	23.12.1973	9	1924–1926	403	100	1	31.00	12	2-20	0/0	43.41	0	
Richardson Jhye Avon	20.9.1996		2	2018	1	1	0	1.00	6	3-26	0/0	20.50	0	12/9
⁴Richardson Victor York OBE	7.9.1894	30.10.1969	19	1924–1935	706	138	1	23.53	–	–	–	–	24	
Rigg Keith Edward	21.5.1906	28.2.1995	8	1930–1936	401	127	1	33.41	–	–	–	–	5	
Ring Douglas Thomas	14.10.1918	23.6.2003	13	1947–1953	426	67	0	22.42	35	6-72	2/0	37.28	5	
Ritchie Gregory Michael	23.1.1960		30	1982–1986	1,690	146	3	35.20	0	0-10	0/0	–	14	44
Rixon Stephen John	25.2.1954		13	1977–1984	394	54	0	18.76	–	–	–	–	42/5	6
Robertson Gavin Ron	28.5.1966		4	1997–1998	140	57	0	20.00	13	4-72	0/0	39.61	1	13
Robertson William Roderick	6.10.1861	24.6.1938	1	1884	2	2	0	1.00	0	0-24	0/0	–	0	
Robinson Richard Daryl	8.6.1946		3	1977	100	34	0	16.66	–	–	–	–	4	2
Robinson Rayford Harold	26.3.1914	10.8.1965	1	1936	5	3	0	2.50	–	–	–	–	1	
Rogers Christopher John Llewellyn (CY 2014)	31.8.1977		25	2007–2015	2,015	173	5	42.87	–	–	–	–	15	
Rorke Gordon Frederick	27.6.1938		4	1958–1959	9	7	0	4.50	10	3-23	0/0	30.00	1	
Rutherford John Walter	25.9.1929		1	1956	30	30	0	30.00	1	1-11	0/0	15.00	0	
Ryder John	8.8.1889	3.4.1977	20	1920–1928	1,394	201*	3	51.62	17	2-20	0/0	43.70	17	
Saggers Ronald Arthur	15.5.1917	17.3.1987	6	1948–1949	30	14	0	10.00	–	–	–	–	16/8	
Saunders John Victor	21.3.1876	21.12.1927	14	1901–1907	39	11*	0	2.29	79	7-34	6/0	22.73	5	
Sayers Chadd James	31.8.1987		1	2017	0	0	0	0.00	2	2-78	0/0	73.00	0	
Scott Henry James Herbert	26.12.1858	23.9.1910	8	1884–1886	359	102	1	27.61	0	0-9	0/0	–	8	
Sellers Reginald Hugh Durning	20.8.1940		1	1964	0	0	0	0.00	0	0-17	0/0	–	1	
Serjeant Craig Stanton	1.11.1951		12	1977–1977	522	124	1	23.72	–	–	–	–	13	3
⁵Sheahan Andrew Paul	30.9.1946		31	1967–1973	1,594	127	2	33.91	–	–	–	–	17	3
Shepherd Barry Kenneth	23.4.1937	17.9.2001	9	1962–1964	502	96	0	41.83	0	0-3	0/0	–	2	

§ *Ponting's figures include 100 runs and one catch for Australia v the ICC World XI in the Super Series Test in 2005-06.*

	Born	Died	Tests	Test Career	Runs	HS	100s	Avge	Wkts	BB	5/10	Avge	Ct/St	O/T
Siddle Peter Matthew	25.11.1984		67	2008–2019	1,164	51	0	14.73	221	6-54	8/0	30.66	19	20/2
Sievers Morris William	13.4.1912	10.5.1968	3	1936	67	25*	0	13.40	9	5-21	1/0	17.88	4	
Simpson Robert Baddeley (CY 1965)	3.2.1936		62	1957–1977	4,869	311	10	46.81	71	5-57	2/0	42.26	110	2
Sincock David John	1.2.1942		3	1964–1965	80	29	0	26.66	8	3-67	0/0	51.25	2	
Slater Keith Nichol	12.3.1936		1	1958	–	1*	0	–	2	2-40	0/0	50.50	1	
Slater Michael Jonathon	21.2.1970		74	1993–2001	5,312	219	14	42.83	1	1-4	0/0	10.00	33	42
Sleep Peter Raymond	4.5.1957		14	1978–1989	483	90	0	24.15	31	5-72	0/0	45.06	4	
Slight James	20.10.1855	9.12.1930	1	1880	11	11	0	5.50					0	
Smith David Bertram Miller	14.9.1884	29.7.1963	2	1912	30	24*	0	15.00					0	
Smith Steven Barry	18.10.1961		3	1983	41	12	0	8.20					1	
Smith Steven Peter Devereux (CY 2016)	2.6.1989		73	2010–2019	7,227	239	26	62.84	17	3-18	0/0	56.47	117	28
Spofforth Frederick Robert	9.9.1853	4.6.1926	18	1876–1886	217	50	0	9.43	94	7-44	7/4	18.41	11	118/36
Stackpole Keith Raymond MBE (CY 1973)	10.7.1940		43	1965–1973	2,807	207	7	37.42	15	2-33	0/0	66.73	47	6
Starc Mitchell Aaron	13.1.1990		57	2011–2019	1,515	99	0	22.27	244	6-50	13/2	26.97	29	85/28
Stevens Gavin Byron	29.2.1932		4	1959	112	28	0	16.00					3	
Symonds Andrew	9.6.1975		26	2003–2008	1,462	162*	2	40.61	24	3-50	0/0	37.33	22	198/14
Tait Shaun William	22.2.1983		3	2005–2007	20	8	0	6.66	5	3-97	0/0	60.40	–	35/21
Tallon Donald (CY 1949)	17.2.1916	7.9.1984	21	1945–1953	394	92	0	17.13					50/8	
Taylor John Morris	10.10.1895	12.5.1971	20	1920–1926	997	108	1	35.60	1	1-25	0/0	45.00	11	
Taylor Mark Anthony (CY 1990)	27.10.1964		104	1988–1998	7,525	334*	19	43.49	1	1-11	0/0	26.00	157	113
Taylor Peter Laurence	22.8.1956		13	1986–1991	431	87	0	26.93	27	6-78	1/0	39.55	10	83
Thomas Grahame	21.3.1938		8	1964–1965	325	61	0	29.54					3	
Thoms George Ronald	22.3.1927	29.8.2003	1	1951	44	28	0	22.00					0	
Thomson Alan Lloyd ("Froggy")	2.12.1945		4	1970	22	12*	0	22.00	12	3-79	0/0	54.50	0	1
Thomson Jeffrey Robert	16.8.1950		51	1972–1985	679	49	0	12.81	200	6-46	8/0	28.00	20	50
Thomson Nathaniel Frampton Davis	29.5.1839	2.9.1896	2	1876	67	41	0	16.75	1	1-14	0/0	31.00	3	
Thurlow Hugh Motley ("Pud")	10.1.1903	3.12.1975	1	1931	–	–	–	0.00	0	0-33	0/0	–	0	
Toohey Peter Michael	20.4.1954		15	1977–1979	893	122	1	31.89	0	0-4	0/0	–	9	5
Toshack Ernest Raymond Herbert	8.12.1914	11.5.2003	12	1945–1948	73	20*	0	14.60	47	6-29	4/1	21.04	4	
Travers Joseph Patrick Francis	10.1.1871	15.9.1942	1	1901	10	9	0	5.00	1	1-14	0/0	14.00	1	
Tribe George Edward (CY 1955)	4.10.1920	5.4.2009	3	1946	35	25*	0	17.50	2	2-48	0/0	165.00	0	
[2]Trott Albert Edwin (CY 1899)	6.2.1873	30.11.1914	3+	1894	205	85*	0	102.50	9	8-43	1/0	21.33	4	
[2]Trott George Henry Stevens (CY 1894)	5.8.1866	10.11.1917	24	1888–1897	921	143	1	21.92	29	4-71	0/0	35.13	21	
[3]Trumble Hugh (CY 1897)	12.5.1867	14.8.1938	32	1890–1903	851	70	0	19.79	141	8-65	9/3	21.78	45	
[3]Trumble John William	16.9.1863	17.8.1944	7	1884–1886	243	59	0	20.25	10	3-29	0/0	22.20	3	

	Born	Died	Tests	Test Career	Runs	HS	100s	Avge	Wkts	BB	5/10	Avge	Ct/St	O/T
Trumper Victor Thomas (CY 1903)	2.11.1877	28.6.1915	48	1899–1916	3,163	214*	8	39.04	8	3-60	0/0	39.62	31	6
Turner Alan	23.7.1950		14	1975–1976	768	136	1	29.53					15	
Turner Charles Thomas Biass (CY 1889)	16.11.1862	1.1.1944	17	1886–1894	323	29	0	11.53	101	7-43	11/2	16.53	8	
Veivers Thomas Robert	6.4.1937		21	1963–1966	813	88	0	31.26	33	4-68	0/0	41.66	7	
Veletta Michael Robert John	30.10.1963		8	1987–1989	207	39	0	18.81					12	20
Voges Adam Charles	4.10.1979		20	2015–2016	1,485	269*	5	61.87	0	0-3			15	31/7
Wade Matthew Scott	26.12.1987		32	2011–2019	1,440	117	4	31.30			0/0		69/11	94/26
Waite Mervyn George	7.1.1911	16.12.1985	2	1938	11	8	0	3.66	1	1-150	0/0	190.00	1	
Walker Maxwell Henry Norman	12.9.1948	28.9.2016	34	1972–1977	586	78*	0	19.53	138	8-143	6/0	27.47	12	17
Wall Thomas Welbourn ("Tim")	13.5.1904	26.3.1981	18	1928–1934	121	20	0	6.36	56	5-14	3/0	35.89	11	
Walters Francis Henry	9.2.1860	1.6.1922	1	1884	12	7	0	6.00					1	
Walters Kevin Douglas MBE	21.12.1945		74	1965–1980	5,357	250	15	48.26	49	5-66	1/0	29.08	43	28
Ward Frederick Anthony	23.2.1906	25.3.1974	4	1936–1938	36	18	0	6.00	11	6-102	1/0	52.18	1	
Warne Shane Keith (CY 1994)	13.9.1969		145§	1991–2006	3,154	99	0	17.32	708	8-71	37/10	25.41	125	193‡
Warner David Andrew	27.10.1986		84	2011–2019	7,244	335*	24	48.94	4	2-45	0/0	67.25	68	116/76
Watkins John Russell	16.4.1943		1	1972	39	36	0	39.00	0	0-21	0/0		0	
Watson Graeme Donald	8.3.1945		5	1966–1972	97	50	0	10.77	6	2-67	0/0	42.33	1	2
Watson Robert	17.6.1981		59§	2004–2015	3,731	176	4	35.19	75	6-33	3/0	33.68	45	190/58
Watson William James	31.1.1931	29.12.2018	4	1954	106	30	0	17.66					2	
[2] Waugh Mark Edward (CY 1991)	2.6.1965		128	1990–2002	8,029	153*	20	41.81	59	5-40	0/0	41.16	181	244
[3] Waugh Stephen Rodger (CY 1989)	2.6.1965		168	1985–2003	10,927	200	32	51.06	92	5-28	3/0	37.44	112	325
Wellham Dirk Macdonald	13.3.1959		6	1981–1986	257	103	1	23.36					5	17
Wessels Kepler Christoffel (CY 1995)	14.9.1957		24†	1982–1985	1,761	179	4	42.95	0	0-2	0/0		18	54‡
Whatmore Davenell Frederick	16.3.1954		7	1978–1979	293	77	0	22.53					13	1
White Cameron Leon	18.8.1983		4	2008	146	46	0	29.20	5	2-71	0/0	68.40	2	91/47
Whitney Michael Roy	24.2.1959		12	1981–1992	68	13	0	6.18	39	7-27	2/1	33.97	2	38
Whitty William James	15.8.1886	30.1.1974	14	1909–1912	161	39*	0	13.41	65	6-17	3/0	21.12	4	
Wiener Julien Mark	1.5.1955		6	1979	281	93	0	25.54	0	0-19	0/0		4	7
Williams Brad Andrew	20.11.1974		4	2003	23	10*	0	7.66	9	4-53	0/0	45.11	4	25
Wilson John William	20.8.1921	13.10.1985	1	1956	–	–	–	–	1	1-25	0/0	64.00	0	
Wilson Paul	12.1.1972		1	1997		0*	0	–	1	0-50	0/0	–	0	11
Wood Graeme Malcolm	6.11.1956		59	1977–1988	3,374	172	9	31.83					41	83
Woodcock Ashley James	27.2.1947		1	1973	27	27	0	27.00					–	
Woodfull William Maldon OBE (CY 1927)	22.8.1897	11.8.1965	35	1926–1934	2,300	161	7	46.00					7	
Woods Samuel Moses James (CY 1889)	13.4.1867	30.4.1931	3†	1888	32	18	0	5.33	5	2-35	0/0	24.20	1	

§ Warne's figures include 12 runs and six wickets, and Watson's 34 runs and no wicket, for Australia v the ICC World XI in the Super Series Test in 2005-06.

	Born	Died	Tests	Test Career	Runs	HS	100s	Avge	Wkts	BB	5/10	Avge	Ct/St	O/T
Woolley Roger Douglas	16.9.1954		2	1982–1983	21	13	0	10.50	–	–	–/–	–	7	4
Worrall John	20.6.1860	17.11.1937	11	1884–1899	478	76	0	25.15	1	1-97	0/0	127.00	13	
Wright Kevin John	27.12.1953		10	1978–1979	219	55*	0	16.84	–	–	–/–	–	31/4	5
Yallop Graham Neil	7.10.1952		39	1975–1984	2,756	268	8	41.13	1	1-21	0/0	116.00	23	30
Yardley Bruce	5.9.1947	27.3.2019	33	1977–1982	978	74	0	19.56	126	7-98	6/1	31.63	31	7
Young Shaun	13.6.1970		1	1997	4	4*	0	4.00	0	0-5		–	0	
Zoehrer Timothy Joseph	25.9.1961		10	1985–1986	246	52*	0	20.50			–/–	–	18/1	22

SOUTH AFRICA (345 players)

	Born	Died	Tests	Test Career	Runs	HS	100s	Avge	Wkts	BB	5/10	Avge	Ct/St	O/T
Abbott Kyle John	18.6.1987		11	2012–2016	95	17	0	6.78	39	7-29	3/0	22.71	4	28/21
Ackerman Hylton Deon	14.2.1973		4	1997	161	57	0	20.12	–		–/–	–	1	
Adams Paul Regan	20.1.1977		45	1995–2003	360	35	0	9.00	134	7-128	4/1	32.87	29	24
Adcock Neil Amwin Treharne (CY 1961)	8.3.1931	6.1.2013	26	1953–1961	146	24	0	5.40	104	6-43	5/0	21.10	4	
Amla Hashim Mahomed (CY 2013)	31.3.1983		124	2004–2018	9,282	311*	28	46.64	0	0-4		–	108	181/41‡
Anderson James Henry	26.4.1874	11.3.1926	1	1902	43	32	0	21.50					0	
Ashley William Hare	10.2.1862	14.7.1930	1	1888	1	1	0	0.50	7	7-95	1/0	13.57	0	
Bacher Adam Marc	29.10.1973		19	1996–1999	833	96	0	26.03	0	0-4		–	11	13
Bacher Aron ('Ali')	24.5.1942		12	1965–1969	679	73	0	32.33					10	
Balaskas Xenophon Constantine	15.10.1910	12.5.1994	9	1930–1938	174	122*	1	14.50	22	5-49	1/0	36.63	5	
Barlow Edgar John	12.8.1940	30.12.2005	30	1961–1969	2,516	201	6	45.74	40	5-85	1/0	34.05	35	
Baumgartner Harold Vane	17.11.1883	8.4.1938	1	1913	29	16	0	9.50	2	2-99		49.50	1	
Bavuma Temba	17.5.1990		40	2014–2019	1,845	102*	1	30.75	1	1-29	0/0	61.00	17	2/2
Beaumont Rolland	4.2.1884	25.5.1958	5	1912–1913	70	31	0	7.77	0	0-0	0/0	–	2	
Begbie Denis Warburton	12.12.1914	10.3.2009	5	1948–1949	138	48	0	19.71	1	1-38	0/0	130.00	2	
Bell Alexander John	15.4.1906	1.8.1985	16	1929–1935	69	26*	0	6.27	48	6-99	4/0	32.64	6	
Bisset Sir Murray	14.4.1876	24.10.1931	3	1898–1909	103	35	0	25.75	–		–/–	–	2/1	
Bisset George Finlay	5.11.1905	14.11.1965	4	1927	38	23	0	19.00	25	7-29	2/0	18.76	0	
Blanckenberg James Manuel	31.12.1892	d unknown	18	1913–1924	455	59	0	19.78	60	6-76	4/0	30.28	9	
Bland Kenneth Colin (CY 1966)	5.4.1938	14.4.2018	21	1961–1966	1,669	144*	3	49.08	2	2-16	0/0	62.50	10	
Bock Ernest George	17.9.1908	5.9.1961	1	1935	11	9*	0	–	0	0-42		–	0	
Boje Nico	20.3.1973		43	1999–2006	1,312	85	0	25.23	100	5-62	3/0	42.65	18	113‡/1
Bond Gerald Edward	5.4.1909	27.8.1965	1	1938	0	0	0	0.00	0	0-16	0/0	–	0	
Bosch Tertius	14.3.1966	14.2.2000	1	1991	5	5*	0	–	3	2-61	0/0	34.66	0	2

	Born	Died	Tests	Test Career	Runs	HS	100s	Avge	Wkts	BB	5/10	Avge	Ct/St	O/T
Botha Johan	2.5.1982	–	5	2005–2010	83	25	0	20.75	17	4-56	0/0	33.70	3	76‡/40
Botten James Thomas ("Jackie")	21.6.1938	14.5.2006	3	1965	65	33	0	10.83	8	2-56	0/0	42.12	1	
Boucher Mark Verdon (CY 2009)	3.12.1976		146‡	1997–2011	5,498	125	5	30.54	1	1-6	0/0	6.00	530/23	290‡/25
Brann William Henry	4.4.1899	22.9.1953	3	1922	71	50	0	14.20	–	–	–/–	–	2	
Briscoe Arthur Wellesley ("Dooley")	6.2.1911	22.4.1941	2	1935–1938	33	16	0	11.00	–	–	–/–	–	1	
Bromfield Harry Dudley	26.6.1932		9	1961–1965	59	21	0	11.80	17	5-88	1/0	35.23	13	
Brown Lennox Sidney	24.11.1910	1.9.1983	2	1931	17	8	0	5.66	3	1-30	0/0	63.00	1	
Burger Christopher George de Villiers	12.7.1935	5.6.2014	2	1957	62	37*	0	20.66	–	–	–/–	–	0	
Burke Sydney Frank	11.3.1934	3.4.2017	2	1961–1964	42	20	0	14.00	11	6-128	2/1	23.36	0	
Buys Isaac Daniel	4.2.1895	d unknown	1	1922	4	4*	0	4.00	0	0-20	0/0	–	0	
Cameron Horace Brakenridge ("Jock") (CY 1936)	5.7.1905	2.11.1935	26	1927–1935	1,239	90	0	30.21	–	–	–/–	–	39/12	
Campbell Thomas	9.2.1882	5.10.1924	5	1909–1912	90	48	0	15.00	–	–	–/–	–	7/1	
Carlstein Peter Rudolph	28.10.1938		8	1957–1963	190	42	0	14.61	–	–	–/–	–	3	
Carter Claude Pagdett	23.4.1881	8.11.1952	10	1912–1924	181	45	0	18.10	28	6-50	2/0	24.78	2	
Catterall Robert Hector (CY 1925)	10.7.1900	3.1.1961	24	1922–1930	1,555	120	3	37.92	7	3-15	0/0	23.14	12	
Chapman Horace William	30.6.1890	1.12.1941	2	1913–1921	39	17	0	13.00	1	1-51	0/0	104.00	1	
Cheetham John Erskine	26.5.1920	21.8.1980	24	1948–1955	883	89	0	23.86	0	0-2	0/0	–	13	
Chevalier Grahame Anton	9.3.1937	14.11.2017	1	1969	0	0*	0	0.00	5	3-68	0/0	20.00	1	
Christy James Alexander Joseph	12.12.1904	1.2.1971	10	1929–1931	618	103	1	34.33	2	1-15	0/0	46.00	3	
Chubb Geoffrey Walter Ashton	12.4.1911	28.8.1982	5	1951	63	15*	0	10.50	21	6-51	2/0	27.47	0	
Cochran John Alexander Kennedy	15.7.1909	15.6.1987	1	1930	4	4	0	4.00	0	0-47	0/0	–	0	
Coen Stanley Keppel ("Shunter")	14.10.1902	29.1.1967	2	1927	101	41*	0	50.50	0	0-7	0/0	–	1	
Commaille John McIlwaine Moore ("Mick")	21.2.1883	28.7.1956	12	1909–1927	355	47	0	16.90	–	–	–/–	–	1	
Commins John Brian	19.2.1965		3	1994	125	45	0	25.00	–	–	–/–	–	2	
Conyngham Dalton Parry	10.5.1897	7.7.1979	1	1922	6	3*	0	–	2	1-40	0/0	51.50	1	
Cook Frederick James	1870	30.11.1915	1	1895	7	7	0	3.50	–	–	–/–	–	1	
Cook Stephen Craig	29.11.1982		11	2015–2016	632	117	3	33.26	0	0-16	0/0	–	6	
Cook Stephen James (CY 1990)	31.7.1953		3	1992–1993	107	43	0	17.83	–	–	–/–	–	6	4
Cooper Alfred Henry Cecil	2.9.1893	18.7.1963	1	1913	6	6	0	3.00	–	–	–/–	–	1	
Cox Joseph Lovell	28.6.1886	4.7.1971	3	1913	17	12*	0	3.40	4	2-74	0/0	61.25	1	
Cripps Godfrey	19.10.1865	27.7.1943	1	1891	21	18	0	10.50	0	0-23	0/0	–	0	
Crisp Robert James	28.5.1911	2.3.1994	9	1935–1935	123	35	0	10.25	20	5-99	1/0	37.35	3	
Cronje Wessel Johannes ("Hansie")	25.9.1969	1.6.2002	68	1991–1999	3,714	135	6	36.41	43	3-14	0/0	29.95	33	188
Cullinan Daryll John	4.3.1967		70	1992–2000	4,554	275*	14	44.21	2	1-10	0/0	35.50	67	138

§ *Boucher's figures exclude 17 runs and two catches for the ICC World XI v Australia in the Super Series Test in 2005-06.*

	Born	Died	Tests	Test Career	Runs	HS	100s	Avge	Wkts	BB	5/10	Avge	Ct/St	O/T
Curnow Sydney Harry	16.12.1907	28.7.1986	7	1930–1931	168	47	0	12.00			–/–	–	5	
Dalton Eric Londesbrough	2.12.1906	3.6.1981	15	1929–1938	698	117	2	31.72	12	4-59	0/0	40.83	5	
Davies Eric Quail	26.8.1909	11.11.1976	5	1935–1938	9	3	0	1.80	7	4-75	0/0	68.71	0	
Dawson Alan Charles	27.11.1969		2	2003	10	10	0	10.00	5	2-20	0/0	23.40	0	19
Dawson Oswald Charles	1.9.1919	22.12.2008	9	1947–1948	293	55	0	20.92	10	2-57	0/0	57.80	10	
Deane Hubert Gouvaine ("Nummy")	21.7.1895	21.10.1939	17	1924–1930	628	93	0	25.12			–/–	–	8	
de Bruyn Theunis Booysen	8.10.1992		12	2016–2019	428	101	1	19.45	0	0-6	0/0	–	11	0/2
de Bruyn Zander	5.7.1975		3	2004	155	83	0	38.75	3	2-32	0/0	30.66	6	
de Kock Quinton	17.12.1992		47	2013–2019	2,934	129*	5	39.12			–/–	–	191/11	115/38
de Lange Marchant	13.10.1990		2	2011	9	9	0	4.50	9	7-81	1/0	30.77	1	4/6
de Villiers Abraham Benjamin	17.2.1984		114	2004–2017	8,765	278*	22	50.66	2	2-49	0/0	52.00	222/5	223‡/78
de Villiers Petrus Stephanus ("Fanie")	13.10.1964		18	1993–1997	359	67*	0	18.89	85	6-23	5/2	24.27	11	83
de Wet Friedel	26.6.1980		2	2009	20	20	0	10.00	6	4-55	0/0	31.00	1	
Dippenaar Hendrik Human ("Boeta")	14.6.1977		38	1999–2006	1,718	177*	3	30.14	0	0-1	0/0	–	27	101‡/1
Dixon Cecil Donovan	12.2.1891	9.9.1969	1	1913	0	0	0	0.00	3	2-62	0/0	39.33	1	
Donald Allan Anthony (CY 1992)	20.10.1966		72	1991–2001	652	37	0	10.68	330	8-71	20/3	22.25	18	164
Dower Robert Reid	4.6.1876	15.9.1964	1	1898	9	9	0	4.50			–/–	–	2	
Draper Ronald George	24.12.1926		2	1949	25	15	0	8.33			–/–	–	1	
Duckworth Christopher Anthony Russell	22.3.1933	16.5.2014	2	1956	28	13	0	7.00			–/–	–	3	
Dumbrill Richard	19.11.1938		5	1965–1966	153	36	0	15.30	9	4-30	0/0	37.33	3	
Duminy Jacobus Petrus	16.12.1897	31.1.1980	3	1927–1929	30	12	0	5.00	1	1-17	0/0	39.00	2	
Duminy Jean-Paul	14.4.1984		46	2008–2011	2,103	166	6	32.85	42	4-47	0/0	38.11	38	199/81
Dunell Owen Robert	15.7.1856	21.10.1929	1	1888	42	26*	0	14.00	0	0-1	0/0	–	1	
du Plessis Francois	13.7.1984		65	2012–2019	3,901	137	9	39.80			–/–	–	59	143/41‡
du Preez John Harcourt	14.11.1942		2	1966	0	0	0	0.00	3	2-22	0/0	17.00	2	
du Toit Jacobus Francois	2.4.1869	10.7.1909	1	1891	2	2*	0	–	1	1-47	0/0	47.00	1	
Dyer Dennis Victor	2.5.1914	16.6.1990	3	1947	96	62	0	16.00			–/–	–	0	
Eksteen Clive Edward	2.12.1966		7	1993–1999	91	22	0	10.11	8	3-12	0/0	61.75	5	6
Elgar Dean	11.6.1987		63	2012–2019	3,888	199	12	38.49	18	4-22	0/0	43.93	67	8
Elgie Michael Kelsey ("Kim")	6.3.1933		3	1961	75	56	0	12.50	0	0-18	0/0	–	4	
Elworthy Steven MBE	23.2.1965		4	1998–2002	72	48	0	18.00	13	4-66	0/0	34.15	1	39
Endean William Russell	31.5.1924	28.6.2003	28	1951–1957	1,630	162*	3	33.95			–/–	–	41	
Farrer William Stephen ("Buster")	8.12.1936		6	1961–1963	221	40	0	27.62			–/–	–	1	
Faulkner George Aubrey	17.12.1881	10.9.1930	25	1905–1924	1,754	204	4	40.79	82	7-84	4/0	26.58	20	
Fellows-Smith Jonathan Payn	3.2.1932	28.9.2013	4	1960	166	35	0	27.66	6	0-13	0/0	–	2	
Fichardt Charles Gustav	20.3.1870	30.5.1923	2	1891–1895	15	10	0	3.75			–/–	–	2	

	Born	Died	Tests	Test Career	Runs	HS	100s	Avge	Wkts	BB	Avge	5/10	Avge	Ct/St	O/T
Finlason Charles Edward	19.2.1860	31.7.1917	1	1888	6	6	0	3.00	0	0-7	–	–/–	–	0	
Floquet Claude Eugene	3.11.1884	22.11.1963	1	1909	12	11*	0	12.00	0	0-24	–	–/–	–	0	
Francis Howard Henry	26.5.1868	7.1.1936	2	1898	39	29	0	9.75	–	–	–	–/–	–	1	
Francois Cyril Matthew	20.6.1897	26.5.1944	5	1922	252	72	0	31.50	6	3-23	37.50	0/0	37.50	5	
Frank Charles Newton	27.1.1891	25.12.1961	3	1921	236	152	1	39.33	–	–	–	–/–	–	0	
Frank William Hughes Bowker	23.11.1872	16.2.1945	1	1895	7	5	0	3.50	1	1-52	52.00	0/0	52.00	0	
Fuller Edward Russell Henry	2.8.1931	19.7.2008	7	1952–1957	64	17	0	8.00	22	5-66	30.36	1/0	30.36	3	
Fullerton George Murray	8.12.1922	19.11.2002	7	1947–1951	325	88	0	25.00	–	–	–	–/–	–	10/2	
Funston Kenneth James	3.12.1925	15.4.2005	18	1952–1957	824	92	0	25.75	–	–	–	–/–	–	7	
Gamsy Dennis	17.2.1940		2	1969	39	30*	0	19.50	–	–	–	–/–	–	5	
Gibbs Herschelle Herman	23.2.1974		90	1996–2007	6,167	228	14	41.95	0	0-4	–	–/–	–	94	248/23
Gleeson Robert Anthony	6.12.1873	27.9.1919	1	1895	4	3	0	4.00	–	–	–	–/–	–	2	
Glover George Keyworth	13.5.1870	15.11.1938	1	1895	21	18*	0	21.00	1	1-28	28.00	0/0	28.00	0	
Goddard Trevor Leslie	1.8.1931	25.11.2016	41	1955–1969	2,516	112	1	34.46	123	6-53	26.22	5/0	26.22	48	
Gordon Norman	6.8.1911	2.9.2014	5	1938	8	7*	0	2.00	20	5-103	40.35	2/0	40.35	1	
Graham Robert	16.9.1877	21.4.1946	2	1898	6	4	0	1.50	3	2-22	42.33	0/0	42.33	2	
Grieveson Ronald Eustace	24.8.1909	24.7.1998	2	1938	114	75	0	57.00	–	–	–	–/–	–	7/3	
Griffin Geoffrey Merton	12.6.1939	16.11.2006	2	1960	25	14	0	6.25	8	4-87	24.00	0/0	24.00	0	
Hall Alfred Ewart	23.1.1896	1.1.1964	7	1922–1930	11	5	0	1.83	40	7-63	22.15	3/1	22.15	4	
Hall Andrew James	31.7.1975		21	2001–2006	760	163	1	26.20	45	3-1	35.93	1/0	35.93	16	88/2
Hall Glen Gordon	24.5.1938	26.6.1987	1	1964	0	0	0	0.00	1	1-94	94.00	0/0	94.00	0	
Halliwell Ernest Austin (CY 1905)	7.9.1864	2.10.1919	8	1891–1902	188	57	0	12.53	–	–	–	–/–	–	10/2	
Halse Clive Gray	28.2.1935	28.5.2002	3	1963	30	19*	0	–	6	3-50	43.33	0/0	43.33	1	
Hamza Mogammad Zubayr	19.6.1995		5	2018–2019	181	62	0	18.10	–	–	–	–/–	–	5	
[2] Hands Philip Albert Myburgh	18.3.1890	27.4.1951	7	1913–1924	300	83	0	25.00	0	0-1	–	–/–	–	3	
[2] Hands Reginald Harry Myburgh	26.7.1888	20.4.1918	1	1913	7	7	0	3.50	–	–	–	–/–	–	0	
Hanley Martin Andrew	10.11.1918	2.6.2000	1	1948	0	0	0	0.00	1	1-57	57.00	0/0	88.00	0	
Harmer Simon Ross (CY 2020)	10.2.1989		5	2014–2015	58	13	0	11.60	20	4-61	29.40	0/0	29.40	16	
Harris Paul Lee	2.11.1978		37	2006–2010	460	46	0	10.69	103	6-127	37.87	3/0	37.87	3	3
Harris Terence Anthony	27.8.1916	7.3.1993	3	1947–1948	100	60	0	25.00	–	–	–	–/–	–	0	
Hartigan Gerald Patrick Desmond	30.12.1884	7.1.1955	5	1912–1913	114	51	0	11.40	1	1-72	141.00	0/0	141.00	0	
Harvey Robert Lyon	14.9.1911	20.7.2000	2	1935	51	28	0	12.75	–	–	–	–/–	–	0	
Hathorn Christopher Maitland Howard	7.4.1878	17.5.1920	12	1902–1910	325	102	0	17.10	–	–	–	–/–	–	5	
Hayward Frank	6.3.1977		1	1999–2004	66	14	0	7.33	54	5-56	29.79	1/0	29.79	0	21
[1,2] Hearne Frank	23.11.1858	14.7.1949	4†	1891–1895	121	30	0	15.12	2	2-40	20.00	1/0	20.00	4	
[1,2] Hearne George Alfred Lawrence	27.3.1888	13.11.1978	3	1922–1924	59	28	0	11.80	–	–	–	–/–	–	3	

	Born	Died	Tests	Test Career	Runs	HS	100s	Avge	Wkts	BB	5/10	Avge	Ct/St	O/T
Heine Peter Samuel	28.6.1928	4.2.2005	14	1955–1961	209	31	0	9.95	58	6-58	4/0	25.08	8	4
Henderson Claude William	14.6.1972		7	2001–2002	65	30	0	9.28	22	4-116	0/0	42.18	2	
Hendricks Beuran Eric	8.6.1990		1	2019	9	5*	0	9.00	6	5-64	1/0	29.16	0	4/11
Henry Omar	23.1.1952		3	1992	53	34	0	17.66	3	2-56	0/0	63.00	2	3
Hime Charles Frederick William	24.10.1869	6.12.1940	1	1895	8	8	0	4.00	1	1-20	0/0	31.00	0	
Hudson Andrew Charles	17.3.1965		35	1991–1997	2,007	163	4	33.45					36	89
Hutchinson Philip	25.1.1862	30.9.1925	2	1888	14	11	0	3.50					—	
Imran Tahir	27.3.1979		20	2011–2015	130	29*	0	9.28	57	5-32	2/0	40.24	8	107/35‡
Ironside David Ernest James	2.5.1925	21.8.2005	3	1953	37	13	0	18.50	15	5-51	1/0	18.33	1	
Irvine Brian Lee	9.3.1944		4	1969	353	102	1	50.42					1	
Jack Steven Douglas	4.8.1970		2	1994	7	7	0	3.50	8	4-69	0/0	24.50	—	2
Johnson Clement Lecky	31.3.1871	31.5.1908	1	1895	10	7	0	5.00	0	0-57	0/0	—	—	
Kallis Jacques Henry (CY 2013)	16.10.1975		165‡	1995–2013	13,206	224	45	55.25	291	6-54	5/0	32.63	196	323‡/25
Keith Headley James	25.10.1927	17.11.1997	8	1952–1956	318	73	0	21.20	0	0-19	0/0	—	9	
Kemp Justin Miles	2.10.1977		5	2000–2005	80	55	0	13.33	9	3-33	0/0	24.66	2	79‡/8
Kempis Gustav Adolph	4.8.1865	19.5.1890	1	1888	2	0*	0	0.00	4	3-53	0/0	19.00	0	
Khan Imraan	27.4.1984		1	2008	20	20	0	20.00					1	
Kirsten Gary (CY 2004)	23.11.1967		101	1993–2003	7,289	275	21	45.27	2	1-0	0/0	71.00	83	185
[2] Kirsten Peter Noel	14.5.1955		12	1991–1994	626	104	1	31.30	2	0-5	0/0	—	8	40
Klaasen Heinrich	30.7.1991		4	2019	11	6	0	5.50					3/1	14/9
Kleinveldt Rory Keith	15.3.1983		4	2012	27	17*	0	9.00	10	3-65	0/0	42.20	2	10/6
Klusener Lance (CY 2000)	4.9.1971		49	1996–2004	1,906	174	4	32.86	80	8-64	1/0	37.91	34	171
Kotze Johannes Jacobus ("Kodgee")	7.8.1879	7.7.1931	3	1902–1907	2	2	0	0.40	6	3-64	0/0	40.50	1	
Kuhn Heino Gunther	1.4.1984		4	2017	113	34	0	14.12					3	0/7
Kuiper Adrian Paul	24.8.1959		1	1991	34	34	0	17.00	—	—			1	25
Kuys Frederick	21.3.1870	12.9.1953	1	1898	26	26	0	13.00	2	2-31	0/0	15.50	0	
Lance Herbert Roy ("Tiger")	6.6.1940	10.11.2010	13	1961–1969	591	70	0	28.14	12	3-30	0/0	39.91	7	
Langeveldt Charl Kenneth	17.12.1974		6	2004–2005	16	10	0	8.00	16	5-46	1/0	37.06	2	72/9
Langton Arthur Chudleigh Beaumont ("Chud")	2.3.1912	27.11.1942	15	1935–1938	298	73*	0	15.68	40	5-58	1/0	45.67	8	
Lawrence Godfrey Bernard	31.3.1932		5	1961	141	43	0	17.62	28	8-53	2/0	18.28	2	
le Roux Frederick Louis	5.2.1882	22.9.1963	1	1913	1	1	0	0.50	0	0-5	0/0	—	0	
Lewis Percy Tyson	2.10.1884	30.11.1976	1	1913	0	0	0	0.00					0	
Liebenberg Gerhardus Frederick Johannes	7.4.1972		5	1997–1998	104	45	0	13.00					0	
Linde George Fredrik	4.12.1991		1	2019	64	37	0	32.00	4	4-133	0/0	33.25	0	4
[1] Lindsay Denis Thomson	4.9.1939	30.11.2005	19	1963–1969	1,130	182	3	37.66					57/2	

§ *Kallis's figures exclude 83 runs, one wicket and four catches for the ICC World XI v Australia in the Super Series Test in 2005-06.*

	Born	Died	Tests	Test Career	Runs	HS	100s	Avge	Wkts	BB	5/10	Avge	Ct/St	O/T
[1]Lindsay John Dixon	8.9.1908	31.8.1990	1	1947	21	9*	0	7.00	–	–	–/–	–	4/1	
Lindsay Nevil Vernon	30.7.1886	2.2.1976	1	1921	35	38	0	17.50	0	0-20	–/–	–	1	
Ling William Victor Stone	3.10.1891	26.9.1960	6	1921–1922	168	38	0	16.80	0	0-6	0/0	–	1	
Llewellyn Charles Bennett (CY 1911)	26.9.1876	7.6.1964	15	1895–1912	544	90	0	20.14	48	6-92	4/1	29.60	7	64/2
Lundie Eric Balfour	15.3.1888	12.9.1917	1	1913	1	1	0	1.00	4	4-101	0/0	26.75	0	
Macaulay Michael John	19.4.1939		1	1964	33	21	0	16.50	2	1-10	0/0	36.50	0	
McCarthy Cuan Neil	24.3.1929	14.8.2000	15	1948–1951	28	5*	0	3.11	36	6-43	2/0	41.94	6	
McGlew Derrick John ("Jackie") (CY 1956)	11.3.1929	9.6.1998	34	1951–1961	2,440	255*	7	42.06	0	0-7	0/0	–	18	
McKenzie Neil Douglas (CY 2009)	24.11.1975		58	2000–2008	3,253	226	5	37.39	0	0-1	0/0	–	54	
McKinnon Atholl Henry	20.8.1932	2.12.1983	8	1960–1966	107	27	0	17.83	26	4-128	0/0	35.57	1	54/12
McLaren Ryan	9.2.1983		2	2009–2011	47	33*	0	23.50	3	2-72	0/0	54.00	0	
McLean Roy Alastair (CY 1961)	9.7.1930	26.8.2007	40	1951–1964	2,120	142	5	30.28	0	0-1	0/0	–	23	
McMillan Brian Mervin	22.12.1963		38	1992–1998	1,968	113	3	39.36	75	4-65	0/0	33.82	49	78
McMillan Quintin	23.6.1904	3.7.1948	13	1929–1931	306	50*	0	18.00	36	5-66	2/0	34.52	8	
Maharaj Keshav Athmanand	7.2.1990		30	2016–2019	643	72	0	15.30	110	9-129	6/1	33.19	8	4
Malan Pieter Jacobus	13.8.1989		3	2019	156	84	0	26.00	0	0-5	0/0	–	3	
Mann Norman Bertram Fleetwood ("Tufty")	28.12.1920	31.7.1952	19	1947–1951	400	52	0	13.33	58	6-59	1/0	33.10	3	
Mansell Percy Neville Frank MBE	16.3.1920	9.5.1995	13	1951–1955	355	90	0	17.75	11	3-58	0/0	66.90	15	
Markham Lawrence Anderson	12.9.1924	5.8.2000	1	1948	20	20	0	20.00	1	1-34	0/0	72.00	–	
Markram Aiden Kyle	4.10.1994		20	2017–2019	1,424	152	4	38.48	0	0-0	0/0	–	15	26/2
Marx Waldemar Frederick Eric	4.7.1895	2.6.1974	3	1921	125	36	0	20.83	4	3-85	0/0	36.00	8	
Matthews Craig Russell	15.2.1965		18	1992–1995	348	62*	0	18.31	52	5-42	2/0	28.88	4	56
Meintjes Douglas James	9.6.1890	17.7.1979	2	1922	43	21	0	14.33	6	3-38	0/0	19.16	3	
Melle Michael George	3.6.1930	28.12.2003	7	1949–1952	68	17	0	8.50	26	6-71	2/0	32.73	4	
Melville Alan (CY 1948)	19.5.1910	18.4.1983	11	1938–1948	894	189	4	52.58	–	–	–/–	–	8	
Middleton James	30.9.1865	23.12.1913	6	1895–1902	52	22	0	7.42	24	5-51	2/0	18.41	5	
Mills Charles Henry	26.11.1867	26.7.1948	1	1891	25	21	0	12.50	2	2-83	0/0	41.50	1	
Milton Sir William Henry	3.12.1854	6.3.1930	3	1888–1891	68	21	0	11.33	2	1-5	0/0	24.00	2	
Mitchell Bruce (CY 1936)	8.1.1909	1.7.1995	42	1929–1948	3,471	189*	8	48.88	27	5-87	1/0	51.11	56	
Mitchell Frank (CY 1902)	13.8.1872	11.10.1935	3†	1912	28	12	0	4.66	–	–	–/–	–	2	
Morkel Denijs Paul Beck	25.1.1906	6.10.1980	16	1927–1931	663	88	0	24.55	18	4-93	0/0	45.61	13	
Morkel Johannes Albertus	10.6.1981		1	2008	58	58	0	58.00	1	1-44	0/0	132.00	1	56‡/50
[2]Morkel Morne	6.10.1984		86	2006–2017	944	40	0	11.65	309	6-23	8/0	27.66	25	114‡/41‡
Morris Christopher Henry	30.4.1987		4	2015–2017	173	69	0	24.71	12	3-38	0/0	38.25	5	42/23
Mulder Peter Wiaan Adriaan	19.2.1998		2	2018	14	9	0	7.00	1	1-6	0/0	12.00	0	10
Murray Anton Ronald Andrew	30.4.1922	17.4.1995	10	1952–1953	289	109	1	22.23	18	4-169	0/0	39.44	3	

	Born	Died	Tests	Test Career	Runs	HS	100s	Avge	Wkts	BB	5/10	Avge	Ct/St	O/T
Muthusamy Senuran	22.2.1994		2	2019	98	49*	0	49.00	2	1-63	0/0	90.00	2	
Nel Andre	15.7.1977		36	2001–2008	337	34	0	9.91	123	6-32	3/1	31.86	16	79/2
Nel John Desmond	10.7.1928	13.1.2018	6	1949–1957	150	38	0	13.63					3	
Newberry Claude	1889	1.8.1916	4	1913	62	16	0	7.75	11	4-72	0/0	24.36	3	
Newson Edward Serrurier OBE	2.12.1910	24.4.1988	3	1930–1938	30	16	0	7.50	4	2-58	0/0	66.25	3	
Ngam Mfuneko	29.1.1979		3	2000	6	0*	0		11	3-26	0/0	17.18	1	
Ngidi Lungisani True-man . .	29.03.1996		15	2017–2019	15	5	0	3.00	50	6-39	–/–	25.06	3	22/7
Nicolson Frank	17.9.1909	30.7.1982	3	1935	76	29	0	10.85	2	0-5	0/0	35.80	3	
Nicolson John Fairless William	19.7.1899	13.12.1935	4	1927	179	78	0	35.80					0	
Nortje Anrich Arno	16.11.1993		6	2019	89	40	0	9.88	19	5-110	0/0	9.88	1	4/1
Norton Norman Ogilvie	11.5.1881	27.6.1968	1	1909	9	7	0	4.50	4	4-47	0/0	11.75	0	
[1] **Nourse** Arthur Dudley (CY 1948)	12.11.1910	14.8.1981	34	1935–1951	2,960	231	9	53.81	0	0-0	0/0		12	
[1] **Nourse** Arthur William (“Dave”)	25.1.1879	8.7.1948	45	1902–1924	2,234	111	1	29.78	41	4-25	0/0	37.87	43	
Ntini Makhaya	6.7.1977		101	1997–2009	699	32*	0	9.84	390	7-37	18/4	28.82	25	172½/10
Nupen Eiulf Peter (“Buster”) .	1.1.1902	29.1.1977	17	1921–1935	348	69	0	14.50	50	6-46	5/1	35.76	9	
Ochse Arthur Edward	11.3.1870	11.4.1918	2	1888	16	8	0	4.00			–/–		0	
Ochse Arthur Lennox	11.10.1899	5.5.1949	3	1927–1929	11	4*	0	3.66	10	4-79	0/0	36.20	1	
O'Linn Sidney	5.5.1927	11.12.2016	7	1960–1961	297	98	0	27.00			–/–		4	
Olivier Duanne	9.5.1992		10	2016–2018	26	10*	0	3.71	48	6-37	3/1	19.25	7	2
Ontong Justin Lee	4.1.1980		2	2001–2004	57	32	0	19.00	1	1-79	0/0	133.00	1	27½/14
Owen-Smith Harold Geoffrey (“Tuppy”) (CY 1930)	18.2.1909	28.2.1990	5	1929	252	129	1	42.00	0	0-3	0/0		4	
Palm Archibald William . . .	8.6.1901	17.8.1966	1	1927	15	13	0	7.50			–/–			
Parker George Macdonald . .	27.5.1899	1.5.1969	2	1924	3	2*	0	1.50	8	6-152	1/0	34.12	0	
Parkin Durant Clifford	20.2.1873	20.3.1936	1	1891	6	6	0	3.00	3	3-82	0/0	27.33	1	
Parnell Wayne Dillon	30.7.1989		6	2009–2017	67	23	0	16.75	44	4-51	0/0	27.60	3	65/40
Partridge Joseph Titus	9.12.1932	6.6.1988	11	1963–1964	73	13*	0	10.42	44	7-91	3/0	31.20	6	
Paterson Dane	4.4.1989		2	2019	43	39*	0	43.00	4	2-86	0/0	41.50	1	4/8
Pearse Charles Ormerod Cato.	10.10.1884	7.5.1953	3	1910	55	31	0	9.16	3	3-56	0/0	35.33	1	
Pegler Sidney James	28.7.1888	10.9.1972	16	1909–1924	356	35*	0	15.47	47	7-65	2/0	33.44	5	21/2
Petersen Alviro Nathan	25.11.1980		36	2009–2014	2,093	182	5	34.88		1-2	0/0	62.00	31	79/21
Petersen Robin John	4.8.1979		15	2003–2013	464	84	0	27.29	38	5-33	1/0	37.26	9	52/23
Phehlukwayo Andile Lucky .	3.3.1996		4	2017	19	74	0	9.50	13	3-13	0/0	13.36	2	30/7
Philander Vernon Darryl . . .	24.6.1985		64	2011–2019	1,779	74	0	24.04	224	6-21	13/2	22.32	17	
Piedt Dane Lee-Roy	6.3.1990		9	2014–2019	131	56	0	11.90	26	5-153	1/0	45.19	5	
[2] **Pithey** Anthony John	17.7.1933	17.11.2006	17	1956–1964	819	154	1	31.50	0	0-5	0/0		3	

	Born	Died	Tests	Test Career	Runs	HS	100s	Avge	Wkts	BB	5/10	Avge	Ct/St	O/T
[2] Pithey David Bartlett.	4.10.1936	21.11.2018	8	1963–1966	138	55	0	12.54	12	6-58	1/0	48.08	6	
Plimsoll Jack Bruce.	27.10.1917	11.11.1999	1	1947	16	8*	0	16.00	3	3-128	0/0	47.66	0	
[1,2] Pollock Peter Maclean (CY 1966).	30.6.1941		28	1961–1969	607	75*	0	21.67	116	6-38	9/1	24.18	9	
[1] Pollock Robert Graeme (CY 1966).	27.2.1944		23	1963–1969	2,256	274	7	60.97	4	2-50	0/0	51.00	17	
[1] Pollock Shaun Maclean (CY 2003).	16.7.1973		108	1995–2007	3,781	111	2	32.31	421	7-87	16/1	23.11	72	294‡/12
[1] Poore Robert Montagu (CY 1900).	20.3.1866	14.7.1938	3	1895	76	20	0	12.66	1	1-4	0/0	4.00	3	
Pothecary James Edward.	6.12.1933	11.5.2016	3	1960	26	12	0	6.50	9	4-58	0/0	39.33	2	
Powell Albert William.	18.7.1873	11.9.1948	1	1898	16	11	0	8.00	1	1-10	0/0	10.00	2	
Pretorius Dewald.	6.12.1977		4	2001–2003	22	9	0	7.33	6	4-115	0/0	71.66	0	
Pretorius Dwaine.	29.3.1989		3	2019	83	37	0	13.83	7	2-26	0/0	36.00	2	22/6
Prince Ashwell Gavin.	28.5.1977		66	2001–2011	3,665	162*	11	41.64	1	1-2	0/0	47.00	47	49‡/1
Prince Charles Frederick Henry.	11.9.1874	2.2.1949	1	1898	6	5	0	3.00	–		–/–		0	
Pringle Meyrick Wayne.	22.6.1966		4	1991–1995	67	33	0	16.75	5	2-62	0/0	54.00	0	17
[2] Procter Michael John (CY 1970).	15.9.1946		7	1966–1969	226	48	0	25.11	41	6-73	1/0	15.02	4	
Promnitz Henry Louis Ernest.	23.2.1904	7.9.1983	2	1927	14	5	0	3.50	8	5-58	1/0	20.12	2	
Quinn Neville Anthony.	21.2.1908	5.8.1934	12	1929–1931	90	28	0	6.00	35	6-92	1/0	32.71	1	
Rabada Kagiso.	25.5.1995		43	2015–2019	606	34	0	11.43	197	7-112	9/4	22.95	22	75/21
Reid Norman.	26.12.1890	6.6.1947	1	1921	17	11	0	8.50	–	2-63	0/0	31.50	3	
[2] Rhodes Jonathan Neil (CY 1999).	27.7.1969		52	1992–2000	2,532	117	3	35.66	0	0-0	–/–	–	34	245
[2] Richards Alfred Renfrew.	14.12.1867	9.1.1904	1	1895	6	6	0	3.00	–		–/–		0	
Richards Barry Anderson (CY 1969).	21.7.1945		4	1969	508	140	2	72.57	1	1-12	0/0	26.00	3	
Richards William Henry Matthews.	26.3.1862	4.1.1903	1	1888	4	4	0	2.00	–		–/–		0	
[2] Richardson David John.	16.9.1959		42	1991–1997	1,359	109	0	24.26	0	3-143	0/0	–	150/2	122
Robertson John Benjamin.	5.6.1906	5.7.1985	3	1935	51	17	0	10.20	6	3-143	0/0	53.50	2	
[2] Rose-Innes Albert.	16.2.1868	22.11.1946	2	1889	14	13	0	3.50	5	5-43	1/0	17.80	2	
[2] Routledge Thomas William.	18.4.1867	9.5.1927	2	1891–1895	72	24	0	9.00	0	0-0	–/–	–	1	
[2] Rowan Athol Matthew Burchell.	7.2.1921	22.2.1998	15	1947–1951	290	41	0	17.05	54	5-68	4/0	38.59	14	
[2] Rowan Eric Alfred Burchell (CY 1952).	20.7.1909	30.4.1993	26	1935–1951	1,965	236	3	43.66	0	0-0	0/0	–	14	
Rowe George Alexander.	15.6.1874	8.1.1950	5	1895–1902	26	13*	0	4.33	15	5-115	1/0	30.40	4	
Rudolph Jacobus Andries.	4.5.1981		48	2003–2012	2,622	222*	6	35.43	4	1-1	0/0	108.00	29	43‡/1
Rushmere Mark Weir.	7.1.1965		1	1991	6	3	0	3.00	–		–/–		0	
Samuelson Sievert Vause.	21.11.1883	18.11.1958	1	1909	22	15	0	11.00	0	0-64	0/0	–	0	4
Schultz Brett Nolan.	26.8.1970		9	1992–1997	9	6	0	1.50	37	5-48	2/0	20.24	1	
Schwarz Reginald Oscar (CY 1908).	4.5.1875	18.11.1918	20	1905–1912	374	61	0	13.85	55	6-47	2/0	25.76	18	
Seccull Arthur William.	14.9.1868	20.7.1945	1	1895	23	17*	0	23.00	2	2-37	0/0	18.50	1	
Seymour Michael Arthur ("Kelly").	5.6.1936	18.2.2019	7	1963–1969	84	36	0	12.00	9	3-80	0/0	65.33	2	

Name	Born	Died	Tests	Test Career	Runs	HS	100s	Avge	Wkts	BB	5/10	Avge	Ct/St	O/T
Shalders William Alfred	12.2.1880	18.3.1917	12	1898-1907	355	42	0	16.13	1	1-6	0/0	6.00	3	
Shamsi Tabraiz	18.2.1990		3	2016-2018	20	18*	0	20.00	6	3-91	0/0	46.33	0	17/16
Shepstone George Harold	9.4.1876	3.7.1940	1	1895-1898	38	21	0	9.50	0	0-8	0/0	–	0	
Sherwell Percy William	17.8.1880	17.4.1948	13	1905-1910	427	115	1	23.72	1	1-7	0/0	7.00	20/16	
Siedle Ivan Julian ("Jack")	11.1.1903	24.8.1982	18	1927-1935	977	141	1	28.73		–	–/–	–	7	
Sinclair James Hugh	16.10.1876	23.2.1913	25	1895-1910	1,069	106	3	23.23	63	6-26	1/0	31.68	9	
Smith Charles James Edward	25.12.1872	27.3.1947	2	1902	106	45	0	21.20		–	–/–	–	2	
Smith Frederick William	31.3.1861	17.4.1914	3	1888-1895	45	12	0	9.00		–	–/–	–	2	
§Smith Graeme Craig (CY 2004)	1.2.1981		116	2001-2013	9,253	277	27	48.70	8	2-145	0/0	110.62	166	196‡/33
Smith Vivian Ian	23.2.1925	25.8.2015	9	1947-1957	39	11*	0	3.90	12	4-143	0/0	64.08	3	
Snell Richard Peter	12.9.1968		5	1991-1994	95	48	0	13.57	19	4-74	0/0	28.31	1	42
[2]Snooke Sibley John ("Tip")	1.2.1881	14.8.1966	26	1905-1922	1,008	103	1	22.40	35	8-70	1/1	20.05	24	
Snooke Stanley de la Courtte	1.11.1878	6.4.1959	1	1907	0	0	0	0.00		–	–/–	–	1	
Solomon William Rodger Thomson	23.4.1872	13.7.1964	1	1898	4	2	0	2.00		–	–/–	–	2	
Stewart Robert Burnard	3.9.1856	12.9.1913	1	1888	13	9	0	6.50		–	–/–	–	1	
Steyn Dale Willem	27.6.1983		93	2004-2018	1,251	76	0	13.59	439	7-51	26/5	22.95	26	123‡/44
Steyn Philippus Jeremia Rudolf	30.6.1967		3	1994	127	46	0	21.16		–	–/–	–	3	1
Stricker Louis Anthony	26.5.1884	5.2.1960	13	1909-1912	344	48	0	14.33	1	1-36	0/0	105.00	3	
Strydom Pieter Coenraad	10.6.1969		2	1999	35	30	0	11.66		–	–/–	–	3	10
Susskind Manfred John	8.6.1891	9.7.1957	5	1924	268	65	0	33.50	0	0-27	0/0	–	1	
Symcox Patrick Leonard	14.4.1960		20	1993-1998	741	108	1	28.50	37	4-69	0/0	43.32	5	80
Taberer Henry Melville	7.10.1870	5.6.1932	1	1902	2	2	0	2.00	1	1-25	0/0	48.00	1	
[2]Tancred Augustus Bernard	20.8.1865	23.11.1911	2	1888	87	29	0	29.00		–	–/–	–	1	
[2]Tancred Louis Joseph	7.10.1876	28.7.1934	14	1902-1913	530	97	0	21.20		–	–/–	–	3	
[2]Tancred Vincent Maximilian	7.7.1875	3.6.1904	1	1898	25	18	0	12.50		–	–/–	–	2	
[2]Tapscott George Lancelot ("Dusty")	7.11.1889	13.12.1940	1	1913	5	4	0	2.50		–	–/–	–	1	
[2]Tapscott Lionel Eric ("Doodles")	18.3.1894	7.7.1934	2	1922	58	50*	0	29.00	0	0-2	0/0	–	1	
Tayfield Hugh Joseph (CY 1956)	30.1.1929	24.2.1994	37	1949-1960	862	75	0	16.90	170	9-113	14/2	25.91	26	
[2]Taylor Alistair Innes ("Scotch")	25.7.1925	7.2.2004	1	1956	18	12	0	9.00		–	–/–	–	1	
[2]Taylor Daniel	9.1.1887	24.1.1957	2	1913	85	36	0	21.25		–	–/–	–	0	
[2]Taylor Herbert Wilfred (CY 1925)	5.5.1889	8.2.1973	42	1912-1931	2,936	176	7	40.77	5	3-15	0/0	31.20	19	
Terbrugge David John	31.1.1977		7	1998-2003	16	4*	0	5.33	20	5-46	1/0	25.85	4	4
Theunissen Nicolaas Hendrik Christiaan de Jong	4.5.1867	9.11.1929	1	1888	2	2*	0	2.00	0	0-51	0/0	–	0	
Thornton George	24.12.1867	31.1.1939	1	1902	1	1*	0	–	1	1-20	0/0	20.00	1	
Tomlinson Denis Stanley	4.9.1910	11.7.1993	2	1935	9	9	0	9.00	0	0-38	0/0	–	1	
Traicos Athanasios John	17.5.1947		3†	1969	8	5*	0	4.00	4	2-70	0/0	51.75	4	0‡

§ *G. C. Smith's figures exclude 12 runs and three catches for the ICC World XI v Australia in the Super Series Test in 2005-06.*

	Born	Died	Tests	Test Career	Runs	HS	100s	Avge	Wkts	BB	5/10	Avge	Ct/St	O/T
Trimborn Patrick Henry Joseph	18.5.1940	—	4	1966–1970	13	11*	0	6.50	11	3-12	0/0	23.36	7	
Tsolekile Thami Lungisa	9.10.1980		3	2004	47	22	0	9.40					6	
Tsotsobe Lonwabo Lennox	7.3.1984		5	2010–2010	19	8*	0	6.33	9	3-43	0/0	49.77	1	61/23
¹**Tuckett** Lindsay Thomas Delville	6.2.1919	5.9.2016	9	1947–1948	131	40*	0	11.90	19	5-68	2/0	51.57	9	
¹**Tuckett** Lindsay Richard ("Len")	19.4.1885	8.4.1963	1	1913	0	0*	0	0.00		0-24	0/0	—	2	
Twentyman-Jones Percy Sydney	13.9.1876	8.3.1954	1	1902	0	0*	0	0.00					1	
van der Bijl Pieter Gerhard Vintcent	21.10.1907	16.2.1973	5	1938	460	125	1	51.11					8	18/9
van der Dussen Hendrik Erasmus ("Rassie")	7.2.1989		7	2019	274	98	0	34.25					3	
van der Merwe Edward Alexander	9.11.1903	26.2.1971	2	1929–1935	27	19	0	9.00					11	
van der Merwe Peter Laurence	14.3.1937	23.1.2013	15	1963–1966	533	76	1	25.38	1	1-6	0/0	22.00	11	11
van Jaarsveld Martin	18.6.1974		9	2002–2004	397	73	0	30.53	17	4-67	0/0	39.47	14	11
van Ryneveld Clive Berrange	19.3.1928	29.1.2018	19	1951–1957	724	83	1	26.81	17	4-67	0/0	24.66	6	
van Zyl Stiaan	19.9.1987		12	2014–2016	395	101*	1	26.33	6	3-20	0/0	—	0	0/1
Varnals George Derek	24.7.1935		3	1964	97	23	0	16.16	0	0-2	-/-	—	13	
Vilas Dane James	10.6.1985		6	2015–2015	94	26	0	10.44					0	
Viljoen G. C. ("Hardus")	6.3.1989		3	2015	26	20*	0	26.00	6	1-79	0/0	94.00	5	
Viljoen Kenneth George	14.5.1910	21.1.1974	27	1930–1948	1,365	124	3	28.43	0	0-10	0/0	—	27	
Vincent Cyril Leverton	16.2.1902	24.8.1968	25	1927–1935	526	60	0	20.23	84	6-51	3/0	31.32	20	
Vintcent Charles Henry	2.9.1866	28.9.1943	3	1888–1891	26	9	0	4.33	4	3-88	0/0	48.25	4	
Vogler Albert Edward Ernest (CY 1908)	28.11.1876	9.8.1946	15	1905–1910	340	65	0	17.00	64	7-94	5/1	22.73	15/2	
²**Wade** Herbert Frederick	14.9.1905	23.11.1980	10	1935–1935	327	40*	0	20.43						
²**Wade** Walter Wareham ("Billy")	18.6.1914	31.5.2003	2	1938–1949	511	125	2	28.38						
Waite John Henry Bickford	19.1.1930	22.6.2011	50	1938–1964	2,405	134	4	30.44					124/17	
Walter Kenneth Alexander	5.11.1939	13.9.2003	2	1961	11	10	0	3.66	6	4-63	0/0	32.83		
Ward Thomas Alfred	2.8.1887	16.2.1936	23	1912–1924	459	64	0	13.90					19/13	
Watkins John Cecil	10.4.1923		15	1949–1956	612	92	1	23.53	29	4-22	0/0	28.13	12	
Wesley Colin	5.9.1937		3	1960	49	35	0	9.80						
Wessels Kepler Christoffel (CY 1995)	19.9.1957		16†	1991–1994	1,027	118	2	38.03	1	0-22	0/0	—	12	55‡
Westcott Richard John	5.2.1882	16.1.2013	5	1953–1957	166	62	0	18.44		0-22	0/0	—	0	
White Gordon Charles	3.12.1974	17.10.1918	17	1905–1912	872	147	2	30.06	9	4-47	0/0	33.44	10	
Willoughby Charl Myles	7.11.1874		2	2003	8	5	0	2.00	2	2-37	0/0	125.00	0	3
Willoughby Joseph Thomas	22.4.1861	11.3.1952	2	1895	5	5	0	0.00	6	1-47	0/0	26.50	0	
Wimble Clarence Skelton	21.5.1929	28.1.1930	1	1891	0	0	0	0.00					1	
Winslow Paul Lyndhurst	1.6.1919	24.5.2011	5	1949–1955	186	108	1	20.66					3	
Wynne Owen Edgar	25.7.1882	13.7.1975	6	1948–1949	219	50	0	18.25					1	
Zondeki Monde	25.7.1882		6	2003–2008	164	59	0	16.40	19	6-39	1/0	25.26	1	3
Zulch Johan Wilhelm	2.1.1886	19.5.1924	16	1909–1921	983	150	2	32.76		0-2	0/0	—	4	11½/1

WEST INDIES (320 players)

	Born	Died	Tests	Test Career	Runs	HS	100s	Avge	Wkts	BB	5/10	Avge	Ct/St	O/T
Achong Ellis Edgar	16.2.1904	30.8.1986	6	1929-1934	81	22	0	8.10	8	2-64	-/-	47.25	6	127
Adams James Clive	9.1.1968		54	1991-2000	3,012	208*	6	41.26	27	5-17	1/0	49.48	48	
Alexander Franz Copeland Murray ("Gerry")	2.11.1928	16.4.2011	25	1957-1960	961	108	1	30.03					85/5	
Ali Imtiaz	28.7.1954		1	1975		1*	0	—	2	2-37	0/0	44.50	0	
Ali Inshan	25.9.1949	24.6.1995	12	1970-1976	172	25	0	10.75	34	5-59	1/0	47.67	7	
Allan David Walter	5.11.1917		5	1961-1966	75	40*	0	12.50				—	15/3	
Allen Ian Basil Alston	6.10.1965		2	1991	5	4*	0	—	5	2-69	0/0	36.00	0	
Ambris Sunil Walford	23.3.1993		6	2017-2018	166	43	0	15.09			-/-		1	9
Ambrose Sir Curtly Elconn Lynwall (CY 1992)	21.9.1963		98	1987-2000	1,439	53	0	12.40	405	8-45	22/3	20.99	18	176
Arthurton Keith Lloyd Thomas	21.2.1965		33	1988-1995	1,382	157*	2	30.71	1	1-17	0/0	183.00	22	105
²**Asgarali** Nyron Sultan	28.12.1920	5.11.2006	2	1957	62	29	0	15.50			-/-		0	
Atkinson Denis St Eval	9.8.1926	9.11.2001	22	1948-1957	922	219	1	31.79	47	7-53	3/0	35.04	11	
²**Atkinson** Eric St Eval	6.11.1927	29.5.1998	8	1957-1958	126	37	0	15.75	25	5-42	1/0	23.56	2	
Austin Richard Arkwright	5.9.1954	7.2.2015	2	1977	22	20	0	11.00	0	0-5	0/0	—	2	1
Austin Ryan Anthony	15.11.1981		1	2009	39	19	0	9.75	3	1-29	0/0	51.66	3	
Bacchus Sheik Faoud Ahamul Fasiel	31.1.1954		19	1977-1981	782	250	1	26.06	0	0-3	0/0	—	17	29
Baichan Leonard	12.5.1946		3	1974-1975	184	105*	1	46.00			-/-		2	
Baker Lionel Sionne	6.9.1984		4	2008-2009	23	17	0	11.50	5	2-39	0/0	79.00	1	10/3
Banks Omari Ahmed Clemente	17.7.1982		10	2002-2005	318	50*	0	26.50	28	4-87	0/0	48.82	6	5
Baptiste Eldine Ashworth Elderfield	12.3.1960		10	1983-1989	233	87*	0	23.30	16	3-31	0/0	35.18	2	43
Barath Adrian Boris	14.4.1990		15	2009-2012	657	104	1	23.46	0	0-3	0/0	—	13	14/2
Barrett Arthur George	4.4.1944	6.3.2018	6	1970-1974	40	19	0	6.66	13	3-43	0/0	46.38	0	
Barrow Ivanhoe Mordecai	16.1.1911	2.4.1979	11	1930-1939	276	105	1	16.23					17/5	
Bartlett Edward Lawson	10.3.1906	21.12.1976	5	1928-1930	131	84	0	18.71					2	
Baugh Carlton Seymour	23.6.1982		21	2002-2011	610	68	0	17.94			-/-		43/5	47/3
Benjamin Kenneth Charlie Griffith	8.4.1967		26	1991-1997	222	43*	0	7.92	92	6-66	4/1	30.27	6	26
Benjamin Winston Keithroy Matthew	31.12.1964		21	1987-1994	470	85	0	18.80	61	4-46	0/0	27.01	12	85
Benn Sulieman Jamaal	22.7.1981		26	2007-2014	486	42	0	14.29	87	6-81	6/0	39.10	14	47/24
Bernard David Eddison	19.7.1981		3	2002-2009	202	69	0	40.40	4	2-30	0/0	46.25	0	20/1
Bess Brandon Jeremy	13.12.1987		1	2010	11	11*	0	11.00	1	1-65	0/0	92.00	0	
Best Carlisle Alonza	14.5.1959		8	1985-1990	342	164	1	28.50	0	0-2	0/0	—	8	24
Best Tino la Bertram	26.8.1981		25	2002-2013	401	95	0	12.53	57	6-40	2/0	40.19	6	26/6
Betancourt Nelson	4.6.1887	12.10.1947	1	1929	52	39	0	26.00			-/-		0	

Name	Born	Died	Test Career	Tests	Runs	HS	100s	Avge	Wkts	BB	5/10	Avge	Ct/St	O/T
Binns Alfred Phillip	24.7.1929	29.12.2017	1952–1955	4	64	27	0	9.14	1	1-16	0/0	71.00	14/3	
Birkett Lionel Sydney	14.4.1905	16.1.1998	1930	4	136	64	0	17.00	—	—	—/—	—	20	
Bishop Devendra	6.11.1985		2010–2018	36	707	45	0	15.36	117	8-49	4/1	37.17	8	42/7
Bishop Ian Raphael	24.10.1967		1988–1997	43	632	48	0	12.15	161	6-40	6/0	24.27	8	84
Black Marlon Ian	7.6.1975		2000–2001	6	21	6	0	2.62	12	4-83	0/0	49.75	2	5
Blackwood Jermaine	20.11.1991		2014–2019	28	1,362	112*	1	30.26	—	—	—/—	—	24	5
Boyce Keith David (CY 1974)	11.10.1943	11.10.1996	1970–1975	21	657	95*	0	24.33	60	6-77	2/1	30.01	3	8
Bradshaw Ian David Russell	9.7.1974		2005	3	96	33	0	13.71	9	3-73	0/0	60.00	3	62/1
Brathwaite Carlos Ricardo	18.7.1988		2015–2016	3	181	69	0	45.25	—	—	—/—	—	0	44/41
Brathwaite Kraigg Clairmonte	1.12.1992		2011–2019	59	3,496	212	8	33.29	1	1-30	0/0	242.00	26	10
Bravo Dwayne John	7.10.1983		2004–2010	40	2,200	113	3	31.42	86	6-55	1/0	39.83	41	164/66
Bravo Darren Michael	6.2.1989		2010–2019	54	3,506	218	8	37.69	—	—	—/—	—	51	110/20
Breese Gareth Rohan	9.1.1976		2002	1	5	5	0	2.50	2	2-108	0/0	67.50	1	
Brooks Sharmarh Shaqad Joshua	1.10.1988		2019–2019	3	174	111	1	34.80	—	—	—/—	—	6	
Browne Courtney Oswald	7.12.1970		1994–2004	20	387	68	0	16.12	—	—	—/—	—	79/2	46
Browne Cyril Rutherford	8.10.1890	12.1.1964	1928–1929	4	176	70*	0	25.14	6	2-72	0/0	48.00	1	
Butcher Basil Fitzherbert (CY 1970)	3.9.1933	16.12.2019	1958–1969	44	3,104	209*	7	43.11	5	5-34	1/0	18.00	15	
Butler Lennox Stephen	9.2.1929	1.9.2009	1954	1	16	16	0	16.00	2	2-151	0/0	75.50	0	
Butts Clyde Godfrey	8.7.1957		1984–1987	7	108	38	0	15.42	10	4-73	0/0	59.50	2	
Bynoe Michael Robin	23.2.1941		1958–1966	4	111	48	0	18.50	—	—	—/—	—	4	
Camacho George Stephen	15.10.1945	2.10.2015	1967–1970	11	640	87	0	29.09	—	—	—/—	—	4	
Cameron Francis James	22.6.1923	10.6.1994	1948	5	151	75*	0	25.16	3	2-74	0/0	92.66	0	
Cameron John Hemsley	8.4.1914	13.2.2000	1939	2	6	5	0	2.00	3	3-66	0/0	29.33	4	
Campbell John Dillon	21.9.1993		2018–2019	6	298	55	0	29.80	—	—	—/—	—	4	6/2
Campbell Sherwin Legay	1.11.1970		1994–2001	52	2,882	208	4	32.38	—	—	—/—	—	47	90
Carew George McDonald	4.6.1910	9.12.1974	1934–1948	4	170	107	1	28.33	—	—	—/—	—	13	
Carew Michael Conrad ("Joey")	15.9.1937	8.1.2011	1963–1971	19	1,127	109	1	34.15	8	1-11	0/0	54.62	0	
Challenor George	28.6.1888	30.7.1947	1928	3	101	46	0	16.83	—	—	—/—	—	2	
Chanderpaul Shivnarine (CY 2008)	16.8.1974		1993–2014	164	11,867	203*	30	51.37	9	1-2	0/0	98.11	66	268/22
Chandrika Rajindra	8.8.1989		2015–2016	5	140	37	0	14.00	—	—	—/—	—	2	
Chang Herbert Samuel	2.7.1952		1978	1	8	6	0	4.00	—	—	—/—	—	4	
Chase Roston Lamar	22.3.1992		2016–2019	32	1,695	137*	5	31.38	59	8-60	2/0	42.37	14	25
Chattergoon Sewnarine	3.4.1981		2007–2008	2	127	46	0	18.14	—	—	—/—	—	4	18
Christiani Cyril Marcel	28.10.1913	4.4.1938	1934	4	98	32*	0	19.60	—	—	—/—	—	6/1	
Christiani Robert Julian OBE	19.7.1920	4.1.2005	1947–1953	22	896	107	1	26.35	3	3-52	0/0	36.00	19/2	
Clarke Carlos Bertram OBE	7.4.1918	14.10.1993	1939	3	3	2	0	1.00	6	3-59	0/0	43.50	0	

	Born	Died	Tests	Test Career	Runs	HS	100s	Avge	Wkts	BB	5/10	Avge	Ct/St	O/T
Clarke Sylvester Theophilus	11.12.1954	4.12.1999	11	1977–1981	172	35*	0	15.63	42	5-126	1/0	27.85	2	10
²**Collins** Pedro Tyrone	12.8.1976		32	1998–2005	235	24	0	5.87	106	6-53	3/0	34.63	7	30
Collymore Corey Dalanelo	21.12.1977		30	1998–2007	197	16*	0	7.88	93	7-57	4/1	32.30	6	84
Constantine *Lord* [Learie Nicholas] MBE														
(CY 1940)	21.9.1901	1.7.1971	18	1928–1939	635	90	0	19.24	58	5-75	2/0	30.10	28	
Cornwall Rahkeem Rashawn Shane	1.2.1993		2	2019–2019	20	14	0	6.66	13	7-75	1/1	22.61	5	30/22
Cottrell Sheldon Shane	19.8.1989		2	2013–2014	11	5	0	2.75	2	1-72	0/0	98.00	0	19
Croft Colin Everton Hunte	15.3.1953		27	1976–1981	158	33	0	10.53	125	8-29	3/0	23.30	8	41
Cuffy Cameron Eustace	8.2.1970		15	1994–2002	58	15	0	4.14	43	4-82	0/0	33.83	5	63‡
Cummins Anderson Cleophas	7.5.1966		5	1992–1994	98	50	0	19.60	8	4-54	0/0	42.75	1	11
Cummins Miguel Lamar	5.9.1990		14	2016–2019	114	24*	0	7.60	27	6-48	1/0	40.14	2	
Da Costa Oscar Constantine	11.9.1907	1.10.1936	5	1929–1934	153	39	0	19.12	3	1-14	0/0	58.33	5	
Daniel Wayne Wendell	16.1.1956		10	1975–1983	46	11	0	6.57	36	5-39	1/0	25.27	4	18
²**Davis** Bryan Allan	2.5.1940		4	1964	245	68	0	30.62					1	
²**Davis** Charles Allan	1.1.1944		15	1968–1972	1,301	183	4	54.20	2	1-27	0/0	165.00	4	
Davis Winston Walter	18.9.1958		15	1982–1987	202	77	0	15.53	45	4-19	0/0	32.71	10	35
de Caires Francis Ignatius	12.5.1909	2.2.1959	3	1929	232	80	0	38.66	0		0/0	–	1	
Deonarine Narsingh	16.8.1983		18	2004–2013	725	82	0	25.89	24	4-37	0/0	29.70	16	31/8
Depeiza Cyril Clairmonte	10.10.1928	10.11.1995	5	1954–1955	187	122	1	31.16	0		0/0	–	7/4	
²**Dewdney** David Thomas	23.10.1933		9	1954–1957	17	5*	0	2.42	21	5-21	1/0	38.42	1	
Dhanraj Rajindra	6.2.1969		4	1994–1995	17	9	0	4.25	8	2-49	0/0	74.37	1	6
Dillon Mervyn	5.6.1974		38	1996–2003	549	43	0	8.44	131	5-71	2/0	33.57	16	108
Dowe Uton George	29.3.1949		4	1970–1972	8	5*	0	8.00	12	4-69	0/0	44.50	3	
Dowlin Travis Montague	24.2.1977		6	2009–2010	343	95	0	31.18	0	0-3	0/0	–	5	11/2
Dowrich Shane Omari	30.10.1991		31	2015–2019	1,444	125*	3	30.08				–	78/5	1
²**Drakes** Vasbert Conniel	5.8.1969		12	2002–2003	386	67	0	21.44	33	5-93	1/0	41.27	4	34
²**Dujon** Peter Jeffrey Leroy (CY 1989.)	28.5.1956		81	1981–1991	3,322	139	5	31.94	–		–/–		267/5	169
²**Edwards** Fidel Henderson	6.2.1982		55	2003–2012	394	30	0	6.56	165	7-87	12/0	37.87	10	50/20
Edwards Kirk Anton	3.11.1984		17	2011–2014	986	121	2	31.80	0	0-19	0/0	–	15	16
Edwards Richard Martin	3.6.1940		5	1968	65	22	0	9.28	18	5-84	1/0	34.77	0	
Ferguson Wilfred	14.12.1917	23.2.1961	8	1947–1953	200	75	0	28.57	34	6-92	3/1	34.26	11	
Fernandes Maurius Pacheco	12.8.1897	8.5.1981	2	1928–1929	49	22	0	12.25	–		–/–		0	
Findlay Thaddeus Michael MBE	19.10.1943		10	1969–1972	212	44*	0	16.30	–		–/–		19/2	
Foster Maurice Linton Churchill	9.5.1943		14	1969–1977	580	125	1	30.52	9	2-41	0/0	66.66	3	
Francis George Nathaniel	11.12.1897	12.1.1942	10	1928–1933	81	19*	0	5.78	23	4-40	0/0	33.17	7	
Frederick Michael Campbell	6.5.1927	18.6.2014	1	1953	30	30	0	15.00	–		–/–		0	

Player	Born	Died	Tests	Test Career	Runs	HS	100s	Avge	Wkts	BB	5/10	Avge	Ct/St	O/T
Fredericks Roy Clifton (CY 1974)	11.11.1942	5.9.2000	59	1968-1976	4,334	169	8	42.49	7	1-12	0/0	78.28	62	12
Fudadin Assad Badyr	1.8.1985		3	2012	122	55	0	30.50	0	0-11	0/0	–	4	
Fuller Richard Livingston	30.1.1913	3.5.1987	1	1934	1	1	0	1.00	0	0-2	0/0	–	0	
Furlonge Hammond Allan	19.6.1934		3	1954-1955	99	64	0	19.80		–			0	
Gabriel Shannon Terry	28.4.1988		45	2012-2019	200	20*	0	4.76	133	8-62	5/1	30.63	16	25/2
Ganga Daren	14.1.1979		48	1998-2007	2,160	135	3	25.71	1	1-20	0/0	106.00	30	35/1
Ganteaume Andrew Gordon	22.1.1921	17.2.2016	1	1947	112	112	1	112.00		–			0	
Garner Joel MBE (CY 1980)	16.12.1952		58	1976-1986	672	60	0	12.44	259	6-56	7/0	20.97	42	98
Garrick Leon Vivian	11.11.1976		1	2000	27	27	0	13.50		–			2	3
Gaskin Berkeley Bertram McGarrell	21.3.1908	2.5.1979	2	1947	17	10	0	5.66	2	1-15	0/0	79.00	1	
Gayle Christopher Henry	21.9.1979		103	1999-2014	7,214	333	15	42.18	73	5-34	2/0	42.73	96	298/58
Gibbs Glendon Lionel	27.12.1925	21.2.1979	1	1954	12	12	0	6.00	0	0-2	0/0	–	1	
Gibbs Lancelot Richard (CY 1972)	29.9.1934		79	1957-1975	488	25	0	6.97	309	8-38	18/2	29.09	52	3
Gibson Ottis Delroy (CY 2008)	16.3.1969		2	1995-1998	93	37	0	23.25	3	2-81	0/0	91.66	1	15
Gilchrist Roy	28.6.1934	18.7.2001	13	1957-1958	60	12	0	5.45	57	6-55	1/0	26.68	4	
Gladstone Morais George	14.11.1901	19.5.1978	1	1929	12	12*	0	–	1	1-139	0/0	189.00	0	
Goddard John Douglas Claude OBE	21.4.1919	26.8.1987	27	1947-1957	859	83*	0	30.67	33	5-31	1/0	31.81	22	
Gomes Hilary Angelo ("Larry") (CY 1985)	13.7.1953		60	1976-1986	3,171	143	9	39.63	15	2-20	0/0	62.00	18	83
Gomez Gerald Eldridge	10.10.1919	6.8.1996	29	1939-1953	1,243	101	1	30.31	58	7-55	1/0	27.41	18	
[2] Grant George Copeland ("Jackie")	9.5.1907	26.10.1978	12	1930-1934	413	71*	0	25.81	0	0-1	0/0	–	10	
[2] Grant Rolph Stewart	15.12.1909	18.10.1977	7	1934-1939	220	77	0	22.00	11	3-68	0/0	32.09	13	
Gray Anthony Hollis	23.5.1963		5	1986	48	12*	0	8.00	22	4-39	0/0	17.13	6	25
Greenidge Alvin Ethelbert	20.8.1956		6	1977-1978	222	69	0	22.20		–			5	1
Greenidge Sir Cuthbert Gordon MBE (CY 1977)	1.5.1951		108	1974-1990	7,558	226	19	44.72	0	0-0	0/0	–	96	128
Greenidge Geoffrey Alan	26.5.1948		5	1971-1972	209	50	0	29.85	0	0-2	0/0	–	3	
Grell Mervyn George	18.12.1899	11.1.1976	1	1929	34	21	0	17.00	0	0-7	0/0	–	1	
Griffith Adrian Frank Gordon	19.11.1971		14	1996-2000	638	114	1	24.53		–			5	9
Griffith Charles Christopher (CY 1964)	14.12.1938		28	1959-1968	530	54	0	16.56	94	6-36	5/0	28.54	16	
Griffith Herman Clarence	1.12.1893	18.3.1980	13	1928-1933	91	18	0	5.05	44	6-103	2/0	28.25	4	
Guillen Simpson Clairmonte ("Sammy")	24.9.1924	2.3.2013	5†	1951	104	54	0	26.00	0	–		–	9/2	
Hall Sir Wesley Winfield	12.9.1937		48	1958-1968	818	50*	0	15.73	192	7-69	9/1	26.38	11	
Hamilton Jahmar Neville	22.9.1990		2	2019	5	5	0	2.50		–			5	
Harper Roger Andrew	17.3.1963		25	1983-1993	535	74	0	18.44	46	6-57	1/0	28.06	36	105
Haynes Desmond Leo (CY 1991)	15.2.1956		116	1977-1993	7,487	184	18	42.29	1	1-2	0/0	8.00	65	238
[3] Headley George Alphonso (CY 1934)	30.5.1909	30.11.1983	22	1929-1953	2,190	270*	10	60.83	0	0-0	0/0	–	14	
[3] Headley Ronald George Alphonso	29.6.1939		2	1973	62	42	0	15.50		–			2	1

	Born	Died	Tests	Test Career	Runs	HS	100s	Avge	Wkts	BB	5/10	Avge	Ct/St	O/T
Hendriks John Leslie	21.12.1933	—	20	1961–1969	447	64	0	18.62	—	—	-/-	—	42/5	—
Hetmyer Shimron Odilon	26.12.1996	—	16	2016–2019	838	93	3	27.93	—	—	-/-	—	7	43/20
Hinds Ryan O'Neal	17.2.1981	—	15	2001–2009	505	84	0	21.04	13	2-45	0/0	66.92	7	14
Hinds Wavell Wayne	7.9.1976	—	45	1999–2005	2,608	213	5	33.01	16	3-79	0/0	36.87	32	119/5
Hoad Edward Lisle Goldsworthy	29.1.1896	5.3.1986	4	1928–1933	98	36	0	12.25	—	—	-/-	—	1	—
Holder Jason Omar	5.11.1991	—	40	2014–2019	1,898	202*	3	32.72	106	6-59	6/1	26.37	33	112/17
Holder Roland Irwin Christopher	22.12.1967	—	11	1996–1998	380	91	0	25.33	—	—	-/-	—	9	37
Holder Vanburn Alonzo	10.10.1945	—	40	1969–1978	682	42	0	14.20	109	6-28	3/0	33.27	16	12
Holding Michael Anthony (CY 1977)	16.2.1954	—	60	1975–1986	910	73	0	13.78	249	8-92	13/2	23.68	22	102
Holford David Anthony Jerome	16.4.1940	—	24	1966–1976	768	105*	1	22.58	51	5-23	1/0	39.39	18	—
Holt John Kenneth Constantine	12.8.1923	3.6.1997	17	1953–1958	1,066	166	2	36.75	1	1-20	0/0	20.00	8	—
Hooper Carl Llewellyn	15.12.1966	—	102	1987–2002	5,762	233	13	36.46	114	5-26	4/0	49.42	115	227
[2]**Hope Kyle Antonio**	20.11.1988	—	5	2017–2017	101	43	0	11.22	—	—	-/-	—	3	—
[2]**Hope Shai Diego (CY 2018)**	10.11.1993	—	31	2014–2019	1,498	147	2	27.23	—	—	-/-	—	44/1	72/13
Howard Anthony Bourne	27.8.1946	—	1	1971	—	—	—	—	2	2-140	0/0	70.00	0	—
Hunte Sir Conrad Cleophas (CY 1964)	9.5.1932	3.12.1999	44	1957–1966	3,245	260	8	45.06	2	1-17	0/0	55.00	16	—
Hunte Errol Ashton Clairmore	3.10.1905	26.6.1967	3	1929	166	58	0	33.20	—	—	-/-	—	5	—
Hylton Leslie George	29.3.1905	17.5.1955	6	1934–1939	70	19	0	11.66	16	4-27	1/0	26.12	—	—
Jacobs Ridley Detamore	26.11.1967	—	65	1998–2004	2,577	118	3	28.31	—	—	-/-	—	207/12	147
Jaggernauth Amit Sheldon	16.11.1983	—	1	2007	0	0*	0	0.00	1	1-74	0/0	96.00	0	—
Johnson Hophnie Hobah Hines	13.7.1910	24.6.1987	3	1947–1950	38	22	0	9.50	13	5-41	2/1	18.30	0	—
Johnson Leon Rayon	8.8.1987	—	9	2014–2016	403	66	0	25.18	—	0-9	0/0	—	1	6
Johnson Tyrell Fabian	10.1.1917	5.4.1985	1	1939	9	9*	0	—	3	2-53	0/0	43.00	3	—
Jones Charles Ernest Llewellyn	3.11.1902	10.12.1959	4	1929–1934	63	19	0	9.00	—	0-2	0/0	—	6	—
Jones Prior Erskine Waverley	6.6.1917	21.11.1991	9	1947–1951	47	10*	0	5.22	25	5-85	1/0	30.04	10	—
Joseph Alzarri Shaheim	20.11.1996	—	9	2016–2018	84	34	0	5.60	25	5-56	1/0	32.84	3	22
Joseph David Rolston Emmanuel	15.11.1969	—	4	1998	141	50	0	20.14	—	0-8	0/0	—	—	—
Joseph Sylvester Cleofoster	5.9.1978	—	5	2004–2007	147	45	0	14.70	—	—	-/-	—	—	13
Julien Bernard Denis	13.3.1950	—	24	1973–1975	866	121	2	30.92	50	5-57	1/0	37.36	14	12
Jumadeen Raphick Rasif	12.4.1948	—	12	1971–1978	84	56	0	21.00	29	4-72	0/0	39.34	4	—
Kallicharran Alvin Isaac BEM (CY 1983)	21.3.1949	—	66	1971–1980	4,399	187	12	44.43	4	2-16	0/0	39.50	51	31
Kanhai Rohan Bholalall (CY 1964)	26.12.1935	—	79	1957–1973	6,227	256	15	47.53	—	0-1	0/0	—	50	7
Kentish Esmond Seymour Maurice	21.11.1916	10.6.2011	2	1947–1953	1	1*	0	1.00	8	5-49	1/0	22.25	—	—
King Collis Llewellyn	11.6.1951	—	9	1976–1980	418	100*	1	32.15	3	1-30	0/0	94.00	5	—
King Frank McDonald	14.12.1926	23.12.1990	14	1952–1955	116	21	0	8.28	29	5-74	1/0	39.96	5	—
King Lester Anthony	27.2.1939	9.7.1998	2	1961–1967	41	20	0	10.25	9	5-46	1/0	17.11	2	—

Name	Born	Died	Tests	Test Career	Runs	HS	100s	Avge	Wkts	BB	Avge	5/10	Ct/St	O/T
King Reon Dane	6.10.1975		19	1998–2004	66	12*	0	3.47	53	5-51	32.69	1/0	2	50
Lambert Clayton Benjamin	10.2.1962		5	1991–1998	284	104	1	31.55	1	1-4	5.00	0/0	8	11‡
Lara Brian Charles (CY 1995)	2.5.1969		130§	1990–2006	11,912	400*	34	53.17	0	0-0	—	0/0	164	295‡
Lashley Patrick Douglas ("Peter")	11.2.1937		4	1960–1966	159	49	0	22.71	1	1-1	1.00	0/0	4	—
Legall Ralph Archibald	1.12.1925	2003	4	1952	50	23	0	10.00	—	—	—	—	8/1	—
Lewis Desmond Michael	21.2.1946	25.3.2018	3	1970	259	88	0	86.33	—	—	—	—	0	—
Lewis Rawl Nicholas	5.9.1974		5	1997–2007	89	40	0	8.90	4	2-42	114.00	0/0	0	28/1
Lewis Sherman Hakim	21.10.1995		2	2018	24	13	0	6.00	—	—	—	—	1	—
Lloyd Sir Clive Hubert CBE (CY 1971)	31.8.1944		110	1966–1984	7,515	242*	19	46.67	10	2-13	62.20	0/0	90	87
Logie Augustine Lawrence	28.9.1960		52	1982–1991	2,470	130	2	35.79	0	0-0	—	0/0	57	158
McGarrell Neil Christopher	12.7.1972		4	2000–2001	61	33	0	15.25	17	4-23	26.64	0/0	2	17
McLean Nixon Alexei McNamara	20.7.1973		19	1997–2000	368	46	0	12.26	44	3-53	42.56	0/0	2	45
McMorris Easton Dudley Ashton St John	4.4.1935	20.7.1997	13	1957–1966	564	125	1	26.85	—	—	—	—	5	—
McWatt Clifford Aubrey	1.2.1922	23.4.2009	6	1953–1954	202	54	0	28.85	1	1-16	16.00	0/0	9/1	—
Madray Ivan Samuel	2.7.1934	11.8.2007	2	1957	3	2	0	1.00	2	—	—	0/0	0	—
Marshall Malcolm Denzil (CY 1983)	18.4.1958	4.11.1999	81	1978–1991	1,810	92	0	18.85	376	7-22	20.94	22/4	25	136
[2]Marshall Norman Edgar	27.2.1924		1	1954	8	8	0	4.00	1	1-22	31.00	0/0	0	—
[2]Marshall Roy Edwin (CY 1959)	25.4.1930	27.10.1992	4	1951–1957	143	30	0	20.42	0	0-3	—	0/0	7	—
Marshall Xavier Melbourne	27.3.1986		7	2005–2008	243	85	0	20.25	0	0-0	—	0/0	7	24/6
Martin Frank Reginald	12.10.1893	23.11.1967	9	1928–1930	486	123*	1	28.58	8	3-91	77.37	0/0	5	—
Martindale Emmanuel Alfred	25.11.1909	17.3.1972	10	1933–1939	58	22	0	5.27	37	5-22	21.72	3/0	5	—
Mattis Everton Hugh	11.4.1957		4	1980	145	71	0	29.00	0	0-4	—	0/0	3	2
Mendonca Ivor Leon	13.7.1934	14.6.2014	2	1961	81	78	0	40.50	—	—	—	—	8/2	—
Merry Cyril Arthur	20.1.1911	19.4.1964	2	1933	34	13	0	8.50	0	0-27	—	0/0	0	—
Miller Nikita O'Neil	16.5.1982		1	2009	5	5	0	2.50	0	0-28	—	0/0	0	50/9
Miller Roy Samuel	24.12.1924	21.8.2014	1	1952	23	23	0	23.00	0	—	—	0/0	0	—
Mohammed Dave	8.10.1979		5	2003–2006	225	52	0	32.14	13	3-98	51.38	0/0	0	7
Moodie George Horatio	26.11.1915	8.6.2002	1	1934	5	5	0	5.00	3	3-23	13.33	0/0	0	—
Morton Runako Shakur	22.7.1978	4.3.2012	15	2005–2007	573	70*	0	22.03	0	0-4	—	0/0	20	56/7
Moseley Ezra Alphonsa	5.1.1958		2	1989	35	26	0	8.75	6	2-70	43.50	0/0	0	9
Murray David Anthony	29.5.1950		19	1977–1981	601	84	0	21.46	—	—	—	—	57/5	10
Murray Deryck Lance	20.5.1943		62	1963–1980	1,993	91	0	22.90	—	—	—	—	181/8	26
Murray Junior Randalph	20.1.1968		33	1992–2001	918	101*	1	22.39	—	—	—	—	99/3	55
Nagamootoo Mahendra Veeren	9.10.1975		5	2000–2002	185	68	0	26.42	12	3-119	53.08	0/0	2	24

§ *Lara's figures exclude 41 runs for the ICC World XI v Australia in the Super Series Test in 2005-06.*

	Born	Died	Tests	Test Career	Runs	HS	100s	Avge	Wkts	BB	5/10	Avge	Ct/St	O/T
Nanan Rangy	29.5.1953		1	1980	16	8	0	8.00	4	2-37	0/0	22.75	2	
Narine Sunil Philip	26.5.1988		6	2012–2013	40	22*	0	8.00	21	6-91	2/0	40.52	2	65/51
Nash Brendan Paul	14.12.1977		21	2008–2011	1,103	114	2	33.42	1	1-21	0/0	123.50	6	9
Neblett James Montague	13.11.1901	28.3.1959	1	1934	16	11*	0	16.00	1	1-44	0/0	75.00	0	
Noreiga Jack Mollinson	15.4.1936	8.8.2003	4	1970	11	9	0	3.66	17	9-95	2/0	29.00	2	
Nunes Robert Karl	7.6.1894	23.7.1958	4	1928–1929	245	92	0	30.62					2	
Nurse Seymour MacDonald (CY 1967)	10.11.1933	6.5.2019	29	1959–1968	2,523	258	6	47.60	0	0-0	–/–		21	
Padmore Albert Leroy	17.12.1946		2	1975–1976	8	8*	0	8.00	1	1-36	0/0	135.00	0	
Pagon Donovan Jomo	13.9.1982		2	2004	37	35	0	12.33					0	
Pairaudeau Bruce Hamilton	14.4.1931		13	1952–1957	454	115	1	21.61	0	0-3	0/0		6	
Parchment Brenton Anthony	24.6.1982		2	2007	55	20	0	13.75					0	7/1
Parry Derick Recaldo	22.12.1954		12	1977–1979	381	65	0	22.41	23	5-15	1/0	40.69	4	6
Pascal Nelon Troy	25.4.1987		1	2010–2010	12	10	0	6.00	0	0-27	0/0			1
Passailaigue Charles Clarence	4.8.1901	7.1.1972	1	1929	46	44	0	46.00	0	0-15	0/0			1
Patterson Balfour Patrick	15.9.1961		28	1985–1992	145	21*	0	6.59	93	5-24	5/0	30.90	5	59
Paul Keemo Mandela Angus	21.2.1998		3	2018–2018	96	47	0	16.00	6	2-25	0/0	31.50	2	16/18
Payne Thelston Rodney O'Neale	13.2.1957		1	1985	5	5	0	5.00			–/–		5	7
Permaul Veerasammy	11.8.1989		6	2012–2015	98	23*	0	12.25	18	3-32	–/–	43.77	2	7/1
Perry Nehemiah Odolphus	16.6.1968		4	1998–1999	74	26	0	12.33	10	5-70	1/0	44.60	1	21
Peters Keon Kenroy	24.2.1982		2	2014	0	0	0	0.00	2	2-69	0/0	34.50	0	
Phillip Norbert	12.6.1948		9	1977–1978	297	47	0	29.70	28	4-48	0/0	37.17	5	1
Phillips Omar Jamel	12.10.1986		2	2009	160	94	0	40.00					1	
Pierre Lancelot Richard	5.6.1921	14.4.1989	1	1947					0	0-9	0/0			
Powell Daren Brentlyle	15.4.1978		37	2002–2008	407	36*	0	7.82	85	5-25	1/0	47.85	8	55/5
Powell Kieran Omar Akeem	6.3.1990		40	2011–2018	2,011	134	3	26.81	0	0-0	0/0		29	46/1
Powell Ricardo Lloyd	16.12.1978		2	1999–2003	53	30	0	17.66	0	0-13	0/0			109
Rae Allan Fitzroy	30.9.1922	27.2.2005	15	1948–1952	1,016	109	4	46.18					10	
Ragonath Suruj	22.3.1968		2	1998	13	9	0	4.33					0	
Ramadhin Sonny (CY 1951)	1.5.1929		43	1950–1960	361	44	0	8.20	158	7-49	10/1	28.98	9	
Ramdass Ryan Rakesh	3.7.1983		1	2005	26	23	0	13.00					2	
Ramdin Denesh	13.3.1985		74	2005–2015	2,898	166	4	25.87					205/12	139/71
Ramnarine Dinanath	4.6.1975		12	1997–2001	106	35*	0	6.23	45	5-78	1/0	30.73	8	4
Rampaul Ravindranath	15.10.1984		18	2009–2012	335	40*	0	14.56	49	4-48	0/0	34.79	3	92/23
Reifer Floyd Lamonte	23.7.1972		6	1996–2009	111	29	0	9.25					6	8/1
Reifer Raymon Anton	11.5.1991		2	2017	52	29	0	52.00	2	1-36	0/0	44.00	2	8/1
Richards Dale Maurice	16.7.1976		3	2009–2010	125	69	0	20.83					0	

	Born	Died	Tests	Test Career	Runs	HS	100s	Avge	Wkts	BB	5/10	Avge	Ct/St	O/T
Richards Sir Isaac Vivian Alexander (CY 1977)	7.3.1952		121	1974–1991	8,540	291	24	50.23	32	2-17	0/0	61.37	122	187
Richardson Sir Richard Benjamin (CY 1992)	12.1.1962		86	1983–1995	5,949	194	16	44.39	0	0-0	0/0	–	90	224
Rickards Kenneth Roy	22.8.1923	21.8.1995	2	1947–1951	104	67	0	34.66	–			–	0	
Roach Clifford Archibald	13.3.1904	16.4.1988	16	1928–1934	952	209	2	30.70	2	1-18	0/0	51.50	5	
Roach Kemar Andre Jamal	30.6.1988		56	2009–2019	890	41	0	12.19	193	6-48	9/1	27.13	13	92/11
Roberts Alphonso Theodore	18.9.1937	24.7.1996	1	1955	28	28	0	14.00	–			–	0	
Roberts Sir Anderson Montgomery Everton CBE (CY 1975)	29.1.1951		47	1973–1983	762	68	0	14.94	202	7-54	11/2	25.61	9	56
Roberts Lincoln Abraham	4.9.1974		1	1998	0	0	0	0.00	0	0-0	–/–	–	0	
Rodriguez William Vicente	25.6.1934		5	1961–1967	96	50	0	13.71	7	3-51	0/0	53.42	3	
Rose Franklyn Albert	1.2.1972		19	1996–2000	344	69	0	13.23	53	7-84	2/0	30.88	4	27
Rowe Lawrence George	8.1.1949		30	1971–1979	2,047	302	7	43.55	0	0-1	0/0	–	17	11
Russell Andre Dwayne	29.4.1988		1	2010	2	2	0	2.00	1	1-73	0/0	104.00	1	56/47
[2] St Hill Edwin Lloyd	9.3.1904	21.5.1957	2	1929	18	12	0	4.50	3	2-110	0/0	73.66	0	
[2] St Hill Wilton H.	6.7.1893	d unknown	3	1928–1929	117	38	0	19.50	0	0-9	–/–	–	1	
Sammy Darren Julius Garvey	20.12.1983		38	2007–2013	1,323	106	1	21.68	84	7-66	4/0	35.79	65	126/66‡
[2] Samuels Marlon Nathaniel (CY 2013)	5.1.1981		71	2000–2016	3,917	260	7	32.64	41	4-13	0/0	59.63	28	207/67
Samuels Robert George	13.3.1971		6	1995–1996	372	125	1	37.20	–			–	4	
Sanford Adam	12.7.1975		11	2001–2003	72	18*	0	4.80	30	4-132	0/0	43.86	1	
Sarwan Ramnaresh Ronnie	23.6.1980		87	1999–2011	5,842	291	15	40.01	23	4-37	0/0	50.56	53	181/18
Scarlett Reginald Osmond	15.8.1934	14.8.2019	3	1959	54	29*	0	18.00	2	1-46	0/0	104.50	2	
[1] Scott Alfred Homer Patrick	29.7.1934	15.6.1961	1	1952	5	5	0	5.00	0	0-52	0/0	–	0	
Sealey Benjamin James	14.8.1892	12.9.1963	1	1933	41	29	0	20.50	1	1-10	0/0	10.00	0	
Sealy James Edward Derrick	11.9.1912	3.1.1982	11	1929–1939	478	92	0	28.11	3	2-7	0/0	31.33	6/1	
Shepherd John Neil (CY 1979)	9.11.1943		5	1969–1970	77	32	0	9.62	19	5-104	1/0	25.21	4	
Shillingford Grayson Cleophas	25.9.1944	23.12.2009	7	1969–1971	57	25	0	8.14	15	3-63	0/0	35.80	2	
Shillingford Irvine Theodore	18.4.1944		4	1976–1977	218	120	1	31.14	0			–	1	2
Shillingford Shane	22.2.1983		16	2010–2014	266	53*	0	13.30	70	6-49	6/2	34.55	9	
Shivnarine Sewdatt	13.5.1952		8	1977–1978	379	63	0	29.15	1	1-13	0/0	167.00	6	1
Simmons Lendl Mark Platter	25.1.1985		8	2008–2011	278	49	0	17.37	1	1-60	0/0	147.00	5	68/49
Simmons Philip Verant (CY 1997)	18.4.1963		26	1987–1997	1,002	110	1	22.26	4	2-34	0/0	64.25	26	143
Singh Charran Kamkaran	27.11.1935	19.11.2015	2	1959	11	11	0	3.66	5	2-28	0/0	33.20	2	
Singh Vishaul Anthony	12.11.1989		3	2016	63	32	0	10.50	–			–	1	
Small Joseph A.	3.11.1892	26.4.1958	3	1928–1929	79	52	0	13.16	3	2-67	0/0	61.33	3	
Small Milton Aster	12.2.1964		2	1983–1984	3	3*	0	–	3	3-40	0/0	38.25	0	2
Smith Cameron Wilberforce	29.7.1933		5	1960–1961	222	55	0	24.66	–			–	4/1	

	Born	Died	Tests	Test Career	Runs	HS	100s	Avge	Wkts	BB	5/10	Avge	Ct/St	O/T
Smith Devon Sheldon	21.10.1981		43	2002-2018	1,760	108	4	23.78	0	0-3	0/0	—	36	47/6
Smith Dwayne Romel	12.4.1983		10	2003-2005	320	105*	1	24.61	7	3-71	0/0	49.14	9	105/33
Smith O'Neil Gordon ("Collie") (CY 1958)	5.5.1933	9.9.1959	26	1954-1958	1,331	168	4	31.69	48	5-90	5/0	33.85	9	1
Sobers Sir Garfield St Aubrun (CY 1964)	28.7.1936		93	1953-1973	8,032	365*	26	57.78	235	6-73	6/0	34.03	109	
Solomon Joseph Stanislaus	26.8.1930		27	1958-1964	1,326	100*	1	34.00	4	1-20	0/0	67.00	13	
Stayers Sven Conrad ("Charlie")	9.6.1937	6.1.2005	4	1961	58	35*	0	19.33	9	3-65	0/0	40.44	0	
[2]**Stollmeyer** Jeffrey Baxter	11.3.1921	10.9.1989	32	1939-1954	2,159	160	4	42.33	13	3-32	0/0	39.00	20	
[2]**Stollmeyer** Victor Humphrey	24.1.1916	21.9.1999	1	1939	96	96	0	96.00	—				0	
Stuart Colin Ellsworth Laurie	28.9.1973		6	2000-2001	24	12*	0	3.42	20	3-33	0/0	31.40	2	5
Taylor Jaswick Ossie	3.1.1932	13.11.1999	3	1957-1958	4	4*	0	2.00	10	5-109	1/0	27.30	2	
Taylor Jerome Everton	22.6.1984		46	2003-2015	856	106	1	12.96	130	6-47	4/0	34.46	8	90/30
Thompson Patterson Ian Chesterfield	26.9.1971		2	1995-1996	17	10*	0	8.50	5	2-58	0/0	43.00	0	5/1
Tonge Gavin Courtney	13.2.1983		1	2009	25	23*	0	25.00	1	1-28	0/0	113.00	0	
Trim John	25.1.1915	12.11.1960	4	1947-1951	21	12	0	5.25	18	5-34	1/0	16.16	2	
Valentine Alfred Louis (CY 1951)	28.4.1930	11.5.2004	36	1950-1961	141	14	0	4.70	139	8-104	8/2	30.32	13	
Valentine Vincent Adolphus	4.4.1908	6.7.1972	2	1933	35	19*	0	11.66	1	1-55	0/0	104.00	0	
Walcott Sir Clyde Leopold (CY 1958)	17.1.1926	26.8.2006	44	1947-1959	3,798	220	15	56.68	11	3-50	0/0	37.09	53/11	
Walcott Leslie Arthur	18.1.1894	27.2.1984	1	1929	40	24	0	40.00	1	1-17	0/0	32.00	1	
Wallace Philo Alphonso	2.8.1970		7	1997-1998	279	92	0	21.46	—				9	33
[1]**Walsh** Courtney Andrew (CY 1987)	30.10.1962		132	1984-2000	936	30*	0	7.54	519	7-37	22/3	24.44	29	205
Walton Chadwick Antonio Kirkpatrick	3.7.1985		2	2009	13	10	0	3.25	—				10	
Warrican Jomel Andrel	20.5.1992		8	2015-2019	142	41	0	28.40	22	4-62	0/0	39.63	3	9/19
Washington Dwight Marlon	5.3.1983		1	2004	7	7*	0	—	0	0-20	0/0	—	3	
Watson Chester Donald	1.7.1938		7	1959-1961	12	5	0	2.40	19	4-62	0/0	38.10	1	
[1]**Weekes** Sir Everton de Courcy (CY 1951)	26.2.1925		48	1947-1957	4,455	207	15	58.61	1	1-8	0/0	77.00	49	
Weekes Kenneth Hunnell	24.1.1912	9.2.1998	2	1939	173	137	2	57.66	—				0	
White Anthony Wilbur	20.11.1938		2	1964	71	57*	0	23.66	3	2-34	0/0	50.66	0	
Wight Claude Vibart	28.7.1902	4.10.1969	2	1928-1929	67	23	0	22.33	0	0-6	0/0	—	0	
Wight George Leslie	28.5.1929	4.1.2004	1	1952	21	21	0	21.00	—				1	
Wiles Charles Archibald	11.8.1892	4.11.1957	1	1933	2	2	0	1.00	—				0	
Willett Elquemedo Tonito	1.5.1953		5	1972-1974	74	26	0	14.80	11	3-33	0/0	43.81	0	
Williams Alvadon Basil	21.11.1949	25.10.2015	7	1977-1978	469	111	2	39.08	—				0	
Williams David	4.11.1963		11	1991-1997	242	65	0	13.44	—				40/2	36
Williams Ernest Albert Vivian ("Foffie")	10.4.1914	13.4.1997	4	1939-1947	113	72	0	18.83	9	3-51	0/0	26.77	0	
Williams Stuart Clayton	12.8.1969		31	1993-2001	1,183	128	1	24.14	0	0-19	0/0	—	27	57
Wishart Kenneth Leslie	28.11.1908	18.10.1972	1	1934	52	52	0	26.00	—				0	
Worrell Sir Frank Mortimer Maglinne (CY 1951)	1.8.1924	13.3.1967	51	1947-1963	3,860	261	9	49.48	69	7-70	2/0	38.72	43	

NEW ZEALAND (278 players)

	Born	Died	Tests	Test Career	Runs	HS	100s	Avge	Wkts	BB	5/10	Avge	Ct/St	O/T
Adams Andre Ryan	17.7.1975		1	2001	18	11	0	9.00	6	3-44	0/0	17.50	1	42/4
Alabaster John Chaloner	11.7.1930		21	1955-1971	272	34	0	9.71	49	4-46	0/0	38.02	7	–
Allcott Cyril Francis Walter	7.10.1896	19.11.1973	6	1929-1931	113	33	0	22.60	6	2-102	0/0	90.16	3	–
Allott Geoffrey Ian	24.12.1971		10	1995-1999	27	8*	0	3.37	19	4-74	0/0	58.47	2	31
Anderson Corey James	13.12.1990		13	2013-2015	683	116	1	32.52	16	3-47	0/0	41.18	7	49/31
Anderson Robert Wickham	2.10.1948		9	1976-1978	423	92	0	23.50	–	–	–	–	1	2
[1]Anderson William McDougall	8.10.1919	21.12.1979	1	1945	5	4	0	2.50	–	–	–	–	–	–
Andrews Bryan	4.4.1945		2	1973	22	17	0	22.00	2	2-40	0/0	77.00	1	–
Arnel Brent John	3.1.1979		6	2009-2011	45	8*	0	5.62	9	4-95	0/0	62.88	3	–
Astle Nathan John	15.9.1971		81	1995-2006	4,702	222	11	37.02	51	3-27	0/0	42.01	70	223/4
Astle Todd Duncan	24.9.1986		5	2012-2019	98	35	0	19.60	7	3-39	0/0	52.57	3	9/3
Badcock Frederick Theodore ("Ted")	9.8.1897	19.9.1982	7	1929-1932	137	64	0	19.57	16	4-80	0/0	38.12	1	–
[1]Barber Richard Trevor	3.6.1925	7.8.2015	1	1955	17	12	0	8.50	–	–	–	–	1	–
Bartlett Gary Alex	3.2.1941		10	1961-1967	263	40	0	15.47	24	6-38	1/0	33.00	8	–
Barton Paul Thomas	9.10.1935		7	1961-1962	285	109	1	20.35	–	–	–	–	4	–
Beard Donald Derek	14.11.1920	15.7.1982	4	1951-1955	101	31	0	20.20	9	3-22	0/0	33.55	0	–
Beck John Edward Francis	1.8.1934	23.4.2000	8	1953-1955	394	99	0	26.26	–	–	–	–	2	–
Bell Matthew David	25.2.1977		18	1998-2007	729	107	2	24.30	2	1-54	0/0	117.50	19	7
Bennett Hamish Kyle	22.2.1987		1	2010	4	4	0	4.00	0	0-47	0/0	–	1	16
Bilby Grahame Paul	7.5.1941	23.7.2002	2	1965	55	28	0	13.75	–	–	–	–	3	–
Blain Tony Elston	17.2.1962		11	1986-1993	456	78	0	26.82	–	–	–	–	19/2	38
Blair Robert William	23.6.1932		19	1952-1963	189	64*	0	6.75	43	4-85	0/0	35.23	5	–
Blundell Thomas Ackland	1.9.1990		4	2017-2019	308	121	2	51.33	0	0-13	0/0	–	3	0/3
Blunt Roger Charles (CY 1928)	3.11.1900	22.6.1966	9	1929-1931	330	96	0	27.50	12	3-17	0/0	39.33	10	–
Bolton Bruce Alfred	31.5.1935		2	1958	59	33	0	19.66	–	–	–	–		–
Bond Shane Edward	7.6.1975		18	2001-2009	168	41*	0	12.92	87	6-51	5/1	22.09	8	82/20
Boock Stephen Lewis	20.9.1951		30	1977-1988	207	37	0	6.27	74	7-87	4/0	34.64	14	14
Boult Trent Alexander	22.7.1989		65	2011-2019	615	52*	0	14.64	256	6-30	8/1	28.01	36	89/27
[1,2]Bracewell Brendon Paul	14.9.1959		6	1978-1984	24	8	0	2.40	14	3-110	0/0	41.78	1	1
[1]Bracewell Douglas Alexander John	28.9.1990		27	2011-2016	568	47	0	13.85	72	6-40	2/0	38.83	10	19/18
[2]Bracewell John Garry	15.4.1958		41	1980-1990	1,001	110	1	20.42	102	6-32	4/1	35.81	31	53
[1]Bradburn Grant Eric	26.5.1966		7	1990-2000	105	30*	0	13.12	6	3-134	0/0	76.66	6	11

	Born	Died	Tests	Test Career	Runs	HS	100s	Avge	Wkts	BB	5/10	Avge	Ct/St	O/T
[1]Bradburn Wynne Pennell	24.11.1938	25.9.2008	2	1963	62	32	0	15.50	–	–	–/–	–	2	39/11
Broom Neil Trevor	20.11.1983		2	2016	32	20	0	10.66					0	3
Brown Vaughan Raymond	3.11.1959		2	1985	51	36*	0	25.50	1	1-17	0/0	176.00	3	16/5
Brownlie Dean Graham	30.7.1984		14	2011–2013	711	109	1	29.62	1	1-13	0/0	52.00	17	3
Burgess Mark Gordon	17.7.1944		50	1967–1980	2,684	119*	5	31.20	6	3-23	0/0	35.33	34	26
Burke Cecil	27.3.1914	4.8.1997	1	1945	4	3	0	2.00	2	2-30	0/0	15.00	0	
Burtt Thomas Browning	22.1.1915	24.5.1988	10	1946–1952	252	42	0	21.00	33	6-162	3/0	35.45	2	
Butler Ian Gareth	24.11.1981		8	2001–2004	76	26	0	9.50	24	6-46	1/0	36.83	4	26/19
Butterfield Leonard Arthur	29.8.1913	5.7.1999	1	1945	0	0	0	0.00	0	0-24	0/0	–	0	
[1]Cairns Bernard Lance	10.10.1949		43	1973–1985	928	64	0	16.28	130	7-74	6/1	32.91	30	78
[1]Cairns Christopher Lance (CY 2000)	13.6.1970		62	1989–2004	3,320	158*	5	33.53	218	7-27	13/1	29.40	14	214½/2
Cameron Francis James MBE	1.6.1932		19	1961–1965	116	27*	0	11.60	62	5-34	3/0	29.82	1	
Cave Henry Butler	10.10.1922	15.9.1989	19	1949–1958	229	22*	0	8.80	34	4-21	0/0	43.14	8	
Chapple Murray Ernest	25.7.1930	31.7.1985	14	1952–1965	497	76	0	19.11	1	1-24	0/0	84.00	10	
Chatfield Ewen John MBE	3.7.1950		43	1974–1988	180	21*	0	8.57	123	6-73	3/1	32.17	7	114
Cleverley Donald Charles	23.12.1909	16.2.2004	2	1931–1945	19	10*	0	19.00	0	0-51	0/0	–	0	
Collinge Richard Owen	2.4.1946		35	1964–1978	533	68*	0	14.40	116	6-63	3/0	29.25	10	15
Colquhoun Ian Alexander	8.6.1924	26.2.2005	2	1954	1	1*	0	0.50	–	–	–/–	–	4	
[2]Coney Jeremy Vernon MBE (CY 1984)	21.6.1952		52	1973–1986	2,668	174*	3	37.57	27	3-28	0/0	35.77	64	88
Congdon Bevan Ernest OBE (CY 1974)	11.2.1938		61	1964–1978	3,448	176	7	32.22	59	5-65	0/0	36.50	44	11
Cowie John OBE	30.3.1912	3.6.1994	9	1937–1949	90	45	0	10.00	45	6-40	4/1	21.53	3	
Craig Mark Donald	23.3.1987		15	2014–2016	589	67	0	36.81	50	7-94	4/1	46.52	14	
Cresswell George Fenwick	22.3.1915	10.1.1966	3	1949–1950	14	12*	0	7.00	13	6-168	1/0	22.46	0	
Cromb Ian Burns	25.6.1905	6.3.1984	5	1931–1932	123	51*	0	20.50	8	3-113	0/0	55.25	1	
Crowe Jeffrey John	14.9.1958		39	1982–1989	1,601	128	3	26.24	0	0-0	0/0	–	41	75
[2]Crowe Martin David MBE (CY 1985)	22.9.1962	3.3.2016	77	1981–1995	5,444	299	17	45.36	14	2-25	0/0	48.28	71	143
Cumming Craig Derek	31.8.1975		11	2004–2007	441	74	0	25.94	–	–	–/–	–	3	13
Cunis Robert Smith	5.1.1941		20	1963–1971	295	51	0	12.82	51	6-76	1/0	37.00	1	
D'Arcy John William	23.4.1936		5	1958	136	33	0	13.60	–	–	–/–	–	0	
Davis Heath Te-Ihi-O-Te-Rangi	30.11.1971		5	1994–1997	20	8*	0	6.66	17	5-63	1/0	29.35	4	11
de Grandhomme Colin	22.7.1986		22	2016–2019	1,116	105	1	37.20	45	6-41	1/0	31.40	15	38/33
de Groen Richard Paul	5.8.1962		5	1993–1994	45	26	0	7.50	11	3-40	0/0	45.90	3	12
Dempster Charles Stewart (CY 1932)	15.11.1903	14.2.1974	10	1929–1932	723	136	2	65.72	0	0-10	0/0	–	2	
Dempster Eric William MBE	25.11.1925	15.8.2011	5	1952–1953	106	47	0	17.66	2	1-24	0/0	109.50	0	
Dick Arthur Edward	10.10.1936		17	1961–1965	370	50*	0	14.23	–	–	–/–	–	47/4	
Dickinson George Ritchie	11.3.1903	17.3.1978	3	1929–1931	31	11	0	6.20	8	3-66	0/0	30.62	3	

	Born	Died	Test Career	Tests	Runs	HS	100s	Avge	Wkts	BB	5/10	Avge	Ct/St	O/T
Donnelly Martin Paterson (CY 1948)	17.10.1917	22.10.1999	1937–1949	7	582	206	1	52.90	0	0-20	0/0	–	7	42
Doull Simon Blair	6.8.1969	–	1992–1999	32	570	46	0	14.61	98	7-65	6/0	29.30	16	–
Dowling Graham Thorne OBE	4.3.1937	–	1961–1971	39	2,306	239	3	31.16	1	1-19	0/0	19.00	23	5
Drum Christopher James	10.7.1974	–	2000–2001	5	10	8	0	3.33	16	3-36	0/0	30.12	4	–
Dunning John Angus	6.2.1903	24.6.1971	1932–1937	4	38	19	0	7.60	5	2-35	0/0	98.60	2	5
Edgar Bruce Adrian	23.11.1956	–	1978–1986	39	1,958	161	3	30.59	0	0-3	0/0	–	14	64
Edwards Graham Neil ("Jock")	27.5.1955	–	1976–1980	8	377	55	0	25.13	–	–	–/–	–	7	–
Elliott Grant David	21.3.1979	–	2007–2009	5	86	25	0	10.75	4	2-8	0/0	35.00	2	83/16‡
Emery Raymond William George	28.3.1915	18.12.1982	1951	2	46	28	0	11.50	5	2-52	0/0	26.00	0	–
Ferguson Lachlan Hammond ("Lockie")	13.6.1991	–	2019	1	1	1*	0	–	0	0-47	0/0	–	0	36/8
Fisher Frederick Eric	28.7.1924	19.6.1996	1952	1	23	14	0	11.50	1	1-78	0/0	78.00	0	–
Fleming Stephen Paul	1.4.1973	–	1993–2007	111	7,172	274*	9	40.06	–	–	–/–	–	171	279‡/5
Flynn Daniel Raymond	16.4.1985	–	2008–2012	24	1,038	95	1	25.95	–	–	–/–	–	10	20/5
Foley Henry	28.1.1906	16.10.1948	1929	1	4	2	0	2.00	0	0-0	0/0	–	–	–
Franklin James Edward Charles	7.11.1980	–	2000–2012	31	808	122*	1	20.71	82	6-119	3/0	33.97	12	110/38
Franklin Trevor Jon	15.3.1962	–	1983–1990	21	828	101	1	23.00	–	–	–/–	–	8	3
Freeman Douglas Linford	8.9.1914	31.5.1994	1932	2	2	1	0	1.00	1	1-91	0/0	169.00	–	–
Fulton Peter Gordon	1.2.1979	–	2005–2014	23	967	136	2	25.44	–	–	–/–	–	25	49/12
Gallichan Norman	3.6.1906	25.3.1969	1937	1	32	30	0	16.00	3	3-99	0/0	37.66	–	–
Gedye Sidney Graham	2.5.1929	10.8.2014	1963–1964	4	193	55	0	24.12	0	–	–/–	–	0	–
Germon Lee Kenneth	4.11.1968	–	1995–1996	12	382	55	0	21.22	–	–	–/–	–	27/2	37
Gillespie Mark Raymond	17.10.1979	–	2007–2011	5	76	27	0	10.85	22	6-113	3/0	28.68	1	32/11
Gillespie Stuart Ross	2.3.1957	–	1985	1	28	28	0	28.00	1	1-79	0/0	79.00	–	19
Gray Evan John	18.11.1954	–	1983–1988	10	248	50	0	15.50	17	3-73	0/0	52.11	6	10
Greatbatch Mark John	11.12.1963	–	1987–1996	41	2,021	146*	3	30.62	0	0-0	0/0	–	27	84
Guillen Simpson Clairmonte ("Sammy")	24.9.1924	2.3.2013	1955	3†	98	41	0	16.33	–	–	–/–	–	4/1	–
Guptill Martin James	30.9.1986	–	2008–2016	47	2,586	189	5	29.38	8	3-11	0/0	37.25	50	179/83
Guy John William	29.8.1934	–	1955–1961	12	440	102	1	20.95	–	–	–/–	–	2	–
Hadlee Dayle Robert [1,2]	6.1.1948	–	1969–1977	26	530	56	0	14.32	71	4-30	0/0	33.64	8	11
Hadlee Sir Richard John (CY 1982) [1,2]	3.7.1951	–	1972–1990	86	3,124	151*	2	27.16	431	9-52	36/9	22.29	39	115
Hadlee Walter Arnold CBE [1]	4.6.1915	29.9.2006	1937–1950	11	543	116	1	30.16	–	–	–/–	–	6	115
Harford Noel Sherwin	30.8.1930	30.3.1981	1955–1958	8	229	93	0	15.26	–	–	–/–	–	–	–
Harford Roy Ivan [1]	30.5.1936	–	1967	3	7	6	0	2.33	–	–	–/–	–	11	–
Harris Chris Zinzan	20.11.1969	–	1992–2002	23	777	71	0	20.44	16	2-16	0/0	73.12	14	250
Harris Parke Gerald Zinzan [1]	18.7.1927	1.12.1991	1955–1964	9	378	101	1	22.23	0	0-14	0/0	–	6	–
Harris Roger Meredith	27.7.1933	–	1958	2	31	13	0	10.33	–	–	–/–	–	–	–

	Born	Died	Tests	Test Career	Runs	HS	100s	Avge	Wkts	BB	5/10	Avge	Ct/St	O/T
[2] Hart Matthew Norman	16.5.1972		14	1993–1995	353	45	0	17.65	29	5-77	1/0	49.58	9	13
[2] Hart Robert Garry	2.12.1974		11	2002–2003	260	57*	0	16.25	–	–	–	–	29/1	2
[2] Hartland Blair Robert	22.10.1966		9	1991–1994	303	52	0	16.83	–	–	–	–	5	16
Haslam Mark James	26.9.1972		4	1992–1995	3	3	0	4.00	2	1-33	0/0	122.50	2	1
Hastings Brian Frederick	23.3.1940		31	1968–1975	1,510	117*	4	30.20	0	0-3	0/0	–	23	11
Hayes John Arthur	11.1.1927	25.12.2007	15	1950–1958	73	19	0	4.86	30	4-36	0/0	40.56	3	
Henderson Matthew	2.8.1895	17.6.1970	1	1929	8	6	0	8.00	2	2-38	0/0	32.00	1	
Henry Matthew James	14.12.1991		12	2015–2019	224	66	0	18.66	30	4-93	0/0	50.16	5	52/6
Hopkins Gareth James	24.11.1976		1	2008–2010	71	15	0	11.83	–	–	–	–	9	25/10
[2] Horne Matthew Jeffery	5.12.1970		35	1996–2003	1,788	157	4	28.38	0	0-4	0/0	–	17	50
[2] Horne Philip Andrew	21.1.1960		4	1986–1990	71	27	0	10.14	–	–	–	–	3	4
Hough Kenneth William	24.10.1928	20.9.2009	2	1958	62	31*	0	62.00	6	3-79	0/0	29.16	1	
How Jamie Michael	19.5.1981		19	2005–2008	772	92	0	22.70	0	0-0	0/0	–	18	41/5
[2] Howarth Geoffrey Philip OBE.	29.3.1951		47	1974–1984	2,531	147	6	32.44	3	1-13	0/0	90.33	29	70
Howarth Hedley John	25.12.1943	7.11.2008	30	1969–1976	291	61	0	12.12	86	5-34	2/0	36.95	33	9
Ingram Peter John	25.10.1978		2	2009	61	42	0	15.25	–	–	–	–	0	8/3
James Kenneth Cecil	12.3.1904	21.8.1976	11	1929–1932	52	14	0	4.72	–	–	–	–	11/5	
Jarvis Terrence Wayne	29.7.1944		13	1964–1972	625	182	1	29.76	0	0-0	0/0	–	3	
Jones Andrew Howard	9.5.1959		39	1986–1994	2,922	186	7	44.27	1	1-40	0/0	194.00	25	87
Jones Richard Andrew	22.10.1973		1	2003	23	16	0	11.50	–	–	–	–	0	5
Kennedy Robert John	3.6.1972		4	1995	28	22	0	7.00	6	3-28	0/0	63.33	2	7
Kerr John Lambert	28.12.1910	27.5.2007	7	1931–1937	212	59	0	19.27	–	–	–	–	4	
Kuggeleijn Christopher Mary	10.5.1956		2	1988	7	7	0	1.75	1	1-50	0/0	67.00	0	16
Larsen Gavin Rolf	27.9.1962		8	1994–1995	127	26*	0	14.11	24	3-57	0/0	28.70	5	121
[1] Latham Rodney Terry	12.6.1961		4	1991–1992	219	119	1	31.28	0	0-6	0/0	–	5	33
[1] Latham Thomas William Maxwell	2.4.1992		50	2013–2019	3,604	264*	11	42.40	–	–	–	–	49	95/13
Lees Warren Kenneth MBE.	19.3.1952		21	1976–1983	778	152	1	23.57	–	–	–	–	52/7	31
Leggat Ian Bruce	7.6.1930		1	1953	0	0	0	0.00	0	0-4	0/0	–	0	
Leggat Jack Gordon	27.5.1926	9.3.1973	9	1951–1955	351	61	0	21.93	–	–	–	–	1	
Lissette Allen Fisher	6.11.1919	24.1.1973	2	1955	2	1*	0	1.00	3	2-73	0/0	41.33	1	
Loveridge Greg Riaka	15.1.1975		1	1995	4	4*	0	–	–	–	–	–	1	
Lowry Thomas Coleman	17.2.1898	20.7.1976	7	1929–1931	223	80	0	27.87	0	0-0	0/0	–	8	
McCullum Brendon Barrie (CT 20/6)	27.9.1981		101	2003–2015	6,453	302	12	38.64	1	1-1	0/0	88.00	198/11	260/71
McEwan Paul Ernest	19.12.1953		4	1979–1984	96	40*	0	16.00	0	0-6	0/0	–	5	17
MacGibbon Anthony Roy	28.8.1924		26	1950–1958	814	66	0	19.85	70	5-64	1/0	30.85	13	
McGirr Herbert Mendelson	5.11.1891	14.4.1964	2	1929	51	51	0	51.00	1	1-65	0/0	115.00	0	

	Born	Died	Tests	Test Career	Runs	HS	100s	Avge	Wkts	BB	5/10	Avge	Ct/St	O/T
McGregor Spencer Noel	18.12.1931	21.11.2007	25	1954–1964	892	111	2	19.82	–	–	–/–	–	9	–
McIntosh Timothy Gavin	4.12.1979		17	2008–2010	854	136	2	27.54	–	–	–/–	–	10	–
McKay Andrew John	17.4.1980		1	2010	25	20*	0	25.00	1	1-120	0/0	120.00	0	19/2
McLeod Edwin George	14.10.1900	14.9.1989	1	1929	18	16	0	18.00	–	–	–/–	–	7/1	–
McMahon Trevor George	8.11.1929		5	1955	7	4*	0	2.33	–	–	–/–	–	22	–
McMillan Craig Douglas	13.9.1976		55	1997–2004	3,116	142	6	38.46	28	3-48	0/0	44.89	22	197/8
McRae Donald Alexander Noel	25.12.1912	10.8.1986	1	1945	8	8	0	4.00	0	0-44	0/0	–	0	–
² Marshall Hamish John Hamilton	15.2.1979		13	2000–2005	652	160	2	38.35	0	0-4	0/0	–	1	66/3
² Marshall James Andrew Hamilton	15.2.1979		7	2004–2008	218	52	0	19.81	–	–	–/–	–	5	10/3
Martin Bruce Philip	25.4.1980		5	2012–2013	74	41	0	14.80	12	4-43	0/0	53.83	1	20/6
Martin Christopher Stewart	10.12.1974		71	2000–2012	123	12*	0	2.36	233	6-26	10/1	33.81	14	26/3
Mason Michael James	27.8.1974		1	2003	3	3	0	1.50	0	0-32	0/0	–	0	–
Matheson Alexander Malcolm	27.2.1906	31.12.1985	2	1929–1931	7	7	0	7.00	2	2-7	0/0	68.00	2	–
Meale Trevor	18.8.1908	21.5.2010	2	1958	21	10	0	5.25	–	–	–/–	–	1	–
Merritt William Edward	18.8.1908	9.6.1977	6	1929–1931	73	19	0	10.42	12	4-104	0/0	51.41	2	–
Meuli Edgar Milton	20.2.1926	15.4.2007	1	1952	38	23	0	19.00	–	–	–/–	–	0	–
Milburn Barry Douglas	24.11.1943		3	1968	8	4*	0	8.00	–	–	–/–	–	6/2	–
Miller Lawrence Somerville Martin	31.3.1923	17.12.1996	13	1952–1958	346	47	0	13.84	0	0-1	0/0	–	1	–
Mills John Ernest	3.9.1905	11.12.1972	7	1929–1932	241	117	1	26.77	2	2-7	0/0	33.02	4	170/42
Mills Kyle David	15.3.1979		19	2004–2008	289	57	0	11.56	44	4-16	0/0	33.02	4	0/9
Mitchell Daryl Joseph	20.5.1991		1	2019	73	73	0	73.00	0	0-69	0/0	–	2	–
Moir Alexander McKenzie	17.7.1919	17.6.2000	17	1950–1958	327	41*	0	14.86	28	6-155	2/0	50.64	2	–
Moloney Denis Andrew Robert ("Sonny")	11.8.1910	15.7.1942	3	1937	156	64	0	26.00	0	0-9	0/0	–	0	–
Mooney Francis Leonard Hugh	26.5.1921	8.3.2004	14	1949–1953	343	46	0	17.15	–	0-0	0/0	–	22/8	–
Morgan Ross Winston	12.2.1941		20	1964–1971	734	97	1	22.24	5	1-16	0/0	121.80	12	–
Morrison Bruce Donald	17.12.1933		1	1962	10	10	0	5.00	2	2-129	0/0	64.50	1	–
Morrison Daniel Kyle	3.2.1966		48	1987–1996	379	42	0	8.42	160	7-89	10/0	34.68	14	96
Morrison John Francis MacLean	27.8.1947		17	1973–1981	656	117	1	22.62	2	2-52	0/0	22.50	9	18
Motz Richard Charles (CY 1966)	12.1.1940	29.4.2007	32	1961–1969	612	60	0	11.54	100	6-63	5/0	31.48	9	57/60
Munro Colin	11.3.1987		1	2012	15	15	0	7.50	2	2-40	0/0	20.00	0	–
Murray Bruce Alexander Grenfell	18.9.1940		13	1967–1970	598	90	0	23.92	1	1-0	0/0	0.00	21	1
Murray Darrin James	4.9.1967	1994	8	1994	303	52	0	20.20	–	–	–/–	–	6	81
Nash Dion Joseph	20.11.1971		32	1992–2001	729	89*	0	23.51	93	6-27	3/1	28.48	13	59/18
Neesham James Douglas Sheehan	17.9.1990		12	2013–2016	709	137*	2	33.76	14	3-42	0/0	48.21	12	–
Newman *Sir* Jack	3.7.1902	23.9.1996	3	1931–1932	33	19	0	8.25	2	2-76	0/0	127.00	0	45/5
Nicholls Henry Michael	15.11.1991		31	2015–2019	1,711	162*	5	40.73	–	–	–/–	–	21	–

	Born	Died	Tests	Test Career	Runs	HS	100s	Avge	Wkts	BB	5/10	Avge	Ct/St	O/T
Nicol Robert James.	28.5.1983		2	2011	28	19	0	7.00	–	0-0	0/0	–	2	22/21
O'Brien Iain Edward.	10.7.1976		22	2004–2009	219	31	0	7.55	73	6-75	1/0	33.27	7	10/4
O'Connor Shayne Barry	15.11.1973		19	1997–2001	103	20	0	5.72	53	5-51	1/0	32.52	6	38
Oram Jacob David Philip . . .	28.7.1978		33	2002–2009	1,780	133	5	36.32	60	4-41	0/0	33.05	15	160/36
O'Sullivan David Robert	16.11.1944		11	1972–1976	158	23*	0	9.29	18	5-148	1/0	67.83	4	3
Overton Guy William Fitzroy.	8.6.1919	7.9.1993	3	1953	8	3*	0	1.60	9	3-65	0/0	28.66	1	
Owens Michael Barry	11.11.1969		8	1992–1994	16	8*	0	2.66	17	4-99	0/0	34.41	3	1
Page Milford Laurenson ("Curly")	8.5.1902	13.2.1987	14	1929–1937	492	104	1	24.60	5	2-21	0/0	46.20	6	
Papps Michael Hugh William.	2.7.1979		8	2003–2007	246	86	0	16.40	–	–	–/–	–	11	6
2 Parker John Morton	21.2.1951		36	1972–1980	1,498	121	3	24.55	1	1-24	0/0	24.00	30	24
Parker Norman Murray.	28.8.1948		3	1976	89	40	0	14.83	–	–	–/–	–	2	
Parore Adam Craig.	23.1.1971		78	1990–2001	2,865	110	2	26.28	–	–	–/–	–	197/7	179
Patel Ajaz Yunus	21.10.1988		7	2018–2019	49	14	0	7.00	22	5-59	2/0	32.18	5	0/2
Patel Dipak Narshibhai	25.10.1958		37	1986–1996	1,200	99	0	20.68	75	6-50	3/0	42.05	15	75
Patel Jeetan Shashi (CY 2015).	7.5.1980		24	2005–2016	381	47	0	12.70	65	5-110	1/0	47.35	13	43/11
Petherick Peter James	25.9.1942	7.6.2015	6	1976	34	13	0	4.85	16	3-90	0/0	42.81	4	
Petrie Eric Charlton	22.5.1927	14.8.2004	14	1955–1965	258	55	0	12.90	–	–	–/–	–	25	
Phillips Glenn Dominic	6.12.1996		1	2019	52	52	0	26.00	–	–	–/–	–	1	0/11
Playle William Rodger.	1.12.1938	27.2.2019	8	1958–1962	151	65	0	10.06	–	–	–/–	–	4	
Pocock Blair Andrew	18.6.1971		15	1993–1997	665	85	0	22.93	0	0-10	0/0	–	5	
Pollard Victor	7.9.1945		32	1964–1973	1,266	116	2	24.34	40	3-3	0/0	46.32	19	3
Poore Matt Beresford	1.6.1930		14	1952–1955	355	45	0	15.43	9	2-28	0/0	40.77	1	
Priest Mark Wellings.	12.8.1961		3	1990–1997	56	26	0	14.00	3	2-42	0/0	52.66	0	18
Pringle Christopher.	26.1.1968		14	1990–1994	175	30	0	10.29	30	7-52	1/1	46.30	3	64
Puna Narotam ("Tom").	28.10.1929	7.6.1996	3	1965	31	18*	0	15.50	4	2-40	0/0	60.00	1	
Rabone Geoffrey Osborne . . .	6.11.1921	19.1.2006	12	1949–1954	562	107	1	31.22	16	6-68	1/0	39.68	5	
Raval Jeet Ashokbhai	22.5.1988		24	2016–2019	1,143	132	1	30.07	1	1-33	0/0	34.00	21	
3 Redmond Aaron James	23.9.1979		8	2008–2013	325	83	0	21.66	3	2-47	0/0	26.66	5	6/7
1 Redmond Rodney Ernest.	29.12.1944		1	1972	163	107	1	81.50	–	–	–/–	–	0	2
Reid John Fulton.	3.3.1956		19	1978–1985	1,296	180	6	46.28	–	–	–/–	–	9	25
Reid John Richard OBE (CY 1959).	3.6.1928		58	1949–1965	3,428	142	6	33.28	85	6-60	1/0	33.35	43/1	
Richardson Mark Hunter	11.6.1971		38	2000–2004	2,776	145	4	44.77	4	1-16	0/0	21.00	26	4
Roberts Albert William	20.8.1909	13.5.1978	5	1929–1937	248	66*	0	27.55	7	4-101	0/0	29.85	4	
Roberts Andrew Duncan Glenn .	6.5.1947	26.10.1989	7	1975–1976	254	84*	0	23.09	4	1-12	0/0	45.50	4	6/7
Robertson Gary Keith.	15.7.1960		1	1985	12	12	0	12.00	1	1-91	0/0	91.00	0	1
Ronchi Luke	23.4.1981		4	2015–2016	319	88	0	39.87	–	–	–/–	–	5	10
													81‡/29‡	

	Born	Died	Tests	Test Career	Runs	HS	100s	Avge	Wkts	BB	5/10	Avge	Ct/St	O/T
Rowe Charles Gordon	30.6.1915	9.6.1995		1945	0	0	0	0.00	–	–	–/–	–	–	
Rutherford Hamish Duncan	27.4.1989		16	2012–2014	755	171	1	26.96	0	0-2	0/0	–	11	4/8
Rutherford Kenneth Robert	26.10.1965		56	1984–1994	2,465	107*	3	27.08	1	1-38	0/0	161.00	32	121
Ryder Jesse Daniel	6.8.1984		18	2008–2011	1,269	201	3	40.93	5	2-7	0/0	56.00	12	48/22
Santner Mitchell Josef	5.2.1992		22	2015–2019	741	126	0	25.55	39	3-53	0/0	44.71	14	69/39
Scott Roy Hamilton	6.3.1917	5.8.2005	1	1946	18	18	0	18.00	1	1-74	0/0	74.00	0	
Scott Verdun John	31.7.1916	2.8.1980	10	1945–1951	458	84	0	28.62	0	0-5	0/0	–	7	
Sewell David Graham	20.10.1977		1	1997	1	1*	0	–	0	0-9	0/0	–	0	
Shrimpton Michael John Froud	23.6.1940	13.6.2015	10	1962–1973	265	46	0	13.94	5	3-35	0/0	31.60	2	
Sinclair Barry Whitley	23.10.1936		21	1962–1967	1,148	138	3	29.43	2	2-32	0/0	16.00	8	
Sinclair Ian McKay	1.6.1933		2	1955	25	18*	0	8.33	1	1-79	0/0	120.00	0	
Sinclair Mathew Stuart	9.11.1975		33	1999–2009	1,635	214	3	32.05	0	0-1	0/0	–	31	54/2
Smith Frank Brunton	13.3.1922	6.7.1997	4	1946–1951	237	96	0	47.40	–	–	–/–	–		
Smith Horace Dennis	8.1.1913	25.11.1986	1	1932	4	4	0	4.00	0	1-113	0/0	113.00		
Smith Ian David Stockley MBE	28.2.1957		63	1980–1991	1,815	173	2	25.56	0	0-5	0/0	–	168/8	98
Snedden Colin Alexander	7.1.1918	23.4.2011	1	1946	–	–	–	–	1	0-46	0/0	–	0	
Snedden Martin Colin	23.11.1958		25	1980–1990	327	33*	–	14.86	58	5-68	1/0	37.91	7	93
Sodhi Inderbir Singh ("Ish")	31.10.1992		17	2013–2018	448	63	0	21.33	41	4-60	0/0	48.58	11	31/40
Somerville William Edgar Richard	9.8.1984		4	2018–2019	72	40*	0	18.00	15	4-75	0/0	32.46	0	
Southee Timothy Grant	11.12.1988		71	2007–2019	1,662	77*	0	17.68	270	7-64	9/1	29.82	52	140/66
Sparling John Trevor	24.7.1938		11	1958–1963	229	50	0	12.72	5	1-9	0/0	65.40	4	
Spearman Craig Murray	4.7.1972		19	1995–2000	922	112	1	26.34	0	–	–/–	–	21	51
Stead Gary Raymond	9.1.1972		5	1998–1999	278	78	0	34.75	–	0-1	0/0	–	2	
Stirling Derek Alexander	5.10.1961		6	1984–1986	108	26	0	15.42	13	4-88	0/0	46.23		6
Styris Scott Bernard	10.7.1975		29	2002–2007	1,586	170	5	36.04	20	3-28	0/0	50.75	23	188/31
Su'a Murphy Logo	7.11.1966		13	1991–1994	165	44	0	12.69	36	5-73	2/0	38.25	8	12
Sutcliffe Bert MBE (CY 1950)	17.11.1923	20.4.2001	42	1946–1965	2,727	230*	5	40.10	4	2-38	0/0	86.00	20	
Taylor Bruce Richard	12.7.1943		30	1964–1973	898	124	2	20.40	111	7-74	4/0	26.60	10	
Taylor Donald Dougald	2.3.1923	5.12.1980	3	1946–1955	159	77	0	31.80	–	–	–/–	–	2	
Taylor Luteru Ross Poutoa Lote	8.3.1984		99	2007–2019	7,174	290	19	46.28	2	2-4	0/0	24.00	145	228/95
Thomson Keith	26.2.1941		2	1967	94	69	0	31.33	–	–	–/–	–	7	
Thomson Shane Alexander	27.1.1969		19	1989–1995	958	120*	2	30.90	19	1-9	0/0	50.15		56
Tindill Eric William Thomas	18.12.1910	1.8.2010	5	1937–1946	73	37*	0	9.12	–	–	–/–	–	6/1	
Troup Gary Bertram	3.10.1952		15	1976–1985	55	13*	0	4.58	39	6-95	1/1	37.28		22
Truscott Peter Bennetts	14.8.1941		1	1964	29	26	0	14.50	–	–	–/–	–		
Tuffey Daryl Raymond	11.6.1978		26	1999–2009	427	80*	0	16.42	77	6-54	2/0	31.75	15	94/3

	Born	Died	Tests	Test Career	Runs	HS	100s	Avge	Wkts	BB	5/10	Avge	Ct/St	O/T
Turner Glenn Maitland (CY 1971)	26.5.1947		41	1968-1982	2,991	259	7	44.64	0	0-5	0/0	–	42	41
Twose Roger Graham	17.4.1968		16	1995-1999	628	94	0	25.12	3	2-36	0/0	43.33	5	87
Vance Robert Howard	31.3.1955		4	1987-1989	207	68	0	29.57	–	–	–/–	–	0	8
Van Wyk Cornelius Francois Kruger	7.2.1980		9	2011-2012	341	71	0	21.31	–	–	–/–	–	23/1	
Vaughan Justin Thomas Caldwell	30.8.1967		6	1992-1996	201	44	0	18.27	11	4-27	0/0	40.90	4	18
Vettori Daniel Luca	27.1.1979		112§	1996-2014	4,523	140	6	30.15	361	7-87	20/3	34.15	58	291±/34
Vincent Lou	11.11.1978		23	2001-2007	1,332	224	3	34.15	0	0-2	0/0	–	19	102/9
Vivian Graham Ellery	28.2.1946		5	1964-1971	110	43	0	18.33	1	1-14	0/0	107.00	3	1
Vivian Henry Gifford	4.11.1912	12.8.1983	7	1931-1937	421	100	1	42.10	17	4-58	0/0	37.23	4	
Wadsworth Kenneth John	30.11.1946	19.8.1976	33	1969-1975	1,010	80	0	21.48	–	–	–/–	–	92/4	13
Wagner Neil	13.3.1986		47	2012-2019	554	47	0	12.31	204	7-39	9/0	26.63	12	
Walker Brooke Graeme Keith	25.3.1977		5	2000-2002	118	27*	0	19.66	5	2-92	0/0	79.80	0	11
Wallace Walter Mervyn	19.12.1916	21.3.2008	13	1937-1952	439	66	0	20.90	0	0-5	0/0	–	5	
Walmsley Kerry Peter	23.8.1973		5	1994-2000	13	5	0	2.60	9	3-70	0/0	43.44	0	2
Ward John Thomas	11.3.1937		8	1963-1967	75	35*	0	12.50	–	–	–/–	–	16/1	
Watling Bradley-John	9.7.1985		68	2009-2019	3,644	205	8	39.18	–	–	–/–	–	229/8	28/5
Watson William	31.8.1965		15	1986-1993	60	11	0	5.00	40	6-78	1/0	34.67	4	61
Watt Leslie	17.9.1924	15.11.1996	1	1954	2	2	0	1.00	–	–	–/–	–	0	
Webb Murray George	22.6.1947		3	1970-1973	12	12	0	6.00	4	2-114	0/0	117.75	0	
Webb Peter Neil	14.7.1957		2	1979	11	5	0	3.66	–	–	–/–	–	2	
Weir Gordon Lindsay	2.6.1908	31.10.2003	11	1929-1937	416	74*	0	29.71	7	3-38	0/0	29.85	3	5
White David John	26.6.1961		2	1990	31	18	0	7.75	0	0-5	0/0	–	0	
Whitelaw Paul Erskine	10.2.1910	28.8.1988	2	1932	64	30	0	32.00	–	–	–/–	–	3	3
Williamson Kane Stuart (CY 2016)	8.8.1990		78	2010-2019	6,379	242*	21	51.44	29	4-44	0/0	40.62	71	149/57
Wiseman Paul John	4.5.1970		25	1997-2004	366	36	0	14.07	61	5-82	2/0	47.59	11	15
Wright John Geoffrey MBE	5.7.1954		82	1977-1992	5,334	185	12	37.82	0	0-1	0/0	–	38	149
Young Bryan Andrew	3.11.1964		35	1993-1998	2,034	267*	2	31.78	–	–	–/–	–	54	74
Young Reece Alan	15.9.1979		5	2010-2011	169	57	0	24.14	–	–	–/–	–	8	
Yuile Bryan William	29.10.1941		17	1962-1969	481	64	0	17.81	34	4-43	0/0	35.67	12	

§ *Vettori's figures exclude eight runs and one wicket for the ICC World XI v Australia in the Super Series Test in 2005-06.*

INDIA (296 players)

	Born	Died	Tests	Test Career	Runs	HS	100s	Avge	Wkts	BB	5/10	Avge	Ct/St	O/T
Aaron Varun Raymond	29.10.1989		9	2011–2015	35	9	0	3.88	18	3-97	0/0	52.61	9	9
Abid Ali Syed	9.9.1941		29	1967–1974	1,018	81	0	20.36	47	6-55	1/0	42.12	32	5
Adhikari Hemchandra Ramachandra	31.7.1919	25.10.2003	21	1947–1958	872	114*	1	31.14	3	3-68	0/0	27.33	8	
Agarkar Ajit Bhalchandra	4.12.1977		26	1998–2005	571	109*	1	16.79	58	6-41	1/0	47.32	6	191/4
Agarwal Mayank Anurag	16.2.1991		7	2018–2019	872	243	3	67.07	–	–	–/–	–	7	
¹,² Amar Singh Ladha	4.12.1910	21.5.1940	7	1932–1936	292	51	0	22.46	28	7-86	2/0	30.64	3	
¹,² Amarnath Mohinder (CY 1984)	24.9.1950		69	1969–1987	4,378	138	11	42.50	32	4-63	0/0	55.68	47	85
¹,² Amarnath Nanik ("Lala")	11.9.1911	5.8.2000	24	1933–1952	878	118	1	24.38	45	5-96	2/0	32.91	13	
¹,² Amarnath Surinder	30.12.1948		10	1975–1978	550	124	1	30.55	1	1-5	0/0	5.00	4	3
Amir Elahi	1.9.1908	28.12.1980	1†	1947	17	13	0	8.50	–	–	–/–	–	0	
Amre Pravin Kalyan	14.8.1968		11	1992–1993	425	103	1	42.50	0	–	–/–	–	9	37
Ankola Salil Ashok	1.3.1968		1	1989	6	6	0	6.00	2	1-35	0/0	64.00	0	20
² Apte Arvindrao Laxmanrao	24.10.1934	5.8.2014	1	1959	15	8	0	7.50	0	–	–/–	–	0	
² Apte Madhavrao Laxmanrao	5.10.1932	23.9.2019	7	1952	542	163*	1	49.27	0	0-3	0/0	–	2	
Arshad Ayub	2.8.1958		13	1987–1989	257	57	0	17.13	41	5-50	3/0	35.07	2	32
Arun Bharathi	14.12.1962		2	1986	4	2*	0	4.00	4	3-76	0/0	29.00	2	4
Arun Lal	1.8.1955		16	1982–1988	729	93	0	26.03	0	0-0	0/0	–	13	13
Ashwin Ravichandran	17.9.1986		70	2011–2019	2,385	124	4	28.73	362	7-59	27/7	25.36	24	111/46
Azad Kirtivardhan	2.1.1959		7	1980–1983	135	24	0	11.25	3	2-84	0/0	124.33	3	25
Azharuddin Mohammad (CY 1991)	8.2.1963		99	1984–1999	6,215	199	22	45.03	0	0-4	0/0	–	105	334
Badani Hemang Kamal	14.11.1976		4	2001	94	38	0	15.66	0	0-17	0/0	–	6	40
Badrinath Subramaniam	30.8.1980		2	2009	63	56	0	21.00	–	–	–/–	–	2	7/1
Bahutule Sairaj Vasant	6.1.1973		2	2000–2001	39	21*	0	13.00	3	1-32	0/0	67.66	1	8
Baig Abbas Ali	19.3.1939		10	1959–1966	428	112	1	23.77	0	0-2	0/0	–	6	
Balaji Lakshmipathy	27.9.1981		8	2003–2004	51	31	0	5.66	27	5-76	1/0	37.18	2	30/5
Banerjee Sarodindu Nath ("Shute")	3.10.1911	14.10.1980	1	1948	13	8	0	6.50	5	4-54	0/0	25.40	0	
Banerjee Subroto Tara	13.2.1969		1	1991	3	3	0	3.00	3	3-47	0/0	15.66	0	6
Banerjee Sudangsu Abinash	1.11.1917	14.9.1992	1	1948	0	0	0	0.00	5	4-120	0/0	36.20	0	
Bangar Sanjay Bapusaheb	11.10.1972		12	2001–2002	470	100*	1	29.37	7	2-23	0/0	49.00	4	15
Baqa Jilani Mohammad	20.7.1911	2.7.1941	1	1936	16	12	0	16.00	0	0-55	0/0	–	0	
Bedi Bishan Singh	25.9.1946		67	1966–1979	656	50*	0	8.98	266	7-98	14/1	28.71	26	10
Bhandari Prakash	27.11.1935		3	1954–1956	77	39	0	19.25	0	0-12	0/0	–	1	10
Bharadwaj Raghvendrarao Vijay	15.8.1975		3	1999	28	22	0	9.33	1	1-26	0/0	107.00	3	10

	Born	Died	Tests	Test Career	Runs	HS	100s	Avge	Wkts	BB	5/10	Avge	Ct/St	O/T
Bhat Adwai Raghuram	16.4.1958		2	1983	6	6	0	3.00	4	2-65	0/0	37.75	0	—
Bhuvneshwar Kumar	5.2.1990		21	2012-2017	552	63*	0	22.08	63	6-82	4/0	26.09	8	114/43
Binny Roger Michael Humphrey	19.7.1955		27	1979-1986	830	83*	0	23.05	47	6-56	2/0	32.63	11	72
Binny Stuart Terence Roger	3.6.1984		6	2014-2015	194	78	0	21.55	3	2-24	0/0	86.00	4	14/3
Borde Chandrakant Gulabrao	21.7.1934		55	1958-1969	3,061	177*	5	35.59	52	5-88	1/0	46.48	37	
Bumrah Jasprit Jasbirsingh	6.12.1993		12	2017-2019	18	6	0	2.00	62	6-27	5/0	19.24	3	58/42
Chandrasekhar Bhagwat Subramanya (CY 1972)	17.5.1945		58	1963-1979	167	22	0	4.07	242	8-79	16/2	29.74	25	1
Chauhan Chetandra Pratap Singh	21.7.1947		40	1969-1980	2,084	97	0	31.57	2	1-4	0/0	53.00	38	7
Chauhan Rajesh Kumar	19.12.1966		21	1992-1997	98	23	0	7.00	47	4-48	0/0	39.51	12	35
Chawla Piyush Pramod	24.12.1988		3	2005-2012	6	4	0	2.00	7	4-69	0/0	38.57	1	25/7
Chopra Aakash	19.9.1977		10	2003-2004	437	60	0	23.00	—	—	—/—	–	15	
Chopra Nikhil	26.12.1973		1	1999	7	4	0	3.50	0	0-78	0/0	–	0	39
Chowdhury Nirode Ranjan	23.5.1923	14.12.1979	2	1948-1951	3	3*	0	3.00	1	1-130	0/0	205.00	0	
Colah Sorabji Hormasji Munchersha	22.9.1902	11.9.1950	2	1932-1933	69	31	0	17.25	—	—	—/—	–	2	
Contractor Nariman Jamshedji	7.3.1934		31	1955-1961	1,611	108	1	31.58	1	1-9	0/0	80.00	18	
Dahiya Vijay	10.5.1973		2	2000	2	2*	0	–	—	—	—/—	–	6	19
Dani Hemchandra Tukaram	24.5.1933		1	1952	—	—	—	–	1	1-9	0/0	19.00	1	
Das Shiv Sunder	5.11.1977		23	2000-2001	1,326	110	2	34.89	0	0-7	0/0	–	34	4
Dasgupta Deep	7.6.1977		8	2001	344	100	1	28.66	—	—	—/—	–	13	5
Desai Ramakant Bhikaji	20.6.1939	27.4.1998	28	1958-1967	418	85	0	13.48	74	6-56	2/0	37.31	9	
Dhawan Shikhar (CY 2014)	5.12.1985		34	2012-2018	2,315	190	7	40.61	0	0-0	0/0	–	28	133/58
Dhoni Mahendra Singh	7.7.1981		90	2005-2014	4,876	224	6	38.09	0	0-1	0/0	–	256/38	347‡/98
Dighe Sameer Sudhakar	8.10.1968		6	2000-2001	141	47	0	15.66	—	—	—/—	–	12/2	23
Dilawar Hussain	19.3.1907	26.8.1967	3	1933-1936	254	59	0	42.33	—	—	—/—	–	6/1	
Divecha Ramesh Vithaldas	18.10.1927	11.2.2003	5	1951-1952	60	26	0	12.00	11	3-102	0/0	32.81	5	
Doshi Dilip Rasiklal	22.12.1947		33	1979-1983	129	20	0	4.60	114	6-102	6/0	30.71	10	15
Dravid Rahul (CY 2000)	11.1.1973		163§	1996-2011	13,265	270	36	52.63	1	1-18	0/0	39.00	209	340‡/1
Durani Salim Aziz	11.12.1934		29	1959-1972	1,202	104	1	25.04	75	6-73	3/1	35.42	14	
Engineer Farokh Maneksha	25.2.1938		46	1961-1974	2,611	121	2	31.08	—	—	—/—	–	66/16	5
Gadkari Chandrasekhar Vaman	3.2.1928	11.1.1998	6	1952-1954	129	50*	0	21.50	0	0-8	0/0	–	6	
Gaekwad Anshuman Dattajirao	23.9.1952		40	1974-1984	1,985	201	2	30.07	2	1-4	0/0	93.50	15	15
Gaekwad Dattajirao Krishnarao	27.10.1928		11	1952-1960	350	52	0	18.42	0	0-4	0/0	–	5	
Gaekwad Hiralal Ghasulal	29.8.1923	2.1.2003	1	1952	22	14	0	11.00	0	0-47	0/0	–	0	
Gambhir Gautam	14.10.1981		58	2004-2016	4,154	206	9	41.95	0	0-4	0/0	–	38	147/37

§ *Dravid's figures exclude 23 runs and one catch for the ICC World XI v Australia in the Super Series Test in 2005-06.*

	Born	Died	Tests	Test Career	Runs	HS	100s	Avge	Wkts	BB	5/10	Avge	Ct/St	O/T
Gandhi Devang Jayant	6.9.1971		4	1999	204	88	0	34.00	0	0-5	0/0	–	3	3
Gandotra Ashok	24.11.1948		2	1969	54	54	0	13.50	0		0/0	–	3	
Ganesh Doddanarasiah	30.6.1973		4	1996	25	8	0	6.25	5	2-28	0/0	57.40	1	1
Ganguly Sourav Chandidas	8.7.1972		113	1996–2008	7,212	239	16	42.17	32	3-28	0/0	52.53	71	308‡
Gavaskar Sunil Manohar (CY 1980)	10.7.1949		125	1970–1986	10,122	236*	34	51.12	1	1-34	0/0	206.00	108	108
Ghavri Karsan Devjibhai	28.2.1951		39	1974–1980	913	86	0	21.23	109	5-33	4/0	33.54	16	19
Chorpade Jayasinghrao Mansinghrao	2.10.1930	29.3.1978	8	1952–1959	229	41	0	15.26	0	0-17	0/0	–	4	
Ghulam Ahmed	4.7.1922	28.10.1998	22	1948–1958	192	50	0	8.72	68	7-49	4/1	30.17	11	
Gopalan Morappakam Joysam	6.6.1909	21.12.2003	1	1933	18	11*	0	18.00	1	1-39	0/0	39.00	3	
Gopinath Coimbatarao Doraikannu	1.3.1930		8	1951–1959	242	50*	0	22.00	1	1-11	0/0	11.00	2	
Guard Ghulam Mustafa	12.12.1925	13.3.1978	2	1958–1959	11	7	0	5.50	3	2-69	0/0	60.66	2	
Guha Subrata	31.1.1946	5.11.2003	4	1967–1969	17	6	0	3.40	3	2-55	0/0	103.66	2	
Gul Mahomed	15.10.1921	8.5.1992	8†	1946–1952	166	34	0	11.06	2	2-21	0/0	12.00	3	
Gupte Balkrishna Pandharinath	30.8.1934	5.7.2005	3	1960–1964	28	17*	0	28.00	3	1-54	0/0	116.33	3	
[2] Gupte Subhashchandra Pandharinath ("Fergie")	11.12.1929	31.5.2002	36	1951–1961	183	21	0	6.31	149	9-102	12/1	29.55	14	
Gursharan Singh	8.3.1963		1	1989	18	18	0	18.00	–	–	–	–	2	1
Hafeez Abdul (see Kardar)														
Hanumant Singh	29.3.1939	29.11.2006	14	1963–1969	686	105	1	31.18	0	0-5	0/0	–	11	
Harbhajan Singh	3.7.1980		103	1997–2015	2,224	115	2	18.22	417	8-84	25/5	32.46	42	234‡/28
Hardikar Manohar Shankar	8.2.1936	4.2.1995	2	1958	56	32*	0	18.66	1	1-9	0/0	55.00	3	
Harvinder Singh	23.12.1977		3	1997–2001	6	6	0	2.00	4	2-62	0/0	46.25	0	16
Hazare Vijay Samuel	11.3.1915	18.12.2004	30	1946–1952	2,192	164*	7	47.65	20	4-29	0/0	61.00	11	
Hindlekar Dattaram Dharmaji	1.1.1909	30.3.1949	4	1936–1946	71	26	0	14.20	0		–/–	–	3	
Hirwani Narendra Deepchand	18.10.1968		17	1987–1996	54	17	0	5.40	66	8-61	4/1	30.10	5	18
Ibrahim Khanmohammad Cassumbhoy	26.1.1919	12.11.2007	4	1948	169	85	0	21.12	–		–/–	–	0	
Indrajitsinhji Kumar Shri	15.6.1937	12.3.2011	4	1964–1969	51	23	0	8.50	–		–/–	–	6/3	
Irani Jamshed Khudadad	18.8.1923	25.2.1982	2	1947	3	2*	0	3.00	–		–/–	–	2/1	
Jadeja Ajaysinhji	1.2.1971		15	1992–1999	576	96	0	26.18	1	1-45	–/–	–	5	196
Jadeja Ravindrasinh Anirudhsinh	6.12.1988		48	2012–2019	1,844	100*	1	35.46	211	7-48	9/1	24.64	34	159/46
Jahangir Khan Mohammad	1.2.1910	23.7.1988	4	1932–1936	39	13	0	5.57	4	4-60	0/0	63.75	4	
[3] Jai Laxmidas Purshottamdas	1.4.1902	29.1.1968	5	1933	19	19	0	9.50	–		–/–	–	0	
Jaisimha Motganhalli Laxmanarsu	3.3.1939	6.7.1999	39	1959–1970	2,056	129	3	30.68	9	2-54	0/0	92.11	17	
Jamshedji Rustomji Jamshedji Dorabji	18.11.1892	5.4.1976	1	1933	5	4*	0	–	3	3-137	0/0	45.66	2	
Jayantilal Kenia	13.1.1948		1	1970	5	5	0	5.00	–		–/–	–	2	
Johnson David Jude	16.10.1971		2	1996	8	5	0	4.00	3	2-52	0/0	47.66	0	
Joshi Padmanabh Govind	27.10.1926	8.1.1987	12	1951–1960	207	52*	0	10.89	–		–/–	–	18/9	

Name	Born	Died	Tests	Test Career	Runs	HS	100s	Avge	Wkts	BB	5/I	Avge	Ct/St	O/T
Joshi Sunil Bandacharya	6.6.1970	—	15	1996–2000	352	92	0	20.70	41	5-142	1/0	35.85	7	69
Kaif Mohammad	1.12.1980	—	13	1999–2005	624	148*	1	32.84	0	0-4	0/0	—	14	125
Kambli Vinod Ganpat	18.1.1972	—	17	1992–1995	1,084	227	4	54.20	—	—	—	—	7	104
Kanitkar Hrishikesh Hemant	14.11.1974	—	2	1999	74	45	0	18.50	0	0-2	0/0	—	1	34
Kanitkar Hemant Shamsunder	8.12.1942	9.6.2015	2	1974	111	65	0	27.75	—	—	—	—	0	—
Kapil Dev (CY 1983)	6.1.1959	—	131	1978–1993	5,248	163	8	31.05	434	9-83	23/2	29.64	64	225
Kapoor Aashish Rakesh	25.3.1971	—	4	1994–1996	97	42	0	19.40	6	2-19	—/—	42.50	2	17
Kardar Abdul Hafeez	17.1.1925	21.4.1996	3†	1946	80	43	0	16.00	—	—	—	—	0	—
Karim Syed Saba	14.11.1967	—	1	2000	15	15	0	15.00	—	—	—	—	3/1	34
Karthik Krishankumar Dinesh	1.6.1985	—	26	2004–2018	1,025	129	2	25.00	—	—	—	—	57/6	94/31‡
Kartik Murali	11.9.1976	—	8	1999–2004	88	43	0	9.77	24	4-44	0/0	34.16	2	37/1
Kenny Kannath Baburao	29.9.1930	21.11.1985	5	1958–1959	245	62	0	27.22	—	—	—	—	2	—
Kirmani Syed Mujtaba Hussein	29.12.1949	—	88	1975–1985	2,759	102	2	27.04	1	1-9	0/0	13.00	160/38	49
Kischenchand Gogumal	14.4.1925	16.4.1997	12	1947–1952	89	44	0	8.90	—	—	—	—	1	—
Kohli Virat (CY 2019)	5.11.1988	—	84	2011–2019	7,202	254*	27	54.97	0	0-0	0/0	—	80	242/75
Kripal Singh Amritsar Govindsingh	6.8.1933	22.7.1987	14	1955–1964	422	100*	1	28.13	10	3-43	0/0	58.40	4	—
Krishnamurthy Pochiah	12.7.1947	28.1.1999	5	1970	33	20	0	5.50	—	—	—	—	7/1	—
Kulkarni Nilesh Moreshwar	3.4.1973	—	3	1997–2000	5	4	0	5.00	2	1-70	0/0	166.00	0	1
Kulkarni Rajiv Ramesh	25.9.1962	—	4	1986	13	7	0	4.33	—	—	—	—	2	10
Kulkarni Umesh Narayan	7.3.1942	—	6	1967	6	6	0	1.00	5	2-37	0/0	47.60	0	—
Kumar Praveen	2.10.1986	—	6	2011	149	40	0	14.90	27	5-106	1/0	25.81	2	68/10
Kumar Vaman Viswanath	22.6.1935	—	2	1960–1961	6	6	0	3.00	7	5-64	1/0	28.85	0	—
Kumble Anil (CY 1996)	17.10.1970	—	132	1990–2008	2,506	110*	1	17.77	619	10-74	35/8	29.65	60	269‡
Kunderan Budhisagar Krishnappa	2.10.1939	23.6.2006	18	1959–1967	981	192	2	32.70	0	0-13	0/0	—	23/7	—
Kuruvilla Abey	8.8.1968	—	10	1996–1997	66	35*	0	6.60	25	5-68	1/0	35.68	5	25
Lall Singh	16.12.1909	19.11.1985	1	1932	44	29	0	22.00	—	—	—	—	1	—
Lamba Raman	2.1.1960	22.2.1998	4	1986–1987	102	53	0	20.40	—	—	—	—	0	32
Laxman Vangipurappu Venkata Sai (CY 2002)	1.11.1974	—	134	1996–2011	8,781	281	17	45.97	2	1-2	0/0	63.00	135	86
Madan Lal	20.3.1951	—	39	1974–1986	1,042	74	0	22.65	71	5-23	4/0	40.08	15	67
Maka Ebrahim Suleman	5.3.1922	7.9.1994	2	1952	2	2*	0	—	—	—	—	—	2/1	—
Malhotra Ashok Omprakash	26.1.1957	—	7	1981–1984	226	72*	0	25.11	0	0-0	—/—	—	2	20
Maninder Singh	13.6.1965	—	35	1982–1992	99	15	0	3.80	88	7-27	3/2	37.36	9	59
Manjrekar Sanjay Vijay	12.7.1965	—	37	1987–1996	2,043	218	4	37.14	—	—	—	—	25/1	74
Manjrekar Vijay Laxman	26.9.1931	18.10.1983	55	1951–1964	3,208	189*	7	39.12	1	1-16	0/0	44.00	19/2	—
Mankad Ashok Vinoo	12.10.1946	1.8.2008	22	1969–1977	991	97	0	25.41	0	0-0	0/0	—	12	1
Mankad Mulvantrai Himmatlal ("Vinoo") (CY 1947)	12.4.1917	21.8.1978	44	1946–1958	2,109	231	5	31.47	162	8-52	8/2	32.32	33	—

	Born	Died	Tests	Test Career	Runs	HS	100s	Avge	Wkts	BB	5/10	Avge	Ct/St	O/T
Mantri Madhav Krishnaji	1.9.1921	23.5.2014	4	1951–1954	67	39	0	9.57	—	—	—/—	—	8/1	
Meherhomji Khershedji Rustomji	9.8.1911	10.2.1982	1	1936	0	0*	0	—	—	—	—/—	—	1/-	
Mehra Vijay Laxman	12.3.1938	25.8.2006	8	1955–1963	329	62	0	25.30	0	0-1	0/0	—	1	
Merchant Vijay Madhavji (CY 1937)	12.10.1911	27.10.1987	10	1933–1951	859	154	3	47.72	0	0-17	0/0	—	7	3
Mhambrey Paras Laxmikant	20.6.1972		2	1996	58	28	0	29.00	2	1-43	0/0	74.00	1	
[2]Milkha Singh Amritsar Govindsingh	31.12.1941	10.11.2017	4	1959–1961	92	35	0	15.33	0	0-2	0/0	—	2	
Mishra Amit	24.11.1982		22	2008–2016	648	84	0	21.60	76	5-71	1/0	35.72	8	36/10
Mithun Abhimanyu	25.10.1989		4	2010–2011	120	46	0	24.00	9	4-105	0/0	50.66		5
Modi Rustomji Sheryar	11.11.1924	17.5.1996	10	1946–1952	736	112	1	46.00	0	0-14	0/0	—	3	
Mohammed Shami	3.9.1990		47	2013–2019	453	51*	0	11.04	175	6-56	4/0	27.09	10	73/8
Mohanty Debasis Sarbeswar	20.7.1976		2	1997	0	0*	0	—	4	4-78	0/0	59.75	0	45
Mongia Nayan Ramlal	19.12.1969		44	1993–2000	1,442	152	1	24.03	—	—	—/—	—	99/8	140
More Kiran Shankar	4.9.1962		49	1986–1993	1,285	73	0	25.70	—	—	—/—	—	110/20	94
Muddiah Venkatappa Musandra	8.6.1929	1.10.2009	2	1959–1960	11	11	0	5.50	3	2-40	0/0	44.66	0	
Mukund Abhinav	6.1.1990		7	2011–2017	320	81	0	22.85	0	0-12	0/0	—	6	
Mushtaq Ali Syed	17.12.1914	18.6.2005	11	1933–1951	612	112	2	32.21	3	1-45	0/0	67.33	7	
Nadeem Shahbaz	12.8.1989		2	2019	1	1*	0	—	4	2-18	0/0	10.00	0	
Nadkarni Rameshchandra Gangaram ("Bapu")	4.4.1933	17.1.2020	41	1955–1967	1,414	122*	1	25.70	88	6-43	1/0	29.07	22	
Naik Sudhir Sakharam	21.2.1945		3	1974–1974	141	77	0	23.50	0	—	—/—	—	0	2
Nair Karun Kaladharan	6.12.1991		6	2016	374	303*	1	62.33	0	0-4	0/0	—	6	2
Naoomal Jeoomal	17.4.1904	28.7.1980	3	1932–1933	108	20*	0	27.00	2	1-4	0/0	34.00	8	
Narasimha Rao Modireddy Venkateshwar	11.8.1954		4	1978–1979	46	13	0	9.20	3	2-46	0/0	75.66	1	4
Navle Janaradan Gyanoba	7.12.1902	7.9.1979	2	1932–1933	42	13	0	10.50	—	—	—/—	—		
Nayak Surendra Vithal	20.10.1954		2	1982	19	11	0	9.50	1	1-16	0/0	132.00	1	
[2]Nayudu Cottari Kanakaiya (CY 1933)	31.10.1895	14.11.1967	7	1932–1936	350	81	0	25.00	9	3-40	0/0	42.88	4	
[2]Nayudu Cottari Subbanna	18.4.1914	22.11.2002	11	1933–1951	147	36	0	9.18	2	1-19	0/0	179.50	4	
Nazir Ali Syed	8.6.1906	18.2.1975	2	1932–1933	30	13	0	7.50	4	4-83	0/0	20.75		
Nehra Ashish	29.4.1979		17	1998–2003	77	19	0	5.50	44	4-72	0/0	42.40	5	117‡27
Nissar Mohammad	1.8.1910	11.3.1963	6	1932–1936	55	14	0	6.87	25	5-90	3/0	28.28	2	
Nyalchand Sukhlal Shah	14.9.1915	3.1.1997	1	1952	7	6*	0	7.00	3	3-97	0/0	32.33	0	
Ojha Naman Vijaykumar	20.7.1983		1	2015	56	35	0	28.00	—	—	—/—	—	4/1	1/2
Ojha Pragyan Prayish	5.9.1986		24	2009–2013	89	18*	0	8.90	113	6-47	7/1	30.26	10	18/6
Pai Ajit Manohar	28.4.1945		1	1969	10	9	0	5.00	2	2-29	0/0	15.50	0	
Palia Phiroze Edulji	5.9.1910	9.9.1981	2	1932–1936	29	16	0	9.66	0	0-2	0/0	—	0	
Pandit Chandrakant Sitaram	30.9.1961		5	1986–1991	171	39	0	24.42	—	—	—/—	—	14/2	36
Pandya Hardik Himanshu	11.10.1993		11	2017–2018	532	108	1	31.29	17	5-28	1/0	31.05	7	54/40

	Born	Died	Tests	Test Career	Runs	HS	100s	Avge	Wkts	BB	5/10	Avge	Ct/St	O/T
Pankaj Singh	6.5.1985		2	2014	10	10	0	3.33	2	2-113	0/0	146.00	2	1
Pant Rishabh Rajendra	4.10.1997		11	2018–2019	754	159*	2	44.35	–	–	–/–	–	51/2	15/26
Parkar Ghulam Ahmed	25.10.1955		1	1982	7	6	0	3.50	–	–	–/–	–	0	10
Parkar Ramnath Dhondu	31.10.1946		2	1972	80	35	0	20.00	–	–	–/–	–	0	
Parsana Dhiraj Devshibhai	2.12.1947	11.8.1999	2	1978	1	1	0	0.50	1	1-32	0/0	50.00	0	
Patankar Chandrakant Trimbak	24.11.1930		1	1955	14	13	0	14.00	–	–	–/–	–	3/1	
Pataudi Iftikhar Ali Khan, Nawab of (CY 1932)	16.3.1910	5.1.1952	3†	1946	55	22	0	11.00	–	–	–/–	–	0	1
Pataudi Mansur Ali Khan, Nawab of (CY 1968)	5.1.1941	22.9.2011	46	1961–1974	2,793	203*	6	34.91	1	1-10	0/0	88.00	27	
Patel Brijesh Pursuram	24.11.1952		21	1974–1977	972	115*	1	29.45	–	–	–/–	–	17	10
Patel Jasubhai Motibhai	26.11.1924	12.12.1992	7	1954–1959	25	12	0	2.77	29	9-69	2/1	21.96	2	
Patel Munaf Musa	12.7.1983		13	2005–2011	60	15*	0	7.50	35	4-25	0/0	38.54	6	70/3
Patel Parthiv Ajay	9.3.1985		25	2002–2017	934	71	0	31.13	–	–	–/–	–	62/10	38/2
Patel Rashid	1.6.1964		1	1988	0	0	0	0.00	0	0-14	0/0	–	0	
Pathan Irfan Khan	27.10.1984		29	2003–2007	1,105	102	1	31.57	100	7-59	7/2	32.26	8	120/24
Patiala Maharajah of (Yadavendra Singh)	17.1.1913	17.6.1974	1	1933	84	60	0	42.00	–	–	–/–	–	2	
Patil Sadashiv Raoji	10.10.1933		1	1955	14	14*	0	–	2	1-15	0/0	25.50	1	
Patil Sandeep Madhusudan	18.8.1956		29	1979–1984	1,588	174	4	36.93	9	2-28	0/0	26.66	12	45
Phadkar Dattatraya Gajanan	12.12.1925	17.3.1985	31	1947–1958	1,229	123	2	32.34	62	7-159	3/0	36.85	21	
Powar Ramesh Rajaram	20.5.1978		2	2007	13	7	0	6.50	6	3-33	0/0	19.66	0	31
Prabhakar Manoj	15.4.1963		39	1984–1995	1,600	120	1	32.65	96	6-132	3/0	37.30	20	130
Prasad Bapu Krishnarao Venkatesh	5.8.1969		33	1996–2001	203	30*	0	7.51	96	6-33	7/1	35.00	6	161
Prasad Mannava Sri Kanth	24.4.1975		6	1999	106	19	0	11.77	–	–	–/–	–	15	17
Prasanna Erapalli Anatharao Srinivas	22.5.1940		49	1961–1978	735	37	0	11.48	189	8-76	10/2	30.38	18	
Pujara Cheteshwar Arvind	25.1.1988		75	2010–2019	5,740	206*	18	49.48	0	0-2	0/0	–	50	5
Punjabi Pananmal Hotchand	20.9.1921	4.10.2011	5	1954	164	33	0	16.40	–	–	–/–	–	5	
Rahane Ajinkya Madhukar	6.6.1988		63	2012–2019	4,112	188	11	43.74	–	–	–/–	–	80	90/20
Rahul Kannur Lokesh	18.4.1992		36	2014–2019	2,006	199	5	34.58	–	–	–/–	–	46	26/34
Rai Singh Kanwar	24.2.1922	12.11.1993	1	1947	26	24	0	13.00	–	–	–/–	–	0	
Raina Suresh Kumar	27.11.1986		18	2010–2014	768	120	1	26.48	13	2-1	0/0	46.38	23	226/78
Rajinder Pal	18.11.1937	9.5.2018	1	1963	6	3*	0	6.00	0	0-3	0/0	–	1	
Rajindernath Vijay	7.1.1928	22.11.1989		1952									0/4	
Rajput Lalchand Sitaram	18.12.1961		2	1985	105	61	0	26.25	–	–	–/–	–	1	4
Raju Sagi Lakshmi Venkatapathy	9.7.1969		28	1989–2000	240	31	0	10.00	93	6-12	5/1	30.72	6	53
Raman Woorkeri Venkat	23.5.1965		11	1987–1996	448	96	0	24.88	2	1-7	0/0	64.50	6	27
Ramaswami Cotar	16.6.1896	1.1990	2	1936	170	60	0	56.66	–	–	–/–	–	0	
Ramchand Gulabrai Sipahimalani	26.7.1927	8.9.2003	33	1952–1959	1,180	109	2	24.58	41	6-49	1/0	46.31	20	

	Born	Died	Test Career	Tests	Runs	HS	100s	Avge	Wkts	BB	5/10	Avge	Ct/St	O/T
Ramesh Sadagoppan	16.10.1975		1998-2001	19	1,367	143	2	37.97	0	0-5	0/0		18	24
[2] Ranji Ladha	10.2.1900	20.12.1948	1933	1			0	0.50	0	0-64	0/0		1	
Rangachari Commandur Rajagopalachari	14.4.1916	9.10.1993	1947-1948	4	8	8*	0	2.66	9	5-107	1/0	54.77	1	
Rangnekar Khanderao Moreshwar	27.6.1917	11.10.1984	1947	3	33	18	0	5.50	0		-/-		1	
Ranjane Vasant Baburao	22.7.1937	22.12.2011	1958-1964	7	40	16	0	6.66	19	4-72	0/0	34.15	1	
Rathore Vikram	26.3.1969		1996-1996	6	131	44	0	13.10					12	7
Ratra Ajay	13.12.1981		2001-2002	6	163	115*	1	18.11	0	0-1	0/0		11/2	12
Razdan Vivek	25.8.1969		1989	2	6	6*	0	6.00	5	5-79	1/0	28.20	0	3
Reddy Bharath	12.11.1954		1979	4	38	21	0	9.50	0		-/-		9/2	3
Rege Madhusudan Ramachandra	18.3.1924	16.12.2013	1948	1	15	15	0	7.50	0		-/-		1	
Roy Ambar	5.6.1945	19.9.1997	1969	4	91	48	0	13.00	0		-/-			
Roy Pankaj	31.5.1928	4.2.2001	1951-1960	43	2,442	173	5	32.56	1	1-6	0/0	66.00	16	
[1] Roy Pranab	10.2.1957		1981	2	71	60*	0	35.50	0		-/-		1	
Saha Wriddhaman Prasanta	24.10.1984		2009-2019	37	1,238	117	3	30.19	0		-/-		92/11	9
Sandhu Balwinder Singh	3.8.1956		1982-1983	8	214	71	0	30.57	10	3-87	0/0	55.70	1	22
Sanghvi Rahul Laxman	3.9.1974		2000	1	0	0*	0	1.00	2	2-67	0/0	39.00		10
Sarandeep Singh	21.10.1979		2000-2001	3	43	39*	0	43.00	10	4-136	0/0	34.00	1	5
Sardesai Dilip Narayan	8.8.1940	2.7.2007	1961-1972	30	2,001	212	5	39.23	0	0-3	0/0		4	
Sarwate Chandrasekhar Trimbak	22.7.1920	23.12.2003	1946-1951	9	208	37	0	13.00	3	1-16	0/0	124.66	0	
Saxena Ramesh Chandra	20.9.1944	16.8.2011	1967	1	25	16	0	12.50	0	0-11	0/0		1	
Sehwag Virender	20.10.1978		2001-2012	103§	8,503	319	23	49.43	40	5-104	1/0	47.35	90	241†/19
Sekhar Thirumalai Ananthanpillai	28.3.1956		1982	2	8	0*	0		0	0-43	-/-			4
Sen Probir Kumar ("Khokhan")	31.5.1926	27.1.1970	1947-1952	14	165	25	0	11.78	0		-/-		20/11	
Sen Gupta Apoorva Kumar	3.8.1939	14.9.2013	1958	1	9	8	0	4.50	0		-/-			
Sharma Ajay Kumar	3.4.1964		1987	1	53	30	0	26.50	0	0-9	0/0		1	31
Sharma Chetan	3.1.1966		1984-1988	23	396	54	0	22.00	61	6-58	4/1	35.45	7	65
Sharma Gopal	3.8.1960		1984-1990	5	11	10*	0	3.66	10	4-88	0/0	41.80	2	11
Sharma Ishant	2.9.1988		2007-2019	96	703	57	0	8.36	292	7-74	10/1	32.68	21	80/14
Sharma Karan Vinod	23.10.1987		2014	1	8	4*	0	8.00	4	2-95	0/0	59.50		2/1
Sharma Parthasarathy Harishchandra	5.1.1948	20.10.2010	1974-1976	5	187	54	0	18.70	0		-/-		1	2
Sharma Rohit Gurunath	30.4.1987		2013-2019	32	2,141	212	6	46.54	2	1-26	0/0	108.00	31	221†/104
Sharma Sanjeev Kumar	25.8.1965		1988-1990	2	56	38	0	28.00	6	3-37	0/0	41.16	1	23
Shastri Ravishankar Jayadritha	27.5.1962		1980-1992	80	3,830	206	11	35.79	151	5-75	2/0	40.96	36	150
Shaw Prithvi Pankaj	9.11.1999		2018	2	237	134	1	118.50					2	
Shinde Sadashiv Ganpatrao	18.8.1923	22.6.1955	1946-1952	7	85	14	0	14.16	12	6-91	1/0	59.75	0	

§ Sehwag's figures exclude 83 runs and one catch for the ICC World XI v Australia in the Super Series Test in 2005-06.

	Born	Died	Tests	Test Career	Runs	HS	100s	Avge	Wkts	BB	5/10	Avge	Ct/St	O/T
Shodhan Roshan Harshadlal ("Deepak")	18.10.1928	16.5.2016	3	1952	181	110	1	60.33	0	0-1	0/0	–	1	–
Shukla Rakesh Chandra	4.2.1948	29.6.2019	1	1982	–	–	–	–	2	2-82	0/0	76.00	0	–
Siddiqui Iqbal Rashid	26.12.1974	–	1	2001	29	24	0	29.00	1	1-32	0/0	48.00	–	–
Sidhu Navjot Singh	20.10.1963	–	51	1983–1998	3,202	201	9	42.13	0	0-9	0/0	–	9	136
Singh Rabindra Ramanarayan ("Robin")	14.9.1963	–	1	1998	27	15	0	13.50	0	0-16	0/0	–	5	136
Singh Robin	1.1.1970	–	1	1998	0	0	0	0.00	3	2-74	0/0	58.66	–	–
Singh Rudra Pratap	6.12.1985	–	14	2005–2011	116	30	0	7.25	40	5-59	1/0	42.05	6	58/10
Singh Vikram Rajvir	17.9.1984	–	5	2005–2007	47	29	0	11.75	8	3-48	0/0	53.37	2	2
Sivaramakrishnan Laxman	31.12.1965	–	9	1982–1985	130	25	0	16.25	26	6-64	3/1	44.03	9	16
Sohoni Sriranga Wasudev	5.3.1918	19.5.1993	4	1946–1951	83	29*	0	16.60	2	1-16	0/0	101.00	2	–
Solkar Eknath Dhondu	18.3.1948	26.6.2005	27	1969–1976	1,068	102	1	25.42	18	3-28	0/0	59.44	53	7
Sood Man Mohan	6.7.1939	19.1.2020	1	1959	3	3	0	1.50	–	–	-/-	–	–	–
Sreesanth Shanthakumaran	6.2.1983	–	27	2005–2011	281	35	0	10.40	87	5-40	3/0	37.59	5	53/10
Srikkanth Krishnamachari	21.12.1959	–	43	1981–1991	2,062	123	2	29.88	0	0-1	0/0	–	40	146
Srinath Javagal	31.8.1969	–	67	1991–2002	1,009	76	0	14.21	236	8-86	10/1	30.49	22	229
Srinivasan Thirumalai Echambadi	26.10.1950	6.12.2010	2	1980	48	29	0	24.00	–	–	-/-	–	0	2
Subramanya Venkataraman	16.7.1936	–	9	1964–1967	263	75	0	18.78	3	2-32	0/0	67.00	9	–
Sunderram Gundibail Rama	29.3.1930	20.6.2010	2	1955	3	3*	0	–	3	2-46	0/0	55.33	–	–
Surendranath Raman	4.1.1937	5.5.2012	11	1958–1960	136	27	0	10.46	26	5-75	2/0	40.50	4	–
Surti Rusi Framroze	25.5.1936	13.1.2013	26	1960–1969	1,263	99	0	28.70	42	5-74	1/0	46.71	26	–
Swamy Venkataraman Narayan	23.5.1924	1.5.1983	1	1955	–	–	–	–	0	0-15	0/0	–	0	–
Tamhane Narendra Shankar	4.8.1931	19.3.2002	21	1954–1960	225	54*	0	10.22	–	–	-/-	–	35/16	–
Tarapore Keki Khurshedji	17.12.1910	15.6.1986	1	1948	2	2	0	2.00	0	0-72	0/0	–	–	–
Tendulkar Sachin Ramesh (CY 1997)	24.4.1973	–	200	1989–2013	15,921	248*	51	53.78	46	3-10	0/0	54.17	115	463/1
Thakur Shardul Narendra	16.10.1991	–	1	2018	4	4*	0	–	0	0-9	0/0	–	–	7/7
Umrigar Pahlanji Ratanji ("Polly")	28.3.1926	7.11.2006	59	1948–1961	3,631	223	12	42.22	35	6-74	2/0	42.08	33	–
Unadkat Jaydev Dipakbhai	18.10.1991	–	1	2010	1	1*	0	–	0	0-101	0/0	–	0	7/10
Vengsarkar Dilip Balwant (CY 1987)	6.4.1956	–	116	1975–1991	6,868	166	17	42.13	0	0-3	0/0	–	78	129
Venkataraghavan Srinivasaraghavan	21.4.1945	–	57	1964–1983	748	64	0	11.68	156	8-72	3/1	36.11	44	15
Venkataramana Margashayam	24.4.1966	–	1	1988	0	0*	0	–	1	1-10	0/0	58.00	–	–
Vihari Gade Hanuma	13.10.1993	–	7	2018–2019	466	111	1	42.36	5	3-37	0/0	36.00	1	–
Vijay Murali	1.4.1984	–	61	2008–2018	3,982	167	12	38.28	1	1-12	0/0	198.00	49	17/9
Vinay Kumar Ranganath	12.2.1984	–	1	2011	11	6	0	5.50	1	1-73	0/0	73.00	0	31/9
Viswanath Gundappa Ranganath	12.2.1949	–	91	1969–1982	6,080	222	14	41.93	1	1-11	0/0	46.00	63	25
Viswanath Sadanand	29.11.1962	–	3	1985	31	20	0	6.20	–	–	-/-	–	11	22
Vizianagram Maharajkumar of (Sir Vijaya Anand)	28.12.1905	2.12.1965	3	1936	33	19*	0	8.25	–	–	-/-	–	1	–

	Born	Died	Tests	Test Career	Runs	HS	100s	Avge	Wkts	BB	5/10	Avge	Ct/St	O/T
Wadekar Ajit Laxman	1.4.1941	15.8.2018	37	1966–1974	2,113	143	1	31.07	–	0-0	000	–	46	2
Wasim Jaffer	16.2.1978		31	1999–2007	1,944	212	5	34.10	2	2-18	000	9.00	27	2
Wassan Atul Satish	23.3.1968		4	1989–1990	94	53	0	23.50	10	4-108	000	50.40	1	9
¹·²Wazir Ali Syed	15.9.1903	17.6.1950	7	1932–1936	237	42	0	16.92	0	0-0	000	–	1	–
Yadav Jayant	22.1.1990		4	2016	228	104	1	45.60	11	3-30	000	33.36	3	1
Yadav Kuldeep	14.12.1994		6	2016–2018	51	26	0	8.50	24	5-57	2/0	24.12	1	56/19
Yadav Nandlal Shivlal	26.1.1957		35	1979–1986	403	43	0	14.39	102	5-76	3/0	35.09	10	7
Yadav Umeshkumar Tilak	25.10.1987		45	2011–2019	339	31	0	12.10	142	6-88	3/1	30.26	16	75/7
Yadav Vijay	14.3.1967		1	1992	30	30	0	30.00	0	–	–/–	–	1/2	19
Yajurvindra Singh	1.8.1952		4	1976–1979	109	43*	0	18.16	0	0-2	000	–	11	–
Yashpal Sharma	11.8.1954		37	1979–1983	1,606	140	2	33.45	1	1-6	000	17.00	16	42
¹Yograj Singh	25.3.1958		1	1980	10	6	0	5.00	1	1-63	000	63.00	–	6
Yohannan Tinu	18.2.1979		3	2001–2002	13	8*	0	–	5	2-56	000	51.20	1	–
¹Yuvraj Singh	12.12.1981		40	2003–2012	1,900	169	3	33.92	9	2-9	000	60.77	31	301½/58
Zaheer Khan (CY 2008)	7.10.1978		92	2000–2013	1,231	75	0	11.95	311	7-87	11/1	32.94	19	194½/17

PAKISTAN (240 players)

	Born	Died	Tests	Test Career	Runs	HS	100s	Avge	Wkts	BB	5/10	Avge	Ct/St	O/T
Aamer Malik	3.1.1963		14	1987–1994	565	117	2	35.31	1	1-0	000	89.00	15/1	24
Aamir Nazir	2.1.1971		6	1992–1995	31	11	0	6.20	20	5-46	1/0	29.85	2	9
Aamir Sohail	14.9.1966		47	1992–1999	2,823	205	5	35.28	25	4-54	000	41.96	36	156
Abdul Kadir	10.5.1944		4	1964	272	95	0	34.00	–	–	–/–	–	0/1	–
Abdul Qadir	15.9.1955	12.3.2002	67	1977–1990	1,029	61	0	15.59	236	9-56	15/5	32.80	15	104
Abdul Razzaq	2.12.1979		46	1999–2006	1,946	134	3	28.61	100	5-35	1/0	36.94	15	261½/32
Abdur Rauf	9.12.1978		3	2009–2009	52	31	0	8.66	6	2-59	000	46.33	0	4/1
Abdur Rehman	1.3.1980		22	2007–2014	395	60	0	14.10	99	6-25	2/0	29.39	8	31/8
Abid Ali	16.10.1987		2	2019	321	174	2	160.50	–	–	–/–	–	0	4
²Adnan Akmal	13.3.1985		21	2010–2013	591	64	0	24.62	0	1-40	000	106.00	66/11	5
Afaq Hussain	31.12.1939	25.2.2002	2	1961–1964	66	35*	0	–	1	0-2	000	–	2	–
Aftab Baloch	1.4.1953		2	1969–1974	97	60*	0	48.50	0	0-4	000	–	0	–
Aftab Gul	31.3.1946		6	1968–1971	182	33	0	22.75	–	–	–/–	–	3	–
Agha Saadat Ali	21.6.1929	25.10.1995	1	1955	8	8*	0	–	–	–	–/–	–	3	–
Agha Zahid	7.1.1953		1	1974	15	14	0	7.50	–	–	–/–	–	0	–
Ahmed Shehzad	23.11.1991		13	2013–2016	982	176	3	40.91	–	0-8	000	–	3	81/59

Name	Born	Died	Test Career	Tests	Runs	HS	100s	Avge	Wkts	BB	5/10	Avge	Ct/St	O/T
Aizaz Cheema	5.9.1979		2011–2012	7	1	1*	0	–	20	4-24	0/0	31.90	1	14/5
Akram Raza	22.11.1964		1989–1994	9	153	32	0	15.30	13	3-46	0/0	56.30	8	49
Ali Hussain Rizvi	6.1.1974		1997	1	–	–	–	–	2	2-72	0/0	36.00	1	
Ali Naqvi	19.3.1977		1997	5	242	115	1	30.25	2	0-11	0/0	–	0	
Alim-ud-Din	15.12.1930	12.7.2012	1954–1962	25	1,091	109	2	25.37	–	–	–	–	8	
Amir Elahi	1.9.1908	28.12.1980	1952	5†	65	47	0	10.83	7	4-134	0/0	75.00	1	15
Anil Dalpat	20.9.1963		1983–1984	9	167	52	0	15.18	–	–	–	–	22/3	
Anwar Hussain	16.7.1920	9.10.2002	1952	4	42	17	0	7.00	1	1-25	0/0	29.00	1	
Anwar Khan	24.12.1955		1978	1	15	12	0	15.00	0	0-12	0/0	–	0	
Aqib Javed	5.8.1972		1988–1998	22	101	28*	0	5.05	54	5-84	1/0	34.70	2	163
Arif Butt	17.5.1944	10.7.2007	1964	3	59	20	0	11.80	14	6-89	1/0	20.57	0	
Arshad Khan	22.3.1971		1997–2004	9	31	9*	0	5.16	32	5-38	1/0	30.00	2	58
Asad Shafiq	28.1.1986		2010–2019	73	4,528	137	12	39.03	2	1-7	0/0	80.00	71	60/10
Ashfaq Ahmed	6.6.1973		1993	1	–	–	0	1.00	2	2-31	0/0	26.50	0	3
Ashraf Ali	22.4.1958		1981–1987	8	229	65	0	45.80	–	–	–/–	–	17/5	16
Asif Iqbal (CY 1968)	6.6.1943		1964–1979	58	3,575	175	11	38.85	53	5-48	2/0	28.33	36	10
Asif Masood	23.1.1946		1968–1976	16	93	30*	0	10.33	38	5-111	1/0	41.26	5	7
Asif Mujtaba	4.11.1967		1986–1996	25	928	65*	0	24.42	4	1-0	0/0	75.75	19	66
Asim Kamal	31.5.1976		2003–2005	12	717	99	0	37.73	–	–	–/–	–	10	
Ata-ur-Rehman	28.3.1975		1992–1996	13	76	19	0	8.44	31	4-50	0/0	34.54	2	30
Atif Rauf	3.3.1964		1993	1	25	16	0	12.50	–	–	–/–	–	0	
Atiq-uz-Zaman	20.7.1975		1999	1	26	25	0	13.00	–	–	–/–	–	5	3
Azam Khan	1.3.1969		1996	1	14	14	0	14.00	–	–	–/–	–	0	6
Azeem Hafeez	29.7.1963		1983–1984	18	134	24	0	8.37	63	6-46	4/0	34.98	5	15
Azhar Ali	19.2.1985		2010–2019	77	5,885	302*	16	42.64	8	2-35	0/0	76.37	61	53
Azhar Khan	7.9.1955		1979	1	14	14	0	14.00	–	1-1	0/0	2.00	0	
Azhar Mahmood	28.2.1975		1997–2001	21	900	136	3	30.00	39	4-50	–/–	35.94	14	143
[2] Azmat Rana	3.11.1951	30.5.2015	1979	1	49	49	0	49.00	–	–	–/–	–	0	2
Babar Azam	15.10.1994		2016–2019	25	1,707	127*	4	42.67	–	0-6	0/0	–	19	74/36
Basit Ali	13.12.1970		1992–1995	19	858	103	0	26.81	0	–	–/–	–	6	50
[3] Bazid Khan	25.3.1981		2004	5	32	23	0	16.00	–	–	–/–	–	2	5
Bilal Asif	24.9.1985		2018	2	73	15	0	9.12	16	6-36	2/0	26.50	2	3
Bilawal Bhatti	17.9.1991		2013	6	70	29	0	35.00	6	3-65	0/0	48.50	3	109
Danish Kaneria	16.12.1980		2000–2010	61	360	29	0	7.05	261	7-77	15/2	34.79	18	18
D'Souza Antao	17.1.1939		1958–1962	6	76	23*	0	38.00	17	5-112	1/0	43.82	3	
Ehsan Adil	15.3.1993		2012–2015	3	21	12	0	5.25	5	2-54	0/0	52.60	0	6

	Born	Died	Tests	Test Career	Runs	HS	100s	Avge	Wkts	BB	5/10	Avge	Ct/St	O/T
Ehtesham-ud-Din	4.9.1950		5	1979–1982	2	2	0	1.00	16	5-47	1/0	23.43	2	23/27
Fahim Ashraf	16.1.1994		4	2018–2018	138	83	0	23.00	11	3-42	0/0	26.09	0	18
Faisal Iqbal	30.12.1981		26	2000–2009	1,124	139	1	26.76	0	0-7	0/0	–	22	46/34
Fakhar Zaman	10.4.1990		3	2018	192	94	0	32.00	–	–	–/–	–	3	
Farhan Adil	25.9.1977		1	2003	33	25	0	16.50	–	–	–/–	–	0	
Farooq Hamid	3.3.1945		1	1964	3	3	0	1.50	1	1-82	0/0	107.00	0	
Farrukh Zaman	2.4.1956		1	1976	–	–	–	–	0	0-7	0/0	–	0	
Fawad Alam	8.10.1985		3	2009–2009	250	168	1	41.66	–	–	–/–	–	3	38/24
Fazal Mahmood (CY 1955)	18.2.1927	30.5.2005	34	1952–1962	620	60	0	14.09	139	7-42	13/4	24.70	11	2
Fazl-e-Akbar	20.10.1980		5	1997–2003	52	25	0	13.00	11	3-85	0/0	46.45	0	2
Ghazali Mohammad Ebrahim Zainuddin	15.6.1924	26.4.2003	2	1954	32	18	0	8.00	0	0-18	0/0	–	0	
Ghulam Abbas	1.5.1947		1	1967	12	12	0	6.00	–	–	–/–	–	0	
Gul Mahomed	15.10.1921	8.5.1992	1†	1956	39	27*	0	39.00	–	–	–/–	–	0	
[1,2] Hanif Mohammad (CY 1968)	21.12.1934	11.8.2016	55	1952–1969	3,915	337	12	43.98		1-1	0/0	95.00	40	41/14
Harris Sohail	9.1.1989		13	2017–2019	744	147	2	35.42	1	1-3	0/0	24.00	10	12
Haroon Rashid	25.3.1953		23	1976–1982	1,217	153	3	34.77	0	0-3	0/0	–	16	53/30
Hasan Ali	7.2.1994		9	2016–2018	155	29	0	15.50	31	5-45	1/0	28.90	4	16
Hasan Raza	11.3.1982		7	1996–2005	235	68	0	26.11	0	0-1	0/0	–	5	
Haseeb Ahsan	15.7.1939	8.3.2013	12	1957–1961	61	14	0	6.77	27	6-202	2/0	49.25	1	
[2] Humayun Farhat	24.1.1981		1	2000	54	28	0	27.00	–	–	–/–	–	3	5
[2] Ibadulla Khalid ("Billy")	20.12.1935		4	1964–1967	253	166	1	31.62	1	1-42	0/0	99.00	3	
Iftikhar Ahmed	3.9.1990		3	2016–2019	48	27	0	9.60	1	1-1	0/0	141.00	1	4/6
Iftikhar Anjum	1.12.1980		1	2005	9	9*	0	–	0	0-8	0/0	–	0	62/2
Ijaz Ahmed snr	20.9.1968		60	1986–2000	3,315	211	12	37.67	2	1-9	0/0	38.50	45	250
Ijaz Ahmed jnr	2.2.1969		2	1995	29	16	0	9.66	0	0-1	0/0	–	1	2
Ijaz Butt	10.3.1938		8	1958–1962	279	58	0	19.92	–	–	–/–	–	5	
Ijaz Faqih	24.3.1956		5	1980–1987	183	105	1	26.14	4	1-38	0/0	74.75	0	27
Imam-ul-Haq	12.12.1995		11	2018–2019	485	76	0	25.52	–	–	–/–	–	7	37/2
[2] Imran Farhat	20.5.1982		40	2000–2012	2,400	128	3	32.00	3	2-69	0/0	94.66	40	58/7
Imran Khan (CY 1983)	25.11.1952		88	1971–1991	3,807	136	6	37.69	362	8-58	23/6	22.81	28	175
Mohammad Imran Khan	15.7.1987		10	2014–2019	16	6	0	2.28	29	5-58	1/0	31.62	4	2
Imran Nazir	16.12.1981		8	1998–2002	427	131	1	32.84	–	–	–/–	–	4	79/25
Imtiaz Ahmed	5.1.1928	31.12.2016	41	1952–1962	2,079	209	3	29.28	0	0-0	0/0	–	77/16	27
Intikhab Alam	28.12.1941		47	1959–1976	1,493	138	1	22.28	125	7-52	5/2	35.95	20	4
Inzamam-ul-Haq (CY 1983)	3.3.1970		119§	1992–2007	8,829	329	25	50.16	0	0-8	0/0	–	81	375‡/1

§ *Inzamam-ul-Haq's figures exclude one run for the ICC World XI v Australia in the Super Series Test in 2005-06.*

	Born	Died	Tests	Test Career	Runs	HS	100s	Avge	Wkts	BB	5/10	Avge	Ct/St	O/T
Iqbal Qasim	6.8.1953		50	1976-1988	549	56	0	13.07	171	7-49	8/2	28.11	42	15
Irfan Fazil	2.11.1981		1	1999	4	3	0	4.00	4	1-30	0/0	32.50	2	1
Israr Ali	1.5.1927	1.2.2016	4	1952-1959	33	10	0	4.71	6	2-29	0/0	27.50	1	
Jalal-ud-Din	12.6.1959		6	1982-1985	4	2*	0	3.00	11	3-77	0/0	48.81	1	8
Javed Akhtar	21.11.1940	8.7.2016	1	1962	2	2*	0	4.00	0	0-52	0/0	—	0	
Javed Burki	8.5.1938		25	1960-1969	1,341	140	3	30.47	0	0-2	0/0	—	7	
Javed Miandad (CY 1982)	12.6.1957		124	1976-1993	8,832	280*	23	52.57	17	3-74	0/0	40.11	93/1	233
Junaid Khan	24.12.1989		22	2011-2015	122	17	0	7.17	71	5-38	5/0	31.73	4	769
Kabir Khan	12.4.1974		4	1994	24	10	0	8.00	9	3-26	0/0	41.11	1	10
[2] Kamran Akmal	13.1.1982		53	2002-2010	2,648	158*	6	30.79			—/—		184/22	157/58
Kardar Abdul Hafeez	17.1.1925	21.4.1996	23†	1952-1957	847	93	0	24.91	21	3-35	0/0	45.42	15	
Khalid Hassan	14.7.1937	3.12.2013	1	1954	17	10	0	17.00	2	2-116	0/0	58.00	0	
[1] Khalid Wazir	27.4.1936		2	1954	14	9*	0	7.00			—/—	—	0	
Khan Mohammad	1.1.1928	4.7.2009	13	1952-1957	100	26*	0	10.00	54	6-21	4/0	23.92	4	
Khurram Manzoor	10.6.1986		16	2008-2014	817	146	1	28.17			—/—	—	8	7/3
Liaqat Ali	21.5.1955		5	1974-1978	28	12	0	7.00	6	3-80	0/0	59.83	0	3
Mahmood Hussain	2.4.1932	25.12.1991	27	1952-1962	336	35	0	10.18	68	6-67	2/0	38.64	5	
[3] Majid Jahangir Khan (CY 1970)	28.9.1946		63	1964-1982	3,931	167	8	38.92	27	4-45	0/0	53.92	70	23
Mansoor Akhtar	25.12.1957		19	1980-1989	655	111	1	25.19			—/—		9	41
[2] Manzoor Elahi	15.4.1963		6	1984-1994	123	52	0	15.37	7	2-38	0/0	27.71	7	54
Maqsood Ahmed	26.3.1925	4.1.1999	16	1952-1955	507	99	0	19.50	3	2-12	0/0	63.66	13	
Masood Anwar	12.12.1967		1	1990	39	37	0	19.50	3	2-59	0/0	34.00	0	
Mathias Wallis	4.2.1935	1.9.1994	21	1955-1962	783	77	0	23.72	0	0-20	0/0	—	22	
Mir Hamza	10.9.1992		1	2018	4	4*	0	—	2	1-40	0/0	67.00	0	
Miran Bux	20.4.1907	8.2.1991	2	1954	1	1*	0	1.00	2	2-82	0/0	57.50	0	
Misbah-ul-Haq (CY 2017)	28.5.1974		75	2000-2016	5,222	161*	10	46.62			—/—	—	50	162/39
Mohammad Abbas	10.3.1990		17	2016-2019	93	29	0	7.15	72	5-33	4/1	20.90	3	3
Mohammad Akram	10.9.1974		9	1995-2000	24	10*	0	2.66	17	5-138	1/0	50.52	4	23
Mohammad Amir (formerly Mohammad Aamer)	13.4.1992		36	2009-2018	751	48	0	13.41	119	6-44	4/0	30.47	5	61/48
Mohammad Asif	20.12.1982		23	2004-2010	141	29	0	5.64	106	6-41	7/1	24.36	3	35/11
Mohammad Aslam Khokhar	5.1.1920	22.1.2011	1	1954	34	18	0	17.00			—/—	—	0	
Mohammad Ayub	13.9.1979		1	2012	47	25	0	23.50			—/—	—	0	
Mohammad Farooq	8.4.1938		7	1960-1964	85	47	0	17.00	21	4-70	0/0	32.47	1	
Mohammad Hafeez	17.10.1980		55	2003-2018	3,652	224	10	37.64	53	4-16	0/0	34.11	45	218/89
Mohammad Hussain	8.10.1976		2	1996-1998	18	17	0	6.00	3	2-66	0/0	29.00	1	14

	Born	Died	Tests	Test Career	Runs	HS	100s	Avge	Wkts	BB	5/10	Avge	Ct/St	O/T
Mohammad Ilyas	19.3.1946		10	1964–1968	441	126	1	23.21	0	0-1	0/0	–	6	60/22
Mohammad Irfan	6.6.1982		4	2012–2013	28	14	0	5.60	10	3-44	0/0	38.90	0	3
Mohammad Khalil	11.11.1982		2	2004	9	5	0	3.00	0	0-38	0/0	–	0	
Mohammad Munaf	2.11.1935	28.1.2020	4	1959–1961	63	19	0	12.60	11	4-42	0/0	31.00	2	3
Mohammad Nawaz	21.3.1994		3	2016	50	25	0	12.50	5	2-32	0/0	29.40	2	15/16
Mohammad Nazir	8.3.1946		14	1969–1983	144	29*	0	18.00	34	7-99	3/0	33.05	4	4
Mohammad Ramzan	25.12.1970		1	1997	36	29	0	18.00	–	–	–/–	–	–	
Mohammad Rizwan	1.6.1992		5	2016–2019	215	95	0	35.83	–	–	–/–	–	14	32/16
Mohammad Salman	7.8.1981		2	2010	25	13	0	6.25	–	–	–/–	–	2/1	7/1
Mohammad Sami	24.2.1981		36	2000–2012	487	49	0	11.59	85	5-36	2/0	52.74	7	87/13
Mohammad Talha	15.10.1988		4	2008–2014	34	19	0	8.50	9	3-65	0/0	56.00	1	3
Mohammad Wasim	8.8.1977		18	1996–2000	783	192	2	30.11	–	–	–/–	–	22/2	25
Mohammad Yousuf (CY 2007) (formerly Yousuf Youhana)	27.8.1974		90	1997–2010	7,530	223	24	52.29	0	0-3	0/0	–	65	281‡/3
Mohammad Zahid	2.8.1976		5	1996–2002	7	6*	0	1.40	15	7-66	1/1	33.46	1	11
Mohsin Kamal	16.6.1963		9	1983–1994	37	13*	0	9.25	24	4-116	0/0	34.25	4	19
Mohsin Khan	15.3.1955		48	1977–1986	2,709	200	7	37.10	0	0-0	0/0	–	34	75
[2] Moin Khan	23.9.1971		69	1990–2004	2,741	137	4	28.55	–	–	–/–	–	128/20	219
[1] Mudassar Nazar	6.4.1956		76	1976–1988	4,114	231	10	38.09	66	6-32	1/0	38.36	48	122
Mufasir-ul-Haq	16.8.1944	27.7.1983	1	1964	8	8*	0	–	3	2-50	0/0	28.00	1	
Munir Malik	10.7.1934	30.11.2012	3	1959–1962	11	4	0	2.33	9	5-128	1/0	39.77	1	
Musa Khan	20.8.2000		1	2019	16	12*	0	–	0	0-114	0/0	–	–	1
[2] Mushtaq Ahmed (CY 1997)	28.6.1970		52	1989–2003	656	59	0	11.71	185	7-56	10/3	32.97	23	144
[2] Mushtaq Mohammad (CY 1963)	22.11.1943		57	1958–1978	3,643	201	10	39.17	79	5-28	3/0	29.22	42	10
Nadeem Abbasi	15.4.1964		1	1989	46	36	0	23.00	–	–	–/–	–	6	
[1] Nadeem Ghauri	12.10.1962		1	1989	0	0	0	0.00	2	0-20	0/0	–	–	6
[2] Nadeem Khan	10.12.1969		2	1992–1998	34	25	0	17.00	2	2-147	0/0	115.00	0	2
Naseem Shah	15.2.2003		3	2019	8	7	0	8.00	8	5-31	1/0	32.75	0	
Nasim-ul-Ghani	14.5.1941		29	1957–1972	747	101	1	16.60	52	6-67	2/0	37.67	11	1
Nasir Jamshed	6.12.1989		2	2012	51	46	0	12.75	–	–	–/–	–	1	48/18
Naushad Ali	1.10.1943		6	1964	156	39	0	14.18	–	–	–/–	–	9	
Naved Anjum	27.7.1963		2	1989–1990	44	22	0	14.66	4	2-57	0/0	40.50	1	13
Naved Ashraf	4.9.1974		2	1998–1999	64	32	0	21.33	–	–	–/–	–	0	
Naved Latif	21.2.1976		1	2001	20	20	0	10.00	–	–	–/–	–	0	11
[1] Naved-ul-Hasan	28.2.1978		9	2004–2006	239	42*	0	19.91	18	3-30	0/0	58.00	3	744/4
[1] Nazar Mohammad	5.3.1921	12.7.1996	5	1952	277	124*	1	39.57	0	0-4	0/0	–	7	

Name	Born	Died	Tests	Test Career	Runs	HS	100s	Avge	Wkts	BB	5/10	Avge	Ct/St	O/T
Niaz Ahmed	11.11.1945	12.4.2000	2	1967-1968	17	16*	0		3	2-72	0/0	31.33	2	
[2]Pervez Sajjad	30.8.1942		19	1964-1972	123	24	0	13.66	59	7-74	3/0	23.89	9	
Qaiser Abbas	7.5.1982		1	2000	2	2	0	2.00	0	0-35	0/0	-	1	
Qasim Omar	9.2.1957		26	1983-1986	1,502	210	3	36.63	0	0-0	0/0	-	15	31
Rahat Ali	12.9.1988		21	2012-2018	136	35*	0	7.55	58	6-127	2/0	39.03	9	14
[2]Ramiz Raja	14.8.1962		57	1983-1996	2,833	122	2	31.83	-	-	-/-	-	34	198
Rashid Khan	15.12.1959		4	1981-1984	155	59	0	51.66	8	3-129	0/0	45.00	2	29
Rashid Latif	14.10.1968		37	1992-2003	1,381	150	1	28.77	-	0-10	0/0	-	119/11	166
Rehman Sheikh Fazalur	11.6.1935		1	1957	10	8	0	5.00	2	1-43	0/0	99.00	1	
Riaz Afridi	21.1.1985		1	2004	9	9	0	9.00	4	2-42	0/0	43.50	0	
Rizwan-uz-Zaman	4.9.1961		11	1981-1988	345	60	0	19.16	4	3-26	0/0	11.50	4	3
[2]Sadiq Mohammad	3.5.1945		41	1969-1980	2,579	166	5	35.81	0	0-0	0/0	-	28	19
Saeed Ahmed	1.10.1937		41	1957-1972	2,991	172	5	40.41	22	4-64	0/0	36.45	13	
Saeed Ajmal	14.10.1977		35	2009-2014	451	50	0	11.00	178	7-55	10/4	28.10	11	113/64
[2]Saeed Anwar (CY 1997)	6.9.1968		55	1990-2001	4,052	188*	11	45.52	6	2-36	0/0		18	247
Salah-ud-Din	14.2.1947		5	1964-1969	117	34*	0	19.50	7	5-40	1/0	26.71	2	
Saleem Jaffer	19.11.1962		14	1986-1991	42	10*	0	5.25	36	4-11	0/0	31.63	3	39
Salim Altaf	19.4.1944		21	1967-1978	276	53*	0	14.52	46		0/0	37.17	3	6
[2]Salim Elahi	21.11.1976		13	1995-2002	436	72	0	18.95	-		-/-	-	10/1	48
[2]Salim Malik (CY 1988)	16.4.1963		103	1981-1998	5,768	237	15	43.69	5	1-3	0/0	82.80	65	283
Salim Yousuf	7.12.1959		32	1981-1990	1,055	91*	0	27.05	-		-/-	-	91/13	86
Salman Butt	7.10.1984		33	2003-2010	1,889	122	3	30.46	1	1-36	0/0	106.00	12	78/24
Sami Aslam	12.12.1995		13	2014-2017	758	91	0	31.58	-		-/-	-	7	
[2]Saqlain Mushtaq (CY 2000)	29.12.1976		49	1995-2002	927	101*	1	14.48	208	8-164	13/3	29.83	15	169
Sarfraz Ahmed	22.5.1987		49	2009-2018	2,657	112	3	36.39	-		-/-	-	146/21	116/58
Sarfraz Nawaz	1.12.1948		55	1968-1983	1,045	90	0	17.71	177	9-86	4/1	32.75	26	45
Shabbir Ahmed	21.4.1976		10	2003-2005	88	24*	0	8.80	51	5-48	2/0	23.03	3	32/1
Shadab Kabir	12.11.1977		5	1996-2001	148	55	0	21.14	-		0/0	-	1	3
Shadab Khan	4.10.1998		5	2016-2018	240	56	0	34.28	12	3-31	0/0	38.83	1	43/38
Shafiq Ahmed	28.3.1949		6	1974-1980	99	27*	0	11.00	-		-/-	-	0	
Shafqat Rana	10.8.1943		5	1964-1969	221	95	0	31.57	1	1-2	0/0	9.00	5	
[2]Shaheen Shah Afridi	6.4.2000		7	2018-2019	39	14	0	4.33	25	5-77	1/0	29.88	0	19/10
[2]Shahid Afridi	1.3.1980		27	1998-2010	1,716	156	5	36.51	48	5-52	1/0	35.60	10	393‡98‡
Shahid Israr	1.3.1950	29.4.2013	1	1976	7	7*	0	-	-		-/-	-	1	
Shahid Mahboob	25.8.1962		1	1989	25	16	0	12.50	2	2-131	0/0	65.50	2	10
Shahid Mahmood	17.3.1939		1	1962					0	0-23	0/0	-	0	

	Born	Died	Tests	Test Career	Runs	HS	100s	Avge	Wkts	BB	5/10	Avge	Ct/St	O/T
Shahid Nazir	4.12.1977		15	1996–2006	194	40	0	12.12	36	5-53	1/0	35.33	5	17
Shahid Saeed	6.1.1966		1	1989	12	12	0	12.00	0	0-7	0/0	–	1	10
Shakeel Ahmed snr.	12.2.1966		1	1998	1	1	0	1.00	4	4-91	0/0	34.75	0	
Shakeel Ahmed jnr.	12.11.1971		3	1992–1994	74	33	0	14.80				–	4	2
Shan Masood	14.10.1989		19	2013–2019	1,089	135	2	29.43	2	1-6	–/–	22.00	11	5
Sharjeel Khan	14.8.1989		1	2016	44	40	0	22.00			–/–	–	0	25/15
Sharpe Duncan Albert	3.8.1937		3	1959	134	56	0	22.33				–	2	
Shoaib Akhtar	13.8.1975		46	1997–2007	544	47	0	10.07	178	6-11	12/2	25.69	12	158‡/15
Shoaib Malik	1.2.1982		35	2001–2015	1,898	245	3	35.14	32	4-33	0/0	47.46	18	287†/110‡
Shoaib Mohammad	8.1.1961		45	1983–1995	2,705	203*	7	44.34	5	2-8	0/0	34.00	22	63
Shuja-ud-Din Butt	10.4.1930	7.2.2006	19	1954–1961	395	47	0	15.19	20	3-18	0/0	40.05	8	
Sikander Bakht	25.8.1957		26	1976–1982	146	22*	0	6.34	67	8-69	3/1	36.00	7	27
Sohail Khan	6.3.1984		9	2008–2016	252	65	0	25.20	27	5-68	2/0	41.66	3	13/5
Sohail Tanvir	12.12.1984		2	2007	17	13	0	5.66	5	3-83	0/0	63.20	2	62/57
Tahir Naqqash	6.6.1959		15	1981–1984	300	57	0	21.42	34	5-40	2/0	41.11	3	40
Talat Ali Malik	29.5.1950		10	1972–1978	370	61	0	23.12	0	0-1	0/0	–	4	
Tanvir Ahmed	20.12.1978		5	2010–2012	170	57	0	34.00	17	6-120	1/0	26.64	2	2/1
Taslim Arif	1.5.1954	13.3.2008	6	1979–1980	501	210*	1	62.62	1	1-28	0/0	28.00	6/3	2
Taufeeq Umar	20.6.1981		44	2001–2014	2,963	236	7	37.98	0	0-0	0/0	–	48	22
Tauseef Ahmed	10.5.1958		34	1979–1993	318	35*	0	17.66	93	6-45	3/0	31.72	9	70
Umar Akmal	26.5.1990		16	2009–2011	1,003	129	1	35.82			–/–	–	12	121/84
Umar Amin	16.10.1989		4	2010	99	33	0	12.37	1	1-7	–/–	21.00	1	16/14
Umar Gul	14.4.1984		47	2003–2012	577	65*	0	9.94	163	6-135	4/0	34.06	11	130/60
Usman Salahuddin	2.12.1990		1	2018	37	33	0	18.50			–/–	–	0	
Wahab Riaz	28.6.1985		27	2010–2018	306	39	0	8.50	83	5-63	2/0	34.50	5	17/16
Wajahatullah Wasti	11.11.1974		6	1998–1999	329	133	2	36.55	0	0-0	0/0	–	7	89/31
Waqar Hassan	12.9.1932	10.2.2020	21	1952–1959	1,071	189	1	31.50	0	0-10	0/0	–	10	15
Waqar Younis (CY 1992)	16.11.1971		87	1989–2002	1,010	45	0	10.20	373	7-76	22/5	23.56	18	262
Wasim Akram (CY 1993)	3.6.1966		104	1984–2002	2,898	257*	3	22.64	414	7-119	25/5	23.62	44	356
Wasim Bari	23.3.1948		81	1967–1983	1,366	85	0	15.88	0	0-2	0/0	–	201/27	51
Wasim Raja	3.7.1952	23.8.2006	57	1972–1984	2,821	125	4	36.16	51	4-50	0/0	35.80	20	54
Wazir Mohammad	22.12.1929		20	1952–1959	801	189	2	27.62	0	0-2	0/0	–	5	
Yasir Ali	15.10.1985		1	2003	1	1*	0	–	2	1-12	0/0	27.50	0	
Yasir Arafat	12.3.1982		3	2007–2008	94	50*	0	47.00	9	5-161	1/0	48.66	0	11/13
Yasir Hameed	28.2.1978		25	2003–2010	1,491	170	2	32.41	0	0-0	0/0	–	20	56

	Born	Died	Tests	Test Career	Runs	HS	100s	Avge	Wkts	BB	5/10	Avge	Ct/St	O/T
Yasir Shah	2.5.1986		38	2014-2016	702	113	1	13.76	209	8-41	16/3	30.43	19	25/2
[2]Younis Ahmed	20.10.1947		4	1969-1986	177	62	0	29.50	0	0-6	0/0	–	2	2
Younis Khan (CY 2017)	29.11.1977		118	1999-2016	10,099	313	34	52.05	9	2-23	0/0	54.55	139	265/25
Yousuf Youhana (see Mohammad Yousuf)														
Zaheer Abbas (CY 1972)	24.7.1947		78	1969-1985	5,062	274	12	44.79	3	2-21	0/0	44.00	34	62
Zahid Fazal	10.11.1973		9	1990-1995	288	78	0	18.00	–	–	–/–	–	5	19
[2]Zahoor Elahi	1.3.1971		2	1996	30	22	0	10.00	–	–	–/–	–	–	14
Zakir Khan	3.4.1963		2	1985-1989	9	9*	0	–	5	3-80	0/0	33.33	1	17
Zulfiqar Ahmed	22.11.1926	3.10.2008	9	1952-1956	200	63*	0	33.33	20	6-42	2/1	18.30	5	17
Zulfiqar Babar	10.12.1978		15	2013-2016	144	56	0	16.00	54	5-74	2/0	39.42	4	5/7
Zulqarnain	25.5.1962		3	1985	24	13	0	6.00	–	–	–/–	–	8/2	16
Zulqarnain Haider	23.4.1986		1	2010	88	88	0	44.00	–	–	–/–	–	2	4/3

SRI LANKA (150 players)

	Born	Died	Tests	Test Career	Runs	HS	100s	Avge	Wkts	BB	5/10	Avge	Ct/St	O/T
Ahangama Franklyn Saliya	14.9.1959		3	1985	11	11	0	5.50	18	5-52	1/0	19.33	3	1
Amalean Kaushik Naginda	7.4.1965		2	1985-1987	9	7*	0	9.00	7	4-97	0/0	22.28	0	8
Amerasinghe Amerasinghe Mudalige Jayantha Gamini	2.2.1954		2	1983	54	34	0	18.00	1	2-73	0/0	50.00	3	1
Amerasinghe Meronna Koralage Don Ishara	5.3.1978		1	2007	0	0*	0	–	1	1-62	0/0	105.00	0	–
Anurasiri Sangarange Don	25.10.1966		18	1985-1997	91	24	0	5.35	41	4-71	0/0	37.75	4	45
Arnold Russel Premakumaran	25.10.1973		44	1996-2004	1,821	123	3	28.01	11	3-76	0/0	54.36	51	180/1
Atapattu Marvan Samson	22.11.1970		90	1990-2007	5,502	249	16	39.02	1	1-9	–/–	24.00	58	268/2
Bandara Herath Mudiyanselage Charitha	31.12.1979		8	1997-2005	124	43	0	15.50	16	3-84	0/0	39.56	4	31/4
Bandaratilleke Mapa Rallage Chandima Malinga	16.5.1975		7	1997-2001	93	25	0	11.62	23	5-36	1/0	30.34	0	3
Chameera Pathira Vasan Dushmantha Niroshan	11.1.1992		7	2015-2018	69	19	0	5.30	24	5-47	1/0	41.00	0	23/19
Chandana Umagiliya Durage Upul	7.5.1972		16	1998-2004	616	92	0	26.78	37	6-179	3/1	41.48	7	147
Chandimal Lokuge Dinesh	18.11.1989		57	2011-2019	3,877	164	11	40.81	–	–	–/–	–	77/10	146/54
Dananjaya Akila (Mahamarakkala Kurukulasooriya Patabendige Akila Dananjaya Perera)	4.10.1993		6	2017-2019	135	43*	0	16.87	33	6-115	4/0	24.81	1	36/22
Dassanayake Pubudu Bathiya	11.7.1970		11	1993-1994	196	36	0	13.06	–	–	–/–	–	19/5	16

	Born	Died	Test Career	Tests	Runs	HS	100s	Avge	Wkts	BB	5/10	Avge	Ct/St	O/T
de Alwis Ronald Guy	15.2.1959	12.1.2013	1982–1987	11	152	28	0	8.00	–	–	–/–	–	21/2	31
de Mel Ashantha Lakdasa Francis	9.5.1959		1981–1986	17	326	34	0	14.17	59	6-109	3/0	36.94	9	57
de Saram Samantha Indika	2.9.1973		1999	4	117	39	0	23.40	–	–	–/–	–	1	15/1
de Silva Ashley Matthew	3.12.1963		1992–1993	4	10	9	0	3.33	–	–	–/–	–	4/1	4
de Silva Dandeniyage Somachandra	11.6.1942		1981–1984	12	406	61	0	21.36	37	5-59	1/0	36.40	4	41
de Silva Dhananjaya Maduranga	6.9.1991		2016–2019	31	1,863	173	6	35.15	21	3-25	0/0	51.95	34	42/13
de Silva Elluwalakankanamge Asoka Ranjit	28.3.1956		1985–1990	10	185	50	0	15.41	8	2-67	0/0	129.00	4	28
de Silva Ginigalgodage Ramba Ajit	12.12.1952		1981–1982	4	41	14	0	8.20	7	2-38	0/0	55.00	0	6
de Silva Karunakalage Sajeewa Chanaka	1.1.1971		1996–1998	4	65	27	0	9.28	16	5-85	1/0	55.56	5	38
de Silva Pinnaduwage Aravinda (CY 1996)	17.10.1965		1984–2002	93	6,361	267	20	42.97	29	3-30	0/0	41.65	43	308
de Silva Sanjeewa Kumara Lanka	29.7.1975		1997	3	36	20*	0	18.00	–	–	–/–	–	1	11
de Silva Weddikkara Ruwan Sujeewa	7.10.1979		2002–2007	3	10	5*	0	10.00	11	4-35	0/0	19.00	1	
Dharmasena Handunnettige Deepthi Priyantha Kumar	24.4.1971		1993–2003	31	868	62*	0	19.72	69	6-72	3/0	42.31	14	141
Dias Roy Luke	18.10.1952		1981–1986	20	1,285	109	3	36.71	0	0-17	0/0	–	6	58
Dickwella Dickwella Patabandige Dilantha Niroshan	23.6.1993		2014–2019	37	1,921	83	0	30.98	–	–	–/–	–	87/23	52/23
Dilshan Tillekeratne Mudiyanselage	14.10.1976		1999–2012	87	5,492	193	16	40.98	39	4-10	0/0	43.87	88	330/80
Dunusinghe Chamara Iroshan	19.10.1970		1994–1995	5	160	91	0	16.00	–	–	–/–	–	13/2	1
Embuldeniya Lasith	20.10.1996		2018–2019	7	56	24	0	6.22	30	5-66	2/0	39.80	1	
Eranga Ranaweera Mudiyanselage Shaminda	23.6.1986		2011–2016	19	193	45*	0	12.86	57	4-49	0/0	37.50	5	19/3
Fernando Athibachchi Nuwan Pradeep Roshan	19.10.1986		2011–2017	28	132	17*	0	4.00	70	6-132	1/0	42.90	5	42/14
Fernando Bodiyabaduge Oshada Piumal	15.4.1992		2018–2019	6	393	102	1	43.66	–	–	–/–	–	4	6/3
Fernando Congenige Randhi Dilhara	19.7.1979		2000–2012	40	249	39*	0	8.30	100	5-42	3/0	37.84	10	146⅔/18
Fernando Ellekuige Rufus Nemesion Susil	19.12.1955		1982–1983	2	112	46	0	11.20	4	3-63	0/0	27.00	0	7
Fernando Kandage Hasantha Ruwan Kumara	14.10.1979		2002	2	38	24	0	9.50	4	1-29	0/0	107.00	1	7
Fernando Kandana Arachchige Dinusha Manoj	10.8.1991		2003	2	56	51*	0	28.00	23	4-62	0/0	33.56	2	8/1
Fernando Muthuthanthrige Vishwa Thilina	18.9.1991		2016–2019	8	54	38	0	9.00	18	4-27	0/0	44.00	4	17
Fernando Thudellage Charitha Buddhika	22.8.1980		2001–2002	9	132	45	0	26.40	10	2-28	0/0	57.30	4	3
Gallage Indika Sanjeewa	22.11.1975		1999	1	6	3	0	3.00	–	–	–/–	–	3	9
Gamage Panagamuwa Lahiru Sampath	5.4.1988		2017–2018	5	177	56	0	22.12	10	2-38	0/0	57.30	3	6
Goonatillake Hettiarachige Mahes	16.8.1952		1981–1982	5	455	116	1	56.87	–	–	–/–	–	10/3	31/12
Gunaratne Downdegedara Asela Sampath	8.1.1986		2016–2017	6	48	23	0	12.00	–	–	–/–	–	6	3
Gunasekera Yohan	8.11.1957		1982	2					–	–	–/–	–	6	
Gunathilleke Masthyage Dhanushka	17.03.1991		2017–2018	8	299	61	0	18.68	1	1-16	0/0	111.00	6	38/21
Gunawardene Dihan Avishka	26.5.1977		1998–2005	6	181	43	0	16.45	–	–	–/–	–	2	61

Name	Born	Died	Tests	Test Career	Runs	HS	100s	Avge	Wkts	BB	5/10	Avge	Ct/St	O/T
Guneratne Roshan Punyajith Wijesinghe	26.1.1962	21.7.2005	1	1982	0	0*	0	–	0	0-84	0/0	–	–	
Gurusinha Asanka Pradeep	16.9.1966		41	1985-1996	2,452	143	7	38.92	20	2-7	0/0	34.05	33	147
Hathurusinghe Upul Chandika	13.9.1968		26	1990-1998	1,274	83	0	29.62	17	4-66	0/0	46.41	7	35
Herath Herath Mudiyanselage Rangana Keerthi Bandara	19.3.1978		93	1999-2018	1,699	80*	0	14.64	433	9-127	34/9	28.07	24	71/17
Hettiarachchi Dinuka Sulaksana	15.7.1976		1	2000	0	0*	0	0.00	2	2-36	0/0	20.50	0	
Jayasekera Rohan Stanley Amarasiriwardene	7.12.1957		1	1981	2	2	0	1.00	–			–	0	2
Jayasundera Madurawelage Don Udara Supeksha	3.1.1991		2	2015	30	26	0	7.50	0	0-12	0/0	–	2	
Jayasuriya Sanath Teran (CY 1997)	30.6.1969		110	1990-2007	6,973	340	14	40.07	98	5-34	2/0	34.34	78	441‡/31
Jayawardene Denagamage Proboth Mahela de Silva (CY 2007)	27.5.1977		149	1997-2014	11,814	374	34	49.84	6	2-32	0/0	51.66	205	443‡/55
Jayawardene Hewasandatchige Asiri Prasanna Wishvanath	9.10.1979		58	2000-2014	2,124	154*	4	29.50	–		–/–	–	124/32	
Jeganathan Sridharan	11.7.1951		2	1982	19	8	0	4.75	0	0-12	0/0	–	0	6
John Vinothen Bede	27.5.1960	14.5.1996	6	1982-1984	53	27*	0	10.60	28	5-60	2/0	21.92	2	5
Jurangpathy Baba Roshan	25.6.1967		2	1985-1986	8	7	0	0.25	1	1-69	–/–	93.00	2	
Kalavitigoda Shantha	23.12.1977		1	2004	7	7	0	4.00	–			–		
Kalpage Ruwan Senani	19.2.1970		11	1993-1998	294	63	0	18.37	12	2-27	0/0	64.50	10	86
Kaluhalamulla H. K. S. R. (see Randiv, Suraj)														
[2] Kaluperuma Lalith Wasantha Silva	25.6.1949		2	1981	12	11*	0	4.00	0	0-24	0/0	–	2	4
[2] Kaluperuma Sanath Mohan Silva	22.10.1961		4	1983-1987	88	23	0	11.00	2	2-17	0/0	62.00	6	2
Kaluwitharana Romesh Shantha	24.11.1969		49	1992-2004	1,933	132*	3	26.12	–		–/–	–	93/26	189
Kapugedera Chamara Kantha	24.2.1987		8	2006-2009	418	96	0	34.83	0	0-9	0/0	–	6	102/43
Karunaratne Chamika	29.5.1996		1	2018	22	22	0	11.00	1	1-130	0/0	148.00		
Karunaratne Frank Dimuth Madushanka	28.4.1988		66	2012-2019	4,524	196	9	36.78	1	1-12	0/0	74.50	52	28
Kaushal Paskuwal Handi Tharindu	5.3.1993		7	2014-2015	106	18	0	10.60	25	5-42	2/0	44.20	3	1
Kulasekara Chamith Kosala Bandara	15.7.1985		1	2011	22	15	0	11.00	1	1-65	0/0	80.00	0	4
Kulasekara Kulasekara Mudiyanselage Dinesh Nuwan	22.7.1982		21	2004-2014	391	64	0	14.48	48	4-21	0/0	37.37	8	184/58
Kumara Chandradasa Brahammana Ralalage Lahiru Sudesh	13.2.1997		21	2016-2019	52	10	0	3.71	67	6-122	1/0	36.58	4	13/3
Kuruppu Don Sardha Brendon Priyantha	5.1.1962		4	1986-1991	320	201*	1	53.33	–		–/–	–	1	54
Kuruppuarachchi Ajith Kosala	1.11.1964		2	1985-1986	0	0*	0	–	8	5-44	1/0	18.62	0	
Labrooy Graeme Fredrick	7.6.1964		9	1986-1990	158	70*	0	14.36	27	5-133	1/0	44.22	3	44
Lakmal Ranasinghe Arachchige Suranga	10.3.1987		61	2010-2019	836	42	0	11.61	151	5-54	3/0	37.42	18	85/11

	Born	Died	Tests	Test Career	Runs	HS	100s	Avge	Wkts	BB	5/10	Avge	Ct/St	O/T
Lakshitha Materba Kanatha Gamage Chamila														
Premanath	4.1.1979		2	2002-2002	42	40	0	14.00	5	2-33	0/0	31.60	1	7
Liyanage Dulip Kapila	6.6.1972		9	1992-2001	84	23	0	7.66	17	4-56	0/0	39.17	1	16
Lokuarrachchi Kaushal Samaraweera	20.5.1982		4	2003-2003	94	28*	0	23.50	5	2-47	0/0	59.00	0	21/2
Madugalle Ranjan Senerath	22.4.1959		21	1981-1988	1,029	103	1	29.40	0	0-0	0/0	–	9	63
Madurasinghe Madurasinghe Arachchige														
Wijayasiri Ranjith	30.1.1961		3	1988-1992	24	11	0	4.80	3	3-60	0/0	57.33	0	12
Mahanama Roshan Siriwardene	31.5.1966		52	1985-1997	2,576	225	4	29.27	0	0-3	0/0	–	56	213
Maharoof Mohamed Farveez	7.9.1984		22	2003-2011	556	72	0	18.53	25	4-52	0/0	37.64	7	109/8
Malinga Separamadu Lasith	28.8.1983		30	2004-2010	275	64	0	11.45	101	5-50	3/0	33.15	7	226/79
Mathews Angelo Davis (CY 2015)	2.6.1987		86	2009-2019	5,981	200*	10	45.31	33	4-44	0/0	52.87	68	214/72
Mendis Balapuwaduge Ajantha Winslo	11.3.1985		19	2008-2014	213	78	0	16.38	70	6-99	4/1	34.77	2	87/39
Mendis Balapuwaduge Kusal Gimhan	2.2.1995		44	2015-2019	2,995	196	7	36.97	1	1-10	0/0	69.00	65	73/24
Mendis Louis Rohan Duleep	25.8.1952		24	1981-1988	1,329	124	4	31.64	–	–	–	–	9	79
Mirando Magina Thilan Thushara	1.3.1981		10	2003-2010	94	15*	0	8.54	28	5-83	1/0	37.14	3	38/6
Mubarak Jehan	10.1.1981		13	2002-2015	385	49	0	17.50	0	0-1	0/0	–	15	40/16
Muralitharan Muttiah (CY 1999)	17.4.1972		132‡	1992-2010	1,259	67	0	11.87	795	9-51	67/22	22.67	70	343‡/12
Nawaz Mohamed Naveed	20.9.1973		1	2002	99	78*	0	99.00	1	1-26	0/0	86.00	0	3
Nissanka Ratnayake Arachchige Prabath	25.10.1980		4	2003	18	12*	0	6.00	10	5-64	1/0	36.60	0	23
Paranavitana Nishad Tharanga	15.4.1982		32	2008-2012	1,792	111	2	32.58	–	–	–	–	27	–
Perera Anhettige Suresh Asanka	16.2.1978		2	1998-2001	77	43*	0	25.66	1	1-104	0/0	180.00	0	20
Perera Mahawaduge Dilruwan Kamalaneth	22.7.1982		41	2013-2019	1,208	95	0	18.58	156	6-32	8/2	35.33	19	13/3
Perera Mathurage Don Kusal Janith	17.8.1990		18	2015-2019	934	153*	2	31.13	–	–	–	–	19/8	98/42
Perera N. K. P. A. D. (see Dananjaya, Akila)														
Perera Narangoda Liyanaarachchige Tissara														
Chirantha	3.4.1989		6	2011-2012	203	75	0	20.30	11	4-63	0/0	59.36	1	161/75‡
Perera Panagodage Don Ruchira Laksiri	6.4.1977		8	1998-2002	33	11*	0	11.00	17	3-40	0/0	38.88	6	19/2
Prasad Kariyawasam Tirana Gamage Dammika	30.5.1983		25	2008-2015	476	47	0	12.86	75	5-50	1/0	35.97	6	24/1
Prasanna Seekkuge	27.6.1985		1	2011	5	5	0	5.00	0	0-80	0/0	–	0	40/20
Pushpakumara Karuppiahyage Ravindra	21.7.1975		23	1994-2001	166	42*	0	8.73	58	7-116	4/0	38.65	10	31
Pushpakumara Paulage Malinda	24.3.1987		4	2017-2018	102	12	0	17.00	14	3-28	0/0	37.14	2	2
Rajitha Chandrasekara Arachchilage Kasun	1.6.1993		2	2018-2019	23	12	0	2.87	25	3-20	0/0	30.52	4	9/10
Ramanayake Champaka Priyadarshana Hewage	8.1.1965		18	1987-1993	143	34*	0	9.53	44	5-82	1/0	42.72	6	62
Ramyakumara Wijekoon Mudiyanselage														
Gayan	21.12.1976		2	2005	38	14	0	12.66	2	2-49	0/0	33.00	0	0/3

‡ *Muralitharan's figures exclude two runs, five wickets and two catches for the ICC World XI v Australia in the Super Series Test in 2005-06.*

	Born	Died	Tests	Test Career	Runs	HS	100s	Avge	Wkts	BB	5/10	Avge	Ct/St	O/T
Ranasinghe Anura Nandana	13.10.1956	9.11.1998		1981–1982	88	77	0	22.00	1	1-23	0/0	69.00	–	9
[2] Ranatunga Arjuna (CY 1999)	1.12.1963		93	1981–2000	5,105	135*	4	35.69	16	2-17	0/0	65.00	47	269
[2] Ranatunga Dammika	12.10.1962		2	1989	87	45	0	29.00	–	–	–/–	–	0	4
[2] Ranatunga Sanjeeva	25.4.1969		9	1994–1996	531	118	2	33.18	–	–	–/–	–	2	13
Randiv Suraj (Hewa Kaluhalamullage Suraj Randiv Kaluhalamulla; formerly M. M. M. Suraj)	30.1.1985		12	2010–2012	147	39	0	9.18	43	5-82	1/0	37.51	1	31/7
Ratnayake Rumesh Joseph	2.1.1964		23	1982–1991	433	56	0	14.43	73	6-66	5/0	35.10	9	70
Ratnayeke Joseph Ravindran	2.5.1960		22	1981–1989	807	93	0	25.21	56	8-83	4/0	35.21	3	78
Samarasekera Maitipage Athula Rohitha	5.8.1961		4	1988–1991	118	57	0	16.85	3	2-38	0/0	34.66	3	39
Samaraweera Dulip Prasanna	12.2.1972		7	1993–1994	211	42	0	15.07	–	–	–/–	–	4	5
[2] Samaraweera Thilan Thusara	22.9.1976		81	2001–2012	5,462	231	14	48.76	15	4-49	0/0	45.93	45	53
Sandakan Paththamperuma Arachchige Don Lakshan Rangika	10.6.1991		11	2016–2018	117	25	0	10.63	37	5-95	2/0	34.48	6	21/14
Sangakkara Kumar Chokshanada (CY 2012)	27.10.1977		134	2000–2015	12,400	319	38	57.40	0	0-4	0/0	–	182/20	397±/56
Senanayake Charith Panduka	19.12.1962		3	1990	97	64	0	19.40	–	–	–/–	–	2	7
Senanayake Senanayake Mudiyanselage Sachithra Madhushanka	9.2.1985		1	2013	5	5	0	5.00	0	0-30	0/0	–	–	49/42
Shanaka Madagamagamage Dasun	9.9.1991		3	2016–2017	29	17	0	5.80	9	3-46	0/0	29.00	1	22/35
Silva Athege Roshen Shivanka	17.11.1988		12	2017–2018	702	109	1	35.10	–	–	–/–	–	2	–
Silva Jayan Kaushal	27.5.1986		39	2011–2018	2,099	139	3	28.36	–	–	–/–	–	34/1	–
Silva Kelaniyage Jayantha	2.6.1973		7	1995–1997	6	6*	0	2.00	20	4-16	0/0	32.35	–	1
Silva Lindamullage Prageeth Chamara	14.12.1979		11	2006–2007	537	152*	1	33.56	1	1-57	0/0	65.00	7	75/16
Silva Sampathawaduge Amal Rohitha	12.12.1960		9	1982–1988	353	111	2	25.21	–	–	–/–	–	33/1	20
Siriwardene Tissa Appuhamilage Milinda	4.12.1985		11	2015–2016	298	68	0	33.11	11	3-25	0/0	23.36	3	27/22
Tharanga Warushavithana Upul	2.2.1985		31	2005–2011	1,754	165	3	31.89	1	0-5	0/0	–	24	234±/26
Thirimanne Hettige Don Rumesh Lahiru	8.9.1989		35	2011–2019	1,404	155*	1	22.64	0	0-5	0/0	–	20	127/26
Tillekeratne Hashan Prasantha	14.7.1967		83	1989–2003	4,545	204*	11	42.87	0	0-0	0/0	–	122/2	200
Udawatte Mahela Lakmal	19.7.1986		2	2018	23	19	0	5.75	–	–	–/–	–	2	9/8
Upashantha Kalutarage Eric Amila	10.6.1972		2	1998–2002	10	6	0	3.33	4	2-41	0/0	50.00	0	12
Vaas Warnakulasuriya Patabendige Ushantha Joseph Chaminda	27.1.1974		111	1994–2009	3,089	100*	1	24.32	355	7-71	12/2	29.58	31	321±/6
Vandort Michael Graydon	19.1.1980		20	2001–2008	1,144	140	4	36.90	–	–	–/–	–	6	1
Vithanage Kasun Disi Kithuruwan	26.2.1991		10	2012–2015	370	103*	1	26.42	1	1-73	0/0	133.00	10	6/3
Warnapura Bandula	1.3.1953		4	1981–1982	96	38	0	12.00	0	0-1	0/0	–	2	12

	Born	Died	Tests	Test Career	Runs	HS	100s	Avge	Wkts	BB	5/10	Avge	Ct/St	O/T
Warnapura Basnayake Shalith Malinda	26.5.1979		14	2007–2009	821	120	2	35.69	0	0-40	0/0	–	14	3
Warnaweera Kahakatchchi Patabandige Jayananda	23.11.1960		10	1985–1994	39	20	0	4.33	32	4-25	0/0	31.90	0	6
Weerasinghe Colombage Don Udesh Sanjeewa	1.3.1968		1	1985	3	3	0	3.00	0	0-8	0/0	–	0	–
Welagedara Uda Walawwe Mahim Bandaralage Chanaka Asanka	20.3.1981		21	2007–2014	218	48	0	9.08	55	5-52	2/0	41.32	5	10/2
[2]Wettimuny Mithra de Silva	11.6.1951	20.1.2019	2	1982	28	17	0	7.00	–	–	–/–	–	2	1
[2]Wettimuny Sidath (CY 1985)	12.8.1956		23	1981–1986	1221	190	2	29.07	0	0-16	0/0	–	10	35
Wickremasinghe Angupulige Gamini Dayantha	27.12.1965		3	1989–1992	17	13*	0	8.50	–	–	–/–	–	9/1	4
Wickremasinghe Gallage Pramodya	14.8.1971		40	1991–2000	555	51	0	9.40	85	6-60	3/0	41.87	18	134
Wijegunawardene Kapila Indaka Weerakkody	23.11.1964		2	1991–1991	14	6*	0	4.66	7	4-51	0/0	21.00	0	26
Wijesuriya Roger Gerard Christopher Ediriweera	18.2.1960		4	1981–1985	22	8	0	4.40	1	1-68	0/0	294.00	1	8
Wijetunge Piyal Kashyapa	6.8.1971		1	1993	10	10	0	5.00	2	1-58	0/0	59.00	0	–
Zoysa Demuni Nuwan Tharanga	13.5.1978		30	1996–2004	288	28*	0	8.47	64	5-20	1/0	33.70	4	9

ZIMBABWE (112 players)

	Born	Died	Tests	Test Career	Runs	HS	100s	Avge	Wkts	BB	5/10	Avge	Ct/St	O/T
Arnott Kevin John	8.3.1961		4	1992	302	101*	1	43.14	–	–	–/–	–	4	13
Bignaut Arnoldus Mauritius ("Andy")	1.8.1978		19	2000–2005	886	92	0	26.84	53	5-73	3/0	37.05	4	54/1
Brain David Hayden	4.10.1964		9	1992–1994	115	28	0	10.45	30	5-42	1/0	30.50	1	23
Brandes Eddo André	5.3.1963		10	1992–1999	121	39	0	10.08	26	3-45	0/0	36.57	4	59
Brent Gary Bazil	13.1.1976		4	1999–2001	35	25	0	5.83	7	3-21	0/0	44.85	0	70/3
Briant Gavin Aubrey	11.4.1969		1	1992	17	16	0	8.50	–	–	–/–	–	0	5
Bruk-Jackson Glen Keith	25.4.1969		2	1993	39	31	0	9.75	–	–	–/–	–	1	–
Burl Ryan Ponsonby	15.4.1994		3	2017	16	16	0	8.00	–	–	–/–	–	0	18/16
Burmester Mark Greville	24.11.1968		3	1992	54	30*	0	27.00	3	3-78	0/0	75.66	1	8
Butchart Iain Peter	9.5.1960		1	1994	23	15	0	11.50	0	0-11	0/0	–	0	20
Campbell Alistair Douglas Ross	23.9.1972		60	1992–2002	2,858	103	2	27.21	0	0-1	0/0	–	60	188
Carlisle Stuart Vance	10.5.1972		37	1994–2005	1,615	118	2	26.91	–	–	–/–	–	34	111
Chakabva Regis Wirirania	20.9.1987		16	2011–2019	758	101	1	25.26	–	–	–/–	–	29/4	38/12
Chari Brian Bara	14.2.1992		7	2014–2018	254	80	0	18.14	–	–	–/–	–	0	11/3
Chatara Tendai Larry	28.2.1991		9	2012–2018	90	22	0	6.42	24	5-61	1/0	27.62	0	70/21

	Born	Died	Tests	Test Career	Runs	HS	100s	Avge	Wkts	BB	5/10	Avge	Ct/St	O/T
Chibhabha Chamunorwa Justice	6.9.1986		3	2016–2017	124	60	0	20.66	1	1-44	0/0	162.00	0	103/33
Chigumbura Elton	14.3.1986		14	2003–2014	569	88	0	21.07	21	5-54	1/0	46.00	6	210½/54
Chinouya Michael Tawanda	9.6.1986		2	2016	1	1	0	0.50	3	1-45	0/0	62.66	0	2
Chisoro Tendai Sam	12.2.1988		1	2017	9	9	0	9.00	3	3-113	0/0	37.66	3	18/12
Coventry Charles Kevin	8.3.1983		2	2005	88	37	0	22.00	–	–	–/–	–	3	39/13
Cremer Alexander Graeme	19.9.1986		19	2004–2017	540	102*	0	16.36	57	5-125	1/0	45.68	12	96/29
² **Crocker** Gary John	16.5.1962		3	1992	69	33	0	23.00	5	2-65	0/0	72.33	0	6
Dabengwa Keith Mbusi	17.8.1980		3	2005	90	35	0	15.00	3	3-127	0/0	49.80	1	37/8
Dekker Mark Hamilton	5.12.1969		14	1993–1996	333	68*	0	15.85	0	0-5	–/–	–	12	23
Duffin Terrence	20.3.1982		2	2005	80	56	0	20.00	–	–	–/–	–	1	23
Ebrahim Dion Digby	7.8.1980		29	2000–2005	1,226	94	0	22.70	–	–	–/–	–	16	82
² **Ervine** Craig Richard	19.8.1985		17	2011–2019	1,058	160	2	33.06	–	–	–/–	–	16	93/22
² **Ervine** Sean Michael	6.12.1982		5	2003–2003	261	86	0	32.62	9	4-146	0/0	43.11	7	42
Evans Craig Neil	29.11.1969		3	1996–2003	52	22	0	8.66	3	0-8	0/0	–	2	53
Ewing Gavin Mackie	21.1.1981		3	2003–2005	108	71	0	18.00	2	1-27	0/0	130.00	1	7
Ferreira Neil Robert	3.6.1979		1	2005	21	16	0	10.50	–	–	–/–	–	0	
² **Flower** Andrew OBE (CY 2002)	28.4.1968		63	1992–2002	4,794	232*	12	51.54	0	0-0	–/–	–	151/9	213
² **Flower** Grant William	20.12.1970		67	1992–2003	3,457	201*	6	29.54	25	4-41	0/0	61.48	43	221
Friend Travis Michael	7.1.1981		13	2001–2003	447	81	0	29.80	25	5-31	1/0	43.60	7	51
Goodwin Murray William	11.12.1972		19	1997–2000	1,414	166*	3	42.84	0	0-3	0/0	–	10	84
Gripper Trevor Raymond	28.12.1975		20	1999–2003	809	112	1	21.86	6	2-91	0/0	84.83	14	8
Hondo Douglas Tafadzwa	7.7.1979		9	2001–2004	83	19	0	9.22	21	6-59	1/0	36.85	5	56
Houghton David Laud	23.6.1957		22	1992–1997	1,464	266	4	43.05	0	0-0	–/–	–	17	63
Huckle Adam George	21.9.1971		8	1997–1998	74	28*	0	6.72	25	6-109	2/1	34.88	3	19
James Wayne Robert	27.8.1965		4	1993–1994	61	33	0	15.25	–	–	–/–	–	16	11
Jarvis Kyle Malcolm	16.2.1989		13	2011–2019	128	39	0	9.14	46	5-54	3/0	29.43	3	49/22
Jarvis Malcolm Peter	6.12.1955		5	1992–1994	4	2*	0	2.00	11	3-30	0/0	35.72	2	12
Johnson Neil Clarkson	24.1.1970		13	1998–2000	532	107	1	24.18	15	4-77	0/0	39.60	12	48
Kamungozi Tafadzwa Paul	8.6.1987		1	2014	5	5	0	2.50	1	1-51	0/0	58.00	0	14/1
Kasuza Kevin Tatenda	20.6.1993		2	2019	101	63	0	50.50	–	–	–/–	–	0	
Lamb Gregory Arthur	4.3.1980		1	2011	46	39	0	23.00	3	3-120	0/0	47.00	2	15/5
Lock Alan Charles Ingram	10.9.1962		1	1995	8	8*	0	8.00	5	3-68	0/0	21.00	0	8
Madondo Trevor Nyasha	22.11.1976	11.6.2001	3	1997–2000	90	74*	0	30.00	–	–	–/–	–	1	13
Mahwire Ngonidzashe Blessing	31.7.1982		5	2002–2005	147	50*	0	13.36	18	4-92	0/0	50.83	1	23
Maregwede Alester	5.8.1981		2	2003	74	28	0	18.50	–	–	–/–	–	3	11
Marillier Douglas Anthony	24.4.1978		5	2000–2001	185	73	0	30.83	11	4-57	0/0	29.27	2	48

	Born	Died	Tests	Test Career	Runs	HS	100s	Avge	Wkts	BB	5/10	Avge	Ct/St	O/T
Maruma Timycen	19.4.1988		2	2012–2019	20	10	0	6.66	16	3-24	–/–	–	1	21/13
²Masakadza Hamilton	9.8.1983		38	2001–2018	2,223	158	5	30.04	16	4-32	00	30.56	29	209/66
²Masakadza Shingirai Winston	4.9.1986		5	2011–2014	88	24	0	11.00	2	2-33	00	32.18	1	16/7
²Masakadza Wellington Pedzisai	4.10.1993		1	2018	21	17	0	10.50	0	0-23	00	27.00	1	17/12
Masvaure Prince Spencer	7.10.1988		4	2016–2019	171	55	0	21.37	0	0-23	00	–	2	2
Matambanadzo Everton Zvikomborero	13.4.1976		3	1996–1999	17	7	0	4.25	4	2-62	00	62.50	0	7
Matsikenyeri Stuart	3.5.1983		8	2003–2004	351	57	0	23.40	2	1-58	00	172.50	7	113/10
Mavuta Brandon Anesu	4.3.1997		2	2018	9	6	0	2.25	4	4-21	00	59.25	3	7/3
Mawoyo Tinotenda Mbiri Kanayi	8.1.1986		11	2011–2016	615	163*	1	29.28	0	–	–/–	–	7	7
Mbangwa Mpumelelo ("Pommie")	26.6.1976		15	1996–2000	34	8	0	2.00	32	3-23	00	31.43	7	29
Meth Keegan Orry	8.2.1988		2	2012	72	31*	0	24.00	4	2-41	00	24.50	0	11/2
Mire Solomon Farai	21.8.1989		7	2017	78	47	0	19.50	1	1-22	00	32.00	2	47/9
Moor Peter Joseph	2.2.1991		8	2016–2018	533	83	0	35.53	0	–	–/–	–	9/1	49/21
Mpofu Christopher Bobby	27.11.1985		15	2004–2017	105	33	0	5.83	29	4-92	00	48.00	4	83/50
Mudzinganyama Brian Simbarashe	9.4.1999		1	2019	16	11*	0	16.00	0	–	–/–	–	0	–
Mumba Carl Tapfuma	6.5.1995		3	2016–2019	25	14	0	8.33	10	4-50	00	35.40	2	2
Mupariwa Tawanda	16.4.1985		1	2003	15	14	0	15.00	0	0-136	00	–	0	40/4
Murphy Brian Andrew	1.12.1976		11	1999–2001	123	30	0	10.25	18	3-32	00	61.83	11	31
Musakanda Tarisai Kenneth	31.10.1994		2	2017	6	6	0	3.00	0	–	–/–	–	0	15/6
Mushangwe Natsai	9.2.1991		2	2014	8	8	0	2.00	7	4-82	00	62.14	0	6/5
Mutendera David Travolta	25.1.1979		1	2000	10	10	0	5.00	0	0-29	00	–	0	9
Mutizwa Forster	24.8.1985		1	2011	24	18	0	12.00	0	–	–/–	–	1	17/3
Mutombodzi Confidence Tinotenda	21.12.1990		1	2019	41	33	0	20.50	0	0-19	00	–	0	11/13
Mutumbami Richmond	11.6.1989		6	2012–2014	217	43	0	19.72	0	–	–/–	–	17/2	33/22
Muzarabani Blessing	2.10.1996		1	2017	14	10	0	14.00	0	0-48	00	–	0	18/6
Mwayenga Waddington	20.6.1984		1	2005	15	14*	0	15.00	1	1-79	00	79.00	0	3
Ncube Njabulo	14.10.1989		1	2011	17	14	0	8.50	1	1-80	00	121.00	1	–
Ndlovu Ainsley	26.1.1996		1	2019	5	5	0	2.50	0	0-107	00	–	0	2/3
Nkala Mluleki Luke	1.4.1981		10	2000–2004	187	47	0	14.38	11	3-82	00	66.09	4	50/1
Nyauchi Victor Munyaradzi	8.7.1992		2	2019	17	11	0	8.50	5	3-69	00	31.60	0	–
Nyumbu John Curtis	1.3.1983		3	2014–2016	38	14	0	7.60	5	5-157	1/0	75.80	2	19/2
Olonga Henry Khaaba	3.7.1976		30	1994–2002	184	24	0	5.41	68	5-70	2/0	38.52	2	50
Panyangara Tinashe	21.10.1985		9	2003–2014	201	40*	0	16.75	31	5-59	1/0	26.22	3	65/14
Peall Stephen Guy	2.9.1969		4	1993–1994	60	30	0	15.00	2	2-89	00	75.75	1	21
Price Raymond William	12.6.1976		22	1999–2012	261	36	0	8.70	80	6-73	5/1	36.06	4	102/16
Pycroft Andrew John	6.6.1956		3	1992	152	60	0	30.40	–	–	–/–	–	2	20

	Born	Died	Tests	Test Career	Runs	HS	100s	Avge	Wkts	BB	5/10	Avge	Ct/St	O/T
Ranchod Ujesh	17.5.1969		1	1992	8	7	0	4.00	1	1-45	0/0	45.00	—	3
2 Rennie Gavin James	12.1.1976		23	1997–2001	1,023	93	0	22.73	1	1-40	0/0	84.00	13	40
2 Rennie John Alexander	29.7.1970		4	1993–1997	62	22	0	12.40	3	2-22	0/0	97.66	1	44
Rogers Barney Guy	20.8.1982		4	2004	90	29	0	11.25	0	0-17	0/0	—	1	15
Shah Ali Hassimshah	7.8.1959		3	1992–1996	122	62	0	24.40	1	1-46	0/0	125.00	1	28
Sibanda Vusimuzi	10.10.1983		14	2003–2014	591	93	0	21.10	—	—	—/–	—	16	125‡/26
Sikandar Raza	24.4.1986		14	2013–2019	982	127	1	35.07	31	7-113	2/0	39.58	3	97/32
Strang Bryan Colin	9.6.1972		26	1994–2001	465	53	0	12.91	56	5-101	1/0	39.33	11	49
2 Strang Paul Andrew	28.7.1970		24	1994–2001	839	106*	1	27.06	70	8-109	4/1	36.02	15	95
Streak Heath Hilton	16.3.1974		65	1993–2005	1,990	127*	1	22.35	216	6-73	7/0	28.14	17	187‡
Taibu Tatenda	14.5.1983		28	2001–2011	1,546	153	1	30.31	1	1-27	0/0	27.00	57/5	149‡/17
Taylor Brendan Ross Murray	6.2.1986		30	2003–2019	2,028	171	6	36.21	0	0-6	0/0	—	28	193/38
1 Tiripano Donald Tatenda	17.3.1988		9	2014–2019	291	49*	0	22.38	15	3-91	0/0	49.40	2	31/10
Traicos Athanasios John	17.5.1947		4†	1992	11	5	0	2.75	14	5-86	1/0	40.14	4	27
Utseya Prosper	26.3.1985		9	2003–2013	107	45	0	15.28	10	3-60	0/0	41.00	4	164/35
Vermeulen Mark Andrew	2.3.1979		9	2002–2014	449	118	1	24.94	0	0-5	0/0	—	6	43
Viljoen Dirk Peter	11.3.1977		2	1997–2000	57	38	0	14.25	1	1-14	0/0	65.00	1	53
Vitori Brian Vitalis	22.2.1990		4	2011–2013	52	19*	0	10.40	12	5-61	1/0	38.66	2	24/11
1 Waller Andrew Christopher	25.9.1959		2	1996	69	50	0	23.00	—	—	—/–	—	2	39
Waller Malcolm Noel	28.9.1984		14	2011–2017	577	72*	0	21.37	8	4-59	0/0	27.25	10	79/32
Watambwa Brighton Tonderai	9.6.1977		6	2000–2001	11	4*	0	3.66	14	4-64	0/0	35.00	2	—
Whittall Andrew Richard	28.3.1973		10	1996–1999	114	17	0	7.60	7	3-73	0/0	105.14	8	63
Whittall Guy James	5.9.1972		46	1993–2002	2,207	203*	4	29.42	51	4-18	0/0	40.94	19	147
Williams Sean Colin	26.9.1986		12	2012–2019	770	119	2	33.47	19	3-20	0/0	48.68	10	131/38
Wishart Craig Brian	9.1.1974		27	1995–2005	1,098	114	1	22.40	—	—	—/–	—	15	90

BANGLADESH (95 players)

	Born	Died	Tests	Test Career	Runs	HS	100s	Avge	Wkts	BB	5/10	Avge	Ct/St	O/T
Abdur Razzak	15.6.1982		13	2005–2017	248	43	0	15.50	28	4-63	0/0	59.75	4	153/34
Abu Jayed	2.8.1993		7	2018–2019	24	7*	0	3.00	17	4-108	0/0	36.35	1	2/3
Abul Hasan	5.8.1992		3	2012	165	113	1	82.50	3	2-80	0/0	123.66	3	7/5
Aftab Ahmed	10.11.1985		16	2004–2009	582	82*	0	20.78	5	2-31	0/0	47.40	7	85/11

	Born	Died	Tests	Test Career	Runs	HS	100s	Avge	Wkts	BB	5/10	Avge	Ct/St	O/T
Akram Khan	1.1.1968		8	2000–2003	259	44	0	16.18	0	–	–/–	–	3	44
Al-Amin Hossain	1.1.1990		7	2013–2019	90	32*	0	22.50	9	3-80	0/0	60.55	3	14/28
Al Sahariar	23.4.1978		15	2000–2003	683	71	0	22.76	0	–	0/0	–	10	29
Alamgir Kabir	10.1.1981		3	2002–2003	8	4	0	2.00	0	0-39	0/0	–	0	–
Alok Kapali	1.1.1984		17	2002–2005	584	85	0	17.69	6	3-3	0/0	118.16	5	69/7
Aminul Islam	2.2.1968		13	2000–2002	530	145	1	21.20	1	1-66	0/0	149.00	5	39
Anamul Haque	16.12.1992		4	2012–2014	73	22	0	9.12	–	–	–/–	–	2	38/13
Anwar Hossain Monir	31.12.1981		3	2003–2005	22	13	0	7.33	0	0-95	0/0	–	0	1
Anwar Hossain Piju	10.12.1981		1	2002	14	12	0	7.00	–	–	–/–	–	0	1
Ariful Haque	18.11.1992		2	2018	88	41*	0	29.33	1	1-10	0/0	24.00	2	1/9
Bikash Ranjan Das	14.7.1982		1	2000	2	2	0	1.00	1	1-64	0/0	72.00	1	–
Ebadat Hossain	7.1.1994		4	2018–2019	2	2	0	0.66	5	3-91	0/0	79.40	0	–
Ehsanul Haque	1.12.1979		1	2002	7	5	0	3.50	0	0-18	0/0	–	0	6
Elias Sunny	2.8.1986		4	2011–2012	38	20*	0	7.60	12	6-94	1/0	43.16	1	4/7
Enamul Haque snr	27.2.1966		10	2000–2003	180	24*	0	12.00	18	4-136	0/0	57.05	7	29
Enamul Haque jnr	5.12.1986		15	2003–2012	59	13	0	5.90	44	7-95	3/1	40.61	3	10
Fahim Muntasir	1.11.1980		3	2001–2002	52	33	0	8.66	5	3-131	0/0	68.40	0	3
Faisal Hossain	26.10.1978		1	2003	7	5	0	3.50	–	–	–/–	–	0	6
Habibul Bashar	17.8.1972		50	2000–2007	3,026	113	3	30.87	0	0-1	0/0	–	22	111
Hannan Sarkar	1.12.1982		17	2002–2004	662	76	1	20.06	0	0-2	0/0	–	7	20
Hasibul Hossain	3.6.1977		5	2000–2001	97	31	0	10.77	6	2-125	0/0	95.16	1	32
Imrul Kayes	2.2.1987		39	2008–2012	1,797	150	3	24.28	0	0-1	0/0	–	35	78/14
Jahurul Islam	12.12.1986		7	2009–2012	347	48	0	26.69	0	0-12	0/0	–	7	14/3
Javed Omar Belim	25.11.1976		40	2000–2007	1,720	119	1	22.05	0	–	–/–	–	10	59
Jubair Hossain	12.9.1995		6	2014–2015	13	7*	0	4.33	16	5-96	1/0	30.81	2	3/1
Junaid Siddique	30.10.1987		19	2007–2012	969	106	1	26.18	0	0-2	0/0	–	11	54/7
Kamrul Islam	10.12.1991		7	2016–2018	51	25*	0	5.66	8	3-87	0/0	63.00	0	2
Khaled Ahmed	20.9.1992		2	2018	4	4*	0	4.00	0	0-45	0/0	–	0	77
Khaled Mahmud	26.7.1971		12	2001–2003	266	45	0	12.09	13	4-37	0/0	64.00	2	–
Khaled Mashud	8.2.1976		44	2000–2007	1,409	103*	0	19.04	0	–	–/–	–	78/9	126
Liton Das	13.10.1994		18	2015–2019	744	94	0	24.80	0	–	–/–	–	27/2	33/25
Mahbubul Alam	1.12.1983		4	2008	5	2	0	1.25	5	2-62	0/0	62.80	0	5
Mahmudullah	4.2.1986		48	2009–2019	2,739	146	4	32.22	43	5-51	1/0	45.18	37/1	185/83
Manjural Islam	7.11.1979		17	2000–2003	81	21	0	3.68	28	6-81	1/0	57.32	4	34
Manjural Islam Rana	4.5.1984	16.3.2007	6	2003–2004	257	69	0	25.70	5	3-84	0/0	80.20	3	25
Marshall Ayub	5.12.1988		3	2013	125	41	0	20.83	0	0-15	0/0	–	2	–

	Born	Died	Tests	Test Career	Runs	HS	100s	Avge	Wkts	BB	5/10	Avge	Ct/St	O/T
Mashrafe bin Mortaza	5.10.1983		36	2001–2009	797	79	0	12.85	78	4-60	0/0	41.52	9	215±/54
Mehedi Hasan	25.10.1997		22	2016–2019	638	68*	0	17.72	90	7-58	7/2	33.12	19	38/13
Mehrab Hossain snr.	22.9.1978		9	2000–2003	241	71	0	13.38	0	0-5	0/0	–	6	18
Mehrab Hossain jnr.	8.7.1987		7	2007–2008	243	83	0	20.25	4	2-29	0/0	70.25	2	18/2
Mithun Ali	3.2.1990		7	2018–2019	228	67	0	17.53	–	–	–	–	6	24/14
Mohammad Ashraful	9.9.1984		61	2001–2012	2,737	190	6	24.00	21	2-42	0/0	60.52	25	175±/23
Mohammad Rafique	5.9.1970		33	2000–2007	1,059	111	1	18.57	100	6-77	7/0	40.76	7	123±/1
Mohammad Salim	15.10.1981		2	2003	49	26	0	16.33	–	–	–/–	–	3/1	1
Mohammad Shahid	1.11.1988		5	2014–2015	57	25	0	11.40	5	2-23	0/0	57.60	1	1
Mohammad Sharif	12.12.1983		10	2000–2007	122	24*	0	7.17	14	4-98	0/0	79.00	5	9
Mominul Haque	29.9.1991		38	2012–2019	2,657	181	8	39.65	4	3-27	0/0	94.00	29	28/6
Mosaddek Hossain	10.12.1995		3	2016–2019	164	75	0	41.00	0	0-1	0/0	–	2	35/14
Mushfiqur Rahim	1.9.1988		69	2005–2019	4,210	219*	6	35.08	–	–	–/–	–	103/15	216/84
Mushfiqur Rahman	1.1.1980		10	2000–2004	232	46*	0	13.64	13	4-65	0/0	63.30	6	28
Mustafizur Rahman	6.9.1995		13	2015–2018	56	16	0	4.30	28	4-37	0/0	35.17	1	56/37
Naeem Islam	31.12.1986		8	2008–2012	416	108	1	32.00	1	1-11	0/0	303.00	2	59/10
[2] Nafis Iqbal	31.1.1985		11	2004–2005	518	121	1	23.54	–	–	–/–	–	2	16
Naimur Rahman	19.9.1974		8	2000–2002	210	48	0	15.00	12	6-132	1/0	59.83	4	29
Nasir Hossain	30.11.1991		19	2011–2017	1,044	100	1	34.80	8	3-52	0/0	55.25	10	65/31
Nayeem Hasan	2.12.2000		4	2018–2019	70	26	0	17.50	10	5-61	1/0	23.70	1	–
Nazimuddin	1.10.1985		3	2011–2012	125	78	0	20.83	–	–	–/–	–	1	117
Nazmul Hossain	5.10.1987		2	2004–2011	16	8*	0	8.00	5	2-61	0/0	38.80	1	38/4
Nazmul Hossain Shanto	25.5.1998		2	2016–2018	48	18	0	12.00	0	0-13	0/0	–	2	3/2
Nazmul Islam	21.3.1991		1	2018	4	4	0	2.00	4	2-27	0/0	19.00	–	5/13
Nurul Hasan	21.11.1993		3	2016–2018	115	64	0	19.16	–	–	–/–	–	5/3	2/9
Rafiqul Islam	7.11.1977		1	2002	7	6	0	3.50	–	–	–/–	–	–	1
Rajin Saleh	20.11.1983		24	2003–2008	1,141	89	0	25.93	2	1-9	0/0	134.00	15	43
Raqibul Hasan	8.10.1987		9	2008–2011	336	65	0	19.76	1	1-0	0/0	17.00	9	55/5
Robiul Islam	20.10.1986		9	2010–2014	99	33	0	9.00	25	6-71	2/0	39.68	5	3/1
Rubel Hossain	1.1.1990		26	2009–2018	259	45*	0	9.96	33	5-166	1/0	80.33	11	101/27
Sabbir Rahman	20.8.1991		11	2016–2017	481	66	0	24.05	3	0-9	0/0	–	3	66/44
Sajidul Islam	18.11.1988		3	2007–2012	18	6	0	3.00	3	2-71	0/0	77.33	–	0/1
Sanjamul Islam	17.1.1990		1	2017	24	24	0	24.00	1	1-153	0/0	153.00	–	–
Sanwar Hossain	5.8.1973		9	2001–2003	345	49	0	19.16	5	2-128	0/0	62.00	1	27
Shadman Islam	18.5.1995		6	2018–2019	275	76	0	25.00	–	–	–/–	–	3	–
Shafiul Islam	6.10.1989		11	2009–2017	211	53	0	10.55	17	3-86	0/0	55.41	2	59/17

	Born	Died	Test Career	Tests	Runs	HS	100s	Avge	Wkts	BB	5/10	Avge	Ct/St	O/T
Shahadat Hossain	7.8.1986		2005–2014	38	521	40	0	10.01	72	6-27	4/0	51.81	9	51/6
Shahriar Hossain	1.6.1976		2000–2003	3	99	48	0	19.80	–	–	–/–	–	0/1	20
Shahriar Nafees	1.5.1985		2005–2012	24	1,267	138	1	26.39	–	–	–/–	–	19	75/1
Shakib Al Hasan	24.3.1987		2007–2019	56	3,862	217	5	39.40	210	7-36	18/2	31.12	24	206/76
Shamsur Rahman	5.6.1988		2013–2014	6	305	106	1	25.41	–	0-5	0/0	–	7	10/9
Shuvagata Hom	11.11.1986		2014–2016	8	244	50	0	22.18	8	2-66	0/0	63.25	8	4/5
Sohag Gazi	5.8.1991		2012–2013	10	325	101*	1	21.66	38	6-74	2/0	42.07	5	20/10
Soumya Sarkar	25.2.1993		2014–2019	15	818	149	1	29.21	3	2-68	0/0	96.00	21	55/46
Subashis Roy	28.11.1988		2016–2017	4	14	12*	0	14.00	9	3-118	0/0	51.66	0	1
Suhrawadi Shuvo	21.11.1988		2011	1	15	15	0	7.50	4	3-73	0/0	36.50	0	17/1
Syed Rasel	3.7.1984		2005–2007	6	37	19	0	4.62	12	4-129	0/0	47.75	0	52/8
Taijul Islam	7.2.1992		2014–2019	27	374	39*	0	9.58	106	8-39	7/1	32.78	15	6/2
Talha Jubair	10.12.1985		2002–2004	7	52	31	0	6.50	14	3-135	0/0	55.07	1	6
²Tamim Iqbal (*CY 2011*)	20.3.1989		2007–2018	58	4,327	206	9	38.98	0	0-1	0/0	–	14	204/71‡
Tapash Baisya	25.12.1982		2002–2005	21	384	66	0	11.29	36	4-72	0/0	59.36	6	56
Tareq Aziz	4.9.1983		2003–2004	3	22	10*	0	11.00	1	1-76	0/0	261.00	0	10
Taskin Ahmed	3.4.1995		2016–2017	5	68	33	0	6.80	7	2-43	0/0	97.42	1	32/19
Tushar Imran	10.12.1983		2002–2007	5	89	28	0	8.90	0	0-48	0/0	–	1	41
Ziaur Rahman	2.12.1986		2012	1	14	14	0	7.00	4	4-63	0/0	17.75	0	13/14

IRELAND (17 players)

	Born	Died	Test Career	Tests	Runs	HS	100s	Avge	Wkts	BB	5/10	Avge	Ct/St	O/T
Adair Mark Richard	27.3.1996		2019	1	11	8	0	5.50	6	3-32	0/0	16.33	1	9/17
Balbirnie Andrew	28.12.1990		2018–2019	3	146	82	0	24.33	–	–	–/–	–	3	64/37
Cameron-Dow James	18.5.1990		2018	1	41	32*	0	41.00	3	2-94	0/0	39.33	2	4
Dockrell George Henry	22.7.1992		2018	1	64	39	0	32.00	2	2-63	0/0	60.50	0	87/73
Joyce Edmund Christopher	22.9.1978		2018	1	47	43	0	23.50	–	–	–/–	–	1	61⅔/16‡
Kane Tyrone Edward	8.7.1994		2018	1	14	14	0	7.00	0	0-17	0/0	–	0	0/7
McBrine Andrew Robert	30.4.1993		2018–2019	2	18	11	0	4.50	3	2-77	0/0	53.00	1	42/19
McCollum James Alexander	1.8.1995		2018–2019	2	73	39	0	18.25	–	–	–/–	–	0	8
Murtagh Timothy James	2.8.1981		2018–2019	3	109	54*	0	27.25	13	5-13	1/0	16.38	0	58/14

	Born	Died	Tests	Test Career	Runs	HS	100s	Avge	Wkts	BB	5/10	Avge	Ct/St	O/T
²O'Brien Kevin Joseph	4.3.1984		3	2018–2019	258	118	1	51.60	–	–	0/0	–	–	142/90
²O'Brien Niall John	8.11.1981		1	2018	18	18	0	9.00	–	–	–/–	–	2	103/30
Porterfield William Thomas Stuart	6.9.1984		3	2018–2019	58	32	0	9.66	–	–	–/–	–	2	136/61
Poynter Stuart William	18.10.1990		1	2018	1	1	0	0.50	–	–	–/–	–	2/1	21/25
Rankin William Boyd	5.7.1984		2†	2018–2019	30	17	0	10.00	7	2-5	0/0	31.85	–	66¾/46¾
Stirling Paul Robert	3.9.1990		3	2018–2019	104	36	0	17.33	–	0-11	0/0	–	4	114/72
Thompson Stuart Robert	15.8.1991		3	2018–2019	64	53	0	10.66	10	3-28	0/0	20.40	–	20/41
Wilson Gary Craig	5.2.1986		2	2018–2019	45	33*	0	15.00	–	–	–/–	–	6	105/78

AFGHANISTAN (19 players)

	Born	Died	Tests	Test Career	Runs	HS	100s	Avge	Wkts	BB	5/10	Avge	Ct/St	O/T
Afsar Zazai	10.8.1993		3	2018–2019	135	48*	0	27.00	–	–	–/–	–	5/1	17/1
Asghar Afghan Stanikzai	27.2.1987		4	2018–2019	249	92	0	35.57	0	0-16	0/0	–	2	111/66
Hamza Hotak	15.8.1991		1	2019	35	34	0	17.50	6	5-74	1/0	13.16	–	31/31
Hashmatullah Shahidi	4.11.1994		3	2018–2019	138	61	0	34.50	–	–	–/–	–	1	39/1
Ibrahim Zadran	12.12.2001		1	2019	148	87	0	37.00	–	–	–/–	–	4	1/3
Ihsanullah Janat	28.12.1997		3	2018–2019	110	65*	0	22.00	–	–	–/–	–	–	16
Ikram Alikhil	29.9.2000		2	2018	7	7	0	7.00	–	–	–/–	–	4/1	12
Javed Ahmadi	2.1.1992		2	2018–2019	105	62	0	26.25	0	0-9	0/0	–	2	44/3
Mohammad Nabi	7.3.1985		3	2018–2019	33	24	0	5.50	8	3-36	0/0	31.75	2	124/75
Mohammad Shahzad	15.7.1991		2	2018–2018	69	40	0	17.25	–	–	–/–	–	–	84/65
Mujeeb Ur Rahman Zadran	28.3.2001		1	2018	18	15	0	9.00	1	1-75	0/0	75.00	0	40/16
Nasir Ahmadzai	21.12.1993		1	2019	17	15	0	8.50	–	–	–/–	–	0	16
Qais Ahmad	15.8.2000		1	2019	23	14	0	11.50	1	1-22	0/0	28.00	0	–
Rahmat Shah	6.7.1993		4	2018–2019	298	102	1	37.25	–	–	–/–	–	2	73
Rashid Khan	20.9.1998		4	2018–2019	106	51	0	15.14	23	6-49	3/1	21.08	2	71/44‡
Wafadar Momand	1.2.2000		2	2018–2018	12	6*	0	6.00	2	2-100	0/0	77.50	0	–
Waqar Salamkheil	2.10.2001		1	2018	–	1*	0	–	4	2-35	0/0	25.25	0	–
Yamin Ahmadzai	25.7.1992		4	2018–2019	31	18	0	4.42	10	3-41	0/0	21.10	0	4/2
Zahir Khan	20.12.1998		2	2019	0	0*	0	0.00	5	3-59	0/0	31.60	0	1

Notes

Family relationships in the above lists are indicated by superscript numbers; the following list contains only those players whose relationship is not apparent from a shared name.

In one Test, A. and G. G. Hearne played for England; their brother, F. Hearne, for South Africa.

The Waughs and New Zealand's Marshalls are the only instance of Test-playing twins.

Adnan Akmal: brother of Kamran and Umar Akmal.

Amar Singh, L.: brother of L. Ramji.

Azmat Rana: brother of Shafqat Rana.

Bazid Khan (Pakistan): son of Majid Khan (Pakistan) and grandson of M. Jahangir Khan (India).

Bravo, D. J. and D. M.: half-brothers.

Chappell, G. S., I. M. and T. M.: grandsons of V. Y. Richardson.

Collins, P. T.: half-brother of F. H. Edwards.

Cooper, W. H.: great-grandfather of A. P. Sheahan.

Edwards, F. H.: half-brother of P. T. Collins.

Hanif Mohammad: brother of Mushtaq, Sadiq and Wazir Mohammad; father of Shoaib Mohammad.

Headley, D. W (England): son of R. G. A. and grandson of G. A. Headley (both West Indies).

Hearne, F. (England and South Africa): father of G. A. L. Hearne (South Africa).

Jahangir Khan, M. (India): father of Majid Khan and grandfather of Bazid Khan (both Pakistan).

Kamran Akmal: brother of Adnan and Umar Akmal.

Khalid Wazir (Pakistan): son of S. Wazir Ali (India).

Kirsten, G. and P. N.: half-brothers.

Majid Khan (Pakistan): son of M. Jahangir Khan (India) and father of Bazid Khan (Pakistan).

Manzoor Elahi: brother of Salim and Zahoor Elahi.

Moin Khan: brother of Nadeem Khan.

Mudassar Nazar: son of Nazar Mohammad.

Murray, D. A.: son of E. D. Weekes.

Mushtaq Mohammad: brother of Hanif, Sadiq and Wazir Mohammad.

Nadeem Khan: brother of Moin Khan.

Nafis Iqbal: brother of Tamim Iqbal.

Nazar Mohammad: father of Mudassar Nazar.

Nazir Ali, S.: brother of S. Wazir Ali.

Pattinson, D. J. (England): brother of J. L. Pattinson (Australia).

Pervez Sajjad: brother of Waqar Hassan.

Ramiz Raja: brother of Wasim Raja.

Ramji, L.: brother of L. Amar Singh.

Riaz Afridi: brother of Shaheen Shah Afridi.

Richardson, V. Y.: grandfather of G. S., I. M. and T. M. Chappell.

Sadiq Mohammad: brother of Hanif, Mushtaq and Wazir Mohammad.

Saeed Ahmed: brother of Younis Ahmed.

Salim Elahi: brother of Manzoor and Zahoor Elahi.

Shafqat Rana: brother of Azmat Rana.

Shaheen Shah Afridi: brother of Riaz Afridi.

Sheahan, A. P.: great-grandson of W. H. Cooper.

Shoaib Mohammad: son of Hanif Mohammad.

Tamim Iqbal: brother of Nafis Iqbal.

Umar Akmal: brother of Adnan and Kamran Akmal.

Waqar Hassan: brother of Pervez Sajjad.

Wasim Raja: brother of Ramiz Raja.

Wazir Ali, S. (India): brother of S. Nazir Ali (India) and father of Khalid Wazir (Pakistan).

Wazir Mohammad: brother of Hanif, Mushtaq and Sadiq Mohammad.

Weekes, E. D.: father of D. A. Murray.

Yograj Singh: father of Yuvraj Singh.

Younis Ahmed: brother of Saeed Ahmed.

Yuvraj Singh: son of Yograj Singh.

Zahoor Elahi: brother of Manzoor and Salim Elahi.

Teams are listed only where relatives played for different sides.

PLAYERS APPEARING FOR MORE THAN ONE TEST TEAM

Fifteen cricketers have appeared for two countries in Test matches, namely:

Amir Elahi (India 1, Pakistan 5)	W. L. Murdoch (Australia 18, England 1)
J. J. Ferris (Australia 8, England 1)	Nawab of Pataudi snr (England 3, India 3)
S. C. Guillen (West Indies 5, New Zealand 3)	W. B. Rankin (England 1, Ireland 2)
Gul Mahomed (India 8, Pakistan 1)	A. J. Traicos (South Africa 3, Zimbabwe 4)
F. Hearne (England 2, South Africa 4)	A. E. Trott (Australia 3, England 2)
A. H. Kardar (India 3, Pakistan 23)	K. C. Wessels (Australia 24, South Africa 16)
W. E. Midwinter (England 4, Australia 8)	S. M. J. Woods (Australia 3, England 3)
F. Mitchell (England 2, South Africa 3)	

Rankin also played seven one-day internationals and two Twenty20 internationals for England and 68 ODIs and 46 T20Is for Ireland; Wessels played 54 ODIs for Australia and 55 for South Africa.

The following players appeared for the ICC World XI against Australia in the Super Series Test in 2005-06: M. V. Boucher, R. Dravid, A. Flintoff, S. J. Harmison, Inzamam-ul-Haq, J. H. Kallis, B. C. Lara, M. Muralitharan, V. Sehwag, G. C. Smith, D. L. Vettori.

In 1970, England played five first-class matches against the Rest of the World after the cancellation of South Africa's tour. Players were awarded England caps, but the matches are no longer considered to have Test status. Alan Jones (born 4.11.1938) made his only appearance for England in this series, scoring 5 and 0; he did not bowl and took no catches.

CONCUSSION SUBSTITUTES

From 2019, Test regulations provided for a full playing substitute to replace a player suffering from concussion. The following substitutions have been made:

Original player	Concussion substitute		
S. P. D. Smith	M. Labuschagne	Australia v England at Lord's	2019
D. M. Bravo	J. Blackwood	West Indies v India at Kingston	2019
D. Elgar	T. B. de Bruyn	South Africa v India at Ranchi.	2019-20
Liton Das	Mehedi Hasan	Bangladesh v India at Kolkata	2019-20
Nayeem Hasan	Taijul Islam	Bangladesh v India at Kolkata	2019-20
K. T. Kasuza	B. S. Mudzinganyama†	Zimbabwe v Sri Lanka (1st Test) at Harare . . .	2019-20
K. T. Kasuza	T. Maruma	Zimbabwe v Sri Lanka (2nd Test) at Harare . .	2019-20

† *Mudzinganyama made his Test debut as a substitute.*

ONE-DAY AND TWENTY20 INTERNATIONAL CRICKETERS

The following players had appeared for Test-playing countries in one-day internationals or Twenty20 internationals by December 31, 2019, but had not represented their countries in Test matches by January 31, 2020. (Numbers in brackets signify number of ODIs for each player: where a second number appears, e.g. (5/1), it signifies the number of T20Is for that player.)

By January 2020, D. A. Miller (126 ODIs/72 T20Is, including three for the World XI) was the most experienced international player never to have appeared in Test cricket. R. G. Sharma held the record for most international appearances before making his Test debut, with 108 ODIs and 36 T20Is. S. Badree had played a record 52 T20Is (including two for the World XI) without a Test or ODI appearance.

England

M. W. Alleyne (10), I. D. Austin (9), T. Banton (0/3), S. W. Billings (15/25), D. R. Briggs (1/7), A. D. Brown (16), D. R. Brown (9), P. R. Brown (0/4), G. Chapple (1), J. W. M. Dalrymple (27/3), S. M. Davies (8/5), J. W. Dernbach (24/34), M. V. Fleming (11), P. J. Franks (1), I. J. Gould (18), A. P. Grayson (2), L. Gregory (0/5), H. F. Gurney (10/2), G. W. Humpage (3), T. E. Jesty (10), E. C. Joyce (17/2), C. Kieswetter (46/25), L. S. Livingstone (0/2), G. D. Lloyd (2), A. G. R. Loudon (1), J. D. Love (3), M. B. Loye (7), M. J. Lumb (3/27), M. A. Lynch (3), S. Mahmood (0/3), A. D. Mascarenhas (20/14), S. C. Meaker (2/2), T. S. Mills (0/4), P. Mustard (10/2), P. A. Nixon (19/1), M. W. Parkinson (0/2), S. D. Parry (2/5), M. J. Smith (5), N. M. K. Smith (7), J. N. Snape (10/1),

V. S. Solanki (51/3), R. J. W. Topley (10/6), J. O. Troughton (6), C. M. Wells (2), V. J. Wells (9), A. G. Wharf (13), D. J. Willey (46/28), L. J. Wright (50/51), M. H. Yardy (28/14).

D. R. Brown also played 16 ODIs for Scotland, and E. C. Joyce one Test, 61 ODIs and 16 T20Is for Ireland.

Australia

S. A. Abbott (1/4), J. P. Behrendorff (11/7), T. R. Birt (0/4), G. A. Bishop (2), S. M. Boland (14/3), C. J. Boyce (0/7), R. J. Campbell (2), A. T. Carey (29/25), D. T. Christian (19/16), M. J. Cosgrove (3), N. M. Coulter-Nile (32/28), B. C. J. Cutting (4/4), M. J. Di Venuto (9), B. R. Dorey (4), B. R. Dunk (0/5), Fawad Ahmed (3/2), P. J. Forrest (15), B. Geeves (2/1), S. F. Graf (11), I. J. Harvey (73), S. M. Harwood (1/3), S. D. Heazlett (1), J. R. Hopes (84/12), D. J. Hussey (69/39), M. Klinger (0/3), B. Laughlin (5/3), S. Lee (45), M. L. Lewis (72/4), C. A. Lynn (4/18), R. J. McCurdy (11), B. R. McDermott (0/12), K. H. MacLeay (16), J. P. Maher (26), J. M. Muirhead (0/5), D. P. Nannes (1/15), M. G. Neser (2), A. A. Noffke (1/2), J. S. Paris (2), L. A. Pomersbach (0/1), G. D. Porter (2), N. J. Reardon (0/2), K. W. Richardson (22/15), B. J. Rohrer (0/1), L. Ronchi (4/3), G. S. Sandhu (2), D. J. M. Short (4/20), J. D. Siddons (1), B. Stanlake (7/19), M. P. Stoinis (41/19), A. M. Stuart (3), M. J. Swepson (0/1), C. P. Tremain (4), G. S. Trimble (2), A. J. Turner (3/11), A. J. Tye (7/26), J. D. Wildermuth (0/2), D. J. Worrall (3), B. E. Young (6), A. Zampa (48/27), A. K. Zesers (2).

R. J. Campbell also played three T20Is for Hong Kong, D. P. Nannes two T20Is for the Netherlands, and L. Ronchi four Tests, 72 ODIs and 26 T20Is for New Zealand.

South Africa

Y. A. Abdulla (0/2), S. Abrahams (1), F. Behardien (59/38), D. M. Benkenstein (23), G. H. Bodi (2/1), L. E. Bosman (13/14), R. E. Bryson (7), D. J. Callaghan (29), G. L. Cloete (0/2), D. N. Crookes (32), C. J. Dala (2/9), H. Davids (2/9), B. C. Fortuin (0/2), R. Frylinck (0/3), T. Henderson (0/1), R. R. Hendricks (18/22), C. A. Ingram (31/9), C. Jonker (2/2), J. C. Kent (2), L. J. Koen (5), G. J-P. Kruger (3/1), E. Leie (0/2), R. E. Levi (0/13), J. Louw (3/2), J. N. Malan (0/2), D. A. Miller (126/72), M. Mosehle (0/7), P. V. Mpitsang (2), S. J. Palframan (7), A. M. Phangiso (21/16), N. Pothas (3), A. G. Puttick (1), S. Qeshile (0/2), C. E. B. Rice (3), M. J. R. Rindel (22), R. R. Rossouw (36/15), D. B. Rundle (2), T. G. Shaw (9), M. Shezi (1), E. O. Simons (23), L. L. Sipamla (0/5), J. T. Smuts (0/8), E. L. R. Stewart (6), R. Telemachus (37/3), J. Theron (4/9), A. C. Thomas (0/1), T. Tshabalala (4), R. E. van der Merwe (13/13), J. J. van der Wath (10/8), V. B. van Jaarsveld (2/3), M. N. van Wyk (17/8), C. J. P. G. van Zyl (2), D. Wiese (6/20), H. S. Williams (7), M. Yachad (1), K. Zondo (5).

R. E. van der Merwe also played two ODIs and 30 T20Is for the Netherlands.

West Indies

F. A. Allen (12/11), H. A. G. Anthony (3), S. Badree (0/50), C. D. Barnwell (0/6), M. C. Bascombe (0/1), R. R. Beaton (2), N. E. Bonner (0/2), D. Brown (3), B. St A. Browne (4), P. A. Browne (5), H. R. Bryan (15), D. C. Butler (5/1), J. L. Carter (33), J. Charles (48/34), D. O. Christian (0/2), R. T. Crandon (1), R. E. Emrit (2/4), S. E. Findlay (9/2), A. D. S. Fletcher (25/42), R. S. Gabriel (11), R. C. Haynes (8), C. Hemraj (6), R. O. Hurley (9), D. P. Hyatt (9/5), K. C. B. Jeremy (6), B. A. King (1/6), E. Lewis (48/29), A. M. McCarthy (0/3), O. C. McCoy (2/2), A. Martin (91), G. E. Mathurin (0/3), J. N. Mohammed (28/9), A. R. Nurse (54/13), W. K. D. Perkins (0/1), K. A. Pierre (2/8), K. A. Pollard (107/68), N. Pooran (19/16), R. Powell (34/23), M. R. Pydanna (3), A. C. L. Richards (1/1), S. E. Rutherford (0/3), K. Santokie (0/12), K. F. Semple (7), R. Shepherd (3), O. F. Smith (0/2), D. C. Thomas (21/3), O. R. Thomas (19/10), C. M. Tuckett (1), H. R. Walsh (4/5), K. O. K. Williams (8/24), L. R. Williams (15).

New Zealand

G. W. Aldridge (2/1), M. D. Bailey (1), M. D. Bates (2/3), B. R. Blair (14), T. C. Bruce (0/15), C. E. Bulfin (4), T. K. Canning (4), M. S. Chapman (3/5), P. G. Coman (3), A. P. Devcich (12/4), B. J. Diamanti (1/1), M. W. Douglas (6), A. M. Ellis (15/5), L. H. Ferguson (19/2), B. G. Hadlee (2), L. J. Hamilton (2), R. T. Hart (1), R. L. Hayes (1), R. M. Hira (0/15), P. A. Hitchcock (14/1), L. G. Howell (12), A. K. Kitchen (0/5), S. C. Kuggeleijn (2/9), M. J. McClenaghan (48/28), N. L. McCullum (84/63), P. D. McGlashan (4/11), B. J. McKechnie (14), E. B. McSweeney (16), A. W. Mathieson (1), J. P. Millmow (5), A. F. Milne (0/47), T. S. Nethula (5), C. J. Nevin (37), A. J. Penn (5), R. G. Petrie (12), G. D. Phillips (0/11), S. H. A. Rance (2/8), K. B. Reid (9), S. J. Roberts (2), T. L. Seifert (3/15), S. L. Stewart (4), L. W. Stott (1), G. P. Sulzberger (3), A. R. Tait (5), E. P. Thompson (1/1),

B. M. Tickner (0/3), M. D. J. Walker (3), R. J. Webb (3), B. M. Wheeler (6/6), J. W. Wilson (6), W. A. Wisneski (3), L. J. Woodcock (4/3), G. H. Worker (10/2).

M. S. Chapman also played 2 ODIs and 19 T20Is for Hong Kong.

India

K. K. Ahmed (11/14), S. Aravind (0/1), P. Awana (0/2), A. C. Bedade (13), A. Bhandari (2), Bhupinder Singh snr (2), G. Bose (1), Y. S. Chahal (50/36), D. L. Chahar (3/10), R. D. Chahar (0/1), V. B. Chandrasekhar (7), U. Chatterjee (3), N. A. David (4), P. Dharmani (1), R. Dhawan (3/1), A. B. Dinda (13/9), S. R. Dube (1/6), F. Y. Fazal (1), R. S. Gavaskar (11), R. S. Ghai (6), S. Gill (2), M. S. Gony (2), Gurkeerat Singh (3), S. S. Iyer (12/14), K. M. Jadhav (71/9), Joginder Sharma (4/4), A. V. Kale (1), S. Kaul (3/3), S. C. Khanna (10), G. K. Khoda (2), A. R. Khurasiya (12), D. S. Kulkarni (12/2), T. Kumaran (8), Mandeep Singh (0/3), M. Markande (0/1), J. J. Martin (10), D. Mongia (57/1), S. P. Mukherjee (3), A. M. Nayar (3), P. Negi (0/1), G. K. Pandey (2), M. K. Pandey (23/32), K. H. Pandya (0/18), J. V. Paranjpe (4), Parvez Rasool (1/1), A. K. Patel (8), A. R. Patel (38/11), Y. K. Pathan (57/22), Randhir Singh (2), S. S. Raul (2), A. T. Rayudu (55/6), N. Saini (1/5), A. M. Salvi (4), S. V. Samson (0/1), V. Shankar (12/9), M. Sharma (26/8), R. Sharma (4/2), S. Sharma (0/2), L. R. Shukla (3), R. P. Singh (2), M. Siraj (1/3), R. S. Sodhi (18), S. Somasunder (2), B. B. Sran (6/2), S. Sriram (8), Sudhakar Rao (1), M. K. Tiwary (12/3), S. S. Tiwary (3), S. Tyagi (4/1), R. V. Uthappa (46/13), P. S. Vaidya (4), Y. Venugopal Rao (16), M. S. Washington Sundar (1/18), Jai P. Yadav (12).

Pakistan

Aamer Hameed (2), Aamer Hanif (5), Aamer Yamin (4/2), Akhtar Sarfraz (4), Anwar Ali (22/16), Arshad Pervez (2), Asad Ali (4/2), Asif Ali (18/25), Asif Mahmood (2), Awais Zia (0/5), Faisal Athar (1), Ghulam Ali (3), Haafiz Shahid (3), Hammad Azam (11/5), Hasan Jamil (6), Hussain Talat (1/14), Imad Wasim (53/41), Imran Abbas (3), Imran Khan jnr (0/3), Iqbal Sikandar (4), Irfan Bhatti (1), Javed Qadir (1), Junaid Zia (4), Kamran Hussain (2), Kashif Raza (1), Khalid Latif (5/13), Khushdil Shah (0/1), Mahmood Hamid (1), Mansoor Amjad (1/1), Mansoor Rana (2), Manzoor Akhtar (7), Maqsood Rana (1), Masood Iqbal (1), Mohammad Hasnain (5/4), Moin-ul-Atiq (5), Mujahid Jamshed (4), Mukhtar Ahmed (0/6), Naeem Ahmed (1), Naeem Ashraf (2), Najaf Shah (1), Naseer Malik (3), Nauman Anwar (0/1), Naumanullah (1), Parvez Mir (3), Rafatullah Mohmand (0/3), Rameez Raja (0/2), Raza Hasan (1/10), Rizwan Ahmed (1), Rumman Raees (9/8), Saad Ali (2), Saad Nasim (3/3), Saadat Ali (8), Saeed Azad (4), Sahibzada Farhan (0/3), Sajid Ali (13), Sajjad Akbar (2), Salim Pervez (1), Samiullah Khan (2), Shahid Anwar (1), Shahzaib Hasan (3/10), Shakeel Ansar (0/2), Shakil Khan (1), Shoaib Khan (0/1), Sohaib Maqsood (26/20), Sohail Fazal (2), Tanvir Mehdi (1), Usman Shinwari (9/13), Waqas Maqsood (0/1),Wasim Haider (3), Zafar Gohar (1), Zafar Iqbal (8), Zahid Ahmed (2).

Sri Lanka

M. A. Aponso (9/3), J. R. M. W. S. Bandara (0/8), K. M. C. Bandara (1/1), J. W. H. D. Boteju (2), D. L. S. de Silva (1), G. N. de Silva (4), P. C. de Silva (7/2), P. W. H. de Silva (12/8), S. N. T. de Silva (0/3), L. H. D. Dilhara (9/2), A. M. Fernando (1), B. Fernando (0/2), E. R. Fernando (3), T. L. Fernando (1), U. N. K. Fernando (2), W. I. A. Fernando (15/10), J. C. Gamage (4), W. C. A. Ganegama (4), F. R. M. Goonatilleke (1), P. W. Gunaratne (23), A. A. W. Gunawardene (1), P. D. Heyn (2), W. S. Jayantha (17), P. S. Jayaprakashdaran (1), C. U. Jayasinghe (0/5), S. A. Jayasinghe (2), G. S. N. F. G. Jayasuriya (12/16), N. G. R. P. Jayasuriya (2), S. H. T. Kandamby (39/5), S. H. U. Karnain (19), H. G. J. M. Kulatunga (0/2), D. S. M. Kumara (1/2), L. D. Madushanka (4/2), B. M. A. J. Mendis (58/22), C. Mendis (1), P. H. K. D. Mendis (2/4), A. M. N. Munasinghe (5), E. M. D. Y. Munaweera (2/13), H. G. D. Nayanakantha (1), A. R. M. Opatha (5), S. P. Pasqual (2), S. S. Pathirana (18/5), A. K. Perera (6/6), K. G. Perera (1), P. A. R. P. Perera (1), H. S. M. Pieris (3), S. M. A. Priyanjan (23/3), W. M. Pushpakumara (3/1), P. B. B. Rajapaksa (0/5), R. L. B. Rambukwella (0/2), M. B. Ranasinghe (1/2), S. K. Ranasinghe (4), N. Ranatunga (2), N. L. K. Ratnayake (2), R. J. M. G. M. Rupasinghe (0/2), A. P. B. Tennekoon (4), M. H. Tissera (3), I. Udana (15/27), J. D. F. Vandersay (12/10), D. M. Vonhagt (1), A. P. Weerakkody (1), D. S. Weerakkody (3), S. Weerakoon (2), K. Weeraratne (15/5), S. R. D. Wettimuny (3), R. P. A. H. Wickremaratne (3).

Zimbabwe

R. D. Brown (7), K. M. Curran (11), S. G. Davies (4), K. G. Duers (6), E. A. Essop-Adam (1), D. A. G. Fletcher (6), T. N. Garwe (1), J. G. Heron (6), R. S. Higgins (11), V. R. Hogg (2), A. J. Ireland (26/1), D. Jakiel (0/2), L. M. Jongwe (22/8), R. Kaia (1), T. S. Kamunhukamwe (5), F. Kasteni (2), A. J. Mackay (3), N. Madziva (12/15), G. C. Martin (5), W. T. Mashinge (0/2),

M. A. Meman (1), T. V. Mufambisi (6), T. T. Munyonga (0/5), R. C. Murray (5), T. K. Musakanda (1), C. T. Mutombodzi (11/5), T. Muzarabani (8/9), R. Ngarava (9/1), I. A. Nicolson (2), G. A. Paterson (10), G. E. Peckover (3), E. C. Rainsford (39/2), P. W. E. Rawson (10), H. P. Rinke (18), L. N. Roche (3), R. W. Sims (3), G. M. Strydom (12), C. Zhuwao (9/7).

Bangladesh

Abu Haider (2/13), Afif Hossain (0/8), Ahmed Kamal (1), Alam Talukdar (2), Aminul Islam (Bhola) (1), Aminul Islam (Biplob) (4), Anisur Rahman (2), Arafat Sunny (16/10), Ather Ali Khan (19), Azhar Hussain (7), Dhiman Ghosh (14/1), Dolar Mahmud (7), Farhad Reza (34/13), Faruq Ahmed (7), Fazle Mahmud (2), Gazi Ashraf (5), Ghulam Faruq (5), Ghulam Nausher (9), Hafizur Rahman (2), Harunur Rashid (2), Jahangir Alam (3), Jahangir Badshah (5), Jamaluddin Ahmed (1), Mafizur Rahman (4), Mahbubur Rahman (1), Mazharul Haque (1), Mehedi Hasan snr (47), Minhazul Abedin (27), Mohammad Naim (3), Mohammad Saifuddin (20/13), Moniruzzaman (2), Morshed Ali Khan (3), Mosharraf Hossain (5), Mukhtar Ali (0/1), Nadif Chowdhury (0/3), Nasir Ahmed (7), Nazmus Sadat (0/1), Neeyamur Rashid (2), Nurul Abedin (4), Rafiqul Alam (2), Raqibul Hasan snr (2), Rony Talukdar (0/1), Saiful Islam (7), Sajjad Ahmed (2), Samiur Rahman (2), Saqlain Sajib (0/1), Shafiuddin Ahmed (11), Shahidur Rahman (2), Shariful Haq (1), Sheikh Salahuddin (6), Tanveer Haider (2), Wahidul Gani (1), Zahid Razzak (3), Zakir Hasan (0/1), Zakir Hassan (2).

Ireland

J. Anderson (8/4), A. C. Botha (42/14), J. P. Bray (15/2), S. A. Britton (1), K. E. D. Carroll (6), P. K. D. Chase (25/12), P. Connell (13/9), A. R. Cusack (59/37), D. C. A. Delany (0/8), G. J. Delany (0/17), P. S. Eaglestone (1/1), M. J. Fourie (7), S. C. Getkate (3/14), P. G. Gillespie (5), R. S. Haire (2), J. D. Hall (3), D. T. Johnston (67/30), N. G. Jones (14/5), D. I. Joyce (3), G. E. Kidd (6/1), D. Langford-Smith (22), J. B. Little (4/11), W. K. McCallan (39/9), R. D. McCann (8/3), G. J. McCarter (1/3), B. J. McCarthy (27/6), J. F. Mooney (64/27), P. J. K. Mooney (4), E. J. G. Morgan (23), J. Mulder (4/8), A. D. Poynter (19/19), D. A. Rankin (0/2), E. J. Richardson (2), J. N. K. Shannon (1/8), S. Singh (15/18), M. C. Sorensen (13/26), R. Strydom (9/4), H. T. Tector (0/14), S. P. Terry (5/1), S. J. Thompson (3/10), L. J. Tucker (5/14), A. van der Merwe (9), R. M. West (10/5), R. K. Whelan (2), A. R. White (61/18), C. A. Young (13/26).

E. J. G. Morgan also played 16 Tests, 210 ODIs and 86 T20Is for England.

Afghanistan

Abdullah Mazari (2), Aftab Alam (27/12), Ahmed Shah (1), Dawlat Ahmadzai (3/2), Dawlat Zadran (82/34), Fareed Ahmad (5/14), Fazal Niazai (0/1), Gulbadeen Naib (65/45), Hamid Hassan (38/22), Hasti Gul (2), Hazratullah Zazai (16/13), Izatullah Dawlatzai (5/4), Karim Janat (1/21), Karim Sadiq (24/36), Khaliq Dad (6), Mirwais Ashraf (46/25), Mohibullah Paak (2), Najeeb Tarakai (1/12), Najibullah Zadran (67/57), Nasim Baras (0/3), Naveen-ul-Haq (4/4), Nawroz Mangal (49/32), Noor Ali Zadran (51/20), Noor-ul-Haq (2), Raees Ahmadzai (5/8), Rahmanullah Gurbaz (0/7), Rokhan Barakzai (1/3), Samiullah Shenwari (84/62), Sayed Shirzad (2/4), Shabir Noori (10/1), Shafiqullah Shinwari (24/46), Shapoor Zadran (44/34), Sharafuddin Ashraf (17/8), Usman Ghani (15/19), Zakiullah (1), Zamir Khan (0/1), Ziaur Rahman (0/1).

PLAYERS APPEARING FOR MORE THAN ONE ONE-DAY/TWENTY20 INTERNATIONAL TEAM

The following players have played ODIs for the **African XI** in addition to their national side:

N. Boje (2), L. E. Bosman (1), J. Botha (2), M. V. Boucher (5), E. Chigumbura (3), A. B. de Villiers (5), H. H. Dippenaar (6), J. H. Kallis (2), J. M. Kemp (6), J. A. Morkel (2), M. Morkel (3), T. M. Odoyo (5), P. J. Ongondo (2), J. L. Ontong (1), S. M. Pollock (5), A. G. Prince (3), J. A. Rudolph (2), V. Sibanda (2), G. C. Smith (1), D. W. Steyn (2), H. H. Streak (2), T. Taibu (1), S. O. Tikolo (4), M. Zondeki (2). (Odoyo, Ongondo and Tikolo played for Kenya, who do not have Test status.)

The following players have played ODIs for the **Asian Cricket Council XI** in addition to their national side:

Abdul Razzaq (4), M. S. Dhoni (3), R. Dravid (1), C. R. D. Fernando (1), S. C. Ganguly (3), Harbhajan Singh (2), Inzamam-ul-Haq (3), S. T. Jayasuriya (4), D. P. M. D. Jayawardene (5), A. Kumble (2), Mashrafe bin Mortaza (2), Mohammad Ashraful (2), Mohammad Asif (3), Mohammad Rafique (2), Mohammad Yousuf (7), M. Muralitharan (4), A. Nehra (3), K. C. Sangakkara (4),

V. Sehwag (7), Shahid Afridi (3), Shoaib Akhtar (3), W. U. Tharanga (1), W. P. U. J. C. Vaas (1), Yuvraj Singh (3), Zaheer Khan (6).

The following players have played ODIs for an **ICC World XI** in addition to their national side:

C. L. Cairns (1), R. Dravid (3), S. P. Fleming (1), A. Flintoff (3), C. H. Gayle (3), A. C. Gilchrist (1), D. Gough (1), M. L. Hayden (1), J. H. Kallis (1), B. C. Lara (4), G. D. McGrath (1), M. Muralitharan (3), M. Ntini (1), K. P. Pietersen (2), S. M. Pollock (3), R. T. Ponting (1), K. C. Sangakkara (3), V. Sehwag (3), Shahid Afridi (2), Shoaib Akhtar (2), D. L. Vettori (4), S. K. Warne (1).

The following players have played T20Is for a **World XI** in addition to their national side:

H. M. Amla (3), S. Badree (2), G. J. Bailey (1), S. W. Billings (1), P. D. Collingwood (1), B. C. J. Cutting (3), F. du Plessis (3), G. D. Elliott (1), Imran Tahir (3), K. D. Karthik (1), S. Lamichhane (1), M. J. McClenaghan (1), D. A. Miller (3), T. S. Mills (1), M. Morkel (3), T. D. Paine (2), N. L. T. C. Perera (4), Rashid Khan (1), L. Ronchi (1), D. J. G. Sammy (2), Shahid Afridi (2), Shoaib Malik (1), Tamim Iqbal (4).

K. C. Wessels played Tests and ODIs for both Australia and South Africa. **D. R. Brown** played ODIs for England plus ODIs and T20Is for Scotland. **C. B. Lambert** played Tests and ODIs for West Indies and one ODI for USA. **E. C. Joyce** played ODIs and T20Is for England and all three formats for Ireland; **E. J. G. Morgan** ODIs for Ireland and all three formats for England; and **W. B. Rankin** all three formats for Ireland and England. **A. C. Cummins** played Tests and ODIs for West Indies and ODIs for Canada. **G. M. Hamilton** played Tests for England and ODIs for Scotland. **D. P. Nannes** played ODIs and T20Is for Australia and T20Is for the Netherlands. **L. Ronchi** played ODIs and T20Is for Australia and all three formats for New Zealand. **G. O. Jones** played all three formats for England and ODIs for Papua New Guinea. **R. E. van der Merwe** played ODIs and T20Is for South Africa and the Netherlands. **R. J. Campbell** played ODIs for Australia and T20Is for Hong Kong. **M. S. Chapman** played ODIs and T20Is for Hong Kong and New Zealand. **Izatullah Dawlatzai** played ODIs and T20Is for Afghanistan and T20Is for Germany. **X. M. Marshall** played all three formats for West Indies and ODIs and T20Is for USA. **G. M. Strydom** played ODIs for Zimbabwe and T20Is for Cayman Islands. **J. Theron** played ODIs and T20Is for South Africa and ODIs for USA. **H. R. Walsh** played ODIs and T20Is for both USA and West Indies.

ELITE TEST UMPIRES

The following umpires were on the ICC's elite panel in February 2020. The figures for Tests, one-day internationals and Twenty20 internationals and the Test Career dates refer to matches in which they officiated as on-field umpires (excluding abandoned games). The totals of Tests are complete up to January 31, 2020, the totals of one-day internationals and Twenty20 internationals up to December 31, 2019.

	Country	Born	Tests	Test Career	ODIs	T20Is
Aleem Dar	P	6.6.1968	131	*2003–2019*	207	46
Dharmasena Handunnettige Deepthi Priyantha Kumar	SL	24.4.1971	65	*2010–2019*	103	22
Erasmus Marais	SA	27.2.1964	62*	*2009–2019*	90	26
Gaffaney Christopher Blair	NZ	30.11.1975	32	*2014–2019*	68	22
Gough Michael Andrew	E	18.12.1979	13	*2016–2019*	60	14
Illingworth Richard Keith	E	23.8.1963	47*	*2012–2019*	65	16
Kettleborough Richard Allan	E	15.3.1973	62	*2010–2019*	88	22
Llong Nigel James	E	11.2.1969	61	*2007–2019*	129	32
Oxenford Bruce Nicholas James	A	5.3.1960	59	*2010–2019*	95	20
Reiffel Paul Ronald	A	19.4.1966	47	*2012–2019*	69	16
Tucker Rodney James	A	28.8.1964	71	*2009–2019*	84	35
Wilson Joel Sheldon	WI	30.12.1966	18	*2015–2019*	64	26

* *Includes one Test where he took over mid-match.*

BIRTHS AND DEATHS

OTHER CRICKETING NOTABLES

The following list shows the births and deaths of cricketers, and people associated with cricket, who have *not* played in men's Test matches.

Criteria for inclusion All non-Test players who have either (1) scored 20,000 first-class runs, or (2) taken 1,500 first-class wickets, or (3) achieved 750 dismissals, or (4) reached both 15,000 runs and 750 wickets. Also included are (5) the leading players who flourished before the start of Test cricket, (6) *Wisden* Cricketers of the Year who did not play Test cricket, and (7) others of merit or interest.

Names Where players were normally known by a name other than their first, this is underlined.

Teams Where only one team is listed, this is normally the one for which the player made most first-class appearances. Additional teams are listed only if the player appeared for them in more than 20 first-class matches, or if they are especially relevant to their career. School and university teams are not given unless especially relevant (e.g. for the schoolboys chosen as wartime Cricketers of the Year in the 1918 and 1919 *Wisdens*).

		Born	Died
Adams Percy Webster	Cheltenham College; *CY 1919*	5.9.1900	28.9.1962
Aird Ronald MC Hampshire; sec. MCC 1953–62, pres. MCC 1968–69		4.5.1902	16.8.1986
Aislabie Benjamin	Surrey, secretary of MCC 1822–42	14.1.1774	2.6.1842
Alcock Charles William	Secretary of Surrey 1872–1907	2.12.1842	26.2.1907
Editor, Cricket magazine, 1882–1907. Captain of Wanderers and England football teams.			
Aleem Dar	Umpire in a record 131 Tests by January 2020	6.6.1968	
Alley William Edward	NSW, Somerset; Test umpire; *CY 1962*	3.2.1919	26.11.2004
Alleyne Mark Wayne	Gloucestershire; *CY 1991*	23.5.1968	
Altham Harry Surtees CBE Surrey, Hants; historian; pres. MCC 1959–60		30.11.1888	11.3.1965
Arlott Leslie Thomas <u>John</u> OBE	Broadcaster and writer	25.2.1914	14.12.1991
Arthur John Michael	Griq. W, OFS; South Africa coach 2005–10,		17.5.1968	
Australia coach 2011–13, Pakistan coach 2016–19, SL coach 2019–			
Ashdown William Henry	Kent	27.12.1898	15.9.1979
The only player to appear in English first-class cricket before and after the two world wars.			
Ash Eileen (*née* Whelan)	England women	30.10.1911	
Ashley-Cooper Frederick Samuel	Historian	22.3.1877	31.1.1932
Ashton *Sir* Hubert KBE MC Cam U, Essex; pres. MCC 1960–61; *CY 1922*		13.2.1898	17.6.1979
Austin *Sir* Harold Bruce Gardiner	Barbados	15.7.1877	27.7.1943
Austin Ian David	Lancashire; *CY 1999*	30.5.1966	
Bailey Jack Arthur	Essex; secretary of MCC 1974–87	22.6.1930	12.7.2018
Bainbridge Philip	Gloucestershire, Durham; *CY 1986*	16.4.1958	
Bakewell Enid (*née* Turton) MBE	England women	16.12.1940	
Bannister John David	Warwickshire; writer and broadcaster	23.8.1930	23.1.2016
Barker Gordon	Essex	6.7.1931	10.2.2006
Bartlett Hugh Tryon	Sussex; *CY 1939*	7.10.1914	26.6.1988
Bates Suzannah Wilson	New Zealand women	16.9.1987	
Bayliss Trevor Harley OBE NSW; SL coach 2007–11; Eng. coach 2015–19		21.12.1962	
Beauclerk *Rev. Lord* Frederick	Middlesex, Surrey, MCC	8.5.1773	22.4.1850
Beaumont Tamsin Tilley MBE	England women; *CY 2019*	11.3.1991	
Beldam George William	Middlesex; photographer	1.5.1868	23.11.1937
Beldham William ("Silver Billy")	Hambledon, Surrey	5.2.1766	26.2.1862
Beloff Michael Jacob QC	Head of ICC Code of Conduct Commission	18.4.1942	
Benkenstein Dale Martin	KwaZulu-Natal, Durham; *CY 2009*	9.6.1974	
Berry Anthony <u>Scyld</u> Ivens	Editor of *Wisden* 2008–11	28.4.1954	
Berry Leslie George	Leicestershire	28.4.1906	5.2.1985
Bird Harold Dennis ("Dickie") OBE Yorkshire, Leics; umpire in 66 Tests		19.4.1933	
Blofeld Henry Calthorpe OBE	Cambridge Univ; broadcaster	23.9.1939	
Bond John David	Lancashire; *CY 1971*	6.5.1932	11.7.2019
Booth Roy	Yorkshire, Worcestershire	1.10.1926	24.9.2018
Bowden Brent Fraser ("Billy")	Umpire in 84 Tests	11.4.1963	
Bowley Frederick Lloyd	Worcestershire	9.11.1873	31.5.1943

		Born	Died
Bradshaw Keith	Tasmania; secretary/chief executive MCC 2006–11	2.10.1963	
Brewer Derek Michael	Secretary/chief executive MCC 2012–17	2.4.1958	
Briers Nigel Edwin	Leicestershire; *CY 1993*	15.1.1955	
Brittin Janette Ann MBE	England women	4.7.1959	11.9.2017
Brookes Wilfrid H.	Editor of Wisden 1936–39	5.12.1894	28.5.1955
Bryan John Lindsay	Kent; *CY 1922*	26.5.1896	23.4.1985
Buchanan John Marshall	Queensland; Australia coach 1999–2007	5.4.1953	
Bucknor Stephen Anthony	Umpire in 128 Tests	31.5.1946	
Bull Frederick George	Essex; *CY 1898*	2.4.1875	16.9.1910
Buller John Sydney MBE	Worcestershire; Test umpire	23.8.1909	7.8.1970
Burnup Cuthbert James	Kent; *CY 1903*	21.11.1875	5.4.1960
Caine Charles Stewart	Editor of Wisden 1926–33	28.10.1861	15.4.1933
Calder Harry Lawton	Cranleigh School; *CY 1918*	24.1.1901	15.9.1995
Cardus Sir John Frederick <u>Neville</u>	Writer	2.4.1888	27.2.1975
Chalke Stephen Robert	Writer	5.6.1948	
Chapple Glen	Lancashire; *CY 2012*	23.1.1974	
Chester Frank	Worcestershire; Test umpire	20.1.1895	8.4.1957
Stood in 48 Tests between 1924 and 1955, a record that lasted until 1992.			
Clark Belinda Jane	Australia women	10.9.1970	
Clark David Graham	Kent; president MCC 1977–78	27.1.1919	8.10.2013
Clarke Charles <u>Giles</u> CBE	Chairman ECB, 2007–15, pres. ECB, 2015–18	29.5.1953	
Clarke William	Nottinghamshire; founded the All-England XI	24.12.1798	25.8.1856
Collier David Gordon OBE	Chief executive of ECB, 2005–14	22.4.1955	
Collins Arthur Edward Jeune	Clifton College	18.8.1885	11.11.1914
Made 628* in a house match in 1899, the highest score in any cricket until 2016.			
Conan Doyle Dr Sir Arthur Ignatius		22.5.1859	7.7.1930
Creator of Sherlock Holmes; his only victim in first-class cricket was W. G. Grace.			
Connor Clare Joanne CBE	England women; administrator	1.9.1976	
Constant David John	Kent, Leics; first-class umpire 1969–2006	9.11.1941	
Cook Thomas Edwin Reed	Sussex	5.1.1901	15.1.1950
Cox George jnr	Sussex	23.8.1911	30.3.1985
Cox George snr	Sussex	29.11.1873	24.3.1949
Cozier Winston <u>Anthony</u> Lloyd	Broadcaster and writer	10.7.1940	11.5.2016
Dalmiya Jagmohan	Pres. BCCI 2001–04, 2015, pres. ICC 1997–2000	30.5.1940	20.9.2015
Davies Emrys	Glamorgan; Test umpire	27.6.1904	10.11.1975
Davison Brian Fettes	Rhodesia, Leics, Tasmania, Gloucestershire	21.12.1946	
Dawkes George Owen	Leicestershire, Derbyshire	19.7.1920	10.8.2006
Day Arthur Percival	Kent; *CY 1910*	10.4.1885	22.1.1969
de Lisle Timothy John March Phillipps	Editor of *Wisden* 2003	25.6.1962	
Dennett Edward <u>George</u>	Gloucestershire	27.4.1880	14.9.1937
Deutrom Warren Robert	Chief executive, Cricket Ireland 2006–	13.1.1970	
Dhanawade Pranav Prashant	K. C. Gandhi English School	13.5.2000	
Made the highest score in any cricket, 1,009*, in a school match in Mumbai in January 2016.			
Di Venuto Michael James	Tas., Derbys, Durham; Surrey coach 2016–	12.12.1973	
Domingo Russell Craig	SA coach 2013–17, Bangladesh coach 2019–	30.8.1974	
Eagar Edward <u>Patrick</u>	Photographer	9.3.1944	
Eddings Earl Robert	Chairman of Cricket Australia 2018–	10.12.1967	
Edwards Charlotte Marie CBE	England women; *CY 2014*	17.12.1979	
Ehsan Mani	President ICC 2003–06; Chairman PCB 2018–	23.3.1945	
Engel Matthew Lewis	Editor of *Wisden* 1993–2000, 2004–07	11.6.1951	
Farbrace Paul	Kent, Middx; SL coach 2014; Eng. asst coach 2014–19	7.7.1967	
"Felix" (Nicholas Wanostrocht)	Kent, Surrey, All-England	4.10.1804	3.9.1876
Batsman, author (Felix on the Bat) and inventor of the Catapulta bowling machine.			
Ferguson William Henry BEM	Scorer	6.6.1880	22.9.1957
Scorer and baggage-master for five Test teams on 43 tours over 52 years and "never lost a bag".			
Findlay William	Oxford U, Lancs; sec. MCC 1926–36	22.6.1880	19.6.1953
Firth John D'Ewes Evelyn	Winchester College; *CY 1918*	21.2.1900	21.9.1957
Fitzpatrick Cathryn Lorraine	Australia women	4.3.1968	
Fletcher Duncan Andrew Gwynne OBE	Zimbabwe; England coach 1999–2007; India coach 2011–15	27.9.1948	

		Born	Died
Ford Graham Xavier	Natal B; South Africa coach 1999–2002;	16.11.1960	
	SL coach 2012–14, 2016–17; Ireland coach 2017–		
Foster Henry Knollys	Worcestershire; *CY 1911*	30.10.1873	23.6.1950
Frindall William Howard MBE	Statistician	3.3.1939	30.1.2009
Frith David Edward John	Writer	16.3.1937	
Gibbons Harold Harry Ian Haywood	Worcestershire	8.10.1904	16.2.1973
Gibson Clement Herbert	Eton, Cam. U, Sussex, Argentina; *CY 1918*	23.8.1900	31.12.1976
Gibson Norman Alan Stanley	Writer	28.5.1923	10.4.1997
Gore Adrian Clements	Eton College; *CY 1919*	14.5.1900	7.6.1990
Gould Ian James	Middlesex, Sussex; Test umpire	19.8.1957	
Grace *Mrs* Martha	Mother and cricketing mentor of WG	18.7.1812	25.7.1884
Grace William Gilbert jnr	Gloucestershire; son of WG	6.7.1874	2.3.1905
Graveney David Anthony	Gloucestershire, Somerset, Durham	2.1.1953	
Chairman of England selectors 1997–2008.			
Graves Colin James CBE	Chairman of ECB, 2015–	22.1.1948	
Gray James Roy	Hampshire	19.5.1926	31.10.2016
Gray Malcolm Alexander	President of ICC 2000–03	30.5.1940	
Green David Michael	Lancashire, Gloucestershire; *CY 1969*	10.11.1939	19.3.2016
Grieves Kenneth James	New South Wales, Lancashire	27.8.1925	3.1.1992
Griffith Mike Grenville	Sussex, Camb. Univ; president MCC 2012–13	25.11.1943	
Haigh Gideon Clifford Jeffrey Davidson	Writer	29.12.1965	
Hair Darrell Bruce	Umpire in 78 Tests	30.9.1952	
Hall Louis	Yorkshire; *CY 1890*	1.11.1852	19.11.1915
Hallam Albert William	Lancashire, Nottinghamshire; *CY 1908*	12.11.1869	24.7.1940
Hallam Maurice Raymond	Leicestershire	10.9.1931	1.1.2000
Hallows James	Lancashire; *CY 1905*	14.11.1873	20.5.1910
Hamilton Duncan	Writer	24.12.1958	
Harper Daryl John	Umpire in 95 Tests	23.10.1951	
Harrison Tom William	Derbyshire; chief executive of ECB 2015–	11.12.1971	
Hartley Alfred	Lancashire; *CY 1911*	11.4.1879	9.10.1918
Harvey Ian Joseph	Victoria, Gloucestershire; *CY 2004*	10.4.1972	
Hedges Lionel Paget	Tonbridge School, Kent, Glos; *CY 1919*	13.7.1900	12.1.1933
Henderson Robert	Surrey; *CY 1890*	30.3.1865	28.1.1931
Hesson Michael James	New Zealand coach 2012–18	30.10.1974	
Hewett Herbert Tremenheere	Somerset; *CY 1893*	25.5.1864	4.3.1921
Heyhoe Flint *Baroness* [Rachael] OBE	England women	11.6.1939	18.1.2017
Hide Mary Edith ("Molly")	England women	24.10.1913	10.9.1995
Hodson Richard <u>Phillip</u>	Cambridge Univ; president MCC 2011–12	26.4.1951	
Horton Henry	Hampshire	18.4.1923	2.11.1998
Howard Cecil <u>Geoffrey</u>	Middlesex; administrator	14.2.1909	8.11.2002
Hughes David Paul	Lancashire; *CY 1988*	13.5.1947	
Huish Frederick Henry	Kent	15.11.1869	16.3.1957
Humpage Geoffrey William	Warwickshire; *CY 1985*	24.4.1954	
Hunter David	Yorkshire	23.2.1860	11.1.1927
Ingleby-Mackenzie Alexander <u>Colin</u> David OBE	Hants; pres. MCC 1996–98	15.9.1933	9.3.2006
Iremonger James	Nottinghamshire; *CY 1903*	5.3.1876	25.3.1956
Isaac Alan Raymond	Chair NZC 2008–10; president ICC 2012–14	20.1.1952	
Jackson Victor Edward	NSW, Leicestershire	25.10.1916	30.1.1965
James Cyril Lionel Robert ("Nello")	Writer	4.1.1901	31.5.1989
Jesty Trevor Edward	Hants, Griq W., Surrey, Lancs; umpire; *CY 1983*	2.6.1948	
Johnson Paul	Nottinghamshire	24.4.1965	
Johnston Brian Alexander CBE MC	Broadcaster	24.6.1912	5.1.1994
Jones Alan MBE	Glamorgan; *CY 1978*	4.11.1938	
Played once for England, against Rest of World in 1970, regarded at the time as a Test match.			
Keightley Lisa Maree	Aust women; England women coach 2019–	26.8.1971	
Kerr Amelia Charlotte	New Zealand women	13.10.2000	
Scored 232*, the highest score in women's ODIs, against Ireland in 2018, aged 17.			
Kilburn James Maurice	Writer	8.7.1909	28.8.1993
King John Barton	Philadelphia	19.10.1873	17.10.1965
"Beyond question the greatest all-round cricketer produced by America" – Wisden.			

		Born	Died
Knight Heather Clare OBE	England women; *CY 2018*	26.12.1990	
Knight Roger David Verdon OBE	Surrey, Glos, Sussex; sec. MCC 1994–2005, pres. MCC 2015–16	6.9.1946	
Knight W. H.	Editor of *Wisden* 1864–79	29.11.1812	16.8.1879
Koertzen Rudolf Eric	Umpire in 108 Tests	26.3.1949	
Lacey *Sir* Francis Eden	Hants; secretary of MCC 1898–1926	19.10.1859	26.5.1946
Lamb Timothy Michael	Middx, Northants; ECB chief exec 1997–2004	24.3.1953	
Langridge John George MBE	Sussex; Test umpire; *CY 1950*	10.2.1910	27.6.1999
Lanning Meghann Moira	Australia women	25.3.1992	
Lavender Guy William	Secretary/chief executive MCC 2017–	8.7.1967	
Lee Peter Granville	Northamptonshire, Lancashire; *CY 1976*	27.8.1945	
Lillywhite Frederick William	Sussex	13.6.1792	21.8.1854
Long Arnold	Surrey, Sussex	18.12.1940	
Lord Thomas	Middlesex; founder of Lord's	23.11.1755	13.1.1832
Lorgat Haroon	Chief executive of ICC 2008–12	26.5.1960	
Lovett Ian Nicholas	President of ECB 2018–	6.9.1944	
Lyon Beverley Hamilton	Gloucestershire; *CY 1931*	19.1.1902	22.6.1970
McEwan Kenneth Scott	Eastern Province, Essex; *CY 1978*	16.7.1952	
McGilvray Alan David MBE	NSW; broadcaster	6.12.1909	17.7.1996
Maclagan Myrtle Ethel	England women	2.4.1911	11.3.1993
MacLaurin *Lord* [Ian Charter]	Chair of ECB 1997–2002, pres. MCC 2017–18	30.3.1937	
Mandhana Smriti Shriniwas	India women	18.7.1996	
Manners John Errol DSC	Hampshire	25.9.1914	

Believed to be the longest-lived first-class cricketer; in 2018 he overtook Jim Hutchinson of Derbyshire (103 years 344 days).

		Born	Died
Manohar Shashank Vyankatesh	Pres. BCCI 2008–11, 2015–16; ICC chairman 2015–20	29.9.1957	
Marlar Robin Geoffrey	Sussex; writer; pres. MCC 2005–06	2.1.1931	
Marshal Alan	Surrey; *CY 1909*	12.6.1883	23.7.1915
Martin-Jenkins Christopher Dennis Alexander MBE	Writer; broadcaster; pres. MCC 2010–11	20.1.1945	1.1.2013
Maxwell James Edward	Commentator	28.7.1950	
Mendis Gehan Dixon	Sussex, Lancashire	20.4.1955	
Mercer John	Sussex, Glamorgan; coach and scorer; *CY 1927*	22.4.1893	31.8.1987
Meyer Rollo John Oliver OBE	Somerset	15.3.1905	9.3.1991
Modi Lalit Kumar	Chairman, Indian Premier League 2008–10	29.11.1963	
Moles Andrew James	Warwickshire, NZ coach 2008–09	12.2.1961	
Moores Peter	Sussex; England coach 2007–09, 2014–15	18.12.1962	
Moorhouse Geoffrey	Writer	29.11.1931	26.11.2009
Morgan Derek Clifton	Derbyshire	26.2.1929	4.11.2017
Morgan Frederick *David* OBE	Chair ECB 2003–07, pres. ICC 2008–10, pres. MCC 2014–15	6.10.1937	
Mynn Alfred	Kent, All-England	19.1.1807	1.11.1861
Neale Phillip Anthony OBE	Worcestershire; England manager; *CY 1989*	5.6.1954	
Newman John Alfred	Hampshire	12.11.1884	21.12.1973
Newstead John Thomas	Yorkshire; *CY 1909*	8.9.1877	25.3.1952
Nicholas Mark Charles Jefford	Hampshire; broadcaster	29.9.1957	
Nicholls Ronald Bernard	Gloucestershire	4.12.1933	21.7.1994
Nixon Paul Andrew	Leicestershire, Kent	21.10.1970	
Nyren John	Hants; author of *The Young Cricketer's Tutor*, 1833	15.12.1764	28.6.1837
Nyren Richard	Hants; Landlord Bat & Ball, Broadhalfpenny Down	1734	25.4.1797
Ontong Rodney Craig	Border, Glamorgan, N. Transvaal	9.9.1955	
Ormrod Joseph *Alan*	Worcestershire, Lancashire	22.12.1942	
Pardon Charles Frederick	Editor of *Wisden* 1887–90	28.3.1850	18.4.1890
Pardon Sydney Herbert	Editor of *Wisden* 1891–1925	23.9.1855	20.11.1925
Parks Henry William	Sussex	18.7.1906	7.5.1984
Parr George	Notts, captain/manager of All-England XI	22.5.1826	23.6.1891
Partridge Norman Ernest	Malvern College, Warwickshire; *CY 1919*	10.8.1900	10.3.1982
Pawar Sharadchandra Govindrao	Pres. BCCI 2005–08, ICC 2010–12	12.12.1940	

		Born	Died
Payton Wilfred Richard Daniel	Nottinghamshire	13.2.1882	2.5.1943
Pearce Thomas Neill	Essex; administrator	3.11.1905	10.4.1994
Pearson Frederick	Worcestershire	23.9.1880	10.11.1963
Perrin Percival Albert ("Peter")	Essex; *CY 1905*	26.5.1876	20.11.1945
Perry Ellyse Alexandra	Australia women; *CY 2020*	3.11.1990	
Pilch Fuller	Norfolk, Kent	17.3.1804	1.5.1870
"The best batsman that has ever yet appeared" – Arthur Haygarth, 1862.			
Porter James Alexander	Essex; *CY 2018*	25.5.1993	
Preston Hubert	Editor of *Wisden* 1944–51	16.12.1868	6.8.1960
Preston Norman MBE	Editor of *Wisden* 1952–80	18.3.1903	6.3.1980
Pritchard Thomas Leslie	Wellington, Warwickshire, Kent	10.3.1917	22.8.2017
Pybus Richard Alexander	Coach Pak 1999–2003, Bang 2012, WI 2019	5.7.1964	
Rait Kerr *Col.* Rowan Scrope	Europeans; sec. MCC 1936–52	13.4.1891	2.4.1961
Raj Mithali Dorai	India women	3.12.1982	
Reeves William	Essex; Test umpire	22.1.1875	22.3.1944
Rheinberg Netta MBE	England women; writer and administrator	24.10.1911	18.6.2006
Rice Clive Edward Butler	Transvaal, Nottinghamshire; *CY 1981*	23.7.1949	28.7.2015
Richardson Alan	Warwicks, Middx, Worcs; *CY 2012*	6.5.1975	
Roberts Kevin Joseph	New South Wales; CEO Cricket Australia 2018–	25.7.1972	
Robertson-Glasgow Raymond Charles	Somerset; writer	15.7.1901	4.3.1965
Robins Derrick Harold	Warwickshire; tour promoter	27.6.1914	3.5.2004
Robinson Mark Andrew OBE	Northants, Yorkshire, Sussex, coach	23.11.1966	
Robinson Raymond John	Writer	8.7.1905	6.7.1982
Roebuck Peter Michael	Somerset; writer; *CY 1988*	6.3.1956	12.11.2011
Rotherham Gerard Alexander	Rugby School, Warwickshire; *CY 1918*	28.5.1899	31.1.1985
Sainsbury Peter James	Hampshire; *CY 1974*	13.6.1934	12.7.2014
Samson Andrew William	Statistician	17.2.1964	
Sawhney Manu	Chief executive of ICC 2019–	1.11.1966	
Sciver Natalie Ruth	England women; *CY 2018*	20.8.1992	
Scott Stanley Winckworth	Middlesex; *CY 1893*	24.3.1854	8.12.1933
Sellers Arthur Brian MBE	Yorkshire; *CY 1940*	5.3.1907	20.2.1981
Seymour James	Kent	25.10.1879	30.9.1930
Shepherd David Robert MBE	Gloucestershire; umpire in 92 Tests	27.12.1940	27.10.2009
Shepherd Donald John	Glamorgan; *CY 1970*	12.8.1927	18.8.2017
Shrubsole Anya MBE	England women; *CY 2018*	7.12.1991	
Silk Dennis Raoul Whitehall CBE	Somerset; pres. MCC 1992–94	8.10.1931	19.6.2019
Simmons Jack MBE	Lancashire, Tasmania; *CY 1985*	28.3.1941	
Skelding Alexander	Leics; first-class umpire 1931–58	5.9.1886	17.4.1960
Smith Sydney Gordon	Northamptonshire; *CY 1915*	15.1.1881	25.10.1963
Smith William Charles ("Razor")	Surrey; *CY 1911*	4.10.1877	15.7.1946
Solanki Vikram Singh	Worcestershire, Surrey, England	1.4.1976	
Southerton Sydney James	Editor of *Wisden* 1934–35	7.7.1874	12.3.1935
Speed Malcolm Walter	Chief executive of ICC 2001–08	14.9.1948	
Spencer Thomas William OBE	Kent; Test umpire	22.3.1914	1.11.1995
Srinivasan Narayanaswami	Pres. BCCI 2011–14; ICC chair 2014–15	3.1.1945	
Stephenson Franklyn Dacosta	Nottinghamshire, Sussex; *CY 1989*	8.4.1959	
Stephenson Harold William	Somerset	18.7.1920	23.4.2008
Stephenson Heathfield Harman	Surrey, All-England	3.5.1832	17.12.1896
Captained first English team to Australia, 1861–62; umpired first Test in England, 1880.			
Stephenson *Lt.-Col.* John Robin CBE	Secretary of MCC 1987–93	25.2.1931	2.6.2003
Studd *Sir* John Edward Kynaston	Middlesex	26.7.1858	14.1.1944
Lord Mayor of London 1928–29; president of MCC 1930.			
Surridge Walter Stuart	Surrey; *CY 1953*	3.9.1917	13.4.1992
Sutherland James Alexander	Victoria; CEO Cricket Australia 2001–18	14.7.1965	
Suttle Kenneth George	Sussex	25.8.1928	25.3.2005
Swanton Ernest William ("Jim") CBE	Middlesex; writer	11.2.1907	22.1.2000
Tarrant Francis Alfred	Victoria, Middlesex; *CY 1908*	11.12.1880	29.1.1951
Taufel Simon James Arnold	Umpire in 74 Tests	21.1.1971	
Taylor Brian ("Tonker")	Essex; *CY 1972*	19.6.1932	12.6.2017
Taylor Samantha Claire MBE	England women; *CY 2009*	25.9.1975	

		Born	Died
Taylor Stafanie Roxann	West Indies women	11.6.1991	
Taylor Tom Launcelot	Yorkshire; *CY 1901*	25.5.1878	16.3.1960
Thornton Charles Inglis ("Buns")	Middlesex	20.3.1850	10.12.1929
Timms John Edward	Northamptonshire	3.11.1906	18.5.1980
Todd Leslie John	Kent	19.6.1907	20.8.1967
Tunnicliffe John	Yorkshire; *CY 1901*	26.8.1866	11.7.1948
Turner Francis Michael MBE	Leicestershire; administrator	8.8.1934	21.7.2015
Turner Robert Julian	Somerset	25.11.1967	
Ufton Derek Gilbert	Kent	31.5.1928	
van der Bijl Vintcent Adriaan Pieter	Natal, Middx, Transvaal; *CY 1981*	19.3.1948	
van Niekerk Dane	South Africa women	14.5.1993	
Virgin Roy Thomas	Somerset, Northamptonshire; *CY 1971*	26.8.1939	
Ward William	Hampshire	24.7.1787	30.6.1849
Scorer of the first recorded double-century: 278 for MCC v Norfolk, 1820.			
Wass Thomas George	Nottinghamshire; *CY 1908*	26.12.1873	27.10.1953
Watson Frank	Lancashire	17.9.1898	1.2.1976
Webber Roy	Statistician	23.7.1914	14.11.1962
Weigall Gerald John Villiers	Kent; coach	19.10.1870	17.5.1944
West George H.	Editor of *Wisden* 1880–86	1851	6.10.1896
Wheatley Oswald Stephen CBE	Warwickshire, Glamorgan; *CY 1969*	28.5.1935	
Whitaker Edgar Haddon OBE	Editor of *Wisden* 1940–43	30.8.1908	5.1.1982
Wight Peter Bernard	Somerset; umpire	25.6.1930	31.12.2015
Wilson Elizabeth Rebecca ("Betty")	Australia women	21.11.1921	22.1.2010
Wilson John Victor	Yorkshire; *CY 1961*	17.1.1921	5.6.2008
Wisden John	Sussex	5.9.1826	5.4.1884
"The Little Wonder"; founder of Wisden Cricketers' Almanack, *1864.*			
Wood Cecil John Burditt	Leicestershire	21.11.1875	5.6.1960
Woodcock John Charles OBE	Writer; editor of *Wisden* 1981–86	7.8.1926	
Wooller Wilfred	Glamorgan	20.11.1912	10.3.1997
Wright Graeme Alexander	Editor of *Wisden* 1987–92, 2001–02	23.4.1943	
Wright Levi George	Derbyshire; *CY 1906*	15.1.1862	11.1.1953
Wright Luke James	Leicestershire, Sussex, England	7.3.1985	
Young Douglas Martin	Worcestershire, Gloucestershire	15.4.1924	18.6.1993

CRICKETERS OF THE YEAR, 1889–2020

1889	*Six Great Bowlers of the Year:* J. Briggs, J. J. Ferris, G. A. Lohmann, R. Peel, C. T. B. Turner, S. M. J. Woods.
1890	*Nine Great Batsmen of the Year:* R. Abel, W. Barnes, W. Gunn, L. Hall, R. Henderson, J. M. Read, A. Shrewsbury, F. H. Sugg, A. Ward.
1891	*Five Great Wicketkeepers:* J. M. Blackham, G. MacGregor, R. Pilling, M. Sherwin, H. Wood.
1892	*Five Great Bowlers:* W. Attewell, J. T. Hearne, F. Martin, A. W. Mold, J. W. Sharpe.
1893	*Five Batsmen of the Year:* H. T. Hewett, L. C. H. Palairet, W. W. Read, S. W. Scott, A. E. Stoddart.
1894	*Five All-Round Cricketers:* G. Giffen, A. Hearne, F. S. Jackson, G. H. S. Trott, E. Wainwright.
1895	*Five Young Batsmen of the Season:* W. Brockwell, J. T. Brown, C. B. Fry, T. W. Hayward, A. C. MacLaren.
1896	W. G. Grace.
1897	*Five Cricketers of the Season:* S. E. Gregory, A. A. Lilley, K. S. Ranjitsinhji, T. Richardson, H. Trumble.
1898	*Five Cricketers of the Year:* F. G. Bull, W. R. Cuttell, N. F. Druce, G. L. Jessop, J. R. Mason.
1899	*Five Great Players of the Season:* W. H. Lockwood, W. Rhodes, W. Storer, C. L. Townsend, A. E. Trott.
1900	*Five Cricketers of the Season:* J. Darling, C. Hill, A. O. Jones, M. A. Noble, Major R. M. Poore.
1901	*Mr R. E. Foster and Four Yorkshiremen:* R. E. Foster, S. Haigh, G. H. Hirst, T. L. Taylor, J. Tunnicliffe.
1902	L. C. Braund, C. P. McGahey, F. Mitchell, W. G. Quaife, J. T. Tyldesley.
1903	W. W. Armstrong, C. J. Burnup, J. Iremonger, J. J. Kelly, V. T. Trumper.
1904	C. Blythe, J. Gunn, A. E. Knight, W. Mead, P. F. Warner.
1905	B. J. T. Bosanquet, E. A. Halliwell, J. Hallows, P. A. Perrin, R. H. Spooner.
1906	D. Denton, W. S. Lees, G. J. Thompson, J. Vine, L. G. Wright.
1907	J. N. Crawford, A. Fielder, E. G. Hayes, K. L. Hutchings, N. A. Knox.
1908	A. W. Hallam, R. O. Schwarz, F. A. Tarrant, A. E. E. Vogler, T. G. Wass.
1909	*Lord Hawke and Four Cricketers of the Year:* W. Brearley, Lord Hawke, J. B. Hobbs, A. Marshal, J. T. Newstead.
1910	W. Bardsley, S. F. Barnes, D. W. Carr, A. P. Day, V. S. Ransford.
1911	H. K. Foster, A. Hartley, C. B. Llewellyn, W. C. Smith, F. E. Woolley.
1912	*Five Members of MCC's team in Australia:* F. R. Foster, J. W. Hearne, S. P. Kinneir, C. P. Mead, H. Strudwick.
1913	*Special Portrait:* John Wisden.
1914	M. W. Booth, G. Gunn, J. W. Hitch, A. E. Relf, Hon. L. H. Tennyson.
1915	J. W. H. T. Douglas, P. G. H. Fender, H. T. W. Hardinge, D. J. Knight, S. G. Smith.
1916–17	No portraits appeared.
1918	*School Bowlers of the Year:* H. L. Calder, J. D. E. Firth, C. H. Gibson, G. A. Rotherham, G. T. S. Stevens.
1919	*Five Public School Cricketers of the Year:* P. W. Adams, A. P. F. Chapman, A. C. Gore, L. P. Hedges, N. E. Partridge.
1920	*Five Batsmen of the Year:* A. Ducat, E. H. Hendren, P. Holmes, H. Sutcliffe, E. Tyldesley.
1921	*Special Portrait:* P. F. Warner.
1922	H. Ashton, J. L. Bryan, J. M. Gregory, C. G. Macartney, E. A. McDonald.
1923	A. W. Carr, A. P. Freeman, C. W. L. Parker, A. C. Russell, A. Sandham.
1924	*Five Bowlers of the Year:* A. E. R. Gilligan, R. Kilner, G. G. Macaulay, C. H. Parkin, M. W. Tate.
1925	R. H. Catterall, J. C. W. MacBryan, H. W. Taylor, R. K. Tyldesley, W. W. Whysall.
1926	*Special Portrait:* J. B. Hobbs.
1927	G. Geary, H. Larwood, J. Mercer, W. A. Oldfield, W. M. Woodfull.
1928	R. C. Blunt, C. Hallows, W. R. Hammond, D. R. Jardine, V. W. C. Jupp.
1929	L. E. G. Ames, G. Duckworth, M. Leyland, S. J. Staples, J. C. White.
1930	E. H. Bowley, K. S. Duleepsinhji, H. G. Owen-Smith, R. W. V. Robins, R. E. S. Wyatt.
1931	D. G. Bradman, C. V. Grimmett, B. H. Lyon, I. A. R. Peebles, M. J. Turnbull.
1932	W. E. Bowes, C. S. Dempster, James Langridge, Nawab of Pataudi snr, H. Verity.
1933	W. E. Astill, F. R. Brown, A. S. Kennedy, C. K. Nayudu, W. Voce.

1934	A. H. Bakewell, G. A. Headley, M. S. Nichols, L. F. Townsend, C. F. Walters.
1935	S. J. McCabe, W. J. O'Reilly, G. A. E. Paine, W. H. Ponsford, C. I. J. Smith.
1936	H. B. Cameron, E. R. T. Holmes, B. Mitchell, D. Smith, A. W. Wellard.
1937	C. J. Barnett, W. H. Copson, A. R. Gover, V. M. Merchant, T. S. Worthington.
1938	T. W. J. Goddard, J. Hardstaff jnr, L. Hutton, J. H. Parks, E. Paynter.
1939	H. T. Bartlett, W. A. Brown, D. C. S. Compton, K. Farnes, A. Wood.
1940	L. N. Constantine, W. J. Edrich, W. W. Keeton, A. B. Sellers, D. V. P. Wright.
1941–46	No portraits appeared.
1947	A. V. Bedser, L. B. Fishlock, V. (M. H.) Mankad, T. P. B. Smith, C. Washbrook.
1948	M. P. Donnelly, A. Melville, A. D. Nourse, J. D. Robertson, N. W. D. Yardley.
1949	A. L. Hassett, W. A. Johnston, R. R. Lindwall, A. R. Morris, D. Tallon.
1950	T. E. Bailey, R. O. Jenkins, John Langridge, R. T. Simpson, B. Sutcliffe.
1951	T. G. Evans, S. Ramadhin, A. L. Valentine, E. D. Weekes, F. M. M. Worrell.
1952	R. Appleyard, H. E. Dollery, J. C. Laker, P. B. H. May, E. A. B. Rowan.
1953	H. Gimblett, T. W. Graveney, D. S. Sheppard, W. S. Surridge, F. S. Trueman.
1954	R. N. Harvey, G. A. R. Lock, K. R. Miller, J. H. Wardle, W. Watson.
1955	B. Dooland, Fazal Mahmood, W. E. Hollies, J. B. Statham, G. E. Tribe.
1956	M. C. Cowdrey, D. J. Insole, D. J. McGlew, H. J. Tayfield, F. H. Tyson.
1957	D. Brookes, J. W. Burke, M. J. Hilton, G. R. A. Langley, P. E. Richardson.
1958	P. J. Loader, A. J. McIntyre, O. G. Smith, M. J. Stewart, C. L. Walcott.
1959	H. L. Jackson, R. E. Marshall, C. A. Milton, J. R. Reid, D. Shackleton.
1960	K. F. Barrington, D. B. Carr, R. Illingworth, G. Pullar, M. J. K. Smith.
1961	N. A. T. Adcock, E. R. Dexter, R. A. McLean, R. Subba Row, J. V. Wilson.
1962	W. E. Alley, R. Benaud, A. K. Davidson, W. M. Lawry, N. C. O'Neill.
1963	D. Kenyon, Mushtaq Mohammad, P. H. Parfitt, P. J. Sharpe, F. J. Titmus.
1964	D. B. Close, C. C. Griffith, C. C. Hunte, R. B. Kanhai, G. S. Sobers.
1965	G. Boycott, P. J. Burge, J. A. Flavell, G. D. McKenzie, R. B. Simpson.
1966	K. C. Bland, J. H. Edrich, R. C. Motz, P. M. Pollock, R. G. Pollock.
1967	R. W. Barber, B. L. D'Oliveira, C. Milburn, J. T. Murray, S. M. Nurse.
1968	Asif Iqbal, Hanif Mohammad, K. Higgs, J. M. Parks, Nawab of Pataudi jnr.
1969	J. G. Binks, D. M. Green, B. A. Richards, D. L. Underwood, O. S. Wheatley.
1970	B. F. Butcher, A. P. E. Knott, Majid Khan, M. J. Procter, D. J. Shepherd.
1971	J. D. Bond, C. H. Lloyd, B. W. Luckhurst, G. M. Turner, R. T. Virgin.
1972	G. G. Arnold, B. S. Chandrasekhar, L. R. Gibbs, B. Taylor, Zaheer Abbas.
1973	G. S. Chappell, D. K. Lillee, R. A. L. Massie, J. A. Snow, K. R. Stackpole.
1974	K. D. Boyce, B. E. Congdon, K. W. R. Fletcher, R. C. Fredericks, P. J. Sainsbury.
1975	D. L. Amiss, M. H. Denness, N. Gifford, A. W. Greig, A. M. E. Roberts.
1976	I. M. Chappell, P. G. Lee, R. B. McCosker, D. S. Steele, R. A. Woolmer.
1977	J. M. Brearley, C. G. Greenidge, M. A. Holding, I. V. A. Richards, R. W. Taylor.
1978	I. T. Botham, M. Hendrick, A. Jones, K. S. McEwan, R. G. D. Willis.
1979	D. I. Gower, J. K. Lever, C. M. Old, C. T. Radley, J. N. Shepherd.
1980	J. Garner, S. M. Gavaskar, G. A. Gooch, D. W. Randall, B. C. Rose.
1981	K. J. Hughes, R. D. Jackman, A. J. Lamb, C. E. B. Rice, V. A. P. van der Bijl.
1982	T. M. Alderman, A. R. Border, R. J. Hadlee, Javed Miandad, R. W. Marsh.
1983	Imran Khan, T. E. Jesty, A. I. Kallicharran, Kapil Dev, M. D. Marshall.
1984	M. Amarnath, J. V. Coney, J. E. Emburey, M. W. Gatting, C. L. Smith.
1985	M. D. Crowe, H. A. Gomes, G. W. Humpage, J. Simmons, S. Wettimuny.
1986	P. Bainbridge, R. M. Ellison, C. J. McDermott, N. V. Radford, R. T. Robinson.
1987	J. H. Childs, G. A. Hick, D. B. Vengsarkar, C. A. Walsh, J. J. Whitaker.
1988	J. P. Agnew, N. A. Foster, D. P. Hughes, P. M. Roebuck, Salim Malik.
1989	K. J. Barnett, P. J. L. Dujon, P. A. Neale, F. D. Stephenson, S. R. Waugh.
1990	S. J. Cook, D. M. Jones, R. C. Russell, R. A. Smith, M. A. Taylor.
1991	M. A. Atherton, M. Azharuddin, A. R. Butcher, D. L. Haynes, M. E. Waugh.
1992	C. E. L. Ambrose, P. A. J. DeFreitas, A. A. Donald, R. B. Richardson, Waqar Younis.
1993	N. E. Briers, M. D. Moxon, I. D. K. Salisbury, A. J. Stewart, Wasim Akram.
1994	D. C. Boon, I. A. Healy, M. G. Hughes, S. K. Warne, S. L. Watkin.
1995	B. C. Lara, D. E. Malcolm, T. A. Munton, S. J. Rhodes, K. C. Wessels.
1996	D. G. Cork, P. A. de Silva, A. R. C. Fraser, A. Kumble, D. A. Reeve.
1997	S. T. Jayasuriya, Mushtaq Ahmed, Saeed Anwar, P. V. Simmons, S. R. Tendulkar.
1998	M. T. G. Elliott, S. G. Law, G. D. McGrath, M. P. Maynard, G. P. Thorpe.
1999	I. D. Austin, D. Gough, M. Muralitharan, A. Ranatunga, J. N. Rhodes.

2000	C. L. Cairns, R. Dravid, L. Klusener, T. M. Moody, Saqlain Mushtaq.

Cricketers of the Century D. G. Bradman, G. S. Sobers, J. B. Hobbs, S. K. Warne, I. V. A. Richards.

2001	M. W. Alleyne, M. P. Bicknell, A. R. Caddick, J. L. Langer, D. S. Lehmann.
2002	A. Flower, A. C. Gilchrist, J. N. Gillespie, V. V. S. Laxman, D. R. Martyn.
2003	M. L. Hayden, A. J. Hollioake, N. Hussain, S. M. Pollock, M. P. Vaughan.
2004	C. J. Adams, A. Flintoff, I. J. Harvey, G. Kirsten, G. C. Smith.
2005	A. F. Giles, S. J. Harmison, R. W. T. Key, A. J. Strauss, M. E. Trescothick.
2006	M. J. Hoggard, S. P. Jones, B. Lee, K. P. Pietersen, R. T. Ponting.
2007	P. D. Collingwood, D. P. M. D. Jayawardene, Mohammad Yousuf, M. S. Panesar, M. R. Ramprakash.
2008	I. R. Bell, S. Chanderpaul, O. D. Gibson, R. J. Sidebottom, Zaheer Khan.
2009	J. M. Anderson, D. M. Benkenstein, M. V. Boucher, N. D. McKenzie, S. C. Taylor.
2010	S. C. J. Broad, M. J. Clarke, G. Onions, M. J. Prior, G. P. Swann.
2011	E. J. G. Morgan, C. M. W. Read, Tamim Iqbal, I. J. L. Trott.
2012	T. T. Bresnan, G. Chapple, A. N. Cook, A. Richardson, K. C. Sangakkara.
2013	H. M. Amla, N. R. D. Compton, J. H. Kallis, M. N. Samuels, D. W. Steyn.
2014	S. Dhawan, C. M. Edwards, R. J. Harris, C. J. L. Rogers, J. E. Root.
2015	M. M. Ali, G. S. Ballance, A. Lyth, A. D. Mathews, J. S. Patel.
2016	J. M. Bairstow, B. B. McCullum, S. P. D. Smith, B. A. Stokes, K. S. Williamson.
2017	B. M. Duckett, Misbah-ul-Haq, T. S. Roland-Jones, C. R. Woakes, Younis Khan.
2018	S. D. Hope, H. C. Knight, J. A. Porter, N. R. Sciver, A. Shrubsole.
2019	T. T. Beaumont, R. J. Burns, J. C. Buttler, S. M. Curran, V. Kohli.
2020	J. C. Archer, P. J. Cummins, S. R. Harmer, M. Labuschagne, E. A. Perry.

From 2001 to 2003 the award was made on the basis of all cricket round the world, not just the English season. This ended in 2004 with the start of Wisden's Leading Cricketer in the World *award. Sanath Jayasuriya was chosen in 1997 for his influence on the English season, stemming from the 1996 World Cup. In 2011, only four were named after the Lord's spot-fixing scandal made the selection of one of the five unsustainable.*

CRICKETERS OF THE YEAR: AN ANALYSIS

The special portrait of John Wisden in 1913 marked the 50th anniversary of his retirement as a player – and the 50th edition of the Almanack. Wisden died in 1884. The special portraits of P. F. Warner in 1921 and J. B. Hobbs in 1926 were in addition to their earlier selection as a Cricketer of the Year in 1904 and 1909 respectively. These three special portraits and the Cricketers of the Century in 2000 are excluded from the following analysis.

The five players selected to be Cricketers of the Year for 2020 bring the number chosen since selection began in 1889 to 605. They have been chosen from 42 different teams, as follows:

Derbyshire	13	Nottinghamshire	29	Australians	75	Cheltenham College	1
Durham	8	Somerset	20	South Africans	28	Cranleigh School	1
Essex	26	Surrey	52	West Indians	27	Eton College	2
Glamorgan	13	Sussex	22	New Zealanders	10	Malvern College	1
Gloucestershire	17	Warwickshire	26	Indians	16	Rugby School	1
Hampshire	16	Worcestershire	17	Pakistanis	14	Tonbridge School	1
Kent	28	Yorkshire	47	Sri Lankans	7	Univ College School	1
Lancashire	35	Oxford Univ	7	Zimbabweans	1	Uppingham School	1
Leicestershire	8	Cambridge Univ	10	Bangladeshis	1	Winchester College	1
Middlesex	30	Berkshire	1	Australia Women	1		
Northamptonshire	15	Staffordshire	1	England Women	6		

Schoolboys were chosen in 1918 and 1919 when first-class cricket was suspended due to war. The total of sides comes to 637 because 32 players appeared for more than one side (excluding England men) in the year for which they were chosen.

Types of Player

Of the 605 Cricketers of the Year, 300 are best classified as batsmen, 165 as bowlers, 100 as all-rounders and 40 as wicketkeepers or wicketkeeper-batsmen.

Research: Robert Brooke

PART TEN

The Almanack

OFFICIAL BODIES

INTERNATIONAL CRICKET COUNCIL

The ICC are world cricket's governing body. They are responsible for managing the playing conditions and Code of Conduct for international fixtures, expanding the game and organising the major tournaments, including World Cups. Their mission statement says the ICC "will lead by providing a world-class environment for international cricket, delivering major events across three formats, providing targeted support to members and promoting the global game".

Twelve national governing bodies are currently Full Members of the ICC; full membership qualifies a nation (or geographic area) to play official Test matches. A candidate for full membership must meet a number of playing and administrative criteria, after which elevation is decided by a vote among existing Full Members. The former categories of associate and affiliate membership merged in 2017; there are currently 92 Associate Members.

The ICC were founded in 1909 as the Imperial Cricket Conference by three Foundation Members: England, Australia and South Africa. Other countries (or geographic areas) became Full Members, and thus acquired Test status, as follows: India, New Zealand and West Indies in 1926, Pakistan in 1952, Sri Lanka in 1981, Zimbabwe in 1992, Bangladesh in 2000, and Afghanistan and Ireland in 2017. South Africa ceased to be a member on leaving the Commonwealth in 1961, but were re-elected as a Full Member in 1991.

In 1965, "Imperial" was replaced by "International", and countries from outside the Commonwealth were elected for the first time. The first Associate Members were Ceylon (later Sri Lanka), Fiji and the USA. Foundation Members retained a veto over all resolutions. In 1989, the renamed International Cricket Council (rather than "Conference") adopted revised rules, aimed at producing an organisation which could make a larger number of binding decisions, rather than simply make recommendations to national governing bodies. In 1993, the Council, previously administered by MCC, gained their own secretariat and chief executive. The category of Foundation Member was abolished.

In 1997, the Council became an incorporated body, with an executive board, and a president instead of a chairman. The ICC remained at Lord's, with a commercial base in Monaco, until August 2005, when after 96 years they moved to Dubai in the United Arab Emirates, which offered organisational and tax advantages.

In 2014, the ICC board approved a new structure, under which they were led by a chairman again, while India, Australia and England took permanent places on key committees. But in 2016 the special privileges given to these three were dismantled and, in early 2017, the board agreed to revise the constitution on more egalitarian lines.

Officers

Chairman: S. V. Manohar. *Deputy Chairman:* I. Khwaja. *Chief Executive:* M. Sawhney.

Chairs of Committees – Chief Executives' Committee: M. Sawhney. *Cricket:* A. Kumble. *Audit:* Y. Narayan. *Finance and Commercial Affairs:* Ehsan Mani. *Nominations Committee:* S. V. Manohar. *Code of Conduct Commission:* M. J. Beloff QC. *Women's Committee:* C. J. Connor. *Development:* I. Khwaja. *Disputes Resolution Committee:* M. J. Beloff QC. *Membership:* I. Khwaja. *Medical Advisory:* Dr P. Harcourt. *Anti-Corruption Oversight:* D. Howman. *HR & Remuneration:* G. J. Barclay. *Anti-Corruption Unit Chairman:* Sir Ronnie Flanagan. *ICC Ethics Officer:* P. Nicholson.

ICC Board: The chairman and chief executive sit on the board *ex officio*. They are joined by I. K. Nooyi (independent female director), G. J. Barclay (New Zealand), A. G. S. Brian (Scotland), E. R. Eddings (Australia), Ehsan Mani (Pakistan), Farhan Yusufzai (Afghanistan), C. J. Graves (England), I. Khwaja (Singapore), R. A. McCollum (Ireland), T. Mukuhlani (Zimbabwe), Nazmul Hassan (Bangladesh), C. Nenzani (South Africa), A. S. S. Silva (Sri Lanka), R. O. Skerritt (West Indies), M. Vallipuram (Malaysia). Indian representative to be confirmed.

Chief Executives' Committee: The chief executive, chairman and the chairs of the committee and women's committees sit on this committee *ex officio*. They are joined by the chief executives of the 12 Full Member boards and three Associate Member boards: S. Damodar (Botswana), A. M. de Silva (Sri Lanka), W. R. Deutrom (Ireland), J. J. Faul (South Africa), J. M. Grave (West Indies), T. W. Harrison (England), W. G. Khan (Pakistan), Lutfullah Stanikzai (Afghanistan), G. Makoni (Zimbabwe), Nizam Uddin Chowdhury (Bangladesh), K. J. Roberts (Australia), J. Shah (India), N. Speight (Bermuda), M. Stafford (Vanuatu), D. J. White (New Zealand).

Cricket Committee: The chief executive and chairman sit on the committee *ex officio*. They are joined by A. Kumble (*chairman*), J. M. Arthur, B. J. Clark, K. J. Coetzer, R. Dravid, R. K. Illingworth, D. P. M. D. Jayawardene, D. Kendix, R. S. Madugalle, T. B. A. May, S. M. Pollock, J. P. Stephenson, A. J. Strauss, D. J. White.

Chief Financial Officer: A. Khanna. *Chief Commercial Officer:* A. Dahiya. *General Counsel/Company Secretary:* J. Hall. *General Manager – Cricket:* G. J. Allardice. *General Manager – Anti-Corruption Unit:* A. J. Marshall. *General Manager – Strategic Communications:* C. Furlong. *General Manager – Development:* W. Glenwright. *Head of Events:* C. M. B. Tetley. *Head of Internal Audit:* Muhammad Ali. *Senior Manager Broadcast/Executive Producer – ICC TV:* A. Ramachandran.

Membership

Full Members (12): Afghanistan, Australia, Bangladesh, England, India, Ireland, New Zealand, Pakistan, South Africa, Sri Lanka, West Indies and Zimbabwe.

Associate Members* (92):

Africa (19): Botswana (2005), Cameroon (2007), Gambia (2002), Ghana (2002), Kenya (1981), Lesotho (2001), Malawi (2003), Mali (2005), Mozambique (2003), Namibia (1992), Nigeria (2002), Rwanda (2003), St Helena (2001), Seychelles (2010), Sierra Leone (2002), Swaziland (2007), Tanzania (2001), Uganda (1998), Zambia (2003).

Americas (16): Argentina (1974), Bahamas (1987), Belize (1997), Bermuda (1966), Brazil (2002), Canada (1968), Cayman Islands (2002), Chile (2002), Costa Rica (2002), Falkland Islands (2007), Mexico (2004), Panama (2002), Peru (2007), Suriname (2002), Turks & Caicos Islands (2002), USA (1965/2019).

Asia (16): Bahrain (2001), Bhutan (2001), China (2004), Hong Kong (1969), Iran (2003), Kuwait (2005), Malaysia (1967), Maldives (2001), Myanmar (2006), Nepal (1996), Oman (2000), Qatar (1999), Saudi Arabia (2003), Singapore (1974), Thailand (2005), United Arab Emirates (1990).

East Asia Pacific (9): Cook Islands (2000), Fiji (1965), Indonesia (2001), Japan (2005), Papua New Guinea (1973), Philippines (2000), Samoa (2000), South Korea (2001), Vanuatu (1995).

Europe (32): Austria (1992), Belgium (2005), Bulgaria (2008), Croatia (2001), Cyprus (1999), Czech Republic (2000), Denmark (1966), Estonia (2008), Finland (2000), France (1998), Germany (1999), Gibraltar (1969), Greece (1995), Guernsey (2005), Hungary (2012), Isle of Man (2004), Israel (1974), Italy (1995), Jersey (2007), Luxembourg (1998), Malta (1998), Netherlands (1966), Norway (2000), Portugal (1996), Romania (2013), Russia (2012), Scotland (1994), Serbia (2015), Slovenia (2005), Spain (1992), Sweden (1997), Turkey (2008).

* *Year of election shown in parentheses. Switzerland (1985) were removed in 2012; Cuba (2002) and Tonga (2000) in 2013; Brunei (1992) in 2014; the USA in 2017, though a new USA body were admitted in 2019; and Morocco (1999) in 2019. Croatia and Zambia were suspended in 2019.*

Full Members are the governing bodies for cricket of a country recognised by the ICC, or nations associated for cricket purposes, or a geographical area, from which representative teams are qualified to play official Test matches.

Associate Members are the governing bodies for cricket of a country recognised by the ICC, or countries associated for cricket purposes, or a geographical area, which does not qualify as a Full Member, but where cricket is firmly established and organised.

Addresses

ICC Street 69, Dubai Sports City, Sh Mohammed Bin Zayed Road, PO Box 500 070, Dubai, United Arab Emirates (+971 4382 8800; www.icc-cricket.com; enquiry@icc-cricket.com).

Afghanistan Afghanistan Cricket Board, Alokozay Kabul International Cricket Stadium, Kabul Nandari, District 8, Kabul (+93 78 813 3144; www.cricket.af; info@afghancricket.af).

Australia Cricket Australia, 60 Jolimont Street, Jolimont, Victoria 3002 (+61 3 9653 9999; www.cricket.com.au; public.enquiries@cricket.com.au).

Bangladesh Bangladesh Cricket Board, Sher-e-Bangla National Cricket Stadium, Mirpur, Dhaka 1216 (+880 2 803 1001; www.tigercricket.com.bd; info@tigercricket.com.bd).

England England and Wales Cricket Board (see below).

India Board of Control for Cricket in India, Cricket Centre, 4th Floor, Wankhede Stadium, D Road, Churchgate, Mumbai 400 020 (+91 22 2289 8800; www.bcci.tv; office@bcci.tv).

Ireland Cricket Ireland, 15c Kinsealy Business Park, Kinsealy, Co Dublin K36 YH61 (+353 1 894 7914; www.cricketireland.ie; info@cricketireland.ie).

New Zealand New Zealand Cricket, PO Box 8353, Level 4, 8 Nugent Street, Grafton, Auckland 1023 (+64 9 393 9700; www.nzc.nz; info@nzcricket.org.nz).

Pakistan Pakistan Cricket Board, Gaddafi Stadium, Ferozpur Road, Lahore 54600 (+92 42 3571 7231; www.pcb.com.pk; inquiry@pcb.com.pk).

South Africa Cricket South Africa, PO Box 55009 Northlands 2116; 86, 5th & Glenhove St, Melrose Estate, Johannesburg (+27 11 880 2810; www.cricket.co.za; info@cricket.co.za).

Sri Lanka Sri Lanka Cricket, 35 Maitland Place, Colombo 07000 (+94 112 681 601; www.srilankacricket.lk; info@srilankacricket.lk).

West Indies West Indies Cricket Board, PO Box 616 W, Factory Road, St John's, Antigua (+1 268 481 2450; www.windiescricket.com; wicb@windiescricket.com).

Zimbabwe Zimbabwe Cricket, PO Box 2739, 28 Maiden Drive, Highlands, Harare (+263 4 788 090; www.zimcricket.org; info@zimcricket.org).

Associate Members' addresses may be found on the ICC website, www.icc-cricket.com.

ENGLAND AND WALES CRICKET BOARD

The England and Wales Cricket Board (ECB) are responsible for the administration of all cricket – professional and recreational – in England and Wales. In 1997, they took over the functions of the Cricket Council, the Test and County Cricket Board and the National Cricket Association, which had run the game since 1968. In 2005, a streamlined constitution replaced a Management Board of 18 with a 12-strong Board of Directors, three appointed by the first-class counties, two by the county boards. In 2010, this expanded to 14, and added the ECB's first women directors. After a governance review, it returned to 12, including four independent non-executive directors, in 2018.

Officers

President: I. N. Lovett. *Chairman:* C. J. Graves. *Chief Executive Officer:* T. W. Harrison.

Board of Directors: K. Bickerstaffe, D. M. Bushell, M. Darlow, A. P. Dickinson, C. J. Graves, T. W. Harrison, B. J. O'Brien, Lord Patel of Bradford, L. C. Pearson, S. A. Smith, B. D. H. Trenowden, J. H. Wood.

Committee Chairs – Anti-Corruption: M. Darlow. *Audit & Risk:* A. P. Dickinson. *Governance:* Lord Patel. *Cricket:* Sir Andrew Strauss. *Discipline:* T. J. G. O'Gorman. *Recreational Assembly:* J. H. Wood. *Regulatory:* N. I. Coward. *Remuneration:* C. J. Graves.

Chief Operating Officer: D. Mahoney. *Chief Financial Officer:* S. A. Smith. *Chief Commercial Officer:* T. Singh. *Managing Director, County Cricket:* N. Snowball. *Managing Director, The Hundred:* S. Patel. *Managing Director, England Men's Cricket:* A. F. Giles. *Managing Director, England Women's Cricket:* C. J. Connor. *Director, Special Projects:* S. Elworthy. *Director, Communications:* K. Miller. *Director, England Cricket Operations:* J. D. Carr. *Director, Participation & Growth:* N. Pryde. *Director, Strategy & Corporate Development:* V. Banerjee. *Commercial Director, The Hundred:* R. Calder. *Performance Director:* M. Bobat. *Head of Information Technology:* D. Smith. *National Selector:* E. T. Smith. *Selector:* J. W. A. Taylor.

ECB: Lord's Ground, London NW8 8QZ (020 7432 1200; www.ecb.co.uk; feedback@ecb.co.uk).

THE MARYLEBONE CRICKET CLUB

The Marylebone Cricket Club evolved out of the White Conduit Club in 1787, when Thomas Lord laid out his first ground in Dorset Square. Their members revised the Laws in 1788 and gradually took responsibility for cricket throughout the world. However, they relinquished control of the game in the UK in 1968, and the International Cricket Council finally established their own secretariat in 1993. MCC still own Lord's, and remain the guardian of the Laws. They call themselves "a private club with a public function", and aim to support cricket everywhere, especially at grassroots level and in countries where the game is least developed.

Patron: HER MAJESTY THE QUEEN

Officers

President: 2019–20 – K. C. Sangakkara. *Club Chairman:* G. M. N. Corbett. *Treasurer:* A. B. Elgood. *Trustees:* P. A. B. Beecroft, M. V. Fleming, R. S. Leigh. *Hon. Life Vice-Presidents:* E. R. Dexter, C. A. Fry, M. G. Griffith, A. R. Lewis, Sir Oliver Popplewell, O. H. J. Stocken, M. O. C. Sturt, J. C. Woodcock.

Chief Executive and Secretary: G. W. Lavender. *Assistant Secretaries – Cricket:* J. P. Stephenson. *Finance:* A. D. Cameron. *Membership and Operations:* J. A. S. Clifford. *Estates:* R. J. Ebdon. *Commercial:* A. N. Muggleton. *Legal:* H. A. Roper-Curzon.

MCC Committee: J. M. Brearley, I. S. Duncan, N. J. C. Gandon, C. Goodson-Wickes, V. K. Griffiths, C. M. Gupte, W. J. House, S. P. Hughes, P. L. O. Leaver, M. C. J. Nicholas, N. E. J. Pocock, G. J. Toogood. The president, club chairman, treasurer and committee chairs are also on the committee.

Chairmen of Committees – Cricket: S. C. Taylor. *Estates:* A. J. Johnston. *Finance:* A. B. Elgood. *Heritage and Collections:* J. O. D. Orders. *Membership and General Purposes:* Sir Ian Magee. *World Cricket:* M. W. Gatting.

MCC: The Chief Executive and Secretary, Lord's Ground, London NW8 8QN (020 7616 8500; www.lords.org; reception@mcc.org.uk. Tickets 020 7432 1000; ticketing@mcc.org.uk).

PROFESSIONAL CRICKETERS' ASSOCIATION

The Professional Cricketers' Association were formed in 1967 (as the Cricketers' Association) to be the collective voice of first-class professional players, and enhance and protect their interests. During the 1970s, they succeeded in establishing pension schemes and a minimum wage. In recent years, their strong commercial operations and greater funding from the ECB have increased their services to current and past players, including education, legal and financial help. In 2011, these services were extended to England's women cricketers.

President: G. A. Gooch. *Chairman:* D. K. H. Mitchell. *President – Professional Cricketers' Trust:* D. A. Graveney. *Non-Executive Chairman:* J. R. Metherell. *Non-Executive Directors:* I. T. Guha and P. G. Read. *Chief Executive:* A. R. Irish. *Director of Development and Welfare:* I. J. Thomas. *Commercial Director:* R. K. Lynch. *Financial Director:* P. Garrett. *Business Development Manager:* G. M. Hamilton. *Commercial Manager:* A. Phipps. *Head of Events and Fundraising:* E. Lewis. *Head of Commercial Rights:* E. M. Reid. *Player Rights Manager:* E. Caldwell. *Communications Manager:* L. Reynolds. *Member Services Manager:* A. Prosser. *Player Operations Manager:* R. Hudson.

PCA: *London Office* – The Bedser Stand, The Oval, Kennington, London SE11 5SS (0207 449 4228); www.thepca.co.uk; communications@thepca.co.uk). *Birmingham Office* – Box 108–9, R. E. S. Wyatt Stand, Edgbaston Stadium, Birmingham B5 7QU.

CRIME AND PUNISHMENT

ICC Code of Conduct – Breaches and Penalties in 2018-19 to 2019-20

S. T. Gabriel   West Indies v England, Third Test at Gros Islet, St Lucia.
Personal comments with abusive intent to batsman J. E. Root. 75% fine/3 demerit pts – J. J. Crowe.

Mahmudullah   Bangladesh v New Zealand, second one-day international at Christchurch.
Smashed his bat against boundary fence after dismissal. 10% fine/1 demerit pt – S. R. Bernard.

T. A. Boult   New Zealand v Bangladesh, second one-day international at Christchurch.
Obscene language audible via stump mike when bowling. 15% fine/1 demerit pt – S. R. Bernard.

Mashrafe bin Mortaza   Bangladesh v New Zealand, third one-day international at Dunedin.
Obscene language audible to umpires and broadcast. 15% fine/1 demerit pt – S. R. Bernard.

E. J. Villani   Australia v New Zealand, third women's one-day international at Adelaide.
Gestured to show dissent when given lbw. Reprimand/1 demerit pt – R. W. Stratford.

J. L. Jonassen   Australia v New Zealand, third women's one-day international at Adelaide.
Gestured at edge of her bat when given lbw. Reprimand/1 demerit pt – R. W. Stratford.

J. M. Bairstow   England v Pakistan, third one-day international at Bristol.
Smashed his bat against stumps on being dismissed. Reprimand/1 demerit pt – R. B. Richardson.

A. Balbirnie   Ireland v Bangladesh, tri-series one-day international at Clontarf.
Lingered at wicket and expressed dissent when given out. Reprimand/1 demerit pt – B. C. Broad.

J. C. Archer   England v Pakistan, World Cup one-day international at Nottingham.
Expressed dissent when umpire called a delivery wide. 15% fine/1 demerit pt – J. J. Crowe.

J. J. Roy   England v Pakistan, World Cup one-day international at Nottingham.
Audible obscenity while fielding. 15% fine/1 demerit pt – J. J. Crowe.

A. Zampa   Australia v West Indies, World Cup one-day international at Nottingham.
Audible obscenity while bowling. Reprimand/1 demerit pt – J. J. Crowe.

C. R. Brathwaite   West Indies v England, World Cup one-day international at Southampton.
Shrugged and expressed dissent when given out. Reprimand/1 demerit pt – D. C. Boon.

V. Kohli   India v Afghanistan, World Cup one-day international at Southampton.
Moved aggressively towards umpire after lbw appeal. 25% fine/1 demerit pt – B. C. Broad.

C. R. Brathwaite   West Indies v India, World Cup one-day international at Manchester.
Gestured and expressed dissent when umpire called wide. 15% fine/1 demerit pt – B. C. Broad.

J. J. Roy   England v Australia, World Cup one-day international at Birmingham.
Shook head, lingered and uttered obscenity when out. 30% fine/2 demerit pts – R. S. Madugalle.

Mushfiqur Rahim   Bangladesh v Sri Lanka, second one-day international at Colombo (RPS).
Demanded review after full-pitched waist-high delivery. 15% fine/1 demerit pt – B. C. Broad.

K. A. Pollard   West Indies v India, first Twenty20 international at Lauderhill.
Ignored protocol of requesting substitute through umpires. 20%/1 demerit pt – J. J. Crowe.

N. Saini   India v West Indies, first Twenty20 international at Lauderhill.
Gave batsman N. Pooran send-off after dismissing him. Reprimand/1 demerit pt – J. J. Crowe.

S. T. Knox (coach)   Scotland v Bangladesh, women's T20 World Cup Qualifier at Dundee.
Criticised umpires after Scotland lost on DLS. Reprimand/1 demerit pt – G. F. Labrooy.

V. Kohli   India v South Africa, third Twenty20 international at Bangalore.
Avoidable shoulder contact with bowler B. E. Hendricks. Reprimand/1 demerit pt – R. B. Richardson.

Aaqib Ilyas   Oman v Ireland, quadrangular Twenty20 international at Al Amerat.
Lingered and expressed dissent when given out. Reprimand/1 demerit pt – W. C. Labrooy.

J. M. Bairstow   England v New Zealand, fifth Twenty20 international at Auckland.
Audible obscenity when given out. Reprimand/1 demerit pt – A. J. Pycroft.

N. Pooran West Indies v Afghanistan, third Twenty20 international at Lucknow.
Tampered with the ball, using a thumbnail. 4 suspension pts, banned for 4 matches – B. C. Broad.

C. N. Nation West Indies v India, third women's Twenty20 international at Providence.
Lingered and gestured after being given out stumped. 10% fine/1 demerit pt – R. D. King.

C. A. Henry West Indies v India, third women's Twenty20 international at Providence.
Turned round and stared at umpires when given lbw. 10% fine/1 demerit pt – R. D. King.

J. C. Buttler England v South Africa, Second Test at Cape Town.
Obscenity to batsman V. D. Philander while keeping wicket. 15% fine/1 demerit pt – A. J. Pycroft.

K. Rabada South Africa v England, Third Test at Port Elizabeth.
Advanced provocatively towards J. E. Root on dismissing him. 15% fine/1 demerit pt, leading to his suspension for one Test for accumulating four demerit pts since February 2018 – A. J. Pycroft.

B. A. Stokes England v South Africa, Fourth Test at Johannesburg.
Obscene language to spectator as he left the field when out. 15% fine/1 demerit pt – A. J. Pycroft.

V. D. Philander South Africa v England, Fourth Test at Johannesburg.
Abusive language towards J. C. Buttler on dismissing him. 15% fine/1 demerit pt – A. J. Pycroft.

S. C. J. Broad England v South Africa, Fourth Test at Johannesburg.
Used inappropriate language to batsman F. du Plessis. 15% fine/1 demerit pt – A. J. Pycroft.

Twenty-one further breaches took place in men's and women's Associate Member or Under-19 internationals during this period.

Under ICC regulations on minor over-rate offences up to July 2019, players were fined 10% of their match fee for every over their side failed to bowl in the allotted time, with the captain fined double that amount. From August 2019, this was changed to a fine of 20% per over for all players, including the captain, who would no longer be suspended for over-rate offences.
    There were 11 instances in this period in men's internationals, and two in women's:

J. O. Holder/West Indies v England, 2nd Test at North Sound, 40%/20% – J. J. Crowe.
    Holder suspended for one Test as it was his second offence within 12 months.

E. J. G. Morgan/England v West Indies, 2nd ODI at Bridgetown, 20%/10% – A. J. Pycroft.

Imad Wasim/Pakistan v Australia, 4th ODI at Dubai, 20%/10% – J. J. Crowe.

E. J. G. Morgan/England v Pakistan, 3rd ODI at Bristol, 40%/20% – R. B. Richardson.
    Morgan suspended for one ODI as it was his second offence within 12 months.

Sarfraz Ahmed/Pakistan v England, World Cup ODI at Nottingham, 20%/10% – J. J. Crowe.

S. R. Taylor/West Indies v England, 2nd women's T20I at Northampton, 20%/10% – P. Whitticase.

K. S. Williamson/New Zealand v WI, World Cup ODI at Manchester, 20%/10% – D. C. Boon.

Tamim Iqbal/Bangladesh v Sri Lanka, 1st ODI at Colombo (RPS), 40%/20% – B. C. Broad.

S. L. Malinga/Sri Lanka v New Zealand, 1st T20I at Pallekele, 40%/40% – A. J. Pycroft.

A. M. C. Jayangani/S Lanka v Australia, 3rd women's T20I at Sydney, 40%/40% – S. R. Bernard.

K. A. Pollard/West Indies v India, 1st ODI at Chennai, 80%/80% – D. C. Boon.

F. du Plessis/South Africa v England, 4th Test at Johannesburg, 60%/60% – A. J. Pycroft.
    South Africa were also fined six points in the World Test Championship.

E. J. G. Morgan/England v South Africa, 3rd T20I at Centurion, 20%/20% – D. C. Boon.

There were two further instances in Associate Member women's T20 internationals.

INTERNATIONAL UMPIRES' PANELS

In 1993, the ICC formed an international umpires' panel, containing at least two officials from each Full Member. A third-country umpire from this panel stood with a home umpire in every Test from 1994 onwards. In 2002, an elite panel was appointed: two elite umpires – both independent – were to stand in all Tests, and at least one in every ODI, where one home umpire was allowed. A supporting panel of international umpires was created to provide cover at peak times in the Test schedule, second umpires in one-day internationals, and third umpires to give rulings from TV replays. There is also a panel of development umpires, mostly drawn from Associate Members but also including several female umpires from Full Members. The panels are sponsored by Emirates Airlines.

The elite panel at the start of 2020: Aleem Dar (P), H. D. P. K. Dharmasena (SL), M. Erasmus (SA), C. B. Gaffaney (NZ), M. A. Gough (E), R. K. Illingworth (E), R. A. Kettleborough (E), N. J. Llong (E), B. N. J. Oxenford (A), P. R. Reiffel (A), R. J. Tucker (A), J. S. Wilson (WI).

The international panel: G. A. Abood (A), Ahmed Shah Durrani (Afg), Ahmed Shah Pakteen (Afg), Ahsan Raza (P), Asif Yaqoob (P), Bismillah Shinwari (Afg), R. E. Black (Ire), G. O. Brathwaite (WI), C. M. Brown (NZ), M. Burns (E), I. Chabi (Z), a. K. Chowdhury (I), S. A. J. Craig (A), N. Duguid (WI), Gazi Sohel (B), S. George (SA), P. A. Gustard (WI), S. B. Haig (NZ), L. E. Hannibal (SL), M. Hawthorne (Ire), A. T. Holdstock (SA), Izatullah Safi (Afg), P. B. Jele (SA), W. R. Knights (NZ), Masudur Rahman (B), N. N. Menon (I), D. J. Millns (E), F. Mutizwa (Z), A. J. Neill (Ire), S. J. Nogajski (A), a. Paleker (SA), R. S. A. Palliyagururge (SL), C. Phiri (Z), R. M. P. J. Rambukwella (SL), Rashid Riaz (P), L. S. Reifer (WI), P. A. Reynolds (Ire), L. Rusere (Z), M. J. Saggers (E), C. Shamsuddin (I), Sharfuddoula (B), V. K. Sharma (I), Shozab Raza (P), Tanvir Ahmed (B), A. G. Wharf (E), P. Wilson (A), R. R. Wimalasiri (SL).

ICC development panel: L. Agenbag (SA), Akbar Ali (UAE), V. R. Angara (Botswana), S. N. Bandekar (USA), E. Carrington (Bermuda), K. D. Cotton (NZ), R. D'Mello (Kenya), A. J. T. Dowdalls (Scotland), H. Grewal (Canada), D. A. Haggo (Scotland), Harikrishna Pillai (Oman), R. Hassan (Italy), Iftikhar Ali (UAE), M. Jameson (Germany), H. K. G. Jansen (Netherlands), J. Jensen (Denmark), V. K. Jha (Nepal), a. Kapa (PNG), H. E. Kearns (Jersey), J. A. Lindo (USA), A. W. Louw (Namibia), D. H. McLean (Scotland), a. R. Maddela (Canada), V. P. Mallela (USA), P. M. Musoke (Uganda), L. Oala (PNG), D. Odhiambo (Kenya), B. Olewale (PNG), I. O. Oyieko (Kenya), C. A. Polosak (A), B. B. Pradhan (Nepal), S. Prasad (Singapore), Rahul Asher (Oman), A. K. Rana (Thailand), S. Redfern (E), Rizwan Akram (Netherlands), F. T. Samura (Sierra Leone), E. Sheridan (A), Shiju Sam (UAE), Shivani Mishra (Qatar), D. N. Subedi (Nepal), S. Subramanian (Indonesia), Tabarak Dar (Hong Kong), I. A. Thomson (Hong Kong), C. H. Thorburn (Namibia), A. van der Dries (Netherlands), W. P. M. van Liemt (Netherlands), Vinod Babu (Oman), K. Viswanadan (Malaysia), M. V. Waldron (Ireland), J. M. Williams (WI).

ICC REFEREES' PANEL

In 1991, the ICC formed a panel of referees to enforce their Code of Conduct for Tests and one-day internationals, and to support the umpires in upholding the game's conduct. In 2002, the ICC launched an elite panel, on full-time contracts, for all international cricket, sponsored by Emirates Airlines. At the start of 2020, it consisted of D. C. Boon (A), B. C. Broad (E), J. J. Crowe (NZ), R. S. Madugalle (SL), A. J. Pycroft (Z), R. B. Richardson (WI), J. Srinath (I).

A further panel of international referees consisted of Akhtar Ahmad (B), Anis Sheikh (P), G. A. V. Baxter (NZ), S. R. Bernard (A), O. Chirombe (Z), D. Cooke (Ire), E. T. Dube (Z), R. A. Dykes (NZ), S. A. Fritz (SA), K. Gallagher (Ire), Hamim Talwar (P), D. O. Hayles (WI), D. T. Jukes (E), R. D. King (WI), G. F. Labrooy (SL), W. C. Labrooy (SL), G. S. Lakshmi (I), Mohammad Javed (P), V. Narayanan Kutty (I), M. Nayyar (I), Neeyamur Rashid (B), W. M. Noon (E), G. H. Pienaar (SA), R. W. Stratford (A), S. Wadvalla (SA), P. Whitticase (E), Zarab Shah Zaheer (Afg).

ENGLISH UMPIRES FOR 2020

First-class: R. J. Bailey, N. L. Bainton, P. K. Baldwin, I. D. Blackwell, M. Burns, N. G. B. Cook, B. J. Debenham, J. H. Evans, M. A. Gough, I. J. Gould, P. J. Hartley, R. K. Illingworth, R. A. Kettleborough, N. J. Llong, D. J. Lloyd, J. W. Lloyds, N. A. Mallender, D. J. Millns, S. J. O'Shaughnessy, P. R. Pollard, R. T. Robinson, M. J. Saggers, B. V. Taylor, R. J. Warren, A. G. Wharf. *Reserves:* H. M. S. Adnan, T. Lungley, J. D. Middlebrook, M. Newell, N. Pratt, I. N. Ramage, C. M. Watts, R. A. White.

MEETINGS AND DECISIONS IN 2019

USA CRICKET

On January 8, the ICC approved USA Cricket's application to join as an Associate Member, bringing the number of Associates to 93, and the total to 105. As an ICC Member, USA Cricket became eligible to receive ICC development funding, and to sanction domestic and international cricket in the United States. The previous governing body, USACA, had been expelled in 2017 after failing to unify the USA cricket community. The new body was established later that year, but initially managed by the ICC Americas regional support programme. The chair of USA Cricket, Paraag Marathe, and the board were to recruit a chief executive and other key managers.

ICC CHIEF EXECUTIVE

On January 15, the ICC announced that Manu Sawhney would become their chief executive officer when David Richardson stood down in July, after seven years in the post. The former chief executive of Singapore Sports Hub and managing director of ESPN Star Sports, Sawhney would join the ICC in February to work alongside Richardson, before formally taking over the job.

On April 1, it was announced that Sawhney was becoming chief executive with immediate effect, after six weeks shadowing the position. Richardson remained with the ICC until July to oversee the men's World Cup.

ENGLAND WOMEN PLAYER CONTRACTS

On February 6, the ECB awarded 21 central contracts to women. There were full contracts for Tammy Beaumont, Katherine Brunt, Kate Cross, Freya Davies, Sophie Ecclestone, Georgia Elwiss, Jenny Gunn, Alex Hartley, Amy Jones, Heather Knight, Laura Marsh, Nat Sciver, Anya Shrubsole, Sarah Taylor, Fran Wilson, Lauren Winfield and Danni Wyatt, and rookie contracts (for players on the fringe of the side) for Alice Davidson-Richards, Katie George, Bryony Smith and Linsey Smith. Compared with 2017 and 2018, Davies and Ecclestone had been added to the main list. Dani Hazell had retired from international cricket, and Tash Farrant and Beth Langston were released.

THE HUNDRED – PLAYING CONDITIONS

On February 21, the ECB announced that the 18 first-class counties had agreed 17–1 to the playing conditions for the new 100-ball format to be known as The Hundred, which had already been endorsed by the ECB Board. The key elements would be: 100 balls per innings; a change of ends after ten balls; bowlers to deliver either five or ten consecutive balls, with a maximum of 20 balls per game; each bowling side to get a strategic timeout of up to two and a half minutes; a 25-ball powerplay start for each team, with two fielders allowed outside the 30-yard circle during the powerplay. The competition would feature eight new city-based teams, with a player draft in autumn 2019; it would be played over five weeks in the height of the summer, from 2020. Sanjay Patel had been appointed managing director for the competition.

ICC BOARD

The ICC Board met in Dubai from February 25–March 2.

Members were reassured about the ECB's security plans ahead of the men's World Cup in 2019, which would continue to be monitored in association with the UK authorities.

The Chief Executives' Committee agreed to introduce an age-group World Cup for girls during the current commercial cycle.

The Board reformed the Women's Committee, with a remit to drive the growth in women and girls playing cricket; grow the female fan-base and fans of women's cricket; promote administrative and leadership opportunities for women; create pathways and events fostering competitive women's cricket with context; and oversee regulations, rankings, the Future Tours Programme and technology. Clare Connor was confirmed as chair of the Women's Committee, to be joined by representatives from two Full Members and one Associate, the Chief Executives' Committee and the media, plus two elected players, an ODI coach and an independent. Meanwhile, Anil Kumble was reappointed chair of the Cricket Committee for a final three-year term.

The ICC Board were updated on the World Anti-Doping Agency's concerns about India's domestic anti-doping programme, and committed to working with the BCCI, WADA and India's NADA to resolve outstanding issues.

The board accepted Sri Lanka Cricket had complied with directions to hold elections (previously delayed by the government), welcomed Shammi Silva, the new SLC president, and removed funding restrictions imposed until the elections were held.

The board approved a new set of safeguarding regulations for children, adults at risk and participants in ICC events. A safeguarding chair and tribunal with specific expertise would be appointed.

NATIONAL COUNTIES

On February 27, the Minor Counties unanimously voted that the Minor Counties Cricket Association should become the National Counties Cricket Association from 2020.

The Western and Eastern divisions of the National Counties competitions would each be divided into two five-team divisions, with one team promoted from each second division, and one relegated from the first every season. Teams would play four three-day games (down from six), before a final between the East and West first-division winners. The 50-over competition would revert from a straight knockout to its previous group format, leading to quarter-finals, semis and a final. The Twenty20 competition would be retained, with four groups of five, whose winners would progress to finals day. The three competitions were to be played in blocks, starting with the 50-over tournament, then the T20 and finally the three-day championship. There would also be a round of 50-over fixtures between first-class and national counties.

The ECB promised at least £450m of direct funding to the county network – including first-class counties, county cricket boards and national counties – over five years from 2020 to 2024.

MCC WORLD CRICKET COMMITTEE

The MCC world cricket committee met in Bangalore on March 8–9, with Shane Warne attending for the first time. There were updates on ICC matters from David Richardson, the outgoing chief executive officer, and on corruption in cricket from Alex Marshall, general manager of the Anti-Corruption Unit.

On March 8 – International Women's Day – there was unanimous support for the inclusion of women's T20 in the 2022 Commonwealth Games in Birmingham.

An MCC survey had attracted over 13,000 responders from more than 100 countries, of whom 86% said Test cricket was the format that interested them most. The survey highlighted challenges of increasing attendances and support for Test cricket, including the cost and availability of tickets; providing half-day tickets to encourage families to attend; and access to Test cricket on free-to-air TV.

The committee felt the World Test Championship, due to begin in 2019, would benefit from the use of a standard ball (except for day/night matches). Currently, the Dukes ball was used for Tests in England and the West Indies, the SG ball in India, and the Kookaburra in all other countries; the pink Kookaburra had been used in day/night Tests, and the white

Kookaburra for all one-day and T20 internationals. The ICC should choose the most suitable ball, but the committee stressed that the balance between ball and bat was crucial.

The committee's concerns about the pace of play had been backed up by the survey: 25% of fans from England, Australia, New Zealand and South Africa (where spinners bowl fewer overs) complained about slow over-rates. ICC statistics from May 2018 showed that over-rates over the past year were the lowest in the 11 years they had been measured, at 13.77 per hour. The Decision Review System was partly responsible, but the committee recommended measures to speed up the game, including a timer on the scoreboard, counting down 45 seconds from the call of "over" (60 seconds for a new batsman on strike, 80 seconds for a change of bowler). If either side were not ready when the clock reached zero, they would be warned, and further infringements would earn five penalty runs. A similar timer could be used when wickets fell. During DRS reviews, the protocol should be cut short by the TV production team informing the TV umpire as soon as they realise the verdict will be "not out"; time is often spent trying to discern an inside edge for lbws, only to find that the ball would have missed the stumps.

The committee recommended introducing free hits after no-balls in Tests, a system which had already led to a marked drop in no-balls in white-ball formats. This would speed up over-rates, as well as provide extra excitement for spectators.

The committee asked MCC to carry out trials of the red Dukes ball in Asian conditions, free hits after a no-ball, and the use of a countdown clock to speed up play.

MCC ANNUAL GENERAL MEETING

The 232nd AGM of the Marylebone Cricket Club was held at Lord's on May 1, with president Anthony Wreford in the chair. He announced that his successor, from October, would be Kumar Sangakkara, the former Sri Lankan Test batsman and captain – MCC's first non-British president.

Members approved the appointment of former England international Claire Taylor as MCC's first female Chairman of Cricket. They voted 96.5% in favour of the £52m project to redevelop the Compton and Edrich stands, after Westminster City Council granted conditional planning permission for the plans by architects WilkinsonEyre. The new stands, to be completed by the summer of 2021, would accommodate 11,600 – increasing the capacity at Lord's by around 2,600, with integrated amenities, wheelchair spaces, additional accessible seating and lift access at all levels.

Members also approved an internal Code of Conduct, providing for the suspension or expulsion of any member failing to show respect for all those visiting or working at Lord's.

Membership on December 31, 2018, totalled 23,422, made up of 17,889 full members, 5,008 associate members, 365 honorary members, 33 senior members and 127 out-match members. There were 12,172 candidates awaiting election to full membership; 466 vacancies arose in 2017.

ECB ANNUAL GENERAL MEETING

On May 7, ECB members (the chairs of the 39 first-class and Minor Counties, and of MCC and the Minor Counties Cricket Association) agreed to extend chairman Colin Graves's term in office by six months, from May to November 2020, so that he could oversee the first season of The Hundred. The process for appointing his successor would begin in September 2019, to be managed by the Nominations Committee; the intention was that the chair-elect would be able to shadow Graves during the 2020 season.

Lord Patel's term as the ECB's senior independent director was also extended, for a further three years.

ICC ANNUAL MEETINGS

The ICC annual conference and associated meetings took place in London on July 15–18.

The ICC Board unanimously decided to suspend Zimbabwe Cricket with immediate effect, for breaching the ICC constitutional requirement that there should be no government interference in any member's administration. Zimbabwe's Sports and Recreation Commission had suspended ZC's board and managing director in June, and appointed an interim committee, after the board ignored their instruction to delay the ZC AGM while the SRC investigated "irregularities of a financial nature". The ICC directed that the elected board should be reinstated within three months. The suspension meant ICC funding to ZC was frozen, and Zimbabwe were unable to take part in any ICC events, including the T20 World Cup qualifying tournaments later in 2019 (they were replaced by Namibia in the women's event, and Nigeria in the men's).

Associate Members Croatia and Zambia were also suspended, and Morocco expelled, for non-compliance with ICC membership criteria; Morocco's expulsion put the number of Associates back to 92.

After a two-year trial of concussion substitutes in domestic cricket, the ICC included concussion replacements in playing conditions for all men's and women's international cricket and first-class cricket worldwide from August 1, 2019. Decisions to replace players would be made by the team medical representative; the substitute should be a like-for-like replacement, who would need approval from the referee.

Following recommendations from the Cricket Committee on the pace of play in international cricket, the ICC agreed that, from August, captains would no longer be suspended for repeated or serious over-rate breaches. All players should be held equally responsible, and fined at the same level as the captain (previously, captains were fined 20% of their match fee for each over not completed on time, and players 10%). In the World Test Championship, starting in August, teams would have two points deducted for each over they fell behind the required rate at the end of a Test. Trials would be conducted on using replays to call no-balls, another Cricket Committee recommendation.

The ICC approved revised medical standards for international cricket, aimed at greater consistency in the medical care of players around the world.

The Women's Committee met for the first time since being reformed in February. Clare Connor, the chair, was joined by Full Member chief executives Warren Deutrom (Ireland) and Wasim Khan (Pakistan); two co-opted representatives from Full Members, Saba Karim (India) and Belinda Clark (Australia); media representative Natalie Germanos (South Africa); players Lisa Sthalekar (Australia), Sana Mir (Pakistan) and Mithali Raj (India); and England women's coach Mark Robinson. An Associate Member representative and an independent representative were to be added later.

MCC WORLD CRICKET COMMITTEE

The MCC world cricket committee met at Lord's on August 11–12.

The committee were pleased by the launch of the World Test Championship, which had begun with the Edgbaston Ashes Test ten days before, with two more series about to follow. They felt it was important to market the championship and to educate audiences around the new system giving context to Test cricket.

They were also pleased that the Commonwealth Games Federation executive had approved the inclusion of women's T20 cricket at the Birmingham 2022 Commonwealth Games; a final vote was about to be taken by the Commonwealth Games Associations. Cricket was due to return to the Asian Games at Hangzhou 2022, probably in the T20 format, which the committee felt would be the perfect opportunity to showcase the sport in China. But there was still much to be done before cricket could be included in the Olympics; Los Angeles 2028 was the earliest likely opportunity.

Wasim Khan, managing director of the Pakistan Cricket Board, attended to speak on the security and political situation in Pakistan. The committee discussed the conditions which would enable touring sides to return, with security analysis a prerequisite. MCC would consider touring in the future.

Committee member Kumar Sangakkara, also president-designate of MCC, spoke on the social and economic importance of supporting cricket in Sri Lanka in the aftermath of a terrorist attack on Easter Sunday 2019; he thanked Pakistan (Under-19s), Bangladesh and New Zealand for touring, and welcomed the England series scheduled for March 2020. The committee planned to hold their next meeting in Sri Lanka during that tour.

As part of their role in monitoring the balance between bat and ball, the committee heard presentations from Dukes and Kookaburra, on both companies' research and development to improve the performance of balls in all conditions.

They renewed calls for measures to speed up play, including a countdown clock between overs and at the fall of wickets. The committee noted the ICC's recent steps – to fine all players more heavily for slow over-rates and deduct World Test Championship points, rather than suspend captains – but felt that in-match five-run penalties would be the best deterrent. With DRS referrals, as well as reviews being cut short as soon as the result was known to be not out, fielders should return to their positions during the review, in readiness for the next ball, and no drinks should be brought on.

The committee discussed Law 19.8 in relation to overthrows, after the men's World Cup final in July; the Law was clear, but it would be reviewed by the Laws subcommittee.

They welcomed the ICC's introduction of concussion replacements, and the announcement of further trials into the automated calling of no-balls. They suggested that ball-tracking software should be used to help on-field umpires judge no-balls over waist height, and wides over the batsman's head.

COMMONWEALTH GAMES FEDERATION

On August 13, the Commonwealth Games Federation voted to include women's T20 cricket in the 2022 games in Birmingham. Eight teams (probably qualifying via the ICC rankings) would compete across eight days, with all matches played at Edgbaston. Cricket last appeared in the Commonwealth Games in 1998, when South Africa won a men's 50-over tournament at Kuala Lumpur.

ENGLAND PLAYER CONTRACTS

The ECB currently award separate contracts for Test and white-ball cricket. Players on Test contracts have their salaries paid in full by the ECB; previously, those on white-ball contracts received a supplement to their county salary, but from February 2020 they will be paid in full by the ECB, like the Test contract players.

On September 20, the ECB awarded ten Test contracts to run for 12 months from October 2019. They went to James Anderson, Jofra Archer, Jonny Bairstow, Stuart Broad, Rory Burns, Jos Buttler, Sam Curran, Joe Root, Ben Stokes and Chris Woakes. They also awarded 12 white-ball contracts, to Archer, Bairstow, Buttler, Root, Stokes, Woakes, plus Moeen Ali, Joe Denly, Eoin Morgan, Adil Rashid, Jason Roy and Mark Wood. Tom Curran retained his incremental contract, and Jack Leach was given one. Burns, Denly and Leach were also awarded retrospective incremental contracts for 2018-19, reflecting their performances during the previous year.

Compared with 2018-19, Archer had gained contracts in both formats, Burns for Tests and Denly for white-ball cricket. Ali and Rashid lost their Test contracts, while Alex Hales, Liam Plunkett and David Willey lost their white-ball contracts.

ENGLAND HEAD COACHES

On October 7, Chris Silverwood was appointed England men's head coach, succeeding Trevor Bayliss, who was standing down after four years in charge. Silverwood, a Yorkshire and Middlesex fast bowler, had played six Tests and seven one-day internationals for England between 1996 and 2002, and later coached Essex to the 2017 Championship title, before becoming England's fast bowling coach under Bayliss.

On October 30, Lisa Keightley was appointed England women's head coach, succeeding Mark Robinson, who resigned after England's defeat in the 2019 Ashes. Keightley had played nine Tests, 82 one-day internationals and one Twenty20 international for Australia, and coached the side from 2007 to 2008. She became the first woman to coach the England women's team since it became a full-time professional job, though Ruth Prideaux was the team's first coach, from 1988 to 1993.

ECB PLAN FOR WOMEN'S CRICKET

On October 8, the ECB launched a plan to transform women's and girls' cricket with the goal of making cricket a gender-balanced sport. They pledged £20m of funding over the next two years, intended to rise to £50m over five, and to fund 40 full-time professional domestic contracts (in line with the Professional Cricketers' Association recommendations for young male cricketers), in addition to the existing 21 central contracts for the England players. The plan had five key objectives:

• Participation: to increase the number of women and girls playing cricket recreationally by inspiring girls to believe "cricket is a game for me", bringing it to more schools, and building a strong, sustainable and inclusive club network;
• Pathway: to develop aspiring female cricketers by raising standards in girls' county age-group cricket;
• Performance: to drive the performance of England women's cricket through a semi-professional, elite domestic eight-region structure and 40 new full-time professional contracts (five per region);
• Profile: to elevate the profile of women's cricket through The Hundred, the England team and the elite game, connecting elite women cricketers to a new generation of fans;
• People: to increase the representation of women across the cricket workforce and support more women to take on leadership roles.

The plan had been developed after two years' consultation with the 38 counties and Cricket Wales, and detailed analysis of thousands of survey responses from the recreational and elite game; the ECB had run pilot programmes with over 600 clubs. Clare Connor, managing director of women's cricket, said that recent initiatives, such as All Stars Cricket for five-to-eight-year-olds, the South Asian female activators programme and the Kia Super League, had given women and girls more opportunities, but to transform the game they must move from targeted standalone programmes to addressing the whole pathway.

ICC BOARD

The ICC Board met in Dubai on October 14, and readmitted Zimbabwe and Nepal as ICC members. Both had been suspended for breaching constitutional rules prohibiting government interference.

Zimbabwe were readmitted after a three-month break, following a meeting between ICC chairman Shashank Manohar and chief executive Manu Sawhney, Zimbabwe Cricket's reinstated chairman Tavengwa Mukuhlani, Zimbabwe sports minister Kirsty Coventry, and Gerald Mlotshwa, the chairman of Zimbabwe's Sports and Recreation Commission. Manohar said Coventry had "unconditionally complied" with the conditions set down by the board. Funding to ZC would continue to be on a controlled basis, but Zimbabwe would now be able to take part in the men's Under-19 World Cup in January 2020 and the ICC Super League (leading to qualification for the 2023 World Cup) later in the year. They had already missed their chance to qualify for the women's and men's Twenty20 World Cups in 2020.

Nepal, suspended in 2016, were readmitted on a conditional basis after the election of a 17-member central working committee, but would be required to follow a transition plan to ensure full compliance with Associate Membership criteria.

The board agreed to increase the prize money for ICC women's tournaments, following a rise in the revenue generated by women's cricket. The winners of the T20 World Cup in early 2020 would receive $1m and the runners-up $500,000, five times the amount on offer in 2018, with an overall 320% increase in the prize pot for all ten competing teams, intended to drive improved standards throughout the game and not just the top end. The total prize money for the World Cup in 2021 would rise from $2m in 2017 to $3.5m. The board also approved a biennial Under-19 T20 World Cup, to start in Bangladesh in 2021. The proposed eight-year cycle of global events from 2023 to 2031 now comprised eight major events for men (including two 50-over World Cups and four T20 World Cups), eight for women, four for Under-19 men and four for Under-19 women. Manohar said that a major men's and women's event each year would bring consistency to the calendar and complement bilateral cricket, though some members felt bilateral cricket would suffer.

On the Cricket Committee's recommendation, the Chief Executives' Committee agreed to retain the super over to decide results at ICC events, including 50-over and T20 World Cups, but in future semi-finals and finals the super over would be repeated until one team scored more; in group stages, a tied super over would mean a tied match.

The board approved $30.5m funding for Associate Members, a 12% increase on 2019.

A Governance Working Group was set up to consider the ICC's structure, chaired by Earl Eddings (Australia) and comprising Greg Barclay (New Zealand), Tony Brian (Scotland), Ehsan Mani (Pakistan), Chris Nenzani (South Africa) and Ricky Skerritt (West Indies).

Indra Nooyi was unanimously reappointed as the ICC independent director for a second two-year term.

ECB SPONSORSHIP

On October 18, the ECB announced that insurance firm Vitality, which sponsors Twenty20 cricket in the UK, from T20 internationals to recreational cricket via the Blast county tournament, would extend their sponsorship to the new franchise competition, The Hundred, which would begin in 2020.

ICC AND UNICEF

On December 19, the ICC announced an extension to their four-year partnership with UNICEF (the United Nations Children's Fund) through the women's T20 World Cup in 2020, with a focus on empowering women and girls through cricket.

During the men's World Cup in 2019, Unicef had raised $180,000 to fund a girls' cricket project in Afghanistan for 12 months, including a competition for school-aged girls, training for 120 teachers and cricket equipment, as well as a community outreach programme working with elders to reinforce the positive impact of girls playing cricket. Money raised during the women's T20 World Cup would fund similar projects in cricket-playing nations, including Sri Lanka. Fans could donate when buying tickets and at the stadiums, while fans watching globally would be able to donate online.

DATES IN CRICKET HISTORY

c. 1550	Evidence of cricket being played in Guildford, Surrey.
1610	Reference to "cricketing" between Weald & Upland and North Downs near Chevening, Kent.
1611	Randle Cotgrave's French–English dictionary translates the French word "crosse" as a cricket staff. Two youths fined for playing cricket at Sidlesham, Sussex.
1624	Jasper Vinall becomes first man known to be killed playing cricket: hit by a bat while trying to catch the ball – at Horsted Green, Sussex.
1676	First reference to cricket being played abroad, by British residents in Aleppo, Syria.
1694	Two shillings and sixpence paid for a "wagger" (wager) on a match at Lewes.
1697	First reference to "a great match" with 11 players a side for 50 guineas, in Sussex.
1700	Cricket match announced on Clapham Common.
1709	First recorded inter-county match: Kent v Surrey.
1710	First reference to cricket at Cambridge University.
1727	Articles of Agreement written governing the conduct of matches between the teams of the Duke of Richmond and Mr Brodrick of Peperharow, Surrey.
1729	Date of earliest surviving bat, belonging to John Chitty, now in the Oval pavilion.
1730	First recorded match at the Artillery Ground, off City Road, central London, still the cricketing home of the Honourable Artillery Company.
1744	Kent beat All-England by one wicket at the Artillery Ground. First known version of the Laws of Cricket, issued by the London Club, formalising the pitch as 22 yards long.
c. 1767	Foundation of the Hambledon Club in Hampshire, the leading club in England for the next 30 years.
1769	First recorded century, by John Minshull for Duke of Dorset's XI v Wrotham.
1771	Width of bat limited to 4$\frac{1}{4}$ inches, which it has remained ever since.
1774	Lbw law devised.
1776	Earliest known scorecards, at the Vine Club, Sevenoaks, Kent.
1780	The first six-seamed cricket ball, manufactured by Dukes of Penshurst, Kent.
1787	First match at Thomas Lord's first ground, Dorset Square, Marylebone – White Conduit Club v Middlesex. Formation of Marylebone Cricket Club by members of the White Conduit Club.
1788	First revision of the Laws of Cricket by MCC.
1794	First recorded inter-school match: Charterhouse v Westminster.
1795	First recorded case of a dismissal "leg before wicket".
1806	First Gentlemen v Players match at Lord's.
1807	First mention of "straight-armed" (i.e. roundarm) bowling: by John Willes of Kent.
1809	Thomas Lord's second ground opened, at North Bank, St John's Wood.
1811	First recorded women's county match: Surrey v Hampshire at Ball's Pond, London.
1814	Lord's third ground opened on its present site, also in St John's Wood.
1827	First Oxford v Cambridge match, at Lord's: a draw.
1828	MCC authorise the bowler to raise his hand level with the elbow.

1833	John Nyren publishes *Young Cricketer's Tutor* and *The Cricketers of My Time*.
1836	First North v South match, for years regarded as the principal fixture of the season.
c. 1836	Batting pads invented.
1841	General Lord Hill, commander-in-chief of the British Army, orders that a cricket ground be made an adjunct of every military barracks.
1844	First official international match: Canada v United States.
1845	First match played at The Oval.
1846	The All-England XI, organised by William Clarke, begin playing matches, often against odds, throughout the country.
1849	First Yorkshire v Lancashire match.
c. 1850	Wicketkeeping gloves first used.
1850	John Wisden bowls all ten batsmen in an innings for North v South.
1853	First mention of a champion county: Nottinghamshire.
1858	First recorded instance of a hat being awarded to a bowler taking wickets with three consecutive balls.
1859	First touring team to leave England, captained by George Parr, draws enthusiastic crowds in the US and Canada.
1864	"Overhand bowling" authorised by MCC. John Wisden's *The Cricketer's Almanack* first published.
1868	Team of Australian Aboriginals tour England.
1873	W. G. Grace becomes the first player to record 1,000 runs and 100 wickets in a season. First regulations restricting county qualifications, regarded by some as the official start of the County Championship.
1877	First Test match: Australia beat England by 45 runs at Melbourne.
1880	First Test in England: a five-wicket win against Australia at The Oval.
1882	Following England's first defeat by Australia in England, an "obituary notice" to English cricket in the *Sporting Times* leads to the tradition of the Ashes.
1889	Work begins on present Lord's Pavilion. South Africa's first Test match. Declarations first authorised, but only on the third day, or in a one-day match.
1890	County Championship officially constituted.
1895	W. G. Grace scores 1,000 runs in May, and reaches his 100th hundred.
1899	A. E. J. Collins scores 628 not out in a junior house match at Clifton College, the highest recorded individual score in any game – until 2016. Selectors choose England team for home Tests, instead of host club issuing invitations.
1900	In England, six-ball over becomes the norm, instead of five.
1909	Imperial Cricket Conference (ICC – now the International Cricket Council) set up, with England, Australia and South Africa the original members.
1910	Six runs given for any hit over the boundary, instead of only for a hit out of the ground.
1912	First and only triangular Test series played in England, involving England, Australia and South Africa.
1915	W. G. Grace dies, aged 67.
1926	Victoria score 1,107 v New South Wales at Melbourne, still a first-class record.
1928	West Indies' first Test match. A. P. Freeman of Kent and England becomes the only player to take more than 300 first-class wickets in a season: 304.

1930   New Zealand's first Test match.
Donald Bradman's first tour of England: he scores 974 runs in five Tests, still a record for any series.

1931   Stumps made higher (28 inches not 27) and wider (nine inches not eight – this was optional until 1947).

1932   India's first Test match.
Hedley Verity of Yorkshire takes ten wickets for ten runs v Nottinghamshire, the best innings analysis in first-class cricket.

1932-33   The Bodyline tour of Australia in which England bowl at batsmen's bodies with a packed leg-side field to neutralise Bradman's scoring.

1934   Jack Hobbs retires, with 197 centuries and 61,237 runs, both records.
First women's Test: Australia v England at Brisbane.

1935   MCC condemn and outlaw Bodyline.

1947   Denis Compton (Middlesex and England) hits a record 3,816 runs in an English season.

1948   First five-day Tests in England.
Bradman concludes Test career with a second-ball duck at The Oval and an average of 99.94 – four runs would have made it 100.

1952   Pakistan's first Test match.

1953   England regain the Ashes after a 19-year gap, the longest ever.

1956   Jim Laker of England takes 19 wickets for 90 v Australia at Manchester, the best match analysis in first-class cricket.

1960   First tied Test: Australia v West Indies at Brisbane.

1963   Distinction between amateurs and professionals abolished in English cricket.
The first major one-day tournament begins in England: the Gillette Cup.

1968   Garry Sobers becomes first man to hit six sixes in an over, for Nottinghamshire against Glamorgan at Swansea.

1969   Limited-over Sunday league inaugurated for first-class counties.

1970   Proposed South African tour of England cancelled; South Africa excluded from international cricket because of their government's apartheid policies.

1971   First one-day international: Australia beat England at Melbourne by five wickets.

1973   First women's World Cup: England are the winners.

1975   First men's World Cup: West Indies beat Australia in final at Lord's.

1976   First women's match at Lord's: England beat Australia by eight wickets.

1977   Centenary Test at Melbourne, with identical result to the first match: Australia beat England by 45 runs.
Australian media tycoon Kerry Packer signs 51 of the world's leading players in defiance of the cricketing authorities.

1978   Graham Yallop of Australia is the first batsman to wear a protective helmet in a Test.

1979   Packer and official cricket agree peace deal.

1981   England beat Australia in Leeds Test, after following on with bookmakers offering odds of 500-1 against them winning.

1982   Sri Lanka's first Test match.

1991   South Africa return, with a one-day international in India.

1992   Zimbabwe's first Test match.
Durham become first county since Glamorgan in 1921 to attain first-class status.

1993   The ICC cease to be administered by MCC, becoming an independent organisation.

1994	Brian Lara becomes the first player to pass 500 in a first-class innings: 501 not out for Warwickshire v Durham.
2000	South Africa's captain Hansie Cronje banned from cricket for life after admitting receiving bribes from bookmakers in match-fixing scandal.
	Bangladesh's first Test match.
	County Championship split into two divisions, with promotion and relegation.
2001	Sir Donald Bradman dies, aged 92.
2003	First Twenty20 game played, in England.
2004	Lara is the first to score 400 in a Test innings, for West Indies v England in Antigua.
2005	England regain the Ashes after 16 years.
2006	Pakistan become first team to forfeit a Test, for refusing to resume at The Oval.
	Shane Warne becomes the first man to take 700 Test wickets.
2007	Australia complete 5–0 Ashes whitewash for the first time since 1920-21.
	Australia win the World Cup for the third time running.
	India beat Pakistan in the final of the inaugural World Twenty20.
2008	Indian Premier League of 20-over matches launched.
	Sachin Tendulkar becomes the leading scorer in Tests, passing Lara.
2009	Terrorists in Lahore attack buses containing Sri Lankan team and match officials.
2010	Tendulkar scores the first double-century in a one-day international, against South Africa; later in the year, he scores his 50th Test century.
	Muttiah Muralitharan retires from Test cricket, after taking his 800th wicket.
	England's men win the World T20, their first global title.
	Pakistan bowl three deliberate no-balls in Lord's Test against England; the ICC ban the three players responsible.
2011	India become the first team to win the World Cup on home soil.
	Salman Butt, Mohammad Asif and Mohammad Amir are given custodial sentences of between six and 30 months for their part in the Lord's spot-fix.
2012	Tendulkar scores his 100th international century, in an ODI against Bangladesh at Mirpur.
2013	150th edition of *Wisden Cricketers' Almanack*.
	Tendulkar retires after his 200th Test match, with a record 15,921 runs.
2014	Australia complete only the third 5–0 Ashes whitewash.
	India's Rohit Sharma hits 264 in one-day international against Sri Lanka at Kolkata.
	Australian batsman Phillip Hughes, 25, dies after being hit on the neck by a bouncer.
2015	Australia win World Cup for fifth time, beating New Zealand in final at Melbourne.
2016	Pranav Dhanawade, 15, makes 1,009 not out – the highest recorded individual score in any match – in a school game in Mumbai.
	Brendon McCullum hits Test cricket's fastest hundred, from 54 balls, in his final match, against Australia at Christchurch.
2017	England women beat India by nine runs to win the World Cup at Lord's.
	England play their first day/night home Test, against West Indies at Edgbaston.
	Australia and England play first day/night Ashes Test, at Adelaide.
2018	Three Australians are banned after sandpaper used on the ball in a Test in South Africa.
	Afghanistan and Ireland's men play their first Test matches.
	Alastair Cook retires from Test cricket with 161 caps, 12,472 runs and 33 centuries.
	James Anderson takes his 564th Test wicket, unprecedented by a pace bowler.
2019	England's men win their first 50-over World Cup, after super over against New Zealand.
	Ireland play a Test at Lord's for the first time.
	England (362-9) complete their record run-chase to win Ashes Test, at Leeds.
2020	The Hundred competition introduced in England and Wales.

ANNIVERSARIES IN 2020–21

Compiled by Steven Lynch

2020

May 8   Michael Bevan (Australia) born, 1970.
Perhaps the first great one-day finisher: averaged 53 in his 232 ODIs.

May 15   Maitland Hathorn (South Africa) dies aged 42, 1920.
Transvaal batsman who hit 102 v England in Johannesburg in 1905-06.

May 26   Jack Cheetham (South Africa) born, 1920.
Popular Test captain of the 1950s, who put the emphasis on his side's fielding.

Jul 16   W. G. Grace scores 215 for Gentlemen v Players at The Oval, 1870.
The first double-century in the fixture's history.

Jul 19   Robert Christiani (West Indies) born, 1920.
Bespectacled batsman from Guyana who was out for 99 on Test debut in 1947-48.

Jul 22   Chandu Sarwate (India) born, 1920.
Shared a last-wicket stand of 249 with No. 11 Shute Banerjee v Surrey at The Oval, 1946.

Jul 26   William Ward (MCC) makes the first double-century in an important match, 1820.
Ward scored 278 at Lord's against Norfolk, whose side included the young Fuller Pilch.

Jul 30   Eddie Barlow (World XI) takes four wickets in five balls against England, 1970.
This unofficial series, won 4–1 by the strong World XI, replaced the South African tour.

Aug 7   Syd Buller (umpire) dies during a match aged 60, 1970.
The best umpire of his time, Buller collapsed during a break in a county game at Edgbaston.

Aug 11   Tom Richardson (England) born, 1870.
Hard-working Surrey fast bowler who took 290 first-class wickets in 1895.

Aug 18   Godfrey Evans (England) born, 1920.
Popular Kent wicketkeeper whose 91 Test caps between 1946 and 1959 was a record.

Aug 26   Percy Fender (Surrey) hits a hundred in 35 minutes, 1920.
Fender's onslaught, at Northampton, is still the fastest authentic century.

Sep 18   Darren Gough (England) born, 1970.
Combative Yorkshire fast bowler whose 229 Test wickets included an Ashes hat-trick.

Oct 4   George Tribe (Australia) born, 1920.
Left-arm wrist-spinner who took over 1,000 wickets for Northamptonshire, 176 in 1955.

Oct 17   Anil Kumble (India) born, 1970.
Leg-spinner who took 619 Test wickets, including all ten v Pakistan at Delhi in 1998-99.

Oct 20   Alec Watson (Lancashire) dies aged 75, 1920.
Long-serving Scottish-born all-rounder who took more than 1,300 wickets for Lancashire.

Nov 21   Joe Darling (Australia) born, 1870.
Left-hand batsman who captained Australia on three Ashes tours – 1899, 1902 and 1905.

Nov 21   Stanley Jackson (England) born, 1870.
Aristocratic batsman who led England to victory in the 1905 Ashes – against Joe Darling.

Dec 14   The first tied Test, Australia v West Indies at Brisbane, 1960.
Joe Solomon's direct-hit run-out brings a tie to start a famous series.

Dec 16   Eric Marx (Transvaal) scores double-century on first-class debut, 1920.
Marx, who later won three Test caps, hits 240 against Griqualand West in Johannesburg.

Dec 28   Norman "Tufty" Mann (South Africa) born, 1920.
Spinner whose dismissal of England's George Mann provoked one of John Arlott's best lines, about "Mann's inhumanity to Mann".

2021

Jan 5 The first one-day international is played at Melbourne, 1971.
A limited-overs game is hastily arranged after an Ashes Test is washed out.

Jan 22 Andy Ganteaume (West Indies) born, 1921.
Trinidad batsman who scored 112 in his only Test innings, in 1947-48.

Jan 29 William Gunn (England) dies aged 62, 1921.
Part of a famous Nottinghamshire family, he played 11 early Tests for England.

Feb 7 Athol Rowan (South Africa) born, 1921.
Off-spinner who took 54 Test wickets, despite a metal leg-brace after a war injury.

Mar 1 Australia complete first Ashes whitewash, 1921.
Captained by Warwick Armstrong, Australia won the first post-WW1 Ashes series 5–0.

Mar 5 Nazar Mohammad (Pakistan) born, 1921.
Pakistan's first Test centurion, at Lucknow in 1952-53; father of Mudassar Nazar.

Mar 16 Leslie "Chuck" Fleetwood-Smith (Australia) dies aged 62, 1971.
Whimsical slow left-armer who took one for 298 in the 1938 Ashes Test at The Oval.

Mar 29 Tom Hayward (England) born, 1871.
Prolific Surrey batsman who once scored four centuries in a week.

Mar 29 Sam Loxton (Australia) born, 1921.
Combative Victorian all-rounder; one of Don Bradman's Invincible tourists in 1948.

Apr 30 First edition of *The Cricketer* magazine published, 1921.
Founded by the former England captain Pelham Warner.

FIFTY YEARS AGO

Wisden Cricketers' Almanack 1971

NOTES BY THE EDITOR [Norman Preston]   When on May 27 [1970], the Test and County Cricket Board announced through the MCC Secretary that the newly arranged series of five Test matches between England and The Rest of the world would be accorded "Test match status" and that England caps would be given to the England players, I never regarded them as anything other than proper Test matches. Here cricket came into line with international Association Football, when England have played the Rest of the World, FIFA and the Rest of Europe. Since 1953 there have been five such matches, some drawing attendances of 100,000 at Wembley, and one has only to look at the football record books to find that such famous players as Billy Wright and Bobby Charlton count their caps in these matches among the hundred and more with which they are credited for their country. No one has ever suggested that these football matches were wrongly classified, yet when a World cricket XI is brought together by events caused by political pressure a small minority have sought to have these splendid matches omitted from the records. At the moment, the Test matches, as the TCCB announced at the time, must be considered unofficial and therefore do not come within the jurisdiction of the International Cricket Conference, the governing body for official Tests. Since South Africa left the Commonwealth, and consequently the International Cricket Conference, there have been no official Tests between England and South Africa, or Australia and South Africa, or New Zealand and South Africa. If one must omit England v The Rest of the World, then all those matches played by South Africa since 1961 would presumably have to go, which to my mind is a ridiculous situation. I would emphasise that the England v The Rest of the World matches were broadcast by the BBC and ITV, and publicised by the newspapers throughout Great Britain, and sold to the public as Test matches as advised by the Test and County Cricket Board of Control. There is no copyright in the term "Test Match".

FIVE CRICKETERS OF THE YEAR: CLIVE LLOYD, by John Kay   Few cricketers in recent years have captured the public imagination in the manner of Clive Hubert Lloyd. This tall, bespectacled all-rounder, short-sighted but by no means handicapped by the affliction, joined Lancashire two years ago and has played a leading part in the revival of cricket at Old Trafford, where crowds are now big again and enthusiasm is ever growing... Clive Lloyd would be the last to proclaim that his signing from the Lancashire League club, Haslingden, had anything more than a passing significance. He would, of course, be wrong. No cricketer has made a greater impact on his county than has Lloyd on Lancashire. He has set an example with the bat, the ball, and in the field, that has inspired every other member of the team and the staff.

OBITUARY   STRUDWICK, HERBERT, who died suddenly on February 14, a few days after his 90th birthday, held the world record for most dismissals in a career by a wicketkeeper. One of the greatest and assuredly one of the most popular players of his time, he helped to get rid of 1,497 batsmen, 73 of them in Test matches... [and he held 1,242 first-class catches]. His stumpings numbered 255... Strudwick figured regularly behind the stumps for Surrey for 25 years and, becoming scorer afterwards, served the county altogether for 60 years. He played 28 times for England between 1910 and 1926 during the period when Australia and South Africa were their only Test match opponents and would doubtless have been chosen more often had he not been contemporary with A. A. Lilley, of Warwickshire, a better batsman... No more genuine sportsman, in every sense of the word, than the teetotal, non-smoking Strudwick ever took the field for Surrey. An idol of the Surrey crowd, he was always ready to proffer helpful advice to young players... S. C. Griffith, MCC Secretary and a former England wicketkeeper, said: "This wonderful man and great cricketer... was the best coach I have ever known... Apart from his ability, he was one of the outstanding figures and personalities of the game."

THE SOUTH AFRICAN TOUR DISPUTE: A RECORD OF CONFLICT, 1970 by Irving Rosenwater   The bitterness of 1970… was moral, political, personal, ideological. Confusion and hate were brought into cricket together with prejudices of race, creed and colour – brought into the very sport which had shown perhaps the greatest tolerance of all sports in the passage of history and where friendly, civilised competition had for so long been paramount… The summer of a general election did not help to cool matters, either. How thankful must have been the village, club and school sides of England who happily played their cricket last year with their traditional blend of innocence, zest and good fellowship… A rare event in British life – a House of Commons emergency debate on a sporting topic – took place, at the insistence of Mr Philip Noel-Baker, on May 14, when for three hours the tour issue was passionately thrashed out… Hot on the heels of the Commons debate came the shattering news for South Africa of her formal expulsion from the Olympic movement – the first nation ever so expelled… The Fair Cricket Campaign… stepped up its activities by sending out 20,000 invitations to organisations and individuals to stop the tour. The Archbishop of Canterbury and the Chief Rabbi added their voices to the wave of opposition. It was even made public that, according to unofficial sources, the Queen, in her personal capacity, was opposed to the tour… The Home Secretary requested that the tour be cancelled "on the grounds of broad public policy"… The cancellation came on May 22… Cricket, and especially Mr Griffith at Lord's, had been subjected to pressures never experienced in the game before. Let us hope that cricket will never know such conflict again.

AUSTRALIANS IN SOUTH AFRICA, 1970 by Geoffrey A. Chettle   The Springboks gained a clean sweep in the four Tests… From the moment the new Springbok captain, Dr Ali Bacher, won the toss at Newlands and elected to bat in the First Test, the series followed an almost stereotyped pattern. Bacher wins the toss; South Africa takes first knock; the visitors' reply is characterised by the abject failure of the majority of the top six batsmen, and the final phase, which always ends in a resounding victory for the Springboks, finds Australia with back to the wall facing a fourth-innings total of 452 (First Test) increasing progressively to a formidable 570 in the final Test. Demoralised by the batting failures and an unbelievable epidemic of dropped catches – totalling almost 30 in the series – the outcome was invariably a foregone conclusion. Individually each member of the Australian Test side was a talented cricketer in his own right, and in attempting to probe the reasons for the humiliation that rocked the cricketing world, one feels that the main contributory factors were the simultaneous failure of the top-class batsmen… deplorable catching failures and the incredible and total loss of form of the leading bowler, Graham McKenzie. This tremendous cricketer was so completely lethargic and listless that in 111 overs during the series he captured only one wicket for 333 runs.

HAMPSHIRE v MIDDLESEX, AT PORTSMOUTH, July 19, 1970   Middlesex won by eight wickets. Parfitt's "pocket computer" and a hard-hit 49 by Russell took Middlesex to victory in a rain-affected match. Parfitt's "computer" – a piece of paper on which he had recorded Hampshire's over-by-over score – was vital for Middlesex. He knew his side not only had to score 135 in 35 overs to win, but they also had to keep ahead of the Hampshire total for each over in case rain ended play abruptly. In fact, they always kept ahead and would have won at any stage after ten overs… Middlesex found the men for the situation in Russell and Parfitt, both of whom paused to consult the "computer" every other over.

WOMEN'S CRICKET, 1970 by Netta Rheinberg   The first unofficial international tour to be arranged by women cricketers gave a pleasant and original start to the year 1970. Rachael Heyhoe, England's captain, took a team of 15, including five internationals, to Jamaica where, during a stay of three weeks they played three one-day and three two-day matches, watched by large and enthusiastic crowds. The tour was made possible through Mr Jack Hayward, a Wolverhampton-born businessman, whose generosity reaches out to a wide variety of activities and acquisitions, including the recent purchase of Lundy for the nation. The standard of cricket played by the Jamaicans was considerably higher than anticipated, and the touring team was not quite strong enough to avoid three draws in the two-day "Tests", in the first of which Heyhoe scored the only century of the tour.

ONE HUNDRED YEARS AGO

Wisden Cricketers' Almanack 1921

PUBLIC SCHOOL CRICKET IN 1920 by E. B. Noel In watching the school matches at Lord's, there were two points which struck one. First, that several of the Marlborough XI, when batting, waited to receive the ball with their bats held quite high in the air… The method entailed the raising of the bat almost shoulder high, and so many of the Marlborough XI did it that it obviously was *malice prépensée*. The idea is no doubt that of being "ready", an admirable precept at all ball games, but it certainly did not meet with the approval of a number of the critics. The second point was that the Tonbridge XI in the match against Clifton at Lord's did not all wear caps of the same colours. The majority of the XI wore the first XI cap, but some of the side, including the captain and second captain, wore the second XI cap, which struck one as a rather extraordinary proceeding to those conversant with the customs in the most Public School Matches.

MIDDLESEX v SURREY, AT LORD'S, AUGUST 28, 30, 31, 1920 This was the match of the season. Middlesex and Lancashire were running neck and neck for the Championship, and as Lancashire on the same days had the simplest of tasks against Worcestershire, Middlesex knew that nothing less than an actual victory would be of real value to them. Never before has a county match proved such an attraction at Lord's. On the Saturday there must have been nearly 25,000 people on the ground, 20,700 paying for admission at the gates. A great fight was looked forward to and, as it happened, all expectations were exceeded. It was a game never to be forgotten, Middlesex in the end winning by 55 runs, and so securing the Championship… In the end, Middlesex won with ten minutes to spare. Warner was carried off the field shoulder high and, before the crowd dispersed, he and Fender had to make speeches.

NORTHAMPTONSHIRE v SURREY, AT NORTHAMPTON, AUGUST 25–27, 1920 Though beaten by eight wickets in a match which produced 1,475 runs – a record in county cricket – the Northamptonshire players had good reason to be pleased with themselves. Scores of 306 and 430 against Surrey were immeasurably above their ordinary form. Surrey's huge total was the more remarkable as Hobbs contributed only three runs to it. The hitting on the second afternoon was some of the fiercest of the season, Fender actually getting his hundred in 35 minutes. Peach and Ducat also played in dazzling style.

Fender's hundred remains the fastest in first-class cricket (excluding those scored in contrived circumstances).

SPECIAL PORTRAIT: P. F. WARNER by Sydney Pardon There have been many greater cricketers than Pelham Warner, but none more devoted to the game. Nothing has ever damped his enthusiasm. Whether winning or losing, he has always been the same. When, having made up his mind to finish with county cricket last season, he had the extreme satisfaction of leading Middlesex to victory in the Championship. It was suggested that, though he had already found a place in the *Wisden* portrait gallery, there could be no more appropriate picture for this year's issue of the Almanack than a special photograph of him at the end of his career. The previous portrait appeared in 1904, Middlesex then, as now, having gained first place among the counties… It was not his batting, but his skill as a captain that made his final season memorable. But for his leadership Middlesex would never have gained in August the wonderful series of victories that culminated with the triumph over Surrey. His great asset as a captain in that month of strenuous matches, counting for even more than his judgment in changing the bowling and placing the field, was his sanguine spirit. He was full of encouragement and got the very best out of his men by making them believe in themselves.

Rather than Five Cricketers of the Year, the 1921 edition of Wisden *had a special portrait of Warner, who had already been in the Five in 1904.*

ONE HUNDRED AND FIFTY YEARS AGO

Wisden Cricketers' Almanack 1871

MCC AND GROUND v NOTTINGHAMSHIRE, AT LORD'S, JUNE 13–15, 1870
A lamentable celebrity will ever attach to this match, through the fatal accident to Summers, whose death resulted from a ball bowled by Platts in the second innings of Nottinghamshire. The wickets were excellent, and the sad mishap universally regretted… Summers's last innings was a good one; at 12.48 he went in one wicket down with the score 29, at dinner call he had made 35 (the score 137), and at 3.30 his wicket fell to a shooter from the same hand that subsequently bowled the fatal ball. The score was 158 when Summers was out for 41 – a fact that tells how steadily and carefully he batted. This his final innings comprised 11 singles, eight twos, three threes, and one five – that five (a fine forward cut down to the Tavern) being the last hit the poor fellow ever made, as he was then bowled by Platts; and the first ball bowled to him in the second innings was the fatal one.

THE MARYLEBONE CLUB IN 1870   At a special general meeting of the members of MCC, held in the Pavilion on May 4, the Hon. F. Ponsonby proposed, Mr F. N. Micklethwait seconded, and (after discussion) it was duly carried, that Law IX should read as follows: "The Bowler shall deliver the ball with one foot on the ground behind the bowling crease, and within the return crease, and shall bowl one over before he change wickets, which he shall be permitted to do twice in the same innings, and no bowler shall bowl more than two overs in succession."

GLOUCESTERSHIRE IN 1870   This shire played a brief but brilliant cricket season in 1870, winning every match the 11 played. There was no county club for Gloucestershire then in existence, the matches being arranged by, and played under, the management of Mr W. G. Grace; however, there is very little doubt but that in 1871 a county cricket club for Gloucestershire will be established on a firm basis.

FORD (Lingfield) v TONBRIDGE SCHOOL AT THE FORD, JULY 29, 1870   Mr Arthur Hoare's (of Edenbridge) score in the above match is far away the largest innings hit in 1870, and it is the highest score ever gained in an uninterrupted innings… Mr Hoare was consequently six hours and ten minutes at wickets, and ran 538 runs. His 302 was made by two sevens, three sixes, eight fives, ten fours, 36 threes, 21 twos, and 40 singles. (The School did not play their full strength.)

ETON v HARROW, AT LORD'S, JULY 8–9, 1870   Their Royal Highnesses the Duchess of Cambridge, and the Prince and Princess of Teck, with a host of the nobility, honoured this match with their presence at Lord's. The Grand Stand was thronged, a large majority of its occupants being ladies. The Pavilion seats and roof were crowded with members and their friends. The Ring was deeper and more densely packed, and the outer ring of carriages more extensive than at any preceding match. Such an assemblage of rank, fashion and numbers had never before been seen, even at Lord's. It was computed that quite 30,000 visitors attended the ground on those memorable two days… Down by Mr Dark's house, up by the north-east corner, and fronting the whole row of well-known dwarf chestnut trees, the accidental but graceful grouping of ladies elegantly attired, added a picturesque brilliancy to the old ground not seen at other matches. Two sights unusual on cricket grounds and curious by contrast, were witnessed at this match: the first occurred on the Friday, when on the boys' retiring to luncheon, the whole playing area of the ground was covered by a gay company promenading; the other on the Saturday when, on rain commencing falling at noon, the youthful cricketers were suddenly surrounded by a dense ring of some thousands of opened umbrellas.)

Compiled by Christopher Lane

HONOURS AND AWARDS IN 2019-20

In 2019-20, the following were decorated for their services to cricket:

Order of Ikhamanga (South Africa), 2019: J. H. Kallis (excellent contribution to the sport of cricket) Silver Award.

Queen's Birthday Honours, 2019: K. A. Beaumont (Buckinghamshire CCC secretary; services to Minor County cricket) BEM; K. J. Coetzer (Durham, Northamptonshire and Scotland; services to cricket) MBE; A. N. Vollans (Anston CC; services to cricket and the community in South Yorkshire and Nottinghamshire) BEM.

Queen's Birthday Honours (Australia), 2019: T. T. Harrison (former chairman of Cricket Tasmania; services to cricket) OAM; L. J. Kausmann (Maccabi Ajax CC; services to sport and the community) OAM; M. H. Klumpp (Bankstown DCC; services to cricket) OAM; A. G. Mellick (Beaumaris CC; services to cricket and rugby union) OAM; C. R. Norris (Preston CC and Victoria Sub District CA; services to cricket and the community) OAM; F. Thomas (South Australia and Australia women; services to cricket and the indigenous community) AM; M. R. Whitney (New South Wales and Australia; services to cricket and the media) AM.

Queen's Birthday Honours (New Zealand), 2019: B. A. Waddle (commentator; services as a broadcaster) MNZM.

Arjuna Awards (India), 2019: R. A. Jadeja (Saurashtra and India); P. Yadav (Uttar Pradesh and India women).

Prime Minister Theresa May's Resignation Honours, September 2019: G. Boycott (Yorkshire and England; services to sport) Knight; A. J. Strauss (Middlesex and England; services to sport) Knight.

New Year's Honours, 2020: R. Bainbridge (World Cup volunteer; services to sport) BEM; T. H. Bayliss (England coach; services to cricket) OBE; J. C. Buttler (Somerset, Lancashire and England; services to cricket) MBE; K. V. Cook (Warwickshire operations manager; services to cricket) BEM; M. Frost (Glamorgan community projects manager/Cricket Wales development manager; services to cricket) BEM; C. J. Graves (ECB chairman; services to cricket) CBE; C. G. Greenidge (Barbados, Hampshire and West Indies; services to cricket and the development of sport) Knight Commander of the Order of St Michael and St George; A. P. E. Knott (Kent and England; services to cricket) MBE; C. H. Lloyd (Guyana, Lancashire and West Indies; services to cricket) Knight; E. J. G. Morgan (Middlesex, Ireland and England; services to cricket) CBE; A. Pradhan (World Cup volunteer; services to cricket) BEM; J. E. Root (Yorkshire and England; services to cricket) MBE; C. Sheldon (World Cup volunteer; services to cricket) BEM; B. A. Stokes (Durham and England; services to cricket) OBE; P. W. Thomas (Norfolk; services to grassroots cricket in Norfolk) BEM; J. Wiles (World Cup volunteer; services to cricket) BEM.

New Year's Honours (New Zealand), 2020: N. R. Crawshaw (Buller CA organiser, coach, umpire, statistician and historian; services to the community and sport) QSM.

Padma Awards (India), 2020: Zaheer Khan (Baroda, Mumbai and India) Padma Shri.

Australia Day Honours, 2020: A. J. Corr (Hightett West CC; services to cricket) OAM; I. A. Healy (Queensland and Australia; services to cricket, media and the community) AO; B. Kimberley (Mount Colah CC; services to cricket) OAM; B. P. McFarlane (Geelong CA; services to cricket) OAM; J. W. Orchard (sports physician; services to sports medicine, particularly cricket) AM; K. N. Slater (Western Australia and Australia; services to cricket, Australian rules and baseball) AM; A. C. Voges (Western Australia and Australia; services to sport and the community) OAM.

ICC AWARDS

The ICC's 16th annual awards, selected by a panel of 43, were announced in January 2020.

Cricketer of the Year (Sir Garfield Sobers Trophy)	**Ben Stokes** (England)
Test Player of the Year	**Pat Cummins** (Australia)
One-Day International Player of the Year	**Rohit Sharma** (India)
Twenty20 International Performance of the Year	**Deepak Chahar** (India)*
Emerging Player of the Year	**Marnus Labuschagne** (Australia)
Associate Player of the Year	**Kyle Coetzer** (Scotland)
Umpire of the Year (David Shepherd Trophy)	**Richard Illingworth** (England)
Spirit of Cricket Award	**Virat Kohli** (India)†

* *For his 6-7 against Bangladesh.* † *For asking a World Cup crowd not to boo Steve Smith.*

The panel also selected two men's World XIs from the previous 12 months:

ICC World Test team		*ICC World one-day team*	
1	Mayank Agarwal (I)	1	Rohit Sharma (I)
2	Tom Latham (NZ)	2	Shai Hope (WI)
3	Marnus Labuschagne (A)	3	*Virat Kohli (I)
4	*Virat Kohli (I)	4	Babar Azam (P)
5	Steve Smith (A)	5	Kane Williamson (NZ)
6	Ben Stokes (E)	6	Ben Stokes (E)
7	†B-J. Watling (NZ)	7	†Jos Buttler (E)
8	Pat Cummins (A)	8	Mitchell Starc (A)
9	Mitchell Starc (A)	9	Trent Boult (NZ)
10	Neil Wagner (NZ)	10	Mohammed Shami (I)
11	Nathan Lyon (A)	11	Kuldeep Yadav (I)

Previous Cricketers of the Year were Rahul Dravid (2004), Andrew Flintoff and Jacques Kallis (jointly in 2005), Ricky Ponting (2006 and 2007), Shivnarine Chanderpaul (2008), Mitchell Johnson (2009 and 2014), Sachin Tendulkar (2010), Jonathan Trott (2011), Kumar Sangakkara (2012), Michael Clarke (2013), Steve Smith (2015), Ravichandran Ashwin (2016) and Virat Kohli (2017 and 2018).

The women's awards and World XIs, selected by a panel of 21, were announced in December 2019:

Women's Cricketer of the Year (Rachael Heyhoe Flint Trophy)	**Ellyse Perry** (Australia)
Women's One-Day International Cricketer of the Year	**Ellyse Perry** (Australia)
Women's Twenty20 International Cricketer of the Year	**Alyssa Healy** (Australia)
Women's Emerging Player of the Year	**Chanida Sutthiruang** (Thailand)

ICC ODI Team of the Year		*ICC T20I Team of the Year*	
1	†Alyssa Healy (A)	1	†Alyssa Healy (A)
2	Smriti Mandhana (I)	2	Danni Wyatt (E)
3	Tammy Beaumont (E)	3	*Meg Lanning (A)
4	*Meg Lanning (A)	4	Smriti Mandhana (I)
5	Stafanie Taylor (WI)	5	Lizelle Lee (SA)
6	Ellyse Perry (A)	6	Ellyse Perry (A)
7	Jess Jonassen (A)	7	Deepti Sharma (I)
8	Shikha Pandey (I)	8	Nida Dar (P)
9	Jhulan Goswami (I)	9	Megan Schutt (A)
10	Megan Schutt (A)	10	Rumana Ahmed (B)
11	Poonam Yadav (I)	11	Radha Yadav (I)

ICC CRICKET HALL OF FAME

The ICC Cricket Hall of Fame was launched in 2009 in association with the Federation of International Cricketers' Associations to recognise legends of the game. In the first year, 60 members were inducted: 55 from the earlier FICA Hall of Fame, plus five players elected in October 2009 by a voting academy made up of the ICC president, 11 ICC member representatives, a FICA representative, a women's cricket representative, ten journalists, a statistician, and all living members of the Hall of Fame. Candidates must have retired from international cricket at least five years ago.

The members elected in 2019 were Allan Donald (South Africa), Cathryn Fitzpatrick (Australia) and Sachin Tendulkar (India), who brought the total to 90.

ICC DEVELOPMENT AWARDS

The ICC announced the global winners of their 2018 Development Awards for Associate Members in July 2019.

Participation Programme	**Cricket Peru**
Female Participation Programme	**Samoa International Cricket Association**
Associate Men's Performance of the Year	**Scotland** (beating England in an ODI)
Associate Women's Performance of the Year	**Thailand** (beating Sri Lanka in the Asia Cup)
Cricket for Change Innovation of the Year	**Bhutan Cricket Council Board** (work with Unicef)
Innovation of the Year	**Cricket Scotland** (CricHIIT women's training initiative)

ALLAN BORDER MEDAL

Pat Cummins won the Allan Border Medal in February 2019, after being voted the best Australian men's international player of the previous 12 months. The award has also been won by Glenn McGrath, Steve Waugh, Matthew Hayden, Adam Gilchrist, Ricky Ponting (four times), Michael Clarke (four times), Brett Lee, Shane Watson (twice), Mitchell Johnson, Steve Smith (twice) and David Warner (twice). The first bowler to win the medal since Johnson in 2014, Cummins received 156 votes from team-mates, umpires and journalists, six ahead of **Nathan Lyon**, who was named Test Player of the Year. The men's One-day International Player of the Year was **Marcus Stoinis**, while **Glenn Maxwell** was Twenty20 International Player of the Year. **Matthew Wade** succeeded Tasmanian team-mate George Bailey as Men's Domestic Player of the Year, and **Will Pucovski** of Victoria was the Bradman Young Cricketer of the Year. Wicketkeeper **Alyssa Healy** dominated the women's awards, claiming the Belinda Clark Award for the leading woman player – winning 125 votes, well ahead of Megan Schutt's 81 – plus the One-Day International and Twenty20 International Player of the Year awards. **Heather Graham** of Western Australia was Women's Domestic Player of the Year, and Victoria's **Georgia Wareham** the Betty Wilson Young Cricketer of the Year. **Moises Henriques** won the inaugural Community Champion Award for his work raising awareness about mental health.

SHEFFIELD SHIELD PLAYER OF THE YEAR

The Sheffield Shield Player of the Year Award for 2018-19 was **Scott Boland**, who took 48 wickets for Victoria. The award, instituted in 1975-76, is adjudicated by umpires over the season. Boland was also named the Taverners Indigenous Cricketer of the Year, and **Paul Wilson** retained his title as Umpire of the Year. Three prizes went to **Tasmania**, with their men's and women's teams picking up the Benaud Spirit of Cricket Awards for fair play, while wicketkeeper **Georgia Redmayne** was the WNCL Player of the Year.

PROFESSIONAL CRICKETERS' ASSOCIATION AWARDS

The following awards were announced at the PCA's annual dinner in October 2019.

Reg Hayter Cup (NatWest PCA Players' Player of the Year)	**Ben Stokes**
John Arlott Cup (PCA Young Player of the Year)	**Tom Banton**
NatWest Women's Player of the Summer	**Sophie Ecclestone**
Specsavers Test Player of the Summer	**Stuart Broad**
Royal London One-Day International Player of the Summer	**Chris Woakes**
Specsavers County Championship Player of the Year	**Simon Harmer**
Vitality Blast Player of the Year	**D'Arcy Short**
Royal London One-Day Cup Player of the Year	**Saqib Mahmood**
ECB Special Award	**Eoin Morgan**
Harold Goldblatt Award (PCA Umpire of the Year)	**Alex Wharf**
Greene King PCA England Masters Player of the Year	**Jonathan Trott**

Greene King Team of the Year: **Billy Godleman, Dom Sibley, Tom Banton, Wayne Madsen, Sam Hain, Ryan Higgins, †Dane Vilas, Lewis Gregory, *Simon Harmer, Kyle Abbott, Ben Sanderson.**

CHRISTOPHER MARTIN-JENKINS SPIRIT OF CRICKET AWARDS

MCC and the BBC introduced the Spirit of Cricket awards in memory of Christopher Martin-Jenkins, the former MCC president and *Test Match Special* commentator, in 2013. In December 2019, the Award went to **Kane Williamson's New Zealand team**, for their sporting conduct throughout the men's World Cup and especially for their "exceptional level of sportsmanship, humility and selflessness in defeat" in the aftermath of the final at Lord's, which they lost to England on boundary count after the match and a super over were both tied.

WALTER LAWRENCE TROPHY

The Walter Lawrence Trophy for the fastest century in 2019 went to **Cameron Delport**, who reached a hundred in 38 balls for Essex against Surrey in a floodlit Vitality Blast game at Chelmsford on

July 19. He won the trophy plus £3,000. Since 2008, the trophy has been available for innings in all senior cricket in England; traditionally, it was reserved for the fastest first-class hundred (in 2019, David Wiese's 80-ball century for Sussex against Cardiff MCCU at Hove). England captain **Heather Knight** won the women's award, for the second time, after an unbeaten 129 as Berkshire beat Wales at Pontarddulais in Division Two of the Royal London One-Day Cup. The MCCU Universities Award went to **Oliver Batchelor**, who made 215 not out for Leeds/Bradford against Cardiff at Usk. Knight and Batchelor each received a silver medallion and £500. **Dani Long-Martinez** won the Schools Award, for the highest score by a schoolboy against MCC; he made a match-winning 158 not out for Norwich School, to earn a medallion and a Gray-Nicolls bat.

CRICKET WRITERS' CLUB AWARDS

The Cricket Writers' Club announced their annual awards in October 2019. **Tom Banton** of Somerset was voted Young Cricketer of the Year; he had made 1,536 runs for the county across all formats, including 1,000 in white-ball games. His 454 runs at 41 helped Somerset win the Royal London One-Day Cup, and he followed up with 549 at 42 and a strike-rate of 161 in the Vitality Blast. **Simon Harmer** was County Championship Player of the Year; his 83 wickets made him the tournament's leading bowler, and ensured a second title in three years for Essex; he took another 17 in the Blast as they completed the double. **Beth Morgan** of Middlesex was named the fourth CWC Women's Cricketer of the Year; she had scored more than 4,000 runs and taken over 100 wickets for the county, and was the only woman to feature in every year of the One-Day County Championship, which ran from 1997 to 2019. The Lord's Taverners Disability Cricketer of the Year was **Callum Flynn** from Manchester, whose 180 runs at 45, plus four wickets, helped England finish as runners-up in the 2019 Physical Disability World Series. The Peter Smith Memorial Award "for services to the presentation of cricket to the public" went to author and publisher **Stephen Chalke**. The Cricket Book of the Year was *Steve Smith's Men* by **Geoff Lemon**.

A list of Young Cricketers from 1950 to 2004 appears in Wisden 2005, page 995. A list of Peter Smith Award winners from 1992 to 2004 appears in Wisden 2005, page 745.

SECOND XI PLAYER OF THE YEAR

The Association of Cricket Statisticians and Historians named **Liam Patterson-White** of Nottinghamshire as the Les Hatton Second XI Player of the Year for 2019. Patterson-White scored 670 at 74 in eight matches in the Second XI Championship, and took 20 wickets at 24 with his left-arm spin. Against Durham, he combined eight wickets with 149, and in the next game, against Warwickshire, followed up with 153. He claimed a further 14 wickets in the Second XI T20 tournament.

GROUNDSMEN OF THE YEAR

The ECB Groundsman of the Year was **Andy Fogarty**, for his four-day pitches at Headingley; **Andy Ward** at Leicester was runner-up, with commendations for Gary Barwell (Edgbaston), Vic Demain (Chester-le-Street), Andy Mackay (Hove) and Matt Merchant (Old Trafford). The one-day award was shared by **Robin Saxton** (Cardiff) and **Simon Lee** (Taunton); Fogarty, Ward, Stuart Kerrison (Chelmsford), Adrian Llong (Canterbury) and Karl McDermott (Lord's) were commended. **John Dodds** (Scarborough) regained the award for the best outground, with **Christian Brain** (Cheltenham) runner-up for the third year in four (he won in 2017); Nick Searle was commended for Radlett, and John Corcoran for Clifton Park in York, which hosted Yorkshire for the first time in 2019. **Lee de Grammont** of Fenner's (Cambridge) was MCC Universities Groundsman of the Year.

SPORTS PERSONALITY OF THE YEAR AWARDS

Ben Stokes was named BBC Sports Personality of the Year in December 2019, for his role in England winning the men's World Cup for the first time, and for steering England to an astonishing victory in the Headingley Ashes Test. He was the first cricketer to win the trophy since Andrew Flintoff in 2005. England's World Cup team were Team of the Year, and the Greatest Sporting Moment was judged to be Jos Buttler breaking the stumps to seal the World Cup win.

GQ SPORTSMEN OF THE YEAR AWARD

In September 2019, the GQ Sportsmen of the Year Award went to **England's one-day team**, for winning the World Cup. Captain Eoin Morgan accepted on behalf of his side.

CRICKET SOCIETY AWARDS

Wetherell Award Leading First-class All-rounder	**Ryan Higgins** (Gloucestershire)
Wetherell Award for Leading Schools All-rounder	**George Hill** (Sedbergh School)
Most Promising Young Male Cricketer	**Zak Crawley** (Kent and England)
Most Promising Young Woman Cricketer	**Freya Davies** (Sussex, Western Storm, England)
Sir John Hobbs Silver Jubilee Memorial Prize (for Outstanding Under-16 Schoolboy)	**James Coles** (Magdalen College School, Oxford)
A. A. Thomson Fielding Prize (for Best Schoolboy Fielder)	**Nafis Shaikh** (Bemrose School, Derby)
Charlotte Edwards Award (for Outstanding Under-16 Schoolgirl)	**Alice Capsey** (Lancing College and Surrey)
Don Rowan Memorial Trophy (for schools promoting cricket for disabled children)	**Garratt Park School, Wandsworth**
Ian Jackson Award for Services to Cricket	**Enid Bakewell** (East Midlands and England)
The Perry-Lewis/Kershaw Memorial Trophy (for contribution to the Cricket Society XI)	**Tom Carmichael**

WOMBWELL CRICKET LOVERS' SOCIETY AWARDS

George Spofforth Cricketer of the Year	**Ben Stokes** (Durham and England)
Brian Sellers Captain of the Year	**Eoin Morgan** (England)
C. B. Fry Young Cricketer of the Year	**Dominic Sibley** (Warwickshire)
Arthur Wood Wicketkeeper of the Year	**Ben Brown** (Sussex)
Learie Constantine Fielder of the Year	**Tom Köhler-Cadmore** (Yorkshire)
Denis Compton Memorial Award for Flair	**Ben Stokes** (Durham and England)
Denzil Batchelor Award for Services to English Cricket	**Marcus Trescothick** (Somerset)
Dr Leslie Taylor Award (best Roses performance)	**Alyssa Healy** (Yorkshire Diamonds)
Les Bailey Most Promising Young Yorkshire Player	**Jack Shutt**
Ted Umbers Award – Services to Yorkshire Cricket	**Geoff Cope***
J. M. Kilburn Cricket Writer of the Year	**Mike Atherton** (*The Times*)
Jack Fingleton Cricket Commentator of the Year	**Charles Dagnall**

* For services as a Yorkshire player from 1966 to 1980, on the club board and as president.

ECB COUNTY JOURNALISM AWARDS

The ECB announced the winners of the eighth annual County Cricket Journalism Awards for the coverage of domestic cricket in March 2019. The *Yorkshire Post* became the first regional title to win the award for Outstanding Newspaper Coverage, with previous winners *The Times* highly commended; the *Post* was also the Regional Newspaper of the Year, ahead of London's *Evening Standard* and the *County Gazette* in Somerset. The Outstanding Online Coverage award went to **thecricketer.com** for expanding its domestic cricket reporting; Cricbuzz and CRICKETher were commended, and the judges also praised the *Yorkshire Post* and *BBC West Midlands*. **Isabelle Westbury** was the Christopher Martin-Jenkins Young Journalist of the Year, 16 months after being named County Broadcaster of the Year; also commended were Charlie Taylor of BBC Somerset, Will Macpherson (*Evening Standard*), Matt Roller (ESPNcricinfo), Ben Gardner (*Wisden Cricket Monthly*) and Paul Martin (*County Gazette*). **Alex Winter** of BBC Radio Northampton was the Christopher Martin-Jenkins County Broadcaster of the Year.

ECB BUSINESS OF CRICKET AWARDS

The ECB announced the 2019 BOCA awards, designed to celebrate marketing and PR excellence, in February 2020. **Nottinghamshire** collected three awards: they won again in the Warmest Welcome category, and added the Inclusivity award and the Blast IT Communications award for a high-profile match venue – for behind-the-scenes access for fans – while **Derbyshire** took the same prize for a first-class venue, for a video campaign which helped sell out their T20 fixture with Nottinghamshire. **Hampshire** won the Best Loyalty Initiative, for an app enabling fans to buy tickets and access live streaming, highlights and scorecards, while Harry Walklin, their head of marketing, was named the year's Rising Star. **Yorkshire** also pulled off a double: Team Awesome, for their Yorkies Match Day Support Team, and Community Engagement Impact (high-profile venue), for a women's charity tournament. **Somerset** won the Community Engagement Impact award (first-class venue), for working with people needing extra support, and the Fan Innovation Award for their new website. **Warwickshire**'s cricket operations manager Keith Cook and head of stadium operations Claire Daniel shared the title of Unsung Hero of Match Operations. **Essex** won the Most Improved Matchday Experience, and **Durham** the Welcome Families award for its family zone roadshow.

ECB OSCAs

The ECB presented the 2019 NatWest Outstanding Service to Cricket Awards to volunteers from recreational cricket in October. The winners were:

Lifetime Achiever **Ernie Brabbins** (Cumbria)
Sixty years as player, umpire, scorer, coach and club officer in Cumbria. Helped raise £800,000 to repair Appleby Eden CC's facilities after devastating floods, and began their All Stars programme.

Heartbeat of the Club **Ian Guppy** (Sussex)
Saved Aldwick CC from extinction after the pavilion burned down in 2017, launching a fund-raising drive and managing the rebuilding, while helping the club connect with the wider community.

Outstanding Contribution to Disability Cricket **Phil Lucas** (Derbyshire)
Founding member of Derbyshire Disabled Cricket in 2005 – the club now have 40 members and have won the National Super 9s title three times – and deliver cricket sessions for community groups.

Most Inspiring and Diverse Cricket Offer **Richard Langdon** (Berkshire)
Doubled participation in Falkland CC's juniors, women's and All Stars programmes, and conducted weekly cricket sessions for adults with special educational needs.

Pro-Active Leadership **Martin Croucher** (Huntingdonshire)
Worked tirelessly to ensure the futures of St Ives Town and Warboys clubs through a merger.

Young volunteer 14–18 **Alicia Smith** (Yorkshire)
Has played in Illingworth St Mary's sides up to senior level, coaches the All Stars, helps with ground maintenance and catering, pioneered electronic scoring in Aire/Wharfe and Halifax leagues.

Young volunteer 19–25 **James Thompson** (Northumberland)
Head groundsman and sponsorship co-ordinator at Berwick CC, who has secured nearly £40,000 in grants for improvements to club facilities, runs the club's All Stars scheme and opens the bowling.

CRICKET COMMUNITY CHAMPION AWARD

MCC and *The Cricketer* introduced a new award in 2017 recognising individuals working to build, maintain and support the game at grassroots level. The third winner, announced in July 2019, was **John Reeve** from Acton CC, who has run a cricket programme to help teach life skills to youngsters at Feltham Young Offenders' Institute, as well as sitting on the Middlesex County Cricket League committee and setting up the West London Cricket Academy for young players. He was invited to ring the bell at Lord's on the second day of England's Test with Ireland.

ACS STATISTICIAN OF THE YEAR

In March 2020, the Association of Cricket Statisticians and Historians awarded the Brooke–Lambert Statistician of the Year trophy to **Eric Midwinter**, for his long record of writing on and around cricket, most recently *His Captain's hand on his shoulder smote*, examining the influence of cricket in schoolboy stories from the 1850s to the 1950s.

2020 FIXTURES

Test	Test match
RL ODI	Royal London one-day international
VT20I	Vitality Twenty20 international
RL WODI	Royal London women's one-day international
WVT20I	Vitality women's T20 international
SSCC D1/2	Specsavers County Championship Division 1/2
Men's/women's 100	The Hundred
RLODC	Royal London One-Day Cup
VB T20	Vitality Blast
Univs	First-class university match
Univs (nfc)	Non-first-class university match
♀	Day/night or floodlit game

Tue Mar 24–Fri 27	Friendly	MCC	v Essex	Galle, Sri Lanka
Thu Apr 2–Sat 4	Univs	Durham	v Durham MCCU	Chester-le-Street
		Gloucestershire	v Cardiff MCCU	Bristol
		Kent	v Oxford MCCU	Canterbury
		Leicestershire	v Loughboro MCCU	Leicester
		Middlesex	v Cambridge MCCU	Northwood
		Yorkshire	v Leeds/Brad MCCU	Leeds
Tue Apr 7–Thu 9	Univs	Cambridge MCCU	v Nottinghamshire	Cambridge
		Lancashire	v Durham MCCU	Manchester
		Leeds/Brad MCCU	v Warwickshire	Weetwood
		Loughboro MCCU	v Worcestershire	Loughborough
		Somerset	v Cardiff MCCU	Taunton
		Sussex	v Oxford MCCU	Hove
Sun Apr 12–Wed 15	SSCC D1	Lancashire	v Kent	Manchester
		Somerset	v Warwickshire	Taunton
		Yorkshire	v Gloucestershire	Leeds
	SSCC D2	Middlesex	v Worcestershire	Lord's
		Nottinghamshire	v Leicestershire	Nottingham
		Sussex	v Durham	Hove
Mon Apr 13–Wed 15	Univs (nfc)	Cambridge MCCU	v Essex	Cambridge
		Glamorgan	v Cardiff MCCU	Cardiff
		Hampshire	v Loughboro MCCU	Southampton
		Northamptonshire	v Leeds/Brad MCCU	Northampton
		Oxford MCCU	v Surrey	Oxford
Tue Apr 14–Thu 16	Univs (nfc)	Derbyshire	v Durham MCCU	Derby
Sun Apr 19–Wed 22	SSCC D1	Essex	v Yorkshire	Chelmsford
		Gloucestershire	v Lancashire	Bristol
		Hampshire	v Kent	Southampton
		Surrey	v Somerset	The Oval
		Warwickshire	v Northamptonshire	Birmingham
	SSCC D2	Derbyshire	v Leicestershire	Derby
		Durham	v Nottinghamshire	Chester-le-Street
		Glamorgan	v Middlesex	Cardiff
Sat Apr 25–Tue 28	SSCC D1	Kent	v Gloucestershire	Canterbury
		Northamptonshire	v Essex	Northampton
		Somerset	v Hampshire	Taunton
		Warwickshire	v Lancashire	Birmingham
		Yorkshire	v Surrey	Leeds
	SSCC D2	Leicestershire	v Glamorgan	Leicester
		Middlesex	v Derbyshire	Lord's
		Worcestershire	v Sussex	Worcester

Fri May 1–Mon 4	**SSCC D1**	Gloucestershire	v Somerset	Bristol
		Hampshire	v Yorkshire	Southampton
		Lancashire	v Essex	Manchester
		Northamptonshire	v Kent	Northampton
		Surrey	v Warwickshire	The Oval
	SSCC D2	Durham	v Middlesex	Chester-le-Street
		Glamorgan	v Worcestershire	Cardiff
		Nottinghamshire	v Derbyshire	Nottingham
		Sussex	v Leicestershire	Hove
Fri May 8–Mon 11	**SSCC D1**	Essex	v Gloucestershire	Chelmsford
		Kent	v Surrey	Beckenham
		Somerset	v Northamptonshire	Taunton
		Warwickshire	v Hampshire	Birmingham
	SSCC D2	Derbyshire	v Durham	Derby
		Leicestershire	v Worcestershire	Leicester
		Middlesex	v Nottinghamshire	Lord's
		Sussex	v Glamorgan	Hove
Thu May 14	**ODI**	**IRELAND**	**v BANGLADESH**	**Belfast**
Fri May 15–Mon 18	**SSCC D1**	Essex	v Hampshire	Chelmsford
		Lancashire	v Somerset	Manchester
		Surrey	v Northamptonshire	Guildford
		Yorkshire	v Kent	Leeds
	SSCC D2	Glamorgan	v Derbyshire	Cardiff
		Leicestershire	v Durham	Leicester
		Nottinghamshire	v Sussex	Nottingham
		Worcestershire	v Middlesex	Worcester
Sat May 16	**ODI**	**IRELAND**	**v BANGLADESH**	**Belfast**
Tue May 19	**ODI**	**IRELAND**	**v BANGLADESH**	**Belfast**
Fri May 22–Mon 25	**Tour**	England Lions	v West Indians	Taunton
	SSCC D1	Gloucestershire	v Surrey	Bristol
		Hampshire	v Lancashire	Southampton
		Kent	v Essex	Canterbury
		Northamptonshire	v Yorkshire	Northampton
		Warwickshire	v Somerset	Birmingham
	SSCC D2	Derbyshire	v Sussex	Derby
		Durham	v Glamorgan	Chester-le-Street
		Middlesex	v Leicestershire	Lord's
		Worcestershire	v Nottinghamshire	Worcester
Thu May 28–Sun 31	**Tour**	Worcestershire	v West Indians	Worcester
Thu May 28	**VB T20**	Surrey	v Middlesex	The Oval ♀
		Sussex	v Kent	Hove ♀
Fri May 29	**VB T20**	Derbyshire	v Leicestershire	Derby ♀
		Essex	v Glamorgan	Chelmsford ♀
		Hampshire	v Sussex	Southampton ♀
		Kent	v Surrey	Canterbury ♀
		Lancashire	v Northamptonshire	Liverpool
		Nottinghamshire	v Warwickshire	Nottingham ♀
		Somerset	v Gloucestershire	Taunton ♀
		Yorkshire	v Durham	Leeds ♀
Sat May 30	**VB T20**	Leicestershire	v Northamptonshire	Leicester
Sun May 31	**VB T20**	Derbyshire	v Lancashire	Derby
		Essex	v Somerset	Chelmsford
		Glamorgan	v Surrey	Cardiff
		Kent	v Hampshire	Canterbury
		Middlesex	v Gloucestershire	Lord's
		Nottinghamshire	v Yorkshire	Nottingham
		Warwickshire	v Durham	Birmingham
Tue Jun 2	**VB T20**	Worcestershire	v Northamptonshire	Worcester

Wed Jun 3	VB T20	Durham	v Leicestershire	Chester-le-Street	♀
		Gloucestershire	v Glamorgan	Bristol	♀
		Sussex	v Somerset	Hove	♀
		Warwickshire	v Yorkshire	Birmingham	♀
Thu Jun 4–Mon 8	1st Test	**ENGLAND**	**v WEST INDIES**	**The Oval**	
Thu Jun 4	VB T20	Middlesex	v Hampshire	Lord's	♀
		Nottinghamshire	v Worcestershire	Nottingham	♀
		Yorkshire	v Lancashire	Leeds	♀
Fri Jun 5	VB T20	Derbyshire	v Nottinghamshire	Derby	♀
		Essex	v Kent	Chelmsford	♀
		Leicestershire	v Worcestershire	Leicester	♀
		Northamptonshire	v Durham	Northampton	♀
		Somerset	v Surrey	Taunton	♀
		Sussex	v Glamorgan	Hove	♀
		Warwickshire	v Lancashire	Birmingham	♀
Sat Jun 6	VB T20	Kent	v Gloucestershire	Canterbury	♀
Sun Jun 7	VB T20	Hampshire	v Gloucestershire	Southampton	
		Lancashire	v Durham	Manchester	
		Leicestershire	v Warwickshire	Leicester	
		Middlesex	v Glamorgan	Richmond	
		Northamptonshire	v Derbyshire	Northampton	
		Somerset	v Essex	Taunton	
		Worcestershire	v Yorkshire	Worcester	
	Varsity (o-d)	Cambridge U	v Oxford U	Lord's	
Wed Jun 10	T20I	**SCOTLAND**	**v NEW ZEALAND**	**Edinburgh**	
	VB T20	Durham	v Nottinghamshire	Chester-le-Street	♀
		Glamorgan	v Kent	Cardiff	♀
		Gloucestershire	v Surrey	Bristol	♀
		Hampshire	v Essex	Southampton	♀
		Lancashire	v Leicestershire	Manchester	♀
		Yorkshire	v Derbyshire	Leeds	♀
Thu Jun 11	VB T20	Middlesex	v Sussex	Lord's	♀
		Northamptonshire	v Worcestershire	Northampton	♀
Fri Jun 12–Tue 16	2nd Test	**ENGLAND**	**v WEST INDIES**	**Birmingham**	
Fri Jun 12	T20I	**SCOTLAND**	**v NEW ZEALAND**	**Edinburgh**	
	VB T20	Durham	v Warwickshire	Chester-le-Street	♀
		Glamorgan	v Somerset	Cardiff	♀
		Gloucestershire	v Middlesex	Bristol	♀
		Lancashire	v Derbyshire	Manchester	♀
		Surrey	v Essex	The Oval	♀
		Sussex	v Hampshire	Hove	♀
		Worcestershire	v Nottinghamshire	Worcester	♀
		Yorkshire	v Northamptonshire	Leeds	♀
Sat Jun 13	VB T20	Nottinghamshire	v Leicestershire	Nottingham	♀
Sun Jun 14–Wed 17	SSCC D1	Essex	v Northamptonshire	Chelmsford	
		Hampshire	v Warwickshire	Southampton	
		Somerset	v Gloucestershire	Taunton	
		Surrey	v Kent	The Oval	
		Yorkshire	v Lancashire	Scarborough	
	SSCC D2	Derbyshire	v Worcestershire	Chesterfield	
		Durham	v Leicestershire	Chester-le-Street	
		Sussex	v Middlesex	Hove	
Mon Jun 15–Thu 18	SSCC D2	Nottinghamshire	v Glamorgan	Nottingham	
Tue Jun 16	W Varsity	Cambridge U	v Oxford U	Wormsley	
Thu Jun 18	VB T20	Hampshire	v Somerset	Southampton	♀
		Middlesex	v Kent	Lord's	♀
		Sussex	v Surrey	Hove	♀

Fri Jun 19	**T20I**	**IRELAND**	**v NEW ZEALAND**	**Bready**
Fri Jun 19–Sun 21	**Tour**	Northamptonshire	v West Indians	Northampton
Fri Jun 19	**VB T20**	Durham	v Yorkshire	Chester-le-Street ♀
		Essex	v Middlesex	Chelmsford ♀
		Glamorgan	v Gloucestershire	Cardiff ♀
		Kent	v Sussex	Canterbury ♀
		Leicestershire	v Nottinghamshire	Leicester ♀
		Surrey	v Somerset	The Oval ♀
		Worcestershire	v Warwickshire	Worcester
Sat Jun 20	**VB T20**	Derbyshire	v Yorkshire	Chesterfield
		Gloucestershire	v Hampshire	Bristol
Sun Jun 21	**T20I**	**IRELAND**	**v NEW ZEALAND**	**Bready**
	VB T20	Durham	v Derbyshire	Chester-le-Street
		Hampshire	v Glamorgan	Southampton
		Kent	v Essex	Canterbury
		Lancashire	v Nottinghamshire	Manchester
		Somerset	v Middlesex	Taunton
		Worcestershire	v Leicestershire	Worcester
Tue Jun 23	**T20I**	**IRELAND**	**v NEW ZEALAND**	**Bready**
	VB T20	Somerset	v Hampshire	Taunton
		Warwickshire	v Northamptonshire	Birmingham ♀
Wed Jun 24	**VB T20**	Essex	v Sussex	Chelmsford ♀
		Northamptonshire	v Lancashire	Northampton ♀
		Nottinghamshire	v Durham	Nottingham ♀
Thu Jun 25–Mon 29	**3rd Test**	**ENGLAND**	**v WEST INDIES**	**Lord's**
Thu Jun 25	**WVT20I**	**ENGLAND WOMEN**	**v INDIA WOMEN**	**Taunton** ♀
	VB T20	Derbyshire	v Worcestershire	Derby ♀
		Leicestershire	v Yorkshire	Leicester ♀
		Surrey	v Glamorgan	The Oval ♀
		Sussex	v Gloucestershire	Hove ♀
Fri Jun 26	**VB T20**	Durham	v Lancashire	Chester-le-Street ♀
		Essex	v Gloucestershire	Chelmsford ♀
		Glamorgan	v Middlesex	Cardiff ♀
		Hampshire	v Surrey	Southampton ♀
		Northamptonshire	v Nottinghamshire	Northampton ♀
		Somerset	v Kent	Taunton ♀
		Yorkshire	v Worcestershire	Leeds ♀
		Warwickshire	v Derbyshire	Birmingham ♀
Sat Jun 27	**WVT20I**	**ENGLAND WOMEN**	**v INDIA WOMEN**	**Bristol** ♀
	ODI	**IRELAND**	**v NEW ZEALAND**	**Belfast**
Sun Jun 28–	**SSCC D1**	Kent	v Somerset	Canterbury
Wed Jul 1		Lancashire	v Warwickshire	Manchester
		Northamptonshire	v Surrey	Northampton
		Yorkshire	v Essex	Leeds
	SSCC D2	Glamorgan	v Durham	Swansea
		Leicestershire	v Middlesex	Leicester
		Nottinghamshire	v Worcestershire	Nottingham
		Sussex	v Derbyshire	Arundel
Mon Jun 29	**T20I**	**SCOTLAND**	**v AUSTRALIA**	**Edinburgh**
Mon Jun 29–	**SSCC D1**	Gloucestershire	v Hampshire	Cheltenham
Thu Jul 2				
Tue Jun 30	**ODI**	**IRELAND**	**v NEW ZEALAND**	**Belfast**
Wed Jul 1	**RL WODI**	**ENGLAND WOMEN**	**v INDIA WOMEN**	**Worcester**

Thu Jul 2	ODI	**IRELAND**	**v NEW ZEALAND**	**Belfast**	
	VB T20	Lancashire	v Worcestershire	Manchester	♀
		Middlesex	v Surrey	Lord's	♀
		Yorkshire	v Warwickshire	Leeds	♀
Fri Jul 3	VT20I	**ENGLAND**	**v AUSTRALIA**	**Chester-le-Street**	♀
	VB T20	Derbyshire	v Warwickshire	Derby	♀
		Glamorgan	v Essex	Cardiff	
		Gloucestershire	v Sussex	Cheltenham	
		Kent	v Somerset	Canterbury	♀
		Northamptonshire	v Leicestershire	Northampton	♀
		Nottinghamshire	v Lancashire	Nottingham	♀
		Surrey	v Hampshire	The Oval	♀
		Worcestershire	v Durham	Worcester	
Sat Jul 4	RL WODI	**ENGLAND WOMEN**	**v INDIA WOMEN**	**Chelmsford**	
	VB T20	Leicestershire	v Derbyshire	Leicester	
Sun Jul 5	VT20I	**ENGLAND**	**v AUSTRALIA**	**Manchester**	
Sun Jul 5–Wed Jul 8	SSCC D1	Essex	v Somerset	Chelmsford	
		Gloucestershire	v Yorkshire	Cheltenham	
		Northamptonshire	v Lancashire	Northampton	
		Surrey	v Hampshire	The Oval	
		Warwickshire	v Kent	Birmingham	
	SSCC D2	Derbyshire	v Nottinghamshire	Derby	
		Leicestershire	v Sussex	Leicester	
		Middlesex	v Glamorgan	Northwood	
		Worcestershire	v Durham	Worcester	
Mon Jul 6	RL WODI	**ENGLAND WOMEN**	**v INDIA WOMEN**	**Canterbury**	♀
Mon Jul 6–Thu 9	Varsity	Oxford U	v Cambridge U	Oxford	
Tue Jul 7	VT T20I	**ENGLAND**	**v AUSTRALIA**	**Leeds**	♀
Thu Jul 9	RL WODI	**ENGLAND WOMEN**	**v INDIA WOMEN**	**Hove**	♀
	VB T20	Gloucestershire	v Kent	Cheltenham	
		Middlesex	v Essex	Northwood	
		Northamptonshire	v Warwickshire	Northampton	♀
		Surrey	v Sussex	The Oval	♀
Fri Jul 10	VB T20	Hampshire	v Middlesex	Southampton	♀
		Lancashire	v Yorkshire	Manchester	♀
		Leicestershire	v Durham	Leicester	♀
		Nottinghamshire	v Derbyshire	Nottingham	♀
		Somerset	v Glamorgan	Taunton	♀
		Surrey	v Kent	The Oval	♀
		Sussex	v Essex	Hove	♀
		Warwickshire	v Worcestershire	Birmingham	♀
Sat Jul 11	RL ODI	**ENGLAND**	**v AUSTRALIA**	**Lord's**	♀
	VB T20	Derbyshire	v Northamptonshire	Derby	
Sun Jul 12	T20I	**IRELAND**	**v PAKISTAN**	**Dublin**	
	VB T20	Durham	v Northamptonshire	Chester-le-Street	
		Essex	v Hampshire	Chelmsford	
		Glamorgan	v Sussex	Cardiff	
		Gloucestershire	v Somerset	Bristol	
		Kent	v Middlesex	Canterbury	
		Warwickshire	v Nottinghamshire	Birmingham	
		Worcestershire	v Lancashire	Worcester	
		Yorkshire	v Leicestershire	Leeds	
Tue Jul 14	RL ODI	**ENGLAND**	**v AUSTRALIA**	**Southampton**	♀
	T20I	**IRELAND**	**v PAKISTAN**	**Dublin**	
Thu Jul 16	RL ODI	**ENGLAND**	**v AUSTRALIA**	**Bristol**	♀

Fri Jul 17	Men's 100	Oval I	v Welsh F	The Oval	♀
Sat Jul 18	Men's 100	Birmingham P	v London S	Birmingham	
		Manchester O	v Northern S	Manchester	♀
Sun Jul 19	Men's 100	Trent R	v Birmingham P	Nottingham	
		Welsh F	v Southern B	Cardiff	♀
	RLODC	Essex	v Kent	Chelmsford	
		Hampshire	v Worcestershire	Southampton	
		Lancashire	v Middlesex	Sedbergh School	
		Surrey	v Northamptonshire	The Oval	
		Sussex	v Durham	Hove	
		Yorkshire	v Nottinghamshire	Scarborough	
Mon Jul 20	Men's 100	Northern S	v Oval I	Leeds	
	RLODC	Warwickshire	v Somerset	Birmingham	
Tue Jul 21	Men's 100	London S	v Trent R	Lord's	♀
	RLODC	Durham	v Gloucestershire	Scarborough	
Wed Jul 22	Men's 100	Southern B	v Manchester O	Southampton	♀
	Women's 100	Birmingham P	v Manchester O	Worcester	
	RLODC	Derbyshire	v Glamorgan	Derby	
		Essex	v Worcestershire	Chelmsford	♀
		Leicestershire	v Surrey	TBC	
		Warwickshire	v Northamptonshire	Edgbaston CSG	
Thu Jul 23–Sun 26	Tour	FCC Xl	v Pakistanis	Northampton	
Thu Jul 23	Women's 100	London S	v Northern S	Lord's	
	Men's 100	London S	v Northern S	Lord's	♀
Fri Jul 24	Women's 100	Birmingham P	v Southern B	Birmingham	
	Men's 100	Birmingham P	v Southern B	Birmingham	♀
	Women's 100	Manchester O	v Oval I	Sedbergh School	
	RLODC	Durham	v Lancashire	Gosforth	
		Glamorgan	v Surrey	Cardiff	
		Gloucestershire	v Essex	Bristol	
		Middlesex	v Hampshire	Radlett	
		Nottinghamshire	v Derbyshire	Grantham	
		Sussex	v Kent	Eastbourne	
		Yorkshire	v Warwickshire	Scarborough	
Sat Jul 25	Men's 100	Oval I	v Manchester O	The Oval	
	Women's 100	Trent R	v Welsh F	Nottingham	
	Men's 100	Trent R	v Welsh F	Nottingham	
Sun Jul 26	Men's 100	Northern S	v Birmingham P	Leeds	♀
		Southern B	v Oval I	Southampton	
	Women's 100	London S	v Southern B	Chelmsford	
		Northern S	v Oval I	Gosforth	
	RLODC	Derbyshire	v Yorkshire	Chesterfield	
		Gloucestershire	v Lancashire	Bristol	
		Kent	v Hampshire	Tunbridge Wells	
		Leicestershire	v Glamorgan	TBC	
		Middlesex	v Durham	Radlett	
		Nottinghamshire	v Northamptonshire	Grantham	
		Surrey	v Somerset	Guildford	
		Worcestershire	v Sussex	Worcester	
Mon Jul 27	Women's 100	Manchester O	v Trent R	Manchester	
	Men's 100	Manchester O	v Trent R	Manchester	♀
Tue Jul 28	Women's 100	Welsh F	v Birmingham P	Cardiff	
	Men's 100	Welsh F	v Birmingham P	Cardiff	♀
	RLODC	Northamptonshire	v Derbyshire	Northampton	
		Sussex	v Middlesex	Hove	
		Warwickshire	v Leicestershire	Edgbaston CSG	

Date	Competition	Home		Away	Venue	
Wed Jul 29	Women's 100	Oval I	v	London S	The Oval	
	Men's 100	Oval I	v	London S	The Oval	💡
	RLODC	Hampshire	v	Essex	Southampton	
		Kent	v	Gloucestershire	Tunbridge Wells	
		Lancashire	v	Worcestershire	Blackpool	
		Somerset	v	Glamorgan	Taunton	
Thu Jul 30– Mon Aug 3	1st Test	**ENGLAND**	**v**	**PAKISTAN**	**Lord's**	
Thu Jul 30	Men's 100	Northern S	v	Southern B	Leeds	💡
	Women's 100	Trent R	v	Birmingham P	Leicester	💡
		Welsh F	v	Northern S	Bristol	💡
Fri Jul 31	Women's 100	Manchester O	v	London S	Manchester	
	Men's 100	Manchester O	v	London S	Manchester	💡
	Women's 100	Southern B	v	Oval I	Hove	
	RLODC	Glamorgan	v	Yorkshire	Newport	
		Hampshire	v	Sussex	Southampton	
		Kent	v	Durham	Tunbridge Wells	
		Northamptonshire	v	Leicestershire	Northampton	
		Somerset	v	Derbyshire	Taunton	💡
		Warwickshire	v	Nottinghamshire	Birmingham	
		Worcestershire	v	Middlesex	Worcester	
Sat Aug 1	Men's 100	Welsh F	v	Northern S	Cardiff	💡
	Women's 100	Trent R	v	Northern S	Derby	
Sun Aug 2	Men's 100	Trent R	v	Oval I	Nottingham	💡
	Women's 100	Oval I	v	Birmingham P	Beckenham	
		Welsh F	v	Southern B	Taunton	
	RLODC	Essex	v	Middlesex	Chelmsford	
		Glamorgan	v	Nottinghamshire	Newport	
		Gloucestershire	v	Hampshire	Bristol	
		Lancashire	v	Sussex	Manchester	
		Leicestershire	v	Yorkshire	Leicester	
		Northamptonshire	v	Somerset	Northampton	
		Surrey	v	Warwickshire	The Oval	
		Worcestershire	v	Kent	Worcester	
Mon Aug 3	Men's 100	Birmingham P	v	Manchester O	Birmingham	💡
Tue Aug 4	Women's 100	Southern B	v	Trent R	Southampton	
	Men's 100	Southern B	v	Trent R	Southampton	💡
	RLODC	Derbyshire	v	Warwickshire	Derby	
		Durham	v	Hampshire	Darlington	
		Gloucestershire	v	Worcestershire	Bristol	
		Lancashire	v	Essex	Liverpool	💡
		Somerset	v	Leicestershire	Taunton	
		Surrey	v	Nottinghamshire	The Oval	
		Yorkshire	v	Northamptonshire	York	
Wed Aug 5	Women's 100	Northern S	v	Manchester O	Leeds	
	Men's 100	Northern S	v	Manchester O	Leeds	💡
Thu Aug 6	Men's 100	London S	v	Oval I	Lord's	💡
	Women's 100	London S	v	Welsh F	Northampton	
	RLODC	Glamorgan	v	Warwickshire	Cardiff	
		Kent	v	Lancashire	Canterbury	
		Worcestershire	v	Durham	Worcester	
		Yorkshire	v	Surrey	York	
Fri Aug 7–Tue 11	2nd Test	**ENGLAND**	**v**	**PAKISTAN**	**Manchester**	
Fri Aug 7	Men's 100	Southern B	v	Welsh F	Southampton	💡
	Women's 100	Trent R	v	Oval I	Derby	💡
	RLODC	Essex	v	Sussex	Chelmsford	
		Leicestershire	v	Derbyshire	Leicester	
		Middlesex	v	Gloucestershire	Radlett	
		Nottinghamshire	v	Somerset	Nottingham	
Sat Aug 8	Men's 100	Birmingham P	v	Trent R	Birmingham	💡
	Women's 100	Welsh F	v	Manchester O	Bristol	

Sun Aug 9	Men's 100	Welsh F	v London S	Cardiff	♀
	Women's 100	Birmingham P	v London S	Worcester	
		Northern S	v Southern B	York	
	RLODC	Derbyshire	v Surrey	Derby	
		Durham	v Essex	Chester-le-Street	
		Hampshire	v Lancashire	Newclose, IoW	
		Middlesex	v Kent	Radlett	
		Northamptonshire	v Glamorgan	Northampton	
		Nottinghamshire	v Leicestershire	Sookholme	
		Somerset	v Yorkshire	Taunton	
		Sussex	v Gloucestershire	Horsham	
Mon Aug 10	Men's 100	Trent R	v Northern S	Nottingham	♀
Tue Aug 11	Men's 100	Oval I	v Birmingham P	The Oval	♀
	Women's 100	London S	v Trent R	Chelmsford	
		Northern S	v Birmingham P	York	
Wed Aug 12	Men's 100	London S	v Southern B	Lord's	♀
	Women's 100	Southern B	v Manchester O	Hove	♀
		Oval I	v Welsh F	Beckenham	
Thu Aug 13	Men's 100	Manchester O	v Welsh F	Manchester	♀
	RLODC	**Quarter-final**			
	RLODC	**Quarter-final**			
Fri Aug 14	Women's 100	**Semi-final and final**		Hove	
Sat Aug 15	Men's 100	**Semi-final and final**		Lord's	
Sun Aug 16	RLODC	**Semi-final**			
	RLODC	**Semi-final**			
	U19 T20	England U19	v West Indies U19	Beckenham	
Tue Aug 18	VB T20	**Quarter-final**			
	U19 ODI	England U19	v West Indies U19	Beckenham	
Wed Aug 19	VB T20	**Quarter-final**			
Thu Aug 20–Mon 24	**3rd Test**	**ENGLAND**	**v PAKISTAN**	**Nottingham**	
Thu Aug 20	VB T20	**Quarter-final**			
	U19 ODI	England U19	v West Indies U19	Beckenham	
Fri Aug 21	VB T20	**Quarter-final**			
Sat Aug 22	U19 ODI	England U19	v West Indies U19	Beckenham	
Sun Aug 23–Wed 26	SSCC D1	Hampshire	v Gloucestershire	Southampton	
		Kent	v Northamptonshire	Canterbury	
		Lancashire	v Surrey	Manchester	
		Somerset	v Essex	Taunton	
		Yorkshire	v Warwickshire	Scarborough	
	SSCC D2	Durham	v Derbyshire	Chester-le-Street	
		Glamorgan	v Nottinghamshire	Colwyn Bay	
		Sussex	v Worcestershire	Hove	
Wed Aug 26	Tour (T20)	Leicestershire	v Pakistanis	Leicester	♀
Thu Aug 27–Sun 30	U19 Test	England U19	v West Indies U19	Bristol	
Sat Aug 29	VT20I	**ENGLAND**	**v PAKISTAN**	**Leeds**	♀
Sat Aug 29–Sep 1	SSCC D1	Essex	v Lancashire	Chelmsford	
		Kent	v Hampshire	Canterbury	
		Somerset	v Yorkshire	Taunton	
		Warwickshire	v Surrey	Birmingham	
	SSCC D2	Derbyshire	v Glamorgan	Derby	
		Durham	v Sussex	Chester-le-Street	
		Nottinghamshire	v Middlesex	Nottingham	
		Worcestershire	v Leicestershire	Worcester	

Sun Aug 30–Sep 2	SSCC D1	Northamptonshire	v Gloucestershire	Northampton	
Mon Aug 31	VT20I	**ENGLAND**	**v PAKISTAN**	**Cardiff**	
Tue Sep 1	WVT20I	**ENGLAND WOMEN**	**v S AFRICA WOMEN**	**Hove**	♀
Wed Sep 2	VT20I	**ENGLAND**	**v PAKISTAN**	**Southampton**	♀
Thu Sep 3–Sep 6	U19 Test	England U19	v West Indies U19	Hove	
Fri Sep 4	WVT20I	**ENGLAND WOMEN**	**v S AFRICA WOMEN**	**Chelmsford**	♀
Sat Sep 5	VB T20	Semi-finals and final		Birmingham	♀
Tue Sep 8	RL WODI	**ENGLAND WOMEN**	**v S AFRICA WOMEN**	**Canterbury**	♀
Tue Sep 8–Fri 11	SSCC D1	Gloucestershire	v Warwickshire	Bristol	
		Hampshire	v Northamptonshire	Southampton	
		Lancashire	v Yorkshire	Manchester	
		Surrey	v Essex	The Oval	
	SSCC D2	Glamorgan	v Sussex	Cardiff	
		Leicestershire	v Nottinghamshire	Leicester	
		Middlesex	v Durham	Lord's	
		Worcestershire	v Derbyshire	Worcester	
Thu Sep 10	RL ODI	**ENGLAND**	**v IRELAND**	**Nottingham**	♀
Fri Sep 11	RL WODI	**ENGLAND WOMEN**	**v S AFRICA WOMEN**	**Derby**	♀
Sat Sep 12	RL ODI	**ENGLAND**	**v IRELAND**	**Birmingham**	♀
Sun Sep 13	RL WODI	**ENGLAND WOMEN**	**v S AFRICA WOMEN**	**Leeds**	
		The Cricketer Village Cup final		Lord's	
Mon Sep 14–Thu 17	SSCC D1	Essex	v Kent	Chelmsford	
		Lancashire	v Gloucestershire	Manchester	
		Northamptonshire	v Warwickshire	Northampton	
		Somerset	v Surrey	Taunton	
		Yorkshire	v Hampshire	Leeds	
	SSCC D2	Derbyshire	v Middlesex	Derby	
		Durham	v Worcestershire	Chester-le-Street	
		Glamorgan	v Leicestershire	Cardiff	
		Sussex	v Nottinghamshire	Hove	
Mon Sep 14		National Club final		Lord's	
Tue Sep 15	RL ODI	**ENGLAND**	**v IRELAND**	**The Oval**	♀
Wed Sep 16	RL WODI	**ENGLAND WOMEN**	**v S AFRICA WOMEN**	**Leicester**	♀
Sat Sep 19	RLODC	**Final**		**Nottingham**	♀
Tue Sep 22–Fri 25	SSCC D1	Gloucestershire	v Northamptonshire	Bristol	
		Hampshire	v Somerset	Southampton	
		Kent	v Lancashire	Canterbury	
		Surrey	v Yorkshire	The Oval	
		Warwickshire	v Essex	Birmingham	
	SSCC D2	Leicestershire	v Derbyshire	Leicester	
		Middlesex	v Sussex	Lord's	
		Nottinghamshire	v Durham	Nottingham	
		Worcestershire	v Glamorgan	Worcester	

CRICKET TRADE DIRECTORY

BOOKSELLERS

CHRISTOPHER SAUNDERS, Kingston House, High Street, Newnham-on-Severn, Glos GL14 1BB. Tel: 01594 516030; **email:** chris@cricket-books.com; **website:** cricket-books.com. Office/bookroom open by appointment. Second-hand/antiquarian cricket books and memorabilia bought and sold. Regular catalogues issued containing selections from over 12,000 items in stock.

GRACE BOOKS AND CARDS (Ted Kirwan), Donkey Cart Cottage, Main Street, Bruntingthorpe, Lutterworth, Leics LE17 5QE. Tel: 0116 247 8417; **email:** ted@gracecricketana.co.uk. Second-hand and antiquarian cricket books, *Wisdens*, autographed material and cricket ephemera of all kinds. Now also modern postcards of current international cricketers.

JOHN JEFFERS, The Old Mill, Aylesbury Road, Wing, Leighton Buzzard LU7 0PG. Tel: 01296 688543 or 07903 028767; **e-mail:** edgwarerover@live.co.uk. *Wisden* specialist. Immediate decision and top settlement for purchase of *Wisden* collections. Why wait for the next auction? Why pay the auctioneer's commission anyway?

J. W. McKENZIE, 12 Stoneleigh Park Road, Ewell, Epsom, Surrey KT19 0QT. Tel: 020 8393 7700; **email:** mckenziecricket@btconnect.com; **website:** mckenzie-cricket.co.uk. Old cricket books and memorabilia specialist since 1971. Free catalogues issued regularly. Large shop premises open 9–4.30 Monday–Friday. Thirty minutes from London Waterloo. Please phone before visiting.

KEN PIESSE CRICKET BOOKS, PO Box 868, Mt Eliza, Victoria 3930, Australia. Tel: (+61) 419 549 458; email: kenpiesse@ozemail.com.au; **website:** cricketbooks.com.au. Australian cricket's internet specialists. Quality limited editions in stock include *Dainty: The Bert Ironmonger Story* and, soon, a centenary biography of Sam Loxton, last of the Invincibles.

ROGER PAGE, 10 Ekari Court, Yallambie, Victoria 3085, Australia. Tel: (+61) 3 9435 6332; email: rpcricketbooks@iprimus.com.au; **website:** rpcricketbooks.com. Australia's only full-time dealer in new and second-hand cricket books. Distributor of overseas cricket annuals and magazines. Agent for Association of Cricket Statisticians and Cricket Memorabilia Society.

ST MARY'S BOOKS & PRINTS, 9 St Mary's Hill, Stamford, Lincolnshire PE9 2DP. Tel: 01780 763033; **email:** info@stmarysbooks.com; **website:** stmarysbooks.com. Dealers in *Wisdens*, second-hand, rare cricket books and *Vanity Fair* prints. Book-search service offered.

SPORTSPAGES, 23 Menin Way, Farnham, Surrey GU9 8DY. Email: info@sportspages.com; **website:** sportspages.com. Large stock of *Wisdens*, fine sports books and sports memorabilia. Books and sports memorabilia also purchased. Visitors welcome to browse by appointment.

TIM BEDDOW, 66 Oak Road, Oldbury, West Midlands B68 0BD. Tel: 0121 421 7117 or 07956 456112; **email:** wisden1864@hotmail.com. Wanted: any items of sporting memorabilia. Cricket, motor racing, TT, F1, stock cars, speedway, ice hockey, football, rugby, golf, boxing, horse racing, athletics and *all* other sports. Top prices paid for vintage items.

WILLIAM H. ROBERTS, Long Low, 27 Gernhill Avenue, Fixby, Huddersfield, West Yorkshire HD2 2HR. Tel: 01484 654463; **email:** william@roberts-cricket.co.uk; **website:** williamroberts-cricket.com. Second-hand/antiquarian cricket books, *Wisdens*, autographs and memorabilia bought and sold. Many thanks for your continued support.

WISDEN DIRECT: wisdenalmanack.com/books. Various editions of *Wisden Cricketers' Almanack* since 2002 (plus 1864–78 and 1916–19 reprints) and other Wisden publications, all at discounted prices.

WISDEN REPRINTS, email: wisdenauction@cridler.com; **website:** wisdenauction.com. Limited-edition Willows *Wisden* reprints still available for various years at wisdenauction.com. Secondhand *Wisdens* also sold (see WisdenAuction entry in Auctioneers section).

WISDENWORLD.COM, Tel: 01480 819272 or 07966 513171; **email:** bill.wisden@gmail.com; **website:** wisdenworld.com. A unique and friendly service; quality *Wisdens* bought and sold at fair prices, along with free advice on the value of your collection. The world's largest *Wisden*-only seller; licensed by Wisden.

AUCTIONEERS

DOMINIC WINTER, Specialist Auctioneers & Valuers, Mallard House, Broadway Lane, South Cerney, Gloucestershire GL7 5UQ. Tel: 01285 860006; website: dominicwinter.co.uk. Check our website for forthcoming specialist sales.

GRAHAM BUDD AUCTIONS in association with Sotheby's, PO Box 47519, London N14 6XD. Tel: 020 8366 2525; website: grahambuddauctions.co.uk. Specialist auctioneer of sporting memorabilia.

KNIGHTS WISDEN, Norfolk. Tel: 01263 768488; email: tim@knights.co.uk; website: knightswisden.co.uk. Respected auctioneers, established in 1993. World-record *Wisden* prices achieved in 2007. Four major cricket/sporting memorabilia auctions per year, including specialist *Wisden* sale day in each auction. Entries invited.

WISDENAUCTION.COM. Tel: 0800 7 999 501; email: wisdenauction@cridler.com; website: wisdenauction.com. A specially designed auction website for buying and selling *Wisdens*. List your spares today and bid live for that missing year. Every original edition for sale, including all hardbacks. Built by collectors for collectors, with the best descriptions on the internet.

CRICKET DATABASES

CRICKETARCHIVE: cricketarchive.com. The most comprehensive searchable database on the internet with scorecards of all first-class, List A, pro T20 and major women's matches, as well as a wealth of league and friendly matches. The database currently has more than 1.25m players and over 700,000 full and partial scorecards.

CRICVIZ: cricviz.com; email: marketing@cricviz.com. CricViz is the largest cricket database, providing predictive modelling and analytics to the ICC, teams and media clients.

CSW DATABASE FOR PCs. Contact Ric Finlay, email: ricf@netspace.net.au; website: tastats.com.au. Men's and women's internationals; major T20 leagues; domestic cricket in Australia, NZ, South Africa and England. Full scorecards and 2,500 searches. Suitable for professionals and hobbyists alike.

WISDEN RECORDS: wisdenrecords.com. Up-to-date and in-depth cricket records from *Wisden*.

CRICKET COLLECTING, MEMORABILIA AND MUSEUMS

CRICKET MEMORABILIA SOCIETY. See entry in Cricket Societies section.

LORD'S TOURS & MUSEUM, Lord's Cricket Ground, St John's Wood, London NW8 8QN. Tel: 020 7616 8595; email: tours@mcc.org.uk; website: lords.org/tours. A tour of Lord's provides a fascinating behind-the-scenes insight into the world's most famous cricket ground. See the original Ashes urn, plus an outstanding collection of art, cricketing memorabilia and much more.

SIR DONALD BRADMAN'S CHILDHOOD HOME, 52 Shepherd Street, Bowral, NSW 2576, Australia. Tel: (+61) 478 779 642; email: hello@52shepherdstreet.com.au; website: 52shepherdstreet.com. The house where Don Bradman developed his phenomenal cricketing skills by throwing a golf ball against the base of a tank stand. Open for tours and special events.

WILLOW STAMPS, 10 Mentmore Close, Harrow, Middlesex HA3 0EA. Tel: 020 8907 4200; email: willowstamps@gmail.com. Standing order service for new cricket stamp issues, comprehensive back stocks of most earlier issues.

WISDEN COLLECTORS' CLUB. Tel: 01480 819272 or 07966 513171; email: bill.wisden@gmail.com; website: wisdencollectorsclub.co.uk. Free and completely impartial advice on *Wisdens*. We also offer *Wisdens* and other cricket books to our members, usually at no charge except postage. Quarterly newsletter, discounts on publications, and a great website. Licensed by Wisden.

WISDENS.ORG. Tel: 07793 060706; email: wisdens@cridler.com; website: wisdens.org; Twitter: @Wisdens. The unofficial *Wisden* collectors' website. Valuations, guide, discussion forum, all free to use. *Wisden* prices updated constantly. We also buy and sell *Wisdens* for our members. Email us for free advice about absolutely anything to do with collecting *Wisdens*.

CRICKET EQUIPMENT

ACUMEN BOOKS, Pennyfields, New Road, Bignall End, Stoke-on-Trent ST7 8QF. Tel: 01782 720753; email: wca@acumenbooks.co.uk; website: acumenbooks.co.uk. Specialist for umpires, scorers, officials, etc. MCC Lawbooks, Tom Smith, other textbooks, Duckworth/Lewis, scorebooks, trousers, over & run counters, gauges, bails (heavy, Hi-Vis and tethered), etc.

BOLA MANUFACTURING LTD, 6 Brookfield Road, Cotham, Bristol BS6 5PQ. Tel: 0117 924 3569; email: info@bola.co.uk; website: bola.co.uk. Manufacturer of bowling machines and ball-throwing machines for all sports. Machines for professional and all recreational levels for sale to the UK and overseas.

CHASE CRICKET, Dummer Down Farm, Basingstoke, Hampshire RG25 2AR. Tel: 01256 397499; email: info@chasecricket.co.uk; website: chasecricket.co.uk. Chase Cricket specialises in handmade bats and hi-tech soft goods. Established 1996. "Support British Manufacturing."

CRICKET SOCIETIES

CRICKET MEMORABILIA SOCIETY, Honorary Secretary: Steve Cashmore, 4 Stoke Park Court, Stoke Road, Bishops Cleeve, Cheltenham, Gloucestershire GL52 8US. Email: cms87@btinternet.com; website: cricketmemorabilia.org. To promote and support the collection and appreciation of all cricket memorabilia. Four meetings annually at first-class grounds, with two auctions. Meetings attended by former Test players. Regular members' magazine. Research and valuations undertaken.

THE CRICKET SOCIETIES' ASSOCIATION, Secretary: Mike Hitchings, 34 Derwent Drive, Mitton, Tewkesbury GL20 8BB. Tel: 07979 464715; email: mikehitchings@aol.com; website: cricketsocietiesassociation.com. For cricket lovers in the winter – join a local society and enjoy speaker evenings with fellow enthusiasts for the summer game.

THE CRICKET SOCIETY, c/o David Wood, Membership Secretary, PO Box 6024, Leighton Buzzard, LU7 2ZS. Email: davidwood@cricketsociety.com; website: cricketsociety.com. A worldwide society which promotes cricket through its awards, acclaimed publications, regular meetings, lunches and special events.

CRICKET TOUR OPERATORS

GULLIVERS SPORTS TRAVEL, Ground Floor, Ashvale 2, Ashchurch Business Centre, Alexandra Way, Tewkesbury, Gloucs GL20 8NB. Tel: 01684 879221; email: gullivers@gulliverstravel.co.uk; website: gulliverstravel.co.uk. The UK's longest-established cricket tour operator offers a great choice of supporter packages for the world's most exciting events – including the Ashes in Australia – and playing tours for schools, clubs, universities and military teams.

PITCHES AND GROUND EQUIPMENT

HUCK NETS (UK) LTD, Gore Cross Business Park, Corbin Way, Bradpole, Bridport, Dorset DT6 3UX. Tel: 01308 425100; email: sales@huckcricket.co.uk; website: huckcricket.co.uk. Alongside manufacturing our unique knotless high-quality polypropylene cricket netting, we offer the complete portfolio of ground and club equipment necessary for cricket clubs of all levels.

NOTTS SPORT, Bridge Farm, Holt Lane, Ashby Magna LE17 5NJ. Tel: 01455 883730; email: info@nottssports.com; website: nottssports.com. With various ECB-approved pitch systems, Notts Sport, the world's leading supplier of artificial grass pitch systems for coaching, practice and matchplay, can provide a solution tailored to suit individual needs and budgets.

PLUVIUS, Willow Cottage, Canada Lane, Norton Lindsey, Warwick CV35 8JH. Tel: 07966 597203; email: pluviusltd@aol.com; website: pluvius.uk.com. Manufacturers of value-for-money pitch covers and sightscreens, currently used on Test, county, school and club grounds throughout the UK.

ERRATA

Wisden 1939	Page 910	Major C. B. Grace, youngest son of WG, collapsed and died while playing at Sidley, near Bexhill-on-Sea, rather than Hawkhurst, where he lived. His last stroke was described as a perfect cover-drive for four, which brought up 300, a record for the Weald Electricity Company CC.
Wisden 1948	Page 624	C. V. L. Marques of Hertfordshire, who was known as Robin, is incorrectly shown as R. C. V. L. Marques. This error is repeated in every *Wisden* from 1950 to 1956.
Wisden 1949	Page 872	R. C. Grellet played for Hertfordshire from 1900 to 1913, not 1911. He also appeared for MCC on their visits to Northumberland and Durham in 1920 and 1921.
Wisden 1964	Page 375	The F. Fletcher who made 1 and 0 for Essex v Yorkshire at Clacton should be K. W. R. Fletcher.
	Page 625	The Roses match in which Geoffrey Boycott scored his maiden century took place on June 1, 3, 4, not June 1, 2, 3; June 2 was a Sunday, and thus a rest day.
	Page 642	Yorkshire's Gillette match against Nottinghamshire was on May 22.
Wisden 1967	Page 92	John Murray's 217-run stand with Tom Graveney against West Indies in the final Test was for the eighth wicket, not the seventh.
Wisden 1980	Page 1090	Sargodha are now believed to have scored 336, not 376, in the first innings v Lahore MC on February 24–27, 1978, making their winning margin 585 runs, not 625.
Wisden 1985	Page 74	Greg Chappell's wretched season against West Indies was in 1981-82, not 1980-81.
Wisden 1988	Page 73	Derek Underwood's unauthorised tour of South Africa was in March 1982. The TCCB banned him from international cricket on March 19 that year, not in 1981.
Wisden 2011	Page 782	The first of the five large totals conceded by Australia in the space of six Tests was 495, not 490, in the Second Test against India.
	Page 839	Pakistan's No. 6 in the Under-19 final was Hammad Azam.
Wisden 2017	Page 208	Mick Harvey's funeral notice states that he died on October 6, not 5.
Wisden 2019	Page 55	Chris Lewis was sentenced to 13 years, but served six and a half.
	Page 137	Enid Bakewell had her teeth removed before she was 21.
	Page 165	K. R. Brown's career average was 26.65, not 46.06 (his strike-rate).
	Page 229	Although John Shaw was educated at St Joseph's College, his uncle Lindsay Hassett attended the nearby Geelong College.
	Page 683	The Overton who played for Somerset v Hampshire was Craig.
	Page 687	In Yorkshire's quarter-final, their captain was Steve Patterson.
	Page 919	Sangakkara and Jayawardene added 357, not 257, on the second day of Sri Lanka's Test v South Africa in Colombo in 2006.
	Page 1016	"Du Plessis had backed his team to bowl, despite most teams at Newlands preferring to chase" – in 40 previous ODIs there, 27 toss-winners had batted first.
	Page 1057	Rovman Powell, not Ricardo, played in the third ODI.
	Page 1091	In Australia A's match v India B on August 27, they were 155-5 in the 29th over.

CHARITIES IN 2019

ARUNDEL CASTLE CRICKET FOUNDATION – more than 300,000 disadvantaged youngsters, many with special needs, mainly from inner-city areas, have benefited from sporting and educational activities at Arundel over the past 30 years. In 2019, there were more than 70 days devoted to activities for over 2,000 young people. Donations can be made at www.justgiving.com/arundelcastlecricket. Director: Tim Shutt, Arundel Park, West Sussex BN18 9LH; 01903 882602; tim@arundelcastlecricket.co.uk; www.arundelcastlecricketfoundation.co.uk.

THE BRIAN JOHNSTON MEMORIAL TRUST supports cricket for the blind, and aims to ease the financial worries of talented young cricketers through scholarships. Registered Charity No. 1045946. Trust administrator: Richard Anstey, 178 Manor Drive North, Worcester Park, Surrey KT4 7RU; raganstey@btinternet.com; www.lordstaverners.org/brian-johnston-memorial-trust.

THE BUNBURY CRICKET CLUB has raised over £17m for national charities, schools cricket and worthwhile causes since 1987. A total of 1,848 boys have appeared in the Bunbury Festival; 1,039 have gone on to play first-class cricket, and 105 for England. The 34th ECB David English Bunbury Festival will be staged at Eastbourne College from August 2–7. The Bunburys also presented the only two Under-15 World Cups (1996 and 2000), while this year sees the 15th match between the Bunbury English Schools Cricket XI and MCC Schools (September 3). Contact: Dr David English CBE, 1 Highwood Cottages, Nan Clark's Lane, London NW7 4HJ; davidenglishbunbury@gmail.com; www.bunburycricket.co.uk.

CAPITAL KIDS CRICKET, which celebrated its 30th anniversary in 2019, aims to improve the physical, social and emotional development of young people in all abilities, including refugee children. It is a fully inclusive organisation providing sporting and social opportunities in the more deprived areas of Greater London, and organises activities in state schools, hospitals, community centres, local parks, refugee camps and residential centres away from London: the Spirit of Cricket is at the heart of what we do. Around 10,000 young people are involved every year. Chairman: Haydn Turner; haydn.turner@yahoo.co.uk. Chief executive: Shahidul Alam Ratan; 07748 114811; shahidul.alam@ckc.london; www.ckc.london.

CHANCE TO SHINE is a national children's charity on a mission to spread the power of cricket throughout schools and communities. Since launching in 2005, Chance to Shine has reached over 4m children across more than 16,000 state schools. Contact: The Kia Oval, London SE11 5SW; 020 7735 2881; www.chancetoshine.org.

THE CHANGE FOUNDATION is an award-winning UK-based charity that uses cricket and other sports to create transformational change in the lives of marginalised and vulnerable young people. The charity has been designing sport-for-development initiatives for 39 years, and has worked in 38 countries with a range of partners, including the ICC and UNICEF. We pioneered disability cricket, including the England Blind team. Our centre in the London Borough of Sutton was built – with the help of our president, Phil Tufnell – to cater for cricketers with a disability, and is home to many projects, including our new "walking cricket" programme. CEO: Andy Sellins, The Cricket Centre, Plough Lane, Wallington, Surrey SM6 8JQ; 020 8669 2177; office@changefdn.org.uk; www.thechangefoundation.org.uk.

CRICKET BUILDS HOPE (formerly Rwanda Cricket Stadium Foundation) completed efforts in 2017 to raise £1m to build a new cricket facility in Rwanda's capital, Kigali. The charity now plans more cricketing projects. Partnership head: Jon Surtees, The Kia Oval, London SE11 5SS; 020 7820 5780.

THE CRICKET SOCIETY TRUST enables disabled and disadvantaged young people to access the benefits of cricket as a physical activity and team sport, by supporting a range of programmes such as the MCC Foundation Hub for state-school girls at Felsted School, and the Arundel Castle Special Needs Programme. Chairman: Ronald Paterson, 3 Orlando Road, London SW4 0LE. Tel: 07710 989004; www.cricketsocietytrust.org.uk.

THE DICKIE BIRD FOUNDATION, set up by the former umpire in 2004, helps financially disadvantaged young people under 18 to participate in the sport of their choice. Grants are made towards the cost of equipment and clothing. Trustee: Ted Cowley, 3 The Tower, Tower Drive, Arthington Lane, Pool-in-Wharfedale, Otley, Yorkshire LS21 1NQ; 07503 641457; www. thedickiebirdfoundation.co.uk.

THE ENGLAND AND WALES CRICKET TRUST was established in 2005 to aid community participation in cricket, with a fund for interest-free loans to amateur clubs. In its last financial year (to January 2019) it spent £18m on charitable activities – primarily grants to cricket charities and amateur clubs, and to county boards to support their programmes. Contact: ECB, Lord's Cricket Ground, London NW8 8QZ; 020 7432 1200; feedback@ecb.co.uk.

THE EVELINA LONDON CHILDREN'S HOSPITAL is the official charity partner of Surrey CCC and The Kia Oval. Ten minutes from the ground, Evelina is one of the country's leading children's hospitals, treating patients from all over south-east England. Partnership head: Jon Surtees, The Kia Oval, London SE11 5SS; 020 7820 5780; www.kiaoval.com.

FIELDS IN TRUST is a UK charity that champions parks and green spaces by protecting them in perpetuity. Green spaces are good, do good, and need to be protected for good. Almost 3,000 spaces have been protected since our foundation in 1925. CEO: Helen Griffiths, 36 Woodstock Grove, London W12 8LE; 020 7427 2110: www.fieldsintrust.org; www.facebook.com/fieldsintrust. Twitter: @FieldsInTrust.

THE HORNSBY PROFESSIONAL CRICKETERS' FUND supports former professional cricketers "in necessitous circumstances", or their dependants, through regular financial help or one-off grants towards healthcare or similar essential needs. Where appropriate, it works closely with the PCA and a player's former county. The Trust was established in 1928 from a bequest from the estate of J. H. J. Hornsby (Middlesex, MCC and the Gentlemen), augmented more recently by a bequest from Sir Alec and Eric Bedser, and by a merger with the Walter Hammond Memorial Fund. Secretary: The Rev. Prebendary Mike Vockins OBE, The Chantry, Charlton Musgrove, Wincanton, Somerset BA9 8HG; 01963 34837.

THE LEARNING FOR A BETTER WORLD (LBW) TRUST, established in 2006, provides tertiary education to disadvantaged students in the cricket-playing countries of the developing world. In 2019, it assisted over 2,000 students in India, Pakistan, Nepal, Uganda, Afghanistan, Sri Lanka, South Africa, Jamaica, Kenya and Tanzania. Chairman: David Vaux, GPO Box 3029, Sydney, NSW 2000, Australia; www.lbwtrust.com.au.

THE LORD'S TAVERNERS is the UK's leading youth cricket and disability sports charity, dedicated to giving disadvantaged and disabled young people a sporting chance. This year, it will donate over £5m to help young people of all abilities and backgrounds to participate in cricket and other sporting activities. Registered Charity No. 306054. The Lord's Taverners, 90 Chancery Lane, London WC2A 1EU; 020 7025 0000; contact@lordstaverners.org; www.lordstaverners.org.

THE MARYLEBONE CRICKET CLUB FOUNDATION's flagship programme is a network of 54 Cricket Hubs that provide a free ten-week coaching programme to state-educated 11–15-year-olds across the country. The Foundation recently launched its first major overseas project in Nepal, building pitches, training coaches and delivering cricket to young people in 15 government schools in Pokhara. Contact: MCC Foundation, Lord's Ground, London NW8 8QN; 020 7616 8529; info@mccfoundation.org.uk; www.lords.org/mccfoundation.

THE PRIMARY CLUB provides sporting facilities for the blind and partially sighted. Membership is nominally restricted to those dismissed first ball in any form of cricket; almost 10,000 belong. In total, the club has raised £3m, helped by sales of its tie, popularised by *Test Match Special*. Hon. secretary: Chris Larlham, PO Box 12121, Saffron Walden, Essex CB10 2ZF; 01799 586507; www.primaryclub.org.

THE PRINCE'S TRUST helps young people get their lives on track. Founded by HRH The Prince of Wales in 1976, it supports 11–30-year-olds who are struggling at school or unemployed. The Trust's programmes use a variety of activities, including cricket, to engage young people and help them gain skills, confidence and qualifications. The Prince's Trust South London Centre, 8 Glade Path, Southwark, London SE1 8EG; 0800 842842, or text "call me" to 07983 385418; www.princes-trust.org.uk.

THE PROFESSIONAL CRICKETERS' TRUST was created to support the lifelong health and wellbeing of PCA members and their immediate families. We look out for players throughout their active careers and long afterwards, funding life-changing medical assistance, crisis helplines and educational programmes in England and Wales. Director of development and welfare: Ian Thomas, PCA, The Kia Oval, Laker Stand, London SE11 5SS; 07920 575578; www.thepca.co.uk.

STREET CHILD OF NEPAL, founded in 2015, has helped over 7,000 children access education and WASH facilities through post-earthquake construction of 160 Transitional Learning Centres with UNICEF. Currently, the charity is working with 10,500 adolescent girls in one of the most marginalised communities in the country, with a literacy rate of less than 4% among females, to improve their educational and employment prospects. Website: www.street-child.org.np.

THE TOM MAYNARD TRUST – formed in 2012 after Tom's death – covers two main areas: helping aspiring young professionals with education projects, currently across six sports; and providing grants to help with travel, kit, coaching, training and education. From 2014 to 2018, we also ran an academy in Spain for young county cricketers. Contact: Mike Fatkin, 67a Radnor Road, Canton, Cardiff CF5 1RA; www.tommaynardtrust.com.

CHRONICLE OF 2019

And now, the rest of the news…

COMPILED BY MATTHEW ENGEL. CARTOONS BY NICK NEWMAN

THE GUARDIAN   January 3

A BBC documentary, *Bats, Balls and Bradford Girls*, has shown Britain's first all-Asian girls' cricket team being reunited for a last match before going their separate ways after GCSEs. Until they got together, the girls – all students at Carlton Bolling College (motto: "Achievement for All") – had merely watched the game on TV. "We are rebels within our community," said 16-year-old Zainab. "We do what Asian girls from Bradford are not supposed to do – and we're good at it." Her team-mate Mariyah said some white opponents had laughed at them and refused to shake their hands: "Because I wear a scarf and cover my arms, people regard me as a terrorist."

THE CITIZEN, JOHANNESBURG   January 11

Qaasim Adams of Western Province has been banned from provincial cricket for 12 playing days after pulling a gun on team-mate Givon Christian during a match against South Western Districts. Christian reported the incident, but refused to take it further. "If I did press charges, he would serve jail time," he said. "I'm happy to forgive him and move on." A season-long ban was expected, but was whittled down after negotiations. Adams could still play for his Cape Town club, United.

SIDMOUTH HERALD   January 16

The seafront ground at Sidmouth, Devon, is to have retractable nets to protect holidaymakers on the Esplanade from stray balls. In 2018, an 80-year-old day tripper needed stitches after being hit by a six (*Wisden 2019*, page 1528). The nets will be taken down between matches.

STUFF.CO.NZ   January 27

Former New Zealand Test bowler Ewen Chatfield ("The Naenae Express") has finally retired, aged 68, having played his last game for Naenae Old Boys, his Wellington club. He had been hoping to finish with a first century, but failed to manage his best score ("fifty-something"). "I got a golden duck, but don't put that in the paper," he said.

SYDNEY MORNING HERALD/ALL AUSTRALIA MEDIA   February 2

Former first-class batsman Cam Merchant appeared on the Australian edition of the reality show *Married at First Sight*, in which participants are matched "scientifically", and expected to get married at once. In some versions, this is an official marriage (usually destined for rapid divorce), but not in Australia. The ceremony with fellow contestant and "bride" Jules Robinson merely expressed commitment. Merchant, 35 and born in Sydney, is a left-handed batsman who plays for Manly-Warringah. He played 26 first-class matches in New Zealand for Wellington and Northern Districts, and decided to go on the show after losing his long-term girlfriend. Merchant said: "With my hours and hours of prioritising cricket, it just got to a stage where her patience had run out, and I lost the love of my life." (See also April 2 and November 17.)

ESPN cricinfo/Bucks Free Press February 21/July 15
Australian international Alyssa Healy claimed a world record for the highest catch of a cricket ball. In a stunt at the Melbourne Cricket Ground, she caught – with the aid of wicketkeeping gloves – a ball dropped by a drone from 80 metres. The previous record of 62 metres was set by Kristan Baumgartner of England in 2016. Less than five months later, club cricketer Sam Norman won the Drone Catch World Cup at Wormsley, Buckinghamshire, with 89.6 metres (294ft), the height of 20 double-decker buses.

Star Weekly, Melton & Moorabool			February 25
Grade cricket umpires in Gisborne, Victoria, are going on strike to protest against player dissent and poor behaviour. They were supported by the competition's board of management.

New Statesman				March 1
Amanda Feilding of the Beckley Foundation, which funds research into the effect of psychoactive substances, said that small doses of LSD have been shown to improve cricketers' ability to bowl accurately.

Cherwell/The Times				March 12/21
Students at Oxford University have expressed outrage after the speaker at Brasenose College's annual sports dinner, former Essex player Don Topley, read an "inappropriate and misogynistic" poem. The couplets of "Never Trust

a Cricketer", an old after-dinner staple, include "Then there's the real stonewaller, girls, he knows what he's about; and if you let him settle in, it's hard to get him out!" One Brasenose student, Sophie Brookes, said Topley asked if the audience knew what sport was growing fastest in popularity. "He then said 'girls' cricket'. Then, without any further comment, he goes on to read the poem. Another student said: "There seemed a general consensus that the poem had been in very poor taste."

THE TIMES   March 20

Australia have beaten England yet again to win the Marmalashes, the annual contest between the two nations at the world marmalade awards. Australia lead 6–2 with one draw since the Marmalashes were instituted in 2011. Although marmalade is considered quintessentially English, head judge Dan Lepard says the Aussies have an advantage. "They grow the trees in their gardens. You go out and pick a lemon, you slice it and you cook it. The way to get the best result is to have the freshest fruit."

SYDNEY MORNING HERALD   April 2

Cricketer Cam Merchant and his TV "bride" Jules Robinson (see February 2) have made their relationship official after Cam dropped to one knee and proposed in the Final Vows section at the end of the *Married at First Sight* TV show. "Some people are a little bit confused," Jules explained. "Like, 'But aren't you married already?' But obviously we're not legally binded in marriage. But we will be, very soon." The successful match – which Cam chalked up to "fate" rather than the show's experts – is said to be a rarity. "There were moments when I just felt embarrassed to be there," Jules added. "All that horrible yelling and screaming and just childish behaviour, that wasn't very normal for being an adult. Overall, Cam and I, we had a great time being part of the show, but there were moments where we were like, 'This is an absolute circus; this is crazy.'" (see also November 17.)

MANCHESTER EVENING NEWS April 5

The pitch at Ashton Ladysmith CC, based in Ashton-under-Lyne, was put out of action for about a month after an intruder dug 150 holes on the square and outfield. Clubhouse manager David Gaskin said there was a similar attack the previous year, but added: "It wasn't as bad, and we thought at the time it may have been kids, but not this time – this is deliberate. It seems like someone has a grievance against the club. They will have had to get over a 6ft metal fence with a spade to get in."

HUDDERSFIELD EXAMINER April 19

Residents of the village of Golcar complained that 40ft netting to protect a new housing estate from sixes was, in the words of one resident, "horrendous – a right monstrosity". Another said: "I'm a big supporter of the cricket club. But no way on God's earth can anyone say that net isn't spoiling my view. It's complete overkill."

YORKSHIRE EVENING POST April 23

Two days after Hall Park CC, Leeds, raised £4,000 from an Easter family fun day, thieves broke in through the roof and stole the safe where the money was stored, as well as the CCTV evidence. "This is not an opportunist," said club secretary Rob Hodson. "They sawed that hole in exactly the right place."

THE TIMES May 2

The cricketing world was transfixed by a video of Nathan Trussler, making his debut for Kirby Portland II against Spondon in the Mansfield & District Sunday League, Section 3 (South). The turf was soft, and a team-mate slid and fell, trying to intercept a ball at mid-on. Trussler backed up from mid-off and aimed for the stumps. Unfortunately, he hit his stricken team-mate flush on the arse. Trussler did score 22, and took a wicket and a catch, but few seemed to notice.

SIDMOUTH HERALD May 2

Sidbury CC in Devon raised funds by releasing three alpacas on to their pitch and inviting people to guess the precise location of the first hint of alpaca poo. The turf was divided into 806 squares for the purpose, and location determined to the nearest millimetre. The club used a cow for similar competitions in the 1970s. The winner, Sharon Davis, gave her £250 prize back to the club.

INDIAN INSTITUTE OF TECHNOLOGY May 6

The first question in the Institute's Material and Energy Balances exam related to the possible role of dew in next day's IPL match between Chennai Super Kings and Mumbai Indians. Professor Vignesh Muthuvijayan asked: "As per the weather forecast for May 7, the relative humidity in Chennai is expected to be 70%. Temperature at the start of the game is predicted to be 39°C, at the beginning of the second innings the temperature is expected to drop to 27°C. Based on this info, if M. S. Dhoni wins the toss, would you recommend batting or fielding first?" Students had to give their reasons. (Dhoni did win the toss, batted first – and lost.)

THE STATESMAN, KOLKATA   May 12

Former Pakistan all-rounder Shahid Afridi has said he refuses to let his four daughters (Ansha, Ajwa, Asmara and Aqsa) play any outdoor sports. In *Game Changer*, his new autobiography, Afridi maintains the stance is motivated by "social and religious reasons". "The feminists can say whatever they want about my decision," he said. "Ajwa and Asmara are the youngest, and love to play dress-up. They have my permission to play any sport, as long as they're indoors. Cricket? No, not for my girls."

ITV   May 17

Against Newport Seconds (Essex), Michael Miller – captain of Royston Thirds – carried his bat for 33. Unfortunately, all his team-mates were out for ducks. The total reached 39 with the help of six extras, but Newport won by ten wickets.

BBC   May 20

A Rainhill batsman was suspended for allegedly headbutting the bowler after being given out caught behind in a Lancashire Cup tie against Eccleston.

EASTERN DAILY PRESS   May 21

A village match in Norfolk between Great Melton C and Old Buckenham B was abandoned because an air ambulance broke down on the outfield after it landed to help a sick woman. She was taken to hospital by road, and was said to be recovering. "You don't worry about the outcome of a cricket match when there is someone battling for their life in the pavilion," said Great Melton chairman Steve Phoenix.

STOKE SENTINEL   May 22

Thieves ripped out a 20ft-long piece of artificial turf from the nets at Porthill Park CC, Staffordshire. Chairman Craig Chorlton was left baffled, as well as upset: "It is specialist flooring, and the part they targeted is used by the young cricketers. I don't know what they will do with it. It's very bizarre how they have cut out one section – but we need to have the whole thing redone."

May 23

HELLO! May 23

A 19-year-old guest at a Buckingham Palace garden party has said the Queen told her that she was nearly hit by a cricket ball in 1994. According to *Hello!*, Lucy Stafford said: "The Queen was very funny; she reminisced about how her bodyguard had caught a cricket ball flying towards her at a match in 1994. She said she would have been dead if it hadn't been caught." (It was not immediately clear when, where or how this incident might have taken place, though the monarch is usually regarded as a reliable source.)

GOOGLE May 30

The animated doodle on Google's home page to mark the start of the World Cup showed a batsman smashing an intended six and getting brilliantly caught. It was pointed out that he might have performed better if he had stood in *front* of the stumps.

THE TIMES June 4

Tom Harrison, ECB chief executive, has met representatives of Google X, the company's experimental division, which says it creates "radical new technologies to solve some of the world's hardest problems". It is thought they discussed whether Project Loon, the company's use of autonomous balloons, might have some value in preventing rain stopping play. Harrison is believed to be particularly concerned about bad weather affecting the ECB's new tournament, The Hundred.

EMERGINGCRICKET.COM June 8

Japan have qualified for the 2020 Under-19 World Cup without having to play a crunch fixture, because their opponents, Papua New Guinea, had suspended 11 of their 14 players. The match between the two unbeaten teams in the East Asia–Pacific section was to have been played on Japan's home ground at Sano. The banned players were suspected of shoplifting.

THE AGE, MELBOURNE/ABC NEWS June 9

The new French Open tennis champion, Ash Barty of Australia, credited a stint with Brisbane Heat in the Women's Big Bash League with rescuing her career. Barty struggled to deal with expectations after winning Junior Wimbledon in 2011, and took a sabbatical. "I met an amazing group of people who couldn't care less whether I could hit a tennis ball or not," she said. "They accepted me, and they got to know Ash Barty." Four first-class cricketers have previously won what are now called tennis grand slams, the last being Tony Wilding of New Zealand, who won Wimbledon in 1913.

FINANCIAL EXPRESS   June 9

Virat Kohli's chauffeur and staff were caught by officials of Gurugram Municipal Corporation washing "six or seven" of his cars with drinking water outside his home. The town controls water in summer to prevent wastage. A fine of 500 rupees was imposed (about £5.35).

NORTHERN ECHO   June 15

Spout House CC have resigned from the Feversham League in mid-season, which may mean the end of cricket on one of the world's most beautiful and eccentric grounds. Spout have played in Bilsdale on the North York Moors for 170 years; visiting players have always complained about the vertiginous and cattle-grazed outfield but, as William Ainsley, club secretary for 62 years before he died in 2012, used to tell them: "It's t'same for both teams. If it lands in t'cow clap for one, it lands in t'cow clap for t'other."

The resignation threatens the League itself, now down to four teams. Audrey Wilson, landlady of The Sun Inn, later said they hoped to arrange a couple of friendlies in 2020, but that it was impossible to return to the League: "We can't get the players."

CRICBUZZ/AGENCE FRANCE-PRESSE   June 19/August 27

Cec Wright, 85, is to retire after 60 years playing league cricket round Lancashire. Wright played a single first-class match as a fast bowler for his native Jamaica in 1958, before coming to England as professional for Crompton. He settled in England, spent more than two decades as a pro at different clubs, then worked for Mars, and carried on just for fun. He has still been taking wickets off a ten-step amble for Uppermill Second XI, bringing his total well over 4,000. "I can't believe it," he heard a batsman say a couple of years ago. "He got me out when I was 17 and he was 70. And he's still getting me out."

NEW FOREST POST   June 20

Waste, thought to have come from a cannabis factory, has been dumped at Bartley CC, Hampshire. Cuttings from the plants were found alongside heaters, radiators and fans.

AGENCE FRANCE-PRESSE   June 30

A leading Bangladeshi paediatrician was sent to a remote rural clinic weeks after criticising the national cricket captain, Mashrafe bin Mortaza, on Facebook. Mortaza, who is also an MP, had censured doctors for being absent when he visited a hospital in his constituency. Rezaul Karim, a child cancer specialist, took issue with Mortaza, and two months later was moved from Chittagong, where he was treating more than 100 young patients, to Rangamati, a small town with no cancer facilities. A Health Ministry official said it was "an administrative decision".

CHURCH TIMES   July 5

The Vatican beat the Archbishop of Canterbury's XI by 75 runs in Rome in what has become a regular clerical fixture. The Anglicans included two women, Thea Smith and Becky Heath-Taylor, an option not available to the Catholics. The Church of England has a 3–2 lead in the series, which began in 2014 and, it is hoped, will go on for eternity.

EVENING STANDARD   July 7

Mitcham Green in South London, believed to be the world's oldest cricket ground (see *Wisden 2019*, page 1523), has been saved for cricket after Merton Council renewed the 116-year-old pavilion's status as an Asset of Community Value for another five years. The pavilion was sold to a developer in 2008, and has been under threat. Tony Burton, secretary of Mitcham Cricket Green Community and Heritage, said: "The decision is a shot in the arm for the club, though by no means the end of the saga."

TWITTER   July 9

The toss in the Asian Under-19 Cup qualifying match between Nepal and Hong Kong at Kinrara, Malaysia, had to be restaged after the coin landed, and apparently became wedged on its side. Nepal won the second toss, the match – and the tournament.

INDIA TODAY   July 12

A severed fingertip belonging to Nilotpal Chakraborty of Kolkata was lost by hospital staff because they were more interested in watching India's World Cup semi-final, his wife alleged. Chakraborty had fallen off his motorcycle, and his finger was wedged under the wheel. The hospital claimed it was not possible to reattach it.

PAKISTAN TIMES   July 14

Pakistan made up for their failure in the real World Cup by winning the first Inter-Parliamentary World Cup in Beckenham. They beat Bangladesh in the final by nine wickets, thanks to 52 not out from the Minister for Kashmir Affairs, Ali Amin Gandapur. Politicians from seven countries took part. The organiser, British MP Chris Heaton-Harris, said in advance that Pakistan were favourites as they had spent "quite some time" in training camps.

THE TIMES   July 17

Despite India's failure in the tournament, their captain will lift the World Cup at Lord's in August, though both captain and trophy are replicas. A Bollywood film is being made about India's win in the 1983 World Cup, and shooting will take place at Lord's. To avoid anachronisms, the portrait of Mike Atherton on the pavilion stairs will be removed, and the director told he should not use female extras as spectators in the Long Room. Before 1999, only the Queen was allowed in.

THE TIMES July 19

Taiwanese pop star Jay Chou has been asked to become a patron of East Dean & Friston CC, near Eastbourne, whose home is threatened by a housing development. Chou has boosted tourism to the area through the video for his hit "What's Wrong", which shows him walking across the nearby clifftops. The club, who need £26,000 to move, have heard nothing from Chou. But they have put up a sign in Mandarin inviting visitors to the ground to ring the "tiger bell" (named after the nearby pub). If the bell rings during play, the team rush to the boundary, pose for a photo op and ask for a £50 donation. This has so far raised £500.

BBC July 19

Russia's sports ministry have refused to include cricket on their register of officially recognised sports. This is not a ban, but it means cricket is ineligible for government grants. Alexander Sorokin, of the Moscow Cricket Sports Federation, said there were errors made in applying, and the federation would reapply in 2020.

THE SUN-HERALD, SYDNEY July 21

Analysis of Cricket Australia's participation statistics has shown that figures have been inflated for years. The latest Australian Cricket Census, published in June, claims 684,356 registered cricketers. However, thousands of players have multiple entries, and a manual count suggests the true figure is 247,060. While Cricket Australia have been reporting increasing participation, club administrators say they have been losing adult males at an alarming rate. The number of clubs has fallen from 4,200 to 3,500 in the past decade, though CA have claimed a rise in "participants" from 600,000 to 1.65m. A senior official admitted: "Any kid who we can get a bat into their hands, we call them a cricketer."

GETSURREY.CO.UK July 29

Stranded motorists played an impromptu game of cricket amid stationary vehicles on the A23 dual carriageway between London and Brighton. The road was closed for eight hours following an accident.

BRISTOL POST   July 29

Six months after moving into her new home, Julie Brodribb, 60, suffered a badly bruised leg, and a patio planter was smashed, when a six was hit out of the W. G. Grace Memorial Ground at Downend, Bristol. According to the victim's daughter, the man who collected the ball did not say sorry, instead suggesting: "That's what you get for buying a house next to the cricket ground." Downend blamed a visiting fielder, and wrote an apologetic letter.

INVERNESS COURIER   July 31

West Indian all-rounder Kacy Clement hit 20 sixes, and dominated an unbroken last-wicket stand of 130, after Northern Counties had reduced Highland CC to 123 for nine in an Inverness derby. No. 11 Anup Shetty was still there at the end of the 40 overs, without scoring; Clement was on 154. Highland won by 73 runs.

WEST SUSSEX COUNTY TIMES   August 2

Denny Pease is still playing club cricket past his 90th birthday, and is now in his 78th season. In his prime, he was a medium-pace swing bowler who once took two hat-tricks in a weekend during a 54-year stint with Eastonians CC in Essex. He now lives in Sussex and plays for Yellow Stump, a wandering team founded in 2017. "He still opens the bowling and usually gets through six or seven overs," said captain Matthew Reynolds. "His control is incredible and he takes amazing slip catches – in 2018 he took four in an afternoon." Pease missed the match on his 90th birthday due to a foot injury, but the club took the opportunity to award him his "baggy", which they reserve for special achievement.

HUDDERSFIELD EXAMINER   August 4/7/10

A group of youths, armed with knives, stumps and a baseball bat, allegedly attacked players at Linthwaite CC during a Huddersfield League match against Kirkheaton. Four players were treated in hospital, including one who suffered a broken leg after being hit with a wooden pole. One of the attackers was said to have shouted: "This is our postcode – we run this postcode." Three boys and a girl, all teenagers, were arrested.

OUTLOOK INDIA   August 9

The fixture in the Global T20 Canada between Toronto Nationals (captained by Yuvraj Singh) and Montreal Tigers (George Bailey) was delayed two hours because the players went on strike over unpaid wages. The official Twitter feed attributed the hold-up to "technical reasons".

DAILY TELEGRAPH/DAILY MAIL   August 13

Earley CC of the Berkshire League are believed to be Britain's first vegan cricket club, after chairman Gary Shacklady successfully campaigned to abandon meat at teatime to make Muslim and Hindu members feel more welcome. Tagines and curries are served instead of sandwiches. Earley are also experimenting with a rubber-based vegan ball. "It does behave like a leather cricket ball, but it bounces more and it's more difficult to grip," said Shacklady. "But we're enthused by it, and we're hopeful of finding a better version."

August 13

GEOLOGYPAGE.COM   August 14

A newly discovered range of about 100 underground volcanoes in the Australian outback has been named "The Warnie Volcanic Province", in Shane Warne's honour. The volcanoes are buried hundreds of metres beneath the rocks in the Cooper–Eromanga Basins, in the oil-and-gas-producing region shared by Queensland and South Australia. They are believed to be about 170m years old. Warne is about to turn 50.

BBC NEWS/TWITTER   August 15/October 23

Gloucester AIW, a mainly Muslim cricket club, were docked 22 points by the Gloucestershire League for refusing to play on the Day of Arafat, one of the holiest Islamic festivals. Club secretary Ahmed Goga said he had told the League about the clash in January, but was ignored. Opponents Redmarley, who said they could not rearrange the fixture, were awarded 20 points. The league said they were acting in accordance with the rules, which mention Eid-Al-Adha (which falls the following day), but not the Day of Arafat. Goga said the officials' ignorance was "shocking". In October, the club said they were "delighted" when the league voted overwhelmingly to amend the rules and prevent a recurrence.

HINDUSTAN TIMES   August 19/20

Former Indian captain M. S. Dhoni has returned home after a 15-day training stint with his Territorial Army unit. Dhoni has been made an honorary lieutenant-colonel, but is not allowed to take part in active operations.

TIMES OF INDIA   August 20

Two boys, aged five and eight, were electrocuted when they touched a live pole while playing cricket near Ahmedabad.

THE TIMES   August 22

Village cricket is becoming an unlikely internet hit. Dan Allen, who set up a YouTube channel for Sanderstead CC, Surrey, says he has had 2.5m views for videos of their fixtures. And the incident at Spondon (see May 2) has passed

3.1m views on Twitter. However, Allen has been astonished by the interest in even routine events. "I only really started uploading the videos so that the players could watch," he said, "but now we are getting thousands of people tuning in every week. I think we offer something that the professional game can't – the warm beer and village green atmosphere that reminds you of your childhood."

DAILY MAIL   August 23

Volunteers drying out the pitch at Castle Cary, Somerset, for a match against Huish & Langport had unexpected help – from an air ambulance. The helicopter landed on the field after being called out to help an elderly person who had fallen. In the event, there was no need to transport the patient – so the pilot helpfully hovered overhead to allow the rotor blades to dry the square.

PRESS ASSOCIATION   August 25

Jack Hughes of Warrington helped his team score a shock win over St Helens in the Rugby League Challenge Cup final at Wembley by wearing a cricket box. He was suffering from a ruptured testicle that put his appearance in doubt, but he produced a starring performance. "It did the job," he said. "It was pretty uncomfortable at the start but, once you get out there, you don't think about it."

UCKFIELD NEWS   August 28

Cricketer Colin Parsons returned to action seven weeks after suffering a cardiac arrest during a match. Parsons collapsed while playing for Nutley against Hadlow Down in Sussex. Fortunately, the Hadlow Down team contained two doctors and a paramedic, who performed CPR. Parsons celebrated his recovery by guesting for Hadlow Down at a special tournament to mark Nutley's 150th anniversary.

PRESS ASSOCIATION   August 28

Calm, a sleep app designed to help insomniacs, has turned to retired commentator Henry Blofeld to narrate a 35-minute audio essay on cricket. The app has previously read out sections of the EU's General Data Protection

Regulations. Its co-founder, Michael Acton Smith, said he thought cricket was a perfect subject thanks to a confusing vocabulary. "Before there was mindfulness, you might say, there was cricket," he said. "And before there were sleeping pills, there were Test matches."

EDINBURGH EVENING NEWS   August 30

Members of Heriot's CC, one of the oldest clubs in Scotland, say it is under threat because their landlords, George Heriot's School, plan to replace the main cricket square with artificial hockey pitches.

GRIMSBY TELEGRAPH   August 31

Barton Town CC in Lincolnshire have had a 300m boundary rope stolen by a group of men in a white van, who pulled it into the bushes and drove off. Barton will use flags instead for today's fixture.

BBC   September 1

Players from Blunham CC, Bedfordshire, have reclaimed the world record for non-stop cricket by completing a full week (168 hours) of play that included hot sunshine and tropical downpours. "Physically shot… mentally shot… great experience," said club captain George Hutson.

THE SUN   September 1

After defeating neighbours Burnham, members of Chesham CC, Buckinghamshire, discovered the away dressing-room had been used for a "dirty protest". Volunteers worked "through the night" to clean up the excrement.

HEREFORD TIMES   September 5

The artificial wicket at Widemarsh Common, Hereford – where cricket dates back to at least 1829 – has been removed to allow more junior football to be played. There is only one cricket ground left in the city.

FARNHAM HERALD   September 5

The I'Anson Cup, said to be the oldest village league in the world, ended in controversy when a batsman changed the destination of the title by refusing to run a single off the last over. Blackheath (Surrey) won their match against Headley (Hampshire) and became champions. But if Headley captain Matt Hall had not chosen to block out the last ten balls, the title would have gone to Grayswood, not Blackheath, on bonus points. Grayswood chairman Malcolm Gloak called the incident a breach of the spirit of cricket; Headley stripped Hall of the captaincy.

THE INDEPENDENT   September 5

Peter Lalor, cricket correspondent of *The Australian*, thought he was paying £5.50 for a bottle of beer in a Manchester hotel bar during the Old Trafford Test. He discovered that he had actually been charged £55,000 (plus a hefty transaction fee) only when the money was removed from his account.

CRICKET.COM.AU   September 6

In 2015, eight-year-old Max Waight of Port Lonsdale, Victoria, announced that he wanted to go to England to watch the Ashes four years later. His father, Damien, agreed – if Max raised $1,500 (about £1,000) towards the cost. From then on, Max ran his own waste management service, shifting neighbours' bins on to the pavement and back again, week after week. In the end, the whole family travelled to the Old Trafford Test. Max, now 12, and his brothers had a ride on the team bus, met the players and received an autographed shirt. His mother, Ali, said: "Four years, he's pretty determined. He's very well organised, too, Max. It's been really good in the community. It's brought us all together." Australia won.

THE TIMES   September 10

Cricketers should be allowed to wear shorts in hot weather, according to a report presented to MCC's world cricket committee. The British Association for Sustainability in Sport also say the game needs to adapt to the changing climate by developing a new generation of gloves, helmets and pads to keep players cool.

THE NEWS LETTER, BELFAST   September 10/11

The future of Sion Mills, perhaps Ireland's most resonant cricket ground, was in doubt after an arson attack destroyed the club's equipment store. Sion Mills, near Strabane in north-west Ulster, is famous for Ireland's stunning win over the 1969 West Indies, who were bowled out for 25. The store was burned out, but fund-raising efforts began immediately. "The last thing I want is to be forced to fold the thing, especially not because of some young hoods," said captain Simon Galloway.

THE GUARDIAN   September 10/13

The knighthood for Geoffrey Boycott has come under fire from women's groups and opposition politicians. This intensified after he said he did not "care a toss" what critics said. He had been convicted for assaulting a girlfriend in France 21 years ago, an offence he has always denied. Adina Claire of

Women's Aid said the honour was "extremely disappointing", and the judge in the case, Dominique Haumant, said: "I cannot believe he's being received by the Queen." Boycott was awarded the honour by Theresa May, a long-standing fan, after her resignation as prime minister. Normally, Downing Street has limited influence over honours, but this particular batch, including a knighthood for Andrew Strauss, is traditionally the departing PM's choice.

IT COULD BE GOWER – HE'S FLASHING HARD

FRANCIS BACON

THE OBSERVER   September 15

Barry Joule, a friend of the late artist Francis Bacon, says he was the model for some of Bacon's most arresting works – a series of paintings from the 1980s showing a full-frontal male lower body wearing only cricket pads and shoes. David Gower had been suggested, though he never met Bacon.

BBC   September 23

John Williams, scorer for Bury St Edmunds CC, Suffolk, for the past 16 years, has decided to spend an unexpected £30,000 inheritance by buying the club a new scorer's box. Williams said he was embarrassed by the current facility – "a draughty garden shed" – when visiting scorers arrive. "Ours will be as good as the best instead of the worst."

PRESS TRUST OF INDIA   October 8

Bharat Soni, 30, was arrested for allegedly stealing over 25kg of gold from his employers, a jewellery firm, to pay his debts from IPL bets. Two accomplices were also held.

THE GUARDIAN   October 11

England team-mates Natalie Sciver and Katherine Brunt have announced their engagement, two years after Brunt asked Sciver out while on the Lord's balcony following their 2017 World Cup success. "We want to be ambassadors and role models for boys and girls who want to be what they want to be," Brunt said. There have already been two married couples in international women's teams – Dane van Niekerk and Marizanne Kapp of South Africa, and Amy Satterthwaite and Lea Tahuhu of New Zealand. There are no known cases in men's cricket yet.

BBC   October 28

Billy Cookson, 23, an amateur cricketer from Wiltshire, has returned to the crease 12 months after a car crash in Australia which led to 18 operations on different parts of his shattered body. The crash happened on his first day working in Melbourne, where he was due to play for Kyabram. He was applauded on to the field when he finally made his debut.

MANCHESTER EVENING NEWS   November 1

A teenager who smashed up a newly renovated pavilion at Springhead CC, Oldham, with his mates, was forced to help clear up the mess – by his mum. The place was left covered in broken glass and paint, and secretary Kyle Green posted a message on Facebook urging parents to see if any of their kids had white paint on their clothes. He took a call from the mother next morning. "Faith in humanity has been restored," he said. "Fantastic parenting."

INDO-ASIAN NEWS SERVICE/DECCAN CHRONICLE November 8/11

Spectators at the T20 series between Afghanistan and West Indies, played in neutral Lucknow, were transfixed by the sight of Sher Khan, a travelling Afghan fan reputedly 8ft 2in tall. Several hotels refused to accommodate him, and Khan needed a police escort to reach the ground to avoid being mobbed. Eventually he moved to a secret location. Later, Khan told the *Deccan Chronicle* he was a bachelor, in the dried fruit business, and – contrary to earlier press reports – a more plausible 7ft 4in. He really does love cricket, though.

DAILY MAIL   November 14

The 2005 Ashes wicketkeeper Geraint Jones, 43, has completed his initial training to be a volunteer firefighter in Kent. He is expected to be on call 50 hours a week, when not doing his day job teaching business studies at St Lawrence College.

DAILY MAIL AUSTRALIA   November 17

Cam Merchant and Jules Robinson (see February 2 and April 2) have been married in Sydney – genuinely.

STUFF.CO.NZ   November 17

New Zealand international Andrew Ellis bowled in a baseball catcher's mask for Canterbury against Central Stags in the 50-over Ford Trophy. He was hit while bowling by a ball that went for six and, though not seriously hurt, called for more protection. "For guys like me who tend to bowl at the death and try to bowl yorkers, it's probably a prudent move." In a T20 game in December 2017, Warren Barnes of Otago bowled in a mask that was a cross between a baseball visor and a track cyclist's helmet.

MID-DAY, MUMBAI   November 21

In the 45-over Harris Shield in Mumbai, 15-year-old Meet Mayekar scored 338 out of 761 for four for SVIS, Borivali. The opposing batsmen, from Children's Welfare Academy, scored no runs between them. Thanks to six wides and a bye, they reached seven all out, restricting the size of the defeat to 754 runs. "I got a lot of full tosses," said Mayekar. "We dropped too many catches," said the vanquished captain, Harsh Mishra.

BBC   November 22

At the age of 105, John Manners, believed to be the last man alive who played pre-war first-class cricket, has been awarded a commemorative medal by Norway for his role in liberating the country from Nazi occupation. Manners was the British naval officer in charge of Trondheim when the Germans surrendered. The Norwegian defence attaché, Colonel John Andreas Olsen, presented the award at the care home in Newbury where Manners lives, and said: "He put his life in danger to defend our values." Manners made 81 for Hampshire on his first-class debut in 1936. (See *Wisden 2016*, page 65.)

THE AGE, MELBOURNE   November 26

The Ashes have gone to Australia, in reality as well as metaphorically. The urn left its home at Lord's, along with curator Neil Robinson, and sat on its own business class seat to Melbourne. It will be displayed at the State Library of Victoria until February, on its third visit to Australia. The first was in 1988 for Australia's bicentennial; the second was during the 2006-07 Ashes. "The urn travelled in an unmarked black case," said Robinson. "Nobody knew what was inside apart from me, and the curious thing is nobody asked. You have to bear in mind not just the possibility of accidents, but even the vibrations during turbulence on an aircraft. With an article this fragile, this delicate and this irreplaceable, you have to be sure every risk has been minimised."

THE CRICKETER   December 2

A Delhi cricketer, Prince Yadav, has been banned for two years for posing as an Under-19 player. His school record revealed he was 23.

AUSTRALIAN ASSOCIATED PRESS   December 21

Sydney Thunder were denied a likely Big Bash League victory over Adelaide Strikers when smoke from bushfires enveloped the ground in Canberra, and the match was called off four balls before there could be a DLS result. "Being able to see the ball is pretty fundamental in our sport, but also the respiratory situation is something that needs to be considered," said Strikers coach Jason Gillespie.

ASIAN AGE   December 22

Samit Dravid, 14-year-old son of Rahul, scored 201 in a Karnataka state inter-zonal Under-14 match.

JERUSALEM POST   December 22

The *Jerusalem Post*, Israel's English-language newspaper, has apologised for muddling their Twitter handles, and reporting that the International Cricket Council had accused the Israelis of war crimes. It was in fact the International Criminal Court.

SOUTH WALES ARGUS   December 26

The community team run by Glamorgan raised the spirits of elderly patients at St Woolos Hospital, Newport, by teaching them clock cricket. The game is played indoors, sitting down, with a foam bat and sponge ball: four if it hits the wall, six for the ceiling. "Patients who wouldn't get out of bed or do anything were suddenly playing clock cricket," said Sean Carey from Glamorgan. "It was inspirational."

THE TRIBUNE, INDIA   December 26

Six years after his retirement, Sachin Tendulkar has had his security downgraded by the Indian government. Henceforth, he will have a police bodyguard only when he has left his house.

BBC   December 31

Prime minister Sir John Major missed the chance to see Britain's only gold in the 1996 Atlanta Olympics, preferring to watch a Test against Pakistan, according to newly released archives. Major's aides tried to convince him that attending the Games would help his "street cred". His planned itinerary would have included the rowing final won by Steve Redgrave and Matthew Pinsent, but he opted for Lord's. He was voted out of office less than a year later.

This is the 26th year of the Chronicle. Highlights of the first 25 have been published in *WHAT Did You Say Stopped Play?* (John Wisden).

Contributions from readers are always welcome. Items must have been previously published in print or online. Please send weblinks/cuttings to hugh.chevallier@wisdenalmanack.com or post them to Matthew Engel at Fair Oak, Bacton, Herefordshire HR2 0AT.

INDEX OF TEST MATCHES

Nine earlier men's Test series in 2018-19 – India v West Indies, Pakistan v Australia, Bangladesh
v Zimbabwe, Sri Lanka v England, Pakistan v New Zealand, Bangladesh v West Indies, Australia
v India, New Zealand v Sri Lanka and South Africa v Pakistan – appeared in *Wisden 2019*. WTC
signifies that a series formed part of the World Test Championship.